One method of reducing a part of the earth's surface is by aerial photography. The two photographs on this page are semi-controlled mosaics and are made by matching together a series of vertical aerial photographs. Although an accurate map cannot be made directly from such a mosaic, it does illustrate one way that a map can be made. Each of the mosaics is approximately the scale of its corresponding map. On a map, cultural and physical features are represented by means of signs, symbols, and certain conventions. By comparing the mosaic with the map in each case, one can ascertain how various features on the earth have been represented on the map and how they, and other features, appear from the air. For example, the darkest areas on the Pittsburgh mosaic are wooded areas which are shown in green on the map. The heavily built-up area of Pittsburgh is depicted by a red screen on the map. The major buildings, roads, and bridges are easily recognized.

The part of the Strasburg, Virginia, Quadrangle selected lies in the folded Appalachians just east of Woodstock, Virginia, and across the "Great Valley" of the Shenandoah River. The valley, occupied by the meanders of both forks of the Shenandoah River, is divided at this point by Massanutten Mountain. The latter is a complex synclinal mass, made mostly of sandstone. The three northeast trending parallel ridges of the mountain can be readily recognized and compared. Notice that the shading on the map and the shadows on the mosaic do not agree. The photographs were taken in the morning, placing the western slopes of the ridges in shadow. The general practice of the cartographer, however, is to render the relief as if the light source was from the northwest. The comparison, nevertheless, facilitates an understanding of how contours and relief shading are used to represent surface configuration.

PITTSBURGH WEST 1:24 000
U.S. GEOLOGICAL SURVEY

GOODE'S

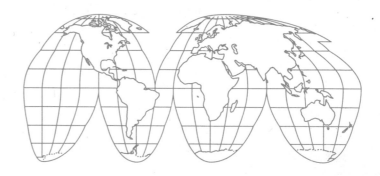

WORLD
ATLAS

TWELFTH EDITION
Revised

edited by
Edward B. Espenshade, Jr.
Professor of Geography, Northwestern University

RAND McNALLY & COMPANY • CHICAGO

CONTENTS

ACKNOWLEDGMENTS

This is the twelfth edition of *Goode's World Atlas* which was first published more than thirty years ago. The name of Dr. Goode, the original editor who was a distinguished cartographer and designed the early editions, is still retained and suggests the high standards which all those who have participated in the preparation of the book have sought to attain. The practice of including systematic improvements and revisions of the maps and data with each new edition is continued.

Sources. Every effort has been made to assemble the latest and most authentic source materials for use in compiling the atlas. For the general physical-political maps, national and state surveys, recent military maps, and hydrographic charts have been utilized. For the specialized maps, the source materials are even more varied. They include both published and unpublished items in the form of maps, descriptions in articles and books, statistics, and correspondence with geographers and others. To the various agencies and organizations, official and unofficial, who have cooperated, appreciation and thanks are expressed. Noteworthy among these organizations and agencies are: Food and Agriculture Organization of The United Nations for production statistics on livestock, crop and forest products, and statistics on world trade; the Office of the Geographer, The Department of State, for the map of Surface Transport Facilities, and other items; the Office of Foreign Agricultural Relations, Department of Agriculture, for information on crop and livestock production and distribution; the Bureau of Mines, Department of the Interior, for information on mineral production; various branches of the National Military Establishment and the Weather Bureau, Department of Commerce, for information on temperature, wind, pressure, and ocean currents; the Maritime Commission and the Department of Commerce, for statistics on ocean trade; the American Geographical Society, for use of its library and permission to use the Miller cylindrical projection; The University of Chicago Press, owners of the copyright, for permission to use Goode's Homolosine equal-area projection; and McGraw-Hill Book Company, for cooperation in permitting the use of Glenn Trewartha's map of climatic regions and Petterson's diagram of zones of precipitation.

Other acknowledgments. The variety and complexity of the problems involved in the preparation of a world atlas make highly desirable the participation of specialists in some of the problems. In the preparation of the new edition of *Goode's World Atlas* the editor has been ably assisted by several such experts. He expresses his deep appreciation and thanks to all of them. He is particularly indebted to the experts listed below who have assumed primary responsibility for certain maps.

The editor's grateful thanks are due to the staff of Rand McNally & Company. It is not possible to cite individual contributions, but the varied skills of geographers, cartographers, and many others are involved. Their faithful and careful work has contributed much to the final result.

EDWARD B. ESPENSHADE, JR.
Northwestern University
May, 1964

Cooperating Experts

A. W. KÜCHLER
Department of Geography
University of Kansas

THOBURN C. LYON
Consultant
Cartography and Air Navigation

A. C. ORVEDAL
Soil Scientist
Division of Soil Survey
United States Department of Agriculture

ERWIN RAISZ
Cartographer
Cambridge, Massachusetts

GLENN T. TREWARTHA
Department of Geography
University of Wisconsin

J. PARKER VAN ZANDT
President
Aviation Research Institute

WALTER H. VOSKUIL
Mineral Economist
Illinois Geological Survey

DERWENT WHITTLESEY
Late Professor of Geography
Harvard University

BOGDAN ZABORSKI
Professor of Geography
University of Ottawa

INTRODUCTION

Utility of maps. There are many kinds of maps, and they are useful in countless ways. It would be difficult to list all the ways in which even a simple road map, for example, is or may be useful. A knowledge of location, relative size, direction, distance, or of other facts which are set down in an atlas is necessary to an understanding of much about which one reads today. The changing world and the widespread commitments of the United States place new emphasis on map study. An atlas has become a prime necessity for understanding the course of world events. Three outstanding attributes may be noted in connection with the maps of this atlas. They are characteristics common to maps of the most varied kinds and utilities.

(1) The maps show facts of areal distribution, both qualitative and quantitative. For example, the world vegetation map (pp. 16-17) is based on observations made by many hundreds of individuals. The map shows hundreds of varied vegetative units and thirty-two types of vegetation. Thousands of words would be required to state the facts portrayed by the map. These facts can be presented best on a map and can be grasped quickly from a map. The information embodied in the world vegetation map is chiefly qualitative. It was reduced from a general, undefined form to a particular, classified form, and so its utility was greatly enhanced. The world rainfall map (pp. 14-15) provides quantitative facts concerning annual precipitation, by means of isohyets (lines connecting points of equal rainfall). Here again, a single map conveys factual information far better than could be done by volumes of words and tables.

(2) The maps in *Goode's World Atlas* also serve to illustrate innumerable facts of significance that are associated with location and areal distribution. For example, the climatic-regions map (pp. 8-9) shows the areal distribution of types of climate which are determined from a synthesis of thousands of rainfall and temperature statistics.

(3) Finally, many useful comparisons may be made between different maps, between two in some instances, between three or more in others, with a view to establishing relationships between the various types of information entered on the maps. Useful comparisons may also be made, of course, between different places on the same map as well as between different aspects of the same place as shown on two or more

maps. For example, compare the areas of dense population (pp. 20-21) with areas which have an intensive subsistence rice or non-rice agriculture (pp. 24-25). There are few agricultural areas in the world, with the exception of those in Europe, which have similar population densities. Note also on the agricultural-regions map the absence of nomadic herding in the Western Hemisphere, whereas extensive areas exist in Asia and Africa.

Reading maps. An ability to read maps is acquired through practice, in the same manner as the ability to read a written text. The effectiveness of any written text depends both on the skill of the writer and on that of the reader. Similarly, the value of a particular map depends both on the effectiveness of the cartography and on the map-reading ability of the user. Of particular importance in reading maps is a knowledge of map scales, projections, and symbolism.

Understanding scales. A function of all maps is to provide a reduced representation of the earth's surface. Since part or all of the earth's surface is depicted on a single page of this atlas, the question arises, "What is the relation of map size to earth size?" This proportional relationship is the scale of a map. The scale is given in three forms on most maps of this atlas to facilitate answering this question.

To aid further in understanding scales, a comparison of scale is given in a series of maps on the next page. A comparison of diagrams A, B, C, and D illustrates how progressively smaller-scale maps (of constant page size) increase the size of the area covered but reduce the detail which can be expressed. On the second map and on each later map, the area covered by the previous map is outlined within the map, to provide a direct comparison of the areas covered. On the first map, individual buildings are shown. On the final map, even many cities are omitted.

To aid the student in acquiring accurate concepts of the relative size of continents and of some countries and regions, uniform scales for comparable areas are used as far as possible. Continental maps are given on a uniform scale of 1:40,000,000 (one inch to 640 miles). In similar fashion, series of regions comparable in area appear in groups of maps on uniform scales of 1:16,000,000 (one inch to 250 miles), 1:12,000,000 (one inch to 190 miles), 1:4,000,000 (one inch to 64 miles), and on larger scales. The maximum size of the scale utilized for any

viii

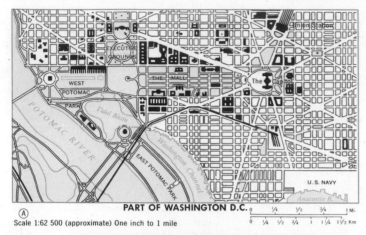

PART OF WASHINGTON D.C.
Scale 1:62 500 (approximate) One inch to 1 mile

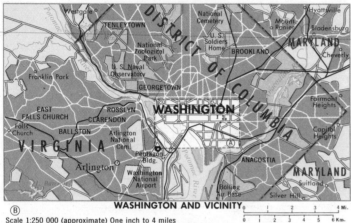

WASHINGTON AND VICINITY
Scale 1:250 000 (approximate) One inch to 4 miles

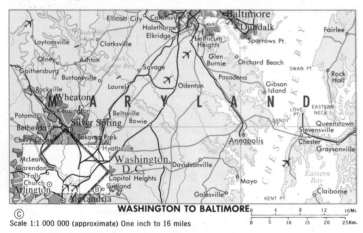

WASHINGTON TO BALTIMORE
Scale 1:1 000 000 (approximate) One inch to 16 miles

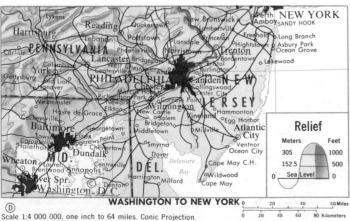

Relief

Meters	Feet
305	1000
152.5	500
0 Sea Level	0

WASHINGTON TO NEW YORK
Scale 1:4 000 000, one inch to 64 miles. Conic Projection

given region is a partial measure of the importance of the region and of interest in it.

Understanding projections. There is no way of representing the curved surface of the globe on a flat surface without some distortion of the useful features desired on flat maps. On large-scale maps covering areas of only a few square miles, this distortion is negligible. In maps representing large areas, as in maps of a large country, a continent, or the whole world, the distortion inevitably is considerable, and, unless understood, it may result in serious misconceptions. The distortion may involve distances, directions, or the shapes and sizes of areas.

A map projection is an orderly system of parallels and meridians on which a map can be drawn. There are hundreds of map projections in use, but none avoids distortion of the spatial relationships that only a globe map can show truthfully. It is not possible to have truth of area, shape, angle, and scale all in the same flat map. It is possible, however, to select from the many types of projections one which is accurate for a particular property or which is a compromise (limiting the distortion of one or more elements at the expense of the others) that is relatively satisfactory for a particular need.

Truth of area is of prime importance in many maps. Most of the maps made for geographical study, particularly those used to show the areal distribution of an item, are drawn on equal-area projections. In an equal-area projection any square inch on the map represents the same number of square miles on the earth's surface as any other square inch on the map. Continents, oceans, islands, states, all are shown in their true relative size. Close to the importance of equality of area is truth of shape. This characteristic is to some extent an esthetic quality, but it is also a practical one. The student becomes familiar with the true shape of a continent or an island or a body of water as it appears on a globe map. Distortion of these shapes almost beyond recognition on a flat map is incongruous and a source of bewilderment to the student. Truth of direction is especially important in the study of the distribution of factors of significance in world relations. To show the latitudinal or zonal distribution of such factors, it is obviously desirable that lines of latitude be parallel, or better, straight lines parallel with the equator.

Most of the maps used in this atlas are drawn on projections that give equality of area, good land and ocean shapes, and parallel latitudinal directions. To provide these and other qualities desired for particular maps, some distortion of other elements is inevitable. The student should make himself aware of the nature of such distortions and make allowances for them in his use of the maps. One of the more practical procedures is to compare the projection grid of the flat map with the grid of the globe map. He should first verify the fundamental characteristics of the globe grid as listed here:

(1) On the globe map all longitude lines are equal in length and meet at the poles.

(2) All latitude lines are parallel.

(3) The length of the latitude lines, that is, the circumference of latitude circles, decreases from the equator to the points representing the poles. At latitude 60°, the circumference of the latitude circle is one-half the circumference of the equatorial circle.

(4) Distances along lines of longitude between any two latitude lines are equal.

(5) All latitude and longitude lines meet at right angles. With item (1) in mind, the student will observe that the projection used on pages 44-45 has latitude lines of equal length. This results in considerable exaggeration of areas in the higher latitudes. With item (5) in mind, he will note that the projection used on pages 6-7 has oblique angles at the junction of latitude and longitude lines in the higher latitudes, and that this partly causes distortion of land shapes in such areas as Alaska and Greenland. In this projection, however, truth of area has been maintained.

Some illustration of the construction of the more commonly used projections and indication of their properties are helpful in making clear the nature of inherent distortions. Pages 2 and 3 are designed to provide this help. They also illustrate the seven projections used in this atlas.

Few of the several hundred projections in use can be constructed graphically by methods of descriptive geometry. Most of them are derived from mathematical formulas designed to afford the properties desired. In some cases it is easier to visualize the general form and characteristics of a projection if the earth's surface is considered to be projected upon a plane, a cone, or a cylinder. The last two surfaces, when they are cut and unrolled, form a plane surface. These surfaces provide one general classification of projections: azimuthal (on a plane), conic, or cylindrical (fig. 1, 2, and 5, pp. 2 and 3). In each class the characteristics of the projections may be changed by varying the systematic arrangement or spacing of the latitude and longitude lines.

Figure 1, A (p. 2) is a true plane projection with the point of projection at the center of the globe. This geometrical projection of the earth grid on a tangent plane is called a gnomonic projection. In the illustration the plane is tangent to the equator, but it could be placed tangent to the poles, or to any other point on the earth's surface. Several other distinctive map projections can be obtained by changing the origin point of the projection. For example, the projection obtained from an origin point on the surface of the globe diametrically opposite the point of contact of the tangent plane is called a stereographic projection, and the projection from an origin point at infinity is called an orthographic projection. None of these perspective projections obtained from projection on a plane is used in this atlas, but the mathematically derived Lambert azimuthal equal-area projection (fig. 1, B, p. 2) may be considered in this general class. The polar aspect of the Lambert azimuthal equal-area projection is used for the map of the Northern Lands and Seas (p. 48); the oblique aspect is used for the series of continental maps. Besides its equal-area quality, the projection gives relatively good shapes to continental areas as a whole.

Conic projections may be thought of as derived from a tangent cone (fig. 2) or from an intersecting cone (fig. 3). In the latter case, the resulting projection is said to have "two standard parallels" along which the scale is exact (since the cone and the sphere coincide throughout the length of the parallels). In maps of areas covering a wide range of longitude, the projection used in this atlas is a modified conic of the latter type

(De Lisle's). In this projection, as here used, the shapes are excellent, and the departure from the equal-area quality is almost negligible. (See Canada, pp. 86-87, and Siberia, pp. 134-135). The scale between the two standard parallels is too small along the parallels, and outside the standard parallels is too great along the parallels. The use of two standard parallels, however, provides a much better opportunity of extending the area within which the scale is reasonably accurate than the use of a single standard parallel, as in the simple conic.

Another modification of the conic principle is the Bonne projection (fig. 3, C, p. 2), used on pages 114-115 for the map of the Mediterranean lands. It has a selected standard parallel, and other parallels are arcs of concentric circles truly divided for points of intersection with the meridians. The scale along all the parallels is true everywhere, but the central meridian is the only one along which it is true. By construction, however, it is equal-area, and reasonably correct representation of shape is obtained in narrow zones along the standard parallel and central meridian, where the intersections are at right angles, or nearly so.

The polyconic projection (fig. 4, p. 2) is used for the United States and some other areas of similar position and size. In the case of the polyconic projection, the earth may be considered as made up of a series of tangent cones. As each base is developed, the result is as shown, somewhat exaggerated, in figure 4, B, page 2. The area of the projection used for the map of the United States (fig. 4, C, page 2) is the central portion of figure 4, B, beneath the word "Pole." In this projection the central meridian crosses all parallels at right angles, as on the globe; other intersections become noticeably oblique only at considerable distance from the central meridian. The scale is true on the central meridian and on each parallel. Shapes, as a result, are very good. Meridian-scale errors, however, increase rapidly with increasing distance from the central meridian. The projection is thus not well adapted to areas of wide longitudinal extent. The departure, however, from equality of area is slight where it has been used for maps in this atlas.

The cylindrical class of projections may be visualized as perspective projections on a tangent or intersecting cylinder (fig. 5, page 3). Many of the cylindrical projections in use, however, are mathematical modifications of the true perspective forms. As a general class, the cylindrical projections have the following characteristics: (1) latitude lines which are straight, parallel, and equal in length; (2) longitude lines which are straight, parallel, equal in length, and equally spaced; (3) meridians and parallels which intersect at right angles (fig. 5, page 3). Since the latitude lines are all drawn equal in length, an increasing distortion of scale occurs along the parallels with increasing distance from the standard parallel or parallels of tangency.

Mercator's projection (fig. 5, C, page 3), which belongs to this general class, is one of the better-known projections. For nearly four hundred years it has been used widely for world distributional maps, in spite of the facts (1) that it is impossible with this projection to show the entire surface of the earth, the poles being at infinity; and (2) that distances and areas grow rapidly larger with increase of latitude, until the distortion becomes enormous in higher latitudes. This is made apparent by

a comparison of the relative size of areas in figures 5, C, and 6. The distortion of area is so great that the use of the Mercator projection for world maps showing areal distributions of most kinds is pedagogically unsound and misleading. The projection was designed by Mercator primarily for use of navigators, and for that use it is incomparable. On it, the navigator can draw a straight line (called a rhumb line) between any two points, read the angle between the rhumb line and any meridian that it crosses, set his compass on that angle, and go direct to his destination without change of compass. This advantage is so great that no other projection has yet taken the place of the Mercator in marine navigation.

A variation of the Mercator is the transverse or oblique Mercator. The grid is derived from a cylinder tangent along a selected great circle (fig. 7). The resulting projection is conformal, but its grid bears no resemblance to that of the ordinary Mercator and may be mistaken for that of a conic projection. Although the transverse Mercator projection is not used in this atlas, it illustrates a special-purpose projection which is being used more and more because of its value in air navigation for maps of great-circle strips.

Miller's projection (fig. 5, D) is a recent "compromise projection." It has been used in the atlas (with permission of the American Geographical Society) for climatic maps showing barometric pressures, winds, and temperatures, and for the map of ocean communications. A continuous grid without interruptions, and straight-line parallels were desirable for the best presentation of the features listed above. Miller's projection meets these requirements and provides a compromise between the distortion of areas and shapes. Mercator's projection was not suitable because of its excessive area distortion, although shapes of areas are excellent. Use of continuous grids for the whole world which were strictly equal-area would result in considerable distortion of shapes. The student will note, however, that even on the Miller projection there is still considerable distortion of areas and shapes in the higher latitudes (cf. fig. 5, D, 5, C, and 6). Changes in scale according to latitude are indicated in the legend of the map and should be carefully noted. For example, compare on the graphic scale (page 44) a distance of one thousand miles at the equator with the same distance at latitude 60° or 80°.

Figure 6 illustrates three projections which are purely conventional in design. They cannot be readily related to the three general classes just discussed. They are not projections in the sense of being projected on a plane, a cone, or a cylinder; rather, they all are based on mathematical formulas. The sinusoidal projection (fig. 6, C, page 3) is used for the large-scale sectional maps of South America and Africa and for the map showing world surface transport facilities. It is an equal-area projection. On these continental maps it is most accurate along the equator where the two continents are widest. The placement of the central meridian through the center of the continents results in relatively little distortion of scale or shapes in the narrower southern parts of the continents. The scale is true along all parallels and the central meridian, but it increases on other meridians in conformity with their increasing obliquity. On the world map (pp. 42-43) the extent of the distortion is reduced by the technique of interrupting the projection and of using a separate central meridian for different land masses.

Mollweide's equal-area projection (fig. 6, A, page 3), designed to show the entire globe as an uninterrupted unit, gives an elliptical picture of the earth. The ellipse is drawn to enclose an area equal to that of a globe on the same scale. The central meridian is divided so that the areas of the bands between the parallels are truthfully proportional. Mollweide's projection is thus an equal-area projection, but there is little uniformity in linear scale. So that the areas of greater distortion in the outer parts of the projection will be eliminated, it, like the sinusoidal projection, may be interrupted and a new central meridian established through each continent (cf. the two forms, fig. 6, A and B, page 3).

Most of the world distribution maps in this atlas are drawn on Goode's homolosine equal-area projection (fig. 6, D, page 3). This projection is derived by combining the sinusoidal projection for latitudes up to 40° north and south with the homolographic projection (Mollweide) for areas poleward of these latitudes. In this manner an equal-area projection is obtained which has some of the better qualities of both the sinusoidal and homolographic. Further improvement of shapes is obtained by application of the principle of interruption, so that extremely oblique intersections are eliminated. The result has a number of distinct advantages: (1) It presents the entire surface of the earth, which Mercator's projection cannot do. (2) It is strictly an equal-area projection, with no distortion of the size of areas. (3) On it the parallels of latitude are represented by straight lines trending with the equator, a real advantage in the study of comparative latitudes. (4) On it the grid is interrupted in the oceans so as to give each continent in turn the advantage of being in the center of the projection, thus providing better shapes for the continents than any uninterrupted world map can give. No map projection has been devised which displays to better advantage the distribution of most world phenomena which are studied best from the equatorial aspect.

Symbolism. The signs, symbols, and conventions shown on maps are a form of "shorthand" indicating a variety of phenomena (page xii). Many of them are self-explanatory. Compare also the aerial mosaics with the adjacent topographic maps of Pittsburgh and Strasburg areas (inside cover). A complete legend (page xii) provides a key to the physical-political reference maps.

Two systems of measurement are used in connection with the maps in this atlas. The English system of measures, which is conventional in this country, is utilized, although admittedly it is somewhat irrational and cumbersome. Since much of the world uses the metric system of measurement and the centigrade thermometer, most measures are given also in these scientific terms, or conversion scales are provided. A linear scale in miles is placed alongside a linear scale in kilometers, with the zero points together. Heights and depths may be read in feet or in meters from opposite scales. Comparative scales in the margins permit ready conversion of temperature and precipitation values from one system to another.

Surface configuration on the continental and regional maps is shown in a different manner from the tenth edition of this

atlas. A combination of two techniques is utilized which gives a striking three-dimensional effect. General elevation above sea level is indicated as previously by layer-tints, altitudinal zones, each of which has a different hue and is defined by a generalized contour line. The hues for the zones, however, have been selected so that their values increases with elevation in preference to the more conventional layer-tint colors. Thus, although shades of green are still used for the lowlands below 1,000 feet, hues of light tan, buff, and yellow are used for successively higher elevations and areas of more than 10,000 feet are left white. Each of the hues increases in value with increasing elevation and thus visually appears closer to the observer.

An oblique shading in gray has been utilized to indicate local relief, particularly the direction and steepness of slopes. This has been superimposed over the layer tints and a much more realistic and readily visualized impression of the surface configuration is obtained. The three-dimensional effect is more noticeable where it is important in the higher mountainous areas whose slopes are steepest, because the shadow contrast is greatest in the very areas where the color values are highest.

This new presentation of relief is designed to overcome some of the serious weaknesses of the layer-tints system used previously. Steepness of slope, the ruggedness of the terrain, and significant relief features which have differences in elevation with a value less than the layer-tint interval are distinguished and can be visualized. No longer should the nearly level high plateau area be confused with an adjacent mountain area. The improved symbolism for representation of surface configuration should facilitate the reading of the maps and should reduce some of the misconceptions obtained when layer-tints alone were utilized.

Place Names. Place names are used to distinguish particular places and features—cities, towns, bays, peninsulas—from other similar features. Many place names consist of two parts —a specific and a generic part. For example, Lake Michigan consists of the specific term "Michigan" modifying the generic term "lake."

If the world used one alphabet and one language, no particular difficulty would arise in the use of place names. Unfortunately, people use many languages and various alphabets. Moreover, some of the people of the world, the Chinese and the Japanese, for example, use non-alphabet languages. In order to make some languages intelligible to American readers, their letters and symbols must be converted into the Roman alphabet. It has been the practice of many people to transform place names further by transcribing or translating part or all of them into English. The recent war, which brought far corners of the earth to our attention, and the increasing facilities for communication in recent years make this practice no longer desirable. In this atlas, a "local-name policy" generally has been used for the cities and towns and for all local topographic and water features. However, for a few major cities the Anglicized form is preferred and the local name is given in parentheses. In countries where more than one official language is used such as South Africa, the spelling of the name is in the form of the dominant local language. The generic parts of local names for topographic and water features are self-explanatory in many cases because of the

associated map symbol or type style. A complete list of foreign generic terms is given in the glossary on page 171, and a short list of "geographical equivalents" is given on pages 6 and 7.

A distinctive feature of *Goode's World Atlas* is the pronouncing index which has been completely revised. The variable vowel sounds of English and the differences among other languages make the correct pronunciation of place names difficult. The correct pronunciation of many names differs from the pronunciation that may seem natural. Under these circumstances, the pronouncing index of more than thirty thousand names should be very helpful to the student.

Economic maps and statistics. The statistics presented in this atlas are not intended to take the place of statistical reference works. Instead of having been planned to present an absolute index to production and trade, they were planned to give a picture of the relative importance of countries and regions in the particulars involved. The maps have been reserved chiefly to present facts of distribution. However, the general magnitude of production is indicated by graded point symbols in the case of minerals, and the density of the uniform dot pattern indirectly provides a similar assessment for crop production. Marginal graphs show the relative importance of different areas by percentage values of world totals.

No single year affords, for this purpose, a satisfactory base for production and trade statistics. For this reason, the percentages and world totals used have been computed with few exceptions, from averages of a period of three or four years. The base period of years varies, but the latest year for which data are available at time of publication has been used. Few realize that there is a necessary gap of several years between the date of a publication such as this and the date of the statistics used. Organizations issuing statistical data of the sort used in the atlas require two or three years to gather, tabulate, and publish their materials. An additional year is required to incorporate and publish the data within this atlas. Publishers often are reluctant to date their statistical materials, since few users understand the reason for the gap in time. The dates of the base period used are indicated on each graph. In general the averages and percentages will provide the student with a sufficiently accurate picture of the relative importance of areas, despite the fact they are not for the current year. An exception occurs in the case of a product which is subject to major or rapid expansion or contraction of production either nationally, regionally, or on a world wide basis. This occurs more commonly in mineral products than in agricultural products. An important example is petroleum where notable shifts in proven reserves, production, and trade movements have occurred within the last five years.

EDWARD B. ESPENSHADE, JR.
Northwestern University
May, 1964

MAP SYMBOLS

CULTURAL FEATURES

Political Boundaries

International
(Demarcated, Undemarcated, and Administrative)

Disputed de facto

Disputed de jure

Indefinite or Undefined

Secondary, State, Provincial, etc. (over water)

Parks, Indian Reservations

City Limits   Built-up Areas

Cities, Towns and Villages

PARIS   1,000,000 and over
(Metropolitan Area Population)

Ufa   500,000 to 1,000,000
(Metropolitan Area Population)

Győr   50,000 to 500,000

Agadir   25,000 to 50,000

Moreno   0 to 25,000

Note: On maps at 1:20,000,000 and smaller, and on maps at 1:1,000,000, the type size indicates the relative importance of cities, not the specific population classification shown above.

TŌKYŌ   National Capitals

Boise   Secondary Capitals

Transportation

Railroads

Railroads
(On 1:1,000,000 scale maps)

Railroad Ferries

Roads

Caravan Routes

Airports

Other Cultural Features

Dams

Pipelines

Pyramids

Ruins

LAND FEATURES

Peaks, Spot Heights

Passes

Sand

Contours

WATER FEATURES

Lakes and Reservoirs

Fresh Water

Fresh Water: Intermittent

Salt Water

Salt Water: Intermittent

Other Water Features

Salt Basins, Flats

Swamps

Ice Caps and Glaciers

Rivers

Intermittent Rivers

Aqueducts and Canals

Ship Channels

Falls

Rapids

Springs

Water Depths

Fishing Banks

Sand Bars

Reefs

The two illustrations below represent the same imaginary area.
The upper illustration demonstrates how the Atlas maps symbolize land and water features.
The lower illustration shows how these same features on the earth's surface would appear if viewed obliquely from an airplane.

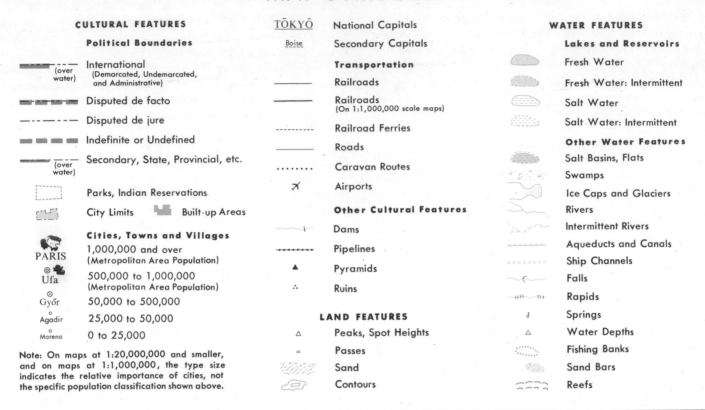

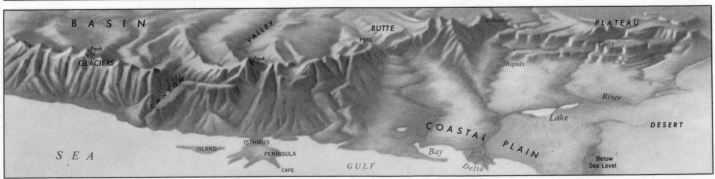

THE SEASONS

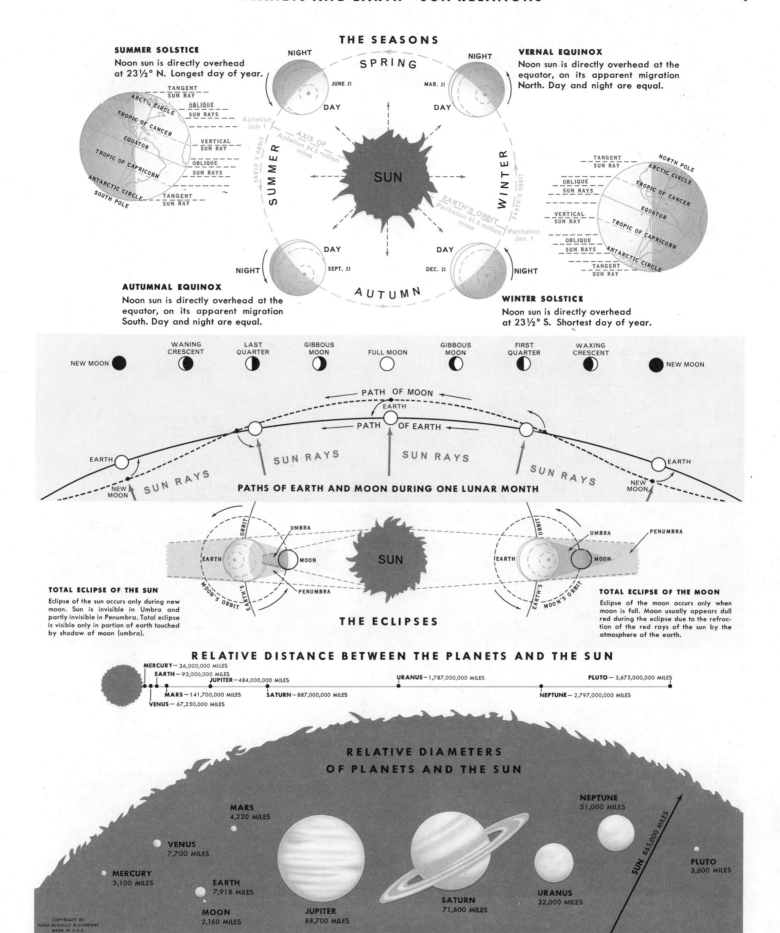

SUMMER SOLSTICE
Noon sun is directly overhead at 23½° N. Longest day of year.

VERNAL EQUINOX
Noon sun is directly overhead at the equator, on its apparent migration North. Day and night are equal.

AUTUMNAL EQUINOX
Noon sun is directly overhead at the equator, on its apparent migration South. Day and night are equal.

WINTER SOLSTICE
Noon sun is directly overhead at 23½° S. Shortest day of year.

PATHS OF EARTH AND MOON DURING ONE LUNAR MONTH

THE ECLIPSES

TOTAL ECLIPSE OF THE SUN
Eclipse of the sun occurs only during new moon. Sun is invisible in Umbra and partly invisible in Penumbra. Total eclipse is visible only in portion of earth touched by shadow of moon (umbra).

TOTAL ECLIPSE OF THE MOON
Eclipse of the moon occurs only when moon is full. Moon usually appears dull red during the eclipse due to the refraction of the red rays of the sun by the atmosphere of the earth.

RELATIVE DISTANCE BETWEEN THE PLANETS AND THE SUN

MERCURY—36,000,000 MILES
EARTH—93,000,000 MILES
JUPITER—484,000,000 MILES
URANUS—1,787,000,000 MILES
PLUTO—3,675,000,000 MILES
MARS—141,700,000 MILES
SATURN—887,000,000 MILES
NEPTUNE—2,797,000,000 MILES
VENUS—67,250,000 MILES

RELATIVE DIAMETERS OF PLANETS AND THE SUN

MARS 4,220 MILES
NEPTUNE 31,000 MILES
VENUS 7,700 MILES
MERCURY 3,100 MILES
EARTH 7,918 MILES
MOON 2,160 MILES
JUPITER 88,700 MILES
SATURN 71,600 MILES
URANUS 32,000 MILES
SUN 865,000 MILES
PLUTO 3,600 MILES

PROJECTIONS

A map projection is merely an orderly system of parallels and meridians on which a flat map can be drawn. There are hundreds of projections, but no one represents the earth's spherical surface without some distortion. The distortion is relatively small for most practical purposes when a small part of the sphere is projected. For larger areas, a sacrifice of some property is necessary.

Most projections are designed to preserve on the flat map some particular property of the sphere. By varying the systematic arrangement or spacing of the latitude and longitude lines, a projection may be made either equal-area or conformal. Although most projections are derived from mathematical formulas, some are easier to visualize if thought of as projected upon a plane, or upon a cone or cylinder which is then unrolled into a plane surface. Thus, many projections are classified as plane (azimuthal), conic, or cylindrical.

For a fuller discussion of map projections, see Preface. Figures with asterisks indicate projections used in this atlas.

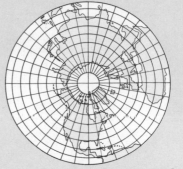

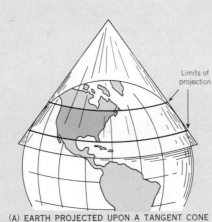

(A) GNOMONIC PROJECTION

A geometric or perspective projection on a tangent plane with the origin point at the center of the globe. Shapes and distances rapidly become increasingly distorted away from the center of the projection. Important in navigation, because all straight lines are great circles.

(B) LAMBERT EQUAL AREA PROJECTION*

A mathematically designed azimuthal equal-area projection. Excellent for continental areas. For larger areas away from the center, distortion of distances and shapes is appreciable.

FIGURE 1.–TYPICAL PLANE PROJECTIONS

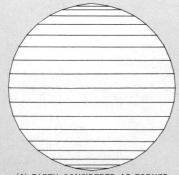

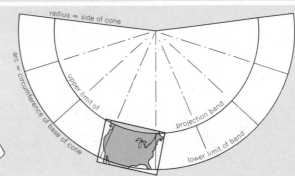

(B) CONE CUT FROM BASE TO APEX

A perspective projection on a tangent cone with the origin point at the center of the globe. At the parallel of tangency, all elements of the map are

(C) CONE DEVELOPED INTO A PLANE SURFACE

true- angles,distances,shapes,areas. Away from the tangent parallel, distances increase rapidly, giving bad distortion of shapes and areas.

(A) EARTH PROJECTED UPON A TANGENT CONE

FIGURE 2 –SIMPLE CONIC PROJECTIONS

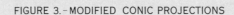

(A) EARTH PROJECTED UPON AN INTERSECTING CONE

This modification of the conic has two standard parallels, or lines of intersection. It is not an equal-area projection, the space being reduced in size between the standard parallels and

(B) CONIC PROJECTION WITH TWO STANDARD PARALLELS*

progressively enlarged beyond the standard parallels. Careful selection of the standard parallels provides, however, good representation for areas of limited latitudinal extent.

(C) BONNE PROJECTION*

An equal-area modification of the conic principle. Distances are true along all parallels and the central meridian; but away from it, increasing obliqueness of intersections and longitudinal distances, with their attendant distortion of shapes, limits the satisfactory area.

FIGURE 3.–MODIFIED CONIC PROJECTIONS

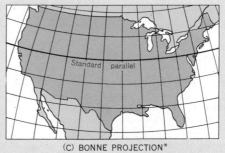

(A) EARTH CONSIDERED AS FORMED BY BASES OF CONES

(B) DEVELOPMENT OF THE CONICAL BASES

This variation is not equal-area. Parallels are non-concentric circles truly divided. Distances along the straight central meridian are also true, but

along the curving meridians are increasingly exaggerated. Representation is good near the central meridian, but away from it there is marked distortion.

(C) POLYCONIC PROJECTION*

FIGURE 4.–POLYCONIC PROJECTION

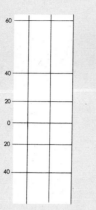

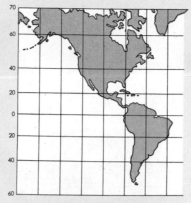

(A) PERSPECTIVE PROJECTION

A perspective projection on a tangent cylinder. Because of rapidly increasing distortion away from the line of tangency and the lack of any special advantage, it is rarely used.

(B) EARTH PROJECTED UPON A CYLINDER

(C) MERCATOR CONFORMAL PROJECTION

Mercator's modification increases the latitudinal distances in the same proportion as longitudinal distances are increased. Thus, at any point shapes are true, but areas become increasingly exaggerated. Of value in navigation, because a line connecting any two points gives the true direction between them.

(D) MILLER PROJECTION*

This recent modification is neither conformal nor equal-area. Whereas shapes are less accurate than on the Mercator, the exaggeration of areas has been reduced somewhat.

FIGURE 5.—CYLINDRICAL PROJECTIONS

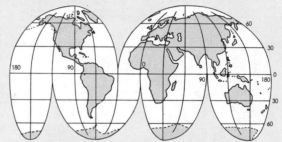

(A) MOLLWEIDE'S HOMOLOGRAPHIC PROJECTION

(B) GOODE'S INTERRUPTED HOMOLOGRAPHIC PROJECTION

(C) SINUSOIDAL PROJECTION*

(D) GOODE'S INTERRUPTED HOMOLOSINE PROJECTION*

Although each of these projections is equal-area, differences in the spacing and arrangement of latitude and longitude lines result in differences in the distribution and relative degree of the shape and distance distortion within each grid. On the homolographic, there is no uniformity in scale. It is different on each parallel and each meridian. On the sinusoidal, only distances along all latitudes and the central meridian are true. The homolosine combines the homolographic, for areas poleward of 40°, with the sinusoidal. The principle of interruption permits each continent in turn the advantage of being in the center of the projection, resulting in better shapes.

FIGURE 6.—EQUAL AREA PROJECTIONS OF THE WORLD

A conformal projection in which a selected great circle of the globe is considered as the "equator" of the ordinary Mercator projection, with the cylinder tangent along the great circle. It is used chiefly for charts of great-circle air routes between distant cities.

FIGURE 7.—TRANSVERSE MERCATOR PROJECTION

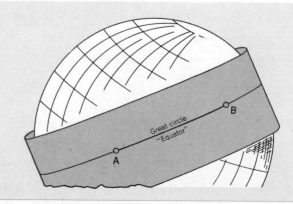

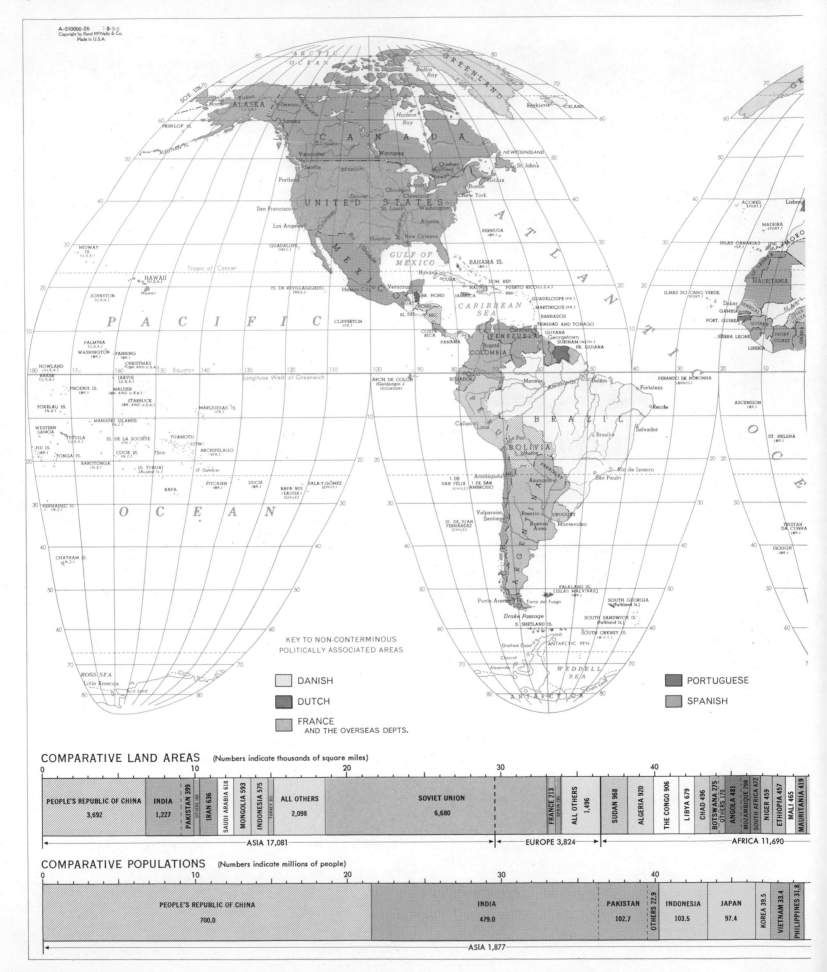

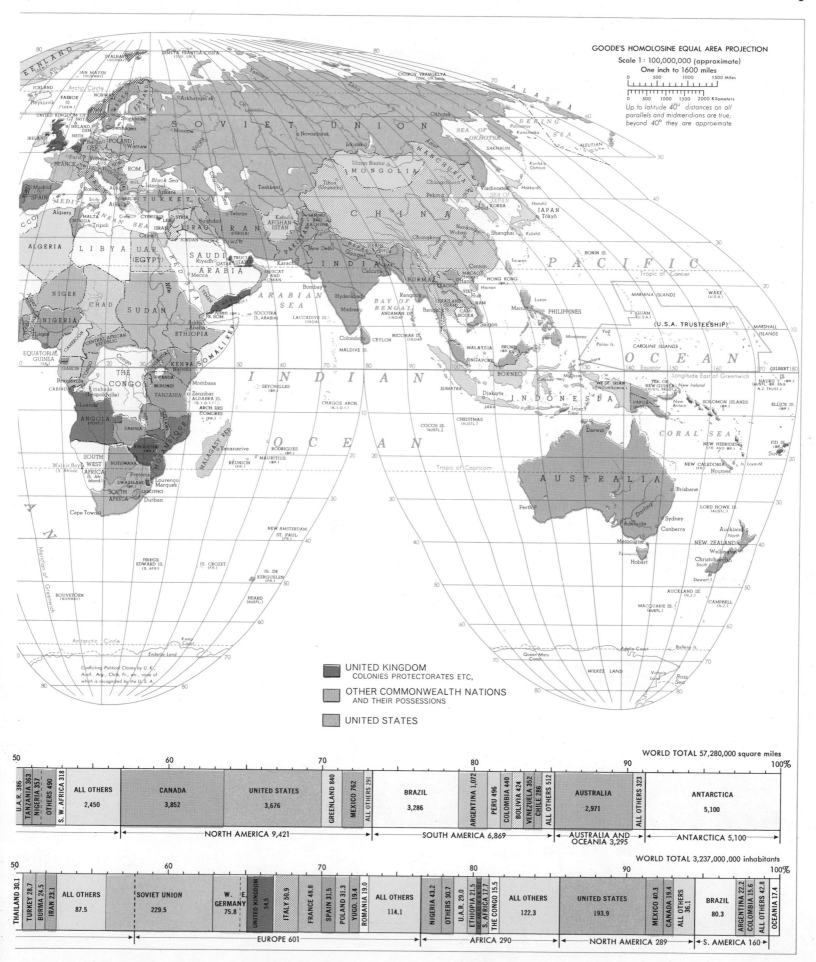

GOODE'S HOMOLOSINE EQUAL AREA PROJECTION

Scale 1 : 100,000,000 (approximate)
One inch to 1600 miles

0   500   1000   1500 Miles

0   500   1000   1500   2000 Kilometers

*Up to latitude 40° distances on all
parallels and midmeridians are true;
beyond 40° they are approximate*

UNITED KINGDOM
COLONIES PROTECTORATES ETC,

OTHER COMMONWEALTH NATIONS
AND THEIR POSSESSIONS

UNITED STATES

WORLD TOTAL 57,280,000 square miles

WORLD TOTAL 3,237,000,000 inhabitants

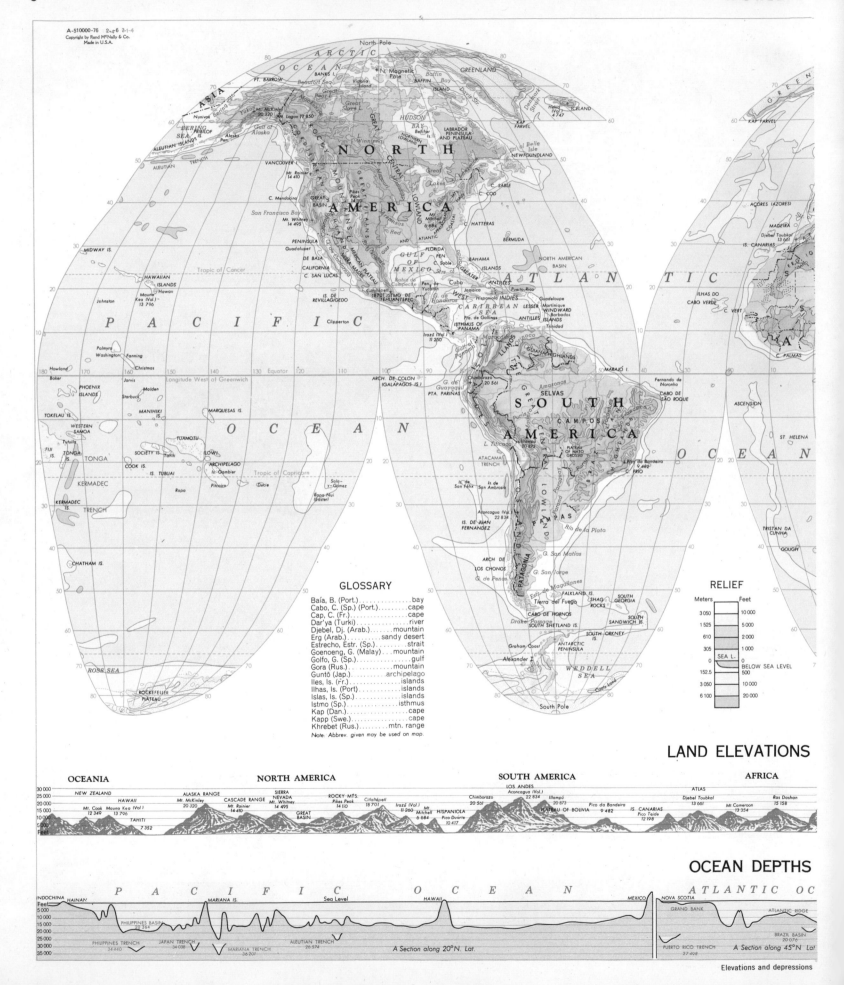

GLOSSARY

Baía, B. (Port.) . . . . bay
Cabo, C. (Sp.) (Port.) . . . . cape
Cap, C. (Fr.) . . . . cape
Dar'ya (Turki) . . . . river
Djebel, Dj. (Arab.) . . . . mountain
Erg (Arab.) . . . . sandy desert
Estrecho, Estr. (Sp.) . . . . strait
Goenoeng, G. (Malay) . . mountain
Golfo, G. (Sp.) . . . . gulf
Gora (Rus.) . . . . mountain
Guntô (Jap.) . . . . archipelago
Iles, Is. (Fr.) . . . . islands
Ilhas, Is. (Port) . . . . islands
Islas, Is. (Sp.) . . . . islands
Istmo (Sp.) . . . . isthmus
Kap (Dan.) . . . . cape
Kapp (Swe.) . . . . cape
Khrebet (Rus.) . . . . mtn. range

Note: Abbrev. given may be used on map.

RELIEF

Meters	Feet
3 050	10 000
1 525	5 000
610	2 000
305	1 000
0 SEA L.	0
	BELOW SEA LEVEL
152.5	500
3 050	10 000
6 100	20 000

LAND ELEVATIONS

OCEAN DEPTHS

Elevations and depressions

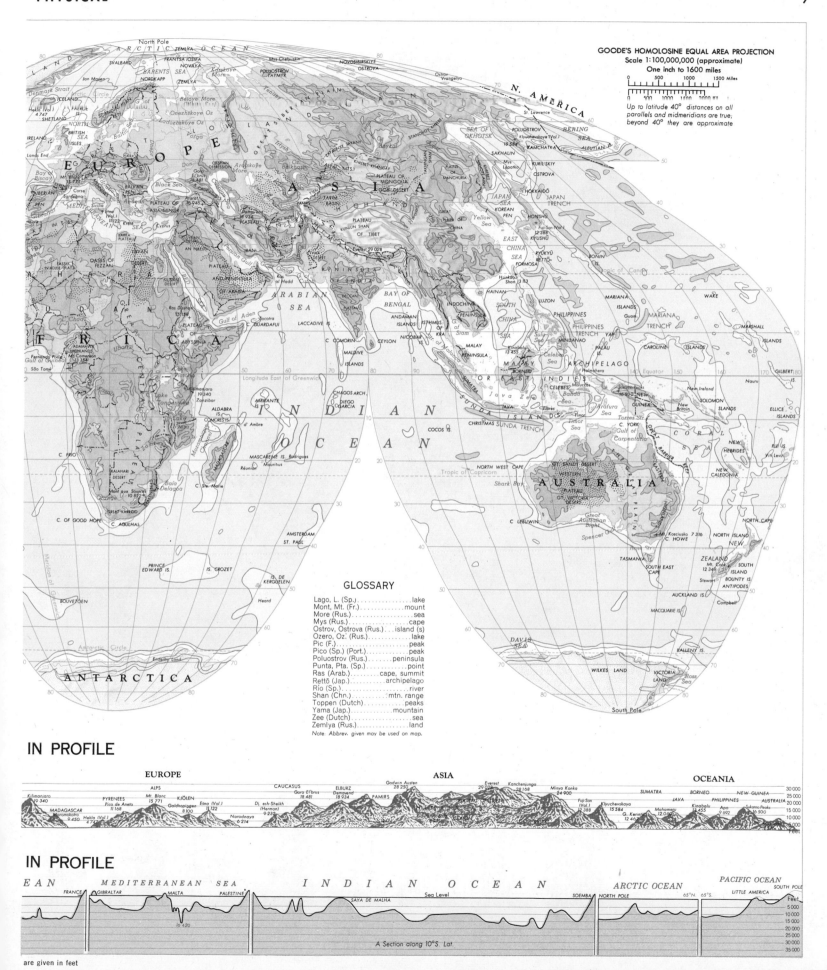

GOODE'S HOMOLOSINE EQUAL AREA PROJECTION
Scale 1:100,000,000 (approximate)
One inch to 1600 miles

0   500   1000   1500 Miles

Up to latitude 40° distances on all
parallels and midmeridians are true;
beyond 40° they are approximate

GLOSSARY

Lago, L. (Sp.)	lake
Mont, Mt. (Fr.)	mount
More (Rus.)	sea
Mys (Rus.)	cape
Ostrov, Ostrova (Rus.)	island (s)
Ozero, Oz. (Rus.)	lake
Pic (Fr.)	peak
Pico (Sp.) (Port.)	peak
Poluostrov (Rus.)	peninsula
Punta, Pta. (Sp.)	point
Ras (Arab.)	cape, summit
Rettō (Jap.)	archipelago
Río (Sp.)	river
Shan (Chn.)	mtn. range
Toppen (Dutch)	peaks
Yama (Jap.)	mountain
Zee (Dutch)	sea
Zemlya (Rus.)	land

Note. Abbrev. given may be used on map.

IN PROFILE

EUROPE   ASIA   OCEANIA

IN PROFILE

EAN   MEDITERRANEAN SEA   INDIAN OCEAN   ARCTIC OCEAN   PACIFIC OCEAN

A Section along 10°S. Lat.

are given in feet

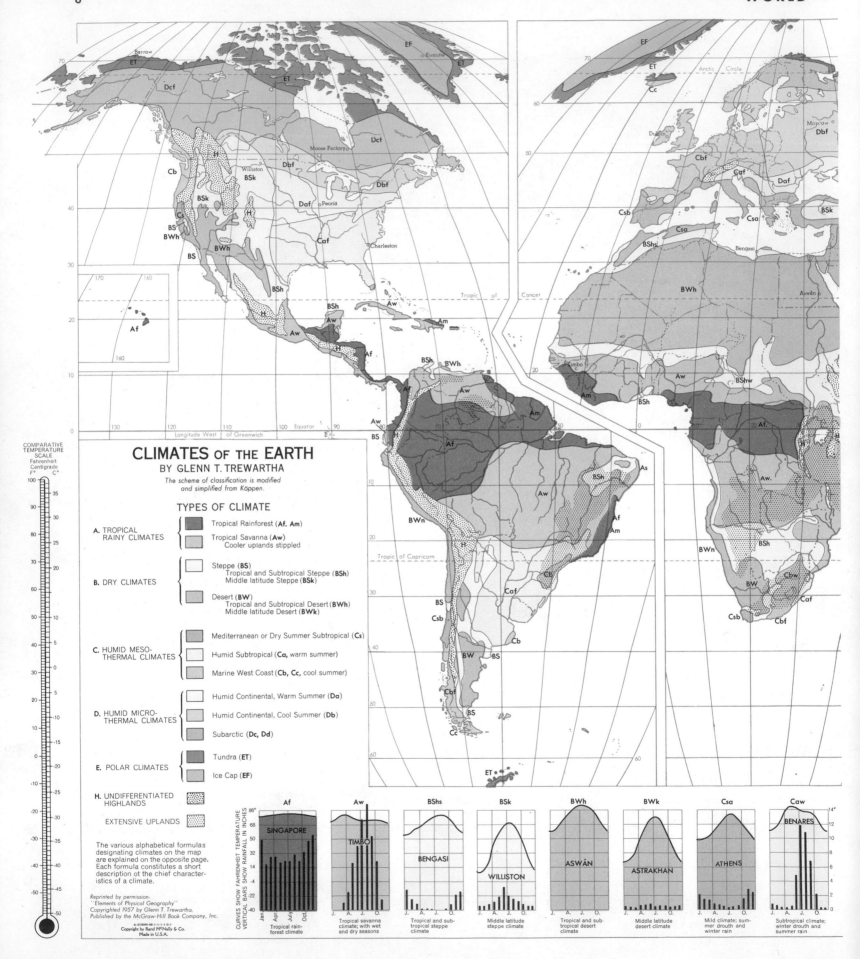

CLIMATES OF THE EARTH
BY GLENN T. TREWARTHA

The scheme of classification is modified
and simplified from Köppen.

TYPES OF CLIMATE

COMPARATIVE
TEMPERATURE
SCALE
Fahrenheit
Centigrade
F°   C°

A. TROPICAL RAINY CLIMATES
- Tropical Rainforest (**Af. Am**)
- Tropical Savanna (**Aw**)
  Cooler uplands stippled

B. DRY CLIMATES
- Steppe (**BS**)
  Tropical and Subtropical Steppe (**BSh**)
  Middle latitude Steppe (**BSk**)
- Desert (**BW**)
  Tropical and Subtropical Desert (**BWh**)
  Middle latitude Desert (**BWk**)

C. HUMID MESO-THERMAL CLIMATES
- Mediterranean or Dry Summer Subtropical (**Cs**)
- Humid Subtropical (**Ca,** warm summer)
- Marine West Coast (**Cb, Cc,** cool summer)

D. HUMID MICRO-THERMAL CLIMATES
- Humid Continental, Warm Summer (**Da**)
- Humid Continental, Cool Summer (**Db**)
- Subarctic (**Dc, Dd**)

E. POLAR CLIMATES
- Tundra (**ET**)
- Ice Cap (**EF**)

H. UNDIFFERENTIATED HIGHLANDS

EXTENSIVE UPLANDS

The various alphabetical formulas
designating climates on the map
are explained on the opposite page.
Each formula constitutes a short
description of the chief characteristics of a climate.

CURVES SHOW FAHRENHEIT TEMPERATURE
VERTICAL BARS SHOW RAINFALL IN INCHES

Af — SINGAPORE
Tropical rain-
forest climate

Aw — TIMBO
Tropical savanna
climate; with wet
and dry seasons

BShs — BENGASI
Tropical and sub-
tropical steppe
climate

BSk — WILLISTON
Middle latitude
steppe climate

BWh — ASWÂN
Tropical and sub-
tropical desert
climate

BWk — ASTRAKHAN
Middle latitude
desert climate

Csa — ATHENS
Mild climate; sum-
mer drouth and
winter rain

Caw — BENARES
Subtropical climate;
winter drouth and
summer rain

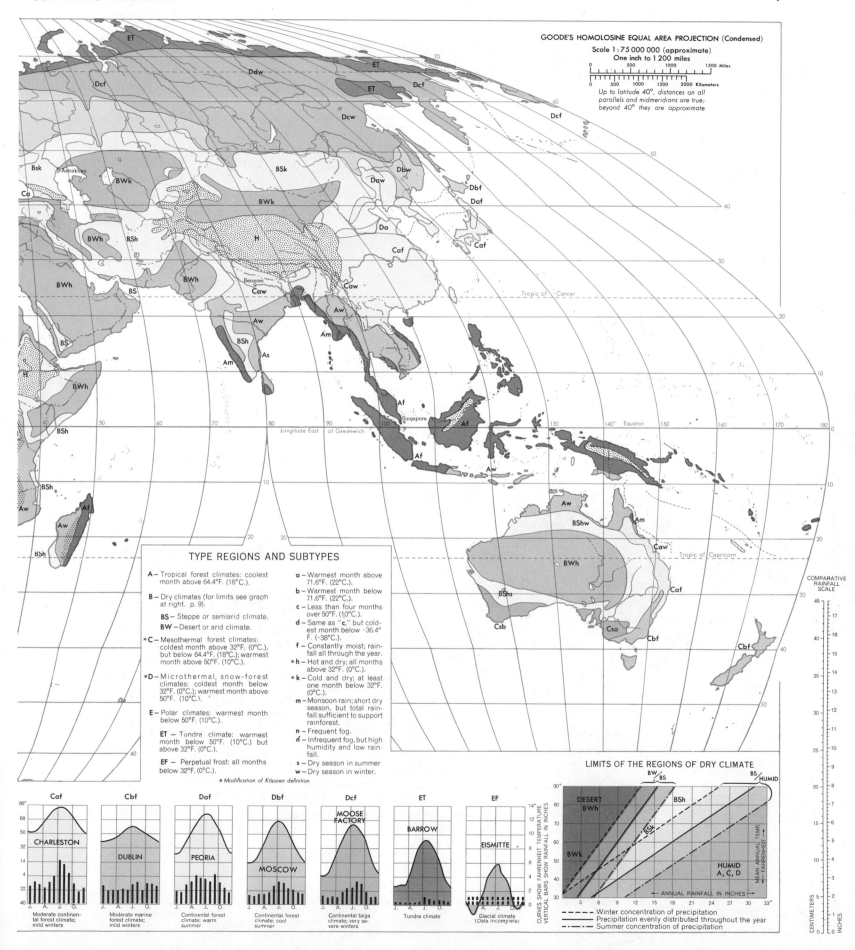

GOODE'S HOMOLOSINE EQUAL AREA PROJECTION (Condensed)
Scale 1 : 75 000 000 (approximate)
One inch to 1 200 miles

Up to latitude 40°, distances on all
parallels and midmeridians are true;
beyond 40° they are approximate

TYPE REGIONS AND SUBTYPES

A – Tropical forest climates: coolest month above 64.4°F. (18°C.).

B – Dry climates (for limits see graph at right. p. 9).

  BS – Steppe or semiarid climate.

  BW – Desert or arid climate.

*C – Mesothermal forest climates: coldest month above 32°F. (0°C.), but below 64.4°F. (18°C.); warmest month above 50°F. (10°C.).

*D – Microthermal, snow-forest climates: coldest month below 32°F. (0°C.); warmest month above 50°F. (10°C.).

E – Polar climates: warmest month below 50°F. (10°C.).

  ET – Tundra climate: warmest month below 50°F. (10°C.) but above 32°F. (0°C.).

  EF – Perpetual frost: all months below 32°F. (0°C.).

a – Warmest month above 71.6°F. (22°C.).

b – Warmest month below 71.6°F. (22°C.).

c – Less than four months over 50°F. (10°C.).

d – Same as "c," but coldest month below -36.4° F. (-38°C.).

f – Constantly moist; rainfall all through the year.

*h – Hot and dry; all months above 32°F. (0°C.).

*k – Cold and dry; at least one month below 32°F. (0°C.).

m – Monsoon rain; short dry season, but total rainfall sufficient to support rainforest.

n – Frequent fog.

n' – Infrequent fog, but high humidity and low rainfall.

s – Dry season in summer

w – Dry season in winter.

*Modification of Köppen definition

COMPARATIVE RAINFALL SCALE

LIMITS OF THE REGIONS OF DRY CLIMATE

DESERT
BWh

BShh

BWk

BShk

BSh

BSk

HUMID
A, C, D

ANNUAL RAINFALL IN INCHES

MEAN ANNUAL TEMP. FAHRENHEIT

------ Winter concentration of precipitation
——— Precipitation evenly distributed throughout the year
—·—·— Summer concentration of precipitation

CURVES SHOW FAHRENHEIT TEMPERATURE
VERTICAL BARS SHOW RAINFALL IN INCHES

Caf
CHARLESTON

Moderate continental forest climate; mild winters

Cbf
DUBLIN

Moderate marine forest climate; mild winters

Daf
PEORIA

Continental forest climate; warm summer

Dbf
MOSCOW

Continental forest climate; cool summer

Dcf
MOOSE FACTORY

Continental taiga climate; very severe winters

ET
BARROW

Tundra climate

EF
EISMITTE

Glacial climate (Data incomplete)

CENTIMETERS

INCHES

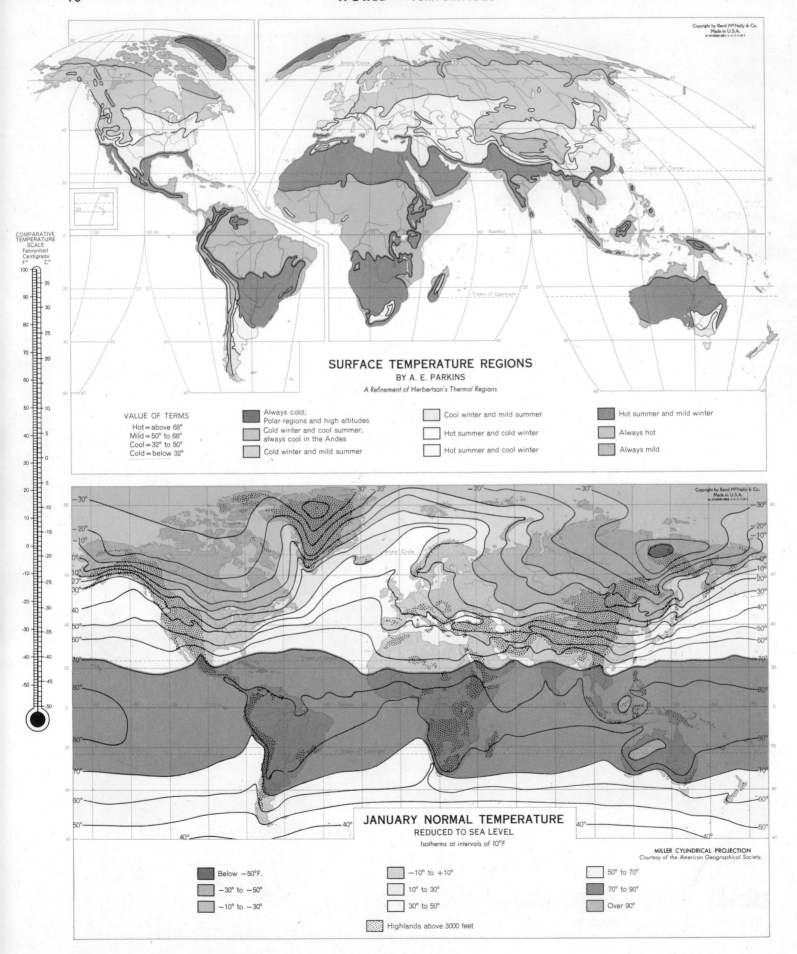

SURFACE TEMPERATURE REGIONS
BY A. E. PARKINS
A Refinement of Herbertson's Thermal Regions

COMPARATIVE
TEMPERATURE
SCALE
Fahrenheit
Centigrade
F°   C°

VALUE OF TERMS

Hot = above 68°
Mild = 50° to 68°
Cool = 32° to 50°
Cold = below 32°

Always cold;
Polar regions and high altitudes

Cold winter and cool summer;
always cool in the Andes

Cold winter and mild summer

Cool winter and mild summer

Hot summer and cold winter

Hot summer and cool winter

Hot summer and mild winter

Always hot

Always mild

JANUARY NORMAL TEMPERATURE
REDUCED TO SEA LEVEL
Isotherms at intervals of 10°F

MILLER CYLINDRICAL PROJECTION
Courtesy of the American Geographical Society.

Below −50°F.

−30° to −50°

−10° to −30°

−10° to +10°

10° to 30°

30° to 50°

50° to 70°

70° to 90°

Over 90°

Highlands above 3000 feet

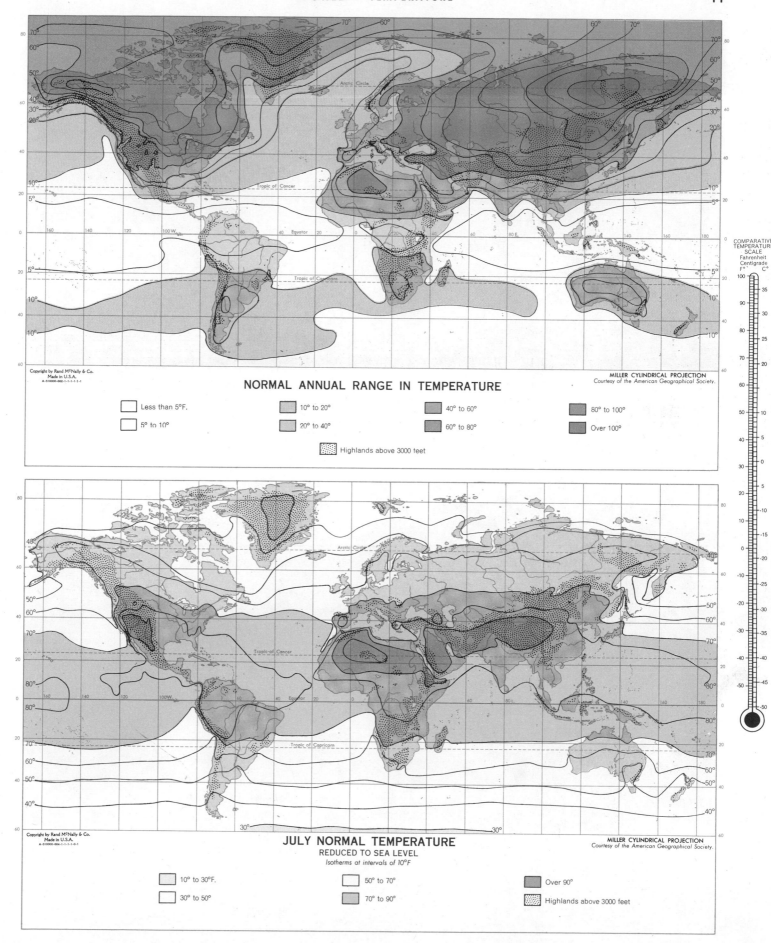

NORMAL ANNUAL RANGE IN TEMPERATURE

Copyright by Rand McNally & Co.
Made in U.S.A.
A-510000-662-1-1-1-1-1

MILLER CYLINDRICAL PROJECTION
Courtesy of the American Geographical Society.

Less than 5°F.

5° to 10°

10° to 20°

20° to 40°

40° to 60°

60° to 80°

80° to 100°

Over 100°

Highlands above 3000 feet

COMPARATIVE
TEMPERATURE
SCALE
Fahrenheit
Centigrade
F° C°

JULY NORMAL TEMPERATURE
REDUCED TO SEA LEVEL
Isotherms at intervals of 10°F

Copyright by Rand McNally & Co.
Made in U.S.A.
A-510000-664-1-1-1-1-0-1

MILLER CYLINDRICAL PROJECTION
Courtesy of the American Geographical Society.

10° to 30°F.

30° to 50°

50° to 70°

70° to 90°

Over 90°

Highlands above 3000 feet

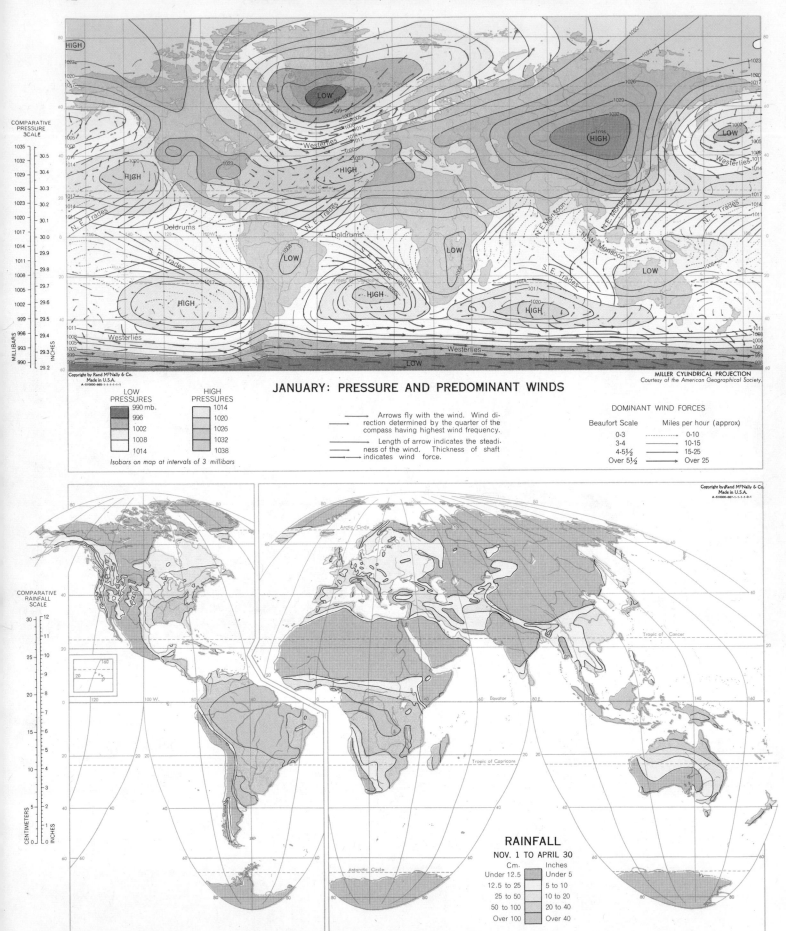

COMPARATIVE
PRESSURE
SCALE

MILLIBARS	INCHES
1035	30.5
1032	30.5
1029	30.4
1026	30.3
1023	30.2
1020	30.1
1017	30.0
1014	29.9
1011	29.8
1008	29.7
1005	29.6
1002	29.5
999	29.4
996	29.3
993	29.3
990	29.2

Copyright by Rand McNally & Co.
Made in U.S.A.
A-510000-665-1-1-1-1-1-1

JANUARY: PRESSURE AND PREDOMINANT WINDS

MILLER CYLINDRICAL PROJECTION
Courtesy of the American Geographical Society.

LOW PRESSURES		HIGH PRESSURES	
	990 mb.		1014
	996		1020
	1002		1026
	1008		1032
	1014		1038

Isobars on map at intervals of 3 millibars

→ Arrows fly with the wind. Wind direction determined by the quarter of the compass having highest wind frequency.

→ Length of arrow indicates the steadiness of the wind. Thickness of shaft indicates wind force.

DOMINANT WIND FORCES

Beaufort Scale	Miles per hour (approx)
0-3	0-10
3-4	10-15
4-5½	15-25
Over 5½	Over 25

Copyright by Rand McNally & Co.
Made in U.S.A.
A-510000-667-1-1-1-1-0-1

COMPARATIVE
RAINFALL
SCALE

CENTIMETERS   INCHES

RAINFALL

NOV. 1 TO APRIL 30

Cm.	Inches
Under 12.5	Under 5
12.5 to 25	5 to 10
25 to 50	10 to 20
50 to 100	20 to 40
Over 100	Over 40

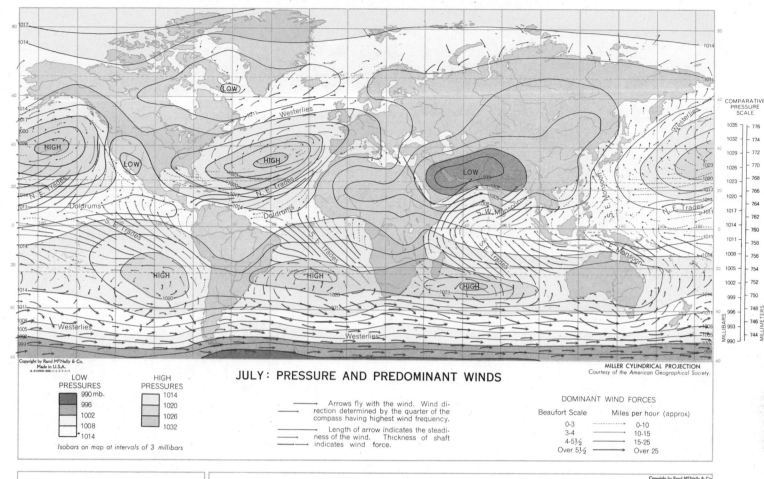

JULY: PRESSURE AND PREDOMINANT WINDS

MILLER CYLINDRICAL PROJECTION
Courtesy of the American Geographical Society.

COMPARATIVE
PRESSURE
SCALE

Copyright by Rand McNally & Co.
Made in U.S.A.
A-510000-868-1-1-1-1-1

LOW PRESSURES	HIGH PRESSURES
990 mb.	1014
996	1020
1002	1026
1008	1032
1014	

Isobars on map at intervals of 3 millibars

Arrows fly with the wind. Wind direction determined by the quarter of the compass having highest wind frequency.

Length of arrow indicates the steadiness of the wind. Thickness of shaft indicates wind force.

DOMINANT WIND FORCES

Beaufort Scale	Miles per hour (approx)
0-3	0-10
3-4	10-15
4-5½	15-25
Over 5½	Over 25

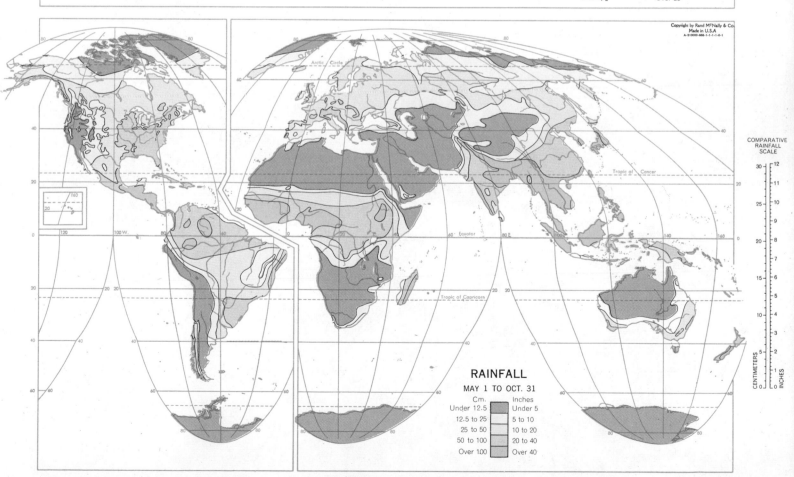

Copyright by Rand McNally & Co.
A-510000-868-1-1-1-1-0-1

COMPARATIVE
RAINFALL
SCALE

RAINFALL

MAY 1 TO OCT. 31

Cm.	Inches
Under 12.5	Under 5
12.5 to 25	5 to 10
25 to 50	10 to 20
50 to 100	20 to 40
Over 100	Over 40

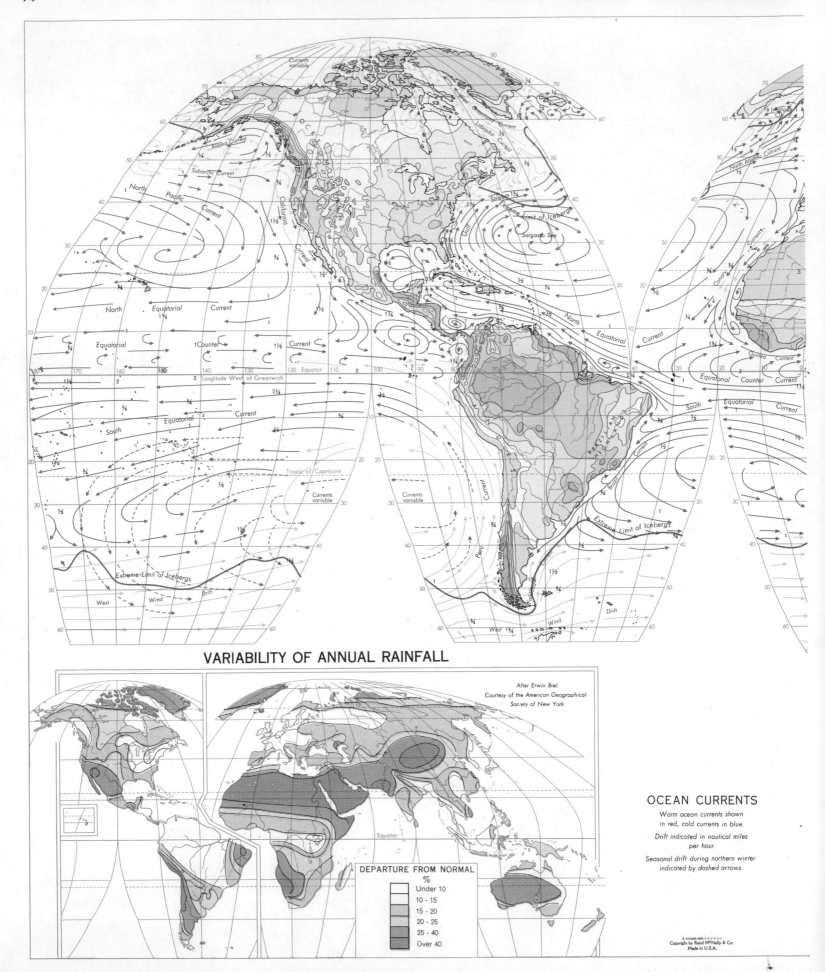

VARIABILITY OF ANNUAL RAINFALL

After Erwin Biel.
Courtesy of the American Geographical
Society of New York

DEPARTURE FROM NORMAL
%
Under 10
10 - 15
15 - 20
20 - 25
25 - 40
Over 40

OCEAN CURRENTS

*Warm ocean currents shown
in red, cold currents in blue.*

*Drift indicated in nautical miles
per hour.*

*Seasonal drift during northern winter
indicated by dashed arrows.*

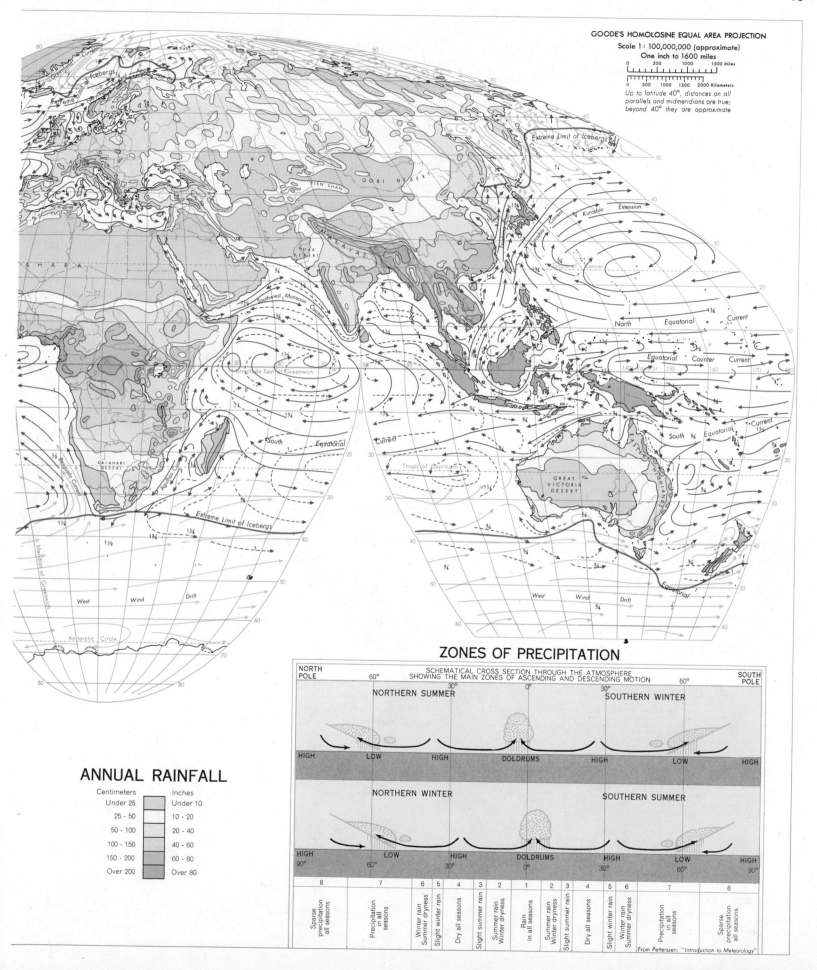

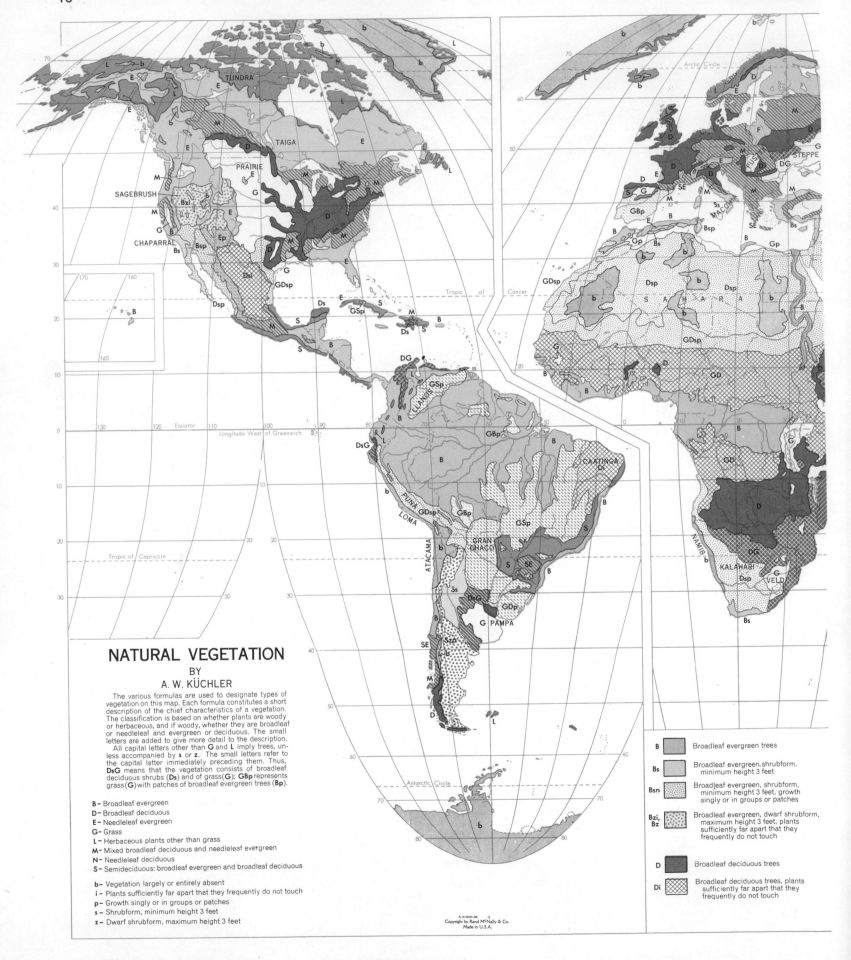

NATURAL VEGETATION

BY
A. W. KÜCHLER

The various formulas are used to designate types of
vegetation on this map. Each formula constitutes a short
description of the chief characteristics of a vegetation.
The classification is based on whether plants are woody
or herbaceous, and if woody, whether they are broadleaf
or needleleaf and evergreen or deciduous. The small
letters are added to give more detail to the description.

All capital letters other than **G** and **L** imply trees, unless accompanied by **s** or **z**. The small letters refer to
the capital letter immediately preceding them. Thus,
DsG means that the vegetation consists of broadleaf
deciduous shrubs (**Ds**) and of grass (**G**); **GBp** represents
grass (**G**) with patches of broadleaf evergreen trees (**Bp**).

B – Broadleaf evergreen
D – Broadleaf deciduous
E – Needleleaf evergreen
G – Grass
L – Herbaceous plants other than grass
M – Mixed broadleaf deciduous and needleleaf evergreen
N – Needleleaf deciduous
S – Semideciduous: broadleaf evergreen and broadleaf deciduous

b – Vegetation largely or entirely absent
i – Plants sufficiently far apart that they frequently do not touch
p – Growth singly or in groups or patches
s – Shrubform, minimum height 3 feet
z – Dwarf shrubform, maximum height 3 feet

B	Broadleaf evergreen trees
Bs	Broadleaf evergreen, shrubform, minimum height 3 feet
Bsn	Broadleaf evergreen, shrubform, minimum height 3 feet, growth singly or in groups or patches
Bzi, Bz	Broadleaf evergreen, dwarf shrubform, maximum height 3 feet, plants sufficiently far apart that they frequently do not touch
D	Broadleaf deciduous trees
Di	Broadleaf deciduous trees, plants sufficiently far apart that they frequently do not touch

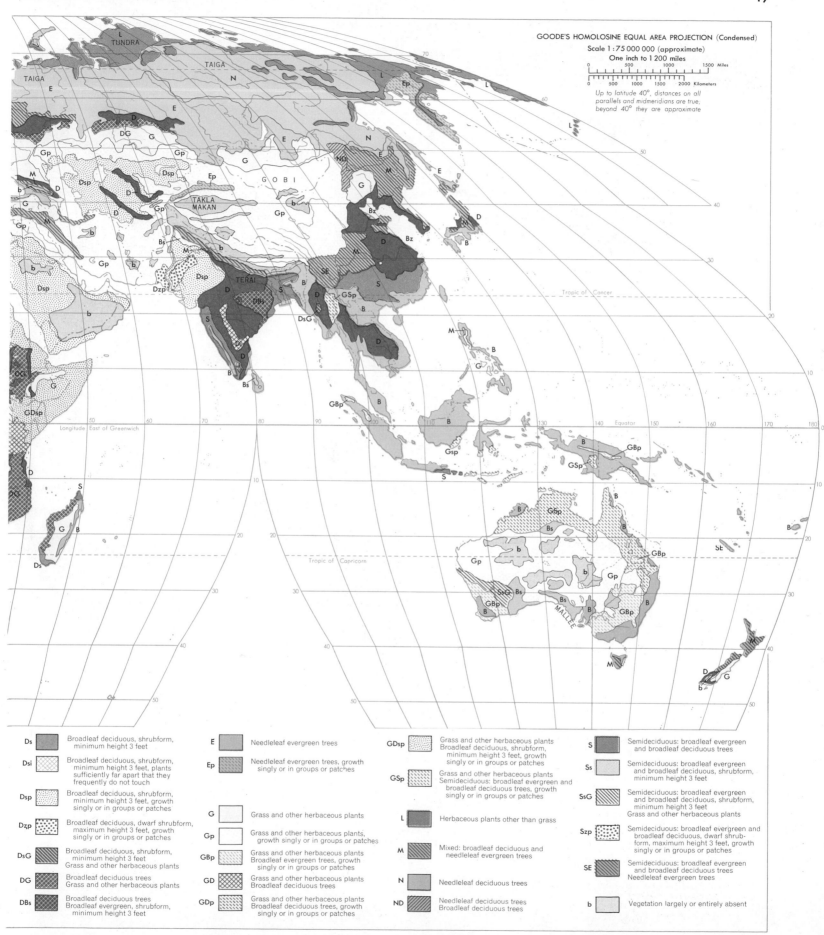

GOODE'S HOMOLOSINE EQUAL AREA PROJECTION (Condensed)
Scale 1 : 75 000 000 (approximate)
One inch to 1 200 miles

Up to latitude 40°, distances on all
parallels and midmeridians are true,
beyond 40° they are approximate

Ds		Broadleaf deciduous, shrubform, minimum height 3 feet
Dsi		Broadleaf deciduous, shrubform, minimum height 3 feet, plants sufficiently far apart that they frequently do not touch
Dsp		Broadleaf deciduous, shrubform, minimum height 3 feet, growth singly or in groups or patches
Dzp		Broadleaf deciduous, dwarf shrubform, maximum height 3 feet, growth singly or in groups or patches
DsG		Broadleaf deciduous, shrubform, minimum height 3 feet Grass and other herbaceous plants
DG		Broadleaf deciduous trees Grass and other herbaceous plants
DBs		Broadleaf deciduous trees Broadleaf evergreen, shrubform, minimum height 3 feet

E		Needleleaf evergreen trees
Ep		Needleleaf evergreen trees, growth singly or in groups or patches
G		Grass and other herbaceous plants
Gp		Grass and other herbaceous plants, growth singly or in groups or patches
GBp		Grass and other herbaceous plants Broadleaf evergreen trees, growth singly or in groups or patches
GD		Grass and other herbaceous plants Broadleaf deciduous trees
GDp		Grass and other herbaceous plants Broadleaf deciduous trees, growth singly or in groups or patches

GDsp		Grass and other herbaceous plants Broadleaf deciduous, shrubform, minimum height 3 feet, growth singly or in groups or patches
GSp		Grass and other herbaceous plants Semideciduous: broadleaf evergreen and broadleaf deciduous trees, growth singly or in groups or patches
L		Herbaceous plants other than grass
M		Mixed: broadleaf deciduous and needleleaf evergreen trees
N		Needleleaf deciduous trees
ND		Needleleaf deciduous trees Broadleaf deciduous trees

S		Semideciduous: broadleaf evergreen and broadleaf deciduous trees
Ss		Semideciduous: broadleaf evergreen and broadleaf deciduous, shrubform, minimum height 3 feet
SsG		Semideciduous: broadleaf evergreen and broadleaf deciduous, shrubform, minimum height 3 feet Grass and other herbaceous plants
Szp		Semideciduous: broadleaf evergreen and broadleaf deciduous, dwarf shrubform, maximum height 3 feet, growth singly or in groups or patches
SE		Semideciduous: broadleaf evergreen and broadleaf deciduous trees Needleleaf evergreen trees
b		Vegetation largely or entirely absent

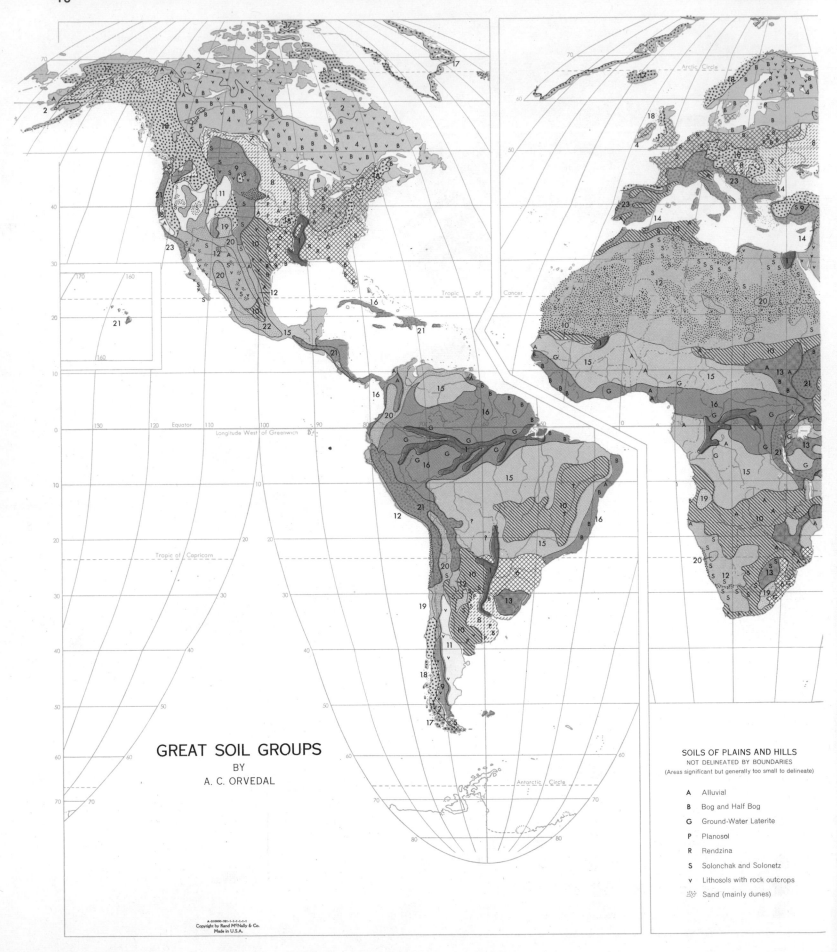

GREAT SOIL GROUPS
BY
A. C. ORVEDAL

SOILS OF PLAINS AND HILLS
NOT DELINEATED BY BOUNDARIES
(Areas significant but generally too small to delineate)

A	Alluvial
B	Bog and Half Bog
G	Ground-Water Laterite
P	Planosol
R	Rendzina
S	Solonchak and Solonetz
v	Lithosols with rock outcrops
░	Sand (mainly dunes)

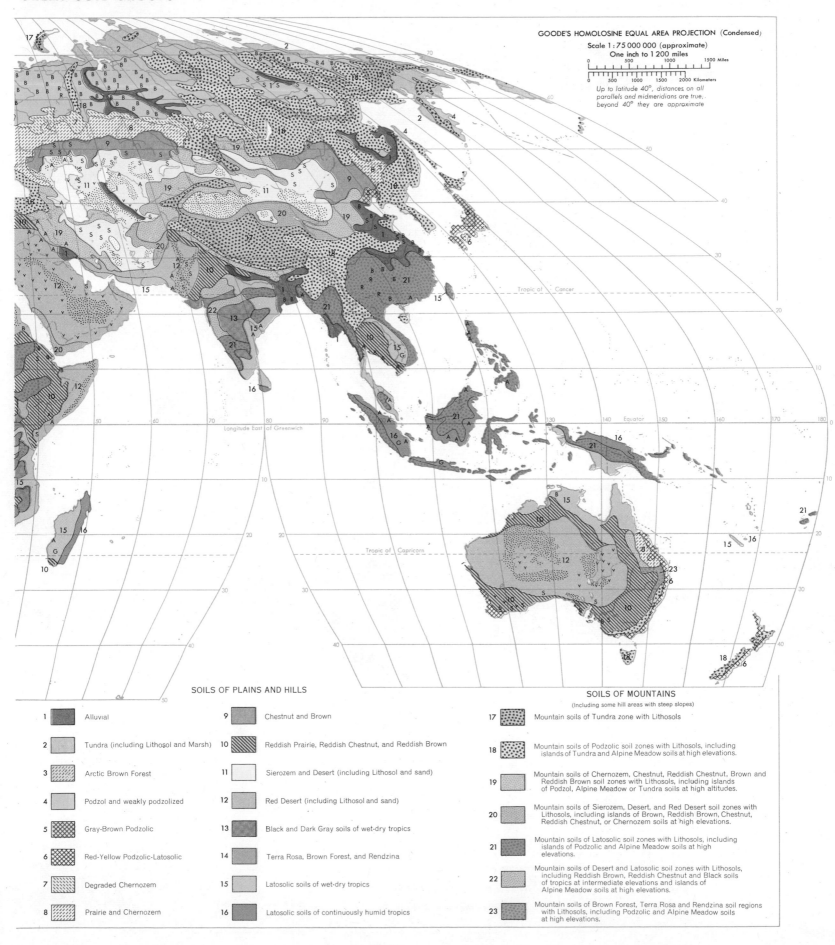

GOODE'S HOMOLOSINE EQUAL AREA PROJECTION (Condensed)

Scale 1 : 75 000 000 (approximate)

One inch to 1 200 miles

Up to latitude 40°, distances on all
parallels and midmeridians are true,
beyond 40° they are approximate

SOILS OF PLAINS AND HILLS

1   Alluvial

2   Tundra (including Lithosol and Marsh)

3   Arctic Brown Forest

4   Podzol and weakly podzolized

5   Gray-Brown Podzolic

6   Red-Yellow Podzolic-Latosolic

7   Degraded Chernozem

8   Prairie and Chernozem

9   Chestnut and Brown

10   Reddish Prairie, Reddish Chestnut, and Reddish Brown

11   Sierozem and Desert (including Lithosol and sand)

12   Red Desert (including Lithosol and sand)

13   Black and Dark Gray soils of wet-dry tropics

14   Terra Rosa, Brown Forest, and Rendzina

15   Latosolic soils of wet-dry tropics

16   Latosolic soils of continuously humid tropics

SOILS OF MOUNTAINS

(Including some hill areas with steep slopes)

17   Mountain soils of Tundra zone with Lithosols

18   Mountain soils of Podzolic soil zones with Lithosols, including islands of Tundra and Alpine Meadow soils at high elevations.

19   Mountain soils of Chernozem, Chestnut, Reddish Chestnut, Brown and Reddish Brown soil zones with Lithosols, including islands of Podzol, Alpine Meadow or Tundra soils at high altitudes.

20   Mountain soils of Sierozem, Desert, and Red Desert soil zones with Lithosols, including islands of Brown, Reddish Brown, Chestnut, Reddish Chestnut, or Chernozem soils at high elevations.

21   Mountain soils of Latosolic soil zones with Lithosols, including islands of Podzolic and Alpine Meadow soils at high elevations.

22   Mountain soils of Desert and Latosolic soil zones with Lithosols, including Reddish Brown, Reddish Chestnut and Black soils of tropics at intermediate elevations and islands of Alpine Meadow soils at high elevations.

23   Mountain soils of Brown Forest, Terra Rosa and Rendzina soil regions with Lithosols, including Podzolic and Alpine Meadow soils at high elevations.

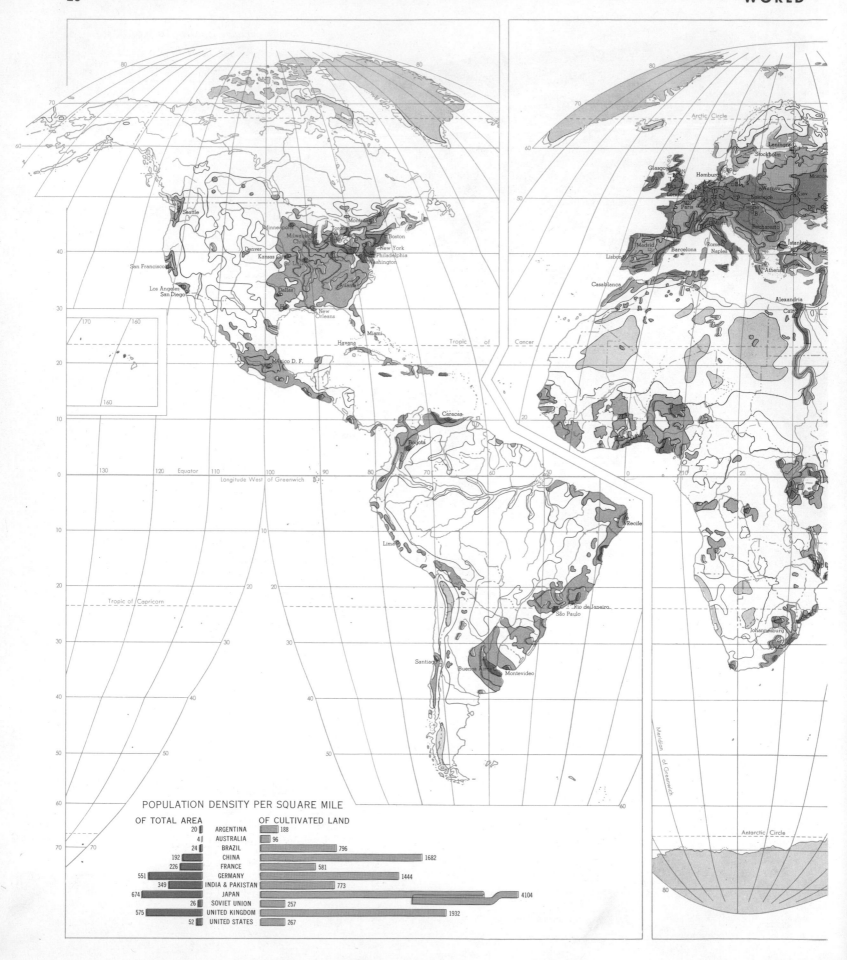

POPULATION DENSITY PER SQUARE MILE

OF TOTAL AREA			OF CULTIVATED LAND		
20		ARGENTINA		188	
4		AUSTRALIA		96	
24		BRAZIL		796	
192		CHINA		1682	
226		FRANCE		581	
551		GERMANY		1444	
349		INDIA & PAKISTAN		773	
674		JAPAN		4104	
26		SOVIET UNION		257	
575		UNITED KINGDOM		1932	
52		UNITED STATES		267	

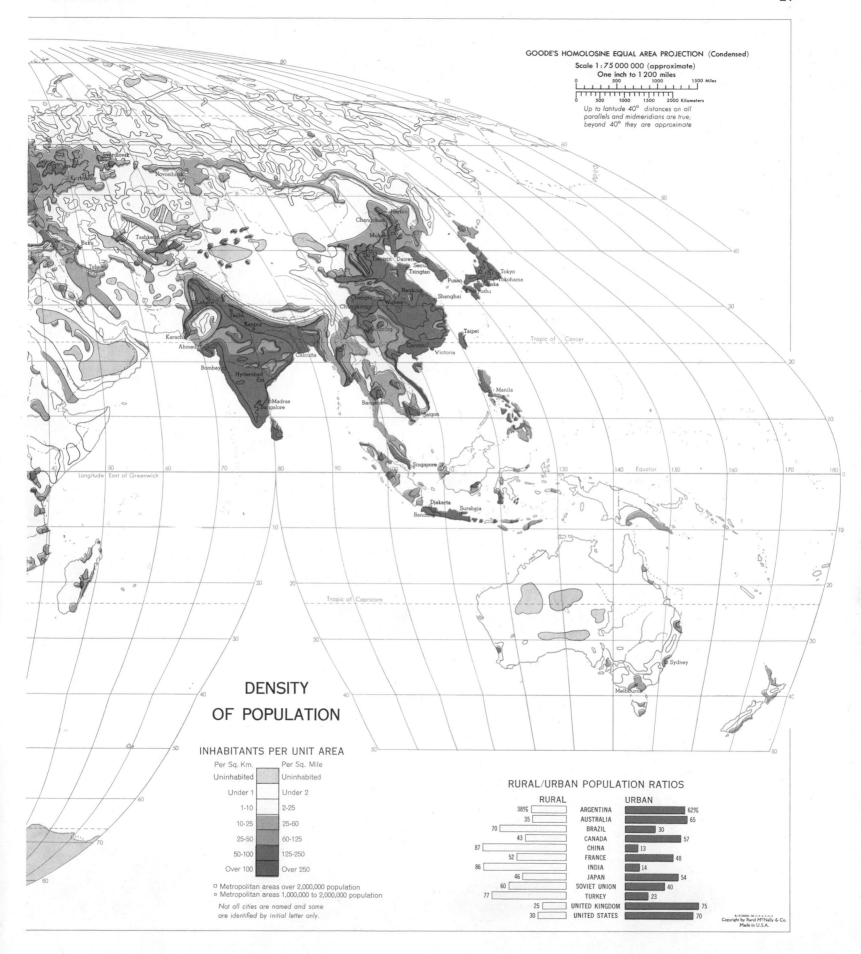

GOODE'S HOMOLOSINE EQUAL AREA PROJECTION (Condensed)
Scale 1 : 75 000 000 (approximate)
One inch to 1 200 miles

Up to latitude 40° distances on all
parallels and midmeridians are true;
beyond 40° they are approximate

DENSITY
OF POPULATION

INHABITANTS PER UNIT AREA

Per Sq. Km.	Per Sq. Mile
Uninhabited	Uninhabited
Under 1	Under 2
1-10	2-25
10-25	25-60
25-50	60-125
50-100	125-250
Over 100	Over 250

□ Metropolitan areas over 2,000,000 population
○ Metropolitan areas 1,000,000 to 2,000,000 population

Not all cities are named and some
are identified by initial letter only.

RURAL/URBAN POPULATION RATIOS

RURAL		URBAN
38%	ARGENTINA	62%
35	AUSTRALIA	65
70	BRAZIL	30
43	CANADA	57
87	CHINA	13
52	FRANCE	48
86	INDIA	14
46	JAPAN	54
60	SOVIET UNION	40
77	TURKEY	23
25	UNITED KINGDOM	75
30	UNITED STATES	70

A-510000-16-1-1-1-1-1
Copyright by Rand McNally & Co.
Made in U.S.A.

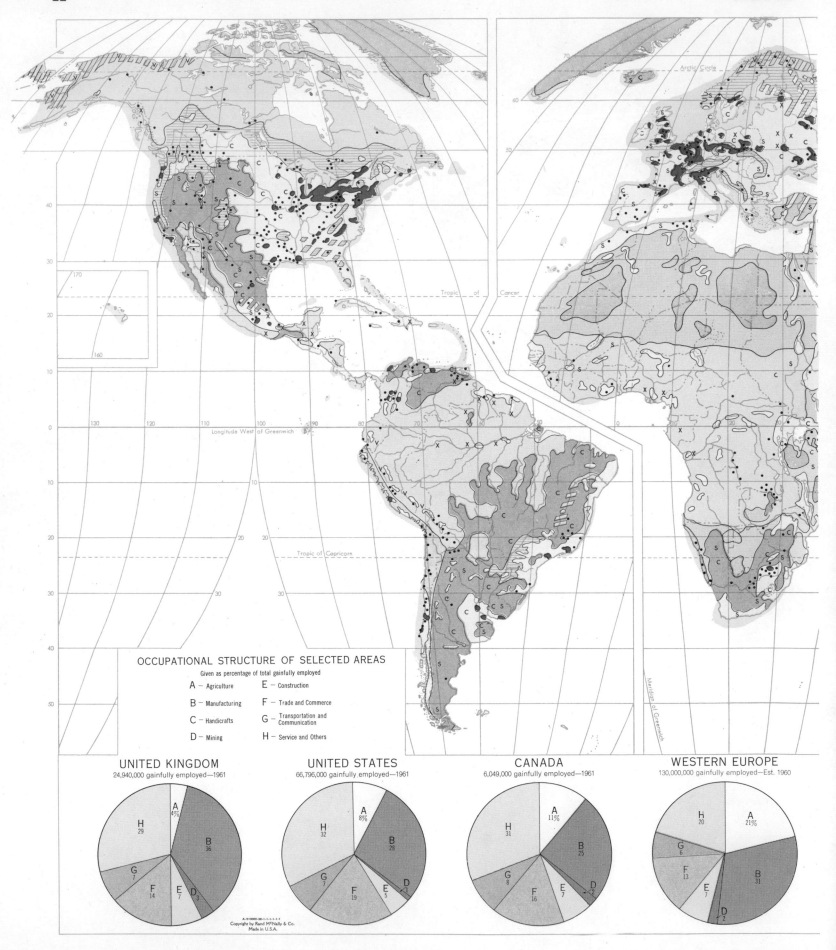

OCCUPATIONAL STRUCTURE OF SELECTED AREAS

Given as percentage of total gainfully employed

A — Agriculture   E — Construction

B — Manufacturing   F — Trade and Commerce

C — Handicrafts   G — Transportation and
                           Communication

D — Mining   H — Service and Others

UNITED KINGDOM
24,940,000 gainfully employed—1961

UNITED STATES
66,796,000 gainfully employed—1961

CANADA
6,049,000 gainfully employed—1961

WESTERN EUROPE
130,000,000 gainfully employed—Est. 1960

UNITED KINGDOM pie: A 4%, B 36, D 3, E 7, F 14, G 7, H 29

UNITED STATES pie: A 8%, B 28, D 1, E 5, F 19, G 7, H 32

CANADA pie: A 11%, B 25, D 2, E 7, F 16, G 8, H 31

WESTERN EUROPE pie: A 21%, B 31, D 2, E 7, F 13, G 6, H 20

A-510000-36-1-1-1-1-1
Copyright by Rand M°Nally & Co.
Made in U.S.A.

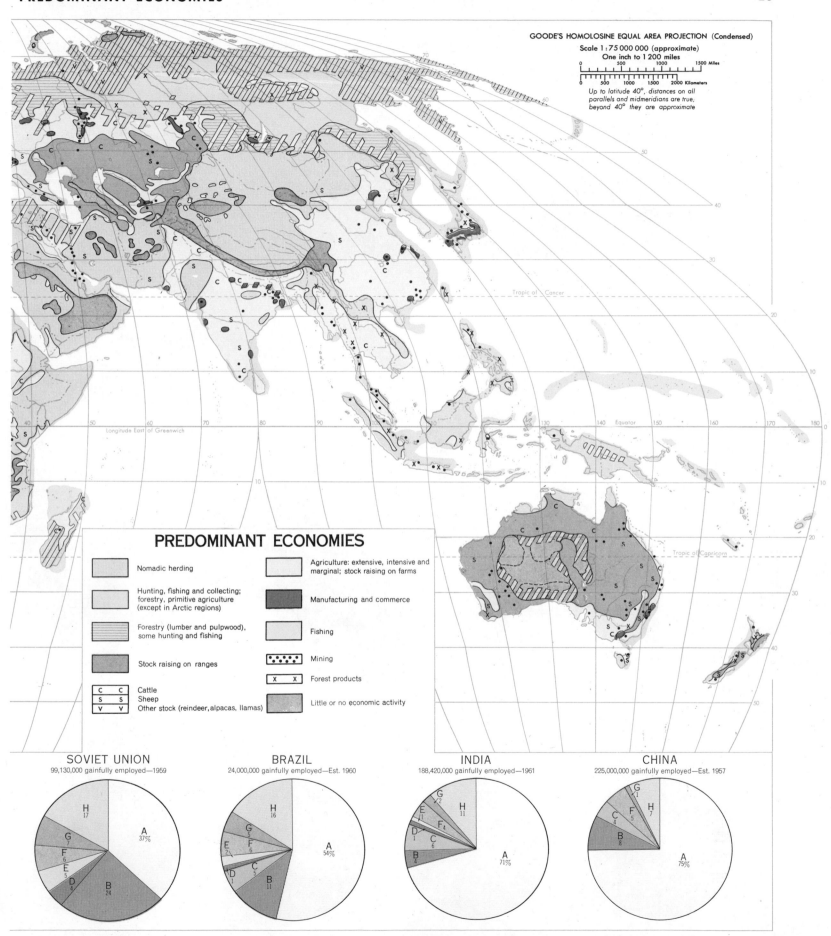

GOODE'S HOMOLOSINE EQUAL AREA PROJECTION (Condensed)
Scale 1:75 000 000 (approximate)
One inch to 1 200 miles

*Up to latitude 40°, distances on all
parallels and midmeridians are true;
beyond 40° they are approximate*

PREDOMINANT ECONOMIES

Nomadic herding

Hunting, fishing and collecting;
forestry, primitive agriculture
(except in Arctic regions)

Forestry (lumber and pulpwood),
some hunting and fishing

Stock raising on ranges

C	C	Cattle
S	S	Sheep
V	V	Other stock (reindeer, alpacas, llamas)

Agriculture: extensive, intensive and
marginal; stock raising on farms

Manufacturing and commerce

Fishing

Mining

Forest products

Little or no economic activity

SOVIET UNION
99,130,000 gainfully employed—1959

H 17 · A 37% · G 7 · F 6 · E 5 · D 4 · B 24

BRAZIL
24,000,000 gainfully employed—Est. 1960

H 16 · A 54% · G 5 · F 6 · E 2 · D 1 · C 5 · B 11

INDIA
188,420,000 gainfully employed—1961

G 2 · H 11 · A 71% · E 1 · F 4 · D 1 · C 6 · B 4

CHINA
225,000,000 gainfully employed—Est. 1957

G 1 · H 7 · F 5 · A 75% · C 4 · B 8

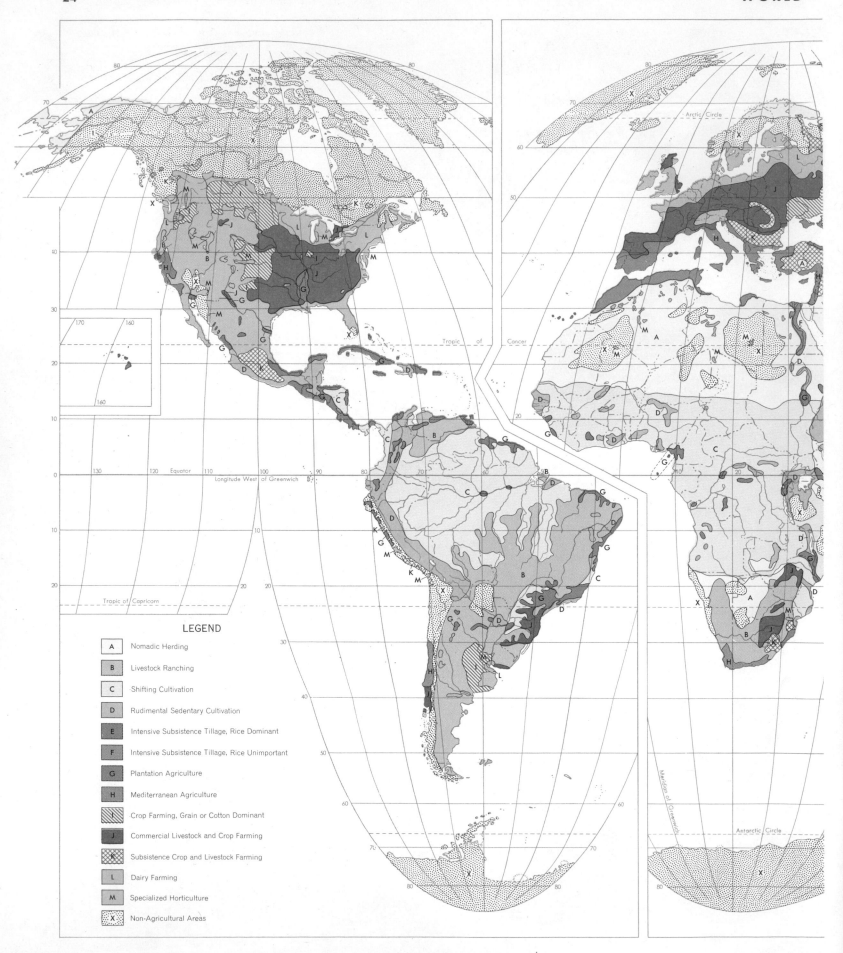

LEGEND

A	Nomadic Herding
B	Livestock Ranching
C	Shifting Cultivation
D	Rudimental Sedentary Cultivation
E	Intensive Subsistence Tillage, Rice Dominant
F	Intensive Subsistence Tillage, Rice Unimportant
G	Plantation Agriculture
H	Mediterranean Agriculture
I	Crop Farming, Grain or Cotton Dominant
J	Commercial Livestock and Crop Farming
K	Subsistence Crop and Livestock Farming
L	Dairy Farming
M	Specialized Horticulture
X	Non-Agricultural Areas

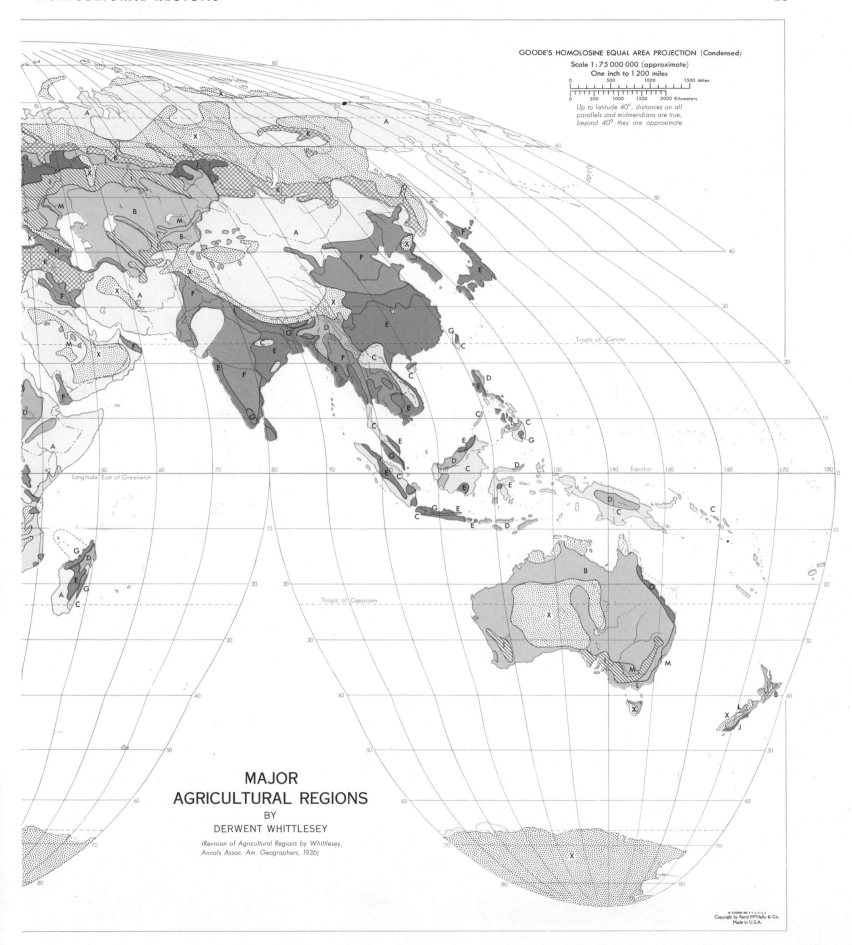

GOODE'S HOMOLOSINE EQUAL AREA PROJECTION (Condensed)
Scale 1 : 75 000 000 (approximate)
One inch to 1 200 miles

*Up to latitude 40°, distances on all
parallels and midmeridians are true;
beyond 40° they are approximate*

MAJOR
AGRICULTURAL REGIONS
BY
DERWENT WHITTLESEY

*(Revision of Agricultural Regions by Whittlesey,
Annals Assoc. Am. Geographers, 1936)*

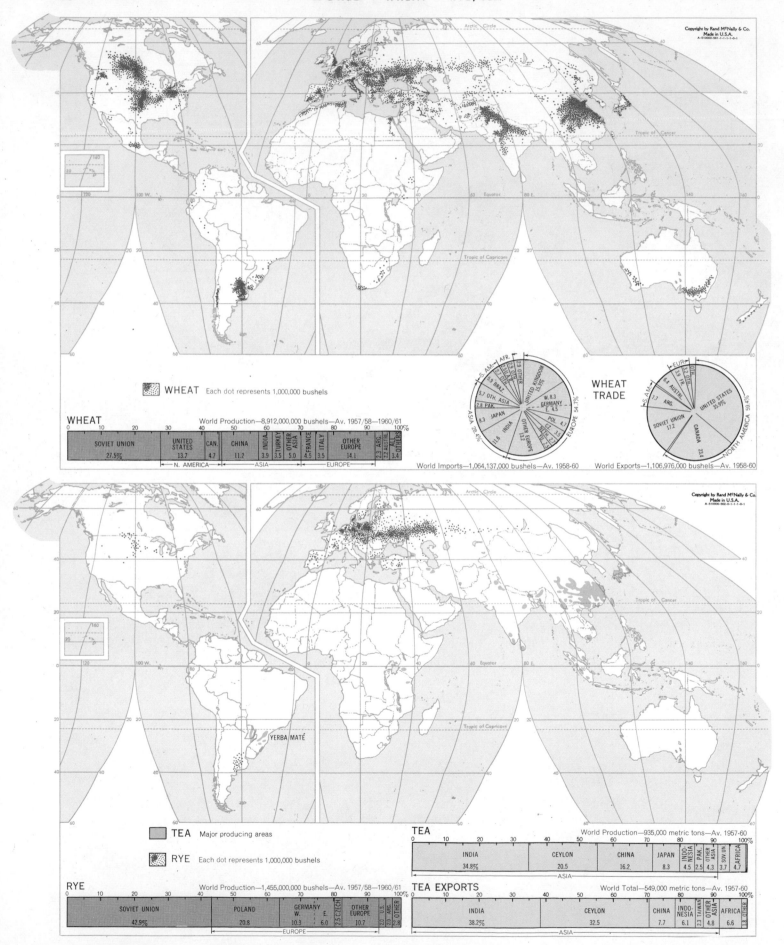

WHEAT   Each dot represents 1,000,000 bushels

WHEAT TRADE

WHEAT
World Production—8,912,000,000 bushels—Av. 1957/58—1960/61

| SOVIET UNION 27.5% | UNITED STATES 13.7 | CAN. 4.7 | CHINA 11.2 | INDIA 3.9 | TURKEY 3.5 | OTHER ASIA 5.0 | FRANCE 4.5 | ITALY | OTHER EUROPE 14.1 | 2.3 ARG. | 2.2 AUSTRL. | ALL OTHERS 3.4 |

N. AMERICA   ASIA   EUROPE

World Imports—1,064,137,000 bushels—Av. 1958-60   World Exports—1,106,976,000 bushels—Av. 1958-60

YERBA MATÉ

TEA   Major producing areas

RYE   Each dot represents 1,000,000 bushels

TEA
World Production—935,000 metric tons—Av. 1957-60

| INDIA 34.8% | CEYLON 20.5 | CHINA 16.2 | JAPAN 8.3 | INDO-NESIA 4.5 | OTHER ASIA 2.5 | PAK. 4.3 | SOV UN 3.7 | AFRICA 4.7 |

ASIA

RYE
World Production—1,455,000,000 bushels—Av. 1957/58—1960/61

| SOVIET UNION 42.9% | POLAND 20.8 | GERMANY W. 10.3 | E. 6.0 | CZECH 2.5 | OTHER EUROPE 10.7 | 2.3 U.S. | ARG. | OTHER 2.8 |

EUROPE

TEA EXPORTS
World Total—549,000 metric tons—Av. 1957-60

| INDIA 38.2% | CEYLON 32.5 | CHINA 7.7 | INDO-NESIA 6.1 | TAIWAN 2.3 | OTHER ASIA 4.8 | AFRICA 6.6 | OTHER 1.8 |

ASIA

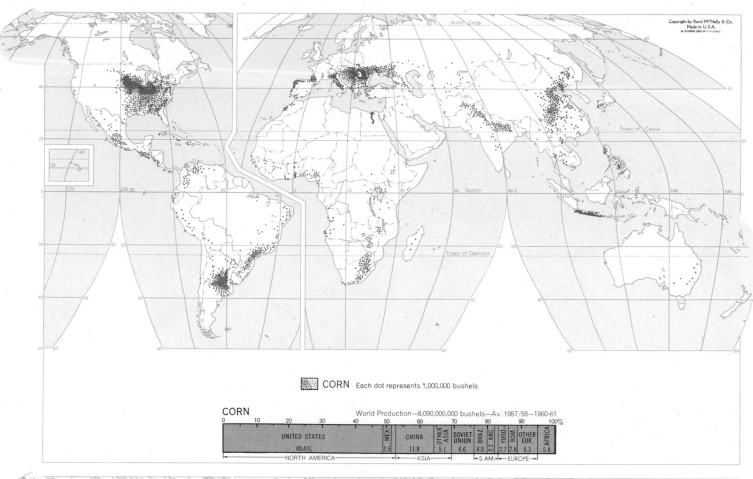

CORN Each dot represents 1,000,000 bushels

CORN World Production—8,090,000,000 bushels—Av. 1957/58—1960-61

0	10	20	30	40	50	60	70	80	90	100%

UNITED STATES 48.4%	MEX. 2.5	CHINA 11.8	OTHER ASIA 5.1	SOVIET UNION 6.6	BRAZ. 4.0	ARG. 2.3	YUGO- 2.7	ROM. 2.6	OTHER EUR. 6.3	AFRICA 5.4

← NORTH AMERICA → ← ASIA → ←S.AM.→ ←EUROPE→

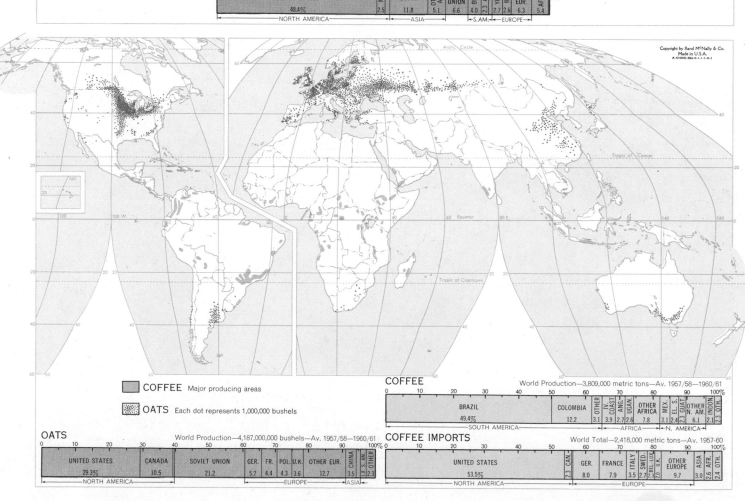

COFFEE Major producing areas

OATS Each dot represents 1,000,000 bushels

COFFEE World Production—3,809,000 metric tons—Av. 1957/58—1960/61

BRAZIL 49.4%	COLOMBIA 12.2	OTHER 3.1	IV. COAST 3.9	ANG. 2.7	UGAN. 2.6	OTHER AFRICA 7.8	MEX. 3.1	EL. S. 2.4	GUAT. 2.3	OTHER N. AM. 6.1	INDON. 2.3	OTH.

←SOUTH AMERICA→ ←AFRICA→ ←N. AMERICA→

OATS World Production—4,187,000,000 bushels—Av. 1957/58—1960/61

UNITED STATES 29.3%	CANADA 10.5	SOVIET UNION 21.2	GER. 5.2	FR. 4.4	POL. 4.3	U.K. 3.6	OTHER EUR. 12.7	CHINA 3.5	S.AM 1.8	OTHER 2.3

←NORTH AMERICA→ ←EUROPE→ ←ASIA→

COFFEE IMPORTS World Total—2,418,000 metric tons—Av. 1957-60

UNITED STATES 53.5%	CAN 2.3	GER. 8.0	FRANCE 7.9	ITALY 3.5	SWED. 2.7	BEL. 2.0	U.K. 1.9	OTHER EUROPE 9.7	ASIA 3.0	AFR. 2.6	OTH. 2.4

←NORTH AMERICA→ ←EUROPE→

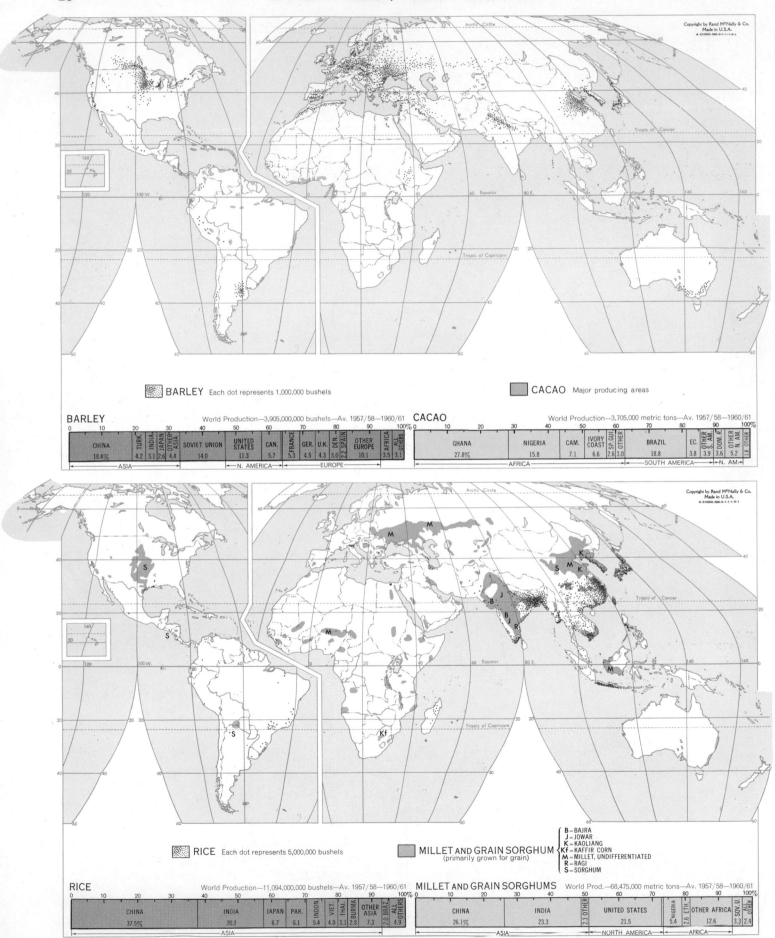

Copyright by Rand McNally & Co.
Made in U.S.A.
A-510000-565-0-1-1-0-1

▦ BARLEY Each dot represents 1,000,000 bushels

▨ CACAO Major producing areas

BARLEY   World Production—3,905,000,000 bushels—Av. 1957/58—1960/61

0	10	20	30	40	50	60	70	80	90	100%
CHINA 18.4%		TURK. 4.2	INDIA 3.1	JAPAN 2.6	OTHER ASIA 4.4	SOVIET UNION 14.0	UNITED STATES 11.3	CAN. 5.7	FRANCE 5.3 / GER. 4.5 / U.K. 4.3 / DEN. 3.0 / SPAIN 2.2	OTHER EUROPE 10.1 / AFRICA 3.5 / ALL OTHERS 3.1

← ASIA → ← N. AMERICA → ← EUROPE →

CACAO   World Production—3,705,000 metric tons—Av. 1957/58—1960/61

0	10	20	30	40	50	60	70	80	90	100%
GHANA 27.8%		NIGERIA 15.8	CAM. 7.1	IVORY COAST 6.6	SP. GUI. 2.6 / OTHER 3.0	BRAZIL 18.8	EC. 3.8	OTHER S. AM. 3.9	DOM. R. 3.6	OTHER N. AM. 5.2 / OTHER 1.8

← AFRICA → ← SOUTH AMERICA → ← N. AM. →

Copyright by Rand McNally & Co.
Made in U.S.A.
A-510000-566-0-1-1-1-0-1

▦ RICE Each dot represents 5,000,000 bushels

▨ MILLET AND GRAIN SORGHUM
(primarily grown for grain)

B = BAJRA
J = JOWAR
K = KAOLIANG
Kf = KAFFIR CORN
M = MILLET, UNDIFFERENTIATED
R = RAGI
S = SORGHUM

RICE   World Production—11,094,000,000 bushels—Av. 1957/58—1960/61

0	10	20	30	40	50	60	70	80	90	100%
CHINA 37.5%		INDIA 20.2	JAPAN 6.7	PAK. 6.1	INDON. 5.4 / VIET. 4.0 / THAI. 3.1 / BURMA 2.8	OTHER ASIA 7.3	BRAZ. 2.0	ALL OTHERS 4.9

← ASIA →

MILLET AND GRAIN SORGHUMS   World Prod.—68,475,000 metric tons—Av. 1957/58—1960/61

0	10	20	30	40	50	60	70	80	90	100%
CHINA 26.1%		INDIA 23.3	OTHER 2.3	UNITED STATES 21.5	NIGERIA 5.4	ETH. 2.6	OTHER AFRICA 12.6	SOV. U. 3.3 / ALL OTHER 2.4

← ASIA → ← NORTH AMERICA → ← AFRICA →

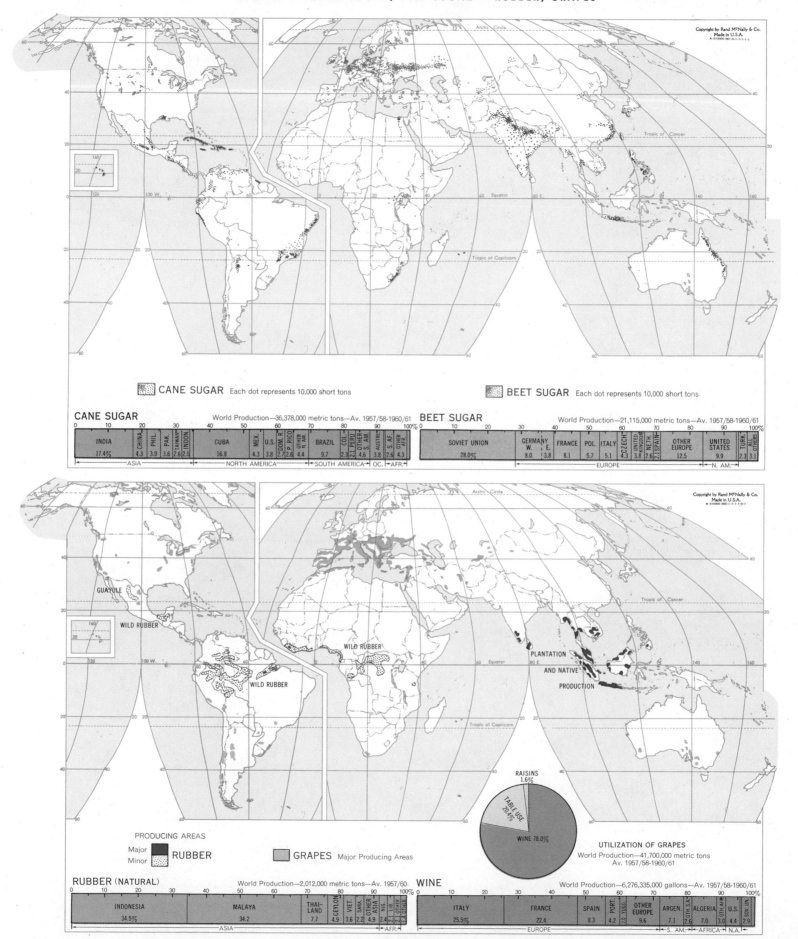

Copyright by Rand McNally & Co.
Made in U.S.A.
A-510000-987-0-1-1-1-1-1

⬛ CANE SUGAR Each dot represents 10,000 short tons

🟫 BEET SUGAR Each dot represents 10,000 short tons

CANE SUGAR   World Production—36,378,000 metric tons—Av. 1957/58-1960/61

	0	10	20	30	40	50	60	70	80	90	100%

| INDIA 17.4% | CHINA 4.3 | PHIL. 3.9 | PAK. 3.6 | TAIWAN 2.6 | INDON. 2.5 | CUBA 16.8 | MEX. 4.3 | U.S. 3.8 | DOM.R. 2.7 | P. RICO 2.6 | OTHER N. AM. 4.4 | BRAZIL 9.7 | COL. 2.3 | PERU 2.1 | OTHER S. AM. 4.6 | AUSTR. 3.8 | S. AF. 2.6 | OTHER AFR. 4.3 |

— ASIA — — NORTH AMERICA — — SOUTH AMERICA — OC. AFR.

BEET SUGAR   World Production—21,115,000 metric tons—Av. 1957/58-1960/61

	0	10	20	30	40	50	60	70	80	90	100%

| SOVIET UNION 28.0% | GERMANY W. 8.0 E. 3.8 | FRANCE 8.1 | POL. 5.7 | ITALY 5.1 | CZECH. 4.3 | UNITED KINGDOM 3.8 | NETH. 2.6 | SPAIN 2.1 | OTHER EUROPE 12.5 | UNITED STATES 9.9 | TURK. 2.3 | OTHERS 3.1 |

— EUROPE — — N. AM. —

GUAYULE
WILD RUBBER
WILD RUBBER
WILD RUBBER
WILD RUBBER
PLANTATION
AND NATIVE
PRODUCTION

Copyright by Rand McNally & Co.
Made in U.S.A.
A-510000-988-1-1-1-1-0-1

PRODUCING AREAS
Major ⬛
Minor ⬛ RUBBER

🟩 GRAPES Major Producing Areas

RAISINS 1.6%
TABLE USE 20.4%
WINE 78.0%

UTILIZATION OF GRAPES
World Production—41,700,000 metric tons
Av. 1957/58-1960/61

RUBBER (NATURAL)   World Production—2,012,000 metric tons—Av. 1957/60

	0	10	20	30	40	50	60	70	80	90	100%

| INDONESIA 34.5% | MALAYA 34.2 | THAILAND 7.7 | CEYLON 4.9 | VIET. 3.6 | SARA. 2.2 | OTHER ASIA 4.9 | NIG. 2.1 | LIB. 2.2 | OTHER 1.7 |

— ASIA — AFR.

WINE   World Production—6,276,335,000 gallons—Av. 1957/58-1960/61

	0	10	20	30	40	50	60	70	80	90	100%

| ITALY 25.5% | FRANCE 22.4 | SPAIN 8.3 | PORT. 4.2 | YUGO. 2.0 | OTHER EUROPE 9.6 | ARGEN. 7.1 | OTH. S.AM. 2.6 | ALGERIA 7.0 | OTH. AFR. 3.0 | U.S. 4.4 | SOV. UN. 2.9 |

— EUROPE — — S. AM. — — AFRICA — N.A.

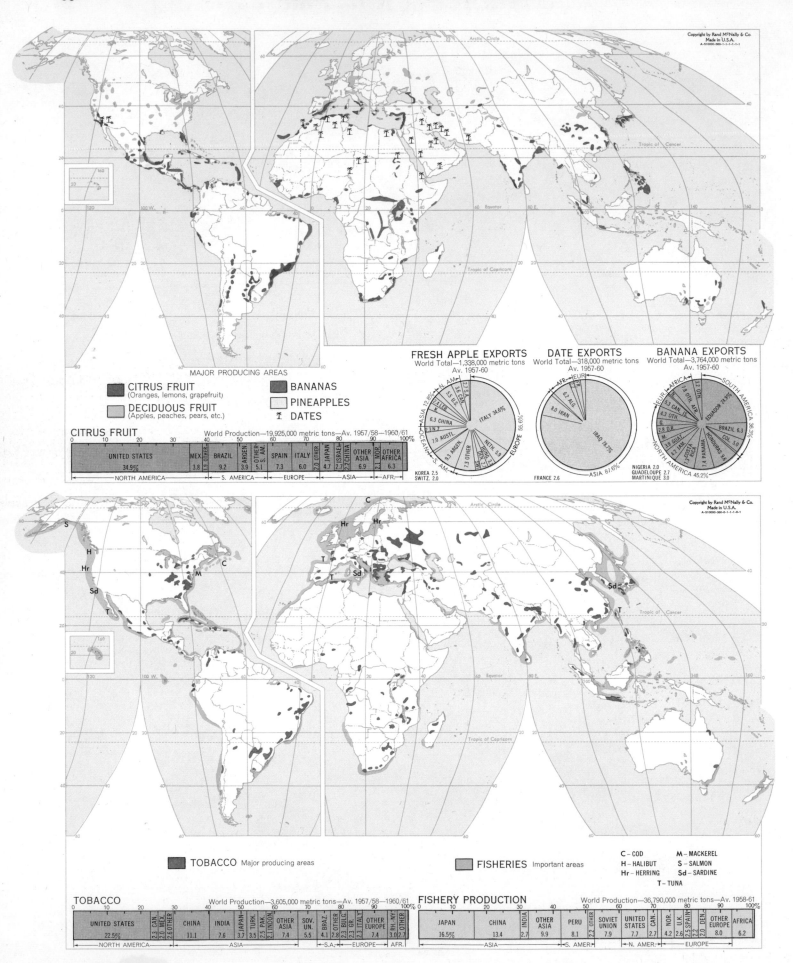

Copyright by Rand McNally & Co.
Made in U.S.A.

MAJOR PRODUCING AREAS

CITRUS FRUIT (Oranges, lemons, grapefruit)

DECIDUOUS FRUIT (Apples, peaches, pears, etc.)

BANANAS

PINEAPPLES

☨ **DATES**

FRESH APPLE EXPORTS
World Total—1,338,000 metric tons
Av. 1957-60

N. AM. 12.9% · 2.7 ALB. · 3.6 GER. · 5.5 U.S. · 2.1 LEB. · 6.3 CHINA · 2.3 N Z · 7.0 AUSTL. · 9.3 OTHER · 7.3 Other · ITALY 34.6% · NETH. 5.9 · EUROPE 55.6% · S. AM. · KOREA 2.5 · SWITZ. 2.0

DATE EXPORTS
World Total—318,000 metric tons
Av. 1957-60

AFR. · FR. · EUR · 6.2 ALG. · 8.0 IRAN · IRAQ 78.7% · ASIA 81.6% · FRANCE 2.6

BANANA EXPORTS
World Total—3,764,000 metric tons
Av. 1957-60

EUR. · AFRICA · 7.8 OTH. · 3.2 OTH. · SOUTH AMERICA · 5.3 CAN. IS. · 4.3 OTH. · 2.8 D.R. · 2.0 · G. · ECUADOR 24.9% · BRAZIL 6.3 · COL. 5.0 · 3.9 GUAT. · 4.2 COSTA RICA · HONDURAS 9.6 · 7.4 PANAMA · SOUTH AMERICA 38.3% · NORTH AMERICA 45.2% · NIGERIA 2.0 · GUADELOUPE 2.7 · MARTINIQUE 3.0

CITRUS FRUIT
World Production—19,925,000 metric tons—Av. 1957/58—1960/61

0	10	20	30	40	50	60	70	80	90	100%

| UNITED STATES 34.9% | MEX. 3.8 | OTHER 1.9 | BRAZIL 9.2 | ARGEN. 3.9 | OTHER S. AM. 5.1 | SPAIN 7.3 | ITALY 6.0 | OTHER 2.0 | JAPAN 4.7 | ISRAEL 2.7 | CHINA 2.2 | OTHER ASIA 6.9 | MOR. 2.1 | OTHER AFRICA 6.3 |

NORTH AMERICA — S. AMERICA — EUROPE — ASIA — AFR.

TOBACCO Major producing areas

FISHERIES Important areas

C – COD   M – MACKEREL
H – HALIBUT   S – SALMON
Hr – HERRING   Sd – SARDINE
T – TUNA

TOBACCO
World Production—3,605,000 metric tons—Av. 1957/58—1960/61

0	10	20	30	40	50	60	70	80	90	100%

| UNITED STATES 22.5% | CAN. 2.3 | MEX. 2.0 | OTHER 2.6 | CHINA 11.1 | INDIA 7.6 | JAPAN 3.7 | TURK. 3.5 | PAK. 2.5 | INDON. 2.1 | OTHER ASIA 7.4 | SOV. UN. 5.5 | BRAZ. 4.1 | OTHER 2.8 | BULG. 2.3 | GR. 2.3 | ITALY 2.3 | OTHER EUROPE 7.4 | RH. NY. 3.0 | OTHER 2.7 |

NORTH AMERICA — ASIA — S.A. — EUROPE — AFR.

FISHERY PRODUCTION
World Production—36,790,000 metric tons—Av. 1958-61

0	10	20	30	40	50	60	70	80	90	100%

| JAPAN 16.5% | CHINA 13.4 | INDIA 2.7 | OTHER ASIA 9.9 | PERU 8.1 | OTHER 2.2 | SOVIET UNION 7.9 | UNITED STATES 7.7 | CAN. 2.7 | NOR. 4.2 | U.K. 2.6 | SPAIN 2.5 | DEN. 2.2 | OTHER EUROPE 8.0 | AFRICA 6.2 |

ASIA — S. AMER. — N. AMER. — EUROPE

Copyright by Rand McNally & Co.
Made in U.S.A.

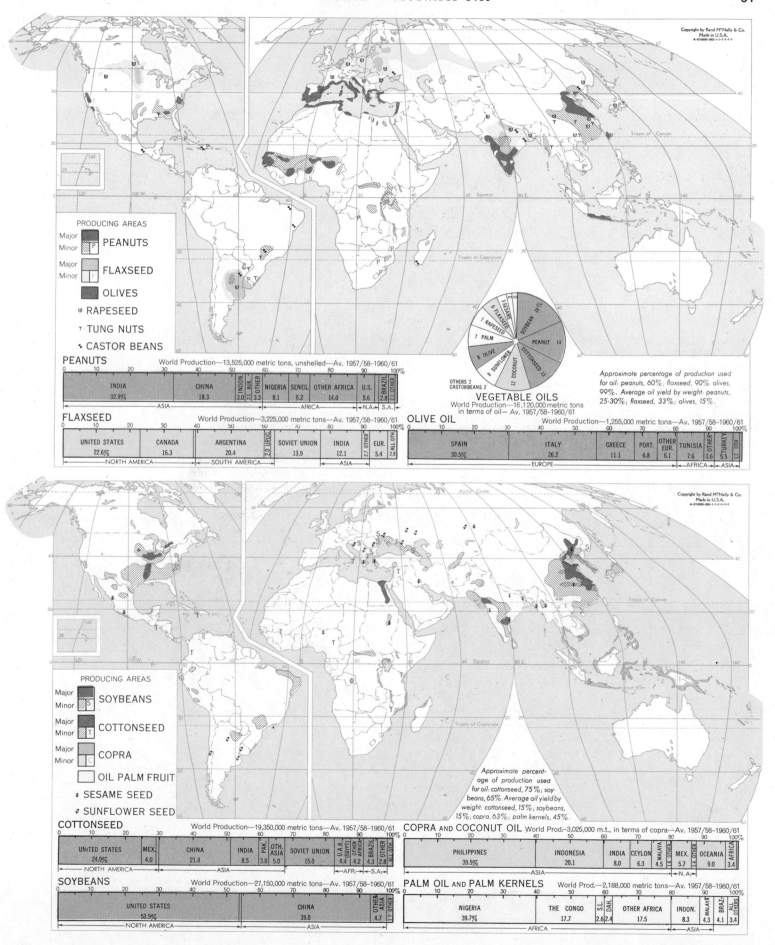

PRODUCING AREAS

- Major / Minor — P — PEANUTS
- Major / Minor — F — FLAXSEED
- OLIVES
- ш RAPESEED
- T TUNG NUTS
- ⸱ CASTOR BEANS

VEGETABLE OILS

World Production—16,120,000 metric tons
in terms of oil— Av. 1957/58–1960/61

Pie chart: SOYBEAN 15%, PEANUT 14, COTTONSEED 13, COCONUT 12, SUNFLOWER, OLIVE 8, PALM 7, RAPESEED 7, FLAXSEED 6, SESAME 3, C, OTHERS 2, CASTORBEANS 2

Approximate percentage of production used for oil: peanuts, 60%; flaxseed, 90% olives, 99%. Average oil yield by weight: peanuts, 25-30%; flaxseed, 33%; olives, 15%.

PEANUTS
World Production—13,525,000 metric tons, unshelled—Av. 1957/58–1960/61

INDIA 32.9%	CHINA 18.3	INDON. 3.0	BUR. 2.1	OTHER 3.3	NIGERIA 8.1	SENEG. 6.2	OTHER AFRICA 14.0	U.S. 5.6	BRAZIL 2.8	OTHER 2.1
ASIA					AFRICA			N.A.	S.A.	

FLAXSEED
World Production—3,225,000 metric tons—Av. 1957/58–1960/61

UNITED STATES 22.6%	CANADA 16.3	ARGENTINA 20.4	URUG. 2.0	SOVIET UNION 13.9	INDIA 12.1	OTHER 2.7	EUR. 5.4	ALL OTH. 2.8
NORTH AMERICA		SOUTH AMERICA		ASIA				

OLIVE OIL
World Production—1,255,000 metric tons—Av. 1957/58–1960/61

SPAIN 30.5%	ITALY 26.2	GREECE 11.1	PORT. 6.8	OTHER EUR. 6.1	TUNISIA 7.6	OTHER 3.6	TURKEY 5.5	OTH 1.7
EUROPE					AFRICA		ASIA	

PRODUCING AREAS

- Major / Minor — S — SOYBEANS
- Major / Minor — T — COTTONSEED
- Major / Minor — C — COPRA
- OIL PALM FRUIT
- ↓ SESAME SEED
- ↷ SUNFLOWER SEED

Approximate percentage of production used for oil: cottonseed, 75%; soybeans, 65%. Average oil yield by weight: cottonseed, 15%; soybeans, 15%; copra, 63%; palm kernels, 45%.

COTTONSEED
World Production—19,350,000 metric tons—Av. 1957/58–1960/61

UNITED STATES 24.9%	MEX. 4.0	CHINA 21.4	INDIA 8.5	PAK. 3.0	OTH. ASIA 5.0	SOVIET UNION 15.0	U.A.R. (EGYPT) 4.4	OTHER AFRICA 4.2	BRAZIL 4.3	OTHER 2.8
NORTH AMERICA		ASIA					AFR.		S.A.	

COPRA AND COCONUT OIL
World Prod.—3,025,000 m.t., in terms of copra—Av. 1957/58–1960/61

PHILIPPINES 39.5%	INDONESIA 20.1	INDIA 8.0	CEYLON 6.3	MALAYA 4.5	OTHER 1.6	MEX. 5.7	OTHER 1.4	OCEANIA 9.0	AFRICA 3.4
ASIA						N.A.			

SOYBEANS
World Production—27,150,000 metric tons—Av. 1957/58–1960/61

UNITED STATES 53.9%	CHINA 39.0	OTHER ASIA 4.7	ALL OTHER 1.7
NORTH AMERICA	ASIA		

PALM OIL AND PALM KERNELS
World Prod.—2,188,000 metric tons—Av. 1957/58–1960/61

NIGERIA 39.7%	THE CONGO 17.7	S.L. 2.6	DAH. 2.4	OTHER AFRICA 17.5	INDON. 8.3	MALAYA 4.3	BRAZ. 4.1	ALL OTHERS 3.4
AFRICA					ASIA			

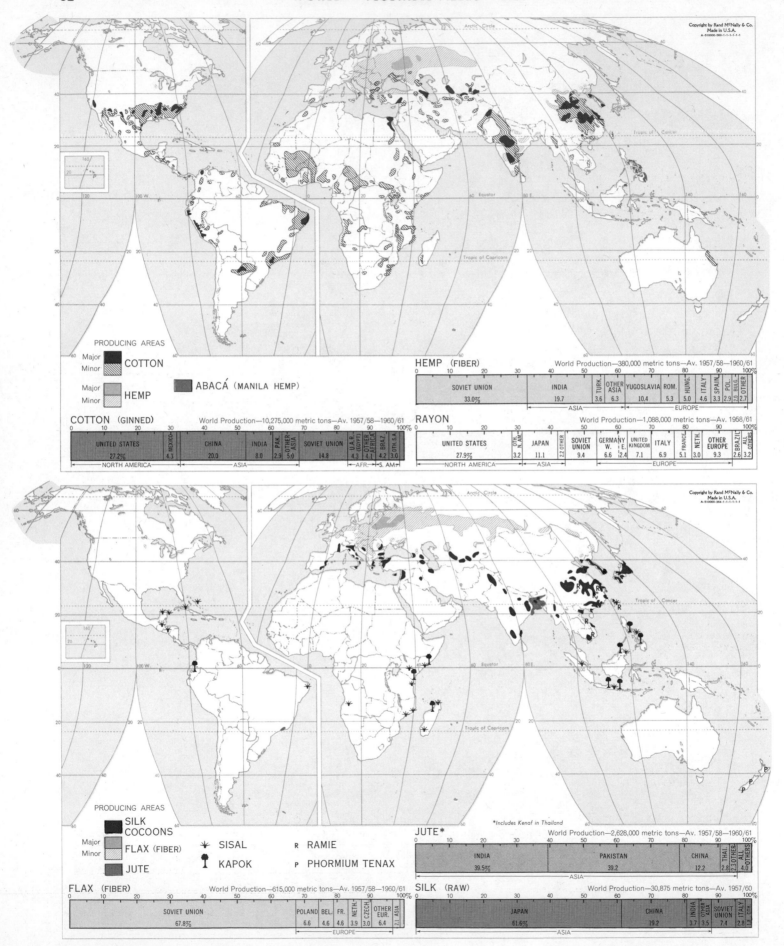

Copyright by Rand McNally & Co.
Made in U.S.A.
A-510000-560-1-1-1-1-1-1

PRODUCING AREAS

Major   ■ **COTTON**
Minor   ⬚

Major   ■ **HEMP**   ■ **ABACÁ** (MANILA HEMP)
Minor   ⬚

HEMP (FIBER)
World Production—380,000 metric tons—Av. 1957/58—1960/61

0	10	20	30	40	50	60	70	80	90	100%

| SOVIET UNION 33.0% | INDIA 19.7 | TURK. 3.6 | OTHER ASIA 6.3 | YUGOSLAVIA 10.4 | ROM. 5.3 | HUNG. 5.0 | ITALY 4.6 | SPAIN 3.3 | POL. 2.9 | BULG. 2.0 | OTHER 2.7 |

ASIA   EUROPE

COTTON (GINNED)
World Production—10,275,000 metric tons—Av. 1957/58—1960/61

0	10	20	30	40	50	60	70	80	90	100%

| UNITED STATES 27.2% | MEXICO 4.3 | CHINA 20.0 | INDIA 8.0 | PAK. 2.9 | OTHER ASIA 5.0 | SOVIET UNION 14.8 | U.A.R. (EGYPT) 4.3 | OTHER AFRICA 4.1 | BRAZ. 4.2 | OTH. S.A. 3.0 |

NORTH AMERICA   ASIA   AFR.   S. AM.

RAYON
World Production—1,088,000 metric tons—Av. 1958/61

0	10	20	30	40	50	60	70	80	90	100%

| UNITED STATES 27.9% | OTH. N. AM. 3.2 | JAPAN 11.1 | OTHER 2.2 | SOVIET UNION 9.4 | GERMANY W. E. 6.6 | UNITED KINGDOM 12.4 | ITALY 7.1 | FRANCE 6.9 | NETH. 5.1 | OTHER EUROPE 3.0 | BRAZIL 9.3 | ALL OTHERS 2.6 3.2 |

NORTH AMERICA   ASIA   EUROPE

Copyright by Rand McNally & Co.
Made in U.S.A.
A-510000-364-1-1-1-1-1-1

PRODUCING AREAS

   ■ **SILK COCOONS**

Major   ⬚ **FLAX** (FIBER)
Minor   ⬚

   ■ **JUTE**

✱ **SISAL**   **R** **RAMIE**

🌳 **KAPOK**   **P** **PHORMIUM TENAX**

*Includes Kenaf in Thailand

JUTE*
World Production—2,628,000 metric tons—Av. 1957/58—1960/61

0	10	20	30	40	50	60	70	80	90	100%

| INDIA 39.5% | PAKISTAN 39.2 | CHINA 12.2 | THAI. 2.8 | OTHER 2.3 | ALL OTHERS 4.0 |

ASIA

FLAX (FIBER)
World Production—615,000 metric tons—Av. 1957/58—1960/61

0	10	20	30	40	50	60	70	80	90	100%

| SOVIET UNION 67.8% | POLAND 6.6 | BEL. 4.6 | FR. 4.6 | NETH. 3.9 | CZECH 3.0 | OTHER EUR. 6.4 | ASIA 2.1 |

EUROPE

SILK (RAW)
World Production—30,875 metric tons—Av. 1957/60

0	10	20	30	40	50	60	70	80	90	100%

| JAPAN 61.6% | CHINA 19.2 | INDIA 3.7 | OTHER ASIA 3.5 | SOVIET UNION 7.4 | ITALY 2.8 | OTH. 1.8 |

ASIA

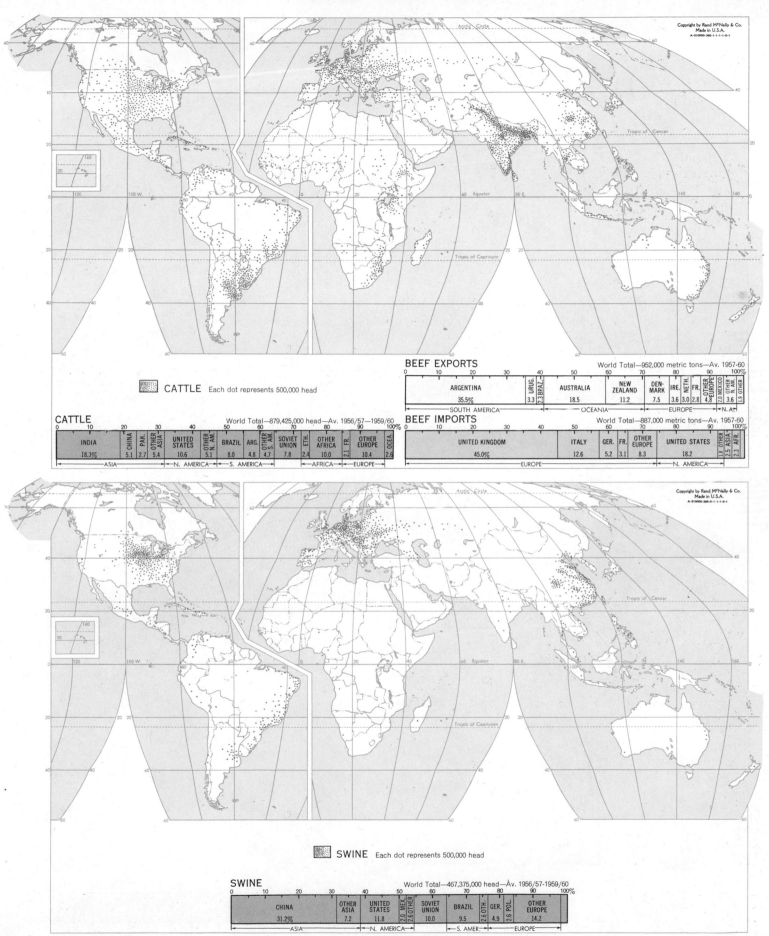

Copyright by Rand M℠Nally & Co.
Made in U.S.A.
A-510000-365-1-1-1-0-1

<table><tbody>
<tr><td>░░</td><td>**CATTLE** Each dot represents 500,000 head</td></tr>
</tbody></table>

BEEF EXPORTS
World Total—952,000 metric tons—Av. 1957-60

0	10	20	30	40	50	60	70	80	90	100%

ARGENTINA	URUG.	BRAZ.	AUSTRALIA	NEW ZEALAND	DEN-MARK	IRE.	NETH.	FR.	OTHER EUROPE	MEXICO	OTHER N. AM.	OTHER
35.5%	3.3	2.3	18.5	11.2	7.5	3.6	3.0	2.8	4.0	2.0	3.6	1.9

SOUTH AMERICA ← | → OCEANIA ← | → EUROPE ← | → N. A.

CATTLE
World Total—879,425,000 head—Av. 1956/57—1959/60

0	10	20	30	40	50	60	70	80	90	100%

INDIA	CHINA	PAK.	OTHER ASIA	UNITED STATES	OTHER N. AM.	BRAZIL	ARG.	OTHER S. AM.	SOVIET UNION	ETH.	OTHER AFRICA	FR.	OTHER EUROPE	OCEA.
18.3%	5.1	2.7	5.4	10.6	5.1	8.0	4.8	4.7	7.8	2.4	10.0	2.1	10.4	2.6

←—ASIA—→ | ←—N. AMERICA—→ | ←—S. AMERICA—→ | ←—AFRICA—→ | ←—EUROPE—→

BEEF IMPORTS
World Total—887,000 metric tons—Av. 1957-60

0	10	20	30	40	50	60	70	80	90	100%

UNITED KINGDOM	ITALY	GER.	FR.	OTHER EUROPE	UNITED STATES	OTHER N. AM.	ASIA	AFR.
45.0%	12.6	5.2	3.1	8.3	18.2	1.8	2.5	2.3

←————————EUROPE————————→ | ←—N. AMERICA—→

Copyright by Rand M℠Nally & Co.
Made in U.S.A.
A-510000-366-0-1-1-1-0-1

<table><tbody>
<tr><td>░░</td><td>**SWINE** Each dot represents 500,000 head</td></tr>
</tbody></table>

SWINE
World Total—467,375,000 head—Av. 1956/57-1959/60

0	10	20	30	40	50	60	70	80	90	100%

CHINA	OTHER ASIA	UNITED STATES	MEX.	OTHER	SOVIET UNION	BRAZIL	OTH.	GER.	POL.	OTHER EUROPE
31.2%	7.2	11.8	2.0	2.6	10.0	9.5	2.6	4.9	2.6	14.2

←——ASIA——→ | ←—N. AMERICA—→ | ←—S. AMER.—→ | ←——EUROPE——→

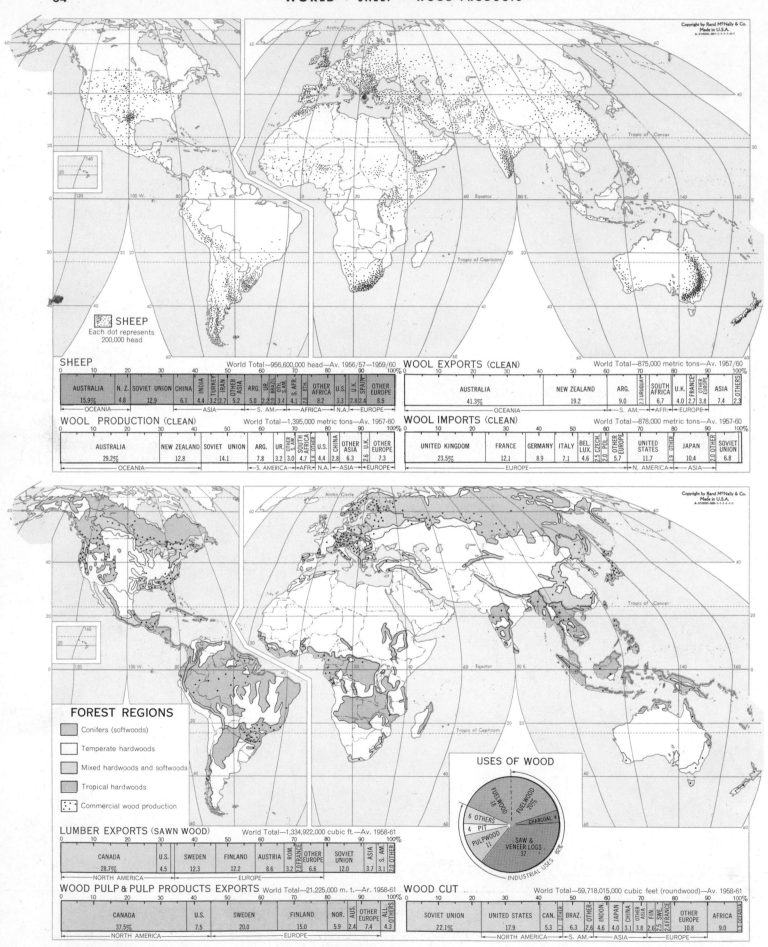

SHEEP
Each dot represents 200,000 head

SHEEP
World Total—956,600,000 head—Av. 1956/57 – 1959/60

AUSTRALIA 15.9%	N.Z. 4.8	SOVIET UNION 12.9	CHINA 6.1	INDIA 4.4	TURKEY 3.2	IRAN 2.7	OTHER ASIA 5.2	ARG. 5.2	UR. 2.2	BRAZIL 3.4	OTH. S.AM. 2.0	S. AFR. 4.1	OTH. AFRICA 8.2	N.A. 3.3	U.S. 2.8	SPAIN 2.4	OTHER EUROPE 8.5

OCEANIA — ASIA — S. AM. — AFRICA — N.A. — EUROPE

WOOL PRODUCTION (CLEAN)
World Total—1,395,000 metric tons—Av. 1957-60

AUSTRALIA 29.2%	NEW ZEALAND 12.8	SOVIET UNION 14.1	ARG. 7.8	UR. 3.2	OTHER S.AM. 3.0	SOUTH AFRICA 4.7	OTHER 4.4	U.S. 2.8	CHINA 6.3	OTHER ASIA 2.6	U.K.	OTHER EUROPE 7.3

OCEANIA — S. AMERICA — AFR. — N.A. — ASIA — EUROPE

WOOL EXPORTS (CLEAN)
World Total—875,000 metric tons—Av. 1957/60

AUSTRALIA 41.3%	NEW ZEALAND 19.2	ARG. 9.0	URUGUAY 2.3	SOUTH AFRICA 6.7	U.K. 4.0	FRANCE 2.7	OTHER EUROPE 3.8	ASIA 7.4	OTHERS 2.3

OCEANIA — S. AM. — AFR. — EUROPE

WOOL IMPORTS (CLEAN)
World Total—878,000 metric tons—Av. 1957-60

UNITED KINGDOM 23.5%	FRANCE 12.1	GERMANY 8.9	ITALY 7.1	BEL. LUX. 4.6	CZECH. 2.5	POL. 2.0	OTHER EUROPE 5.7	UNITED STATES 11.7	JAPAN 10.4	OTHER 2.0	SOVIET UNION 6.8

EUROPE — N. AMERICA — ASIA

FOREST REGIONS
- Conifers (softwoods)
- Temperate hardwoods
- Mixed hardwoods and softwoods
- Tropical hardwoods
- Commercial wood production

USES OF WOOD
- FUELWOOD 18
- FUELWOOD 20%
- CHARCOAL 4
- 6 OTHERS
- 4 PIT
- PULPWOOD 11
- SAW & VENEER LOGS 37
- INDUSTRIAL USES 62

LUMBER EXPORTS (SAWN WOOD)
World Total—1,334,922,000 cubic ft.—Av. 1958-61

CANADA 28.7%	U.S. 4.5	SWEDEN 12.3	FINLAND 12.2	AUSTRIA 8.6	ROM. 3.2	FRANCE 2.0	OTHER EUROPE 6.6	SOVIET UNION 12.0	ASIA 3.7	S. AM. 3.1	OTHER 2.0

NORTH AMERICA — EUROPE

WOOD PULP & PULP PRODUCTS EXPORTS
World Total—21,225,000 m. t.—Av. 1958-61

CANADA 37.5%	U.S. 7.5	SWEDEN 20.0	FINLAND 15.0	NOR. 5.9	AUS. 2.4	OTHER EUROPE 7.4	ALL OTHERS 4.3

NORTH AMERICA — EUROPE

WOOD CUT
World Total—59,718,015,000 cubic feet (roundwood)—Av. 1958-61

SOVIET UNION 22.1%	UNITED STATES 17.9	CAN. 5.3	OTHER 1.7	BRAZ. 6.3	OTHER 2.6	INDON. 4.6	JAPAN 4.0	CHINA 3.1	FIN. 3.8	SWE. 2.6	FRANCE 2.5	OTHER EUROPE 10.8	AFRICA 9.0	ALL OCEANIA

NORTH AMERICA — S. AM. — ASIA — EUROPE

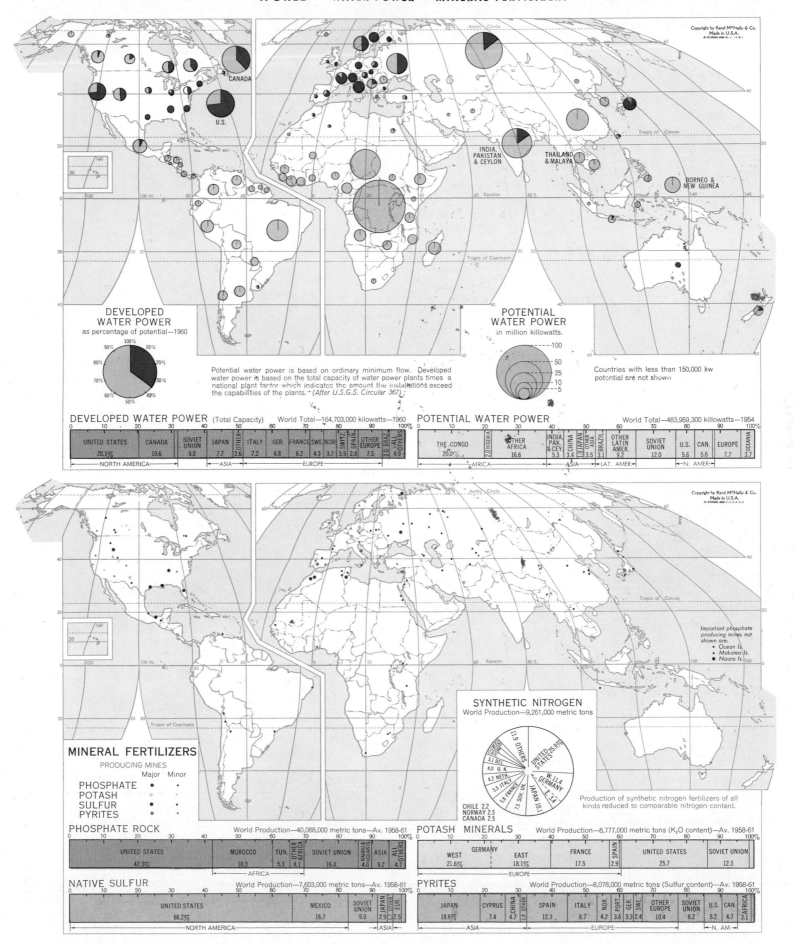

Copyright by Rand McNally & Co.
Made in U.S.A.
A-510000-468-0- | -1-0 |

CANADA

U.S.

INDIA, PAKISTAN & CEYLON

THAILAND & MALAYA

BORNEO & NEW GUINEA

DEVELOPED WATER POWER
as percentage of potential—1960

100%
90%   10%
80%   20%
70%   30%
60%   40%
50%

Potential water power is based on ordinary minimum flow. Developed water power is based on the total capacity of water power plants times a national plant factor which indicates the amount the installations exceed the capabilities of the plants." (After U.S.G.S. Circular 367)

POTENTIAL WATER POWER
in million killowatts.

——— 100
——— 50
——— 25
——— 10
——— 5

Countries with less than 150,000 kw potential are not shown

DEVELOPED WATER POWER (Total Capacity) World Total—164,703,000 kilowatts—1960

0	10	20	30	40	50	60	70	80	90	100%
UNITED STATES 20.1%			CANADA 10.6	SOVIET UNION 9.0	JAPAN 7.7	OTHER 2.6	ITALY 7.2	GER. 6.8	FRANCE 6.2	SWE. 4.3	NOR. 3.7	SWITZ. 3.5	SPAIN 2.8	OTHER EUROPE 7.5	2.0 BRAZIL	ALL OTHERS 4.9

NORTH AMERICA — ASIA — EUROPE

POTENTIAL WATER POWER World Total—483,959,300 killowatts—1954

0	10	20	30	40	50	60	70	80	90	100%
THE CONGO 20.0%	2.2 NIGERIA	OTHER AFRICA 16.6	INDIA, PAK. & CEY. 5.3	CHINA 3.4	OTHER ASIA 3.5	1.9 JAPAN	BRAZIL 3.1	OTHER LATIN AMER. 9.2	SOVIET UNION 12.0	U.S. 5.6	CAN. 5.6	EUROPE 7.7	OCEANIA 3.7

AFRICA — ASIA — LAT. AMER. — N. AMER.

Copyright by Rand McNally & Co.
Made in U.S.A.
A-510000-468-1-1-1-1-1

Important phosphate producing mines not shown are:
• Ocean Is.
• Makatea Is.
• Nauru Is.

MINERAL FERTILIZERS
PRODUCING MINES

	Major	Minor
PHOSPHATE	•	·
POTASH	•	·
SULFUR	•	·
PYRITES	•	·

SYNTHETIC NITROGEN
World Production—9,261,000 metric tons

11.9 OTHERS
3.1 BEL.
4.0 U.K.
4.2 NETH.
5.5 ITALY
5.8 FRANCE
7.3 SOV. UN.
JAPAN 10.1
E. 3.4
W. 11.4 GERMANY
UNITED STATES 25.9%

CHILE 2.2
NORWAY 2.5
CANADA 2.5

Production of synthetic nitrogen fertilizers of all kinds reduced to comparable nitrogen content.

PHOSPHATE ROCK World Production—40,088,000 metric tons—Av. 1958-61

0	10	20	30	40	50	60	70	80	90	100%
UNITED STATES 42.3%				MOROCCO 18.0	TUN. 5.3	OTHER AFRICA 4.1	SOVIET UNION 16.4	NAURU & OCEANIA 4.0	ASIA 5.2	ALL OTHERS 4.7

AFRICA

POTASH MINERALS World Production—8,777,000 metric tons (K₂O content)—Av. 1958-61

0	10	20	30	40	50	60	70	80	90	100%
WEST 21.6%	GERMANY	EAST 18.1%	FRANCE 17.5	SPAIN 2.9	UNITED STATES 25.7	SOVIET UNION 12.3

EUROPE

NATIVE SULFUR World Production—7,603,000 metric tons—Av. 1958-61

0	10	20	30	40	50	60	70	80	90	100%
UNITED STATES 66.2%						MEXICO 16.7	SOVIET UNION 9.0	JAPAN 2.9	OTHER EUR. 2.5

NORTH AMERICA — ASIA

PYRITES World Production—8,078,000 metric tons (Sulfur content)—Av. 1958-61

0	10	20	30	40	50	60	70	80	90	100%
JAPAN 18.6%	CYPRUS 7.4	CHINA 4.7	1.8 OTHER	SPAIN 12.3	ITALY 8.7	NOR. 4.2	PORT. 3.6	GER. 3.3	SWE. 2.4	OTHER EUROPE 10.4	SOVIET UNION 8.2	U.S. 5.2	CAN. 4.7	AFRICA 3.1

ASIA — EUROPE — N. AM.

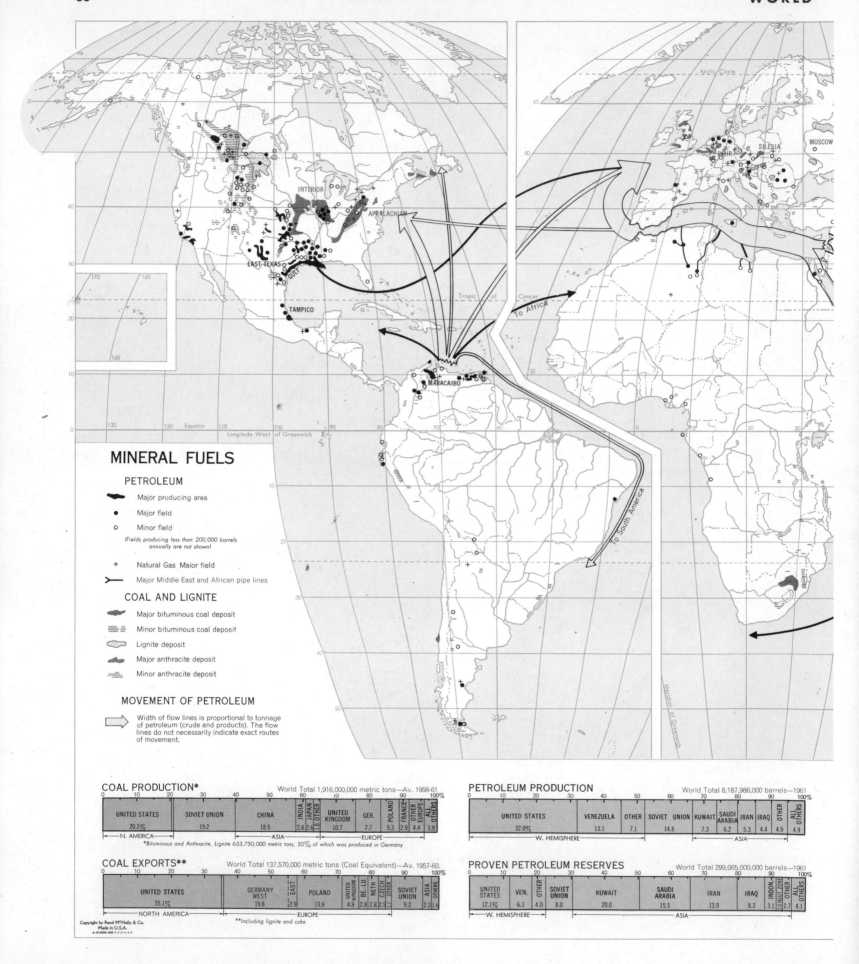

MINERAL FUELS

PETROLEUM

Major producing area

● Major field

○ Minor field

(Fields producing less than 200,000 barrels annually are not shown)

+ Natural Gas Major field

⟩ Major Middle East and African pipe lines

COAL AND LIGNITE

Major bituminous coal deposit

Minor bituminous coal deposit

Lignite deposit

Major anthracite deposit

Minor anthracite deposit

MOVEMENT OF PETROLEUM

Width of flow lines is proportional to tonnage of petroleum (crude and products). The flow lines do not necessarily indicate exact routes of movement.

INTERIOR
APPALACHIAN
EAST TEXAS
GULF
TAMPICO
MARACAIBO
RUHR
SILESIA
MOSCOW
To Africa
To South America
Tropic of Cancer
Equator
Longitude West of Greenwich
Meridian of Greenwich
Arctic Circle

COAL PRODUCTION*

World Total 1,916,000,000 metric tons—Av. 1958-61

UNITED STATES 20.2%	SOVIET UNION 19.2	CHINA 18.5	INDIA 2.6	JAPAN 2.6	OTHER 1.6	UNITED KINGDOM 10.7	GER. 7.7	POLAND 5.3	FRANCE 2.9	OTHER EUROPE 4.4	ALL OTHERS 3.8

— N. AMERICA — ——— ASIA ——— ——————— EUROPE ———————

*Bituminous and Anthracite, Lignite 633,750,000 metric tons, 50% of which was produced in Germany.

PETROLEUM PRODUCTION

World Total 8,187,986,000 barrels—1961

UNITED STATES 32.0%	VENEZUELA 13.1	OTHER 7.1	SOVIET UNION 14.8	KUWAIT 7.3	SAUDI ARABIA 6.2	IRAN 5.3	IRAQ 4.4	OTHER 4.9	ALL OTHERS 4.9

——————— W. HEMISPHERE ——————— ——————— ASIA ———————

COAL EXPORTS**

World Total 137,570,000 metric tons (Coal Equivalent)—Av. 1957-60.

UNITED STATES 35.1%	GERMANY WEST 19.6	EAST 2.9	POLAND 13.9	UNITED KINGDOM 4.9	BE.-LU. 2.8	NETH. 2.8	CZECH 2.5	OTHER 1.7	SOVIET UNION 9.2	ASIA 2.3	OTHERS 1.8

— NORTH AMERICA — ——————— EUROPE ———————

**Including lignite and coke

PROVEN PETROLEUM RESERVES

World Total 299,065,000,000 barrels—1961

UNITED STATES 12.1%	VEN. 6.3	OTHER 4.0	SOVIET UNION 8.0	KUWAIT 20.0	SAUDI ARABIA 15.5	IRAN 13.9	IRAQ 8.3	INDON. 3.1	NEUT. ZONE 2.0	OTHER 2.7	ALL OTHERS 4.1

——— W. HEMISPHERE ——— ——————————— ASIA ———————————

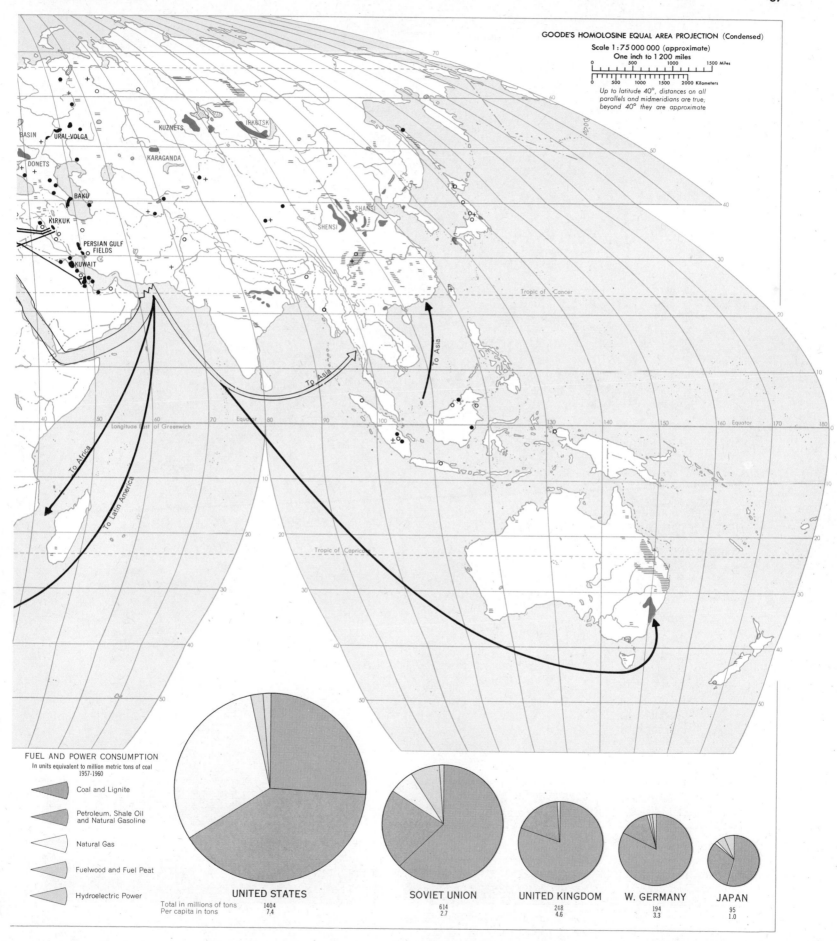

GOODE'S HOMOLOSINE EQUAL AREA PROJECTION (Condensed)
Scale 1 : 75 000 000 (approximate)
One inch to 1 200 miles

Up to latitude 40°, distances on all
parallels and midmeridians are true;
beyond 40° they are approximate

BASIN
URAL-VOLGA
DONETS
BAKU
KIRKUK
PERSIAN GULF
FIELDS
KUWAIT

KUZNETS
KARAGANDA
IRKUTSK
SHANSI
SHENSI

To Africa
To Latin America
To Asia
To Asia
To Asia

Tropic of Cancer
Longitude East of Greenwich
Equator
Tropic of Capricorn
Equator

FUEL AND POWER CONSUMPTION

In units equivalent to million metric tons of coal
1957-1960

Coal and Lignite

Petroleum, Shale Oil
and Natural Gasoline

Natural Gas

Fuelwood and Fuel Peat

Hydroelectric Power

	UNITED STATES	SOVIET UNION	UNITED KINGDOM	W. GERMANY	JAPAN
Total in millions of tons	1404	614	248	194	95
Per capita in tons	7.4	2.7	4.6	3.3	1.0

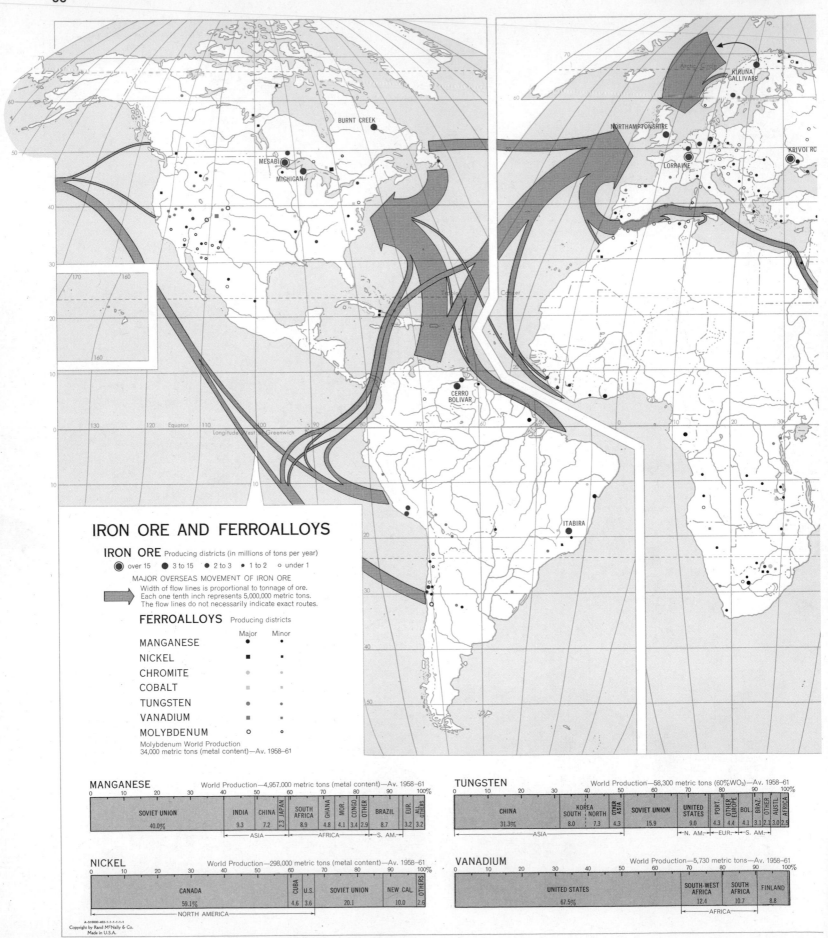

KIRUNA
GALLIVARE

BURNT CREEK

NORTHAMPTONSHIRE

LORRAINE

KRIVOI RO

MESABI

MICHIGAN

CERRO
BOLIVAR

ITABIRA

IRON ORE AND FERROALLOYS

IRON ORE Producing districts (in millions of tons per year)

⊙ over 15   ● 3 to 15   ● 2 to 3   • 1 to 2   ○ under 1

MAJOR OVERSEAS MOVEMENT OF IRON ORE

Width of flow lines is proportional to tonnage of ore.
Each one tenth inch represents 5,000,000 metric tons.
The flow lines do not necessarily indicate exact routes.

FERROALLOYS   Producing districts

	Major	Minor
MANGANESE	●	•
NICKEL	■	▪
CHROMITE	●	•
COBALT	■	▪
TUNGSTEN	●	•
VANADIUM	■	▪
MOLYBDENUM	○	○

Molybdenum World Production
34,000 metric tons (metal content)—Av. 1958–61

MANGANESE   World Production—4,957,000 metric tons (metal content)—Av. 1958–61

| SOVIET UNION 40.0% | INDIA 9.3 | CHINA 7.2 | JAPAN 2.3 | SOUTH AFRICA 8.9 | GHANA 4.8 | MOR. 4.1 | CONGO 3.4 | OTHER 2.9 | BRAZIL 8.7 | EUR. 3.2 | ALL OTHERS 3.2 |

—ASIA—   —AFRICA—   —S. AM.—

NICKEL   World Production—298,000 metric tons (metal content)—Av. 1958–61

| CANADA 59.1% | CUBA 4.6 | U.S. 3.6 | SOVIET UNION 20.1 | NEW CAL. 10.0 | OTHERS 2.6 |

—NORTH AMERICA—

TUNGSTEN   World Production—58,300 metric tons (60%WO₃)—Av. 1958–61

| CHINA 31.3% | KOREA SOUTH 8.0 | KOREA NORTH 7.3 | OTHER ASIA 4.3 | SOVIET UNION 15.9 | UNITED STATES 9.0 | PORT. 4.3 | OTHER EUROPE 4.4 | BOL. 4.1 | BRAZ. 3.1 | OTHER 2.1 | AUSTL. 3.0 | AFRICA 2.5 |

—ASIA—   —N. AM.—   —EUR.—   —S. AM.—

VANADIUM   World Production—5,730 metric tons—Av. 1958–61

| UNITED STATES 67.5% | SOUTH-WEST AFRICA 12.4 | SOUTH AFRICA 10.7 | FINLAND 8.8 |

—AFRICA—

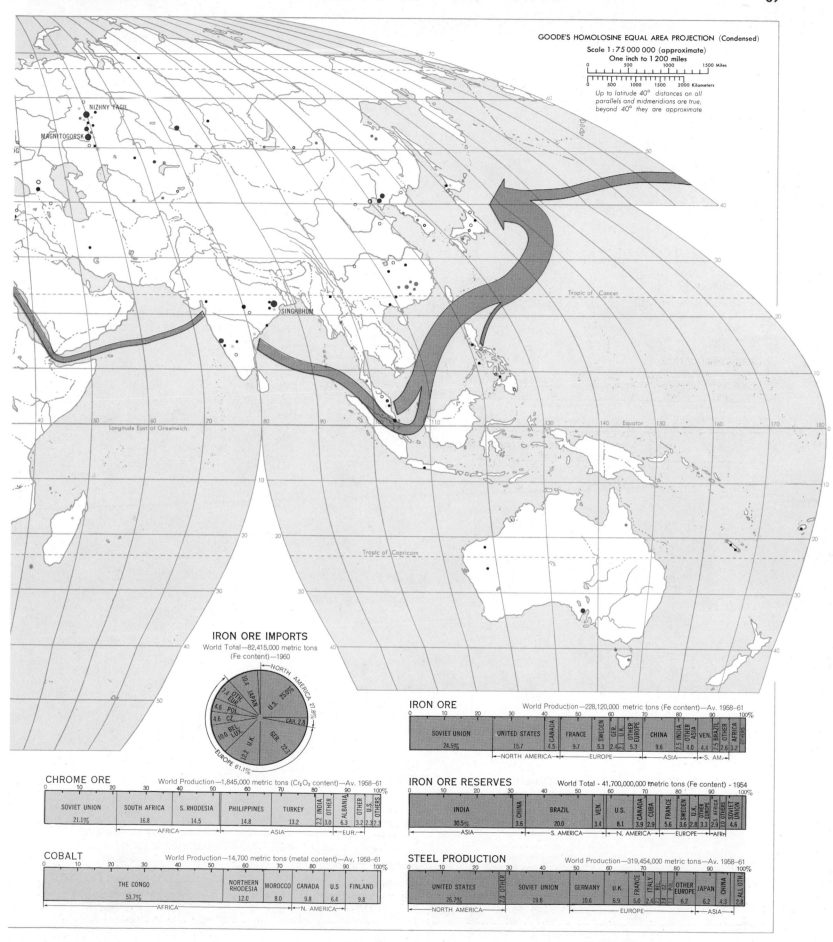

GOODE'S HOMOLOSINE EQUAL AREA PROJECTION (Condensed)
Scale 1 : 75 000 000 (approximate)
One inch to 1 200 miles

Up to latitude 40° distances on all parallels and midmeridians are true, beyond 40° they are approximate

NIZHNY TAGIL

MAGNITOGORSK

SINGHBHUM

Tropic of Cancer

Longitude East of Greenwich

Equator

Tropic of Capricorn

IRON ORE IMPORTS
World Total—82,415,000 metric tons
(Fe content)—1960

NORTH AMERICA 27.8%

10.4 JAPAN
7.4 OTH. EUR.
4.6 POL.
4.6 CZ.
10.0 BEL LUX.
12.2 U.K.
U.S. 25.0%
CAN. 2.8
GER. 22.2

EUROPE 61.1%

IRON ORE
World Production—228,120,000 metric tons (Fe content)—Av. 1958–61

SOVIET UNION 24.5%	UNITED STATES 15.7	CANADA 4.5	FRANCE 9.7	SWEDEN 5.3	GER. 2.4	OTHER EUROPE 5.3	CHINA 9.6	INDIA 2.5	OTHER ASIA 4.0	VEN. 4.4	BRAZIL 2.5	OTHER AFRICA 3.2	OTHERS 3.2

NORTH AMERICA — EUROPE — ASIA — S. AM.

CHROME ORE
World Production—1,845,000 metric tons (Cr₂O₃ content)—Av. 1958–61

SOVIET UNION 21.1%	SOUTH AFRICA 16.8	S. RHODESIA 14.5	PHILIPPINES 14.8	TURKEY 13.2	INDIA 2.2	OTHER 3.0	ALBANIA 6.3	OTHER 3.2	U.S. 2.3	OTHERS 2.3

AFRICA — ASIA — EUR.

IRON ORE RESERVES
World Total - 41,700,000,000 metric tons (Fe content) - 1954

INDIA 30.5%	CHINA 3.6	BRAZIL 20.0	VEN. 3.4	U.S. 8.1	CANADA 3.6	CUBA 2.8	FRANCE 5.6	SWEDEN 2.8	U.K. 3.3	OTHER EUROPE 3.3	S. AFRICA 2.9	OTHERS	SOVIET UNION 4.6

ASIA — S. AMERICA — N. AMERICA — EUROPE — AFR.

COBALT
World Production—14,700 metric tons (metal content)—Av. 1958–61

THE CONGO 53.7%	NORTHERN RHODESIA 12.0	MOROCCO 8.0	CANADA 9.8	U.S 6.4	FINLAND 9.8

AFRICA — N. AMERICA

STEEL PRODUCTION
World Production—319,454,000 metric tons—Av. 1958–61

UNITED STATES 26.7%	OTHER 2.0	SOVIET UNION 19.6	GERMANY 10.6	U.K. 6.9	FRANCE 5.0	ITALY 2.4	BEL.	CZ.	POL. 2.5	OTHER EUROPE 6.2	JAPAN 6.2	CHINA 4.3	ALL OTH. 2.8

NORTH AMERICA — EUROPE — ASIA

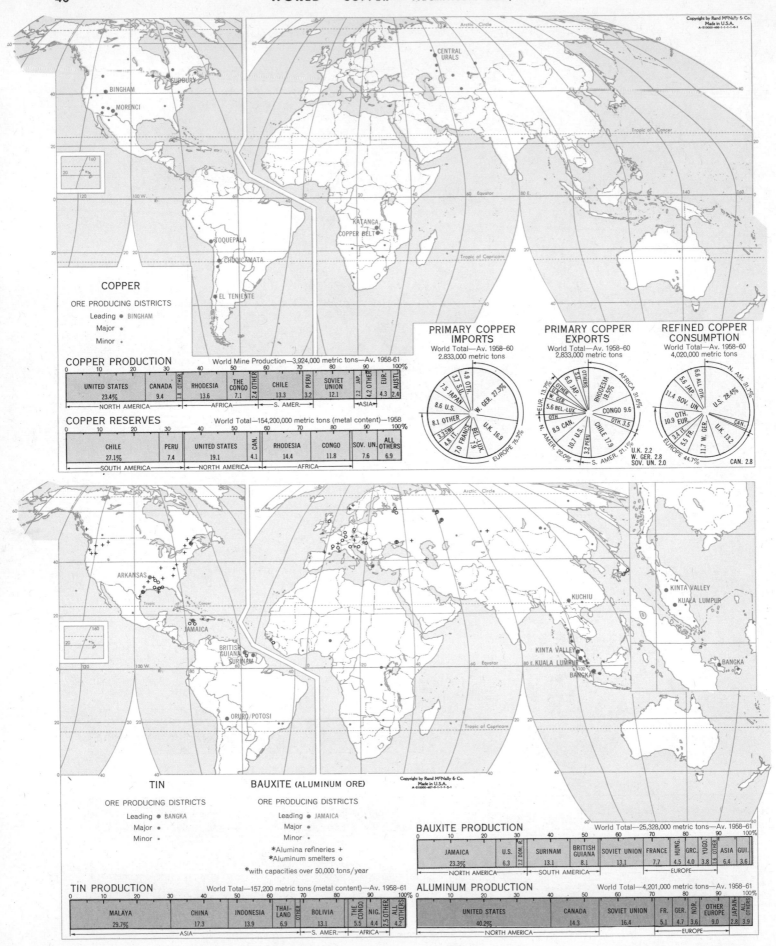

COPPER

ORE PRODUCING DISTRICTS

Leading ● BINGHAM
Major ●
Minor ·

COPPER PRODUCTION
World Mine Production—3,924,000 metric tons—Av. 1958-61

0	10	20	30	40	50	60	70	80	90	100%

| UNITED STATES 23.4% | CANADA 9.4 | OTHER 1.8 | RHODESIA 13.6 | THE CONGO 7.1 | OTHER 2.4 | CHILE 13.3 | PERU 3.2 | SOVIET UNION 12.1 | JAP. 2.2 | OTHER 4.2 | EUR. 4.3 | AUSTL. 2.4 |

NORTH AMERICA — AFRICA — S. AMER. — ASIA —

COPPER RESERVES
World Total—154,200,000 metric tons (metal content)—1958

0	10	20	30	40	50	60	70	80	90	100%

| CHILE 27.1% | PERU 7.4 | UNITED STATES 19.1 | CAN. 4.1 | RHODESIA 14.4 | CONGO 11.8 | SOV. UN. 7.6 | ALL OTHERS 6.9 |

SOUTH AMERICA — NORTH AMERICA — AFRICA —

PRIMARY COPPER IMPORTS
World Total—Av. 1958-60
2,833,000 metric tons

W. GER. 27.3%
4.9 OTH.
3.7 S.U.
7.5 JAPAN
8.6 U.S.
8.1 OTHER
3.3 SWE.
4.8 IT.
7.0 FRANCE
BEL.-LUX. .9
U.K. 16.9
EUROPE 75.3%

PRIMARY COPPER EXPORTS
World Total—Av. 1958-60
2,833,000 metric tons

AFRICA 31.6%
RHODESIA 18.5%
CONGO 9.6
OTH. 3.5
CHILE 17.9
S. AMER. 21.1%
13.7% EUR.
6.0 JAP.
OTHER
W. GER.
5.6 BEL.-LUX.
OTH.
8.9 CAN.
10.7 U.S.
N. AMER. 22.0%
3.2 PERU
U.K. 2.2
W. GER. 2.8
SOV. UN. 2.0

REFINED COPPER CONSUMPTION
World Total—Av. 1958-60
4,020,000 metric tons

N. AM. 31.1%
6.6 ALL OTH.
5.6 JAP.
11.4 SOV. UN.
10.9 OTH. EUR.
EUROPE 44.7%
U.S. 28.4%
CAN.
U.K. 13.2
3.4 IT.
11.7 W. GER.
5.5 FR.
CAN. 2.8

TIN

ORE PRODUCING DISTRICTS

Leading ● BANGKA
Major ●
Minor ·

BAUXITE (ALUMINUM ORE)

ORE PRODUCING DISTRICTS

Leading ● JAMAICA
Major ●
Minor ·
*Alumina refineries +
*Aluminum smelters o
*with capacities over 50,000 tons/year

BAUXITE PRODUCTION
World Total—25,328,000 metric tons—Av. 1958-61

0	10	20	30	40	50	60	70	80	90	100%

| JAMAICA 23.3% | U.S. 6.3 | DOM. R. 2.2 | SURINAM 13.1 | BRITISH GUIANA 8.1 | SOVIET UNION 13.1 | FRANCE 7.7 | HUNG. 4.5 | GRC. 4.0 | YUGO. 3.8 | OTHER 1.6 | ASIA 6.4 | GUI. 3.6 |

NORTH AMERICA — SOUTH AMERICA — EUROPE —

TIN PRODUCTION
World Total—157,200 metric tons (metal content)—Av. 1958-61

0	10	20	30	40	50	60	70	80	90	100%

| MALAYA 29.7% | CHINA 17.3 | INDONESIA 13.9 | THAILAND 6.9 | OTHER | BOLIVIA 13.1 | THE CONGO 5.5 | NIG. 4.4 | ALL OTHERS 4.2 |

ASIA — S. AMER. — AFRICA —

ALUMINUM PRODUCTION
World Total—4,201,000 metric tons—Av. 1958-61

0	10	20	30	40	50	60	70	80	90	100%

| UNITED STATES 40.2% | CANADA 14.3 | SOVIET UNION 16.4 | FR. 5.1 | GER. 4.7 | NOR. 3.6 | OTHER EUROPE 9.0 | JAPAN 2.8 | ALL OTHERS 3.9 |

NORTH AMERICA — EUROPE —

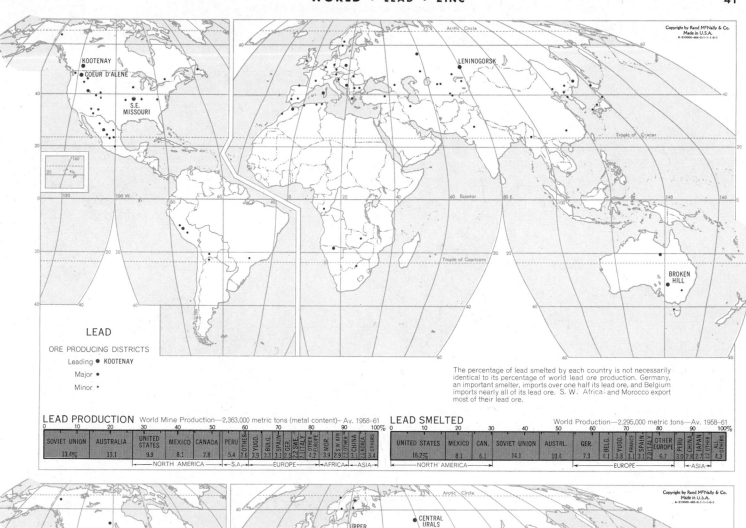

LEAD

ORE PRODUCING DISTRICTS

Leading ● KOOTENAY

Major ●

Minor ·

The percentage of lead smelted by each country is not necessarily identical to its percentage of world lead ore production. Germany, an important smelter, imports over one half its lead ore, and Belgium imports nearly all of its lead ore. S. W. Africa and Morocco export most of their lead ore.

LEAD PRODUCTION World Mine Production—2,363,000 metric tons (metal content)— Av. 1958–61

SOVIET UNION	AUSTRALIA	UNITED STATES	MEXICO	CANADA	PERU	OTHER N.A.	YUGO.	BULG.	SPAIN	GER.	SWE.	ITALY	OTHER EUROPE	MOR.	S.W AFR	CHINA	KOREA	OTHERS
13.4%	13.1	9.9	8.1	7.8	5.4	2.6	3.9	3.3	3.1	2.2	4.2	2.1		3.9	2.9	3.1	2.2	3.4

NORTH AMERICA — S.A. — EUROPE — AFRICA — ASIA —

LEAD SMELTED World Production—2,295,000 metric tons— Av. 1958–61

UNITED STATES	MEXICO	CAN.	SOVIET UNION	AUSTRL.	GER.	BELG.	YUGO.	FRANCE	SPAIN	ITALY	OTHER EUROPE	PERU	CHINA	JAPAN	ALL OTHERS
16.2%	8.1	6.1	14.1	10.4	7.3	4.1	3.8	3.1	2.1		6.7	3.0	2.8	2.2	4.3

NORTH AMERICA — EUROPE — ASIA —

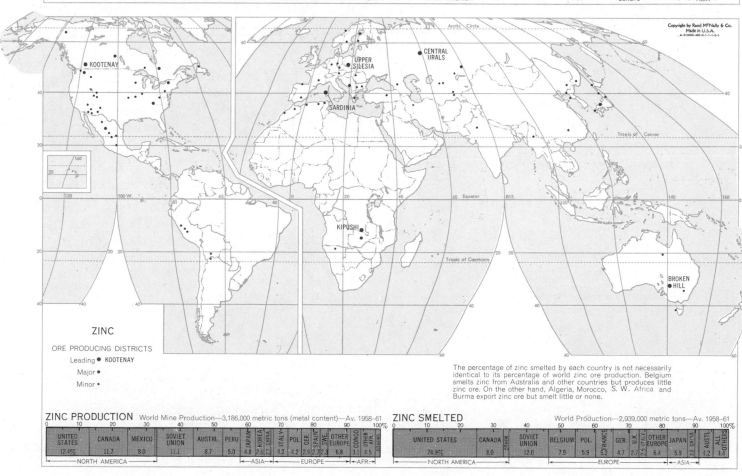

ZINC

ORE PRODUCING DISTRICTS

Leading ● KOOTENAY

Major ●

Minor ·

The percentage of zinc smelted by each country is not necessarily identical to its percentage of world zinc ore production. Belgium smelts zinc from Australia and other countries but produces little zinc ore. On the other hand, Algeria, Morocco, S. W. Africa and Burma export zinc ore but smelt little or none.

ZINC PRODUCTION World Mine Production—3,186,000 metric tons (metal content)— Av. 1958–61

UNITED STATES	CANADA	MEXICO	SOVIET UNION	AUSTRL.	PERU	JAPAN	KOREA	CHINA	ITALY	POL.	GER.	SPAIN	SWE.	OTHER EUROPE	CONGO	OTHER AFR.	OTHERS
12.4%	11.7	8.0	11.1	8.7	5.0	4.8	2.6	2.3	4.2	4.2	2.7	2.3			3.1		4.5

NORTH AMERICA — ASIA — EUROPE — AFR. —

ZINC SMELTED World Production—2,939,000 metric tons— Av. 1958–61

UNITED STATES	CANADA	OTHER	SOVIET UNION	BELGIUM	POL.	FRANCE	GER.	U.K.	ITALY	OTHER EUROPE	JAPAN	CHINA	AUSTL.	ALL OTHERS
24.9%	8.0		12.0	7.9	5.9	5.2	4.7	2.7		6.4	5.9		4.2	4.4

NORTH AMERICA — EUROPE — ASIA —

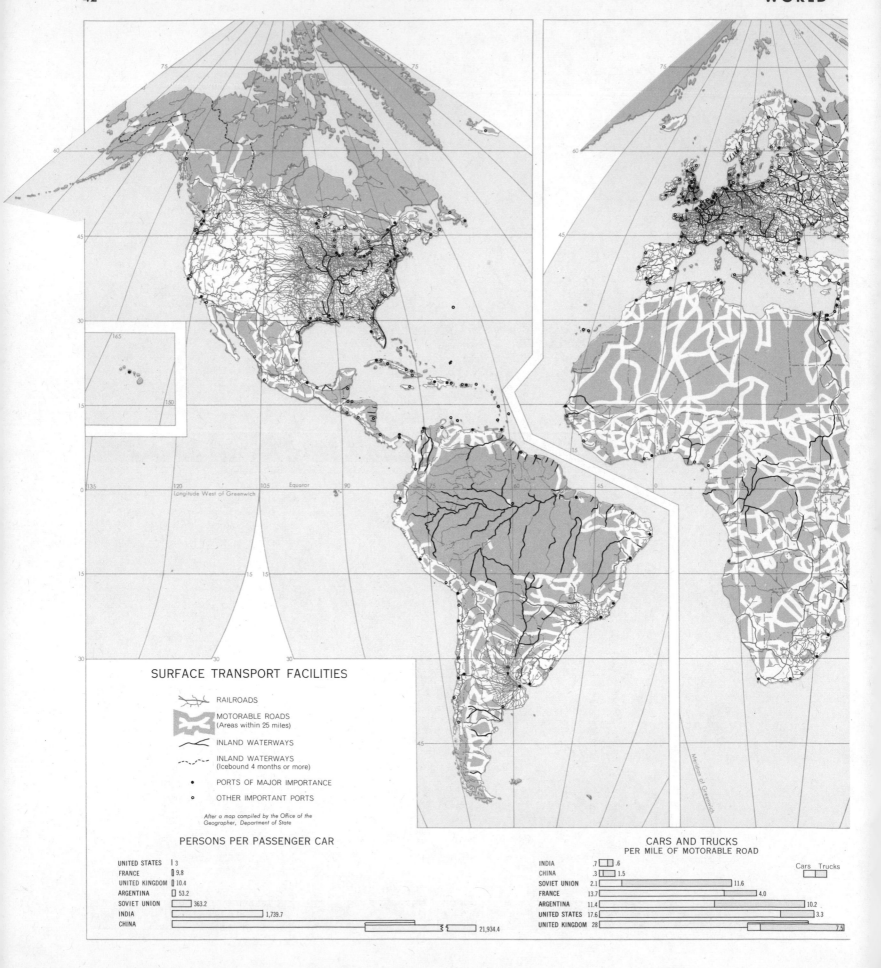

SURFACE TRANSPORT FACILITIES

RAILROADS

MOTORABLE ROADS
(Areas within 25 miles)

INLAND WATERWAYS

INLAND WATERWAYS
(Icebound 4 months or more)

●   PORTS OF MAJOR IMPORTANCE

○   OTHER IMPORTANT PORTS

*After a map compiled by the Office of the
Geographer, Department of State*

PERSONS PER PASSENGER CAR

UNITED STATES	3
FRANCE	9.8
UNITED KINGDOM	10.4
ARGENTINA	53.2
SOVIET UNION	363.2
INDIA	1,739.7
CHINA	21,934.4

CARS AND TRUCKS
PER MILE OF MOTORABLE ROAD

Cars   Trucks

	Cars	Trucks
INDIA	.7	.6
CHINA	.3	1.5
SOVIET UNION	2.1	11.6
FRANCE	13.7	4.0
ARGENTINA	11.4	10.2
UNITED STATES	17.6	3.3
UNITED KINGDOM	28	7.5

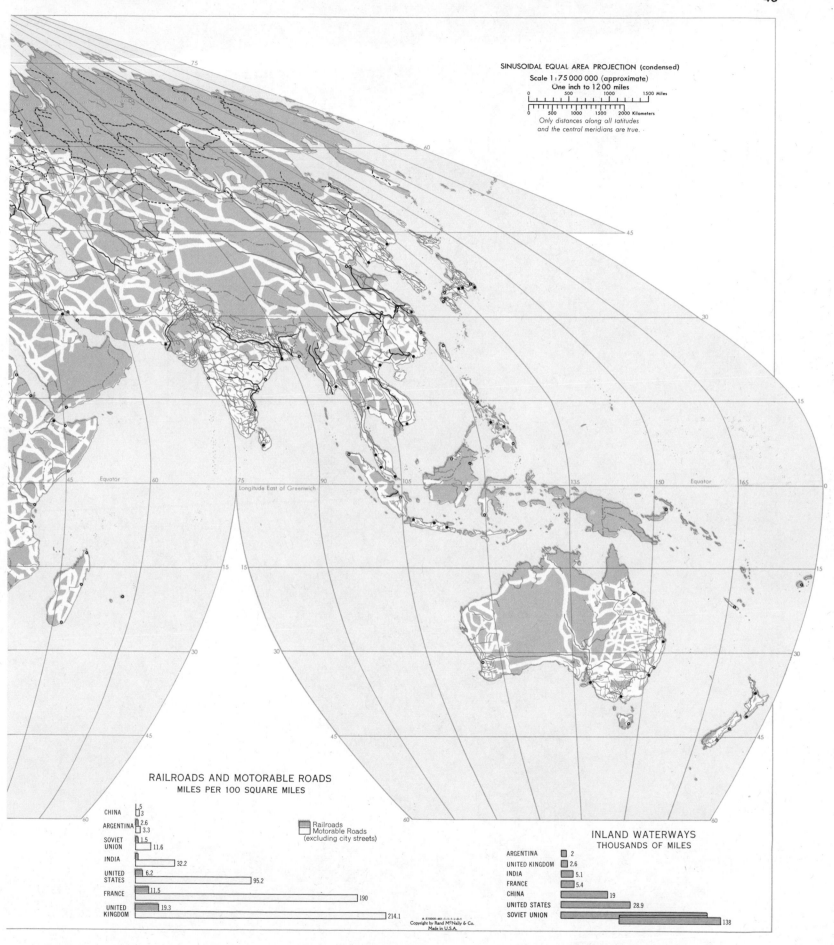

SINUSOIDAL EQUAL AREA PROJECTION (condensed)
Scale 1 : 75 000 000 (approximate)
One inch to 1200 miles

Only distances along all latitudes
and the central meridians are true.

RAILROADS AND MOTORABLE ROADS
MILES PER 100 SQUARE MILES

Railroads
Motorable Roads
(excluding city streets)

	Railroads	Motorable Roads
CHINA	.5	3
ARGENTINA	2.6	3.3
SOVIET UNION	1.5	11.6
INDIA		32.2
UNITED STATES	6.2	95.2
FRANCE	11.5	190
UNITED KINGDOM	19.3	214.1

INLAND WATERWAYS
THOUSANDS OF MILES

ARGENTINA	2
UNITED KINGDOM	2.6
INDIA	5.1
FRANCE	5.4
CHINA	19
UNITED STATES	28.9
SOVIET UNION	138

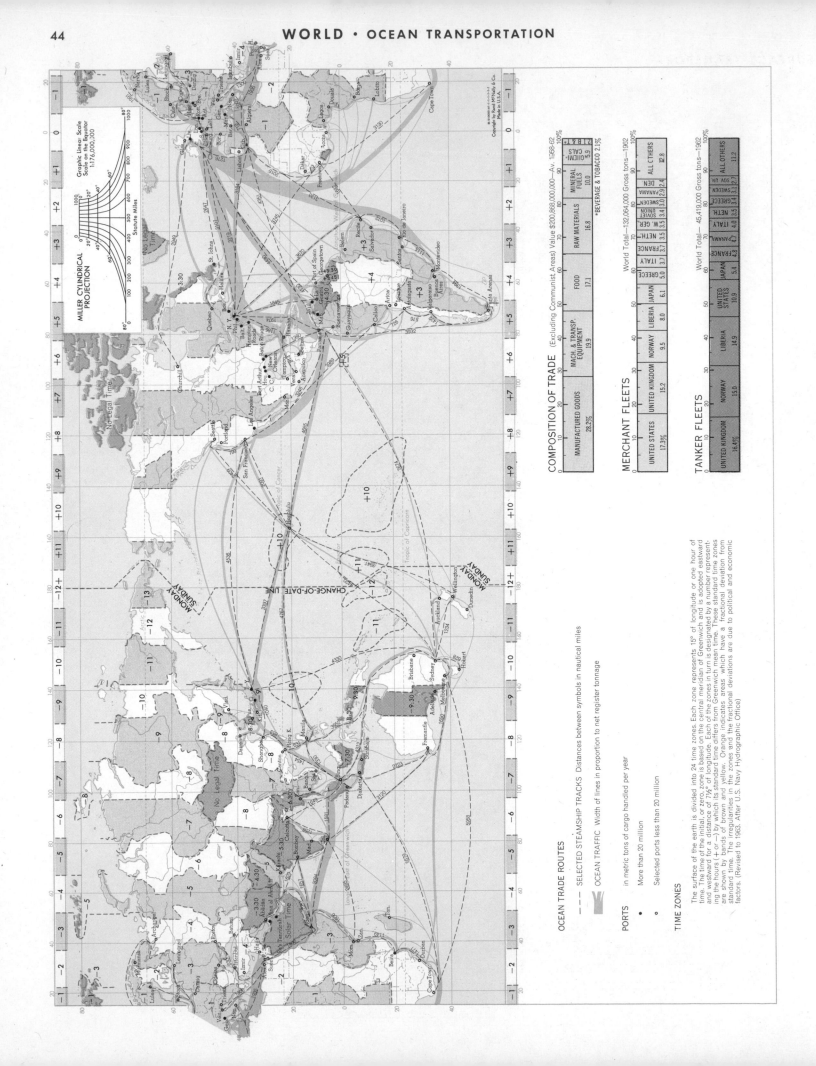

WORLD • EXPORTS • IMPORTS

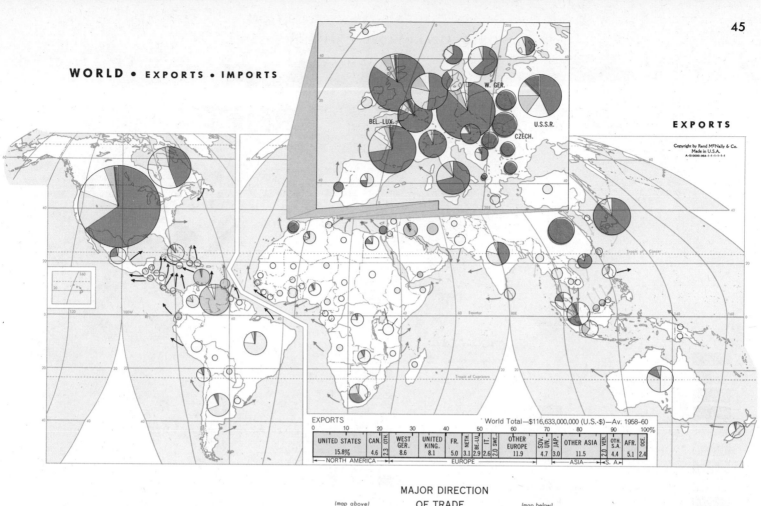

EXPORTS

Copyright by Rand McNally & Co.
Made in U.S.A.
A-510000-964-1-1-1-1-1-1

EXPORTS															World Total—$116,633,000,000 (U.S.-$)—Av. 1958–60
0	10	20	30	40	50	60	70	80	90	100%				
UNITED STATES 15.8%	CAN. 4.6	OTH. 2.3	WEST GER. 8.6	UNITED KING. 8.1	FR. 5.0	NETH. 3.1	BE.-LU. 2.9	IT. 2.6	SWE. 2.0	OTHER EUROPE 11.9	SOV. UN. 4.7	JAP. 3.0	OTHER ASIA 11.5	VEN. 2.0	OTH. S.A. 4.4	AFR. 5.1	OCE. 2.4
← NORTH AMERICA →			← EUROPE →								← ASIA →			← S. A. →		

COMPOSITION OF TRADE
(Data based on 3 year averages—mostly 1958–1960)

Manufactured Articles   Food, bev. & tobacco   Raw Materials   Fuel & Related Prod.   All other or undifferentiated

If volume of trade is less than $400,000,000 color indicates major class only.

MAJOR DIRECTION OF TRADE

(map above)
EXPORTS TO
Europe ←
N. America ←
Asia ←

Color of arrows beside selected countries in-dicates direction of major trade alignment.

(map below)
IMPORTS FROM
Europe →
N. America →
Asia →

VOLUME OF TRADE
in millions of U.S. dollars

20,000
10,000
5,000
2,500
1,000
0–100

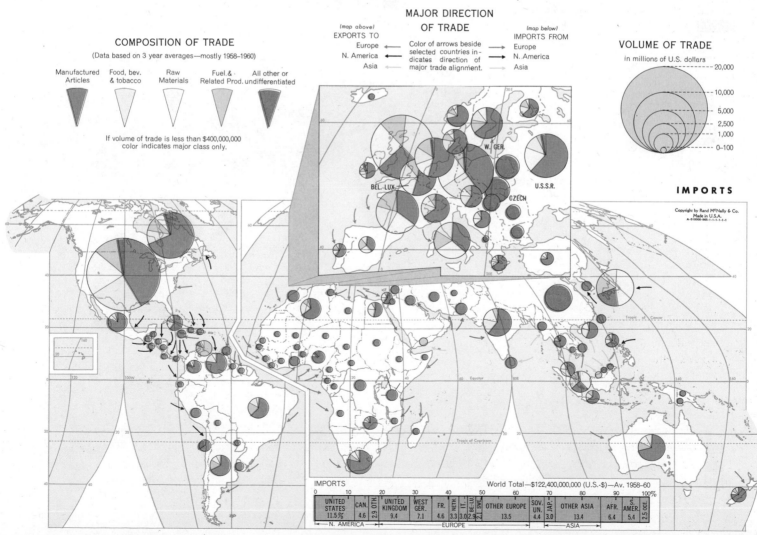

IMPORTS

Copyright by Rand McNally & Co.
Made in U.S.A.
A-510000-965-1-1-1-1-1-1

IMPORTS															World Total—$122,400,000,000 (U.S.-$)—Av. 1958–60
0	10	20	30	40	50	60	70	80	90	100%				
UNITED STATES 11.5%	CAN. 4.6	OTH. 2.9	UNITED KINGDOM 9.4	WEST GER. 7.1	FR. 4.6	NETH. 3.3	IT. 3.0	BE.-LU. 2.9	SWE. 2.5	OTHER EUROPE 13.5	SOV. UN. 4.4	JAP. 3.0	OTHER ASIA 13.4	AFR. 6.4	S. AMER. 5.4	OCE. 2.5
← N. AMERICA →			← EUROPE →								← ASIA →					

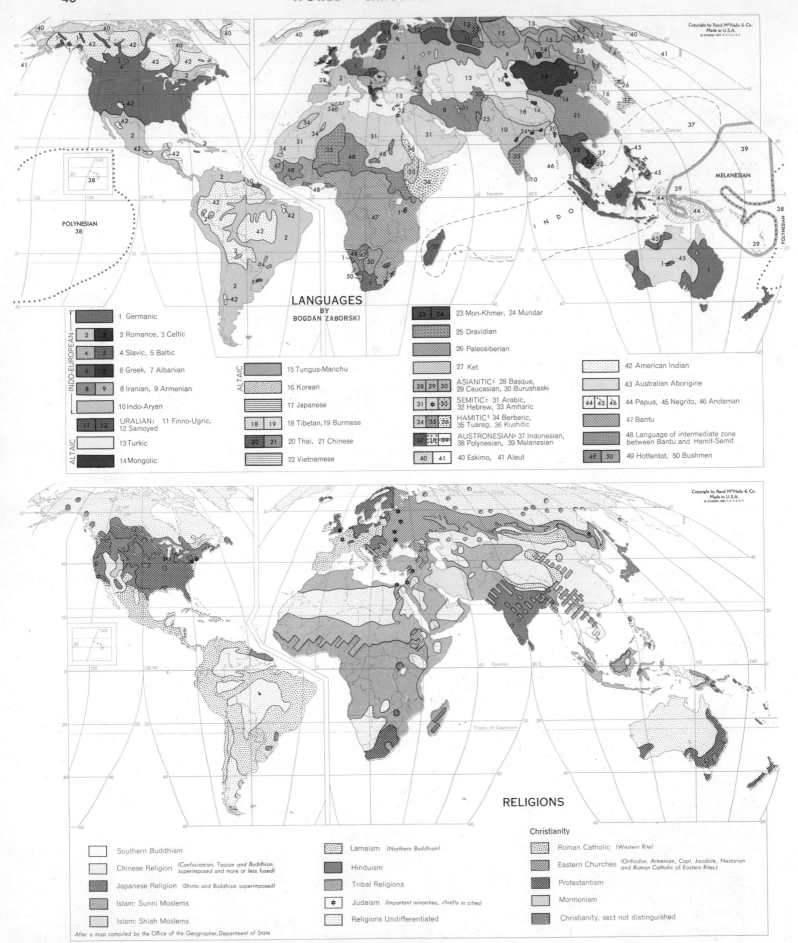

LANGUAGES
BY
BOGDAN ZABORSKI

INDO-EUROPEAN
1 Germanic
2 Romance, 3 Celtic
4 Slavic, 5 Baltic
6 Greek, 7 Albanian
8 Iranian, 9 Armenian
10 Indo-Aryan
URALIAN: 11 Finno-Ugric, 12 Samoyed
ALTAIC
13 Turkic
14 Mongolic
15 Tungus-Manchu
16 Korean
17 Japanese
18 Tibetan, 19 Burmese
20 Thai, 21 Chinese
22 Vietnamese

23 Mon-Khmer, 24 Mundar
25 Dravidian
26 Paleosiberian
27 Ket
ASIANITIC: 28 Basque, 29 Caucasian, 30 Burushaski
SEMITIC: 31 Arabic, 32 Hebrew, 33 Amharic
HAMITIC: 34 Berberic, 35 Tuareg, 36 Kushitic
AUSTRONESIAN: 37 Indonesian, 38 Polynesian, 39 Melanesian
40 Eskimo, 41 Aleut

42 American Indian
43 Australian Aborigine
44 Papua, 45 Negrito, 46 Andaman
47 Bantu
48 Language of intermediate zone between Bantu and Hamit-Semit
49 Hottentot, 50 Bushmen

RELIGIONS

Southern Buddhism
Chinese Religion (Confucianism, Taoism and Buddhism, superimposed and more or less fused)
Japanese Religion (Shinto and Buddhism superimposed)
Islam: Sunni Moslems
Islam: Shiah Moslems

Lamaism (Northern Buddhism)
Hinduism
Tribal Religions
Judaism (Important minorities, chiefly in cities)
Religions Undifferentiated

Christianity
Roman Catholic (Western Rite)
Eastern Churches (Orthodox, Armenian, Copt, Jacobite, Nestorian and Roman Catholic of Eastern Rites.)
Protestantism
Mormonism
Christianity, sect not distinguished

After a map compiled by the Office of the Geographer, Department of State

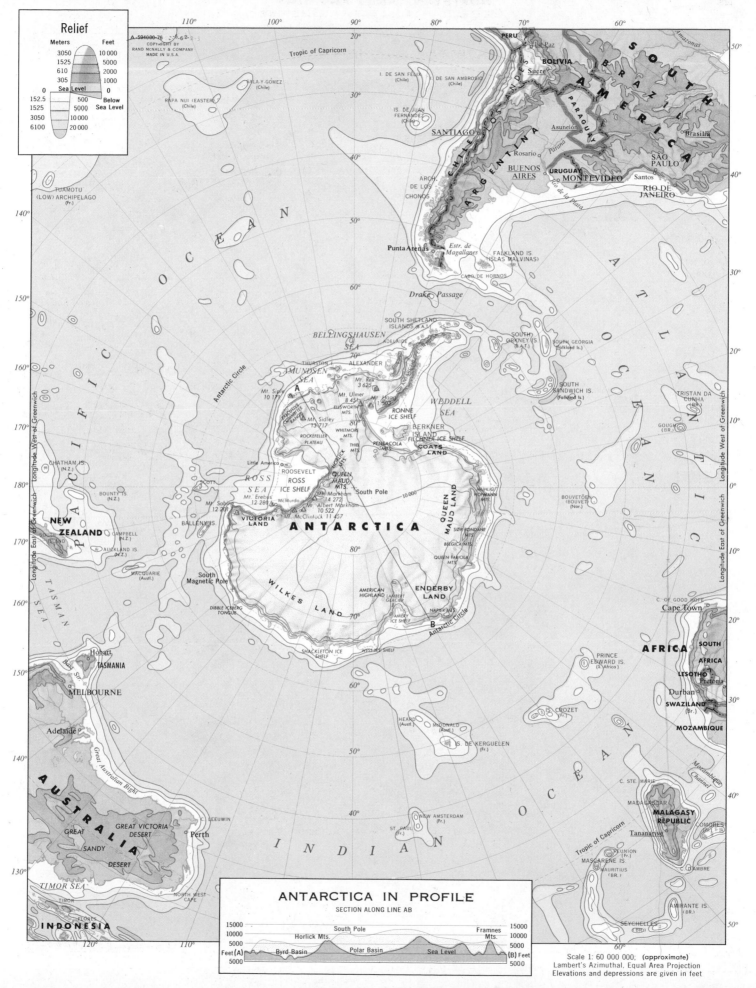

Relief

Meters	Feet
3050	10 000
1525	5000
610	2000
305	1000
Sea Level	Sea Level
152.5	500 Below
1525	5000 Sea Level
3050	10 000
6100	20 000

A-594000-76
COPYRIGHT BY
RAND MCNALLY & COMPANY
MADE IN U.S.A.

Tropic of Capricorn

PERU

Tropic of Capricorn

SOUTH AMERICA

BRAZIL

BOLIVIA
La Paz
Sucre

Amazonas

I. DE SAN FELIX (Chile)
DE SAN AMBROSIO (Chile)

SALA-Y-GÓMEZ (Chile)

RAPA NUI (EASTER) (Chile)

IS. DE JUAN FERNÁNDEZ (Chile)

SANTIAGO
CHILE
ANDES
LOS ANDES

PARAGUAY
Asunción
Paraná

Brasília

SÃO PAULO

TUAMOTU (LOW) ARCHIPELAGO (Fr.)

ARGENTINA
Rosario
Paraná

BUENOS AIRES
URUGUAY
MONTEVIDEO
Santos
RIO DE JANEIRO
Río de la Plata

ARCH. DE LOS CHONOS

Punta Arenas
Estr. de Magallanes
FALKLAND IS. ISLAS MALVINAS (BR.)

CABO DE HORNOS

Drake Passage

P A C I F I C   O C E A N

SOUTH SHETLAND ISLANDS (B.A.T.)

BELLINGSHAUSEN SEA
ADELAIDE

SOUTH ORKNEY IS. (B.A.T.)

SOUTH GEORGIA (Falkland Is.)

A T L A N T I C   O C E A N

Antarctic Circle

THURSTON I.
ALEXANDER I.

AMUNDSEN SEA

Mt. Sipie 10 171

A
Mt. Rex 3 625
Mt. Ulmer 8 451
Mt. Haag 1 925

SENTINEL GRANITE RANGES
Mt. Sidley 13 717
ELLSWORTH MTS.

WHITMORE MTS.

ROCKEFELLER PLATEAU

THIEL MTS.

WEDDELL SEA

RONNE ICE SHELF

PENSACOLA MTS.

BERKNER ISLAND
FILCHNER ICE SHELF
COATS LAND

SOUTH SANDWICH IS. (Falkland Is.)

TRISTAN DA CUNHA

GOUGH I. (BR.)

CHATHAM IS. (N.Z.)

Little America

ROOSEVELT I.

ROSS ICE SHELF

ROSS SEA

QUEEN MAUD MTS.

South Pole

10 000

QUEEN MAUD LAND

MÜHLIG HOFMANN MTS.

BOUVETÖEN (BOUVET) (Nor.)

SCOTT

Mt. Erebus 12 280
McMurdo
Mt. Sabine 12 201

BOUNTY IS. (N.Z.)

BALLENY IS.

VICTORIA LAND

Mt. Markham 14 272
Albert Markham 10 522
Mt. McClintock 11 457

A N T A R C T I C A

SÖR RONDANE MTS.
BELGICA MTS.
QUEEN FABIOLA MTS.

NEW ZEALAND

CAMPBELL I. (N.Z.)

AUCKLAND IS. (N.Z.)

South Magnetic Pole

WILKES LAND

AMERICAN HIGHLAND
LAMBERT GLACIER
AMERY ICE SHELF

ENDERBY LAND

NAPIER MTS.

Antarctic Circle

C. OF GOOD HOPE
Cape Town

AFRICA
SOUTH AFRICA
LESOTHO
Pretoria

MACQUARIE I. (Austl.)

DIBBLE ICEBERG TONGUE

SHACKLETON ICE SHELF
WEST ICE SHELF

PRINCE EDWARD IS. (S. Africa)

Durban
SWAZILAND (Br.)

T A S M A N   S E A

Hobart
TASMANIA
Bass Str.

CROZET

MOZAMBIQUE

MELBOURNE

HEARD (Austl.)
McDONALD (Austl.)

IS. DE KERGUELEN (Fr.)

C. STE MARIE

Adelaide

MADAGASCAR
MALAGASY REPUBLIC

Mozambique Channel

AUSTRALIA

Great Australian Bight

I N D I A N   O C E A N

NEW AMSTERDAM (Fr.)

ST PAUL (Fr.)

Tropic of Capricorn

RÉUNION
MASCARENE IS.
MAURITIUS (BR.)

Tananarive

C. D'AMBRE
COMORES

GREAT VICTORIA DESERT
C. LEEUWIN
Perth

GREAT SANDY DESERT

AMIRANTE IS. (BR.)

TIMOR SEA

TIMOR
NORTH WEST CAPE

SEYCHELLES (BR.)

FLORES
INDONESIA

ANTARCTICA IN PROFILE
SECTION ALONG LINE AB

Feet (A)						(B) Feet
15000		South Pole			Framnes Mts.	15000
10000	Horlick Mts.					10000
5000						5000
Sea Level	Byrd Basin	Polar Basin	Sea Level			Sea Level
5000						5000

Scale 1: 60 000 000; (approximate)
Lambert's Azimuthal, Equal Area Projection
Elevations and depressions are given in feet

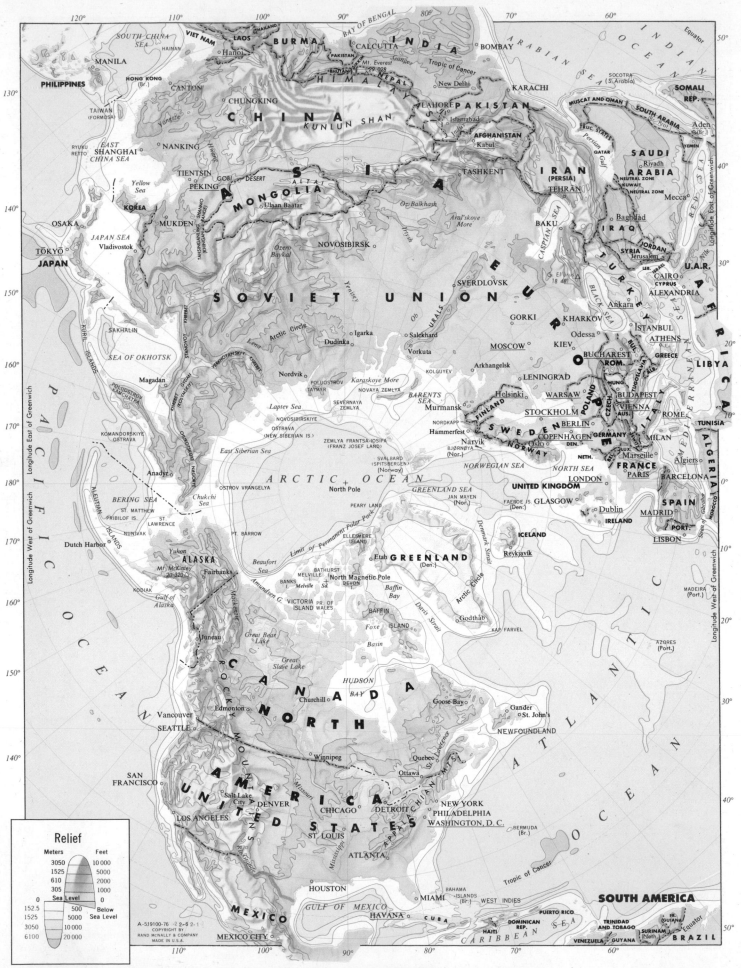

Relief

Meters	Feet
3050	10 000
1525	5000
610	2000
305	1000
Sea Level	0
0	500 Below
152.5	Sea Level
1525	5000
3050	10 000
6100	20 000

A-519100-76 -2 2-6 2-1
COPYRIGHT BY
RAND McNALLY & COMPANY
MADE IN U.S.A.

Scale 1: 60 000 000; (approximate)
Lambert's Azimuthal, Equal Area Projection
Elevations and depressions are given in feet

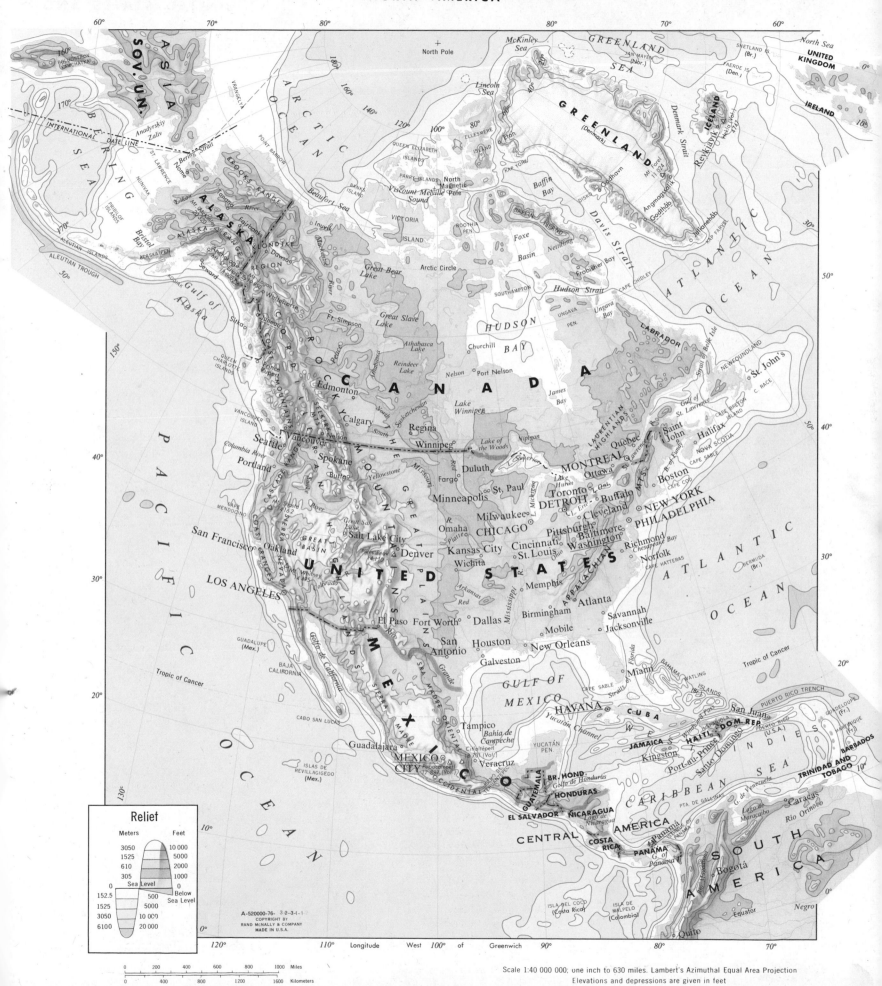

Relief

Meters		Feet
3050		10 000
1525		5000
610		2000
305		1000
0	Sea Level	0
		Below
152.5		500 Sea Level
1525		5000
3050		10 000
6100		20 000

A-520000-76- 3-2-3-1-1
COPYRIGHT BY
RAND MCNALLY & COMPANY
MADE IN U.S.A.

Scale 1:40 000 000; one inch to 630 miles. Lambert's Azimuthal Equal Area Projection
Elevations and depressions are given in feet

Miles				
0	200	400	600	800	1000

Kilometers			
0	400	800	1200	1600

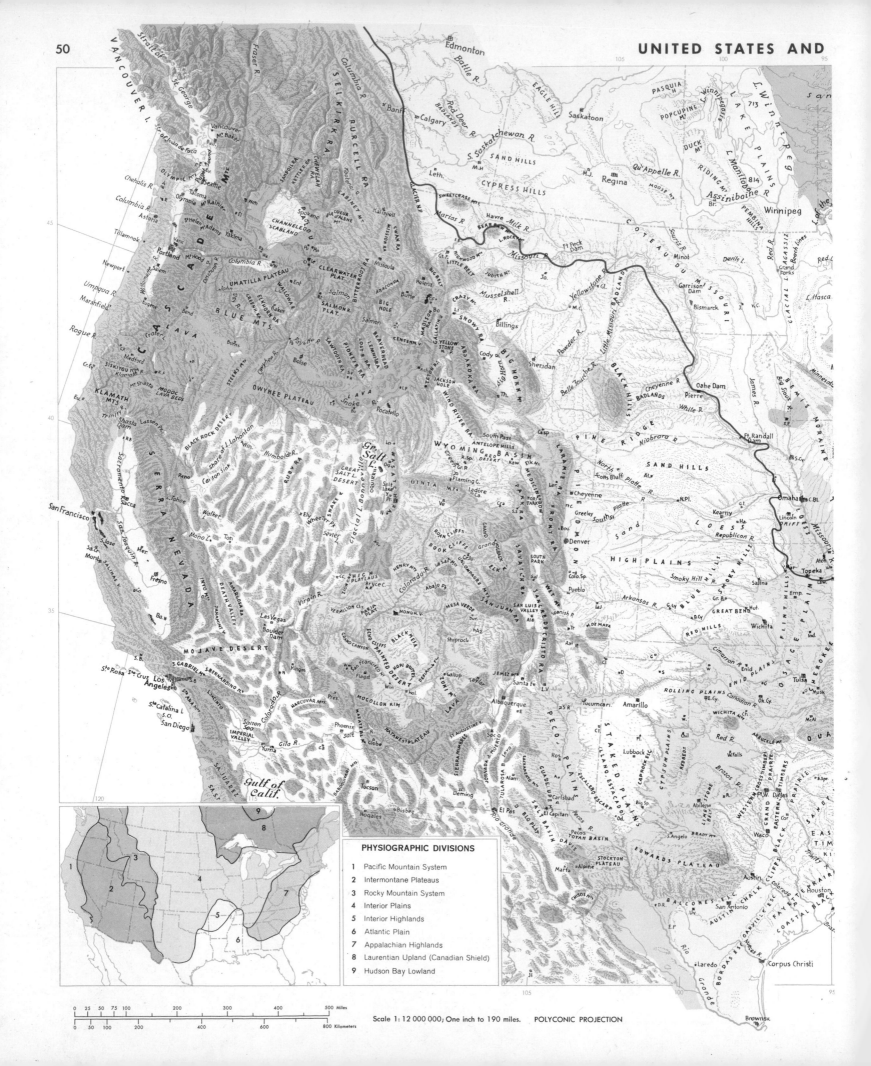

PHYSIOGRAPHIC DIVISIONS

1 Pacific Mountain System
2 Intermontane Plateaus
3 Rocky Mountain System
4 Interior Plains
5 Interior Highlands
6 Atlantic Plain
7 Appalachian Highlands
8 Laurentian Upland (Canadian Shield)
9 Hudson Bay Lowland

Scale 1: 12 000 000; One inch to 190 miles.   POLYCONIC PROJECTION

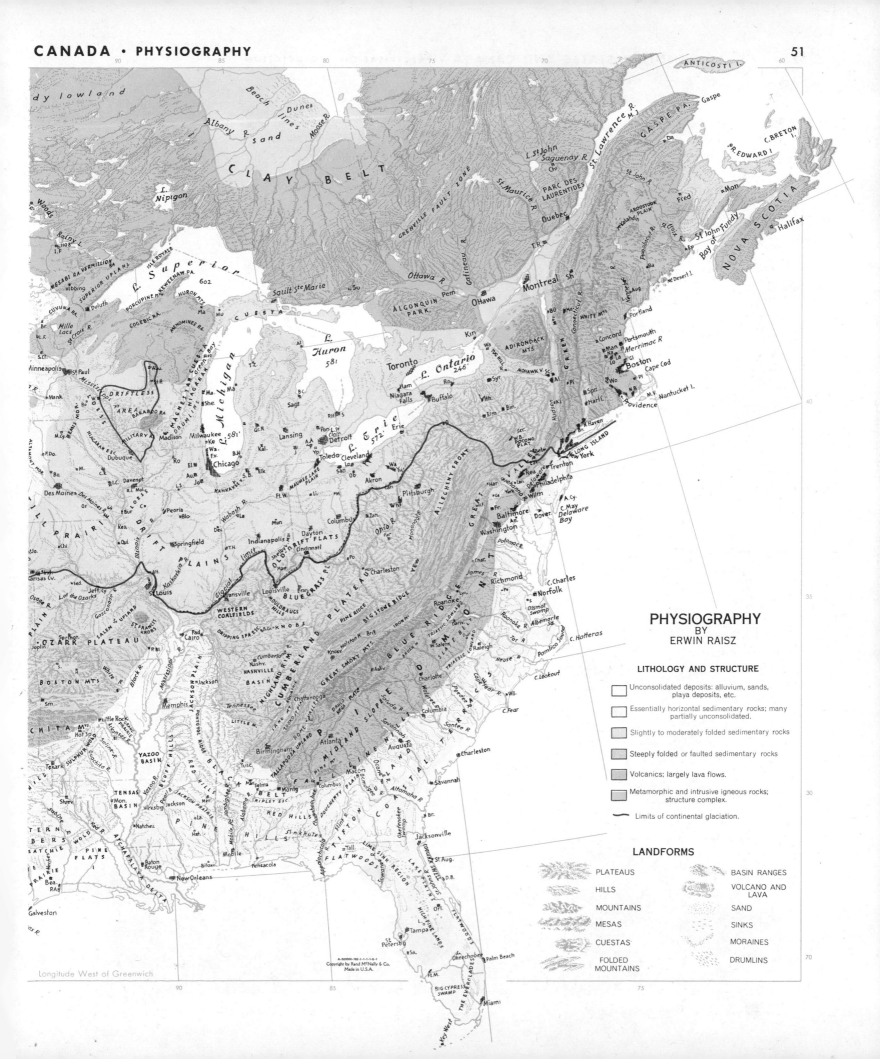

PHYSIOGRAPHY
BY
ERWIN RAISZ

LITHOLOGY AND STRUCTURE

Unconsolidated deposits: alluvium, sands, playa deposits, etc.

Essentially horizontal sedimentary rocks; many partially unconsolidated.

Slightly to moderately folded sedimentary rocks

Steeply folded or faulted sedimentary rocks

Volcanics; largely lava flows.

Metamorphic and intrusive igneous rocks; structure complex.

Limits of continental glaciation.

LANDFORMS

PLATEAUS	BASIN RANGES
HILLS	VOLCANO AND LAVA
MOUNTAINS	SAND
MESAS	SINKS
CUESTAS	MORAINES
FOLDED MOUNTAINS	DRUMLINS

Longitude West of Greenwich

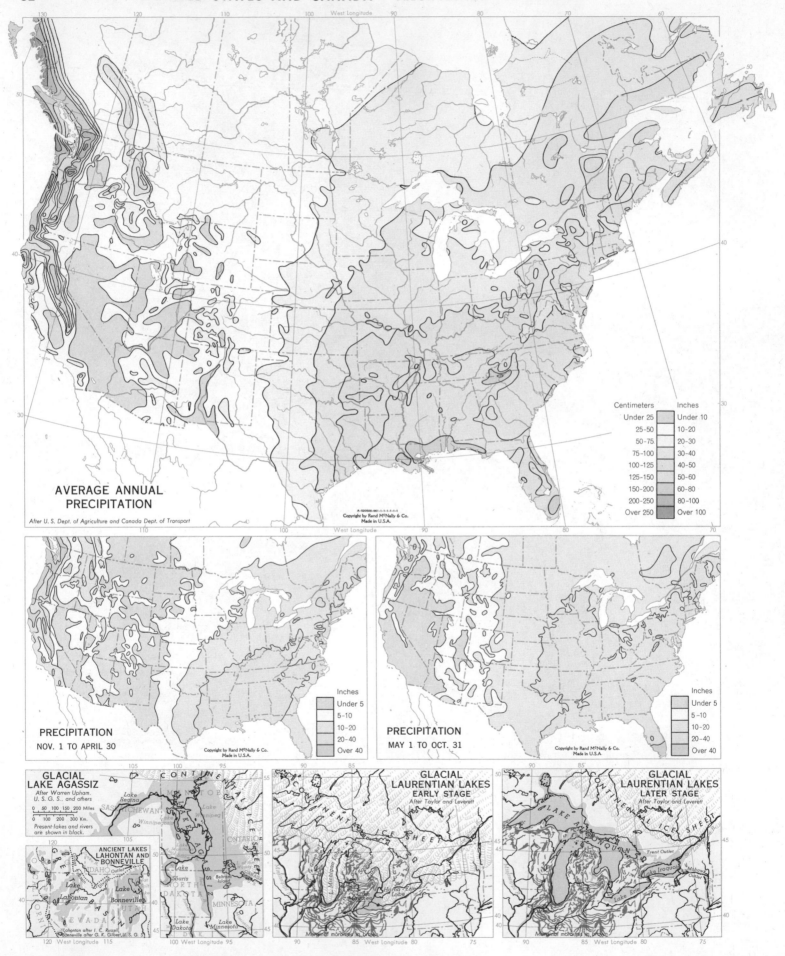

AVERAGE ANNUAL PRECIPITATION

After U. S. Dept. of Agriculture and Canada Dept. of Transport

A-520500-961-1-1-1-1-1
Copyright by Rand McNally & Co.
Made in U.S.A.

Centimeters	Inches
Under 25	Under 10
25-50	10-20
50-75	20-30
75-100	30-40
100-125	40-50
125-150	50-60
150-200	60-80
200-250	80-100
Over 250	Over 100

PRECIPITATION
NOV. 1 TO APRIL 30

Copyright by Rand McNally & Co.
Made in U.S.A.

Inches
Under 5
5-10
10-20
20-40
Over 40

PRECIPITATION
MAY 1 TO OCT. 31

Copyright by Rand McNally & Co.
Made in U.S.A.

Inches
Under 5
5-10
10-20
20-40
Over 40

GLACIAL LAKE AGASSIZ
After Warren Upham,
U. S. G. S., and others

0 50 100 150 200 Miles
0 100 200 300 Km.

Present lakes and rivers
are shown in black.

ANCIENT LAKES LAHONTAN AND BONNEVILLE

Lahontan after I. C. Russell.
Bonneville after G. K. Gilbert, U. S. G. S.

GLACIAL LAURENTIAN LAKES
EARLY STAGE
After Taylor and Leverett

Marginal moraines in brown

GLACIAL LAURENTIAN LAKES
LATER STAGE
After Taylor and Leverett

Marginal moraines in brown

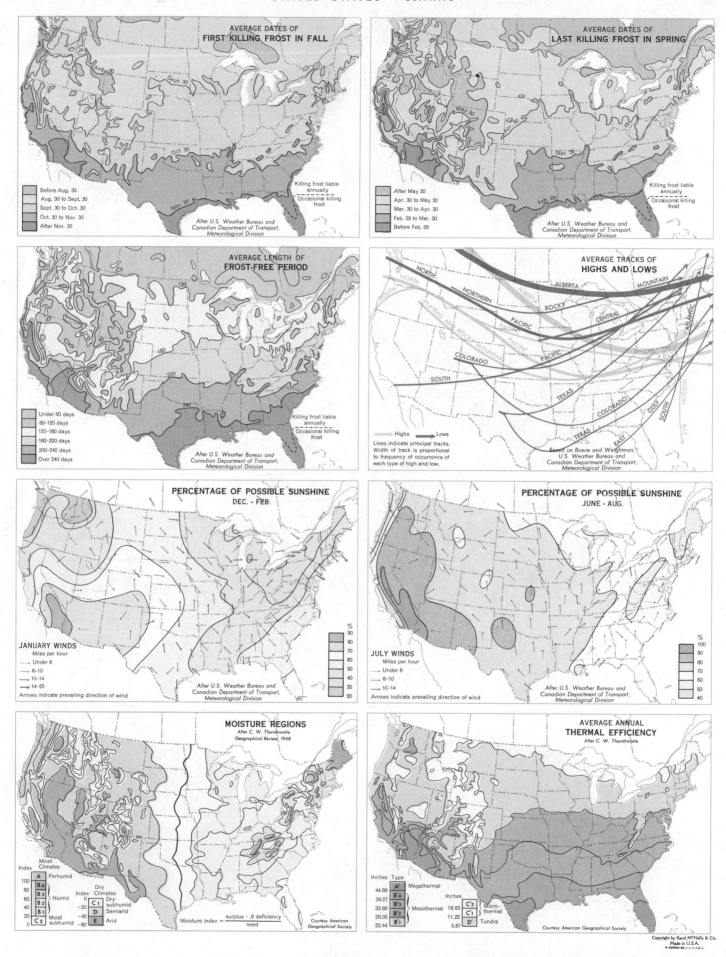

AVERAGE DATES OF
FIRST KILLING FROST IN FALL

Before Aug. 30
Aug. 30 to Sept. 30
Sept. 30 to Oct. 30
Oct. 30 to Nov. 30
After Nov. 30

Killing frost liable
annually
Occasional killing
frost

After U.S. Weather Bureau and
Canadian Department of Transport,
Meteorological Division

AVERAGE DATES OF
LAST KILLING FROST IN SPRING

After May 30
Apr. 30 to May 30
Mar. 30 to Apr. 30
Feb. 28 to Mar. 30
Before Feb. 28

Killing frost liable
annually
Occasional killing
frost

After U.S. Weather Bureau and
Canadian Department of Transport,
Meteorological Division

AVERAGE LENGTH OF
FROST-FREE PERIOD

Under 80 days
80-120 days
120-160 days
160-200 days
200-240 days
Over 240 days

Killing frost liable
annually
Occasional killing
frost

After U.S. Weather Bureau and
Canadian Department of Transport,
Meteorological Division

AVERAGE TRACKS OF
HIGHS AND LOWS

Highs   Lows
Lines indicate principal tracks.
Width of track is proportional
to frequency of occurrence of
each type of high and low.

Based on Bowie and Weightman,
U.S. Weather Bureau and
Canadian Department of Transport,
Meteorological Division

PERCENTAGE OF POSSIBLE SUNSHINE
DEC. - FEB.

JANUARY WINDS
Miles per hour
Under 6
6-10
10-14
14-20
Arrows indicate prevailing direction of wind

%
90
80
70
60
50
40
30
20

After U.S. Weather Bureau and
Canadian Department of Transport,
Meteorological Division

PERCENTAGE OF POSSIBLE SUNSHINE
JUNE - AUG.

JULY WINDS
Miles per hour
Under 6
6-10
10-14
Arrows indicate prevailing direction of wind

%
100
90
80
70
60
50
40

After U.S. Weather Bureau and
Canadian Department of Transport,
Meteorological Division

MOISTURE REGIONS
After C. W. Thornthwaite
Geographical Review, 1948

Index   Moist
         Climates
100   A   Perhumid
80   B4
60   B3   Humid
40   B2
20   B1   Moist
0   C2   subhumid

Index   Dry
         Climates
0   C1   Dry
-20   subhumid
-40   D   Semiarid
-60   E   Arid

Moisture index = surplus - .6 deficiency / need

Courtesy American
Geographical Society

AVERAGE ANNUAL
THERMAL EFFICIENCY
After C. W. Thornthwaite

Inches Type
44.88   A'   Megathermal
39.27   B'4
33.66   B'3   Mesothermal
28.05   B'2
22.44   B'1

Inches
16.83   C'2   Micro-
11.22   C'1   thermal
5.61   D'   Tundra

Courtesy American
Geographical Society

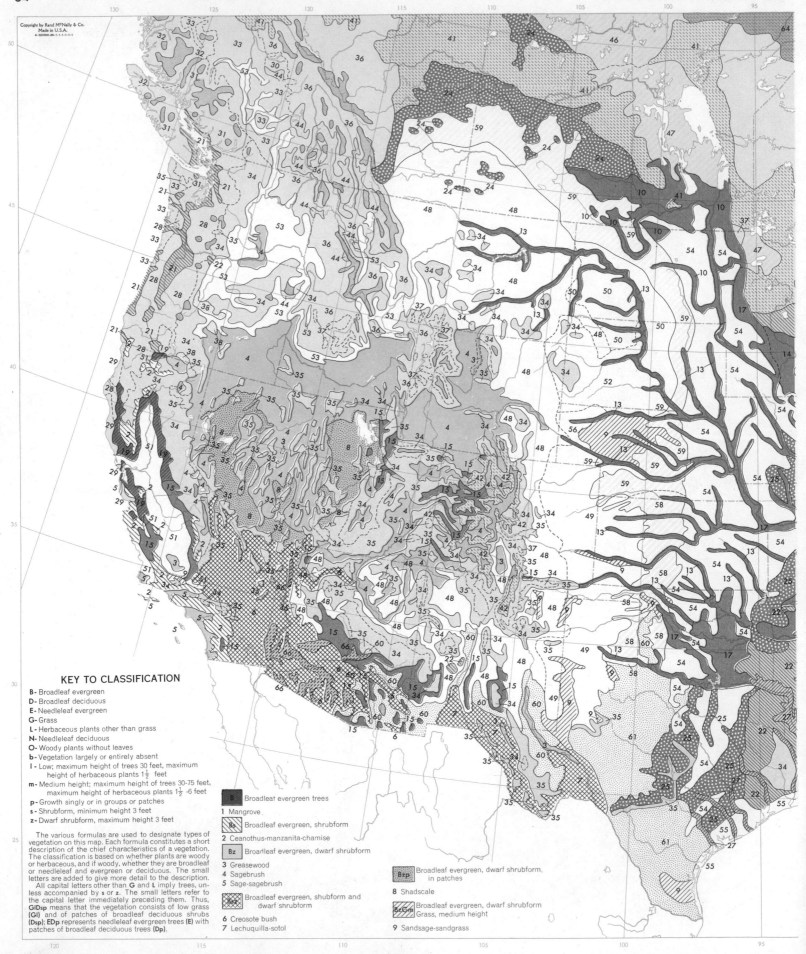

Copyright by Rand McNally & Co.
Made in U.S.A.
A-520500-86-1-1-1-1-1-1

KEY TO CLASSIFICATION

B- Broadleaf evergreen
D- Broadleaf deciduous
E- Needleleaf evergreen
G- Grass
L- Herbaceous plants other than grass
N- Needleleaf deciduous
O- Woody plants without leaves
b- Vegetation largely or entirely absent
l- Low; maximum height of trees 30 feet, maximum
    height of herbaceous plants 1½ feet
m- Medium height; maximum height of trees 30-75 feet,
    maximum height of herbaceous plants 1½ -6 feet
p- Growth singly or in groups or patches
s- Shrubform, minimum height 3 feet
z- Dwarf shrubform, maximum height 3 feet

The various formulas are used to designate types of
vegetation on this map. Each formula constitutes a short
description of the chief characteristics of a vegetation.
The classification is based on whether plants are woody
or herbaceous, and if woody, whether they are broadleaf
or needleleaf and evergreen or deciduous. The small
letters are added to give more detail to the description.

All capital letters other than **G** and **L** imply trees, unless accompanied by **s** or **z**. The small letters refer to
the capital letter immediately preceding them. Thus,
GlDsp means that the vegetation consists of low grass
(**Gl**) and of patches of broadleaf deciduous shrubs
(**Dsp**); **EDp** represents needleleaf evergreen trees (**E**) with
patches of broadleaf deciduous trees (**Dp**).

B Broadleaf evergreen trees

1 Mangrove

Bs Broadleaf evergreen, shrubform

2 Ceanothus-manzanita-chamise

Bz Broadleaf evergreen, dwarf shrubform

3 Greasewood
4 Sagebrush
5 Sage-sagebrush

Bsz Broadleaf evergreen, shubform and
    dwarf shrubform

6 Creosote bush
7 Lechuquilla-sotol

Bzp Broadleaf evergreen, dwarf shrubform,
    in patches

8 Shadscale

Bz/Gm Broadleaf evergreen, dwarf shrubform
    Grass, medium height

9 Sandsage-sandgrass

0 25 50 75 100   200   300   400   500 Miles

0 50 100   200   400   600   800 Kilometers

Scale 1:14 000 000;   One inch to 220 miles.

NATURAL VEGETATION

BY A. W. KÜCHLER

Based on "A Physiognomic Classification of Vegetation"
Annals of the Assoc. of American Geographers, Vol. 39, September, 1949

Longitude West of Greenwich

D Broadleaf deciduous trees

10 Aspen-oak
11 Beech-maple
12 Beech-tulip tree-maple-basswood
13 Cottonwood-willow
14 Maple-basswood
15 Oak
16 Oak-ash-maple
17 Oak-hickory
18 Oak-tulip tree

DB Broadleaf deciduous trees
Broadleaf evergreen trees

19 Oak-madrone

DE Broadleaf deciduous trees
Needleleaf evergreen trees

20 Maple-yellow birch-hemlock-pine
21 Oak-Douglas fir
22 Oak-pine
23 Maple-beech-hemlock

D / Gpp Broadleaf deciduous trees
Grass, medium height, in patches

24 Aspen-needle grass-wheat grass
25 Oak-hickory-bluestem

DN Broadleaf deciduous trees
Needleleaf deciduous trees

26 Bay trees-bald cypress
27 Tupelo-gum-bald cypress

E Needleleaf evergreen trees

28 Douglas fir
29 Douglas fir-redwood
30 Hemlock-arbor vitae
31 Hemlock-arbor vitae-Douglas fir
32 Hemlock-arbor vitae-fir
33 Hemlock-spruce
34 Pine
35 Pine-juniper
36 Pine-spruce
37 Spruce-fir

Esp Needleleaf evergreen, shrubform,
in patches

38 Juniper

EDp Needleleaf evergreen trees
Broadleaf deciduous trees, in patches

39 Douglas fir-pine-aspen
40 Pine-spruce-birch
41 Spruce-aspen
42 Spruce-fir-aspen
43 Spruce-poplar-birch

EN Needleleaf evergreen trees
Needleleaf deciduous trees

44 Hemlock-arbor vitae-Douglas fir-larch
45 Pine-bald cypress
46 Pine-spruce-larch
47 Spruce-larch

Gl Grass, low

48 Grama grass
49 Grama grass-buffalo grass
50 Grama grass-needle grass
51 Needle grass-blue grass
52 Wheat grass
53 Wheat grass-blue grass

Gm Grass, medium height

54 Bluestem
55 Broom grass-water grass
56 Marsh grass
57 Saw grass

Gml Grass, medium and low height

58 Bluestem-bunch grass
59 Needle grass-wheat grass

Gl / Dsp Grass, low
Broadleaf deciduous, shrubform, in patches

60 Bunch grass-oak

Gm / Dsp Grass, medium height
Broadleaf deciduous, shrubform, in patches

61 Mesquite grass-mesquite

L Herbaceous plants other than grass

62 Lichens, etc.

LEp Herbaceous plants other than grass
Needleleaf evergreen trees, in patches

63 Lichens-spruce

LEp / Np Herbaceous plants other than grass
Needleleaf evergreen trees, in patches
Needleleaf deciduous trees, in patches

64 Lichens-spruce-larch

N Needleleaf deciduous trees

65 Bald cypress

Op Woody plants without leaves, in patches

66 Palo verde-cacti-ocotillo

b Vegetation largely or entirely absent

CROPLAND HARVESTED

1—dot—25,000 acres

Total acreage
(1959)
311,476,141

U. S. Dept. of Commerce
Bureau of Census

A-520500-361-1-1-1-1-1-1
Copyright by Rand McNally & Co.
Made in U.S.A.

0 25 50 75 100   200   300   400   500 Miles

0 50 100   200   400   600   800 Kilometers

Scale: 1:12 000 000; One inch to 190 miles.

LAMBERT CONFORMAL CONIC PROJECTION

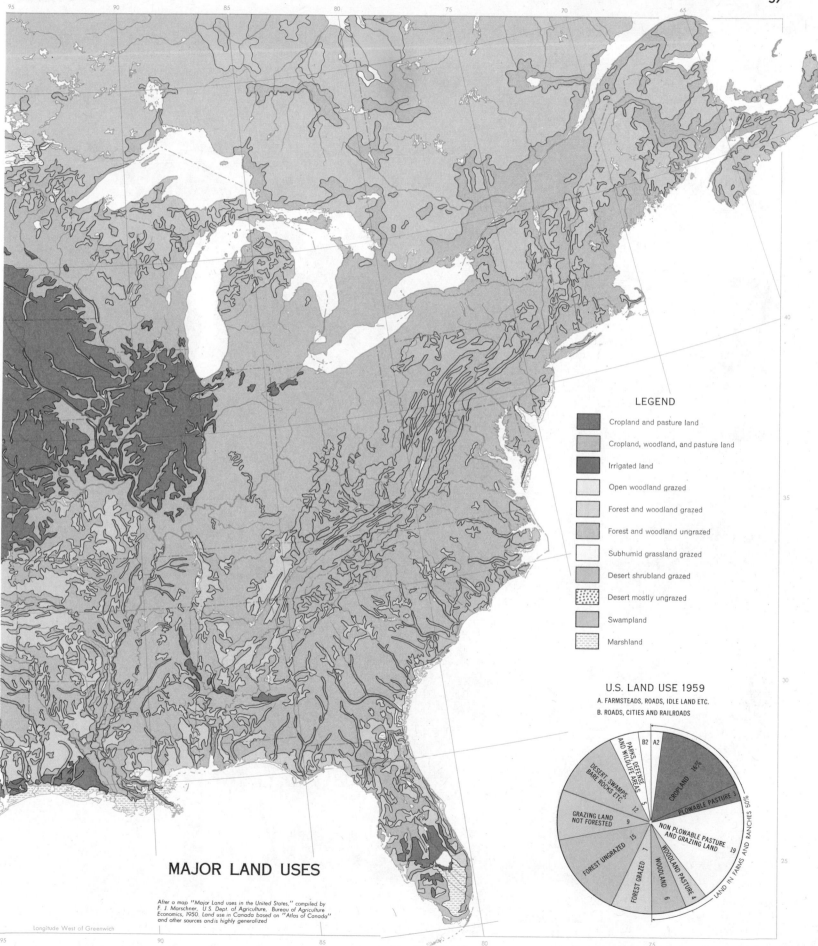

LEGEND

Cropland and pasture land

Cropland, woodland, and pasture land

Irrigated land

Open woodland grazed

Forest and woodland grazed

Forest and woodland ungrazed

Subhumid grassland grazed

Desert shrubland grazed

Desert mostly ungrazed

Swampland

Marshland

U.S. LAND USE 1959

A. FARMSTEADS, ROADS, IDLE LAND ETC.
B. ROADS, CITIES AND RAILROADS

B2 A2

PARKS, DEFENSE AND WILDLIFE AREAS.

DESERT SWAMPS, BARE ROCKS ETC.   5

GRAZING LAND NOT FORESTED   9

FOREST UNGRAZED   15

FOREST GRAZED   7

WOODLAND PASTURE 4

WOODLAND   6

12

CROPLAND   16%

PLOWABLE PASTURE 3

NON PLOWABLE PASTURE AND GRAZING LAND   19

LAND IN FARMS AND RANCHES 50%

MAJOR LAND USES

After a map "Major Land uses in the United States," compiled by
F. J. Marschner, U.S. Dept. of Agriculture, Bureau of Agriculture
Economics, 1950. Land use in Canada based on "Atlas of Canada"
and other sources and is highly generalized

Longitude West of Greenwich

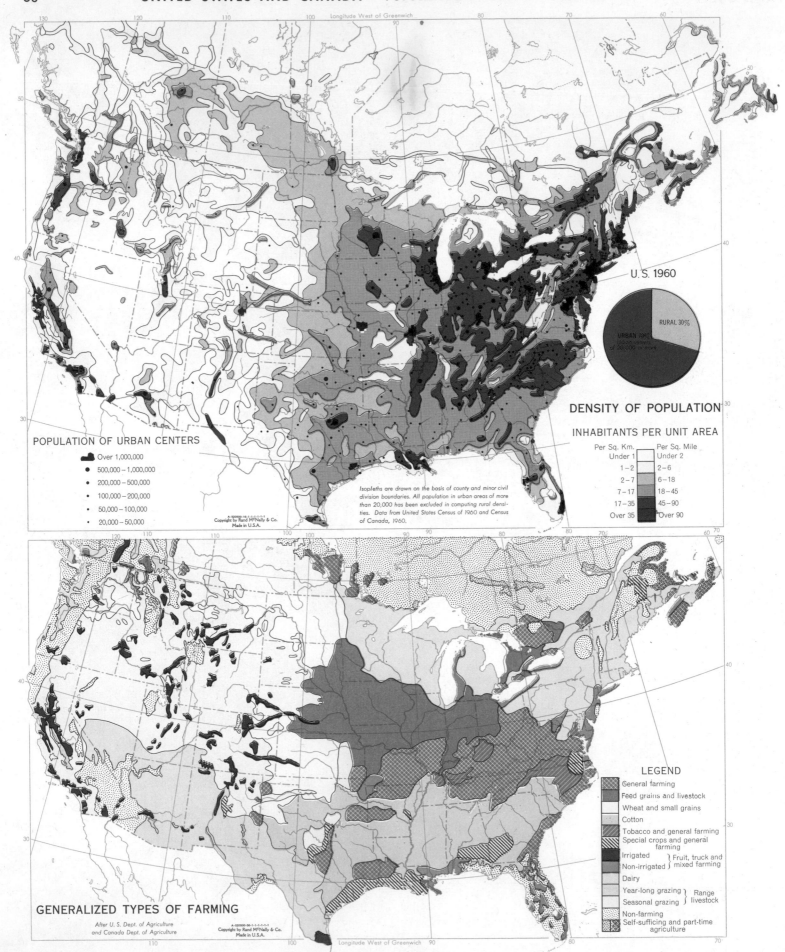

U. S. 1960

RURAL 30%

URBAN 70%
Urban centers
of 20,000 or more

DENSITY OF POPULATION

INHABITANTS PER UNIT AREA

Per Sq. Km.	Per Sq. Mile
Under 1	Under 2
1 – 2	2 – 6
2 – 7	6 – 18
7 – 17	18 – 45
17 – 35	45 – 90
Over 35	Over 90

POPULATION OF URBAN CENTERS

Over 1,000,000
500,000 – 1,000,000
200,000 – 500,000
100,000 – 200,000
50,000 – 100,000
20,000 – 50,000

Isopleths are drawn on the basis of county and minor civil division boundaries. All population in urban areas of more than 20,000 has been excluded in computing rural densities. Data from United States Census of 1960 and Census of Canada, 1960.

Copyright by Rand McNally & Co.
Made in U.S.A.

LEGEND

General farming
Feed grains and livestock
Wheat and small grains
Cotton
Tobacco and general farming
Special crops and general farming
Irrigated ⎫ Fruit, truck and
Non-irrigated ⎭ mixed farming
Dairy
Year-long grazing ⎫ Range
Seasonal grazing ⎭ livestock
Non-farming
Self-sufficing and part-time agriculture

GENERALIZED TYPES OF FARMING

*After U. S. Dept. of Agriculture
and Canada Dept. of Agriculture*

Copyright by Rand McNally & Co.
Made in U.S.A.

Longitude West of Greenwich

Scale 1: 28 000 000; One inch to 440 miles.   LAMBERT CONFORMAL CONIC PROJECTION

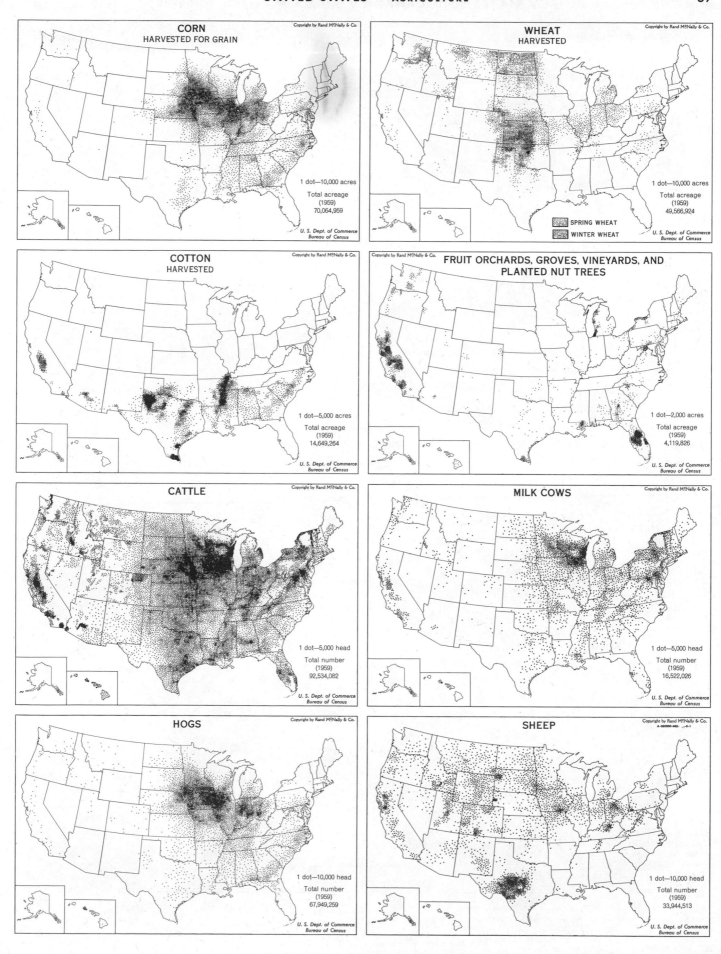

CORN
HARVESTED FOR GRAIN

Copyright by Rand M?Nally & Co.

1 dot—10,000 acres

Total acreage
(1959)
70,064,959

U. S. Dept. of Commerce
Bureau of Census

WHEAT
HARVESTED

Copyright by Rand M?Nally & Co.

1 dot—10,000 acres

Total acreage
(1959)
49,566,924

SPRING WHEAT
WINTER WHEAT

U. S. Dept. of Commerce
Bureau of Census

COTTON
HARVESTED

Copyright by Rand M?Nally & Co.

1 dot—5,000 acres

Total acreage
(1959)
14,649,264

U. S. Dept. of Commerce
Bureau of Census

FRUIT ORCHARDS, GROVES, VINEYARDS, AND PLANTED NUT TREES

Copyright by Rand M?Nally & Co.

1 dot—2,000 acres

Total acreage
(1959)
4,119,826

U. S. Dept. of Commerce
Bureau of Census

CATTLE

Copyright by Rand M?Nally & Co.

1 dot—5,000 head

Total number
(1959)
92,534,082

U. S. Dept. of Commerce
Bureau of Census

MILK COWS

Copyright by Rand M?Nally & Co.

1 dot—5,000 head

Total number
(1959)
16,522,026

U. S. Dept. of Commerce
Bureau of Census

HOGS

Copyright by Rand M?Nally & Co.

1 dot—10,000 head

Total number
(1959)
67,949,259

U. S. Dept. of Commerce
Bureau of Census

SHEEP

Copyright by Rand M?Nally & Co.
A-529000-962-   -0-1

1 dot—10,000 head

Total number
(1959)
33,944,513

U. S. Dept. of Commerce
Bureau of Census

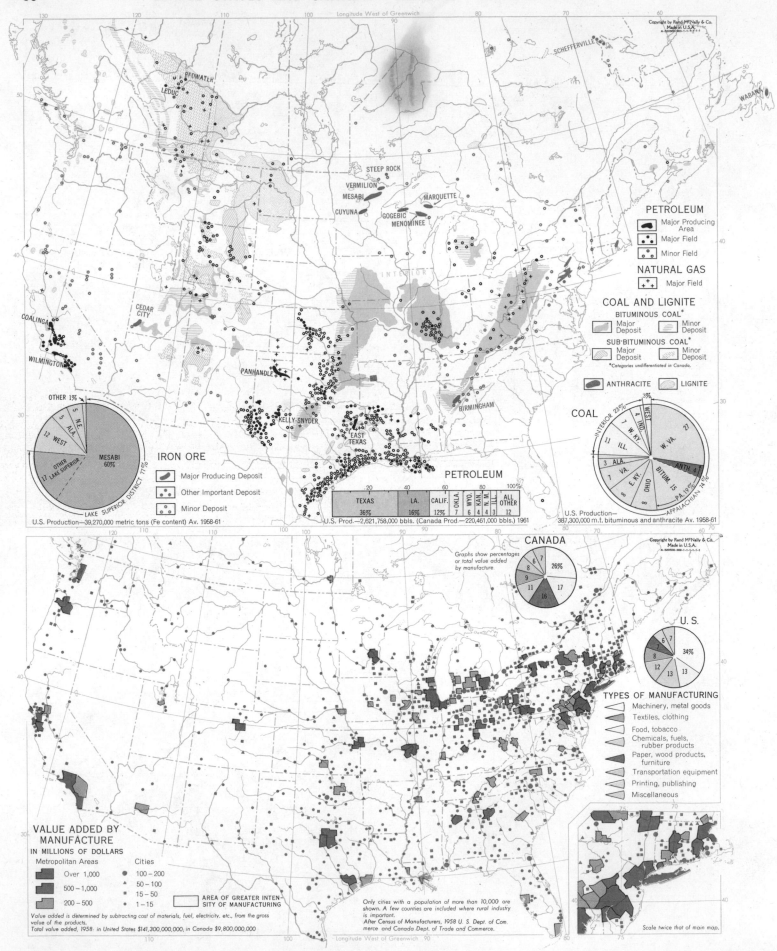

Copyright by Rand McNally & Co.
Made in U.S.A.
A-520000-963-1-1-1-1-1-1

PETROLEUM

Major Producing Area

Major Field

Minor Field

NATURAL GAS

Major Field

COAL AND LIGNITE

BITUMINOUS COAL*

Major Deposit

Minor Deposit

SUB-BITUMINOUS COAL*

Major Deposit

Minor Deposit

*Categories undifferentiated in Canada.

ANTHRACITE   LIGNITE

IRON ORE

Major Producing Deposit

Other Important Deposit

Minor Deposit

U.S. Production—39,270,000 metric tons (Fe content) Av. 1958-61

OTHER 1%
5 N.E.
5 ALA.
12 WEST
OTHER
17 LAKE SUPERIOR
MESABI 60%
LAKE SUPERIOR DISTRICT 17%

PETROLEUM

TEXAS 36%	LA. 16%	CALIF. 12%	OKLA. 7	WYO. 6	KAN. 4	N.M. 4	ILL. 3	ALL OTHER 12

U.S. Prod.—2,621,758,000 bbls. (Canada Prod.—220,461,000 bbls.) 1961

COAL

INTERIOR 23%
WEST 4
W. IND. 7
W. KY. 7
ILL. 11
ALA. 3
VA. 7
E. KY. 8
OHIO 8
W. VA. 27
ANTH. 4
BITUM. 15
PA. 19%
APPALACHIAN 74%
3%

U.S. Production—387,300,000 m.t. bituminous and anthracite Av. 1958-61

Copyright by Rand McNally & Co.
Made in U.S.A.
A-520000-368-1-1-1-1-1-1

CANADA

Graphs show percentages or total value added by manufacture.

7
6
8
9
11
16
17
26%

U.S.

6 7
7
8
12
13
13
34%

TYPES OF MANUFACTURING

Machinery, metal goods

Textiles, clothing

Food, tobacco

Chemicals, fuels, rubber products

Paper, wood products, furniture

Transportation equipment

Printing, publishing

Miscellaneous

VALUE ADDED BY MANUFACTURE

IN MILLIONS OF DOLLARS

Metropolitan Areas

Over 1,000

500 – 1,000

200 – 500

Cities

100 – 200

50 – 100

15 – 50

1 – 15

AREA OF GREATER INTENSITY OF MANUFACTURING

Value added is determined by subtracting cost of materials, fuel, electricity, etc., from the gross value of the products.
Total value added, 1958: in United States $141,300,000,000, in Canada $9,800,000,000

Only cities with a population of more than 10,000 are shown. A few counties are included where rural industry is important.
After Census of Manufacturers, 1958 U.S. Dept. of Commerce and Canada Dept. of Trade and Commerce.

Scale twice that of main map.

Scale 1: 28 000 000; One inch to 440 miles.   LAMBERT CONFORMAL CONIC PROJECTION

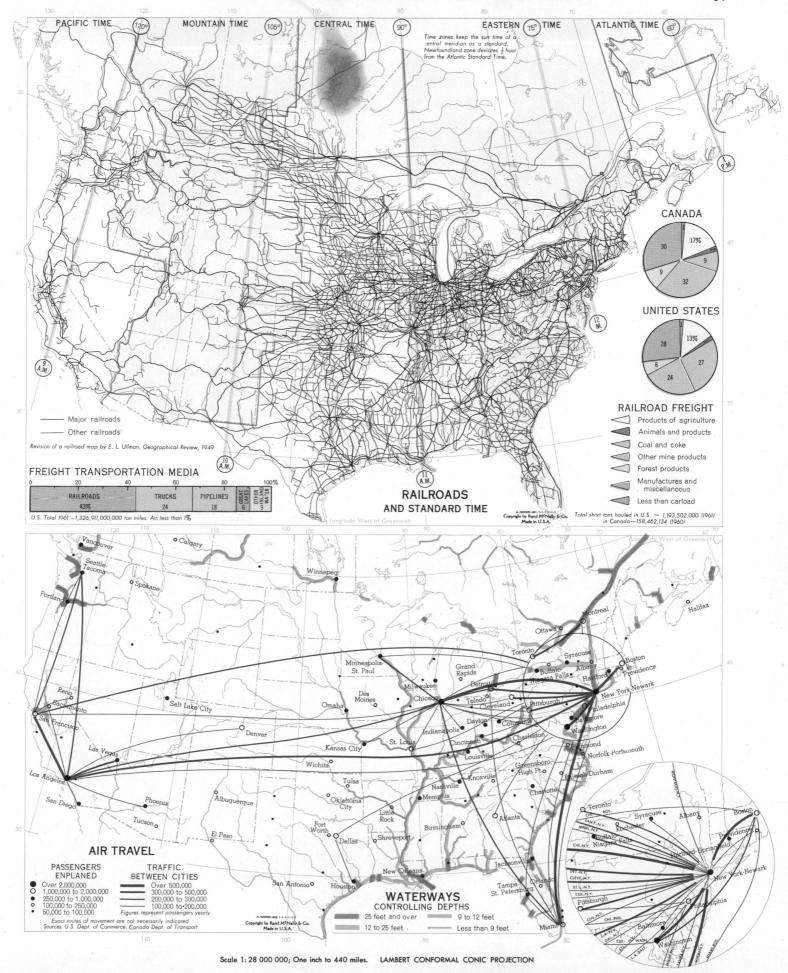

PACIFIC TIME   (120°)   MOUNTAIN TIME   (105°)   CENTRAL TIME   (90°)   EASTERN (75°) TIME   ATLANTIC TIME   (60°)

Time zones keep the sun time of a
central meridian as a standard.
Newfoundland zone deviates ½ hour
from the Atlantic Standard Time.

CANADA

17%
30
9
9
32

UNITED STATES

13%
28
27
6
24

RAILROAD FREIGHT

- Products of agriculture
- Animals and products
- Coal and coke
- Other mine products
- Forest products
- Manufactures and miscellaneous
- Less than carload

— Major railroads
— Other railroads

Revision of a railroad map by E. L. Ullman, Geographical Review, 1949

FREIGHT TRANSPORTATION MEDIA

0	20	40	60	80	100%

RAILROADS 43%   TRUCKS 24   PIPELINES 18   GREAT LAKES 6   OTHER WATER 9

U.S. Total 1961—1,326,911,000,000 ton miles. Air, less than 1%

RAILROADS
AND STANDARD TIME

A-520500-481-1-1-1-1-1-1-1
Copyright by Rand M?Nally & Co.
Made in U.S.A.

Total short tons hauled in U.S. — 1,193,502,000 (1961)
in Canada—158,462,134 (1960)

Longitude West of Greenwich

Vancouver   Calgary   Winnipeg   Halifax
Seattle-Tacoma   Spokane
Portland
Reno   Salt Lake City   Minneapolis-St. Paul   Grand Rapids   Montreal   Ottawa   Toronto   Syracuse   Boston
Sacramento   Des Moines   Milwaukee   Detroit   Buffalo   Albany   Providence   Hartford
San Francisco   Omaha   Chicago   Toledo   Cleveland   Niagara Falls   New York-Newark
Las Vegas   Denver   Indianapolis   Dayton   Pittsburgh   Philadelphia
Los Angeles   Kansas City   St. Louis   Cincinnati   Columbus   Baltimore   Washington
San Diego   Phoenix   Wichita   Louisville   Charleston   Richmond   Norfolk-Portsmouth
Tucson   Albuquerque   Tulsa   Oklahoma City   Nashville   Knoxville   Greensboro High Pt.   Raleigh-Durham
El Paso   Fort Worth   Little Rock   Memphis   Birmingham   Charlotte   Atlanta
Dallas   Shreveport

AIR TRAVEL

PASSENGERS ENPLANED
- ● Over 2,000,000
- ○ 1,000,000 to 2,000,000
- ○ 250,000 to 1,000,000
- ○ 100,000 to 250,000
- • 50,000 to 100,000

TRAFFIC BETWEEN CITIES
- Over 500,000
- 300,000 to 500,000
- 200,000 to 300,000
- 100,000 to 200,000

Figures represent passengers yearly

Exact routes of movement are not necessarily indicated
Sources: U.S. Dept. of Commerce; Canada Dept. of Transport

San Antonio   Houston   New Orleans   Jacksonville   Tampa-St. Petersburg   Orlando   Miami

A-520500-482-1-1-1-1-1-1
Copyright by Rand M?Nally & Co.
Made in U.S.A.

WATERWAYS
CONTROLLING DEPTHS
- 25 feet and over
- 12 to 25 feet
- 9 to 12 feet
- Less than 9 feet

Toronto   Syracuse   Albany   Boston
BOS.
Rochester   Providence
Buffalo   Niagara Falls   Hartford-Springfield
New York-Newark
Pittsburgh   Philadelphia
Baltimore
Washington
Miami

Scale 1: 28 000 000; One inch to 440 miles.   LAMBERT CONFORMAL CONIC PROJECTION

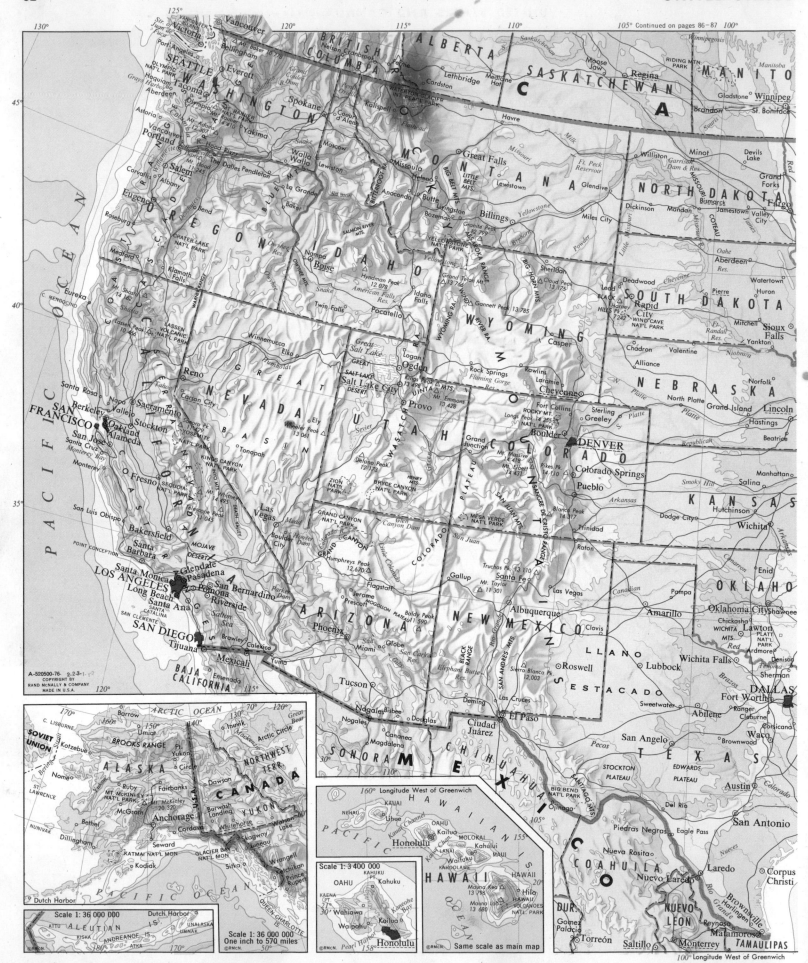

Scale 1:12 000 000; one inch to 190 miles. Polyconic Projection
Elevations and depressions are given in feet

Relief

Meters		Feet
3050		10 000
1525		5000
610		2000
305		1000
152.5		500
0	Sea Level	0
152.5		Below Sea Level
1525		500
3050		5 000
6100		10 000
		20 000

0 25 50 75 100   200   300   400   500 Miles
0   100   200   300   400   600   800 Kilometers

STATE OF ALASKA

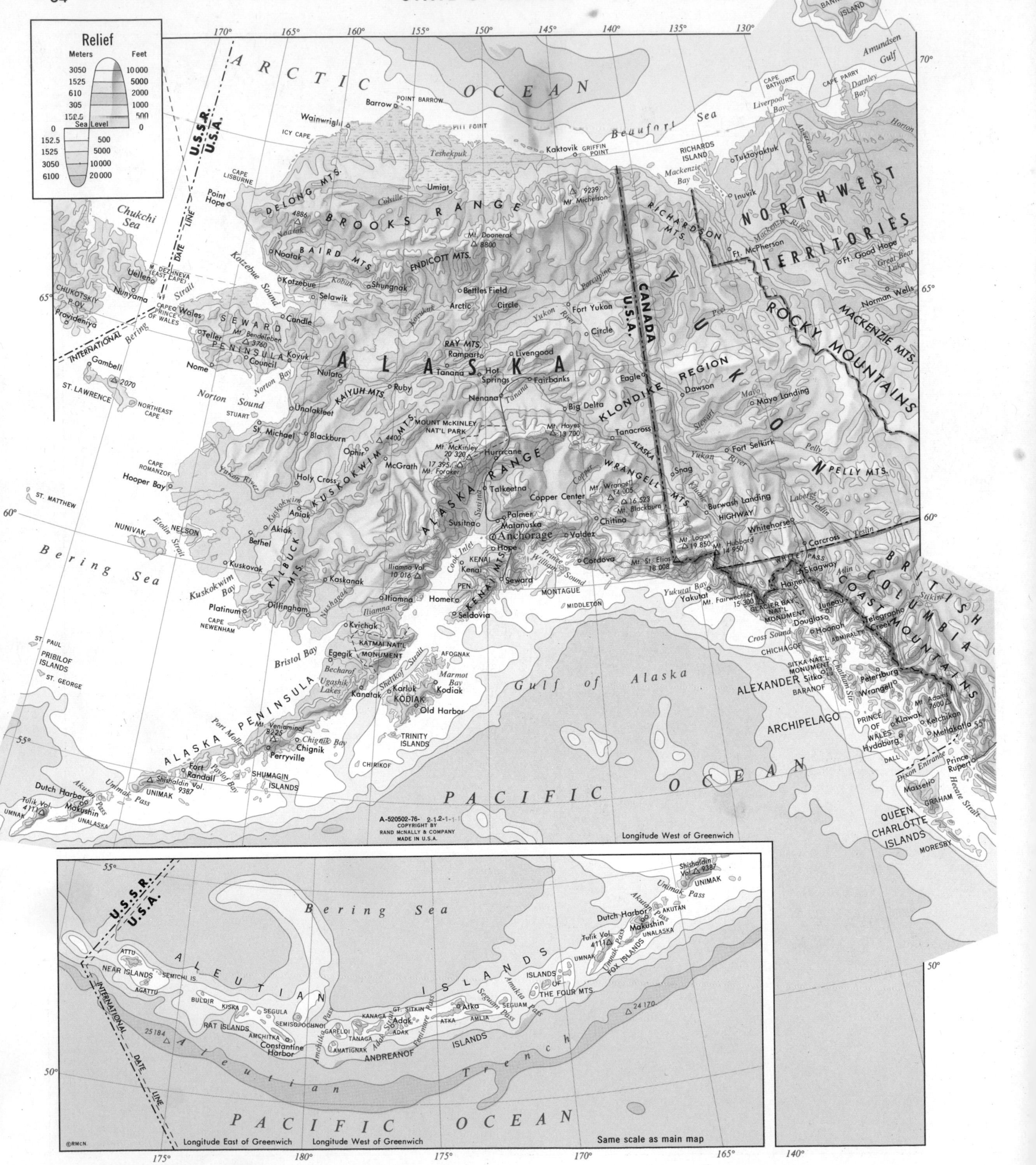

Relief

Meters	Feet
3050	10 000
1525	5000
610	2000
305	1000
152.5	500
0 Sea Level	0
152.5	500
1525	5000
3050	10000
6100	20 000

ARCTIC OCEAN

U.S.S.R.
U.S.A.

DATE LINE

Chukchi Sea

Point Barrow
Barrow
Wainwright
ICY CAPE
PITT POINT
Teshekpuk
Kaktovik GRIFFIN POINT
Beaufort Sea
RICHARDS ISLAND
CAPE BATHURST
CAPE PARRY
Darnley Bay
Liverpool Bay
Amundsen Gulf
BANKS ISLAND
Horton
Aklavik
Mackenzie Bay
Tuktoyaktuk
Inuvik

CAPE LISBURNE
Point Hope
DELONG MTS.
4886
Noatak
BROOKS RANGE
Mt. Doonerak 8800
9239 Mt. Michelson
RICHARDSON MTS.
Ft. McPherson
Ft. Good Hope
NORTHWEST TERRITORIES
Great Bear Lake
Mackenzie River

Kotzebue Sound
Noatak
BAIRD MTS.
Kobuk
Shungnak
Selawik
ENDICOTT MTS.
Bettles Field
Arctic Circle
Fort Yukon
Porcupine
CANADA U.S.A.
YUKON
Peel
ROCKY MOUNTAINS
MACKENZIE MTS.
Norman Wells

CHUKOTSKIY P.O.V.
Provideniya
M. DESHNEVA (EAST CAPE)
Uelleno
Nunyama
CAPE PRINCE OF WALES
Kotzebue
Candle
Circle
Eagle
KLONDIKE REGION
Dawson
Mayo
Mayo Landing
Stewart

INTERNATIONAL
Bering Strait
CAPE PRINCE OF WALES
Teller
Mt. Bendeleben 3760
SEWARD PENINSULA
Koyuk
Council
Nome
Gambell
ST. LAWRENCE
2070
NORTHEAST CAPE
Nulato
KAIYUH MTS.
RAY MTS.
Ramparto
Tanana
Livengood
Hot Springs
Fairbanks
Nenana
Tanana
Yukon River
Fort Selkirk
Yukon River
Pelly
PELLY MTS.

ALASKA

Norton Sound
Norton Bay
St. Michael
Blackburn
Stuart
Ruby
Ophir
McGrath
MOUNT McKINLEY NAT'L PARK
4400
Mt. McKinley 20 320
17 395 Mt. Foraker
Hurricane
Big Delta
Mt. Hayes 13 700
Tanacross
ALASKA
Snag
BRITISH COLUMBIA
COAST MOUNTAINS

St. Matthew
NELSON
NUNIVAK
Bethel
Akiak
Aniak
Holy Cross
KUSKOKWIM
Talkeetna
ALASKA RANGE
Susitna
Palmer
Matanuska
WRANGELL MTS.
Mt. Wrangell 14 005
16 523 Mt. Blackburn
Chitina
Copper Center
Copper River
Kluane
Burwash Landing
ALASKA HIGHWAY
Whitehorse
Teslin
Atlin

Bering Sea
ST. PAUL
PRIBILOF ISLANDS
ST. GEORGE
Hooper Bay
CAPE ROMANZOF
Kuskokwim Bay
KILBUCK MTS.
Dillingham
Platinum
CAPE NEWENHAM
Iliamna Vol 10 016
KENAI MTS.
Anchorage
Hope
Kenai
KENAI PEN.
Homer
Seldovia
Cook Inlet
Valdez
Cordova
Prince William Sound
Seward
MONTAGUE
MIDDLETON
Mt. St. Elias 18 008
Mt. Logan 19 850
Mt. Hubbard 14 950
Yakutat
Yukutat Bay
Mt. Fairweather 15 300
GLACIER BAY NAT'L MONUMENT
Haines
Skagway
WHITE PASS
Carcross
SUMMIT PASS

Kuskokwim River
Kvichak
KATMAI NAT'L MONUMENT
Egegik
Becharof
Ugashik Lakes
Kanatak
Karluk
KODIAK
Old Harbor
Kodiak
Marmot Bay
AFOGNAK
Shelikof Strait
TRINITY ISLANDS
CHIRIKOF

Bristol Bay
ALASKA PENINSULA
Port Moller
Mt. Veniaminof 8225
Chignik
Perryville
Chignik Bay
SHUMAGIN ISLANDS
Port Pavlof Bay
Fort Randall
Shishaldin Vol. 9387
UNIMAK

Gulf of Alaska

PACIFIC OCEAN

Dutch Harbor
Tulik Vol 4111
Makushin
UMNAK
UNALASKA
Akutan Pass
Unimak Pass

Cross Sound
CHICHAGOF
SITKA NAT'L MONUMENT
Sitka
BARANOF
ALEXANDER ARCHIPELAGO
PRINCE OF WALES
Hydaburg
Juneau
Douglas
Hoonah
ADMIRALTY
Petersburg
Wrangell
Telegraph Creek
Stikine
Mt. Ada 7600
Klawak
Ketchikan
Metlakatla
BALL
Hecate Strait
QUEEN CHARLOTTE ISLANDS
Dixon Entrance
Prince Rupert
Masseto
GRAHAM
MORESBY

A-520502-76- 2-1-2-1-1
COPYRIGHT BY
RAND McNALLY & COMPANY
MADE IN U.S.A.

Longitude West of Greenwich

Inset map (Aleutian Islands)

U.S.S.R.
U.S.A.
INTERNATIONAL DATE LINE

Bering Sea

ATTU
NEAR ISLANDS
SEMICHI IS.
AGATTU
BULDIR
KISKA
RAT ISLANDS
AMCHITKA
25 184
Constantine Harbor
SEGULA
SEMISOPOCHNOI
GARELOI
TANAGA
AMATIGNAK
KANAGA
GT. SITKIN
Adak
ANDREANOF ISLANDS
ATKA
AMLIA
SEGUAM
Seguam Pass
ISLANDS OF THE FOUR MTS.
24 170
ALEUTIAN ISLANDS
FOX ISLANDS
UMNAK
Tulik Vol 4111
Makushin
UNALASKA
Dutch Harbor
AKUTAN
Akutan Pass
Unimak Pass
UNIMAK
Shishaldin Vol 9387

Aleutian Trench

PACIFIC OCEAN

Longitude East of Greenwich
Longitude West of Greenwich
Same scale as main map

0 50 100 200 300 400 Miles
0 100 200 300 400 500 600 Kilometers

Scale 1: 12 000 000; one inch to 190 miles.   Conic Projection

Elevations and depressions are given in feet

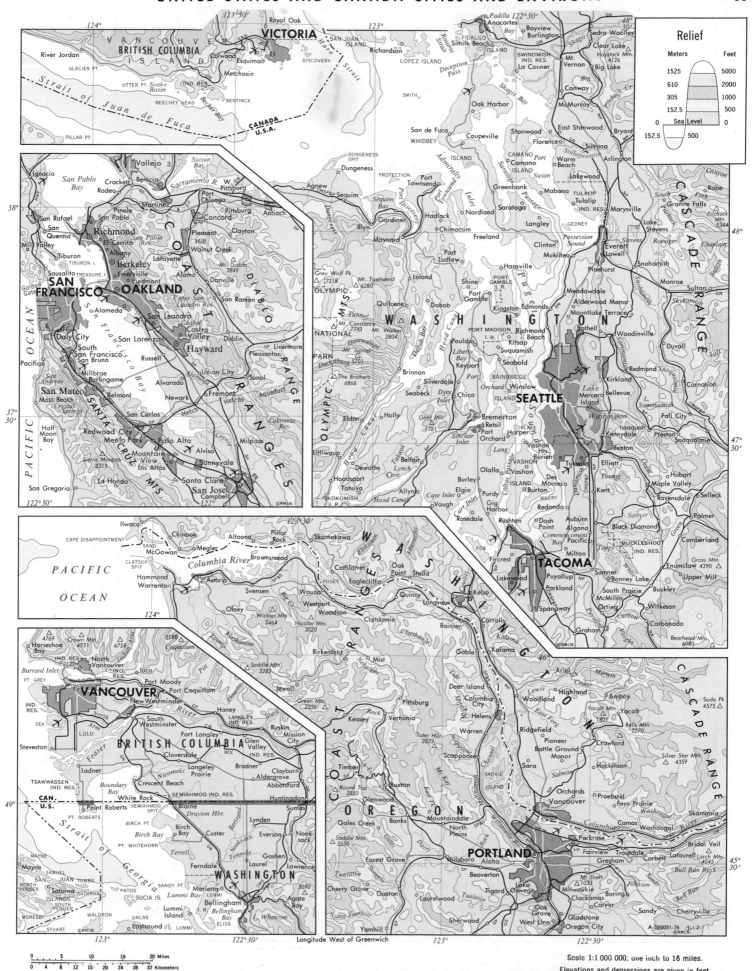

Relief

Meters	Feet
1525	5000
610	2000
305	1000
152.5	500
0	Sea Level	0
152.5	500

Longitude West of Greenwich

Scale 1:1 000 000, one inch to 16 miles.
Elevations and depressions are given in feet.

0   5   10   15   20 Miles
0 4 8 12 16 20 24 28 32 Kilometers

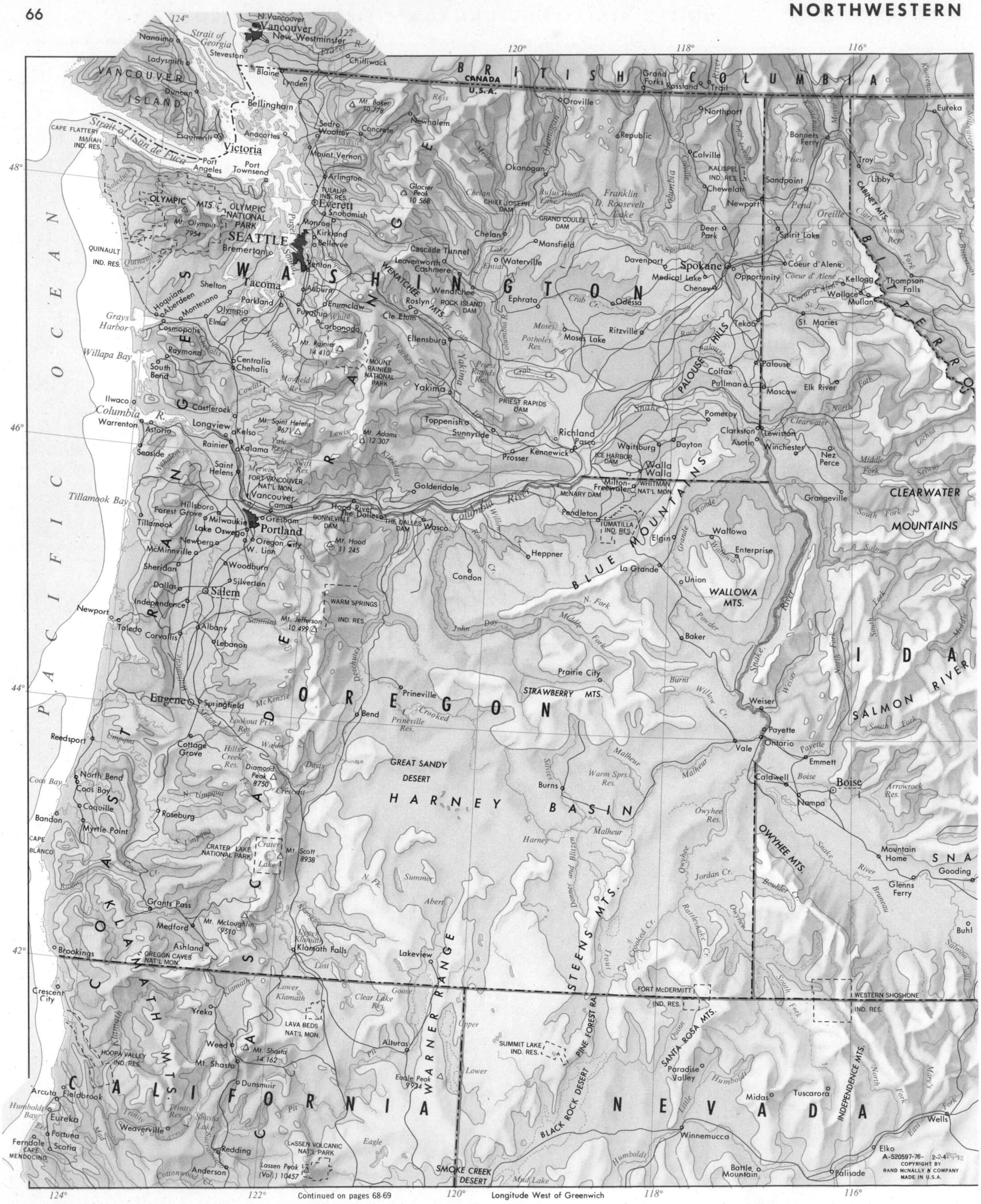

PACIFIC OCEAN

BRITISH COLUMBIA
CANADA
U.S.A.

VANCOUVER ISLAND

Strait of Georgia

Strait of Juan de Fuca

CAPE FLATTERY

WASHINGTON

OLYMPIC MTS.
OLYMPIC NATIONAL PARK
Mt. Olympus 7954

QUINAULT IND. RES.

N. Vancouver
Vancouver
New Westminster
Steveston
Blaine
Lynden
Chilliwack
Nanaimo
Ladysmith
Duncan
Esquimalt
Victoria
Bellingham
Anacortes
Sedro Woolley
Concrete
Newhalem
Ross
Oroville
Northport
Grand Forks
Rossland
Trail
Euteka
Port Angeles
Port Townsend
Mount Vernon
Arlington
Glacier Peak 10 568
Chelan
CHIEF JOSEPH DAM
Okanogan
Republic
Colville
KALISPEL IND. RES.
Chewelah
Sandpoint
Bonners Ferry
Troy
Libby
Mt. Baker 10,778
Newport
Deer Park
Spirit Lake
CABINET MTS.
Noxon Res.

Everett
Snohomish
Monroe
Kirkland
Bellevue
Renton
SEATTLE
Bremerton
Tacoma
Shelton
Auburn
Enumclaw
Puyallup
Carbonado
Cascade Tunnel
Leavenworth
Cashmere
Wenatchee
Rock Island Dam
GRAND COULEE DAM
Waterville
Mansfield
Davenport
Spokane
Medical Lake
Cheney
Opportunity
Coeur d'Alene
Kellogg
Wallace
Mullan
Thompson Falls
GRAND COULEE DAM
St. Joe
St. Maries

Hoquiam
Aberdeen
Montesano
Olympia
Elma
Cosmopolis
Grays Harbor
Willapa Bay
Raymond
South Bend
Centralia
Chehalis
Parkland
Roslyn
Cle Elum
Ellensburg
Ephrata
Moses Lake
Ritzville
Odessa
PALOUSE HILLS
Tekoa
Palouse
Colfax
Pullman
Moscow
Elk River

Ilwaco
Columbia R.
Warrenton
Astoria
Castlerock
Longview
Kelso
Kalama
Mt. Saint Helens 9671
Yale
Mt. Adams 12 307
Yakima
Toppenish
Sunnyside
Priest Rapids Dam
Richland
Kennewick
Prosser
Pasco
Waitsburg
Dayton
Clarkston
Lewiston
Asotin
Winchester
Nez Perce
Pomeroy
Grangeville
CLEARWATER MOUNTAINS

Seaside
Rainier
Saint Helens
Merwin
FORT VANCOUVER NAT'L MON.
Vancouver
Camas
Hood River
The Dalles
BONNEVILLE DAM
THE DALLES DAM
Wasco
Goldendale
McNARY DAM
Milton-Freewater
WHITMAN NAT'L MON.
Walla Walla
ICE HARBOR DAM
Pendleton
TUMATILLA IND. RES.
Elgin
Wallowa
Enterprise

Tillamook Bay
Tillamook
Hillsboro
Forest Grove
Milwaukie
Gresham
PORTLAND
Lake Oswego
Oregon City
W. Linn
McMinnville
Newberg
Sheridan
Dallas
Salem
Independence
Silverton
Woodburn
Albany
Lebanon
Corvallis
WARM SPRINGS IND. RES.
Mt. Jefferson 10 499
Condon
Heppner
Prairie City
STRAWBERRY MTS.
La Grande
Union
WALLOWA MTS.
Baker

Newport
Toledo
Eugene
Springfield
Lookout Pt.
Prineville
Bend
Prineville Res.
Crooked
OREGON
John Day
N. Fork
Middle Fork
Willow Cr.
Powder
Payette
Vale
Ontario
SALMON RIVER
IDAHO

Reedsport
Cottage Grove
Hills Creek Res.
Diamond Peak 8750
Crescent
Davis
Waldo
GREAT SANDY DESERT
Burns
Warm Sprs. Res.
Malheur
HARNEY BASIN
Harney
Malheur
Caldwell
Boise
BOISE
Nampa
Emmett
Arrowrock Res.
Mountain Home
SNA

Coos Bay
North Bend
Coos Bay
Coquille
Bandon
Myrtle Point
Roseburg
N. Umpqua
S. Umpqua
CAPE BLANCO
CRATER LAKE NATIONAL PARK
Crater Lake
Mt. Scott 8938
Summer
Abert
OWYHEE MTS.
Owyhee Res.
Jordan Cr.
Boulder
Glenns Ferry
Gooding
Buhl

Grants Pass
Medford
Mt. McLoughlin 9510
Ashland
OREGON CAVES NAT'L MON.
KLAMATH MTS.
Upper Klamath Lake
Klamath Falls
Lost
Lakeview
WARNER RANGE
STEENS MTS.
Donner and Blitzen
Trout
FORT McDERMITT IND. RES.
WESTERN SHOSHONE IND. RES.

Brookings
Crescent City
Lower Klamath
Clear Lake Res.
Goose
LAVA BEDS NAT'L MON.
Weed
Alturas
Upper
SUMMIT LAKE IND. RES.
PINE FOREST RA.
SANTA ROSA MTS.
Paradise Valley
Humboldt
INDEPENDENCE MTS.
Wells

Arcata
Fieldbrook
Humboldt Bay
Eureka
Fortuna
Scotia
Ferndale
CAPE MENDOCINO
Yreka
Mt. Shasta 14 162
Dunsmuir
Weaverville
Redding
Anderson
Trinity Res.
Shasta Lake
LASSEN VOLCANIC NATIONAL PARK
Lassen Peak (Vol.) 10457
Eagle Peak 9934
Eagle
CALIFORNIA
Lower
SMOKE CREEK DESERT
Mud Lake
BLACK ROCK DESERT
Quinn
Rattlesnake Cr.
Paradise Valley
Midas
Tuscarora
NEVADA
Winnemucca
Humboldt
Battle Mountain
Palisade
Elko

Continued on pages 68-69

Longitude West of Greenwich

A-520597-76- 2-2-4-   '12
COPYRIGHT BY
RAND McNALLY & COMPANY
MADE IN U.S.A.

Scale 1: 4 000 000; one inch to 64 miles. Conic Projection
Elevations and depressions are given in feet

124°   122°   120°   118°   116°
48°   46°   44°   42°

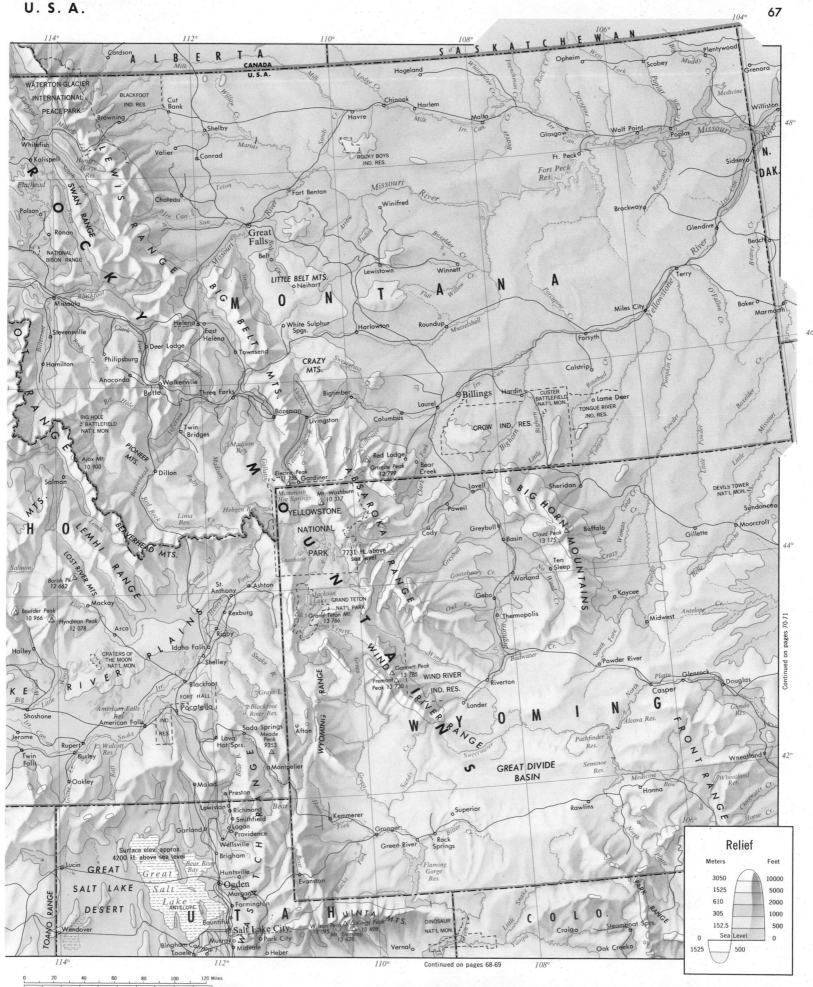

ALBERTA

CANADA
U.S.A.

SASKATCHEWAN

WATERTON-GLACIER
INTERNATIONAL
PEACE PARK

BLACKFOOT
IND. RES.

Cardson

Milk

Opheim

West

Fork

Plentywood

Muddy

Cr.

Grenora

Hogeland

Whitewater

Cr.

Rock

Cr.

Frenchman

Cr.

Poplar

Medicine

Scobey

Williston

Cut
Bank

Willow

Cr.

Chinook

Harlem

Milk

River

Malta

Cr.

Bear

Cr.

Glasgow

Can.

Wolf Point

Poplar

Missouri

N.
DAK.

48°

Browning

Shelby

Havre

Irr.

Ft. Peck

Sidney

Whitefish

Valier

Conrad

Marias

ROCKY BOYS
IND. RES.

Fort Peck
Res.

Redwater

River

Kalispell

Teton

Missouri

River

Brockway

Glendive

Beach

Polson

Flathead

Fort Benton

Winifred

Beaver

Cr.

Ronan

Sun

Irr. Can.

Winnett

NATIONAL
BISON RANGE

Great
Falls

Belt

LITTLE BELT MTS.

Lewistown

Terry

Missoula

Blackfoot

Neihart

Winnett

Judith

Flat

Willow

Miles City

Baker

Marmarth

46°

Helena

East
Helena

White Sulphur
Spgs.

Harlowton

Roundup

Musselshell

Forsyth

O'Fallon

Cr.

Stevensville

Deer Lodge

Townsend

Yellowstone

River

Hamilton

Philipsburg

CRAZY
MTS.

Sweetgrass

Porcupine

Cr.

Anaconda

Walkerville

Three Forks

Shields

Bigtimber

Billings

Hardin

CUSTER
BATTLEFIELD
NAT'L MON.

Lame Deer

Butte

Bozeman

Livingston

Laurel

Pumpkin

Cr.

Boxelder

Cr.

BIG HOLE
BATTLEFIELD
NAT'L MON.

PIONEER
MTS.

Columbus

CROW IND. RES.

TONGUE RIVER
IND. RES.

Dillon

Madison
Res.

Red Lodge

Bear
Creek

Bighorn

Little

Powder

Missouri

Ajax Mt.
10 900

Twin
Bridges

Electric Peak
11 155

Granite Peak
12 799

Lovell

Sheridan

DEVILS TOWER
NAT'L MON.

44°

Salmon

Gardiner

Mammoth
Hot Springs

Mt. Washburn
10 317

Powell

BIG HORN

Buffalo

Syndanceo

Borah Pk.
12 662

Lima
Res.

Hebgen Res.

Yellowstone

NATIONAL

Cody

Greybull

Basin

Cloud Peak
13 175

MOUNTAINS

Gillette

Moorcroft

Boulder Peak
10 966

Hyndman Peak
12 078

Mackay

Snoshone

PARK

7731 ft. above
sea level

Greybull

Ten
Sleep

No Wood

Crazy

Hailey

Arco

St.
Anthony

Ashton

Worland

Midwest

Antelope

Jackson
Lake

GRAND TETON
NAT'L PARK

Gebo

Gooseberry Cr.

Kaycee

Powder River

Rexburg

Grand Teton Mt.
13 766

Thermopolis

Idaho Falls

Rigby

Gros Ventre

Wind

Owl

Cr.

Badwater

Cr.

South

Fork

CRATERS OF
THE MOON
NAT'L MON.

Gannett Peak
13 785

WIND RIVER
IND. RES.

Riverton

Casper

Glenrock

42°

Shelley

Fremont
Peak 13 730

Lander

North

Platte

Douglas

Blackfoot

FORT HALL

Pocatello

Grays L.

Afton

Alcova Res.

FRONT RANGE

Blackfoot
River Res.

IND.
RES.

Soda Springs

Meade
Peak
9353

Pathfinder
Res.

American Falls
Res.

Lava
Hot Sprs.

GREAT DIVIDE
BASIN

Seminoe
Res.

Wheatland
Res.

Jerome

American Falls

Montpelier

Sweetwater

Hanna

Medicine

Bow

Twin
Falls

Rupert

Walcott
Res.

Malad

Preston

Superior

Rawlins

Wheatland

Oakley

Lewiston

Richmond

Smithfield

Kemmerer

Grangee

Green River

Rock
Springs

Bear

North

Platte

Logan

Providence

Horse

Cr.

Wellsville

Brigham

Flaming
Gorge
Res.

Lucin

Surface elev. approx.
4200 ft. above sea level

Bear River
Bay

Huntsville

Evanston

GREAT

Great
Salt
Lake

Antelope

Ogden

Morgan

SALT LAKE
DESERT

UTAH

Farmington

DINOSAUR
NAT'L MON.

COLO.

Wendover

Bountiful

Wilson Peak
13 095

Kings Peak
13 498

Salt Lake City

Uinta

MTS.

Park City

Mt. Emmons
13 428

Craigo

Steamboat Sprs.

Murray

Bingham Cyn.

Tooele

Midvale

Heber

Vernal

Oak Creeko

Continued on pages 70-71
Continued on pages 68-69

Relief

Meters		Feet
3050		10000
1525		5000
610		2000
305		1000
152.5		500
0	Sea Level	0
1525		500

0 20 40 60 80 100 120 Miles
0 20 40 60 80 100 120 140 160 180 200 Kilometers

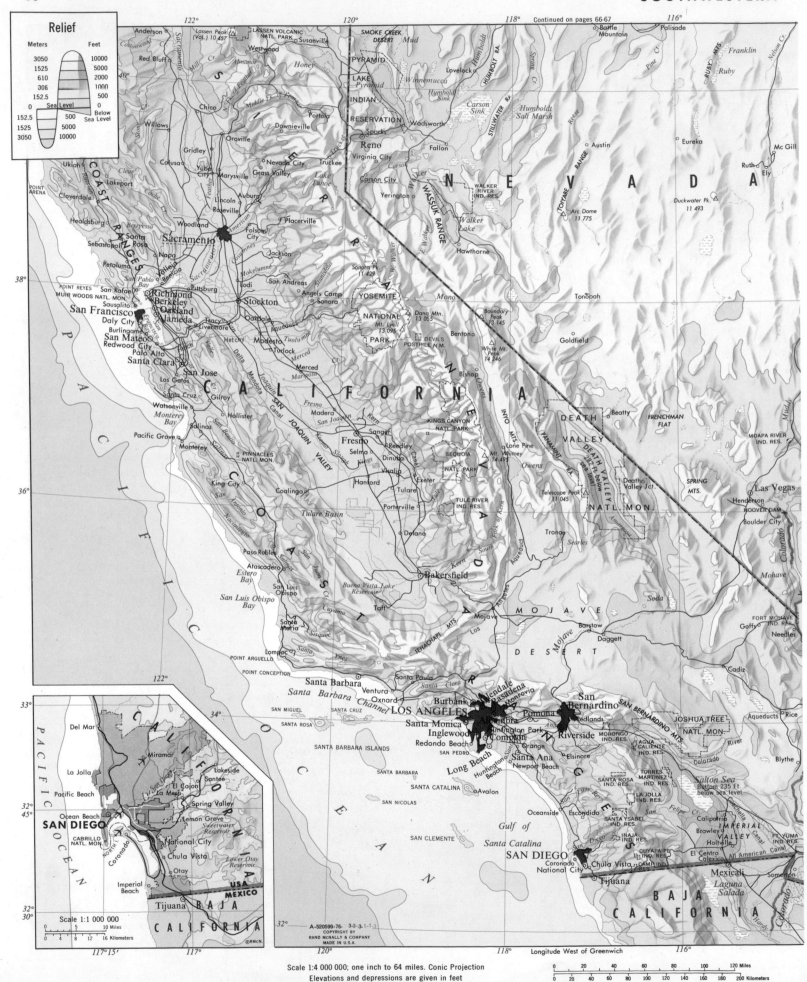

Relief

Meters	Feet
3050	10000
1525	5000
610	2000
306	1000
152.5	500
0 Sea Level	0 Below
152.5	500 Sea Level
1525	5000
3050	10000

Continued on pages 66-67

San Diego

Scale 1:1 000 000

Scale 1:4 000 000; one inch to 64 miles. Conic Projection
Elevations and depressions are given in feet

Longitude West of Greenwich

A-520599-76- 3-3-3-1-1
COPYRIGHT BY
RAND McNALLY & COMPANY
MADE IN U.S.A.

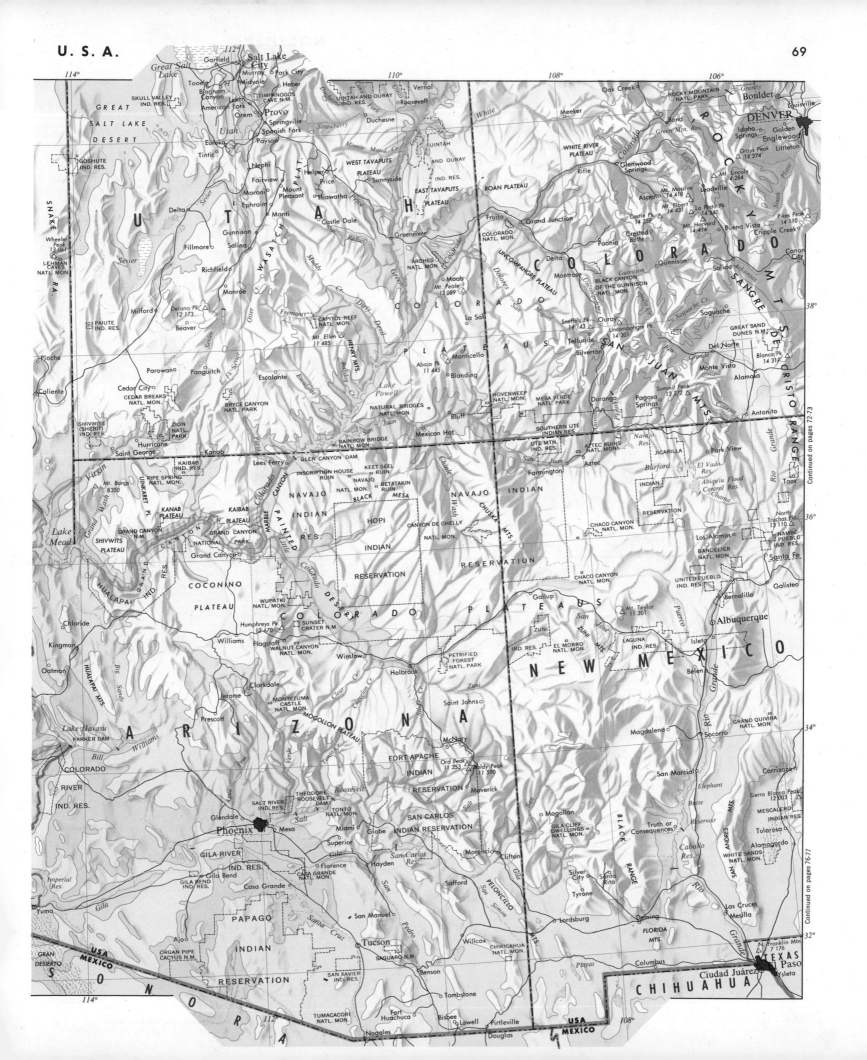

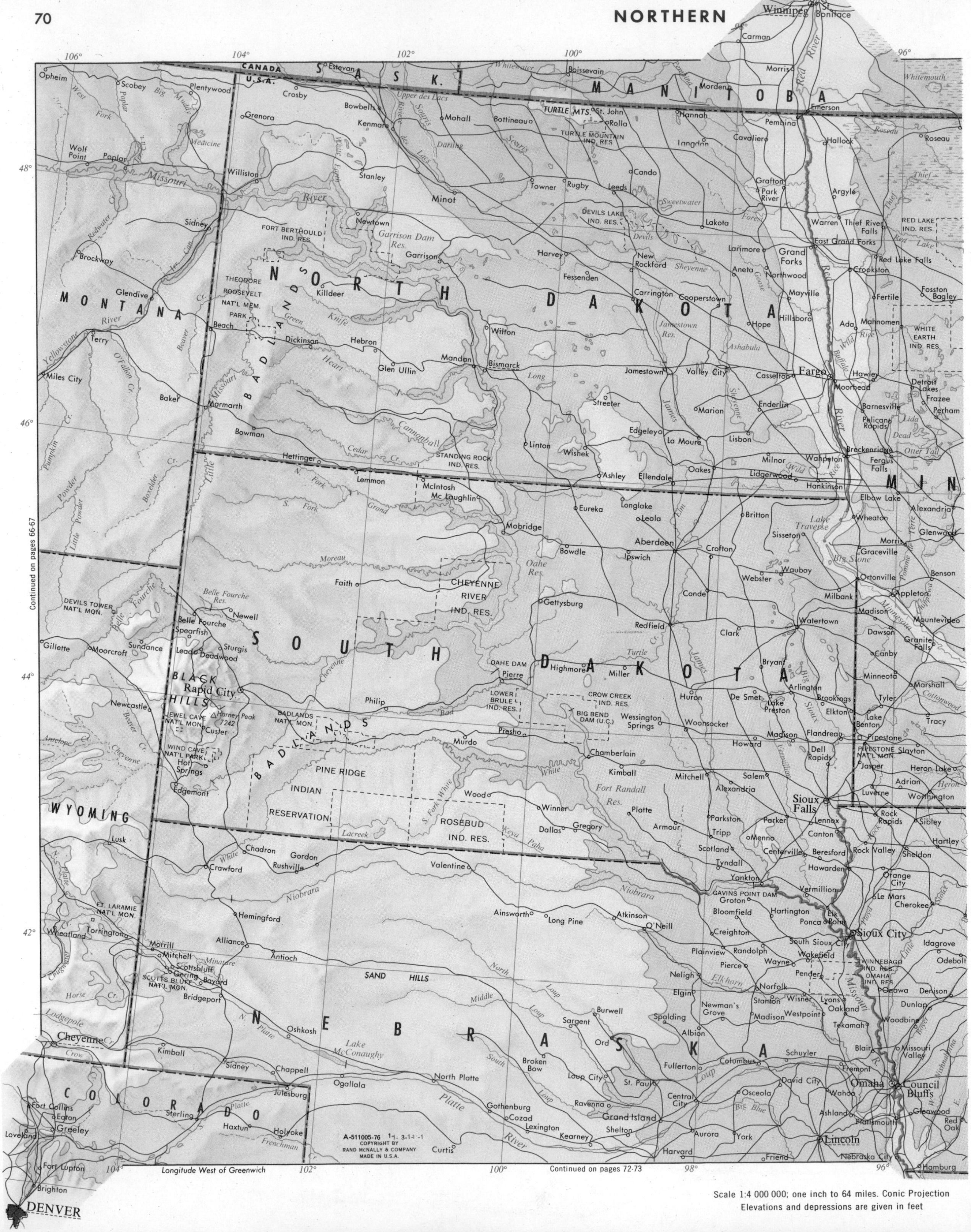

CANADA
U.S.A.
S A S K.

M A N I T O B A

Winnipeg · St. Boniface
Carman · Morris · Whitemouth
Estevan · Boissevain · Mordena · Emerson · Roseau · Whitemouth
Crosby · Bowbells · Mohall · Bottineau · TURTLE MTS. · St. John · Rolla · Hannah · Pembina · Hallock
Opheim · Scobey · Plentywood · Crenora · Kenmare · Darling · TURTLE MOUNTAIN IND. RES. · Cavalier · Langdon · RED LAKE IND. RES.
Wolf Point · Poplar · Williston · Stanley · Minot · Towner · Rugby · Leeds · Cando · Grafton · Park River · Argyle · Thief River Falls
Sidney · Newtown · Garrison Dam Res. · Harvey · DEVILS LAKE IND. RES. · Lakota · Warren · Red Lake Falls
Brockway · Glendive · FORT BERTHOULD IND. RES. · Killdeer · New Rockford · Sheyenne · Larimore · Grand Forks · East Grand Forks · Crookston · Fosston · Bagley

M O N T A N A
THEODORE ROOSEVELT NAT'L MEM. PARK · Beach · Dickinson · Hebron · Wilton · Carrington · Cooperstown · Mayville · Hillsboro · Fertile · WHITE EARTH IND. RES.

N O R T H   D A K O T A

Terry · Miles City · Baker · Marmarth · Glen Ullin · Mandan · Bismarck · Jamestown · Valley City · Casselton · Fargo · Moorhead · Detroit Lakes · Frazee · Perham
Bowman · Hettinger · Streeter · Edgeley · La Moure · Marion · Enderlin · Lisbon · Breckenridge · Pelican Rapids
Lemmon · STANDING ROCK IND. RES. · Linton · Wishek · Ashley · Ellendale · Oakes · Milnor · Wahpeton · Fergus Falls
McIntosh · Mc Laughlin · Eureka · Longlake · Leola · Britton · Lidgerwood · Hankinson · Elbow Lake

M I N

Mobridge · Aberdeen · Sisseton · Lake Traverse · Wheaton · Morris · Glenwood
Faith · CHEYENNE RIVER IND. RES. · Bowdle · Ipswich · Conde · Webster · Waubay · Ortonville · Graceville · Appleton · Benson
Gettysburg · Redfield · Clark · Watertown · Milbank · Madison · Montevideo · Granite Falls

S O U T H   D A K O T A

DEVILS TOWER NAT'L MON. · Belle Fourche Res. · Newell · Belle Fourche · Spearfish · Lead · Deadwood · Sturgis
Gillette · Moorcroft · Sundance · Newcastle
BLACK HILLS · Rapid City · OAHE DAM · Pierre · Highmore · Miller · Huron · De Smet · Arlington · Brookings · Tyler
JEWEL CAVE NAT'L MON. · Custer · Harney Peak 7242 · BADLANDS NAT'L MON. · Philip · LOWER BRULE IND. RES. · CROW CREEK IND. RES. · Wessington Springs · Woonsocket · Madison · Flandreau · Lake Benton · Pipestone · Tracy
WIND CAVE NAT'L PARK · Hot Springs · BAD LANDS · Murdo · Presho · BIG BEND DAM (U.C.) · Howard · Dell Rapids · PIPESTONE NAT'L MON. · Slayton
Edgemont · PINE RIDGE · INDIAN · RESERVATION · Wood · Winner · Chamberlain · Kimball · Mitchell · Salem · Heron Lake · Adrian · Worthington
ROSEBUD IND. RES. · Fort Randall Res. · Dallas · Gregory · Platte · Parkston · Lennox · Canton · Rock Rapids · Sibley

W Y O M I N G

Lusk · Chadron · Gordon · Valentine · Tripp · Scotland · Centerville · Beresford · Rock Valley · Sheldon · Hartley
Crawford · Rushville · Tyndall · Yankton · Hawarden · Orange City
Newcastle · Hemingford · Ainsworth · Long Pine · Atkinson · O'Neill · GAVINS POINT DAM · Groton · Vermillion · Le Mars · Cherokee
Morrill · Alliance · Antioch · Bloomfield · Hartington · Ponca · SIOUX CITY · Idagrove
Wheatland · Torrington · Mitchell · Scottsbluff · Gering · Bayard · Creighton · Plainview · Randolph · South Sioux City · Wakefield · Odebolt
SCUTTS BLUFF NAT'L MON. · Bridgeport · WINNEBAGO IND. RES. · Wayne · Pender · OMAHA IND. RES. · Lyons · Denison

N E B R A S K A

Oshkosh · SAND HILLS · Burwell · Spalding · Neligh · Elgin · Norfolk · Stanton · Wisner · Oakland · Westpoint · Tekamah · Woodbine
Cheyenne · Kimball · Sidney · Chappell · Lake McConaughy · North Platte · Broken Bow · Loup City · St. Paul · Albion · Columbus · Schuyler · Blair · Missouri Valley
Julesburg · Ogallala · Gothenburg · Cozad · Lexington · Kearney · Ravenna · Grand Island · Aurora · York · Fullerton · Central City · Osceola · David City · Wahoo · Omaha · Council Bluffs · Glenwood

C O L O R A D O

Fort Collins · Eaton · Greeley · Sterling · Haxtun · Holyoke · Curtis · Shelton · Harvard · Friend · Lincoln · Nebraska City · Hamburg
Loveland · Fort Lupton · Brighton

DENVER

A-511005-76
COPYRIGHT BY
RAND McNALLY & COMPANY
MADE IN U.S.A.

Continued on pages 66-67
Continued on pages 72-73

Longitude West of Greenwich

Scale 1:4 000 000; one inch to 64 miles. Conic Projection
Elevations and depressions are given in feet

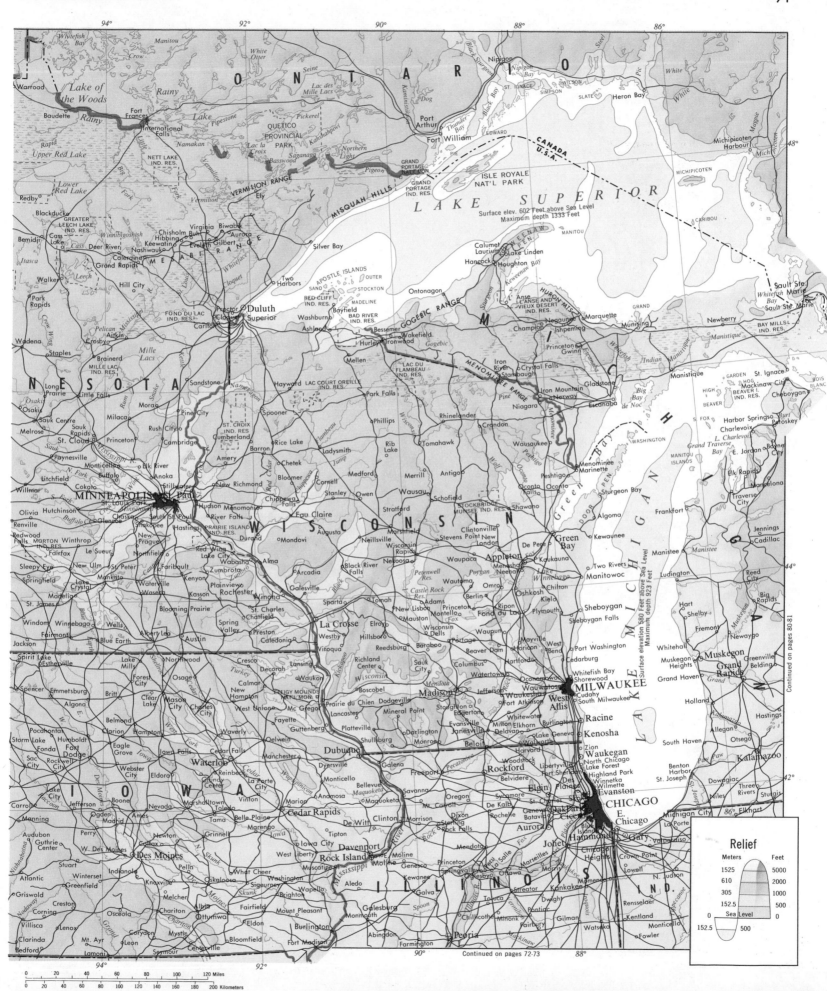

Continued on pages 80-81

Continued on pages 72-73

Relief

Meters	Feet
1525	5000
610	2000
305	1000
152.5	500
0	Sea Level
152.5	500

LAKE SUPERIOR
Surface elev. 602 Feet above Sea Level
Maximum depth 1333 Feet

LAKE MICHIGAN
Surface elevation 580 Feet above Sea Level
Maximum depth 923 Feet

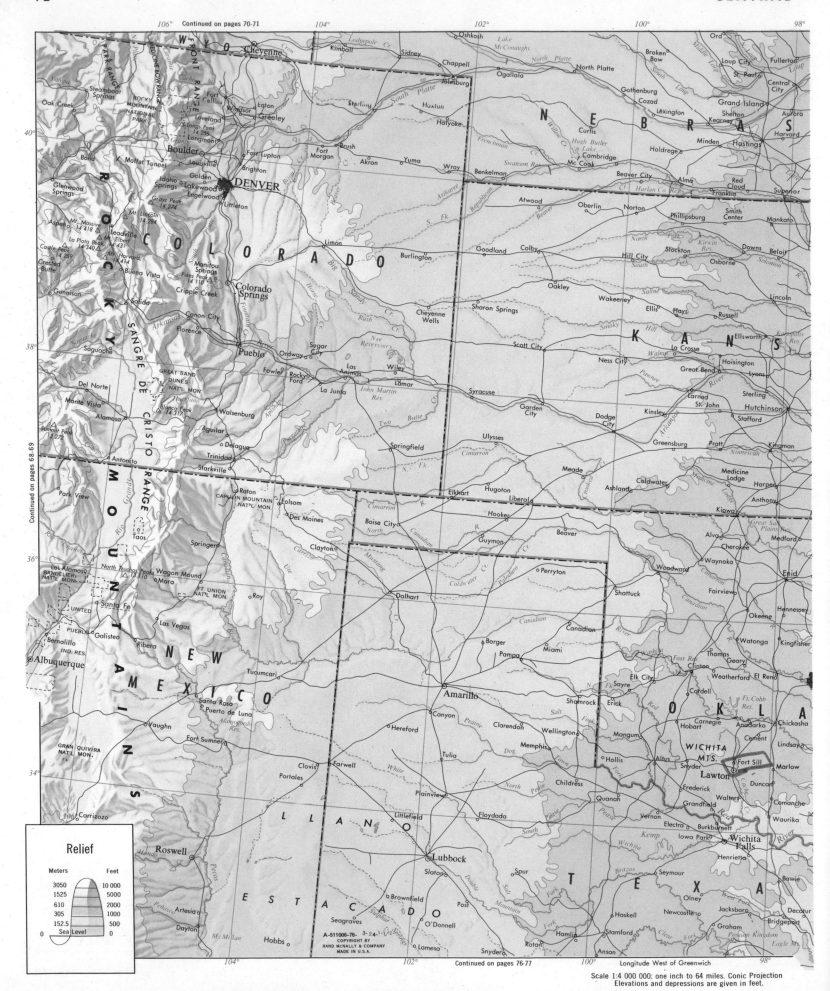

Continued on pages 70-71

Continued on pages 68-69

Continued on pages 76-77

Longitude West of Greenwich

Scale 1:4 000 000; one inch to 64 miles. Conic Projection
Elevations and depressions are given in feet.

Relief

Meters	Feet
3050	10 000
1525	5000
610	2000
305	1000
152.5	500
Sea Level	0
0	0

A-511006-76- 3-2-1-
COPYRIGHT BY
RAND McNALLY & COMPANY
MADE IN U.S.A.

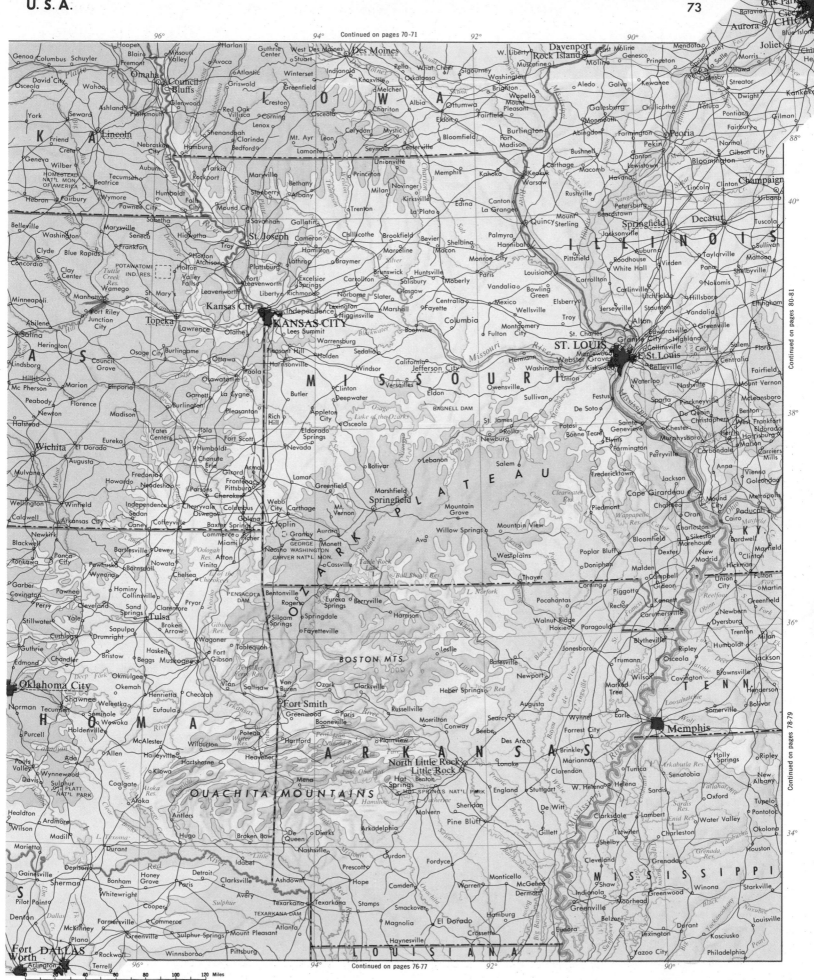

Continued on pages 70-71
Continued on pages 80-81
Continued on pages 78-79
Continued on pages 76-77

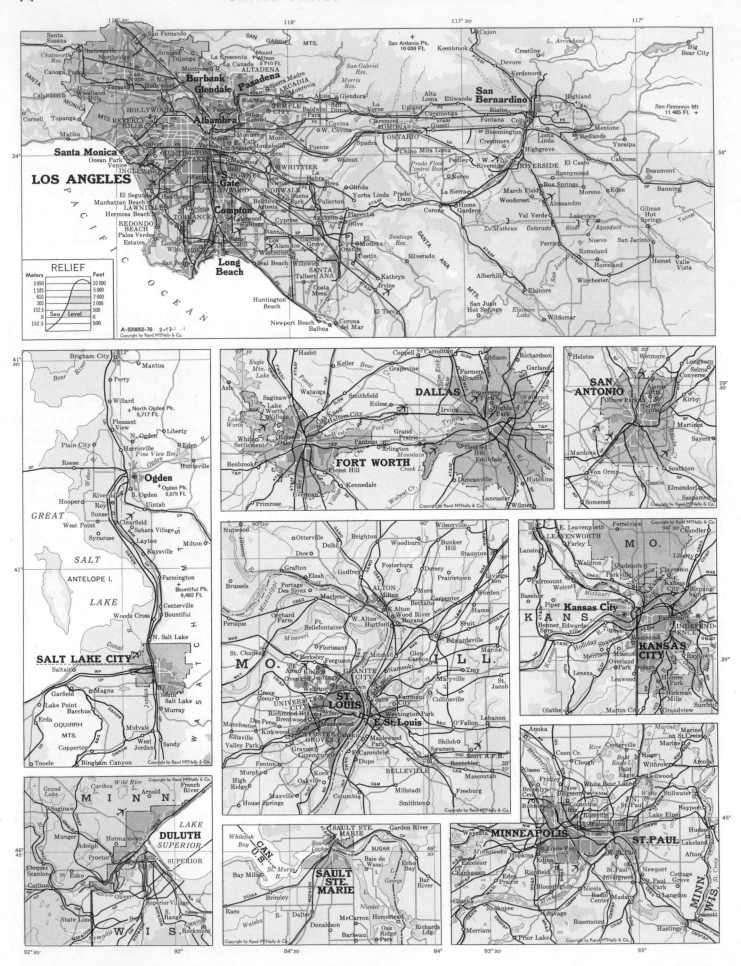

Scale 1:1 000 000; One inch to 16 miles.
Elevations and depressions are given in feet.

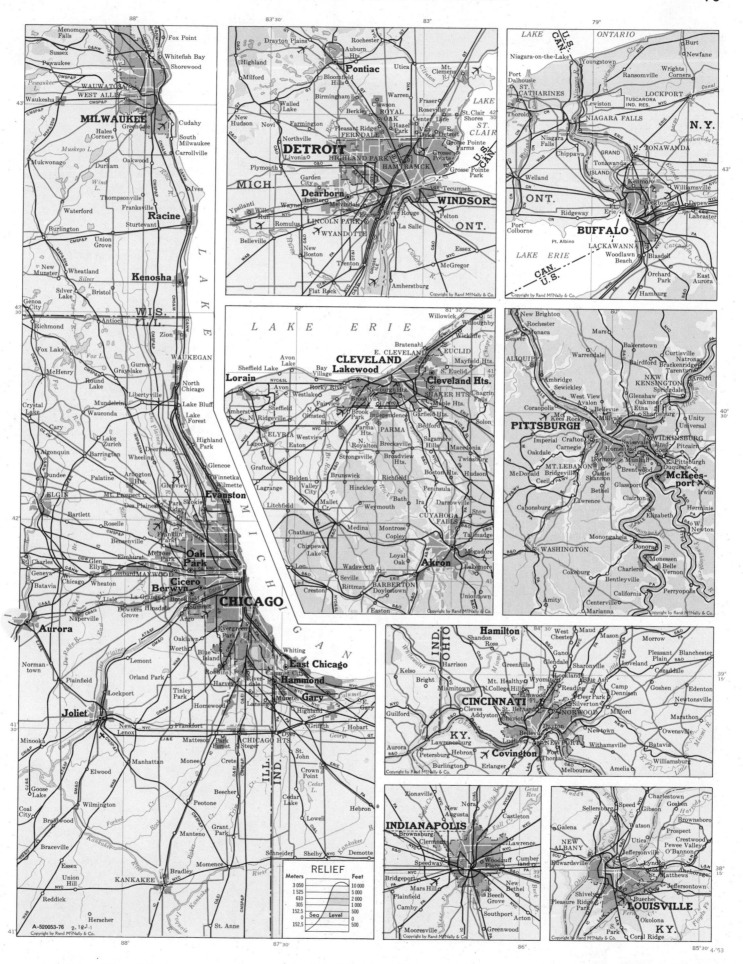

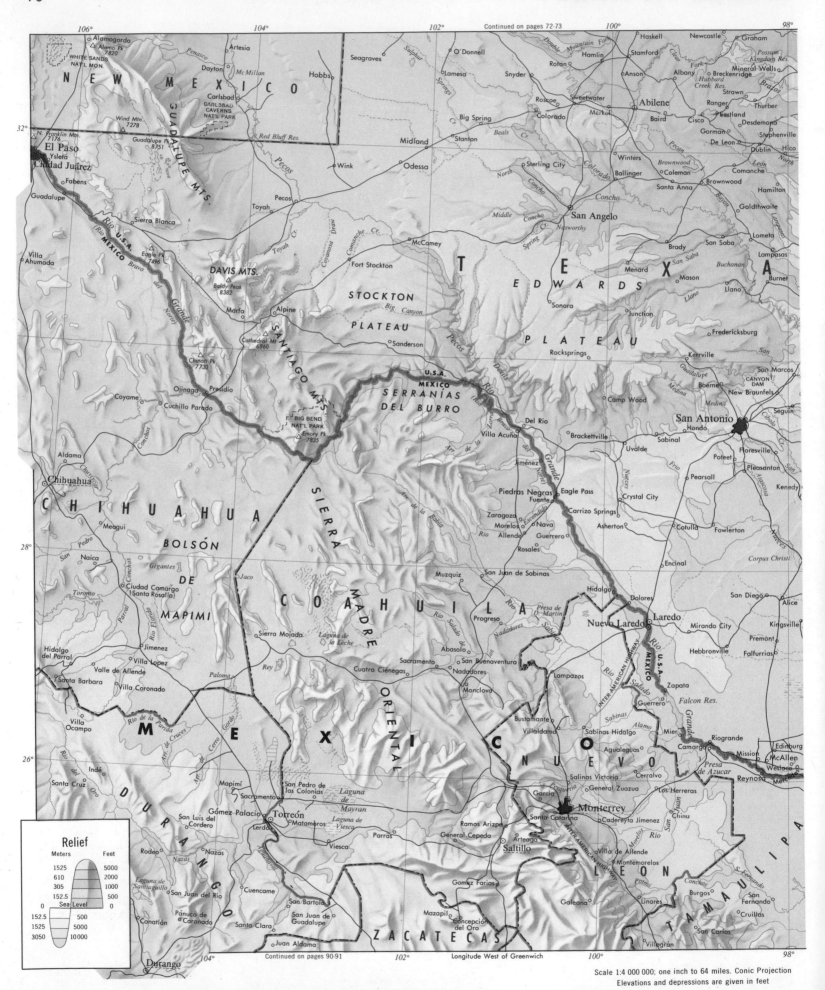

Continued on pages 72-73

Continued on pages 90-91

Longitude West of Greenwich

Scale 1:4 000 000; one inch to 64 miles. Conic Projection
Elevations and depressions are given in feet

Relief

Meters	Feet
1525	5000
610	2000
305	1000
152.5	500
0	Sea Level 0
152.5	500
1525	5000
3050	10000

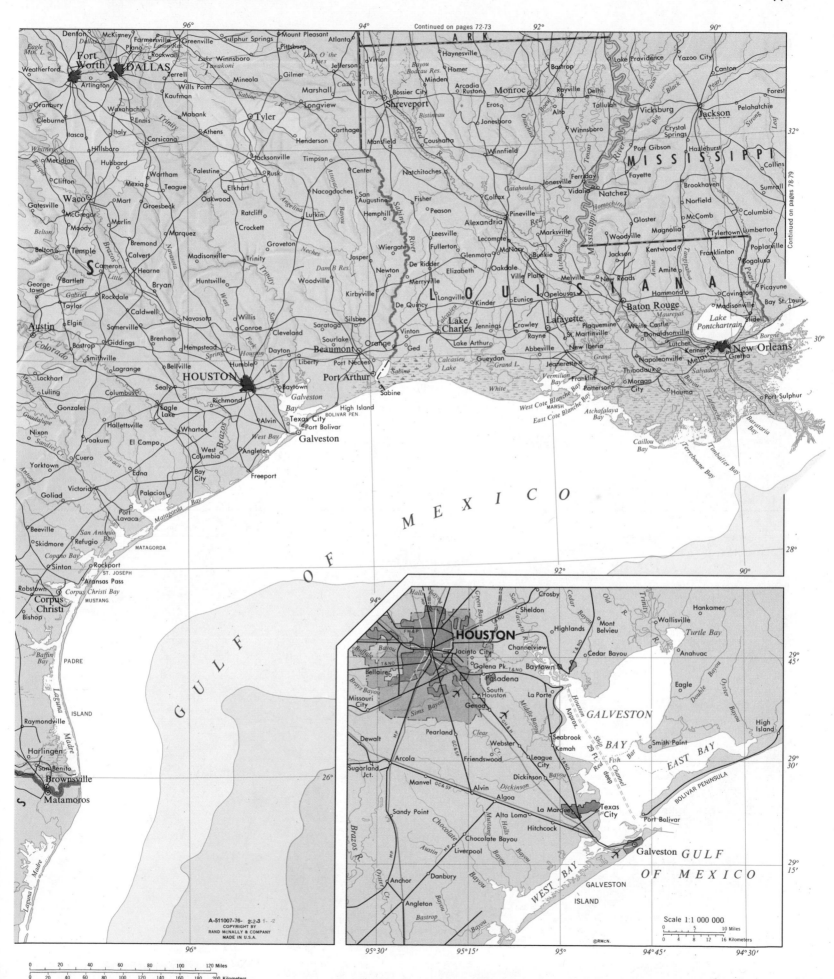

Continued on pages 72-73

Continued on pages 78-79

Scale 1:1 000 000

A-511007-76-
COPYRIGHT BY
RAND McNALLY & COMPANY
MADE IN U.S.A.

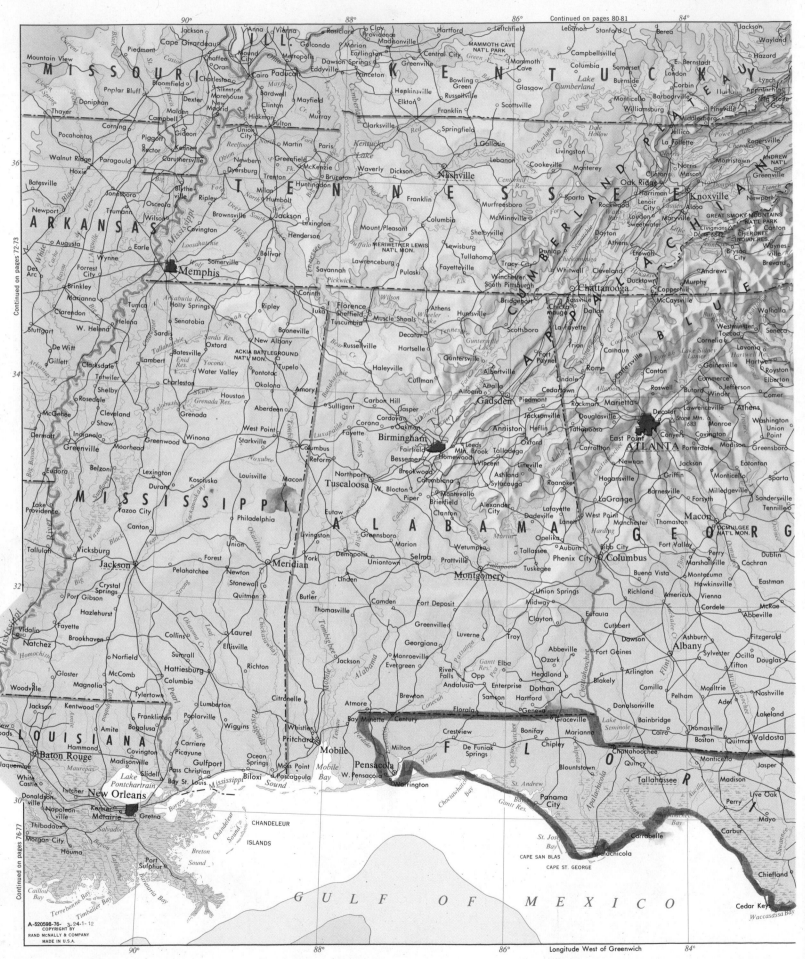

Continued on pages 80-81

Continued on pages 72-73

Continued on pages 76-77

GULF OF MEXICO

A-520598-76-
COPYRIGHT BY
RAND MCNALLY & COMPANY
MADE IN U.S.A.

3-24-1-12

Longitude West of Greenwich

Scale 1:4 000 000; one inch to 64 miles. Conic Projection
Elevations and depressions are given in feet

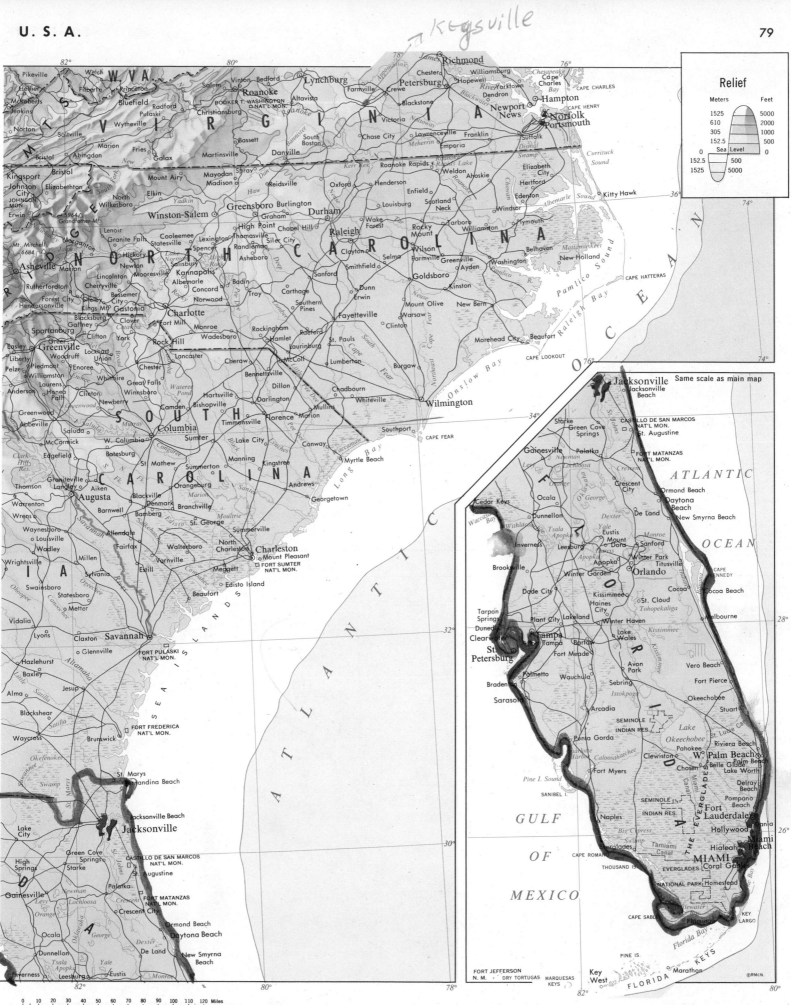

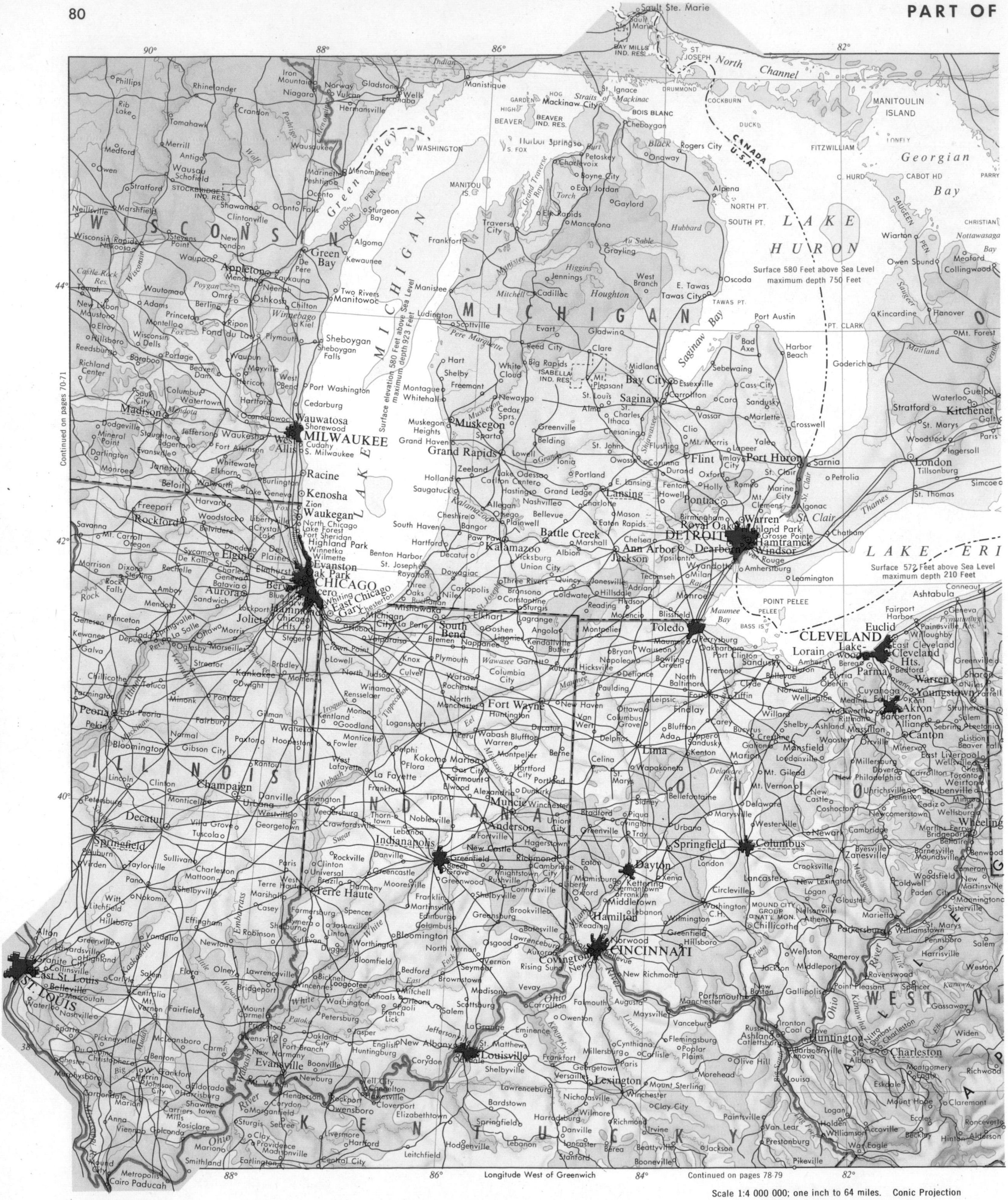

90°　　　88°　　　86°　　　82°

WISCONSIN

MICHIGAN

Lake Huron
Surface 580 Feet above Sea Level
maximum depth 750 Feet

Georgian Bay

MANITOULIN ISLAND

North Channel

CANADA
U.S.A.

Sault Ste. Marie

Straits of Mackinac

Green Bay

Surface elevation 580 Feet above Sea Level
maximum depth 923 Feet

Saginaw Bay

Milwaukee

Grand Rapids

Muskegon

Lansing

Battle Creek

Kalamazoo

Flint

Port Huron

Saginaw

Bay City

Pontiac

DETROIT

Royal Oak
Warren
Hamtramck
Dearborn
Windsor

Lake Erie
Surface 572 Feet above Sea Level
maximum depth 210 Feet

POINT PELEE

CLEVELAND
Euclid
Lakewood
East Cleveland
Cleveland Hts.
Parma

Lorain

Toledo

Akron
Barberton
Canton

Warren
Youngstown

44°

42°

ILLINOIS

Rockford

Chicago
Evanston
Oak Park
Cicero
Gary
Hammond
Joliet
Aurora
Elgin

South Bend

Fort Wayne

INDIANA

Peoria

Bloomington

Champaign

Springfield

Decatur

Terre Haute

Indianapolis

Muncie
Anderson

OHIO

Lima

Springfield
Columbus

Dayton

Hamilton

CINCINNATI

40°

St. Louis
East St. Louis

Evansville

Louisville

Lexington

KENTUCKY

WEST VIRGINIA

Charleston
Huntington

38°

Cairo Paducah

88°　　　86°　Longitude West of Greenwich　84°　　Continued on pages 78-79　　82°

Scale 1:4 000 000; one inch to 64 miles.　Conic Projection
Elevations and depressions are given in feet

Continued on pages 70-71

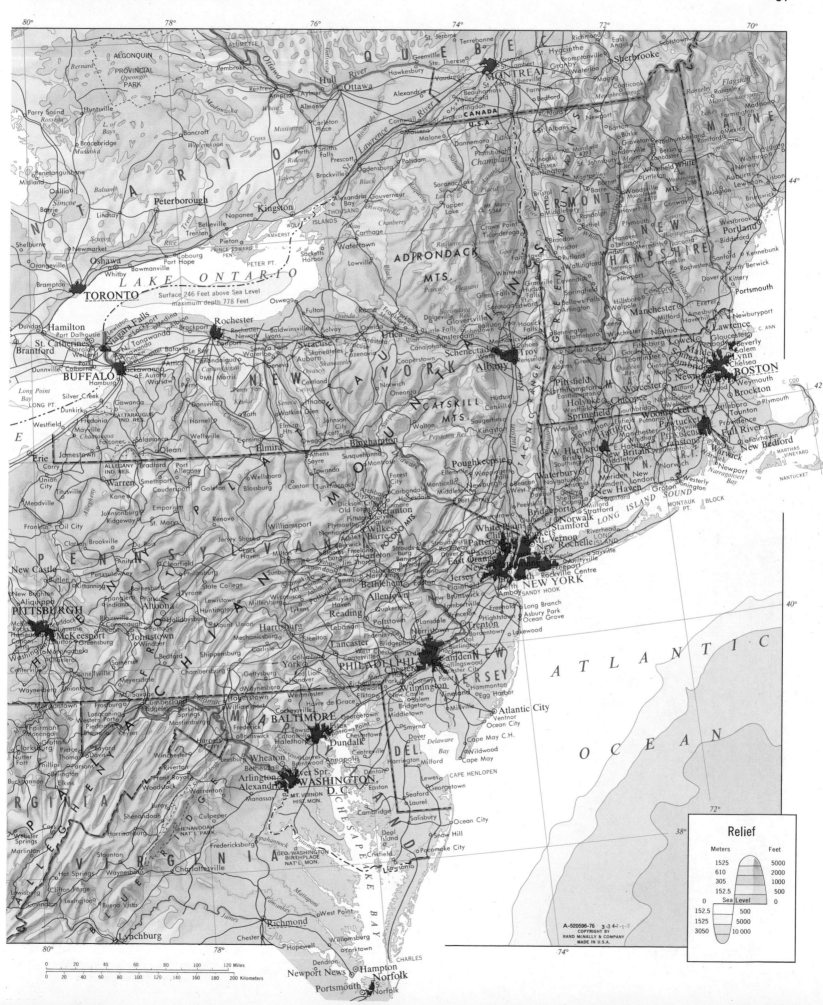

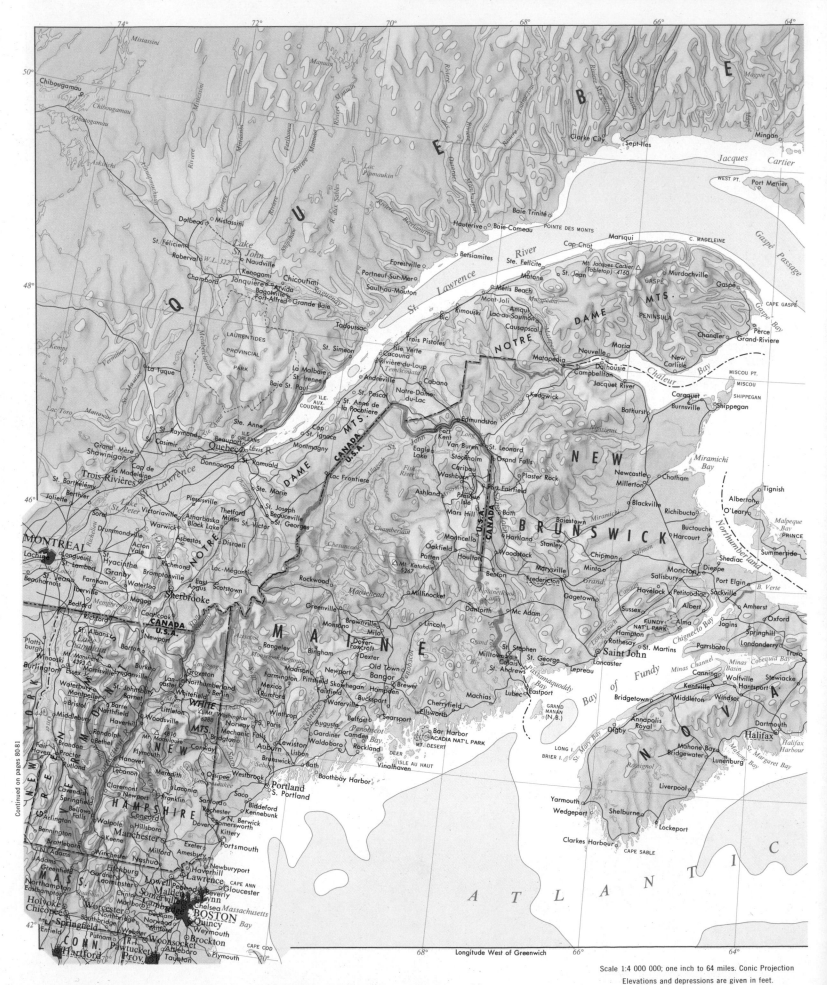

Scale 1:4 000 000; one inch to 64 miles. Conic Projection
Elevations and depressions are given in feet.

Longitude West of Greenwich

Continued on pages 80-81

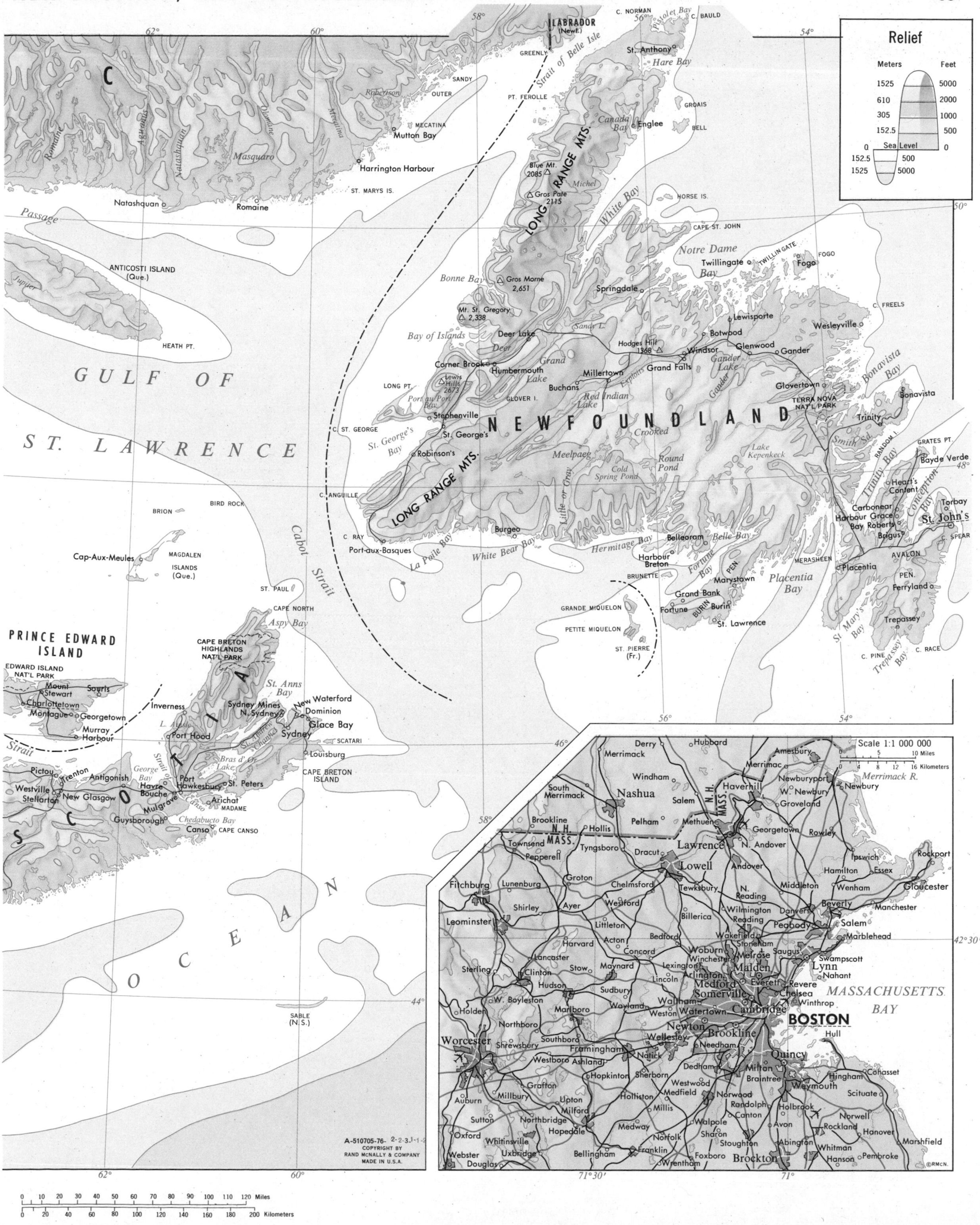

Relief

Meters		Feet
1525		5000
610		2000
305		1000
152.5		500
0	Sea Level	0
152.5		500
1525		5000

C. NORMAN

LABRADOR (Newf.)

C. BAULD

Pistolet Bay

GREENLY

St. Anthony

Hare Bay

Strait of Belle Isle

SANDY

OUTER

PT. FEROLLE

GROAIS

Robertson

MECATINA

Mutton Bay

Canada Bay

Englee

BELL

Harrington Harbour

Blue Mt. 2085

LONG RANGE MTS.

Michel

ST. MARYS IS.

Gros Pate 2115

HORSE IS.

White Bay

Natashquan

Romaine

CAPE ST. JOHN

Passage

Notre Dame Bay

Twillingate

TWILLINGATE

FOGO

ANTICOSTI ISLAND (Que.)

Jupiter

Springdale

Botwood

Glenwood

Wesleyville

Gander

Bonne Bay

Gros Morne 2,651

Lewisporte

C. FREELS

HEATH PT.

Mt. St. Gregory 2,338

Deer Lake

Sandy L.

Hodges Hill 1368

Windsor

GULF OF

Bay of Islands

Deer

Grand

Lake

Grand Falls

Gander Lake

Gander

Glovertown

Bonavista Bay

Corner Brook

Humbermouth

Humber

Millertown

Lake

Bonavista

Long Pt.

Lewis Hills 2673

Buchans

GLOVER I.

Red Indian Lake

Exploits

TERRA NOVA NAT'L PARK

Trinity

ST. LAWRENCE

Port au Port Bay

Stephenville

St. George's

Gander

Smith Sd.

RANDOM I.

GRATES PT.

Bayde Verde

Torbay

SPEAR

C. ST. GEORGE

St. George's Bay

Meelpaeg

Crooked

Lake Kepenkeck

Trinity Bay

Heart's Content

Carbonear

Robinson's

Cold Spring Pond

Round Pond

NEWFOUNDLAND

Harbour Grace

Brigus

Roberts

St. John's

C. ANGUILLE

LONG RANGE MTS.

AVALON

Cabot

C. RAY

Burgeo

White Bear Bay

Hermitage Bay

Belleoram

Belle Bay

MERASHEEN

Placentia

PEN.

BRION

BIRD ROCK

Port-aux-Basques

La Poile Bay

Fortune Bay

BURIN PEN.

Placentia Bay

Ferryland

Cap-Aux-Meules

MAGDALEN ISLANDS (Que.)

Harbour Breton

GRANDE MIQUELON

BRUNETTE

Grand Bank

Marystown

Strait

ST. PAUL

Fortune

Burin

St. Mary's Bay

Trepassey

CAPE NORTH

Aspy Bay

PETITE MIQUELON

St. Lawrence

C. PINE

Trepassey Bay

C. RACE

St. PIERRE (Fr.)

PRINCE EDWARD ISLAND

CAPE BRETON HIGHLANDS NAT'L PARK

EDWARD ISLAND NAT'L PARK

Mount Stewart

Souris

St. Anns Bay

New Waterford

Charlottetown

Georgetown

Inverness

Sydney Mines

N. Sydney

Dominion

Glace Bay

Montague

Murray Harbour

Port Hood

Sydney

SCATARI

Strait

L. Ainslie

Bras d'Or Lake

Louisburg

Pictou

George Bay

Port Hawkesbury

St. Peters

CAPE BRETON ISLAND

Westville

Antigonish

Havre Bouche

Stellarton

New Glasgow

Mulgrave

Arichat

MADAME

Guysborough

Chedabucto Bay

Canso

CAPE CANSO

GULF OF ST. LAWRENCE

SCOTIA

ATLANTIC OCEAN

SABLE (N.S.)

A-510705-76- 2-2-3J-1-1
COPYRIGHT BY
RAND McNALLY & COMPANY
MADE IN U.S.A.

Scale 1:1 000 000

Derry

Hubbard

Amesbury

Merrimack

Merrimac

Newburyport

Newbury

Windham

W. Newbury

Merrimack R.

South Merrimack

Nashua

Salem

Haverhill

Groveland

Brookline

Pelham

Methuen

Georgetown

Rowley

N.H.

MASS.

Hollis

Townsend

Tyngsboro

Lawrence

N. Andover

Ipswich

Essex

Rockport

Pepperell

Dracut

Andover

Hamilton

Fitchburg

Lunenburg

Groton

Lowell

Tewksbury

Middleton

Wenham

Gloucester

Chelmsford

N. Reading

Beverly

Manchester

Leominster

Shirley

Ayer

Westford

Wilmington

Danvers

Salem

Billerica

Reading

Peabody

Littleton

Acton

Bedford

Wakefield

Marblehead

Lancaster

Concord

Woburn

Stoneham

Melrose

Saugus

Swampscott

Sterling

Clinton

Stow

Maynard

Lexington

Winchester

Malden

Lynn

Nahant

Holden

Hudson

Lincoln

Arlington

Everett

Revere

Chelsea

W. Boylston

Marlboro

Sudbury

Wayland

Medford

Somerville

Winthrop

MASSACHUSETTS BAY

Northboro

Weston

Watertown

Cambridge

Worcester

Shrewsbury

Southboro

Framingham

Newton

Brookline

BOSTON

Hull

Westboro

Ashland

Natick

Wellesley

Needham

Auburn

Millbury

Upton

Hopkinton

Sherborn

Dedham

Milton

Quincy

Hingham

Cohasset

Sutton

Northbridge

Milford

Holliston

Westwood

Norwood

Braintree

Weymouth

Scituate

Oxford

Whitinsville

Hopedale

Medfield

Millis

Canton

Randolph

Holbrook

Norwell

Webster

Uxbridge

Medway

Norfolk

Sharon

Walpole

Avon

Rockland

Hanover

Douglas

Bellingham

Franklin

Stoughton

Foxboro

Abington

Whitman

Marshfield

Wrentham

Brockton

Hanson

Pembroke

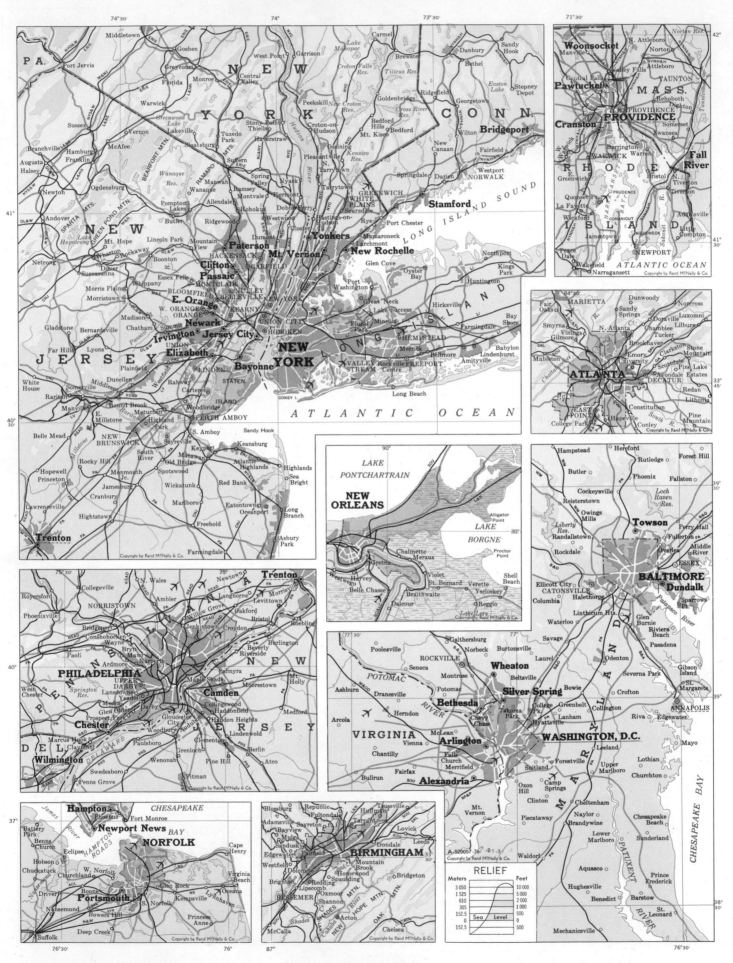

Scale 1:1 000 000; One inch to 16 miles.
Elevations and depressions are given in feet.

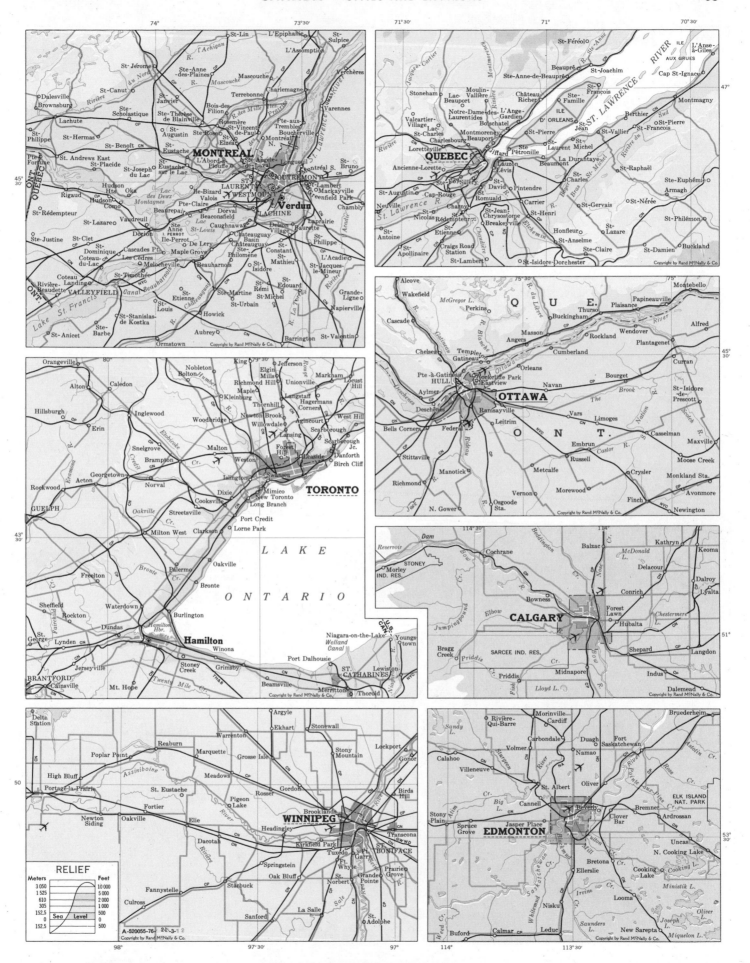

Scale 1:1 000 000; One inch to 16 miles.
Elevations and depressions are given in feet.

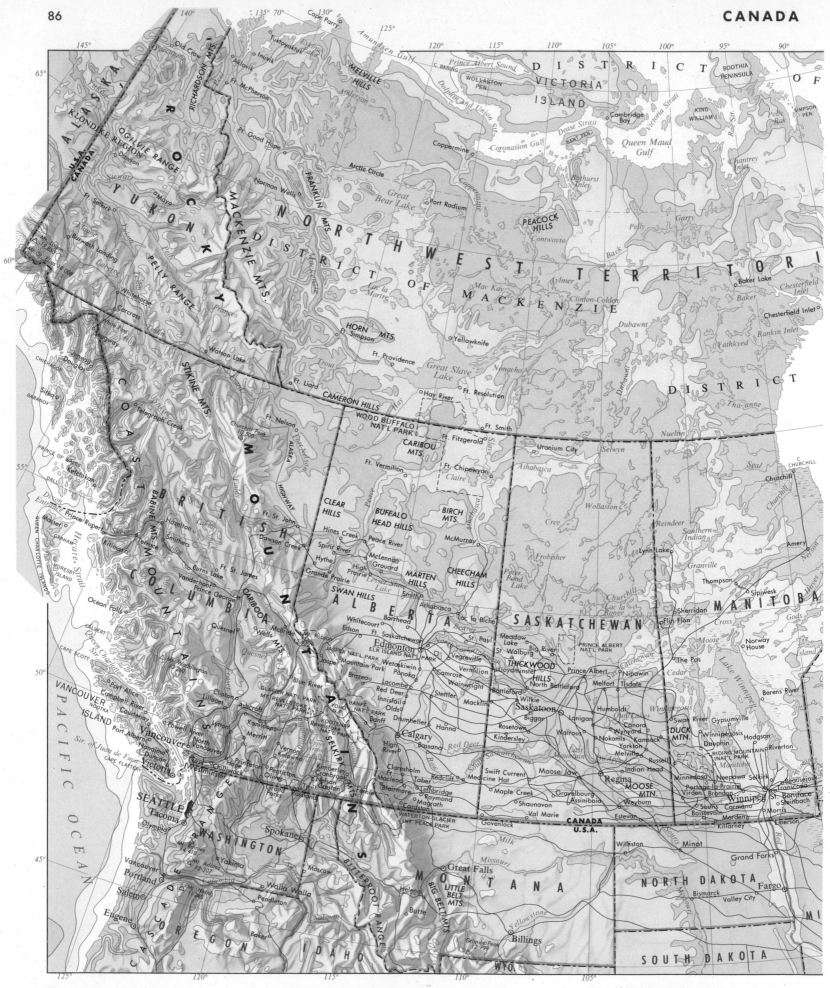

Scale 1: 12 000 000; one inch to 190 miles. Conic Projection
Elevations and depressions are given in feet

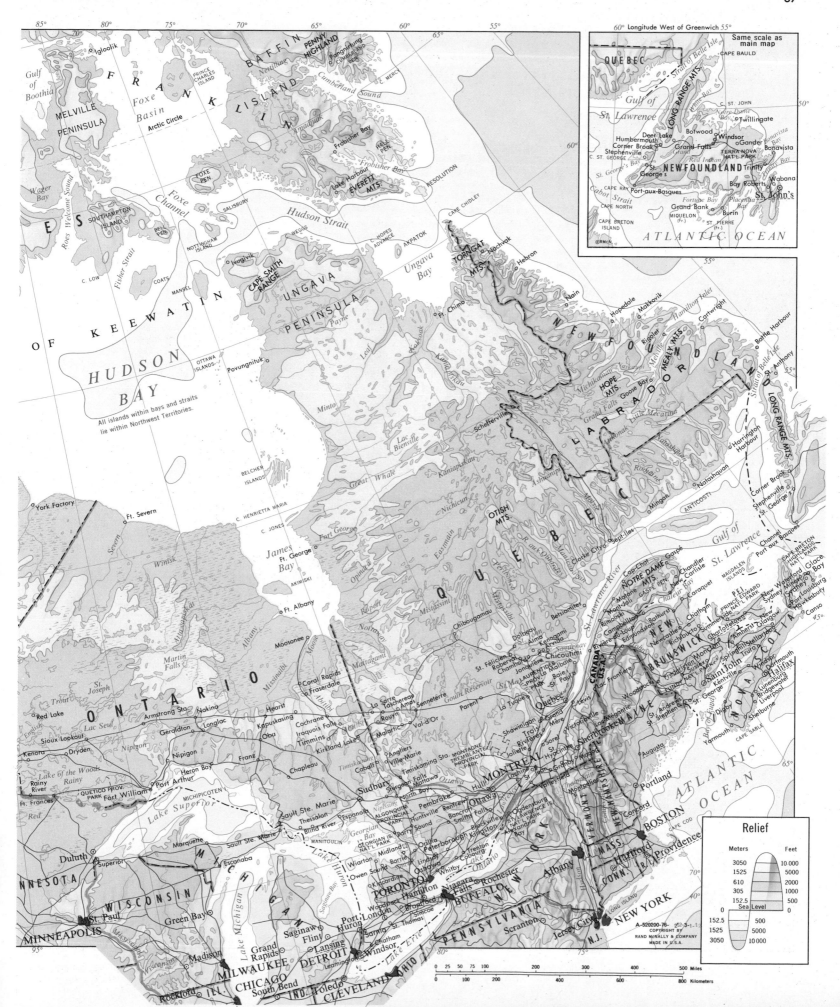

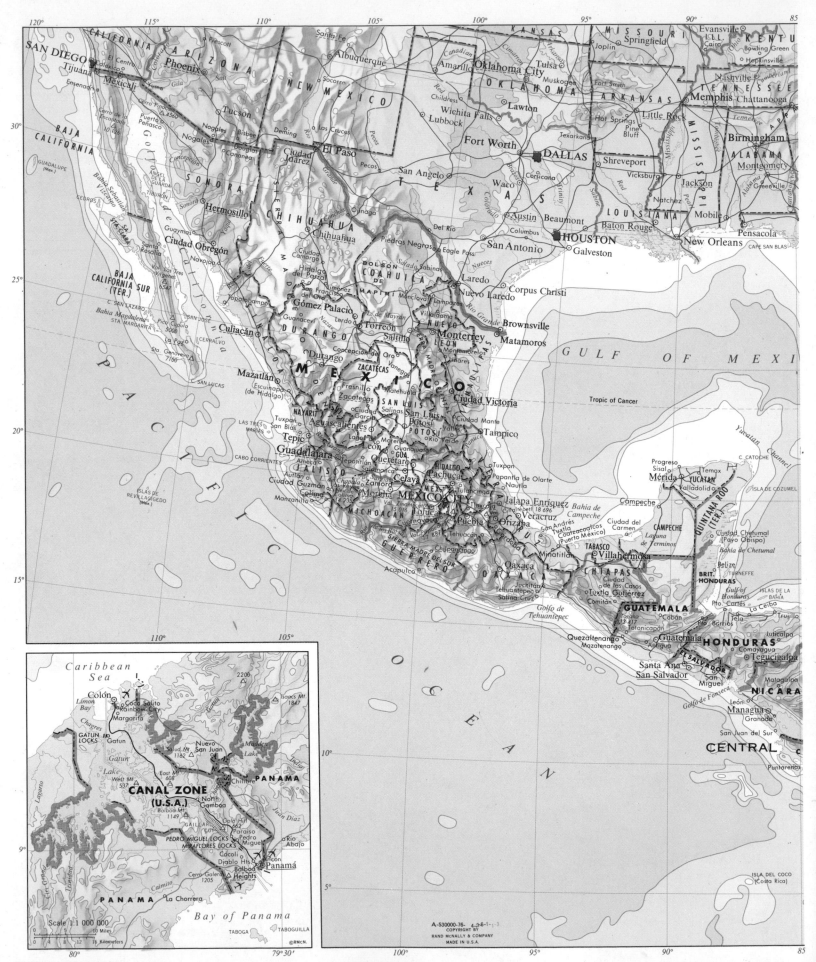

Scale 1:16 000 000; one inch to 250 miles. Polyconic Projection
Elevations and depressions are given in feet

A-530000-76- 4-3-6-1-3
COPYRIGHT BY
RAND McNALLY & COMPANY
MADE IN U.S.A.

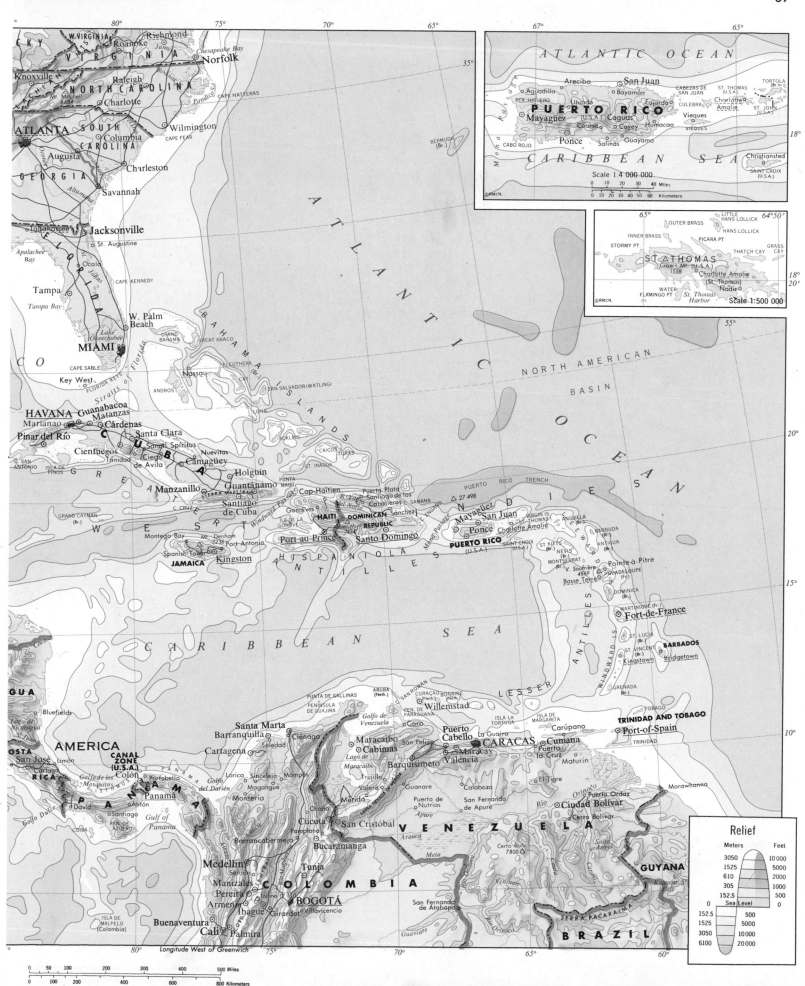

Relief

Meters	Feet
3050	10 000
1525	5000
610	2000
305	1000
152.5	500
0	Sea Level 0
152.5	500
1525	5000
3050	10 000
6100	20 000

Scale 1:4 000 000

Scale 1:500 000

Longitude West of Greenwich

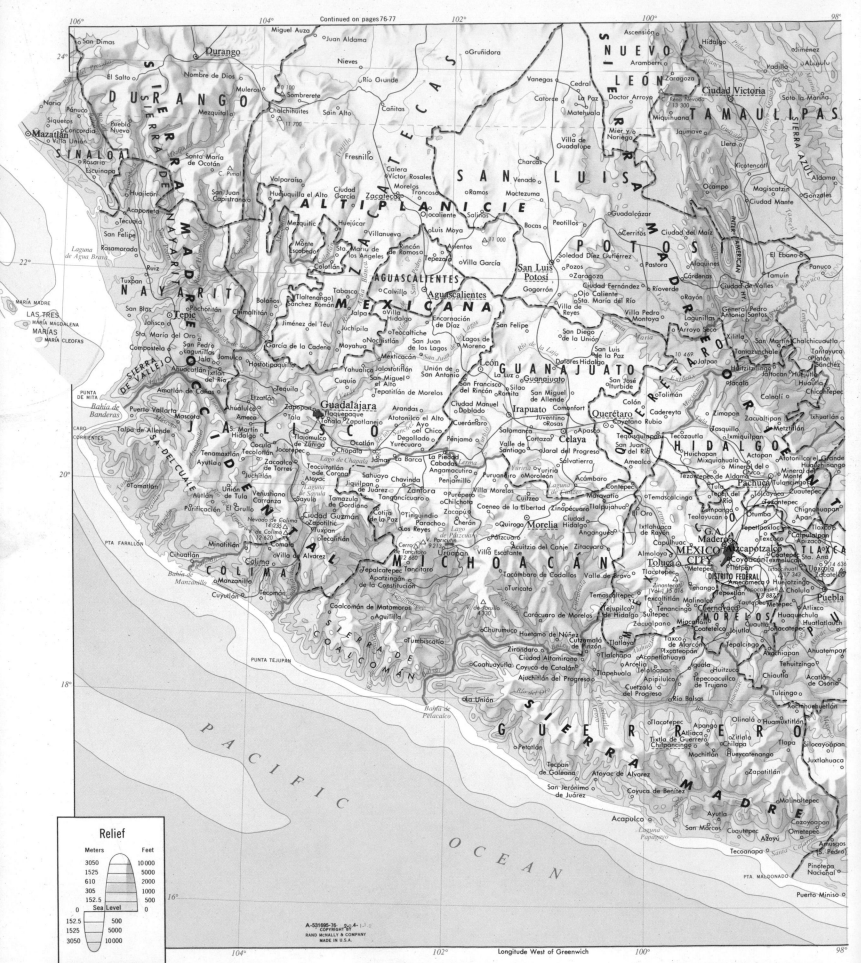

Relief

Meters		Feet
3050		10000
1525		5000
610		2000
305		1000
152.5		500
0	Sea Level	0
152.5		500
1525		5000
3050		10000

A-531695-76 COPYRIGHT BY
RAND McNALLY & COMPANY
MADE IN U.S.A.

Longitude West of Greenwich

Scale 1:4 000 000; one inch to 64 miles. Conic Projection
Elevations and depressions are given in feet

Continued on pages 76-77

GULF OF MEXICO

BAHÍA DE CAMPECHE

Golfo de Tehuantepec

Continued on pages 92-93

Continued on page 91

Continued in inset below

A-539200-76 -2-1-4-1-1
COPYRIGHT BY
RAND McNALLY & COMPANY
MADE IN U.S.A.

Same scale as main map

Longitude West of Greenwich

Scale 1:4 000 000; one inch to 64 miles. Sinusoidal Projection

Elevations and depressions are given in feet

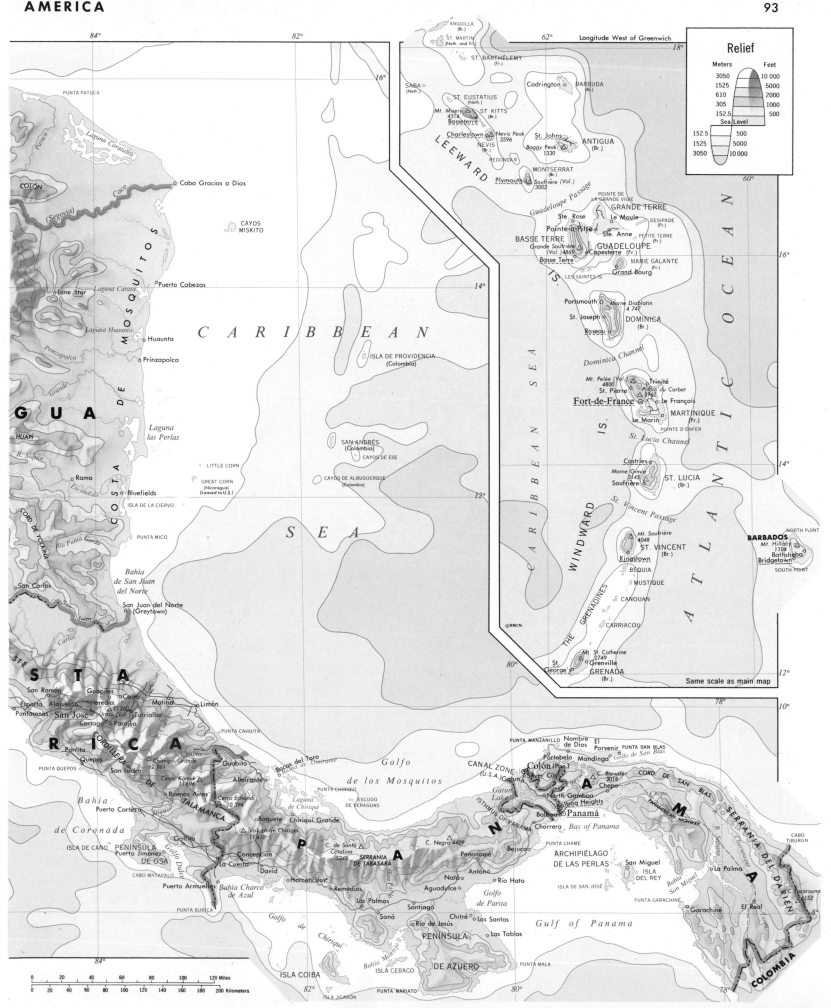

Relief

Meters	Feet
3050	10 000
1525	5000
610	2000
305	1000
152.5	500

Sea Level

152.5	500
1525	5000
3050	10 000

Longitude West of Greenwich

ANGUILLA (Br.)
ST. MARTIN (Neth. and Fr.)
ST. BARTHÉLEMY (Fr.)
SABA (Neth.)
ST. EUSTATIUS (Neth.)
ST. KITTS (Br.)
Mt. Misery 4314
Basseterre
Charlestown △ Nevis Peak 3596
NEVIS (Br.)
REDONDA
Codrington BARBUDA (Br.)
St. Johns
Boggy Peak 1330 △ ANTIGUA (Br.)
MONTSERRAT (Br.)
Plymouth Soufrière (Vol.) 3002
LEEWARD IS.

POINTE DE LA GRANDE VIGIE
Ste. Rose Le Moule GRANDE TERRE
Pointe-à-Pitre DÉSIRADE (Fr.)
Ste. Anne PETITE TERRE (Fr.)
BASSE TERRE
Grande Soufrière (Vol.) 4869 △ GUADELOUPE
Basse Terre Capesterre (Fr.)
MARIE GALANTE (Fr.)
LES SAINTES IS. Grand Bourg

Guadeloupe Passage

Portsmouth Morne Diablotin 4 747 △
St. Joseph DOMINICA (Br.)
Roseau

Dominica Channel

Mt. Pelée (Vol.) 4800 △ Trinité
St. Pierre Pitons du Carbet 3960 △
Fort-de-France Le François
Le Marin MARTINIQUE (Fr.)
POINTE D'ENFER

St. Lucia Channel

Castries
Morne Gimie 3145 △ ST. LUCIA (Br.)
Soufrière

St. Vincent Passage

Mt. Soufrière 4048 △
ST. VINCENT (Br.)
Kingstown
BEQUIA
MUSTIQUE
CANOUAN
CARRIACOU

BARBADOS
Mt. Hillaby 1104 △ Bathsheba
NORTH POINT
Bridgetown
SOUTH POINT

Mt. St. Catherine 2749 △
St. George's Grenville
GRENADA (Br.)

C A R I B B E A N   S E A

WINDWARD IS.

THE GRENADINES

A T L A N T I C   O C E A N

©RMcN

Same scale as main map

PUNTA PATUCA
COLÓN
Laguna Caratasca
Cabo Gracias a Dios
Patuca
Coco
(Segovia)
CAYOS MISKITO
Lone Star
Laguna Carata
Puerto Cabezas
Huaunta
Laguna Huaunta
Prinzapolca
C A R I B B E A N
GUA
HUAPÍ
Laguna las Perlas
ISLA DE PROVIDENCIA (Colombia)
S E A
COSTA DE MOSQUITOS
Rama
Escondido
Bluefields
SAN ANDRÉS (Colombia)
CAYOS DE ESE
LITTLE CORN
GREAT CORN
CAYOS DE ALBUQUERQUE (Colombia)
ISLA DE LA CIERVO
PUNTA MICO
Río Punta Gorda
CORD. DE YOLAINA
Bahía de San Juan del Norte
San Carlos
San Juan del Norte (Greytown)
San Carlos
San Juan
STE
STA
RICA
CORDILLERA DE TALAMANCA
San Ramón
Guapiles Cairo
Esparta Alajuela Heredia Irazú Vol.) 11 260
Puntarenas San José Turrialba
Cartago Paraíso
Matina
Limón
Puerto Cahuita
San Isidro
Cerro Kámuk 11 696 △
Buenos Aires
Cerro Echandi 10 394 △
Puerto Cortés
Bahía de Coronada
PENÍNSULA DE OSA
ISLA DE CAÑO
Puerto Jiménez
Golfito
Golfo Dulce
Volcán de Chiriquí 11 410 △
CABO MATAPALO
Boquete Chiriquí Grande
Concepción
La Cuesta David
Puerto Armuelles
Bahía Charco de Azul
PUNTA BURICA
Golfo de Chiriquí
Chirripó Grande 12 861
Guabito
Almirante
Bocas del Toro
Isla de Almirante
PUNTA CHIRIQUÍ
Laguna de Chiriquí
ESCUDO DE VERAGUAS
Golfo de los Mosquitos
Horconcitos
Remedios
Las Palmas
Soná
ISLA COIBA
ISLA JICARÓN
ISLA CEBACO
Bahía Montijo
Chitré
Río de Jesús
Los Santos
Las Tablas
PENÍNSULA DE AZUERO
PUNTA MALA
Santiago
Natá
Antón
Aguadulce
Río Hato
Golfo de Parita
SERRANÍA DE TABASARA
C. de Santa Catalina 5249
C. Negro 4429 △
Penonomé
Bejuco
PUNTA CHAME
Chorrera
Bay of Panama
Gulf of Panama
PUNTA MANZANILLO Nombre de Dios
El Porvenir PUNTA SAN BLAS
Portobelo Mandinga Golfo de San Blas
CANAL ZONE (U.S.A.)
Colón (Pan.) Gatun
Silver City
C. Brewster 3018 Chepo
North Gamboa
Balboa Heights
Balboa Panamá
ISTHMUS OF PANAMA
Gatun Lake
PANAMA
CORD. DE SAN BLAS
Chepo
Río Chepo
PANAMERICAN HIGHWAY
SERRANÍA DEL DARIEN
ARCHIPIÉLAGO DE LAS PERLAS
San Miguel ISLA DEL REY
ISLA DE SAN JOSÉ
Bahía San Miguel
PUNTA GARACHINÉ
La Palma
Garachiné
El Real
Río Tuira
CABO TIBURÓN
C. Jacarouna 4152 △
COLOMBIA

Scale

0 20 40 60 80 100 120 Miles
0 20 40 60 80 100 120 140 160 180 200 Kilometers

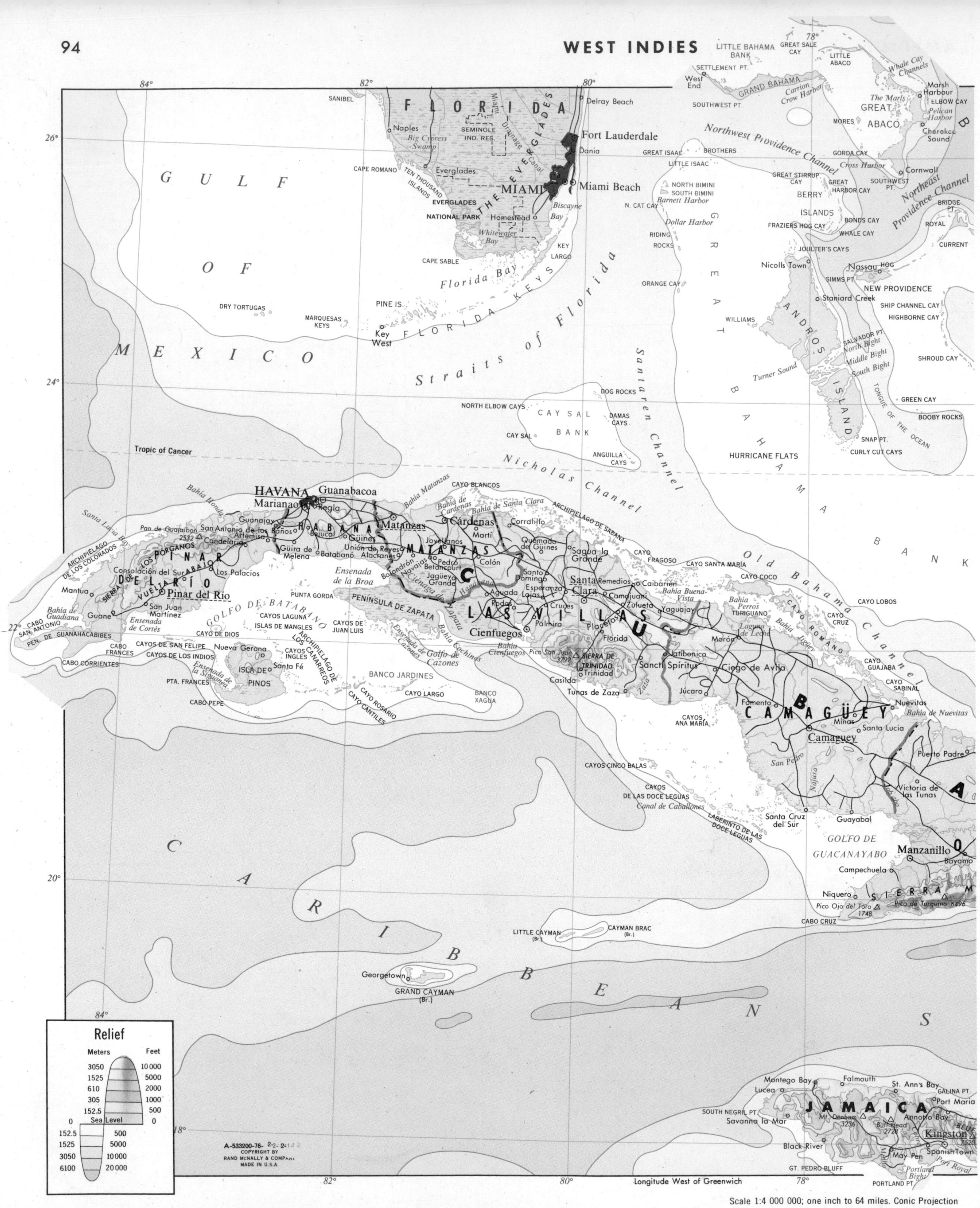

LITTLE BAHAMA BANK
GREAT SALE CAY
LITTLE ABACO
78°
Whale Cay Channels
Marsh Harbour
GREAT ABACO
Pelican Harbor
ELBOW CAY

SETTLEMENT PT.
West End
GRAND BAHAMA
Carrion Crow Harbor
GORDA CAY
Cross Harbor
Cornwall
SOUTHWEST PT.

F L O R I D A
SANIBEL
82°
80°
Delray Beach
Northwest Providence Channel
Cherokee Sound

26°
Naples
Big Cypress Swamp
SEMINOLE IND. RES.
THE EVERGLADES
Fort Lauderdale
Dania
GREAT ISAAC
BROTHERS
LITTLE ISAAC
GREAT STIRRUP CAY
Whale Cay
SOUTHWEST PT.
Northeast Providence Channel
BRIDGE PT.
ROYAL

CAPE ROMANO
Everglades
TEN THOUSAND ISLANDS
MIAMI
Miami Beach
N. CAT CAY
NORTH BIMINI
SOUTH BIMINI
Barnett Harbor
GREAT HARBOR CAY
BERRY
BONDS CAY
CURRENT

EVERGLADES NATIONAL PARK
Homestead
Biscayne Bay
Dollar Harbor
ISLANDS
FRAZIERS HOG CAY
WHALE CAY
JOULTER'S CAYS

CAPE SABLE
Whitewater Bay
KEY LARGO
RIDING ROCKS
Nicolls Town
SHIP CHANNEL CAY
HIGHBORNE CAY

Florida Bay
NEW PROVIDENCE
Nassau
HOG
SIMMS PT.

DRY TORTUGAS
PINE IS.
KEY WEST
FLORIDA KEYS
Straits of Florida
ORANGE CAY
WILLIAMS
Staniard Creek
SALVADOR PT.
North Bight

24°
MARQUESAS KEYS
Turner Sound
Middle Bight
SHROUD CAY

M E X I C O
G R E A T
TONGUE OF THE OCEAN
South Bight

DOG ROCKS
NORTH ELBOW CAYS
CAY SAL
DAMAS CAYS
A N D R O S
GREEN CAY

CAY SAL
BANK
HURRICANE FLATS
SNAP PT.
CURLY CUT CAYS
BOOBY ROCKS

Tropic of Cancer
ANGUILLA CAYS
Santaren Channel
I S L A N D

Nicholas Channel

Bahía Honda
HAVANA
Guanabacoa
CAYO BLANCOS
Bahía Matanzas
CAYO
ARCHIPIÉLAGO DE SABANA
B A H A M A

Santa Lucía
Marianao
Regla
Bahía de Cárdenas
Bahía de Santa Clara

Guanajay
Pan de Guajaibón
San Antonio de los Baños
HABANA
Matanzas
Cárdenas
Martí
Corralillo

2532
Artemisa
Güines
Joyellanos
Quemado de Güines
Sagua la Grande
CAYO
CAYO SANTA MARÍA

P I N A R
Candelaria
Güira de Melena
Unión de Reyes
M A T A N Z A S
Colón
Santo Domingo
FRAGOSO
CAYO COCO

Consolación del Sur
Los Palacios
Batabanó
Alacranes
C
Esperanza
Santa Clara
Remedios
Caibarién
Bahía Buena Vista
CAYO LOBOS

ARCHIPIÉLAGO DE LOS COLORADOS
D E L R Í O
Bolondrón
Navajas
Pedro Betancourt
Jagüey Grande
Aguada
Rodas
Lajas
Camajuaní
Bahía Perros
TURIGUANO
Old Bahama

Mantua
SIERRA
BAHÍA
Pinar del Río
PUNTA GORDA
Ciénaga de Zapata
Cruces
Palmira
L A S   V I L L A S
Yaguajay
Laguna de Leche
CAYO CRUZ

22°
Guane
ABAJO
San Juan y Martínez
GOLFO DE BATABANÓ
PENÍNSULA DE ZAPATA
Cienfuegos
Florida
CAYO ROMANO

CABO SAN ANTONIO
Ensenada de Cortés
CAYOS LAGUNA
ISLAS DE MANGLES
CAYOS DE JUAN LUIS
Bahía Cochinos
Bahía Cienfuegos
Pico San Juan
1792
SIERRA DE TRINIDAD
Jatibonica
Marón
CAYO GUAJABA

PEN. DE GUANAHACABIBES
CAYO DE DIOS
Trinidad
Zaza
Sancti Spíritus
Ciego de Ávila
CAYO SABINAL

CABO FRANCÉS
CAYOS DE SAN FELIPE
Nueva Gerona
ARCHIPIÉLAGO DE LOS CANARREOS
Casilda
Tunas de Zaza
Júcaro
Bahía de Nuevitas

CABO CORRIENTES
CAYOS DE LOS INDIOS
CAYOS INGLÉS
Santa Fé
Fomento
Nuevitas

ISLA DE PINOS
BANCO JARDINES
B A G Ü E Y
Minas
Santa Lucía

PTA. FRANCÉS
Ensenada de la Siguanea
CAYO ROSARIO
CAYO LARGO
BANCO XAGUA
Camagüey
Puerto Padre

CABO PEPE
CAYO CANTILES
CAYOS ANA MARÍA
San Pedro
Victoria de las Tunas

CAYOS CINCO BALAS
Najasa

C A R I B B E A N
CAYOS DE LAS DOCE LEGUAS
Canal de Caballones
Santa Cruz del Sur
Guayabal
GOLFO DE GUACANAYABO
Manzanillo
Bayamo

20°
LABERINTO DE LAS DOCE LEGUAS
Campechuela

Niquero
SIERRA M
Pico Ojo del Toro
1748
Pico de Turquino 6496
CABO CRUZ

Relief

Meters	Feet
3050	10 000
1525	5000
610	2000
305	1000
152.5	500
0	Sea Level 0
152.5	500
1525	5000
3050	10 000
6100	20 000

CAYMAN BRAC (Br.)
LITTLE CAYMAN (Br.)

Georgetown
GRAND CAYMAN (Br.)

84°
Montego Bay
Falmouth
St. Ann's Bay
GALINA PT.

Lucea
Port Maria

SOUTH NEGRIL PT.
J A M A I C A
Annotto Bay

Savanna la Mar
Mt. Denham
3236

18°
Black River
May Pen
Spanish Town
Kingston

A-533200-76-
COPYRIGHT BY
RAND McNALLY & COMPANY
MADE IN U.S.A.
GT. PEDRO BLUFF
PORTLAND PT.

82°
80°
Longitude West of Greenwich
78°

Scale 1:4 000 000; one inch to 64 miles. Conic Projection
Elevations and depressions are given in feet.

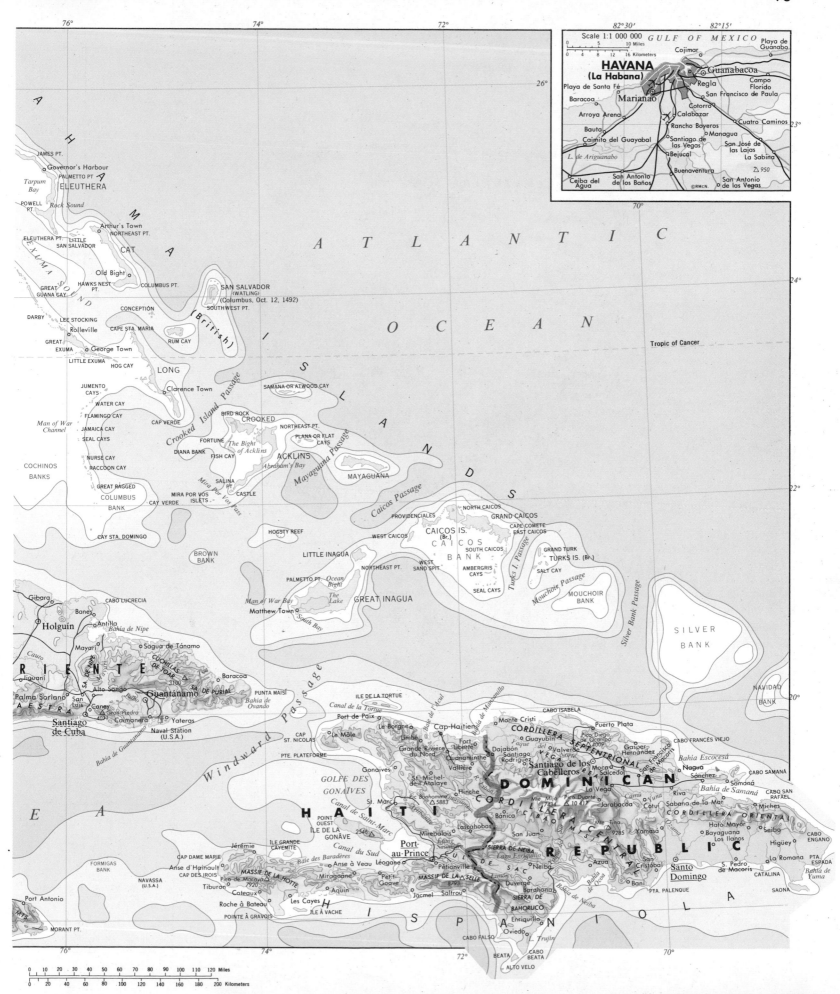

HAVANA
CUBA
Bahía de Campeche
PEN. DE YUCATÁN
Gulf of Honduras
CENTRAL
AMÉRICA
Lago de Nicaragua
Panamá
ISLA DEL COCO (Costa Rica)
ISLA DE MALPELO (Colombia)
ARCHIPIÉLAGO DE COLÓN (GALÁPAGOS ISLANDS) (Ec.)

HISPANIOLA
JAMAICA
PUERTO RICO TRENCH
San Juan
PUERTO RICO (U.S.A.)
CARIBBEAN SEA
WEST INDIES
NORTH AMERICAN BASIN
GUADELOUPE (Fr.)
MARTINIQUE (Fr.)
BARBADOS
TRINIDAD AND TOBAGO
Port-of-Spain

PUNTA DE GALLINAS
Golfo de Venezuela
Barranquilla
Cartagena
Golfo del Darien
Maracaibo
La Guaira
Valencia
CARACAS
Medellín
BOGOTÁ
Nevado del Tolima 17 110
Cerro Icutú 7800
Ciudad Bolívar
Orinoco
VENEZUELA
GUYANA
Georgetown
Paramaribo
SURINAM (Neth.)
Cayenne
FR. GUIANA
COLOMBIA
Guaviare
Boa Vista do Rio Branco
GUIANA HIGHLANDS

Quito
ECUADOR
Cotopaxi 19 344
Chimborazo 20 561
Guayaquil
Golfo de Guayaquil
Iquitos
Leticia
Rio Negro
Japurá
Putumayo
Manaus (Manáos)
Rio Amazonas
ILHA DE MARAJÓ
Belém (Pará)
São Luís (Maranhão)
Equator
ROCEDOS SÃO PEDRO E SÃO PAULO (Brazil)

Chiclayo
Trujillo
Nevs. Huascarán 22 205
PERU
Callao
LIMA
Cuzco
El Misti 19 144
Arequipa
Mollendo
Lago Titicaca
La Paz
Nev. Illimani
BOLIVIA
Sucre
Potosí
Rio Branco
Rio Solimões (Amazonas)
Juruá
Purús
Pôrto Velho
Rio Madeira
Beni
Mamoré
Guaporé
Rooseveit
Tapajós
Xingú
Tocantins
Araguaia
BRAZIL
CHAPADA DE MATO GROSSO
Cuiabá
Diamantina
Belo Horizonte
Rio São Francisco
Brasília
SERRA DO PIAUÍ
Teresina
Fortaleza (Ceará)
Natal
João Pessoa (Paraíba)
RECIFE (Pernambuco)
Maceió
Salto Paulo Afonso
Salvador (Bahia)
ARQUIPÉLAGO FERNANDO DE NORONHA (Brazil)
CABO DE SÃO ROQUE
BRAZILIAN HIGHLANDS

Antofagasta
CHACO
PARAGUAY
Salta
Gran Chaco
Tucumán
Asunción
Corrientes
Pilcomayo
Rio Paraguay
São Paulo
Santos
RIO DE JANEIRO
Vitória
Pico da Bandeira 9482
CABO FRIO
ILHA DA TRINDADE (Brazil)
Cerro Azufre Copiapó 19 947
Copiapó
Coquimbo
Córdoba
Mendoza
Cerro Aconcagua 22 835
Valparaíso
SANTIAGO
ISLAS DE JUAN FERNÁNDEZ (Chile)
ISLA DE SAN FÉLIX (Chile)
ISLA DE SAN AMBROSIO (Chile)
Tropic of Capricorn
ATACAMA
DESIERTO DE ATACAMA
Iquique

Concepción
Valdivia
Rosario
Santa Fe
Salado
Salto
URUGUAY
Rio Grande
Pôrto Alegre
Florianópolis
BUENOS AIRES
MONTEVIDEO
La Plata
Rio de la Plata
PAMPAS
Colorado
Bahía Blanca
Negro
Viedma
Golfo San Matías
ARGENTINA
Chubut
Puerto Montt
ISLA DE CHILOÉ
ARCHIPIÉLAGO DE LOS CHONOS
Monte San Valentín 13 314
Comodoro Rivadavia
Golfo San Jorge
WELLINGTON
HANOVER
Río Gallegos
FALKLAND IS. (ISLAS MALVINAS) (Br.)
Stanley
Punta Arenas
DESOLACIÓN
Estrecho de Magallanes
TIERRA DEL FUEGO
ISLA DE LOS ESTADOS
Mt. Sarmiento 8100
CABO DE HORNOS (CAPE HORN)
Drake Passage

PACIFIC OCEAN

ATLANTIC OCEAN

Tropic of Cancer

SOUTH GEORGIA (Falkland Is.)
SOUTH SANDWICH ISLANDS (B.A.T.)
SOUTH ORKNEY IS. (B.A.T.)
SOUTH SHETLAND ISLANDS (B.A.T.)
JOINVILLE
ANTARCTIC PENINSULA
JAMES ROSS
Antarctic Circle
SOUTH SANDWICH TRENCH

Longitude West of Greenwich

A-540000-76- 2-2-5
COPYRIGHT BY
RAND McNALLY & COMPANY
MADE IN U.S.A.

Relief		
Meters		Feet
3050		10 000
1525		5000
610		2000
305		1000
0	Sea Level	0
152.5		500
1525		5000
3050		10 000
6100		20 000

	Miles
0 200 400 600 800	1000
0 400 800 1200	1600 Kilometers

Scale 1:40 000 000; one inch to 630 miles. Lambert's Azimuthal, Equal Area Projection
Elevations and depressions are given in feet

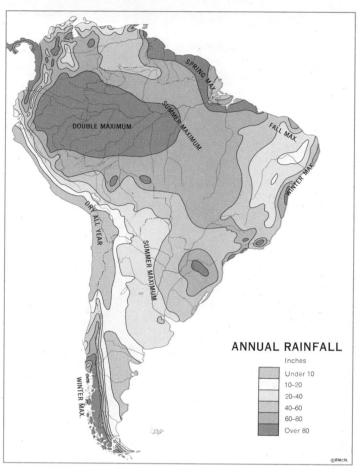

DOUBLE MAXIMUM
SPRING MAX.
SUMMER MAXIMUM
FALL MAX.
WINTER MAX.
DRY ALL YEAR
SUMMER MAXIMUM
WINTER MAX.

ANNUAL RAINFALL

Inches

- Under 10
- 10–20
- 20–40
- 40–60
- 60–80
- Over 80

©RMCN.

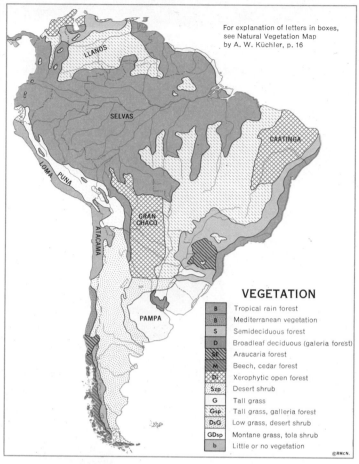

For explanation of letters in boxes,
see Natural Vegetation Map
by A. W. Küchler, p. 16

LLANOS
SELVAS
CAATINGA
LOMA
PUNA
GRAN CHACO
ATACAMA
PAMPA

VEGETATION

B	Tropical rain forest
B	Mediterranean vegetation
S	Semideciduous forest
D	Broadleaf deciduous (galeria forest)
BE	Araucaria forest
M	Beech, cedar forest
Di	Xerophytic open forest
Szp	Desert shrub
G	Tall grass
Gsp	Tall grass, galleria forest
DsG	Low grass, desert shrub
GDsp	Montane grass, tola shrub
b	Little or no vegetation

©RMCN.

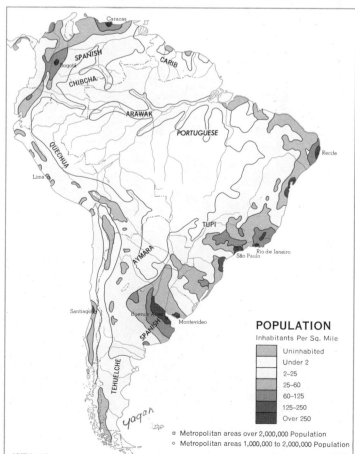

Caracas
SPANISH
CARIB
Bogotá
CHIBCHA
ARAWAK
PORTUGUESE
QUECHUA
Recife
Lima
TUPI
AYMARA
Rio de Janeiro
São Paulo
Santiago
Buenos Aires
Montevideo
SPANISH
TEHUELCHE
Yagan

POPULATION

Inhabitants Per Sq. Mile

- Uninhabited
- Under 2
- 2–25
- 25–60
- 60–125
- 125–250
- Over 250

□ Metropolitan areas over 2,000,000 Population
○ Metropolitan areas 1,000,000 to 2,000,000 Population

A-540000-16   ©RMCN.

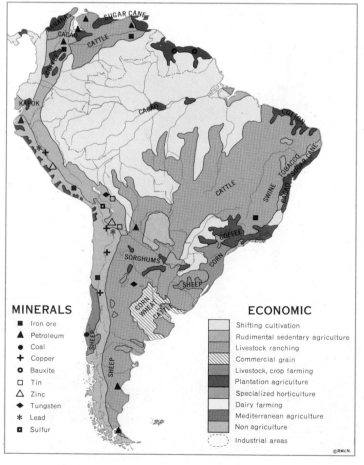

BANANAS
SUGAR CANE
CACAO
CATTLE
KAPOK
CACAO
COTTON
SUGAR CANE
CATTLE
SWINE TOBACCO
COFFEE
SORGHUMS
CORN
SHEEP
SHEEP
CORN WHEAT
CATTLE
SHEEP

MINERALS

- ■ Iron ore
- ▲ Petroleum
- ● Coal
- ＋ Copper
- ○ Bauxite
- □ Tin
- △ Zinc
- ◆ Tungsten
- ✳ Lead
- ▪ Sulfur

ECONOMIC

- Shifting cultivation
- Rudimental sedentary agriculture
- Livestock ranching
- Commercial grain
- Livestock, crop farming
- Plantation agriculture
- Specialized horticulture
- Dairy farming
- Mediterranean agriculture
- Non agriculture
- Industrial areas

©RMCN.

CARIBBEAN SEA

PACIFIC OCEAN

VENEZUELA

COLOMBIA

ECUADOR

PERU

BOLIVIA

AMAZO SELVAS

ARCHIPIELAGO DE COLON (GALÁPAGOS ISLANDS) (Ecuador)

A-549100-76- 3-34- 1-1-1
COPYRIGHT BY
RAND MCNALLY & COMPANY
MADE IN U.S.A.

Tropic of Capricorn

Scale 1:4 000 000
Scale 1:16 000 000; one inch to 250 miles. Sinusoidal Projection
Elevations and depressions are given in feet

65° Longitude West of

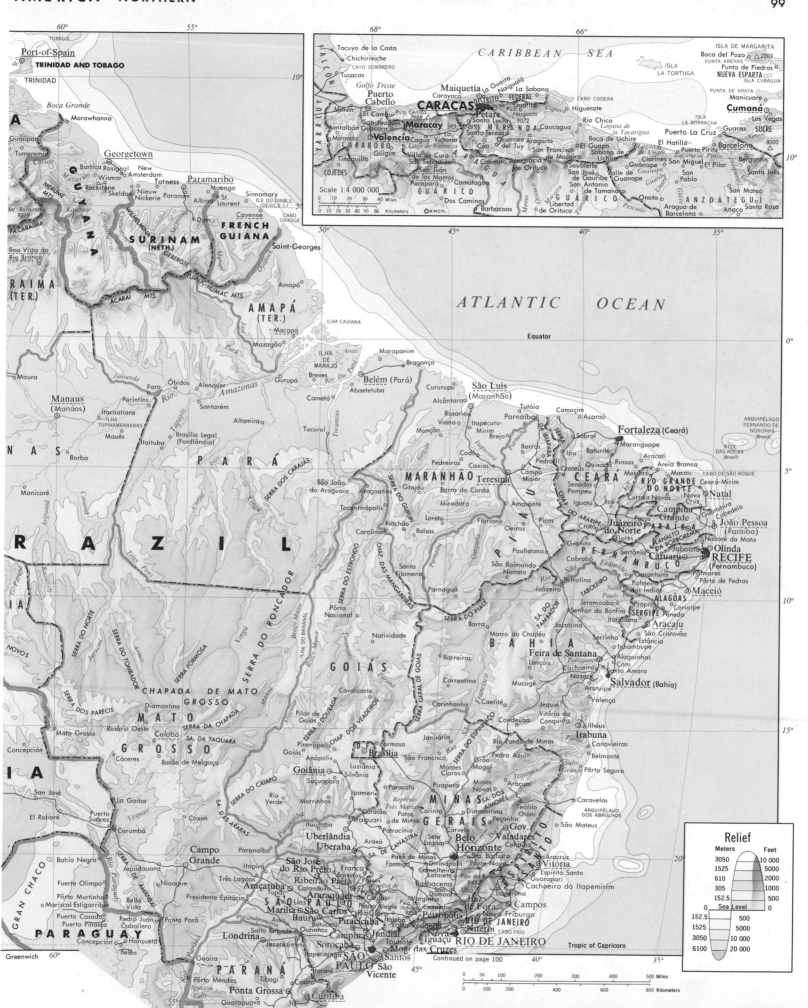

Port-of-Spain
TRINIDAD AND TOBAGO
TRINIDAD
TOBAGO

Boca Grande
Morawhanna
Guasipati
Tumeremo
Bartica Rosignol New
Wismar Amsterdam
Rockstone Nieuw Totness
Skeldon Nickerie Paranam
Georgetown
Paramaribo
Moengo
Albina St.
Laurent
Sinnamary
ILE DU DIABLE
(DEVILS I.)
Cayenne

MERUME MTS.
Mt. Roraima
9219
KAIETEUR
FALLS
GUYANA
SURINAM
(NETH.)
FRENCH
GUIANA
Saint-Georges

PACARAIMA
Boa Vista do
Rio Branco
RORAIMA
(TER.)
ACARAI MTS.
TUMUC-HUMAC MTS.
GEBERGTE
WILHELMINA MTS.

Tocuyo de la Costa
Chichiriviche
CAYO SOMBRERO
Tucacas
Golfo Triste
Puerto
Cabello
Morón
El Cambur
San Joaquín
Montalbán Guacara
Miranda
Tinaquillo
CARABOBO
Güigue
COJEDES
Valencia
Maiquetía
Carayaca
La Guaira
Naiguatá
La Sabana
Guatire
ESP. FEDERAL
CARACAS
Petare
Pico Ceniza
2988
Pico Naiguatá
9072
Santa Lucía
Los Teques
MIRANDA
Villa de Cura
Cagua
Victoria
La
Victoria
San
Casimiro
Altagracia
de Orituco
San
Sebastián
Tinaco
San Juan
de los Morros
Parapara
GUARICO
Dos Caminos
Libertad
de Orituco
Barbacoas
Camatagua
San Francisco
de Macaira
Ocumare
del Tuy
Araguita
Río Chico
Higuerote
Caucagua
Santa
Teresa
CABO CODERA
El Guapo
Sabana de
Uchire
Boca de Uchire
El Guarico
San José
de Guanape
San Antonio
Valle de
Guanape
Onoto
Aragua de
Barcelona
ISLA DE MARGARITA
Boca del Pozo 2303
PUNTA ARENAS
Punta de Piedras
NUEVA ESPARTA
ISLA CUBAGUA
PUNTA DE ARAYA
Manicuare
Cumaná
SUCRE
Neveri
8000
ISLA
LA TORTUGA
LA BORRACHA
Puerto Pirítu
Puerto La Cruz
Guanta
Piritu
Clarines
El Pilar
Soublette
San Miguel
San Mateo
San Pablo
Barcelona
Bergantin
Santa Inés
Santa Rosa
Anaco
ANZOATEGUI

Scale 1:4 000 000
0 10 20 30 40 Miles
0 10 20 30 40 50 60 Kilometers
©R.M.C.N.

ATLANTIC OCEAN

Equator

Moura
Manaus
(Manáos)
Itacoatiara
ILHA
TUPINAMBARANAS
Manicoré
Maués
Borba
Parintins
Óbidos
Santarém
Alenquer
Faro
Juruná
Gurupá
Breves
ILHA
DE
MARAJÓ
Belém (Pará)
Abaetetuba
Cametá
Bragança
Curuçá
Marapanim
Cururupu
Alcântara
São Luís
(Maranhão)
Tutóia
Camocim
Acaraú
Viana
Rosário
Itapecurú-
Mirim
Brejo
Parnaíba
Maranguape
Fortaleza (Ceará)
Sobral
Ipu
Baturité
Aracati
Quixadá
Russas
Areia Branca
CEARÁ
RIO GRANDE
DO NORTE
Ceará-Mirim
Natal
ARQUIPÉLAGO
FERNANDO DE
NORONHA
(Brazil)
ATOL
DAS ROCAS
(Brazil)
CABO DE SÃO ROQUE

BRAZIL
PARÁ
Brasília Legal
(Fordlândia)
Itaituba
Altamira
Tucuruí
São João
do Araguaia
Araguatins
Tocantinópolis
Carolina
Riachão
MARANHÃO
Grajaú
Barra do Corda
Teresina
Miradór
Floriano
Loreto
Balsas
Oeiras
Picos
Amarante
Caxias
Codó
Pedreiras
Mançāo
Campo
Maior
Pedro II
Crateús
Senador
Pompeu
PIAUÍ
Paulistana
São Raimundo
Nonato
São
Filomena
Santa
Quixadá
Iguatu
Crateús
Juazeiro
do Norte
Crato
Flores
Sertânia
Granito
Cabrobó
PERNAMBUCO
Caruarú
Campina
Grande
PARAÍBA
João Pessoa
(Paraíba)
Nazaré da Mata
Jaboatão
Olinda
RECIFE
(Pernambuco)
Palmares
Pôrto de Pedras
CANAL DE
BORBOREMA
Cobedel

Serra dos Carajás
SERRA DO GURUPI
SERRA DO ESTRONDO
SERRA DO RONCADOR
SERRA DO PIAUI
SERRA DA IBIAPABA
CHAP. DAS MANGABEIRAS

Parnaguá
Juàzeiro
Remanso
Rio São Francisco
Parnaíba

ALAGOAS
Penedo
Propriá
Corúripe
Maceió
SERGIPE
Aracaju
Estância
São Cristóvão
Estância
Inhambupe
Alagoinhas
Catu
Santo Amaro
Salvador (Bahia)
Cachoeira
Nazaré
Aratuípe
Valença
BAHIA
Feira de Santana
Senhor do Bonfim
Jacobina
Serrinha
Morro do Chapéu
Lençóis
Barra
Itaberaba
Mucugê
Caetité
Jequié
Vitória da
Conquista
Itabuna
Ilhéus
Canavieiras
Belmonte

SERRA DO NORTE
SERRA DO TOMBADOR
SERRA DOS PARECIS
SERRA FORMOSA
SERRA DA CHAPADA
SA. DA TAQUARA
CHAPADA DE MATO
GROSSO
MATO
GROSSO
Mato Grosso
Rosário Oeste
Cuiabá
Barão de Melgaço
Cáceres
SERRA DO CAIAPÓ
SA. DAS ARARAS
SERRA DO CAIAPÓ

GOIÁS
Barreiras
Correntina
Cavalcante
Natividade
Pôrto
Nacional
ILHA DO BANANAL
Pilar
de Goiás
Goiás
Januária
Corinto
Pirenópolis
Anápolis
Formosa
D.F.
Brasília
Luziânia
Silvânia
Goiânia
Suçuapara
Ipameri
Morrinhos
Catalão
Paracatú
Patos
de Minas
SERRA GERAL DE GOIÁS
SERRA GERAL DO ESPINHAÇO

MINAS
GERAIS
Montes
Claros
Pedra Azul
Araçuaí
Teófilo
Otoni
Peçanha
Curvelo
Diamantina
Pirapora
São Francisco
Januária
Rio Pardo de Minas
Mogi
Minas
Novas
SA. DOS
AIMORÉS
Gov.
Valadares
Coldina
Nanuque
Caravelas
ARQUIPÉLAGO
DOS ABROLHOS
Pôrto Seguro
Salto
Grande

BOLIVIA
San José
La Gaiba
El Roboré
Puerto Suárez
Corumbá
Concepción
PARAGUAY
GRAN CHACO
Fuerte Olimpo
Mariscal Estigarribia
Pôrto Murtinho
Bahía Negra
Puerto Casado
Pedro Juan
Caballero
Concepción
Horqueta
Belén

Bella
Vista
Ponta Porã
Presidente Epitácio
MATO GROSSO
Aquidauana
Campo
Grande
Três Lagoas
Nioaque
Coxim
Rio
Verde
Paranaíba
Uberlândia
Uberaba
Araguari
Ituiutaba
Paranaíba
SÃO PAULO
Araçatuba
Tupã
Marília
Bauru
Assis
Lins
Catanduva
São Carlos
São José
do Rio Prêto
Ribeirão Prêto
Franca
Bebedouro
Barretos
Araxá
SA. DE CANASTRA
SA. DA MANTIQUEIRA
Formiga
Divinópolis
Pará de Minas
Patos
de Minas
Patrocínio
Belo
Horizonte
Sete
Lagoas
Conselheiro
Lafaiete
Barbacena
Juiz
de Fora
Ubá
Ponte Nova
Sta. Bárbara
Pico da Bandeira
9482
Vitória
Guarapari
Aracruz
Linhares
Espírito Santo
Cachoeiro do Itapemirim
ESPÍRITO SANTO
Gov.
Campos
Nova Friburgo
Petrópolis
Nova
Iguaçu
RIO DE JANEIRO
Niterói
CABO FRIO
Vitória
Itaperuna
Volta
Redonda
Resende
Campos
Pouso Alegre
Itajubá
Cruzeiro
Virgínia
Taubaté
Piracicaba
Campinas
Jundiaí
Mogi das Cruzes
Santos
São
Vicente
SÃO PAULO
Sorocaba
Itapetininga
Itararé
PARANÁ
Curitiba
Ponta Grossa
Guarapuava
Londrina
Presidente Prudente
Marília
Ourinhos
Botucatú
Jacarèzinho
Guaíra
Pôrto Mendes
Iguassú Falls
Tibají

PARANÁ

Tropic of Capricorn

Greenwich

Continued on page 100

0 50 100 200 300 400 500 Miles
0 100 200 400 600 800 Kilometers

Relief
Meters   Feet
3050   10 000
1525   5000
610   2000
305   1000
152.5   500
0   Sea Level   0
152.5   500
1525   5000
3050   10 000
6100   20 000

SOUTH AMERICA · SOUTHERN

Continued on pages 98-99

BOLIVIA

PARAGUAY

GRAN CHACO

CHACO

FORMOSA

MATO GROSSO

Asunción

Tropic of Capricorn

ARGENTINA

CHILE

PACIFIC OCEAN

ATLANTIC OCEAN

PUNA DE ATACAMA

Antofagasta

Salta

TUCUMÁN

SANTIAGO DEL ESTERO

CATAMARCA

LA RIOJA

CÓRDOBA

SAN JUAN

Mendoza

MENDOZA

SANTIAGO

Valparaíso

SAN LUIS

SANTA FE

Rosario

ENTRE RÍOS

Paraná

URUGUAY

MONTEVIDEO

BUENOS AIRES

La Plata

Cerro Aconcagua

LA PAMPA

Bahía Blanca

Mar del Plata

RÍO NEGRO

NEUQUÉN

Golfo San Matías

PENÍNSULA VALDÉS

Golfo San Jorge

CHUBUT

PATAGONIA

SANTA CRUZ

Golfo de Penas

Comodoro Rivadavia

Puerto Deseado

Puerto Santa Cruz

Río Gallegos

FALKLAND IS. (ISLAS MALVINAS) (Br.)

Stanley

Bahía Grande

MESETA DE LAS VIZCACHAS

ISLA DE CHILOÉ

ARCHIPIÉLAGO DE LOS CHONOS

ARCHIPIÉLAGO MADRE DE DIOS

WELLINGTON

HANOVER

PENÍNSULA DE TAITAO

Punta Arenas

Estrecho de Magallanes

TIERRA DEL FUEGO

CABO DE HORNOS (Cape Horn)

ISLAS DIEGO RAMÍREZ

BANCO BURDWOOD

ISLA DE LOS ESTADOS

BRASIL

São Paulo

RIO DE JANEIRO

SÃO PAULO

PARANÁ

SANTA CATARINA

RIO GRANDE DO SUL

Pôrto Alegre

Florianópolis

Curitiba

MINAS GERAIS

Belo Horizonte

Relief

Meters	Feet
3050	10 000
1525	5000
610	2000
305	1000
152.5	500
0	Sea Level
Sea Level	0
152.5	500
1525	5000
3050	10 000
6100	20 000

Below Sea Level

BUENOS AIRES

RÍO DE LA PLATA

San Fernando

San Isidro

Vicente López

Olivos

San Miguel

General San Martín

Morón

San Justo

Avellaneda

Lanús

Quilmes

Lomas de Zamora

Canal Punta Indio

Scale 1:1 000 000

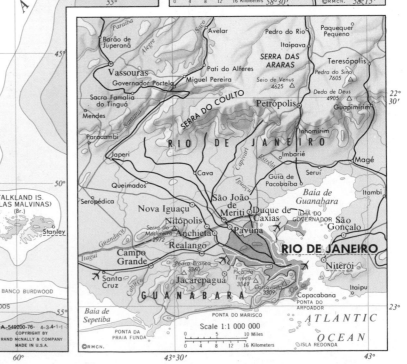

RIO DE JANEIRO

SERRA DAS ARARAS

Petrópolis

Teresópolis

RIO DE JANEIRO

Baía de Guanabara

Nova Iguaçu

Niterói

Duque de Caxias

São Gonçalo

GUANABARA

Copacabana

ATLANTIC OCEAN

Scale 1:1 000 000

A-549200-76- 4-3.4-1-1
COPYRIGHT BY
RAND McNALLY & COMPANY
MADE IN U.S.A.

Longitude West of Greenwich

Scale 1:16 000 000, one inch to 250 miles. Sinusoidal Projection
Elevations and depressions are given in feet

0 50 100 200 400 500 Miles
0 100 200 400 800 Kilometers

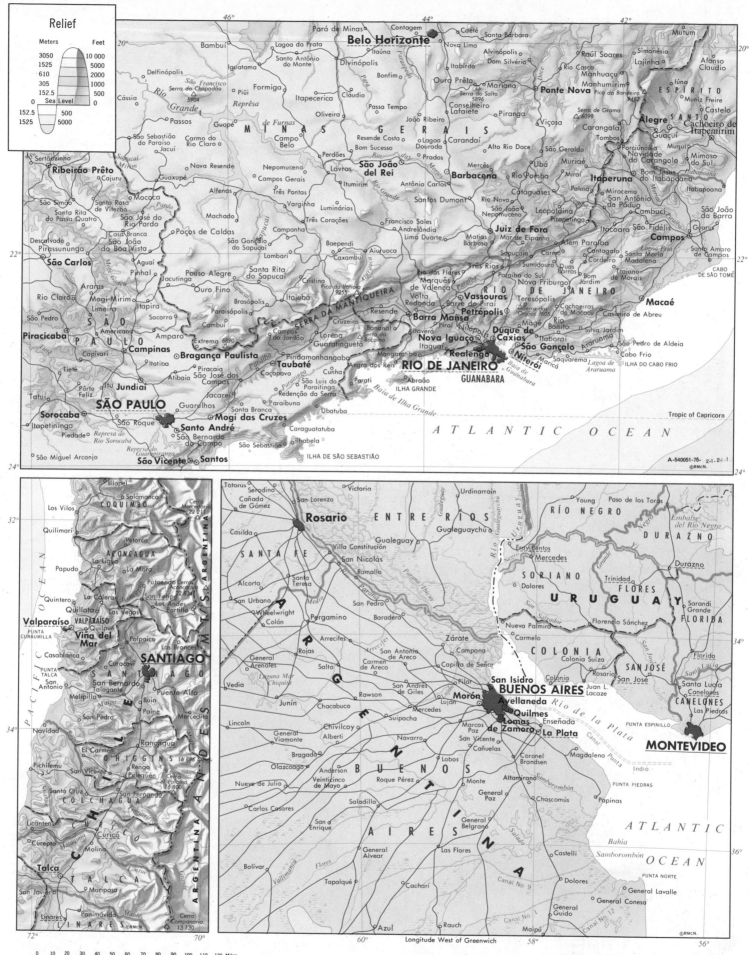

Relief

Meters	Feet
3050	10 000
1525	5000
610	2000
305	1000
152.5	500
0	Sea Level 0
152.5	500
1525	5000

Belo Horizonte

Pará de Minas Contagem Caeté Santa Barbara Mutum
Bambuí Lagoa da Prata Nova Lima Simonésia Lajinha
Delfinópolis Iguatama Santo Antônio do Monte Divinópolis Itaúna Itabirito Alvinópolis Dom Silvério Raúl Soares Afonso Claudio
Serra do Chapadão 5904 Piúi Formiga Itapecirica Cláudio Passa Tempo Bonfim Ouro Prêto Mariana Ponte Nova Manhuaçu Manhumirim ESPIRITO
Cássia Santo Antônio São Francisco M I N A S G E R A I S Conselheiro Lafaiete Serra do Salto 5896 Piranga Pico da Bandeira 9482 Muniz Freire SANTO
Passos Carmo do Rio Claro Oliveira Resende Costa Bom Sucesso Alto Rio Doce Carandaí São Geraldo Viçosa Carangola Castelo Alegre Cachoeiro de Itapemirim
São Sebastião do Paraiso Jacuí Guapé Nepomuceno Lavras Campo Belo Lagoa Dourada Prados Mercês Rio Pomba Tombos Porciúncula Navidade do Carangola Mimoso do Sul
Sertãozinho Ribeirão Prêto Cajuru Nova Resende Campos Gerais São João del Rei Antônio Carlos Santos Dumont Muriaé Itaperuna Bom Jesus do Itabápoana São João da Barra
São Simão Santa Rosa de Viterbo Mocóca Alfenas Itumirim Barbacena Rio Novo Leopoldina Miracema San Antônio de Pádua Itabapoana
Santa Rita do Passa Quatro São José do Rio Pardo Machado Três Pontas Varginha Luminárias Cataguases Mirai Palma Cambuci
Casa Branca Descalvado Poços de Caldas Campanha Três Corações Francisco Sales Juiz de Fora Mar de Espanha Além Paraíba Guarus
Pirassununga São João da Boa Vista Andrelândia Matias Barbosa Campos
São Carlos Pinhal Pouso Alegre Santa Rita do Sapucaí Lima Duarte Cabo DE São Tomé
São Pedro Mogi Mirim Aguaí Ouro Fino Lambari Baependi Sapucaia Carmo Cantagalo Santa Maria Madalena
Rio Claro Limeira Itapira Socorro Brasópolis Santa Rita do Sapucai Aiuruoca Sumidouro Duas Barras Santo Amaro de Campos
Piracicaba Americana Amparo Paraisópolis Caxambu Rio das Flores Três Rios Paraíba do Sul Trajano de Morais
Campinas Extrema 6890 Cambuí Itajubá Pico do Itatiaia 9255 Marquês de Valença Nova Friburgo Bom Jardim Macaé
Bragança Paulista Piracaia S E R R A D A M A N T I Q U E I R A Resende Volta Redonda Teresópolis Casimiro de Abreu
Itatiba São José dos Campos Serra da Bocaina Cruzeiro Lorena Barra do Piraí Vassouras Serra dos Órgãos 7605 Silva Jardim
Tietê Jundiaí Atibaia Taubaté Guaratinguetá Barra Mansa Petrópolis Rio Bonito São Pedro de Aldeia
Pôrto Feliz Pindamonhangaba Itavera Itaguaí Magé Cabo Frio
Tatuí Jacareí Cunha Angra dos Reis Nova Iguaçu Itaborai São Gonçalo Maricá Saquarema ILHA DO CABO FRIO
SÃO PAULO Guarulhos Paraibuna São Luis do Paraitinga Parati Realengo Duque de Caxias Lagoa de Araruama
Sorocaba São Roque Santa Branca Redenção da Serra Mangaratiba Itaguaí RIO DE JANEIRO Niterói RIO DE JANEIRO
Mogi das Cruzes Caraguatatuba Ubatuba Abraão GUANABARA Baía de Guanabara
Itapetininga Santo André São Bernardo do Campo ILHA GRANDE
Piedade São Miguel Arcanjo Represa do Rio Sorocaba São Sebastião Baía de Ilha Grande Tropic of Capricorn
Represa do Guarapiranga São Vicente Santos Ilhabela
ILHA DE SÃO SEBASTIÃO A T L A N T I C   O C E A N
A-540051-76- 2-1-24-1 ©RMCN.

Valparaíso **VALPARAÍSO**
Illapel Salamanca Cerro Mercedario 22 211
Los Vilos COQUIMBO Totoras Serodino Victoria Young Paso de los Toros
Quilimarí ACONCAGUA Cañada de Gómez San Lorenzo E N T R E   R I O S Urdinarrain RÍO NEGRO Embalse del Rio Negro
Petorca Rosario Gualeguaychú Fray Bentos DURAZNO
La Ligua La Mora Casilda Gualeguay Mercedes
Papudo Putaendo Cerro Aconcagua 22 834 Villa Constitución SORIANO Trinidad Durazno
Quintero Los Andes San Felipe Partillo SANTA FE San Nicolás Dolores URUGUAY FLORES
Quillota La Calera Las Vegas Alcorta Santa Teresa Ramallo Nueva Palmira Florencio Sánchez FLORIDA
Viña del Mar Quilpué San Urbano San Pedro Carmelo Sarandí Grande
PUNTA CURAUMILLA Casablanca Wheelwright COLONIA Rosario Florida
Colón Pergamino Zárate Colonia Suiza SAN JOSÉ
Polpaico Vedia Rojas Arrecifes Campana Colonia San José Santa Lucia
SANTIAGO Curacaví General Arenales San Antonio de Areco Capilla de Señor San Isidro Juan L. Lacaze Canelones
San Bernardo Salto Carmen de Areco BUENOS AIRES CANELONES
Talagante S A N T I A G O Junín Chacabuco Mercedes Pilar Avellaneda Río de la Plata Las Piedras
Melipilla Puente Alto Lincoln General Viamonte Suipacha Rawson Lobos Luján Morón Quilmes PUNTA ESPINILLO
San Antonio Buin Alberti Chivilcoy Navarro San Andrés de Giles Lomas de Zamora Ensenada La Plata
Paine Mercedita Bragado Marcos Paz San Vicente Cañuelas MONTEVIDEO
San Pedro O'HIGGINS 16 886 Nueve de Julio Veinticinco de Mayo Olazcoaga Roque Pérez Monte Coronel Brandsen Canal Indio
Navidad El Carmen Cerro El Paloma 16 900 Carlos Casares Saladillo General Paz Magdalena PUNTA PIEDRAS
Pichilemu COLCHAGUA Renga Bolívar Anderson General Alvear Las Flores Altamirano Chascomús Papinas
San Vicente Peleqúen San Fernando San Enrique Monte General Belgrano PUNTA PIEDRAS
Santa Cruz Rancagua Tapalqué Las Flores Castelli B U E N O S Bahia Samborombón
Cerro Companario 13 130 TALCA Cachari Canal No. 9 Dolores A I R E S ATLANTIC PUNTA NORTE
Licantén Curepto Curicó Molina Azul Rauch Maipú General Conesa OCEAN
San Javier TALCA Panimávida Mariposa Tapalqué General Guido
Linares LINARES Canal No. 1 Canal No. 12 General Lavalle ©RMCN.

Longitude West of Greenwich

0 10 20 30 40 50 60 70 80 90 100 110 120 Miles
0 20 40 60 80 100 120 140 160 180 200 Kilometers

Scale 1:4 000 000; one inch to 64 miles.
Elevations and depressions are given in feet.

Relief

Meters	Feet
3050	10 000
1525	5000
610	2000
305	1000
152.5	500
0 Sea Level	0
152.5	500 Below Sea Level
1525	5000
3050	10 000

ATLANTIC OCEAN

ICELAND
Reykjavík
Reykjanes
Vík
Eskifjörður

Tórshavn
FÆRØE IS.
(Den.)

Arctic Circle

ARCTIC

NORD KAPP
Hammerfest
Vardö
Varangerfjord
Pechenga
Murmansk
LOFOTEN IS.
Narvik
Vestfjord
LAPLAND
Monchegorsk
Kirovsk
Kandalaksha

Mt. Kebnekaise
6962

NORWAY
SWEDEN
FINLAND

DOVRE FJELL
Galdhøpiggen
8100

Trondheim
(Nidaros)

Luleå
Tornio
Oulu

Sognefjord
Sundsvall
Umeå
Umeå

Bergen
Gulf of Bothnia
Vaasa

Gävle
Turku
Helsinki
Vyborg
Kronstadt

Oslo
Uppsala
Hangö
LENINGRAD
Narva

Stavanger
Kristiansand
Norrköping
STOCKHOLM
Tallinn
ESTONIAN S.S.R.
Novgorod

SHETLAND IS.
(Scot.)
Lerwick

Álborg
Karlstad
GÖTLAND
Visby
ÖLAND
Gulf of Riga
Tartu
Pskov

ORKNEY IS.
Göteborg
Riga
Velikiye Luki

NORTH
SEA
Skagerrak
Kattegat

DENMARK
COPENHAGEN
(København)
Malmö
BORNHOLM
(Den.)
Klaipéda
LATVIAN S.S.R.
Jelgava
Daugavpils
Dvina

LITHUANIAN S.S.R.
Kaunas
Vitebsk

IRELAND
Galway
(Baile Átha Cliath)

GLASGOW
BRITISH
Dundee
Firth of Forth
Edinburgh
ISLES
NEWCASTLE
KINGDOM

SCOTLAND
Grampians
Aberdeen

UNITED

NORTHERN IRELAND
Belfast
Carlisle

LIVERPOOL
IRISH SEA
LEEDS
Hull

Dublin
Cobh
Cork
MANCHESTER

CAPE CLEAR
St. George's Chan.

BIRMINGHAM
Leicester
AMSTERDAM
NETHERLANDS

LANDS END
SCILLY IS.
Southampton
The Hague
('s Gravenhage)
ROTTERDAM

LONDON
Dover
ANTWERP
BELGIUM
ESSEN
COLOGNE
Bonn

Helgoland
(Ger.)
Kiel
HAMBURG
Lübeck
Bremen
Hannover
BERLIN
Magdeburg
Leipzig
Dresden

RÜGEN
Szczecin
Gdańsk
GERMANY
Poznań
POLAND
WARSAW
Brest

Torún
Białystok
Łódź
Lublin

Kaliningrad
R.S.F.S.R.
Vilnius
BELORUSSIAN
S.S.R.
Grodno
Minsk
Mogilëv
Baranovichi
Bobruysk
Pinsk
Pripyat

English Channel
Cherbourg
CHANNEL IS.
(Br.)
Le Havre
Calais
Lille
BRUSSELS
LUX.
Mainz
FRANKFURT
PRAGUE
CZECHOSLOVAKIA
Ostrava
Kraków
Przemyśl

Brest
Rennes
PARIS
Rouen
Reims
Nürnberg
STUTTGART
Plzeň
Brno
SUDETEN
Wrocław
L'vov
UKRAINE
Rovno
Zhitomir
Berdichev
Ternopol

St. Nazaire
Orléans
Tours
Strasbourg
MUNICH
Danube
Bodensee
VIENNA
(Wien)
Bratislava
Miskolc
Drogobych
Ivano-Frankovsk
Chernovtsy

La Rochelle
Nantes
FRANCE
Dijon
Lausanne
Bern
Zürich
LIECHT.
AUSTRIA
Graz
BUDAPEST
HUNGARY
Oradea
Cluj
Iasi
MOLD.
S.S.R.
Kishinev

Bay of Biscay
Clermont-Ferrand
Lyon
Geneva
SWITZERLAND
Mont Blanc
15 771
Maribor
Ljubljana
Zagreb
Szeged
Subotica
ROMANIA
Galati

El Ferrol
La Coruña
C. DE FINISTERRE
Santander
S. Sebastián
Bayonne
MASSIF
CENTRAL
Gironde
Dordogne
Nîmes
MILAN
TURIN
Venice
Trieste
Novi Sad
CARPATI MERIDIONALI
(TRANSYLVANIAN ALPS)
Brăila
Ploesti

Vigo
Oviedo
Gijón
CORD. CANTÁBRICA
Bilbao
PYRENEES
Pic d'Aneto
11 168
Toulouse
Genoa
La Spezia
Bologna
Golfo di Genova
YUGOSLAVIA
Belgrade
BUCHAREST
Ruse

Pôrto
(Oporto)
Coimbra
Salamanca
Valladolid
Douro
SIERRA DE GUADARRAMA
ANDORRA
Marseille
Golfe du Lion
Toulon
Nice
MONACO
Livorno
(Leghorn)
Florence
SAN MARINO
Ancona
Zadar
Split
Sarajevo
Niš
Sofia
(Sofiya)
STARA PLANINA
(BALKAN MTS.)
Varna
(Stalin)

LISBON
(Lisboa)
PORTUGAL
MADRID
SPAIN
Zaragoza
BARCELONA
Tarragona
Tortosa
CORSICA
(Fr.)
Ajaccio
ROME
(Roma)
ITALY
NAPLES
(Napoli)
Bari
Brindisi
Dubrovnik
Cetinje
ALBANIA
Shkoder
Tirane
Durrës
Skopje
Bitola
BULGARIA
Plovdiv
RHODOPE MTS.
Edirne

Guadiana
SIERRA MORENA
Guadalquivir
Valencia
Murcia
ISLAS BALEARES
DE MEIIORCA
(Sp.)
Palma de Mallorca
DE IBIZA
C. DE LA NAO
SARDINIA
(It.)
Cagliari
TYRRHENIAN
SEA
ADRIATIC SEA
Golfo di Taranto
KÉRKIRE
GREECE
ATHENS
(Athinai)
Izmir

C. DE SÃO VICENTE
Cádiz
Sevilla
SIERRA NEVADA
Almería
Cartagena
C. SPARTIVENTO
C. BON
Palermo
Messina
Mts. Etna
11 122
SICILY
(It.)
Catania
IONIAN
SEA
Kalámai
AKR. TAINARON
CRETE
(Gr.)
Iráklion
Khaniá

Rabat
Fès
Tanger
Ceuta (Sp.)
Straits of Gibraltar
Gibraltar
(Br.)
Málaga
Oran
(Ouahran)
Algiers
(Alger)
Constantine
Tunis
(Tunis)
Bizerte
C. BON
MALTA
MEDITERRANEAN SEA

MOROCCO
Casablanca
ATLAS MOUNTAINS
ALGERIA
TUNISIA

MEDITERRANEAN

Scale 1: 16 000 000; one inch to 250 miles. Conic Projection

Elevations and depressions are given in feet

0	50	100	200	300	400	500 Miles
0	100	200	400	600		800 Kilometers

Continued on pages 134-135

Continued on pages 144-145

A-519697-76 22- 5-
COPYRIGHT BY
RAND McNALLY & COMPANY
MADE IN U.S.A.

COPYRIGHT BY
RAND MCNALLY & COMPANY
MADE IN U.S.A.

Scale 1:16 000 000; one inch to 250 miles. Conic Projection
Elevations and depressions are given in feet.

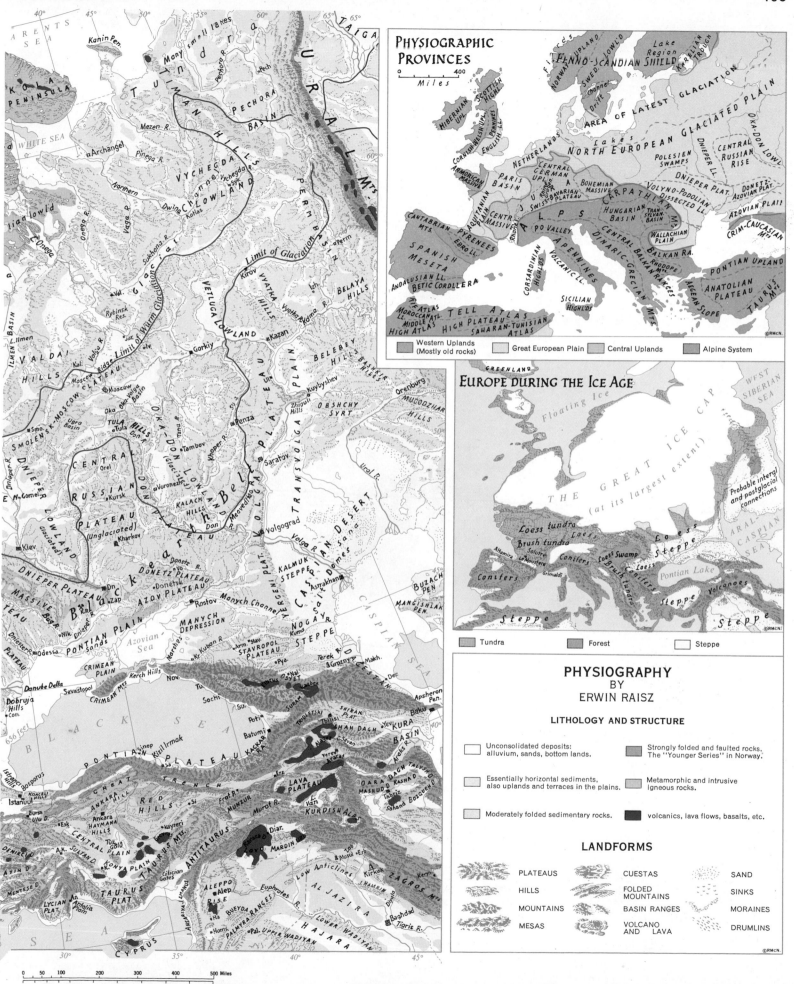

COPYRIGHT BY
RAND McNALLY & COMPANY
MADE IN U.S.A.

MAJOR LAND USES

Cropland-wheat important	Oases and important cotton areas
Cropland-rye important	Chiefly pasture land (meadow, alpine pastures) with some cropland
Cropland-corn important	Sparse pasture land (heath, maquis, steppe)
Cropland-oats and barley important	Sparse grass, desert shrub; seasonally grazed
Cropland and pasture with some woodland	Tundra; seasonally grazed
Intensive grape culture for wine	Forest and woodland
Mediterranean agriculture (including olives, grapes, grains and specialized vegetables)	Waste and unproductive areas

0 100 200 300 400 500 600 Miles

0   200   400   600   800   1000 Kilometers

Scale 1:20,000,000; one inch to 315 miles Conic Projection

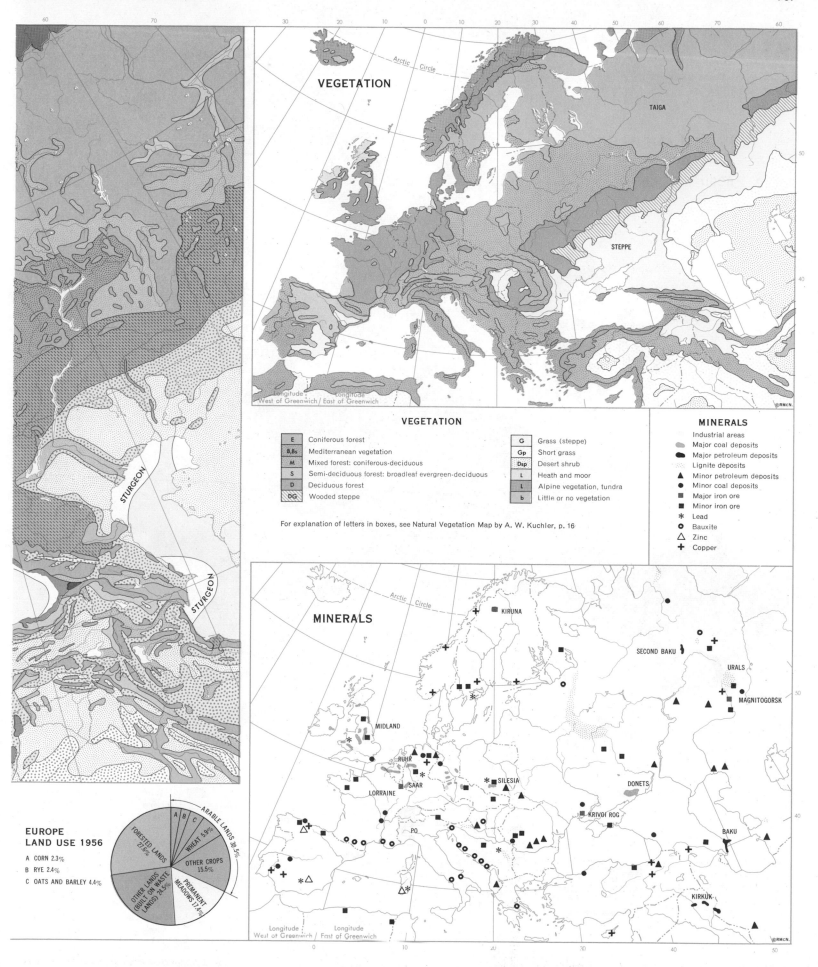

VEGETATION

E	Coniferous forest	G	Grass (steppe)	
B,Bs	Mediterranean vegetation	Gp	Short grass	
M	Mixed forest: coniferous-deciduous	Dsp	Desert shrub	
S	Semi-deciduous forest: broadleaf evergreen-deciduous	L	Heath and moor	
D	Deciduous forest	L	Alpine vegetation, tundra	
DG	Wooded steppe	b	Little or no vegetation	

For explanation of letters in boxes, see Natural Vegetation Map by A. W. Kuchler, p. 16

MINERALS

- Industrial areas
- Major coal deposits
- Major petroleum deposits
- Lignite deposits
- ▲ Minor petroleum deposits
- ● Minor coal deposits
- ■ Major iron ore
- ■ Minor iron ore
- ✳ Lead
- ○ Bauxite
- △ Zinc
- + Copper

EUROPE
LAND USE 1956

A CORN 2.3%
B RYE 2.4%
C OATS AND BARLEY 4.4%

ARABLE LANDS 30.5%
WHEAT 5.9%
OTHER CROPS 15.5%
PERMANENT MEADOWS 17.4%
OTHER LANDS (BUILT ON WASTE LANDS) 24.5%
FORESTED LANDS 27.6%

STURGEON

TAIGA
STEPPE

KIRUNA
SECOND BAKU
URALS
MAGNITOGORSK
MIDLAND
RUHR
SAAR
LORRAINE
SILESIA
DONETS
KRIVOI ROG
BAKU
PO
KIRKUK

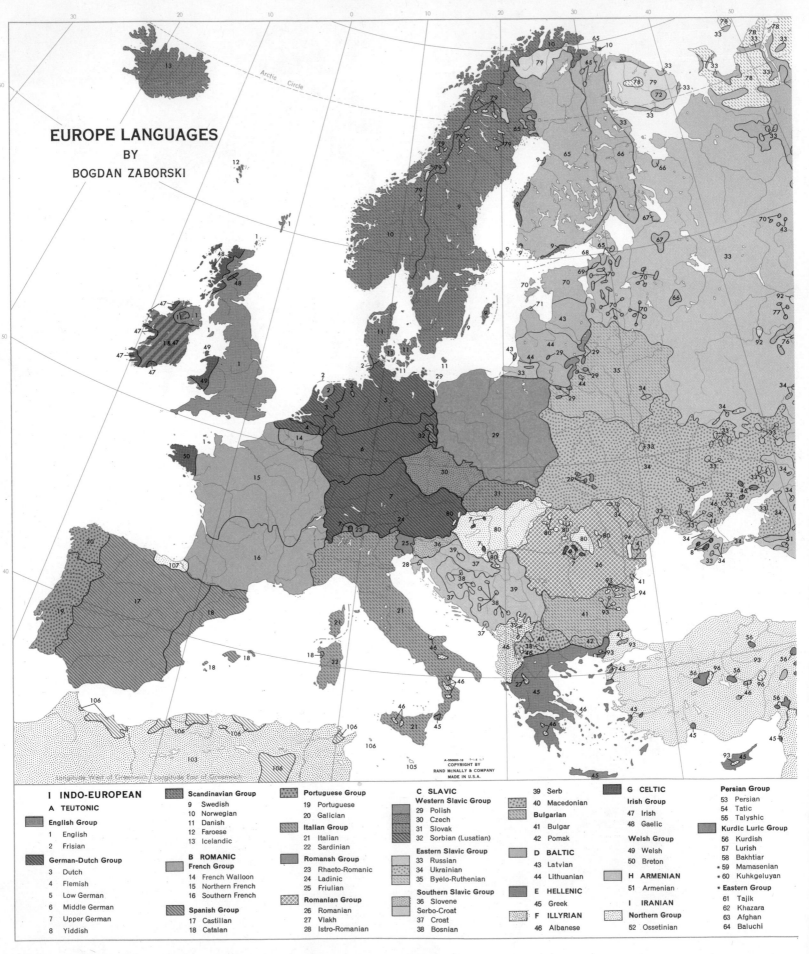

EUROPE LANGUAGES
BY
BOGDAN ZABORSKI

COPYRIGHT BY
RAND MCNALLY & COMPANY
MADE IN U.S.A.

I INDO-EUROPEAN	Scandinavian Group	Portuguese Group	C SLAVIC	39 Serb	G CELTIC	Persian Group
A TEUTONIC	9 Swedish	19 Portuguese	Western Slavic Group	40 Macedonian	Irish Group	53 Persian
English Group	10 Norwegian	20 Galician	29 Polish	Bulgarian	47 Irish	54 Tatic
1 English	11 Danish	Italian Group	30 Czech	41 Bulgar	48 Gaelic	55 Talyshic
2 Frisian	12 Faroese	21 Italian	31 Slovak	42 Pomak	Welsh Group	Kurdic Luric Group
	13 Icelandic	22 Sardinian	32 Sorbian (Lusatian)		49 Welsh	56 Kurdish
German-Dutch Group	B ROMANIC	Romansh Group	Eastern Slavic Group	D BALTIC	50 Breton	57 Lurish
3 Dutch	French Group	23 Rhaeto-Romanic	33 Russian	43 Latvian	H ARMENIAN	58 Bakhtiar
4 Flemish	14 French Walloon	24 Ladinic	34 Ukrainian	44 Lithuanian	51 Armenian	* 59 Mamasenian
5 Low German	15 Northern French	25 Friulian	35 Byelo-Ruthenian	E HELLENIC	I IRANIAN	* 60 Kuhkgeluyan
6 Middle German	16 Southern French	Romanian Group	Southern Slavic Group	45 Greek	Northern Group	* Eastern Group
7 Upper German	Spanish Group	26 Romanian	36 Slovene	F ILLYRIAN	52 Ossetinian	61 Tajik
8 Yiddish	17 Castilian	27 Vlakh	Serbo-Croat	46 Albanese		62 Khazara
	18 Catalan	28 Istro-Romanian	37 Croat			63 Afghan
			38 Bosnian			64 Baluchi

Scale 1:20,000,000; one inch to 315 miles Conic Projection

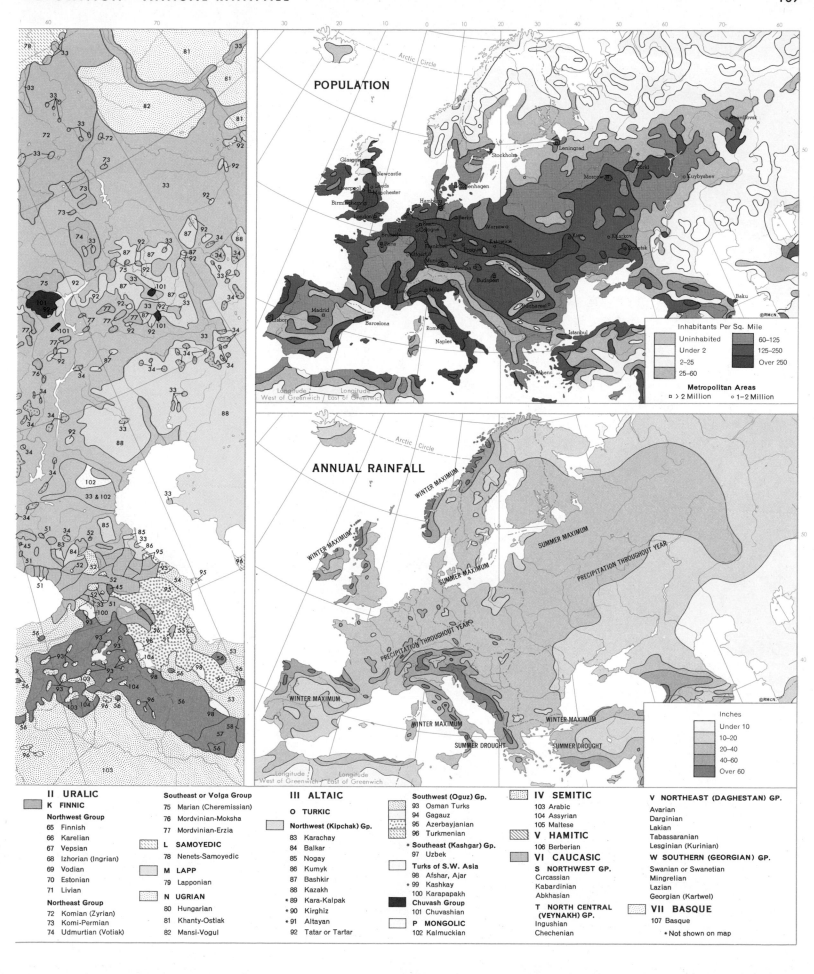

POPULATION

Inhabitants Per Sq. Mile

Uninhabited	60–125
Under 2	125–250
2–25	Over 250
25–60	

Metropolitan Areas
□ > 2 Million   ○ 1–2 Million

©RMCN.

ANNUAL RAINFALL

WINTER MAXIMUM
WINTER MAXIMUM
WINTER MAXIMUM
SUMMER MAXIMUM
SUMMER MAXIMUM
SUMMER MAXIMUM
PRECIPITATION THROUGHOUT YEAR
PRECIPITATION THROUGHOUT YEAR
PRECIPITATION THROUGHOUT YEAR
WINTER MAXIMUM
WINTER MAXIMUM
WINTER MAXIMUM
SUMMER DROUGHT
SUMMER DROUGHT

Inches

Under 10
10–20
20–40
40–60
Over 60

©RMCN.

II URALIC

K FINNIC

Northwest Group
65 Finnish
66 Karelian
67 Vepsian
68 Izhorian (Ingrian)
69 Vodian
70 Estonian
71 Livian

Northeast Group
72 Komian (Zyrian)
73 Komi-Permian
74 Udmurtian (Votiak)

Southeast or Volga Group
75 Marian (Cheremissian)
76 Mordvinian-Moksha
77 Mordvinian-Erzia

L SAMOYEDIC
78 Nenets-Samoyedic

M LAPP
79 Lapponian

N UGRIAN
80 Hungarian
81 Khanty-Ostiak
82 Mansi-Vogul

III ALTAIC

O TURKIC

Northwest (Kipchak) Gp.
83 Karachay
84 Balkar
85 Nogay
86 Kumyk
87 Bashkir
88 Kazakh
* 89 Kara-Kalpak
* 90 Kirghiz
* 91 Altayan
92 Tatar or Tartar

Southwest (Oguz) Gp.
93 Osman Turks
94 Gagauz
95 Azerbayjanian
96 Turkmenian

Southeast (Kashgar) Gp.
97 Uzbek

Turks of S.W. Asia
98 Afshar, Ajar
* 99 Kashkay
100 Karapapakh

Chuvash Group
101 Chuvashian

P MONGOLIC
102 Kalmuckian

IV SEMITIC
103 Arabic
104 Assyrian
105 Maltese

V HAMITIC
106 Berberian

VI CAUCASIC

S NORTHWEST GP.
Circassian
Kabardinian
Abkhasian

**T NORTH CENTRAL
(VEYNAKH) GP.**
Ingushian
Chechenian

V NORTHEAST (DAGHESTAN) GP.
Avarian
Darginian
Lakian
Tabassaranian
Lesginian (Kurinian)

W SOUTHERN (GEORGIAN) GP.
Swanian or Swanetian
Mingrelian
Lazian
Georgian (Kartwel)

VII BASQUE
107 Basque

* Not shown on map

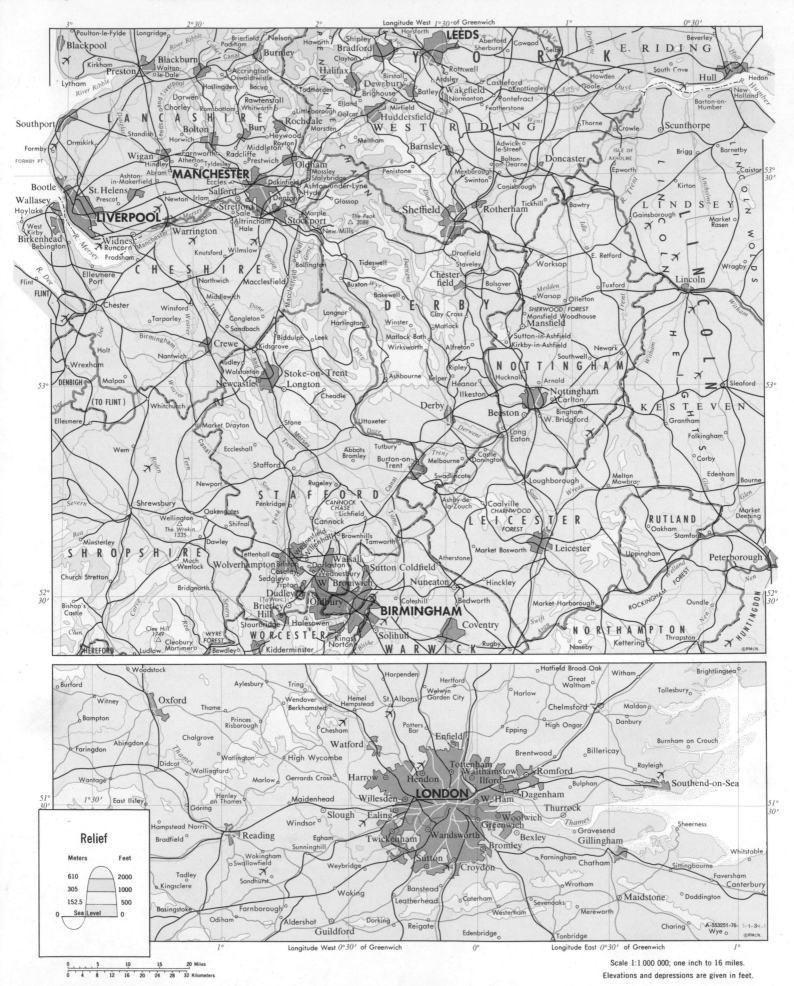

Relief

Meters	Feet
610	2000
305	1000
152.5	500
0	Sea Level	0

0   5   10   15   20 Miles
0 4 8 12 16 20 24 28 32 Kilometers

Scale 1:1 000 000; one inch to 16 miles.
Elevations and depressions are given in feet.

A-553251-76- 1-1-3-
Wye
©RMcN.

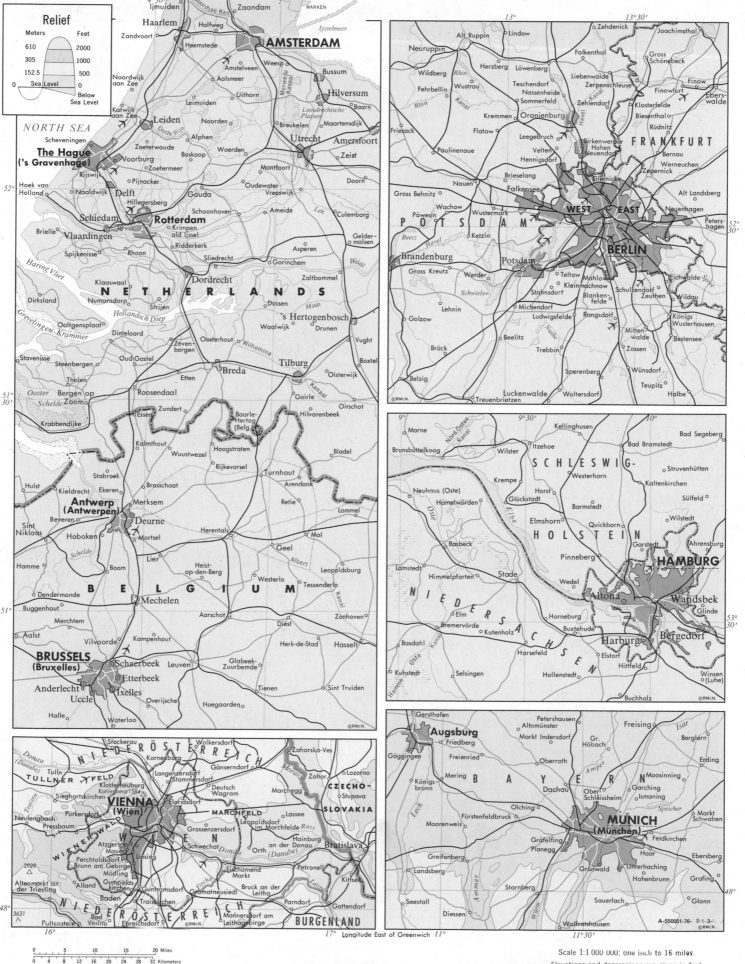

Relief

Meters	Feet
610	2000
305	1000
152.5	500
0 Sea Level	0
	Below Sea Level

NORTH SEA

AMSTERDAM

IJmuiden Zaandam MARKEN
Haarlem Halfweg
Zandvoort Heemstede
Noordwijk aan Zee Amstelveen Weesp
Aalsmeer Bussum
Katwijk aan Zee Leimuiden Uithorn **Hilversum**
Leiden Noorden Baarn
Zoeterwoude Alphen Breukelen Maartensdijk
The Hague Voorburg Woerden Loosdrechtsche Plassen
('s Gravenhage) Boskoop Amersfoort
Rijswijk Zoetermeer **Utrecht**
Hoek van Holland Naaldwijk Delft Gouda Oudewater Zeist Doorn
Schiedam Hillegersberg Schoonhoven Vreeswijk Montfoort
Brielle **Rotterdam** Krimpen aid Ijssel Ameide Culemborg Geldermalsen
Vlaardingen Rhoon Ridderkerk Sliedrecht Gorinchem
Spijkenisse Asperen
Haring Vliet **Dordrecht** Zaltbommel
Klaaswaal Dussen Waal
Dirksland **NETHERLANDS** Maas
Numansdorp Strijen 's Hertogenbosch
Oltgensplaat Hollandsch Diep Waalwijk Drunen Vught
Krammer Dinteloord Zevenbergen Oosterhout Wilhemina Kanaal Boxtel
Stavenisse Oud Gastel **Tilburg** Oisterwijk
Steenbergen Etten Oirschot
Tholen **Breda** Kanaal
Bergen op Zoom Roosendaal Goirle Hilvarenbeek
Krabbendijke Zundert Baarle-Hertog (Belg.) Bladel
Essen Wuustwezel Hoogstraten
Kalmthout Rijkevorsel Turnhout Arendonk
Hulst Stabroek Brasschaat Retie Lommel
Kieldrecht Ekeren Merksem
Sint Niklaas **Antwerp** Herentals Mol
(Antwerpen) Deurne Albert Kanaal Geel Leopoldsburg
Beveren Mortsel Lier Heist-op-den-Berg Westerlo Tessenderlo
Hoboken Boom Schelde
Hamme **BELGIUM** Aarschot Zonhoven
Dendermonde Mechelen Diest Herk-de-Stad Hasselt
Buggenhout Merchtem Kampenhout Sint Truiden
Aalst Vilvoorde Glabeek-Zuurbemde
BRUSSELS Schaerbeek Leuven Tienen
(Bruxelles) Etterbeek Hoegaarden
Anderlecht Ixelles Overijsche
Uccle Halle Waterloo

FRANKFURT

Alt Ruppin Lindow Zehdenick Joachimsthal
Neuruppin Herzberg Löwenberg Falkenthal Gross Schönebeck
Wildberg Rhin Wustrau Teschendorf Liebenwalde Finowfurt Finow Eberswalde
Fehrbellin Nassenheide Zerpenschleuse Klosterfelde
Rhin Kremmen Sommerfeld Zehlendorf Rüdnitz Biesenthal
Friesack Flatow Oranienburg Birkenwerder Bernau
Paulinenaue Leegebruch Hohen Neuendorf Werneuchen
Nauen Velten Zepernick
Brieselang Hennigsdorf Glienicke
Gross Behnitz Falkensee Alt Landsberg
Päwesin Wustermark **WEST** **EAST** Neuenhagen
POTSDAM Wachow Petershagen
Beetz Ketzin Teltow Mahlow Eichwalde Spree
Brandenburg Havel **Potsdam** Kleinmachnow **BERLIN** Wildau
Gross Kreutz Werder Stahnsdorf Blankenfelde Schulzendorf Zeuthen Königs Wusterhausen
Schwielow Michendorf Rangsdorf
Lehnin Golzow Ludwigsfelde Mittenwalde Bestensee
Brück Nuthe Beelitz Zossen Wünsdorf Teupitz
Belzig Trebbin Sperenberg Halbe
Luckenwalde Woltersdorf
Treuenbrietzen

SCHLESWIG-HOLSTEIN

Marne Kellinghusen Bad Segeberg
Brunsbüttelkoog Nord-Ostsee Kanal Wilster Itzehoe Bad Bramstedt
Struvenhütten
Neuhaus (Oste) Krempe Westerhorn Kaltenkirchen
Hamelwörden Glückstadt Horst Sülfeld
Oste Barmstedt Quickborn Wilstedt
Basbeck Elmshorn Ahrensburg
HOLSTEIN Pinneberg Garstedt
Lamstedt **HAMBURG**
Himmelpforten Stade Wedel Altona Wandsbek
NIEDERSACHSEN Glinde
Bremervörde Horneburg Buxtehude
Basdahl Kutenholz **Harburg** **Bergedorf**
Harsefeld Elstorf
Kuhstedt Selsingen Hollenstedt Hittfeld Winsen (Luhe)
Buchholz

Vienna / Wien

Stockerau Wolkersdorf Zahorska-Ves
NIEDERÖSTERREICH Korneuburg Gänserndorf Lozorno
Donau (Danube) Tulln Langenzersdorf Stammersdorf Zohor Stupava
TULLNER FELD Klosterneuburg Deutsch Wagram Marchegg **CZECHO-**
Sieghartskirchen Kohlenberg 1584 Floridsdorf **MARCHFELD** **SLOVAKIA**
Purkersdorf **VIENNA** Leopoldsdorf Lassee
Neulengbach Pressbaum **(Wien)** im Marchfelde Bratislava
Atzgersdorf Grossenzersdorf Hainburg an der Donau (Danube)
WIENERWALD Mauer Schwechat Orth Fischamend Markt
Perchtoldsdorf Liesing Donau Petronell
2929 Brunn am Gebirge Russ
Mödling Fischamend Kittsee
Gumpoldskirchen Gramatneusiedl Leitha
Alland Guntramsdorf Bruck an der Leitha
3631 Traiskirchen Mannersdorf am Parndorf
Altenmarkt an der Triesting Leithagebirge Gattendorf
NIEDERÖSTERREICH **BURGENLAND**
Pottenstein Ebreichsdorf

MUNICH

Gersthofen Petershausen Freising Isar
Augsburg Altomünster Berglern
Göggingen Friedberg Markt Indersdorf Gr. Höbach
Freienried Oberroth Moosinning
Königsbrunn Mering **BAYERN** Garching Erding
Dachau Ismaning Speicher
Moorenweis Olching Ober-Schleissheim
Fürstenfeldbruck Markt Schwaben
Landsberg Gräfelfing **MUNICH** Haar
Greifenberg Planegg **(München)** Feldkirchen
Lech Grünwald Unterhaching Ebersberg
Starnberg Hohenbrunn Grafing
Ammer Seestall Würm
Diessen Sauerlach Glonn
Wolfratshausen

0 5 10 15 20 Miles
0 4 8 12 16 20 24 28 32 Kilometers

Scale 1:1 000 000; one inch to 16 miles.
Elevations and depressions are given in feet.

A-550051-76 2-1-3-1

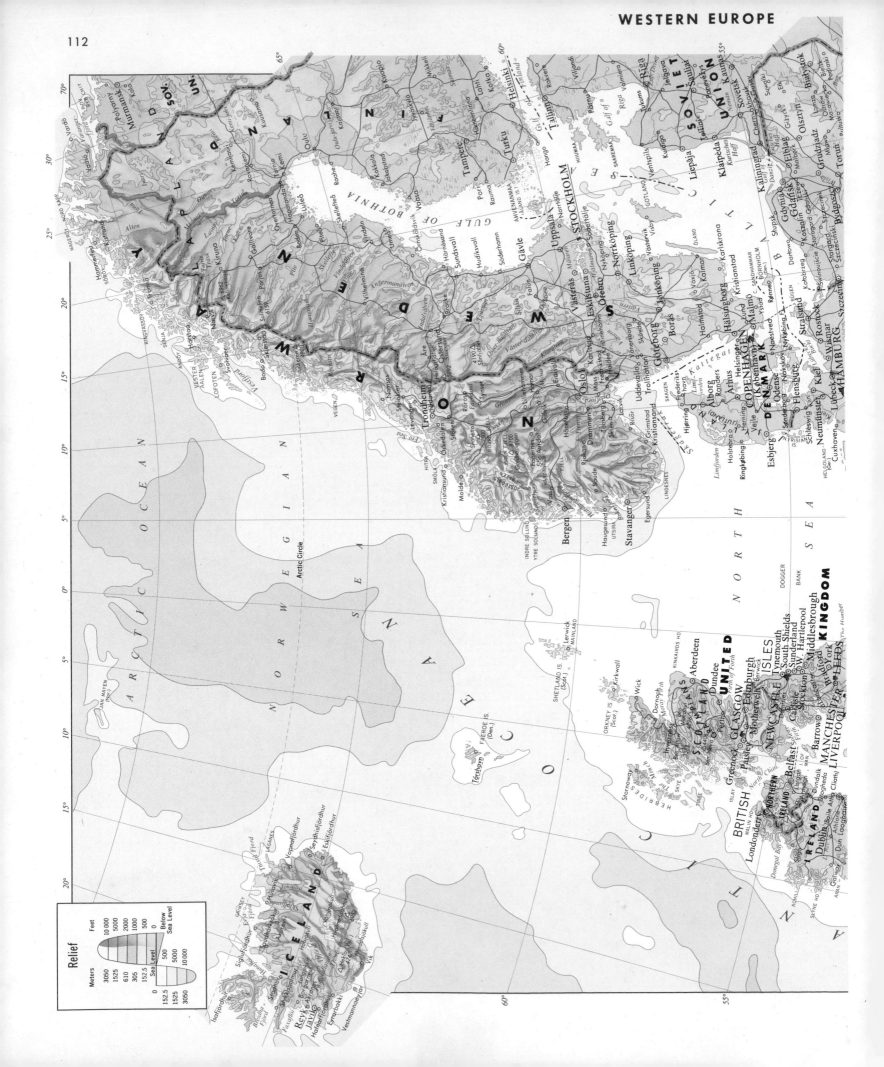

WESTERN EUROPE

SOVIET UNION

FINLAND

Murmansk

Helsinki

Tampere
Turku

GULF OF BOTHNIA

STOCKHOLM

SWEDEN

NORWAY

Trondheim

Bergen

Stavanger

Oslo

DENMARK
COPENHAGEN

NORTH SEA

HAMBURG

NORWEGIAN SEA

ARCTIC OCEAN

Arctic Circle

JAN MAYEN (Nor.)

FÆROE IS. (Den.)

SHETLAND IS. (Scot.)
Lerwick

ORKNEY IS. (Scot.)
Kirkwall

UNITED KINGDOM

SCOTLAND
GLASGOW
Edinburgh

NEWCASTLE

BRITISH ISLES

NORTHERN IRELAND
Belfast
Londonderry

IRELAND
Dublin

MANCHESTER
LEEDS
LIVERPOOL

HEBRIDES

ATLANTIC OCEAN

ICELAND
Reykjavik

Relief

Meters	Feet
3050	10 000
1525	5000
610	2000
305	1000
152.5	500
0	Sea Level
	Below
	Sea Level
152.5	500
1525	5000
3050	10 000

113

Scale 1: 10 000 000; one inch to 160 miles. Conic Projection

Elevations and depressions are given in feet

A-559400-76 · 2½ · 4-1-1½
COPYRIGHT BY
RAND M^cNALLY & COMPANY
MADE IN U.S.A.

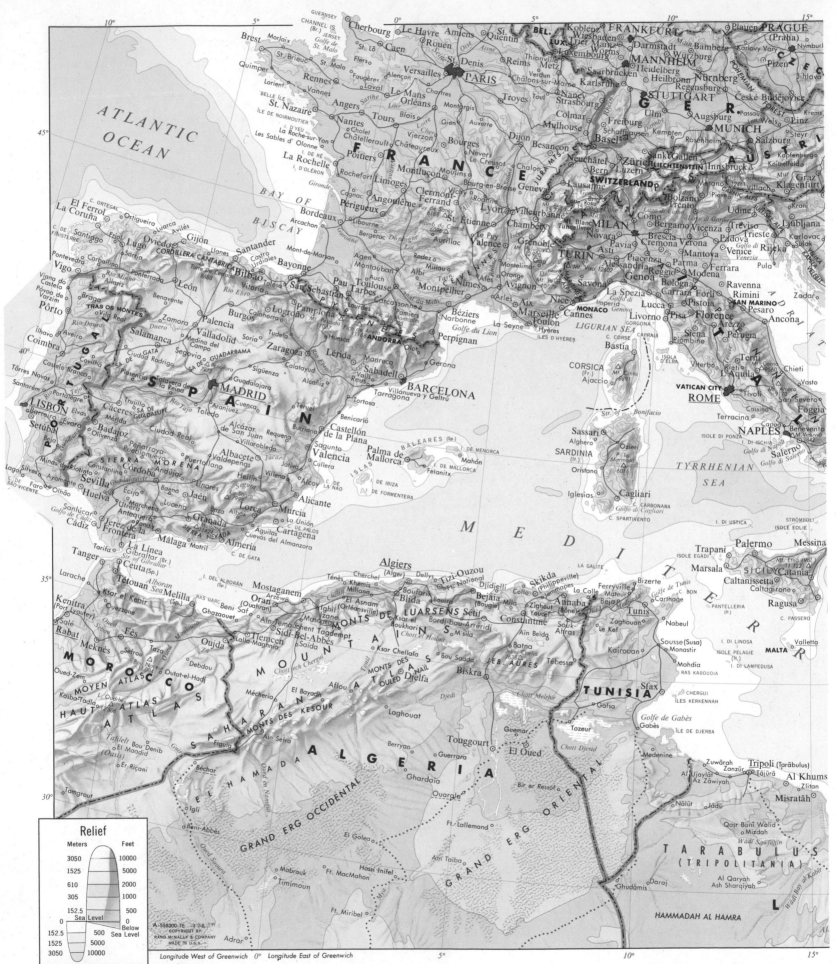

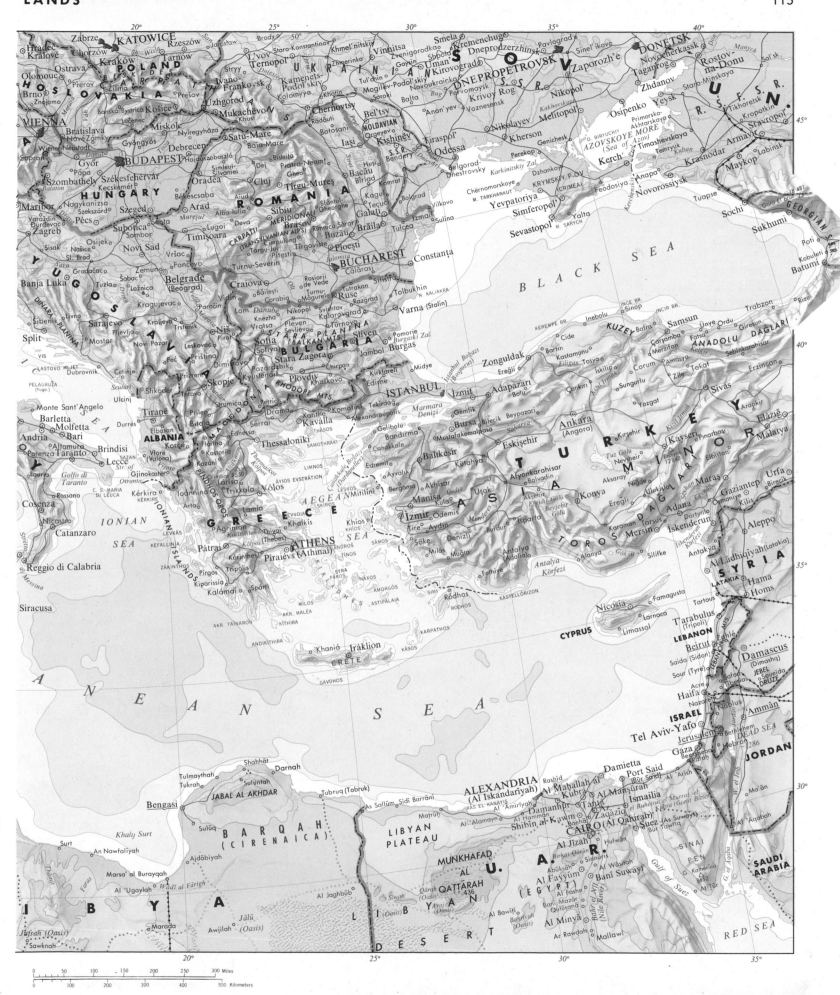

KATOWICE
Hradec Zabrze
Králové Chorzów
Olomouc Ostrava POLAND
Brno Přerov BESKID KARPATY
Znojmo

VIENNA Bratislava
Wiener Neustadt Nové Zámky
Sopron Győr
Szombathely Székesfehérvár BUDAPEST
Szombathely Pápa
Maribor Nagykanizsa Kecskemét
Varaždin Durdevac Pécs Szeged
Zagreb Subotica
Sisak Osijek Sombor
Sl. Brod Novi Sad
Gradačac Vršac
Banja Luka Tuzla Zemun
Loznica Šabac Belgrade
(Beograd)

YUGOSLAVIA

HUNGARY

ROMANIA

U K R A I N I A N S. S. R.

DNEPROPETROVSK

DONETSK

R. S. F. S. R.

MOLDAVIAN
S. S. R.

B L A C K   S E A

A E G E A N
S E A

I O N I A N
S E A

M E D I T E R R A N E A N   S E A

GREECE

TURKEY

ASIA MINOR

ALBANIA

BULGARIA

ATHENS
(Athínai)

ISTANBUL

Ankara
(Angora)

SYRIA

LEBANON

ISRAEL

JORDAN

CYPRUS

CRETE

L I B Y A

U. A. R.
(EGYPT)

SAUDI
ARABIA

LIBYAN
PLATEAU

LIBYAN
DESERT

BARQAH
(CIRENAICA)

RED SEA

Scale 1: 4 000 000; one inch to 64 miles. Conic Projection

Elevations and depressions are given in feet

Relief

Meters	Feet
610	2000
305	1000
152.5	500
0	Sea Level
152.5	500
1525	5000
	Below Sea Level

A-559700-76 -3 24-1 -2
COPYRIGHT BY
RAND McNALLY & COMPANY
MADE IN U.S.A.

Longitude West of Greenwich

NORWAY

Egersund
Sogndal
Flekkefjord
Farsund
LINDESNES
Kristiansand
Mandal

Arendal
Grimstad
Lillesand

SWEDEN

Kungäl Mjörn
Alingsås
Ulricehamn
Göteborg
Borås
Mölndal

Varberg
Bolmen
Falkenberg
Oskarström

S k a g e r r a k

Skagen
Skagen

Hjørring
Frederikshavn
LÆSØ
Brønderslev

Halmstad
Ängelholm
Laholm
Lagan

Thisted
Ålborg
Limfjorden
Løgstør
Hobro
Mariager
Mariager Fjord
ANHOLT

Helsingborg

K
a
t
t
e
g
a
t

Nykøbing
Skive
Viborg
Randers
Grenå
Skälderviken

Limfjorden
JYLLAND
Silkeborg
Århus

Helsingør
Lådskrobå

Struer
Holstebro
Herning
Skanderborg

N O R T H

Nissum
Fjord

Ringkøbing

Ringkøbing
Fjord

Vejle
Horsens
Skern

Skern

Varde
Fredericia
Esbjerg
Kolding
BLÅVANDS HUK
FANØ
Ribe
Haderslev
RØMØ
Åbenrå
SYLT
Tønder
FØHR
Flensburg
SCHLESWIG
Schleswig
Husum

COPENHAGEN (København)
Hillerød
Roskilde
SJAELLAND
Holbaek
Ringsted
Køge
Kalundborg
Slagelse
Korsør
Naestved
Bogense
Odense
Assens
Nyborg
Fåborg
Svendborg
Vordingborg
Rudkøbing
ALS
Sønderborg
AERØ
Langeland
LOLLAND
Nakskov
Maribo
Nykøbing Fl.
FEHMARN
(Ger.)

Malmö
Trelleborg

MØN
FALSTER

DENMARK

DOGGER

BANK

60—120 Ft.

S E A

HELGOLAND
(Ger.)

NORTH FRISIAN IS.

Tønning
Heide
Eckernförde
Rendsburg
Kiel
RENDSBURG
HOLSTEIN
Neustadt
Itzehoe
Neumünster
Lübeck
Ratzeburg
Bad Oldesloe
Elmshorn
Schweriner

BALTIC SEA

Kiel Bay
Lübecker Bucht

Rostock
Wismar
Güstrow
Teterow
Schwerin
Parchim
MECKLENBURG
Ludwigslust
Pritzwalk
Perleberg

FRISIAN ISLANDS
NORDERNEY LANGEOOG
JUIST
BØRKUM
Norden
Wilhelmshaven
Emden
Leer

Cuxhaven
Stade
Bremerhaven
HAMBURG
Lüneburg
LÜNEBURGER
HEIDE

Elbe
Bergedorf
Osté
Wittenberge
Ülzen
Salzwedel
Stendal
Tangermünde
Gardelegen

GERMANY
Havel

TERSCHELLING
AMELAND
Delfzijl
Groningen
Papenburg
Oldenburg
Delmenhorst
Bremen
Weser
Verden HEIDE
Soltau
Celle

VLIELAND
Leeuwarden
Harlingen
TEXEL
Den Helder
Waddenzee

Emmen
Meppen
Lingen
Nordhorn
Rheine
Osnabrück
Nienburg
Minden
Hannover
Gifhorn
Braunschweig
Helmstedt
Neuhaldensleben
Magdeburg
Schönebeck

IJsselmeer
Meppel
Zwolle
Almelo
Hengelo
NETHERLANDS
Alkmaar
Zaandam
AMSTERDAM
Haarlem
Apeldoorn
Almelo
Deventer
Enschede
Gronau
Münster
Herford
Bielefeld
Detmold
Hameln
Hildesheim
Wolfenbüttel
Goslar
Holzminden
Stassfurt
Bernburg
Quedlinburg
Blankenburg
Halberstadt
Aschersleben

The Hague
('s Gravenhage)
Delft
Vlaardingen
Leiden
Utrecht
Rheden
Arnhem
Coesfeld
Gütersloh
Paderborn
Lippstadt
Soest
Northeim
Einbeck
Göttingen
Nordhausen
Heiligenstadt
Sangerhausen
Eisleben
Halle
Merseburg

Colchester
Harwich
Chelmsford
ROTTERDAM
Dordrecht
Nijmegen
Waal
Maas
Bergen
op Zoom
Breda
Hertogenbosch
Wesel
Bocholt
Hamm
WEST GERMANY
Gelsenkirchen
Dortmund
Arnsberg
Iserlohn
Kassel
Eschwege
THÜRINGEN
Göttingen
Kreuz
Merseburg

Southend-
on-Sea
Gillingham
Chatham
Canterbury
Margate
Ramsgate
DOWNS
Dover
Folkestone
Hastings
Bexhill
Eastbourne
BEACHY
HEAD
Boulogne-
sur-Mer
Étaples

Vlissingen
W. Schelde
Zeebrugge
Oostende
Brugge
Gent
ANTWERP
Mechelen
Tilburg
Helmond
Eindhoven
Weert
Mönchengladbach
DÜSSELDORF
Oberhausen
Duisburg
ESSEN
Mülheim
Wuppertal
Solingen
Remscheid
Lüdenscheid
Siegen
COLOGNE
(Köln)
Siegburg
Marburg
Bad Hersfeld
Schmalkalden
Zella-Mehlis
Eisenach
Gotha
Erfurt
Weimar
Jena
Arnstadt
Rudolstadt

Dunkerque
Calais
Strait of Dover
NORTH FORELAND
FLANDERS
Torhout
Roeselare
Ieper
Kortrijk
Aalst
Anderlecht
BRUSSELS
Leuven
Maastricht
Heerlen
Aachen
Eupen
Düren
Bonn
BELGIUM
Liège
Herstal
Verviers
Malmedy
Euskirchen
Ahrweiler
Neuwied
Limburg
Giessen
FRANKFURT
AM MAIN
Bad Homburg
Hanau
Offenbach

Bad Kissingen
Schweinfurt
Sonneberg
Coburg
Kulmbach
Kitzingen

St. Omer
Lille
Roubaix
Tourcoing
Armentières
Béthune
Douai
Arras
Hesdin
Denain
Valenciennes
Nivelles
La Louvière
Charleroi
Namur
Dinant
Givet
ARDENNES
Bastogne
LUX.
EIFEL
Mayen
Koblenz
Andernach
Bad Kreuznach
Kirn
Bingen
Mainz
Wiesbaden
Höchst
TAUNUS
HUNSRÜCK
Wittlich
Bad
Kreuznach
Darmstadt
Aschaffenburg
Bayreuth
Bamberg
Forchheim
Erlangen
Würzburg

FRANCE
St. Valéry
Le Tréport
Abbeville
Crécy
Cambrai
Somme
Maubeuge
Hautmont
Fourmies

Kings Lynn
The Wash
Wensum
Norwich
Great
Yarmouth
Lowestoft
Thetford
Ely
Bury
St. Edmunds
Stour
Ipswich
Waveney

Longitude East of Greenwich

0 10 20 30 40 50 60 70 80 90 100 110 120 Miles
0 20 40 60 80 100 120 140 160 180 200 Kilometers

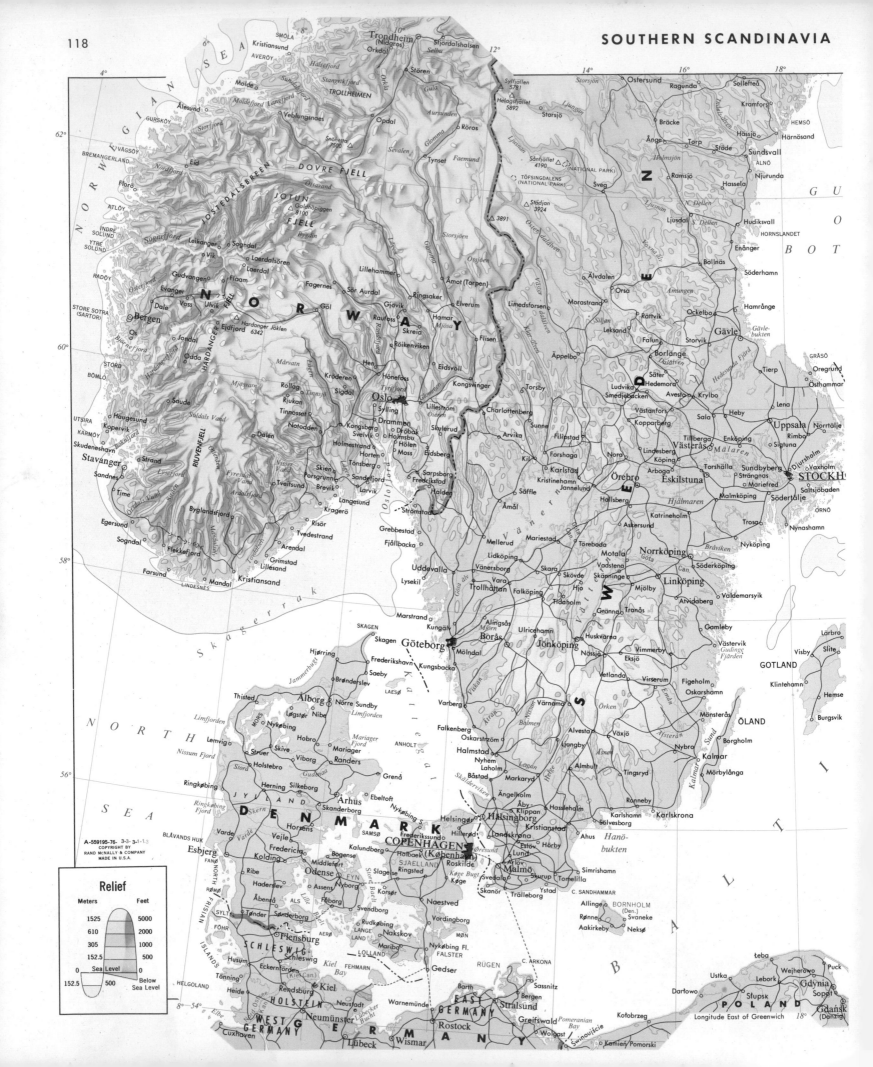

Relief

Meters	Feet
1525	5000
610	2000
305	1000
152.5	500
0	Sea Level
152.5	500 Below Sea Level

A-559195-76- 3-3- 3-1-1.3
COPYRIGHT BY
RAND McNALLY & COMPANY
MADE IN U.S.A.

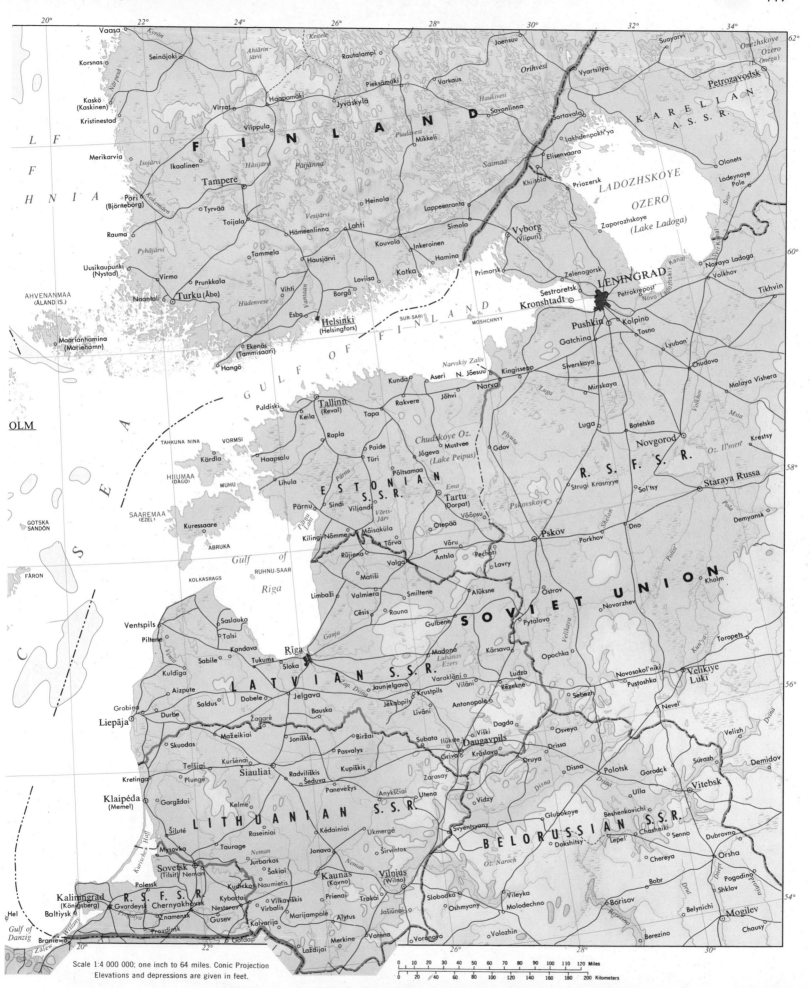

62°

Vaasa
Korsnas
Seinäjoki
Kyrön
Keitele
Rautalampi
Joensuu
Suoyarvi
Onezhskoye
Ozero
(Onega)

KARELIAN
A.S.S.R.

Orihvesi
Vyartsilya
Petrozavodsk

Kaskö
(Kaskinen)
Kristinestad
Virrat
Vilppula
Ahtärin-järvi
Haapamaki
Jyväskylä
Pieksämäki
Varkaus

F I N L A N D

Lakhdenpokh'ya
Olonets
Lodeynoye
Pole

L
F
F
N
I
A

Merikarvia
Isojärvi
Ikaalinen
Hasijärvi
Tampere
Päijänne
Mikkeli
Haukivesi
Savonlinna
Sortavala
Elisenvaara
Khiitola
Priozersk

LADOZHSKOYE
OZERO
(Lake Ladoga)

Zaporozhskoye

Pori
(Björneborg)
Tyrvää
Kokemäen
Toijala
Vesijärvi
Heinola
Lahti
Lappeenranta
Simola
Vyborg
(Viipuri)

Rauma
Pyhäjärvi
Hämeenlinna
Kouvola
Inkeroinen
Primorsk

Novaya Ladoga
60°
Volkhov
Tikhvin

Uusikaupunki
(Nystad)
Tammela
Hausjärvi
Loviisa
Kotka
Hamina
Zelenogorsk
Sestroretsk
LENINGRAD
Petrokrepost'
Kronshtadt

AHVENANMAA
(ÅLAND IS.)
Virmo
Prunkkala
Vihti
Borgå
Pushkin
Kolpino
Gatchina
Tosno
Lyuban'

Naantali
Turku (Åbo)
Hüdenvese
Esbo
Helsinki
(Helsingfors)
SUR-SARI
MOSHCHNYY
Siverskaya
Chudovo

Maarianhamina
(Mariehamn)
Ekenäs
(Tammisaari)
Hangö
G U L F   O F   F I N L A N D
Kingisepp
Siverskaya
Malaya Vishera

OLM

Paldiski
Tallinn
(Reval)
Keila
Narvskiy Zaliv
Aseri
N. Jõesuu
Narva
Luga
Minskaya

S E A

TAHKUNA NINA
VORMSI
Tapa
Rakvere
Jõhvi
Kunda

Kärdla
HIIUMAA
(DAGO)
Rapla
Paide
Chudskoye Oz.
Jõgeva
Mustvee
Gdov

R. S. F. S. R.

Novgorod
58°

MUHU
Haapsalu
Türi
Põltsamaa
(Lake Peipus)
Strugi Krasnyye
Sol'tsy
Staraya Russa

GOTSKA
SANDÖN
Lihula
ESTONIAN
S.S.R.
Pärnu
Sindi
Viljandi
Vörts-Järv
Tartu
(Dorpat)
Ema
Vööpsu
Pskovskoye

Kuressaare
SAAREMAA
(EZEL)
ABRUKA
Pärnu
Kilingi-Nõmme
Mõisaküla
Otepää
Võru
Pechori
Lavry
Pskov
Porkhov
Dno
Demyansk

FÅRON
Gulf of
RUHNU-SAAR
Pärnu Laht
Torva
Valga
Antsla

KOLKASRAGS
Riga
Rūjiena
Valga
Matiši
Alūksne
Ostrov
Kholm

Ventspils
Saslauka
Limbaži
Valmiera
Smiltene
Rauna
Gulbene
Pytalovo
Novorzhev

S O V I E T   U N I O N

Piltene
Talsi
Cēsis
Rauna
Madona
Lubānas Ezers
Kārsava
Opochka
Novosokol'niki
Velikiye
Luki
Toropets

Kuldīga
Kandava
Sabile
Rīga
Tukums
Sloka
LATVIAN S.S.R.
Zap. Dvina
Jaunjelgava
Varakļāni
Vilāni
Ludza
Rēzekne
Pustoshka
Nevel'
56°

Grobiņa
Aizpute
Saldus
Dobele
Jelgava
Jēkabpils
Krustpils
Līvāni
Antonopole
Sebezh
Osveya
Velizh

Liepāja
Durbe
Žagarē
Bauska
Subata
Ilūkste
Viški
Dagda
Drissa

Mažeikiai
Joniškis
Birži
Daugavpils
Griva
Krāslava
Druya
Disna
Polotsk
Gorodok
Vitebsk

Skuodas
Telšiai
Kuršenai
Pasvalys
Zarasay
Surazh
Demidov

Kretinga
Plungė
Šiauliai
Radviliškis
Kupiškis
Utena
Vidzy
Disna
Dvina
Ulla

Klaipéda
(Memel)
Gargždai
Kelmė
Šeduva
Panevėžys
Anykščiai
Glubokoye
Beshenkovichi

LITHUANIAN   S.S.R.
Šilutė
Raseiniai
Kédainiai
Ukmergė
Svyentsyany
Dokshitsy
Lepel'
Chashniki
Senno
Dubrovna

Mysovka
Taurage
Šakiai
Jonava
Širvintos
Oz. Naroch
Cherëya
Orsha

Sovetsk
(Tilsit)
Neman
Jurbarkas
Kaunas
(Kovno)
Vilnius
(Wilno)
Vileyka
Dnepr
Shklov

Kalinigrad
(Königsberg)
Polessk
Kudirkos-Naumiestis
Priena
Trakai
Slobodka
Molodechno
Bobr

BELORUSSIAN   S.S.R.
Baltiysk
Gvardeysk
Chernyakhovsk
Znamensk
Kybartai
Vilkaviškis
Virbalis
Marijampole
Jašiūnai
Oshmyany
Volozhin
Berezino

Hel
Gusev
Nesterov
Kalvarija
Voronovo
Vileyka
Belynichi

R.S.F.S.R.
Pravdinsk
54°
Mogilev

Gulf of
Danzig
Braniewo
Wisly
Gołdap
Merkine
Varena
Lazdijai
Oshmyany
Chausy

Scale 1:4 000 000; one inch to 64 miles. Conic Projection
Elevations and depressions are given in feet.

0 10 20 30 40 50 60 70 80 90 100 110 120 Miles
0 20 40 60 80 100 120 140 160 180 200 Kilometers

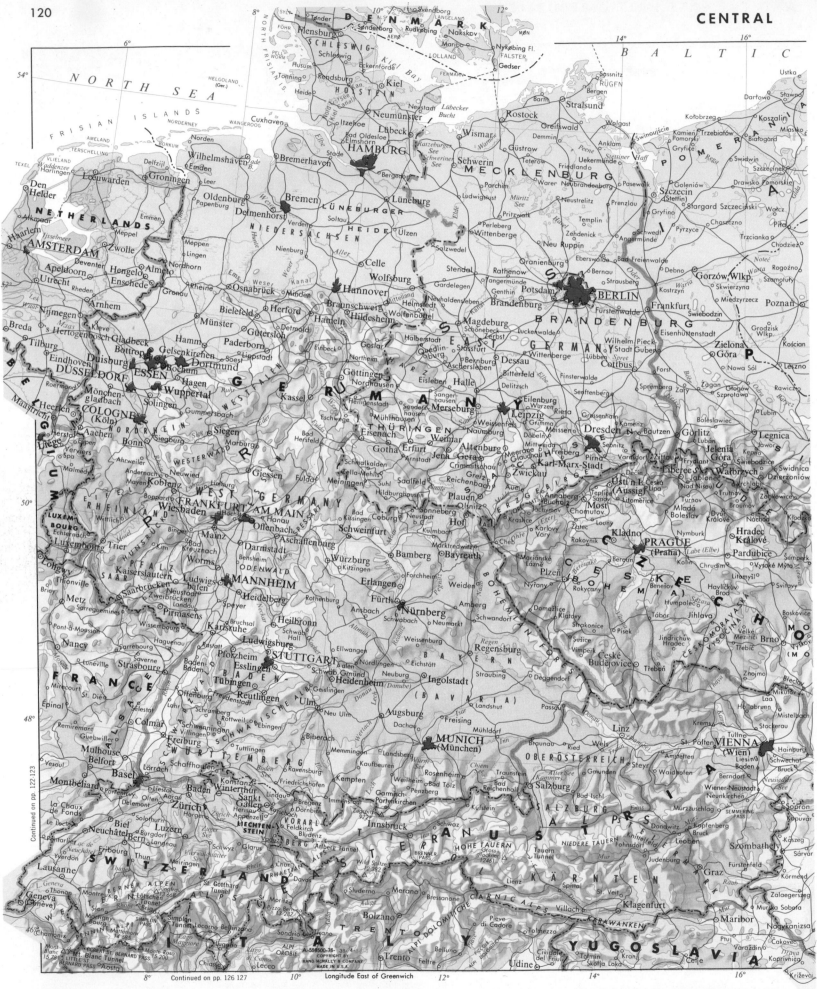

Scale 1:4 000 000; one inch to 64 miles. Conic Projection
Elevations and depressions are given in feet.

S E A

Relief

Meters	Feet
3050	10 000
1525	5000
610	2000
305	1000
152.5	500
0 Sea Level	0
	Below Sea Level

Kurisches Haff

Gulf of Danzig

Zalew Wiślany

Neman Jurbarkas Vilkija 24°

Sovetsk (Tilsit) Ragnit Šakiai Kaunas (Kovno) 26° 28°

Kaliningrad (Königsberg) Pravdinsk Chernyakhovsk Gusev Polessk Kudirkos (Naumiestis) LITHUANIAN S.S.R. Vilnius Slobódka Vileyka

Baltiysk Pregolya Znamensk Nesterov Kybartai Virbalis Marijampolé Prienai Trakai Jašiūnai Molodechno

Braniewo Bartoszyce Manych Gołdap Trakiszki Lazdijai Kalvarija Alytus Varéna Merkine Voronovo Oshmyany Volozhin

Puck Hel Elbląg Orneta Lidzbark Węgorzewo Olecko Suwałki Merkys Lida Minsk

Gdynia Wejherowo Tczew Malbork Ketrzyn Giżycko Ełk Augustów Gradno Novogrudok Mir Dzerzhinsk

Słupsk Gdańsk (Danzig) Olsztyn Mrągowo Sniardwy Grajewo Dabrowa Sokółka Krynki Volkovysk Baranovichi Nesvizh Slutsk

Lębork Bytów Kościerzyna Kwidzyn Iława Ostróda Nidzica Kolno Szczuczyn Knyszyn Wasilków Grodno Ruzhany Kletsk

Chojnice Czersk Starograd Gdański Lubawa Mrawa Łomża Białystok Semionówka Shereshevo Bereza BELORUSSIAN S.S.R. Oz. Chervonnoye

Nakło n. Notecia Brda Świecie Chełmno Brodnica Rypin Przedbórz Maków Mazowiecki Ostrów Mazowiecka Wysokie Mazowieckie Bielsk Podlaski Brańsk Kobrin Drogichin Pinsk PRIPYAT

Bydgoszcz Toruń Aleksandrów Kujawski Inowrocław Lipno Ciechanów Narew Wyszków Zambrów Siemiatycze Brest Piitch'

Wągrowiec Mogilno Strzelno Włocławek Płock Nasielsk Bug Sokołów Podlaski Biała Podlaska Kobrin Drogichin David-Gorodok Luninets 52°

Gniezno Września Konin Koło Gostynin Nw. Dwór Maz. (Vistula) WARSAW (Warszawa) Wołomin Mińsk Mazowiecki Siedlce Bug Stolin MARSHE

Środa Śrem Jarocin Kalisz Kutno Łowicz Pruszków Grodzisk Maz. Otwock Garwolin Łuków Radzyń Podlaski Włodawa Tomashevka Kovel Sarny Korosten

O L A N D Żyrardów Skierniewice Grójec Żelechów Parczew Ostrów Lubelski Pripyat' S O V I E T

Pleszew Kalisz Ostrów Wlkp. Zgierz Łódź Pabianice Tomaszów Mazowiecki Rawa Mazowiecka Kozienice Dęblin Lubartów Chełm Vladimir-Volynskiy Lutsk Rovno Zdolbunov Korets Novograd-Volynskiy Polonnoye

Ostrzeszów Kepno Sieradz Zduńska Wola Piotrków Trybunalski Opoczno Radom Puławy Lublin Krasnystaw Hrubieszów Zamość Dubno Kremenets Slavuta Lyubar 50°

Wrocław (Breslau) Oława Oleśnica Kluczbork Radomsko Przedbórz Szydłowiec Opole Lubelskie Janów Lubelski Szczebrzeszyn Sokal Rava-Russkaya Brody Zolochëv Khmel'nitskiy Staro-Konstantinov Khmel'nik

Strzelin Opole Strzelce Opol. Zawiercie Częstochowa Kielce Włoszczowa Chmielnik Sandomierz Nisko Biłgoraj Tomaszów Lubelski UKRAINIAN U N I O N Zbarazh Podvolochisk Medzhibozh Letichev

Nysa Prudnik Kozle Bytom Chorzów Będzin Olkusz Działoszyce Pińczów Staszów Opatów Ostrowiec Świętokrzyski Janów Lubelski Krasnik Lubaczów L'vov Busk S. S. R.

Racibórz Zabrze Gliwice KATOWICE Sosnowiec Jaworzno Kraków Nowa Huta Tarnów Mielec Leżajsk Jarosław Yavorov Gorodok Komarno Bóberka Berezhany Ternapol Zbarazh Khmel'nitskiy

Ostrava Karviná Frýdek Nový Jičín Oświęcim Wieliczka Bochnia Rzeszów Rzozów Przemyśl Sambor Rogatin Terebovlya

Šternberk Hranice Rybnik Kety Wadowice Sucha Nowy Sącz Gorlice Krosno Drogobych Borislav Stryy Bóberka Kalush Buchach Chortkóv Zastavna Dunayevtsy Bar Zhmerinka

Olomouc Přerov Cieszyn Żywiec Stary Sącz Jasło G A L I C I A Dolina Ivano-Frankovsk Gorodenka Borshchëv Kamenets-Podol'skiy Mogilëv-Podol'skiy

MORAVA Kroměříž Vsetín BESKID EAS Zakopane Nowy Targ Bardejov DUKLA PASS Sanok Turka Skole Nadvornaya Kolomyya Khotin

Prostejov JABLUNKÓV PASS TATRA MTS. Gerlachovka 8737 Kežmarok Levoča Prešov Michalovce Uzhgorod RUTHENIA Kuty Storozhinets Chernovtsy Dărăbani MOLDAVIAN

Uherské Hradiště Trenčín Žilina Vrútky Svätý Martin LOW TATRA MTS. Spišská Nová Ves Košice Trebišov Mukachevo Latoritsa YABLONITSKIY PEREVAL Yasinya BUKOVINA Dorohoi A. S. S. R.

Hodonín Nové Mesto (Nad Váhom) Myjava Bánská Bystrica Hnilov Dobšiná Rožňava S L O V A K I A Velkiy Bychkov Storozhinets Rădăuti Bel'tsy 48°

Holíč Piešťany Zvolen Detva Rimavská Sobota Kazincbarcika Satoraljaujhely Sárospatak Tokaj Beregovo Khust Tyachev Rakhov Sighet Suceava Făleşti

MALÉ KARPATH Trnava Sered Nitra Levice Lučenec Salgótarján Miskolc Tisza Nyíregyháza Satu-Mare MUNTII RODNEI Pietrosul Câmpulung Moldovenesc Botoşani

Bratislava Nové Zámky Kolárovo Komárno Šurany Farkasd Balassagyarmat Eger Polgár Tiszapolkonya Hajdunánás Carei Baia-Mare Lăpuşul Vatra Dornei Tîrgu Neamţ Roman Iaşi

Mosonmagyaróvár Győr Komárom Esztergom Vác Szentendre Gyöngyös Mezőkövesd Hajdúböszörmény Hajdúhádház Baia-Mare Bistriţa MUNTII CĂLIMAN Piatra Neamţ Bîrlad

Csorna Pápa Mór Bicske BUDAPEST Jászberény Jászapáti Hajduszoboszló Debrecen Berettyóújfalu Oradea Dej Gherla Reghin Tîrgu-Mureş Gheorghieni Vaslui

Raba Székesfehérvár Abony Szolnok Karcag Kisújszállás Zalău Simleul-Silvaniei Cluj Turda MUNTII HARGHITA Vatra Dornei

Veszprém Mór Cegléd Nagykőrös Mezőtúr Devaványa Veszto Salonta Bistriţa ROMANIA Mureşul Tîrgu-Ocna Adjud

Sümeg Balaton Dunaújváros Sárbogárd H U N G A R Y Kecskemét Szarvas Békés Gyula BIHOR MUNTII Tîrnăveni Tîrnava Mica Odorhei Tecuci

Keszthely Siófok Dunaföldvár Dunapataj Kiskunfélegyháza Csongrád Békéscsaba TRANSYLVANIA Aiud Sighişoara Sfîntul Gheorghe

Tapolca Paks Kalocsa Kiskunmajsa Hódmezővásárhely Orosháza Gyula Cpul Alb MUNTII ZARANDULUI Alba Iulia Mediaş Braşov

Kaposvár Szekszárd Tolna Jánoshalma Szeged Makó Nagylak Arad Baia-de-Criş Sebeş Ocna Sibiului Făgăraş Olt Odobeşti 46°

Dombóvár Bátaszék Baja Bácsalmás Mélykút Nădlac Lipova Timişoara Deva Sibiu Focşani

Barcs Szigetvár Pécs Mohács Subotica Senta Kikinda Zimbolia Vršac 22° 24° 26°

Đurđevac Y U G O Osijek Bačka Topola Bečej Bečkerek Bosut

Continued on pp 132–133

0 10 20 30 40 50 60 70 80 90 100 110 120 Miles

0 20 40 60 80 100 120 140 160 180 200 Kilometers

Relief

Meters		Feet
3050		10 000
1525		5000
610		2000
305		1000
152.5		500
0	Sea Level	0
152.5		500
1525		5000

A-550900-76- 3- 2-4.1-1 .2
COPYRIGHT BY
RAND McNALLY & COMPANY
MADE IN U.S.A.

Scale 1:1 000 000

Scale 1:4 000 000; one inch to 64 miles. Conic Projection
Elevations and depressions are given in feet

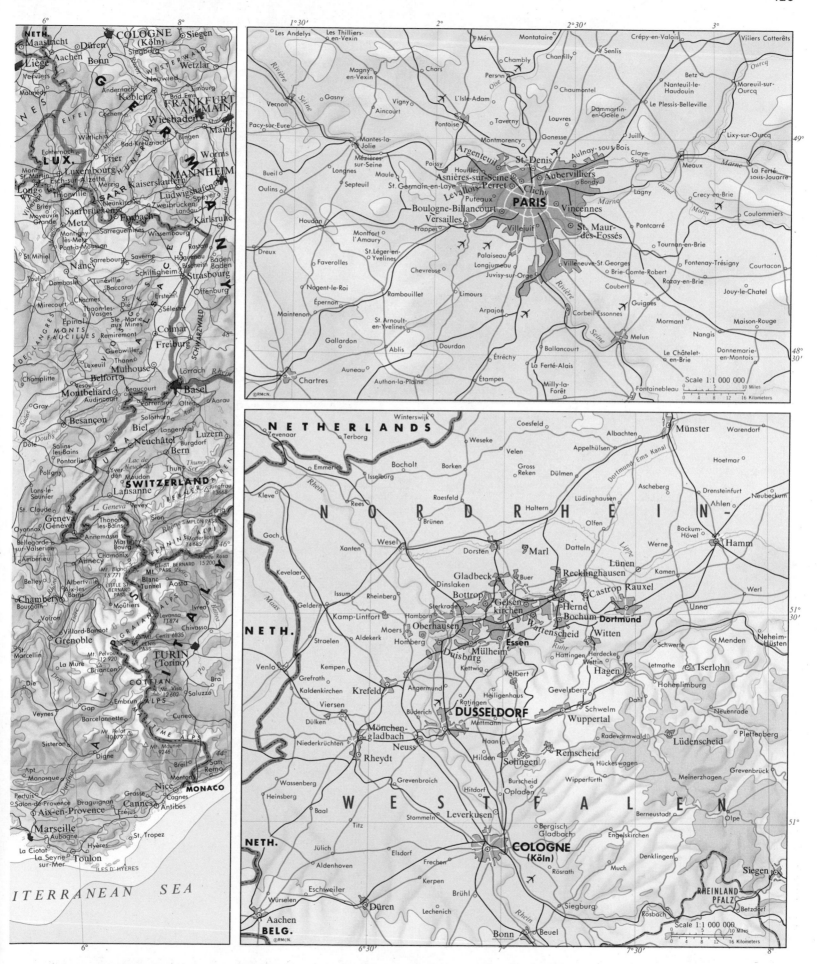

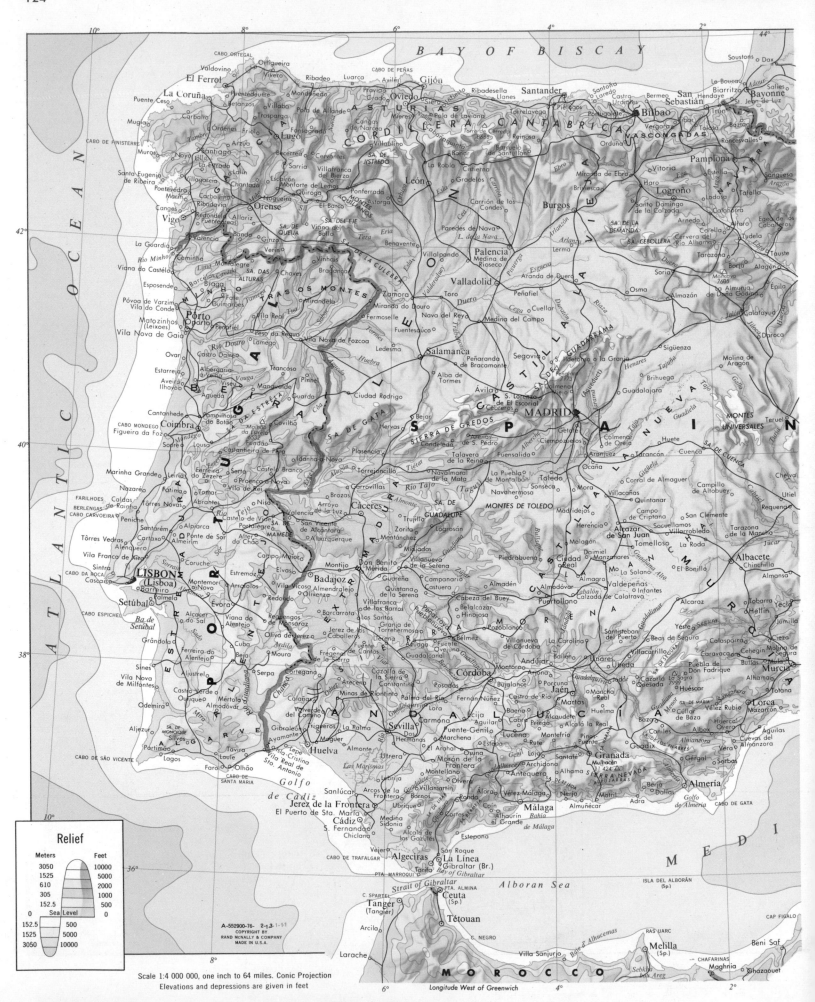

Scale 1:4 000 000, one inch to 64 miles. Conic Projection
Elevations and depressions are given in feet

Longitude West of Greenwich

Relief

Meters	Feet
3050	10000
1525	5000
610	2000
305	1000
152.5	500
0	Sea Level	0
152.5	500
1525	5000
3050	10000

A-552900-76- 2-1.3-1-1-1
COPYRIGHT BY
RAND McNALLY & COMPANY
MADE IN U.S.A.

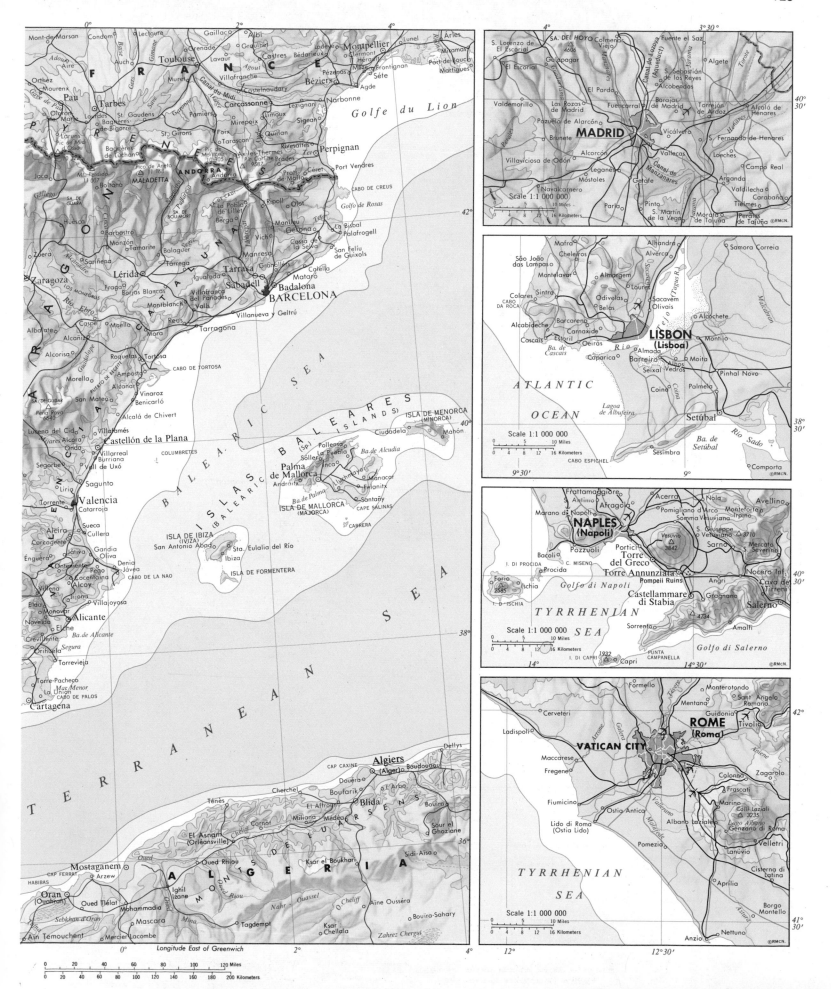

Continued on pp. 120-121

Continued on pp. 122-123

SWITZERLAND

AUSTRIA

SLOVENIJA

HUN

YUG

CROATIA (HRVATSKA)

BOSN

D A L M A T I A

A D R I A T I C   S E A

TURIN (Torino)

FRANCE

MONACO

MILAN (Milano)

LOMBARDIA

PIEMONTE

LIGURIA

Genoa (Genova)

VENETO

Venice (Venezia)

Golfo di Venezia

TRENTO

EMILIA

ROMAGNA

Bologna

Ravenna

MARCHE

SAN MARINO

Ancona

TOSCANA

Florence (Firenze)

UMBRIA

LAZIO

ABRUZZI E MOLISE

Pescara

L I G U R I A N

S E A

CORSICA (FR.)

Ajaccio

Bastia

ISOLA D'ELBA

VATICAN CITY

ROME (Roma)

Naples (Napoli)

CAMPANIA

PUGLIA

Bari

Foggia

Taranto

BASILICATA

SARDINIA

Sassari

Cagliari

Golfo di Cagliari

T Y R R H E N I A N

S E A

CALABRIA

Cosenza

Catanzaro

Reggio di Calabria

Palermo

Trapani

Marsala

Messina

Catania

SICILY

Golfo di Squillace

ISOLE EOLIE

AEGEAN SEA

Same scale as main map

CRETE (Greece)

Iráklion (Candia)

Khaniá (Canea)

MEDITERRANEAN SEA

Scale 1:4 000 000; one inch to 64 miles. Conic Projection
Elevations and depressions are given in feet

Relief

Meters		Feet
3050		10 000
1525		5000
610		2000
305		1000
152.5		500
0	Sea Level	0
152.5		500
1525		5000
3050		10 000

BLACK SEA

ROMANIA

VALACHIA

BUCHAREST (Bucureşti)

BULGARIA

Sofia (Sofiya)

YUGOSLAVIA

Belgrade (Beograd)

Sarajevo

CRNA GORA (MONTENEGRO)

ALBANIA

Tiranë

Durrës

MACEDONIA

Skopje

THRACE

TURKEY

Marmara Denizi

Thessaloníki

ÁYION ÓROS (MOUNT ATHOS)

EPEIRUS

THESSALIA

GREECE

AEGEAN SEA

IONIAN SEA

ATHENS (Athinai)

Piraévs (Piraeus)

PELOPONNISOS

DHODHEKANISOS (DODECANESE)

A-558396-76- 2-2 3-1-1 2
COPYRIGHT BY
RAND McNALLY & COMPANY
MADE IN U.S.A.

Longitude East of Greenwich

0 10 20 30 40 50 60 70 80 90 100 110 120 Miles
0 20 40 60 80 100 120 140 160 180 200 Kilometers

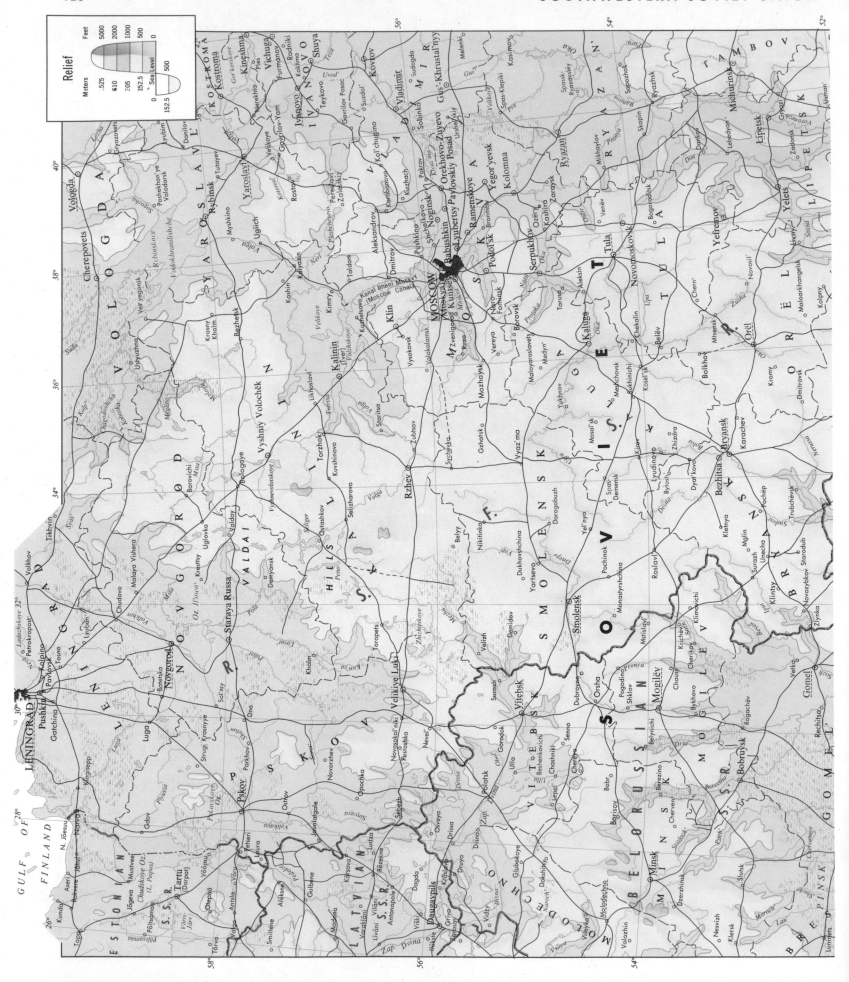

Relief

Meters	Feet
1525	5000
610	2000
305	1000
152.5	500
0 Sea Level	0
152.5	500

GULF OF FINLAND

ESTONIAN S.S.R.

LATVIAN S.S.R.

LENINGRAD

NOVGOROD

PSKOV

VOLOGDA

YAROSLAVL'

KOSTROMA

IVANOVO

VLADIMIR

VALDAI HILLS

KALININ

MOSCOW

MOSKVA

SMOLENSK

BELORUSSIAN S.S.R.

MINSK S.S.R.

BRYANSK

OREL

TULA

KALUGA

RYAZAN'

TAMBOV

LIPETSK

PINSK

GOMEL'

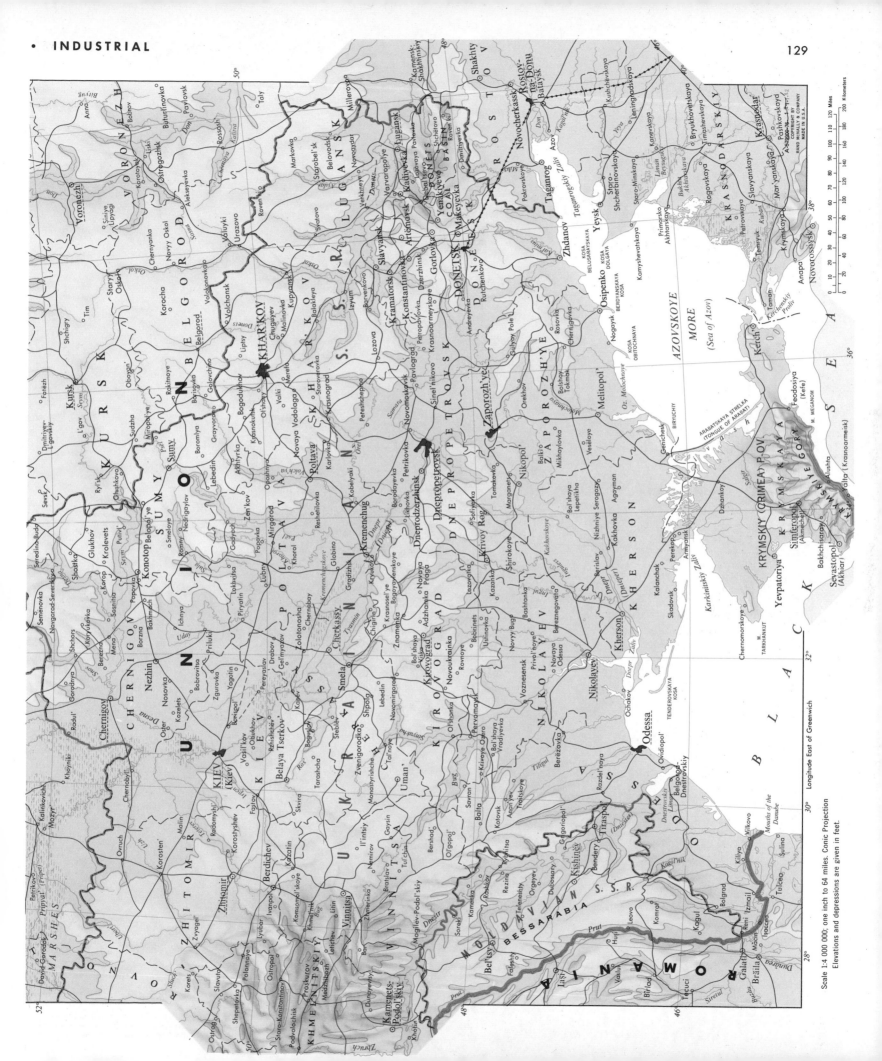

Scale 1:4 000 000; one inch to 64 miles. Conic Projection
Elevations and depressions are given in feet.

Longitude East of Greenwich

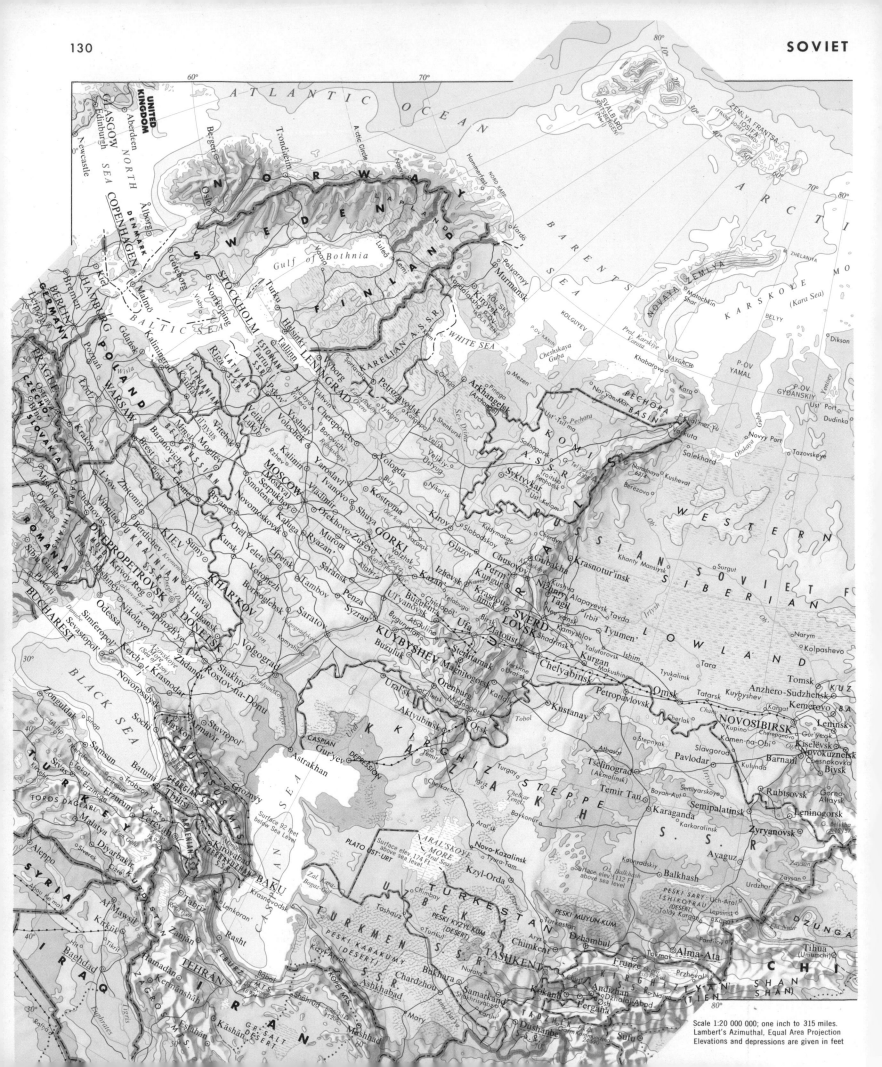

Scale 1:20 000 000; one inch to 315 miles.
Lambert's Azimuthal, Equal Area Projection
Elevations and depressions are given in feet

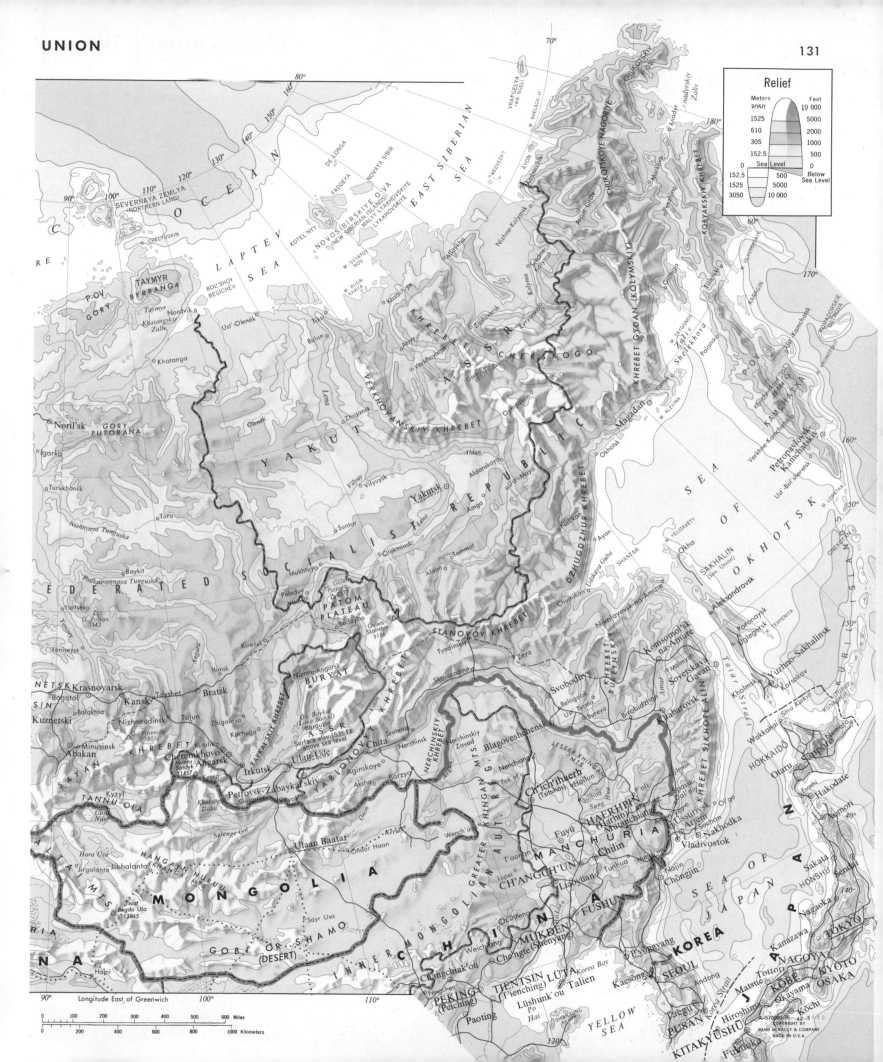

Relief

Meters		Feet
3050		10 000
1525		5000
610		2000
305		1000
152.5		500
0	Sea Level	0
152.5		500	Below
1525		5000	Sea Level
3050		10 000

ARCTIC OCEAN

SEVERNAYA ZEMLYA
(NORTHERN LAND)

LAPTEV SEA

EAST SIBERIAN SEA

CHUKOTSKOYE NAGORYE

P-OV
GORY

TAYMYR
BYRRANGA

KORYAKSKIY KHREBET

KHREBET GYDAN (KOLYMSKIY)

KAMCHATKA

KHREBET SCHERSKOGO

VERKHOYANSKIY KHREBET

Petropavlovsk-
Kamchatskiy

YAKUT

Y A K U T

A.S.S.R.

Yakutsk

SOCIALIST REPUBLIC

DZHUGDZHUR KHREBET

SEA OF OKHOTSK

GORY PUTORANA

Noril'sk

Igarka

SAKHALIN
(Sov. Union)

Aleksandrovsk

EDERATED

PATOM
PLATEAU

STANOVOY KHREBET

Yuzhno-Sakhalinsk

KURIL ISLANDS

NETSK
Krasnoyarsk

BURYAT

A.S.S.R.

KHREBET BUREINSKIY

Komsomol'sk
na-Amure

Kansk

Kuznetski

SIN

Oz. Baykal
(Lake Baikal)

Chita

NERCHINSKIY KHREBET

Khabarovsk

KHREBET SIKHOTE ALIN

HOKKAIDO

Sapporo

Irkutsk

Ulan-Ude

YABLONOVYY KHREBET

Blagoveshchensk

Abakan

SAYAN

TANNU-OLA

Petrovsk-Zabaykal'skiy

AMUR

LESSER KHINGAN MTS.

HAKODATE

J A P A N

Vladivostok

MONGOLIA

HANGAYN NURUU
KHANGAI MTS.

Ulaan Baatar

GREATER KHINGAN AUT'R RG.

MONGOLIAN AUT'R RG.

MANCHURIA

HAERHPIN
(Harbin)

CH'ANGCH'UN

FUSHUN

SEA OF JAPAN

HONSHU

GOBI OR SHAMO
(DESERT)

INNER

CHINA

MUKDEN
(Shenyang)

KOREA

SEOUL

TOKYO

NAGOYA

KYOTO
OSAKA

PEKING
(Peiching)

TIENTSIN
(Fienching)

LÜTA
(Lüshun)

P'yongyang

PUSAN

KITAKYUSHU

YELLOW
SEA

0 100 200 300 400 500 600 Miles

0 200 400 600 800 1000 Kilometers

A-570000-76   42-5 1/12
COPYRIGHT BY
RAND McNALLY & COMPANY
MADE IN U.S.A.

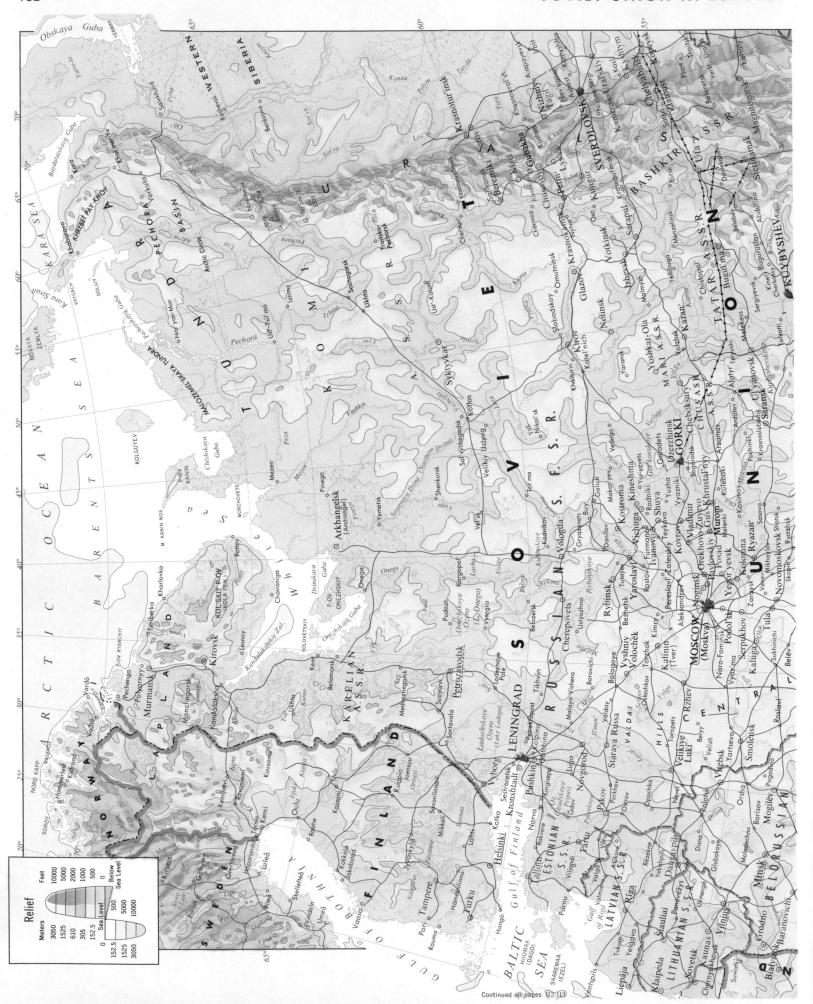

Relief

Meters	Feet
3050	10000
1525	5000
610	2000
305	1000
152.5	500
0	Sea Level
	Below
	Sea Level

Sea Level	
152.5	500
1525	5000
3050	10000

Continued on pages 112-113

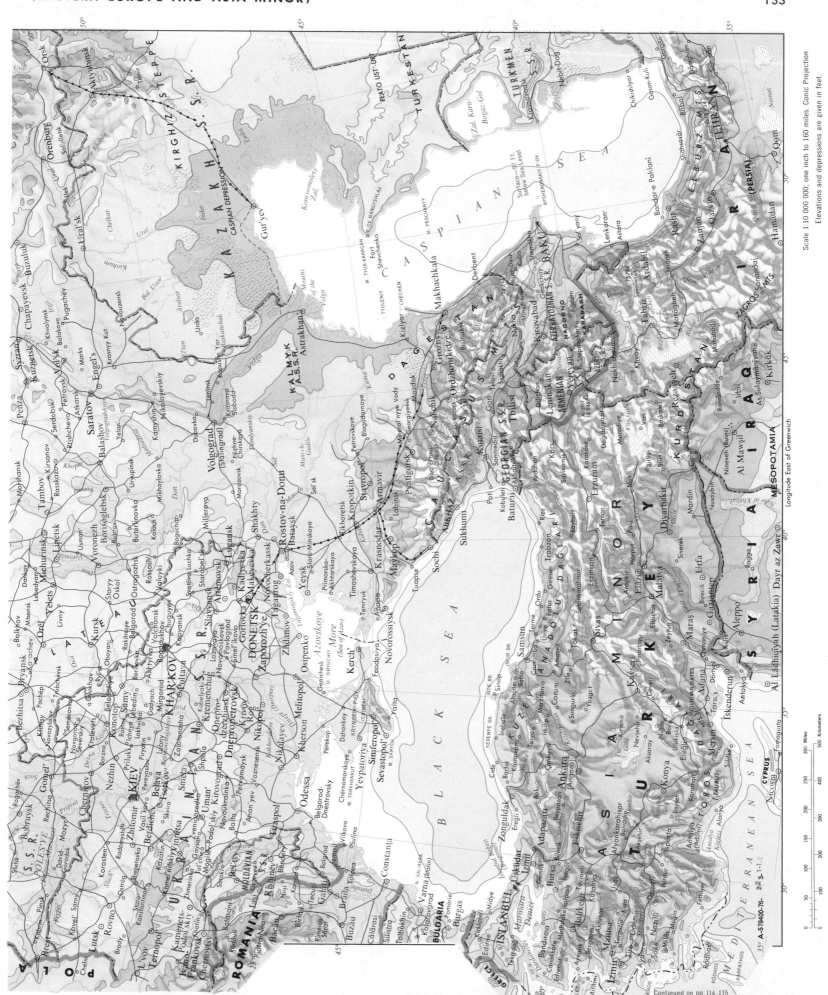

Scale 1:10 000 000; one inch to 160 miles. Conic Projection

Elevations and depressions are given in feet.

Continued on pp. 114-115

Scale 1:16 000 000; one inch to 250 miles Conic Projection
Elevations and depressions are given in feet.

Continued on pp. 102-103

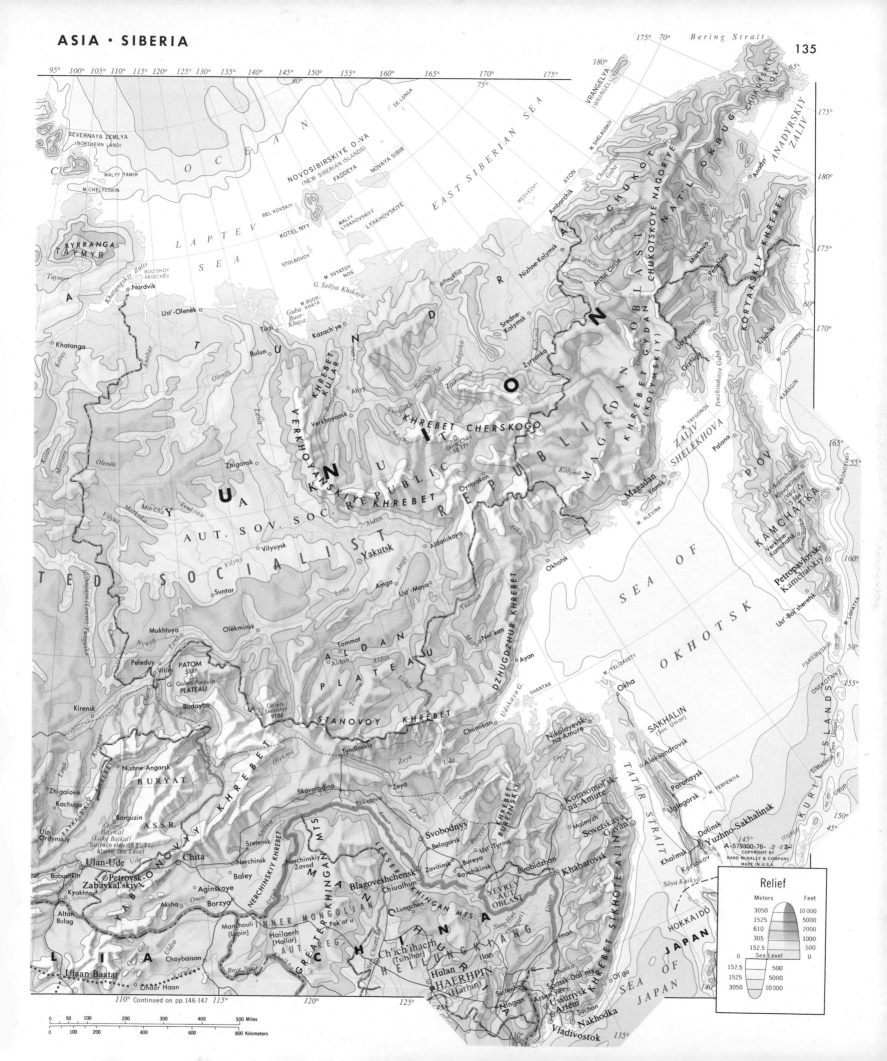

Bering Strait

175° 70°

180°

VRANGELYA
(WRANGEL)

CHUKOT NATL OKRUG

CHUKOTSKOYE NAGORYE

ANADYRSKIY ZALIV

Anadyr'

Arctic Circle

KORYAKSKIY KHREBET

SEVERNAYA ZEMLYA
(NORTHERN LAND)

MALYY TAYMIR

M. CHELYUSKIN

NOVOSIBIRSKIYE O-VA
(NEW SIBERIAN ISLANDS)

DE LONGA

FADDEYA

NOVAYA SIBIR

EAST SIBERIAN SEA

C   O   C   E   A   N

BYRRANGA
TAYMYR

LAPTEV   SEA

BOL'SHOY
BEGICHEV

Khatangskiy Zaliv

Taymyr

Nordvik

Khatanga

Kotuy

Ust'-Olenek

STOLBOVOY

BEL'KOVSKIY

KOTEL'NYY

MALYY
LYAKHOVSKIY

BOL'SHOY
LYAKHOVSKIY

G. Sellya Khskaya

M. SVYATOY
NOS

MEDVEZH'I

AYON

Chaunskaya
Guba

M SHELAGSKIY

Ambarchik

Ambarchik

Bol Anyuy

Nizhne-Kolymsk

Malyy Anyuy

M. OLYUTORSKIY

Tilichiki

Markovo

Penzhino

Ust'Penzhino

Olenek

Anabar

Bulun

Kazach ye

Guba
Buor-
Khaya

M BUOR
KHAYA

Tiksi

Sredne-
Kolymsk

Zyryanka

Kolyma

Oroton

ZALIV
SHELEKHOVA

Penzhinskaya Guba

Gizhiga

M TAYGONOS

KAMCHATKA

KHREBET KULAR

VERKHOYANSKIY

Zhigansk

Verkhoyansk

Adycha

KHREBET CHERSKOGO

Gora Chen
10 171

Indigirka

Selennyakh

Oymyakon

KHREBET

Omolon

(KOLYMSKIY)

Kolyma

Magadan

MAGADAN

Palana

Verkhne-
Kamchatsk

KARAGIN

M KRONOTSKIY

Y   A   K   U   T

Zhiganskiy

Vilyuy

Markha

Olenek

Vilyuysk

Vilyuy

Yakutsk

Aldan

Amga

Aldanskaya

Amga

Ust'-Maya

Yudoma

Arka

Yamsk

M ALEVINA

Yam

Okhotsk

Verkhne-
Kamchatsk

Petropavlovsk-
Kamchatskiy

Klyuchevskaya
Volc.
15 584

NUNGUS   REPUBLIC

AUT. SOV. SOC.   REPUBLIC

SOCIALIST

Suntar

Vilyuy

Lena

Lena

Tunguska

Nyuya

Mukhtuya

Olekminsk

Aldan

ALDAN

Tommot

Aldan

Timptan

PLATEAU

Maya

Nel'kan

DZHUGDZHUR KHREBET

Udskaya G.

Ayan

SHANTAR

SEA   OF

OKHOTSK

Okha

M YELIZAVETY

Okha

SAKHALIN
(Sov. Union)

Ust'-Bol'sheretsk

PARAMUSHIR

ONEKOTAN

KURIL ISLANDS

SIMUSHIR (Sov. Union)

URUP

TED   SOCIALIST

Peleduy

Vitim

Bol. Chuya

Kirensk

PATOM
5377

G. Golets-Purpula

PLATEAU

Bodaybo

Golets-
Skalistyy
9186

STANOVOY   KHREBET

Olekma

Uchur

Uda

Zeya

Tynda

Tyndinskiy

Chumikan

Nikolayevsk-
na-Amure

Amgun

Selemdzha

KHREBET
BUREINSKIY

Komsomol'sk
na-Amure

TATAR STRAIT

Aleksandrovsk

Poronaysk

M TERPENIYA

Uglegorsk

ITURUP (Sov. Union)

Nizhne-Angarsk

BURYAT

BAYKAL'SKIY KHREBET

Lena

Zhigalova

Kachuga

Ust'-
Ordynskiy

Ozero
Baykal
(Lake Baikal)
Surface elev. 1535 Ft.
above Sea Level

A.S.S.R.

Barguzin

Sretensk

Nerchinsk

Baley

Aginskoye

YABLONOVYY KHREBET

Skovorodino

Bekelova

Zeya

Zeya

Svobodnyy

Belogorsk

Ust Tyrma

Bureya

Zavitinsk

Roychikinsk

Birobidzhan

Khabarovsk

Sovetskaya
Gavan'

Dolinsk

Yuzhno-Sakhalinsk

Kholmsk

Korsakov

A-579300-76- -2 -22-
COPYRIGHT BY
RAND MCNALLY & COMPANY
MADE IN U.S.A.

Ulan-Ude

Petrovsk-
Zabaykal'skiy

Babushkin

Kyakhta

Altan
Bulag

Chita

Uda

Ingoda

Onon

Borzya

Aksha

NERCHINSKIY KHREBET

Nerchinskiy
Zavod

Shilka

Argun

GREATER KHINGAN MTS

Manchouli
(Lupin)

Hailaerh
(Hailar)

Pok'ot'u

INNER MONGOLIAN

AUT REG

GREATER

KHINGAN MTS

Argun

LESSER KHINGAN MTS

Blagoveshchensk

Chiualhun

Lungchen

C   H   I   N   A

HEILUNGKIANG

Sungari

Sung Hua

SIKHOTE ALIN

USSURIYSK KHREBET

Ussuri

Iman

Sôya Kaikyô

YEVREY
AUT
OBLAST

Bireya

SEA OF

JAPAN

HOKKAIDO

JAPAN

Choybalsan

Kerulen

Buyr Nuur

Ch'ich'ihaerh
(Tsitsihar)

Ilan

Hulan

HAERHPIN
(Harbin)

Ningan

Suifenho

Spassk-Dal'niy

Khanka

Ol ga

Ussuriysk

Arsen yevo

Artëm

Suchan

Nakhodka

Vladivostok

Ulaan Baatar

Ohoor Haan

Onon Gol

Uldza

Khalkin

Kerulen

L   I   A

Continued on pp. 146-147

110°   115°   120°   125°   130°   135°

0   50   100   200   300   400   500 Miles

0   100   200   300   400   500   600   800 Kilometers

Relief		
Meters		Feet
3050		10 000
1525		5000
610		2000
305		1000
152.5		500
Sea Level		0
152.5		500
1525		5000
3050		10000

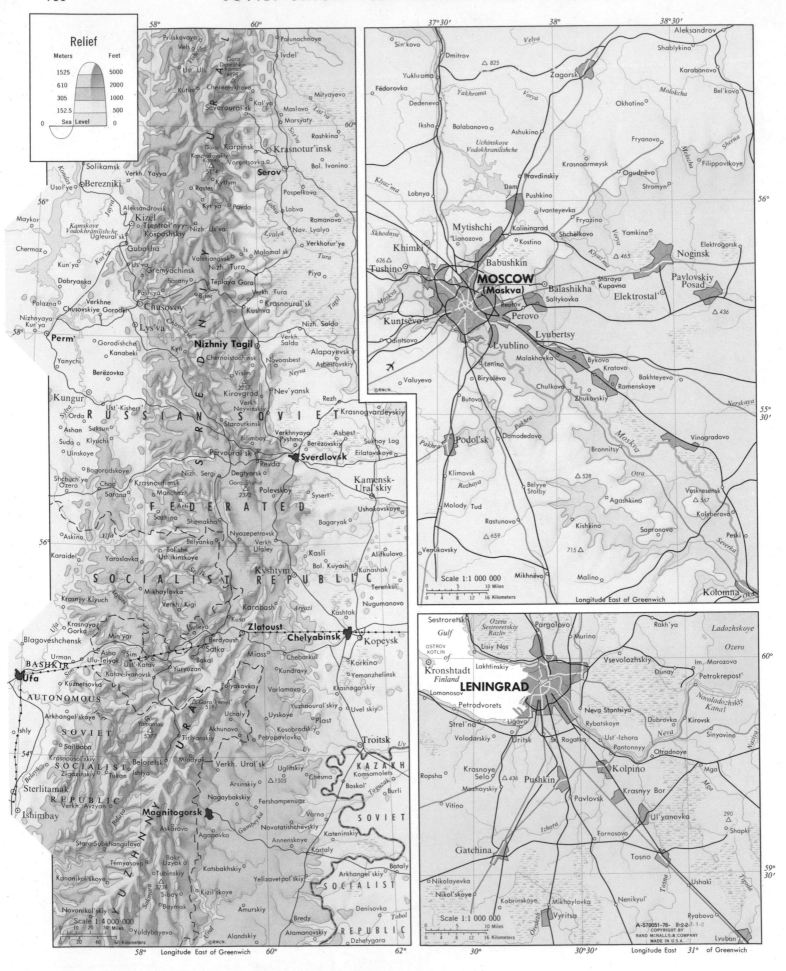

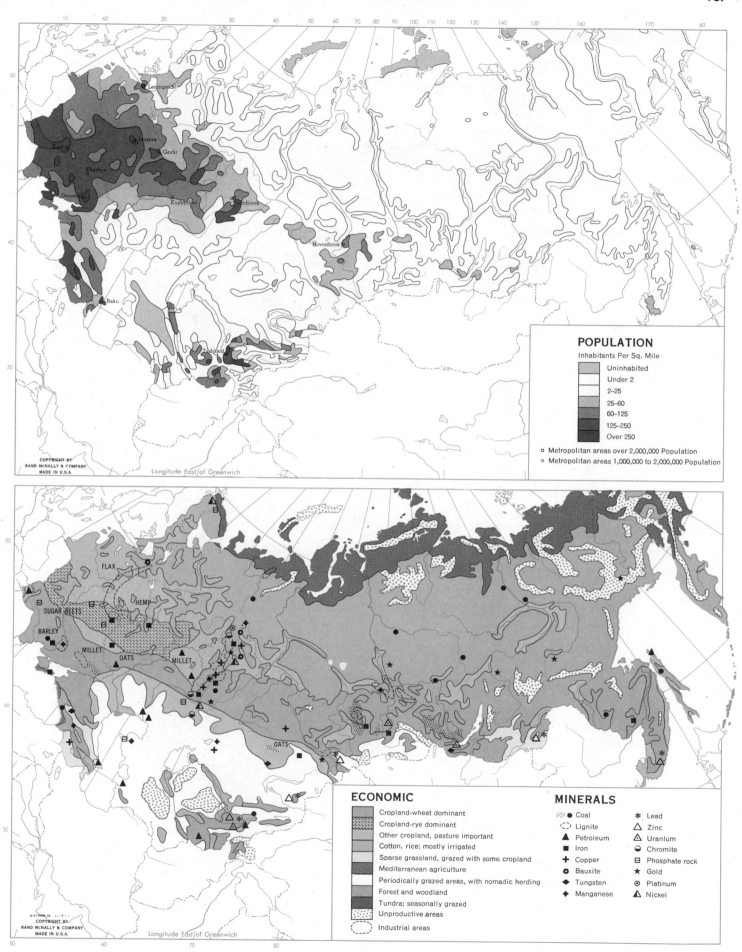

POPULATION

Inhabitants Per Sq. Mile

- Uninhabited
- Under 2
- 2–25
- 25–60
- 60–125
- 125–250
- Over 250

▫ Metropolitan areas over 2,000,000 Population

○ Metropolitan areas 1,000,000 to 2,000,000 Population

Longitude East/of Greenwich

ECONOMIC

- Cropland-wheat dominant
- Cropland-rye dominant
- Other cropland, pasture important
- Cotton, rice; mostly irrigated
- Sparse grassland, grazed with some cropland
- Mediterranean agriculture
- Periodically grazed areas, with nomadic herding
- Forest and woodland
- Tundra; seasonally grazed
- Unproductive areas
- Industrial areas

MINERALS

●	Coal	✳	Lead
◌	Lignite	△	Zinc
▲	Petroleum	△	Uranium
■	Iron	◠	Chromite
✚	Copper	⊟	Phosphate rock
◎	Bauxite	★	Gold
◆	Tungsten	⊙	Platinum
◆	Manganese	△	Nickel

Longitude East/of Greenwich

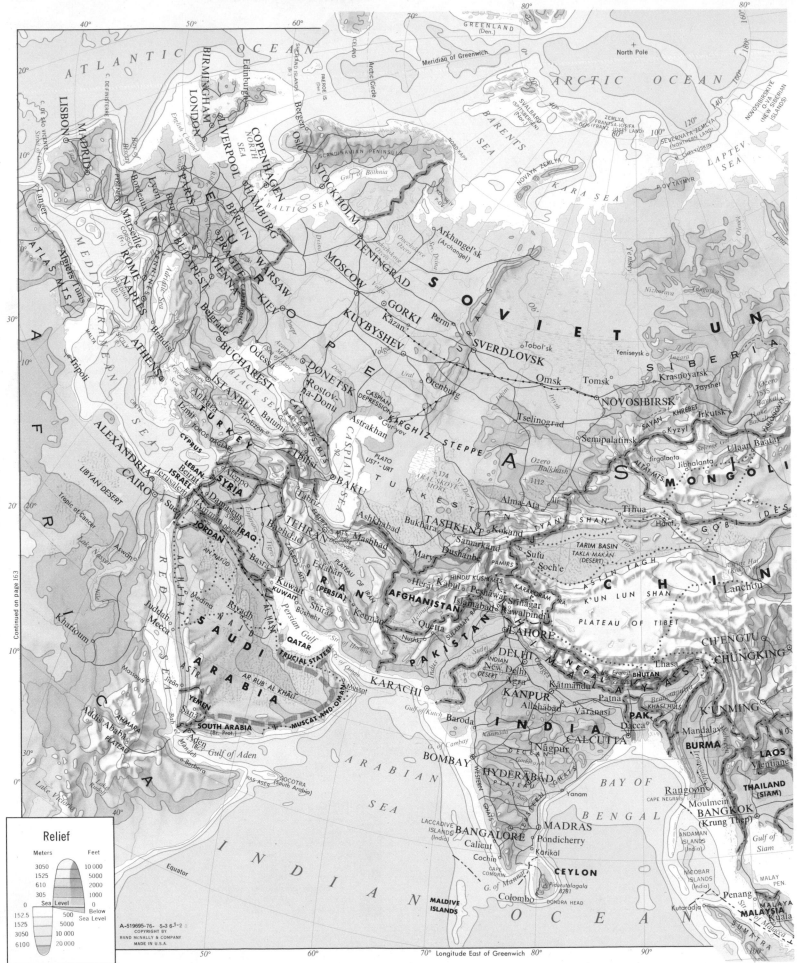

ARCTIC OCEAN

ATLANTIC OCEAN

GREENLAND (Den.)

North Pole

Meridian of Greenwich

Arctic Circle

ICELAND

BARENTS SEA

KARA SEA

LAPTEV SEA

SCANDINAVIAN PENINSULA

BIRMINGHAM
LONDON
EDINBURGH
LISBON
MADRID
LIVERPOOL
COPENHAGEN
HAMBURG
BERLIN
PARIS
ROME
NAPLES
ATHENS
BUDAPEST
PRAGUE
VIENNA
WARSAW
BUCHAREST
KIEV
BELGRADE
ISTANBUL
ANKARA
TURKEY
CYPRUS

MEDITERRANEAN SEA

ATLAS MTS.

AFRICA

LIBYAN DESERT

ALEXANDRIA
CAIRO
ISRAEL
BEIRUT
DAMASCUS
LEBANON
SYRIA
ALEPPO

MOSCOW
LENINGRAD
GORKI
KUYBYSHEV
SVERDLOVSK
DONETSK
Rostov-na-Donu
CASPIAN DEPRESSION
KARGHIZ STEPPE
Astrakhan
CASPIAN SEA
BAKU
TURKESTAN
Orenburg
Omsk
Tomsk
NOVOSIBIRSK
SIBERIA

SOVIET UNION

MONGOLIA

GOBI (DESERT)

CHINA

TASHKENT
Samarkand
Bukhara
Alma-Ata
TIAN SHAN
TARIM BASIN
TAKLA MAKAN (DESERT)
ASTIN TAGH
K'UN LUN SHAN
PLATEAU OF TIBET

TEHRAN
IRAN (PERSIA)
IRAQ
Baghdad
Basra
Esfahan
AFGHANISTAN
Herat
Kabul
Peshawar
Srinagar
Rawalpindi
Islamabad
HINDU KUSH MTS.
KARAKORAM RA.
PAMIRS
Mashhad
Ashkhabad
Mary
Dushanbe
SULAIMAN RANGE

JORDAN
KUWAIT
QATAR
TRUCIAL STATES
SAUDI ARABIA
NAJD
AL HASA
RED SEA
Riyadh
Mecca
Medina
Juddah
AR RUB' AL KHALI
Muscat
MUSCAT AND OMAN
YEMEN
SOUTH ARABIA
Aden
Gulf of Aden
SOCOTRA (South Arabia)

PAKISTAN
KARACHI
Quetta
Nushki
Kerman
Shiraz
Bushehr
Persian Gulf
Str. of Hormuz
Gulf of Oman

LAHORE
DELHI
New Delhi
KANPUR
Agra
Allahabad
Varanasi
NEPAL
BHUTAN
Mt. Everest
Katmandu
Patna
HIMALAYAS
Lhasa
CH'ENGTU
CHUNGKING
K'UNMING
Lanchow

INDIA
BOMBAY
HYDERABAD
DECCAN PLATEAU
Nagpur
Baroda
WESTERN GHATS
EASTERN GHATS
CALCUTTA
Dacca
PAK.
BURMA
Mandalay
KHASI HILLS
Brahmaputra

BANGALORE
MADRAS
Pondicherry
Calicut
Cochin
Karikal
CAPE COMORIN
CEYLON
Colombo
Pidurutalagala 8281
Dondra Head

ARABIAN SEA

BAY OF BENGAL

LACCADIVE ISLANDS (India)

MALDIVE ISLANDS

ANDAMAN ISLANDS (India)

NICOBAR ISLANDS (India)

RANGOON
CAPE NEGRAIS
Moulmein
BANGKOK (Krung Thep)
THAILAND (SIAM)
LAOS
Vientiane
Gulf of Siam
MALAY PEN.
Penang
MALAYA
KUALA
SUMATRA
Str. of Malacca

INDIAN OCEAN

Equator

Lake Victoria
Khartoum
Addis Ababa
AMHARA PLATEAU

Continued on page 163

Relief

Meters		Feet
3050		10 000
1525		5000
610		2000
305		1000
0	Sea Level	0
152.5		500 Below
1525		5000 Sea Level
3050		10 000
6100		20 000

A-519695-76- 5-3 6-1-2
COPYRIGHT BY
RAND MCNALLY & COMPANY
MADE IN U.S.A.

Scale 1:40 000 000; one inch to 630 miles. Lambert's Azimuthal, Equal Area Projection
Elevations and depressions are given in feet

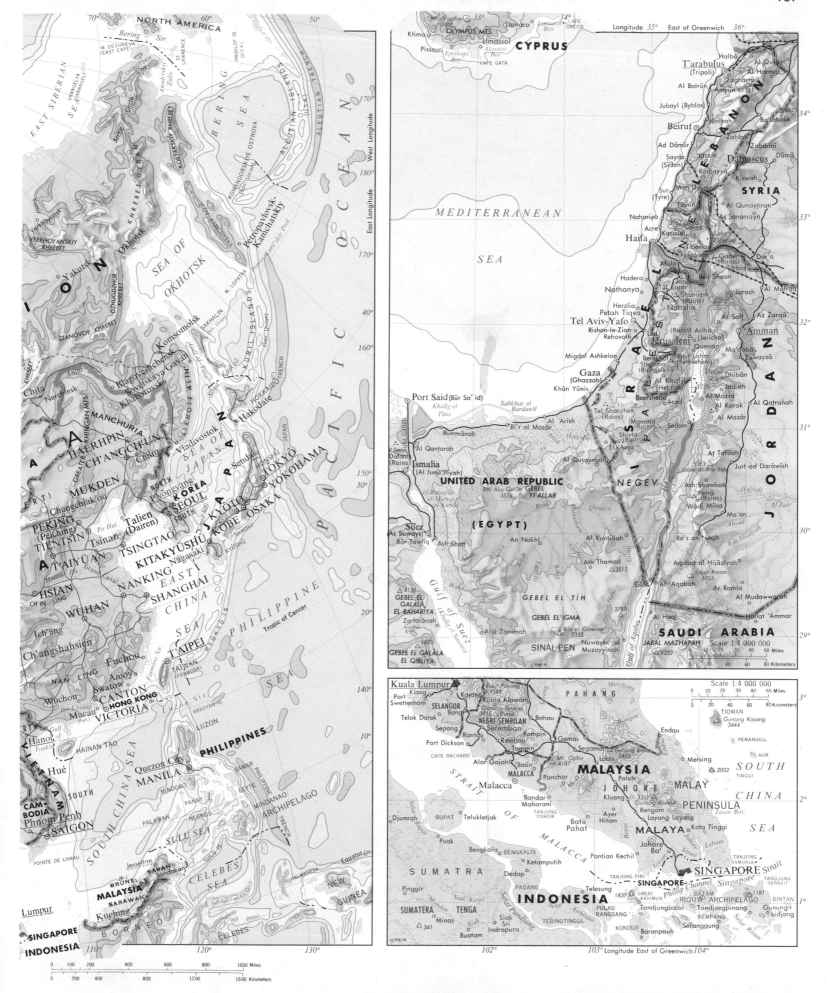

Main map (left)

NORTH AMERICA

Bering Str.
M. DEZHNEVA
(EAST CAPE)
Arctic Circle

EAST SIBERIAN SEA

WRANGELYA
(WRANGEL)

PRIBILOF IS. (U.S.A.)
ST. LAWRENCE I.

70° 60° 50°

West Longitude
East Longitude
180°
170°

KOMANDORSKIYE OSTROVA (Sov. Union)

ALEUTIAN ISLANDS

ALEUTIAN TRENCH

U N I O N

EAST SIBERIAN SEA

VERKHOYANSK
Verkhoyansk

SE. AYUWSKANGEL

ANADYRSKIY ZALIV
Anadyr'
CHUKOTSKIY

KHREBET GYDA

KORYAKSKIY KHREBET

KHREBET DZHUGDZHUR

Okhotsk

SEA OF OKHOTSK

M. LOPATRA

Petropavlovsk-
Kamchatskiy

P. KAMCHATKA

KURIL ISLANDS (Sov. Union)

PACIFIC OCEAN

Yakutsk
Yakutsk

VERKHOYANSKIY KHREBET

STANOVOY KHREBET

Komsomolsk

SAKHALIN

PEROUSE STR.

160°
40°

Chita
Nerchinsk

Blagoveshchensk
Svobodnyy
Sovetskaya Gavan'
Khabarovsk

Amur

SIKHOTE ALIN

SEA OF JAPAN

HOKKAIDO
Hakodate

HOKKAIDO TRENCH

150°
30°

MANCHURIA
GREATER KHINGAN MTS.

HAERHPIN
CH'ANGCHUN
Chilin

Vladivostok

Sungari

Sendai

HONSHU

TOKYO
YOKOHAMA

JAPAN

JAPAN TRENCH

PEKING (Peiching)
TIENTSIN
Changchiak'ou
MUKDEN

Po Hai
Talien (Dairen)
KOREA
Pyongyang
SEOUL
NORTH
SOUTH

KYOTO
KOBE OSAKA
SHIKOKU

KYUSHU
KITAKYUSHU
Nagasaki

140°
20°

T'AIYÜAN
Tsinan
Grand Canal
Hwang Ho
TSINGTAO

NANKING
SHANGHAI

EAST CHINA SEA

RYUKYU IS.

Tropic of Cancer

HSIAN
CH'IN LING
WUHAN

Ich'ang
Ch'angshahsien

CHINA

T'AIPEI
TAIWAN (FORMOSA)

PHILIPPINE SEA

130°
10°

NAN LING
Fuchou
Amoy
Swatow
Wuchou
CANTON
HONG KONG
VICTORIA
Macau (Port.)

Hsi Chiang

LUZON STR.
BABUYAN IS.

PHILIPPINES

LUZON

Hanoi
Gulf of Tonkin
HAINAN TAO

Hué

Quezon City
MANILA

MINDORO
SAMAR
LEYTE

120°
Equator

CAMBODIA
Phnom Penh
SAIGON

VIETNAM

SOUTH CHINA SEA

PALAWAN
PANAY
NEGROS

MINDANAO
ARCHIPELAGO

PHILIPPINE TRENCH

POINTE DE CAMAU

SULU SEA
SULU IS.

Jesselton
SABAH
Sandakan

CELEBES SEA

HALMAHERA

NEW GUINEA

110°

Lumpur

MALAYSIA
BRUNEI (Br.)
SARAWAK

Kuching

BORNEO

CELEBES

SINGAPORE

INDONESIA

100 200 400 600 800 1000 Miles
200 400 800 1200 1600 Kilometers

Upper right map — Israel / Lebanon / Jordan

CYPRUS

Mt. Troodos 33° 1900
OLYMPUS MTS.
Ktima
Pissouri
Episkopi Bay
Akrotiri
CAPE GATA
Limassol
Larnaca
Larnaca Bay
CAPE GRECO

34°

Longitude 35° East of Greenwich 36°

T'arabulus (Tripoli)
Al Qusayr
Al Harmal
Zagharta
Al Batrun
Amyun 1013
Jubayl (Byblos)

LEBANON

Ba'labakk

34°

Beirut
Ad Damur
Zahle
Zabdani
Damascus
Duma

Sayda (Sidon)
Jazzin
Rashayya
Kiswah

SYRIA

Sur (Tyre)
Mari 'Uyun
Tibnin
Al Qunaytirah
As Sanamayn

33°

Nahariya
Acre
Karmiel
Tiberias
Gader (Ruins)
Dar'a

Haifa
Nazareth
Irbid

MEDITERRANEAN SEA

Afula
Beit Shean
Jarash
Al Mafraq

Hadera
Janin
Karm
Shomron (Ruins)
Nablus

Nathanya
Herzlia
Petah Tiqva
As Salt
Az Zarqa

Tel Aviv-Yafo
(Ruins) Ariha (Jericho)
Amman

Rishon-le-Zion
Rehovoth
Jerusalem
Qumran
Ma'daba
Zuwayza

Migdal Ashkelon
Bereikot
Shelomo (Ruins)
Bayt Lahm (Bethlehem)
Al Khalil (Hebron)
Dhiban
Jad'ah

ISRAEL
JORDAN

Gaza (Ghazzah)
Khan Yunis
Beersheba
Arad
Al Mazra'
Al Karak
Al Qatranah

Port Said (Bur Sa'id)
Khalig el Tina
Sabkhat al Bardawil
Al 'Arish
Tel Sharuhen (Ruins)
Sedom
Al Mazar

Rummanah
Bi'r al Mazar
Shiya (Ruins)
Mamshit (Ruins)

Suez Canal
Al Qantarah
El 'Auja
At Tafilah
Jurf ad Darawish

Ismalia (Al Isma'iliyah)
Damas (Ruins)
Al Qusaymah
NEGEV
Ash Shawbak
Petra (Ruins)
Al Jufr

UNITED ARAB REPUBLIC

el Buheirat el-Murrat el-Kubra
Ras Abu Qurun
GEBEL YI'ALLAR 3578

Wadi Musa
Ma'an
Abyad

Suez (As Suways)
Bur Tawfiq
Ash Shaft
An Nakhl
Al Kuntillah
Ra's an Naqb
Ash Shidiyah

(EGYPT)
Ath Thamad
Aqabat al Hijaziyah
Al Mudawwarah

Wakdan
Eilat
Al 'Aqabah
Ar Ramla

GEBEL EL GALALA EL BAHARIYA 4136
Za'faranah
GEBEL EL TIH
Jabal Kamm 5755
Hallat 'Ammar

GEBEL EL'IGMA
3789
Al Haql

Abu Zanimah
Ras el Gineina 5335
SAUDI ARABIA

Nuwaybi' al Muzayyinah
JABAL MAZHAFAH

GEBEL EL GALALA EL QIBLIYA 4833
SINAI PEN
6232

Scale 1:4 000 000
10 20 30 40 50 Miles
20 40 60 80 Kilometers

Lower right map — Malaya / Singapore

Scale 1:4 000 000
10 20 30 40 50 Miles
20 40 60 80 Kilometers

Kuala Lumpur
Port Swettenham
Klang
Kajang
Bukit Payong 3349
Kuala Klawang
PAHANG
Merchong
3°

SELANGOR
Bangi
Gunung Telapa 3915
Burak
Bahau
Rompin

Telok Datok
Sepang
NEGRI SEMBILAN
Seremban
Gemas
Endau
TIOMAN
Gunung Kajang 3444

Port Dickson
Rantau
Rembau
Segamat
PEMANGGIL

CAPE RACHADO
Tampin
MALAYSIA
Mt. Ophir 4187
Labis
Gunong Besar 3493
Mersing
AUR
2002
SOUTH TINGGI

Alor Gajah
Jasin
JOHORE
MALAY

MALACCA
Panchor
Kluang 3312
Rengam
PENINSULA
CHINA
2°

Malacca
Bandar Maharani
TANJONG TOHOR
Ayer Hitam
Layang Layang
MALAYA
Kota Tinggi
Jason Bay
SEA

STRAIT OF MALACCA

Djumrah
Teluk Djetak
Batu Pahat
Pontian Kechil
Johore Ba'
Leban

SUMATRA
RUPAT
Puak
Bengkalis
BENGKALIS
Ketamputih
Dedap
TANJONG PIAI
Tanjong Piai
SINGAPORE
TANJONG RAMUNIA

Pinggir
PADANG
Telesung
SINGAPORE
Phillip Channel
BATAM
TANJUNG HERAKIT

INDONESIA
1837
GREAT KARIMUN
Singapore Strait
BINTAN

SUMATERA TENGA
Minas 341
Siak Ketjil
PULAU RANGSANG
Tandjungbalai
Tandjungpinang
RIOUW ARCHIPELAGO
REMPANG
Gunung-kidjang 1181

Siak Sri Indrapura
Selat pandjang
Serangung

KUNDUR
Buatam
Baranpauh

102° 103° Longitude East of Greenwich 104°

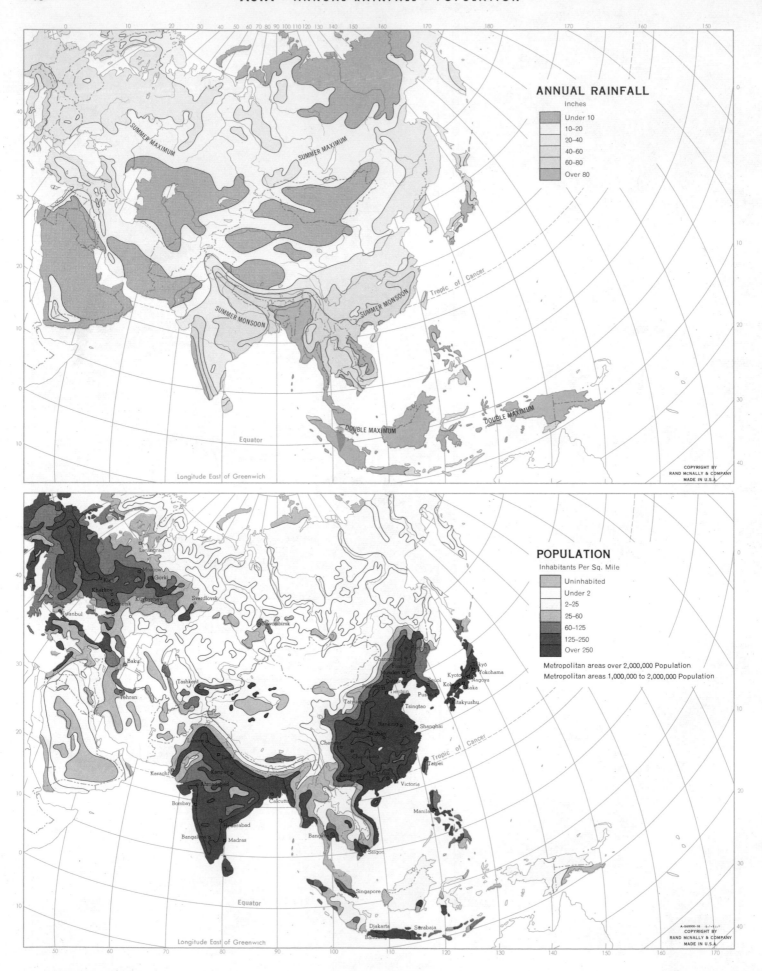

ANNUAL RAINFALL

Inches

- Under 10
- 10–20
- 20–40
- 40–60
- 60–80
- Over 80

SUMMER MAXIMUM

SUMMER MAXIMUM

SUMMER MONSOON

SUMMER MONSOON

Tropic of Cancer

DOUBLE MAXIMUM

DOUBLE MAXIMUM

Equator

Longitude East of Greenwich

POPULATION

Inhabitants Per Sq. Mile

- Uninhabited
- Under 2
- 2–25
- 25–60
- 60–125
- 125–250
- Over 250

Metropolitan areas over 2,000,000 Population
Metropolitan areas 1,000,000 to 2,000,000 Population

Leningrad

Kiev
Moscow
Gorki
Kharkov
Donetsk
Kuybyshev
Sverdlovsk
Istanbul
Novosibirsk
Baku
Tashkent
Tehran
Changchun
Mukden
Dairen
Tōkyō
Kyoto
Yokohama
Nagoya
Seoul
Osaka
Kobe
Pusan
Taiyuan
Tientsin
Tsingtao
Kitakyushu
Nanking
Sian
Wuhan
Shanghai
Chengtu
Chungking
Lahore
Karachi
Kanpur
Ahmadabad
Canton
Taipei
Victoria
Bombay
Hyderabad
Calcutta
Bangalore
Madras
Manila
Bangkok
Saigon
Singapore
Equator
Djakarta
Surabaja
Bandung

Tropic of Cancer

Longitude East of Greenwich

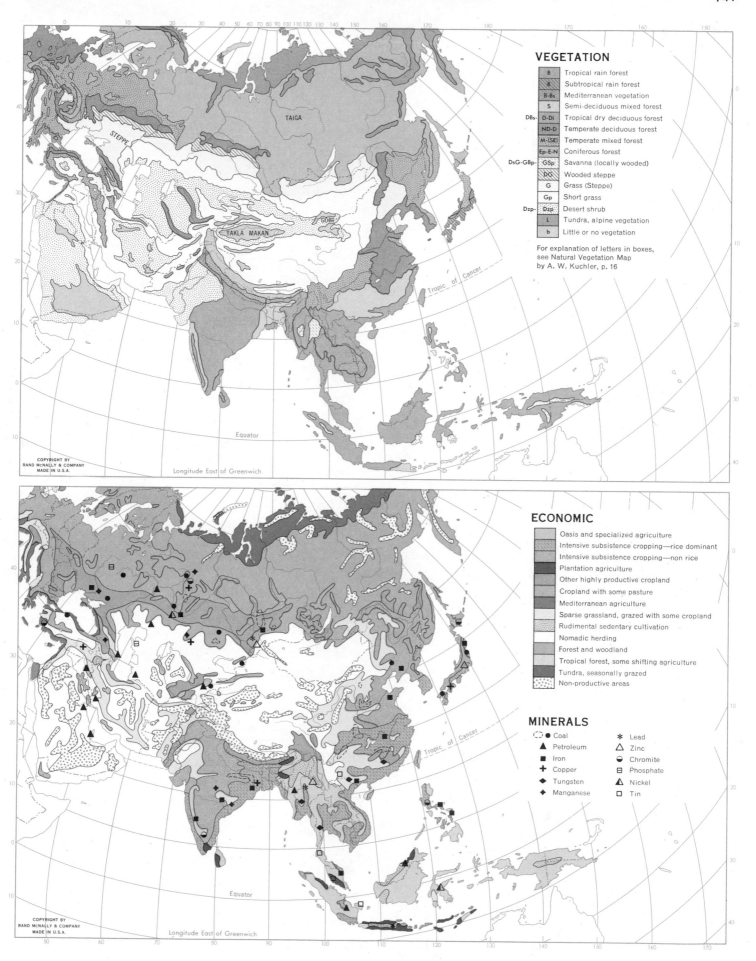

VEGETATION

B	Tropical rain forest
ß	Subtropical rain forest
B-Bs	Mediterranean vegetation
S	Semi-deciduous mixed forest
DBs- D-Di	Tropical dry deciduous forest
ND-D	Temperate deciduous forest
M-(SE)	Temperate mixed forest
Ep-E-N	Coniferous forest
DsG-GBp- GSp	Savanna (locally wooded)
DG	Wooded steppe
G	Grass (Steppe)
Gp	Short grass
Dzp- Dzp	Desert shrub
L	Tundra, alpine vegetation
b	Little or no vegetation

For explanation of letters in boxes,
see Natural Vegetation Map
by A. W. Kuchler, p. 16

TAIGA

STEPPE

TAKLA MAKAN

GOBI

Tropic of Cancer

Equator

Longitude East of Greenwich

ECONOMIC

	Oasis and specialized agriculture
	Intensive subsistence cropping—rice dominant
	Intensive subsistence cropping—non rice
	Plantation agriculture
	Other highly productive cropland
	Cropland with some pasture
	Mediterranean agriculture
	Sparse grassland, grazed with some cropland
	Rudimental sedentary cultivation
	Nomadic herding
	Forest and woodland
	Tropical forest, some shifting agriculture
	Tundra, seasonally grazed
	Non-productive areas

MINERALS

●	Coal	✳	Lead
▲	Petroleum	△	Zinc
■	Iron	◡	Chromite
✛	Copper	⊟	Phosphate
◆	Tungsten	◮	Nickel
◆	Manganese	☐	Tin

Tropic of Cancer

Equator

Longitude East of Greenwich

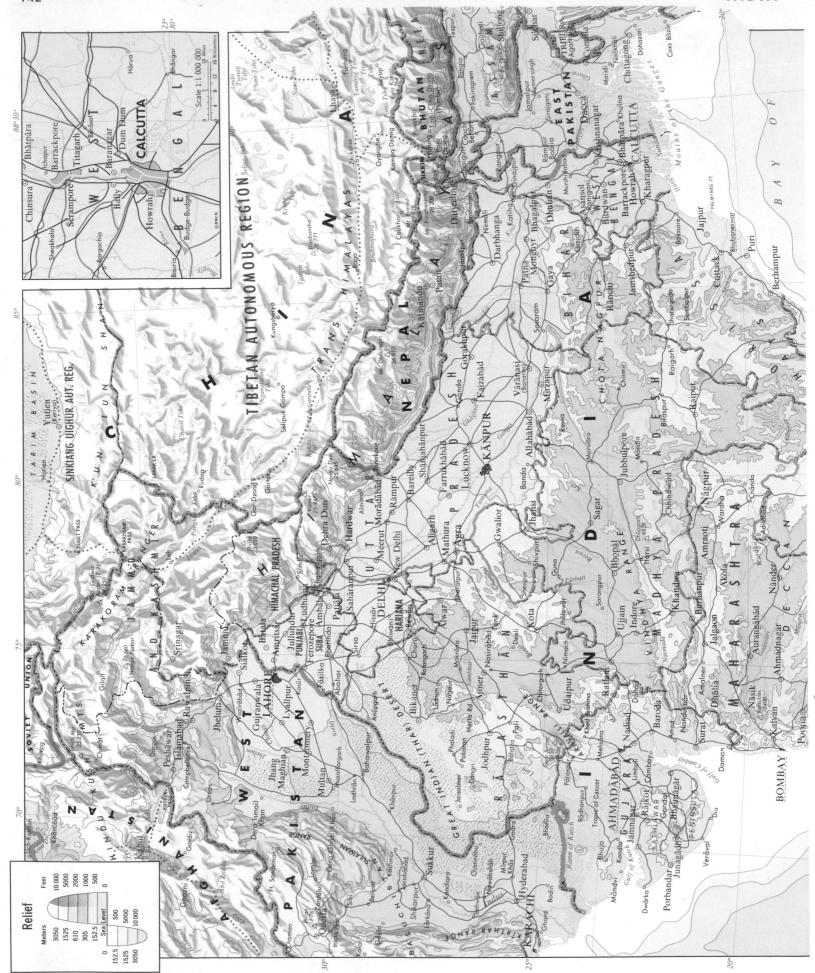

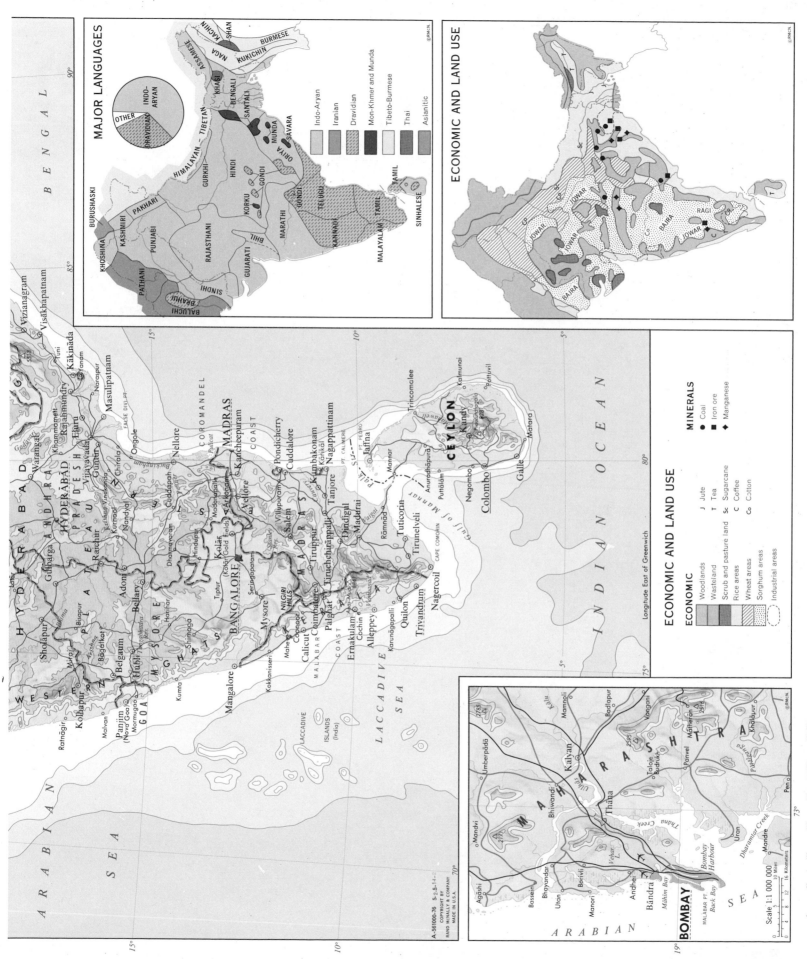

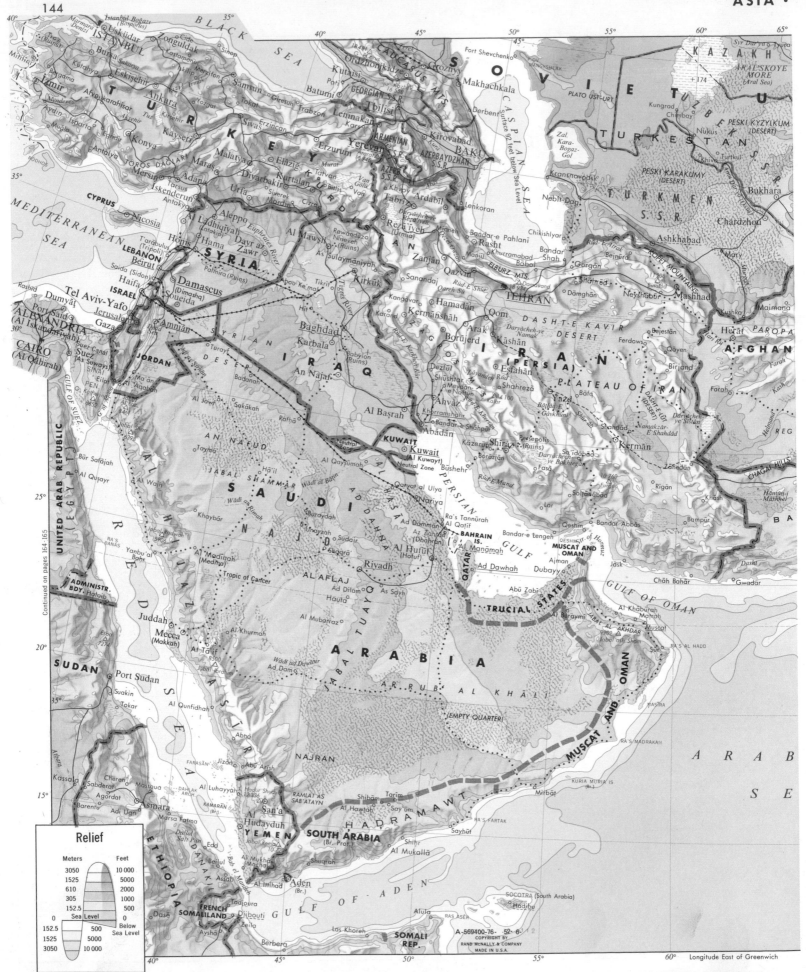

Relief

Meters	Feet
3050	10 000
1525	5000
610	2000
305	1000
152.5	500
0 Sea Level	0
Below	
152.5	500
1525	5000
3050	10 000

Continued on pages 164-165

A-569400-76-   52- 6-
COPYRIGHT BY
RAND McNALLY & COMPANY
MADE IN U.S.A.

Scale 1:16 000 000; one inch to 250 miles. Polyconic Projection
Elevations and depressions are given in feet

Longitude East of Greenwich

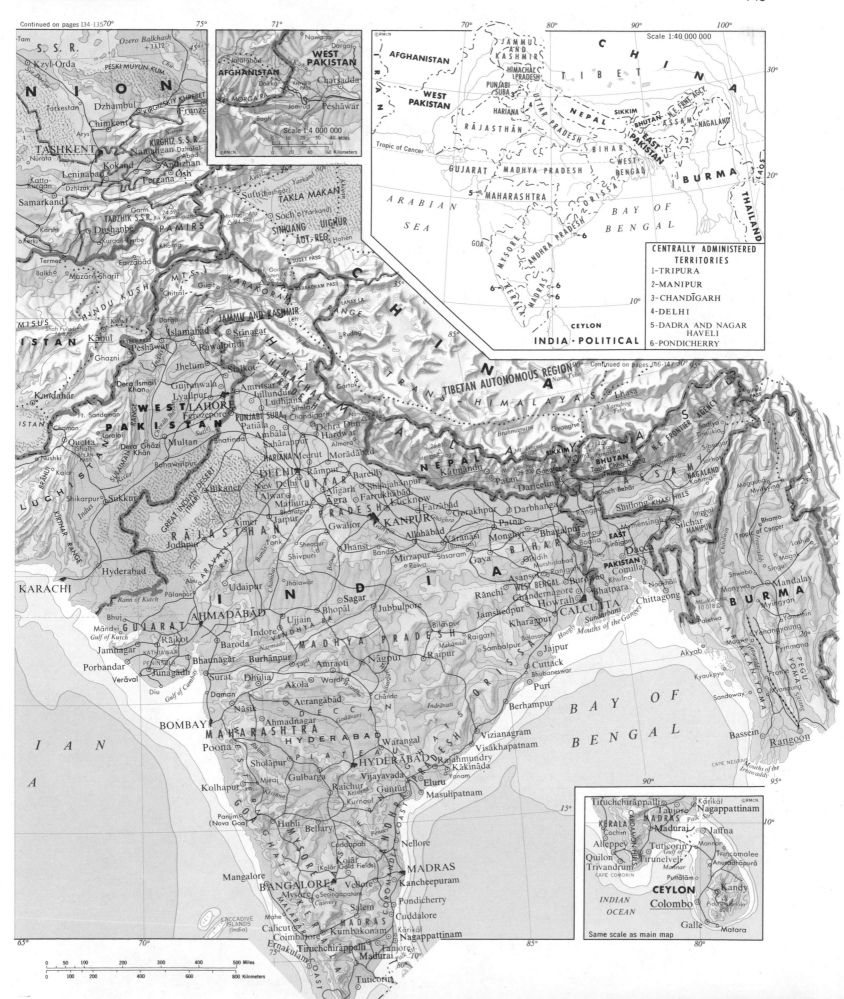

Continued on pages 134-135

71°

WEST PAKISTAN

AFGHANISTAN

Scale 1:4 000 000

0   10   20   30   40 Miles
0   20   40   60 Kilometers

Scale 1:40 000 000

CHINA

AFGHANISTAN

JAMMU AND KASHMIR

HIMACHAL PRADESH

WEST PAKISTAN

PUNJABI SUBA

HARIANA

TIBET

NEPAL   SIKKIM

BHUTAN

N.E. FRONT. AGCY.

ASSAM   NAGALAND

RĀJASTHĀN

UTTAR PRADESH

EAST

PAKISTAN

Tropic of Cancer

GUJARAT   MADHYA PRADESH

BIHAR

WEST BENGAL

ORISSA

BURMA

ARABIAN SEA

MAHARASHTRA

GOA

MYSORE   ANDHRA PRADESH

BAY OF BENGAL

THAILAND

KERALA   MADRAS

CEYLON

INDIA · POLITICAL

CENTRALLY ADMINISTERED TERRITORIES
1-TRIPURA
2-MANIPUR
3-CHANDĪGARH
4-DELHI
5-DADRA AND NAGAR HAVELI
6-PONDICHERRY

CEYLON
Colombo

Same scale as main map

0   50   100   200   300   400   500 Miles
0   100   200   400   600   800 Kilometers

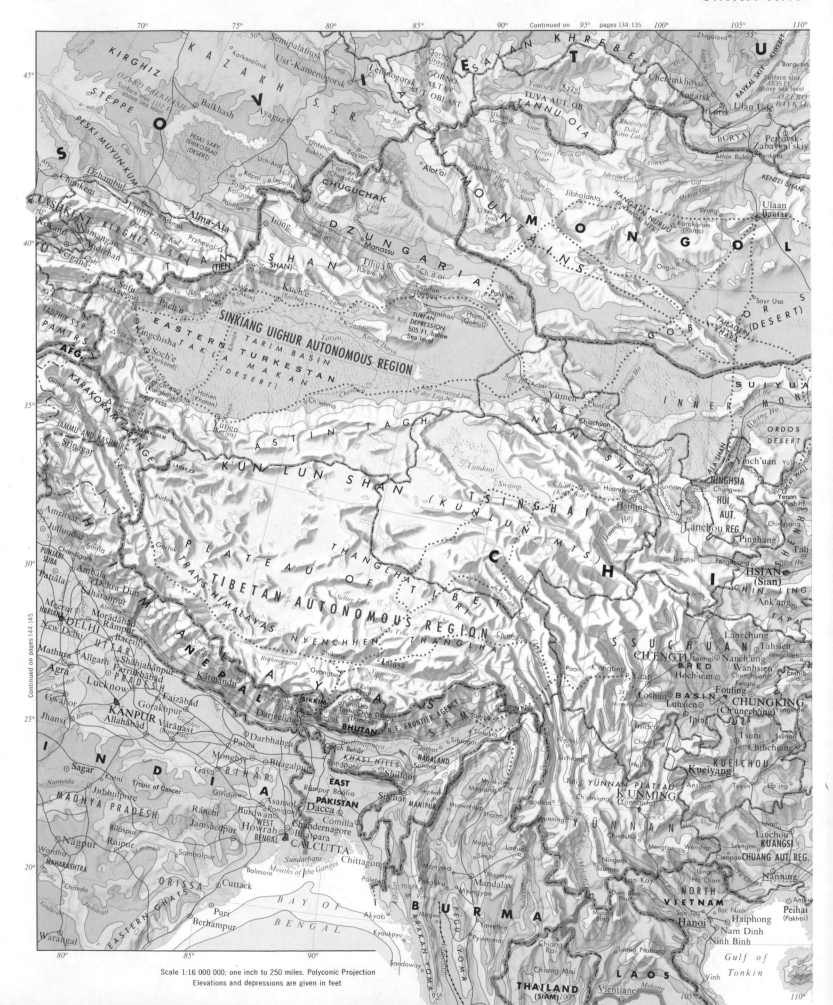

Continued on pages 134-135

Continued on pages 144, 145

S O V I E T

KIRGHIZ

KAZAKH

STEPPE

OZERO BALKHASH
Surface elev. 1112 Ft.
above sea level

PESKI MUYUN-KUM

Balkhash

Ayaguz

Karkaralinsk

Ust'-Kamenogorsk

Semipalatinsk

PESKI SARY-
ISHIKOTRAU
(DESERT)

Dzhambul

Chimkent

Frunze

Alma-Ata

TASHKENT

Kokand

Samarkand

Andizhan

TADZHIK S.S.R.

AFG.

PAMIRS

KARAKORAM RANGE

JAMMU AND KASHMIR

Srinagar

Gilgit

Leh

Amritsar

Jullundur

Simla

Ambala

PUNJABI
SUBA

Patiala

Chandigarh

Dehra Dun

Saharanpur

Meerut

Morādābad

Rāmpur

Bareilly

New Delhi

DELHI

UTTAR

Mathura

Aligarh

Agra

Gwalior

PRADESH

Shāhjahānpur

Farrukhābād

Lucknow

Gorakhpur

Faizābād

MADHYA PRADESH

Jhansi

Jubbulpore

Nāgpur

Wardha

MAHARASHTRA

Raipur

Bilaspur

Sagar

Jhansi

Katni

Narmada

Chanda

Ranchi

Jamshedpur

Sambalpur

ORISSA

Cuttack

EASTERN GHATS

Warangal

Puri

Berhampur

BAY OF
BENGAL

NEPAL

Katmandu

HIMALAYA

TRANS-HIMALAYAS

NYENCHHEN

SIKKIM

Darjeeling

BHUTAN

Thimbu

N.E. FRONTIER AGENCY

KIRGHIZ S.S.R.

TYAN SHAN
(TIEN SHAN)

Sufu
(Kashgar)

Yingchisha

Soch'e
(Yarkand)

Pach'u

Aksu
(Uch Turfan)

Wen-su

Kuch'e
(Kucha)

Yenchi

K'uerhlo

Kara Shahr

Hotien
(Khotan)

Yutien
(Keriya)

Chechen

ASTIN TAGH

KUN-LUN SHAN (KUNLUN MTS.)

PLATEAU OF TIBET

TIBETAN AUTONOMOUS REGION

THANGLHA TBI

Gartok

Rudog

Seling Tsho

Nam Tsho

Zhikatse

Gyangtse

Lhasa

Yamdrog
Tsho

Brahmaputra

SINKIANG UIGHUR AUTONOMOUS REGION

TARIM BASIN

EASTERN TURKESTAN

TAKLA MAKAN
(DESERT)

Tarim

DZUNGARIA

CHUGUCHAK

Kuldja

Ining

Manassu

Tihua
(Urumchi)

Chi t'ai

TURFAN DEPRESSION
505 Ft. below
sea level

Turfan

Hami
(Qomul)

Shanshan

Salt incrusted bed
of dry Lop-Nor

ALTAY

Fuhai

Alot'ai

GORNO
ALTAY
AUT. OBLAST

SAYAN
KHREBET

TUVA AUT. OB.

TANNU OLA

Kyzyl

Yenisey

HANGAYN NURUU

M O N G O L

G O B I

OZERO
BAYKAL

BURYAT

Ulan Ude

Irkutsk

KENTEI SHAN

Ulaan Baatar

Karakorum
(Ruins)

ORDOS
(DESERT)

INNER MON-

SUIYUA

NAN SHAN

Yümen

Chiuchuan

Anhsi

Ch'ing-Hai
(Koko Nor)

TSAIDAM

Swamp

Hsining

Huangyüan

Lanchou REG.

ALA SHAN

Yinch'uan

NINGHSIA

HUI
AUT.

Chungwei

Pinghiang

Lunghsi

Fengsiang

Yenan
(Fushih)

Chingyang

GREAT WALL

ORDOS
DESERT

Huang Ho

HSIAN
(Sian)

CHIN LING

Ank'ang

C H I N

TSINGHAI

THANGLHATBRI

Ch'angtu

CH'ENGTU

RED
BASIN

SSUCH'UAN

CHUNGKING
(Ch'ungch'ing)

K'angting

P.Yaan

Hoch'uan

Nanch'ung

Wanhsien

Fouling

Fengtu

Luhsien

Ipin

Loshan

Tsuni

KUEICHOU

Kueiyang

Anshun

YÜNNAN PLATEAU

K'UNMING
(Yünnanfu)

Y Ü N N A N

Tali

Paoshan

Ch'uhsiung

Mengtzu

KUANGSI
CHUANG AUT. REG.

Nanning

Lungchow

I N D I A

BIHAR

Patna

Darbhanga

Monghyr

Bhāgalpur

Gaya

Giridih

Rānchi

Asansol

Burdwan

Chandernagore

Bhātpara

Howrah

CALCUTTA

WEST
BENGAL

EAST
PAKISTAN

Dacca

Comilla

Chittagong

Sundarbans

Mouths of the Ganges

Balasore

KHASI HILLS

Shillong

Silchar

NAGALAND

MANIPUR

Imphal

B U R M A

Mandalay

Myitkyina

Bhamo

Lashio

Maymyo

ARAKAN YOMA

BEGU YOMA

Akyab

N O R T H

VIETNAM

Hanoi

Haiphong

Nam Dinh

Ninh Binh

Peihai
(Pakhoi)

Gulf of
Tonkin

L A O S

Vientiane

THAILAND
(SIAM)

Chiang Mai

Luang Prabang

N
(Lake Baikal)
U. S. S. R.
YABLONOVYY KHREBET
Skovorodino
Komsomol'sk-
da-na-Amure
SEA
Chita
Skovorodino
Beketova
Svobodnyy
Blagoveshchensk
Goszan
OF
Aginskoye
Ingoda
Nerchinsk
Chiuchichien
Zavitinsk
Moho
SAKHALIN
(Sov. Un.)
OKHOTSK
SMUSHIR
Nerchinsk
NERCHINSKIY KHREBET
HSIAOHSINGANLING SHANMO
(LESSER KHINGAN MTS.)
Khabarovsk
Sovetskaya
Gavan'
Dolinsk
URUP
Aksha
Nerchinski
Zavod
Chuchhun
Khabarovsk
Yuzhno-
Sakhalinsk
Korsakov
KURIL ISLANDS
(Sov. Union)
Choybalsan
Manchouli
(Lupin)
Dalai
Nor
Hailaerh
(Hailar)
Pok'o t'u
Nenchiang
Hailun
Wuyün
K'oshan
T'ungchiang
Sungari
SIKHOTE ALIN
ITURUP
Ozümiin Üüde
Buyr
Nuur
Wench'üan
Solun
Ch'ich'iharh
(Tsitsihar)
Angangchi
Suihua
HEILUNGKIANG
Sung Hua
Soya Kaikyo M. ANIVA
Wakkanai
KUNASHIR
Ondör Haan
Kerulen
HAMO
Taonan
HAERHPIN
(Harbin)
Spassk-Dal'niy
O'ga
Asahigawa
Kushiro
Nemuro
Fuyu
Hulan
Ningan
N
CH'AHAERH
CH'ANGCH'UN
Chilin
(Kirin)
Tunhua
Ussuriysk
Vladivostok
Otaru
Sapporo
HOKKAIDO
ERIMO SAKI
YAHSINGANLING SHANMO
(GREATER KHINGAN) AUTON. REG.
Liaoyüan
Yenchi
Vladimiro
Aleksandrovskoye
Muroran
Hakodate
Esashi
Lupei
Chihfeng
T'iehling
Tungliao
Najin
Chöngjin
Hamhüng
Hirosaki
Aomori
Kuji
Tolun
Weich'ang
FUSHUN
MUKDEN
(Shenyang)
PAI-T'OU
SHAN
MUSU-DAN
SEA
OF
Akita
Morioka
Ishinomaki
Changpai
Ch'engte
Chaoyang
Liaoyang
Yingk'ou
Kanggye
Uiju
Sinüiju
Wönsan
JAPAN
SADO
Sakata
Yamagata
Sendai
Paot'ou
Fengchen
Kalgan
(Kalgan)
PEICHING-SHIH
Linyü
Antung
Sinüiju
NORTH
Chinnampo
P'yöngyang
NOTO HANTO
Toyama
Niigata
Nagaoka
Nagano
Utsunomiya
PEKING
(Peiching)
HOPEH
TIENTSIN
(Tienching)
LÜTA
Talien
(Dairen)
Lüshunk'ou
(Port Arthur)
KOREA
Kaesöng
(Kaijo)
SEOUL
(Söul)
SOUTH
Kanazawa
Fukui
Gifu
Maebashi
TOKYO
Chiba
YOKOHAMA
Paoting
Chengting
Po Hai
Yent'ai (Chefoo)
Inch'ön
Andong
OKI GUNTO
Tottori
KYOTO
NAGOYA
HONSHU
T'AIYÜAN
SHANSI
Laichou
Wan
Weihai
Kunsan
Kyöngju
Matsue
Nara
OSAKA
KOBE
Wakayama
IZU
SHICHITO
Fenyang
Linch'ing
SHANTUNG PANTAO
Weifang
Chuahsien
TSINGTAO
(Ch'ingtao)
YELLOW
Taegu
Masan
Okayama
Kure
Takamatsu
Kochi
SHIKOKU
Matsuyama
Tsinan
(Tsinan)
Tzuyang
Chiaochou
Wan
Kunsan
PUSAN
Hiroshima
Shimonoseki
Tokushima
Anyang
Linfen
Poshan
Lini
SEA
Mokpo
TSU SHIMA
KITAKYUSHU
Fukuoka
Chinyang
Chining
KOREAN ARCHIPELAGO
Korea Str.
Tsushima Str.
Kurume
Loyang
Tung-Kuan
K'aifeng
Lienyün
CHE JU I
(QUELPART)
Saseho
Nagasaki
Kumamoto
KYUSHU
Chengchou
HONAN
Hsüchou
CHIANGSU
EAST
CHINA
Kagoshima
OSUMI
GUNTO
TANEGA
Nanyang
Huaiyin
Huang Ho
TAKU
TOKARA GUNTO
Hsinyang
Nanyang
Fouyang
Yangchou
Ch'angchou
NANKING
(Nanking)
Chenchiang
Soochow
SHANGHAI
SHANGHAI-SHIH
SEA
RYUKYU RETTO
TAPIEH SHAN
ANHUI
Hofei
Wuhsi
Sungchiang
AMAMI
GUNTO
Kominato
SHAN
HUPEH
Ich'ang
Hanyang
WUHAN
Wuch'ang
Anching
Wuhsing
Chiahsing
Hangchou
CHOUSAN
ARCHIPELAGO
TOKUNO
Chiangling
Shashih
Chuchiang
Shaohsing
CHECHIANG
Ningpo
Chinhua
Ch'uhsien
OKINAWA
GUNTO
OKINAWA
HUNAN
CHIANGSI
Nanch'ang
Lishui
Ch'angshahsien
Hsiangt'an
Wenchou
Naha
PHILIPPINE
Shaoyang
Hengyang
Kanchou
Nanp'ing
Hsiap'u
Ningte
Chian
Kweilin
HUNAN
FUCHIEN
Fuchou
(Foochow)
SEA
Chilung
IRIOMOTE
JIMA
SAKISHIMA
GUNTO
Tropic of Cancer
Shaokuan
KUANGTUNG
Meihsien
Ch'aoan
Chinchiang
Amoy
(Hsiamen)
Lungch'i
T'AIPEI
T'aichung
Swatow
(Shant'ou)
Chichyang
T'ainan
TAIWAN
(FORMOSA)
NATIONALIST
CHINA
CANTON
(Kuangchou)
Kowloon
VICTORIA
HONG KONG
(Br.)
Kaohsiung
Bashi
Channel
BATAN
IS.
Foshan
Hsinhui
Macau
SEA
Chanchiang
(Ft. Bayard)
LEICHOU
PAN-TAO
SOUTH CHINA SEA
HAINAN TAO

Continued on pages 154-155

Longitude East of Greenwich

55° 115° 120° 125° 130° 135° 140° 145° 150°
50°
45°
40°
35°
30°
25°
20°

Relief

Meters		Feet
3050		10 000
1525		5000
610		2000
305		1000
152.5		500
Sea Level	0	0 Sea Level
152.5		500 Below Sea Level
1525		5000
3050		10 000
6100		20 000

A-569700-76- 5-2-6-1-1
COPYRIGHT BY
RAND McNALLY & COMPANY
MADE IN U.S.A.

0 50 100 200 300 400 500 Miles
0 200 400 600 800 Kilometers

PART OF EASTERN CHINA

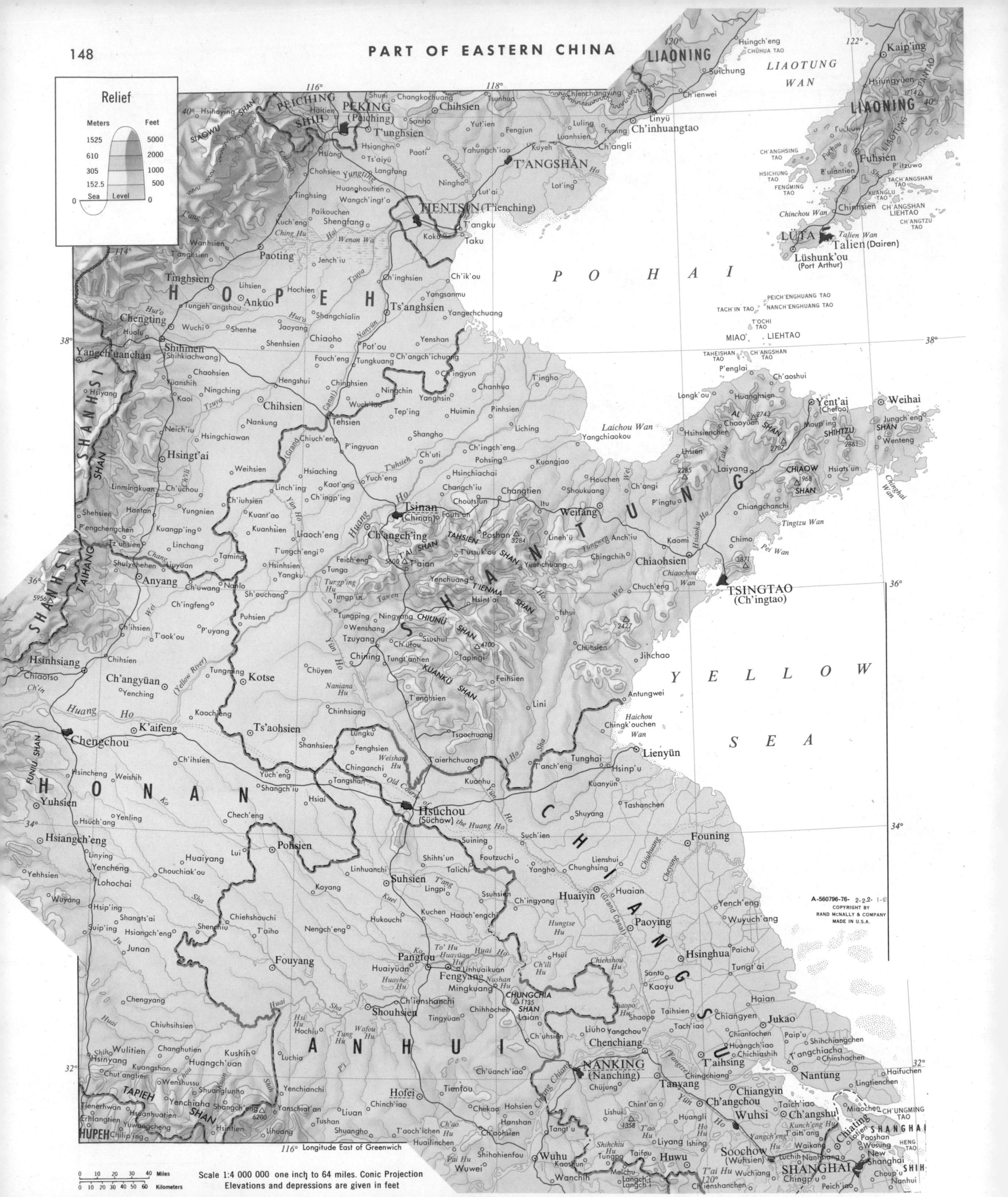

Relief

Meters	Feet
1525	5000
610	2000
305	1000
152.5	500
Sea	Level
0	0

LIAONING

LIAOTUNG WAN

PEICHING SHIH

PEKING (Peiching)

T'ANGSHAN

TIENTSIN (T'ienching)

POHAI

LÜTA — Talien (Dairen)
Lüshunk'ou (Port Arthur)

HOPEH

Paoting

Tinghsien

Chengting

Shihmen (Shihkiachwang)

Yangch'uanchan

SHANSI

TAIHANG SHAN

Tsinan (Chinan)

T'AI SHAN

SHANTUNG

Weifang

Yent'ai (Chefoo)

Weihai

TSINGTAO (Ch'ingtao)

Laichou Wan

CHIAOW SHAN

SHIHTZU SHAN

HONAN

K'aifeng

Chengchou

FUNIU SHAN

Hsüchou (Süchow) the Huang Ho

YELLOW SEA

Lienyün

CHIANGSU

Huaiyin

Paoying

Hsinghua

ANHUI

Pangfou

Fengyang

Fouyang

Shouhsien

TAPIEH SHAN

HUPEH

NANKING (Nanching)

Hofei

Wuhu

Soochow (Wuhsien)

SHANGHAI

SHIH

A-560796-76- 2-2.2- 1-?
COPYRIGHT BY
RAND McNALLY & COMPANY
MADE IN U.S.A.

Scale 1:4 000 000 one inch to 64 miles. Conic Projection
Elevations and depressions are given in feet

Longitude East of Greenwich

0 10 20 30 40 Miles
0 10 20 30 40 50 60 Kilometers

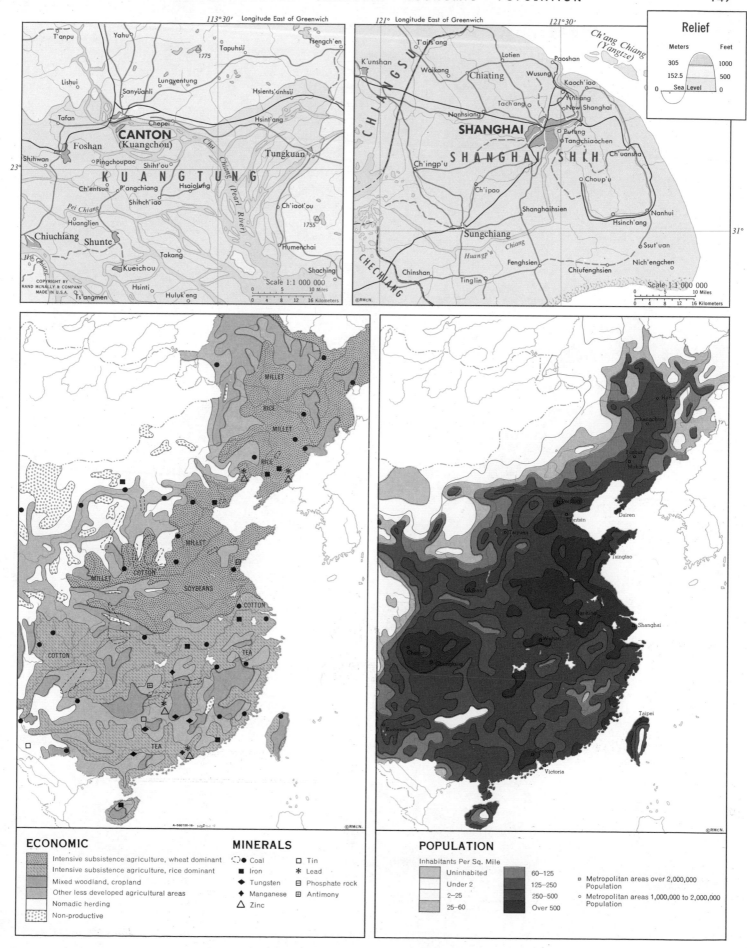

Relief

Meters		Feet
305		1000
152.5		500
0	Sea Level	0

Scale 1:1 000 000

Scale 1:1 000 000

ECONOMIC

- Intensive subsistence agriculture, wheat dominant
- Intensive subsistence agriculture, rice dominant
- Mixed woodland, cropland
- Other less developed agricultural areas
- Nomadic herding
- Non-productive

MINERALS

- ● Coal
- ■ Iron
- ◆ Tungsten
- △ Zinc
- □ Tin
- ✳ Lead
- ⊟ Phosphate rock
- ⊞ Antimony

POPULATION

Inhabitants Per Sq. Mile

- Uninhabited
- Under 2
- 2–25
- 25–60
- 60–125
- 125–250
- 250–500
- Over 500

- □ Metropolitan areas over 2,000,000 Population
- ○ Metropolitan areas 1,000,000 to 2,000,000 Population

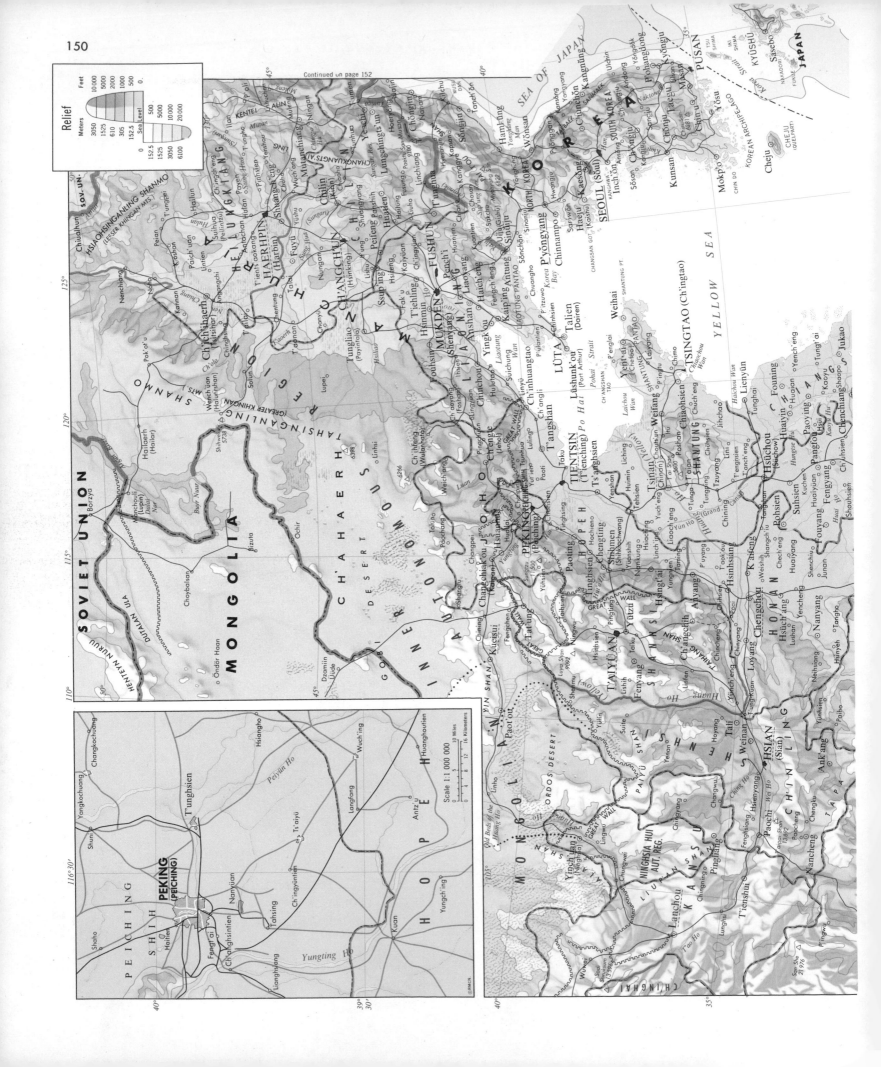

Continued on page 152

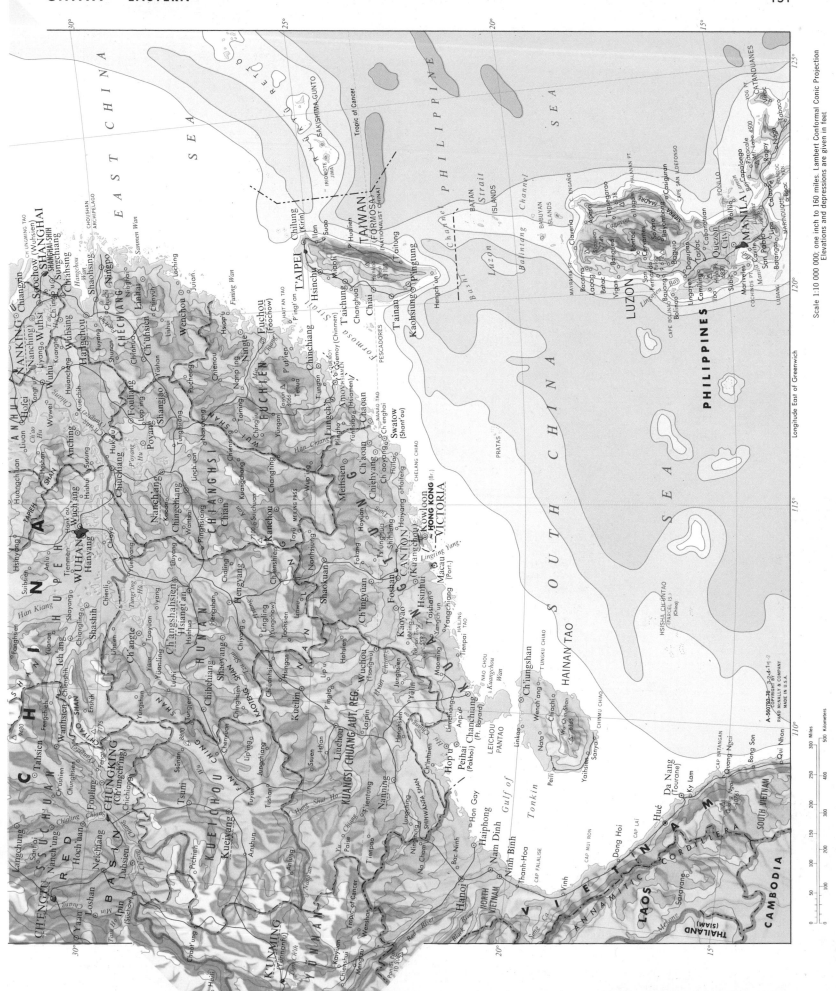

Scale 1:10 000 000; one inch to 160 miles. Lambert Conformal Conic Projection
Elevations and depressions are given in feet

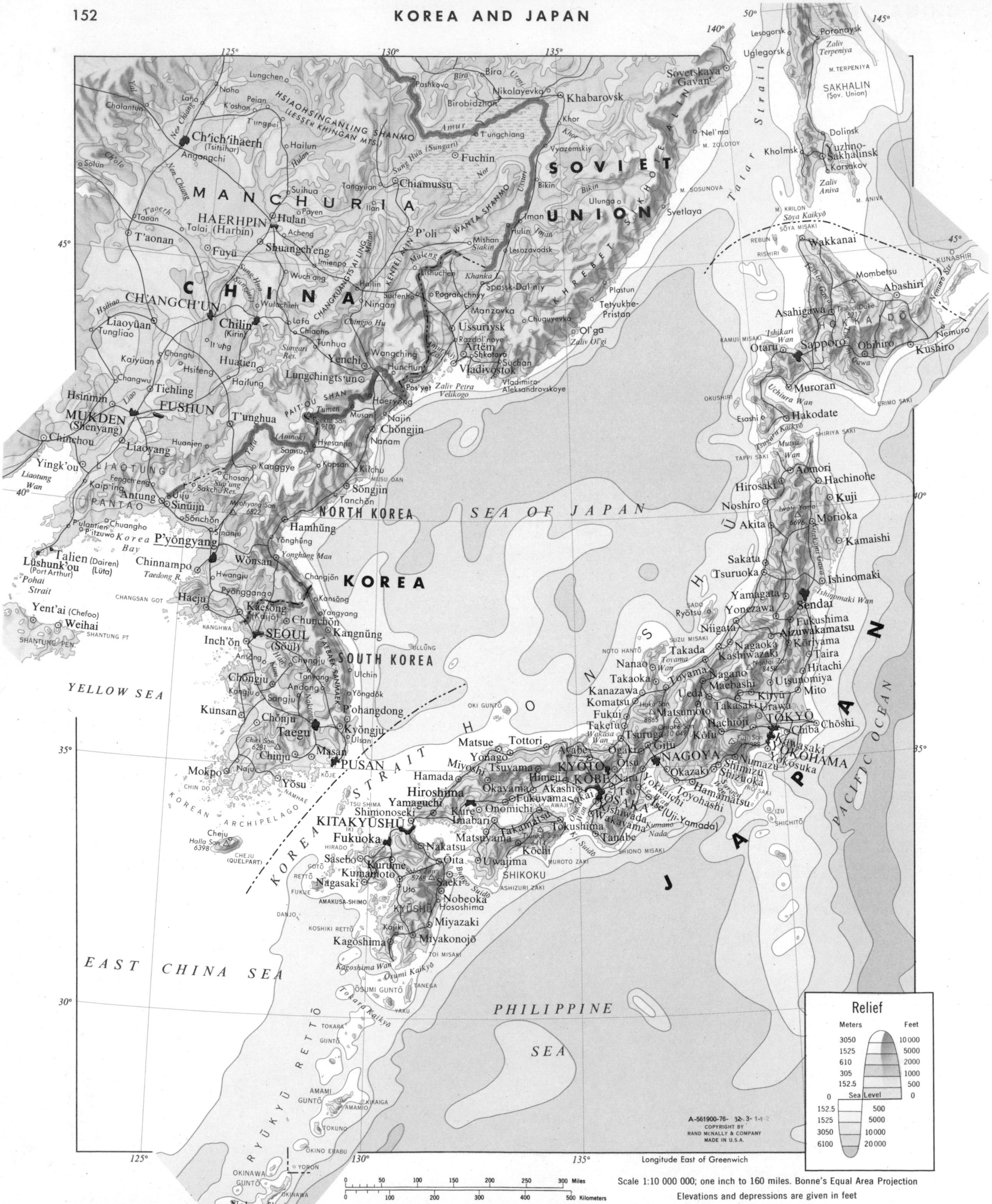

SOVIET UNION

MANCHURIA

CHINA

HAERHPIN
Talai (Harbin)

CH'ANGCH'UN
Chilin (Kirin)

MUKDEN (Shenyang)
FUSHUN

LIAOTUNG
PANTAO

Talien (Dairen) (Lüta)
Lüshunk'ou (Port Arthur)

Yent'ai (Chefoo)
Weihai

SHANTUNG PEN.
SHANTUNG PT.

YELLOW SEA

Khabarovsk

Amur

Ussuriysk
Vladivostok

SAKHALIN (Sov. Union)
Yuzhno-Sakhalinsk
Korsakov

Wakkanai
HOKKAIDO
Asahigawa
Sapporo
Otaru
Obihiro
Kushiro
Muroran
Hakodate
Nemuro

NORTH KOREA

P'yŏngyang
Chinnampo
Wŏnsan
Hamhŭng

Korea Bay

KOREA

SEA OF JAPAN

Aomori
Hachinohe
Hirosaki
Kuji
Noshiro
Akita
Morioka
Kamaishi
Sakata
Tsuruoka
Ishinomaki
Yamagata
Yonezawa
Sendai
Niigata
Fukushima
Aizuwakamatsu

SEOUL (Sŏul)
Inch'ŏn
Chunch'ŏn
Kangnŭng

SOUTH KOREA

Chŏngju
Taejŏn
Taegu
Chinju
Masan
PUSAN

Mokpo
Kunsan
Chŏnju
Kwangju

CHEJU (QUELPART)
Halla San 6398

Nagaoka
Nagano
Takada
Toyama
Takaoka
Kanazawa
Komatsu
Fukui
Matsumoto
Takasaki
Maebashi
Utsunomiya
Mito
KYŌTO
NAGOYA
TŌKYŌ
YOKOHAMA
Kawasaki
Chiba
Chōshi

Matsue
Tottori
Yonago
Tsuyama
KŌBE
ŌSAKA
Wakayama

Hamada
Hiroshima
Yamaguchi
Okayama
Fukuyama
Onomichi
Kure
Shimonoseki

KITAKYŪSHŪ
Fukuoka
Sasebo
Kurume
Kumamoto
Nagasaki

KOREA STRAIT

KOREAN ARCHIPELAGO

Matsuyama
Takamatsu
Tokushima
Kōchi
SHIKOKU

Ōita
Nobeoka
Miyazaki
Miyakonojō
Kagoshima
KYŪSHŪ

EAST CHINA SEA

PACIFIC OCEAN

PHILIPPINE SEA

RYŪKYŪ RETTŌ

AMAMI GUNTŌ

OKINAWA GUNTŌ
Naha

Longitude East of Greenwich

Scale 1:10 000 000; one inch to 160 miles. Bonne's Equal Area Projection
Elevations and depressions are given in feet

Relief		
Meters		Feet
3050		10 000
1525		5000
610		2000
305		1000
152.5		500
0	Sea Level	0
152.5		500
1525		5000
3050		10 000
6100		20 000

A-561900-76- 32-3- 1-1-2
COPYRIGHT BY
RAND McNALLY & COMPANY
MADE IN U.S.A.

0   50   100   150   200   250   300 Miles
0   100   200   300   400   500 Kilometers

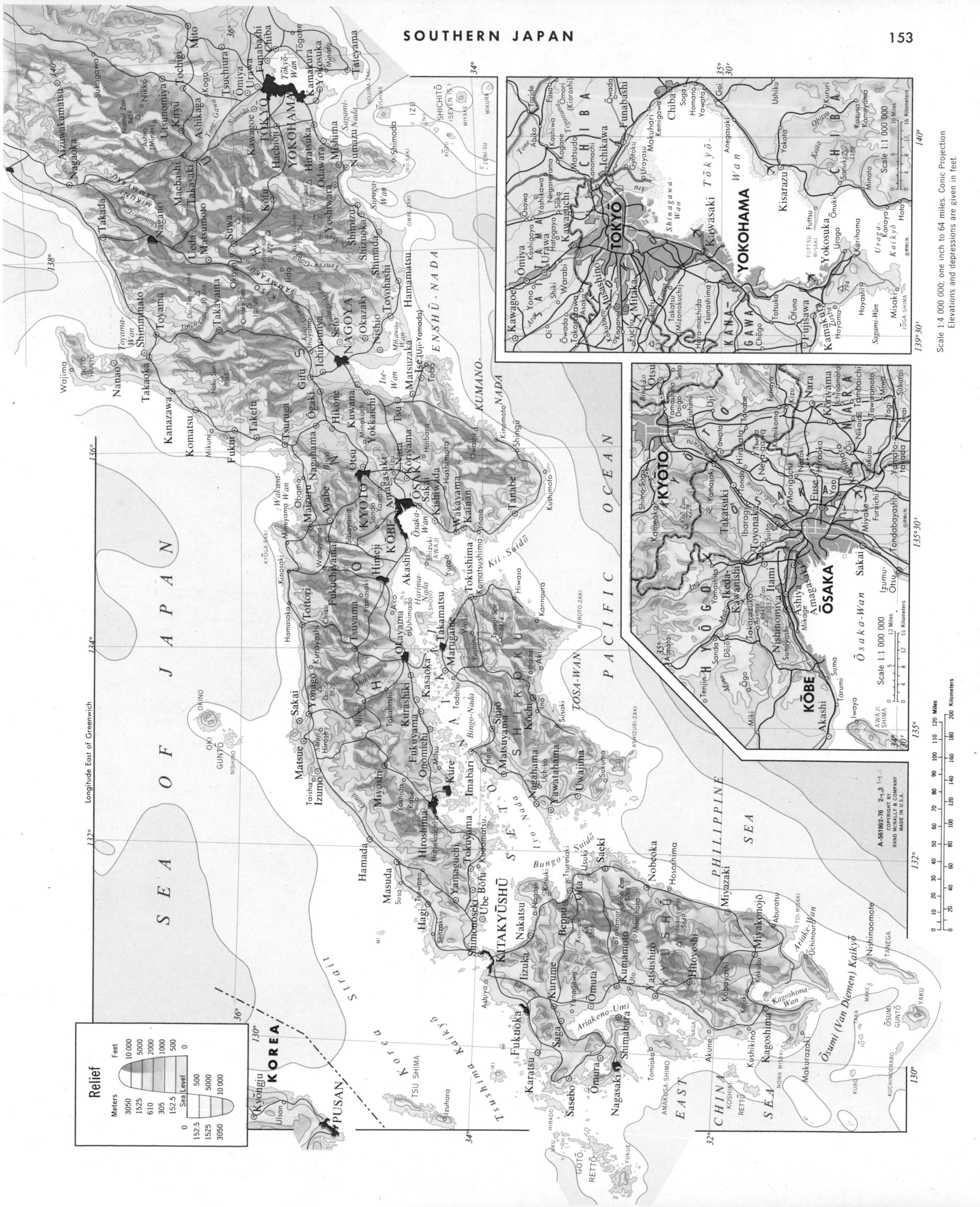

Scale 1:4 000 000; one inch to 64 miles. Conic Projection
Elevations and depressions are given in feet.

TOKYO
YOKOHAMA
Scale 1:1 000 000

KYŌTO
ŌSAKA
KŌBE
Scale 1:1 000 000

SEA OF JAPAN

PACIFIC OCEAN

PHILIPPINE SEA

EAST CHINA SEA

KOREA

PUSAN

Longitude East of Greenwich

Relief

Meters	Feet
3050	10 000
1525	5000
610	2000
305	1000
152.5	500
0	Sea Level
152.5	500
1525	5000
3050	10 000

Miles
Kilometers

A-561962-76
COPYRIGHT BY
RAND McNALLY & COMPANY
MADE IN U.S.A.

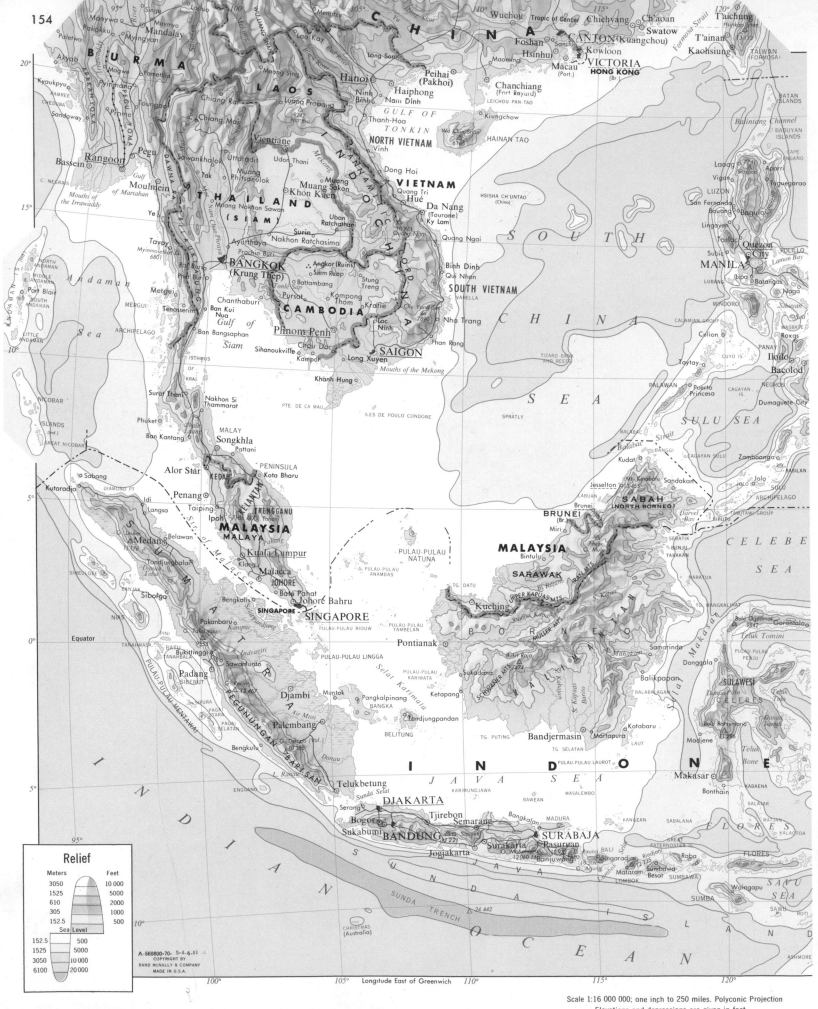

154

Scale 1:16 000 000; one inch to 250 miles. Polyconic Projection
Elevations and depressions are given in feet

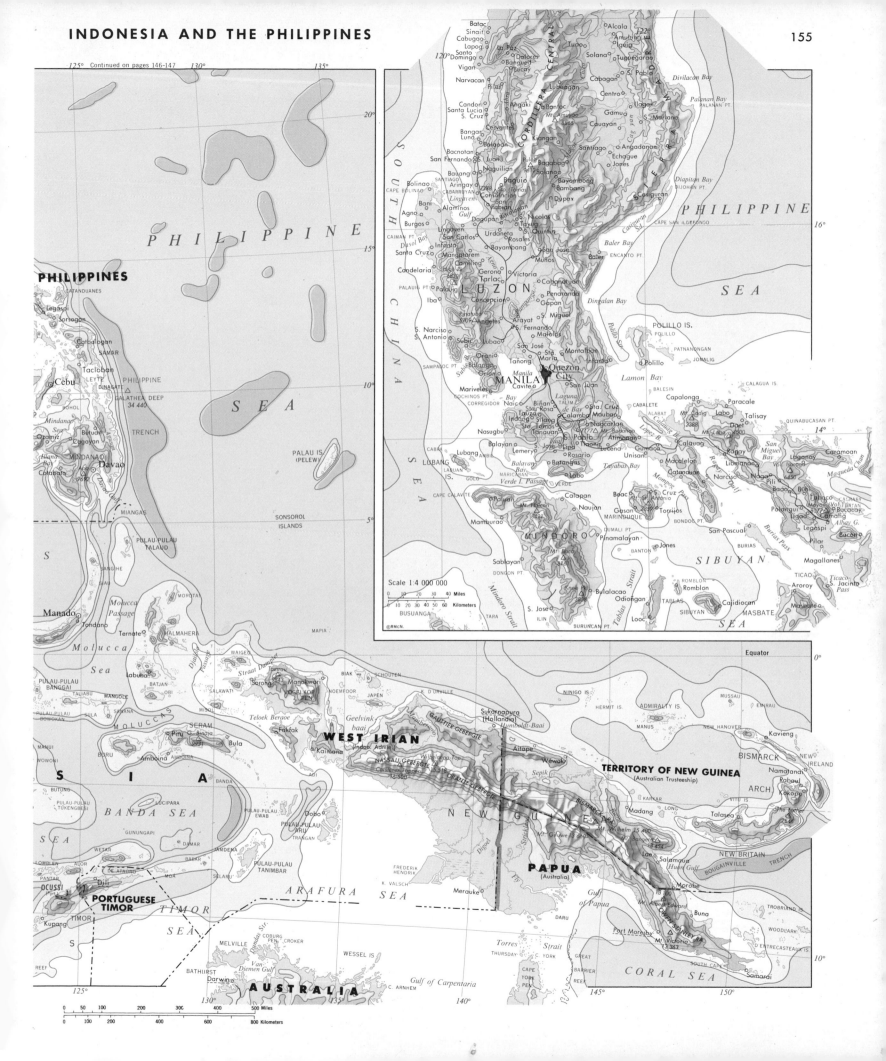

Continued on pages 146-147

PHILIPPINES

P H I L I P P I N E

S E A

PHILIPPINE SEA

CORDILLERA CENTRAL

SOUTH CHINA SEA

LUZON

MANILA
Quezon City

MINDORO

SIBUYAN SEA

MASBATE

Scale 1:4 000 000

0   10   20   30   40 Miles

0 10 20 30 40 50 60 Kilometers

©RMcN.

SAMAR

LEYTE

Cebu

Tacloban

PHILIPPINE TRENCH

GALATHEA DEEP
34 440

BOHOL

Mindanao Sea

MINDANAO

Davao

PALAU IS.
(PELEW)

SONSOROL
ISLANDS

MIANGAS

PULAU-PULAU
TALAUD

SANGIHE

Manado

Molucca
Passage

Molucca
Sea

HALMAHERA

MOROTAI

MAPIA

Equator

0°

WEST IRIAN
(Indon. Admin.)

VOGELKOP
PEN.

BIAK

SCHOUTEN

Sukarnapura
(Hollandia)

NINIGO IS.

HERMIT IS.

ADMIRALTY IS.

MUSSAU

EMIRAU

NEW HANOVER

Kavieng

BISMARCK
ARCH.

NEW
IRELAND

Namatanai

Rabaul
Kokopo

MANUS

TERRITORY OF NEW GUINEA
(Australian Trusteeship)

N E W   G U I N E A

Madang

VITU IS.

NEW BRITAIN

BISMARCK SEA

BOUGAINVILLE TRENCH

PAPUA
(Australia)

Port Moresby

OWEN STANLEY RA.

Mt. Victoria
13 363

Buna

TROBRIAND IS.

WOODLARK

D'ENTRECASTEAUX IS.

CORAL SEA

Samarai

Torres Strait

Gulf of Papua

S I A

BANDA SEA

MOLUCCAS

SERAM

BURU

Amboina

BANDA

PULAU-PULAU
TUKENGBESI

PULAU-PULAU
ARU

Dobo

ARAFURA SEA

PORTUGUESE
TIMOR

Dili

OCUSSI
(Port.)

Kupang

TIMOR

TIMOR SEA

Darwin

AUSTRALIA

Gulf of Carpentaria

WESSEL IS.

C. ARNHEM

MELVILLE

BATHURST

0   50   100   200   300   400   500 Miles

0   100   200   400   600   800 Kilometers

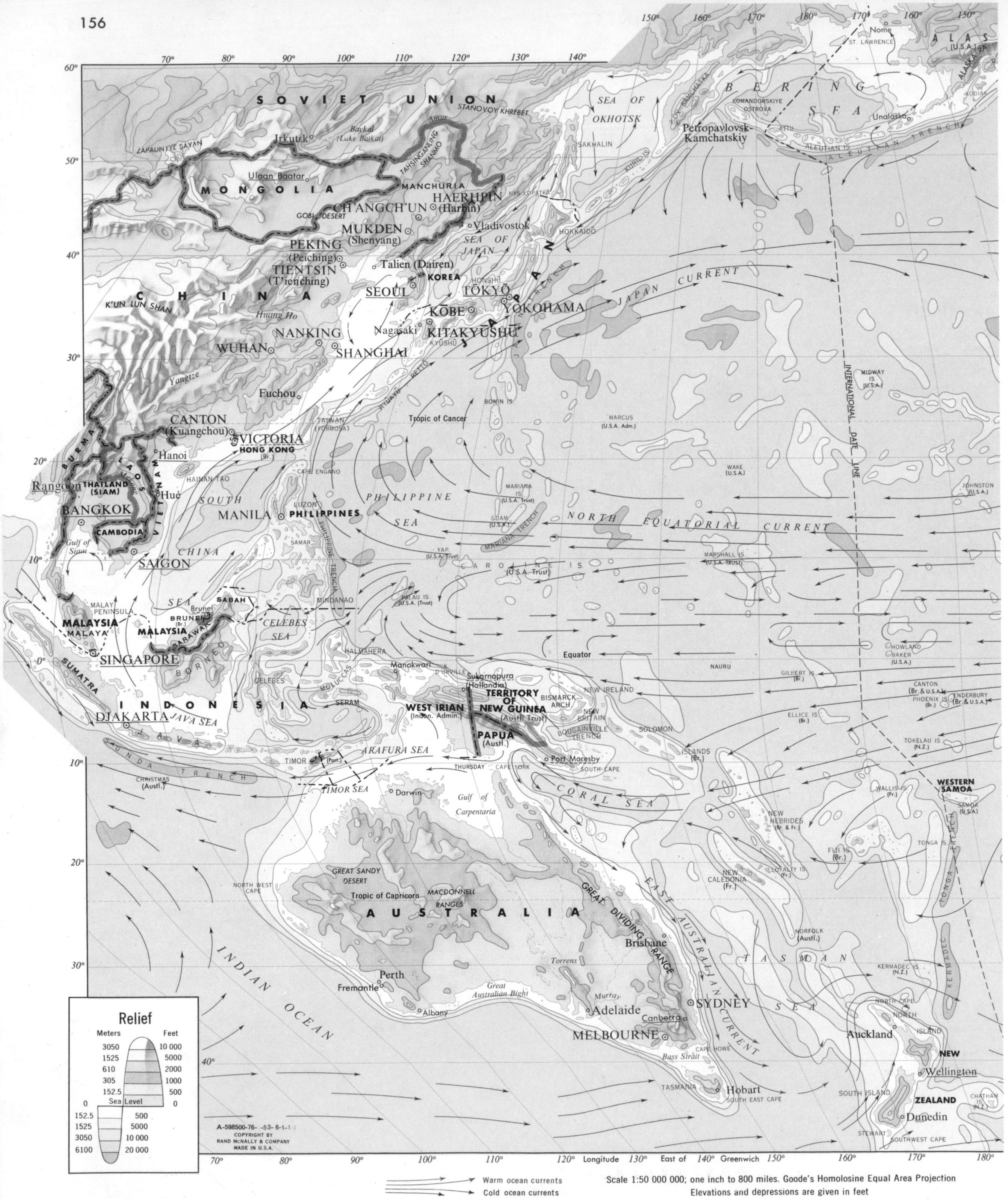

SOVIET UNION

150° 160° 170° 180° 170° 160° 150°

Nome
ST. LAWRENCE
ALASKA
U.S.A

70° 80° 90° 100° 110° 120° 130° 140°

60°

ZAPADNYYE SAYAN
Irkutsk
Baykal (Lake Baikal)
Amur
STANOVOY KHREBET
SEA OF OKHOTSK
B E R I N G   S E A
KOMANDORSKIYE OSTROVA
Petropavlovsk-Kamchatskiy
MYS LOPATKA
ATTU
Unalaska
KODIAK
ALEUTIAN TRENCH

50°

Ulaan Baatar
M O N G O L I A
TAHSINGANLING SHANNO
MANCHURIA
HAERHPIN (Harbin)
CH'ANGCH'UN
SAKHALIN
KURIL IS.

GOBI DESERT
MUKDEN (Shenyang)
Vladivostok
HOKKAIDO

PEKING (Peiching)
Talien (Dairen)
SEA OF JAPAN

40°

C H I N A
TIENTSIN (T'ienching)
KOREA
SEOUL
TOKYO
YOKOHAMA
HONSHU
J A P A N
JAPAN CURRENT

MIDWAY IS. (U.S.A.)

K'UN LUN SHAN
Huang Ho
KOBE
Nagasaki
KITAKYUSHU
KYUSHU
NANKING
WUHAN
SHANGHAI

30°

Yangtze
Fuchou
RYUKYU RETTO
BONIN IS.
MARCUS (U.S.A. Adm.)

INTERNATIONAL DATE LINE

CANTON (Kuangchou)
Tropic of Cancer
TAIWAN (FORMOSA)

WAKE (U.S.A.)

JOHNSTON (U.S.A.)

20°

VICTORIA
HONG KONG (Br.)
Hanoi
CAPE ENGANO
P H I L I P P I N E   S E A
MARIANA IS. (U.S.A. Trust)

BURMA
HAINAN TAO
Hué
LAOS
VIETNAM
SOUTH
LUZON
MANILA
PHILIPPINES
GUAM (U.S.A.)

MARSHALL IS. (U.S.A. TRUST)

Rangoon
THAILAND (SIAM)
BANGKOK
CAMBODIA
CHINA
SEA
SAMAR
MARIANA TRENCH
N O R T H   E Q U A T O R I A L   C U R R E N T

10°

Gulf of Siam
SAIGON
PHILIPPINE TRENCH
MINDANAO
YAP (U.S.A. Trust)
C A R O L I N E   I S.
(U.S.A. Trust)

MALAY PENINSULA
SABAH
CELEBES SEA
PALAU IS. (U.S.A. Trust)
MARSHALL IS.

CANTON (Br. & U.S.A.)
ENDERBURY (Br. & U.S.A.)
PHOENIX (Br.)

MALAYSIA (MALAYA)
BRUNEI (Br.)
MALAYSIA
SARAWAK
Equator
NAURU
HOWLAND BAKER (U.S.A.)
GILBERT IS. (Br.)

0°

SINGAPORE
SUMATRA
BORNEO
CELEBES
MOLUCCAS
SERAM
HALMAHERA
Manokwari
D'URVILLE
Sukarnopura (Hollandia)
TERRITORY OF NEW GUINEA (Austl. Trust)
NEW IRELAND
BISMARCK ARCH.
NEW BRITAIN
SOLOMON
ELLICE IS. (Br.)
TOKELAU IS. (N.Z.)

INDONESIA
DJAKARTA
JAVA SEA
WEST IRIAN (Indon. Admin.)
PAPUA (Austl.)
BOUGAINVILLE TRENCH
ISLANDS (Br.)

10°

JAVA
SUNDA TRENCH
TIMOR (Port.)
ARAFURA SEA
Port Moresby
THURSDAY
CAPE YORK
SOUTH CAPE
C O R A L   S E A
WALLIS IS. (Fr.)
WESTERN SAMOA
SAMOA (U.S.A.)

CHRISTMAS (Austl.)
TIMOR SEA
Darwin
Gulf of Carpentaria
NEW HEBRIDES (Br. & Fr.)
FIJI IS. (Br.)
TONGA IS.

20°

NORTH WEST CAPE
GREAT SANDY DESERT
Tropic of Capricorn
MACDONNELL RANGES
GREAT DIVIDING RANGE
NEW CALEDONIA (Fr.)
LOYALTY IS. (Fr.)

A U S T R A L I A
EAST AUSTRALIAN CURRENT
NORFOLK (Austl.)
KERMADEC IS. (N.Z.)

30°

I N D I A N   O C E A N
Brisbane
Torrens
T A S M A N   S E A

Perth
Fremantle
Murray
Adelaide
Canberra
SYDNEY
NORTH CAPE
NORTH ISLAND
Auckland

Albany
Great Australian Bight
MELBOURNE
CAPE HOWE
Bass Strait
NEW

40°

TASMANIA
Hobart
SOUTH EAST CAPE
SOUTH ISLAND
ZEALAND
Wellington
CHATHAM (N.Z.)
Dunedin
STEWART
SOUTHWEST CAPE

70° 80° 90° 100° 110° 120° 130° Longitude East of 140° Greenwich 150° 160° 170° 180°

Relief

Meters	Feet
3050	10 000
1525	5000
610	2000
305	1000
152.5	500
0 Sea Level	0
152.5	500
1525	5000
3050	10 000
6100	20 000

A-598500-76- -53-6-1-1
COPYRIGHT BY
RAND McNALLY & COMPANY
MADE IN U.S.A.

→ Warm ocean currents
→ Cold ocean currents

Scale 1:50 000 000; one inch to 800 miles. Goode's Homolosine Equal Area Projection
Elevations and depressions are given in feet

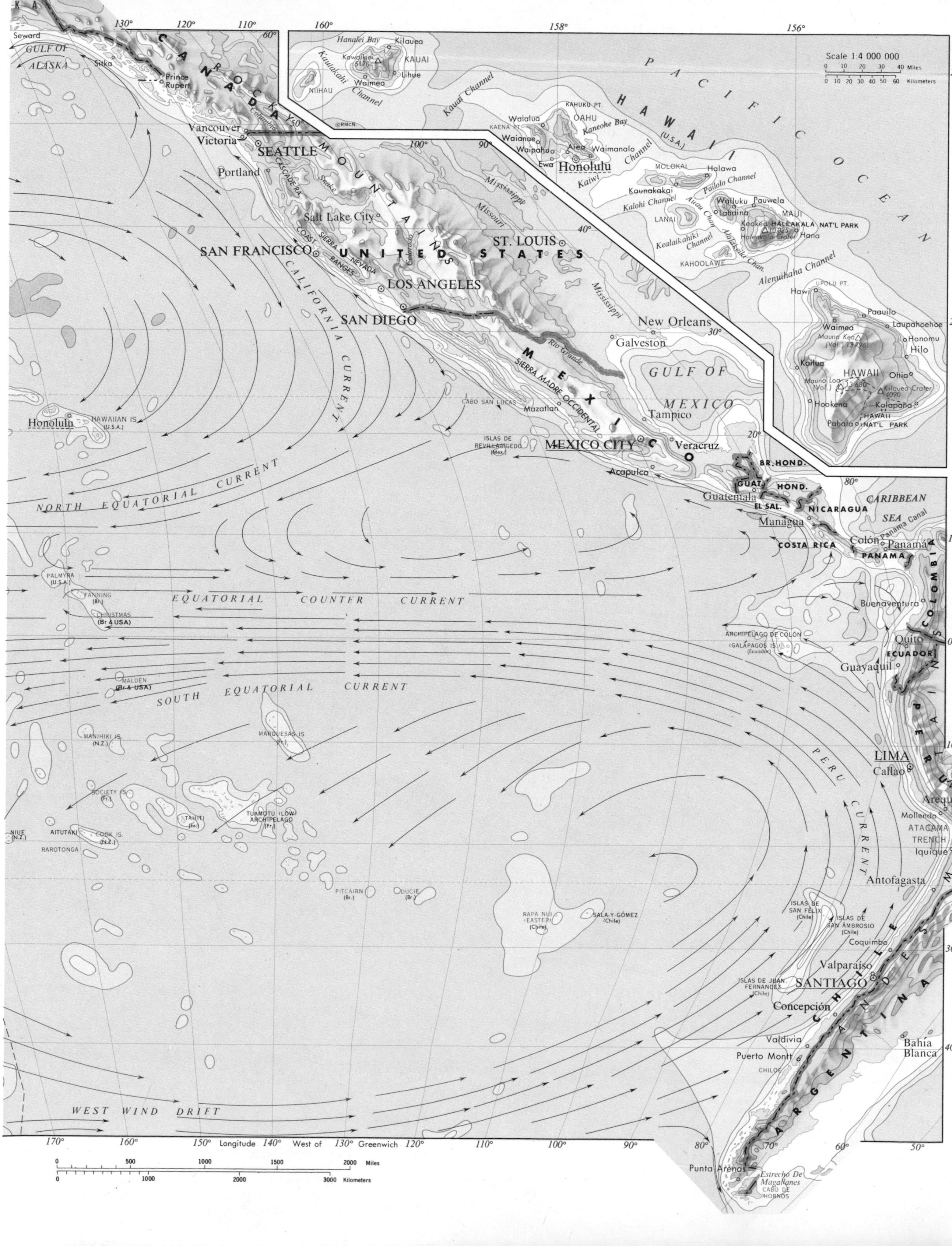

GULF OF ALASKA
Seward
Sitka
Prince Rupert
CANADA
ROCKY MOUNTAINS
Vancouver
Victoria
SEATTLE
Portland
CASCADE RA.
Salt Lake City
SAN FRANCISCO
COAST RANGES
SIERRA NEVADA
UNITED STATES
ST. LOUIS
LOS ANGELES
SAN DIEGO
Mississippi
Missouri
Colorado
Snake
Columbia
New Orleans
Galveston
Rio Grande
GULF OF MEXICO
Tampico
MEXICO
SIERRA MADRE OCCIDENTAL
Mazatlan
CABO SAN LUCAS
ISLAS DE REVILLAGIGEDO (Mex.)
MEXICO CITY
Veracruz
Acapulco
CALIFORNIA CURRENT
NORTH EQUATORIAL CURRENT
Honolulu
HAWAIIAN IS. (U.S.A.)
BR. HOND.
GUAT.
HOND.
Guatemala
EL SAL.
NICARAGUA
Managua
CARIBBEAN SEA
COSTA RICA
PANAMA
Colón
Panamá
Panama Canal
PALMYRA (U.S.A.)
FANNING (Br.)
CHRISTMAS (Br & USA)
EQUATORIAL COUNTER CURRENT
Buenaventura
COLOMBIA
ARCHIPELAGO DE COLON (GALAPAGOS IS.) (Ecuador)
Quito
ECUADOR
Guayaquil
MALDEN (Br & USA)
SOUTH EQUATORIAL CURRENT
MANIHIKI IS. (N.Z.)
MARQUESAS IS. (Fr.)
PERU
LIMA
Callao
PERU CURRENT
Arequipa
Mollendo
ATACAMA TRENCH
Iquique
Antofagasta
SOCIETY IS. (Fr.)
TAHITI (Fr.)
TUAMOTU (LOW) ARCHIPELAGO (Fr.)
NIUE (N.Z.)
AITUTAKI
COOK IS. (N.Z.)
RAROTONGA
PITCAIRN (Br.)
DUCIE (Br.)
RAPA NUI (EASTER) (Chile)
SALA-Y-GOMEZ (Chile)
ISLAS DE SAN FELIX (Chile)
ISLAS DE SAN AMBROSIO (Chile)
Coquimbo
Valparaíso
SANTIAGO
ISLAS DE JUAN FERNANDEZ (Chile)
Concepción
CHILE
ANDES MOUNTAINS
ARGENTINA
Valdivia
Puerto Montt
CHILOE
Bahía Blanca
WEST WIND DRIFT
Punta Arenas
Estrecho De Magallanes
CABO DE HORNOS
170° 160° 150° Longitude 140° West of 130° Greenwich 120° 110° 100° 90° 80° 70° 60° 50°
10° 0° 10° 20° 30° 40°
0 500 1000 1500 2000 Miles
0 1000 2000 3000 Kilometers
Hanalei Bay
Kilauea
Kawaikini 5170
KAUAI
Lihue
Waimea
NIIHAU
Kaulakahi Channel
Kauai Channel
PACIFIC OCEAN
HAWAII (U.S.A.)
Scale 1:4 000 000
0 10 20 30 40 Miles
0 10 20 30 40 50 60 Kilometers
KAHUKU PT.
Waialua
OAHU
KAENA PT.
Kaneohe Bay
Waianae
Waipahu
Aiea
Waimanalo
Ewa
Honolulu
Kaiwi Channel
MOLOKAI
Halawa
Kaunakakai
Pailolo Channel
Kalohi Channel
LANAI
Auau Chan.
Wailuku
Pauwela
Lahaina
MAUI
Keokea
HALEAKALA NAT'L PARK
Haleakala Crater 10025
Hana
Kealaikahiki Channel
Alalakeiki Chan.
KAHOOLAWE
Alenuihaha Channel
UPOLU PT.
Hawi
Paauilo
Waimea
Laupahoehoe
Mauna Kea (Vol.) 13796
Honomu
Hilo
Kailua
HAWAII
Mauna Loa (Vol.) 13680
Ohia
Kilauea Crater 4090
Hookena
Kalapana
Pahala
HAWAII NAT'L PARK
160° 158° 156° 22° 20°
©RMcN.

Continued on pages 154-155

Relief

Meters		Feet
3050		10 000
1525		5000
610		2000
305		1000
152.5		500
0	Sea Level	0
		Below
152.5		500	Sea Level
1525		5000
3050		10 000
6100		20 000

A-590200-76-   2-24-1-42
COPYRIGHT BY
RAND McNALLY & COMPANY
MADE IN U.S.A.

Longitude   115°   East of Greenwich   120°

Scale 1:16 000 000; one inch to 250 miles. Lambert's Azimuthal, Equal Area Projection
Elevations and depressions are given in feet

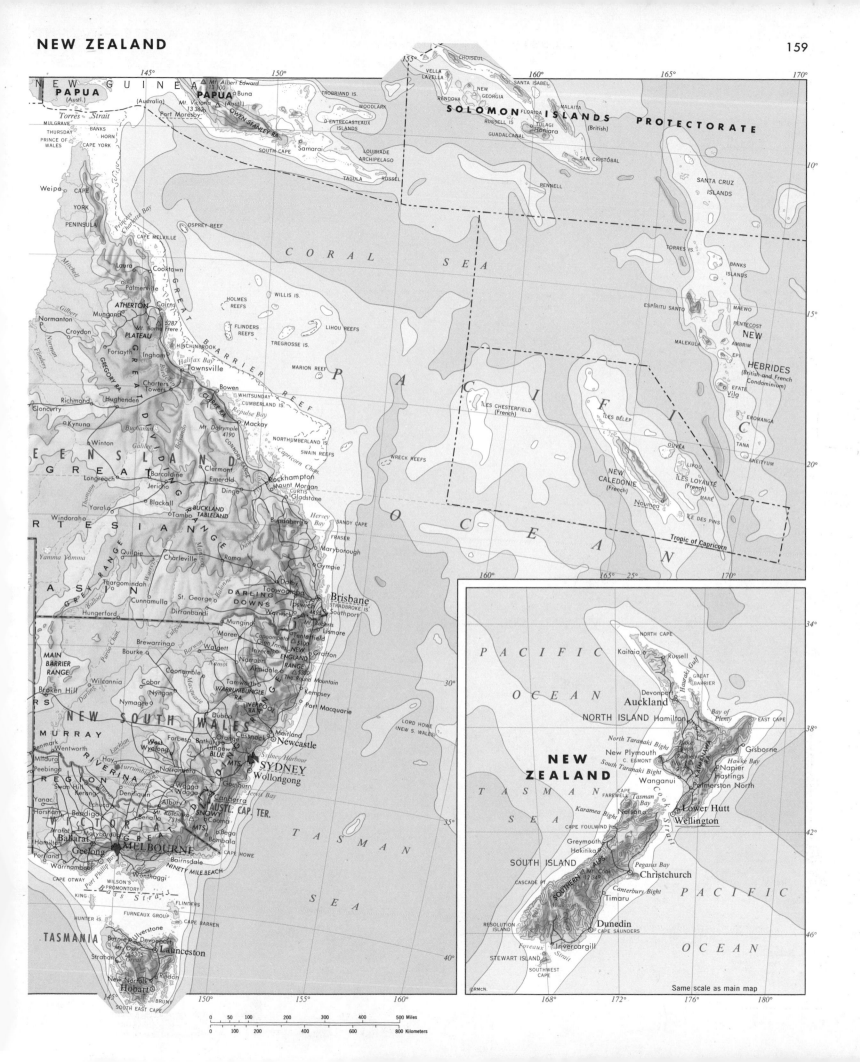

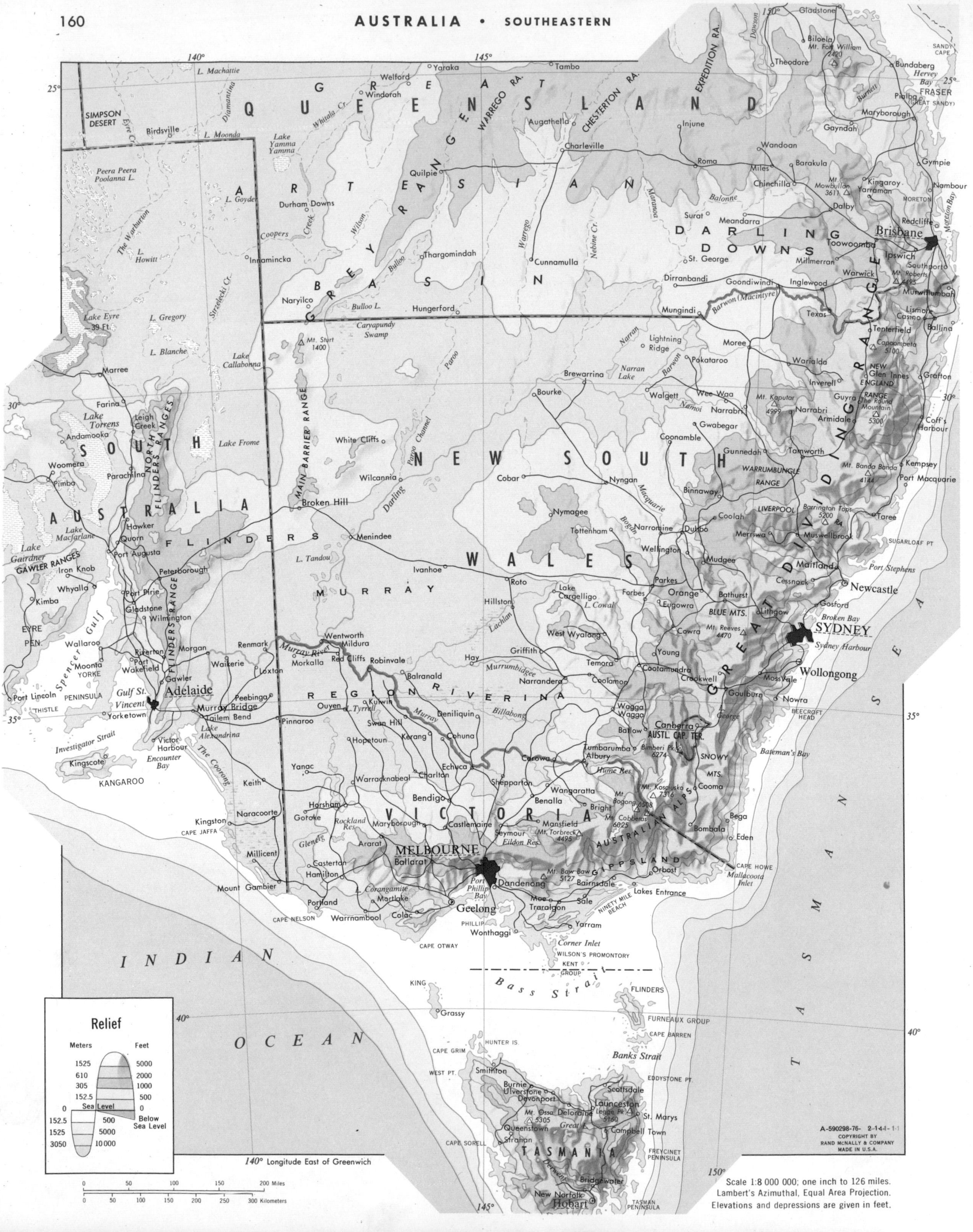

Relief

Meters	Feet
1525	5000
610	2000
305	1000
152.5	500
0 Sea Level	Sea Level 0
152.5	500
1525	5000
3050	10 000

Below Sea Level

0   50   100   150   200 Miles
0   50   100   150   200   250   300 Kilometers

140° Longitude East of Greenwich

Scale 1:8 000 000; one inch to 126 miles.
Lambert's Azimuthal, Equal Area Projection.
Elevations and depressions are given in feet.

A-590298-76- 2-14-1-1
COPYRIGHT BY
RAND McNALLY & COMPANY
MADE IN U.S.A.

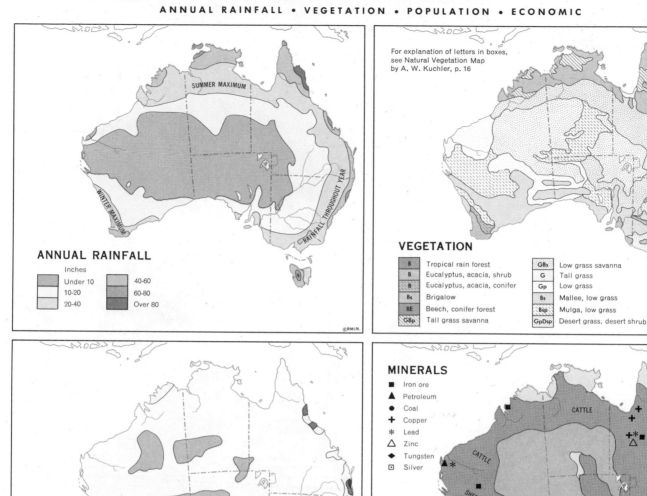

ANNUAL RAINFALL

SUMMER MAXIMUM

WINTER MAXIMUM

RAINFALL THROUGHOUT YEAR

Inches

- Under 10
- 10-20
- 20-40
- 40-60
- 60-80
- Over 80

VEGETATION

For explanation of letters in boxes,
see Natural Vegetation Map
by A. W. Kuchler, p. 16

B	Tropical rain forest	GBs	Low grass savanna
B	Eucalyptus, acacia, shrub	G	Tall grass
B	Eucalyptus, acacia, conifer	Gp	Low grass
Bs	Brigalow	Bs	Mallee, low grass
BE	Beech, conifer forest	Bsp	Mulga, low grass
GBp	Tall grass savanna	GpDsp	Desert grass, desert shrub

©RMcN.

POPULATION

Inhabitants Per Sq. Mile

- Uninhabited
- Under 2
- 2-25
- 25-60
- 60-125

□ Metropolitan areas over 2,000,000 Population

○ Metropolitan areas 1,000,000 to 2,000,000 Population

Sydney

Melbourne

A-590200-16- 1- -0-1- -2   ©RMcN.

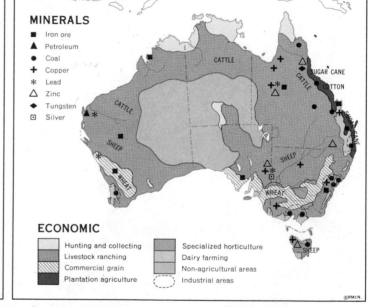

MINERALS

- ■ Iron ore
- ▲ Petroleum
- ● Coal
- + Copper
- ✳ Lead
- △ Zinc
- ◆ Tungsten
- ⊡ Silver

CATTLE

CATTLE

CATTLE

SUGAR CANE

COTTON

SUGAR CANE

SHEEP

SHEEP

WHEAT

WHEAT

SHEEP

ECONOMIC

- Hunting and collecting
- Livestock ranching
- Commercial grain
- Plantation agriculture
- Specialized horticulture
- Dairy farming
- Non-agricultural areas
- Industrial areas

©RMcN.

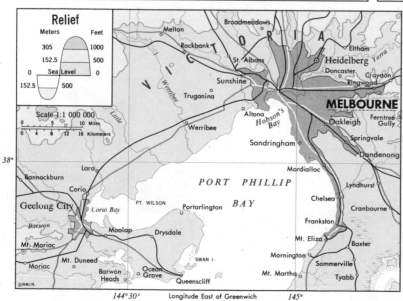

Relief

Meters		Feet
305		1000
152.5		500
0	Sea Level	0
152.5		500

Scale 1:1 000 000

0 5 10 Miles

0 4 8 12 16 Kilometers

VICTORIA

Broadmeadows

Melton

Rockbank

St. Albans

Heidelberg

Eltham

Yarra

Doncaster

Sunshine

Ringwood

Croydon

Truganina

Ferntree Gully

MELBOURNE

Altona

Hobson's Bay

Oakleigh

Springvale

Werribee

Sandringham

Dandenong

Lara

Mordialloc

Bannockburn

Corio

Chelsea

Geelong City

Corio Bay

PT. WILSON

Portarlington

Cranbourne

Barwon

PORT PHILLIP BAY

Frankston

Mt. Moriac

Moolap

Drysdale

Mt. Eliza

Moriac

Mt. Duneed

SWAN I.

Mornington

Baxter

Barwon Heads

Ocean Grove

Sommerville

Queenscliff

Mt. Martha

Tyabb

©RMcN.

38°

144°30'   Longitude East of Greenwich   145°

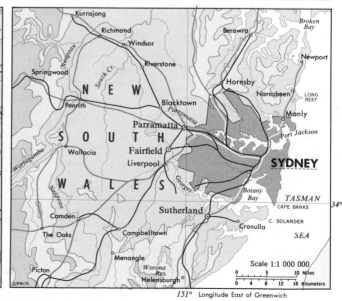

Kurrajong

Richmond

Broken Bay

Windsor

Berowra

Springwood

Riverstone

Newport

Nepean

South Cr.

NEW

Penrith

Blacktown

Hornsby

Narrabeen

LONG REEF

Parramatta

Parramatta

Manly

SOUTH

Fairfield

Port Jackson

Wallacia

Liverpool

SYDNEY

Warragamba

Georges

WALES

Botany Bay

TASMAN

Camden

Sutherland

CAPE BANKS

The Oaks

Campbelltown

Cronulla

C. SOLANDER

34°

Menangle

Worona Res.

SEA

Picton

Helensburgh

Scale 1:1 000 000

0 5 10 Miles

0 4 8 12 16 Kilometers

©RMcN.

151°   Longitude East of Greenwich

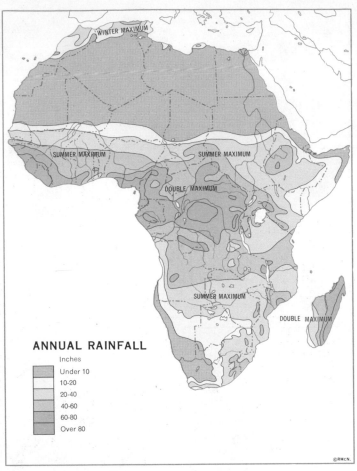

ANNUAL RAINFALL

Inches

- Under 10
- 10-20
- 20-40
- 40-60
- 60-80
- Over 80

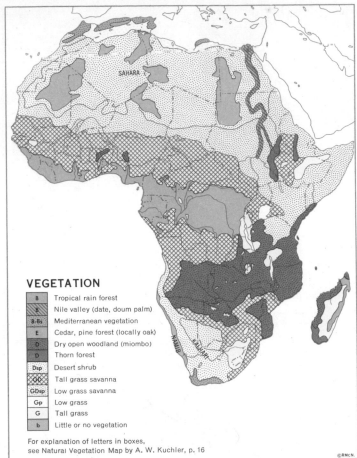

VEGETATION

B	Tropical rain forest
B	Nile valley (date, doum palm)
B-Bs	Mediterranean vegetation
E	Cedar, pine forest (locally oak)
D	Dry open woodland (miombo)
D	Thorn forest
Dsp	Desert shrub
	Tall grass savanna
GDsp	Low grass savanna
Gp	Low grass
G	Tall grass
b	Little or no vegetation

For explanation of letters in boxes,
see Natural Vegetation Map by A. W. Kuchler, p. 16

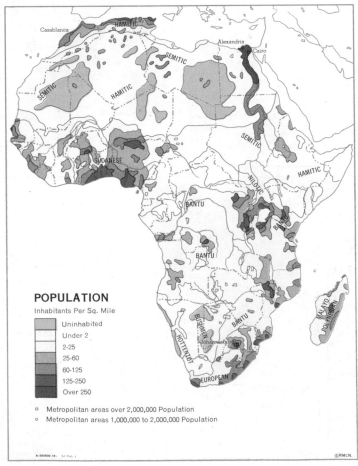

POPULATION

Inhabitants Per Sq. Mile

- Uninhabited
- Under 2
- 2-25
- 25-60
- 60-125
- 125-250
- Over 250

○ Metropolitan areas over 2,000,000 Population
○ Metropolitan areas 1,000,000 to 2,000,000 Population

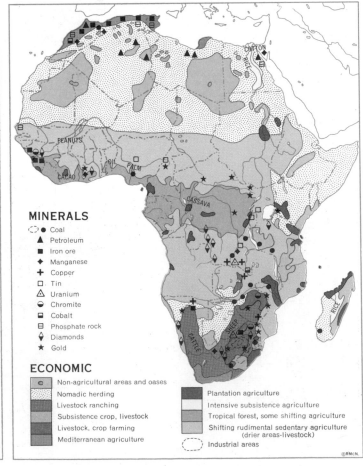

MINERALS

- ⬤ Coal
- ▲ Petroleum
- ■ Iron ore
- ◆ Manganese
- ✚ Copper
- ☐ Tin
- △ Uranium
- ◖ Chromite
- ▭ Cobalt
- ⊟ Phosphate rock
- ◈ Diamonds
- ★ Gold

ECONOMIC

- Non-agricultural areas and oases
- Nomadic herding
- Livestock ranching
- Subsistence crop, livestock
- Livestock, crop farming
- Mediterranean agriculture
- Plantation agriculture
- Intensive subsistence agriculture
- Tropical forest, some shifting agriculture
- Shifting rudimental sedentary agriculture (drier areas-livestock)
- Industrial areas

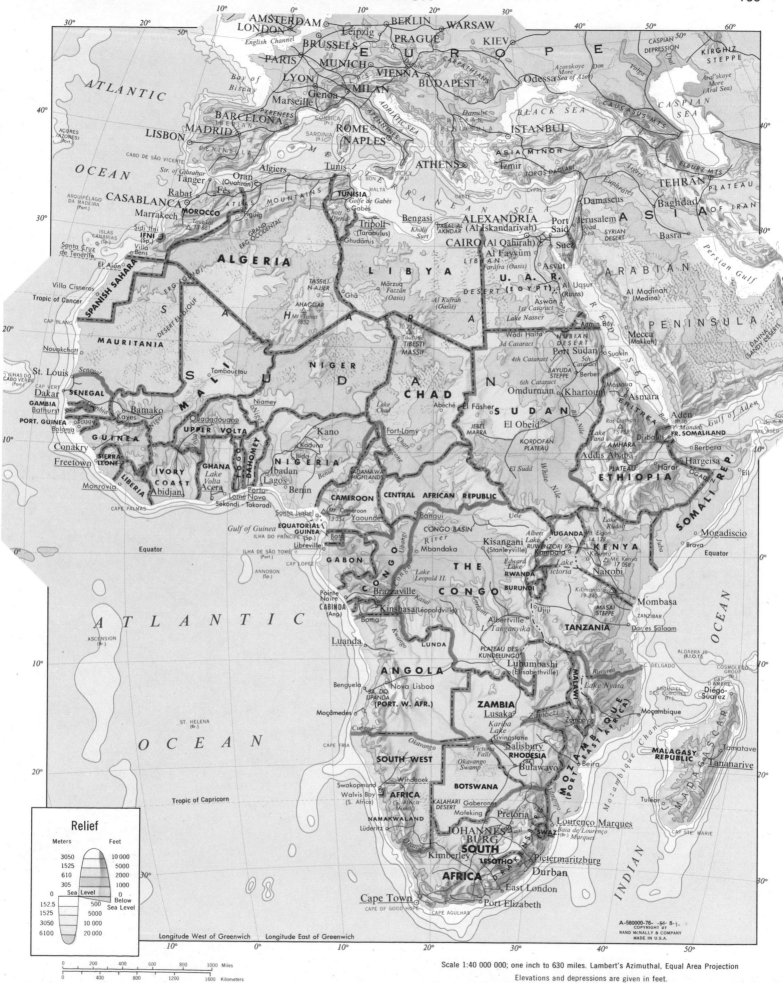

A-580000-76- -54- 8-1
COPYRIGHT BY
RAND McNALLY & COMPANY
MADE IN U.S.A.

Scale 1:40 000 000; one inch to 630 miles. Lambert's Azimuthal, Equal Area Projection
Elevations and depressions are given in feet.

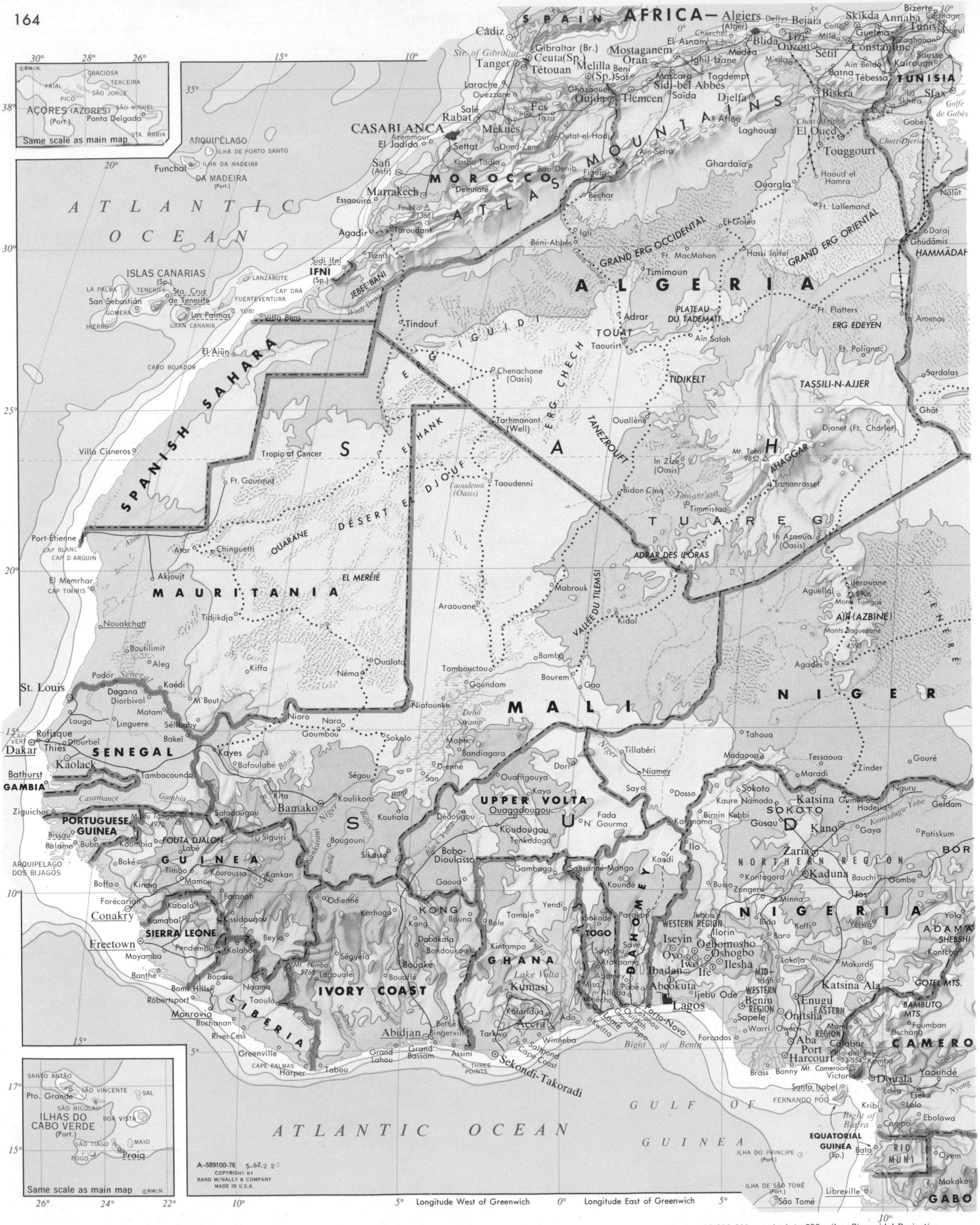

AFRICA—

Oceans and Seas
ATLANTIC OCEAN

ATLANTIC OCEAN

GULF OF GUINEA

Sir. of Gibraltar
Golfe de Gabès
Bight of Benin
Bight of Biafra

Countries and Regions
SPAIN
MOROCCO
ALGERIA
TUNISIA
SPANISH SAHARA
MAURITANIA
MALI
NIGER
SENEGAL
GAMBIA
PORTUGUESE GUINEA
GUINEA
SIERRA LEONE
LIBERIA
IVORY COAST
GHANA
UPPER VOLTA
TOGO
DAHOMEY
NIGERIA
CAMEROON
EQUATORIAL GUINEA
RIO MUNI
GABON
IFNI (Sp.)

SAHARA

ATLAS MOUNTAINS
AHAGGAR
TUAREG
HAGGAR

GRAND ERG OCCIDENTAL
GRAND ERG ORIENTAL
ERG CHECH
ERG IGUIDI
ERG EDEYEN
HAMMADAH
TANEZROUFT
TIDIKELT
TOUAT
PLATEAU DU TADEMAIT
TASSILI-N-AJJER
EL HANK
EL DJOUF
DÉSERT EL DJOUF
OUARANE
EL MERÉIÉ
ADRAR DES IFÓRAS
VALLÉE DU TILEMSI
AÏR (AZBINE)
TÉNÉRÉ
NORTHERN REGION
WESTERN REGION
EASTERN REGION
MID-WESTERN REGION
FOUTA DJALON
KONG
ADAMAWA
SHEBSHI
GOTEL MTS.
BAMBUTO MTS.

Inset Maps
AÇORES (AZORES) (Port.)
FAIAL PICO GRACIOSA TERCEIRA SÃO JORGE
SÃO MIGUEL STA. MARIA
Ponta Delgada
Same scale as main map

ILHAS DO CABO VERDE (Port.)
SANTO ANTÃO SÃO VICENTE SAL
Pto. Grande SÃO NICOLAU
BOA VISTA MAIO SÃO TIAGO FOGO
Praia
Same scale as main map

Cities and Towns
Cádiz Ceuta (Sp.) Tanger Tétouan Melilla (Sp.)
Larache Ouezzane Fès Taza Meknès Rabat Salé
CASABLANCA El Jadida Settat Oued-Zem Kasba Tadla
Safi (Asfi) Marrakech Demnate Essaouira Agadir
Taroudant Tiznit Sidi Ifni IFNI (Sp.)
Algiers (Alger) Dellys Bejaia Collo Skikda Annaba
Bizerte Tunis Blida Tizi Mila Guelma Constantine
Médéa M'sila Sétif Aïn Beïda Souk Ahras Sousse
Oran Mostaganem Mascara Saïda Tlemcen Sidi-bel-Abbès
Tagdempt Laghouat Djelfa Aflou Biskra El Oued Sfax
Ghardaïa Ouargla Touggourt Gabès Nalut Ghudâmis
Béchar Figuig Igli Béni-Abbès Ft. MacMahon Timimoun
Adrar Taourirt Aïn Salah Ft. Flatters In Aménas
Chenachane Ouallène In Ziza (Oasis) Bidon Cinq
Mt. Tahat Tamanrasset Djanet (Ft. Charlet) Ghât
Tindouf Villa Bens El Aiūn Cabo Bojador Villa Cisneros
Tarhmanant (Well) Taoudenni (Oasis) Taoudenni
Port-Étienne Cap Blanc Cap d'Arguin Atar Chinguetti
El Memrhar Cap Timiris Akjoujt Nouakchott Boutilimit
Tidjikdja Kiffa Néma Oualâta Araouane Mabrouk
Tombouctou Gao Bamba Bourem Gourma
Aguellal Iférouane Monts Bagzane Agadès
St. Louis Dagana Diorbivol Podor Kaédi Matam
Louga Linguère Sélibaby M'Bout Nara Nioro
Goumbou Sokolo Niafunké Débo Swamp Dakar Thiès
Diourbel Kaolack Tambacounda Kayes Bafoulabé
Ségou Djenné San Mopti Bandiagara Tillabéri
Tahoua Madaoua Tessaoua Maradi Zinder Gouré Nguru
Bathurst Ziguinchor Bissau Bolama Buba Koumbia Boké
Labé Timbo Siguiri Kita Bamako Koulikoro Koutiala
Dédougou Ouagadougou Koudougou Tenkodogo Kaya Dori
Say Niamey Dosso Birnin Kebbi Kaura Namoda Sokoto
Katsina Gumel Hadeija Kano Gaya Potiskum Gusau Zaria
Kaduna Bauchi Gombe Boffa Kindia Conakry Forécariah
Kamabaï Kissidougou Kankan Kouroussa Mamou Faranah
Freetown Moyamba Banthe Bopara Bomi Hills Ngama
Robertsport Monrovia Buchanan River Cess Greenville
Harper Cape Palmas Pendembu Kolahun Kabala Beyla
Odienné Korhogo Bouna Bole Tamale Yendi Ferkessédougou
Bobo-Dioulasso Sikasso Bougouni Séguéla Bouaké
Dabakala Bondoukou Kintampo Kumasi Bouaflé Lagoualé
Mt. Nimba Taoulo Gagnoa Abidjan Grand Lahou Grand Bassam
Assini Tabou Sekondi-Takoradi Accra Winneba Cape Coast
Tarkwa Keta Lomé Porto-Novo Cotonou Lagos Abeokuta
Ibadan Ife Oyo Oshogbo Ilesha Ogbomosho Iseyin Ilorin
Jebba Bida Baro Lokoja Makurdi Ibi Yola Garoua
Enugu Onitsha Aba Calabar Warri Sapele Benin Ado
Ijebu Ode Bonny Brass Port Harcourt Fernando Póo
Santa Isabel Rio del Rey Mt. Cameroon Victoria Douala
Kribi Ebolowa Edéa Yaoundé Libreville São Tomé
ILHA DO PRÍNCIPE (Port.) ILHA DE SÃO TOMÉ (Port.)
Bata Oyem Makokou Kumba Fumban Dschang

Tropic of Cancer

Longitude West of Greenwich Longitude East of Greenwich

Scale 1:16 000 000; one inch to 250 miles. Sinusoidal Projection
Elevations and depressions are given in feet

A-589100-76 5-67-2
COPYRIGHT BY
RAND McNALLY & COMPANY
MADE IN U.S.A.

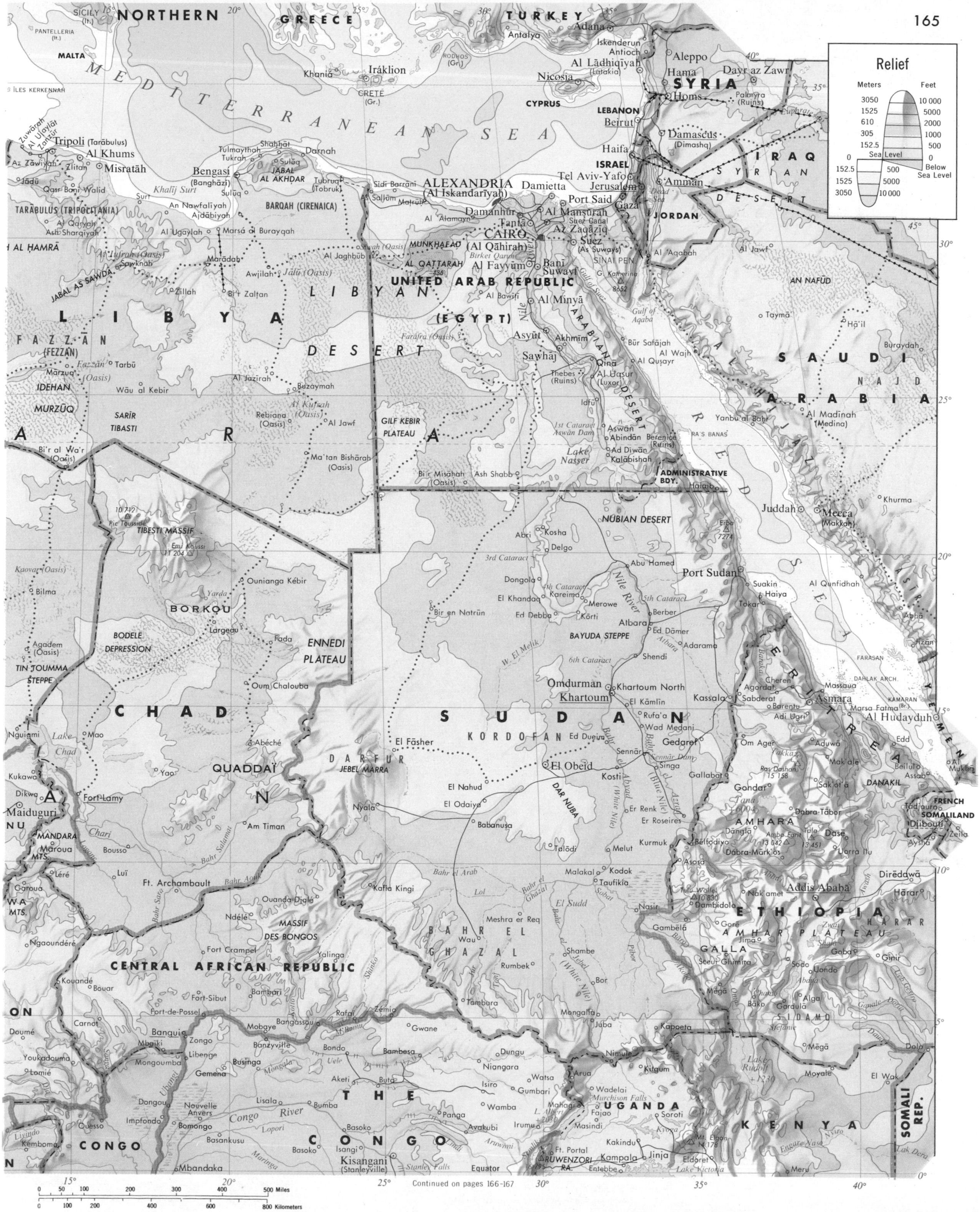

SICILY (It.)
NORTHERN
GREECE
TURKEY
Antalya
Adana
Iskenderun
Antioch
Aleppo
Dayr az Zawr
PANTELLERIA (It.)
MALTA
ÎLES KERKENNAH
Khaniá
Iráklion
CRETÉ (Gr.)
RODHOS (Gr.)
Nicosia
CYPRUS
Al Lādhiqīyah (Latakia)
Hama
Homs
SYRIA
Palmyra (Ruins)
Euphrates
IRAQ
SYRIAN
DESERT

Relief
Meters   Feet
3050   10 000
1525   5000
610   2000
305   1000
152.5   500
0   Sea Level   0
152.5   500
1525   5000
3050   10 000   Below Sea Level

MEDITERRANEAN SEA
Zuwārah
Al Ujaylāt
Tripoli (Tarābulus)
Al Khums
Az Zāwiyah
Zlitan
Misrātah
Jādū
Qasr Bani Walid
TARĀBULUS (TRIPOLITANIA)
Al Qaryah
Ash Shaqīqah
Shahhāt
Tūlmaythoh
Sulūq
Darnah
Bengasi (Banghāzī)
JABAL AL AKHDAR
Tukrah
Tubruq (Tobruk)
BARQAH (CIRENAICA)
Ajdābiyah
An Nawfalīyah
Sūrt
Khalīj Surt
LEBANON
Beirut
Haifa
Tel Aviv-Yafo
ISRAEL
Jerusalem
Damascus (Dimashq)
Amman
JORDAN
Al 'Aqabah
Al Jawf
AN NAFŪD
Taymā'
Hā'il
Buraydah

Sīdī Barrānī
As Sallūm
Maţrūh
ALEXANDRIA (Al Iskandarīyah)
Damietta
Damanhūr
Ţanţā
Al Mansūrah
Az Zaqāzīq
Port Said
Suez Canal
Suez (As Suways)
SINAI PEN
St. Katherine 8652
Gulf of Aqaba
RAS
SAUDI ARABIA
NAJD
Al Madīnah (Medina)

H AL HAMRĀ
JABAL AS SAWDĀ
LIBYA
FAZZĀN (FEZZAN)
Fazzān (Oasis)
Tarbū
Mārzuq
IDEHAN MURZŪQ
Al 'Ugaylah
Marsá al Burayqah
Marādah
Sawknah
Zillah
Bi'r Zaltan
Al Jaghbūb
Awjilah
Jālū (Oasis)
LIBYAN DESERT
Sīwah (Oasis)
MUNKHAFAD
AL QATTARAH
Birket Qarūn
Al Fayyūm
CAIRO (Al Qāhirah)
Banī Suwayf
UNITED ARAB REPUBLIC
(EGYPT)
Al Bawīţī
Al Minyā
Asyūţ
Akhmīm
Sawhāj
Qinā
Thebes (Ruins)
Al Uqsur (Luxor)
Idfū
Aswān
Aswān Dam
Lake Nasser
ARABIAN DESERT
Būr Safājah
Al Wajh
Al Qusayr
Yanbu' al Bahr
Abindān
Berenice (Ruins)
RA'S BANAS
Ad Diwān
Kalābishah
Juddah
Mecca (Makkah)
Khurma

SAHARA
Bi'r al Wa'r (Oasis)
Al Jazirah
Buzaymah
Al Kufrah (Oasis)
Al Jawf
GILF KEBIR PLATEAU
Rebiana (Oasis)
Ma'tan Bishārah (Oasis)
1st Cataract
Bi'r Misāhah (Oasis)
Ash Shabb
ADMINISTRATIVE BDY.
Halaib
NUBIAN DESERT
Jebel Erba 7274
Al Qunfidhah

Pic Toussidé 10 712
TIBESTI MASSIF
Emi Koussi 11 204
SARĪR TIBASTI
Abri
Kosha
Delgo
Dongola
El Khandaq
Kareima
Merowe
Abu Hamed
Port Sudan
Suakin
Haiya
Tokar
3rd Cataract
4th Cataract
Nile River
5th Cataract
Berber
Ed Dāmer
Adarama
FARASAN

Kaovar (Oasis)
Bilma
Yarda
Ounianga Kébir
BORKOU
BODELE DEPRESSION
Largeau
Fada
ENNEDI PLATEAU
Oum Chalouba
Bir en Natrūn
W. El Melik
BAYUDA STEPPE
6th Cataract
Shendi
Atbara
Omdurman
Khartoum North
Khartoum
El Kāmlīn
Kassala
Cheren
Agordat
Sabderat
Adi Ugri
Asmara
DAHLAK ARCH.
Massaua
KAMARAN
YEMEN
Al Hudaydah

TIN TOUMMA STEPPE
Agadem (Oasis)
Nguigmi
Lake Chad
Mao
CHAD
Abéché
QUADDAÏ
DARFUR
Jebel Marra
JEBEL MARRA
El Fāsher
Kordofan
Ed Dueim
El Obeid
Rufa'a
Wad Medani
Gedaref
Om Ager
Aduwā
Mak'ale
DANAKIL
FRENCH SOMALILAND
Djibouti
Zeila
Aysha

Kukawa
Dikwa
Maiduguri
MANDARA MTS.
Maroua
Bousso
Léré
Luï
Fort-Lamy
Yao
Am Timan
Nyala
El Nahud
El Odaiya
Babanusa
DAR NUBA
Talōdi
Melut
Kurmuk
Er Roseires
Asosa
AMHARA
Dāngla
Ambo Fenti 13 042
Dabra-Tābor
Dase
Tana
Lake Tana
Gandar
Ras Dashan 15 158
Gallabat
Singa
Sennār
Sennar Dam
Er Renk
Kosti
DAR NUBA

Garoua
WA MTS.
Ngaoundéré
Ft. Archambault
Bahr Aouk
Ndélé
MASSIF DES BONGOS
Kafia Kingi
Lol
Bahr el Arab
Wau
BAHR EL GHAZAL
Meshra er Req
El Sudd
Malakal
Kodok
Taufikia
Nasir
Sobat
Gambéla
Tulu Wallel 10 830
Nak'amet
ETHIOPIA
AMHAR PLATEAU
Dire Dawa
Harar
HARAR
Dābra-Mārk'os
Qora

CENTRAL AFRICAN REPUBLIC
Carnot
Bouar
Fort-Sibut
Bambari
Bangassou
Rafaï
Zémio
Gwane
Tambura
Mongalla
Juba
Kapoeta
Rumbek
Bor
Shambe
Pibor
GALLA
GINIR
SIDAMO
Sodo
Uondo
Abaya
Mēga

Doumé
Kouandé
Banqui
Zongo
Mbaïki
Libenge
Mobaye
Banzyville
Bondo
Bambesa
Dungu
Niangara
Watsa
Arua
Wadelai
Kitgum
Moyale
El Wak

Youkadouma
Lomié
Quesso
Impfondo
Nouvelle Anvers
Lisala
Bumba
Aketi
Buta
Isiro
Gumbari
Wamba
Fajao
Murchison Falls
Lake Albert
Panga
Niangara
Soroti
Lake Rudolf
Mt. Elgon 14 178

CONGO
Bomongo
Basoko
Isangi
Stanley Falls
Kisangani (Stanleyville)
THE CONGO
Basankusu
Mbandaka
Lopori
Maringa
Aruwimi
Irumu
Ft. Portal
RUWENZORI RA.
Kakindu
Entebbe
Kampala
Jinja
Lake Victoria
Eldoret
Meru
UGANDA
Nimule
Equator
KENYA
SOMALI REP.

Continued on pages 166-167

0 50 100 200 300 400 500 Miles
0 100 200 400 600 800 Kilometers

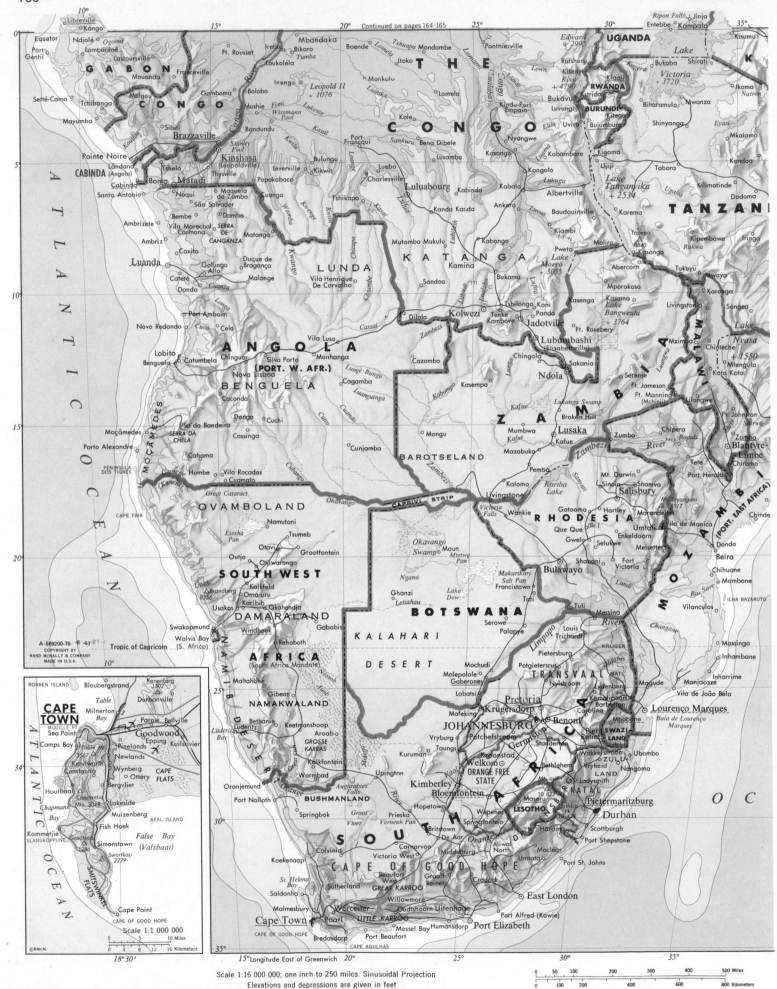

Continued on pages 164·165

Scale 1:16 000 000; one inch to 250 miles. Sinusoidal Projection
Elevations and depressions are given in feet

CAPE TOWN

Scale 1:1 000 000

CAPE OF GOOD HOPE

A-589200-76 -6 47-21
COPYRIGHT BY
RAND McNALLY & COMPANY
MADE IN U.S.A.

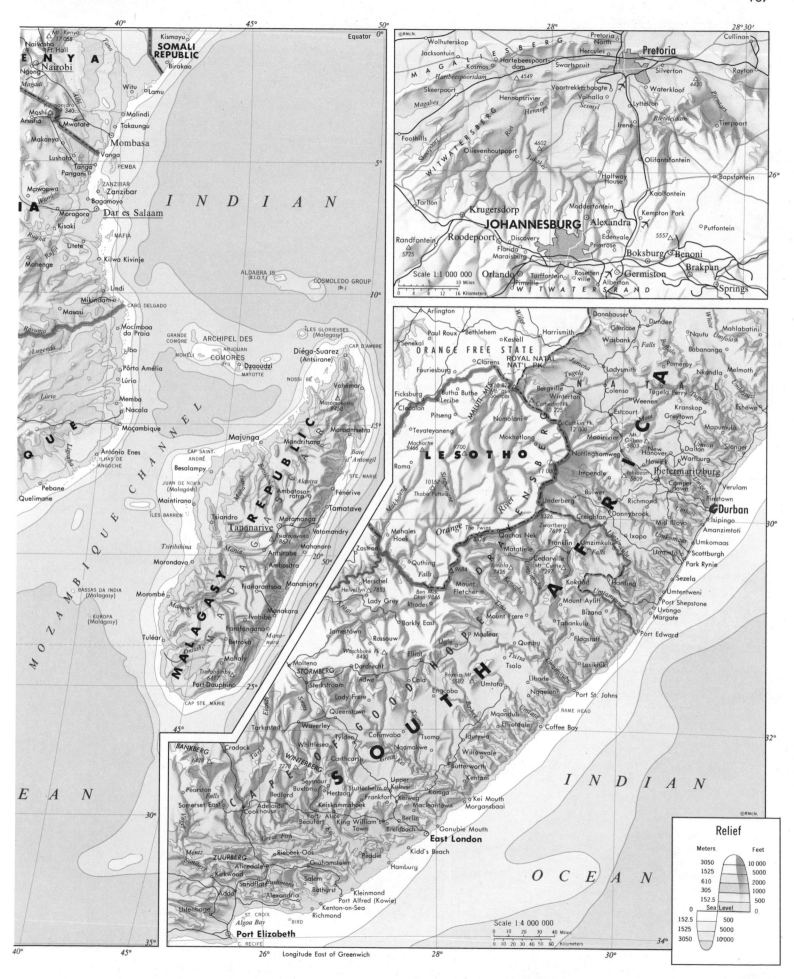

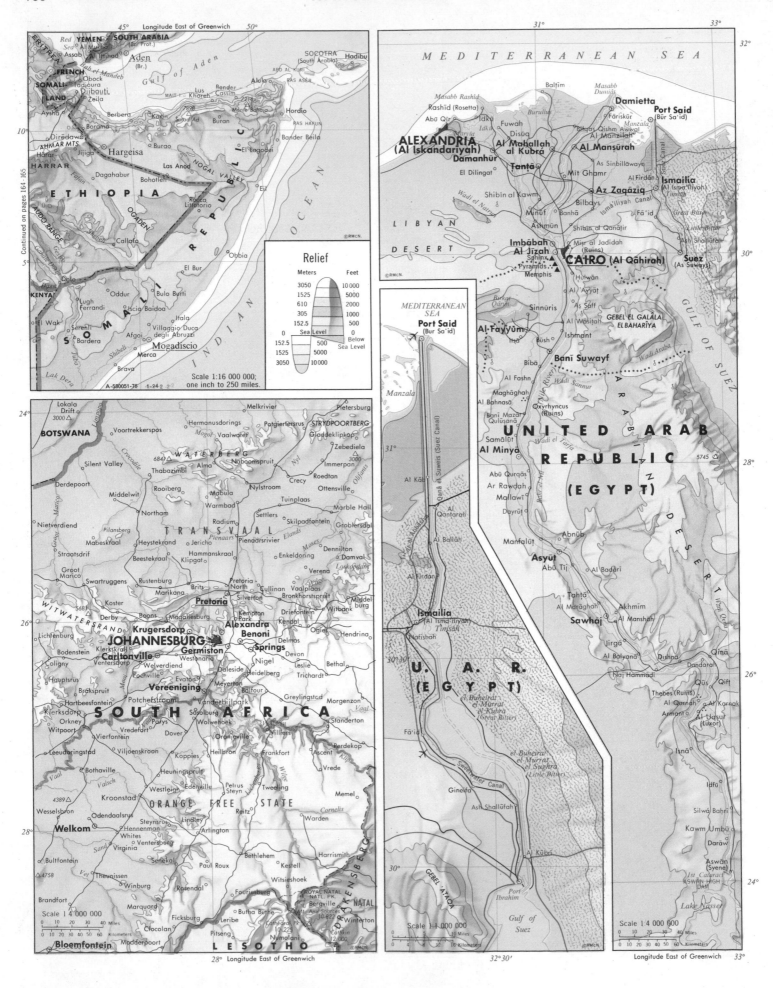

Relief

Meters	Feet
3050	10 000
1525	5000
610	2000
305	1000
152.5	500
0 Sea Level	0
152.5	500 Below
1525	5000 Sea Level
3050	10000

Scale 1:16 000 000;
one inch to 250 miles.

A-580051-78 · 1-24-2 · 1

Scale 1:4 000 000

Scale 1:1 000 000

Scale 1:4 000 000

WORLD COMPARISONS

General Information

Equatorial diameter of the earth, 7,926.68 miles
Polar diameter of the earth, 7,899.99 miles
Diameter of the mean sphere of the earth, 7,918.78 miles
Equatorial circumference of the earth, 24,902.45 miles
Polar circumference of the earth, 24,818.60 miles
Mean distance from the earth to the sun, 92,900,000 miles
Mean distance from the earth to the moon, 238,857 miles
Total area of the earth, 196,940,400 square miles

Highest elevation on the earth's surface, Mt. Everest, Asia, 29,028 feet
Lowest elevation on the earth's land surface, shores of the Dead Sea, Asia.—1,286 feet
Greatest known depth of the ocean, south of the Mariana Islands, Pacific Ocean, 36,198 feet
Total land area of the earth, including inland water and Antarctica, 57,280,000 square miles

Area of Africa, 11,685,000 square miles
Area of Antarctica, 5,100,000 square miles
Area of Asia, 17,085,000 square miles
Area of Europe, 3,825,000 square miles
Area of North America, 9,420,000 square miles
Area of Oceania, incl. Australia, 3,295,000 square miles
Area of South America, 6,870,000 square miles
Population of the earth (est. 1/1/1965), 3,237,000,000

Principal Islands and Their Areas

Island	Area Sq. Miles
Baffin, Arctic Region	183,810
Banks, Arctic Region	23,230
Borneo, Asia	286,967
Bougainville, Oceania	3,880
Celebes, Indonesia	72,986
Ceylon, Indian Ocean	25,332
Corsica, Mediterranean Sea	3,352
Crete, Mediterranean Sea	3,217
Cuba, West Indies	44,218
Cyprus, Mediterranean Sea	3,572
Devon, Arctic Region	20,861
Ellesmere, Arctic Region	82,119
Formosa, China Sea	13,885

Island	Area Sq. Miles
Great Britain, Europe	88,756
Greenland, Arctic Region	840,000
Hainan, South China Sea	13,127
Hawaii, Oceania	4,030
Hispaniola, West Indies	29,530
Hokkaidō, Japan	29,950
Honshū, Japan	88,930
Iceland, Arctic Region	39,800
Ireland, Europe	32,596
Jamaica, West Indies	4,411
Java, Indonesia	50,745
Kyūshū, Japan	16,215
Luzon, Philippines	40,814

Island	Area Sq. Miles
Madagascar, Indian Ocean	227,800
Melville, Arctic Region	16,141
Mindanao, Philippines	36,906
Mindoro, Philippines	3,794
Negros, Philippines	4,903
New Britain, Oceania	14,592
Newfoundland, Canada	43,359
New Guinea, Oceania	316,856
North East Land, Arctic Region	6,350
North Island (New Zealand), Oceania	44,281

Island	Area Sq. Miles
New Caledonie, Oceania	5,671
Novaya Zemlya, Arctic Region	31,390
Palawan, Philippines	4,500
Panay, Philippines	4,448
Prince of Wales, Arctic Region	12,830
Puerto Rico, West Indies	3,435
Sakhalin, Soviet Union	29,344
Samar, Philippines	5,124
Sardinia, Mediterranean Sea	9,301
Seram, Indonesia	6,046
Sicily, Mediterranean Sea	9,926

Island	Area Sq. Miles
Shikoku, Japan	7,245
Somerset, Arctic Region	9,370
Southampton, Hudson Bay	15,700
South Island (New Zealand) Oceania	58,093
Sumatra, Indonesia	182,860
Tasmania, Australia	26,383
Tierra del Fuego, S.A.	18,600
Timor, Asia	13,094
Vancouver, Canada	12,408
Victoria, Arctic Region	81,930
Vrangelya, Arctic Region	2,819
West Spitsbergen, Arctic Region	15,260

Principal Lakes, Oceans, Seas, and Their Areas

Lake Country	Area Sq. Miles
Aral'skoye More (Aral Sea) Sov. Un.	26,518
Arctic O.	5,427,000
Athabasca, L., Can.	3,120
Atlantic O.	31,744,000
Balkhash, Ozero (L.), Sov. Un.	6,678
Baltic Sea, Eur	163,000
Baykal, Ozero (L.), Sov. Un.	12,159
Bering Sea. Asia-N.A.	876,000

Lake Country	Area Sq. Miles
Black Sea, Eur.-Asia	178,000
Caribbean Sea, N.A.-S.A.	750,000
Caspian Sea, Sov. Un.	152,084
Chad, L., Chad-Cam.-Nig.	6,300
Ch'ing Hai (Koko Nor) (L.), China	1,650
East China Sea, Asia	482,000
Erie, L., U. S.-Can	9,940
Eyre, L., Austl.	3,700
Gairdner, L., Austl.	1,500
Great Bear L., Can.	12,275
Great Salt L., U. S.	1,700

Lake Country	Area Sq. Miles
Great Slave L., Can.	10,980
Hudson Bay, Can.	476,000
Huron, L., U. S.-Can	23,010
Indian O.	28,371,000
Japan, Sea of, Asia	389,000
Ladozhskoye Ozero (Lake Ladoga), Sov. Un.	7,092
Leopold II, L., Con. K.	1,700
Manitoba, L., Can.	1,817
Mediterranean Sea, Eur.-Afr.-Asia	967,000
Mexico, G. of, N. A.	596,000

Lake Country	Area Sq. Miles
Michigan, L., U. S.	22,400
Nicaragua, Lago de (L.), Nic.	2,972
North Sea, Eur	222,000
Nyasa, L., Mwi.-Moz.-Tan.	10,900
Okhotsk, Sea of, Pac. O.	590,000
Onezhskoye Ozero (Lake Onega), Sov. Un.	3,821
Ontario, L., U. S.-Can	7,540
Pacific O.	63,855,000
Red Sea, Afr.-Asia	169,000
Rudolf, L., Ken.-Eth.	2,473
Superior, L., U. S.-Can	31,820

Lake Country	Area Sq. Miles
Tanganyika, L., Tan.-Con. K.-Bdi.-Zam.	10,965
Titicaca, Lago (L.), Bol.-Peru	3,500
Torrens, L., Austl	2,200
Vänern, L., Swe	2,156
Van Gölü (L.), Tur	1,470
Victoria, L., Tan.-Ken.-Ug.	26,828
Winnipeg, L., Can	9,465
Winnipegosis, L., Can	2,103
Yellow Sea, China	480,000

Principal Mountains and Their Heights

Mountain Country	Height in Feet
Aconcagua, Argentina	22,834
Albert Edward, Papua	13,100
Altar, Ecuador	17,451
Annapurna, Nepal	26,504
Antisana, Ecuador	18,717
Antofalla, Argentina	21,129
Apo, Philippines	9,692
Ararat, Turkey	16,946
Azufre (Copiapó), Chile	19,947
Balbi, Solomon I.	10,170
Bandeira, Brazil	9,482
Belukha, Soviet Union	15,157
Blanc, France-Italy	15,771
Blanca, Colorado, U. S.	14,317
Bolívar (La Columna), Venezuela	16,411
Bona, Alaska, U. S.	16,421
Borah, Idaho, U. S.	12,062
Cameroon, Cam	13,354
Cano, Cape Verde Is.	9,760
Cayambe, Ecuador	19,170
Chimborazo, Ecuador	20,561
Citlaltépetl, Mexico	18,701
Colima, Mexico	14,235
Cook, New Zealand	12,349
Cotopaxi, Ecuador	19,344
Cristobal Colón, Colombia	18,947
Demavand, Iran	18,934
Dhaulagiri, Nepal	26,810
Dos Conos, Argentina	22,507
Dykh-Tau, Soviet Union	17,054
Elbert, Colorado, U. S.	14,431

Mountain Country	Height in Feet
El'brus, Soviet Union	18,481
Elgon, Kenya	14,178
El Misti, Peru	19,144
Emi Koussi, Chad	11,204
Erebus, Antarctica	12,280
Etna, Italy	11,122
Everest, Nepal-China	29,028
Finsteraarhorn, Switzerland	14,026
Foraker, Alaska, U. S.	17,395
Fuji San, Japan	12,388
Galdhöpiggen, Norway	8,100
Gasherbrum, Pak	26,470
Godwin Austen (K-2), Pak	28,250
Gosainthan, China	26,291
Gran Paradiso, Italy	13,323
Gunnbjörn, Greenland	12,139
Gurla Mandhata, China	25,355
Hekla, Iceland	4,747
Hood, Oregon, U. S.	11,245
Hsinkao, Taiwan	13,113
Huascarán, Peru	22,205
Huila, Colombia	18,865
Hvannadalshnukur, Iceland	6,952
Illampu, Bolivia	21,490
Illimani, Bolivia	21,151
Incahuasi, Argentina-Chile	21,719
Ixtacihuatl, Mexico	17,343
Jabal Al Loz, Saudi Arabia	8,461
Jabal Razih, Saudi Arabia	11,999
Juliana-Top, West Iran	15,426
Jungfrau, Switzerland	13,668

Mountain Country	Height in Feet
Kailas, China (Tibet)	22,028
Kāmet, India	25,447
Kanchenjunga, Nepal-Sikkim	28,208
Karisimbi, Con. K.-Rwanda	14,787
Kazbek, Soviet Union	16,558
Kenya, Kenya	17,058
Kerintji, Indonesia	12,467
Kilimanjaro, Tanzania	19,340
Kinabalu, Malaysia	13,455
Klyuchevskaya, Soviet Union	15,584
Kommunizma, Soviet Union	24,590
Korab, Albania	9,068
Kosciusko, Australia	7,316
Krakatoa (Rakata), Indonesia	2,667
Kwanmo, Korea	8,307
Lassen, California, U. S.	10,457
Lenin Pk., Soviet Union	23,382
Leuser, Indonesia	11,178
Llullaillaco, Argentina-Chile	22,146
Logan, Canada	19,850
McKinley, Alaska, U. S.	20,320
Makalu, China-Nepal	27,790
Markham, Antarctica	14,272
Maromokotro, Malagasy Rep.	9,450
Matterhorn, Switz.-Italy	14,685
Mauna Kea, Hawaii, U. S.	13,796
Mauna Loa, Hawaii, U. S.	13,680
Mercedario, Argentina	22,211

Mountain Country	Height in Feet
Minya Konka, China	24,900
Mitchell, North Carolina, U. S.	6,684
Musala, Bulgaria	9,592
Muztagh Ata, China	24,388
Namcha Barwa, China	25,445
Nanda Devi, India	25,645
Nanga Parbat, Pak	26,660
Negoi, Romania	8,344
Neiges, Piton des, Reunion	10,069
Ojos del Salado, Argentina-Chile	22,590
Ólimbos, Greece	9,550
Orohena, Tahiti	7,618
Paricutín, Mexico	9,213
Pelée, Martinique	4,800
Pic du Midi d'Ossau, France	10,322
Pidurutalagala, Ceylon	8,281
Pikes Peak, Colorado, U. S.	14,110
Pissis, Argentina	22,546
Pobeda, China-Soviet Union	24,409
Popocatépetl, Mexico	17,887
Pulog, Philippines	9,612
Qurnet es Sa'uda, Lebanon	10,131
Rainier, Washington, U. S	14,410
Rakaposhi, Pak	25,551
Ras Dashan, Ethiopia	15,158
Rindjani, Indonesia	12,225
Rosa, Monte, Italy-Switzerland	15,200

Mountain Country	Height in Feet
Ruapehu, New Zealand	9,175
Ruwenzori, Con. K.-Uganda	16,795
St. Elias, U.S.-Canada	18,008
Sajama, Bolivia	21,391
Sanford, Alaska, U. S.	16,208
Sangay, Ecuador	17,159
Semeru, Indonesia	12,060
Shasta, California, U. S.	14,162
Shkhara, Soviet Union	17,059
Sources, Mt. aux, Lesotho-S. Afr.	10,822
Sukarno Peaks, West Irian	16,500
Tengri Khan, Soviet Union	22,940
Thabana Ntlenyana, Lesotho	11,425
Tina, Dominican Republic	9,285
Tirich Mir, Pak	25,230
Tocorpuri, Bolivia-Chile	22,162
Toubkal, Morocco	13,661
Tupungato, Argentina-Chile	22,310
Ulugh Muztagh, China	25,340
Vesuvio (Vesuvius), Italy	3,842
Victoria, Papua	13,363
Vinson Massif, Ant.	16,864
Weisshorn, Switzerland	14,803
Whitney, California, U. S.	14,495
Wilhelmina-Top, West Irian	15,518
Wrangell, Alaska, U. S.	14,005
Yerupaja, Peru	21,758

Principal Rivers and Their Lengths

River Continent	Length in Miles
Albany, North America	610
Aldan, Asia	1,392
Amazonas, South America	3,900
Amu Dar'ya (Oxus), Asia	1,628
Amur, Asia	2,802
Araguaia, South America	1,630
Arkansas, North America	1,450
Athabasca, North America	765
Back, North America	605
Brahmaputra, Asia	1,800
Branco, South America	580
Brazos, North America	870
Canadian, North America	906
Churchill, North America	1,000
Colorado, North America	1,450
Columbia, North America	1,214
Congo, Africa	2,900
Cumberland, North America	687
Danube, Europe	1,770
Darling, Australia	1,750
Dnepr (Dnieper), Europe	1,420
Dnestr (Dniester), Europe	876

River Continent	Length in Miles
Don, Europe	1,224
Donets, Europe	735
Elbe, Europe	720
Euphrates, Asia	1,675
Fraser, North America	850
Gambia, Africa	680
Ganges, Asia	1,550
Gila, North America	630
Godāvari, Asia	930
Hsi Chiang, Asia	1,590
Huang Ho (Yellow), Asia	2,903
Indus, Asia	1,980
Irrawaddy, Asia	1,425
Japurá, South America	1,400
Juruá, South America	1,250
Kama, Europe	1,261
Kolyma, Asia	1,615
Lena, Asia	2,653
Loire, Europe	625
Mackenzie, North America	2,635
Madeira, South America	2,060
Magdalena, South America	950

River Continent	Length in Miles
Marañón, South America	1,000
Mekong, Asia	2,600
Meuse, Europe	575
Mississippi, North America	2,348
Mississippi-Missouri-Red Rock, N. A.	3,860
Missouri-Red Rock, N. A.	2,683
Murray, Australia	1,600
Negro, South America	1,305
Nelson, North America	1,600
Neman, Europe	582
Niger, Africa	2,590
Nile, Africa	4,132
Ob'-Irtysh, Asia	3,461
Oder, Europe	565
Ohio, N. A.	981
Oka, Europe	920
Orange, Africa	1,155
Orinoco, South America	1,800
Ottawa, North America	696
Paraguay, South America	1,290
Paraná, South America	2,450

River Continent	Length in Miles
Parnaíba. South America	850
Peace, North America	1,195
Pechora, Europe	1,118
Pecos, North America	735
Pilcomayo, South America	1,550
Plata-Paraguay, S. America	2,300
Purús, South America	1,900
Red, North America	1,018
Rhein, Europe	820
Rhône, Europe	500
Rio Grande, North America	1,885
Roosevelt, South America	950
St. Lawrence, North America	1,900
Salado, South America	870
Salween, Asia	1,730
São Francisco, South America	1,800
Saskatchewan, North America	1,205
Sava, Europe	585
Sénégal, Africa	1,000
Snake, North America	1,038

River Continent	Length in Miles
Sung Hua (Sungari), Asia	1,140
Syr-Dar'ya, Asia	1,653
Tajo (Tagus), Europe	625
Tennessee, N. A.	652
Tigris, Asia	1,150
Tisza, Europe	607
Tobol, Asia	1,093
Tocantins, South America	1,640
Ucayali, South America	1,220
Ural, Europe	1,522
Uruguay, South America	1,025
Verkhnyaya Tunguska (Angara), Asia	1,549
Vilyuy, Asia	1,513
Volga, Europe	2,293
White, North America	690
Wisla (Vistula), Europe	630
Xingú, South America	1,230
Yangtze, Asia	3,430
Yellowstone, North America	671
Yenisey, Asia	2,566
Yukon, North America	1,800
Zambezi, Africa	1,650

PRINCIPAL COUNTRIES AND REGIONS OF THE WORLD

Political Division or Region	Area in sq. miles	Population 1/1/65 est.	Pop. per sq. mi.
Aden............(U.K.)	80	250,000	3,125
Afghanistan	251,000	15,200,000	61
Africa	11,685,000	290,200,000	25
Alabama........(U.S.)	51,609	3,462,000	67
Alaska........(U.S.)	586,400	247,000	0.4
Albania	11,099	1,846,000	166
Alberta........(Can.)	255,285	1,449,000	5.7
Algeria	919,595	10,700,000	12
American Samoa..(U.S.)	76	21,000	276
Andorra	175	12,000	69
Angola........(Port.)	481,351	5,125,000	11
Antarctica	5,100,000	....	....
Antigua (incl. Barbuda)........(U.K.)	171	59,000	345
Argentina	1,072,070	22,200,000	21
Arizona........(U.S.)	113,909	1,635,000	14
Arkansas........(U.S.)	53,104	1,889,000	36
Asia	17,085,000	1,877,000,000	110
Australia...(Br. Comm.)	2,971,081	11,335,000	3.8
Austria	32,374	7,235,000	223
Azores Is........(Port.)	894	332,000	371
Bahama Is........(U.K.)	4,375	136,000	31
Bahrain	231	166,000	719
Barbados...(Br. Comm.)	166	242,000	1,458
Belgium	11,778	9,400,000	798
Bermuda........(U.K.)	21	60,000	2,857
Bhutan	19,300	750,000	39
Bolivia	424,163	3,675,000	8.7
Bonin Is..(U.S. Admin.)	40	200	5.0
Botswana..(Br. Comm.)	275,000	555,000	2.0
Brazil	3,286,478	80,250,000	24
Br. Antarctic Territory (excl. Antarctic mainland)........(U.K.)	2,040	No perm. pop.	....
British Columbia..(Can.)	366,255	1,770,000	4.8
Br. Comm. of Nations...	10,890,845	796,403,000	73
British Indian Ocean Territory........(U.K.)	29	1,400	48
British Honduras.(U.K.)	8,866	105,000	12
Brunei........(U.K.)	2,226	105,000	47
Bulgaria	42,829	8,175,000	191
Burma	261,789	24,500,000	94
Burundi (Urundi)	10,747	2,775,000	258
California........(U.S.)	158,693	18,338,000	116
Cambodia	66,606	6,100,000	92
Cameroon	183,569	4,750,000	26
Canada....(Br. Comm.)	3,851,809	19,445,000	5.0
Canal Zone........(U.S.)	558	50,000	90
Canary Is........(Sp.)	2,808	1,005,000	358
Cape Verde Is....(Port.)	1,538	229,000	149
Cayman Is........(U.K.)	100	9,000	90
Central African Republic	238,200	1,350,000	5.7
Central America	200,412	13,800,000	69
Ceylon.....(Br. Comm.)	25,332	11,000,000	434
Chad	495,800	2,900,000	5.8
Channel Is........(U.K.)	75	112,000	1,493
Chile	286,397	8,450,000	30
China (excl. Taiwan)....	3,691,500	700,000,000	190
Colombia	439,513	15,600,000	35
Colorado........(U.S.)	104,247	2,003,000	19
Congo (Republic of Congo; capital Brazzaville)......	132,000	1,050,000	8.0
Congo, The (Republic of the Congo; capital Kinshasa)......	905,565	15,500,000	17
Connecticut........(U.S.)	5,009	2,752,000	549
Cook Is........(N.Z.)	93	19,000	204
Costa Rica	19,600	1,425,000	73
Cuba	44,217	7,100,000	161
Cyprus...(Br. Comm.)	3,572	590,000	165
Czechoslovakia	49,370	14,100,000	286
Dahomey	44,696	2,300,000	51
Delaware........(U.S.)	2,057	494,000	240
Denmark	16,619	4,740,000	285
Denmark and Possessions	857,159	4,817,000	5.6
Dist. of Columbia (U.S.)	69	810,000	11,739
Dominica........(U.K.)	305	65,000	213
Dominican Republic	18,704	3,500,000	187
Ecuador	104,506	4,950,000	47
El Salvador	8,260	2,875,000	348
England & Wales.(U.K.)	58,344	47,825,000	820
Equatorial Guinea..(Sp.)	10,830	266,000	25
Ethiopia	457,267	21,500,000	47
Europe	3,825,000	601,900,000	157
Faeroe Is........(Den.)	540	37,000	69
Falkland Is. (excl. Deps.)...(U.K.)	4,618	2,200	0.5
Fiji........(U.K.)	7,040	455,000	65
Finland	130,119	4,600,000	35
Florida........(U.S.)	58,560	5,913,000	101
France	212,822	48,800,000	229
France and Possessions	276,238	50,366,000	182
French Guiana........(Fr.)	35,100	36,000	1.0
French Polynesia...(Fr.)	1,550	89,000	57
French Somaliland..(Fr.)	8,500	80,000	9.4
Gabon	103,100	465,000	4.5
Gambia....(Br. Comm.)	4,008	320,000	80
Georgia........(U.S.)	58,876	4,312,000	73
Germany (Entire)......	137,743	75,800,000	550
Germany, East......	41,815	17,250,000	413
Germany, West (incl. West Berlin)......	95,928	58,550,000	610
Ghana....(Br. Comm.)	91,843	7,600,000	83
Gibraltar........(U.K.)	2	25,000	12,500
Gilbert & Ellice Is.(U.K.)	369	51,000	138
Greece	50,547	8,500,000	168
Greenland........(Den.)	840,000	40,000	0.05
Grenada........(U.K.)	133	93,000	699
Guadeloupe........(Fr.)	687	308,000	448
Guam........(U.S.)	212	70,000	330
Guatemala	42,042	4,375,000	104
Guinea	94,925	3,500,000	37
Guyana....(Br. Comm.)	83,000	631,000	7.6
Haiti	10,714	4,600,000	429
Hawaii........(U.S.)	6,424	710,000	111
Honduras	43,277	2,125,000	49
Hong Kong........(U.K.)	398	3,750,000	9,422
Hungary	35,919	10,135,000	282
Iceland	39,800	190,000	4.8
Idaho........(U.S.)	83,557	702,000	8.4
Ifni........(Sp.)	580	51,000	88
Illinois........(U.S.)	56,400	10,584,000	188
India (incl. part of Kashmir).(Br. Comm.)	1,227,275	479,000,000	390
Indiana........(U.S.)	36,291	4,914,000	135
Indonesia	574,670	103,350,000	180
Iowa........(U.S.)	56,290	2,783,000	49
Iran	636,300	23,100,000	36
Iraq	173,260	7,050,000	41
Ireland	27,135	2,855,000	105
Isle of Man........(U.K.)	227	48,000	211
Israel	7,993	2,520,000	315
Italy	116,303	50,900,000	438
Ivory Coast	124,504	3,775,000	30
Jamaica........(Br. Comm.)	4,411	1,750,000	397
Japan	142,726	97,400,000	682
Jordan	37,301	1,900,000	51
Kansas........(U.S.)	82,264	2,251,000	27
Kentucky........(U.S.)	40,395	3,138,000	77
Kenya........(Br. Comm.)	224,960	9,200,000	41
Korea (Entire)	84,540	39,500,000	467
Korea, North	46,540	11,500,000	247
Korea, South	38,000	28,000,000	737
Kuwait	6,000	405,000	68
Laos	91,400	2,000,000	22
Lebanon	4,000	2,265,000	566
Lesotho...(Br. Comm.)	11,716	740,000	63
Liberia	43,000	1,050,000	24
Libya	679,362	1,580,000	2.3
Liechtenstein	61	18,000	295
Louisiana........(U.S.)	48,523	3,480,000	72
Luxembourg	998	332,000	333
Macao........(Port.)	6	175,000	29,167
Madeira Is........(Port.)	308	270,000	877
Maine........(U.S.)	33,215	989,000	30
Malagasy Republic	227,800	6,200,000	27
Malawi...(Br. Comm.)	45,747	3,900,000	85
Malaysia..(Br. Comm.)	128,431	9,310,000	72
Maldive Is..(Br. Comm.)	115	95,000	826
Mali	464,874	4,550,000	9.8
Malta........(Br. Comm.)	122	325,000	2,664
Manitoba........(Can.)	251,000	963,000	3.8
Martinique........(Fr.)	425	312,000	734
Maryland........(U.S.)	10,577	3,480,000	329
Massachusetts....(U.S.)	8,257	5,387,000	652
Mauritania	419,230	1,000,000	2.4
Mauritius (incl. Deps.)........(U.K.)	808	752,000	931
Mexico	761,602	40,250,000	53
Michigan........(U.S.)	58,216	8,269,000	142
Midway Is........(U.S.)	2	2,500	1,250
Minnesota........(U.S.)	84,068	3,613,000	43
Mississippi........(U.S.)	47,716	2,320,000	49
Missouri........(U.S.)	69,686	4,446,000	64
Monaco	0.8	22,000	27,500
Mongolia	592,700	1,079,000	1.8
Montana........(U.S.)	147,138	717,000	4.9
Montserrat........(U.K.)	32	13,000	406
Morocco	171,305	13,150,000	77
Mozambique........(Port.)	297,846	6,900,000	23
Muscat & Oman	82,000	580,000	7.1
Nauru........(Austl.)	8	5,000	625
Nebraska........(U.S.)	77,227	1,507,000	20
Nepal	54,362	9,900,000	182
Netherlands	12,950	12,200,000	942
Netherlands and Poss...	68,464	12,793,000	187
Neth. Antilles....(Neth.)	371	208,000	561
Nevada........(U.S.)	110,540	426,000	3.9
New Brunswick...(Can.)	28,354	620,000	22
New Caledonia (incl. Deps.)........(Fr.)	6,531	85,000	13
Newfoundland........(Can.)	156,185	495,000	3.2
New Guinea Ter.(Austl.)	94,430	1,575,000	17
New Hampshire..(U.S.)	9,304	639,000	69
New Hebrides..(Fr.-U.K.)	5,700	65,000	11
New Jersey........(U.S.)	7,836	6,587,000	841
New Mexico........(U.S.)	121,666	1,048,000	8.6
New York........(U.S.)	49,576	17,834,000	360
New Zealand........(Br. Comm.)	103,736	2,625,000	25
Nicaragua	48,600	1,620,000	33
Niger	458,995	3,275,000	7.1
Nigeria........(Br. Comm.)	356,669	43,200,000	121
Niue........(N.Z.)	100	5,000	50
Norfolk I........(Austl.)	13	1,000	77
North America	9,420,000	289,700,000	31
North Carolina...(U.S.)	52,712	4,877,000	93
North Dakota........(U.S.)	70,665	642,000	9.1
Northern Ireland.(U.K.)	5,459	1,460,000	267
Northwest Ters...(Can.)	1,304,903	25,000	0.02
Norway	125,181	3,710,000	30
Nova Scotia........(Can.)	21,425	761,000	36
Oceania	3,295,000	17,400,000	5.3
Ohio........(U.S.)	41,222	10,372,000	252
Oklahoma........(U.S.)	69,919	2,512,000	36
Ontario........(Can.)	412,582	6,670,000	16
Oregon........(U.S.)	96,981	1,896,000	20
Pacific Is. Tr. Ter.(U.S.)	672	90,000	134
Pakistan (incl. part of Kashmir).(Br. Comm.)	399,373	102,700,000	257
Panama	29,209	1,225,000	42
Papua (excl. N. Gui. Ter.)........(Austl.)	90,600	560,000	6.2
Paraguay	157,048	1,920,000	12
Pennsylvania........(U.S.)	45,333	11,511,000	254
Peru	496,224	11,500,000	23
Philippines	115,831	31,800,000	275
Pitcairn (excl. Deps.)...(U.K.)	2	100	50
Poland	120,359	31,350,000	260
Portugal	35,340	9,140,000	259
Portugal and Possessions	837,733	22,697,000	27
Portuguese Guinea......(Port.)	13,948	525,000	38
Portuguese Timor (Port.)	7,332	548,000	75
Prince Edward I..(Can.)	2,184	108,000	49
Puerto Rico........(U.S.)	3,435	2,600,000	757
Qatar	8,500	65,000	7.6
Quebec........(Can.)	594,860	5,620,000	9.4
Reunion........(Fr.)	969	385,000	397
Rhode Island........(U.S.)	1,214	897,000	739
Rhodesia........(U.K.)	150,333	4,200,000	28
Romania	91,698	19,025,000	207
Rwanda (Ruanda)	10,169	2,800,000	275
St. Helena (incl. Deps.)...(U.K.)	160	4,600	29
St. Kitts-Nevis-Anguilla........(U.K.)	153	64,000	418
St. Lucia........(U.K.)	238	94,000	395
St. Pierre & Miquelon........(Fr.)	93	5,000	54
St. Vincent........(U.K.)	150	85,000	567
San Marino	23	17,000	739
Sao Tome & Principe........(Port.)	372	55,000	148
Saskatchewan........(Can.)	251,700	947,000	3.8
Saudi Arabia	617,800	7,000,000	11
Scotland........(U.K.)	30,411	5,215,000	171
Senegal	76,124	3,480,000	46
Seychelles........(U.K.)	156	47,000	301
Sierra Leone (Br. Comm.)	27,925	2,250,000	81
Sikkim	2,744	170,000	62
Singapore..(Br. Comm.)	224	1,840,000	8,214
Solomon Is........(Austl.)	4,320	62,000	14
Solomon Is., Br....(U.K.)	11,500	133,000	12
Somali Republic	246,202	2,350,000	9.5
South Africa	472,359	17,700,000	37
South America	6,870,000	160,800,000	23
South Arabia........(U.K.)	111,000	1,050,000	9.5
South Carolina...(U.S.)	31,055	2,524,000	81
South Dakota........(U.S.)	77,047	711,000	9.2
S. W. Africa........(S. Afr.)	317,725	555,000	1.7
Soviet Union	8,599,300	229,500,000	27
Spain	194,884	31,500,000	162
Spain and Possessions	309,079	32,020,000	104
Spanish Sahara........(Sp.)	102,703	45,000	0.4
Sudan	967,500	13,350,000	14
Surinam........(Neth.)	55,143	385,000	7.0
Svalbard........(Nor.)	24,101	No perm. pop.	...
Swaziland........(U.K.)	6,705	295,000	44
Sweden	173,666	7,675,000	44
Switzerland	15,941	6,075,000	381
Syria	71,498	5,100,000	71
Taiwan (Formosa) (Nationalist China)...	13,884	12,250,000	882
Tanzania...(Br. Comm.)	362,820	10,425,000	29
Tennessee........(U.S.)	42,244	3,737,000	88
Texas........(U.S.)	267,339	10,669,000	40
Thailand	198,500	30,100,000	152
Togo	21,850	1,620,000	74
Tokelau Is........(N.Z.)	4	2,000	500
Tonga........(U.K.)	270	72,000	267
Trinidad & Tobago........(Br. Comm.)	1,980	960,000	485
Trucial States	32,300	120,000	3.7
Tunisia	48,332	4,600,000	95
Turkey	301,381	31,300,000	104
Turks & Caicos Is.(U.K.)	166	6,000	36
Uganda........(Br. Comm.)	92,525	7,450,000	81
United Arab Republic (Egypt)	386,000	29,000,000	75
United Kingdom	94,214	54,500,000	578
United Kingdom and Poss.	412,295	66,957,000	163
United States	3,675,633	193,850,000	53
United States and Poss.	3,680,757	196,723,000	53
Upper Volta	105,869	4,775,000	45
Uruguay	72,172	2,600,000	36
Utah........(U.S.)	84,916	1,008,000	12
Vatican City	0.2	1,000	5,000
Venezuela	352,143	8,600,000	24
Vermont........(U.S.)	9,609	396,000	41
Vietnam (Entire)	127,574	33,400,000	262
Vietnam, North	61,294	17,500,000	286
Vietnam, South	66,280	15,900,000	240
Virgin Is...(U.S.-U.K.)	192	46,000	239
Virginia........(U.S.)	40,815	4,400,000	108
Wales (incl. Monmouthshire)........(U.K.)	8,017	2,675,000	334
Washington........(U.S.)	68,192	3,051,000	45
Western Samoa	1,133	124,000	111
West Irian (Indon. Admin.)	160,600	775,000	4.8
West Virginia........(U.S.)	24,181	1,797,000	74
Wisconsin........(U.S.)	56,154	4,166,000	74
World	57,280,000	3,237,000,000	57
Wyoming........(U.S.)	97,914	355,000	3.6
Yemen	75,300	5,000,000	66
Yugoslavia	98,766	19,400,000	196
Yukon........(Can.)	207,076	17,000	0.08
Zambia....(Br. Comm.)	290,537	3,650,000	13

GLOSSARY OF FOREIGN GEOGRAPHICAL TERMS

Annam ... Annamese
Arab ... Arabic
Bantu ... Bantu
Bur ... Burmese
Camb ... Cambodian
Celt ... Celtic
Chn ... Chinese
Czech ... Czech
Dan ... Danish
Du ... Dutch
Fin ... Finnish
Fr ... French
Ger ... German
Gr ... Greek
Hung ... Hungarian
Ice ... Icelandic
India ... India
Indian ... American Indian
Indon ... Indonesian
It ... Italian
Jap ... Japanese
Kor ... Korean
Mal ... Malayan
Mong ... Mongolian
Nor ... Norwegian
Per ... Persian
Pol ... Polish
Port ... Portuguese
Rom ... Romanian
Rus ... Russian
Siam ... Siamese
So. Slav ... Southern Slavonic
Sp ... Spanish
Swe ... Swedish
Tib ... Tibetan
Tur ... Turkish
Yugo ... Yugoslav

å, *Nor., Swe* ... brook, river
aa, *Dan., Nor* ... brook
aas, *Dan., Nor* ... ridge
ab, *Per* ... water, river
abad, *India, Per* ... town, city
ada, *Tur* ... island
adrar, *Arab* ... mountain
air, *Indon* ... stream
akrotírion, *Gr* ... cape
älf, *Swe* ... river
alp, *Ger* ... mountain
altipiano, *It* ... plateau
alto, *Sp* ... height
archipel, *Fr* ... archipelago
archipiélago, *Sp* ... archipelago
arquipélago, *Port* ... archipelago
arroyo, *Sp* ... brook, stream
ås, *Nor., Swe* ... ridge
austral, *Sp* ... southern
baai, *Du* ... bay
bab, *Arab* ... gate, port
bach, *Ger* ... brook, stream
backe, *Swe* ... hill
bad, *Ger* ... bath, spa
bahía, *Sp* ... bay, gulf
bahr, *Arab* ... sea, lake
baia, *It* ... bay, gulf
baía, *Port* ... bay
baie, *Fr* ... bay, gulf
bajo, *Sp* ... depression
bak, *Indon* ... stream
bakke, *Dan., Nor* ... hill
balkan, *Tur* ... mountain range
bana, *Jap* ... point, cape
banco, *Sp* ... bank
bandar, *Mal., Per.* ... town, port, harbor
bang, *Siam* ... village
bassin, *Fr* ... basin
batang, *Indon., Mal* ... river
ben, *Celt* ... mountain, summit
bender, *Arab* ... harbor, port
bereg, *Rus* ... coast, shore
berg, *Du., Ger., Nor., Swe.* ... mountain, hill
bir, *Arab* ... well
birket, *Arab* ... pond, pool
bit, *Arab* ... house
bjaerg, *Dan., Nor* ... mountain
bocche, *It* ... mouth
bogaz, *Tur* ... strait
bois, *Fr* ... forest, wood
boloto, *Rus* ... marsh
bolsón, *Sp* flat-floored desert valley
boreal, *Sp* ... northern
borg, *Dan., Nor., Swe* castle, town
borgo, *It* ... town, suburb
bosch, *Du* ... forest, wood
bouche, *Fr* ... river mouth
bourg, *Fr* ... town, borough
bro, *Dan., Nor., Swe* ... bridge
brücke, *Ger* ... bridge
bucht, *Ger* ... bay, bight
bugt, *Dan., Nor., Swe* ... bay, gulf
bulu, *Indon* ... mountain
burg, *Du., Ger* ... castle, town
buri, *Siam* ... town
burun, burnu, *Tur* ... cape
by, *Dan., Nor., Swe* ... village
caatinga, *Port.* (*Brazil*) ... open brushland
cabezo, *Sp* ... summit
cabo, *Port., Sp* ... cape
campo, *It., Port., Sp* ... field
campos, *Port.* (*Brazil*) ... plains
cañon, *Sp* ... canyon
cap, *Fr* ... cape
capo, *It* ... cape
casa, *It., Port., Sp* ... house
castello, *It., Port* ... castle, fort
castillo, *Sp* ... castle
càte, *Fr* ... hill
çay, *Tur* ... stream, river
cayo, *Sp* ... rock, shoal, islet
cerro, *Sp* ... hill
champ, *Fr* ... field
chang, *Chn* ... village, middle
château, *Fr* ... castle
chen, *Chn* ... market town
chiang, *Chn* ... river
chott, *Arab* ... salt lake
chou, *Chn* capital of district; island
chu, *Tib* ... water, stream
cidade, *Port* ... town, city
cima, *Sp* ... summit, peak
città, *It* ... town, city
ciudad, *Sp* ... town, city
cochilha, *Port* ... ridge
col, *Fr* ... pass
colina, *Sp* ... hill
cordillera, *Sp* ... mountain chain
costa, *It., Port., Sp* ... coast
côte, *Fr* ... coast
cuchilla, *Sp* ... mountain ridge
dag, *Tur* ... mountain
dake, *Jap* ... peak, summit
dal, *Dan., Du., Nor., Swe* ... valley
dan, *Kor* ... point, cape
danau, *Indon* ... lake
dar, *Arab* ... house, abode, country
darya, *Per* ... river, sea
dasht, *Per* ... plain, desert
deniz, *Tur* ... sea
désert, *Fr* ... desert
deserto, *It* ... desert
desierto, *Sp* ... desert
détroit, *Fr* ... strait
dijk, *Du* ... dam, dike
djebel, *Arab* ... mountain
do, *Kor* ... island
dorf, *Ger* ... village
dorp, *Du* ... village
duin, *Du* ... dune
dzong, *Tib.* ... fort, administrative capital
eau, *Fr* ... water
ecuador, *Sp* ... equator
eiland, *Du* ... island
elv, *Dan., Nor* ... river, stream
embalse, *Sp* ... reservoir
erg, *Arab* ... dune, sandy desert
est, *Fr., It* ... east
estado, *Sp* ... state
este, *Port., Sp* ... east
estrecho, *Sp* ... strait
étang, *Fr* ... pond, lake
état, *Fr* ... state
eyjar, *Ice* ... islands
feld, *Ger* ... field, plain
festung, *Ger* ... fortress
fiume, *It* ... river
fjäll, *Swe* ... mountain
fjärd, *Swe* ... bay, inlet
fjeld, *Nor* ... mountain, hill
fjord, *Dan., Nor* ... fiord, inlet
fjördur, *Ice* ... fiord, inlet
fleuve, *Fr* ... river
flod, *Dan., Swe* ... river
flói, *Ice* ... bay, marshland
fluss, *Ger* ... river
foce, *It* ... river mouth
fontein, *Du* ... a spring
forêt, *Fr* ... forest
fors, *Swe* ... waterfall
forst, *Ger* ... forest
fos, *Dan., Nor* ... waterfall
fu, *Chn* ... town, residence
fuente, *Sp* ... spring, fountain
fuerte, *Sp* ... fort
furt, *Ger* ... ford
gang, *Kor* ... stream, river
gangri, *Tib* ... mountain
gat, *Dan., Nor* ... channel
gàve, *Fr* ... stream
gawa, *Jap* ... river
gebergte, *Du* ... mountain range
gebiet, *Ger* ... district, territory
gebirge, *Ger* ... mountains
ghat, *India* ... pass, mountain range
gobi, *Mong* ... desert
goenoeng, *Mal* ... mountain
gol, *Mong* ... river
göl, gölü, *Tur* ... lake
golf, *Du., Ger* ... gulf, bay
golfe, *Fr* ... gulf, bay
golfo, *It., Port., Sp* ... gulf, bay
gomba, gompa, *Tib* ... monastery
gora, *Rus., So. Slav* ... mountain
góra, *Pol* ... mountain
gorod, *Rus* ... town
grad, *Rus., So. Slav* ... town
guba, *Rus* ... bay, gulf
gundung, *Indon* ... mountain
guntō, *Jap* ... archipelago
haf, *Swe* ... sea, ocean
hafen, *Ger* ... port, harbor
haff, *Ger* ... gulf, inland sea
hai, *Chn* ... sea, lake
hama, *Jap* ... beach, shore
hamada, *Arab* ... rocky plateau
hamn, *Swe* ... harbor
hamun, *Per* ... swampy lake, plain
hantō, *Jap* ... peninsula
hassi, *Arab* ... well, spring
haus, *Ger* ... house
haut, *Fr* ... summit, top
hav, *Dan., Nor* ... sea, ocean
havn, *Dan., Nor* ... harbor, port
havre, *Fr* ... harbor, port
háza, *Hung* ... house, dwelling of
heim, *Ger* ... hamlet, home
hem, *Swe* ... hamlet, home
higashi, *Jap* ... east
hisar, *Tur* ... fortress
hissar, *Arab* ... fort
ho, *Chn* ... river
hoek, *Du* ... cape
hof, *Ger* ... court, farm house
höfn, *Ice* ... harbor
hoku, *Jap* ... north
holm, *Dan., Nor., Swe* ... island
hora, *Czech* ... mountain
horn, *Ger* ... peak
hoved, *Dan., Nor* ... cape
hsien, *Chn* district, district capital
hu, *Chn* ... lake
hügel, *Ger* ... hill
huk, *Dan., Swe* ... point
hus, *Dan., Nor., Swe* ... house
île, *Fr* ... island
ilha, *Port* ... island
indsö, *Dan., Nor* ... lake
insel, *Ger* ... island
insjö, *Swe* ... lake
irmak, irmagi, *Tur* ... river
isla, *Sp* ... island
isola, *It* ... island
istmo, *It., Sp* ... isthmus
istrova, *Rus* ... islands
järvi, jaur, *Fin* ... lake
jebel, *Arab* ... mountain
jima, *Jap* ... island
jökel, *Nor* ... glacier
joki, *Fin* ... river
jökull, *Ice* ... ice-covered mountain
kaap, *Du* ... cape
kai, *Jap* ... bay, gulf, sea
kaikyō, *Jap* ... channel, strait
kalat, *Per* ... castle, fortress
kale, *Tur* ... fort
kali, *Mal* ... river
kand, *Per* ... village
kang, *Chn* mountain ridge; village
kap, *Dan., Ger* ... cape
kapp, *Nor., Swe* ... cape
kasr, *Arab* ... fort, castle
kawa, *Jap* ... river
kefr, *Arab* ... village
kei, *Jap* ... creek, river
ken, *Jap* ... prefecture
khor, *Arab* ... bay, inlet
khrebet, *Rus* ... mountain range
kiang, *Chn* ... large river
king, *Chn* ... capital city, town
kita, *Jap* ... north
ko, *Jap* ... lake
köbstad, *Dan* ... market-town
kol, *Mong* ... lake
kólpos, *Gr* ... gulf
kong, *Chn* ... river
kopf, *Ger* ... head, summit, peak
köpstad, *Swe* ... market-town
korfezi, *Tur* ... gulf
kosa, *Rus* ... cape
kou, *Chn* ... river mouth
köy, *Tur* ... village
kraal, *Du.* (*Africa*) ... native village
ksar, *Arab* ... fortified village
kuala, *Mal* ... river mouth
kuh, *Per* ... mountain
kum, *Tur* ... sand
kuppe, *Ger* ... summit
küste, *Ger* ... coast
kyo, *Jap* ... town, capital
la, *Tib* ... mountain pass
labuan, *Mal* ... anchorage, port
lac, *Fr* ... lake
lago, *It., Port., Sp* ... lake
lagoa, *Port* ... lake, marsh
laguna, *It., Port., Sp* ... lagoon, lake
lahti, *Fin* ... bay, gulf
län, *Swe* ... county
landsby, *Dan., Nor* ... village
liehtao, *Chn* ... archipelago
liman, *Tur* ... bay, port
ling, *Chn* ... pass, ridge, mountain
llanos, *Sp* ... plains
loch, *Celt.* (*Scotland*) ... lake, bay
loma, *Sp* ... long, low hill
lough, *Celt.* (*Ireland*) ... lake, bay
machi, *Jap* ... town
man, *Kor* ... bay
mar, *Port., Sp* ... sea
mare, *It., Rom* ... sea
marisma, *Sp* ... marsh, swamp
mark, *Ger* ... boundary, limit
massif, *Fr* ... block of mountains
mato, *Port* ... forest, thicket
me, *Siam* ... river
meer, *Du., Ger* ... lake, sea
mer, *Fr* ... sea
mesa, *Sp* ... flat-topped mountain
meseta, *Sp* ... plateau
mina, *Port., Sp* ... mine
minami, *Jap* ... south
minato, *Jap* ... harbor, haven
misaki, *Jap* ... cape, headland
mont, *Fr* ... mount, mountain
montagna, *It* ... mountain
montagne, *Fr* ... mountain
montaña, *Sp* ... mountain
monte, *It., Port., Sp.* ... mount, mountain
more, *Rus., So. Slav* ... sea
morro, *Port., Sp* ... hill, bluff
mühle, *Ger* ... mill
mund, *Ger* ... mouth, opening
mündung, *Ger* ... river mouth
mura, *Jap* ... township
myit, *Bur* ... river
mys, *Rus* ... cape
nada, *Jap* ... sea
nadi, *India* ... river, creek
naes, *Dan., Nor* ... cape
nafud, *Arab* ... desert of sand dunes
nagar, *India* ... town, city
nahr, *Arab* ... river
nam, *Siam* ... river, water
nan, *Chn., Jap* ... south
näs, *Nor., Swe* ... cape
nez, *Fr* ... point, cape
nishi, nisi, *Jap* ... west
njarga, *Fin* ... peninsula
nong, *Siam* ... marsh
noord, *Du* ... north
nor, *Mong* ... lake
nord, *Dan., Fr., Ger., It., Nor., Swe* ... north
norte, *Port., Sp* ... north
nos, *Rus* ... cape
nyasa, *Bantu* ... lake
ö, *Dan., Nor., Swe* ... island
occidental, *Sp* ... western
ocna, *Rom* ... salt mine
odde, *Dan., Nor* ... point, cape
oedjoeng, *Mal* ... point, cape
oeste, *Port., Sp* ... west
oka, *Jap* ... hill
oost, *Du* ... east
oriental, *Sp* ... eastern
óros, *Gr* ... mountain
ost, *Ger., Swe* ... east
öster, *Dan., Nor., Swe* ... eastern
ostrov, *Rus* ... island
oued, *Arab* ... river, stream
ouest, *Fr* ... west
ozero, *Rus* ... lake
pää, *Fin* ... mountain
padang, *Mal* ... plain, field
pampas, *Sp.* (*Argentina*) ... grassy plains
pará, *Indian* (*Brazil*) ... river
pas, *Fr* ... channel, passage
paso, *Sp* ... passage
passo, *It., Port* ... passage, strait
patam, *India* ... city, town
pei, *Chn* ... north
pélagos, *Gr* ... open sea
pegunungan, *Indon* ... mountains
peña, *Sp* ... rock
peresheyek, *Rus* ... isthmus
pertuis, *Fr* ... strait
peski, *Rus* ... desert
pic, *Fr* ... mountain peak
pico, *Port., Sp* ... mountain peak
piedra, *Sp* ... stone, rock
ping, *Chn* ... plain, flat
planalto, *Port* ... plateau
planina, *Yugo* ... mountains
playa, *Sp* ... shore, beach
pnom, *Camb* ... mountain
poelau, *Mal* ... island
pointe, *Fr* ... point
polder, *Du., Ger* ... reclaimed marsh
polje, *So. Slav* ... field
poluostrov, *Rus* ... peninsula
pont, *Fr* ... bridge
ponta, *Port* ... point, headland
ponte, *It., Port* ... bridge
pore, *India* ... city, town
porthmós, *Gr* ... strait
porto, *It., Port* ... port, harbor
potamós, *Gr* ... river
p'ov, *Rus* ... peninsula
prado, *Sp* ... field, meadow
presqu'île, *Fr* ... peninsula
proliv, *Rus* ... strait
pu, *Chn* ... commercial village
pueblo, *Sp* ... town, village
puerto, *Sp* ... port, harbor
pulau, *Mal* ... island
punkt, *Ger* ... point
punt, *Du* ... point
punta, *It., Sp* ... point
pur, *India* ... city, town
puy, *Fr* ... peak
qal'a, qal'at, *Arab* ... fort, village
qasr, *Arab* ... fort, castle
rann, *India* ... wasteland
ras, *Arab* ... cape, head
reka, *Rus., So. Slav* ... river
represa, *Port* ... reservoir
rettō, *Jap* ... island chain
ría, *Sp* ... estuary
ribeira, *Port* ... stream
riberão, *Port* ... river
rio, *It., Port* ... stream, river
río, *Sp* ... river
rivière, *Fr* ... river
roca, *Sp* ... rock
rt, *Yugo* ... cape
rud, *Per* ... river
saari, *Fin* ... island
sable, *Fr* ... sand
sahara, *Arab* ... desert, plain
saki, *Jap* ... cape
sal, *Sp* ... salt
salar, *Sp* ... salt flat, salt lake
salto, *Sp* ... waterfall
san, *Jap., Kor* ... mountain, hill
sat, satul, *Rom* ... village
schloss, *Ger* ... castle
sebkha, *Arab* ... salt marsh
see, *Ger* ... lake, sea
şehir, *Tur* ... town, city
selat, *Indon* ... stream
selvas, *Port.* (*Brazil*) ... tropical rain forests
seno, *Sp* ... bay
serra, *Port* ... mountain chain
serranía, *Sp* ... mountain ridge
seto, *Jap* ... strait
severnaya, *Rus* ... northern
shahr, *Per* ... town, city
shan, *Chn* ... mountain, hill, island
shatt, *Arab* ... river
shi, *Jap* ... city
shima, *Jap* ... island
shōtō, *Jap* ... archipelago
si, *Chn* ... west, western
sierra, *Sp* ... mountain range
sjö, *Nor., Swe* ... lake, sea
sö, *Dan., Nor* ... lake, sea
söder, södra, *Swe* ... south
soengai, soengei, *Mal* ... river
song, *Annam* ... river
sopka, *Rus* ... peak, volcano
source, *Fr* ... a spring
spitze, *Ger* ... summit, point
staat, *Ger* ... state
stad, *Dan., Du., Nor., Swe.* ... city, town
stadt, *Ger* ... city, town
stato, *It* ... state
step, *Rus* ... treeless plain, steppe
straat, *Du* ... strait
strand, *Dan., Du., Ger., Nor., Swe* ... shore, beach
stretto, *It* ... strait
strom, *Ger* ... river, stream
ström, *Dan., Nor., Swe* stream, river
stroom, *Du* ... stream, river
su, suyu, *Tur* ... water, river
sud, *Fr., Sp* ... south
süd, *Ger* ... south
suidō, *Jap* ... channel
sul, *Port* ... south
sund, *Dan., Nor., Swe* ... sound
sungai, sungei, *Indon., Mal* ... river
sur, *Sp* ... south
syd, *Dan., Nor., Swe* ... south
tafelland, *Ger* ... plateau
take, *Jap* ... peak, summit
tal, *Ger* ... valley
tandjoeng, tanjong, *Mal* ... cape
tao, *Chn* ... island
târg, târgul, *Rom* ... market, town
tell, *Arab* ... hill
teluk, *Indon* ... bay, gulf
terra, *It* ... land
terre, *Fr* ... earth, land
thal, *Ger* ... valley
tierra, *Sp* ... earth, land
tō, *Jap* ... east; island
tonle, *Camb* ... river, lake
top, *Du* ... peak
torp, *Swe* ... hamlet, cottage
tsangpo, *Tib* ... river
tsi, *Chn* ... village, borough
tso, *Tib* ... lake
tsu, *Jap* ... harbor, port
tundra, *Rus* ... treeless arctic plains
tung, *Chn* ... east
tuz, *Tur* ... salt
udde, *Swe* ... cape
ufer, *Ger* ... shore, river bank
umi, *Jap* ... sea, gulf
ura, *Jap* ... bay, coast, creek
ust'ye, *Rus* ... river mouth
valle, *It., Port., Sp* ... valley
vallée, *Fr* ... valley
valli, *It* ... lake
vár, *Hung* ... fortress
város, *Hung* ... town
varoš, *So. Slav* ... town
veld, *Du* ... open plain, field
verkh, *Rus* ... top, summit
ves, *Czech* ... village
vest, *Dan., Nor., Swe* ... west
vik, *Swe* ... cove, bay
vila, *Port* ... town
villa, *Sp* ... town
villar, *Sp* ... village, hamlet
ville, *Fr* ... town, city
vostok, *Rus* ... east
wad, wadi, *Arab.* ... intermittent stream
wald, *Ger* ... forest, woodland
wan, *Chn., Jap* ... bay, gulf
weiler, *Ger* ... hamlet, village
westersch, *Du* ... western
wüste, *Ger* ... desert
yama, *Jap* ... mountain
yarimada, *Tur* ... peninsula
yug, *Rus* ... south
zaki, *Jap* ... cape
zaliv, *Rus* ... bay, gulf
zapad, *Rus* ... west
zee, *Du* ... sea
zemlya, *Rus* ... land
zuid, *Du* ... south

ABBREVIATIONS OF
GEOGRAPHICAL NAMES AND TERMS

Afg............Afghanistan
Afr................Africa
Ala...............Alabama
Alb...............Albania
Alg.,,,............Algeria
Alsk...............Alaska
Am. Sam...American Samoa
And..............Andorra
Ang...............Angola
Ant.............Antarctica
Arc. O........Arctic Ocean
Arch.........Archipelago
Arg.............Argentina
Ariz.............Arizona
Ark.............Arkansas
A. S. S. R.
   Autonomous Soviet
   Socialist Republic
Atl. O........Atlantic Ocean
Aus...............Austria
Austl...........Australia
Aut...........Autonomous

B............Bay, Bahia
Ba. Is......Bahama Is.
Barb............Barbados
Bdy............Boundary
Bel..............Belgium
Bg................Berg
Bhu..............Bhutan
Bk................Bank
Bol..............Bolivia
Bots...........Botswana
Br...............British
Braz..............Brazil
Br. Comm.
   British Commonwealth
   of Nations
Br. Hond...British Honduras
Brit. Prot..British Protectorate
Bru...............Brunei
Bul.............Bulgaria
Bur...............Burma

C...........Cerro, Cape
Calif...........California
Cam...........Cameroon
Camb..........Cambodia
Can....Canal, Canada
Can. Is....Canary Is.
Cen. Afr. Rep.
   Central African Republic
Cen. Am.....Central America
C. H.......Court House
Chan...........Channel
Co................County
Col.............Colombia
Colo............Colorado
Con. B.
   Congo; capital Brazzaville
Con. K...Congo, The; capital;
   Kinshasa
Conn..........Connecticut
Cor.............Corsica
C. R.........Costa Rica
Cr................Creek
C. V. Is.......Cape Verde Is.
C. Z..........Canal Zone
Czech.......Czechoslovakia

D. C.....District of Columbia
Del.............Delaware
Den.............Denmark
Dept.........Department
Des..............Desert
D. F....Distrito Federal
Dist.............District
Div.............Division
Dom. Rep.
   Dominican Republic

E..................East
Ec..............Ecuador
Elec.............Electric
Eng.............England
E. Pak......East Pakistan
Equat. Gui..Equatorial Guinea
Eth.............Ethiopia
Eur..............Europe

Faer............Faeroe Is.
Falk. Is......Falkland Is.
Fd................Fjord
Fin..............Finland
Fk................Fork
Fla..............Florida
For..............Forest
Fr.................France
Fr. Gu.....French Guiana
Fr. Som....French Somaliland
Ft................Fort

G..................Gulf
Ga..............Georgia
Gam............Gambia
Ger............Germany
Gib............Gibraltar
Grc..............Greece
Grnld.........Greenland
Gt................Great
Gt. Brit....Great Britain

Guad..........Guadeloupe
Guat..........Guatemala
Gui..............Guinea
Guy............Guyana

Hai................Haiti
Har., Hbr...Harbor, Harbour
Hd.................Head
Hond..........Honduras
Hts.............Heights
Hung..........Hungary

I..................Island
Ice..............Iceland
Ill................Illinois
In..................Inset
Ind...............Indiana
Ind. O......Indian Ocean
Indon.........Indonesia
Ind. Res...Indian Reservation
Int., Intl....International
Ire...............Ireland
Is................Islands
Isr................Israel
Isth............Isthmus
It....................Italy

Jam.............Jamaica
Jap................Japan
Jc..............Junction

Kans............Kansas
Ken..............Kenya
Km....Kilometer, Kilometers
Kor................Korea
Kur. Is.......Kuril Is.
Kuw.............Kuwait
Ky..............Kentucky

L........Lake, Loch, Lough
La.............Louisiana
Lat.............Latitude
Leb............Lebanon
Le. Is.......Leeward Is.
Leso............Lesotho
Lib..............Liberia
Liech.......Liechtenstein
Long............Longitude
Lux..........Luxembourg

M.........Mile, Miles
Mad. Is.....Madeira Islands
Mala...........Malaysia
Malag. Rep.
   Malagasy Republic
Mand............Mandate
Mart.........Martinique
Mass......Massachusetts
Max.........Maximum
Max. surf. elev.
   Maximum surface
   elevation
Md.............Maryland
Medit......Mediterranean
Mex..............Mexico
Mi.........Mile, Miles
Mich..........Michigan
Minn..........Minnesota
Miss.........Mississippi
Mo.............Missouri
Mong..........Mongolia
Mont..........Montana
Mor............Morocco
Moz..........Mozambique
Mt................Mount
Mtn...........Mountain
Mts..........Mountains
Mus. & Om...Muscat & Oman

N.................North
N. A.......North America
Natl...........National
Natl. Mon.
   National Monument
N. C........North Carolina
N. Cal......New Caledonia
N. D.......North Dakota
Nebr.........Nebraska
Nep.............Nepal
Neth........Netherlands
Nev..............Nevada
New Hebr....New Hebrides
N. Gui. Ter...New Guinea Ter.
N. H......New Hampshire
Nic............Nicaragua
Nig.............Nigeria
N. Ire....Northern Ireland
N. J.........New Jersey
N. Mex.....New Mexico
Nor...............Norway
N. Y..........New York
N. Z..........New Zealand

O..................Ocean
Obs.........Observatory
Okla..........Oklahoma
Ore..............Oregon

P...................Pass
Pa..........Pennsylvania
Pac. O....Pacific Ocean

Pan.............Panama
Pap...............Papua
Par.............Paraguay
Pass............Passage
Pen.............Peninsula
Phil.........Philippines
Pk.........Peak, Park
Plat............Plateau
Pln................Plain
Pol...............Poland
Port.............Portugal
Port. Gui...Portuguese Guinea
Port. Tim...Portuguese Timor
Poss.........Possession
P. R........Puerto Rico
Prot........Protectorate
Prov..........Province
Pt.................Point
Pta................Punta
Pte...............Pointe

R.......River, Rio, Rivière
Ra....Range, Ranges
Reg.............Region
Rep.............Republic
Res....Reservation, Reservoir
Rf..................Reef
Rh..............Rhodesia
R. I.......Rhode Island
Rom............Romania
R. R............Railroad
R. S. F. S. R....Russian Soviet
   Federated Socialist
   Republic
Rw.............Rwanda
Ry..............Railway
Rys...........Railways

S......San, Santo, South
Sa......Serra, Sierra
S. A........South America
Sal........El Salvador
Sard............Sardinia
Sau. Ar......Saudi Arabia
S. C........South Carolina
Scot...........Scotland
S. D........South Dakota
Sd................Sound
S. L.........Sierra Leone
Sol. Is......Solomon Is.
Som......Somali Republic
S. Ar........South Arabia
Sov. Un......Soviet Union
Sp.................Spain
Sp. Gui....Spanish Guinea
Spr., Sprs...Spring, Springs
Sp. Sah....Spanish Sahara
S. S. R.....Soviet Socialist
   Republic
St..................Saint
Sta...............Santa
Ste...............Sainte
Str................Strait
Strm.............Stream
Sud................Sudan
Sur.............Surinam
S. Afr.......South Africa
S. W. Afr...South West Africa
Swaz.........Swaziland
Swe............Sweden
Switz.......Switzerland
Swp..............Swamp
Syr.................Syria

Tan............Tanzania
Tas............Tasmania
Tenn.........Tennessee
Ter............Territory
Tex..............Texas
Thai..........Thailand
Trin...Trinidad and Tobago
Tr. State......Trucial State
Tun..............Tunisia
Tur..............Turkey

U. A. R. United Arab Republic
Ug...............Uganda
U. K........United Kingdom
   of Gt. Brit. and N. Ire.
Ur..............Uruguay
U. S., U. S. A.
   United States of America

Va..............Virginia
Val................Valley
Ven...........Venezuela
Viet.............Vietnam
Vir. Is........Virgin Is.
Vol.............Volcano
Vt................Vermont

W..................West
Wash.........Washington
W. I..........West Indies
Wind. Is...Windward Islands
W. Irian......West Irian
Wis...........Wisconsin
W. Pak....West Pakistan
W. Sam....Western Samoa
W. Va....West Virginia
Wyo...........Wyoming

Yugo........Yugoslavia

PRONUNCIATION OF
GEOGRAPHICAL NAMES

Key to the Sound Values of Letters and Symbols
Used in the Index to Indicate Pronunciation

ă—ăt, căt, băttle
ȧ—ȧppeal, finȧl
ā—rāte, elāte
â—inanimâte, senâte
ä—cälm, ärm
à—àsk, bàth
a̠—ma̠rine, sofa̠ (short neutral or indeterminate sound)
å—fåre, prepåre
ch—church, choose
dh—as th in other, either
ē—bē, ēve
ê—crêate, êvent
ĕ—bĕt, ĕnd
ḝ—recḝnt (short neutral or indeterminate sound)
ẽ—cratẽr, cindẽr
g—gō, gāme
gh—guttural g
ĭ—wĭll, bĭt
ḭ—short neutral or indeterminate sound
ī—rīde, bīte
к—guttural k as ch in German ich
ng—sing
ŋ—baŋk, liŋger
N—indicates nasalized preceding vowel
ŏ—nŏd, ŏdd
ọ—cọmmit, cọnnect
ō—ōld, bōld
ô—ôbey, hôtel
ô—ôrder, nôrth
oi—boil
ōō—fōōd, rōōt
ŏŏ—fŏŏt, wŏŏd
ou—thou, out
s—as in soft, so, sane
sh—dish, finish
th—thin, thick
ū—pūre, cūre
û—ûnite, ûsurp
û—ûrn, fûr
ŭ—stŭd, ŭp
ü—as in French tu or as "y" in study
u̇—circu̇s, su̇bmit
zh—as z in azure
'—indeterminate vowel sound

In many cases the spelling of foreign geographic names does not even remotely indicate the pronunciation to an American, i. e., Slupca in Poland is pronounced swŏŏp'tsȧ; Jujuy in Argentina is pronounced hōō-hwē'; Spezia in Italy is spät'sē-ä.

This condition is hardly surprising, however, when we consider that in our own language Worcester, Massachusetts, is pronounced wŏŏs'tẽr; Sioux City, Iowa, sōō sĭ'tĭ; Schuylkill Haven, Pennsylvania, skōōl'kĭl; Poughkeepsie, New York, pȯ-kĭp'sē.

The indication of pronunciation of geographic names presents several peculiar problems:

(1) Many foreign tongues use sounds that are not present in the English language and which an American cannot normally articulate. Thus, though the nearest English equivalent sound has been indicated, only approximate results are possible.

(2) There are several dialects in each foreign tongue which cause variation in the local pronunciation of names. This also occurs in identical names in the various divisions of a great language group, as the Slavic or the Latin.

(3) Within the United States there are marked differences in pronunciation, not only of local geographic names, but also of common words, indicating that the sound and tone values for letters as well as the placing of the emphasis vary considerably from one part of the country to another.

(4) A number of different letter and diacritical combinations could be used to indicate essentially the same or approximate pronunciations.

Some variation in pronunciation other than that indicated in this index may be encountered, but such a difference does not necessarily indicate that either is in error, and in many cases it is a matter of individual choice as to which is preferred. In fact, an exact indication of pronunciation of many foreign names using English letters and diacritical marks is extremely difficult and sometimes impossible.

A PRONOUNCING INDEX

of over 30,000 Geographical Names

This universal index includes in a single alphabetical list all important names that appear on the reference maps. Each place name is preceded by the page number of the map on which it appears. Place names are followed by the pronunciation of the name (see facing page for an explanation of the pronunciation system); the location; and the approximate geographic coordinates.

State locations are listed for all places in the United States. All other place name entries show only country locations. When a name is only shown on an inset map the name of the inset on which it appears is listed.

All minor political divisions are followed by a descriptive term (Dist., Reg., Prov., State, etc.) and by the country in which they are located.

The names of physical features and points of interest that are shown on the maps are listed in the index. Each entry is followed by a descriptive term (Bay, Hill, Mtn., Is., Plat., etc.) to indicate its nature.

The system of alphabetizing used in the index is standard. When more than one name with the same spelling is shown, including both political and physical names, the order of precedence is as follows: *first*, place names, *second*, political divisions, and *third*, physical features.

Local official names are used on the maps for nearly all cities and towns, with the exception of about fifty major world cities for which Anglicized conventional names have been preferred. For these exceptions the index gives a cross reference to the official local name.

Page	Name Pronunciation Region	Lat. °′	Long. °′
123	Aachen (ä′kĕn) . . . Ger. (Ruhr In.)	50·46 N	6·07 E
118	Aakirkeby (ô-kĭr′kĕ-bü) . . . . . Den.	55·04 N	15·00 E
120	Aalen (ä′lĕn) . . . . Ger.	48·49 N	10·08 E
111	Aalsmeer . . Neth. (Amsterdam In.)	52·16 N	4·44 E
111	Aalst . . . . Bel. (Brussels In.)	50·58 N	4·00 E
120	Aarau (är′ou) . . . . Switz.	47·22 N	8·03 E
111	Aarschot . . . . . . Bel. (Brussels In.)	50·59 N	4·51 E
164	Aba . . . . Nig.	5·13 N	7·14 E
144	Ābādān (ä-bŭ-dän′) . . . . Iran	30·15 N	48·30 E
99	Abaetetuba (ä′bȧĕ-tĕ-tōō′bȧ) Braz.	1·44 S	48·45 W
69	Abajo Pk. (ä-bȧ′-hŏ) . . . . Utah	38·50 N	109·35 W
134	Abakan (ŭ-bȧ-kän′) . . . . . Sov. Un.	53·43 N	91·28 E
134	Abakan (R.) . . . . Sov. Un.	53·00 N	91·06 E
98	Abancay (ä-bän-kä′ê) . . . . Peru	13·44 S	72·46 W
152	Abashiri (ä-bä-shē′rê) . . . . Jap.	44·00 N	144·13 E
90	Abasolo (ä-bä-sō′lô) . . . . Mex.	24·05 N	98·24 W
76	Abasolo . . . . Mex.	27·13 N	101·25 W
165	Abaya L. (ȧ-bä′yȧ) . . . . Eth.	6·24 N	38·22 E
165	Abbai R. (ȧ-bä′ê) . . . . Eth.	9·45 N	37·23 E
78	Abbeville (ăb′ê-vĭl) . . . . Ala.	31·35 N	85·15 W
122	Abbeville (ȧb-vēl′) . . . . Fr.	50·08 N	1·49 E
78	Abbeville (ăb′ê-vĭl) . . . . Ga.	31·53 N	83·23 W
77	Abbeville . . . . La.	29·59 N	92·07 W
79	Abbeville . . . . S. C.	34·09 N	82·25 W
126	Abbiategrasso (äb-byä′tȧ-gräs′sō) It.	45·23 N	8·52 E
110	Abbots Bromley (ăb′ŭts brŭm′lê) . Eng.	52·49 N	1·52 W
65	Abbotsford (ăb′ŭts-fērd) Can. (Vancouver In.)	49·03 N	122·17 W
168	Abd Al Kuri (I.) (ăbd-ĕl-kōō′rê) S. Ar. (Horn of Afr. In.)	12·21 N	51·00 E
132	Abdulino (äb-dōō-lē′nō) . . Sov. Un.	53·40 N	53·45 E
165	Abéché (ȧ-bĕ-shā′) . . . . Chad	13·48 N	20·39 E
118	Åbenrå (ô′bĕn-rô) . . . . Den.	55·03 N	9·20 E
164	Abeokuta (ä-bȧ-ô-kōō′tä) . . . . Nig.	7·14 N	3·19 E
166	Abercorn (ăb′ēr-kôrn) . . . . . Zambia	8·45 S	31·23 E
116	Aberdare (ăb-ēr-dâr′) . . . . Wales	51·45 N	3·35 W
116	Aberdeen (ăb-ēr-dēn′) . . . . Scot.	57·10 N	2·05 W
78	Aberdeen . . . . Miss.	33·49 N	88·33 W
70	Aberdeen . . . . S. D.	45·28 N	98·29 W
66	Aberdeen . . . . Wash.	47·00 N	123·48 W
110	Aberford (ăb′ēr-fērd) . . . . Eng.	53·49 N	1·21 W
116	Abergavenny (ăb′ēr-gȧ-vĕn′ĭ) Wales	51·45 N	3·05 W
66	Abert L. (ā′bērt) . . . . Ore.	42·39 N	120·24 W
116	Aberystwyth (ă-bēr-ĭst′wĭth) Wales	52·25 N	4·04 W
136	Abestovskiy (ä-bĕs′tôv-skĭ) Sov. Un. (Urals In.)	57·46 N	61·23 E
144	Abhā . . . . Sau. Ar.	17·47 N	42·29 E
164	Abidjan (ä-bêd-zhäɴ′) . Ivory Coast	5·26 N	4·06 W
153	Abiko (ä-bē-kō) . Jap. (Tōkyō In.)	35·53 N	140·01 E
73	Abilene (ăb′ĭ-lēn) . . . . Kans.	38·54 N	97·12 W
76	Abilene . . . . Tex.	32·25 N	99·45 W
110	Abingdon . . . . . . Eng. (London In.)	51·38 N	1·17 W
71	Abingdon (ăb′ĭng-dŭn) . . . . Ill.	40·48 N	90·21 W
79	Abingdon . . . . Va.	36·42 N	81·57 W
83	Abington (ăb′ĭng-tŭn) Mass. (Boston In.)	42·07 N	70·57 W
69	Abiquiu Res . . . . N. Mex.	36·26 N	106·42 W
87	Abitibi (L.) (ăb-ĭ-tĭb′ĭ) . . . . . . Can.	48·27 N	80·20 W
87	Abitibi (R.) . . . . Can.	49·30 N	81·10 W
133	Abkhaz A.S.S.R. . . . . Sov. Un.	43·10 N	40·45 E
123	Ablis (ȧ-blē′) . . . . . . Fr. (Paris In.)	48·31 N	1·50 E
168	Abnūb (ȧb-nōōb′) U. A. R. (Nile In.)	27·18 N	31·11 E
	Åbo, see Turku		
142	Abohar . . . . India	30·12 N	74·13 E
164	Abomey (ȧb-ô-mā′) . . . . . Dahomey	7·13 N	2·04 E
121	Abony (ŏ′bô-ny′) . . . . Hung.	47·12 N	20·00 E
144	Abou Ke′mal (ä′bōō kĕ′mȧl) . . Syr.	34·45 N	40·46 E
155	Abra (R.) (ä′brä) Phil. (Manila In.)	17·16 N	120·38 E
101	Abraão (äbrȧ-ouɴ′) Braz. (Rio de Janeiro In.)	23·10 S	44·10 W
95	Abraham′s B. . . . . Ba. Is.	22·20 N	73·50 W
110	Abram (ā′brăm) . . . . Eng.	53·31 N	2·36 W
124	Abrantes (ȧ-brän′tĕs) . . . . Port.	39·28 N	8·13 W
165	Abri . . . . Sud.	20·36 N	29·57 E
99	Abrolhos, Arquipélago dos (Arch.) (ä-rōōê-pĕ′lä-gô-dôs-ä-brô′l-yōs) Braz.	17·58 S	38·40 W
119	Abruka (I.) (ȧ-brōō′kȧ) . . Sov. Un.	58·09 N	22·30 E
126	Abruzzi and Molise (Reg.) (ä-brōōt′sē, mô′lê-zā) . . . . It.	42·10 N	13·55 E
67	Absaroka Ra. (Mts.) (ȧb-sȧ-rō′kȧ) . Wyo.	44·50 N	109·47 W
142	Abu (ȧ′bōō) . . . . India	24·38 N	72·45 E
144	Abū Arīsh (ä′bōō ȧ-rēsh′) . Sau. Ar.	16·48 N	43·00 E
165	Abu Hamed (ä′bōō hä′mĕd) . . Sud.	19·37 N	33·21 E
115	Abūksāh . . . . U. A. R.	29·29 N	30·40 E
98	Abunã (R.) (ȧ-bōō-nä′) . Bol-Braz. .	10·25 S	67·00 W
168	Abū Qīr (ä′bōō kēr′) U. A. R. (Nile In.)	31·18 N	30·06 E
168	Abū Qurqāṣ (ä′bōō kōōr-käs′) U. A. R. (Nile In.)	27·57 N	30·51 E
139	Abu Qurûn, Ras (Mt.) U. A. R. (Palestine In.)	30·22 N	33·32 E
153	Aburatsu (ä′bōō-rät′sōō) . . . . . Jap.	31·33 N	131·20 E
168	Abū Tīj . . . . U. A. R. (Nile In.)	27·03 N	31·19 E
144	Abū Zabī . . . . Tr. States	24·15 N	54·28 E
139	Abū Zanīmah U. A. R. (Palestine In.)	29·03 N	33·08 E
139	Abyad (R.) . Jordan (Palestine In.)	30·07 N	36·01 E
118	Åby-Klippan (ô′bü klĭp′pȧn) . Swe.	56·08 N	13·09 E
135	Abyy . . . . Sov. Un.	68·24 N	134·00 E
98	Acacias (ȧ-kȧ′sēäs) . . . . . Col. (In.)	3·59 N	73·44 W
82	Acadia Natl. Park (ȧ-kā′dĭ-ȧ) Maine	44·19 N	68·01 W
92	Acajutla (ä-kä-hōōt′lä) . . . . Sal.	13·37 N	89·50 W
91	Acala (ä-kä′-lä) . . . . Mex.	16·38 N	92·49 W
90	Acȧmbaro (ä-käm′bä-rō) . . . . Mex.	20·03 N	100·42 W
92	Acancéh (ä-kän-sĕ′) Mex. (Yucatan In.)	20·50 N	89·27 W
90	Acapetlahuaya (ä-kä-pĕt′lä-hwä′yä) . Mex.	18·24 N	100·04 W
90	Acaponeta (ä-kä-pô-nā′tȧ) . . . Mex.	22·31 N	105·25 W
90	Acaponeta (R.) . . . . Mex.	22·47 N	105·23 W
90	Acapulco (ä-kä-pōōl′kō) . . . . . Mex.	16·49 N	99·57 W
99	Acaraí Mts. . . . . Braz.	1·30 N	57·40 W
99	Acaraú (ä-kȧrhȧ-ōō′) . . . . Braz.	2·55 S	40·04 W
98	Acarigua (äkȧ-rē′gwä) . . . . Ven.	9·29 N	69·11 W
90	Acatlán de Osorio (ä-kät-län′dā ô-sō′rē-ō) . Mex.	18·11 N	98·04 W
91	Acatzingo de Hidalgo (ä-kät-zĭŋ′gō dā ê-dhäl′gō) . Mex.	18·58 N	97·47 W
91	Acayucan (ä-kä-yōō′kän) . . . . Mex.	17·56 N	94·55 W
80	Accoville (äk′kô-vĭl) . . . . . . W. Va.	37·45 N	81·50 W
164	Accra (ă′krȧ) . . . . Ghana	5·40 N	0·15 W
110	Accrington (ăk′rĭng-tŭn) . . . . . Eng.	53·45 N	2·22 W
125	Acerra (ä-chĕ′r-rä) . It. (Naples In.)	40·42 N	14·22 E
98	Achacachi (ä-chä-kä′chê) . . . . . Bol.	16·11 S	68·32 W
152	Acheng (ä′chĕng′) . . . . China	45·32 N	126·59 E
116	Achill (ă-chĭl′) . . . . Ire.	53·55 N	10·05 W
134	Achinsk (ȧ-chênsk′) . . . . . Sov. Un.	56·13 N	90·32 E
126	Acireale (ä-chê-rā-ä′lā) . . . . It.	37·37 N	15·12 E
78	Ackia Battle Ground Natl. Mon. (ă-ᴋyŭ′) . Miss.	34·22 N	89·05 W
95	Acklins (I.) (ăk′lĭns) . . . . . . Ba. Is.	22·30 N	73·55 W
95	Acklins, The Bight of (B.) . Ba. Is.	22·35 N	74·20 W
91	Acolman (ä-kôl-mȧ′n) Mex. (Mexico City In.)	19·38 N	98·56 W
101	Aconcagua (ä-kôn-kä′gwä) (Prov.) Chile (Santiago In.)	32·20 S	71·00 W
101	Aconcagua, Cerro (Mtn.) Arg. (Santiago In.)	32·38 S	70·00 W
101	Aconcagua (R.) Chile (Santiago In.)	32·43 S	70·53 W
164	Açores (Azores) Is. (ä-zô′rês) (ȧ-zōrz′) . Atl. O.	37·44 N	29·25 W
92	Acoyapa (ä-kô-yä′pä) . . . . Nic.	11·54 N	85·11 W
126	Acqui (äk′kwē) . . . . It.	44·41 N	8·22 W
139	Acre (ä′kēr) . . . Isr. (Palestine In.)	32·56 N	35·05 E
98	Acre (State) (ä′krā) . . . . Braz.	8·40 S	70·45 W
98	Acre (R.) . . . . Braz.	10·33 S	68·34 W
84	Acton (ăk′tŭn) Ala. (Birmingham In.)	33·21 N	86·49 W
85	Acton . . . . Can. (Toronto In.)	43·38 N	80·02 W
75	Acton . . . . . Ind. (Indianapolis In.)	39·39 N	85·58 W
83	Acton . . . . Mass. (Boston In.)	42·29 N	71·26 W
82	Acton Vale . . . . Can.	45·39 N	72·33 W
90	Actopan (äk-tô-pän′) . . . . Mex.	20·16 N	98·57 W
91	Actópan (R.) (äk-tŏ′pän) . . . . Mex.	19·25 N	96·31 W
90	Acuitzio del Canje (ä-kwēt′zê-ō dĕl kän′hȧ) . Mex.	19·28 N	101·21 W
95	Acul, Baie de l′ (B.) (ä-kōōl′) . Hai.	19·55 N	72·20 W
164	Ada (ä′dä) . . . . Ghana	5·57 N	0·31 E
70	Ada (ā′dŭ) . . . . Minn.	47·17 N	96·32 W
80	Ada . . . . Ohio	40·45 N	83·45 W
73	Ada . . . . Okla.	34·45 N	96·43 W
127	Ada (ä′dä) . . . . Yugo.	45·48 N	20·06 E
64	Adak (ă-dăk′) . . . . Alaska	56·50 N	176·48 W
64	Adak (I.) . . . . Alaska	51·40 N	176·28 W
64	Adak Str. . . . . Alaska	51·42 N	177·16 W
	Adalia, see Antalya		
164	Adamawa (Reg.) (ä-dä-mä′wä) Nig.-Cam.	8·39 N	11·58 E
81	Adams (ăd′ămz) . . . . Mass.	42·35 N	73·10 W
71	Adams . . . . Wis.	43·55 N	89·48 W
64	Adams, Mt. . . . . Alaska	55·40 N	130·25 W
66	Adams, Mt. . . . . Wash.	46·15 N	121·19 W
84	Adamsville (ăd′ămz-vĭl) Ala. (Birmingham In.)	33·36 N	86·57 W
84	Adamsville . . . . . Ga. (Atlanta In.)	33·45 N	84·31 W
84	Adamsville, R. I. (Providence In.)	41·33 N	71·04 W
133	Adana (ä′dä-nä) . . . . Tur.	37·05 N	35·20 E
133	Adapazarı (ä-dä-pä-zä′rê) . . . . Tur.	40·45 N	30·20 E
165	Adarama (ä-dä-rä′mä) . . . . Sud.	17·11 N	34·56 E
126	Adda (R.) (äd′dä) . . . . It.	45·43 N	9·31 E
144	Ad Dahna (Des.) . . . . Sau. Ar.	26·05 N	47·15 E
144	Ad Dam (äd däm′) . . . . . . Sau. Ar.	20·45 N	44·12 E
144	Ad Dammān . . . . Sau. Ar.	26·27 N	49·59 E
139	Ad Damur . . . . Leb. (Palestine In.)	33·44 N	35·27 E
144	Ad Dawhah . . . . Qatar	25·02 N	51·28 E
144	Ad Dilam . . . . Sau. Ar.	23·47 N	47·03 E
165	Addis Ababā . . . . Eth.	9·00 N	38·44 E
74	Addison (ă′dĭ-sŭn) Tex. (Dallas, Fort Worth In.)	32·58 N	96·50 W
165	Ad Dīwān . . . . U. A. R.	23·30 N	33·10 E
167	Addo (ădō) . . . . S. Afr. (Natal In.)	33·33 S	25·43 E
75	Addyston (ăd′ê-stŭn) Ohio (Cincinnati In.)	39·09 N	84·42 W
78	Adel (ā-dĕl′) . . . . Ga.	31·08 N	83·55 W
167	Adelaide (ăd-ĕl′ād) S. Afr. (Natal In.)	32·41 S	26·07 E
160	Adelaide (ăd′ê-lād) . . . . Austl.	34·46 S	139·08 E
47	Adelaide I. . . . . Ant.	67·15 S	68·40 W
144	Aden (ä′dĕn) . . . . Aden	12·48 N	45·00 E
144	Aden, G. of . . . . Asia	11·45 N	45·45 E
155	Adi (I.) (ä′dē) . . . . W. Irian	4·25 S	133·52 E
114	Adige R. (ä′dê-jā) . . . . . Aus.-Switz.	46·34 N	10·51 E
126	Adige, Fiume (R.) (fyōō′mĕ-ä′dê-jā) . It.	46·38 N	10·43 E
142	Ādilābād (ŭ-dĭl-ä-bäd′) . . . . . India	19·47 N	78·30 E
143	Adini . . . . India	15·42 N	77·18 E
81	Adirondack, Mts. (ăd-ĭ-rŏn′dăk) N. Y.	43·45 N	74·40 W
165	Adi Ugri (ä-dē ōō′grē) . . . . Eth.	14·54 N	38·52 E
121	Adjud (äd′zhōōd) . . . . Rom.	46·05 N	27·12 E
64	Admiralty (I.) . . . . Alaska	57·50 N	133·50 W
65	Admiralty Inlet (ăd′mĭrȧl-tê) Wash. (Seattle In.)	48·10 N	122·45 W
155	Admiralty Is. . . . . N. Gui. Ter.	1·40 S	146·45 E
74	Adolph (ā′dolf) Minn. (Duluth In.)	46·47 N	92·17 W
122	Adour (R.) (ȧ-dōōr′) . . . . Fr.	43·43 N	0·38 W
124	Adra (ä′drä) . . . . Sp.	36·45 N	3·02 W
126	Adrano (ä-drä′nō) . . . . It.	37·42 N	14·52 E
164	Adrar des Iforas (Reg.) (ä-drär′) Alg.	20·22 N	1·44 E
126	Adria (ä′drê-ä) . . . . It.	45·03 N	12·01 E
80	Adrian (ā′drĭ-ăn) . . . . Mich.	41·55 N	84·00 W
70	Adrian . . . . Minn.	43·39 N	95·56 W
	Adrianople, see Edirne		
126	Adriatic Sea . . . . Eur.	41·30 N	14·27 E
164	Adrir . . . . Alg.	27·53 N	0·15 W
100	Adrogué (ȧdrō-gā′) . . . . . Arg. (In.)	34·33 S	58·24 W
165	Aduwā . . . . Eth.	14·02 N	38·58 E
110	Adwick-le-Street (ăd′wĭk-lê-strēt′) Eng.	53·35 N	1·11 W
135	Adycha (R.) (ä′dĭ-chȧ) . . Sov. Un.	66·11 N	136·45 E
129	Adzhamka (ȧd-zhäm′kȧ) . Sov. Un.	48·33 N	32·28 E
132	Adz′va (R.) (ädz′vȧ) . . . . Sov. Un.	67·00 N	59·20 E
115	Aegean Sea (ê-jē′ăn) . . . . Eur.-Asia	39·04 N	24·56 E
118	Aerø (I.) (âr′ö) . . . . Den.	54·52 N	10·22 E
138	Afghanistan (ăf-găn-ĭ-stăn′) . . Asia	33·00 N	63·00 E
168	Afgoi (äf-gô′ĭ) Som. (Horn of Afr. In.)	2·08 N	45·08 E
164	Aflou (ä-flōō′) . . . . Alg.	33·59 N	2·04 E
64	Afognak (I.) (ä-fŏg-nȧk′) . . Alaska	58·28 N	151·35 W
125	Afragola (ä-frȧ′gō-lä) It. (Naples In.)	40·40 N	14·19 E
7	Africa (ăf′rĭ-kȧ)		
74	Afton (ăf′tŭn) . . . . Minn. (Minneapolis, St. Paul In.)	44·54 N	92·47 W

174 Afton–Alcaudete PRONOUNCING INDEX

Page Name Pronunciation Region Lat. °′ Long. °′

73 Afton....................Okla. 36·42 N 94·56 W
67 Afton....................Wyo. 42·42 N 110·52 W
139 'Afula (ä-fōō'lȧ) Isr. (Palestine In.) 32·36 N 35·17 E
133 Afyonkarahisar (ä-fê-ŏn-kä-rȧ-hê-sär'). Tur. 38·45 N 30·20 E
165 Agadem (Oasis) (ä'gȧ-dĕm). Niger 16·50 N 13·15 E
164 Agadès (ä'gȧ-dĕs)..........Niger 17·01 N 7·55 E
164 Agadir (ä-gȧ-dēr)...........Mor. 30·30 N 9·37 W
92 Agalta, Cord. de (Mts.) (kôr-dēl-yĕ'rä-dĕ-ä-gä'l-tä).......Hond. 15·15 N 85·42 W
136 Agapovka (ä-gä-pôv'kȧ) Sov. Un. (Urals In.) 53·18 N 59·10 E
142 Agartala...................India 23·53 N 91·22 E
143 Agāshi......India (Bombay In.) 19·28 N 72·46 E
136 Agashkino (ȧ-gȧsh'kĭ-nô) Sov. Un. (Moscow In.) 55·18 N 38·13 E
65 Agate Bay (ăg'ĭt) (ăg'ȧt) Wash. (Vancouver In.) 48·45 N 122·20 W
64 Agattu (I.) (ȧ'gä-tōō)....Alaska 52·14 N 173·40 E
129 Agayman (ȧ-gä-ē-män')..Sov. Un. 46·39 N 34·20 E
133 Agdam (äg'dām)........Sov. Un. 40·00 N 47·00 E
122 Agde (ägd)..................Fr. 43·19 N 3·30 E
122 Agen (ȧ-zhäN')..............Fr. 44·13 N 0·31 E
85 Agincourt (ä'zhĕN-kōōr') Can. (Toronto In.) 43·47 N 79·16 W
135 Aginskoye (ä-hĭn'skô-yĕ).Sov. Un. 51·15 N 113·15 E
65 Agnew (ăg'nū).Wash. (Seattle In.) 48·06 N 123·15 W
155 Agno (äg'nō)...Phil. (Manila In.) 16·07 N 119·49 E
155 Agno (R.)......Phil. (Manila In.) 15·42 N 120·28 E
126 Agnone (än-yō'nä)...........It. 41·49 N 14·23 E
165 Agordat (ä-gōr'dät).........Eth. 15·34 N 37·54 E
142 Agra (ä'grä)...............India 27·18 N 78·00 E
126 Agri (R.) (ä'grē).............It. 40·15 N 16·21 E
127 Agrínion (ȧ-grē'nyôn)........Grc. 38·38 N 21·06 E
92 Agua (Vol.) (ä'gwä).......Guat. 14·28 N 90·43 W
90 Agua Blanca, Río (R.) (rê'ō-ä-gwä-blä'n-kä). Mex. 21·46 N 102·54 W
90 Agua Brava, Laguna de (L.) (lä-gōō'nä-dĕ-ä'gwä-brä'vä)...Mex. 22·04 N 105·40 W
68 Agua Caliente Ind. Res. (ä'gwä kal-yĕn'tä). Calif. 33·50 N 116·24 W
94 Aguada (ä-gwä'dȧ).........Cuba 22·25 N 80·50 W
92 Aguada L....Mex. (Yucatan In.) 18·46 N 89·40 W
98 Aguadas (ä-gwä'-däs)...Col. (In.) 5·37 N 75·27 W
89 Aguadilla (ä-gwä-dēl'yä) P. R. (Puerto Rico In.) 18·27 N 67·10 W
93 Aguadulce (ä-gwä-dōōl'sä)...Pan. 8·15 N 80·33 W
91 Agua Escondida, Meseta de (Plat.) (mĕ-sĕ'tä-dĕ-ä'gwä-ĕs-kôn-dē'dä). Mex. 16·54 N 91·35 W
69 Agua Fria (R.) (ä'gûä frĭ'ä)..Ariz. 33·43 N 112·22 W
101 Aguai (ägwä-ē') Braz. (Rio de Janeiro In.) 22·04 S 46·57 W
76 Agualeguas (ä-gwä-lä'gwäs).Mex. 26·19 N 99·33 W
76 Aguanaval, R. (ä-guä-nä-väl'). Mex. 25·12 N 103·28 W
92 Aguán R. (ä-gwä'n).........Hond. 15·22 N 87·00 W
83 Aguanus (R.) (ä-gwä'nŭs)...Can. 50·45 N 62·03 W
90 Aguascalientes (ä'gwäs-käl-yĕn'täs). Mex. 21·52 N 102·17 W
124 Agueda (ä-gwä'dȧ).........Port. 40·36 N 8·26 W
124 Agueda (R.) (ä-gĕ-dä)........Sp. 40·50 N 6·44 W
164 Aguellal (ä-gĕl-yäl).........Niger 19·05 N 8·10 E
72 Aguilar (ä-gē-lär')..........Colo. 37·24 N 104·38 W
124 Aguilar.......................Sp. 37·32 N 4·39 W
124 Aguilas (ä'gē-läs)............Sp. 37·26 N 1·35 W
90 Aguililla (ä-gē-lēl-yä).......Mex. 18·44 N 102·44 W
98 Aguja, Pta. (Pt.) (pŭn'tä ȧ-gōō' hä). Peru 6·00 S 81·15 W
166 Agulhas, C. (ä-gōōl'yäs)...S. Afr. 34·47 S 20·00 E
154 Agung, Gunung (Mtn.) (ä-gōōng'). Indon. 8·41 S 115·07 E
155 Agusan (R.) (ä-gōō'sän).....Phil. 8·12 N 126·07 E
164 Ahaggar (Mts.) (ȧ-hȧ-gär')...Alg. 23·14 N 6·00 E
123 Ahlen (ä'lĕn).....Ger. (Ruhr In.) 51·45 N 7·52 E
142 Ahmadābād (ŭ-mĕd-ä-bäd'). India 23·04 N 72·38 E
142 Ahmadnagar (ä'mûd-nû-gûr).India 19·09 N 74·45 E
168 Ahmar Mts. Eth. (Horn of Afr. In.) 9·22 N 42·00 E
165 Ahmara Plat..................Eth. 10·09 N 37·21 E
79 Ahoskie (ā-hŏs'kē).........N. C. 36·15 N 77·00 W
111 Ahrensburg (ä'rĕns-bōōrg) Ger. (Hamburg In.) 53·40 N 10·14 E
120 Ahrweiler (är'vī-lĕr).........Ger. 50·34 N 7·05 E
119 Ahtärin-järvi (L.)...........Fin. 62·46 N 24·25 E
90 Ahuacatlán (ä-wä-kät-län')..Mex. 21·05 N 104·28 W
92 Ahuachapan (ä-wä-chä-pän')..Sal. 13·57 N 89·53 W
90 Ahualulco (ä-wä-lōōl'kō)....Mex. 20·43 N 103·57 W
90 Ahuatempan (ä-wä-tĕm-pän).Mex. 18·11 N 98·02 W
118 Ahus (ô'hōōs)...............Swe. 55·56 N 14·19 E
144 Ahvāz.......................Iran 31·15 N 48·54 E
118 Ahvenanma (Åland Is.) (ä'vĕ-nȧn-mô) (ô'länd). Fin. 60·36 N 19·55 E
157 Aiea..............Hawaii (In.) 21·18 N 157·52 W
79 Aiken (ā'kĕn)...............S. C. 33·32 N 81·43 W
99 Aimorés, Serra dos (Mts.) (sĕ'r-rä-dôs-ī-mō-rĕ's). Braz. 17·40 S 42·38 W
153 Aimoto (ī-mô-tō). Jap. (Ōsaka In.) 34·59 N 135·09 E
164 Aïn Beida (ä'ēn bā-dā')......Alg. 35·57 N 7·25 E
123 Aincourt (ăN-kōō'r). Fr. (Paris In.) 49·04 N 1·47 E
125 Aïne Ousséra (ĕn ōō-sä-rȧ)....Alg. 35·25 N 2·50 E
164 Aïn Salah.....................Alg. 27·13 N 2·22 E
164 Aïn Sefra (ä'ēn sĕf'rȧ)......Alg. 32·49 N 0·39 W
83 Ainsle, L. (ăn'slē)..........Can. 46·08 N 61·23 W
70 Ainsworth (ānz'wûrth)......Nebr. 42·32 N 99·51 W
114 Aïn Taïba (ä'ēn tä'ē-bä)....Alg. 30·20 N 5·30 E
113 Aïn-Temouchent (ä'ēntĕ-mōō-shäN'). Alg. 35·20 N 1·23 W
98 Aipe (ī'-pĕ)..........Col. (In.) 3·13 N 75·15 W
122 Aire (âr).....................Fr. 43·42 N 0·17 W
110 Aire (R.)...................Eng. 53·42 N 1·00 W
139 Airhitam, Selat (Str.) Indon. (Singapore In.) 0·58 N 102·38 E
164 Aïr ou Azbine (Mts.).......Niger 18·28 N 7·51 E
122 Aisne (R.) (ĕn)...............Fr. 49·28 N 3·32 E
155 Aitape (ä-ê-tä'pȧ)....N. Gui. Ter. 3·00 S 142·10 E
71 Aitkin (ăt'kĭn)............Minn. 46·32 N 93·43 W
127 Aitolikón (ȧ-tō'lĭ-kôn).......Grc. 38·27 N 21·21 E
127 Aitos (ä-ē'tōs)..............Bul. 42·42 N 27·17 E
157 Aitutaki (I.) (ī-tōō-tä'kē). Cook Is. 19·00 S 162·00 W
121 Aiud (ä'ē-ōōd)..............Rom. 46·19 N 23·40 E
101 Aiuruoca (äē'ōō-rōōô'-kȧ) Braz. (Rio de Janeiro In.) 21·57 S 44·36 W
101 Aiuruoca (R.) Braz. (Rio de Janeiro In.) 22·11 S 44·35 W
122 Aix-en-Provence (ĕks-prô-vȧNs) Fr. (Marseille In.) 43·32 N 5·27 E
123 Aix-les-Bains (ĕks'-lā-băN')....Fr. 45·42 N 5·56 E
127 Aiyien.......................Grc. 37·37 N 22·12 E
127 Aíyina (I.)..................Grc. 37·43 N 23·35 E
127 Aíyion.......................Grc. 38·13 N 22·04 E
119 Aizpute (ä'ēz-pōō-tĕ)....Sov. Un. 56·44 N 21·37 E
153 Aizuwakamatsu...............Jap. 37·27 N 139·51 E
126 Ajaccio (ä-yät'chō)...........Fr. 41·55 N 8·42 E
91 Ajalpan (ä-häl'pän)........Mex. 18·21 N 97·14 W
158 Ajana (äj-än'ĕr)...........Austl. 28·00 S 114·45 E
67 Ajax Mt. (ā'jăks)..........Mont. 45·19 N 113·43 W
165 Ajdabiyah...................Libya 30·56 N 20·16 E
144 Ajman....................Tr. States 25·15 N 54·30 E
142 Ajmer (ŭj-mēr')............India 26·26 N 74·42 E
69 Ajo (ä'hō)...................Ariz. 32·20 N 112·55 W
90 Ajuchitlán del Progreso (ä-hōō-chet-lân). Mex. 18·11 N 100·32 W
91 Ajusco (ä-hōō's-kō) Mex. (Mexico City In.) 19·13 N 99·12 W
91 Ajusco, Cerro (sĕ'r-rô-ä-hōō's-kō) Mex. (Mexico City In.) 19·12 N 99·16 W
153 Akaishi-dake (Mtn.) (ä-kī-shē dä'kä). Jap. 5·30 N 138·00 E
153 Akashi (ä'kä-shē). Jap. (Ōsaka In.) 34·38 N 134·59 E
165 Aketi (ä-kȧ-tē)...........Con. K. 2·58 N 23·57 E
133 Akhaltsikhe (äkȧ'l-tsĭ-kĕ) Sov. Un. 41·40 N 42·50 E
165 Akhdar, Jabal al (Mts.)....Libya 32·45 N 21·52 E
144 Akhdar, Jabal al (Mts.) Mus. & Om.-Sau. Ar. 23·30 N 56·43 E
127 Akhelóös (R.) (ä-hĕ'lô-ōs)...Grc. 38·45 N 21·26 E
133 Akhisar (äk-hĭs-sär')........Tur. 38·58 N 27·58 E
129 Akhtarskaya, Bukhta (B.) (bōōk'tä äK-tär'skä-yȧ). Sov. Un. 45·53 N 38·22 E
127 Akhtopol (äK'tô-pōl)........Bul. 42·08 N 27·54 E
129 Akhtyrka (äK-tür'kȧ)....Sov. Un. 50·18 N 34·53 E
136 Akhunovo (ä-kû'nô-vô) Sov. Un. (Urals In.) 54·13 N 59·36 E
153 Aki (ä'kē)...................Jap. 33·31 N 133·51 E
64 Akiak (äk'yȧk)...........Alaska 61·00 N 161·02 W
87 Akimiski (I.) (ä-kĭ-mĭ'skĭ)...Can. 52·54 N 80·22 W
152 Akita (ä'kē-tä)...............Jap. 39·40 N 140·12 E
164 Akjoujt...............Mauritania 19·45 N 14·30 W
86 Aklavik (äk'lä-vĭk).........Can. 68·28 N 135·26 W
153 Ako (ä'kō)....................Jap. 34·44 N 134·22 E
142 Akola (ä-kô'lä)............India 20·47 N 77·00 E
87 Akpatok (I.) (äk'pȧ-tŏk)....Can. 60·30 N 67·10 W
112 Akranes.......................Ice. 64·18 N 21·40 W
127 Akrítas, Akr. (C.)...........Grc. 37·45 N 23·53 E
72 Akron (ăk'rŭn)...............Colo. 40·09 N 103·14 W
75 Akron......Ohio (Cleveland In.) 41·05 N 81·30 W
139 Akrotiri B.. Cyprus (Palestine In.) 34·38 N 33·18 E
133 Aksaray (äk-sä-rī')..........Tur. 38·30 N 34·05 E
133 Akşehir (äk'shä-hēr)........Tur. 38·20 N 31·20 E
133 Aksehir (L.)..................Tur. 38·40 N 31·30 E
135 Aksha (äk'shä).........Sov. Un. 50·28 N 113·00 E
Aksu, see Wensu
146 Ak Su (R.)..................China 40·34 N 77·15 E
133 Aktyubinsk (äk'tyōō-bĕnsk) Sov. Un. 50·20 N 57·00 E
153 Akune (ä'kōō-nȧ)............Jap. 32·03 N 130·16 E
112 Akureyri (ä-kōō-rȧ'rē)........Ice. 65·39 N 18·01 W
64 Akutan (I.) (ä-kōō-tän')....Alaska 53·58 N 169·54 W
63 Alabama (State)(ăl-ȧ-băm'ȧ).U. S. 32·50 N 87·30 W
78 Alabama (R.).................Ala. 31·20 N 87·39 W
155 Alabat (I.) (ä-lä-bät') Phil. (Manila In.) 14·14 N 122·05 E
155 Alaca (ä-lä-kä). Phil. (Manila In.) 17·56 N 121·39 E
133 Alacam (ä-lä-chäm')..........Tur. 41·30 N 35·40 E
94 Alacranes (ä-lä-krä'nȧs)....Cuba 22·45 N 81·35 W
144 Alaflau (Des.)..........Sau. Ar. 24·00 N 44·47 E
99 Alagôas (ä-lä-gō'äzh)........Braz. 9·50 S 36·33 W
99 Alagoinhas (ä-lä-gō-ēn'yäzh). Braz. 12·13 S 38·12 W
124 Alagón (ä-lä-gōn')............Sp. 41·46 N 1·07 W
124 Alagón (R.)...................Sp. 39·53 N 6·42 W
90 Alahuatán (R.) (ä-lä-wä-tä'n).Mex. 18·30 N 100·00 W
93 Alajuela (ä-lä-hwä'lä)........C.R. 10·01 N 84·14 W
134 Alakol (L.)................Sov. Un. 45·45 N 81·13 E
157 Alalakeiki Chan. (ä-lä-lä-kä'kē) Hawaii (In.) 20·40 N 156·30 W
165 Al 'Alamayn...............U. A. R. 30·53 N 28·52 E
65 Alameda (ăl-ȧ-mā'dȧ) Calif. (San Francisco In.) 37·46 N 122·15 W
65 Alameda (R.) Calif. (San Francisco In.) 37·36 N 122·02 W
155 Alaminos (ä-lä-mē'nôs) Phil. (Manila In.) 16·09 N 119·58 E
115 Al 'Amirīyah...............U. A. R. 31·01 N 29·52 E
65 Alamo (ă'lȧ-mō) Calif. (San Francisco In.) 37·51 N 122·02 W
91 Alamo (ä'lä-mô)...............Mex. 21·07 N 99·35 W
76 Alamo, R. (ä'lä-mô)..........Mex. 26·33 N 99·35 W
69 Alamogordo (ăl-ȧ-mō-gôr'dō) N. Mex. 32·55 N 106·00 W
74 Alamo Heights (ă'lȧ-mō) Tex. (San Antonio In.) 29·28 N 98·27 W
76 Alamo Pk. (ă'lȧ-mō pēk)..N. Mex. 32·50 N 105·55 W
69 Alamosa (ăl-ȧ-mō'sȧ)........Colo. 37·25 N 105·50 W
136 Alandskiy (ä-länt'skĭ) Sov. Un. (Urals In.) 52·14 N 59·48 E
133 Alanya.......................Tur. 36·40 N 32·10 E
167 Alaotra (L.) (ä-lä-ō'trä) Malag. Rep. 17·15 S 48·17 E
136 Alapayevsk (ä-lä-pä'yĕfsk) Sov. Un. (Urals In.) 57·50 N 61·35 E
139 Al 'Aqabah. Jordan (Palestine In.) 29·32 N 35·00 E
90 Alaquines (ä-lȧ-kē'nȧs).....Mex. 22·07 N 99·35 W
139 Al 'Arīsh (ä-resh') U. A. R. (Palestine In.) 31·08 N 33·48 E
150 Ala Shan (Mtns.) (ä'lä-shän') China 38·02 N 105·20 E
62 Alaska (State) (ȧ-lăs'kȧ).....U. S. 65·00 N 158·00 W
64 Alaska, G. of.............Alaska 57·42 N 147·40 W
64 Alaska Hy................Alaska 63·00 N 142·00 W
64 Alaska Pen...............Alaska 55·50 N 162·10 W
64 Alaska Ra.................Alaska 62·00 N 152·18 W
132 Alatyr' (ä'lä-tür)........Sov. Un. 54·55 N 46·30 E
98 Alausí (ä-lou-sē')............Ec. 2·15 S 78·45 W
168 Al 'Ayyāţ (ä-ê-yät') U. A. R. (Nile In.) 29·38 N 31·18 E
126 Alba (äl'bä)..................It. 44·41 N 8·02 E
124 Albacete (äl-bä-thä'tä)........Sp. 39·00 N 1·49 W
123 Albachten (äl-bä'K-tĕn) Ger. (Ruhr In.) 51·55 N 7·31 E
168 Al Badārī.....U. A. R. (Nile In.) 26·59 N 31·29 E
124 Alba de Tormes (äl-bȧ dā tôr'mās) Sp. 40·48 N 5·28 W
168 Al Bahnasā...U. A. R. (Nile In.) 28·35 N 30·30 E
121 Alba Iulia (äl-bä yōō'lyȧ)...Rom. 46·05 N 23·32 E
125 Albalate (äl-bä-lä'tä).........Sp. 41·07 N 0·34 W
168 Al Ballāḩ (bä'lȧ) U. A. R. (Suez In.) 30·46 N 32·20 E
168 Al Balyanā....U. A. R. (Nile In.) 26·12 N 32·00 E
102 Albania (ăl-bā'nĭ-ȧ).........Eur. 41·45 N 20·00 E
125 Albano, Lago (L.) (lä'-gō-äl-bä'nō) It. (Rome In.) 41·45 N 12·44 E
125 Albano Laziale (äl-bä'nō lät-zē-ä'lä). It. (Rome In.) 41·44 N 12·43 E
158 Albany (ôl'bȧ-nĭ)..........Austl. 35·00 S 118·00 E
65 Albany. Calif. (San Francisco In.) 37·54 N 122·18 W
78 Albany......................Ga. 31·35 N 84·10 W
73 Albany......................Mo. 40·14 N 94·18 W
81 Albany.....................N. Y. 42·40 N 73·50 W
66 Albany.....................Ore. 44·38 N 123·06 W
76 Albany.....................Tex. 32·43 N 99·17 W
87 Albany (R.)................Can. 51·45 N 83·30 W
144 Al Başrah...................Iraq 30·27 N 47·52 E
139 Al Batrūn (bä-trōōn') Leb. (Palestine In.) 34·16 N 35·39 E
165 Al Bawīţī...............U. A. R. 28·19 N 29·00 E
155 Albay G. (äl-bä'ē) Phil. (Manila In.) 13·09 N 123·52 E
79 Albemarle (ăl'bē-märl)......N. C. 35·24 N 80·36 W
79 Albemarle Sd...............N. C. 36·00 N 76·17 W
126 Albenga (äl-bĕn'gä)...........It. 44·04 N 8·13 E
124 Alberche (R.) (äl-bĕr'chä).....Sp. 40·08 N 4·19 W
158 Alberga, The (R.) (ăl-bûr'gȧ) Austl. 27·15 S 135·00 E
124 Albergaria a-Velha (äl-bĕr-gȧ-rē'-ȧ-ä-väl'yȧ). Port. 40·47 N 8·31 W
74 Alberhill (ăl'bĕr-hĭl) Calif. (Los Angeles In.) 33·43 N 117·23 W
82 Albert (ăl'bērt)..............Can. 45·44 N 64·46 W
122 Albert (äl-bâr')...............Fr. 50·00 N 2·49 E
86 Alberta (Prov.) (ăl-bûr'tȧ)...Can. 54·33 N 117·10 W
155 Albert Edward, Mt. (ăl'bērt ĕd'wērd). Austl. 8·25 S 147·25 E
101 Alberti (äl-bĕ'r-tē) Arg. (Buenos Aires In.) 35·01 S 60·16 W
111 Albert Kanal (can.) Bel. (Brussels In.) 51·07 N 5·07 E
165 Albert L. (ăl'bērt) (äl-bâr') Con. K.-Ug. 2·00 N 30·16 E
71 Albert Lea (ăl'bērt lē')......Minn. 43·38 N 93·24 W
82 Alberton (ăl'bēr-tŭn).........Can. 46·50 N 64·02 W
167 Alberton..................S. Afr. (Johannesburg & Pretoria In.) 26·16 S 28·08 E
78 Albertville (ăl'bērt-vĭl).......Ala. 34·15 N 86·10 W
166 Albertville (äl-bêr-vēl')...Con. K. 5·59 S 29·12 E
123 Albertville...................Fr. 45·42 N 6·25 E
122 Albi (äl-bē')..................Fr. 43·54 N 2·07 E
71 Albia (ăl bĭ-ȧ)..............Iowa 41·01 N 92·44 W
99 Albina (äl-bē'nä).............Sur. 5·30 N 54·33 W
75 Albino, Pt. (äl-bē'nō) Can. (Buffalo In.) 42·50 N 79·05 W
80 Albion (ăl'bĭ-ŭn)...........Mich. 42·15 N 84·50 W
70 Albion......................Nebr. 41·42 N 99·00 W
81 Albion......................N. Y. 43·15 N 78·10 W
124 Alboran, Isla del (I.) (ê's-lä-dĕl-äl-bō-rä'n). Sp. 35·58 N 3·02 W
124 Alboran Sea...............Medit. 35·54 N 4·26 W
118 Ålborg (ôl'bŏr)..............Den. 57·02 N 9·55 E
124 Albox (äl-bōk')...............Sp. 37·23 N 2·08 W
69 Albuquerque (ăl-bû-kûr'kē) N. Mex. 35·05 N 106·40 W
93 Albuquerque, Cayus de (I.) (äl-bû-kûr'kē). Col. 12·12 N 81·24 W
144 Al Buraymi.........Mus. & Om. 23·45 N 55·39 E
124 Alburquerque (äl-bōōr-kĕr'kä).Sp. 39·13 N 6·58 W
160 Albury (ôl'bēr-ē)...........Austl. 36·00 S 147·00 E
125 Alcabideche (äl-kä-bē-dä'chä) Port. (Lisbon In.) 38·43 N 9·24 W
124 Alcacer do Sal (äl-kä'sĕr dōō säl') Port. 38·24 N 8·33 W
125 Alcalá de Chivert (äl-kä-lä'dä chē-vĕrt'). Sp. 40·18 N 0·12 E
125 Alcalá de Henares (äl-kä-lä' dä ā nä'räs). Sp. (Madrid In.) 40·29 N 3·22 W
124 Alcalá de los Gazules (äl-kä-lä' dä lōs gä-thōō'läs). Sp. 36·29 N 5·44 W
124 Alcalá la Real (äl-kä-lä'lä rä-äl'). Sp. 37·27 N 3·57 W
126 Alcamo (äl'kä-mō)..............It. 37·58 N 13·03 E
125 Alcanadre (R.) (äl-kä-nä'drȧ)..Sp. 41·41 N 0·18 W
125 Alcanar (äl-kä-när')...........Sp. 40·35 N 0·27 E
125 Alcañiz (äl-kän-yēth')........Sp. 41·03 N 0·08 W
99 Alcântara (äl-kän'tȧ-rȧ).....Braz. 2·17 S 44·29 W
124 Alcaraz (äl-kä-räth')..........Sp. 38·39 N 2·28 W
124 Alcaudete (äl-kou-dhä'tä).....Sp. 37·38 N 4·05 W

ăt; finăl; rate; senâte; ārm; ȧsk; sofȧ; fâre; ch-choose; dh-as th in other; bē; ēvent; bĕt; recĕnt; cratēr; g-go; gh-guttural g; bĭt; ĭ-short neutral; rīde; K-guttural k as ch in German ich;

PRONOUNCING INDEX Alcazar de San Juan–Alta Gracia 175

Page	Name Pronunciation Region	Lat. °′	Long. °′
124	Alcázar de San Juan (äl-kä'thär dā sän hwän').Sp.	39·22 N	3·12 W
125	Alcira (ä-thē'rä)............Sp.	39·09 N	0·26 W
78	Alcoa (ăl-kō'ȧ)............Tenn.	35·45 N	84·00 W
125	Alcobendas (äl-kō-bĕn'dås) Sp. (Madrid In.)	40·32 N	3·39 W
125	Alcochete (äl-kō-chā'ta) Port. (Lisbon In.)	38·45 N	8·58 W
125	Alcora (äl-kō'rä)............Sp.	40·05 N	0·12 W
125	Alcorisa (äl-kō-rē'sä)...........Sp.	40·53 N	0·20 W
125	Alcorón (äl-kô-rô'n) Sp. (Madrid In.)	40·22 N	3·50 W
101	Alcorta (àl-kôr'tä) Arg. (Buenos Aires In.)	33·32 S	61·08 W
67	Alcova Res. (ăl-kō'vȧ)......Wyo.	42·31 N	106·33 W
85	Alcove (ăl-kōv')Can. (Ottawa In.)	45·41 N	75·55 W
125	Alcoy (äl-koi')..............Sp.	38·42 N	0·30 W
125	Alcudia, Ba. de (B.) (bä-ē'ä-dĕ-äl-kōō-dhē'ä).Sp.	39·48 N	3·20 E
167	Aldabra Is. (äl-dä'brä).......Afr.	9·16 S	46·17 E
90	Aldama (äl-dä'mä).........Mex.	22·54 N	98·04 W
76	Aldama..................Mex.	28·50 N	105·54 W
135	Aldan...............Sov. Un.	58·46 N	125·19 E
135	Aldan (R.)............Sov. Un.	63·30 N	132·14 E
135	Aldan Plat............Sov. Un.	57·42 N	130·28 E
135	Aldanskaya............Sov. Un.	61·52 N	135·29 E
123	Aldekerk (äl'dĕ-kĕ'rk) Ger. (Ruhr In.)	51·26 N	6·26 E
123	Aldenhoven (äl'dĕn-hō'vĕn) Ger. (Ruhr In.)	50·54 N	6·18 E
65	Aldergrove (ôl'dēr-grōv) Can. (Vancouver In.)	49·03 N	122·28 W
122	Alderney (I.) (ôl'dēr-nĭ)..Guernsey	49·43 N	2·11 W
110	Aldershot (ôl'dēr-shŏt) Eng. (London In.)	51·14 N	0·46 W
80	Alderson (ôl-dēr-sŭn)......W. Va.	37·40 N	80·40 W
65	Alderwood Manor (ôl'dēr-wŏŏd măn'ŏr).Wash. (Seattle In.)	47·49 N	122·18 W
73	Aledo (ȧ-le'dō)...............Ill.	41·12 N	90·47 W
164	Aleg................Mauritania	17·10 N	13·57 W
101	Alegre (àlĕ'-grĕ) Braz. (Rio de Janeiro In.)	20·41 S	41·32 W
100	Alegre (R.)...........Braz. (In.)	22·22 S	43·34 W
100	Alegrete (ä-lå-grā'tä).......Braz.	29·46 S	55·44 W
136	Aleksandrov (ä-lyĕk-sän' drôf) Sov. Un. (Moscow In.)	56·24 N	38·45 E
136	Aleksandrovsk (ä-lyĕk-sän'drôfsk) Sov. Un. (Urals In.)	59·11 N	57·36 E
135	Aleksandrovsk..........Sov. Un.	51·02 N	142·21 E
121	Aleksandrow Kujawski (ä-lĕk-säh'drōōv kōō-yav'skē) Pol.	52·54 N	18·45 E
129	Alekseyevka (ä-lyĕk-sā-yĕf'kȧ) Sov. Un.	50·39 N	38·40 E
128	Aleksin (ä-lyĕk-sēn).....Sov. Un.	54·31 N	37·07 E
127	Aleksinac (å-lyĕk-sē-näk')..Yugo.	43·33 N	21·42 E
101	Alem Paraíba (ä-lĕ'm-pà-räē'bà) Braz. (Rio de Janeiro In.)	21·54 S	42·40 W
122	Alençon (à-läɴ-sôɴ')..........Fr.	48·26 N	0·08 E
99	Alenquer (ä-lĕŋ-kĕr')........Braz.	1·58 S	54·44 W
124	Alenquer.................Port.	39·04 N	9·01 W
124	Alentjo (Reg.) (ä-lĕŋ-tä'zhōō) Port.	38·05 N	7·45 W
157	Alenuihaha Chan. (ä'lä-nōō-ê-hä'hä).Hawaii (In.)	20·20 N	156·05 W
115	Aleppo (ȧ-lĕp-ō)...........Syria	36·10 N	37·18 E
122	Alès (ä-lĕs')................Fr.	44·07 N	4·06 E
126	Alessandria (ä-lĕs-sän'drê-ä)...It.	44·53 N	8·35 E
74	Alessandro (ä-lĕs-san'drō) Calif. (Los Angeles In.)	33·52 N	117·16 W
	Alessio, see Lesh		
118	Ålesund (ô'lĕ-sōōn')........Nor.	62·28 N	6·14 E
64	Aleutian Is. (ȧ-lu'shăn)....Alaska	52·40 N	177·30 E
64	Aleutian Trench..........Alaska	50·40 N	177·10 E
135	Alevina, Mys (C.).......Sov. Un.	58·49 N	151·44 E
64	Alexander Arch. (ăl-ĕg-zăn'dēr) Alaska	57·05 N	138·10 W
78	Alexander City.............Ala.	32·55 N	85·55 W
47	Alexander I...............Ant.	71·00 S	71·00 W
167	Alexandra (ăl-ex-ăn'-drȧ) S. Afr. (Johannesburg & Pretoria In.)	26·07 S	28·07 E
158	Alexandria (ăl-ĕg-zăn'drĭ-ȧ).Austl.	19·00 S	136·56 E
81	Alexandria...............Can.	45·50 N	74·35 W
80	Alexandria...............Ind.	40·20 N	85·20 W
77	Alexandria.................La.	31·18 N	92·28 W
70	Alexandria...............Minn.	45·53 N	95·23 W
127	Alexandria...............Rom.	43·55 N	25·21 E
70	Alexandria...............S. D.	43·39 N	97·45 W
167	Alexandria (ăl-ĕx-ăn-drĭ-ȧ) S. Afr. (Natal In.)	33·40 S	26·26 E
84	Alexandria (ăl-ĕg-zăn'drĭ-ȧ) Va. (Washington D.C. In.)	38·50 N	77·05 W
	Alexandria, see Al Iskandarīyah		
81	Alexandria Bay............N. Y.	44·20 N	75·55 W
127	Alexandroúpolis (Dedeagats) (ä-lĕk-sän-drōō'pō-lĭs) (dĕ'dĕ-ä-gäts).Grc.	40·51 N	25·51 E
124	Alfaro (äl-färō)..............Sp.	42·08 N	1·43 W
168	Al Fashn......U. A. R. (Nile In.)	28·47 N	30·53 E
165	Al Fayyūm...........U. A. R.	29·14 N	30·48 E
101	Alfenas (äl-fĕ'nàs) Braz. (Rio de Janeiro In.)	21·26 S	45·55 W
127	Alfiós (R.)................Grc.	37·33 N	21·50 E
168	Al Firdān (fer-dän') U. A. R. (Nile In.)	30·43 N	32·20 E
101	Alfonso Claudio (äl-fōn'sô-klou'dēō) Braz. (Rio de Janeiro In.)	20·05 S	41·05 W
85	Alfred (ăl'frĕd).Can. (Ottawa In.)	45·34 N	74·52 W
110	Alfreton (ăl'fēr-tŭn).........Eng.	53·06 N	1·23 W
165	Alga.......................Eth.	5·56 N	38·09 E
124	Algarve (Reg.) (äl-gär'vĕ)...Port	37·15 N	8·12 W
124	Algeciras (äl-hä-thē'räs).......Sp.	36·08 N	5·25 W
164	Alger (Algiers) (äl-zhā') (ăl-jēr) Alg.	36·51 N	2·56 E
163	Algeria (ăl-gē'rĭ-ȧ)...........Afr.	34·58 N	4·00 E
125	Algete (äl-hā'tā).Sp. (Madrid In.)	40·36 N	3·30 W
126	Alghero (äl-gâ'rō)............It.	40·32 N	8·22 E
	Algiers, see Alger		
77	Algoa (ăl-gō'ȧ).........Tex. (In.)	29·24 N	95·11 W
167	Algoa B. (ăl'gôȧ) S. Afr. (Natal In.)	33·51 S	24·50 E
65	Algoma.......Wash. (Seattle In.)	47·17 N	122·15 W
71	Algoma...................Wis.	44·38 N	87·29 W
71	Algona....................Iowa	43·04 N	94·11 W
80	Algonac (ăl'gô-năk)........Mich.	42·35 N	82·30 W
75	Algonquin (ăl-gŏŋ'kwĭn) Ill. (Chicago In.)	42·10 N	88·17 W
81	Algonquin Provincial Park...Can.	45·50 N	78·20 W
124	Alhama (äl-hä'mä)..........Sp.	37·00 N	3·59 W
124	Alhama....................Sp.	37·50 N	1·24 W
74	Alhambra (ăl-hăm'brȧ) Calif. (Los Angeles In.)	34·05 N	118·08 W
115	Al Ḩammām...........U. A. R.	30·46 N	29·42 E
125	Alhandra (äl-yän'drȧ) Port. (Lisbon In.)	38·55 N	9·01 W
139	Al Haql...Sau. Ar. (Palestine In.)	29·15 N	34·57 E
139	Al Harmal....Leb. (Palestine In.)	34·23 N	36·22 E
144	Al Hasā (Plain).........Sau. Ar.	27·00 N	47·48 E
124	Alhaurín el Grande (ä-lou-rēn'ĕl-grä'n-dĕ).Sp.	36·40 N	4·40 W
144	Al Hijaz (Reg.)..........Sau. Ar.	23·45 N	39·08 E
125	Alhos Vedros (äl'yōs-vā'drōs) Port. (Lisbon In.)	38·39 N	9·02 W
124	Alhucemas, Baie d' (B.).....Mor.	35·18 N	5·50 W
144	Al Hudayduh..............Yemen	14·43 N	43·03 E
144	Al Hufūf (Hofuf) (hô-fōōf') Sau. Ar.	25·15 N	49·43 E
127	Aliákmon (R.) (äl-ê-äk'-mōn) Grc.	40·26 N	22·17 E
125	Alicante (ä-lê-kän'tä)........Sp.	38·20 N	0·30 W
125	Alicante, Bahia de (B.) (bä-ē'ä-dĕ-ä-lê-kän'tä).Sp.	38·12 N	0·22 W
76	Alice (ăl'ĭs)................Tex.	27·45 N	98·04 W
167	Alice (ăl-ĭs)....S. Afr. (Natal In.)	32·47 S	26·51 E
167	Alicedale (ăl'ĭs-dāl) S. Afr. (Natal In.)	33·18 S	26·04 E
158	Alice Springs (ăl'ĭs)........Austl.	23·38 S	133·56 E
126	Alicudi (I.) (ä-lē-kōō'dē).......It.	38·34 N	14·21 E
136	Alifkulovo (ä-lĭf-kû'lô-vô) Sov. Un. (Urals In.)	55·57 N	62·06 E
142	Aligarh (ä-lê-gŭr')..........India	27·58 N	78·08 E
118	Alingsås (å'lĭŋ-sōs)..........Swe.	57·57 N	12·30 E
75	Aliquippa (ăl-ĭ-kwĭp'ȧ) Pa. (Pittsburgh In.)	40·37 N	80·15 W
168	Al Iskandarīyah (Alexandria) U. A. R. (Nile In.)	31·12 N	29·58 E
	Al Isma'īlīyah, see Ismailia		
166	Aliwal North (ä-lê-wäl')....S. Afr.	31·09 S	28·26 E
139	Al Jafr (L.).Jordan (Palestine In.)	30·17 N	36·20 E
165	Al Jaghbūb................Libya	29·46 N	24·32 E
165	Al Jawf..................Libya	24·14 N	23·15 E
144	Al Jawf................Sau. Ar.	29·45 N	39·30 E
165	Al Jazirah...............Libya	25·47 N	21·25 E
124	Aljezur (äl-zhä-zōōr')......Port.	37·18 N	8·52 W
168	Al Jīzah......U. A. R. (Nile In.)	30·01 N	31·12 E
165	Al Jufrah (Oasis)...........Libya	29·30 N	15·16 E
124	Aljustrel (äl-zhōō-strĕl')......Port.	37·44 N	8·23 W
168	Al Kāb.......U. A. R. (Suez In.)	30·56 N	32·19 E
139	Al Karak (kĕ-räk') Jordan (Palestine In.)	31·11 N	35·42 E
168	Al Karnak (kär'nak) U. A. R. (Nile In.)	25·42 N	32·43 E
144	Al Khābūrah........Mus. & Om.	23·45 N	57·30 E
139	Al Khalīl (Hebron) Jordan (Palestine In.)	31·31 N	35·07 E
165	Al Khums................Libya	32·35 N	14·10 E
144	Al Khurmah.............Sau. Ar.	21·37 N	41·44 E
117	Alkmaar (älk-mär')........Neth.	52·39 N	4·42 E
168	Al Kūbrī (kōō'brē) U. A. R. (Suez In.)	30·01 N	32·35 E
165	Al Kufrah (Oasis)...........Libya	24·45 N	22·45 E
139	Al Kuntillah U. A. R. (Palestine In.)	29·59 N	34·42 E
144	Al Kuwayt (Kuwait) (koō-wit) Kuw.	29·04 N	47·59 E
164	Allada (äl-lä'dä)........Dahomey	6·44 N	2·08 E
115	Al Lādhiqīyah (Latakia).....Syr.	35·32 N	35·51 E
82	Allagash (R.) (ăl'ȧ-găsh)...Maine	46·50 N	69·24 W
142	Allahābād (ŭl-ŭ-hä-bäd').....India	25·32 N	81·53 E
68	All American can. (âl ȧ-mĕr'ĭ-kăn) Calif.	32·43 N	115·12 W
111	Alland.........Aus. (Vienna In.)	48·04 N	16·05 E
124	Allariz (äl-yä-rēth')..........Sp.	42·10 N	7·48 W
78	Allatoona (R.) (ăl'ȧ-tōōn'ȧ)...Ga.	34·05 N	84·57 W
122	Allauch (ä-lĕ'ōō) Fr. (Marseille In.)	43·21 N	5·30 E
135	Allaykha (ä-lī'kȧ).......Sov. Un.	70·32 N	148·53 E
80	Allegan (ăl'ê-găn)..........Mich.	42·30 N	85·55 W
81	Allegany Ind. Res. (ăl-ê-gā'nĭ) N. Y.	42·05 N	78·55 W
81	Allegheny (R.)..............Pa.	41·10 N	79·20 W
63	Allegheny Mts..............U. S.	37·35 N	81·55 W
80	Allegheny Plat..............U. S.	39·00 N	81·15 W
81	Allegheny Front (Mts.).......U. S.	38·12 N	80·03 W
73	Allen (ăl'ĕn)................Okla.	34·51 N	96·26 W
116	Allen, Lough (B.) (lŏk ăl'ĕn)..Ire.	54·07 N	8·09 W
84	Allendale (ăl'ĕn-dāl) N. J. (New York In.)	41·02 N	74·08 W
79	Allendale..................S. C.	33·00 N	81·19 W
91	Allende (äl-yĕn'dā)........Mex.	18·23 N	92·49 W
76	Allende...................Mex.	28·20 N	100·50 W
81	Allentown (ăl'en-toun)........Pa.	40·35 N	75·30 W
143	Alleppey (ȧ-lĕp'ē)..........India	9·33 N	76·22 E
120	Aller R. (äl'ēr)..............Ger.	52·43 N	9·50 E
70	Alliance (ȧ-lī'ăns)..........Nebr.	42·06 N	102·53 W
80	Alliance..................Ohio	40·55 N	81·10 W
122	Allier (R.) (ȧ-lyā')...........Fr.	46·43 N	3·03 E
84	Alligator Pt. (al'ĭ-gā-tēr) La. (New Orleans In.)	30·57 N	89·41 W
118	Allinge (äl'ĭŋ-ĕ)............Den.	55·16 N	14·48 E
92	All Pines (ôl pīnz) Br. Hond. (Yucatan In.)	16·55 N	88·15 W
144	Al Luhayyah.............Yemen	15·58 N	42·48 E
65	Allyn (ăl'ĭn)..Wash. (Seattle In.)	47·23 N	122·51 W
82	Alma (ăl'mȧ)..............Can.	45·36 N	65·01 W
79	Alma.......................Ga.	31·33 N	82·31 W
80	Alma.....................Mich.	43·25 N	84·40 W
72	Alma.....................Nebr.	40·08 N	99·21 W
87	Alma......................Can.	48·29 N	71·42 W
168	Alma....S. Afr. (Johannesburg & Pretoria In.)	24·30 S	28·05 E
71	Alma......................Wis.	44·21 N	91·57 W
134	Alma-Ata (ăl'mà à'tà)...Sov. Un.	43·19 N	77·08 E
125	Almada (äl-mä'dä) Port. (Lisbon In.)	38·40 N	9·09 W
124	Almadén (äl-mȧ-dhän')......Sp.	38·47 N	4·50 W
144	Al Madīnah (Medina)....Sau. Ar.	24·26 N	39·42 E
139	Al Mafraq.Jordan (Palestine In.)	32·21 N	36·13 E
91	Almagre, Laguna (L.) (lä-gōō'nä-äl-mä'grĕ)......Mex.	22·48 N	97·45 W
124	Almagro (äl-mä'grō)..........Sp.	38·52 N	3·41 W
168	Al Mahallah al Kubrá U. A. R. (Nile In.)	31·00 N	31·10 E
144	Al Manāmah............Bahrain	26·01 N	50·33 E
68	Almanor (R.) (ăl-măn'ôr)...Calif.	40·11 N	121·20 W
124	Almansa (äl-män'sä).........Sp.	38·52 N	1·09 W
168	Al Manshāh...U. A. R. (Nile In.)	26·31 N	31·46 E
124	Almansor (R.) (äl-män-sôr)..Port.	38·41 N	8·27 W
168	Al Manşūrah..U. A. R. (Nile In.)	31·02 N	31·25 W
168	Al Manzilah (măn'za-la) U. A. R. (Nile In.)	31·09 N	32·05 E
124	Almanzora (R.) (äl-män-thō'rä) Sp.	37·20 N	2·25 W
168	Al Marāghah..U. A. R. (Nile In.)	26·41 N	31·35 E
125	Almargem (äl-mär-zhĕɴ) Port. (Lisbon In.)	38·51 N	9·16 W
144	Al Mawsil.................Iraq	36·00 N	42·53 E
124	Almazán (äl-mä-thän')........Sp.	41·30 N	2·33 W
139	Al Mazār...Jordan (Palestine In.)	31·04 N	35·41 E
139	Al Mazra'..Jordan (Palestine In.)	31·17 N	35·33 E
124	Almeirim (äl-māĭ-rêɴ')......Port.	39·13 N	8·31 W
117	Almelo (äl'mē-lō)..........Neth.	52·20 N	6·42 E
124	Almendralejo (äl-män-drä-lä'hō) Sp.	38·43 N	6·24 W
124	Almería (äl-mā-rē'ä).........Sp.	36·52 N	2·28 W
124	Almeria, Golfo de (G.) (gôl-fô-dĕ-äl-māĭ-reɴ').Sp.	36·45 N	2·26 W
124	Almería (R.)...............Sp.	37·00 N	2·40 W
118	Almhult (älm'hōōlt)........Swe.	56·35 N	14·08 E
124	Almina, Pta. (äl-mē'nä).....Mor.	35·58 N	5·17 W
168	Al Minyā.....U. A. R. (Nile In.)	28·04 N	30·45 E
93	Almirante (äl-mē-rän'tä).....Pan.	9·18 N	82·24 W
93	Almirante, Bahia de (B.) (bä-ē'ä-dĕ-äl-mē-rän'tä).Pan.	9·22 N	82·07 W
127	Almirós....................Grc.	39·13 N	22·47 E
124	Almodóvar (äl-mo-dhō'vär)...Sp.	38·43 N	4·10 W
142	Almoi....................India	29·41 N	79·42 E
90	Almoloya (äl-mō-lō'yä)......Mex.	19·32 N	99·44 W
91	Almoloya.Mex. (Mexico City In.)	19·11 N	99·28 W
81	Almonte (ăl-mŏn'tê)..........Can.	45·15 N	76·15 W
124	Almonte (äl-mōn'tä).........Sp.	37·16 N	6·32 W
124	Almonte (R.)...............Sp.	39·35 N	5·50 W
142	Almora...................India	29·20 N	79·40 E
144	Al Mubarraz.............Sau. Ar.	22·31 N	46·27 E
139	Al Mudawwarah Jordan (Palestine In.)	29·20 N	36·01 E
144	Al Mukallā..................S. Ar.	14·27 N	49·05 E
144	Al Mukhā.................Yemen	13·43 N	43·27 E
124	Almuñécar (äl-mōōn-yā'kär)...Sp.	36·44 N	3·43 W
118	Alnö (I.)..................Swe.	62·20 N	17·39 E
65	Aloha (ä'lô-hä) Ore. (Portland In.)	45·29 N	122·52 W
155	Alor (I.) (ä'lôr)...........Indon.	8·07 S	125·00 E
124	Álora (ä'lô-rä)..............Sp.	36·49 N	4·42 W
139	Alor Gajah..Mala (Singapore In.)	2·23 N	102·13 E
154	Alor Star (ä'lôr stär).......Mala.	6·24 N	100·08 E
146	Alot'ai (ä'lŏt'ī)............China	47·52 N	86·50 E
65	Alouette (R.) (ä-lōō-ĕt') Can. (Vancouver In.)	49·16 N	122·32 W
80	Alpena (ăl-pē'nȧ).........Mich.	45·05 N	83·30 W
111	Alphen....Neth. (Amsterdam In.)	52·07 N	4·38 E
124	Alpiarca (äl-pyär'sȧ)........Port.	39·38 N	8·37 W
76	Alpine (ăl'pīn)..............Tex.	30·21 N	103·41 W
114	Alps (Mts.) (ălps)..........Eur.	46·18 N	8·42 E
98	Alpujarra (äl-pōō-ká'r'rà) Col. (In.)	3·23 N	74·56 W
124	Alpujarras (Mts.) (äl-pōō-här'räs) Sp.	36·55 N	3·25 W
168	Al Qāhirah (Cairo) U. A. R. (Nile In.)	30·03 N	31·17 E
168	Al Qanţarah..U. A. R. (Suez In.)	30·51 N	32·20 E
165	Al Qaryah ash Shargiyah...Libya	30·36 N	13·13 E
144	Al Qaţif................Sau. Ar.	26·30 N	50·00 E
139	Al Qaţranah.Jordan (Palestine In.)	31·15 N	36·04 E
144	Al Qayşūmah............Sau. Ar.	28·30 N	46·27 E
139	Al Quarayyah Sau. Ar. (Palestine In.)	28·43 N	36·11 E
139	Al Qunaytirah.Syr. (Palestine In.)	33·09 N	35·49 E
144	Al Qunfidhah............Sau. Ar.	18·48 N	41·20 E
168	Al Qurnah (kōōr'na) U. A. R. (Nile In.)	25·44 N	32·39 E
139	Al Quşaymah U. A. R. (Palestine In.)	30·40 N	34·23 E
165	Al Quşayr...............U. A. R.	26·14 N	34·11 E
139	Al Quşayr.U. A. R. (Palestine In.)	34·32 N	36·33 E
118	Als (äls)...................Den.	55·06 N	9·40 E
123	Alsace (Reg.) (äl-sà's)........Fr.	48·25 N	7·24 E
148	Al Shan (Mts.) (äĭ'shän)...China	37·27 N	120·35 E
118	Alsterån (R.)..............Swe.	56·54 N	15·50 E
74	Altadena (ăl-tȧ-dē'nä) Calif. (Los Angeles In.)	34·12 N	118·08 W
100	Alta Gracia (äl'tä grä'sê-ä)...Arg.	31·41 S	64·19 W

ng-sing; ŋ-baŋk; ɴ-nasalized n; nŏd; cŏmmit; ōld; ôbey; ôrder; fōōd; fŏŏt; ou-out; s-soft; sh-dish; th-thin; pūre; ûnite; ûrn; stŭd; circŭs; ü-as "y" in study; '-indeterminate vowel.

Page	Name Pronunciation Region	Lat. °′	Long. °′
98	Altagracia . . . . Ven.	10·42 N	71·34 W
99	Altagracia de Orituco (ä′l-tȧ-grȧ′ sēȧ-dĕ-ôrē-to͞o′kô). Ven. (In.)	9·53 N	66·22 W
134	Altai Ter . . . . Sov. Un.	53·39 N	78·52 E
146	Altai Mts. (äl′tī′) . . . . Asia	49·11 N	87·15 E
74	Alta Loma (ăl′tă lō′mä) Calif. (Los Angeles In.)	34·07 N	117·35 W
77	Alta Loma (ăl′tȧ lō-mȧ) Tex. (In.)	29·22 N	95·05 W
79	Altamaha (R.) (ôl-tȧ-mȧ-hô′). . Ga.	31·50 N	82·00 W
99	Altamira (äl-tä-mē′rä) . . . . . . Braz.	3·13 S	52·14 W
91	Altamira . . . . Mex.	22·25 N	97·55 W
100	Altamirano (äl-tä-mê-rā′nō) . . Arg.	35·26 S	58·12 W
126	Altamura (äl-tä-mo͞o′rä) . . . . It.	40·40 N	16·35 E
135	Altan Bulag . . . . Mong.	50·18 N	106·31 E
79	Altavista (äl-tä-vēs′tȧ) . . . . Va.	37·08 N	79·14 W
112	Alten (R.) (äl′tĕn) . . . . Nor.	69·40 N	24·09 E
120	Altenburg (äl-tĕn-bo͝orgh) . . . . Ger.	50·59 N	12·27 E
111	Altenmarkt an der Triesting Aus. (Vienna In.)	48·02 N	16·00 E
124	Alter do Chão (äl-tĕr′do͝o shäN′ōN). Port.	39·13 N	7·38 W
90	Altiplanicie Mexicana (Plat.) (äl-tē-plä-nē′syĕ-mĕ-Kē-kȧ-nä) Mex.	22·38 N	102·33 W
98	Altiplano (Plat.) (äl-tē-plȧ′nō) Bol.	18·38 S	68·20 W
111	Alt Landsberg (ält länts′bĕrgh) Ger. (Berlin In.)	52·34 N	13·44 E
77	Alto (ăl′tō) . . . . La.	32·21 N	91·52 W
98	Alto Marañón, Rio (R.) (rê′ō-ȧl′tô-mä-rän-yŏ′n) . Peru	8·18 S	77·13 W
111	Altomünster (äl′tō-mün′stĕr) Ger. (Munich In.)	48·24 N	11·16 E
85	Alton (ôl′tŭn) . Can. (Toronto In.)	43·52 N	80·05 W
74	Alton . . . . Ill. (St. Louis In.)	38·53 N	90·11 W
161	Altona . . . . Austl. (Melbourne In.)	37·52 S	144·50 E
111	Altona (äl′tō-nȧ) Ger. (Hamburg In).	53·33 N	9·54 E
78	Altoona (ăl-to͞o′nȧ) . . . . Ala.	34·01 N	86·15 W
81	Altoona . . . . Pa.	40·25 N	78·25 W
65	Altoona . . . . . Wash. (Portland In.)	46·16 N	123·39 W
101	Alto Rio Doce (äl′tô-rē′ô-dō′sĕ) Braz. (Rio de Janeiro In.)	21·02 S	43·23 W
95	Alto Songo (äl-fō-sôŋ′gō) . . . . Cuba	20·10 N	75·45 W
91	Altotonga (äl-tō-tôŋ′gä) . . . . . Mex.	19·44 N	97·13 W
95	Alto Velo (I.) (äl-tô-vĕ′lō) Dom. Rep.	17·30 N	71·35 W
110	Altrincham (ôl′trĭng-ăm) . . . . . Eng.	53·18 N	2·21 W
111	Alt Ruppin (ält ro͞o′ppēn) Ger. (Berlin In.)	54·56 N	12·48 E
66	Alturas (ăl-to͞o′rȧs) . . . . Calif.	41·29 N	120·33 W
72	Altus (ăl′tŭs) . . . . Okla.	34·38 N	99·20 W
165	Al ‘Ugaylah . . . . Libya	30·15 N	19·07 E
165	Al Ujaylāt . . . . Libya	32·45 N	12·27 E
128	Alūksne (ä′lo͝oks-nĕ) . . . . . Sov. Un.	57·24 N	27·04 E
168	Alula (ä-lo͞o′lä) Som. (Horn of Afr. In.)	11·53 N	50·40 E
81	Alumette I. (ȧ-lü-mĕt′) . . . . . . Can.	45·50 N	77·00 W
168	Al Uqşur (Luxor) U. A. R. (Nile In.)	25·38 N	32·59 E
129	Alushta (ä′lo͝osh-tȧ) . . . . . Sov. Un.	44·39 N	34·23 E
72	Alva (ăl′vȧ) . . . . Okla.	36·46 N	98·41 W
65	Alvarado (ăl-vȧ-rā′dō) Calif (San Francisco In.)	37·35 N	122·05 W
91	Alvarado (äl-vä-rä′dhō) . . . . . Mex.	18·48 N	95·45 W
91	Alvarado, Luguna de (L.) (lä-go͝o′nä-dĕ-äl-vä-rȧ′dô) . . Mex.	18·44 N	96·45 W
118	Älvdalen (ĕlv′dä-lĕn) . . . . Swe.	61·14 N	14·04 E
125	Alverca (al-vĕr′kȧ) Port. (Lisbon In.)	38·53 N	9·02 W
118	Alvesta (äl-vĕs′tä) . . . . Swe.	56·55 N	14·29 E
77	Alvin (ăl′vĭn) . . . . Tex. (In.)	29·25 N	95·14 W
101	Alvinópolis (äl-vēnō′pō-lês) Braz. (Rio de Janeiro In.)	20·07 S	43·03 W
65	Alviso (ăl-vī′sō) Calif. (San Francisco In.)	37·26 N	121·59 W
144	Al Wajh . . . . Sau. Ar.	26·15 N	36·32 E
142	Alwar (ŭl′wŭr) . . . . India	27·39 N	76·39 E
168	Al Wāsiţah . . . . U. A. R. (Nile In.)	29·21 N	31·15 E
119	Alytus (ä′lê-to͝os) . . . . Sov. Un.	54·25 N	24·05 E
118	Åmå (ô′môl) . . . . Swe.	59·05 N	12·40 E
90	Amacuzac (R.) (ä-mä-ko͞o-zȧk) Mex.	18·00 N	99·03 W
158	Amadeus, (L.) (ăm-ȧ-dē′ŭs) . Austl.	24·30 S	131·25 E
87	Amadjuak (L.) (ä-mädj′wäk). Can.	64·50 N	69·20 W
153	Amagasaki (ä′mä-gä-sä′kê) Jap. (Osaka In.)	34·43 N	135·25 E
153	Amakusa-Shimo (I.) (ämä-ko͞o′sä shē-mō) . Jap.	32·24 N	129·35 E
98	Amalfi (ä′mȧ′l-fē) . . . . . . Col. (In.)	6·55 N	75·04 W
125	Amalfi (ä-mä′l-fê) . It. (Naples In.)	40·23 N	14·36 E
127	Amaliás (ȧ-mäl′yȧs) . . . . Grc.	37·48 N	21·23 E
142	Amalner . . . . India	21·07 N	75·06 E
99	Amambay, Cordillera de (Mts.) Braz.	20·06 S	57·08 W
152	Amami Guntō (Is.) (ä′mä′mē go͝on′tō′) . Jap.	28·25 N	129·00 E
152	Amamio (I.) (ä-mä′mē-ō) . . . . Jap.	28·10 N	129·55 E
167	Amanzimtoti . . . S. Afr. (Natal In.)	30·02 S	30·54 E
99	Amapá (ä-mä-pȧ′) . . . . Braz.	2·14 N	50·48 W
99	Amapá (Ter.) . . . . Braz.	1·15 N	52·15 W
92	Amapala (ä-mä-pä′lä) . . . . . . Hond.	13·16 N	87·39 W
99	Amarante (ä-mä-rän′tā) . . . . . Braz.	6·17 S	42·43 W
68	Amargosa (R.) (ȧ′mär-gō′sȧ) Calif.	35·55 N	116·45 W
72	Amarillo (ăm-ȧ-rĭl′ō) . . . . Tex.	35·14 N	101·49 W
126	Amaro, Mt. (ä-mä′rō) . . . . It.	42·07 N	14·07 E
133	Amasya (ä-mä′sê-ȧ) . . . . Tur.	40·40 N	35·50 E
91	Amatenango (ä-mä-tā-naŋ′gō) Mex.	16·30 N	92·29 W
64	Amatignak (I.) (ä-mȧ′tê-näk) Alaska	51·12 N	178·30 W
92	Amatique, Bahía de (B.) (bä-ē′ä-dĕ-ä-mä-tē′kā) . Guat.-Br. Hond.	15·58 N	88·50 W
92	Amatitlán (ä-mä-tê-tlän′) . . Guat.	14·27 N	90·39 W
90	Amatlán de Cañas (ä-mät-län′dā kän-yäs) . Mex.	20·50 N	104·22 W
98	Amazonas Selvas (Reg.) (ä mä-thō′näs) . Braz.	4·15 S	64·30 W
99	Amazonas, Rio (R.) (rē′ō-ä-mä-thō′näs) . Braz.	2·03 S	53·18 W
142	Ambāla (ŭm-bä′lŭ) . . . . India	30·31 N	76·48 E
98	Ambalema (äm-bä-lā′mä) Col. (In.)	4·47 N	74·45 W
135	Ambarchik (ŭm-bär′chĭk) Sov. Un.	69·39 N	162·18 E
98	Ambato (äm-bä′tō) . . . . Ec.	1·15 S	78·30 W
167	Ambatosoratra (ämbä′to͞o-so͞or-ä′trŭ) . Malag. Rep.	17·44 S	48·41 E
120	Amberg (äm′bĕrgh) . . . . Ger.	49·26 N	11·51 E
95	Ambergris Cays (Is.) (ăm′bẽr-grēs kāz) Caicos	21·20 N	71·40 W
92	Ambergris I. Br. Hond. (Yucatan In.)	18·04 N	87·43 W
123	Ambérieu (äN-bā-rê-û′) . . . . Fr.	45·57 N	5·21 E
122	Ambert (äN-bĕr′) . . . . Fr.	45·32 N	3·41 E
155	Ambil (I.) (äm′bēl) Phil. (Manila In.)	13·51 N	120·25 E
84	Ambler (ăm′blẽr) Pa. (Philadelphia In.)	40·09 N	75·13 W
155	Amboina (ăm-boi′nȧ) . . . . . . Indon.	3·45 S	128·17 E
155	Amboina (I.) . . . . Indon.	4·50 S	128·45 E
122	Amboise (äN-bwăz′) . . . . Fr.	47·25 N	0·56 E
167	Ambositra (äN-bô-sē′trä) Malag. Rep.	20·31 S	47·28 E
80	Amboy (ăm′boi) . . . . Ill.	41·41 N	89·15 W
65	Amboy . . . . . Wash. (Portland In.)	45·55 N	122·27 W
167	Ambre, Cap d′ (C.) . . Malag. Rep.	12·06 S	49·15 E
75	Ambridge (ăm′brĭdj) Pa. (Pittsburgh In.)	40·36 N	80·13 W
159	Ambrim (I.) . . . . New Heb.	16·28 S	158·17 E
166	Ambriz . . . . Ang.	7·50 S	15·10 E
166	Ambrizete . . . . Ang.	7·15 S	12·50 E
64	Amchitka P. (ăm-chĭt′kȧ) . . Alaska	51·30 N	179·36 W
90	Amealco (ä-mā-äl′kō) . . . . Mex.	20·12 N	100·08 W
90	Ameca (ä-mĕ′kä) . . . . Mex.	20·34 N	104·02 W
91	Amecameca (ä-mȧ-kä-mā′kä) Mex. (Mexico City In.)	19·06 N	98·46 W
111	Ameide . . . Neth. (Amsterdam In.)	51·57 N	4·57 E
117	Ameland (I.) . . . . Neth.	53·29 N	5·54 E
75	Amelia (ȧ-mēl′yā) Ohio (Cincinnati In.)	39·01 N	84·12 W
68	American (R.) (ȧ-mĕr′ĭ-kăn) Calif.	38·37 N	121·19 W
101	Americana (ä-mĕ-rê-kȧ′nȧ) Braz. (Rio de Janeiro In.)	22·46 S	47·19 W
67	American Falls (ȧ-mĕr-ĭ-kăn) . Idaho	42·45 N	112·53 W
67	American Falls Res . . . . Idaho	42·56 N	113·18 W
69	American Fork . . . . Utah	40·20 N	111·50 W
47	American Highland . . . . Ant.	72·00 S	79·00 E
78	Americus (ȧ-mĕr′ĭ-kŭs) . . . . Ga.	32·04 N	84·15 W
111	Amersfoort (ä′mĕrz-fōrt) Neth. (Amsterdam In.)	52·08 N	5·23 E
86	Amery (ā′mẽr-ê) . . . . Can.	56·32 N	93·58 W
71	Amery . . . . Wis.	45·19 N	92·24 W
71	Ames (āmz) . . . . Iowa	42·00 N	93·36 W
83	Amesbury (āmz′bẽr-ê) Mass. (Boston In.)	42·51 N	70·56 W
127	Ámfissa (ȧm-fĭ′sȧ) . . . . Grc.	38·32 N	22·26 E
135	Amga (ŭm-gä′) . . . . Sov. Un.	61·08 N	132·09 E
135	Amga (R.) . . . . Sov. Un.	61·41 N	133·11 E
135	Amgun (R.) . . . . Sov. Un.	53·33 N	137·57 E
165	Amhara (Prov.) (äm-hä′rä) . . Eth.	11·30 N	36·45 E
82	Amherst (ăm′hẽrst) . . . . Can.	45·49 N	64·14 W
75	Amherst . . . . . Ohio (Cleveland In.)	41·24 N	82·13 W
81	Amherst (I.) . . . . Can.	44·10 N	76·40 W
122	Amiens (ä-myäN′) . . . . Fr.	49·54 N	2·18 E
142	Amio Tsönag Tsho (L.) . . . . China	31·38 N	91·18 E
47	Amirante Is . . . . Ind. O.	6·02 S	52·30 E
77	Amite (ă-mēt′) . . . . La.	30·43 N	90·32 W
77	Amite R . . . . La.	30·45 N	90·48 W
75	Amity (ăm′ĭ-tĭ) Pa. (Pittsburgh In.)	40·02 N	80·11 W
84	Amityville (ăm′ĭ-tĭ-vĭl) N. Y. (New York In.)	40·41 N	73·24 W
64	Amlia (I.) (ȧ′m-lêä) . . . . Alaska	52·00 N	173·28 W
139	‘Ammān (äm′ mȧn) Jordan (Palestine In.)	31·57 N	35·57 E
111	Ammer L. (äm′mĕr) Ger. (Munich In.)	48·00 N	11·08 E
74	Amnicon R. (ăm′nė-kŏn) Wis. (Duluth In.)	46·35 N	91·56 W
	Amnok, see Yalu		
	Amnok, see Yalu (R.)		
142	Amod . . . . India	21·47 N	72·58 E
127	Amorgós (I.) (ä-môr′gōs) . . . . . Grc.	36·47 N	25·47 E
78	Amory (ām′o-rē) . . . . Miss.	33·58 N	88·27 W
87	Amos (ā′mŭs) . . . . Can.	48·31 N	78·04 W
118	Åmot (Torpen) (ô′mōt) (tôr′pĕn) Nor.	61·08 N	11·17 E
	Amoy, see Hsiamen		
101	Amparo (äm-pȧ′-rô) Braz. (Rio de Janeiro In.)	22·43 S	46·44 W
111	Amper R. (äm′pĕr) Ger. (Munich In.)	48·18 N	11·32 E
125	Amposta (äm-pōs′tä) . . . . Sp.	40·42 N	0·34 E
82	Amqui . . . . Can.	48·27 N	67·27 W
142	Amraoti (ŭm-rŭ-ō′tê) . . . . India	20·58 N	77·47 E
142	Amritsar (ŭm-rĭt′sŭr) . . . . India	31·43 N	74·52 E
111	Amstelveen Neth. (Amsterdam In.)	52·18 N	4·51 E
111	Amsterdam (äm-stẽr-däm′) Neth. (Amsterdam In.)	52·21 N	4·52 E
81	Amsterdam (ăm′stẽr-dăm) . . N. Y.	42·55 N	74·10 W
47	Amsterdam (I.) . . . . . Fr. (Ind. O.)	37·52 S	77·32 E
120	Amstetten (äm′stĕt-ĕn) . . . . . . Aus.	48·09 N	14·53 E
165	Am Timan (äm′tê-män′) . . . . Chad	11·18 N	20·30 E
144	Amu Dar′ya (Oxus) (R.) (ä-mo͝o-dä′rēä) . Asia	40·40 N	62·47 E
142	Amu Dar′ye (R.) (ä-mo͞o dä′rēä) Afg.-Sov. Un.	36·50 N	66·58 E
64	Amukta P. (ä-mook′tȧ) . . . . Alaska	52·30 N	172·00 W
155	Amulung (ä′mo͞o′lo͞ong) Phil. (Manila In.)	17·51 N	121·43 E
86	Amundsen G. (ä′mŭn-sĕn) . . . Can.	70·17 N	23·28 W
47	Amundsen Sea . . . . Ant.	72·00 S	110·00 W
118	Amungen (L.) . . . . Swe.	61·07 N	16·00 E
150	Amur R. (ä-mo͝or′) China and Sov. Un.	49·38 N	127·25 E
136	Amurskiy (ä-mûr′skĭ) Sov. Un. (Urals In.)	52·35 N	59·36 E
152	Amurskiy, Zaliv (B.) (zä′lĭf ä-mo͝or′skĭ) . Sov. Un.	43·20 N	131·40 E
90	Amusgos (San Pedro) (ä-mo͞o′s-gôs) (sän-pĕ′drō) . Mex.	16·39 N	98·09 W
155	Amuyao, Mt. (ä-mo͞o-yä′ō) Phil. (Manila In.)	17·04 N	121·09 E
127	Amvrakikos Kólpos (G.) . . . . . Grc.	39·00 N	21·00 E
139	Amyun . . . . Leb. (Palestine In.)	34·18 N	35·48 E
135	Anabar (R.) (ăn-ȧ-bär′) . . Sov. Un.	71·15 N	113·00 E
99	Anaco (ä-nȧ′kô) . . . . Ven. (In.)	9·29 N	64·27 W
67	Anaconda (ăn-ȧ-kŏn′dȧ) . . . . Mont.	46·07 N	112·55 W
65	Anacortes (ăn-ȧ-kôr′tĕz) Wash. (Seattle In.)	48·30 N	122·37 W
72	Anadarko (ăn-ȧ-där′kō) . . . . . Okla.	35·05 N	98·14 W
135	Anadyr (ŭ-nȧ-dĭr′) . . . . . . Sov. Un.	64·47 N	177·01 E
135	Anadyr (R.) . . . . Sov. Un.	65·30 N	172·45 E
139	Anadyrskiy Zaliv (B.) . . . Sov. Un.	64·10 N	178·00 W
74	Anaheim (ăn′ȧ-hīm) Calif. (Los Angeles In.)	33·50 N	117·55 W
77	Anahuac (ä-nä′wäk) . . . . Tex. (In.)	29·46 N	94·41 W
143	Anai Mudi Mt . . . . India	15·28 N	77·10 E
94	Ana María, Cayos (Is.) (kä′yōs-ä′nȧ mȧ-rē′ȧ) . Cuba	21·55 N	78·50 W
154	Anambas, Pulau-Pulau (Is.) (ä-näm-bäs) . Indon.	2·41 N	106·38 E
71	Anamosa (ăn-ȧ-mō′sȧ) . . . . . . Iowa	42·06 N	91·18 W
129	Anan′yev (ȧ-nä′nyĕf) . . . . Sov. Un.	47·43 N	29·59 E
129	Anapa (ȧ-nä′pä) . . . . Sov. Un.	44·54 N	37·19 E
99	Anápolis (ä-nȧ′pō-lês) . . . . Braz.	16·17 S	48·47 W
100	Añatuya (ȧ-nyä-to͞o′yȧ) . . . . . . Arg.	28·22 S	62·45 W
122	Ancenis (äN-sē-nē′) . . . . Fr.	47·24 N	1·12 W
100	Anchieta (ȧn-chyĕ′tä) . . Braz. (In.)	22·49 S	43·24 W
151	Anching (än′kĭng′) . . . . China	30·32 N	117·00 E
64	Anchitka (I.) (än-chĕ′t-kä) . Alaska	51·25 N	178·10 E
148	Anch′ iu (än′chê) . . . . China	36·26 N	119·12 E
110	Ancholme (R.) (ăn′chŭm) . . . Eng.	53·28 N	0·27 W
77	Anchor (ăŋ′kẽr) . . . . Tex. (In.)	29·13 N	95·28 W
64	Anchorage (ăŋ′kẽr-ȧj) . . . . . Alaska	61·12 N	149·48 W
75	Anchorage . . . . Ky. (Louisville In.)	38·16 N	85·32 W
85	Ancienne-Lorette (äN-syĕn′ lō-rĕt′) . Can. (Quebec In.)	46·48 N	71·21 W
88	Ancon (äŋ-kōn′) C. Z. (Panama Canal In.)	8·55 N	79·32 W
126	Ancona (än-kō′nä) . . . . It.	43·37 N	13·32 E
100	Ancud (äŋ-ko͞odh′) . . . . Chile	41·52 S	73·45 W
100	Ancud, G. de (gôl-fô-dĕ-äŋ-ko͞odh′) . Chile	41·15 S	73·00 W
100	Andalgalá (ȧ′n-däl-gȧ-lȧ′) . . . . Arg.	27·35 S	66·14 W
124	Andalucia (Reg.) (än-dä-lo͞o-sê′ä) . Sp.	37·35 N	5·40 W
78	Andalusia (ăn-dȧ-lo͞o′zhĭȧ) . . . . Ala.	31·19 N	86·19 W
154	Andaman Is. (ăn-dȧ-măn′) . . India	11·38 N	92·17 E
154	Andaman Sea . . . . Asia	12·44 N	95·45 E
111	Anderlecht (än′dẽr-lĕkt) Bel. (Brussels In.)	50·49 N	4·16 E
120	Andernach (än′dẽr-näK) . . . . . . Ger.	50·25 N	7·23 E
101	Anderson (ȧ′n-dĕr-sōn) Arg. (Buenos Aires In.)	35·15 S	60·15 W
66	Anderson (ăn′dẽr-sŭn) . . . . . . Calif.	40·28 N	122·19 W
80	Anderson . . . . Ind.	40·05 N	85·50 W
79	Anderson . . . . S. C.	34·30 N	82·40 W
86	Anderson (R.) . . . . Can.	68·32 N	125·12 W
98	Andes (ăn′dēz) (än′dās) . Col. (In.)	5·40 N	75·54 W
96	Andes Mts. . . . . S. A.	13·00 S	75·00 W
143	Andhei . . . . . . India (Bombay In.)	19·08 N	72·50 E
143	Andhra Pradesh (State) . . . . . India	22·00 N	78·50 E
115	Andikíthira (I.) . . . . Grc.	35·50 N	23·20 E
134	Andizhan (än-dê-zhän′) . . Sov. Un.	40·51 N	72·39 E
152	Andong (än′dŭng′) . . . . Kor.	36·31 N	128·42 E
125	Andorra (än-dôr′rä) . . . . And.	42·38 N	1·30 E
125	Andorra . . . . Eur.	42·32 N	1·18 E
83	Andover (ăn′dô-vẽr) Mass. (Boston In.)	42·39 N	71·08 W
84	Andover . . . . N. J. (New York In.)	40·59 N	74·45 W
112	Andöy (I.) (änd-ûê) . . . . Nor.	69·12 N	14·58 E
125	Andraitx (än-drȧ-ĭtsh′) . . . . Sp.	39·34 N	2·25 E
64	Andreanof Is. (än-drȧ-ä′nôf) Alaska	51·10 N	177·00 W
101	Andrelândia (än-drĕ-lȧ′n-dyȧ) Braz. (Rio de Janeiro In.)	21·45 S	44·18 W
82	Andréville . . . . Can.	47·40 N	69·44 W
78	Andrew Johnson Natl Mon. (ăn′dro͞o jŏn′sŭn) . Tenn.	36·15 N	82·55 W
78	Andrews (ăn′dro͞oz) . . . . N. C.	35·12 N	83·48 W
79	Andrews . . . . S. C.	33·25 N	79·32 W
129	Andreyevka (än-drȧ-yĕf′kȧ) Sov. Un.	48·03 N	37·03 E
126	Andria (än′drê-ä) . . . . It.	41·17 N	15·55 E
127	Andros (ȧn′dhrôs) . . . . Grc.	37·50 N	24·54 E
94	Andros I. (ăn′drŏs) . . . . Ba. Is.	24·30 N	78·00 W
127	Andrós (I.) (ȧn′dhrôs) . . . . Grc.	37·59 N	24·55 E
82	Androscoggin (R.) (ăn-drŭs-kŏg′ĭn) . Maine	44·25 N	70·45 W
124	Andújar (än-do͝o′här) . . . . Sp.	38·04 N	4·03 W
164	Anécho (ȧ-nā′chō) . . . . Togo	6·25 N	1·36 E
153	Anegasaki (ä′mȧ-gä-sä′kê) Jap. (Tōkyō In.)	35·29 N	140·02 E
159	Aneityum (I.) (ä-nȧ-ē′tê-ŭm) New Hebr.	20·15 S	169·49 E
70	Aneta (ă-nē′tȧ) . . . . N. D.	47·41 N	97·57 W
155	Angadanan (äŋ-gȧ-dä′nȧn) Phil. (Manila In.)	16·45 N	121·45 E
155	Angaki (än-gä′kê) Phil. (Manila In.)	17·10 N	120·40 E

ăt: finăl; rāte; senâte; ärm; ȧsk; sofȧ; fâre; ch-choose; dh-as th in other; bē; êvent; bĕt; recĕnt; cratẽr; g-go; gh-guttural g; bĭt; ĭ-short neutral; rīde; K-guttural k as ch in German ich;

PRONOUNCING INDEX

Angamacutiro–Arctic Ocean 177

Page	Name Pronunciation Region	Lat. °′	Long. °′
90	Angamacutiro (än'gä-mä-kōō-tē'rō) Mex.	20·08 N	101·44 W
150	Angangchi (än'gäng'kē') China	47·05 N	123·58 E
90	Angangueo (än-gäŋ'gwā-ō) Mex.	19·36 N	100·18 W
	Angara (R.), see Verkhnyaya Tunguska		
134	Angarsk Sov. Un.	52·48 N	104·15 E
118	Ånge (ông'ĕ) Swe.	62·31 N	15·39 E
99	Angel, Salto (Falls) (säl'tō-á'n-hĕl) Ven.	5·44 N	62·27 W
88	Angel De La Guarda (I.) (á'n-hĕl-dĕ-lä-gwä'r-dä) Mex.	29·30 N	113·00 W
155	Angeles (än'hâ-läs) Phil. (Manila In.)	15·09 N	120·35 E
118	Ängelholm (ĕng'ĕl-hôlm) Swe.	56·14 N	12·50 E
77	Angelina R. (ăn-jē lē'nȧ) Tex.	31·30 N	94·53 W
68	Angels Camp (ān'jĕls kămp') Calif.	38·03 N	120·33 W
112	Angermanälven (R.) Swe.	64·02 N	17·15 E
123	Angermund (án'ngĕr-mũnd) Ger. (Ruhr In.)	51·20 N	6·47 E
120	Angermünde (äng'ĕr-mûn-dĕ) Ger.	53·02 N	14·00 E
85	Angers (äN-zhā') Can. (Ottawa In.)	41·31 N	75·29 W
122	Angers Fr.	47·29 N	0·36 W
154	Angkor (Ruins) (äng'kôr) Camb.	13·52 N	103·50 E
116	Anglesey (I.) (ăŋ'g'l-sē) Wales	52·28 N	4·35 W
77	Angleton (aŋ'g'l-tŭn) Tex. (In.)	29·10 N	95·25 W
87	Angliers Can.	47·29 N	79·16 W
49	Angmagssalik (âŋ-mä'sä-lĭk) Grnld.	65·40 N	37·40 W
167	Angoche, Ilhas de (Is.) (ē'läs-dĕ-än-gō'châ) Moz.	16·03 S	40·17 E
100	Angol (äŋ-gōl') Chile	37·47 S	72·43 W
80	Angola (ăŋ-gō'lȧ) Ind.	41·35 N	85·00 W
163	Angola (Portuguese West Africa) Afr.	14·15 S	16·00 E
	Angora, see Ankara		
122	Angoulême (äŋ-gōō-lâm') Fr.	45·40 N	0·09 E
101	Angra dos Reis (aŋ'-grä dōs rā'ēs) Braz. (Rio de Janeiro In.)	23·01 S	44·17 W
125	Angri (ä'n-grē) It. (Naples In.)	40·30 N	14·35 E
94	Anguilla, Cays (Is.) (ăŋ-gwĭl'ȧ) Ba. Is.	23·30 N	79·35 W
93	Anguilla I. St. Kitts-Nevis-Anguilla (Le. & Wind. Is. In.)	18·15 N	62·54 W
83	Anguille, C. (äŋ-gē'yē) Can.	47·58 N	59·35 W
118	Anholt (I.) (än'hŏlt) Den.	56·43 N	11·34 E
146	Anhsi China	40·36 N	95·49 E
147	Anhui (Anhwei) (Prov.) China	31·23 N	116·53 E
64	Aniak (ä-nyà'k) Alaska	61·32 N	159·35 W
125	Aniene (ä-nyĕ'nĕ) It. (Rome In.)	41·54 N	12·49 E
69	Animas (R.) (ä'nê-mäs) Colo.	37·03 N	107·50 W
127	Anina (ä-nē'nä) Rom.	45·03 N	21·50 E
81	Anita (ȧ-ne'ȧ) Pa.	41·05 N	79·00 W
152	Aniva, Mys (Pt.) (mĭs à-nē'vȧ) Sov. Un.	46·08 N	143·13 E
152	Aniva, Zaliv (B.) (zä'lĭf à-nē'và) Sov. Un.	46·28 N	143·30 E
167	Anjouan (I.) (äN-zhwäN) Comores, Arch. des	12·14 S	44·47 E
150	Ank'ang China	32·38 N	109·10 E
133	Ankara (Angora) (än'kȧ-rȧ) (ăn-gō'rȧ) Tur.	39·55 N	32·50 E
120	Anklam (än'kläm) Ger.	53·52 N	13·43 E
166	Ankoro (äŋ-kō'rō) Con. K.	6·48 S	26·45 E
148	Ankou (an'gōō ŭ) China	38·27 N	115·19 E
151	Anlu (än'lōō') China	31·18 N	113·40 E
151	Anlung China	25·01 N	105·32 E
81	Ann, C. (ăn) Mass.	42·40 N	70·40 W
73	Anna (ăn'ȧ) Ill.	37·28 N	89·15 W
129	Anna (än'ä) Sov. Un.	51·31 N	40·27 E
164	Annaba (Bône) Alg.	36·57 N	7·39 E
120	Annaberg-Buchols (än'ä-bĕrgh) Ger.	50·35 N	13·02 E
144	An Nafud (Des.) Sau. Ar.	28·23 N	39·30 E
144	An Najaf (än nä-jäf') Iraq	31·30 N	44·31 E
139	An Nakhl. U. A. R. (Palestine In.)	29·55 N	33·45 E
154	Annamitic Cord. Mts. (ă-nà-mĭt'ĭk kôr-dĭl-yä'rȧ) Laos-Viet.	17·34 N	105·38 E
84	Annapolis (ă-năp'ô-lĭs) Md. (Baltimore In.)	39·00 N	76·25 W
82	Annapolis Royal Can.	44·44 N	65·32 W
80	Ann Arbor (ăn är'bēr) Mich.	42·15 N	83·45 W
165	An Nawfalīyah Libya	30·57 N	17·38 E
123	Annecy (än sē') Fr.	45·54 N	6·07 E
123	Annemasse (än'mäs') Fr.	46·09 N	6·13 E
136	Annenskoye (ä-nĕn'skô-yĕ) Sov. Un. (Urals In.)	53·09 N	60·25 E
78	Anniston (ăn'ĭs-tŭn) Ala.	33·39 N	85·47 W
163	Annobon (I.) (än-nō-bôn') Atl. O.	2·00 S	3·30 E
122	Annonay (ȧ-nô-nĕ') Fr.	45·16 N	4·36 E
94	Annotto Bay (än-nō'tō) Jam.	18·15 N	76·45 W
74	Anoka (ȧ-nō'kȧ) Minn. (Minneapolis, St. Paul In.)	45·12 N	93·24 W
98	Anori (ȧ-nō'rē) (Col. In.)	7·01 N	75·09 W
127	Áno Theológos Grc.	40·37 N	24·41 E
126	Áno Viánnos Grc. (Inset)	35·52 N	25·26 E
151	Anp'u China	21·28 N	110·00 E
120	Ansbach (äns'bäk) Ger.	49·18 N	10·35 E
95	Anse à Veau (äNs' ȧ-vō') Hai.	18·30 N	73·25 W
95	Anse d' Hainault (äNs'dĕnō) Hai	18·45 N	74·25 W
98	Anserma (á'n-sĕ'r-mä) Col. (In.)	5·13 N	75·47 W
98	Ansermanuevo (á'n-sĕ'r-mä-nwĕ'vō) Col. (In.)	4·47 N	75·59 W
150	Anshan China	41·00 N	123·00 E
151	Anshun (än-shōōn') China	26·12 N	105·50 E
76	Anson (ăn'sŭn) Tex.	32·45 N	99·52 W
158	Anson B. Austl.	13·10 S	34·25 E
152	Ansŏng (än'sŭng') Kor.	37·00 N	127·12 E
81	Ansonia (ăn-sō'nĭ-ȧ) Conn.	41·20 N	73·05 W
150	Antachan China	41·20 N	125·20 E
133	Antakya (än-täk'yä) Tur.	36·20 N	36·10 E
133	Antalya (Adalia) (än-tä'lē-ä) (ä-dä'lē-ä) Tur.	37·00 N	30·50 E
133	Antalya Körfezi (G.) Tur.	36·40 N	31·20 E
47	Antarctica	80·15 S	127·00 E
47	Antartic Pen. Ant.	70·00 S	65·00 W
67	Antelope Cr. (ăn'tē-lōp) Wyo.	43·29 N	105·42 W
74	Antelope I. Utah (Salt Lake City In.)	40·39 N	112·07 W
124	Antequera (än-tĕ-kĕ'rä) Sp.	37·01 N	4·34 W
72	Anthony (ăn'thô-nē) Kans.	37·08 N	98·01 W
123	Antibes (äN-tēb') Fr.	43·36 N	7·12 E
83	Anticosti I. (ăn-tĭ-kŏs'tē) Can.	49·40 N	62·00 W
71	Antigo (ăn'tĭ-gō) Wis.	45·09 N	89·11 W
83	Antigonish (ăn-tĭ-gô-nēsh') Can.	45·39 N	61·59 W
92	Antigua (än-tē'gwä) Guat.	14·32 N	90·43 W
91	Antigua (R.) Mex.	19·16 N	96·36 W
93	Antigua I. N. A. (Le. & Wind. Is. In.)	17·07 N	61·32 W
91	Antigua Veracruz (än-tē'gwä vā-rä-krōōz') Mex.	19·18 N	96·17 W
95	Antilla (än-tē'lyä) Cuba	20·50 N	75·50 W
89	Antilles, Greater (Is.) N. A.	20·30 N	79·15 W
89	Antilles, Lesser (Is.) N. A.	12·15 N	65·00 W
65	Antioch (ăn'tĭ-ŏk) Calif. (San Francisco In.)	38·00 N	121·48 W
75	Antioch Ill. (Chicago In.)	42·29 N	88·06 W
70	Antioch Nebr.	42·05 N	102·36 W
98	Antioquia (än-tē-ō'kēä) Col. (In.)	6·34 N	75·49 W
98	Antioquia (Dept.) Col. (In.)	6·48 N	75·42 W
73	Antlers (ănt'-lērz) Okla.	34·14 N	95·38 W
100	Antofagasta (än-tô-fä-gäs'tä) Chile	23·32 S	70·21 W
100	Antofalla, Salar de (Des.) (sä-lär'de än'tō-fä'lä) Arg.	26·00 S	67·52 W
93	Antón (än-tōn') Pan.	8·24 N	80·15 W
167	Antongil, Baie d' (B.) (äN-tôN-zhēl') Malagasy	16·15 S	50·15 E
101	Antonio Carlos (än-tō'nēōō-kà'r-lôs) Braz. (Rio de Janeiro In.)	21·19 S	43·45 W
167	António Enes (än-to'nyō ĕn'ēs) Moz.	16·13 S	39·58 E
72	Antonito (ăn-tô-nē'tō) Colo.	37·04 N	106·01 W
128	Antonopole (än'tô-nô-pō lyĕ) Sov. Un.	56·19 N	27·11 E
116	Antrim Mts. (ăn'trĭm) N. Ire.	54·60 N	6·15 W
167	Antsirabe (änt-sê-rä'bā) Malag. Rep.	19·49 S	47·16 E
	Antsirane, see Diégo-Suarez		
128	Antsla (änt'slȧ) Sov. Un.	57·49 N	26·29 E
100	Antuco (Vol.) (än-tōō'kō) Chile	37·30 S	72·30 W
150	Antung (än'tōōng') China	40·10 N	124·30 E
148	Antungwei (ändōōngwā) China	35·08 N	119·19 E
	Antwerp, see Antwerpen		
111	Antwerpen (Antwerp) (änt'wĕrpĕn) Bel. (Brussels In.)	51·13 N	4·24 E
150	Antz'u China (Peking In.)	39·23 N	116·44 E
142	Anun (R.) Nepal	27·18 N	86·51 E
142	Anūpgarh (ŭ-nōōp'-gŭr) India	29·22 N	73·20 E
143	Anurādhapura (ŭ-nōō'rä-dŭ-pōō'rŭ) Ceylon	8·24 N	80·25 E
148	Anyang (än'yäng) China	36·05 N	114·22 E
119	Anykščiai (anĭksh-chä'ē) Sov. Un.	55·34 N	25·04 E
98	Anzá (än-zä') Col. (In.)	6·19 N	75·51 W
134	Anzhero-Sudzhensk ((än'zhâ-rô-sōōd'zhĕnsk) Sov. Un.	56·08 N	86·08 E
125	Anzio (änt'zē-ō) It. (Rome In.)	41·28 N	12·39 E
99	Anzoategui (State) (än-zôä'tĕ-gē) Ven. (In.)	9·38 N	64·45 W
152	Aomori (äô-mō'rē) Jap.	40·45 N	140·52 E
126	Aosta (ä-ôs'tä) It.	45·45 N	7·20 E
165	Aouk, Bahr (R.) (ä-ōōk') Chad	9·30 N	20·45 E
78	Apalachicola (ăp-ȧ-lăch-ĭ-kō'lȧ) Fla.	29·43 N	84·59 W
91	Apan (ä-pä'n) Mex. (Mexico City In.)	19·43 N	98·27 W
90	Apango (ä-päŋ'gō) Mex.	17·41 N	99·22 W
98	Apaporis (R.) (ä-pä-pô'rĭs) Col.	0·48 N	72·32 W
154	Aparri (ä-pär'rē) Phil.	18·15 N	121·40 E
90	Apasco (ä-pà's-kō) Mex.	20·33 N	100·43 W
127	Apatin (ŏ'pŏ-tĭn) Yugo.	45·40 N	19·00 E
90	Apatzingán de la Constitución (ä-pät-zĭŋ-gän'dä lä cōn-stĭ-tōō-sē-ōn') Mex.	19·07 N	102·21 W
117	Apeldoorn (ä'pĕl-dōrn) Neth.	52·14 N	5·55 E
98	Apía (ä-pē'ä) Col. (In.)	5·07 N	75·58 W
90	Apipilulco (ä-pĭ-pĭ-lōōl'kō) Mex.	18·09 N	99·40 W
127	Apíranthos Grc.	37·07 N	25·32 E
72	Apishapa (R.) (ăp-ĭ-shä'pȧ) Colo.	37·40 N	104·08 W
90	Apizaco (ä-pē-zä'kō) Mex.	19·18 N	98·11 W
155	Apo (Mtn.) (ä'pō) Phil.	6·56 N	125·05 E
79	Apoka (ä-pŏp'kȧ) Fla. (In.)	28·37 N	81·30 W
79	Apoka (L.) Fla. (In.)	28·38 N	81·50 W
71	Apostle Is. (ȧ-pŏs'l) Wis.	97·03 N	90·55 W
78	Appalachia (ăpȧ-lăch'ĭ-ȧ) Va.	36·54 N	82·49 W
63	Appalachian Mts. (ăp-ȧ-lăch'ĭ-ȧn) U. S.	37·20 N	82·00 W
78	Appalachicola R. (ăpȧ-lăch'ĭ-cōlä) Fla.	30·11 N	85·00 W
118	Äppelbo (ĕp-ĕl-bōō) Swe.	60·30 N	14·02 E
123	Appelhülsen (ä'pĕl-hül'-sĕn) Ger. (Ruhr In.)	51·55 N	7·26 E
126	Appennino (Mts.) (äp-pĕn-nē'nō) It.	43·48 N	11·06 E
120	Appenzell (äp'ĕn-tsĕl) Switz.	47·19 N	9·22 E
70	Appleton (ăp' l-tŭn) Minn.	45·10 N	96·01 W
71	Appleton Wis.	44·14 N	88·27 W
73	Appleton City Mo.	38·10 N	94·02 W
79	Appomattox (R.) (ăp-ô-măt'ŭks) Va.	37·22 N	78·09 W
125	Aprília (ȧ-prē'lyȧ) It. (Rome In.)	41·36 N	12·40 E
133	Apsheronskiy, P-Ov. (pen.) Sov. Un.	40·20 N	50·30 E
123	Apt (äpt) Fr.	43·54 N	5·19 E
	Apulia (Reg.), see Puglia		
98	Apure (R.) (ä-pōō'rä) Ven.	8·08 N	68·46 W
98	Apurimac (R.) (ä-pōō-rê-mäk') Peru	11·39 S	73·48 W
115	Aqaba, G. of (ä'kȧ-bȧ) Asia	28·30 N	34·40 E
139	Aqaba (R.) U. A. R. (Palestine In.)	29·58 N	34·05 E
139	Aqabat al Hijaziyah Jordan (Palestine In.)	29·45 N	35·55 E
84	Aquasco (ȧ'gwā'scō) Md. (Baltimore In.)	38·35 N	76·44 W
99	Aquidauana (ä-kē-däwä'nä) Braz.	20·24 S	55·46 W
84	Aquidneck (ȧ-kwĭd'nĭk) R. I. (Providence In.)	41·31 N	71·14 W
124	Aquilianos, Montes (Mts.) (mô'n-tĕs-ä-kē-lyä'nôs) Sp.	42·27 N	6·35 W
95	Aquin (ä-kăn') Hai.	18·20 N	73·25 W
153	Ara (R.) (ä-rä) Jap. (Tōkyō In.)	35·40 N	139·52 E
	Araba, see Ha'arava (R.)		
168	Araba, Wadi U. A. R. (Nile In.)	29·02 N	32·10 E
129	Arabatskaya Strelka (Spit) (Tongue of Arabat) (ä-rä-bat' skȧ-yȧ strĕl'kȧ) (ä-rȧ-băt') Sov. Un.	45·50 N	35·05 E
165	Arabian Des. (ȧ-rā'bĭ-ăn) U. A. R.	27·06 N	32·49 E
163	Arabian Pen. Asia	28·00 N	40·00 E
138	Arabian Sea (ȧ-rā'bĭ-ăn) Asia	16·00 N	65·15 E
99	Aracaju (ä-rä'kä-zhōō') Braz.	11·00 S	37·01 W
99	Aracati (ä-rä'kä-tē') Braz.	4·31 S	37·41 W
99	Araçatuba (ä-rä-sä-tōō'bȧ) Braz.	21·14 S	50·19 W
99	Aracruz (ä-rä-krōō's) Braz.	19·58 S	40·11 W
99	Araçuaí (ä-rä-sōō-ä-ē') Braz.	16·57 S	41·56 W
139	Arad Isr. (Palestine In.)	31·20 N	35·15 E
121	Arad (ŏ'rŏd) Rom.	46·10 N	21·18 E
156	Arafura Sea (ä-rä-fōō'rä) Oceania	8·40 S	130·00 E
125	Aragon (Reg.) (ä-rä-gōn') Sp.	40·55 N	0·45 W
124	Aragón (R.) Sp.	42·35 N	1·10 W
99	Aragua (State) (ä-rä'gwä) Ven. (In.)	10·00 N	67·05 W
99	Aragua de Barcelona (ä-rä'gwä dā bär-thä-lō'nä) Ven. (In.)	9·29 N	64·48 W
99	Araguaía (R.) (ä-rä-gwä'yä) Braz.	8·37 S	49·43 W
99	Araguari (ä-rä-gwä'rē) Braz.	18·43 S	48·03 W
98	Araguatins (ä-rä-gwä-tēns) Braz.	5·41 S	48·04 W
99	Aragüita (ärà-gwē'tä) Ven. (In.)	10·13 N	66·28 W
115	Araj (Oasis) (ä-räj') U. A. R.	29·05 N	26·51 E
144	Arak Iran	34·08 N	49·57 E
146	Arakanyoma (Mts.) (ŭ-rŭ-kŭn'yō'mà) Bur.	19·51 N	94·13 E
127	Arakhthos (R.) (är'äk-thôs) Grc.	39·10 N	21·05 E
	Aral Sea, see Aral'skoye More		
134	Aral'sk (ȧ-rälsk') Sov. Un.	46·47 N	62·00 E
103	Aral'skoye More (Aral Sea) Sov. Un.	45·17 N	60·02 E
133	Aralsor (L.) (ȧ-räl'sôr') Sov. Un.	49·00 N	48·20 E
90	Aramberri (ä-ràm-bĕr-rē') Mex.	24·05 N	99·47 W
116	Aran (I.) (ăr'ăn) Ire.	53·04 N	9·59 W
116	Aran (I.) Ire.	54·60 N	8·25 W
124	Aranda de Duero (ä-rän'dä dā dwā'rō) Sp.	41·43 N	3·45 W
90	Arandas (ä-rän'däs) Mex.	20·43 N	102·18 W
124	Aranjuez (ä-rän-hwāth') Sp.	40·02 N	3·24 W
77	Aransas Pass (ȧ-răn'sȧs pȧs) Tex.	27·55 N	97·09 W
142	Aransol India	23·45 N	86·58 E
164	Araouane Mali	18·54 N	3·33 W
133	Arapkir (ä-räp-kēr') Tur.	39·00 N	38·10 E
99	Araraquara (ä-rä-rä-kwä'rä) Braz.	21·47 S	48·08 W
101	Araras (ä-rä'räs) Braz. (Rio de Janeiro In.)	22·21 S	47·22 W
99	Araras, Serra das (Mts.) (sĕ'r-rä-däs-ä-rä'räs) Braz.	18·03 S	53·23 W
100	Araras, Serra das (Mts.) Braz.	23·30 S	53·00 W
100	Araras, Serra das (Mts.) Braz. (In.)	22·24 S	43·15 W
160	Ararat (ăr'ărăt) Austl.	37·12 S	38·00 E
133	Ararat (Mtn.) Tur.	39·50 N	44·20 E
99	Arari (L.) (ä-rä'rē) Braz.	0·30 S	48·50 W
99	Araripe, Chapadodo (Plain) (shä-pä'dä-dō-ä-rä-rē'pĕ) Braz.	5·55 S	40·42 W
101	Araruama (ä-rä-rōō-ä'mä) Braz. (Rio de Janeiro In.)	22·53 S	42·19 W
101	Araruama, Lagoa de (L.) (lä-gôä-dĕ-ä-rä-rōō-ä'mä) Braz. (Rio de Janeiro In.)	23·00 S	42·15 W
133	Aras (R.) (ä-räs) Iran-Sov. Un.	39·15 N	47·10 E
99	Aratuípe (ä-rä-tōō-ē'pĕ) Braz.	13·12 S	38·58 W
98	Arauca (ä-rou'kä) Col.	6·56 N	70·45 W
98	Arauca (R.) Ven.	7·13 N	68·43 W
142	Aravalli Ra. (ä-rä'vŭ-lē) India	29·15 N	72·59 E
99	Araxá (ä-rä-shà') Braz.	19·41 S	46·46 W
99	Araya, Punta de (Pt.) (pŭn'tä-dĕ-ä-rä'yȧ) Ven. (In.)	10·40 N	64·15 W
155	Arayat (ä-rä'yät) Phil. (Manila In.)	15·10 N	120·44 E
118	Arboga (är-bō'gä) Swe.	59·26 N	15·50 E
126	Arborea (är-bō-rĕ'ä) It.	39·50 N	8·36 E
116	Arbroath (är-brōth') Scot.	56·36 N	2·25 W
123	Arc (R.) (ärk) Fr. (Marseille In.)	43·32 N	5·17 E
122	Arcachon (ar-kȧ-shôN') Fr.	44·39 N	1·12 W
122	Arcachon, Bassin d' (Basin) (bä-sĕn' där-kä-shôN') Fr.	44·42 N	1·50 W
74	Arcadia (är-kā'dĭ-ȧ) Calif. (Los Angeles In.)	34·08 N	118·02 W
79	Arcadia Fla. (In.)	27·12 N	81·51 W
77	Arcadia La.	32·33 N	92·56 W
71	Arcadia Wis.	44·15 N	91·30 W
66	Arcata (är-kȧ'tȧ) Calif.	40·54 N	124·05 W
68	Arc Dome Mtn. (ärk dōm) Nev.	38·51 N	117·21 W
90	Arcelia (är-sä'lē-ä) Mex.	18·19 N	100·14 W
81	Archbald (ärch'bôld) Pa.	41·30 N	75·35 W
69	Arches Natl. Mon. (är'chĕs) Utah	38·45 N	109·35 W
98	Archidona (är-chē-do'nä) Ec.	1·01 S	77·49 W
124	Archidona (är-chē-dô'nä) Sp.	37·08 N	4·24 W
157	Archipelago (I.) Oceania	16·50 S	142·00 W
124	Arcila (är-sē'lä) Mor.	35·30 N	6·05 W
122	Arcis-sur-Aube (är-sēs'sûr-ōb') Fr.	48·31 N	4·04 E
67	Arco (är'kō) Idaho	43·39 N	113·15 W
74	Arcola (är'kō'lȧ) Minn. (Minneapolis, St. Paul In.)	45·07 N	92·46 W
84	Arcola (är'cōlä) Va. (Washington D.C. In.)	38·57 N	77·32 W
77	Arcola Tex. (In.)	29·30 N	95·28 W
124	Arcos de la Frontera (är'kōs-dĕ-lä-frôn-tĕ'rä) Sp.	36·44 N	5·48 W
48	Arctic Ocean (ärk'tĭk)		

ng-sing; ŋ-baŋk; N-nasalized n; nŏd; cŏmmit; ōld; ôbey; ôrder; fōōd; fŏŏt; ou-out; s-soft; sh-dish; th-thin; pūre; ûnite; ûrn; stŭd; circŭs; ü-as "y" in study; '-indeterminate vowel.

Page	Name Pronunciation Region	Lat. °′	Long. °′
127	Arda (R.) (är'dä)..........Bul.	41·36 N	25·18 E
144	Ardabīl..................Iran	38 15 N	48·00 E
133	Ardahan (är-dà-hän')........Tur.	41·10 N	42·40 E
118	Ardals Fd. (är-däls).........Nor.	58·53 N	7·55 E
132	Ardatov (är-dä-tôf')......Sov. Un.	54·58 N	46·10 E
117	Ardennes (Mts.) (år-děn')....Bel.	50·01 N	5·12 E
124	Ardila (R.) (är-dē'lä).......Port.	38·12 N	9·20 W
73	Ardmore (ärd'mōr).........Okla.	34·10 N	97·08 W
84	Ardmore...Pa. (Philadelphia In.)	40·01 N	75·18 W
85	Ardrossan (är-dros'ăn) Can. (Edmonton In.)	53·33 N	113·08 W
110	Ardsley (ärdz'lē)..........Eng.	53·43 N	1·33 W
112	Åre......................Swe.	63·12 N	13·12 E
124	Arecena (ä-rě-sě'nä).........Sp.	37·53 N	6·34 W
89	Arecibo (ä-rā-sē'bō) P. R. (Puerto Rico In.)	18·28 N	66·45 W
99	Areia Branca (ä-rě'yä-brä'n-kă) Braz.	4·58 S	37·02 W
68	Arena, Pt. (ä-rā'nȧ)........Calif.	38·57 N	123·40 W
99	Arenas, Punta (Pt.) (pōōn'tä-rě'näs).Ven. (In.)	10·57 N	64·24 W
124	Arenas de San Pedro (ä-rā'nàs dā sän pā'drō).Sp.	40·12 N	5·04 W
118	Arendal (ä'rĕn-däl).........Nor.	58·29 N	8·44 E
111	Arendonk......Bel. (Brussels In.)	51·19 N	5·07 E
98	Arequipa (ä-rå-kē'pä).......Peru	16·27 S	71·30 W
126	Arezzo (ä-rět'sō)............It.	43·28 N	11·54 E
124	Arga (R.) (är'gä)............Sp.	42·35 N	1·55 W
125	Arganda (är-gän'dä) Sp. (Madrid In.)	40·18 N	3·27 W
136	Argazi L. (är'gä-zĭ) Sov. Un. (Urals In.)	55·24 N	60·37 E
136	Argazi R.....Sov. Un. (Urals In.)	55·33 N	57·30 E
122	Argentan (àr-zhäN-täN')......Fr.	48·45 N	0·01 W
122	Argentat (är-zhäN-tä')........Fr.	45·07 N	1·57 E
123	Argenteuil (är-zhäN-tû'y') Fr. (Paris In.)	48·56 N	2·15 E
96	Argentina (är-jěn-tē'nȧ).....S. A.	35·30 S	67·00 W
100	Argentino (L.) (är-kěn-tē'nō).Arg.	50·15 S	72·45 W
122	Argenton-sur-Creuse (är-zhäN'tôN-sür-krôs).Fr.	46·34 N	1·28 E
127	Arges (R.) (àr'zhěsh).......Rom.	44·27 N	25·22 E
75	Argo (är'go).....Ill. (Chicago In.)	41·47 N	87·49 W
127	Argolikos Kólpos (G.).......Grc.	37·20 N	23·00 E
122	Argonne (Mts.) (ä'r-gôn)......Fr.	49·21 N	5·54 E
127	Argos (är'gŏs)..............Grc.	37·38 N	22·45 E
127	Argostólion (är-gŏs-tô'lē-ŏn)..Grc.	38·10 N	20·30 E
68	Arguello, Pt. (är-gwāl'yō)...Calif.	34·35 N	120·40 W
135	Argun R. (år-gōōn') Sov. Un.-China	50·15 N	118·45 E
85	Argyle (år'gīl).Can. (Winnipeg In.)	50·11 N	97·27 W
70	Argyle..................Minn.	48·21 N	96·48 W
118	Århus (ôr'hōōs).............Den.	56·09 N	10·10 E
153	Ariakeno-Uni (Sea) (ä-rē'ä-kä'nō ōō'nē).Jap.	33·03 N	130·18 E
153	Ariake-Wan (B.) (ä'rē-ä'kȧ wän) Jap.	31·18 N	131·15 E
126	Ariano (ä-rē-ä'nō)............It.	41·09 N	15·11 E
98	Ariari (ä-ryà'rē) (R.)....Col. (In.)	3·34 N	73·42 W
98	Arica (ä-rē'kä).............Chile	18·34 S	70·14 W
83	Arichat (ä-rĭ-shät')..........Can.	45·33 N	61·03 W
122	Ariège (R.) (ȧ-rê-ĕzh')........Fr.	43·26 N	1·29 E
65	Ariel (â'rĭ-ĕl) Wash. (Portland In.)	45·57 N	122·34 W
121	Ariesul R. (ä-rê-ā'shōōl)....Rom.	46·25 N	23·15 E
95	Ariguanabo, L. de (lä'gô-dě-ä-rē-gwä-nä'bô) Cuba (Havana In.)	22·17 N	82·33 W
139	Arīḥā (Jericho) Jordan (Palestine In.)	31·51 N	35·28 E
72	Arikaree (R.) (ă-rĭ-kȧ-rē')...Colo.	39·51 N	102·18 W
153	Arima (ä'rē-mä').Jap. (Ōsaka In.)	34·17 N	135·16 E
155	Aringay (ä-rĭṉ-gä'ē) Phil. (Manila In.)	16·25 N	120·20 E
99	Arinos (R.) (ä-rē'nôzsh).......Braz.	12·09 S	56·49 W
99	Aripuanã (R.) (à-rê-pwän'yȧ) Braz.	7·06 S	60·29 W
139	Arish (R.) (ȧ-rēsh') U. A. R. (Palestine In.)	29·53 N	33·39 E
62	Arizona (State) (ăr-ĭ-zō'nȧ)..U. S.	34·00 N	113·00 W
124	Arjona (är-hō'nä)............Sp.	37·58 N	4·03 W
135	Arka (R.)..........Sov. Un.	60·12 N	142·30 E
78	Arkabutla Res. (är-kȧ-bŭt'lȧ) Miss.	34·48 N	88·53 W
73	Arkadelphia (är-kȧ-děl'fĭ-ȧ)..Ark.	34·06 N	93·05 W
63	Arkansas (State) (är'kăn-sô) (är-kăn'sȧs).U. S.	34·50 N	93·40 W
73	Arkansas City.............Kans.	37·04 N	97·02 W
73	Arkansas R................Okla.	35·20 N	94·56 W
132	Arkhangelsk (Archangel) (är-kän'gělsk).Sov. Un.	64·30 N	40·25 E
136	Arkhangel'skiy (är-kän-gěl'skĭ) Sov. Un. (Urals In.)	52·52 N	61·53 E
136	Arkhangel'skoye (är-kän-gěl' skô-yě).Sov. Un. (Urals In.)	54·25 N	56·48 E
116	Arklow (ärk'lō).............Ire.	52·47 N	6·10 W
118	Arkona, C. (är'kō-nä).......Ger.	54·43 N	13·43 E
143	Arkonam (är-kō-nām')......India	13·05 N	79·43 E
124	Arlanza (R.) (är-län-thä')....Sp.	42·08 N	3·45 W
124	Arlanzón (R.) (är-län-thōn')...Sp.	42·12 N	3·58 W
120	Arlberg Tun. (ärl'běrgh).....Aus.	47·05 N	10·15 E
122	Arles (ärl).................Fr.	43·42 N	4·38 E
78	Arlington (är'lĭng-tun').......Ga.	31·25 N	84·42 W
83	Arlington.....Mass. (Boston In.)	42·26 N	71·13 W
70	Arlington (är'-lěng-tŭn)......S. D.	44·23 N	97·09 W
74	Arlington (är'lĭng-tŭn) Tex. (Dallas, Fort Worth In.)	32·44 N	97·07 W
168	Arlington.S. Afr. (Johannesburg & Pretoria In.)	28·02 S	27·52 E
81	Arlington..................Vt.	43·05 N	73·05 W
84	Arlington Va. (Washington D.C. In.)	38·55 N	77·10 W
65	Arlington.....Wash. (Seattle In.)	48·11 N	122·08 W
75	Arlington Heights (är'lěng-tŭn-hī'ts).Ill. (Chicago In.)	42·05 N	87·59 W
118	Arlöv (är'lûf)..............Swe.	55·38 N	13·05 E
158	Arltunga (ärl-tōōṉ'gȧ)......Austl.	23·19 S	134·45 E
73	Arma (är'mȧ)...............Kans.	37·34 N	94·43 W
85	Armagh (är-mä') (är-mäk') Can. (Quebec In.)	46·45 N	70·36 W
116	Armagh..................N. Ire.	54·21 N	6·25 W
168	Armant (är-mänt') U. A. R. (Nile In.)	25·37 N	32·32 E
98	Armaro (är-mà'rō)......Col. (In.)	4·58 N	74·54 W
133	Armavir (ár-mà-vĭr')....Sov. Un.	45·00 N	41·00 E
98	Armenia (är-mě'nēȧ)....Col. (In.)	4·33 N	75·40 W
92	Armenia (är-mā'nē-ä).........Sal.	13·44 N	89·31 W
130	Armenian, S. S. R.......Sov. Un.	41·00 N	44·39 E
122	Armentières (är-mäN-tyâr')....Fr.	50·43 N	2·53 E
90	Armeria, Rio de (R.) (rē'ō-dě-är-mȧ-rē'ä).Mex.	19·36 N	104·10 W
75	Armherstburg (ärm'hěrst-bōōrgh) Can. (Detroit In.)	42·06 N	83·06 W
160	Armidale (är'mĭ-dāl).......Austl.	30·27 S	151·50 E
70	Armour (är'mēr)...........S. D.	43·18 N	98·21 W
87	Armstrong Station (ärm'strŏng).Can.	50·21 N	89·00 W
129	Armyansk (ärm'yȧnsk)..Sov. Un.	46·06 N	33·42 E
124	Arnedo (är-nā'dō)............Sp.	42·12 N	2·03 W
117	Arnhem (ärn'hěm).........Neth.	51·58 N	5·56 E
158	Arnhem, C................Austl.	12·15 S	137·00 E
158	Arnhem Land, (Reg.) (ärn'hěm-lănd).Austl.	13·15 S	133·00 E
126	Arno (R.) (ä'r-nō)............It.	43·45 N	10·42 E
110	Arnold (är'nŭld)............Eng.	53·00 N	1·08 W
74	Arnold (ár'nŭld) Minn. (Duluth In.)	46·53 N	92·06 W
75	Arnold.......Pa. (Pittsburgh In.)	40·35 N	79·45 W
81	Arnprior (ärn-prī'ẽr)........Can.	45·25 N	76·20 W
117	Arnsberg (ärns'běrgh).......Ger.	51·25 N	8·02 E
120	Arnstadt (ärn'shtät).........Ger.	50·51 N	10·57 E
166	Aroab (är'ō-àb)..........S. W. Afr.	25·40 S	19·45 E
82	Aroostook (ȧ-rōōs'tōōk)....Maine	46·44 N	68·15 W
155	Aroroy (ä-rô-rō'ê) Phil. (Manila In.)	12·30 N	123·24 E
123	Arpajon (ăr-pä-jŏ'n) Fr. (Paris In.)	48·35 N	2·15 E
100	Arpoador, Ponta do (Pt.) (pô'n-tä-dō-är'pôä-dō'r).Braz. (In.)	22·59 S	43·11 W
124	Arraiolos (är-rī-ō'lōzh)......Port.	38·47 N	7·59 W
139	Ar Ramta.Jordan (Palestine In.)	29·31 N	35·57 E
116	Arran (I.) (ă'rȧn)...........Scot.	55·39 N	5·30 W
122	Arras (ȧ-räs')................Fr.	50·21 N	2·40 E
168	Ar Rawḍah....U. A. R. (Nile In.)	27·47 N	30·52 E
101	Arrecifes (är-rå-sē'fäs) Arg. (Buenos Aires In.)	34·03 S	60·05 W
101	Arrecifes (R.) Arg. (Buenos Aires In.)	34·07 S	59·50 W
122	Arrée, Mts. d' (är-rā')........Fr.	48·27 N	4·00 W
91	Arriaga (är-rēä'gä).........Mex.	16·15 N	95·00 W
125	Arrone (R.).......It. (Rome In.)	41·57 N	12·17 E
74	Arrowhead, L. (läk ăr'ōhěd) Calif. (Los Angeles In.)	34·17 N	117·13 W
67	Arrow R. (ăr'ō)............Mont.	47·29 N	109·53 W
66	Arrowrock Res. (ăr'ō-rŏk)..Idaho	43·40 N	115·30 W
95	Arroya Arena (är-rō'yä-rě'nä) Cuba (Havana In.)	23·01 N	82·30 W
91	Arroy Caribe (R.) (är-ro'i-kä-rē'bě).Mex.	18·18 N	90·38 W
124	Arroyo de la Luz (är-rō'yō-dě-lä-lōō'z).Sp.	39·39 N	6·46 W
90	Arroyo Grande (R.) (är-rô'yō-grä'n-dě).Mex.	23·30 N	98·45 W
90	Arroyo Seco (är-rō'yō-sä'kō).Mex.	21·31 N	99·44 W
144	Ar Rub Al Khālī (Empty Quarter) (Des.).Sau. Ar.	20·30 N	51·45 E
135	Arsen'yev..............Sov. Un.	44·13 N	133·32 E
136	Arsinskiy (är-sĭn'skĭ) Sov. Un. (Urals In.)	53·46 N	59·54 E
127	Árta (är'tä).................Grc.	39·08 N	21·02 E
76	Arteaga (är-tä-ä'gä).........Mex.	25·28 N	100·50 W
135	Artëm (ȧr-tyôm').......Sov. Un.	43·28 N	132·29 E
94	Artemisa (är-tä-mē'sä)......Cuba	22·50 N	82·45 W
129	Artëmovsk (ȧr-työm'ôfsk) Sov. Un.	48·37 N	38·00 E
72	Artesia (är-tē'sĭ-ȧ).......N. Mex.	32·44 N	104·23 W
160	Artesian Basin, The (är-tē'zhăn).Austl.	26·45 S	141·40 E
95	Arthur's Town...........Ba. Is.	24·40 N	74·30 W
136	Arti (är'tĭ)...Sov. Un. (Urals In.)	56·20 N	58·38 E
95	Artibonite (R.) (är-tē-bō-nē'tā) Hai.	19·00 N	72·25 W
155	Aru, Pulau-Pulau (Is.).....Indon.	6·20 S	133·00 E
165	Arua (ä'rōō-ä)..............Ug.	3·04 N	31·01 E
98	Aruba (ä-rōō'bȧ) (I.) Neth. Antilles	12·29 N	70·00 W
167	Arusha (ä-rōō'shä)..........Tan.	3·18 S	36·43 E
165	Aruwimi R. (ä-rōō-wē'mē) Con. K.	1·04 N	28·31 E
82	Arvida....................Can.	48·25 N	71·11 W
118	Arvika (är-vē'kȧ)...........Swe.	59·41 N	12·35 E
132	Arzamas (är-zä-mäs')....Sov. Un.	55·20 N	43·52 E
125	Arzew (är-zȧ-ōō')...........Alg.	35·50 N	0·20 W
124	Arzua (är-thōō'ä)............Sp.	42·54 N	8·19 W
120	As (äsh')..................Czech.	50·12 N	12·13 E
152	Asahigawa (ä-sä'hê-gä'wä)..Jap.	43·50 N	142·09 E
153	Asahi-Gawa (Strm.) (ä-sä'hê-gä'wä).Jap.	35·01 N	133·40 E
153	Asaka (ä-sä'kä)..Jap. (Tōkyō In.)	35·47 N	139·36 E
136	Asbest (äs- bĕst') Sov. Un. (Urals In.)	57·02 N	61·28 E
82	Asbestos (ăs bĕs'tŏs)........Can.	45·49 N	71·52 W
84	Asbury Park (ăz'bĕr-ĭ) N. J. (New York In.)	40·13 N	74·01 W
92	Ascencion, Bahía de la (B.) (bä-ē'ä-dě-lä-äs-sěn-sē-ōn') Mex. (Yucatan In.)	19·39 N	87·30 W
90	Ascensión (äs-sěn-sê-ōn')....Mex.	24·21 N	99·54 W
163	Ascension (I.) (ȧ-sĕn'shŭn).Atl. O.	8·00 S	13·00 W
168	Ascent (ăs-ĕnt')....S. Afr. (Johannesburg & Pretoria In.)	27·14 S	29·06 E
120	Aschaffenburg (ä-shäf'ěn-bōōrgh) Ger.	49·58 N	9·12 E
123	Ascheberg (ä'shě-běrg) Ger. (Ruhr In.)	51·47 N	7·38 E
120	Aschersleben (äsh'ērs-lā-běn).Ger.	51·46 N	11·28 E
126	Ascoli Piceno (äs'kô-lēpê-chā'nō) It.	42·50 N	13·55 E
127	Asenovgrad...............Bul.	42·00 N	24·49 E
168	Aser, Ras (C.) Som. (Horn of Afr. In.)	11·55 N	51·30 E
128	Aseri (á'sě-rĭ)..........Sov. Un.	59·26 N	26·58 E
	Asfi, see Safi		
136	Asha (ä'shä).Sov. Un. (Urals In.)	55·01 N	57·17 E
70	Ashabula (L.) (ăsh'ȧ-bū-lă)..N. D.	47·07 N	97·51 W
136	Ashan (ä'shän) Sov. Un. (Urals In.)	57·08 N	56·25 E
110	Ashbourne (ăsh'bŭrn).......Eng.	53·01 N	1·44 W
78	Ashburn (ăsh'bŭrn)..........Ga.	31·42 N	83·42 W
84	Ashburn Va. (Washington D.C. In.)	39·02 N	77·30 W
158	Ashburton (R.) (ăsh'bûr-tŭn) Austl.	22·30 S	115·30 E
110	Ashby-de-la-Zouch (ăsh'bĭ-dê-lȧ zōōsh').Eng.	52·44 N	1·23 W
86	Ashcroft....................Can.	50·47 N	121·02 W
73	Ashdown (ăsh'doun).........Ark.	33·41 N	94·07 W
79	Asheboro (ăsh'bŭr-ô).......N. C.	35·41 N	79·50 W
76	Asherton (ăsh'ēr-tŭn)........Tex.	28·26 N	99·45 W
79	Asheville (ăsh'vĭl)..........N. C.	35·35 N	82·35 W
153	Ashikaga (ä'shē-kä'gȧ).......Jap.	36·22 N	139·26 E
153	Ashiya (ä'shê-yä')...........Jap.	33·54 N	130·40 E
153	Ashiya..........Jap. (Ōsaka In.)	34·44 N	135·18 E
153	Ashizuri-Zaki (Pt.) (ä-shē-zōō-rē zä-kē).Jap.	32·43 N	133·04 E
103	Ashkhabad (ŭsh-kä-bät').Sov. Un.	39·45 N	58·13 E
78	Ashland (ăsh'lȧnd)..........Ala.	33·15 N	85·50 W
72	Ashland..................Kans.	37·11 N	99·46 W
80	Ashland....................Ky.	38·25 N	82·40 W
82	Ashland..................Maine	46·37 N	68·26 W
83	Ashland.......Mass. (Boston In.)	42·16 N	71·28 W
70	Ashland..................Nebr.	41·02 N	96·23 W
80	Ashland..................Ohio	40·50 N	82·15 W
66	Ashland....................Ore.	42·12 N	122·42 W
81	Ashland....................Pa.	40·45 N	76·20 W
71	Ashland...................Wis.	46·34 N	90·55 W
70	Ashley (ăsh'lē).............N. D.	46·03 N	99·23 W
81	Ashley.....................Pa.	41·15 N	75·55 W
154	Ashmore Rf. (ăsh'mōr)....Indon.	12·08 S	122·45 E
168	Ashmūn (ash-mōōn') U. A. R. (Nile In.)	30·19 N	30·57 E
165	Ash Shabb (Shěb).......U. A. R.	22·34 N	29·52 E
168	Ash Shallūfah (Shăl'lōō-fä) U. A. R. (Suez In.)	30·09 N	32·33 E
139	Ash Shaṭṭ U. A. R. (Palestine In.)	29·58 N	32·36 E
139	Ash Shawbak Jordan (Palestine In.)	30·31 N	35·35 E
139	Ash Shīdīyah (R.) Jordan (Palestine In.)	29·53 N	36·49 E
80	Ashtabula (ăsh-tȧ-bū'lȧ).....Ohio	41·55 N	80·50 W
67	Ashton (ăsh'tŭn)............Idaho	44·04 N	111·28 W
110	Ashton-in-Makerfield (ăsh'tŭn-ĭn-māk'ēr-fēld).Eng.	53·29 N	2·39 W
110	Ashton-under-Lyne (ăsh'tŭn-ŭn-dēr-līn').Eng.	53·29 N	2·04 W
87	Ashuanipi (L.) (ăsh-wȧ-nĭp'ĭ).Can.	52·40 N	67·42 W
82	Ashuapmuchuan (R.) (ăsh-wăp-mōō-chwăn').Can.	49·10 N	73·10 W
136	Ashukino (ȧ-shōō'ki-nô) Sov. Un. (Moscow In.)	56·10 N	37·57 E
7	Asia (ā'zhȧ)		
103	Asia Minor (ā'zhȧ)..........Asia	38·18 N	31·18 E
90	Asientos (ä-sē-ěn'tōs)........Mex.	22·13 N	102·05 W
126	Asinara, Golfo di (G.) (gôl'fô-dē-ä-sē-nä'rä)..It.	40·58 N	8·28 E
126	Asinara (I.) (ä-sē-nä'rä).......It.	41·02 N	8·22 E
144	Asīr (Reg.) (ä-sēr')........Sau. Ar.	19·30 N	21·27 E
136	Askarovo (äs-kä-rō'vô) Sov. Un. (Urals In.)	53·21 N	58·32 E
118	Askersund (äs'kěr-sōōnd)....Swe.	58·43 N	14·53 E
136	Askino (äs'kĭ-nô) Sov. Un. (Urals In.)	56·06 N	56·29 E
82	Askitichi (L.) (ăs-kĭ-tĭ'chĭ)...Can.	49·15 N	73·55 W
165	Asmara (äs-mä'rȧ)...........Eth.	15·17 N	38·56 E
123	Asnières-sur-Seine (ä-nyâr'-sür-sě'n).Fr. (Paris In.)	48·55 N	2·18 E
165	Asosā.....................Eth.	10·13 N	34·28 E
66	Asotin (ȧ-sō'tĭn)...........Wash.	46·19 N	117·01 W
69	Aspen (ăs'pěn)..............Colo.	39·15 N	106·55 W
111	Asperen...Neth. (Amsterdam In.)	51·52 N	5·07 E
83	Aspy B. (ăs'pê)............Can.	46·26 N	60·17 W
168	Assab (ȧs-säb') Eth. (Horn of Afr. In.)	12·52 N	42·39 E
168	Aṣ Ṣaff.......U. A. R. (Nile In.)	29·33 N	31·23 E
165	As Sallūm..............U. A. R.	31·34 N	25·09 E
139	As Salt.....Jordan (Palestine In.)	32·02 N	35·44 E
142	Assam (State) (ăs-săm').....India	30·45 N	90·55 E
144	As Sayh.................Sau. Ar.	24·00 N	47·45 E
118	Assens (äs'sĕns)............Den.	55·16 N	9·54 E
168	As Sinbillāwayn U. A. R. (Nile In.)	30·53 N	31·37 E
164	Assini (ȧ-sê-nē')......Ivory Coast	4·52 N	3·16 W
86	Assiniboia..................Can.	49·36 N	106·10 W
85	Assiniboine R. (ă-sĭn'ĭ-boin) Can. (Winnipeg In.)	50·02 N	97·56 W
99	Assis (ȧ-sě's)...............Braz.	22·39 S	50·21 W
144	As Sulaymānīyah............Iraq	35·47 N	45·23 E
168	As Suways (Suez) U.A.R. (Suez In.)	29·58 N	32·34 E
127	Astakós (äs'tä-kôs)..........Grc.	38·42 N	21·00 E
133	Astara.................Sov. Un.	38·30 N	48·50 E
126	Asti (äs'tē)...................It.	44·54 N	8·12 E
146	Astin Tagh (Mts.)..........China	36·58 N	85·09 E
115	Astipálaia (I.)..............Grc.	36·31 N	26·19 E
124	Astorga (äs-tôr'gä)............Sp.	42·28 N	6·03 W
65	Astoria (ăs-tō'rĭ-ȧ) Ore. (Portland In.)	46·11 N	123·51 W

ăt; finȧl; rāte; senâte; ärm; ȧsk: sofȧ; fâre; ch-choose; dh-as th in other; bē; ēvent; bĕt; recĕnt; cratẽr; g-go; gh-guttural g; bĭt; ĭ-short neutral; rīde; K-guttural k as ch in German ich:

Page	Name Pronunciation Region	Lat. °′	Long. °′
85	Astotin Cr. (ăs-tō-tĕɴ') Can. (Edmonton In.)	53·43 N	113·00 W
133	Astrakhan' (ăs-trȧ-kän') Sov. Un.	46·15 N	48·00 E
166	Astrida (ăs-trē'dȧ) Rw.	2·37 S	29·48 E
124	Asturias (Reg.) (ăs-tōō'ryăs) Sp.	43·21 N	6·00 W
100	Asunción (ä-sōōn-syōn') Par.	25·25 S	57·30 W
	Asuncion, see Ixtaltepec		
	Asunción, see Nochixtlán		
92	Asuncion Mita (ä-sōōn-syō'n-mē'tä) Guat.	14·19 N	89·43 W
117	Åsunden (L.) (ô'sōōn-dĕn) Swe.	57·46 N	13·16 E
168	Aswān (Syene) (ä-swän') (sē-ā'nē) U. A. R. (Nile In.)	24·05 N	32·57 E
165	Aswān Dam U. A. R.	23·50 N	31·30 E
168	Aswān High Dam U. A. R. (Nile In.)	23·58 N	32·53 E
168	Asyūt (ä-syōōt') U. A. R. (Nile In.)	27·10 N	31·10 E
100	Atacama, Puna de (Reg.) (pōō'nä-dĕ-ätä-kä'mä) Chile	23·15 S	68·45 W
98	Atacama, Puna de (Plat.) (pōō'nä-dĕ-ä-tä-kä'mä) Bol.	21·35 S	66·58 W
96	Atacama, Desierto de (Des.) (dĕ-syĕ'r-tô-dĕ-ä-tä-kä'mä) Chile-Peru	23·50 S	69·00 W
100	Atacama, Salar de (L.) (sȧ-lär'dĕ-ätä-kä'mä) Chile	23·38 S	68·15 W
98	Ataco (ä-tȧ'kŏ) Col. (In.)	3·36 N	75·22 W
139	'Ata'Itah, Jabal al (Mts.) Jordan (Palestine In.)	30·48 N	35·19 E
164	Atakpamé (ä'täk-pȧ-mā') Togo	7·37 N	1·09 E
136	Atamanovskiy (ä-tä-mä'nôv-skĭ) Sov. Un. (Urals In.)	52·15 N	60·47 E
168	Ataqa Gebel (Plat.) U. A. R. (Suez In.)	29·59 N	32·20 E
164	Atar (ä-tär') Mauritania	20·45 N	13·16 W
68	Atascadero (ăt-ăs-kȧ-dâ'rō) Calif.	35·29 N	120·40 W
76	Atascosa R. (ăt-ăs-kō'sȧ) Tex.	28·50 N	98·17 W
165	Atbara (ät'bȧ-rä) Sud.	17·45 N	30·01 E
165	Atbara R. Sud.	17·14 N	34·27 E
134	Atbasar (ät'bä-sär') Sov. Un.	51·42 N	68·28 E
77	Atchafalaya B. (ăch-ȧ-fȧ-lī'ȧ) La.	29·25 N	91·30 W
77	Atchafalaya R. La.	30·53 N	91·51 W
73	Atchison (ăch'ĭ-sŭn) Kans.	39·33 N	95·08 W
84	Atco (ăt'kō) N. J. (Philadelphia In.)	39·46 N	74·53 W
91	Atempan (ä-tĕm-pä'n) Mex.	19·49 N	97·25 W
90	Atenguillo (R.) (ä-tĕn-gē'l-yô) Mex.	20·18 N	104·35 W
86	Athabasca (ăth-ȧ-băs'kȧ) Can.	54·41 N	113·11 W
86	Athabasca (L.) Can.	59·04 N	109·10 W
86	Athabasca (R.) Can.	57·21 N	112·02 W
82	Atharbaska (ăth-ȧr-băs'kȧ) Can.	46·03 N	71·54 W
78	Athens (ăth'ĕnz) Ala.	34·47 N	86·58 W
78	Athens Ga.	33·55 N	83·24 W
80	Athens Ohio	39·20 N	82·10 W
81	Athens Pa.	42·00 N	76·30 W
78	Athens Tenn.	35·26 N	84·36 W
77	Athens Tex.	32·13 N	95·51 W
	Athens, see Athinai		
110	Atherstone (ăth'ĕr-stŭn) Eng.	52·34 N	1·33 W
110	Atherton (ăth'ĕr-tŭn) Eng.	53·32 N	2·29 W
159	Atherton Plat. (ădh-ĕr-tŏn) Austl.	17·00 S	144·30 E
167	Athi (R.) (ä'tē) Ken.	2·31 S	35·28 E
127	Athinai (Athens) (ä-thē'nĕ) Grc.	38·00 N	23·38 E
116	Athlone (ăth-lōn') Ire.	53·24 N	7·30 W
127	Athos (Mtn.) (ăth'ŏs) Grc.	40·10 N	24·15 E
139	Ath Thamad U. A. R. (Palestine In.)	29·41 N	34·17 E
116	Athy (ȧ-thī) Ire.	52·59 N	7·08 W
101	Atibaia (ä-tē-bä'yȧ) Braz. (Rio de Janeiro In.)	23·08 S	46·32 W
87	Atikonak (L.) Can.	52·34 N	63·49 W
85	Atim Cr. Can. (Edmonton In.)	53·34 N	113·59 W
155	Atimonan (ä-tē-mō'nän) Phil. (Manila In.)	13·59 N	121·56 E
92	Atiquizaya (ä'tē-kē-zä'yä) Sal.	14·00 N	89·42 W
92	Atitlan (Vol.) (ä-tē-tlän') Guat.	14·35 N	91·11 W
92	Atitlan L. (ä-tē-tlän') Guat.	14·38 N	91·23 W
91	Atizapán (ä'tē-zȧ-pän') Mex. (Mexico City In.)	19·33 N	99·16 W
64	Atka (ăt'kȧ) Alaska	52·18 N	174·18 W
64	Atka (I.) Alaska	51·58 N	174·30 W
133	Atkarsk (ät-kärsk') Sov. Un.	51·50 N	45·00 E
70	Atkinson (ăt'kĭn-sŭn) Nebr.	42·32 N	98·58 W
84	Atlanta (ăt-lăn'tȧ) Ga. (Atlanta In.)	33·45 N	84·23 W
73	Atlanta Tex.	33·09 N	94·09 W
71	Atlantic (ăt-lăn'tĭk) Iowa	41·23 N	94·58 W
84	Atlantic Highlands N. J. (New York In.)	40·25 N	74·04 W
81	Atlantic City N. J.	39·20 N	74·30 W
6	Atlantic Ocean		
164	Atlas Mts. (ăt'lăs) Alg.-Mor.	31·22 N	4·57 W
90	Atliaca (ät-lē-ä'kä) Mex.	17·38 N	99·24 W
86	Atlin (L.) (ăt'lĭn) Can.	59·34 N	133·20 W
90	Atlixco (ät-lēz'kō) Mex.	18·52 N	98·27 W
118	Atlöy (I.) (ät-lûê) Nor.	61·24 N	4·46 E
78	Atmore (ăt'mōr) Ala.	31·01 N	87·31 W
73	Atoka (ȧ-tō'kȧ) Okla.	34·23 N	96·07 W
73	Atoka Res. Okla.	34·30 N	96·05 W
90	Atotonilco el Alto (ä'tō-tô-nēl'kō ĕl äl'tō) Mex.	20·35 N	102·32 W
90	Atotonilco el Grande (ä'tō-tô-nēl-kō ĕl grän'dä) Mex.	20·17 N	98·41 W
164	Atoui R. (ȧ-tōō-ē') Mauritania-Sp. Sah.	21·00 N	15·32 W
90	Atoyac (ä-tô-yäk') Mex.	20·01 N	103·28 W
91	Atoyac (R.) Mex.	16·27 N	97·28 W
90	Atoyac (R.) Mex.	18·35 N	98·16 W
90	Atoyac de Alvarez (ä-tô-yäk'dā äl'vä-rāz) Mex.	17·13 N	100·29 W
91	Atoyatempan (ä-tō'yä-tĕm-pän') Mex.	18·47 N	97·54 W
144	Atrak, Rud-e (R.) Iran	37·42 N	55·30 E
118	Atran (R.) Swe.	57·02 N	12·43 E
99	Atrato, Rio (R.) (rê'ō-ä-trä'tō) Col.	7·00 N	77·12 W
98	Atrato (R.) (ä-trä'tō) Col. (In.)	5·48 N	76·19 W
139	Aṭ Tafilah (tȧ-fē'la) Jordan (Palestine In.)	30·50 N	35·36 E
144	At Tāif Sau. Ar.	21·03 N	41·00 E
78	Attalla (ȧ-tăl'yȧ) Ala.	34·01 N	86·05 W
87	Attawapiskat (R.) (ăt'ȧ-wȧ-pĭs'kăt) Can.	52·31 N	86·22 W
120	Atter See (L.) (Kammer) Aus.	47·57 N	13·25 E
81	Attica (ăt'ĭ-kȧ) N. Y.	42·55 N	78·15 W
84	Attleboro (ăt''l-bŭr-ô) Mass. (Providence In.)	41·56 N	71·15 W
116	Attow, Ben (Mtn.) (bĕn ăt'tô) Scot.	57·15 N	5·25 W
77	Attoyac Bay (ă-toi'yăk) Tex.	31·45 N	94·23 W
64	Attu (I.) (ät-tōō') Alaska	53·08 N	173·18 E
115	Aṭ Ṭūr U. A. R.	28·09 N	33·47 E
118	Atvidaberg (ôt-vē'dä-bĕrgh) Swe.	58·12 N	15·55 E
72	Atwood (ăt'wŏŏd) Kans.	39·48 N	101·06 W
91	Atzcapotzalco (ät'zkä-pô-tzäl'kō) Mex. (Mexico City In.)	19·29 N	99·11 W
111	Atzgersdorf Aus. (Vienna In.)	48·10 N	16·17 E
157	Auau Chan (ä'ōō-ä'ōō) Hawaii (In.)	20·55 N	156·50 W
123	Aubagne (ō-bän'y') Fr.	43·18 N	5·34 E
122	Aube (R.) (ōb) Fr.	48·42 N	3·49 E
122	Aubenas (ōb'-nä') Fr.	44·37 N	4·22 E
123	Aubervilliers (ō-bĕr-vē-yā') Fr. (Paris In.)	48·54 N	2·23 E
122	Aubin (ō-băɴ') Fr.	44·29 N	2·12 E
85	Aubrey (ô-brē') Can. (Montreal In.)	45·08 N	73·47 W
78	Auburn (ô'bŭrn) Ala.	32·35 N	85·26 W
68	Auburn Calif.	38·52 N	121·05 W
73	Auburn Ill.	39·36 N	89·46 W
80	Auburn Ind.	41·20 N	85·05 W
82	Auburn Maine	44·04 N	70·24 W
83	Auburn Mass. (Boston In.)	42·11 N	71·51 W
73	Auburn Nebr.	40·23 N	95·50 W
81	Auburn N. Y.	42·55 N	76·35 W
65	Auburn Wash. (Seattle In.)	47·18 N	122·14 W
75	Auburn Hts. Mich. (Detroit In.)	42·37 N	83·13 W
122	Aubusson (ō-bü-sôɴ') Fr.	45·57 N	2·10 E
122	Auch (ōsh) Fr.	43·38 N	0·35 E
78	Aucilla (R.) (ô-sĭl'ȧ) Fla.-Ga.	30·15 N	83·55 W
159	Auckland (ôk'lănd) N. Z. (In.)	37·43 S	174·53 E
47	Auckland Is. N. Z.	50·30 S	166·30 E
122	Aude (ōd) Fr.	42·55 N	2·08 E
122	Audierne (ō-dyĕrn') Fr.	48·02 N	4·31 W
123	Audincourt (ō-dăn-kōōr') Fr.	47·30 N	6·49 E
110	Audley (ôd'lĭ) Eng.	53·03 N	2·18 W
168	Audo Ra. Eth. (Horn of Afr. In.)	6·58 N	41·18 E
71	Audubon (ô'dōō-bŏn) Iowa	41·43 N	94·57 W
84	Audubon N. J. (Philadelphia In.)	39·54 N	75·04 W
120	Aue (ou'ĕ) Ger.	50·35 N	12·44 E
160	Augathella (ôr'gȧ'thĕ-lȧ) Austl.	25·49 S	146·40 E
166	Aughrabies Falls (ô-grä'bēs) S. Afr.	28·30 S	20·00 E
111	Augsburg (ouks'bŏŏrgh) Ger. (Munich In.)	48·23 N	10·55 E
73	Augusta (ô-gŭs'tȧ) Ark.	35·16 N	91·21 W
79	Augusta Ga.	33·26 N	82·00 W
73	Augusta Kans.	37·41 N	96·58 W
80	Augusta Ky.	38·45 N	84·00 W
82	Augusta Maine	44·19 N	69·42 W
84	Augusta N. J. (New York In.)	41·07 N	74·44 W
71	Augusta Wis.	44·40 N	91·09 W
121	Augustow (ou-gŏŏs'tŏŏf) Pol.	53·52 N	23·00 E
123	Aulnay-sous-Bois (ō-nĕ'sōō-bwä') Fr. (Paris In.)	48·56 N	2·30 E
122	Aulne (R.) (ōn) Fr.	48·08 N	3·53 W
123	Auneau (ō-nō') Fr. (Paris In.)	48·28 N	1·45 E
166	Auob (R.) (ä'wŏb) S. W. Afr.	25·00 S	19·00 E
139	Aur (I.) Mala. (Singapore In.)	2·27 N	104·51 E
142	Aurangābād (ou-rŭŋ-gä-bäd') India	19·56 N	75·19 E
122	Auray (ō-rĕ') Fr.	47·42 N	3·00 W
122	Aurillac (ō-rē-yäk') Fr.	44·57 N	2·27 E
75	Aurora (ô-rō'rȧ) Ill. (Chicago In.)	41·45 N	88·18 W
75	Aurora Ind. (Cincinnati In.)	39·04 N	84·55 W
71	Aurora Minn.	47·31 N	92·17 W
73	Aurora Mo.	36·58 N	93·42 W
72	Aurora Nebr.	40·54 N	98·01 W
118	Aursunden (L.) (äûr-sûndĕn) Nor.	62·42 N	11·10 E
80	Au Sable (R.) (ô-sä'b'l) Mich.	44·40 N	84·25 W
81	Ausable (R.) N. Y.	44·25 N	73·50 W
	Aussig, see Usti nad Labem		
71	Austin (ôs'tĭn) Minn.	43·40 N	92·58 W
68	Austin Nev.	39·30 N	117·05 W
77	Austin Tex.	30·15 N	97·42 W
158	Austin (L.) Austl.	27·45 S	117·30 E
77	Austin Bay (ôs'tĭn bī-ōō') Tex. (In.)	29·17 N	95·21 W
7	Australia (ôs-trā'lĭ-ȧ)		
160	Australian Alps (Mts.) Austl.	37·10 S	147·55 E
160	Australian Capital Ter. (ôs-trā'lĭ-ăn) Austl.	35·30 S	148·40 E
102	Austria (ôs'trĭ-ȧ) Eur.	47·15 N	11·53 E
123	Authon-la-Plaine (ō-tôɴ-lȧ-plĕ'n) Fr. (Paris In.)	48·27 N	1·58 E
90	Autlán (ä-ōōt-län') Mex.	19·47 N	104·24 W
122	Autun (ō-tŭɴ') Fr.	46·58 N	4·14 E
122	Auvergne (Mts.) (ō-vĕrn'y') Fr.	45·12 N	2·31 E
122	Auxerre (ō-sâr') Fr.	47·48 N	3·32 E
85	Aux Grues, Ile (I.) (ō grü) Can. (Quebec In.)	47·05 N	70·32 W
73	Ava (ā'vȧ) Mo.	36·56 N	92·40 W
165	Avakubi (ä-vȧ-kōō'bē) Con. K.	1·19 N	27·32 E
122	Avallon (ȧ-vȧ-lôɴ') Fr.	47·30 N	3·58 E
75	Avalon (ăv'ȧ-lŏn) Pa. (Pittsburgh In.)	40·31 N	80·05 W
68	Avalon Calif.	33·21 N	118·22 W
83	Avalon Pen. Can.	47·23 N	53·10 W
124	Aveiro (ä-vā'rŏŏ) Port.	40·38 N	8·38 W
100	Avelar (ȧ'vĕ-lȧ'r) Braz. (In.)	22·20 S	43·25 W
100	Avellaneda (ä-vĕl-yä-nā'dhä) Arg. (In.)	34·25 S	58·23 W
125	Avellino (ä-vĕl-lē'nō) It. (Naples In.)	40·40 N	14·46 E
118	Averöy (I.) (ävĕr-ûê) Nor.	63·40 N	7·16 E
126	Aversa (ä-vĕr'sä) It.	40·58 N	14·13 E
73	Avery (ā'vēr-ĭ) Tex.	33·34 N	94·46 W
118	Avesta (ä-vĕs'tä) Swe.	60·16 N	16·09 E
122	Aveyron (R.) (ä-vâ-rôɴ) Fr.	44·07 N	1·45 E
126	Avezzano (ä-vât-sä'nō) It.	42·03 N	13·27 E
126	Avigliano (ä-vēl-yä'nō) It.	40·45 N	15·44 E
122	Avignon (ȧ-vē-nyôɴ') Fr.	43·55 N	4·50 E
124	Avila (ä-vē-lä) Sp.	40·39 N	4·42 W
124	Avilés (ä-vē-lās') Sp.	43·33 N	5·55 W
73	Avoca (ȧ-vō'kȧ) Iowa	41·29 N	95·16 W
81	Avon (ā'vŏn) Conn.	41·40 N	72·50 W
116	Avon (R.) (ā'vŭn) Eng.	52·05 N	1·55 W
83	Avon (ā'vŏn) Mass. (Boston In.)	42·08 N	71·03 W
75	Avon Ohio (Cleveland In.)	41·27 N	82·02 W
84	Avondale Ga. (Atlanta In.)	33·47 N	84·16 W
75	Avon Lake Ohio (Cleveland In.)	41·31 N	82·01 W
85	Avonmore (ā'vŏn-mōr) Can. (Ottawa In.)	45·11 N	74·58 W
79	Avon Park (ā'vŏn pärk') Fla. (In.)	27·35 N	81·29 W
122	Avranches (ȧ-vräɴsh') Fr.	48·43 N	1·34 W
153	Awaji (ä'wä-jê) Jap.	34·23 N	135·00 E
153	Awaji-Shima (I.) (ä'wä-jê shē-mä) Jap. (Osaka In.)	34·32 N	135·02 E
165	Awash R. (ȧ-wäsh') Eth.	9·19 N	40·30 E
116	Awe, Loch (L.) (lŏk ôr) Scot.	56·22 N	5·04 W
165	Awjilah Libya	29·07 N	21·21 E
122	Ax-les-Thermes (äks'lā tĕrm') Fr.	42·43 N	1·50 E
90	Axochiapan (äks-ō-chyä'pän) Mex.	18·29 N	98·49 W
122	Ay (ä'ē) Fr.	49·05 N	3·58 E
132	Ay (R.) Sov. Un.	55·55 N	57·55 E
153	Ayabe (ä'yä-bĕ) Jap.	35·16 N	135·17 E
100	Ayacucho (ä-yȧ-kōō'chō) Arg.	37·05 S	58·30 W
98	Ayacucho Peru	12·12 S	74·03 W
134	Ayaguz (ä-yȧ-gōōz') Sov. Un.	48·00 N	80·12 E
124	Ayamonte (ä-yä-mō'n-tĕ) Sp.	37·14 N	7·28 W
135	Ayan (ȧ-yän') Sov. Un.	56·26 N	138·18 E
98	Ayata (ä-yä'tä) Bol.	15·17 S	68·43 W
98	Ayaviri (ä-yä-vē'rē) Peru	14·46 S	70·38 W
129	Aydar (R.) (ī-där') Sov. Un.	49·15 N	38·48 E
79	Ayden (ā'dĕn) N. C.	35·27 N	77·25 W
133	Aydın (āĭy-dĕn) Tur.	37·40 N	27·40 E
83	Ayer (âr) Mass. (Boston In.)	42·33 N	71·36 W
139	Ayer Hitam Mala. (Singapore In.)	1·55 N	103·11 E
127	Ayiá (ä-yē'ä) Grc.	39·42 N	22·47 E
127	Ayiassos Grc.	39·06 N	26·25 E
127	Áyion Óros (Mount Athos) (Reg.) Grc.	40·20 N	24·15 E
127	Áyios Evstrátion (I.) Grc.	39·30 N	24·58 E
110	Aylesbury (ālz'bĕr-ĭ) Eng. (London In.)	51·47 N	0·49 W
85	Aylmer (āl'mēr) Can. (Ottawa In.)	45·24 N	75·50 W
86	Aylmer (L.) Can.	64·27 N	108·22 W
90	Ayo el Chico (ä'yō el chē'kō) Mex.	20·31 N	102·21 W
135	Ayon (I.) (ī-ôn') Sov. Un.	70·04 N	168·33 E
91	Ayotla (ä-yōt'lä) Mex. (Mexico City In.)	19·18 N	98·55 W
116	Ayr (âr) Scot.	55·27 N	4·40 W
116	Ayr (L.) Scot.	55·25 N	4·20 W
168	Ayshā Eth. (Horn of Afr. In.)	10·48 N	42·32 E
92	Ayutla (ä-yōōt'lä) Guat.	14·44 N	92·11 W
90	Ayutla Mex.	16·50 N	99·16 W
90	Ayutla Mex.	20·09 N	104·20 W
154	Ayutthaya (ä-yōōt'hē'ä) Thai.	14·16 N	100·37 E
127	Ayvalık (āĭy-wä-lĭk) Tur.	39·19 N	26·40 E
164	Azemmour (ä-zē-mōōr') Mor.	33·20 N	8·21 W
130	Azerbaydzhan (Azerbaijan) (S. S. R.) (ä'zĕr-bä-ē-jän') Sov. Un.	40·38 N	47·25 E
82	Aziscoos (L.) (ăz'ĭ kōōs') Maine	45·03 N	70·50 W
74	Azle (ăz'lē) Tex. (Dallas, Fort Worth In.)	35·54 N	97·33 W
98	Azogues (ä-sō'gās) Ec.	2·47 S	78·45 W
	Azores, see Açores		
129	Azov (ȧ-zôf') (ä'zôf) Sov. Un.	47·07 N	39·19 E
	Azov, Sea of, see Azovskoye More		
129	Azovskoye More (Sea of Azov) (ȧ-zôf'skô-yĕ mô'rĕ) Sov. Un.	46·00 N	36·20 E
90	Azoyú (ä-zō-yōō') Mex.	16·42 N	98·46 W
69	Aztec (ăz'tĕk) N. Mex.	36·40 N	108·00 W
69	Aztec Ruins Natl. Mon. N. Mex.	36·50 N	108·00 W
95	Azua (ä'swä) Dom. Rep.	18·30 N	70·45 W
124	Azuaga (ä-thwä'gä) Sp.	38·15 N	5·42 W
93	Azuero, Peninsula de (Pen.) (ä-swā'rō) Pan.	7·30 N	80·34 W
76	Azucar, Presa de (Res.) (prĕ'sä-dĕ-ä-zōō'kär) Mex.	26·06 N	98·44 W
100	Azufre, Cerro (Copiapó) (Vol.) (sĕr'rō ä-sōō'frä) (kō-pē-ä-pō') Chile	26·10 S	69·00 W
101	Azul (ä-sōōl') Arg. (Buenos Aires In.)	36·46 S	59·51 W
90	Azul, Sierra (Mts.) (sē-ĕ'r-rä-zōō'l) Mex.	23·20 N	98·28 W
98	Azul, Cordillera (Mts.) (kô'r-dē-lyĕ'rä zōō'l) Peru	7·15 S	75·30 W
74	Azusa (ä-zōō'sȧ) Calif. (Los Angeles In.)	34·08 N	117·55 W
144	Aẓ Ẓahrān (Dhahran) (dä-rän') Sau. Ar.	26·13 N	50·00 E
168	Az Zaqāzīq U. A. R. (Nile In.)	30·36 N	31·36 E
139	Az Zarqā' Jordan (Palestine In.)	32·03 N	36·07 E
165	Az Zawiyah Libya	32·28 N	11·55 E
123	Baal (bäl) Ger. (Ruhr In.)	51·02 N	6·17 E
155	Baao (bä'ō) Phil. (Manila In.)	13·27 N	123·22 E
111	Baarle-Hertog Bel. (Brussels In.)	51·26 N	4·57 E
111	Baarn Neth. (Amsterdam In.)	52·12 N	5·18 E
127	Babaeski (bä'bä-ĕs'kĭ) Tur.	41·25 N	27·05 E
98	Babahoyo (bä-bä-ō'yō) Ec.	1·56 S	79·24 W
167	Babanango S. Afr. (Natal In.)	28·24 S	31·11 E
165	Babanusa Sud.	11·30 N	27·55 E
155	Babar (I.) (bä'bär) Indon.	7·50 S	129·15 E

180 Babel–Bandeira PRONOUNCING INDEX

Page	Name Pronunciation Region	Lat. °′	Long. °′
144	Bābel . . . . Iran	36·30 N	52·48 E
165	Bab-el-Mandeb, Str. of (băb′ĕl măn-dĕb′) . Afr.-Asia	13·17 N	42·49 E
76	Babia, Arroyo de la (är-rō′yō dā lä bä′bê-ȧ) . Mex.	28·26 N	101·50 W
86	Babine (L.) (băb′ēn) . . . . Can.	54·34 N	126·47 W
86	Babine Mts. . . . . Can.	55·35 N	128·26 W
135	Babushkin (bä′bo͝osh-kĭn) Sov. Un.	51·47 N	106·08 E
136	Babushkin . Sov. Un. (Moscow In.)	55·52 N	37·42 E
154	Babuyan Is. (bä-bo͞o-yän′) . . . Phil.	4·30 N	122·38 E
127	Babyak (bäb′zhȧk) . . . . Bul.	41·59 N	23·42 E
84	Babylon (băb′ĭ-lŏn) N. Y. (New York In.)	40·42 N	73·19 W
144	Babylon (Ruins) . . . . Iraq	32·15 N	45·23 E
155	Bacacay (bä-kä-kī′) Phil. (Manila In.)	13·17 N	123·48 E
92	Bacalar, Laguna de (L.) (lä-go͞o-nä-dĕ-bä-kä-lär′) Mex. (Yucatan In.)	18·50 N	88·31 W
151	Bacarra (bä-kär′rä) . . . . Phil.	18·22 N	120·40 E
121	Bacău . . . . Rom.	46·34 N	27·00 E
123	Baccarat (bȧ-kȧ-rȧ′) . . . . Fr.	48·29 N	6·42 E
74	Bacchus (băk′ŭs) Utah (Salt Lake City In.)	40·40 N	112·06 W
91	Bachajón (bä-chä-hōn′) . . . . Mex.	17·08 N	92·18 W
127	Bačka Topola (Bäch′kä Tô′pô-lä′) Yugo.	45·48 N	19·38 E
143	Back Bay (băk) India (Bombay In.)	18·55 N	72·45 E
158	Backstairs Pass. (băk-stârs′) Austl.	35·50 S	138·15 E
151	Bac Ninh (bäk′nên″) . . . . Viet.	21·10 N	106·02 E
155	Bacnotan (bäk-nô-tän′) Phil. (Manila In.)	16·43 N	120·21 E
155	Baco, Mt. (bä′kô) Phil. (Manila In.)	12·50 N	121·11 E
125	Bacoli (bä-kō-lē′) It. (Naples In.)	40·33 N	14·05 E
154	Bacolod (bä-kō′lôd) . . . . Phil.	10·42 N	123·03 E
155	Bacon (bä-kōn′) . Phil. (Manila In.)	13·02 N	124·04 E
121	Bácsalmás (bäch′ôl-mäs) . . . Hung.	46·07 N	19·18 E
110	Bacup (băk′ŭp) . . . . Eng.	53·42 N	2·12 W
70	Bad (R.) (băd) . . . . S. D.	44·04 N	100·58 W
124	Badajoz (bȧ-dhä-hōth′) . . . . Sp.	38·52 N	6·56 W
125	Badalona (bä-dhä-lō′nä) . . . . Sp.	41·27 N	2·15 E
144	Badanah . . . . Sau. Ar.	30·49 N	40·45 E
80	Bad Axe (băd′ ăks) . . . . Mich.	43·50 N	82·55 W
111	Bad Bramstedt (bät bräm′shtĕt) Ger. (Hamburg In.)	53·55 N	9·53 E
123	Bad Ems (bät ĕms) . . . . Ger.	50·20 N	7·45 E
111	Baden (bä′dĕn) . . Aus. (Vienna In.)	48·00 N	16·14 E
120	Baden . . . . Switz.	47·28 N	8·17 E
120	Baden-Baden (bä′dĕn-bä′dĕn) . Ger.	48·46 N	8·11 E
120	Baden Württemberg (State) (bä′dĕn vür′tĕm-bĕrgh) . Ger.	48·38 N	9·00 E
120	Bad Freienwalde (bät frī′ĕn-väl′dĕ) . Ger.	52·47 N	14·00 E
120	Bad Hersfeld (bät hĕrsh′fĕlt) . Ger.	50·53 N	9·43 E
117	Bad Homberg (bät hōm′bĕrgh) Ger.	50·14 N	8·35 E
79	Badin (bă′dĭn) . . . . N. C.	35·23 N	80·08 W
120	Bad Ischl (bät ĭsh″l) . . . . Aus.	47·46 N	13·37 E
120	Bad Kissingen (bät kĭs′ĭng-ĕn) . Ger.	50·12 N	10·05 E
120	Bad Kreuznach (bät kroits′näk) Ger.	49·52 N	7·53 E
70	Badlands (Reg.) (băd′ lănds) N. D.	46·43 N	103·22 W
70	Badlands (Reg.) . . . . S. D.	43·43 N	102·36 W
70	Badlands Natl. Mon. . . . . S. D.	43·56 N	102·37 W
143	Badlapur . . . . India (Bombay In.)	19·12 N	73·12 E
120	Bad Oldesloe (bät ôl′dĕs-lōē) . Ger.	53·48 N	10·21 E
120	Bad Reichenhall (bät rī′ĸĕn-häl) Ger.	47·43 N	12·53 E
71	Bad River Ind. Res. (băd) . . . Wis.	46·41 N	90·36 W
111	Bad Segeburg (bät sĕ′gĕ-bo͞orgh) Ger. (Hamburg In.)	53·56 N	10·18 E
120	Bad Tölz (bät tûltz) . . . . Ger.	47·46 N	11·35 E
111	Bad Vöslau . . . . Aus. (Vienna In.)	47·58 N	16·13 E
67	Badwater Cr. (băd′wô-tĕr) . . Wyo.	43·13 N	107·55 W
124	Baena (bä-ā′nä) . . . . Sp.	37·38 N	4·20 W
101	Baependi (bä-å-pĕn′dĭ) Braz. (Rio de Janeiro In.)	21·57 S	44·51 W
49	Baffin B. (băf′ĭn) . . . . Can.	72·00 N	65·00 W
77	Baffin B. . . . . Tex.	27·11 N	97·35 W
49	Baffin I. . . . . Can.	67·20 N	71·00 W
164	Bafoulabe (bä-fo͞o-lä-bā′) . . . . Mali	13·58 N	10·51 W
144	Bāfq (bäfk) . . . . Iran	31·48 N	55·23 E
133	Bafra (bäf′rä) . . . . Tur.	41·30 N	35·50 E
155	Bagabag (bä-gä-bäg′) Phil. (Manila In.)	16·38 N	121·16 E
143	Bāgalkot . . . . India	16·14 N	75·40 E
167	Bagamoyo (bä-gä-mō′yō) . . . . Tan.	6·28 S	38·49 E
136	Bagaryak (bȧ-gȧr-yäk′) Sov. Un. (Urals In.)	56·13 N	61·32 E
100	Bagé (bä-zhā′) . . . . Braz.	31·17 S	54·07 W
145	Bagh (bäk) . Afg. (Khyber Pass In.)	33·47 N	70 45 E
144	Baghdad (bȧgh-dăd′) (băg′dăd) Iraq	33·14 N	44 22 E
126	Bagheria (bä-gå-rē′ä) . . . . It.	38·03 N	13·32 E
70	Bagley (băg′lê) . . . . Minn.	47·31 N	95·24 W
126	Bagnara (bän-yä′rä) . . . . It.	38·17 N	15·52 E
73	Bagnell Dam (băg′nĕl) . . . . Mo.	38·13 N	92·40 W
122	Bagnères-de-Bigorre (bän-yâr′dĕ-bê-gor′) . Fr.	43·40 N	0·70 E
122	Bagnères-de-Luchon (bän-yâr′ dĕ-lü chôɴ′) . Fr.	42·46 N	0·36 E
122	Bagnols (bä-nyôl′) . . . . Fr.	44·09 N	4·37 E
164	Bagoe R. (bȧ-gō′å) . . . . Mali	12·22 N	6·34 W
82	Bagotville (bȧ-gô-vēl′) . . . . Can.	48·20 N	70·58 W
146	Bagrash Köl (L.) . . . . China	42·06 N	88·01 E
164	Baguezane, Monts (Mt.) (bȧ-gē-zän′) . Niger	17·45 N	8·40 E
155	Baguio (bä-gê-ō′) Phil. (Manila In.)	16·24 N	120·36 E
168	Bahaja, Monte (Mt.) Som. (Horn of Afr. In.)	11·00 N	49·38 E
89	Bahama Is. (bȧ-hā′mȧ) . . . . N. A.	26·15 N	76·00 W
139	Bahau . . . . Mala. (Singapore In.)	2·48 N	102·25 E
142	Bahawalpur (bŭ-hä′wŭl-po͞or) W. Pak.	29·29 N	71·41 E
	Bahia, see Salvador		
88	Bahía, Islas de la (I.) (ê′s-läs-dĕ-lä-bä-ē′ä) . Hond.	16·15 N	86·30 W
100	Bahia Blanca (bä-ē′ä bläŋ′kä) Arg.	38·45 S	62·07 W
98	Bahía de Caraquez (bä-e′ä dā kä-rä′kĕz) . Ec.	0·45 S	80·29 W
99	Bahía Negra (bä-ē′ä nā′grä) . . Par.	20·11 S	58·05 W
100	Bahias, Cabo dos (C.) (kȧ′bô-dôs-bä-ē′äs) . Arg.	44·55 S	65·35 W
95	Bahoruco, Sierra de (Mts.) (sē-ĕ′r-rä-dĕ-bä-ō-ro͞o′kô) Dom. Rep.	18·10 N	71·25 W
144	Bahrain Is. (bä-rān′) . . . . Asia	26·15 N	51·17 E
165	Bahr el Ghazal (Prov.) (bär ĕl ghä-zäl′) . Sud.	7·56 N	27·15 E
115	Baḩrīyah (Oasis) (bȧ-hȧ-rē′yȧ) U. A. R.	28·34 N	29·01 E
121	Baia de Cris (bä′yä dā krēs′) Rom.	46·11 N	22·40 E
121	Baia-Mare (bä′yä-mä′rā) . . . Rom.	47·40 N	23·35 E
82	Baie-Comeau . . . . Can.	49·15 N	68·12 W
74	Baie de Wasai (bā dē wä-sä′ê) Mich. (Sault Ste. Marie In.)	46·27 N	84·15 W
82	Baie St. Paul (bā′sånt-pôl′) . . Can.	47·26 N	70·33 W
82	Baie Trinite . . . . Can.	49·24 N	67·21 W
	Baikal, see Baykal'skiy Khrebet		
	Baikal, L., see Baykal Ozero		
	Baile Atha Cliath, see Dublin		
124	Bailén (bä-ê-lān′) . . . . Sp.	38·05 N	3·48 W
127	Băileşti (bă-ĭ-lĕsh′tê) . . . . Rom.	44·01 N	23·21 E
78	Bainbridge (bān′brĭj) . . . . Ga.	30·52 N	84·35 W
65	Bainbridge I. . . Wash. (Seattle In.)	47·39 N	122·32 W
76	Baird (bârd) . . . . Tex.	32·22 N	99·28 W
75	Bairdford (bârd′fŏrd) Pa. (Pittsburgh In.)	40·37 N	79·53 W
64	Baird Mts. . . . . Alaska	67·35 N	160·10 W
160	Bairnsdale (bârnz′dāl) . . . . Austl.	137·50 S	47·39 E
122	Baïse (R.) (bä-ēz′) . . . . Fr.	43·52 N	0·23 E
121	Baja (bŏ′yŏ) . . . . Hung.	46·11 N	18·55 E
88	Baja California (State) (bä-hä) . Mex.	30·15 N	117·25 W
88	Baja California (Ter.) . . . . Mex.	26·00 N	113·30 W
154	Bajak (I.) . . . . Indon.	2·08 N	97·15 E
136	Bakal (bä′kȧl) . Sov. Un. (Urals In.)	54·57 N	58·50 E
164	Bakel (bä-kĕl′) . . . . Senegal	14·52 N	12·26 W
67	Baker (bā′kẽr) . . . . Mont.	46·21 N	104·12 W
66	Baker . . . . Ore.	44·46 N	117·52 W
156	Baker (I.) . . . . Oceania	1·00 N	176·00 W
86	Baker (L.) . . . . Can.	63·51 N	96·10 W
66	Baker, Mt. . . . . Wash.	48·46 N	121·52 W
75	Baker Cr. . . . . Ill. (Chicago In.)	41·13 N	87·47 W
86	Baker Lake . . . . Can.	64·18 N	96·26 W
68	Bakersfield (bā′kẽrz-fēld) . . Calif.	35·23 N	119·00 W
75	Bakerstown (bā′kerz-toun) Pa. (Pittsburgh In.)	40·39 N	79 56 W
110	Bakewell (bāk′wĕl) . . . . Eng.	53·12 N	1·40 W
129	Bakhchisaray (bȧĸ′chê-sȧ-rī′) Sov. Un.	44·46 N	33·54 E
129	Bakhmach (bȧĸ-mäch′) . . Sov. Un.	51·09 N	32·47 E
144	Bakhtegān, Daryachch-ye (L.) Iran	29·29 N	54·31 E
136	Bakhteyevo (bȧk-tyĕ′yĕ-vô) Sov. Un. (Moscow In.)	55·35 N	38·32 E
165	Bāko (bä′kö) . . . . Eth.	5·47 N	36·39 E
121	Bakony-Erdo (Mts.) (bȧ-kōn′y′) Hung.	46·57 N	17·30 E
164	Bakoy R. (bȧ-kô′ê) . . . . Mali	12·49 N	9·51 W
136	Bakr Uzyak (bȧkr o͞oz′yȧk) Sov. Un. (Urals In.)	52·59 N	58·43 E
133	Baku (bȧ-ko͞o′) . . . . Sov. Un.	40·28 N	49·45 E
154	Balabac (I.) (bä′lä-bäk) . . . . Phil.	8·00 N	116·28 E
154	Balabac Str. . . . . Indon.-Phil.	7·23 N	116·30 E
139	Ba'labakk . . . . Leb. (Palestine In.)	34·00 N	36·13 E
154	Balabalagan (I.) (bä-lȧ-bä′lȧ-gän) Indon.	2·00 S	117·15 E
136	Balabanovo (bȧ-lȧ-bä′nô-vô) Sov. Un. (Moscow In.)	56·10 N	37·44 E
134	Balagansk (bä-lä-gänsk′) Sov. Un.	53·58 N	103·09 E
125	Balaguer (bä-lä-gĕr′) . . . . Sp.	41·48 N	0·50 E
134	Balakhta (bȧ′lȧk-tȧ′) . . . . Sov. Un.	55·22 N	91·43 E
129	Balakleya (bȧ′lȧ-klā′yȧ) . Sov. Un.	49·28 N	36·51 E
133	Balakovo (bȧ′lȧ-kô′vô) . . . Sov. Un.	52·00 N	47·40 E
91	Balancán (bä-läŋ-kän′) . . . . Mex.	17·47 N	91·32 W
155	Balanga (bä-läŋ′gä) Phil. (Manila In.)	14·41 N	120·31 E
155	Balaoan (bȧ-lou′än) Phil. (Manila In.)	16·49 N	120·24 E
136	Balashikha (bȧ-lä′shĭ-kȧ) Sov. Un. (Moscow In.)	55·48 N	37·58 E
133	Balashov (bȧ′lȧ-shôf) . . . . Sov. Un.	51·30 N	43·00 E
142	Balasore (bä-lȧ-sōr′) . . . . India	21·38 N	86·59 E
121	Balassagyarmat (bô′lôsh-shô-dyôr′môt) . Hung.	48·04 N	19·19 E
121	Balaton L. (bô′lô-tôn) . . . . Hung.	46·47 N	17·55 E
155	Balayan (bä-lä-yān′) Phil. (Manila In.)	13·56 N	120·44 E
155	Balayan B. . . . . Phil. (Manila In.)	13·46 N	120·46 E
74	Balboa (băl-bō′ȧ) Calif. (Los Angeles In.)	33·36 N	117·54 W
88	Balboa (bäl-bô′ä) C. Z. (Panama Canal In.)	8·55 N	79·34 W
93	Balboa Heights . . . . C. Z.	8·59 N	79·33 W
88	Balboa Mt. C. Z. (Panama Canal In.)	9·05 N	79·44 W
100	Balcarce (bäl-kär′sā) . . . . Arg.	37·49 S	58·17 W
127	Balchik . . . . Bul.	43·24 N	28·13 E
74	Bald Eagle (bôld ē′g′l) Minn. (Minneapolis, St. Paul In.)	45·06 N	93·01 W
74	Bald Eagle L. Minn. (Minneapolis, St. Paul In.)	45·08 N	93·03 W
142	Baldin . . . . W. Pak.	24·47 N	69·51 E
74	Baldwin Park (bôld′wĭn) Calif. (Los Angeles In.)	34·05 N	117·58 W
81	Baldwinsville (bôld′wĭns-vĭl) . N. Y.	43·10 N	76·20 W
69	Baldy Pk. (bôl′dê) . . . . Ariz.	33·55 N	109·35 W
76	Baldy Pk. (bôl′dê pēk) . . . . Tex.	30·38 N	104·11 W
125	Baleares, Islas (Balearic Is.) (e′s-läs bä-lĕ-ä′rĕs) . Sp.	39·25 N	1·28 E
	Balearic Is., see Baleares, Islas		
125	Balearic Sea (băl-ê-ăr′ĭk) . . . . Eur.	39·40 N	1·05 E
155	Baler (bä-lâr′) . . Phil. (Manila In.)	15·46 N	121·33 E
155	Baler B. . . . . Phil. (Manila In.)	15·51 N	121·40 E
155	Balesin (I.) . . . . Phil. (Manila In.)	14·28 N	122·10 E
135	Baley (bȧl-yā′) . . . . Sov. Un.	51·29 N	116·12 E
92	Balfate (bäl-fä′tē) . . . . Hond.	15·48 N	86·24 W
168	Balfour (băl′fo͝or) . S. Afr. (Johannesburg & Pretoria In.)	26·41 S	28·37 E
154	Bali (I.) (bä′lê) . . . . Indon.	8·00 S	115·22 E
133	Balıkesir (balĭk′ĭysīr) . . . . Tur.	39·40 N	27·50 E
154	Balikpapan (bä′lêk-pä′pän) . Indon.	1·13 N	116·52 E
154	Balintang Chan. (bā-lĭn-täng′) Phil.	19·50 N	121·08 E
	Balkan Mts., see Stara Planina		
142	Balkh (bälk) . . . . Afg.	36·48 N	66·50 E
134	Balkhash (bȧl-kăsh′) . . . . Sov. Un.	46·58 N	75·00 E
134	Balkhash, Ozero (L.) . . . . Sov. Un.	45·58 N	72·15 E
129	Balki (bäl′kĭ) . . . . Sov. Un.	47·22 N	34·56 E
123	Ballancourt (bä-äɴ-ko͝or′) Fr. (Paris In.)	48·31 N	2·23 E
160	Ballarat (băl′ȧ-răt) . . . . Austl.	37·37 S	144·00 E
158	Ballard (I.) (băl′ȧrd) . . . . Austl.	29·15 S	120·45 E
116	Ballater (băl′ȧ-tẽr) . . . . Scot.	57·05 N	3·06 W
47	Balleny Is. (băl′ĕ nê) . . . . Ant.	67·00 S	164·00 E
160	Ballina (băl-ĭ-nä′) . . . . Austl.	28·50 S	153·35 E
116	Ballina . . . . Ire.	54·06 N	9·05 W
116	Ballinasloe (băl′ĭ-nȧ-slō′) . . . . Ire.	53·20 N	8·09 W
76	Ballinger (băl′ĭn-jẽr) . . . . Tex.	31·45 N	99·58 W
81	Ballston Spa (bôls′tŭn spä′) . N. Y.	43·05 N	73·50 W
142	Bally . . . . India (Calcutta In.)	22·38 N	88·20 E
121	Balmazújváros (bŏl′mŏz-o͞o′y′vä′rôsh) . Hung.	47·35 N	21·23 E
160	Balonne (R.) (băl-ōn′) . . . . Austl.	27·00 S	149·10 E
142	Balotra . . . . India	25·56 N	72·12 E
160	Balranald (băl′-rȧn-ăld) . . . . Austl.	34·42 S	143·30 E
127	Balş (bälsh) . . . . Rom.	44·21 N	24·05 E
81	Balsam (L.) (bôl′sȧm) . . . . Can.	44·30 N	78·50 W
99	Balsas (bäl′säs) . . . . Braz.	7·09 S	46·04 W
90	Balsas (R.) . . . . Mex.	18·15 N	102·08 W
129	Balta (bȧl′tȧ) . . . . Sov. Un.	47·57 N	29·38 W
112	Baltic Sea (bôl′tĭk) . . . . Eur.	55·20 N	16·50 E
168	Balţīm (bȧl-tēm′) U. A. R. (Nile In.)	31·33 N	31·04 E
84	Baltimore (bôl′tĭ-môr) Md. (Baltimore In.)	39·20 N	76·38 W
119	Baltiysk (bäl-tēysk′) . . . . Sov. Un.	54·40 N	19·55 E
145	Baluchistan (Reg.) (bȧ-lo͝o-chĭ-stän′) . W. Pak.	27·45 N	66·58 E
90	Balurte, Río del (rê′ō-dĕl-bä-lo͞o′r-tĕ) . Mex.	23·09 N	105·42 W
85	Balzac (bôl′zăk) . Can. (Calgary In.)	51·13 N	114·00 W
164	Bamako (bä-mā-kō′) . . . . Mali	12·45 N	7·50 W
164	Bamba (bȧm-bä′) . . . . Mali	17·13 N	1·30 W
155	Bambang (bäm-bäng′) Phil. (Manila In.)	16·24 N	121·08 E
165	Bambari (bäm-bȧ-rē) Cen. Afr. Rep.	5·44 N	20·40 E
120	Bamberg (bäm′bĕrgh) . . . . Ger.	49·53 N	10·52 E
79	Bamberg (băm′bûrg) . . . . S. C.	33·17 N	81·04 W
165	Bambesa (bäm-bĕ′sä) . . . . Con. K.	3·46 N	26·09 E
101	Bambuí (bä′m-bo͞o′-ê) Braz. (Rio de Janeiro In.)	20·01 S	45·59 W
164	Bambuto Mts. (bäm-bo͞o′tō) Nig.-Cam.	6·22 N	11·14 E
110	Bampton (băm′tŭn) Eng. (London In.)	51·42 N	1·33 W
144	Bampūr (bŭm-po͞or′) . . . . Iran	27·15 N	60·22 E
155	Banahao, Mt. (bä-nä-hä′ô) Phil. (Manila In.)	14·04 N	121·45 E
101	Bananal (bä-nä-näl′) Braz. (Rio de Janeiro In.)	22·42 S	44·17 W
99	Bananal, Ilha do (I.) (ē′lä-dô-bä-nä-näl′) . Braz.	12·09 S	50·27 W
	Banaras, see Vārānasi		
142	Banās (R.) (bän-äs′) . . . . India	25·20 N	74·51 E
165	Banas, Ra's (C.) . . . . U. A. R.	23·48 N	36·39 E
127	Banat (Reg.) (bä-nät′) Yugo.-Rom.	45·35 N	21·05 E
154	Ban Bangsaphan . . . . Thai.	11·19 N	99·27 E
81	Bancroft (băn′krŏft) . . . . Can.	45·05 N	77·55 W
142	Banda (bän′dä) . . . . India	25·36 N	80·21 E
155	Banda (I.) . . . . Indon.	4·40 S	129·56 E
160	Banda Banda, Mt. (băn′dȧ băn′dȧ) . Austl.	31·09 S	152·15 E
164	Bandama R. (bän-dä′mä) Ivory Coast	6·19 N	5·40 W
144	Bandar Abbās (Hbr.) (bän-där′ ȧb-bäs′) . Iran	27·04 N	56·22 E
144	Bandar-e Lengeh (Hbr.) . . . . Iran	26·44 N	54·47 E
133	Bandar-e Pahlanī (bän-där′) . Iran	37·30 N	49·30 E
144	Bandar-e-Shāhpūr (Hbr.) . . . . Iran	30·27 N	48·45 E
139	Bandar Maharani (bän-där′ mä-hä-rä′nê) Mala. (Singapore In.)	2·02 N	102·34 E
144	Bandar Shah (Hbr.) . . . . Iran	37·00 N	54·08 E
155	Banda Sea (bän′dä) . . . . Indon.	6·05 S	127·28 E
101	Bandeira, Pico da (Pk.) (pē′ko͝o dā bän-dā′rä) . Braz. (Rio de Janeiro In.)	20·27 S	41·47 W

ăt; finăl; rāte; senâte; ärm; ȧsk; sofȧ; fâre; ch-choose; dh-as th in other; bē; êvent; bĕt; recĕnt; cratẽr; g-go; gh-guttural g; bĭt; ĭ-short neutral; rīde; ĸ-guttural k as ch in German ich;

PRONOUNCING INDEX Bandelier–Bathsheba 181

Page Name Pronunciation Region Lat. °' Long. °'

69 Bandelier Natl. Mon. (băn-dĕ-lēr') N. Mex. 35·50 N 106·45 W
90 Banderas, Bahía de (B.) (bä-ē'ä-dĕ-bän-dĕ'räs). Mex. 20·38 N 103·25 W
168 Bander Beila Som. (Horn of Afr. In.) 9·40 N 50·45 E
164 Bandiagara (bän-dē-à-gä'rä). Mali 14·19 N 3·39 W
133 Bandırma (bän-dĭr'mà) Tur. 40·25 N 27·50 E
154 Bandjermasin (bän-jĕr-mä'sĕn) Indon. 3·18 S 114·32 E
124 Bando (bä'n-dô) Sp. 42·02 N 7·58 W
66 Bandon (băn'dŭn) Ore. 43·06 N 124·25 W
143 Bāndra India (Bombay In.) 19·04 N 72·49 E
166 Bandundu Con. K. 3·19 S 17·28 E
154 Bandung Indon. 7·00 S 107·22 E
95 Banes (bä'näs) Cuba 21·00 N 75·45 W
86 Banff (bănf) Can. 51·17 N 115·30 W
116 Banff Scot. 57·39 N 2·37 W
86 Banff Natl. Park Can. 51·45 N 116·04 W
100 Bánfield (bà'n-fyĕ'ld) Arg. (In.) 34·30 S 58·24 W
143 Bangalore (băŋ'gà'lôr) India 13·03 N 77·39 E
155 Bangar (bäŋ-gär') Phil. (Manila In.) 16·54 N 120·24 E
165 Bangassou (bäɴ-gà-sōō') Cen. Afr. Rep. 4·47 N 22·49 E
155 Bangeta, Mt. N. Gui. Ter. 6·20 S 147·00 E
155 Banggai, Pulau-Palau (Is.) (bäng-gī'). Indon. 1·05 S 123·45 E
154 Banggi (I.) Mala. 7·12 N 117·10 E
165 Banghāzī (Bengasi) (bĕn-gä'zē) Libya 32·08 N 20·06 E
139 Bangi Mala. (Singapore In.) 2·54 N 101·48 E
154 Bangka (I.) (băŋ'kà) Indon. 2·24 S 106·55 E
154 Bangkalan (bäng-kà-län') Indon. 6·07 S 112·50 E
Bangkok, see Krung Thep
82 Bangor (băn'gẽr) Maine 44·47 N 68·47 W
80 Bangor Mich. 42·20 N 86·05 W
81 Bangor Pa. 40·55 N 75·10 W
116 Bangor (băŋ'ẽr) (băŋ'ŏr) Wales 53·13 N 4·05 W
69 Bangs, Mt. (băngs) Ariz. 36·45 N 113·50 W
155 Bangued (bän-gād') Phil. (Manila In.) 17·36 N 120·38 E
165 Bangui (bäɴ-gē'). Cen. Afr. Rep. 4·28 N 18·35 E
166 Bangweulu, L. (băng-wē-ōō'lōō) Zambia 10·30 S 30·15 E
168 Banhā U. A. R. (Nile In.) 30·24 N 31·11 E
95 Bani (bä'-nē) Dom. Rep. 18·15 N 70·25 W
155 Bani (bä'nē) Phil. (Manila In.) 16·11 N 119·51 E
164 Bani (R.) Mali 13·00 N 5·36 W
164 Bani, Jebel (Mts.) (jĕb'ĕl bä'nē) Mor. 28·39 N 9·33 W
95 Bánica (bä'-nē-kä) Dom. Rep. 19·00 N 71·35 W
168 Banī Mazār U. A. R. (Nile In.) 28·29 N 30·48 E
168 Banī Suwayf U. A. R. (Nile In.) 29·05 N 31·06 E
126 Banja Luka (bän-yä-lōō'kà). Yugo. 44·45 N 17·11 E
154 Banjuwangi (bän-jōō-wäŋ'gē) Indon. 8·15 S 114·15 E
154 Ban Kantang (bän-kän'täng') Thai. 7·26 N 99·28 E
167 Bankberg (Mts.) (bäŋk'bûrg) S. Afr. (Natal In.) 32·10 S 25·11 E
65 Banks (bănks). Ore. (Portland In.) 45·37 N 123·07 W
159 Banks (Is.) Austl. 10·10 S 143·08 E
161 Banks, C. Austl. (Sydney In.) 34·01 S 151·17 E
49 Banks I. Can. 73·00 N 123·00 W
159 Banks Is. New Hebr. 13·38 S 168·23 E
160 Banks Str. Austl. 40·45 S 148·00 E
154 Ban Kui Nua Thai. 12·04 N 99·50 E
116 Bann (R.) (băn) N. Ire. 54·50 N 6·29 W
74 Banning (băn'ĭng) Calif. (Los Angeles In.) 33·56 N 116·53 W
79 Bannister (R.) (băn'ĭs-tẽr) Va. 36·45 N 79·17 W
161 Bannockburn Austl. (Melbourne In.) 38·03 S 144·11 E
98 Baños (bä'-nyôs) Ec. 1·30 S 78·22 W
121 Banská Bystrica (bän'skä bē'strē-tzä). Czech. 48·46 N 19·10 E
127 Bansko (bän'skō) Bul. 41·51 N 23·33 E
110 Banstead (băn'stĕd) Eng. (London In.) 51·18 N 0·09 W
164 Banthe (băn'thĕ) S. L. 7·36 N 12·34 W
155 Banton (bän-tōn') Phil. (Manila In.) 12·54 N 121·55 E
116 Bantry (băn'trĭ) Ire. 51·39 N 9·30 W
116 Bantry B. Ire. 51·25 N 10·09 W
165 Banzyville (bäɴ-zē-vēl') Con. K. 4·14 N 21·11 E
164 Baoule R. (bà-ōō-lā') Mali 14·00 N 9·08 W
167 Bapsfontein (băps-fŏn-tān') S. Afr. (Johannesburg & Pretoria In.) 26·01 S 28·26 E
98 Baqueroncito (bä-kĕ-rô-n-sē-tô) Col. (In.) 3·18 N 74·40 W
129 Bar (bär) Sov. Un. 49·02 N 27·44 E
127 Bar Yugo. 42·05 N 19·09 E
134 Barabinsk (bȧ'rà-bĭnsk). Sov. Un. 55·18 N 78·00 E
71 Baraboo (bâr'ȧ-bōō) Wis. 43·29 N 89·44 W
95 Baracoa (bä-rä-kō'ä) Cuba 20·20 N 74·25 W
95 Baracoa Cuba (Havana In.) 23·03 N 82·34 W
101 Baradeo (bä-rä-dĕ'ō) Arg. (Buenos Aires In.) 33·50 S 59·30 W
95 Baradères, Baie des (B.) (bä-rä-dâr'). Hai. 18·35 N 73·35 W
95 Barahona (bä-rä-ô'nä). Dom. Rep. 18·15 N 71·10 W
125 Barajas de Madrid (bä-rä'häs dā mä-drēdh'). Sp. (Madrid In.) 40·28 N 3·35 W
165 Baraka R. (bȧ-rä'kä) Eth. 16·44 N 37·34 E
142 Baranagar India (Calcutta In.) 22·38 N 88·25 E
92 Baranco (bä-räŋ'kō) Br. Hond. 16·01 N 88·55 W
64 Baranof (I.) (bä-rä'nôf) Alaska 56·48 N 136·08 W
121 Baranovichi (bä'rä-nô-vē'chē) Sov. Un. 53·08 N 25·59 E
139 Baranpauh. Indon. (Singapore In.) 0·40 N 103·28 E
100 Barão de Juperanã (bä-rouɴ-dĕ-zhōō-pe-rà'nȧ). Braz. (In.) 22·21 S 43·41 W
99 Barão de Melgaço (bä-rouɴ-dĕ-mĕl-gä'sō). Braz. 16·12 S 55·48 W
142 Bārāsat India (Calcutta In.) 22·42 N 88·29 E
77 Barataria B. La. 29·13 N 89·90 W
98 Baraya (bä-rä'yä) Col. (In.) 3·10 N 75·04 W
101 Barbacena (bär-bä-sā'nȧ) Braz. (Rio de Janeiro In.) 21·15 S 43·46 W
98 Barbacoas (bär-bä-kō'äs) Col. 1·39 N 78·12 W
99 Barbacoas (bär-bä-kô'äs) Ven. (In.) 9·30 N 66·58 W
93 Barbados (bär-bā'dōz) N. A. (Le. & Wind. Is. In.) 13·30 N 59·48 W
125 Barbastro (bär-bäs'trō) Sp. 42·05 N 0·05 E
74 Barbeau (bȧr-bō') Mich. (Sault Ste. Marie In.) 46·17 N 84·16 W
75 Barberton (bär'bẽr-tŭn) Ohio (Cleveland In.) 41·01 N 81·37 W
166 Barberton S. Afr. 25·48 S 31·04 E
122 Barbezieux (bärb'zyû') Fr. 45·30 N 0·11 W
78 Barboorville (bär'bẽr-vĭl) Ky. 36·52 N 83·58 W
98 Barbosa (bär-bô'-sà) Col. (In.) 6·26 N 75·19 W
80 Barboursville (bär'bẽrs-vĭl). W. Va. 38·20 N 82·20 W
93 Barbuda I. (bär-bōō'dȧ) Antigua (Le. & Wind. Is. In.) 17·40 N 61·37 W
159 Barcaldine (bär'kôl-dĭn) Austl. 28·30 S 145·43 E
125 Barcarena (bär-kä-rē'-nä) Port. (Lisbon In.) 38·29 N 9·17 W
124 Barcarrota (bär-kär-rō'tä) Sp. 38·31 N 6·50 W
126 Barcellona (bär-chĕl-lō'nä) It. 38·07 N 15·15 E
125 Barcelona (bär-thȧ-lō'nä) Sp. 41·25 N 2·08 E
99 Barcelona (bär-sä-lō'nä). Ven. (In.) 10·09 N 64·41 W
123 Barcelonnette (bär-sĕ-lô-nĕt'). Fr. 44·24 N 6·42 E
98 Barcelos (bär-sĕ'lôs) Braz. 1·04 S 63·00 W
124 Barcélos (bär-thȧ'lōs) Port. 41·34 N 8·39 W
144 Bardar-e Pahlant Iran 37·16 N 49·15 E
139 Bardawīl, Sabkhat al (B.) U. A. R. (Palestine In.) 31·20 N 33·24 E
121 Bardejov (bär'dyĕ-yôf) Czech. 49·18 N 21·18 E
168 Bardera (bär-dā'rä) Som. (Horn of Afr. In.) 2·13 N 42·24 E
116 Bardsey (I.) (bärd'sē) Wales 52·45 N 4·50 W
80 Bardstown (bärds'toun) Ky. 37·50 N 85·30 W
78 Bardwell (bärd'wĕl) Ky. 36·51 N 88·57 W
130 Barents Sea (bä'rĕnts) Sov. Un. 72·14 N 37·28 E
165 Barentu (bä-rĕn'tōō) Eth. 15·06 N 37·39 E
122 Barfleur, Pte. de (Pt.) (bär-flûr') Fr 49·43 N 1·17 W
142 Bargāchia India (Calcutta In.) 22·39 N 88·07 E
135 Barguzin (bär'gōō-zĭn). Sov. Un. 53·44 N 109·28 E
82 Bar Harbor (bär här'bẽr). Maine 44·22 N 68·13 W
126 Bari (bä'rē) It. 41·08 N 16·53 E
98 Barinas (bä-rē'näs) Ven. 8·36 N 70·14 W
86 Baring, C. (bâr'ĭng) Can. 70·07 N 119·48 W
154 Barisan, Pegunungan (Mts.) (bä-rē-sän'). Indon. 2·38 S 101·45 E
154 Barito (Strm.) (bä-rē'tō) Indon. 2·10 S 114·38 E
167 Barkly East (bärk'lē ēst) S. Afr. (Natal In.) 30·58 S 27·37 E
158 Barkly Tableland (Reg.) (bär'klē) Austl. 18·15 S 145·55 E
122 Bar-le-Duc (bär-lē-dük') Fr. 48·47 N 5·05 E
158 Barlee (L.) (bär-lē') Austl. 29·45 S 119·00 E
126 Barletta (bär-lĕt'tä) It. 41·19 N 16·20 E
111 Barmstedt (bärm'shtĕt) Ger. (Hamburg In.) 53·47 N 9·46 E
134 Barnaul (bär-nä-ōōl') Sov. Un. 53·18 N 83·23 E
81 Barnesboro (bärnz'bẽr-ô) Pa. 40·45 N 78·50 W
78 Barnesville (bärnz'vĭl) Ga. 33·03 N 84·10 W
70 Barnesville Minn. 46·38 N 96·25 W
80 Barnesville Ohio 39·55 N 81·10 W
81 Barnet (bär'nĕt) Vt. 44·20 N 72·00 W
110 Barnetby (bär'nĕt-bĭ) Eng. 53·34 N 0·26 W
94 Barnett Hbr. Ba. Is. 25·40 N 79·20 W
73 Barnsdall (bärnz'dôl) Okla. 36·38 N 96·14 W
110 Barnsley (bärnz'lĭ) Eng. 53·33 N 1·29 W
116 Barnstaple (bärn'stä-p'l) Eng. 51·06 N 4·05 W
79 Barnwell (bärn'wĕl) S. C. 33·14 N 81·23 W
164 Baro (bä'rō) Nig. 8·34 N 6·25 E
142 Baroda (bär-rō'dä) India 22·21 N 73·12 E
165 Baro R. Eth. 7·40 N 34·17 E
166 Barotseland (Reg.) (bȧ-rŏt'sĕ-lănd) Zambia 16·00 S 22·52 E
165 Barqah (Cirenaica) (Prov.). Libya 31·09 N 21·45 E
98 Barquisimeto (bär-kē-sē-mā'tō) Ven. 10·04 N 69·16 W
99 Barra (bär'rä) Braz. 11·04 S 43·11 W
142 Barrackpore India (Calcutta In.) 22·46 N 88·22 E
99 Barra do Corda (bär'rä dōō cōr-dä) Braz. 5·33 S 45·13 W
116 Barra Is. (băr'rȧ) Scot. 56·57 N 6·85 W
101 Barra Mansa (bär'rä män'sä) Braz. (Rio de Janeiro In.) 22·35 S 44·09 W
98 Barrancabermeja (bär-räŋ'kä-bẽr-mā'hä). Col. 7·06 N 73·49 W
98 Barranquilla (bär-rän-kēl'yä). Col. 10·57 N 75·00 W
99 Barras (bà'r-räs) Braz. 4·13 S 42·14 W
81 Barre (băr'ē) Vt. 44·15 N 72·30 W
101 Barre do Piraí (bär'rĕ-dō-pē'rä-ē') Braz. (Rio de Janeiro In.) 22·30 S 43·49 W
99 Barreiras (bär-rā'-räs) Braz. 12·13 S 44·59 W
125 Barreiro (bär-rĕ'ê-rōō) Port. (Lisbon In.) 38·39 N 9·05 W
160 Barren, C. (băr'ĕn) Austl. 40·20 S 149·00 E
167 Barren, Îles (Is.) Malag. Rep. 18·18 S 43·57 E
78 Barren (R.) Ky. 37·00 N 86·20 W
99 Barretos (bär-rā'tōs) Braz. 20·40 S 48·36 W
86 Barrhead (băr-hĕd) (băr'ĭd). Can. 54·10 N 114·20 W
81 Barrie (băr'ĭ) Can. 44·25 N 79·45 W
85 Barrington (bă-rĕng-tŏn) Can. (Montreal In.) 45·07 N 73·35 W
75 Barrington Ill. (Chicago In.) 42·09 N 88·08 W
84 Barrington. R. I. (Providence In.) 41·44 N 71·16 W
160 Barrington Tops (Mtn.) Austl. 32·00 S 151·25 E
74 Bar River (bär) Can. (Sault Ste. Marie In.) 46·27 N 84·02 W
71 Barron (băr'ŭn) Wis. 45·24 N 91·51 W
64 Barrow (băr'ō) Alaska 71·20 N 156·00 W
116 Barrow Eng. 54·10 N 3·15 W
158 Barrow (I.) Austl. 21·05 S 11·30 E
64 Barrow, Pt. Alaska 71·20 N 156·00 W
158 Barrow Creek Austl. 21·23 S 133·55 E
116 Barrow R. (bȧ-rȧ) Ire. 52·35 N 7·05 W
124 Barruelo de Santullán (bär-rōō-ā-lō dā sän-tōō-lyän'). Sp. 42·55 N 4·19 W
74 Barry (băr'ĭ) Mo. (Kansas City In.) 39·14 N 94·36 W
68 Barstow (bär'stō) Calif. 34·53 N 117·03 W
84 Barstow Md. (Baltimore In.) 38·32 N 76·37 W
120 Barth (bärt) Ger. 54·20 N 12·43 E
73 Bartholomew Bay. (bär-thŏl'ō-mū bī-ōō'). Ark. 33·53 N 91·45 W
82 Barthurst (băr-thŭrst') Can. 47·38 N 65·40 W
99 Bartica (bär'tĭ-kȧ) Guy. 6·23 N 58·32 W
133 Bartın (bär'tĭn) Tur. 41·35 N 32·12 E
159 Bartle Frere, Mt. (bärt''l frēr') Austl. 17·30 S 145·46 E
73 Bartlesville (bär'tlz-vĭl) Okla. 36·44 N 95·58 W
75 Bartlett (bärt'lĕt). Ill. (Chicago In.) 41·59 N 88·11 W
77 Bartlett Tex. 30·48 N 97·25 W
81 Barton (bär'tŭn) Vt. 44·45 N 72·05 W
110 Barton-on-Humber (bär'tŭn-ŏn-hŭm'bẽr). Eng. 53·41 N 0·26 W
121 Bartoszyce (bär-tô-shĭ'tsȧ) Pol. 54·15 N 20·50 E
79 Bartow (bär'tō) Fla. (In.) 27·51 N 81·50 W
129 Barvenkovo (bär'vĕn-kô'vô) Sov. Un. 48·55 N 36·59 E
160 Barwon (R.) (bär'wŭn) Austl. 29·45 S 148·25 E
161 Barwon Heads Austl. (Melbourne In.) 38·17 S 144·59 E
120 Barycz R. (bä'rĭch) Pol. 51·30 N 16·38 E
165 Basankusu (bä-sän-kōō'sōō) Con. K. 1·14 N 19·45 E
111 Basbeck (bäs'bĕk) Ger. (Hamburg In.) 53·40 N 9·11 E
111 Basdahl (bäs'däl) Ger. (Hamburg In.) 53·27 N 9·00 E
74 Basehor (bās'hôr) Kans. (Kansas City In.) 39·08 N 94·55 W
120 Basel (bä'z'l) Switz. 47·32 N 7·35 E
167 Bashee (R.) (bȧ-shē') S. Afr. (Natal In.) 31·47 S 28·25 E
151 Bashi Chan (băsh'ē) Phil. 21·20 N 120·22 E
132 Bashkir (A.S.S.R.) (bȧsh-kēr') Sov. Un. 54·12 N 57·15 E
129 Bashtanka (bȧsh-tän'kȧ). Sov. Un. 47·32 N 32·31 E
154 Basilan (I.) Phil. 6·37 N 122·07 E
126 Basilicata (Reg.) (bä-zē-lē-kä'tä) It. 40·30 N 15·55 E
67 Basin (bā'sĭn) Wyo. 44·22 N 108·02 W
110 Basingstoke (bā'zĭng-stōk) Eng. (London In.) 51·14 N 1·06 W
126 Baška (bäsh'ka) Yugo. 44·58 N 14·44 E
133 Baskale (bäsh-kä'lĕ) Tur. 38·10 N 44·00 E
133 Baskunchak (L.) Sov. Un. 48·20 N 46·40 E
165 Basoko (nȧ-sō'kō) Con. K. 0·52 N 23·50 E
165 Basoko Con. K. 1·22 N 23·40 E
86 Bassano (băs-săn'ō) Can. 50·44 N 112·35 W
126 Bassano It. 45·46 N 11·44 E
167 Bassas da India (I.) (bäs'sȧs dȧ ēn'dē-ȧ). Malag. Rep. 21·23 S 39·42 E
154 Bassein (bŭ-sēn') Bur. 16·46 N 94·47 E
143 Bassein India (Bombay In.) 19·20 N 72·47 E
79 Basset (băs'sĕt) Va. 36·45 N 81·58 W
93 Basse Terre (bäs' târ') Basse Terre (Le. & Wind. Is. In.) 16·00 N 61·43 W
93 Basseterre St. Kitts-Nevis-Anguilla (Le. & Wind. Is. In.) 17·20 N 62·42 W
93 Basse Terre I. Guad. (Le. & Wind. Is. In.) 16·10 N 62·14 W
80 Bass Is. (băs) Ohio 41·40 N 82·50 W
160 Bass Str. Austl. 39·40 S 145·40 E
71 Basswood (L.) (băs'wŏŏd) Can.-Minn. 48·10 N 91·36 W
118 Båstad (bô'stät) Swe. 56·26 N 12·46 E
126 Bastia (bäs'tē-ä) Fr. 42·43 N 9·27 E
117 Bastogne (bäs-tôn'y') Bel. 50·02 N 5·45 E
77 Bastrop (băs'trŭp) La. 32·47 N 91·55 W
77 Bastrop Tex. 30·08 N 97·18 W
77 Bastrop Bay Tex. (In.) 29·07 N 95·22 W
164 Bata (bä'tä) Equat. Gui. 1·53 N 9·48 E
94 Batabanó (bä-tä-bä-nō') Cuba 22·45 N 82·20 W
94 Batabano, Golfo de (G.) (gôl-fô-dĕ-bä-tä-bä'nô). Cuba 22·10 N 83·05 W
155 Batac Phil. (Manila In.) 17·56 N 120·29 E
142 Batala India 31·54 N 75·18 E
136 Bataly (bȧ-tä'lĭ) Sov. Un. (Urals In.) 52·51 N 62·03 E
139 Batam I. (bä-täm') Indon. (Singapore In.) 1·03 N 104·00 E
155 Batan (bä-tän'). Phil. (Manila In.) 13·20 N 124·00 E
151 Batan Is. Phil. 20·58 N 122·20 E
151 Batangan, C. Viet. 15·18 N 109·10 E
155 Batangas (bä-tän'gäs) Phil. (Manila In.) 13·45 N 121·04 E
121 Bataszék (bä'tȧ-sĕk) Hung. 46·07 N 18·40 E
75 Batavia (bȧ-tā'vĭ-ȧ) Ill. (Chicago In.) 41·51 N 88·18 W
81 Batavia N. Y. 43·00 N 78·15 W
75 Batavia Ohio (Cincinnati In.) 39·05 N 84·10 W
129 Bataysk (bȧ-tīsk') Sov. Un. 47·08 N 39·44 E
79 Batesburg (bāts'bûrg) S. C. 33·53 N 81·34 W
73 Batesville (bāts'vĭl) Ark. 35·46 N 91·39 W
80 Batesville Ind. 39·15 N 85·15 W
78 Batesville Miss. 34·17 N 89·55 W
128 Batetska (bȧ-tĕ'tskȧ) Sov. Un. 58·36 N 30·21 E
82 Bath (bȧth) Can. 46·31 N 67·36 W
116 Bath Eng. 51·24 N 2·20 W
82 Bath Maine 43·54 N 69·50 W
81 Bath N. Y. 42·25 N 77·20 W
75 Bath Ohio (Cleveland In.) 41·11 N 81·38 W
93 Bathsheba Barb. (Le. & Wind. Is. In.) 13·13 N 60·30 W

182 Bathurst–Bellingham PRONOUNCING INDEX

Page	Name Pronunciation Region	Lat. °′	Long. °′
159	Bathurst (bȧth'ŭrst)........Aust.	33·28 s	149·30 e
164	Bathurst..................Gam.	13·23 n	16·45 w
167	Bathurst (băt-hûrst) S. Afr. (Natal In.)	33·26 s	26·53 e
64	Bathurst, C. (bȧth'ŭrst).....Can.	70·33 n	127·55 w
158	Bathurst (I.)..............Austl.	11·19 s	130·13 e
86	Bathurst Inlet.............Can.	67·25 n	106·50 w
155	Batian (I.)................Indon.	1·07 s	127·52 e
144	Batin, Wādī al (R.)......Sau. Ar.	27·17 n	44·13 e
155	Batjan (I.) (bät-jän')......Indon.	1·07 s	127.52 e
144	Bātlaq-E Gāvkhūn (L.)......Iran	31·40 n	52·48 e
110	Batley (băt'lĭ).............Eng.	53·43 n	1·37 w
164	Batna (bät'nȧ)..............Alg.	35·41 n	6·12 e
77	Baton Rouge (băt'ŭn rōōzh')..La.	30·28 n	91·10 w
154	Battambang (bȧt-tȧm-bäng') Camb.	13·14 n	103·15 e
84	Battery Park (băt'ēr-ĭ) Va. (Norfolk In.)	36·59 n	76·36 w
80	Battle Creek (băt''l krēk')..Mich.	42·20 n	85·15 w
86	Battleford (băt''l-fērd)......Can.	52·44 n	108·30 w
65	Battle Ground (băt''l ground) Wash. (Portland In.)	45·47 n	122·32 w
87	Battle Harbour (băt''l här'bēr) Can.	52·17 n	55·33 w
66	Battle Mountain...........Nev.	40·40 n	116·56 w
121	Battonya (bät-tô'nyä).....Hung.	46·17 n	21·00 e
154	Batu (I.) (bä'tōō).........Indon.	0·10 s	99·55 e
133	Batumi (bŭ-tōō'mē).....Sov. Un.	41·40 n	41·30 e
139	Batu Pahat..Mala (Singapore In.)	1·51 n	102·56 e
99	Baturité (bä-tōō-rē-tā').....Braz.	4·16 s	38·47 w
155	Bauang (bä'wäng) Phil. (Manila In.)	16·31 n	120·19 e
164	Bauchi (bȧ-ōō'chē)..........Nig.	10·19 n	9·51 e
166	Baudouinville (bō-dwăn-vēl') Con. K.	7·12 s	29·39 e
83	Bauld, C..................Can.	51·38 n	55·10 w
85	Baurette (bō-rĕt') Can. (Montreal In.)	45·24 n	73·32 w
142	Bāuria.......India (Calcutta In.)	22·29 n	88·08 e
99	Bauru (bou-rōō')..........Braz.	22·21 s	48·57 w
119	Bauska (bou'skȧ).......Sov. Un.	56·24 n	24·12 e
95	Bauta (bä'ōō-tä) Cuba (Havana In.)	22·14 n	82·33 w
120	Bautzen (bout'sĕn)..........Ger.	51·11 n	14·27 e
	Bavaria, see Bayern		
160	Baw Baw, Mt. (bȧ-bȧ).....Austl.	37·50 s	146·17 e
154	Bawean (I.) (bȧ'vē-än)....Indon.	5·50 s	112·40 e
110	Bawtry (bô'trĭ).............Eng.	53·26 n	1·01 w
79	Baxley (băks'lĭ).............Ga.	31·47 n	82·22 w
161	Baxter (băks'tēr) Austl. (Melbourne In.)	38·12 s	145·10 e
73	Baxter Springs (băks'tēr springs') Kans.	37·01 n	94·44 w
95	Bayaguana (bä-yä-gwä'nä) Dom. Rep.	18·45 n	69·40 w
114	Bay al Kabīr Wadi (R.)....Libya	29·52 n	14·28 e
155	Bayambang (bä-yȧm-bäng') Phil. (Manila In.)	15·50 n	120·26 e
94	Bayamo (bä-yä'mō)........Cuba	20·25 n	76·35 w
89	Bayamón . P. R. (Puerto Rico In.)	18·27 n	66·13 w
134	Bayan-Aul (bȧ'yȧn-oul').Sov. Un.	50·43 n	75·37 e
70	Bayard (bā'ērd)..........Nebr.	41·45 n	103·20 w
81	Bayard...................W. Va.	39·15 n	79·20 w
133	Bayburt (bā'ĭ-bŏŏrt)........Tur.	40·15 n	40·10 e
80	Bay City (bā)............Mich.	43·35 n	83·55 w
77	Bay City..................Tex.	28·59 n	95·58 w
146	Baydarag Gol (R.)........Mong.	46·09 n	98·52 e
132	Baydaratskaya Guba (B.) Sov. Un.	69·20 n	66·10 e
83	Bayde Verde...............Can.	48·06 n	52·50 w
120	Bayern (Bavaria) (State) (bī'ērn) (bȧ-vâ-rĭ-ȧ).Ger.	49·00 n	11·16 e
122	Bayeux (bȧ-yû')............Fr.	49·19 n	0·41 w
71	Bayfield (bā'fēld)..........Wis.	46·48 n	90·51 w
135	Baykal, Ozero (Baikal, L.) (bī'käl') (bī'kôl).Sov. Un.	53·00 n	109·28 e
135	Baykals'kiy Khrebet (Baikal Mts.).Sov. Un.	53·30 n	102·00 e
134	Baykit (bī-kēt')........Sov. Un.	61·43 n	96·39 e
134	Baykonur (bī-kô-nōōr')..Sov. Un.	47·46 n	66·11 e
136	Baymak (bȧy'mȧk) Sov. Un. (Urals In.)	52·35 n	58·21 e
78	Bay Minette (bā'mĭn-ĕt')....Ala.	30·52 n	87·44 w
74	Bay Mills (bā mĭlls) Mich. (Sault Ste. Marie In.)	46·27 n	84·36 w
71	Bay Mills Ind. Res.........Mich.	46·19 n	85·03 w
155	Bayombong (bä-yôm-bŏng') Phil. (Manila In.)	16·28 n	121·09 e
122	Bayonne (bȧ-yôn')..........Fr.	43·28 n	1·30 w
84	Bayonne (bā-yōn') N. J. (New York In.)	40·40 n	74·07 w
77	Bayou Bodcau Res. (bī'yōō bŏd'kō).La.	32·49 n	93·22 w
74	Bayport (bā'pōrt) Minn. (Minneapolis, St. Paul In.)	45·02 n	92·46 w
127	Bayramiç.................Tur.	39·48 n	26·35 e
120	Bayreuth (bī-roit')..........Ger.	49·56 n	11·35 e
83	Bay Roberts (bā rŏb'ērts)...Can.	47·36 n	53·12 w
81	Bays, L. of (bās)...........Can.	45·15 n	79·00 w
78	Bay St. Louis (bā' sânt lōō'ĭs) Miss.	30·19 n	89·20 w
84	Bay Shore (bā' shôr) N. Y. (New York In.)	40·44 n	73·15 w
139	Bayt Lahm (Bethlehem) (bĕth'lē-hĕm).Jordan (Palestine In.)	31·42 n	35·13 e
77	Baytown (bā'town)....Tex. (In.)	29·44 n	95·01 w
165	Bayuda Steppe (bä-yōō'dä)..Sud.	17·27 n	31·43 e
84	Bayview (bā'vū) Ala. (Birmingham In.)	33·34 n	86·59 w
65	Bayview.....Wash. (Seattle In.)	48·29 n	122·28 w
75	Bay Village (bā) Ohio (Cleveland In.)	41·29 n	81·56 w
124	Baza (bä'thä)..............Sp.	37·29 n	2·46 w
133	Bazar-Dyuzi, Gora (Mt.) (bä'zär-dyōōz'ĕ).Sov. Un.	41·20 n	47·40 e
166	Bazaruto, Ilha (I.) (ē'lä-bä-zȧ-rōō'tō).Moz.	21·42 s	36·10 e
167	Bazeia Mt. (bă-zēȧ) S. Afr. (Natal In.)	31·33 s	28·23 e
124	Baztán (bäth-tän')..........Sp.	43·12 n	1·30 w
70	Beach (bēch)...............N. D.	46·55 n	104·00 w
117	Beachy Head (bēchē hĕd)....Eng.	50·40 n	·25 e
81	Beacon (bē'kŭn)............N. Y.	41·30 n	73·55 w
85	Beaconsfield (bē'kŭnz-fēld) Can. (Montreal In.)	45·26 n	73·51 w
84	Beafort Mtn. (bē'fōrt) N. J. (New York In.)	41·08 n	74·23 w
76	Beals Cr. (bēls)............Tex.	32·10 n	101·14 w
85	Beamsville....Can. (Toronto In.)	43·10 n	79·29 w
67	Bear Creek (bâr krēk).....Mont.	45·11 n	109·07 w
78	Bear Cr. (bâr).............Ala.	34·27 n	88·00 w
74	Bear Cr. Tex. (Dallas, Fort Worth In.)	32·56 n	97·09 w
73	Beardstown (bērds'toun)......Ill.	40·01 n	90·26 w
65	Bearhead Mtn. (bâr'hĕd) Wash. (Seattle In.)	47·01 n	121·49 w
67	Bear L...........Idaho-Utah	41·56 n	111·10 w
67	Bear R..................Idaho	42·17 n	111·42 w
74	Bear R.Utah (Salt Lake City In.)	41·28 n	112·10 w
67	Bear River B.............Utah	41·25 n	112·20 w
124	Beas de Segura (bā'äs dā sā-gōō'rä) Sp.	38·16 n	2·53 w
95	Beata (I.) (bĕ-ä'tä)....Dom. Rep.	17·40 n	71·40 w
95	Beata, Cabo (C.) (kä'bô-bĕ-ä'tä) Dom. Rep.	17·40 n	71·20 w
73	Beatrice (bē'ȧ-trĭs).........Nebr.	40·16 n	96·45 w
68	Beatty (bēt'ē)..............Nev.	36·58 n	116·48 w
80	Beattyville (bēt'ē-vĭl)........Ky.	37·35 n	83·40 w
122	Beaucaire (bō-kâr')...........Fr.	43·49 n	4·37 e
82	Beauceville (bōs'vĕl)........Can.	46·12 n	70·46 w
123	Beaucourt (bō-kōōr')..........Fr.	47·30 n	6·54 e
79	Beaufort (bō'fērt)..........N. C.	34·43 n	76·40 w
79	Beaufort...................S. C.	32·25 n	80·40 w
64	Beaufort Sea.............Alaska	70·30 n	138·40 w
166	Beaufort West............S. Afr.	32·20 s	22·45 e
85	Beauharnois (bō-är-nwä') Can. (Montreal In.)	45·23 n	73·52 w
74	Beaumont (bō'mŏnt) Calif. (Los Angeles In.)	33·57 n	116·57 w
85	Beaumont......Can. (Quebec In.)	46·50 n	71·01 w
77	Beaumont..................Tex.	30·05 n	94·06 w
122	Beaune (bōn)................Fr.	47·02 n	4·49 e
85	Beauport (bō-pôr') Can. (Quebec In.)	46·52 n	71·11 w
85	Beaupré (bō-prā') Can. (Quebec In.)	47·03 n	70·53 w
85	Beaurepaire (bōr-pĕr') Can. (Montreal In.)	45·25 n	73·53 w
86	Beausejour.................Can.	50·07 n	96·39 w
122	Beauvais (bō-vĕ')............Fr.	49·25 n	2·05 e
72	Beaver (bē'vēr).............Okla.	36·46 n	100·31 w
75	Beaver.......Pa. (Pittsburgh In.)	40·42 n	80·18 w
69	Beaver.....................Utah	38·15 n	112·40 w
80	Beaver (I.)................Mich.	45·40 n	85·30 w
86	Beaver (R.)................Can.	54·21 n	111·50 w
72	Beaver City................Nebr.	40·08 n	99·52 w
72	Beaver Cr..................Colo.	39·42 n	103·37 w
72	Beaver Cr..................Kans.	39·44 n	101·05 w
70	Beaver Cr..................Mont.	46·45 n	104·18 w
67	Beaver Cr..................Wyo.	43·46 n	104·25 w
71	Beaver Dam.................Wis.	43·29 n	88·50 w
67	Beaverhead Mts. (bē'vēr-hĕd) Mont.	44·33 n	112·59 w
67	Beaverhead R.............Mont.	45·05 n	112·50 w
80	Beaver Ind. Res..........Mich.	45·40 n	85·30 w
65	Beaverton (bē'vēr-tŭn) Ore. (Portland In.)	45·29 n	122·49 w
98	Bebara' (bĕ-bä-rä')....Col. (In.)	6·07 n	76·39 w
110	Bebington (bē'bĭng-tŭn).....Eng.	53·20 n	2·59 w
91	Becal (bā-käl')..............Mex.	20·25 n	90·04 w
127	Bečej (bĕ'chā)..............Yugo.	45·36 n	20·03 e
124	Becerreá (bā-thā'rē-ä)........Sp.	42·49 n	7·12 w
164	Béchar......................Alg.	31·39 n	2·14 w
64	Becharof (L.) (bĕk ȧ rôf)..Alaska	57·58 n	156·58 w
65	Becher B. (bēch'ēr) Can. (Seattle In.)	48·18 n	123·37 w
80	Beckley (bĕk'lĭ)...........W. Va.	37·40 n	81·15 w
122	Bédarieux (bā-dȧ-ryû')........Fr.	43·36 n	3·11 e
85	Beddington Cr. (bĕd'ĕng tŭn) Can. (Calgary In.)	51·14 n	114·13 w
81	Bedford (bĕd'fērd)..........Can.	45·10 n	73·00 w
116	Bedford....................Eng.	52·10 n	0·25 w
80	Bedford....................Ind.	38·50 n	86·30 w
71	Bedford....................Iowa	40·40 n	94·41 w
83	Bedford.......Mass. (Boston In.)	42·30 n	71·17 w
84	Bedford....N. Y. (New York In.)	41·12 n	73·38 w
75	Bedford.....Ohio (Cleveland In.)	41·23 n	81·32 w
81	Bedford.....................Pa.	40·05 n	78·20 w
167	Bedford.......S. Afr. (Natal In.)	32·43 s	26·19 e
79	Bedford.....................Va.	37·19 n	79·27 w
84	Bedford Hill.N. Y. (New York In.)	41·14 n	73·41 w
110	Bedworth (bĕd'wērth).......Eng.	52·29 n	1·28 w
121	Bedzin (băn-jēn')............Pol.	50·19 n	19·10 w
73	Beebe (bē'bē)...............Ark.	35·04 n	91·54 w
75	Beecher (bē'chŭr) Ill. (Chicago In.)	41·20 n	87·38 w
65	Beechey Hd. (bē'chĭ hĕd) Can. (Seattle In.)	48·19 n	123·40 w
75	Beech Grove (bēch grōv) Ind. (Indianapolis In.)	39·43 n	86·05 w
160	Beecroft Hd. (bē'krŭft).....Austl.	35·03 s	151·15 e
111	Beelitz (bē'lētz)..Ger. (Berlin In.)	52·14 n	12·59 e
139	Beer (R.).......Isr. (Palestine In.)	31·23 n	34·30 e
139	Beersheba (bēr-shē'bȧ) Isr. (Palestine In.)	31·15 n	34·48 e
168	Beestekraal....S. Afr. (Johannesburg & Pretoria In.)	25·22 s	27·34 e
110	Beeston (bēs't'n)...........Eng.	52·55 n	1·11 w
111	Beetz R. (bĕtz)..Ger. (Berlin In.)	52·28 n	12·37 e
77	Beeville (bē'vĭl).............Tex.	28·24 n	97·44 w
160	Bega (bā'gȧ)...............Austl.	36·50 s	149·49 e
73	Beggs (bĕgz)...............Okla.	35·46 n	96·06 w
122	Bègles (bĕ'gl')...............Fr.	44·47 n	0·34 w
142	Behampur..................India	20·19 n	85 53 e
165	Beilul......................Eth.	13·15 n	42·21 e
166	Beira (bā'rȧ)...............Moz.	19·46 s	34·58 e
124	Beira (Reg.) (bĕ'y-rä).......Port.	40·38 n	8·00 w
139	Beirut (bā-rōōt') Leb. (Palestine In.)	33·53 n	35·30 e
139	Beit Shean....Isr. (Palestine In.)	32·30 n	35·30 e
124	Beja (bā'zhȧ)...............Port.	38·03 n	7·53 w
113	Béja........................Tun.	36·52 n	9·20 e
164	Bejaia (Bougie).............Alg.	36·46 n	5·00 e
124	Bejar........................Sp.	40·25 n	5·43 w
144	Bejestān....................Iran	34·30 n	58·22 e
144	Bejnurd....................Iran	37·29 n	57·13 e
95	Bejucal (bā-hōō-käl') Cuba (Havana In.)	22·08 n	82·23 w
93	Bejuco (bĕ-kōō'kō)..........Pan.	8·37 n	79·54 w
121	Békés (bā'kāsh)............Hung.	46·45 n	21·08 e
121	Békéscsaba (bā'kāsh-chô'bô) Hung.	46·39 n	21·06 e
147	Beketova (bĕk'e-to'vȧ)..Sov. Un.	53·23 n	125·21 e
127	Bela Crkva (bĕ'lä tsĕrk'vä).Yugo.	44·53 n	21·25 e
124	Belalcázar (bāl-ál-kä'thär)....Sp.	38·35 n	5·12 w
125	Belas (bĕ'-läs).Port. (Lisbon In.)	38·47 n	9·16 w
127	Bela-Slatina (byä'la slä'tēnä).Bul.	43·26 n	23·56 e
154	Belawan (bä-lä'wän)......Indon.	3·43 n	98·43 e
132	Belaya (R.) (byĕ'lĭ-yȧ).Sov. Un.	52·45 n	61·15 e
129	Belaya Tserkov' (byĕ'lĭ-yȧ tsĕr'kôf).Sov. Un.	49·48 n	30·09 e
87	Belcher Is. (bĕl'chēr)........Can.	56·20 n	80·40 w
75	Belden (bĕl'dĕn) Ohio (Cleveland In.)	41·14 n	82·01 w
80	Belding (bĕl'dĭng).........Mich.	43·05 n	85·25 w
132	Belebey (byĕ'lĕ-bā'ĭ).....Sov. Un.	54·00 n	54·10 e
99	Belém (Pará) (bā-lĕn') (pä-rä') Braz.	1·18 s	48·27 w
69	Belen (bĕ-lăn')..........N. Mex.	34·40 n	106·45 w
100	Belén (bā-lān')..............Par.	23·30 s	57·09 w
159	Bélep, Isles...............N. Cal.	19·30 s	160·32 e
128	Belëv (byĕl'yĕf)........Sov. Un.	53·49 n	36·06 e
65	Belfair (bĕl'fâr) Wash. (Seattle In.)	47·27 n	122·50 w
116	Belfast (bĕl'fást).........N. Ire.	54·36 n	5·45 w
82	Belfast....................Maine	44·25 n	69·01 w
116	Belfast, Lough (B.) (lŏk bĕl'fást) Ire.	54·45 n	7·40 w
165	Bēlfodiyo...................Eth.	10·45 n	39·27 e
123	Belfort (bā-fôr')..............Fr.	47·40 n	7·50 e
143	Belgaum....................India	15·57 n	74·32 e
102	Belgium (bĕl'jĭ-ŭm).........Eur.	51·00 n	2·52 e
129	Belgorod (byĕl'gŭ-rŭt)...Sov. Un.	50·36 n	36·32 e
129	Belgorod (Oblast)........Sov. Un.	50·40 n	36·42 e
129	Belgorod Dnestrovskiy (byĕl'gŭ-rŭd nyĕs-trôf'skē).Sov. Un.	46·09 n	30·19 e
	Belgrade, see Beograd		
79	Belhaven (bĕl'hā-vĕn)......N. C.	35·33 n	76·37 w
81	Belington (bĕl'ĭng-tŭn)....W. Va.	39·00 n	79·55 w
127	Beli Timok (R.) (Bĕ'lē Tē'môk) Yugo.	43·35 n	22·13 e
154	Belitung (I.)...............Indon.	3·30 s	107·30 e
92	Belize (bĕ-lēz') Br. Hond. (Yucatan In.)	17·31 n	88·10 w
92	Belize R.Br. Hond. (Yucatan In.)	17·16 n	88·56 w
136	Bel'kovo (byĕl'kô-vô) Sov. Un. (Moscow In.)	56·15 n	38·49 e
135	Bel'kovskiy (I.) (byĕl-kôf'skĭ) Sov. Un.	75·52 n	133·00 e
74	Bell (bĕl).Calif. (Los Angeles In.)	33·59 n	118·11 w
83	Bell (I.)....................Can.	50·45 n	55·35 w
80	Bellaire (bĕl-âr')............Ohio	40·00 n	80·45 w
77	Bellaire...............Tex. (In.)	29·43 n	95·28 w
143	Bellary (bĕl-lä'rē)..........India	15·15 n	76·56 e
100	Bella Union (bĕ'l-yȧ-ōō-nyô'n).Ur.	30·18 s	57·26 w
100	Bella Vista (bä'lyȧ vēs'tä)....Arg.	27·07 s	65·14 w
100	Bella Vista..................Arg.	28·35 s	58·53 w
100	Bella Vista............Arg. (In.)	34·18 s	58·41 w
99	Bella Vista..................Braz.	22·16 s	56·14 w
83	Belle B. (bĕl)................Can.	47·35 n	55·15 w
84	Belle Chasse (bĕl shäs') La. (New Orleans In.)	29·52 n	90·00 w
80	Bellefontaine (bĕl-fŏn'tān).. Ohio	40·25 n	83·50 w
70	Belle Fourche (bĕl' fōōrsh')..S. D.	44·28 n	103·50 w
70	Belle Fourche (R.).........Wyo.	44·29 n	104·40 w
70	Belle Fourche Res...........S. D.	44·51 n	103·44 w
123	Bellegarde-sur-Valserine (bĕl-gärd'sür-väl-sȧ-rēn').Fr.	46·06 n	6 50 e
79	Belle Glade (bĕl glād)...Fla. (In.)	26·39 n	80·37 w
122	Belle Île (I.) (bĕl-ēl')...........Fr.	47·15 n	3·30 w
87	Belle Isle, Str. of............Can.	51·21 n	55·56 w
84	Belle Mead (bĕl mēd) N. J. (New York In.)	40·28 n	74·40 w
83	Belleoram...................Can.	47·29 n	55·50 w
71	Belle Plaine (bĕl plān').......Iowa	41·52 n	92·19 w
75	Belle Vernon (bĕl vûr'nŭn) Pa. (Pittsburgh In.)	40·08 n	79·52 w
81	Belleville (bĕl'vĭl)...........Can.	44·15 n	77·25 w
74	Belleville......Ill. (St. Louis In.)	38·31 n	89·59 w
73	Belleville....................Kans.	39·49 n	97·37 w
75	Belleville.....Mich. (Detroit In.)	42·12 n	83·29 w
84	Belleville....N. J. (New York In.)	40·47 n	74·09 w
71	Bellevue (bĕl'vū).............Iowa	42·14 n	90·26 w
75	Bellevue.....Ky. (Cincinnati In.)	39·06 n	84·29 w
80	Bellevue.....................Mich.	42·30 n	85·00 w
80	Bellevue.....................Ohio	41·15 n	82·45 w
75	Bellevue......Pa. (Pittsburgh In.)	40·30 n	80·04 w
65	Bellevue.......Wash. (Seattle In.)	47·37 n	122·12 w
123	Belley (bĕ-lē')..................Fr.	45·46 n	5·41 e
74	Bellflower (bĕl-flou'ēr) Calif. (Los Angeles In.)	33·53 n	118·08 w
83	Bellingham (bĕl'ĭng-hăm) Mass. (Boston In.)	42·05 n	71·28 w
65	Bellingham.Wash. (Vancouver In.)	48·46 n	122·29 w
65	Bellingham B. Wash. (Vancouver In.)	48·44 n	122·34 w

ăt; finăl; rāte; senāte; ärm; ȧsk; sofȧ; fâre; ch-choose; dh-as th in other; bē; ēvent; bĕt; recĕnt; cratēr; g-go; gh-guttural g; bĭt; ĭ-short neutral; rīde; ĸ-guttural k as ch in German ich;

ng-sing; ŋ-baŋk; N-nasalized n; nŏd; cŏmmit; ōld; ôbey; ôrder; fōōd; fŏŏt; ou-out; s-soft; sh-dish; th-thin; pūre; únite; ûrn; stŭd; circŭs; ū-as "y" in study; '-indeterminate vowel.

184 Biak–Blooming Prairie PRONOUNCING INDEX

Page	Name Pronunciation Region	Lat. °′	Long. °′
155	Biak (I.) (bē'āk) ....W. Irian	0·45 S	135·00 E
121	Biała Podlaska (byä'wä pōd-läs'kä) . Pol.	52·01 N	23·08 E
120	Białogard (byä-wō'gärd) .....Pol.	54·00 N	16·01 E
121	Białystok (byä-wĭs'tōk) ......Pol.	53·08 N	23·12 E
122	Biarritz (byä-rēts') ....Fr.	43·27 N	1·39 W
168	Bibā (bē'bä) . . U. A. R. (Nile In.)	28·54 N	30·59 E
78	Bibb City (bĭb' sĭ'tē) ....Ga.	32·31 N	84·56 W
120	Biberach (bē'bĕrāk) ....Ger.	48·06 N	9·49 E
82	Bic (bĭk) ....Can.	48·21 N	68·44 W
80	Bicknell (bĭk'nĕl) ....Ind.	38·45 N	87·20 W
121	Bicske (bĭsh'kē) ....Hung.	47·29 N	18·38 E
164	Bida (bē'dä) ....Nig.	9·05 N	6·04 E
82	Biddeford (bĭd'ē-fērd) ......Maine	43·29 N	70·29 W
110	Biddulph (bĭd'ŭlf) ....Eng.	53·07 N	2·10 W
164	Bidon Cing ....Alg.	22·22 N	0·33 E
121	Biebrza R. (byĕb'zhà) ....Pol.	53·18 N	22·25 E
120	Biel (bēl) ....Switz.	47·09 N	7·12 E
120	Bielefeld (bē'lē-fĕlt) ....Ger.	52·01 N	8·35 E
127	Bieljina (bē-yĕ'lyē-nä) .....Yugo.	44·44 N	19·15 E
126	Biella (byĕl'lä) ....It.	45·34 N	8·05 E
121	Bielsk Podlaski (byĕlsk pŭd-lä'skĭ) Pol.	52·47 N	23·14 E
87	Bienville, Lac (L.) ....Can.	55·32 N	72·45 W
111	Biesenthal (bē'sĕn-täl) Ger. (Berlin In.)	52·46 N	13·38 E
126	Biferno (R.) (bē-fĕr'nō) ....It.	41·49 N	14·46 E
82	Big (L.) (bĭg) ....Can.	45·06 N	67·43 W
65	Big (L.) ....Wash. (Seattle In.)	48·23 N	122·14 W
78	Big (R.) ....Ark.	35·55 N	90·10 W
127	Biga (bē'ghà) ....Tur.	40·13 N	27·14 E
73	Big Bay (bĭg' bī'yōō) ....Ark.	33·04 N	91·28 W
71	Big Bay de Noc (bĭg bā dē nok') Mich.	45·48 N	86·41 W
74	Big Bear City (bĭg bâr) Calif. (Los Angeles In.)	34·16 N	116·51 W
74	Big Bear Lake (bĭg bâr lāk) Calif. (Los Angeles In.)	34·14 N	116·54 W
67	Big Belt Mts. (bĭg bĕlt) ....Mont.	46·53 N	111·43 W
70	Big Bend Dam (bĭg bĕnd) ...S. D.	44·11 N	99·33 W
76	Big Bend Natl. Park ....Tex.	29·15 N	103·15 W
78	Big Black (R.) (bĭg blăk) ...Miss.	32·05 N	90·49 W
73	Big Blue (R.) (bĭg blōō) ....Nebr.	40·53 N	97·00 W
76	Big Canyon (bĭg kăn'yŭn) ...Tex.	30·27 N	102·19 W
79	Big Cypress Swp. (bĭg sī'prĕs) Fla. (In.)	26·02 N	81·20 W
64	Big Delta (bĭg dĕl'tà) .....Alaska	64·08 N	145·48 W
71	Big Fork (R.) (bĭg fôrk) ....Minn.	48·08 N	93·47 W
86	Biggar ....Can.	52·09 N	108·10 W
67	Big Hole R. (bĭg 'hōl) ......Mont.	45·53 N	113·15 W
67	Big Hole Battlefield Natl. Mon. (bĭg hōl băt''l-fēld) . Mont.	45·44 N	113·35 W
67	Big Horn Mts. (bĭg hôrn) ....Wyo.	44·47 N	107·40 W
67	Bighorn R. ....Mont.	45·17 N	107·53 W
65	Big Lake (bĭg lāk) Wash. (Seattle In.)	48·24 N	122·14 W
85	Big L. (bĭg lāk) Can. (Edmonton In.)	53·35 N	113·47 W
80	Big Muddy (R.) ....Ill.	37·55 N	89·10 W
67	Big Muddy Cr. (bĭg mud'ĭ) . Mont.	48·53 N	105·02 W
80	Big Rapids (bĭg răp'ĭdz) ....Mich.	43·40 N	85·30 W
86	Big River ....Can.	53·50 N	107·20 W
	Big Sandy, see Fraser I.		
69	Big Sandy (R.) (bĭg sănd'ē) . Ariz.	34·59 N	113·36 W
80	Big Sandy (R.) ....Ky.-W. Va.	38·15 N	82·35 W
72	Big Sandy Cr. ....Colo.	39·08 N	103·36 W
70	Big Sioux (R.) (bĭg sōō) .....S. D.	44·34 N	97·00 W
76	Big Spring (bĭg spring) ....Tex.	32·15 N	101·28 W
70	Big Stone (L.) (bĭg stōn) Minn.-S. Dak.	45·29 N	96·40 W
78	Big Stone Gap ....Va.	36·50 N	82·50 W
67	Bigtimber (bĭg'tĭm-bēr) ....Mont.	45·50 N	109·57 W
67	Big Wood R. (bĭg wŏŏd) ....Idaho	43·02 N	114·30 W
126	Bihać (bē'hāch) ....Yugo.	44·48 N	15·52 E
142	Bihar (State) (bē-hār') ......India	23·48 N	84·57 E
166	Biharamulo (bē-hä-rä-mōō'lō) Tan.	2·38 S	31·39 E
121	Bihor, Muntii (Mts.) (bē'hôr) Rom.	46·37 N	22·37 E
164	Bijagós, Arquipelago dos (Is.) (är-kē-pā'lä-gō dôs bē-zhä-gôs') Port. Gui.	10·58 N	16·39 W
143	Bijapur ....India	16·53 N	75·42 E
127	Bijelo Polje (bē'yĕ-lō pō'lyĕ) Yugo.	43·02 N	19·48 E
72	Bijou Cr. (bē'zhōō) ....Colo.	39·41 N	104·13 W
142	Bikaner (bĭ-kă'nûr) ....India	28·07 N	73·19 E
152	Bikin (bē-kēn') ....Sov. Un.	46·41 N	134·29 E
152	Bikin (R.) ....Sov. Un.	46·37 N	135·55 E
166	Bikoro (bē-kō'rō) ....Con. K.	0·45 S	18·51 E
142	Bilāspur (bē-läs'pōōr) ....India	22·08 N	82·12 E
154	Bilauktaung Ra. ....Thai.	14·27 N	98·53 E
124	Bilbao (bĭl-bä'ō) ....Sp.	43·12 N	2·48 W
168	Bilbays.......U. A. R. (Nile In.)	30·26 N	31·37 E
127	Bileća (bē'lĕ-chä) ....Yugo.	42·52 N	18·26 E
133	Bilecik (bē-lĕd-zhĕk') ....Tur.	40·10 N	29·58 E
121	Bilé Karpaty (Mts.) ....Czech.	48·53 N	17·35 E
121	Biłgoraj (bēw-gō'rī) ....Pol.	50·31 N	22·43 E
136	Bilimbay (bē'lĭm-bày) Sov. Un. (Urals In.)	56·59 N	59·53 E
160	Billabong (R.) (bĭl'ă-bŏng) . Austl.	35·15 S	145·20 E
83	Billerica (bĭl'rĭk-à) Mass. (Boston In.)	42·33 N	71·46 W
110	Billericay ......Eng. (London In.)	51·38 N	0·25 E
67	Billings (bĭl'ĭngz) ....Mont.	45·47 N	108·29 W
69	Bill Williams (L.) (bĭl-wĭl'yumz) Ariz.	34·10 N	113·50 W
165	Bilma (bēl'mä) ....Niger.	18·41 N	13·20 E
78	Biloxi (bĭ-lŏk'sĭ) ....Miss.	30·24 N	88·50 W
168	Bilqas Qishm Awwal U. A. R. (Nile In.)	31·14 N	31·25 E
110	Bilston (bĭl'stŭn) ....Eng.	52·34 N	2·04 W
160	Bimberi Pk. (bĭm'bĕrĭ) ......Austl.	35·45 S	148·50 W
155	Binaja, Gunung (Mtn.) ....Indon.	3·07 S	129·25 E
155	Binalonan (bē-nä-lō'nän) Phil. (Manila In.)	16·03 N	120·35 E

Page	Name Pronunciation Region	Lat. °′	Long. °′
144	Binalud (Mtn.) ....Iran	36·32 N	58·34 E
155	Biñan (bē'nän) . Phil. (Manila In.)	14·20 N	121·06 E
120	Bingen (bĭn'gĕn) ....Ger.	49·57 N	7·54 E
164	Bingerville (băn-zhā-vēl') Ivory Coast	5·24 N	3·56 W
110	Bingham (bĭng'ăm) ....Eng.	52·57 N	0·57 W
82	Bingham ....Maine	45·03 N	69·51 W
74	Bingham Canyon Utah (Salt Lake City In.)	40·33 N	112·09 W
81	Binghamton (bĭng'ăm-tŭn) . . N. Y.	42·05 N	75·55 W
153	Bingo-Nada (Sea) (bĭn'gō nä-dä) Jap.	34·06 N	133·14 E
154	Binh Dinh (bĭng'dĭng') ......Viet.	13·55 N	109·00 E
160	Binnaway (bĭn'ă-wā) ....Austl.	31·42 S	149·22 E
139	Bintan, Palau (I.) (bĭn'tän) Indon. (Singapore In.)	1·09 N	104·43 E
154	Bintulu (bēn'tōō-lōō) ....Mala.	3·07 N	113·06 E
152	Bira (bē'rà) ....Sov. Un.	49·00 N	133·18 E
152	Bira (R.) ....Sov. Un.	48·55 N	132·25 E
167	Birakao ....Som.	1·14 S	41·47 E
139	Bi'r al Mazār U. A. R. (Palestine In.)	31·03 N	33·24 E
165	Bi'r al Wa'r (Oasis) ....Libya	22·51 N	14·22 E
142	Biratnagar (bĭ-rät'nŭ-gŭr) . . . Nep.	26·35 N	87·18 E
65	Birch Bay . Wash. (Vancouver In.)	48·55 N	122·45 W
65	Birch B. (bûrch) Wash. (Vancouver In.)	48·55 N	122·52 W
85	Birch Cliff (bĕrch klĭf) Can. (Toronto In.)	43·41 N	79·16 W
86	Birch Mts. ....Can.	57·36 N	113·10 W
65	Birch Pt. . . Wash. (Vancouver In.)	48·57 N	122·50 W
167	Bird (I.) (bĕrd) S. Afr. (Natal In.)	33·51 S	26·21 E
95	Bird Rock (I.) (bûrd) .....Ba. Is.	22·50 N	74·20 W
83	Bird Rock (I.) ....Can.	47·53 N	61·00 W
85	Birds Hill (bûrds) Can. (Winnipeg In.)	49·58 N	97·00 W
160	Birdsville (bûrdz'vĭl) ....Aust.	22·50 S	139·31 E
158	Birdum (bûrd'ŭm) ....Austl.	15·45 S	133·25 E
133	Birecik (bē-rĕd-zhĕk') ....Tur.	37·10 N	37·50 E
165	Bir en Natrūn ....Sud.	18·13 N	26·44 E
114	Bir er Ressof (bēr-ĕr-rĕ-sôf') . . Alg.	32·19 N	7·58 E
144	Bīrjand (bēr'jänd) ....Iran	33·07 N	59·16 E
65	Birkenfeld . . . . Ore. (Portland In.)	49·59 N	123·20 W
110	Birkenhead (bûr'kĕn-hĕd) . . . Eng.	53·23 N	3·02 W
111	Birkenwerder (bĕr'kĕn-vĕr-dĕr) Ger. (Berlin In.)	52·41 N	13·22 E
121	Bîrlad ....Rom.	46·15 N	27·43 E
84	Birmingham (bûr'mĭng-häm) Ala. (Birmingham In.)	33·31 N	86·49 W
110	Birmingham ....Eng.	52·29 N	1·53 W
75	Birmingham . . Mich. (Detroit In.)	42·32 N	83·13 W
74	Birmingham Mo. (Kansas City In.)	39·10 N	94·22 W
110	Birmingham, Can. ....Eng.	53·07 N	2·40 W
165	Bi'r Misāḥah (Oasis) . . . . U. A. R.	22·16 N	28·04 E
164	Birnin Kebbi ....Nig.	12·26 N	4·04 E
135	Birobidzhan (bē'rô-bê-jän') Sov. Un.	48·42 N	133·28 E
132	Birsk (bĭrsk) ....Sov. Un.	55·25 N	55·30 E
110	Birstall (bûr'stôl) ....Eng.	53·44 N	1·39 W
129	Biryuchiy (I.) (bĭr-yōō'chĭ) Sov. Un.	46·07 N	35·12 E
136	Biryulëvo (bēr-yōōl'yô-vô) Sov. Un. (Moscow In.)	55·35 N	37·39 E
134	Biryusa (R.) (bēr-yōō'sä) Sov. Un.	56·43 N	97·30 E
118	Biržai (bĕr-zhä'ē) ......Sov. Un.	56·11 N	24·45 E
165	Bi'r Zaltan ....Libya	28·20 N	19·40 E
69	Bisbee (bĭz'bē) ....Ariz.	31·30 N	109·55 W
113	Biscay, B. of (bĭs'kā') ....Eur.	45·19 N	3·51 W
79	Biscayne B. (bĭs-kān') . . . Fla. (In.)	25·22 N	80·15 W
123	Bischeim (bĭsh'hĭm) ....Fr.	48·40 N	7·48 E
136	Biser (bē'sĕr) . Sov. Un. (Urals In.)	58·24 N	58·54 E
126	Biševo (Is.) (bē'shĕ-vō) .....Yugo.	43·58 N	15·41 E
68	Bishop (bĭsh'ŭp) ....Calif.	37·22 N	118·25 W
77	Bishop ....Tex.	27·35 N	97·46 W
110	Bishop's Castle (bĭsh'ŏps käs''l) Eng.	52·29 N	2·57 W
79	Bishopville (bĭsh'ŭp-vĭl) .....S. C.	34·11 N	80·13 W
164	Biskra (bēs'krà) ....Alg.	34·52 N	5·39 E
70	Bismarck (bĭz'märk) ....N. D.	46·48 N	100·46 W
155	Bismarck Arch. .....N. Gui. Ter.	3·15 S	150·45 E
155	Bismarck Ra. ....N. Gui. Ter.	5·15 S	144·15 E
164	Bissau (bē-sä'ōō) ....Port. Gui.	11·52 N	15·47 W
77	Bistineau L. (bĭs-tĭ-nō') ....La.	32·19 N	93·45 W
121	Bistrita (bĭs'trĭt-sà) ....Rom.	47·09 N	24·29 E
121	Bistrita R. ....Rom.	47·08 N	25·47 E
133	Bitlis (bĭt-lēs') ....Tur.	38·30 N	42·00 E
127	Bitola (Monastir) (bē'tō-lä) (mô'nä-stêr) . Yugo.	41·02 N	21·22 E
126	Bitonto (bē-tôn'tō) ....It.	41·08 N	16·42 E
67	Bitter Cr. (bĭt'ĕr) ....Wyo.	41·36 N	108·29 W
120	Bitterfeld (bĭt'ĕr-fĕlt) ....Ger.	51·39 N	12·19 E
66	Bitterroot Ra. (bĭt'ĕr-ōōt) . . Mont.	47·15 N	115·13 W
67	Bitterroot R. ....Mont.	46·28 N	114·10 W
129	Bityug (R.) (bĭt'yōōg) . . . Sov. Un.	51·23 N	40·33 E
71	Biwabik (bē-wä'bĭk) ....Minn.	47·32 N	92·24 W
153	Biwa-ko (L.) (bē-wä'kō) Jap. (Ōsaka In.)	35·03 N	135·51 E
134	Biya (R.) (bĭ'yà) ....Sov. Un.	52·22 N	87·28 E
134	Biysk (bēsk) ....Sov. Un.	52·32 N	85·28 E
167	Bizana (bĭz-änä) S. Afr. (Natal In.)	30·51 S	29·54 E
164	Bizerte (bē-zĕrt') ....Tun.	37·23 N	9·52 E
150	Bizuta ....Mong.	41·28 N	115·10 E
126	Bjelovar (byĕ-lō'vär) ....Yugo.	45·54 N	16·53 E
	Bjorneborg, see Pori		
118	Bjorne Fd. (byûr'nĕ fyôrd) . . . Nor.	60·11 N	5·26 E
80	Black (L.) (blăk) ....Mich.	45·25 N	84·15 W
81	Black (L.) ....N. Y.	44·30 N	75·35 W
73	Black (R.) ....Ark.	35·47 N	91·22 W
81	Black (R.) ....N. Y.	43·45 N	75·20 W
79	Black (R.) ....S. C.	34·55 N	80·08 W
71	Black (R.) ....Wis.	44·07 N	90·56 W
159	Blackall (blăk'ăl) ....Austl.	24·23 S	145·37 E
71	Black B. (blăk) ....Can.	48·36 N	88·32 W

Page	Name Pronunciation Region	Lat. °′	Long. °′
64	Blackburn (blăk'bûrn) .....Alaska	63·20 N	159·45 W
110	Blackburn ....Eng.	53·45 N	2·28 W
64	Blackburn, Mt. ....Alaska	61·50 N	143·12 W
69	Black Canyon of the Gunnison Natl. Mon. (blăk kăn'yŭn) . Colo.	38·35 N	107·45 W
65	Black Diamond (dī'mŭnd) Wash. (Seattle In.)	47·19 N	122·00 W
116	Blackdown Hills (blăk'doun) . Eng.	50·58 N	3·19 W
71	Blackduck (blăk'dŭk) ......Minn.	47·41 N	94·33 W
67	Blackfoot (blăk'fŏŏt) ....Idaho	43·11 N	112·23 W
67	Blackfoot Ind. Res. ....Mont.	48·49 N	112·53 W
67	Blackfoot R. ....Mont.	46·53 N	113·33 W
67	Blackfoot River Res. ....Idaho	42·53 N	111·23 W
70	Black Hills (Reg.) ....S. D.	44·08 N	103·47 W
82	Black Lake ....Can.	46·02 N	71·24 W
69	Black Mesa (blăk māsá) .....Ariz.	36·33 N	110·40 W
85	Blackmud Cr. (blăk'mŭd) Can. (Edmonton In.)	53·28 N	113·34 W
110	Blackpool (blăk'pōōl) ....Eng.	53·49 N	3·02 W
69	Black Ra. ....N. Mex.	33·15 N	107·55 W
94	Black River (blăk') ....Jam.	18·00 N	77·50 W
75	Black R. . . . . Ohio (Cleveland In.)	41·26 N	82·08 W
151	Black R. ....Viet.	20·56 N	104·30 E
71	Black River Falls ....Wis.	44·18 N	90·51 W
66	Black Rock Des. (rŏk) ......Nev.	40·55 N	119·00 W
79	Blacksburg (blăks'bûrg) .....S. C.	35·09 N	81·30 W
103	Black Sea ....Eur.-Asia	43·01 N	32·16 E
79	Blackshear (blăk'shĭr) ....Ga.	31·20 N	82·15 W
79	Blackstone (blăk'stôn) ....Va.	37·04 N	78·00 W
71	Black Sturgeon (R.) (stû'jŭn) . Can.	49·12 N	88·41 W
161	Blacktown (blăk'toun) Austl. (Sydney In.)	33·47 S	150·55 E
82	Blackville (blăk'vĭl) ....Can.	46·44 N	65·50 W
79	Blackville ....S. C.	33·21 N	81·19 W
164	Black Volta R. (vōl'tà) Upper Volta	11·21 N	4·21 W
78	Black Warrior (R.) (blăk wŏr'ĭ-ēr) Ala.	32·37 N	87·42 W
78	Black Warrior (R.), Locust Fk. Ala.	34·06 N	86·27 W
78	Black Warrior (R.), Mulberry Fk. Ala.	34·06 N	86·32 W
116	Blackwater (blăk-wô'tēr) .....Ire.	52·05 N	9·02 W
73	Blackwater (R.) ....Mo.	38·53 N	93·22 W
79	Blackwater (R.) ....Va.	37·07 N	77·10 W
73	Blackwell (blăk'wĕl) ....Okla.	36·47 N	97·19 W
111	Bladel . . . . Neth. (Amsterdam In.)	51·22 N	5·15 E
133	Blagodarnoye (blä'gô-där-nō'yĕ) Sov. Un.	45·00 N	43·30 E
127	Blagoevgrad (Gorna Dzhumaya) Bul.	42·01 N	23·06 E
135	Blagoveshchensk (blä'gŏ-vyĕsh'-chĕnsk) . Sov. Un.	50·16 N	127·47 E
136	Blagoveshchensk Sov. Un. (Urals In.)	55·03 N	56·00 E
65	Blaine (blān) Wash. (Vancouver In.)	48·59 N	122·49 W
81	Blaine ....W. Va.	39·25 N	79·10 W
70	Blair (blâr) ....Nebr.	41·33 N	96·09 W
86	Blairmore (blâr-mōr) ....Can.	49·38 N	114·20 W
81	Blairsville (blârs'vĭl) ....Pa.	40·30 N	79·40 W
65	Blake (I.) (blāk) . Wash. (Seattle In.)	47·37 N	122·28 W
78	Blakely (blāk'lē) ....Ga.	31·22 N	84·55 W
164	Blanc, Cap (C.) ....Mauritania	20·39 N	18·08 W
123	Blanc, Mt. (môn blän) . . . . . Fr.-It.	45·50 N	6·53 E
100	Blanca, Bahia (B.) (bä-ē'ä-blàn'kä) . Arg.	39·30 S	61·00 W
72	Blanca Pk. (blăŋ'kà) ....Colo.	37·36 N	105·22 W
160	Blanch, L. (blănch) ....Austl.	29·20 S	139·12 E
85	Blanche, R. . . . Can. (Ottawa In.)	45·34 N	75·38 W
75	Blanchester (blăn'chĕs-tēr) Ohio (Cincinnati In.)	39·18 N	83·58 W
100	Blanco, C. (blăŋ'kō) ....Arg.	47·08 S	65·47 W
92	Blanco, Cabo (C.) (kä'bô-blăŋ'kō) C. R.	9·29 N	85·15 W
66	Blanco, C. (blăn'kō) ....Ore.	42·53 N	124·38 W
91	Blanco (R.) ....Mex.	18·42 N	96·03 W
90	Blanco (R.) ....Mex.	24·05 N	99·21 W
94	Blancos, Cayo (I.) (kä'yō-blăŋ'kōs) . Cuba	23·15 N	80·55 W
69	Blanding ....Utah	37·40 N	109·31 W
117	Blankenburg (blăŋ'kĕn-bōōrgh) Ger.	51·45 N	13·07 E
111	Blankenfelde (blăn'kĕn-fĕl-dĕ) Ger. (Berlin In.)	52·20 N	13·24 E
91	Blanquilla, Arrecife (Reef) (är-rĕ-sē'fĕ-blän-kē'l-yä) . Mex.	21·32 N	97·14 W
166	Blantyre-Limbe (blăn-tīyr-lĭmb) Malawi	15·48 S	35·07 E
75	Blasdell (blăz'dĕl) N. Y. (Buffalo In.)	42·48 N	78·51 W
126	Blato (blä'tō) ....Yugo.	42·55 N	16·47 E
118	Blåvands Huk (cape) (blŏ'văns-hōk) Den.	55·36 N	7·35 E
122	Blaye-et-Ste. Luce (blā'ā-sănt-lüs') . Fr.	45·08 N	0·40 W
121	Błazowa (bwä-zhō'vä) ....Pol.	49·51 N	22·05 E
164	Blida ....Alg.	36·33 N	2·45 E
87	Blind River (blīnd) ....Can.	46·10 N	83·09 W
80	Blissfield (blĭs-fēld) ....Mich.	41·50 N	83·50 W
110	Blithe (R.) (blĭth) ....Eng.	52·22 N	1·49 W
81	Block (I.) (blŏk) ....R. I.	41·05 N	71·35 W
168	Bloemfontein (blōōm'fŏn-tān) S. Afr. (Johannesburg & Pretoria In.)	29·09 S	26·16 E
122	Blois (blwä) ....Fr.	47·36 N	1·21 E
71	Bloomer (blōōm'ēr) ....Wis.	45·07 N	91·30 W
80	Bloomfield (blōōm'fēld) ......Ind.	39·00 N	86·55 W
71	Bloomfield ....Iowa	40·44 N	92·21 W
73	Bloomfield ....Mo.	36·54 N	89·55 W
70	Bloomfield ....Nebr.	42·36 N	97·40 W
84	Bloomfield . N. J. (New York In.)	40·48 N	74·12 W
75	Bloomfield Hills Mich. (Detroit In.)	42·35 N	83·15 W
71	Blooming Prairie (blōōm'ĭng prâ'rĭ) . Minn.	43·52 N	93·04 W

ăt; finăl; rāte; senāte; ärm; åsk; sofá; fâre; ch-choose; dh-as th in other; bē; ēvent; bĕt; recĕnt; cratēr; g-go; gh-guttural g; bĭt; ĭ-short neutral; rīde; ĸ-guttural k as ch in German ich;

Page	Name	Pronunciation	Region	Lat. °'	Long. °'
74	Bloomington	(bloom'ĭng-tŭn) Calif. (Los Angeles In.)		34·04 N	117·24 W
80	Bloomington		Ill.	40·30 N	89·00 W
80	Bloomington		Ind.	39·10 N	86·35 W
74	Bloomington		Minn. (Minneapolis, St. Paul In.)	44·50 N	93·18 W
81	Bloomsburg	(bloomz'bûrg)	Pa.	41·00 N	76·25 W
84	Blossburg	(blŏs'bûrg) Ala. (Birmingham In.)		33·38 N	86·57 W
81	Blossburg		Pa.	41·45 N	77·00 W
166	Bloubergstrand		S. Afr. (Cape Town In.)	33·48 S	18·28 E
78	Blountstown	(blŭnts'tun)	Fla.	30·24 N	85·02 W
120	Bludenz	(bloo-děnts')	Aus.	47·09 N	9·50 E
83	Blue, Mt.		Can.	50·28 N	57·11 W
75	Blue Ash	(bloo ăsh) Ohio (Cincinnati In.)		39·14 N	84·23 W
71	Blue Earth	(bloo ûrth)	Minn.	43·38 N	94·05 W
71	Blue Earth (R.)		Minn.	43·55 N	94·16 W
79	Bluefield	(bloo'feld)	W. Va.	37·15 N	81·11 W
93	Bluefields	(bloo'feldz)	Nic.	12·03 N	83·45 W
75	Blue Island		Ill. (Chicago In.)	41·39 N	87·41 W
160	Blue Mts.		Austl.	33·35 S	149·00 E
94	Blue Mts.		Jam.	18·05 N	76·35 W
66	Blue Mts.		Ore.	45·15 N	118·50 W
158	Blue Mud B.	(bloo mŭd)	Austl.	13·20 S	136·45 E
	Blue Nile, see El Azraq, Bahr				
73	Blue Rapids	(bloo răp'ĭdz)	Kans.	39·40 N	96·41 W
63	Blue Ridge (Mts.)	(bloo rĭj)	U. S.	35·30 N	82·50 W
86	Blue River		Can.	52·09 N	119·21 W
74	Blue R.		Mo. (Kansas City In.)	38·55 N	94·33 W
69	Bluff		Utah	37·18 N	109·34 W
80	Bluffton	(blŭf-tŭn)	Ind.	40·40 N	85·15 W
80	Bluffton	(blŭf-tŭn)	Ohio	40·50 N	83·55 W
100	Blumenau	(bloo'měn-ou)	Braz.	26·53 S	48·58 W
139	Blumut, Gunong (Mt.)		Mala. (Singapore In.)	2·03 N	103·34 E
65	Blyn	(blĕn)	Wash. (Seattle In.)	48·01 N	123·00 W
116	Blyth	(blĭth)	Eng.	55·03 N	1·34 W
68	Blythe		Calif.	33·37 N	114·37 W
73	Blytheville	(blĭth'vĭl)	Ark.	35·55 N	89·51 W
155	Boac		Phil. (Manila In.)	13·26 N	121·50 E
92	Boaco	(bō-ä'kō)	Nic.	12·24 N	85·41 W
99	Boa Vista do Rio Branco	(bō'ä vēsh'tä dōō rē'ōō brän'kōō)	Braz.	2·46 N	60·45 W
164	Boa Vista I.	(bō-ä-vēsh'tä)	C. V. Is. (In.)	16·01 N	23·52 W
121	Boberka	(bō'bĕr-kà)	Sov. Un.	49·36 N	24·18 E
164	Bobo-Dioulasso	(bō'bō-dyōō-läs-sō')	Upper Volta	11·13 N	4·13 W
128	Bobr	(bō'b'r)	Sov. Un.	54·19 N	29·11 E
129	Bobrinets	(bō'brē-nyĭts)	Sov. Un.	48·04 N	32·10 E
120	Bóbr R.	(bŭ'br)	Pol.	51·44 N	15·13 E
129	Bobrov	(bō-rōf')	Sov. Un.	51·07 N	40·01 E
129	Bobrovitsa	(bŭb-rô'vē-tsà)	Sov. Un.	50·43 N	31·27 E
128	Bobruysk	(bŏ-broo'ĭsk)	Sov. Un.	53·07 N	29·13 E
99	Boca del Pozo	(bō-kä-děl-pō'zō)	Ven. (In.)	11·00 N	64·21 W
99	Boca de Uchire	(bô-kä-dě-ōō-chē'rě)	Ven. (In.)	10·09 N	65·27 W
101	Bocaina, Serra da (Mtn.)	(sě'r-rä-dä-bô-kä'ē-nä)	Braz. (Rio de Janeiro In.)	22·47 S	44·39 W
90	Bocas	(bō'käs)	Mex.	22·29 N	101·03 W
93	Bocas del Toro	(bō'käs děl tō'rō)	Pan.	9·24 N	82·15 W
121	Bochnia	(bōĸ'nyä)	Pol.	49·58 N	20·28 E
123	Bocholt	(bō'ĸōlt)	Ger. (Ruhr In.)	51·50 N	6·37 E
123	Bochum	(bō'ĸōōm)	Ger. (Ruhr In.)	51·29 N	7·13 E
123	Bockum-Hövel	(bō'ĸōōm-hû'fĕl)	Ger. (Ruhr In.)	51·41 N	7·45 E
135	Bodaybo	(bō-dī'bō)	Sov. Un.	57·12 N	114·46 E
165	Bodele Depression	(bō-dā-lā')	Chad	17·21 N	16·38 E
112	Boden		Swe.	65·51 N	21·29 E
120	Boden See (L.)	(bō'děn zā)	Ger.	47·48 N	9·22 E
168	Bodenstein	(bō'děn-stān)	S. Afr. (Johannesburg & Pretoria In.)	26·20 S	26·27 E
116	Boderg	(bō'dûrg)	Ire.	53·51 N	8·06 W
116	Bodmin	(bŏd'mĭn)	Eng.	50·29 N	4·45 W
116	Bodmin Moor	(bŏd'mĭn mōōr)	Eng.	50·36 N	4·43 W
112	Bodø	(bŏd'ŭ)	Nor.	67·13 N	14·19 E
166	Boende	(bō-ĕn'dà)	Con. K.	0·21 S	21·06 E
76	Boerne	(bō'ĕrn)	Tex.	29·49 N	98·44 W
77	Boeuf R.	(běf)	La.	32·23 N	91·57 W
164	Boffa	(bō'fä)	Gui.	10·13 N	14·06 W
153	Bōfu	(bō'fōō)	Jap.	34·03 N	131·35 E
77	Bogalusa	(bō-gä-loo'sä)	La.	30·48 N	89·52 W
160	Bogan (R.)	(bō'gĕn)	Austl.	32·10 S	147·40 E
118	Bogense	(bō'gĕn-sě)	Den.	55·34 N	10·09 E
93	Boggy Pk.	(bŏg'ĭ-pēk)	Antigua (Le. & Wind. Is. In.)	17·03 N	61·50 W
129	Bogodukhov	(bō-gŏ-dōō'ĸōf)	Sov. Un.	50·10 N	35·31 E
160	Bogong, Mt.		Austl.	36·50 S	147·15 E
154	Bogor		Indon.	6·45 S	106·45 E
128	Bogoroditsk	(bō-gŏ'rō-dĭtsk)	Sov. Un.	53·48 N	38·06 E
132	Bogorodsk		Sov. Un.	56·02 N	43·40 E
136	Bogorodskoye	(bō-gŏ-rŏd'skō-yě)	Sov. Un. (Urals In.)	56·43 N	56·53 E
98	Bogotá	(bō-gō-tä')	Col. (In.)	4·38 N	74·06 W
98	Bogotá, Rio (R.)	(rē'ō-bō-gō-tä')	Col. (In.)	4·27 N	74·38 W
134	Bogotol	(bŏ'gô-tŏl)	Sov. Un.	56·13 N	89·13 E
129	Bogoyavlenskoye	(bō-gō-yäf'lěn-skō'yě)	Sov. Un.	48·46 N	31·49 E
133	Boguchar	(bō'gōō-chär)	Sov. Un.	49·40 N	41·00 E
93	Boguete	(bō'gā'tě)	Pan.	8·54 N	82·29 W
129	Boguslav	(bō'gōō-släf)	Sov. Un.	49·34 N	30·51 E
122	Bohain-en-Vermandois	(bô-ăN-ŏN-vâr-mäN-dwä')	Fr.	49·58 N	3·22 E
	Bohemia, see Ceske				
120	Bohemian For.	(bō-hē'mǐ-ăn)	Ger.	49·35 N	12·27 E
155	Bohol (I.)	(bō-hōl')	Phil.	9·28 N	124·35 E
91	Bohom	(bō-ō'm)	Mex.	16·47 N	92·42 W
168	Bohotleh	(bō-hŏt'lě)	Som. (Horn of Afr. In.)	8·15 N	46·20 E
82	Boiestown	(boiz'toun)	Can.	46·27 N	66·25 W
127	Boin (R.)	(bō'ěn)	Yugo.	44·19 N	17·54 E
80	Bois Blanc (I.)	(boi' blänk)	Mich.	45·45 N	84·30 W
85	Boischatel	(bwä-shä-těl')	Can. (Quebec In.)	46·54 N	71·08 W
85	Bois-des-Filion	(bōō-ä'dě-fě-yōN')	Can. (Montreal In.)	45·40 N	73·46 W
66	Boise	(boi'zē)	Idaho	43·38 N	116·12 W
72	Boise City		Okla.	36·42 N	102·30 W
66	Boise R.		Idaho	43·43 N	116·30 W
86	Boissevain	(bois'vān)	Can.	49·11 N	100·01 W
145	Boizabād		Afg.	37·13 N	70·38 E
164	Bojador, Cabo (C.)	(kä'bō-bō-hä-dōr') (bōj-à-dôr')	Sp. Sah.	26·21 N	16·08 W
164	Boké	(bō-kā')	Gui.	10·58 N	14·15 W
118	Bokn Fd.	(bôk''n fyôrd)	Nor.	59·12 N	5·37 E
167	Boksburg	(bōĸs'bûrgh)	S. Afr. (Johannesburg & Pretoria In.)	26·13 S	28·15 E
164	Bolama	(bō-lä'mä)	Port. Gui.	11·34 N	15·41 W
142	Bolan Mt.	(bō-län')	W. Pak.	35·13 N	67·09 E
90	Bolaños	(bō-län'yōs)	Mex.	21·40 N	103·48 W
90	Bolaños (R.)		Mex.	21·26 N	103·54 W
142	Bolan P.		W. Pak.	34·50 N	67·10 E
122	Bolbec	(bōl-běk')	Fr.	49·37 N	0·26 E
164	Bole	(bō'lä)	Ghana	9·02 N	2·28 W
120	Boleslawiec	(bō-lě-slä'vyěts)	Pol.	51·15 N	15·35 E
129	Bolgrad	(bōl-grät')	Sov. Un.	45·41 N	28·38 E
155	Bolinao	(bō-lē-nä'ō)	Phil. (Manila In.)	16·24 N	119·53 E
155	Bolinao, C.		Phil. (Manila In.)	16·24 N	119·42 E
101	Bolívar	(bō-lē'vär)	Arg. (Buenos Aires In.)	36·15 S	61·05 W
98	Bolívar		Col.	1·46 N	76·58 W
73	Bolivar	(bŏl'ĭ-vàr)	Mo.	37·37 N	93·22 W
78	Bolivar		Tenn.	35·14 N	88·56 W
98	Bolívar (La Columna) (Mtn.)	(bō-lē'vär) (lä-kō-loo'm-nä)	Ven.	8·44 N	70·54 W
77	Bolivar Pen.	(bŏl'ĭ-vàr)	Tex. (In.)	29·25 N	94·40 W
96	Bolivia	(bō-lĭv'ĭ-à)	S. A.	17·00 S	64·00 W
128	Bolkhov	(bōl-ĸōf')	Sov. Un.	53·27 N	35·59 E
110	Bollin (R.)	(bŏl''n)	Eng.	53·18 N	2·11 W
110	Bollington	(bŏl'ĭng-tŭn)	Eng.	53·18 N	2·06 W
118	Bollnäs	(bŏl'něs)	Swe.	61·22 N	16·20 E
118	Bolmen (L.)	(bŏl'měn)	Swe.	56·58 N	13·25 E
166	Bolobo	(bō'lō-bō)	Con. K.	2·14 S	16·18 E
126	Bologna	(bō-lōn'yä)	It.	44·30 N	11·18 E
128	Bologoye	(bō-lŏ-gô'yě)	Sov. Un.	57·52 N	34·02 E
92	Bolonchenticul	(bō-lōn-chěn-tē-kōō'l)	Mex. (Yucatan In.)	20·03 N	89·47 W
94	Bolondrón	(bō-lōn-drōn')	Cuba	22·45 N	81·25 W
126	Bolseno, Lago di (L.)	(lä'gō-dē-bōl-sā'nō)	It.	42·35 N	11·40 E
132	Bol'shaya Kinel' (R.)		Sov. Un.	53·20 N	52·40 E
129	Bol'shaya Lepetikha	(bōl-shà'yà lyě'pyě-tē'ĸä)	Sov. Un.	47·11 N	33·58 E
129	Bol'shaya Viska	(vĭs-kä')	Sov. Un.	48·34 N	31·54 E
129	Bol'shaya Vradiyevka	(vrä-dyěf'kà)	Sov. Un.	47·51 N	30·38 E
136	Bol'she Ust'ikinskoye	(bōl'she ōōs-tyĭ-kēn'skô-yě)	Sov. Un. (Urals In.)	55·58 N	58·18 E
135	Bolshoy Anyuy (R.)		Sov. Un.	67·58 N	161·15 E
135	Bol'shoy Begichëv (I.)		Sov. Un.	74·30 N	114·40 E
135	Bolshoy Chuva (R.)		Sov. Un.	58·15 N	111·13 E
136	Bol'shoye Ivonino	(ǐ-vô'nǐ-nô)	Sov. Un. (Urals In.)	59·41 N	61·12 E
136	Bol'shoy Kuyash	(bōl'-shôy kōō'yäsh)	Sov. Un. (Urals In.)	55·52 N	61·07 E
129	Bolshoy Tokmak	(bōl-shôy' tôk-mäk')	Sov. Un.	47·17 N	35·48 E
76	Bolson de Mapimi	(bôl-sŏ'n-dě-mä-pē'mē)	Mex.	28·07 N	104·30 W
110	Bolsover	(bōl'zô-věr)	Eng.	53·14 N	1·17 W
125	Boltana	(bōl-tä'nä)	Sp.	42·28 N	0·03 E
85	Bolton	(bōl'tŭn)	Can. (Toronto In.)	43·53 N	79·44 W
110	Bolton		Eng.	53·35 N	2·26 W
110	Bolton-on-Dearne	(bōl'tŭn-ŏn-dûrn)	Eng.	53·31 N	1·19 W
133	Bolu	(bō'lōō)	Tur.	40·45 N	31·45 E
128	Bolva (R.)	(bōl'vä)	Sov. Un.	53·30 N	34·30 E
133	Bolvadin	(bōl-vä-děn')	Tur.	38·50 N	30·50 E
126	Bolzano	(bōl-tsä'nō)	It.	46·29 N	9·22 E
166	Boma	(bō'mä)	Con. K.	5·45 S	13·05 E
160	Bombala	(bŭm-bä'lä)	Austl.	36·55 S	149·07 E
143	Bombay	(bŏm-bā')	India (Bombay In.)	18·58 N	72·50 E
142	Bombay (State)		India	20·27 N	72·56 E
143	Bombay Hbr.		India (Bombay In.)	18·55 N	72·52 E
164	Bomi Hills		Lib.	7·00 N	11·00 W
101	Bom Jardim	(bôn zhär-dēN')	Braz. (Rio de Janeiro In.)	22·10 S	42·25 W
101	Bom Jesus do Itabapoana	(bōN-zhě-sōō's-dô-ē-tä'bä-pô-ä'nä)	Braz. (Rio de Janeiro In.)	21·08 S	41·51 W
118	Bömlo (I.)	(bûmlô)	Nor.	59·47 N	4·57 E
165	Bomongo		Con. K.	1·35 N	18·20 E
101	Bom Sucesso	(bôn-sōō-sě'sō)	Braz. (Rio de Janeiro In.)	21·02 S	44·44 W
113	Bon, C.	(bŏn)	Tun.	37·04 N	11·13 E
98	Bonaire (I.)	(bô-nâr')	Neth. Antilles	12·10 N	68·15 W
124	Boñar	(bō-nyär')	Sp.	42·53 N	5·18 W
83	Bonavista	(bō-nä-vǐs'tä)	Can.	48·40 N	53·09 W
83	Bonavista B.		Can.	48·48 N	53·20 W
72	Bond	(bŏnd)	Colo.	39·53 N	106·40 W
165	Bondo	(bōn'dō)	Con. K.	3·49 N	23·43 E
155	Bondoc Pen.	(bŏn-dōk')	Phil. (Manila In.)	13·24 N	122·30 E
155	Bondoc Pt.		Phil. (Manila In.)	13·11 N	122·20 E
164	Bondoukou	(bŏn-dōō'kōō)	Ivory Coast	8·06 N	3·47 W
94	Bonds Cay (I.)	(bŏnds kē)	Ba. Is.	25·30 N	77·45 W
	Bône, see Annaba				
154	Bone, Teluk (L.)		Indon.	4·09 S	121·00 E
100	Bonete, Cerro (Mt.)	(bō'nětěh çěrrō)	Arg.	27·50 S	68·35 W
101	Bonfim	(bōn-fē'n)	Braz. (Rio de Janeiro In.)	20·20 S	44·15 W
165	Bongos, Massif des (Mts.)		Cen. Afr. Rep.	8·04 N	21·59 E
151	Bong Son		Viet.	14·20 N	109·10 E
73	Bonham	(bŏn'ăm)	Tex.	33·35 N	96·09 W
95	Bonhomme, Pic (Pk.)		Hai.	19·10 N	72·20 W
126	Bonifacio	(bō-nē-fä'chō)	It.	41·23 N	9·10 E
126	Bonifacio, Str. of		Eur.	41·14 N	9·02 E
78	Bonifay	(bŏn-ĭ-fā')	Fla.	30·46 N	85·40 W
156	Bonin Is.	(bō'nǐn)	Asia	26·30 N	141·00 E
123	Bonn	(bŏn)	Ger. (Ruhr In.)	50·44 N	7·06 E
66	Bonners Ferry	(bon'erz fěr'ǐ)	Idaho	48·41 N	116·19 W
74	Bonner Springs	(bŏn'ěr sprǐngz)	Kans. (Kansas City In.)	39·04 N	94·52 W
73	Bonne Terre	(bŏn tär')	Mo.	37·55 N	90·32 W
66	Bonneville Dam	(bŏn'ě-vǐl)	Wash.-Ore.	45·37 N	121·57 W
83	Bonnie B.	(bŏn'ě)	Can.	49·38 N	58·15 W
164	Bonny	(bŏn'ě)	Nig.	4·29 N	7·13 E
65	Bonny Lake	(bŏn'ě lǎk)	Wash. (Seattle In.)	47·11 N	122·11 W
126	Bonorva	(bō-nôr'vä)	It.	40·26 N	8·46 E
154	Bonthain	(bōn-tīn')	Indon.	5·30 S	119·52 E
155	Bontoc	(bōn-tŏk')	Phil. (Manila In.)	17·10 N	121·01 E
94	Booby Rocks (I.)	(bōō'bǐ rŏks)	Ba. Is.	25·55 N	77·00 W
79	Booker T. Washington Natl. Mon.	(bōōk'ěr tē wŏsh'ĭng-tŭn)	Va.	37·07 N	79·45 W
111	Boom		Bel. (Brussels In.)	51·05 N	4·22 E
71	Boone	(bōōn)	Iowa	42·04 N	93·51 W
84	Boone		Va. (Norfolk In.)	36·50 N	76·26 W
73	Boone		N. C.	36·09 N	81·42 W
80	Booneville	(bōōn'vǐl)	Ark.	35·09 N	93·54 W
80	Booneville		Ky.	37·25 N	83·40 W
78	Booneville		Miss.	34·37 N	88·35 W
168	Boons		S. Afr. (Johannesburg & Pretoria In.)	25·59 S	27·15 E
84	Boonton	(bōōn'tŭn)	N. J. (New York In.)	40·54 N	74·24 W
80	Boonville		Ind.	38·00 N	87·15 W
73	Boonville		Mo.	38·57 N	92·44 W
82	Boothbay Harbor	(bōōth'bä här'běr)	Maine	43·51 N	69·39 W
87	Boothia, G. of	(bōō'thǐ-à)	Can.	69·04 N	86·04 W
49	Boothia Pen.		Can.	73·30 N	95·00 W
110	Bootle	(bōōt'l)	Eng.	53·29 N	3·02 W
164	Boporo	(bō-pô'rō)	Lib.	7·13 N	10·47 W
120	Boppard	(bŏp'ärt)	Ger.	50·14 N	7·35 E
165	Bor	(bor)	Sud.	6·13 N	31·35 E
133	Bor	(bôr)	Tur.	37·50 N	34·40 E
67	Borah Pk.	(bō'rä)	Idaho	44·12 N	113·47 W
168	Borama	(bôr-á-mä)	Som. (Horn of Afr. In.)	10·05 N	43·08 E
118	Borås	(bō-rôs')	Swe.	57·43 N	12·55 E
144	Borāzjān	(bō-räz-jän')	Iran	29·13 N	51·13 E
99	Borba	(bôr'bä)	Braz.	4·23 S	59·31 W
99	Borborema, Planalto da (Plat.)	(plä-näl'tô-dä-bôr-rě'mä)	Braz.	7·35 S	36·40 W
122	Bordeaux	(bôr-dō')	Fr.	44·50 N	0·37 W
81	Bordentown	(bôr'děn-toun)	N. J.	40·05 N	74·40 W
113	Bordj-bou-Arréridj	(bôrj-bōō-à-rä-rēj')	Alg.	36·03 N	4·48 E
119	Borgå	(bôr'gō)	Fin.	60·26 N	25·41 E
112	Borgarnes		Ice.	64·31 N	21·40 W
72	Borger	(bôr'gēr)	Tex.	35·40 N	101·23 W
118	Borgholm	(bôrg-hôlm')	Swe.	56·52 N	16·40 E
77	Borgne L.	(bôrn'y')	La.	30·03 N	89·36 W
126	Borgomanero	(bôr'gō-mä-nā'rō)	It.	45·40 N	8·28 E
125	Borgo Montello	(bô'r-zhō-môn-tě'lō)	It. (Rome In.)	41·31 N	12·48 E
126	Borgo Val di Taro	(bô'r-zhō-väl-dē-tä'rō)	It.	44·29 N	9·44 E
65	Boring	(bōr'ǐng)	Ore. (Portland In.)	45·26 N	122·22 W
121	Borislav	(bō'rǐs-lôf)	Sov. Un.	49·17 N	23·24 E
133	Borisoglebsk	(bō-rē-sō-glyěpsk')	Sov. Un.	51·23 N	42·00 E
128	Borisov	(bō-rē'sôf)	Sov. Un.	54·16 N	28·33 E
129	Borisovka	(bō-rē-sôf'kä)	Sov. Un.	50·38 N	36·00 E
129	Borispol'	(bo-rǐs'pol)	Sov. Un.	50·17 N	30·54 E
143	Borivli		India (Bombay In.)	19·15 N	72·48 E
124	Borja	(bôr'hä)	Sp.	41·50 N	1·33 W
125	Borjas Blancas	(bô'r-käs-blä'n-käs)	Sp.	41·29 N	0·53 E
123	Borken	(bôr'kěn)	Ger. (Ruhr In.)	51·50 N	6·51 E
165	Borkou (Reg.)	(bôr-kōō')	Chad.	18·18 N	18·28 E
120	Borkum I.	(bôr'kōōm)	Ger.	53·31 N	6·50 E
118	Borlänge	(bôr-lěŋ'ě)	Swe.	60·30 N	15·24 E
154	Borneo (I.)	(bôr'ně-ō)	Asia	0·25 N	112·39 E
118	Bornholm (I.)	(bôrn-hôlm')	Den.	55·16 N	15·15 E
124	Bornos	(bôr'nōs)	Sp.	36·48 N	5·45 W
129	Borodayevka		Sov. Un.	48·44 N	34·09 E
129	Boromlya	(bō-rôm''l-yä)	Sov. Un.	50·38 N	34·59 E
127	Borovan	(bō-rô-vän')	Bul.	43·24 N	23·47 E
128	Borovichi	(bō-rō-vē'chē)	Sov. Un.	58·23 N	33·56 E
128	Borovsk	(bō'rôvsk)	Sov. Un.	55·13 N	36·26 E
99	Borracha, Isla la (I.)	(ě's-lä-lä-bôr-rä'chä)	Ven. (In.)	10·18 N	64·44 W
158	Borroloola	(bō-rō-loo'lä)	Austl.	16·15 S	136·19 E
121	Borshchëv	(bôrsh-chyôf')	Sov. Un.	48·47 N	26·04 E
122	Bort-les-Orgues	(bôr-lā-zôrg)	Fr.	45·26 N	2·26 E
144	Borūjerd		Iran	33·45 N	48·53 E

ng-sing; ŋ-baŋk; N-nasalized n; nŏd; cŏmmit; ōld; ōbey; ôrder; fōōd; fŏŏt; ou-out; s-soft; sh-dish; th-thin; pūre; ūnite; ûrn; stŭd; circŭs; ü-as "y" in study; '-indeterminate vowel.

186 Borzna – Bridlington PRONOUNCING INDEX

Page	Name Pronunciation Region	Lat. °′	Long. °′
129	Borzna (bôrz'ná) ....Sov. Un.	51·15 N	32·26 E
135	Borzya (bôrz'yà) ....Sov. Un.	50·37 N	116·53 E
126	Bosa (bō'sä) ....It.	40·18 N	8·34 E
126	Bosanska Dubica (bō'sän-skä		
	dōō'bĭt-sä) . Yugo.	45·10 N	16·49 E
126	Bosanska Gradiška (bō'sän-skä		
	gra-dĭsh'kä) . Yugo.	45·08 N	17·15 E
126	Bosanski Novi (bō's sän-skĭ nō'vē)		
	Yugo.	45·00 N	16·22 E
126	Bosanski Petrovac (bō'sän-skĭ		
	pĕt'rō-väts) . Yugo.	44·33 N	16·23 E
127	Bosanski Šamac		
	(bō'sän-skĭ shä'mȧts) . Yugo.	45·03 N	18·30 E
71	Boscobel (bŏs'kō-bĕl) ....Wis.	43·08 N	90·44 W
136	Boskol' (bás-kôl')		
	Sov. Un. (Urals In.)	53·45 N	61·17 E
111	Boskoop . . Neth. (Amsterdam In.)	52·04 N	4·39 E
120	Boskovice (bŏs'kō-vē-tsĕ) . . Czech.	49·26 N	16·37 E
127	Bosnia (Reg.) (bŏs'nĭ-ȧ) . . . . Yugo.	44·17 N	16·58 E
	Bosporous, see İstanbul Boğazı		
77	Bossier City (bŏsh'ēr) ....La.	32·31 N	93·42 W
78	Boston (bôs'tŭn) ....Ga.	30·47 N	83·47 W
83	Boston........Mass. (Boston In.)	42·15 N	71·07 W
75	Boston Heights		
	Ohio (Cleveland In.)	41·15 N	81·30 W
73	Boston Mts. ....Ark.	35·46 N	93·32 W
161	Botany B. (bŏt'ȧ-nĭ)		
	Austl. (Sydney In.)	33·58 S	151·11 E
127	Botevgrad ....Bul.	42·54 N	23·41 E
168	Bothaville (bō'tä-vĭl) ......S. Afr.		
	(Johannesburg & Pretoria In.)	27·24 S	26·38 E
65	Bothell (bŏth'ĕl)		
	Wash. (Seattle In.)	47·46 N	122·12 W
112	Bothnia, G. of (bŏth'nĭ-ȧ) . . . . Eur.	61·45 N	19·45 E
121	Botosani (bô-tô-shán'ĭ) ......Rom.	47·46 N	26·40 E
163	Botswana (bŏtswănä) ....Afr.	22·10 S	23·13 E
70	Bottineau (bŏt-ĭ-nō') ....N. D.	48·48 N	100·28 W
123	Bottrop (bōt'trōp) . Ger. (Ruhr In.)	51·31 N	6·56 E
99	Botucatú (bô-tōō-kä-tōō') . . . Braz.	22·50 S	48·23 W
83	Botwood (bŏt'wŏŏd) ....Can.	49·10 N	55·23 W
164	Bouaflé (bōō-ȧ-flā') . . Ivory Coast	7·23 N	5·32 W
164	Bouaké (bōō-ȧ-kā') . . . Ivory Coast	7·45 N	5·08 W
165	Bouar (bōō-är) . . . . Cen. Afr. Rep.	6·04 N	15·34 E
83	Bouche ....Can.	45·37 N	61·25 W
85	Boucherville (bōō-shä-vēl')		
	Can. (Montreal In.)	45·37 N	73·27 W
164	Bou Denib (bōō-dĕ-nēb') . . . . Mor.	32·14 N	3·04 W
71	Boudette (bōō-dĕt) ....Minn.	48·42 N	94·34 W
113	Bou Dia, C. (bōō dē'ȧ) ......Tun.	35·18 N	11·17 E
125	Boudouaou ....Alg.	36·44 N	1·27 E
125	Boufarik (bōō-fȧ-rēk') ....Alg.	36·35 N	2·55 E
156	Bougainville Trench		
	(bōō-găN-vēl') . Oceania	7·00 S	152·00 E
	Bougie, see Bejaia		
164	Bougouni (bōō-gōō-nē') ......Mali	11·27 N	7·30 W
114	Bouira (boo-ē'rȧ) ....Alg.	36·25 N	3·55 W
125	Bouïra-Sahary (bwē-rȧ sȧ'ȧ-rē)		
	Alg.	35·16 N	3·23 E
158	Boulder (bōl'dēr) ....Austl.	31·00 S	121·40 E
72	Boulder ....Colo.	40·02 N	105·19 W
68	Boulder City ....Nev.	35·57 N	114·50 W
66	Boulder Cr. ....Idaho	42·53 N	116·49 W
67	Boulder Pk. ....Idaho	43·53 N	114·33 W
67	Boulder R. ....Mont.	46·10 N	112·07 W
164	Boulé R. (bōō-lā') ....Mali	10·53 N	7·30 W
123	Boulogne-Billancourt (bōō-lôn'y'-		
	bē-yäN-kōōr') . Fr. (Paris In.)	48·50 N	2·14 E
122	Boulogne-sur-Mer		
	(bōō-lôn'y-sür-mâr') . Fr.	50·44 N	1·37 E
125	Bou-Mort, Sierra de (Mts.)		
	(sē-ĕ'r-rä-dĕ-bō-ō-mō'rt) . Sp.	42·11 N	1·05 E
164	Bouna (bōō-nä') ......Ivory Coast	9·14 N	3·56 W
65	Boundary B. (boun'dȧ-rĭ)		
	Can. (Vancouver In.)	49·03 N	122·59 W
68	Boundary Pk. ....Nev.	37·52 N	118·20 W
84	Bound Brook (bound brŏŏk)		
	N. J. (New York In.)	40·34 N	74·32 W
74	Bountiful (boun'tĭ-fŏŏl)		
	Utah (Salt Lake City In.)	40·55 N	111·53 W
75	Bountiful Pk. (boun'tĭ-fŏŏl)		
	Utah (Salt Lake City In.)	40·58 N	111·49 W
47	Bounty Is. ....N. Z.	47·42 S	179·05 E
164	Bourem (bōō-rĕm') ....Mali	16·43 N	0·15 W
122	Bourg-en-Bresse (bōōr-gĕN-brĕs')		
	Fr.	46·12 N	5·13 E
122	Bourges (bōōrzh) ....Fr.	47·06 N	2·22 E
85	Bourget (bōōr-zhĕ')		
	Can. (Ottawa In.)	45·26 N	75·09 W
123	Bourgoin (bōōr-gwăN') ....Fr.	45·46 N	5·17 E
160	Bourke (bûrk) ....Austl.	30·10 S	146·00 E
135	Bour Khaya, Guba (B.) . Sov. Un.	71·45 N	131·00 E
110	Bourne (bôrn) ....Eng.	52·46 N	0·22 W
116	Bournemouth (bôrn'mŭth) . . . Eng.	50·44 N	1·55 W
114	Bou Saada (bōō-sä'dä) ....Alg.	35·13 N	4·17 E
165	Bousso (bōō-sō') ....Chad	10·33 N	16·45 E
164	Boutilimit (bōō-tē-lē-mē')		
	Mauritania	17·30 N	14·54 W
	Bouvet (I.), see Bouvetøya		
47	Bouvetøya (Bouvet) (I.) . . . Atl. O.	54·26 S	3·24 E
126	Bovino (bō-vē'nō) ....It.	41·14 N	15·21 E
86	Bow (R.) (bō) ....Can.	50·33 N	112·25 W
70	Bowbells (bō'bĕls) ....N. D.	48·50 N	102·16 W
70	Bowdle (bōd''l) ....S. D.	45·28 N	99·42 W
159	Bowen (bō'ĕn) ....Austl.	20·02 S	148·14 E
84	Bowers Hill (bou'ērs)		
	Va. (Norfolk In.)	36·47 N	76·25 W
84	Bowie (bōō'ĭ) (bō'ē)		
	Md. (Baltimore In.)	39·01 N	76·48 W
72	Bowie ....Tex.	33·34 N	97·50 W
78	Bowling Green (bōlĭng grēn) . . Ky.	37·00 N	86·26 W
73	Bowling Green ....Mo.	39·19 N	91·09 W
80	Bowling Green ....Ohio	41·25 N	83·40 W
70	Bowman (bō'măn) ....N. D.	46·11 N	103·23 W
81	Bowmanville (bō'măn-vĭl) . . . Can.	43·50 N	78·40 W
85	Bowness.......Can. (Calgary In.)	51·06 N	114·13 W
155	Bowokan, Pulau-Pulau (Is.) . Indon.	2·20 S	123·45 E
70	Boxelder Cr. (bŏks'ĕl-dēr) . . Mont.	45·35 N	104·28 W
67	Boxelder Cr. ....Mont.	47·17 N	108·37 W
74	Box Springs (bŏks sprĭngz)		
	Calif (Los Angeles In.)	33·55 N	117·17 W
111	Boxtel . . . . Neth. (Amsterdam In.)	51·40 N	5·21 E
85	Boyer, R. (boi'ēr)		
	Can. (Quebec In.)	46·46 N	70·56 W
70	Boyer (R.) ....Iowa	41·45 N	95·36 W
116	Boyle (boil) ....Ire.	53·59 N	8·15 W
80	Boyne City ....Mich.	45·15 N	85·05 W
116	Boyne R. (boin) ....Ire.	53·40 N	6·40 W
127	Bozcaada (Tenedos) (bōz-cä'dä)		
	(tĕ'nĕ-dŏs) . Tur.	39·50 N	26·05 E
127	Bozcaada (I.) (bōz-cä'dä) . . . . Tur.	39·50 N	26·00 E
67	Bozeman (bōz'măn) ....Mont.	45·41 N	111·00 W
126	Bra (brä) ....It.	44·41 N	7·52 E
126	Brač (I.) (bräch) ....Yugo.	43·18 N	16·36 E
126	Bracciano, Lago di (L.)		
	(lä'gō-dē-brä-chä'nō) . It.	42·05 N	12·00 E
81	Bracebridge (brās'brĭj) ......Can.	45·05 N	79·20 W
75	Braceville (brās'vĭl)		
	Ill. (Chicago In.)	41·13 N	88·16 W
118	Bräcke (brĕk'kĕ) ....Swe.	62·44 N	15·28 E
75	Brackenridge (brăk'ĕn-rĭj)		
	Pa. (Pittsburgh In.)	40·37 N	79·44 W
76	Brackettville (brăk'ĕt-vĭl) . . . . Tex.	29·19 N	100·24 W
99	Braço Maior (R.) ....Braz.	11·00 S	51·00 W
99	Braço Menor (R.) (brä'zō-		
	mĕ-nō'r) . Braz.	11·38 S	50·00 W
126	Brádano (R.) (brä-dä'nō) ......It.	40·43 N	16·22 E
75	Braddock (brăd'ŭk)		
	Pa. (Pittsburgh In.)	40·24 N	79·52 W
79	Bradenton (brā'dĕn-tŭn) . Fla. (In.)	27·28 N	82·35 W
110	Bradfield (brăd-fēld)		
	Eng. (London In.)	51·25 N	1·08 W
110	Bradford (brăd'fērd) ....Eng.	53·47 N	1·44 W
80	Bradford ....Ohio	40·10 N	84·30 W
81	Bradford ....Pa.	42·00 N	78·40 W
75	Bradley (brăd'lĭ) . Ill. (Chicago In.)	41·09 N	87·52 W
65	Bradner (brăd'nēr)		
	Can. (Vancouver In.)	49·05 N	122·26 W
76	Brady (brā'dĭ) ....Tex.	31·09 N	99·21 W
124	Braga (brä'gä) ....Port.	41·20 N	8·25 W
101	Bragado (brä-gä'dō)		
	Arg. (Buenos Aires In.)	35·07 S	60·28 W
99	Bragança (brä-gän'sä) ....Braz.	1·02 S	46·50 W
124	Bragança ....Port.	41·48 N	6·46 W
101	Bragança Paulista (brä-gän'sä-		
	pä'ōō-lē's-tȧ)		
	Braz. (Rio de Janeiro In.)	22·58 S	46·31 W
85	Bragg Creek (brăg)		
	Can. (Calgary In.)	50·57 N	114·35 W
145	Brahmaputra (R.) (brä'mȧ-		
	pōō'trȧ) . India	26·45 N	92·45 E
145	Brahui (Reg.) ....W. Pak.	28·32 N	66·15 E
75	Braidwood (brād'wŏŏd)		
	Ill. (Chicago In.)	41·16 N	88·13 W
129	Brăila (brē'ēlä) ....Rom.	45·15 N	27·58 E
71	Brainerd (brān'ērd) ....Minn.	46·20 N	94·09 W
83	Braintree (brān'trē)		
	Mass. (Boston In.)	42·14 N	71·00 W
84	Braithwaite (brĭth'wĭt)		
	La. (New Orleans In.)	29·52 N	89·57 W
167	Brakpan (brăk'păn) ....S. Afr.		
	(Johannesburg & Pretoria In.)	26·15 S	28·22 E
168	Brakspruit . S. Afr.		
	(Johannesburg & Pretoria In.)	26·41 S	26·34 E
85	Brampton (brămp'tŭn)		
	Can. (Toronto In.)	43·41 N	79·46 W
100	Branca, Pedra (Mtn.)		
	(pĕ'drä-brä'N-kä) . Braz. (In.)	22·55 S	43·28 W
84	Branchville (brănch'vĭl)		
	N. J. (New York In.)	41·09 N	74·44 W
79	Branchville ....S. C.	33·17 N	80·48 W
99	Branco (R.) (brăn'kō) ......Braz.	2·21 N	60·38 W
166	Brandberg (Mtn.) ......S. W. Afr.	21·15 S	14·15 E
111	Brandenburg (brăn'dĕn-bŏŏrgh)		
	Ger. (Berlin In.)	52·25 N	12·33 E
120	Brandenburg (Reg.) ....Ger.	52·12 N	13·31 E
168	Brandfort (brăn'd-fôrt)		
	S. Afr. (Johannesburg &		
	Pretoria In.)	28·42 S	26·29 E
86	Brandon (brăn'dŭn) ....Can.	49·42 N	99·53 W
81	Brandon ....Vt.	43·45 N	73·05 W
116	Brandon Hill (brăn-dŏn) . . . . . Ire.	52·15 N	10·12 W
84	Brandywine (brăndĭ'wīn)		
	Md. (Baltimore In.)	38·42 N	76·51 W
81	Branford (brăn'fērd) ....Conn.	41·15 N	72·50 W
121	Braniewo (brä-nyĕ'vô) ....Pol.	54·23 N	19·50 E
168	Brankhorstspruit		
	S. Afr. (Johannesburg &		
	Pretoria In.)	24·47 S	28·45 E
121	Brańsk (brän' sk) ....Pol.	52·44 N	22·51 E
85	Brantford (brănt'fērd)		
	Can. (Toronto In.)	43·09 N	80·17 W
83	Bras d'Or L. (brä-dôr') ......Can.	45·53 N	60·47 W
99	Brasília (brä-sē'lyä) ....Braz.	15·49 S	47·39 W
99	Brasília Legal (Fordlândia)		
	(brä-sē'lyä-lĕ-gäl) (fô'rd-län-dyä)		
	Braz.	3·45 S	55·46 W
101	Brasópolis (brä-sô'pô-lēs)		
	Braz. (Rio de Janeiro In.)	22·30 S	45·36 W
127	Brașov (Orașul-Stalin) ......Rom.	45·39 N	25·35 E
164	Brass (brăs) ....Nig.	4·28 N	6·28 E
111	Brasschaat (bräs'κät)		
	Bel. (Brussels In.)	51·19 N	5·30 E
75	Bratenahl (bră'tĕn-ôl)		
	Ohio (Cleveland In.)	41·34 N	81·36 W
111	Bratislava (brä'tĭs-lȧ-vä)		
	Czech (Vienna In.)	48·09 N	17·07 E
134	Bratsk (brätsk) ....Sov. Un.	56·10 N	102·04 E
129	Bratslav (brät'slȧf) ......Sov. Un.	48·48 N	28·59 E
81	Brattleboro (brăt''l-bŭr-ô) . . . . Vt.	42·50 N	72·35 W
120	Braunau (brou'nou) ....Aus.	48·15 N	13·05 E
120	Braunschweig (broun'shvīgh) . Ger.	52·16 N	10·32 E
168	Brava (brä'vä)		
	Som. (Horn of Afr. In.)	1·20 N	44·00 E
118	Bråviken (R.) ....Swe.	58·40 N	16·40 E
	Bravo del Norte, Rio, see Grande,		
	Rio		
68	Brawley (brô'lĭ) ....Calif.	32·59 N	115·32 W
116	Bray (brā) ....Ire.	53·10 N	6·05 W
73	Braymer (brā'mēr) ....Mo.	39·34 N	93·47 W
77	Brays Bay . (brās'bī'yōō) . Tex. (In.)	29·41 N	95.33 W
86	Brazeau ....Can.	52·31 N	116·00 W
80	Brazil (brȧ-zĭl') ....Ind.	39·30 N	87·00 W
96	Brazil ....S. A.	9·00 S	53·00 W
96	Brazilian Highlands (Mts.)		
	(brȧ zĭl yăn hī-lăndz . Braz.	14·00 S	48·00 W
62	Brazos (R.) (brä'zōs) ....U. S.	33·10 N	98·50 W
76	Brazos (R.), Clear Fk. ....Tex.	32·56 N	99·14 W
72	Brazos (R.), Double Mountain Fk.		
	Tex.	33·23 N	101·21 W
72	Brazos (R.), Salt Fk. (sôlt fôrk)		
	Tex.	33·20 N	100·57 E
166	Brazzaville (brȧ-zȧ-vēl') . . . Con. B.	4·10 S	15·18 E
127	Brčko (bĕrch'kō) ....Yugo.	44·54 N	18·46 E
121	Brda R. (bĕr-dä') ....Pol.	53·18 N	17·55 E
74	Brea (brē'ȧ)		
	Calif. (Los Angeles In.)	33·55 N	117·54 W
85	Breakeyville . . . . Can. (Quebec In.)	46·40 N	71·13 W
70	Breckenridge (brĕk'ĕn-rĭj) . . Minn.	46·17 N	96·35 W
76	Breckenridge ....Tex.	32·46 N	98·53 W
75	Brecksville (brĕks'vĭl)		
	Ohio (Cleveland In.)	41·19 N	81·38 W
120	Břeclav (brzhĕl'läf) ....Czech.	48·46 N	16·54 E
116	Brecon Beacons (brĕk'ŭn bē kŭns)		
	Wales	52·00 N	3·55 W
111	Breda (brā-dä')		
	Neth. (Amsterdam In.)	51·35 N	4·47 E
166	Bredasdorp (brā'das-dôrp) . S. Afr.	34·15 S	20·00 E
136	Bredy (brĕ'dĭ) . Sov. Un. (Urals In.)	52·25 N	60·23 E
120	Bregenz (brā'gĕnts) ....Aus.	47·30 N	9·46 E
127	Bregovo (brĕ'gô-vô) ....Bul.	44·07 N	22·45 E
167	Breidbach (brēd'băk)		
	S. Afr. (Natal In.)	32·54 S	27·26 E
112	Breidha Fd. (brā'dĭ) ....Ice.	65·15 N	22·50 W
123	Breil (brĕ'y') ....Fr.	43·57 N	7·36 E
99	Brejo (brå'zhŏŏ) ....Braz.	3·33 S	42·46 W
118	Bremangerland (I.)		
	(brĕ-mängĕr-lănd) . Nor.	61·51 N	4·25 E
120	Bremen (brā-mĕn) ....Ger.	53·05 N	8·50 E
80	Bremen (brē'mĕn) ....Ind.	41·25 N	86·05 W
120	Bremerhaven (brām-ēr-hä'fĕn) . Ger.	53·33 N	8·38 E
65	Bremerton (brĕm'ēr-tŭn)		
	Wash. (Seattle In.)	47·34 N	122·38 W
111	Bremervörde (brĕ'mĕr-fûr-dĕ)		
	Ger. (Hamburg In.)	53·29 N	9·09 E
85	Bremner (brĕm'nēr)		
	Can (Edmonton In.)	53·34 N	113·14 W
77	Bremond (brĕm'ŭnd) ....Tex.	31·11 N	96·40 W
77	Brenham (brĕn'ăm) ....Tex.	30·10 N	96·24 W
120	Brenner P. (brĕn'ēr) ......Aus.-It.	47·00 N	11·30 E
110	Brentwood (brĕnt'wŏŏd)		
	Eng. (London In.)	51·37 N	0·18 E
81	Brentwood ....Md.	39·00 N	76·55 W
74	Brentwood . . . . Mo. (St. Louis In.)	38·37 N	90·21 W
75	Brentwood . . . Pa. (Pittsburgh In.)	40·22 N	79·59 W
126	Brescia (brā'shä) ....It.	45·33 N	10·15 E
	Breslau, see Wrocław		
126	Bressanone (brĕs-sä-nō'nā) . . . . It.	46·42 N	11·40 E
122	Bressuire (brĕ-swēr') ....Fr.	46·49 N	0·14 W
122	Brest (brĕst) ....Fr.	48·24 N	4·30 W
121	Brest ....Sov. Un.	52·06 N	23·43 E
128	Brest (Oblast) ....Sov. Un.	52·30 N	26·50 E
122	Bretagne, Monts de (Mts.) (mŏN-		
	dĕ-brĕ-tăN'yĕ) . Fr.	48·25 N	3·36 W
122	Breton, Pertvis (Str.)		
	(pâr-twē'brĕ-tôN') . Fr.	46·18 N	1·43 W
78	Breton Sd. (brĕt'ŭn) ....La.	29·38 N	89·15 W
85	Bretona (brĕ-tō'nä)		
	Can. (Edmonton In.)	53·27 N	113·20 W
111	Breukelen Neth. (Amsterdam In.)	52·09 N	5·00 E
79	Brevard (brē-värd') ....N. C.	35·14 N	82·45 W
99	Breves (brā'vĕzh) ....Braz.	1·32 S	50·13 W
118	Brevik (brĕ'vĕk) ....Nor.	59·04 N	9·39 E
160	Brewarrina (brōō-ēr-rē'nȧ) . . Austl.	29·54 S	146·50 E
82	Brewer (brōō'ēr) ....Maine	44·46 N	68·46 W
84	Brewster (brōō'stēr)		
	N. Y. (New York In.)	41·23 N	73·38 W
93	Brewster, Cerro (Mt.) (sĕ'r-rô-		
	brōō'stēr) . Pan.	9·19 N	79·15 W
78	Brewton (brōō'tŭn) ....Ala.	31·06 N	87·04 W
126	Brežice (brĕ'zhē-tsĕ) ....Yugo.	45·55 N	15·37 E
127	Breznik (brĕs'nêk) ....Bul.	42·44 N	22·55 E
123	Briancon (brē-äN-sôN') ....Fr.	44·54 N	6·39 E
122	Briare (brē-är') ....Fr.	47·40 N	2·46 E
65	Bridal Veil (brīd'ăl vāl)		
	Ore. (Portland In.)	45·33 N	122·10 W
94	Bridge Pt. (brĭj) ....Ba. Is.	25·35 N	76·40 W
78	Bridgeport (brĭj'pôrt) ....Ala.	34·55 N	85·42 W
84	Bridgeport . Conn. (New York In.)	41·12 N	73·12 W
80	Bridgeport ....Ill.	38·40 N	87·45 W
75	Bridgeport . Ind. (Indianapolis In.)	39·44 N	86·18 W
70	Bridgeport ....Nebr.	41·40 N	103·06 W
80	Bridgeport ....Ohio	40·00 N	80·45 W
84	Bridgeport . Pa. (Philadelphia In.)	40·06 N	75·21 W
72	Bridgeport ....Tex.	33·13 N	97·46 W
84	Bridgeton (brĭj'tŭn)		
	Ala. (Birmingham In.)	33·27 N	86·39 W
81	Bridgeton ....N. J.	39·30 N	75·15 W
82	Bridgetown ....Can.	44·51 N	65·21 W
93	Bridgetown (brĭj' toun)		
	Barb. (Le. & Wind. Is. In.)	13·08 N	59·37 W
75	Bridgeville (brĭj'vĭl)		
	Pa. (Pittsburgh In.)	40·22 N	80·07 W
160	Bridgewater (brĭj'wô-tēr) . . . Austl.	42·50 S	147·28 E
82	Bridgewater ....Can.	44·24 N	64·34 W
110	Bridgnorth (brĭj'nôrth) ......Eng.	52·32 N	2·25 W
82	Bridgton (brĭj'tŭn) ....Maine	44·04 N	70·45 W
116	Bridlington (brĭd'lĭng-tŭn) . . . Eng.	54·06 N	0·10 W

ăt; finăl; rāte; senāte; ärm; åsk; sofȧ; fâre; ch-choose; dh-as th in other; bē; ēvent: bĕt; recĕnt; cratēr; g-go; gh-guttural g; bĭt; ĭ-short neutral; rīde; κ-guttural k as ch in German ich;

PRONOUNCING INDEX Brie-Comte-Robert—Burdur 187

Page	Name Pronunciation Region	Lat. °'	Long. °'
123	Brie-Comte-Robert (brē-kôɴt-ē-rō-bâr') . Fr. (Paris In.)	48·42 N	2·37 E
111	Brielle.... Neth. (Amsterdam In.)	51·54 N	4·08 E
82	Brier (I.) (brī'ẽr)........... Can.	44·16 N	66·24 W
78	Brierfield (brī'ẽr-fēld)........ Ala.	33 01 N	86·55 W
110	Brierfield (brī'ẽr fēld)........ Eng.	53·49 N	2·14 W
110	Brierley Hill (brī'ẽr-lē hĭl).... Eng.	52·28 N	2·07 W
111	Brieselang (brē'zĕ-läng) Ger. (Berlin In.)	52·36 N	12·59 E
123	Briey (brē-ĕ')................ Fr.	49·15 N	5·57 E
120	Brig (brēg).............. Switz.	46·17 N	7·59 E
110	Brigg (brĭg).............. Eng.	53·33 N	0·29 W
74	Brigham City (brĭg'ăm) Utah (Salt Lake City In.)	41·31 N	112·01 W
110	Brighouse (brĭg'hous)....... Eng.	53·42 N	1·47 W
160	Bright (brīt)............... Austl.	36·43 S	147·00 E
75	Bright (brīt) . Ind. (Cincinnati In.)	39·13 N	84·51 W
110	Brightlingsea (brī't-lĭng-sē) Eng. (London In.)	51·50 N	1·00 E
84	Brighton (brīt'ŭn) Ala. (Birmingham In.)	33·27 N	86·56 W
72	Brighton................. Colo.	39·58 N	104·49 W
116	Brighton................. Eng.	50·47 N	0·07 W
74	Brighton....... Ill. (St. Louis In.)	39·03 N	90·08 W
71	Brighton................. Iowa	41·11 N	91·47 W
83	Brigus (brĭg'ŭs)........... Can.	47·31 N	53·11 W
124	Brihuega (brē-wā'gä)......... Sp.	40·32 N	2·52 W
74	Brimley (brĭm lē) Mich. (Sault Ste. Marie In.)	46·24 N	84·34 W
127	Brindisi (brēn'dē-zē).......... It.	40·38 N	17·57 E
126	Brinje (brēn'yĕ).......... Yugo.	45·00 N	15·08 E
73	Brinkley (brĭŋk'lĭ).......... Ark.	34·52 N	91·12 W
65	Brinnon (brĭn'ŭn) Wash. (Seattle In.)	47·41 N	122·54 W
83	Brion (brē-ôɴ')............ Can.	47·47 N	61·26 W
122	Brioude (brē-ōōd')............ Fr.	45·18 N	3·22 E
160	Brisbane (brĭz' bān)....... Austl.	27·30 S	153·10 E
81	Bristol (brĭs' tŭl).......... Conn.	41·40 N	72·55 W
116	Bristol.................... Eng.	51·29 N	2·39 W
84	Bristol..... Pa. (Philadelphia In.)	40·06 N	74·51 W
84	Bristol...... R.I. (Providence In.)	41·41 N	71·14 W
79	Bristol.................. Tenn.	36·35 N	82·10 W
81	Bristol...................... Vt.	44·10 N	73·00 W
79	Bristol..................... Va.	36·36 N	82·12 W
75	Bristol...... Wis. (Milwaukee In.)	42·32 N	88·04 W
64	Bristol B................ Alaska	58·08 N	158·54 W
116	Bristol Chan.............. Eng.	51·20 N	3·47 E
73	Bristow (brĭs'tō).......... Okla.	35·50 N	96·25 W
86	British Columbia (Prov.) (brĭt'ĭsh kŏl'ŭm-bĭ-ȧ) . Can.	56·00 N	124·53 W
88	British Honduras (hŏn-dōō'rȧs) N. A.	17·00 N	88·40 W
168	Brits . S. Afr. (Johannesburg & Pretoria In.)	25·39 S	27·47 E
166	Britstown (brĭts'toun)..... S. Afr.	30·30 S	23·40 E
71	Britt (brĭt)................ Iowa	43·05 N	93·47 W
70	Britton (brĭt'ŭn).......... S. D.	45·47 N	97·44 W
122	Brive-la-Gaillarde (brēv-lä-gī-yärd'ĕ) . Fr.	45·10 N	1·31 E
124	Briviesca (brē-vyās'kȧ)........ Sp.	42·34 N	3·21 W
120	Brno (b'r'nô)............ Czech.	49·18 N	16·37 E
94	Broa, Ensenada de la (B.) (ĕn-sĕ-nä'-dä-dĕ-lä-brō'ȧ) . Cuba	22·30 N	82·00 W
78	Broad (R.) (brôd)............ Ga.	34·15 N	83·14 W
79	Broad (R.)................ N. C.	35·38 N	82·40 W
161	Broadmeadows (brôd'mĕd-ōz) Austl. (Melbourne In.)	37·40 S	144·53 E
75	Broadview Heights (brôd'vū) Ohio (Cleveland In.)	41·18 N	81·41 W
81	Brockport (brŏk'pōrt)........ N. Y.	43·15 N	77·55 W
83	Brockton (brŏk'tŭn) Mass. (Boston In.)	42·04 N	71·01 W
81	Brockville (brŏk'vĭl)........ Can.	44·35 N	75·40 W
67	Brockway (brŏk'wā)....... Mont.	47·24 N	105·41 W
121	Brodnica (brôd'nĭt-sȧ)........ Pol.	53·16 N	19·26 E
121	Brody (brô'dĭ)......... Sov. Un.	50·05 N	25·10 E
73	Broken Arrow (brō'kĕn ăr'ō) . Okla.	36·03 N	95·48 W
161	Broken B..... Austl. (Sydney In.)	33·34 S	151·20 E
70	Broken Bow (brō'kĕn bō).... Nebr.	41·24 N	99·37 W
73	Broken Bow.............. Okla.	34·02 N	94·43 W
160	Broken Hill (brōk'ĕn)...... Austl.	31·55 S	141·35 E
166	Broken Hill............ Zambia	14·18 S	28·28 E
110	Bromley (brŭm'lĭ) Eng. (London In.)	51·23 N	0·01 E
81	Bromptonville (brŭmp'tŭn-vĭl) Can.	45·30 N	72·00 W
118	Brønderslev (brûn'dẽr-slĕv).. Den.	57·15 N	9·56 E
136	Bronnitsy (brô-nyĭ'tsĭ) Sov. Un. (Moscow In.)	55·26 N	38·16 E
80	Bronson (brŏn'sŭn)........ Mich.	41·55 N	85·15 W
85	Bronte (brōɴt) Can. (Toronto In.)	43·24 N	79·43 W
85	Bronte Cr..... Can. (Toronto In.)	43·25 N	79·53 W
79	Brood (R.) (brōōd).......... S. C.	34·46 N	81·25 W
85	Brook, The (R.) Can. (Ottawa In.)	45·25 N	75·09 W
75	Brookfield (brŏŏk'fēld) Ill. (Chicago In.)	41·49 N	87·51 W
73	Brookfield................. Mo.	39·45 N	93·04 W
84	Brookhaven (brŏŏk'hāv'n) Ga. (Atlanta In.)	33·52 N	84·21 W
78	Brookhaven.............. Miss.	31·35 N	90·26 W
66	Brookings (brŏŏk'ĭngs)....... Ore.	42·04 N	124·16 W
70	Brookings................ S. D.	44·18 N	96·47 W
85	Brooklands (brŏŏk'lăndz) Can. (Winnipeg In.)	49·56 N	97·12 W
83	Brookline (brŏŏk'lĭn) Mass. (Boston In.)	42·20 N	71·08 W
83	Brookline..... N. H. (Boston In.)	42·44 N	71·37 W
75	Brooklyn (brŏŏk'lĭn) Ohio (Cleveland In.)	41·26 N	81·44 W
74	Brooklyn Center Minn. (Minneapolis, St. Paul In.)	45·05 N	93·21 W
75	Brook Park (brŏŏk) Ohio (Cleveland In.)	41·24 N	81·50 W
64	Brooks Range (brŏŏks).... Alaska	68·20 N	159·00 W
79	Brooksville (brŏŏks'vĭl) . Fla. (In.)	28·32 N	82·28 W
80	Brookville (brŏŏk'vĭl)........ Ind.	39·20 N	85 00 W
81	Brookville.................. Pa.	41·10 N	79·00 W
78	Brookwood (brŏŏk'wŏŏd)..... Ala.	33·15 N	87·17 W
116	Broom (L.) (brōōm)........ Scot.	57·59 N	5·32 W
158	Broome (brōōm)........... Austl.	18·00 S	122·15 E
94	Brothers (Is.) (brŭd'hẽrs).. Ba. Is.	26·05 N	79·00 W
120	Broumov (brōō'môf)...... Czech.	50·33 N	15·55 E
95	Brown Bk............... Ba. Is.	21·30 N	74·35 W
72	Brownfield (broun'fēld)...... Tex.	33·11 N	102·16 W
110	Brownhills (broun'hĭlz)...... Eng.	52·38 N	1·55 W
67	Browning (broun'ĭng)...... Mont.	48·37 N	113·05 W
75	Brownsboro (brounz'bô-rô) Ky. (Louisville In.)	38·22 N	85·30 W
85	Brownsburg (brouns'bûrg) Can. (Montreal In.)	45·40 N	74·24 W
75	Brownsburg Ind. (Indianapolis In.)	39·51 N	86·23 W
65	Brownsmead (brounz'-mēd) Ore. (Portland In.)	46·13 N	123·33 W
80	Brownstown (brounz'toun)... Ind.	38·50 N	86·00 W
78	Brownsville (brounz'vĭl).... Tenn.	35·35 N	89·15 W
77	Brownsville................ Tex.	25·55 N	97·30 W
82	Brownville (broun'vĭl)..... Maine	45·20 N	69·04 W
76	Brownwood (broun'wŏŏd).... Tex.	31·44 N	98·58 W
76	Brownwood L............... Tex.	31·55 N	99·15 W
124	Brozas (brō'thäs)............ Sp.	39·37 N	6·44 W
158	Bruce, Mt. (brōōs).......... Austl.	22·35 S	118·15 E
78	Bruceton (brōōs'tŭn)....... Tenn.	36·02 N	88·14 W
120	Bruchsal (brŏŏk'zäl)........ Ger.	49·08 N	8·34 E
120	Bruck (brŏŏk).............. Aus.	47·25 N	15·14 E
111	Brück (brük).... Ger. (Berlin In.)	52·12 N	12·45 E
111	Bruck an der Leitha Aus. (Vienna In.)	48·01 N	16·47 E
85	Bruederheim (brōō'dẽr-hīm) Can. (Edmonton In.)	53·47 N	113·56 W
117	Brugge.................... Bel.	51·13 N	3·05 E
123	Brühl (brül)...... Ger. (Ruhr In.)	50·49 N	6·54 E
66	Bruneau R. (brōō-nō')...... Idaho	42·47 N	115·43 W
154	Brunei..................... Asia	4·52 N	113·38 E
154	Brunei (brōō-nī')............ Bru.	5·00 N	114·59 E
123	Brünen (brü'nĕn) . Ger. (Ruhr In.)	51·43 N	6·41 E
125	Brunete (brōō-nā'tȧ) Sp. (Madrid In.)	40·24 N	4·00 W
83	Brunette (I.) (brōō-nĕt')..... Can.	47·17 N	55·55 W
111	Brunn am Gebirge (brōōn'äm gĕ-bĭr'gĕ) Aus. (Vienna In.)	48·07 N	16·18 E
111	Brunsbüttelkoog (brōōns'büt-tĕl-kōg) . Ger. (Hamburg In.)	53·58 N	9·10 E
79	Brunswick (brŭnz'wĭk)....... Ga.	31·08 N	81·30 W
82	Brunswick............... Maine	43·54 N	69·57 W
81	Brunswick................. Md.	39·20 N	77·35 W
73	Brunswick................. Mo.	39·25 N	93·07 W
75	Brunswick... Ohio (Cleveland In.)	41·14 N	81·50 W
100	Brunswick, Pen. de.......... Chile	53·25 S	71·15 W
59	Bruny (I.) (brōō'nē)....... Austl.	43·30 S	47·50 E
72	Brush (brŭsh).............. Colo.	40·14 N	103·40 W
100	Brusque (brōō's-kōōĕ)....... Braz.	27·15 S	48·45 W
74	Brussels (brŭs'ĕls) Ill. (St. Louis In.)	38·57 N	90·36 W
	Brussels, see Bruxelles		
111	Bruxelles (Brussels) (brü-sĕl') (brŭs'ĕls) . Bel. (Brussels In.)	50·51 N	4·21 E
80	Bryan (brī'ăn).............. Ohio	41·25 N	84·30 W
77	Bryan..................... Tex.	30·40 N	96·22 W
128	Bryansk (b'r-yänsk')..... Sov. Un.	53·12 N	34·23 E
128	Bryansk (Oblast)...... Sov. Un.	52·43 N	32·25 E
70	Bryant (brī'ănt)............ S. D.	44·35 N	97·29 E
65	Bryant....... Wash. (Seattle In.)	48·14 N	122·10 W
69	Bryce Canyon Natl. Park (brīs) Utah	37·35 N	112·15 W
84	Bryn Mawr (brĭn mär') Pa. (Philadelphia In.)	40·02 N	75·20 W
78	Bryson City (brīs'ŭn)...... N. C.	35·25 N	83·25 W
129	Bryukhovetskaya (b'ryŭk'ô-vyĕt-skä'yä) . Sov. Un.	45·56 N	38·58 E
139	Buatam.... Indon. (Singapore In.)	0·45 N	101·49 E
164	Buba (bōō'bȧ)......... Port. Gui.	11·39 N	14·58 W
98	Bucaramanga (bōō-kä'rä-mäŋ'gä) Col.	7·12 N	73·14 W
155	Bucay (bōō-kī') . Phil. (Manila In.)	17·32 N	120·42 E
158	Buccaneer Arch. (bŭk-ȧ-nẽr') Austl.	16·05 S	122·00 E
121	Buchach (bŏŏ'chäch).... Sov. Un.	49·04 N	25·25 E
164	Buchanan (bû-kăn'ăn)....... Lib.	6·05 N	10·10 W
80	Buchanan................. Mich.	41·50 N	86·25 W
159	Buchanan (L.) (bû-kân'nŏn) . Austl.	21·45 S	21·02 E
76	Buchanan L. (bû-kăn'ăn).... Tex.	30·55 N	98·40 W
83	Buchans................... Can.	48·49 N	56·54 W
	Bucharest, see București		
111	Buchholtz (bōōk'hōltz) Ger. (Hamburg In.)	53·19 N	9·53 E
75	Buck Cr. (bŭk) Ind. (Indianapolis In.)	39·43 N	85·58 W
81	Buckhannon (bŭk-hăn'ŭn) W. Va.	39·00 N	80·10 W
116	Buckhaven (bŭk-hā'v'n).... Scot.	56·10 N	3·10 W
116	Buckie (bŭk'ĭ).............. Scot.	57·40 N	2·50 W
85	Buckingham (bŭk'ĭng-ăm) Can. (Ottawa In.)	45·35 N	75·25 W
142	Buckingham (R.) (bŭk'ĭng-ăm) India	15·18 N	79·50 E
85	Buckland (bŭk'lănd) Can. (Quebec In.)	46·37 N	70·33 W
159	Buckland Tableland, (Reg.) Austl.	24·31 S	148·00 E
65	Buckley (bŭk'lē) Wash. (Seattle In.)	47·10 N	122·02 W
82	Bucksport (bŭks'pôrt)..... Maine	44·35 N	68·47 W
82	Buctouche (bŭk-tōōsh')...... Can.	46·30 N	64·42 W
127	București (Bucharest) (bōō-kōō-rĕsh'tĭ) (bōō-kȧ-rĕst') . Rom.	44·23 N	26·10 E
80	Bucyrus (bû-sī'rŭs).......... Ohio	40·50 N	82·55 W
121	Budapest (bōō'dȧ-pĕsht')... Hung.	47·30 N	19·05 E
123	Büderich (bü'dĕ-rēк) Ger. (Ruhr In.)	51·15 N	6·41 E
142	Budge-Budge . India (Calcutta In.)	22·28 N	88·08 E
75	Buechel (bē-chŭl') Ky. (Louisville In.)	38·12 N	85·38 W
123	Bueil (bwā')....... Fr. (Paris In.)	48·55 N	1·27 E
74	Buena Park (bwā'nȧ pärk) Calif. (Los Angeles In.)	33·52 N	118·00 W
98	Buenaventura (bwā'nä-vĕn-tōō'rȧ) Col.	3·46 N	77·09 W
95	Buenaventura Cuba (Havana In.)	22·08 N	82·22 W
98	Buenaventura, Bahia de (B.) (bä-ē'ä-dĕ-bwā'nä-vĕn-tōō'rȧ) Col.	3·45 N	79·23 W
72	Buena Vista (bū'nȧ vĭs'tȧ).. Colo.	38·51 N	106·07 W
78	Buena Vista................ Ga.	32·15 N	84·30 W
81	Buena Vista................ Va.	37·45 N	79·20 W
94	Buena Vista, Bahía (B.) (bä-ē'ä-bwĕ-nä-vē's-tä) . Cuba	22·30 N	79·10 W
68	Buena Vista Lake Res. (bū'nȧ vĭs'tȧ) Calif.	35·14 N	119·17 W
100	Buenos Aires (bwā'nōs ī'rās) Arg. (In.)	34·20 S	58·30 W
98	Buenos Aires.......... Col. (In.)	3·01 N	76·34 W
93	Buenos Aires............. C. R.	9·10 N	83·21 W
100	Buenos Aires (Prov.)........ Arg.	36·15 S	61·45 W
100	Buenos Aires (L.)...... Arg.-Chile	46·30 S	72·15 W
123	Buer (bür)...... Ger. (Ruhr In.)	51·35 N	7·03 E
71	Buffalo (bŭf'ȧ lō).......... Minn.	45·10 N	93·50 W
75	Buffalo....... N. Y. (Buffalo In.)	42·54 N	78·51 W
67	Buffalo.................. Wyo.	44·19 N	106·42 W
73	Buffalo (R.)............... Ark.	35·56 N	92·58 W
167	Buffalo (R.).... S. Afr. (Natal In.)	28·35 S	30·27 E
78	Buffalo (R.).............. Tenn.	35·24 N	87·10 W
77	Buffalo Bay.......... Tex. (In.)	29·46 N	95·32 W
71	Buffalo Cr................ Minn.	44·46 N	94·28 W
86	Buffalo Head Hills.......... Can.	57·16 N	116·18 W
85	Buford (bū'fûrd) Can. (Edmonton In.)	53·15 N	113·55 W
78	Buford (bū'fẽrd)............ Ga.	34·05 N	84·00 W
69	Buford (L.).............. N. Mex.	36·37 N	107·12 W
129	Bug (R.) (bŏŏk)........ Sov. Un.	48·12 N	30·13 E
98	Buga (bōō'gä).......... Col. (In.)	3·54 N	76·17 W
111	Buggenhout.... Bel. (Brussels In.)	51·01 N	4·10 E
126	Bugojno (bōō-gō ĭ nō)...... Yugo.	44·03 N	17·28 E
121	Bug R. (bōōg)............... Pol.	52·29 N	21·20 E
132	Bugul'ma (bōō-gōōl'mȧ) . Sov. Un.	54·40 N	52·40 E
132	Buguruslan (bōō-gōō-rōōs-lȧn') Sov. Un.	53·30 N	52·32 E
155	Buhi (bōō'ē).... Phil. (Manila In.)	13·26 N	123·31 E
66	Buhl (bŭl)................. Idaho	42·36 N	114·45 W
71	Buhl..................... Minn.	47·28 N	92·49 W
101	Buin (bōō-ēn') Chile (Santiago In.)	33·44 S	70·44 W
133	Buinaksk (bōō'ē-näksk).. Sov. Un.	42·40 N	47·20 E
124	Bujalance (bōō-hä-län'thā)... Sp.	37·54 N	4·22 W
166	Bujumbura............. Burundi	3·19 S	29·28 E
166	Bukama (bōō-kä'mä)..... Con. K.	9·08 S	26·00 E
166	Bukavu.................. Con. K.	2·39 S	28·50 E
103	Bukhara (bōō-kä'rä)..... Sov. Un.	39·31 N	64·22 E
154	Bukittingg.............. Indon.	0·25 S	100·28 E
166	Bukoba.................... Tan.	1·19 S	31·49 E
121	Bukovina (Reg.) (bōō-kô'vĭ-nȧ) Sov. Un.	48·06 N	25·20 E
155	Bula (bōō'lä)............ Indon.	3·00 S	13·30 E
155	Bulalacao (bōō-lä-lä'kä-ō) Phil. (Manila In.)	12·32 N	121·25 E
166	Bulawayo (bōō-lȧ-wä'yō)..... Rh.	20·12 S	28·43 E
64	Buldir (I.) (bŭl dĭr)........ Alaska	52·22 N	175·50 E
102	Bulgaria (bŏŏl-gā'rĭ-ă)....... Eur.	42·12 N	24·13 E
124	Bullaque (R.) (bōō-lä'kȧ).... Sp.	39·15 N	4·13 W
124	Bullas (bōōl'yäs)............ Sp.	38·07 N	1·48 W
69	Bulldog Cr. (bŏŏl'dŏg')...... Utah	37·45 N	110·55 W
94	Bull Head (Mtn.)........... Jam.	18·10 N	77·15 W
159	Bulloo (R.) (bŭ-lōō')....... Austl.	25·23 S	143·30 E
84	Bullrun Va. (Washington D.C. In.)	38·50 N	77·29 W
65	Bull Run (R.) (bŏŏl) Ore. (Portland In.)	45·26 N	122·11 W
65	Bull Run Res. (bŏŏl) Ore. (Portland In.)	45·29 N	122·11 W
73	Bull Shoals Res. (bŏŏl shōlz) Ark.-Mo.	36·35 N	92·57 W
168	Bulo Burti (bōō'lō bōōr'tĭ) Som. (Horn of Afr. In.)	3·53 N	45·30 E
110	Bulphan (bŏŏl'făn) Eng. (London In.)	51·33 N	0·21 E
168	Bultfontein (bŏŏlt'fŏn-tān') S. Afr. (Johannesburg & Pretoria In.)	28·18 S	26·10 E
135	Bulun (bōō-lōōn')...... Sov. Un.	70·48 N	127·27 E
166	Bulungu (bōō-lōōŋ'gōō)... Con. K.	4·58 S	18·57 E
167	Bulwer (bŏŏl-wẽr) S. Afr. (Natal In.)	29·49 S	29·48 E
165	Bumba (bŏŏm'bȧ)........ Con. K.	2·15 N	22·32 E
155	Buna (bōō'nȧ).............. Pap.	8·58 S	148·38 E
158	Bunbury (bŭn'bŭrĭ)........ Austl.	33·25 S	115·45 E
160	Bundaberg (bŭn'dȧ-bûrg).... Austl.	24·45 S	152·18 E
153	Bungo-Suidō (Chan.) (bōōŋ'gō sōō-ē'dō) . Jap.	33·26 N	131·54 E
74	Bunker Hill (bŭnk'ẽr hĭl) Ill. (St. Louis In.)	39·03 N	89·57 W
77	Bunkie (bŭŋ'kĭ)............ La.	30·55 N	92·10 W
135	Buor Khaya, Mys (C.) . . Sov. Un.	71·47 N	133·22 E
168	Buran (bûr'ăn) Som. (Horn of Afr. In.)	10·38 N	48·30 E
168	Burao.... Som. (Horn of Afr. In.)	9·20 N	45·45 E
144	Buraydah.............. Sau. Ar.	26·23 N	44·14 E
74	Burbank (bûr'bănk) Calif. (Los Angeles In.)	34·11 N	118·19 W
159	Burdekin (R.) (bûr'dē-kĭn) . Austl.	19·22 S	145·07 E
133	Burdur (bōōr-dōōr')........ Tur.	37·50 N	30·15 E

ng-sing; ŋ-baŋk; ɴ-nasalized n; nŏd; cŏmmit; ōld; ôbey; ôrder; fōōd; fŏŏt; ou-out; s-soft; sh-dish; th-thin; pūre; ûnite; ûrn; stŭd; circŭs; ü-as "y" in study; '-indeterminate vowel.

188 Burdwan–Calcasieu PRONOUNCING INDEX

Page	Name Pronunciation Region	Lat. °′	Long. °′
142	Burdwan (bŏŏrd-wän′)......India	23·29 N	87·53 E
100	Burdwood, Banco (Bk.)...Atl. O.	54·00 S	60·45 W
135	Bureinskiy, Khrebet (Mts.) Sov. Un.	51·15 N	133·30 E
135	Bureya (bŏŏrā′ȧ)........Sov. Un.	49·55 N	130·00 E
135	Bureya (R.) (bŏŏ-rā′yä)..Sov. Un.	51·00 N	130·14 E
110	Burford (bûr-fĕrd) Eng. (London In.)	51·46 N	1·38 W
127	Burgas (bŏŏr-gäs′)...........Bul.	42·29 N	27·30 E
127	Burgaski Zaliv (G.).........Bul.	42·30 N	27·40 E
79	Burgaw (bûr′gô)...........N. C.	34·31 N	77·56 W
120	Burgdorf (bŏŏrg′dôrf)......Switz.	47·04 N	7·37 E
111	Burgenland (State) Aus. (Vienna In.)	47·58 N	16·57 E
83	Burgeo...................Can.	47·36 N	57·39 W
76	Burgos (bŏŏr′gōs)..........Mex.	24·57 N	98·47 W
155	Burgos........Phil. (Manila In.)	16·03 N	119·52 E
124	Burgos (bōō′r-gôs)...........Sp.	42·20 N	3·44 E
118	Burgsvik (bŏŏrgs′vĭk).......Swe.	57·04 N	18·18 E
142	Burhānpur (bŏŏr′hȧn-pōōr).India	21·26 N	76·08 E
155	Burias I. (bōō′rê-äs) Phil. (Manila In.)	12·56 N	122·56 E
155	Burias Pass (bōō′rê-äs) Phil. (Manila In.)	13·04 N	123·11 E
93	Burica, Punta (Pt.) (pōō′n-tä-bōō′rē-kä).Pan.	8·02 N	83·12 W
65	Burien (bū′rĭ-ĕn) Wash. (Seattle In.)	47·28 N	122·20 W
83	Burin (bûr′ĭn).............Can.	47·03 N	55·33 W
83	Burin Pen..................Can.	47·04 N	55·14 W
72	Burkburnett (bûrk-bûr′nĕt)..Tex.	34·04 N	98·35 W
81	Burke (bûrk)...............Vt.	44·40 N	72·00 W
158	Burketown (bûrk′toun).....Austl.	17·50 S	139·30 E
67	Burley (bûr′lĭ)............Idaho	42·31 N	113·48 W
65	Burley........Wash. (Seattle In.)	47·25 N	122·38 W
136	Burli........Sov. Un. (Urals In.)	53·36 N	61·55 E
65	Burlingame (bûr′lĭn-gām) Calif. (San Francisco In.)	37·35 N	122·22 W
73	Burlingame...............Kans.	38·45 N	95·49 W
85	Burlington (bûr′lĭng-tŭn) Can. (Toronto In.)	43·19 N	79·48 W
72	Burlington...............Colo.	39·17 N	102·26 W
71	Burlington...............Iowa	40·48 N	91·05 W
73	Burlington...............Kans.	38·10 N	95·46 W
75	Burlington...Ky. (Cincinnati In.)	39·01 N	84·44 W
84	Burlington.N. J. (Philadelphia In.)	40·04 N	74·52 W
79	Burlington...............N. C.	36·05 N	79·26 W
81	Burlington...............Vt.	44·30 N	73·15 W
65	Burlington....Wash. (Seattle In.)	48·28 N	122·20 W
75	Burlington..Wis. (Milwaukee In.)	42·41 N	88·16 W
138	Burma (bûr′mȧ)............Asia	21·00 N	95·15 E
76	Burnet (bûrn′ĕt)...........Tex.	30·46 N	98·14 W
110	Burnham on Crouch (bûrn′ăm-ŏn-krouch) Eng. (London In.)	51·38 N	0·48 E
160	Burnie (bûr′nê)...........Austl.	41·15 S	146·05 E
110	Burnley (bûrn′lĕ)...........Eng.	53·47 N	2·19 W
66	Burns (bûrnz)..............Ore.	43·35 N	119·05 W
78	Burnside (bûrn′sīd).........Ky.	36·57 N	84·33 W
86	Burns Lake (bûrnz lăk).....Can.	54·12 N	125·38 W
82	Burnsville (bûrnz′vĭl).......Can.	47·44 N	65·07 W
66	Burnt R. (bûrnt)...........Ore.	44·26 N	117·53 W
65	Burrard Inlet (bûr′ȧrd) Can. (Vancouver In.)	49·19 N	123·15 W
125	Burriana (bōōr-rê-ä′nä).......Sp.	39·53 N	0·05 W
133	Bursa (bōōr′sȧ).............Tur.	40·10 N	28·10 E
165	Būr Safājah...........U. A. R.	26·57 N	33·56 E
168	Būr Sa′id (Port Said) U. A. R. (Suez In.)	31·15 N	32·19 E
123	Burscheid (bōōr′shīd) Ger. (Ruhr In.)	51·05 N	7·07 E
75	Burt (bŭrt)...N. Y. (Buffalo In.)	43·19 N	78·45 W
80	Burt (L.) (bŭrt)...........Mich.	45·25 N	84·45 W
139	Būr Tawfīq U. A. R. (Palestine In.)	29·58 N	32·33 E
65	Burton (bûr′tŭn) Wash. (Seattle In.)	47·24 N	122·28 W
110	Burton-on-Trent (bŭr′tŭn-ŏn-trĕnt).Eng.	52·48 N	1·37 W
78	Burton Res..................Ga.	34·46 N	83·40 W
84	Burtonsville (bûrtŏns-vil) Md. (Baltimore In.)	39·07 N	76·57 W
155	Buru (I.)...............Indon.	3·30 S	126·30 E
168	Burullus L.....U. A. R. (Nile In.)	31·20 N	30·58 E
155	Buruncan Pt. (bōō-rōōn′kän) Phil. (Manila In.)	12·11 N	121·23 E
166	Burundi...................Afr.	3·00 S	29·30 E
86	Burwash Landing (bûr wăsh).Can.	61·20 N	139·12 W
70	Burwell (bûr′wĕl)..........Nebr.	41·46 N	99·08 W
110	Bury (bĕr′ĭ)...............Eng.	53·36 N	2·17 W
135	Buryat A.S.S.R.........Sov. Un.	54·15 N	111·22 E
117	Bury St. Edmunds (bĕr′ī-sānt ĕd′mŭndz).Eng.	52·14 N	0·44 E
100	Burzaco (bōōr-zȧ′kô)...Arg. (In.)	34·35 S	58·23 W
168	Būsh (bŏŏsh).U. A. R. (Nile In.)	29·13 N	31·08 E
144	Būshehr...................Iran	28·48 N	50·53 E
166	Bushmanland (Reg.) (bŏŏsh-măn lănd).S. Afr.	29·15 S	18·45 E
167	Bushmans (R.) (bŏŏsh′mănz) S. Afr. (Natal In.)	33·29 S	26·09 E
73	Bushnell (bŏŏsh′nĕl).........Ill.	40·33 N	90·28 W
165	Businga (bōō-siŋ′gȧ)......Con. K.	3·15 N	21·00 E
121	Busk (bōō′sk)..........Sov. Un.	49·58 N	24·39 E
164	Bussa (bōō′sȧ)...............Nig.	10·11 N	4·20 E
158	Busselton (bûs″l-tŭn)......Austl.	33·40 S	115·30 E
111	Bussum...Neth. (Amsterdam In.)	52·16 N	5·10 E
76	Bustamante (bōōs-tȧ-män′tȧ).Mex.	26·34 N	100·30 W
126	Busto Arsizio (bōōs′tō är-sēd′zê-ō).It.	45·47 N	8·51 E
155	Busuanga (I.) (bōō-swäŋ′gä).Phil.	12·20 N	119·43 E
165	Buta (bōō′tȧ)...........Con. K.	2·47 N	24·46 E
167	Butha Buthe (bōō-thȧ-bōō′thȧ) Leso. (Natal In.)	28·49 S	28·16 E
78	Butler (bŭt′lĕr).............Ala.	32·05 N	88·10 W
80	Butler....................Ind.	41·25 N	84·50 W
84	Butler.......Md. (Baltimore In.)	39·32 N	76·46 W
73	Butler....................Mo.	38·16 N	94·19 W
84	Butler......N. J. (New York In.)	41·00 N	74·20 W
81	Butler....................Pa.	40·50 N	79·55 W
136	Butovo (bŏŏ-tô′vô) Sov. Un. (Moscow In.)	55·33 N	37·36 E
78	Buttahatchie (R.) (bŭt-ȧ-hăch′ê) Ala.-Miss.	34·02 N	88·05 W
67	Butte (būt)...............Mont.	46·00 N	112·31 W
167	Butterworth (bŭ tĕr′wûrth) S. Afr. (Natal In.)	32·20 S	28·09 E
116	Butt of Lewis (C.) (bŭt ŏv lū′ĭs) Scot.	58·34 N	6·15 W
155	Butuan (bōō-tōō′än)........Phil.	8·40 N	125·33 E
155	Butung (I.)...............Indon.	5·15 S	124·15 E
129	Buturlinovka (bōō-tōō′lê-nôf′ka) Sov. Un.	50·47 N	40·35 E
111	Buxtehude (bŏŏks-tĕ-hōō′dĕ) Ger. (Hamburg In.)	53·29 N	9·42 E
110	Buxton (bŭks′t′n)..........Eng.	53·15 N	1·55 W
65	Buxton.......Ore. (Portland In.)	45·41 N	123·11 W
167	Buxton........S. Afr. (Natal In.)	32·36 S	26·39 E
132	Buy (bwē)..............Sov. Un.	58·30 N	41·48 E
150	Buyr Nuur (bōō′yĕr nôr)..Mong.	47·50 N	117·00 E
127	Buzău (bōō-zĕ′ŏŏ)..........Rom.	45·09 N	26·51 E
129	Buzău (R.)................Rom.	45·17 N	27·22 E
165	Buzaymah.................Libya	25·14 N	22·13 E
133	Buzuluk (bŏŏ-zŏŏ-lŏŏk′).Sov. Un.	52·50 N	52·10 E
127	Byala......................Bul.	43·26 N	25·44 E
	Byblos, see Jubayl		
121	Bydgoszcz (bĭd′gôshch)......Pol.	53·07 N	18·00 E
80	Byesville (bīz-vĭl)..........Ohio	39·55 N	81·35 W
118	Bygdin (bügh-dên′).........Nor.	61·24 N	8·31 E
118	Byglandsfjord (bügh′lănds-fyôr) Nor.	58·40 N	7·49 E
128	Bykhovo (bĭ-ĸô′vô).....Sov. Un.	53·32 N	30·15 E
136	Bykovo (bĭ-kô′vô) Sov. Un. (Moscow In.)	55·38 N	38·05 E
134	Byrranga, Gory (Mts.)..Sov. Un.	74·15 N	94·28 E
135	Bytantay (R.) (byăn′tăy).Sov. Un.	68·15 N	132·15 E
121	Bytom (bĭ′tŭm).............Pol.	50·21 N	18·55 E
128	Bytosh′ (bī-tôsh′).......Sov. Un.	53·48 N	34·06 E
121	Bytow (bĭ′tŭf)..............Pol.	54·10 N	17·30 E
127	Buzîu (R.)................Rom.	45·18 N	26·29 E
100	Caazapa′ (kä-zä-pä′)........Par.	26·14 S	56·18 W
155	Cabagan (kä-bä-gän′) Phil. (Manila In.)	17·27 N	12·46 E
155	Cabalete (I.) (kä-bä-lā′tȧ) Phil. (Manila In.)	14·19 N	122·00 E
94	Caballones, Canal de (Chan.) (kä-nä′l-dĕ-kä-bäl-yô′nĕs).Cuba	20·45 N	79·20 W
69	Caballo Res. (kä-bä-lyō′).N. Mex.	33·00 N	107·20 W
124	Cabañaquinta (kä-bän-yä-kê′n-tä) Sp.	43·10 N	5·37 W
155	Cabanatuan (kä-bä-nä-twän′) Phil. (Manila In.)	15·30 N	120·56 E
82	Cabano (kă-bă-nō′).........Can.	47·41 N	68·55 W
160	Cabar (kă′bĕr)............Austl.	31·28 S	145·50 E
155	Cabarruyan (I.) (kä-bä-rōō′yän) Phil. (Manila In.)	16·21 N	120·10 E
99	Cabedelo (kä-bē-dā′lŏŏ).....Braz.	6·58 S	34·49 W
91	Cabeza, Arrecife (Reef) (är-rĕ-sē′fĕ-kä-bĕ-zä).Mex.	19·07 N	95·52 W
124	Cabeza del Buey (kȧ-bā′thä dĕl bwā′).Sp.	38·43 N	5·18 W
98	Cabimas (kä-bê′mäs)........Ven.	10·21 N	71·27 W
166	Cabinda (kä-bĭn′dȧ)........Ang.	5·45 S	12·10 E
163	Cabinda (kä-bĭn′dȧ)........Ang.	5·10 S	10·00 E
66	Cabinet Mts. (kăb′ĭ-nĕt)..Mont..	48·13 N	115·52 W
101	Cabo Frio (kä′bô-frē′ô) Braz. (Rio de Janeiro In.)	22·53 S	42·02 W
101	Cabo Frio, Ilha do (ē′lä-dô-kä′bô frē′ô).Braz. (Rio de Janeiro In.)	23·01 S	42·00 W
80	Cabot Hd. (kăb′ŭt).........Can.	45·15 N	81·20 W
83	Cabot Str. (kăb′ŭt).........Can.	47·35 N	60·00 W
164	Cabo Verde, Ilhas do....Afr. (In.)	15·48 N	26·02 W
124	Cabra (käb′rä)...............Sp.	37·28 N	4·29 W
155	Cabra (I.)......Phil. (Manila In.)	13·55 N	119·55 E
125	Cabrera (I.) (kä-brā′rä).......Sp.	39·08 N	2·57 E
124	Cabriel (R.) (kä-brē-ĕl′)......Sp.	39·41 N	1·32 W
68	Cabrillo Natl. Mon. (kä-brēl′yō) Calif. (San Diego In.)	32·41 N	117·03 W
99	Cabrobo′ (kä-brō-bô′)......Braz.	8·34 S	39·13 W
100	Cabuçu (R.) (kä-bōō′-sōō) Braz. (In.)	22·57 S	43·36 W
155	Cabugao (kä-bōō′gä-ô) Phil. (Manila In.)	17·48 N	120·28 E
127	Čačak (chä′chȧk)..........Yugo.	43·51 N	20·22 E
101	Caçapava (kä′sä-pȧ′vä) Braz. (Rio de Janeiro In.)	23·05 S	45·42 W
99	Cáceres (kȧ′-sĕ-rĕs).........Braz.	16·11 S	57·32 W
124	Cáceres (kȧ′thȧ-rās)..........Sp.	39·28 N	6·20 W
101	Cachapoal (R.) (kä-chä-pô-ȧ′l) Chile (Santiago In.)	34·23 S	70·19 W
101	Cacharí (kä-chä-rē′) Arg. (Buenos Aires In.)	36·23 S	59·29 W
73	Cache (R.) (kȧsh)...........Ark.	35·24 N	91·12 W
68	Cache Cr. (kăsh)..........Calif.	38·53 N	122·24 W
72	Cache la Poudre (R.) (kȧsh lȧ pōōd′r′).Colo.	40·43 N	105·39 W
100	Cachi, Nevados de (Pk.) (nĕ-vȧ′dôs-dĕ-kȧ′chē).Arg.	25·05 S	66·40 W
100	Cachinal (kä-chē-näl′)......Chile	24·57 S	69·33 W
99	Cachoeira (kä-shô-ā′rä).....Braz.	12·32 S	38·47 W
100	Cachoeira do Sul (kä-shô-ā′rä-dô-sōō′l).Braz.	30·02 S	52·49 W
101	Cachoeiras de Macacu (kä-shô-ā′räs-dĕ-mä-kȧ′kōō) Braz. (Rio de Janeiro In.)	22·28 S	42·39 W
101	Cachoeiro de Itapemirim (kä-shô-ā′rô-dĕ-ē′tä-pĕmē-rē′ɴ) Braz. (Rio de Janeiro In.)	20·51 S	41 06 W
166	Caconda (kä-kōn′dä)......Ang.	13·40 S	15·05 E
77	Caddo L. (kăd′ō)........La.-Tex.	32·37 N	94·15 W
90	Cadereyta (kä-dȧ-rā′tä).....Mex.	20·42 N	99·47 W
76	Cadereyta Jimenez (kä-dä-rā′tä hê-mā′nāz).Mex.	25·36 N	99·59 W
125	Cadi, Sierra de (Mts.) (sē-ĕ′r-rä-dĕ-kä′dē).Sp.	42·17 N	1·34 E
155	Cadig, Mt. (kä′dêg) Phil. (Manila In.)	14·11 N	122·26 E
80	Cadillac (kăd′ĭ-lăk)........Mich.	44·15 N	85·25 W
68	Cadiz (kā′dĭz).............Calif.	34·33 N	115·30 W
80	Cadiz.....................Ohio	40·15 N	81·00 W
124	Cádiz (kȧ′dēz)...............Sp.	36·34 N	6·20 W
124	Cádiz, Golfo de (G.) (gôl-fô-dĕ-kȧ′dēz).Sp.	36·50 N	7·00 W
122	Caen (käɴ)..................Fr.	49·13 N	0·22 W
101	Caeté (kä′ĕ-tĕ′) Braz. (Rio de Janeiro In.)	19·53 S	43·41 W
99	Caetité (kä-ȧ-tê-tā′).........Braz.	14·02 S	42·14 W
166	Cagamba (kä-gä′m-bä)......Ang.	13·20 S	19·55 E
155	Cagayan (kä-gä-yän′).......Phil.	8·13 N	124·30 E
154	Cagayan (R.)...............Phil.	16·45 N	121·55 E
154	Cagayan Is.................Phil.	9·40 N	120·30 E
154	Cagayan Sulu (I.) (kä-gä-yän sōō′lōō).Phil.	7·00 N	118·30 E
126	Cagli (käl′yē)................It.	42·33 N	12·38 E
126	Cagliari (käl′yä-rē)...........It.	39·16 N	9·08 E
126	Cagliari, Golfo di (G.) (gôl-fô-dē-käl′yä-rē).It.	39·08 N	9·12 E
123	Cagnes (kän′y′)..............Fr.	43·40 N	7·14 E
99	Cagua (kä′-gwä).......Ven. (In.)	10·12 N	67·27 W
89	Caguas (kä′gwäs) P. R. (Puerto Rico In.)	18·12 N	66·01 W
78	Cahaba (R.) (kȧ hä-bä)......Ala.	32·50 N	87·15 W
166	Cahama (kä-ȧ′mä)..........Ang.	16·15 S	14·15 E
74	Cahokia (kȧ-hō′kĭ-ȧ) Ill. (St. Louis In.)	38·34 N	90·11 W
122	Cahors (kȧ-ôr′)..............Fr.	44·27 N	1·27 E
91	Cahuacán (kä-wä-kä′n) Mex. (Mexico City In.)	19·38 N	99·25 W
93	Cahuita, Punta (Pt.) (pōō′n-tä-kä-wē′tȧ).C. R.	9·47 N	82·41 W
99	Caiapó, Serra do (Mts.) (sĕ′r-rä-dô-kä-yä-pô′).Braz.	17·52 S	52·37 W
94	Caibarién (kī-bä-rê-ĕn′).....Cuba	22·35 N	79·30 W
98	Caicedonia (kī-sĕ-dô-nêä) Col. (In.)	4·21 N	75·48 W
95	Caicos Bk. (kī′kōs)........Ba. Is.	21·35 N	72·00 W
95	Caicos Is......Turks & Caicos Is.	21·45 N	71·50 W
95	Caicos Passage (Str.)......Ba. Is.	21·55 N	72·45 W
77	Caillou B. (kȧ-yōō′)..........La.	29·07 N	91·00 W
95	Caimanera (kī-mä-nā′rä)....Cuba	20·00 N	75·10 W
90	Caimanere, Laguna del (lä-gŏŏ′nä-dĕl-kä-ē-mä-nĕ-rĕ) Mex.	22·57 N	106·07 W
155	Caiman Pt. (kī′mȧn) Phil. (Manila In.)	15·56 N	119·33 E
88	Caimito, (R.) (kä-ē-mē′tô) Pan. (Panama Canal In.)	8·50 N	79·45 W
95	Caimito del Guayabal (kä-ē-mê′tō-dĕl-gwä-yä-bä′l) Cuba (Havana In.)	22·12 N	82·36 W
85	Cainsville (kānz′vĭl) Can. (Toronto In.)	43·09 N	80·13 W
159	Cairns (kârnz).............Austl.	17·02 S	145·49 E
93	Cairo (kī′-rô)..............C. R.	10·06 N	83·47 W
78	Cairo (kā′rō).................Ga.	30·48 N	84·12 W
73	Cairo.......................Ill.	36·59 N	89·11 W
	Cairo, see Al Qāhirah		
110	Caistor (kâs′tĕr)............Eng.	53·30 N	0·20 W
98	Cajamarca (kä-ĸä-mȧ′r-kä) Col. (In.)	4·25 N	75·25 W
98	Cajamarca (kä-hä-mär′kä)...Peru	7·16 S	78·30 W
155	Cajidiocan (kä-hē-dyô′kän) Phil. (Manila In.)	12·22 N	122·41 E
127	Čajniče (chī′nĭ-chĕ)........Yugo.	43·32 N	19·04 E
74	Cajon (kȧ-hōn′) Calif. (Los Angeles In.)	34·18 N	117·28 W
101	Cajuru (kȧ-zhōō′-rōō) Braz. (Rio de Janeiro In.)	21·17 S	47·17 W
126	Čakovec (chȧ′kō-vĕts)......Yugo.	46·23 N	16·27 E
167	Cala (cā-lȧ)....S. Afr. (Natal In.)	31·33 S	27·41 E
	(Natal In.)	31·33 S	27·41 E
164	Calabar (kăl-ȧ-bär′).........Nig.	4·58 N	8·21 E
74	Calabasas (kä-lä-bäs′äs) Calif. (Los Angeles In.)	34·09 N	118·39 W
95	Calabazar (kä-lä-bä-zä′r) Cuba (Havana In.)	23·02 N	82·25 W
98	Calabozo (kä-lä-bō′zō).......Ven.	8·48 N	67·27 W
126	Calabria (Reg.) (kä-lä′brê-ä)...It.	39·26 N	16·23 E
127	Calafat (kȧ-lȧ-fȧt′).........Rom.	43·59 N	22·56 E
155	Calagua Is. (kä-läg′wä) Phil. (Manila In.)	14·30 N	123·06 E
85	Calahoo (kă-lȧ-hōō′) Can. (Edmonton In.)	53·42 N	113·58 W
124	Calahorra (kä-lä-ôr′rä)........Sp.	42·18 N	1·58 W
82	Calais (kȧ-lĕ′)............Maine	45·11 N	67·15 W
122	Calais......................Fr.	50·56 N	1·51 E
100	Calama (kä-lä′mä).........Chile	22·17 S	68·58 W
98	Calamar (kä-lä-mär′)........Col.	10·24 N	75·00 W
98	Calamar....................Col.	1·55 N	72·33 W
155	Calamba (kä-läm′bä) Phil. (Manila In.)	14·12 N	121·10 E
154	Calamian Group (Is.) (kä-lä-myän′).Phil.	12·14 N	118·38 E
124	Calañas (kä-län′yäs)..........Sp.	37·41 N	6·52 W
155	Calapan (kä-lä-pän′) Phil. (Manila In.)	13·25 N	121·11 E
115	Călărasi (kŭ-lŭ-rȧsh′ĭ)......Rom.	44·09 N	27·20 E
114	Calasparra (kä-lä-spär′rä).....Sp.	38·13 N	1·40 W
124	Calatayud (kä-lä-tä-yōōdh′)...Sp.	41·23 N	1·37 W
155	Calauag (kä-lä-wäg′) Phil. (Manila In.)	13·56 N	122·16 E
155	Calauag B.....Phil. (Manila In.)	14·07 N	122·10 E
65	Calaveras Res. (kăl-ȧ-vĕr′ăs) Calif. (San Francisco In.)	37·29 N	121·47 W
155	Calavite, C. (kä-lä-vē′tā) Phil. (Manila In.)	13·29 N	120·00 E
77	Calcasieu L. (kăl′kȧ-shū)......La.	29·58 N	93·08 W
77	Calcasieu R..................La.	30·22 N	93·08 W

ăt; finăl; rāte; senâte; ärm; ȧsk; sofȧ; fâre; ch-choose; dh-as th in other; bē; êvent; bĕt; recĕnt; cratẽr; g-go; gh-guttural g; bĭt; ĭ-short neutral; rīde; ĸ-guttural k as ch in German ich;

PRONOUNCING INDEX Calcutta–Cape Flats 189

Page	Name Pronunciation Region	Lat. °′	Long. °′
142	Calcutta (kăl-kŭt'ȧ) India (Calcutta In.)	22·32 N	88·22 E
98	Caldas (kȧ'l-däs) Col. (In.)	6·06 N	75·38 W
98	Caldas (Dept.) Col. (In.)	5·20 N	75·38 W
124	Caldas de Rainha (käl'däs dä rīn'yȧ) Port.	39·25 N	9·08 W
110	Calder (R.) (kôl'dẽr) Eng.	53·39 N	1·30 W
110	Calder (R.) Eng.	53·48 N	2·25 W
100	Caldera (käl-dä'rä) Chile	27·02 S	70·53 W
66	Caldwell (kôld'wĕl) Idaho	43·40 N	116·43 W
73	Caldwell Kans.	37·04 N	97·36 W
80	Caldwell Ohio	39·40 N	81·30 W
77	Caldwell Tex.	30·30 N	96·40 W
85	Caledon (kăl'ē-dŏn) Can. (Toronto In.)	43·52 N	79·59 W
71	Caledonia (kăl-ē-dō'nĭ-ȧ) Minn.	43·38 N	91·31 W
116	Caledonian Can. (kăl-ē-dō'nĭ-ăn) Scot.	56·58 N	4·05 W
125	Calella (kä-lĕl'yä) Sp.	41·37 N	2·39 E
90	Calera Victor Rosales (kä-lā'rä-vē'k-tôr-rô-sä'lĕs) Mex.	22·57 N	102·42 W
68	Calexico (kȧ-lĕk'sĭ-kō) Calif.	32·41 N	115·30 W
85	Calgary (kăl'gȧ-rĭ) Can. (Calgary In.)	51·03 N	114·05 W
78	Calhoun (kăl-hōōn') Ga.	34·30 N	84·56 W
98	Cali (kä'lē) Col. (In.)	3·26 N	76·30 W
143	Calicut (kăl'ĭ-kŭt) India	11·19 N	75·49 E
69	Caliente (käl-yĕn'tä) Nev.	37·38 N	114·30 W
73	California (kăl-ĭ-fôr'nĭ-ȧ) Mo.	38·38 N	92·38 W
75	California.... Pa. (Pittsburgh In.)	40·03 N	79·53 W
62	California (State) U. S.	38·10 N	121·20 W
88	California, Golfo de (G.) (gôl-fô-dĕ-kä-lē-fôr-nyä) Mex.	30·30 N	113·45 W
121	Căliman, Muntii (Mts.) Rom.	47·05 N	24·47 E
143	Calimere, Pt India	15·25 N	80·05 E
74	Calimesa (kă-lĭ-mā'sȧ) Calif. (Los Angeles In.)	34·00 N	117·04 W
68	Calipatria (kăl-ĭ-păt'rĭ-ȧ) Calif.	33·03 N	115·30 W
91	Calkini (käl-kē-nē') Mex.	20·21 N	90·06 W
160	Callabonna, L. (călă'bŏnȧ) Austl.	29·35 S	140·28 E
168	Callafo.... Eth. (Horn of Afr. In.)	5·40 N	44·00 E
98	Callao (käl-yä'ō) Peru	12·80 S	77·07 W
85	Calmar (kăl'mär) Can. (Edmonton In.)	53·16 N	113·49 W
71	Calmar Iowa	43·12 N	91·54 W
90	Calnali (käl-nä-lē') Mex.	20·53 N	98·34 W
79	Calooshatchee (R.) (kȧ-loo-sȧ-hăch'ē) Fla. (In.)	26·45 N	81·41 W
92	Calotmul (kä-lôt-mōōl) Mex. (Yucatan In.)	20·58 N	88·11 W
90	Calpulalpan (käl-pōō-läl'pän) Mex.	19·35 N	98·33 W
126	Caltagirone (käl-tä-jē-rō'nā) It.	37·14 N	14·32 E
126	Caltanissetta (käl-tä-nē-sĕt'tä) It.	37·30 N	14·02 E
71	Calumet (kă-lū-mĕt') Mich.	47·15 S	88·29 W
75	Calumet, L..... Ill. (Chicago In.)	41·43 N	87·36 W
75	Calumet City .. Ill. (Chicago In.)	41·37 N	87·33 W
77	Calvert (kăl'vẽrt) Tex.	30·59 N	96·41 W
86	Calvert (I.) Can.	51·40 N	129·02 W
126	Calvi (käl'vē) Fr.	42·33 N	8·35 E
90	Calvillo (käl-vēl'yō) Mex.	21·51 N	102·44 W
166	Calvinia (kăl-vĭn'ĭ-ȧ) S. Afr.	31·20 S	19·50 E
124	Calzada de Calatrava (käl-zä'dä-dĕ-kä-lä-trä'vä) Sp.	38·42 N	3·44 W
116	Cam (R.) (kăm) Eng.	52·15 N	0·05 E
94	Camaguey (kä-mä-gwā') Cuba	21·25 N	78·00 W
94	Camaguey (State) Cuba	21·30 N	78·10 W
94	Camajuani (kä-mä-hwä'nē) Cuba	22·25 N	79·50 W
155	Camalig (kä-mä'lēg) Phil. (Manila In.)	13·11 N	123·36 E
98	Camaná (kä-mä'nä) Peru	16·37 S	72·33 W
65	Camano (kä-mä'no) Wash. (Seattle In.)	48·10 N	122·32 W
65	Camano I.... Wash. (Seattle In.)	48·11 N	122·29 W
76	Camargo (kä-mär'gō) Mex.	26·19 N	98·49 W
92	Camaron, Cabo (C.) (kȧ'bô-kä-mä-rōn') Hond.	16·06 N	85·05 W
65	Camas (kăm'ȧs) Wash. (Portland In.)	45·35 N	122·54 W
67	Camas Cr. Idaho	44·10 N	112·09 W
99	Camatagua (kä-mä-tä'gwä) Ven. (In.)	9·49 N	66·55 W
154	Ca Mau, Pte de Viet.	8·42 N	103·11 E
142	Cambay (kăm-bā') India	22·22 N	72·39 E
142	Cambay, G. of India	21·05 N	71·58 E
64	Cambell (kămbĕl') Alaska	63·48 N	171·58 W
139	Cambodia (kăm-bō'dĭ-ȧ) Asia	14·00 N	105·45 E
116	Camborne (kăm'bôrn) Eng.	50·15 N	5·28 W
122	Cambrai (käN-brĕ') Fr.	50·10 N	3·15 E
116	Cambrian (Mts.) (kăm'brĭ-ăn) Wales	52·05 N	4·05 W
116	Cambridge (kām'brĭj) Eng.	52·12 N	0·11 E
81	Cambridge Md.	38·35 N	76·10 W
83	Cambridge.... Mass. (Boston In.)	42·23 N	71·07 W
71	Cambridge Minn.	45·35 N	93·14 W
72	Cambridge Nebr.	40·17 N	100·10 W
80	Cambridge Ohio	40·00 N	81·35 W
86	Cambridge Bay Can.	69·15 N	105·00 W
80	Cambridge City Ind.	39·45 N	85·15 W
101	Cambuci (käm-bōō'sē) Braz. (Rio de Janeiro In.)	21·35 S	41·54 W
101	Cambuí (käm-bōō-ē') Braz. (Rio de Janeiro In.)	22·38 S	46·02 W
75	Camby (kăm'bē) Ind. (Indianapolis In.)	39·40 N	86·19 W
78	Camden (kăm'dĕn) Ala.	31·58 N	87·15 W
73	Camden Ark.	33·36 N	92·49 W
161	Camden...... Austl. (Sydney In.)	34·03 S	150·42 E
82	Camden Maine	44·11 N	69·05 W
84	Camden N. J. (Philadelphia In.)	39·56 N	75·06 W
79	Camden S. C.	34·14 N	80·37 W
73	Cameron (kăm'ẽr-ŭn) Mo.	39·44 N	94·14 W
77	Cameron Tex.	30·52 N	96·57 W
80	Cameron W. Va.	39·40 N	80·35 W
86	Camerons Hills Can.	60·13 N	120·20 W
163	Cameroon Afr.	5·48 N	11·00 E
164	Cameroon, Mt. Cam.	4·15 N	9·01 E
99	Cametá (kä-mā-tä') Braz.	1·14 S	49·30 W
155	Camiling (kä-mē-lĭng') Phil. (Manila In.)	15·42 N	120·24 E
78	Camilla (kȧ-mĭl'ȧ) Ga.	31·13 N	84·12 W
124	Caminha (kä-mĭn'yȧ) Port.	41·52 N	8·44 W
99	Camoçim (kä-mô-sēN') Braz.	2·56 S	40·55 W
158	Camooweal Austl.	20·00 S	138·13 E
101	Campana (käm-pä'nä) Arg. (Buenos Aires In.)	34·10 S	58·58 W
100	Campana (I.) (käm-pän'yä) Chile	48·20 S	75·15 W
124	Campanario (käm-pä-nä'rē-ō) Sp.	38·51 N	5·36 W
125	Campanella, Punta (C.) (pōō'n-tä-käm-pä-nĕ'lä) It. (Naples In.)	40·20 N	14·21 E
101	Campanha (käm-pän-yäN') Braz. (Rio de Janeiro In.)	21·51 S	45·24 W
126	Campania (Reg.) (käm-pän'yä) It.	43·00 N	14·40 E
65	Campbell (kăm'bĕl) Calif. (San Francisco In.)	37·17 N	121·57 W
73	Campbell Mo.	36·29 N	90·04 W
47	Campbell Is. N. Z.	52·30 S	169·00 E
142	Campbellpore W. Pak.	33·49 N	72·24 E
86	Campbell River Can.	50·00 N	125·24 W
78	Campbellsville (kăm'bĕlz-vĭl) Ky.	37·19 N	85·20 W
82	Campbellton (kăm'bĕl-tŭn) Can.	48·00 N	66·43 W
161	Campbelltown (kăm'bĕl-toun) Austl. (Sydney In.)	34·04 S	150·49 E
116	Campbelltown (kăm'b'l-toun) Scot.	55·25 N	5·50 W
75	Camp Dennison (dĕ'nĭ-sŏn) Ohio (Cincinnati In.)	39·12 N	84·17 W
91	Campeche (käm-pā'chä) Mex.	19·51 N	90·32 W
88	Campeche (State) Mex.	18·55 N	90·20 W
88	Campeche, Bahía de (B.) (bä-ē'ä-dĕ-käm-pā'chä) Mex.	19·30 N	93·40 W
94	Campechuela (käm-pȧ-chwā'lä) Cuba	20·15 N	77·15 W
167	Camperdown (kăm'pẽr-doun) S. Afr. (Natal In.)	29·14 S	30·33 E
124	Campillo de Altobuey (käm-pēl'yō dä äl-tō-bōō'ā) Sp.	39·37 N	1·50 W
99	Campina Grande (käm-pē'nä grän'dĕ) Braz.	7·15 S	35·49 W
101	Campinas (käm-pē'näzh) Braz. (Rio de Janeiro In.)	22·53 S	47·03 W
68	Camp Ind. Res. (kămp) Calif.	32·39 N	116·26 W
164	Campo (käm'pō) Cam.	2·32 N	9·54 E
98	Campoalegre (kä'm-pô-ȧlĕ'grĕ) Col.	2·34 N	75·20 W
126	Campobasso (käm'pô-bäs'sō) It.	41·35 N	14·39 E
101	Campo Belo Braz. (Rio de Janeiro In.)	20·52 S	45·15 W
124	Campo de Criptana (käm'pō dä krēp-tä'nä) Sp.	39·24 N	3·09 W
95	Campo Florido (kä'm-pô flô-rē'dō) Cuba (Havana In.)	23.07 N	82.07 W
99	Campo Grande (käm-pōō grän'dĕ) Braz.	20·28 S	54·32 W
100	Campo Grande Braz. (In.)	22·54 S	43·33 W
99	Campo Maior (käm-pōō mä-yôr') Braz.	4·48 S	42·12 W
124	Campo Maior Port.	39·03 N	7·06 W
125	Campo Real (käm'pô rȧ-äl') Sp. (Madrid In.)	40·21 N	3·23 W
164	Campo R. Cam.	2·23 N	11·07 E
101	Campos (käm-pôs) Braz. (Rio de Janeiro In.)	21·46 S	41·19 W
101	Campos do Jordão (kä'm-pôs-dô-zhôr-douN) Braz. (Rio de Janeiro In.)	22·45 S	45·35 W
101	Campos Gerais (kä'm-pôs-zhĕ-rä'es) Braz. (Rio de Janeiro In.)	21·17 S	45·43 W
166	Camps Bay (kămps) S. Afr. (Cape Town In.)	33·57 S	18·22 E
84	Camp Springs (cămp sprĭngz) Md.	38·48 N	76·55 W
76	Camp Wood (kămp wŏŏd) Tex.	29·39 N	100·02 W
86	Camrose (kăm-rōz) Can.	53·08 N	112·50 W
95	Camu (R.) (kä'mōō) Dom. Rep.	19·05 N	70·15 W
82	Canaan (R.) (kā'năn) Can.	45·55 N	65·45 W
49	Canada (kăn'ȧ-dȧ) N. A.	50·00 N	100·00 W
83	Canada B. Can.	50·51 N	56·22 W
101	Cañada de Gomez (kä-nyä'dä-dĕ-gô'mĕz) Arg. (Buenos Aires In.)	32·49 S	61·24 W
72	Canadian (kȧ-nā'dĭ-ăn) Tex.	35·54 N	100·24 W
73	Canadian R. Okla.	34·53 N	97·06 W
81	Canajoharie (kăn-ȧ-jō-hăr'ē) N. Y.	42·55 N	74·35 W
127	Çanakkale (chä-näk-kä'lĕ) Tur.	40·10 N	26·26 E
127	Çanakkale Boğazı (Dardanelles) (Str.) (chä-näk-kä'lĕ) (där-dȧ-nĕlz') Tur.	40·05 N	25·50 E
88	Canal Zone N. A. (Panama Canal In.)	9·08 N	80·30 W
81	Canandaigua (kăn-ăn-dā'gwȧ) N. Y.	42·55 N	77·20 W
81	Canandaigua (L.) N. Y.	42·45 N	77·20 W
88	Cananea (kä-nä-nĕ'ä) Mex.	31·00 N	110·20 W
75	Canard R..... Can. (Detroit In.)	42·10 N	83·04 W
164	Canarias, Islas (Is.) (ē's-läs-kä-nä'ryȧs) Sp.	29·15 N	16·30 W
94	Canarreos, Arch. de los (Is.) (är-chē-pyĕ'lä-gô-dĕ-lôs-kä-när-rĕ'ōs) Cuba	21·35 N	82·20 W
92	Cañas (kä'-nyȧs) C. R.	10·26 N	85·06 W
98	Cañasgordas (kä'nyäs-gô'r-däs) Col. (In.)	6·44 N	76·01 W
92	Cañas R. C. R.	10·20 N	85·21 W
81	Canastota (kăn-ȧs-tō'tȧ) N. Y.	43·05 N	75·45 W
99	Canastra, Serra de (Mts.) (sĕ'r-rä-dĕ-kä-nä's-trä) Braz.	19·53 S	46·57 W
76	Canatlán (kä-nät-län') Mex.	24·30 N	104·45 W
	Canaveral, C., see Kennedy, C.		
99	Canavieiras (kä-nȧ-vē-ā'räs) Braz.	15·40 S	38·49 W
160	Canberra (kăn'bĕr-ȧ) Austl.	35·21 S	149·10 E
70	Canby (kăn'bĭ) Minn.	44·43 N	96·15 W
98	Canchuaya, Cerros de (Mts.) (sĕ'r-rôs-dĕ-kän-chōō-ȧ'īä) Peru	7·30 S	74·30 W
91	Cancuc (kän-kōōk) Mex.	16·58 N	92·17 W
94	Candelaria (kän-dĕ-lä'ryä) Cuba	22·45 N	82·55 W
155	Candelaria (kän-dȧ-lä'rē-ä) Phil. (Manila In.)	15·39 N	119·55 E
91	Candelaria (R.) (kän-dĕ-lä-ryä) Mex.	18·25 N	91·21 W
124	Candeleda (kän-dhȧ-lā'dhä) Sp.	40·09 N	5·18 W
	Candia, see Kráklion		
64	Candle (kăn'd'l) Alaska	65·00 N	162·04 W
70	Cando (kăn'dō) N. D.	48·27 N	99·13 W
155	Candon (kän-dōn') Phil. (Manila In.)	17·13 N	120·26 E
	Canea, see Khaniá		
101	Canelones (kä-nĕ-lô-nĕs) Ur. (Buenos Aires In.)	34·32 S	56·19 W
101	Canelones (Dept.) Ur. (Buenos Aires In.)	34·34 S	56·15 W
98	Cañete (kän-yā'tā) Peru	13·06 S	76·17 W
95	Caney (kä-nā') (kā'nĭ) Cuba	20·05 N	75·45 W
73	Caney (kā'nĭ) Kans.	37·00 N	95·57 W
78	Caney (R.) Tenn.	36·10 N	85·50 W
166	Canganza, Sierra de (Mts.) (sĕr'rȧ dä kän-gän'zȧ) Ang.	7·35 S	15·30 E
124	Cangas (kän'gäs) Sp.	42·15 N	8·43 W
124	Cangas de Narcea (kä'n-gäs-dĕ-när-sĕ-ä) Sp.	43·08 N	6·36 W
126	Canicatti (kä-nē-kät'tē) It.	37·18 N	13·58 E
124	Caniles (kä-nē'läs) Sp.	37·26 N	2·43 W
90	Cañitas (kän-yē'täs) Mex.	23·38 N	102·44 W
133	Cankırı (chän-kē'rē) Tur.	40·40 N	33·40 E
85	Cannell..... Can. (Edmonton In.)	53·35 N	113·38 W
80	Cannelton (kăn'ĕl-tŭn) Ind.	37·55 N	86·45 W
123	Cannes (kȧn) Fr.	43·34 N	7·05 E
82	Canning (kăn'ĭng) Can.	45·11 N	64·26 W
110	Cannock (kăn'ŭk) Eng.	52·41 N	2·02 W
110	Cannock Chase (Reg.) (kăn'ŭk chās) Eng.	52·43 N	1·54 W
71	Cannon (R.) (kăn'ŭn) Minn.	44·18 N	93·24 W
70	Cannonball (R.) (kăn'ŭn-bäl) N. D.	46·17 N	101·35 W
93	Caño, Isla de (I.) (ē's-lä-dĕ-kä'nō) C. R.	8·38 N	84·00 W
74	Canoga Park (kä-nō'gȧ) Calif. (Los Angeles In.)	34·07 N	118·36 W
72	Canon City (kăn'yŭn) Colo.	38·27 N	105·16 W
75	Canonsburg (kăn'ŭnz-bûrg) Pa. (Pittsburgh In.)	40·16 N	80·11 W
79	Canoochee (R.) (kȧ-nōō'chē) Ga.	32·25 N	82·11 W
86	Canora (kȧ-nōrȧ) Can.	51·43 N	102·32 W
126	Canosa (kä-nō'sä) It.	41·14 N	16·03 E
93	Canouan I. N. A. (Le. & Wind. Is. In.)	12·44 N	61·10 W
92	Cansaheab (kän-sä-ĕ-äb) Mex. (Yucatan In.)	21·11 N	89·05 W
83	Canso (kăn'sō) Can.	45·23 N	60·59 W
83	Canso, C. Can.	45·21 N	60·46 W
83	Canso, Str. of Can.	45·50 N	61·35 W
101	Cantagalo (kän-tä-gá'lo) Braz. (Rio de Janeiro In.)	21·59 S	42·22 W
124	Cantanhede (kän-täN-yā'dä) Port.	40·22 N	8·35 W
110	Canterbury (kăn'tẽr-bẽr-ē) Eng. (London In.)	51·17 N	1·06 E
159	Canterbury Bght...... N. Z. (In.)	44·17 S	172·38 E
94	Cantiles, Cayo (I.) (ky-ō-kän-tē'läs) Cuba	21·40 N	82·00 W
78	Canton Ga.	34·13 N	84·29 W
73	Canton Ill.	40·34 N	90·02 W
83	Canton....... Mass. (Boston In.)	42·09 N	71·09 W
78	Canton Miss.	32·36 N	90·01 W
73	Canton Mo.	40·08 N	91·33 W
78	Canton N. C.	35·32 N	82·50 W
80	Canton Ohio	40·50 N	81·25 W
81	Canton Pa.	41·50 N	76·45 W
70	Canton S. D.	43·17 N	96·37 W
	Canton, see Kuangchou		
156	Canton (I.) Oceania	3·50 S	174.00 W
126	Cantu (kän-tōō') It.	45·43 N	9·09 E
101	Cañuelas (kä-nyōōĕ'-läs) Arg. (Buenos Aires In.)	35·03 S	58·45 W
99	Canumã (R.) (kä-nōō-mȧ') Braz.	6·20 S	58·57 W
72	Canyon (kăn'yŭn) Tex.	34·59 N	101·57 W
65	Canyon (R.) Wash. (Seattle In.)	48·09 N	121·48 W
76	Canyon Dam Tex.	29·51 N	98·20 W
69	Canyon De Chelly Natl. Mon. Ariz.	36·14 N	110·00 W
155	Capalonga (kä-pä-lôŋ'gä) Phil. (Manila In.)	14·20 N	122·30 E
126	Capannori (kä-pän'nō-rē) It.	43·50 N	10·30 E
125	Caparica (kä-pä-rē'kä) Port. (Lisbon In.)	38·40 N	9·12 W
83	Cap-Aux-Meules Can.	47·25 N	61·51 W
99	Capaya (R.) (kä-pä-īä) Ven. (In.)	10·28 N	66·15 W
82	Cap-Chat (kăp shä') Can.	49·07 N	66·42 W
82	Cap de la Madeleine (kăp dē lȧ mȧ-d'lĕn') Can.	46·23 N	72·30 W
83	Cape Breton (I.) (kāp brĕt'ŭn) Can.	45·48 N	59·53 W
83	Cape Breton Highlands Natl. Park Can.	46·45 N	61·05 W
79	Cape Charles (kāp chärlz) Va.	37·13 N	76·02 W
164	Cape Coast Ghana	5·14 N	1·19 W
81	Cape Cod B. (kāp kŏd) Mass.	41·50 N	70·20 W
79	Cape Fear (R.) (kāp fēr) N. C.	34·43 N	78·41 W
166	Cape Flats S. Afr. (Cape Town In.)	34·01 S	18·37 E

ng-sing; ŋ-baŋk; N-nasalized n; nŏd; cŏmmit; ōld; ôbey; ôrder; fōōd; fŏŏt; ou-out; s-soft; sh-dish; th-thin; pūre; ûnite; ûrn; stŭd; circŭs; ü-as "y" in study; '-indeterminate vowel.

190 Cape Girardeau–Castellammare di Stabia PRONOUNCING INDEX

Page	Name Pronunciation Region	Lat. °′	Long. °′
73	Cape Girardeau (jē-rär-dō′) . . Mo.	37·17 N	89·32 W
84	Cape Henry (hĕn′rē) Va. (Norfolk In.)	36·55 N	76·00 W
81	Cape May (kāp mā) . . . . N. J.	38·55 N	74·50 W
81	Cape May C. H. (kāp mā) . . N. J.	39·05 N	75·00 W
166	Cape of Good Hope (Prov.) (kāp ŏv gŏŏd hōp) . S. Afr.	31·50 S	21·15 E
86	Cape Parry (kāp păr′ē) . . . . . Can.	70·29 N	127·41 W
166	Cape Point . S. Afr. (Cape Town In.)	34·21 S	18·29 E
87	Cape Smith Ra. (kāp smĭth) . Can.	61·23 N	76·32 W
93	Capesterre Basse Terre (Le. & Wind Is. In.)	16·02 N	61·37 W
166	Cape Town (kāp toun) S. Afr. (Cape Town In.)	33·48 S	18·28 E
159	Cape York Pen. (kāp yôrk) . Austl.	12·30 S	142·35 E
95	Cap-Haïtien (kȧp ȧ-ē-syăn′) . . Hai.	19·45 N	72·15 W
101	Capilla de Señor (kä-pēl′yä dā sān-yōr′) . Arg. (Buenos Aires In.)	34·18 S	59·07 W
69	Capitol Reef Natl. Mon. (kăp′ĭ-tŏl) . Utah	38·15 N	111·10 W
101	Capivari (kä-pē-vá′rē) Braz. (Rio de Janeiro In.)	22·59 S	47·29 W
100	Capivari . . . . Braz. (In.)	22·39 S	43·19 W
160	Capoompeta (Mtn.) (kȧ-pōōm-pē′tȧ) . Austl.	29·15 S	152·12 E
126	Caporetto (kä-pō-rĕt′tō) . . . Yugo.	46·15 N	13·34 E
126	Capraia (I.) (kä-prä′yä) . . . . It.	43·02 N	9·51 E
126	Caprara Pt. (kä-prä′rä) . . . . . . It.	41·08 N	8·20 E
126	Caprera (I.) (kä-prā′rä) . . . . It.	41·12 N	9·28 E
125	Capri . . . . It. (Naples In.)	40·18 N	14·16 E
125	Capri, I. di (ē′-sō-lä-dē-kä′prē) It. (Naples In.)	40·19 N	14·10 E
159	Capricorn Chan. (kăp′rĭ-kôrn) Austl.	22·27 S	151·24 E
166	Caprivi Strip (Reg.) . . . . S. W. Afr.	18·00 S	22·00 E
85	Cap-Rouge (kȧp rōōzh′) Can. (Quebec In.)	46·45 N	71·21 W
85	Cap St. Ignace (kĭp săN-tē-nyȧs′) Can. (Quebec In.)	47·02 N	70·27 W
126	Capua (kä′pwä) . . . . It.	41·07 N	14·14 E
90	Capulhuac (kä-pōōl-hwäk′) . . Mex.	19·33 N	99·43 W
72	Capulin Mountain Natl. Mon. (kȧ-pū′lĭn) . N. Mex.	36·15 N	103·58 W
91	Capultitlán (kä-pōō′l-tē-tlȧ′n) Mex. (Mexico City In.)	19·15 N	99·40 W
98	Caquetá (R.) (kä-kä-tȧ′) . . . . . Col.	0·23 S	73·22 W
125	Carabaña (kä-rä-bän′yä) Sp. (Madrid In.)	40·16 N	3·15 W
99	Carabobo (State) (kä-rä-bô′-bô) Ven. (In.)	10·07 N	68·06 W
127	Caracal (kȧ-rȧ-kȧl′) . . . . Rom.	44·06 N	24·22 E
99	Caracas (kä-rä′käs) . . . . Ven. (In.)	10·30 N	66·58 W
90	Carácuaro de Morelos (kä-rä′kwä-rō-dĕ-mô-rĕ-lôs) . Mex.	18·44 N	101·04 W
101	Caraguatatuba (kä-rä-gwä-tȧ-tōō′bȧ) . Braz. (Rio de Janeiro In.)	23·37 S	45·26 W
99	Carajás, Serra dos (Mts.) (sĕ′r-rä-dôs-kä-rä-zhá′s) . Braz.	5·58 S	51·45 W
98	Caramanta, Cerro (Mtn.) (sĕ′r-rô-kä-rä-mȧ′n-tä) . Col. (In.)	5·29 N	76·01 W
100	Caramarca (kä-rä-mȧ′r-kä) . . . Arg.	28·29 S	65·45 W
155	Caramoan (kä-rä-mō′än) Phil. (Manila In.)	13·46 N	123·52 E
101	Carandaí (kä-rän-dȧē′) Braz. (Rio de Janeiro In.)	20·57 S	43·47 W
101	Carangola (kä-rȧn′gŏ′lȧ) Braz. (Rio de Janeiro In.)	20·46 S	42·02 W
127	Caransebes (kȧ-rȧn-sā′bĕsh) . Rom.	45·24 N	22·13 E
82	Caraquet (kă-rȧ-kĕt′) . . . . Can.	47·47 N	64·56 W
93	Carata, Laguna (L.) (lä-gōō′nä-kä-rä′tä) . Nic.	13·59 N	83·41 W
93	Caratasca, Laguna (L.) (lä-gōō′nä-kä-rä-täs′kä) . Hond.	15·20 N	83·45 W
124	Caravaca (kä-rä-vä′kä) . . . . . . Sp.	38·05 N	1·51 W
99	Caravelas (kȧ-rä-vĕl′äzh) . . . . . Braz.	17·46 S	39·06 W
99	Carayaca (kȧ-rä-īȧ′kä) . . Ven. (In.)	10·32 N	67·07 W
100	Caràzinho (kä-rȧ′zē-nyŏ) . . . Braz.	28·22 S	52·33 W
124	Carballino (kär-bäl-yē′nō) . . . . . Sp.	42·26 N	8·04 W
124	Carballo (kär-bäl′yō) . . . . Sp.	43·13 N	8·40 W
65	Carbon (R.) (kär′bŏn) Wash. (Seattle In.)	47·06 N	122·08 W
65	Carbonado (kär-bō-nä′dō) Wash. (Seattle In.)	47·05 N	122·03 W
126	Carbonara, C. (kär-bō-nä′rä) . . . It.	39·08 N	9·33 E
85	Carbondale (kär′bŏn-dāl) Can. (Edmonton In.)	53·45 N	113·32 W
73	Carbondale . . . . Ill.	37·42 N	89·12 W
81	Carbondale . . . . Pa.	41·35 N	75·30 W
83	Carbonear (kär-bô-nēr′) . . . . . Can.	47·43 N	53·16 W
78	Carbon Hill (kär′bŏn hĭl) . . . . . Ala.	33·53 N	87·34 W
78	Carbur (kär′bûr) . . . . Fla.	29·55 N	83·25 W
125	Carcagente (kär-kä-hĕn′tä) . . . . Sp.	39·09 N	0·29 W
122	Carcans, Étang de (L.) (ā-taN-dĕ-kär-käN) . Fr.	45·12 N	1·00 W
122	Carcassonne (kȧr-kȧ-sôn′) . . . . Fr.	43·12 N	2·23 E
86	Carcross (kär′krŏs) . . . . Can.	60·18 N	134·54 W
145	Cardamon Hills (kär′dȧ-mŭm) Ceylon (In.)	9·45 N	77·28 E
94	Cárdenas (kär′dȧ-näs) . . . . . . Cuba	23·00 N	81·10 W
91	Cárdenas (kȧ′r-dĕ-näs) . . . . . . Mex.	17·59 N	93·23 W
90	Cárdenas . . . . Mex.	22·01 N	99·38 W
95	Cardenas, Bahía de (B.) (bä-ē′ä-dĕ-kär′dȧ-näs) . Cuba	23·10 N	81·10 W
85	Cardiff (kär′dĭf) Can. (Edmonton In.)	53·46 N	113·36 W
116	Cardiff . . . . Wales	51·30 N	3·18 W
116	Cardigan (kär′dĭ-gȧn) . . . . Wales	52·05 N	4·40 W
116	Cardigan B . . . . Wales	52·35 N	4·40 W
86	Cardston (kärds′tŭn) . . . . Can.	49·14 N	113·23 W
121	Carei (kä-rĕ′) . . . . Rom.	47·42 N	22·28 E
122	Carentan (kä-rôN-täN′) . . . . Fr.	49·19 N	1·14 W
80	Carey (kā′rē) . . . . Ohio	40·55 N	83·25 W
158	Carey (I.) (kâr′ē) . . . . Austl.	29·20 S	123·35 E
122	Carhaix (kär-ĕ′) . . . . Fr.	48·17 N	3·37 W
89	Caribbean Sea (kăr-ĭ-bē′ăn) N. A.-S. A.	14·30 N	75·30 W
86	Cariboo Mts. (kă′rĭ-bōō) . . . . Can.	53·51 N	122·13 W
82	Caribou . . . . Maine	46·51 N	68·01 W
71	Caribou (I.) . . . . Can.	47·22 N	85·42 W
74	Caribou L . . . . Minn. (Duluth In.)	46·54 N	92·16 W
86	Caribou Mts . . . . Can.	59·20 N	115·30 W
99	Carinhanha (kä-rĭ-nyăn′yä) . Braz.	14·14 S	43·44 W
126	Carini (kä-rē′nē) . . . . It.	38·09 N	13·10 E
	Carinthia, see Kärnten		
81	Carleton Place (kärl′tŭn) . . . . Can.	45·15 N	76·10 W
73	Carlinville (kär′lĭn-vĭl) . . . . Ill.	39·16 N	89·52 W
116	Carlisle (kär-līl′) . . . . Eng.	54·54 N	3·03 W
80	Carlisle . . . . Ky.	38·20 N	84·00 W
81	Carlisle . . . . Pa.	40·10 N	77·15 W
122	Carlitte, Pic (Pk.) (pēk′-kär-lēt′) Fr.	42·33 N	1·56 E
126	Carloforte (kär′lō-fôr-tȧ) . . . . . . It.	39·11 N	8·18 E
101	Carlos Casares (kär-lôs-kä-sȧ′rĕs) Arg. (Buenos Aires In.)	35·38 S	61·17 W
116	Carlow (kär′lō) . . . . Ire.	52·50 N	7·00 W
76	Carlsbad (kärlz′băd) . . . . . N. Mex.	32·24 N	104·12 W
76	Carlsbad Caverns Natl. Park N. Mex.	32·08 N	104·30 W
110	Carlton (kärl′tŭn) . . . . Eng.	52·58 N	1·05 W
74	Carlton . . . . Minn. (Duluth In.)	46·40 N	92·26 W
80	Carlton Center (kärl′tŭn sĕn′tĕr) Mich.	42·45 N	85·20 W
168	Carltonville S. Afr. (Johannesburg & Pretoria In.)	26·20 S	27·23 E
73	Carlyle (kär-līl′) . . . . Ill.	38·37 N	89·23 W
126	Carmagnola (kär-mä-nyô′lä) . . . It.	44·52 N	7·48 E
86	Carman (kär′mȧn) . . . . Can.	49·30 N	98·02 W
116	Carmarthen (kär-mär′thĕn) . Wales	51·50 N	4·20 W
116	Carmarthen B. (kär-mär′thĕn) Wales	51·33 N	4·50 W
122	Carmaux (kȧr-mō′) . . . . Fr.	44·05 N	2·09 E
84	Carmel (kär′mĕl) N. Y. (New York In.)	41·25 N	73·42 W
101	Carmelo (kär-mĕ′lo) Ur. (Buenos Aires In.)	33·59 S	58·15 W
90	Carmen, Isla del (I.) (ē′s-lä-dĕl-kä′r-mĕn) . Mex.	18·43 N	91·40 W
91	Carmen, Laguna del (L.) (lä-gōō′nä-dĕl-kä′r-mĕn) . Mex.	18·15 N	93·26 W
101	Carmen de Areco (kär′mĕn′ dā ä-rä′kō) . Arg. (Buenos Aires In.)	34·21 S	59·50 W
100	Carmen de Patagones (kä′r-mĕn-dĕ-pä-tä-gô′-nĕs) . Arg.	41·00 S	63·00 W
80	Carmi (kär′mī) . . . . Ill.	38·05 N	88·10 W
101	Carmo (kä′r-mô) Braz. (Rio de Janeiro In.)	21·57 S	42·06 W
101	Carmo do Rio Clara (kä′r-mô-dō-rē′ō-klä′-rä) Braz. (Rio de Janeiro In.)	20·57 S	46·04 W
124	Carmona (kär-mō′nä) . . . . Sp.	37·28 N	5·38 W
158	Carnarvon (kär-när′vŭn) . . . Austl.	24·45 S	113·45 E
166	Carnarvon . . . . S. Afr.	31·00 S	22·15 E
116	Carnarvon . . . . Wales	53·08 N	4·17 W
116	Carnarvon Bay . . . . Wales	53·09 N	4·56 W
65	Carnation (kär-nā′shŭn) Wash. (Seattle In.)	47·39 N	121·55 W
125	Carnaxide (kär-nä-shē′dĕ) Port. (Lisbon In.)	38·44 N	9·15 W
116	Carndonagh (kärn-dō-nä′) . . . . Ire.	54·75 N	6·75 W
72	Carnegie (kär-nĕg′ĭ) . . . . Okla.	35·06 N	98·38 W
75	Carnegie . . . . . Pa. (Pittsburgh In.)	40·24 N	80·06 W
81	Carneys Point (kär′nês) . . . . . N. J.	39·45 N	75·25 W
120	Carnic Alps (Mts.) . . . . Aus.-It.	46·43 N	12·38 E
125	Carnot (kär nō′) . . . . Alg.	36·15 N	1·40 E
165	Carnot . . . . Cen. Afr. Rep.	4·56 N	16·00 E
116	Carnsore Pt. (kärn′sôr) . . . . Ire.	52·10 N	6·16 W
80	Caro (kâ′rō) . . . . Mich.	43·30 N	83·25 W
99	Carolina (kä-rô-lē′nä) . . . . Braz.	7·26 S	47·16 W
166	Carolina (kă-rô-lī′nȧ) . . . . . . S. Afr.	26·07 S	30·09 E
92	Carolina L. (kä-rô-lē′-nä) Mex. (Yucatan In.)	18·41 N	89·40 W
156	Caroline Is. (kăr′ô-līn) Pac. Is. Trust Ter.	9·30 N	143·00 E
98	Caroni (R.) (kä-rō′nē) . . . . Ven.	5·49 N	62·57 W
98	Carora (kä-rō′rä) . . . . Ven.	10·09 N	70·12 W
115	Carpathians Mts. (kär-pā′thĭ-ăn) Eur.	49·23 N	20·14 E
127	Carpatii Meridionali (Transylvanian Alps) (Mts.) . Rom.	45·30 N	23·30 E
158	Capentaria, G. of (kär-pĕn-târ′ĭȧ) . Austl.	14·45 S	138·50 E
74	Carpenter (kär′pĕn-tĕr) Ill. (St. Louis In.)	38·54 N	89·54 W
122	Carpentras (kär-päN-träs′) . . . . Fr.	44·04 N	5·01 E
126	Carpi . . . . It.	44·48 N	10·54 E
78	Carrabelle (kăr′ȧ-bĕl) . . . . Fla.	29·50 N	84·40 W
116	Carrantuohill (kă-răn-tōō′ĭl) . Ire.	52·01 N	9·48 W
126	Carrara (kä-rä′rä) . . . . It.	44·05 N	10·05 E
98	Carretas, Punta (Pt.) (pōō′n-tä-kär-rĕ′tĕ′räs) . Peru	14·15 S	76·25 W
93	Carriacou I. (kăr-ê-ȧ-kōō′) N. A. (Le. & Wind. Is. In.)	12·28 N	61·20 W
116	Carrick (kăr′ĭk) . . . . Ire.	52·20 N	7·35 W
85	Carrier (kăr′ĭ-ĕr) Can. (Quebec In.)	46·43 N	71·05 W
78	Carriere (kȧ-rēr′) . . . . Miss.	30·37 N	89·37 W
80	Carriers Mills (kăr′ĭ-ĕrs) . . . . . . Ill.	37·40 N	88·40 W
70	Carrington (kăr′ĭng-tŭn) . . . . N. D.	47·26 N	99·06 W
65	Carr Inlet (kär ĭn′lĕt) Wash. (Seattle In.)	47·20 N	122·42 W
124	Carrion (kär-rē-ōn′) . . . . Sp.	42·36 N	6·42 W
94	Carrion Crow Hbr. (kăr′ĭŭn krō) Ba. Is.	26·35 N	77·55 W
124	Carrión de los Condes (kär-rê-ōn′ dā lōs kōn′dȧs) . Sp.	42·20 N	4·35 W
72	Carrizo Cr. (kär-rē′zō) . . . N. Mex.	36·22 N	103·39 W
76	Carrizo Springs . . . . Tex.	28·32 N	99·51 W
69	Carrizozo (kär-rē-zō′zō) . . N. Mex.	33·40 N	105·55 W
71	Carroll (kăr′ŭl) . . . . Iowa	42·03 N	94·51 W
78	Carrollton (kăr-ŭl-tŭn) . . . . Ga.	33·35 N	84·05 W
73	Carrollton . . . . Ill.	39·18 N	90·22 W
80	Carrollton . . . . Ky.	38·45 N	85·15 W
80	Carrollton . . . . Mich.	43·30 N	83·55 W
73	Carrollton . . . . Mo.	39·21 N	93·29 W
80	Carrollton . . . . Ohio	40·35 N	81·10 W
74	Carrollton Tex. (Dallas, Fort Worth In.)	32·58 N	96·53 W
75	Carrollville (kăr′ŭl vĭl) Wis. (Milwaukee In.)	42·53 N	87·52 W
65	Carrols (kăr′ŭlz) Wash. (Portland In.)	46·05 N	122·51 W
116	Carron (L.) (kȧ′rŭn) . . . . Scot.	57·25 N	5·25 W
122	Carry-le-Rouet (kä-rē′lĕ-rōō-ā′) Fr. (Marseille In.)	43·20 N	5·10 E
133	Çarşamba (chär-shäm′bä) . . . . Tur.	41·05 N	36·40 E
68	Carson (R.) (kär′sŭn) . . . . Nev.	39·15 N	119·25 W
68	Carson City . . . . Nev.	39·10 N	119·45 W
68	Carson Sink . . . . Nev.	39·51 N	118·25 W
155	Carstensz-Toppen (Pk.) (kärs′tĕns) W. Irian	4·00 S	137·10 E
98	Cartagena (kär-tä-hā′nä) . . . . . Col.	10·30 N	75·40 W
125	Cartagena (kär-tä-κē′nä) . . . . . . Sp.	37·46 N	1·00 W
98	Cartago (kär-tä′gō) . . . . . Col. (In.)	4·44 N	75·54 W
93	Cartago . . . . C. R.	9·52 N	83·56 W
124	Cartaxo (kär-tä′shō) . . . . Port.	39·10 N	8·48 W
84	Carteret (kär′tē-rĕt) N. J. (New York In.)	40·35 N	74·13 W
78	Cartersville (kär′tĕrs-vĭl) . . . . . Ga.	34·09 N	84·47 W
73	Carthage (kär′thȧj) . . . . Ill.	40·27 N	91·09 W
73	Carthage . . . . Mo.	37·10 N	94·18 W
81	Carthage . . . . N. Y.	44·00 N	75·45 W
79	Carthage . . . . N. C.	35·22 N	79·25 W
77	Carthage . . . . Tex.	32·09 N	94·20 W
164	Carthage . . . . Tun.	37·04 N	10·18 E
167	Carthcart (cärth-cȧ′t) S. Afr. (Natal In.)	32·18 S	27·11 E
87	Cartwright (kärt′rīt) . . . . Can.	53·36 N	57·00 W
99	Caruaru (kä-rōō-ȧ-rōō′) . . . . . Braz.	8·19 S	35·52 W
98	Carúpano (kä-rōō′pä-nō) . . . . . Ven.	10·45 N	63·21 W
73	Caruthersville (kȧ-rŭdh′ērz-vĭl) Mo	36·09 N	89·41 W
65	Carver (kärv′ĕr) Ore. (Portland In.)	45·24 N	122·30 W
124	Carvoeira, Cabo (C.) (kȧ′bō-kär-vô-ĕ′y-rä) . Port.	39·22 N	9·24 W
75	Cary (kā′rē) . . . . Ill. (Chicago In.)	42·13 N	88·14 W
101	Casablanca (kä-sä-blăŋ′kä) Chile (Santiago In.)	33·19 S	71·24 W
164	Casablanca . . . . Mor.	33·32 N	7·41 W
101	Casa Branca (kȧ′sä-brȧ′N-kȧ) Braz. (Rio de Janeiro In.)	21·47 S	47·04 W
69	Casa Grande (kä′sä grăn′dā) . Ariz.	32·50 N	111·45 W
69	Casa Grande Natl. Mon. . . . . Ariz.	33·00 N	111·33 W
126	Casale (kä-sä′lā) . . . . It.	45·08 N	8·26 E
126	Casalmaggiore (kä-säl-mäd-jō′rä) . It.	45·00 N	10·24 E
164	Casamance R. (kä-sä-mäNs′) Senegal	12·58 N	15·15 W
85	Cascade (kăs-kād′) Can. (Ottawa In.)	45·35 N	75·51 W
159	Cascade Pt. . . . . N. Z. (In.)	43·59 S	168·23 E
62	Cascade Ra . . . . U. S.	42·50 N	122·20 W
85	Cascades Point (kăs-kādz′) Can. (Montreal In.)	45·19 N	73·58 W
66	Cascade Tun . . . . Wash.	47·41 N	120·53 W
125	Cascais (käs-kȧ-ēzh) Port. (Lisbon In.)	38·42 N	9·25 W
125	Cascais, Ba. de (B.) (bä-ē′ä-dĕ-käs-kī′s) Port. (Lisbon In.)	38·41 N	9·24 W
65	Case Inlet (kās) Wash. (Seattle In.)	47·22 N	122·47 W
100	Caseros (kä-sā′rôs) . . . . . Arg. (In.)	34·21 S	58·34 W
126	Caserta (kä-zĕr′tä) . . . . It.	41·04 N	14·21 E
80	Casey (kā′sĭ) . . . . Ill.	39·20 N	88·00 W
66	Cashmere (kăsh′mĭr) . . . . Wash.	47·30 N	120·28 W
155	Casiguran (kä-sē-gōō′rän) Phil. (Manila In.)	16·15 N	122·10 E
155	Casiguran Sd . . Phil. (Manila In.)	16·02 N	121·51 E
101	Casilda (kä-sē′l-dä) Arg. (Buenos Aires In.)	33·02 S	61·11 W
94	Casilda . . . . Cuba	21·50 N	80·00 W
101	Casimiro de Abreu (kä′sē-mē′ro-(dĕ-ȧ-brĕ′ōō) . Braz. (Rio de Janeiro In.)	22·30 S	42·11 W
160	Casino (kȧ-sē′nō) . . . . Austl.	28·35 S	153·10 E
98	Casiquiare (R.) (kä-sê-kyä′rä) Ven.	2·11 N	66·15 W
125	Caspe (käs′pȧ) . . . . Sp.	41·18 N	0·02 W
67	Casper (kăs′pĕr) . . . . Wyo.	42·51 N	106·18 W
132	Caspian Dep. (kăs′pĭ-ȧn) . Sov. Un.	47·40 N	51·40 E
130	Caspian Sea . . . . Sov. Un.	39·30 N	52·00 E
81	Cass (kăs) . . . . W. Va.	38·25 N	79·55 W
71	Cass (L.) . . . . Minn.	47·23 N	94·28 W
125	Cassá de la Selva (käs-sä′dĕ-lä-sĕl-vä) . Sp.	41·52 N	2·52 E
166	Cassai (R.) (kä-sä′ē) . . . . Ang.	11·15 S	21·00 E
80	Cass City (kăs) . . . . Mich.	43·35 N	83·10 W
85	Casselman (kăs′′l-mȧn) Can. (Ottawa In.)	45·18 N	75·05 W
70	Casselton (kăs′′l-tŭn) . . . . N. D.	46·53 N	97·14 W
101	Cássia (kȧ′syä) Braz. (Rio de Janeiro In.)	20·36 S	46·53 W
74	Cassin (kăs′ĭn) Tex. (San Antonio In.)	29·16 N	98·29 W
166	Cassinga (kä-sĭŋ′gȧ) . . . . Ang.	15·05 S	16·15 E
126	Cassino (käs-sē′nō) . . . . It.	41·30 N	13·50 E
71	Cass Lake (kăs) . . . . Minn.	47·23 N	94·37 W
80	Cassopolis (kăs-ŏ′pô-lĭs) . . . . Mich.	41·55 N	86·00 W
73	Cassville (kăs′vĭl) . . . . Mo.	36·41 N	93·52 W
124	Castanheira de Pêra (käs-tän-yā′rä-dĕ-pĕ′rä) . Port.	40·00 N	8·07 W
122	Casteljaloux (käs-tĕl-zhä-lōō′) . Fr.	44·20 N	0·04 E
125	Castellammare di Stabia (käs-tĕl-läm-mä′rä-dē-stä′byä) It. (Naples In.)	40·26 N	14·29 E

ăt; finȧl; rāte; senȧte; ärm; ȧsk; sofȧ; fâre; ch-choose; dh-as th in other; bē; ēvent; bĕt; recĕnt; cratēr; g-go; gh-guttural g; bĭt; ĭ-short neutral; rīde; κ-guttural k as ch in German ich;

PRONOUNCING INDEX Castelli–Chalons-sur-Marne 191

Page	Name Pronunciation Region	Lat. °′	Long. °′
101	Castelli (käs-tĕ'zhē) Arg. (Buenos Aires In.)	36·07 S	57·48 W
125	Castellón de la Plana (käs-tĕl-yô'n-dĕ-lä-plä'nä). Sp.	39·59 N	0·05 W
122	Castelnaudary (käs'tĕl-nō-dà-rē') Fr.	43·20 N	1·57 E
101	Castelo (käs-tĕ'lô) Braz. (Rio de Janeiro In.)	21·37 S	41·13 W
124	Castelo Branco (käs-tä'lōō brän'kōō). Port.	39·48 N	7·37 W
124	Castelo de Vide (käs-tä'lōō dĭ vē'dĭ). Port.	39·25 N	7·25 W
122	Castelsarrasin (kàs'tĕl-sà-rà-zăN'). Fr.	44·03 N	1·05 E
126	Castelvetrano (käs'tĕl-vē-trä'nō) It.	37·43 N	12·50 E
98	Castilla (kàs-tē'l-yä) Peru	5·18 S	80·40 W
124	Castilla La Nueva (Reg.) (käs-tē'lyä lä nwä'vä). Sp.	39·15 N	3·55 W
124	Castilla La Vieja (Reg.) (käs-tē'lyä lä vyā'hä). Sp.	40·48 N	4·24 W
79	Castillo De San Marcos Natl. Mon. (käs-tē'lyä de-sän mär-kōs) Fla.	29·55 N	81·25 W
95	Castle (I.) (kàs''l) Ba. Is.	22·05 N	74·20 W
116	Castlebar (kàs''l-bär) Ire.	53·55 N	9·15 W
69	Castle Dale (kàs''l dāl) Utah	39·15 N	111·00 W
110	Castle Donington (dŏn'ĭng-tŭn) Eng.	52·50 N	1·21 W
110	Castleford (kàs''l-fērd) Eng.	53·43 N	1·21 W
160	Castlemaine (käs''l-mān) Austl.	37·05 S	144·14 E
69	Castle Pk. Colo.	39·00 N	106·50 W
66	Castlerock (kàs''l-rŏk) Wash.	46·17 N	122·53 W
71	Castle Rock Res. Wis.	44·03 N	89·48 W
75	Castle Shannon (shăn'ŭn) Pa. (Pittsburgh In.)	40·22 N	80·02 W
75	Castleton (kàs''l-tŭn) Ind. (Indianapolis In.)	39·54 N	86·03 W
85	Castor R. (kăs'tôr) Can (Ottawa In.)	45·16 N	75·14 W
73	Castor (R.) Mo.	36·59 N	89·53 W
122	Castres (kàs'tr') Fr.	43·36 N	2·13 E
93	Castries (kàs-trē') St. Lucia (Le. & Wind. Is. In.)	14·01 N	61·00 W
100	Castro (käs'trōō) Braz.	24·56 S	50·00 W
100	Castro (käs'tro) Chile	42·27 S	73·48 W
124	Castro Daire (käs'trōō dīr'ĭ). Port.	40·56 N	7·57 W
124	Castro de Río (käs-trô-dĕ-rē'ō) Sp.	37·42 N	4·28 W
123	Castrop Rauxel (käs'trōp rou'ksĕl). Ger. (Ruhr In.)	51·33 N	7·19 E
124	Castro Urdiales (käs'trō ōōr-dyä'läs). Sp.	43·23 N	3·11 W
65	Castro Valley Calif. (San Francisco In.)	37·42 N	122·05 W
124	Castro Verde (käs-trō vĕr'dĕ). Port.	37·43 N	8·05 W
126	Castrovillari (käs'tro-vēl-lyä'rē). It.	39·48 N	16·11 E
124	Castuera (käs-tōō-ā'rä) Sp.	38·43 N	5·33 W
95	Cat (I.) Ba. Is.	25·30 N	75·30 W
92	Catacamas (kä-tä-kà'màs). Hond.	14·52 N	85·55 W
101	Cataguases (kä-tä-gwà'sĕs) Braz. (Rio de Janeiro In.)	21·23 S	42·42 W
77	Catahoula L. (kăt-à-hōō'là) La.	31·35 N	92·20 W
99	Catalão (kä-tä-louN') Braz.	18·09 S	47·42 W
95	Catalina (I.) (kä-tä-lē'nä) Dom. Rep.	18·20 N	69·00 W
125	Cataluma (Reg.) (kä-tä-lōō'mä) Sp.	41·23 N	0·50 E
100	Catamarca (Prov.) (kä-tä-mär'kä) Arg.	27·15 S	67·15 W
155	Catanduanes (I.) (kä-tän-dwä'nĕs) Phil.	13·55 N	125·00 E
99	Catanduva (kä-tàn-dōō'vä). Braz.	21·12 S	48·47 W
126	Catania (kä-tä'nyä) It.	37·30 N	15·09 E
126	Catania, Golfo di (G.) (gôl-fô-dē-kä-tä'nyä). It.	37·24 N	15·28 E
155	Catanuan (kä-tä-nä'wän) Phil.	13·36 N	122·20 E
126	Catanzaro (kä-tän-dzä'rō) It.	38·53 N	16·34 E
125	Catarroja (kä-tär-rō'hä) Sp.	39·24 N	0·25 W
79	Catawba (L.) S. C.	35·02 N	81·21 W
79	Catawba (R.) (kȧ-tô'bȧ) N. C.	35·25 N	80·55 W
91	Catazajá, Laguna de (L.) (lä-gōō'nä-dĕ-kä-tä-zä-hà'). Mex.	17·45 N	92·03 W
155	Catbalogan (kät-bä-lō'gän) Phil.	11·45 N	124·52 E
91	Catemaco (kä-tä-mä'kō) Mex.	18·26 N	95·06 W
91	Catemaco, Lago (L.) (lä'gô-kä-tä-mä'kō). Mex.	18·23 N	95·04 W
110	Caterham (kā'tēr-ŭm) Eng. (London In.)	51·16 N	0·04 W
166	Catete (kä-tĕ'tĕ) Ang.	9·05 S	13·38 E
76	Cathedral Mt. (kȧ-thē'drăl). Tex.	30·09 N	103·46 W
167	Cathedral Pk. (kă-thē'drăl) S. Afr. (Natal In.)	28·53 S	29·04 E
73	Catherine, L. (kă-thĕr-ĭn) Ark.	34·26 N	92·47 W
167	Cathkin Pk. (kăth'kĭn) S. Afr. (Natal In.)	29·08 S	29·22 E
65	Cathlamet (kăth-lăm'ĕt) Wash. (Portland In.)	46·12 N	123·53 W
80	Catlettsburg (kăt'lĕts-bûrg) Ky.	38·20 N	82·35 W
88	Catoche, C. (kä-tô'chĕ) Mex.	21·30 N	87·15 W
84	Catonsville (kā'tŭnz-vĭl) Md. (Baltimore In.)	39·16 N	76·45 W
90	Catorce (kä-tôr'sà) Mex.	23·41 N	100·51 W
81	Catskill (kăts'kĭl) N. Y.	42·15 N	73·50 W
81	Catskill Mts. N. Y.	42·20 N	74·35 W
81	Cattaraugus Ind. Res. (kăt'tà-rô-gŭs). N. Y.	42·30 N	79·05 W
99	Catu (kà-tōō) Braz.	12·26 S	38·12 W
166	Catumbela (kä'tŏm-bĕl'à) Ang.	12·30 S	13·35 E
155	Cauayan (kou-ä'yän) Phil. (Manila In.)	16·56 N	121·46 E
98	Cauca (R.) (kou'kä) Col.	7·30 N	75·26 W
99	Caucagua (käōō-kä'gwä) Ven. (In.)	10·17 N	66·22 W
133	Caucasus Mts. (kô'kȧ-sŭs). Sov. Un.	43·20 N	42·00 E
122	Cauderan (kō-dā-räN') Fr.	44·50 N	0·40 W
85	Caughnawaga. Can. (Montreal In.)	45·24 N	73·41 W
126	Caulonia (kou-lō'nyä) It.	38·24 N	16·22 E
100	Cauquenes (kou-kā'nās) Chile	35·54 S	72·14 W
98	Caura (R.) (kou'rä) Ven.	6·48 N	64·40 W
82	Causapscal Can.	48·19 N	67·18 W
95	Cauto (R.) (kou'tō) Cuba	18·35 N	76·20 W
142	Cauvery (R.) India	11·15 N	78·06 E
100	Cava (kà'vä) Braz. (In.)	22·41 S	43·26 W
125	Cava de' Tirreni (kä'vä-dĕ-tēr-rĕ'nē). It. (Naples In.)	40·27 N	14·43 E
124	Cavado (R.) (kä-vä'dō) Port.	41·43 N	8·08 W
99	Cavalcante (kä-väl-kän'tā). Braz.	13·45 S	47·33 W
70	Cavalier (kăv-à-lēr') N. D.	48·45 N	97·39 W
164	Cavally (R.) Lib.-Ivory Coast	6·06 N	8·09 W
116	Cavan (kăv'ăn) Ire.	54·01 N	7·00 W
126	Cavarzere (kä-vär'dzā-rā) It.	45·08 N	12·06 E
81	Cavendish (kăv'ĕn-dĭsh) Vt.	43·25 N	72·35 W
99	Caviana, Ilha (I.) (kä-vyä'nä) Braz.	0·45 N	49·33 W
155	Cavite (kä-vē'tä) Phil. (Manila In.)	14·30 N	120·54 E
110	Cawood (kā'wŏŏd) Eng.	53·49 N	1·07 W
101	Caxambu (kä-shä'm-bōō) Braz. (Rio de Janeiro In.)	22·00 S	44·45 W
99	Caxias (kä'shē-äzh) Braz.	4·48 S	43·16 W
100	Caxias do Sul (kä'shē-äzh-dô-sōō'l). Braz.	29·13 S	51·03 W
125	Caxine, Cap (C.) (kăp kăk'sēn) Alg.	36·47 N	2·52 E
166	Caxito (kä-shē'tōō) Ang.	8·20 S	13·35 E
98	Cayambe (kä-īä'm-bĕ) Ec.	0·03 N	79·09 W
99	Cayenne (kā-ĕn') Fr. Gu.	4·56 N	52·18 W
90	Cayetano Rubio (kä-yĕ-tà-nô-rōō'byô). Mex.	20·37 N	100·21 W
89	Cayey. P. R. (Puerto Rico In.)	18·05 N	66·12 W
94	Cayman Brac (I.) (kī-män' bràk) Cayman Is.	19·45 N	79·50 W
92	Cayo (kī'yō) Br. Hond. (Yucatan In.)	17·11 N	89·04 W
94	Cay Sal Bk. (kē-săl) Ba. Is.	23·55 N	80·20 W
81	Cayuga (L.) (kā-yōō'gȧ) N. Y.	42·35 N	76·35 W
124	Cazalla de la Sierra (kä-thäl'yä-dĕ-lä-sē-ĕ'r-rä). Sp.	37·55 N	5·48 W
122	Cazaux, Étang de (L.) (ā-tăN' dĕ kä-zō'). Fr.	44·32 N	0·59 W
81	Cazneovia (kăz-ê-nō'vĭ-ä) N. Y.	42·55 N	75·50 W
75	Cazenovia Cr. N. Y. (Buffalo In.)	42·49 N	78·45 W
126	Čazma (chäz'mä) Yugo.	45·44 N	16·39 E
166	Cazombo (kä-zô'm-bô) Ang.	12·25 S	22·40 E
91	Cazones (R.) (kä-zô'nĕs) Mex.	20·37 N	97·28 W
94	Cazones, Ensenada de (B.) (ĕn-sĕ-nä-dä-dĕ-kä-zō'nås). Cuba	22·05 N	81·30 W
94	Cazones, Golfo de (G.) (gôl-fô-dĕ-kä-zō'nås). Cuba	23·55 N	81·15 W
124	Cazorla (kä-thôr'lä) Sp.	37·55 N	2·58 W
124	Cea (R.) (thā'ä) Sp.	42·18 N	5·10 W
	Ceará, see Fortaleza		
99	Ceará (State) (sä-ä-rä') Braz.	5·13 S	39·43 W
99	Ceará-Mirim (sä-ä-rä'mē-rē'N) Braz.	6·00 S	35·13 W
93	Cebaco, Isla (I.) (ē's-lä--sä-bä'kō) Pan.	7·27 N	81·08 W
69	Cebolla Cr. (sē-bōl'yä) Colo.	38·15 N	107·10 W
124	Cebollera, Sierra (Mts.) (sē-ĕ'r-rä-sĕ-bôl-yĕ-rä). Sp.	42·03 N	2·53 W
124	Cebreros (sĕ-brĕ'rôs) Sp.	40·28 N	4·28 W
155	Cebu (sā-bōō') Phil.	10·22 N	123·49 E
75	Cecil (sē'sĭl). Pa. (Pittsburgh In.)	40·20 N	80·10 W
86	Cedar (L.) Can.	53·18 N	101·08 W
71	Cedar (R.) Iowa	42·23 N	92·07 W
65	Cedar (R.). Wash. (Portland In.)	45·56 N	122·32 W
71	Cedar (R.) West Fk. Iowa	42·49 N	93·10 W
77	Cedar Bay Tex. (In.)	29·54 N	94·58 W
77	Cedar Bayou Tex. (In.)	29·46 N	94·56 W
69	Cedar Breaks Natl. Mon. Utah	37·35 N	112·55 W
71	Cedarburg (sē'dēr bûrg) Wis.	43·23 N	88·00 W
69	Cedar City Utah	37·40 N	113·10 W
70	Cedar Cr. N. D.	46·05 N	102·10 W
71	Cedar Falls Iowa	42·31 N	92·29 W
78	Cedar Keys Fla.	29·06 N	83·03 W
75	Cedar Lake. Ind. (Chicago In.)	41·22 N	87·27 W
75	Cedar L. Ind. (Chicago In.)	41·23 N	87·25 W
71	Cedar Rapids Iowa	42·00 N	91·43 W
80	Cedar Springs Mich.	43·15 N	85·40 W
78	Cedartown (sē'dēr-toun) Ga.	34·00 N	85·15 W
167	Cedarville (cē-dȧr'vĭl) S. Afr. (Natal In.)	30·23 S	29·04 E
90	Cedral (sā-dräl') Mex.	23·47 N	100·42 W
92	Cedros (sā'drōs) Hond.	14·36 N	87·07 W
88	Cedros (I.) Mex.	28·10 N	115·10 W
158	Ceduna (sē-dōō'nȧ) Austl.	32·15 S	133·55 E
126	Cefalù (chā-fä-lōō') It.	38·01 N	14·01 E
124	Cega (R.) (thā'gä) Sp.	41·25 N	4·27 W
121	Cegléd (tsā'glād) Hung.	47·10 N	19·49 E
127	Ceglie (chĕ'lyĕ) It.	40·39 N	17·32 E
124	Cehegín (thā-ä-hēn') Sp.	38·05 N	1·48 W
95	Ceiba del Agua (sā'-bä-dĕl-ä'gwä) Cuba (Havana In.)	22·08 N	82·38 W
166	Cela (sĕ-là) Ang.	11·10 S	15·07 E
90	Celaya (sā-lä'yä) Mex.	20·33 N	100·49 W
154	Celebes (Is.) (sĕl'ê-bēz) (sĕl-ā'bĕs). Indon.	2·15 S	120·30 E
154	Celebes Sea Indon.	3·45 N	121·52 E
92	Celestún (sĕ-lĕs-tōō'n) Mex. (Yucatan In.)	20·57 N	90·18 W
80	Celina (sê-lī'nȧ) Ohio	40·30 N	84·35 W
126	Celje (tsĕl'yĕ) Yugo.	46·13 N	15·17 E
120	Celle (tsĕl'ĕ) Ger.	52·37 N	10·05 E
72	Cement (sê-mĕnt') Okla.	34·56 N	98·07 W
99	Ceniza, Pico (Mtn.) (pē'-kô-sĕ-nē'zä). Ven. (In.)	10·24 N	67·26 W
122	Cenon (sĕ-nôN') Fr.	44·51 N	0·33 W
77	Center (sĕn'tēr) Tex.	31·50 N	94·10 W
78	Centerhill Res. (sĕn'tēr-hĭl). Tenn.	36·02 N	86·00 W
75	Center Line (sĕn'tēr līn) Mich. (Detroit In.)	42·29 N	83·01 W
71	Centerville (sĕn'tēr-vĭl) Iowa	40·44 N	92·48 W
74	Centerville. Minn. (Minneapolis, St. Paul In.)	45·10 N	93·03 W
75	Centerville. Pa. (Pittsburgh In.)	40·02 N	79·58 W
70	Centerville S. D.	43·70 N	96·56 W
74	Centerville Utah (Salt Lake City In.)	40·55 N	111·53 W
98	Central, Cordillera (Mts.) (kôr-dēl-yĕ'-rä-sĕn-trä'l). Bol.	19·18 S	65·29 W
98	Central, Cordillera (Mts.) Col. (In.)	3·58 N	75·55 W
95	Central, Cordillera (Cibao Mts.) (kôr-dēl-yā'rä sĕn'träl) (sê-bä'ô) Dom. Rep.	19·05 N	71·30 W
163	Central African Republic Afr.	7·50 N	21·00 E
88	Central America (ȧ-mĕr'ĭ-kȧ) N. A.	10·45 N	87·15 W
78	Central City (sĕn'trȧl) Ky.	37·15 N	87·09 W
70	Central City (sĕn'trȧl sĭ'tĭ). Nebr.	41·07 N	98·00 W
84	Central Falls (sĕn'trȧl fôlz) R. I. (Providence In.)	41·54 N	71·23 W
80	Centralia (sĕn-trā'lĭ-ȧ) Ill.	38·35 N	89·05 W
73	Centralia Mo.	39·11 N	92·07 W
66	Centralia Wash.	46·42 N	122·58 W
133	Central Plat Sov. Un.	55·00 N	33·30 E
84	Central Valley N. Y. (New York In.)	41·19 N	74·07 W
81	Centreville (sĕn'tēr-vĭl) Md.	39·05 N	76·05 W
155	Centro (sĕ'n-trô). Phil. (Manila In.)	17·16 N	121·48 E
78	Century (sĕn'tû-rĭ) Fla.	30·57 N	87·15 W
	Cephalonia, see Kefallinéa		
122	Céret (sā-rĕ') Fr.	42·29 N	2·47 E
98	Cereté (sĕ-rĕ-tĕ') Col.	8·56 N	75·58 W
126	Cerignola (chā-rē-nyô'lä) It.	41·16 N	15·55 E
126	Cerknica (tsĕr'knē-tsȧ) Yugo.	45·48 N	14·21 E
76	Cerralvo (sĕr-räl'vō) Mex.	26·05 N	99·37 W
88	Cerralvo (I.) Mex.	24·00 N	109·59 W
98	Cerrito (sĕr-rē'-tô) Col. (In.)	3·41 N	76·17 W
90	Cerritos (sĕr-rē'tôs) Mex.	22·26 N	100·16 W
98	Cerro de Pasco (sĕr'rō dā päs'kō) Peru	10·45 S	76·14 W
76	Cerro Gordo, Arroyo de (är-rô-yô-dĕ-sĕ'r-rô-gôr-dô) Mex.	26·12 N	104·06 W
98	Certegui (sĕr-tĕ'gē) Col. (In.)	5·21 N	76·35 W
155	Cervantes (sĕr-vän'tās) Phil. (Manila In.)	16·59 N	120·42 E
124	Cervantes (thĕr-vän'tās) Sp.	42·43 N	7·04 W
124	Cervera del Río Alhama (thĕr-vă'rä dĕl rē'ō-äl-ä'mä). Sp.	42·02 N	1·55 W
125	Cerveteri (chĕr-vĕ'tĕ-rē) It. (Rome In.)	42·00 N	12·06 E
126	Cesena (chĕ'sĕ-nä) It.	44·08 N	12·16 E
119	Cēsis (sā'sĭs) Sov. Un.	57·19 N	25·17 E
120	Česká Lípa (chĕs'kä lē'pa). Czech.	50·41 N	14·31 E
120	Ceske (Bohemia) (Prov.) (chĕs'kä) (bô-hē'mĭ-ȧ). Czech.	49·51 N	13·55 E
120	České Budějovice (chĕs'kä bōō'dyĕ-yô-vēt-sĕ). Czech.	49·00 N	14·30 E
120	Ceskomoravaska Vysočina (Hts.) Czech.	49·21 N	15·40 E
127	Cesme (chĕsh'mĕ) Tur.	38·20 N	26·20 E
160	Cessnock Austl.	32·58 S	151·15 E
127	Cetinje (tsĕt'in-yĕ) Yugo.	42·23 N	18·55 E
164	Ceuta (Sp.) (thā-ōō'tä) Afr.	36·04 N	5·36 W
122	Cévennes (sā-vĕn') Fr.	44·20 N	3·48 E
115	Ceyhan (R.) Tur.	37·19 N	36·06 E
138	Ceylon (sê-lŏn') Asia	8·45 N	82·30 E
65	Chabot (L.) (sha'bŏt) Calif. (San Francisco In.)	37·44 N	122·06 W
101	Chacabuco (chä-kä-bōō'kō) Arg. ((Buenos Aires In.)	34·37 S	60·27 W
91	Chacaltianguis (chä-käl-tē-äŋ'-gwēs). Mex.	18·18 N	95·50 W
98	Chachapoyas (chä-chä-poi'yäs) Peru	6·16 S	77·48 W
100	Chaco (Prov.) (chä'kō) Arg.	26·00 S	60·45 W
69	Chaco Can. Natl. Mon. (chä'kô) N. Mex.	35·38 N	108·06 W
136	Chad (chăd). Sov. Un. (Urals In.)	56·33 N	57·11 E
163	Chad Afr.	17·48 N	19·00 E
165	Chad, L. Chad.	14·00 N	14·28 E
79	Chadbourn (chăd'bŭrn) N. C.	34·19 N	78·55 W
70	Chadron (chăd'rŭn) Nebr.	42·50 N	103·10 W
124	Chafarinas (C.) Mor.	35·08 N	2·20 W
73	Chaffee (chăf'ê) Mo.	37·10 N	89·39 W
144	Chāgal Hills Afg.-Pak.	29·15 N	63·28 E
128	Chagodoshcha (R.) (chä-gō-dôsh-chä). Sov. Un.	59·08 N	35·13 E
93	Chagres R. (chä'grĕs) Pan.	9·18 N	79·22 W
75	Chagrin R. (shȧ'grĭn) Ohio (Cleveland In.)	41·34 N	81·24 W
75	Chagrin Falls (shȧ'grĭn fôls) Ohio (Cleveland In.)	41·26 N	81·23 W
150	Ch'ahaerh (Reg.) (chä'här). China	44·25 N	115·00 E
144	Chāh Bahār (chä'h' bä'här). Iran	25·18 N	60·45 E
152	Chalantun (chä'län-tōōn'). China	47·59 N	122·56 E
92	Chalatenango (chäl-ä-tĕ-näŋ'gō) Sal.	14·04 N	88·54 W
91	Chalcatongo (chäl-kä-tôŋ'gō) Mex.	17·04 N	97·41 W
90	Chalchihuites (chäl-chê-wē'tās) Mex.	23·28 N	103·57 W
92	Chalchuapa (chäl-chwä'pä) Sal.	14·01 N	89·39 W
91	Chalco (chäl-kō) Mex. (Mexico City In.)	19·15 N	98·54 W
82	Chaleur Bay (shȧ-lûr') Can.	48·07 N	64·50 W
110	Chalgrove (chăl'grōv) Eng. (London In.)	51·38 N	1·05 W
151	Chaling (chä'lĭng) China	27·00 N	118·30 E
84	Chalmette (shăl-mĕt') La. (New Orleans In.)	29·57 N	89·57 W
122	Châlons-sur-Marne (shȧ-lôN'-sür-märn). Fr.	48·57 N	4·23 E

ng-sing; ŋ-baŋk; N-nasalized n; nŏd; cŏmmit; ōld; ôbey; ôrder; fōōd; fŏŏt; ou-out; s-soft; sh-dish; th-thin; pūre; ûnite; ûrn; stŭd; circŭs; ü-as "y" in study; '-indeterminate vowel.

Page	Name Pronunciation Region	Lat. °′	Long. °′
122	Châlon-sur-Saône............Fr.	46·47 N	4·54 E
100	Chaltel, Cerro (Mtn.) (sě'r-rô-chäl'těl) . Arg.-Chile	48·10 S	73·18 W
69	Chama (R.) (chä'mä)....N. Mex.	36·19 N	106·31 W
92	Chama, Sierra de (Mts.) (sē-ě'r-rä-dě-chä-mä) . Guat.	15·48 N	90·20 W
122	Chamalières (shä-mä-lyår')....Fr.	45·45 N	3·59 E
142	Chaman (chŭm,-än')....W. Pak.	30·58 N	66·21 E
142	Chambal (R.) (chŭm-bäl')..India	26·05 N	76·37 E
70	Chamberlain (chām'bēr-lĭn) .S. D.	43·48 N	99·21 W
82	Chamberlain (L.).........Maine	46·15 N	67·05 W
81	Chambersburg (chām'bērz-bûrg) Pa.	40·00 N	77·40 W
123	Chambéry (shäm-bā-rē')......Fr.	45·35 N	5·54 E
84	Chamblee (chăm-blē') Ga. (Atlanta In.)	33·53 N	84·18 W
85	Chambly (shäɴ-blē') Can. (Montreal In.)	45·27 N	73·17 W
123	Chambly..........Fr. (Paris In.)	49·11 N	2·14 E
87	Chambord..................Can.	48·22 N	72·01 W
93	Chame, Punta (Pt.) (po͝o'n-tä-chä'må) . Pan.	8·41 N	79·27 W
92	Chamelecón R. (chä-mě-lě-kô'n) Hond.	15·09 N	88·42 W
165	Chamo L. (chä'mō).........Eth.	5·58 N	37·00 E
123	Chamonix (shå-mô-nē').......Fr.	45·55 N	6·50 E
122	Champagne (Reg.) (shäm-pän'-yē) . Fr.	48·53 N	4·48 E
80	Champaign (shăm-pān').......Ill.	40·10 N	88·15 W
92	Champerico (chăm-på-rē'kō) Guat.	14·18 N	91·55 W
71	Champion (chăm'pĭ-ŭn)....Mich.	46·30 N	87·59 W
81	Champlain, L. (shăm-plān') N. Y.-Vt.	44·45 N	73·20 W
123	Champlitte (shäɴ-plēt').......Fr.	47·38 N	5·28 E
91	Champotón (chäm-pō-tōn')..Mex.	19·21 N	90·43 W
91	Champotón (R.)...........Mex.	19·19 N	90·15 W
100	Chañaral (chän-yä-räl').....Chile	26·20 S	70·46 W
124	Chanca (R.) (chäŋ'kä)..Sp.-Port.	38·15 N	7·22 W
151	Chanchiang (Fort Bayard) China	21·20 N	110·28 E
142	Chanda (chăn'dŭ)..........India	19·58 N	79·21 E
78	Chandeleur Is. (shăn-dē-lo͞or') . La.	29·53 N	88·35 W
78	Chandeleur Sd..............La.	29·47 N	89·08 W
142	Chandīgarh...............India	30·51 N	77·13 E
82	Chandler (chăn'dlēr)........Can.	48·24 N	64·40 W
74	Chandler..Mo. (Kansas City In.)	39·18 N	94·24 W
73	Chandler..................Okla.	35·42 N	96·52 W
148	Chang (R.) (jäng) .... China	36·17 N	114·31 E
166	Changane (R.).............Moz.	22·42 S	32·46 E
148	Ch'angch'ichuang (chäng'chē'zho͝oäng) . China	37·59 N	116·57 E
150	Ch'angchih..............China	35·58 N	112·58 E
148	Ch'angch'ing (chäng'chĭng) . China	36·33 N	116·42 E
148	Changch'iu (zhängchĭû)....China	36·50 N	117·29 E
148	Ch'angchou...............China	31·47 N	119·56 E
150	Ch'angch'un (Hsinking) (chäng'cho͞on') (hsĭn'kĭng) China	43·55 N	125·25 E
148	Ch'anghsing Tao (I.) (chängsĭng dou) . China	39·38 N	121·10 E
150	Ch'anghsintien China (Peking In.)	39·49 N	116·12 E
151	Changhua (chäng'hwä')...Taiwan	24·02 N	120·32 E
148	Changhutien (jang'ho͞o'dĭan) China	32·07 N	114·44 E
148	Ch'angi (jäng'yē)..........China	36·51 N	119·23 E
152	Changjōn (chäng'jŭn')......Kor.	38·38 N	128·02 E
150	Changkochuang China (Peking In.)	40·09 N	116·56 E
150	Changkuangts'ai Ling (Mts.) China	43·50 N	127·55 E
148	Ch'angli (chäng'lē')........China	39·46 N	119·10 E
150	Changpei (chäng'pě').......China	41·12 N	114·50 E
152	Changsan Cot (I.)..........Kor.	38·06 N	124·50 E
148	Ch'angshan Liehtao (Is.) (chäng'shän' lĭĕdou) . China	39·08 N	122·26 E
148	Ch'angshan Tao (I.) (chäng'shän' dou) . China	37·56 N	120·42 E
148	Ch'angshu (chäng'sho͞o')....China	31·40 N	120·45 E
151	Ch'angte (chäng'tě').......China	29·00 N	111·38 E
148	Changtien (jäng'dĭan)......China	36·48 N	118·04 E
151	Changting................China	25·50 N	116·18 E
146	Ch'angtu (chäng'to͞o')......China	31·06 N	96·30 E
152	Changtu..................China	43·00 N	124·02 E
148	Ch'angtzu Tao (I.) (chäng'zho͞o dou) . China	39·02 N	122·44 E
150	Changwu (chäng'wo͞o').....China	35·12 N	107·45 E
152	Changwu..................China	42·21 N	123·00 E
146	Changyeh.................China	38·46 N	101·00 E
148	Ch'angyüan (chäng'yü-än') . China	35·10 N	114·41 E
74	Chanhassen (shăn'hăs-sĕn) Minn. (Minneapolis, St. Paul In.)	44·52 N	93·32 W
148	Chanhua (jän'ho͝oå)........China	37·42 N	117·49 E
122	Channel Is. (chăn'ĕl)........Eur.	49·20 N	2·40 W
77	Channelview (chăn'elvū) Tex. (In.)	29·46 N	95·07 W
150	Chanping.................China	40·12 N	116·10 E
124	Chantada (chän-tä'dä)........Sp.	42·38 N	7·36 W
154	Chanthaburi..............Thai.	12·37 N	102·04 E
123	Chantilly (shäɴ-tê-yē') Fr. (Paris In.)	49·12 N	2·30 E
84	Chantilly (shăn'tĭlē) Va. (Washington D.C. In.)	38·53 N	77·26 W
86	Chantrey Inlet (chăn-trē)....Can.	67·49 N	94·30 W
73	Chanute (shȧ-no͞ot')........Kans.	37·41 N	95·27 W
134	Chany (L.) (chä'nê).....Sov. Un.	54·15 N	77·31 E
150	Chanyü...................China	44·30 N	122·30 E
151	Ch'aoan (chä'ō-än')........China	23·48 N	117·10 E
148	Ch'aohsien (chou'sĭän).....China	31·37 N	117·50 E
148	Chaohsien................China	37·46 N	114·48 E
154	Chao Phraya, Mae Nam (R.) Thai.	16·13 N	99·33 E
148	Ch'aoshui (jĭouso͞oĭ)........China	37·43 N	120·56 E
151	Chaot'ung (chä'ō-to͝ong)....China	27·18 N	103·50 E
151	Ch'aoyang (chä'ō-yäng')....China	23·18 N	116 32 E
150	Ch'aoyang (Foshan).......China	41·32 N	120·20 E
148	Chaoyüan (chä'ō-yü-än')...China	37·22 N	120·23 E
99	Chapada, Serra da (Mts.) (sě'r-rä-dä-shä-pä'dä) . Braz.	14·57 S	54·34 W
101	Chapadão, Serra do (Mtn.) (sě'r-rä-dô-shä-på-dou'ɴ) Braz. (Rio de Janeiro In.)	20·31 S	46·20 W
90	Chapala, Lago de (L.) (lä'gô-dě-chä-pä'lä) . Mex.	20·14 N	103·02 W
90	Chapalagana (R.) (chä-pä-lä-gå'nä) . Mex.	22·11 N	104·09 W
98	Chaparral (chä-pär-rå'l) . Col. (In.)	3·44 N	75·28 W
90	Chapata (chä-på'tä)........Mex.	20·18 N	103·10 W
133	Chapayevsk (châ-pī'ĕfsk) .Sov. Un.	53·00 N	49·30 E
79	Chapel Hill (chăp''l hĭl)....N. C.	35·55 N	79·05 W
65	Chaplain (L.) (chăp'lĭn) Wash. (Seattle In.)	47·58 N	121·50 W
87	Chapleau (chăp-lō').........Can.	47·43 N	83·28 W
166	Chapmans B. (chăp'măns bă) S. Afr. (Cape Town In.)	34·06 S	18·17 E
70	Chappell (chă-pĕl').........Nebr.	41·06 N	102·29 W
91	Chapultenango (chä-po͝ol-tē-näŋ'gō) . Mex.	17·19 N	93·08 W
90	Charcas (chär'käs)..........Mex.	23·09 N	101·09 W
93	Charco de Azul, Bahia (B.) (bä-ē'ä-chä'r-kô-dě-ä-zo͞o'l) . Pan.	8·14 N	82·45 W
103	Chardzhou (chēr-jô'o͝o)..Sov. Un.	38·52 N	63·37 E
122	Charente (shå-räɴt')..........Fr.	45·48 N	0·28 W
165	Chari (R.) (shä-rē')........Chad	11·02 N	15·46 E
110	Charing (chă'rĭng) Eng. (London In.)	51·13 N	0·49 E
71	Chariton (châr'ĭ-tŭn)........Iowa	41·02 N	93·16 W
73	Chariton (R.)...............Mo.	40·24 N	92·38 W
85	Charlemagne (shårl-mäny') Can. (Montreal In.)	45·43 N	73·29 W
117	Charleroi (shår-lē-rwä')......Bel.	50·25 N	4·35 E
75	Charleroi (shär'lē-roi) Pa. (Pittsburgh In.)	40·08 N	79·54 W
79	Charles, C. (chärlz)..........Va.	37·05 N	75·48 W
85	Charlesbourg (shårl-bo͞or') Can. (Quebec In.)	46·51 N	71·16 W
71	Charles City (chärlz)........Iowa	43·03 N	92·40 W
80	Charleston (chärlz'tŭn).......Ill.	39·30 N	88·10 W
78	Charleston................Miss.	34·00 N	90·02 W
73	Charleston.................Mo.	36·53 N	89·20 W
79	Charleston.................S. C.	32·47 N	79·56 W
80	Charleston..............W. Va.	38·20 N	81·35 W
75	Charlestown (chärlz'toun) Ind. (Louisville In.)	38·46 N	85·39 W
93	Charlestown St. Kitts-Nevis-Anguilla (Le. & Wind. Is. In.)	17·10 N	62·32 W
166	Charlesville.............Con. K.	5·19 S	30·59 E
160	Charleville (chär'lê-vĭl).....Austl.	26·16 S	146·28 E
122	Charleville (shärl-vēl').......Fr.	49·48 N	4·41 E
80	Charlevoix (shär'lē-voi).....Mich.	45·20 N	86·15 W
71	Charlevoix, L.............Mich.	45·17 N	85 43 W
80	Charlotte (shär'lŏt)........Mich.	42·35 N	84·50 W
79	Charlotte.................N. C.	35·15 N	80·50 W
89	Charlotte Amalie (St. Thomas) (shär-lŏt'ĕ ä-mä'lĭ-å) . Virgin Is. (U. S. A.) (St. Thomas In.)	18·21 N	64·54 W
79	Charlotte Hbr..........Fla. (In.)	26·47 N	81·58 W
118	Charlottenberg (shär-lŭt'ĕn-bĕrg) Swe.	59·53 N	12·17 E
81	Charlottesville (shär'lŏtz-vĭl)..Va.	38·00 N	78·25 W
83	Charlottetown (shär'lŏt-toun) Can.	46·14 N	63·08 W
158	Charlotte Waters (shär'lŏt) . Austl.	26·00 S	134·50 E
123	Charmes (shärm).............Fr.	48·23 N	6·19 E
110	Charnwood Forest (chärn'wo͝od) Eng.	52·42 N	1·15 W
85	Charny (shär-nē') Can. (Quebec In.)	46·43 N	71·16 W
142	Charol Tsho (L.)..........China	34·00 N	81·47 E
123	Chars (shär).......Fr. (Paris In.)	49·09 N	1·57 E
145	Charsadda (chŭr-sä'dä) W. Pak. (Khyber Pass In.)	34·17 N	71·43 E
159	Charters Towers (chär'tērz) Austl.	20·03 S	146·20 E
123	Chartres (shärt'r') . Fr. (Paris In.)	48·26 N	1·29 E
101	Chascomús (chäs-kō-mo͞os') Arg. (Buenos Aires In.)	35·32 S	58·01 W
79	Chase City (chās)............Va.	36·45 N	78·27 W
128	Chashniki (chäsh'nyê-kē) .Sov. Un.	54·51 N	29·08 E
74	Chaska (chăs'kå) Minn.(Minneapolis,St.Paul In.)	44·48 N	93·36 W
122	Châteaubriant (shå-tō-brē-äɴ') . Fr.	47·43 N	1·23 W
122	Châteaudun (shä-tō-dåɴ').....Fr.	48·04 N	1·23 E
122	Château-Gontier (chå-tō' gôɴ' tyā') .Fr.	47·48 N	0·43 W
85	Chateauguay (chå-tō-gā') Can. (Montreal In.)	45·22 N	73·45 W
85	Châteauguay, R. Can. (Montreal In.)	45·13 N	73·51 W
85	Chateauguay Basin Can. (Montreal In.)	45·22 N	73·44 W
122	Chateauneuf-les-Martigues (shä-tō-nûf'lā-mär-tēg'ĕ) Fr. (Marseille In.)	43·23 N	5·11 E
122	Château-Renault (shå-tō-rē-nō') Fr.	47·36 N	0·57 E
85	Château-Richer (shå-tō'rē-shā') Can. (Quebec In.)	46·58 N	71·01 W
122	Châteauroux (shå-tō-ro͞o').....Fr.	46·47 N	1·39 E
122	Château-Thierry (shå-tō'tyĕr-rē') Fr.	49·03 N	3·22 E
122	Châtellerault (shä-tĕl-rō').....Fr.	46·48 N	0·31 E
71	Chatfield (chăt'fēld).......Minn.	43·50 N	92·10 W
80	Chatham (chăt'ȧm).........Can.	42·25 N	82·10 W
82	Chatham..................Can.	47·01 N	65·28 W
110	Chatham (chăt'ŭm) Eng. (London In.)	51·21 N	0·27 E
84	Chatham (chăt'ȧm) N. J. (New York In.)	40·44 N	74·23 W
75	Chatham....Ohio (Cleveland In.)	41·06 N	82·01 W
156	Chatham Is................N. Z.	44·00 S	178·00 W
64	Chatham Str.............Alaska	57·00 N	134·40 W
74	Chatsworth (chătz'wûrth) Calif. (Los Angeles In.)	34·16 N	118·36 W
74	Chatsworth Res. Calif. (Los Angeles In.)	34·15 N	118·41 W
78	Chattahoochee (chăt-tå-ho͞o' chēē) Fla.	30·42 N	84·47 W
78	Chattahoochee (R.)......Ala.-Ga.	31·17 N	85·10 W
78	Chattanooga (chăt-ȧ-no͞o'gȧ) Tenn.	35·01 N	85·15 W
78	Chattooga (R.) (chă-to͞o'gȧ) Ga.-S. C.	34·47 N	83·13 W
82	Chaudiere (R.) (shō-dyĕr')...Can.	46·26 N	71·10 W
154	Chau Doc (shō-dôk')......Camb.	10·49 N	104·57 E
122	Chaumont (shō-môɴ').........Fr.	48·08 N	5·07 E
123	Chaumontel (shô-mŏɴ-tĕl') Fr. (Paris In.)	49·07 N	2·26 E
135	Chaunskaya Guba (B.)..Sov. Un.	69·15 N	170·00 E
122	Chauny (shō-nē')............Fr.	49·40 N	3·09 E
128	Chausy (chou'sĭ)........Sov. Un.	53·57 N	30·58 E
81	Chautauqua (L.) (shȧ-tô'kwȧ) N. Y.	42·10 N	79·25 W
132	Chavaniga.............Sov. Un.	66·02 N	37·50 E
124	Chaves (chä'vĕzh)..........Port.	41·44 N	7·30 W
90	Chavinda (chä-vē'n-dä).....Mex.	20·01 N	102·27 W
91	Chazumba (chä-zo͝om'bä)...Mex.	18·11 N	97·41 W
110	Cheadle (chē'd'l)...........Eng.	52·59 N	1·59 W
81	Cheat (R.) (chēt).........W. Va.	39·35 N	79·40 W
120	Cheb (ᴋĕb)...............Czech.	50·05 N	12·23 E
136	Chebarkul (chĕ-bår-kûl') Sov. Un. (Urals In.)	54·59 N	60·22 E
132	Cheboksary (chyĕ-bôk-sä'rê) Sov. Un.	56·00 N	47·20 E
80	Cheboygan (shê-boi'găn)...Mich.	45·40 N	84·30 W
164	Chech, Erg (Dune)..........Alg.	24·45 N	2·07 W
133	Chechen' (I.) (chyĕch'ĕn) . Sov. Un.	44·00 N	48·10 E
148	Chech'eng (jĭŭcheng)......China	34·05 N	115·19 E
147	Chechiang (Chekiang) (Prov.) China	29·28 N	119·33 E
73	Checotah (chê-kō'tȧ).......Okla.	35·27 N	95·32 W
83	Chedabucto B. (chĕd-ȧ-bŭk-tō) Can.	45·25 N	61·05 W
154	Cheduba (I.)...............Bur.	18·45 N	93·01 E
86	Cheecham Hills (chēē'hăm)..Can.	55·56 N	112·06 W
75	Cheektowaga (chēk-tŏ-wä'gȧ) N. Y. (Buffalo In.)	42·54 N	78·46 W
	Chefoo, see Yent'ai		
66	Chehalis (chê-hā'lĭs).......Wash.	46·39 N	122·58 W
66	Chehalis R...............Wash.	46·47 N	123·17 W
152	Cheju (chĕ'jo͞o')............Kor.	33·29 N	126·40 E
152	Cheju (Quelpart) (I.)........Kor.	33·20 N	126·25 E
128	Chekalin (chĕ-kä'lĭn)....Sov. Un.	54·05 N	36·13 E
148	Chekao (jĭŭgou)...........China	31·47 N	117·44 E
	Chekiang, see Chechiang		
166	Chela, Serrada (Mts.) (sĕr'rȧ dā shā'lȧ) . Ang.	15·30 S	13·30 E
66	Chelan (chê-lăn')..........Wash.	47·51 N	119·59 W
151	Chelang Chiao (Pt.).......China	22·38 N	116·00 E
66	Chelan R.................Wash.	48·09 N	120·20 W
125	Cheleiros (shĕ-la'rōzh) Port. (Lisbon In.)	38·54 N	9·19 W
113	Chelic (Mt.) (shĕl-ĭk)........Alg.	35·22 N	6·47 E
125	Chéliff, Oued (R.) (o͞o-ĕd shā-lēf) Alg.	36·17 N	1·22 E
134	Chelkar (chyĕl'kär)......Sov. Un.	47·52 N	59·41 E
133	Chelkar (L.)............Sov. Un.	50·30 N	51·30 E
134	Chelkar Tengiz (L.) (chyĕl'kär tĕn'yēz) .Sov. Un.	47·42 N	61·45 E
121	Chełm (ᴋĕlm)..............Pol.	51·08 N	23·30 E
121	Chełmno (ᴋĕlm'nō).........Pol.	53·20 N	18·25 E
110	Chelmsford (chĕlm's-fērd) Eng. (London In.)	51·44 N	0·28 E
83	Chelmsford....Mass. (Boston In.)	42·36 N	71·21 W
84	Chelsea (chĕl'sê) Ala. (Birmingham In.)	33·20 N	86·38 W
161	Chelsea...Austl. (Melbourne In.)	38·05 S	145·08 E
85	Chelsea........Can. (Ottawa In.)	45·30 N	75·46 W
83	Chelsea.......Mass. (Boston In.)	42·23 N	71·02 W
80	Chelsea...................Mich.	42·20 N	84·00 W
73	Chelsea...................Okla.	36·32 N	95·23 W
116	Cheltenham (chĕlt''nŭm)....Eng.	51·57 N	2·06 W
84	Cheltenham (chĕltēn-hăm) Md. (Baltimore In.)	38·45 N	76·50 W
125	Chelva (chĕl'vä).............Sp.	39·43 N	1·00 W
136	Chelyabinsk (chĕl-yä-bênsk') Sov. Un. (Urals In.)	55·10 N	61·25 E
135	Chelyuskin, Mys (C.) (chĕl-yo͝os'-kĭn) . Sov. Un.	77·45 N	104·45 E
122	Chemillé (shē-mê-yā')........Fr.	47·13 N	0·46 W
	Chemnitz, see Karl-Marx-Stadt		
81	Chemung (R.) (shê-mŭng)..N. Y.	42·20 N	77·25 W
135	Chën, Gora (Mtn.)......Sov. Un.	65·13 N	142·12 E
142	Chenāb (R.) (chê-näb)...W. Pak.	31·33 N	72·28 E
164	Chenachane (Oasis) (shē-nȧ-shän') Alg.	26·14 N	4·14 W
148	Chenchiang (jienjäng)......China	32·13 N	119·24 E
66	Cheney (chē'nå)...........Wash.	47·29 N	117·34 W
148	Chengchou (jengjō)........China	34·46 N	113·42 E
151	Ch'enghai.................China	23·22 N	116·40 E
151	Chengku..................China	33·05 N	107·25 E
150	Ch'engte (Jehol) (chĕng'tĕ') (rē-hōl') . China	40·50 N	117·50 E
148	Chengting (chengding).....China	38·10 N	114·35 E
151	Ch'engtu (chĕng'to͞o')......China	30·30 N	104·10 E
148	Chengyang (chĕn'yäng')...China	32·34 N	114·22 E
151	Ch'enshien................China	25·40 N	113·00 E
149	Ch'entsun....China (Canton In.)	22·58 N	113·14 E
150	Chentung.................China	45·28 N	123·42 E
151	Chenyüan (chĕn'yü-an')....China	27·08 N	108·30 E
149	Chepei.......China (Canton In.)	23·07 N	113·23 E
98	Chepén (chĕ-pĕ'n)..........Peru	7·17 S	79·24 W
93	Chepo (chā'pō).............Pan.	9·12 N	79·06 W

Page	Name Pronunciation Region	Lat. °'	Long. °'
93	Chepo R. . . . . .Pan.	9·10 N	78·36 W
122	Cher (R.) (shâr). . . . . .Fr.	47·14 N	1·34 E
90	Cheran (chā-rän') . . . . .Mex.	19·41 N	101·54 W
79	Cheraw (chē'rô). . . . . .S. C.	34·40 N	79·52 W
122	Cherbourg (shär-bōōr') . . . . .Fr.	49·39 N	1·43 W
164	Cherchel (shĕr-shĕl') . . . . .Alg.	36·38 N	2·09 E
146	Cherchen (R.) (chĕr-chĕn') .China	39·00 N	87·19 E
132	Cherdyn' (chĕr-dyĕn') . . .Sov. Un.	60·25 N	56·32 E
134	Cheremkhovo (chĕr'yĕm-kô-vō) Sov. Un.	52·58 N	103·18 E
136	Cherëmukhovo (chĕr-yĕ-mû-kô-vô) .Sov. Un. (Urals In.)	60·20 N	60·00 E
165	Cheren (chĕr'ĕn) . . . . .Eth.	15·46 N	38·28 E
134	Cherepanovo (chĕr'yĕ pä-nô'vō) Sov. Un.	54·13 N	83·18 E
128	Cherepovets (chĕr-yĕ-pô'vyĕtz) Sov. Un.	59·08 N	35·54 E
128	Chereya (chĕr-ā'yä) . . . . .Sov. Un.	54·38 N	29·16 E
114	Chergui, Chott ech (L.) (chĕr gē) Alg.	34·12 N	0·10 W
114	Chergui I. . . . . .Tun.	34·48 N	11·41 E
128	Cherikov (chĕ'rē-kôf) . . . .Sov. Un.	53·34 N	31·22 E
129	Cherkassy (chĕr-kȧ'sĭ) . . .Sov. Un.	49·26 N	32·03 E
129	Cherkassy (Oblast) . . . . .Sov. Un.	48·58 N	30·55 E
134	Cherlak (chĭr-läk') . . . . . .Sov. Un.	54·04 N	74·28 E
136	Chermoz (chĕr-môz') Sov. Un. (Urals In.)	58·47 N	56·08 E
128	Chern' (chĕrn) . . . . .Sov. Un.	53·28 N	36·49 E
129	Chërnaya Kalitva (R.) (chôr'nȧ yȧ kȧ-lēt'vȧ) .Sov. Un.	50·15 N	39·16 E
129	Chernigov (chĕr-nē'gôf) . .Sov. Un.	51·28 N	31·18 E
129	Chernigov (Oblast) (chĕr-nē'gôf) Sov. Un.	51·23 N	31·15 E
129	Chernobay (chĕr-nō-bī') . .Sov. Un.	49·41 N	32·24 E
129	Chernobyl' (chĕr-nō-bĭl') .Sov. Un.	51·17 N	30·14 E
134	Chernogorsk (chĕr-nŏ-gôrsk') Sov. Un.	54·01 N	91·07 E
129	Chernogovka (chĕr-nô-gôf'kȧ) Sov. Un.	47·08 N	36·20 E
136	Chernoistochinsk (chĕr-nôy-stô'chĭnsk) .Sov. Un. (Urals In.)	57·44 N	59·55 E
129	Chërnomorskoye (chĕr-nô-môr'skô-yĕ) .Sov. Un.	45·29 N	32·43 E
121	Chernovtsy (Cernăuti) (chĭr-nôf'tsē) (chĕr-nou'tsĕ) Sov. Un.	48·18 N	25·56 E
119	Chernyakhovsk (chĕr-nyä'ĸôfsk) .Sov. Un.	55·38 N	21·17 E
129	Chernyanka (chĕrn-yäŋ'kȧ) Sov. Un.	50·56 N	37·48 E
70	Cherokee (chĕr-ô-kē') . . . . . . .Iowa	42·43 N	95·33 W
73	Cherokee . . . . .Kans.	37·21 N	94·50 W
72	Cherokee . . . . .Okla.	36·44 N	98·22 W
78	Cherokee (R.) . . . . .Tenn.	36·22 N	83·22 W
78	Cherokee Indian Res. . . . . . .N. C.	35·33 N	83·12 W
94	Cherokee Sd. . . . . .Ba. Is.	26·15 N	76·55 W
73	Cherokees, L. of the (chĕr-ô-kēz') .Okla.	36·32 N	95·14 W
82	Cherryfield (chĕr'ĭ-fēld) . . .Maine	44·37 N	67·56 W
65	Cherry Grove . .Ore. (Portland In.)	45·27 N	123·15 W
73	Cherryvale . . . . .Kans.	37·16 N	95·33 W
79	Cherryville (chĕr'ĭ-vĭl) . . . . . .N. C.	35·32 N	81·22 W
65	Cherryville . . . .Ore. (Portland In.)	45·22 N	122·08 W
135	Cherskogo, Khrebet (Mts.) Sov. Un.	66·15 N	138·30 E
128	Cherven' (chĕr'vyĕn) . . . .Sov. Un.	53·43 N	28·26 E
128	Chervonoye (L.) (chĕr-vô'nô-yĕ) Sov. Un.	52·24 N	28·12 E
80	Chesaning (chĕs'ȧ-nĭng) . . . .Mich.	43·10 N	84·10 W
81	Chesapeake B. (chĕs'ȧ-pēk bā) Md.	38·20 N	76·15 W
84	Chesapeake Beach Md. (Baltimore In.)	38·42 N	76·33 W
110	Chesham (chĕsh'ŭm) Eng. (London In.)	51·41 N	0·37 W
80	Cheshire (chĕsh'ĭr) . . . . .Mich.	42·25 N	86·00 W
110	Cheshire (Co.) . . . . .Eng.	53·16 N	2·30 W
132	Chëshskaya Guba (B.) . . .Sov. Un.	67·25 N	46·00 E
136	Chesma (chĕs'mȧ) Sov. Un. (Urals In.)	53·50 N	60·42 E
134	Chesnokovka (chĕs-nŏ-kôf'kȧ) Sov. Un.	53·28 N	83·41 E
110	Chester (chĕs'tĕr) . . . . .Eng.	53·12 N	2·53 W
73	Chester . . . . .Ill.	37·54 N	89·48 W
84	Chester . . . .Pa. (Philadelphia In.)	39·51 N	75·22 W
79	Chester . . . . .S. C.	34·42 N	81·11 W
79	Chester .Va.	37·20 N	77·24 W
80	Chester . . . . .W. Va.	40·35 N	80·30 W
110	Chesterfield (chĕs'tĕr-fēld) . . .Eng.	53·14 N	1·26 W
159	Chesterfield, Isles . . . . .N. Cal.	19·38 S	160·08 E
86	Chesterfield (Inlet) . . . . .Can.	63·59 N	92·09 W
86	Chesterfield Inlet . . . . .Can.	63·19 N	91·11 W
85	Chestermere L. (chĕs'tĕr-mēr) Can. (Calgary In.)	51·03 N	113·45 W
80	Chesterton (chĕs'tĕr-tŭn) . . . .Ind.	41·35 N	87·05 W
81	Chestertown (chĕs'tĕr-toun) . .Md.	39·15 N	76·05 W
82	Chesuncook (chĕs'ŭn-kŏŏk) .Maine	46·03 N	69·40 W
71	Chetek (chĕ'tĕk) . . . . .Wis.	45·18 N	91·41 W
92	Chetumal, Bahia de (B.) (bä-ē-ä dĕ chĕt-ōō-mäl') Br. Hond. (Yucatan In.)	18·07 N	88·05 W
69	Chevelon Cr. (shĕv'ȧ-lŏn) . . . .Ariz.	34·35 N	111·00 W
75	Cheviot (shĕv'ĭ-ŭt) Ohio (Cincinnati In.)	39·10 N	84·37 W
116	Cheviot Hills . . . . .Scot., Eng.	55·20 N	2·40 W
123	Chevreuse (shĕ-vrûz') Fr. (Paris In.)	48·42 N	2·02 E
84	Chevy Chase (shĕvĭ chās) Md. (Baltimore In.)	38·58 N	77·06 W
66	Chewelah (chē-wē'lȧ) . . . . . .Wash.	48·17 N	117·42 W
148	Cheyang (R.) (Sĭyang) . . . . . .China	33·42 N	119·40 E
70	Cheyenne (shī-ĕn') . . . . .Wyo.	41·10 N	104·49 W
70	Cheyenne (R.) . . . . .S. D.	44·20 N	102 15 W
70	Cheyenne River Ind. Res. . . .S. D.	45·07 N	100·46 W
72	Cheyenne Wells . . . . .Colo.	38·46 N	102·21 W
151	Chiachi . . . . .China	19·10 N	110·28 E
151	Chiahsing . . . . .China	30·45 N	120·50 E
151	Chiai (chĭ'ī') . . . . .Taiwan	23·28 N	120·28 E
151	Chialing (R.) . . . . .China	30·30 N	106·20 E
151	Chian . . . . .China	27·12 N	115·10 E
150	Chian . . . . .China	41·00 N	126·04 E
148	Chiangchanchi . . . . .China	36·39 N	120·31 E
83	Chianghsi (Kiangsi) (Prov.) .China	28·16 N	115·34 E
151	Chiangling . . . . .China	30·30 N	112 10 E
146	Chiang Mai . . . . .Thai.	18·38 N	99 48 E
154	Chiang Rai . . . . .Thai.	19·53 N	99 48 E
147	Chiangsu (Kiangsu) (Prov.) .China	33·51 N	120·09 E
148	Chiangyen (jiäng'yĭn) . . . . . .China	32·33 N	120·07 E
148	Chiangyin (jiäng'in) . . . . .China	31·54 N	120·15 E
148	Chiantochen (jĭäng'tô'jĕn) . .China	32·23 N	120·14 E
148	Chiaochou Wan (B.) (jĭou'zhēō wän) .China	36·10 N	119·55 E
148	Chiaoho (jēou'hŭ) . . . . .China	38·03 N	116·18 E
150	Chiaoho . . . . .China	43·40 N	127·20 E
148	Chiaohsien (jēou'sĭän) . . . . . .China	36·18 N	120·01 E
149	Ch'iaot'ou . . . .China (Canton In.)	22·55 N	113·39 E
148	Chiaotso (jēou'zhōōŭ) . . . . . .China	35·17 N	113·11 E
148	Chiaow Shan (Mts.) (jēou shän) China	36·59 N	121·15 E
92	Chiapa, Rio de (R.) (rê-ô-dĕ-chê-ä'pä) .Mex.	16·00 N	92·20 W
91	Chiapa de Corzo (chê-ä'pä dā kôr'zō) .Mex.	16·44 N	93·01 W
88	Chiapas (State) (chê-ä'päs) . .Mex.	17·10 N	93·00 W
91	Chiapas, Cordilla de (Mts.) (kôr-dēl-yĕ'rä-dĕ-chyȧ'räs) Mex.	15·55 N	93·15 W
126	Chiari (kyä'rē) . . . . .It.	45·31 N	9·57 E
120	Chiasso . . . . .Switz.	45·50 N	8·57 E
149	Chiating . . . .China (Shanghai In.)	31·23 N	121·15 E
90	Chiautla (chyä-ōōt'lȧ) . . . . . . .Mex.	18·16 N	98·37 W
126	Chiavari (kyä-vä'rē) . . . . .It.	44·18 N	9·21 E
151	Chiayü . . . . .China	33·00 N	114·00 E
153	Chiba (chē'bȧ) . . Jap. (Tōkyō In.)	35·37 N	140·08 E
153	Chiba (Pref.) . . . .Jap. (Tōkyō In.)	35·47 N	140·02 E
87	Chibougamau (chē-bōō'gȧ-mou) Can.	49·57 N	74·23 W
75	Chicago (shĭ-kô-gō) (chĭ-kȧ'gō) Ill. (Chicago In.)	41·49 N	87·37 W
75	Chicago Heights (shĭ-kô'gō) (chĭ-kä'gō) . Ill. (Chicago In.)	41·30 N	87·38 W
166	Chicapa (R.) (chē-kä'pȧ) . . . .Ang.	8·15 S	20·15 E
91	Chicbul (chēk-bōō'l) . . . . .Mex.	18·45 N	90·56 W
64	Chichagof (I.) (chê-chä'gôf) Alaska	57·50 N	137·00 W
92	Chichâncanab, Lago de (L.) (lä'-gô-dĕ-chē-chän-kä-nä'b) Mex. (Yucatan In.)	19·50 N	88·28 W
92	Chichen Itzá (Ruins) (chē-chĕ'n-ē-tsä') . Mex. (Yucatan In.)	20·38 N	88·35 W
116	Chichester (chĭch'ĕs-tēr) . . . . .Eng.	50·50 N	0·55 W
151	Chichiang . . . . .China	29·05 N	106·40 E
148	Chichiashih (jĭ'jĭä'shĕ) . . . . .China	32·10 N	120·17 E
150	Ch'ich'ihaerh (Tsitsihar) . . .China	47·18 N	124·00 E
92	Chichimila (chē-chē-mē'lȧ) Mex. (Yucatan In.)	20·36 N	88·14 W
99	Chichiriviche (chē-chē-rē-vē-chĕ) Ven. (In.)	10·56 N	68·17 W
78	Chickamauga (chĭk-ȧ-mô'gȧ) . .Ga.	34·50 N	85·15 W
79	Chickamauga, (R.) . . . . .Tenn.	35·18 N	85·22 W
78	Chickasawhay (R.) (chĭk-ȧ-sô'wā) Miss.	31·45 N	88·45 W
72	Chickasha (chĭk'ȧ-shā) . . . . . .Okla.	35·04 N	97·56 W
124	Chiclana (chê-klä'nä) . . . . .Sp.	36·25 N	6·09 W
98	Chiclayo (chê-klä'yō) . . . . .Peru	6·46 S	79·50 W
68	Chico (chē'kō) . . . . .Calif.	39·43 N	121·51 W
65	Chico . . . . .Wash. (Seattle In.)	47·37 N	122·43 W
100	Chico (R.) . . . . .Arg.	44·30 S	66·00 W
100	Chico (R.) . . . . .Arg.	49·15 S	69·30 W
155	Chico (R.) . . . . . .Phil. (Manila In.)	17·33 N	121·24 E
91	Chicoloapan (chê-kō-lwä'pän) Mex. (Mexico City In.)	19·24 N	98·54 W
91	Chiconautla (chê-kō-nä-ōō'tlȧ) Mex. (Mexico City In.)	19·39 N	99·01 W
90	Chicontepec (chê-kōn'tĕ-pĕk') Mex.	20·58 N	98·08 W
81	Chicopee (chĭk'ô-pē) . . . . .Mass.	42·10 N	72·35 W
82	Chicoutimi (shē-kōō'tē-mē') . .Can.	48·27 N	71·03 W
92	Chicxulub (chēk-sōō-lōō'b) Mex. (Yucatan In.)	21·10 N	89·30 W
87	Chidley, C. (chĭd'lĭ) . . . . .Can.	60·32 N	63·56 W
66	Chief Joseph Dam . . . . .Wash.	48·00 N	119·39 W
78	Chiefland (chēf'lănd) . . . . .Fla.	29·30 N	82·50 W
146	Ch'iehmo . . . . .China	38·02 N	85·16 E
148	Chiehshou Hu (L.) (jĭeh'shō hōō) China	32·59 N	119·04 E
151	Chiehyang . . . . .China	23·38 N	116·20 E
120	Chiem See (L.) (Kēm zā) . . . .Ger.	47·58 N	12·20 E
148	Chienchangying (jĭan'chang'yĭng) China	40·09 N	118·47 E
148	Chienkan (R.) (jĭan'gän) . . . China	39·35 N	117·34 E
151	Chienli . . . . .China	29·50 N	112·52 E
151	Chienning . . . . .China	26·50 N	116·55 E
151	Chienou . . . . .China	27·10 N	118·18 E
148	Ch'ienshanchen (chĭan'shän'jen) China	31·05 N	120·24 E
148	Ch'ienshanchi (chĭan'shan'jĭ) China	32·38 N	117·02 E
151	Chienshih . . . . .China	30·40 N	109·45 E
151	Chienshui . . . . .China	23·32 N	102·50 E
148	Ch'ienwei (chĭăn'wā) . . . . . . .China	40·11 N	120·05 E
126	Chieri (kyâ'rē) . . . . .It.	45·03 N	7·48 E
126	Chieti (kyĕ'tē) . . . . .It.	42·22 N	14·22 E
129	Chigirin (chê-gē'rĕn) . . . . .Sov. Un.	49·02 N	32·39 E
90	Chignanuapan (chē'g-nä-nwä-pä'n) Mex.	19·49 N	98·02 W
82	Chignecto B. (shĭg-nĕk'tō) . . . .Can.	45·33 N	64·50 W
64	Chignik (chĭg'nĭk) . . . . .Alaska	56·14 N	158·12 W
64	Chignik B. . . . . .Alaska	56·18 N	157·22 W
151	Chihchiang . . . . .China	27·25 N	109·45 E
150	Ch'ihfeng (chĭ'fŭng) . . . . .China	42·18 N	118·52 E
148	Chihhochen (zhĭ'hŭ'jen) . . . .China	32·32 N	117·57 E
148	Ch'ihsien (chĭ'hsyĕn') . . . . . .China	34·33 N	114·47 E
148	Chihsien . . . . .China	35·25 N	114·03 E
148	Ch'ihsien . . . . .China	35·36 N	114·13 E
148	Chihsien . . . . .China	37·37 N	115·33 E
148	Chihsien . . . . .China	40·03 N	117·25 E
76	Chihuahua (chê-wä'wä) . . . . .Mex.	28·37 N	106·06 W
88	Chihuahua (State) . . . . .Mex.	29·00 N	107·30 W
166	Chihuane (chē-wä'nȧ) . . . . . . .Moz.	20·43 S	34·57 E
133	Chikishlyar (chê-kêsh-lyär') Sov. Un.	37·40 N	53·50 E
148	Ch'ik'ou (chē'kō) . . . . .China	38·37 N	117·33 E
90	Chilapa (chê-lä'pä) . . . . .Mex.	17·34 N	99·14 W
90	Chilchota (chêl-chō'tä) . . . . . .Mex.	19·40 N	102·04 W
72	Childress (chīld'rĕs) . . . . .Tex.	34·26 N	100·11 W
96	Chile (chē'lā) . . . . .S.A.	35·00 S	72·00 W
100	Chilecito (chê-lâ-sē'tō) . . . . . . .Arg.	29·06 S	67·25 W
98	Chilí, Pico de (Pk.) (pē'kô-dĕ chē-lē') . Col. (In.)	4·14 N	75·38 W
88	Chilibre (chē-lē'brĕ) Pan. (Panama Canal In.)	9·09 N	79·37 W
148	Ch'ili Hu (L.) (chē'lē hōō) . .China	32·57 N	118·26 E
150	Chilin (Kirin) (chĭl'ĭn') (kĭr'ĭn) China	43·58 N	126·40 E
147	Chilin (Prov.) . . . . .China	44·36 N	124·23 E
148	Chilip'ing (chē'lē'pĭng) . . . . .China	31·28 N	114·41 E
142	Chilka (L.) . . . . .India	19·26 N	85·42 E
100	Chillán (chēl-yän') . . . . .Chile	36·44 S	72·06 W
80	Chillicothe (chĭl-ĭ-kŏth'ê) . . . . . .Ill.	41·55 N	89·30 W
73	Chillicothe . . . . .Mo.	39·46 N	93·32 W
80	Chillicothe . . . . .Ohio	39·20 N	83·00 W
86	Chilliwack (chĭl'ĭ-wăk) . . . . . .Can.	49·09 N	121·59 W
100	Chiloé, Isla de (I.) (ē's-lä-dĕ-chē-lô-ā') .Chile	43·00 S	76·30 W
90	Chilpancingo (chēl-pän-sēŋ'gō) Mex.	17·32 N	97·30 W
71	Chilton (chĭl'tŭn) . . . . .Wis.	44·00 N	88·12 W
151	Chilung (Kirin) (chĭ'lŭng) .Taiwan	25·02 N	121·48 E
65	Chimacum (chĭm'ä-kŭm) Wash. (Seattle In.)	48·01 N	122·47 W
91	Chimalpa (chē-mäl'pä) Mex. (Mexico City In.)	19·26 N	99·22 W
92	Chimaltenango (chê-mäl-tȧ-näŋ'gō) Guat.	14·39 N	90·48 W
90	Chimaltitan (chêmäl-tē-tän') Mex.	21·36 N	103·50 W
103	Chimbay (chĭm-bī') . . . . .Sov. Un.	43·00 N	59·44 E
98	Chimborazo (Mtn.) (chêm-bô-rä'zō) Ec.	1·35 S	78·45 W
98	Chimbote (chêm-bō'tȧ) . . . . . .Peru	9·02 S	78·33 W
134	Chimkent (chĭm-kĕnt) . . .Sov. Un.	42·17 N	69·42 E
148	Chimo (gē'mŭ) . . . . .China	36·22 N	120·28 E
138	China (chī'nȧ) . . . . .Asia	36·45 N	93·00 E
76	China (chē'nä) . . . . .Mex.	25·43 N	99·13 W
92	Chinameca (chē-nä-mā'kȧ) . . . .Sal.	13·31 N	88·18 W
	Chinan, see Tsinan		
92	Chinandega (chē-nän-dā'gä) . .Nic.	12·38 N	87·08 W
76	Chinati Pk. (chĭ-nä'tē) . . . . . .Tex.	92·56 N	104·29 W
145	Chinawin (R.) . . . . .Bur.	23·30 N	94·30 E
98	Chincha Alta (chĭn'chȧ äl'tä) Peru	13·24 S	76·04 W
98	Chinchas, Islas (Is.) (ē's-läs-chē'n-chäs) .Peru	11·27 S	79·05 W
150	Chincheng . . . . .China	35·30 N	112·50 E
151	Chinchiang . . . . .China	24·58 N	118·40 E
148	Chinch'iao (jĭnchĭou) . . . . . . .China	31·46 N	116·46 E
160	Chinchilla (chĭn-chĭl'ȧ) . . . . .Austl.	26·44 S	150·36 E
124	Chinchilla (chên-chē'lyä) . . . . . .Sp.	38·54 N	1·43 W
92	Chinchorro, Banco (Bk.) (bä'n-kô-chēn-chô'r-rŏ) Mex. (Yucatan In.)	18·43 N	87·25 W
150	Chinchou . . . . .China	41·00 N	121·00 E
148	Chinchou Wan (B.) (jĭn'zhō wän) .China	39·07 N	121·17 E
166	Chinde (shēn'dĕ) . . . . .Moz.	17·39 S	36·34 E
152	Chin Do (I.) . . . . .Kor.	34·30 N	125·43 E
142	Chindwara . . . . .India	22·08 N	78·57 E
146	Chindwin R. (chĭn-dwĭn) . . . . .Bur.	23·30 N	94·34 E
148	Chinganchi (jing'än'jĭ) . . . . . .China	34·30 N	116·55 E
148	Ch'ingcheng (chĭng'cheng) . .China	37·12 N	117·43 E
150	Ch'ingch'eng . . . . .China	46·50 N	127·30 E
151	Chingchiang (jĭng'jĭang) . . . . .China	28·00 N	115·30 E
148	Chingchiang . . . . .China	32·02 N	120·15 E
148	Chingchih (jing'jē) . . . . .China	36·19 N	119·23 E
148	Ch'ingfeng (chingfeng) . . . . . .China	35·52 N	115·05 E
146	Ch'ing Hai (Koko Nor) (L.) (kō'kô nor) .China	37·26 N	98·30 E
148	Chinghai Wan (B.) (jĭng'hăĭ wän) .China	36·47 N	122·10 E
150	Ching Ho (R.) (chĭng'hō') . . .China	34·40 N	108·20 E
151	Chinghsien (jĭng'sĭan) . . . . . .China	26·32 N	109·45 E
148	Chinghsien . . . . .China	37·43 N	116·17 E
148	Ch'inghsien (chingsĭan) . . . . .China	38·37 N	116·48 E
150	Chinghsing . . . . .China	47·00 N	123·00 E
148	Ching Hu (L.) (chĭng hōō) . . .China	39·00 N	115·45 E
148	Chingk'ouchen (chĭng'kō'jĕn) China	34·52 N	119·07 E
151	Chingliu . . . . .China	26·15 N	116·50 E
150	Chingning . . . . .China	35·28 N	105·50 E
166	Chingola (chĭng-gōlä) . . . . .Zambia	12·32 S	27·35 E
148	Ch'ingp'ing (chĭng'pĭng) . . . .China	36·46 N	116·03 E
150	Chingpo Hu (L.) . . . . .China	44·10 N	129·00 E
149	Ch'ingp'u . . . .China (Shanghai In.)	31·08 N	121·06 E
148	Ch'ingtao (Tsingtao) (tsĭng'dou) China	36·05 N	120·10 E
166	Chinguar (chĭng-gär) . . . . .Ang.	12·35 S	16·15 E
164	Chinguetti (chĕŋ-gĕt'ĕ) Mauritania	20·34 N	12·34 W
148	Ch'ingyang (chĭng'yäng) . . . China	33·25 N	118·13 E
150	Chingyang . . . . .China	36·02 N	107·42 E
151	Ch'ingyüang . . . . .China	23·43 N	113·10 E
148	Ch'ingyun (chĭng'yōōn) . . . . .China	37·52 N	117·26 E
150	Chingyütien . . .China (Peking In.)	39·41 N	116·31 E
148	Chinhsiang (jĭn'sĭang) . . . . . .China	35·03 N	116·20 E

ng-sing; ŋ-baŋk; ɴ-nasalized n; nŏd; cŏmmit; ōld; ôbey; ôrder; fōōd; fŏŏt; ou-out; s-soft; sh-dish; th-thin; pūre; ûnite; ûrn; stŭd; circŭs; ü-as "y" in study; '-indeterminate vowel.

PRONOUNCING INDEX Ciudad Juarez–Coldwater 195

Page	Name	Pronunciation	Region	Lat. °′	Long. °′
76	Ciudad Juárez	(syōō-dhädh hwä'rāz)	Mex.	31·44 N	106·28 W
91	Ciudad Madero	(syōō-dä'd-mä-dĕ'-rô)	Mex.	22·16 N	97·52 W
90	Ciudad Mante	(syōō-dä'd-mân'tĕ)	Mex.	22·34 N	98·58 W
90	Ciudad Manuel Doblado	(syōō-dä'd-män-wāl' dō-blä'dō)	Mex.	20·43 N	101·57 W
88	Ciudad Obregon	(syōō-dhädh-ô-brĕ-gô'n)	Mex.	27·40 N	109·58 W
124	Ciudad Real	(thyōō-dhädh'rā-äl')	Sp.	38·59 N	3·55 W
124	Ciudad Rodrigo	(thyōō-dhädh'rô-drē'gō)	Sp.	40·38 N	6·34 W
91	Ciudad Serdán	(syōō-dä'd-sĕr-dâ'n)	Mex.	18·58 N	97·26 W
90	Ciudad Victoria	(syōō-dhädh'vêk-tō'rê-ä)	Mex.	23·43 N	99·09 W
126	Civadale del Friuli	(chē-vê-dä'lā-dĕl-frē-ōō'lē)	It.	46·06 N	13·24 E
126	Civitavecchia	(chē'vê-tä-vĕk'kyä)	It.	42·06 N	11·49 E
65	Clackamas	(klăc-kȧ'măs)	Ore. (Portland In.)	42·25 N	122·34 W
86	Claire (L.)	(klâr)	Can.	58·33 N	113·16 W
75	Clairton	(klârtŭn)	Pa. (Pittsburgh In.)	40·17 N	79·53 W
78	Clanton	(klăn'tŭn)	Ala.	32·50 N	86·38 W
80	Clare	(klâr)	Mich.	43·50 N	84·45 W
116	Clare (I.)		Ire.	53·46 N	9·60 W
74	Claremont	(klâr'mŏnt)	Calif. (Los Angeles In.)	34·06 N	117·43 W
81	Claremont	(klâr'mŏnt)	N. H.	43·20 N	72·20 W
80	Claremont		W. Va.	37·55 N	81·00 W
73	Claremore	(klâr'mōr)	Okla.	36·16 N	95·37 W
116	Claremorris	(klâr-mŏr'ĭs)	Ire.	53·46 N	9·05 W
158	Clarence Str.	(klăr'ĕns)	Austl.	12·15 S	130·05 E
95	Clarence Town		Ba. Is.	23·05 N	75·00 W
73	Clarendon	(klâr'ĕn-dŭn)	Ark.	34·42 N	91·17 W
72	Clarendon		Tex.	34·55 N	100·52 W
167	Clarens	(clâ-rĕns)	S. Afr. (Natal In.)	28·34 S	28·26 E
86	Claresholm	(klâr'ĕs-hōlm)	Can.	50·01 N	113·30 W
71	Clarinda	(klȧ-rĭn'dȧ)	Iowa	40·42 N	95·00 W
99	Clarines	(klä-rē'nĕs)	Ven. (In.)	9·57 N	65·10 W
71	Clarion	(klăr'i-ŭn)	Iowa	42·43 N	93·45 W
81	Clarion		Pa.	41·10 N	79·25 W
70	Clark	(klärk)	S. D.	44·52 N	97·45 W
80	Clark, Pt.		Can.	44·05 N	81·50 W
82	Clark City		Can.	50·12 N	66·38 W
69	Clarkdale	(klärk-dāl)	Ariz.	34·45 N	112·05 W
159	Clarke Ra.		Austl.	20·30 S	148·00 E
82	Clarkes Harbour	(klärks)	Can.	43·28 N	65·37 W
67	Clark Fork R.		Mont.	47·50 N	115·35 W
79	Clark Hill Res.	(klärk-hĭl)	Ga.-S. C.	33·50 N	82·35 W
81	Clarksburg	(klärkz'bûrg)	W. Va.	39·15 N	80·20 W
78	Clarksdale	(klärks-dāl)	Miss.	34·10 N	90·31 W
85	Clarkson		Can. (Toronto In.)	43·31 N	79·38 W
84	Clarkston	(klärks'-tŭn)	Ga. (Atlanta In.)	33·49 N	84·15 W
66	Clarkston		Wash.	46·24 N	117·01 W
73	Clarksville	(klärks-vĭl)	Ark.	35·28 N	93·26 W
78	Clarksville		Tenn.	36·30 N	87·23 W
73	Clarksville		Tex.	33·37 N	95·02 W
65	Clatskanie		Oreg. (Portland In.)	46·06 N	123·11 W
65	Clatskanie (R.)	(klăt-skā'nê)	Ore. (Portland In.)	46·06 N	123·11 W
65	Clatsop Spit	(klăt-sŏp)	Ore. (Portland In.)	46·13 N	124·04 W
101	Cláudio	(klou'-dēō)	Braz. (Rio de Janeiro In.)	20·26 S	44·44 W
151	Claveria	(klä-vå-rē'ä)	Phil.	18·38 N	121·08 E
75	Clawson	(klô's'n)	Mich. (Detroit In.)	42·32 N	83·09 W
79	Claxton	(klăks'tŭn)	Ga.	32·07 N	81·54 W
78	Clay	(klā)	Ky.	37·28 N	87·50 W
65	Clayburn	(klā'bûrn)	Can. (Vancouver In.)	49·05 N	122·17 W
73	Clay Center	(klā sĕn'tẽr)	Kans.	39·23 N	97·08 W
80	Clay City	(klā sĭ'tĭ)	Ky.	37·50 N	83·55 W
74	Claycomo	(kla-kō'mo)	Mo. (Kansas City In.)	39·12 N	94·30 W
110	Clay Cross	(klā krŏs)	Eng.	53·10 N	1·25 W
123	Claye-Souilly	(klĕ-sōō-yē')	Fr. (Paris In.)	48·56 N	2·43 E
84	Claymont	(klā-mŏnt)	Del. (Philadelphia In.)	39·48 N	75·28 W
78	Clayton	(klā'tŭn)	Ala.	31·52 N	85·25 W
65	Clayton		Calif. (San Francisco In.)	37·56 N	122·56 W
110	Clayton		Eng.	53·47 N	1·49 W
74	Clayton		Mo. (St. Louis In.)	38·39 N	90·20 W
72	Clayton		N. Mex.	36·26 N	103·12 W
79	Clayton		N. C.	35·40 N	78·27 W
68	Clear, (L.)		Calif.	39·05 N	122·50 W
116	Clear, C.	(klēr)	Ire.	51·24 N	9·15 W
73	Clear Boggy Cr.	(klēr bŏg'ĭ krēk)	Okla.	34·21 N	96·22 W
69	Clear Cr.		Ariz.	34·40 N	111·05 W
67	Clear Cr.		Wyo.	44·35 N	106 20 W
81	Clearfield	(klēr-fēld)	Pa.	41·00 N	78·25 W
74	Clearfield		Utah (Salt Lake City In.)	41·07 N	112·01 W
86	Clear Hills		Can.	57·11 N	119·20 W
71	Clear Lake		Iowa	43·09 N	93·23 W
65	Clear Lake		Wash. (Seattle In.)	48·27 N	122·14 W
66	Clear Lake Res.		Calif.	41·53 N	121·00 W
77	Clear R.		Tex. (In.)	29·34 N	95·13 W
79	Clearwater	(klēr-wô'tẽr)	Fla. (In.)	27·43 N	82·45 W
66	Clearwater Mts.		Idaho	45·56 N	115·15 W
73	Clearwater Res.		Mo.	37·20 N	91·04 W
66	Clearwater R.		Idaho	46·27 N	116·33 W
66	Clearwater R., Middle Fork		Idaho	46·10 N	115·48 W
66	Clearwater R., North Fork		Idaho	46·34 N	116·08 W
66	Clearwater R., South Fork		Idaho	45·46 N	115·53 W
77	Cleburne	(klē'bŭrn)	Tex.	32·21 N	97·23 W
110	Clee Hill	(klē)	Eng.	52·24 N	2·37 W
66	Cle Elum	(klē ĕl'ŭm)	Wash.	47·12 N	120·55 W
84	Clementon	(klē'mĕn-tŭn)	N. J. (Philadelphia In.)	39·49 N	75·00 W
110	Cleobury Mortimer	(klē'ô-bĕr'ĭ môr'tĭ-mĕr)	Eng.	52·22 N	2·29 W
159	Clermont	(klẽr'mŏnt)	Austl.	23·02 S	147·46 E
75	Clermont		Ind. (Indianapolis In.)	39·48 N	86·19 W
122	Clermont-Ferrand	(klĕr-môɴ'fĕr-răɴ')	Fr.	45·47 N	3·03 E
122	Clermont l'Herault	(klĕr-mŏɴ' lā-rō')	Fr.	43·38 N	3·22 E
78	Cleveland	(klēv'lănd)	Miss.	33·45 N	90·42 W
75	Cleveland		Ohio (Cleveland In.)	41·30 N	81·42 W
73	Cleveland		Okla.	36·18 N	96·28 W
78	Cleveland		Tenn.	35·09 N	84·52 W
77	Cleveland		Tex.	30·18 N	95·05 W
75	Cleveland Heights		Ohio (Cleveland In.)	41·30 N	81·35 W
75	Cleves	(klē'vĕs)	Ohio (Cincinnati In.)	39·10 N	84·45 W
116	Clew (B.)	(klōō)	Ire.	53·47 N	9·45 W
79	Clewiston	(klē'wĭs-tŭn)	Fla. (In.)	26·44 N	80·55 W
123	Clichy	(klē-shē)	Fr. (Paris In.)	48·54 N	2·18 E
116	Clifden	(klĭf'dĕn)	Ire.	53·31 N	10·04 W
69	Clifton	(klĭf'tŭn)	Ariz.	33·05 N	109·20 W
84	Clifton		N. J. (New York In.)	40·35 N	74·09 W
79	Clifton		S. C.	35·00 N	81·47 W
77	Clifton		Tex.	31·45 N	97·31 W
81	Clifton Forge		Va.	37·50 N	79·50 W
78	Clinch Res.	(klĭnch)	Tenn.-Va.	36·30 N	83·19 W
78	Clingmans Dome, (Mtn.)	(klĭng'măns dōm)	N. C.	35·37 N	83·26 W
86	Clinton	(klĭn-tŭn)	Can.	51·09 N	121·40 W
80	Clinton		Ill.	40·10 N	88·55 W
80	Clinton		Ind.	39·40 N	87·25 W
71	Clinton		Iowa	41·50 N	90·13 W
78	Clinton		Ky.	36·39 N	88·56 W
83	Clinton		Mass. (Boston In.)	42·25 N	71·41 W
84	Clinton		Md. (Baltimore In.)	38·46 N	76·54 W
73	Clinton		Mo.	38·23 N	93·46 W
79	Clinton		N. C.	35·58 N	78·20 W
72	Clinton		Okla.	35·31 N	98·56 W
79	Clinton		S. C.	34·27 N	81·53 W
78	Clinton		Tenn.	36·05 N	84·08 W
65	Clinton		Wash. (Seattle In.)	47·59 N	122·22 W
86	Clinton-Colden (L.)		Can.	63·58 N	106·34 W
75	Clinton R.		Mich. (Detroit In.)	42·36 N	83·00 W
71	Clintonville	(klĭn'tŭn-vĭl)	Wis.	44·37 N	88·46 W
80	Clio	(klē'ō)	Mich.	43·10 N	83·45 W
158	Cloates, Pt.	(klōts)	Austl.	22·47 S	113·45 E
168	Clocolan		S. Afr. (Johannesburg & Pretoria In.)	28·56 S	27·35 E
116	Clonakilty B.	(klŏn-ȧ-kĭltē)	Ire.	51·30 N	8·50 W
158	Cloncurry	(klŏn-kŭr'ê)	Austl.	20·58 S	140·42 E
116	Clonmel	(klŏn-mĕl)	Ire.	52·21 N	7·45 W
74	Cloquet	(klô-kā')	Minn. (Duluth In.)	46·28 N	92·28 W
71	Cloquet (R.)		Minn.	47·02 N	92·17 W
84	Closter	(clōs'tẽr)	N. J. (New York In.)	40·58 N	74·57 W
67	Cloud Pk.	(kloud)	Wyo.	44·23 N	107·11 W
74	Clough	(klou'h)	Minn. (Minneapolis, St. Paul In.)	45·08 N	93·14 W
79	Clover	(klō'vẽr)	S. C.	35·08 N	81·08 W
85	Clover Bar	(klō'vẽr bār)	Can. (Edmonton In.)	53·34 N	113·20 W
68	Cloverdale	(klō'vẽr-dāl)	Calif.	38·47 N	123·03 W
65	Cloverdale		Can. (Vancouver In.)	49·06 N	122·44 W
80	Cloverport	(klō'vẽr pōrt)	Ky.	37·50 N	86·35 W
72	Clovis	(klō'vĭs)	N. Mex.	34·24 N	103·11 W
121	Cluj	(klo͝ozh)	Rom.	46·46 N	23·34 E
110	Clun (R.)	(klŭn)	Eng.	52·25 N	2·56 W
122	Cluny	(klü-nē')	Fr.	46·27 N	4·40 E
159	Clutha (R.)	(klōō'thȧ)	N. Z. (In.)	45·26 S	169·15 E
73	Clyde	(klīd)	Kans.	39·34 N	97·23 W
80	Clyde		Ohio	41·15 N	83·00 W
116	Clyde (L.)		Scot.	55·35 N	3·50 W
116	Clyde, Firth of	(fûrth ŏv klīd)	Scot.	55·28 N	5·01 W
116	Clydebank		Scot.	55·56 N	4·20 W
124	Côa (R.)	(kô'ä)	Port.	40·28 N	6·55 W
91	Coacalco	(kō-ä-käl'kō)	Mex. (Mexico City In.)	19·37 N	99·06 W
68	Coachella, Can.	(kō'chĕl-lȧ)	Calif.	30·10 N	115·23 W
90	Coahuayana, Rio de (R.)	(rê'ō-dĕ-kô-ä-wä-yȧ'nä)	Mex.	19·00 N	103·33 W
90	Coahuayutla	(kō-ä-wē'lȧ	Mex.	18·19 N	101·44 W
88	Coahuila (State)	(kō-ä-wē'lȧ)	Mex.	27·30 N	103·00 W
75	Coal City	(kōl sĭ'tĭ)	Ill. (Chicago In.)	41·17 N	88·17 W
90	Coalcomán, Sierra de (Mts.)	(syĕr'rä dā kō-äl-kō-män')	Mex.	18·30 N	102·45 W
90	Coalcomán, Rio de (R.)	(rê'ō-dĕ-kō-äl-kō-män')	Mex.	18·30 N	102·48 W
90	Coalcomán de Matamoros	(kō-äl-kō-män' dä mä-tä-mō'rôs)	Mex.	18·46 N	103·10 W
73	Coalgate	(kōl'gāt)	Okla.	34·33 N	96·13 W
80	Coal Grove	(kōl grōv)	Ohio	38·20 N	82·40 W
68	Coalinga	(kō-ȧ-lĭŋ'gȧ)	Calif.	36·09 N	120·23 W
110	Coalville	(kōl'vĭl)	Eng.	52·43 N	1·21 W
89	Coamo	(kō-ä'mō)	P. R. (Puerto Rico In.)	18·05 N	66·21 W
98	Coari	(kō-är'ê)	Braz.	4·06 S	63·10 W
86	Coast Mts.	(kōst)	Can.	57·10 N	131·05 W
62	Coast Ranges, (Mts.)		U. S.	41·28 N	123·30 W
90	Coatepec	(kō-ä-tā-pĕk)	Mex.	19·23 N	98·44 W
91	Coatepec		Mex.	19·26 N	96·56 W
91	Coatepec		Mex. (Mexico City In.)	19·08 N	99·25 W
92	Coatepeque	(kō-ä-tå-pā'kå)	Guat.	14·40 N	91·52 W
92	Coatepeque		Sal.	13·56 N	89·30 W
81	Coatesville	(kōts'vĭl)	Pa.	40·00 N	75·50 W
90	Coatetelco	(kō-ä-tå-tĕl'kō)	Mex.	18·43 N	99·47 W
81	Coaticook	(kō'tĭ-ko͝ok)	Can.	45·10 N	71·55 W
91	Coatlinchán	(kô-ä-tlē'n-chä'n)	Mex. (Mexico City In.)	19·26 N	98·52 W
87	Coats (I.)	(kōts)	Can.	62·23 N	82·11 W
47	Coats Land (Reg.)		Ant.	74·00 S	12·00 W
91	Coatzacoalcos (Puerto Mexico)	kô-ät'zä-kô-äl'kōs) (pwĕ'r-tô-mĕ'-kē-kô)	Mex.	18·09 N	94·26 W
91	Coatzacoalcos (R.)		Mex.	17·40 N	94·41 W
92	Coba (Ruins)	(kô'bä)	Mex. (Yucatan In.)	20·23 N	87·23 W
87	Cobalt	(kō'bôlt)	Can.	47·21 N	79·40 W
92	Cobán	(kō-bän')	Guat.	15·28 N	90·19 W
160	Cobberas, Mt.	(cŏ-bẽr-ăs)	Austl.	36·45 S	148·15 E
82	Cobequid B.	(kŏb'ê-kwĭd)	Can.	45·22 N	63·50 W
116	Cobh	(kôv)	Ire.	51·52 N	8·09 W
98	Cobija	(kô-bē'hä)	Bol.	11·12 S	68·49 W
81	Cobourg	(kō'bo͝orgh)	Can.	43·55 N	78·05 W
94	Cobre (R.)	(kō'brā)	Jam.	18·05 N	77·00 W
120	Coburg	(kō'bōōrg)	Ger.	50·16 N	10·57 E
125	Cocentaina	(kō-thân-tä-ē'nȧ)	Sp.	38·44 N	0·27 W
98	Cochabamba	(kō-chä-bäm'bȧ)	Bol.	17·28 S	65·43 W
123	Cochem	(kō'ĸĕm)	Ger.	50·10 N	7·06 E
143	Cochin	(kō-chĭn')	India	9·58 N	76·19 E
94	Cochinos, Bahia (B.)	(bä-ē'ä-kô-chê'nōs)	Cuba	22·05 N	81·10 W
95	Cochinos Bks.		Ba. Is.	22·20 N	76·15 W
155	Cochinos Pt.	(kô-chē'-nôs)	Phil. (Manila In.)	14·25 N	120·15 E
78	Cochran	(kŏk'răn)	Ga.	32·23 N	83·23 W
87	Cochrane	(kŏk'răn)	Can.	49·01 N	81·06 W
85	Cochrane		Can. (Calgary In.)	51·11 N	114·28 W
80	Cockburn (I.)	(kŏk-bûrn)	Can.	45·55 N	83·25 W
84	Cockeysville	(kŏk'ĭz-vĭl)	Md. (Baltimore In.)	39·30 N	76·40 W
74	Cockrell Hill	(kŏk'rēl)	Tex. (Dallas, Fort Worth In.)	32·44 N	96·53 W
98	Coco, Isla del (I.)	(ê's-lä-dĕl-kô-kô)	C. R.	5·33 N	87·02 W
94	Coco, Cayo (I.)	(kä'yō-kô'kô)	Cuba	22·30 N	78·30 W
79	Cocoa	(kō'kō)	Fla. (In.)	28·21 N	80·44 W
79	Cocoa Beach		Fla. (In.)	28·20 N	80·35 W
88	Cocoli	(kŏ-kô'lē)	C. Z. (Panama Canal In.)	8·58 N	79·36 W
69	Coconino, Plat.	(kō kō nê'nō)	Ariz.	35·45 N	112·28 W
93	Coco R. (Segovia)	(kô-kô) (sĕ-gô'vyä)	Hond.	14·55 N	83·45 W
7	Cocos (Keeling)	(kō'kôs) (kē'ling)	Is. Oceania	11·50 S	90·50 E
88	Coco Solito	(kô-kô-sŏ-lē'tŏ)	C. Z. (Panama Canal In.)	9·21 N	79·53 W
82	Cocouna		Can.	47·54 N	69·31 W
90	Cocula	(kō-kōō'lä)	Mex.	20·23 N	103·47 W
90	Cocula (R.)		Mex.	18·17 N	99·11 W
98	Codajás	(kō-dä-häzh')	Braz.	3·44 S	62·09 W
99	Codera, Cabo (C.)	(kȧ'bô-kō-dĕ'rä)	Ven. (In.)	10·35 N	66·06 W
99	Codó	(kō'dō)	Braz.	4·21 S	43·52 W
126	Codogno	(kô-dō'nyō)	It.	45·08 N	9·43 E
93	Codrington	(kŏd'rĭng-tŭn)	Barbuda (Le. & Wind. Is. In.)	17·39 N	61·49 W
67	Cody	(kō'dĭ)	Wyo.	44·31 N	109·02 W
123	Coesfeld	(kûs'fĕld)	Ger. (Ruhr In.)	51·56 N	7·10 E
66	Coeur d' Alene	(kûr dȧ-lān')	Idaho	47·43 N	116·35 W
66	Coeur d' Alene L.		Idaho	47·32 N	116·39 W
66	Coeur d' Alene R.		Idaho	47·26 N	116·35 W
167	Coffee Bay	(cŏfē bā)	S. Afr. (Natal In.)	31·58 S	29·10 E
73	Coffeyville	(kŏf'ĭ-vĭl)	Kans.	37·01 N	95·38 W
160	Coff's Harbour		Austl.	30·20 S	153·10 E
167	Cofimvaba	(căfĭm'vä-bȧ)	S. Afr. (Natal In.)	32·01 S	27·37 E
126	Coghinas (R.)	(kō'gē-nȧs)	It.	40·31 N	9·00 E
122	Cognac	(kôn-yak')	Fr.	45·41 N	0·22 W
83	Cohasset	(kô-hăs'ĕt)	Mass. (Boston In.)	42·14 N	70·48 W
81	Cohoes	(kô-hōz')	N. Y.	42·50 N	73·40 W
100	Coig	(kô'êk) (R.)	Arg.	51·15 S	71·00 W
143	Coimbatore	(kô-ēm-bȧ-tôr')	India	11·03 N	76·56 E
124	Coimbra	(kô-ēm'brä)	Port.	40·14 N	8·23 W
124	Coín	(kô-ēn')	Sp.	36·40 N	4·45 W
125	Coina	(kô-ē'nȧ)	Port. (Lisbon In.)	38·35 N	9·03 W
125	Coina (R.)	(kô'y-nä)	Port. (Lisbon In.)	38·35 N	9·02 W
98	Coipasa, Salar de (Salt Flat)	(sä-lä'r-dĕ-koi-pä'-sä)	Chile	19·12 S	69·13 W
91	Coixtlahuaca	(kō-ēks'tlä-wä'kä)	Mex.	17·42 N	97·17 W
99	Cojedes (State)	(kô-kĕ'dĕs)	Ven. (In.)	9·50 N	68·21 W
95	Cojimar	(kō-hê-mär')	Cuba (Havana In.)	23·10 N	82·19 W
92	Cojutepeque	(kô-ho͝o-tĕ-pā'kå)	Sal.	13·45 N	88·50 W
71	Cokato	(kô-kā'tō)	Minn.	45·03 N	94·11 W
75	Cokeburg	(kōk bûgh)	Pa. (Pittsburgh In.)	40·06 N	80·03 W
160	Colac	(kŏ'lȧc)	Austl.	38·25 S	143·40 E
125	Colares	(kô-lä'rĕs)	Port. (Lisbon In.)	38·47 N	9·27 W
99	Colatina	(kô-lä-tê'nä)	Braz.	19·33 S	40·42 W
72	Colby	(kōl'bĭ)	Kans.	39 23 N	101·04 W
101	Colchagua (Prov.)	(kôl-chȧ'gwä)	Chile (Santiago In.)	36·42 S	71·24 W
117	Colchester	(kōl'chĕs-tẽr)	Eng.	51·52 N	0·50 E
83	Cold Spring Pd.	(kōld)	Can.	48·08 N	56·25 W
72	Coldwater	(kōld'wô-tẽr)	Kans.	37·14 N	99·21 W
80	Coldwater		Mich.	41·55 N	85·00 W
78	Coldwater (R.)		Miss.	34·25 N	90·12 W
72	Coldwater Cr.		Tex.	36·10 N	101·45 W

n-sing ŋ-baŋk; ɴ-nasalized n; nŏd; cŏmmit; ōld; ôbey; ôrder; fōōd; fo͝ot; ou-out; s-soft; sh-dish; th-thin; pūre; ûnite; ûrn; stŭd; circŭs; ü-as "y" in study; '-indeterminate vowel.

PRONOUNCING INDEX Coracora–Crisul Alb 197

Page	Name Pronunciation Region	Lat. °′	Long. °′
98	Coracora (kō′rä-kō′rä) . . . . Peru	15·12 s	73·42 w
79	Coral Gables . . . . Fla. (In.)	25·43 n	80·14 w
94	Coralillo (kô-rä-lē-yō) . . . . Cuba	73·00 n	80·40 w
87	Coral Rapids (kŏr′ăl) . . . . Can.	50·18 n	81·49 w
75	Coral Ridge (kŏr′ăl) Ky. (Louisville In.)	38·05 n	85·42 w
156	Coral Sea (kŏr′ăl) . . . . Oceania	13·30 s	150·00 e
160	Corangamite, L. (cŏr-ăŋg′ȧ-mīt) Austl.	38·05 s	142·55 e
75	Coraopolis (kō-rä-ŏp′ô-lĭs) Pa. (Pittsburgh In.)	40·31 n	80·10 w
126	Corato (kô′rä-tô) . . . . It.	41·08 n	16·28 e
123	Corbeil-Essonnes (kôr-bā′yĕ-sŏn′) Fr. (Paris In.)	48·31 n	2·29 e
65	Corbett (kôr′bĕt) Ore. (Portland In.)	45·31 n	122·17 w
122	Corbie (kôr-bē′) . . . . Fr.	49·55 n	2·27 e
78	Corbin (kôr′bĭn) . . . . Ky.	36·55 n	84·06 w
110	Corby (kôr′bĭ) . . . . Eng.	52·50 n	0·32 w
100	Corcovado (Mtn.) (kôr-kô-vä′do͞o) Braz. (In.)	22·57 s	43·13 w
100	Corcovado, Golfo (G.) (kôr-kô-vä′dhō) . Chile	43·40 s	75·00 w
101	Cordeiro (kôr-dā′rō) Braz. (Rio de Janeiro In.)	22·03 s	42·22 w
78	Cordele (kôr-dēl′) . . . . Ga.	31·55 n	83·50 w
72	Cordell (kôr-dĕl′) . . . . Okla.	35·19 n	98·58 w
124	Cordillera Cantabrica (Mts.) (kôr-dēl-yĕ′rä-kän-tä′brē-kä) . Sp.	43·05 n	6·05 w
155	Cordillera Central (Mts.) (kôr-dēl-yĕ′rä-sĕn′träl) Phil. (Manila In.)	17·05 n	120·55 e
49	Cordilleran Highlands (Reg.) (kōr dĭl′lŭr ȧn) . N. A.	55·00 n	125·00 w
100	Córdoba (kôr′dô-vä) . . . . Arg.	30·20 s	64·03 w
91	Córdoba (kô′r-dô-bä) . . . . Mex.	18·53 n	96·54 w
124	Córdoba (kô′r-dô-bä) . . . . Sp.	37·55 n	4·45 w
100	Córdoba (Prov.) (kôr′dô-vä) . Arg.	32·00 s	64·00 w
100	Córdoba, Sa. de (Mts.) . . . . . . Arg.	31·15 s	64·30 w
78	Cordova (kôr′dô-ȧ) . . . . Ala.	33·45 n	86·11 w
64	Cordova (kôr′dô-vä) . . . . Alaska	60·34 n	145·38 w
124	Corella (kô-rĕl-yä) . . . . Sp.	42·07 n	1·48 w
126	Corigliano (kō-rē-lyä′nō) . . . . . . It.	39·35 n	16·30 e
78	Corinth (kŏr′ĭnth) . . . . Miss.	34·55 n	88·30 w
	Corinth, see Korinthos		
99	Corinto (kô-rē′n-tō) . . . . Braz.	18·20 s	44·16 w
98	Corinto . . . . Col. (In.)	3·09 n	76·12 w
92	Corinto (kōr-ĭn′to) . . . . Nic.	12·30 n	87·12 w
161	Corio . . . . . Austl. (Melbourne In.)	38·05 s	144·22 e
161	Corio B . . . Austl. (Melbourne In.)	38·07 s	144·25 e
116	Cork (kôrk) . . . . Ire.	51·54 n	8·25 w
116	Cork Hbr . . . . Ire.	51·44 n	8·15 w
126	Corleone (kôr-lå-ō′nā) . . . . It.	37·48 n	13·18 e
127	Corlu (chôr′lo͞o) . . . . Tur.	41·09 n	27·48 e
78	Cornelia (kôr-nē′lyȧ) . . . . Ga.	34·31 n	83·30 w
168	Cornelis R. (kôr-nē′lĭs) . . . . S. Afr. (Johannesburg & Pretoria In.)	27·48 s	29·15 e
74	Cornell (kôr-nĕl′) Calif. (Los Angeles In.)	34·06 n	118·46 w
71	Cornell . . . . Wis.	45·10 n	91·10 w
83	Corner Brook (kôr′nẽr) . . . . . . Can.	48·58 n	57·49 w
160	Corner Inlet . . . . Austl.	38·55 s	146·45 e
	Corneta, see Targuinia		
73	Corning (kôr′nĭng) . . . . Ark.	36·26 n	90·35 w
71	Corning . . . . Iowa	40·58 n	94·40 w
81	Corning . . . . N. Y.	42·10 n	77·05 w
126	Corno, M. (Mtn.) (kôr′nō) . . . . . It.	42·28 n	13·37 e
94	Cornwall . . . . Ba. Is.	25·55 n	77·15 w
81	Cornwall (kôrn′wôl) . . . . Can.	45·05 n	74·35 w
116	Cornwall Pen. (kôrn′wăl) . . . . Eng.	50·25 n	5·04 w
98	Coro (kō′rô) . . . . Ven.	11·22 n	69·43 w
98	Corocoro (kō-rô-kō′rô) . . . . Bol.	17·15 s	68·21 w
143	Coromandel Coast (kŏr-ô-man′dĕl) India	17·50 n	80·14 e
78	Corona (kô-rō′nȧ) . . . . Ala.	33·42 n	87·28 w
74	Corona . . . Calif. (Los Angeles In.)	33·52 n	117·34 w
93	Coronada, Bahia de (B.) (bä-ē′ä-dĕ-kô-rô-nä′dō) . C.R.	8·47 n	84·04 w
74	Corona del Mar (kô-rō′nȧ dēl măr) Calif. (Los Angeles In.)	33·36 n	117·53 w
68	Coronado (kŏr-ô-nä′dō) Calif. (San Diego In.)	32·42 n	117·12 w
86	Coronation G. (kŏr-ô-nā′shŭn) Can.	68·07 n	112·50 w
100	Coronel (kō-rô-nĕl′) . . . . Chile	37·00 s	73·10 w
101	Coronel Brandsen (kŏ-rô-nĕl-brȧ′nd-sĕn) Arg. (Buenos Aires In.)	35·09 s	58·15 w
100	Coronel Dorrego (kŏ-rô-nĕl-dôr-rĕ′gô) . Arg.	38·43 s	61·16 w
100	Coronel Oviedo (kŏ-rô-nĕl-ô-vêĕ′dô) . Par.	25·28 s	56·22 w
100	Coronel Pringles (kŏ-rô-nĕl-prēn′glĕs) . Arg.	37·54 s	61·22 w
100	Coronel Suárez (kŏ-rô-nĕl-swă′rās) . Arg.	37·24 s	66·49 w
160	Corowa (cŏr-ôwă) . . . . Austl.	36·02 s	146·23 e
92	Corozal (cŏr-ŏth-ăl′) Br. Hond. (Yucatan In.)	18·25 n	88·23 w
77	Corpus Christi (kôr′pŭs krĭs′tê) Tex.	27·48 n	97·24 w
77	Corpus Christi B. . . . . Tex.	27·47 n	97·14 w
76	Corpus Christi L. . . . . Tex.	28·08 n	98·20 w
100	Corral (kô-räl′) . . . . Chile	39·57 s	73·15 w
124	Corral de Almaguer (kô-räl′dā ăl-mă-gâr′) . Sp.	39·45 n	3·10 w
155	Corregidor (I.) (kô-rā-hē-dōr′) Phil. (Manila In.)	14·21 n	120·25 e
99	Correntina (kô-rĕn-tē-nȧ) . . . Braz.	13·18 s	44·33 w
116	Corrib, Lough (B.) (lŏk kŏr′ĭb) Ire.	53·56 n	9·19 w
100	Corrientes (kō-ryĕn′tās) . . . . . Arg.	27·25 s	58·39 w
100	Corrientes (Prov.) . . . . Arg.	28·45 s	58·00 w
98	Corrientes, Cabo (kȧ′bô-kō-ryĕn′tās) . Col.	5·34 n	77·35 w
94	Corrientes, Cabo (C.) (kȧ′bô-kôr-rē-ĕn′tĕs) . Cuba	21·50 n	84·25 w
94	Corrientes, Ensenada de (B.) (ĕn-sĕ-nă-dä-dĕ-kō-ryĕn′tās) Cuba	21·45 n	84·45 w
90	Corrientes, Cabo (C.) . . . . Mex.	20·25 n	105·41 w
81	Cory (kŏr′ĭ) . . . . Pa.	41·55 n	79·40 w
126	Corse, C. (kôrs) . . . . Fr.	42·59 n	9·19 e
126	Corsica (I.) (kô′r-sē-kä) . . . . Fr.	42·10 n	8·55 e
77	Corsicana (kôr-sĭ-kăn′ȧ) . . . . . Tex.	32·06 n	96·28 w
90	Cortazar (kôr-tä-zär′) . . . . Mex.	20·30 n	100·57 w
126	Corte (kôr′tå) . . . . Fr.	42·18 n	9·10 e
124	Cortegana (kôr-tå-gä′nä) . . . . . . Sp.	37·54 n	6·48 w
124	Cortes (kôr-tās′) . . . . Sp.	36·38 n	5·20 w
94	Cortés, Ensenada de (B.) (ĕn-sĕ-nä-dä-dĕ-kôr-tās′) . Cuba	22·05 n	83·45 w
81	Cortland (kôrt′lănd) . . . . N. Y.	42·35 n	76·10 w
126	Cortona (kôr-tō′nä) . . . . It.	43·16 n	12·00 e
124	Coruche (kô-ro͞o′she) . . . . Port.	38·58 n	8·34 w
133	Coruh (R.) (chō-ro͞ok′) . . . . . . Tur.	40·30 n	41·10 e
133	Corum (chô-ro͞om′) . . . . Tur.	39·30 n	34·50 e
99	Corumbá (kō-ro͝om-bä′) . . . . . Braz.	19·01 s	57·28 w
80	Corunna (kô-rŭn′ȧ) . . . . Mich.	43·00 n	84·05 w
99	Coruripe (kō-ro͝o-rē′pĭ) . . . . . . Braz.	10·09 s	36·13 w
66	Corvallis (kŏr-văl′ĭs) . . . . Ore.	44·34 n	123·17 w
110	Corve (R.) (kôr′vê) . . . . Eng.	52·28 n	2·43 w
80	Corydon (kŏr′ĭ-dŭn) . . . . Ind.	38·10 n	86·05 w
71	Corydon . . . . Iowa	40·45 n	93·20 w
80	Corydon . . . . Ky.	37·45 n	87·40 w
91	Cosamaloápan (kô-sȧ-mă-lwă′pän) Mex.	18·21 n	95·48 w
91	Coscomatepec (kôs′kōmă-tĕ-pĕk′) Mex.	19·04 n	97·03 w
110	Coseley (kôs′lē) . . . . Eng.	52·33 n	2·10 w
126	Cosenza (kô-zĕnt′să) . . . . It.	39·18 n	16·15 e
80	Coshocton (kô-shŏk′tŭn) . . . . Ohio	40·15 n	81·55 w
92	Cosigüina (Vol.) . . . . Nic.	12·59 n	83·35 w
167	Cosmoledo Group (Is.) (kŏs-mô-lā′dō) . Afr.	9·42 s	47·45 e
66	Cosmopolis (kŏz-mŏp′ô-lĭs) . Wash.	46·58 n	123·47 w
122	Cosne-sur-Loire (kōn-sür-lwär′) Fr.	47·25 n	2·57 e
91	Cosoleacaque (kō sō lā-ȧ-kă′kē) Mex.	18·01 n	94·38 w
74	Costa Mesa (kŏs′tȧ mā′sȧ) Calif. (Los Angeles In.)	33·39 n	118·54 w
89	Costa Rica (kŏs′tȧ rē′kȧ) . . . N. A.	10·30 n	84·30 w
68	Cosumnes (R.) (kŏ-sŭm′nêz) . Calif.	38·21 n	121·17 w
98	Cotabambas (kô-tä-bȧm′bäs) Peru	13·49 s	72·17 w
155	Cotabato (kō-tä-bä′tō) . . . . . . Phil.	7·06 n	124·13 e
91	Cotaxtla (kō-täs′tlä) . . . . Mex.	18·49 n	96·22 w
91	Cotaxtla (R.) . . . . Mex.	18·54 n	96·21 w
85	Coteau-du-Lac (cō-tō′dü-läk) Can. (Montreal In.)	45·17 n	74·11 w
85	Coteau Landing Can. (Montreal In.)	45 15 n	74·13 w
95	Coteaux . . . . Hai.	18·15 n	74·05 w
122	Côte d'Or (hill) (kōt-dŏr′) . . . . . Fr.	47·02 n	4·35 e
90	Cotija de la Paz (kô-tē′-ĸä-dĕ-lä-pȧ′z) . Mex.	19·46 n	102·43 w
164	Cotonou (kô-tô-no͞o′) . . . Dahomey	6·26 n	2·19 e
98	Cotopaxi (Mtn.) (kō-tô-păk′sê) Ec.	0·40 s	78·26 w
95	Cotorro (kô-tôr-rō) Cuba (Havana In.)	23·03 n	82·17 w
116	Cotswold Hills (kŭtz′wōld) . . Eng.	51·35 n	2·16 w
74	Cottage Grove (kŏt′åj grōv) Minn. (Minneapolis, St. Paul In.)	44·50 n	92·52 w
66	Cottage Grove . . . . Ore.	43·48 n	123·04 w
120	Cottbus (kōtt′bo͞os) . . . . Ger.	51·47 n	14·20 e
123	Cottian Alps (Mts.) (kŏ′tē-ŭn-ălps) . Fr.-It.	44·46 n	7·02 e
70	Cottonwood (R.) (kŏt′ŭn-wo͝od) Minn.	44·25 n	95·35 w
66	Cottonwood Cr. . . . . Calif.	40·24 n	122·50 w
95	Cotui (kô-to͞o′-ê) . . . . . . Dom. Rep.	19·05 n	70·10 w
76	Cotulla (kŏ-tŭl′lȧ) . . . . Tex.	28·26 n	99·14 w
123	Coubert (ko͞o-bâr′) . Fr. (Paris In.)	48·40 n	2·43 e
81	Coudersport (koŭ′dẽrz-port) . . . Pa.	41·45 n	78·00 w
82	Coudres, Ile-aux . . . . Can.	47·25 n	70·25 w
122	Couéron (ko͞o-å-rôɴ′) . . . . Fr.	47·16 n	1·45 w
123	Coulommiers (ko͞o-lô-myā′) Fr. (Paris In.)	48·49 n	3·05 e
100	Coulto, Serra do (Mts.) (sĕ′r-rä-dô-kô-o͝o′tô) . Braz. (In.)	22·33 s	43·27 w
64	Council (koun′sĭl) . . . . Alaska	64·55 n	163·40 w
70	Council Bluffs (koun′sĭl blūf) Iowa	41·16 n	95·53 w
73	Council Grove (koun′sĭl grōv) Kans.	38·39 n	96·30 w
65	Coupeville (ko͞op′vĭl) Wash. (Seattle In.)	48·13 n	122·41 w
99	Courantyne (R.) (kôr′ăntĭn) Guy-Sur.	4·28 n	57·42 w
86	Courtenay (co͞ort-nā′) . . . . Can.	49·51 n	125·07 w
77	Coushatta (kou-shăt′ȧ) . . . . La.	32·02 n	93·21 w
122	Coutras (ko͞o-trȧ′) . . . . Fr.	45·02 n	0·07 w
110	Coventry (kŭv′ĕn-trĭ) . . . . Eng.	52·25 n	1·29 w
124	Covilhã (kô-vēl′yăɴ) . . . . Port.	40·18 n	7·29 w
74	Covina (kô-vē′nȧ) Calif. (Los Angeles In.)	34·06 n	117·54 w
78	Covington (kŭv′ĭng-tŭn) . . . . . . Ga.	33·36 n	83·50 w
80	Covington . . . . Ind.	40·10 n	87·15 w
75	Covington . . Ky. (Cincinnati In.)	39·05 n	84·31 w
77	Covington . . . . La.	30·30 n	90·06 w
80	Covington . . . . Ohio	40·10 n	84·20 w
73	Covington . . . . Okla.	36·18 n	97·32 w
78	Covington . . . . Tenn.	35·33 n	89·40 w
81	Covington . . . . Va.	37·50 n	80·00 w
160	Cowal, L. (kou′ăl) . . . . Austl.	33·30 s	147·10 e
158	Cowan, (L.) (kou′ȧn) . . . . Austl.	32·00 s	122·30 e
66	Cow Cr. (kou) . . . . Ore.	42·45 n	123·35 w
116	Cowes (kouz) . . . . Eng.	50·43 n	1·25 w
66	Cowlitz R. (kou′lĭts) . . . . Wash.	46·30 n	122·45 w
160	Cowra (kou′rȧ) . . . . Austl.	33·50 s	148·33 e
99	Coxim (kō-shēɴ′) . . . . Braz.	18·32 s	54·43 w
91	Coxquihui (kōz-kē-wē′) . . . . . Mex.	20·10 n	97·34 w
142	Coxs Bazar . . . . E. Pak.	21·32 n	92·00 e
98	Coyaima (kô-yȧê′-mä) . . Col. (In.)	3·48 n	75·11 w
76	Coyame (kō-yä′mā) . . . . Mex.	29·26 n	105·05 w
76	Coyanosa Draw (kŏ yȧ-nō′sä) . Tex.	30·55 n	103·07 w
91	Coyoacàn (kô-yô-ȧ-kän′) Mex. (Mexico City In.)	19·21 n	99·10 w
65	Coyote (R.) (kī′ōt) Calif. (San Francisco In.)	37·27 n	121·57 w
90	Coyuca de Benítez (kō-yo͞o′kä dā bā-nē′tāz) . Mex.	17·04 n	100·06 w
90	Coyuca de Catalán (kō-yo͞o′kä dā kä-tä-län′) . Mex.	18·19 n	100·41 w
91	Coyutla (kō-yo͞o′tlä) . . . . Mex.	20·13 n	97·40 w
72	Cozad (kō′zăd) . . . . Nebr.	40·53 n	99·59 w
75	Cozaddale (kô-zăd-dāl) Ohio (Cincinnati In.)	39·16 n	84·09 w
90	Cozoyoapan (kô-zō-yô-ä-pȧ′n) Mex.	16·45 n	98·17 w
92	Cozumel (kŏ-zo͞o-mĕ′l) Mex. (Yucatan In.)	20·31 n	86·55 w
92	Cozumel, Isla de (I.) (ê′s-lä-dĕ-kŏ-zo͞o-mĕ′l) Mex. (Yucatan In.)	20·26 n	87·10 w
66	Crab Cr. (krăb) . . . . Wash.	46·47 n	119·43 w
66	Crab Cr . . . . Wash.	47·21 n	119·09 w
167	Cradock (kră′dŭk) S. Afr. (Natal In.)	32·12 s	25·38 e
75	Crafton (krăf′tŭn) Pa. (Pittsburgh In.)	40·26 n	80·04 w
67	Craig (krāg) . . . . Colo.	40·32 n	107·31 w
85	Craigs Road Station (krāgz) Can. (Quebec In.)	46·37 n	71·22 w
127	Craiova (krȧ-yō′vȧ) . . . . Rom.	44·18 n	23·50 e
81	Cranberry (L.) (krăn′bĕr-ĭ) . . N. Y.	44·10 n	74·50 w
161	Cranbourne Austl. (Melbourne In.)	38·07 s	145·16 e
86	Cranbrook (krăn′bro͝ok) . . . . . Can.	49·43 n	115·47 w
84	Cranbury (krăn′bē-rĭ) N. J. (New York In.)	40·19 n	74·31 w
71	Crandon (krăn′dŭn) . . . . Wis.	45·35 n	88·55 w
122	Cransac (kräɴ-zȧk′) . . . . Fr.	44·28 n	2·19 e
84	Cranston (krăns′tŭn) R. I. (Providence In.)	41·46 n	71·25 w
66	Crater L. (krā′tẽr) . . . . Ore.	43·00 n	122·08 w
66	Crater Lake Natl. Park . . . . . . Ore.	4258· n	122·40 w
67	Craters of the Moon Natl. Park (krā′tẽr) . Idaho	43·28 n	113·15 w
99	Crateús (krä-tå-o͞ozh′) . . . . . . Braz.	5·09 s	40·35 w
99	Crato (krä′to͝o) . . . . Braz.	7·19 s	39·13 w
70	Crawford (krô′fẽrd) . . . . Nebr.	42·41 n	103·25 w
65	Crawford . . . . Wash. (Portland In.)	45·49 n	122·24 w
80	Crawfordsville (krô′fẽrdz-vĭl) . Ind.	40·00 n	86·55 w
67	Crazy Mts. (krā′zĭ) . . . . Mont.	46·11 n	110·25 w
67	Crazy Woman Cr . . . . Wyo.	44·08 n	106·40 w
122	Crécy (krā-sē′) . . . . Fr.	50·13 n	1·48 e
168	Crecy (krĕ-sê) S. Afr. (Johannesburg & Pretoria In.)	24·38 s	28·52 e
123	Crecy-en-Brie (krā-sē′-ĕɴ-brē′) Fr. (Paris In.)	48·52 n	2·55 e
85	Credit R . . . . . . Can. (Toronto In.)	43·41 n	79·55 w
86	Cree (L.) (krē) . . . . Can.	57·35 n	107·52 w
70	Creighton (krā′tŭn) . . . . Nebr.	42·27 n	97·54 w
167	Creighton (cre-tŏn) S. Afr. (Natal In.)	30·02 s	29·52 e
122	Creil (krĕ′y′) . . . . Fr.	49·18 n	2·28 e
126	Crema (krā′mä) . . . . It.	45·21 n	9·53 e
126	Cremona (krā-mō′nä) . . . . It.	45·09 n	10·02 e
126	Crépy-en-Valois (krā-pē′-ĕɴ-vä-lwä′) Fr. (Paris In.)	49·14 n	2·53 e
126	Cres (Tsrĕs) . . . . Yugo.	44·58 n	14·21 e
126	Cres (I.) . . . . Yugo.	44·50 n	14·31 e
79	Crescent (R.) (krĕs′ĕnt) . . . . . . Fla.	29·33 n	81·30 w
65	Crescent Beach Can. (Vancouver In.)	49·03 n	122·58 w
79	Crescent City . . . . Fla.	29·26 n	81·35 w
66	Crescent L. . . . . Ore.	43·25 n	121·58 w
71	Cresco (krĕs′kō) . . . . Iowa	43·23 n	92·07 w
66	Cresent City (krĕs′ĕnt) . . . . . Calif.	41·46 n	124·13 w
69	Crested Butte (krĕst′ĕd būt) . Colo.	38·50 n	107·00 w
74	Crestline (krĕst-līn) Calif. (Los Angeles In.)	34·15 n	117·17 w
80	Crestline . . . . Ohio	40·50 n	82·40 w
74	Crestmore (krĕst′môr) Calif. (Los Angeles In.)	34·02 n	117·23 w
86	Creston (krĕs′tŭn) . . . . Can.	49·09 n	116·32 w
71	Creston . . . . Iowa	41·04 n	94·22 w
75	Creston . . . . . Ohio (Cleveland In.)	40·59 n	81·54 w
78	Crestview (krĕst′vū) . . . . Fla.	30·44 n	86·35 w
75	Crestwood (krĕst′wo͝od) Ky. (Louisville In.)	38·20 n	85·28 w
75	Crete (krēt) . . . . . Ill. (Chicago In.)	41·26 n	87·38 w
73	Crete . . . . Nebr.	40·38 n	96·56 w
126	Crete (I.) . . . . Grc. (Inset)	35·15 n	24·30 e
125	Creus, Cabo de (C.) (kā′-bô-dĕ-krĕ-o͞os) . Sp.	42·16 n	3·18 e
122	Creuse (krûz) . . . . Fr.	46·51 n	0·49 e
74	Creve Coeur (krēv ko͝or) Mo. (St. Louis In.)	38·40 n	90·27 w
125	Crevillente (krå-vê-lyĕn′tå) . . . . Sp.	38·12 n	0·48 w
110	Crewe (kro͞o) . . . . Eng.	53·06 n	2·27 w
79	Crewe . . . . Va.	37·09 n	78·08 w
	Crimea Poluostrov (Pen.), see Krymskiy		
120	Crimmitschau (krĭm′ĭt-shou) . Ger.	50·49 n	12·22 e
72	Cripple Creek (krĭp′′l) . . . . . . Colo.	38·44 n	105·12 w
81	Crisfield (krĭs-fēld) . . . . Md.	38·00 n	78·50 w
101	Cristina (krês-tē′-nä) Braz. (Rio de Janeiro In.)	22·13 s	45·15 w
98	Cristobal Colón, Pico (Pk.) (pē′kô-krēs-tô′bäl-kō-lôn′) . . Col.	11·00 n	74·00 w
121	Crisul Alb R. (krē′sho͞ol älb) Rom.	46·20 n	22·15 e

ng-sing; ŋ-baŋk; ɴ-nasalized n; nŏd; cŏmmit; ōld; ôbey; ôrder; fo͞od; fo͝ot; ou-out; s-soft; sh-dish; th-thin; pūre; ûnite; ûrn; stŭd; circŭs; ü-as "y" in study; ′-indeterminate vowel.

198 Crna–Dalesville PRONOUNCING INDEX

Page	Name Pronunciation Region	Lat. °′	Long. °′
127	Crna (R.) (ts'r'nȧ) Yugo.	41·03 N	21·46 E
127	Črna Gora (Montenegro) (Reg.) (ts'r-nȧ-gō'rȧ) (mōn-tȧ-nā'grō) (mōn-tê-nē'grō). Yugo.	42·55 N	18·52 E
126	Črnomelj (ch'r'nō-māl') Yugo.	45·35 N	15·11 E
	Croatia, see Hrvatska		
65	Crockett (krŏk'ĕt) Calif. (San Francisco In.)	38·03 N	122·14 W
77	Crockett Tex.	31·19 N	95·28 W
168	Crocodile R. (krŏ'kō-dīl) S. Afr. (Johannesburg & Pretoria In.)	24·25 S	27·08 E
84	Crofton Md. (Baltimore In.)	39·01 N	76·43 W
70	Crofton (krôf'tŭn) S. D.	45·25 N	98·04 W
71	Croix, Lac la (L.) (krōō-ä' läk lä). Can.-Minn.	48·19 N	91·53 W
158	Croker (krō'kȧ) Austl.	10·45 S	132·25 E
161	Cronulla (krō-nŭl'ȧ) Austl. (Sydney In.)	34·03 S	151·09 E
95	Crooked (I.) Ba. Is.	22·45 N	74·10 W
83	Crooked (L.) Can.	48·24 N	56·00 W
73	Crooked Cr. (krŏŏk'ĕd) Ill.	40·21 N	90·49 W
66	Crooked Cr. Ore.	42·23 N	118·14 W
95	Crooked Island Passage (Str.) Ba. Is.	22·40 N	74·50 W
66	Crooked R. Ore.	44·07 N	120·30 W
70	Crookston (krŏŏks'tŭn) Minn.	47·44 N	96·35 W
80	Crooksville (krŏŏks'vĭl) Ohio	39·45 N	82·05 W
71	Crosby (krôz'bĭ) Minn.	46·29 N	93·58 W
70	Crosby N. D.	48·55 N	103·18 W
77	Crosby Tex. (In.)	29·55 N	95·04 W
81	Cross (L.) (krôs) Can.	44·55 N	76·55 W
86	Cross (L.) Can.	54·40 N	98·47 W
73	Crossett (krôs'ĕt) Ark.	33·08 N	91·56 W
94	Cross Hbr. Ba. Is.	25·55 N	77·15 W
77	Cross L. La.	32·33 N	93·58 W
84	Cross River Res. (krôs) N. Y. (New York In.)	41·14 N	73·34 W
64	Cross Sd. (krŏs) Alaska	58·12 N	137·20 W
80	Crosswell (krŏz'wĕl) Mich.	43·15 N	82·35 W
127	Crotone (krō-tô'nĕ) It.	39·05 N	17·08 E
84	Croton Falls Res. (krōtŭn) N. Y. (New York In.)	41·22 N	73·44 W
84	Croton-on-Hudson (krō'tŭn-ŏn hŭd'sŭn). N. Y. (New York In.)	41·12 N	73·53 W
71	Crow (L.) Can.	49·13 N	93·29 W
72	Crow Cr. Colo.	41·08 N	104·25 W
70	Crow Creek Ind. Res. S. D.	44·17 N	99·17 W
67	Crow Ind. Res. (krō) Mont.	45·26 N	108·12 W
110	Crowle (kroul) Eng.	53·36 N	0·49 W
77	Crowley (krou'lē) La.	30·13 N	92·22 W
89	Crown, Mt. Vir. Is. (U. S. A.) (St. Thomas In.)	18·22 N	64·58 W
65	Crown Mtn. (kroun) Can. (Vancouver In.)	49·24 N	123·05 W
75	Crown Point (kroun point') Ind. (Chicago In.)	41·25 N	87·22 W
81	Crown Point N. Y.	44·00 N	73·25 W
71	Crow Wing (R.) (krō) Minn.	44·50 N	94·01 W
71	Crow Wing (R.) Minn.	46·42 N	94·48 W
71	Crow Wing (R.), North Fork. Minn.	45·16 N	94·28 W
71	Crow Wing (R.), South Fork Minn.	44·59 N	94·42 W
159	Croydon (kroi'dŭn) Austl.	18·15 S	142·15 E
161	Croydon Austl. (Melbourne In.)	37·48 S	145·17 E
110	Croydon Eng. (London In.)	51·22 N	0·06 W
84	Croydon Pa. (Philadelphia In.)	40·05 N	74·55 W
47	Crozet I. (krô-zĕ') Ind. O.	46·20 S	51·30 E
94	Cruces (krōō'sås) Cuba	22·20 N	80·20 W
76	Cruces, Arroyo de (är-rŏ'yô-dĕ-krōō'sĕs). Mex.	26·17 N	104·32 W
76	Cruillas (krōō-ēl'yäs) Mex.	24·45 N	98·31 W
94	Cruz, Cabo (C.) (kä'-bô-krōōz) Cuba	19·50 N	77·45 W
94	Cruz, Cayo (I.) (kä'yō-krōōz) Cuba	22·15 N	77·50 W
100	Cruz Alta (krōōz äl'tä) Braz.	28·41 S	54·02 W
100	Cruz del Eje (krōō's-dĕl-ĕ-kĕ). Arg.	30·46 S	64·45 W
101	Cruzeiro (krōō-zā'rŏŏ) Braz. (Rio de Janeiro In.)	22·36 S	44·57 W
98	Cruzeiro do Sul (krōō-zā'rŏŏ dōō sōōl). Braz.	7·34 S	72·40 W
85	Crysler Can. (Ottawa In.)	45·13 N	75·09 W
76	Crystal City (krĭs'tăl sĭ'tĭ) Tex.	28·40 N	99·90 W
71	Crystal Falls (krĭs'tăl fôls) Mich.	46·06 N	88·21 W
75	Crystal Lake (krĭs'tăl lăk) Ill. (Chicago In.)	42·15 N	88·18 W
78	Crystal Springs (krĭs'tăl springz) Miss.	31·58 N	90·20 W
65	Crystal Spr. (krĭs'tăl) Calif. (San Francisco In.)	37·31 N	122·26 W
121	Csongrád (chôn'gräd) Hung.	46·42 N	20·09 E
121	Csorna (chôr'nä) Hung.	47·39 N	17·11 E
99	Cúa (kōō'ä) Ven. (In.)	10·10 N	66·54 W
91	Cuajimalpa (kwä-hē-mäl'pä) Mex. (Mexico City In.)	19·21 N	99·18 W
90	Cuale, Sierra del (Mts.) (sē-ĕ'r-rä-dĕl-kwä'lĕ). Mex.	20·20 N	104·58 W
166	Cuamato (kwä-mä'tō) Ang.	17·05 S	15·15 E
166	Cuando (R.) (kwän'dō) Ang.	14·15 S	20·00 E
166	Cuango (kwäŋ'gō) Ang.	6·15 S	16·53 E
166	Cuanza (R.) (kwän'zä) Ang.	9·45 S	15·00 E
100	Cuarto Saladillo (R.) (kwär'tō-sä-lä-dē'l-yō). Arg.	33·00 S	63·25 W
95	Cuatro Caminos (kwä'trō-kä-mē'nōs). Cuba (Havana In.)	23·01 N	82·13 W
76	Cuatro Ciénegas (kwä'trō syā'nā-gäs). Mex.	26·59 N	102·03 W
92	Cuauhtemoc (kwä-ōō-tĕ-mŏk') Mex.	15·43 N	91·57 W
90	Cuautepec (kwä-ōō-tĕ-pĕk) Mex.	16·41 N	99·04 W
90	Cuautepec Mex.	20·01 N	98·19 W
91	Cuautitlán (kwä-ōō-têt-län') Mex. (Mexico City In.)	19·40 N	99·12 W
90	Cuautla (kwä-ōō'tlä) Mex.	18·47 N	98·57 W
124	Cuba (kōō'bä) Port.	38·10 N	7·55 W
89	Cuba (kū'bȧ) N. A.	22·00 N	79·00 W
99	Cubagua, Isla (ē's-lä-kōō-bä'gwä) Ven. (In.)	10·48 N	64·10 W
166	Cubango (R.) (kōō bäŋ'gō) Ang.	15·45 S	18·00 E
74	Cucamonga (kōō-kȧ-mŏŋ'gȧ) Calif. (Los Angeles In.)	34·05 N	117·35 W
166	Cuchi Ang.	14·40 S	16·50 E
76	Cuchillo Parado (kōō-chē'lyô pä-rä'dō). Mex.	29·26 N	104·52 W
92	Cuchumatanes, Sierra de los (Mts.) Guat.	16·02 N	91·50 W
98	Cúcuta (kōō'kōō-tä) Col.	7·56 N	72·30 W
75	Cudahy (kŭd'ȧ-hī) Wis. (Milwaukee In.)	42·57 N	87·52 W
143	Cuddalore (kŭd ȧ-lōr') India	11·49 N	79·46 E
143	Cuddapah (kŭd'ȧ-pä) India	14·31 N	78·52 E
158	Cue (kū) Austl.	27·30 S	118·10 E
124	Cuellar (kwā'lyär') Sp.	41·24 N	4·15 W
98	Cuenca (kwĕn'kä) Ec.	2·52 S	78·54 W
124	Cuenca Sp.	40·05 N	2·07 W
124	Cuenca, Sierra de (Mts.) (sē-ĕ'r-rä-dĕ-kwĕ'n-kä). Sp.	40·02 N	1·50 W
76	Cuencame (kwĕn-kä-mā') Mex.	24·52 N	103·42 W
90	Cuerámaro (kwā-rä'mä-rō) Mex.	20·39 N	101·44 W
91	Cuernavaca (kwĕr-nä-vä'kä) Mex. (Mexico City In.)	18·55 N	99·15 W
77	Cuero (kwā'rō) Tex.	29·05 N	97·16 W
90	Cuetzalá del Progreso (kwĕt-zä-lä dĕl prō-grā'sō). Mex.	18·07 N	99·51 W
91	Cuetzalan del Progreso (kwĕt-zä-län dĕl prō-grā'sō). Mex.	20·02 N	97·33 W
124	Cuevas del Almanzora (kwĕ'väs-dĕl-äl-män-zō-rä). Sp.	37·19 N	1·54 W
126	Cuglieri (kōō-lyâ'rê) It.	40·11 N	8·37 E
99	Cuiabá (kōō-yä-bä') Braz.	15·33 S	56·03 W
91	Cuicatlan (kwē-kä-tlän') Mex.	17·46 N	96·57 W
92	Cuilapa (kōō-ē-lä'pä) Guat.	14·16 N	90·20 W
116	Cuillin Sd. Scot.	57·09 N	6·20 W
166	Cuito (R.) (kōō-ē'tō) Ang.	14·30 S	19·10 E
90	Cuitzeo (kwēt'zā-ō) Mex.	19·57 N	101·11 W
90	Cuitzeo, Laguna de (L.) (lä-ōō'nä-dĕ-kwēt'zā-ō). Mex.	19·58 N	101·05 W
95	Cul de Sac (Val.) (kōō'l-dĕ-sä'k) Dom. Rep.-Hai.	18·35 N	72·05 W
89	Culebra (I.) (kōō-lā'brä) P. R. (Puerto Rico In.)	18·19 N	65·32 W
111	Culemborg Neth. (Amsterdam In.)	51·57 N	5·14 E
159	Culgoa (R.) (kŭl-gō'ȧ) Austl.	29·21 S	147·00 E
88	Culiacán (kōō-lyä-kä'n) Mex.	24·45 N	107·30 W
154	Culion (kōō-lê-ōn') Phil.	11·43 N	119·58 E
124	Cúllar de Baza (kōō'l-yär-dĕ-bä'zä). Sp.	37·36 N	2·35 W
125	Cullera (kōō-lyā'rä) Sp.	39·12 N	0·15 W
167	Cullinan (kōō'lĭ-nán) S. Afr. (Johannesburg & Pretoria In.)	25·41 S	28·32 E
78	Cullman (kŭl'măn) Ala.	34·10 N	86·50 W
81	Culpeper (kŭl'pĕp-ēr) Va.	38·30 N	77·55 W
85	Culross (kŭl'rŏs) Can. (Winnipeg In.)	49·43 N	97·54 W
80	Culver (kŭl'vēr) Ind.	41·15 N	86·25 W
74	Culver City Calif. (Los Angeles In.)	34·00 N	118·23 W
99	Cumaná (kōō-mä-nä') Ven. (In.)	10·28 N	64·10 W
85	Cumberland (kŭm'bēr-lănd) Can. (Ottawa In.)	45·31 N	75·25 W
75	Cumberland Ind. (Indianapolis In.)	39·46 N	85·57 W
81	Cumberland Md.	39·40 N	78·40 W
65	Cumberland Wash. (Seattle In.)	47·17 N	121·55 W
71	Cumberland Wis.	45·31 N	92·01 W
78	Cumberland, L. Ky.	36·55 N	85·20 W
63	Cumberland (R.) U. S.	36·30 N	87·40 W
159	Cumberland Is. Austl.	20·29 S	149·46 E
87	Cumberland Pen. Can.	65·59 N	64·05 W
78	Cumberland Plat. Tenn.	35·25 N	85·30 W
87	Cumberland Sd. Can.	65·27 N	65·44 W
98	Cundinamarca (Dept.) (kōōn-dē-nä-mä'r-kä). Col. (In)	4·57 N	74·27 W
91	Cunduacán (kōōn-dōō-ä-kän') Mex.	18·04 N	93·23 W
166	Cunene (Kunene) (R.) Ang.-S. W. Afr.	17·00 S	13·00 E
126	Cuneo (kōō'nā-ō) It.	44·24 N	7·31 E
101	Cunha (kōō'nyä) Braz. (Rio de Janeiro In.)	23·05 S	44·56 W
166	Cunjamba (kōōn-kä'm-bä) Ang.	15·45 S	20·15 E
160	Cunnamulla (kŭn-ȧ-mŭl-ȧ). Austl.	28·00 S	145·55 E
88	Cupula, Pico (Mtn.) (pē'kō-kōō'pōō-lä). Mex.	24·45 N	111·10 W
90	Cuquío (kōō-kē'ō) Mex.	20·55 N	103·03 W
98	Curaçao (kōō-rä-sä'ō) (I.) Neth. Antilles	12·12 N	68·58 W
100	Curacautín (kä-rä-käōō-tē'n) Chile	38·25 S	71·53 W
101	Curacaví (kōō-rä-kä-vē') Chile (Santiago In.)	33·23 S	71·09 W
101	Curaumilla, Punta (Pt.) (kōō-rou-mē'lyä). Chile (Santiago In.)	33·05 S	71·44 W
101	Curepto (kōō-rĕp-tō) Chile (Santiago In.)	35·06 S	72·02 W
101	Curicó (kōō-rē-kō') Chile (Santiago In.)	34·57 S	71·14 W
101	Curicó (Prov.) Chile (Santiago In.)	34·55 S	71·15 W
100	Curitiba (kōō-rē-tē'bä) Braz.	25·20 S	49·15 W
94	Curly Cut Cays (Is.) Ba. Is.	23·40 N	77·40 W
99	Currais Novos (kōōr-rä'ēs nō-vōs). Braz.	6·02 S	36·39 W
85	Curran (kŭ-răN') Can. (Ottawa In.)	45·30 N	74·00 W
94	Current (I.) (kŭ-rĕnt) Ba. Is.	25·20 N	76·50 W
73	Current (R.) (kûr'ĕnt) Mo.	37·18 N	91·21 W
167	Currie, Mt. (cŭ-rē) S. Afr. (Natal In.)	30·28 S	29·23 E
79	Currituck Sd. (kûr'ĭ-tŭk) N. C.	36·27 N	75·42 W
127	Curtea de Argeş (kŏŏr'tē-ä dĕ är'zhĕsh). Rom.	45·09 N	24·40 E
72	Curtis (kûr'tĭs) Nebr.	40·36 N	100·29 W
159	Curtis (I.) Austl.	23·38 S	151·43 E
75	Curtisville (kûr'tĭs-vĭl) Pa. (Pittsburgh In.)	40·38 N	79·50 W
99	Curuá (R.) (kōō-rōō-ä') Braz.	6·26 S	54·39 W
127	Ćurug (chōō'rŏŏg) Yugo.	45·27 N	20·06 E
98	Curupira, Serra (Mts.) (sĕr'rȧ kōō-rōō-pē'rȧ) Braz.-Ven.	1·00 N	65·30 W
99	Cururupu (kōō-rōō-rōō-pōō') Braz.	1·40 S	44·56 W
100	Curuzú Cuatiá (kōō-rōō-zōō' kwä-tē-ä'). Arg.	29·45 S	57·58 W
99	Curvelo (kŏŏr-vĕl'ŏŏ) Braz.	18·47 S	44·14 W
73	Cushing (kŭsh'ĭng) Okla.	35·58 N	96·46 W
122	Cusset (kü-sĕ') Fr.	46·08 N	3·29 E
70	Custer (kŭs'tēr) S. D.	43·46 N	103·36 W
65	Custer Wash. (Vancouver In.)	48·55 N	122·39 W
67	Custer Battlefield Nat'l. Mon. (kŭs'tēr băt''l-fēld). Mont.	45·44 N	107·15 W
67	Cut Bank (kŭt bănk) Mont.	48·38 N	112·19 W
78	Cuthbert (kŭth'bērt) Ga.	31·47 N	84·48 W
142	Cuttack (kŭ-tăk') India	20·38 N	85·53 E
90	Cutzamala (R.) (kōō-tzä-mä-lä') Mex.	18·57 N	100·41 W
90	Cutzamalá de Pinzón (kōō-tzä-mä-lä'dĕ-pēn-zō'n). Mex.	18·28 N	100·36 W
166	Cuvo (R.) (kōō'vō) Ang.	11·15 S	14·15 E
120	Cuxhaven (kŏŏks' hä-fĕn) Ger.	53·51 N	8·43 E
75	Cuyahoga Falls Ohio (Cleveland In.)	41·08 N	81·29 W
75	Cuyahoga R. (kī-ȧ-hō'gȧ) Ohio (Cleveland In.)	41·22 N	81·38 W
68	Cuyapaire Ind. Res. (kū-yȧ-pâr) Calif.	32·46 N	116·20 W
154	Cuyo Is. (kōō'yō) Phil.	10·54 N	120·08 E
92	Cuyotenango (kōō-yô-tĕ-näŋ'gô) Guat.	14·30 N	91·35 W
99	Cuyuni (R.) (kōō-yōō'nē) Guy.-Ven.	6·40 N	60·44 W
90	Cuyutlán (kōō-yōō-tlän') Mex.	18·54 N	104·04 W
98	Cuzco Peru	13·36 S	71·52 W
80	Cynthiana (sĭn-thĭ-ăn'ȧ) Ky.	38·20 N	84·20 W
74	Cypress (sī'prĕs) Calif. (Los Angeles In.)	33·50 N	118·03 W
77	Cypress Cr. Tex.	32·49 N	94·35 W
115	Cyprus (sī'prŭs) Asia	34·56 N	31·28 E
102	Czechoslovakia (chĕk'ō-slō-vä'kĭ-ȧ). Eur.	49·28 N	16·00 E
121	Czersk (chĕrsk) Pol.	53·47 N	17·58 E
121	Częstochowa (chăN-stô kô'vȧ). Pol.	50·49 N	19·10 E
164	Dabakala (dä-bä-kä'lä) Ivory Coast	8·16 N	4·36 W
98	Dabeiba (dȧ-bā'bä) Col. (In.)	7·01 N	76·16 W
65	Dabob (dā'bŏb) Wash. (Seattle In.)	47·50 N	122·49 W
65	Dabob B. Wash. (Seattle In.)	47·44 N	122·50 W
165	Dabra-Mārk'os Eth.	10·15 N	37·45 E
165	Dabra-Tābor Eth.	11·57 N	38·09 E
121	Dabrowa (dôN-brō'vä) Pol.	53·37 N	23·18 E
142	Dacca (dä'kä) (dăk'ȧ) E. Pak.	23·45 N	90·29 E
111	Dachau (dä'kou). Ger. (Munich In.)	48·16 N	11·26 E
85	Dacotah (dȧ-kō'tȧ) Can. (Winnipeg In.)	49·52 N	97·38 W
79	Dade City (dād) Fla. (In.)	28·22 N	82·09 W
78	Dadeville (dād'vĭl) Ala.	32·48 N	85·44 W
155	Daet (Mtn.) (dä'āt) Phil. (Manila In.)	14·07 N	122·59 E
74	Dafter (dăf'tēr) Mich. (Sault Ste. Marie In.)	46·21 N	84·26 W
168	Dagahabur. Eth. (Horn of Afr. In.)	8·10 N	43·25 E
164	Dagana (dä-gä'nä) Senegal	16·27 N	15·28 W
128	Dagda (däg'dȧ) Sov. Un.	56·04 N	27·30 E
110	Dagenham (dăg'ĕn-ăm) Eng. (London In.)	51·32 N	0·09 E
133	Dagestan (Reg.) (dä-gĕs-tän') Sov. Un.	43·40 N	46·10 E
68	Daggett (dăg'ĕt) Calif.	34·50 N	116·52 W
155	Dagupan (dä-gōō'pän) Phil. (Manila In.)	16·02 N	120·20 E
123	Dahl (däl) Ger. (Ruhr In.)	51·18 N	7·33 E
163	Dahomey (dȧ-hō-mā') Afr.	8·00 N	2·00 E
153	Daigo (dī-gō) Jap. (Ōsaka In.)	34·57 N	135·49 E
124	Daimiel Manzanares (dī-myĕl' män-zä-nä'rĕs). Sp.	39·05 N	3·36 W
	Dairen, see Talien		
65	Dairy (R.) (dâr'ĭ) Ore. (Portland In.)	45·33 N	123·04 W
65	Dairy (R.) East Fk. Ore. (Portland In.)	45·40 N	123·03 W
153	Dai-Sen (Mtn.) (dī'sĕn') Jap.	35·22 N	133·35 E
153	Dai-Tenjo-dake (Mtn.) (dī-tĕn'jō dä-kä). Jap.	36·21 N	137·38 E
95	Dajabón (dä-kä-bō'n) Dom. Rep.	19·35 N	71·40 W
158	Dajarra (dȧ-jăr'ȧ) Austl.	21·45 S	139·30 E
164	Dakar (dȧ-kär') Senegal	14·39 N	17·28 W
145	Dakka (däk'ȧ) Afg. (Khyber Pass In.)	34·13 N	71·02 E
127	Dakovica (dyä'kō-vē-tsa) Yugo.	42·23 N	20·28 E
150	Dalai Nor (L.) (dä-lī'nōr) China	48·50 N	116·45 E
118	Dalälven (R.) Swe.	60·26 N	15·50 E
160	Dalby (dôl'bē) Austl.	27·10 S	151·15 E
84	Dalcour (dăl-kour) La. (New Orleans In.)	29·49 N	89·59 W
118	Dale (dä'lĕ) Nor.	60·34 N	5·46 E
78	Dale Hollow (L.) (dāl hŏl'ō). Tenn.	36·33 N	85·03 W
85	Dalemead (dä'lĕ-mēd) Can. (Calgary In.)	50·53 N	113·38 W
118	Dalen (dä'lĕn) Nor.	59·28 N	8·01 E
168	Daleside (dāl'sīd) S. Afr. (Johannesburg & Pretoria In.)	26·30 S	28·03 E
85	Dalesville (dālz'vĭl) Can. (Montreal In.)	45·42 N	74·23 W

PRONOUNCING INDEX

Daley–Dem'yanka 199

Page	Name Pronunciation Region	Lat. °′	Long. °′
158	Daley (L.) (dā'lĭ) ... Austl.	14·15 S	131·15 E
158	Daley Waters (dā-lē) ... Austl.	16·15 S	133·30 E
72	Dalhart (dăl'härt) ... Tex.	36·04 N	102·32 W
82	Dalhousie (dăl-hōō'zĕ) ... Can.	48·03 N	66·24 W
124	Dalías (dä-lĕ'äs) ... Sp.	36·49 N	2·50 W
64	Dall (I.) (dăl) ... Alaska	54·50 N	133·10 W
66	Dallas (dăl'lȧs) ... Ore.	44·55 N	123·20 W
70	Dallas ... S. D.	43·13 N	99·34 W
74	Dallas Tex. (Dallas Fort Worth In.)	32·45 N	96·48 W
73	Dallas (L.) ... Tex.	33·16 N	96·54 W
66	Dalles Dam ... Ore.	45·36 N	121·08 W
126	Dalmacija (Reg.) (däl-mä'tsē-yä) Yugo.	43·25 N	16·37 E
85	Dalroy (dăl'roi) . Can. (Calgary In.)	51·08 N	113·40 W
159	Dalrymple, Mt. (dăl'rĭm-p'l) Austl.	21·14 S	148·46 E
78	Dalton (dôl'tŭn) ... Ga.	34·46 N	84·58 W
167	Dalton (dŏl'tŏn) S. Afr. (Natal In.)	29·21 S	30·41 E
65	Daly City (dā'lē) Calif. (San Francisco In.)	37·42 N	122·27 W
99	Dam (dăm) ... Sur.	4·36 N	54·54 W
142	Daman ... India	20·32 N	72·53 E
168	Damanhūr (dä-män-hōōr') U. A. R. (Nile In.)	30·59 N	30·31 E
155	Damar (I.) ... Indon.	7·15 S	129·15 E
166	Damaraland (Reg.) (dă'mȧ-rȧ-lănd) . S. W. Afr.	22·15 S	16·15 E
94	Damas Cays (Is.) (dä'mȧs) . Ba. Is.	23·50 N	79·50 W
	Damascus, see Dimashq		
133	Damavand (Mtn.) ... Iran	36·05 N	52·05 E
166	Damba (däm'bä) ... Ang.	6·50 S	15·20 E
165	Dambidolo ... Eth.	8·46 N	34·46 E
77	Dam B Res. (dăm) ... Tex.	30·52 N	94·30 W
95	Dame Marie, Cap (C.) (dām mȧrē') . Hai.	18·35 N	74·50 W
144	Dāmghān (dām-gān') ... Iran	35·50 N	54·15 E
168	Damietta (dăm-ĭ-ĕt'ȧ) U. A. R. (Nile In.)	31·22 N	31·50 E
123	Dammartin-en-Goële (däN-mär-tăN-äN-gō-ĕl') . Fr. (Paris In.)	49·03 N	2·40 E
155	Dampier, Straat (Str.) (dăm'pēr) W. Irian	0·40 N	131·15 E
158	Dampier Arch. (däN-pyâr') . Austl.	20·15 S	116·25 E
79	Dan (R.) (dȧn) ... N. C.	36·26 N	79·40 W
165	Danakil Des ... Eth.	12·45 N	41·01 E
151	Da Nang (Tourane) ... Viet.	16·08 N	108·22 E
154	Danau (R.) ... Indon.	4·17 S	105·00 E
84	Danbury (dăn'bĕr-ĭ) Conn. (New York In.)	41·23 N	73·27 W
110	Danbury ... Eng. (London In.)	51·42 N	0·34 E
77	Danbury ... Tex. (In.)	29·14 N	95·22 W
168	Dandarah (dĕn'dȧ-rȧ) U. A. R. (Nile In.)	26·08 N	32·42 E
161	Dandenong (dăn'dē-nông) Austl. (Melbourne In.)	37·59 S	145·13 E
110	Dane (R.) (dān) ... Eng.	53·11 N	2·14 W
85	Danforth (dăn'fŭrth) Can. (Toronto In.)	43·42 N	79·15 W
82	Danforth ... Maine	45·38 N	67·53 W
165	Dānglā ... Eth.	11·17 N	36·69 E
142	Dangri ... India	26·43 N	71·32 E
79	Dania (dā'nĭ-ȧ) ... Fla. (In.)	26·01 N	80·10 W
128	Danilov (dä'nē-lôf) ... Sov. Un.	58·12 N	40·08 E
127	Danilov Grad (dä'nē-lôf'gräd) Yugo.	42·31 N	19·08 E
128	Dankov (däŋ'kôf) ... Sov. Un.	53·17 N	39·09 E
92	Danlí (dän'lē) ... Hond.	14·02 N	86·35 W
81	Dannemora (dăn-ē-mō'rȧ) . . N. Y.	44·45 N	73·45 W
167	Dannhauser (dän'hou-zēr) . . S. Afr. (Natal In.)	28·07 S	30·04 E
81	Dansville (dănz'vĭl) ... N. Y.	42·30 N	77·40 W
129	Danube, Mouths of the (dăn'ub) Rom.	45·13 N	29·37 E
115	Danube R ... Eur.	43·41 N	23·35 E
83	Danvers (dăn'vērz) Mass. (Boston In.)	42·34 N	70·57 W
65	Danville (dăn'vĭl) Calif. (San Francisco In.)	37·49 N	122·00 W
80	Danville ... Ill.	40·10 N	87·35 W
80	Danville ... Ind.	39·45 N	86·30 W
80	Danville ... Ky.	37·35 N	84·50 W
81	Danville ... Pa.	41·00 N	76·35 W
79	Danville ... Va.	36·35 N	79·24 W
	Danzig, see Gdańsk		
112	Danzig, G. of (dȧn'tsĭk) ... Pol.	54·41 N	19·01 E
139	Dar'a ... Syria (Palestine In.)	32·37 N	36·07 E
121	Dărăbani (dă-ră-bän'ĭ) ... Rom.	48·13 N	26·38 E
164	Daraj ... Libya	30·12 N	10·14 E
168	Darāw (dȧ-rä'ōō) U. A. R. (Nile In.)	24·24 N	32·56 E
142	Darbhanga (dŭr-bŭŋ'gä) ... India	26·03 N	85·09 E
84	Darby (där'bĭ) Pa. (Philadelphia In.)	39·55 N	75·16 W
95	Darby (I.) ... Ba. Is.	23·50 N	76·20 W
	Dardanelles (Str.), see Çanakkale Boğazi		
167	Dar es Salaam (där ĕs sȧ-läm') Tan.	6·58 S	39·13 E
165	Darfur (Prov.) (där-fōōr') ... Sud.	13·21 N	23·46 E
145	Dargai (dŭr-gä'ē) W. Pak. (Khyber Pass In.)	34·35 N	72·00 E
164	D'Arguin, Cap (C.) ... Mauritania	20·28 N	17·46 W
98	Darien (dā-rĭ-ĕn') ... Col. (In.)	3·56 N	76·30 W
84	Darien (dâ-rē-ĕn') Conn. (New York In.)	41·04 N	73·28 W
	Dairen, see Talien		
92	Darien, Cordillera de (Mts.) . . Nic.	13·00 N	85·42 W
98	Darién, Golfo del (G.) (gôl-fô-dĕl-dā-rĭ-ĕn') . N. A.-S. A.	9·36 N	77·54 W
93	Darien, Serrania del (Ra.) (sĕr-ä-nē'ä dĕl dä-rē-ĕn') . Pan.	8·13 N	77·28 W
142	Darjeeling (dŭr-jē'lĭng) ... India	27·05 N	88·16 E
110	Darlaston (där'lȧs-tŭn) ... Eng.	52·34 N	2·02 W
70	Darling (L.) (där'lĭng) ... N. D.	48·35 N	101·25 W
160	Darling (R.) ... Austl.	31·50 S	143·20 E
160	Darling Downs (Reg.) ... Austl.	27·22 S	150·50 E
158	Darling Ra ... Austl.	30·30 S	115·45 E
116	Darlington (där'lĭng-tŭn) ... Eng.	54·32 N	1·35 W
79	Darlington ... S. C.	34·15 N	79·52 W
71	Darlington ... Wis.	42·41 N	90·06 W
120	Darlowo (där-lô'vô) ... Pol.	24·25 N	16·21 E
120	Darmstadt (därm'shtät) ... Ger.	49·53 N	8·40 E
165	Darnah ... Libya	32·44 N	22·41 E
64	Darnley B. (därn'lē) ... Alaska	70·00 N	124·00 W
165	Dar Nuba (Reg.) ... Sud.	12·22 N	30·39 E
124	Daroca (dä-rō-kä) ... Sp.	41·08 N	1·24 W
75	Darrowville (dâr'rō-vĭl) Ohio (Cleveland In.)	41·12 N	81·27 W
116	Dartmoor (därt'mōōr) ... Eng.	50·35 N	4·05 W
82	Dartmouth (därt'mŭth) ... Can.	44·41 N	63·36 W
116	Dartmouth ... Eng.	50·33 N	3·28 W
155	Daru (I.) (dä'rōō) ... Pap.	9·17 S	143·13 E
126	Daruvar (där'rōō-vär) ... Yugo.	45·37 N	17·16 E
154	Darvel B. (där'vĕl) ... Mala.	4·50 N	118·40 E
110	Darwen (där'wĕn) ... Eng.	53·42 N	2·28 W
158	Darwin (där'wĭn) ... Austl.	12·25 S	131·00 E
100	Darwin, Cordillera (Mts.) (kôr-dēl-yĕ'rä-där'wēn) Chile-Arg.	54·40 S	69·30 W
144	Daryācheh-ye Rezācheh (L.) . Iran	38·07 N	45·17 E
124	Das Alturas, Serra (Mts.) (sĕ'r-rä-däs-äl-tōō'räs) . Port.	40·43 N	7·48 W
165	Dasē ... Eth.	11·00 N	39·51 E
65	Dash Point (dăsh) Wash. (Seattle In.)	47·19 N	122·25 W
144	Dasht (R.) (dŭsht) ... W. Pak.	25·47 N	63·01 E
144	Dasht-e-Kavir Des. (dŭsht-ē-ka-vēr') . Iran	34·43 N	53·30 E
144	Dasht-e-Lūt (Des.) (dă'sht-ē-lōōt) Iran	31·47 N	58·38 E
155	Dasol B. (dä-sōl') Phil. (Manila In.)	15·53 N	119·40 E
123	Datteln (dät'tĕln) . Ger. (Ruhr In.)	51·39 N	7·20 E
154	Datu, Tandjung (C.) ... Indon.	2·08 N	110·15 E
165	Daua R. (dä'wä) ... Eth.	4·34 N	41·34 E
128	Daugavpils (dä'ŏŏ-gäv-pēls) Sov. Un.	55·52 N	25·32 E
86	Dauphin (dô'fĭn) ... Can.	51·09 N	100·01 W
155	Davao (dä'vä-ô) ... Phil.	7·05 N	125·30 E
155	Davao Gulf ... Phil.	6·30 N	125·45 E
71	Davenport (dăv'ĕn-pōrt) ... Iowa	41·34 N	90·38 W
159	Davenport ... N. Z. (In.)	37·29 S	174·47 E
66	Davenport ... Wash.	47·39 N	118·07 W
93	David (dȧ-vēdh') ... Pan.	8·27 N	82·27 W
70	David City (dā'vĭd) ... Nebr.	41·15 N	97·10 W
121	David-Gorodok (dȧ-vēt' gô-rō'dôk) Sov. Un.	52·02 N	27·14 E
73	Davis (dā'vĭs) ... Okla.	34·34 N	97·08 W
81	Davis ... W. Va.	39·15 N	79·25 W
66	Davis L ... Ore.	43·38 N	121·43 W
76	Davis Mts ... Tex.	30·45 N	104·17 W
47	Davis Sea ... Ant.	66·00 S	92·00 E
49	Davis Str ... Can.	66·00 N	60·00 W
120	Davos (dä'vōs) ... Switz.	46·47 N	9·50 E
144	Dawāsir, Wādī ad (R.) . Sau. Ar.	20·48 N	44·07 E
110	Dawley (dô'lĭ) ... Eng.	52·38 N	2·28 W
154	Dawna Ra. (dô'nȧ) ... Bur.	17·02 N	98·01 E
86	Dawson (dô'sŭn) ... Can.	64·04 N	139·22 W
78	Dawson ... Ga.	31·45 N	84·29 W
70	Dawson ... Minn.	44·54 N	96·03 W
160	Dawson (R.) ... Austl.	24·20 S	149·45 E
86	Dawson Creek ... Can.	55·49 N	120·21 W
78	Dawson Springs ... Ky.	37·10 N	87·40 W
122	Dax (dȧks) ... Fr.	43·42 N	1·06 W
144	Dayr az Zawr (dâ-ēr'ez-zôr') . . Syr.	35·15 N	40·01 E
168	Dayrūţ ... U. A. R. (Nile In.)	27·33 N	30·48 E
75	Dayton (dā'tŭn) Ky. (Cincinnati In.)	39·07 N	84·28 W
72	Dayton ... N. Mex.	32·44 N	104·23 W
80	Dayton ... Ohio	39·45 N	84·15 W
78	Dayton ... Tenn.	35·30 N	85·00 W
77	Dayton ... Tex.	30·03 N	94·53 W
66	Dayton ... Wash.	46·18 N	117·59 W
79	Daytona Beach (dā-tō'nȧ) ... Fla.	29·11 N	81·02 W
81	Dayville (dā'vĭl) ... Conn.	41·50 N	71·55 W
166	De Aar (dē-är') ... S. Afr.	30·45 S	24·05 E
70	Dead (L.) (dĕd) ... Minn.	46·28 N	96·00 W
70	Deadwood (dĕd'wŏŏd) ... S. D.	44·23 N	103·43 W
81	Deal Island (dēl-ī'lănd) ... Md.	38·10 N	75·55 W
100	Deán Funes (dĕ-ȧ'n-fōō-nĕs) . Arg.	30·26 S	64·12 W
75	Dearborn (dēr'bŭrn) Mich. (Detroit In.)	42·18 N	83·15 W
116	Dearg, Ben (Mtn.) (bĕn dŭrg) Scot.	57·48 N	4·59 W
86	Dease Str. (dēz) ... Can.	68·50 N	108·20 W
155	De Atauro (I.) (dĕ-ä-tä'ōō-rô) Port. Timor	8·20 S	126·15 E
68	Death Valley ... Calif.-Nev.	36·55 N	117·12 W
68	Death Valley Junction ... Calif.	36·18 N	116·26 W
68	Death Valley Natl. Mon. ... Calif.	36·34 N	117·00 W
129	Debal'tsevo (dyĕb'ȧl-tsyĕ'vô) Sov. Un.	48·23 N	38·29 E
127	Debar (Dibra) (dĕ'bär) (dā'brä) Yugo.	41·31 N	20·32 E
114	Debdou (dĕb-dōō') ... Mor.	34·01 N	2·50 W
121	Deblin (dăN'blĭn) ... Pol.	51·34 N	21·49 E
121	Debno (dĕb-nô') ... Sov. Un.	50·24 N	25·44 E
164	Debo Swp. (dā'bō) ... Mali	15·33 N	3·28 W
121	Debrecen (dĕ'brĕ-tsĕn) ... Hung.	47·32 N	21·40 E
78	Decatur (dē-kā'tŭr) ... Ala.	34·35 N	87·00 W
84	Decatur ... Ga. (Atlanta In.)	33·47 N	84·18 W
73	Decatur ... Ill.	39·50 N	88·59 W
80	Decatur ... Ind.	40·50 N	84·55 W
80	Decatur ... Mich.	42·10 N	86·00 W
72	Decatur ... Tex.	33·14 N	97·33 W
122	Decazeville (dē-käz'vēl') ... Fr.	44·33 N	2·16 E
143	Decean Plat. (dĕk'ăn) ... India	26·36 N	76·35 E
65	Deception P. (dē-sĕp'shŭn) Wash. (Seattle In.)	48·24 N	122·44 W
120	Decin (dyĕ'chēn) ... Czech.	50·47 N	14·14 E
71	Decorah (dē-kō'rȧ) ... Iowa	43·18 N	91·48 W
139	Dedap ... Indon. (Singapore In.)	1·19 N	102·22 E
	Dedeagats, see Alexandroupolis		
136	Dedenevo (dyĕ-dyĕ'nyĕ-vô) Sov. Un. (Moscow In.)	56·14 N	37·31 E
83	Dedham (dĕd'ăm) Mass. (Boston In.)	42·15 N	71·11 W
100	Dedo do Deus (Mt.) (dĕ-dô-dô-dĕ'ōōs) . Braz. (In.)	22·30 S	43·02 W
164	Dédougou (dā-dŏŏ-gōō') Upper Volta	12·28 N	3·21 W
116	Dee (R.) ... Wales	53·00 N	3·10 W
116	Dee (R.) ... Scot.	57·05 N	2·25 W
79	Deep (R.) (dēp) ... N. C.	35·36 N	79·32 W
84	Deep Creek ... Va. (Norfolk In.)	36·44 N	76·22 W
73	Deep Fk. (R.) ... Okla.	35·35 N	96·42 W
73	Deepwater (dep-wô-tēr) ... Mo.	38·15 N	93·46 W
83	Deer (dēr) ... Can.	49·06 N	57·45 W
82	Deer ... Maine	44·07 N	68·38 W
75	Deerfield (dēr'fēld) Ill. (Chicago In.)	42·10 N	87·51 W
65	Deer Island . . . Ore. (Portland In.)	45·56 N	122·51 W
83	Deer Lake ... Can.	49·09 N	57·26 W
67	Deer Lodge (dēr lŏj) ... Mont.	46·23 N	112·42 W
75	Deer Park . . Ohio (Cincinnati In.)	39·12 N	84·24 W
66	Deer Park ... Wash.	47·58 N	117·28 W
71	Deer River ... Minn.	47·20 N	93·49 W
80	Defiance (dē-fī'ăns) ... Ohio	41·15 N	84·20 W
78	DeFuniak Springs (dē fū'nĭ-ăk) Fla.	30·42 N	86·06 W
120	Deggendorf (dĕ'ghĕn-dôrf) . . . Ger.	48·50 N	12·59 E
90	Degollado (dā-gô-lyä'dō) ... Mex.	20·27 N	102·11 W
158	DeGrey (R.) (dē grā') ... Austl.	20·20 S	119·25 E
136	Degtyarsk (dĕg-ty'arsk) Sov. Un. (Urals In.)	56·42 N	60·05 E
142	Dehra Dun (dā'rŭ) ... India	30·09 N	78·07 E
121	Dej (dāzh) ... Rom.	47·09 N	23·53 E
71	De Kalb (dē kălb') ... Ill.	41·54 N	88·46 W
85	Delacour (dĕ-lä-kōōr') Can. (Calgary In.)	51·09 N	113·45 W
72	Delagua (dĕl-ä'gwä) ... Colo.	37·19 N	104·42 W
79	De Land (dē lănd') ... Fla.	29·00 N	81·19 W
68	Delano (dĕl'ȧ-nō) ... Calif.	35·47 N	119·15 W
69	Delano, Pk ... Utah	38·25 N	112·25 W
71	Delavan (dĕl'ȧ-văn) ... Wis.	42·39 N	88·38 W
80	Delaware (dĕl'ȧ-wâr) ... Ohio	40·15 N	83·05 W
63	Delaware (State) ... U. S.	38·40 N	75·30 W
73	Delaware (R.) ... Kans.	39·45 N	95·47 W
81	Delaware (R.) ... N. J.-Pa.	41·50 N	75·20 W
81	Delaware B ... Del.-N. J.	39·05 N	75·10 W
80	Delaware Res ... Ohio	40·30 N	83·05 W
124	Del Eje, Sierra (Mts.) (sē-ĕ'r-rä-dĕl-ĕ'Kĕ) . Sp.	42·15 N	6·45 W
120	Delemont (dē-lā-môN') ... Switz.	47·21 N	7·18 E
76	De Leon (dē lē-ŏn') ... Tex.	32·06 N	98·33 W
85	De Léry (dā lā-rī') Can. (Montreal In.)	45·21 N	73·49 W
101	Delfínópolis (dĕl-fē'nô'pō-lēs) Braz. (Rio de Janeiro In.)	20·20 S	46·50 W
111	Delft (dĕlft) Neth. (Amsterdam In.)	52·01 N	4·20 E
117	Delfzijl ... Neth.	53·20 N	6·50 E
100	Delgada Pta. (Pt.) (pōō'n-tä-dĕl-gä'dä) . Arg.	43·46 S	63·46 W
167	Delgado, Cabo (C.) (kȧ'bô-dĕl-gä'dō) . Moz.	10·30 S	41·00 E
165	Delgo (dĕl'gō) ... Sud.	20·07 N	30·41 E
74	Delhi (dĕl'hī) . . Ill. (St. Louis In.)	39·03 N	90·16 W
142	Delhi ... India	28·54 N	77·13 E
77	Delhi ... La.	32·26 N	91·29 W
125	Del Hoyo, Sierra (Mtn.) (sē-ĕ'r-rä-dĕl-ô'yô) Sp. (Madrid In.)	40·39 N	3·56 W
120	Delitzsch (dā'lĭch) ... Ger.	51·32 N	12·18 E
127	Dell Alice, Pt. (dĕl-ä-lē'chĕ) ... It.	39·23 N	17·10 E
70	Dell Rapids (dĕl) ... S. D.	43·50 N	96·43 W
74	Dellwood (dĕl'wŏŏd) Minn. (Minneapolis, St. Paul In.)	45·05 N	92·58 W
164	Dellys (dĕ'lēs') ... Alg.	36·59 N	3·40 E
68	Del Mar (dĕl mär') Calif. (San Diego In.)	32·57 N	117·16 W
168	Delmas (dĕl'mȧs) S. Afr. (Johannesburg & Pretoria In.)	26·08 S	28·43 E
120	Delmenhorst (dĕl'mĕn-hôrst) . Ger.	53·03 N	8·38 E
69	Del Norte (dĕl nôrt') ... Colo.	37·40 N	106·25 W
135	De-Longa (I.) ... Sov. Un.	176·58 N	157·39 E
64	Delong Mts. (dē'lŏng) ... Alaska	68·30 N	163·25 W
160	Deloraine (dĕ-lŭ-rān') ... Austl.	41·30 S	146·40 E
80	Delphi (dĕl'fī) ... Ind.	40·35 N	86·40 W
80	Delphos (dĕl'fŏs) ... Ohio	40·50 N	84·20 W
79	Delray Beach (dĕl-rā') . . Fla. (In.)	26·27 N	80·05 W
76	Del Rio (dĕl rē'ō) ... Tex.	29·21 N	100·52 W
85	Delson Village (dĕl'sŭn) Can. (Montreal In.)	45·24 N	73·32 W
69	Delta ... Colo.	38·45 N	108·05 W
69	Delta ... Utah	39·20 N	112·35 W
68	Delta Mendota can ... Calif.	37·10 N	121·02 W
85	Delta Station . Can. (Winnipeg In.)	50·10 N	98·20 W
127	Delvine (dĕl'vē-nȧ) ... Alb.	39·58 N	20·10 E
132	Dëma (R.) (dyĕm'ä) ... Sov. Un.	53·40 N	54·30 E
128	Demidov (dzyĕ'mē-dô'f) . Sov. Un.	55·16 N	31·32 E
69	Deming (dĕm'ĭng) ... N. Mex.	32·15 N	107·45 W
120	Demmin (dĕm'mĕn) ... Ger.	53·54 N	13·04 E
164	Demnate (dĕm-nät) ... Mor.	31·58 N	7·03 W
78	Demopolis (dē-mŏp'ō-lĭs) ... Ala.	32·30 N	87·50 W
75	Demotte (dē'mŏt) Ind. (Chicago In.)	41·12 N	87·13 W
154	Dempo, Gunung (Vol.) (dĕm'pô) Indon.	4·04 S	103·11 E
134	Dem'yanka (R.) (dyĕm-yän'kä) Sov. Un.	59·07 N	72·58 E

ng-sing; ŋ-baŋk; N-nasalized n; nŏd; cŏmmit; ōld; ôbey; ôrder; fōōd; fŏŏt; ou-out; s-soft; sh-dish; th-thin; pūre; ûnite; ûrn; stŭd; circŭs; ü-as "y" in study; '-indeterminate vowel.

200 Demyansk–Dogubayazit PRONOUNCING INDEX

Page	Name Pronunciation Region	Lat. °′	Long. °′
128	Demyansk (dyĕm-yänsk') Sov. Un.	57·39 N	32·26 E
122	Denain (dē-năN') Fr.	50·23 N	3·21 E
116	Denbigh (dĕn'bĭ) Wales	53·15 N	3·25 W
110	Denbigh (Co.) Wales	53·01 N	2·59 W
111	Dendermonde. Bel. (Brussels In.)	51·02 N	4·04 E
79	Dendron (dĕn'drŭn) Va.	37·02 N	76·53 W
136	Denezhkin Kamen, Gora (Mtn.) (dzyĕ-ŋĕ'zhkĕn kăm'iĕŋ) Sov. Un. (Urals In.)	60·26 N	59·35 E
93	D'Enfer, Pointe (Pt.) Mart. (Le. & Wind. Is. In.)	14·21 N	60·48 W
94	Denham, Mt. Jam.	18·20 N	77·30 W
117	Den Helder (dĕn hĕl'dĕr) Neth.	52·55 N	5·45 E
125	Denia (dā'nyä) Sp.	38·48 N	0·06 E
160	Deniliquin (dĕ-nĭl'ĭ-kwĭn) Austl.	35·20 S	144·52 E
70	Denison (dĕn'ĭ-sŭn) Iowa	42·01 N	95·22 W
73	Denison Tex.	33·45 N	97·02 W
136	Denisovka (dĕ-nē'sof-kȧ) Sov. Un. (Urals In.)	52·26 N	61·45 E
133	Denizli (dĕn-ĭz-lē') Tur.	37·40 N	29·10 E
123	Denklingen (dĕn'klĕn-gĕn) Ger. (Ruhr In.)	50·54 N	7·40 E
79	Denmark (dĕn'märk) S. C.	33·18 N	81·09 W
102	Denmark Eur.	56·14 N	8·30 E
49	Denmark Str. Grnld.	66·30 N	27·00 W
168	Dennilton (dĕn-ĭl-tŭn) S. Afr. (Johannesburg & Pretoria In.)	25·18 S	29·13 E
80	Dennison (dĕn'ĭ-sŭn) Ohio	40·25 N	81·20 W
81	Denton (dĕn'tŭn) Md.	38·55 N	75·50 W
73	Denton Tex.	33·12 N	97·06 W
158	D'entrecasteaux, Pt. (dăN-tr'kȧs-tō') Austl.	34·50 S	114·45 E
155	D'entrecasteaux Is. (dăN-tr'-kȧs-tō') Pap.	9·45 S	152·00 E
72	Denver (dĕn'vĕr) Colo.	39·44 N	104·59 W
142	Deoli India	25·52 N	75·23 E
71	De Pere (dē pēr') Wis.	44·25 N	88·04 W
75	Depew (dē-pū') N. Y. (Buffalo In.)	42·55 N	78·43 W
80	Depue (dē pū) Ill.	41·15 N	89·55 W
73	De Queen (dē kwēn') Ark.	34·02 N	94·21 W
77	De Quincy (dē kwĭn'sĭ) La.	30·27 N	93·27 W
142	Dera Ghāzi Khān (dā'rŭ gä-zē' кän') W. Pak.	30·09 N	70·39 E
142	Dera Ismail Khan (dā'rŭ ĭs-mä-ēl' кän') W. Pak.	31·55 N	70·51 E
133	Derbent (dĕr-bĕnt') Sov. Un.	42·00 N	48·10 E
158	Derby (där'bē) (dûr'bē) Austl.	17·20 S	123·40 E
81	Derby (dûr'bē) Conn.	41·20 N	73·05 W
110	Derby (där'bē) Eng.	52·55 N	1·29 W
168	Derby (där'bĭ) S. Afr. (Johannesburg & Pretoria In.)	25·55 S	27·02 E
110	Derby (Co.) (där'bē) Eng.	53·11 N	1·30 W
168	Derdepoort S. Afr. (Johannesburg & Pretoria In.)	24·39 S	26·21 E
116	Derg, Lough (B.) (lŏk dĕrg) Ire.	53·00 N	8·09 W
77	De Ridder (dē rĭd'ēr) La.	30·50 N	93·18 W
73	Dermott (dûr'mŏt) Ark.	33·32 N	91·24 W
83	Derry (dâr'ĭ) N. H. (Boston In.)	45·52 N	71·22 W
127	Derventa (dĕr'ven-tȧ) Yugo.	45·58 N	17·58 E
160	Derwent (R.) (dûr'wĕnt) Austl.	42·21 S	146·30 E
110	Derwent (R.) (dĕr'wĕnt) Eng.	52·54 N	1·24 W
73	Des Arc (dāz ärk') Ark.	34·59 N	91·31 W
101	Descalvado (dĕs-käl-vȧ-dō) Braz. (Rio de Janeiro In.)	21·55 S	47·37 W
85	Deschenes Can. (Ottawa In.)	45·23 N	75·47 W
85	Deschenes, L. Can. (Ottawa In.)	54·25 N	75·53 W
66	Deschutes R. (dā-shōōt') Ore.	44·25 N	121·21 W
76	Desdemona (dĕz-dē-mō'nȧ) Tex.	32·16 N	98·33 W
100	Deseado, Rio (R.) (rē'-ō-dā-sä-ä'dhō) Arg.	46·50 S	67·45 W
93	Desirade I. (dā-zē-rȧs') N. A. (Le. & Wind. Is. In.)	16·21 N	60·51 W
70	De Smet (dē smĕt') S. D.	44·23 N	97·33 W
71	Des Moines (dē moin') Iowa	41·35 N	93·37 W
72	Des Moines N. Mex.	36·42 N	103·48 W
65	Des Moines Wash. (Seattle In.)	46·24 N	122·20 W
63	Des Moines (R.) U. S.	43·45 N	94·20 W
129	Desna (R.) (dyĕs-nȧ') Sov. Un.	51·05 N	31·03 E
100	Desolación (dĕ-sô-lä-syô'n) (I.) Chile	53·05 S	74·00 W
73	De Soto (dē sō'tō) Mo.	38·07 N	90·32 W
74	Des Peres (dĕs pĕr'ĕs) Mo. (St. Louis In.)	38·36 N	90·26 W
75	Des Plaines (dĕs plānz') Ill. (Chicago In.)	42·02 N	87·54 W
75	Des Plaines R. Ill. (Chicago In.)	41·39 N	88·05 W
120	Dessau (dĕs'ou) Ger.	51·50 N	12·15 E
120	Detmold (dĕt'mōld) Ger.	51·57 N	8·55 E
75	Detroit (dē-troit') Mich. (Detroit In.)	42·22 N	83·10 W
73	Detroit Tex.	33·41 N	95·16 W
70	Detroit Lakes (dē-troit' lăkz) Minn.	46·48 N	95·51 W
75	Detroit R. U. S.-Can. (Detroit In.)	42·08 N	83·07 W
121	Detva (dyĕt'vȧ) Czech.	48·32 N	19·21 E
111	Deurne Bel. (Brussels In.)	51·13 N	4·27 E
111	Deutsch Wagram Aus. (Vienna In.)	48·19 N	16·34 E
85	Deux Montagnes, Lac des (dû mōN-tăny') Can. (Montreal In.)	45·28 N	74·00 W
127	Deva (dā'vä) Rom.	45·52 N	22·52 E
121	Dévaványa (dā'vô-vän-yô) Hung.	47·01 N	20·58 E
133	Develi (dĕ'vȧ-lē) Tur.	38·20 N	35·10 E
117	Deventer (dĕv'ĕn-tĕr) Neth.	52·14 N	6·07 E
70	Devils (L.) (dĕv''lz) N. D.	47·57 N	99·04 W
76	Devils (R.) Tex.	29·55 N	101·10 W
	Devils I., see Diable, Ile du		
62	Devils Lake N. D.	48·10 N	98·55 W
70	Devils Lake Ind. Res. N. D.	48·08 N	99·40 W
68	Devils Postpile Natl. Mon. Calif.	37·42 N	119·12 W
67	Devils Tower Natl. Mon. Wyo.	44·38 N	105·07 W
127	Devoll (R.) Alb.	40·55 N	20·10 E
168	Devon (dĕv'ŭn) S. Afr. (Johannesburg & Pretoria In.)	26·23 S	28·47 E
160	Devonport (dĕv'ŭn-pŏrt) Austl.	41·20 S	146·30 E
74	Devore (dē-vôr') Calif. (Los Angeles In.)	34·13 N	117·24 W
77	Dewalt (dū'ôlt) Tex. (In.)	29·33 N	95·33 W
65	Dewatto (dē-wăt'ō) Wash. (Seattle In.)	47·27 N	123·04 W
73	Dewey (dū'ĭ) Okla.	36·48 N	95·55 W
73	De Witt (dē wĭt') Ark.	34·17 N	91·22 W
71	De Witt Iowa	41·46 N	90·34 W
110	Dewsbury (dūz'bĕr-ĭ) Eng.	53·42 N	1·39 W
82	Dexter (dĕks'tĕr) Maine	45·01 N	69·19 W
73	Dexter Mo.	36·46 N	89·56 W
79	Dexter (L.) Fla.	29·07 N	81·24 W
144	Dezfūl Iran	32·14 N	48·37 E
139	Dezhneva, Mys (East Cape) (dyĕzh'nyĭf) Sov. Un.	68·00 N	172·00 W
	Dhahran, see AzZahrān		
143	Dharamtar Cr. India (Bombay In.)	18·49 N	72·54 E
143	Dharmavaram India	14·32 N	77·43 E
142	Dhaulagiri, Mt. (dou-lȧ-gē'rē) Nep.	33·50 N	83·32 E
127	Dhenoúsa (I.) Grc.	37·09 N	25·53 E
139	Dhibān Jordan (Palestine In.)	31·30 N	35·46 E
127	Dhidhimótikhon Grc.	41·20 N	26·27 E
127	Dhodhekánisos (Dodecanese) (Is.) Grc.	38·00 N	26·10 E
142	Dhūlia (dōōl'yȧ) India	20·58 N	74·43 E
142	Dhupgarth (Mt.) India	27·30 N	78·27 E
126	Dia (I.) (dē'ȧ) Grc. (Inset)	35·27 N	25·17 E
99	Diable, Île du (Devils I.) Fr. Gu.	5·15 N	57·10 W
65	Diablo, Mt. (dyȧ'blō) Calif. (San Francisco In.)	37·52 N	121·55 W
88	Diablo Heights (dyȧ'blō) C. Z. (Panama Canal In.)	8·58 N	79·34 W
65	Diablo Range (Mts.) Calif. (San Francisco In.)	37·47 N	121·50 W
99	Diamantina Braz.	18·14 S	43·32 W
158	Diamantina (R.) (dī'man-tē'nȧ) Austl.	25·38 S	139·53 E
99	Diamantino (dē-ȧ-män-tē'no) Braz.	14·22 S	56·23 W
66	Diamond Pk. Ore.	43·32 N	122·08 W
154	Diamond Pt. (dī'mŭnd) Indon.	5·30 N	96·45 E
95	Diana Bk. (dī'ăn'ȧ) Ba. Is.	22·30 N	74·45 W
155	Diapitan B. (dyȧ-pē-tä'n) Phil. (Manila In.)	16·28 N	122·25 E
	Dibra, see Debar		
70	Dickinson (dĭk'ĭn-sŭn) N. D.	46·52 N	102·49 W
77	Dickinson (dĭk'ĭn-sŭn) Tex. (In.)	29·28 N	95·02 W
77	Dickinson Bay Tex. (In.)	29·26 N	95·08 W
78	Dickson (dĭk'sŭn) Tenn.	36·03 N	87·24 W
81	Dickson City Pa.	41·25 N	75·40 W
133	Dicle (R.) (dĭj'lȧ) Tur.	37·50 N	40·40 E
110	Didcot (dĭd'cŏt) Eng. (London In.)	51·35 N	1·15 W
123	Die (dē) Fr.	44·45 N	5·22 E
95	Diego de Ocampo, Pico (Pk.) (pē'-kō-dyĕ'gō-dĕ-ō-kä'm-pō) Dom. Rep.	19·40 N	70·45 W
100	Diego Ramirez, Islas (Is.) (dē ȧ'gō rȧ-mē'rāz) Chile	56·15 S	70·15 W
167	Diégo-Suarez (Antsirane) (dē-ā'gō-swȧ'rāz) (änt-sē-rän') Malag. Rep.	12·18 S	49·16 E
146	Dien Bien Phan Viet.	21·38 N	102·49 E
82	Dieppe (dē-ĕp') Can.	46·08 N	64·45 W
122	Dieppe Fr.	49·54 N	1·05 E
73	Dierks (dērks) Ark.	34·06 N	94·02 W
111	Diessen (dēs'sĕn) Ger. (Munich In.)	47·57 N	11·06 E
111	Diest Bel. (Brussels In.)	50·59 N	5·05 E
82	Digby (dĭg'bĭ) Can.	44·37 N	65·48 W
84	Dighton (dī-tŭn) Mass. (Providence In.)	41·49 N	71·05 W
123	Digne (dēn'y') Fr.	44·07 N	6·16 E
155	Digoel (R.) W. Irian	7·00 S	140·25 E
122	Digoin (dē-gwăN') Fr.	46·28 N	4·06 E
155	Dijohan Pt. (dē-kō-än) Phil. (Manila In.)	16·24 N	122·25 E
122	Dijon (dē-zhôN') Fr.	47·21 N	5·02 E
134	Dikson (dĭk'sŏn) Sov. Un.	72·47 N	79·20 E
165	Dikwa (dē'kwȧ) Nig.	12·06 N	13·53 E
155	Dili (dĭl'ē) Port. Timor	8·35 S	125·35 E
114	Di Linosa I. (dē-lē-nō'sȧ) Medit. Sea	36·01 N	12·43 E
133	Dilizhan Sov. Un.	40·45 N	45·00 E
64	Dillingham (dĭl'ĕng-hăm) Alaska	59·10 N	158·38 W
67	Dillon (dĭl'ŭn) Mont.	45·12 N	112·40 W
79	Dillon S. C.	34·24 N	79·28 W
166	Dilolo (dē-lō'lō) Con. K.	10·19 S	22·23 E
139	Dimashq (Damascus) (dȧ-măs'kŭs) Syria (Palestine In.)	33·31 N	36·18 E
127	Dimbovita (R.) Rom.	44·43 N	25·41 E
127	Dimitrovo (Pernik) (pĕr-nēk') Bul.	42·36 N	23·04 E
155	Dinagat I. (dē-nä'gät) Phil.	10·15 N	126·15 E
142	Dinājpur India	25·38 N	87·39 E
122	Dinan (dē-näN') Fr.	48·27 N	2·03 W
117	Dinant (dē-näN') Bel.	50·17 N	4·50 E
126	Dinara Planina (Mts.) (dē'nä-rä plä'nē-nä) Yugo.	43·50 N	16·15 E
143	Dindigul India	10·25 N	78·03 E
155	Dingalan B. (dĭŋ-gä'län) Phil. (Manila In.)	15·19 N	121·33 E
116	Dingle (dĭng''l) Ire.	52·10 N	10·13 W
116	Dingle B. Ire.	52·02 N	10·15 W
159	Dingo (dĭŋ'gō) Austl.	23·45 S	149·26 E
116	Dingwall (dĭng'wôl) Scot.	57·37 N	4·23 W
67	Dinosaur Natl. Mon. (dī'nō-sŏr) Utah-Colo.	40·45 N	109·17 W
123	Dinslaken (dēns'lä-kĕn) Ger. (Ruhr In.)	51·33 N	6·44 E
111	Dinterloord Neth. (Amsterdam In.)	51·38 N	4·21 E
68	Dinuba (dĭ-nū'bȧ) Calif.	36·33 N	119·29 W
164	Diorbivol (dē-ŏr-bē-vôl') Senegal	16·07 N	13·52 W
94	Dios, Cayo de (I.) (kä'yō-dĕ-dē-ōs') Cuba	22·05 N	83·05 W
164	Diourbel (dē-ōōr-bĕl') Senegal	14·37 N	16·28 W
145	Diphu Pass (dĭ-pōō) China	28·15 N	96·45 E
93	Diquis R. (dē-kēs') C. R.	8·59 N	83·24 W
168	Dirēdawā Eth. (Horn of Afr. In.)	9·40 N	41·47 E
92	Diriamba (dēr-yäm'bä) Nic.	11·52 N	86·15 W
158	Dirk Hartog (I.) Austl.	26·25 S	113·15 E
111	Dirksland Neth. (Amsterdam In.)	51·45 N	4·04 E
160	Dirranbandi (dĭ-rȧ-băn'dē) Austl.	28·24 S	148·29 E
69	Dirty Devil (R.) (dûr'tĭ dĕv''l) Utah	38·20 N	110·30 W
158	Disappointment (L.) Austl.	23·20 S	120·20 E
65	Disappointment, C. (dĭs'ȧ-point'ment) Wash. (Portland In.)	46·16 N	124·11 W
125	D'Ischia, I. (dē'sh-kyȧ) It. (Naples In.)	40·26 N	13·55 E
167	Discovery (dĭs-cŭv'ēr-ĭ) S. Afr. (Johannesburg & Pretoria In.)	26·10 S	27·53 E
65	Discovery Is. (dĭs-kŭv'ĕr-ē) Can. (Seattle In.)	48·25 N	123·13 W
168	Dishnā (dêsh'nȧ) U. A. R. (Nile In.)	26·08 N	32·27 E
49	Disko (dĭs'kō) (I.) Grnld.	70·00 N	54·00 W
79	Dismal Swp. (dĭz'măl) N. C.-Va.	36·35 N	76·34 W
128	Disna (dēs'nȧ) Sov. Un.	55·34 N	28·15 E
82	Disraeli (dĭs-rā'lĭ) Can.	45·53 N	71·23 W
81	District of Columbia U. S.	38·50 N	77·00 W
91	Distrito Federal (Dist.) (dēs-trē'tô-fĕ-dĕ-rä'l) Mex.	19·14 N	99·08 W
168	Disūq (dē-sōōk') U. A. R. (Nile In.)	31·07 N	30·41 E
142	Diu (dē'ōō) India	20·48 N	70·58 E
122	Dives (dēv) Fr.	49·18 N	0·05 W
155	Divilacan B. (dē-vē-lä'kän) Phil.	17·26 N	122·25 E
101	Divinópolis (dē-vē-nô'pō-lēs) Braz. (Rio de Janeiro In.)	20·10 S	44·53 W
85	Dixie (dĭk'sĭ) Can. (Toronto In.)	43·36 N	79·35 W
71	Dixon (dĭks'ŭn) Ill.	41·50 N	89·30 W
86	Dixon Ent. Alaska-Can.	54·36 N	132·32 W
133	Diyarbakir (dē-yär-bĕk'ĭr) Tur.	38·00 N	40·10 E
165	Dja R. Cam.	2·40 N	14·11 E
155	Djailolo Pass Indon.	0·05 S	129·08 E
154	Djakarta (yä-kär'tä) Indon.	6·17 S	106·45 E
154	Djambi (jäm'bē) Indon.	1·45 S	103·28 E
164	Djanet (Fort Charlet) Alg.	24·29 N	9·26 E
114	Djedi R. Alg.	34·18 N	4·39 E
164	Djelfa (jĕl'fä) Alg.	34·40 N	3·17 E
164	Djenné (jĕn-nā') Mali	13·55 N	4·26 W
114	Djerba, Ile de (I.) Tun.	33·53 N	11·26 E
164	Djerid, Chott (L.) (jĕr'ĭd) Tun.	33·15 N	8·29 E
168	Djibouti (jē-bōō-tē') Fr. Som. (Horn of Afr. In.)	11·34 N	43·00 E
113	Djidjelli (jē-jĕ-lē') Alg.	36·49 N	5·47 E
139	Djumrah Indon. (Singapore In.)	1·48 N	101·04 E
118	Djursholm (djōōrs'hōlm) Swe.	59·26 N	18·01 E
129	Dmitriyevka (d'mē-trē-yĕf'kȧ) Sov. Un.	47·57 N	38·56 E
129	Dmitriyev L'govskiy (d'mē'trĭ-yĕf l'gôf'skĭ) Sov. Un.	52·07 N	35·05 E
136	Dmitrov (d'mē'trôf) Sov. Un. (Moscow In.)	56·21 N	37·32 E
128	Dmitrovsk (d'mē'trôfsk) Sov. Un.	52·30 N	35·10 E
129	Dnepr (Dnieper) (R.) (nē'pĕr) Sov. Un.	46·47 N	32·57 E
129	Dneprodzerzhinsk (d'nyĕp'rô-zĕr-shĭnsk) Sov. Un.	48·32 N	34·38 E
129	Dnepropetrovsk (d'nyĕp'rô-pä-trôfsk) Sov. Un.	48·23 N	34·10 E
129	Dnepropetrovsk (Oblast) Sov. Un.	48·15 N	34·08 E
129	Dnepr Zaliv (B.) (dnyĕp'r zȧ'lĭf) Sov. Un.	46·33 N	31·45 E
129	Dnestr (Dniester) (R.) (nēst'rōōl) (nēs'tĕr) Sov. Un.	48·21 N	28·10 E
129	Dnestrovskiy Líman (B.) Sov. Un.	46·13 N	29·50 E
	Dnieper (R.), see Dnepr		
	Dniester (R.), see Dnestr		
128	Dno (d'nô') Sov. Un.	57·49 N	29·59 E
84	Dobbs Ferry (dŏbz' fĕ'rē) N. Y. (New York In.)	41·01 N	73·53 W
158	Dobbyn (dôb'ĭn) Austl.	19·45 S	140·02 E
119	Dobele (dô'bĕ-lĕ) Sov. Un.	56·37 N	23·18 E
120	Döbeln (dû'bĕln) Ger.	51·08 N	13·07 E
155	Dobo Indon.	6·00 S	134·18 E
127	Doboj (dō'boi) Yugo.	44·42 N	18·04 E
136	Dobryanka (dôb-ryän'kȧ) Sov. Un. (Urals In.)	58·27 N	56·26 E
121	Dobšina (dôp'shē-nä) Czech.	48·48 N	20·25 E
99	Doce (R.) (dō'sȧ) Braz.	19·01 S	42·14 W
94	Doce Leguas, Cayos de las (Is.) (kä'yōs-dĕ-läs-dō-sĕ-lĕ'gwäs) Cuba	20·55 N	79·05 W
90	Doctor Arroyo (dōk-tōr' är-rō'yō) Mex.	23·41 N	100·10 W
110	Doddington (dŏd'dĭng-tŏn) Eng. (London In.)	51·17 N	0·47 E
	Dodecanese (Is.), see Dhodhekánisos		
72	Dodge City (dŏj) Kans.	37·44 N	100·01 W
81	Dodgeville (dŏj'vĭl) N. Y.	43·10 N	74·45 W
71	Dodgeville Wis.	42·58 N	90·07 W
166	Dodoma (dō'dō-mȧ) Tan.	6·13 S	35·36 E
74	Dodson (dŏd's'n) Mo. (Kansas City In.)	38·48 N	94·33 W
71	Dog (L.) (dŏg) Can.	48·42 N	89·24 W
117	Dogger Bk. (dŏg'gĕr) Eur.	55·07 N	2·25 E
94	Dog Rocks (I.) Ba. Is.	24·05 N	79·50 W
133	Dogubayazit Tur.	39·35 N	44·00 E

ăt; finăl; rāte; senâte; ärm; ȧsk; sofȧ; fâre; ch-choose: dh-as th in other; bē; ĕvent; bĕt; recĕnt; cratĕr; g-go; gh-guttural g; bĭt; ĭ-short neutral; rīde; к-guttural k as ch in German ich;

Page	Name Pronunciation Region	Lat. °'	Long. °'
142	Dohad .... India	22·52 N	74·18 E
127	Doiran (L.) .... Grc.	41·10 N	23·00 E
153	Dōjō (dō-jō) ..... Jap. (Osaka In.)	34·51 N	135·14 E
128	Dokshitsy (dôk-shēt'sē) .. Sov. Un.	54·53 N	27·49 E
82	Dolbeau .... Can.	48·52 N	72·16 W
123	Dôle (dōl) .... Fr.	47·07 N	5·28 E
129	Dolgaya, Kosa (C.) (kô'sà dôl-gä'yà) . Sov. Un.	46·42 N	37·42 E
132	Dolgiy (I.) .... Sov. Un.	69·20 N	59·20 E
121	Dolina (dô-lyē'nä) .... Sov. Un.	48·57 N	24·01 E
152	Dolinsk (dà-lēnsk') ...... Sov. Un.	47·29 N	142·31 E
94	Dollar Hbr. .... Ba. Is.	25·30 N	79·15 W
165	Dolo .... Som.	4·01 N	42·14 E
84	Dolomite (dŏl'ô-mīt) Ala. (Birmingham In.)	33·28 N	86·57 W
126	Dolomitiche, Alpi (Mts.) (äl-pē-dô-lô'mē-tē'chĕ) . It.	46·16 N	11·43 E
101	Dolores (dô-lō'rĕs) Arg. (Buenos Aires In.)	36·20 S	57·42 W
98	Dolores .... Col. (In.)	3·33 N	74·54 W
155	Dolores (dô-lô-rĕs) Phil. (Manila In.)	17·40 N	120·43 E
76	Dolores (dô-lō'rĕs) .... Tex.	27·42 N	99·47 W
101	Dolores.... Ur. (Buenos Aires In.)	33·32 S	58·15 W
69	Dolores (R.) .... Colo.-Utah	38·35 N	108·50 W
90	Dolores Hidalgo (dô-lô'rĕs-ē-däl'gō) . Mex.	21·09 N	100·56 W
86	Dolphin and Union Str. (dŏl'fĭn ūn'yŭn) . Can.	69·22 N	117·10 W
120	Domažlice (dō'mäzh-lē-tsĕ) Czech.	49·27 N	12·55 E
123	Dombasle (dôN-bäl') .... Fr.	48·38 N	6·18 E
121	Dombóvár (dōm'bō-vär) ... Hung.	46·22 N	18·08 E
122	Dôme, Puy de (Pk.) (pwē'dĕ-dôm') . Fr.	45·47 N	2·54 E
98	Domeyko, Cordillera (Mts.) (kôr-dēl-yĕ'rä-dô-mä'kō) . Chile	20·50 S	69·02 W
93	Dominica Chan. (dŏ-mĭ-nē'kà) N. A. (Le. & Wind. Is. In.)	15·00 N	61·30 W
93	Dominica I. N. A. (Le. & Wind. Is. In.)	15·24 N	61·05 W
88	Dominican Republic (dô-mĭn'ĭ-kăn) . N. A.	18·59 N	70·40 W
83	Dominion (dô-mĭn'yŭn) ..... Can.	46·13 N	60·01 W
136	Domodedovo (dô-mô-dyĕ'do-vô) Sov. Un. (Moscow In.)	55·27 N	37·45 E
101	Dom Silvério (doN-sēl-vĕ'ryō) Braz. (Rio de Janeiro In.)	20·09 S	42·57 W
110	Don (R.) (dŏn) .... Eng.	53·27 N	1·34 W
110	Don (R.) .... Eng.	53·39 N	0·58 W
116	Don (R.) .... Scot.	57·19 N	2·39 W
74	Donaldson (dŏn'ăl-săn) Mich. (Sault Ste. Marie In.)	46·19 N	84·22 W
77	Donaldsonville (dŏn'ăld-săn-vĭl) La.	30·05 N	90·58 W
78	Donalsonville .... Ga.	31·02 N	84·50 W
120	Donawitz (dō'nà-vĭts) .... Aus.	47·23 N	15·05 E
142	Donazari .... E. Pak.	22·18 N	91·52 E
124	Don Benito Mérida (dōn' bā-nē'tō-mĕ'rē-dä) . Sp.	38·55 N	6·08 W
161	Doncaster (doŋ'kăs-tēr) Austl. (Melbourne In.)	37·47 S	145·08 E
110	Doncaster (doŋ'kăs-tēr) ..... Eng.	53·32 N	1·07 W
166	Dondo (dōn'dō) .... Ang.	9·35 S	14·25 E
166	Dondo .... Moz.	19·33 S	34·47 E
116	Donegal (dŏn-ê-gôl') .... Ire.	54·44 N	8·05 W
116	Donegal, Mts. of (dŏn-ê-gôl') . Ire.	54·44 N	8·10 W
116	Donegal Bay (dŏn-ĕ-gôl') .. N. Ire.	54·35 N	8·36 W
129	Donets (R.) (dô-nyĕts') .. Sov. Un.	48·48 N	38·42 E
129	Donets Coal Basin (Reg.) (dô-nyĕts') . Sov. Un.	48·15 N	38·50 E
133	Donetsk (Stalino) (dô-nyĕts'k) (stä'lĭ-nō) . Sov. Un.	48·00 N	37·35 E
158	Dongara (dôŋ-gă'rà) .... Austl.	29·15 S	115·00 E
154	Donggala (dôŋ-gä'lä) ...... Indon.	0·45 S	119·32 E
151	Dong Hoi (dông-hô-ē') ...... Viet.	17·25 N	106·42 E
166	Dongo (dôŋ'gō) .... Ang.	14·45 S	15·30 E
165	Dongola (dŏŋ'gô-là) .... Sud.	19·21 N	30·19 E
155	Dongon Pt. (dŏng-ŏn') Phil. (Manila In.)	12·43 N	120·35 E
165	Dongou (dôŋ-gōō') ...... Con. B.	2·12 N	18·08 E
73	Doniphan (dŏn'ĭ-făn) .... Mo.	36·37 N	90·50 W
126	Donji Vakuf (dōn'yĭ väk'ŏŏf) Yugo.	44·08 N	17·25 E
76	Don Martin, Presa de (Res.) (prĕ'sä-dĕ-dôn-mär-tē'n) . Mex.	27·35 N	100·38 W
82	Donnacona .... Can.	46·40 N	71·46 W
123	Donnemarie-en-Montois (dôn-mä-rē'ĕN-môN-twä') Fr. (Paris In.)	48·29 N	3·09 E
66	Donner und Blitzen R. (dŏn'ēr ŏŏnt blĭ'tsĕn) . Ore.	42·45 N	118·57 W
167	Donnybrook (dŏ-nĭ-brŏŏk) S. Afr. (Natal In.)	29·56 S	29·54 E
75	Donora (dŏ-nō'ră) Pa. (Pittsburgh In.)	40·10 N	79·51 W
64	Doonerak (dōō'nē-răk) .... Alaska	68·00 N	150·34 W
111	Doorn.... Neth. (Amsterdam In.)	52·02 N	5·21 E
71	Door Pen. (dōr) .... Wis.	44·40 N	87·36 W
126	Dora Baltea (dō'rä bäl'tä-ä) ... It.	45·40 N	7·34 E
84	Doraville (dō'rà-vĭ.) Ga. (Atlanta In.)	33·54 N	84·17 W
116	Dorchester (dôr'chĕs-tēr) .... Eng.	50·45 N	2·34 W
122	Dordogne (R.) (dôr-dôn'yĕ) ... Fr.	44·53 N	0·16 E
111	Dordrecht (dôr'drĕKt) Neth. (Amsterdam In.)	51·48 N	4·39 E
167	Dordrecht (dô'drĕkt) S. Afr. (Natal In.)	31·24 S	27·06 E
126	Dorgali (dôr'gä-lē) .... Sard.	40·18 N	9·37 E
164	Dori (dō-rē') .... Upper Volta	13·56 N	0·01 W
85	Dorion (dôr-yō) Can. (Montreal In.)	45·23 N	74·01 W
110	Dorking (dôr'kĭng) Eng. (London In.)	51·12 N	0·20 W
85	D'Orleans, Ile (I.) (dōr-lē-äN', yl) Can. (Quebec In.)	46·56 N	70·27 W
75	Dormont (dôr'mŏnt) Pa. (Pittsburgh In.)	40·24 N	80·02 W
120	Dornbirn (dôrn'bērn) .... Aus.	47·24 N	9·45 E
116	Dornoch (dôr'nŏK) .... Scot.	57·55 N	4·01 W
116	Dornoch Firth (dôr'nŏK fûrth) Scot.	57·55 N	3·55 W
128	Dorogobuzh (dôrôgô'-bōō'zh) Sov. Un.	54·57 N	33·18 E
121	Dorohoi (dō-rô-hoi') .... Rom.	47·57 N	26·28 E
	Dorpat, see Tartu		
158	Dorre (I.) (dôr) .... Austl.	25·19 S	113·10 E
74	Dorsey (dôrsĭ) .. Ill. (St. Louis In.)	38·59 N	90·00 W
123	Dorsten (dōr'stĕn) . Ger. (Ruhr In.)	51·40 N	6·58 E
123	Dortmund (dôrt'mŏŏnt) Ger. (Ruhr In.)	51·31 N	7·28 E
123	Dortmund-Ems Kanal (can.) (dōrt'mŏŏnd-ĕms' kä-näl') Ger. (Ruhr In.)	51·50 N	7·25 E
133	Dörtyal (dûrt'yôl) .... Tur.	36·50 N	36·20 E
85	Dorval (dôr-vál') Can. (Montreal In.)	45·26 N	73·44 W
99	Dos Caminos (dôs-kä-mê'nôs) Ven. (In.)	9·38 N	67·17 W
65	Dosewallips (R.) (dō'sê-wăl'lĭps) Wash. (Seattle In.)	47·45 N	123·04 W
124	Dos Hermanas (dōsĕr-mä'näs) . Sp.	37·17 N	5·56 W
164	Dosso (dôs-ō') .... Niger	13·03 N	3·09 E
78	Dothan (dō'thăn) .... Ala.	31·13 N	85·23 W
122	Douai (dōō-å') .... Fr.	50·23 N	3·04 E
164	Douala (dōō-ä'lä) .... Cam.	4·00 N	9·37 E
122	Douarnenez (dōō-är nē-nĕs') ... Fr.	48·06 N	4·18 W
77	Double Bay. (dŭb''l bī'yōō) Tex. (In.)	29·40 N	94·38 W
125	Douéra (dōō-ā'rà) .... Alg.	36·40 N	2·55 E
64	Douglas (dŭg'lăs) .... Alaska	58·18 N	134·35 W
69	Douglas .... Ariz.	31·20 N	109·30 W
78	Douglas .... Ga.	31·30 N	82·53 W
116	Douglas (dŭg'lăs) ..... Isle of Man	54·10 N	4·24 W
83	Douglas (dŭg'lăs) Mass. (Boston In.)	42·04 N	71·45 W
67	Douglas (dŭg'lăs) .... Wyo.	42·45 N	105·21 W
110	Douglas (R.) (dŭg'lăs) .... Eng.	53·38 N	2·48 W
78	Douglas (R.) (dŭg'lăs) ...... Tenn.	36·00 N	83·35 W
78	Douglasville (dŭg'lăs-vĭl) ..... Ga.	33·45 N	84·47 W
165	Doumé (dōō-mā') .... Cam.	4·14 N	13·26 E
99	Dourada, Serra (Mts.) (sĕ'r-rä-dōōō-rà'dä) . Braz.	15·11 S	49·57 W
123	Dourdan (dōōr-däN') Fr. (Paris In.)	48·32 N	2·01 E
124	Douro, Rio (R.) (rē'ō-dô'ōō-rô) Port.	41·03 N	8·12 W
110	Dove (R.) (dŭv) .... Eng.	52·53 N	1·47 W
81	Dover (dō vēr) .... Del.	39·10 N	75·30 W
117	Dover .... Eng.	51·08 N	1·19 E
81	Dover .... N. H.	43·15 N	71·00 W
84	Dover...... N. J. (New York In.)	40·53 N	74·33 W
80	Dover .... Ohio	40·35 N	81·30 W
168	Dover... S. Afr. (Johannesburg & Pretoria In.)	27·05 S	27·44 E
117	Dover, Str. of .... Eur.	50·50 N	1·15 W
82	Dover-Foxcroft (dō'vēr fŏks'krôft) Maine	45·10 N	69·15 W
132	Dovlekanovo (dŏv'lyĕk-à-nô-vô) Sov. Un.	54·15 N	55·05 E
118	Dovre Fjell (Plat.) (dŏv'rĕ fyĕl') Nor.	62·03 N	8·36 E
74	Dow (dou) ..... Ill. (St. Louis In.)	39·01 N	90·20 W
166	Dow, L. .... Bots.	21·22 S	24·52 E
80	Dowagiac (dô-wô'jăk) ...... Mich.	42·00 N	86·05 W
75	Downers Grove (dou'nērz grōv) Ill. (Chicago In.)	41·48 N	88·00 W
74	Downey (dou'nĭ) Calif. (Los Angeles In.)	33·56 N	118·08 W
68	Downieville (dou'nĭ-vĭl) ..... Calif.	39·35 N	120·48 W
72	Downs (dounz) .... Kans.	39·29 N	98·32 W
75	Doylestown (doilz'toun) Ohio (Cleveland In.)	40·58 N	81·43 W
164	Draa, C. (drà) .... Mor.	28·39 N	12·15 W
164	Draa, Wadi R. (wä-dĭ drä') .. Mor.	28·00 N	9·31 W
129	Drabov (drä'bôf) ...... Sov. Un.	49·57 N	32·14 E
123	Drac (R.) (dräk) .... Fr.	44·50 N	5·47 E
83	Dracut (drā'kŭt) Mass. (Boston In.)	42·40 N	71·19 W
127	Draganovo (drä-gä-nô'vô) .... Bul.	43·13 N	25·45 E
127	Drăgăsani (drä-gà-shän'ĭ) ... Rom.	44·39 N	24·18 E
123	Draguignan (drä-gēn-yäN') ... Fr.	43·35 N	6·28 E
166	Drakensberg (Mts.) (drä'kĕnz-bĕrgh) . Leso.-S. Afr.	29·15 S	29·07 E
96	Drake Passage (drāk păs'ĭj) S. A.-Ant.	57·00 S	65·00 W
127	Dráma (drä'mä) .... Grc.	41·09 N	24·10 E
118	Drammen (dräm'ĕn) .... Nor.	59·45 N	10·15 E
84	Dranesville (drānz-vĭl) Va. (Washington D.C. In.)	39·00 N	77·21 W
120	Drau R. (drou) .... Aus.	46·44 N	13·45 E
126	Drava (R.) (Drä'vä) .... Yugo.	46·37 N	15·17 E
126	Dravograd (Drä'vô-gräd') .. Yugo.	46·37 N	15·01 E
120	Drawsko Pomorskie (dräv'skō pō-mōr'skyĕ) . Pol.	53·31 N	15·50 E
65	Drayton Hbr. (drā'tŭn) Wash. (Vancouver In.)	48·58 N	122·40 W
75	Drayton Plains Mich. (Detroit In.)	42·41 N	83·23 W
146	Dre Chu (R.) .... China	34·11 N	96·08 E
123	Drensteinfurt (drĕn'shtīn-fōōrt) Ger. (Ruhr In.)	51·47 N	7·44 E
120	Dresden (drās'dĕn) .... Ger.	51·05 N	13·45 E
123	Dreux (drû) ..... Fr. (Paris In.)	48·44 N	1·24 E
168	Driefontein S. Afr. (Johannesburg & Pretoria In.)	25·53 S	29·10 E
127	Drin (R.) (drēn) .... Alb.	42·13 N	20·13 E
127	Drina (R.) (drē'nä) .... Yugo.	44·09 N	19·30 E
127	Drinit, Pellg I (Bght.) ...... Alb.	41·42 N	19·17 E
128	Drissa (drĭs'sä) .... Sov. Un.	55·48 N	27·59 E
128	Drissa (R.) .... Sov. Un.	55·44 N	28·58 E
84	Driver .... Va. (Norfolk In.)	36·50 N	76·30 W
118	Dröbak (drû'bäk) .... Nor.	59·40 N	10·35 E
116	Drogheda (drŏ'hē-dà) .... Ire.	53·43 N	6·15 W
121	Drogichin (drō-gē'chĭn) .. Sov. Un.	52·10 N	25·11 E
121	Drogobych (drô-hô'bĭch) . Sov. Un.	49·21 N	23·31 E
122	Drôme (R.) (drōm) .... Fr.	44·42 N	4·53 E
110	Dronfield (drŏn'fēld) .... Eng.	53·18 N	1·28 W
86	Drumheller (drŭm-hĕl-ēr) ... Can.	51·30 N	112·42 W
80	Drummond (I.) (drŭm'ŭnd) Mich.	46·00 N	83·50 W
82	Drummondville (drŭm'ŭnd-vĭl) Can.	45·53 N	72·33 W
73	Drumright (drŭm'rīt) .... Okla.	35·59 N	96·37 W
111	Drunen... Neth. (Amsterdam In.)	51·41 N	5·10 E
128	Drut' (R.) (drōōt) ...... Sov. Un.	53·40 N	29·45 E
128	Druya (drŏŏ'yá) .... Sov. Un.	55·45 N	27·26 E
115	Druze, Jebel (Mts.) .... Syria	32·40 N	36·58 E
121	Drweca R. (d'r-văn'tsà) ...... Pol.	53·06 N	19·13 E
87	Dryden (drī-dĕn) .... Can.	49·50 N	92·47 W
161	Drysdale.. Austl. (Melbourne In.)	38·11 S	144·34 E
79	Dry Tortugas (I.) (tôr-tōō'gäz) Fla. (In.)	24·37 N	82·45 W
164	Dschang (dshäng) .... Cam.	5·34 N	10·09 E
85	Duagh...... Can. (Edmonton In.)	53·43 N	113·24 W
95	Duarte, Pico (Pk.) (dŭĭ'ärtĕh pêcô) . Dom. Rep	19·05 N	70·55 W
101	Duas Barras (dōō'äs-bà'r-räs) Braz. (Rio de Janeiro In.)	22·03 S	42·30 W
86	Dubawnt (L.) (dōō-bônt') .... Can.	63·27 N	103·30 W
86	Dubawnt (R.) .... Can.	61·30 N	103·49 W
144	Dubayy .... Tr. States	25·18 N	55·26 E
160	Dubbo (dŭb'ō) .... Austl.	32·20 S	148·42 E
65	Dublin (dŭb'lĭn) Calif. (San Francisco In.)	37·42 N	121·56 W
78	Dublin .... Ga.	32·33 N	82·55 W
116	Dublin (Baile Atha Cliath) (dŭb'lĭn) (bŏ'lĕō'hŏclē'ōh) .. Ire.	53·20 N	6·15 W
76	Dublin .... Tex.	32·05 N	98·20 W
121	Dubno (dōō'b-nô) ...... Sov. Un.	50·24 N	25·44 E
81	Du Bois (dōō-bois') .... Pa.	41·10 N	78·45 W
129	Dubossary (dōō-bŏ-sä'rĭ) . Sov. Un.	47·16 N	29·11 E
133	Dubovka (dōō-bôf'kà) ... Sov. Un.	49·00 N	44·50 E
136	Dubrovka (dōō-brôf'kà) Sov. Un. (Leningrad In.)	59·51 N	30·56 E
127	Dubrovnik (Ragusa) (dōō'brôv-nēk) (rä-gōō'sä) Yugo.	42·40 N	18·10 E
128	Dubrovno (dōō-brôf'nō) .. Sov. Un.	54·39 N	30·54 E
71	Dubuque (dŏŏ-būk') .... Iowa	42·30 N	90·43 W
69	Duchesne (dōō-shän') .... Utah	40·12 N	110·23 W
69	Duchesne (R.) .... Utah	40·20 N	110·50 W
158	Duchess (dŭch'ĕs) .... Austl.	21·30 S	139·55 E
157	Ducie I. (dü-sē') .... Oceania	25·30 S	126·20 W
80	Duck (I.) (dŭk) .... Can.	45·35 N	83·00 W
78	Duck (R.) .... Tenn.	35·55 N	87·40 W
65	Duckabush (R.) (dŭk'ā-bōōsh) Wash. (Seattle In.)	47·41 N	123·09 W
86	Duck Mtn. .... Can.	51·43 N	101·07 W
78	Ducktown (dŭk'toun) ...... Tenn.	35·03 N	84·20 W
68	Duckwater Pk. (dŭk-wô-tēr) . Nev.	39·00 N	115·31 W
98	Duda (dōō'dä) (R.) ..... Col. (In.)	3·25 N	74·23 W
134	Dudinka (dōō-dĭn'kà) .... Sov. Un.	69·15 N	85·42 E
110	Dudley (dŭd'lĭ) .... Eng.	52·31 N	2·04 W
124	Duero (R.) (dwĕ'rô) .... Sp.	41·30 N	5·10 W
80	Dugger (dŭg'ēr) .... Ind.	39·00 N	87·10 W
126	Dugi Otok (I.) (dōō'gē O'tôk) Yugo.	44·03 N	14·40 E
123	Duisburg (dōō'ĭs-bōōrgh) Ger. (Ruhr In.)	51·26 N	6·46 E
98	Duitama (dōōē-tä'mä) .... Col.	5·48 N	73·09 W
128	Dukhovshchina (dōō-Kôfsh'chēnä) Sov. Un.	55·13 N	32·26 E
110	Dukinfield (dŭk'ĭn-fēld) ..... Eng.	53·28 N	2·05 W
121	Dukla P. (dōō'klä) .... Pol.	49·25 N	21·44 E
93	Dulce, Golfo (G.) (gōl'fô dōōl'sä) C. R.	8·25 N	83·13 W
	Dulcigno, see Ulčinj		
123	Dülken (dül'kĕn) .. Ger. (Ruhr In.)	51·15 N	6·21 E
123	Dülmen (dül'mĕn) Ger. (Ruhr In.)	51·50 N	7·17 E
74	Duluth (dōō-lōōth') Minn. (Duluth In.)	46·50 N	92·07 W
139	Dūmă .... Syria (Palestine In.)	33·34 N	36·17 E
155	Dumaguete City (dōō-mä-gä'tä) Phil.	9·14 N	123·15 E
168	Dumaît, Masabb (R. Mth.) U. A. R. (Nile In.)	31·36 N	31·45 E
155	Dumali Pt. (dōō-mä'lē) Phil. (Manila Pt.)	13·07 N	121·42 E
116	Dumbarton (dŭm'băr-tŭn) .. Scot.	56·00 N	4·35 W
142	Dum Dum... India (Calcutta In.)	22·37 N	88·25 E
116	Dumfries (dŭm-frēs') .... Scot.	54·05 N	3·40 W
84	Dumont (dōō'mŏnt) N. J. (New York In.)	40·56 N	74·00 W
77	Dumont .... Tex. (In.)	29·40 N	95·14 W
121	Dunaföldvar (dōō'nô-fûld'vär) Hung.	46·48 N	18·55 E
121	Dunajec R. (dōō-nä'yĕts) ..... Pol.	49·52 N	20·53 E
121	Dunapataj (doo'nô-pô-toi) . Hung.	46·42 N	19·03 E
121	Duna R. (dōō'nä) .... Hung.	46·07 N	18·45 E
121	Dunaujvaros .... Hung.	46·57 N	18·55 E
136	Dunay (dōō'nī) Sov. Un. (Leningrad In.)	59·59 N	30·57 E
129	Dunayevtsy (dōō-nä'yĕf-tsĭ) Sov. Un.	48·52 N	26·51 E
116	Dunbar (dŭn'bär) .... Scot.	56·00 N	2·25 W
80	Dunbar .... W. Va.	38·20 N	81·45 W
66	Duncan (dŭŋ'kăn) .... Can.	48·46 N	123·42 W
72	Duncan .... Okla.	34·29 N	97·56 W
116	Duncansby Hd. (dŭn'kănz-bĭ) Scot.	58·40 N	3·01 W
74	Duncanville (dŭn'kăn-vĭl) Tex. (Dallas, Fort Worth In.)	32·39 N	96·55 W
116	Dundalk (dŭn'dôk) .... Ire.	54·00 N	6·18 W
84	Dundalk.... Md. (Baltimore In.)	39·16 N	76·31 W
116	Dundalk B. (dŭn'dôk) .... Ire.	53·55 N	6·15 W

ng-sing; ŋ-baŋk; N-nasalized n; nŏd; cŏmmit; ōld; ôbey; ôrder; fōōd; fŏŏt; ou-out; s-soft; sh-dish; th-thin; pūre; ûnite; ûrn; stŭd; circŭs; ü-as "y" in study; '-indeterminate vowel.

Page	Name Pronunciation Region	Lat. °′	Long. °′
85	Dundas (dŭn-dăs′) Can. (Toronto In.)	43·16 N	79·58 W
75	Dundee (dŭn-dē′) . Ill. (Chicago In.)	42·06 N	88·17 W
116	Dundee.................Scot.	56·30 N	2·55 W
167	Dundee.......S. Afr. (Natal In.)	28·14 S	30·16 E
158	Dundras (L.) (dŭn-drȧs)....Austl.	32·15 S	132·00 E
158	Dundras Str. (dŭn′drȧs)....Austl.	10·35 S	131·15 E
116	Dundrum B. (dŭn-drŭm′).....Ire.	54·13 N	5·47 W
79	Dunedin (dŭn-ē′dĭn)....Fla. (In.)	28·00 N	82·43 W
159	Dunedin..............N. Z. (In.)	45·48 S	170·32 E
84	Dunellen (dŭn-ĕl′l′n) N. J. (New York In.)	40·36 N	74·28 W
116	Dunfermline (dŭn-fĕrm′lĭn)..Scot.	56·05 N	3·30 W
116	Dungarvin (dŭn-gȧr′văn).....Ire.	52·06 N	7·50 W
65	Dungeness (dŭnj-nĕs′) Wash. (Seattle In.)	48·09 N	123·07 W
65	Dungeness (R.) . Wash. (Seattle In.)	48·03 N	123·10 W
65	Dungeness Spit Wash. (Seattle In.)	48·11 N	123·03 W
165	Dungu (do͞oŋ-go͞o′)......Con. K.	3·48 N	28·32 E
122	Dunkerque (dŭɴ-kĕrk′).......Fr.	51·02 N	2·37 E
80	Dunkirk (dŭn′kûrk).........Ind.	40·20 N	85·25 W
81	Dunkirk..................N. Y.	42·30 N	79·20 W
116	Dun Laoghaire (dŭn-lā′rĕ)....Ire.	53·16 N	6·09 W
70	Dunlap (dŭn′lăp)..........Iowa	41·53 N	95·33 W
78	Dunlap..................Tenn.	35·23 N	85·23 W
81	Dunmore (dŭn′mōr)..........Pa.	41·25 N	75·30 W
79	Dunn (dŭn)...............N. C.	35·18 N	78·37 W
79	Dunnellon (dŭn-ĕl′ŏn)........Fla.	29·02 N	82·28 W
81	Dunnville (dŭn′vĭl).........Can.	42·55 N	79·40 W
66	Dunsmuir (dŭnz′mūr)......Calif.	41·08 N	122·17 W
84	Dunwoody (dŭn-wo͝od′ĭ) Ga. (Atlanta In.)	33·57 N	84·20 W
75	Du Page R. (do͞o pāj) Ill. (Chicago In.)	41·41 N	88·11 W
75	Du Page R., E. Br. Ill. (Chicago In.)	41·49 N	88·05 W
75	Du Page R., W. Br. Ill. (Chicago In.)	41·48 N	88·10 W
155	Dupax (do͞o′päks) Phil. (Manila In.)	16·16 N	121·06 E
127	Dupnitsa (do͝op′nê-tsȧ)......Bul.	42·15 N	23·07 E
74	Dupo (dū′pō)..Ill. (St. Louis In.)	38·31 N	90·12 W
166	Duque de Bragança (do͞o′kȧ dȧ brä-gäɴ′sä).Ang.	8·55 S	16·10 E
100	Duque de Caxias (do͞o′kĕ-dĕ-kȧ′shyȧs) Braz. (In.)	22·46 S	43·18 W
75	Duquesne (do͞o-kān′) Pa. (Pittsburgh In.)	40·22 N	79·51 W
73	Du Quoin (do͞o-kwoin′).......Ill.	38·01 N	89·14 W
123	Durance (R.) (dü-räɴs′)......Fr.	43·46 N	5·52 E
80	Durand (dů-rănd′).........Mich.	42·50 N	84·00 W
71	Durand...................Wis.	44·37 N	91·58 W
69	Durango (do͞o-răŋ′gō).......Colo.	37·15 N	107·55 W
90	Durango (do͞o-rä′n-gô)......Mex.	24·02 N	104·42 W
88	Durango (State)...........Mex.	25·00 N	106·00 W
78	Durant (dů-rănt′)..........Miss.	33·05 N	89·50 W
73	Durant..................Okla.	33·59 N	96·23 W
124	Duratón (R.) (do͞o-rä-tōn′)....Sp.	41·55 N	3·55 W
101	Durazno (do͞o-räz′nō) Ur. (Buenos Aires In.)	33·21 S	56·31 W
101	Durazno (Dept.) Ur. (Buenos Aires In.)	33·00 S	56·35 W
167	Durban (dûr′băn) S. Afr. (Natal In.)	29·48 S	31·00 E
166	Durbanville (dûr-băn′vĭl) S. Afr. (Cape Town In.)	33·50 S	18·39 E
119	Durbe (do͞or′bĕ)........Sov. Un.	56·36 N	21·24 E
126	Đurđevac (dūr′dyĕ-vȧts′)...Yugo.	46.03 N	17·03 E
123	Düren (dü′rĕn)...Ger. (Ruhr In.)	50·48 N	6·30 E
116	Durham (dûr′ăm)..........Eng.	54·47 N	1·46 W
79	Durham..................N. C.	36·00 N	78·55 W
75	Durham....Wis. (Milwaukee In.)	42·52 N	88·04 W
160	Durham Downs...........Austl.	27·30 S	141·55 E
127	Durrës (do͝or′ĕs)............Alb.	41·19 N	19·27 E
155	D'urville, Kap (C.) (dûr′vĭl) W. Irian	1·20 S	138·45 E
81	Duryea (do͞or-yā′)...........Pa.	41·20 N	75·50 W
144	Dushanbe..............Sov. Un.	38·41 N	68·43 E
123	Düsseldorf (düs′ĕl-dôrf) Ger. (Ruhr In.)	51·14 N	6·47 E
111	Dussen...Neth. (Amsterdam In.)	51·43 N	4·58 E
150	Dutalan Ula (Mtn.).......Mong.	49·25 N	112·40 E
64	Dutch Harbor (dŭch här′bĕr) Alaska	53·58 N	166·30 W
65	Duvall (do͞o′vâl) Wash. (Seattle In.)	47·44 N	121·59 W
95	Duvergé (do͞o-vĕr-hĕ′) . Dom. Rep.	18·20 N	71·20 W
65	Duwamish (do͞o-wăm′ĭsh) Wash. (Seattle In.)	47·24 N	122·18 W
	Dvina, Western, R., see Zapadnaya Dvina		
132	Dvinskaya Guba (G.)...Sov. Un.	65·10 N	38·40 E
120	Dvůr Králové nad Labem (dvo͞or′ krä′lô-vā) . Czech.	50·28 N	15·43 E
142	Dwārka..................India	22·18 N	68·59 E
80	Dwight (dwīt)..............Ill.	41·00 N	88·20 W
128	Dyat'kovo (dyät′kō-vō)..Sov. Un.	53·36 N	34·19 E
75	Dyer (dī′ĕr)....Ind. (Chicago In.)	41·30 N	87·31 W
78	Dyersburg (dī′ĕrz-bûrg)....Tenn.	36·02 N	89·23 W
71	Dyersville (dī′ĕrz-vĭl).......Iowa	42·28 N	91·09 W
65	Dyes Inlet (dīz) Wash. (Seattle In.)	47·37 N	122·45 W
146	Dzabhan Gol (R.).........Mong.	48·19 N	94·08 E
150	Dzamiin Üüde............Mong.	44·38 N	111·32 E
167	Dzaoudzi (dzou′dzĭ) Comores, Arch. des	12·44 S	45·15 E
103	Dzaudzhikau (dzou-jĭ-kou′) Sov. Un.	48·00 N	44·52 E
129	Dzerzhinsk (dzhĕr-zhĭnsk′) Sov. Un.	48·24 N	37·58 E
128	Dzerzhinsk.............Sov. Un.	53·41 N	27·14 E
132	Dzerzhinsk.............Sov. Un.	56·20 N	43·50 E
134	Dzhalal-Abad (jȧ-läl′ȧ-bät′) Sov. Un.	41·13 N	73·35 E
134	Dzhambul (dzhäm-bo͝ol′) Sov. Un.	42·51 N	71·29 E
129	Dzhankoy (dzhän′koi)...Sov. Un.	45·43 N	34·22 E
136	Dzhetygara (dzhĕt′-gä′rȧ) Sov. Un. (Urals In.)	52·12 N	61·18 E
134	Dzhizak (dzhê′zäk)......Sov. Un.	40·13 N	67·58 E
135	Dzhugdzhur Khrebet (Mts.) (jo͝og-jo͞or′) . Sov. Un.	56·15 N	137·00 E
121	Działoszyce (jyä-wō-shē′tsĕ).. Pol.	50·21 N	20·22 E
92	Dzibalchén (zē-bäl-chĕ′n) Mex. (Yucatan In.)	19·25 N	89·39 W
93	Dzidzantún (zēd-zän-to͞o′n) Mex. (Yucatan In.)	21·18 N	89·00 W
120	Dzierzoniów (dzyĕr-zhôn′yŭt) . Pol.	50·44 N	16·38 E
92	Dzilam Gonzalez (zē-lä′m-gôn-zä′lĕz) . Mex. (Yucatan In.)	21·21 N	88·53 W
92	Dzitás (zē-tȧ′s) . Mex. (Yucatan In.)	20·47 N	88·32 W
92	Dzitbalché (dzēt-bäl-chā′) Mex. (Yucatan In.)	20·18 N	90·03 W
146	Dzungaria (Reg.) (dzo͝oŋ-gä′rĭ-ȧ) . China	44·39 N	86·13 E
64	Eagle (ē′g′l).............Alaska	64·42 N	141·20 W
77	Eagle...............Tex. (In.)	29·40 N	94·40 W
80	Eagle..................W. Va.	38·10 N	81·20 W
69	Eagle (R.)................Colo.	39·32 N	106·28 W
65	Eaglecliff (ē′g′l-klĭf) Wash. (Portland In.)	46·10 N	123·13 W
75	Eagle Cr..Ind. (Indianapolis In.)	39·54 N	86·17 W
74	Eagle Ford (ē′g′l fĕrd) Tex. (Dallas, Fort Worth In.)	32·47 N	96·52 W
71	Eagle Grove..............Iowa	42·39 N	93·55 W
82	Eagle Lake..............Maine	47·03 N	68·38 W
77	Eagle Lake................Tex.	29·37 N	96·20 W
66	Eagle L..................Calif.	40·45 N	120·52 W
74	Eagle Mountain L. Tex. (Dallas, Fort Worth In.)	32·56 N	97·27 W
76	Eagle Pass................Tex.	28·49 N	100·30 W
66	Eagle Pk.................Calif.	41·18 N	120·11 W
110	Ealing (ē′lĭng) . Eng. (London In.)	51·29 N	0·19 W
73	Earle (ûrl).................Ark.	35·14 N	90·28 W
78	Earlington (ûr′lĭng-tŭn).....S. C.	37·15 N	87·31 W
79	Easley (ēz′lĭ)..............S. C.	34·48 N	82·37 W
88	East, Mt. C. Z. (Panama Canal In.)	9·09 N	79·16 W
74	East Alton (ôl′tŭn) Ill. (St. Louis In.)	38·53 N	90·08 W
81	East Angus (ăŋ′gŭs)........Can.	45·35 N	71·40 W
75	East Aurora (ô-rō′rȧ) N. Y. (Buffalo In.)	42·46 N	78·38 W
77	East B...............Tex. (In.)	29·30 N	94·41 W
111	East Berlin (bĕr-lēn′) Ger. (Berlin In.)	52·31 N	13·28 E
78	East Bernstadt (bûrn′stȧt)...Ky.	37·09 N	84·08 W
65	Eastbound (ēst-bound) Wash. (Vancouver In.)	48·42 N	122·42 W
117	Eastbourne (ēst′bôrn).......Eng.	50·48 N	0·16 E
95	East Caicos (I.) (kī′kōs)...Caicos	21·40 N	71·35 W
159	East C...............N. Z. (In.)	37·37 S	178·33 E
	East Cape, see Dezhneva, Mys		
74	East Carondelet (kȧ-rŏn′dĕ-lĕt) Ill. (St. Louis In.)	38·33 N	90·14 W
75	East Chicago (shĭ-kô′gō) Ind. (Chicago In.)	41·39 N	87·29 W
147	East China Sea.............Asia	30·28 N	125·52 E
75	East Cleveland (klēv′lănd) Ohio (Cleveland In.)	41·33 N	81·35 W
77	East Cote Blanche B. (kōt bläɴsh′) . La.	29·30 N	92·07 W
71	East Des Moines (R.) (dē moin′) Iowa	42·57 N	94·17 W
75	East Detroit (dê-troit′) Mich. (Detroit In.)	42·28 N	82·57 W
	Easter (I.), see Rapa Nui		
120	Eastern Alps (Mts.)...Aus.-Switz.	47·03 N	10·55 E
143	Eastern Ghats (Mts.).......India	19·35 N	78·08 E
164	Eastern Region (Div.).......Nig.	6·00 N	7·00 E
146	Eastern Turkestan (Reg.) (to͝or-kĕ-stän′) (tûr-kĕ-stăn′) China	38·23 N	80·41 E
75	East Gary (gā′rĭ) Ind. (Chicago In.)	41·34 N	87·15 W
70	East Grand Forks (grănd fôrks) Minn.	47·56 N	97·02 W
84	East Greenwich (grĭn′ĭj) R. I. (Providence In.)	41·40 N	71·27 W
81	Easthampton (ēst-hămp′tŭn) Mass.	42·15 N	72·45 W
81	East Hartford (härt′fĕrd)...Conn.	41·45 N	72·35 W
67	East Helena (hĕ-lē′nȧ).....Mont.	46·31 N	111·50 W
110	East Ilsley (ĭl′slē) Eng. (London In.)	51·30 N	1·18 W
80	East Jordan (jôr′dăn)......Mich.	45·05 N	85·05 W
74	East Kansas City (kăn′zȧs) Mo. (Kansas City In.)	39·09 N	94·30 W
76	Eastland (ēst′lănd)..........Tex.	32·24 N	98·47 W
80	East Lansing (lăn′sĭng).....Mich.	42·45 N	84·30 W
74	East Leavenworth (lĕv′ĕn-wûrth) Mo. (Kansas City In.)	39·18 N	94·50 W
80	East Liverpool (lĭv′ĕr-po͞ol)..Ohio	40·40 N	80·35 W
167	East London (lŭn′dŭn) S. Afr. (Natal In.)	33·02 S	27·54 E
74	East Los Angeles (lōs ăŋ′hȧ-lās) Calif. (Los Angeles In.)	34·01 N	118·09 W
87	Eastmain (R.) (ēst′mān).....Can.	52·12 N	73·19 W
78	Eastman (ēst-măn)...........Ga.	32·10 N	83·11 W
84	East Millstone (mĭl′stōn) N. J. (New York In.)	40·30 N	74·35 W
71	East Moline (mô-lēn′)........Ill.	41·31 N	90·28 W
73	East Nishnabotna (R.) (nĭsh-nȧ-bŏt′nȧ) . Iowa	40·53 N	95·23 W
81	Easton (ēs′tŭn).............Md.	72·45 N	76·05 W
75	Easton (ēst′ŭn) Ohio (Cleveland In.)	40·57 N	81·45 W
81	Easton......................Pa.	40·45 N	75·15 W
84	Easton L...Conn. (New York In.)	41·18 N	73·17 W
84	East Orange (ŏr′ĕnj) N. J. (New York In.)	40·46 N	74·12 W
80	East Peoria (pē-ō′rĭ-ȧ)........Ill.	40·40 N	89·30 W
75	East Pittsburgh (pĭts′bûrg) Pa. (Pittsburgh In.)	40·24 N	79·50 W
84	East Point.....Ga. (Atlanta In.)	33·41 N	84·27 W
82	Eastport (ēst-pōrt)........Maine	44·53 N	67·01 W
84	East Providence (prŏv′ĭ-dĕns) R. I. (Providence In.)	41·49 N	71·22 W
110	East Retford (rĕt′fĕrd)......Eng.	53·19 N	0·56 W
110	East Riding (Co.) (rīd′ĭng)..Eng.	53·47 N	0·36 W
81	East Rochester (rŏch′ĕs-tĕr) . N. Y.	43·10 N	77·30 W
74	East St. Louis (sānt lo͞o′ĭs) (lo͞o-ĭ) Ill. (St. Louis In.)	38·38 N	90·10 W
130	East Siberian Sea (sī-bĭr′y′n) Sov. Un.	73·00 N	153·28 E
65	East Stanwood (stăn′wo͝od) Wash. (Seattle In.)	48·14 N	122·21 W
81	East Stroudsburg (stroudz′bûrg) Pa.	41·00 N	75·10 W
81	East Syracuse (sĭr′ȧ-kūs)...N. Y.	43·05 N	76·00 W
69	East Tavaputs Plat. (tă-vă′-pŭts) Utah	39·25 N	109·45 W
80	East Tawas (tô′wăs).......Mich.	44·15 N	83·30 W
85	Eastview (ēst′vyo͞o) Can. (Ottawa In.)	45·27 N	75·39 W
68	East Walker (R.) (wôk′ĕr)...Nev.	38·36 N	119·02 W
75	Eaton (ē′tŭn)..............Colo.	40·31 N	104·42 W
80	Eaton.....................Ohio	39·45 N	84·40 W
75	Eaton.......Ohio (Cleveland In.)	41·19 N	82·01 W
80	Eaton Rapids (răp′ĭdz).....Mich.	42·30 N	84·40 W
78	Eatonton (ē′tŭn-tŭn).........Ga.	33·20 N	83·24 W
84	Eatontown (ē′tŭn-toun) N. J. (New York In.)	40·18 N	74·04 W
71	Eau Claire (ō klâr′).........Wis.	44·47 N	91·32 W
118	Ebeltoft (ĕ′bĕl-tŭft).........Den.	56·11 N	10·39 E
111	Ebersberg (ĕ′bĕrs-bĕrgh) Ger. (Munich In.)	48·05 N	11·58 E
120	Ebingen (ā′bĭng-ĕn).........Ger.	48·13 N	9·04 E
146	Ebi Nuur (L.) (ā′bê).......China	45·09 N	83·15 E
126	Eboli (ĕb′ô-lē)...............It.	40·38 N	15·04 E
164	Ebolowa..................Cam.	2·54 N	11·09 E
111	Ebreichsdorf....Aus. (Vienna In.)	47·58 N	16·24 E
125	Ebro, Río (R.) (rê′-ô-ā′brō)...Sp.	41·22 N	0·17 W
110	Eccles (ĕk′′lz)..............Eng.	53·29 N	2·20 W
80	Eccles..................W. Va.	37·45 N	81·10 W
110	Eccleshall (ĕk′′lz-hôl).......Eng.	52·51 N	2·15 W
127	Eceabat (Maidos)...........Tur.	40·10 N	26·21 E
155	Echague (ā-chä′gwā) Phil. (Manila In.)	16·43 N	121·40 E
93	Echandi, Cerro (Mt.) (sĕ′r-rô-ĕ-chä′nd) . Pan.	9·05 N	82·51 W
74	Echo Bay (ĕk′ō) Can. (Sault Ste. Marie In.)	46·29 N	84·04 W
123	Echternach (ĕk′tĕr-näk).....Lux.	49·48 N	6·25 E
160	Echuca (ê-cho͝o′kȧ)........Austl.	36·10 S	144·47 E
124	Écija (ā′thê-hä)..............Sp.	37·20 N	5·07 W
120	Eckernförde................Ger.	54·27 N	9·51 E
84	Eclipse (ê-klĭps′) . Va. (Norfolk In.)	36·55 N	76·29 W
75	Ecorse (ê-kôrs′) Mich. (Detroit In.)	42·15 N	83·09 W
96	Ecuador (ĕk′wȧ-dôr)........S. A.	0·00 N	78·30 W
165	Edd......................Eth.	13·57 N	41·37 E
165	Ed Dāmer (ĕd dä′mĕr)......Sud.	17·38 N	33·57 E
165	Ed Debba (dĕb′ȧ)...........Sud.	18·04 N	30·58 E
165	Ed Dueim (do͝o-ām′)........Sud.	13·56 N	32·22 E
78	Eddyville (ĕd′ĭ-vĭl)...........Ky.	37·03 N	88·03 W
164	Edéa (ĕ-dā′ä)..............Cam.	3·45 N	10·08 E
74	Eden (ē′d′n) Calif. (Los Angeles In.)	33·54 N	117·05 W
74	Eden...Utah (Salt Lake City In.)	41·18 N	111·49 W
116	Eden (R.) (ē′dĕn)...........Eng.	54·40 N	2·35 W
110	Edenbridge (ē′dĕn-brĭj) Eng. (London In.)	51·11 N	0·05 E
110	Edenham (ē′d′n-ăm)........Eng.	52·46 N	0·25 W
74	Eden Prairie (prâr′ĭ) Minn. (Minneapolis, St. Paul In.)	44·51 N	93·29 W
79	Edenton (ē′dĕn-tŭn)........N. C.	36·02 N	76·37 W
75	Edenton....Ohio (Cincinnati In.)	39·14 N	84·02 W
167	Edenvale (ēd′ĕn-vāl)......S. Afr. (Johannesburg & Pretoria In.)	29·06 S	28·10 E
168	Edenville (ē′d′n-vĭl) S. Afr. (Johannesburg & Pretoria In.)	27·33 S	27·42 E
120	Eder R. (ā′dĕr).............Ger.	51·05 N	8·52 E
164	Edeyen, Erg (Dunes) (ĕ-dā′yĕn) Alg.	27·30 N	7·30 E
79	Edgefield (ĕj′fēld)..........S. C.	33·52 N	81·55 W
70	Edgeley (ĕj′lĭ).............N. D.	46·24 N	98·43 W
70	Edgemont (ĕj′mŏnt)........S. D.	43·19 N	103·50 W
71	Edgerton (ĕj′ĕr-tŭn).........Wis.	42·49 N	89·06 W
84	Edgewater (ĕj-wô-tĕr) Ala. (Birmingham In.)	33·31 N	86·52 W
84	Edgewater...Md. (Baltimore In.)	38·58 N	76·35 W
127	Édhessa...................Grc.	40·48 N	22·04 E
74	Edina (ê-dī′nȧ) Minn. (Minneapolis, St. Paul In.)	44·55 N	93·20 W
73	Edina......................Mo.	40·10 N	92·11 W
80	Edinburg (ĕd′′n-bûrg).......Ind.	39·20 N	85·55 W
76	Edinburg..................Tex.	26·18 N	98·08 W
116	Edinburgh (ĕd′′n-bŭr-ô).....Scot.	55·57 N	3·10 W
127	Edirne (Adrianople) (ĕ-dĭr′nĕ) (ā-drĭ-ăn-ō′p′l) . Tur.	41·41 N	26·35 E
79	Edisto, (R.) (ĕd′ĭs-tō).......S. C.	33·10 N	80·50 W
79	Edisto (R.), North Fk.......S. C.	33·42 N	81·24 W
79	Edisto (R.), South Fk.......S. C.	33·43 N	81·35 W
79	Edisto Island..............S. C.	32·32 N	80·20 W
73	Edmond (ĕd′mŭnd)........Okla.	35·39 N	97·29 W
65	Edmonds (ĕd′mŭndz) Wash. (Seattle In.)	47·49 N	122·23 W
85	Edmonton..Can. (Edmonton In.)	53·30 N	113·45 W
82	Edmundston (ĕd′mŭn-stŭn)..Can.	47·23 N	68·20 W
77	Edna (ĕd′nȧ)...............Tex.	28·59 N	96·39 W
127	Edremit (ĕd-rĕ-mēt′).........Tur.	39·35 N	27·00 E
127	Edremit Körfezi (G.)........Tur.	39·28 N	26·35 E
86	Edson (ĕd′sŭn).............Can.	53·40 N	116·40 W

PRONOUNCING INDEX

Edward–Ems-Weser 203

Page	Name Pronunciation Region	Lat. °′	Long. °′
71	Edward (I.) (ĕd'wẽrd) Can.	48·21 N	88·29 W
166	Edward (L.) Con. K.	0·15 S	28·32 E
74	Edwardsville (ĕd'wẽrdz-vĭl) Ill. (St. Louis In.)	38·49 N	89·58 W
75	Edwardsville . Ind. (Louisville In.)	38·17 N	85·53 W
74	Edwardsville Kans. (Kansas City In.)	39·04 N	94·49 W
66	Eel R. (ēl) Calif.	40·39 N	124·15 W
80	Eel (R.) Ind.	40·50 N	85·55 W
159	Efate (I.) (å-fä'tā) New Hebr.	18·02 S	168·29 E
71	Effigy Mounds Natl. Mon. (ĕf'ĭ-jŭ mounds) Iowa	43·04 N	91·15 W
80	Effingham (ĕf'ĭng-hăm) Ill.	39·05 N	88·30 W
124	Ega (R.) (ā'gä) Sp.	42·40 N	2·20 W
126	Egadi, Isole (Is.) (ē'sō-lĕ-ĕ'gä-dē) It.	38·01 N	12·00 E
124	Egea de los Caballeros (å-kā'å dā lōs kä-bäl-yā'rōs) Sp.	42·07 N	1·05 W
64	Egegik (ĕg'ĕ-jĭt) Alaska	58·10 N	157·22 W
121	Eger (ĕ gĕr) Hung.	47·53 N	20·24 E
	Eger, see Ohre R.		
118	Egersund (ĕ'ghĕr-sŏŏn') Nor.	58·29 N	6·01 E
81	Egg Harbor (ĕg här'bẽr) N. J.	39·30 N	74·35 W
110	Egham (ĕg'ŭm) Eng. (London In.)	51·24 N	0·33 W
146	Egiin Gol (R.) (å-gēn') Mong.	49·41 N	100·40 E
159	Egmont, C. (ĕg'mŏnt) N. Z. (In.)	39·18 S	173·49 E
133	Egridir Gölü (L.) (ā-rĭ-dĭr') Tur.	38·10 N	30·00 E
122	Eguilles (ĕ-gwē') Fr. (Marseille In.)	43·34 N	5·21 E
	Egypt, see United Arab Republic		
124	Eibar (ā'ê-bär) Sp.	43·12 N	2·20 W
120	Eichstätt (īk'shtät) Ger.	48·54 N	11·14 E
111	Eichwalde (īĸ'väl-dĕ) Ger. (Berlin In.)	52·22 N	13·37 E
118	Eid (īdh) Nor.	61·54 N	6·01 E
118	Eidsberg (īdhs'bĕrgh) Nor.	59·32 N	11·16 E
118	Eidsvoll (īdhs'vôl) Nor.	60·19 N	11·15 E
120	Eifel (Plat.) (ī'fĕl) Ger.	50·08 N	6·30 E
168	Eil Som. (Horn of Afr. In.)	7·53 N	49·45 E
139	Eilat Jordan (Palestine In.)	29·34 N	34·57 E
120	Eilenburg (ī'lĕn-bŏŏrgh) Ger.	51·27 N	12·38 E
167	Eilliot S. Afr. (Natal In.)	31·19 S	27·52 E
120	Einbeck (īn'bĕk) Ger.	51·49 N	9·52 E
117	Eindhoven (īnd'hō-vĕn) Neth.	51·29 N	5·20 E
98	Eirunepé (ā-rōō-nĕ-pĕ') Braz.	6·37 S	69·58 W
120	Eisenach (ī'zĕn-äĸ) Ger.	50·58 N	10·18 E
120	Eisenhuttenstadt Ger.	52·08 N	14·40 E
120	Eisleben (īs'lā'bĕn) Ger.	51·31 N	11·33 E
118	Ejdfjord (ĕīd'fyōr) Nor.	60·28 N	7·04 E
91	Ejutla de Crespo (å-hōōt'lä dā krās'pō) Mex.	16·34 N	96·44 W
119	Ekenäs (Tammisaari) (ĕ'kĕ-nâs) (tåm'ĭ-sä'rĭ) Fin.	59·59 N	23·25 E
111	Ekeren Bel. (Brussels In.)	51·17 N	4·27 E
85	Ekhart (ĕk'årt) Can. (Winnipeg In.)	50·08 N	97·26 W
118	Eksjö (ĕk'shû) Swe.	57·41 N	14·55 E
165	El Abyad, Bahr (R.) (White Nile) (bär ĕl ä-byäd') Sud.	14·09 N	32·27 E
125	El Affroun (ĕl åf-froun') Alg	36·28 N	2·38 E
164	El Aiún (ĕl å-ē-ōō'n) Sp. Sah.	26·45 N	13·15 W
167	Elands (R.) S. Afr. (Natal In.)	31·48 S	26·09 E
168	Elands R. (ê'lånds) S. Afr. (Johannesburg & Pretoria In.)	25·11 S	28·52 E
165	El Arab, Buhr (R.) Sud.	9·46 N	26·52 E
124	El Arahal (ĕl ä-rä-äl') Sp.	37·17 N	5·32 W
114	El Asnam (Orléansville) Alg.	36·14 N	1·32 E
139	El 'Auja (ăl oujå) Isr.-U. A. R. (Palestine In.)	30·53 N	34·28 E
133	Elâzıg (ĕl-ä'zêz) Tur.	38·30 N	39·10 E
165	El Azrag, Bahr (R.) (Blue Nile) (bär ĕläz-räk') Sud.	13·59 N	33·45 E
78	Elba (ĕl'bȧ) Ala.	31·25 N	86·01 W
126	Elba, Isola di (I.) (ê-sō-lä-dē-ĕl'bȧ) It.	42·42 N	10·25 E
98	El Banco (ĕl băn'cô) Col.	8·58 N	74·01 W
124	El Barco (ĕl bär'kô) Sp.	42·26 N	6·58 W
127	Elbasan (ĕl-bä-sän'') Alb.	41·08 N	20·05 E
114	El Bayadh Alg.	33·42 N	1·06 E
	Elbe, see Labe R.		
120	Elbe R. (ĕl'bĕ) Ger.	53·47 N	9·20 E
69	Elbert, Mt. (ĕl'bẽrt) Colo.	39·05 N	106·25 W
78	Elberton (ĕl'bẽr-tŭn) Ga.	34·05 N	82·53 W
122	Elbeuf (ĕl-bûf') Fr.	49·16 N	0·59 E
133	Elbistan (ēl-bē-stän') Tur.	38·20 N	37·10 E
121	Elblag (ĕl'blăŋg) Pol.	54·11 N	19·25 E
124	El Bonillo (ĕl bō-nēl'yô) Sp.	38·56 N	2·31 W
94	Elbow Cay (I.) Ba. Is.	26·25 N	77·55 W
70	Elbow Lake Minn.	46·00 N	95·59 W
85	Elbow R. (ĕl'bō). Can. (Calgary In.)	51·03 N	114·24 W
133	El'brus, Gora (Mt.) (ĕl'brŏŏs') Sov. Un.	43·20 N	42·25 E
168	El Buheirat el Murrat el Kubra (Great Bitter). U. A R. (Suez In.)	30·24 N	32·27 E
168	El Buheirat el Murrat el Sughra (Little Bitter). U. A. R. (Suez In.)	30·10 N	32·36 E
168	El Bur Som. (Horn of Afr. In.)	4·35 N	46·40 E
133	Elburz Mts. (ĕl'bŏŏrz') Iran	36·30 N	51·00 E
68	El Cajon Calif. (San Diego In.)	32·48 N	116·58 W
98	El Cajon (ĕl-kä-kô'n) Col. (In.)	4·50 N	76.35 W
99	El Cambur (käm-bōōr'). Ven. (In.)	10·24 N	68·06 W
77	El Campo (kăm'pō) Tex.	29·13 N	96·17 W
101	El Carmen (kȧ'r-mĕn) Chile (Santiago In.)	34·14 S	71·23 W
98	El Carmen (kȧ'r-mĕn) Col.	9·54 N	75·12 W
74	El Casco (kăs'kô) Calif. (Los Angeles In.)	33·59 N	117·08 W
68	El Centro (sĕn'trô) Calif.	32·47 N	115·33 W
65	El Cerrito (sĕr-rē'tō) Calif. (San Francisco In.)	37·55 N	122·19 W
125	Elche (ĕl'chā) Sp.	38·15 N	0·42 W
92	El Cuyo Mex. (Yucatan In.)	21·30 N	87·42 W
125	Elda (ĕl'dä) Sp.	38·28 N	0·44 W
120	Elde R. (ĕl'dĕ) Ger.	53·11 N	11·30 E
168	El Dilingat U. A. R. (Nile In.)	30·48 N	30·32 E
164	El Djouf (Des.) (ĕl djōōf) Mauritania	21·38 N	7·44 W
71	Eldon (ĕl-dŭn) Iowa	40·55 N	92·15 W
73	Eldon Mo.	38·21 N	92·36 W
65	Eldon Wash. (Seattle In.)	47·33 N	123·02 W
71	Eldora (ĕl-dō'rȧ) Iowa	42·21 N	93·08 W
73	El Dorado (ĕl dô-rä'dō) Ark.	33·13 N	92·39 W
80	Eldorado Ill.	37·50 N	88·30 W
73	El Dorado Kans.	37·49 N	96·51 W
73	Eldorado Springs (sprĭngz) Mo.	37·51 N	94·02 W
165	Eldoret (ĕl-dô-rĕt') Ken.	00·31 N	35·18 E
90	El Ebano (ā-bä'nō) Mex.	22·13 N	98·26 W
72	Electra (ê-lĕk'trȧ) Tex.	34·02 N	98·54 W
67	Electric Pk. (ê-lĕk'trĭk) Mont.	45·03 N	110·52 W
136	Elektrogorsk (ĕl-yĕk'trô-gôrsk) Sov. Un. (Moscow In.)	55·53 N	38·48 E
136	Elektrostal (ĕl-yĕk'trô-stål) Sov. Un. (Moscow In.)	55·47 N	38·27 E
69	Elephant Butte Res. (ĕl'ê-fănt būt). N. Mex.	33·25 N	107·10 W
125	El Escorial (ĕl-ĕs-kô-ryä'l) Sp. (Madrid In.)	40·38 N	4·08 W
92	El Espino (ĕl-ĕs-pē'nŏ) Nic.	13·26 N	86·48 W
95	Eleuthera (I.) (ê-lū'thẽr-ȧ) Ba. Is.	25·05 N	76·10 W
95	Eleuthera Pt. Ba. Is.	24·35 N	76·05 W
73	Eleven Point (R.) (ê-lĕv'ĕn) Mo.	36·53 N	91·39 W
165	El Fāsher (fä'shẽr) Sud.	13·38 N	25·21 E
124	El Ferrol (fā-rōl') Sp.	43·30 N	8·12 W
75	Elgin (ĕl'jĭn) Ill. (Chicago In.)	42·03 N	88·16 W
70	Elgin Nebr.	41·58 N	98·04 W
66	Elgin Ore.	45·34 N	117·58 W
116	Elgin Scot.	57·40 N	3·30 W
77	Elgin Tex.	30·21 N	97·22 W
65	Elgin Wash. (Seattle In.)	47·23 N	122·42 W
85	Elgin Mills (mĭls) Can. (Toronto In.)	43·54 N	79·26 W
164	El Goléa (gô-lā-ä') Alg.	30·39 N	2·52 E
165	Elgon, Mt. (ĕl'gŏn) Ken.	1·07 N	34·37 E
90	El Grullo (grōōl-yô) Mex.	19·46 N	104·10 W
99	El Guapo (gwȧ'pô) Ven. (In.)	10·07 N	66·00 W
114	El Hamada (Plat.) (häm'ä-dä) Alg.	30·53 N	1·52 W
164	El Hank (Bluffs) Mauritania-Mali	23·44 N	6·45 W
99	El Hatillo (ä-tē'l-yô) Ven. (In.)	10·08 N	65·13 W
85	Elic (ē'lē) Can. (Winnipeg In.)	49·55 N	97·45 W
166	Elila (R.) (ĕ-lē'lȧ) Con. K.	3·38 S	27·48 E
65	Elisa (I.) (ê-lĭ'sȧ) Wash. (Vancouver In.)	48·43 N	122·37 W
	Élisabethville, see Lubumbashi		
119	Elisenvaara (ā-lē'sĕn-vä'rȧ) Sov. Un.	61·25 N	29·46 E
77	Elizabeth (ê-lĭz'ȧ-bĕth) La.	30·50 N	92·47 W
84	Elizabeth N. J. (New York In.)	40·40 N	74·13 W
75	Elizabeth Pa. (Pittsburgh In.)	40·16 N	79·53 W
79	Elizabeth City N. C.	36·15 N	76·15 W
79	Elizabethton (ê-lĭz-ȧ-bĕth'tŭn) Tenn.	36·19 N	82·12 W
80	Elizabethtown (ê-lĭz'ȧ-bĕth-toun) Ky.	37·40 N	85·55 W
164	El Jadida Mor.	33·14 N	8·34 W
121	Ełk (ĕlk) Pol.	53·53 N	22·23 E
78	Elk (R.) Tenn.	35·05 N	86·36 W
80	Elk (R.) W. Va.	38·30 N	81·05 W
165	El Kāmlīn (käm-lēn') Sud.	15·09 N	33·06 E
72	Elk City (ĕlk) Okla.	35·23 N	99·23 W
165	El Khandaq (ĸän-dåk') Sud.	18·38 N	30·29 E
80	Elkhart (ĕlk'härt) Ind.	41·40 N	86·00 W
72	Elkhart Kans.	37·00 N	101·54 W
77	Elkhart Tex.	31·38 N	95·35 W
71	Elkhorn (ĕlk'hôrn) Wis.	42·39 N	88·32 W
70	Elkhorn (R.) Nebr.	42·06 N	97·46 W
79	Elkin (ĕl'kĭn) N. C.	36·15 N	80·50 W
81	Elkins (ĕl'kĭnz) W. Va.	38·55 N	79·50 W
86	Elk Island Natl. Park (ĕlk ī'lănd) Can.	53·21 N	115·47 W
66	Elko (ĕl'kō) Nev.	40·51 N	115·46 W
70	Elk Point S. D.	42·41 N	96·41 W
80	Elk Rapids (răp'ĭdz) Mich.	44·55 N	85·25 W
66	Elk River (rĭv'ẽr) Idaho	46·47 N	116·11 W
71	Elk River Minn.	45·17 N	93·33 W
78	Elkton (ĕlk'tŭn) Ky.	36·47 N	87·08 W
81	Elkton Md.	39·35 N	75·50 W
70	Elkton S. D.	44·15 N	96·28 W
168	El Lagodei Som. (Horn of Afr. In.)	9·20 N	49·09 E
110	Elland (el'ănd) Eng.	53·41 N	1·50 W
69	Ellen, Mt. (ĕl'ĕn) Utah	38·05 N	110·50 W
70	Ellendale (ĕl'ĕn-dāl) N. D.	46·01 N	98·33 W
66	Ellensburg (ĕl'ĕnz-bûrg) Wash.	47·00 N	120·31 W
81	Ellenville (ĕl'ĕn-vĭl) N. Y.	41·40 N	74·25 W
85	Ellerslie (ĕl'ẽrz-lê) Can. (Edmonton In.)	53·25 N	113·30 W
110	Ellesmere (ĕlz'mẽr) Eng.	52·55 N	2·54 W
49	Ellesmere I. Can.	81·00 N	80·00 W
110	Ellesmere Port Eng.	53·17 N	2·54 W
156	Ellice Is. (ĕl'lês) Oceania	5·20 S	174·00 E
84	Ellicott City (ĕl'ĭ-kŏt sĭ'tê) Md. (Baltimore In.)	39·16 N	76·48 W
75	Ellicott Cr. N. Y. (Buffalo In.)	43·00 N	78·46 W
167	Elliotdale (ĕl-ĭ ŏt'dāl) S. Afr. (Natal In.)	31·58 S	28·42 E
65	Elliott (el'ĭ-ŭt). Wash. (Seattle In.)	47·28 N	122·08 W
72	Ellis (ĕl'ĭs) Kans.	38·56 N	99·34 W
78	Ellisville (ĕl'ĭs-vĭl) Miss.	31·37 N	89·10 W
74	Ellisville Mo. (St. Louis In.)	38·35 N	90·35 W
72	Ellsworth (ĕlz'wûrth) Kans.	38·43 N	98·14 W
82	Ellsworth Maine	44·33 N	68·26 W
47	Ellsworth Highland Ant.	77·00 S	90·00 W
120	Ellwangen (ĕl'väŋ-gĕn) Ger.	48·57 N	10·08 E
111	Elm (ĕlm) Ger. (Hamburg In.)	53·31 N	9·13 E
70	Elm (R.) S. D.	45·47 N	98·28 W
80	Elm (R.) W. Va.	38·30 N	81·05 W
66	Elma (ĕl'mȧ) Wash.	47·02 N	123·20 W
114	El Maadid Mor.	31·32 N	4·30 W
73	Elm Cr. Tex.	33·34 N	97·03 W
164	El Memrhar Mauritania	19·30 N	16·18 W
74	Elmendorf (ĕl'mĕn-dôrf) Tex. (San Antonio In.)	29·16 N	98·20 W
164	El Meréié (Des.) Mauritania	19·45 N	8·00 W
74	Elm Fork (ĕlm fôrk) Tex. (Dallas, Fort Worth In.)	32·55 N	96·56 W
75	Elmhurst (ĕlm'hûrst) Ill. (Chicago In.)	41·54 N	87·56 W
81	Elmira (ĕl-mī'rȧ) N. Y.	42·05 N	76·50 W
81	Elmira Heights N. Y.	42·10 N	76·50 W
98	El Misti (Vol.) (mē's-tē) Peru	16·04 S	71·20 W
74	El Modena (mô-dē'nô) Calif. (Los Angeles In.)	33·47 N	117·48 W
74	El Monte (mōn'tȧ) Calif. (Los Angeles In.)	34·04 N	118·02 W
69	El Morro Natl. Mon. N. Mex.	35·05 N	108·20 W
111	Elmshorn (ĕlms'hôrn) Ger. (Hamburg In.)	53·45 N	9·39 E
75	Elmwood Place (ĕlm'wŏŏd plās) Ohio (Cincinnati In.)	39·11 N	84·30 W
165	El Nahud (nä'hŏŏd) Sud.	12·39 N	28·18 E
165	El Obeid (ô-bād') Sud.	13·15 N	30·15 E
165	El Odaiya (ô-dī'yȧ) Sud.	12·06 N	28·16 E
65	Elokomin (R.) (ê-lō'kô-mĭn) Wash. (Portland In.)	46·16 N	123·16 W
90	El Oro (ô-rô) Mex.	19·49 N	100·04 W
164	El Oued (wĕd') Alg.	33·23 N	6·49 E
98	El Pao (ĕl pȧ'ō) Ven.	8·08 N	62·37 W
92	El Paraíso (pä-rä-ē'sō) Hond.	13·55 N	86·35 W
125	El Pardo (pä'r-dô) Sp. (Madrid In.)	40·31 N	3·47 W
76	El Paso (pas'ō) Tex.	31·47 N	106·27 W
99	El Pilar (pē-lä'r) Ven. (In.)	9·56 N	64·48 W
93	El Porvenir (pôr-vȧ-nēr') Pan.	9·34 N	78·55 W
124	El Puerto de Sta. María (pwĕr tō dā sän tä mä-rē'ä) Sp.	36·36 N	6·18 W
93	El Real (rā-äl) Pan.	8·07 N	77·43 W
72	El Reno (rē'nō) Okla.	35·31 N	97·57 W
99	El Roboré (rô-bō-rĕ') Bol.	18·23 S	59·43 W
71	Elroy (ĕl'roi) Wis.	43·44 N	90·17 W
74	Elsah (ĕl'zȧ) Ill. (St. Louis In.)	38·57 N	90·22 W
90	El Salto (säl'tō) Mex.	22·48 N	105·22 E
88	El Salvador N. A.	14·00 N	89·30 W
92	El Sauce (ĕl-sȧ'ŏŏ-sĕ) Nic.	13·00 N	86·40 W
73	Elsberry (ēlz'bĕr-ĭ) Mo.	39·09 N	90·44 W
123	Elsdorf (ĕls'dōrf) Ger. (Ruhr In.)	50·56 N	6·35 E
74	El Segundo (sêgŭn'dō) Calif. (Los Angeles In.)	33·55 N	118·24 W
74	Elsinore (ĕl'sĭ-nôr) Calif. (Los Angeles In.)	33·40 N	117·19 W
74	Elsinore L. Calif. (Los Angeles In.)	33·38 N	117·21 W
111	Elstorf (ĕls'tōrf) Ger. (Hamburg In.)	53·25 N	9·48 E
165	El Sudd (Swp.) Sud.	8·45 N	30·45 E
161	Eltham (ĕl'thăm) Austl. (Melbourne In.)	37·43 S	145·08 E
98	El Tigre (tē'grĕ) Ven.	8·49 N	64·15 W
133	El'ton (L.) Sov. Un.	49·10 N	47·00 E
74	El Toro (tō'rō) Calif. (Los Angeles In.)	33·37 N	117·42 W
92	El Triunfo (ĕl-trē-ōō'n-fô) Hond.	13·06 N	87·00 W
92	El Triunfo Sal.	13·17 N	88·32 W
145	Eluru India	16·44 N	80·09 E
69	El Vado Res. N. Mex.	36·37 N	106·30 W
124	Elvas (ĕl'väzh) Port.	38·53 N	7·11 W
118	Elverum (ĕl'vĕ-rŏŏm) Nor.	60·53 N	11·33 E
92	El Viego (ĕl-vyĕ'ĸŏ) Nic.	12·44 N	87·03 W
92	El Viejo (Vol.) Nic.	12·44 N	87·03 W
73	Elvins (ĕl'vĭnz) Mo.	37·49 N	90·31 W
165	El Wak (wäk') Ken.	3·00 N	41·00 E
75	Elwood (ĕl'wŏŏd) Ill. (Chicago In.)	41·24 N	88·07 W
80	Elwood Ind.	40·15 N	85·50 W
117	Ely (ē'lĭ) Eng.	52·25 N	0·17 E
71	Ely Minn.	47·54 N	91·53 W
68	Ely Nev.	39·16 N	114·53 W
75	Elyria (ê-lĭr'ĭ-ȧ) Ohio (Cleveland In.)	41·22 N	82·07 W
119	Ema (R.) (å'mȧ) Sov. Un.	58·25 N	27·00 E
118	Emån (R.) Swe.	57·15 N	15·46 E
133	Emba (R.) (yĕm'bȧ) Sov. Un.	46·50 N	54·10 E
80	Embarrass (R.) (ĕm-băr'ăs) Ill.	39·15 N	88·05 W
85	Embrun (ĕm'brŭn) Can. (Ottawa In.)	45·16 N	75·17 W
123	Embrun (äɴ-brûɴ') Fr.	44·35 N	6·32 E
120	Emden (ĕm'dĕn) Ger.	53·21 N	7·15 E
159	Emerald (ĕm'ẽr-ăld) Austl.	28·34 S	148·00 E
86	Emerson (ĕm'ẽr-sŭn) Can.	49·00 N	97·18 W
65	Emeryville (ĕm'ẽr-ĭ-vĭl) Calif. (San Francisco In.)	37·50 N	122·17 W
165	Emi Koussi (Mtn.) (ā'mê ĸōō-sē') Chad	19·50 N	18·30 E
126	Emilia (Reg.) (ā-mēl'yä) It.	44·35 N	10·48 E
91	Emiliano Zapata (ĕ-mē-lyȧ'nô-zä-pȧ'tȧ). Mex.	17·45 N	91·46 W
80	Eminence (ĕm'ĭ-nĕns) Ky.	38·25 N	85·15 W
155	Emirau (I.) (ā-mê-rä'ŏŏ) N. Gui. Ter.	1·40 S	150·28 E
117	Emmen (ĕm'ĕn) Neth.	52·48 N	6·55 E
123	Emmerich (ĕm'ẽr-ĭk) Ger. (Ruhr In.)	51·51 N	6·16 E
71	Emmetsburg (ĕm'ĕts-bûrg) Ia.	43·07 N	94·41 W
66	Emmett (ĕm'ĕt) Idaho	43·53 N	116·30 W
67	Emmons Mt. (ĕm'ŭnz) Utah	40·43 N	110·20 W
76	Emory Pk. (ĕ'mŏ-rē pēk) Tex.	29·13 N	103·20 W
126	Empoli (ām'pô-lē) It.	43·43 N	10·55 E
73	Emporia (ĕm-pō'rĭ-ȧ) Kans.	38·24 N	96·11 W
79	Emporia Va.	37·40 N	77·34 W
81	Emporium (ĕm-pō'rĭ-ŭm) Pa.	41·30 N	78·15 W
	Empty Quarter, see Ar Al Khālī		
120	Ems R. (ĕms) Ger.	52·52 N	7·16 E
120	Ems-Weser (Can.) (vā'zĕr) Ger.	52·23 N	8·11 E

ng-sing; ŋ-baŋk; ɴ-nasalized n; nŏd; cŏmmit; ōld; ôbey; ôrder; fōōd; fŏŏt; ou-out; s-soft; sh-dish; th-thin; pūre; ûnite; ûrn; stŭd; circŭs; ü-as "y" in study; '-indeterminate vowel.

Page	Name Pronunciation Region	Lat. °′	Long. °′
118	Enånger (ĕn-ôŋ′gĕr) ... Swe.	61·36 N	16·55 E
88	Encantada, Cerro de la (Mtn.) (sĕ′r-rô-dĕ-lä-ĕn-kän-tä′dä) Mex.	31·58 N	115·15 W
155	Encanto Pt. (ĕn-kän′tō) Phil. (Manila In.)	15·44 N	121·46 E
100	Encarnación (ĕn-kär-nä-syōn′) Par.	27·26 S	55·52 W
90	Encarnación de Diaz (ĕn-kär-nä-syōn dȧ dē′ȧz) . Mex.	21·34 N	102 15 W
76	Encinal (ĕn′sĭ-nôl) ... Tex.	28·02 N	99·22 W
98	Encontrados (ĕn-kōn-trä′dōs) Ven.	9·01 N	72·10 W
160	Encounter B. (ĕn-koun′tẽr) . Austl.	35·50 S	138·45 E
139	Endau ... Mala. (Singapore In.)	2·39 N	103·38 E
139	Endau (R.) . Mala. (Singapore In.)	2·29 N	103·40 E
156	Enderbury (I.) (ĕn′dẽr-bûrĭ) Oceania	2·00 S	170·50 W
47	Enderby Land (Reg.) (ĕn′dĕr bĭ) Ant.	72·00 S	52·00 E
70	Enderlin (ĕn′dẽr-lĭn) ... N. D.	46·38 N	97·37 W
81	Endicott (ĕn′dĭ-kŏt) ... N. Y.	42·05 N	76·00 W
64	Endicott Mts. ... Alaska	67·30 N	153·45 W
127	Enez ... Tur.	40·42 N	26·05 E
81	Enfield (ĕn′fēld) ... Conn.	41·55 N	72·35 W
110	Enfield ... Eng. (London In.)	51·38 N	0·06 W
79	Enfield ... N. C.	36·10 N	77·41 W
95	Engano, Cabo (C.) (kȧ′-bô-ĕn-gä-nô) . Dom. Rep.	18·40 N	68·30 W
154	Engaño, C. (ĕn-gän′yō) ... Phil.	18·40 N	122·45 E
165	Engare Vaso Nyiro R. (ĕn-gä′rā wä′sô nyē′rô) . Ken.	0·59 N	37·47 E
167	Engcobo (ĕŋg-cô-bô) S. Afr. (Natal In.)	31·41 S	27·59 E
133	Engel's (ĕn′gēls) ... Sov. Un.	51·20 N	45·40 E
123	Engelskirchen (ĕn′gĕls-kẽr′ĸĕn) Ger. (Ruhr In.)	50·59 N	7·25 E
72	Engelwood (ĕn′g′l-wo͝od) ... Colo.	39·39 N	105·00 W
154	Enggano (ĕng-gä′nō) ... Indon.	5·22 S	102·18 E
73	England (ĭŋ′glănd) ... Ark.	34·33 N	91·58 W
116	England (Reg.) (ĭŋ′glănd) . . U. K.	51·35 N	1·40 W
83	Englee (ĕn-glee) ... Can.	50·46 N	56·07 W
80	English (ĭn′glĭsh) ... Ind.	38·15 N	86·25 W
87	English (R.) ... Can.	50·31 N	94·12 W
113	English Chan. ... Eng.	49·45 N	3·06 W
125	Enguera (ān′gārä) ... Sp.	38·58 N	0·42 W
72	Enid (ē′nĭd) ... Okla.	36·25 N	97.52 W
78	Enid Res. ... Miss.	34·13 N	89·47 W
166	Enkeldoorn (ĕŋ′k′l-do͞orn) ... Rh.	19·59 S	30·58 E
168	Enkeldoring (ĕŋ′k′l-dôr-ĭng) S. Afr. (Johannesburg & Pretoria In.)	25·24 S	28·43 E
118	Enköping (ĕn′kû-pĭng) ... Swe.	59·39 N	17·05 E
165	Ennedi Plat. (ĕn-nĕd′ē) ... Chad.	17·15 N	22·45 W
116	Ennis (ĕn′ĭs) ... Ire.	52·54 N	9.05 W
77	Ennis ... Tex.	32·20 N	96·38 W
116	Enniscorthy (ĕn-ĭs-kôr′thĭ) ... Ire.	52·33 N	6·27 W
116	Enniskillen (ĕn-ĭs-kĭl′ĕn) ... N. Ire.	54·20 N	7·25 W
120	Enns R. (ĕns) ... Aus.	47·37 N	14·35 E
79	Enoree (ē-nō′rē) ... S. C.	34·43 N	81·58 W
79	Enoree, (R.) ... S. C.	34·35 N	81·55 W
95	Enriquillo (ĕn-rē-kē′l-yô) Dom. Rep.	17·55 N	71·15 W
95	Enriquillo, Lago (L.) (lä′gô-ĕn-rē-kē′l-yô) . Dom. Rep.	18·35 N	71·35 W
117	Enschede (ĕns′ĸȧ-dĕ) ... Neth.	52·10 N	6·50 E
88	Ensenada (ĕn-sĕ-nä′dä) ... Mex.	32·00 N	116·30 W
101	Enseñada . Arg. (Buenos Aires In.)	34·50 S	57·55 W
151	Enshih ... China	30·18 N	109·25 E
153	Enshū-Nada (Sea) (ĕn′sho͞o nä-dä) . Jap.	34·25 N	137·14 E
165	Entebbe (ĕn-tĕb′ē) ... Ug.	0·01 N	32·29 E
78	Enterprise (ĕn′tẽr-prīz) ... Ala.	31·20 N	85·50 W
66	Enterprise ... Ore.	45·25 N	117·16 W
66	Entiat, L ... Wash.	45·43 N	120·11 W
122	Entraygues (ĕɴ-trĕg′) ... Fr.	44·39 N	2·33 E
100	Entre Ríos (Prov.) (ĕn-trā rē′ōs) Arg.	31·30 S	59·00 W
164	Enugu (ĕ-no͞o′go͞o) ... Nig.	6·13 N	7·18 E
65	Enumclaw (ĕn′ŭm-klô) Wash. (Seattle In.)	47·12 N	121·59 W
98	Envigado (ĕn-vē-gȧ′dō) . . Col. (In.)	6·10 N	75·34 W
126	Eolie, Isole (Is.) (ē′sō-lĕ-ĕ-ô′lyĕ) . It.	38·43 N	14·43 E
127	Epeirus (Reg.) ... Grc.	39·35 N	20·45 E
122	Epernay (ā-pĕr-nĕ′) ... Fr.	49·02 N	3·54 E
123	Épernon (ā-pĕr-nôɴ′) Fr. (Paris In.)	48·36 N	1·41 E
69	Ephraim (ē′frȧ-ĭm) ... Utah	39·20 N	111·40 W
66	Ephrata (ē frā′tȧ) ... Wash.	47·18 N	119·35 W
159	Epi (ā′pē) ... New Hebr.	16·59 S	168·29 E
124	Épila (ā′pē-lä) ... Sp.	41·38 N	1·15 W
123	Épinal (ā-pē-nȧl′) ... Fr.	48·11 N	6·27 E
139	Episkopi B. Cyprus (Palestine In.)	34·34 N	32·41 E
110	Epping (ĕp′ĭng) . Eng. (London In.)	51·41 N	0·06 E
166	Epping . . . S. Afr. (Cape Town In.)	33·56 S	18·35 E
110	Epworth (ĕp′wûrth) ... Eng.	53·31 N	0·50 W
163	Equatorial Guinea ... Afr.	2·20 N	7·37 E
122	Equeurdreville (ā-kûr-dr′vēl′) . . Fr.	49·38 N	1·42 W
85	Eramosa R. (ĕr-ȧ-mō′sȧ) Can. (Toronto In.)	43·39 N	80·08 W
165	Erba (Mt.) (ĕr′bȧ) ... Sud.	20·53 N	36·45 E
115	Erciyas (Mtn.) ... Tur.	38·30 N	35·36 E
74	Erda (ẽr′dä) Utah (Salt Lake City In.)	40·41 N	112·17 W
111	Erding (ĕr′dēng) Ger. (Munich In.)	48·19 N	11·54 E
100	Erechim (ĕ-rĕ-shē′ɴ) ... Braz.	27·43 S	52·11 W
133	Ereğli (ĕ-rȧ′ĭ-le) ... Tur.	37·40 N	34·00 E
133	Ereğli ... Tur.	41·15 N	31·25 E
120	Erfurt (ĕr′fo͝ort) ... Ger.	50·59 N	11·04 E
127	Ergene (R.) (ĕr′gĕ-nĕ) ... Tur.	41·17 N	26·50 E
124	Erges (R.) (ĕr′-zhĕs) ... Port.-Sp.	39·45 N	7·01 W
148	Erhlangtien (ē′läng′diän) ... China	31·33 N	114·07 E
124	Eria (R.) (ā-rē′ä) ... Sp.	42·10 N	6·08 W
72	Erick (âr′ĭk) ... Okla.	35·14 N	99·51 W
73	Erie (ē′rĭ) ... Kans.	37·35 N	95·17 W
81	Erie ... Pa.	42·05 N	80·05 W
63	Erie, L. ... U. S.-Can.	42·15 N	81·25 W
152	Erimo Saki (C.) (ā′rē-mō sä-kē) Jap.	41·53 N	143·20 E
85	Erin (ĕ′rĭn) ... Can. (Toronto In.)	43·46 N	80·04 W
165	Eritrea (Reg.) (ā-rē-trā′ȧ) ... Eth.	16·15 N	38·30 E
120	Erlangen (ĕr′läng-ĕn) ... Ger.	49·36 N	11·03 E
75	Erlanger (ẽr′lăng-ẽr) Ky. (Cincinnati In.)	39·01 N	84·36 W
	Ermoúpolis, see Síros		
143	Ernakulam ... India	9·58 N	76 23 E
116	Erne, Upper, Lough (B.) (lŏĸ ûrn) . N. Ire.	54·20 N	7·24 W
116	Erne, Lough (B.) ... N. Ire.	54·30 N	7·40 W
159	Eromanga (I.) ... New Hebr.	18·58 S	169·18 E
77	Eros (ē′rōs) ... La.	32·23 N	92·22 W
165	Er Renk (ẽr rĕnk′) ... Sud.	11·45 N	32·53 E
114	Er Ricani ... Mor.	31·09 N	4·20 W
116	Errigal, Mt. (ĕr-ĭ-gôl′) ... Ire.	54·60 N	8·13 W
165	Er Roseires (rô-sā′rĕs) ... Sud.	11·38 N	34·42 E
123	Erstein (ĕr′shtīn) ... Fr.	48·27 N	7·40 E
79	Erwin (ûr′wĭn) ... N. C.	35·16 N	78·40 W
79	Erwin ... Tenn.	36·07 N	82·25 W
120	Erzgebirge (Ore Mts.) (ĕrts′gĕ-bē′gĕ) . Ger.	50·29 N	12·40 E
133	Erzincan (ĕr-zĭn-jän′) ... Tur.	39·50 N	39·30 E
133	Erzurum (ĕrz′ro͞om′) ... Tur.	39·55 N	41·10 E
152	Esashi (ĕs′ä-shē) ... Jap.	41·50 N	140·10 E
118	Esbjerg (ĕs′byĕrgh) ... Den.	55·29 N	8·25 E
119	Esbo (ĕs′bô) ... Fin.	60·13 N	24·41 E
124	Escairón (ĕs-kī-rô′n) ... Sp.	42·34 N	7.40 W
69	Escalante (ĕs-kȧ-lăn′tē) ... Utah	37·50 N	111·40 W
69	Escalante (R.) ... Utah	37·40 N	111·20 W
78	Escambia (R.) (ĕs-kăm′bĭ-ȧ) . . Fla	30·38 N	87·20 W
71	Escanaba (ĕs-kȧ-nô′bȧ) ... Mich.	45·44 N	87·05 W
71	Escanaba (R.) ... Mich.	46·10 N	87·22 W
123	Esch-sur-Alzette ... Lux.	49·32 N	6·21 E
120	Eschwege (ĕsh′vā-gē) ... Ger.	51·11 N	10·02 E
123	Eschweiler (ĕsh′vī-lẽr) Ger. (Ruhr In.)	50·49 N	6·15 E
95	Escocesá, Bahia (B.) (bä-ē′ä-ĕs-kō-sĕ′sä) . Dom. Rep.	19·25 N	69·40 W
68	Escondido (ĕs-kŏn-dē′dō) ... Calif.	33·07 N	117·07 W
76	Escondido, Rio (R.) (rē′ō-ĕs-kōn-dē′dô) . Mex.	28·30 N	100·45 W
93	Escondido R ... Nic.	12·04 N	84·09 W
93	Escudo de Veraguas I. (ĕs-ko͞o′dä dā vā-rä′gwäs) . Pan.	9·07 N	81·25 W
90	Escuinapa (ĕs-kwē-nä′pä) ... Mex.	22·49 N	105·44 W
92	Escuintla (ĕs-kwēn′tlä) ... Guat.	14·16 N	90·47 W
91	Escuintla ... Mex.	15·20 N	92·45 W
93	Ese, Cayos de (I.) ... Col.	12·24 N	81·07 W
164	Eséka (ĕ-sā′kȧ) ... Cam.	3·40 N	11·08 E
144	Esfahān ... Iran	32·38 N	51·30 E
124	Esgueva (R.) (ĕs-gĕ′vä) ... Sp.	41·48 N	4·10 W
167	Eshowe (ĕsh′ô-wē) S. Afr. (Natal In.)	28·54 S	31·28 E
80	Eskdale (ĕsk′dāl) ... W. Va.	38·05 N	81·25 W
112	Eskifjördhur (ĕs′kē-fyŭr′do͞or) . Ice.	65·04 N	14·01 W
118	Eskilstuna (ȧ′shēl-stü-na) ... Swe.	59·23 N	16·28 E
86	Eskimo L. (es′kĭ-mō) ... Can.	69·29 N	129·57 W
133	Eskişehir (ĕs-kē-shĕ′h′r) ... Tur.	39·40 N	30·20 E
74	Esko (ĕs′kô) . . Minn. (Duluth In.)	46·27 N	92·22 W
124	Esla (R.) (ĕs-lä) ... Sp.	41·50 N	5·48 W
118	Eslöv (ĕs′lûv) ... Swe.	55·50 N	13·17 E
98	Esmeraldas (ĕs-mȧ-räl′däs) ... Ec.	0·58 N	79·45 W
95	Espada, Punta (Pt.) (po͞o′n-tä-ĕs-pä′dä) . Dom. Rep.	18·30 N	68·30 W
87	Espanola (ĕs-pȧ-nō′lȧ) ... Can.	46·11 N	81·59 W
93	Esparta (ĕs-pär′tä) ... C. R.	9·59 N	84·40 W
158	Esperance (ĕs′pē-răns) ... Austl.	33·45 S	122·07 E
94	Esperenza (ĕs-pĕ-rä′n-zä) ... Cuba	22·30 N	80·10 W
125	Espichel, Cabo (C.) (kȧ′bō-ĕs-pē-shĕl′) . Port. (Lisbon In.)	38·25 N	9·13 W
98	Espinal (ĕs-pē-näl′) ... Col. (In.)	4·10 N	74·53 W
99	Espinhaço, Serra do (Mts.) (sĕ′r-rä-dô-ĕs-pē-nȧ-sô) . Braz.	16·06 S	44·56 W
101	Espinillo, Punta (Pt.) (po͞o′n-tä-ĕs-pē-nē′l-yô) Ur. (Buenos Aires In.)	34·49 S	56·27 W
99	Espirito Santo (ĕs-pē′rē-tô-sȧn′tô) . Braz.	20·27 S	40·18 W
99	Espírito Santo (State) ... Braz.	19·57 S	40·58 W
92	Espíritu Santo, Bahia del (B.) (bä-ē′ä-dĕl-ĕs-pē′rē-to͞o-sän′tô) Mex. (Yucatan In.)	19·25 N	87·28 W
159	Espiritu Santo (I.) (ĕs-pē′rē-to͞o sän′tō) . New Hebr.	15·45 S	166·50 E
92	Espita (ĕs-pē′tä) Mex. (Yucatan In.)	20·57 N	88·22 W
124	Esposende (ĕs-pō-zĕn′dā) ... Port.	41·33 N	8·45 W
100	Esquel (ĕs-kĕ′l) ... Arg.	42·47 S	71·22 W
65	Esquimalt (ĕs-kwī′mŏlt) Can. (Seattle In.)	48·26 N	123·25 W
164	Essaouira ... Mor.	31·34 N	9·44 W
111	Essen ... Bel. (Brussels In.)	51·28 N	4·27 E
123	Essen (ĕs′sĕn) . . . Ger. (Ruhr In.)	51·26 N	6·59 E
99	Essequibo (R.) (ĕs-ā-kē′bō) . . . Guy.	4·26 N	58·17 W
75	Essex (ĕs′ĕks) . . Can. (Detroit In.)	42·10 N	82·50 W
75	Essex ... Ill. (Chicago In.)	41·11 N	88·11 W
84	Essex ... Md. (Baltimore In.)	39·19 N	76·29 W
83	Essex ... Mass. (Boston In.)	42·38 N	70·47 W
81	Essex ... Vt.	44·30 N	73·05 W
84	Essex Fells (ĕs′ĕks fĕlz) N. J. (New York In.)	40·50 N	74·16 W
80	Essexville (ĕs′ĕks-vĭl) ... Mich.	43·35 N	83·50 W
120	Esslingen (ĕs′slēn-gĕn) ... Ger.	48·45 N	9·19 E
62	Estacado, Llano (Plain) (yȧ-nō ĕs-tȧ-cȧ-dō′) . U. S.	33·50 N	103·20 W
100	Estados, Isla de los ... S. A.	55·05 S	63·00 W
99	Estância (ĕs-tän′sĭ-ä) ... Braz.	11·17 S	37·18 W
124	Estarreja (ĕs-tär-rā′zhä) ... Port.	40·44 N	8·39 W
167	Estcourt (ĕst-coort) S. Afr. (Natal In.)	29·04 S	29·53 E
126	Este (ĕs′tā) ... It.	45·13 N	11·40 E
92	Estelí (ĕs-tā-lē′) ... Nic.	13·10 N	86·23 W
124	Estella (ĕs-tāl′yä) ... Sp.	42·40 N	2·01 W
124	Estepa (ĕs-tā′pä) ... Sp.	37·18 N	4·54 W
124	Estepona (ĕs-tȧ-pō′nä) ... Sp.	36·26 N	5·08 W
68	Esteros, B. (ĕs-tā′rōs) ... Calif.	35·22 N	121·04 W
86	Estevan (ĕ-stē′văn) ... Can.	49·11 N	102·57 W
71	Estherville (ĕs′tẽr-vĭl) ... Iowa	43·24 N	94·49 W
79	Estill (ĕs′tĭl) ... S. C.	32·46 N	81 15 W
130	Estonian S. S. R. (ĕs-tō′nĭ-ä) Sov. Un.	59·10 N	25·00 E
125	Estoril (ĕs-tô-rēl′) Port. (Lisbon In.)	38·45 N	9·24 W
100	Estrêla (R.) (ĕs-trĕ′lȧ) . Braz. (In.)	22·39 S	43·16 W
124	Estrêla, Serra da (Mts.) (sĕr′rȧ dä ĕs-trā′lȧ) . Port.	40·25 N	7 45 W
124	Estremadura (Reg.) (ĕs-trā-mä-do͞o′rȧ) . Port.	41·35 N	8·36 W
124	Estremoz (ĕs-trā-mōzh′) ... Port.	38·50 N	7·35 W
99	Estrondo, Serra do (Mts.) (sĕr′rȧ do͞o ĕs-trôn′do͞o) . Braz.	9·52 S	48·56 W
121	Esztergom (ĕs′tẽr-gōm) ... Hung.	47·46 N	18·45 E
49	Etah (ē′tă) ... Grnld.	78·20 N	72·42 W
123	Étampes (ā-täɴp′) . Fr. (Paris In.)	48·26 N	2·09 E
122	Étaples (ā-täp′l′) ... Fr.	50·32 N	1·38 E
85	Etchemin, R. (ĕch′ĕ-mĭn) Can. (Quebec In.)	46·39 N	71·03 W
163	Ethiopia (ē-thē-ō′pē-ȧ) ... Afr.	7·53 N	37·55 E
74	Etiwanda (ĕ-tĭ-wän′dȧ) Calif. (Los Angeles In.)	34·07 N	117·31 W
	Etlatongo, see San Mateo		
75	Etna (ĕt′nȧ) . . Pa. (Pittsburgh In.)	40·30 N	79·55 W
126	Etna, Mt. (Vol.) ... It.	37·48 N	15·00 E
85	Etobicoke Cr . . Can. (Toronto In.)	43·44 N	79·48 W
64	Etolin Str. (ĕt ō lĭn) ... Alaska	60·35 S	165·40 W
166	Etosha Pan (ētō′shä) . . . S. W. Afr.	19·07 S	15·30 E
78	Etowah (ĕt′ô-wä) ... Tenn.	35·18 N	84·31 W
78	Etowah (R.) ... Ga.	34·23 N	84·19 W
123	Étréchy (ā-trā-shē′) . Fr. (Paris In.)	48·29 N	2·12 E
111	Etten ... Neth. (Amsterdam In.)	51·34 N	4·38 E
111	Etterbeek (ĕt′ẽr-bāk) Bel. (Brussels In.)	50·51 N	4·24 E
90	Etzatlán (ĕt-zä-tlän′) ... Mex.	20·44 N	104·04 W
158	Eucla (ū′klȧ) ... Austl.	31·45 S	128·50 E
75	Euclid (ū′klĭd) Ohio (Cleveland In.)	41·34 N	81·32 W
73	Eudora (u-dō′rȧ) ... Ark.	33·07 N	91·16 W
78	Eufaula (û-fô′lȧ ... Ala.	31·53 N	85·09 W
73	Eufaula ... Okla.	35·16 N	95·35 W
66	Eugene (û-jēn′) ... Ore.	44·02 N	123·06 W
74	Euless (ū′lĕs) Tex. (Dallas, Fort Worth In.)	32·50 N	97·05 W
77	Eunice (ū′nĭs) ... La.	30·30 N	92·25 W
117	Eupen (oi′pĕn) ... Bel.	50·39 N	6·05 E
144	Euphrates, R. (û-frā′tēz) ... Asia	35·52 N	39·53 E
122	Eure (R.) (ûr) ... Fr.	49·03 N	1·22 E
66	Eureka (û-rē′kȧ) ... Calif.	40·45 N	124·10 W
73	Eureka ... Kans.	37·48 N	96·17 W
66	Eureka ... Mont.	48·53 N	115·07 W
68	Eureka ... Nev.	39·33 N	115·58 W
70	Eureka ... S. D.	45·46 N	99·38 W
69	Eureka ... Utah	39·55 N	112·10 W
73	Eureka Springs ... Ark.	36·24 N	93·43 W
144	Eurgun (Mtn.) ... Iran	28·47 N	57·00 E
7	Europe (ū′rŭp)		
79	Eustis (ūs′tĭs) ... Fla.	28·50 N	81·41 W
78	Eutaw (ū-tȧ) ... Ala.	32·48 N	87·50 W
118	Evanger (ĕ-väŋ′gĕr) ... Nor.	60·40 N	6·06 E
75	Evanston (ĕv′ănz-tūn) Ill. (Chicago In.)	42·03 N	87·41 W
67	Evanston ... Wyo.	41·17 N	111·02 W
80	Evansville (ĕv′ănz-vĭl) ... Ind.	38·00 N	87·30 W
71	Evansville ... Wis.	42·46 N	89·19 W
80	Evart (ĕv′ẽrt) ... Mich.	43·55 N	85·10 W
168	Evaton (ĕv′ȧ-tŏn) ... S. Afr. (Johannesburg & Pretoria In.)	26·32 S	27·53 E
71	Eveleth (ĕv′ē-lĕth) ... Minn.	47·27 N	92·35 W
158	Everard (L.) (ĕv′ẽr-ȧrd) ... Austl.	36·20 S	134·10 E
158	Everard Ra. ... Austl.	27·15 S	132·00 E
142	Everest, Mt. (ĕv′ẽr-ĕst) Nep.-China	32·58 N	86·57 E
83	Everett (ĕv′ẽr-ĕt) Mass. (Boston In.)	42·24 N	71·03 W
65	Everett (ĕv′ẽr-ĕt) Wash. (Seattle In.)	47·59 N	122·11 W
87	Everett Mts. ... Can.	62·34 N	68·00 W
79	Everglades (ĕv′ẽr-glādz) . Fla. (In.)	25·50 N	81·25 W
94	Everglades, The (Swp.) ... Fla.	25·35 N	80·55 W
79	Everglades Natl. Park . . Fla. (In.)	25·39 N	80·57 W
78	Evergreen (ĕv′ẽr-grēn) ... Ala.	31·25 N	87·56 W
75	Evergreen Park . . Ill. (Chicago In.)	41·44 N	87·42 W
74	Everman (ĕv′ẽr-măn) Tex. (Dallas, Fort Worth In.)	32·38 N	97·17 W
65	Everson (ĕv′ẽr-sŭn) Wash. (Vancouver In.)	48·55 N	122·21 W
124	Évora (ĕv′ô-rä) ... Port.	38·35 N	7·54 W
122	Évreux (ā-vrû′) ... Fr.	49·02 N	1·11 E
127	Evrotas (R.) (ĕv-rō′täs) ... Grc.	37·15 N	22·17 E
127	Evvoia (Pen.) ... Grc.	38·38 N	23·45 E
157	Ewa (ē′wä) ... Hawaii (In.)	21·17 N	158·03 E
155	Ewab, Palau-Palan Is. ... Indon.	5·55 S	131·30 E
74	Excelsior (ĕk-sel′sĭ-ŏr) Minn. (Minneapolis, St. Paul In.)	44·54 N	93·35 W
73	Excelsior Springs ... Mo.	39·20 N	94·13 W
116	Exe (R.) (ĕks) ... Eng.	50·57 N	3·37 W
68	Exeter (ĕk′sē-tẽr) ... Calif.	36·18 N	119·09 W
116	Exeter ... Eng.	50·45 N	3·33 W
81	Exeter ... N. H.	43·00 N	71·00 W
116	Exmoor (ĕks′mo͝or) ... Eng.	51·10 N	3·55 W
116	Exmouth (ĕks′mŭth) ... Eng.	50·40 N	3·20 W
158	Exmouth, G. ... Austl.	21·45 S	114·30 E
83	Exploits (R.) (ĕks-ploits′) ... Can.	48·50 N	56·15 W
90	Extórrax (R.) (ĕx-tó′rȧx) ... Mex.	21·04 N	99·39 W
101	Extrema (ĕsh-trĕ′mä) Braz. (Rio de Janeiro In.)	22·52 S	46·19 W

ăt; finăl; rāte; senȧte; ärm; ȧsk; sofȧ; fâre; ch-choose; dh-as th in other; bē; ēvent; bĕt; recĕnt; cratẽr; g-go; gh-guttural g; bĭt; ĭ-short neutral; rīde; ĸ-guttural k as ch in German ich;

PRONOUNCING INDEX Extremadura–Finch 205

Page	Name Pronunciation Region	Lat. °′	Long. °′
124	Extremadura (Reg.) (ĕks-trā-mä-doo'rä) . Sp.	38·43 N	6·30 W
95	Exuma Sd. (ĕk-sōō'mä) . . . . Ba. Is.	24·20 N	76·20 W
166	Eyasi (L.) (ā-yä'sē) . . . . Tan.	3·41 S	34·14 E
112	Eyja Fd. . . . . Ice.	66·21 N	18·20 W
112	Eyrarbakki . . . . Ice.	63·51 N	20·52 W
158	Eyre (âr) . . . . Austl.	32·15 S	126·20 E
160	Eyre (L.) . . . . Austl.	28·43 S	137·50 E
158	Eyre Pen. . . . . Austl.	33·30 S	136·00 E
100	Ezeiza (ĕ-zā'zä) . . . . Arg. (In.)	34·36 S	58·31 W
127	Ezine (å'zĭ-nā) . . . . Tur.	39·47 N	26·18 E
76	Fabens (fā'bĕnz) . . . . Tex.	31·30 N	106·07 W
118	Fåborg (fô'bôrg) . . . . Den.	55·06 N	10·19 E
126	Fabriano (fä-brē-ä'nô) . . . . It.	43·20 N	12·55 E
98	Facatativá (fä-kä-tä-tē-vá') Col (In.)	4·49 N	74·09 W
165	Fada (fä'dä) . . . . Chad	17·06 N	21·18 E
164	Fada N'Gourma (fä'dä'’n gōōr'mä) . Upper Volta	12·11 N	00·21 E
135	Faddeya (I.) (fåd-yä') . . . Sov. Un.	76·12 N	145·00 E
118	Faemund (L.) (fä'mōōn') . . . . . Nor.	62·17 N	11·40 E
126	Faenza (fä-ĕnd'zä) . . . . It.	44·16 N	11·53 E
112	Faeroe Is. (fâ'rō) . . . . Eur.	61·53 N	5·58 W
168	Fafan R. . . . Eth. (Horn of Afr. In.)	8·15 N	42·40 E
124	Fafe (fä'fä) . . . . Port.	41·30 N	8·10 W
127	Făgăras (fă-gă'rash) . . . . Rom.	45·50 N	24·55 E
118	Fagerness (fä'ghĕr-nĕs) . . . . . . Nor.	61·00 N	9·10 E
100	Fagnano (fäk-nä'nō) (L.) Arg.-Chile	54·35 S	68·20 W
164	Faial I. (fä-yä'l) . . . . . Açores (In.)	38·40 N	29·19 W
168	Fā'id (fä-yēd') . U. A. R. (Suez In.)	30·19 N	32·18 E
116	Fair (I.) (fâr) . . . . Scot.	59·34 N	1·41 W
64	Fairbanks (fâr'bănks) . . . . . Alaska	64·50 N	147·48 W
80	Fairbury (fâr'bĕr-ĭ) . . . . Ill.	40·45 N	88·25 W
73	Fairbury . . . . Nebr.	40·09 N	97·11 W
85	Fairchild Cr. (fâr'chīld) Can. (Toronto In.)	43·18 N	80·10 W
71	Fairfax (fâr'făks) . . . . Minn.	44·29 N	94·44 W
79	Fairfax . . . . S. C.	32·29 N	81·13 W
84	Fairfax . Va. (Washington D.C. In.)	38·51 N	77·20 W
84	Fairfield (fâr'fēld) Ala. (Birmingham In.)	33·30 N	86·50 W
161	Fairfield . . . . . . Austl. (Sydney In.)	33·52 S	150·57 E
84	Fairfield . . . Conn. (New York In.)	41·08 N	73·22 W
80	Fairfield . . . . Ill.	38·25 N	88·20 W
71	Fairfield . . . . Iowa	41·00 N	91·59 W
82	Fairfield . . . . Maine	44·35 N	69·38 W
81	Fairhaven (fâr-hā'vĕn) . . . . . . Mass.	41·35 N	70·55 W
81	Fair Haven . . . . Vt.	43·35 N	73·15 W
71	Fairmont . . . . Minn.	43·39 N	94·26 W
81	Fairmont . . . . W. Va.	39·30 N	80·10 W
74	Fairmont City . . Ill. (St. Louis In.)	38·39 N	90·05 W
80	Fairmount . . . . Ind.	40·25 N	85·45 W
74	Fairmount Kans. (Kansas City In.)	39·12 N	95·55 W
74	Fairmount . Mo. (Kansas City In.)	39·06 N	94·28 W
84	Fair Oaks (fâr ōks) Ga. (Atlanta In.)	33·56 N	84·33 W
81	Fairport (fâr'pōrt) . . . . N. Y.	43·05 N	77·30 W
80	Fairport Harbor . . . . Ohio	41·45 N	81·15 W
75	Fairview (fâr'vū) Ohio (Cleveland In.)	41·27 N	81·52 W
72	Fairview . . . . Okla.	36·16 N	98·28 W
65	Fairview . . . . . . Ore. (Portland In.)	45·32 N	122·26 W
69	Fairview . . . . Utah	39·35 N	111·30 W
64	Fairweather, Mt. (fâr-wĕdh'ēr) Can.	59·12 N	137·22 W
70	Faith (fāth) . . . . S. D.	45·02 N	120·02 W
142	Faizābād . . . . India	26·50 N	82·17 E
165	Fajao (fä-jä'ō) . . . . Ug.	2·13 N	31·44 E
89	Fajardo . . . P. R. (Puerto Rico In.)	18·20 N	65·40 W
155	Fakfak . . . . W. Irian	2·56 S	132·25 E
142	Fakiragram . . . . India	26·28 N	90·16 E
150	Fak'u . . . . China	42·28 N	123·20 E
151	Falalise, C. . . . . Viet.	19·20 N	106·18 E
99	Falcón (fäl-kô'n) (State) . Ven. (In.)	11·00 N	68·28 W
81	Falconer (fô'k'n-ēr) . . . . N. Y.	42·10 N	79·10 W
74	Falcon Heights (fô'k'n) Minn. (Minneapolis, St. Paul In.)	44·59 N	93·10 W
76	Falcon Res. (fôk'n) . . . . Tex.	26·47 N	99·03 W
164	Faleme R. (fà-lā-mä') . Mali-Senegal	13·15 N	11·27 W
129	Faleshty (fä-lăsh'tĭ) . . . . . Sov. Un.	47·33 N	27·46 E
76	Falfurrias (făl'fōō-rē'ás) . . . . . . Tex.	27·15 N	98·08 W
118	Falkenberg (fäl'kĕn-bĕrgh) . . . Swe.	56·54 N	12·25 E
111	Falkensee (fäl'kĕn-zā) Ger. (Berlin In.)	52·34 N	13·05 E
111	Falkenthal (fäl'kĕn-täl) Ger. (Berlin In.)	52·54 N	13·18 E
116	Falkirk (fôl'kûrk) . . . . Scot.	55·59 N	3·55 W
100	Falkland Is. (fôk'lănd) . . . . . . S. A.	50·45 S	61·00 W
118	Falköping (fäl'chûp-ĭng) . . . . . Swe.	58·09 N	13·30 E
65	Fall City . . . . . Wash. (Seattle In.)	47·34 N	121·53 W
75	Fall Cr. (fôl) Ind. (Indianapolis In.)	39·52 N	86·04 W
68	Fallon (făl'ŭn) . . . . Nev.	39·30 N	118·48 W
84	Fall River . Mass. (Providence In.)	41·42 N	71·07 W
84	Falls Church (fălz chûrch) Va. (Washington D.C. In.)	38·53 N	77·10 W
73	Falls City . . . . Nebr.	40·04 N	95·37 W
84	Fallston (făls'tŏn) Md. (Baltimore In.)	39·32 N	76·26 W
116	Falmouth (făl'mŭth) . . . . Eng.	50·08 N	3·04 W
94	Falmouth . . . . Jam.	18·30 N	77·40 W
80	Falmouth . . . . Ky.	38·40 N	84·20 W
166	False B. (Valsbaai) S. Afr. (Cape Town In.)	34·14 S	18·35 E
143	False Divi Pt. . . . . India	20·43 N	81·06 E
95	Falso, Cabo (C.) (kä'bō-fäl-sō) Dom. Rep.	17·45 N	71·55 W
118	Falster (I.) (fäls'tĕr) . . . . Den.	54·43 N	12·16 E
121	Fălticeni (fŭl-tē-chān'y') . . . . Rom.	47·27 N	26·17 E
118	Falun (fä-lōōn') . . . . Swe.	60·38 N	15·35 E
115	Famagusta (fä-mä-gōōs'tä) . Cyprus	35·08 N	33·59 E
100	Famatina, Sierra de (Mts.) (sē-ĕ'r-rä-dĕ-fä-mä-tē'-nä) . Arg.	29·00 S	67·50 W
151	Fan Ching Shan (Mts.) . . . . China	26·46 N	107·42 E
151	Fanghsien . . . . China	32·05 N	110·45 E
157	Fanning (I.) (făn'ĭng) Gilbert & Ellice Is.	4·20 N	159·00 W
85	Fannystelle (făn'ĭ-stĕl) Can. (Winnipeg In.)	49·45 N	97·46 W
126	Fano (fä'nō) . . . . It.	43·49 N	13·01 E
118	Fanø (I.) (făn'û) . . . . Den.	55·24 N	8·10 E
167	Farafangana (fä-rä-fäŋ-gä'nä) Malag. Rep.	21·18 S	47·59 E
165	Farâfra (Oasis) (fà-rä'frà) . U. A. R.	27·04 N	28·13 E
144	Farah (fä-rä') . . . . Afg.	32·15 N	62·13 E
90	Farallón, Punta (Pt.) (pōō'n-tä-fä-rä-lōn) . Mex.	19·21 N	105·03 W
164	Faranah (fä-rä'nä) . . . . Gui.	10·02 N	10·52 W
165	Farasan Dahlak Arch. . . . . Eth.	16·45 N	41·08 E
115	Faras R. . . . . Libya	30·18 N	17·19 E
115	Faregh, Wadi al (R.) (wädē ĕl fä-rĕg') . Libya	30·10 N	19·34 E
159	Farewell, C. (fâr-wĕl') . N. Z. (In.)	40·37 S	171·46 E
70	Fargo (fär'gō) . . . . N. D.	46·53 N	96·48 W
84	Far Hills (fär hĭlz) N. J. (New York In.)	40·41 N	74·38 W
71	Faribault (fâ'rĭ-bō) . . . . Minn.	44·19 N	93·16 W
124	Farilhoes (Is.) (fä-rē-lyônzh') Port.	39·28 N	9·32 W
160	Farina (fà-rē'nȧ) . . . . Austl.	30·03 S	138·20 E
110	Faringdon (fâ'rĭng-dŏn) Eng. (London In.)	51·38 N	1·35 W
168	Fārīskūr (fä-rēs-kōōr') U. A. R. (Nile In.)	31·19 N	31·46 E
165	Farit, Amba (Mt.) . . . . Eth.	10·51 N	37·52 E
121	Farkašd (fär'käsht) . . . . Czech.	48·00 N	17·43 E
74	Farley (fär'lē) Mo. (Kansas City In.)	39·16 N	94·49 W
74	Farmers Branch (fär'mērz brănch) Tex. (Dallas, Fort Worth In.)	32·56 N	96·53 W
80	Farmersburg (fär'mērz-bûrg) . Ind.	39·15 N	87·25 W
73	Farmersville (fär'mērz-vĭl) . . . Tex.	33·11 N	96·22 W
84	Farmingdale (färm'ĕng-dāl) N. J. (New York In.)	40·11 N	74·10 W
84	Farmingdale N. Y. (New York In.)	40·44 N	73·26 W
83	Farmingham (färm-ĭng-hăm) Mass. (Boston In.)	42·17 N	71·25 W
73	Farmington (färm-ĭng-tŭn) . . . . Ill.	40·42 N	90·01 W
82	Farmington . . . . Maine	44·40 N	70·10 W
75	Farmington . . . Mich. (Detroit In.)	42·28 N	83·23 W
73	Farmington . . . . Mo.	37·46 N	90 26 W
69	Farmington . . . . N. Mex.	36·40 N	108·10 W
74	Farmington Utah (Salt Lake City In.)	40·59 N	111·53 W
79	Farmville (färm-vĭl) . . . . N. C.	35·35 N	77·35 W
79	Farmville . . . . Va.	37·15 N	78·23 W
110	Farnborough (färn'bŭr-ô) Eng. (London In.)	51·15 N	0·45 W
116	Farne (I.) (färn) . . . . Eng.	55·40 N	1·32 W
81	Farnham (fär'nȧm) . . . . Can.	45·15 N	72·55 W
110	Farningham (fär'nĭng-ŭm) . . . Eng.	51·22 N	0·14 E
110	Farnworth (färn'wŭrth) . . . . . Eng.	53·34 N	2·24 W
99	Faro (fä'rōō) . . . . Braz.	2·05 S	56·32 W
124	Faro . . . . Port.	37·01 N	7·57 W
118	Fåron (I.) . . . . Swe.	57·57 N	19·10 E
158	Farquhar, C. (fär'kwȧr) . . . . Austl.	23·50 S	112·55 E
80	Farrell (făr'ĕl) . . . . Pa.	41·10 N	80·30 W
142	Farrukhābād (fŭ-rōōk-hä-bäd') India	27·29 N	79·35 E
127	Fársala (Pharsalus) . . . . Grc.	39·18 N	22·25 E
118	Farsund (fär'sōōn) . . . . Nor.	58·05 N	6·47 E
100	Fartura, Serra da (Mts.) (sĕ'r-rä-dä-fär-tōō'rä) . Braz.	26·40 S	53·15 W
49	Farvel, Kap (C.) . . . . Grnld.	60·00 N	44·00 W
72	Farwell (fär'wĕl) . . . . Tex.	34·24 N	103·03 W
144	Fasā (fŭ-sä') . . . . Iran	28·59 N	53·44 E
127	Fasano (fä-zä'nō) . . . . It.	40·50 N	17·22 E
129	Fastov (fäs'tôf) . . . . Sov. Un.	50·04 N	29·57 E
129	Fatëzh . . . . Sov. Un.	52·06 N	35·51 E
124	Fatima . . . . Port.	39·36 N	9·36 E
133	Fatsa (fät'sä) . . . . Tur.	40·50 N	37·30 E
123	Faucilles, Monts (Mts.) (môɴ' fō-sēl') . Fr.	48·07 N	6·13 E
126	Favara (fä-vä'rä) . . . . It.	37·19 N	13·50 E
123	Faverolles (fä-vrōl') . Fr. (Paris In.)	48·42 N	1·34 E
110	Faversham (fă'vēr-sh'm) Eng. (London In.)	51·19 N	0·54 E
112	Faxaflói (B.) . . . . Ice.	64·33 N	22·40 W
78	Fayette (fā-yĕt') . . . . Ala.	33·40 N	87·54 W
71	Fayette . . . . Iowa	42·49 N	91·49 W
78	Fayette . . . . Miss.	31·43 N	91·00 W
73	Fayette . . . . Mo.	39·09 N	92·41 W
73	Fayetteville (fā-yĕt'vĭl) . . . . . . Ark.	36·03 N	94·08 W
79	Fayetteville . . . . N. C.	35·02 N	78·54 W
78	Fayetteville . . . . Tenn.	35·10 N	86·33 W
142	Fazilka . . . . India	30·30 N	74·02 E
165	Fazzān (Fezzan) Prov. . . . . . . Libya	26·45 N	13·01 E
165	Fazzān (Oasis) . . . . Libya	26·06 N	15·00 E
79	Fear, C. (fēr) . . . . N. C.	33·52 N	77·48 W
68	Feather (R.) (fĕth'ēr) . . . . Calif.	38·56 N	121·41 W
68	Feather, Middle Fk. of (R.) . Calif.	39·49 N	121·10 W
68	Feather, North Fk. of (R.) . . Calif.	40·00 N	121·20 W
110	Featherstone (fĕdh'ēr stŭn) . . Eng.	53·39 N	1·21 W
122	Fécamp (fā-käɴ') . . . . Fr.	49·45 N	0·20 E
85	Federal (fĕd'ēr-ăl) Can. (Ottawa In.)	45·20 N	75·42 W
99	Federal, Distrito (Dist.) (dēs-trē'tô-fĕ-dĕ-rä'l) Ven. (In.)	10·34 N	66·55 W
142	Federal Capital Dist. . . . . W. Pak.	29·55 N	67·01 E
136	Fëdorovka (fyô'dô-rôf-kȧ) Sov. Un. (Moscow In.)	56·15 N	37·14 E
120	Fehmarn I. (fā'märn) . . . . Ger.	54·28 N	11·15 E
111	Fehrbellin (fĕr'bĕl-lēn) Ger. (Berlin In.)	52·49 N	12·46 E
101	Feia, Logoa (L.) (lô-gôä-fĕ'yä) Braz. (Rio de Janeiro In.)	21·54 S	41·45 W
148	Feich'eng (fā'chĕng) . . . . China	36·18 N	116·45 E
148	Feihsien (fā'ē-hsyĕn') . . . . China	35·17 N	117·59 E
99	Feira de Santana (fĕ'ê-rä dä sänt-än'ä) . Braz.	12·16 S	38·46 W
125	Felanitx (fā-lä-nēch') . . . . Sp.	39·29 N	3·09 E
120	Feldkirch (fĕlt'kĭrk) . . . . Aus.	47·15 N	9·36 E
111	Feldkirchen (fĕld'kēr-kĕn) Ger. (Munich In.)	48·09 N	11·44 E
92	Felipe Carrillo Puerto (fĕ-lē'pĕ-kär-rē'l-yô-pwĕ'r-tô) Mex. (Yucatan In.)	19·36 N	88·04 W
126	Feltre (fĕl'trā) . . . . It.	46·02 N	11·56 E
167	Fénérive (fĕ-nā-rēv') . Malag. Rep.	17·30 S	49·31 E
150	Fengchen (fŭng'chĕn') . . . . . . China	40·28 N	113·20 E
150	Fengch'eng (fŭng'chŭng') . . . China	40·28 N	124·03 E
151	Fengchieh . . . . China	31·02 N	109·30 E
150	Fenghsiang . . . . China	34·25 N	107·20 E
149	Fenghsien (fŭng'hsyĕn') China (Shanghai In.)	30·55 N	121·26 E
148	Fenghsien . . . . China	34·41 N	116·36 E
148	Fengjun (fĕng'yĕn) . . . . China	39·51 N	118·06 E
148	Fengming Tao (I.) (fĕng'mĭng dou) . China	39·19 N	121·15 E
150	Fengt'ai (fŭng'tī') China (Peking In.)	39·51 N	116·19 E
151	Fengtu (fŭng'tōō') . . . . China	29·58 N	107·50 E
148	Fengyang (fŭng'yäng') . . . . . China	32·55 N	117·32 E
64	Fenimore P. (fĕn ĭ mōr) . . . Alaska	51·40 N	175·38 W
80	Fenton (fĕn-tŭn) . . . . Mich.	42·50 N	83·40 W
74	Fenton . . . . Mo. (St. Louis In.)	38·31 N	90·27 W
150	Fenyang . . . . China	37·20 N	111·48 E
129	Feodosiya (Kefe) (fĕ-ô-dô'sē'yȧ) (kyĕ'fĕ) . Sov. Un.	45·02 N	35·21 E
144	Ferdows . . . . Iran	34·00 N	58·13 E
126	Ferentino (fā-rĕn-tē'nō) . . . . It.	41·42 N	13·18 E
134	Fergana . . . . Sov. Un.	40·16 N	72·07 E
70	Fergus Falls (fûr'gŭs) . . . . . . Minn.	46·17 N	96·03 W
74	Ferguson (fûr-gŭ-sŭn) Mo. (St. Louis In.)	38·45 N	90·18 W
126	Fermo (fĕr'mō) . . . . It.	43·10 N	13·43 E
124	Fermoselle (fĕr-mō-säl'yā) . . . . Sp.	41·20 N	6·23 W
116	Fermoy (fûr-moi') . . . . Ire.	52·05 N	8·06 W
79	Fernandina Beach (fûr-năn-dē'nȧ) . Fla.	30·38 N	81·29 W
99	Fernando de Noronha, Arquipélago (Arch.) (är-kē-pĕ'lä-gô-fĕr-nän-dô-dĕ-nô-rô'n-yä) . Braz.	3·50 S	33·15 W
164	Fernando Póo (Reg.) (fĕr-nän'dō-pō'ō) . Equat. Gui.	3·22 N	7·37 E
124	Fernān-Núñez (fĕr-nän'nōōn'yāth) Sp.	37·42 N	4·43 W
66	Ferndale (fûrn'dāl) . . . . Calif.	40·34 N	124·18 W
75	Ferndale . . . . . Mich. (Detroit In.)	42·27 N	83·08 W
65	Ferndale . . . . Wash. (Vancouver In.)	48·51 N	122·36 W
86	Fernie (fûr'nĭ) . . . . Can.	49·29 N	114·56 W
65	Fern Prairie (fûrn prâr'ĭ) Wash. (Portland In.)	45·38 N	122·25 W
161	Ferntree Gully Austl. (Melbourne In.)	37·53 S	145·18 E
83	Ferolle, Pt. (fē-rōl') . . . . Can.	51·01 N	57·04 W
142	Ferozepore (fē-rōz-pōr') . . . . . India	30·58 N	74·39 E
126	Ferrara (fĕr-rä'rä) . . . . It.	44·50 N	11·37 E
125	Ferrat, Cap (C.) (kăp fĕr-rät) . Alg.	35·49 N	0·29 W
124	Ferreira do Alentejo (fĕr-rĕ'ê-rä dōō ä-lĕN-tā'zhōō) Port.	38·03 N	8·06 W
124	Ferreira do Zezere (fĕr-rĕ'ê-rä dōō zā-zā'rĕ) . Port.	39·49 N	8·17 W
74	Ferrelview (fĕr'rĕl-vū) Mo. (Kansas City In.)	39 18 N	94·40 W
98	Ferreñafe (fĕr-rĕn-yä'fĕ) . . . . . Peru	6·38 S	79·48 W
77	Ferriday (fĕr'ĭ-dā) . . . . La.	31·38 N	91·33 W
83	Ferryland (fĕr'ē-lănd) . . . . Can.	46·50 N	47·06 W
113	Ferryville (fĕr-ê-vēl') . . . . Tun.	37·12 N	9·51 E
136	Fershampenuaz (fĕr-shäm'pĕn-wäz) Sov. Un. (Urals In.)	53·32 N	59·50 E
70	Fertile (fûr'tĭl) . . . . Minn.	47·33 N	96·18 W
164	Fès (fĕs) . . . . Mor.	34·08 N	5·00 W
70	Fessenden (fĕs'ĕn-dĕn) . . . . . . N. D.	47·39 N	99·40 W
116	Festiniog (fĕs-tĭn-ĭ-ŏg) . . . . . Wales	52·59 N	3·58 W
73	Festus (fĕst'ŭs) . . . . Mo.	38·12 N	90·22 W
133	Fethiye (fĕt-hē'yĕ) . . . . Tur.	36·40 N	29·05 E
	Fezzan, see Fazzān		
167	Fianarantsoa (fyȧ-nä'rȧn-tsō'ȧ) Malag. Rep.	21·21 S	47·15 E
168	Ficksburg (fĭks'bûrg) S. Afr. (Johannesburg & Pretoria In.)	28·53 S	27·53 E
65	Fidalgo I. (fĭ-dăl'gō) Wash. (Seattle In.)	48·28 N	122·39 W
66	Fieldbrook (fēld'brŏŏk) . . . . . Calif.	40·59 N	124·02 W
127	Fier (fyĕr) . . . . Alb.	40·43 N	19·34 E
116	Fife Ness (C.) (fīf'nes') . . . . . Scot.	56·15 N	2·19 W
165	Fifth Cataract . . . . Sud.	18·27 N	33·38 E
124	Figalo, Cap (C.) (kăp fē-gä-lô) . Alg.	35·35 N	1·12 W
122	Figeac (fē-zhäk') . . . . Fr.	44·37 N	2·02 E
118	Figeholm (fē-ghĕ-hōlm) . . . . . . Swe.	57·24 N	16·33 E
124	Figueira da Foz (fē-gwĕy-rä-dä-fô'z) . Port.	40·10 N	8·50 W
164	Figuig . . . . Mor.	32·20 N	1·30 W
156	Fiji Is. (fē'jē) . . . . Oceania	18·50 S	175·00 E
92	Filadelfia (fĭl-ȧ-dĕl'fĭ-ȧ) . . . . . C. R.	10·26 N	85·37 W
136	Filatovskoye (fĭ-lä'tôf-skô-yĕ) Sov. Un. (Urals In.)	56·49 N	62·20 E
79	Filbert (fĭl'bērt) . . . . W. Va.	37·18 N	81·29 W
47	Filchner Ice Shelf (fĭlk'nēr) . . Ant.	80·00 S	35·00 W
127	Filiatrá . . . . Grc.	37·10 N	21·35 E
126	Filicudi (I.) (fē'le-kōō'dē) . . . . . It.	38·34 N	14·39 E
115	Filigas (R.) . . . . Tur.	41·10 N	32·53 E
136	Filippovskoye (fĭ-lĭ-pôf'skô-yĕ) Sov. Un. (Moscow In.)	56·06 N	38·38 E
118	Filipstad (fĭl'ĭps-städh) . . . . . . Swe.	59·44 N	14·09 E
69	Fillmore (fĭl'mōr) . . . . Utah	39·00 N	112·20 W
166	Fimi (R) . . . . Con. K.	2·46 S	17·30 E
85	Finch (fĭnch) . . . Can. (Ottawa In.)	45·09 N	75·06 W

ng-sing; ŋ-baŋk; ɴ-nasalized n; nŏd; cŏmmit; ōld; ôbey; ôrder; fōōd; fŏŏt; ou-out; s-soft; sh-dish; th-thin; pūre; ûnite; ûrn; stŭd; circŭs; ü-as "y" in study; '-indeterminate vowel.

206 Findlay–Fort Portal PRONOUNCING INDEX

Page	Name Pronunciation Region	Lat. °'	Long. °'
80	Findlay (fĭnd'lā) Ohio	41·05 N	83·40 W
124	Finisterre, Cabo de (C.) (kä'bō-dĕ-fĭn-ĭs-târ'). Sp.	42·52 N	9·48 W
158	Finke (R.) (fĭŋ'kē) Austl.	25·25 S	134·30 E
102	Finland (fĭn'lănd) Eur.	62·45 N	26·13 E
119	Finland, G. of (fĭn'lănd) Eur.	59·35 N	23·35 E
98	Finlandia (fēn-lä'n-dēä). Col. (In.)	4·38 N	75·39 W
86	Finlay (R.) (fĭn'lā) Can.	56·57 N	124·40 W
111	Finofurt (fē'nō-fōōrt) Ger. (Berlin In.)	52·50 N	13·41 E
111	Finow (fē'nōv). Ger. (Berlin In.)	52·50 N	13·44 E
120	Finsterwalde (fĭn'stēr-väl-dĕ). Ger.	51·38 N	13·42 E
133	Firat (R.) (fē-rät') Tur.	39·40 N	38·30 E
65	Fircrest (fûr'krĕst) Wash. (Seattle In.)	47·14 N	122·31 W
126	Firenze (Florence) (fē-rĕnt'sä). It.	43·47 N	11·15 E
126	Firenzuola (fē-rĕnt-swô'lä) It.	44·08 N	11·21 E
165	First Cataract U. A. R.	24·00 N	32·52 E
111	Fischa (R.) Aus. (Vienna In.)	48·04 N	16·33 E
111	Fischamend Markt Aus. (Vienna In.)	48·07 N	16·37 E
95	Fish Cay (I.) Ba. Is.	22·30 N	74·20 W
85	Fish Cr. (fĭsh). Can. (Calgary In.)	50·52 N	114·21 W
77	Fisher (fĭsh'ēr) La.	31·28 N	93·30 W
87	Fisher Str. Can.	62·43 N	84·28 W
166	Fish Hoek (fĭsh'hōōk) S. Afr. (Cape Town In.)	34·13 S	18·26 E
83	Fitchburg (fĭch'bûrg) Mass. (Boston In.)	42·35 N	71·48 W
78	Fitzgerald (fĭts-jĕr'ăld) Ga.	31·42 N	83·17 W
158	Fitzroy (R.) (fĭts-roi') Austl.	18·00 S	124·05 E
159	Fitzroy (R.) Austl.	23·45 S	150·02 E
158	Fitzroy Crossing Austl.	18·08 S	126·00 E
80	Fitzwilliam (I.) (fĭts-wĭl'yŭm) Can.	45·30 N	81·45 W
	Fiume, see Rijeka		
125	Fiumicino (fyōō-mē-chē'nô) It. (Rome In.)	41·47 N	12·19 E
118	Fjällbacka (fyĕl'băk-å) Swe.	58·37 N	11·17 E
118	Flaam (flôm) Nor.	60·51 N	7·01 E
69	Flagstaff (flăg-stâf) Ariz.	35·15 N	111·40 W
167	Flagstaff (flăg'stâf) S. Afr. (Natal In.)	31·06 S	29·31 E
81	Flagstaff (L.) (flăg-stâf) Maine	45·05 N	70·30 W
111	Flalow (flä'lōv). Ger. (Berlin In.)	52·44 N	12·58 E
71	Flambeau (R.) (flăm-bō') Wis.	45·32 N	91·05 W
67	Flaming Gorge Res. Wyo.	41·13 N	109·30 W
79	Flamingo (flȧ-mĭŋ'gō) Fla.	25·10 N	80·55 W
95	Flamingo Cay (I.) (flȧ-mĭŋ'gō) Ba. Is.	22·50 N	75·50 W
89	Flamingo Pt. Vir. Is. (U. S. A.) (St. Thomas In.)	18·19 N	65·00 W
117	Flanders (Reg.) Fr.	50·53 N	2·29 E
70	Flandreau (flăn'drō) S. D.	44·02 N	96·35 W
116	Flannan (Is.) (flăn'ăn) Scot.	58·13 N	8·14 W
67	Flathead L. (flăt'hĕd) Mont.	47·57 N	114·20 W
67	Flathead R. Mont.	48·45 N	114·20 W
67	Flathead R., Middle Fork. Mont.	48·30 N	113·47 W
67	Flathead R., South Fork. Mont.	48·05 N	113·45 W
75	Flat Rock (flăt rŏk) Mich. (Detroit In.)	42·06 N	83·17 W
66	Flattery C. (flăt'ēr-ĭ) Wash.	48·22 N	125·10 W
67	Flat Willow Cr. (flat wĭl'ô). Mont.	46·45 N	108·47 W
118	Flekkefjord (flĕk'kē-fyôr) Nor.	58·19 N	6·38 E
80	Flemingsburg (flĕm'ĭngz-bûrg) Ky.	38·25 N	83·45 W
120	Flensburg (flĕns'bōōrgh) Ger.	54·48 N	9·27 E
122	Flers-del-l'Orne (flĕr-dĕ-lôrn'). Fr.	48·43 N	0·37 W
158	Flinders (Reg.) (flĭn'dērz) Austl.	32·15 S	138·45 E
160	Flinders (I.) Austl.	39·35 S	148·10 E
159	Flinders (R.) Austl.	18·48 S	141·07 E
160	Flinders Ra. Austl.	34·09 S	138·56 E
159	Flinders Rfs. Austl.	17·30 S	149·02 E
86	Flin Flon Can.	54·50 N	101·52 W
110	Flint Wales	53·15 N	3·07 W
80	Flint Mich.	43·00 N	83·45 W
110	Flint (Co.) Wales	53·13 N	3·06 W
78	Flint (R.) (flĭnt) Ga.	31·25 N	84·15 W
118	Flisen (flē'sĕn) Nor.	60·35 N	12·03 E
80	Flora (flō'rȧ) Ill.	38·40 N	88·25 W
80	Flora Ind.	40·25 N	86·30 W
78	Florala (flŏr-ăl'ȧ) Ala.	31·01 N	86·19 W
84	Floral Park (flôr'ăl pärk) N. Y. (New York In.)	40·42 N	73·42 W
78	Florence (flŏr'ĕns) Ala.	34·46 N	87·40 W
69	Florence Ariz.	33·00 N	111·25 W
72	Florence Colo.	38·23 N	105·08 W
73	Florence Kans.	38·14 N	96·56 W
79	Florence S. C.	34·10 N	79·45 W
65	Florence Wash. (Seattle In.)	48·13 N	122·21 W
	Florence, see Firenze		
98	Florencia (flō-rĕn'sē-ȧ) Col.	1·31 N	75·13 W
101	Florencio Sánchez (flō-rĕn-sēō-sä'n-chĕz). Ur. (Buenos Aires In.)	33.52 S	57·24 W
100	Florencio Varela (flō-rĕn'sē-o vä-rä'lä). Arg. (In.)	34·34 S	58·16 W
99	Flores (flō'rĕzh) Braz.	7·57 S	37·48 W
92	Flores Guat. (Yucatan In.)	16·53 N	89·54 W
101	Flores (Dept.) Ur. (Buenos Aires In.)	33·33 S	57·00 W
154	Flores (I.) Indon.	8·14 S	121·08 E
101	Flores (R.) Arg. (Buenos Aires In.)	36·13 S	60·28 W
154	Flores Sea Indon.	7·09 N	120·30 E
76	Floresville (flō'rĕs-vĭl) Tex.	29·10 N	98·08 W
99	Floriano (flō-rē-ä'nō) Braz.	6·17 S	42·58 W
100	Florianópolis (flō-rē-ä-nō'pō-lēs) Braz.	27·30 S	48·30 W
98	Florida (flō-rē'-dä) Col. (In.)	3·20 N	76·12 W
94	Florida Cuba	22·10 N	79·50 W
84	Florida (flŏr'ĭ-dȧ) N. Y. (New York In.)	41·20 N	74·21 W
167	Florida S. Afr. (Johannesburg & Pretoria In.)	26·11 S	27·56 E
101	Florida (flō-rē-dhä) Ur. (Buenos Aires In.)	34·06 S	56·14 W
63	Florida (State) (flŏr'ĭ-dȧ) U. S.	30·30 N	84·40 W
101	Florida (Dept.) (flō-rē'dhä) Ur. (Buenos Aires In.)	33·48 S	56·15 W
159	Florida (I.) Sol. Is.	8·56 S	159·45 E
94	Florida, Strs. of N. A.	24·10 N	81·00 W
79	Florida B. (flŏr'ĭ-dȧ) Fla. (In.)	24·55 N	80·55 W
79	Florida Keys (Is.) Fla. (In.)	24·33 N	81·20 W
69	Florida Mts. N. Mex.	32·10 N	107·35 W
76	Florido, R. (flō-rē'dō) Mex.	27·21 N	104·48 W
111	Floridsdorf (flō'rĭds-dôrf) Aus. (Vienna In.)	48·16 N	16·25 E
127	Florina (flō-rē'nä) Grc.	40·48 N	21·24 E
74	Florissant (flŏr'ĭ-sănt) Mo. (St. Louis In.)	38·47 N	90·20 W
118	Florö (flôr'ü) Nor.	61·36 N	5·01 E
70	Floyd (R.) (floid) Iowa	42·38 N	96·15 W
72	Floydada (floi-dā'dȧ) Tex.	33·59 N	101·19 W
75	Floyds Fk. (R.) (floi-dz) Ky. (Louisville In.)	38·08 N	85·30 W
126	Flumendosa, R. (flōō-mĕn-dô'sä) It.	39·45 N	9·18 E
80	Flushing (flŭsh'ĭng) Mich.	43·05 N	83·50 W
155	Fly (R.) (flī) Austl.	8·00 S	141·45 E
127	Foča (fō'chä) Yugo.	43·29 N	18·48 E
168	Fochville (fŏk'vĭl) S. Afr. (Johannesburg & Pretoria In.)	26·29 S	27·29 E
121	Focsani (fôk-shä'nē) Rom.	45·41 N	27·17 E
126	Foggia (fôd'jä) It.	41·30 N	15·34 E
83	Fogo (fō'gō) Can.	49·43 N	54·14 W
83	Fogo (I.) Can.	49·44 N	53·53 W
164	Fogo I. C. V. Is. (In.)	14·46 N	24·51 W
120	Fohnsdorf (fōns'dôrf) Aus.	47·13 N	14·40 E
120	Föhr I. (fûr) Ger.	54·47 N	8·30 E
122	Foix (fwä) Fr.	42·58 N	1·34 E
151	Fokang China	23·50 N	113·35 E
126	Foligno (fō-lēn'yō) It.	42·58 N	12·41 E
110	Folkingham (fō'kĭng-ăm) Eng.	52·53 N	0·24 W
117	Folkstone (fōk'stŭn) Eng.	51·05 N	3·04 W
72	Folsom (fŏl'sŭm) N. Mex.	36·47 N	103·56 W
68	Folsom City Calif.	38·40 N	121·10 W
94	Fomento (fō-mĕ'n-tō) Cuba	21·35 N	78·20 W
98	Fómeque (fô'mĕ-kĕ) Col. (In.)	4·29 N	73·52 W
71	Fonda (fŏn'dȧ) Iowa	42·33 N	94·51 W
71	Fond du Lac (fŏn dū lăk') Wis.	43·47 N	88·29 W
71	Fond du Lac Ind. Res. Minn.	46·44 N	93·04 W
126	Fondi (fōn'dē) It.	41·23 N	13·25 E
124	Fonsagrada (fôn-sä-grä'dhä) Sp.	43·08 N	7·07 W
92	Fonseca, Golfo de (G.) (gôl-fô-dĕ-fôn-sā'kä). Hond.	13·09 N	87·55 W
123	Fontainebleau (fôN-tĕn-blō') Fr. (Paris In.)	48·24 N	2·42 E
74	Fontana (fŏn-tă'nȧ) Calif. (Los Angeles In.)	34·06 N	117·27 W
98	Fonte Boa (fōn'tā bō'ȧ) Braz.	2·32 S	66·05 W
122	Fontenay-le-Comte (fôNt-nĕ'lē-kôNt'). Fr.	46·28 N	0·53 W
123	Fontenay-Trésigny (fôN-tē-hā' tra-sēn-yē'). Fr. (Paris In.)	48·43 N	2·53 E
91	Fontera, Punta (Pt.) (pōō'n-tä-fôn-tĕ'rä). Mex.	18·36 N	92·43 W
98	Fontibón (fōn-tē-bôn'). Col. (In.)	4·42 N	74·09 W
	Foochow, see Fuchou		
167	Foothills (fōōt-hĭls) S. Afr. (Johannesburg & Pretoria In.)	25·55 S	27·36 E
64	Foraker, Mt. (fôr'ȧ-kēr) Alaska	62·40 N	152·40 W
123	Forbach (fôr'bäK) Fr.	49·12 N	6·54 E
160	Forbes (fôrbz) Austl.	33·24 S	148·05 E
164	Forcados (fôr-kä'dōs) Nig.	5·19 N	5·26 E
120	Forchheim (fôrK'hīm) Ger.	49·43 N	11·05 E
	Fordlândia, see Brasília Legal		
73	Fordyce (fôr'dīs) Ark.	33·48 N	92·24 W
164	Forecariah (fōr-kȧ-rē'ȧ') Gui.	9·31 N	13·14 W
49	Forel, Mt. Grnld.	65·50 N	37·41 W
78	Forest (fŏr'ĕst) Miss.	32·22 N	89·29 W
70	Forest (R.) N. D.	48·08 N	97·45 W
71	Forest City Iowa	43·14 N	93·40 W
79	Forest City N. C.	35·20 N	81·52 W
81	Forest City Pa.	41·35 N	75·30 W
65	Forest Grove (grōv) Ore. (Portland In.)	45·31 N	123·07 W
85	Forest Hill (hĭl) Can. (Toronto In.)	43·42 N	79·25 W
84	Forest Hill. Md. (Baltimore In.)	39·35 N	76·26 W
74	Forest Hill Tex. (Dallas, Fort Worth In.)	32·40 N	97·16 W
85	Forest Lawn (lôn) Can. (Calgary In.)	51·02 N	113·59 W
82	Forestville (fŏr'ĕst-vĭl) Can.	48·46 N	69·05 W
84	Forestville. Md. (Baltimore In.)	38·51 N	76·55 W
122	Forez, Mts. du (môN dü fō-rā'). Fr.	44·55 N	3·43 E
116	Forfar (fôr'fȧr) Scot.	57·10 N	2·55 W
125	Forio (Mtn.) (fô'ryō) It. (Naples In.)	40·29 N	13·55 E
75	Forked Cr. (fôrk'd) Ill. (Chicago In.)	41·16 N	88·01 W
78	Forked Deer (R.) Tenn.	35·53 N	89·29 W
126	Forli (fôr-lē') It.	44·13 N	12·03 E
110	Formby (fôrm'bē) Eng.	53·34 N	3·04 W
110	Formby Pt. Eng.	53·33 N	3·06 W
125	Formello (fôr-mĕ'lō) It. (Rome In.)	42·04 N	12·25 E
125	Formentera, Isla de (I.) (ē's-lä-dĕ-fôr-mĕn-tā'rä). Sp.	38·43 N	1·25 E
101	Formiga (fôr-mē'gä) Braz. (Rio de Janeiro In.)	20·27 S	45·25 W
95	Formigas Bk. (fōr-mē'gäs). N. A.	18·30 N	75·40 W
100	Formosa (fôr-mō'sä) Arg.	27·25 S	58·12 W
99	Formosa Braz.	15·32 S	47·10 W
100	Formosa (Prov.) Arg.	24·30 S	60·45 W
	Formosa, see Taiwan (I.)		
99	Formosa, Serra (Mts.) (sĕ'r-rä) Braz.	12·59 S	55·11 W
139	Formosa Str. (fŏr-mō'sȧ) Asia	24·30 N	120·00 E
136	Fornosovo (fôr-nô'sô vô) Sov. Un. (Leningrad In.)	59·35 N	30·34 E
73	Forrest City (fŏr'ĕst sĭ'tĭ) Ark.	35·00 N	90·46 W
159	Forsayth (fôr-sīth') Austl.	18·33 S	143·42 E
118	Forshaga (fôrs'hä'gä) Swe.	59·34 N	13·25 E
201	Forst (fôrst) Ger.	51·45 N	14·38 E
78	Forsyth (fôr-sīth') Ga.	33·02 N	83·56 W
67	Forsyth Mont.	46·15 N	106·41 W
87	Fort Albany (fôrt ôl'bȧ nĭ) Can.	52·20 N	81·20 W
99	Fortaleza (Ceará) (fôr'tä-lā'zȧ) (sā-ä-rä'). Braz.	3·35 S	38·31 W
69	Fort Apache Ind. Res. (ȧ-păch'ē) Ariz.	34·02 N	110·27 W
165	Fort-Archambault (är-chaN-bō') Chad	9·04 N	18·17 E
71	Fort Atkinson (ăt'kĭn-sŭn) Wis.	42·55 N	88·46 W
	Fort Bayard, see Chanchiang		
167	Fort Beaufort (bō'fôrt) S. Afr. (Natal In.)	32·47 S	26·39 E
74	Fort Bellefontaine (bĕl-fōn-tān') Mo. (St. Louis In.)	38·50 N	90·15 W
67	Fort Benton (bĕn'tŭn) Mont.	47·51 N	110·40 W
70	Fort Berthould Ind. Res. (bērth'ōld). N. D.	47·47 N	103·28 W
80	Fort Branch (brănch) Ind.	38·15 N	87·35 W
	Fort Charlet, see Djanet		
87	Fort Chimo Can.	58·18 N	68·08 W
86	Fort Chipewyan Can.	58·46 N	111·15 W
72	Fort Cobb Res. Okla.	35·12 N	98·28 W
72	Fort Collins (kŏl'ĭns) Colo.	40·36 N	105·04 W
165	Fort Crampel (kräm-pĕl') Cen. Afr. Rep.	7·10 N	19·07 E
167	Fort-Dauphin (dō-făN') Malag. Rep.	24·59 S	46·58 E
93	Fort-de-France (dē fräNs) Mart. (Le. & Wind. Is. In.)	14·37 N	61·06 W
78	Fort Deposit (dē-pŏz'ĭt) Ala.	31·58 N	86·35 W
165	Fort de Possel (dē pô-sĕl') Cen. Afr. Rep.	5·03 N	19·11 E
71	Fort Dodge (dŏj) Iowa	42·31 N	94·10 W
81	Fort Edward (wērd) N. Y.	43·15 N	73·30 W
75	Fort Erie (ē'rĭ) Can. (Buffalo In.)	42·55 N	78·56 W
158	Fortescue (R.) (fôr'tĕs-kū). Austl.	21·25 S	116·50 E
82	Fort Fairfield (fâr'fēld) Maine	46·46 N	67·53 W
86	Fort Fitzgerald (fĭts-jĕr'ăld). Can.	59·48 N	111·50 W
164	Fort Flatters (flȧ-târ') Alg.	28·06 N	6·34 E
87	Fort Frances (frăn'sĕs) Can.	48·41 N	94·29 W
79	Fort Frederica Natl. Mon. (frĕd'ĕ-rĭ-kȧ). Ga.	31·12 N	85·25 W
78	Fort Gaines (gānz) Ga.	31·35 N	85·03 W
85	Fort Garry (gă'rē) Can. (Winnipeg In.)	49·50 N	97·09 W
87	Fort George (jôrj) Can.	53·40 N	78·58 W
87	Fort George (R.) Can.	53·50 N	78·34 W
73	Fort Gibson (gĭb'sŭn) Okla.	35·50 N	95·13 W
86	Fort Good Hope (gŏŏd hōp). Can.	66·19 N	128·52 W
164	Fort Gouraud Mauritania	22·45 N	12·38 W
116	Forth, Firth of (fûrth ôv fôrth) Scot.	56·04 N	3·03 W
167	Fort Hall (hôl) Ken.	0·47 S	37·13 E
67	Fort Hall Ind. Res. Idaho	43·02 N	112·21 W
69	Fort Huachuca (wä-chōō'kä). Ariz.	31·30 N	110·25 W
85	Fortier (fôr-tyā') Can. (Winnipeg In.)	49·56 N	97·55 W
166	Fort Jameson (jăm'sŭn). Zambia	13·35 S	32·43 E
79	Fort Jefferson Natl. Mon. (jĕf'ēr-sŭn). Fla. (In.)	24·42 N	83·02 W
166	Fort Johnston Malawi	14·16 S	35·14 E
82	Fort Kent (kĕnt) Maine	47·14 N	68·37 W
164	Fort Lallemand (lȧ-lĕ-mäN'). Alg.	31·17 N	6·13 E
165	Fort-Lamy (lȧ-mē') Chad	12·15 N	15·04 E
65	Fort Langley (lăng'lĭ) Can. (Vancouver In.)	49·10 N	122·35 W
70	Fort Laramie Natl. Mon. (fôrt lăr'ȧ-mĭ). Wyo.	42·10 N	104·34 W
79	Fort Lauderdale (lō'dēr-dāl) Fla. (In.)	26·07 N	80·09 W
86	Fort Liard Can.	60·16 N	123·34 W
95	Fort Liberté (lē-bĕr-tā') Hai.	19·40 N	71·50 W
78	Fort Louden (R.) (fôrt lou'dĕn) Tenn.	35·52 N	84·10 W
72	Fort Lupton (lŭp'tŭn) Colo.	40·04 N	104·45 W
66	Fort McDermitt Ind. Res. (măk Dĕr'mĭt). Ore.	42·04 N	118·07 W
86	Fort Macleod (mȧ-Kloud') Can.	49·40 N	113·22 W
164	Fort MacMahon (mȧk mȧ-ôN') Alg.	29·55 N	1·49 E
86	Fort McPherson (mȧk-fŭr's'n) Can.	67·37 N	134·59 W
71	Fort Madison (măd'ĭ-sŭn) Iowa	40·40 N	91·17 W
166	Fort Manning (Mchinji) (măn'ĭng). Malawi	13·42 S	33·00 E
79	Fort Matanzas (mä-tän'zäs). Fla.	29·39 N	81·17 W
79	Fort Meade (mēd) Fla. (In.)	27·45 N	81·48 W
79	Fort Mill (mĭl) S.C.	35·03 N	80·57 W
114	Fort Miribel (mē-rē-bĕl') Alg.	28·50 N	2·51 E
68	Fort Mohave Ind. Res. (mō-hä'vā) Calif.	34·59 N	115·02 W
84	Fort Monroe (mŏn-rō') Va. (Norfolk In.)	37·00 N	76·19 W
72	Fort Morgan (môr'gȧn) Colo.	40·14 N	103·49 W
79	Fort Myers (mī'ĕrz) Fla. (In.)	26·36 N	81·45 W
114	Fort National (fô nȧ-syō-nȧl') Alg.	36·45 N	4·15 E
86	Fort Nelson (nĕl'sŭn) Can.	58·57 N	122·30 W
86	Fort Nelson (R.) (nĕl'sŭn). Can.	58·44 N	122·20 W
78	Fort Payne (pān) Ala.	34·26 N	85·41 W
67	Fort Peck (pĕk) Mont.	47·58 N	106·30 W
67	Fort Peck Res. Mont.	47·52 N	106·59 W
79	Fort Pierce (pērs) Fla. (In.)	27·25 N	80·20 W
164	Fort Polignac (pō-lē-nyäk') Alg.	26·35 N	8·24 E
165	Fort Portal (pôr'tăl) Ug.	00·40 N	30·16 E

ăt; finăl; rāte; senâte; ärm; åsk; sofȧ; fâre; ch-choose; dh-as th in other; bē; ēvent; bĕt; recĕnt; cratēr; g-go; gh-guttural g; bĭt; ĭ-short neutral; rīde; K-guttural k as ch in German ich;

PRONOUNCING INDEX Fort Providence–Fulda 207

Page	Name Pronunciation Region	Lat. °′	Long. °′
86	Fort Providence (prŏv'ĭ-dĕns) Can.	61·27 N	117·59 W
79	Fort Pulaski Natl. Mon. (pu-lăs'kĭ) . Ga.	31·59 N	80·56 W
64	Fort Randall (răn'd'l) ..... Alaska	55·12 N	162·38 W
62	Fort Randall Dam .... U. S.	43·05 N	100·15 W
70	Fort Randall Res. .... S. D.	43·35 N	99·12 W
86	Fort Resolution (rĕz'ô-lū'shŭn) Can.	61·08 N	113·42 W
73	Fort Riley (rī'lĭ) .... Kans.	39·05 N	96·46 W
166	Fort Rosebery (rōz'bēr-ĭ) . . Zambia	11·14 S	28·58 E
166	Fort Rousset (fôr rōō-sĕ') . . Con. B.	0·23 S	15·42 E
86	Fort St. James (fôrt sānt jāmz) Can.	54·28 N	124·19 W
86	Fort St. John (sānt jŏn) ..... Can.	56·28 N	120·57 W
142	Fort Sandeman (săn'da-măn) W. Pak.	31·28 N	69·29 E
85	Fort Saskatchewan (săs-kăt'chōō-ân) Can. (Edmonton In.)	53·42 N	113·14 W
73	Fort Scott (skŏt) .... Kans.	37·50 N	94·43 W
86	Fort Selkirk (sĕl-kûrk') ...... Can.	62·43 N	137·40 W
87	Fort Severn (sĕv'ērn) .... Can.	56·58 N	87·50 W
133	Fort Shevchenko (shĕv-chĕn'kô) Sov. Un.	44·30 N	50·18 E
165	Fort Sibut (fôr sē-bü') Cen. Afr. Rep.	5·52 N	19·01 E
72	Fort Sill (fôrt sĭl) .... Okla.	34·41 N	98·25 W
86	Fort Simpson (sĭmp'sŭn) .... Can.	61·52 N	121·48 W
73	Fort Smith (smĭth) .... Ark.	35.23 N	94·24 W
86	Fort Smith .... Can.	60·09 N	112·08 W
76	Fort Stockton (stŏk'tŭn) ..... Tex.	30·54 N	102·51 W
72	Fort Sumner (sŭm'nēr) . . . N. Mex.	34·30 N	104·17 W
79	Fort Sumter Natl. Mon. (sŭm'tēr) . S. C.	32·43 N	79·54 W
75	Fort Thomas (tŏm'ăs) Ky. (Cincinnati In.)	39·05 N	84·27 W
66	Fortuna (fŏr-tū'nȧ) .... Calif.	40·36 N	124·10 W
83	Fortune (fôr'tûn) .... Can.	47·04 N	55·51 W
95	Fortune (I.) .... Ba. Is.	22·35 N	74·20 W
83	Fortune B .... Can.	47·25 N	55·30 W
72	Fort Union Natl. Mon. (ūn'yŭn) N. Mex.	35·51 N	104·57 W
78	Fort Valley (văl'ĭ) .... Ga.	32·33 N	83·53 W
66	Fort Vancouver Natl. Mon. (văn-kōō'vēr) . Wash.	45·50 N	122·36 W
86	Fort Vermilion (vēr-mĭl'yŭn) . Can.	58·23 N	115·50 W
166	Fort Victoria .... Rh.	20·07 S	30·47 E
80	Fortville (fôrt-vĭl) .... Ind.	40·00 N	85·50 W
80	Fort Wayne (wān) .... Ind.	41·00 N	85·10 W
85	Fort Whyte (whīt) Can. (Winnipeg In.)	49·49 N	97·13 W
87	Fort William (wĭl'yŭm) ...... Can.	48·20 N	89·20 W
116	Fort William (wĭl'yŭm) ..... Scot.	56·50 N	3·00 W
160	Fort William, Mt. (wĭ 'l-ăm) Austl.	24·45 S	151·15 E
74	Fort Worth (wûrth) Tex. (Dallas, Fort Worth In.)	32·45 N	97·20 W
64	Fort Yukon (yōō'kŏn) ..... Alaska	66·30 N	145·00 W
68	Fort Yuma Ind. Res. (yōō'mä) Calif.	32·54 N	114·47 W
122	Fos, Golfe de (G.) (gôlf'dĕ-fôs') Fr. (Marseille In.)	43·22 N	4·55 E
149	Foshan ...... China (Canton In.)	23·02 N	113·07 E
	Foshan, see Ch'aoyang		
126	Fossano (fôs-sä'nō) .... It.	44·34 N	7·42 E
74	Fossil Cr. (fŏs-ĭl) Tex. (Dallas, Fort Worth In.)	32·53 N	97·19 W
126	Fossombrone (fôs-sôm-brō'nā) . . It.	43·41 N	12·48 E
72	Foss Res. .... Okla.	35·38 N	99·11 W
70	Fosston (fôs'tŭn) .... Minn.	47·34 N	95·44 W
74	Fosterburg (fŏs'tēr-bûrg) Ill. (St. Louis In.)	38·58 N	90·04 W
80	Fostoria (fŏs-tō'rĭ-ȧ) .... Ohio	41·10 N	83·20 W
148	Fouch'eng (fōō'chĕng) ...... China	37·53 N	116·08 E
122	Fougères (fōō-zhâr') .... Fr.	48·23 N	1·14 W
150	Fouhsin .... China	42·05 N	121·40 E
116	Foula (I.) (fou'lȧ) .... Scot.	60·08 N	2·04 W
151	Fouliang .... China	29·18 N	117·18 E
151	Fouling .... China	29·40 N	107·30 E
159	Foulwind, C. (foul'wĭnd) N. Z. (In.)	41·45 S	171·37 E
164	Foumban (fōōm-bȧn') ...... Cam.	5·49 N	10·52 E
148	Founing (fōō'nĭng) .... China	33·55 N	119·54 E
72	Fountain Cr. (foun'tĭn) ..... Colo.	38·36 N	104·37 W
73	Fourche la Fave (R.) (fōōrsh lä fȧv') . Ark.	34·46 N	93·45 W
168	Fouriesburg (fōō'rēz-bûrg) S. Afr. (Johannesburg & Pretoria In.)	28·38 S	28·13 E
122	Fourmies (fōōr-mē') .... Fr.	50·01 N	4·01 E
64	Four Mts., Is. of the (fōr) . . Alaska	52·58 N	170·40 W
165	Fourth Cataract .... Sud.	18·52 N	32·07 E
164	Fouta Djalon (Mts.) (fōō'tä jā-lôɴ) . Gui.	11·37 N	12·29 W
148	Fouts'un (fōō'tsŏŏn) .... China	36·38 N	117·26 E
148	Foutzuchi (fōō'tzĕ'jē) ...... China	33·48 N	118·13 E
148	Fouyang (fōō'yäng) .... China	32·53 N	115·48 E
159	Foveaux Str. (fô-vō') . . N. Z. (In.)	46·30 S	167·43 E
72	Fowler (foul'ēr) .... Colo.	38·04 N	104·02 W
80	Fowler .... Ind.	40·35 N	87·20 W
158	Fowler, Pt. .... Austl.	32·05 S	132·30 E
76	Fowlerton (foul'ēr-tŭn) ...... Tex.	28·26 N	98·48 W
65	Fox (I.) (fŏks) . Wash. (Seattle In.)	47·15 N	122·08 W
71	Fox (R.) .... Ill.	41·35 N	88·43 W
71	Fox (R.) .... Wis.	44·18 N	88·23 W
83	Foxboro (fŏks'bŭrô) Mass. (Boston In.)	42·04 N	71·15 W
86	Foxe Basin (fŏks) .... Can.	67·35 N	79·21 W
87	Foxe Chan .... Can.	64·30 N	79·23 W
87	Foxe Pen .... Can.	64·57 N	77·26 W
64	Fox Is. (fŏks) .... Alaska	53·04 N	167·30 W
75	Fox Lake (lăk) . . Ill. (Chicago In.)	42·24 N	88·11 W
75	Fox L. .... Ill. (Chicago In.)	42·24 N	88·07 W
75	Fox Point . . . Wis. (Milwaukee In.)	43·10 N	87·54 W
116	Folye, Lough (B.) (lŏk foil') . . Ire.	54·69 N	6·75 W
125	Fraga (frä'gä) .... Sp.	41·31 N	0·20 E
94	Fragoso, Cayo (I.) (kä'yō-frä-gō'sô) . Cuba	22·45 N	79·30 W
99	Franca (frä'n-kä) .... Braz.	20·28 S	47·20 W
127	Francavilla (fräŋ-kä-vēl'lä) .... It.	40·32 N	17·37 E
102	France (frȧns) .... Eur.	46·39 N	0·47 E
86	Frances (L.) (frăn'sĭs) .... Can.	61·27 N	128·28 W
94	Frances, Cabo (C.) (kä'bô-frän-sĕ's) . Cuba	21·55 N	84·05 W
94	Frances, Punta (Pt.) (pōō'n-tä-frän-sĕ's) . Cuba	21·45 N	83·10 W
95	Frances Viejo, Cabo (C.) (kȧ'bô-frän'sȧs vyā'hô) Dom. Rep.	19·40 N	69·35 W
166	Franceville (fräɴs-vēl') .... Gabon.	1·37 S	13·37 E
101	Francisco Sales (frän-sē's-kô-sȧ'lĕs) . Braz. (Rio de Janeiro In.)	21·42 S	44·26 W
166	Francistown (frȧn'sis-toun) . . Bots.	21·17 S	27·28 E
75	Frankfort (frăŋk'fŭrt) Ill. (Chicago In.)	41·30 N	87·51 W
80	Frankfort .... Ind.	40·15 N	86·30 W
73	Frankfort .... Kans.	39·42 N	96·27 W
80	Frankfort .... Ky.	38·10 N	84·55 W
80	Frankfort .... Mich.	44·40 N	86·15 W
81	Frankfort .... N. Y.	43·05 N	75·05 W
168	Frankfort . S. Afr. (Johannesburg & Pretoria In.)	27·17 S	28·30 E
167	Frankfort (frănk'fŏrt) S. Afr. (Natal In.)	32·43 S	27·28 E
120	Frankfurt (fräŋk'fŏŏrt) ...... Ger.	52·20 N	14·31 E
111	Frankfurt (Dist.) . Ger. (Berlin In.)	52·42 N	13·37 E
120	Frankfurt am Main .... Ger.	50·07 N	8·40 E
80	Franklin (frănk'lĭn) .... Ind.	39·25 N	86·00 W
78	Franklin .... Ky.	36·42 N	86·34 W
77	Franklin .... La.	29·47 N	91·31 W
83	Franklin ...... Mass. (Boston In.)	42·05 N	71·24 W
72	Franklin .... Nebr.	40·06 N	99·01 W
81	Franklin .... N. H.	43·25 N	71·40 W
84	Franklin .... N. J. (New York In.)	41·08 N	74·35 W
80	Franklin .... Ohio	39·30 N	84·20 W
81	Franklin .... Pa.	41·25 N	79·50 W
78	Franklin .... Tenn.	35·54 N	86·54 W
167	Franklin ...... S. Afr. (Natal In.)	30·19 S	29·28 E
79	Franklin .... Va.	36·41 N	76·57 W
86	Franklin, Dist. of .... Can.	70·46 N	105·22 W
68	Franklin (L.) .... Nev.	40·23 N	115·10 W
66	Franklin D. Roosevelt L. . . Wash.	48·12 N	118·43 W
86	Franklin Mts .... Can.	65·36 N	125·55 W
75	Franklin Park . . . Ill. (Chicago In.)	41·56 N	87·53 W
77	Franklinton (frăŋk'lĭn-tŭn) .... La.	30·49 N	90·09 W
161	Frankston . Austl. (Melbourne In.)	38·09 S	145·08 E
75	Franksville (frănkz'vĭl) Wis. (Milwaukee In.)	42·46 N	87·55 W
87	Franz (frȧnz) .... Can.	48·27 N	84·28 W
	Franz Josef Land (Is.), see Zemlya Frantsa Iosifa		
125	Frascati (fräs-kä'tē) It. (Rome In.)	41·49 N	12·45 E
75	Fraser (frā'zēr) Mich. (Detroit In.)	42·32 N	82·57 W
160	Fraser (Great Sandy) (I.) (frā'zēr) Austl.	25·12 S	153·00 E
86	Fraser (R.) .... Can.	51·41 N	122·19 W
116	Fraserburgh (frā'zēr-bûrg) . . . Scot.	57·40 N	2·01 W
87	Fraserdale (frā'zēr-dāl) ...... Can.	49·51 N	81·40 W
125	Frattamaggiore (frät-tä-mäg-zhyô'rĕ) . It. (Naples In.)	40·41 N	14·16 E
101	Fray Bentos (frī bĕn'tōs) Ur. (Buenos Aires In.)	33·10 S	58·19 W
70	Frazee (frȧ-zē') .... Minn.	46·42 N	95·43 W
94	Fraziers Hog Cay (I.) ..... Ba. Is.	25·25 N	77·55 W
123	Frechen (frĕ'ĸĕn) . . Ger. (Ruhr In.)	50·54 N	6·49 E
118	Fredericia (frĕdh-ĕ-rē'tsē-ȧ) . . Den.	55·35 N	9·45 E
81	Frederick (frĕd'ēr-ĭk) .... Md.	39·25 N	77·25 W
72	Frederick .... Okla.	34·23 N	99·01 W
76	Fredericksburg (frĕd'ēr-ĭkz-bûrg) . Tex.	30·16 N	98·52 W
81	Fredericksburg .... Va.	38·20 N	77·30 W
73	Fredericktown (frĕd'ēr-ĭk-toun) . Mo.	37·32 N	90·16 W
82	Fredericton (frĕd'ēr-ĭk-tŭn) . . Can.	45·58 N	66·40 W
155	Frederik Hendrik (I.) (frĕd'ēr-ĭk hĕn'drēk) . W. Irian	7·45 S	137·30 E
118	Frederikshavn (frĕdh'ĕ-rêks-houn) . Den.	57·27 N	10·31 E
118	Frederikssund (frĕdh'ĕ-rêks-sŏŏn) Den.	55·51 N	12·04 E
98	Fredonia (frĕ-dō'nyȧ) . . . Col. (In.)	5·55 N	75·40 W
73	Fredonia (frê-dō'nĭ-ȧ) ...... Kans.	36·31 N	95·50 W
81	Fredonia .... N. Y.	42·25 N	79·20 W
118	Fredrikstad (frȧdh'rêks-städ) . Nor.	59·14 N	10·58 E
74	Freeburg (frē'bûrg) Ill. (St. Louis In.)	38·26 N	89·59 W
84	Freehold (frē'hōld) N. J. (New York In.)	40·15 N	74·16 W
81	Freeland (frē'lȧnd) .... Pa.	41·00 N	75·50 W
65	Freeland ...... Wash. (Seattle In.)	48·01 N	122·32 W
83	Freels, C. (frēlz) .... Can.	49·18 N	53·10 W
85	Freelton (frēl'tŭn) Can. (Toronto In.)	43·24 N	80·02 W
71	Freeport (frē'pōrt) .... Ill.	42·19 N	89·30 W
84	Freeport . . . N. Y. (New York In.)	40·39 N	73·35 W
77	Freeport .... Tex.	28·56 N	95·21 W
164	Freetown (frē'toun) .... S. L.	8·29 N	13·16 W
124	Fregenal de la Sierra (frā-hȧ-näl' dā lä syĕr'rä) . Sp.	38·09 N	6·40 W
125	Fregene (frĕ-zhĕ'-nĕ) It. (Rome In.)	41·52 N	12·12 E
120	Freiberg (frī'bĕrgh) .... Ger.	50·54 N	13·18 E
120	Freiburg .... Ger.	48·00 N	7·50 E
111	Freienried (frī'ĕn-rēd) Ger. (Munich In.)	48·20 N	11·08 E
100	Freirina (frȧ-ĭ-rē'nä) .... Chile	28·35 S	71·26 W
111	Freising (frī'zĭng) Ger. (Munich In.)	48·25 N	11·45 E
123	Fréjus (frā-zhüs') .... Fr.	43·28 N	6·46 E
158	Fremantle (frē'măn-t'l) ..... Austl.	32·03 S	116·05 E
65	Fremont (frê-mŏnt') Calif, (San Francisco In.)	37·33 N	122·00 W
80	Fremont .... Mich.	43·25 N	85·55 W
70	Fremont .... Nebr.	41·26 N	96·30 W
80	Fremont .... Ohio	41·20 N	83·05 W
69	Fremont (R.) .... Utah	38·20 N	111·30 W
67	Fremont Pk. .... Wyo.	43·05 N	109·35 W
	French, see Loyaute, Iles.		
78	French Broad (R.) (frĕnch brôd) Tenn.-N. C.	35·59 N	83·01 W
99	French Guiana (gē-ä'nä) .... S. A.	4·20 N	53·00 W
80	French Lick (frĕnch lĭk) ...... Ind.	38·35 N	86·35 W
67	Frenchman Cr. (frĕnch-măn) Mont.	48·51 N	107·20 W
72	Frenchman Cr. .... Nebr.	40·24 N	101·50 W
68	Frenchman F. .... Nev.	36·55 N	116·11 W
74	French River . Minn. (Duluth In.)	46·54 N	91·54 W
	French, see Loyaute, Iles		
163	French Somaliland .... Afr.	11·35 N	45·08 E
90	Fresnillo (frȧs-nēl'yô) .... Mex.	23·10 N	102·52 W
68	Fresno (frĕz'nō) .... Calif.	36·43 N	119·47 W
98	Fresno (frĕs'-nô) .... Col. (In.)	5·10 N	75·01 W
68	Fresno (R.) (frĕz'nō) .... Calif.	37·00 N	120·24 W
68	Fresno Slough .... Calif.	36·39 N	120·12 W
120	Freudenstadt (froi'den-shtät) . Ger.	48·28 N	8·26 E
160	Freycinet Pen. (frā-sē-nĕ') . . Austl.	42·13 S	148·56 E
69	Fria (R.) (frê-ä) .... Ariz.	34·03 N	112·12 W
166	Fria, C. (frĭȧ) .... S. W. Afr.	18·15 S	12·10 E
100	Frias (frē-äs) .... Arg.	28·43 S	65·03 W
120	Fribourg (frē-bōōr') .... Switz.	46·48 N	7·07 E
74	Fridley (frĭd'lĭ) Minn. (Minneapolis, St. Paul In.)	45·05 N	93·16 W
120	Frieburg (frī'bōōrgh) .... Ger.	47·59 N	7·50 E
111	Friedberg (frēd'bĕrgh) Ger. (Munich In.)	48·22 N	11·00 E
120	Friedland (frēt'länt) .... Ger.	53·39 N	13·34 E
120	Friedrichshafen (frē-drēks-häf'ĕn) Ger.	47·39 N	9·28 E
73	Friend (frĕnd) .... Nebr.	40·40 N	97·16 W
77	Friendswood (frĕnds'-wŏŏd) Tex. (In.)	29·31 N	95·11 W
79	Fries (frēz) .... Va.	36·42 N	80·59 W
111	Friesack (frē'säk) Ger. (Berlin In.)	52·44 N	12·35 E
99	Frio, Cabo (C.) (kä'bō-frê'ō) Braz.	22·58 S	42·08 W
76	Frio R. .... Tex.	29·00 N	99·15 W
124	Friol (frê-ōl') .... Sp.	43·02 N	7·48 W
117	Frisian (Is.) (frē'zhăn) ...... Neth.	53·30 N	5·20 E
86	Frobisher (L.) (frŏb'ĭsh-ēr) . . . Can.	56·33 N	107·57 W
87	Frobisher Bay .... Can.	63·48 N	68·31 W
87	Frobisher B. .... Can.	62·49 N	66·41 W
110	Frodsham (frŏdz'ăm) .... Eng.	53·18 N	2·48 W
160	Frome, L. (frōōm) .... Austl.	30·40 S	140·13 E
73	Frontenac (frŏn'tê-năk) .... Kans.	37·27 N	94·41 W
91	Frontera (frôn-tā'rä) .... Mex.	18·34 N	92·38 W
122	Frontignan (frôɴ-tê-nyäɴ') .... Fr.	43·26 N	3·45 E
67	Front Ra. (frŭnt) .... Wyo.	42·17 N	105·53 W
81	Front Royal (frŭnt) .... Va.	38·55 N	78·10 W
112	Fro Sea (frô) .... Nor.	63·49 N	9·12 E
126	Frosinone (frō-zê-nō'nȧ) .... It.	41·38 N	13·22 E
81	Frostburg (frôst'bûrg) .... Md.	39·40 N	78·55 W
74	Fruit (frōōt) .... Ill. (St. Louis In.)	38·50 N	89·51 W
69	Fruita (frōōt-ȧ) .... Colo.	39·10 N	108·45 W
74	Fruitdale (frōōt'dāl) Tex. (Dallas, Fort Worth In.)	32·43 N	96·46 W
134	Frunze (frōōn'zĕ) .... Sov. Un.	42·49 N	74·42 E
136	Fryanovo (f'ryä'nô-vô) Sov. Un. (Moscow In.)	56·08 N	38·28 E
136	Fryazino (f'ryä'zĭ-nô) Sov. Un. (Moscow In.)	55·58 N	38·05 E
121	Frýdek (frē'dĕk) .... Czech.	49·43 N	18·22 E
120	Frydlant (frēd'länt) .... Czech.	50·56 N	15·05 E
147	Fuchien (Fukien) (Prov.) . . . China	25·39 N	117·21 E
147	Fuchin (fōō'chĭn') .... China	47·13 N	132·11 E
151	Fuchou (Foochow) (fōō'chó) China	26·02 N	119·18 E
148	Fuchow (fōō'chō') .... China	39·46 N	121·44 E
153	Fuchu (fōō'chōō) . Jap. (Tōkyō In.)	35·41 N	139·29 E
151	Fuch'un (R.) .... China	29·50 N	120·00 E
92	Fuego (Vol.) (fwā'gō) ...... Guat.	14·29 N	90·52 W
125	Fuencarral (fuān-kär-räl') Sp. (Madrid In.)	40·29 N	3·42 W
124	Fuensalida (fwān-sä-lē'dä) .... Sp.	40·04 N	4·15 W
76	Fuente (fwĕ'n-tĕ) .... Mex.	28·39 N	100·34 W
124	Fuente de Cantos (fwĕn'tȧ dā kän'tōs) . Sp.	38·15 N	6·18 W
125	Fuente el Saz (fwĕn'tȧ ĕl säth') Sp. (Madrid In.)	40·39 N	3·30 W
124	Fuente-Ovejuna (fwĕn'tȧ-ōvȧ-hōō'nä) . Sp.	38·15 N	5·30 W
124	Fuentesaúco (fwĕn-tȧ-sä-ōō'kō) Sp.	41·18 N	5·25 W
88	Fuerte, Rio del (R.) (rê'ō-dĕl-fōō-ĕ'r-tĕ) . Mex.	26·15 N	108·50 W
99	Fuerte Olimpo (fwĕr'tȧ ō-lēm-pō) Par.	21·10 S	57·49 W
164	Fuerteventura I. (fwĕr'tȧ-vĕn-tōō'rä) . Can. Is.	28·24 N	13·21 W
146	Fuhai .... China	47·01 N	87·07 E
148	Fuhsien (fōō'sĭăn) .... China	39·36 N	121·59 E
153	Fuji (R.) .... Jap.	35·20 N	138·23 E
153	Fuji-san (Mtn.) (fōō'jê sän) . . Jap.	35·23 N	138·44 E
153	Fujisawa (fōō'jê-sä'wa) Jap. (Tōkyō In.)	35·20 N	139·29 E
	Fukien (Prov.), see Fuchien		
153	Fukuchiyama (fŏŏ'kŏŏ-chê-yä'mä) . Jap.	35·18 N	135·07 E
153	Fukue (I.) (fŏŏ-kōō'ā) .... Jap.	32·40 N	129·02 E
153	Fukui (fōō'kōō-ê) .... Jap.	36·05 N	136·14 E
153	Fukuoka (fōō'kŏŏ-ō'kȧ) ...... Jap.	33·35 N	130·23 E
152	Fukushima (fōō'kŏŏ-shē'mȧ) . . Jap.	37·45 N	140·29 E
153	Fukuyama (fōō'kŏŏ-yä'mȧ) . . . Jap.	34·31 N	133·21 E
120	Fulda R. (fŏŏl'dä) .... Ger.	51·05 N	9·40 E

ng-sing; ŋ-baŋk: ɴ-nasalized n; nŏd; cŏmmit; ōld; ôbey; ôrder; fōōd; fŏŏt; ou-out; s-soft; sh-dish; th-thin; pūre; ûnite; ûrn; stŭd; circŭs; ü-as "y" in study; '-indeterminate vowel.

208 Fullerton–Gemlik PRONOUNCING INDEX

Page	Name Pronunciation Region	Lat. °′	Long. °′
74	Fullerton (fŏŏl′ẽr-tŭn) Calif. (Los Angeles In.)	33·53 N	117·56 W
77	Fullerton … La.	31·00 N	93·00 W
84	Fullerton … Md. (Baltimore In.)	39·22 N	76·31 W
70	Fullerton … Nebr.	41·21 N	97·59 W
78	Fulton (fŭl′tŭn) … Ky.	36·30 N	88·53 W
73	Fulton … Mo.	38·51 N	91·56 W
81	Fulton … N. Y.	43·20 N	76·25 W
85	Fulton Cr. … Can. (Edmonton In.)	53·30 N	113·24 W
84	Fultondale (fŭl′tŭn-dāl) Ala. (Birmingham In.)	33·37 N	86·48 W
153	Funabashi (fōō′nȧ-bä′shē) Jap. (Tōkyō In.)	35·43 N	139·59 E
153	Funaya (fōō-nä′yä) Jap. (Osaka In.)	34·45 N	135·52 E
164	Funchal (fŏŏn-shäl′) … Mad. Is.	32·41 N	16·15 W
98	Fundación (fōōn-dä-syō′n) … Col.	10·43 N	74·13 W
124	Fundão (fŏŏn-douɴ′) … Port.	40·08 N	7·32 W
82	Fundy, B. of (fŭn′dĭ) … Can.	44·50 N	66·05 W
82	Fundy Natl. Park … Can.	45·38 N	65·25 W
148	Funing (fōō′nĭng′) … China	39·55 N	119·16 E
151	Funing Wan (B.) (fōō′nĭng′) . China	26·48 N	120·35 E
148	Funiu Shan (Mts.) (fōō′nēo shän) China	34·25 N	113·28 E
91	Furbero (fōōr-bĕ′rô) … Mex.	20·21 N	97·32 W
128	Furmanov (fûr-mä′nôf) . . Sov. Un.	57·14 N	41·11 E
101	Furnas, Represa de (Res.) Braz. (Rio de Janeiro In.)	21·00 S	46·00 W
159	Furneaux Group (Is.) (fûr′nō) Austl.	40·15 S	146·27 E
120	Fürstenfeld (für′stĕn-fĕlt) … Aus.	47·02 N	16·03 E
111	Fürstenfeldbruck (fur′stĕn-fĕld′ brōōk) . Ger. (Munich In.)	48·11 N	11·16 E
120	Fürstenwalde (für′stĕn-väl-dĕ) Ger.	52·21 N	14·04 E
120	Fürth (fürt) … Ger.	49·28 N	11·03 E
153	Furuichi (fōō′rŏŏ-ē′chê) Jap. (Ōsaka In.)	34·33 N	135·37 E
153	Fusa (fōō′sä) … Jap. (Tōkyō In.)	35·52 N	140·08 E
98	Fusagasugá (fōō-sä-gä-sōō-gȧ′) Col. (In.)	4·22 N	74·22 W
153	Fuse (fōō′sȧ) … Jap. (Ōsaka In.)	34·39 N	135·35 E
	Fushih, see Yenan		
153	Fushimi (fōō′shē-mê) Jap. (Osaka In.)	34·57 N	135·47 E
150	Fushun (fōō′shōōn′) … China	41·50 N	124·00 E
150	Fusung … China	42·12 N	127·12 E
153	Futtsu (fōōt′tsōō′) Jap. (Tōkyō In.)	35·19 N	139·49 E
153	Futtsu Misaki (C.) (fōōt′tsōō′ mê-sä′kē) . Jap. (Tōkyō In.)	35·19 N	139·46 E
168	Fuwah (fōō′wȧ) . U. A. R. (Nile In.)	31·13 N	30·35 E
151	Fuyang … China	30·10 N	119·58 E
150	Fuyü (fōō′yōō′) … China	45·20 N	125·00 E
118	Fyn (fü″n) … Den.	55·24 N	10·33 E
116	Fyne (L.) (fīn) … Scot.	56·14 N	5·10 W
118	Fyresdal Vand (L.) (fü′rĕs-däl vän) . Nor.	59·04 N	7·55 E
166	Gaberones (gù-bē-rō′nōz) … Bots.	24·28 S	25·59 E
164	Gabès (gä′bĕs) … Tun.	33·51 N	10·04 E
164	Gabès, Golfe de (G.) … Tun.	32·22 N	10·59 E
121	Gabin (gŏɴ′bên) … Pol.	52·23 N	19·47 E
163	Gabon (gȧ-bôɴ′) … Afr.	0·30 S	10·45 E
77	Gabriel R. (gā′brĭ-ĕl) … Tex.	30·38 N	97·15 W
127	Gabrovo (gäb′rô-vō) … Bul.	42·52 N	25·19 E
98	Gachetá (gä-chā′tä) … Col (In.)	4·50 N	73·36 W
127	Gacko (gäts′kô) … Yugo.	43·10 N	18·34 E
139	Gader … Jordan (Palestine In.)	32·39 N	35·41 E
78	Gadsden (gădz′dĕn) … Ala.	34·00 N	86·00 W
129	Gadyach (gäd-yäch′) … Sov. Un.	50·22 N	33·59 E
127	Gaesti (gä-yĕsh′tê) … Rom.	44·43 N	25·21 E
126	Gaeta (gä-ā′tä) … It.	41·18 N	13·34 E
79	Gaffney (găf′nĭ) … S. C.	35·04 N	81·47 W
164	Gafsa (gäf′sä) … Tun.	34·16 N	8·37 E
82	Gagetown (gāj′toun) … Can.	45·47 N	66·09 W
155	Gagrary (I.) (gä-grä-rê) Phil. (Manila In.)	13·23 N	123·58 E
126	Gaidhouronísi (I.) … Grc. (Inset)	34·53 N	25·45 E
122	Gaillac-sur-Tarn (gȧ-yäk′sür-tärn′) . Fr.	43·54 N	1·52 E
88	Gaillard Cut (gä-êl-yä′rd) C. Z. (Panama Canal In.)	9·03 N	79·42 W
79	Gainesville (gānz′vĭl) … Fla.	28·43 N	82·25 W
78	Gainesville … Ga.	34·16 N	83·48 W
73	Gainesville … Tex.	33·38 N	97·08 W
110	Gainsborough (gānz′bŭr-ô) … Eng.	53·23 N	0·46 W
160	Gairdner, L. (gȧrd′nẽr) … Austl.	32·20 S	136·30 E
84	Gaithersburg (gā′thẽrs′bûrg) … Md. (Baltimore In.)	39·08 N	77·13 W
142	Gajan … W. Pak.	28·45 N	67·30 E
139	Galala, Gebel el (Mts.) U. A. R. (Palestine In.)	28·51 N	32·14 E
125	Galapagar (gä-lä-pä-gär′) Sp. (Madrid In.)	40·36 N	4·00 W
	Galápagos Is., see Colon, Archip. de		
116	Galashiels (găl-ȧ-shēlz) … Scot.	55·40 N	2·57 W
129	Galati (gȧ-lätz′ĭ) … Rom.	45·25 N	28·05 E
127	Galatina (gä-lä-tē′nä) … It.	40·10 N	18·12 E
127	Galaxidhion … Grc.	38·26 N	22·22 E
118	Galdhöpiggen (Mtn.) (gäld-hû-pĭggĕn) . Nor.	61·39 N	8·12 E
76	Galeana (gä-lȧ-ä′nä) … Mex.	24·50 N	100·04 W
71	Galena (gȧ-lē′nȧ) … Ill.	42·26 N	90·27 W
75	Galena … Ind. (Louisville In.)	38·21 N	85·55 W
73	Galena … Kans.	37·06 N	94·39 W
77	Galena Pk. … Tex. (In.)	29·44 N	95·14 W
88	Galera, Cerro (Mtn.) (sĕ′r-rô-gä-lĕ′rä) C. Z. (Panama Canal In.)	8·55 N	79·38 W
125	Galera (R.) (gä-lĕ′-rä) It. (Rome In.)	41·58 N	12·21 E
98	Galeras (Vol.) (gä-lĕ′räs) … Col.	0·57 N	77·27 W
65	Gales (R.) (gālz) Ore. (Portland In.)	45·33 N	123·11 W
73	Galesburg (gālz′bûrg) … Ill.	40·56 N	90·21 W
71	Galesville (gālz′vĭl) … Wis.	44·04 N	91·22 W
81	Galeton (gāl′tŭn) … Pa.	41·45 N	77·40 W
127	Galibolu (Gallipoli) (gĕ-lĭb′ô-lŏŏ) (gȧ-lĭp′ô-lē) . Tur.	40·25 N	26·40 E
132	Galich (gȧl′ĭch) … Sov. Un.	58·20 N	42·38 E
121	Galicia (Reg.) (gȧ-lĭsh′ĭ-ȧ) Pol.-Sov. Un.	49·48 N	21·05 E
124	Galicia (Reg.) (gȧ-lē′thyä) … Sp.	43·35 N	8·03 W
159	Galilee (L.) (găl′ĭ-lē) … Austl.	22·23 S	145·09 E
94	Galina Pt. (gä-lē′nä) … Jam.	18·25 N	76·50 W
80	Galion (găl′ĭ-ŭn) … Ohio	40·45 N	82·50 W
69	Galisteo (gā-lĭs-tā′ō) … N. Mex.	35·20 N	106·00 W
113	Galite, I. La (gä-lēt) … Alg.	37·36 N	8·03 E
165	Galla (Prov.) (gäl′lä) … Eth.	7·22 N	35·28 E
165	Gallabat (găl′ȧ-băt) … Sud.	12·55 N	36·12 E
126	Gallarate (gäl-lä-rä′tā) … It.	45·37 N	8·48 E
123	Gallardon (gä-lär-dôɴ′) Fr. (Paris In.)	48·31 N	1·40 E
73	Gallatin (găl′ȧ-tĭn) … Mo.	39·55 N	93·58 W
78	Gallatin … Tenn.	36·23 N	86·28 W
67	Gallatin R … Mont.	45·12 N	111·10 W
143	Galle (gäl) … Ceylon	6·13 N	80·10 E
125	Gállego (R.) (gäl-yā′gō) … Sp.	42·27 N	0·37 W
98	Gallinas, Pta. de (Pt.) (gä-lyē′näs) Col.	12·10 N	72·10 W
127	Gallipoli (gäl-lē′pô-lē) … It.	40·03 N	17·58 E
	Gallipoli, see Galibolu		
80	Gallipolis (găl-ĭ-pô-lēs) … Ohio	38·50 N	82·10 W
112	Gällivare (yĕl-ĭ-vär′ĕ) … Swe.	68·06 N	20·29 E
124	Gallo (R.) (gäl′yō) … Sp.	40·43 N	1·42 W
69	Gallup (găl′ŭp) … N. Mex.	35·30 N	108·45 W
165	Galnale Doria R … Eth.	5·35 N	40·26 E
116	Galty Mts … Ire.	52·19 N	8·20 W
73	Galva (găl′vȧ) … Ill.	41·11 N	90·02 W
77	Galveston (găl′vĕs-tŭn) . Tex. (In.)	29·18 N	94·48 W
77	Galveston B … Tex.	29·39 N	94·45 W
77	Galveston I … Tex. (In.)	29·12 N	94·53 W
116	Galway … Ire.	53·16 N	9·05 W
116	Galway B. (gôl′wā) … Ire.	53·10 N	9·47 W
164	Gambaga (gäm-bä′gä) … Ghana	10·37 N	0·20 W
165	Gambēlā (gäm-bā′lȧ) … Eth.	8·15 N	34·33 E
163	Gambia (găm′bê-ȧ) … Afr.	13·38 N	19·38 W
164	Gambia R … Gam.-Senegal	12·58 N	12·58 W
166	Gamboma (gäm-bō′mä) … Con. B.	2·30 S	16·00 E
118	Gamleby (gäm′lĕ-bü) … Swe.	57·54 N	16·20 E
155	Gamu (gä-mōō′) . Phil. (Manila In.)	17·05 N	121·50 E
142	Gandak (R.) … India	26·37 N	84·22 E
83	Gander (găn′dẽr) … Can.	48·59 N	54·32 W
83	Gander (R.) … Can.	48·45 N	55·13 W
83	Gander L … Can.	48·57 N	55·10 W
125	Gandia (gän-dē′ä) … Sp.	38·56 N	0·10 W
142	Ganges, Mouths of (găn′jēz) . India	21·18 N	88·40 E
142	Ganges (R.) (găn′jēz) … India	24·32 N	87·58 E
126	Gangi (gän′jē) … It.	37·48 N	14·15 E
146	Gangtok … Sikkim	27·15 N	88·30 E
67	Gannett Pk. (găn′ĕt) … Wyo.	43·10 N	109·38 W
75	Gano (ğ′nô) . Ohio (Cincinnati In.)	39·18 N	84·24 W
111	Gänserndorf … Aus. (Vienna In.)	48·21 N	16·43 E
164	Gao (gä′ō) … Mali	16·17 N	0·00
164	Gaoua (gȧ-ōō-ȧ′) … Upper Volta	10·21 N	3·11 W
123	Gap (gȧp) … Fr.	44·34 N	6·08 E
155	Gapan (gä-pän) . Phil. (Manila In.)	15·18 N	120·56 E
93	Garachiné (gä-rä-chē′nȧ) … Pan.	8·02 N	78·22 W
93	Garachiné, Punta (Pt.) (pŏŏ′n-tä-gä-rä-chē′nȧ) . Pan.	8·08 N	78·35 W
99	Garanhuns (gä-rän-yŏŏɴsh′) . Braz.	8·49 S	36·28 W
73	Garber (gȧr′bẽr) … Okla.	36·28 N	97·35 W
111	Garching (gär′ᴋĕng) Ger. (Munich In.)	48·15 N	11·39 E
76	Garcia (gär-sē′ä) … Mex.	25·90 N	100·37 W
90	Garcia de la Cadena (dĕ-lä-kä-dĕ-nä) . Mex.	21·14 N	103·26 W
126	Garda, Lago di (L.) (lä′gō-dē-gär′dä) . It.	45·43 N	10·26 E
122	Gardanne (gȧr-dȧn′) Fr. (Marseille In.)	43·28 N	5·29 E
120	Gardelegen (gär-dē-lȧ′ghĕn) . Ger.	52·32 N	11·22 E
80	Garden (I.) (gär′d′n) … Mich.	45·50 N	85·50 W
74	Gardena (gär-dē′nȧ) Calif. (Los Angeles In.)	33·53 N	118·19 W
75	Garden City . . Mich. (Detroit In.)	42·20 N	83·21 W
72	Garden City … Kan.	37·58 N	100·52 W
74	Garden Grove (gär′d′n grōv) Calif. (Los Angeles In.)	33·47 N	117·56 W
74	Garden River Can. (Sault Ste. Marie In.)	46·33 N	84·10 W
82	Gardiner (gärd′nẽr) … Maine	44·12 N	69·46 W
67	Gardiner … Mont.	45·03 N	110·43 W
65	Gardiner … Wash. (Seattle In.)	48·03 N	122·55 W
142	Gardiz … Afg.	33·43 N	69·09 E
81	Gardner … Mass.	42·35 N	72·00 W
165	Gardulā … Eth.	5·43 N	37·40 E
142	Gar Dzong … China	32·28 N	79·50 E
64	Gareloi (I.) (gär-lōō-ä′) … Alaska	51·40 N	178·48 W
84	Garfield (gär′fēld) N. J. (New York In.)	40·53 N	74·06 W
74	Garfield Utah (Salt Lake City In.)	40·45 N	112·10 W
75	Garfield Heights Ohio (Cleveland In.)	41·25 N	81·36 W
127	Gargaliánoi (gȧr-gä-lyä′nē) … Grc.	37·07 N	21·50 E
119	Gargždai (gärgzh′dī) … Sov. Un.	55·43 N	20·09 E
100	Garin (gä-rē′n) … Arg. (In.)	34·10 S	58·44 W
74	Garland (gär′lănd) Tex. (Dallas, Fort Worth In.)	32·55 N	96·39 W
67	Garland … Utah	41·45 N	112·10 W
134	Garm … Sov. Un.	39·12 N	70·28 E
120	Garmisch-Partenkirchen (gär′ mēsh pär′tĕn-kēr′ᴋĕn) . Ger.	47·38 N	11·10 E
73	Garnett (gär′nĕt) … Kans.	38·16 N	95·15 W
122	Garonne Rivière (R.) (gȧ-rôn) Fr.	44·43 N	0·25 W
165	Garoua (gär′wä) … Cam.	9·16 N	13·24 E
80	Garrett (găr′ĕt) … Ind.	41·20 N	85·10 W
84	Garrison (găr′ĭ-sŭn) N. Y. (New York In.)	41·23 N	73·57 W
70	Garrison … N. D.	47·38 N	101·24 W
70	Garrison Dam Res … N. D.	47·49 N	101·58 W
124	Garrovillas (gä-rô-vēl′yäs) … Sp.	39·42 N	6·30 W
86	Garry (L.) (găr′ĭ) … Can.	66·16 N	99·23 W
111	Garstedt (gär′shtĕt) Ger. (Hamburg In.)	53·40 N	9·58 E
142	Gartok (gär-tŏk′) … China	31·11 N	80·35 E
121	Garwolin (gär-vō′lên) … Pol.	51·54 N	21·40 E
75	Gary (gā′rĭ) … Ind. (Chicago In.)	41·35 N	87·21 W
98	Garzón (gär-thōn′) … Col.	2·13 N	75·44 W
155	Gasan (gä-sän′) . Phil. (Manila In.)	13·19 N	121·52 E
133	Gasan-Kuli … Sov. Un.	37·25 N	53·55 E
80	Gas City (găs) … Ind.	40·30 N	85·40 W
122	Gascogne (Reg.) (gäs-ᴋôn′yĕ) . Fr.	43·45 N	1·49 W
73	Gasconade (R.) (găs-kô-nād′) . Mo.	37·46 N	92·15 W
158	Gascoyne (R.) (găs-koin′) . . Austl.	25·15 S	117·00 E
74	Gashland (găsh′-lănd) Mo. (Kansas City In.)	39·15 N	94·35 W
123	Gasny (gäs-nē′) … Fr. (Paris In.)	49·05 N	1·36 E
82	Gaspé, C … Can.	48·44 N	64·00 W
82	Gaspe (I.) … Can.	48·52 N	65·45 W
82	Gaspé B. (gas′pā) (gȧs-pā′) . . Can.	48·40 N	64·07 W
82	Gaspé Pass … Can.	49·21 N	64·16 W
82	Gaspé Pen … Can.	48·51 N	64·32 W
95	Gasper Hernandez (gäs-pär′ ĕr-nän′dāth) … Dom. Rep.	19·40 N	70·15 W
80	Gassaway (găs′ȧ-wā) … W. Va.	38·40 N	80·45 W
65	Gaston (găs′tŭn) Ore. (Portland In.)	45·26 N	123·08 W
79	Gastonia (găs-tô′nĭ-ȧ) … N. C.	35·15 N	81·14 W
100	Gastre (gäs-trĕ) … Arg.	42·12 S	68·50 W
139	Gata, C … Cyprus (Palestine In.)	34·31 N	33·08 E
124	Gata, Cabo de (C.) (kȧ′bô-dĕ-gä′tä) . Sp.	36·42 N	2·00 W
124	Gata, Sierra de (Mts.) (syĕr′rȧ dā gȧ′tä) . Sp.	40·12 N	6·39 W
136	Gatchina (gä-chē′nȧ) Sov. Un. (Leningrad In.)	59·33 N	30·08 E
116	Gateshead (gāts′hĕd) … Eng.	54·56 N	1·38 W
77	Gatesville (gāts′vĭl) … Mex.	31·26 N	97·43 W
85	Gatineau (gȧ′tê-nō) Can. (Ottawa In.)	45·29 N	75·38 W
81	Gatineau (R.) … Can.	45·45 N	75·50 W
166	Gatooma (gä-tōō′mä) … Rh.	18·14 S	29·46 E
111	Gattendorf … Aus. (Vienna In.)	48·01 N	17·00 E
88	Gatun (gä-tōōn′) C. Z. (Panama Canal In.)	9·16 N	79·25 W
88	Gatun, L. Pan.-C. Z. (Panama Canal In.)	9·13 N	79·24 W
88	Gatun (R.) Pan. (Panama Canal In.)	9·21 N	79·10 W
88	Gatun Locks C. Z. (Panama Canal In.)	9·16 N	79·27 W
142	Gauhati … India	26·09 N	91·51 E
119	Gauja (R.) (gå′ŏŏ-yå) … Sov. Un.	57·10 N	24·30 E
155	Gauttier-Gebergte (Mts.) (gō-tyā′) W. Irian	2·30 S	138·45 E
126	Gávdhos (I.) (gäv′dôs) . . Grc. (In.)	34·48 N	24·08 E
70	Gavins Point Dam (gă′-vĭns) Nebr.	42·47 N	97·47 W
118	Gävle (yĕv′lĕ) … Swe.	60·40 N	17·07 E
118	Gavle-bukten (B.) … Swe.	60·45 N	17·30 E
128	Gavrilov Posad (gȧ′vrê-lôf′ka po-sȧt) . Sov. Un.	56·34 N	40·09 E
128	Gavrilov-Yam (gȧ′vrê-lôf yäm′) Sov. Un.	57·17 N	39·49 E
160	Gawler (gô′lẽr) … Austl.	34·35 S	138·47 E
160	Gawler Ra … Austl.	32·35 S	136·30 E
142	Gaya (gŭ′yä) (gī′ȧ) … India	24·53 N	85·04 E
164	Gaya (gä′yä) … Nig.	11·58 N	9·05 E
80	Gaylord (gā′lôrd) … Mich.	45·00 N	84·35 W
160	Gayndah (gān′däh) … Austl.	25·43 S	151·33 E
129	Gaysin … Sov. Un.	48·46 N	29·22 E
	Gaza, see Ghazzah		
133	Gaziantep (gä-zē-än′tĕp) … Tur.	37·10 N	37·30 E
121	Gdańsk (Danzig) (g′dänsk) (dän′tsēg) . Pol.	54·20 N	18·40 E
128	Gdov (g′dôf′) … Sov. Un.	58·44 N	27·51 E
121	Gdynia (g′dēn′yȧ) … Pol.	54·29 N	18·30 E
72	Geary (gē′rĭ) … Okla.	35·36 N	98·19 W
168	Gebel el Galala el Bahariya (Plat.) U. A. R. (Nile In.)	29·23 N	31·50 E
67	Gebo (gĕb′ō) … Wyo.	43·49 N	108·13 W
77	Ged (gĕd) … La.	30·07 N	93·36 W
165	Gedaref … Sud.	14·03 N	35·11 E
115	Gediz (R.) … Tur.	38·44 N	28·45 E
65	Gedney (I.) (gĕd-nê) Wash. (Seattle In.)	48·01 N	122·18 W
120	Gedser … Den.	54·35 N	12·08 E
111	Geel … Bel. (Brussels In.)	51·09 N	5·01 E
161	Geelong (jē-lông′) Austl. (Melbourne In.)	38·06 S	144·13 E
155	Geelvink-baai (B.) (gäl′vĭŋk) W. Irian	2·20 S	135·30 E
164	Geidam … Nig.	12·49 N	11·49 E
158	Geikie Ra. (gē′kê) … Austl.	17·35 S	125·32 E
120	Geislingen (gis′lĭng-ĕn) … Ger.	48·37 N	9·52 E
75	Geist Res. (gēst) Ind. (Indianapolis In.)	39·57 N	85·59 W
111	Geldermalsen Neth. (Amsterdam In.)	51·53 N	5·18 E
123	Geldern (gĕl′dĕrn) Ger. (Ruhr In.)	51·31 N	6·20 E
127	Gelibolu, Yarimada (Pen.) (gĕ-lĭb′ô-lŏŏ) . Tur.	40·23 N	25·10 E
129	Gel′myazov … Sov. Un.	49·49 N	31·54 E
123	Gelsenkirchen (gĕl-zĕn-kĭrk-ĕn) Ger. (Ruhr In.)	51·31 N	7·05 E
139	Gemas (jĕm′ȧs) Mala. (Singapore In.)	2·35 N	102·37 E
165	Gemena … Con. K.	3·20 N	19·45 E
133	Gemlik (gĕm′lĭk) … Tur.	40·30 N	29·10 E

ăt; finăl; rāte; senâte; ärm; ȧsk; sofȧ; fâre; ch-choose; dh-as th in other; bē; êvent; bĕt; recĕnt; cratẽr; g-go; gh-guttural g; bĭt; ĭ-short neutral; rīde; ᴋ-guttural k as ch in German ich;

PRONOUNCING INDEX General Alvear–Goggingen 209

Page	Name Pronunciation Region	Lat. °′	Long. °′
101	General Alvear (gĕ-nĕ-räl'äl-vĕ-â'r). Arg. (Buenos Aires In.)	36·04 s	60·02 W
101	General Arenales (ä-rĕ-nä'lĕs) Arg. (Buenos Aires In.)	34·19 s	61·16 W
101	General Belgrano (bĕl-grá'nô) Arg. (Buenos Aires In.)	35·45 s	58·32 W
76	General Cepeda (sĕ-pĕ'dä) ... Mex.	25·24 N	101·29 W
101	General Conesa (kô-nĕ'sä) Arg. (Buenos Aires In.)	36·30 s	57·19 W
101	General Guido (gē'dô) Arg. (Buenos Aires In.)	36·41 s	57·48 W
101	General Lavalle (lä-vá'l-yĕ) Arg. (Buenos Aires In.)	36·25 s	56·55 W
100	General Madariaga (män-dä-rēä'gä). Arg.	36·59 s	57·14 W
101	General Paz (pá'z) Arg. (Buenos Aires In.)	35·30 s	58·20 W
90	General Pedro Antonio Santios (pĕ'drô-än-tô'nyô-sän-tyōs). Mex.	21·37 N	98·58 W
100	General Pico (pē'kô) ... Arg.	36·46 s	63·44 W
100	General Roca (rô-kä) ... Arg.	39·01 s	67·31 W
100	General San Martín (sän-mär-tē'n) Arg. (In.)	34·19 s	58·32 W
101	General Viamonte (vēä'môn-tĕ) Arg. (Buenos Aires In.)	35·01 s	60·59 W
76	General Zuazua (zwä'zwä). Mex.	25·54 N	100·07 W
81	Genesee (R.) (jĕn-ē-sē') ... N. Y.	42·25 N	78·10 W
80	Geneseo (jē-nĕs'eō) ... Ill.	41·28 N	90·11 W
78	Geneva (jē-nē'vá) ... Ala.	31·03 N	85·50 W
75	Geneva ... Ill. (Chicago In.)	41·53 N	88·18 W
73	Geneva ... Nebr.	40·32 N	97·37 W
81	Geneva ... N. Y.	42·50 N	77·00 W
80	Geneva ... Ohio	41·45 N	80·55 W
	Geneva, see Génève		
120	Geneva, L. ... Switz.	46·28 N	6·30 E
120	Génève (Geneva) (zhĕ-nĕv'). Switz.	46·14 N	6·04 E
129	Genichesk (gå'nĕ-chyĕsk') Sov. Un.	46·11 N	34·47 E
124	Genil (R.) (hå-nēl') ... Sp.	37·12 N	4·30 W
73	Genoa (jen'ô-à) ... Nebr.	41·26 N	97·43 W
77	Genoa ... Tex. (In.)	29·37 N	95·11 W
	Genoa, see Genova		
75	Genoa City. Wis. (Milwaukee In.)	42·31 N	88·19 W
126	Genova (Genoa) (jĕn'ō-vä) ... It.	44·23 N	9·52 E
126	Genova, Golfo di (G.) (gôl-fô-dē-jĕn'ō-vä). It.	44·10 N	8·45 E
98	Genovesa (I.) (ĕ's-lä-gĕ-nō-vĕ-sä) Ec.	0·08 N	90·15 W
117	Gent ... Bel.	51·05 N	3·40 E
120	Genthin (gĕn-tēn') ... Ger.	52·24 N	12·10 E
125	Genzano di Roma (gzhĕnt-zä'-nô-dē-rô'-mä) It. (Rome In.)	41·43 N	12·49 E
158	Geographe B. (jē-ô-grăf') ... Austl.	33·00 s	114·00 E
158	Geographic Chan. (jēō'gră-fĭk) Austl.	24·15 s	112·50 E
133	Geokchay (gĕ-ôk'chī) ... Sov. Un.	40·40 N	47·40 E
79	George (L.) (jôr-ĭj) ... Fla.	29·10 N	81·50 W
81	George (L.) (jôrj) ... N. Y.	43·40 N	73·30 W
83	George B. (jôr-ĭj) ... Can.	45·46 N	61·45 W
74	George L. (jôrg) Can.-U. S. (Sault Ste. Marie In.)	46·26 N	84·09 W
75	George, L. ... Ind. (Chicago In.)	41·31 N	87·17 W
161	Georges (R.) .. Austl. (Sydney In.)	33·57 s	151·00 E
95	George Town ... Ba. Is.	23·30 N	75·50 W
99	Georgetown (jôrj'toun) ... Guy.	7·45 N	58·04 W
83	Georgetown (jôr-ĭj-toun) ... Can.	46·09 N	62·32 W
85	Georgetown (jôrg-toun) Can. (Toronto In.)	43·39 N	79·56 W
84	Georgetown. Conn. (New York In.)	41·15 N	73·25 W
81	Georgetown ... Del.	38·40 N	75·20 W
94	Georgetown ... Cayman Is.	19·20 N	81·20 W
80	Georgetown ... Ill.	40·00 N	87·40 W
80	Georgetown ... Ky.	38·10 N	84·35 W
81	Georgetown ... Md.	39·25 N	75·55 W
83	Georgetown (jôrg-toun) Mass. (Boston In.)	42·43 N	71·00 W
79	Georgetown (jôr-ĭj-toun) ... S. C.	33·22 N	79·17 W
77	Georgetown (jôrg-toun) ... Tex.	30·37 N	97·40 W
81	George Washington Birthplace Natl. Mon. (jôrj wŏsh'ĭng-tŭn) Va.	38·10 N	77·00 W
73	George Washington Carver Natl. Mon. (jôrg wăsh-ĭng-tŭn kär'-vĕr). Mo.	36·58 N	94·21 W
63	Georgia (State) (jôr'ji-ă) ... U. S.	32·40 N	83·50 W
65	Georgia, Str. of Wash. (Vancouver In.)	48·56 N	123·06 W
130	Georgian (S. S. R.) ... Sov. Un.	42·17 N	43·00 E
78	Georgiana (jôr-jē-ăn'á) ... Ala.	31·39 N	86·44 W
87	Georgian Is. Natl. Park (jôr'ji-ăn). Can.	45·15 N	81·10 W
158	Georgina (R.) (jôr-jē'ná) ... Austl.	22·00 s	138·15 E
133	Georgiyevsk (gyôr-gyĕfsk') Sov. Un.	44·05 N	43·30 E
120	Gera (gā'rä) ... Ger.	50·52 N	12·06 E
100	Geral, Serra (Mts.) (sĕr'rá zhä-räl'). Braz.	28·30 s	51·00 W
99	Geral de Goiás, Serra (Mts.) (zhä-räl'-dĕ-gô-yá's). Braz.	14·22 s	45·40 W
158	Geraldton (jĕr'ăld-tŭn) ... Austl.	28·40 s	114·35 E
87	Geraldton ... Can.	49·43 N	87·00 W
124	Gérgal (gĕr'gäl) ... Sp.	37·08 N	2·29 W
70	Gering (gē'rĭng) ... Nebr.	41·49 N	103·41 W
121	Gerlachovka Pk. ... Czech.	49·12 N	20·05 E
80	Germantown (jûr'măn-toun). Ohio	39·35 N	84·25 W
102	Germany (jûr'má-nĭ) ... Eur.	51·44 N	8·46 E
167	Germiston (jûr'mĭs-tŭn) ... S. Afr. (Johannesburg & Pretoria In.)	26·19 s	28·11 E
155	Gerona (hä-rō'nä) Phil. (Manila In.)	15·36 N	120·36 E
124	Gerona (hĕ-rô'-nä) ... Sp.	41·55 N	2·48 E
110	Gerrards Cross (jĕr'ărds krŏs) Eng. (London In.)	51·34 N	0·33 W
125	Gers (R.) (zhĕr) ... Fr.	43·25 N	0·30 E
111	Gersthofen (gĕrst-hō'fĕn) Ger. (Munich In.)	48·26 N	10·54 E
168	Gestro R. .Eth. (Horn of Afr. In.)	5·18 N	41·50 E
125	Getafe (hā-tä'fā). Sp. (Madrid In.)	40·19 N	3·44 W
81	Gettysburg (gĕt'ĭs-bûrg) ... Pa.	39·50 N	77 15 W
70	Gettysburg ... S. D.	45·01 N	99·59 W
123	Gevelsberg (gĕ-fĕls'bĕrgh) Ger. (Ruhr In.)	51·18 N	7·20 E
142	Ghāghra (R.) ... India	27·19 N	81·22 E
163	Ghana (gän'ä) ... Afr.	8·00 N	2·00 W
166	Ghanzi (găn'zē) ... Bots.	21·30 s	22·00 E
142	Ghard ... W. Pak.	24·50 N	68·35 E
164	Ghardaïa (gär-dä'ē-ä) ... Alg.	32·29 N	3·38 E
164	Ghāt ... Libya	24·52 N	10·16 E
165	Ghazal, Bahr el (R.) (bär ĕl ghä-zäl'). Sud.	9·11 N	29·37 E
113	Ghazaouet ... Alg.	35·19 N	1·09 W
142	Ghazni (gŭz'nē) ... Afg.	33·43 N	68·18 E
139	Ghazzah (Gaza) Gaza Area (Palestine In.)	31·30 N	34·29 E
121	Gheorghieni ... Rom.	46·48 N	25·30 E
121	Gherla (gĕr'lä) ... Rom.	47·01 N	23·55 E
164	Ghudāmis ... Alg.	30·07 N	9·26 E
126	Giannutri, I. di (jän-nōō'trē) ... It.	42·15 N	11·06 E
95	Gibara (hē-bä'rä) ... Cuba	21·05 N	76·10 W
166	Gibeon (gĭb'ē-ŭn) ... S. W. Afr.	24·45 s	16·40 E
124	Gibraleón (hē-brä-lā-ōn') ... Sp.	37·24 N	7·00 W
124	Gibraltar (hē-bräl-tä'r) ... Eur.	36·08 N	5·22 W
124	Gibraltar, Bay of ... Sp.	35·04 N	5·10 W
124	Gibraltar, Strait of ... Afr.-Eur.	35·55 N	5·45 W
75	Gibson (gĭb'sŭn) Ind. (Louisville In.)	38·24 N	85·40 W
80	Gibson City ... Ill.	40·25 N	88·20 W
158	Gibson Des. ... Austl.	24·45 s	123·15 E
84	Gibson Island. Md. (Baltimore In.)	39·05 N	76·26 W
73	Gibson Res. ... Okla.	36·07 N	95·08 W
77	Giddings (gĭd'ĭngz) ... Tex.	30·11 N	96·55 W
73	Gideon (gĭd'ē-ŭn) ... Mo.	36·27 N	89·56 W
122	Gien (zhē-ăN') ... Fr.	47·43 N	2·37 E
120	Giessen (gēs'sĕn) ... Ger.	50·35 N	8·40 E
85	Giffard (zhē-färd') Can. (Quebec In.)	46·51 N	71·12 W
153	Gifu (gē'fōō) ... Jap.	35·25 N	136·45 E
65	Gig Harbor (gĭg) Wash. (Seattle In.)	47·20 N	122·36 W
126	Giglio, I. di (jēl'yō) ... It.	42·23 N	10·55 E
124	Gigüela (R.) (hē-gā'lä) ... Sp.	39·53 N	2·54 W
124	Gijón (hē-hōn') ... Sp.	43·33 N	5·37 W
69	Gila (R.) (hē'lá) ... Ariz.	32·41 N	113·50 W
69	Gila Bend ... Ariz.	32·59 N	112·41 W
69	Gila Bend Ind. Res. ... Ariz.	33·02 N	112·48 W
69	Gila Cliff Dwellings Natl. Mon. N. Mex.	33·15 N	108·20 W
69	Gila River Ind. Res. ... Ariz.	33·11 N	112·38 W
71	Gilbert (gĭl'bērt) ... Minn.	47·27 N	92·29 W
159	Gilbert (R.) (gĭl'bērt) ... Austl.	17·15 s	142·09 E
156	Gilbert Is. ... Oceania	1·30 s	173·00 E
167	Gilboa, Mt. (gĭl-bôá) S. Afr. (Natal In.)	29·13 s	30·17 E
165	Gilf Kebir Plat. ... U. A. R.	24·09 N	25·29 E
142	Gilgit (gĭl'gĭt) ... Pak.	35·58 N	73·48 E
158	Gillen (L.) (jĭl'ĕn) ... Austl.	26·15 s	125·15 E
73	Gillett (jĭ-lĕt') ... Ark.	34·07 N	91·22 W
67	Gillette ... Wyo.	44·17 N	105·30 W
110	Gillingham (gĭl'ĭng ăm) Eng. (London In.)	51·23 N	0·33 E
80	Gilman (gĭl'măn) ... Ill.	40·45 N	87·55 W
74	Gilman Hot Springs Calif. (Los Angeles In.)	33·49 N	116·57 W
77	Gilmer (gĭl'mēr) ... Tex.	32·43 N	94·57 W
84	Gilmore (gĭl'môr). Ga. (Atlanta In.)	33·51 N	84·29 W
68	Gilroy (gĭl-roi') ... Calif.	37·00 N	121·34 W
155	Giluwe, Mt. ... N. Gui. Ter.	6·04 s	144·00 E
122	Gimone (R.) (zhē-mōn') ... Fr.	43·26 N	0·36 E
168	Gineifa (jē-nā'fä) U. A. R. (Suez In.)	30·11 N	32·26 E
139	Gineina, Ras el (Mt.) U. A. R. (Palestine In.)	29·02 N	33·58 E
165	Ginir ... Eth.	7·13 N	40·44 E
126	Ginosa (jē-nō'zä) ... It.	40·35 N	16·48 E
124	Ginzo (hēn-thō') ... Sp.	42·03 N	7·43 W
126	Gioja del Colle (jô'yä dĕl kôl'lā) It.	40·48 N	16·55 E
99	Gi-Paraná (R.) (zhē-pä-rä-nä') Braz.	9·33 s	61·35 W
139	Girâfi (R.). U. A. R. (Palestine In.)	29·48 N	34·43 E
73	Girard (jĭ-rärd') ... Kans.	37·30 N	94·50 W
98	Girardot (hē-rär-dōt') ... Col. (In.)	4·19 N	75·47 W
133	Giresun (ghĕr'ĕ-sōōn') ... Tur.	40·55 N	38·20 E
142	Giridih (jē'rē-dē) ... India	24·12 N	81·18 E
122	Gironde (Est.) (zhē-rôNd') ... Fr.	45·31 N	1·00 W
116	Girvan (gûr'văn) ... Scot.	55·15 N	5·01 W
159	Gisborne (gĭz'bŭrn) ... N. Z. (In.)	38·40 s	178·08 E
122	Gisors (zhē-zôr') ... Fr.	49·19 N	1·47 E
127	Giurgiu (jōōr'jōō) ... Rom.	43·53 N	25·58 E
122	Givet (zhē-vĕ') ... Fr.	50·80 N	4·47 E
122	Givors (zhē-vôr') ... Fr.	45·35 N	4·46 E
135	Gizhiga (gē'zhi-gá) ... Sov. Un.	61·59 N	160·46 E
121	Gizycko (gĭ'zhĭ-ko) ... Pol.	54·03 N	21·48 E
127	Gjinokastër ... Alb.	40·04 N	20·10 E
118	Gjövik (gyû'vĕk) ... Nor.	60·47 N	10·36 E
111	Glabeek-Zuurbemde Bel. (Brussels In.)	50·52 N	4·59 E
64	Glacier Bay Natl. Mon. (glā'shēr) Alaska	58·40 N	136·50 W
86	Glacier Natl. Park ... Can.	51·35 N	120·00 W
66	Glacier Pk. ... Wash.	48·07 N	121·10 W
65	Glacier Pt. ... Can. (Seattle In.)	48·24 N	123·59 W
123	Gladbeck (gläd'bĕk) Ger. (Ruhr In.)	51·35 N	6·59 E
168	Gladdeklipkop S. Afr. (Johannesburg & Pretoria In.)	24·17 s	29·36 E
160	Gladstone (glăd'stŏn) ... Austl.	23·45 s	150·00 E
160	Gladstone ... Austl.	33·15 s	138·20 E
62	Gladstone ... Can.	50·20 N	99·00 W
71	Gladstone ... Mich.	45·50 N	87·04 W
84	Gladstone .. N. J. (New York In.)	40·43 N	74·39 W
65	Gladstone ... Ore. (Portland In.)	45·23 N	122·36 W
80	Gladwin (glăd'wĭn) ... Mich.	44·00 N	84·25 W
126	Glamoč (gläm'ôch) ... Yugo.	44·03 N	16·51 E
120	Glarus (glä'rōōs) ... Switz.	47·02 N	9·03 E
78	Glasgow ... Ky.	37·00 N	85·55 W
73	Glasgow ... Mo.	39·14 N	92·48 W
67	Glasgow ... Mont.	48·14 N	106·39 W
116	Glasgow (glás'gō) ... Scot.	55·54 N	4·25 W
83	Glass B. (glás) ... Can.	46·12 N	59·57 W
75	Glassport (glás'pōrt) Pa. (Pittsburgh In.)	40·19 N	79·53 W
120	Glauchau (glou'kou) ... Ger.	50·51 N	12·28 E
132	Glazov (glä'zôf) ... Sov. Un.	58·05 N	52·52 E
120	Glda R. (g'l'dá) ... Pol.	53·27 N	16·52 E
110	Glen (R.) (glĕn) ... Eng.	52·44 N	0·18 W
122	Glénans, Iles de (Is.) (ēl-dĕ-glā-näN'). Fr.	47·43 N	4·42 W
84	Glen Burnie (bûr'nē) Md. (Baltimore In.)	39·10 N	76·38 W
69	Glen Canyon Dam (glĕn kăn'yŭn) Ariz.	36·57 N	111·25 W
74	Glen Carbon (kär'bŏn) Ill. (St. Louis In.)	38·45 N	89·59 W
75	Glencoe ... Ill. (Chicago In.)	42·08 N	87·45 W
71	Glencoe (glĕn'kō) ... Minn.	44·44 N	94·07 W
167	Glencoe (glĕn-cô) S. Afr. (Natal In.)	28·14 s	30·09 E
84	Glen Cove (kōv) N. Y. (New York In.)	40·51 N	73·38 W
69	Glendale (glĕn'dāl) ... Ariz.	33·30 N	112·15 W
74	Glendale ... Calif. (Los Angeles In.)	34·09 N	118·15 W
75	Glendale ... Ohio (Cincinnati In.)	31·16 N	84·22 W
67	Glendive (glĕn'dīv) ... Mont.	47·08 N	104·41 W
67	Glendo ... Wyo.	42·32 N	104·54 W
74	Glendora (glĕn-dō'rá) Calif. (Los Angeles In.)	34·08 N	117·52 W
160	Glenelg (R.) ... Austl.	37·20 s	141·30 E
75	Glen Ellyn (glĕn ĕl'-lĕn) Ill. (Chicago In.)	41·53 N	88·04 W
160	Glen Innes (ĭn'ĕs) ... Austl.	29·45 s	152·02 E
77	Glenmora (glĕn-mō'rá) ... La.	30·58 N	92·36 W
66	Glenns Ferry (fĕr'ĭ) ... Idaho	42·58 N	115·21 W
79	Glennville (glĕn'vĭl) ... Ga.	31·55 N	81·56 W
84	Glen Olden (ōl'd'n) Pa. (Philadelphia In.)	39·54 N	75·17 W
84	Glen Rock (rŏk). Va. (Norfolk In.)	36·50 N	76·13 W
67	Glenrock (glĕn'rŏk) ... Wyo.	42·50 N	105·53 W
81	Glens Falls (glĕnz fôlz) ... N. Y.	43·20 N	73·40 W
75	Glenshaw (glĕn'shô) Pa. (Pittsburgh In.)	40·33 N	79·57 W
70	Glen Ullin (glĕn'ŭl'ĭn) ... N. D.	46·47 N	101·49 W
65	Glen Valley. Can. (Vancouver In.)	49·09 N	122·30 W
75	Glenview (glĕn'vū) Ill. (Chicago In.)	42·04 N	87·48 W
83	Glenwood (glĕn-wŏŏd) ... Can.	48·59 N	54·51 W
70	Glenwood ... Iowa	41·03 N	95·44 W
70	Glenwood ... Minn.	45·39 N	95·23 W
69	Glenwood Springs ... Colo.	39·35 N	107·20 W
111	Glienicke (glē'nē-kĕ) Ger. (Berlin In.)	52·38 N	13·19 E
111	Glinde (glĕn'dĕ) Ger. (Hamburg In.)	53·32 N	10·13 E
121	Gliwice (gwĭ-wĭt'sĕ) ... Pol.	50·18 N	18·40 E
69	Globe (glōb) ... Ariz.	33·20 N	110·50 W
129	Globino (glôb'ē-nô) ... Sov. Un.	49·22 N	33·17 E
120	Głogów (gwō'gōōv) ... Pol.	51·40 N	16·04 E
118	Glomma (R.) (glômmä) ... Nor.	61·22 N	11·02 E
118	Glommen (R.) (glôm'ĕn) ... Nor.	60·03 N	11·15 E
111	Glonn (glōnn) .. Ger. (Munich In.)	47·59 N	11·52 E
167	Glorieuses, Îles (Is.) .. Malag. Rep.	11·28 s	47·50 E
110	Glossop (glŏs'ŭp) ... Eng.	53·26 N	1·57 W
78	Gloster (glŏs'tēr) ... Miss.	31·10 N	91·00 W
116	Gloucester (glŏs'tēr) ... Eng.	51·54 N	2·11 W
83	Gloucester ... Mass. (Boston In.)	42·37 N	70·40 W
84	Gloucester City N. J. (Philadelphia In.)	39·53 N	75·08 W
80	Glouster (glŏs'tēr) ... Ohio	39·35 N	82·05 W
83	Glover I. (glŭv'ēr) ... Can.	48·41 N	57·30 W
81	Gloversville (glŭv'ērz-vĭl) ... N. Y.	43·05 N	74·20 W
83	Glovertown (glŭv'ēr-toun) ... Can.	48·42 N	54·01 W
128	Glubokoye (glōō-bô-kō'yĕ) Sov. Un.	55·08 N	27·44 E
111	Glückstadt (glük-shtät) Ger. (Hamburg In.)	53·47 N	9·25 E
129	Glukhov (glōō'kôf') ... Sov. Un.	51·42 N	33·52 E
129	Glushkovo (glōōsh'kô-vō). Sov. Un.	51·21 N	34·43 E
120	Gmünden (g'mōōn'dĕn) ... Aus.	47·57 N	13·47 E
121	Gniezno (g'nyăz'nô) ... Pol.	52·32 N	17·34 E
127	Gnjilane (gnyē'lá-nĕ) ... Yugo.	42·28 N	21·27 E
143	Goa (Ter.) (gō'á) ... India	15·45 N	74.00 E
92	Goascorán (gō-äs'kō-rän') ... Hond.	13·37 N	87·43 W
165	Goba (gō'bä) ... Eth.	7·17 N	39·58 E
166	Gobabis (gō-bä'bĭs) ... S. W. Afr.	22·25 s	18·50 E
146	Gobi or Shamo (Des.) (gō'be) Mong.	43·29 N	103·15 E
65	Goble (gō'b'l) .. Ore. (Portland In.)	46·01 N	122·53 W
123	Goch (gōk) ... Ger. (Ruhr In.)	51·35 N	6·10 E
142	Godāvari (R.) (gō-dä'vŭ-rē). India	17·42 N	81·15 E
158	Goddards Soak (Swp.) (gŏd'ărdz) Austl.	31·20 s	123·30 E
80	Goderich (gōd'rĭch) ... Can.	43·45 N	81·45 W
74	Godfrey (gŏd'frē) Ill. (St. Louis In.)	38·57 N	90·12 W
49	Godhavn (gōdh'hâvn) ... Grnld.	69·15 N	53·30 W
86	Gods (L.) (gŏdz) ... Can.	54·38 N	95·23 W
49	Godthåb (gŏt'hōōb) ... Grnld.	64·10 N	51·32 W
146	Godwin Austen, Mt. (gŏd wĭn ôs'tĕn). Pak.	36·06 N	76·38 E
68	Goffs (gôfs) ... Calif.	34·57 N	115·06 W
71	Gogebic (L.) (gō-gē'bĭk) ... Mich.	46·24 N	89·25 W
71	Gogebic Ra. ... Mich.	46·37 N	89·48 W
111	Goggingen (gûg'gĕn-gĕn) Ger. (Munich In.)	48·21 N	10·53 E

ng-sing; ŋ-baŋk; N-nasalized n; nŏd; cŏmmit; ōld; ôbey; ôrder; fōōd; fŏŏt; ou-out; s-soft; sh-dish; th-thin; pūre; ûnite; ûrn; stŭd; circŭs; ü-as "y" in study; '-indeterminate vowel.

210 Gogorron–Grangeville PRONOUNCING INDEX

Page	Name Pronunciation Region	Lat. °′	Long. °′
90	Gogorrón (gō-gô-rōn')......Mex.	21·51 N	100·54 W
153	Goi (gō'ê).......Jap. (Tōkyō In.)	35·31 N	140·05 E
99	Goiânia (gô-yä'nyä)........Braz.	16·41 S	48·57 W
99	Goiás (gô-yà's)............Braz.	15·57 S	50·10 W
99	Goiás (State)..............Braz.	12·35 S	48·38 W
111	Goirle....Neth. (Amsterdam In.)	51·31 N	5·06 E
133	Göksu (R.) (gûk'sōō').......Tur.	36·40 N	33·30 E
118	Göl (gûl)..................Nor.	60·58 N	8·54 E
79	Golax (gō'lăks)............Va.	36·41 N	80·56 W
110	Golcar (gōl'kȧr)...........Eng.	53·38 N	1·52 W
73	Golconda (gŏl-kŏn'dȧ)........Ill.	37·21 N	88·32 W
121	Gołdap (gôl'dăp)...........Pol.	54·17 N	22·17 E
72	Golden....................Colo.	39·44 N	105·15 W
84	Goldenbridge (gōl'dĕn-brĭj) N. Y. (New York In.)	41·17 N	73·41 W
66	Goldendale (gōl'dĕn-dāl)...Wash.	45·49 N	120·48 W
65	Golden Gate (Str.) (gōl'dĕn gāt) Calif. (San Francisco In.)	37·48 N	122·32 W
68	Goldfield (gōld-fēld)........Nev.	37·42 N	117·15 W
88	Gold Hill (Mtn.) C. Z. (Panama Canal In.)	9·03 N	79·08 W
65	Gold Mtn. (gōld) Wash. (Seattle In.)	47·33 N	122·48 W
79	Goldsboro (gōldz-bûr'ō).....N. C.	35·23 N	77·59 W
76	Goldthwaite (gōld'thwāt)....Tex.	31·27 N	98·34 W
120	Goleniów (gô-lĕ-nyŭf')......Pol.	53·33 N	14·51 E
135	Golets-Purpula, Gol'tsy (Mtn.) Sov. Un.	59·08 N	115·22 E
93	Golfito (gôl-fē'tō)..........C. R.	8·40 N	83·12 W
	Golfo Dulce, see Izabal, L.		
77	Goliad (gō-lĭ-ăd')..........Tex.	28·40 N	97·21 W
155	Golo (gō'lō)....Phil. (Manila In.)	13·38 N	120·17 E
126	Golo (R.)..................Cor.	42·28 N	9·18 E
129	Golovchino (gō-lôf'chē-nō) Sov. Un.	50·34 N	35·52 E
166	Golungo Alto (gô-lōōŋ'gô äl'tō) Ang.	9·10 S	14·40 E
127	Golyamo Konare (gō'lä-mō-kō'nä-rĕ).Bul.	42·16 N	24·33 E
111	Golzow (gōl'tsōv) Ger. (Berlin In.)	52·17 N	12·36 E
164	Gombe....................Nig.	10·23 N	11·08 E
128	Gomel' (gô'mĕl')........Sov. Un.	52·20 N	31·03 E
128	Gomel' (Oblast)........Sov. Un.	52·18 N	29·00 E
164	Gomera I. (gô-mā'rä)....Can. Is.	28·00 N	18·01 W
76	Gomez Farias (gō'māz fä-rē'äs) Mex.	24·59 N	101·02 W
76	Gómez Palacio (pä-lä'syō)...Mex.	25·35 N	103·30 W
95	Gonaïves (gō-nà-ēv')........Hai.	19·25 N	72·45 W
95	Gonaïves, Golfe des (G.) (gō-nà-ēv').Hai.	19·20 N	73·20 W
95	Gonâve, Ile De La (I.) (gô-nàv') Hai.	18·50 N	73·30 W
142	Gonda....................India	27·13 N	82·00 E
142	Gondal...................India	22·02 N	70·47 E
165	Gondar (gŏn'dȧr)...........Eth.	12·39 N	37·30 E
123	Gonesse (gô-nĕs')..Fr. (Paris In.)	48·59 N	2·28 E
153	Gonō (R.) (gô'nō)...........Jap.	35·00 N	132·25 E
85	Gonor (gō'nŏr) Can. (Winnipeg In.)	50·04 N	96·57 W
167	Gonubie Mouth (gŏn'ōō-bē mouth).S. Afr. (Natal In.)	32·56 S	28·02 E
90	Gonzales (gôn-zà'lĕs).......Mex.	22·47 N	98·26 W
77	Gonzales (gŏn-zä'lĕz)........Tex.	29·31 N	97·25 W
100	González Catán (gōn-zà'lĕz-kä-tà'n).Arg. (In.)	34·31 S	58·39 W
166	Good Hope, C. of (kāp ov gŏŏd hōp).S. Afr. (Cape Town In.)	34·21 S	18·29 E
66	Gooding (gŏŏd'ĭng)........Idaho	42·55 N	114·43 W
80	Goodland (gŏŏd'lănd)........Ind.	40·50 N	87·15 W
72	Goodland..................Kans.	39·19 N	101·43 W
166	Goodwood (gŏŏd'wŏŏd) S. Afr. (Cape Town In.)	33·54 S	18·33 E
110	Goole (gōōl)..............Eng.	53·42 N	0·52 W
70	Goose (R.)................N. D.	47·40 N	97·41 W
87	Goose Bay.................Can.	53·19 N	60·33 W
67	Gooseberry Cr. (gōōs-bĕr'ĭ)..Wyo.	44·04 N	108·35 W
67	Goose Cr. (gōōs)..........Idaho	42·07 N	113·53 W
75	Goose Lake (gōōs lāk) Ill. (Chicago In.)	41·21 N	88·18 W
66	Goose L..................Calif.	41·56 N	120·35 W
142	Gorakhpur (gō'rŭk-pōōr)....India	26·45 N	82·39 E
94	Gorda, Punta (Pt.) (pōō'n-tä-gôr-dä).Cuba	22·25 N	82·10 W
94	Gorda Cay (gôr'dä).......Ba. Is.	26·05 N	77·30 W
85	Gordon (gôr'dŭn) Can. (Winnipeg In.)	50·00 N	97·20 W
70	Gordon....................Nebr.	42·47 N	102·14 W
165	Gorē (gō'rē)...............Eth.	8·12 N	35·34 E
144	Gorgān....................Iran	36·44 N	54·30 E
126	Gorgona (I.) (gôr-gō'nä).......It.	43·27 N	9·55 E
133	Gori (gō'rê)..........Sov. Un.	42·00 N	44·08 E
111	Gorinchem (gō'rĭn-kĕm) Neth. (Amsterdam In.)	51·50 N	4·59 E
110	Goring (gôr'ĭng) Eng. (London In.)	51·30 N	1·08 W
126	Gorizia (gô-rē'tsē-yä)........It.	45·56 N	13·40 E
132	Gorki (gôr'kē)..........Sov. Un.	56·15 N	44·05 E
132	Gor'kovskoye...........Sov. Un.	56·38 N	43·40 E
128	Gor'kovskoye (Gorkov) (L.) (gôr'kôf-skô-yĕ).Sov. Un.	57·38 N	41·18 E
121	Gorlice (gôr-lē'tsĕ)..........Pol.	49·38 N	21·11 E
120	Görlitz (gŭr'lĭts)...........Ger.	51·10 N	15·01 E
129	Gorlovka (gôr'lôf-kȧ)....Sov. Un.	48·17 N	38·03 E
76	Gorman (gôr'măn)..........Tex.	32·13 N	98·40 W
127	Gorna-Oryakhovitsa (gôr'nä-ôr-yĕk'ō-vē-tsȧ).Bul.	43·08 N	25·40 E
127	Gornji Milanovac (gôrn'yē-mē'la-nō-väts).Yugo.	44·02 N	20·29 E
134	Gorno-Altay Aut. Oblast.Sov. Un.	51·00 N	86·00 E
134	Gorno-Altaysk (gôr'nŭ-ŭl-tīsk') Sov. Un.	52·28 N	82·45 E
121	Gorodënka (gō-rô-deŋ'kä) Sov. Un.	48·40 N	25·30 E
132	Gorodets (Res.).........Sov. Un.	57·00 N	43·55 E
136	Gorodishche (gô-rô'dĭsh-chĕ) Sov. Un. (Urals In.)	57·57 N	57·03 E
129	Gorodnya (gô-rôd''nyä)..Sov. Un.	51·54 N	31·31 E
121	Gorodok (gō-rô-dôk')....Sov. Un.	49·37 N	23·40 E
134	Gorodok..............Sov. Un.	50·30 N	103·58 E
128	Gorodok...............Sov. Un.	55·27 N	29·58 E
154	Gorontalo (gō-rōn-tä'lo)...Indon.	0·40 N	123·04 E
121	Goryn' R. (gō'rĕn')......Sov. Un.	50·55 N	26·07 E
120	Gorzow Wielkopolski (gō-zhōōv'vyĕl-ko-pōl'skē).Pol.	53·44 N	15·15 E
80	Goshen (gō'shĕn)...........Ind.	41·35 N	85·50 W
75	Goshen.......Ky. (Louisville In.)	38·24 N	85·34 W
84	Goshen....N. Y. (New York In.)	41·24 N	74·19 W
75	Goshen.....Ohio (Cincinnati In.)	39·14 N	84·09 W
65	Goshen....Wash. (Vancouver In.)	48·52 N	122·20 W
69	Goshute Ind. Res. (gō-shōōt') Utah	39·50 N	114·00 W
120	Goslar (gôs'lär)............Ger.	51·55 N	10·25 E
99	Gospa (R.) (gôs-pä).....Ven. (In.)	9·43 N	64·23 W
126	Gospić (gôs'pĭch)..........Yugo.	44·31 N	15·03 E
127	Gostivar (gos'tē-vär).......Yugo.	41·46 N	20·58 E
121	Gostynin (gôs-tē'nĭn)........Pol.	52·24 N	19·30 E
118	Göta älv (R.) (gōĕtȧ ĕĕl'v)..Swe.	58·11 N	12·03 E
118	Göta Can. (yû'tȧ)...........Swe.	58·35 N	15·24 E
118	Göteborg (yû'tĕ-bôrgh).......Swe.	57·39 N	11·56 E
164	Gotel Mts............Nig.-Cam.	7·04 N	11·28 E
92	Gotera (gō-tā'rä)...........Sal.	13·41 N	88·06 W
120	Gotha (gō'tȧ)..............Ger.	50·57 N	10·43 E
72	Gothenburg (gŏth'ĕn-bûrg).Nebr.	40·57 N	100·08 W
118	Gotland (I.)...............Swe.	57·35 N	17·35 E
153	Gotō-Rettō (Is.) (gō'tō rĕt'tō) Jap.	33·06 N	128·54 E
119	Gotska Sandön (I.).........Swe.	58·24 N	19·15 E
120	Göttingen (gût'ĭng-ĕn).......Ger.	51·32 N	9·57 E
111	Gouda (gou'dä) Neth. (Amsterdam In.)	52·00 N	4·42 E
47	Gough (I.) (gŏf)..........Atl. O.	40·00 S	10·00 W
87	Gouin Res..................Can.	77·12 N	75·34 W
160	Goulburn (gōl'bŭrn).......Austl.	34·47 S	149·40 E
164	Goumbou (gōōm-bōō')......Mali	15·02 N	7·35 W
164	Goundam (gōōn-däN')......Mali	16·29 N	3·37 W
164	Gouré (gōō-rā')...........Niger	13·53 N	10·44 E
81	Gouverneur (gŭv-ĕr-nōōr')..N. Y.	44·20 N	75·25 W
86	Govenlock (gŭvĕn-lŏk)......Can.	49·09 N	109·42 W
100	Governador Ilhado (I.) (gô-vĕr-nä-dō'r-ē-lä'dô).Braz. (In.)	22·48 S	43·13 W
100	Governador Portela (pōr-tĕ'lȧ) Braz. (In.)	22·28 S	43·30 W
99	Governador Valadares (vä-lä-dā'rĕs).Braz.	18·47 S	41·45 W
95	Governor's Harbour.......Ba. Is.	25·15 N	76·15 W
81	Gowanda (gô-wŏn'dȧ).......N. Y.	42·30 N	78·55 W
100	Goya (gō'yä)...............Arg.	29·06 S	59·12 W
110	Goyt (R.) (goit)............Eng.	53·19 N	2·03 W
166	Graaff-Reinet (gräf'rī'nĕt)..S. Afr.	32·10 S	24·40 E
126	Gračac (grä'chäts)..........Yugo.	44·16 N	15·50 E
127	Gračanica (grà-chän''i-tsä).Yugo.	44·42 N	18·19 E
78	Graceville (grās'vĭl).........Fla.	30·57 N	85·30 W
70	Graceville.................Minn.	45·33 N	96·25 W
92	Gracias (grä'sē-äs).........Hond.	14·35 N	88·37 W
93	Gracias a Dios, Cabo (C.) (kà'bô-grä-syäs-ä-dyō's)..Hond.	15·00 N	83·13 W
164	Graciosa I. (grä-syō'sä) Açores (In.)	39·07 N	27·30 W
127	Gradačac (gra-dä'chats)....Yugo.	44·50 N	18·28 E
124	Gradelos (grä-dĕ-lôs).........Sp.	42·38 N	5·15 W
129	Gradizhsk (grä-dēzhsk').Sov. Un.	49·12 N	33·06 E
124	Grado (grä'dō)..............Sp.	43·24 N	6·04 W
111	Grafelfing (grä'fĕl-fēng) Ger. (Munich In.)	48·07 N	11·27 E
111	Grafing (grä'fēng) Ger. (Munich In.)	48·03 N	11·58 E
160	Grafton (graf'tŭn)..........Austl.	29·38 S	153·05 E
74	Grafton........Ill. (St. Louis In.)	38·58 N	90·26 W
83	Grafton.......Mass. (Boston In.)	42·13 N	71·41 W
70	Grafton....................N. D.	48·24 N	97·25 W
75	Grafton.....Ohio (Cleveland In.)	41·16 N	82·04 W
81	Grafton..................W. Va.	39·20 N	80·00 W
125	Gragnano (grän-yä'nô) It. (Naples In.)	40·27 N	14·32 E
79	Graham (grā'ăm)...........N. C.	36·03 N	79·23 W
72	Graham....................Tex.	33·07 N	98·34 W
65	Graham......Wash. (Seattle In.)	47·03 N	122·18 W
86	Graham (I.)................Can.	53·37 N	131·47 W
167	Grahamstown (grā'ăms'toun) S. Afr. (Natal In.)	33·19 S	26·33 E
123	Graian Alps (Mts.) (grā'yăn) Fr.-It.	45·17 N	6·52 E
99	Grajaú (grà-zhä-ōō')........Braz.	5·59 S	46·03 W
99	Grajaú (R.)..................Braz.	4·24 S	46·04 W
121	Grajewo (grä-yā'vo).........Pol.	53·38 N	22·28 E
101	Grama, Serra de (Mtn.) (sĕ'r-rä-dĕ-grá'mà) Braz. (Rio de Janeiro In.)	23·42 S	42·28 W
127	Gramada (grä'mä-dä).........Bul.	43·46 N	22·41 E
111	Gramatneusiedl.Aus. (Vienna In.)	48·02 N	16·29 E
126	Grammichele (gräm-mê-kĕ'lā)..It.	37·15 N	14·40 E
116	Grampian Mts. (grăm'pĭ-ăn) Scot.	56·30 N	4·55 W
92	Granada (grä-nä'dhä)........Nic.	11·55 N	85·58 W
124	Granada (grä-nä'dä).........Sp.	37·13 N	3·37 W
100	Gran Bajo (Pln.) (grà'n'bà'kō) Arg.	47·35 S	68·45 W
77	Granbury (grăn'bĕr-ĭ).......Tex.	32·26 N	97·45 W
81	Granby (grăn'bĭ)............Can.	45·30 N	72·40 W
73	Granby......................Mo.	36·54 N	94·15 W
72	Granby (L.)................Colo.	40·07 N	105·40 W
164	Gran Canaria I. (grän'kä-nä'rê-ä).Can. Is.	27·39 N	15·39 W
100	Gran Chaco (Reg.) (grän'chà'kō) Arg.-Par.	25·30 S	62·15 W
71	Grand (I.).................Mich.	46·31 N	86·38 W
82	Grand (L.).................Can.	45·17 N	67·42 W
82	Grand (L.).................Can.	66·15 N	45·59 W
80	Grand (R.).................Can.	43·45 N	80·20 W
80	Grand (R.)................Mich.	42·58 N	85·13 W
73	Grand (R.).................Mo.	39·50 N	93·52 W
70	Grand (R.)................S. D.	45·40 N	101·55 W
70	Grand (R.), North Fork....S. D.	45·52 N	102·49 W
70	Grand (R.), South Fork.....S. D.	45·38 N	102·56 W
94	Grand Bahama (I.)..........Ba. Is.	26·35 N	78·30 W
83	Grand Bank (grănd băngk)..Can.	47·05 N	55·44 W
164	Grand Bassam (gräN bà-säN') Ivory Coast	5·14 N	3·51 W
93	Grand Bourg (gräN bōōr') Marie Galante (Le. & Wind. Is. In.)	15·54 N	61·20 W
95	Grand Caicos (I.) (grănd kä-ē'kōs).Caicos	21·45 N	71·50 W
116	Grand Canal................Ire.	53·21 N	7·15 W
	Grand Canal, see Yün Ho		
69	Grand Canyon (grănd kăn'yŭn) Ariz.	36·05 N	112·10 W
69	Grand Canyon..............Ariz.	35·50 N	113·16 W
69	Grand Canyon Natl. Mon...Ariz.	36·18 N	113·26 W
69	Grand Canyon Natl. Park..Ariz.	36·15 N	112·20 W
94	Grand Cayman (I.) (kā'măn) Cayman Is.	19·15 N	81·15 W
66	Grand Coulee Dam (kōō'lē).Wash.	47·58 N	119·28 W
100	Grande, Bahia (B.) (bä-ē'ä-grän'dĕ).Arg.	50·45 S	68·00 W
100	Grande, Salinas (F.) (sä-lē'näs) Arg.	29·45 S	65·00 W
98	Grande, Rio (R.)............Bol.	16·49 S	63·19 W
99	Grande, Rio (R.)...........Braz.	19·48 S	49·54 W
101	Grande, Ilha (I.) (grän'dĕ) Braz. (Rio de Janeiro In.)	23·11 S	44·14 W
99	Grande, Salto (Falls) (säl-tô) Braz.	16·18 S	39·38 W
101	Grande (R.)..Chile (Santiago In.)	35·25 S	70·14 W
91	Grande (R.)................Mex.	17·37 N	96·41 W
88	Grande, Ciri (R.) (sē'rē-grän'dĕ) Pan. (Panama Canal In.)	8·55 N	80·04 W
62	Grande, Rio (Bravo del Norte, Rio) (R.) (grän'dä)..U. S.-Mex.	26·50 N	99·10 W
101	Grande (R.)..Ur.(Buenos Aires In.)	33·19 S	57·15 W
100	Grande, Cuchilla (Mts.) (kōō-chē'l-yä).Ur.	33·00 S	55·15 W
99	Grande, Boca (Est.) (bŏ'kä-grä'n-dĕ).Ven.	8·46 N	60·17 W
82	Grande Baie (gräNd bā')......Can.	48·17 N	70·53 W
95	Grande Cayemite, Ile (I.)....Hai.	18·45 N	73·55 W
167	Grande Comore (grä'n-dĕ-kô-mō-rĕ).Comores, Arch. des	11·44 S	42·38 E
92	Grande de Otoro (grän'dȧ dā ô-tō'rô).Hond.	14·42 N	88·21 W
164	Grande Erg Occidental (Dunes) Alg.	29·37 N	6·04 E
85	Grande-Ligne (lēn'y') Can. (Montreal In.)	45·13 N	73·17 W
85	Grande Pointe (grănd point') Can. (Winnipeg In.)	49·47 N	97·03 W
86	Grande Prairie (prâr'ĭ)......Can.	55·09 N	118·48 W
93	Grande R. (grän'dĕ)..........Nic.	13·01 N	84·21 W
95	Grande Rivière du Nord (rē-vyâr' dü nôr').Hai.	19·35 N	72·10 W
66	Grande Ronde R. (rônd')....Ore.	45·32 N	117·52 W
68	Gran Desierto (Des.) (grän-dĕ-syĕ'r-tô).Mex.	32·14 N	114·28 W
93	Grande Soufrière Vol. (sōō-frê-ăr') Guad. (Le. & Wind. Is. In.)	16·06 N	61·42 W
93	Grande Terre I. (târ') Guad. (Le. & Wind. Is. In.)	16·28 N	61·13 W
93	Grande Vigie, Pointe de la (Pt.) (gräNd vē-gē') Grande Terre (Le. & Wind. Is. In.)	16·32 N	61·25 W
82	Grand Falls (fôlz)...........Can.	47·02 N	67·46 W
87	Grand Falls................Can.	53·34 N	64·23 W
79	Grandfather, Mt. (grănd-fä-thēr) N. C.	36·07 N	81·48 W
72	Grandfield (grănd'fēld).....Okla.	34·13 N	98·39 W
86	Grand Forks (fôrks).........Can.	49·00 N	118·27 W
70	Grand Forks...............N. D.	47·55 N	97·05 W
80	Grand Haven (hā'v'n).......Mich.	43·05 N	86·15 W
72	Grand Island (ī'lănd).......Nebr.	40·56 N	98·20 W
75	Grand I......N. Y. (Buffalo In.)	43·03 N	78·58 W
69	Grand Junction (jŭngk'shŭn) Colo.	39·05 N	108·35 W
164	Grand Lahou (lȧ-ōō').Ivory Coast	5·08 N	5·06 W
83	Grand Lake (lāk)...........Can.	49·00 N	57·10 W
77	Grand L....................La.	29·57 N	91·25 W
74	Grand L......Minn. (Duluth In.)	46·54 N	92·26 W
80	Grand Ledge (lĕj)..........Mich.	42·45 N	84·50 W
122	Grand-Lieu, L. de (gräN'-lyû).Fr.	46·00 N	1·45 W
82	Grand Manan (I.) (mȧ-năn).Can.	44·42 N	66·50 W
82	Grand'Mère (gräN mâr')......Can.	46·36 N	72·43 W
123	Grand Morin (R.) (mô-răN') Fr. (Paris In.)	48·23 N	2·19 E
124	Grândola (grăN'dô-lȧ).......Port.	38·10 N	8·36 W
164	Grand-Popo (pô-pō')....Dahomey	6·27 N	1·52 E
71	Grand Portage Ind. Res. (pōr'tĭj) Minn.	47·54 N	89·34 W
71	Grand Portage Nat'l Mon...Mich.	47·59 N	89·47 W
74	Grand Prairie (prē'rê) Tex. (Dallas, Fort Worth In.)	32·45 N	97·00 W
69	Grand Quivira Natl. Mon. (kē-vē'rȧ).N. Mex.	34·10 N	106·05 W
80	Grand Rapids (răp'ĭdz).....Mich.	43·00 N	85·45 W
71	Grand Rapids..............Minn.	47·16 N	93·33 W
82	Grand-Riviere..............Can.	48·26 N	64·30 W
67	Grand Teton Mt...........Wyo.	43·46 N	110·50 W
67	Grand Teton Natl. Park (tē'tŏn) Wyo.	43·54 N	110·15 W
80	Grand Traverse B. (trăv'ērs) Mich.	45·00 N	85·30 W
95	Grand Turk (I.) (tûrk)..Turks Is.	21·30 N	71·10 W
74	Grandview (grănd'vyōō) Mo. (Kansas City In.)	38·53 N	94·32 W
69	Grand Wash (R.) (wŏsh)....Ariz.	36·20 N	113·52 W
67	Granger (grān'jēr)...........Wyo.	41·37 N	109·58 W
66	Grangeville (grānj'vĭl)......Idaho	45·56 N	116·08 W

PRONOUNCING INDEX | Granite City–Grottaglie | 211

Page	Name Pronunciation Region	Lat. °′	Long. °′
74	Granite City Ill. (St. Louis In.)	38·42 N	90·09 W
70	Granite Falls (fôlz) Minn.	44·46 N	95·34 W
79	Granite Falls N. C.	35·49 N	81·25 W
65	Granite Falls Wash. (Seattle In.)	48·05 N	121·59 W
67	Granite Pk. Mont.	45·13 N	109·48 W
79	Graniteville (grăn'ĭt-vĭl) S. C.	33·35 N	81·50 W
99	Granito (grä-nē'tō) Braz.	7·39 S	39·34 W
124	Granja de Torrehermosa (grän'hä dā tôr'rā-ĕr-mō'sä) Sp.	38·21 N	5·38 W
118	Grånna (grĕn'å) Swe.	58·02 N	14·28 E
125	Granollérs (grä-nôl-yĕrs') Sp.	41·36 N	2·19 E
98	Gran Pajonal (Marsh) (grä'n-pä-κô-näl') Peru	11·14 S	71·45 W
95	Gran Piedra (Mtn.) (grän-pyĕ'drä) Cuba	20·00 N	75·40 W
110	Grantham (grăn'tăm) Eng.	52·54 N	0·38 W
75	Grant Park (grănt pärk) Ill. (Chicago In.)	41·14 N	87·39 W
66	Grants Pass (grànts pàs) Ore.	42·26 N	123·20 W
122	Granville (grän-vēl') Fr.	48·52 N	1·35 W
81	Granville (grăn'vĭl) N. Y.	43·25 N	73·15 W
86	Granville (L.) Can.	56·18 N	99·39 W
99	Grão Mogol (grouN' mōō-gôl') Braz.	16·34 S	42·35 W
74	Grapevine (grāp'vīn) Tex. (Dallas, Fort Worth In.)	32·56 N	97·05 W
118	Gräsö (I.) Swe.	60·30 N	18·35 E
81	Grass (R.) N. Y.	44·45 N	75·10 W
89	Grass Cay (I.) Vir. Is. (U.S.A.) (St. Thomas In.)	18·22 N	64·50 W
123	Grasse (gräs) Fr.	43·39 N	6·57 E
65	Grass Mtn. (gràs) Wash. (Seattle In.)	47·13 N	121·48 W
68	Grass Valley Calif.	39·12 N	121·04 W
83	Grates Pt. (grāts) Can.	48·14 N	52·45 W
122	Graulhet (grō-lĕ') Fr.	43·46 N	1·58 E
86	Gravelbourg (gràv'ĕl-bôrg) Can.	49·55 N	106·53 W
110	Gravesend (grāvz'ĕnd') Eng. (London In.)	51·26 N	0·22 E
126	Gravina (grä-vē'nä) It.	40·48 N	16·27 E
74	Gravois (grav'ois) Mo. (St. Louis In.)	38·33 N	90·20 W
95	Gravois, Pte. (grà-vwä') Hai.	18·00 N	74·20 W
123	Gray (grā) Fr.	47·26 N	5·35 E
80	Grayling (grā'lĭng) Mich.	44·40 N	84·40 W
75	Grayslake (grāz'lāk) Ill. (Chicago In.)	42·20 N	88·20 W
72	Grays Pk. (grāz) Colo.	39·29 N	105·52 W
129	Grayvoron (grà-ē'vô-rôn) Sov. Un.	50·28 N	35·41 E
120	Graz (gräts) Aus.	47·05 N	15·26 E
94	Great Abaco (I.) (ă'bà-kō) Ba. Is.	26·30 N	77·05 W
159	Great Artesian Basin (Reg.) (är-tēzh-ăn bā-sĭn) Austl.	23·16 S	143·37 E
158	Great Australian Bight (ôs-trā'-lĭ-ăn bīt) Austl.	33·30 S	127·00 E
94	Great Bahama Bk. (bȧ-hā'mȧ) Ba. Is.	25·00 N	78·50 W
159	Great Barrier (I.) (băr'ĭ-ẽr) N. Z. (In.)	37·00 S	175·31 E
159	Great Barrier Rf. (bȧ-rĭ-ẽr rēf) Austl.	16·43 S	146·34 E
62	Great Basin (grāt bā's'n) U. S.	40·08 N	117·10 W
86	Great Bear L. (bâr) Can.	66·10 N	119·53 W
72	Great Bend (bĕnd) Kans.	38·41 N	98·46 W
	Great Bitter, see el Buheirat el Murrat el Kubra		
116	Great Blasket (Is.) (blăs'kĕt) Ire.	52·05 N	10·55 W
102	Great Britain (brĭt'n) U. K.	56·53 N	0·02 W
166	Great Cataract (Falls) (căt'ȧ-răkt) Ang.-S. W. Afr.	17·25 S	14·20 E
93	Great Corn I. Nic.	12·10 N	82·54 W
67	Great Divide Basin (dĭ-vīd' bā's'n) Wyo.	42·10 N	108·10 W
159	Great Dividing Ra. (dĭ-vī-dĭng rānj) Austl.	35·16 S	146·38 E
	Greater Khingan Mts., see Tahsinganling Shanmo		
71	Greater Leech Ind. Res. (grāt'ẽr lēch) Minn.	47·39 N	94·27 W
95	Great Exuma (I.) (ĕk-sōō'mä) Ba. Is.	23·35 N	76·00 W
83	Great Falls Can.	48·58 N	55·37 W
67	Great Falls (fôlz) Mont.	47·30 N	111·15 W
79	Great Falls S. C.	34·32 N	80·53 W
166	Great Fish (R.) (fĭsh) S. W. Afr.	28·00 S	17·45 E
167	Great Fish (R.) S. Afr. (Natal In.)	33·04 S	26·08 E
95	Great Guana Cay (I.) (gwä'nä) Ba. Is.	24·00 N	76·20 W
94	Great Harbor Cay (I.) (kē) Ba. Is.	25·45 N	77·50 W
95	Great Inagua (I.) (ê-nä'gwä) Ba. Is.	21·00 N	73·15 W
142	Great Indian (Thar) Des. (tŭr) India	32·04 N	70·25 E
94	Great Isaac (I.) (ī'zăk) Ba. Is.	26·05 N	79·05 W
139	Great Karimun (Is.) Indon. (Singapore In.)	1·11 N	103·12 E
166	Great Karroo (Mts.) (grāt kȧ'rōō) S. Afr.	32·45 S	22·00 E
167	Great Kei (R.) (kē) S. Afr. (Natal In.)	32·17 S	27·30 E
84	Great Neck (nĕk) N. Y. (New York In.)	40·48 N	73·44 W
154	Great Nicobar I. (nĭk-ô-bär') India	7·00 N	94·18 E
154	Great Paternoster Is. (pā'tẽr-nŏs-tẽr) Indon.	7·35 S	118·00 E
94	Great Pedro Bluff (Hd.) Jam.	17·50 N	78·05 W
49	Great Plains, The (Reg.) (plāns) N. A.	45·00 N	104·00 W
95	Great Ragged (I.) Ba. Is.	22·10 N	75·45 W
126	Great St. Bernard Pass (sănt bẽr-närd') Switz.-It.	45·53 N	7·15 E
94	Great Sale Cay (I.) (sāl kē) Ba. Is.	27·00 N	78·15 W
67	Great Salt L. (sôlt lāk) Utah	41·19 N	112·48 W
62	Great Salt Lake Des. U. S.	41·00 N	113·30 W
72	Great Salt Plains Res. Okla.	36·56 N	98·14 W
72	Great Sand Dunes Natl. Mon. Colo.	37·56 N	105·25 W
158	Great Sandy Des. (săn'dē) Austl.	21·50 S	123·10 E
66	Great Sandy Des. (săn'dĭ) Ore.	43·43 N	120·44 W
64	Great Sitkin (I.) (sĭt-kĭn) Alaska	52·18 N	176·22 W
86	Great Slave (L.) (slāv) Can.	61·37 N	114·58 W
78	Great Smoky Mts. Natl. Park (smōk-ē) N. C.	35·43 N	83·20 W
94	Great Stirrup Cay (I.) (stĭr-ŭp) Ba. Is.	25·50 N	77·55 W
158	Great Victoria Des. (vĭk-tō'rĭ-ȧ) Austl.	29·45 S	124·30 E
110	Great Waltham (wôl'thŭm) Eng.	51·47 N	0·27 E
87	Great Whale (R.) (hwāl) Can.	54·57 N	75·51 W
117	Great Yarmouth (yär-mŭth) Eng.	52·35 N	1·45 E
118	Grebbestad (grĕb-bĕ-städh) Swe.	58·42 N	11·15 E
139	Greco, C. Cyprus (Palestine In.)	34·57 N	34·11 E
124	Gredos, Sierra de (Mts.) (syĕr'rä dā grā'dōs) Sp.	40·13 N	5·30 W
102	Greece (grēs) Eur.	39·00 N	21·30 E
72	Greeley (grē'lĭ) Colo.	40·25 N	104·41 W
78	Green (R.) Ky.	37·13 N	86.30 W
70	Green (R.) N. D.	47·05 N	103·05 W
62	Green (R.) (grēn) U. S.	38·30 N	110·10 W
65	Green (R.) Wash. (Seattle In.)	47·17 N	121·57 W
65	Greenbank (grēn'bănk) Wash. (Seattle In.)	48·06 N	122·35 W
77	Green Bay Tex. (In.)	29·53 N	95·13 W
71	Green Bay Wis.	44·30 N	88·04 W
63	Green B. U. S.	44·55 N	87·40 W
84	Greenbelt (grēn'bĕlt) Md. (Baltimore In.)	38·59 N	76·53 W
80	Greencastle (grēn-kȧs''l) Ind.	39·40 N	86·50 W
94	Green Cay (I.) Ba. Is.	24·05 N	77·10 W
79	Green Cove Springs (kōv) Fla.	29·56 N	81·42 W
75	Greendale (grēn'dāl) Wis. (Milwaukee In.)	42·56 N	87·59 W
80	Greenfield (grēn'fēld) Ind.	39·45 N	85·40 W
71	Greenfield Iowa	41·16 N	94·30 W
81	Greenfield Mass.	42·35 N	72·35 W
73	Greenfield Mo.	37·23 N	93·48 W
80	Greenfield Ohio	39·15 N	83·25 W
78	Greenfield Tenn.	36·08 N	88·45 W
85	Greenfield Park Can. (Montreal In.)	45·29 N	73·29 W
75	Greenhills (grēn-hĭls) Ohio (Cincinnati In.)	39·16 N	84·31 W
49	Greenland (grēn'lănd) N. A.	74·00 N	40·00 W
83	Greenly (I.) (grēn'lē) Can.	51·23 N	57·15 W
65	Green Mtn. Ore. (Portland In.)	45·52 N	123·24 W
69	Green Mountain Res. Colo.	39·50 N	106·20 W
81	Green Mts. Vt.	43·10 N	73·05 W
116	Greenock (grēn'ŭk) Scot.	55·55 N	4·45 W
84	Green Pond Mtn. (pŏnd) N. J. (New York In.)	41·00 N	74·32 W
69	Greenriver (grēn-rĭv'ẽr) Utah	39·00 N	110·05 W
67	Green River Wyo.	41·32 N	109·26 W
67	Green R., Blacks Fk. Wyo.	41·08 N	110·27 W
67	Green R., Hams Fk. Wyo.	41·55 N	110·40 W
78	Greensboro (grēnz'bŭro) Ala.	32·42 N	87·36 W
78	Greensboro (grēns-bûr'ô) Ga.	33·34 N	83·11 W
79	Greensboro N. C.	36·04 N	79·45 W
80	Greensburg (grēnz'bûrg) Ind.	39·20 N	85·30 W
72	Greensburg (grēns-bûrg) Kans.	37·36 N	99·17 W
81	Greensburg Pa.	40·20 N	79·30 W
78	Greenville (grēn'vĭl) Ala.	31·49 N	86·39 W
78	Greenville Ill.	38·52 N	89·22 W
78	Greenville Ky.	37·11 N	87·11 W
164	Greenville Lib.	5·06 N	8·44 W
82	Greenville Maine	45·26 N	69·35 W
80	Greenville Mich.	43·10 N	85·25 W
78	Greenville Miss.	33·25 N	91·00 W
79	Greenville N. C.	35·35 N	77·22 W
80	Greenville Ohio	40·05 N	84·35 W
80	Greenville Pa.	41·20 N	80·25 W
79	Greenville S. C.	34·50 N	82·25 W
78	Greenville Tenn.	36·08 N	82·50 W
73	Greenville Tex.	33·09 N	96·07 W
84	Greenwich Conn. (New York In.)	41·01 N	73·37 W
110	Greenwich (grĭn'ĭj) Eng. (London In.)	51·28 N	0·00
73	Greenwood (grēn-wŏŏd) Ark.	35·13 N	94·15 W
75	Greenwood Ind. (Indianapolis In.)	39·37 N	86·07 W
78	Greenwood Miss.	33·30 N	90·09 W
79	Greenwood S. C.	34·10 N	82·10 W
79	Greenwood (R.) S. C.	34·17 N	81·55 W
84	Greenwood L. N. Y. (New York In.)	41·13 N	74·20 W
79	Greer (grēr) S. C.	34·55 N	81·56 W
123	Grefrath (grĕf'rät) Ger. (Ruhr In.)	51·20 N	6·21 E
70	Gregory (grĕg'ô-rĭ) S. D.	43·12 N	99·27 W
160	Gregory, L. (grĕg'ô-rê) Austl.	29·47 S	139·15 E
159	Gregory Ra. Austl.	19·23 S	143·45 E
111	Greifenberg (grī'fĕn-bĕrgh) Ger. (Munich In.)	48·04 N	11·06 E
120	Greifswald (grīfs'vält) Ger.	54·05 N	13·24 E
120	Greiz (grīts) Ger.	50·39 N	12·14 E
136	Gremyachinsk (grâ'myȧ chĭnsk) Sov. Un. (Urals In.)	58·35 N	57·53 E
118	Grenå (grĕn'ô) Den.	56·25 N	10·51 E
78	Grenada (grê-nä'da) Miss.	33·45 N	89·47 W
93	Grenada I. N. A. (Le. & Wind. Is. In.)	12·02 N	61·27 W
78	Grenada Res. Miss.	33·52 N	89·30 W
122	Grenade (grē-näd') Fr.	43·46 N	1·15 E
93	Grenadines, The (Is.) (grĕn'ȧ-dēnz) Grenada-St. Vincent (Le. & Wind. Is. In.)	12·37 N	61·35 W
84	Grenloch (grĕn-lŏk) N. J. (Philadelphia In.)	39·48 N	75·04 W
123	Grenoble (grē-nō'bl') Fr.	45·14 N	5·45 E
70	Grenora (grê-nō'rȧ) N. D.	48·38 N	103·55 W
81	Grenville (grĕn'vĭl) Can.	45·40 N	74·35 W
93	Grenville Grenada (Le. & Wind. Is. In.)	12·07 N	61·38 W
65	Gresham (grĕsh'ăm) Ore. (Portland In.)	45·30 N	122·25 W
84	Gretna (grĕt'nȧ) La. (New Orleans In.)	29·56 N	90·03 W
111	Grevelingen Krammer, R. Neth. (Amsterdam In.)	51·42 N	4·03 E
127	Grevená (grĕ'vä-nä) Grc.	40·02 N	21·30 E
123	Grevenbroich (grĕ'fĕn-broik) Ger. (Ruhr In.)	51·05 N	6·36 E
123	Grevenbrück (grĕ'fĕn-brük) Ger. (Ruhr In.)	51·08 N	8·01 E
65	Grey, Pt. (grā) Can. (Vancouver In.)	49·22 N	123·16 W
67	Greybull (grā'bŏŏl) Wyo.	44·28 N	108·05 W
67	Greybull R. Wyo.	44·13 N	108·43 W
84	Greycourt (grā-kōrt) N. Y. (New York In.)	41·22 N	74·16 W
168	Greylingstad (grā-lĭng'shtȧt) S. Afr. (Johannesburg & Pretoria In.)	26·40 S	29·13 E
159	Greymouth (grā'mouth) N. Z. (In.)	42·27 S	171·17 E
160	Grey Ra. Austl.	28·40 S	142·05 E
66	Greys Hbr. (grās) Wash.	46·55 N	124·23 W
167	Greytown (grā'toun) S. Afr. (Natal In.)	29·07 S	30·38 E
	Greytown, see San Juan del Norte		
65	Grey Wolf Pk. (grā wŏŏlf) Wash. (Seattle In.)	48·53 N	123·12 W
68	Gridley (grĭd'lĭ) Calif.	39·22 N	121·43 W
78	Griffin (grĭf'ĭn) Ga.	33·15 N	84·16 W
64	Griffin Pt. Alaska	70·05 N	143·21 W
160	Griffith (grĭf-ĭth) Austl.	34·16 S	146·10 E
75	Griffith Ind. (Chicago In.)	41·31 N	87·26 W
129	Grigoriopol' (grĭ'gor-i-ô'pôl) Sov. Un.	47·09 N	29·18 E
91	Grijalva (R.) (grē-häl'vä) Mex.	18·15 N	92·45 W
160	Grim, C. (grĭm) Austl.	40·43 S	144·30 E
120	Grimma (grĭm'ȧ) Ger.	51·14 N	12·43 E
85	Grimsby (grĭmz'bĭ) Can. (Toronto In.)	43·11 N	79·33 W
112	Grimsey (I.) (grĭms'ȧ) Ice.	66·30 N	17·50 W
118	Grimstad (grĭm-städh) Nor.	58·21 N	8·30 E
71	Grinnel (grĭ-nĕl') Iowa	41·44 N	92·44 W
71	Griswold (grĭz'wŭld) Iowa	41·11 N	95·05 W
128	Griva (grē'vä) Sov. Un.	55·51 N	26·31 E
83	Groais (I.) Can.	50·56 N	55·35 W
119	Grobina (grō'bĭŋia) Sov. Un.	56·35 N	21·10 E
168	Groblersdal S. Afr. (Johannesburg & Pretoria In.)	25·11 S	29·25 E
121	Grodno (grôd'nŏ) Sov. Un.	53·40 N	23·49 E
121	Grodzisk Masowieki (grō'jēsk mä-zō-vyĕts'ke) Pol.	52·06 N	20·40 E
120	Grodzisk Wielkopolski (grō'jēsk vyĕl-ko-pōl'skē) Pol.	52·14 N	16·22 E
77	Groesbeck (grōs'bĕk) Tex.	31·32 N	96·31 W
122	Groix, I. de (ēl dē grwä') Fr.	47·39 N	3·28 W
121	Grójec (grōō'yĕts) Pol.	51·53 N	20·52 E
120	Gronau (grō'nou) Ger.	52·12 N	7·05 E
117	Groningen (grō'nĭng-ĕn) Neth.	53·13 N	6·30 E
158	Groote Eyelandt (I.) (grō'tē ī'lănt) Austl.	13·50 S	137·30 E
166	Grootfontein (grōt'fŏn-tān') S. W. Afr.	18·15 S	19·30 E
166	Grootkop (Mtn.) S. Afr. (Cape Town In.)	34·11 S	18·23 E
168	Groot Marico S. Afr. (Johannesburg & Pretoria In.)	25·36 S	26·23 E
168	Groot R. S. Afr. (Johannesburg & Pretoria In.)	25·13 S	26·20 E
166	Groot Vloer (L.) (grōt' vlōōr') S. Afr.	30·00 S	20·16 E
83	Gros Morne (Mtn.) (grō môrn') Can.	49·37 N	57·45 W
83	Gros Pate (Mtn.) Can.	50·16 N	57·25 W
111	Gross Behnitz (grōss bĕ'nētz) Ger. (Berlin In.)	52·35 N	12·45 E
75	Grosse I. (grōs) Mich. (Detroit In.)	42·08 N	83·09 W
85	Grosse Isle (īl') Can. (Winnipeg In.)	50·04 N	97·27 W
166	Grosse Karras (Mts.) S. W. Afr.	27·10 S	18·30 E
120	Grossenhain (grōs'ĕn-hīn) Ger.	51·17 N	13·33 E
111	Grossenzersdorf Aus. (Vienna In.)	48·13 N	16·33 E
75	Grosse Pointe (point') Mich. (Detroit In.)	42·23 N	82·54 W
75	Grosse Pointe Farms (färm) Mich. (Detroit In.)	42·25 N	82·53 W
75	Grosse Pointe Park (pärk) Mich. (Detroit In.)	42·23 N	82·55 W
126	Grosseto (grôs-sā'tō) It.	42·46 N	11·09 E
120	Grossglockner Pk. (glôk'nẽr) Aus.	47·06 N	12·45 E
111	Gross Höbach (hû'bäk) Ger. (Munich In.)	48·21 N	11·36 E
111	Gross Kreutz (kroitz) Ger. (Berlin In.)	52·24 N	12·47 E
123	Gross Reken (rĕ'kĕn) Ger. (Ruhr In.)	51·50 N	7·20 E
111	Gross Schonebeck (shō'nĕ-bĕk) Ger. (Berlin In.)	52·54 N	13·32 E
67	Gros Ventre R. (grōvĕn't'r) Wyo.	43·38 N	110·34 W
81	Groton (grôt'ŭn) Conn.	41·20 N	72·00 W
83	Groton Mass. (Boston In.)	42·37 N	71·34 W
70	Groton Nebr.	42·44 N	97·32 W
127	Grottaglie (grôt-täl'yä) It.	40·32 N	17·26 E

ng-sing; ŋ-baŋk; N-nasalized n; nŏd; cŏmmit; ōld; ôbey; ôrder; fōōd; fŏŏt; ou-out; s-soft; sh-dish; th-thin; pūre; ûnite; ûrn; stŭd; circŭs; ü-as "y" in study; '-indeterminate vowel.

Page	Name Pronunciation Region	Lat. °'	Long. °'
86	Grouard ... Can.	55·35 N	116·11 W
83	Groveland (grōv'lănd) Mass. (Boston In.)	42·45 N	71·02 W
81	Groveton (grōv'tŭn) ... N. H.	44·35 N	71·30 W
77	Groveton ... Tex.	31·04 N	95·07 W
133	Groznyy (grôz'nĭ) ... Sov. Un.	43·20 N	45·40 E
121	Grudziadz (grōō'jyônts) ... Pol.	53·30 N	18·48 E
111	Grumpholds-Kirchen Aus. (Wien In.)	48·03 N	16·17 E
71	Grundy Center (grŭn'dĭ sĕn'tẽr) Iowa	42·22 N	92·45 W
90	Gruñidora (grōō-nyē-dō'rō) .. Mex.	24·10 N	101·49 W
111	Grunwald (grōōn'väld) Ger. (Munich In.)	48·04 N	11·34 E
128	Gryazi (gryä'zĭ) ... Sov. Un.	52·31 N	39·59 E
128	Gryazovets (gryä'zô-vĕts) Sov. Un.	58·52 N	40·14 E
120	Gryfice (grĭ'fĭ-tsĕ) ... Pol.	53·55 N	15·11 E
120	Gryfino (grĭ'fē-nō) ... Pol.	53·16 N	14·30 E
93	Guabito (gwä-bē'tō) ... Pan.	9·30 N	82·33 W
94	Guacanayabo, Golfo de (G.) (gôl-fô-dĕ-gwä-kä-nä-yä'bō) ... Cuba	20·30 N	77·40 W
99	Guacara (gwá'-kä-rä) ... Ven. (In.)	10·16 N	67·48 W
98	Guacarí (gwä-kä-rē') ... Col. (In.)	3·45 N	76·20 W
101	Guaçuí (gwä'-sōō-ē') Braz. (Rio de Janeiro In.)	20·47 S	41·40 W
90	Guadalajara (gwä-dhä-lä-hä'rä) Mex.	20·41 N	103·21 W
124	Guadalajara (gwä-dä-lä-kä'-rä) Sp.	40·37 N	3·10 W
124	Guadalcanal (gwä-dhäl-kä-näl') Sp.	38·05 N	5·48 W
159	Guadalcanal (I.) ... Sol. Is.	9·48 S	158·43 E
90	Guadalcázar (gwä-dhäl-kä'zär) Mex.	22·38 N	100·24 W
124	Guadalete (R.) (gwä-dhä-lā'tå) . Sp.	38·53 N	5·38 W
124	Guadalhorce (R.) (gwä-dhäl-ôr'thā) . Sp.	37·05 N	4·50 W
124	Guadalimar (R.) (gwä-dhä-lē-mär') . Sp.	38·29 N	2·53 W
125	Guadalope (R.) (gwä-dä-lô-pĕ) . Sp.	40·48 N	0·10 W
124	Guadalquivir, Río (R.) (rē'-ō-gwä-dhäl-kē-vēr') . Sp.	5·57 N	6·00 W
76	Guadalupe ... Mex.	31·23 N	106·06 W
124	Guadalupe, Sierra de (Mts.) (syĕr'rä dā gwä-dhä-lōō'pä) . Sp.	39·30 N	5·25 W
88	Guadalupe I. ... Mex.	29·00 N	118·45 W
76	Guadalupe Mts. ... N. Mex.-Tex.	32·00 N	104·55 W
76	Guadalupe Pk. ... Tex.	31·55 N	104·55 W
76	Guadalupe R. (gwä-dhä-lōō'pä) Tex.	29·54 N	99·03 W
124	Guadarrama, Sierra de (Mts.) (gwä-dhär-rä'mä) . Sp.	41·00 N	3·40 W
125	Guadarrama (R.) (gwä-dhär-rä'mä) Sp. (Madrid In.)	40·34 N	3·58 W
93	Guadeloupe (Is.) (gwä-dĕ-lōōp') N. A. (Le. & Wind. Is. In.)	16·07 N	61·19 W
93	Guadeloupe Pass. N. A. (Le. & Wind. Is. In.)	16·26 N	62·00 W
94	Guadiana, Bahía de (B.) (bä-ē'ä-dĕ-gwä-dhē-ä'nä) . Cuba	22·10 N	84·35 W
124	Guadiana, Rio (R.) (rē'ō-gwä-dvä'nä) . Port.	37·43 N	7·43 W
124	Guadiana Alto (R.) (äl'tō) ... Sp.	39·02 N	2·52 W
124	Guadiana Menor (R.) (mā'nôr) Sp.	37·43 N	2·45 W
124	Guadiaro (R.) (gwä-dhē-ä'rō) .. Sp.	37·38 N	5·25 W
125	Guadiato (R.) (gwä-dhē-ä'tō) .. Sp.	38·10 N	5·05 W
124	Guadiela (R.) (gwä-dhē-ā'lä) .. Sp.	40·23 N	2·23 W
124	Guadix (gwä-dhēsh') ... Sp.	37·18 N	3·09 W
99	Guaira (gwä-ē-rä) ... Braz.	24·03 S	44·02 W
99	Guaire (R.) (gwī'-rĕ) ... Ven. (In.)	10·25 N	66·43 W
94	Guajaba, Cayo (I.) (kä'yō-gwä-hä'bä) . Cuba	21·50 N	77·35 W
98	Guajará Mirim (gwä-zhä-rä'mē-rēɴ' . Braz.	10·58 S	65·12 W
98	Guajira, Pen. de (Pen.) (pĕ-nē'ng-sōō-lä-dĕ-gwä-ĸē'rä) Col.-Ven.	12·35 N	73·00 W
92	Gualán (gwä-län') ... Guat.	15·08 N	89·21 W
101	Gualeguay (gwä-lĕ-gwä'y) Arg. (Buenos Aires In.)	33·10 S	59·20 W
101	Gualeguay (R.) Arg. (Buenos Aires In.)	32·49 S	59·05 W
101	Gualeguaychú (gwä-lå-gwī-chōō') Arg. (Buenos Aires In.)	33·01 S	58·32 W
101	Gualeguaychú (R.) Arg. (Buenos Aires In.)	32·58 S	58·27 W
100	Gualicho, Salina (F.) (sä-lē'nä-gwä-lē'chō) . Arg.	40·20 S	65·15 W
156	Guam (I.) (gwäm) ... Oceania	14·00 N	143·20 E
100	Guaminí (gwä-mē-nē') ... Arg.	37·02 S	62·21 W
98	Guamo (gwá'mō) ... Col. (In.)	4·02 N	74·58 W
95	Guanabacoa (gwä-nä-bä-kō'ä) Cuba (Havana In.)	23·08 N	82·19 W
100	Guanabara (gwä-nä-bä'rä) .. Braz.	23·03 N	43·32 W
100	Guanabara, Baia de (B.) Braz. (In.)	22·44 S	43·09 W
92	Guanacaste Cord. (Mts.) (kôr-dēl-yĕ'rä-gwä-nä-käs'tā) C. R.	10·54 N	85·27 W
88	Guanacevi (gwä-nä-sĕ-vē') .. Mex.	25·30 N	105·45 W
94	Guanahacabibes, Pen. de (pĕ-nĕn-sōō-lä-dĕ-gwä-nä hä-kä-bē'bås) Cuba	21·55 N	84·35 W
94	Guanajay (gwä-nä-hī') ... Cuba	22·55 N	82·40 W
90	Guanajuato (gwä-nä-hwä'tō) Mex.	21·01 N	101·16 W
88	Guanajuato (State) ... Mex.	21·00 N	101·00 W
99	Guanape (gwä-nä'pĕ) ... Ven. (In.)	9·55 N	65·32 W
99	Guanape (R.) ... Ven. (In.)	9·52 N	65·20 W
98	Guanare (gwä-nä'rä) ... Ven.	8·57 N	69·47 W
100	Guanduçu (R.) (gwä'n-dōō'sōō) Braz. (In.)	22·50 S	43·40 W
94	Guane (gwä'nå) ... Cuba	22·10 N	84·05 W
99	Guanta (gwän'tä) ... Ven. (In.)	10·15 N	64·35 W
95	Guantánamo (gwän-tä'nä-mō) Cuba	20·10 N	75·10 W
95	Guantanamo, Bahía de (B.) (bä-ē'ä-dĕ) . Cuba	19·35 N	75·35 W
101	Guapé (gwå-pĕ') Braz. (Rio de Janeiro In.)	20·45 S	45·55 W
93	Guapiles (gwä-pē'lĕs) ... C. R.	10·05 N	83·54 W
100	Guapimirim (gwä-pē-mē-rē'ɴ) Braz. (In.)	22·31 S	42·59 W
98	Guaporé (R.) (gwä-pô-rā') Bol.-Braz.	12·11 S	63·47 W
98	Guaqui (guä'kē) ... Bol.	16·42 S	68·47 W
125	Guara, Sierra de (Mts.) (sē-ĕ'r-rä-dĕ-gwä'rä) . Sp.	42·24 N	0·15 W
99	Guarabira (gwä-rä-bē'rå) ... Braz.	6·49 S	35·27 W
98	Guaranda (gwä-rän'dä) ... Ec.	1·39 S	78·57 W
99	Guarapari (gwä-rä-pä'rē) ... Braz.	20·34 S	40·31 W
101	Guarapiranga, Represa do (Res.) (r'ĕ-prĕ-sä-dô-gwä'rä-pē-rà'n-gä) Braz. (Rio de Janeiro In.)	23·45 S	46·44 W
100	Guarapuava (gwä-rä-pwä'vå) Braz.	25·29 S	51·26 W
101	Guaratinguetá (guä-rä-tĭɴ-gå-tä') Braz. (Rio de Janeiro In.)	22·49 S	45·10 W
124	Guarda (gwär'dä) ... Port.	40·32 N	7·17 W
124	Guareña (gwä-rā'nyä) ... Sp.	38·52 N	6·08 W
99	Guaribe (R.) (gwä-rē'bĕ) Ven. (In.)	9·48 N	65·17 W
99	Guarico (State) ... Ven. (In.)	9·42 N	67·25 W
99	Guárico (R.) ... Ven. (In.)	9·50 N	67·07 W
101	Guarulhos (gwä-rōō'l-yôs) Braz. (Rio de Janeiro In.)	32·28 S	46·30 W
101	Guarus (gwà'rōōs) Braz. (Rio de Janeiro In.)	21·44 S	41·19 W
98	Guasca (gwäs'kä) ... Col. (In.)	4·52 N	73·52 W
99	Guasipati (gwä-sē-pä'tē) ... Ven.	7·26 N	61·57 W
126	Guastalla (gwäs-täl'lä) ... It.	44·53 N	10·39 E
74	Guasti (gwäs'tĭ) Calif. (Los Angeles In.)	34·04 N	117·35 W
92	Guatemala (guä-tå-mä'lä) .. Guat.	14·37 N	90·32 W
88	Guatemala ... N. A.	15·45 N	91·45 W
99	Guatire (gwä-tē'rĕ) ... Ven. (In.)	10·28 N	66·34 W
101	Guaxupé (gwä-shōō-pĕ') Braz. (Rio de Janeiro In.)	21·18 S	46·42 W
94	Guayabal (gwä-yä-bä'l) ... Cuba	20·40 N	77·40 W
90	Guayalejo (R.) (gwä-yä-lĕ'hō) Mex.	23·24 N	99·09 W
89	Guayama (gwä-yä'mä) P. R. (Puerto Rico In.)	18·00 N	66·08 W
95	Guayamouc (R.) ... Hai.	19·05 N	72·00 W
92	Guayape R. ... Hond.	14·39 N	86·37 W
98	Guayaquil (gwī-ä-kēl') ... Ec.	2·16 S	79·53 W
98	Guayaquil, Golfo de (G.) (gôl-fô-dĕ) . Ec.	3·03 S	82·12 W
98	Guayiare (R.) (gwä-yä'rĕ) ... Col.	3·35 N	69·28 W
88	Guaymas (gwä'y-mäs) ... Mex.	27·49 N	110·58 W
95	Guayubin (gwä-yōō-bē'n) Dom. Rep.	19·40 N	71·25 W
92	Guazacapán (gwä-zä-kä-pän') Guat.	14·04 N	90·26 W
136	Gubakha (gōō-bä'kå) Sov. Un. (Urals In.)	58·53 N	57·35 E
126	Gubbio (gōōb'byō) ... It.	43·23 N	12·36 E
125	Gudar, Sierra de (Mts.) (syĕr'rä dā gōō'dhär) . Sp.	40·28 N	0·47 W
118	Gudenaa (R.) ... Den.	56·20 N	9·47 E
118	Gudinge Fjärden (Fd.) ... Swe.	57·43 N	16·55 E
118	Gudvangen (gōōdh'văŋ-gĕn) . Nor.	60·52 N	6·45 E
123	Guebwiller (gĕb-vē-lâr') ... Fr.	47·53 N	7·10 E
164	Guelma (gwĕl'mä) ... Alg.	36·32 N	7·17 E
85	Guelph (gwĕlf) . Can. (Toronto In.)	43·33 N	80·15 W
114	Guemar (gē-mär') ... Alg.	33·32 N	6·42 E
99	Güere (gwĕ'rĕ) (R.) ... Ven. (In.)	9·39 N	65·00 W
122	Guéret (gā-rĕ') ... Fr.	46·09 N	1·52 E
122	Guernsey (I.) (gûrn'zĭ) ... Eur.	49·27 N	2·36 W
114	Guerrara (gĕr-rä'rä) ... Alg.	32·50 N	4·26 E
76	Guerrero (gĕr-rā'rō) ... Mex.	26·47 N	99·20 W
76	Guerrero ... Mex.	28·20 N	100·24 W
122	Gueugnon (gû-nyôɴ') ... Fr.	46·35 N	4·01 E
77	Gueydan (gā'dăn) ... La.	30·01 N	92·31 W
100	Guia de Pacobaíba (gwē'ä-dĕ-pä'kō-bī'bä) . Braz. (In.)	22·42 S	43·10 W
96	Guiana Highlands (Mts.) ... Braz.	3·20 N	60·00 W
91	Guichicovi (San Juan) (gwē-chē-kō'vē) . Mex.	16·58 N	95·10 W
125	Guidonia (gwē-dō'nyä) It. (Rome In.)	42·00 N	12·45 E
123	Guignes (gēɴ'yĕ) ... Fr. (Paris In.)	48·38 N	2·48 E
99	Güigüe (gwē'gwĕ) ... Ven. (In.)	10·05 N	67·48 W
92	Guija, L. (gē'hä) ... Sal.	14·16 N	89·21 W
110	Guildford (gĭl'fĕrd) Eng. (London In.)	51·13 N	0·34 W
75	Guilford (gĭl'fĕrd) Ind. (Cincinnati In.)	39·10 N	84·55 W
124	Guimarães (gē-mä-räɴsh') ... Port.	41·27 N	8·22 W
163	Guinea (gĭn'ē) ... Afr.	10·48 N	12·28 W
163	Guinea, G. of ... Afr.	2·00 N	1·00 E
94	Güines (gwē'näs) ... Cuba	22·50 N	82·05 W
122	Guingamp (găɴ-gäɴ') ... Fr.	48·35 N	3·10 W
94	Güira de Melena (gwē'rä dā må-lā'nå) . Cuba	22·45 N	82·30 W
98	Güiria (gwê-rē'ä) ... Ven.	10·43 N	62·16 W
114	Guir R. ... Mor.-Alg.	31·55 N	2·48 W
123	Guise (guēz) ... Fr.	49·54 N	3·37 E
92	Guisisil (Vol.) (gê-sê-sēl') ... Nic.	12·40 N	86·11 W
142	Gujarat (State) ... India	22·54 N	79·00 E
142	Gujranwala (gōōj-rän'va-lå) W. Pak.	32·08 N	74·14 E
118	Gula (R.) (gōō'lå) ... Nor.	62·55 N	10·45 E
143	Gulbarga (gōōl-bŭr'gå) ... India	17·25 N	76·52 E
128	Gulbene (gōōl-bă'nĕ) ... Sov. Un.	57·09 N	26·49 E
78	Gulfport (gŭlf'pōrt) ... Miss.	30·24 N	89·05 W
129	Gulyay Pole ... Sov. Un.	47·39 N	36·12 E
155	Gumaca (gōō-mä-kä') Phil. (Manila In.)	13·55 N	122·06 E
165	Gumbari (gōōm-bä-rē) ... Con. K.	2·45 N	29·00 E
136	Gumbeyka R. (gōōm-bĕy'kå) Sov. Un. (Urals In.)	53·20 N	59·42 E
164	Gumel ... Nig.	12·43 N	9·19 E
120	Gummersbach (gōōm'ĕrs-bäk) . Ger.	51·02 N	7·34 E
111	Gumpoldskirchen ... Aus.	48·04 N	16·15 E
142	Guna ... India	24·44 N	77·17 E
160	Gunnedah (gŭ'nē-dä) ... Austl.	31·00 S	150·10 E
69	Gunnison (gŭn'ĭ-sŭn) ... Colo.	38·30 N	107·00 W
69	Gunnison ... Utah	39·10 N	111·50 W
69	Gunnison (R.) ... Colo.	38·50 N	108·00 W
78	Guntersville (gŭn'tẽrz-vĭl) ... Ala.	34·20 N	86·19 W
78	Guntersville L. ... Ala.	34·30 N	86·20 W
111	Guntramsdorf .. Aus. (Vienna In.)	48·04 N	16·19 E
143	Guntūr (gōōn'tōōr) ... India	16·22 N	80·29 E
155	Gunungapi (I.) (gōō'nōōng ä'pē) Indon.	6·52 S	127·15 E
139	Gunungkidjang Indon. (Singapore In.)	0·55 N	104·39 E
73	Gurdon (gûr'dŭn) ... Ark.	33·56 N	93·10 W
99	Gurgucia (R.) (gōōr-gōō'syä) Braz.	8·12 S	43·49 W
75	Gurnee (gûr'nē) . Ill. (Chicago In.)	42·22 N	87·55 W
118	Gurskøy (I.) (gōōrskûê) ... Nor.	62·18 N	5·20 E
99	Gurupá (gōō-rōō-pä') ... Braz.	1·28 S	51·32 W
99	Gurupi, Serra do (Mts.) (sĕ'r-rä-dô-gōō-rōō-pē') . Braz.	5·32 S	47·02 W
99	Gurupí (R.) (gōō-rōō-pē') ... Braz.	2·37 S	46·45 W
142	Guru Sikhar Mt. ... India	29·42 N	72·50 E
133	Gur'yev (gōōr'yĕf) ... Sov. Un.	47·10 N	51·50 E
134	Gur'yevsk (gōōr-yĭfsk') .. Sov. Un.	54·14 N	86·07 E
164	Gusau (gōō-zä'ōō) ... Nig.	12·11 N	6·40 E
119	Gusev (gōō'sĕf) ... Sov. Un.	54·35 N	22·15 E
127	Gusinje (gōō-sēn'yĕ) ... Yugo.	42·34 N	19·54 E
128	Gus'-Khrustal'nyy (gōōs-ĸrōō-stäl'ny') . Sov. Un.	55·39 N	40·41 E
91	Gustavo A. Madero (gōōs-tä'vô-ä-mä-dĕ'rô) Mex. (Mexico City In.)	19·29 N	99·07 W
120	Güstrow (güs'trō) ... Ger.	53·48 N	12·12 E
120	Gütersloh (gü'tĕrs-lo) ... Ger.	51·54 N	8·22 E
73	Guthrie (gŭth'rĭ) ... Okla.	35·52 N	97·26 W
71	Guthrie Center ... Iowa	41·41 N	94·33 W
91	Gutiérrez Zamora (gōō-tĭ-âr'räz zä-mō'rä) . Mex.	20·27 N	97·17 W
71	Guttenberg (gŭt'ĕn-bûrg) ... Iowa	42·48 N	91·09 W
99	Guyana (gŭy'ănă) ... S. A.	7·00 N	59·40 W
72	Guymon (gī'mŏn) ... Okla.	36·41 N	101·29 W
83	Guysborough (gīz'bŭr-ô) ... Can.	45·25 N	61·30 W
119	Gvardeysk (gvăr-dĕysk') . Sov. Un.	54·39 N	21·11 E
144	Gwadar (gwä'dŭr) ... W. Pak.	25·15 N	62·29 E
165	Gwane (gwän) ... Con. K.	4·49 N	26·46 E
166	Gwelo (gwā'lō) ... Rh.	19·15 S	29·48 E
71	Gwinn (gwĭn) ... Mich.	46·15 N	87·30 W
146	Gyangtse (gyäng'tsĕ') ... China	29·00 N	89·28 E
142	Gyangtse ... China	28·53 N	89·39 E
135	Gydan, Khrebet (Kolymskiy) (Mts.) . Sov. Un.	61·45 N	155·00 E
134	Gydanskiy, P-Ov (Pen.) . Sov. Un.	70·42 N	76·03 E
160	Gympie (gĭm'pē) ... Austl.	26·20 S	152·50 E
121	Gyöngyös (dyûn'dyûsh) ... Hung.	47·47 N	19·55 E
121	Györ (dyûr) ... Hung.	47·40 N	17·37 E
153	Gyōtoku (gyō'tō-kōō') Jap. (Tōkyō In.)	35·42 N	139·56 E
86	Gypsumville (jĭp'sŭm'vĭl) ... Can.	51·49 N	98·42 W
121	Gyula (dyōō'lä) ... Hung.	46·38 N	21·18 E
128	Gzhatsk (g'zhätsk) ... Sov. Un.	55·32 N	34·58 E
123	Haan (hän) ... Ger. (Ruhr In.)	51·12 N	7·00 E
119	Haapamäki (häp'ä-mĕ-kē) ... Fin.	62·16 N	24·20 E
119	Haapsalu (häp'sä-lōō) .. Sov. Un.	58·56 N	23·33 E
111	Haar (här) ... Ger. (Munich In.)	48·06 N	11·44 E
139	Ha'arava (R.) (Araba) Isr. (Palestine In.)	30·32 N	35·16 E
111	Haarlem (här'lĕm) Neth. (Amsterdam In.)	52·22 N	4·37 E
94	Habana (State) (hä-vä'nä) .. Cuba	22·55 N	82·15 W
125	Habibas (C.) (hä-bē'bås) ... Alg.	35·50 N	0·45 W
152	Hachinohe (hä'chē-nō'hå) ... Jap.	40·29 N	141·40 E
153	Hachiōji (hä'chē-ō'jē) ... Jap.	35·39 N	139·18 E
84	Hackensack (hăk'ĕn-săk) N. J. (New York In.)	40·54 N	74·03 W
84	Haddonfield (hăd'ŭn-fēld) N. J. (Philadelphia In.)	39·53 N	75·02 W
84	Haddon Heights (hăd'ŭn hīts) N. J. (Philadelphia In.)	39·53 N	75·03 W
164	Hadejia (hä-dā'jē-ä) ... Nig.	12·32 N	10·04 E
139	Hadera (ĸå-dĕ'rå) Isr. (Palestine In.)	32·26 N	34·55 E
118	Haderslev (hä'dhĕrs-lĕv) ... Den.	55·17 N	9·28 E
168	Hadibu ... S. Ar. (Horn of Afr. In.)	12·40 N	53·50 E
65	Hadlock (hăd'lŏk) Wash. (Seattle In.)	48·02 N	122·46 W
144	Hadramawt (Reg.) ... S. Ar.	15·15 N	48·32 E
152	Haeju (hä'ĕ-jŭ) ... Kor.	38·03 N	125·42 E
150	Haerhpin (Harbin) (här-bēn') China	45·40 N	126·30 E
112	Hafnarfjördhur ... Ice.	64·02 N	21·32 W
168	Hafun, Ras (C.) (hä-fōōn') Som. (Horn of Afr. In.)	10·15 N	51·35 E
67	Hageland (hăge'lănd) ... Mont.	48·53 N	108·43 W
123	Hagen (hä'gĕn) ... Ger. (Ruhr In.)	51·21 N	7·29 E
85	Hagermans Corners (hăg'ẽr-măns kôr'nẽr) . Can. (Toronto In.)	43·51 N	79·19 W
80	Hagerstown (hā'gĕrz-toun) ... Ind.	39·55 N	85·10 W
81	Hagerstown ... Md.	39·40 N	77·45 W
153	Hagi (hä'gē) ... Jap.	34·25 N	131·25 E
122	Hague, C. de la (dĕ lä åg') ... Fr.	49·44 N	1·55 W
	Hague, The, see 's Gravenhagen		
123	Haguenau (åg'nō') ... Fr.	48·47 N	7·48 E
148	Haian (hăi'äɴ) ... China	32·35 N	120·25 E
153	Haibara (hä'ē-bä-rä) ... Jap.	34·29 N	135·57 E
150	Haich'eng ... China	40·58 N	122·45 E
148	Haichou Wan (B.) (hăi'jō wän) China	34·58 N	119·27 E
139	Haifa (hä'ē-få) . Isr. (Palestine In.)	32·48 N	35·00 E
151	Haifeng (hä'ē-fĕng') ... China	23·00 N	115·20 E

ăt; finăl; rāte; senâte; ärm; àsk; sofá; fâre; ch-choose; dh-as th in other; bē; êvent; bĕt; recĕnt; cratẽr; g-go; gh-guttural g; bĭt; ĭ-short neutral; rīde; ĸ-guttural k as ch in German ich;

Page	Name Pronunciation Region	Lat. °′	Long. °′
148	Haifuchen (hāī′fōō′jĕn) . . . . . China	31·57 N	121·48 E
144	Hā′il (hāl) . . . . Sau. Ar.	27·30 N	41·57 E
150	Hailaerh (Hailar) (hä-ê-lär′) China	49·10 N	118·40 E
	Hailar, see Hailaerh		
67	Hailey (hā′lĭ) . . . . Idaho	43·31 N	114·19 W
73	Haileyville (hā′lĭ-vĭl) . . . . Okla.	34·51 N	95·34 W
152	Hailin (hä′ê-lēn′) . . . . China	44·31 N	129·11 E
151	Hailing Tao (I.) . . . . China	21·30 N	112·15 E
150	Hailun (hä′ê-lōōn′) . . . . China	47·18 N	126·50 E
150	Hailung (hä′ê-lōōng′) . . . . . . China	42·32 N	125·52 E
151	Hainan Tao (I.) (hä′e-nän′dou) China	19·00 N	111·10 E
111	Hainburg an der Donau Aus. (Vienna In.)	48·09 N	16·57 E
64	Haines (hānz) . . . . Alaska	59·10 N	135·38 W
79	Haines City . . . . Fla. (In.)	28·05 N	81·38 W
151	Haiphong (hī′fông′) (hä′ēp-hŏng) Viet.	20·52 N	106·40 E
89	Haiti (hā′tĭ) . . . . N. A.	19·00 N	72·15 W
150	Haitien (hī′tyĕn′) China (Peking In.)	39·59 N	116·17 E
165	Haiya . . . . Sud.	18·40 N	37·45 E
121	Hajdúböszörmény (hôl′dōō-bû′sûr-mān′) . Hung.	47·41 N	21·30 E
121	Hajduhadház (hô′ĭ-dōō-hôd′häz) Hung.	47·32 N	21·32 E
121	Hajdunánás (hô′ĭ-dōō-nä′näsh) Hung.	47·52 N	21·27 E
121	Hajduszoboszló (hô′ĭ-dōō-sô′bôs-lō) . Hung.	47·24 N	21·25 E
152	Hakodate (hä-kō-dä′tå) . . . . . . Jap.	41·46 N	140·42 E
153	Haku-San (Mtn.) (hä′kōō-sän′) Jap.	36·11 N	136·45 E
91	Halachó (ä-lä-chō′) . . . . Mex.	20·28 N	90·06 W
165	Halaib (hä-lä′êb) . . . . U. A. R.	22·10 N	36·40 E
157	Halawa (hä-lä′wä) . . . Hawaii (In.)	21·12 N	156·55 E
139	Halbā . . . . Leb. (Palestine In.)	34·33 N	36·03 E
111	Halbe (häl′bĕ) . . . Ger. (Berlin In.)	52·07 N	13·43 E
120	Halberstadt (häl′bĕr-shtät) . . . Ger.	51·54 N	11·07 E
155	Halcon, Mt. (häl-kōn′) Phil. (Manila In.)	13·19 N	120·55 E
118	Halden (häl′dĕn) . . . . Nor.	59·10 N	11·21 E
110	Hale (hāl) . . . . Eng.	53·22 N	2·20 W
157	Haleakala Crater (hä′lä-ä′kä-lä) Hawaii (In.)	20·44 N	156·15 W
157	Haleakala Natl. Park . Hawaii (In.)	20·46 N	156·00 W
75	Hales Corners (hälz kŏr′nērz) Wis. (Milwaukee In.)	42·56 N	88·03 W
110	Halesowen (hālz′ô-wĕn) . . . . . Eng.	52·26 N	2·03 W
84	Halethorpe (hāl-thôrp) Md. (Baltimore In.)	39·15 N	76·40 W
78	Haleyville (hā′lĭ-vĭl) . . . . Ala.	34·11 N	87·36 W
65	Half Moon Bay (häf′mōōn) . Calif. (San Francisco In.)	37·28 N	122·26 W
167	Halfway House (häf-wā hous) S. Afr. (Johannesburg & Pretoria In.)	26·00 S	28·08 E
111	Halfweg . . Neth. (Amsterdam In.)	52·23 N	4·45 E
82	Halifax (hăl′ĭ-făks) . . . . Can.	44·40 N	63·36 W
110	Halifax . . . . Eng.	53·44 N	1·52 W
159	Halifax B. (hăl′ĭ-făx) . . . . Austl.	18·56 S	147·07 E
82	Halifax Hbr . . . . Can.	44·35 N	63·25 W
139	Halīlah (R.) Jordan (Palestine In.)	30·28 N	35·57 E
152	Halla San (Mt.) (häl′lä-sän) . Kor.	33·20 N	126·37 E
139	Hallat ′Ammar Sau. Ar. (Palestine In.)	29·09 N	36·05 E
111	Halle (häl′lĕ) . . . Bel. (Brussels In.)	50·45 N	4·13 E
120	Halle . . . . Ger.	51·30 N	11·59 E
77	Hallettsville (hăl′ĕts-vĭl) . . . . Tex.	29·26 N	96·55 W
70	Hallock (hăl′ŭk) . . . . Minn.	48·46 N	96·57 W
87	Hall Pen (hôl) . . . . Can.	63·14 N	65·40 W
77	Halls Bay . . . . Tex. (In.)	29·55 N	95·23 W
118	Hallsberg (häls′bĕrgh) . . . . . . Swe.	59·04 N	15·04 E
158	Halls Creek (hôlz) . . . . Austl.	18·15 S	127·45 E
82	Halls Strm. (hôls) . . . . Can.-Maine	45·07 N	71·34 W
155	Halmahera (I.) (häl-mä-hä′rä) Indon.	0·45 N	128·45 E
118	Halmstad (hälm′städ) . . . . Swe.	56·40 N	12·46 E
118	Halse Fd. (häl′sĕ fyôrd) . . . . . Nor.	63·03 N	8·23 E
84	Halsey (hôl′zê) N. J. (New York In.)	41·06 N	74·45 W
118	Hälsingborg (hĕl′sĭng-bôrgh) . Swe.	56·04 N	12·40 E
73	Halstead (hôl′stĕd) . . . . Kans.	38·02 N	97·36 W
151	Halt′an Tao (I.) . . . . China	25·40 N	119·45 E
123	Haltern (häl′tĕrn) Ger. (Ruhr In.)	51·45 N	7·10 E
74	Haltom City (hôl′tŏm) Tex. (Dallas, Fort Worth In.)	32·48 N	97·17 W
	Halunrshan, see Wenchüan		
111	Halvarenbeek Neth. (Amsterdam In.)	51·29 N	5·10 E
115	Hama (hä′mä) . . . . Syr.	35·08 N	36·53 E
144	Hamadān (hŭ-mŭ-dän′) . . . . . Iran	34·45 N	48·07 E
153	Hamamatsu (hä′mä-mät′sōō) . Jap.	34·41 N	137·43 E
118	Hamar (hä′mär) . . . . Nor.	60·49 N	11·05 E
153	Hamasaka (hä′mä-sä′kä) . . . . Jap.	35·37 N	134·27 E
123	Hamborn (häm′bōrn) Ger. (Ruhr In.)	51·30 N	6·43 E
73	Hamburg (hăm′bûrg) . . . . Ark.	33·15 N	91·49 W
11	Hamburg (häm′bōōrgh) Ger. (Hamburg In.)	53·34 N	10·02 E
70	Hamburg . . . . Iowa	40·39 N	95·40 W
84	Hamburg . . . N. J. (New York In.)	41·09 N	74·35 W
75	Hamburg . . . . . N. Y. (Buffalo In.)	42·44 N	78·51 W
167	Hamburg (hăm′bûrg) S. Afr. (Natal In.)	33·18 S	27·28 E
81	Hamden (hăm′dĕn) . . . . Conn.	41·20 N	72·55 W
119	Hämeenlinna (hĕ′mân-lĭn-nä) . Fin.	61·00 N	24·29 E
74	Hamel (hăm′ĕl) . Ill. (St. Louis In.)	38·53 N	89·51 W
120	Hameln (hä′mĕln) . . . . Ger.	52·06 N	9·23 E
111	Hamelwörden (hä′mĕl-vûr-dĕn) Ger. (Hamburg In.)	53·47 N	9·19 E
158	Hamersley Ra. (hăm′ērz-lê) . Austl.	22·15 S	117·50 E
152	Hamhŭng (häm′hōōng′) . . . . . Kor.	39·57 N	127·35 E
146	Hami (Qomul) (hä′mê) (kô-mōōl′) China	42·58 N	93·14 E
160	Hamilton (hăm′ĭl-tŭn) . . . . . Austl.	37·50 S	142·10 E
85	Hamilton . . . . . Can. (Toronto In.)	43·15 N	79·52 W
83	Hamilton . . . . . Mass. (Boston In.)	42·37 N	70·52 W
73	Hamilton . . . . Mo.	39·43 N	93·59 W
67	Hamilton . . . . Mont.	46·15 N	114·09 W
159	Hamilton . . . . N. Z. (In.)	37·45 S	175·28 E
75	Hamilton . . . Ohio (Cincinnati In.)	39·22 N	84·33 W
76	Hamilton . . . . Tex.	31·42 N	98·07 W
73	Hamilton, L . . . . Ark.	34·25 N	93·32 W
85	Hamilton Hbr . Can. (Toronto In.)	43·17 N	79·50 W
87	Hamilton Inlet . . . . Can.	54·20 N	56·57 W
119	Hamina (hä′mê-nä) . . . . Fin.	60·34 N	27·15 E
79	Hamlet (hăm′lĕt) . . . . N. C.	35·52 N	79·46 W
72	Hamlin (hăm′lĭn) . . . . Tex.	32·54 N	100·08 W
123	Hamm (häm) . . . . Ger. (Ruhr In.)	51·40 N	7·48 E
168	Hammanskraal (hä-mȧns-kräl′) S. Afr. (Johannesburg & Pretoria In.)	25·24 S	28·17 E
111	Hamme . . . . Bel. (Brussels In.)	51·06 N	4·07 E
111	Hamme-Oste Kanal (Can.) (hä′mĕ-ōs′tĕ kä-näl) Ger. (Hamburg In.)	53·20 N	8·59 E
112	Hammerfest (häm′mĕr-fĕst) . . Nor.	70·38 N	23·59 E
75	Hammond (hăm′ŭnd) Ind. (Chicago In.)	41·37 N	87·31 W
77	Hammond . . . . La.	30·30 N	90·28 W
65	Hammond . . . . Ore. (Portland In.)	46·12 N	123·57 W
81	Hammonton (hăm′ŭn-tŭn) . . N. J.	39·40 N	74·45 W
82	Hampden (hăm′dĕn) . . . . Maine	44·44 N	68·51 W
116	Hampshire Downs (hămp′shĭr dounz) . Eng.	51·01 N	1·05 W
84	Hampstead . . . Md. (Baltimore In.)	39·36 N	76·54 W
110	Hampstead Norris (hămp-stĕd nŏ′rĭs) . Eng. (London In.)	51·27 N	1·14 W
82	Hampton (hămp′tŭn) . . . . Can.	45·34 N	65·50 W
71	Hampton . . . . Iowa	42·43 N	93·15 W
84	Hampton . . . . Va. (Norfolk In.)	37·02 N	76·21 W
84	Hampton Roads (Inlet) Va. (Norfolk In.)	36·56 N	76·23 W
164	Ḩamrā, Ḩammādah al (Plat.) Libya	29·39 N	10·53 E
118	Hamrånge (häm′rông′ĕ) . . . . . Swe.	60·56 N	17·00 E
75	Hamtramck (hăm-trăm′ĭk) Mich. (Detroit In.)	42·24 N	83·03 W
144	Hāmūn-i Māshkel (L.) (hä-mōōn′ē māsh-kĕl′) . W. Pak.	28·28 N	64·13 E
152	Han (R.) . . . . Kor.	37·10 N	127·40 E
157	Hana (hä′nä) . . . . Hawaii (In.)	20·43 N	155·59 W
94	Hanábana (R.) (hä-nä-bä′nä) Cuba	22·30 N	80·55 W
157	Hanalei B. (hä-nä-lā′ê) Hawaii (In.)	22·15 N	159·40 W
120	Hanau (hä′nou) . . . . Ger.	50·08 N	8·56 E
151	Han Chiang (R.) . . . . China	25·00 N	116·35 E
71	Hancock (hăn′kŏk) . . . . Mich.	47·08 N	88·37 W
65	Haney (hă-nê) Can. (Vancouver In.)	49·13 N	122·36 W
68	Hanford (hăn′fērd) . . . . Calif.	36·20 N	119·38 W
146	Hangayn Nuruu (Khangai Mts.) Mong.	48·03 N	99·45 E
151	Hangchou (hăng′chō′) . . . . . . China	30·17 N	120·12 E
151	Hangchou Wan (B.) (hăng′chō′) China	30·20 N	121·25 E
119	Hangö (häŋ′gû) . . . . Fin.	59·49 N	22·56 E
77	Hankamer (hăŋ′kȧ-mẽr) . Tex. (In.)	29·52 N	94·42 W
151	Han Kiang (R.) (hän′kyäng′) China	31·40 N	112·04 E
70	Hankinson (hăŋ′kĭn-sŭn) . . . N. D.	46·04 N	96·54 W
151	Hank′ou (hän′kō′) . . . . China	30·42 N	114·22 E
158	Hann, Mt. (hän) . . . . Austl.	16·05 S	126·07 E
86	Hanna (hăn′ ȧ) . . . . Can.	51·36 N	111·58 W
67	Hanna . . . . Wyo.	41·51 N	106·34 W
70	Hannah . . . . N. D.	48·58 N	98·42 W
73	Hannibal (hăn′ĭ bǎl) . . . . Mo.	39·42 N	91·22 W
120	Hannover (hän-ō′vĕr) . . . . Ger.	52·22 N	9·45 E
118	Hanö-bukten (B.) . . . . Swe.	55·54 N	14·55 E
151	Hanoi (hä-noi′) . . . . Viet.	21·04 N	105·50 E
82	Hanover (hăn′ô-vēr) . . . . Can.	44·10 N	81·05 W
83	Hanover . . . . . . Mass. (Boston In.)	42·07 N	70·49 W
81	Hanover . . . . N. H.	43·45 N	72·15 W
81	Hanover . . . . Pa.	39·50 N	77·00 W
100	Hanover (I.) . . . . Chile	51·00 S	74·45 W
148	Hanshan (hän′shän′) . . . . China	31·43 N	118·06 E
89	Hans Lollick (I.) (häns′lôl′ĭk) Vir. Is. (U. S. A.) (St. Thomas In.)	18·24 N	64·55 W
83	Hanson (hăn′sŭn) Mass. (Boston In.)	42·04 N	70·53 W
65	Hansville (hăns′-vĭl) Wash. (Seattle In.)	47·55 N	122·33 W
148	Hantan (hän′tän′) . . . . China	36·37 N	114·30 E
82	Hantsport (hănts′pōrt) . . . . . . Can.	45·05 N	64·12 W
151	Hanyang (han′yäng′) . . . . China	30·30 N	114·10 E
148	Haoch′engchi (hou′chĕng′jē) . China	33·19 N	117·33 E
112	Haparanda (hä-pä-rän′dä) . . . Swe.	65·54 N	23·57 E
84	Hapeville (hăp′vĭl) Ga. (Atlanta In.)	33·39 N	84·25 W
153	Hara-machida (hä-rä mä-chê′dä) Jap. (Tōkyō In.)	35·32 N	139·28 E
124	Harana, Sierra (Mts.) (sē-ĕ′r-rä-rä′nä) . Sp.	37·17 N	3·28 W
146	Hara Nuur (L.) . . . . Mong.	47·47 N	94·01 E
168	Hārar (hȧ-rär′) Eth. (Horn of Afr. In.)	9·43 N	42·10 E
165	Harar (Prov.) . . . . Eth.	8·15 N	41·00 E
146	Hara Usa (L.) . . . . Mong.	48·00 N	92·32 E
	Harbin, see Haerhpin		
80	Harbor Beach (här′bēr bēch) Mich.	43·50 N	82·40 W
80	Harbor Springs . . . . Mich.	45·25 N	85·05 W
83	Harbour Breton (brĕt′ŭn) (brē-tôɴ′) . Can.	47·28 N	55·50 W
83	Harbour Grace (grās) . . . . Can.	47·39 N	53·15 W
111	Harburg (här-bōōrgh) Ger. (Hamburg In.)	53·28 N	9·58 E
82	Harcourt (här′côrt) (ȧr-kōōr′) Can.	46·28 N	65·14 W
118	Hardanger Fd. (här-däng′ĕr fyôrd) . Nor.	59·58 N	6·30 E
118	Hardanger Fjell (Mts.) (fyĕl′) Nor.	60·15 N	6·56 E
118	Hardanger Jöklen (Mtn.) (yû′kōōl-ĕn) . Nor.	60·33 N	7·23 E
67	Hardin (här′dĭn) . . . . Mont.	45·44 N	107·36 W
167	Harding (här′dĭng) S. Afr. (Natal In.)	30·34 S	29·54 E
78	Harding (L.) . . . . Ala.-Ga.	32·43 N	85·00 W
142	Hardwar (hŭr′dvär) . . . . India	29·56 N	78·06 E
68	Hardy (R.) (här′dĭ) . . . . Mex.	32·04 N	115·10 W
83	Hare B. (hâr) . . . . Can.	51·21 N	55·45 W
168	Hargeisa (här-gä′ê-sȧ) Som. (Horn of Afr. In.)	9·20 N	43·57 E
121	Harghita, Muntii (Mts.) . . . . Rom.	46·25 N	25·40 E
142	Hariāna (State) . . . . India	29·30 N	75·00 E
153	Harima-Nada (Sea) (hä′rē-mä nä-dä) . Jap.	34·34 N	134·37 E
111	Haring Vliet (R.) Neth. (Amsterdam In.)	51·49 N	4·03 E
73	Harlan (här′lăn) . . . . Iowa	41·40 N	95·10 W
78	Harlan . . . . Ky.	36·50 N	83·19 W
72	Harlan Co. Res . . . . Nebr.	40·03 N	99·51 W
67	Harlem (hâr′lĕm) . . . . Mont.	48·33 N	108·50 W
143	Harlhar . . . . India	14·32 N	75·41 E
117	Harlingen (här′lĭng-ĕn) . . . . . Neth.	53·10 N	5·24 E
77	Harlingen . . . . Tex.	26·12 N	97·42 W
110	Harlow (här′lō) . Eng. (London In.)	51·46 N	0·08 E
67	Harlowton (här′lô-tun) . . . . . Mont.	46·26 N	109·50 W
80	Harmony (här′mô-nĭ) . . . . Ind.	39·35 N	87·00 W
66	Harney Basin (här′nĭ) . . . . Ore.	43·26 N	120·19 W
66	Harney L . . . . Ore.	43·11 N	119·23 W
70	Harney Pk . . . . S. D.	43·52 N	103·32 W
118	Härnösand (hĕr-nû-sänd) . . . . Swe.	62·37 N	17·54 E
124	Haro (ä′rō) . . . . Sp.	42·35 N	2·49 W
65	Haro Str. (hă′rō) . . . . . . Can.-U. S.	48·27 N	123·11 W
110	Harpenden (här′pĕn-d′n) Eng. (London In.)	51·48 N	0·22 W
72	Harper (här′pēr) . . . . Kans.	37·17 N	98·02 W
164	Harper . . . . Lib.	4·28 N	7·52 W
65	Harper . . . . Wash. (Seattle In.)	47·31 N	122·32 W
81	Harpers Ferry (här′pērz) . . W. Va.	39·20 N	77·45 W
133	Harput (kär-pōōt′) . . . . Tur.	38·45 N	39·10 E
78	Harriman (hăr′ĭ-mǎn) . . . . . . Tenn.	35·55 N	84·34 W
81	Harrington (hăr′ĭng-tŭn) . . . . . Del.	38·55 N	75·35 W
87	Harrington Harbour (här′bēr) . Can.	50·30 N	59·19 W
144	Harri Rud (R.) . . . . Afg.	34·29 N	61·16 E
116	Harris (I.) (hăr′ĭs) . . . . Scot.	57·55 N	6·40 W
79	Harris (L.) . . . . Fla. (In.)	28·43 N	81·40 W
80	Harrisburg (hăr′ĭs-bûrg) . . . . Ill.	37·45 N	88·35 W
81	Harrisburg . . . . Pa.	40·15 N	76·50 W
168	Harrismith (hă-rĭs′mĭth) S. Afr. (Johannesburg & Pretoria In.)	28·17 S	29·08 E
73	Harrison (hăr′ĭ-sŭn) . . . . Ark.	36·13 N	93·06 W
75	Harrison . . . . Ohio (Cincinnati In.)	39·16 N	84·45 W
81	Harrisonburg (hăr′-ĭ-sŭn-bûrg) Va.	38·30 N	78·50 W
73	Harrisonville (hăr-ĭ-sŭn-vĭl) . . . Mo.	38·39 N	94·21 W
74	Harrisville (hăr′ĭs-vĭl) Utah (Salt Lake City In.)	41·17 N	112·00 W
80	Harrisville . . . . W. Va.	39·10 N	81·05 W
80	Harrodsburg (hăr′ŭdz-bûrg) . . Ky.	37·45 N	84·50 W
75	Harrods Cr. (hăr′ŭdz) Ky. (Louisville In.)	38·24 N	35·33 W
110	Harrow (hăr′ō) . Eng. (London In.)	51·34 N	0·21 W
111	Harsefeld (här′zĕ-fĕld′) Ger. (Hamburg In.)	53·27 N	9·30 E
112	Harstad (här′städh) . . . . Nor.	68·49 N	16·10 E
80	Hart (härt) . . . . Mich.	43·40 N	86·25 W
168	Hartbeesfontein S. Afr. (Johannesburg & Pretoria In.)	26·46 S	26·25 E
167	Hartbeespoortdam (L.) . . . . S. Afr. (Johannesburg & Pretoria In.)	25·47 S	27·43 E
167	Hartebeespoortdam S. Afr. (Johannesburg & Pretoria In.)	25·44 S	27·51 E
78	Hartford (härt′fērd) . . . . Ala.	31·05 N	85·42 W
73	Hartford . . . . Ark.	35·01 N	94·21 W
81	Hartford . . . . Conn.	41·45 N	72·40 W
74	Hartford . . . . Ill. (St. Louis In.)	38·50 N	90·06 W
78	Hartford . . . . Ky.	37·25 N	86·50 W
80	Hartford . . . . Mich.	42·15 N	86·15 W
71	Hartford . . . . Wis.	43·19 N	88·25 W
80	Hartford City . . . . Ind.	40·35 N	85·25 W
110	Hartington (härt′ĭng-tŭn) . . . . Eng.	53·08 N	1·48 W
70	Hartington . . . . Nebr.	42·37 N	97·18 W
82	Hartland (härt′lǎnd) . . . . Can.	46·19 N	67·32 W
116	Hartland Pt . . . . Eng.	51·03 N	4·40 W
166	Hartley . . . . Rh.	18·11 S	30·08 E
70	Hartley (härt′lĭ) . . . . Iowa	43·12 N	95·29 W
78	Hartselle (härt′sĕl) . . . . Ala.	34·24 N	86·55 W
73	Hartshorne (härts′hôrn) . . . . . Okla.	34·49 N	95·34 W
79	Hartsville (härts′vĭl) . . . . S. C.	34·20 N	80·04 W
78	Hartwell (härt′wĕl) . . . . Ga.	34·21 N	82·56 W
78	Hartwell Res . . . . Ga.	34·30 N	83·00 W
142	Hārua . . . . India (Calcutta In.)	22·36 N	88·40 E
71	Harvard (här′vȧrd) . . . . Ill.	42·25 N	88·39 W
83	Harvard . . . . . . Mass. (Boston In.)	42·30 N	71·35 W
72	Harvard . . . . Nebr.	40·36 N	98·08 W
69	Harvard, Mt . . . . Colo.	38·55 N	106·20 W
67	Harve (här′vĭ) . . . . Mont.	48·34 N	109·42 W
75	Harvey . . . . Ill. (Chicago In.)	41·37 N	87·39 W
84	Harvey . . . . La. (New Orleans In.)	29·54 N	90·05 W
70	Harvey . . . . N. D.	47·46 N	99·55 W
117	Harwich (här′wĭch) . . . . Eng.	51·53 N	1·13 E
120	Harz Mts. (härts) . . . . Ger.	51·42 N	10·50 E
139	Hasa (R.) . . . Jordan (Palestine In.)	30·57 N	35·51 E
153	Hashimoto (hä′shê-mō′tō) . . . . Jap.	34·19 N	135·37 E
119	Häsijärvi (L.) (hĕ′sê-yĕr′vê) . . Fin.	61·42 N	24·05 E

ng-sing; ŋ-baŋk; ɴ-nasalized n; nŏd; cŏmmit; ōld; ôbey; ôrder; fōōd; fŏŏt; ou-out; s-soft; sh-dish; th-thin; pūre; ûnite; ûrn; stŭd; circŭs; ü-as "y" in study; ′-indeterminate vowel.

214 Haskell–Highland Park PRONOUNCING INDEX

Page	Name Pronunciation Region	Lat. °′	Long. °′
73	Haskell (hăs'kĕl) . . . . Okla.	35·49 N	95·41 W
72	Haskell . . . . Tex.	33·09 N	99·43 W
74	Haslet (hăs'lĕt) Tex. (Dallas, Fort Worth In.)	32·58 N	97·21 W
110	Haslingden (hăz'lĭng dĕn) . . . . Eng.	53·43 N	2·19 W
118	Hassela (häs'ĕl-ô) . . . . Swe.	62·05 N	16·46 E
111	Hasselt (häs'ĕlt) Bel. (Brussels In.)	50·56 N	5·23 E
164	Hassi Inifel . . . . Alg.	29·54 N	3·47 E
118	Hässjö (hĕs'shû) . . . . Swe.	62·36 N	17·33 E
118	Hassleholm (häs'lĕ-hōlm) . . . . Swe.	56·10 N	13·44 E
117	Hastings (hās'tĭngz) . . . . Eng.	50·52 N	0·28 E
80	Hastings . . . . Mich.	42·40 N	85·20 W
74	Hastings Minn. (Minneapolis, St. Paul In.)	44·44 N	92·51 W
72	Hastings . . . . Nebr.	40·34 N	98·42 W
159	Hastings . . . . N. Z. (In.)	39·33 S	176·53 E
84	Hastings-on-Hudson (ōn-hŭd'sŭn) N. Y. (New York In.)	40·59 N	73·53 W
78	Hatchie (R.) (hăch'ē) . . . . . . Tenn.	35·28 N	89·14 W
127	Hateg (kät-säg') . . . . Rom.	45·35 N	22·57 E
110	Hatfield Broad Oak (hăt-fēld brôd ōk) . Eng.	51·50 N	0·14 E
153	Hatogaya (hä'tō-gä-yä) Jap. (Tōkyō In.)	35·50 N	139·45 E
153	Hatsukaichi (hät'sōō-kä'ê-chê) Jap.	34·22 N	132·19 E
79	Hatteras, C. (hăt'ēr-ăs) . . . . . N. C.	35·15 N	75·24 W
78	Hattiesburg (hăt'ĭz-bûrg) . . Miss.	31·20 N	89·18 W
123	Hattingen (hä'tēn-gĕn) Ger. (Ruhr In.)	51·24 N	7·11 E
121	Hatvan (hôt'vôn) . . . . Hung.	47·39 N	19·44 E
118	Haugesund (hou'gē-soon') . . . . Nor.	59·26 N	5·20 E
119	Haukivesi (L.) (hou'kê-vĕ'sê) . Fin.	62·02 N	29·02 E
168	Hauptsrus S. Afr. (Johannesburg & Pretoria In.)	26·35 S	26·16 E
159	Hauraki, G. (hä-ōō-rä'kê) N. Z. (In.)	36·44 S	175·15 E
119	Hausjärvi (hä'ōōs-yĕr'vê) . . . . Fin.	60·44 N	24·44 E
82	Haut, Isle au (hō) . . . . Maine	44·03 N	68·13 W
144	Hauta (hou'tä) . . . . Sau. Ar.	23·12 N	45·38 E
114	Haut Atlas (Mts.) . . . . Mor.	32·10 N	5·49 W
82	Hauterive . . . . Can.	49·12 N	68·15 W
122	Hautmont (ō-môN') . . . . Fr.	50·14 N	3·50 E
73	Havana (hȧ-vă'nȧ) . . . . Ill.	40·17 N	90·02 W
	Havana, see La Habana		
69	Havasu L. (hăv'ȧ-sōō) . . . . . . Ariz.	34·26 N	114·09 W
82	Havelock (hăv'lŏk) . . . . Can.	56·58 N	65·20 W
120	Havel R. (hä'fĕl) . . . . Ger.	53·09 N	13·10 E
81	Haven (hā-vĕn) . . . . Pa.	40·31 N	76·14 W
83	Haverhill (hā'vēr-hĭl) Mass. (Boston In.)	42·46 N	71·05 W
81	Haverhill . . . . N. H.	44·00 N	72·05 W
84	Haverstraw (hā'vēr-strô) N. Y. (New York In.)	41·11 N	73·58 W
120	Havlíčkův Brod . . . . Czech.	49·38 N	15·34 E
83	Havre (hăv'rȧ) . . . . Can.	45·42 N	61·30 W
81	Havre de Grace (hăv'ēr dē gräs') Md.	39·35 N	76·05 W
79	Haw (R.) (hô) . . . . N. C.	36·17 N	79·46 W
62	Hawaii (State) . . . . U. S.	20·00 N	157·40 W
157	Hawaii (I.) . . . . Hawaii (In.)	19·35 N	155·30 W
62	Hawaiian Is. (hä-wī'ăn) . . . Oceania	22·00 N	158·00 W
157	Hawaii Vol. Natl. Park (hä-wī'ē) Hawaii (In.)	19·15 N	155·20 W
70	Hawarden (hā'wȧr-dĕn) . . . . . Iowa	43·00 N	96·28 W
157	Hawi (hä'wē) . . . . Hawaii (In.)	20·16 N	155·48 W
116	Hawick (hô'ĭk) . . . . Scot.	55·25 N	2·55 W
159	Hawke B. (hôk) . . . . N. Z. (In.)	39·17 S	177·58 E
160	Hawker (hô'kēr) . . . . Austl.	31·58 S	138·12 E
81	Hawkesbury (hôks'bēr-ĭ) . . . . Can.	45·35 N	74·35 W
83	Hawkesbury, Port . . . . Can.	45·39 N	60·48 W
78	Hawkinsville (hô'kĭnz-vĭl) . . . . Ga.	32·15 N	83·30 W
95	Hawks Nest Pt. . . . . Ba. Is.	24·05 N	75·30 W
70	Hawley (hô'lĭ) . . . . Minn.	46·52 N	96·18 W
110	Haworth (hä'wûrth) . . . . Eng.	53·50 N	1·57 W
144	Hawtah . . . . Sau. Ar.	15·58 N	48·26 E
74	Hawthorne (hô'thôrn) Calif. (Los Angeles In.)	33·55 N	118·22 W
68	Hawthorne . . . . Nev.	38·33 N	118·39 W
72	Haxtun (hăks'tŭn) . . . . Colo.	40·39 N	102·38 W
158	Hay (R.) (hā) . . . . Austl.	123·00 S	136·45 E
86	Hay (R.) . . . . Can.	60·21 N	117·14 W
153	Hayama (hä-yä'mä) Jap. (Tōkyō In.)	35·16 N	139·35 E
153	Hayashi (hä-yä'shē) Jap. (Tōkyō In.)	35·13 N	139·38 E
69	Hayden (hā'dĕn) . . . . Ariz.	33·00 N	110·50 W
64	Hayes, Mt. (hāz) . . . . Alaska	63·32 N	146·40 W
86	Hayes (R.) . . . . Can.	55·30 N	94·00 W
77	Haynesville (hānz'vĭl) . . . . La.	32·55 N	93·08 W
127	Hayrabolu . . . . Tur.	41·14 N	27·05 E
86	Hay River . . . . Can.	60·50 N	115·53 W
72	Hays (hāz) . . . . Kans.	38·51 N	99·20 W
65	Haystack Mtn. (hā-stăk') Wash. (Seattle In.)	48·26 N	122·07 W
65	Hayward (hā'wērd) Calif. (San Francisco In.)	37·40 N	122·06 W
71	Hayward . . . . Wis.	46·01 N	91·31 W
78	Hazard (hăz'ȧrd) . . . . Ky.	37·13 N	83·10 W
79	Hazelhurst (hā'z'l-hûrst) . . . . . Ga.	31·50 N	82·36 W
78	Hazelhurst . . . . Miss.	31·52 N	90·23 W
75	Hazel Park . . . Mich. (Detroit In.)	42·28 N	83·06 W
86	Hazelton (hā'z'l-tŭn) . . . . Can.	55·18 N	127·11 W
81	Hazleton . . . . Pa.	41·00 N	76·00 W
85	Headingley (hĕd'ĭng-lĭ) Can. (Winnipeg In.)	49·53 N	97·25 W
78	Headland (hĕd'lănd) . . . . Ala.	31·22 N	85·20 W
68	Healdsburg (hēldz'bûrg) . . . . Calif.	38·37 N	122·52 W
73	Healdton (hēld'tŭn) . . . . Okla.	34·13 N	97·28 W
110	Heanor (hēn'ŏr) . . . . Eng.	53·01 N	1·22 W
47	Heard I. (hûrd) . . . . Ind. O.	53·10 S	74·35 E
77	Hearne (hûrn) . . . . Tex.	30·53 N	96·35 W
87	Hearst (hûrst) . . . . Can.	49·36 N	83·40 W
70	Heart (R.) (härt) . . . . N. D.	46·46 N	102·34 W
83	Heart's Content (härts kŏn'tĕnt) Can.	47·55 N	53·20 W
83	Heath Pt. (hēth) . . . . Can.	49·06 N	61·45 W
73	Heavener (hēv'nēr) . . . . Okla.	34·52 N	94·36 W
76	Hebbronville (hē'brŭn-vĭl) . . . Tex.	27·18 N	98·40 W
69	Heber (hē'bēr) . . . . Utah	40·30 N	111·25 W
73	Heber Springs . . . . Ark.	35·28 N	91·59 W
67	Hebgen Res. (hĕb'gĕn) . . . . . Mont.	44·47 N	111·38 W
116	Hebrides, Sea of . . . . Scot.	56·63 N	6·41 W
87	Hebron (hē'brŭn) . . . . Can.	58·11 N	62·56 W
75	Hebron . . . . Ind. (Chicago In.)	41·19 N	87·13 W
75	Hebron . . . . . Ky. (Cincinnati In.)	39·04 N	84·43 W
73	Hebron . . . . Nebr.	40·11 N	97·36 W
70	Hebron . . . . N. D.	46·54 N	102 01 W
	Hebron, see Al Khalil		
118	Heby (hĭ'bü) . . . . Swe.	59·56 N	16·48 E
86	Hecate Str. (hĕk'ȧ-tē) . . . . Can.	53·34 N	130·53 W
91	Hecelchakán (ā-sĕl-chä-kän') . Mex.	20·10 N	90·09 W
118	Hedemora (hĭ-dĕ-mō'rä) . . . . . Swe.	60·16 N	15·55 E
118	Hedesunda Fd. (hi-de-sōōn'dä) Swe.	60·22 N	16·50 E
110	Hedon (hĕd'ŭn) . . . . Eng.	53·44 N	0·12 W
111	Heemstede Neth. (Amsterdam In.)	52·20 N	4·36 E
117	Heerlen . . . . Neth.	50·55 N	5·58 E
78	Heflin (hĕf'lĭn) . . . . Ala.	33·40 N	85·33 W
120	Heide (hī'dē) . . . . Ger.	54·13 N	9·06 E
161	Heidelberg (hī'dĕl-bûrg) Austl. (Melbourne In.)	37·45 S	145·04 E
120	Heidelberg (hīdĕl-bĕrgh) . . . . . Ger.	49·24 N	8·43 E
120	Heidenheim (hī'dĕn-hīm) . . . . . Ger.	48·41 N	10·09 E
168	Heilbron (hīl'brōn) . . . . S. Afr. (Johannesburg & Pretoria In.)	27·17 S	27·58 E
120	Heilbronn (hīl'brōn) . . . . Ger.	49·09 N	9·16 E
123	Heiligenhaus (hī'lē-gĕn-houz) Ger. (Ruhr In.)	51·19 N	6·58 E
120	Heiligenstadt (hī'lē-gĕn-shtät) Ger.	51·21 N	10·10 E
147	Heilungkiang (Prov.) (hā-lōōng' kyăng') . China	46·36 N	128·07 E
119	Heinola (hā-nō'lä) . . . . Fin.	61·13 N	26·03 E
123	Heinsberg (hīnz'bĕrgh) Ger. (Ruhr In.)	51·04 N	6·07 E
139	Heisi (R.) . U. A. R. (Palestine In.)	29·21 N	34·30 E
111	Heist-op-den-Berg Bel. (Brussels In.)	51·05 N	4·14 E
112	Hekla (Vol.) (hĕk'lȧ) . . . . Ice.	63·53 N	19·37 W
121	Hel (hāl) . . . . Pol.	54·37 N	18·53 E
118	Helagsfjället (M.) . . . . Swe.	62·54 N	12·24 E
73	Helena (hē-lē'nȧ) . . . . Ark.	34·33 N	90·35 W
67	Helena (hĕ-lĕ'nȧ) . . . . Mont.	46·35 N	112·01 W
161	Helensburgh (hĕl'ĕnz-bŭr-ô) Austl. (Sydney In.)	34·11 S	150·59 E
116	Helensburgh . . . . Scot.	56·01 N	4·53 W
118	Helge (R.) (hĕl'gĕ) . . . . Swe.	56·31 N	13·47 E
120	Helgoland I. (hĕl'gô-länd) . . . . Ger.	54·13 N	7·30 E
79	Hellier (hĕl'yēr) . . . . Ky.	37·16 N	82·27 W
124	Hellín (ĕl-yēn') . . . . Sp.	38·30 N	1·40 W
144	Helmand (R.) (hĕl'mŭnd) . . . . Afg.	31·00 N	63·48 E
117	Helmond (hĕl'mōnt) (ĕl'môN') Neth.	51·35 N	5·04 E
120	Helmstedt (hĕlm'shtĕt) . . . . . . Ger.	52·14 N	11·03 E
74	Helotes (hē'-lōts) Tex. (San Antonio In.)	29·35 N	98·41 W
69	Helper (hĕlp'ēr) . . . . Utah	39·40 N	110·55 W
	Helsingfors, see Helsinki		
118	Helsingør (hĕl-sĭng-ûr') . . . . . . Den.	56·03 N	12·33 E
119	Helsinki (Helsingfors) (hĕl'sĕn-kê) (hĕl'sĭng-fôrs') . Fin.	60·10 N	24·53 E
167	Helvellyn (Mts.) (hĕl-vĕl-lĭn) S. Afr. (Natal In.)	30·32 S	27·18 E
110	Hemel Hempstead (hĕm'ĕl hĕmp'stĕd) Eng. (London In.)	51·43 N	0·29 W
74	Hemet (hĕm'ĕt) Calif. (Los Angeles In.)	33·45 N	116·57 W
70	Hemingford (hĕm'ĭng-fērd) . . Nebr.	42·21 N	103·30 W
77	Hemphill (hĕmp'hĭl) . . . . Tex.	31·20 N	93·48 W
84	Hempstead (hĕmp'stĕd) N. Y. (New York In.)	40·42 N	73·37 W
77	Hempstead . . . . Tex.	30·07 N	96·05 W
118	Hemse (hĕm'sĕ) . . . . Swe.	57·15 N	18·25 E
118	Hemsö (I.) . . . . Swe.	62·43 N	18·22 E
118	Hen (hĭn) . . . . Nor.	60·14 N	10·10 E
124	Henares (R.) (å-nä'räs) . . . . Sp.	40·50 N	2·55 W
122	Hendaye (äN-dā') . . . . Fr.	43·20 N	1·46 W
80	Henderson (hĕn'dēr-sŭn) . . . . . Ky.	37·50 N	87·30 W
68	Henderson . . . . Nev.	36·09 N	115·04 W
79	Henderson . . . . N. C.	36·18 N	78·24 W
78	Henderson . . . . Tenn.	35·25 N	88·40 W
77	Henderson . . . . Tex.	32·09 N	94·48 W
79	Hendersonville (hĕn'dēr-sŭn-vĭl) N. C.	35·17 N	82·28 W
110	Hendon (hĕn'dŭn) Eng. (London In.)	51·34 N	0·13 W
168	Hendrina (hĕn-drē'nȧ) . . . . . S. Afr. (Johannesburg & Pretoria In.)	26·10 S	29·44 E
151	Hengch'un (hĕng'chŭn') . . Taiwan	22·00 N	120·42 E
117	Hengelo (hĕng'ĕ-lō) . . . . Neth.	52·20 N	6·45 E
151	Henghsien . . . . China	22·40 N	104·20 E
151	Hengshan (hĕng'shän') . . . . . China	27·20 N	112·40 E
148	Hengshui (hĕng'shōō-ē') . . . . China	37·43 N	115·42 E
151	Hengyang . . . . China	26·58 N	112·30 E
110	Henley on Thames (hĕn'lē ŏn tĕmz) . Eng. (London In.)	51·31 N	0·54 W
81	Henlopen, C. (hĕn-lō'pĕn) . . . . Del.	38·45 N	75·05 W
122	Hennebont (ĕn-bôN') . . . . Fr.	47·47 N	3·16 W
168	Hennenman . . . . S. Afr. (Johannesburg & Pretoria In.)	27·59 S	27·03 E
77	Hennessey (hĕn'ĕ-sĭ) . . . . Okla.	36·04 N	97·53 W
111	Hennigsdorf (hĕ'nĕngz-dōrf) Ger. (Berlin In.)	52·39 N	13·12 E
167	Hennops (R.) (hĕn'ŏps) . . . . S. Afr. (Johannesburg & Pretoria In.)	25·51 S	27·57 E
167	Hennopsrivier . . . . S. Afr. (Johannesburg & Pretoria In.)	25·50 S	27·59 E
73	Henrietta (hĕn-rĭ-ĕt'ȧ) . . . . . Okla.	35·25 N	95·58 W
72	Henrietta (hen-rĭ-ĕ'tȧ) . . . . . . Tex.	33·47 N	98·11 W
87	Henrietta Maria, C. (hĕn-rĭ-ĕt'ȧ) Can.	55·10 N	82·20 W
69	Henry Mts. (hĕn'rĭ) . . . . Utah	38·55 N	110·45 W
150	Henteyn Nuruu (Mts.) . . Sov. Un.	49·40 N	111·00 E
66	Heppner (hĕp'nēr) . . . . Ore.	45·21 N	119·33 W
144	Herāt (hĕ-rät') . . . . Afg.	34·28 N	62·13 E
127	Hercegovina (Reg.) (hĕr-tsĕ-gô'vê-nȧ) . Yugo.	43·23 N	17·52 E
167	Hercules (hēr'ku-lēs) . . . . . S. Afr. (Johannesburg & Pretoria In.)	25·43 S	28·10 E
123	Herdecke (hĕr'dĕ-kĕ) Ger. (Ruhr In.)	51·24 N	7·26 E
93	Heredia (ā-rā'dhê-ä) . . . . C. R.	10·04 N	84·06 W
116	Hereford (hĕrĕ'fērd) . . . . Eng.	52·05 N	2·44 W
110	Hereford (Co.) . . . . Eng.	52·22 N	2·52 W
84	Hereford . . . . . Md. (Baltimore In.)	39·36 N	76·43 W
72	Hereford (hĕr'ê-fērd) . . . . Tex.	34·47 N	102·25 W
139	Hereidin (R.) U. A. R. (Palestine In.)	31·02 N	34·03 E
124	Herencia (å-rān'thê-ä) . . . . Sp.	39·23 N	3·22 W
111	Herentals . . . . . . Bel. (Brussels In.)	51·10 N	4·51 E
120	Herford (hĕr'fōrt) . . . . Ger.	52·06 N	8·42 E
73	Herington (hĕr'ĭng-tŭn) . . . . Kans.	38·41 N	96·57 W
120	Herisau (hā'rê-zou) . . . . Switz.	47·23 N	9·18 E
111	Herk-de-Stad . . Bel. (Brussels In.)	50·56 N	5·13 E
81	Herkimer (hûr'kĭ-mēr) . . . . N. Y.	43·05 N	75·00 W
116	Herma Ness (Prom.) (hûr'mȧ nĕs) Scot.	60·50 N	1·10 W
73	Hermann (hûr'mŭn) . . . . Mo.	38·41 N	91·27 W
80	Hermansville (hûr'mŭns-vĭl) . Mich.	45·40 N	87·35 W
74	Hermantown (hēr'mȧn-toun) Minn. (Duluth In.)	46·46 N	92·12 W
168	Hermanusdorings . . . . S. Afr. (Johannesburg & Pretoria In.)	24·08 S	27·46 E
75	Herminie (hûr-mĭ'nē) Pa. (Pittsburgh In.)	40·16 N	79·45 W
83	Hermitage B. (hûr'mĭ-tĕj) . . . Can.	47·31 N	56·30 W
155	Hermit Is. (hûr'mĭt) . . N. Gui. Ter.	1·48 S	144·55 E
74	Hermosa Beach (hēr-mō'sȧ) Calif. (Los Angeles In.)	33·51 N	118·24 W
88	Hermosillo (ĕr-mô-sē'l-yō) . . . Mex.	29·00 N	110·57 W
84	Herndon (hērn'dŏn) Va. (Washington D.C. In.)	38·58 N	77·22 W
123	Herne (hĕr'nĕ) . . . . Ger. (Ruhr In.)	51·32 N	7·13 E
118	Herning (hĕr'nĭng) . . . . Den.	56·08 N	8·55 E
70	Heron (L.) (hĕr'ŭn) . . . . Minn.	43·42 N	95·23 W
87	Heron Bay . . . . Can.	48·32 N	86·20 W
70	Heron Lake . . . . Minn.	43·48 N	95·20 W
92	Herrero, Punta (pt.) (pōō'n-tä-ĕr-rĕ'rô) . Mex. (Yucatan In.)	19·18 N	87·24 W
80	Herrin (hĕr'ĭn) . . . . Ill.	37·50 N	89·00 W
167	Herschel (hēr'-shĕl) S. Afr. (Natal In.)	30·37 S	27·12 E
75	Herscher (hēr'shēr) Ill. (Chicago In.)	41·03 N	88·06 W
117	Herstal (hĕr'stäl) . . . . Bel.	50·42 N	5·32 E
110	Hertford (hûrt'fērd) . . . . Eng.	51·46 N	0·05 W
79	Hertford . . . . N. C.	36·10 N	76·30 W
111	Hertzberg (hĕrtz'bĕrgh) Ger. (Berlin In.)	52·54 N	12·58 E
167	Hertzog (hĕrt'zŏg) S. Afr. (Natal In.)	32·36 S	26·46 E
139	Herzlia . . . . Isr. (Palestine In.)	32·10 N	34·49 E
122	Hesdin (ē-dăN') . . . . Fr.	50·24 N	1·59 E
120	Hessen (State) (hĕs'ĕn) . . . . . . Ger.	50·16 N	8·48 E
68	Hetch Hetchy Aqueduct (hĕtch hĕt'-chĭ ăk'wê-dŭkt) . Calif.	37·27 N	120·54 W
70	Hettinger (hĕt'ĭn-jēr) . . . . N. D.	45·58 N	102·36 W
168	Heuningspruit . . . . S. Afr. (Johannesburg & Pretoria In.)	27·28 S	27·26 E
168	Heystekrand . . . . S. Afr. (Johannesburg & Pretoria In.)	25·16 S	27·14 E
110	Heywood (hā'wŏŏd) . . . . Eng.	53·36 N	2·12 W
79	Hialeah (hī-ȧ-lē'-ăh) . . . Fla. (In.)	25·49 N	80·18 W
73	Hiawatha (hī-ȧ-wô'thȧ) . . . . . Kans.	39·50 N	95·33 W
69	Hiawatha . . . . Utah	39·25 N	111·05 W
71	Hibbing (hĭb'ĭng) . . . . Minn.	47·26 N	92·58 W
78	Hickman (hĭk'mŭn) . . . . Ky.	34·33 N	89·10 W
74	Hickman Mills Mo. (Kansas City In.)	38·56 N	94·32 W
79	Hickory (hĭk'ō-rĭ) . . . . N. C.	35·43 N	81·21 W
84	Hicksville (hĭks'vĭl) N. Y. (New York In.)	40·47 N	73·25 W
80	Hicksville . . . . Ohio	41·15 N	84·45 W
76	Hico (hī'kō) . . . . Tex.	32·00 N	98·02 W
90	Hidalgo (ê-dhäl'gō) . . . . Mex.	24·14 N	99·25 W
76	Hidalgo . . . . Mex.	27·49 N	99·53 W
88	Hidalgo (State) . . . . Mex.	20·45 N	99·30 W
76	Hidalgo del Parral (ê-dä'l-gō-dĕl-pär-rä'l) . Mex.	26·55 N	105·40 W
91	Hidalgo Yalalag (ê-dhäl'gō-yä-lä-läg) . Mex.	17·12 N	96·11 W
168	Hiedelberg . . . . S. Afr. (Johannesburg & Pretoria In.)	26·32 S	28·22 E
164	Hierro I. (yĕ'r-rō) . . . . Can. Is.	27·37 N	18·29 W
80	Higgins (L.) (hĭg'ĭnz) . . . . Mich.	44·20 N	84·45 W
73	Higginsville (hĭg'ĭnz-vĭl) . . . . . . Mo.	39·05 N	93·44 W
80	High (I.) . . . . Mich.	45·45 N	85·45 W
85	High Bluff . . . Can. (Winnipeg In.)	50·01 N	98·08 W
94	Highborne Cay (hī'bôrn kē) . Ba. Is.	24·45 N	76·50 W
74	Highgrove (hī'grōv) Calif. (Los Angeles In.)	34·01 N	117·20 W
77	High Island . . . . Tex. (In.)	29·34 N	94·24 W
74	Highland (hī'lănd) Calif. (Los Angeles In.)	34·08 N	117·13 W
73	Highland . . . . Ill.	38·44 N	89·41 W
75	Highland . . . . Ind. (Chicago In.)	41·33 N	87·28 W
75	Highland . . . . . Mich. (Detroit In.)	42·38 N	83·37 W
65	Highland . . . . . Wash. (Portland In.)	45·55 N	122·37 W
75	Highland Park . . Ill. (Chicago In.)	42·11 N	87·47 W
75	Highland Park Mich. (Detroit In.)	42·24 N	83·06 W
84	Highland Park N. J. (New York In.)	40·30 N	74·25 W

ăt; finăl; rāte; senåte; ärm; ȧsk; sofȧ; fâre; ch-choose; dh-as th in other; bē; ėvent; bĕt; recĕnt; cratēr; g-go; gh-guttural g; bĭt; ĭ-short neutral; rīde: K-guttural k as ch in German ich;

PRONOUNCING INDEX Highland Park–Horten 215

Page	Name / Pronunciation	Region	Lat. °′	Long. °′
74	Highland Park	Tex. (Dallas, Fort Worth In.)	32·49 N	96·48 W
84	Highlands (hī-lǎndz)	N. J. (New York In.)	40·24 N	73·59 W
77	Highlands	Tex. (In.)	29·49 N	95·01 W
70	Highmore (hī'-mōr)	S. D.	44·30 N	99·26 W
110	High Ongar (ŏn'gẽr)	Eng. (London In.)	51·43 N	0·15 E
155	High Pk.	Phil. (Manila In.)	15·38 N	120·05 E
79	High Point	N. C.	35·55 N	80·00 W
86	High Prairie	Can.	55·30 N	116·47 W
74	High Ridge	Mo. (St. Louis In.)	38·27 N	90·32 W
86	High River	Can.	50·40 N	113·47 W
79	Highrock (R.) (hī'-rŏk)	N. C.	35·40 N	80·15 W
79	High Springs	Fla.	29·48 N	82·38 W
84	Hightstown (hīts-toun)	N. J. (New York In.)	40·16 N	74·32 W
110	High Wycombe (wĭ-kŭm)	Eng. (London In.)	51·36 N	0·45 W
89	Higuero, Pta. (Pt.)	P. R. (Puerto Rico In.)	18·21 N	67·11 W
99	Higuerote (ē-gĕ-rô'-tĕ)	Ven. (In.)	10·29 N	66·06 W
95	Higüey (ē-gwĕ'y)	Dom. Rep.	18·40 N	68·45 W
119	Hiiumaa (D'Ago) (hē'ōōm-ô)	Sov. Un.	58·47 N	22·05 E
153	Hikone (hē'kô-nĕ)	Jap.	35·15 N	136·15 E
120	Hildburghausen (hĭld'bōōrg hou-zĕn)	Ger.	50·26 N	10·45 E
123	Hilden (hēl'dĕn)	Ger. (Ruhr In.)	51·10 N	6·56 E
120	Hildesheim (hĭl'dĕs-hīm)	Ger.	52·08 N	9·56 E
93	Hillaby, Mt. (hĭl'à-bĭ)	Barb. (Le. & Wind. Is. In.)	13·15 N	59·35 W
72	Hill City (hĭl)	Kans.	39·22 N	99·54 W
71	Hill City	Minn.	46·58 N	93·38 W
111	Hillegersberg	Neth. (Amsterdam In.)	51·57 N	4·29 E
118	Hillerød (hē'lĕ-rûdh)	Den.	55·56 N	12·17 E
73	Hillsboro (hĭlz'bŭr-ō)	Ill.	39·09 N	89·28 W
73	Hillsboro	Kans.	38·22 N	97·11 W
81	Hillsboro	N. H.	43·05 N	71·55 W
70	Hillsboro	N. D.	47·23 N	97·05 W
80	Hillsboro	Ohio	39·10 N	83·40 W
65	Hillsboro	Ore. (Portland In.)	45·31 N	122·59 W
77	Hillsboro	Tex.	32·01 N	97·06 W
71	Hillsboro	Wis.	43·39 N	90·20 W
85	Hillsburgh (hĭlz'bûrg)	Can. (Toronto In.)	43·48 N	80·09 W
66	Hills Creek Res.	Ore.	43·41 N	122·26 W
80	Hillsdale (hĭls-dāl)	Mich.	41·55 N	84·35 W
157	Hilo (hē'lō)	Hawaii (In.)	19·44 N	155·01 W
111	Hilversum (hĭl'vẽr-sŭm)	Neth. (Amsterdam In.)	52·13 N	5·10 E
142	Himachal Pradesh (Ter.)	India	36·03 N	77·41 E
145	Himalaya Mts. (hĭ-mä'là-yà)	Asia	29·30 N	85·02 E
153	Himeji (hē'mà-jē)	Jap.	34·50 N	134·42 E
111	Himmelpforten (hē'mĕl-pfōr-tĕn)	Ger. (Hamburg In.)	53·37 N	9·19 E
95	Hinche (hēn'chå) (ăNsh)	Hai.	19·10 N	72·05 W
159	Hinchinbrook (I.) (hĭn-chĭn-brŏŏk)	Austl.	18·23 S	146·57 W
110	Hinckley (hĭnk'lĭ)	Eng.	52·32 N	1·21 W
110	Hindley (hĭnd'lĭ)	Eng.	53·32 N	2·35 W
145	Hindu Kush Mts. (hĭn'dōō kōōsh')	Asia	35·15 N	68·44 E
143	Hindupur (hĭn'dōō-pōōr)	India	13·52 N	77·34 E
86	Hines Creek (hīnz)	Can.	56·15 N	118·33 W
83	Hingham (hĭng'ăm)	Mass. (Boston In.)	42·14 N	70·53 W
75	Hinkley (hĭnk'-lĭ)	Ohio (Cleveland In.)	41·14 N	81·45 W
124	Hinojosa (ē-nô-kō'sä)	Sp.	38·30 N	5·09 W
75	Hinsdale (hĭnz'dāl)	Ill. (Chicago In.)	41·48 N	87·56 W
80	Hinton (hĭn'tŭn)	W. Va.	37·40 N	80·55 W
153	Hirado (I.) (hē'rä-dō)	Jap.	33·19 N	129·18 E
153	Hirakata (hē'rä-kä'tä)	Jap. (Ōsaka In.)	34·49 N	135·40 E
153	Hiraoka (hē'rä-ō'kä)	Jap. (Ōsaka In.)	34·40 N	135·39 E
153	Hiratsuka (hē-rät-sōō'kà)	Jap.	35·20 N	139·19 E
146	Hirgis Nuur (L.)	Mong.	49·18 N	94·21 E
152	Hirosaki (hē'rô-sä'kê)	Jap.	40·31 N	140·38 E
153	Hirose (hē'rô-sä)	Jap.	35·20 N	133·11 E
153	Hiroshima (hē-rô-shē'mà)	Jap.	34·22 N	132·25 E
122	Hirson (ēr-sôN')	Fr.	49·54 N	4·00 E
89	Hispaniola (I.) (hĭ'spăn-ĭ-ō-là)	N. A.	17·30 N	73·15 W
142	Hissar	India	29·15 N	75·47 E
144	Hīt (hĭt)	Iraq	33·32 N	42·35 E
152	Hitachi (hē-tä'chē)	Jap.	36·42 N	140·47 E
77	Hitchcock (hĭch'kŏk)	Tex. (In.)	29·21 N	95·01 W
123	Hitdorf (hēt'dōrf)	Ger. (Ruhr In.)	51·04 N	6·56 E
153	Hitoyoshi (hē'tô-yō'shê)	Jap.	32·13 N	130·45 E
112	Hitra (I.) (hĭtrà)	Nor.	63·34 N	7·37 E
111	Hittefeld (hē'tĕ-fĕld)	Ger. (Hamburg In.)	53·23 N	9·59 E
153	Hiwasa (hē'wà-sä)	Jap.	33·44 N	134·31 E
78	Hiwassee (R.) (hī-wôs'sē)	Tenn.	35·10 N	84·35 W
118	Hjälmaren (L.)	Swe.	59·07 N	16·05 E
118	Hjo (yō)	Swe.	58·19 N	14·11 E
118	Hjørring (jûr'ĭng)	Den.	57·27 N	9·59 E
121	Hlohovec (hlō'hô-vĕts)	Czech.	48·24 N	17·49 E
160	Hobart (hō'bàrt)	Austl.	43·00 S	147·30 E
75	Hobart	Ind. (Chicago In.)	41·31 N	87·15 W
72	Hobart	Okla.	35·02 N	99·06 W
65	Hobart	Wash. (Seattle In.)	47·25 N	121·58 W
72	Hobbs (hŏbs)	N. Mex.	32·41 N	104·04 W
146	Hobdo Gol (R.)	Mong.	49·06 N	91·16 E
111	Hoboken (hō'bō-kĕn)	Bel. (Brussels In.)	51·11 N	4·20 E
84	Hoboken	N. J. (New York In.)	40·43 N	74·03 W
118	Hobro (hô-brô')	Den.	56·38 N	9·47 E
84	Hobson (hŏb'-sŭn)	Va. (Norfolk In.)	36·54 N	76·31 W
161	Hobson's B. (hŏb'sŭnz)	Austl. (Melbourne In.)	37·54 S	144·45 E
148	Hochien (hŭ'jĭän)	China	38·28 N	116·05 E
148	Hochiu	China	32·19 N	116·17 E
120	Höchst (hûKst)	Ger.	50·06 N	8·37 E
151	Hoch'uan	China	30·00 N	106·20 E
65	Hockinson (hŏk'-ĭn-sŭn)	Wash. (Portland In.)	45·44 N	122·29 W
92	Hoctún (ôk-tōō'n)	Mex. (Yucatan In.)	20·52 N	89·10 W
80	Hodgenville (hŏj'ĕn-vĭl)	Ky.	37·35 N	85·45 W
83	Hodges Hill (hŏj'ĕz)	Can.	49·03 N	55·54 W
86	Hodgson (hŏj-sŭn)	Can.	51·16 N	97·40 W
121	Hódmezövásárhely (hōd'mĕ-zû-vô' shôr-hĕl-y')	Hung.	46·24 N	20·21 E
121	Hodonin (hē'dô-nén)	Czech.	48·50 N	17·06 E
111	Hoegaarden	Bel. (Brussels In.)	50·46 N	4·55 E
111	Hoek van Holland	Neth. (Amsterdam In.)	51·59 N	4·05 E
152	Hoeryŏng (hwĕr'yŭng)	Kor.	42·28 N	129·39 E
123	Hoetmar (hût'mär)	Ger. (Ruhr In.)	51·52 N	7·54 E
120	Hof (hōf)	Ger.	50·19 N	11·55 E
148	Hofei (hŏ'fā)	China	31·51 N	117·15 E
112	Hofsjökull (Gl.) (hôfs'yü'kōōl)	Ice.	64·55 N	18·40 W
	Hofuf, see Al Hufūf			
94	Hog (I.) (hŏg)	Ba. Is.	25·05 N	77·20 W
80	Hog (I.)	Mich.	45·50 N	85·20 W
78	Hogansville (hō'gănz-vĭl)	Ga.	33·10 N	84·54 W
95	Hog Cay (I.)	Ba. Is.	23·35 N	75·30 W
95	Hogsty Rf	Ba. Is.	21·45 N	73·50 W
111	Hohenbrunn (hō'hĕn-brōōn)	Ger. (Munich In.)	48·03 N	11·42 E
123	Hohenlimburg (hō'hĕn lĕm'bōōrg)	Ger. (Ruhr In.)	51·20 N	7·35 E
111	Hohen Neuendorf (hō'hĕn noi'ĕn-dōrf)	Ger. (Berlin In.)	52·40 N	13·22 E
120	Hohe Tauern (Mts.) (hō'ĕ tou'ĕrn)	Aus.	47·11 N	12·12 E
84	Hohokus (hō-hō-kŭs)	N. J. (New York In.)	41·01 N	74·08 W
151	Hohsien	China	24·20 N	24·20 E
148	Hohsien (hō'syĕn')	China	31·44 N	118·20 E
148	Ho Hu (L.) (hŭ'hoo)	China	31·37 N	119·57 E
72	Hoisington (hoi'zĭng-tŭn)	Kans.	38·30 N	98·46 W
153	Hojo (hō'jō)	Jap.	33·58 N	132·50 E
159	Hokitika (hō-kĭ-tē'kä)	N. Z. (In.)	42·43 S	171·12 E
152	Hokkaido (I.) (hôk'kĭ-dō)	Jap.	43·30 N	142·45 E
151	Hokou (hō'kō')	China	29·58 N	116·20 E
118	Holbaek (hôl'bĕk)	Den.	55·42 N	11·40 E
92	Holbox (ôl-bŏ'x)	Mex. (Yucatan In.)	21·33 N	87·19 W
92	Holbox, Isla (I.) (ē's-là-ôl-bŏ'x)	Mex. (Yucatan In.)	21·40 N	87 21 W
69	Holbrook (hōl'brŏŏk)	Ariz.	34·55 N	110·15 W
83	Holbrook	Mass. (Boston In.)	42·10 N	71·01 W
83	Holden (hōl'dĕn)	Mass. (Boston In.)	42·21 N	71·51 W
73	Holden	Mo.	38·42 N	94·00 W
80	Holden	W. Va.	37·45 N	82·05 W
73	Holdenville (hōl'dĕn-vĭl)	Okla.	35·05 N	96·25 W
72	Holdrege (hōl'drĕj)	Nebr.	40·25 N	99·28 W
118	Hölen (hûl'ĕn)	Nor.	59·34 N	10·40 E
95	Holguín (ôl-gēn')	Cuba	20·55 N	76·15 W
81	Holidaysburg (hŏl'ĭ-dāz-bûrg)	Pa.	40·30 N	78·30 W
120	Hollabrunn	Aus.	48·33 N	16·04 E
80	Holland (hŏl'ănd)	Mich.	42·45 N	86·10 W
	Hollandia, see Sukarnapura			
111	Hollandsch Diep (Chan.)	Neth. (Amsterdam In.)	51·43 N	4·25 E
111	Hollenstedt (hō'lĕn-shtĕt)	Ger. (Hamburg In.)	53·22 N	9·43 E
74	Holliday (hŏl'ĭ-dā)	Kans. (Kansas City In.)	39·02 N	94·48 W
83	Hollis (hŏl'ĭs)	N. H. (Boston In.)	42·30 N	71·29 W
72	Hollis	Okla.	34·39 N	99·56 W
68	Hollister (hŏl'ĭs-tẽr)	Calif.	36·50 N	121·25 W
83	Holliston (hŏl'ĭs-tŭn)	Mass. (Boston In.)	42·12 N	71·25 W
80	Holly (hŏl'ĭ)	Mich.	42·45 N	83·30 W
65	Holly	Wash. (Seattle In.)	47·34 N	122·58 W
78	Holly Springs (hŏl'ĭ sprĭngz)	Miss.	34·45 N	89·28 W
74	Hollywood (hŏl'ē-wŏŏd)	Calif. (Los Angeles In.)	34·06 N	118·20 W
79	Hollywood	Fla. (In.)	26·00 N	80·11 W
74	Holmes Park	Mo. (Kansas City In.)	38·57 N	94·33 W
159	Holmes Rfs. (hōmz)	Austl.	16·33 S	148·43 E
118	Holmestrand (hôl'mĕ-strän)	Nor.	59·29 N	10·17 E
118	Holmsbu (hôlms'bōō)	Nor.	59·36 N	10·26 E
118	Holmsjön (L.)	Swe.	62·23 N	15·43 E
118	Holstebro (hôl'stĕ-brô')	Den.	56·22 N	8·39 E
78	Holston (R.) (hōl'stŭn)	Tenn.	36·02 N	83·42 W
110	Holt (hōlt)	Eng.	53·05 N	2·53 W
73	Holton (hōl'tŭn)	Kans.	39·27 N	95·43 W
116	Holy (I.) (hō'lĭ)	Wales	53·45 N	4·45 W
116	Holy (I.)	Eng.	55·43 N	1·48 W
64	Holy Cross (hō'lĭ krôs)	Alaska	62·10 N	159·40 W
116	Holyhead (hŏl'ē-hĕd)	Wales	53·48 N	4·45 W
72	Holyoke (hōl'yōk)	Colo.	40·36 N	102·18 W
81	Holyoke	Mass.	42·10 N	72·40 W
153	Homano (hō-mä'nō)	Jap. (Tōkyō In.)	35·33 N	140·08 E
123	Homberg (hōm'bĕrgh)	Ger. (Ruhr In.)	51·27 N	6·42 E
74	Home Gardens (hōm gär'd'nz)	Calif. (Los Angeles In.)	33·53 N	117·32 W
74	Homeland (hōm'lănd)	Calif. (Los Angeles In.)	33·44 N	117·07 W
64	Homer (hō'mẽr)	Alaska	59·42 N	151·30 W
77	Homer	La.	32·46 N	93·05 W
79	Homestead (hōm'stĕd)	Fla. (In.)	25·27 N	80·28 W
74	Homestead	Mich. (Sault Ste. Marie In.)	46·20 N	84·07 W
75	Homestead	Pa. (Pittsburgh In.)	40·29 N	79·55 W
73	Homestead Natl. Mon. of America	Nebr.	40·16 N	96·51 W
84	Homewood (hōm'wŏŏd)	Ala. (Birmingham In.)	33·28 N	86·48 W
75	Homewood	Ill. (Chicago In.)	41·34 N	87·40 W
73	Hominy (hŏm'ĭ-nĭ)	Okla.	36·25 N	96·24 W
78	Homochiho (R.) (hō-mō-chĭt'ō)	Miss.	31·23 N	91·15 W
115	Homs (hōms)	Syr.	34·42 N	36·52 E
147	Honan (Prov.) (hō'nän')	China	33·58 N	112·33 E
98	Honda (hōn'dà)	Col. (In.)	5·13 N	74·45 W
94	Honda, Bahía (B.) (bä-ē'ä-ô'n-dä)	Cuba	23·10 N	83·20 W
76	Hondo	Tex.	29·20 N	99·08 W
92	Hondo, Rio (R.) (hon-dō')	Br. Hond. (Yucatan In.)	18·16 N	88·32 W
72	Hondo (R.)	N. Mex.	33·22 N	105·06 W
88	Honduras (hŏn-dōō'ràs)	N. A.	14·30 N	88·00 W
88	Honduras, Gulf of	N. A.	16·30 N	87·30 W
79	Honea Path (hŭn'ĭ păth)	S. C.	34·25 N	82·16 W
118	Hönefoss (hē'nē-fôs)	Nor.	60·10 N	10·15 E
81	Honesdale (hōnz'dāl)	Pa.	41·30 N	75·15 W
68	Honey (R.) (hŭn'ĭ)	Calif.	40·11 N	120·34 W
73	Honey Grove (hŭn'ĭ grōv)	Tex.	33·35 N	95·54 W
85	Honfleur (ôN-flûr')	Can. (Quebec In.)	46·39 N	70·53 W
122	Honfleur (ôN-flûr')	Fr.	49·26 N	0·13 E
151	Hon Gay	Viet.	20·58 N	107·10 E
159	Honiara	Austl.	9·15 S	159·45 E
116	Honiton (hŏn'ĭ-tŏn)	Eng.	50·49 N	3·10 W
151	Hong Kong (hŏng' kŏng')	Asia	22·15 N	114·40 E
157	Honolulu (hŏn-ô-lōō'lōō)	Hawaii (In.)	21·18 N	157·50 W
157	Honomu (hŏn'ô-mōō)	Hawaii (In.)	19·50 N	155·04 W
152	Honshū (I.) (hŏn'shōō)	Jap.	36·50 N	135·20 E
66	Hood, Mt.	Ore.	45·20 N	121·43 W
65	Hood Can. (hŏŏd)	Wash. (Seattle In.)	47·45 N	122·45 W
66	Hood River	Ore.	45·42 N	121·30 W
65	Hoodsport (hŏŏdz'pōrt)	Wash. (Seattle In.)	47·25 N	123·09 W
142	Hoogly (R.) (hōōg'lĭ)	India	21·30 N	87·28 E
111	Hoogstraten	Bel. (Brussels In.)	51·24 N	4·46 E
157	Hookena (hōō'kĕ-nà)	Hawaii (In.)	19·23 N	155·51 W
72	Hooker (hŏŏk'ẽr)	Okla.	36·49 N	101·13 W
92	Hool (ōō'l)	Mex. (Yucatan In.)	19·32 N	90·22 W
64	Hoonah (hōō'nä)	Alaska	58·05 N	135·25 W
66	Hoopa Valley Ind. Res. (hōō'pà)	Calif.	41·18 N	123·35 W
73	Hooper (hŏŏp'ẽr)	Nebr.	41·37 N	96·31 W
74	Hooper	Utah (Salt Lake City In.)	41·10 N	112·08 W
64	Hooper Bay	Alaska	61·32 N	166·02 W
80	Hoopeston (hōōps'tŭn)	Ill.	40·35 N	87·40 W
81	Hoosick Falls (hōō'sĭk)	N. Y.	42·55 N	73·15 W
68	Hoover Dam (hōō'vẽr)	Nev.	36·00 N	115·06 W
84	Hopatcong, L. (hō-păt'kong)	N. J. (New York In.)	40·57 N	74·38 W
64	Hope (hōp)	Alaska	60·54 N	149·48 W
73	Hope	Ark.	33·41 N	93·35 W
86	Hope	Can.	49·25 N	121·10 W
70	Hope	N. D.	47·17 N	97·45 W
87	Hopedale (hōp'dāl)	Can.	55·26 N	60·11 W
83	Hopedale (hōp'dāl)	Mass. (Boston In.)	42·08 N	71·33 W
147	Hopeh (Prov.)	China	39·09 N	115·22 E
92	Hopelchén (o-pĕl-chĕ'n)	Mex. (Yucatan In.)	19·47 N	89·51 W
87	Hope Mts.	Can.	53·58 N	62·29 W
87	Hopes Advance, C. (hōps ăd-văns')	Can.	61·00 N	69·12 W
158	Hopetoun (hōp'toun)	Austl.	33·50 S	120·15 E
84	Hopewell (hōp'wĕl)	N. J. (New York In.)	40·23 N	74·45 W
79	Hopewell	Va.	37·14 N	77·15 W
166	Hopetown (hōp'toun)	S. Afr.	29·35 S	24·10 E
69	Hopi Ind. Res. (hō'pē)	Ariz.	36·20 N	110·30 W
74	Hopkins (hŏp'-kĭns)	Minn. (Minneapolis, St. Paul In.)	44·55 N	93·24 W
78	Hopkinsville (hŏp'-kĭns-vĭl)	Ky.	36·50 N	87·28 W
83	Hopkinton (hŏp'-kĭn-tŭn)	Mass. (Boston In.)	42·14 N	71·31 W
151	Hop'u	China	21·28 N	109·10 E
66	Hoquiam (hō'kwĭ-ăm)	Wash.	47·00 N	123·53 W
118	Horby (hûr'bü)	Swe.	55·50 N	13·41 E
93	Horconcitos (ŏr-kôn-sē'-tōs)	Pan.	8·18 N	82·11 W
168	Hordio	Som. (Horn of Afr. In.)	10·43 N	51·05 E
120	Horgen (hôr'gĕn)	Switz.	47·16 N	8·35 E
71	Horicon (hŏr'ĭ-kŏn)	Wis.	43·26 N	88·40 W
144	Hormuz, Str. of (hôr'mŭz')	Asia	26·37 N	15·27 E
	Horn, C., see Hornos, Cabo de			
159	Horn (Is.) (hôrn)	Austl.	10·30 S	143·30 E
112	Hornavan (L.)	Swe.	65·54 N	16·17 E
111	Horneburg (hôr'nĕ-bŏŏrgh)	Ger. (Hamburg In.)	53·30 N	9·35 E
81	Hornell (hôr-nĕl')	N. Y.	42·10 N	77·40 W
86	Horn Mts.	Can.	62·12 N	120·29 W
100	Hornos, C. de (Horn, C.) (kä'-bô-dĕ-ô'r-nôs) (kă'p-hŏr'n)	Chile	56·00 S	67·00 W
161	Hornsby (hôrnz' bĭ)	Austl. (Sydney In.)	33·43 S	151·06 E
118	Hornslandet (I.)	Swe.	61·40 N	17·58 E
100	Horqueta (ŏr-kĕ'tä)	Par.	23·20 S	57·00 W
72	Horse Cr. (hôrs)	Colo.	38·49 N	103·48 W
70	Horse Cr.	Wyo.	41·33 N	104·39 W
83	Horse Is.	Can.	50·11 N	55·45 W
118	Horsens (hôrs'ĕns)	Den.	55·50 N	9·49 E
65	Horseshoe B. (hôrs-shōō)	Can. (Vancouver In.)	49·23 N	123·16 W
110	Horsforth (hôrs'fŭrth)	Eng.	53·50 N	1·38 W
160	Horsham (hôr'shăm) (hôrs'ăm)	Austl.	36·42 S	142·17 E
111	Horst (hôrst)	Ger. (Hamburg In.)	53·49 N	9·37 E
118	Horten (hôr'tĕn)	Nor.	59·26 N	10·27 E

ng-sing; ŋ-baŋk; N-nasalized n; nŏd; cŏmmit; ōld; ôbey ôrder; fōōd; fŏŏt; ou-out; s-soft; sh-dish; th-thin; pūre; ûnite; ûrn; stŭd; circŭs; ü-as "y" in study; '-indeterminate vowel.

ăr; fĭnăl; rāte; senâte; ârm; àsk; sofá; fâre; ch-choose; dh-as th in other; bē; ĕvent; bĕt; recĕnt; cratēr; g-go; gh-guttural g; bĭt; ĭ-short neutral; rīde; ᴋ-guttural k as ch in German ich;

PRONOUNCING INDEX Huntingdon–Inner Brass 217

Page	Name Pronunciation Region	Lat. °′	Long. °′
78	Huntingdon..........Tenn.	36·00 N	88·23 W
110	Huntingdon (Co.)..........Eng.	52·26 N	0·19 W
80	Huntington..........Ind.	40·55 N	85·30 W
84	Huntington.N. Y. (New York In.)	40·51 N	73·25 W
81	Huntington..........Pa.	40·30 N	78·00 W
80	Huntington..........W. Va.	38·25 N	82·25 W
74	Huntington Beach Calif. (Los Angeles In.)	33·39 N	118·00 W
74	Huntington Park Calif. (Los Angeles In.)	33·59 N	118·14 W
78	Huntsville (hŭnts′-vĭl)..........Ala.	35·43 N	86·36 W
81	Huntsville..........Can.	45·20 N	79·15 W
73	Huntsville..........Mo.	39·24 N	92·32 W
77	Huntsville..........Tex.	30·44 N	95·34 W
74	Huntsville Utah (Salt Lake City In.)	41·16 N	111·46 W
91	Hunucmá (hōō-nōōk-mä′)...Mex.	21·01 N	89·54 W
148	Huolu (hōōŭ lōō)..........China	38·05 N	114·20 E
155	Huon G..........N. Gui. Ter.	7·15 S	147·45 E
147	Hupeh (Prov.)..........China	31·20 N	111·58 E
80	Hurd, C. (hûrd)..........Can.	45·15 N	81·45 W
71	Hurley (hûr′lĭ)..........Wis.	46·26 N	90·11 W
100	Hurlingham (ōō′r-lēn-gäm) Arg. (In.)	34·20 S	58·38 W
80	Huron (hū′rŏn)..........Ohio	41·20 N	82·35 W
70	Huron..........S. D.	44·22 N	98·15 W
63	Huron, L. (hū′rŏn)....U. S.-Can.	45·15 N	82·40 W
71	Huron Mts.(hū′rŏn)..........Mich.	46·47 N	87·52 W
75	Huron R......Mich. (Detroit In.)	42·12 N	83·26 W
64	Hurricane (hŭr′ĭ-kān).....Alaska	63·00 N	149·30 W
69	Hurricane..........Utah	37·10 N	113·20 W
94	Hurricane Flats (Shoal) (hŭ-rĭ-kăn flăts).Ba. Is.	23·35 N	78·30 W
112	Húsavik..........Ice.	66·00 N	17·10 W
129	Huşi (kōōsh′)..........Sov. Un.	46·52 N	28·04 E
118	Huskvarna (hōōsk-vär′nȧ)...Swe.	57·48 N	14·16 E
120	Husum (hōō′zōōm)..........Ger.	54·29 N	9·04 E
74	Hutchins (hŭch′ĭnz) Tex. (Dallas, Fort Worth In.)	32·38 N	96·43 W
72	Hutchinson (hŭch′ĭn-sŭn)...Kans.	38·02 N	97·56 W
71	Hutchinson..........Minn.	44·53 N	94·23 W
150	Hut′o Ho (R.) (hōō′tō′hō′).China	38·10 N	114·00 E
148	Huwu (hōō wōō)..........China	31·17 N	119·48 E
117	Huy (û-ē′) (hû′ē)..........Bel.	50·33 N	5·14 E
112	Hvannadalshnukur (Mtn.)....Ice.	64·09 N	16·46 W
147	Hwang Ho (Yellow R.) (hwäng′hō′).China	35·06 N	113·39 E
146	Hwang Ho, Old beds of the.China	40 28 N	106·34 E
126	Hvar (I.) (кhvär)..........Yugo.	43·08 N	16·28 E
152	Hwangju (hwäng′jōō′).......Kor.	38·39 N	125·49 E
84	Hyattsville (hī′ăt′s-vĭl) Md. (Baltimore In.)	38·57 N	76·58 W
64	Hydaburg (hī-dă′bûrg)....Alaska	55·18 N	132·40 W
110	Hyde (hīd)..........Eng.	53·27 N	2·05 W
143	Hyderābād (hī-dēr-ȧ-băd′)..India	17·29 N	79·28 E
142	Hyderabad (hī-dēr-ȧ-băd′) W. Pak.	25·29 N	68·28 E
143	Hyderabad (State)..........India	23·29 N	76·50 E
123	Hyères (ē-âr′)..........Fr.	43·09 N	6·08 E
123	Hyères, Iles d′ (Is.) (ēl′dyâr′)..Fr.	42·57 N	6·17 E
152	Hyesanjin (hyĕ′sän-jĭn′).....Kor.	41·11 N	128·12 E
80	Hymera (hī-mē′rȧ)..........Ind.	39·10 N	87·20 W
67	Hyndman Pk. (hīnd′măn)..Idaho	43·38 N	114·04 W
153	Hyōgo (Pref.) (hĭyō′gō) Jap. (Ōsaka In.)	34·54 N	135·15 E
86	Hythe..........Can.	55·18 N	119·34 W
153	Ia (R.) (ē′ä)....Jap. (Ōsaka In.)	34·54 N	135·34 E
121	Iaşi (yä′shē)..........Rom.	47·10 N	27·40 E
155	Iba (ē′bä)......Phil. (Manila In.)	15·20 N	119·59 E
164	Ibadan (ē-bä′dän)..........Nig.	7·26 N	3·48 E
98	Ibagué (ē-bä-gā′).......Col. (In.)	4·27 N	75·13 W
127	Ibar (R.) (ē′bär)..........Yugo.	43·22 N	20·35 E
153	Ibaragi (ē-bä′rä-gē) Jap. (Ōsaka In.)	34·49 N	135·35 E
98	Ibarra (ē-bär′rä)..........Ec.	0·19 N	78·08 W
163	Iberian Pen..........Port.-Sp.	41·00 N	0·07 W
82	Iberville (ē-bâr-vēl′) (ī′bēr-vĭl) Can.	45·14 N	73·01 W
164	Ibi (ē′bē)..........Nig.	8·08 N	9·45 E
99	Ibiapaba, Serra da (Mts.) (sĕ′r-rä-dä-ē-byä-pä′bä).Braz.	3·30 S	40·55 W
125	Ibiza (ē-bē′thä)..........Sp.	38·55 N	1·24 E
125	Ibiza, Isla de (Iviza I.) (ē′s-lä-dĕ-ē-bē′zä).Sp.	39·07 N	1·05 E
167	Ibo (ē′bō)..........Moz.	12·17 S	40·35 E
144	Ibrahim, Jabal (Mtn.)...Sau. Ar.	20·31 N	41·17 E
168	Ibrahim, Port.U. A. R. (Suez In.)	29·57 N	32·33 E
98	Ica (ē′kä)..........Peru	14·09 S	75·42 W
98	Icá (R.) (ē-kä′)..........Braz.	2·56 S	69·12 W
98	Içana (ē-sä′nä)..........Braz.	0·15 N	67·19 W
66	Ice Harbor Dam..........Wash.	46·15 N	118·54 W
102	Iceland (īs′lănd)..........Eur.	65·12 N	19·45 W
151	Ich′ang (ē′chäng′)..........China	30·38 N	111·22 E
142	Ichāpur......India (Calcutta In.)	22·47 N	88·21 E
153	Ichibusayama (Mt.) (ē′chē-bōō′sȧ-yä′mä).Jap.	32·19 N	131·08 E
153	Ichikawa (ē′chē-kä′wä) Jap. (Tōkyō In.)	35·44 N	139·54 E
153	Ichinomiya (ē′chē-nō-mē′yȧ).Jap.	35·19 N	136·49 E
153	Ichinomoto (ē-chē′nō-mō-tō) Jap. (Ōsaka In.)	34·37 N	135·50 E
129	Ichnya (ĭch′nyä)..........Sov. Un.	50·47 N	32·23 E
99	Icó (ē-kō′)..........Braz.	6·25 S	38·43 W
98	Icutú, Cerro (Mtn.) (sĕ′r-rô-ē-kōō-tōō′) Ven.	7·07 N	65·30 W
64	Icy C. (ī′sĭ)..........Alaska	70·20 N	161·40 W
73	Idabel (ī′dȧ-bĕl)..........Okla.	33·52 N	94·47 W
70	Idagrove (ī′dȧ-grōv)..........Iowa	42·22 N	95·29 W
164	Idah (ē′dä)..........Nig.	7·08 N	6·45 E
62	Idaho (State) (ī′dȧ-hō).....U. S.	44·00 N	115·10 W
67	Idaho Falls..........Idaho	43·30 N	112·01 W
72	Idaho Springs..........Colo.	39·43 N	105·32 W
124	Idanha-a-Nova (ē-dän′yȧ-ä-nō′vȧ).Port.	39·58 N	7·13 W
146	Ideriin Gol (R.)..........Mong.	48·58 N	98·38 E
168	Idfū (ĕd′fōō)..U. A. R. (Nile In.)	24·57 N	32·53 E
127	Idhra (I.)..........Grc.	37·20 N	23·30 E
154	Idi (ē′dē)..........Indon.	4·58 N	97·47 E
168	Idkū (ĕd′kōō).U. A. R. (Nile In.)	31·18 N	30·20 E
168	Idkū L..........U. A. R. (Nile In.)	31·13 N	30·22 E
110	Idle (R.) (īd′'l)..........Eng.	53·22 N	0·56 W
126	Idrija (ē′drē-ȧ)..........Yugo.	46·01 N	14·01 E
167	Idutywa (ē-dōō-tĭ′wȧ) S. Afr. (Natal In.)	32·06 S	28·18 E
117	Ieper..........Bel.	50·50 N	2·53 E
126	Ierápetra..........Grc. (Inset)	35·01 N	25·48 E
126	Iesi (yā′sē)..........It.	43·37 N	13·20 E
164	Ife..........Nig.	7·36 N	4·38 E
164	Iferouane (ēf′rōō-än′).......Niger	19·23 N	8·24 E
163	Ifni (ēf′nē)..........Afr.	29·45 N	10·00 W
134	Igarka (ē-gär′kȧ)........Sov. Un.	67·22 N	86·16 E
125	Ighil Izane..........Alg.	35·43 N	0·43 E
126	Iglesias (ē-lĕ′syôs)..........It.	39·20 N	8·34 E
164	Igli (ē-glē′)..........Alg.	30·32 N	2·15 W
87	Igloolik..........Can.	69·33 N	81·18 W
139	′Igma, Gebel el (Mts.) U. A. R. (Palistine In.)	29·12 N	33·42 E
65	Ignacio (ĭg-nä′cĭ-ō) Calif. (San Francisco In.)	38·05 N	122·32 W
100	Iguaçu (R.) (ē-gwä-sōō′).Braz.(In.)	22·42 S	43·19 W
90	Iguala (ē-gwä′lä)..........Mex.	18·18 N	99·34 W
125	Igualada (ē-gwä-lä′dä)..........Sp.	41·35 N	1·38 E
100	Iguassu (R.) (ē-gwä-sōō′)....Braz.	25·45 S	52·30 W
100	Iguassu Falls (Falls)........Braz.	25·40 S	54·16 W
101	Iguatama (ē-gwä-tá′mä) Braz (Rio de Janeiro In.)	20·13 S	45·40 W
99	Iguatu (ē-gwä-tōō′)..........Braz.	6·22 S	39·17 W
164	Iguidi, Erg (Dune)..........Alg.	26·22 N	6·53 W
155	Iguig (ē-gēg′).Phil. (Manila In.)	17·46 N	121·44 E
150	Ihsien..........China	41·30 N	121·15 E
148	I Ho (R.) (yē′hŭ)..........China	34·38 N	118·07 E
150	Iian..........China	46·10 N	129·40 E
153	Iida (ē′ē-dȧ)..........Jap.	35·39 N	137·53 E
132	Iijoki (R.) (ē′yō′kĭ)..........Fin.	65·28 N	27·00 E
153	Iizuka (ē′ē-zōō-kȧ)..........Jap.	33·39 N	130·39 E
164	Ijebu Ode (ē-jĕ′bōō ōdȧ).....Nig.	6·46 N	3·59 E
117	IJsselmeer (L.) (ī′sĕl-mär)....Neth.	52·46 N	5·14 E
119	Ikaalinen (ē′kä-lĭ-nĕn)........Fin.	61·47 N	22·55 E
127	Ikaría (I.) (ē-kä′ryȧ)........Grc.	37·43 N	26·07 E
153	Ikeda-Kawanishi (ē′kȧ-dȧ kä-wä′nē-shē).Jap. (Ōsaka In.)	34·49 N	135·26 E
127	Ikhtiman (ēk′tē-män)........Bul.	42·26 N	23·49 E
153	Iki (I.) (ē′kē)..........Jap.	33·46 N	129·44 E
166	Ikoma (ē-kō′mä)..........Tan.	2·08 S	34·47 E
136	Ikshа (ĭk′shȧ) Sov. Un. (Moscow In.)	56·10 N	37·30 E
155	Ilagen (ē-lä′gän).Phil. (Manila In.)	17·09 N	121·52 E
151	Ilan (ē′län′)..........Taiwan	24·50 N	121·42 E
121	Iława (ē-lä′vȧ)..........Pol.	53·35 N	19·36 E
85	Ile-Bizard Valois (yl-bē-zär vä-lōō-ä′).Can. (Montreal In.)	45·29 N	73·53 W
133	Ilek (ē′lyĕk)..........Sov. Un.	51·30 N	53·10 E
133	Ilek (R.)..........Sov. Un.	51·20 N	53·10 E
85	Ile-Perrot (yl-pĕ-rōt′) Can. (Montreal In.)	45·21 N	73·54 W
164	Ilesha..........Nig.	7·45 N	4·50 E
110	Ilford (ĭl′fērd)..Eng. (London In.)	51·33 N	0·06 E
116	Ilfracombe (ĭl-frȧ-kōōm′)....Eng.	51·13 N	4·08 W
101	Ilhabela (ē′lä-bĕ′lä) Braz. (Rio de Janeiro In.)	23·47 S	45·21 W
101	Ilha Grande, Baia de (B.) (ēl′yä grän′dĕ) Braz. (Rio de Janeiro In.)	23·17 S	44·25 W
124	Ilhavo (ēl′yȧ-vō)..........Port.	40·36 N	8·41 W
99	Ilhéus (ē-lĕ′ōōs)..........Braz.	14·52 S	39·00 W
64	Iliamna (ē-lē-ăm′nȧ)......Alaska	59·45 N	155·05 W
64	Iliamna (L.)..........Alaska	59·25 N	155·30 W
64	Iliamna Vol.)..........Alaska	60·18 N	153·25 W
134	Ilim (R.) (ē-lyēm′)......Sov. Un.	57·28 N	103·00 E
134	Ilimsk (ē-lyēmsk′)......Sov. Un.	56·47 N	103·43 E
155	Ilin (I.) (ē-lyēn′).Phil. (Manila In.)	12·16 N	120·57 E
129	Il′intsiy..........Sov. Un.	49·07 N	29·13 E
127	Iliodhrómia (I.)..........Grc.	39·18 N	23·35 E
81	Ilion (ĭl′ĭ-ŭn)..........N. Y.	43·00 N	75·05 W
146	Ili R. (ē′lē′)..........Sov. Un.	43·46 N	77·41 E
110	Ilkeston (ĭl′kĕs-tŭn)..........Eng.	52·58 N	1·19 W
98	Illampu, Nevado (Pk.) (nĕ-vá′dô-ēl-yäm-pōō′).Bol.	15·50 S	68·15 W
155	Illana B. (ēl-yä-nō)..........Phil.	7·38 N	123·41 E
101	Illapel (ē-zhä-pĕ′l) Chile (Santiago In.)	31·37 S	71·10 W
120	Iller R. (ĭl′er)..........Ger.	47·52 N	10·06 E
98	Illimani, Nevado (Pk.) (nĕ-vá′dô-ēl-yē-mä′nē).Bol.	16·50 S	67·38 W
63	Illinois (State) (ĭl-ĭ-noi′) (ĭl-ĭ-noiz′) U. S.	40·25 N	90·40 W
73	Illinois (R.)..........Ill.	40·52 N	89·31 W
128	Il′men′, Ozero (L.) (ô′zĕ-rô el″men″) (ĭl′mĕn).Sov. Un.	58·18 N	32·00 E
117	Ilmenau (ēl′mē-nou)..........Ger.	50·37 N	13·02 E
117	Ilmenau (R.)..........Ger.	53·20 N	10·20 E
164	Ilo (ē′lō)..........Nig.	11·30 N	3·41 E
98	Ilo..........Peru	17·46 S	71·13 W
92	Ilobasco (ē-lō-bäs′kō)........Sal.	13·57 N	88·46 W
154	Iloilo (ē-lō-ē′lō)..........Phil.	10·49 N	122·33 E
92	Ilopango, L. (ē-lō-päŋ′gō).....Sal.	13·48 N	88·50 W
164	Ilorin (ē-lō-rēn′)..........Nig.	8·32 N	4·30 E
128	Ilūkste..........Sov. Un.	55·59 N	26·20 E
65	Ilwaco (ĭl-wä′kō) Wash. (Portland In.)	46·19 N	124·02 W
132	Ilych (R.) (ē′l′ĭch)......Sov. Un.	62·30 N	57·30 E
153	Imabari (ē′mä-bä′rē)..........Jap.	34·05 N	132·58 E
153	Imai (ē-mī′)....Jap. (Ōsaka In.)	34·30 N	135·47 E
152	Iman (R.) (ē-män′).....Sov. Un.	45·40 N	134·31 E
135	Iman..........Sov. Un.	46·07 N	133·21 E
132	Imandra (L.) (ē-män′drȧ).Sov. Un.	67·40 N	32·30 E
168	Imbābah (ēm-bä′bȧ) U. A. R. (Nile In.)	30·06 N	31·09 E
100	Imbarié (ēm-bä-ryĕ′)..Braz. (In.)	22·38 S	43·13 W
136	Imeni Morozova (ĭm-yĕ′nyĭ mô rô′zô vȧ) Sov. Un. (Leningrad In.)	59·58 N	31·02 E
128	Imeni Moskvy, Kanal (Moscow Can.) (kȧ-näl′ĭm-yă′nĭ mŏs-kvĭ).Sov. Un.	56·33 N	37·15 E
152	Imienpo (yēmĭänpŭ).......China	44·59 N	127·56 E
80	Imlay City (ĭm′lā)..........Mich.	43·00 N	83·15 W
120	Immenstadt (ĭm′ĕn-shtät)....Ger.	47·34 N	10·12 E
168	Immerpan (ĭmĕr-pän).....S. Afr. (Johannesburg & Pretoria In.)	24·29 S	29·14 E
126	Imola (ē′mō-lä)..........It.	44·19 N	11·43 E
126	Imotski (ē-mōts′kē)........Yugo.	43·25 N	17·15 E
99	Impameri..........Braz.	17·44 S	48·03 W
167	Impendle (ĭm-pĕnd′lȧ) S. Afr. (Natal In.)	29·38 S	29·54 E
126	Imperia (ēm-pä′rē-ä)..........It.	43·52 N	8·00 E
75	Imperial (ĭm-pē′rĭ-ăl) Pa. (Pittsburgh In.)	40·27 N	80·15 W
68	Imperial Beach Calif. (San Diego In.)	32·34 N	117·08 W
69	Imperial Res..........Ariz.	32·57 N	114·19 W
68	Imperial Valley..........Calif.	33·00 N	115·22 W
165	Impfondo (ĭmp-fōn′dō)...Con. B.	1·46 N	17·53 E
145	Imphal (ĭmp′hŭl)..........India	24·42 N	94·00 E
127	Imroz (I.) (ĭm′rŏz)..........Tur.	40·10 N	25·27 E
153	Ina (R.) (ē-nä′).Jap. (Ōsaka In.)	34·56 N	135·21 E
68	Inaja Ind. Res. (ē-nä′hä)....Calif.	32·56 N	116·37 W
112	Inari (L.)..........Fin.	69·02 N	26·22 E
164	In Azaoua (Oasis) (ēn-ȧ-zou′ȧ).Alg.	20·57 N	7·24 E
125	Inca (ēŋ′kä)..........Sp.	39·43 N	2·53 E
133	Ince Burun (C.) (ĭn′jȧ)......Tur.	42·00 N	35·00 E
152	Inch′ŏn (ĭn′chŭn)..........Kor.	37·26 N	126·46 E
126	Incudine, Mt. (Mtn.) (ēn-kōō-dē′nȧ) (ăN-kü-dēn′).Cor.	41·53 N	9·17 E
118	Indals-älven (R.)..........Swe.	62·50 N	16·50 E
155	Indang (ēn′däng′) Phil. (Manila In.)	14·11 N	120·53 E
76	Indé (ēn′dā)..........Mex.	25·53 N	105·15 W
73	Independence (ĭn-dē-pĕn′dĕns) Kans.	37·14 N	95·42 W
74	Independence Mo. (Kansas City In.)	39·06 N	94·26 W
75	Independence Ohio (Cleveland In.)	41·23 N	81·39 W
66	Independence..........Ore.	44·49 N	123·13 W
66	Independence Mts..........Nev.	41·15 N	116·02 W
133	Inder (L.)..........Sov. Un.	48·20 N	52·10 E
138	India (ĭn′dĭ-ȧ)..........Asia	23·00 N	77·30 E
71	Indian (L.) (ĭn′dĭ-ăn)......Mich.	46·04 N	86·34 W
81	Indian (R.)..........N. Y.	44·05 N	75·45 W
81	Indiana (ĭn-dĭ-ăn′ȧ)..........Pa.	40·40 N	79·10 W
63	Indiana (State)..........U. S.	39·50 N	86·45 W
75	Indianapolis (ĭn-dĭ-ăn-ăp′ō-lĭs) Ind. (Indianapolis In.)	39·45 N	86·08 W
65	Indian Arm (R.) (ĭn′dĭ-ăn ärm) Can. (Vancouver In.)	49·21 N	122·55 W
86	Indian Head (ĭn′dĭ-ăn hĕd)..Can.	50·36 N	103·42 W
7	Indian Ocean		
71	Indianola (ĭn-dĭ-ăn-ō′lȧ).....Iowa	41·22 N	93·33 W
78	Indianola..........Miss.	33·29 N	90·35 W
135	Indigirka (R.) (ēn-dē-gēr′kȧ) Sov. Un.	67·45 N	145·45 E
88	Indio (R.) (ē′n-dyô) Pan. (Panama Canal In.)	9·13 N	78·28 W
154	Indochina (Reg.) (ĭn-dô-chī′nȧ) Asia	17·22 N	105·18 E
154	Indonesia (ĭn′dô-nē-zhȧ).....Asia	4·38 S	118·45 E
142	Indore (ĭn-dōr′)..........India	22·48 N	76·51 E
154	Indragiri (R.) (ĭn-drȧ-jē′rē).Indon.	0·27 S	102·05 E
142	Indrāvati (R.) (ĭn-drŭ-vä′tē) India	19·15 N	80·54 E
122	Indre (R.) (ăN′dr′)..........Fr.	47·13 N	0·29 E
118	Indre Solund (I.) (ĭndrĕ-sô-lŭnd) Nor.	61·09 N	4·37 E
85	Indus (ĭn′dŭs).Can. (Calgary In.)	50·55 N	113·45 W
142	Indus (R.)..........W. Pak.	26·43 N	67·41 E
167	Indwe (ĭnd′wȧ).S. Afr. (Natal In.)	31·30 S	27·21 E
133	Inebolu (ē-nȧ-bō′lōō)........Tur.	41·50 N	33·40 E
133	Inego (ē′nȧ-gŭ)..........Tur.	40·05 N	29·20 E
155	Infanta (ēn-fän′tä) Phil. (Manila In.)	14·44 N	121·39 E
155	Infanta......Phil. (Manila In.)	15·50 N	119·53 E
124	Infantes (ēn-fän′tås)..........Sp.	38·44 N	3·00 W
91	Inferror, Laguna (L.) (lä-gōō′nä-ēn-fĕr-rôr).Mex.	16·18 N	94·40 W
124	Infiesto (ēn-fyĕ′s-tō)..........Sp.	43·21 N	5·24 W
80	Ingersoll (ĭn′gēr-sōl)..........Can.	43·05 N	81·00 W
159	Ingham (ĭng′ăm)..........Austl.	18·45 S	146·14 E
94	Ingles, Cayos (Is.) (kä′yōs-ĕ′n-glĕ′s).Cuba	21·55 N	82·35 W
74	Inglewood (ĭn′g′l-wŏŏd) Calif. (Los Angeles In.)	33·57 N	118·22 W
85	Inglewood..Can. (Toronto In.)...	43·48 N	79·56 W
135	Ingoda (R.) (ēn-gô′dȧ)...Sov. Un.	51·29 N	112·32 E
120	Ingolstadt (ĭŋ′gôl-shtät).....Ger.	48·46 N	11·27 E
129	Ingul (R.) (ēn-gōōl′).....Sov. Un.	47·22 N	32.52 E
129	Ingulets (R.) (ēn-gōōl′yĕts′) Sov. Un.	47·12 N	33·12 E
133	Ingur (R.) (ēn-gōōr′)....Sov. Un.	42·30 N	42·00 E
166	Inhambane (ēn′äm-bä′-nĕ)...Moz.	23·47 S	35·28 E
99	Inhambupe (ēn-yäm-bōō′pä) Braz.	11·47 S	38·13 W
166	Inharrime (ēn-yär-rē′mä)....Moz.	24·17 S	35·07 E
100	Inhomirim (ē-nô-mē-rē′N) Braz. (In.)	22·34 S	43·11 W
167	Inhiuzan (Mtn.) S. Afr. (Natal In.)	29·34 S	30·03 E
146	Ining (ē′nĭng′)..........China	43·58 N	80·49 E
98	Inirida (R.) (ē-nē-rē′dä).....Col.	2·25 N	70·38 W
160	Injune (ĭn′jōōn)..........Austl.	25·52 S	148·30 E
119	Inkeroinem (ĭn′kĕr-oi-nĕn)....Fin.	60·42 N	26·50 E
75	Inkster (ĭngk′stēr) Mich. (Detroit In.)	42·18 N	83·19 W
160	Innamincka (ĭnn-ȧ′mĭn-kȧ).Austl.	27·50 S	140·48 E
89	Inner Brass (I.) (bräs) Vir. Is. (U. S. A.) (St. Thomas In.)	18·23 N	64·58 W

ng-sing; ŋ-baŋk; N-nasalized n; nŏd; cŏmmit; ōld; ōbey; ôrder; fōōd; fŏŏt; ou-out; s-soft; sh-dish; th-thin; pūre; ûnite; ûrn; stŭd; circŭs; ü as "y" in study; ′-indeterminate vowel.

ăt; fīnăl; rāte; senăte; ârm; ȧsk; sofá; fâre; ch-choose; dh-as th in other; bē; ĕvent; bĕt; recĕnt; cratēr; g-go; gh-guttural g; bĭt; ĭ-short neutral; rīde; ĸ-guttural k as ch in German ich;

PRONOUNCING INDEX Izhevsk–John Day 219

Page Name Pronunciation Region Lat. °′ Long. °′

132 Izhevsk (ē-zhyĕfsk')..........Sov. Un. 56·50 N 53·15 E
132 Izhma (ĭzh'mȧ)..........Sov. Un. 65·00 N 54·05 E
132 Izhma (R.)..........Sov. Un. 64·00 N 53·00 E
136 Izhora R. (ēz'hô-rȧ) Sov. Un. (Leningrad In.) 59·36 N 30·20 E
129 Izmail (ēz-mȧ-ēl)..........Sov. Un. 45·00 N 28·49 E
133 İzmir (ĭz-mēr')..........Tur. 38·25 N 27·05 E
127 Izmir Körfezi (G.)..........Tur. 38·43 N 26·37 E
133 Izmit (ĭz-mēt')..........Tur. 40·45 N 29·45 E
153 Izu (I.) (ē'zōō)..........Jap. 34·32 N 139·25 E
153 Izuhara (ē'zōō-hä'rä)..........Jap. 34·11 N 129·18 E
153 Izumo (ē'zōō-mō)..........Jap. 35·22 N 132·45 E
153 Izumu-Otsu (ē'zōō-mōō ō'tsōō) Jap. (Ōsaka In.) 34·30 N 135·24 E
111 Jaachimsthal (yä'kēm-stäl) Ger. (Berlin In.) 52·58 N 13·45 E
144 Jabal Rema (Mtn.)..........Yemen 14·13 N 44·38 E
120 Jablonec (Nad Nisou) (yäb'lô-nyĕts).Czech. 50·43 N 15·12 E
121 Jablunkov P. (yäb'lōōn-kôf).Czech. 49·31 N 18·35 E
99 Jaboatão (zhä-bô-ȧ-touɴ)...Braz. 8·14 S 35·08 W
144 Jabul Hadur Shuayb (Mtn.) Yemen 15·45 N 43·45 E
125 Jaca (hä'kä)..........Sp. 42·35 N 0·30 W
90 Jacala (hä-kä'lä)..........Mex. 21·01 N 99·11 W
92 Jacaltenango (hä-käl-tĕ-näŋ'gō) Guat. 15·39 N 91·41 W
101 Jacareí (zhä-kȧ-rĕ-ē') Braz. (Rio de Janeiro In.) 23·19 S 45·57 W
100 Jacarepaguá (zhä-kä-rȧ'pä-gwä') Braz. (In.) 22·55 S 43·22 W
99 Jacarézinho (zhä-kä-rĕ'zē-nyô) Braz. 23·13 S 49·58 W
120 Jachymov (yä'chĭ-môf)....Czech. 50·22 N 12·51 E
77 Jacinto City (hä-sēn'tō) (jȧ-sĭn'tō) Tex. (In.) 29·45 N 95·14 W
72 Jacksboro (jăks'bŭr-ô)..........Tex. 33·13 N 98·11 W
78 Jackson (jăk'sŭn)..........Ala. 31·31 N 87·52 W
68 Jackson..........Calif. 38·22 N 120·47 W
78 Jackson..........Ga. 33·19 N 83·55 W
78 Jackson..........Ky. 37·32 N 83·17 W
77 Jackson..........La. 30·50 N 91·13 W
80 Jackson..........Mich. 42·15 N 84·25 W
71 Jackson..........Minn. 43·37 N 95·00 W
78 Jackson..........Miss. 32·17 N 90·10 W
73 Jackson..........Mo. 37·23 N 89·40 W
80 Jackson..........Ohio 39·00 N 82·40 W
78 Jackson..........Tenn. 35·37 N 88·49 W
161 Jackson, Port.Austl. (Sydney In.) 33·50 S 151·18 E
67 Jackson L..........Wyo. 43·57 N 110·28 W
167 Jacksontuin..........S. Afr. (Johannesburg & Pretoria In.) 25·44 S 27·45 E
78 Jacksonville (jăk'sŭn-vĭl).....Ala. 33·52 N 85·45 W
79 Jacksonville..........Fla. 30·20 N 81·40 W
73 Jacksonville..........Ill. 39·43 N 90·12 W
77 Jacksonville..........Tex. 31·58 N 95·18 W
79 Jacksonville Beach..........Fla. 31·18 N 81·25 W
95 Jacmel (zhȧk-mĕl')..........Hai. 18·15 N 72·30 W
76 Jaco, L. (hä'kō)..........Mex. 27·51 N 103·50 W
142 Jacobābad..........W. Pak. 28·22 N 28·27 E
99 Jacobina (zhä-kô-bē'nȧ).....Braz. 11·13 S 40·30 W
82 Jacques Cartier, Mt. (Tabletop) (zhȧk'kär-tyā').Can. 48·59 N 65·59 W
85 Jacques-Cartier, R. Can. (Quebec In.) 47·04 N 71·28 W
83 Jacques Cartier Pass..........Can. 50·04 N 63·43 W
82 Jacquet River (zhȧ-kĕ') (jăk'ĕt) Can. 47·54 N 66·01 W
101 Jacuí (zhä-kōō-ē') Braz. (Rio de Janeiro In.) 21·03 S 46·43 W
101 Jacutinga (zhä-kōō-tēn'gä) Braz. (Rio de Janeiro In.) 21·17 S 46·36 W
139 Jad'ah.....Jordan (Palestine In.) 31·23 N 35·45 E
120 Jade B. (yä'dĕ)..........Ger. 53·28 N 8·17 E
166 Jadotville..........Con. K. 11·01 S 26·52 E
165 Jādū..........Libya 31·57 N 12·04 E
98 Jaén (kä-ĕ'n)..........Peru 5·38 S 78·49 W
124 Jaén..........Sp. 37·45 N 3·48 W
160 Jaffa, C. (jăf'ȧ)..........Austl. 36·58 S 139·29 E
143 Jaffna (jäf'nȧ)..........Ceylon 9·44 N 80·09 E
94 Jagüey Grande (hä'gwā grän'dā) Cuba 22·35 N 81·05 W
139 Jahore Str...Mala. (Singapore In.) 1·22 N 103·37 E
95 Jaibo (R.) (hä-ē'bō)..........Cuba 20·10 N 75·20 W
142 Jaipur..........India 27·00 N 75·50 E
142 Jaisamer..........India 27·00 N 70·54 E
126 Jajce (yī'tsĕ)..........Yugo. 44·20 N 17·19 E
112 Jakobstad (yȧ'kôb-stȧdh)....Fin. 63·33 N 22·31 E
91 Jalacingo (hä-lä-sĭŋ'gō).....Mex. 97·16 N 19·47 W
145 Jalālābād (jŭ-lä-lȧ-bäd') Afg. (Khyber Pass In.) 34·25 N 70·27 E
92 Jalapa (hä-lä'pȧ)..........Guat. 14·38 N 89·58 W
91 Jalapa de Diaz (San Felipe) (dā dē-äz') (sän fē-lē'pā).Mex. 18·06 N 96·33 W
91 Jalapa del Marqués (dĕl mär-kās').Mex. 16·30 N 95·29 W
91 Jalapa Enriquez (ĕn-rē'kāz)..Mex. 19·32 N 96·53 W
142 Jalgaon..........India 21·08 N 75·33 E
90 Jalisco (hä-lēs'kō)..........Mex. 21·27 N 104·54 W
88 Jalisco (State)..........Mex. 20·07 N 104·45 W
127 Jalomita (R.)..........Rom. 44·37 N 26·42 E
124 Jalón (R.) (hä-lōn')..........Sp. 41·22 N 1·46 W
90 Jalostotitlán (hä-lōs-tē-tlän')..Mex. 21·09 N 102·30 W
91 Jalpa (häl'pä)..........Mex. 18·12 N 93·06 W
90 Jalpa (häl'pä)..........Mex. 21·40 N 103·04 W
90 Jalpan (häl'pän)..........Mex. 21·13 N 99·31 W
142 Jalpur..........India 20·49 N 86·37 E
91 Jaltepec (häl-tȧ-pĕk')..........Mex. 17·20 N 95·15 W
91 Jaltipan (häl-tȧ-pän')..........Mex. 17·59 N 94·42 W
90 Jaltocan (häl-tô-kän')..........Mex. 21·08 N 98·32 W
165 Jālū (Oasis)..........Libya 28·58 N 21·45 E
94 Jamaica (I.)..........N. A. 18·21 N 77·31 W
95 Jamaica Cay (I.)..........Ba. Is. 22·45 N 75·55 W
142 Jamalpur..........E. Pak. 24·56 N 89·58 E
90 Jamay (hä-mī')..........Mex. 20·16 N 103·43 W
127 Jambol (yȧm'bôl)..........Bul. 42·28 N 26·31 E
155 Jamdena (I.)..........Indon. 7·23 S 130·30 E
73 James (R.)..........Mo. 36·51 N 93·22 W
79 James (R.)..........N. C. 36·07 N 81·48 W
62 James (R.)..........U. S. 46·25 N 98·55 W
81 James (R.)..........Va. 37·35 N 77·50 W
87 James B. (jāmz)..........Can. 53·53 N 80·40 W
84 Jamesburg (jāmz'bûrg) N. J. (New York In.) 40·21 N 74·26 W
95 James Pt..........Ba. Is. 25·20 N 76·30 W
158 James Ra..........Austl. 24·15 S 133·30 E
96 James Ross (I.)..........Ant. 64·20 S 58·20 W
81 Jamestown (jāmz'toun).....N. Y. 42·05 N 79·15 W
70 Jamestown..........N. D. 46·54 N 98·42 W
84 Jamestown.R. I. (Providence In.) 41·30 N 71·21 W
167 Jamestown....S. Afr. (Natal In.) 31·07 S 26·49 E
70 Jamestown Res..........N. D. 47·16 N 98·40 W
91 Jamiltepec (hä-mēl-tȧ-pĕk)..Mex. 16·16 N 97·54 W
118 Jammerburgt (B.)..........Den. 57·20 N 9·28 E
142 Jammu..........India 32·50 N 32·51 E
142 Jammu and Kashmīr (disputed reg.) (kȧsh-mēr').India & Pak. 39·10 N 75·05 E
142 Jamnagar (jäm-nŭ'gŭr).....India 22·33 N 70·03 E
145 Jamrud (jäm'rōōd) W. Pak. (Khyber Pass In.) 34·00 N 71·22 E
142 Jamshedpur (jäm'shĕd-pōōr) India 22·52 N 86·11 E
98 Jamundí (hä-mōō'n-dē').Col. (In.) 3·15 N 76·32 W
142 Janakpur..........Nep. 26·50 N 85·55 E
124 Jándula (R.) (hän'dōō-lä).....Sp. 38·28 N 3·52 W
71 Janesville (jānz'vĭl)..........Wis. 42·41 N 89·03 W
139 Janin.......Jordan (Palestine In.) 32·27 N 35·19 E
112 Jan Mayen (I.) (yän mī'ĕn)..Nor. 70·59 N 8·05 W
118 Jannelund (yän'ĕ-lōōnd).....Swe. 59·14 N 14·24 E
121 Jánoshalma (yä'nôsh-hôl-mô) Hung. 46·17 N 19·18 E
121 Janów Lubelski (yä'nōōf lŭ-bĕl'skĭ) Pol. 50·40 N 22·25 E
99 Januária (zhä-nwä'rē-ä).....Braz. 15·31 S 44·17 W
148 Jaoyang (jä'ō-yäng').........China 38·16 N 115·45 E
139 Japan (jȧ-păn')..........Asia 36·30 N 133·30 E
152 Japan, Sea of (jȧ-păn')......Asia 40·08 N 132·55 W
155 Japen (I.) (yä'pĕn).....W. Irian 1·30 S 136·15 E
100 Japeri (zhä-pĕ'rē).....Braz. (In.) 22·38 S 43·40 W
98 Japurá (R.) (zhä-pōō-rä')...Braz. 1·30 S 67·54 W
95 Jarabacoa (ĸä-rä-bä-kô'ä) Dom. Rep. 19·05 N 70·40 W
90 Jaral del Progreso (hä-räl dĕl prô-grā'sō).Mex. 20·21 N 101·05 W
124 Jarama (R.) (hä-rä'mä).......Sp. 40·33 N 3·30 W
139 Jarash.....Jordan (Palestine In.) 32·17 N 35·53 E
94 Jardines, Banco (Bk.) (bä'n-kō-här-dē'nȧs).Cuba 21·45 N 81·40 W
99 Jari (R.) (zhä-rē)..........Braz. 0·28 N 53·00 W
122 Jarnac (zhȧr-nȧk')..........Fr. 45·42 N 0·09 W
121 Jarocin (yȧ-rō'tsyēn)..........Pol. 51·58 N 17·31 E
121 Jarosław (yȧ-rôs-wȧf)........Pol. 50·01 N 22·41 E
139 Jasin.......Mala. (Singapore In.) 2·19 N 102·26 E
119 Jašiūnai (dzȧ-shōō-nȧ'yĕ) Sov. Un. 54·27 N 25·25 E
144 Jāsk (jäsk)..........Iran 25·46 N 57·48 E
121 Jasło (yȧs'wō)..........Pol. 49·44 N 21·28 E
139 Jason B.....Mala. (Singapore In.) 1·53 N 104·14 E
80 Jasonville (jā'sŭn-vĭl)..........Ind. 39·10 N 87·15 W
78 Jasper (jăs'pēr)..........Ala. 33·50 N 87·17 W
86 Jasper..........Can. 52·54 N 118·18 W
78 Jasper..........Fla. 30·30 N 82·56 W
80 Jasper..........Ind. 38·20 N 86·55 W
70 Jasper..........Minn. 43·51 N 96·22 W
77 Jasper..........Tex. 30·55 N 93·59 W
86 Jasper Natl. Park..........Can. 53·09 N 117·45 W
85 Jasper Place.Can. (Edmonton In.) 53·32 N 113·36 W
121 Jászapáti (yäs'ô-pä-tē).....Hung. 47·29 N 20·10 E
91 Jatate (R.) (hä-tä-tā').....Mex. 16·30 N 91·29 W
94 Jatibonico (hä-tē-bô-nē'kô)..Cuba 22·00 N 79·15 W
125 Játiva (hä'tē-vä)..........Sp. 38·58 N 0·31 W
100 Jau' (zhȧ-ōō')..........Braz. 22·16 S 48·31 W
98 Jauja (kä-ōō'ĸ)..........Peru 11·43 S 75·32 W
90 Jaumave (hou-mä'vȧ).......Mex. 23·23 N 99·24 W
119 Jaunjelgava (youn'yĕl'gȧ-vȧ) Sov. Un. 56·37 N 25·06 E
128 Jaunlatgale (youn'lat'gä-lĕ) Sov. Un. 57·04 N 27·54 E
154 Java (I.) (jä'vȧ) (jȧ'vȧ)....Indon. 8·35 S 111·11 E
98 Javari (R.) (ĸä-vä-rē)....Col.-Peru 4·25 S 72·07 W
154 Java Sea (jä'vȧ) (jȧ'vȧ)....Indon. 5·10 S 110·30 E
125 Jávea (hȧ-vā'ä)..........Sp. 38·45 N 0·07 E
120 Jawor (yä'vôr)..........Pol. 51·04 N 16·12 E
121 Jaworzno (yä-vôzh'nô)........Pol. 50·11 N 19·18 E
136 Jayva R. (yäy'vȧ) Sov. Un. (Urals In.) 59·13 N 57·17 E
121 Jászberény (yäs'bĕ-rān')....Hung. 47·30 N 19·56 E
139 Jazzin........Leb. (Palestine In.) 33·34 N 35·37 E
77 Jeanerette (jĕn-ēr-et') (zhän-rĕt') La. 29·54 N 91·41 W
114 Jebal Aures (Mts.)..........Alg. 35·16 N 5·53 E
164 Jebba (jĕb'ȧ)..........Nig. 9·07 N 4·46 E
165 Jebel, Bahr el (R.)..........Sud. 28·22 N 30·31 E
121 Jędrzejów (yăɴ-dzhā'yŏŏf)....Pol. 50·38 N 20·18 E
85 Jefferson (jĕf'ēr-sŭn) Can. (Toronto In.) 43·55 N 79·26 W
78 Jefferson..........Ga. 34·05 N 83·35 W
71 Jefferson..........Iowa 42·10 N 94·22 W
77 Jefferson..........Tex. 32·47 N 94·21 W
71 Jefferson..........Wis. 42·59 N 88·45 W
66 Jefferson, Mt..........Ore. 44·41 N 121·50 W
73 Jefferson City..........Mo. 38·34 N 92·10 W
67 Jefferson R..........Mont. 45·37 N 112·22 W
75 Jeffersontown (jĕf'ēr-sŭn-toun) Ky. (Louisville In.) 38·11 N 85·34 W
75 Jeffersonville (jĕf'ēr-sŭn-vĭl) Ind. (Louisville In.) 38·17 N 85·44 W
Jehol, see Ch'engte
115 Jeib, Wadi el (R.).....Jordan-Isr. 30·30 N 35·20 E
119 Jēkabpils (yĕk'ȧb-pĭls)...Sov. Un. 56·29 N 25·50 E
120 Jelenia Góra (yĕ-lĕn'yȧ gōō'rȧ) Pol. 50·53 N 15·43 E
119 Jelgava (yĕl'gȧ-vȧ)......Sov. Un. 56·39 N 23·40 E
78 Jellico (jĕl'ĭ-kō)..........Tenn. 36·34 N 84·06 W
113 Jemmapes (zhĕ-map')........Alg. 36·43 N 7·21 E
120 Jena (yā'nä)..........Ger. 50·55 N 11·37 E
148 Jench'iu (rĕnchēō)..........China 38·44 N 116·05 E
79 Jenkins (jĕŋ'kĭnz)..........Ky. 37·09 N 82·38 W
84 Jenkintown (jĕŋ'kĭn-toun) Pa. (Philadelphia In.) 40·06 N 75·08 W
77 Jennings (jĕn'ĭngz)..........La. 30·14 N 92·40 W
80 Jennings..........Mich. 44·20 N 85·20 W
74 Jennings......Mo. (St. Louis In.) 38·43 N 90·16 W
99 Jequié (zhĕ-kyĕ')..........Braz. 13·53 S 40·06 W
99 Jequitinhonha (R.) (zhĕ-kē-tēŋ-ō'n-yä).Braz. 16·47 S 41·19 W
95 Jérémie (zhā-rā-mē')........Hai. 18·40 N 74·10 W
99 Jeremoabo (zhĕ-rā-mō-ȧ'bō).Braz. 10·03 S 38·13 W
91 Jerez, Punta (Pt.) (pōō'n-tä-ĸĕ-räz').Mex. 23·04 N 97·44 W
124 Jerez de la Frontera (ĸĕ-räth' dā lä frôn-tā'rä).Sp. 36·42 N 6·09 W
124 Jerez de los Caballeros (ĸĕ-rath' dā lōs kä-väl-yä'rôs).Sp. 38·20 N 6·45 W
159 Jericho (jĕr'ĭ-kō)..........Austl. 28·38 S 146·24 E
168 Jericho (jĕr-ĭkô) S. Afr. (Johannesburg & Pretoria In.) 25·16 S 27·47 E
Jericho, see Arīhā
69 Jerome (jē-rōm')..........Ariz. 34·45 N 112·10 W
67 Jerome..........Idaho 42·44 N 114·31 W
122 Jersey (I.) (jûr'zĭ)..........Eur. 49·13 N 2·07 W
84 Jersey City.N. J. (New York In.) 40·43 N 74·05 W
81 Jersey Shore..........Pa. 41·10 N 77·15 W
85 Jerseyville (jĕr'zē-vĭl) Can. (Toronto In.) 43·12 N 80·08 W
73 Jerseyville..........Ill. 39·07 N 90·18 W
139 Jerusalem (jē-rōō'sȧ-lĕm) Isr.-Jordan (Palestine In.) 31·46 N 35·14 E
154 Jesselton..........Mala. 5·55 N 116·05 E
79 Jesup (jĕs'ŭp)..........Ga. 31·36 N 81·53 W
91 Jesús Carranza (hē-sōō's-kär-rȧ'n-zä).Mex. 17·26 N 95·01 W
70 Jewel Cave Natl. Mon.......S. D. 43·44 N 103·52 W
65 Jewell (jū'ĕl)...Ore. (Portland In.) 45·56 N 123·30 W
142 Jhālawār..........India 24·29 N 79·09 E
142 Jhang Maghian.........W. Pak. 31·21 N 72·19 E
142 Jhansi (jän'sē)..........India 25·29 N 78·32 E
142 Jharsuguda..........India 22·51 N 86·13 E
142 Jhelum (R.) (jā'lŭm).....W. Pak. 31·40 N 71·51 E
146 Jibhalanta..........Mong. 47·49 N 97·00 E
69 Jicarilla Ind. Res. (kē-kȧ-rēl'yȧ) N. Mex. 36·45 N 107·00 W
93 Jicaron, Isla (I.) (ĸē-kä-rōn').Pan. 7·14 N 81·41 W
121 Jiffa R..........Rom. 47·35 N 27·02 E
158 Jiggalong (jĭg'ȧ-lông).......Austl. 23·20 S 120·45 E
95 Jiguani (ĸē-gwä-nē')........Cuba 20·20 N 76·30 W
94 Jigüey, Bahía (B.) (bä-ē'ä-ĸē'gwā).Cuba 22·15 N 78·10 W
148 Jihchao (rē'jou)..........China 35·27 N 119·28 E
120 Jihlava (yē'hlȧ-vȧ)........Czech. 49·23 N 15·33 E
168 Jijiga.....Eth. (Horn of Afr. In.) 9·15 N 42·48 E
125 Jijona (ĸē-hō'nä)..........Sp. 38·31 N 0·29 W
142 Jikyop..........China 28·41 N 91·42 E
124 Jiloca (R.) (ĸē-lō'kȧ)..........Sp. 41·13 N 1·30 W
92 Jilotepeque (ĸē-lô-tĕ-pĕ'kĕ) Guat. 14·39 N 89·36 W
165 Jima..........Eth. 7·41 N 36·52 E
127 Jimbolia (zhĭm-bô'lyȧ)......Rom. 45·45 N 20·44 E
90 Jiménez (ĸē-mä'nȧz)........Mex. 24·12 N 98·29 W
76 Jimenez..........Mex. 27·09 N 104·55 W
76 Jiménez..........Mex. 29·03 N 100·42 W
90 Jiménez del Téul (tĕ-ōō'l)...Mex. 21·28 N 103·51 W
81 Jim Thorpe (jĭm' thôrp')......Pa. 40·50 N 75·45 W
120 Jindřichov Hradec (yēn'd'r-zhĭ-kōōf hrä'dĕts).Czech. 49·09 N 15·02 E
165 Jinja (jĭn'jä)..........Ug. 0·29 N 33·11 E
92 Jinotega (kē-nô-tā'gä)........Nic. 13·07 N 86·00 W
92 Jinotepe (kē-nô-tā'pā)........Nic. 11·52 N 86·12 W
153 Jinzū-Gawa (Strm.) (jēn'zōō gä'wä).Jap. 36·26 N 137·18 E
98 Jipijapa (ĸē-pē-hä'pä)........Ec. 1·36 S 80·52 W
92 Jiquilisco (ĸē-kē-lē's-kô).......Sal. 13·18 N 88·32 W
90 Jiquilpan de Juarez (ĸē-kēl'pän dā hwä'räz).Mex. 20·00 N 102·43 W
91 Jiquipilco (hē-kē-pē'l-kô) Mex. (Mexico City In.) 19·32 N 99·37 W
168 Jirgā (jĕr'gȧ)..U. A. R. (Nile In.) 26·20 N 31·51 E
146 Jirgalanta..........Mong. 48·08 N 91·40 E
124 Jistredo, Sierra de (Mts.) (sē-ĕ'r-rä-dĕ-ĸēs-trĕ'dô).Sp. 42·50 N 6·15 W
91 Jitotol (ĸē-tô-tōl')..........Mex. 17·03 N 92·54 W
99 João Pessoa (Paraíba) (shô-ouɴ' pĕ-sōȧ') (pä-rä-ē'bȧ).Braz. 7·09 S 34·45 W
101 João Ribeiro (zhô-uɴ-rē-bä'rō) Braz. (Rio de Janeiro In.) 20·42 S 44·03 W
94 Jobabo (R.) (hō-bä'bä).......Cuba 20·50 N 77·15 W
85 Jock R. (jŏk)...Can. (Ottawa In.) 45·08 N 75·51 W
90 Jocotepec (hô-kō-tä-pĕk')....Mex. 20·17 N 103·26 W
124 Jodar (hō'där)..........Sp. 37·54 N 3·20 W
142 Jodhpur (jōd'pōōr)..........India 26·23 N 83·00 E
119 Joensuu (yô-ĕn'sōō)..........Fin. 62·35 N 29·46 E
153 Jōga-Shima (I.) (jō'gä shē'mä) Jap. (Tōkyō In.) 35·07 N 139·37 E
128 Jōgeva (yû'gĕ-vȧ)........Sov. Un. 58·45 N 26·23 E
82 Jogins..........Can. 45·41 N 64·27 W
154 Jogjakarta (yŏg-yȧ-kär'tȧ).Indon. 7·50 S 110·20 E
167 Johannesburg (yô-hän'ĕs-bōōrgh) S. Afr. (Johannesburg & Pretoria In.) 26·08 S 27·54 E
66 John Day R. (jŏn dā).......Ore. 44·46 N 120·15 W
66 John Day R., Middle Fork...Ore. 44·53 N 119·04 W
66 John Day R., North Fork....Ore. 45·03 N 118·50 W

220 John Martin–Kamenz PRONOUNCING INDEX

Page	Name Pronunciation Region	Lat. °′	Long. °′
72	John Martin Res. (jŏn mär′tĭn) Colo.	37·57 N	103·04 W
65	Johnson (R.) (jŏn′sŭn) Ore. (Portland In.)	45·27 N	122·20 W
81	Johnsonburg (jŏn′sŭn-bûrg)...Pa.	41·30 N	78·40 W
80	Johnson City (jŏn′sŭn)........Ill.	37·50 N	88·55 W
81	Johnson City..............N. Y.	42·10 N	76·00 W
79	Johnson City..............Tenn.	36·17 N	82·23 W
156	Johnston (I.) (jŏn′stŭn)...Oceania	17·00 N	168·00 W
81	Johnstown (jonz′toun)......N. Y.	43·00 N	74 20 W
81	Johnstown..................Pa.	40·20 N	78·50 W
147	Joho (Prov.)..............China	42·31 N	118·12 E
154	Johore (State) (jŭ-hōr′).....Mala.	2·15 N	103·00 E
139	Johore (R.) (jŭ-hōr′) Mala. (Singapore In.)	1·39 N	103·52 E
139	Johore Bahru (bȧ-hŭ-rōō′) Mala. (Singapore In.)	1·28 N	103·46 E
128	Jōhvi (yû′vĭ)...........Sov. Un.	59·21 N	27·21 E
122	Joigny (zhwȧn-yē′)...........Fr.	47·58 N	3·26 E
100	Joinville (zhwăN-vēl′).......Braz.	26·18 S	48·47 W
122	Joinville....................Fr.	48·28 N	5·05 E
96	Joinville (I.)..............Ant.	63·80 S	53·80 W
90	Jojutla (hō-hōō′tlȧ).........Mex.	18·39 N	99·11 W
112	Jökullsá (R.) (yû′kōōls-ô).....Ice.	65·38 N	16·08 W
90	Jola (Kô′lä)...............Mex.	21·08 N	104·26 W
75	Joliet (jō-lĭ-ĕt′)..Ill. (Chicago In.)	41·37 N	88·05 W
82	Joliette (zhô-lyĕt′)..........Can.	46·01 N	73·30 W
154	Jolo (hō-lô)................Phil.	5·59 N	121·05 E
154	Jolo (I.)...................Phil.	5·55 N	121·15 E
155	Jomalig (I.) (hô-mä′lêg) Phil. (Manila In.)	14·44 N	122·34 E
90	Jomulco (hô-mōōl′kô).......Mex.	21·08 N	104·24 W
90	Jonacatepec (hō-nä-kä-tȧ-pĕk′) Mex.	18·39 N	98·46 W
119	Jonava (yō-nä′vȧ).......Sov. Un.	55·05 N	24·15 E
118	Jondal (yōn′däl)............Nor.	60.16 N	6·16 E
155	Jones (jōnz)....Phil. (Manila In.)	13·56 N	122·05 E
155	Jones..........Phil. (Manila In.)	16·35 N	121·39 E
87	Jones, C...................Can.	54·35 N	79·51 W
73	Jonesboro (jōnz′bûro).......Ark.	35·49 N	90·42 W
77	Jonesboro..................La.	32·14 N	92·43 W
77	Jonesville (jōnz′vĭl)..........La.	31·35 N	91·50 W
80	Jonesville.................Mich.	42·00 N	84·45 W
119	Joniškis (yô′nĭsh-kĭs)....Sov. Un.	56·14 N	23·36 E
118	Jönköping (yûn′chû-pĭng)....Swe.	57·47 N	14·10 E
82	Jonquiere (zhôN-kyâr′)......Can.	48·24 N	71·16 W
91	Jonuta (hô-nōō′tä).........Mex.	18·07 N	92·09 W
122	Jonzac (zhôN-zȧk′)...........Fr.	45·27 N	0·27 W
73	Joplin (jŏp′lĭn).............Mo.	37·05 N	94·31 W
138	Jordan (jôr′dăn)............Asia	30·15 N	38·00 E
139	Jordan (R.).Jordan (Palestine In.)	31·58 N	35·36 E
74	Jordan R. Utah (Salt Lake City In.)	40·42 N	111·56 W
145	Jorhat (jôr-hät′)...........India	26·43 N	94·16 E
90	Jorullo, Vol. de (vôl-kȧ′n-dĕ-hô-rōōl′yō).Mex.	18·54 N	101·38 W
164	Jos (jôs)..................Nig.	9·53 N	8·56 E
158	Joseph Bonaparte, G. (jô′sĕf bô′nȧ-pärt).Austl.	13·30 S	128·40 E
85	Joseph L. (jô′sĕf lāk) Can. (Edmonton In.)	53·18 N	113·06 W
68	Joshua Tree Natl. Mon. (jô′shū-ȧ trē).Calif.	34·02 N	115·53 W
118	Jostedalsbreen (Gl.) (yôstĕ-däls-brėĕn).Nor.	61·40 N	6·55 E
118	Jotun Fjell (Mts.) (yō′tōōn fyel′) Nor.	61·44 N	8·11 E
94	Joulter's Cays (Is.) (jōl′tẽrz).Ba. Is.	25·20 N	78·10 W
123	Jouy-le-Chatel (zhwē-lĕ-shä-tĕl′) Fr. (Paris In.)	48·40 N	3·07 E
94	Jovellanos (hō-vĕl-yä′nōs)...Cuba	22·50 N	81·10 W
148	Ju (R.) (rōō)..............China	33·07 N	114·18 E
90	Juan Aldama (kōōȧ′n-äl-dȧ′mä) Mex.	24·16 N	103·21 W
66	Juan de Fuca, Str. of (hwän′ dā fōō′kä).Wash.-Can.	48·25 N	124·37 W
167	Juan de Nova (I.)...Malag. Rep.	17·18 S	43·07 E
88	Juan Diaz, (R.) (Kōōȧ′n-dê′-äz) Pan. (Panama Canal In.)	9·05 N	79·30 W
96	Juan Fernández, Islasde (Is.) (ê′s-läs-dĕ-hwän′ fĕr-nän′däth) Chile	33·30 S	79·00 W
101	Juan L. Lacaze (hōōȧ′n-ĕ′lĕ-lä-kä′zĕ).Ur. (Buenos Aires In.)	34·25 S	57·28 W
94	Juan Luis, Cayos de (Is.) (ka-yōs-dĕ-hwän lōō-ēs′).Cuba	22·15 N	82·00 W
99	Juàzeiro (zhōōȧ′zā′rô)......Braz.	9·27 S	40·28 W
99	Juazeiro do Norte (zhōōȧ′zā′rô-dô-nôr-tĕ).Braz.	7·16 S	38·57 W
100	Juárez (hōōȧ′rĕz)...........Arg.	37·42 S	59·46 W
165	Juba.......................Sud.	4·58 N	31·37 E
168	Juba R. (jōō′bȧ) Som. (Horn of Afr. In.)	1·30 N	42·25 E
139	Jubayl (Byblos) (jōō-bīl′) Leb. (Palestine In.)	34·07 N	35·38 E
142	Jubbulpore (jŭb-ŭl-pōr′)....India	23·18 N	79·59 E
124	Júcar (R.) (hōō′kär)........Sp.	39·10 N	1·22 W
94	Júcaro (hōō′kȧ-rô)..........Cuba	21·40 N	78·50 W
90	Juchipila (hōō-chê-pē′lȧ)....Mex.	21·26 N	103.09 W
88	Juchitan (hōō-chê-tän′).....Mex.	16·15 N	95·00 W
91	Juchitán de Zaragoza (hōō-chê-tän′ dā thä-rä-gō′thä).Mex.	16·27 N	95·03 W
90	Juchitlán (hōō-chē-tlän).....Mex.	20·05 N	104·07 W
92	Jucuapa (Kōō-kwä′pä)........Sal.	13·30 N	88·24 W
144	Juddah...............Sau. Ar.	21·30 N	39·15 E
120	Judenburg (jōō′dĕn-bûrg)....Aus.	47·10 N	14·40 E
67	Judith R. (jōō′dĭth).......Mont.	47·20 N	109·36 W
127	Jui........................Rom.	44·45 N	23·17 E
151	Juian (jwĭ′än′)............China	27·48 N	120·40 E
92	Juigalpa (hwê-gäl′pä)........Nic.	12·02 N	85·24 W
123	Juilly (zhwē-yē′).Fr. (Paris In.)..	49·01 N	2·41 E
117	Juist (I.) (yōō′ēst)..........Ger.	53·41 N	6.50 E
101	Juiz de Fora (zhōō-ēzh′ dā fō′rä) Braz. (Rio de Janeiro In.)	21·47 S	43·20 W
100	Jujuy (hōō-hwē′)...........Arg.	24·14 S	65·15 W
100	Jujuy (Prov.) (hōō-hwē′).....Arg.	23·00 S	65·45 W
148	Jukao (rōōgou)............China	32·24 N	120·33 E
167	Jukskei (R.)..............S. Afr. (Johannesburg & Pretoria In.)	25·58 S	27·58 E
72	Julesburg (jōōlz′bûrg).......Colo.	40·59 N	102·16 W
98	Juliaca (hōō-lê-ä′kä)........Peru	15·26 S	70·12 W
49	Julianehåb...............Grnld.	60·70 N	46·20 W
123	Jülich (yü′lĕk)....Ger. (Ruhr In.)	50·55 N	6 22 E
126	Julijske Alpe (Mts.) (û′lêy-skĕ′ äl′pĕ).Yugo.	46·05 N	14 05 E
142	Jullundur.................India	31·29 N	75·39 E
142	Julpaiguri................India	26·35 N	88·48 E
167	Jumbla (Mtn.) (jum′blȧ) S. Afr. (Natal In.)	30·29 S	28·52 E
95	Jumento Cays (Is.) (hōō-mĕn′tō) Ba. Is.	23·05 N	75·40 W
117	Jumet (zhü-mĕ′)............Bel.	50·28 N	4·30 E
124	Jumilla (hōō-mēl′yä).........Sp.	38·28 N	1·20 W
71	Jump (R.) (jŭmp)..........Wis.	45·18 N	90·53 W
85	Jumpingpound Cr. (jŭmp-ĭng-pound).Can. (Calgary In.)	51·01 N	114·34 W
99	Jumundá (R.) (zhōō-mōō′n-dä′) Braz.	1·33 S	57·42 W
142	Junagādh (jōō-nä′gŭd)......India	21·33 N	70·25 E
148	Junan (rōō Nän)..........China	32·59 N	114·22 E
76	Junction (jŭŋk′shŭn)........Tex.	30·29 N	99·48 W
73	Junction City.............Kans.	39·01 N	96·49 W
101	Jundiaí (zhōō′n-dyä-ē′) Braz. (Rio de Janeiro In.)	23·12 S	46·52 W
64	Juneau (jōō′nō)..........Alaska	58·25 N	134·30 W
148	Jungch'eng (jōōng′chĕng′)..China	37·23 N	122·31 E
151	Jungchiang...............China	25·52 N	108·45 E
120	Jungfrau Pk. (yōōng′frou)..Switz.	46·30 N	7·59 E
151	Junghsien................China	22·48 N	110·38 E
101	Junín (hōō-nē′n) Arg. (Buenos Aires In.)	34·35 S	60·56 W
98	Junín................Col. (In.)	4·47 N	73·39 W
139	Juniyah (jōō-nē′ĕ) Leb. (Palestine In.)	33·59 N	35·38 E
112	Junkeren (Mtn.) (yōōn′kĕ-rĕn) Nor.	66·29 N	14·58 E
83	Jupiter (jōō′pĭ-tẽr)..........Can.	49·30 N	63·25 W
65	Jupiter, Mt....Wash. (Seattle In.)	47·42 N	123·04 W
116	Jura (I.) (jōō′rȧ)...........Scot.	56·09 N	6·45 W
123	Jura (Mts.) (zhü-rȧ′).......Switz.	46·55 N	6·49 E
116	Jura, Sd. of (jōō′rȧ)........Scot.	55·45 N	5·55 W
119	Jurbarkas (yōōr-bär′kȧs) Sov. Un.	55·06 N	22·50 E
139	Jurf ad Darāwīsh Jordan (Palestine In.)	30·41 N	35·51 E
165	Jur R. (jōōr)...............Sud.	6·38 N	27·52 E
98	Juruá (R.) (zhōō-rōō-ä′)....Braz.	5·27 S	67·39 W
99	Juruena (R.) (zhōō-rōōĕ′nä) Braz.	12·22 S	58·34 W
98	Jutaí (R.) (zhōō-tȧy).......Braz.	4·26 S	68·16 W
92	Jutiapa (hōō-tê-ä′pä).......Guat.	14·16 N	89·55 W
92	Juticalpa (hōō-tê-käl′pä)...Hond.	14·35 N	86·17 W
90	Juventino Rosas (Kōō-vĕn-tē′-nô-rŏ-säs).Mex.	20·38 N	101·02 W
123	Juvisy-sur-Orge (zhü-vê-sē′sür ôrzh′).Fr. (Paris In.)	48·41 N	2·22 E
90	Juxtahuaca (hōōs-tlȧ-hwä′kä) Mex.	17·20 N	98·02 W
127	Južna Morava (R.) (û′zhnȧ mô′rȧ-vȧ).Yugo.	42·30 N	22·00 E
118	Jylland (Reg.).............Den.	56·04 N	9·00 E
119	Jyväskylä (yû′vĕs-kû-lĕ).....Fin.	62·14 N	25·46 E
167	Kaalfontein (kärl-fŏn-tān)..S. Afr. (Johannesburg & Pretoria In.)	26·02 S	28·16 E
154	Kabaena (I.) (kä-bȧ-ā′nȧ).Indon.	5·35 S	121·07 E
164	Kabala (kȧ-bȧ′lȧ)..........S. L.	9·43 N	11·39 W
166	Kabalo (kä-bä′lō).......Con. K.	6·09 S	26·52 E
166	Kabambare (kä-bäm-bä′rȧ) Con. K.	4·47 S	27·45 E
153	Kabe (kä′bā)...............Jap.	34·32 N	132·30 E
166	Kabinda (kä-bēN′dä).....Con. K.	6·13 S	24·16 E
139	Kabir (R.) Leb. (Palestine In.)	34·40 N	36·06 E
166	Kabompo (R.) (kȧ-bôm′pō) Zambia	13·52 S	23·45 E
166	Kabongo (kȧ-bông′ô).....Con. K.	7·58 S	25·10 E
114	Kaboudia, Ras (C.).........Tun.	35·17 N	11·28 E
142	Kābul (kä′bōōl)............Afg.	34·39 N	69·14 E
145	Kabul (R.) (kä′bōōl)........Asia	34·44 N	69·43 E
135	Kachuga (kȧ-chōō-gȧ)...Sov. Un.	54·09 N	105·43 E
129	Kadiyevka (kȧ-dĭ-yĕf′kȧ).Sov. Un.	48·34 N	38·37 E
132	Kadnikov (käd′nê-kôf)..Sov. Un.	59·30 N	40·10 E
164	Kaduna (kä-dōō′nä).........Nig.	10·29 N	7·32 E
164	Kaédi (kä-ā-dē′)......Mauritania	16·20 N	13·32 W
157	Kaena Pt. (kä′ȧ-nä)..Hawaii (In.)	21·33 N	158·19 W
152	Kaesŏng (Kaijo) (kä′ĕ-sŭng) (kī′jō).Kor.	38·00 N	126·35 E
165	Kafia Kingi (kä′fê-ȧ kĭŋ′gê)..Sud.	9·17 N	24·28 E
166	Kafue (kä′fōō-*).........Zambia	15·45 S	28·17 E
166	Kafue (R.)...............Zambia	15·31 S	26·33 E
129	Kagal'nik (R.) (kä-gäl″nêk) Sov. Un.	46·58 N	39·25 E
166	Kagera (R.) (kä-gā′rȧ)......Tan.	1·17 S	31·04 E
153	Kagoshima (kä′gô-shē′mȧ)...Jap.	31·35 N	130·31 E
153	Kagoshima-Wan (B.) (kä′gô-shē′mȧ wăn).Jap.	31·24 N	130·39 E
129	Kagul (ka-gōōl′)........Sov. Un.	45·49 N	28·17 E
154	Kahajan (R.).............Indon.	1·45 S	113·40 E
73	Kahoka (kȧ-hō′kȧ)...........Mo.	40·26 N	91·42 W
157	Kahoolawe (I.) (kä-hōō-lä′wē) Hawaii (In.)	20·28 N	156·48 W
71	Kahshahpiwi (R.)...........Can.	48·24 N	90·56 W
157	Kahuku Pt. (kä-hōō′kōō) Hawaii (In.)	21·50 N	157·50 W
139	Kaiang.....Mala. (Singapore In.)	3·00 N	101·47 E
69	Kaibab Ind. Res. (kä′ē-bȧb).Ariz.	36·55 N	112·45 W
69	Kaibab Plat...............Ariz.	36·30 N	112·10 W
99	Kaieteur Fall (kī-ĕ-tōōr′)....Guy.	4·48 N	59·24 W
148	K'aifeng (käī′fĕng).........China	34·48 N	114·22 E
	Kaijo, see Kaesong		
152	Kaikyo, Sōya (Str.) (sô′yȧ kȧ-ē′kĭ-ô).Sov. Un.	45·45 N	141·20 E
157	Kailua (kä′ē-lōō′ä).Hawaii (In.)	19·49 N	155·59 W
155	Kaimana...............W. Irian	3·32 S	133·47 E
159	Kaimanawa Ra. (kä′ê-mȧ-nä′wȧ) N. Z. (In.)	39·13 S	176·02 E
153	Kainan (kä′ē-nȧn′)..........Jap.	34·09 N	135·14 E
148	Kaip'ing (kī-pĭng′).........China	40·25 N	122·20 E
164	Kairouan (kĕr-ōō-äN′).......Tun.	35·46 N	10·04 E
120	Kaiserslautern (kī-zĕrs-lou′tẽrn) Ger.	49·26 N	7·46 E
159	Kaitaia (kä-ê-tä′ê-ȧ)...N. Z. (In.)	35·30 S	173·28 E
157	Kaiwi Chan (kä′ê-wē).Hawaii (In.)	21·10 N	157·38 W
151	Kaiyüan (kī′yōō-än′).......China	23·42 N	103·20 E
150	Kaiyuan (kī′yōō-än′).......China	42·30 N	124·00 E
64	Kaiyuh Mts. (kī-yōō′).....Alaska	64·25 N	157·38 W
112	Kajaani (kä′yȧ-nê)..........Fin.	64·15 N	27·16 E
154	Kajan, Sungai (Strm.).....Indon.	1·45 N	115·38 E
139	Kajang, Gunong (Mt.) Mala. (Singapore In.)	2·47 N	104·05 E
153	Kajiki (kä′jē-kê)............Jap.	31·44 N	130·41 E
129	Kakhovka (kä-Kôf′kȧ)...Sov. Un.	46·46 N	33·32 E
129	Kakhovskoye (L.) (kȧ-Kôf′skô-yĕ) Sov. Un.	47·21 N	33·33 E
145	Kākināda..................India	16·58 N	82·18 E
165	Kakindu (kȧ-kĭn′dōō)........Ug.	1·06 N	32·59 E
64	Kaktovik (kăk-tō′vĭk).....Alaska	70·08 N	143·51 W
133	Kalach (kȧ-lȧch′).......Sov. Un.	50·15 N	40·55 E
146	Kaladan (R.)...............Bur.	21·07 N	93·04 E
166	Kalahari Des. (kä-lä-hä′rê)..Bots.	23·00 S	22·03 E
65	Kalama (kȧ-lăm′ȧ) Wash. (Portland In.)	46·01 N	122·50 W
65	Kalama (R.).Wash. (Portland In.)	46·03 N	122·47 W
127	Kalámai (kä-lä-mī′).........Grc.	37·04 N	22·08 E
80	Kalamazoo (kăl-ȧ-mȧ-zōō′).Mich.	42·20 N	85·40 W
80	Kalamazoo (R.)...........Mich.	42·35 N	86·00 W
129	Kalanchak (kä-län-chäk′) Sov. Un.	46·17 N	33·14 E
157	Kalapana (kä-lä-pȧ′nä) Hawaii (In.)	19·25 N	155·00 W
144	Kalar (Mtn.)...............Iran	31·43 N	51·41 E
142	Kalat (kŭ-lät′)..........W. Pak.	29·05 N	66·36 E
154	Kalatoa (I.)..............Indon.	7·22 S	122·30 E
123	Kaldenkirchen (käl′dĕn-kēr-Kĕn) Ger. (Ruhr In.)	51·19 N	6·13 E
150	Kalgan (käl-gän′)..........China	40·45 N	114·58 E
158	Kalgoorlie (kăl-gōōr′lê).....Austl.	30·45 S	121·35 E
115	Kaliakra, Nos (Pt.)........Rom.	43·25 N	28·42 E
154	Kalimantan (Prov.).......Indon.	1·00 S	113·48 E
128	Kalinin (Tver) (kȧ′lê-nên) (tvĕr).Sov. Un.	56·52 N	35·57 E
128	Kalinin (Oblast).......Sov. Un.	56·50 N	33·08 E
119	Kaliningrad (Königsberg) (kä-lē-nēn′grät) (kû′nēks-bĕrgh) Sov. Un.	54·42 N	20·32 E
136	Kaliningrad (kä-lê-nēn′grät) Sov. Un. (Moscow In.)	55·55 N	37·49 E
129	Kalinkovichi (kä-lēn-ko-vē′chê) Sov. Un.	52·07 N	29·19 E
66	Kalispel Ind. Res. (kăl-ĭ-spĕl′) Wash.	48·25 N	117·30 W
67	Kalispell (kăl′ĭ-spĕl).......Mont.	48·12 N	114·18 W
121	Kalisz (kä′lēsh)............Pol.	51·45 N	18·05 E
112	Kalix (R.) (kä′lēks).........Swe.	67·12 N	21·41 E
166	Kalkfeld (kälk′fĕlt)....S. W. Afr.	21·05 S	16·05 E
166	Kalkfontein (kälk′fŏn-tān) S. W. Afr.	27·50 S	18·40 E
118	Kalmar (käl′mär)...........Swe.	56·40 N	16·19 E
118	Kalmar Sund (Sd.) (käl′mär) Swe.	56·30 N	16·17 E
129	Kal'mius (R.) (käl″myōōs) Sov. Un.	47 15 N	37·38 E
111	Kalmthout.....Bel. (Brussels In.)	51·23 N	4·28 E
143	Kalmunai................Ceylon	7·22 N	81·49 E
133	Kalmyk A. S. S. R. (kȧl′mĭk) Sov. Un.	46·56 N	46·00 E
121	Kalocsa (kä′lô-chä)........Hung.	46·32 N	19·00 E
157	Kalohi Chan. (kä-lō′hĭ) Hawaii (In.)	20·55 N	157·15 W
166	Kalomo (kä-lō′mō).......Zambia	17·06 S	26·22 E
142	Kalsubai Mt..............India	24·43 N	73·47 E
111	Kaltenkirchen (käl′tĕn-kēr-Kĕn) Ger. (Hamburg In.)	53·50 N	9·57 E
143	Kālu (R.)....India (Bombay In.)	19·18 N	73·14 E
128	Kaluga (kȧ-lōō′gä)......Sov. Un.	54·29 N	36·12 E
128	Kaluga (Oblast).........Sov. Un.	54·10 N	34·30 E
118	Kalundborg (kȧ-lōōn″bôr′)..Den.	55·42 N	11·07 E
121	Kalush (kä′lōōsh).......Sov. Un.	49·02 N	24·24 E
119	Kalvarija (käl-vä-rē′yȧ).Sov. Un.	54·24 N	23·17 E
136	Kal'ya (käl′yȧ) Sov. Un. (Urals In.)	60·17 N	59·58 E
143	Kalyān......India (Bombay In.)	19·16 N	73·07 E
128	Kalyazin (käl-yȧ′zēn)....Sov. Un.	57·13 N	37·55 E
135	Kalyma (R.)............Sov. Un.	66·32 N	152·46 E
132	Kama (L.)..............Sov. Un.	55·28 N	51·00 E
132	Kama (R.) (kä′mä)......Sov. Un.	56·52 N	54·35 E
164	Kamabai (kä-mä-bä′ê)......S. L.	9·13 N	11·56 W
152	Kamaishi (kä′mä-ē′shê)......Jap.	39·16 N	142·03 E
153	Kamakura (kä′mä-kōō′rä) Jap. (Tōkyō In.)	35·19 N	139·33 E
144	Kamarān (I.) (Br.).........Aden	15·19 N	41·47 E
166	Kambove (käm-bō′vĕ)....Con. K.	10·58 S	26·43 E
135	Kamchatka, P-Ov (Pen.).Sov. Un.	55·19 N	157·45 E
135	Kamchatka (R.)........Sov. Un.	54·15 N	158·38 E
123	Kamen (kä′mĕn).Ger. (Ruhr In.)	51·35 N	7·40 E
129	Kamenets-Podol'skiy (kȧ-mă′nĕts pô-dôl′skĭ).Sov. Un.	48·41 N	26·34 E
126	Kamenjak, Rt (C.) (Kä′mĕ-nyäk) Yugo.	44·45 N	13·57 E
129	Kamenka (kä-mĕŋ′kȧ)...Sov. Un.	48·02 N	28·43 E
121	Kamenka...............Sov. Un.	50·06 N	24·20 E
134	Kamen'-na-Obi (kä-mĭny′nŭ ô′bē) Sov. Un.	53·43 N	81·28 E
129	Kamensk-Shakhtinskiy (kä′mĕnsk shäk′tĭn-skĭ).Sov. Un.	48·17 N	40·16 E
136	Kamensk-Ural'skiy (kä′mĕn-skĭ ōō-räl′skĭ) Sov. Un. (Urals In.)	56·27 N	61·55 E
120	Kamenz (kä′mĕnts).........Ger.	51·16 N	14·05 E

ăt; finăl; rāte; senâte; ärm; ȧsk; sofȧ; fâre; ch-choose; dh-as th in other; bē; êvent; bĕt; recĕnt; cratẽr; g-go; gh-guttural g; bĭt; ĭ-short neutra ; rīde; K-guttural k as ch in German ich;

Page	Name Pronunciation Region	Lat. °′	Long. °′
153	Kameoka (kä'mä-ōkä) Jap. (Osaka In.)	35·01 N	135·35 E
142	Kámet (Mt.) India	35·50 N	79·42 E
120	Kamień Pomorski Pol.	53·57 N	14·48 E
153	Kamikoma (kä'mē-kō'mä) Jap. (Ōsaka In.)	34·45 N	135·50 E
166	Kamina Con. K.	8·41 S	25·01 E
71	Kaministikwia (R.) (kà-mǐ-nǐ-stǐk'wǐ-à). Can.	48·40 N	89·41 W
86	Kamloops (kăm'lōōps) Can.	50·41 N	120·19 W
	Kammer, see Atter See		
142	Kampa Dzong China	28·23 N	89·42 E
165	Kampala (käm-pä'lä) Ug.	0·14 N	32·34 E
154	Kampar (Strm.) (käm'pär) Indon.	0·30 N	101·30 E
111	Kampenhout Bel. (Brussels In.)	50·56 N	4·33 E
123	Kamp-Lintfort (kämp-lēnt'fōrt) Ger. (Ruhr In.)	51·30 N	6·34 E
154	Kampot (käm'pōt) Camb.	10·41 N	104·07 E
120	Kamp R. (kămp) Aus.	48·30 N	15·45 E
86	Kamsack (kăm'săk) Can.	51·32 N	102·00 W
103	Kamskoye (Res.) Sov. Un.	59·08 N	56·30 E
136	Kamskoye Vodokranilishche (L.) Sov. Un. (Urals In.)	59·03 N	56·48 E
93	Kamuk, Cerro (Mt.) (sĕ'r-rô-kä-mōō'k). C. R.	9·18 N	83·02 W
152	Kamu Misaki (C.) (kä'mōō mē-sä'kē). Jap.	43·25 N	139·35 E
129	Kamyshevatskaya (kà-mwēsh'ĕ-vät'skä-yà). Sov. Un.	46·24 N	37·58 E
133	Kamyshin (kä-mwēsh'ĭn) Sov. Un.	50·08 N	45·20 E
132	Kamyshlov (kä-mēsh'lôf) Sov. Un.	56·50 N	62·32 E
151	Kan (R.) (kän) China	26·50 N	115·00 E
134	Kan (R.) Sov. Un.	56·30 N	94·17 E
69	Kanab (kăn'ăb) Utah	37·00 N	112·30 W
69	Kanab Plat. Ariz.	36·31 N	112·55 W
136	Kanabeki (kà-nä'byĕ-kĭ) Sov. Un. (Urals In.)	57·48 N	57·16 E
64	Kanaga (I.) (kă-nă'gă) Alaska	52·02 N	177·38 W
153	Kanagawa (Pref.) (kä'nä-gä'wä) Jap. (Tōkyō In.)	35·29 N	139·32 E
153	Kanamachi (kä-nä-mä'chē) Jap. (Tōkyō In.)	35·46 N	139·52 E
136	Kananikol'skoye (kà-nà-nǐ-kôl'skô-yě). Sov. Un. (Urals In.)	52·48 N	57·29 E
92	Kanasín (kä-nä-sē'n) Mex. (Yucatan In.)	20·54 N	89·31 W
64	Kanatak (kă-nă'tŏk) Alaska	57·35 N	155·48 W
63	Kanawha (R.) (kà-nô'wà) U. S.	37·55 N	81·50 W
153	Kanaya (kä-nä'yä) Jap. (Tōkyō In.)	35·10 N	139·49 E
115	Kanayis, Rasel (C.) U. A. R.	31·14 N	28·08 E
153	Kanazawa (kä'nà-zä'wà) Jap.	36·34 N	136·38 E
143	Kancheepuram India	12·55 N	79·43 E
142	Kanchenjunga, Mt. (kĭn-chĭn-jōōŋ'gà). Nep.	32·40 N	88·18 E
151	Kanchou (kăn'chou) China	25·50 N	115·00 E
145	Kandahār (kŭn-dŭ-här') Afg.	31·43 N	65·58 E
166	Kanda Kanda (kän'dà kän'dà) Con. K.	6·51 S	23·27 E
132	Kandalaksha (kàn-dà-làk'shà) Sov. Un.	67·10 N	33·05 E
132	Kandalakshskiy Zaliv (B.) Sov. Un.	66·20 N	35·00 E
119	Kandava (kän'dà-và) Sov. Un.	57·03 N	22·45 E
164	Kandi (käN-dē') Dahomey	11·09 N	3·02 E
142	Kandiaro W. Pak.	27·09 N	68·12 E
142	Kandla (kŭnd'lŭ) India	23·00 N	70·20 E
143	Kandy (kän'dē) Ceylon	7·18 N	80·42 E
81	Kane (kān) Pa.	41·40 N	78·50 W
157	Kaneohe B. (kä-nā-ō'hā) Hawaii (In.)	21·32 N	157·40 W
129	Kanëv (kä-nyôf') Sov. Un.	49·46 N	31·27 E
129	Kanevskaya (kà-nyěf'skà-yà) Sov. Un.	46·07 N	38·58 E
160	Kangaroo (I.) (kăŋ-gà-rōō') Austl.	36·05 S	137·05 E
144	Kangāvar (kŭŋ'gä-vär) Iran	34·37 N	46·45 E
154	Kangean (I.) (käŋ'gē-än) Indon.	6·50 S	116·22 E
152	Kanggye (käng'gyĕ) Kor.	40·55 N	126·40 E
152	Kanghwa (I.) (käng'hwä) Kor.	37·28 N	126·00 E
152	Kangnŭng(käng'nōōng) Kor.	37·42 N	128·50 E
166	Kango (käN-gō') Gabon	0·14 N	10·07 E
146	K'angting China	30·15 N	101·58 E
87	Kaniapiskau (L.) (kă-nǐ-ăp'ĭs-kô) Can.	54·04 N	71·20 W
87	Kaniapiskau (R.) Can.	56·52 N	68·53 W
132	Kanin, P-Ov. (Pen.) (kà-nēn') Sov. Un.	68·00 N	45·00 E
132	Kanin Nos, Mys (C.) Sov. Un.	68·40 N	44·00 E
127	Kanjiža (kä'nyē-zhä) Yugo.	46·05 N	20·02 E
75	Kankakee (kăŋ-kà-kē') Ill. (Chicago In.)	41·07 N	87·53 W
80	Kankakee (R.) Ill.	41·15 N	88·15 W
164	Kankan (käN-käN) (kän-kän'). Gui	10·20 N	9·16 W
150	Kannan China	47·50 N	123·30 E
79	Kannapolis (kăn-ăp'ô-lĭs) N. C.	35·30 N	80·38 W
153	Kannoura (kä'nō-ōō'rä) Jap.	33·34 N	134·18 E
164	Kano (kä'nō) Nig.	12·03 N	8·32 E
166	Kanonberg (Mtn.) S. Afr. (Cape Town In.)	33·49 S	18·37 E
72	Kanopolis Res. (kăn-ŏp'ô-lĭs) Kans.	38·44 N	98·01 W
142	Kānpur (kän'pûr) India	26·00 N	82·45 E
62	Kansas (State) (kăn'zàs) U. S.	38·30 N	99·40 W
73	Kansas (R.) Kans.	39·08 N	95·52 W
74	Kansas City Kans. (Kansas City In.)	39·06 N	94·39 W
74	Kansas City. Mo. (Kansas City In.)	39·05 N	94·35 W
134	Kansk Sov. Un.	56·14 N	95·43 E
152	Kansŏng Kor.	38·09 N	128·29 E
146	Kansu (Prov.) (kän'sōō') China	38·00 N	102·06 E
154	Kan Tang (kän'täng') Thai.	7·26 N	99·28 E
92	Kantunilkin (kän-tōō-nēl-kē'n) Mex. (Yucatan In.)	21·07 N	87·30 W
136	Kanzhakovskiy Kamen Gora (kàn-zhă'kôvs-kēē kămiēn) Sov. Un. (Urals In.)	59·38 N	59·12 E
151	Kaoan China	28·30 N	115·02 E
148	Kaoch'eng (kä'ō-chěng') China	34·56 N	114·57 E
149	Kaoch'iao China (Shanghai In.)	31·21 N	121·35 E
151	Kaohsiung (kä'ô-syōōng'). Taiwan	22·35 N	120·25 E
148	Kaoi (gou'yē) China	37·37 N	114·39 E
164	Kaolack Senegal	14·02 N	16·16 W
148	Kaomi (gou'mē) China	36·23 N	119·46 E
148	Kaoshun (gou'shōōn) China	31·22 N	118·50 E
148	Kaot'ang (kä'ō-täng') China	36·52 N	116·12 E
151	Kaoteng Shan (Mtns.) China	26·30 N	110·00 E
165	Kaovar (Oasis) Niger	19·16 N	13·09 E
151	Kaoyao China	23·08 N	112·25 E
148	Kaoyu (gou'yû) China	32·46 N	119·26 E
151	Kaoyu Hu (L.) (kä'ō-yōō'hōō) China	32·42 N	118·40 E
134	Kapal (kà-päl') Sov. Un.	45·13 N	79·08 E
120	Kapfenberg (käp'fĕn-bĕrgh) Aus.	47·27 N	15·16 E
165	Kapoeta Sud.	4·45 N	33·35 E
121	Kaposvár (kô'pôsh-vär) Hung.	46·21 N	17·45 E
152	Kapsan (käp'sän') Kor.	40·59 N	128·22 E
154	Kapuas, Sungai (Strm.) (kä'pōō-äs). Indon.	2·05 S	114·15 E
87	Kapuskasing Can.	49·28 N	82·22 W
133	Kapustin Yar (kä'pōōs-tēn yär') Sov. Un.	48·30 N	45·40 E
160	Kaputar, Mt. (kă-pû-tăr) Austl.	30·11 S	150·11 E
120	Kapuvár (kô'pōō-vär) Hung.	47·35 N	17·02 E
134	Kara (kärà) Sov. Un.	68·42 N	65·30 E
132	Kara (R.) Sov. Un.	68·30 N	65·20 E
136	Karabanovo (kä'rà-bà-nō-vô) Sov. Un. (Moscow In.)	56·19 N	38·43 E
136	Karabash (kó-rà-băsh') Sov. Un. (Urals In.)	55·27 N	60·14 E
133	Kara-Bogaz-Gol, Zaliv (B.) (kàrä' bŭ-gäs'). Sov. Un.	41·30 N	53·40 E
128	Karachev (kà-rà-chôf') Sov. Un.	53·08 N	34·54 E
142	Karachi W. Pak.	24·59 N	68·56 E
103	Karacumy (Des.) Sov. Un.	39·08 N	59·53 E
134	Karaganda (kà-rà-gän'dä) Sov. Un.	49·42 N	73·18 E
136	Karaidel (kä'rĭ-dĕl) Sov. Un. (Urals In.)	55·52 N	56·54 E
133	Kara-Khobda (R.) (kä-rà kôb'dà). Sov. Un.	50·40 N	55·00 E
145	Karakoram Pass India & Pak.	35·35 N	77·45 E
146	Karakoram Ra. (kä'rä kō'rōōm) India & Pak.	35·24 N	76·38 E
146	Karakorum (Ruins) Mong.	47·25 N	102·22 E
133	Karaköse (kä-rä-kŭ'sĕ) Tur.	39·50 N	43·10 E
130	Karakumy (kara-kum) (Des.) Sov. Un.	40·00 N	57·00 E
133	Karaman (kä-rä-män') Tur.	37·10 N	33·00 E
159	Karamea Bght. (kà-rà-mē'à bīt) N. Z. (In.)	41·10 S	170·42 E
144	Karand Iran	34·08 N	46·19 E
	Kara Sea, see Karskoye More		
153	Karatsu (kä'rà-tsōō) Jap.	33·28 N	129·59 E
134	Karaul (kä-rä-ōōl') Sov. Un.	70·13 N	83·46 E
120	Karawanken Mts. Aus.	46·32 N	14·07 E
144	Karbala (kŭr'bà-lä) Iraq	32·31 N	43·58 E
121	Karcag (kär'tsäg) Hung.	47·18 N	20·58 E
127	Kardhítsa Grc.	39·23 N	21·57 E
119	Kärdla (kĕrd'là) Sov. Un.	58·59 N	22·44 E
165	Kareima (kä-rā'mà) Sud.	18·34 N	31·49 E
132	Karelian (A. S. S. R.) Sov. Un.	62·30 N	32·35 E
166	Karema Tan.	6·47 S	30·29 E
134	Kargat (kär-gät') Sov. Un.	55·17 N	80·07 E
	Karghalik, see Yehch'eng		
132	Kargopol' (kär-gō-pōl'') Sov. Un.	61·30 N	38·50 E
127	Kariaí Grc.	40·14 N	24·15 E
166	Kariba L. Zambia	17·30 S	28·06 E
166	Karibib (kär'à-bĭb) S. W. Afr.	21·55 S	15·50 E
143	Kārikāl (kä-rē-käl') India	10·58 N	79·49 E
164	Karimama (kä-rē-mä'mà) Dahomey	12·04 N	3·09 E
154	Karimata, Pulau-Pulau (Is.) (kä-rē-mä'tà). Indon.	1·08 S	108·10 E
154	Karimata, Selat (Str.) Indon.	1·15 S	107·10 E
154	Karimundjawa (I.) (kä'rē-mōōn-yä'vä). Indon.	5·36 S	110·15 E
168	Karin (kär'ĭn) Som. (Horn of Afr. In.)	10·43 N	45·50 E
155	Karkar (I.) (kär'kär). N. Gui. Ter.	4·50 S	146·45 E
134	Karkaralinsk (kär-kär-ä-lēnsk') Sov. Un.	49·18 N	75·28 E
129	Karkinitskiy Zailv (B.) (kär-kē-net'skĭ-ē zä'lĭf). Sov. Un.	45·50 N	32·45 E
120	Karl-Marx-Stadt (Chemnitz). Ger.	50·48 N	12·53 E
126	Karlobag (kär-lō-bäg') Yugo.	44·30 N	15·03 E
126	Karlovac (kär'lō-våts) Yugo.	45·29 N	15·16 E
129	Karlovka (kär'lôv-kà) Sov. Un.	49·26 N	35·08 E
127	Karlovo (kär'lō-vō) Bul.	42·39 N	24·48 E
120	Karlovy Vary (kär'lô-vē vä'rē) Czech.	50·13 N	12·53 E
118	Karlshamn (kärls'häm) Swe.	56·11 N	14·50 E
118	Karlskrona (kärls'krō-nà) Swe.	56·10 N	15·33 E
120	Karlsruhe (kärls'rōō-ē) Ger.	49·00 N	8·23 E
118	Karlstad (kärl'städ) Swe.	59·25 N	13·28 E
64	Karluk (kär'lŭk) Alaska	57·30 N	154·22 W
118	Karmöy (I.) (kärm-ûe) Nor.	59·14 N	5·00 E
127	Karnobat (kär-nô'bät) Bul.	42·39 N	26·59 E
120	Kärnten (Carinthia) (State) (kĕrn'tĕn). Aus.	46·55 N	13·42 E
166	Karonga (kà-rōŋ'gà) Malawi	9·52 S	33·57 E
115	Kárpathos (I.) Grc.	35·34 N	27·26 E
136	Karpinsk (kär'pĭnsk) Sov. Un. (Urals In.)	59·46 N	60·00 E
133	Kars (kärs) Tur.	40·35 N	43·00 E
134	Karsakpay (kär-säk-pī') Sov. Un.	47·47 N	67·07 E
128	Kārsava (kär'sà-vä) Sov. Un.	56·46 N	27·39 E
145	Karshi (kär'shē) Sov. Un.	38·30 N	66·08 E
134	Karskiye Vorota, Proliv (Str.) Sov. Un.	70·30 N	58·07 E
134	Karskoye More (Kara Sea) Sov. Un.	74·00 N	68·00 E
136	Kartaly (kàr'tá lē) Sov. Un. (Urals In.)	53·05 N	60·40 E
143	Karunagapalli India	9·09 N	76·34 E
121	Karvina Czech.	49·50 N	18·30 E
166	Kasai (R.) Con. K.	3·45 S	19·07 E
166	Kasama (kà-sä'mà) Zambia	10·15 S	31·13 E
166	Kasanga (kà-säŋ'gà) Tan.	8·27 S	31·13 E
153	Kasaoka (kä'sà-ō'kà) Jap.	34·33 N	133·29 E
164	Kasba-Tadla (käs'bà-täd'là). Mor.	32·37 N	5·57 W
166	Kasempa (kà-sĕm'pà) Zambia	13·15 S	25·41 E
166	Kasenga (kà-sĕŋ'gà) Con. K.	10·27 S	28·42 E
144	Kash (R.) (kŭsh) Afg.	32·27 N	64·15 E
144	Kāshān (kä-shän') Iran	33·52 N	51·15 E
	Kashqar, see Sufu		
153	Kashihara (kä'shē-hä'rä) Jap. (Ōsaka In.)	34·35 N	135·38 E
128	Kashin (kä-shēn') Sov. Un.	57·20 N	37·38 E
128	Kashira (kä-shē'rà) Sov. Un.	54·49 N	38·11 E
153	Kashiwa (kä'shē-wä) Jap. (Tōkyō In.)	35·51 N	139·58 E
152	Kashiwazaki (kä'shē-wä-zä'kē) Jap.	37·06 N	138·17 E
	Kashmir, see Jammu and Kashmir		
142	Kashmor W. Pak.	28·33 N	69·34 E
136	Kashtak (käsh'ták) Sov. Un. (Urals In.)	55·18 N	61·25 E
128	Kasimov (kà-sē'môf) Sov. Un.	54·56 N	41·23 E
64	Kaskanak (kăs-kă'năk) Alaska	60·00 N	158·00 W
80	Kaskaskia (R.) (kăs-kăs'kĭ-à) Ill.	38·45 N	89·15 W
	Kaskinem, see Kaskö		
119	Kaskö (Kaskinen) (käs'kû) (käs'kē-nĕn). Fin.	62·24 N	21·18 E
136	Kasli (käs'lĭ). Sov. Un. (Urals In.)	55·54 N	60·46 E
166	Kasongo (kä-sôŋ'gō) Con. K.	4·31 S	26·42 E
115	Kásos (I.) Grc.	35·20 N	26·55 E
165	Kassala (kä-sä'lä) Sud.	15·26 N	36·28 E
120	Kassel (käs'ĕl) Ger.	51·19 N	9·30 E
71	Kasson (kăs'ŭn) Minn.	44·01 N	92·45 W
133	Kastamonu (kä-stà-mō'nōō) Tur.	41·20 N	33·50 E
126	Kastélli Grc. (Inset)	35·13 N	24·11 E
115	Kastellórizon (C.) Tur.	36·01 N	30·00 E
127	Kastoría (kàs-tō'rĭ-à) Grc.	40·28 N	21·17 E
127	Kastron (käs'trôn) Grc.	39·52 N	25·01 E
142	Kasur W. Pak.	31·10 N	74·29 E
82	Katahdin, Mt. (kà-tä'dĭn) Maine	45·56 N	68·57 W
166	Katanga (Reg.) (kà-täŋ'gà) Con. K.	8·35 S	23·59 E
158	Katanning (kà-tăn'ĭng) Austl.	33·45 S	117·45 E
136	Katav-Ivanovsk (kä'tăf ĭ-vä'nôfsk). Sov. Un. (Urals In.)	54·46 N	58·13 E
136	Kateninskiy (kàtyĕ'nĭs-kĭ) Sov. Un. (Urals In.)	53·12 N	61·05 E
127	Katerini Grc.	40·18 N	22·36 E
165	Katherina, G. (Pk.) U. A. R.	28·43 N	34·00 E
158	Katherine (kăth'ĕr-ĭn) Austl.	14·15 S	132·20 E
142	Kathiawar Pen. (kä'tyà-wär') India	27·18 N	70·32 E
85	Kathryn (kăth'rĭn) Can. (Calgary In.)	51·13 N	113·42 W
74	Kathryn. Calif. (Los Angeles In.)	33·42 N	117·45 W
142	Katiha India	25·39 N	87·39 E
64	Katmai Natl. Mon. (kăt'mī) Alaska	58·38 N	155·00 W
142	Kātmāndu (kät-män-dōō') Nep.	27·49 N	85·21 E
121	Katowice Pol.	50·15 N	19·00 E
118	Katrineholm (kà-trē'nĕ-hōlm) Swe.	59·01 N	16·10 E
136	Katsbakhskiy (kàts-băk'skĭ) Sov. Un. (Urals In.)	52·57 N	59·37 E
164	Katsina (kăt'sē-nà) Nig.	13·03 N	7·39 E
164	Katsina Ala (ä'lä) Nig.	7·15 N	9·12 E
153	Katsura (R.) (kä'tsōō-rä) Jap. (Ōsaka In.)	34·55 N	135·43 E
134	Katta-Kurgan (kà-tà-kōōr-gän') Sov. Un.	39·45 N	66·42 E
118	Kattegat (Str.) (kăt'ĕ-gät) Eur.	56·57 N	11·25 E
134	Katun' (R.) (kà-tōōn') Sov. Un.	51·30 N	86·18 E
111	Katwijkaan Zee Neth. (Amsterdam In.)	52·12 N	4·23 E
157	Kauai (I.) Hawaii (In.)	22·09 N	159·15 W
157	Kauai Chan. (kä-ōō-ä'ē) Hawaii (In.)	21·35 N	158·52 W
120	Kaufbeuren (kouf'boi-rĕn) Ger.	47·52 N	10·38 E
77	Kaufman (kôf'măn) Tex.	32·36 N	96·18 W
71	Kaukauna (kô-kô'nà) Wis.	44·17 N	88·15 W
157	Kaulakahi Chan. (kä'ōō-lä-kä'hē) Hawaii (In.)	22·00 N	159·55 W
157	Kaunakakai (kä'ōō-nà-kä'kī) Hawaii (In.)	21·06 N	156·59 E
119	Kaunas (Kovno) (kou'nàs) (kôv'nô). Sov. Un.	54·52 N	23·54 E
164	Kaure Namoda Nig.	12·41 N	7·32 E
127	Kavajë (kà-vä'yŭ) Alb.	41·11 N	19·36 E
127	Kavála (kä-vä'lä) Grc.	40·55 N	24·24 E
127	Kavallas, Kólpos (G.) Grc.	40·45 N	24·20 E
155	Kavieng (kä-vē-ĕng'). N. Gui. Ter.	2·44 S	151·02 E
153	Kawagoe (kä-wă-gō'ā) Jap. (Tōkyō In.)	35·55 N	139·29 E
153	Kawaguchi (kä-wä-gōō-chē) Jap. (Tōkyō In.)	35·48 N	139·44 E
157	Kawaikini (Mtn.) (kä-wä'ē-kĭ-nĭ). Hawaii (In.)	22·05 N	159·33 W
153	Kawasaki (kä-wä-sä'kē) Jap. (Tōkyō In.)	35·32 N	139·43 E

ng-sing; ŋ-baŋk; N-nasalized n; nŏd; cŏmmit; ōld; ôbey; ôrder; fōōd; fŏŏt; ou-out; s-soft; sh-dish; th-thin; pūre; ûnite; ûrn; stŭd; circŭs; ü-as "y" in study; '-indeterminate vowel.

222 Kawm Umbu–Killdeer PRONOUNCING INDEX

Page	Name Pronunciation Region	Lat. °′	Long. °′
168	Kawm Umbū . . U. A. R. (Nile In.)	24·30 N	32·59 E
164	Kaya (kä'yä) . . . Upper Volta	12·59 N	1·21 W
67	Kaycee (kā-sē') . . . Wyo.	43·43 N	106·38 W
164	Kayes (kāz) . . . Mali	14·20 N	11·33 W
133	Kayseri (kī'sĕ-rē) . . . Tur.	38·45 N	35·20 E
74	Kaysville (kāz'vĭl) Utah (Salt Lake City In.)	41·02 N	111·56 W
135	Kazach'ye . . . Sov. Un.	70·46 N	135·47 E
130	Kazakh S. S. R. (kà-zäk') . Sov. Un.	48·45 N	59·00 E
132	Kazan' (kà-zän') . . . Sov. Un.	55·50 N	49·18 E
129	Kazanka (kà-zän'kà) . . . Sov. Un.	47·49 N	32·50 E
127	Kazanlŭk (kà'zàn-lĕk) . . . Bul.	42·47 N	25·23 E
129	Kazatin . . . Sov. Un.	49·43 N	28·50 E
133	Kazbek, Gora (Mt.) (kàz-bĕk') Sov. Un.	42·45 N	44·30 E
144	Kāzerūn . . . Iran	29·37 N	51·44 E
121	Kazincbarcika (kô'zĭnts-bôr-tsĭ-ko) . Hung.	48·15 N	20·39 E
153	Kazusa Kameyama (kä-zōō-sä kä-mā'yä-mä) . Jap. (Tōkyō In.)	35·14 N	140·06 E
134	Kazym (R.) (kä-zēm') . . . Sov. Un.	63·30 N	67·41 E
127	Kéa (I.) . . . Grc.	37·36 N	24·13 E
157	Kealaikahiki Chan. (kā-ä'lä-ē-kä-hē'kē) Hawaii (In.)	20·38 N	157·00 W
84	Keansburg (kēnz'bûrg) N. J. (New York In.)	40·26 N	74·08 W
72	Kearney (kär'nĭ) . . . Nebr.	40·42 N	99·05 W
84	Kearny . . . N. J. (New York In.)	40·46 N	74·09 W
65	Keasey (kēz'ĭ) . Ore. (Portland In.)	45·51 N	123·20 W
112	Kebnekaise (Mtn.) (kĕp'nĕ-kà-ēs'ĕ) . Swe.	67·53 N	18·10 E
121	Kecskemét (kĕch'kĕ-māt) . . Hung.	46·52 N	19·42 E
154	Kedah State (kä'dä) . . . Mala.	6·08 N	100·31 E
119	Kédainiai (kē-dī'nĭ-ī) . . . Sov. Un.	55·16 N	23·58 E
82	Kedgwick (kĕdj'wĭk) . . . Can.	47·42 N	67·24 W
74	Keenbrook (kēn'brŏŏk) Calif. (Los Angeles In.)	34·16 N	117·29 W
81	Keene (kēn) . . . N. H.	42·55 N	72·15 W
166	Keetmanshoop (kāt'mäns-hōp) S. W. Afr.	26·30 S	18·05 E
69	Keet Seel Ruin (kēt sēl) . . . Ariz.	36·46 N	110·32 W
71	Keewatin (kē-wä'tĭn) . . . Minn.	47·24 N	93·03 W
86	Keewatin, Dist. of . . . Can.	61·26 N	97·54 W
127	Kefallinía (Cephalonia) (I.) . . Grc.	38·08 N	20·58 E
	Kefe, see Feodosiya		
164	Keffi (kĕf'ē) . . . Nig.	8·52 N	7·49 E
167	Kei (R.) (kā) . . S. Afr. (Natal In.)	32·57 S	26·50 E
119	Keila (kā'là) . . . Sov. Un.	59·19 N	24·25 E
167	Kei Mouth . . . S. Afr. (Natal In.)	32·40 S	28·23 E
167	Keiskammahoek (käs'kämä-hŏŏk') S. Afr. (Natal In.)	32·42 S	27·11 E
119	Keitele (L.) (kā'tĕ-lĕ) . . . Fin.	62·50 N	25·40 E
167	Keiweg . . . S. Afr. (Natal In.)	32·43 S	27·34 E
154	Kelatan State (kĕ-làn-tän') . Mala.	5·11 N	101·51 E
115	Kelkit (R.) . . . Tur.	40·38 N	37·03 E
74	Keller (kĕl'ĕr) Tex. (Dallas, Fort Worth In.)	32·56 N	97·15 W
111	Kellinghusen (kĕ'lĕng-hōō-zĕn) Ger. (Hamburg In.)	53·57 N	9·43 E
66	Kellogg (kĕl'ŏg) . . . Idaho	47·32 N	116·07 W
119	Kelme' (kĕl-mà) . . . Sov. Un.	55·36 N	22·53 E
86	Kelowna . . . Can.	49·49 N	119·17 W
65	Kelso . . . Wash. (Portland In.)	46·09 N	122·54 W
132	Kem' (kĕm) . . . Sov. Un.	65·00 N	34·48 E
77	Kemah (kē'mà) . . . Tex. (In.)	29·32 N	95·01 W
165	Kemboma (kĕm-bō-mä') . . . Gabon	0·43 N	13·34 E
112	Kemi (kā'mē) . . . Fin.	65·48 N	24·38 E
112	Kemi (R.) . . . Fin.	67·02 N	27·50 E
153	Kemigawa (kĕ'mē-gä'wä) Jap. (Tōkyō In.)	35·38 N	140·07 E
112	Kemijarvi (kā'mē-yĕr-vē) . . . Fin.	66·48 N	27·21 E
112	Kemi-joki (L.) . . . Fin.	66·37 N	28·13 E
67	Kemmerer (kĕm'ĕr-ĕr) . . . Wyo.	41·48 N	110·36 W
72	Kemp (L.) (kĕmp) . . . Tex.	33·55 N	99·22 W
123	Kempen (kĕm'pĕn) . Ger. (Ruhr In.)	51·22 N	6·25 E
160	Kempsey (kĕmp'sē) . . . Austl.	30·59 S	152·50 E
84	Kempsville (kĕmps'vĭl) Va. (Norfolk In.)	36·49 N	76·10 W
82	Kempt (L.) (kĕmpt) . . . Can.	47·28 N	74·00 W
120	Kempten (kĕmp'tĕn) . . . Ger.	47·44 N	10·17 E
167	Kempton Park (kĕmp'tŏn pärk) S. Afr. (Johannesburg & Pretoria In.)	26·07 S	28·29 E
142	Ken (R.) . . . India	25·00 N	79·55 E
64	Kenai (kĕ-nī') . . . Alaska	60·38 N	151·18 W
64	Kenai Mts. . . . Alaska	60·00 N	150·00 W
64	Kenai Pen. . . . Alaska	64·40 N	150·18 W
116	Kendal (kĕn'dăl) . . . Eng.	54·20 N	1·48 W
168	Kendal . . . S. Afr. (Johannesburg & Pretoria In.)	26·03 S	28·58 E
80	Kendallville (kĕn'dăl-vĭl) . . . Ind.	41·25 N	85·20 W
77	Kenedy (kĕn'ĕ-dĭ) . . . Tex.	28·49 N	97·50 W
167	Kenegha (R.) . . S. Afr. (Natal In.)	30·37 S	28·52 E
166	Kenilworth (kĕn'ĭl-wûrth) S. Afr. (Cape Town In.)	33·59 S	18·28 E
114	Kenitra (Port Lyautey) (kĕ-nē'trà) . Mor.	34·21 N	6·34 W
70	Kenmare (kĕn-mâr') . . . N. D.	48·41 N	102·05 W
75	Kenmore (kĕn'mōr) N. Y. (Buffalo In.)	42·58 N	78·53 W
82	Kennebec (R.) (kĕn-ē-bĕk') . Maine	44·23 N	69·48 W
82	Kennebunk (kĕn-ē-bŭnk') . . Maine	43·24 N	70·33 W
74	Kennedale (kĕn'-ē-dāl) Tex. (Dallas, Fort Worth In.)	32·38 N	97·13 W
79	Kennedy, C. . . . Fla. (In.)	28·30 N	80·23 W
77	Kenner (kĕn'ĕr) . . . La.	29·58 N	90·15 W
73	Kennett (kĕn'ĕt) . . . Mo.	36·14 N	90·01 W
66	Kennewick (kĕn'ē-wĭk) . . . Wash.	46·12 N	119·06 W
65	Kennydale (kĕn-nē'-dāl) Wash. (Seattle In.)	47·31 N	122·12 W
82	Kenogami (kĕn-ŏ'gä-mē) . . . Can.	48·27 N	71·15 W
87	Kenora (kē-nō'rà) . . . Can.	49·47 N	94·22 W
75	Kenosha (kĕ-nō'shà) Wis. (Milwaukee In.)	42·34 N	87·50 W
80	Kenova (kē-nō'và) . . . W. Va.	38·20 N	82·35 W

Page	Name Pronunciation Region	Lat. °′	Long. °′
84	Kensico Res. (kĕn'sĭ-kō) N. Y. (New York In.)	41·08 N	73·45 W
80	Kent (kĕnt) . . . Ohio	41·05 N	81·20 W
65	Kent . . . Wash. (Seattle In.)	47·23 N	122·14 W
167	Kentani (kĕnt-änĭ') S. Afr. (Natal In.)	32·31 S	28·19 E
147	Kentei Alin (Mts.) (kĕn'tā'ā-lēn') China	45·54 N	131·45 E
146	Kentei Shan (Mts.) (kĕn'tĭ'shän') Mong.	49·25 N	107·51 E
80	Kentland (kĕnt'lănd) . . . Ind.	40·50 N	87·25 W
80	Kenton (kĕn'tŭn) . . . Ohio	40·40 N	83·35 W
167	Kenton-on-Sea (kĕn'tŏn ŏn sē) S. Afr. (Natal In.)	33·41 S	26·42 E
86	Kent Pen. . . . Can.	68·28 N	108·10 W
63	Kentucky (State) (kĕn-tŭk'ĭ) U. S.	37·30 N	87·35 W
63	Kentucky (L.) . . . U. S.	36·20 N	88·50 W
63	Kentucky (R.) . . . U. S.	38·15 N	85·01 W
82	Kentville (kĕnt'vĭl) . . . Can.	45·04 N	64·31 W
77	Kentwood (kĕnt'wŏŏd) . . . La.	30·56 N	90·31 W
163	Kenya (kĕn'yà) . . . Afr.	1·00 N	36·53 E
167	Kenya, Mt. . . . Ken.	0·15 S	37·16 E
71	Kenyon (kĕn'yŭn) . . . Minn.	44·15 N	92·58 W
157	Keokea . . . Hawaii (In.)	20·44 N	156·26 W
73	Keokuk (kē'ō-kŭk) . . . Iowa	40·24 N	91·34 W
85	Keoma (kē-ō'mà) Can. (Calgary In.)	51·13 N	113·39 W
83	Kepenkeck, L. . . . Can.	48·15 N	54·57 W
121	Kepno (kăɴ'pnō) . . . Pol.	51·17 N	17·59 E
143	Kerala (State) . . . India	16·38 N	76·00 E
160	Kerang (kē-răng') . . . Austl.	35·32 S	143·58 E
129	Kerch' (kĕrch) . . . Sov. Un.	45·20 N	36·26 E
129	Kerchenskiy Proliv (Str.) (Kerch Str.) (kĕr-chĕn'skĭ prô'lĭf) . Sov. Un.	45·08 N	36·35 E
133	Kerempe Burun (C.) . . . Tur.	42·00 N	33·20 E
47	Kerguelen, Is. de (kĕr'gà-lĕn) Ind. O.	49·50 S	69·30 E
154	Kerintji, Gunung (Mtn.) . . . Indon.	1·45 S	101·18 E
146	Keriya (R.) (kē'rē-yä) . . . China	37·13 N	81·59 E
	Keriya, see Yutien		
165	Kerkennah, Îles (I.) (kĕr'kĕn-nä) Tun.	34·49 N	11·37 E
145	Kerki (kĕr'kē) . . . Sov. Un.	37·52 N	65·15 E
127	Kérkira . . . Grc.	39·36 N	19·56 E
127	Kérkira (I.) . . . Grc.	39·33 N	19·36 E
156	Kermadec Is. (kĕr-măd'ĕk) . . N. Z.	30·30 S	177·00 E
156	Kermadec Tonga Trench (kĕr-măd'ĕk tŏŋ'gà) . Oceania	23·00 S	172·30 W
144	Kermān (kĕr-män') . . . Iran	30·23 N	57·08 E
144	Kermānshāh (kĕr-män-shä') . . Iran	34·01 N	47·00 E
134	Kemerovo . . . Sov. Un.	55·31 N	86·05 E
68	Kern (R.) . . . Calif.	35·31 N	118·37 W
68	Kern, South Fork of (R.) . . . Calif.	35·40 N	118·15 W
68	Kern Can. (kûrn) . . . Calif.	36·57 N	119·37 W
123	Kerpen (kĕr'pĕn) . Ger. (Ruhr In.)	50·52 N	6·42 E
79	Kerr Res. (kĕr) . . . N. C.-Va.	36·30 N	78·38 W
76	Kerrville (kûr'vĭl) . . . Tex.	30·02 N	99·07 W
116	Kerry, Mts. (kĕr'ĭ) . . . Ire.	51·48 N	10·02 W
147	Kerulen (R.) (kĕr'ōō-lĕn) . . . Mong.	47·52 N	113·22 E
127	Kesan (kĕ'shàn) . . . Tur.	40·50 N	26·37 E
114	Kesour, Monts des (Mts.) . . . Alg.	32·51 N	0·30 W
168	Kestell (kĕs'tĕl) S. Afr. (Johannesburg & Pretoria In.)	28·19 S	28·43 E
110	Kesteven (Co.) (kĕs'tē-vĕn) . . Eng.	52·57 N	0·30 W
121	Keszthely (kĕst'hĕl-lĭ) . . . Hung.	46·46 N	17·12 E
134	Ket' (R.) (kyĕt) . . . Sov. Un.	58·30 N	84·15 E
139	Ketamputih Indon. (Singapore In.)	1·25 N	102·19 E
154	Ketapang (kĕ-tà-päng') . . . Indon.	2·00 S	109·57 E
64	Ketchikan (kĕch-ĭ-kăn') . . . Alaska	55·26 N	131·40 W
121	Ketrzyn (kăŋ't'r-zĭn) . . . Pol.	54·04 N	21·24 E
110	Kettering (kĕt'ĕr-ĭng) . . . Eng.	52·23 N	0·43 W
80	Kettering . . . Ohio	39·40 N	84·15 W
71	Kettle (R.) (kĕt''l) . . . Minn.	46·20 N	92·57 W
123	Kettwig (kĕt'vēg) . Ger. (Ruhr In.)	51·22 N	6·56 E
121	Kety (kăŋ tĭ) . . . Pol.	49·54 N	19·16 E
111	Ketzin (kĕ'tzēn) . . Ger. (Berlin In.)	52·29 N	12·51 E
81	Keuka (L.) (kē-ū'kà) . . . N. Y.	42·30 N	77·10 W
123	Kevelaer (kĕ'fĕ-lăr) Ger. (Ruhr In.)	51·35 N	6·15 E
71	Kewanee (kē-wä'nē) . . . Ill.	41·15 N	89·55 W
71	Kewaunee (kē-wô'nē) . . . Wis.	44·27 N	87·33 W
71	Keweenaw B. (kē'wē-nô) . . . Mich.	46·59 N	88·15 W
71	Keweenaw Pen. . . . Mich.	47·28 N	88·12 W
70	Keya Paha (R.) (kē-yà pä'hä) S. D.	43·11 N	100·10 W
79	Key Largo (I.) . . . Fla. (In.)	25·11 N	80·15 W
84	Keyport (kē'pōrt) N. J. (New York In.)	40·26 N	74·12 W
65	Keyport . . . Wash. (Seattle In.)	47·42 N	122·38 W
81	Keyser (kī'zĕr) . . . W. Va.	39·25 N	79·00 W
79	Key West (kē wĕst') . . . Fla. (In.)	24·31 N	81·47 W
121	Kežmarok (kĕzh'mà-rôk) . . . Czech.	49·10 N	20·27 E
134	Khabarovo (ᴋŭ-bár-ôvô) . Sov. Un.	69·31 N	60·41 E
135	Khabarovsk (ᴋä-bä'rôfsk) Sov. Un.	48·35 N	135·12 E
146	Khaidik Gol (R.) (ᴋī'dĕk gôl) China	42·35 N	84·04 E
134	Khakass Aut. Oblast . . . Sov. Un.	52·32 N	89·33 E
143	Khālāpur . . . India (Bombay In.)	18·48 N	73·17 E
168	Khalig El Tina (G.) U. A. R. (Nile In.)	31·12 N	32·42 E
135	Khalkha (R.) . . . China-Mong.	48·00 N	118·45 E
127	Khalkidhiki Khers (Pen.) . . . Grc.	40·30 N	23·18 E
127	Khalkís (käl'kĭs) . . . Grc.	38·28 N	23·38 E
134	Khal'mer-Yu (kŭl-myĕr'-yōō') Sov. Un.	67·52 N	64·25 E
132	Khalturin (ᴋál'tōō-rēn) . . Sov. Un.	58·28 N	49·00 E
143	Khammameth . . . India	17·09 N	80·13 E
142	Khānābād . . . Afg.	36·43 N	69·11 E
142	Khandwa . . . India	21·53 N	76·22 E
	Khangai Mts., see Hangayn Nuruu		
154	Khanh Hung . . . Viet.	9·45 N	105·50 E

Page	Name Pronunciation Region	Lat. °′	Long. °′
126	Khaniá (Canea) (kä-nē'ä) (kä-nĕ'ä) . Grc. (In.)	35·29 N	24·04 E
126	Khaniōn, Kólpos (G.) . . . Grc. (In.)	35·35 N	23·55 E
147	Khanka (L.) (kän'kà) . . . Sov. Un.	45·09 N	133·28 E
142	Khānpur . . . W. Pak.	28·42 N	70·42 E
146	Khan Tengri (kän'tĕn'grē) . . China	42·10 N	80·20 E
134	Khanty-Mansiysk (ᴋŭn-te' mŭn-sēsk') . Sov. Un.	61·02 N	69·01 E
139	Khān Yūnis . . . Isr. (Palestine In.)	31·21 N	34·19 E
142	Kharagpur (kŭ-rŭg'pŏŏr) . . . India	22·26 N	87·21 E
129	Khar'kov (ᴋär'kôf) . . . Sov. Un.	50·00 N	36·10 E
129	Kharkov (Oblast) . . . Sov. Un.	49·33 N	35·55 E
132	Kharlovka . . . Sov. Un.	68·47 N	37·20 E
127	Kharmanli (ᴋàr-män'lē) . . . Bul.	41·54 N	25·55 E
165	Khartoum (kär-tōōm') . . . Sud.	15·34 N	32·36 E
165	Khartoum North . . . Sud.	15·43 N	32·41 E
144	Khāsh . . . Iran	28·08 N	61·08 E
142	Khasi Hills . . . Bur.	30·56 N	91·19 E
127	Khaskovo (ᴋás'kô-vô) . . . Bul.	41·56 N	25·32 E
135	Khatanga (ᴋà-tän'gà) . . . Sov. Un.	71·48 N	101·47 E
135	Khatangskiy Zaliv (B.) (kà-täŋ'g-skē) . Sov. Un.	73·45 N	108·30 E
142	Khed Brahma (kād brä'mà) . India	24·00 N	73·05 E
113	Khemis Miliana . . . Alg.	36·19 N	1·56 E
144	Khersan, Rud-E (R.) . . . Iran	31·17 N	50·38 E
129	Kherson (ᴋĕr-sôn') . . . Sov. Un.	46·38 N	32·34 E
129	Kherson (Oblast) . . . Sov. Un.	46·32 N	32·55 E
142	Khetan (R.) . . . India	10·57 N	78·23 E
119	Khiitola (ᴋhē'tō-là) . . . Sov. Un.	61·14 N	29·40 E
136	Khimki (kēm'kĭ) Sov. Un. (Moscow In.)	55·54 N	37·27 E
127	Khíos (kē'ôs) . . . Grc.	38·23 N	26·09 E
127	Khíos (I.) . . . Grc.	38·20 N	25·45 E
103	Khiva (kē'vá) . . . Sov. Un.	41·15 N	60·30 E
129	Khmel'nik . . . Sov. Un.	49·34 N	27·58 E
133	Khmel'nitskiy (kmĭĕ'lnē'ts-kēē) Sov. Un.	49·29 N	26·54 E
129	Khmel'nitskiy (Oblast) (ᴋmĕl-nēt'skĭ ôb'lâst') . Sov. Un.	49·27 N	26·30 E
146	Khōbsōgol Dalai (Koso Lake) Mong.	51·11 N	99·11 E
128	Kholm (ᴋôlm) . . . Sov. Un.	57·09 N	31·07 E
135	Kholmsk (ᴋŭlmsk) . . . Sov. Un.	47·09 N	142·33 E
133	Khopër (R.) (ᴋô'pēr) . . . Sov. Un.	52·00 N	43·00 E
152	Khor (ᴋôr') . . . Sov. Un.	47·50 N	134·52 E
152	Khor (R.) . . . Sov. Un.	47·23 N	135·20 E
126	Khóra Sfakión . . . Grc. (In.)	35·12 N	24·10 E
134	Khorog (ᴋôr'ôg) . . . Sov. Un.	37·30 N	71·47 E
147	Khorog . . . Sov. Un.	37·10 N	71·43 E
129	Khorol (ᴋô'rôl) . . . Sov. Un.	49·48 N	33·17 E
129	Khorol (R.) . . . Sov. Un.	49·50 N	33·21 E
144	Khorramshahr (kô-ram'shär) . Iran	30·36 N	48·15 E
146	Khotan (R.) (kō-tän') . . . China	39·09 N	81·08 E
	Khotan, see Hotien		
129	Khotin (ᴋô'tēn) . . . Sov. Un.	48·29 N	26·32 E
144	Khoybar . . . Sau. Ar.	25·45 N	39·28 E
129	Khoyniki . . . Sov. Un.	51·54 N	30·00 E
142	Khulna . . . E. Pak.	22·50 N	89·38 E
144	Khurramabad (ᴋōō-rä-mä-bäd') Iran	36·57 N	50·30 E
121	Khust (ᴋōōst) . . . Sov. Un.	48·10 N	23·18 E
133	Khvalynsk (ᴋvà-lĭnsk') . . Sov. Un.	52·30 N	48·00 E
144	Khvoy . . . Iran	38·32 N	45·01 E
145	Khyber Pass (kī'bĕr) W. Pak. (Khyber Pass In.)	34·28 N	71·18 E
166	Kiambi (kyäm'bē) . . . Con. K.	7·23 S	27·59 E
73	Kiamichi (R.) (kyà-mē'chē) . Okla.	34·31 N	95·34 W
155	Kiangan (kyäŋ'gän) Phil. (Manila In.)	16·48 N	121·11 E
	Kiangsi, see Chianghsi		
	Kiangsu, see Chiangsu		
132	Kianta (L.) (kyàn'tà) . . . Fin.	65·00 N	28·15 E
127	Kičevo (kē'chĕ-vô) . . . Yugo.	41·30 N	20·59 E
71	Kickapoo (R.) (kĭk'á-pōō) . . . Wis.	43·20 N	90·55 W
164	Kidal (kē-dàl') . . . Mali	18·33 N	1·00 E
110	Kidderminster (kĭd'ĕr-mĭn-stĕr) Eng.	52·23 N	2·14 W
167	Kidd's Beach (kĭdz) S. Afr. (Natal In.)	33·09 S	27·43 E
110	Kidsgrove (kĭdz'grōv) . . . Eng.	53·05 N	2·30 W
120	Kiel (kēl) . . . Ger.	54·19 N	10·08 E
71	Kiel . . . Wis.	43·52 N	88·04 W
120	Kiel B. . . . Ger.	54·33 N	10·19 E
	Kiel Can., see Nord-Ostsee Can.		
121	Kielce (kyĕl'tsĕ) . . . Pol.	50·50 N	20·41 E
111	Kieldrecht (kēl'drĕᴋt) Bel. (Brussels In.)	51·17 N	4·09 E
	Kiev, see Kiyev		
164	Kiffa (kēf'á) . . . Mauritania	16·52 N	10·53 W
166	Kigali (kē-gä'lē) . . . Rw.	1·59 S	30·05 E
166	Kigoma (kē-gō'mä) . . . Tan.	4·44 S	29·41 E
153	Kii-Suido (Chan.) (kē sōō-ē'dō) Jap.	33·53 N	134·55 E
152	Kikaiga (I.) . . . Jap.	28·25 N	130·10 E
127	Kikinda (ᴋē'kēn-dä) . . . Yugo.	45·49 N	20·30 E
127	Kikladhes (Is.) . . . Grc.	37·30 N	24·45 E
166	Kikwit (kē'kwēt) . . . Con. K.	5·18 S	18·48 E
118	Kil (kēl) . . . Swe.	59·30 N	13·15 E
157	Kilauea (kē-lä-ōō-ā'ä) . Hawaii (In.)	22·12 N	159·25 W
157	Kilauea Crater . . . Hawaii (In.)	19·28 N	155·18 W
64	Kilbuck Mts. (kĭl-bŭk) . . . Alaska	60·05 N	160·00 W
152	Kilchu (kĭl'chōō) . . . Kor.	40·59 N	129·23 E
116	Kildare (kĭl-dâr') . . . Ire.	53·09 N	7·05 W
167	Kilimanjaro (Mtn.) (k -ē-măn-jä'rō) . Tan.	3·09 S	37·19 E
166	Kilimatinde (kĭl-ē-mä-tĭn'dä) . Tan.	5·48 S	34·58 E
119	Kilingi-Nōmme (kē'lĭŋ-gē-nôm'mĕ) . Sov. Un.	58·08 N	25·03 E
133	Kilis (kē'lēs) . . . U. A. R.	36·50 N	37·20 E
129	Kiliya (kē'lyà) . . . Sov. Un.	45·28 N	29·17 E
116	Kilkenny (kĭl-kĕn-ĭ) . . . Ire.	52·40 N	7·30 W
127	Kilkís (kĭl'kĭs) . . . Grc.	40·59 N	22·51 E
116	Killala (kĭ-lä'lá) . . . Ire.	54·11 N	9·10 W
86	Killarney (kĭ-lär'nē) . . . Can.	49·02 N	99·34 W
116	Killarney . . . Ire.	52·03 N	9·05 W
70	Killdeer (kĭl'dēr) . . . N. D.	47·22 N	102·45 W

ăt; finăl; rāte; senāte; ärm; ȧsk; sofȧ; fâre; ch-choose; dh-as th in other; bē; ēvent; bĕt; recĕnt; cratēr; g-go; gh-guttural g; bĭt; ĭ-short neutral; rīde; ᴋ-guttural k as ch in German ich;

PRONOUNCING INDEX Kilmarnock–Kolyma 223

Page	Name Pronunciation Region	Lat. °′	Long. °′
116	Kilmarnock (kĭl-mär′nŭk) ... Scot.	55·38 N	4·25 W
116	Kilrush (kĭl′rŭsh) ... Ire.	52·40 N	9·16 W
167	Kilwa Kivinje ... Tan.	8·43 S	39·18 E
160	Kimba (kĭm′bȧ) ... Austl.	33·08 S	136·25 E
70	Kimball (kĭm-bȧl) ... Nebr.	41·14 N	103·41 W
70	Kimball ... S. D.	43·44 N	98·58 W
86	Kimberley (kĭm′bẽr-lĭ) ... Can.	49·48 N	115·55 W
166	Kimberley ... S. Afr.	28·40 S	24·50 E
127	Kími ... Grc.	38·38 N	24·05 E
127	Kímolos (I.) (kē′mō-lôs) ... Grc.	36·52 N	24·20 E
128	Kimry (kĭm′rê) ... Sov. Un.	56·53 N	37·24 E
154	Kinabalu, Mt ... Mala.	5·45 N	115·26 E
80	Kincardine (kĭn-kär′dĭn) ... Can.	44·10 N	81·15 W
77	Kinder (kĭn′dẽr) ... La.	30·30 N	92·50 W
86	Kindersley (kĭn′dẽrz-lê) ... Can.	51·30 N	109·10 W
164	Kindia (kĭn′dê-ȧ) ... Gui.	10·02 N	12·49 W
166	Kindu-Port-Empain ... Con. K.	2·59 S	25·59 E
132	Kinel′-Cherkassy ... Sov. Un.	53·32 N	51·32 E
128	Kineshma (kê-nĕsh′mȧ) .. Sov. Un.	57·27 N	41·02 E
85	King (kĭng) ... Can. (Toronto In.)	43·56 N	79·32 W
160	King (I.) ... Austl.	39·35 S	143·40 E
160	Kingaroy (kĭŋ′gă-roi) ... Austl.	26·37 S	151·50 E
68	King City (kĭng sĭ′tĭ) ... Calif.	36·12 N	121·08 W
72	Kingfisher (kĭng′fĭsh-ẽr) ... Okla.	35·51 N	97·55 W
158	King George Sd. (jôrj) ... Austl.	35·17 S	118·30 E
128	Kingisepp (kĭŋ-gê-sep′) .. Sov. Un.	59·22 N	28·38 E
158	King Leopold Ranges (lē′ô-pōld) Austl.	16·35 S	125·00 E
69	Kingman (kĭng′măn) ... Ariz.	35·10 N	114·05 W
72	Kingman (kĭng′măn) ... Kans.	37·38 N	98·07 W
68	Kings (R.) ... Calif.	36·28 N	119·43 W
68	Kings Canyon Natl. Park (kăn′yŭn) Calif.	36·52 N	118·53 W
110	Kingsclere (kĭngs-clēr) Eng. (London In.)	51·18 N	1·15 W
160	Kingscote (kĭngz′kŭt) ... Austl.	35·45 S	137·32 E
117	Kings Lynn (kĭngz lĭn′) ... Eng.	52·45 N	0·20 E
79	Kings Mt ... N. C.	35·13 N	81·30 W
110	Kings Norton (nôr′tŭn) ... Eng.	52·25 N	1·54 W
158	King Sd ... Austl.	16·50 S	123·35 E
84	Kings Park (kĭngz pärk) N. Y. (New York In.)	40·53 N	73·16 W
67	Kings Pk ... Utah	40·46 N	110·20 W
79	Kingsport (kĭngz′pōrt) ... Tenn.	36·33 N	82·36 W
160	Kingston (kĭngz′tŭn) ... Austl.	37·52 S	139·52 E
81	Kingston ... Can.	44·15 N	76·30 W
94	Kingston ... Jam.	18·00 N	76·45 W
81	Kingston ... N. Y.	42·00 N	74·00 W
81	Kingston ... Pa.	41·15 N	75·50 W
65	Kingston ... Wash. (Seattle In.)	47·04 N	122·29 W
93	Kingstown (kĭngz′toun) ... St. Vincent (Le. & Wind. Is. In.)	13·10 N	61·14 W
79	Kingstree (kĭngz′trē) ... S. C.	33·30 N	79·50 W
76	Kingsville (kĭngz′vĭl) ... Tex.	27·32 N	97·52 W
86	King William I. (kĭng wĭl′yăm) Can.	69·25 N	97·00 W
167	King William's Town (kĭng-wĭl′-yŭmz-toun) . S. Afr. (Natal In.)	32·53 S	27·24 E
74	Kinloch (kĭn-lŏk) Mo. (St. Louis In.)	38·44 N	90·19 W
116	Kinnairds Hd. (kĭn-årdś hĕd) . Scot.	57·42 N	3·55 W
153	Kinomoto (kē′nō-mōtō) ... Jap.	33·53 N	136·07 E
153	Kinosaki (kē′nō-sä′kê) ... Jap.	35·38 N	134·47 E
116	Kinsale Hbr. (kĭn-sāl′) ... Ire.	51·35 N	8·17 W
166	Kinshasa (Léopoldville) .. Cong. K.	4·28 S	15·16 E
72	Kinsley (kĭnz′lĭ) ... Kans.	37·55 N	99·24 W
79	Kinston (kĭnz′tŭn) ... N. C.	35·15 N	77·35 W
164	Kintampo (kēn-täm′pō) ... Ghana	8·05 N	1·44 W
116	Kintyre Pen ... Scot.	55·50 N	5·40 W
	Kiorashi, see Ōmori		
72	Kiowa (kī′ô-wȧ) ... Kans.	37·01 N	98·30 W
73	Kiowa ... Okla.	34·42 N	95·53 W
127	Kiparissía ... Grc.	37·17 N	21·43 E
127	Kiparissiakós Kólpos (G.) ... Grc.	37·28 N	21·15 E
166	Kipembawe (kê-pĕm-bä′wå) . Tan.	7·43 S	33·22 E
74	Kirby (kŭr′bĭ) Tex. (San Antonio In.)	29·29 N	98·23 W
77	Kirbyville (kŭr′bĭ-vĭl) ... Tex.	30·39 N	93·54 W
135	Kirenga (R.) (kê-rĕŋ′gȧ) . Sov. Un.	56·30 N	103·18 E
135	Kirensk (kē-rĕnsk′) ... Sov. Un.	57·47 N	108·22 E
130	Kirghiz S. S. R. (kĭr-gēz′) . Sov. Un.	41·45 N	74·38 E
130	Kirghiz Steppe (Plain) ... Sov. Un.	49·28 N	57·07 E
145	Kirgizskiy Khrebet (Kirgiz) (Mts.) . Sov. Un.	37·58 N	72·23 E
	Kirin, see Chilin		
	Kirin, see Chilung		
110	Kirkby-in-Ashfield (kûrk′bē-ĭn-ăsh′fēld) .. Eng.	53·06 N	1·16 W
116	Kirkcaldy (kẽr-kô′dĭ) ... Scot.	56·06 N	3·15 W
85	Kirkfield Park (kûrk-fēld) Can. (Winnipeg In.)	49·53 N	97·16 W
110	Kirkham (kûrk′ăm) ... Eng.	53·47 N	2·53 W
65	Kirkland (kûrk′lănd) Wash. (Seattle In.)	47·41 N	122·12 W
87	Kirkland Lake ... Can.	48·14 N	80·06 W
127	Kirklareli (kêrk′lär-ĕ′lê) ... Tur.	41·44 N	27·15 E
73	Kirksville (kûrks′vĭl) ... Mo.	40·12 N	92·35 W
144	Kirkūk (kĭr-kōōk′) ... Iraq	35·28 N	44·22 E
116	Kirkwall (kûrk′wôl) ... Scot.	58·58 N	2·59 W
74	Kirkwood (kûrk′wŏŏd) Mo. (St. Louis In.)	38·35 N	90·24 W
167	Kirkwood ... S. Afr. (Natal In.)	33·26 S	25·24 E
120	Kirn (kêrn) ... Ger.	49·47 N	7·23 E
128	Kirov ... Sov. Un.	54·04 N	34·19 E
132	Kirov ... Sov. Un.	58·35 N	49·35 E
133	Kirovabad (kē-rŭ-vŭ-bät′) Sov. Un.	40·40 N	46·20 E
136	Kirovgrad (kē′rŭ-vŭ-grad) Sov. Un. (Urals In.)	57·26 N	60·03 E
129	Kirovograd (kē-rŭ-vŭ-grät′) Sov. Un.	48·33 N	32·17 E
129	Kirovograd (Oblast) ... Sov. Un.	48·23 N	31·10 E
132	Kirovsk ... Sov. Un.	67·40 N	33·58 E
136	Kirovsk (kê-rôfsk′) Sov. Un. (Leningrad In.)	59·52 N	30·59 E

Page	Name Pronunciation Region	Lat. °′	Long. °′
133	Kirsanov (kêr-sȧ′nôf) ... Sov. Un.	52·40 N	42·40 E
133	Kırşehir (kêr-shĕ′hēr) ... Tur.	39·10 N	34·00 E
142	Kirthar Ra. (kĭr-tŭr) ... W. Pak.	30·40 N	67·20 E
110	Kirton (kûr′tŭn) ... Eng.	53·29 N	0·35 W
112	Kiruna (kē-rōō′nä) ... Swe.	67·49 N	20·08 E
72	Kirwin Res. (kûr′wĭn) ... Kans.	39·34 N	99·04 W
153	Kiryū (kē′rĭ-ōō) ... Jap.	36·26 N	139·18 E
128	Kirzhach (kêr-zhȧk′) ... Sov. Un.	56·08 N	38·53 E
167	Kisaki (kē-sȧ′kē) ... Tan.	7·37 S	37·43 E
126	Kisámou, Kólpos (G) ... Grc. (In.)	35·40 N	23·37 E
165	Kisangani (Stanleyville) .. Con. K.	0·32 N	25·14 E
153	Kisarazu (kē′sȧ-rȧ′zōō) Jap. (Tōkyō In.)	35·23 N	139·55 E
134	Kiselëvsk (kē-sĭ-lyôfsk′) .. Sov. Un.	54·05 N	86·19 E
166	Kisenyi (kē′sĕn′yē) ... Rw.	1·43 S	29·15 E
129	Kishinëv (ke-shê-nyôf′) .. Sov. Un.	47·02 N	28·52 E
153	Kishiwada (kē′shê-wä′dä) ... Jap.	34·25 N	135·18 E
136	Kishkino (kēsh′kĭ-nô) Sov. Un. (Moscow In.)	55·15 N	38·04 E
64	Kiska (I.) (kĭs′kä) ... Alaska	52·08 N	177·10 E
121	Kiskunfélegyháza (kĭsh′kŏŏn-fā′lĕd-y′hä′zô) . Hung.	46·42 N	19·52 E
121	Kiskunhalas (kĭsh′kŏŏn-hô′lôsh) Hung.	46·24 N	19·26 E
121	Kiskunmajsa (kĭsh′kŏŏn-mī′shô) Hung.	46·29 N	19·42 E
167	Kismayu ... Som.	0·18 S	42·30 E
153	Kiso-Gawa (Strm.) (kē′sō-gä′wä) Jap.	35·29 N	137·12 E
153	Kiso-Sammyaku (Mts.) (kê′sō säm′myȧ-kōō) . Jap.	35·47 N	137·39 E
164	Kissidougou (kē′sê-dōō′gōō) .. Gui.	9·19 N	10·26 W
79	Kissimmee (kĭ-sĭm′ê) ... Fla. (In.)	28·17 N	81·25 W
79	Kissimmee (L.) ... Fla. (In.)	27·58 N	81·17 W
79	Kissimmee (R.) ... Fla. (In.)	27·45 N	81·07 W
112	Kistrand (kē′stränd) ... Nor.	70·29 N	25·01 E
121	Kisujszallás (kĭsh′ŏŏ′y′sä′läsh) Hung.	47·12 N	20·47 E
166	Kisumu (kē′sōō-mōō) ... Ken.	0·05 S	34·49 E
139	Kiswah ... Syr. (Palestine In.)	33·31 N	36·13 E
164	Kita (kē′tȧ) ... Mali	13·05 N	9·33 W
152	Kitakami Gawa (R.) (kê′tȧ-kä′mē gä-wä) . Jap.	39·20 N	141·10 E
153	Kitakyūshū (kē′tȧ-kyōō′shōō′) Jap.	34·15 N	130·23 E
80	Kitchener (kĭch′ĕ-nẽr) ... Can.	43·25 N	80·35 W
166	Kitega (kê-tā′gȧ) ... Burundi	3·39 S	30·05 E
165	Kitgum (kĭt′gŏŏm) ... Ug.	3·29 N	33·04 E
115	Kíthira (I.) ... Grc.	36·15 N	22·56 E
127	Kíthnos (I.) ... Grc.	37·24 N	24·10 E
86	Kitimat ... Can.	54·01 N	128·11 W
65	Kitsap (kĭt-săp) Wash. (Seattle In.)	47·45 N	122·32 W
153	Kitsuki (kêt′sōō-kê) ... Jap.	33·24 N	131·35 E
81	Kittaning (kĭ-tăn′ĭng) ... Pa.	40·50 N	79·30 W
84	Kittatinny Mts. (kĭ-tŭ-tĭ′nê) N. J. (New York In.)	41·16 N	74·44 W
82	Kittery (kĭt′ẽr-ĭ) ... Maine	43·07 N	70·45 W
111	Kittsee ... Aus. (Vienna In.)	48·05 N	17·05 E
79	Kitty Hawk (kĭt′tê hôk) ... N. C.	36·04 N	75·42 W
120	Kitzingen (kĭt′zĭng-ĕn) ... Ger.	49·44 N	10·08 E
166	Kivu (L.) ... Con. K.	2·00 S	28·30 E
133	Kiyev (Kiev) (kē′yĕf) ... Sov. Un.	50·27 N	30·30 E
136	Kizel (kē′zĕl) . Sov. Un. (Urals In.)	59·05 N	57·42 E
133	Kızıl Irmak (R.) (kĭz′ĭl ĭr-mäk′) Tur.	40·15 N	34·00 E
136	Kizil'skoye (kĭz′ĭl-skô-yĕ) Sov. Un. (Urals In.)	52·43 N	58·53 E
133	Kizlyar (kĭz-lyär′) ... Sov. Un.	44·00 N	46·50 E
153	Kizu (kē′zōō) ... Jap. (Ōsaka In.)	34·43 N	135·49 E
103	Kizyl-Arvat (kē′zĭl-ŭr-vät′) Sov. Un.	38·55 N	56·33 E
111	Klaaswaal . Neth. (Amsterdam In.)	51·46 N	4·25 E
120	Kladno (kläd′nō) ... Czech.	50·10 N	14·05 E
120	Klagenfurt (klä′gĕn-fŏŏrt) ... Aus.	46·38 N	14·19 E
119	Klaipéda (Memel) (klī′pȧ-dȧ) (mā′mĕl) . Sov. Un.	55·43 N	21·10 E
66	Klamath Falls ... Ore.	42·13 N	121·49 W
66	Klamath Mts. ... Calif.	42·00 N	123·25 W
66	Klamath R. ... Calif.	41·27 N	123·35 W
139	Klang ... Mala. (Singapore In.)	3·02 N	101·27 E
139	Klang (R.) . Mala. (Singapore In.)	3·00 N	101·38 E
118	Klar-älven (R.) ... Swe.	60·40 N	13·00 E
65	Klaskanine (R.) (klăs′kȧ-nīn) Ore. (Portland In.)	46·02 N	123·43 W
120	Klatovy (klȧ′tô-vê) ... Czech.	49·23 N	13·18 E
64	Klawak (klā′wăk) ... Alaska	55·32 N	133·10 W
85	Kleinburg (klīn-bûrg) Can. (Toronto In.)	43·51 N	79·38 W
111	Kleinmachnow (klīn-mäĸ′nō) Ger. (Berlin In.)	52·22 N	13·12 E
167	Kleinmond ... S. Afr. (Natal In.)	33·33 S	27·04 E
168	Klerksdorp (klẽrks′dôrp) ... S. Afr. (Johannesburg & Pretoria In.)	26·52 S	26·40 E
168	Klerkskraal (klẽrks′kräl) ... S. Afr. (Johannesburg & Pretoria In.)	26·15 S	27·10 E
128	Kletnya (klyĕt′nyȧ) ... Sov. Un.	52·19 N	33·14 E
128	Kletsk (klĕtsk) ... Sov. Un.	53·04 N	26·43 E
123	Kleve (klĕ′fĕ) ... Ger. (Ruhr In.)	51·47 N	6·09 E
66	Klickitat R. ... Wash.	46·01 N	121·07 W
128	Klimovichi (klē-mô-vē′chê) Sov. Un.	53·37 N	31·21 E
136	Klimovsk (klĭ′môfsk) Sov. Un. (Moscow In.)	55·21 N	37·32 E
128	Klin (klên) ... Sov. Un.	56·18 N	36·43 E
118	Klintehamn (klēn′tē-häm) ... Swe.	57·24 N	18·14 E
128	Klintsy (klĭn′tsĭ) ... Sov. Un.	52·46 N	32·14 E
168	Klipgat ... S. Afr. (Johannesburg & Pretoria In.)	25·26 S	27·57 E
168	Klip R. (klĭp) ... S. Afr. (Johannesburg & Pretoria In.)	27·18 S	29·25 E
126	Ključ (klyōōch) ... Yugo.	44·32 N	16·48 E
120	Kłodzko (klôd′skô) ... Pol.	50·26 N	16·38 E
64	Klondike Reg. (klŏn′dīk) Alaska-Can.	64·12 N	142·38 W

Page	Name Pronunciation Region	Lat. °′	Long. °′
111	Klosterfelde (klōs′tĕr-fĕl-dĕ) Ger. (Berlin In.)	52·47 N	13·29 E
111	Klosterneuburg (klōs-tēr-noi′bŏŏrgh) . Aus. (Vienna In.)	48·19 N	16·20 E
139	Kluang ... Mala. (Singapore In.)	2·01 N	103·19 E
121	Kluczbork (klōōch′bōrk) ... Pol.	50·59 N	18·15 E
128	Klyaz′ma (R.) (klyäz′mȧ) . Sov. Un.	55·49 N	39·19 E
135	Klyuchevskaya (Vol.) (klyōō-chĕfskä′yä) . Sov. Un.	56·13 N	160·00 E
136	Klyuchi (klyōō′chĭ) Sov. Un. (Urals In.)	57·03 N	57·20 E
127	Knezha (knyā′zhȧ) ... Bul.	43·27 N	24·03 E
70	Knife (R.) (nīf) ... N. D.	47·06 N	102·33 W
80	Knightstown (nīts′toun) ... Ind.	39·45 N	85·30 W
126	Knin (knēn) ... Yugo.	44·02 N	16·14 E
120	Knittelfeld ... Aus.	47·13 N	14·50 E
155	Knob Pk. (nŏb) . Phil. (Manila In.)	12·30 N	121·20 E
116	Knockmealdown Mts. (nŏk-mēl′doun) . Ire.	52·13 N	8·09 W
110	Knottingley (nŏt′ĭng-lĭ) ... Eng.	53·42 N	1·14 W
80	Knox (nŏks) ... Ind.	41·15 N	86·40 W
71	Knoxville (nŏks′vĭl) ... Iowa	41·19 N	93·05 W
78	Knoxville ... Tenn.	35·58 N	83·55 W
110	Knutsford (nŭts′fẽrd) ... Eng.	53·18 N	2·22 W
121	Knyszyn (knĭ′shĭn) ... Pol.	53·16 N	22·59 E
148	Ko (R.) (gōōŭ) ... China	33·04 N	117·16 E
153	Kobayashi (kō′bȧ-yä′shê) ... Jap.	31·58 N	130·59 E
153	Kōbe (kō′bĕ) ... Jap. (Ōsaka In.)	34·30 N	135·10 E
129	Kobelyaki (kō-bĕl-yä′kê) . Sov. Un.	49·11 N	34·12 E
118	København (Copenhagen) (kû-b′n-houn′) . Den.	55·43 N	12·27 E
120	Koblenz (kō′blĕntz) ... Ger.	50·18 N	7·36 E
128	Kobozha (R.) (kô-bō′zhȧ) . Sov. Un.	58·55 N	35·18 E
121	Kobrin (kō′brên′) ... Sov. Un.	52·13 N	24·23 E
136	Kobrinskoye (kô-brĭn′skô-yĕ) Sov. Un. (Leningrad In.)	59·25 N	30·07 E
64	Kobuk (R.) (kō′bŭk) ... Alaska	66·58 N	158·48 W
133	Kobuleti (kô-bŏŏ-lyā′tê) . Sov. Un.	41·50 N	41·40 E
127	Kocani (kô′chä-nĕ) ... Yugo.	41·54 N	22·25 E
126	Kočevje (kô′chāv-ye) ... Yugo.	45·38 N	14·51 E
74	Koch (kōk) ... Mo. (St. Louis In.)	38·28 N	90·17 W
120	Kocher R. (kôĸ′ĕr) ... Ger.	49·00 N	9·52 E
153	Kōchi (kō′chê) ... Jap.	33·35 N	133·32 E
64	Kodiak (kō′dyăk) ... Alaska	57·50 N	152·30 W
64	Kodiak (I.) ... Alaska	57·24 N	153·32 W
165	Kodok (ko′dŏk) ... Sud.	9·57 N	32·08 E
166	Koekenaap ... S. Afr.	31·25 S	18·20 E
164	Koforidua (kō fô-rĭ-dōō′ȧ) .. Ghana	6·12 N	0·30 W
153	Kōfu (kō′fōō′) ... Jap.	35·41 N	138·34 E
153	Koga (kō′gȧ) ... Jap.	36·13 N	139·40 E
153	Kogane (kō′gä-nå) . Jap. (Tōkyō In.)	35·50 N	139·56 E
153	Koganei (kō′gä-nā) Jap. (Tōkyō In.)	35·42 N	139·31 E
118	Køge (kû′gĕ) ... Den.	55·27 N	12·09 E
118	Køge Bugt (B.) ... Den.	55·30 N	12·25 E
129	Kogil′nik (R.) (kô-gêl-nēk′) Sov. Un.	46·08 N	29·10 E
142	Koh-i Baba Mt. ... Afg.	39·39 N	67·09 E
145	Kohima (kô-ē′mȧ) ... India	25·45 N	94·41 E
153	Koito (R.) (kô′ê-tō) Jap. (Tōkyō In.)	35·19 N	139·58 E
152	Kŏje (I.) (kû′jĕ) ... Kor.	34·53 N	129·00 E
134	Kokand (kô-känt′) ... Sov. Un.	40·27 N	71·07 E
134	Kokchetav (kôk′chĕ-tȧf) . Sov. Un.	53·15 N	69·13 E
119	Kokemäen (R.) (kô′kē-må′ĕn) . Fin.	61·23 N	22·03 E
128	Kokhma (kôĸ′mȧ) ... Sov. Un.	56·57 N	41·08 E
143	Kokkanisseri ... India	12·08 N	74·14 E
112	Kokkola (kô′kô-lȧ) ... Fin.	63·47 N	22·58 E
80	Kokomo (kō′kô-mô) ... Ind.	40·30 N	86·20 W
	Koko Nor, see Ch′ing Hai		
155	Kokopo (kô-kô′pō) ... N. Gui. Ter.	4·25 S	152·27 E
87	Koksoak (R.) (kôk′sô-ăk) ... Can.	57·42 N	69·50 W
167	Kokstad (kôk′shtät) S. Afr. (Natal In.)	30·33 S	29·27 E
148	Koku (gŏ′gōō) ... China	39·00 N	117·30 E
153	Kokubu (kō′kōō-bōō) ... Jap.	31·42 N	130·46 E
153	Kokubunji (kō′kōō-bŏŏn′jê) Jap. (Tōkyō In.)	35·43 N	139·29 E
153	Kokuou (kô′kōō-ô′ōō) Jap. (Ōsaka In.)	34·34 N	135·39 E
164	Kolahun (kô-lä′hōōn) ... Lib.	8·24 N	10·11 W
	Kola Pen., see Kol′skiy P-Ov.		
143	Kolār (kôl-är′) ... India	13·39 N	78·33 E
143	Kolār Gold Fields (kôl-är′) .. India	13·45 N	79·55 E
121	Kolárvo (kōl-árōvō) ... Czech.	47·54 N	17·59 E
127	Kolarovgrad ... Bul.	43·15 N	26·54 E
128	Kol′chugino (kôl-chŏŏ′gê-nô) Sov. Un.	56·19 N	39·29 E
118	Kolding (kŭl′dĭng) ... Den.	55·29 N	9·24 E
166	Kole (kō′lå) ... Con. K.	3·19 S	22·46 E
132	Kolguyev (I.) (kôl-gŏŏ′yĕf) Sov. Un.	69·00 N	49·00 E
120	Kolin (kō′lēn) ... Czech.	50·01 N	15·11 E
119	Kolkasrags (Pt.) (kôl-käs′rȧgz) Sov. Un.	57·46 N	22·39 E
123	Köln (Cologne) ... Ger. (Ruhr In.)	50·56 N	6·57 E
121	Kolno (kôw′nô) ... Pol.	53·23 N	21·56 E
121	Koło (kô′wô) ... Pol.	52·11 N	18·37 E
120	Kołobrzeg (kô-lôb′zhĕk) ... Pol.	54·10 N	15·35 E
136	Kolomna (kȧl-ôm′nȧ) Sov. Un. (Moscow In.)	55·06 N	38·47 E
121	Kolomyya (kō′lô-mē′yȧ) . Sov. Un.	48·32 N	25 04 E
128	Kolp′ (R.) (kôlp) ... Sov. Un.	59·29 N	35·32 E
134	Kolpashevo (kŭl pȧ shô′vȧ) Sov. Un.	58·16 N	82·43 E
136	Kolpino (kôl′pê-nô) Sov. Un. (Leningrad In.)	59·45 N	30·37 E
128	Kolpny (kôlp′nyê) ... Sov. Un.	52·14 N	36·54 E
132	Kol′skiy P-Ov. (Kola Pen.) Sov. Un.	67·15 N	37·40 E
132	Kolva (R.) ... Sov. Un.	61·00 N	57·00 E
166	Kolwezi (kōl-wĕ′zē) ... Con. K.	10·40 S	25·30 E
136	Kolyberovo (kô-lĭ-byå′rô-vô) Sov. Un. (Moscow In.)	55·16 N	38·45 E
135	Kolyma (R.) ... Sov. Un.	66·30 N	151·45 E

ng-sing; ŋ-baŋk; ɴ-nasalized n; nŏd; cŏmmit; ōld; ôbey; ôrder; fōōd; fŏŏt; ou-out; s-soft; sh-dish; th-thin; pūre; ûnite; ûrn; stŭd; circŭs; ü-as "y" in study; ′-indeterminate vowel.

224 Kolymskiy–Krymskaya PRONOUNCING INDEX

Page	Name Pronunciation Region	Lat. °′	Long. °′
	Kolymskiy (Mts.), see Gydan, Khrebet		
134	Kolyvan' (kôl-ê-vän')...Sov. Un.	55·28 N	82·59 E
130	Komadorskie Ostrova (Is.) Sov. Un.	55·40 N	167·13 E
164	Komadugu-Yobe R..........Nig.	12·14 N	10·00 E
121	Komárno (kô'mär-nô).....Czech.	47·46 N	18·08 E
121	Komarno...............Sov. Un.	49·38 N	23·43 E
121	Komaron (kô'mä-rôm).....Hung.	47·45 N	18·06 E
166	Komatipoort (kō-mä'tê-pōrt) S. Afr.	25·21 S	32·00 E
153	Komatsu (kō-mät'sōō).......Jap.	36·23 N	136·26 E
153	Komatsushima (kō-mät'sōō-shê'mä).Jap.	34·04 N	134 32 E
167	Komga (kōm'gȧ) S. Afr. (Natal In.)	32·36 S	27·54 E
130	Komi (A. S. S. R.) (kômê) Sov. Un.	61·31 N	53·15 E
166	Kommetijie S. Afr. (Cape Town In.)	34·09 S	18·19 E
146	Kommunizma, Pik (Pk.).Sov. Un.	39·46 N	71·23 E
127	Komotiní..................Grc.	41·07 N	25·22 E
154	Kompong Thom (kŏm'pŏng-tŏm) Camb.	12·41 N	104·39 E
129	Komrat (kôm-rät')......Sov. Un.	46·17 N	28·38 E
136	Komsomolets (kôm-sô-mô'lĕts) Sov. Un. (Urals In.)	53·45 N	63·04 E
133	Komsomolets Zaliv (B.)..Sov. Un.	45·40 N	52·00 E
135	Komsomol'sk-na-Amure (kŭm-sŭ-môlsk'nŭ-ŭ-mōōr'yĭ).Sov. Un.	50·46 N	137·14 E
129	Komsomol'skoye (kôm-sô-môl'skô-yĕ).Sov. Un.	48·42 N	28·44 E
132	Konda (R.) (kôn'dȧ)....Sov. Un.	60·50 N	64·00 E
136	Kondas R. (kôn'dȧs) Sov. Un. (Urals In.)	59·30 N	56·28 E
166	Kondoa (kôn-dō'ȧ)..........Tan.	4·52 S	36·00 E
164	Kong (kông).........Ivory Coast	9·05 N	4·41 W
164	Kong (Reg.).........Ivory Coast	9·19 N	4·03 W
166	Kongolo (kôŋ'gō'lō)......Con. K.	5·20 S	26·58 E
118	Kongsberg (kŭngs'bĕrg).....Nor.	59·40 N	9·36 E
118	Kongsvinger (kŭngs'vĭŋ-gĕr).Nor.	60·12 N	12·00 E
166	Koni (kō'nē).............Con. K.	10·32 S	27·27 E
	Königsberg, see Kaliningrad		
111	Königsbrunn (kû'nēgs-brōōn) Ger. (Munich In.)	48·16 N	10·53 E
111	Königs Wusterhausen (kû'nēgs vōōs'tĕr-hou-zĕn) Ger. (Berlin In.)	52·18 N	13·38 E
121	Konin (kô'nyên).............Pol.	52·11 N	18·17 E
127	Kónitsa (kô'nyē'tsȧ).........Grc.	40·03 N	20·46 E
127	Konjic (kôn'yēts)..........Yugo.	43·38 N	17·59 E
152	Konju.....................Kor.	36·21 N	127·05 E
129	Konotop (kô-nô-tôp')....Sov. Un.	51·13 N	33·14 E
121	Końskie (koin''skyĕ).........Pol.	51·12 N	20·26 E
129	Konstantinovka (kôn-stȧn-tē'nôf-kȧ).Sov. Un.	48·33 N	37·42 E
120	Konstanz (kôn'-shtänts).....Ger.	47·39 N	9·10 E
164	Kontagora (kōn-tȧ-gō'rä)....Nig.	10·27 N	5 30 E
164	Kontcha (kōn'chȧ).........Cam.	8·03 N	12·21 E
133	Konya (kōn'yȧ)............Tur.	36·55 N	32·25 E
86	Kootenay Natl. Park (kōō'tê-nâ) Can.	51·06 N	117·02 W
86	Kootenay (R.) (kōō'tê-nâ)...Can.	50·28 N	115·50 W
153	Kōō-zan (Mtn.) (kōō'zän) Jap. (Ōsaka In.)	34·53 N	135·32 E
118	Kopervik (kô'pĕr-vêk).......Nor.	59·18 N	5·20 E
144	Kopet, Mts................Iran	37·28 N	58·29 E
136	Kopeysk (kô-pāsk') Sov. Un. (Urals In.)	55·07 N	61·36 E
118	Köping (chû'pĭng)..........Swe.	59·32 N	15·58 E
118	Kopparberg (kŏp'pȧr-bĕrgh)..Swe.	59·53 N	15·00 E
168	Koppies..S. Afr. (Johannesburg & Pretoria In.)	27·15 S	27·35 E
126	Koprivnica (kô'prēv-nê'tsȧ).Yugo.	46·10 N	16·48 E
121	Kopychintsy (kô-pê-chēn'tsĕ) Sov. Un.	49·06 N	25·55 E
127	Korçë (kôr'chĕ).............Alb.	40·37 N	20·48 E
126	Korčula (I.) (kôr'chōō-lȧ)...Yugo.	42·50 N	17·05 E
165	Kordofan (Prov.) (kôr-dô-fän') Sud.	14·08 N	28·39 E
152	Korea B.............China-Kor.	39·18 N	123·50 E
139	Korea (kô-rē'ȧ).............Asia	38·45 N	130·00 E
152	Korean Arch...............Kor.	39·05 N	125·35 E
152	Korea Str.............Kor.-Jap.	33·30 N	128·30 E
121	Korets (kô-rĕts')........Sov. Un.	50·35 N	27·13 E
164	Korhogo (kôr-hō'gō)..Ivory Coast	9·22 N	5·21 W
127	Korinthiakós Kólpos (G.)....Grc.	38·15 N	22·33 E
127	Korinthos (Corinth) (kô-rên'thôs) (kŏr'ĭnth).Grc.	37·56 N	22·54 E
152	Kōriyama (kō'rê-yä'mä).....Jap.	37·18 N	140·25 E
153	Kōriyama.......Jap. (Osaka In.)	34·39 N	135·48 E
136	Korkino (kôr'kē-nŭ) Sov. Un. (Urals In.)	54·53 N	61·25 E
120	Körmend (kûr'mĕnt).......Hung.	47·02 N	16·36 E
126	Kornat (I.) (kôr-nät')......Yugo.	43·46 N	15·10 E
111	Korneuburg (kôr'noi-bŏŏrgh) Aus. (Vienna In.)	48·22 N	16·21 E
129	Korocha (kô-rō'chȧ).....Sov. Un.	50·50 N	37·13 E
129	Korop (kō'rôp).........Sov. Un.	51·33 N	33·54 E
129	Korosten' (kô'rôs-tĕn)...Sov. Un.	50·51 N	28·39 E
129	Korostyshev (kô-rôs'tê-shôf) Sov. Un.	50·19 N	29·05 E
129	Korotoyak (kô'rô-tô-yȧk') Sov. Un.	51·00 N	39·06 E
135	Korsakov (kôr'sȧ-kôf')...Sov. Un.	46·42 N	143·16 E
119	Korsnas (kôrs'nĕs)...........Fin.	62·51 N	21·17 E
118	Korsør (kôrs'ûr')...........Den.	55·19 N	11·08 E
165	Kōrti (kôr'tê)...............Sud.	18·08 N	31·39 E
117	Kortrijk...................Bel.	50·49 N	3·10 E
135	Koryakskiy Khrebet (Mts.) Sov. Un.	62·00 N	168·45 E
129	Koryukovka (kôr-yōō-kôf'kȧ) Sov. Un.	51·44 N	32·24 E
120	Kościan (kŭsh'tsyȧn)........Pol.	52·05 N	16·38 E
121	Kościerzyna (kŭsh-tsyĕ-zhē'nȧ) Pol.	54·08 N	17·59 E
78	Kosciusko (kŏs-ĭ-ŭs'kō).....Miss.	33·04 N	89·35 W
160	Kosciusko, Mt............Austl.	36·26 S	148·20 E
128	Kosel'sk (kô-zĕlsk')......Sov. Un.	54·01 N	35·49 E
165	Kosha (kō'shä).............Sud.	20·49 N	30·27 E
150	K'oshan (kō'shän').........China	48·00 N	126·30 E
153	Koshigaya (kô'shê-gä'yä) Jap. (Tōkyō In.)	35·53 N	139·48 E
153	Koshiki-Rettō (Is.) (kō-shē'kê rât'tō).Jap.	31·51 N	129·40 E
142	Kosi (R.) (kô'sē)...........India	26·00 N	86·20 E
121	Košice (kō'shê-tsĕ').......Czech.	48·43 N	21·17 E
167	Kosmos (kŏz'mŏs) S. Afr. (Johannesburg & Pretoria In.)	25·45 S	27·51 E
136	Kosobrodskiy (kä-sô'brôd-skĭ) Sov. Un. (Urals In.)	54·14 N	60·53 E
	Koso Lake, see Khöbsögol Dalai		
127	Kosovska Mitrovica (kô'sôv-skä' mê'trô-vê-tsä').Yugo.	42·51 N	20·50 E
126	Kostajnica (kôs'tä-ê-nē'tsȧ).Yugo.	45·14 N	16·32 E
168	Koster...S. Afr. (Johannesburg & Pretoria In.)	25·52 S	26·52 E
165	Kosti (kôs'tê)..............Sud.	13·09 N	32·39 E
136	Kostino (kôs'tĭ-nô) Sov. Un. (Moscow In.)	55·54 N	37·51 E
128	Kostroma (kôs-trô-mȧ')..Sov. Un.	57·46 N	40·55 E
128	Kostroma (Oblast).......Sov. Un.	57·50 N	41·10 E
120	Kostrzyn' (kôst'chên)........Pol.	52·35 N	14·38 E
136	Kos'va R. (kôs'vȧ) Sov. Un. (Urals In.)	58·44 N	57·08 E
120	Koszalin (kô-shä'lĭn).........Pol.	54·12 N	16·10 E
120	Köszeg (kû'sĕg)...........Hung.	47·21 N	16·32 E
142	Kota....................India	25·17 N	75·49 E
154	Kotabaru................Indon.	3·22 S	116·15 E
154	Kota Bharu (kō'tä bä'rōō)..Mala.	6·15 N	102·23 E
166	Kota Kota (kō-tȧ kō-tȧ)..Malawi	12·52 S	34·16 E
139	Kota Tinggi Mala. (Singapore In.)	1·43 N	103·54 E
127	Kotel (kō-tĕl')..............Bul.	42·54 N	26·28 E
132	Kotel'nich (kô-tyĕl'nêch).Sov. Un.	58·15 N	48·20 E
135	Kotel'nyy (I.) (kô-tyĕl'nê) Sov. Un.	74·51 N	134·09 E
143	Kothapur.................India	16·48 N	74·15 E
119	Kotka (kŏt'kȧ)..............Fin.	60·28 N	26·56 E
132	Kotlas (kôt'lȧs).........Sov. Un.	61·10 N	46·50 E
136	Kotlin, Ostrov (I.) (ôs-trôf' kôt'lĭn) Sov. Un. (Leningrad In.)	60·02 N	29·49 E
127	Kotor (kō'tôr)............Yugo.	42·26 N	18·48 E
128	Kotorosl' (R.) (kô-tô'rôsl) Sov. Un.	57·18 N	39·08 E
126	Kotor Varoš (kô'tôr vä'rôsh).Yugo.	44·37 N	17·23 E
129	Kotovsk (kô-tôfsk').....Sov. Un.	47·49 N	29·31 E
148	Kotse (hŏ'zhē)............China	35·13 N	115·28 E
165	Kotto R.........Cen. Afr. Rep.	5·17 N	22·04 E
135	Kotuy (R.) (kô-tōō')....Sov. Un.	71·00 N	103·15 E
64	Kotzebue (kôt'sē-bōō).....Alaska	66·48 N	162·42 W
64	Kotzebue Sd.............Alaska	67·00 N	164·28 W
165	Kouandé (kwän-dā') Cen. Afr. Rep.	6·08 N	14·32 E
164	Koudougou (kōō-dōō'gōō) Upper Volta	12·02 N	2·15 W
164	Koulikoro (kōō-lê-kō'rô).....Mali	13·00 N	7·29 W
166	Kouilou (R.).............Con. B.	4·10 S	11·45 E
164	Koumbia (kōōm'bĭ-ä)........Gui.	11·35 N	13·01 W
164	Koundé (kōōn-dā').....Dahomey	10·19 N	1·42 E
134	Kounradskiy (kŭ-ōōn-rät'skē) Sov. Un.	47·25 N	75·10 E
164	Kouroussa (kōō-rōō'sä)......Gui.	10·43 N	9·59 W
165	Koussi, Emi (Mt.) (ā'mê kōō-sē') Chad	19·56 N	18·34 E
164	Koutiala (kōō-tê-ä'lä).......Mali	12·29 N	5·29 W
119	Kouvola (kō'ŏŏ-vô-lä).......Fin.	60·51 N	26·40 E
132	Kovda (L.) (kôv'dȧ).....Sov. Un.	66·45 N	32·00 E
121	Kovel' (kō'vĕl)..........Sov. Un.	51·13 N	24·45 E
	Kovno, see Kaunas		
128	Kovrov (kôv-rôf').......Sov. Un.	56·23 N	41·21 E
	Kowie, see Port Alfred		
151	Kowloon (kō'lōōn')...Hong Kong	22·28 N	114·20 E
148	Koyang (gōōŭ'yäng).......China	33·32 N	116·10 E
127	Koynare...................Bul.	43·23 N	24·07 E
64	Koyuk (kô-yōōk').........Alaska	65·00 N	161·18 W
64	Koyukuk (R.) (kô-yōō'kŏŏk) Alaska	66·25 N	153·50 W
127	Kozáni....................Grc.	40·16 N	21·51 E
129	Kozelets (kôzĕ-lyĕts)....Sov. Un.	50·53 N	31·07 E
121	Kozienice (kō-zyĕ-nē'tsĕ).....Pol.	51·34 N	21·35 E
121	Koźle (kôzh'lĕ)..............Pol.	50·19 N	18·10 E
127	Kozloduy (kŭz'lô-dwē).......Bul.	43·45 N	23·42 E
153	Kōzu (I.) (kō'zōō).........Jap.	34·16 N	139·03 E
154	Kra, Isth. of..............Thai.	9·30 S	99·45 E
167	Kraai (R.) (krā'ê) S. Afr. (Natal In.)	30·50 S	27·03 E
111	Krabbendijke Neth. (Amsterdam In.)	51·26 N	4·05 E
118	Kragerö (krä'gĕr-û).........Nor.	58·53 N	9·21 E
127	Kragujevac (krä'gōō'yĕ-vȧts) Yugo.	44·01 N	20·55 E
121	Kraków (krä'kŏŏf)..........Pol.	50·05 N	20·00 E
113	Kraljevo (kräl'ye-vô)......Yugo.	43·39 N	20·48 E
129	Kramatorsk (krȧ-mä'tôrsk) Sov. Un.	48·43 N	37·32 E
118	Kramfors (kräm'fôrs).......Swe.	62·54 N	17·49 E
126	Kranj (krän')..............Yugo.	46·16 N	14·23 E
167	Kranskop (kränz'kŏp) S. Afr. (Natal In.)	28·57 S	30·54 E
128	Krāslava (kräs'lä-vä)....Sov. Un.	55·53 N	27·12 E
120	Kraslice (kräs'lê-tsĕ).......Czech.	50·19 N	12·30 E
136	Krasnaya Gorka (kräs'nȧ-yȧ gôr'kȧ).Sov. Un. (Urals In.)	55·13 N	56·43 E
133	Krasnaya Sloboda.......Sov. Un.	48·25 N	44·35 E
121	Kraśnik (kräsh'nĭk)..........Pol.	50·53 N	22·15 E
136	Krasnoarmeysk (kräs'nô-ȧr-maśk') Sov. Un. (Moscow In.)	56·06 N	38·09 E
129	Krasnoarmeyskoye......Sov. Un.	48·19 N	37·04 E
129	Krasnodar (kräs'nô-dȧr).Sov. Un.	45·03 N	38·55 E
129	Krasnodarskiy (Oblast) Province (krȧs-nô-där'skĭ ôb'lȧst) Sov. Un.	47·28 N	38·13 E
136	Krasnogorskiy (kräs-nô-gôr'skĭ) Sov. Un. (Urals In.)	54·36 N	61·25 E
129	Krasnograd (kräs'nô-grät) Sov. Un.	49·23 N	35·26 E
136	Krasnogvardeyskiy (krâ'sno-gvăr-dzyē ês-kēê) Sov. Un. (Urals In.)	57·17 N	62·05 E
132	Krasnokamsk (kräs-nô-kämsk') Sov. Un.	58·00 N	55·45 E
129	Krasnokutsk (krȧs-nô-kōōtsk') Sov. Un.	50·03 N	35·05 E
129	Krasnosel'ye (kräs'nô-sĕl'yĕ) Sov. Un.	48·44 N	32·24 E
132	Krasnoslobodsk (kräs'nô-slôbôtsk') Sov. Un.	54·20 N	43·50 E
136	Krasnotur'insk (krŭs-nŭ-tōō-rensk') Sov. Un. (Urals In.)	59·47 N	60·15 E
136	Krasnoufimsk (krŭs-nŭ-ōō-fēmsk') Sov. Un. (Urals In.)	56·38 N	57·46 E
136	Krasnoural'sk (kräs'nô-ōō-rälsk') Sov. Un. (Urals In.)	58·21 N	60·05 E
136	Krasnousol'skiy (kräs-nô-ŏŏ-sôl'skĭ) Sov. Un. (Urals In.)	53·53 N	56·30 E
132	Krasnovishersk (kräs-nô-vêshersk').Sov. Un.	60·22 N	57·20 E
133	Krasnovodsk (krȧs-nô-vôtsk') Sov. Un.	40·00 N	52.50 E
134	Krasnoyarsk (kräs-nô-yȧrsk') Sov. Un.	56·13 N	93·12 E
136	Krasnoye Selo (kräs'nŭ-yŭ sâ'lō) Sov. Un. (Leningrad In.)	59·44 N	30·06 E
128	Krasny Kholm (kräs'nê кōlm) Sov. Un.	58·03 N	37·11 E
121	Krasnystaw (kräs-nê-stȧf')...Pol.	50·59 N	23·11 E
136	Krasnyy Bor (kräs'nê bôr) Sov. Un. (Leningrad In.)	59·41 N	30·40 E
136	Krasnyy Klyuch (kräs'nê klyûch') Sov. Un. (Urals In.)	55·24 N	56·43 E
133	Krasnyy Kut (krȧs-nê kōōt') Sov. Un.	50·50 N	47·00 E
154	Kratie (krȧ-tyā')..........Camb.	12·28 N	106·06 E
136	Kratovo (krä'tô-vô) Sov. Un. (Moscow In.)	55·35 N	38·10 E
127	Kratovo (krä'tô-vô)........Yugo.	42·04 N	22·12 E
123	Krefeld (krā'fĕlt).Ger. (Ruhr In.)	51·20 N	6·34 E
129	Kremenchug (krĕm'ĕn-chōōgh') Sov. Un.	49·04 N	33·26 E
129	Kremenchugskoye (Res.) (krĕm-ĕn-chōōgh'skô-ye) Sov. Un.	49·20 N	32·45 E
121	Kremenets (krĕ-mĕn-yĕts') Sov. Un.	50·06 N	25·43 E
111	Kremmen (krĕ'mĕn) Ger. (Berlin In.)	52·45 N	13·02 E
111	Krempe (krĕm'pĕ) Ger. (Hamburg In.)	53·50 N	9·29 E
120	Krems (krĕms).............Aus.	48·25 N	15·36 E
119	Krestsy...............Sov. Un.	58·18 N	32·26 E
128	Kresttsy (krâst'sê)......Sov. Un.	58·16 N	32·25 E
119	Kretinga (krĕ-tĭŋ'gȧ)....Sov. Un.	55·55 N	21·17 E
164	Kribi (krē'bê).............Cam.	3·03 N	9·58 E
128	Krichëv (krē'chôf)......Sov. Un.	53·44 N	31·39 E
152	Krillon, Mys (Pt.) (mĭs krĭl' ôn) Sov. Un.	45·58 N	142·00 E
111	Krimpenald Ijssel Neth. (Amsterdam In.)	51·55 N	4·34 E
142	Krishnanagar..............India	23·29 N	88·33 E
118	Kristiansand (krĭs-tyȧn-sän'').Nor.	58·09 N	7·59 E
118	Kristianstad(krĭs-tyȧn-städ').Swe.	56·02 N	14·09 E
118	Kristiansund (krĭs-tyȧn-sŏŏn'') Nor.	63·07 N	7·49 E
118	Kristinehamn (krês-tē'nĕ-häm') Swe.	59·20 N	14·05 E
119	Kristinestad (krĭs-tē'nĕ-städh).Fin.	62·16 N	21·28 E
127	Kriva-Palanka (krē-vȧ-pȧ-läŋ'kȧ) Yugo.	42·12 N	22·21 E
129	Krivoy Rog (krê-voi' rôgh') Sov. Un.	47·54 N	33·22 E
129	Krivoye Ozero..........Sov. Un.	47·57 N	30·21 E
126	Križevci (krē'zhĕv-tsĭ).....Yugo.	46·02 N	16·30 E
126	Krk (I.) (k'rk)............Yugo.	45·06 N	14·33 E
121	Krnov (k'r'nôf)...........Czech.	50·05 N	17·41 E
118	Kröderen (krû'dĕ-rĕn).......Nor.	60·07 N	9·49 E
129	Krolevets (krô-lĕ'vyĕts)..Sov. Un.	51·33 N	33·21 E
121	Kroměříž (krô'myĕr-zhēzh).Czech.	49·18 N	17·23 E
128	Kromy (krô'mê)........Sov. Un.	52·44 N	35·41 E
135	Kronotskiy, Mys (C.) (krô'nôt'skĭ-ê).Sov. Un.	54·58 N	163·15 E
136	Kronshtadt (krōn'shtät) Sov. Un. (Leningrad In.)	59·59 N	29·47 E
168	Kroonstad (krōn'shtät)....S. Afr. (Johannesburg & Pretoria In.)	27·40 S	27·15 E
133	Kropotkin (krȧ-pôt'kĭn).Sov. Un.	45·25 N	40·30 E
121	Krosno (krôs'nô)............Pol.	49·41 N	21·46 E
121	Krotoszyn (krô-tō'shĭn)......Pol.	51·41 N	17·25 E
126	Krško (k'rsh'kô)...........Yugo.	45·58 N	15·30 E
166	Kruger Natl. Park (krōō'gĕr) (krü'gĕr).S. Afr.	23·22 S	30·18 E
167	Krugersdorp (krōō'gĕrz-dôrp) S. Afr. (Johannesburg & Pretoria In.)	26·06 S	27·46 E
127	Krujë (krōō'yȧ).............Alb.	41·32 N	19·49 E
154	Krung Thep (Bangkok).....Thai.	13·50 N	100·29 E
127	Kruševac (krŏŏ'shĕ-vȧts)...Yugo.	43·34 N	21·21 E
127	Krušovo (krōō'shô-vô).....Yugo.	41·20 N	21·15 E
119	Krustpils (krŏŏst'pêls)...Sov. Un.	56·31 N	25·51 E
118	Krylbo (krŭl'bô)...........Swe.	60·07 N	16·14 E
129	Krymskaya (krĭm'skȧ-yȧ).Sov. Un.	44·58 N	38·01 E
129	Krymskaya (Oblast).....Sov. Un.	45·08 N	34·05 E

ăt; finăl; rāte; senâte; ärm; ȧsk; sofȧ; fâre; ch-choose; dh-as th in other; bē; êvent; bĕt; recĕnt; cratẽr; g-go; gh-guttural g; bĭt; ĭ-short neutral; rīde; к-guttural k as ch in German ich;

PRONOUNCING INDEX

Krymskiye Gory–La Cresenta 225

Page	Name Pronunciation Region	Lat. °′	Long. °′
129	Krymskiye Gory (Mts.) (krēm′skĭ-yě gô′rĭ). Sov. Un.	65·21 N	117·13 E
129	Krymskiy (Crimea) Poluostrov (Pen.) (krēm′skĭ pô-lo͝o-ôs′trôf) Sov. Un.	45·18 N	33·30 E
121	Krynki (krĭn′kė)............Pol.	53·15 N	23·47 E
129	Kryukov (k′r′yo͞o-kôf′)..Sov. Un.	49·02 N	33·26 E
125	Ksar Chellala...............Alg.	35·12 N	2·20 E
125	Ksar el Boukhari............Alg.	35·50 N	2·48 E
114	Ksar el Kebir..............Mor.	35·01 N	5·48 W
139	Ktima.....Cyprus (Palestine In.)	34·46 N	32·27 E
139	Kuala Klawang Mala. (Singapore In.)	2·57 N	102·04 E
139	Kuala Lumpur (kwä′lä lo͞om-po͞or′) Mala. (Singapore In.)	3·08 N	101·42 E
150	Kuan (ko͞o′än′).China (Peking In.)	39·25 N	116·18 E
148	Kuan (R.) (go͞oäɴ)........China	31·56 N	115·19 E
151	Kuangchang..............China	25·50 N	116·18 E
149	Kuangchou (Canton) (kăn′tŏn′) China (Canton In.)	23·07 N	113·15 E
151	Kuangchou Wan (B.)......China	20·40 N	111·00 E
	Kuanghsi, see Kwangsi Chuang		
148	Kuangjao (go͞oäɴg′rou).....China	37·04 N	118·24 E
148	Kuanglu Tao (I.) (go͞oäng′lo͞o dou) China	39·13 N	122·21 E
148	Kuangp′ing (go͞oäɴg′pĭng).China	36.30 N	114·57 E
148	Kuangshan (go͞oäɴg′shan)..China	32·02 N	114·53 E
146	Kuangsi Chuang (Aut. Reg.) (go͞oäɴg′sē jwäng).China	23·52 N	108·30 E
151	Kuangte.................China	30·40 N	119·20 E
147	Kuangtung (Kwangtung) (Prov.) China	23·49 N	113·02 E
148	Kuanhsien (go͞oäɴ′sĭäɴ)....China	36·30 N	115·28 E
148	Kuanhu (go͞oäɴ′hoo).......China	34·26 N	117·59 E
148	Kuankü Shan (Mts.) (go͞oäɴ′go͞o shäɴ).China	35·20 N	117·27 E
148	Kuant′ao (go͞oäɴ′tou)......China	36·39 N	115·25 E
150	Kuantien................China	40·40 N	24·50 E
148	Kuanyün (go͞oän′yün).....China	34·28 N	119·16 E
133	Kuba (ko͞o′bȧ)..........Sov. Un.	41·05 N	48·30 E
129	Kuban′ (R.) (ko͝o-bȧn″).Sov. Un.	45·10 N	37·55 E
133	Kuban (R.)............Sov. Un.	45·20 N	40·05 E
115	Kuban R...............Sov. Un	45·14 N	38·20 E
132	Kubenskoye (L.)........Sov. Un.	59·40 N	39·40 E
	Kucha, see Kuch′e		
146	Kuch′e (Kucha) (ko͞o′chĕ′) (kō′chä′).China	41·34 N	82·44 E
148	Kuchen (ko͞o′jĕn)..........China	33·20 N	117·18 E
148	Kuch′eng (ko͞o′chĕng′).....China	39·09 N	115·43 E
154	Kuching (ko͞o′chĭng).......Mala.	1·30 N	110·26 E
153	Kuchinoerabo (I.) (ko͞o′chė nō ĕr′ȧ-bō).Jap.	30·31 N	129·53 E
153	Kudamatsu (ko͞o′dȧ-mä′tso͞o).Jap.	34·00 N	131·51 E
154	Kudat (ko͞o-dät′).........Mala.	6·56 N	116·48 E
119	Kudirkos Naumiestis (ko͞odĭr-kôs nȧ′o͞o-mě′stĭs).Sov. Un.	54·51 N	23·00 E
134	Kudymakar (ko͞o-dĭm-kär′) Sov. Un.	58·43 N	54·52 E
148	Kuei (R.) (ko͞oä)..........China	33·30 N	116·56 E
151	Kueichih................China	30·35 N	117·28 E
149	Kueichou.....China (Canton In.)	22·46 N	113·15 E
146	Kueichou (Kweichow) (Prov.) China	27·03 N	106·31 E
151	Kueilin.................China	25·18 N	110·22 E
150	Kueisui.................China	41·05 N	111·50 E
151	Kueiyang................China	26·45 N	107·00 E
146	K′uerhlo................China	41·37 N	86·03 E
120	Kufstein (ko͞of′shtīn)........Aus.	47·34 N	12·11 E
111	Kuhstedt (ko͞o′shtĕt) Ger. (Hamburg In.)	53·23 N	8·58 E
	Kuibyshev, see Kuybyshev		
166	Kuilsrivier.S. Afr. (Cape Town In.)	33·56 S	18·41 E
153	Kuji....................Jap.	33·57 N	131·18 E
153	Kujū-san (Mt.) (ko͞o′jo͝o-sän′).Jap.	33·07 N	131·14 E
165	Kukawa (ko͞o-kä′wä)........Nig.	12·55 N	13·35 E
127	Kukës (ko͞o′kĕs)............Alb.	42·03 N	20·25 E
127	Kula (ko͞o′lȧ)...............Bul.	43·52 N	23·13 E
133	Kula.......................Tur.	38·32 N	28·30 E
142	Kula Kangri Mt...........China	33·11 N	90·36 E
135	Kular, Khrebet (Mts.) (ko͝o-lär′) Sov. Un.	69·00 N	131·45 E
119	Kuldīga (ko͝ol′dė-gȧ).....Sov. Un.	56·59 N	21·59 E
132	Kulebaki (ko͞o-lě-bäk′ĭ)..Sov. Un.	55·22 N	42·30 E
120	Kulmbach (klo͝olm′bäĸ).....Ger.	50·07 N	11·28 E
126	Kulpa (R.) (ko͝ol′pȧ).......Yugo.	45·32 N	14·50 E
134	Kulunda (ko͝o-lo͝on′dȧ)...Sov. Un.	52·38 N	74·00 E
134	Kulundinskoye (L.).....Sov. Un.	52·45 N	77·18 E
152	Kum (R.) (ko͝om)..........Kor.	36·50 N	127·30 E
133	Kuma (R.) (ko͞o′mä)....Sov. Un.	44·50 N	45·10 E
153	Kumamoto (ko͞o′mä-mō′tô)..Jap.	32·49 N	130·40 E
153	Kumano-Nada (Sea) (ko͞o-mä′nō nä-dä).Jap.	34·03 N	136·36 E
127	Kumanovo (ko͝o-mä′nô-vô).Yugo.	42·10 N	21·41 E
164	Kumasi (ko͞o-mä′sė).......Ghana	6·45 N	1·39 W
164	Kumba (ko͝om′bȧ).........Cam.	4·41 N	9·26 E
143	Kumbakonam (ko͝om′bŭ-kō′nŭm) India	10·59 N	79·25 E
127	Kumkale..................Tur.	39·59 N	26·10 E
143	Kumta...................India	14·19 N	75·28 E
136	Kunashak (kû-nä′shȧk) Sov. Un. (Urals In.)	55·43 N	61·35 E
152	Kunashir (I.) (ko͞o-nŭ-shēr′) Sov. Un.	44·40 N	145·45 E
148	Kunch′eng Hu (L.) (ko͞oɴ′chĕng hoo).China	31·36 N	120·57 E
128	Kunda (ko͝o′dȧ)........Sov. Un.	59·30 N	26·28 E
163	Kundelungu, Plateau des (Plat). Con. K.	9·00 S	25·30 E
136	Kundravy (ko͞on′drȧ-vĭ) Sov. Un. (Urals In.)	54·50 N	60·14 E
139	Kundur (I.).Indon. (Singapore In.)	0·49 N	103·20 E
	Kunene (R.), see Cunene		
118	Kungälv (kŭng′ĕlf).........Swe.	57·53 N	12·01 E
136	Kungur (ko͝on-go͞or′) Sov. Un. (Urals In.)	57·27 N	56·53 E
103	Kungrad (ko͝on-grät′)...Sov. Un.	42·59 N	59·00 E
118	Kungsbacka (kŭngs′bä-kȧ)...Swe.	57·31 N	12·04 E
142	Kungsherya..............China	31·33 N	84·38 E
146	K′un Lun Shan (Mts.) (ko͝on′lo͞on′ shän′).China	35·26 N	83·09 E
151	K′unming (Yünnanfu) (ko͝on′ mĭng′) (yûn′nän′fo͞o′).China	25·10 N	102·50 E
152	Kunsan (ko͝on′sän′).........Kor.	35·54 N	126·46 E
149	K′unshan (ko͞on′shän′) China (Shanghai In.)	31·23 N	120·57 E
136	Kuntsëvo (ko͝on-tsyô′vô) Sov. Un. (Moscow In.)	55·43 N	37·27 E
136	Kun′ya.......Sov. Un. (Urals In.)	58·42 N	56·47 E
128	Kun′ya (R.) (ko͝on′yȧ)...Sov. Un.	56·45 N	30·53 E
112	Kuopio (ko͝o-ô′pê-ŏ).........Fin.	62·48 N	28·30 E
155	Kupang..................Indon.	10·14 S	123·37 E
134	Kupino (ko͞o-pĭ′nô)......Sov. Un.	54·00 N	77·47 E
119	Kupiškis (ko͝o-pĭsh′kĭs)..Sov. Un.	55·50 N	24·55 E
129	Kupyansk (ko͞op-yänsk′).Sov. Un.	49·44 N	37·38 E
133	Kura (R.) (ko͞o′rȧ)......Sov. Un.	41·10 N	45·40 E
146	Kurak Darya (R.).........China	41·09 N	87·46 E
153	Kurashiki (ko͞o′rä-shē′kė)....Jap.	34·37 N	133·44 E
153	Kurayoshi (ko͞o′rȧ-yō′shė)....Jap.	35·25 N	133·49 E
133	Kurdistan (Reg.) (kûrd′ĭ-stăn) Tur.-Iran	37·40 N	43·30 E
127	Kŭrdzhali.................Bul.	41·39 N	25·21 E
153	Kure (ko͞o′rĕ)..............Jap.	34·17 N	132·35 E
119	Kuressaare (ko͝o′rĕ-sä′rĕ).Sov. Un.	58·15 N	22·26 E
134	Kurgan (ko͝or-găn′)......Sov. Un.	55·28 N	65·14 E
134	Kurgan Tyube (ko͝or-gän′ tyo͝o′bĕ) Sov. Un.	38·00 N	68·49 E
144	Kuria Muria Is. (Br.) (ko͞o-rė-ȧ mo͞o′rė-ȧ).Aden	17·27 N	56·02 E
153	Kurihama (ko͞o-rē-hä′mä) Jap. (Tōkyō In.)	35·14 N	139·42 E
135	Kuril Is. (ko͞o′rĭl).......Sov. Un.	46·20 N	149·30 E
119	Kurisches Haff (Bay)....Sov. Un.	55·10 N	21·08 E
165	Kurmuk (ko͝or′mo͞ok)........Sud.	10·40 N	34·13 E
143	Kurnool (ko͝or-no͞ol′).......India	16·00 N	78·04 E
153	Kuro (I.) (ko͞o′rô)...........Jap.	30·49 N	129·56 E
161	Kurrajong Austl. (Sydney In.)	33·33 S	150·40 E
119	Kuršenai (ko͝or′shȧ-nī)...Sov. Un.	56·01 N	22·56 E
129	Kursk (ko͝orsk).........Sov. Un.	51·44 N	36·08 E
129	Kursk (Oblast) (ko͝orsk).Sov. Un.	51·30 N	35·13 E
127	Kuršumlija (ko͝or′sho͝om′lĭ-yȧ) Yugo.	43·08 N	21·18 E
166	Kuruman (ko͞o-ro͞o-măn′)..S. Afr.	27·25 S	23·30 E
153	Kurume (ko͞o′ro͞o-mĕ).......Jap.	33·10 N	130·30 E
153	Kururi (ko͞o′ro͝o-rė) Jap. (Tōkyō In.)	35·17 N	140·05 E
136	Kusa (ko͞o′sȧ) Sov. Un. (Urals In.)	55·19 N	59·27 E
129	Kushchëvskaya.........Sov. Un.	46·34 N	39·40 E
134	Kushevat..............Sov. Un.	65·05 N	65·28 E
148	Kushih (go͞o′sēĭ)...........China	32·11 N	115·39 E
153	Kushikino (ko͞o′shĭ-kē′nō)....Jap.	31·44 N	130·19 E
153	Kushimoto (ko͞o′shĭ-mō′tō)...Jap.	33·29 N	135·47 E
152	Kushiro (ko͞o′shē-rō).........Jap.	43·00 N	144·22 E
134	Kush-Murun (L.) (ko͞osh-mo͞o-ro͞on′).Sov. Un.	52·30 N	64·15 E
133	Kushum (R.) (ko͝o-sho͝om′) Sov. Un.	50·30 N	50·40 E
136	Kushva (ko͞osh′vȧ) Sov. Un. (Urals In.)	58·18 N	59·51 E
64	Kuskokwim (R.)..........Alaska	61·32 N	160·36 W
64	Kuskokwim B. (kŭs′kô-kwĭm) Alaska	59·25 N	163·14 W
64	Kuskokwim Mts.........Alaska	62·08 N	158·00 W
64	Kuskovak (kŭs-kō′văk)...Alaska	60·10 N	162·50 W
134	Kustanay (ko͝os-tȧ-nī′)...Sov. Un.	53·10 N	63·39 E
133	Kütahya (kû-tä′hyȧ)........Tur.	39·20 N	29·50 E
133	Kutaisi (ko͞o-tŭ-ē′sē).....Sov. Un.	42·15 N	42·40 E
154	Kutaradja...............Indon.	5·30 N	95·20 E
142	Kutch, Gulf of............India	22·45 N	68·33 E
142	Kutch, Rann of (Swp.).....India	23·59 N	69·13 E
111	Kutenholz (ko͞o′tĕn-hōlts) Ger. (Hamburg In.)	53·29 N	9·20 E
136	Kutim (ko͞o′tĭm) Sov. Un. (Urals In.)	60·22 N	58·51 E
126	Kutina (ko͞o′tė-nȧ).........Yugo.	45·29 N	16·48 E
121	Kutno (ko͝ot′nô)............Pol.	52·14 N	19·22 E
132	Kutno (L.).............Sov. Un.	65·15 N	31·30 E
134	Kutulik (ko͝o to͞o′lyĭk)...Sov. Un.	53·12 N	102·51 E
121	Kuty (ko͞o′tė)...........Sov. Un.	48·16 N	25·12 E
112	Kuusamo (ko͞o′sȧ-mô).......Fin.	65·59 N	29·10 E
128	Kuvshinovo (ko͝ov-shē′nô-vô) Sov. Un.	57·01 N	34·09 E
	Kuwait, see Al Kuwayt		
138	Kuwait....................Asia	29·00 N	48·45 E
153	Kuwana (ko͞o′wȧ-nȧ).........Jap.	35·02 N	136·40 E
132	Kuybyshev (Kuibyshev) (ko͞o′ē-bĭ-shĭf).Sov. Un.	53·10 N	50·05 E
134	Kuybyshev.............Sov. Un.	55·00 N	44·25 E
132	Kuybyshevskoye (Res.)..Sov. Un.	53·40 N	49·00 E
148	Kuyeh (go͞o′yĕ)............China	39·46 N	118·23 E
133	Kuzey Anadolu Dağ′ari (Mts.) Tur.	41·20 N	34·30 E
133	Kuznetsk (ko͞oz-nyĕtsk′).Sov. Un.	53·00 N	46·30 E
134	Kuznetsk Basin.........Sov Un.	57·15 N	86·15 E
136	Kuznetsovka (ko͝oz-nyĕt′sôf-kȧ) Sov. Un. (Urals In.)	54·41 N	56·40 E
128	Kuznetsovo (ko͝oz-nyĕt-sô′vô) Sov. Un.	56·39 N	36·55 E
126	Kvarnerski Zaliv (B.) (kvär′nĕr-skė′ zä′lêv).Yugo.	44·41 N	14·05 E
64	Kvichak (vĭc′-hăk)........Alaska	59·00 N	156·48 W
166	Kwango (R.) (kwäng′ō′).....Ang.	8·30 S	18·00 E
	Kwangtung, see Kuangtung		
	Kweichow, see Kueichou		
	Kweitun, see Wusu		
166	Kwenge (R.) (kwĕŋ′gĕ)...Con. K.	6·45 S	18·34 E
121	Kwidzyń (kvē′dzĭn′)........Pol.	53·45 N	18·56 E
166	Kwilu (R.) (kwē′lo͞o).....Con. K.	7·00 S	19·20 E
164	Kwitta (kwĭt′ȧ)..........Ghana	6·00 N	1·00 E
135	Kyakhta (kyäĸ′ta)......Sov. Un.	51·00 N	107·30 E
142	Kyang Tsho (L.)..........China	30·37 N	88·33 E
142	Kyayisu (R.)..............India	38·05 N	74·36 E
146	Kyaukpyu (chouk′pyoo′)....Bur.	19·19 N	93·33 E
119	Kybartai (kē′bär-tī′)....Sov. Un.	54·40 N	22·46 E
151	Ky Lam...................Viet.	15·48 N	108·30 E
136	Kyn (kĭn′)...Sov. Un. (Urals In.)	51·52 N	58·42 E
159	Kynuna (kī-no͞o′nȧ)........Austl.	21·30 S	142·12 E
165	Kyoga L....................Ug.	1·27 N	33·51 E
153	Kyōga-Saki (C.) (kyō′gä sa′kė) Jap.	35·46 N	135·14 E
152	Kyŏngju (kyŭng′yo͞o).......Kor.	35·48 N	129·12 E
153	Kyōto (kyō′tō′)..Jap. (Ōsaka In.)	35·00 N	135·46 E
153	Kyōto (Pref.)....Jap. (Ōsaka In.)	34·56 N	135·42 E
134	Kyren (kĭ-rĕn′).........Sov. Un.	51·46 N	102·13 E
119	Kyrön (R.) (kû′rô)..........Fin.	63·03 N	22·20 E
136	Kyrya (kēr′yȧ) Sov. Un. (Urals In.)	59·18 N	59·03 E
136	Kyshtym (kĭsh-tĭm′) Sov. Un. (Urals In.)	55·43 N	60·33 E
136	Kytlym (kĭt′lĭm) Sov. Un. (Urals In.)	59·30 N	59·15 E
153	Kyūshū (I.) (kyo͞o′sho͞o′).....Jap.	32·27 N	131·03 E
127	Kyustendil (kyo͝os-tĕn-dĭl′)...Bul.	42·16 N	22·39 E
134	Kyzyl (kĭ zĭl)...........Sov. Un.	51·37 N	93·38 E
103	Kyzylkum (Des.) (kĭ zĭl ko͞om) Sov. Un.	42·47 N	64·45 E
146	Kyzylsu (R.)..............China	39·26 N	74·30 E
134	Kzyl-Orda (kzėl-ôr′dȧ)...Sov. Un.	44·58 N	65·45 E
120	Laa.......................Aus.	48·42 N	16·23 E
124	La Almunia de Doña Godina (lä′äl-mo͞on′yä dā dō nyä gô-dē′nä).Sp.	41·29 N	1·22 W
98	La Asunción (lä ä-so͞on-syōn′).Ven.	11·02 N	63·57 W
100	La Banda (lä bän′dä).......Arg.	27·48 S	64·12 W
90	La Barca (lä bär′kȧ)........Mex.	20·17 N	102·33 W
164	Labé (lȧ-bā′)...............Gui.	11·15 N	12·16 W
120	Labe (Elbe) R. (lä′bĕ) (ĕl′bĕ) Czech.	50·05 N	15·20 E
86	Laberge (R.) (lȧ-bĕrzh′).....Can.	61·08 N	136·42 W
94	Laberinto de las Doce Leguas (Is.) (lä-bȧ-rēn tô dā läs dō′sȧ lā′gwäs).Cuba	20·40 N	78·35 W
133	Labinsk...............Sov. Un.	44·30 N	40·40 E
139	Labis (läb′ĭs) Mala. (Singapore In.)	2·23 N	103·01 E
125	La Bisbal (lä bēs-bäl′)........Sp.	41·55 N	3·00 E
155	Labo (lä′bô)....Phil. (Manila In.)	13·39 N	121·14 E
155	Labo..........Phil. (Manila In.)	14·11 N	122·49 E
155	Labo, Mt......Phil. (Manila In.)	14·00 N	122·47 E
85	L′Abord-a-Plouffe (lä-bōr′dä-plo͞of).Can. (Montreal In.)	45·32 N	73·45 W
122	Labouheyre (lȧ-bo͞o-âr′).......Fr.	44·14 N	0·58 W
100	Laboulaye (lä-bô′o͞o-lä-yĕ)...Arg.	34·01 S	63·10 W
87	Labrador (Reg.) (lăb′rȧ-dôr)..Can.	53·05 N	63·30 W
98	Lábrea (lä-brā′ä)...........Braz.	7·28 S	64·39 W
155	Labuan (lä-bwä′n) Phil. (Manila In.)	13·43 N	120·07 E
154	Labuan (I.) (lä-bo͝o-än′)....Mala.	5·28 N	115·11 E
155	Labuha..................Indon.	0·43 S	127·35 E
85	L′Acadie (lȧ-kȧ-dē′) Can. (Montreal In.)	45·18 N	73·22 W
85	L′Acadie, Riviére (rė-vyâr′) Can. (Montreal In.)	45·24 N	73·21 W
101	La Calera (lä-kä-lĕ-rä) Chile (Santiago In.)	32·47 S	71·11 W
98	La Calera............Col. (In.)	4·43 N	73·58 W
113	La Calle (lȧ kȧl′)............Alg.	36·52 N	8·23 E
74	La Canada (lä kän-yä′dä) Calif. (Los Angeles In.)	34·13 N	118·12 W
91	Lacantum (R.) (lä-kän-to͞o′m) Mex.	16·13 N	90·52 W
124	La Carolina (lä kä-rô-lē′nä)...Sp.	38·16 N	3·48 W
91	La Catedral, Cerro (Mtn.) (sĕ′r-rô-lä-kä-tĕ-drȧ′l) Mex. (Mexico City In.)	19·32 N	99·31 W
82	Lac-au-Saumon.............Can.	48·24 N	67·23 W
85	Lac-Beauport (läk-bō-pōr′) Can. (Quebec In.)	46·58 N	71·17 W
143	Laccadive Is. (lăk′ȧ-dīv)....India	11·00 N	73·02 E
142	Laccadive Sea..............Asia	9·10 N	75·17 E
71	Lac Court Oreille Ind. Res. (lāk kôrt-ô-rēl) (lȧk ko͞or tô-rā′y′).Wis.	46·04 N	91·18 W
71	Lac du Flambeau Ind. Res...Wis.	46·12 N	89·50 W
92	La Ceiba (lȧ sēbä).........Hond.	15·45 N	86·52 W
98	La Ceja (lä-sĕ-ĸä)......Col. (In.)	6·02 N	75·25 W
87	Lac Frontiere..............Can.	46·41 N	70·04 W
132	Lacha (L.) (lȧ′chä)......Sov. Un.	61·15 N	39·05 E
120	La Chaux de Fonds (lȧ shō-dē-fôɴ′).Switz.	47·07 N	6·47 E
85	L′Achigan, R. (lä-shē-gäɴ) Can. (Montreal In.)	45·49 N	73·48 W
85	Lachine (lȧ-shēn′) Can. (Montreal In.)	45·26 N	73·40 W
160	Lachlan (R.) (läk′lăn)......Austl.	33·54 S	145·15 E
88	La Chorrera (lȧchôr-rā′rä) Pan. (Panama Canal In.)	8·54 N	79·47 W
85	Lachute (lȧ-sho͞ot′) Can. (Montreal In.)	45·39 N	74·20 W
123	La Ciotat (lȧ syô-tȧ′).........Fr.	43·13 N	5·35 E
75	Lackawanna (lak-ȧ-wŏn′á) N. Y. (Buffalo In.)	42·49 N	78·50 W
86	Lac la Biche..............Can.	54·46 N	112·04 W
82	Lac-Mégantic.............Can.	45·34 N	70·53 W
	La Columna, see Bolivar		
86	Lacombe..................Can.	52·29 N	113·41 W
91	La Concordia (lä-kōn-kô′r-dyä) Mex.	16·07 N	92·40 W
81	Laconia (lȧ-kō′nĭ-ȧ)........N. H.	43·30 N	71·30 W
65	La Conner (lȧ kŏn′ēr) Wash. (Seattle In.)	48·23 N	122·30 W
124	La Coruña (lȧ kô-ro͞on′yä)....Sp.	43·20 N	8·20 W
70	Lacreek (L.) (lȧ′krēk).......S. D.	43·04 N	101·46 W
74	La Cresenta (lȧ krĕs′ĕnt-ȧ) Calif. (Los Angeles In.)	34·14 N	118·13 W

ng-sing; ŋ-baŋk; ɴ-nasalized n; nŏd; cŏmmit; ōld; ôbey; ôrder; fo͞od; fo͝ot; ou-out; s-soft; sh-dish; th-thin; pūre; ûnite; ûrn; stŭd; circŭs; ü-as "y" in study; ′-indeterminate vowel.

226 La Cross–Lansing PRONOUNCING INDEX

Page	Name Pronunciation Region	Lat. °′	Long. °′
72	La Cross (lȧ-krôs') Kans.	38·30 N	99·20 W
71	La Crosse Wis.	43·48 N	91·14 W
92	La Cruz (lä-krōō'z) C. R.	11·05 N	85·37 W
98	La Cruz (lȧ krōōz') Col.	1·37 N	77·00 W
70	Lacs, Riviere des (R.) (rē-vyĕr' de läk). N. D.	48·30 N	101·45 W
85	Lac-St-Charles (läk-sĕn-shärl) Can. (Quebec In.)	46·55 N	71·23 W
93	La Cuesta (lä-kwĕ's-tä) C. R.	8·32 N	82·51 W
124	La Culebra, Sierra de (Mts.) (sē-ĕ'r-rä-dĕ-lä-kōō-lĕ-brä). Sp.	41·52 N	6·21 W
73	La Cygne (lȧ-sēn'y')(lȧ-sēn'). Kans.	38·20 N	94·45 W
80	Ladd (lăd) Ill.	41·25 N	89·25 W
124	La Demanda, Sierra de (Mts.) (sē-ĕ'r-rä-dĕ-lä-dĕ-mä'n-dä). Sp.	42·10 N	2·35 W
125	Ladíspoli (lä-dê's-pô-lē) It. (Rome In.)	41·57 N	12·05 E
65	Ladner (lăd'nēr) Can. (Vancouver In.)	49·05 N	123·06 W
142	Lādnun (läd'nōōn) India	27·45 N	74·20 E
	Ladoga, Lake, see Ladozhskoye Ozero		
98	La Dorado (lä dô-rä'dä). Col. (In.)	5·28 N	74·42 W
119	Ladozhskoye Ozero (Lake Ladoga) (lȧ-dôsh'skô-yē ô'zĕ-rô). Sov. Un.	60·59 N	31·30 E
85	La Durantaye (lä dü-rän-tā') Can. (Quebec In.)	46·51 N	70·51 W
167	Lady Frere (lā-dē frâ'r') S. Afr. (Natal In.)	31·48 S	27·16 E
167	Lady Grey S. Afr. (Natal In.)	30·44 S	27·17 E
66	Ladysmith (lā'dĭ-smĭth) Can.	48·59 N	123·50 W
167	Ladysmith S. Afr. (Natal In.)	28·38 S	29·48 E
71	Ladysmith Wis.	45·27 N	91·07 W
155	Lae (lä'ā) N. Gui. Ter.	6·15 S	146·57 E
118	Laerdal (lâr'däl) Nor.	61·03 N	7·24 E
118	Laerdalsören (lâr'däls-û'rĕn). Nor.	61·08 N	7·26 E
118	Laesø (I.) (lâs'û) Den.	57·17 N	10·57 E
92	La Esperanza (lä ĕs-pä-rän'zä) Hond.	14·20 N	88·21 W
124	La Estrada (lä ĕs-trä'dä) Sp.	42·42 N	8·29 W
152	Lafa (lä'fä) China	43·49 N	127·19 E
122	La-Fare-les-Oliviers (lȧ-fär'lā-ô-lē-vyā) Fr. (Marseille In.)	43·33 N	5·12 E
78	Lafayette Ala.	32·52 N	85·25 W
65	Lafayette Calif. (San Francisco In.)	37·53 N	122·07 W
78	Lafayette (lă-fâ-yĕt') Ga.	34·41 N	85·19 W
80	La Fayette Ind.	40·25 N	86·55 W
77	Lafayette La.	30·15 N	92·02 W
84	La Fayette. R. I. (Providence In.)	41·34 N	71·29 W
123	La Ferté-Alais (lȧ-fĕr-tā'-ȧ-lā') Fr. (Paris In.)	48·29 N	2·19 E
123	La Ferté-sous-Jouarre (lȧ fĕr-tā'sōō-zhōō-är') Fr. (Paris In.)	48·56 N	3·07 E
122	La Flèche (lȧ flâsh') Fr.	47·43 N	0·03 W
122	La Flotte (lȧ flôt') Fr.	46·09 N	1·20 W
78	La Follette (lä-fŏl'ĕt) Tenn.	36·23 N	84·07 W
77	Lafourche, Bay. (bȧ-yōō'lȧ-fōōrsh'). La.	29·25 N	90·15 W
99	La Gaiba (lä-gī'bä) Braz.	17·54 S	57·32 W
116	Lagan (lă'gȧn) N. Ire.	54·30 N	6·00 W
118	Lagan (R.) Swe.	56·34 N	13·25 E
112	Laganes (Pt.) Ice.	66·21 N	14·02 W
88	Lagarto, R. (lä-gä'r-tô) Pan. (Panama Canal In.)	9·08 N	80·05 W
92	Lagartos L. (lä-gä'r-tôs) Mex. (Yucatan In.)	21·32 N	88·15 W
118	Lågen (R.) (lô'ghĕn) Nor.	59·15 N	9·47 E
164	Laghouat (lä-gwät') Alg.	33·45 N	2·49 E
123	Lagny (län-yē') Fr. (Paris In.)	48·53 N	2·41 E
101	Lagoa da Prata (lä-gô'ä-dä-prä'tä) Braz. (Rio de Janeiro In.)	20·04 S	45·33 W
101	Lagoa Dourada (lä-gô'ä-dōō-rä'dä) Braz. (Rio de Janeiro In.)	20·55 S	44·03 W
155	Lagonoy (lä-gô-noi') Phil. (Manila In.)	13·44 N	123·31 E
155	Lagonoy G. Phil. (Manila In.)	13·34 N	123·46 E
164	Lagos (lä'gōs) Nig.	6·31 N	3·15 E
124	Lagos (lä'gōzh) Port.	37·08 N	8·43 W
90	Lagos de Moreno (lä'gōs dā mô-rā'nō). Mex.	21·21 N	101·55 W
122	La Grand' Combe (lȧ grän kanb') Fr.	44·12 N	4·03 E
66	La Grande (lȧ grănd') Ore.	45·20 N	118·06 W
158	La Grange (lȧ grānj) Austl.	18·40 S	122·00 E
78	La Grange (lȧ-grānj') Ga.	33·01 N	85·00 W
75	La Grange Ill. (Chicago In.)	41·49 N	87·53 W
80	Lagrange Ind.	41·40 N	85·25 W
80	La Grange Ky.	38·20 N	85·25 W
73	La Grange Mo.	40·04 N	91·30 W
75	Lagrange Ohio (Cleveland In.)	41·14 N	82·07 W
77	Lagrange Tex.	29·55 N	96·50 W
98	La Grita (lä grē'tä) Ven.	8.02 N	71·59 W
99	La Guaira (lä gwä'ē-rä). Ven. (In.)	10·36 N	66·54 W
124	La Guardia (lä gwär'dē-ä) Sp.	41·55 N	8·48 W
100	Laguna (lä-gōō'nä) Braz.	28·19 S	48·42 W
94	Laguna, Cayos (Is.) (kä'yōs-lä-gōō'nä). Cuba	22·15 N	82·45 W
155	Laguna de Bay (L.) (lä-gōō'nä dā bä'ē). Phil. (Manila In.)	14·24 N	121·13 E
69	Laguna Ind. Res. N. Mex.	35·00 N	107·30 W
98	Lagunillas (lä-gōō-nēl'yäs) Bol.	19·42 S	63·38 W
90	Lagunillas (lä-gōō-nē'l-yäs). Mex.	21·34 N	99·41 W
95	La Habana (Havana) (lä-ä-bä'nä) Cuba (Havana In.)	23·08 N	82·23 W
74	La Habra (lȧ hăb'rȧ) Calif. (Los Angeles In.)	34·56 N	117·57 W
157	Lahaina (lä-hä'ē-nä). Hawaii (In.)	20·52 N	156·39 W
122	La Haye-Descartes (lȧ ȧ-dā-kärt') Fr.	46·58 N	0·42 E
120	Lahn R. (län) Ger.	50·21 N	7·54 E
118	Laholm (lä'hôlm) Swe.	56·30 N	13·00 E
65	La Honda (lä hôn'dă) Calif. (San Francisco In.)	37·20 N	122·16 W
142	Lahore (lä-hōr') W. Pak.	32·00 N	80·00 E
120	Lahr (lär) Ger.	48·19 N	7·52 E
119	Lahti (lä'tē) Fin.	60·59 N	27·39 E
151	Lai, C. Viet.	17·08 N	107·30 E
148	Laian (läī'än) China	32·27 N	118·25 E
148	Laichou Wan (B.) (läī'jō wän) China	37·22 N	119·19 E
122	Laigle (lĕ'gl') Fr.	48·45 N	0·37 E
151	Laipin (lī'pĭn') China	23·42 N	109·20 E
148	Laiyang (läī'yäng) China	36·59 N	120·42 E
90	Laja, Río de la (R.) (rê'ō-dĕ-lä-lä'кä). Mex.	20·17 N	100·57 W
94	Lajas (lä'häs) Cuba	22·25 N	80·20 W
100	Lajeado (lä-zhĕä'dô) Braz.	29·24 S	51·46 W
100	Lajes (lȧ'-zhĕs) Braz.	27·47 S	50·17 W
101	Lajinha (lä-zhē'nyä) Braz. (Rio de Janeiro In.)	20·08 S	41·36 W
68	La Jolla (lȧ hōl'yȧ) Calif. (San Diego In.)	32·51 N	117·16 W
68	La Jolla Ind. Res. Calif.	33·19 N	116·21 W
72	La Junta (lȧ hōōn'tȧ) Colo.	37·59 N	103·35 W
168	Lak Dera (R.) (läk dā'rä) Som. (Horn of Afr. In.)	0·45 N	41·26 E
77	Lake Arthur (är'thŭr) La.	30·06 N	92·40 W
70	Lake Benton (bĕn'tŭn) Minn.	44·15 N	96·17 W
75	Lake Bluff (blŭf). Ill. (Chicago In.)	42·17 N	87·50 W
158	Lake Brown (broun) Austl.	31·03 S	118·30 E
77	Lake Charles (chärlz') La.	30·15 N	93·14 W
79	Lake City Fla.	30·09 N	82·40 W
71	Lake City Iowa	42·14 N	94·43 W
71	Lake City Minn.	44·28 N	92·19 W
79	Lake City S. C.	33·57 N	79·45 W
71	Lake Crystal (krĭs'tȧl) Minn.	44·05 N	94·12 W
116	Lake Dist. (läk) Eng.	54·25 N	3·20 W
74	Lake Elmo (ĕlmō) Minn. (Minneapolis, St. Paul In.)	45·00 N	92·53 W
75	Lake Forest (fŏr'ĕst) Ill. (Chicago In.)	42·16 N	87·50 W
69	Lake Fork (R.) Utah	40·30 N	110·25 W
71	Lake Geneva (jĕ-nē'vȧ) Wis.	42·36 N	88·28 W
87	Lake Harbour (här'bēr) Can.	62·43 N	69·40 W
74	Lake June (jōōn) Tex. (Dallas, Fort Worth In.)	32·43 N	96·45 W
79	Lakeland (läk'lănd) Fla. (In.)	28·02 N	81·58 W
78	Lakeland Ga.	31·02 N	83·02 W
74	Lakeland Minn. (Minneapolis, St. Paul In.)	44·57 N	92·47 W
71	Lake Linden (lĭn'dĕn) Mich.	47·11 N	88·26 W
71	Lake Mills (mĭlz') Iowa	43·25 N	93·32 W
75	Lakemore (läk-mōr) Ohio (Cleveland In.)	41·01 N	81·24 W
80	Lake Odessa Mich.	42·50 N	85·15 W
65	Lake Oswego (ŏs-wē'go) Ore. (Portland In.)	45·25 N	122·40 W
74	Lake Point Utah (Salt Lake City In.)	40·41 N	112·16 W
68	Lakeport (läk'pōrt) Calif.	39·03 N	122·54 W
70	Lake Preston (prēs'tŭn) S. D.	44·21 N	97·23 W
77	Lake Providence (prŏv'ĭ-dĕns). La.	32·48 N	91·12 W
68	Lakeside (läk'sīd) Calif. (San Diego In.)	32·52 N	116·55 W
166	Lakeside. S. Afr. (Cape Town In.)	34·05 S	18·28 E
65	Lake Stevens. Wash. (Seattle In.)	48·01 N	122·04 W
84	Lake Success (sŭk-sĕs') N. Y. (New York In.)	40·46 N	73·43 W
74	Lakeview (läk-vū') Calif. (Los Angeles In.)	33·50 N	117·07 W
66	Lakeview Ore.	42·11 N	120·21 W
84	Lakeville (läk'vĭl) N. Y. (New York In.	41·12 N	74·16 W
67	Lake Walcott Res. Idaho	42·35 N	113·15 W
79	Lake Wales (wälz') Fla. (In.)	27·54 N	81·35 W
72	Lakewood (läk'wŏŏd) Colo.	39·44 N	105·06 W
75	Lakewood Ohio (Cleveland In.)	41·29 N	81·48 W
81	Lakewood Pa.	40·05 N	74·10 W
65	Lakewood Wash. (Seattle In.)	47·10 N	122·31 W
65	Lakewood Wash. (Seattle In.)	48·09 N	122·13 W
74	Lakewood Village Calif. (Los Angeles In.)	33·50 N	118·09 W
79	Lake Worth (wûrth') Fla. (In.)	26·37 N	80·04 W
74	Lake Worth Village Tex. (Dallas, Fort Worth In.)	32·49 N	97·26 W
75	Lake Zürich (tsü'rĭk) Ill. (Chicago In.)	42·11 N	88·05 W
119	Lakhdenpokh'ya (l'äк-die'npökyä) Sov. Un.	61·33 N	30·10 E
136	Lakhtinskiy (lȧk-tĭn'skĭ) Sov. Un. (Leningrad In.)	59·59 N	30·10 E
127	Lakonikós Kólpos (G.) Grc.	36·38 N	22·40 E
70	Lakota (lȧ-kō'tȧ) N. D.	48·04 N	98·21 W
92	La Libertad (lä lē-bĕr-tädh'). Guat.	15·31 N	91·44 W
92	La Libertad. Guat. (Yucatan In.)	16·46 N	90·12 W
92	La Libertad Sal.	13·29 N	89·20 W
101	La Ligua (lä lē'gwä) Chile (Santiago In.)	32·21 S	71·13 W
124	Lalín (lä-lē'n) Sp.	42·40 N	8·05 W
124	La Línea (lä lē'nä-ä) Sp.	36·11 N	5·22 W
114	Lalla-Maghnia (lä'lä-mäg'nēä) Alg.	34·52 N	1·40 W
117	La Louviere (lȧ lōō-vyâr') Bel.	50·30 N	4·10 E
90	La Luz (lä lōōz') Mex.	21·04 N	101·19 W
122	La Machine (lȧ mȧ-shēn') Fr.	46·53 N	3·26 E
82	La Malbaie (lä mäl-bā') Can.	47·39 N	70·11 W
124	La Mancha (Mts.) (lä män'chä) Sp.	38·55 N	4·20 W
72	Lamar (lȧ-mär') Colo.	38·04 N	102·44 W
73	Lamar Mo.	37·28 N	94·15 W
126	La Marmora, Pta. (Mtn.) (lä-mä'r-mô-rä). It.	40·00 N	9·28 E
77	La Marque (lȧ-märk) Tex. (In.)	29·23 N	94·58 W
98	Lamas (lä'mȧs) Peru	6·24 S	76·41 W
122	Lamballe (län-bäl') Fr.	48·29 N	2·36 W
166	Lambaréné (län-bȧ-rȧ-nā'). Gabon	0·48 S	10·07 E
101	Lambari (läm-bȧ'rē) Braz. (Rio de Janeiro In.)	21·58 S	45·22 W
98	Lambayeque (läm-bä-yä'kā). Peru	6·41 S	79·58 W
78	Lambert (lăm'bērt) Miss.	34·10 N	90·16 W
81	Lambertville (lăm'bērt-vĭl) N. J.	40·20 N	75·00 W
67	Lame Deer (lām dēr') Mont.	45·36 N	106·40 W
124	Lamego (lä-mā'gō) Port.	41·07 N	7·47 W
68	La Mesa (lä mā'sä) Calif. (San Diego In.)	32·46 N	117·01 W
98	La Mesa Col. (In.)	4·38 N	74·27 W
72	Lamesa Tex.	32·44 N	101·54 W
127	Lamía (lȧ-mē'ȧ) Grc.	38·54 N	22·25 E
155	Lamon B. (lä-mōn') Phil. (Manila In.)	14·35 N	121·52 E
101	La Mora (lä-mō'rä) Chile (Santiago In.)	32·28 S	70·56 W
70	La Moure (lȧ mōōr') N. D.	46·23 N	98·17 W
101	Lampa (R.) (lä'm-pä) Chile (Santiago In.)	33·15 S	70·55 W
76	Lampasas (lăm-păs'ȧs) Tex.	31·06 N	98·10 W
76	Lampasas R. Tex.	31·18 N	98·08 W
76	Lampazos (läm-pä'zōs) Mex.	27·03 N	100·30 W
113	Lampedusa (I.) (läm-pȧ-dōō'sä) It.	35·29 N	12·58 E
111	Lamstedt (läm'shtĕt) Ger. (Hamburg In.)	53·38 N	9·06 E
167	Lamu (lä'mōō) Ken.	2·17 S	41·07 E
123	La Mure (lȧ mür') Fr.	44·55 N	5·50 E
128	Lan' (R.) (län') Sov. Un.	52·38 N	27·05 E
157	Lanai (I.) (lä-nä'ē) Hawaii (In.)	20·48 N	157·06 W
142	Lanak La (P.) China	34·40 N	79·50 E
125	La Nao, Cabo de (C.) (kȧ'bô-dĕ-lä-nä'ō). Sp.	38·43 N	0·14 E
116	Lanark (lăn'ȧrk) Scot.	55·40 N	3·50 W
110	Lancashire (Co.) (lăŋ'kȧ-shĭr) Scot.	53·38 N	2·30 W
82	Lancaster (lăŋ'kȧs-tēr) Can.	45·16 N	66·06 W
116	Lancaster Eng.	54·04 N	2·55 W
80	Lancaster Ky.	37·35 N	84·30 W
83	Lancaster Mass. (Boston In.)	42·28 N	71·40 W
81	Lancaster N. H.	44·25 N	71·30 W
75	Lancaster N. Y. (Buffalo In.)	42·54 N	78·42 W
80	Lancaster Ohio	39·40 N	82·35 W
81	Lancaster Pa.	40·05 N	76·20 W
79	Lancaster S. C.	34·42 N	80·45 W
74	Lancaster Tex. (Dallas, Fort Worth In.)	32·36 N	96·45 W
71	Lancaster Wis.	42·51 N	90·44 W
150	Lanchou (län'chōō) China	35·55 N	103·55 E
122	Lançon-Provence (läN-sôN'prô-vĕNs') Fr. (Marseille In.)	43·35 N	5·08 E
166	Lândana (län-dä'nä) Ang.	5·15 S	12·07 E
120	Landau (län'dou) Ger.	49·13 N	8·07 E
67	Lander (lăn'dēr) Wyo.	42·49 N	108·24 W
122	Landerneau (läN-dĕr-nō') Fr.	48·28 N	4·14 W
122	Landes (Moorland) (Plain) (läNd) Fr.	44·22 N	0·52 W
111	Landsberg (länds'bōōrgh) Ger. (Munich In.)	48·03 N	10·53 E
116	Lands End Pt. Eng.	50·03 N	5·45 W
120	Landshut (länts'hōōt) Ger.	48·32 N	12·09 E
118	Landskrona (läns-krōō'nȧ) Swe.	55·51 N	12·47 E
78	Lanett (lȧ-nĕt') Ala.	32·52 N	85·13 W
150	Lanfang China (Peking In.)	39·31 N	116·42 E
127	Langadhás Grc.	40·44 N	24·10 E
139	Langat (R.). Mala. (Singapore In.)	2·46 N	101·33 E
148	Langch'i (läng'che) China	31·10 N	119·09 E
151	Langchung China	31·40 N	106·05 E
85	Langdon (lăng'dŭn) Can. (Calgary In.)	50·58 N	113·40 W
74	Langdon Minn. (Minneapolis, St. Paul In.)	44·49 N	92·56 W
85	L'Ange-Gardien (läNzh gär-dyăN') Can. (Quebec In.)	46·55 N	71·06 W
118	Lange Land Den.	54·52 N	10·46 E
65	Langeley Prairie (lăng'lĭ prâr'ĭ) Can. (Vancouver In.)	49·06 N	122·40 W
123	Langenthal Switz.	47·11 N	7·50 E
111	Langenzersdorf. Aus. (Vienna In.)	48·30 N	16·22 E
118	Langesund (läng'ĕ-sōōn') Nor.	58·59 N	9·38 E
118	Lang Fd. (läng'fyôr') Nor.	62·40 N	7·45 E
84	Langhorne (lăng'hôrn) Pa. (Philadelphia In.)	40·10 N	74·55 W
112	Langjökoll (Gl.) (läng-yû'kōōl). Ice.	64·40 N	20·31 W
83	Langlade (I.) St. Pierre & Miquelon	46·50 N	56·20 W
79	Langley (lăng'lĭ) S. C.	33·32 N	81·52 W
65	Langley Wash. (Seattle In.)	48·02 N	122·25 W
65	Langley Ind. Res. Can. (Vancouver In.)	49·12 N	122·31 W
120	Langnau (läng'nou) Switz.	46·56 N	7·46 E
122	Langogne (laN-gōn'y') Fr.	44·43 N	3·50 E
122	Langon (läN-gôN') Fr.	44·33 N	0·16 W
122	Langres (läN'gr') Fr.	47·53 N	5·20 E
122	Langres, Plateaux de (Plat.) (plȧ-tō'dĕ-läN'grĕ). Fr.	47·39 N	5·00 E
154	Langsa (läng'sä) Indon.	4·33 N	97·52 E
154	Lang Son (lăng'sŏn') Viet.	21·52 N	106·42 E
85	Langstaff (lăng'stăf) Can. (Toronto In.)	43·51 N	79·25 W
73	L'Anguille (R.) (läN-gē'y') Ark.	35·23 N	90·52 W
84	Lanham (lăn'ăm) Md. (Batimore In.)	38·58 N	76·54 W
86	Lanigan (lăn'ĭ-gȧn) Can.	51·53 N	105·04 W
146	Lanisung Chiang (Mekong). China	24·45 N	100·31 E
81	Lansdale (lănz'dāl) Pa.	40·20 N	75·15 W
84	Lansdowne. Pa. (Philadelphia In.)	39·57 N	75·17 W
71	L'Anse (läns) Mich.	46·43 N	88·28 W
85	L'Anse-a-Giles (läNz-ä-zhēl) Can. (Quebec In.)	47·05 N	70·26 W
71	L'Anse and Vieux Desert Ind. Res. Mich.	46·41 N	88·12 W
81	Lansford (lănz'fērd) Pa.	40·50 N	75·50 W
85	Lansing (lăn'sĭng) Can. (Toronto In.)	43·46 N	79·24 W
75	Lansing Ill. (Chicago In.)	41·34 N	87·33 W
71	Lansing Iowa	43·22 N	91·16 W

ăt; finȧl; rāte; senȧte; ärm; ȧsk; sofȧ; fâre; ch-choose; dh-as th in other; bē; ēvent; bĕt; recĕnt; cratẽr; g-go; gh-guttural g; bĭt; ĭ-short neutral; rīde; κ-guttural k as ch in German ich;

PRONOUNCING INDEX Lansing–Legnano 227

Page	Name Pronunciation Region	Lat. °′	Long. °′
74	Lansing...Kans. (Kansas City In.)	39·15 N	94·53 W
80	Lansing...Mich.	42·45 N	84·35 W
100	Lanús (lä-nōōs')...Arg. (In.)	34·27 S	58·24 W
126	Lanusei (lä-nōō-sě'y)...It.	39·51 N	9·34 E
125	Lanúvio (lä-nōō'vyô) It. (Rome In.)	41·41 N	12·42 E
164	Lanzarote I. (län-zȧ-rō'tä).Can. Is.	29·04 N	13·03 W
154	Laoag (lä-wäg')...Phil.	18·13 N	120·38 E
147	Lao Ho (R.) (lä'ō hō')...China	43·37 N	120·05 E
154	Lao Kay (lä'ōkä'ē)...Viet.	22·30 N	102·32 E
122	Laon (läN)...Fr.	49·36 N	3·35 E
98	La Oroya (lä-ô-rō'yä)...Peru	11·30 S	76·00 W
138	Laos (lä'ōs) (là-ōs')...Asia	19·30 N	102·45 E
93	La Palma (lä-päl'mä)...Pan.	8·25 N	78·07 W
124	La Palma...Sp.	37·24 N	6·36 W
164	La Palma I...Can. Is.	28·42 N	19·03 W
100	La Pampa (Prov.)...Arg.	37·25 S	67·00 W
100	Lapa Rio Negro (lä-pä-rē'ō-nē'grô).Braz.	26·12 S	49·56 W
100	La Paz (lä päz')...Arg.	30·48 S	59·47 W
98	La Paz...Bol.	16·31 S	68·03 W
92	La Paz...Hond.	14·15 N	87·40 W
90	La Paz (lä-pà'z)...Mex.	23·39 N	100·44 W
88	La Paz...Mex.	24·00 N	110·15 W
155	La Paz...Phil. (Manila In.)	17·41 N	120·41 E
80	Lapeer (lȧ-pēr')...Mich.	43·05 N	83·15 W
122	La-Penne-sur-Huveaune (la-pěn'sür-ü-vōn') Fr. (Marseille In.)	43·18 N	5·33 E
90	La Piedad Cabadas (lä pyå-dhädh' kä-bä'dhäs).Mex.	20·20 N	102·04 W
112	Lapland (Reg.) (lăp'lănd)...Eur.	68·20 N	22·00 E
101	La Plata (lä plä'tä) Arg. (Buenos Aires In.)	34·54 S	57·57 W
73	La Plata (lȧ plā'tȧ)...Mo.	40·03 N	92·28 W
69	La Plata Pk...Colo.	39·00 N	106·25 W
125	La Pobla de Lillet (lä-pô'blä-dě-lēl-yě't).Sp.	42·14 N	1·58 E
155	Lapog (lä-pôg') Phil. (Manila In.)	17·44 N	120·28 E
83	La Poile B. (lȧ pwäl')...Can.	47·28 N	58·35 W
80	La Porte (lȧ pōrt')...Ind.	41·35 N	86·45 W
75	Laporte...Ohio (Cleveland In.)	41·19 N	82·05 W
77	La Porte...Tex. (In.)	29·40 N	95·01 W
71	La Porte City...Iowa	42·20 N	92·10 W
119	Lappeenranta (lä'pěn-rän'tä)..Fin.	61·04 N	28·08 E
85	Laprairie (lä-prâ-rē') Can. (Montreal In.)	45·24 N	73·30 W
127	Lapseki (läp'sȧ-kē)...Tur.	40·20 N	26·41 E
130	Laptev Sea (läp'tyĭf)...Sov. Un.	75·39 N	120·00 E
125	La Puebla (lä pwä'blä)...Sp.	39·46 N	3·02 E
124	La Puebla de Montalbán (lä pwā'blä dā mōnt-äl-bän') Sp.	39·54 N	4·21 W
121	Lapusul R. (lä'pōō-shōōl)...Rom.	47·29 N	23·46 E
100	La Quiaca (lä kē-ä'kä)...Arg.	22·15 S	65·44 W
126	L'Aquila (lȧ'kē-lä)...It.	42·22 N	13·24 E
144	Lar (lär)...Iran	27·31 N	54·12 E
161	Lara...Austl. (Melbourne In.)	38·02 S	144·24 E
164	Larache (lä-räsh')...Mor.	35·15 N	6·09 W
62	Laramie (lăr'ȧ-mĭ)...Wyo.	41·20 N	105·40 W
72	Laramie (R.)...Colo.	40·56 N	105·55 W
125	L'Arba (l'är'bȧ)...Alg.	36·35 N	3·10 E
84	Larchmont (lärch'mŏnt) N. Y. (New York In.)	40·56 N	73·46 W
65	Larch Mtn. (lärch) Ore. (Portland In.)	45·32 N	122·06 W
124	Laredo (lȧ-rā'dhō)...Sp.	43·24 N	3·24 W
76	Laredo...Tex.	27·31 N	99·29 W
122	La Réole (lȧ rȧ-ōl')...Fr.	44·37 N	0·03 W
165	Largeau (lär-zhō')...Chad	17·45 N	19·26 E
94	Largo, Cayo (kä'yō-lär'gō)..Cuba	21·40 N	81·30 W
70	Larimore (lăr'ĭ-môr)...N. D.	47·53 N	97·38 W
126	Larino (lä-rē'nô)...It.	41·48 N	14·54 E
100	La Rioja (lä rē-ōhä)...Arg.	29·18 S	67·42 W
100	La Rioja (Prov.) (lä-rē-ô'-kä).Arg.	28·45 S	68·00 W
127	Lárisa (lä'rê-sȧ)...Grc.	39·38 N	22·25 E
142	Lārkāma...W. Pak.	27·40 N	68·12 E
139	Larnaca (lär'nȧ-kä) Cyprus (Palestine In.)	34·55 N	33·37 E
139	Larnaca (B.) Cyprus (Palestine In.)	34·55 N	33·51 E
72	Larned (lär'nĕd)...Kans.	38·09 N	99·07 W
124	La Robla (lä rōb'lä)...Sp.	42·48 N	5·36 W
122	La Rochelle (lȧ rô-shěl')...Fr.	46·10 N	1·09 W
122	La Roche-sur-Yon (lȧ rôsh'sûr-yôN').Fr.	46·39 N	1·27 W
124	La Roda (lä rō'dä)...Sp.	39·13 N	2·08 W
95	La Romona (lä-rä-mô'nä) Dom. Rep.	18·25 N	69·00 W
158	Larrey Pt. (lăr'ē)...Austl.	19·15 S	118·15 E
122	Laruns (lȧ-răNs')...Fr.	42·58 N	0·28 W
118	Larvik (lär'vēk)...Nor.	59·06 N	10·03 E
99	La Sabana (lä-sä-bȧ'nä).Ven. (In.)	10·38 N	66·24 W
95	La Sabina (lä-sä-bē'nä) Cuba (Havana In.)	22·10 N	82·07 W
124	La Sagra (Mtn.) (lä sä'grä)...Sp.	37·56 N	2·35 E
69	La Sal (lȧ săl')...Utah	38·10 N	109·20 W
75	La Salle (lȧ săl') Can. (Detroit In.)	42·14 N	83·06 W
85	La Salle...Can. (Winnipeg In.)	49·41 N	97·16 W
80	La Salle...Ill.	41·20 N	89·05 W
72	Las Animas (lăs ă'nĭ-mȧs)...Colo.	38·03 N	103·16 W
168	Las Anod (läs ăn'ŏd) Som. (Horn of Afr. In.)	8·24 N	47·20 E
87	La Sarre...Can.	48·43 N	79·12 W
95	Lascahobas (läs-kä-ō'bás)...Hai.	19·00 N	71·55 W
91	Las Cruces (läs-krōō'-sěs)...Mex.	16·37 N	93·54 W
69	Las Cruces...N. Mex.	32·20 N	106·50 W
95	La Selle, Massif De (Mts.) (lä sěl').Hai.	18·25 N	72·05 W
100	La Serena (lä-sě-rě'nä)...Chile	29·55 S	71·24 W
123	La Seyne-sur-Mer (lä-sån'sür-měr').Fr.	43·07 N	5·52 E
101	Las Flores (läs flo'rěs) Arg. (Buenos Aires In.)	36·01 S	59·07 W

Page	Name Pronunciation Region	Lat. °′	Long. °′
146	Lashio (lăsh'ē-ō)...Bur.	22·58 N	98·03 E
74	La Sierra (lȧ sĭ-ĕr'ȧ) Calif. (Los Angeles In.)	33·54 N	117·29 W
92	Las Juntas (läs-Kōō'n-täs)...C. R.	10·15 N	85·00 W
168	Las Khoreh (läs Kō'rā) Som. (Horn of Afr. In.)	11·13 N	48·19 E
124	Las Maismas (Reg.) (läs-mī's-mäs).Sp.	37·05 N	6·25 W
124	La Solano (lä-sô-lä-nō)...Sp.	38·56 N	3·13 W
164	Las Palmas (läs päl'mäs).Can. Is.	28·07 N	15·28 W
93	Las Palmas...Pan.	8·08 N	81·30 W
126	La Spezia (lä-spě'zyä)...It.	44·07 N	9·48 E
101	Las Piedras (läs-pyě'dräs) Ur. (Buenos Aires In.)	34·42 S	56·08 W
92	Las Pilas (Vol.) (läs-pē'läs)...Nic.	12·32 N	86·43 W
91	Las Rosas (läs rō thäs)...Mex.	16·24 N	92·23 W
125	Las Rozas de Madrid (läs rō'thas dā mä-dhrēdh').Sp. (Madrid In.)	40·29 N	3·53 W
111	Lassee...Aus. (Vienna In.)	48·14 N	16·50 E
66	Lassen Pk. (lăs'ĕn)...Calif.	40·30 N	121·32 W
66	Lassen Volcanic Natl. Park..Calif.	40·43 N	121·35 W
85	L'Assomption (làs-sôm-syôN) Can. (Montreal In.)	45·50 N	73·25 W
93	Las Tablas (läs tä'bläs)...Pan.	7·48 N	80·16 W
86	Last Mountain (L.) (làst moun'tĭn).Can.	51·07 N	105·50 W
166	Lastoursville (làs-tōōr-vēl') Gabon	1·00 S	12·49 E
88	Las Tres Marías (I.) (läs-trě's mä-rē'äs).Mex.	21·30 N	106·40 W
88	Las Tres Virgenes, Vol. (vē'r-hě-něs).Mex.	26·00 N	111·45 W
91	Las Vacas (läs-vȧ'käs)...Mex.	16·24 N	95·48 W
101	Las Vegas (läs-vě'gäs) Chile (Santiago In.)	30·50 S	70·59 W
68	Las Vegas (läs vā'gȧs)...Nev.	36·12 N	115·10 W
72	Las Vegas...N. Mex.	35·36 N	105·13 W
99	Las Vegas (läs-vě'gäs)..Ven. (In.)	10·26 N	64·08 W
90	Las Vigas...Mex.	19·38 N	97·03 W
94	Las Villas (State) (läs-vê'l-läs) Cuba	22·15 N	80·50 W
100	Las Vizcachas, Meseta de (Plat.) (mě-sě'tä-dě-läs-vēz-kä'-chàs) Arg.	49·35 S	71·00 W
98	Latacunga (lä-tä-kōōŋ'gä)...Ec.	1·02 S	78·33 W
	Latakia, see El Ladhiqiya		
115	Latakia (Reg.) (lä-tä-kē'ä) U. A. R.	35·10 N	35·49 E
122	La Teste-de-Buch (lä-těst-dě-büsh).Fr.	44·38 N	1·11 W
73	Lathrop (lā'thrŭp)...Mo.	39·32 N	94·21 W
	Latium (Reg.), see Lazio		
121	Latoritsa R. (là-tô'rĭ-tsà) Sov. Un.	48·27 N	22·30 E
85	La Tortue, R. (lä tōr-tü') Can. (Montreal In.)	45·12 N	73·32 W
65	Latourell (là-tou'rĕl) Ore. (Portland In.)	45·32 N	122·13 W
122	La Tremblade (lä-trěN-bläd')..Fr.	45·45 N	1·12 W
81	Latrobe (lȧ-trōb')...Pa.	40·25 N	79·15 W
84	La Tuque (lȧ tük')...Can.	47·27 N	72·49 W
143	Latūr (lä-tōōr')...India	18·20 N	76·35 E
130	Latvian (S. S. R.)...Sov. Un.	57·28 N	24·29 E
160	Launceston (lôn'sěs-tŭn)...Austl.	41·35 S	147·22 E
116	Launceston (lôrn'stŏn)...Eng.	50·38 N	4·26 W
100	La Unión (lä-ōō-nyô'n)...Chile	40·15 S	73·04 W
90	La Unión (lä ōōn-nyōn')...Mex.	17·59 N	101·48 W
92	La Unión...Sal.	13·18 N	87·51 W
125	La Unión...Sp.	37·38 N	0·50 W
157	Laupahoehoe (lä'ōō-pä-hō'ē-hō-ē) Hawaii (In.)	19·58 N	155·13 W
159	Laura (lôrȧ)...Austl.	15·40 S	144·45 E
128	Laura (lou'rä)...Sov. Un.	57·36 N	27·29 E
81	Laurel (lô'rĕl)...Del.	38·30 N	75·40 W
84	Laurel...Md. (Baltimore In.)	39·06 N	76·51 W
78	Laurel...Miss.	31·42 N	89·07 W
67	Laurel...Mont.	45·41 N	108·45 W
65	Laurel...Wash. (Vancouver In.)	48·52 N	122·29 W
65	Laurelwood (lô'rĕl-wŏŏd) Ore. (Portland In.)	45·25 N	123·05 W
79	Laurens (lô'rĕnz)...S. C.	34·29 N	82·03 W
49	Laurentian Highlands (Reg.) (lô'rĕn-tĭ-ǎn).Can.	49·00 N	74·50 W
82	Laurentides Provincial Park (lô'rěn-tīdz).Can.	47·53 N	71·26 W
126	Lauria (lou'rê-ä)...It.	40·03 N	15·02 E
79	Laurinburg (lô'rĭn-bûrg)...N. C.	34·45 N	79·27 W
71	Laurium (lô'rĭ-ŭm)...Mich.	47·13 N	88·28 W
154	Laurot Pulau-Pulau Is...Indon.	4·44 S	115·43 E
120	Lausanne (lō-zȧn')...Switz.	46·32 N	6·35 E
154	Laut (I.)...Indon.	3·39 S	116·07 E
100	Lautaro (lou-tä'rô)...Chile	38·40 S	72·24 W
85	Lauzon (lō-zōN') Can. (Quebec In.)	46·50 N	71·10 W
66	Lava Beds Natl. Mon. (lä'vȧ běds).Calif.	41·38 N	121·44 W
77	Lavaca R. (lȧ-väk'ȧ)...Tex.	29·05 N	96·50 W
67	Lava Hot Springs...Idaho	42·37 N	111·58 W
122	Laval (lä-väl')...Fr.	48·05 N	0·47 W
122	Lavaur (là-vōr')...Fr.	43·41 N	1·48 E
122	Lavaveix-les-Mines (lȧ-vȧ-vě'lā-mēn').Fr.	46·05 N	2·05 E
95	La Vega (lä-vě'-gä)...Dom. Rep.	19·15 N	70·35 W
159	Lavella (I.)...Sol. Is.	7·50 S	155·45 E
126	Lavello (lä-věl'lô)...It.	41·05 N	15·50 E
74	La Verne (lȧ vûrn') Calif. (Los Angeles In.)	34·06 N	117·46 W
158	Laverton (lā'vēr-tŭn)...Austl.	28·45 S	122·30 E
99	La Victoria (lä věk-tō'rē-ä) Ven. (In.)	10·14 N	67·20 W
78	Lavonia (lȧ-vō'nĭ-ȧ)...Ga.	34·26 N	83·05 W
77	Lavon Res...Tex.	33·06 N	96·20 W
101	Lavras (lä'vräzh) Braz. (Rio de Janeiro In.)	21·15 S	44·59 W
127	Lávrion (läv'rĭ-ôn)...Grc.	37·44 N	24·05 E

Page	Name Pronunciation Region	Lat. °′	Long. °′
74	Lawndale (lôn'dāl) Calif. (Los Angeles In.)	33·54 N	118·22 W
75	Lawrence (lô'rĕns) Ind. (Indianapolis In.)	39·59 N	86·01 W
73	Lawrence...Kans.	38·57 N	95·13 W
83	Lawrence...Mass. (Boston In.)	42·42 N	71·09 W
75	Lawrence...Pa. (Pittsburgh In.)	40·18 N	80·07 W
65	Lawrence..Wash. (Vancouver In.)	48·52 N	122·18 W
75	Lawrenceburg (lô'rĕns-bûrg) Ind. (Cincinnati In.)	39·06 N	84·47 W
80	Lawrenceburg...Ky.	38·00 N	85·00 W
78	Lawrenceburg...Tenn.	35·13 N	87·20 W
78	Lawrenceville (lô-rĕns-vĭl)...Ga.	33·56 N	83·57 W
80	Lawrenceville...Ill.	38·45 N	87·45 W
84	Lawrenceville N. J. (New York In.)	40·17 N	74·44 W
79	Lawrenceville...Va.	36·43 N	77·52 W
81	Lawsonia (lô-sō'nĭ-ȧ)...Md.	38·00 N	75·50 W
72	Lawton (lô'tŭn)...Okla.	34·36 N	98·25 W
139	Layang Layang (lâ-yäng' lä-yäng').Mala. (Singapore In.)	1·49 N	103·28 E
74	Layton (lā'tŭn) Utah (Salt Lake City In.)	41·04 N	111·58 W
119	Lazdijai (läzh'dē-yī')...Sov. Un.	54·12 N	23·35 E
126	Lazio (Latium) (Reg.) (lä'zyô) (lä't-zēōōm).It.	42·05 N	12·25 E
70	Lead (lēd)...S. D.	44·22 N	103·47 W
72	Leadville (lĕd'vĭl)...Colo.	39·14 N	106·18 W
87	Leaf (R.) (lēf)...Can.	59·12 N	72·50 W
78	Leaf (R.)...Miss.	31·43 N	89·20 W
77	League City (lēg)...Tex. (In.)	29·31 N	95·05 W
80	Leamington (lěm'ĭng-tŭn)...Can.	42·05 N	82·35 W
116	Leamington (lě'mĭng-tŭn)...Eng.	52·17 N	1·25 W
85	Leaside (lē'sīd) Can. (Toronto In.)	43·42 N	79·22 W
110	Leatherhead (lĕdh'ēr-hĕd') Eng. (London In.)	51·17 N	0·20 W
74	Leavenworth (lěv'ěn-wûrth) Kans. (Kansas City In.)	39·19 N	94·54 W
66	Leavenworth...Wash.	47·35 N	120·39 W
74	Leawood (lē'wŏŏd) Kans. (Kansas City In.)	38·58 N	94·37 W
121	Leba (lā'bä)...Pol.	54·45 N	17·34 E
139	Lebam R...Mala. (Singapore In.)	1·35 N	104·09 E
74	Lebanon (lěb'ȧ-nŭn) Ill. (St. Louis In.)	38·36 N	89·49 W
80	Lebanon...Ind.	40·00 N	86·30 W
78	Lebanon...Ky.	37·32 N	85·15 W
73	Lebanon...Mo.	37·40 N	92·43 W
81	Lebanon...N. H.	43·40 N	72·15 W
80	Lebanon...Ohio	39·25 N	84·10 W
66	Lebanon...Ore.	44·31 N	122·53 W
81	Lebanon...Pa.	40·20 N	76·20 W
78	Lebanon...Tenn.	36·10 N	86·16 W
138	Lebanon...Asia	34·00 N	35·00 E
115	Lebanon Mts...Leb.	33·30 N	35·32 E
129	Lebedin (lyě'bě-děn)...Sov. Un.	48·56 N	31·35 E
129	Lebedin...Sov. Un.	50·34 N	34·27 E
128	Lebedyan' (lě'bě-dyän') Sov. Un.	53·03 N	39·08 E
122	Le Blanc (lě-bläN')...Fr	46·38 N	0·59 E
95	Le Borgne (lē bōrn'y')...Hai.	19·50 N	72·30 W
121	Lebork (lăN bōōrk')...Pol.	54·33 N	17·46 E
122	Le Boucau (lě-bōō-kō')...Fr.	43·33 N	1·28 W
122	Le Bouscat (lē bōōs-kȧ)...Fr.	44·53 N	0·38 W
124	Lebrija (lâ-brē'hä)...Sp.	36·55 N	6·06 W
100	Lebú (lě-bōō')...Chile	37·35 S	73·37 W
127	Lecce (lět'chā)...It.	40·22 N	18·11 E
126	Lecco (lěk'kō)...It.	45·52 N	9·28 E
123	Le Châtelet-en-Brie (lě-shä-tě-lā' ěN-brē').Fr. (Paris In.)	48·29 N	2·50 E
94	Leche, Laguna de (L.) (lä-gōō'nä-dě-lě'chě).Cuba	22·10 N	78·30 W
76	Leche, Laguna de la (L.)...Mex.	27·16 N	102·45 W
123	Lechenich (lě'kě-nēK) Ger. (Ruhr In.)	50·47 N	6·46 E
120	Lech R. (lěk)...Ger.	47·41 N	10·52 E
77	Lecompte...La.	31·06 N	92·25 W
122	Le Coteau (lē kō-tō')...Fr.	46·01 N	4·06 E
122	Le Creusot (lěkrû-zô')...Fr.	46·48 N	4·23 E
122	Lectoure (lěK-tōōr')...Fr.	43·56 N	0·38 E
124	Ledesma (lå-děs'mä)...Sp.	41·05 N	5·59 W
85	Leduc (lě-dōōk') Can. (Edmonton In.)	53·16 N	113·34 W
71	Leech (L.) (lēch)...Minn.	47·06 N	94·16 W
84	Leeds (lēdz) Ala. (Birmingham In.)	33·33 N	86·33 W
110	Leeds...Eng.	53·48 N	1·33 W
70	Leeds...N. D.	48·18 N	99·24 W
110	Leeds and Liverpool Can. (lĭv'ēr-pōōl).Eng.	53·36 N	2·38 W
111	Leegebruch (lěh'gěn-brōōK) Ger. (Berlin In.)	52·43 N	13·12 E
110	Leek (lēk)...Eng.	53·06 N	2·01 W
84	Leeland (lē'lănd) Md. (Baltimore In.)	38·53 N	76·46 W
120	Leer (lār)...Ger.	53·14 N	7·27 E
116	Lee R. (lē)...Ire.	51·52 N	8·30 W
79	Leesburg (lēz'bûrg)...Fla.	28·49 N	81·53 W
81	Leesburg...Va.	39·10 N	77·30 W
69	Lees Ferry...Ariz.	36·55 N	111·45 W
74	Lees Summit Mo. (Kansas City In.)	38·55 N	94·23 W
95	Lee Stocking (I.)...Ba. Is.	23·45 N	76·05 W
77	Leesville (lēz'vĭl)...La.	31·09 N	93·17 W
80	Leetonia (lē-tō'nĭ-ȧ)...Ohio	40·50 N	80·45 W
117	Leeuwarden (lā'wär-děn)...Neth.	53·12 N	5·50 E
158	Leeuwin, C. (lōō'wĭn)...Austl.	34·15 S	114·30 E
89	Leeward Is. (lē'wērd)...N. A.	12·25 N	62·15 W
93	Le Francois Mart. (Le. & Wind. Is. In.)	14·37 N	60·55 W
158	Lefroy (L.) (lē-froi')...Austl.	31·30 S	122·00 E
125	Leganés (lå-gä'nås) Sp. (Madrid In.)	40·20 N	3·46 W
155	Legaspi (lå-gäs'pê) Phil. (Manila In.)	13·09 N	123·44 E
160	Legge Pk. (lĕg)...Austl.	41·33 S	148·10 E
	Leghorn, see Livorno		
126	Legnano (lå-nyä'nō)...It.	45·35 N	8·53 E

Page	Name Pronunciation Region	Lat. °′	Long. °′
120	Legnica (lĕk-nĭt'sȧ) Pol.	51·13 N	16·10 E
142	Leh (lā) India	34·10 N	77·40 E
122	Le Havre (lē àv'r') Fr.	49·31 N	0·07 E
69	Lehi (lē'hī) Utah	40·25 N	111·55 W
69	Lehman Caves Natl. Mon. (lē'mȧn) Nev.	38·54 N	114·08 W
111	Lehnin (lĕh'nēn) Ger. (Berlin In.)	52·19 N	12·45 E
110	Leicester (lĕs'tẽr) Eng.	52·37 N	1·08 W
110	Leicester (Co.) Eng.	52·40 N	1·12 W
158	Leichhardt, (R.) (līk'härt) Austl.	18·30 S	139·45 E
111	Leiden (lī'dĕn) Neth. (Amsterdam In.)	52·09 N	4·29 E
160	Leigh Creek (lē krēk) Austl.	30·33 S	138·30 E
118	Leikanger (lī'käŋ'gẽr) Nor.	61·11 N	6·51 E
111	Leimuiden Neth. (Amsterdam In.)	52·13 N	4·40 E
120	Leine R. (lī'nĕ) Ger.	51·58 N	9·56 E
116	Leinster (lĕn-stẽr) Ire.	52·45 N	7·19 W
80	Leipsic (līp'sĭk) Ohio	41·05 N	84·00 W
120	Leipzig (līp'tsĭk) Ger.	51·20 N	12·24 E
124	Leiria (lā-rē'ä) Port.	39·45 N	8·50 W
78	Leitchfield (lēch'fēld) Ky.	37·28 N	86·20 W
111	Leitha (R.) Aus. (Vienna In.)	48·04 N	16·57 E
85	Leitrim Can. (Ottawa In.)	45·20 N	75·36 W
	Leixoes, see Matozinhos		
117	Lek (R.) (lĕk) Neth.	51·59 N	5·30 E
113	Lekef (lĕkĕf') Tun.	36·14 N	8·42 E
118	Leksand (lĕk'sänd) Swe.	60·45 N	14·56 E
65	Leland (lē'lȧnd) Wash. (Seattle In.)	47·54 N	122·53 W
120	Le Locle (lē lô'kl') Switz.	47·03 N	6·43 E
100	Le Maire, Estrecho de (Str.) (ĕs-trĕ'chô-dĕ-lĕ-mī'rĕ) Arg.	55·15 S	65·30 W
122	Le Mans (lē mäɴ') Fr.	48·01 N	0·12 E
93	Le Marin Mart. (Le. & Wind. Is. In.)	14·28 N	60·55 W
70	Le Mars (lē märz') Iowa	42·46 N	96·09 W
155	Lemery (lā-mā-rē') Phil. (Manila In.)	13·51 N	120·55 E
67	Lemhi Ra. (Mts.) (lĕm'hī) Idaho	44·35 N	113·33 W
67	Lemhi R. Idaho	44·40 N	113·27 W
70	Lemmon (lĕm'ŭn) S. D.	45·55 N	102·10 W
95	Le Môle (lē mōl') Hai.	19·50 N	73·20 W
68	Lemon Grove (lĕm'ŭn-grōv) Calif. (San Diego In.)	32·44 N	117·02 W
75	Lemont (lē'-mŏnt) Ill. (Chicago In.)	41·40 N	87·59 W
93	Le Moule (lē mōōl') Grande Terre (Le. & Wind. Is. In.)	16·19 N	61·22 W
92	Lempa R. (lĕm'pä) Sal.	13·20 N	88·46 W
118	Lemvig (lĕm'vēgh) Den.	56·33 N	8·16 E
118	Lena (lī'nä) Swe.	60·01 N	17·40 E
135	Lena (R.) Sov. Un.	68·39 N	124·15 E
100	Lençóes Paulista (lĕɴ-sôɴs' pou-lēs'tà) Braz.	22·30 S	48·45 W
99	Lençóis (lĕn-sóis) Braz.	12·38 S	41·28 W
74	Lenexa (lē-nĕx'ǎ) Kans. (Kansas City In.)	38·58 N	94·44 W
103	Lenger (lyĭn'gyĕr) Sov. Un.	41·38 N	70·00 E
139	Lenik (R.) Mala. (Singapore In.)	1·59 N	102·51 E
134	Leninabad (lĕ-nyē-nȧ bät') Sov. Un.	40·15 N	69·49 E
133	Leninakan (lĕ-nyē-nȧ-kän') Sov. Un.	40·40 N	43·50 E
136	Leningrad (lyĕ-nēn-grät') Sov. Un. (Leningrad In.)	59·57 N	30 20 E
128	Leningrad (Oblast) Sov. Un.	59·15 N	30·30 E
129	Leningradskaya (lyĕ-nĭn-grȧd'skȧ-yȧ) Sov. Un.	46·19 N	39·23 E
136	Lenino (lyĕ'nĭ-nô) Sov. Un. (Moscow In.)	55·37 N	47·41 E
134	Leninogorsk (lyĕ-nĭn ŭ gôrsk') Sov. Un.	50·29 N	83·25 E
133	Leninsk (lyĕ-nēnsk') Sov. Un.	48·40 N	45·10 E
134	Leninsk-Kuznetski (lyĕ-nênsk' kōōz-nyĕt'skĭ) Sov. Un.	54·28 N	86·48 E
133	Lenkoran' (lĕn-kô-rän') Sov. Un.	38·52 N	48·58 E
70	Lennox (lĕn'ŭks) S. D.	43·22 N	96·53 W
79	Lenoir (lē-nōr') N. C.	35·54 N	81·35 W
78	Lenoir City Tenn.	35·47 N	84·16 W
71	Lenox Iowa	40·51 N	94·29 W
120	Leoben (lâ-ō'bĕn) Aus.	47·22 N	15·09 E
95	Léogane (lā-ô-gan') Hai.	18·30 N	72·35 W
70	Leola (lē-ō'lȧ) S. D.	45·43 N	99·55 W
83	Leominster (lĕm'ĭn-stẽr) Mass. (Boston In.)	42·32 N	71·45 W
71	Leon (lē'ŏn) Iowa	40·43 N	93·44 W
90	León (lā-ōn') Mex.	21·08 N	101·41 W
92	León (lĕ-ô'n) Nic.	12·28 N	86·53 W
124	León (lĕ-ô'n) Sp.	42·38 N	5·33 W
124	Leon (Reg.) (lĕ-ô'n) Sp.	41·18 N	5·50 W
126	Leonforte (lā-ôn-fôr'tä) It.	37·40 N	14·27 E
76	Leon R. (lē'ŏn) Tex.	31·54 N	98·20 W
101	Leopoldina (lā-ô-pôl-dē'nä) Braz. (Rio de Janeiro In.)	21·32 S	42·38 W
111	Leopoldsburg Bel. (Brussels In.)	51·07 N	5·18 E
111	Leopoldsdorf im Marchfelde (lā'ô-pôlts-dôrf') Aus. (Vienna In.)	48·14 N	16·42 E
166	Leopold II (L.) (lā'ô-pōld) Con.K.	2·16 S	19·00 E
	Léopoldville, see Kinshasa		
129	Leovo (lâ-ō'vô) Sov. Un.	46·30 N	28·16 E
124	Lepe (lā'pā) Sp.	37·15 N	7·12 W
128	Lepel' (lyĕ-pĕl') Sov. Un.	54·52 N	28·41 E
85	L'Epiphanie (lā-pē-fā-nē') Can. (Montreal In.)	45·51 N	73·29 W
123	Le Plessis-Belleville (lĕ-plĕ-sē' bĕl-vēl') Fr. (Paris In.)	49·05 N	2·46 E
120	Lepontine Alpi (Mts.) (lê-pŏn'tĭn) Switz.	46·28 N	8·38 E
82	Lepreau (lê-prō') Can.	45·10 N	66·28 W
134	Lepsinsh Sov. Un.	45·32 N	80·47 E
122	Le Puy-en-Velay (lē pwē') Fr.	45·02 N	3·54 E
126	Lercara (lĕr-kä'rä) It.	36·47 N	13·36 E
76	Lerdo (lĕr'dō) Mex.	25·31 N	103·30 W
165	Léré (lā-rā') Chad	9·42 N	14·14 E
167	Leribe Leso. (Natal In.)	28·53 S	28·02 E
125	Lérida (lā'rē-dhä) Sp.	41·38 N	0·37 E
91	Lerma (lĕr'mä) Mex.	19·49 N	90·34 W
91	Lerma Mex. (Mexico City In.)	19·17 N	99·30 W
124	Lerma (lĕ'r-mä) Sp.	42·03 N	3·45 W
90	Lerma (R.) Mex.	20·14 N	101·50 W
81	Le Roy (lē roi') N. Y.	43·00 N	78·00 W
116	Lerwick (lĕr'ĭk) (lûr'wĭk) Scot.	60·08 N	1·27 W
84	Lery, L. (lĕ'rē) La. (New Orleans In.)	29·48 N	89·45 W
123	Les Andelys (lā-zäɴ-dē-lē') Fr. (Paris In.)	49·15 N	1·25 E
95	Les Cayes Hai.	18·15 N	73·45 W
85	Les Cèdres (lā-sĕdr'') Can. (Montreal In.)	45·18 N	74·03 W
127	Lesh (Alessio) (lĕshĕ) (ä-lā'sē-ō) Alb.	41·47 N	19·40 E
126	Lésina, Lago di (L.) (lä'gō dē lā'zē-nä) It.	41·48 N	15·12 E
127	Leskovac (lĕs'kô-vȧts) Yugo.	43·00 N	21·58 E
73	Leslie (lĕz'lĭ) Ark.	35·49 N	92·32 W
168	Leslie S. Afr. (Johannesburg & Pretoria In.)	26·23 S	28·57 E
132	Lesnoy (lĕs'noi) Sov. Un.	66·45 N	34·45 E
152	Lesogorsk (lyĕs'ō-gôrsk) Sov. Un.	49·28 N	141·59 E
166	Lesotho (lĕsō'thō) Afr.	29·45 S	28·07 E
152	Lesozavodsk (lyĕ-sô-zȧ-vôdsk') Sov. Un.	45·21 N	133·19 E
122	Lesparre (lĕ-spär) Fr.	45·18 N	0·57 W
122	Les-Pennes-Mirabeau (lā-pĕn' mĭ-rä-bō') Fr. (Marseille In.)	43·25 N	5·19 E
122	Les Sables-d'Olonne (lā sä'bl'dô-lŭn') Fr.	46·30 N	1·47 W
93	Les Saintes Is. (lā-săɴt') Guad. (Le. & Wind. Is. In.)	15·50 N	61·40 W
	Lesser Khingan Mts. see Hsiaohsinganling Shanmo		
86	Lesser Slave L. (lĕs'ẽr slāv) Can.	55·10 N	116·18 W
122	L'Estaque (lĕs-tâl) Fr. (Marseille In.)	43·22 N	5·20 E
123	Les Thilliers-en-Vexin (lā-tē-yā' ĕɴ-vĕ-săɴ') Fr. (Paris In.)	49·19 N	1·36 E
71	Le Sueur (lē sōōr') Minn.	44·27 N	93·53 W
127	Lésvos (I.) Grc.	39·15 N	25·40 E
120	Leszno (lĕsh'nô) Pol.	51·51 N	16·35 E
122	Le Teil (lĕ tā'y') Fr.	44·34 N	4·39 E
86	Lethbridge (lĕth'brĭj) Can.	49·40 N	112·39 W
166	Letiahau (R.) Bots.	21·16 S	22·17 E
129	Letichev (lyĕ-tē-chĕf') Sov. Un.	49·22 N	27·29 E
98	Leticia (lĕ-tē'syȧ) Col.	4·04 S	69·57 W
123	Letmathe (lĕt'mät-hĕ) Ger. (Ruhr In.)	51 22 N	7·37 E
122	Le Tréport (lē-trā-pôr') Fr.	50·03 N	1·21 E
154	Leuser, Gulung (Mtn.) Indon.	3·36 N	97·17 E
111	Leuven Bel. (Brussels In.)	50·53 N	4·42 E
127	Levádhia Grc.	38·25 N	22·51 E
123	Levallois-Perret (lē-vȧl-wä'pĕ-rĕ') Fr. (Paris In.)	48·53 N	2·17 E
112	Levanger (lĕ-väng'ẽr) Nor.	63·42 N	11·01 E
126	Levanna (Mtn.) (lå-vä'nä) Fr.-It.	45·25 N	7·14 E
158	Leveque, C. (lê-vĕk') Austl.	16·25 S	123·08 E
123	Leverkusen (lĕ'fĕr-kōō-zĕn) Ger. (Ruhr In.)	51·01 N	6·59 E
166	Leverville (lē-vä-vēl') Con. K.	5·13 S	18·43 E
121	Levice (lā'vêt-sĕ) Czech.	48·13 N	18·37 E
126	Levico (lā'vê-kō) It.	46·02 N	11·20 E
122	Le Vigan (lē vē-gäɴ') Fr.	43·59 N	3·36 E
85	Lévis (lā-vē') (lē'vĭs) Can. (Quebec In.)	46·48 N	71·11 W
84	Levittown (lĕ'vĭt-toun) Pa. (Philadelphia In.)	40·08 N	74·50 W
127	Levkás (lyĕfkäs') Grc.	38·49 N	20·43 E
127	Levkás (I.) Grc.	38·42 N	20·22 E
121	Levoča (lā'vô-chȧ) Czech.	49·03 N	20·38 E
79	Levy (L.) (lē'vĭ) Fla.	29·31 N	82·23 W
81	Lewes (lōō'ĭs) Del.	38·45 N	75·10 W
116	Lewes Eng.	50·51 N	0·01 E
116	Lewis (I.) (lōō'ĭs) Scot.	58·05 N	6·07 W
65	Lewis (R.) East Fk. Wash. (Portland In.)	45·52 N	122·40 E
78	Lewisburg (lū'ĭs-bûrg) Tenn.	35·27 N	86·47 W
80	Lewisburg (lū'ĭs-bûrg) W. Va.	37·50 N	80·20 W
83	Lewis Hills Can.	48·49 N	58·28 W
83	Lewisporte (lū'ĭs-pōrt) Can.	49·15 N	55·06 W
67	Lewis Ra. (lū'ĭs) Mont.	48·05 N	113·06 W
66	Lewis R. Wash.	46·05 N	122·09 W
66	Lewiston (lū'ĭs-tŭn) Idaho	46·24 N	116·59 W
82	Lewiston Maine	44·05 N	70·14 W
75	Lewiston N. Y. (Buffalo In.)	43·11 N	79·02 W
67	Lewiston Utah	41·58 N	111·51 W
73	Lewistown (lū'ĭs-toun) Ill.	40·23 N	90·06 W
67	Lewistown Mont.	47·05 N	109 25 W
81	Lewistown Pa.	40·35 N	77·30 W
80	Lexington (lĕk'sĭng-tŭn) Ky.	38·05 N	84·30 W
83	Lexington Mass. (Boston In.)	42·27 N	71·14 W
78	Lexington Miss.	33·08 N	90·02 W
73	Lexington Mo.	39·11 N	93·52 W
72	Lexington Nebr.	40·46 N	99·44 W
79	Lexington N. C.	35·47 N	80·15 W
78	Lexington Tenn.	35·37 N	88·24 W
81	Lexington Va.	37·45 N	79·20 W
155	Leyte (I.) (lā'tä) Phil.	10·35 N	125·35 E
121	Lezajsk (lĕ'zhä-ĭsk) Pol.	50·14 N	22·25 E
128	Lezha (R.) (lĕ-zhä') Sov. Un.	58·59 N	40·27 E
122	Lézignan (lā-zē-nyäɴ') Fr.	43·13 N	2·48 E
129	L'gov (lgôf) Sov. Un.	51·42 N	35·15 E
142	Lhasa (läs'ä) China	29·41 N	91·12 E
148	Lhsien (lē'sĭäɴ) China	37·09 N	119·57 E
150	Lianghsiang (lyäng'syän') China (Peking In.)	39·43 N	116·08 E
136	Lianozovo (lĭ-á-nô'zô-vô) Sov. Un. (Moscow In.)	55·54 N	37·36 E
148	Liaoch'eng (lĭou'chĕng) China	36·27 N	115·56 E
150	Liao Ho (R.) (lyä'ō hō') China	41·40 N	122·40 E
147	Liaoning (Prov.) China	41·31 N	122·11 E
148	Liaotung Pantao (Pen.) (lĭou'dōōng bäɴ'dou) China	39·45 N	122·22 E
150	Liaotung Wan (B.) China	40·25 N	121·15 E
150	Liaoyang (lyä'ō-yäng') China	41·18 N	123·10 E
147	Liaoyüan (lyä'ō-yü-än') China	43·37 N	123·30 E
86	Liard (R.) (lē-är') Can.	59·43 N	126·42 W
98	Libano (lē'-bá-nô) Col. (In.)	4·55 N	75·05 W
124	Libar, Sierra de (Mts.) (sē-ĕ'r-rä-dĕ-lē-bär) Sp.	39·42 N	5·28 W
66	Libby (lĭb'ê) Mont.	48·27 N	115·35 W
165	Libenge (lê-bĕŋ'gä) Con. K.	3·39 N	18·40 E
72	Liberal (lĭb'ẽr-ǎl) Kans	37·01 N	100·56 W
120	Liberec (lē'bĕr-ĕts) Czech.	15·47 N	15·06 E
163	Liberia (lī-bē'rĭ-ȧ) Afr.	6·30 N	9·55 W
92	Liberia C. R.	10·38 N	85·28 W
99	Libertad de Orituco (lē-bĕr-tä'd-dĕ-ô-rē-tōō'kô) Ven. (In.)	9·32 N	66·24 W
80	Liberty (lĭb'ẽr-tĭ) Ind.	39·35 N	84·55 W
74	Liberty Mo. (Kansas City In.)	39·15 N	94·25 W
79	Liberty S. C.	34·47 N	82·41 W
77	Liberty Tex.	30·03 N	94·46 W
74	Liberty Utah (Salt Lake City In.)	41·20 N	111·52 W
65	Liberty B. Wash. (Seattle In.)	47·43 N	122·41 W
84	Liberty Res. Md. (Baltimore In.)	39·25 N	76·56 W
75	Libertyville (lĭb'ẽr-tĭ-vĭl) Ill. (Chicago In.)	42·17 N	87·57 W
155	Libmanan (lĭb-mä'nän) Phil. (Manila In.)	13·42 N	123·04 E
167	Libode (lĭ-bō'dĕ) S. Afr. (Natal In.)	31·33 S	29·03 E
95	Libón, R. Hai.	19·30 N	71·45 W
122	Libourne (lē-bōōrn') Fr.	44·55 N	0·12 W
91	Libres (lē'brās) Mex.	19·26 N	97·41 W
164	Libreville (lē-br'vēl') Gabon	0·29 N	9·26 E
84	Liburn (lĭb'ûrn) Ga. (Atlanta In.)	33·53 N	84·09 W
163	Libya (lĭb'ê-ä) Afr.	27·38 N	15·00 E
165	Libyan Des. (lĭb'ê-ǎn) Libya	28·23 N	23·34 E
115	Libyan Plat. U. A. R.	30·58 N	26·20 E
100	Licancábur, Cerro (Mtn.) (sĕ'r-rô-lē-kän-kä'bōōr) Chile	22·45 S	67·45 W
101	Licanten (lē-kän-tĕ'n) Chile (Santiago In.)	34 58 S	72·00 W
110	Lichfield (lĭch'fēld) Eng.	52·41 N	1·49 W
146	Lichiang China	27·06 N	100·08 E
148	Liching (lē'jĭn) China	37·24 N	118·12 E
168	Lichtenburg (lĭk'tĕn-bĕrgh) S. Afr. (Johannesburg & Pretoria In.)	26·09 S	26·10 E
75	Lick Cr. (lĭk) Ind. (Indianapolis In.)	39·43 N	86·06 W
80	Licking (R.) (lĭk'ĭng) Ky.	38·30 N	84·10 W
126	Licosa, Pt. (lê-kō'sä) It.	40·17 N	14·40 E
121	Lida (lē'dȧ) Sov. Un.	53·53 N	25·19 E
70	Lidgerwood (lĭj'ẽr-wood) N. D.	46·04 N	97·10 W
118	Lidköping (lēt'chû-pĭng) Swe.	58·31 N	13·06 E
125	Lido di Roma (Ostia Lido) (lē'dô-dē-rô'mä) (ô's-tyä-lē-dô) It. (Rome In.)	41·19 N	12·17 E
121	Lidzbark (lĭts'bärk) Pol.	54·07 N	20·36 E
168	Liebenbergs R. S. Afr. (Johannesburg & Pretoria In.)	27·35 S	28·25 E
111	Liebenwalde (lē'bĕn-väl-dĕ) Ger. (Berlin In.)	52·52 N	13·24 E
151	Liechou Pan-Tao (Pen.) China	20·40 N	109·25 E
120	Liechtenstein (lĕk'tĕn-shtīn) Eur.	47·14 N	9·15 E
117	Liège (lê-āzh') Bel.	50·40 N	5·30 E
151	Lienchiang China	21·38 N	110·15 E
148	Lienshui (lĭaɴ'sōōĭ) China	33·46 N	119·15 E
147	Lienyün China	33·10 N	120·01 E
148	Lienyun (lĭaɴ'yüɴ) China	34·43 N	119·27 E
120	Lienz (lê-ĕnts') Aus.	46·49 N	12·45 E
119	Liepāja (le'pȧ-yä') Sov. Un.	56·31 N	20·59 E
111	Lier Bel. (Brussels In.)	5·08 N	4·34 E
111	Liesing (lē'sĭng) Aus. (Vienna In.)	48·09 N	16·17 E
120	Liestal (lēs'täl) Switz	47·28 N	7·44 E
81	Lievre, Rivière du (R.) Can.	45·00 N	75·25 W
116	Liffey R. (lĭf'ĭ) Ire.	53·21 N	6·35 W
159	Lifou, (I.) N. Cal. Is.	21·15 S	167·32 E
155	Ligao (lē-gä'ō) Phil. (Manila In.)	13·14 N	123·33 E
160	Lightning Ridge Austl.	29·23 S	147·50 E
167	Ligonha (R.) (lē-gō'nyȧ) Moz.	16·14 S	39·00 E
80	Ligonier (lĭg-ô-nēr') Ind.	41·30 N	85·35 W
136	Ligovo (lē'gô-vô) Sov. Un. (Leningrad In.)	59·51 N	30·13 E
126	Liguria (Reg.) (lē-gōō-rê-ä) It.	44·24 N	8·27 E
126	Ligurian Sea (lĭ-gū'rĭ-ǎn) Eur.	43·42 N	8·32 E
159	Lihou Rfs. (lē-hōō') Austl.	17·23 S	152·43 E
151	Lihsien (lē'hsyĕn') China	29·42 N	111·40 E
148	Lihsien China	38·30 N	115·38 E
148	Lihuang (lē'hōōäng) China	31·32 N	115·46 E
157	Lihue (lê-hōō'ā) Hawaii (In.)	21·59 N	159·23 W
119	Lihula (lē'hōō-lȧ) Sov. Un.	58·41 N	23·50 E
128	Likhoslavl' (lyê-kôslȧv''l) Sov. Un.	57·07 N	35·27 E
129	Likhovka (lyê-ĸôf'kȧ) Sov. Un.	48·52 N	33 57 E
122	Lille (lēl) Fr.	50·38 N	3·01 E
118	Lille Baelt (str.) Den.	55·09 N	9·53 E
118	Lillehammer (lēl'ĕ-häm'mĕr) Nor.	61·07 N	10·25 E
118	Lillesand (lēl'ĕ-sän') Nor.	58·16 N	8·19 E
118	Lilleström (lēl'ĕ-strûm) Nor.	59·56 N	11·04 E
65	Lilliwaup (lĭl'ĭ-wŏp) Wash. (Seattle In.)	47·28 N	123·07 W
86	Lillooet Can.	50·49 N	122·02 W
166	Lilongwe (lê-lô-än) Malawi	13·51 S	33·47 E
80	Lima (lī'mȧ) Ohio	40·40 N	84·05 W
98	Lima (lē'mä) Peru	12·06 S	76·55 W
124	Lima (R.) Port.	41·45 N	8·22 W
101	Lima Duarte (dwä'r-tĕ) Braz. (Rio de Janeiro In.)	21·52 S	43·47 W
67	Lima Res. Mont.	44·45 N	112·15 W
139	Limassol (lē-mä-sōl') Cyprus (Palestine In.)	34·39 N	33·02 E
100	Limay (lē-mä'ê) (R.) Arg.	39·50 S	69·15 W
119	Limbaži (lēm'bä-zĭ) Sov. Un.	57·32 N	24·44 E
95	Limbé Hai.	19·45 N	72·30 W

ăt; finǎl; rāte; senâte; ärm; ȧsk; sofȧ; fâre; ch-choose; dh-as th in other; bē; êvent; bĕt; recĕnt; cratẽr; g-go; gh-guttural g; bĭt· ĭ-short neutral; rīde; ĸ-guttural k as ch in German ich;

ng-sing; ŋ-baŋk; N-nasalized n; nŏd; cǒmmit; ōld; ôbey; ôrder; fōōd; fŏŏt; ou-out; s-soft; sh-dish; th-thin; pūre; ûnite; ûrn; stŭd; circǔs; ū-as "y" in study; '-indeterminate vowel.

Page	Name Pronunciation Region	Lat. °′	Long. °′
70	McLaughlin (mȧk-lŏf′lĭn) . . . S. D.	45·48 N	100·45 W
84	McLean (mȧc′lān) Va. (Washington In.)	38·56 N	77·11 W
80	McLeansboro (mȧ-klānz′bŭr-ȯ) Ill.	38·10 N	88·35 W
167	Macleantown (măk-lān′toun) S. Afr. (Natal In.)	32·48 S	27·48 E
167	Maclear (mȧ-klēr′) S. Afr. (Natal In.)	31·06 S	28·23 E
86	McLennan (măk-lĭn′nȧn) . . . . Can.	55·51 N	117·10 W
66	McLoughlin, Mt. (mȧk-lŏk′lĭn) Ore.	42·27 N	122·20 W
76	McMillan L. (măk-mĭl′ȧn) . . . Tex.	32·40 N	104·09 W
65	McMillin (mȧk-mĭl′ĭn) Wash. (Seattle In.)	47·08 N	122·14 W
66	McMinnville (măk-mĭn′vĭl) . . Ore.	45·13 N	123·13 W
78	McMinnville . . . . Tenn.	35·41 N	85·47 W
86	McMurray (mȧk-mŭr′ĭ) . . . . . Can.	56·45 N	111·15 W
65	McMurray . . . . Wash. (Seattle In.)	48·19 N	122·15 W
69	McNary (mȧk-nâr′ê) . . . . Ariz.	34·10 N	109·55 W
77	McNary . . . . La.	30·58 N	92·32 W
66	McNary Dam . . . . Ore.-Wash.	45·57 N	119·15 W
73	Macomb (mȧ-ko͞om′) . . . . Ill.	40·27 N	90·40 W
122	Mâcon (mä-kôɴ) . . . . Fr.	46·19 N	4·51 E
78	Macon (mā′kŏn) . . . . Ga.	32·49 N	83·39 W
78	Macon . . . . Miss.	32·07 N	88·31 W
73	Macon . . . . Mo.	39·42 N	92·29 W
73	McPherson (mȧk-fŭr′s′n) . . . Kans.	38·21 N	97·41 W
160	Macquarie (R.) . . . . Austl.	31·43 S	148·04 E
47	Macquarie Is. (mȧ-kwŏr′ê) . Austl.	54·36 S	158·45 E
78	McRae (mȧk-rā′) . . . . Ga.	32·02 N	82·55 W
78	McRoberts (mȧk-rŏb′ērts) . . . . Ky.	37·12 N	82·40 W
92	Macuelizo (mä-kwĕ-lē′zô) . . Hond.	15·22 N	88·32 W
139	Ma′dabā) . . Jordan (Palestine In.)	31·43 N	35·47 E
163	Madagascar (I.) (măd-ȧ-găs′kȧr) Malag. Rep.	23·30 S	46·00 E
83	Madame (I.) (mȧ-dȧm′) . . . . . Can.	45·31 N	60·45 W
143	Madanapalle . . . . India	13·06 N	78·09 E
155	Madang (mä-däng′) . N. Gui. Ter.	5·15 S	145·45 E
164	Madaoua (mȧ-dou′ȧ) . . . . Niger	14·04 N	6·03 E
74	Madart (mȧ′därt) Minn. (Minneapolis, St. Paul In.)	44·48 N	93·02 W
81	Madawaska (R.) (măd-ȧ-wôs′kȧ) Can.	45·20 N	77·25 W
88	Madden, L. C. Z. (Panama Canal In.)	9·15 N	79·34 W
164	Madeira, Ilha da (I.) (mä-dā′rä) Mad. Is.	32·41 N	16·15 W
164	Madeira, Arquipelago da (Is.) (är-kē-pĕ′lä-gō-dä-mä-dĕý-rä) Port.	33·26 N	16·44 W
98	Madeira (R.) . . . . Braz.	6·48 S	62·43 W
82	Madeleine, C. (mȧd′lĕn′) . . . . Can.	49·15 N	65·20 W
71	Madelia (mȧ-dē′lĭ-ȧ) . . . . Minn.	44·03 N	94·23 W
71	Madeline (I.) (măd′ĕ-lĭn) . . . . Wis.	46·47 N	91·30 W
68	Madera (mȧ-dā′rȧ) . . . . Calif.	36·57 N	120·04 W
92	Madera (Vol.) . . . . Nic.	11·27 N	85·30 W
142	Madhya Pradesh (State) ((mŭd′vŭ prŭ-dāsh′) . India	27·04 N	77·48 E
73	Madill (mȧ-dĭl′) . . . . Okla.	34·04 N	96·45 W
78	Madison (măd′ĭ-sŭn) . . . . Fla.	30·25 N	85·25 W
78	Madison . . . . Ga.	33·34 N	83·29 W
74	Madison . . . . Ill. (St. Louis In.)	38·40 N	90·09 W
80	Madison . . . . Ind.	38·45 N	85·25 W
73	Madison . . . . Kans.	38·08 N	96·07 W
82	Madison . . . . Maine	44·47 N	69·52 W
70	Madison . . . . Minn.	44·59 N	96·13 W
70	Madison . . . . Nebr.	41·49 N	97·27 W
84	Madison . . . . N. J. (New York In.)	40·46 N	74·25 W
79	Madison . . . . N. C.	36·22 N	79·59 W
70	Madison . . . . S. D.	44·01 N	97·08 W
71	Madison . . . . Wis.	43·05 N	89·23 W
67	Madison Res . . . . Mont.	45·25 N	111·28 W
67	Madison R . . . . Mont.	45·15 N	111·30 W
80	Madisonville (măd′ĭ-sŭn-vĭl) . . Ky.	37·20 N	87·30 W
77	Madisonville . . . . La.	30·22 N	90·10 W
77	Madisonville . . . . Tex.	30·57 N	95·55 W
154	Madjene . . . . Indon.	3·34 S	119·00 E
128	Madona (mȧ′dō′nȧ) . . . . . Sov. Un.	56·50 N	26·14 E
143	Madras (mȧ-drȧs′) (mŭ-drŭs′) . India	13·08 N	80·15 E
143	Madras (State) (mŭ-drŭs′) (mȧ-drȧs′) . India	15·20 N	78·20 E
77	Madre, Laguna L. (lä-go͞o′nä mä′drȧ) . Mex.	25·08 N	97·41 W
90	Madre, Sierra (Mts.) (sē-ĕ′r-rä-mȧ′drĕ) . Mex.	15·55 N	92·40 W
155	Madre, Sierra (Mts.) Phil. (Manila In.)	16·40 N	122·10 E
100	Madre de Dios, Arch. (mȧ′drȧ dā dê-ōs′) . Chile	50·40 S	76·30 W
98	Madre de Dios, Rio (R.) (rê′ō-mä′drȧ dā dê-ōs′) . Bol.	12·07 S	68·20 W
90	Madre del Sur, Sierra (Mts.) (sē-ĕ′r-rä-mä′drȧ dĕlso͞or′) . Mex.	17·35 N	100·35 W
71	Madrid (măd′rĭd) . . . . Iowa	41·51 N	93·48 W
125	Madrid (mä-drê′d) Sp. (Madrid In.)	40·26 N	3·42 W
124	Madridejos (mä-dhrê-dhā′hōs) . Sp.	39·29 N	3·32 W
66	Mad R. (măd) . . . . Calif.	40·38 N	123·37 W
154	Madura (I.) (mȧ-do͞o′rä) . . . Indon.	6·45 S	113·30 E
143	Madurai (mä-do͞o′rä) . . . . India	9·57 N	78·04 E
100	Madureira, Serra do (Mtn.) (sĕ′r-rä-dô-mä-do͞o-rā′rȧ) . Braz. (In.)	22·49 S	43·30 W
153	Maebashi (mä-ĕ-bä′shê) . . . . . . Jap.	36·26 N	139·04 E
125	Maella (mä-āl′yä) . . . . Sp.	41·10 N	0·07 E
94	Maestra, Sierra (Mts.) (sē-ĕ′r-rȧ-mä-ās′trä) . Cuba	20·05 N	77·05 W
159	Maewo (I.) . . . . New Hebr.	15·17 S	168·16 E
166	Mafeking (mȧf′ê-kĭng) . . . . S. Afr.	25·46 S	24·45 E
167	Mafia (I.) (mä-fē′ä) . . . . Tan.	7·45 S	39·45 E
100	Mafra (mä′frä) . . . . Braz.	26·21 S	49·59 W
125	Mafra (mäf′rȧ) . Port. (Lisbon In.)	38·56 N	9·20 W
135	Magadan (mȧ-gȧ-dän′) . . Sov. Un.	59·39 N	150·43 E
135	Magadan Oblast . . . . Sov. Un.	63·00 N	170·30 E
167	Magadi (L.) (mȧ-gä′dê) . . . . . Ken.	2·12 S	37·32 E
167	Magalies (R.) (mä-gä′lyĕs) S. Afr. (Johannesburg & Pretoria In.)	25·51 S	27·42 E
167	Magaliesberg (Mts.) S. Afr. (Johannesburg & Pretoria In.)	25·45 S	27·43 E
168	Magaliesburg . . . . S. Afr. (Johannesburg & Pretoria In.)	26·01 S	27·32 E
155	Magallanes (mä-gäl-yä′nās) Phil. (Manila In.)	12·48 N	123·52 E
100	Magallanes, Estrecho de (Str.) (ĕs-trĕ′chô-dĕ-mä-gäl-yä′nĕs) Arg.-Chile	52·30 S	68·45 W
98	Magangué (mä-gän′ga) . . . . Col.	9·08 N	74·56 W
155	Magat (R.) (mä-gät′) Phil. (Manila In.)	16·45 N	121·16 E
101	Magdalena (mäg-dä-lā′nä) Arg. (Buenos Aires In.)	35·05 S	57·32 W
98	Magdalena . . . . Bol.	13·17 S	63·57 W
62	Magdalena . . . . Mex.	30·34 N	110·50 W
69	Magdalena . . . . N. Mex.	34·10 N	107·45 W
100	Magdalena (I.) . . . . Chile	44·45 S	73·15 W
88	Magdalena, Bahia (B.) (bä-ē′ä-mäg-dä-lā′nä) . Mex.	24·30 N	114·00 W
98	Magdalena, Rio (R.) . . . . Col.	7·45 N	74·04 W
83	Magdalen Is. (măg′dȧ-lĕn) . . . Can.	47·27 N	61·25 W
120	Magdeburg (mäg′dĕ-bo͝orgh) . Ger.	52·07 N	11·39 E
100	Magé (mä-zhā′) . . . . Braz. (In.)	22·39 S	43·02 W
126	Magenta (mȧ-jĕn′tȧ) . . . . It.	45·26 N	8·53 E
112	Mageröy (I.) (mä′ghĕr-ûê) . . . Nor.	71·10 N	24·11 E
126	Maggiore, Lago di (L.) . . . . It.	46·03 N	8·25 E
124	Maghnia . . . . Alg.	35·07 N	2·10 W
168	Maghāghah . . . U. A. R. (Nile In.)	28·38 N	30·50 E
90	Magiscatzin (mä-kês-kät-zēn′) Mex.	22·48 N	98·42 W
127	Maglaj (mȧ′glä-ê) . . . . Yugo.	44·34 N	18·12 E
127	Maglić (mäg′lêch) . . . . Yugo.	43·36 N	20·36 E
127	Maglie (mäl′yā) . . . . It.	40·06 N	18·20 E
74	Magna (măg′nȧ) Utah (Salt Lake City In.)	40·43 N	112·06 W
136	Magnitogorsk (mȧg-nyē′tô-gôrsk) . Sov. Un. (Urals In.)	53·26 N	59·05 E
73	Magnolia (măg-nō′lĭ-ȧ) . . . . . . Ark.	33·16 N	93·13 W
78	Magnolia . . . . Miss.	31·08 N	90·27 W
123	Magny-en-Vexin (mä-nyē′ ĕɴ-vĕ-sȧɴ′) . Fr. (Paris In.)	49·09 N	1·45 E
81	Magog (mȧ-gŏg′) . . . . Can.	45·15 N	72·10 W
82	Magpie (L.) (măg′pī) . . . . Can.	50·56 N	64·30 W
71	Magpie (R.) . . . . Can.	48·13 N	84·50 W
86	Magrath . . . . Can.	49·22 N	112·52 W
166	Magude (mä-go͞o′dȧ) . . . . Moz.	24·58 S	32·39 E
146	Magwe (mŭg-wā′) . . . . Bur.	20·19 N	94·57 E
133	Mahabād . . . . Iran	36·55 N	45·50 E
165	Mahagi (mä-hä′gê) . . . . Con. K.	2·14 N	31·12 E
154	Mahakam, Sungai (Strm.) . . Indon.	0·30 S	116·15 E
167	Mahaly (mȧ-hȧl-ē′) . . Malag. Rep.	24·09 S	46·20 E
154	Mahameru, Gunung (Mtn.) . . Java	8·00 S	112·50 E
142	Mahānadi (R.) (mŭ-hä-nŭd′ê) India	20·50 N	84·27 E
167	Mahanoro (mȧ-hȧ-nô′rō) Malag. Rep.	19·57 S	48·47 E
81	Mahanoy City (mä-hȧ-noi′) . . . Pa.	40·50 N	76·10 W
142	Maharashtra (State) . . . . India	20·25 N	75·00 E
139	Mahasham (R.) U. A. R. (Palestine In.)	30·08 N	34·09 E
167	Mahavavy (R.) (mä-hä-vä′vê) Malag. Rep.	17·42 S	46·06 E
142	Mahaweli (R.) . . . . India	7·47 N	80·43 E
113	Mahdia (mä-dē′ȧ) (mä′dê-ȧ) . Tun.	35·30 N	11·09 E
143	Mahe (mä-ā′) . . . . India	11·42 N	75·39 E
167	Mahenge (mä-hĕŋ′gȧ) . . . . Tan.	8·41 S	36·43 E
142	Mahi (R.) . . . . India	23·16 N	73·20 E
143	Māhīm Bay . . India (Bombay In.)	19·03 N	72·45 E
167	Mahlabatini (mä′lȧ-bȧ-tē′nê) S. Afr. (Natal In.)	28·15 S	31·29 E
111	Mahlow (mä′lōv) . Ger. (Berlin In.)	52·23 N	13·24 E
70	Mahnomen (mô-nō′mĕn) . . . Minn.	47·18 N	95·58 W
125	Mahón (mä-ōn′) . . . . Sp.	39·52 N	4·15 E
82	Mahone Bay (mȧ-hōn′) . . . . . . Can.	44·27 N	64·24 W
82	Mahone B. . . . . Can.	44·27 N	64·05 W
84	Mahopac, L. (mā-hō′păk) N. Y. (New York In.)	41·24 N	73·45 W
84	Mahwah (mȧ-wä′) N. J. (New York In.)	41·05 N	74·09 W
110	Maidenhead (mād′ĕn-hĕd) Eng. (London In.)	51·30 N	0·44 W
	Maidos, see Eceabat		
110	Maidstone (mād′stŭn) Eng. (London In.)	51·17 N	0·32 E
165	Maiduguri (mä′ē-dȧ-go͞o′rê) . . Nig.	11·53 N	13·12 E
98	Maigualida Sierra (Mts.) (sē-ĕ′r-rȧ-mī-gwä′lē-dĕ) . Ven.	6·30 N	65·50 W
142	Maijdi . . . . E. Pak.	22·59 N	91·08 E
	Maikop, see Maykop		
144	Maimana (mī-mȧ-nä′) . . . . Afg.	35·53 N	64·38 E
160	Main Barrier Ra. (băr″ĕr) . Austl.	31·25 S	141·40 E
63	Maine (State) (mān) . . . . U. S.	45·25 N	69·50 W
116	Mainland (I.) (mān-lănd) Scot. (In.)	60·19 N	2·40 W
120	Main R. (mīn) . . . . Ger.	49·49 N	9·20 E
123	Maintenon (mȧɴ-tĕ-nŏɴ′) Fr. (Paris In.)	48·35 N	1·35 E
167	Maintirano (mä′ên-tê-rä′nō) Malag. Rep.	18·05 S	44·08 E
120	Mainz (mīnts) . . . . Ger.	49·59 N	8·16 E
164	Maio I. (mä′yō) . . . . C. V. Is. (In.)	15·15 N	22·50 W
101	Maipo (mī′pô) (R.) Chile (Santiago In.)	33·45 S	71·08 W
100	Maipo (Vol.) . . . . Arg.	34·08 S	69·51 W
101	Maipú (mī′po͞o′) Arg. (Buenos Aires In.)	36·51 S	57·54 W
99	Maiquetía (mī-kĕ-tê′ä) . Ven. (In.)	10·37 N	66·56 W
95	Maisí, Punta (Pt.) (po͞on′n-tä-mī-sē′) . Cuba	20·10 N	74·00 W
123	Maison-Rouge (mȧ-zŏɴ-ro͞ozh′) Fr. (Paris In.)	48·34 N	3·09 E
168	Mait I. (māt) Som. (Horn. of Afr. In.)	11·24 N	46·38 E
160	Maitland (māt′lănd) . . . . Austl.	32·45 S	151·40 E
80	Maitland (R.) . . . . Can.	45·50 N	81·10 W
153	Maizuru (mä-ĭ′zo͞o-ro͞o) . . . . . . Jap.	35·26 N	135·15 E
	Majorca I., see Mallorca, Isle de		
167	Majunga (mȧ-jŭŋ′gä) Malag. Rep.	15·12 S	46·26 E
66	Makah Ind. Res. (mȧ kī′) . . Wash.	48·17 N	124·52 W
165	Mak′alē . . . . Eth.	13·31 N	39·19 E
167	Makanya (mä-kän′yä) . . . . Tan.	4·15 S	37·49 E
166	Makarikari Salt Pan (L.) . . . Bots.	20·38 S	21·31 E
126	Makarska (mȧ′kär-skȧ) . . . . Yugo.	43·17 N	17·05 E
132	Makar′yev . . . . Sov. Un.	57·50 N	43·48 E
154	Makasar . . . . Indon.	5·08 S	119·28 E
154	Makasar, Selat (Str.) (mȧ-käs′ĕr) Indon.	2·00 S	118·07 E
153	Make (I.) (mä′kȧ) . . . . Jap.	30·43 N	130·49 E
129	Makeyevka (mŭk-yā′ŭf-kŭ) Sov. Un.	48·03 N	38·00 E
133	Makhachkala (mäκ′äch-kä′lä) Sov. Un.	43·00 N	47·40 E
167	Makhaleng (R.) . Leso. (Natal In.)	29·53 S	27·33 E
127	Makhlata (mäκ′lä-tä) . . . . Bul.	43·27 N	24·16 E
144	Makkah (Mecca) (mĕk′ä) . Sau. Ar.	21·27 N	39·45 E
87	Makkovik . . . . Can.	55·01 N	59·10 W
121	Makó (mô′kō) . . . . Hung.	46·13 N	20·30 E
164	Makokou (mȧ-kô-ko͞o′) . . . . Gabon	0·39 N	12·46 E
121	Maków Mazowiecki (mä′ko͞ov mä-zō-vyĕts′kē) . Pol.	52·51 N	21·07 E
153	Makuhari (mä-ko͞o-hä′rē) Jap. (Tōkyō In.)	35·39 N	140·04 E
153	Makurazaki (mä′ko͞o-rä-zä′kê) Jap.	31·16 N	130·18 E
164	Makurdi . . . . Nig.	7·44 N	8·34 E
64	Makushin (mȧ-ko͞o′shĭn) . . . Alaska	53·57 N	166·28 W
134	Makushino (mȧ-ko͞o-shên′ô) Sov. Un.	55·03 N	67·43 E
143	Malabar Coast (măl′ȧ-bär) . . India	16·30 N	75·33 E
139	Malacca (mȧ-lăk′ȧ) Mala. (Singapore In.)	2·11 N	102·15 E
139	Malacca (State) Mala. (Singapore In.)	2·19 N	102·09 E
154	Malacca, Str. of (mȧ-lăk′ȧ) . . Asia	4·15 N	99·44 E
67	Malad (mȧ-läd′) . . . . Idaho	42·11 N	112·15 W
125	Maladetta (Mts.) (mä-lä-dĕt′tä) Sp.	42·30 N	0·38 E
125	Malafede (R.) (mä-lä-fĕ′dĕ) It. (Rome In.)	41·43 N	12·28 E
98	Málaga (mȧ′lä-gȧ) . . . . Col.	6·41 N	72·46 W
124	Málaga . . . . Sp.	36·45 N	4·25 W
124	Málaga, Bahía de (B.) (bä-ē′ä-dĕ-mȧ′lä-gä) . Sp.	36·35 N	4·10 W
163	Malagasy Republic . . . . Afr.	18·05 S	43·12 E
124	Malagón (mä-lä-gōn′) . . . . Sp.	39·12 N	3·52 W
159	Malaita (I.) (mȧ-lä′ê-tȧ) . . . Sol. Is.	8·38 S	161·15 E
165	Malakal (mȧ-lȧ-käl′) . . . . Sud.	9·46 N	31·54 E
136	Malakhovka (mȧ-läk′ôf-kȧ) Sov. Un. (Moscow In.)	55·38 N	38·01 E
166	Malange (mȧ-läŋ′gȧ) . . . . Ang.	9·30 S	16·25 E
82	Malapedia (R.) . . . . Can.	48·11 N	67·08 W
93	Mala Punta (Pt.) (po͝o′n-tä-mä′lä) Pan.	7·32 N	79·44 W
118	Mälaren (L.) . . . . Swe.	59·38 N	16·55 E
87	Malartic . . . . Can.	48·07 N	78·11 W
133	Malatya (mȧ-lä′tyȧ) . . . . Tur.	38·30 N	38·15 E
166	Malawi . . . . Afr.	11·15 S	33·45 E
154	Malaya (Reg.) (mȧ-lā′yä) . . . Mala.	3·35 N	101·30 E
128	Malaya Vishera (vê-shā′rä) Sov. Un.	58·51 N	32·13 E
154	Malay Pen. (mȧ-lā′) (mā′lā) . . Asia	7·46 N	101·06 E
154	Malaysia (mȧ-lā′zhȧ) . . . . Asia	4·10 N	101·22 E
116	Mal B. (măl) . . . . Ire.	52·51 N	9·45 E
158	Malbon (măl′bŭn) . . . . Austl.	21·15 S	140·30 E
121	Malbork (mäl′bŏrk) . . . . Pol.	54·02 N	19·04 E
125	Malcabran (R.) (mäl-kä-brän′) Port. (Lisbon In.)	38·47 N	8·46 W
83	Malden (môl′dĕn) Mass. (Boston In.)	42·26 N	71·04 W
73	Malden . . . . Mo.	36·32 N	89·56 W
157	Malden (I.) . . . . Oceania	4·20 S	154·30 W
138	Maldive Is. (măl′dīv) . . . . Asia	4·30 N	71 30 E
110	Maldon (môrl′dŏn) Eng. (London In.)	51·44 N	0·39 E
100	Maldonado (mäl-dŏ-nȧ′dô) . . . . Ur.	34·54 S	54·57 W
90	Maldonado, Punta (Pt.) (po͞o′n-tä) . Mex.	16·18 N	98·34 W
127	Maléa, Akr. (C.) . . . . Grc.	37·31 N	23·13 E
121	Male Karpaty (Mts.) . . . . . . Czech.	48·31 N	17·15 E
159	Malekula (I.) (mä-lā-ko͞o′lä) New Hebr.	16·44 S	167·45 E
124	Malhão da Estrêla (Mtn.) (mäl-you′ɴ-dä-ĕs-trĕ′lä) . Sp.	40·20 N	7·38 W
66	Malheur L. (mȧ-lo͞or′) . . . . Ore.	43·16 N	118·37 W
66	Malheur R. (mȧ-lo͞or′) . . . . Ore.	43·45 N	117·41 W
164	Mali . . . . Afr.	15·45 N	0·15 W
74	Malibu (mă′lĭ-bo͞o) Calif. (Los Angeles In.)	34·03 N	118·38 W
129	Malin (mȧ-lên′) . . . . Sov. Un.	50·44 N	29·15 E
90	Malinalco (mä-lê-näl′kō) . . . . Mex.	18·54 N	99·31 W
90	Malinaltepec (mä-lê-näl-tȧ-pĕk′) Mex.	17·01 N	98·41 W
167	Malindi (mä-lēn′dê) . . . . Ken.	3·14 S	40·04 E
121	Málinec (mä′lê-nyets′) . . . . . Czech.	48·31 N	19·40 E
116	Malin Hd . . . . N. Ire.	54·84 N	6·70 W
116	Malinmore Hd, (mȧ′lĭn-mōr) . . Ire.	54·45 N	8·30 W
136	Malino (mä′lĭ-nô) Sov. Un. (Moscow In.)	55·07 N	38·12 E
129	Malinovka (mȧ-lê-nôf′kȧ) . Sov. Un.	49·50 N	36·43 E
127	Malkara (mäl′κȧ-rȧ) . . . . Tur.	40·51 N	26·52 E
127	Malko Tŭrnovo (mäl′kō-t′r′nô-vȧ) . Bul.	41·59 N	27·28 E
116	Mallaig (măl′ăg) . . . . Scot.	56·59 N	5·55 W
168	Mallawī (mȧ-lä′wê) U. A. R. (Nile In.)	27·43 N	30·49 E
75	Mallet Creek (măl′ĕt) Ohio (Cleveland In.)	41·10 N	81·55 W

ăt; finăl; rāte; senâte; ärm; ȧsk; sofȧ; fâre; ch-choose; dh-as th in other; bē; êvent; bĕt; recĕnt; cratẽr; g-go; gh-guttural g; bĭt; ĭ-short neutral; rīde; κ-guttural k as ch in German ich;

PRONOUNCING INDEX Mallorca–Marennes 233

Page	Name Pronunciation Region	Lat. °′	Long. °′
125	Mallorca, Isla de (Majorca I.) (ê's-lä-dĕ-mäl-yô'r-kä) . Sp.	39·18 N	2·22 E
116	Mallow (măl'ō) .... Ire.	52·07 N	9·04 W
117	Malmédy (mȧl-mā-dē') .... Bel.	50·25 N	6·01 E
166	Malmesbury (mämz'bēr-ĭ) .. S. Afr.	33·30 S	18·35 E
118	Malmköping (mälm'chû'pĭng) Swe.	59·09 N	16·39 E
118	Malmö (mälm'û) .... Swe.	55·36 N	12·58 E
135	Malmyzh (mȧl-mêzh') ... Sov. Un.	49·58 N	137·07 E
132	Malmyzh .... Sov. Un.	56·30 N	50·48 E
128	Maloarkhangelsk (mä'lô-ȧr-ᴋäŋ'gĕlsk) . Sov. Un.	52·26 N	36·29 E
155	Malolos (mä-lô'lôs) Phil. (Manila In.)	14·58 N	120·53 E
136	Malomal'sk (mȧ-lô-mälsk'') Sov. Un. (Urals In.)	58·47 N	59·55 E
81	Malone (mȧ-lōn') .... N. Y.	44·50 N	74·20 W
128	Maloyaroslavets (mä'lô-yä-rô-slä-vyĕts) . Sov. Un.	55·01 N	36·25 E
132	Malozemel'skaya Tundra (Plains) Sov. Un.	67·30 N	50·00 E
110	Malpas (măl'pȧz) .... Eng.	53·01 N	2·46 W
98	Malpelo, Isla de (I.) (mäl-pā'lō) Col.	3·55 N	81·30 W
82	Malpeque B. (môl-pĕk') ..... Can.	46·41 N	63·40 W
67	Malta (môl'tȧ) .... Mont.	48·20 N	107·50 W
113	Malta .... Eur.	35·52 N	14·26 E
166	Maltahöhe (mäl'tä-hō'ĕ) . S. W. Afr.	24·45 S	16·45 E
85	Malton (môl'tŭn) Can. (Toronto In.)	43·42 N	79·39 W
91	Maltrata (mäl-trä'tä) .... Mex.	18·48 N	97·16 W
167	Maluti Mts. (mȧ-lōō-tĭ) Leso. (Natal In.)	29·00 S	28·29 E
143	Malvan .... India	16·08 N	73·32 E
73	Malvern (măl'vērn) .... Ark.	34·21 N	92·47 W
135	Malyy Anyuy (R.) ...... Sov. Un.	67·52 N	164·30 E
135	Malyy Lyakhovskiye (I.) . Sov. Un.	74·15 N	142·30 E
135	Malyy Tamir (I.) .... Sov. Un.	78·10 N	107·30 E
91	Mamantel (mä-mȧn-tĕl') .... Mex.	18·36 N	91·06 W
84	Mamaroneck (măm'ȧ-rō-nĕk) N. Y (New York In.)	40·57 N	73·44 W
164	Mamau .... Gui.	10·26 N	12·07 W
155	Mamberamo (R.) (mäm-bȧ-rä'mō) W. Irian	2·30 S	138·00 E
166	Mambone (mȧm-bŏ'nĕ) ..... Moz.	21·04 S	35·13 E
155	Mamburao (mäm-bōō'rä-ō) Phil. (Manila In.)	13·14 N	120·35 E
124	Mamede, Serra de (Mts.) (sĕ'r-rä-dĕ-mä-mĕ'dĕ) . Port.	39·29 N	7·11 W
164	Mamfe (mäm'fĕ) .... Cam.	9·06 E	5·52 N
153	Mamihara (mä'mê-hä-rä) .... Jap.	32·41 E	131·12 N
78	Mammoth Cave (măm'ŏth) ... Ky.	37·10 N	86·04 W
78	Mammoth Cave Natl. Park .. Ky.	37·20 N	86·21 W
67	Mammoth Hot Springs (măm'ŭth hôt sprĭngz) . Wyo.	44·55 N	110·50 W
143	Mamnoli ..... India (Bombay In.)	19·17 N	73·15 E
98	Mamoré (R.) (mä-mô-rā') .... Bol.	13·19 S	65·27 W
121	Mamry L. (mäm'rĭ) .... Pol.	54·10 N	21·28 E
139	Mamshit ...... Isr. (Palestine In.)	31·02 N	35·04 E
125	Manacor (mä-nä-kôr') .... Sp.	39·35 N	3·15 E
155	Manado .... Indon.	1.29 N	124·50 E
95	Managua (mä-nä'gwä) Cuba (Havana In.)	22·14 N	82·17 W
92	Managua .... Nic.	12·10 N	86·16 W
92	Managua, Lago de (L.) (lȧ'gô-dĕ) Nic.	12·28 N	86·10 W
167	Manakara (mä-nä-kä'rŭ) Malag. Rep.	22·17 S	48·06 E
167	Mananara (R.) (mä-nä-nä'rŭ) Malag. Rep.	23·15 S	48·15 E
167	Mananjary (mä-nän-zhä'rê) Malag. Rep.	20·16 S	48·13 E
	Manáos, see Manaus		
142	Manasaroar (L.) .... China	30·40 N	81·58 E
81	Manassas (mȧ-năs'ȧs) .... Va.	38·45 N	77·30 W
146	Manassu .... China	44·30 N	86·00 E
99	Manaus (Manáos) (mä-nä'ŏŏzh) Braz.	3·01 S	60·00 W
80	Mancelona (măn-sê-lō'nȧ) .. Mich.	44·50 N	85·05 W
124	Mancha Real (män'chä rā-äl') . Sp.	37·48 N	3·37 W
136	Manchazh (män'chȧsh) Sov. Un. (Urals In.)	56·30 N	58·10 E
81	Manchester (măn'chĕs-tēr) .. Conn.	41·45 N	72·30 W
110	Manchester .... Eng.	53·28 N	2·14 W
78	Manchester .... Ga.	32·50 N	84·37 W
71	Manchester .... Iowa	42·30 N	91·30 W
83	Manchester ... Mass. (Boston In.)	42·35 N	70·47 W
74	Manchester ... Mo. (St. Louis In.)	38·36 N	90·31 W
81	Manchester .... N. H.	43·00 N	71·30 W
80	Manchester .... Ohio	38·40 N	83·35 W
110	Manchester Ship Canal ...... Eng.	53·20 N	2·40 W
150	Manchouli (Lupin) (män-chōō'lê) (lōō'pĭn) . China	49·25 N	117·15 E
147	Manchuria (Reg.) (măn-chōō'rē-ȧ) China	48·00 N	124·58 E
144	Mand, Rud-e (R.) .... Iran	28·30 N	51·43 E
118	Mandal (män'däl) .... Nor.	58·03 N	7·28 E
146	Mandalay (măn'dȧ-lā) ...... Bur.	22·00 N	96·08 E
118	Mandalselv (R.) (män'dälsĕlv) Nor.	58·25 N	7·30 E
70	Mandan (măn'dăn) .... N. D.	46·49 N	100 54 W
165	Mandara Mts. (män-dä'rä) .. Cam.	10·55 N	14·10 E
139	Mandau Siak (R.) Indon. (Singapore In.)	1·03 N	101·25 E
93	Mandinga (män-dĭŋ'gä) ..... Pan.	9·32 N	79·04 W
142	Mandla .... India	22·43 N	80·23 E
127	Mándra (män'drä) .... Grc.	38·06 N	23·32 E
167	Mandritsara (mȧn-drēt-sä'rȧ) Malag. Rep.	15·49 S	48·47 E
127	Manduria (män-dōō'rê-ä) ...... It.	40·23 N	17·41 E
143	Mandve ..... India (Bombay In.)	18·47 N	72·52 E
143	Māndvi (mŭnd'vē) India (Bombay In.)	19·29 N	72·53 E
142	Māndvi (mŭnd'vē) .... India	22·54 N	69·23 E
168	Manfalūţ (män-fȧ-loot') U. A. R. (Nile In.)	27·18 N	30·59 E
126	Manfredonia (män-frȧ-dô'nyä) . It.	41·39 N	15·55 E
126	Manfredónia, Golfo di (G.) (gôl-fô-dē) . It.	41·34 N	16·05 E
99	Mangabeiras, Chap. das (Plains) (shä-pä'däs-däs-mäŋ-gä-bā'ê-räzh) . Braz.	8·05 S	47·32 W
143	Mangalore (mŭŋ-gŭ-lōr') .... India	12·53 N	74·52 E
101	Mangaratiba (män-gä-rä-tē'bȧ) Braz. (Rio de Janeiro In.)	22·56 S	44·03 W
155	Mangatarem (män'gȧ-tä'rĕm) Phil. (Manila In.)	15·48 N	120·18 E
154	Mangkalihat, Tandjoeng (C.) (mäng'kȧ-lē-hät') . Indon.	1·25 N	119·55 E
94	Mangles, Islas de (ê's-läs-dĕ-mäŋ'gläs) (măn'g'lz) Cuba	22·05 N	83·50 W
167	Mangoky (R.) (män-gō'kē) Malag. Rep.	22·02 S	44·11 E
155	Mangole (I.) .... Indon.	1·35 S	126·22 E
124	Mangualde (män-gwäl'dĕ) ... Port.	40·38 N	7·44 W
100	Mangueira, L. da (L.) (män-gā'ê-rȧ) . Braz.	33·15 S	52·45 W
72	Mangum (măŋ'gŭm) .... Okla.	34·52 N	99·31 W
133	Mangyshlak, P.-ov. (Pen.) Sov. Un.	44·30 N	50·40 E
75	Manhattan ..... Ill. (Chicago In.)	41·25 N	87·29 W
73	Manhattan (măn-hăt'ăn) ... Kans.	39·11 N	96·34 W
74	Manhattan Beach Calif. (Los Angeles In.)	33·53 N	118·24 W
101	Manhuaçu (män-ŏŏȧ'sōō) Braz. (Rio de Janeiro In.)	20·17 S	42·01 W
101	Manhumirim (män-ōō-mê-rē'ɴ) Braz. (Rio de Janeiro In.)	20·22 S	41·57 W
167	Mania (R.) (män'yä) . Malag. Rep.	19·52 S	46·02 E
99	Manicoré (mä-nê-kō-rā') .... Braz.	5·53 S	61·13 W
87	Manicouagan (R.) .... Can.	50·24 N	68·29 W
99	Manicuare (mä-nē-kwä'rĕ) Ven. (In.)	10·35 N	64·10 W
157	Manihiki Is. (mä'nē-hē'kê) . Oceania	9·40 S	158·00 W
155	Manila (mȧ-nĭl'ȧ) Phil. (Manila In.)	14·37 N	121·00 E
155	Manila B ...... Phil. (Manila In.)	14·38 N	120·46 E
133	Manisa (mä'nê-sȧ) .... Tur.	38·40 N	27·30 E
80	Manistee (măn-ĭs-tē') ...... Mich.	44·15 N	86·20 W
80	Manistee (R.) .... Mich.	44·25 N	85·45 W
71	Manistique (măn-ĭs-tēk') ... Mich.	45·58 N	86·16 W
71	Manistique (L.) .... Mich.	46·14 N	85·30 W
71	Manistique (R.) .... Mich.	46·05 N	86·09 W
86	Manitoba (Prov.) (măn-ĭ-tō'bȧ) Can.	55·12 N	97·29 W
86	Manitoba (L.) .... Can.	50·38 N	98·40 W
71	Manitou (I.) (măn'ĭ-tōō) .... Mich.	47·21 N	87·33 W
71	Manitou (L.) .... Can.	49·21 N	93·01 W
80	Manitou Is .... Mich.	45·05 N	86·00 W
80	Manitoulin I. (măn-ĭ-tōō'lĭn) . Can.	45·45 N	81·30 W
72	Manitou Springs .... Colo.	38·51 N	104·58 W
71	Manitowoc (măn-ĭ-tô-wŏk') .. Wis.	44·05 N	87·42 W
98	Manizales (mä-nê-zä'lȧs) . Col. (In.)	5·05 N	75·31 W
166	Manjacaze (man'yä-kä'zĕ) ... Moz.	24·37 S	33·49 E
144	Manjīl (mŭn-jēl') .... Iran	36·45 N	49·15 E
142	Mānjra (R.) .... India	18·18 N	77·00 E
72	Mankato (măn-kā'tō) ...... Kans.	39·45 N	98·12 W
71	Mankato .... Minn.	44·10 N	93·59 W
125	Manlleu (män-lyā'ōō) .... Sp.	42·00 N	2·16 E
161	Manly (măn'lĭ) Austl. (Sydney In.)	33·48 S	151·16 E
143	Mannar (mȧ-när') .... Ceylon	9.48 N	80·03 E
142	Mannar, G. of .... India	8·47 N	78·33 E
111	Mannersdorf am Leithagebirge Aus. (Vienna In.)	47·58 N	16·36 E
120	Mannheim (män'hīm) .... Ger.	49·30 N	8·31 E
71	Manning (măn'ĭng) .... Iowa	41·53 N	95·04 W
79	Manning .... S. C.	33·41 N	80·12 W
80	Mannington (măn'ĭng-tŭn) . W. Va.	39·30 N	80·55 W
126	Mannu (R.) (mä'n-nōō) .... It.	39·32 N	9·03 E
95	Man of War B .... Ba. Is.	21·05 N	74·05 W
95	Man of War Chan .... Ba. Is.	22·45 N	76·10 W
155	Manokwari (mȧ-nŏk-wä'rê) W. Irian	0·56 S	134·10 E
65	Manor (măn'ēr) Wash. (Portland In.)	45·45 N	122·36 W
143	Manori ...... India (Bombay In.)	19·13 N	72·43 E
123	Manosque (mȧ-nôsh') .... Fr.	43·51 N	5·48 E
85	Manotick ...... Can. (Ottawa In.)	45·13 N	75·41 W
125	Manresa (män-rā'sä) .... Sp.	41·44 N	1·52 E
87	Mansel (I.) (măn'sĕl) ...... Can.	61·56 N	81·10 W
98	Manseriche, Pongo de (Water Gap) (pŏ'n-gô-dĕ-män-sĕ-rê'chĕ) . Peru	4·15 S	77·45 W
110	Mansfield (mănz'fēld) .... Eng.	53·08 N	1·12 W
77	Mansfield .... La.	32·02 N	93·43 W
80	Mansfield .... Ohio	40·45 N	82·30 W
66	Mansfield .... Wash.	47·48 N	119·39 W
81	Mansfield, Mt .... Vt.	44·30 N	72·45 W
110	Mansfield Woodhouse (wŏŏd-hous) . Eng.	53·08 N	1·12 W
99	Manso (R.) .... Braz.	13·30 S	51·45 W
98	Manta (män'tä) .... Ec.	1·03 S	80·16 W
75	Manteno (măn-tē-nō) Ill. (Chicago In.)	41·15 N	87·50 W
123	Mantes-la-Jolie (mäɴt-ĕ-lä-zhŏ-lē') Fr. (Paris In.)	48·59 N	1·42 E
69	Manti (măn'tī) .... Utah	39·15 N	111·40 W
101	Mantiqueira, Serra da (Mts.) (sĕr'rä dä män-tê-kā'ê-rȧ) Braz. (Rio de Janeiro In.)	22·40 S	45·12 W
126	Mantova (Mantua) (män'tô-vä) (măn'tû-ȧ) . It.	45·09 N	10·47 E
94	Mantua (män-tōō'ȧ) .... Cuba	22·20 N	84·15 W
74	Mantua (măn'tû-ȧ) Utah (Salt Lake City In.)	41·30 N	111·57 W
	Mantua, see Mantova		
82	Manuan (L.) (mä-nōō'ȧn) ... Can.	50·36 N	70·50 W
82	Manuan, Riviere (R.) .... Can.	49·50 N	70·55 W
155	Manui (Is.) (mä-nōō'ē) .... Indon.	3·35 S	123·38 E
155	Manus (I.) (mä'nōōs) . N. Gui. Ter.	2·22 S	146·22 E
77	Manvel (măn'vel) ...... Tex. (In.)	29·28 N	95·22 W
84	Manville (măn'vĭl) N. J. (New York In.)	40·33 N	74·36 W
84	Manville ... R. I. (Providence In.)	41·57 N	71·27 W
133	Manych (R.) (mä-nĭch') . Sov. Un.	47·00 N	41·10 E
103	Manych Dep .... Sov. Un.	46·32 N	42·44 E
133	Manych-Gudilo (Lake) .. Sov. Un.	46·40 N	42·50 E
168	Manzala L .... U. A. R. (Nile In.)	31·14 N	32·04 E
98	Manzanares (män-sä-nä'rĕs) Col. (In.)	5·15 N	75·09 W
125	Manzanares (R.) (mänz-nä'rĕs) Sp. (Madrid In.)	40·36 N	3·48 W
125	Manzanares, Canal de (kä-nä'l-dĕ-män-thä-nä'rĕs) Sp. (Madrid In.)	40·20 N	3·38 W
94	Manzanillo (män'zä-nēl'yō) .. Cuba	20·20 N	77·05 W
90	Manzanillo .... Mex.	19·02 N	104·21 W
95	Manzanillo, Bahía de (B.) .... Hai.	19·55 N	71·50 W
90	Manzanillo, Bahía de (B.) (bä-ē'ä-dĕ-män-zä-nê'l-yō) . Mex.	19·00 N	104·38 W
93	Manzanillo, Punta (Pt.) ..... Pan.	9·40 N	79·33 W
152	Manzovka (mȧn-zhô'f-kȧ) Sov. Un.	44·16 N	132·13 E
165	Mao (mä'ô) .... Chad	14·07 N	15·15 E
151	Maoming .... China	21·55 N	110·40 E
91	Mapastepec (ma-päs-tȧ-pĕk') . Mex.	15·24 N	92·52 W
155	Mapia (I.) (mä'pē-ȧ) ..... W. Irian	0·57 N	134·22 E
76	Mapimi (mä-pê-mē') .... Mex.	25·50 N	103·50 W
85	Maple (mā'p'l) . Can. (Toronto In.)	43·51 N	79·30 W
86	Maple Creek (crēk) .... Can.	49·52 N	109·32 W
85	Maple Grove (grōv) Can. (Montreal In.)	45·19 N	73·51 W
75	Maple Heights Ohio (Cleveland In.)	41·25 N	81·34 W
84	Maple Shade (shād) N. J. (Philadelphia In.)	39·57 N	75·01 W
65	Maple Valley (văl'ê) Wash. (Seattle In.)	47·24 N	122·02 W
74	Maplewood (wŏŏd) Mo. (St. Louis In.)	38·37 N	90·20 W
74	Maplewood Park (wŏŏd pärk) Ill. (St. Louis In.)	38·34 N	90·11 W
167	Mapumulo (mä-pä-mōō'lō) S. Afr. (Natal In.)	29·12 S	31·05 E
155	Maqueda Chan. (mä-kā'dä) Phil. (Manila In.)	13·40 N	123·52 E
166	Maquela do Zombo (mȧ-kā'lȧ dŏŏ zôm'bŏŏ) . Ang.	6·08 S	15·15 E
71	Maquoketa (mȧ-kō-kê-tȧ) ... Iowa	42·04 N	90·42 W
71	Maquoketa (R.) .... Iowa	42·08 N	90·40 W
100	Mar, Serra do (Mts.) (sĕr'rȧ dŏŏ mär') . Braz.	26·30 S	49·15 W
98	Maracaibo (mä-rä-kī'bō) ..... Ven.	10·38 N	71·45 W
98	Maracaibo, Lago de (L.) (lä'gô-dĕ-mä-rä-kī'bō) . Ven.	9·55 N	72·13 W
99	Maracay (mä-rä-käy') .. Ven. (In.)	10·15 N	67·35 W
165	Marādah .... Libya	29·10 N	19·07 E
164	Maradi (mȧ-rȧ-dē') .... Niger	13·30 N	7·11 E
133	Marāgheh .... Iran	37·20 N	46·10 E
167	Maraisburg S. Afr. (Johannesburg & Pretoria In.)	26·12 S	27·57 E
99	Marajó, Ilha de (I.) (mă-rä-zhō') Braz.	0·30 S	50·00 W
166	Marandelles (mä-rȧn-dāl'ȧs) .. Rh.	18·08 S	31·36 E
99	Maranguape (mä-rȧŋ-gwä'pĕ) Braz.	3·48 S	38·38 W
	Maranhão, see São Luis		
99	Maranhão (State) (mä-rän-youɴ) Braz.	5·15 S	45·52 W
160	Maranoa (R.) (mä-rä-nō'ä) . Austl.	27·01 S	148·03 E
125	Marano di Napoli (mä-rä'nô-dē-nȧ'pô-lē) It. (Naples In.)	40·39 N	14·12 E
98	Marañón, Rio (R.) (rê'ō-mä-rä-nyōn') . Peru	4·26 S	75·08 W
99	Marapanim (mä-rä-pä-nê'ɴ) . Braz.	0·45 S	47·42 W
133	Maraş (mä-räsh') .... Tur.	37·40 N	36·50 E
79	Marathon (măr'ȧ-thŏn) . Fla. (In.)	24·41 N	81·06 W
75	Marathon ... Ohio (Cincinnati In.)	39·09 N	83·59 W
154	Maratua (I.) .... Indon.	2·14 N	118·30 E
90	Maravatio (mä-rȧ-vä'tê-ō) ... Mex.	19·54 N	100·25 W
158	Marble Bar (märb''l bär) ... Austl.	21·15 S	119·15 E
69	Marble Can. (mär'b'l) .... Ariz.	36·21 N	111·48 W
168	Marble Hall (hâll) S. Afr. (Johannesburg & Pretoria In.)	24·59 S	29·19 E
83	Marblehead (mär'b'l-hĕd) Mass. (Boston In.)	42·30 N	70·51 W
120	Marburg (mär'bŏŏrgh) .... Ger.	50·49 N	8·46 E
92	Marcala (mär-kä-lä) .... Hond.	14·08 N	88·01 W
126	Marche (Reg.) (mär'kā) .... It.	43·35 N	12·33 E
111	Marchegg ...... Aus. (Vienna In.)	48·18 N	16·55 E
124	Marchena (mär-chā'nä) .... Sp.	37·20 N	5·25 W
98	Marchena (I.) (ê's-lä-mär-chĕ'nä) Ec.	0·29 N	90·31 W
111	Marchfeld (Reg.) Aus. (Vienna In.)	48·14 N	16·37 E
74	March Field (märch) Calif. (Los Angeles In.)	33·54 N	117·17 W
73	Marceline (mär-sê-lēn') ...... Mo.	39·42 N	92·56 W
101	Marcos Paz (mär-kōs' päz) Arg. (Buenos Aires In.)	34·49 S	58·51 W
156	Marcus (I.) (mär'kŭs) .... Asia	24·00 N	155·00 E
84	Marcus Hook (mär'kŭs hŏŏk) Pa. (Philadelphia In.)	39·49 N	75·25 W
81	Marcy, Mt. (mär'sê) .... N. Y.	44·10 N	73·55 W
101	Mar de Espanha (mär-dĕ-ĕs-pȧ'nyȧ) Braz. (Rio de Janeiro In.)	21·53 S	43·00 W
100	Mar del Plata (mär dĕl plä'ta) Arg.	37·59 S	57·35 W
133	Mardin (mär-dēn') .... Tur.	37·25 N	40·40 E
159	Mare (I.) (mȧ-rā') .... N. Cal.	21·53 S	168·30 E
116	Maree (L.) (mă-rē') ...... Scot.	57·40 N	5·44 W
71	Marengo (mȧ-rĕŋ'gō) .... Iowa	41·47 N	92·04 W
122	Marennes (mȧ-rĕn') .... Fr.	45·49 N	1·08 W

ng-sing; ŋ-baŋk; ɴ-nasalized n; nŏd; cŏmmit; ōld; ôbey; ôrder; fōōd; fŏŏt; ou-out; s-soft; sh-dish; th-thin; pūre; ûnite; ûrn; stŭd; circŭs; ü-as "y" in study; '-indeterminate vowel.

234 Mareuil-sur-Ourcq – Mataro PRONOUNCING INDEX

Page	Name Pronunciation	Region	Lat. °'	Long. °'
123	Mareuil-sur-Ourcq (mä-rû'yĕ-sür-ōōrk')	Fr. (Paris In.)	49·08 N	2·04 E
76	Marfa (mär'fȧ)	Tex.	30·19 N	104·01 W
129	Marganets	Sov. Un.	47·41 N	34·33 E
88	Margarita (mär-gōō-rē'tä)	C.Z. (Panama Canal In.)	9·20 N	79·55 W
99	Margarita, Isla de (I.) (mär-gȧ-rē'tȧ)	Ven. (In.)	11·00 N	64·15 W
116	Margate (mär'gāt)	Eng.	51 21 N	1·17 E
167	Margate (mär-gāt')	S. Afr. (Natal In.)	30·52 S	30·21 E
82	Marguerite, Riviere (R.)	Can.	50·36 N	66·40 W
132	Mari (A. S. S. R.) (mä'rē)	Sov. Un.	56·20 N	48·00 E
82	Maria (mȧ-rē'ȧ)	Can.	48·10 N	66·04 W
124	Maria, Sierra de (Mts.) (sē-ĕ'r-rä-dĕ-mä-ryä)	Sp.	37·42 N	2·25 W
90	María Cleofas (I.) (mä-rē'ä klā'ō-fäs)	Mex.	21·17 N	106·14 W
118	Mariager (mä-rē-ägh'ĕr)	Den.	56·38 N	10·00 E
118	Mariager Fd.	Den.	56·44 N	10·32 E
90	María Madre	Mex.	21·43 N	106·17 W
90	María Magdalena (I.) (mä rē'ä mäg-dä-lā'nä)	Mex.	21·25 N	106·23 W
101	Mariana (mä-ryä'nä)	Braz. (Rio de Janeiro In.)	20·23 S	43·24 W
156	Mariana Is. (mä-rē-ä'nä)	Pac. Is. Trust. Ter.	17·20 N	145·00 E
156	Mariana Trench	Oceania	12·00 N	144·00 E
95	Marianao (mä-rē-ä-nä'ō)	Cuba (Havana In.)	23·05 N	82·26 W
73	Marianna (mā-rĭ-ăn'ȧ)	Ark.	34·45 N	90·45 W
78	Marianna	Fla.	30·46 N	85·14 W
75	Marianna	Pa. (Pittsburgh In.)	40·01 N	80·05 W
100	Mariano Acosta (mä-rēä'nō-ȧ-kōs'tä)	Arg. (In.)	34·28 S	58·48 W
120	Mariánské Lázně (mär'yán-skě'läz'nyě)	Czech.	49·58 N	12·42 E
67	Marias R. (mȧ-rī'ȧz)	Mont.	48·17 N	111·47 W
93	Mariato, Punta (Pt.)	Pan.	7·17 N	81·09 W
118	Maribo (mä'rē-bō)	Den.	54·46 N	11·29 E
126	Maribor (mä're-bôr)	Yugo.	46·33 N	15·37 E
101	Maricá (mä-rē-kä')	Braz. (Rio de Janeiro In.)	22·55 S	42·49 W
155	Maricaban (I.) (mä-rē-kä-bän')	Phil. (Manila In.)	13·40 N	120·44 E
168	Marico R. (mä'rĭ-cō)	S. Afr. (Johannesburg & Pretoria In.)	24·53 S	26·22 E
47	Marie Byrd Land (mȧ rē' bûrd')	Ant.	78·00 S	130·00 W
118	Mariefred (mä-rē'ĕ-frēd)	Swe.	59·17 N	17·09 E
93	Marie Galante I. (mȧ-rē' gȧ-lȧnt')	Guad. (Le. & Wind. Is. In.)	15·58 N	61·05 W
	Mariehamn, see Maarianhamina			
118	Mariestad (mä-rē'ĕ-städ')	Swe.	58·43 N	13·45 E
84	Marietta (mā-rĭ-ĕt'ȧ)	Ga. (Atlanta In.)	33·57 N	84·33 W
80	Marietta	Ohio	39·25 N	81·30 W
73	Marietta	Okla.	33·53 N	97·07 W
65	Marietta	Wash. (Vancouver In.)	48·48 N	122·35 W
134	Mariinsk (mȧ-re'ĭnsk)	Sov. Un.	56·15 N	87·28 E
119	Marijampole (mä-rē-yäm-pô'lĕ)	Sov. Un.	54·33 N	23·26 E
168	Marikana (mă'-rĭ-kä-nȧ)	S. Afr. (Johannesburg & Pretoria In.)	25·40 S	27·28 E
99	Marília (mä-rē'lyä)	Braz.	22·02 S	49·48 W
155	Marinduque (I.) (mä-rēn-dōō'kä)	Phil. (Manila In.)	13·14 N	121·45 E
74	Marine (mȧ-rēn')	Ill. (St. Louis In.)	38·48 N	89·47 W
74	Marine	Minn. (Minneapolis, St. Paul In.)	45·11 N	92·51 W
80	Marine City	Mich.	42·45 N	82·30 W
74	Marine L.	Minn. (Minneapolis, St. Paul In.)	45·13 N	92·55 W
74	Marine on St. Croix (äɴ sĕɴ krōō-ä)	Minn. (Minneapolis, St. Paul In.)	45·11 N	92·47 W
71	Marinette (măr-ĭ-nĕt')	Wis.	45·05 N	87·40 W
165	Maringa R. (mă-riŋ'gä)	Con. K.	0·30 N	21·08 E
124	Marinha Grande (mä-rēn'yȧ grän'dĕ)	Port.	39·49 N	8·53 W
78	Marion (măr'ĭ-ŭn)	Ala.	32·36 N	87·19 W
80	Marion	Ill.	37·40 N	88·55 W
80	Marion	Ind.	40·35 N	85·45 W
71	Marion	Iowa	42·01 N	91·39 W
73	Marion	Kans.	38·21 N	97·02 W
78	Marion	Ky.	37·19 N	88·05 W
79	Marion	N. C.	35·40 N	82·00 W
70	Marion	N. D.	46·37 N	98·20 W
80	Marion	Ohio	40·35 N	83·10 W
79	Marion	S. C.	34·08 N	79·23 W
79	Marion	Va.	36·48 N	81·33 W
79	Marion (R.)	S. C.	33·25 N	80·35 W
159	Marion Rf.	Austl.	18·57 S	151·31 E
101	Mariposa (mä-rē-pō'sä)	Chile (Santiago In.)	35·33 S	71·21 W
68	Mariposa Cr.	Calif.	37·14 N	120·30 W
98	Mariquita (mä-rē-kē'tä)	Col. (In.)	5·13 N	74·52 W
99	Mariscal Estigarribia (mä-rēs-käl'ĕs-tē-gär-rē'byä)	Par.	22·03 S	60·28 W
100	Marisco, Ponta do (Pt.) (pô'n-tä-dō-mä-rē's-kō)	Braz. (In.)	23·01 S	43·17 W
123	Maritime Alps (Mts.) (mä'rĭ-tĭm ălps)	Fr.-It.	44·20 N	7·02 E
127	Maritsa (R.) (mä'rē-tsȧ)	Gr.-Tur.	40·43 N	26·19 E
155	Mariveles	Phil. (Manila In.)	14·27 N	120·29 E
139	Marj Uyan	Leb. (Palestine In.)	33·21 N	35·36 E
146	Marka Kul' (L.)	Sov. Un.	49·15 N	85·48 E
118	Markaryd (mär'kä-rüd)	Swe.	56·30 N	13·34 E
73	Marked Tree (märkt trē)	Ark.	35·31 N	90·26 W
111	Marken, I.	Neth. (Amsterdam In.)	52·26 N	5·08 E
110	Market Bosworth (bŏz'wûrth)	Eng.	52·37 N	1·23 W
110	Market Deeping (dēp'ĭng)	Eng.	52·40 N	0·19 W
110	Market Drayton (drā'tŭn)	Eng.	52·54 N	2·29 W
110	Market Harborough (här'bŭr-ō)	Eng.	52·28 N	0·55 W
110	Market Rasen (rā'zĕn)	Eng.	53·23 N	0·21 W
85	Markham (märk'ȧm)	Can. (Toronto In.)	43·53 N	79·15 W
47	Markham, Mt.	Ant.	82·59 S	159·30 E
129	Markovka (mȧr-kôf'kȧ)	Sov. Un.	49·32 N	39·34 E
135	Markovo (mär'kō-vō)	Sov. Un.	64·46 N	170·48 E
142	Markrāna	India	27·08 N	74·43 E
133	Marks	Sov. Un.	51·40 N	46 40 E
77	Marksville (märks'vĭl)	La.	31·09 N	92·05 W
111	Markt Indersdorf (märkt ēn'dĕrs-dōrf)	Ger. (Munich In.)	48·22 N	11·23 E
120	Marktredwitz (märk-rĕd'vēts)	Ger.	50·02 N	12·05 E
111	Markt Schwaben (märkt shvä'bĕn)	Ger. (Munich In.)	48·12 N	11·52 E
123	Marl (märl)	Ger. (Ruhr In.)	51·40 N	7·05 E
83	Marlboro (märl'bŭr-ō)	Mass. (Boston In.)	42·21 N	71·33 W
84	Marlboro	N. J. (New York In.)	40·18 N	74·15 W
80	Marlette (mär-lĕt')	Mich.	43·25 N	83·05 W
77	Marlin (mär'lĭn)	Tex.	31·18 N	96·52 W
81	Marlinton (mär'lĭn-tŭn)	W. Va.	38·15 N	80·10 W
110	Marlow (mär'lō)	Eng. (London In.)	51·33 N	0·46 W
72	Marlow	Okla.	34·38 N	97·56 W
94	Marls, The (Shoals) (märls)	Ba. Is.	26·30 N	77·15 W
122	Marmande (mȧr-mäɴd')	Fr.	44·30 N	0·10 E
127	Marmara (I.) (mär'mȧ-rȧ)	Tur.	40·38 N	27·35 E
133	Marmara Denizi (Sea)	Tur.	40·40 N	28·00 E
70	Marmarth (mär'märth)	N. D.	46·19 N	103·57 W
91	Mar Muerto (L.) (mär-mōōĕ'r-tō)	Mex.	16·13 N	94·22 W
111	Marne (mär'nĕ)	Ger. (Hamburg In.)	53·57 N	9·01 E
122	Marne (R.) (märn)	Fr.	49·08 N	3·39 E
98	Maroa (mä-rō'ä)	Ven.	2·43 N	67·37 W
167	Maroantsetra (mȧ-rō-äŋ-tsā'trȧ)	Malag. Rep.	15·18 S	49·48 E
98	Maro Jarapeto (Mtn.) (mä-rō-hä-rä-pĕ'tō)	Col. (In.)	6·29 N	76·39 W
167	Maromokotro (Mtn.)	Malag. Rep.	14·00 S	49·11 E
99	Maroni (R.) (mȧ-rō'nē)	Fr. Gu.-Sur.	3·02 N	53·54 W
165	Maroua (mär'wä)	Cam.	10·41 N	14·14 E
110	Marple (mär'p'l)	Eng.	53·24 N	2·04 W
168	Marquard	S. Afr. (Johannesburg & Pretoria In.)	28·41 S	27·26 E
157	Marquesas Is. (mär-kĕ'säs)	Fr. Polynesia	8·50 S	141·00 W
79	Marquesas Keys (Is.) (mär-kē'zȧs)	Fla. (In.)	24·37 N	82·15 W
101	Marquês de Valença (mȧr-kĕ's-dĕ-vä-lĕ'n-sȧ)	Braz. (Rio de Janeiro In.)	22·16 S	43·42 W
85	Marquette (mär-kĕt')	Can. (Winnipeg In.)	50·04 N	97·43 W
71	Marquette	Mich.	46·32 N	87·25 W
77	Marquez (mär-kāz')	Tex.	31·14 N	96·15 W
165	Marra, Jebel (Mt.) (jĕb'ĕl mär'ä)	Sud.	13·00 N	23·47 E
164	Marrakech (mȧr-rä'kĕsh)	Mor.	31·38 N	8·00 W
160	Marree (măr'rē)	Austl.	29·38 S	137·55 E
124	Marroqui, Pta. (mä-rō-kē')	Sp.	36·03 N	5·36 W
75	Mars (märz)	Pa. (Pittsburgh In.)	40·42 N	80·01 W
165	Marsá al Burayqah	Libya	30·25 N	19·20 E
165	Marsa Fatma	Eth.	14·54 N	40·14 E
126	Marsala (mär-sä'lä)	It.	37·48 N	12·28 E
110	Marsden (märz'dĕn)	Eng.	53·36 N	1·55 W
122	Marseille (mȧr-sâ'y')	Fr. (Marseille In.)	43·18 N	5·25 E
122	Marseille, Canal de (mȧr-sâ-yäɴ')	Fr. (Marseille In.)	43·34 N	5·16 E
80	Marseilles (mär-sĕlz')	Ill.	41·20 N	88·40 W
80	Marshall (mär'shȧl)	Ill.	39·20 N	87·40 W
80	Marshall	Mich.	42·20 N	84·55 W
70	Marshall	Minn.	44·28 N	95·49 W
73	Marshall	Mo.	39·07 N	93·12 W
77	Marshall	Tex.	32·33 N	94·22 W
156	Marshall Is.	Pac. Is. Trust Ter.	10·00 N	165·00 E
71	Marshalltown (mär'shȧl-toun)	Iowa	42·02 N	92·55 W
78	Marshallville (mär'shȧl-vĭl)	Ga.	32·29 N	83·55 W
83	Marshfield (märsh'fēld)	Mass. (Boston In.)	42·06 N	70·43 W
73	Marshfield	Mo.	37·20 N	92·53 W
71	Marshfield	Wis.	44·40 N	90·10 W
94	Marsh Harbour	Ba. Is.	26·30 N	77·00 W
75	Mars Hill (märz' hĭl')	Ind. (Indianapolis In.)	39·43 N	86·15 W
82	Mars Hill	Maine	46·34 N	67·54 W
85	Marsqui	Can.	49·13 N	66·08 W
118	Marstrand (mär'stränd)	Swe.	57·54 N	11·33 E
136	Marsyaty (märs'yȧ-tĭ)	Sov. Un. (Urals In.)	60·03 N	60·28 E
77	Mart (märt)	Tex.	31·32 N	96·49 W
154	Martaban, G. of (mär-tŭ-bän')	Bur.	16·34 N	96·58 E
154	Martapura	Indon.	3·19 S	114·45 E
86	Marten Hills	Can.	55·40 N	114·09 W
81	Marthas Vineyard (I.) (mär'thȧz vĭn'yȧrd)	Mass.	41·25 N	70·35 W
94	Martí (mär-tē')	Cuba	23·00 N	80·55 W
120	Martigny-Bourg (mȧr-tē-nyē')	Switz.	46·06 N	7·00 E
122	Martigues (mȧr-tēg')	Fr. (Marseille In.)	43·24 N	5·05 E
78	Martin (mär'tĭn)	Tenn.	36·20 N	88·45 W
78	Martin (R.)	Ala.	32·40 N	86·05 W
127	Martina Franca (mär-tē'nä fräŋ'kä)	It.	40·43 N	17·21 E
74	Martin City (mär-tĭn sĭ'tĭ)	Mo. (Kansas City In.)	38·53 N	94·35 W
65	Martinez (mär-tē'nĕz)	Calif. (San Francisco In.)	38·01 N	122·08 W
74	Martinez	Tex. (San Antonio In.)	29·25 N	98·20 W
87	Martin Falls (mär'tĭn)	Can.	51·35 N	86·40 W
93	Martinique I. (mȧr-tē-nēk')	N. A. (Le. & Wind. Is. In.)	14·30 N	60·37 W
81	Martinsburg (mär'tĭnz-bûrg)	W. Va.	39·30 N	78·00 W
80	Martins Ferry (mär'tĭnz)	Ohio	40·05 N	80·45 W
80	Martinsville (mär'tĭnz-vĭl)	Ind.	39·25 N	86·25 W
79	Martinsville	Va.	36·40 N	79·53 W
124	Martos (mär'tōs)	Sp.	37·43 N	3·58 W
86	Martre, Lac la (L.) (läk la märtr)	Can.	63·24 N	119·58 W
153	Marugame (mä'rōō-gä'mä)	Jap.	34·19 N	133·48 E
118	Mårvatn (L.) (môr-vät'n)	Nor.	60·10 N	8·28 E
124	Marvín (mär-vē'n)	Sp.	42·24 N	8·40 W
103	Mary (mä'rē)	Sov. Un.	37·45 N	61·47 E
129	Mar'yanskaya (mȧr-yȧn'skȧ-yȧ)	Sov. Un.	45·04 N	38·39 E
160	Maryborough (mä'rĭ-bŭr-ō)	Austl.	25·35 S	152·40 E
160	Maryborough	Austl.	37·00 S	143·50 E
63	Maryland (State) (mĕr'ĭ-lȧnd)	U. S.	39·10 N	76·25 W
66	Mary's R. (mā'rĭz)	Nev.	41·25 N	115·10 W
83	Marystown (mā'rĭz-toun)	Can.	47·11 N	55·11 W
82	Marysville	Can.	45·59 N	66·40 W
68	Marysville (mā'rĭz-vĭl)	Calif.	39·09 N	121·37 W
73	Marysville	Kans.	39·49 N	96·38 W
80	Marysville	Ohio	40·15 N	83·25 W
65	Marysville	Wash. (Seattle In.)	48·03 N	122·11 W
168	Maryūt (L.)	U. A. R. (Nile In.)	31·09 N	30·10 E
74	Maryville (mā'rĭ-vĭl)	Ill. (St. Louis In.)	38·44 N	89·57 W
73	Maryville	Mo.	40·21 N	94·51 W
78	Maryville	Tenn.	35·44 N	83·59 W
165	Marzuq	Libya	26·00 N	14·09 E
163	Masai Steppe	Tan.	5·05 S	36·16 E
154	Masalembo (I.)	Indon.	5·40 S	114·28 E
152	Masan (mä-sän')	Kor.	35·10 N	128·31 E
167	Masasi (mä-sä'sē)	Tan.	10·41 S	38·05 E
92	Masatepe (mä-sä-tē'pĕ)	Nic.	11·57 N	86·10 W
92	Masaya (mä-sä'yä)	Nic.	11·58 N	86·05 W
155	Masbate (mäs-bä'tä)	Phil. (Manila In.)	12·21 N	123·38 E
155	Masbate (I.)	Phil. (Manila In.)	12·19 N	123·03 E
164	Mascara (mäs'kä-rä) (mȧs-kȧ-rä')	Alg.	35·25 N	0·08 E
47	Mascarene Is.	Afr.	20·20 S	56·40 E
78	Mascot (măs'kŏt)	Tenn.	36·04 N	83·45 W
90	Mascota (mäs-kō'tä)	Mex.	20·33 N	104·45 W
90	Mascota (R.)	Mex.	20·33 N	104·52 W
85	Mascouche (mȧs-kōōsh')	Can. (Montreal In.)	45·45 N	73·36 W
85	Mascouche (R.)	Can. (Montreal In.)	45·44 N	73·45 W
74	Mascoutah (măs-kū'tā)	Ill. (St. Louis In.)	38·29 N	89·48 W
166	Maseru (măz'ēr-ōō)	Leso.	29·09 S	27·11 E
144	Mashhad	Iran	36·17 N	59·30 E
165	Masindi (mä-sēn'dē)	Ug.	1·44 N	31·43 E
144	Masīra (I.)	Mus. & Om.	20·43 N	58·58 E
116	Mask, Lough (B.) (lŏk mȧsk)	Ire.	53·35 N	9·23 W
136	Maslovo (mȧs'lô-vô)	Sov. Un. (Urals In.)	60·08 N	60·28 E
80	Mason (mā'sŭn)	Mich.	42·35 N	84·25 W
75	Mason	Ohio (Cincinnati In.)	39·22 N	84·18 W
76	Mason	Tex.	30·46 N	99·14 W
71	Mason City	Iowa	43·08 N	93·14 W
83	Masquaro (L.)	Can.	50·34 N	60·40 W
126	Massa (mäs'sä)	It.	44·02 N	10·08 E
63	Massachusetts (State) (măs-ȧ-chōō'sĕts)	U. S.	42·20 N	72·30 W
82	Massachusetts B.	Mass.	42·26 N	70·20 W
126	Massafra (mäs-sä'frä)	It.	40·35 N	17·05 E
126	Massa Maritima (mäs'sä mä-rē'tē-mä)	It.	43·03 N	10·55 E
165	Massaua (mäs-sä'wä)	Eth.	15·40 N	39·19 E
81	Massena (mă-sē'nȧ)	N. Y.	44·55 N	74·55 W
86	Massett (măs'ĕt)	Can.	54·03 N	132·11 W
122	Massif Central (Plat.) (mȧ-sēf' säɴ-trȧl')	Fr.	45·12 N	3·02 E
80	Massillon (măs'ĭ-lŏn)	Ohio	40·50 N	81·35 W
166	Massinga (mä-sĭn'gä)	Moz.	23·18 S	35·18 E
69	Massive, Mt. (măs'ĭv)	Colo.	39·05 N	106·30 W
85	Masson (mȧs-sŭn)	Can. (Ottawa In.)	45·33 N	75·25 W
153	Masuda (mä-sōō'dä)	Jap.	34·42 N	131·53 E
121	Masuria (Reg.)	Pol.	53·40 N	21·10 E
166	Matadi (mȧ-tä'dē)	Con. K.	5·48 S	13·35 E
92	Matagalpa (mä-tä-gäl'pä)	Nic.	12·52 N	85·57 W
77	Matagorda B. (măt-ȧ-gôr'dȧ)	Tex.	28·32 N	96·13 W
77	Matagorda I.	Tex.	28·13 N	96·27 W
164	Matam (mä-tăm')	Senegal	15·41 N	13·20 W
76	Matamoros (mä-tä-mō'rōs)	Mex.	25·32 N	103·13 W
77	Matamoros	Mex.	25·52 N	97·30 W
82	Matane (mȧ-tȧn')	Can.	48·49 N	67·35 W
166	Matanga (mä-täŋ'gä)	Ang.	7·35 S	17·25 E
64	Matanuska (mä-tä-nōōs'kȧ)	Alaska	61·32 N	149·38 W
94	Matanzas (mä-tän'zäs)	Cuba	23·00 N	81·40 W
94	Matanzas (State)	Cuba	22·45 N	81·20 W
94	Matanzas, Bahía (B.) (bä-ē'-ä)	Cuba	23·10 N	81·30 W
93	Matapalo, Cabo (C.) (kä'bô-mä-tä-pä'lō)	C. R.	8·22 N	83·25 W
82	Matapedia (mă-tȧ-pē'dĭ-ȧ)	Can.	48·00 N	66·55 W
82	Matapedia (L.)	Can.	48·36 N	67·20 W
101	Mataquito (R.) (mä-tä-kē'tô)	Chile (Santiago In.)	35·08 S	71·35 W
143	Matara (mä-tä'rä)	Ceylon	5·59 N	80·35 E
154	Mataram	Indon.	8·45 S	116·15 E
125	Mataró (mä-tä-rō')	Sp.	41·33 N	2·27 E

ăt; finȧl; rāte; senȧte; ärm; ȧsk; sofȧ; fâre; ch-choose; dh-as th in other; bē; ėvent; bĕt; recĕnt; cratẽr; g-go; gh-guttural g; bĭt; ĭ-short neutral; rīde; ĸ-guttural k as ch in German ich;

PRONOUNCING INDEX Matatiele–Mendes 235

Page	Name Pronunciation Region	Lat. °′	Long. °′
167	Matatiele (mä-tä-tyā'lā) S. Afr. (Natal In.)	30·21 S	28·49 E
84	Matawana (mȧ-tȧ-wŏn'ȧ) N. J. (New York In.)	40·24 N	74·13 W
90	Matehuala (mä-tå-wä'lä)....Mex.	23·38 N	100·39 W
126	Matera (mä-tâ'rä)............It.	40·42 N	16·37 E
113	Mateur (må-tûr')...........Tun.	37·09 N	9·43 E
143	Mātherān....India (Bombay In.)	18·58 N	73·16 E
74	Mathews, L. (măth'ūz) Calif. (Los Angeles In.)	33·50 N	117·24 W
142	Mathura (mu-tōō'rŭ).......India	27·39 N	77·39 E
101	Matias Barbosa (mä-tē'äs-bär-bô-sä) Braz. (Rio de Janeiro In.)	21·53 S	43·19 W
91	Matillas, Laguna (L.) (lä-gōō'nä-mä-tē'l-yäs).Mex.	18·02 N	92·36 W
93	Matina (mä-tē'nä).........C. R.	10·06 N	83·20 W
119	Matiši (mä'tē-sē)........Sov. Un.	57·43 N	25·09 E
154	Matjan (I.)..............Indon.	6·52 S	121·45 E
90	Matlalcueyetl, Cerra (sĕ'r-rä-mä-tläl-kwĕ'yĕtl).Mex.	19·13 N	98·02 W
110	Matlock (măt'lŏk)..........Eng.	53·08 N	1·33 W
110	Matlock Bath (măt'lŏk bàth) Eng.	53·06 N	1·34 W
134	Matochkin Shar (mä'tŏch-kĭn) Sov. Un.	73·57 N	56·16 E
99	Mato Grosso (mät'ōō grōs'ōō) Braz.	15·04 S	59·58 W
99	Mato Grosso (State)........Braz.	14·38 S	55·36 W
99	Mato Grosso, Chapada de (Plain) (shä-pä'dä-dĕ).Braz.	13·39 S	55·42 W
124	Matozinhos (Leixoes) (mä-tô-zēn'yōzh) (lĕ'y-shô'-ĕs) Port.	41·10 N	8·48 W
144	Matrah (må-trä')....Mus. & Om.	23·36 N	58·27 E
165	Maṭrūḥ................U.A.R.	31·19 N	27·14 E
153	Matsudo (mät'sōō-dō) Jap. (Tōkyō In.)	35·48 N	139·55 E
153	Matsue (mät'sōō-ĕ)..........Jap.	35·29 N	133·04 E
153	Matsumoto (mät'sōō-mō'tō)..Jap.	36·15 N	137·59 E
153	Matsuyama (mät'sōō-yä'mä).Jap.	33·48 N	132·45 E
153	Matsuzaka (mät'sōō-zä'kä)...Jap.	34·35 N	136·34 E
87	Mattagami (L.) (må-tä-gä'mē) Can.	50·10 N	78·49 W
79	Mattamuskeet (R.) (măt-tȧ-mŭs'kēt).N. C.	35·34 N	76·03 W
81	Mattaponi (R.) (măt'ȧ-pō-nī').Va.	37·45 N	77·00 W
87	Mattawa (măt'ȧ-wȧ).......Can.	46·15 N	78·49 W
82	Mattawin (R.) (măt'ȧ-wĭn)..Can.	46·55 N	73·20 W
120	Matterhorn Mt. (mät'ĕr-hôrn) Switz.	45·57 N	7·36 E
75	Matteson (măt't'ĕ-sŭn) Ill. (Chicago In.)	41·30 N	87·42 W
95	Matthew Town (măth'ū toun) Ba. Is.	21·00 N	73·40 W
80	Mattoon (mă-tōōn')...........Ill.	39·30 N	88·20 W
98	Maturín (mä-tōō-rēn').......Ven.	9·48 N	63·16 W
155	Mauban (mä'ōō-bän') Phil. (Manila In.)	14·11 N	121·44 E
122	Maubeuge (mō-bûzh')........Fr.	50·18 N	3·57 E
75	Maud (môd) Ohio (Cincinnati In.)	39·21 N	84·23 W
111	Mauer (mou'ĕr).Aus. (Vienna In.)	48·09 N	16·16 E
99	Maués (mà-wĕ's)...........Braz.	3·34 S	57·30 W
157	Maui (I.) (mä'ōō-ē)..Hawaii (In.)	20·52 N	156·02 W
101	Maule (R.) (mà'ōō-lĕ) Chile (Santiago In.)	35·45 S	70·50 W
80	Maumee (mô-mē').........Ohio	41·30 N	83·40 W
80	Maumee (R.)..........Ind.-Ohio	41·10 N	84·50 W
80	Maumee B..................Ohio	41·50 N	83·20 W
166	Maun (mä-ōōn')...........Bots.	19·52 S	23·40 E
157	Mauna Kea (Vol.) (mä'ōō-näkä'ä) Hawaii (In.)	19·52 N	155·30 W
157	Mauna Loa (Vol.) (mä'ōō-nälō'ä) Hawaii (In.)	19·28 N	155·38 W
154	Maung Nakhon Sawan.....Thai.	16·00 N	99·52 E
77	Maurepas L. (mō-rē-pä')......La.	30·18 N	90·40 W
163	Mauritania (mô-rē-tā'nĭ-ȧ)...Afr.	19·38 N	13·30 W
47	Mauritius I. (mô-rĭsh'ĭ-ŭs)....Afr.	20·18 S	57·36 E
65	Maury (mô'rĭ).Wash. (Seattle In.)	47·22 N	122·23 W
71	Mauston (môs'tŭn)...........Wis.	43·46 N	90·05 W
69	Maverick, (R.) (mă-vûr'ĭk)..Ariz.	33·40 N	109·30 W
91	Maxcanú (mäs-kä-nōō').....Mex.	20·35 N	89·59 W
85	Maxville (măks'vĭl) Can. (Ottawa In.)	45·17 N	74·52 W
74	Maxville......Mo. (St. Louis In.)	38·26 N	90·24 W
135	Maya (R.) (mä'yä)......Sov. Un.	58·00 N	135·45 E
95	Mayaguana (I.)..........Ba. Is.	22·25 N	73·00 W
95	Mayaguana Passage (Str.).Ba. Is.	22·20 N	73·25 W
89	Mayagüez (mä-yä-gwāz') P. R. (Puerto Rico In.)	18·12 N	67·10 W
95	Mayarí (mä-yä-rē').........Cuba	20·45 N	75·40 W
95	Mayari (R.)................Cuba	20·25 N	75·35 W
92	Mayas, Montañas (Mts.) (môn-tăn'yäs mä'äs) Br. Hond. (Yucatan In.)	16·43 N	89·00 W
120	Mayen (mī'ĕn).............Ger.	50·19 N	7·14 E
122	Mayenne (må-yĕn')...........Fr.	48·19 N	0·35 W
122	Mayenne (R.).................Fr.	48·14 N	0·45 W
78	Mayfield (mā'fēld)...........Ky.	36·44 N	88·19 W
79	Mayfield Cr.................Ky.	36·54 N	88·47 W
75	Mayfield Heights Ohio (Cleveland In.)	41·31 N	81·26 W
66	Mayfield Res...........Wash.	46·31 N	122·34 W
133	Maykop (Maikop) (mī-kôp') Sov. Un.	44·35 N	40·10 E
136	Maykor (mī-kôr') Sov. Un. (Urals In.)	59·01 N	55·52 E
146	Maymyo (mī'myō').........Bur.	22·14 N	96·32 E
83	Maynard (mā'nȧrd) Mass. (Boston In.)	42·25 N	71·27 W
65	Maynard.....Wash. (Seattle In.)	47·59 N	122·54 W
65	Mayne (mān) Can. (Vancouver In.)	48·51 N	123·18 W
65	Mayne (I.)..Can. (Vancouver In.)	48·52 N	123·14 W
86	Mayo (mä-yō')............Can.	63·40 N	135·51 W
78	Mayo.......................Fla.	30·02 N	83·08 W
84	Mayo.......Md. (Baltimore In.)	38·54 N	76·31 W
64	Mayo (L.)...............Alaska	63·50 N	135·30 W
116	Mayo, Mts. of.............Ire.	54·01 N	9·01 W
79	Mayodan (mā-yō'dăn)......N. C.	36·25 N	79·59 W
155	Mayon (Vol.) (mä-yōn') Phil. (Manila In.)	13·21 N	123·43 E
167	Mayotte (I.) (mà-yŏt') Comores, Arch. des	13·07 S	45·32 E
94	May Pen..................Jam.	18·00 N	77·25 W
151	Mayraira Pt...............Phil.	18·40 N	120·45 E
76	Mayran, Laguna de (L.) (lä-ōō'nä-dĕ-mī-rän')......Mex.	25·40 N	102·35 W
80	Maysville (māz'vĭl).........Ky.	38·35 N	83·45 W
166	Mayumba................Gabon	3·15 S	10·10 E
81	Mayville (mā'vĭl)..........N. Y.	42·15 N	79·30 W
70	Mayville..................N. D.	47·30 N	97·20 W
71	Mayville...................Wis.	43·30 N	88·45 W
74	Maywood (mā'wŏŏd) Calif. (Los Angeles In.)	33·59 N	118·11 W
75	Maywood.........Ill. (Chicago In.)	41·53 N	87·51 W
166	Mazabuka (mä-zä-bōō'kä).Zambia	16·00 S	27·43 E
99	Mazagão (mä-zà-gou'N).....Braz.	0·05 S	51·27 W
76	Mazapil (mä-zä-pēl').......Mex.	24·40 N	101·30 W
142	Mazār-i-Sharif (mà-zär'-ē-shà-rēf').Afg.	36·48 N	67·12 E
124	Mazarrón (mä-zär-rō'n).......Sp.	36·37 N	1·29 W
99	Mazaruni (R.) (mä-zä-rōō'nē) Guy.	5·58 N	59·37 W
92	Mazatenango (mä-zä-tå-näŋ'gō) Guat.	14·30 N	91·30 W
91	Mazatla..Mex. (Mexico City In.)	19·30 N	99·24 W
91	Mazatlán (San Juan) (mä-zä-tlän') (sän hwän').Mex.	17·05 N	95·26 W
90	Mazatlán...................Mex.	23·14 N	106·27 W
119	Mažeikiai (mà-zhā'kē-ī)..Sov. Un.	56·19 N	22·24 E
139	Mazhafah, Jabal (Mts.) Sau. Ar. (Palestine In.)	28·56 N	35·05 E
126	Mazzara del Vallo (mät-sä'rä dĕl väl'lō).It.	37·40 N	12·37 E
126	Mazzarino (mät-sä-rē'nō)......It.	37·16 N	14·15 E
166	Mbabane (m'bä-bä'nĕ).....Swaz.	26·18 S	31·14 E
165	Mbaiki (m'bȧ-ē'kē).Cen. Afr. Rep.	3·54 N	17·57 E
165	Mbandaka...............Con. K.	0·01 N	18·17 E
165	Mbigou (m-bē-gōō').......Con. B.	2·07 S	12·07 E
165	M'Bomu R. (m'bō'mōō)..Con. K.	4·38 N	23·48 E
164	M'Bout (m'bōō').....Mauritania	16·03 N	12·31 W
	Mchinji, see Fort Manning		
72	Meade (mēd).............Kans.	37·17 N	100·21 W
69	Meade, L............Nev.-Ariz.	36·20 N	114·14 W
67	Meade Pk.................Idaho	42·19 N	111·16 W
65	Meadowdale (mĕd'ō-dāl) Wash. (Seattle In.)	47·51 N	122·20 W
86	Meadow Lake (mĕd'ō lāk)...Can.	54·10 N	108·30 W
85	Meadows (mĕd'ōz) Can. (Winnipeg In.)	50·02 N	97·35 W
81	Meadville (mēd'vĭl)..........Pa.	41·40 N	80·10 W
80	Meaford (mē'fērd)..........Can.	44·35 N	80·40 W
87	Mealy Mts. (mē'lē).........Can.	53·32 N	57·58 W
160	Meandarra (mē-ăn-dă'rȧ).....Austl.	27·47 S	149·40 E
123	Meaux (mō).......Fr. (Paris In.)	48·58 N	2·53 E
91	Mecapalapa (mā-kä-pä-lä'pä) Mex.	20·32 N	97·52 W
83	Mecatina (I.) (mā-kȧ-tē'nȧ).Can.	50·50 N	58·33 W
83	Mecatina (R.) (mā-kȧ-tē'nȧ).Can.	50·50 N	59·45 W
	Mecca, see Makkah		
82	Mechanic Falls (mē-kăn'ĭk).Maine	44·05 N	70·23 W
81	Mechanicsburg (mē-kăn'ĭks-bûrg).Pa.	40·15 N	77·00 W
84	Mechanicsville (mē-kăn'ĭks-vĭl) Md. (Baltimore In.)	38·27 N	76·45 W
81	Mechanicsville..............N.Y.	42·55 N	73·45 W
111	Mechelen......Bel. (Brussels In.)	51·01 N	4·28 E
114	Mecheria..................Mor.	33·30 N	0·13 W
120	Mecklenburg (Reg.) (mĕk'lĕn-bŏŏrgh). Ger.	53·34 N	12·18 E
154	Medan (mā-dän').........Indon.	3·35 N	98·35 E
100	Medanosa, Punta (Pt.) (pōō'n-tä-mĕ-dä-nô'sä).Arg.	47·50 S	65·53 W
110	Medden (R.) (mĕd'ĕn)......Eng.	53·14 N	1·05 W
125	Médéa (mā-dā'ä)..............Alg.	36·18 N	2·40 E
98	Medellín (må-dhĕl-yēn').Col. (In.)	6·15 N	75·34 W
91	Medellín (mĕ-dĕl-yē'n)......Mex.	19·03 N	96·08 W
114	Medenine (mā-dĕ-nēn')......Tun.	33·22 N	10·33 E
83	Medfield (mĕd'fēld) Mass. (Boston In.)	42·11 N	71·19 W
83	Medford (mĕd'fērd) Mass. (Boston In.)	42·25 N	71·07 W
84	Medford..N. J. (Philadelphia In.)	39·54 N	74·50 W
72	Medford....................Okla.	36·47 N	97·44 W
66	Medford.....................Ore.	42·19 N	122·52 W
71	Medford.....................Wis.	45·09 N	90·22 W
84	Media (mē'dĭ-ȧ) Pa. (Philadelphia In.)	39·55 N	75·24 W
121	Medias (mĕd-yäsh')...........Rom.	46·09 N	24·21 E
66	Medical Lake (mĕd'ĭ-kăl)...Wash.	47·34 N	117·40 W
72	Medicine Bow Ra. (mĕd'ĭ-sĭn bō).Colo.-Wyo.	40·55 N	106·02 W
67	Medicine Bow R...........Wyo.	41·58 N	106·30 W
86	Medicine Hat (mĕd'ĭ-sĭn hăt).Can.	50·09 N	110·50 W
67	Medicine L. (mĕd'ĭ-sĭn)....Mont.	48·24 N	104·15 W
72	Medicine Lodge..........Kans.	37·17 N	98·37 W
72	Medicine Lodge (R.).......Kans.	37·20 N	98·57 W
81	Medina (mē-dī'nȧ)...........N. Y.	43·15 N	78·20 W
75	Medina.....Ohio (Cleveland In.)	41·08 N	81·52 W
	Medina, see Al Mādīnah		
124	Medina del Campo (mȧ-dē'nä dĕl käm'pō).Sp.	41·18 N	4·54 W
124	Medina de Rioseco (mȧ-dē'nä dā rē-ō-sā'kō).Sp.	41·53 N	5·05 W
76	Medina L....................Tex.	29·36 N	98·47 W
76	Medina R....................Tex.	29·45 N	99·13 W
124	Medina Sidonia (sē-dō'nyä)...Sp.	36·28 N	5·58 W
101	Medio (mĕ'dyō) (R.) Arg. (Buenos Aires In.)	33·40 S	60·30 W
114	Mediterranean Sea (mĕd-ĭ-tēr-ā'nē-ăn).Afr.-Asia-Eur.	36·22 N	13·25 E
113	Medjerda, Oued (R.) (wĕd mĕ-jĕr'dȧ).Tun.	36·43 N	9·54 E
134	Mednogorsk............Sov. Un.	51·27 N	57·22 E
133	Medveditsa (R.) (mĕd-vyĕ'dē tsȧ).Sov. Un.	50·10 N	43·40 E
132	Medvezhegorsk (mĕd-vyĕzh'yĕ-gôrsk').Sov. Un.	63·00 N	34·20 E
135	Medvezh'y (Is.).........Sov. Un.	71·00 N	161·25 E
83	Medway (mĕd'wā) Mass. (Boston In.)	42·08 N	71·23 W
128	Medyn' (mĕ-dēn').......Sov. Un.	54·58 N	35·53 E
129	Medzhibozh (mĕd-zhē-bōzh') Sov. Un.	49·23 N	27·29 E
158	Meekatharra (mē-kȧ-thăr'ȧ).Austl.	26·30 S	118·38 E
69	Meeker (mēk'ĕr)...........Colo.	40·00 N	107·55 W
120	Meerane (mā-rä'nĕ).........Ger.	50·51 N	12·27 E
142	Meerut (mē'rŏŏt)..........India	28·59 N	77·43 E
165	Mēgā......................Eth.	6·14 N	35·34 E
127	Megalópolis (mĕg-ȧ lŏ'pō-lĭs).Grc.	37·22 N	22·08 E
129	Meganom, M. (C.) (mĭs mĕ-gà-nôm').Sov. Un.	44·48 N	35·17 E
127	Mégara (mĕg'ȧ-rȧ)...........Grc.	37·59 N	23·21 E
79	Megget (mĕg'ĕt)...........S. C.	32·44 N	80·15 W
65	Megler (mĕg'lēr) Wash. (Portland In.)	46·15 N	123·52 W
128	Meglino (L.) (mä-glē'nō).Sov. Un.	58·32 N	35·27 E
79	Meherrin (R.) (mē-hĕr'ĭn)....Va.	36·40 N	77·49 W
142	Mehsāna..................India	23·42 N	72·23 E
122	Mehun-sur-Yèvre (mĕ-ŭN-sür-yĕvr').Fr.	47·11 N	2·14 E
148	Meichu (mā'jēōō).........China	31·17 N	119·12 E
151	Meihsien.................China	24·20 N	116·10 E
151	Meiling Pass (mā'lĭng').....China	25·22 N	115·00 E
123	Meinerzhagen (mī'nĕrts-hä-gĕn) Ger. (Ruhr In.)	51·06 N	7·39 E
120	Meiningen (mī'nĭng-ĕn)......Ger.	50·35 N	10·25 E
120	Meiringen................Switz.	46·45 N	8·11 E
100	Mejillones (må-κē-lyō'nås)..Chile	23·07 S	70·31 W
164	Meknés (mĕk'nĕs) (mĕk-nĕs').Mor.	33·56 N	5·44 W
	Mekong, see Lanisung Chiang		
154	Mekong, Mouths of the (mē'kông')...Viet.	10·09 N	107·15 E
154	Mekong R............Thai.-Laos	17·53 N	103·57 E
161	Melbourne (mĕl'bŭrn) Austl. (Melbourne In.)	37·52 S	145·08 E
79	Melbourne.............Fla. (In.)	28·02 N	28·37 W
110	Melbourne.................Eng.	52·49 N	1·26 W
75	Melbourne...Ky. (Cincinnati In.)	39·02 N	84·22 W
71	Melcher (mĕl'chēr).........Iowa	41·13 N	93·11 W
132	Melekess (mĕl-yĕk ĕs)....Sov. Un.	54·20 N	49·30 E
128	Melenki (mĕ-lyĕŋ'kē)....Sov. Un.	55·25 N	41·34 E
86	Melfort (mĕl'fôrt)..........Can.	52·55 N	104·31 W
165	Melik, Wadi el (R.).........Sud.	16·48 N	29·30 E
164	Melilla (Sp.) (mā-lēl'yä)......Afr.	35·24 N	3·03 W
101	Melipilla (mā-lē-pē'lyä) Chile (Santiago In.)	33·40 S	71·12 W
129	Melitopol' (mā-lē-tô'pōl-y') Sov. Un.	46·49 N	35·19 E
168	Melkrivier...............S. Afr. (Johannesburg & Pretoria In.)	24·01 S	28·23 E
71	Mellen (mĕl'ĕn).............Wis.	46·20 N	90·40 W
118	Mellerud (mål'ĕ-rōōdh)......Swe.	58·43 N	12·25 E
167	Melmoth.......S. Afr. (Natal In.)	28·38 S	31·26 E
100	Melo (mā'lō)..................Ur.	32·18 S	54·07 W
85	Melocheville (mĕ-lōsh-vēl') Can. (Montreal In.)	45·24 N	73·56 W
136	Melozha R. (myĕ'lô-zhȧ) Sov. Un. (Moscow In.)	56·06 N	38·34 E
164	Melrhir Chott (L.) (mĕl'rēr)..Alg.	33·52 N	5·22 E
83	Melrose (mĕl'rōz) Mass. (Boston In.)	42·29 N	71·06 W
71	Melrose...................Minn.	45·39 N	94·49 W
75	Melrose Park....Ill. (Chicago In.)	41·54 N	87·52 W
166	Melsetter (mĕl-sĕt'ĕr)........Rh.	19·44 S	32·51 E
110	Meltham (mĕl'thăm).........Eng.	53·35 N	1·51 W
161	Melton (mĕl'tŭn) Austl. (Melbourne In.)	37·41 S	144·35 E
110	Melton Mowbray (mō'brȧ)..Eng.	52·45 N	0·52 W
123	Melun (mĕ-lŭN')...Fr. (Paris In.)	48·32 N	2·40 E
165	Melut (må-lōōt')............Sud.	10·30 N	32·17 E
86	Melville (mĕl'vĭl)............Can.	51·00 N	102·52 W
77	Melville......................La.	30·39 N	91·45 W
159	Melville, C................Austl.	14·15 S	145·50 E
158	Melville (I.)...............Austl.	11·30 S	131·12 E
87	Melville (R.)................Can.	53·46 N	59·31 W
86	Melville Hills...............Can.	69·18 N	124·57 W
86	Melville Pen................Can.	67·44 N	84·09 W
75	Melvindale (mĕl'vĭn-dāl) Mich. (Detroit In.)	42·17 N	83·11 W
121	Mélykút (mā'l'kōōt).......Hung.	46·14 N	19·21 E
168	Memal (mĕ'mĕl) S. Afr. (Johannesburg & Pretoria In.)	27·42 S	29·35 E
167	Memba (mĕm'bȧ)..........Moz.	14·12 S	40·35 E
	Memel, see Klaipéda		
120	Memmingen (mĕm'ĭng-ĕn)...Ger.	47·59 N	10·10 E
99	Memo (R.) (mĕ'mō)....Ven. (In.)	9·32 N	66·30 W
73	Memphis (mĕm'fĭs)...........Mo.	40·27 N	92·11 W
78	Memphis (mĕm'fĭs)........Tenn.	35·07 N	90·03 W
72	Memphis....................Tex.	34·42 N	100·33 W
168	Memphis (Ruins) U. A. R. (Nile In.)	29·50 N	31·12 E
81	Memphremagog (L.) (mĕm'frē-mā'gŏg).Can.	45·05 N	72·10 W
73	Mena (mē'nȧ)................Ark.	34·35 N	94·09 W
129	Mena (mā-nȧ')..........Sov. Un.	51·31 N	32·14 E
161	Menangle.....Austl. (Sydney In.)	34·08 S	150·48 E
76	Menard (mē-närd')..........Tex.	30·56 N	99·48 W
71	Menasha (mē-năsh'ȧ).......Wis.	44·12 N	88·29 W
122	Mende (mănd)................Fr.	44·31 N	3·30 E
123	Menden (mĕn'dĕn) Ger. (Ruhr In.)	51·26 N	7·47 E
133	Menderes (R.) (mĕn'dĕr-ĕs)..Tur.	37·50 N	28·20 E
100	Mendes (mĕ'n-dĕs)....Braz. (In.)	22·32 S	43·44 W

ng-sing; ŋ-baŋk; N-nasalized n; nŏd; cŏmmit; ōld; ôbey; ôrder; fōōd; fŏŏt; ou-out; s-soft; sh-dish; th-thin; pūre; ûnite; ûrn; stŭd; circŭs; ü-as "y" in study; '-indeterminate vowel.

236 Mendocino–Mikuni PRONOUNCING INDEX

Page	Name Pronunciation Region	Lat. °′	Long. °′
66	Mendocino, C. (měn'dô-sē'nō) Calif.	40·25 N	124·22 W
71	Mendota (měn-dō'tȧ) Ill.	41·34 N	89·06 W
71	Mendota (L.) Wis.	43·09 N	89·41 W
100	Mendoza (měn-dō'sä) Arg.	32·48 S	68·45 W
100	Mendoza (Prov.) Arg.	35·10 S	69·00 W
151	Mengtzu China	23·22 N	103·20 E
160	Menindee (mě-nĭn-dē) Austl.	32·23 S	142·30 E
65	Menlo Park (měn'lō pȧrk) Calif. (San Francisco In.)	37·27 N	122·11 W
70	Menno (měn'ô) S. D.	43·14 N	97·34 W
71	Menominee (mê-nŏm'ĭ-nē) Mich.	45·08 N	87·40 W
71	Menominee (R.) Mich.-Wis.	45·37 N	87·54 W
75	Menomonee Falls (fôls) Wis. (Milwaukee In.)	43·11 N	88·06 W
71	Menominee Ra. Mich.	46·07 N	88·53 W
75	Menomonee R. Wis. (Milwaukee In.)	43·09 N	88·06 W
71	Menomonie Wis.	44·53 N	91·55 W
125	Menorca, Isla de (Minorca) (I.) (ē's-lä-dě-mě-nô'r-kä) Sp.	40·05 N	3·58 E
125	Mentana (měn-tȧ'nä) It. (Rome In.)	42·02 N	12·40 E
154	Mentawai, Pulau-Pulau (Is.) (měn-tä-vī') Indon.	1·08 S	98·10 E
123	Menton (mäN-tôN') Fr.	43·46 N	7·37 E
74	Mentone (měn'tōne) Calif. (Los Angeles In.)	34·05 N	117·08 W
167	Mentz (R.) (měnts) S. Afr. (Natal In.)	33·13 S	25·15 E
132	Menzelinsk (měn'zyě-lênsk') Sov. Un.	55·40 N	53·15 E
158	Menzies (měn'zēz) Austl.	29·45 S	122·15 E
76	Meogui (mā-ō'gē) Mex.	28·17 N	105·28 W
117	Meppel (měp'ěl) Neth.	52·41 N	6·08 E
120	Meppen (měp'ěn) Ger.	52·40 N	7·18 E
126	Merabéllou, Kólpos (G.) Grc. (In.)	35·16 N	25·55 E
73	Meramec (R.) (měr'ȧ-měk) Mo.	38·06 N	91·06 W
126	Merano (mā-rä'nō) It.	46·39 N	11·10 E
83	Merasheen (I.) (mē'rä-shēn) Can.	47·23 N	54·15 W
155	Merauke (mâ-rou'kä) W. Irian	8·32 S	140·17 E
84	Meraux (mě-rō') La. (New Orleans In.)	29·56 N	89·56 W
168	Merca (měr'kä) Som. (Horn of Afr. In.)	1·45 N	44·47 E
125	Mercato San Severino (měr-kä'tō sän sě-vě-rē'nō) It. (Naples In.)	40·34 N	14·38 E
68	Merced (mēr-sěd') Calif.	37·17 N	120·30 W
68	Merced (R.) Calif.	37·25 N	120·31 W
101	Mercedario, Cerro (Mtn.) (měr-sȧ-dhä'rê-ō) Chile (Santiago In.)	31·58 S	70·07 W
100	Mercedes (měr-sā'dhās) Arg.	29·04 S	58·01 W
101	Mercedes Arg. (Buenos Aires In.)	34·41 S	59·26 W
76	Mercedes Tex.	26·09 N	97·55 W
101	Mercedes Ur. (Buenos Aires In.)	33·17 S	58·04 W
101	Mercedita (měr-sě-dē'tä) Chile (Santiago In.)	33·51 S	71·10 W
65	Mercer Island (mûr'sēr) Wash. (Seattle In.)	47·35 N	122·15 W
101	Mercês (měr-sě's) Braz. (Rio de Janeiro In.)	21·13 S	43·20 N
139	Merchong (R.) Mala. (Singapore In.)	3·08 N	103·13 E
111	Merchtem Bel. (Brussels In.)	50·57 N	4·13 E
125	Mercier-Lacombe (měr-syā' lȧ-kônb) Alg.	35·18 N	0·11 W
87	Mercy, C. Can.	64·48 N	63·22 W
81	Meredith (měr'ê-dĭth) N. H.	43·35 N	71·35 W
129	Merefa (mâ-rěf'ȧ) Sov. Un.	49·49 N	36·04 E
92	Merendón, Serrania de (Mts.) (sěr-rä-nē'ä-dā mâ-rěn-dōn') Hond.	15·01 N	89·05 W
110	Mereworth (mě-rě'wûrth) Eng. (London In.)	51·15 N	0·23 E
154	Mergui (měr-gē') Bur.	12·29 N	98·39 E
154	Mergui Archip. Asia	12·04 N	97·02 E
91	Mérida (mā'rē-dhä) Mex. (Yucatan In.)	20·57 N	89·38 W
98	Mérida Ven.	8·30 N	71·15 W
98	Mérida, Sierra Nevada de (Mts.) (sē-ě'r-rä-ně-vä'dä-dě-mě'rê-dhä) Ven.	8·30 N	70·45 W
81	Meriden (měr'ĭ-děn) Conn.	41·30 N	72·50 W
78	Meridian (mê-rĭd-ĭ-ǎn) Miss.	32·21 N	88·41 W
77	Meridian Tex.	31·56 N	97·37 W
119	Merikarvia (mā'rē-kär'vē-ä) Fin.	61·51 N	21·30 E
111	Mering (mě'rěng) Ger. (Munich In.)	48·16 N	11·00 E
78	Meriwether Lewis Natl. Mon. (měr'ĭ-wěth-ēr lōō'ĭs) Tenn.	35·25 N	87·25 W
76	Merkel (mûr'kěl) Tex.	32·26 N	100·02 W
119	Merkine (měr'kĭ-nê) Sov. Un.	54·09 N	24·10 E
111	Merksem Bel. (Brussels In.)	51·15 N	4·27 E
121	Merkys R. (mär'kĭs) Sov. Un.	54·23 N	25·00 E
100	Merlo (měr-lô) Arg. (In.)	34·25 S	58·44 W
165	Merowe Sud.	18·07 N	31·57 E
74	Merriam (měr-rĭ-yǎm) Kans. (Kansas City In.)	39·01 N	94·42 W
74	Merriam Minn. (Minneapolis, St. Paul In.)	44·44 N	93·36 W
84	Merrick (měr'ĭk) N. Y. (New York In.)	40·40 N	73·33 W
84	Merrifield (měr'ĭ-fēld) Va. (Washington D.C. In.)	38·50 N	77·12 W
71	Merrill (měr'ĭl) Wis.	45·11 N	89·42 W
83	Merrimac (měr'ĭ-mǎk) Mass. (Boston In.)	42·50 N	71·00 W
83	Merrimack N. H. (Boston In.)	42·51 N	71·25 W
81	Merrimack (R.) (měr'ĭ-mǎk) Mass.-N. H.	43·10 N	71·30 W
83	Merrimack R. Mass. (Boston In.)	42·49 N	70·44 W
86	Merritt (měr'ĭt) Can.	50·10 N	120·48 W
85	Merritton (měr'ĭt-tǔn) Can. (Toronto In.)	43·14 N	79·13 W
77	Merryville (měr'ĭ-vĭl) La.	30·46 N	93.34 W
120	Merseburg (měr'zě-bōōrgh) Ger.	51·21 N	11·59 E
110	Mersey (R.) (mûr'zê) Eng.	52·52 N	2·04 W
116	Mersey (R.) Eng.	53·15 N	2·51 W
133	Mersin (měr-sēn') Tur.	37·00 N	34·40 E
139	Mersing Mala. (Singapore In.)	2·25 N	103·51 E
142	Merta Road (mār'tǔ rōd) India	26·50 N	73·54 E
116	Merthyr Tydfil (mûr'thēr tĭd'vĭl) Wales	51·46 N	3·30 W
124	Mértola Almodóvar (měr-tô-lȧ-äl-mô-dô'vär) Port.	37·39 N	8·04 W
123	Méru (mā-rü') Fr. (Paris In.)	49·14 N	2·08 E
165	Meru (mā'rōō) Ken.	00·01 N	37·45 E
99	Merume Mts. (měr-ü'mě) Guy.	5·45 N	60·15 W
111	Merwerde, Kanal (Can.) Neth. (Amsterdam In.)	52·15 N	5·01 E
65	Merwin (L.) (měr'wĭn) Wash. (Portland In.)	45·58 N	122·27 W
133	Merzifon (měr'ze-fōn) Tur.	40·50 N	35·30 E
123	Merzig (měr'tsēg) Ger.	49·27 N	6·54 E
69	Mesa (mā'sȧ) Ariz.	33·25 N	111·50 W
71	Mesabi Ra. (mā-sŏb'bē) Minn.	47·17 N	93·04 W
127	Mesagne (mā-sän'yâ) It.	40·34 N	17·51 E
69	Mesa Verde Natl. Park. (vēr'dē) Colo.	37·22 N	108·27 W
69	Mescalero Ind. Res. (měs-kä-lā'rō) N. Mex.	33·10 N	105·45 W
128	Meshchovsk (myěsh'chěfsk) Sov. Un.	54·17 N	35·19 E
165	Meshra er Req Sud.	8·28 N	29·15 E
69	Mesilla (mā-sē'yä) N. Mex.	32·15 N	106·45 W
127	Mesolóngion (mě-sô-lôn'gê-ŏn) Grc.	38·23 N	21·28 E
126	Messina (mě-sē'nȧ) It.	38·11 N	15·34 E
166	Messina S. Afr.	22·17 S	30·13 E
126	Messina, Stretto di (Str.) (strě't-tô dē) It.	38·10 N	15·34 E
127	Messíni Grc.	37·05 N	22·00 E
127	Méssiniakós Kólpos (G.) Grc.	36·59 N	22·00 E
127	Mesta (R.) (mě-stä') Bul.	41·42 N	23·40 E
126	Mestre (měs'trā) It.	45·29 N	12·15 E
98	Meta (Dept.) (mě'tä) Col. (In.)	3·28 N	74·07 W
98	Meta (R.) Col.	4·33 N	72·09 W
83	Metabetchouan (R.) (mě-tȧ-bět-chōō-ǎn') Can.	47·45 N	72·00 W
77	Metairie (mě-trâr'ĭ) La.	30·00 N	90·11 W
100	Metán (mě-tä'n) Arg.	25·32 S	64·51 W
92	Metapán (mâ-tä-pän') Sal.	14·21 N	89·26 W
85	Metcalfe (mět-käf) Can. (Ottawa In.)	45·14 N	75·27 W
65	Metchosin Can. (Seattle In.)	48·22 N	123·33 W
90	Metepec (mâ-tě-pěk') Mex.	18·56 N	98·31 W
91	Metepec Mex. (Mexico City In.)	19·15 N	99·36 W
66	Methow R. (mět'hou) (mět hou') Wash.	48·26 N	120·15 W
83	Methuen (mê-thū'ěn) Mass. (Boston In.)	42·44 N	71·11 W
82	Metis Beach (mâ-tē') (mā-tĭs') Can.	48·40 N	68·04 W
127	Metkovic' (mět'kô-vĭch) Yugo.	43·02 N	17·40 E
64	Metlakatla (mět-lȧ-kǎt'lȧ) Alaska	55·10 N	131·30 W
73	Metropolis (mê-trŏp'ô-lĭs) Ill.	37·09 N	88·46 W
79	Metter (mět'ēr) Ga.	32·21 N	82·05 W
123	Mettmann (mět'män) Ger. (Ruhr In.)	51·15 N	6·58 E
84	Metuchen (mě-tŭ'chěn) N. J. (New York In.)	40·32 N	74·21 W
123	Metz (mětz) Fr.	49·08 N	6·10 E
90	Metztitlán (mětz-têt-län') Mex.	20·36 N	98·45 W
122	Meuse (R.) (mûz) (müz) Eur.	50·32 N	5·22 E
110	Mexborough (měks'bŭr-ô) Eng.	53·30 N	1·17 W
77	Mexia (mâ-hē'ȧ) Tex.	31·32 N	96·29 W
91	Mexicalcingo (mě-kē-käl-sēn'go) Mex. (Mexico City In.)	19·13 N	99·34 W
68	Mexicali (mâk-sē-kä'lê) Mex.	32·28 N	115·29 W
69	Mexican Hat (měk'sĭ-kǎn hǎt) Utah	37·10 N	109·55 W
82	Mexico (měk'sĭ-kō) Maine	44·34 N	70·33 W
73	Mexico Mo.	39·09 N	91·51 W
88	Mexico (State) (mâk'sê-kō) Mex.	19·50 N	99·50 W
49	Mexico N. A.	23·45 N	104·00 W
88	Mexico, G. of N. A.	25·15 N	93·45 W
91	Mexico City (měk'sĭ-kō) Mex. (Mexico City In.)	19·28 N	99·09 W
90	Mexticacán (měs'tê-kä-kän') Mex.	21·12 N	102·43 W
144	Meydān-e Naftūn Iran	31·45 N	49·17 E
81	Meyersdale (mī'ērz-dāl) Pa.	39·55 N	79·00 W
168	Meyerton (mī'ēr-tǔn) S. Afr. (Johannesburg & Pretoria In.)	26·35 S	28·01 E
132	Mezen' Sov. Un.	65·50 N	44·05 E
132	Mezen' (R.) Sov. Un.	65·20 N	44·45 E
122	Mézenc, Mt. (mŏN-mä-zěN') Fr.	44·55 N	4·12 E
128	Mezha (R.) (myā'zhȧ) Sov. Un.	55·53 N	31·44 E
122	Mézières (mā-zyâr') Fr.	49·45 N	4·40 E
123	Mézières-sur-Seine (mā-zyâr'sür-sân') Fr. (Paris In.)	48·58 N	1·49 E
121	Mezőkövesd (mě'zû-kû'věsht) Hung.	47·49 N	20·36 E
121	Mezőtur (mě'zû-tōōr) Hung.	47·00 N	20·36 E
90	Mezquital (mâz-kê-täl') Mex.	23·30 N	104·20 W
90	Mezquital (R.) Mex.	23·07 N	104·52 W
90	Mezquitic (mâz-kê-tēk') Mex.	22·25 N	103·43 W
90	Mezquitic (R.) Mex.	22·25 N	103·45 W
136	Mga (m'gȧ) Sov. Un. (Leningrad In.)	59·45 N	31·04 E
128	Mglin (m'glēn') Sov. Un.	53·03 N	32·52 E
90	Miacatlán (mê'ä-kä-tlän') Mex.	18·42 N	99·17 W
91	Miahuatlán (mê'ä-wä-tlän') Mex.	16·20 N	96·38 W
124	Miajadas (mê-ä-hä'däs) Sp.	39·10 N	5·53 W
69	Miami (mī-ǎm'ĭ) Ariz.	33·20 N	110·55 W
79	Miami Fla. (In.)	25·45 N	80·11 W
73	Miami Okla.	36·51 N	94·51 W
72	Miami Tex.	35·41 N	100·39 W
80	Miami (R.) Ohio	39·20 N	84·40 W
79	Miami Beach Fla. (In.)	25·47 N	80·07 W
94	Miami Drainage Can. Fla.	26·25 N	80·50 W
80	Miamisburg (mī-ǎm'ĭz-bûrg) Ohio	39·40 N	84·20 W
75	Miamitown (mī-ǎm'ĭ-toun) Ohio (Cincinnati In.)	39·13 N	84·43 W
144	Mīāneh Iran	37·15 N	47·13 E
155	Miangas (I.) (myä'n-gäs) Phil.	5·30 N	127·00 E
148	Miaochen (mĭou'zhen) China	31·44 N	121·28 E
151	Miaoli (mê-ou'lĭ) Taiwan	24·30 N	120·48 E
148	Miao Liehtao (Is.) (miou' lĭědou) China	38·06 N	120·35 E
136	Miass (mī-ǎs') Sov. Un. (Urals In.)	55·00 N	60·03 E
120	Miastko (myäst'kô) Pol.	54·01 N	17·00 E
121	Michalovce (mē'Kä-lôf'tsě) Czech.	48·44 N	21·56 E
83	Michel (L.) (mê-shěl') (mĭch'ěl) Can.	50·21 N	56·45 W
64	Michelson, Mt. (mĭch'ěl-sǔn) Alaska	69·11 N	144·12 W
111	Michendorf (mē'Kěn-dōrf) Ger. (Berlin In.)	52·19 N	13·02 E
95	Miches (mē'-chěs) Dom. Rep.	19·00 N	69·05 W
63	Michigan (State) (mĭsh'ĭ-gǎn) U. S.	45·55 N	87·00 W
63	Michigan, L. U. S.	43·20 N	87·10 W
80	Michigan City Ind.	41·40 N	86·55 W
87	Michikamau (L.) Can.	54·11 N	63·21 W
71	Michipicoten (I.) (mě-shĭ-pĭ-kō'těn) Can.	47·49 N	85·50 W
71	Michipicoten (R.) Can.	47·56 N	84·42 W
71	Michipicoten Harbour Can.	47·58 N	84·58 W
128	Michurinsk (mĭ-chōō-rĭnsk') Sov. Un.	52·53 N	40·32 E
93	Mico, Punta (Pt.) (pōō'n-tä-mē'kô) Nic.	11·38 N	83·24 W
66	Midas (mī'dǎs) Nev.	41·15 N	116·50 W
166	Middelburg (mĭd'ěl-bûrg) S. Afr.	31·30 S	25·00 E
168	Middelburg S. Afr. (Johannesburg & Pretoria In.)	25·47 S	29·30 E
168	Middelwit (mĭd'l'wĭt) S. Afr. (Johannesburg & Pretoria In.)	24·50 S	27·00 E
154	Middle Andaman I. (ǎn-dȧ-mǎn') Andaman Is.	12·44 N	93·21 E
77	Middle Bay (mĭd''l bā) Tex. (In.)	29·38 N	95·06 W
94	Middle Bight (B.) (bīt) Ba. Is.	24·20 N	77·35 W
81	Middlebury (mĭd''l-běr-ĭ) Vt.	44·00 N	73·10 W
76	Middle Concho (kōn'chō) Tex.	31·21 N	100·50 W
118	Middlefart (měd''l-färt) Den.	55·30 N	9·45 E
70	Middle Loup (R.) (lōōp) Nebr.	41·49 N	100·20 W
80	Middleport (mĭd''l-pōrt) Ohio	39·00 N	82·05 W
84	Middle River Md. (Baltimore In.)	39·20 N	76·27 W
78	Middlesboro (mĭd''lz-bŭr-ô) Ky.	36·36 N	83·42 W
116	Middlesbrough (mĭd''lz-brŭ) Eng.	54·35 N	1·18 W
84	Middlesex (mĭd''l-sěks) N. J. (New York In.)	40·34 N	74·30 W
110	Middleton (mĭd''l-tǔn) Eng.	53·04 N	2·12 W
64	Middleton (I.) Alaska	59·35 N	146·35 W
82	Middletown (mĭd''l-toun) Can.	44·56 N	65·03 W
81	Middletown Conn.	41·35 N	72·40 W
81	Middletown Del.	39·30 N	75·40 W
83	Middletown Mass. (Boston In.)	42·35 N	71·01 W
84	Middletown N. Y. (New York In.)	41·26 N	74·25 W
80	Middletown Ohio	39·30 N	84·25 W
110	Middlewich (mĭd''l-wĭch) Eng.	53·11 N	2·27 W
125	Midi, Canal du (kä-näl-dü-mê-dē') Fr.	43·22 N	1·35 E
167	Mid Illovo (mĭd ĭl'ô-vō) S. Afr. (Natal In.)	29·59 S	30·32 E
81	Midland (mĭd'lǎnd) Can.	44·45 N	79·50 W
80	Midland Mich.	43·40 N	84·20 W
76	Midland Tex.	32·00 N	102·04 W
85	Midnapore (mĭd'-nȧ-pōr) Can. (Calgary In.)	50·56 N	114·04 W
74	Midvale (mĭd'vāl) Utah (Salt Lake City In.)	40·37 N	111·54 W
78	Midway (mĭd'wā) Ala.	32·03 N	85·30 W
156	Midway Is. Pac. O.	28·00 N	179·00 W
67	Midwest (mĭd-wěst') Wyo.	43·25 N	106·15 W
164	Midwestern Region (Div.) Nig.	7·00 N	6·00 E
133	Midye (mēd'yě) Tur.	41·35 N	28·10 E
120	Miedzyrzecz (myǎn-dzû'zhěch) Pol.	52·26 N	15·35 E
121	Mielec (myě'lěts) Pol.	50·17 N	21·27 E
76	Mier (myâr) Mex.	26·26 N	99·08 W
124	Mieres (myā'rās) Sp.	43·14 N	5·45 W
90	Mier y Noriega (myâr'ē nô-rê-ā'gä) Mex.	22·28 N	100·08 W
120	Miessen (mē'sěn) Ger.	51·11 N	13·28 E
139	Migdal Ashkelon (mĭg'dǎl ǎsh'kě-lōn) Isr. (Palestine In.)	31·40 N	34·36 E
129	Migorod Sov. Un.	49·56 N	33·36 E
90	Miguel Auza (mē-gě'l-ä-ōō'zä) Mex.	24·17 N	103·27 W
100	Miguel Pereira (pě-rā'-rä) Braz. (In.)	22·27 S	43·28 W
95	Mija, Monte (Mtn.) (mô'n-tě-mē'kä) Dom. Rep.	19·10 N	71·15 W
125	Mijares (R.) (mē-hä'räs) Sp.	40·05 N	0·42 W
153	Mikage (mē'kä-gȧ) Jap. (Ōsaka In.)	34·42 N	135·15 E
153	Mikawa-Wan (B.) (mē'kä-wä wän) Jap.	34·43 N	137·09 E
128	Mikhaylov (mē-Käy'lôf) Sov. Un.	54·14 N	39·03 E
129	Mikhaylovka Sov. Un.	47·16 N	35·12 E
133	Mikhaylovka Sov. Un.	50·05 N	43·10 E
136	Mikhaylovka (mē-kä'ē-lôf-kȧ) Sov. Un. (Urals In.)	55·35 N	57·57 E
136	Mikhaylovka Sov. Un. (Leningrad In.)	59·20 N	30·21 E
136	Mikhnëvo (mĭk-nyô'vô) Sov. Un. (Moscow In.)	55·08 N	37·57 E
153	Miki (mē'kê) Jap. (Ōsaka In.)	34·47 N	134·59 E
167	Mikindani (mē-kēn-dä'nê) Tan.	10·17 S	40·06 E
119	Mikkeli (měk'ě-lĭ) Fin.	61·42 N	27·14 E
127	Míkonos (I.) Grc.	37·26 N	25·30 E
120	Mikulov (mĭ'koo-lôf) Czech.	48·47 N	16·39 E
153	Mikuni (mē'kōō-nê) Jap.	36·09 N	136·14 E

ǎt; finǎl; rāte; senâte; ärm; àsk; sofȧ; fâre; ch-choose; dh-as th in other; bē; êvent; bět; recěnt; cratēr; g-go; gh-guttural g; bĭt; ĭ-short neutral; rīde; K-guttural k as ch in German ich;

PRONOUNCING INDEX

Mikuni-Sammyaku–Moapa River 237

Page	Name Pronunciation Region	Lat. °′	Long. °′
153	Mikuni-Sammyaku (Mts.) (säm'myä-kōō) . Jap.	36·51 N	138·38 E
153	Mikura (I.) (mē'kōō-rä) . Jap.	33·53 N	139·26 E
164	Mila (mē'lä) . Alg.	36·30 N	6.16 E
71	Milaca mê-lăk'à) . Minn.	45·45 N	93·41 W
80	Milan (mī'lăn) . Mich.	42·05 N	83·40 W
73	Milan . Mo.	40·13 N	93·07 W
78	Milan . Tenn.	35·54 N	88·47 W
	Milan, see Milano		
126	Milano (Milan) (mê-lä'nō) . It.	45·29 N	9·12 E
133	Milâs (mê'läs) . Tur.	37·10 N	27·25 E
126	Milazzo (mê-lät'sô) . It.	38·13 N	15·17 E
70	Milbank (mĭl'băŋk) . S. D.	45·13 N	96·38 W
160	Mildura (mĭl-dū'rȧ) . Austl.	34·10 S	142·18 E
67	Miles City (mīlz) . Mont.	46·24 N	105·50 W
81	Milford (mĭl'fērd) . Conn.	41·15 N	73·05 W
81	Milford . Del.	38·55 N	75·25 W
83	Milford . Mass. (Boston In.)	42·09 N	71·31 W
75	Milford . Mich. (Detroit In.)	42·35 N	83·36 W
81	Milford . N. H.	42·50 N	71·40 W
75	Milford . Ohio (Cincinnati In.)	39·11 N	84·18 W
69	Milford . Utah	38·20 N	113·05 W
116	Milford Haven (hāv'n) . Wales	51·40 N	5·10 W
158	Miling (mīl'ng) . Austl.	30·30 S	116·25 E
65	Milipitas (mĭl-ĭ-pĭ'tăs) Calif. (San Francisco In.)	37·26 N	121·54 W
67	Milk R. (mĭlk) . Mont.	48·25 N	108·45 W
68	Mill Cr. . Calif.	40·07 N	121·55 W
85	Mill Cr. (mĭl).Can. (Edmonton In.)	53·13 N	113·25 W
122	Millau (mē-yō') . Fr.	44·06 N	3·04 E
65	Millbrae (mĭl'brā) Calif. (San Francisco In.)	37·36 N	122·23 W
83	Millbury (mĭl'bĕr-ĭ) Mass. (Boston In.)	42·12 N	71·46 W
78	Milledgeville (mĭl'ĕj-vĭl) . Ga.	33·05 N	83·15 W
85	Mille Iles, R. des (rê-vyâr' dā mīl'īl') Can. (Montreal In.)	45·41 N	73·40 W
71	Mille Lac Ind. Res. (mĭl lăk') Minn.	46·14 N	94·13 W
71	Mille Lacs (L.) . Minn.	46·25 N	93·22 W
71	Mille Lacs, Lac des (L.) (läk dĕ mēl läks) . Can.	48·52 N	90·53 W
79	Millen (mĭl'ĕn) . Ga.	32·47 N	81·55 W
70	Miller (mĭl'ēr) . S. D.	44·31 N	99·00 W
129	Millerovo (mĭl'ĕ-rô-vô) . Sov. Un.	48·58 N	40·27 E
80	Millersburg (mĭl'ērz-bûrg) . Ky.	38·15 N	84·10 W
80	Millersburg . Ohio	40·35 N	81·55 W
81	Millersburg . Pa.	40·35 N	76·55 W
82	Millerton (mĭl'ēr-tŭn) . Can.	46·56 N	65·40 W
83	Millertown (mĭl'ēr-toun) . Can.	48·48 N	56·33 W
160	Millicent (mĭl-ĭ'sĕnt) . Austl.	37·30 S	140·20 E
82	Millinocket (mĭl-ĭ-nŏk'ĕt) . Maine	45·40 N	68·44 W
83	Millis (mĭl'ĭs) Mass. (Boston In.)	42·10 N	71·22 W
74	Millstadt (mĭl'stăt) Ill. (St. Louis In.)	38·27 N	90·06 W
84	Millstone R. (mĭl'stōn) N. J. (New York In.)	40·27 N	74·38 W
158	Millstream (mĭl'strēm) . Austl.	21·45 S	117·10 E
82	Milltown (mĭl'toun) . Can.	45·13 N	67·19 W
75	Millvale (mĭl'vāl) Pa. (Pittsburgh In.)	40·29 N	79·58 W
65	Mill Valley (mĭl) Calif. (San Francisco In.)	37·54 N	122·32 W
81	Millville (mĭl'vĭl) . N. J.	39·25 N	75·00 W
123	Milly-la-Forêt (mē-yē'-la-fŏ-rĕ') Fr. (Paris In.)	48·24 N	2·28 E
166	Milnerton (mĭl'nēr-tŭn) S. Afr. (Cape Town In.)	33·52 S	18·30 E
70	Milnor (mĭl'nēr) . N. D.	46·17 N	97·29 W
82	Milo (mī'lō) . Maine	44·16 N	69·01 W
	Milo (I.), see Mílos		
127	Mílos (Milo) (I.) (mē'lŏs) . Grc.	36·45 N	24·35 E
91	Milpa Alta (mē'l-pä-ä'l-tä) Mex. (Mexico City In.)	19·11 N	99·01 W
78	Milton (mĭl'tŭn) . Fla.	30·37 N	87·02 W
74	Milton . Ill. (St. Louis In.)	38·54 N	90·08 W
83	Milton . Mass. (Boston In.)	42·16 N	71·03 W
81	Milton . Pa.	41·00 N	76·50 W
74	Milton . Utah (Salt Lake City In.)	41·04 N	111·44 W
65	Milton . Wash. (Seattle In.)	47·15 N	122·20 W
71	Milton . Wis.	42·45 N	89·00 W
66	Milton-Freewater . Ore.	45·57 N	118·25 W
85	Milton West . Can. (Toronto In.)	43·31 N	79·53 W
75	Milwaukee . Wis. (Milwaukee In.)	43·03 N	87·55 W
75	Milwaukee R. Wis. (Milwaukee In.)	43·10 N	87·56 W
65	Milwaukie (mĭl-wô'kē) Ore. (Portland In.)	45·27 N	122·38 W
91	Mimiapan (mē-myä-pän') Mex. (Mexico City In.)	19·26 N	99·28 W
85	Mimico (mĭ'mĭ-kō) Can. (Toronto In.)	43·37 N	79·30 W
101	Mimoso do Sul (mē-mô'sō-dô-sōō'l) Braz. (Rio de Janeiro In.)	21·03 S	41·21 W
125	Mina (R.) (mē'nȧ) . Alg.	35·24 N	0·51 E
153	Minakuchi (mē'nä-kōō'chê) . Jap.	34·59 N	136·06 E
94	Minas (mē'näs) . Cuba	21·30 N	77·35 W
139	Minas . Indon. (Singapore In.)	0·52 N	101·29 E
100	Minas (mē'näs) . Ur.	34·18 S	55·12·W
92	Minas, Sierra de las (Mts.) (syĕr'rä dā läs mē'näs) . Guat.	15·08 N	90·25 W
82	Minas Basin (mī'nȧs) . Can.	45·19 N	64·10 W
82	Minas Chan. . Can.	45·13 N	64·55 W
92	Minas de Oro (mē'-näs-dĕ-ŏ-rō) Hond.	14·52 N	87·19 W
124	Minas de Ríontinto (mē'näs dā rē-ô-tēn'tō) . Sp.	37·43 N	6·35 W
99	Minas Gerais (State) (mē'näzh-zhĕ-rä'ēs) . Braz.	17·45 S	43·50 W
99	Minas Novas (mē'näzh nō'vázh) Braz.	17·20 S	42·19 W
70	Minatare (L.) (mĭn'á-târ) . Nebr.	41·56 N	103·07 W
91	Minatitlán (mē-nä-tē-tlän') . Mex.	17·59 N	94·33 W
90	Minatitlán . Mex.	19·21 N	104·02 W
153	Minato (mē'nȧ-tô) Jap. (Tōkyō In.)	35·13 N	139·52 E
116	Minch, The (Chan.) . Scot.	58·04 N	6·04 W
116	Minch, The Little (Chan.) (mĭnch) . Scot.	56·85 N	6·42 W
151	Min Chiang (R.) . China	26·30 N	118·30 E
151	Min Chiang (R.) . China	29·30 N	104·00 E
155	Mindanao (I.) (mĭn-dä-nou') . Phil.	7·30 N	125·10 E
155	Mindanao Sea . Phil.	8·55 N	124·00 E
120	Minden (mĭn'dĕn) . Ger.	52·17 N	8·58 E
77	Minden . La.	32·36 N	93·19 W
72	Minden . Nebr.	40·30 N	98·54 W
155	Mindoro (I.) (mĭn-dō'rō) Phil. (Manila In.)	13·04 N	121·06 E
155	Mindoro Str. . Phil. (Manila In.)	12·28 N	120·33 E
136	Mindyak (mĕn'dyȧk) Sov. Un. (Urals In.)	54·01 N	58·48 E
84	Mineola (mĭn-ē-ō'lȧ) N. Y. (New York In.)	40·43 N	73·38 W
77	Mineola . Tex.	32·39 N	95·31 W
90	Mineral del Chico (mê-nȧ-räl'dĕl chē'kô) . Mex.	20·13 N	98·46 W
90	Mineral del Monte (mê-nȧ-räl dĕl mōn'tȧ) . Mex.	20·18 N	98·39 W
133	Mineral'nyye Vody . Sov. Un.	44·10 N	43·15 E
71	Mineral Point (mĭn'ēr-ăl) . Wis.	42·50 N	90·10 W
76	Minerál Wells (mĭn'ēr-ăl wĕlz) Tex.	32·48 N	98·06 W
80	Minerva (mĭ-nûr'vȧ) . Ohio	40·45 N	81·10 W
126	Minervino (mē-nĕr-vē'nô) . It.	41·07 N	16·05 E
153	Mineyama (mē-nĕ-yä'mä) . Jap.	35·38 N	135·05 E
82	Mingan (mĭŋ'gȧn) . Can.	50·19 N	64·02 W
133	Mingechaur (R.) . Sov. Un.	41·00 N	47·20 E
158	Mingenew (mĭn'gĕ-nû) . Austl.	29·15 S	115·45 E
148	Mingkuang (mĭng'gōōäng) . China	32·41 N	118·00 E
80	Mingo Junction (mĭŋ'gō) . Ohio	40·15 N	80·40 W
124	Minho (Reg.) (mēn yōō) . Port.	41·32 N	8·13 W
94	Minho (R.) . Jam.	17·55 N	77·20 W
124	Minho, Rio (R.) (rē'ō-mē'n-yō) Port.	41·48 N	9·05 W
85	Ministik L. (mĭ-nĭs'tĭk) Can. (Edmonton In.)	53·23 N	113·05 W
164	Minna (mĭn'ȧ) . Nig.	9·40 N	6·34 E
73	Minneapoli (mĭn-ē-ăp'ô-lĭ) . Kans.	39·07 N	97·41 W
74	Minneapolis (mĭn-ê-ăp'ô-lĭs) Minn. (Minneapolis, St. Paul In.)	44·58 N	93·15 W
86	Minnedosa (mĭn-ē-dō'sȧ) . Can.	50·16 N	99·50 W
70	Minneota (mĭn-ê-ō'tȧ) . Minn.	44·34 N	95·59 W
63	Minnesota (State) (mĭn-ê-sō'tȧ) U. S.	46·10 N	90·20 W
70	Minnesota (R.) . Minn.	45·04 N	96·03 W
71	Minnetonka (L.) (mĭn-ê-tŏŋ'kȧ) Minn.	44·52 N	93·34 W
69	Minnie Maud Cr. (mĭn'ĭmôd') Utah	39·50 N	110·30 W
153	Mino (R.) (mē'nō) Jap. (Osaka In.)	34·56 N	135·06 E
124	Miño (R.) (mē'nyō) . Sp.	42·28 N	7·48 W
80	Minonk (mī'nŏnk) . Ill.	40·55 N	89·00 W
75	Minooka (mĭ-nōō'kȧ) Ill. (Chicago In.)	41·27 N	88·15 W
	Minorca (I.), see Menorca, Isla de		
70	Minot (mī'nŏt) . N. D.	48·13 N	101·16 W
128	Minsk (mēnsk) . Sov. Un.	53·54 N	27·35 E
128	Minsk (Oblast) . Sov. Un.	53·50 N	27·43 E
121	Mińsk Mazowiecki (mēn'sk mä-zō-vyĕt'skĭ) . Pol.	52·10 N	21·35 E
110	Minsterley (mĭnstēr-lē) . Eng.	52·38 N	2·55 W
82	Minto (mĭn'tô) . Can.	46·05 N	66·05 W
87	Minto (L.) . Can.	57·18 N	75·50 W
126	Minturno (mên-tōōr'nō) . It.	41·17 N	13·44 E
168	Minūf (mê-nōōf') U. A. R. (Nile In.)	30·26 N	30·55 E
134	Minusinsk (mē-nōō-sĕnsk') Sov. Un.	53·47 N	91·45 E
146	Minya Konka (Mt.) (mĕn'yȧ kôŋ'kȧ) . China	29·16 N	101·46 E
136	Min'yar (mēn'yȧr) Sov. Un. (Urals In.)	55·06 N	57·33 E
83	Miquelon (I.) (mĭk-ē-lôn') St. Pierre & Miquelon	47·03 N	56·20 W
85	Miquelon L. (mĭ'kē-lôn) Can. (Edmonton In.)	53·16 N	112·55 W
90	Miquihuana (mê-kê-wä'nä) . Mex.	23·36 N	99·45 W
121	Mir (mēr) . Sov. Un.	53·27 N	26·25 E
124	Mira (R.) (mē'rä) . Port.	37·29 N	8·15 W
101	Miracema (mē-rä-sĕ'mä) Braz. (Rio de Janeiro In.)	21·24 S	42·10 W
99	Mirador (mê-rä-dōr') . Braz.	6·19 S	44·12 W
98	Miraflores (mē-rä-flō'räs) . Col.	5·10 N	73·13 W
98	Miraflores . Peru	16·19 S	71·20 W
88	Miraflores Locks C. Z. (Panama Canal In.)	9·00 N	79·35 W
95	Miragoâne (mê-rä-gwän') . Hai.	18·25 N	73·05 W
101	Miraí (mē-rä-ē') Braz. (Rio de Janeiro In.)	21·13 S	42·36 W
143	Miraj (mê-rŭj') . India	16·55 N	74·40 E
74	Mira Loma (mĭ'rȧ lō'mȧ) Calif. (Los Angeles In.)	34·01 N	117·32 W
68	Miramar (mĭr'ȧ-mär) Calif. (San Diego In.)	32·53 N	117·08 W
122	Miramas . Fr. (Marseille In.)	43·35 N	5·00 E
82	Miramichi (R.) . Can.	46·36 N	66·08 W
82	Miramichi B. (mĭr'ȧ-mē'shē) . Can.	47·14 N	64·45 W
98	Miranda (mē-rä'n-dä) . Col. (In.)	3·14 N	76·11 W
99	Miranda . Ven. (In.)	10·09 N	68·24 W
99	Miranda (State) . Ven. (In.)	10·17 N	66·41 W
124	Miranda de Ebro (mē-rä'n-dä-dĕ-ĕ'l-brô) . Sp.	42·42 N	2·59 W
124	Miranda de Ebro (mê-rän'dä dōō-dwĕ'rô) . Port.	41·30 N	6·17 W
124	Mirandela (mê-rän-dā'lȧ) . Port.	41·28 N	7·10 W
76	Mirando City (mĭr-ăn'dō) . Tex.	27·25 N	99·03 W
95	Mira Por Vos Islets (Is.) (mē'rä pôr vōs') . Ba. Is.	22·05 N	74·30 W
95	Mira Por Vos Pass (Str.) . Ba. Is.	22·10 N	74·35 W
144	Mirbāt . Mus. & Om.	16·58 N	54·42 E
95	Mirebalais (mēr-bȧ-lĕ') . Hai.	18·50 N	72·05 W
123	Mirecourt (mēr-kōōr') . Fr.	48·20 N	6·08 E
122	Mirepoix (mēr-pwä') . Fr.	43·06 N	1·52 E
110	Mirfield (mûr'fēld) . Eng.	53·41 N	1·42 W
154	Miri (mē'rē) . Mala.	4·13 N	113·56 E
100	Mirim, L. (mê-rēN') . Braz.-Ur.	33·00 S	53·15 W
129	Miropol'ye (mē-rō-pôl'yĕ) Sov. Un.	51·02 N	35·13 E
142	Mīrpur Khās (mēr'pōōr kās) W. Pak.	25·36 N	69·10 E
142	Mirzapur (mēr'zä-pōōr) . India	25·12 N	82·38 E
164	Misa . Togo	7·00 N	00·34 E
153	Misaki (mē'sȧ-kê) Jap. (Tōkyō In.)	35·08 N	139·37 E
91	Misantla (mê-sän'tlä) . Mex.	19·55 N	96·49 W
82	Miscou (I.) (mĭs'kō) . Can.	47·58 N	64·35 W
82	Miscou Pt. . Can.	48·04 N	64·25 W
125	Miseno, C. (mē-zĕ'nō) It. (Naples In.)	40·33 N	14·12 E
93	Misery, Mt. (mĭz'rē-ĭ) St. Christopher (Le. & Wind. Is. In.)	17·28 N	62·47 W
152	Mishan (mĭ'shäN) . China	45·32 N	132·19 E
80	Mishawaka (mĭsh-ȧ-wô'kȧ) . Ind.	41·45 N	86·15 W
153	Mishima (mē'shê-mä) . Jap.	35·09 N	138·56 E
100	Misiones (Prov.) (mê-syō'näs) Arg.	27·00 S	54·30 W
93	Miskito, Cayos (Is.) . Nic.	14·34 N	82·30 W
121	Miskolc (mĭsh'kôlts) . Hung.	48·07 N	20·50 E
155	Misol (I.) (mê-sōl') . W. Irian	2·00 S	130·05 E
71	Misquah Hills (mĭs-kwä' hĭlz) Minn.	47·50 N	90·30 W
168	Miṣr al Jadīdah (Ruins) U. A. R. (Nile In.)	30·06 N	31·35 E
165	Misratāh . Libya	32·23 N	14·58 E
87	Missinaibi (R.) (mĭs'ĭn-ă'ê-bê) Can.	50·27 N	83·01 W
74	Mission (mĭsh'ŭn) Kans. (Kansas City In.)	39·02 N	94·39 W
76	Mission . Tex.	26·14 N	98·19 W
65	Mission City (sĭ'tĭ) Can. (Vancouver In.)	49·08 N	122·19 W
80	Mississinewa (R.) (mĭs-ĭ-sĭn'ê-wä) Ind.	40·30 N	85·45 W
63	Mississippi (State) (mĭs-ĭ-sĭp'ê) U. S.	32·30 N	89·45 W
81	Mississippi (L.) . Can.	45·05 N	76·15 W
63	Mississippi (R.) . U. S.	31·50 N	91·30 W
78	Mississippi Sd. . Miss.	34·16 N	89·10 W
67	Missoula (mĭ-zōō'lȧ) . Mont.	46·52 N	114·00 W
63	Missouri (State) (mĭ-sōō'rê) . U. S.	38·00 N	93·40 W
63	Missouri (R.) . U. S.	40·40 N	96·00 W
77	Missouri City . Tex. (In.)	29·37 N	95·32 W
62	Missouri Coteau, (Plat.) . U. S.	47·30 N	101·00 W
70	Missouri Valley . Iowa	41·35 N	95·53 W
65	Mist (mĭst) . Ore. (Portland In.)	46·00 N	123·15 W
82	Mistassibi (R.) (mĭs-tȧ-sĭ'bê) . Can.	49·45 N	71·58 W
82	Mistassini (mĭs-tȧ-sĭ'nê) . Can.	48·56 N	71·55 W
87	Mistassini (L.) (mĭs-tȧ-sĭ'nê) . Can.	50·48 N	75·00 W
120	Mistelbach (mĭs'tĕl-bäk) . Aus.	48·34 N	16·33 E
92	Misteriosa, L. (mēs-tĕ-ryō'sä) Mex. (Yucatan In.)	18·05 N	90·15 W
126	Mistretta (mê-strĕt'tä) . It.	37·54 N	14·22 E
90	Mita, Punta de (Pt.) (pōō'n-tä-dĕ-mē'tä) . Mex.	20·44 N	105·34 W
153	Mitaka (mē'tä-kä) Jap. (Tōkyō In.)	35·42 N	139·34 E
74	Mitchell (mĭch'ĕl) Ill. (St. Louis In.)	38·46 N	90·05 W
80	Mitchell . Ind.	38·45 N	86·25 W
70	Mitchell . Nebr.	41·56 N	103·49 W
70	Mitchell . S. D.	43·42 N	98·01 W
159	Mitchell (R.) . Austl.	15·30 S	142·15 E
79	Mitchell, Mt . N. C.	35·47 N	82·15 W
168	Mīt Ghamr . U. A. R. (Nile In.)	30·43 N	31·20 E
127	Mitilíni . Grc.	39·09 N	26·35 E
153	Mito (mē'tô') . Jap.	36·20 N	140·23 E
153	Mitsu (mēt'sōō) . Jap.	34·21 N	132·49 E
120	Mittelland (can.) (mĭt'ĕl-länd) Ger.	52·18 N	10·42 E
111	Mittenwalde (mē'tĕn-väl-dĕ) Ger. (Berlin In.)	52·16 N	13·33 E
120	Mittweida (mĭt-vī'dä) . Ger.	50·59 N	12·58 E
136	Mityayevo (mĭt-yä'yĕ-vô) Sov. Un. (Urals In.)	60·17 N	61·02 E
129	Mius (R.) (mê-ōōs') . Sov. Un.	47·30 N	38·48 E
153	Miwa (mē'wä) . Jap. (Osaka In.)	34·32 N	135·51 E
92	Mixico (mēs'kô) . Guat.	14·37 N	90·37 W
90	Mixquiahuala (mēs-kê-wä'lä) . Mex.	20·12 N	99·13 W
90	Mixteco (R.) (mēs-tä'kō) . Mex.	17·45 N	98·10 W
153	Miyake (mē'yä-kä) Jap. (Ōsaka In.)	34·35 N	135·34 E
153	Miyake (I.) (mē'yä-kā) . Jap.	34·06 N	139·21 E
153	Miyakonojō (mē'yȧ-kô'nô-jō) . Jap.	31·42 N	131·03 E
153	Miyazaki (mē'yä-zä'kē) . Jap.	31·55 N	131·27 E
153	Miyoshi (mê-yō'shê') . Jap.	34·48 N	132·49 E
114	Mizdah (mēz'dä) . Libya	31·29 N	13·09 E
127	Mizil (mē'zēl) . Rom.	45·01 N	26·30 E
	Mizonokuchi, see Takatsu		
118	Mjölby (myûl'bü) . Swe.	58·20 N	15·09 E
118	Mjörn (L.) . Swe.	57·55 N	12·22 E
118	Mjösa (myûsä) . Nor.	60·41 N	11·25 E
118	Mjösvatn (myûs-vät'n) . Nor.	59·55 N	7·50 E
166	Mkalamo (m'kä-lä'mō) . Tan.	4·07 S	34·38 E
120	Mladá Boleslav (mlä'dä bô'lĕ-släf) Czech.	50·26 N	14·52 E
121	Mława (mwä'vȧ) . Pol.	53·07 N	20·25 E
127	Mljet (I.) (mlyĕt) . Yugo.	42·40 N	17·45 E
155	Moa (I.) . Indon.	8·30 S	128·30 E
69	Moab (mō'ăb) . Utah	38·35 N	109·35 W
68	Moapa River Ind. Res. (mō-ăp'ȧ) Nev.	36·44 N	115·01 W

ng-sing; ŋ-baŋk; N-nasalized n; nŏd; cŏmmit; ōld; ôbey; ôrder; fōōd; fŏŏt; ou-out; s-soft; sh-dish; th-thin; pūre; ûnite; ûrn; stŭd; circŭs; ü-as "y" in study; '-indeterminate vowel.

238 Mobaye–Montmorency PRONOUNCING INDEX

Page Name Pronunciation Region Lat. °′ Long. °′

165 Mobaye (mô-bä'y') . Cen. Afr. Rep. 4·30 N 21·10 E
73 Moberly (mō'bẽr-lĭ) . . . . Mo. 39·24 N 92·25 W
78 Mobile (mô-bēl') . . . . Ala. 30·42 N 88·03 W
78 Mobile (R.) . . . . Ala. 31·15 N 88·00 W
78 Mobile B. . . . . Ala. 30·26 N 87·56 W
70 Mobridge (mō'brĭj) . . . . S. D. 45·32 N 100·26 W
95 Moca (mô'kä) . . . . Dom. Rep. 19·25 N 70·35 W
167 Moçambique (mō-ṣăN-bē'kĕ) . Moz. 15·07 S 40·48 E
166 Moçamedes . . . . Ang. 15·10 S 12·15 E
166 Moçâmedes (Reg.) (mô-zä-mĕ-dĕs) Ang. 16·00 S 12·15 E
144 Mocha (mō'kä) . . . . Yemen 13·11 N 43·20 E
90 Mochitlán (mō-chē-tlän') . . . . Mex. 17·10 N 99·19 W
166 Mochudi (mō-chōō'dē) . . . . . . Bots. 24·13 S 26·07 E
167 Mocímboa da Praia (mô-sē'ēm-bô-ȧ dȧ prä'ēȧ) . Moz. 11·25 S 40·18 E
101 Mococa (mô-kô'kȧ) Braz. (Rio de Janeiro In.) 21·29 S 46·58 W
90 Moctezuma (môk'tā-zōō'mä) . Mex. 22·44 N 101·06 W
167 Modderfontein . . . . S. Afr. (Johannesburg & Pretoria In.) 26·06 S 28·10 E
168 Modderpoort . . . . S. Afr. (Johannesburg & Pretoria In.) 29·08 S 27·27 E
126 Modena (mô'dĕ-nä) . . . . It. 44·38 N 10·54 E
68 Modesto (mô-dĕs'tō) . . . . Calif. 37·39 N 121·00 W
113 Modica (mô'dē-kä) . . . . It. 36·50 N 14·43 E
111 Mödling (mûd'lĭng) Aus. (Vienna In.) 48·06 N 16·17 E
99 Moengo . . . . Sur. 5·43 N 54·19 W
166 Moero, L. . . . . . . Con. K.-Zambia. 8·45 S 27·45 E
123 Moers (mûrs) . . . . . Ger. (Ruhr In.) 51·27 N 6·38 E
72 Moffat Tun. (môf'ăt) . . . . Colo. 39·52 N 106·20 W
168 Mogadiscio (mô-gȧ-dē'shō) Som. (Horn of Afr. In.) 2·08 N 45·22 E
75 Mogadore (mŏg-ȧ-dōr') Ohio (Cleveland In.) 41·04 N 81·23 W
146 Mogaung (mô-gä'ōōng) . . . . . . Bur. 25·30 N 96.52 E
101 Mogi das Cruzes (mô-gê-däs-krōō'sĕs) Braz. (Rio de Janeiro In.) 23·33 S 46·10 W
101 Mogi-Guaçu (R.) (mô-gê-gwä'sōō) Braz. (Rio de Janeiro In.) 22·06 S 47·12 W
128 Mogilëv (mô-gê-lyôf') . . . . Sov. Un. 53·53 N 30·22 E
128 Mogilëv (Oblast) (mô-gê-lyôf') Sov. Un. 53·28 N 30·15 E
129 Mogilëv-Podol'skiy (mô-gê-lyôf) (pô-dôl'skĭ) Sov. Un. 48·27 N 27·51 E
121 Mogilno (mô-gēl'nô) . . . . Pol. 52·38 N 17·58 E
101 Mogi-Mirim (mô-gê-mē-rē'N) Braz. (Rio de Janeiro In.) 22·26 S 46·57 W
146 Mogok (mô-gōk') . . . . Bur. 23·14 N 96.38 E
69 Mogollon (mō-gô-yōn') . . . N. Mex. 33·25 N 108·45 W
69 Mogollon, Plat. (mō-gô-yōn') Ariz. 34·26 N 111·17 W
168 Mogol R. (mô-gŏl) . . . . S. Afr. (Johannesburg & Pretoria In.) 24·12 S 27·55 E
124 Moguer (mō-gĕr') . . . . Sp. 37·15 N 6.50 W
121 Mohács (mô'häch) . . . . Hung. 45·59 N 18·38 E
167 Mohales Hoek . . . Leso. (Natal In.) 30·09 S 27·28 E
70 Mohall (mō'hôl) . . . . N. D. 48·46 N 101·29 W
125 Mohammadia . . . . Alg. 35·35 N 0·05 E
68 Mohave (L.) (mô-hä'vä) . . . . Nev. 35·23 N 114·40 W
81 Mohawk (R.) (mō'hôk) . . . N. Y. 43·15 N 75·20 W
167 Mohéli (I.) (mô-ā-lē') (mô-hā'lē) Comores, Arch. des 12·23 S 43·38 E
147 Moho (mō'hō') . . . . China 53·33 N 122·30 E
119 Mõisaküla (mẽē'sȧ-kü'lȧ) . Sov. Un. 58·07 N 25·12 E
87 Moisie (R.) (mwȧ-zē') . . . . Can. 51·24 N 66·11 W
122 Moissac (mwȧ-sȧk') . . . . Fr. 44·07 N 1·05 E
125 Moita (mō-ē'tȧ) . Port. (Lisbon In.) 38·39 N 9·00 W
68 Mojave . . . . Calif. 35·06 N 118·09 W
68 Mojave (R.) (mô-hä'vä) . . . . Calif. 34·46 N 117·24 W
68 Mojave Desert . . . . Calif. 35·05 N 117·30 W
68 Mokelumne (R.) (mō-kĕ-lŭm'nē) Calif. 38·12 N 121·09 W
167 Mokhotlong . . . . . Leso. (Natal In.) 29·18 S 29·06 E
152 Mokpo (mōk'pō') . . . . Kor. 34·50 N 126·30 E
132 Moksha (R.) (môk-shä') . Sov. Un. 54·50 N 43·20 E
111 Mol . . . . Bel. (Brussels In.) 51·21 N 5·09 E
126 Molat (I.) (mô'lät) . . . . Yugo. 44·15 N 14·40 E
121 Moldavia (Reg.) . . . . Rom. 47·20 N 27·12 E
118 Molde (môl'dĕ) . . . . Nor. 62·44 N 7·15 E
118 Molde Fd. (môl'dĕ fyôrd) . . . . Nor. 62·40 N 7·05 E
121 Moldova R. . . . . Rom. 47·17 N 26·27 E
166 Molepolole (mō-lȧ-pô-lō'lȧ) . . Bots. 24·15 S 25·33 E
126 Molfetta (môl-fĕt'tä) . . . . It. 41·11 N 16·38 E
101 Molina (mŏ-lē'nä) Chile (Santiago In.) 35·07 S 71·17 W
124 Molina de Aragón (mô-lē'nä dĕ ä-rä-gô'n) . . Sp. 41·40 N 1·54 W
124 Molína de Segura (mô-lē'nä dĕ sĕ-gōō'rä) . . . Sp. 38·03 N 1·07 W
71 Moline (mô-lēn') . . . . Ill. 41·31 N 90·34 W
166 Moliro . . . . Con. K. 8·08 S 30·30 E
126 Moliterno (mōl-ē-tĕr'nō) . . . . . . It. 40·13 N 15·54 E
98 Mollendo (mô-lyĕn'dō) . . . . . . Peru 17·02 S 71·59 W
64 Moller, Port (pōrt mōl'ĕr) . . Alaska 56·18 N 161·30 W
118 Mölndal (mûln'däl) . . . . Swe. 57·39 N 12·01 E
129 Molochnaya (R.) (mô-lôch'nȧ-yȧ) (rĕ-kä') Sov. Un. 47·05 N 35·22 E
129 Molochnoye, Ozero (L.) (ô'zĕ-rô mô-lôch'nô-yĕ) Sov. Un. 46·35 N 35·32 E
128 Molodechno (mô-lô-dĕch'nô) Sov. Un. 54·18 N 26·57 E
128 Molodechno (Oblast) . . . . Sov. Un. 54·27 N 27·38 E
136 Molody Tud (mō-lō-dô'ê tōō'd) Sov. Un. (Moscow In.) 55·17 N 37·31 E
128 Mologa (R.) (mô-lô'gȧ) . Sov. Un. 58·05 N 35·43 E
157 Molokai (I.) (mō-lô kä'ē) Hawaii (In.) 21·15 N 157·05 E
136 Molokcha R. (mô'lôk-chä) Sov. Un. (Moscow In.) 56·15 N 38·29 E
166 Molopo (R.) (mō-lō-pō) . . . . S. Afr. 27·45 S 20·45 E

167 Molteno (môl-tā'nô) S. Afr. (Natal In.) 31·24 S 26·23 E
155 Molucca Pass. (mô-lŭk'ȧ) . . Indon. 1·55 N 126·30 E
155 Moluccas (Is.) (mô-lŭk'ȧz) . Indon. 2·40 S 127·15 E
155 Molucca Sea . . . . Indon. 0·15 N 125·41 E
167 Mombasa (mōm-bä'sä) . . . . . . Ken. 4·01 S 39·43 E
152 Mombetsu (môm'bĕt-sōō') . . . Jap. 44·21 N 142·48 E
75 Momence (mô-mĕns') Ill. (Chicago In.) 41·09 N 87·40 W
92 Momostenango (mô-môs-tā-näŋ'gô) . Guat. 15·02 N 91·25 W
92 Momotombo . . . . Nig. 12·25 N 86·43 W
155 Mompog Pass (mōm-pōg') Phil. (Manila In.) 13·35 N 122·09 E
98 Mompos (mōm-pōs') . . . . Col. 8·05 N 74·30 W
118 Møn (I.) (mûn) . . . . Den. 54·54 N 12·30 E
75 Monaca (mŏ-nȧ'kō) Pa. (Pittsburgh In.) 40·41 N 80·17 W
123 Monaco (mŏn'ȧ-kō) . . . . Eur. 43·43 N 7·47 E
116 Monaghan (mŏn'ȧ-găn) . . . . . . Ire. 54·16 N 7·20 W
89 Mona Pass. (mō'nȧ) . . . . N. A. 18·00 N 68·10 W
113 Monastir (mōn-ȧs-tēr') . . . . . . Tun. 35·49 N 10·56 E
Monastir, see Bitola
129 Monastyrishche (mô-nȧs-tē-rēsh'chȧ) . Sov. Un. 48·57 N 29·53 E
128 Monastyrshchina (mô-nȧs-tērsh'chĭ-nȧ) . Sov. Un. 54·19 N 31·49 E
99 Monção (moŋ-souN') . . . . Braz. 3·39 S 45·23 W
124 Moncayo (Mtn.) (môn-kä'yō) . Sp. 41·44 N 1·48 W
132 Monchegorsk (mōn'chĕ-gôrsk) Sov. Un. 69·00 N 33·35 E
123 Mönchengladbach (mûn'kĕn gläd'bäK) Ger. (Ruhr In.) 51·12 N 6·28 E
124 Moncique, Serra de (Mts.) (sĕr'rä dä môn-chē'kĕ) . Port. 37·22 N 8.37 W
76 Monclova (môn-klō'vä) . . . . . . Mex. 26·53 N 101·25 W
82 Moncton (mŭŋk'tŭn) . . . . Can. 46·06 N 64·49 W
124 Mondego, Cabo (C.) (kä'bō mōn-dā'gōō) . Port. 40·12 N 8·55 W
124 Mondêgo (R.) (mōn-dĕ'gō) . . Port. 40·10 N 8·36 W
166 Mondombe (môn-dôm'bā) . Con. K. 0·45 S 23·06 E
124 Mondoñedo (môn-dô-nyā'dō) . . Sp. 43·35 N 7·18 W
126 Mondovì (mōn-dō-vē') . . . . It. 44·23 N 7·53 E
71 Mondovi (mŏn-dō'vĭ) . . . . Wis. 44·35 N 91·42 W
75 Monee (mŏ-nĭ) . . Ill. (Chicago In.) 41·25 N 87·45 W
75 Monessen (mŏ-nĕs'sen) Pa. (Pittsburgh In.) 40·09 N 79·53 W
73 Monett (mō-nĕt') . . . . Mo. 36·55 N 93·55 W
124 Monforte de Lemos (môn-fôr'tä dĕ lĕ'môs) . . Sp. 42·30 N 7·30 W
165 Mongala R. (mŏn-găl'ȧ) . . Con. K. 3·20 N 21·30 E
165 Mongalla . . . . Sud. 5·11 N 31·46 E
142 Monghyr (mōn-gēr') . . . . India 25·23 N 86·34 E
138 Mongolia (mŏŋ-gō'lĭ-ȧ) . . . . Asia 46·00 N 100·00 E
165 Mongoumba (mŏŋ-gōōm'bȧ) Con. B. 3·41 N 18·21 E
166 Mongu (mŏŋ-gōō') . . . . Zambia 15·14 S 23·07 E
92 Monkey River (mŭŋ'kĭ) Br. Hond. (Yucatan In.) 16·22 N 88·33 W
85 Monkland Sta. (mŭngk-lănd) Can. (Ottawa In.) 45·12 N 74·52 W
166 Monkoto (môn-kō'tō) . . . . Con. K. 1·45 S 20·51 E
73 Monmouth (mŏn'mŭth) (mŏn'mouth) . Ill. 40·54 N 90·38 W
84 Monmouth Junction (mŏn'mouth jŭngk'shŭn) N. J. (New York In.) 40·23 N 74·33 W
68 Mono (L.) (mō'nō) . . . . Calif. 38·04 N 119·00 W
80 Monon (mō'nŏn) . . . . Ind. 40·55 N 86·55 W
81 Monongah (mô-nŏŋ'gȧ) . . . W. Va. 39·25 N 80·10 W
75 Monongahela (mô-nōn-gȧ-hē'lȧ) Pa. (Pittsburgh In.) 40·11 N 79·55 W
81 Monongahela (R.) . . . . W. Va. 39·30 N 80·10 W
127 Monopoli (mô-nô'pô-lē) . . . . . . It. 40·55 N 17·17 E
125 Monovar (mô-nō'vär) . . . . Sp. 38·26 N 0·50 W
126 Monreale (môn-rā-ä'lā) . . . . It. 38·04 N 13·15 E
78 Monroe (mŭn-rō') . . . . Ga. 33·47 N 83·43 W
77 Monroe . . . . La. 32·30 N 92·06 W
80 Monroe . . . . Mich. 41·55 N 83·25 W
84 Monroe . . . . N. Y. (New York In.) 41·19 N 74·11 W
79 Monroe . . . . N. C. 34·58 N 80·34 W
69 Monroe . . . . Utah 38·35 N 112·10 W
65 Monroe . . . . . . Wash. (Seattle In.) 47·52 N 121·58 W
71 Monroe . . . . Wis. 42·35 N 89·40 W
79 Monroe (L.) . . . . Fla. 28·50 N 81·15 W
73 Monroe City . . . . Mo. 39·38 N 91·41 W
78 Monroeville (mŭn-rō'vĭl) . . . . . Ala. 31·33 N 87·19 W
74 Monrovia (mŏn-rō'vĭ-ȧ) Calif. (Los Angeles In.) 34·09 N 118·00 W
164 Monrovia . . . . Lib. 6·21 N 10·59 W
117 Mons (môN') . . . . Bel. 50·29 N 3·55 E
82 Monson (mŏn'sŭn) . . . . Maine 45·17 N 69·28 W
118 Mönsterås (mŭn'stĕr-ôs) . . . . . Swe. 57·04 N 16·24 E
146 Montagh Ata (Mt.) . . . . China 38·26 N 75·23 E
87 Montagne Tremblante Provincial Park, Can. 46·30 N 75·51 W
83 Montague (mŏn'tȧ-gū) . . . . . . Can. 46·11 N 62·35 W
80 Montague . . . . Mich. 43·30 N 86·25 W
64 Montague (I.) . . . . Alaska 60·10 N 147·00 W
155 Montalban (mŏnt-ăl-băn) Phil. (Manila In.) 14·47 N 121·11 E
99 Montalbán . . . . Ven. (In.) 10·14 N 68·19 W
126 Montalcone (môn-tăl-kô'nĕ) . . . It. 45·49 N 13·30 E
124 Montalegre (mōn-tä-lā'grĕ) . . Port. 41·49 N 7·48 W
62 Montana (State) (mŏn-tăn'ȧ) U. S. 47·10 N 111·50 W
124 Montánchez (môn-tän'chāth) . . Sp. 39·18 N 6·09 W
122 Montargis (môN-tȧr-zhē') . . . . . Fr. 47·59 N 2·42 E
123 Montataire (môN-tȧ-târ) Fr. (Paris In.) 49·15 N 2·26 E
122 Montauban (môN-tō-bäN') . . . . Fr. 44·01 N 1·22 E
81 Montauk Pt. (mŏn-tôk') . . . . N. Y. 41·05 N 71·55 W
125 Montbanch (mônt-bän'ch) . . . . Sp. 41·20 N 1·08 E
122 Montbard (môN-bȧr') . . . . Fr. 47·40 N 4·19 E
123 Montbéliard (môN-bā-lyȧr') . . . . Fr. 47·32 N 6·45 E

77 Mont Belvieu (mŏnt bĕl'vū) Tex. (In.) 29·51 N 94·53 W
123 Mont Blanc Tunnel (môN bläN) Fr.-It. 45·53 N 6·53 E
122 Montbrison (môN-brê-zôN') . . . . Fr. 45·38 N 4·06 E
122 Montcalm, Pic de (Pk.) (pēk dē môN-kȧm') . Fr. 42·43 N 1·13 E
122 Montceau-les-Mines (môN-sō'lā-mēn') . Fr. 46·39 N 4·22 E
84 Montclair (mŏnt-klâr') N. J. (New York In.) 40·49 N 74·13 W
122 Mont-de-Marsan (môN-dē-mȧr-säN') . Fr. 43·54 N 0·32 W
122 Montdidier (môN-dē-dyā') . . . . . Fr. 49·42 N 2·33 E
101 Monte (mŏ'n-tĕ) Arg. (Buenos Aires In.) 35·25 S 58·49 W
98 Monteagudo (môn'tȧ-ä-gōō'dhō) Bol. 19·49 S 63·48 W
74 Montebello (mŏn-tê-bĕl'ō) Calif. (Los Angeles In.) 34·01 N 118·06 W
85 Montebello . . . . . Can. (Ottawa In.) 45·40 N 74·56 W
158 Monte Bello (Is.) . . . . Austl. 20·30 S 114·10 E
100 Monte Caseros (mŏ'n-tĕ-kä-sĕ'rôs) . Arg. 30·16 S 57·39 W
92 Mont Ecillos, Cord. de (Mts.) (kôr-dēl-yĕ'rä dĕ mŏ'nt ĕ-sē'l-yōs) . Hond. 14·19 N 87·52 W
95 Monte Cristi (mŏ'n-tĕ-krē's-tē) Dom. Rep. 19·50 N 71·40 W
126 Montecristo, I. di (mōn'tȧ-krēs'tō) . It. 42·20 N 10·19 E
90 Monte Escobedo (mōn'tȧ ĕs-kô-bā'dhō) . Mex. 22·18 N 103·34 W
125 Monteforte Irpino (môn-tĕ-fô'r-tĕ ē'r-pē'nō) It. (Naples In.) 40·39 N 14·42 E
124 Montefrío (mōn-tȧ-frē'ō) . . . . . Sp. 37·20 N 4·02 W
94 Montego Bay (mŏn-tē'gō) . . . Jam. 18·30 N 77·55 W
100 Monte Grande (mŏ'n-tĕ grän'dĕ) Arg. (In.) 34·34 S 58·28 W
125 Montelavar (mōn-tĕ-lȧ-vär') Port. (Lisbon In.) 38·51 N 9·20 W
122 Montélimar (môN-tā-lē-mär') . . Fr. 44·33 N 4·47 E
124 Montellano (mōn-tȧ-lyä'nō) . . . Sp. 37·00 N 5·34 W
71 Montello (mŏn-tĕl'ō) . . . . Wis. 43·47 N 89·20 W
76 Montemorelos (mōn'tȧ-mō-rā'lōs) Mex. 25·14 N 99·50 W
124 Montemor-o-Novo (môn-tĕ-môr'ōō-nô'vōō) . . . Port. 38·39 N 8·11 W
Montenegro (Reg.), see Crna Gora
126 Montepulciano (môn'tȧ-pōōl-chä'nō) . It. 43·05 N 11·48 E
122 Montereau-faut-Yonne (môN-t'rō'fō-yôn') . Fr. 48·24 N 2·57 E
68 Monterey (mŏn-tĕ-rā') . . . . . . Calif. 36·36 N 121·53 W
78 Monterey . . . . Tenn. 36·06 N 85·15 W
68 Monterey B. . . . . Calif. 36·48 N 122·01 W
74 Monterey Park Calif. (Los Angeles In.) 34·04 N 118·08 W
98 Montería (mōn-tȧ-rā'ä) . . . . . . Col. 8·47 N 75·57 W
100 Monteros (môn-tĕ'rôs) . . . . . . Arg. 27·14 S 65·29 W
125 Monterotondo (môn-tĕ-rô-tô'n-dō) It. (Rome In.) 42·03 N 12·39 E
76 Monterrey (mōn-tĕr-rā') . . . . Mex. 25·43 N 100·19 W
126 Monte Sant' Angelo (mô'n-tĕ sän ä'n-gzhĕ-lô) . It. 41·43 N 15·59 E
66 Montesano (mŏn-tĕ-sä'nō) . . Wash. 46·59 N 123·35 W
99 Montes Claros (môn-tĕs-klä'rôs) Braz. 16·44 S 43·41 W
78 Montevallo (môn-tê-văl'ō) . . . . Ala. 33·05 N 86·49 W
126 Montevarchi (mōn-tȧ-vär'kē) . . . It. 43·30 N 11·45 E
101 Montevideo (mōn'tȧ-vê-dhā'ō) Ur. (Buenos Aires In.) 34·50 S 56·10 W
69 Monte Vista (mŏn'tē vĭs'tȧ) . Colo. 37·35 N 106·10 W
78 Montezuma (mŏn-tê-zōō'mȧ) . . Ga. 32·17 N 84·00 W
69 Montezuma Castle Natl. Mon. Ariz. 34·38 N 111·50 W
111 Montfoort . Neth. (Amsterdam In.) 52·02 N 4·56 E
123 Montfort l'Amaury (môN-fôr'lā-mō-rē') Fr. (Paris In.) 48·47 N 1·49 E
122 Montfort-sur-Meu (môN-fôr-sür-mû') . Fr. 48·09 N 1·58 W
78 Montgomery (mŏnt-gŭm'ẽr-ĭ) . Ala. 32·23 N 86·17 W
142 Montgomery . . . . W. Pak. 30·43 N 73·04 E
80 Montgomery . . . . W. Va. 38·10 N 81·25 W
73 Montgomery City . . . . Mo. 38·58 N 91·29 W
73 Monticello (mŏn-tĭ-sĕl'ō) . . . . Ark. 33·38 N 91·47 W
78 Monticello . . . . Fla. 30·32 N 83·53 W
78 Monticello . . . . Ga. 33·00 N 83·11 W
80 Monticello . . . . Ill. 40·05 N 88·35 W
80 Monticello . . . . Ind. 40·40 N 86·50 W
71 Monticello . . . . Iowa 42·14 N 91·13 W
78 Monticello . . . . Ky. 36·47 N 84·50 W
82 Monticello . . . . Maine 46·19 N 67·53 W
71 Monticello . . . . Minn. 45·18 N 93·48 W
81 Monticello . . . . N. Y. 41·35 N 74·40 W
69 Monticello . . . . Utah 37·55 N 109·25 W
123 Montigny-lès-Metz (môN-tēn-yē'lā-mĕts') . Fr. 49·06 N 6·07 E
125 Montijo (môn-tē'zhō) Port. (Lisbon In.) 38·42 N 8·58 W
124 Montijo (môn-tē'hō) . . . . Sp. 38·55 N 6·35 W
93 Montijo, Bahia (B.) (bä-ē'ä môn-tē'hō) . Pan. 7·36 N 81·11 W
82 Mont-Joli (môN zhō-lē') . . . . . Can. 48·37 N 68·09 W
122 Montluçon (môN-lü-sôN') . . . . . Fr. 46·20 N 2·35 E
85 Montmagny (môN-män-yē') Can. (Quebec In.) 46·59 N 70·33 W
85 Montmorency (mŏnt-mô-rĕn'sĭ) Can. (Quebec In.) 46·53 N 71·09 W
123 Montmorency (môN'mô-räN-sē') Fr. (Paris In.) 48·59 N 2·19 E
85 Montmorency, Rivière (R.) (rê-vyâr' mŏnt-mô-rĕn'sĭ) Can (Quebec In.) 47·04 N 71·12 W

ăt; finăl; rāte; senāte; ärm; ȧsk; sofȧ; fâre; ch-choose; dh-as th in other; bē; ēvent; bĕt; recĕnt; cratẽr; g-go; gh-guttural g; bĭt; ĭ-short neutral; rīde; K-guttural k as ch in German ich;

PRONOUNCING INDEX Montmorillon–Mount Rainier 239

Page	Name Pronunciation	Region	Lat. °′	Long. °′
122	Montmorillon (môn'mô-rê-yôn')	Fr.	46·26 N	0·50 E
126	Montone (R.) (môn-tô'nĕ)	It.	44·03 N	11·45 E
124	Montoro (môn-tō'rô)	Sp.	38·01 N	4·22 W
80	Montpelier (mŏnt-pēl'yẽr)	Ind.	40·35 N	85·20 W
67	Montpelier	Idaho	42·19 N	111·19 W
80	Montpelier	Ohio	41·35 N	84·35 W
81	Montpelier	Vt.	44·20 N	72·35 W
122	Montpellier (môn-pĕ-lyā')	Fr.	43·38 N	3·53 E
85	Montreal (mŏn-trê-ôl')	Can. (Montreal In.)	45·30 N	73·35 W
85	Montreal North	Can. (Montreal In.)	45·36 N	73·38 W
85	Montreal South	Can. (Montreal In.)	45·31 N	73·30 W
120	Montreux (môn-trû')	Switz.	46·26 N	6·52 E
74	Montrose (mŏnt-rōz)	Calif. (Los Angeles In.)	34·13 N	118·13 W
69	Montrose (mŏn-trōz')	Colo.	38·30 N	107·55 W
84	Montrose	Md. (Baltimore In.)	39·03 N	77·08 W
75	Montrose	Ohio (Cleveland In.)	41·08 N	81·38 W
81	Montrose (mŏnt-rōz')	Pa.	41·50 N	75·50 W
116	Montrose	Scot.	56·45 N	2·25 W
82	Monts, Pointe des (Pt.) (pwănt' dā môn')	Can.	49·19 N	67·22 W
123	Mont St. Martin (môn sân mär-tân')	Fr.	49·34 N	6·13 E
93	Montserrat I. (mŏnt-sĕ-răt')	N. A. (Le. & Wind. Is. In.)	16·48 N	62·00 W
84	Montvale (mŏnt-vāl')	N. J. (New York In.)	41·02 N	74·01 W
154	Monywa (mŏn'yōō-wà)	Bur.	22·02 N	95·16 E
126	Monza (mōn'tsä)	It.	45·34 N	9·17 E
125	Monzón (mōn-thōn')	Sp.	41·54 N	1·09 E
77	Moody (mōō'dĭ)	Tex.	31·18 N	97·20 W
168	Mooi (R.) (mōō'ĭ)	S. Afr. (Johannesburg & Pretoria In.)	26·34 S	27·03 E
167	Mooi (R.)	S. Afr. (Natal In.)	29·00 S	30·15 E
167	Mooirivier	S. Afr. (Natal In.)	29·14 S	29·59 E
161	Moolap	Austl. (Melbourne In.)	38·11 S	144·26 E
160	Moonta (mōōn'tà)	Austl.	34·05 S	137·42 E
158	Moora (mŏŏr'à)	Austl.	30·35 S	116·12 E
67	Moorcroft (mōr'krôft)	Wyo.	44·17 N	104·59 W
158	Moore (L.) (mōr)	Austl.	29·50 S	128·12 E
111	Moorenweis (mō'rĕn-vīz)	Ger. (Munich In.)	48·10 N	11·05 E
81	Moore Res.	Vt.-N. H.	44·20 N	72·10 W
84	Moorestown (morz'toun)	N. J. (Philadelphia In.)	39·58 N	74·56 W
75	Mooresville (mōrz'vĭl)	Ind. (Indianapolis In.)	39·37 N	86·22 W
79	Mooresville (mōrz'vĭl)	N. C.	35·34 N	80·48 W
70	Moorhead (mōr'hĕd)	Minn.	46·52 N	96·44 W
78	Moorhead	Miss.	33·25 N	90·30 W
	Moorland, see Landes			
86	Moose (L.) (mōōs)	Can.	54·14 N	99·28 W
87	Moose (R.)	Can.	51·01 N	80·42 W
85	Moose Creek	Can. (Ottawa In.)	45·16 N	74·58 W
82	Moosehead (mōōs'hĕd)	Maine	45·37 N	69·15 W
86	Moose Jaw (mōōs jô)	Can.	50·26 N	105·40 W
82	Mooselookmeguntic (L.) (mōō-sĕ-lŏŏk-mē-gŭn'tĭk)	Maine	44·54 N	70·20 W
86	Moose Mtn.	Can.	50·10 N	102·54 W
81	Moosilauke (Mtn.) (mōō-sĭ-là'kē)	N. H.	44·00 N	71·50 W
111	Moosinning (mō'zē-nēng)	Ger. (Munich In.)	48·17 N	11·51 E
87	Moosonee (mōō'sô-nê)	Can.	51·20 N	80·44 W
164	Mopti (mŏp'tē)	Mali	14·27 N	3·56 W
98	Moquegua (mô-kā'gwä)	Peru	17·15 S	70·54 W
121	Mór (mōr)	Hung.	47·51 N	18·14 E
71	Mora (mō'rȧ)	Minn.	45·52 N	93·18 W
72	Mora	N. Mex.	35·58 N	105·17 W
124	Mora (mô-rä)	Sp.	39·42 N	3·45 W
125	Mora	Sp.	41·06 N	0·25 E
142	Morādābād (mô-rä-dä-bäd')	India	28·57 N	78·48 E
92	Morales (mô-rä'lĕs)	Guat.	15·29 N	88·46 W
167	Moramanga (mō-rä-mäŋ'gä)	Malag. Rep.	18·48 S	48·09 E
95	Morant Pt. (mô-rănt')	Jam.	17·55 N	76·10 W
118	Morastrand (mō'rä-strănd)	Swe.	61·00 N	14·29 E
125	Morata de Tajuña (mô-rä'tä dā tä-hōō'nyä)	Sp. (Madrid In.)	40·14 N	3·27 W
121	Morava (Moravia) (Prov.) (mô'rä-vä) (mô-rā'vĭ-ȧ)	Czech.	49·21 N	16·57 E
120	Morava R.	Czech.	49·53 N	16·53 E
	Moravia, see Morava			
99	Morawhanna (mô-rà-hwä'nà)	Guy.	8·12 N	59·33 W
116	Moray Firth (mŭr'å)	Scot.	57·41 N	3·55 W
118	Mörbylånga (mûr'bü-lôŋ'gå)	Swe.	56·32 N	16·23 E
86	Morden (môr'dĕn)	Can.	49·08 N	98·19 W
161	Mordialloc (môr-dĭ-ăl'ŏk)	Austl. (Melbourne In.)	38·00 S	145·05 E
116	More, Ben (Mtn.) (bĕn môr)	Scot.	58·09 N	5·01 W
70	Moreau (R.) (mô-rō')	S. D.	45·13 N	102·22 W
116	Morecambe B. (mōr'kăm)	Eng.	53·55 N	3·25 W
160	Moree (mō'rē)	Austl.	29·20 S	149·50 E
80	Morehead	Ky.	38·10 N	83·25 W
79	Morehead City (mōr'hĕd)	N. C.	34·43 N	76·43 W
73	Morehouse (mōr'hous)	Mo.	36·49 N	89·41 W
90	Morelia (mô-rā'lyä)	Mex.	19·43 N	101·12 W
125	Morella (mô-rāl'yä)	Sp.	40·38 N	0·07 W
90	Morelos (mô-rā'lōs)	Mex.	22·46 N	102·36 W
76	Morelos	Mex.	28·24 N	100·51 W
91	Morelos	Mex. (Mexico City In.)	19·41 N	99·29 W
76	Morelos, R.	Mex.	25·27 N	99·35 W
65	Morena, Sierra (Mt.) (syĕr'rä mô-rā'nä)	Calif. (San Francisco In.)	37·24 N	122·19 W
124	Morena, Sierra (Mts.) (syĕr'rä mô-rā'nä)	Sp.	38·15 N	5·45 W
69	Morenci (mô-rĕn'sĭ)	Ariz.	33·05 N	109·25 W
80	Morenci	Mich.	41·50 N	84·05 W
100	Moreno (mô-rĕ'nō)	Arg. (In.)	34·25 S	58·47 W
74	Moreno	Calif. (Los Angeles In.)	33·55 N	117·09 W

Page	Name Pronunciation	Region	Lat. °′	Long. °′
94	Mores (I.) (mōrz)	Ba. Is.	26·20 N	77·35 W
65	Moresby (I.) (mōrz'bĭ)	Can. (Vancouver In.)	48·43 N	123·15 W
86	Moresby I.	Can	52·54 N	131·00 W
160	Moreton (I.) (môr'tŭn)	Austl.	26·53 S	152·42 E
160	Moreton B. (môr'tŭn)	Austl.	27·12 S	153·10 E
85	Morewood (mōr'wŏŏd)	Can. (Ottawa In.)	45·11 N	75·17 W
67	Morgan (môr'găn)	Utah	41·04 N	111·42 W
77	Morgan City	La.	29·41 N	91·11 W
80	Morganfield (môr'găn-fēld)	Ky.	37·40 N	87·55 W
167	Morgansbaai	S. Afr. (Natal In.)	32·42 S	28·19 E
79	Morganton (môr'găn-tŭn)	N. C.	35·44 N	81·42 W
81	Morgantown (môr'găn-toun)	W. Va.	39·40 N	79·55 W
168	Morganzon (môr'gănt-sŏn)	S. Afr. (Johannesburg & Pretoria In.)	26·44 S	29·39 E
145	Morga Ra.	Afg. (Khyber Pass In.)	34·02 N	70·38 E
161	Moriac	Austl. (Melbourne In.)	38·15 S	144·12 E
153	Moriguchi (mō'rê-gōō'chê)	Jap. (Ōsaka In.)	34·44 N	135·34 E
85	Morinville (mō'-rĭn-vĭl)	Can. (Edmonton In.)	53·47 N	113·40 W
152	Morioka (mō'rê-ō'kà)	Jap.	39·40 N	141·21 E
135	Morkoka (R.) (môr-kô'kà)	Sov. Un.	65·35 N	111·00 E
122	Morlaix (mŏr-lĕ')	Fr.	48·36 N	3·48 W
85	Morley (mŏr'lê)	Can. (Calgary In.)	51·10 N	114·51 W
123	Mormant	Fr. (Paris In.)	48·35 N	2·54 E
143	Mormugao	India	15·09 N	73·58 E
93	Morne Diablotin, Mt. (môrn dê-à-blô-tăn')	Dominica (Le. & Wind. Is. In.)	15·31 N	61·24 W
93	Morne Gimie, Mt. (môrn' zhê-mē')	St. Lucia (Le. & Wind. Is. In.)	13·53 N	61·03 W
161	Mornington	Austl. (Melbourne In.)	38·13 S	145·02 E
74	Moro (mō'rō)	Ill. (St. Louis In.)	38·56 N	90·01 W
155	Morobe	N. Gui. Ter.	8·03 S	147·45 E
165	Morocco (mô-rŏk'ō)	Afr.	32·00 N	7·00 W
167	Morogoro (mō-rô-gō'rō)	Tan.	6·49 S	37·46 E
90	Moroleón (mō-rō-lā-ōn')	Mex.	20·07 N	101·15 W
167	Morombé (mōō-rōōm'bā)	Malag. Rep.	21·39 S	43·34 E
100	Morón (mō-rō'n)	Arg. (In.)	34·24 S	58·37 W
94	Morón (mô-rōn')	Cuba	22·05 N	78·35 W
99	Morón (mô-rō'n)	Ven. (In.)	10·29 N	68·11 W
167	Morondava (mō-rōn-dä'vä)	Malag. Rep.	20·17 S	44·18 E
124	Morón de la Frontera (mô-rōn'dā lăf rōn-tā'rä)	Sp.	37·08 N	5·20 W
68	Morongo Ind. Res. (mō-rôŋ'gō)	Calif.	33·54 N	116·47 W
69	Moroni (mô-rō'nĭ)	Utah	39·30 N	111·40 W
155	Morotai (I.) (mō-rô-tä'ê)	Indon.	2·12 N	128·30 E
133	Morozovsk	Sov. Un.	48·20 N	41·50 E
70	Morrill (mŏr'ĭl)	Nebr.	41·59 N	103·54 W
73	Morrilton (mŏr'ĭl-tŭn)	Ark.	35·09 N	92·42 W
99	Morrinhos (mô-rēn'yōzh)	Braz.	17·45 S	48·56 W
86	Morris (mŏr'ĭs)	Can.	49·19 N	97·32 W
80	Morris	Ill.	41·20 N	88·25 W
70	Morris	Minn.	45·35 N	95·53 W
71	Morrison (mŏr'ĭ-sŭn)	Ill.	41·48 N	89·58 W
84	Morris Plains (mŏr'ĭs pláns)	N. J. (New York In.)	40·49 N	74·29 W
74	Morris Res.	Calif. (Los Angeles In.)	34·11 N	117·49 W
84	Morristown (mŏr'rĭs-toun)	N. J. (New York In.)	40·48 N	74·29 W
78	Morristown	Tenn.	36·10 N	83·18 W
84	Morrisville (mŏr'ĭs vĭl)	Pa. (Philadelphia In.)	40·12 N	74·46 W
82	Morrisville	Vt.	44·33 N	72·39 W
99	Morro do Chapéu (môr-ōō dōō-shä-pĕ'ōō)	Braz.	11·34 S	41·03 W
75	Morrow (mŏr'ō)	Ohio (Cincinnati In.)	39·21 N	84·07 W
133	Morshansk (môr-shànsk')	Sov. Un.	53·25 N	41·35 E
118	Mors (I.)	Den.	56·46 N	8·38 E
126	Mortara (môr-tä'rä)	It.	45·13 N	8·47 E
100	Morteros (môr-tĕ'rôs)	Arg.	30·47 S	62·00 W
101	Mortes, Rio das (R.) (rē'-o-däs-mô'r-tĕs)	Braz. (Rio de Janeiro In.)	21·04 S	44·29 W
71	Morton Ind. Res. (mŏr'tŭn)	Minn.	44·35 N	94·48 W
111	Mortsel (môr-sĕl')	Bel. (Brussels In.)	51·10 N	4·28 E
122	Morvan, Mts. du (môr-vän')	Fr.	46·45 N	4·00 E
132	Morzhovets (I.) (môr'zhô-vyĕts')	Sov. Un.	66·40 N	42·30 E
128	Mosal'sk (mō-zàlsk')	Sov. Un.	54·27 N	34·57 E
66	Moscow (mŏs'kō)	Idaho	46·44 N	116·57 W
	Moscow, see Moskva			
	Moscow Canal, see Imeni Moskvy, Kanal			
120	Mosel R. (mō'sĕl) (mô-zĕl)	Ger.	49·49 N	7·00 E
66	Moses Lake	Wash.	47·08 N	119·15 W
66	Moses L. (mō'zĕz)	Wash.	47·09 N	119·30 W
168	Moses R.	S. Afr. (Johannesburg & Pretoria In.)	25·17 S	29·04 E
119	Moshchnyy (Is.) (môsh'chnĭ)	Sov. Un.	59·56 N	28·07 E
167	Moshi (mō'shê)	Tan.	3·17 S	37·18 E
136	Moskva (Moscow) (mŏs-kvä')	Sov. Un. (Moscow In.)	55·45 N	37·37 E
128	Moskva (Oblast)	Sov. Un.	55·38 N	36·48 E
128	Moskva (R.)	Sov. Un.	55·50 N	37·05 E
121	Mosonmagyaróvár	Hung.	47·51 N	17·16 E
93	Mosquitos, Costa de (kôs-tä-dĕ-mŏs-kē'tō)	Nic.	12·05 N	83·49 W
93	Mosquitos, Gulfo de los (G.) (gōō'l-fô-dĕ-lôs-mŏs-kē'tōs)	Pan.	9·17 N	80·59 W
118	Moss (mŏs)	Nor.	59·29 N	10·39 E
65	Moss Beach (mŏs bēch)	Calif. (San Francisco In.)	37·32 N	122·31 W

Page	Name Pronunciation	Region	Lat. °′	Long. °′
166	Mossel Bay (mô'sŭl bā)	S. Afr.	34·06 S	22·23 E
110	Mossley (mŏs'lĭ)	Eng.	53·31 N	2·02 W
99	Mossoró (mō-sô-rōō')	Braz.	5·13 S	37·14 W
78	Moss Point (mŏs)	Miss.	30·25 N	88·32 W
120	Most (mŏst)	Czech.	50·32 N	13·37 E
164	Mostaganem (mŏs'tä-gä-nĕm')	Alg.	36·04 N	0·11 E
127	Mostar (môs'tär)	Yugo.	43·20 N	17·51 E
125	Móstoles (môs-tō'lās)	Sp. (Madrid In.)	40·19 N	3·52 W
92	Motagua R. (mō-tä'gwä)	Guat.	15·29 N	88·39 W
118	Motala (mō-tô'lä)	Swe.	58·34 N	15·00 E
116	Motherwell (mŭdh'ẽr-wĕl)	Scot.	55·45 N	4·05 W
124	Motril (mō-trēl')	Sp.	36·44 N	3·32 W
92	Motul (mō-tōō'l)	Mex. (Yucatan In.)	21·07 N	89·14 W
166	Mouanda	Gabon	1·37 S	13·09 E
95	Mouchoir Bk. (mōō-shwär')	Ba. Is.	21·35 N	70·40 W
95	Mouchoir Passage (Str.)	Ba. Is.	21·05 N	71·05 W
123	Moudon	Switz.	46·40 N	6·47 E
166	Mouille Pt.	S. Afr. (Cape Town In.)	33·54 S	18·19 E
122	Moulins (mōō-lăn')	Fr.	46·34 N	3·19 E
85	Moulin Vallie're (mōō-lĕn' vä-lē-ĕr')	Can. (Quebec In.)	46·58 N	71·12 W
154	Moulmein (mōl-mān')	Bur.	16·30 N	97·39 E
114	Moulouya Oued (R.) (mōō-lōō'yȧ)	Mor.	34·07 N	3·27 W
78	Moultrie (mōl'trĭ)	Ga.	31·10 N	83·48 W
79	Moultrie (Dam)	S. C.	33·12 N	80·00 W
73	Mound City (mound)	Ill.	37·06 N	89·13 W
73	Mound City	Mo.	40·08 N	95·13 W
80	Mound City Group Natl. Mon.	Ohio	39·25 N	83·00 W
80	Moundsville (moundz'vĭl)	W. Va.	39·50 N	80·50 W
123	Mounier, Mt. (mōō-nyā')	Fr.	44·10 N	6·59 E
84	Mountain Brook (moun'tĭn brŏŏk)	Ala. (Birmingham In.)	33·30 N	86·45 W
74	Mountain Creek L.	Tex. (Dallas, Fort Worth In.)	32·43 N	97·03 W
65	Mountaindale (dāl)	Ore. (Portland In.)	45·37 N	123·02 W
73	Mountain Grove (grōv)	Mo.	37·07 N	92·16 W
66	Mountain Home (hōm)	Idaho	43·08 N	115·43 W
86	Mountain Park (pärk)	Can.	52·57 N	117·22 W
65	Mountain View (moun'tĭn vū)	Calif. (San Francisco In.)	37·25 N	122·07 W
73	Mountain View	Mo.	36·59 N	91·46 W
84	Mountain View	N. J. (New York In.)	40·55 N	74·17 W
79	Mount Airy (âr'ĭ)	N. C.	36·28 N	80·37 W
	Mount Athos (Reg.), see Áyion Óros			
167	Mount Ayliff (ā'lĭf)	S. Afr. (Natal In.)	30·48 S	29·24 E
71	Mount Ayr (âr)	Iowa	40·43 N	94·06 W
80	Mount Carmel (kär'mĕl)	Ill.	38·25 N	87·45 W
81	Mount Carmel	Pa.	40·50 N	76·25 W
71	Mount Carroll	Ill.	42·05 N	89·55 W
75	Mount Clemens (klĕm'ĕnz)	Mich. (Detroit In.)	42·36 N	82·52 W
166	Mount Darwin	Rh.	15·44 S	31·40 E
82	Mount Desert (I.) (dê-zûrt')	Can.	44·15 N	68·08 W
79	Mount Dora (dō'rà)	Fla. (In.)	28·45 N	81·38 W
161	Mount Duneed	Austl. (Melbourne In.)	38·15 S	144·20 E
161	Mount Eliza	Austl. (Melbourne In.)	38·11 S	145·05 E
70	Mountevideo (mōn'tà-vê-dhā'ō)	Minn.	44·56 N	95·42 W
167	Mount Fletcher (flĕ'chẽr)	S. Afr. (Natal In.)	30·42 S	28·32 E
80	Mount Forest (fŏr'ĕst)	Can.	44·00 N	80·45 W
167	Mount Frere (frâr')	S. Afr. (Natal In.)	30·54 S	29·02 E
160	Mount Gambier (găm'bēr)	Austl.	37·30 S	140·53 E
80	Mount Gilead (gĭl'ĕăd)	Ohio	40·30 N	82·50 W
75	Mount Healthy (hĕlth'ê)	Ohio (Cincinnati In.)	39·14 N	84·32 W
84	Mount Holly (hŏl'ĭ)	N. J. (Philadelphia In.)	39·59 N	74·47 W
85	Mount Hope	Can. (Toronto In.)	43·09 N	79·55 W
84	Mount Hope (hōp)	N. J. (New York In.)	40·55 N	74·32 W
80	Mount Hope	W. Va.	37·55 N	81·10 W
158	Mount Isa (ī'zà)	Austl.	21·00 S	139·45 E
84	Mount Kisco (kĭs'ko)	N. Y. (New York In.)	41·12 N	73·44 W
65	Mountlake Terrace (mount lāk tĕr'ĭs)	Wash. (Seattle In.)	47·48 N	122·19 W
75	Mount Lebanon (lĕb'á-nŭn)	Pa. (Pittsburgh In.)	40·22 N	80·03 W
64	Mount McKinley Natl. Park (mȧ-kĭn'lĭ)	Alaska	63·48 N	153·02 W
158	Mount Magnet (măg-nĕt)	Austl.	28·00 S	118·00 E
161	Mount Martha	Austl. (Melbourne In.)	38·17 S	145·01 E
159	Mount Morgan (môr-găn)	Austl.	23·42 S	150·45 E
161	Mount Moriac	Austl. (Melbourne In.)	38·13 S	144·12 E
80	Mount Morris (mŏr'ĭs)	Mich.	43·10 N	83·45 W
81	Mount Morris	N. Y.	42·45 N	77·50 W
79	Mount Olive (ŏl'ĭv)	N. C.	35·11 N	78·05 W
69	Mount Peale	Utah	38·26 N	109·16 W
71	Mount Pleasant (plĕz'ănt)	Iowa	40·59 N	91·34 W
80	Mount Pleasant	Mich.	43·35 N	84·45 W
79	Mount Pleasant	S. C.	32·46 N	79·51 W
78	Mount Pleasant	Tenn.	35·31 N	87·12 W
73	Mount Pleasant	Tex.	33·10 N	94·56 W
69	Mount Pleasant	Utah	39·35 N	111·20 W
75	Mount Prospect (prŏs'pĕkt)	Ill. (Chicago In.)	42·03 N	87·56 W
66	Mount Rainier Natl. Park (rà-nēr')	Wash.	46·47 N	121·17 W

ng-sing; ŋ-baŋk: n-nasalized n; nŏd; cŏmmit; ōld; ôbey; ôrder; fōōd; fŏŏt; ou-out; s-soft; sh-dish; th-thin; pūre; ûnite; ûrn; stŭd; circŭs; ü-as "y" in study; '-indeterminate vowel.

240 Mount Revelstoke–Nagua PRONOUNCING INDEX

Page	Name Pronunciation Region	Lat. °′	Long. °′
86	Mount Revelstoke Natl. Park (rĕv′ĕl-stōk). Can.	51·22 N	120·15 W
81	Mount Savage (săv′āj) . . . . . Md.	39·45 N	78·55 W
66	Mount Shasta (shăs′tȧ) . . . . . Calif.	41·18 N	122·17 W
73	Mount Sterling (stûr′lĭng) . . . . . Ill.	39·59 N	90·44 W
80	Mount Sterling . . . . Ky.	38·05 N	84·00 W
83	Mount Stewart (stū′ărt) . . . . . Can.	46·21 N	62·54 W
81	Mount Union (ūn′yŭn) . . . . Pa.	40·25 N	77·50 W
80	Mount Vernon (vûr′nŭn) . . . . . . Ill.	38·20 N	88·50 W
80	Mount Vernon . . . . Ind.	37·55 N	87·50 W
73	Mount Vernon . . . . Mo.	37·09 N	93·48 W
84	Mount Vernon N. Y. (New York In.)	40·55 N	73·51 W
80	Mount Vernon . . . . Ohio	40·25 N	82·30 W
84	Mount Vernon Va. (Washington D.C. In.)	38·43 N	77·06 W
65	Mount Vernon. Wash. (Seattle In.)	48·25 N	122·20 W
155	Mount Wilhelm . . . . New Guinea	5·45 S	144·30 E
148	Moup′ing (mō′pĭng) . . . . China	37·23 N	121·36 E
99	Moura (mō′rȧ) . . . . Braz.	1·33 S	61·38 W
124	Moura . . . . Port.	38·08 N	7·28 W
122	Mourenx (mōō-rän) . . . . Fr.	43·24 N	0·40 W
116	Mourne, Mts. (môrn) . . . . . N. Ire.	54·10 N	6·09 W
123	Moûtiers (mōō-tyâr′) . . . . Fr.	45·31 N	6·34 E
160	Mowbullan, Mt. (mō′bōō-lȧn) Austl.	26·50 S	151·34 E
90	Moyahua (mô-yä′wä) . . . . Mex.	21·16 N	103·10 W
165	Moyale (mô-yä′lä) . . . . Ken.	3·28 N	39·04 E
164	Moyamba (mô-yäm′bä) . . . . . S. L.	8·11 N	12·27 W
114	Moyen Atlas (Mts.) . . . . Mor.	32·49 N	5·28 W
123	Moyeuvre Grande . . . . Fr.	49·15 N	6·26 E
66	Moyie R. (moi′yē) . . . . Idaho	48·50 N	116·10 W
98	Moyobamba (mō-yô-bäm′bä). Peru	6·12 S	76·56 W
92	Moyuta (mô-ē-ōō′tä) . . . . Guat.	14·01 N	90·05 W
135	Moyyero (R.) . . . . Sov. Un.	67·15 N	104·10 E
163	Mozambique (Portuguese East Africa) (mō-zȧm-bēk′). Afr.	20·15 S	33·53 E
167	Mozambique Chan. (mō-zȧm-bek′) Afr.	24·00 S	38·00 E
133	Mozdok (môz-dôk′) . . . . . Sov. Un.	43·45 N	44·35 E
128	Mozhaysh (mô-zhäysh′). Sov. Un.	55·31 N	36·02 E
136	Mozhayskiy (mô-zhay′skĭ) Sov. Un. (Leningrad In.)	59·42 N	30·08 E
129	Mozyr′ (mô-zür′) . . . . Sov. Un.	52·03 N	29·14 E
166	Mporokoso (′m-pō-rô-kō′sō) Zambia	9·28 S	30·06 E
167	Mpwapwa (′m-pwä′pwä) . . . . . Tan.	6·20 S	36·39 E
167	Mqanduli (′m-kän′dōō-lē) S. Afr. (Natal In.)	31·50 S	28·42 E
121	Mragowo (mräŋ′gô-vô) . . . . Pol.	53·52 N	21·18 E
164	M′sila (m′sē′lȧ) . . . . Alg.	35·47 N	4·34 E
128	Msta (R.) (m′stȧ′) . . . . . . Sov. Un.	58·33 N	32·08 E
128	Mstislavl′ (m′stē-slävl′) . . Sov. Un.	54·01 N	31·42 E
166	Mtengula (′m-tĕŋ-gōō′lȧ) . . . . Moz.	12·42 S	34·48 E
166	Mtetwe Pan (Basin) (′m-tĕt′wē) Bots.	20·00 S	24·18 E
128	Mtsensk (m′tsĕnsk) . . . . Sov. Un.	53·17 N	36·33 E
154	Muang Khon Kaen . . . . Thai.	16·37 N	102·41 E
154	Muang Lamphum . . . . Thai.	18·40 N	98·59 E
154	Muang Phitsanulok . . . . Thai.	16·51 N	100·15 E
154	Muang Sakon . . . . Thai.	17·00 N	104·06 E
139	Muar (R.) . . Mala. (Singapore In.)	2·18 N	102·43 E
123	Much (mōōκ). Ger. (Ruhr In.)	50·54 N	7·24 E
110	Much Wenlock (mŭch wĕn′lŏk) Eng.	52·35 N	2·33 W
78	Muckalee Cr. (mŭk′ȧ lē) . . . . . . Ga.	31·55 N	84·10 W
65	Muckleshoot Ind. Res. (mŭck′′l-shōōt) Wash. (Seattle In.)	47·21 N	122·04 W
99	Mucugê (mōō-kōō-zhĕ′) . . . . . Braz.	13·02 S	41·19 W
71	Mud (L.) (mŭd) . . . . Mich.	46·12 N	84·32 W
68	Mud (L.) . . . . Nev.	40·28 N	119·11 W
68	Muddy (R.) (mŭd′ĭ) . . . . Nev.	36·56 N	114·42 W
73	Muddy Boggy Cr. (mud′ĭ bôg′ĭ) Okla.	34·42 N	96·11 W
69	Muddy Cr. (mŭd′ĭ) . . . . Utah	38·45 N	111·10 W
160	Mudgee (mŭ-jē) . . . . Austl.	32·47 S	149·10 E
124	Mugia (mōō-kē′ä) . . . . Sp.	43·05 N	9·14 W
133	Muğla (mōōg′lä) . . . . Tur.	37·10 N	28·20 E
120	Mühldorf (mül-dôrf) . . . . Ger.	48·15 N	12·33 E
120	Mühlhausen (mül′hou-zĕn) . . . . Ger.	51·13 N	10·25 E
119	Muhu (I.) (mōō′hōō) . . . . Sov. Un.	58·41 N	22·55 E
151	Mui Ron, C . . . . Viet.	18·05 N	106·45 E
68	Muir Woods Natl. Mon. (mūr) Calif.	37·54 N	123·22 W
166	Muizenberg (mwĭz-ĕn-bûrg′) S. Afr. (Cape Town In.)	34·07 S	18·28 E
121	Mukachĕvo (mōō-kȧ-chyô′vô) Sov. Un.	48·25 N	22·43 E
	Mukden, see Shenyang		
135	Mukhtuya (mōōk-tōō′yȧ). Sov. Un.	61·00 N	113·00 E
65	Mukilteo (mū-kĭl-tā′ō) Wash. (Seattle In.)	47·57 N	122·18 W
153	Muko (R.) (mōō′kô) Jap. (Ōsaka In.)	34·52 N	135·17 E
75	Mukwonago (mū-kwō-nȧ′gō) Wis. (Milwaukee In.)	42·52 N	88·19 W
124	Mula (mōō′lä) . . . . Sp.	38·05 N	1·12 W
120	Mulde R. (mōōl′dĕ) . . . . Ger.	50·30 N	12·30 E
150	Muleng . . . . China	44·32 N	130·18 E
150	Muleng (R.) . . . . China	44·40 N	130·30 E
90	Muleros (mōō-lā′rōs) . . . . . . Mex.	23·44 N	104·00 W
84	Mulga (mŭl′gȧ) Ala. (Birmingham In.)	33·33 N	86·59 W
83	Mulgrave (mŭl′grāv) . . . . Can.	45·37 N	61·22 W
159	Mulgrave (I.) . . . . Austl.	10·08 S	142·14 E
124	Mulhacén (Mtn.) . . . . Sp.	37·04 N	3·18 W
123	Mülheim (mül′hīm) Ger. (Ruhr In.)	51·25 N	6·53 E
123	Mulhouse (mü-lōōz′) . . . . Fr.	47·46 N	7·20 E
116	Mull (I.) (mŭl) . . . . Scot.	56·40 N	6·19 W
66	Mullan (mŭl′ăn) . . . . Idaho	47·26 N	115·50 W
154	Müller Mts. (mül′ĕr) . . . . . . Indon.	0·22 N	113·05 E
116	Mullet Pen . . . . Ire.	54·15 N	10·12 W
116	Mullinger (mŭl-ĭn-gär) . . . . Ire.	53·31 N	7·26 W
79	Mullins (mŭl′ĭnz) . . . . S. C.	34·11 N	79·13 W
92	Mullins River Br. Hond. (Yucatan In.)	17·08 N	88·18 W
142	Multan (mōōl-tän′) . . . . . . W. Pak.	30·17 N	71·13 E
65	Multnomah Chan. (mŭl nō mȧ) Ore. (Portland In.)	45·41 N	122·53 W
154	Mulu, Gunung (Mtn.) . . . . . . Mala.	3·56 N	115·11 E
73	Mulvane (mŭl-vān′) . . . . Kans.	37·30 N	97·13 W
166	Mumbwa (mōōm′bwä) . . . . Zambia	14·58 S	27·06 E
92	Muna (mōō′nä) Mex. (Yucatan In.)	20·28 N	89·42 W
111	München (Munich) (mün′kĕn) Ger. (Munich In.)	48·08 N	11·35 E
80	Muncie (mŭn′sĭ) . . . . Ind.	40·10 N	85·30 W
75	Mundelein (mŭn-dê-lĭn′) Ill. (Chicago In.)	42·16 N	88·00 W
98	Mundonueva, Pico de (Pk.) (pē′kô-dĕ-mōō′n-dô-nwĕ′vä) Col. (In.)	4·18 N	74·12 W
91	Muneco, Cerro (Mtn.) (sĕ′r-rô-mōō-nĕ′kō) Mex. (Mexico City In.)	19·13 N	99·20 W
159	Mungana (mŭn-găn′ȧ) . . . . . Austl.	17·15 S	144·18 E
74	Munger (mŭn′gĕr) Minn. (Duluth In.)	46·48 N	92·20 W
160	Mungindi (mŭn-gĭn′dē) . . . . . Austl.	32·00 S	148·45 E
75	Munhall (mŭn′hôl) Pa. (Pittsburgh In.)	40·24 N	79·53 W
166	Munhanga (mōōn-häŋ′gȧ) . . . Ang.	12·15 S	18·55 E
	Munich, see München		
71	Munising (mū′nĭ-sĭng) . . . . . . Mich.	46·24 N	86·41 W
134	Munku Sardyk (Mtn.) (mōōn′kōō sär-dĭk′) Sov. Un.-Mong.	51·45 N	100·30 E
155	Muños (mōōn-nyōth′) Phil. (Manila In.)	15·44 N	120·53 E
123	Münster (mün′stĕr). Ger. (Ruhr In.)	51·57 N	7·38 E
75	Munster (mŭn′stĕr) Ind. (Chicago In.)	41·34 N	87·31 W
116	Munster (mŭn-stĕr) . . . . Ire.	52·30 N	9·24 W
154	Muntok (mōōn-tŏk′) . . . . Indon.	2·05 S	105·11 E
101	Munzi Freire (mōō-nē′z-frā′rĕ) Braz. (Rio de Janeiro In.)	20·29 S	41·25 W
154	Muong Sing (mōō′ông-sĭng′) . Laos	21·06 N	101·17 E
112	Muonio (R.) . . . . Fin.-Swe.	68·15 N	23·00 E
101	Muqui (mōō-kōōē) Braz. (Rio de Janeiro In.)	20·56 S	41·20 W
133	Muradiye (mōō-rä′dê-yĕ) . . . . Tur.	39·00 N	43·40 E
122	Murat (mü-rȧ′) . . . . Fr.	45·05 N	2·56 E
133	Murat (R.) (mōō-rät′) . . . . Tur.	38·50 N	40·40 E
158	Murchison (R.) (mûr′chĭ-sŭn) Austl.	26·45 S	116·15 E
165	Murchison Falls (mûr′chĭ-sŭn). Ug.	2·19 N	31·50 E
124	Murcia (mōōr′thyä) . . . . Sp.	38·00 N	1·10 W
124	Murcia (Reg.) . . . . Sp.	38·35 N	1·51 W
70	Murdo (mûr′dô) . . . . S. D.	43·53 N	100·42 W
82	Murdochville (mûr-dŏk′vĭl) . . Can.	48·56 N	65·37 W
121	Muresul R. (mōō′rĕsh-ōōl) . . Rom.	46·02 N	21·50 E
122	Muret (mü-rĕ′) . . . . Fr.	43·28 N	1·17 E
78	Murfreesboro (mûr′frēz-bŭr-ô) Tenn.	35·50 N	86·19 W
103	Murgab (R.) (mōōr-gäb′). Sov. Un.	37·07 N	62·32 E
101	Muriaé (mōō-ryä-ĕ′) Braz. (Rio de Janeiro In.)	21·10 S	42·21 W
101	Muriaé (R.) Braz. (Rio de Janeiro In.)	21·20 S	41·40 W
136	Murino (mōō′rĭ-nô) Sov. Un. (Leningrad In.)	60·03 N	30·28 E
120	Müritz See (L.) (mür′ĭts) . . . . Ger.	53·20 N	12·33 E
146	Murku Sardyk (Pk.) Sov. Un.-Mong.	51·56 N	100·21 E
132	Murmansk (mōōr-mänsk′). Sov. Un.	69·00 N	33·20 E
132	Murom (mōō′rôm) . . . . . . Sov. Un.	55·30 N	42·00 E
152	Muroran (mōō′rô-rän) . . . . Jap.	42·21 N	141·05 E
124	Muros (mōō′rōs) . . . . Sp.	42·48 N	9·00 W
153	Muroto-Zaki (Pt.) (mōō′rô-tō zä′kē). Jap.	33·14 N	134·12 E
74	Murphy (mûr′fĭ) Mo. (St. Louis In.)	38·29 N	90·29 W
78	Murphy . . . . N. C.	35·05 N	84·00 W
73	Murphysboro (mŭr′fĭz-bŭr-ô) . . Ill.	37·46 N	89·21 W
78	Murray (mŭr′ĭ) . . . . Ky.	36·39 N	88·17 W
74	Murray. Utah (Salt Lake City In.)	40·40 N	111·53 W
79	Murray (R.) (mŭr′ĭ) . . . . S. C.	34·07 N	81·18 W
160	Murray Bridge . . . . Austl.	35·10 S	139·35 E
159	Murray Reg. (mŭ′rē) . . . . Austl.	33·20 S	142·30 E
160	Murray R . . . . Austl.	34·12 S	141·20 E
120	Mur R. (mōōr) . . . . Aus.	47·10 N	14·08 E
160	Murrumbidgee (R.) (mŭr-ŭm-bĭd′jē). Austl.	34·30 S	145·20 E
142	Murshidabad (mōōr′shē-dä-bäd′) India	24·08 N	87·11 E
126	Murska Sobota (mōōr′skä sô′bô-tä). Yugo.	46·40 N	16·14 E
142	Murwāra . . . . India	23·54 N	80·23 E
160	Murwillumbah (mŭr-wĭl′lŭm-bŭ) Austl.	28·15 S	153·30 E
120	Mürz R. (mürts) . . . . Aus.	47·30 N	15·21 E
165	Murzūg . . . . Libya	26·00 N	14·09 E
120	Murzzuschlag (mürts′tsōō-shlägh) Aus.	47·37 N	15·41 E
133	Mus (mōōsh) . . . . Tur.	38·55 N	41·30 E
127	Musala (Mtn.) . . . . Bul.	42·05 N	23·24 E
152	Musan (mōō′sän) . . . . Kor.	41·11 N	129·10 E
153	Musashino (mōō-sä′shē-nō) Jap. (Tōkyō In.)	35·43 N	139·35 E
144	Muscat (mŭs-kăt′) . . . Mus. & Om.	23·23 N	58·30 E
144	Muscat & Oman . . . . Asia	18·50 N	56·45 E
71	Muscatine (mŭs-kȧ-tēn′) . . . . Iowa	41·26 N	91·00 W
78	Muscle Shoals (mŭs′′l shōlz) . . Ala.	34·44 N	87·38 W
158	Musgrave Ra. (mŭs′grāv) . . . Austl.	26·15 S	131·15 E
166	Mushie (mŭsh′ē) . . . . Con. K.	3·04 S	16·50 E
154	Musi, Air (Strm.) (mōō′sē). Indon.	2·40 S	103·42 E
98	Musinga, Alto (Ht.) (ä′l-tô-mōō-sē′n-gä). Col. (In.)	6·40 N	76·13 W
75	Muskego L. (mŭs-kē′gō) Wis. (Milwaukee In.)	42·53 N	88·10 W
80	Muskegon (mŭs-kē′gŭn) . . . . Mich.	43·15 N	86·20 W
80	Muskegon (R.) . . . . Mich.	43·20 N	85·55 W
80	Muskegon Heights . . . . Mich.	43·10 N	86·20 W
80	Muskingum (R.) (mŭs-kĭŋ′gŭm) Ohio	39·45 N	81·55 W
73	Muskogee (mŭs-kō′gē) . . . . . . Okla.	35·44 N	95·21 W
81	Muskoka (L.) (mŭs-kō′kȧ) . . . Can.	45·00 N	79·30 W
155	Mussau (I.) (mōō-sä′ōō) N. Gui. Ter.	1·30 S	149·32 E
116	Musselburgh (mŭs′′l-bŭr-ô) . . Scot.	55·55 N	3·08 W
67	Musselshell R. (mŭs′′l-shĕl) . Mont.	46·25 N	108·20 W
133	Mustafakemalpasa . . . . Tur.	40·05 N	28·30 E
77	Mustang Bay . . . . Tex. (In.)	29·22 N	95·12 W
72	Mustang Cr. (mŭs′tăng) . . . . . Tex.	36·22 N	102·46 W
77	Mustang I . . . . Tex.	27·43 N	97·00 W
93	Mustique I. (mŭs-tēk′) N. A. (Le. & Wind. Is. In.)	12·53 N	61·03 W
128	Mustvee (mōōst′vĕ-ĕ) . . . . Sov. Un.	58·50 N	26·54 E
147	Musu Dan (C.) (mōō′sōō dän). Kor.	40·51 N	130·00 E
152	Musu Dan (Pt.) (mōō′sōō dän) Sov. Un.	40·48 N	129·50 E
160	Muswellbrook (mŭs′wŭl-brŏŏk) Austl.	32·15 S	150·50 E
150	Mutan (R.) . . . . China	45·30 N	129·40 E
150	Mutanchiang . . . . China	44·28 N	129·38 E
166	Mutombo Mukulu (mōō-tôm′bō mōō-kōō′lōō) Con. K.	8·12 S	23·56 E
152	Mutsu Wan (B.) (mōōt′sōō wän) Jap.	41·20 N	140·55 E
83	Mutton B. (mŭt′′n) . . . . Can.	50·47 N	58·58 W
101	Mutum (mōō-tōō′m) Braz. (Rio de Janeiro In.)	19·48 S	41·24 W
134	Muyun-Kum, Peski (Des.) (mōō-yōōn′ kōōm′). Sov. Un.	44·30 N	70·00 E
142	Muzaffargarh . . . . W. Pak.	30·09 N	71·15 E
76	Muzquiz (mōōz′kēz) . . . . Mex.	27·53 N	101·31 W
166	Mwanza (mwän′zä) . . . . Tan.	2·31 S	32·52 E
167	Mwatate (mwä-tä′tä) . . . . Ken.	3·28 S	38·19 E
166	Mwaya (mwä′yä) . . . . Tan.	9·19 S	33·51 E
114	Mya R. (myä′) . . . . Alg.	29·26 N	3·15 E
146	Myingyan (myĭng-yŭn′) . . . . . Bur.	21·37 N	95·26 E
154	Myinmoletkat (Pk.) . . . . Bur.	13·58 N	98·34 E
146	Myitkyina (myĭ′chē-nȧ) . . . . . Bur.	25·33 N	97·25 E
121	Myjava (mûē′yȧ-vä) . . . . . . Czech.	48·45 N	17·33 E
142	Mymensingh (mī-mŭn-sĭng′) E. Pak.	24·48 N	90·28 E
152	Myohyang San (Mtn.) (myō′hyang). Kor.	40·00 N	126·12 E
112	Mýrdalsjökull (Gl.) (mür′dâls-yû′kōōl). Ice.	63·34 N	18·04 W
79	Myrtle Beach (mûr′t′l) . . . . . . S. C.	33·42 N	78·53 W
66	Myrtle Point . . . . Ore.	43·04 N	124·08 W
128	Myshkino (mēsh′kē-nô) . . Sov. Un.	57·48 N	38·21 E
143	Mysore (mī-sōr′) . . . . India	12·31 N	76·42 E
143	Mysore (State) . . . . India	20·15 N	75·32 E
119	Mysovka (mē′ sôf-kȧ) . . . Sov. Un.	55·11 N	21·17 E
71	Mystic (mĭs′tĭk) . . . . Iowa	40·47 N	92·54 W
136	Mytishchi (mê-tēsh′chĭ) Sov. Un. (Moscow In.)	55·55 N	37·46 E
166	Mzimba (′m-zĭm′bä) . . . . . . Malawi	11·41 S	33·39 E
120	Naab R. (näp) . . . . Ger.	49·38 N	12·15 E
111	Naaldwijk. Neth. (Amsterdam In.)	52·00 N	4·11 E
164	Naama (nä′ä-mä) . . . . Lib.	7·18 N	9·31 W
119	Naantali (nän′tȧ-lē) . . . . Fin.	60·29 N	22·03 E
158	Nabberu (L.) (năb′ĕr-ōō) . . . Austl.	26·05 S	120·35 E
164	Nabeul (nā-bûl′) . . . . Tun.	36·34 N	10·45 E
168	Naboomspruit . . . . S. Afr. (Johannesburg & Pretoria In.)	24·32 S	28·43 E
139	Nābulus . . . . Jordan (Palestine In.)	32·13 N	35·16 E
167	Nacala (nä-kȧ′lä) . . . . Moz.	14·33 S	40·52 E
92	Nacaome (nä-kä-ō′mä) . . . . . Hond.	13·32 N	87·28 W
114	Naceur, Bou Mt . . . . Mor.	33·50 N	3·55 W
151	Na Cham (nä chäm′) . . . . Viet.	22·02 N	106·30 E
66	Naches R. (năch′ĕz) . . . . Wash.	46·51 N	121·03 W
120	Náchod (näk′ōt) . . . . Czech.	50·25 N	16·08 E
87	Nachvak . . . . Can.	59·08 N	63·57 W
68	Nacimiento (R.) (nȧ-sĭ-myĕn′tô) Calif.	35·50 N	121·00 W
77	Nacogdoches (năk′ô-dō′chĕz). Tex.	31·36 N	94·40 W
76	Nadadores (nä-dä-dō′räs) . . . . Mex.	27·04 N	101·36 W
142	Nadaid . . . . India	22·45 N	72·51 E
89	Nadir . . . . Vir. Is. (U. S. A.) (St. Thomas In.)	18·19 N	64·53 W
127	Nădlac . . . . Rom.	46·09 N	20·52 E
	Nad Nisou, see Jablonec		
	Nad Vahom, see Nové Mesto		
121	Nadvornaya (nád-vôr′ná-yȧ) Sov. Un.	48·37 N	24·35 E
134	Nadym (R.) (nȧ′dĭm) . . . . Sov. Un.	64·30 N	72·48 E
118	Naestved (nĕst′vĭdh) . . . . Den.	55·14 N	11·46 E
168	Nafishah . . . . U. A. R.	30·34 N	32·15 E
155	Naga (nä′gä) . . . Phil. (Manila In.)	13·37 N	123·12 E
153	Naga (I.) . . . . Jap.	32·09 N	130·16 E
153	Nagahama (nä′gä-hä′mä) . . . . Jap.	33·32 N	132·29 E
153	Nagahama . . . . Jap.	35·23 N	136·16 E
146	Nagaland (State) . . . . India	25·47 N	94·15 E
153	Nagano (nä′gä-nô) . . . . Jap.	36·42 N	138·12 E
153	Nagaoka (nä′gȧ-ō′kȧ) . . . . Jap.	37·22 N	138·49 E
143	Nagappattinam . . . . India	10·48 N	79·51 E
92	Nagarote (nä-gä-rô′tē) . . . . . . Nic.	12·17 N	86·35 W
153	Nagasaki (nä′gä-sä′kē) . . . . . . Jap.	32·48 N	129·53 E
153	Nagasu (nä′gäs-ōō) . . . . Jap.	33·31 N	131·22 E
142	Nāgaur . . . . India	27·19 N	73·41 E
136	Nagaybakskiy (nä-gáy-bäk′skĭ) Sov. Un. (Urals In.)	53·33 N	59·33 E
155	Nagcarlan (näg-kär-län′) Phil. (Manila In.)	14·07 N	121·24 E
143	Nagercoil . . . . India	8·15 N	77·29 E
133	Nagornokarabakh (Reg.) (nu-gôr′nŭ-kŭ-rŭ-bäk′) Sov. Un.	40·10 N	46·50 E
153	Nagoya (nä′gō′yȧ) . . . . Jap.	35·09 N	136·53 E
142	Nāgpur (näg′pōōr) . . . . India	21·12 N	79·09 E
95	Nagua (nȧ′gwä) . . . . . . Dom. Rep.	19·20 N	69·40 W

ăt; finăl; rāte; senāte; ärm; ȧsk; sofȧ; fâre; ch-choose; dh-as th in other; bē; ēvent; bĕt; recĕnt; cratēr; g-go; gh-guttural g; bĭt; ĭ-short neutral; rīde; κ-guttural k as ch in German ich;

PRONOUNCING INDEX Naguilian–Negrais 241

Page	Name Pronunciation Region	Lat. °′	Long. °′
155	Naguilian (nä-gwē-lē'än) Phil. (Manila In.)	16·33 N	120·23 E
120	Nagykanizsa (nôd'y'kô'nē-shô) Hung.	46·27 N	17·00 E
121	Nagykörös (nôd'y'kŭ'rŭsh) Hung.	47·02 N	19·46 E
147	Naha (nä'hä) Ryūkyū Is.	26·02 N	127·43 E
83	Nahant (nȧ-hănt) Mass. (Boston In.)	42·26 N	70·55 W
139	Nahariya Isr. (Palestine In.)	33·01 N	35·06 E
133	Nahr al Khābur (R.) U. A. R.	35·50 N	41·00 E
125	Nahr-Ouassel (R.) (när-wä-sĕl') Alg.	35·30 N	1·55 E
100	Nahuel Huapi (L.) (nä'wĕl wä'pē) Arg.	41·00 S	71·30 W
92	Nahuizalco (nä-wē-zäl'kō) Sal.	13·50 N	89·43 W
155	Naic (nä'ēk) Phil. (Manila In.)	14·20 N	120·46 E
76	Naica (nä-ē'kä) Mex.	27·53 N	105·30 W
99	Naiguatá (nī-gwä-tä') Ven. (In.)	10·37 N	66·44 W
99	Naiguata, Pico (Mtn.) (pē'kô) Ven. (In.)	10·32 N	66·44 W
142	Naihāti India (Calcutta In.)	22·54 N	88·25 E
87	Nain (nīn) Can.	56·29 N	61·52 W
116	Nairn (nârn) Scot.	57·35 N	3·54 W
167	Nairobi (nī-rō'bē) Ken.	1·18 S	36·47 E
167	Naivasha (nī-vä'shȧ) Ken.	0·47 S	36·29 E
144	Najd (Des.) Sau. Ar.	25·18 N	42·38 E
168	Naj 'Ḥammādi (nág'hä-mä'dē) U. A. R. (Nile In.)	26·02 N	32·12 E
152	Najin (nä'jĭn) Kor.	42·04 N	136·06 E
144	Najran (Des.) (nŭj-rän') Sau. Ar.	17·29 N	45·30 E
152	Naju (nä'jōō) Kor.	35·02 N	126·42 E
94	Najusa (R.) (nä-hōō'sä) Cuba	21·55 N	77·55 W
150	Nakadorishima (I.) (nä'kä'dô'rē-shē'mä) Jap.	33·00 N	128·20 E
165	Nak'amet Eth.	9·09 N	36·29 E
153	Nakatsu (nä'käts-ōō) Jap.	33·34 N	131·10 E
133	Nakhichevan (nȧ-kē-chĕ-vän') Sov. Un.	39·10 N	45·30 E
135	Nakhodka (nŭ-kôt'kŭ) Sov. Un.	43·03 N	133·08 E
154	Nakhon Ratchasima Thai.	14·56 N	102·14 E
154	Nakhon Si Thammarat Thai.	8·27 N	99·58 E
87	Nakina Can.	50·10 N	86·40 W
118	Nakskov (näk'skou) Den.	54·51 N	11·06 E
121	Nakto nad Notecia (näk'wō näd nō-tĕ'chōn) Pol.	53·10 N	17·35 E
152	Naktong (R.) (näk'tŭng) Kor.	36·10 N	128·30 E
133	Nal'chik (nál-chēk') Sov. Un.	43·30 N	43·35 E
124	Nalón (R.) (nä-lōn') Sp.	43·15 N	5·38 W
164	Nālūt (nä-lōōt') Libya	31·51 N	10·49 E
144	Namak, Daryacheh-ye (L.) Iran	34·58 N	51·33 E
71	Namakan (L.) (nă'mȧ-kȧn) Minn.	48·20 N	92·43 W
166	Namakwaland (Reg.) (nă-mä'kwȧ'lănd) S. W. Afr.	25·30 S	16·30 E
144	Namakzār E Shahdād (L.) (nŭ-mŭk-zär') Iran	31·20 N	57·59 E
134	Namangan (nȧ-mán-gän') Sov. Un.	41·08 N	71·59 E
85	Namao Can. (Edmonton In.)	53·43 N	113·30 W
155	Namatanai (nä'mä-tȧ-nä'ē) N. Gui. Ter.	3·43 S	152·26 E
69	Nambe Pueblo Ind. Res. (näm'bâ pwĕb'lō) N. Mex.	35·52 N	105·39 W
160	Nambour (năm'bōōr) Austl.	26·48 S	153·00 E
154	Nam Dinh (näm dēnk') Viet.	20·30 N	106·10 E
74	Nameoki (nă'mē-ō-kē) Ill. (St. Louis In.)	38·44 N	90·07 W
152	Namhae (I.) (näm'hī') Kor.	34·23 N	128·05 E
166	Namib Des. (nä-mēb') S. W. Afr.	24·00 S	15·00 E
160	Namoi (R.) (năm'oi) Austl.	30·10 S	148·43 E
114	Namous, Oued en (R.) (nȧ-mōōs') Alg.	31·48 N	00·19 W
66	Nampa (năm'pȧ) Idaho	43·35 N	116·35 W
112	Namsos (näm'sôs) Nor.	64·28 N	11·14 E
142	Nam Tsho (L.) China	30·30 N	91·10 E
117	Namur (nȧ-mür') Bel.	50·29 N	4·55 E
166	Namutoni (nä-mōō-tō'nē) S. W. Afr.	18·45 S	17·00 E
154	Nan, Mae Nam (R.) Thai.	18·11 N	100·29 E
91	Nanacamilpa (nä-nä-kä-mē'l-pä) Mex. (Mexico City In.)	19·30 N	98·33 W
66	Nanaimo (nȧ-nī'mō) Can.	49·09 N	123·57 W
152	Nanam (nä'nän') Kor.	41·38 N	129·37 E
153	Nanao (nä'nä-ō) Jap.	37·03 N	136·59 E
151	Nanao Tao (I.) (nä'nä-ō dou) China	23·30 N	117·30 E
151	Nanch'ang (nän'chäng') China	28·38 N	115·48 E
151	Nancheng China	26·50 N	116·40 E
150	Nancheng China	33·02 N	107·00 E
148	Nanch'enghuang Tai (I.) (nan'chĕng'hōōäng'dou) China	38·22 N	120·54 E
148	Nanching (Nanking) (nän'jĭng) (nän'kĭng) China	32·04 N	118·46 E
151	Nanch'ung China	30·45 N	106·05 E
123	Nancy (nän-sē') Fr.	48·42 N	6·11 E
84	Nancy Cr. (năn'cē) Ga. (Atlanta In.)	33·51 N	84·25 W
142	Nanda Devi (Mt.) (năn'dä dā'vē) India	30·30 N	80·25 E
142	Nander India	19·13 N	77·21 E
142	Nandurbār India	21·29 N	74·13 E
142	Nandyal India	15·54 N	78·09 E
142	Nanga Parbat (Pk.) India	40·05 N	74·35 E
123	Nangis (nän-zhē') Fr. (Paris In.)	48·33 N	3·01 E
149	Nanhsiang China (Shanghai In.)	31·17 N	121·17 E
151	Nanhsiung China	25·10 N	114·20 E
149	Nanhui China (Shanghai In.)	31·03 N	121·45 E
148	Naniana China	35·14 N	116·24 E
151	Nani Dinh Viet.	20·25 N	106·08 E
148	Nani Hu (L.) (nän'yi' hōō) China	31·12 N	119·05 E
	Nanking, see Nanching		
148	Nankung (nän'kōōng') China	37·22 N	115·22 E
151	Nan Ling (Mtns.) China	25·15 N	111·40 E
148	Nanlo (nän'lō') China	36·03 N	115·13 E
158	Nannine (nă-nēn') Austl.	26·50 S	118·30 E
151	Nanning (nän'nĭng') China	22·56 N	108·10 E
151	Nanp'an (R.) China	24·50 N	105·30 E
151	Nanp'ing China	26·40 N	118·05 E
84	Nansemond (năn'sē-mŭnd) Va. (Norfolk In.)	36·46 N	76·32 W
84	Nansemond R. Va. (Norfolk In.)	36·50 N	76·34 W
146	Nan Shan (Mts.) (nän'shän') China	38·43 N	98·00 E
153	Nantai Zan (Mtn.) (nän-täē zän) Jap.	36·47 N	139·28 E
122	Nantes (nänt') Fr.	47·13 N	1·37 W
123	Nanteuil-le-Haudouin (nän-tû-lĕ-ō-dwăn') Fr. Paris In.)	49·08 N	2·49 E
81	Nanticoke (năn'tĭ-kōk) Pa.	41·10 N	76·00 W
81	Nantucket (I.) (năn-tŭk'ĕt) Mass.	41·15 N	70·05 W
148	Nantung (nän'tōōng') China	32·02 N	120·51 E
110	Nantwich (nănt'wĭch) Eng.	53·04 N	2·31 W
150	Nanyang China	33·00 N	112·42 E
150	Nanyüan China (Peking In.)	39·48 N	116·24 E
148	Nanyün (nän'yün') China	38·11 N	116·37 E
151	Nao Chou (I.) China	20·58 N	110·58 E
91	Naolinco (nä-ō-lēŋ'kō) Mex.	19·39 N	96·50 W
127	Náousa (nä'ōō-sȧ) Grc.	40·38 N	22·05 E
68	Napa (năp'ȧ) Calif.	38·20 N	122·17 W
81	Napanee (năp'ȧ-nē) Can.	44·15 N	77·00 W
75	Naperville (nā'pēr-vĭl) Ill. (Chicago In.)	41·46 N	88·09 W
159	Napier (nā'pĭ-ēr) N. Z. (In.)	39·30 S	177·00 E
85	Napierville (nā'pĭ-ēr-vĭl) Can. (Montreal In.)	45·11 N	73·24 W
79	Naples (nă'p'lz) Fla. (In.)	26·07 N	81·46 W
	Naples, see Napoli		
98	Napo (R.) (nä'pō) Peru	1·49 S	74·20 W
80	Napoleon (nȧ-pō'lē-ŭn) Ohio	41·20 N	84·10 W
77	Napoleonville (nȧ-pō'lē-ŭn-vĭl) La.	29·56 N	91·03 W
125	Napoli (Naples) (nä'pō-lē) It. (Naples In.)	40·37 N	14·12 E
125	Napoli, Golfo di (G.) (gôl-fô-dē) It. (Napoli In.)	40·29 N	14·08 E
80	Nappanee (năp'ȧ-nē) Ind.	41·30 N	86·00 W
153	Nara (nä'rä) Jap. (Osaka In.)	34·41 N	135·50 E
164	Nara Mali	15·09 N	7·27 W
153	Nara (Pref.) Jap. (Osaka In.)	34·36 N	135·49 E
128	Nara (R.) Sov. Un.	55·05 N	37·16 E
160	Naracoorte (nȧ-rȧ-kōōn'tē) Austl.	36·50 S	140·50 E
143	Naraspur India	16·32 N	81·43 E
84	Narberth (när'bûrth) Pa. (Philadelphia In.)	40·01 N	75·17 W
122	Narbonne (nár-bôn') Fr.	43·12 N	3·00 E
127	Nardò (när-dô') It.	40·11 N	18·02 E
98	Nare (nä'rē) Col. (In.)	6·12 N	74·37 W
121	Narew R. (nä'rĕf) Pol.	52·43 N	21·19 E
142	Narmada (R.) India	22·17 N	74·45 E
128	Naroch' (L.) (nä'rôch) Sov. Un.	54·51 N	27·00 E
132	Narodnaya, Gora (Mtn.) (nȧ-rôd'nȧ-yȧ) Sov. Un.	65·10 N	60·10 E
128	Naro Fominsk (nä'rô-fô-mēnsk') Sov. Un.	55·23 N	36·43 E
119	Närpesä (R.) Fin.	62·35 N	21·24 E
161	Narrabeen (năr-ȧ-bĭn) Austl. (Sydney In.)	33·44 S	151·18 E
160	Narrabri (nä-rä'brē) Austl.	30·17 S	149·46 E
84	Narragansett (năr-ȧ-găn'sĕt) R. I. (Providence In.)	41·26 N	71·27 W
81	Narragansett B. R. I.	41·20 N	71·15 W
160	Narrandera (nȧ-rȧn-dē'rȧ) Austl.	34·40 S	146·40 E
158	Narrogin (năr'ō-gĭn) Austl.	33·00 S	117·15 E
128	Narva (nàr'vȧ) Sov. Un.	59·24 N	28·12 E
155	Narvacan (när-vä-kän') Phil. (Manila In.)	17·27 N	120·29 E
128	Narva Jõesuu (nàr'vȧ ōō-ô-ă'sōō-ōō) Sov. Un.	59·26 N	28·02 E
112	Narvik (när'vēk) Nor.	68·21 N	17·18 E
119	Narvskiy Zaliv (B.) (nàr'vskĭ zä'lĭf) Sov. Un.	59·35 N	27·25 E
132	Nar'yan-Mar (när'yȧn mär') Sov. Un.	67·42 N	53·30 E
160	Naryilco (năr-ĭl'kō) Austl.	28·40 S	141·50 E
134	Narym (nä-rēm') Sov. Un.	58·47 N	82·05 E
145	Naryn (R.) (nŭ-rĭn') Sov. Un.	41·46 N	73·00 E
110	Naseby (nāz'bĭ) Eng.	52·23 N	0·59 W
74	Nashua (năsh'ŭ-ȧ) Mo. (Kansas City In.)	39·18 N	94·34 W
83	Nashua N. H. (Boston In.)	42·47 N	71·23 W
73	Nashville (năsh'vĭl) Ark.	33·56 N	93·50 W
78	Nashville Ga.	31·12 N	83·15 W
73	Nashville Ill.	38·21 N	89·42 W
80	Nashville Mich.	42·35 N	85·05 W
78	Nashville Tenn.	36·10 N	86·48 W
71	Nashwauk (năsh'wôk) Minn.	47·21 N	93·12 W
127	Našice (nä'shē-tsĕ) Yugo.	45·29 N	18·06 E
121	Nasielsk (nä'syĕlsk) Pol.	52·35 N	20·50 E
142	Nāsik (nä'sĭk) India	20·02 N	73·49 E
165	Nasir (nä-zēr') Sud.	8·30 N	33·06 E
142	Nasirabād India	26·13 N	74·48 E
87	Naskaupi (R.) (năs'kô-pĭ) Can.	53·59 N	61·10 W
94	Nassau (năs'ô) Ba. Is.	25·05 N	77·20 W
155	Nassau-Gebergte (Mts.) W. Irian	3·48 S	136·45 E
111	Nassenheide (nä'sĕn-hī-dĕ) Ger. (Berlin In.)	52·49 N	13·13 E
168	Nasser, L. U. A. R.	23·50 N	32·50 E
118	Nässjö (nĕs'shû) Swe.	57·39 N	14·39 E
155	Nasugbu (nȧ-sōōg-bōō') Phil. (Manila In.)	14·05 N	120·37 E
76	Nasworthy L. (năz'wûr-thē) Tex.	31·17 N	100·30 W
151	Nata China	19·30 N	109·38 E
93	Natá (nä-tä') Pan.	8·20 N	8·30 W
153	Natagaima (nä-tä-gī'mä) Col. (In.)	3·38 N	75·07 W
99	Natal (nä-täl') Braz.	6·00 S	35·13 W
166	Natal (Prov.) (nȧ-täl') S. Afr.	28·50 S	30·07 E
83	Natashquan (nä-tȧsh'kwän) Can.	50·09 N	61·46 W
87	Natashquan (R.) Can.	51·34 N	61·46 W
78	Natchez (năch'ĕz) Miss.	31·35 N	91·20 W
77	Natchitoches (năk'ĭ-tŏsh) (nȧch-ĭ-tŏsh') La.	31·46 N	93·06 W
139	Nathanya Isr. (Palestine In.)	32·19 N	34·52 E
83	Natick (nā'tĭk) Mass. (Boston In.)	42·17 N	71·21 W
135	National·Area (Reg.) Sov. Un.	66·30 N	170·30 E
67	National Bison Ra. (Mts.) (năsh'ŭn-ăl bī's'n) Mont.	47·18 N	113·58 W
68	National City Calif. (San Diego In.)	32·38 N	117·01 W
85	Nation R. (nā'shŭn) Can. (Ottawa In.)	45·21 N	75·07 W
99	Natividade (nä-tē-vē-dä'dĕ) Braz.	11·43 S	47·34 W
75	Natrona (nā'trō nä) Pa. (Pittsburgh In.)	40·38 N	79·43 W
166	Natron L. (nā'trŏn) Tan.	2·29 S	35·17 E
168	Natrum, Wadi el (Val.) U. A. R. (Nile In.)	30·33 N	30·12 E
154	Natuna, Pulau-Pulau (Is.) Indon.	3·22 N	108·00 E
69	Natural Bridges Natl. Mon. (năt'ū-răl brĭj'ĕs) Utah	37·20 N	110·20 W
158	Naturaliste, C. (năt-û-rȧ-lĭst') Austl.	33·30 S	115·10 E
91	Naucalpan (nä'ōō-käl-pä'n) Mex. (Mexico City In.)	19·28 N	99·14 W
91	Nauchampatepetl (Mtn.) (näōō-chäm-pä-tĕ'pĕtl) Mex.	19·32 N	97·09 W
82	Naudville Can.	48·36 N	71·40 W
111	Nauen (nou'ĕn) Ger. (Berlin In.)	52·36 N	12·53 E
81	Naugatuck (nô'gȧ-tŭk) Conn.	41·25 N	73·05 W
155	Naujan (nä-ōō-hän') Phil. (Manila In.)	13·19 N	121·17 E
120	Naumburg (noum'bōōrgh) Ger.	51·10 N	11·50 E
156	Nauru I. Oceania	0·30 S	167·00 E
91	Nautla (nä-ōōt'lä) Mex.	20·14 N	96·44 W
76	Nava (nä'vä) Mex.	28·25 N	100·44 W
124	Nava, L. de la Sp.	42·05 N	4·42 W
124	Nava del Rey (nä-vä dĕl rā'ē) Sp.	41·22 N	5·04 W
124	Navahermosa (nä-vä-ēr-mō'sä) Sp.	39·39 N	4·28 W
94	Navajas (nä-vä-häs') Cuba	22·40 N	81·20 W
69	Navajo Ind. Res. (năv'ȧ-hō) Ariz.-N. Mex.	36·31 N	109·24 W
69	Navajo Natl. Mon. Ariz.	36·43 N	110·39 W
69	Navajo Res. N. Mex.	36·57 N	107·26 W
125	Navalcarnero (nä-väl'kär-nä'rō) Sp. (Madrid In.)	40·17 N	4·05 W
124	Navalmoral de la Mata (nä-väl'mōräl' dā lä mä'tä) Sp.	39·53 N	5·32 W
85	Navan (nă'vȧn) Can. (Ottawa In.)	45·25 N	75·26 W
100	Navarino (nä-vä-rē'nō) (I.) Chile	55·30 S	68·15 W
124	Navarra (Reg.) (nä-vär'rä) Sp.	42·40 N	1·35 W
101	Navarro (nä-vä'r-rō) Arg. (Buenos Aires In.)	35·00 S	59·16 W
77	Navasota (năv-ȧ-sō'tȧ) Tex.	30·24 N	96·05 W
77	Navasota R. Tex.	31·03 N	96·11 W
95	Navassa (I.) (nȧ-văs'ȧ) N. A.	18·25 N	75·15 W
124	Navia (R.) (nä-vē'ä) Sp.	43·10 N	6·45 W
101	Navidad (nä-vē-dä'd) Chile (Santiago In.)	34·57 S	71·51 W
95	Navidad Bk. (nä-vē-dädh') Ba. Is.	20·05 N	69·00 W
101	Navidade do Carangola (nȧ-vē-dä'dĕ-dô-kȧ-rän-gô'la) Braz. (Rio de Janeiro In.)	21·04 S	41·58 W
88	Navojoa (nä-vô-kô'ä) Mex.	27·00 N	109 40 W
127	Návplion Grc.	37·33 N	22·46 E
142	Nawābshāh (nȧ-wäb'shä) W. Pak.	26·20 N	68·30 E
145	Nawagai (nŭ-wŭ-gī') W. Pak. (Khyber Pass In.)	34·40 N	71·18 E
127	Náxos (I.) (näk'sôs) Grc.	37·15 N	25·20 E
88	Nayarit (State) (nä-yä-rēt') Mex.	22·00 N	105·15 W
90	Nayarit, Sierra de (Mts.) (sē-ĕ'r-rä-dĕ) Mex.	23·20 N	105·07 W
84	Naylor (nā'lōr) Md. (Baltimore In.)	38·43 N	76·46 W
99	Nazaré (nä-zä-rĕ') Braz.	13·04 S	38·49 W
124	Nazaré (nä-zä-rā') Port.	39·38 N	9·04 W
99	Nazaré da Mata (dä-mä-tä) Braz.	7·46 S	35·13 W
139	Nazareth (năz'ȧ-rĕth) Isr. (Palestine In.)	32·43 N	35·19 E
76	Nazas (nä'zäs) Mex.	25·14 N	104·08 W
76	Nazas, R. Mex.	25·08 N	104·20 W
133	Nazilli (nä-zĭ-lē') Tur.	37·40 N	28·10 E
136	Naziya R. (nä-zē'yȧ) Sov. Un. (Leningrad In.)	59·48 N	31·18 E
165	Ndélé (n'dā-lā') Cen. Afr. Rep.	8·21 N	20·43 E
166	Ndjolé (n'dzhō-lā') Gabon	0·15 S	10·45 E
166	Ndola (n'dō'lä) Zambia	12·52 S	28·44 E
116	Neagh Lough (B.) (lŏk nā) N. Ire.	54·40 N	6·47 W
161	Neapean (R.) Austl. (Sydney In.)	33·40 S	150·39 E
127	Neápolis (nā-ŏp' ô-lĭs) Grc.	36·35 N	23·08 E
126	Neápolis Grc. (In.)	35·17 N	25·37 E
64	Near Is. (nēr) Alaska	52·20 N	172·40 E
116	Neath (nēth) Wales	51·41 N	3·50 W
160	Nebine Cr. (nĕ-bēne') Austl.	27·50 S	147·00 E
133	Nebit-Dag (nyĕ-bĕt'däg') Sov. Un.	39·30 N	54·20 E
62	Nebraska (State) (nē-brăs'kȧ) U. S.	41·45 N	101·30 W
73	Nebraska City Nebr.	40·40 N	95·50 W
77	Neches R. (nĕch'ĕz) Tex.	31·03 N	94·40 W
120	Neckar R. (nĕk'är) Ger.	49·16 N	9·06 E
100	Necochea (nā-kō-chā'ä) Arg.	38·30 S	58·45 W
129	Nedrigaylov (nĕ-drĭ-gī'lôf) Sov. Un.	50·49 N	33·52 E
83	Needham (nēd'ăm) Mass. (Boston In.)	42·17 N	71·14 W
68	Needles (nē'd'lz) Calif.	34·51 N	114·39 W
71	Neenah (nē'nȧ) Wis.	44·10 N	88·30 W
86	Neepawa Can.	50·17 N	99·31 W
72	Nee Res. (nē) Colo.	38·26 N	102·56 W
117	Neetze (R.) (nĕ'tzĕ) Ger.	53·04 N	11·00 E
153	Negareyama (nä'gä-rä-yä'mä) Jap. (Tōkyō In.)	35·52 N	139·54 E
71	Negaunee (nē-gô'nē) Mich.	46·30 N	87·37 W
139	Negev (Des.) (nĕ'gĕv) Isr. (Palestine In.)	30·34 N	34·43 E
127	Negoi (Mtn.) (nā-goi') Rom.	45·33 N	24·38 E
143	Negombo Ceylon	7·39 N	79·49 E
127	Negotin (nĕ'gô-tēn) Yugo.	44·13 N	22·33 E
154	Negrais, C. (nĕ'grīs) Bur.	16·08 N	93·34 E

ng-sing; ŋ-baŋk; N-nasalized n; nŏd; cŏmmit; ōld; ôbey; ôrder; fōōd; fŏŏt; ou-out; s-soft; sh-dish; th-thin; pūre; ûnite; ûrn; stŭd; circŭs; ü-as "y" in study; '-indeterminate vowel.

242 Negri Sembilan–Newton PRONOUNCING INDEX

Page	Name Pronunciation Region	Lat. °′	Long. °′
139	Negri Sembilan (State) (nā'grē sĕm-bē-län') Mala. (Singapore In.)	2·46 N	101·54 E
100	Negro (R.) Arg.	39·50 S	65·00 W
98	Negro, Rio (R.) (rē'ō nā'grōō) Braz.	0·18 S	63·21 W
124	Negro, C. (na'grô) Mor.	35·25 N	4·51 W
93	Negro, Cerro (Mt.) (sě'r-rô-nā'grô) Pan.	8·44 N	80·37 W
101	Negro (R.) Ur. (Buenos Aires In.)	33·17 S	58·18 W
92	Negro R. Nic.	13·01 N	87·10 W
154	Negros (I.) (nā'grōs) Phil.	9·50 N	121·45 E
98	Neguá (nā-gwá') Col. (In.)	5·51 N	76·36 W
66	Nehalem R. (nē-hăl'ĕm) Ore.	45·52 N	123·37 W
123	Neheim-Hüsten (ně'hīm) Ger. (Ruhr In.)	51·28 N	7·58 E
95	Neiba (nå-ē'bä) Dom. Rep.	18·30 N	71·20 W
95	Neiba, Bahai de (B.) (bå-ä'ē-dě) Dom. Rep.	18·10 N	71·00 W
95	Neiba, Sierra de (Mts.) (sē-ĕr'rä-dě) Dom. Rep.	18·40 N	71·40 W
151	Neichiang China	29·38 N	105·01 E
148	Neich'iu (nā'chĭō) China	37·17 N	114·32 E
67	Neihart (nī'hàrt) Mont.	46·54 N	110·39 W
150	Neihsiang China	33·00 N	111·54 E
71	Neillsville (nēlz'vĭl) Wis.	44·35 N	90·37 W
98	Neira (nā'rä) Col. (In.)	5·10 N	75·32 W
98	Neiva (nå-ē'vä) (nā'vä) Col. (In.)	2·55 N	75·16 W
71	Nekoosa (nē-kōō'sȧ) Wis.	44·19 N	89·54 W
118	Neksø (něk'sû) Den.	55·05 N	15·05 E
70	Neligh (nē'lĭg) Nebr.	42·06 N	98·02 W
135	Nel'kan (něl-kän') Sov. Un.	57·45 N	136·36 E
143	Nellore (něl-lōr') India	14·28 N	79·59 E
152	Nel'ma (něl-mä') Sov. Un.	47·34 N	139·05 E
86	Nelson (něl'sŭn) Can.	49·27 N	117·24 W
110	Nelson Eng.	53·50 N	2·13 W
159	Nelson N. Z. (In.)	41·15 S	173·22 E
64	Nelson (I.) Alaska	60·38 N	164·42 W
160	Nelson, C. Austl.	38·29 S	141·20 E
86	Nelson (R.) Can.	56·20 N	93·59 W
68	Nelson Cr. Nev.	40·22 N	114·43 W
80	Nelsonville (něl'sŭn-vĭl) Ohio	39·30 N	82·15 W
164	Néma (nā'mä) Mauritania	16·46 N	7·03 W
74	Nemadji R. (nĕ-măd'jē) Wis. (Duluth In.)	46·33 N	92·16 W
119	Neman (ŋĕ'-mån) Sov. Un.	55·02 N	22·01 E
121	Neman R. Sov. Un.	53·28 N	24·45 E
129	Nemirov (nyå-mē'rôf) Sov. Un.	48·56 N	28·51 E
122	Nemours Fr.	48·16 N	2·41 E
152	Nemuro (nā'mōō-rō) Jap.	43·13 N	145·10 E
152	Nemuro Str. Jap.	43·07 N	145·10 E
110	Nen (R.) (nĕn) Eng.	52·32 N	0·19 W
116	Nenagh (nē'nȧ) Ire.	52·50 N	8·05 W
64	Nenana (nå-nä'nȧ) Alaska	64·28 N	149·18 W
150	Nenchiang China	49·02 N	125·15 E
147	Nen Chiang (R.) China	47·07 N	123·28 E
148	Nengcheng China	33·15 N	116·34 E
136	Nenikyul' (nĕ-nyē'kyûl) Sov. Un. (Leningrad In.)	59·26 N	30·40 E
73	Neodesha (nē-ô-dĕ-shô') Kans.	37·24 N	95·41 W
73	Neosho Mo.	36·51 N	94·22 W
73	Neosho (R.) (nē-ō'shō) Kans.	38·21 N	95·53 W
138	Nepal (nĕ-pôl') Asia	28·45 N	83·00 E
69	Nephi (nē'fī) Utah	39·40 N	111·50 W
101	Nepomuceno (nĕ-pô-mōō-sĕ'no) Braz. (Rio de Janeiro In.)	21·15 S	45·13 W
126	Nera (R.) (nā'rä) It.	42·45 N	12·54 E
122	Nérac (nā-råk') Fr.	44·08 N	0·19 E
135	Nerchinsk (nyĕr' chĕnsk) Sov. Un.	51·47 N	116·17 E
135	Nerchinskiy Khrebet (Mts.) Sov. Un.	50·30 N	118·30 E
135	Nerchinskiy Zavod (nyĕr'chĕn-skĭzå-vôt') Sov. Un.	51·35 N	119·46 E
128	Nerekhta (nyĕ-rĕκ'tå) Sov. Un.	57·29 N	40·34 E
127	Neretva (R.) (nĕ'rĕt-vå) Yugo.	43·08 N	17·50 E
124	Nerja (nĕr'hä) Sp.	36·45 N	3·53 W
128	Nerl' (R.) (nyĕrl) Sov. Un.	56·59 N	37·57 E
136	Nerskaya R. (nyĕr'skå-yå) Sov. Un. (Moscow In.)	55·31 N	38·46 E
128	Nerussa (R.) (nyå-rōō'så) Sov. Un.	52·24 N	34·20 E
116	Ness, Loch (L.) (lŏκ nĕs) Scot.	57·23 N	4·20 W
72	Ness City (nĕs) Kans.	38·27 N	99·55 W
121	Nesterov (ŋĕs'-tzhyé-rôf) Sov. Un.	50·03 N	23·58 E
119	Nesterov (nyĕs-tă'rôf) Sov. Un.	54·39 N	22·38 E
127	Néstos (R.) (nās'tōs) Grc.	41·25 N	24·12 E
128	Nesvizh (nyĕs'vēsh) Sov. Un.	53·13 N	26·44 E
84	Netcong (nĕt'cŏnj) N. J. (New York In.)	40·54 N	74·42 W
102	Netherlands (nĕdh'ēr-lăndz) Eur.	53·01 N	3·57 E
	Netherlands Guiana, see Surinam		
71	Nett Lake Ind. Res. (nĕt lāk) Minn.	48·23 N	93·19 W
125	Nettuno (nĕt-tōō'nô) It. (Rome In.)	41·28 N	12·40 E
123	Neubeckum (noi'bĕ-kōōm) Ger. (Ruhr In.)	51·48 N	8·01 E
120	Neubrandenburg (noi-brän'dĕn-bōōrgh) Ger.	53·33 N	13·16 E
120	Neuburg (noi'bōōrgh) Ger.	48·43 N	11·12 E
120	Neuchâtel (nû-shå-tĕl') Switz.	47·00 N	6·52 E
120	Neuchatel, Lac de (L.) Switz.	46·48 N	6·53 E
111	Neuenhagen (noi'ĕn-hä-gĕn) Ger. (Berlin In.)	52·31 N	13·41 E
123	Neuenrade (noi'ĕn-rä-dĕ) Ger. (Ruhr In.)	51·17 N	7·47 E
122	Neufchâtel-en-Bray (nû-shä-tĕl'ĕɴ-brā') Fr.	49·43 N	1·25 E
120	Neuhaldensleben (noi-häl'dĕns-lā'bĕn) Ger.	52·18 N	11·23 E
111	Neuhaus (Oste) (noi' houz) (ōz'tĕ) Ger. (Hamburg In.)	53·48 N	9·02 E
111	Neulengbach Aus. (Vienna In.)	48·13 N	15·55 E
120	Neumarkt (noi'märkt) Ger.	49·17 N	11·30 E
120	Neumünster (noi'münstēr) Ger.	54·04 N	10·00 E
120	Neunkirchen (noin'kĭrκ-ĕn) Aus.	47·43 N	16·05 E
123	Neunkirchen Ger.	49·21 N	7·20 E
100	Neuquén (nĕ-ōō-kān') Arg.	38·52 S	68·12 W
100	Neuquen (Prov.) Arg.	39·40 S	70·45 W
100	Neuquén (R.) Arg.	38·45 S	69·00 W
111	Neuruppin (noi'rōō-pēn) Ger. (Berlin In.)	52·55 N	12·48 E
79	Neuse (R.) (nūz) N. C.	36·12 N	78·50 W
120	Neusiedler See (L.) (noi-zēd'lēr) Aus.	47·54 N	16·31 E
123	Neuss (nois) Ger. (Ruhr In.)	51·12 N	6·41 E
130	Neustadt (noi'shtät) Ger.	49·21 N	8·08 E
120	Neustadt Ger.	54·06 N	10·50 E
120	Neustadt bei Coburg (bī kō'bōōrgh) Ger.	50·20 N	11·09 E
120	Neustrelitz (noi-strā'lĭts) Ger.	53·21 N	13·05 E
120	Neu Ulm (noi ōō lm') Ger.	48·23 N	10·01 E
85	Neuville (nū'vĭl) Can. (Quebec In.)	46·39 N	71·35 W
120	Neuwied (noi'vēdt) Ger.	50·26 N	7·28 E
71	Nevada (nē-vä'dȧ) Iowa	42·01 N	93·27 W
73	Nevada Mo.	37·49 N	94·21 W
62	Nevada (State) U. S.	39·30 N	117·00 W
124	Nevada, Sierra (Mts.) (syĕr'rä nā-vä'dhä) Sp.	37·01 N	3·28 W
62	Nevada, Sierra (Mts.) (sē-ĕ'r-rä nē-vä'då) U. S.	39·20 N	120·25 W
68	Nevada City Calif.	39·16 N	120·01 W
98	Nevado, Cerro el (Mtn.) (sĕ'r-rô-ĕl-nĕ-vä'dô) Col. (In.)	4·02 N	74·08 W
90	Nevado de Colima (Mtn.) (nå-vä'dhô dā kô-lē'mä) Mex.	19·34 N	103·39 W
136	Neva R. (nyĕ-vä') Sov. Un. (Leningrad In.)	59·49 N	30·54 E
136	Neva Stantsiya (nyĕ-vä' stän'tsĭ-yå) Sov. Un. (Leningrad In.)	59·53 N	30·30 E
128	Nevel' (nyĕ'vĕl) Sov. Un.	56·03 N	29·57 E
99	Neveri (nĕ-vĕ-rē) (R.) Ven. (In.)	10·13 N	64·18 W
122	Nevers (nē-vâr') Fr.	46·59 N	3·10 E
127	Nevesinje (nĕ-vĕ'sēn-yĕ) Yugo.	43·15 N	18·08 E
116	Nevis, Ben (Mtn.) (bĕn) Scot.	56·47 N	5·00 W
93	Nevis I. (nē'vĭs) St. Kitts-Nevis-Anguilla (Le. & Wind. Is. In.)	17·05 N	62·38 W
93	Nevis Pk. Nevis (Le. & Wind. Is. In.)	17·11 N	62·33 W
127	Nevrokop (nĕv'rō-kôp') Bul.	41·35 N	23·46 E
133	Nevşehir (nĕv-shĕ'hēr) Tur.	38·40 N	34·35 E
136	Nev'yansk (nĕv-yänsk') Sov. Un. (Urals In.)	57·29 N	60·14 E
79	New (R.) (nū) Va.	37·20 N	80·35 W
79	New (R.), South Fork Va.-N. C.	36·37 N	81·15 W
75	New Albany (nû ôl'bȧ-nĭ) Ind. (Louisville In.)	38·17 N	85·49 W
78	New Albany Miss.	34·28 N	89·00 W
99	New Amsterdam (ăm'stēr-dăm) Guy.	6·14 N	57·30 W
65	Newark (nū'ērk) Calif. (San Francisco In.)	37·32 N	122·02 W
81	Newark (nōō'ärk) Del.	39·40 N	75·45 W
110	Newark (nū'ērk) Eng.	53·04 N	0·49 W
84	Newark (nōō'ûrk) N. J. (New York In.)	40·44 N	74·10 W
81	Newark (nū'ērk) N. Y.	43·05 N	77·10 W
80	Newark Ohio	40·05 N	82·25 W
75	New Augusta (ô-gŭs'tȧ) Ind. (Indianapolis In.)	39·53 N	86·14 W
80	Newaygo (nū'wā-go) Mich.	43·25 N	85·50 W
81	New Bedford (bĕd'fērd) Mass.	41·35 N	70·55 W
80	Newberg (nū'bûrg) Ore.	45·17 N	122·58 W
79	New Bern (bûrn) N. C.	35·05 N	77·05 W
78	Newbern Tenn.	36·05 N	89·12 W
71	Newberry (nū'bĕr-ĭ) Mich.	46·22 N	85·31 W
79	Newberry S. C.	34·15 N	81·40 W
75	New Bethel (bĕth'ĕl) Ind. (Indianapolis In.)	39·30 N	86·00 W
75	New Boston (bôs'tŭn) Mich. (Detroit In.)	42·10 N	83·24 W
80	New Boston Ohio	38·45 N	82·55 W
76	New Braunfels (nū broun'fĕls) Tex.	29·43 N	98·07 W
74	New Brighton (brī'tŭn) Minn. (Minneapolis, St. Paul In.)	45·04 N	93·12 W
75	New Brighton Pa. (Pittsburgh In.)	40·34 N	80·18 W
81	New Britain (brĭt''n) Conn.	41·40 N	72·45 W
155	New Britain (I.) N. Gui. Ter.	6·45 S	149·38 E
84	New Brunswick (brŭnz'wĭk) N. J. (New York In.)	40·29 N	74·27 W
87	New Brunswick (Prov.) Can.	47·14 N	66·30 W
80	Newburg Ind.	38·00 N	87·25 W
73	Newburg Mo.	37·54 N	91·53 W
81	Newburgh N. Y.	41·30 N	74·00 W
75	Newburgh Heights Ohio (Cleveland In.)	41·27 N	81·40 W
116	Newbury (nū'bēr-ĭ) Eng.	51·24 N	1·26 W
83	Newbury Mass. (Boston In.)	42·48 N	70·52 W
83	Newburyport (nū'bēr-ĭ-pōrt) Mass. (Boston In.)	42·48 N	70·53 W
159	New Caledonia (I.) Oceania	21·28 S	164·15 E
84	New Canaan (kā-nȧn) Conn. (New York In.)	41·06 N	73·30 W
82	New Carlisle (kär-līl') Can.	48·01 N	65·22 W
160	Newcastle (nū-kås''l) Austl.	33·00 S	151·55 E
82	Newcastle Can.	47·00 N	65·36 W
81	New Castle Del.	39·40 N	75·35 W
110	Newcastle (nû-kås''l) (nû-käs''l) Eng.	53·01 N	2·14 W
116	Newcastle Eng.	55·00 N	1·45 W
80	New Castle Ind.	39·55 N	85·25 W
80	New Castle Ohio	40·20 N	82·10 W
80	New Castle Pa.	41·00 N	80·25 W
72	Newcastle Tex.	33·13 N	98·44 W
70	Newcastle Wyo.	43·51 N	104·11 W
158	Newcastle Waters (wô'tērz) Austl.	17·10 S	133·25 E
80	Newcomerstown (nū'kŭm-ērz-toun) Ohio	40·15 N	81·40 W
84	New Croton Res. (krŏ'tôn) N. Y. (New York In.)	41·15 N	73·47 W
142	New Delhi (dĕl'hī) India	28·43 N	77·18 E
70	Newell (nū'ĕl) S. D.	44·43 N	103·26 W
159	New England Ra. (nû ĭŋ'glănd) Austl.	29·32 S	152·30 E
64	Newenham, C. (nū-ĕn-hăm) Alaska	58·40 N	162·32 W
75	Newfane (nū-fān) N. Y. (Buffalo In.)	43·17 N	78·44 W
87	Newfoundland (Prov.) (nû-fŭn'lănd') (nū'fŭnd-lănd) (nû'found-lănd') Can. (Newfoundland In.)	48·15 N	56·53 W
159	New Georgia (I.) (jôr'jĭ-ȧ) Sol. Is.	8.08 S	158·00 E
83	New Glasgow (glås'gō) Can.	45·36 N	62·40 W
155	New Guinea, Territory of Oceania	3·45 S	145·45 E
155	New Guinea (I.) (gĭne) N. Gui. Ter.	5·45 S	140·00 E
66	Newhalem (nū hā'lŭm) Wash.	48·44 N	121·11 W
63	New Hampshire (State) (hămp'shĭr) U. S.	43·55 N	71·40 W
71	New Hampton (hămp'tŭn) Iowa	43·03 N	92·20 W
167	New Hanover (hăn'ôvēr) S. Afr. (Natal In.)	29·23 S	30·32 E
155	New Hanover (I.) N. Gui. Ter.	2·37 S	150·15 E
80	New Harmony (nū här'mô-nĭ) Ind.	38·10 N	87·55 W
81	New Haven (hā'vĕn) Conn.	41·20 N	72·55 W
117	Newhaven Eng.	50·45 N	0·10 E
80	New Haven (nū hāv''n) Ind.	41·05 N	85·00 W
159	New Hebrides (Is.) (hĕb'rĭ-dēz) Oceania	16·02 S	169·15 E
110	New Holland (hŏl'ănd) Eng.	53·42 N	0·21 W
79	New Holland N. C.	35·27 N	76·14 W
84	New Hope Mtn. (hōp) Ala. (Birmingham In.)	33·23 N	86·45 W
75	New Hudson (hŭd'sŭn) Mich. (Detroit In.)	42·30 N	83·36 W
77	New Iberia (ī-bē'rĭ-ȧ) La.	30·00 N	91·50 W
85	Newington (nū'ĕŋg-tŏn) Can. (Ottawa In.)	45·07 N	75·00 W
155	New Ireland (I.) (īr'lănd) N. Gui. Ter.	3·15 S	152·30 E
63	New Jersey (State) (jûr'zĭ) U. S.	40·30 N	74·50 W
75	New Kensington (kĕn'zĭng-tŭn) Pa. (Pittsburgh In.)	40·34 N	79·35 W
73	Newkirk (nū'kûrk) Okla.	36·52 N	97·03 W
166	Newlands (nû'lănds) S. Afr. (Cape Town In.)	33·58 S	18·28 E
75	New Lenox (lĕn'ŭk) Ill. (Chicago In.)	41·31 N	87·58 W
80	New Lexington (lĕk'sĭng-tŭn) Ohio	39·40 N	82·10 W
71	New Lisbon (lĭz'bŭn) Wis.	43·52 N	90·11 W
81	New London (lŭn'dŭn) Conn.	41·20 N	72·05 W
71	New London Wis.	44·24 N	88·45 W
73	New Madrid (măd'rĭd) Mo.	36·34 N	89·31 W
79	Newman (L.) Fla.	29·41 N	82·13 W
70	Newman's Grove (nū'măn grōv) Nebr.	41·46 N	97·44 W
81	Newmarket (nū'mär-kĕt) Can.	44·00 N	79·30 W
80	New Martinsville (mär'tĭnz-vĭl) W. Va.	39·35 N	80·50 W
62	New Mexico (State) (mĕk'sĭ-kō) U. S.	34·30 N	107·10 W
110	New Mills (mĭlz) Eng.	53·22 N	2·00 W
75	New Munster (mŭn'stēr) Wis. (Milwaukee In.)	42·35 N	88·13 W
78	Newnan (nū'năn) Ga.	33·22 N	84·47 W
160	New Norfolk (nôr'fŏk) Austl.	42·50 S	147·17 E
84	New Orleans (ôr'lē-ănz) La. (New Orleans In.)	30·00 N	90·05 W
80	New Philadelphia (fĭl-ȧ-dĕl'fĭ-ȧ) Ohio	40·30 N	81·30 W
159	New Plymouth (plĭm'ŭth) N. Z. (In.)	39·04 S	174·13 E
73	Newport (nū'pōrt) Ark.	35·35 N	91·16 W
161	Newport Austl. (Sydney In.)	33·39 S	151·19 E
116	Newport (nū-pôrt) Eng.	50·41 N	1·25 W
116	Newport Wales	51·36 N	3·05 W
110	Newport Eng.	52·46 N	2·22 W
75	Newport Ky. (Cincinnati In.)	39·05 N	84·30 W
82	Newport Maine	44·49 N	69·20 W
74	Newport Minn. (Minneapolis, St. Paul In.)	44·52 N	92·59 W
81	Newport N. H.	43·20 N	72·10 W
66	Newport Ore.	44·39 N	124·02 W
84	Newport R. I. (Providence In.)	41·29 N	71·16 W
78	Newport Tenn.	35·55 N	83·12 W
81	Newport Vt.	44·55 N	72·15 W
66	Newport Wash.	48·12 N	117·01 W
74	Newport Beach (bēch) Calif. (Los Angeles In.)	33·36 N	117·55 W
84	Newport News Va. (Norfolk In.)	36·59 N	76·24 W
71	New Prague (nū prāg) Minn.	44·33 N	93·35 W
94	New Providence (I.) (prŏv'ĭ-dĕns) Ba. Is.	25·00 N	77·25 W
80	New Richmond (rĭch'mŭnd) Ohio	38·55 N	84·15 W
71	New Richmond Wis.	45·07 N	92·34 W
77	New Roads (rōds) La.	30·42 N	91·26 W
84	New Rochelle (rû-shĕl') N. Y. (New York In.)	40·55 N	73·47 W
70	New Rockford (rŏk'fōrd) N. D.	47·40 N	99·08 W
116	New Ross (rôs) Ire.	52·25 N	6·55 W
85	New Sarepta Can. (Edmonton In.)	53·17 N	113·09 W
149	New Shanghai China (Shanghai In.)	31·18 N	121·31 E
	New Siberian Is., see Novosibirskiye O-va		
79	New Smyrna Beach (smûr'nȧ) Fla.	29·00 N	80·57 W
159	New South Wales (State) (wālz) Austl.	32·45 S	146·14 E
110	Newton (nû'tŭn) Eng.	53·27 N	2·37 W
80	Newton Ill.	39·00 N	88·10 W
71	Newton Iowa	41·42 N	93·04 W
73	Newton Kans.	38·03 N	97·22 W
83	Newton Mass. (Boston In.)	42·21 N	71·13 W

ăt; finăl; rāte; senåte; ärm; åsk: sofȧ; fâre; ch-choose; dh-as th in other; bē; ēvent; bĕt; recĕnt; cratēr; g-go; gh-guttural g; bĭt; ĭ-short neutral; rīde; κ-guttural k as ch in German ich;

Page	Name Pronunciation Region	Lat. °′	Long. °′
78	Newton Miss.	32·18 N	89·10 W
84	Newton N. J. (New York In.)	41·03 N	74·45 W
79	Newton N. C.	35·40 N	81·19 W
77	Newton Tex.	30·47 N	93·45 W
85	Newton Brook (brŏŏk) Can. (Toronto In.)	43·48 N	79·25 W
85	Newton Siding (sīd'ĭng) Can. (Winnipeg In.)	49·56 N	98·04 W
75	Newtonsville (nū'tŭnz-vĭl) Ohio (Cincinnati In.)	39·11 N	84·04 W
85	New Toronto (tō-rŏn'tō) Can. (Toronto In.)	43·37 N	79·30 W
70	Newtown (nū'toun) N. D.	47·57 N	102·25 W
75	Newtown Ohio (Cincinnati In.)	39·08 N	84·22 W
84	Newtown Pa. (Philadelphia In.)	40·13 N	74·56 W
116	Newtownards (nu-t'n-ardz') Ire.	54·35 N	5·39 W
71	New Ulm (ŭlm) Minn.	44·18 N	94·27 W
83	New Waterford (wô'tēr-fērd) Can.	46·14 N	60·04 W
65	New Westminster (wĕst'mĭn-stēr) Can. (Vancouver In.)	49·12 N	122·55 W
84	New York (yôrk) N. Y. (New York In.)	40·40 N	73·58 W
63	New York (State) U. S.	42·45 N	78·05 W
159	New Zealand (zē'lănd) Oceania	39·14 S	169·30 E
90	Nexapa (R.) (nĕks-ä'pä) Mex.	18·32 N	98·29 W
153	Neya-gawa (nā'yä gä'wä) Jap. (Ōsaka In.)	34·47 N	135·38 E
144	Neyshābūr Iran	36·06 N	58·45 E
136	Neyva R. (nēy'vȧ) Sov. Un. (Urals In.)	57·39 N	60·37 E
129	Nezhin (nyĕzh'ēn) Sov. Un.	51·03 N	31·52 E
66	Nez Perce (nĕz' pûrs') Idaho	46·16 N	116·15 W
166	Ngami (R.) (n'gä'mē) Bots.	20·56 S	22·31 E
142	Nganglaring Tsho (L.) China	31·42 N	82·53 E
165	Ngaoundéré (n'gôn-dâ-rā') Cam.	7·19 N	13·30 E
167	Ngong ('n-gông) Ken.	1·27 S	36·39 E
167	Ngqeleni ('ng-kĕ-lā'nē) S. Afr. (Natal In.)	31·41 S	29·04 E
165	Nguigmi ('n-gēg'mē) Niger	14·14 N	13·04 E
164	Nguru ('n-gōō'rōō) Nig.	12·53 N	10·26 E
154	Nha Trang (nyä-träng') Viet.	12·08 N	108·56 E
164	Naifounke Mali	16·03 N	4·17 W
71	Niagara (nī-ăg'ȧ-rȧ) Wis.	45·45 N	88·05 W
75	Niagara Falls Can. (Buffalo In.)	43·05 N	79·05 W
75	Niagara Falls N. Y. (Buffalo In.)	43·06 N	79·02 W
85	Niagara-on-the-Lake Can. (Toronto In.)	43·16 N	79·05 W
75	Niagara R. U. S.-Can. (Buffalo In.)	43·12 N	79·03 W
164	Niamey (nē-ä-mā') Niger	13·33 N	2·08 E
165	Niangara (nē-äŋ-gä'rä) Con. K.	3·36 N	28·00 E
73	Niangua (R.) (nī-ăŋ'gwȧ) Mo.	37·45 N	92·56 W
154	Nias (I.) (nē'äs') Indon.	0·58 N	97·43 E
118	Nibe (nē'bĕ) Den.	56·57 N	9·36 E
88	Nicaragua (nĭk-ȧ-rä'gwȧ) N. A.	12·45 N	86·15 W
92	Nicaragua, Lago de (L.) (lä'gô dĕ) Nic.	11·45 N	85·28 W
126	Nicastro (nê-käs'trō) It.	38·39 N	16·15 E
92	Nicchehabin, Punta (Pt.) (pōō'n-tä-nê-kĕ-chĕ-ä-bē'n) Mex. (Yucatan In.)	19·50 N	87·20 W
123	Nice (nēs) Fr.	43·42 N	7·21 E
149	Nich'engchen China (Shanghai In.)	30·54 N	121·48 E
87	Nichicun (L.) (nĭch'ĭ-kŭn) Can.	53·07 N	72·10 W
95	Nicholas Chan. (nĭk'ô-lȧs) Ba. Is.	23·30 N	80·20 W
80	Nicholasville (nĭk'ô-lȧs-vĭl) Ky.	37·55 N	84·35 W
154	Nicobar Is. (nĭk-ô-bär') India	8·28 N	94·04 E
65	Nicolai Mtn. (nē-cō lī') Ore. (Portland In.)	46·05 N	123·27 W
91	Nicolás Romero (nē-kô-lä's-rô-mĕ'rô) Mex. (Mexico City In.)	19·38 N	99·20 W
74	Nicolet, L. (nĭ'kō-lĕt) Mich. (Sault Ste. Marie In.)	46·22 N	84·14 W
94	Nicolls Town Ba. Is.	25·10 N	78·00 W
74	Nicols (nĭk'ĕls) Minn. (Minneapolis, St. Paul In.)	44·50 N	93·12 W
65	Nicomeki (R.) Can. (Vancouver In.)	49·04 N	122·47 W
115	Nicosia (nē-kô-sē'ȧ) Cyprus	35·10 N	33·22 E
92	Nicoya (nē-kō'yä) C. R.	10·08 N	85·27 W
92	Nicoya, Golfo de (G.) (gôl-fô-dĕ) C. R.	10·03 N	85·04 W
92	Nicoya, Pen. de C. R.	10·05 N	86·00 W
	Nidaros, see Trondheim		
121	Nidzica (nê-jĕt'sȧ) Pol.	53·21 N	20·30 E
120	Niedere Tauern (Mts.) Aus.	47·15 N	13·41 E
123	Niederkrüchten (nē'dĕr-krük-tĕn) Ger. (Ruhr In.)	51·12 N	6·14 E
111	Niederösterreich (Lower Austria) (State) Aus. (Vienna In.)	48·24 N	16·20 E
120	Niedersachsen (Lower Saxony) (State) (nē'dĕr-zäk-sĕn) Ger.	52·52 N	8·27 E
120	Nienburg (nē'ĕn-bŏŏrgh) Ger.	52·40 N	9·15 E
120	Niesse (R.) (nēs) Pol.	51·30 N	15·00 E
168	Nietverdiend S. Afr. (Johannesburg & Pretoria In.)	25·02 S	26·10 E
99	Nieuw Nickerie (nê-nē'kĕ-rē') Sur.	5·51 N	57·00 W
90	Nieves (nyā'vås) Mex.	24·00 N	102·57 W
133	Niğde (nĭg'dĕ) Tur.	37·55 N	34·40 E
168	Nigel (nī'jĕl) S. Afr. (Johannesburg & Pretoria In.)	26·26 S	28·27 E
163	Niger (nī'jēr) Afr.	18·02 N	8·30 E
164	Niger R. Afr.	8·22 N	6·11 E
163	Nigeria (nī-jē'rĭ-ȧ) Afr.	8·57 N	6·30 E
153	Nii (I.) (nē) Jap.	34·26 N	139·23 E
152	Niigata (nē'ē-gä'tä) Jap.	37·47 N	139·04 E
157	Niihau (nē'ē-hä'ōō) Hawaii (In.)	21·50 N	160·05 W
157	Niihau (I.) Hawaii (In.)	21·50 N	160·05 W
153	Niimi (nē'mē) Jap.	34·59 N	133·28 E
117	Nijmegen (nī'mä-gĕn) Neth.	51·50 N	5·52 E
153	Nikaidō (nē'ki-dō) Jap. (Osaka In.)	34·36 N	135·48 E
128	Nikitinka (nê-kĭ'tĭn-kȧ) Sov. Un.	55·33 N	33·19 E
153	Nikkō (nēk'kō) Jap.	36·44 N	139·35 E
129	Nikolayev (nē-kô-lä'yĕf) Sov. Un.	46·58 N	32·02 E
129	Nikolayev (Oblast) (ôb'lȧst) Sov. Un.	47·27 N	31·25 E
152	Nikolayevka Sov. Un.	48·37 N	134·49 E
136	Nikolayevka (nē-kô-lä'yĕf-kȧ) Sov. Un. (Leningrad In.)	59·29 N	29·48 E
133	Nikolayevskiy Sov. Un.	50·00 N	45·30 E
135	Nikolayevsk-na-Amure Sov. Un.	53·18 N	140·49 E
132	Nikol'sk (nê-kôlsk') Sov. Un.	59 30 N	45·40 E
136	Nikol'skoye (nê-kôl'skô-yĕ) Sov. Un. (Leningrad In.)	59·27 N	30·00 E
127	Nikopol (nē'kô-pŏl') Bul.	43·41 N	24·52 E
129	Nikopol' Sov. Un.	47·36 N	34·24 E
127	Nikšić (nēk'shēch) Yugo.	42·45 N	18·57 E
101	Nilahue (R.) (nē-lä'wĕ) Chile (Santiago In.)	36·36 S	71·50 W
163	Nile (R.) (nīl) Afr.	23·00 N	33·00 E
80	Niles (nīlz) Mich.	41·50 N	86·15 W
80	Niles Ohio	41·15 N	80·45 W
143	Nilgiri Hills India	17·05 N	76·22 E
100	Nilópolis (nē-lô'pō-lēs) Braz. (In.)	22·48 S	43·25 W
142	Nimach India	24·32 N	74·51 E
164	Nimba, Mt. (nĭm'bȧ) Ivory Coast	7·40 N	8·33 W
122	Nîmes (nēm) Fr.	43·49 N	4·22 E
73	Nimrod Res. (nĭm'rŏd) Ark.	34·58 N	93·46 W
165	Nimule (nê-mōō'lā) Sud.	3·38 N	32·12 E
160	Ninety Mile Bch. Austl.	38·20 S	147·30 E
133	Nineveh (Ruins) (nĭn'ê-vȧ) Iraq	36·30 N	43·10 E
150	Ningan (nĭng'gän') China	44·20 N	129·20 E
148	Ningchin (nĭng'jĭn) China	37·39 N	116·47 E
148	Ningching (nĭng'jĭn) China	37·37 N	114·55 E
146	Ningerh China	23·14 N	101·14 E
151	Ninghai (nĭng'hī') China	29·20 N	121·20 E
148	Ningho (nĭng'hō') China	39·27 N	117·44 E
	Ninghsia, see Yinch'uan		
146	Ninghsia Hui Aut. Reg. China	37·45 N	106·30 E
151	Ningming China	22·22 N	107·06 E
151	Ningpo (nĭng-pō') China	29·56 N	121·30 E
151	Ningte China	26·38 N	119·33 E
150	Ningwu (nĭng'wōō') China	39·00 N	112·12 E
148	Ningyang (nĭng'yäng') China	35·46 N	116·48 E
151	Ninh Binh (nēn bĕnk') Viet.	20·22 N	106·00 E
155	Ninigo Is. N. Gui. Ter.	1·15 S	143·30 E
72	Ninnescah (R.) (nĭn'ĕs-kä) Kans.	37·37 N	98·31 W
99	Nioaque (nēô-ä'-kĕ) Braz.	21·14 S	55·41 W
70	Niobrara (R.) (nī-ô-brâr'ȧ) Nebr.	42·46 N	98·46 W
164	Nioro (nê-ō'rō) Mali	15·16 N	9·22 W
122	Niort (nê-ôr') Fr.	46·17 N	0·28 W
86	Nipawin Can.	53·24 N	103·52 W
95	Nipe, Bahía de (B.) (bä-ē'ä-dĕ-nē'pā) Cuba	20·50 N	75·30 W
95	Nipe, Sierra de (Mts.) (sē-ĕ'r-rä-dĕ) Cuba	20·20 N	75·50 W
87	Nipigon (nĭp'ĭ-gŏn) Can.	48·58 N	88·17 W
87	Nipigon (L.) Can.	49·37 N	89·55 W
71	Nipigon B. Can.	48·56 N	88·00 W
82	Nipisiguit (R.) (nĭ-pĭ'sĭ-kwĭt) Can.	47·26 N	66·15 W
87	Nipissing (L.) (nĭp'ĭ-sĭng) Can.	45·59 N	80·19 W
94	Niquero (nē-kā'rō) Cuba	20·00 N	77·35 W
142	Nirmāli India	26·30 N	86·43 E
127	Niš (nēsh) Yugo.	43·18 N	21·55 E
124	Nisa (nē'sȧ) Port.	39·32 N	7·41 W
127	Nišava (R.) (nē'shȧ-vȧ) Yugo.	43·17 N	22·17 E
153	Nishino (I.) (nēsh'ê-nō) Jap.	36·06 N	132·49 E
153	Nishinomiya (nēsh'ê-nô-mē'yȧ) Jap. (Osaka In.)	34·44 N	135·21 E
153	Nishinoomote (nēsh'ê-nô-ô-mō'tō) Jap.	30·44 N	130·59 E
153	Nishio (nēsh'ê-ô) Jap.	34·50 N	137·01 E
121	Nisko (nēs'kô) Pol.	50·30 N	22·07 E
85	Nisku (nĭs-kū') Can. (Edmonton In.)	53·21 N	113·33 W
66	Nisqually R. (nĭs-kwôl'ĭ) Wash.	46·51 N	122·33 W
118	Nissan (R.) Swe.	57·06 N	13·22 E
118	Nisser Vand (L.) (nĭs'ĕr vän) Nor.	59·14 N	8·35 E
118	Nissum Fd. Den.	56·24 N	7·35 E
100	Niterói (nē-tĕ-rô'ĭ) Braz. (In.)	22·53 S	43·07 W
116	Nith (R.) (nĭth) Scot.	55·13 N	3·55 W
121	Nitra (nē'trȧ) Czech.	48·18 N	18·04 E
121	Nitra R. Czech.	48·13 N	18·14 E
80	Nitro (nī'trô) W. Va.	38·25 N	81·50 W
156	Niue (I.) (nĭ'ōō) Oceania	19·50 S	167·00 W
117	Nivelles (nē'vĕl') Bel.	50·33 N	4·17 E
122	Nivernais, Côtes de (hills) (nē-vĕr-nĕ') Fr.	47·40 N	3·09 E
77	Nixon (nĭk'sŭn) Tex.	29·16 N	97·48 W
135	Nizhne-Angarsk (nyēzh'nyĭ-ŭngärsk') Sov. Un.	55·49 N	108·46 E
133	Nizhne-Chirskaya (nyĭ-ŭn-gärsk') Sov. Un.	48·20 N	42·50 E
135	Nizhne-Kolymsk (kô-lêmsk') Sov. Un.	68·32 N	160·56 E
134	Nizhneudinsk (nêzh'nyĭ-ōōdēnsk') Sov. Un.	54·58 N	99·15 E
136	Nizhniye Sergi (nyēzh'[nyē] sĕr'gē) Sov. Un. (Urals In.)	56·41 N	59·19 E
129	Nizhniye Serogozy (nyēzh'nyĭ sĕ-rô-gô'zĭ) Sov. Un.	46·51 N	34·25 E
136	Nizhniy Tagil (tŭgēl') Sov. Un. (Urals In.)	57·54 N	59·59 E
136	Nizhnyaya Kur'ya (nyĕ'zhnyȧ-yȧ koor'yȧ) Sov. Un. (Urals In.)	58·01 N	56·00 E
136	Nizhnyaya Salda (nyĕ'zh[nya'ya] säl'da') Sov. Un. (Urals In.)	58·05 N	60·43 E
134	Nizhnyaya Taymyra (R.) Sov. Un.	72·30 N	95·18 E
134	Nizhnyaya (Lower) Tunguska (R.) (tōōn-gōōs'kȧ) Sov. Un.	64·13 N	91·30 E
136	Nizhnyaya Tura (tōō'rȧ) Sov. Un. (Urals In.)	58·38 N	59·50 E
136	Nizhnyaya Us'va (ōōs'vȧ) Sov. Un. (Urals In.)	59·05 N	58·53 E
118	Njurunda (nyōō-rōōn'dȧ) Swe.	62·15 N	17·24 E
167	Nkandla ('n-känd'lä) S. Afr. (Natal In.)	28·40 S	31·06 E
142	Noākhāli E. Pak.	22·52 N	91·08 E
64	Noatak (nô-ȧ'tăk) Alaska	67·22 N	163·28 W
64	Noatak (R.) Alaska	67·58 N	162·15 W
153	Nobeoka (nō-bå-ō'kȧ) Jap.	32·36 N	131·41 E
80	Noblesville (nō'bl'z-vĭl) Ind.	40·00 N	86·00 W
85	Nobleton (nō'bl'tŭn) Can. (Toronto In.)	43·54 N	79·39 W
125	Nocero Inferiore (nô-chĕ'rô-ēn-fĕ-ryô'rĕ) It. (Naples In.)	40·30 N	14·38 E
90	Nochistlán (nô-chēs-tlän') Mex.	21·23 N	102·52 W
91	Nochixtlan (Asunción) (ä-sōōn-syōn') Mex.	17·28 N	97·12 W
155	Noemfoor (I.) (nōōm'fōr) W. Irian	1·20 S	134·48 E
69	Nogales (nô-gä'lĕs) Ariz.	31·20 N	110·55 W
91	Nogales (nô-gä'lĕs) Mex.	18·49 N	97·09 W
88	Nogales Mex.	31·15 N	111·00 W
168	Nogal Val. (nō'găl) Som. (Horn of Afr. In.)	8·30 N	47·50 E
129	Nogaysk (nô-gīsk') Sov. Un.	46·43 N	36·21 E
123	Nogent-le-Roi (nô-zhŏn-lĕ-rwä') Fr. (Paris In.)	48·39 N	1·32 E
122	Nogent-le-Rotrou (rō-trōō') Fr.	48·22 N	0·47 E
136	Noginsk (nô-gēnsk') Sov. Un. (Moscow In.)	55·52 N	38·28 E
124	Nogueira (nô-gā'rä) Sp.	42·25 N	7.43 W
125	Nogueira Pallaresa (R.) (nô-gĕ'y-rä-päl-yä-rĕ-sä) Sp.	42·18 N	1·03 E
150	Noho (nô'hô') China	48·23 N	124·58 E
122	Noires, Mts. (nwär) Fr.	48·07 N	3·42 W
122	Noirmoutier, Île de (I.) (nwär-mōō-tyā') Fr.	47·03 N	3·08 W
153	Nojimā-Zaki (Pt.) (nō'jē-mä zä-kē) Jap.	34·54 N	139·48 E
86	Nokomis (nô-kō'mĭs) Can.	51·30 N	104·58 W
80	Nokomis Ill.	39·15 N	89·10 W
125	Nola (nō'lä) It. (Naples In.)	40·41 N	14·32 E
79	Nolichucky (nŏl-ĭ-chŭck'ĭ) N. C.	39·59 N	82·20 W
132	Nolinsk (nô-lēnsk') Sov. Un.	57·32 N	49·50 E
153	Noma Misaki (C.) (nō'mä mē'sä-kē) Jap.	31·25 N	130·09 E
90	Nombre de Dios (nôm-brĕ-dĕ-dyô's) Mex.	23·50 N	104·14 W
93	Nombre de Dios (nô'm-brĕ) Pan.	9·34 N	79·28 W
64	Nome (nōm) Alaska	64·30 N	165·20 W
86	Nonacho (L.) Can.	61·48 N	111·20 W
166	Nongoma (nŏn-gō'mȧ) S. Afr.	27·48 S	31·45 E
65	Nooksack (nŏŏk'săk) Wash. (Vancouver In.)	48·55 N	122·19 W
65	Nooksack (R.) Wash. (Vancouver In.)	48·54 N	122·31 W
111	Noorden Neth. (Amsterdam In.)	52·09 N	4·49 E
111	Noordwijk aan Zee Neth. (Amsterdam In.)	52·14 N	4·25 E
111	Noordzee, Kanal, (Can.) Neth. (Amsterdam In.)	52·27 N	4·42 E
86	Nootka (I.) (nōōt'kȧ) Can.	49·38 N	127·38 W
166	Noqui (nô-kē') Ang.	5·50 S	13·35 E
152	Nor (R.) (nou') China	46·55 N	132·45 E
75	Nora (nō'rä) Ind. (Indianapolis In.)	39·54 N	86.08 W
118	Nora Swe.	59·32 N	14·56 E
84	Norbeck (nôr'bĕk) Md. (Baltimore In.)	39·06 N	77·05 W
73	Norborne (nôr'bôrn) Mo.	39·17 N	93·39 W
74	Norco (nôr'kô) Calif. (Los Angeles In.)	33·57 N	117·33 W
84	Norcross (nôr'krôs) Ga. (Atlanta In.)	33·56 N	84·13 W
85	Nord, Riviere du (rēv-yĕr' dü nōr) Can. (Montreal In.)	45·45 N	74·02 W
120	Norden (nôr'dĕn) Ger.	53·35 N	7·14 E
120	Norderney I. (nōr'dĕr-nĕy) Ger.	53·45 N	6·58 E
118	Nord Fd. (nôr'fyôr) Nor.	61·50 N	5·35 E
120	Nordhausen (nôrt'hau-zĕn) Ger.	51·30 N	10·48 E
120	Nordhorn (nôrt'hôrn) Ger.	52·26 N	7·05 E
112	Nord Kapp (C.) (nôr-kapp) Nor.	71·07 N	25·57 E
65	Nordland (nôrd'lȧnd) Wash. (Seattle In.)	48·03 N	122·41 W
120	Nördlingen (nûrt'lĭng-ĕn) Ger.	48·51 N	10·30 E
120	Nord-Ostsee (Kiel) Can. (nōrd-ōzt-zā) (kēl) Ger.	54·03 N	9·23 E
120	Nordrhein-Westfalen (North Rhine-Westphalia) (State) (nōrd'hīn-vĕst-fä-lĕn) Ger.	50·50 N	6.53 E
135	Nordvik (nôrd'vēk) Sov. Un.	73·57 N	111·15 E
116	Nore R. (nōr) Ire.	52·34 N	7·15 W
78	Norfield (nôr'fēld) Miss.	31·24 N	90·25 W
83	Norfolk (nôr'fŏk) Mass. (Boston In.)	42·07 N	71·19 W
70	Norfolk Nebr.	42·10 N	97·25 W
84	Norfolk Va. (Norfolk In.)	36·55 N	76·15 W
156	Norfolk (I.) Oceania	27·10 S	166·50 E
73	Norfork, L. Ark.	36·25 N	92·09 W
90	Noria (nō'rē-ȧ) Mex.	23·04 N	106·20 W
134	Noril'sk (nô rēlsk') Sov. Un.	69·00 N	87·11 E
80	Normal (nôr'mȧl) Ill.	40·35 N	89·00 W
73	Norman (nôr'mȧn) Okla.	35·13 N	97·25 W
79	Norman, L. N. C.	35·30 N	80·53 W
159	Norman (R.) Austl.	18·27 S	141·29 E
122	Normandie (Reg.) (nŏr-mäN-dē') Fr.	49·02 N	0·17 E
122	Normandie, Collines de (Hills) (kō-lēn'dĕ-nŏr-män-dē') Fr.	48·35 N	0·30 W
159	Normanton (nôr'mȧn-tŭn) Austl.	17·45 S	141·10 E
110	Normanton Eng.	53·40 N	1·21 W
75	Normantown (nôr'mȧn toun) Ill. (Chicago In.)	41·39 N	88·14 W
86	Norman Wells Can.	65·26 N	127·00 W
158	Nornalup (nôr-năl'ŭp) Austl.	35·00 S	117·00 E
118	Norra Dellen (L.) Swe.	61·57 N	16·25 E
118	Norre Sundby (nû-rĕ-sōōn'bü) Den.	57·04 N	9·55 E
78	Norris (nŏr'ĭs) Tenn.	36·09 N	84·05 W
78	Norris (R.) Tenn.	36·17 N	84·10 W
84	Norristown (nŏr'ĭs-town) Pa. (Philadelphia In.)	40·07 N	75·21 W
118	Norrköping (nôr'chûp'ĭng) Swe.	58·37 N	16·10 E
118	Norrtälje (nôr-tĕl'yĕ) Swe.	59·47 N	18·39 E

ng-sing; ŋ-baŋk; N-nasalized n; nŏd; cŏmmit; ōld; ôbey; ôrder; fōōd; fŏŏt; ou-out; s-soft; sh-dish; th-thin; pūre; ûnite; ûrn; stŭd; circŭs; ü-as "y" in study; '-indeterminate vowel.

Page	Name Pronunciation Region	Lat. °′	Long. °′
158	Norseman (nôrs'măn) . . . . . Austl.	32·15 S	122·00 E
101	Norte, Punta (Pt.) (pōō'n-tä-nŏr'tĕ) Arg. (Buenos Aires In.)	36·17 S	56·46 W
99	Norte, Serra do (Mts.) (sĕ'r-rä-dô-nôr'te) . Braz.	12·04 S	59·08 W
83	North, C. . . . . Can.	47·05 N	60·15 W
159	North, C. . . . . N. Z. (In.)	34·31 S	173·02 E
68	North, I. . . . Calif. (San Diego In.)	32·39 N	117·14 W
159	North, I. . . . . N. Z. (In.)	37·34 S	171·12 E
81	North Adams (ăd'ămz) . . . . . Mass.	42·40 N	73·05 W
158	Northam (nôr-dhăm) . . . . . Austl.	31·50 S	116·45 E
168	Northam (nôr'thăm) . . . . . S. Afr. (Johannesburg & Pretoria In.)	24·52 S	27·16 E
6	North America (á-mĕr'ĭ-ká)		
89	North American Basin (á-mĕr'ĭ-kăn) . Atl. O.	23·45 N	62·45 W
158	Northampton (nôr-thămp'tŭn) Austl.	28·22 S	114·45 E
116	Northampton (nôrth-ămp'tŭn) Eng.	52·14 N	0·56 W
81	Northampton . . . . Mass.	42·20 N	72·45 W
81	Northampton . . . . Pa.	40·45 N	75·30 W
110	Northampton (Co.) . . . . Eng.	52·25 N	0·47 W
154	North Andaman I. (ăn-dá-măn') Andaman Is.	13·15 N	93·30 E
83	North Andover (ăn'dô-vēr) Mass. (Boston In.)	42·42 N	71·07 W
65	North Arm (ärm) Can. (Vancouver In.)	49·13 N	123·01 W
84	North Atlanta (ăt-lăn'tá) Ga. (Atlanta In.)	33·52 N	84·20 W
84	North Attleboro (ăt''l-bŭr-ô) Mass. (Providence In.)	41·59 N	71·18 W
80	North Baltimore (bôl'tĭ-môr) . Ohio	41·10 N	83·40 W
76	North Basque (băsk) . . . . Tex.	31·56 N	98·01 W
86	North Battleford (băt''l-fērd) . Can.	52·52 N	108·22 W
87	North Bay . . . . Can.	46·13 N	79·26 W
66	North Bend (bĕnd) . . . . Ore.	43·23 N	124·13 W
82	North Berwick (bûr'wĭk) . . . Maine	43·18 N	70·46 W
94	North Bght. (bīt) . . . . Ba. Is.	24·30 N	77·40 W
94	North Bimini (I.) (bĭ'mĭ-nē) Ba. Is.	25·45 N	79·20 W
	North Borneo, see Sabah		
83	Northboro (nôrth'bûr-ô) Mass. (Boston In.)	42·19 N	71·39 W
83	Northbridge (nôrth'brĭj) Mass. (Boston In.)	42·09 N	71·39 W
95	North Caicos (I.) (kī'kōs) . Turks & Caicos	21·55 N	72·00 W
72	North Canadian R. (cá nā'dĭ-ăn) Okla.	36·22 N	99·17 W
63	North Carolina (State) (kăr-ô-lī'ná) . U. S.	35·40 N	81·30 W
94	North Cat Cay (I.) . . . . Ba. Is.	25·35 N	79·20 W
80	North Channel (B.) (chăn'ĕl) . Can.	46·10 N	83·20 W
116	North Chan. . . . . N. Ire.-Scot.	55·15 N	7·56 W
79	North Charleston (chärlz'tŭn) S. C.	32·49 N	79·57 W
75	North Chicago (shĭ-kô'gō) Ill. (Chicago In.)	42·19 N	87·51 W
75	North College Hill (kŏl'ĕj hĭl) Ohio (Cincinnati In.)	39·13 N	84·33 W
76	North Concho (kŏn'chō) . . . . . Tex.	31·40 N	100·48 W
85	North Cooking Lake (kŏŏk'ĭng lāk) Can. (Edmonton In.)	53·28 N	112·57 W
62	North Dakota (State) (dá-kō'tá) U. S.	47·20 N	101·55 W
116	North Downs (dounz) . . . . Eng.	51·11 N	0·01 W
64	Northeast C. (nôrth-ēst) . . . Alaska	63·15 N	169·04 W
146	Northeast Frontier Agency (State) India	27·35 N	92·56 E
95	Northeast Pt. . . . . Ba. Is.	21·25 N	73·00 W
95	Northeast Pt. . . . . Ba. Is.	22·45 N	73·50 W
94	Northeast Providence Chan. (prŏv'ĭ-dĕns) . Ba. Is.	25·45 N	77·00 W
120	Northeim (nôrt'hīm) . . . . Ger.	51·42 N	9·59 E
94	North Elbow Cays (Is.) . . . Ba. Is.	23·55 N	80·30 W
	Northern Dvina, see Severnaya Dvina		
102	Northern Ireland (īr'lănd) . . U. K.	54·56 N	8·58 W
	Northern Land (Is.), see Severnaya Zemlya		
71	Northern Light (L.) (nôr'thērn līt) . Can.	46·16 N	90·25 W
164	Northern Region (Div.) . . . . . Nig.	10·54 N	6·37 E
158	Northern Territory (State) . Austl.	18·15 S	133·00 E
71	Northfield (nôrth'fēld) . . . . . Minn.	44·28 N	93·11 W
82	Northfield . . . . Vt.	44·10 N	72·39 W
160	North Flinders, Ra. (flĭn'dērz) Austl.	31·55 S	138·45 E
117	North Foreland (fōr'lănd) . . . Eng.	51·20 N	1·30 E
76	North Franklin Mt. (frăŋ'klĭn) Tex.	31·55 N	106·30 W
118	North Frisian Is. . . . . Den.	55·16 N	8·15 E
88	North Gamboa (găm-bô'ă) C. Z. (Panama Canal In.)	9·07 N	79·40 W
85	North Gower (gŏw'ēr) Can. (Ottawa In.)	45·08 N	75·43 W
74	North Hollywood (hŏl'ē-wŏŏd) Calif. (Los Angeles In.)	34·10 N	118·23 W
80	North Judson (jŭd'sŭn) . . . . . . Ind.	41·15 N	86·50 W
74	North Kansas City (kăn'zás) Mo. (Kansas City In.)	39·08 N	94·34 W
73	North Little Rock (lĭt''l rŏk) . Ark.	34·46 N	92·13 W
70	North Loup (R.) (lōōp) . . . . Nebr.	42·05 N	100·10 W
80	North Manchester (măn'chĕs-tēr) Ind.	41·00 N	85·45 W
74	Northmoor (nôrth'mōōr) Mo. (Kansas City In.)	39·10 N	94·37 W
74	North Ogden (ŏg'dĕn) Utah (Salt Lake City In.)	41·18 N	111·58 W
74	North Ogden Pk. Utah (Salt Lake City In.)	41·23 N	111·59 W
75	North Olmsted (ōlm-stĕd) Ohio (Cleveland In.)	41·25 N	81·55 W
72	North Pease (R.) (pēz) . . . . . . Tex.	34·19 N	100·58 W
65	North Pender (I.) (pĕn'dēr) Can. (Vancouver In.)	48·48 N	123·16 W
65	North Plains (plānz) Ore. (Portland In.)	45·36 N	123·00 W
70	North Platte (plăt) . . . . Nebr.	41·08 N	100·45 W
62	North Platte, (R.) . . . . U. S.	41·20 N	102·40 W
80	North Pt. . . . . Mich.	45·00 N	83·20 W
93	North Pt. Barb. (Le. & Wind. Is. In.)	13·22 N	59·36 W
78	Northport (nôrth'pōrt) . . . . Ala.	33·12 N	87·35 W
84	Northport . . N. Y. (New York In.)	40·53 N	73·20 W
66	Northport . . . . Wash.	48·53 N	117·47 W
83	North Reading (rĕd'ĭng) Mass. (Boston In.)	42·34 N	71·04 W
	North Rhine-Westphalia, see Nordrhein-Westfalen		
74	Northridge (nôrth'ridj) Calif. (Los Angeles In.)	34·14 N	118·32 W
75	North Ridgeville (rĭj-vĭl) Ohio (Cleveland In.)	41·23 N	82·01 W
75	North Royalton (roi'ăl-tŭn) Ohio (Cleveland In.)	41·19 N	81·44 W
74	North St. Paul (sânt pôl') . . Minn. (Minneapolis, St. Paul In.)	45·01 N	92·59 W
74	North Salt Lake (sôlt lāk) Utah (Salt Lake City In.)	40·50 N	111·55 W
86	North Saskatchewan (R.) (săs-kăch'ē-wăn) . Can.	53·54 N	112·37 W
112	North Sea . . . . Eur.	56·09 N	3·16 E
71	North Skunk (R.) (skŭnk) . . . Iowa	41·39 N	92·46 W
83	North Sydney (sĭd'nē) . . . . Can.	46·14 N	60·28 W
159	North Taranaki Bght. (tä-rá-nä'kĭ bīt) . N. Z. (In.)	38·23 S	172·03 E
84	North Tarrytown (tăr'ĭ-toun) N. Y. (New York In.)	41·05 N	73·52 W
84	North Tiverton (tĭv'ēr-tŭn) R. I. (Providence In.)	41·40 N	71·08 W
75	North Tonawanda (tŏn-á-wŏn'dá) N. Y. (Buffalo In.)	43·02 N	78·53 W
69	North Truchas Pks. (Mts.) (trōō'chäs) . N. Mex.	35·58 N	105·37 W
116	North Uist (I.) (ū'ĭst) . . . . Scot.	56·99 N	6·56 W
82	Northumberland Str. (nôr thŭm'bēr-lănd) . Can.	46·25 N	64·20 W
81	Northumberland . . . . N. H.	44·30 N	71·30 W
159	Northumberland, Is. . . . . Austl.	21·42 S	151·30 E
66	North Umpqua R. (ŭmp'kwá) Ore.	43·20 N	122·50 W
65	North Vancouver (văn-kōō'vēr) Can. (Vancouver In.)	49·19 N	123·05 W
80	North Vernon (vûr'nŭn) . . . . . Ind.	39·05 N	85·45 W
75	Northville (nôrth-vĭl) Mich. (Detroit In.)	42·26 N	83·28 W
84	North Wales (wālz) Pa. (Philadelphia In.)	40·12 N	75·16 W
158	North West, C. (nôrth'wĕst) Austl.	21·50 S	112·25 E
79	Northwest Cape Fear, (R.) (cāp fēr) . N. C.	34·34 N	79·46 W
116	Northwest Highlands . . . . Scot.	56·50 N	5·20 W
94	Northwest Providence Chan. (prŏv'ĭ-dĕns) . Ba. Is.	26·15 N	78·45 W
86	Northwest Territories (tĕr'ĭ-tō'rĭs) . Can.	64·42 N	119·09 W
117	Northwich (nôrth'wĭch) . . . . . Eng.	53·15 N	2·31 W
79	North Wilkesboro (wĭlks'bûrô) N. C.	36·08 N	81·10 W
71	Northwood (nôrth'wŏŏd) . . . . Iowa	43·26 N	93·13 W
70	Northwood . . . . N. D.	47·44 N	97·36 W
67	North Wood Cr. . . . . Wyo.	44·02 N	107·37 W
65	North Yamhill (R.) (yăm' hĭl) Ore. (Portland In.)	45·22 N	123·21 W
116	North York Moors (yôrk mōōrz') Eng.	54·20 N	0·40 W
72	Norton (nôr'tŭn) . . . . Kans.	39·40 N	99·54 W
84	Norton . . . . Mass. (Providence In.)	41·58 N	71·08 W
79	Norton . . . . Va.	36·54 N	82·36 W
64	Norton B. . . . . Alaska	64·22 N	162·18 W
84	Norton Res. Mass. (Providence In.)	42·01 N	71·07 W
64	Norton Sd. . . . . Alaska	63·48 N	164·50 W
85	Norval (nôr'vâl) Can. (Toronto In.)	43·39 N	79·52 W
74	Norwalk (nôr'wôk) Calif. (Los Angeles In.)	33·54 N	118·05 W
84	Norwalk . . . Conn. (New York In.)	41·06 N	73·25 W
80	Norwalk . . . . Ohio	41·15 N	82·35 W
102	Norway (nôr'wā) . . . . Eur.	63·48 N	11·17 E
82	Norway . . . . Maine	44·11 N	70·35 W
71	Norway . . . . Mich.	45·47 N	87·55 W
86	Norway House . . . . Can.	54·00 N	97·54 W
112	Norwegian Sea (nôr-wē'jăn) . . Eur.	66·54 N	1·43 E
83	Norwell (nôr'wĕl) Mass. (Boston In.)	42·10 N	70·47 W
81	Norwich (nôr'wĭch) . . . . Conn.	41·20 N	72·00 W
117	Norwich . . . . Eng.	52·40 N	1·15 E
81	Norwich . . . . N. Y.	42·35 N	75·30 W
83	Norwood (nôr'wŏŏd) Mass. (Boston In.)	42·11 N	71·13 W
79	Norwood . . . . N. C.	35·15 N	80·08 W
75	Norwood . . . . Ohio (Cincinnati In.)	39·10 N	84·27 W
85	Nose Cr. (nōz) . Can. (Calgary In.)	51·09 N	114·02 W
152	Noshiro (nō'shē-rô) . . . . Jap.	40·09 N	140·02 E
129	Nosovka (nô'sôf-ká) . . . . . Sov. Un.	50·54 N	31·35 E
167	Nossi Bé (B.) (nōō'sē bā) Malag. Rep.	13·14 S	47·28 E
166	Nossob (R.) (nô'sŏb) . . . S. W. Afr.	24·15 S	19·10 E
120	Noteć R. (nô'tĕch) . . . . Pol.	52·50 N	16·19 E
113	Noto (nô'tô) . . . . It.	36·49 N	15·08 E
118	Notodden (nôt'ôd'n) . . . . Nor.	59·35 N	9·15 E
153	Noto-Hantō (Pen.) (nô'tō hän'tō) Jap.	37·18 N	137·03 E
83	Notre Dame B. (nō't'r dām') . Can.	49·48 N	55·27 W
85	Notre-Dame-des-Laurentides (dĕ-lō-räN-tēd') . Can. (Quebec In.)	46·55 N	71·20 W
82	Notre-Dame-du-Lac . . . . Can.	47·37 N	68·51 W
82	Notre Dame Mts. . . . . Can.	48·10 N	67·40 W
80	Nottawasaga B. (nŏt'á-wá-sâ'gá) Can.	44·45 N	80·35 W
87	Nottaway (R.) (nôt'á-wā) . . . Can.	50·58 N	78·02 W
110	Nottingham (nŏt'ĭng-ăm) . . . . Eng.	52·58 N	1·09 W
110	Nottingham (Co.) . . . . Eng.	53·03 N	1·05 W
87	Nottingham I. . . . . Can.	62·58 N	78·53 W
167	Nottinghamweg (nŏt ĭng hăm vĕg) S. Afr. (Natal In.)	29·21 S	30·00 E
79	Nottoway, (R.) (nŏt'á-wā) . . . . Va.	36·53 N	77·47 W
164	Nouakchott . . . . Mauritania	18·15 N	15·56 W
159	Noumea (nōō-mā'ä) . . . . . . N. Cal.	22·18 S	166·48 E
82	Nouvelle (nōō-vĕl') . . . . Can.	48·08 N	66·19 W
165	Nouvelle Anvers (äN-vâr') . Con. K.	1·42 N	19·08 E
122	Nouzonville (nōō-zôN-vēl') . . . . Fr.	49·51 N	4·43 E
99	Nova Cruz (nō'vá-krōō'z) . . . Braz.	6·22 S	35·20 W
101	Nova Friburgo (frē-bōōr'gōō) Braz. (Rio de Janeiro In.)	22·18 S	42·31 W
	Nova Goa, see Panjim		
100	Nova Iguaçu (nō'vä-ē-gwä-sōō') Braz. (In.)	22·45 S	43·27 W
101	Nova Lima (lē'mä) Braz. (Rio de Janeiro In.)	19·59 S	43·51 W
166	Nova Lisboa (lĕzh-bô'á) . . . . . Ang.	12·45 S	15·45 E
126	Novara (nô-vä'rä) . . . . It.	45·24 N	8·38 E
101	Nova Resende Braz. (Rio de Janeiro In.)	21·12 S	46·25 W
87	Nova Scotia (Prov.) (skō'shá) Can.	44·28 N	65·00 W
127	Nova Varoš (nō'vá vä'rôsh) . Yugo.	43·24 N	19·53 E
119	Novaya Ladoga (nô'vá-yá lá-dô-gô) . Sov. Un.	60·06 N	32·16 E
136	Novaya Lyalya (lyá'lyá) Sov. Un. (Urals In.)	59·03 N	60·36 E
129	Novaya Odessa (ô-dĕs'ä) . Sov. Un.	47·18 N	31·48 E
129	Novaya Praga (prä'gá) . . Sov. Un.	48·34 N	32·54 E
135	Novaya Sibir (I.) (sē-bēr') Sov. Un.	75·42 N	150·00 E
129	Novaya Vodolaga (vô-dôl'á-gá) Sov. Un.	49·43 N	35·51 E
134	Novaya Zemlya (I.) (zĕm-lyá') Sov. Un.	72·00 N	54·46 E
127	Nova Zagora (zä'gô-rá) . . . . . . Bul.	42·30 N	26·01 E
125	Novelda (nō-vĕl'dá) . . . . Sp.	38·22 N	0·46 W
121	Nové Mesto (Nad Váhom) (nô'vĕ myĕs'tō) . Czech.	48·44 N	17·47 E
121	Nové Zámky (zäm'kĕ) . . . . . Czech.	47·58 N	18·10 E
128	Novgorod (nôv'gô-rŏt) . . Sov. Un.	58·32 N	31·16 E
128	Novgorod (Oblast) . . . . . . Sov. Un.	58·27 N	31·55 E
126	Novi (nô'vē) . . . . It.	44·43 N	8·48 W
75	Novi (nō'vĭ) . . Mich. (Detroit In.)	42·29 N	83·28 W
126	Novi Grad (gräd) . . . . Yugo.	44·09 N	15·34 E
73	Novinger (nŏv'ĭn-jēr) . . . . Mo.	40·14 N	92·43 W
127	Novi-Pazar (pá-zär') . . . . Bul.	43·22 N	27·26 E
127	Novi Pazar (pá-zär') . . . . Yugo.	43·08 N	20·30 E
127	Novi Sad (säd') . . . . Yugo.	45·15 N	19·53 E
136	Novoasbest (nô-vô-ä-bĕst') Sov. Un. (Urals In.)	57·43 N	60.14 E
129	Novoaydar (nô'vô-ī-där') Sov. Un.	48·57 N	39·01 E
129	Novocherkassk (nô'vô-chĕr-käsk') Sov. Un.	47·25 N	40·04 E
129	Novogorod-Severskiy . . . . Sov. Un.	52·01 N	33·14 E
121	Novogrudok (nô-vô-grōō'dôk) Sov. Un.	53·35 N	25·51 E
103	Novo-Kazalinsk (nô-vŭ-kŭ-zá-lyĕnsk') . Sov. Un.	45·47 N	62·00 E
134	Novokuznetsk (Stalinsk) (nō'vô-kōō'z-nyĕ'tsk) (stá'lênsk) . Sov. Un.	53·43 N	86·59 E
136	Novoladozhskiy Kanal (Can.) (nô-vô-lä'dôzh-skĭ ká-näl') Sov. Un. (Leningrad In.)	59·54 N	31·19 E
126	Novo Mesto (nôvô mäs'tô) . Yugo.	45·48 N	15·13 E
129	Novomirgorod (nô'vô-mēr'gô-rôt) Sov. Un.	48·46 N	31·44 E
128	Novomoskossk . . . . Sov. Un.	54·06 N	38·08 E
129	Novomoskovsk (nô'vô-môs-kôfsk') Sov. Un.	48·37 N	35·12 E
136	Novonikol'skiy (nô'vô-nyĭ-kôl'skĭ) Sov. Un. (Urals In.)	52·28 N	57·12 E
166	Novo Redondo (nô'vōō rä-dôn'dōō) . Ang.	11·15 S	13·50 E
129	Novorossiysk (nô'vô-rô-sēsk') Sov. Un.	44·43 N	37·48 E
128	Novorzhev (nô'vô-rzhêv') Sov. Un.	57·01 N	29·17 E
127	Novo-Selo (nô'vô-sĕ'lô) . . . . . . Bul.	44·09 N	22·46 E
134	Novosibirsk (nô'vô-sē-bērsk') Sov. Un.	55·09 N	82·58 E
135	Novosibirskiye O-va (New Siberian Is.) (no'vŭ-sĭ-bĭr'skē-ĕ) . Sov. Un.	76·45 N	140·30 E
128	Novosil' (nô'vô-sĭl) . . . . . . Sov. Un.	52·58 N	37·03 E
128	Novosokol'niki (nô'vô-sô-kôl'nē-kē) . Sov. Un.	56·18 N	30·07 E
136	Novotatishchevskiy (nô'vô-tá-tyĭsh'chĕv-skĭ) Sov. Un. (Urals In.)	53·22 N	60·24 E
129	Novoukrainka (nōvō-ōō'krá) Sov. Un.	48·18 N	31·33 E
133	Novouzensk (nô-vô-ōō-zĕnsk') Sov. Un.	50·40 N	48·08 E
128	Novozybkov (nô'vô-zĕp'kôf) Sov. Un.	52·31 N	31·54 E
121	Nový Jičín (nô'vē yē'chēn) . Czech.	49·36 N	18·02 E
129	Novyy Bug (bōōĸ) . . . . . . Sov. Un.	47·43 N	32·33 E
129	Novyy Oskol (ôs-kôl') . . . . Sov. Un.	50·46 N	37·53 E
134	Novyy Port (nô'vē) . . . . . Sov. Un.	67·19 N	72·28 E
121	Nowa Huta (nô'vä hōō'tä) . . . . Pol.	50·04 N	20·20 E
120	Nowa Sól (nô'vá sŭl') . . . . Pol.	51·49 N	15·41 E
73	Nowata (nô-wä'tá) . . . . Okla.	36·42 N	95·38 W
160	Nowra (nou'rá) . . . . Austl.	34·55 S	150·45 E

ăt; finăl; rāte; senâte; ärm; ȧsk; sofȧ; fâre; ch-choose; dh-as th in other; bē; ėvent; bĕt; recĕnt; cratẽr; g-go; gh-guttural g; bĭt; ĭ-short neutral; rīde; ĸ-guttural k as ch in German ich;

PRONOUNCING INDEX Nowy Dwor Mazowiecki–Oglio 245

Page Name Pronunciation Region Lat. °' Long. °'

121 Nowy Dwór Mazowiecki (nō'vĭ dvōōr mä-zō-vyĕts'ke) Pol. 52·26 N 20·46 E
121 Nowy Sącz (nô'vê sôɴch') Pol. 49·36 N 20·42 E
121 Nowy Targ (tärk') Pol. 49·29 N 20·02 E
66 Noxon Res. Mont. 47·50 N 115·40 W
78 Noxubee (R.) (nŏks'ū-bē) Miss. 33·20 N 88·55 W
124 Noya (nō'yä) Sp. 42·46 N 8·50 W
153 Nozaki (nō'zä-kê) Jap. (Osaka In.) 34·43 N 135·39 E
167 Nqamakwe ('n-gä-mä'kwä) S. Afr. (Natal In.) 32·13 S 27·57 E
167 Nqutu ('n-kōō'tōō) S. Afr. (Natal In.) 28·17 S 30·41 E
165 Nubian Des. (nōō'bĭ-ăn) Sud. 21·13 N 33·09 E
98 Nudo Coropuna (Mt.) (nōō'dô kō-rō-pōō'nä) Peru 15·53 S 72·04 W
98 Nudo de Pasco (Mt.) (dĕ päs'kô) Peru 10·34 S 76·12 W
76 Nueces R. (nû-ā'sås) Tex. 28·20 N 98·08 W
86 Nueltin (L.) (nwĕl'tin) Can. 60·14 N 101·00 W
92 Nueva Armenia (nwā'vä är-mā'nê-ä) Hond. 15·47 N 86·32 W
99 Nueva Esparta (State) (nwĕ'vä ĕs-pä'r-tä) Ven. In. 10·50 N 64·35 W
94 Nueva Gerona (ĸĕ-rô'nä) Cuba 21·55 N 82·45 W
101 Nueva Palmira (päl-mē'rä) Ur. (Buenos Aires In.) 33·53 S 58·23 W
62 Nueva Rosita (nōōĕ'vä rô-sē'tä) Mex. 27·55 N 101·10 W
92 Nueva San Salvador (Santa Tecla) (sän' säl-vä-dōr) (sän'tä tĕ'klä) Sal. 13·41 N 89·16 W
101 Nueve de Julio (nwā'vä dā hōō'lyô) Arg. (Buenos Aires In.) 35·26 S 60·51 W
94 Nuevitas (nwā-vē'täs) Cuba 21·35 N 77·15 W
94 Nuevitas, Bahía de (bä-ē'ä dĕ nwā-vē'täs) Cuba 21·30 N 77·05 W
74 Nuevo (nwā'vō) Calif. (Los Angeles In.) 33·48 N 117·09 W
76 Nuevo Laredo (lä-rā'dhō) Mex. 27·29 N 99·30 W
88 Nuevo Leon (State) (lā-ōn') Mex. 26·00 N 100·00 W
88 Nuevo San Juan (nwĕ'vô sän ĸōō-ä'n) Pan. (Panama Canal In.) 9·14 N 79·43 W
136 Nugumanovo (nû-gû-mä'nô-vô) Sov. Un. (Urals In.) 55·28 N 61·50 E
133 Nukha (nōō'kä) Sov. Un. 41·10 N 47·10 E
64 Nulato (nōō-lä'tō) Alaska 64·40 N 158·18 W
158 Nullagine (nŭ-lă'jēn) Austl. 22·00 S 120·07 E
158 Nullarbor Plain, (Reg.) (nŭ-lär'bôr) Austl. 31·45 S 126·30 E
111 Numansdorp Neth. (Amsterdam In.) 51·43 N 4·25 E
153 Numazu (nōō'mä-zōō) Jap. 35·06 N 138·55 E
101 No. 1, Canal Arg. (Buenos Aires In.) 36·43 S 58·14 W
101 No. 9, Canal Arg. (Buenos Aires In.) 36·22 S 58·19 W
101 No. 12, Canal Arg. (Buenos Aires In.) 36·47 S 57·20 W
167 Numolani Leso. (Natal In.) 29·06 S 28·59 E
110 Nuneaton (nŭn'ē-tŭn) Eng. 52·31 N 1·28 W
150 Nungan China 44·25 N 125·10 E
64 Nunivak (I.) (nōō'nĭ-văk) Alaska 60·25 N 167·42 W
92 Nunkiní (nōōn-kē-nē') Mex. (Yucatan In.) 20·19 N 90·14 W
64 Nunyama (nûn-yä'mà) Sov. Un. 65·49 N 170·32 W
126 Nuoro (nwô'rō) It. 40·29 N 9·20 E
134 Nura (R.) (nōō'rä) Sov. Un. 49·48 N 73·54 E
134 Nurata (nōōr'ät'ä) Sov. Un. 40·33 N 65·28 E
120 Nürnberg (nürn'bĕrgh) Ger. 49·28 N 11·07 E
95 Nurse Cay (I.) Ba. Is. 22·30 N 75·50 W
133 Nusabyin (nōō'sĭ-bēn) Tur. 37·05 N 41·10 E
64 Nushagak (R.) (nū-shă-găk') Alaska 59·28 N 157·40 W
148 Nushan Hu (L.) (nü'shän hōō) China 32·50 N 117·59 E
145 Nushki (nŭsh'kê) W. Pak. 29·30 N 66·02 E
111 Nuthe R. (nōō'tê) Ger. (Berlin In.) 52·15 N 13·11 E
84 Nutley (nŭt'lê) N. J. (New York In.) 40·49 N 74·09 W
81 Nutter Fort (nŭt'ĕr fôrt) W. Va. 39·15 N 80·15 W
74 Nutwood (nŭt'wŏŏd) Ill. (St. Louis In.) 39·05 N 90·34 W
139 Nuwaybi 'al Muzayyinah U. A. R. (Palestine In.) 28·59 N 34·40 E
84 Nyack (nī'ăk) N. Y. (New York In.) 41·05 N 73·55 W
165 Nyala Sud. 12·00 N 24·52 E
166 Nyangwe (nyăng'wä) Con. K. 4·09 S 26·16 E
166 Nyasa, L. (nyä'sä) Malawi-Tan. 11·32 S 35·15 E
136 Nyazepetrovsk (nyä'zĕ-pĕ-trôvsk') Sov. Un. (Urals In.) 56·04 N 59·38 E
118 Nyborg (nü'bôr'') Den. 55·20 N 10·45 E
118 Nybro (nü'brô) Swe. 56·44 N 15·56 E
146 Nyenchhen Thanglha (Mts.) China 29·55 N 88·08 E
118 Nyhem (nü'hĕm) Swe. 56·39 N 12·50 E
121 Nyíregyháza (nyē'rĕd-y'hä'zä) Hung. 47·58 N 21·45 E
118 Nykøbing (nü'kû-bĭng) Den. 56·46 N 8·47 E
118 Nykøbing Falster Den. 54·45 N 11·54 E
118 Nykøbing Sjaelland Den. 55·55 N 11·37 E
118 Nyköping (nü'chû-pĭng) Swe. 58·46 N 16·58 E
168 Nyl R. (nĭl) S. Afr. (Johannesburg & Pretoria In.) 24·30 S 28·55 E
168 Nylstroom (nĭl'strōm) S. Afr. (Johannesburg & Pretoria In.) 24·42 S 28·25 E
160 Nymagee (nī-mà-gē') Austl. 32·17 S 146·18 E
120 Nymburk (nĕm'bŏŏrk) Czech. 50·12 N 15·03 E
116 Nymphe Bk. (nĭmpf) Ire. 51·36 N 7·35 W
118 Nynashamn (nü-nĕs-häm'n) Swe. 58·53 N 17·55 E
160 Nyngan (nĭŋ'găn) Austl. 31·31 S 147·25 E
164 Nyong R. (nyông) Cam. 3·41 N 12·21 E
120 Nyrány (nêr-zhä'nê) Czech. 49·43 N 13·13 E
121 Nysa (nē'sä) Pol. 50·29 N 17·20 E
Nystad, see Uusikaupunki
132 Nytva Sov. Un. 58·00 N 55·10 E
135 Nyuya (R.) (nyōō'yä) Sov. Un. 60·30 N 111·45 E
70 Oahe Dam (ō-ä-hē) S. D. 44·28 N 100·34 W
70 Oahe Res. S. Dak. 45·20 N 100·00 W
157 Oahu (I.) (ō-ä'hōō) (ō-ä'hû) Hawaii (In.) 21·38 N 157·48 W
85 Oak Bluff (ōk blŭf) Can. (Winnipeg In.) 49·47 N 97·21 W
67 Oak Creek (ōk krēk') Colo. 40·20 N 106·50 W
68 Oakdale (ōk'dāl) Calif. 37·45 N 120·52 W
80 Oakdale Ky. 38·15 N 85·50 W
77 Oakdale La. 30·49 N 92·40 W
75 Oakdale Pa. (Pittsburgh In.) 40·24 N 80·11 W
110 Oakengates (ōk'ĕn-gāts) Eng. 52·41 N 2·27 W
70 Oakes (ōks) N. D. 46·10 N 98·50 W
82 Oakfield (ōk'fēld) Maine 46·08 N 68·10 W
84 Oakford (ōk'fŏrd) Pa. (Philadelphia In.) 40·08 N 74·58 W
65 Oak Grove (grōv) Ore. (Portland In.) 45·25 N 122·38 W
110 Oakham (ōk'ăm) Eng. 52·40 N 0·38 W
80 Oakharbor (ōk'här'bĕr) Ohio 41·30 N 83·05 W
65 Oak Harbor Wash. (Seattle In.) 48·18 N 122·39 W
74 Oak Knoll (nōl) Tex. (Dallas, Fort Worth In.) 32·47 N 97·17 W
65 Oakland (ōk'lănd) Calif. (San Francisco In.) 37·48 N 122·16 W
70 Oakland Nebr. 41·50 N 96·28 W
80 Oakland City Ind. 38·20 N 87·20 W
75 Oaklawn (ōk'lôn) Ill. (Chicago In.) 41·43 N 87·45 W
161 Oakleigh (ōk'lâ) Austl. (Melbourne In.) 37·54 S 145·05 E
67 Oakley (ōk'lĭ) Idaho 42·15 N 113·53 W
72 Oakley Kans. 39·08 N 100·49 W
78 Oakman (ōk'măn) Ala. 33·42 N 87·20 W
75 Oakmont (ōk'mōnt) Pa. (Pittsburgh In.) 40·31 N 79·50 W
84 Oak Mtn. Ala. (Birmingham In.) 33·22 N 86·42 W
75 Oak Park (pärk) Ill. (Chicago In.) 41·53 N 87·48 W
65 Oak Point Wash. (Portland In.) 46·11 N 123·11 W
78 Oak Ridge (rĭj) Tenn. 36·01 N 84·15 W
74 Oak Ridge Park Mich. (Sault Ste. Marie In.) 46·18 N 84·12 W
85 Oakville (ōk'vĭl) Can. (Toronto In.) 43·27 N 79·40 W
85 Oakville Can. (Winnipeg In.) 49·56 N 98·00 W
74 Oakville Mo. (St. Louis In.) 38·27 N 90·18 W
85 Oakville Cr. Can. (Toronto In.) 43·34 N 79·54 W
77 Oakwood (ōk'wŏŏd) Tex. 31·36 N 95·48 W
75 Oakwood Wis. (Milwaukee In.) 42·51 N 88.30 W
69 Oatman (ōt'măn) Ariz. 34·00 N 114·25 W
88 Oaxaca (State) (wä-hä'kä) Mex. 16·45 N 97·00 W
91 Oaxaca, Sierra de (Mts.) (sē-ĕ'r-rä dĕ) Mex. 16·15 N 97·25 W
91 Oaxaca de Juárez (ĸōōä'rĕz) Mex. 17·03 N 96·42 W
134 Ob' (R.) Sov. Un. 62·15 N 67·00 E
87 Oba (ō'bà) Can. 48·58 N 84·09 W
153 Obama (ō'bä-mä) Jap. 35·29 N 135·44 E
116 Oban (ō'băn) Scot. 56·25 N 5·35 W
75 O'Bannon (ō-băn'nŏn) Ky. (Louisville In.) 38·17 N 85·30 W
82 Obatogamau (L.) (ō-bà-tō'găm-ô) Can. 49·38 N 74·10 W
168 Obbia (ôb'byä) Som. (Horn of Afr. In.) 5·24 N 48·28 E
123 Oberhausen (ō'bĕr-hou'zĕn) Ger. (Ruhr In.) 51·27 N 6·51 E
72 Oberlin (o'bĕr-lĭn) Kans. 39·49 N 100·30 W
80 Oberlin Ohio 41.15 N 82·15 W
120 Oberösterreich (Prov.) Aus. 48·05 N 13·15 E
111 Oberroth (ō'bĕr-rōt) Ger. (Munich In.) 48·19 N 11·20 E
111 Ober-Schleissheim (ō'bĕr-shlīs-hēm) Ger. (Munich In.) 48·15 N 11·34 E
155 Obi (I.) (ō'bê) Indon. 1·25 S 128·15 E
99 Óbidos (ō'bê-dŏŏzh) Braz. 1·57 S 55·32 W
152 Obihiro (ō'bē-hē'rō) Jap. 42·55 N 142·50 E
78 Obion (R.) Tenn. 36·10 N 89·25 W
78 Obion (R.), North Fk. (ô-bī'ŏn) Tenn. 35·49 N 89·06 W
129 Obitochnaya, Kosa (C.) (kô-sä' ô-bē-tôch'ná-yä) Sov. Un. 46·32 N 36·07 E
153 Obitsu (R.) (ō'bēt'sōō) Jap. (Tōkyō In.) 35·19 N 140·03 E
168 Obock (ō-bŏk') Fr. Som. (Horn of Afr. In.) 11·55 N 43·15 E
128 Obol' (R.) (ô-bŏl') Sov. Un. 55·24 N 29·24 E
129 Oboyan' (ō-bô-yän') Sov. Un. 51·14 N 36·16 E
134 Obskaya Guba (R.) Sov. Un. 67·13 N 73·45 E
129 Obukhov (ō'bōō-kôf) Sov. Un. 50·07 N 30·36 E
79 Ocala (ô-kä'lá) Fla. 29·11 N 82·09 W
90 Ocampo (ō-käm'pō) Mex. 22·49 N 99·23 W
98 Ocaña (ō-kän'yä) Col. 8·15 N 73·37 W
124 Ocaña (ō-kä'n-yä) Sp. 39·58 N 3·31 W
164 Occidental, Grand Erg (Dunes) Alg. 29·30 N 00·45 W
98 Occidental, Cordillera (Mts.) (kôr-dēl-yĕ'rä ŏk-sē-dĕn-täl') Col. (In.) 5·05 N 76·04 W
98 Occidental, Cordillera (Mts.) Peru 10·12 S 76·58 W
88 Occidental, Sierra Madre, (Mts.) (sē-ĕ'r-rä-mä'drĕ-ŏk-sē-dĕn-tä'l) Mex. 29·30 N 107·30 W
84 Oceana (ō'shĕ'ăn-à) Va. (Norfolk In.) 36·51 N 76·01 W
68 Ocean Beach (ō'shăn bēch) Calif. (San Diego In.) 32·44 N 117·14 W
95 Ocean Bight (B.) Ba. Is. 21·15 N 73·15 W
81 Ocean City Md. 38·20 N 75·10 W
81 Ocean City N. J. 39·15 N 74·35 W
86 Ocean Falls (Fôls) Can. 52·27 N 127·50 W
161 Ocean Grove Austl. (Melbourne In.) 38·16 S 144·32 E
81 Ocean Grove (grōv) N. J. 40·10 N 74·00 W
74 Ocean Park (pärk) Calif. (Los Angeles In.) 34·00 N 118·28 W
84 Oceanport (ō'-shăn-pōrt) N. J. (New York In.) 40·18 N 74·02 W
68 Oceanside (ō'shăn-sīd) Calif. 33·11 N 117·22 W
78 Ocean Springs (sprĭngs) Miss. 30·25 N 88·49 W
127 Ocenele Mari Rom. 45·05 N 24·17 E
129 Ochakov (ô-chä'kôf) Sov. Un. 46·38 N 31·33 E
146 Ochina Ho (R.) China 41·15 N 100·46 E
150 Ochir China 45·38 N 115·35 E
78 Ochlockonee R. (ŏk-lô-kō'nē) Fla.-Ga. 30·10 N 84·38 W
78 Ocilla (ô-sĭl'à) Ga. 31·36 N 83·15 W
118 Ockelbo (ôk'ĕl-bô) Swe. 60·54 N 16·35 E
79 Ocmulgee, (R.) Ga. 32·35 N 83·30 W
78 Ocmulgee Natl. Mon. (ôk-mŭl'gē) Ga. 32·45 N 83·28 W
127 Ocna-Sibiului (ōk'ná-sê-byōō-lōō-ê) Rom. 45·52 N 24·04 E
95 Ocoa, Bahai de (B.) (bä-ä'ē-ô-kō'ä) Dom. Rep. 18·20 N 70·40 W
91 Ococingo (ô-kô-sê'n-gō) Mex. 17·03 N 92·18 W
92 Ocom, L. (ô-kō'm) Mex. (Yucatan In.) 19·26 N 88·18 W
78 Oconee, (R.) (ô-kō'nē) Ga. 32·45 N 83·00 W
71 Oconomowoc (ô-kŏn'ô-mô-wŏk') Wis. 43·06 N 88·24 W
71 Oconto (ô-kŏn'tō) Wis. 44·54 N 87·55 W
71 Oconto (R.) Wis. 45·08 N 88·24 W
71 Oconto Falls Wis. 44·53 N 88·11 W
92 Ocós (ô-kōs') Guat. 14·31 N 92·12 W
92 Ocotal (ō-kô-täl') Nic. 13·36 N 86·31 W
92 Ocotepeque (ô-kō-tä-pā'kå) Hond. 14·25 N 89·13 W
90 Ocotlán (ō-kô-tlän') Mex. 20·19 N 102·44 W
91 Ocotlán de Morelos (dā mô-rā'lōs) Mex. 16·46 N 96·41 W
91 Ocozocoautla (ô-kō'zô-kwä-ōō'tlä) Mex. 16·44 N 93·22 W
99 Ocumare del Tuy (ō-kōō-mä'rä del twē') Ven. (In.) 10·07 N 66·47 W
155 Ocussi Port. Tim. 9·00 S 128·53 E
153 Odawara (ō'dà-wä'rä) Jap. 35·15 N 139·10 E
118 Odda (ôdh-à) Nor. 60·04 N 6·30 E
168 Oddur Som. (Horn of Afr. In.) 3·55 N 43·45 E
70 Odebolt (ō'dê-bōlt) Iowa 42·20 N 95·14 W
124 Odemira (ō-dà-mē'rà) Port. 37·35 N 8·40 W
133 Ödemis (ů'dĕ-mēsh) Tur. 38·12 N 28·00 E
168 Odendaalsrus (ō'dĕn-däls-rûs') S. Afr. (Johannesburg & Pretoria In.) 27·52 S 26·41 E
118 Odense (ō'dhĕn-sĕ) Den. 55·24 N 10·20 E
84 Odenton (ō'dĕn-tŭn) Md. (Baltimore In.) 39·05 N 76·43 W
120 Odenwald (For.) (ō'dĕn-väld) Ger. 49·39 N 8·55 E
120 Oder R. (ō'dĕr) Ger. 52·40 N 14·19 E
129 Odessa (ô-dĕs'sä) Sov. Un. 46·28 N 30·44 E
76 Odessa (ô-dĕs'à) Tex. 31·52 N 102·21 W
66 Odessa Wash. 47·20 N 118·42 W
129 Odessa (Oblast) Sov. Un. 46·05 N 29·48 E
124 Odiel (R.) (ō-dē-ĕl') Sp. 37·47 N 6·42 W
164 Odienné (ô-dê-ĕn-nā') Ivory Coast 9·47 N 7·32 W
110 Odiham (ŏd'ē-ăm) Eng. (London In.) 51·14 N 0·56 W
138 Odintsovo (ô-dēn'tsô-vô) Sov. Un. (Moscow In.) 55·40 N 37·16 E
155 Odioñgan (ō-dê-ōŋ'gän) Phil. (Manila In.) 12·24 N 121·59 E
125 Odivelas (ō-dê-vā'lyäs) Port. (Lisbon In.) 38·47 N 9·11 W
121 Odobesti (ō-dô-bĕsh't') Rom. 45·46 N 27·08 E
70 O'Donnell (ō-dŏn'ĕl) Tex. 32·59 N 101·51 W
121 Odorhei (ō-dôr-hā') Rom. 46·18 N 25·17 E
121 Odra R. (ô'drà) Pol. 50·28 N 17·55 E
99 Oeiras (wä-ê-räzh') Braz. 7·05 S 42·01 W
125 Oeirás (ô-ĕ'y-rà's) Port. (Lisbon In.) 38·42 N 9·18 W
71 Oelwein (ōl'wīn) Iowa 42·40 N 91·56 W
74 O'Fallon (ō-făl'ŭn) Ill. (St. Louis In.) 38·36 N 89·55 W
67 O'Fallon Cr. Mont. 46·25 N 104·47 W
126 Ofanto (R.) (ô-făn'tō) It. 41·08 N 15·33 E
120 Offenbach (ôf'ĕn-bäk) Ger. 50·06 N 8·50 E
120 Offenburg (ôf'ĕn-bŏŏrgh) Ger. 48·28 N 7·57 E
153 Ofuna (ō'fōō-nä) Jap. (Tōkyō In.) 35·21 N 139·32 E
168 Ogaden Plat. Eth. (Horn of Afr. In.) 6·45 N 44·53 E
153 Ōgaki Jap. 35·21 N 136·36 E
70 Ogallala (ō-gä-lä'lä) Nebr. 41·80 N 101·44 W
164 Ogbomosho (ŏg-bô-mō'shō) Nig. 8·06 N 4·04 E
71 Ogden (ŏg'dĕn) Iowa 42·10 N 94·20 W
74 Ogden Utah (Salt Lake City In.) 41·14 N 111·58 W
74 Ogden Pk. Utah (Salt Lake City In.) 41·11 N 111·51 W
74 Ogden R. Utah (Salt Lake City In.) 41·16 N 111·54 W
84 Ogdensburg (ŏg'dĕnz-bûrg) N. J. (New York In.) 41·05 N 74·36 W
81 Ogdensburg N. Y. 44·40 N 75·30 W
79 Ogeechee, (R.) (ō-gē'chē) Ga. 32·35 N 81·50 W
168 Ogies S. Afr. (Johannesburg & Pretoria In.) 26·03 S 29·04 E
86 Ogilvie Ra. (ō'g'l-vĭ) Can. 64·43 N 138·36 W
80 Oglesby (ō'g'lz-bĭ) Ill. 41·20 N 89·00 W
126 Oglio (R.) (ōl'yō) It. 45·15 N 10·19 E

ng-sing; ŋ-baŋk; ɴ-nasalized n; nŏd; cŏmmit; ōld; ôbey; ôrder; fōōd; fŏŏt; ou-out; s-soft; sh-dish; th-thin; pūre; ûnite; ûrn; stŭd; circŭs; ü-as "y" in study; '-indeterminate vowel.

Page	Name	Pronunciation	Region	Lat. °'	Long. °'
153	Ōgo	(ō'gō)	Jap. (Ōsaka In.)	34·49 N	135·06 E
154	Ogoamas, Bulu (Mtn.)		Indon.	0·45 N	120·15 E
166	Ogooué (R.)		Gabon	0·20 S	11·07 E
136	Ogudnévo	(ŏg-ŏŏg-nyô'vô)	Sov. Un. (Moscow In.)	56·04 N	38·17 E
126	Ogulin	(ō-gŏŏ-lēn')	Yugo.	45·17 N	15·11 E
157	Ohia	(ō-hī'ä)	Hawaii (In.)	19·35 N	155·01 W
101	O'IIigginsz (Prov.)	(ô-kē'gĕns)	Chile (Santiago In.)	34·17 S	70·52 W
63	Ohio, (State)	(ō'hī'ō)	U.S.	40·30 N	83·15 W
80	Ohio R.		U.S.	37·25 N	88·05 W
79	Ohoopee	(ō-hōō'pē)	Ga.	32·32 N	82·38 W
120	Ohre (Eger) R.	(ōr'zhĕ) (ā'gĕr)	Czech.	50·08 N	12·45 E
127	Ohrid	(ō'krēd)	Yugo.	41·08 N	20·46 E
127	Ohrid (L.)		Alb.-Yugo.	40·58 N	20·35 E
153	Ōi	(oi')	Jap. (Tōkyō In.)	35·51 N	139·31 E
118	Oieren (L.)	(ůĭ'ĕrĕn)	Nor.	59·50 N	11·25 E
153	Oi-Gawa (Strm.)	(ô'ē-gä'wä)	Jap.	35·09 N	138·05 E
81	Oil City	(oil sĭ'tĭ)	Pa.	41·25 N	79·40 W
111	Oirschot		Neth. (Amsterdam In.)	51·30 N	5·20 E
122	Oise (R.)	(wäz)	Fr.	49·30 N	2·56 E
111	Oisterwijk		Neth. (Amsterdam In.)	51·34 N	5·13 E
153	Oita	(ô'ē-tä)	Jap.	33·14 N	131·38 E
153	Oji	(ō'jĕ)	Jap. (Ōsaka In.)	34·36 N	135·43 E
76	Ojinaga	(ō-Kē-nä'gä)	Mex.	29·34 N	104·26 W
91	Ojitlán (San Lucas)	(ōkē-tlän') (sän-lōō'käs)	Mex.	18·04 N	96·23 W
90	Ojo Caliente	(ōkō-kä-lyĕn'tä)	Mex.	21·50 N	100·43 W
90	Ojocaliente	(ō-kō-kä-lyĕ'n-tĕ)	Mex.	22·39 N	102·15 W
94	Ojo del Toro, Pico (Pk.)	(pē'kō-ô-ô-dĕl-tō'rō)	Cuba	19·55 N	77·25 W
85	Oka	(ō-kä)	Can. (Montreal In.)	45·28 N	74·05 W
133	Oka (R.)	(ô-kä')	Sov. Un.	52·10 N	35·20 E
134	Oka (R.)	(ô-kä')	Sov. Un.	53·28 N	101·09 E
132	Oka (R.)	(ô-kä')	Sov. Un.	55·10 N	42·10 E
166	Okahandja		S. W. Afr.	21·55 S	16·45 E
86	Okanagan	(ō'kä-năg'ăn)	Can.	49·56 N	120·23 W
66	Okanogan		Wash.	48·20 N	119·34 W
66	Okanogan R.		Wash.	48·36 N	119·33 W
164	Okano R.	(ō'kä'nō)	Gabon	0·15 N	11·08 E
78	Okatibbee (R.)	(ō'kä-tĭb'ē)	Miss.	32·37 N	88·54 W
78	Okatoma Cr.	(ō-kä-tō'mä)	Miss.	31·43 N	89·34 W
166	Okavango (R.)		Ang.-S. W. Afr.	17·50 S	19·30 E
166	Okavango Swp		Bots.	19·30 S	23·02 E
153	Okaya	(ō'kä-yä)	Jap.	36·04 N	138·01 E
153	Okayama	(ō'kä-yä'mä)	Jap.	34·39 N	133·54 E
153	Okazaki	(ō'kä-zä'kē)	Jap.	34·58 N	137·09 E
79	Okeechobee	(ō-kē-chō'bē)	Fla. (In.)	27·15 N	80·48 W
79	Okeechobee, L.		Fla. (In.)	27·00 N	80·49 W
72	Okeene	(ō-kēn')	Okla.	36·06 N	98·19 W
79	Okefenokee Swp.	(ō'kĕ-fē-nō'kē)	Ga.	30·54 N	82·20 W
73	Okemah	(ō-kē'mä)	Okla.	35·26 N	96·18 W
117	Oker	(ō'kĕr)	Ger.	52·23 N	10·00 E
135	Okha	(ŭ-kä')	Sov. Un.	53·44 N	143·12 E
136	Okhotino	(ô-kō'tĭ-nô)	Sov. Un. (Moscow In.)	56·14 N	38·24 E
135	Okhotsk	(ô-kōtsk')	Sov. Un.	59·28 N	143·32 E
139	Okhotsk, Sea of	(ô-kōtsk')	Asia	56·45 N	146·00 E
153	Oki-Guntō (Arch.)	(ō'kē gŏŏn'tō)	Jap.	36·17 N	133·05 E
152	Okinawa (I.)	(ō'kē-nä'wä)	Ryūkyū Is.	26·30 N	128·30 E
152	Okinawa Guntō (Is.)	(gŏŏn'tō')	Ryūkyū Is.	26·50 N	127·25 E
153	Okino (I.)	(ō'kē-nô)	Jap.	36·22 N	133·27 E
152	Ōkino Erabu (I.)	(ō-kē'nô-ä-rä'bōō)	Jap.	27·18 N	129·00 E
62	Oklahoma (State)	(ô-klä-hō'mä)	U. S.	36·00 N	98·20 W
73	Oklahoma City		Okla.	35·27 N	97·32 W
79	Oklawaha (R.)	(ôk-lá-wô'hô)	Fla.	29·13 N	82·00 W
73	Okmulgee	(ôk-mŭl'gē)	Okla.	35·37 N	95·58 W
75	Okolona	(ō-kō-lō'nà)	Ky. (Louisville In.)	38·08 N	85·41 W
78	Okolona		Miss.	33·59 N	88·43 W
152	Okushiri (I.)	(ō'koo-shē'rē)	Jap.	42·12 N	139·30 E
65	Olalla	(ō-lä'lä)	Wash. (Seattle In.)	47·26 N	122·33 W
92	Olanchito	(ō'län-chē'tô)	Hond.	15·28 N	86·35 W
118	Öland (I.)	(ŭ-länd')	Swe.	57·03 N	17·15 E
74	Olathe	(ô-lä'thĕ)	Kans. (Kansas City In.)	38·53 N	94·49 W
100	Olavarría	(ō-lä-vär-rē'ä)	Arg.	36·49 S	60·15 W
121	Olawa	(ō-lä'vä)	Pol.	50·57 N	17·18 E
101	Olazcoago	(ō-läz-kôä'gō)	Arg. (Buenos Aires In.)	35·14 S	60·37 W
126	Olbia	(ō'l-byä)	It.	40·55 N	9·28 E
111	Olching	(ōl'kēng)	Ger. (Munich In.)	48·13 N	11·21 E
94	Old Bahama Chan.	(bá-hä'má)	N. A.	22·45 N	78·30 W
95	Old Bight		Ba. Is.	24·15 N	75·20 W
84	Old Bridge	(brĭj)	N. J. (New York In.)	40·24 N	74·22 W
110	Oldbury	(ōld'bĕr-ĭ)	Eng.	52·30 N	2·01 W
86	Old Crow	(crō)	Can.	67·51 N	139·58 W
120	Oldenburg	(ōl'dĕn-bŏŏrgh)	Ger.	53·09 N	8·13 E
81	Old Forge	(fōrj)	Pa.	41·20 N	75·50 W
110	Oldham	(ōld'ám)	Eng.	53·32 N	2·07 W
64	Old Harbor	(här'bĕr)	Alaska	57·18 N	153·20 W
116	Old Head of Kinsale	(ōld hĕd ŏv kĭn-sāl')	Ire.	51·35 N	8·35 W
77	Old R.		Tex. (In.)	29·54 N	94·52 W
86	Olds	(ōldz)	Can.	51·50 N	114·00 W
82	Old Town	(toun)	Maine	44·55 N	68·42 W
81	Olean	(ō-lē-ăn')	N. Y.	42·05 N	78·25 W
82	O'Leary	(ō-lĕr'ē)	Can.	46·43 N	64·10 W
121	Olecko	(ō-lĕt'skō)	Pol.	54·02 N	22·29 E
135	Olekma (R.)	(ô-lyĕk-má')	Sov. Un.	55·41 N	121·15 E
135	Olëkminsk	(ô-lyĕk-mĕnsk')	Sov. Un.	60·39 N	120·40 E
135	Olenëk (R.)	(ô-lyĕ-nyōk')	Sov. Un.	70·18 N	121·15 E
122	Oléron Île, d' (I.)	(ēl' dō lā-rôN')	Fr.	45·52 N	1·58 W
121	Oleśnica	(ō-lĕsh-nĭ'tsä)	Pol.	51·13 N	17·24 E
123	Olfen	(ōl'fĕn)	Ger. (Ruhr In.)	51·43 N	7·22 E
135	Ol'ga	(ōl'gä)	Sov. Un.	43·48 N	135·44 E
152	Ol'gi, Zaliv (B.)	(zä'lĭf ōl'gĭ)	Sov. Un.	43·43 N	135·25 E
129	Ol'gopol	(ōl-gô-pôl'y)	Sov. Un.	48·11 N	29·28 E
124	Olhão	(ōl-youn')	Port.	37·02 N	7·54 W
167	Olievenhoutpoort		S. Afr. (Johannesburg & Pretoria In.)	25·58 S	27·55 E
166	Olifants (R.)	(ōl'ī-fänts)	S. Afr.	23·58 S	31·00 E
167	Olifantsfontein		S. Afr. (Johannesburg & Pretoria In.)	25·58 S	28·19 E
127	Ólimbos	(ōl'ĭm-bōs)	Grc.	40·03 N	22·22 E
90	Olinalá	(ô-lē-nä-lä')	Mex.	17·47 N	98·51 W
99	Olinda	(ô-lē'n-dä)	Braz.	8·00 S	34·58 W
74	Olinda	(ô-lĭn'dä)	Calif. (Los Angeles In.)	33·55 N	117·51 W
125	Oliva	(ô-lē'vä)	Sp.	38·54 N	0·07 W
124	Oliva de Jerez	(ô-lē'vä dä hä'rĕth)	Sp.	38·33 N	6·55 W
125	Olivais	(ô-lē-vä'ys)	Port. (Lisbon In.)	38·46 N	9·06 W
74	Olive	(ōl'ĭv)	Calif. (Los Angeles In.)	33·50 N	117·51 W
80	Olive Hill		Ky.	38·15 N	83·10 W
101	Oliveira	(ō-lē-vā'rä)	Braz. (Rio de Janeiro In.)	20·42 S	44·49 W
124	Olivenza	(ō-lē-vĕn'thä)	Sp.	38·42 N	7·06 W
86	Oliver	(ô'lĭ-vēr)	Can.	49·09 N	119·36 W
85	Oliver		Can. (Edmonton In.)	53·38 N	113·21 W
74	Oliver	(ō'lĭvēr)	Wis. (Duluth In.)	46·39 N	92·12 W
85	Oliver L.		Can. (Edmonton In.)	53·19 N	113·00 W
71	Olivia	(ō-lĭv'ē-á)	Minn.	44·46 N	95·00 W
100	Olivos	(ōlē'vōs)	Arg. (In.)	34·15 S	58·29 W
121	Olkusz	(ōl'kŏŏsh)	Pol.	50·16 N	19·41 E
98	Ollagüe	(ô-lyä'gä)	Chile	21·17 S	68·17 W
110	Ollerton	(ōl'ĕr-tŭn)	Eng.	53·12 N	1·02 W
74	Olmos Park	(ōl'mŭs pärk')	Tex. (San Antonio In.)	29·27 N	98·32 W
80	Olney	(ōl'nĭ)	Ill.	38·45 N	88·05 W
65	Olney	(ōl'nē)	Ore. (Portland In.)	46·06 N	123·45 W
72	Olney		Tex.	33·24 N	98·43 W
83	Olomane (R.)	(ō'lô mà'nĕ)	Can.	50·50 N	60·30 W
121	Olomouc	(ō'lô-mōts)	Czech.	49·37 N	17·15 E
119	Olonets	(ô-lō'nĕts)	Sov. Un.	60·58 N	32·54 E
122	Oloron, Gave d' (Strm.)	(gäv-lô-ŏr-ôN')	Fr.	43·21 N	0·44 W
122	Oloron-Ste. Marie	(ō-lô-rôNt'säNt má-rē')	Fr.	43·11 N	1·37 W
125	Olot	(ô-lōt')	Sp.	42·09 N	2·30 E
123	Olpe	(ōl'pĕ)	Ger. (Ruhr In.)	51·02 N	7·51 E
129	Ol'shanka	(ōl'shän-kä)	Sov. Un.	48·14 N	30·52 E
129	Ol'shany	(ōl'shän-ē)	Sov. Un.	50·02 N	30·54 E
120	Olsnitz	(ōlz'nētz)	Ger.	50·25 N	12·11 E
121	Olsztyn	(ōl'shtĕn)	Pol.	53·47 N	20·28 E
120	Olten	(ōl'tĕn)	Switz.	47·20 N	7·53 E
127	Oltenita	(ōl-tā'nĭ-tsä)	Rom.	44·05 N	26·39 E
115	Olt R.		Rom.	44·09 N	24·40 E
124	Olvera	(ōl-vĕ'rä)	Sp.	36·55 N	7·16 W
66	Olympia	(ō-lĭm'pĭ-á)	Wash.	47·02 N	122·52 W
66	Olympic Mts.		Wash.	47·54 N	123·58 W
66	Olympic Natl. Park	(ô-lĭm'pĭk)	Wash.	47·54 N	123·00 W
66	Olympus Mt.	(ô-lĭm'pŭs)	Wash.	47·43 N	123·30 W
139	Olympus Mts.		Cyprus (Palestine In.)	34·50 N	32·44 E
81	Olyphant	(ōl'ī-fänt)	Pa.	41·30 N	75·40 W
135	Olyutorskiy, Mys (C.)	(ŭl-yōō'tôr-skē)	Sov. Un.	59·49 N	167·16 E
153	Omae-Zaki (Pt.)	(ō'mä-ä zä'kē)	Jap.	34·37 N	138·15 E
165	Om Ager		Eth.	14·06 N	36·46 E
116	Omagh	(ō'mä)	N. Ire.	54·35 N	7·25 W
70	Omaha	(ō'mä-hä)	Nebr.	41·18 N	95·57 W
70	Omaha Ind. Res.		Nebr.	42·09 N	96·08 W
144	Oman, G. of		Asia	24·24 N	58·58 E
166	Omaruru	(ō-mä-rōō'rōō)	S. W. Afr.	21·25 S	16·50 E
126	Ombrone (R.)	(ôm-brō'nä)	It.	42·48 N	11·18 E
165	Omdurman	(ô-dōōr-män')	Sud.	15·45 N	32·30 E
91	Omealca	(ōmä-äl'kō)	Mex.	18·44 N	96·45 W
90	Ometepec	(ô-mä-tä-pĕk')	Mex.	16·41 N	98·27 W
153	Ōmiya	(ō'mē-yä)	Jap. (Tōkyō In.)	35·54 N	139·38 E
92	Omoa	(ô-mō'rä)	Hond.	15·43 N	88·03 W
135	Omolon (R.)	(ō'mō)	Sov. Un.	67·43 N	159·15 E
153	Ōmori (Kioroshi)	(ō'mō-rē) (kē'ô-rō'shē)	Jap. (Tōkyō In.)	35·50 N	140·09 E
165	Omo R.	(ō'mō)	Eth.	5·54 N	36·09 E
92	Omotepe, Isla de (I.)	(ē's-lä-dĕ-ō-mô-tā'pä)	Nic.	11·32 N	85·30 W
71	Omro	(ŏm'rō)	Wis.	44·01 N	89·46 W
134	Omsk	(ômsk)	Sov. Un.	55·12 N	73·19 E
153	Ōmura	(ō'mōō-rä)	Jap.	32·56 N	129·57 E
153	Ōmuta	(ō-mōō-tä)	Jap.	33·02 N	130·28 E
132	Omutninsk	(ō'mōō-tēnsk)	Sov. Un.	58·38 N	52·10 E
70	Onawa	(ŏn-á-wá)	Iowa	42·02 N	96·05 W
80	Onaway	(ŏn'á-wā)	Mich.	45·25 N	84·10 W
125	Onda	(ōn'dä)	Sp.	39·58 N	0·13 W
121	Ondava R.	(ōn'dä-vä)	Czech.	48·51 N	21·40 E
150	Öndör Haan		Mong.	47·20 N	110·40 E
132	Onega	(ō-nyĕ'gä)	Sov. Un.	63·50 N	38·08 E
132	Onega (R.)		Sov. Un.	63·20 N	39·20 E
132	Onega, L., see Onezhskoye Ozero				
81	Oneida	(ō-nī'dá)	N. Y.	43·05 N	75·40 W
81	Oneida (L.)		N. Y.	43·10 N	76·00 W
70	O'Neill	(ō-nēl')	Nebr.	42·28 N	98·38 W
135	Onekotan	(ŭ-nyĕ-kŭ-tän')	Sov. Un.	49·45 N	153·45 E
81	Oneonta	(ō-nē-ŏn'tá)	N. Y.	42·25 N	75·05 W
132	Onezhskaja Guba (B.)		Sov. Un.	64·30 N	36·00 E
132	Onezhskiy, P-ov. (Pen.)		Sov. Un.	64·30 N	37·40 E
132	Onezhskoye Ozero (L. Onega)	(ō-nĕsh'skô-yĕ ō'zĕ-rō)	Sov. Un.	62·02 N	34·35 E
146	Ongin	(ŏn'gĭn')	Mong.	46·00 N	102·46 E
143	Ongole		India	15·36 N	80·03 E
167	Onilahy (R.)		Malag. Rep.	23·41 S	45·00 E
164	Onitsha	(ō-nĭt'shä)	Nig.	6·13 N	5·47 E
153	Onomichi	(ō'nô-mē'chē)	Jap.	34·27 N	133·12 E
135	Onon (R.)	(ō'nŏn)	Sov. Un.	50·33 N	114·18 E
135	Onon Gol (R.)	(ô'nŏn)	Sov. Un.	48·30 N	110·38 E
99	Onoto	(ô-nō'tō)	Ven. (In.)	9·38 N	65·03 W
158	Onslow	(ōnz'lō)	Austl.	21·53 S	115·00 E
79	Onslow B.	(ŏnz'lō)	N. C.	34·22 N	77·35 W
153	Ontake San (Mtn.)		Jap.	35·55 N	137·29 E
74	Ontario	(ŏn-tā'rĭ-ō)	Calif. (Los Angeles In.)	34·04 N	117·39 W
66	Ontario		Ore.	44·02 N	116·57 W
87	Ontario (Prov.)		Can.	50·47 N	88·50 W
63	Ontario, L.		U.S.-Can.	43·35 N	79·05 W
125	Onteniente	(ōn-tä-nyĕn'tä)	Sp.	38·48 N	0·35 W
71	Ontonagon	(ŏn-tô-năg'ŏn)	Mich.	46·50 N	89·20 W
153	Ōnuki	(ō'nōō-kē)	Jap. (Tōkyō In.)	35·17 N	139·51 E
158	Oodnadatta	(ōōd'nä-dä'tä)	Austl.	27·38 S	135·40 E
158	Ooldea Station	(ōōl-dā'á)	Austl.	30·35 S	132·08 E
73	Oologah Res.		Okla.	36·43 N	95·32 W
111	Ooltgensplaat		Neth. (Amsterdam In.)	51·41 N	4·19 E
78	Oostanaula (R.)	(ōō-stä-nô'lä)	Ga.	34·25 N	85·10 W
117	Oostende	(ōst-ĕn'dĕ)	Bel.	51·14 N	2·55 E
111	Oosterhout		Neth. (Amsterdam In.)	51·38 N	4·52 E
117	Ooster Schelde (R.)		Neth.	51·40 N	3·40 E
92	Opalaca, Sierra de (Mts.)	(sē-ĕ'r-rä-dĕ-ō-pä-lä'kä)	Hond.	14·30 N	88·29 W
121	Opatow	(ō-pä'tŏŏf)	Pol.	50·47 N	21·25 E
121	Opava	(ō'pä-vä)	Czech.	49·56 N	17·52 E
118	Opdal	(ōp'däl)	Nor.	62·37 N	9·41 E
78	Opelika	(ŏp-ē-lī'ká)	Ala.	32·39 N	85·23 W
77	Opelousas	(ŏp-ē-lōō'sás)	La.	30·33 N	92·04 W
81	Opeongo (L.)	(ŏp-ē-ŏŋ'gō)	Can.	45·40 N	78·20 W
67	Opheim	(ŏ-fīm')	Mont.	48·51 N	106·19 W
64	Ophir	(ō'fēr)	Alaska	63·10 N	156·28 W
139	Ophir, Mt.		Mala. (Singapore In.)	2·22 N	102·37 E
92	Opico	(ô-pē'kō)	Sal.	13·50 N	89·23 W
87	Opinaca (R.)	(ŏp-ĭ-nä'ká)	Can.	52·28 N	77·40 W
123	Opladen		Ger. (Ruhr In.)	51·04 N	7·00 E
128	Opochka	(ō-pôch'kä)	Sov. Un.	56·43 N	28·39 E
121	Opoczno	(ō-pôch'nô)	Pol.	51·22 N	20·18 E
121	Opole	(ō-pôl'ä)	Pol.	50·42 N	17·55 E
121	Opole Lubelskie	(ō-pō'lä lōō-bĕl'skyĕ)	Pol.	51·09 N	21·58 E
	Oporto, see Pôrto				
66	Oportunity	(ŏp-ŏr tū'nĭ tĭ)	Wash.	47·37 N	117·20 W
129	Oposhnya	(ô-pôsh'nyá)	Sov. Un.	49·57 N	34·34 E
78	Opp	(ŏp)	Ala.	31·18 N	86·15 W
74	Oquirrh Mts.		Utah (Salt Lake City In.)	40·38 N	112·11 W
121	Oradea	(ô-räd'yä)	Rom.	47·02 N	21·55 E
114	Oran (Ouahran)	(ō-rän) (ô-rän')	Alg.	35·46 N	0·45 W
100	Orán	(ō-rä'n)	Arg.	23·15 S	64·17 W
73	Oran	(ôr'án)	Mo.	37·05 N	89·39 W
160	Orange	(ōr'ĕnj)	Austl.	33·15 S	149·08 E
74	Orange		Calif. (Los Angeles In.)	33·48 N	117·51 W
81	Orange		Conn.	41·15 N	73·00 W
122	Orange	(ô-raNzh')	Fr.	44·08 N	4·48 E
84	Orange		N. J. (New York In.)	40·46 N	74·14 W
77	Orange		Tex.	30·07 N	93·44 W
99	Orange, Cabo (C.)	(kä-bô-rà'n-zhĕ)	Braz.	4·25 N	51·30 W
79	Orange (L.)		Fla.	29·30 N	82·12 W
166	Orange (R.)		Br. W. Afr.-S. Afr.	29·15 S	17·30 E
79	Orangeburg	(ŏr'ĕnj-bûrg)	S. C.	33·30 N	80·50 W
94	Orange Cay (I.)	(ŏr-ĕnj kē)	Ba. Is.	24·55 N	79·05 W
70	Orange City		Iowa	43·01 N	96·06 W
166	Orange Free State (Prov.)		S. Afr.	28·15 S	26·00 E
85	Orangeville	(ŏr'ĕnj-vĭl)	Can. (Toronto In.)	43·55 N	80·06 W
168	Orangeville		S. Afr. (Johannesburg & Pretoria In.)	27·05 S	28·13 E
92	Orange Walk	(wôl'k)	Br. Hond. (Yucatan In.)	18·09 N	88·32 W
155	Orani	(ō-rä'nē)	Phil. (Manila In.)	14·47 N	120·32 E
111	Oranienburg	(ō-rä'nē-ĕn-bŏŏrgh)	Ger. (Berlin In.)	52·45 N	13·14 E
155	Oranje-Gebergte (Mts.)		W. Irian	4·22 S	139·25 E
166	Oranjemund		S. W. Afr.	28·33 S	16·20 E
127	Orastie	(ô-rûsh'tyä)	Rom.	45·50 N	23·14 E
	Oraşul-Stalin, see Braşov				
126	Orbetello	(ōr-bä-tĕl'lō)	It.	42·27 N	11·15 E
124	Orbigo (R.)	(ôr-bē'gō)	Sp.	42·59 N	5·32 W
160	Orbost	(ôr'bŭst)	Austl.	37·43 S	148·20 E
65	Orcas (I.)	(ôr'käs)	Wash. (Vancouver In.)	48·43 N	122·52 W
74	Orchard Farm	(ôr'chĕrd färm)	Mo. (St. Louis In.)	38·53 N	90·27 W
75	Orchard Park		N. Y. (Buffalo In.)	42·46 N	78·46 W
65	Orchards	(ôr'chĕdz)	Wash. (Portland In.)	45·40 N	122·33 W
98	Orchilla	(ôr-kēl'-á)	Ven.	11·47 N	66·34 W
70	Ord	(ôrd)	Nebr.	41·35 N	98·57 W
158	Ord (R.)		Austl.	17·30 S	128·40 E
136	Orda	(ōr'dä)	Sov. Un. (Urals In.)	56·50 N	57·12 E
124	Órdenes	(ōr'dä-näs)	Sp.	43·46 N	8·24 W
150	Ordos Des		China	39·12 N	108·10 E
69	Ord Pk.		Ariz.	33·55 N	109·40 W
133	Ordu	(ôr'dōō)	Tur.	40·10 N	37·50 E
124	Orduña	(ôr-dōō'nyä)	Sp.	42·59 N	3·01 W
72	Ordway	(ôrd'wā)	Colo.	38·11 N	103·46 W
133	Ordzhonikidze	(Ora ghō nĭ' kĭd ze)	Sov. Un.	43·05 N	44·35 E
118	Örebro	(ů'rē-brō)	Swe.	59·16 N	15·11 E
136	Oredezh R.	(ô'rē-dĕzh)	Sov. Un. (Leningrad In.)	59·23 N	30·21 E
71	Oregon	(ŏr'ē-gŏn)	Ill.	42·01 N	89·21 W
62	Oregon (State)		U. S.	43·40 N	121·50 W
66	Oregon Caves Natl. Mon.	(cāvz)	Ore.	42·05 N	123·13 W

PRONOUNCING INDEX
Oregon City–Owyhee 247

Page	Name Pronunciation Region	Lat. °′	Long. °′
65	Oregon City...Ore. (Portland In.)	45·21 N	122·36 W
118	Oregrund (û'rĕ-grŏŏnd)......Swe.	60·20 N	18·26 E
129	Orekhov (ôr-yĕ'κôf).....Sov. Un.	47·34 N	35·51 E
128	Orekhovo-Zuyevo (ôr-yĕ'κô-vô zŏŏ'yĕ-vô).Sov Un.	55·46 N	39·00 E
128	Orël (ôr-yôl')...........Sov. Un.	52·54 N	36·03 E
128	Orël (Oblast)...........Sov. Un.	52·35 N	36·08 E
129	Orel' (R.)..............Sov. Un.	49·08 N	34·55 E
69	Orem (ŏ'rĕm).............Utah	40·15 N	111·50 W
	Ore Mts., see Erzgebirge		
133	Orenburg (ô'rĕn-bŏŏrg)..Sov. Un.	51·50 N	55·05 E
124	Orense (ô-rĕn'sā).............Sp.	42·20 N	7·52 W
94	Organos, Sierra de los (Mts.) (sē-ĕ'r-rä-dĕ-lôs-ŏ'r-gä-nôs).Cuba	22·20 N	84·10 W
69	Organ Pipe Cactus Natl. Mon. (ôr'găn pīp kăk'tŭs).Ariz.	32·14 N	113·05 W
101	Orgãos, Serra das (Mtn.) (sĕ'r-rä-däs-ôr-gouN's) Braz. (Rio de Janeiro In.)	22·30 S	43·01 W
129	Orgeyev (ôr-gyĕ'yĕf).....Sov. Un.	47·27 N	28·49 E
146	Orhon Gol (R.)...........Mong.	48·33 N	103·07 E
98	Oriental, Cordillera (Mts.) (kôr-dēl-yĕ'rä ō-rê-ĕn-täl').Bol.	14·00 S	68·33 W
98	Oriental, Cordillera (Mts.) (kôr-dēl-yĕ'rä).Col. (In.)	3·30 N	74·27 W
95	Oriental, Cordillera (Mts.) (kôr-dēl-yĕ'rä-ô-ryĕ'n-täl) Dom. Rep.	18·55 N	69·40 W
88	Oriental, Sierra Madre, (Mts.) (sē-ĕ'r-rä-mä'drĕ-ô-ryĕ'n-täl') Mex.	25·30 N	100·45 W
95	Oriente (State) (ō-rê-ĕn'tà)..Cuba	20·25 N	76·15 W
125	Orihuela (ō'rê-wā'lä).........Sp.	38·04 N	0·55 W
119	Orihvesi (L.) (ô'rĭ-vĕ-sĭ)......Fin.	62·15 N	29·55 E
81	Orillia (ô-rĭl'ĭ-ȧ)............Can.	44·35 N	79·25 W
98	Orinoco, Rio (R.) (rê'ō-ô-rĭ-nō'kô).Ven.	8·32 N	63·13 W
155	Orion (ō-rê-ōn').Phil. (Manila In.)	14·37 N	120·34 E
142	Orissa (State) (ŏ-rĭs'ȧ)......India	25·09 N	83·50 E
126	Oristano (ô-rês-tä'nō).........It.	39·53 N	8·38 E
126	Oristano, Golfo di (G.) (gôl-fô-dē-ô-rês-tä'nō).It.	39·53 N	8·12 E
99	Orituco (R.) (ô-rē-tōō'kō) Ven. (In.)	9·37 N	66·25 W
99	Oriuco (ô-rêōō'kō) (R.).Ven. (In.)	9·36 N	66·25 W
91	Orizaba (ô-rê-zä'bä)........Mex.	18·52 N	97·05 W
118	Orkdal (ôr'k-däl)...........Nor.	63·19 N	9·54 E
112	Örkedalen (ûr'kĕ-dä-lĕn).....Nor.	63·13 N	9·53 E
118	Örken (L.) (ûr'kĕn).........Swe.	57·11 N	14·45 E
118	Orkla (R.) (ôr'klȧ)..........Nor.	62·55 N	9·50 E
168	Orkney (ôrk'nĭ)...........S. Afr. (Johannesburg & Pretoria In.)	26·58 S	26·39 E
116	Orkney (Is.)..............Scot.	59·01 N	2·08 W
79	Orlando (ôr-lăn'dō).....Fla. (In.)	28·32 N	81·22 W
167	Orlando (ôr-lăn-dô).......S. Afr. (Johannesburg & Pretoria In.)	26·15 S	27·56 E
75	Orland Park (ôr-lăn') Ill. (Chicago In.)	41·38 N	87·52 W
85	Orleans (ôr-lȧ-äN') Can. (Ottawa In.)	45·28 N	75·31 W
122	Orléans (ôr-lā-äN')...........Fr.	47·55 N	1·56 E
80	Orleans (ôr-lēnz')...........Ind.	38·40 N	86·25 W
	Orléansville, see El Asnam		
79	Ormond Beach (ôr'mŏnd)....Fla.	29·15 N	81·05 W
110	Ormskirk (ôrms'kērk).......Eng.	53·34 N	2·53 W
85	Ormstown (ôrms'toun) Can. (Montreal In.)	45·07 N	74·00 W
122	Orne (R.) (ôrn')............Fr.	49·05 N	0·32 W
121	Orneta (ôr-nyĕ'tä)...........Pol.	54·07 N	20·10 E
118	Ornö (I.)..................Swe.	59·02 N	18·35 E
112	Örnsköldsvik (ûrn'skôlts-vēk).Swe.	63·10 N	18·32 E
90	Oro, Rio del (R.) (rē'ō dĕl ō'rō) Mex.	18·04 N	100·59 W
76	Oro, Rio del (R.)...........Mex.	26·04 N	105·40 W
126	Orobie, Alpi (Mts.) (äl'pē-ô-rŏ'byĕ).It.	46·05 N	9·47 E
98	Orocué (ô-rô-kwā')..........Col.	4·48 N	71·26 W
116	Oronsay, Pass. of (ō'rŏn-sȧ)..Scot.	55·55 N	6·25 W
126	Orosei, Golfo di (G.) (gôl-fô-dē-ō-rô-sā'ē).It.	40·12 N	9·45 E
121	Orosháza (ô-rôsh-hä'sô)....Hung.	46·33 N	20·31 E
92	Orosi Vol. (ō-rō'sē).........C. R.	11·00 N	85·30 W
68	Oroville (ōr'ô-vĭl)..........Calif.	39·29 N	121·34 W
66	Oroville..................Wash.	48·55 N	119·25 W
80	Orrville (ôr'vĭl)............Ohio	40·45 N	81·50 W
118	Orsa (ōr'sä)................Swe.	61·08 N	14·35 E
118	Örsdals Vand (L.) (ûrs-däls vän) Nor.	58·39 N	6·06 E
128	Orsha (ôr'shȧ)..........Sov. Un.	54·29 N	30·28 E
133	Orsk (ôrsk)............Sov. Un.	51·15 N	58·50 E
127	Orşova (ôr'shô-vȧ).........Rom.	44·43 N	22·26 E
98	Ortega (ôr-tĕ'gä).......Col. (In.)	3·56 N	75·12 W
124	Ortegal, Cabo (C.) (kȧ'bô-ôr-tȧ-gäl').Sp.	43·46 N	8·15 W
111	Orth..........Aus. (Vienna In.)	48·09 N	16·42 E
125	Orthez (ôr-tĕz')...............Fr.	43·29 N	0·43 W
124	Ortigueira (ôr-tê-gā'ê-rä)......Sp.	43·40 N	7·50 W
65	Orting (ôrt'ĭng) Wash. (Seattle In.)	47·06 N	122·12 W
126	Ortona (ôr-tō'nä)..............It.	42·22 N	14·22 E
70	Ortonville (ôr-tŭn-vĭl)......Minn.	45·18 N	96·26 W
98	Oruro (ô-rōō'rō)..............Bol.	17·57 S	66·59 W
126	Orvieto (ôr-vyȧ'tō)............It.	42·43 N	12·08 E
127	Oryakhovo..................Bul.	43·43 N	23·59 E
118	Os (ôs)....................Nor.	60·24 N	5·22 E
132	Osa (ô'sȧ).............Sov. Un.	57·18 N	55·25 E
93	Osa, Pen. de (ō'sä)........C. R.	8·30 N	83·25 W
71	Osage (ō'sāj)...............Iowa	43·16 N	92·49 W
73	Osage (R.)..................Mo.	38·10 N	93·12 W
73	Osage City (ō'sāj sĭ'tĭ).....Kans.	38·28 N	95·53 W
153	Ōsaka (ō'sä-kä)..Jap. (Ōsaka In.)	34·40 N	135·27 E
153	Ōsaka (Pref.)....Jap. (Ōsaka In.)	34·45 N	135·36 E
153	Ōsaka-Wan (B.) (wän).......Jap.	34·34 N	135·16 E
71	Osakis (ô-sā'kĭs)..........Minn.	45·51 N	95·09 W
71	Osakis (L.)...............Minn.	45·55 N	94·55 W
153	Ōsawa (ō'sä-wä).Jap. (Tōkyō In.)	35·54 N	129·48 E
73	Osawatomie (ŏs-ȧ-wăt'ô-mê).Kans.	38·29 N	94·57 W
72	Osborne (ŏz'bŭrn).........Kans.	39·25 N	98·42 W
73	Osceola (ŏs-ê-ō'lȧ)..........Ark.	35·42 N	89·58 W
71	Osceola...................Iowa	41·04 N	93·45 W
73	Osceola....................Mo.	38·02 N	93·41 W
70	Osceola...................Nebr.	41·11 N	97·34 W
73	Osceola...................Tenn.	35·42 N	89·58 W
80	Oscoda (ŏs-kō'dȧ).........Mich.	44·25 N	83·20 W
128	Osëtr (R.) (ô'sĕt'r)......Sov. Un.	54·27 N	38·15 E
80	Osgood (ŏz'gŏŏd)...........Ind.	39·10 N	85·20 W
85	Osgoode Sta....Can. (Ottawa In.)	45·09 N	75·37 W
134	Osh (ôsh).............Sov. Un.	40·28 N	72·47 E
81	Oshawa (ŏsh'ȧ-wȧ)..........Can.	43·50 N	78·50 W
153	Ōshima (I.) (ō'shē'mä).......Jap.	34·47 N	139·35 E
70	Oshkosh (ŏsh'kŏsh).........Nebr.	41·24 N	102·22 W
71	Oshkosh...................Wis.	44·01 N	88·35 W
119	Oshmyany (ôsh-myä'nĭ)..Sov. Un.	54·27 N	25·55 E
164	Oshogbo...................Nig.	7·53 N	4·23 E
127	Osijek (ôs'ĭ-yĕk)...........Yugo.	45·33 N	18·48 E
134	Osinniki (ŭ-sē'nyĭ-kē)....Sov. Un.	53·29 N	85·19 E
129	Osipenko (ŭ-sē'pyĭn-kō)..Sov. Un.	46·45 N	36·47 E
71	Oskaloosa (ŏs-kȧ-lōō'sȧ).....Iowa	41·16 N	92·40 W
118	Oskarshamn (ôs'kärs-häm'n).Swe.	57·16 N	16·24 E
118	Oskarstrzöm (ôs'kärs-strûm).Swe.	56·48 N	12·55 E
129	Oskol (R.) (ôs-kôl')......Sov. Un.	49·25 N	37·41 E
118	Oslo (ôs'lō)................Nor.	59·56 N	10·41 E
118	Oslo Fd (fyôrd).............Nor.	59·03 N	10·35 E
124	Osma (ōs'mä)................Sp.	41·35 N	3·02 W
133	Osmaniye...................Tur.	37·10 N	36 30 E
120	Osnabrück (ôs-nä-brük').....Ger.	52·16 N	8·05 E
100	Osorno (ô-sō'r-nō)..........Chile	40·42 S	73·13 W
159	Osprey Reef (I.) (ŏs'prȧ)...Austl.	14·00 S	146·45 E
160	Ossa, Mt. (ŏsȧ)...........Austl.	41·45 S	146·05 E
74	Osseo (ŏs'sĕ-ō)............Minn. (Minneapolis, St. Paul In.)	45·07 N	93·24 W
84	Ossining (ŏs'ĭ-nĭng) N. Y. (New York In.)	41·09 N	73·51 W
82	Ossipee (ŏs'ĭ-pê)...........N. H.	43·42 N	71·08 W
118	Ossjöen (L.) (ôs-syûĕn)......Nor.	61·20 N	12·00 E
128	Ostashkov (ôs-täsh'kôf)..Sov. Un.	57·07 N	33·04 E
117	Oste (R.) (ōz'tĕ)............Ger.	53·20 N	9·19 E
129	Oster (ōs'tĕr)..........Sov. Un.	50·55 N	30·52 E
118	Oster-daläven (R.)..........Swe.	61·40 N	13·00 E
118	Oster Fd. (ûs'tēr fyôr')......Nor.	60·40 N	5·25 E
118	Ostersund (ûs'tĕr-sōōnd).....Swe.	63·09 N	14·49 E
118	Östhammar (ûst'häm'är).....Swe.	60·16 N	18·21 E
125	Ostia Antica (ô's-tyä-än-tê'kä) It. (Rome In.)	41·46 N	12·24 E
	Ostia Lido, see Lido di Roma		
121	Ostrava..................Czech.	49·51 N	18·18 E
121	Ostróda (ôs'trōōt-ȧ).........Pol.	53·41 N	19·58 E
129	Ostróg (ŏs-trôk')........Sov. Un.	50·21 N	26·40 E
129	Ostrogozhsk (ôs-trô-gôzhk') Sov. Un.	50·53 N	39·03 E
121	Ostrołeka (ôs-trô-woN'kȧ)....Pol.	53·04 N	21·35 E
129	Ostropol' (ôs-trô-pôl')...Sov. Un.	49·48 N	27·32 E
128	Ostrov (ôs-trôf')........Sov. Un.	57·21 N	28·22 E
121	Ostrowiec Świętokrzyski (ōs-trō'vyĕts shvyĕN-tō-kzhĭ'ske) Pol.	50·55 N	21·24 E
121	Ostrów Lubelski (ôs'trōōf lōō'bĕl-skĭ).Pol.	51·32 N	22·49 E
121	Ostrów Mazowiecka (mä-zô-vyĕt'skȧ).Pol.	52·47 N	21·54 E
121	Ostrów Wielkopolski (ōs'trōōv vyĕl-kō-pōl'skē).Pol.	51·38 N	17·49 E
121	Ostrzeszów (ôs-tzhā'shōōf)....Pol.	51·26 N	17·56 E
127	Ostuni (ôs-tōō'nē)............It.	40·44 N	17·35 E
127	Osum (R.) (ō'sōōm).........Alb.	40·37 N	20·00 E
153	Ōsumi-Guntō (Arch.) (ō'sōō-mê gōōn'tō).Jap.	30·34 N	130·30 E
153	Ōsumi (Van Diemen) Kaikyō (Str.) (văn dē'mĕn) (käê'kyô) Jap.	31·02 N	130·10 E
124	Osuna (ô-sōō'nä).............Sp.	37·18 N	5·05 W
128	Osveya (ôs'vĕ-yȧ).......Sov. Un.	56·00 N	28·08 E
110	Oswaldtwistle (ŏz-wȧld-twĭs''l) Eng.	53·44 N	2·23 W
81	Oswegatchie (R.) (ŏs-wê-găch'ĭ) N. Y.	44·15 N	75·20 W
73	Oswego (ŏs-wē'gō).........Kans.	37·10 N	95·08 W
81	Oswego...................N. Y.	43·25 N	76·30 W
121	Oswiecim (ôsh-vyăN'tsyĭm)...Pol.	50·02 N	19·17 E
152	Otaru (ô'tȧ-rōō).............Jap.	43·07 N	141·00 E
98	Otavalo (ōtä-vä'lō)...........Ec.	0·14 N	78·16 W
166	Otavi (ô-tä'vê)........S. W. Afr.	19·35 S	17·20 E
68	Otay (ō'tā)..Calif. (San Diego In.)	32·36 N	117·04 W
128	Otepää (ô'tĕ-pȧ)........Sov. Un.	58·03 N	26·31 E
127	Othonoí (I.)................Grc.	40·51 N	19·26 E
127	Óthris, Óros (Mts.)..........Grc.	39·00 N	22·15 E
87	Otish Mts. (ô-tĭsh')........Can.	52·24 N	70·01 W
166	Otjiwarongo (ŏt-jê-wȧ-rôŋ'gō).Ang.	20·20 S	16·25 E
126	Otočac (ō'tô-chȧts)........Yugo.	44·53 N	15·15 E
136	Otradnoye (ô-trȧ'd-nôyĕ) Sov. Un. (Leningrad In.)	59·46 N	30·50 E
127	Otranto (ô'trän-tô) (ô-trän'tō)..It.	40·07 N	18·30 E
127	Otranto, C. di...............It.	40·06 N	18·32 E
127	Otranto, Strait of........It.-Alb.	40·30 N	18 45 E
136	Otra R. (ôt'rȧ) Sov. Un. (Moscow In.)	55·22 N	38·20 E
80	Otsego (ŏt-sē'gō).........Mich.	42·25 N	85·45 W
153	Otsu (ō'tsōō)....Jap. (Ōsaka In.)	35·00 N	135·54 E
118	Ottavand (L.) (ôt'tȧ-vän)....Nor.	61·53 N	8·40 E
85	Ottawa (ŏt'ȧ-wȧ) Can. (Ottawa In.)	45·25 N	75·43 W
80	Ottawa....................Ill.	41·20 N	88·50 W
73	Ottawa...................Kans.	38·37 N	95·16 W
80	Ottawa...................Ohio	41·00 N	84·00 W
87	Ottawa (R.)................Can.	46·05 N	77·20 W
87	Ottawa Is..................Can.	59·50 N	81·00 W
168	Ottensville (ŏt'ĕns-vĭl).....S. Afr. (Johannesburg & Pretoria In.)	24·46 S	29·34 E
118	Otteråen (ôt'ĕr-ôĕn).........Nor.	59·13 N	7·20 E
69	Otter Cr. (ŏt'ēr)............Utah	38·20 N	111·55 W
81	Otter Cr....................Vt.	44·05 N	73·15 W
65	Otter Pt.......Can. (Seattle In.)	48·21 N	123·50 W
70	Otter Tail (L.)............Minn.	46·21 N	95·52 W
74	Otterville (ôt'ĕr-vĭl) Ill. (St. Louis In.)	39·03 N	90·24 W
166	Ottery (ŏt'ēr-ĭ) S. Afr. (Cape Town In.)	34·02 S	18·31 E
71	Ottumwa (ô-tŭm'wȧ).......Iowa	41·00 N	92·26 W
91	Otumba (ô-tŭm'bä) Mex. (Mexico City In.)	19·41 N	98·46 W
160	Otway, C. (ŏt'wā).........Austl.	38·55 S	153·40 E
100	Otway, Seno (B.) (sĕ'nō-ô't-wä'y) Chile	53·00 S	73·00 W
121	Otwock (ôt'vôtsk)...........Pol.	52·05 N	21·18 E
63	Ouachita, (R.).............U. S.	33·25 N	92·30 W
73	Ouachita Mts. (wŏsh'ĭ-tô)...Okla.	34·29 N	95·01 W
165	Ouaddai (Reg.) (wä-dī')....Chad	13·04 N	20·00 E
164	Ouagadougou (wä'gȧ-dōō'gōō) Upper Volta	12·20 N	1·43 W
164	Ouahigouya (wä-ê-gōō'yä) Upper Volta	13·34 N	2·22 W
	Ouahran, see Oran		
164	Oualata (wä-lä'tä)....Mauritania	17·11 N	6·50 W
164	Ouallène (wäl-lân')..........Alg.	24·43 N	1·15 E
95	Ouanaminthe..............Hai.	19·35 N	71·45 W
165	Ouanda-Djalé (wän'dȧ jä-lā') Cen. Afr. Rep.	8·56 N	22·46 E
164	Ouarane (Dunes).....Mauritania	20·44 N	10·27 W
164	Ouargla (wär'glä)...........Alg.	32·00 N	5·18 E
111	Oude Rijn (R.) Neth. (Amsterdam In.)	52·09 N	4·33 E
111	Oudewater.Neth. (Amsterdam In.)	52·01 N	4·52 E
111	Oud-Gastel.Neth. (Amsterdam In.)	51·35 N	4·27 E
114	Oudrhes, L. (Mt.)..........Mor.	32·33 N	4·49 W
166	Oudtshoorn (outs'hōrn)....S. Afr.	33·33 S	23·36 E
125	Oued Rhiou.................Alg.	35·55 N	0·57 E
125	Oued Tiélat.................Alg.	35·33 N	0·28 W
164	Oued-Zem (wĕd-zĕm').......Mor.	33·05 N	5·49 W
122	Ouessant, I. d' (ēl-dwĕ-säN')..Fr.	48·28 N	5·00 W
165	Ouesso..................Con. B.	1·38 N	16·04 E
95	Ouest, Pt..................Hai.	19·00 N	73·25 W
164	Ouezzane (wĕ-zan').........Mor.	34·48 N	5·40 W
116	Oughter (L.) (lôK oK'tĕr).....Ire.	54·02 N	7·40 W
164	Ouidah (wē-dä').......Dahomey	6·25 N	2·05 E
114	Ouled Naïl, Montes des (Mts.).Alg.	34·43 N	2·44 E
123	Oulins (ōō-lȧN')....Fr. (Paris In.)	48·52 N	1·27 E
122	Oullins (ōō-lăN')............Fr.	45·44 N	4·46 E
112	Oulu (ō'lōō)................Fin.	64·58 N	25·43 E
112	Oulu-jarvi (L.).............Fin.	64·20 N	25·48 E
165	Oum Chalouba (ōōm shä-lōō'bä) Chad	15·48 N	20·30 E
112	Ounas (R.) (ō'nȧs)..........Fin.	67·46 N	24·40 E
110	Oundle (ôn'd'l).............Eng.	52·28 N	0·28 W
165	Ounianga Kébir (ōō-nê-äŋ'gȧ kē-bēr').Chad	19·04 N	20·22 E
69	Ouray (ōō-rā')..............Colo.	38·00 N	107·40 W
99	Ourinhos (ôōō-rê'nyôs)......Braz.	23·04 S	49·45 W
124	Ourique (ō-rē'kĕ)...........Port.	37·39 N	8·10 W
101	Ouro Fino (ōŭ-rô-fē'nō) Braz. (Rio de Janeiro In.)	22·18 S	46·21 W
101	Ouro Prêto (ō'rōō prā'tōō) Braz. (Rio de Janeiro In.)	20·24 S	43·30 W
116	Ouse (R.)..................Eng.	53·45 N	1·09 W
87	Outardes, R. aux (ōō-tȧrdz').Can.	50·33 N	69·10 W
164	Outat el Hadj..............Mor.	33·25 N	3·44 W
83	Outer (I.) (out'ēr).........Can.	51·06 N	58·23 W
71	Outer (I.) (out'ēr)..........Wis.	47·03 N	90·20 W
89	Outer Brass (I.) (bräs)....Vir. Is. (U. S. A.) (St. Thomas In.)	18·24 N	64·58 W
116	Outer Hebrides (Is.)........Scot.	57·20 N	7·50 W
166	Outjo (ōt'yō).........S. W. Afr.	20·05 S	17·10 E
85	Outremont (ōō-trē-môN') Can. (Montreal In.)	45·31 N	73·36 W
160	Ouyen (ōō-ĕn)............Austl.	35·05 S	142·10 E
100	Ovalle (ō-väl'yā)...........Chile	30·43 S	71·16 W
166	Ovamboland (Reg.)....S. W. Afr.	18·10 S	15·00 E
95	Ovando, Bahía de (B.) (bä-ē'ä-dĕ-ô-vä'n-dō).Cuba	20·10 N	74·05 W
124	Ovar (ô-vär')..............Port.	40·52 N	8·38 W
111	Overijsche.....Bel. (Brussels In.)	50·46 N	4·32 E
74	Overland (ō'vēr-lănd) Mo. (St. Louis In.)	38·42 N	90·22 W
74	Overland Park Kans. (Kansas City In.)	38·59 N	94·40 W
84	Overlea (ō'vēr-lā) (ō'vēr-lē) Md. (Baltimore In.)	39·21 N	76·31 W
112	Overtornea.................Swe.	66·19 N	23·31 E
129	Ovidiopol' (ô-vê-dê-ô'pôl').Sov. Un.	46·15 N	30·28 E
95	Oviedo (ô-vyĕ'dō).....Dom. Rep.	17·50 N	71·25 W
124	Oviedo (ō-vê-ā'dhō)..........Sp.	43·22 N	5·50 W
129	Ovruch (ôv'rōōch).......Sov. Un.	51·19 N	28·51 E
153	Owada (ō'wä-dȧ).Jap. (Tōkyō In.)	35·43 N	140·06 E
153	Owada.........Jap. (Tōkyō In.)	35·49 N	139·33 E
81	Owasco (L.) (ō-wăs'kō).....N. Y.	42·50 N	76·30 W
153	Owashi (ō'wä-shê)............Jap.	34·03 N	136·12 E
81	Owego (ō-wē'gō)...........N. Y.	42·05 N	76·15 W
71	Owen (ō'ĕn)................Wis.	44·56 N	90·35 W
68	Owens (L.) (ō'ĕnz)..........Calif.	36·27 N	117·45 W
68	Owens (R.)................Calif.	37·13 N	118·20 W
80	Owensboro (ō'ĕnz-bŭr-ô)......Ky.	37·45 N	87·05 W
80	Owen Sound (ō'ĕn)..........Can.	44·30 N	80·55 W
155	Owen Stanley Ra. (stăn'lê)..Pap.	9·00 S	147·30 E
80	Owensville (ō'ĕnz-vĭl)........Ind.	38·15 N	87·40 W
73	Owensville..................Mo.	38·20 N	91·29 W
75	Owensville..Ohio (Cincinnati In.)	39·08 N	84·07 W
80	Owenton (ō'ĕn-tŭn)..........Ky.	38·35 N	84·55 W
164	Owerri (ô-wĕr'ê)............Nig.	5·26 N	7·04 E
84	Owings Mill (ōwĭngz mĭl) Md. (Baltimore In.)	39·25 N	76·50 W
67	Owl Cr. (oul)..............Wyo.	43·45 N	108·46 W
80	Owosso (ô-wŏs'ō)..........Mich.	43·00 N	84·15 W
66	Owyhee Mts. (ô-wī'hê).....Idaho	43·15 N	116·48 W
66	Owyhee Res.................Ore.	43·27 N	117·30 W
66	Owyhee R...................Ore.	43·04 N	117·45 W

ng-sing; ŋ-baŋk; N-nasalized n; nŏd; cŏmmit; ōld; ôbey; ôrder; fōōd; fŏŏt; ou-out; s-soft; sh-dish; th-thin; pūre; ûnite; ûrn; stŭd; circŭs; ü-as "y" in study; '-indeterminate vowel.

248 Owyhee–Paraguay PRONOUNCING INDEX

Page	Name Pronunciation Region	Lat. °′	Long. °′
66	Owyhee R., South Fork....Idaho	42·07 N	116·43 W
91	Oxchuc (ôs-chōōk')........Mex.	16·47 N	92·24 W
78	Oxford (ŏks'fẽrd)...........Ala.	33·38 N	8·46 W
82	Oxford (ŏks'fẽrd)..........Can.	45·44 N	63·51 W
110	Oxford........Eng. (London In.)	51·43 N	1·16 W
83	Oxford........Mass. (Boston In.)	42·07 N	71·52 W
80	Oxford.................Mich.	42·50 N	83·15 W
78	Oxford.................Miss.	34·22 N	89·30 W
79	Oxford.................N. C.	36·17 N	78·35 W
80	Oxford.................Ohio	39·30 N	84·45 W
92	Oxkutzcab (ôx-kōō'tz-käb) Mex. (Yucatan In.)	20·18 N	89·22 W
84	Oxmoor (ŏks'mŏŏr) Ala. (Birmingham In.)	33·25 N	86·52 W
116	Ox Mts. (ŏks)..............Ire.	54·05 N	9·05 W
68	Oxnard (ŏks'närd).........Calif.	34·08 N	119·12 W
84	Oxon Hill (ōks'ōn hĭl) Md. (Baltimore In.)	38·48 N	77·00 W
91	Oxtotepec (ôx-tô-tĕ'pĕk) Mex. (Mexico City In.)	19·10 N	99·04 W
168	Oxyrhyncus (Ruins) U. A. R. (Nile In.)	28·37 N	30·48 E
99	Oyapock (ō-yȧ-pŏk').Braz.-Fr. Gu.	2·45 N	52·15 W
164	Oyem (ô-yĕm) (ô-yăɴ')....Gabon	1·42 N	11·38 E
135	Oymyakon (oi-myŭ-kôn').Sov. Un.	63·14 N	142·58 E
164	Oyo (ō'yō)................Nig.	7·52 N	3·51 E
123	Oyonnax (ô-yô-nȧks').........Fr.	46·16 N	5·40 E
84	Oyster Bay. N. Y. (New York In.)	40·52 N	73·32 W
77	Oyster Bay...........Tex. (In.)	29·41 N	94·33 W
77	Oyster Cr. (ois'tẽr).....Tex. (In.)	29·13 N	95·29 W
95	Ozama (R.) (ô-zä'mä) . Dom. Rep.	18·45 N	69·55 W
155	Ozamiz (ô-zä'mêz).........Phil.	8·06 N	123·43 E
78	Ozark (ō'zärk).............Ala.	31·28 N	85·28 W
73	Ozark....................Ark.	35·29 N	93·49 W
73	Ozarks, L. of the (ō'zärkz)...Mo.	38·06 N	93·26 W
73	Ozark Plat.................Mo.	36·37 N	93·56 W
128	Ozëry (ô-zyô'rê).........Sov. Un.	54·53 N	38·31 E
126	Ozieri....................Sard.	40·38 N	8·53 E
121	Ozorków (ô-zôr'kŏŏf)........Pol.	51·58 N	19·20 E
91	Ozuluama (ō'zōō-lōō-ä'mä)..Mex.	21·34 N	97·52 W
91	Ozumba (ô-zōō'm-bä) Mex. (Mexico City In.)	19·02 N	98·48 W
146	Paan.....................China	30·08 N	99·00 E
166	Paarl (pärl)..............S. Afr.	33·45 S	18·55 E
157	Paauilo (pä-ä-ōō'ê-lō).Hawaii (In.)	20·03 N	155·25 W
121	Pabianice (pä-byȧ-nē'tsĕ)....Pol.	51·40 N	19·29 E
98	Pacaás Novos, Massiço de (Mts.) (mä-sē'sô-dĕ-pä-kȧ's-nô'vōs) Braz.	11·03 S	64·02 W
98	Pacaraima, Serra (Mts.) (sĕr'rȧ pä-kä-rä-ē'mȧ) Braz. -Ven.	3·45 N	62·30 W
98	Pacasmayo (pä-käs-mä'yō)...Peru	7·24 S	79·30 W
146	Pach'u (pä'chōō')..........China	39·50 N	78·23 E
90	Pachuca (pä-chōō'kä).......Mex.	20·07 N	98·43 W
65	Pacific (pȧ-sĭf'ĭk) Wash. (Seattle In.)	47·16 N	122·15 W
65	Pacifica (pȧ-sĭf'ĭ-kä) Calif. (San Francisco In.)	37·38 N	122·29 W
68	Pacific Beach. Calif. (San Diego In.)	32·47 N	117·22 W
68	Pacific Grove.............Calif.	36·37 N	121·54 W
157	Pacific O.		
79	Pacolet (R.) (pā'cō-lēt)......S. C.	34·55 N	81·49 W
123	Pacy-sur-Eure (pä-sē-sür-ûr') Fr. (Paris In.)	49·01 N	1·24 E
154	Padang (pä-däng').......Indon.	1·01 S	100·28 E
139	Padang, Palau (I.) Indon. (Singapore In.)	1·12 N	102·21 E
80	Paden City (pā'dĕn)......W. Va.	39·30 N	80·55 W
120	Paderborn (pä-dĕr-bôrn')....Ger.	51·43 N	8·46 E
110	Padiham (păd'ĭ-hăm).......Eng.	53·48 N	2·19 W
90	Padilla (pä-dēl'yä)..........Mex.	24·00 N	98·45 W
65	Padilla B. (pä-dĕl'lȧ) Wash. (Seattle In.)	48·31 N	122·34 W
126	Padova (Padua) (pä'dô-vä) (păd'û-ȧ). It.	45·24 N	11·53 E
77	Padre I. (pä'drā)...........Tex.	27·09 N	97·15 W
	Padua, see Padova		
78	Paducah (pȧ-dū'kȧ)..........Ky.	37·05 N	88·36 W
152	Paektu San (Mt.) (pâk'tōō-sän') China-Kor.	42·00 N	128·03 E
126	Pag (I.) (päg).............Yugo.	44·30 N	14·48 E
154	Pagai Selatan (I.).........Indon.	2·48 S	100·22 E
154	Pagai Utara (I.)..........Indon.	2·45 S	100·02 E
127	Pagasitikós Kólpos (G.)......Grc.	39·15 N	23·00 E
69	Pagosa Springs (pȧ-gō'sȧ)...Colo.	37·15 N	107·05 W
157	Pahala (pä-hä'lä)....Hawaii (In.)	19·11 N	155·28 W
139	Pahang (State) Mala. (Singapore In.)	3·02 N	102·57 E
154	Pahang R................Mala.	3·39 N	102·41 E
79	Pahokee (pȧ-hō'kē).....Fla. (In.)	26·45 N	80·40 W
148	Paichü (bäī'gü)...........China	33·04 N	120·17 E
150	Paich'uan...............China	47·22 N	126·00 E
119	Paide (pī'dĕ).........Sov. Un.	58·54 N	25·30 E
150	Paiho...................China	32·30 N	110·15 E
148	Pai Hu (L.) (bäī' hōō).....China	31·22 N	117·38 E
119	Päijänna (L.) (pĕ'ē-yĕn-nĕ)...Fin.	61·38 N	25·05 E
148	Paikouchen (bäī'gō'jen)....China	39·08 N	116·02 E
157	Pailolo Chan. (pä-ê-lō'lō) Hawaii (In.)	21·05 N	156·41 W
101	Paine (pī'nĕ). Chile (Santiago In.)	33·49 S	70·44 W
80	Painesville (pānz'vĭl)........Ohio	41·40 N	81·15 W
69	Painted Des. (pānt'ĕd)......Ariz.	36·15 N	111·35 W
80	Paintsville (pānts'vĭl)........Ky.	37·50 N	82·50 W
148	Paip'u (bäī'pōō)...........China	32·15 N	120·47 E
151	Paise....................China	24·00 N	106·38 E
116	Paisley (pāz'lĭ).............Scot.	55·50 N	4·30 W
98	Paita (pä-ē'tä).............Peru	5·11 S	81·12 W
150	Pai T'ou Shan (Mts.)......Korea	40·30 N	127·20 E
69	Paiute Ind. Res............Utah	38·17 N	113·50 W
150	Paiyü Shan (Mtns.)........China	37·02 N	108·30 E
91	Pajápan (pä-hä'pän).......Mex.	18·16 N	94·41 W
154	Pakanbaru...............Indon.	0·43 N	101·15 E
	Pakhoi, see Peihai		
136	Pakhra R. (päĸ'rá) Sov. Un. (Moscow In.)	55·29 N	37·51 E
138	Pakistan..................Asia	28·00 N	67·30 E
142	Pakistan, East.............Asia	24·15 N	89·50 E
142	Pakistan, West............Asia	32·20 N	71·30 E
154	Pakokku (pȧ-kŏk'kŏŏ).......Bur.	21·29 N	95·00 E
126	Pakrac (pä'krȧts).........Yugo.	45·25 N	17·13 E
121	Paks (pôksh).............Hung.	46·38 N	18·53 E
77	Palacios (pȧ-lä'syōs).........Tex.	28·42 N	96·12 W
125	Palafrogell (pä-lä-frô-gĕl).....Sp.	41·55 N	3·09 E
126	Palagruža (Is.) (pä'lä-grōō'zhä) Yugo.	42·20 N	16·23 E
123	Palaiseau (pȧ-lĕ-zō'). Fr. (Paris In.)	48·44 N	2·16 E
135	Palana.................Sov. Un.	59·07 N	159·58 E
155	Palanan B. (pä-lä'nän) Phil. (Manila In.)	17·14 N	122·35 E
155	Palanan Pt.....Phil. (Manila In.)	17·12 N	122·40 E
127	Palanka (pä'län-kä)........Yugo.	45·14 N	19·24 E
142	Pālanpur (pä'lŭn-pōōr).....India	24·08 N	73·29 E
166	Palapye (pȧ-läp'yĕ)........Bots.	22·34 S	27·28 E
75	Palatine (păl'â-tīn) Ill. (Chicago In.)	42·07 N	88·03 W
79	Palatka (pȧ-lăt'kȧ)..........Fla.	29·39 N	81·40 W
155	Palau (Pelew) Is. (pä-lä'ŏŏ) Pac. Is. Trust. Ter.	7·15 N	134·30 E
155	Palauig (pȧ-lou'êg) Phil. (Manila In.)	15·27 N	119·54 E
155	Palauig Pt......Phil. (Manila In.)	15·28 N	119·41 E
154	Palawan (I.) (pä-lä'wȧn).....Phil.	9·50 N	117·38 E
119	Paldiski (päl'dĭ-skĭ).....Sov. Un.	59·22 N	24·04 E
154	Palembang (pä-lĕm-bäng'). Indon.	2·57 S	104·40 E
92	Palencia (pä-lĕn'sê-ȧ).......Guat.	14·40 N	90·22 W
124	Palencia (pä-lĕ'n-syä)........Sp.	42·02 N	4·32 W
91	Palenque (pä-lĕŋ'kȧ).......Mex.	17·34 N	91·58 W
95	Palenque, Punta (Pt.) (pōō'n-tä) Dom. Rep.	18·10 N	70·10 W
85	Palermo (pä-lĕr'mô) Can. (Toronto In.)	43·26 N	79·47 W
98	Palermo..............Col. (In.)	2·53 N	75·26 W
126	Palermo...................It.	38·08 N	13·24 E
77	Palestine.................Tex.	31·46 N	95·38 W
139	Palestine (Reg.) (păl'ĕs-tīn) Asia (Palestine In.)	31·33 N	35·00 E
146	Paletwa (pŭ-lĕt'wä).........Bur.	21·19 N	92·52 E
143	Palghāt..................India	10·49 N	76·40 E
142	Pali.....................India	25·53 N	73·18 E
146	Palik'un.................China	43·43 N	92·50 E
92	Palín (pä-lēn')............Guat.	14·42 N	90·42 W
66	Palisade (păl-ĭ-sād').........Nev.	40·39 N	116·11 W
91	Palizada (pä-lê-zä'dä).......Mex.	18·17 N	92·04 W
142	Palk Str. (pôk)............India	10·00 N	79·23 E
101	Palma (päl'mä) Braz. (Rio de Janeiro In.)	21·23 S	42·18 W
125	Palma, Ba. de (B.) (bä-ē'ä-dĕ). Sp.	39·24 N	2·37 E
124	Palma del Río (dĕl rē'ō)......Sp.	37·43 N	5·19 W
125	Palma de Mallorca (dĕ-mäl-yô'r-kä). Sp.	39·35 N	2·38 E
99	Palmares (päl-mȧ'rĕs).......Braz.	8·46 S	35·28 W
100	Palmas (päl'mäs)..........Braz.	26·20 S	51·56 W
164	Palmas, C.................Lib.	4·30 N	9·20 W
95	Palma Soriano (sô-ré-ä'nō)..Cuba	20·15 N	76·00 W
79	Palm Beach (päm bēch'). Fla. (In.)	26·43 N	80·03 W
99	Palmeira dos Índios (päl-mā'rä-dôs-ē'n-dyôs). Braz.	9·26 S	36·33 W
125	Palmela (päl-mā'lä) Port. (Lisbon In.)	38·34 N	8·54 W
64	Palmer (päm'ẽr)..........Alaska	61·38 N	149·15 W
65	Palmer.......Wash. (Seattle In.)	47·19 N	121·53 W
159	Palmerston North (päm'ẽr-stŭn) N. Z. (In.)	40·21 S	175·43 E
159	Palmerville (päm'ẽr-vĭl)....Austl.	16·08 S	144·15 E
79	Palmetto (pȧl-mĕt'ô)....Fla. (In.)	27·32 N	82·34 W
95	Palmetto Pt.............Ba. Is.	21·15 N	73·25 W
126	Palmi (päl'mē)..............It.	38·21 N	15·54 E
98	Palmira (päl-mē'rä).....Col. (In.)	3·33 N	76·17 W
94	Palmira..................Cuba	22·15 N	80·25 W
73	Palmyra (păl-mī'rȧ).........Mo.	39·45 N	91·32 W
84	Palmyra..N. J. (Philadelphia In.)	40·01 N	75·00 W
157	Palmyra (I.)............Oceania	6·00 N	162·20 W
142	Palmyras Pt..............India	25·42 N	87·45 E
103	Palmyre..................Syr.	30·35 N	37·58 E
65	Palo Alto (pä'lō äl'tō) Calif. (San Francisco In.)	37·27 N	122·09 W
72	Paloduro Cr. (pā-lô-dōō'rô)..Tex.	36·16 N	101·12 W
139	Paloh......Mala. (Singapore In.)	2·11 N	103·12 E
76	Paloma, L. (pä-lō'mä)......Mex.	26·53 N	104·02 W
101	Palomo, Cerro el (Mtn.) (sĕ'r-rô-ĕl-pä-lô'mô) Chile (Santiago In.)	34·36 S	70·20 W
125	Palos, Cabo de (C.) (kȧ'bô-dĕ-pä'lôs). Sp.	39·38 N	0·43 W
74	Palos Verdes Estates (pă'lŭs vûr'dĭs) Calif. (Los Angeles In.)	33·48 N	118·24 W
66	Palouse (pȧ-lōōz').........Wash.	46·54 N	117·04 W
66	Palouse Hills............Wash.	46·48 N	117·47 W
66	Palouse R...............Wash.	47·02 N	117·35 W
133	Palu (pä-loo')..............Tur.	38·55 N	40·10 E
98	Palúa (pȧ-lōō'ȧ)...........Ven.	8·30 N	62·30 W
155	Paluan (pä-lōō'än) Phila. (Manila In.)	13·25 N	120·29 E
135	Pamamushir (I.)........Sov. Un.	50·42 N	153·45 E
122	Pamiers (pȧ-myā')..........Fr.	43·07 N	1·34 E
145	Pamirs (Plat.)..........Sov. Un.	38·14 N	72·27 E
79	Pamlico R. (păm'lĭ-kō).....N. C.	35·25 N	76·59 W
79	Pamlico Sd..............N. C.	35·10 N	76·10 W
72	Pampa (păm'pȧ)............Tex.	35·32 N	100 56 W
100	Pampa de Castillo (Plat.) (pä'm-pä-dĕ-käs-tē'l-yô). Arg.	45·30 S	67·30 W
155	Pampanga (R.) (päm-päŋ'gä) Phil. (Manila In.)	15·20 N	120·48 E
100	Pampas (Reg.) (päm'päs)....Arg.	37·00 S	64·30 W
124	Pampilhosa do Botão (päm-pê-lyō'sȧ-dô-bō-to'uɴ) Port.	40·21 N	8·23 W
98	Pamplona (päm-plō'nä)......Col.	7·19 N	72·41 W
124	Pamplona (päm-plô'nä).......Sp.	42·49 N	1·39 W
81	Pamunkey (R.) (pȧ-mŭŋ'kĭ)...Va.	37·40 N	77·20 W
80	Pana (pā'nȧ)...............Ill.	39·25 N	89·05 W
92	Panabá (pä-nä-bȧ') Mex. (Yucatan In.)	21·18 N	88·15 W
127	Panagyurishte (pȧ-nȧ-gyōō'rêsh-tĕ)..Bul.	42·30 N	24·11 E
89	Panamá (păn-ȧ-mä') N. A. (Panama Canal In.)	8·35 N	81·08 W
89	Panama, G. of............Pan.	7·45 N	79·20 W
89	Panama, Isth. of..........Pan.	9·00 N	81·00 W
93	Panama, B. of............Pan.	8·50 N	79·08 W
78	Panama City (păn-ȧ mä' sĭ'tĭ). Fla.	30·08 N	85·39 W
68	Panamint Ra. (păn-ȧ-mĭnt') Calif.	36·40 N	117·30 W
126	Panaria (Is.) (pä-nä'rê-á)......It.	38·37 N	15·05 E
126	Panaro (R.) (pä-nä'rô)........It.	44·47 N	11·06 E
154	Panay (I.) (pä-nī')..........Phil.	11·15 N	121·38 E
127	Pančevo (pȧn'chĕ-vô)......Yugo.	44·52 N	20·42 E
139	Panchor....Mala. (Singapore In.)	2·10 N	102·43 E
166	Panda (pän'dä')..........Con. K.	10·59 S	27·24 E
94	Pan de Guajaibon (Mtn.) (pän dā gwä-jȧ-bōn'). Cuba	22·50 N	83·20 W
154	Pandjang, Selat (Str.).....Indon.	1·00 N	102·00 E
119	Panevėžys (pä'nyĕ-vāzh'ēs) Sov. Un.	55·44 N	24·21 E
134	Panfilov (pŭn-fē'lŏf).....Sov. Un.	44·12 N	79·58 E
165	Panga (päŋ'gä)..........Con. K.	1·58 N	26·45 E
167	Pangani (pän-gä'nē).........Tan.	5·28 S	38·58 E
149	P'angchiang..China (Canton In.)	22·57 N	113·15 E
148	Pangfou (bäng'fōō).......China	32·54 N	117·22 E
154	Pangkalpinang (päng-käl'pê-näng') Indon.	2·11 S	106·04 E
142	Pangkong Tsho (L.).......China	33·40 N	79·30 E
87	Pangnirtung..............Can.	66·08 N	65·26 W
69	Panguitch (päŋ'gwĭch)......Utah	37·50 N	112·30 W
101	Panimávida (pä-nē-mȧ'vē-dä) Chile (Santiago In.)	36·44 S	71·26 W
143	Panjim (Nova Goa)........India	15·33 N	73·52 E
150	Panshih.................China	42·50 N	126·48 E
151	Pan Si Pan (Mtn.)..........Viet.	22·25 N	103 50 E
155	Pantar (I.) (pän'tär)......Indon.	8·40 S	123·45 E
74	Pantego (păn'tĭ-gō) Tex. (Dallas, Fort Worth In.)	32·45 N	97·06 W
113	Pantelleria (I.) (pän-tĕl-lå-rē'ä) It.	36·43 N	11·59 E
91	Pantepec (pän-tå-pĕk')......Mex.	17·11 N	93·04 W
90	Panuco (pä'nōō-kô).........Mex.	22·04 N	98·11 W
90	Pánuco (pä'nōō-kô).........Mex.	29·47 N	105·55 W
90	Panuco (R.)..............Mex.	21·59 N	98·20 W
76	Pánuco de Coronado (pä'nōō-kô dā kō-rô-nä'dhō) Mex.	24·33 N	104·20 W
143	Panvel.......India (Bombay In.)	18·59 N	73·06 E
92	Panzós (pän-zós')..........Guat.	15·26 N	89·40 W
99	Pao (pȧ'ō) (R.).........Ven. (In.)	9·52 N	67·57 W
150	Paochang................China	41·52 N	115·25 E
150	Paocheng................China	33·15 N	106·58 E
150	Paochi..................China	34·10 N	106·58 E
73	Paola (pȧ-ō'lȧ)............Kans.	38·34 N	94·51 W
80	Paoli (pȧ-ō'lī)...............Ind.	38·35 N	86·30 W
84	Paoli.......Pa. (Philadelphia In.)	40·03 N	75·29 W
69	Paonia (pā-ō'nyȧ)..........Colo.	38·50 N	107·40 W
146	Paoshan (pä'ô-shän')........China	25·14 N	99·03 E
149	Paoshan....China (Shanghai In.)	31·25 N	121·29 E
148	Paoti (pä'ô-tē')............China	39·44 N	117·19 E
148	Paoting.................China	38·52 N	115·31 E
150	Paoting.................China	42·04 N	125·00 E
150	Paot'ou.................China	40·28 N	110·10 E
148	Paoying (pä'ô-yĭng)........China	33·14 N	119·20 E
121	Pápa (pä'pô)..............Hung.	47·18 N	17·27 E
92	Papagayo, Golfo del (G.) (gôl-fô-dĕl-pä-pä-gȧ'yō). C. R.	10·44 N	85·56 W
90	Papagayo, Laguna (L.) (lä-ŏŏ-nä).....Mex.	16·44 N	99·44 W
90	Papagayo (R.) (pä-pä-gä'yō) Mex.	16·52 N	99·41 W
69	Papago Ind. Res. (pä'pä-gō). Ariz.	32·33 N	112·12 W
88	Papantla de Olarte (pä-pän'tlä dā-ô-lä'r-tĕ). Mex.	20·30 N	97·15 W
91	Papatoapan (R.) (pä-pä-tô-ā-pȧ'n). Mex.	18·00 N	96·22 W
120	Papenburg (päp'ĕn-bŏŏrgh). Ger.	53·05 N	7·23 E
101	Papinas (pä-pē'näs) Arg. (Buenos Aires In.)	35·30 S	57·19 W
85	Papineauville (pä-pē-nō'vēl) Can. (Ottawa In.)	45·38 N	75·01 W
155	Papua (păp'ōōȧ).........Oceania	7·30 S	142·30 E
155	Papua, Gulf of (păp-ōō-ȧ)...Pap.	8·20 S	144·45 E
101	Papudo (pä-pōō'dô) Chile (Santiago In.)	32·30 S	71·25 W
100	Paquequer Pequeno (pä-kĕ-kĕ'r-pĕ-kĕ'nô). Braz. (In.)	22·19 S	43·02 W
	Pará, see Belém		
99	Pará (State) (pä-rä').......Braz.	4·45 S	53·30 W
101	Pará (pä-rä') (R.) Braz. (Rio de Janeiro In.)	20·21 S	44·38 W
99	Pará, Rio do (R.) (rē'ō-dô-pä-rä') Braz.	1·09 S	48·48 W
128	Para (R.)..............Sov. Un.	53·45 N	40·58 E
155	Paracale (pä-rä-kä'lȧ) Phil. (Manila In.)	14·17 N	122·47 E
100	Paracambi (pä-rä-kȧ'm-bē) Braz. (In.)	22·36 S	43·43 W
99	Paracatu (pä-rä-kä-tōō')....Braz.	17·17 S	46·43 W
160	Parachilna (pȧ-rȧ-chĭl'nȧ)..Austl.	31·09 S	138·20 E
127	Paraćin (pȧ'rä-chên).......Yugo.	43·51 N	21·26 E
101	Para de Minas (pä-rä-dĕ-mē'näs) Braz. (Rio de Janeiro In.)	19·52 S	44·37 W
66	Paradise Valley (păr'á-dīs)...Nev.	41·28 N	117·32 W
98	Parados, Cerro de los (Mtn.) (sĕ'r-rô-dĕ-lôs-pä-rä'dōs) Col. (In.)	5·44 N	75·13 W
73	Paragould (păr'ȧ-gōōld).....Ark.	36·03 N	90·29 W
99	Paraguaçu (R.) (pä-rä-gwä-zōō') Braz.	12·25 S	39·46 W
98	Paraguaná, Pen. de (Pen.) (pĕ-nê'ng-sōō-lä-dĕ-pä-rä-gwȧ-nȧ'). Ven.	12·00 N	69·55 W
96	Paraguay (păr'á-gwā).......S. A.	24·00 S	57·00 W

ăt; finăl; rāte; senâte; ärm; ȧsk; sofȧ; fâre; ch-choose; dh-as th in other; bē; êvent; bĕt; recĕnt; cratẽr; g-go; gh-guttural g; bĭt; ĭ-short neutral; rīde; ĸ-guttural k as ch in German ich;

PRONOUNCING INDEX Paraguay–Peekskill 249

Page	Name Pronunciation Region	Lat. °′	Long. °′
99	Paraguay, Rio (R.) (rē'ō-pä-rä-gwä'y) .S. A.	21·12 S	57·31 W
	Paraíba, see João Pessoa		
99	Paraíba (State) (pä-rä-ē'bä) . Braz.	7·11 S	37·05 W
101	Paraiba (R.) Braz. (Rio de Janeiro In.)	23·02 S	45·43 W
101	Paraíba do Sul (dô-sōō'l) Braz. (Rio de Janeiro In.)	22·10 S	43·18 W
101	Paraibuna (pä-räē-bōō'nä) Braz. (Rio de Janeiro In.)	23·23 S	45·38 W
88	Paraiso (pä-rä-ē'sō) C. Z. (Panama Canal In.)	9·02 N	79·38 W
93	Paraíso C. R.	9·50 N	83·53 W
91	Paraíso Mex.	18·24 N	93·11 W
101	Paraisópolis (pä-räē-sô'pō-lēs) Braz. (Rio de Janeiro In.)	22·35 S	45·45 W
101	Paraitinga (pä-rä-ē-tē'n-gä) (R.) Braz. (Rio de Janeiro In.)	23·15 S	45·24 W
164	Parakou (pȧ-rȧ-kōō') Dahomey	9·16 N	2·37 E
99	Paramaribo (pȧ-rȧ-mä'rê-bō) .Sur.	5·50 N	55·15 W
161	Paramatta (păr-ȧ-măt'ȧ) Austl. (Sydney In.)	33·49 S	150·59 E
122	Paramé (pȧ-rȧ-mā') Fr.	48·40 N	1·58 W
98	Paramillo (Mtn.) (pä-rä-mê'l-yō) Col. (In.)	7·06 N	75·55 W
135	Paramushir (I.) Sov. Un.	50·45 N	154·00 E
139	Paran (R.) Isr. (Palestine In.)	30·05 N	34·50 E
100	Paraná (pä-rä-nä') Arg.	31·44 S	60·29 W
100	Paraná (State) Braz.	24·25 S	52·00 W
100	Paraná, Rio (R.) Arg.	32·15 S	60·55 W
99	Paraná (R.) Braz.	13·05 S	47·11 W
100	Paranaguá (pä-rä'nä-gwà') Braz.	25·39 S	48·42 W
99	Paranaíba (pä-rä-nȧ-ē'bȧ) Braz.	19·43 S	51·13 W
99	Paranaíba (R.) Braz.	18·58 S	50·44 W
101	Parana Ibicuy (R.) (ē-bē-kōō'ē) Arg. (Buenos Aires In.)	33·27 S	59·26 W
99	Paranam Sur.	5·39 N	55·13 W
100	Paránápanema (R.) (pä-rä'nȧ'pä-nĕ-mä) . Braz.	22·28 S	52·15 W
101	Paraopeba (R.) (pä-rä-o-pĕ'dä) Braz. (Rio de Janeiro In.)	20·09 S	44·14 W
99	Parapara (pä-rä-pä-rä) . Ven. (In.)	9·44 N	67·17 W
101	Parati (pä-rätē) Braz. (Rio de Janeiro In.)	23·14 S	44·43 W
122	Paray-le-Monial (pȧ-rĕ'lē-mô-nyȧl') . Fr.	46·27 N	4·14 E
142	Pārbati (R.) India	24·50 N	76·44 E
	Parcel Is., see Hsisha Ch'üntao		
120	Parchim (pȧr'kĭm) Ger.	53·25 N	11·52 E
121	Parczew (pär'chĕf) Pol.	51·38 N	22·53 E
99	Pardo (R.) (pär'dō) Braz.	15·25 S	39·40 W
101	Pardo (R.) Braz. (Rio de Janeiro In.)	21·32 S	46·40 W
120	Pardubice (pär'dōō-bĭt-sĕ) . Czech.	50·02 N	15·47 E
99	Parecis, Serra dos (Mts.) (sĕr'rȧ dōs pä-rä-sēzh') . Braz.	13·45 S	59·28 W
124	Paredes de Nava (pä-rā'dås dā nä'vä) . Sp.	42·10 N	4·41 W
87	Parent Can.	47·56 N	74·30 W
136	Pargolovo (pȧr-gô'lô vô) Sov. Un. (Leningrad In.)	60·04 N	30·18 E
98	Paria, Golfo de (G.) (gôl-fô-dĕ-pä'rê-ä) . Ven.	10·33 N	62·14 W
69	Paria (R.) Utah-Ariz.	37·07 N	111·51 W
90	Paricutín, Vol. (pä-rē-kōō-tē'n) Mex.	19·27 N	102·14 W
76	Parida, Rio de la (R.) (rê'ō-dĕ-lä-pä-rē'dä) . Mex.	26·23 N	104·40 W
98	Parima, Serra (Mts.) (sĕr'rȧ pä-rē'mȧ) . Braz.-Ven.	3·45 N	64·00 W
98	Pariñas, Punta (Pt.) (pōō'n-tä-pä-rê'n-yäs) . Peru	4·30 S	81·23 W
99	Parintins (pä-rĭn-tĭnzh') Braz.	2·34 S	56·30 W
74	Paris (păr'ĭs) Ark.	35·17 N	93·43 W
80	Paris Can.	43·15 N	82·20 W
123	Paris (pȧ-rē') Fr. (Paris In.)	48·51 N	2·20 E
80	Paris Ill.	39·35 N	87·40 W
80	Paris Ky.	38·15 N	84·15 W
73	Paris Mo.	39·27 N	91·59 W
78	Paris Tenn.	36·16 N	88·20 W
73	Paris Tex.	33·39 N	95·33 W
93	Parita, Golfo de (G.) (gôl-fô-dĕ-pä-rē'tä) . Pan.	8·06 N	80·10 W
67	Park City Utah	40·39 N	111·33 W
70	Parker (pär'kēr) S. D.	43·24 N	97·10 W
69	Parker Dam Calif.-Ariz.	34·20 N	114·00 W
80	Parkersburg (pär'kērz-bûrg) W. Va.	39·15 N	81·35 W
160	Parkes (pärks) Austl.	33·10 S	148·10 E
71	Park Falls (pärk) Wis.	45·55 N	90·29 W
75	Park Forest Ill. (Chicago In.)	41·29 N	87·41 W
65	Parkland (pärk'lănd) Wash. (Seattle In.)	47·09 N	122·26 W
67	Park Ra Colo.	40·54 N	106·40 W
71	Park Rapids Minn.	46·53 N	95·05 W
75	Park Ridge Ill. (Chicago In.)	42·00 N	87·50 W
70	Park River N. D.	48·22 N	97·43 W
65	Parkrose (pärk'rōz) Ore. (Portland In.)	45·33 N	122·33 W
167	Park Rynie S. Afr. (Natal In.)	30·22 S	30·43 E
70	Parkston (pärks'tŭn) S. D.	43·22 N	97·59 W
69	Park View (vū) N. Mex.	36·45 N	106·30 W
74	Parkville Mo. (Kansas City In.)	39·12 N	94·41 W
125	Parla (pär'lä) Sp. (Madrid In.)	40·14 N	3·46 W
126	Parma (pär'mä) It.	44·48 N	10·20 E
75	Parma Ohio (Cleveland In.)	41·23 N	81·44 W
75	Parma Heights Ohio (Cleveland In.)	41·23 N	81·36 W
99	Parnaguá (pär-nä-gwà') Braz.	9·52 S	44·27 W
99	Parnaíba (pär-nä-ē'bä) Braz.	3·00 S	41·42 W
99	Parnaiba (R.) Braz.	3·57 S	42·30 W
127	Parnassós (Mtn.) Grc.	38·33 N	22·35 E
111	Parndorf Aus. (Vienna In.)	48·00 N	16·52 E
119	Pärnu (pĕr'nōō) Sov. Un.	58·24 N	24·29 E
119	Pärnu (R.) Sov. Un.	58·40 N	25·05 E
119	Pärnu Laht (B.) (läkt) . Sov. Un.	58·15 N	24·17 E
142	Paro Dzong (pä'rô dzông') Bhu.	27·30 N	89·30 E
160	Paroo (R.) (pä'rōō) Austl.	29·40 S	144·24 E
144	Paropamisus (Mts.) Afg.	34·45 N	63·58 E
127	Páros (pä'rôs) (pă'rŏs) Grc.	37·05 N	25·14 E
127	Páros (I.) Grc.	37·11 N	25·00 E
166	Parow (pă'rô) S. Afr. (Cape Town In.)	33·54 S	18·36 E
69	Parowan (păr'ô-wăn) Utah	37·50 N	112·50 W
100	Parral (pär-rä'l) Chile	36·07 S	71·47 W
76	Parral, R. Mex.	27·25 N	105·08 W
161	Parramatta (R.) (păr-ȧ-măt'ȧ) Austl. (Sydney In.)	33·42 S	150·58 E
76	Parras (pär-räs') Mex.	25·28 N	102·08 W
93	Parrita (pär-rē'tä) C. R.	9·32 N	84·17 W
82	Parrsboro (pärz'bŭr-ô) Can.	45·25 N	64·20 W
80	Parry (I.) Can.	45·15 N	80·00 W
64	Parry, C. (păr'ĭ) Can.	70·20 N	124·31 W
49	Parry Is Can.	75·30 N	110·00 W
81	Parry Sound Can.	45·20 N	80·00 W
73	Parsons (pär's'nz) Kans.	37·20 N	95·16 W
81	Parsons W. Va.	39·05 N	79·40 W
122	Parthenay (pȧr-t'nĕ') Fr.	46·39 N	0·16 W
126	Partinico (pär-tē'nê-kô) It.	38·02 N	13·11 E
168	Parys (pȧ-rĭs') S. Afr. (Johannesburg & Pretoria In.)	26·53 S	27·28 E
74	Pasadena (păs-ȧ-dē'nȧ) Calif. (Los Angeles In.)	34·09 N	118·09 W
84	Pasadena Md. (Baltimore In.)	39·06 N	76·35 W
77	Pasadena Tex. (In.)	29·43 N	95·13 W
78	Pascagoula (păs-kȧ-gōō'lȧ) Miss.	30·22 N	88·33 W
78	Pascagoula (R.) Miss.	30·52 N	88·48 W
121	Paşcani (päsh-kän'') Rom.	47·46 N	26·42 E
66	Pasco (păs'kō) Wash.	46·13 N	119·04 W
120	Pasewalk (pä'zĕ-välk) Ger.	53·31 N	14·01 E
136	Pashiya (pä'shĭ-yȧ) Sov. Un. (Urals In.)	58·27 N	58·17 E
152	Pashkovo (pȧsh-kô'vô) Sov. Un.	48·52 N	131·09 E
129	Pashkovskaya (pȧsh-kôf'skȧ-yȧ) Sov. Un.	45·29 N	39·04 E
92	Pasión, Rio de la (R.) (rê'ō-dĕ-lä-pä-syōn') Guat. (Yucatan In.)	16·31 N	90·11 W
100	Paso de los Libres (pä-sô-dĕ-lôs-lē'brĕs) . Arg.	29·33 S	57·05 W
101	Paso de los Toros (tŏ'rôs) Ur. (Buenos Aires In.)	32·43 S	56·33 W
68	Paso Robles (pă'sō rō'blĕs) Calif.	35·38 N	120·44 W
84	Passaic (pă-sā'ĭk) N. J. (New York In.)	40·52 N	74·08 W
84	Passaic R. N. J. (New York In.)	40·42 N	74·26 W
82	Passamaquoddy B. (păs'ȧ-mȧ-kwŏd'ĭ) . Can.	45·00 N	66·45 W
101	Passa Tempo (pä's-sä-tĕ'm-pô) Braz. (Rio de Janeiro In.)	21·40 S	44·29 W
120	Passau (päs'ou) Ger.	48·34 N	13·27 E
78	Pass Christian (pȧs krĭs'tyĕn) Miss.	30·20 N	89·15 W
113	Passero, C. (päs-sĕ'rô) It.	36·34 N	15·13 E
100	Passo Fundo (pä'sŏ fōōn'dōō) Braz.	28·16 S	52·13 W
101	Passos (pä's-sōs) Braz. (Rio de Janeiro In.)	20·45 S	46·37 W
98	Pastaza (R.) (päs-tä'zä) Peru	3·05 S	76·18 W
98	Pasto (päs'tō) Col.	1·15 N	77·19 W
90	Pastora (päs-tô-rä) Mex.	22·08 N	100·04 W
154	Pasuruan Indon.	7·45 S	112·50 E
119	Pasvalys (päs-vä-lēs') Sov. Un.	56·04 N	24·23 E
100	Patagonia (Reg.) (păt-ȧ-gō'nĭ-ȧ) Arg.	46·45 S	69·30 W
143	Pātālganga (R.) India (Bombay In.)	18·52 N	73·08 E
142	Patan (pä'tŭn) Nep.	27·23 N	85·24 E
84	Patapsco R. (pȧ-tăps'kō) Md. (Baltimore In.)	39·12 N	76·30 W
126	Paternò (pä-tĕr-nô') It.	37·35 N	14·58 E
84	Paterson (păt'ēr-sŭn) N. J. (New York In.)	40·55 N	74·10 W
67	Pathfinder Res. (păth'fīn-dēr) Wyo.	42·22 N	107·10 W
142	Patiāla (pŭt-ê-ā'lŭ) India	30·25 N	76·28 E
100	Pati do Alferes (pä-tē-dô-ål-fĕ'rĕs) . Braz. (In.)	22·25 S	43·25 W
142	Patna (pŭt'nŭ) India	25·33 N	85·18 E
155	Patnanongan (pät-nä-nôŋ'gän) Phil. (Manila In.)	14·50 N	122·25 E
80	Patoka (R.) (pȧ-tō'kȧ) Ind.	38·25 N	87·25 W
135	Patom Plat Sov. Un.	59·30 N	115·00 E
99	Patos (pä'tōzh) Braz.	7·03 S	37·14 W
65	Patos (pä'tōs) Wash. (Vancouver In.)	48·47 N	122·57 W
100	Patos, Lago dos (L.) (lä'gō-ä dozh pä'tōzh) . Braz.	31·15 S	51·30 W
99	Patos de Minas (dĕ-mē'nāzh) Braz.	18·39 S	46·31 W
127	Pátrai (Patras) (pä-trī') (pȧ-trȧs') Grc.	38·15 N	21·48 E
127	Patraïkós Kólpos (G.) Grc.	38·16 N	21·19 E
	Patras, see Pátrai		
99	Patrocínio (pä-trō-sē'nê-ōō) Braz.	18·48 S	46·47 W
154	Pattani (păt'ȧ-nê) Thai.	6·56 N	101·13 E
82	Patten (păt''n) Maine	45·59 N	68·27 W
77	Patterson (păt'ēr-sŭn) La.	29·41 N	91·20 W
81	Patton Pa.	40·40 N	78·45 W
93	Patuca, Punta (Pt.) (pōō'n-tä-pä-tōō'kä) . Hond.	15·23 N	84·05 W
93	Patuca R. Hond.	15·22 N	84·31 W
81	Patuxent (R.) (pȧ-tŭk'sĕnt) . Md.	39·10 N	77·10 W
90	Pátzcuaro (päts'kwä-rō) Mex.	19·30 N	101·36 W
90	Pátzcuaro, Lago de (L.) (lä'gô-dĕ) . Mex.	19·36 N	101·38 W
92	Patzicia (pät-zē'syä) Guat.	14·36 N	90·57 W
92	Patzún (pät-zōōn') Guat.	14·40 N	91·00 W
122	Pau (pō) Fr.	43·18 N	0·23 W
122	Pau, Gave de (strm.) (gȧv-dĕ) . Fr.	43·33 N	0·51 W
122	Pauillac (pō-yȧk') Fr.	45·12 N	0·46 W
80	Paulding (pôl'dĭng) Ohio	41·05 N	84·35 W
111	Paulinenaue (pou'lē-nĕ-nou-ĕ) Ger. (Berlin In.)	52·40 N	12·43 E
99	Paulistana (pá'ōō-lēs-tá-nä) Braz.	8·13 S	41·06 W
99	Paulo Afonso, Salto (falls) (säl-tô-pou'lōō äf-fōn'sōō) . Braz.	9·33 S	38·32 W
168	Paul Roux (pôrl rōō) S. Afr. (Johannesburg & Pretoria In.)	28·18 S	27·57 E
84	Paulsboro (pôlz'bĕ-rô) N. J. (Philadelphia In.)	39·50 N	75·16 W
73	Pauls Valley (pôlz văl'ê) Okla.	34·43 N	97·13 W
157	Pauwela (pä-ōō-wä'lä). Hawaii (In.)	20·58 N	156·19 W
98	Pavarandocito (pä-vä-rän-dô-sē'tô) Col. (In.)	7·18 N	76·32 W
136	Pavda (päv'dá) . Sov. Un. (Urals In.)	59·16 N	59·32 E
126	Pavia (pä-vē'ä) It.	45·12 N	9·11 E
134	Pavlodar (pȧv-lô-dȧr') Sov. Un.	52·17 N	77·23 E
64	Pavlo'f B. (păv-lōf) Alaska	55·20 N	161·20 W
129	Pavlograd (pȧv-lô-grȧt') . Sov. Un.	48·32 N	35·52 E
129	Pavlovsk (pȧv-lôfsk') Sov. Un.	50·28 N	40·05 E
136	Pavlovsk . Sov. Un. (Leningrad In.)	59·41 N	30·27 E
136	Pavlovskiy Posad (pȧv-lôf'skĭ pô-sȧt') Sov. Un. (Moscow In.)	55·47 N	38·39 E
100	Pavuna (pä-vōō'nȧ) Braz. (In.)	22·48 S	43·21 W
111	Päwesin (pă'vĕ-zēn) Ger. (Berlin In.)	52·31 N	12·44 E
73	Pawhuska (pô-hŭs'kȧ) Okla.	36·41 N	96·20 W
73	Pawnee (pô-nē') Okla.	36·20 N	96·47 W
72	Pawnee (R.) Kans.	38·18 N	99·42 W
73	Pawnee City Nebr.	40·08 N	96·09 W
80	Paw Paw (pô'pô) Mich.	42·15 N	85·55 W
71	Paw Paw (R.) Mich.	42·14 N	86·21 W
84	Pawtucket (pô-tŭk'ĕt) R. I. (Providence In.)	41·53 N	71·23 W
127	Paxoi (I.) Grc.	39·14 N	20·15 E
80	Paxton (păks'tŭn) Ill.	40·35 N	88·00 W
150	Payen (pä'yĕn') China	46·00 N	127·20 E
66	Payette (pȧ-ĕt') Idaho	44·05 N	116·55 W
66	Payette R. Idaho	43·57 N	116·26 W
66	Payette R., North Fork Idaho	44·35 N	116 10 W
66	Payette R., South Fork Idaho	44·07 N	115·43 W
	Payintala, see Tungliao		
132	Pay-Khoy, Khrebet (Mts.) Sov. Un.	68·08 N	63·04 E
87	Payne (L.) (pān) Can.	59·22 N	73·16 W
71	Paynesville (pānz'vĭl) Minn.	45·23 N	94·43 W
139	Payong, Bukit (Mt.) Mala. (Singapore In.)	3·04 N	101·58 E
	Payo Obispo, see Ciudad Chetumal		
100	Paysandú (pī-sän-dōō') Ur.	32·16 S	57·55 W
69	Payson (pā's'n) Utah	40·05 N	111·45 W
127	Pazardzhik (pä-zȧr-dzhek') Bul.	42·10 N	24·22 E
126	Pazin (pä'zēn) Yugo.	45·14 N	13·57 E
73	Peabody (pē'bŏd-ĭ) Kans.	38·09 N	97·09 W
83	Peabody Mass. (Boston In.)	42·32 N	70·56 W
86	Peace (R.) Can.	57·29 N	117·32 W
79	Peace Cr. (pēs) Fla. (In.)	27·16 N	81·53 W
84	Peace Dale (dāl) R. I. (Providence In.)	41·27 N	71·30 W
86	Peace River (rĭv'ēr) Can.	56·19 N	117·22 W
86	Peacock Hills (pe-kŏk' hĭlz) . Can.	66·08 N	109·55 W
110	Peak, The (Mt.) (pēk) Eng.	53·23 N	1·52 W
158	Peak Hill Austl.	25·38 S	118·50 E
78	Pearl (R.) (pûrl) Miss.-La.	31·06 N	89·44 W
77	Pearland (pûrl'ănd) Tex. (In.)	29·34 N	95·17 W
	Pearl R., see Chu Chiang		
76	Pearsall (pēr'sôl) Tex.	28·53 N	99·06 W
167	Pearston (pē'ērstŏn) S. Afr. (Natal In.)	32·36 S	25·09 E
48	Peary Land (Reg.) (pēr'ĭ) Grnld.	82·00 N	40·00 W
72	Pease (R.) (pēz) Tex.	34·07 N	99·53 W
77	Peason (pēz''n) La.	31·25 N	93·19 W
167	Pebane (pĕ-bá'nē) Moz.	17·23 S	37·45 E
127	Peć (pĕch) Yugo.	42·39 N	20·18 E
76	Pecan Bay (pê-kăn') Tex.	32·04 N	99·15 W
99	Peçanha (pā-kän'yȧ) Braz.	18·37 S	42·26 W
71	Pecatonica (R.) (pĕk-ȧ-tŏn-ĭ-kȧ) Ill.	42·21 N	89·28 W
132	Pechenga (pyĕ'chĕŋ-gȧ) Sov. Un.	69·30 N	31·10 E
132	Pechora (R.) Sov. Un.	66·00 N	52·30 E
134	Pechora Basin (pyĕ-chô'rȧ) Sov. Un.	67·55 N	58·37 E
132	Pechorskaya Guba (B.) Sov. Un.	68·40 N	55·00 E
76	Pecos (pā'kôs) Tex.	31·26 N	103·30 W
62	Pecos (R.) U. S.	31·10 N	103·10 W
121	Pécs (pāch) Hung.	46·04 N	18·15 E
167	Peddie S. Afr. (Natal In.)	33·13 S	27·09 E
128	Pededze (R.) (pă'dĕd-zĕ) . Sov. Un.	57·18 N	27·13 E
74	Pedley (pĕd'lē) Calif. (Los Angeles In.)	33·59 N	117·29 W
99	Pedra Azul (pä'drä-zōō'l) Braz.	16·03 S	41·13 W
99	Pedreiras (pĕ-drā'räs) Braz.	4·30 S	44·31 W
143	Pedro, Pt. (pē'drō) Cey.	15·05 N	80·28 E
92	Pedro Antonio Santos (Sta. Cruz Chico) (pā'drô än-tō'nê-ô sän'tōs) (sän'tä krōōz' chē'kô) Mex. (Yucatan In.)	18·55 N	88·13 W
94	Pedro Betancourt (bā-täŋ-kōrt') Cuba	22·40 N	81·15 W
100	Pedro de Valdivia (pĕ'drô-dĕ-väl-dē'vê-ä) . Chile	22·32 S	69·55 W
100	Pedro do Rio (dô-rē'ô) . Braz. (In.)	22·20 S	43·09 W
99	Pedro Juan Caballero (hōōá'n-kä-bäl-yĕ'rō) . Par.	22·40 S	55·42 W
88	Pedro Miguel (mê-gāl') C. Z. (Panama Canal In.)	9·01 N	79·36 W
88	Pedro Miguel Locks (mê-gāl') C. Z. (Panama Canal In.)	9·01 N	79·36 W
99	Pedro II (pä'drōō sā-gōōn'dōō) Braz.	4·20 S	41·27 W
160	Peebinga (pê-bĭng'ȧ) Austl.	34·43 S	140·55 E
116	Peebles (pē'b'lz) Scot.	55·40 N	3·15 W
79	Pee Dee (R.) (pē-dē') . S. C.-N. C.	34·01 N	79·26 W
84	Peekskill (pēks'kĭl) N. Y. (New York In.)	41·17 N	73·55 W

ng-sing; ŋ-baŋk; N-nasalized n; nŏd; cŏmmit; ōld; ôbey; ôrder; fōōd; fŏŏt; ou-out; s-soft; sh-dish; th-thin; pūre; ûnite; ûrn; stŭd; circŭs; ü-as "y" in study; '-indeterminate vowel.

250 Pegasus–Petrus Steyn PRONOUNCING INDEX

Page	Name Pronunciation Region	Lat. °′	Long. °′
159	Pegasus B. (pĕg′ȧ-sŭs)......N. Z.	43·18 S	173·37 E
120	Pegnitz R. (pĕgh-nēts).......Ger.	49·38 N	11·40 E
125	Pego (pā′gō)................Sp.	38·50 N	0·09 W
154	Pegu (pĕ-gōō′).............Bur.	17·17 N	96·29 E
146	Pegu Yoma (Mts.) (pĕ-gōō′yō′mä) Bur.	19·16 N	95·59 E
127	Pehčevo (pĕκ′chĕ-vô)......Yugo.	41·42 N	22·57 E
150	Peian (pĕ′ê-än′)...........China	48·05 N	126·26 E
149	Pei-Chiang (R.) China (Canton In.)	22·54 N	113·08 E
148	Peich′iao (bā′chiou)........China	31·03 N	121·27 E
148	Peich′enghuang Tao (I.) (bā′chĕng′hōōäng′ dou).China	38·23 N	120·55 E
150	Peiching (Peking) China (Peking In.)	39·55 N	116·23 E
148	Peiching Shih (City) (bā′jĭng′ shē).China	40·07 N	115·56 E
150	Peifeng...................China	43·00 N	124·59 E
151	Peihai (Pakhoi)...........China	21·30 N	109·10 E
151	Peili.....................China	19·08 N	108·42 E
	Peilintzu, see Suihua		
	Peipus, L., see Chudskoye Oz.		
148	Pei Wan (B.) (bā′wäɴ).....China	36·21 N	120·48 E
150	Peiyün Ho (R.) China (Peking In.)	39·42 N	116·48 E
80	Pekin (pē′kĭn)..............Ill.	40·35 N	89·30 W
	Peking, see Peiching		
114	Pelagie, Isole I..............It.	35·46 N	12·32 E
127	Pélagos (I.)................Grc.	39·17 N	24·05 E
78	Pelahatchee (pĕl-ȧ-hăch′ê)...Miss.	32·17 N	89·48 W
123	Pelat, Mt. (pē-lȧ′)...........Fr.	44·16 N	6·43 E
135	Peleduy (pyĕl-yĭ-dōō′ē)..Sov. Un.	59·50 N	112·47 E
93	Pelee, Mt. (Vol.) (pē-lā′) Mart. (Le. & Wind. Is. In.)	14·49 N	61·10 W
80	Pelee, Pt...................Can.	41·55 N	82·30 W
80	Pelee I. (pē′lê).............Can.	41·45 N	82·30 W
101	Pelequén (pĕ-lĕ-kĕ′n) Chile (Santiago In.)	34·26 S	71·52 W
	Pelew, see Palau		
78	Pelham (pĕl′hăm)...........Ga.	31·07 N	84·10 W
83	Pelham.......N. H. (Boston In.)	42·43 N	71·22 W
71	Pelican (L.)...............Minn.	46·36 N	94·00 W
94	Pelican Hbr. (pĕl′ĭ-kăn)....Ba. Is.	26·20 N	76·45 W
70	Pelican Rapids (pĕl′ĭ-kăn)..Minn.	46·34 N	96·05 W
71	Pella (pĕl′ȧ)................Iowa	41·25 N	92·50 W
120	Pell-Worm I. (pĕl′vôrm).....Ger.	54·33 N	8·25 E
86	Pelly (L.)..................Can.	66·08 N	102·57 W
86	Pelly (R.)..................Can.	62·20 N	133·26 W
86	Pelly B. (pĕl-ĭ)............Can.	68·57 N	91·05 W
86	Pelly Ra....................Can.	61·47 N	133·32 W
69	Peloncillo Mts. (pĕl-ôn-sĭl′lō).Ariz.	32·40 N	109·20 W
127	Peloponnisos (Reg.).........Grc.	37·28 N	22·14 E
100	Pelotas (pȧ-lō′tăzh)........Braz.	31·45 S	52·18 W
75	Pelton (pĕl-tŭn) Can. (Detroit In.)	42·15 N	82·57 W
123	Pelvoux, Mt. (pĕl-vōō′).......Fr.	44·56 N	6·24 E
132	Pelym (R.).............Sov. Un.	60·20 N	63·05 E
79	Pelzer (pĕl′zẽr).............S. C.	34·38 N	82·30 W
139	Pemanggil (I.) Mala. (Singapore In.)	2·37 N	104·41 E
166	Pemba (pĕm′bȧ).........Zambia	15·29 S	27·22 E
167	Pemba (I.)..................Tan.	5·13 S	40·05 E
70	Pembina (pĕm′bĭ-nȧ).......N. D.	48·58 N	97·15 W
70	Pembina (R.)...............Can.	49·16 N	98·38 W
81	Pembroke (pĕm′ brōk)......Can.	45·50 N	77·00 W
83	Pembroke (pĕm′brōk) Mass. (Boston In.)	42·05 N	70·49 W
116	Pembroke.................Wales	51·40 N	5·00 W
143	Pen.........India (Bombay In.)	18·44 N	73·06 E
124	Penafiél (pā-nȧ-fyĕl′).......Port.	41·12 N	8·19 W
124	Penafiel (pā-nyȧ-fyĕl′)........Sp.	41·38 N	4·08 W
124	Peñalara (Mtn.) (pā-nyä-lä′rä).Sp.	40·52 N	3·57 W
90	Pena Nevada, Cerro........Mex.	23·47 N	99·52 W
154	Penang (pê-năng′).........Mala.	5·21 N	100·09 E
155	Penaranda (pā-nyä-rän′dä) Phil. (Manila In.)	15·20 N	120·59 E
124	Peñaranda de Bracamonte (pā-nyä-rän′dä dā brä-kä-mōn′tȧ).Sp.	40·54 N	5·11 W
125	Peña Roya (Mtn.) (pā′nyä rō′yä) Sp.	40·18 N	0·42 W
124	Peñarroya-Pueblonuevo (pĕn-yär-rô′yä-pwĕ′blô-nwĕ′vô) Sp.	38·18 N	5·18 W
124	Peñas, Cabo de (C.) (kȧ′bô-dĕ-pā′nyäs).Sp.	43·42 N	6·12 W
100	Penas, Golfo de (gôl-fô-dĕ-pĕ′n-äs).Chile	47·15 S	77·30 W
76	Penasco R. (pā-nȧs′kō)......Tex.	32·50 N	104·45 W
150	Pench′i....................China	41·25 N	123·50 E
164	Pendembu (pĕn-dĕm′bōō)...S. L.	8·14 N	10·52 W
70	Pender (pĕn′dẽr)..........Nebr.	42·08 N	96·43 W
98	Penderisco (R.) (pĕn-dĕ-rē′s-kô) Col. (In.)	6·30 N	76·21 W
66	Pendleton (pĕn′d′l-tŭn)......Ore.	45·41 N	118·47 W
66	Pend Oreille L. (pŏn-dô-rā′) (pĕn-dô-rĕl′).Idaho	48·09 N	116·38 W
66	Pend Oreille R............Wash.	48·44 N	117·20 W
99	Penedo (pȧ-nā′dōō)........Braz.	10·17 S	36·28 W
81	Penetanguishene (pĕn′ê-tăŋ-gĭ-shēn′).Can.	44·45 N	79·55 W
148	P′engchengchen (pĕng′chĕng′jĕn).China	36·24 N	114·11 E
148	P′englai (pĕng′lāī)........China	37·49 N	120·45 E
124	Peniche (pĕ-nē′chȧ).........Port.	39·22 N	9·24 W
75	Peninsula (pĕn-ĭn′sû-lȧ) Ohio (Cleveland In.)	41·14 N	81·32 W
110	Penistone (pĕn′ĭ-stŭn).......Eng.	53·31 N	1·38 W
90	Penjamillo (pĕn-hä-mēl′yō)..Mex.	20·06 N	101·56 W
90	Penjamo (pān′hä-mō).......Mex.	20·27 N	101·43 W
154	Penju, Pulau-Pulau (Is.)...Indon.	0·18 S	120·43 E
110	Penk (R.) (pĕnk)...........Eng.	52·41 N	2·10 W
110	Penkridge (pĕnk′rĭj)........Eng.	52·43 N	2·07 W
126	Penne (pĕn′nā)...............It.	42·28 N	13·57 E
142	Penner (R.) (pĕn′ẽr)........India	14·43 N	79·09 E
120	Pennine Alpi (Mts.).......Switz.	46·02 N	7·07 E
116	Pennine Chain (Mts.) (pĕn-īn′) Eng.	53·44 N	1·59 W
80	Pennsboro (pĕnz′bŭr-ô)....W. Va.	39·10 N	81 00 W
84	Penns Grove (pĕnz grōv) N. J. (Philadelphia In.)	39·44 N	75·28 W
63	Pennsylvania (State) (pĕn-sĭl-vā′nĭ-ȧ).U. S.	41·00 N	78·10 W
81	Penn Yan (pĕn yăn′).......N. Y.	42·40 N	77·00 W
87	Penny Highland (pĕnz hī′lănd) Can.	66·55 N	65·30 W
128	Peno (L.) (pā′nô).......Sov. Un.	56·55 N	32·28 E
82	Penobscot (R.)............Maine	45·00 N	68·36 W
82	Penobscot B. (pê-nŏb′skŏt).Maine	44·20 N	69·00 W
158	Penong (pê-nông′).........Austl.	32·00 S	133·00 E
93	Penonomé (pā-nō-nô-mā′)....Pan.	8·32 N	80·21 W
161	Penrith.......Austl. (Sydney In.)	33·45 S	150·42 E
78	Pensacola (pĕn-sȧ-kō′lȧ)......Fla.	30·25 N	87·13 W
73	Pensacola Dam............Okla.	36·27 N	95·02 W
98	Pensilvania (pĕn-sêl-vȧ′nyä) Col. (In.)	5·31 N	75·05 W
159	Pentecost (I.) (pĕn′tê-kŏst) New Hebr.	16·05 S	168·28 E
86	Penticton..................Can.	49·29 N	119·28 W
116	Pentland Firth (pĕnt′lănd)..Scot.	58·44 N	3·25 W
133	Penza (pĕn′zȧ).........Sov. Un.	53·10 N	45·00 E
116	Penzance (pĕn-zăns′)........Eng.	50·07 N	5·40 W
120	Penzberg (pĕnts′bĕrgh).......Ger.	47·43 N	11·21 E
135	Penzhina (R.) (pyĭn-zē-nŭ) Sov. Un.	62·15 N	166·30 E
135	Penzhino..............Sov. Un.	63·42 N	168·00 E
135	Penzhinskay′a Guba (B.).Sov. Un.	60·30 N	161·30 E
80	Peoria (pē-ō′rĭ-ȧ).............Ill.	40·45 N	89·35 W
90	Peotillos (pȧ-ō-tel′yōs)......Mex.	22·30 N	100·39 W
75	Peotone (pē′ŏ-tôn) Ill. (Chicago In.)	41·20 N	87·47 W
81	Pepacton Res. (pĕp-ȧc′tŭn).N. Y.	42·05 N	74·40 W
94	Pepe, Cabo (kä′bô-pĕ′pĕ) (C.) Cuba	21·30 N	83·10 W
83	Pepperell (pĕp′ẽr-ĕl) Mass. (Boston In.)	42·40 N	71·36 W
127	Peqin (pĕ-kēn′).............Alb.	41·03 N	19·48 E
125	Perales (R.) (pā-rä′lās).......Sp.	40·24 N	4·07 W
125	Perales de Tajuña (dā tä-hōō′nyä) Sp. (Madrid In.)	40·14 N	3·22 W
82	Percé (pĕr-sā′).............Can.	48·32 N	64·15 W
111	Perchtoldsdorf (pĕrk′tôlts-dôrf) Aus. (Vienna In.)	48·07 N	16·17 E
168	Perdekop................S. Afr. (Johannesburg & Pretoria In.)	27·11 S	29·38 E
125	Perdido, Mt. (pĕr-dē′dō)......Sp.	42·40 N	0·00
78	Perdido (R.) (pĕr-dī′dō)..Ala.-Fla.	30·45 N	87·38 W
101	Perdões (pĕr-dô′ĕs) Braz. (Rio de Janeiro In.)	21·05 S	45·05 W
98	Pereira (pȧ-rā′rä).......Col. (In.)	4·49 N	75·42 W
129	Perekop (pĕr-ȧ-kôp′).....Sov. Un.	46·08 N	33·39 E
80	Pere Marquette............Mich.	43·55 N	86·10 W
129	Pereshchepino (pȧ′rȧsh-chē′pê-nô).Sov. Un.	49·02 N	35·19 E
128	Pereslavl′-Zalesskiy (pȧ-rȧ-slȧv″l zȧ-lyĕs′kĭ).Sov. Un.	56·43 N	38·52 E
129	Pereyaslav (pĕ-rȧ-yäs′ läv) Sov. Un.	50·05 N	31·25 E
101	Pergamino (pĕr-gä-mē′nō) Arg. (Buenos Aires In.)	33·53 S	60·36 W
70	Perham (pẽr′hăm).........Minn.	46·37 N	95·35 W
87	Peribonca (R.) (pĕr-ĭ-bŏŋ′kȧ).Can.	50·57 N	71·19 W
122	Périgueux (pā-rê-gû′).........Fr.	45·12 N	0·43 E
98	Perija, Sierra de (Mts.) (sē-ĕ′r-rȧ-dĕ-pĕ-rē′κä).Col.	9·25 N	73·30 W
85	Perkins (pĕr′kĕns) Can. (Ottawa In.)	45·37 N	75·37 W
93	Perlas, Arch. de Las (är-chē-pyĕ′lä-gô-dĕ-läs-pĕr′läs) Pan.	8·29 N	79·15 W
93	Perlas, Laguna las (L.) (lä-gōō′nä-dĕ-läs).Nic.	12·34 N	83·19 W
120	Perleberg (pĕr′lĕ-bĕrg).......Ger.	53·06 N	11·51 E
136	Perm′ (pĕrm).Sov. Un. (Urals In.)	58·00 N	56·15 E
	Pernambuco, see Recife		
99	Pernambuco (State) (pĕr-näm-bōō′kō).Braz.	8·08 S	38·54 W
	Pernik, see Dimitrovo		
122	Peronne (pā-rôn′)............Fr.	49·57 N	2·49 E
91	Perote (pĕ-rô′tĕ)...........Mex.	19·33 N	97·13 W
136	Perovo (pâ′rô-vô) Sov. Un. (Moscow In.)	55·43 N	37·47 E
122	Perpignan (pĕr-pē-nyäɴ′)......Fr.	42·42 N	2·48 E
74	Perris (pĕr′ĭs) Calif. (Los Angeles In.)	33·46 N	117·14 W
94	Perros, Bahía (B.) (bä-ē′ä-pā′rōs) Cuba	22·25 N	78·35 W
85	Perrot I. (pĕr′ŭt) Can. (Montreal In.)	45·23 N	73·57 W
78	Perry (pĕr′ĭ)................Ga.	32·27 N	83·44 W
78	Perry.......................Fla.	30·06 N	83·35 W
71	Perry......................Iowa	41·49 N	94·40 W
81	Perry......................N. Y.	42·45 N	78·00 W
73	Perry......................Okla.	36·17 N	97·18 W
74	Perry...Utah (Salt Lake City In.)	41·27 N	112·02 W
84	Perry Hall...Md. (Baltimore In.)	39·25 N	76·27 W
75	Perryopolis (pĕ-rê-ŏ′pô-lĭs) Pa. (Pittsburgh In.)	40·05 N	79·45 W
80	Perrysburg (pĕr ĭz-bûrg).....Ohio	41·35 N	83·35 W
72	Perryton (pĕr′ĭ-tŭn)........Tex.	36·23 N	100·48 W
64	Perryville (pĕr ĭ-vĭl).......Alaska	55·58 N	159·28 W
73	Perryville...................Mo.	37·41 N	89·52 W
123	Persan (pĕr-säɴ′)...Fr. (Paris In.)	49·09 N	2·15 E
103	Persepolis (Ruins) (pẽr-sĕp′o-lĭs) Iran	30·15 N	53·08 E
	Persia, see Iran		
144	Persian G. (pûr′zhȧn).......Asia	27·38 N	50·30 E
158	Perth (pûrth).............Austl.	31·50 S	116·10 E
81	Perth......................Can.	44·40 N	76 15 W
116	Perth.....................Scot.	56·24 N	3·25 W
84	Perth Amboy (äm′boi) N. J. (New York In.)	40·31 N	74·16 W
123	Pertuis (pĕr-tüē′)............Fr.	43·43 N	5·29 E
80	Peru (pê-rōō′)...............Ill.	41·20 N	89·10 W
80	Peru.......................Ind.	40·45 N	86·00 W
96	Peru.......................S. A.	10·00 S	75·00 W
126	Perugia (pā-rōō′jä)............It.	43·08 N	12·24 E
74	Peruque (pĕ rō′kĕ) Mo. (St. Louis In.)	38·52 N	90·36 W
129	Pervomaysk (pĕr-vô-mīsk′) Sov. Un.	48·04 N	30·52 E
136	Pervoural′sk (pĕr-vô-ōō-rálsk′) Sov. Un. (Urals In.)	56·54 N	59·58 E
135	Pervyy Kuril′skiy Proliv (Str.) Sov. Un.	51·43 N	154·32 E
126	Pesaro (pā′zä-rō).............It.	43·54 N	12·55 E
99	Pescado (pĕs-kä′dō) (R.) Ven. (In.)	9·33 N	65·32 W
126	Pescara (pās-kä′rä)...........It.	42·26 N	14·15 E
126	Pescara (R.).................It.	42·18 N	13·22 E
133	Peschanyy, Mys (C.)....Sov. Un.	43·10 N	51·20 E
126	Pescia (pā′shä)..............It.	43·53 N	11·42 E
145	Peshāwar (pĕ-shä′wŭr) W. Pak. (Khyber Pass In.)	34·01 N	71·34 E
127	Peshtera...................Bul.	42·03 N	24·19 E
71	Peshtigo (pĕsh′tê-gō)........Wis.	45·03 N	87·46 W
71	Peshtigo (R.)...............Wis.	45·15 N	88·14 W
103	Peski................Sov. Un.	39·46 N	59·47 E
103	Peski................Sov. Un.	44·07 N	63·17 E
136	Peski (pyâs′kĭ) Sov. Un. (Moscow In.)	55·13 N	38·48 E
124	Pêso da Régua (pā-sōō-dä-rā′gwä).Port.	41·09 N	7·47 W
92	Pespire (pȧs-pē′rȧ)........Hond.	13·35 N	87·20 W
76	Pesqueria, R. (pȧs-kȧ-rē′ȧ)..Mex.	25·55 N	100·25 W
90	Petacalco, Bahía de (B.) (bä-ē′ä-dĕ-pĕ-tä-kȧl′kô).Mex.	17·55 N	102·00 W
139	Petah Tiqva (pĕ′tak tĭk′vȧ) Isr. (Palestine In.)	32·05 N	34·53 E
68	Petaluma (pét-ȧ- lōō′mȧ)...Calif.	38·15 N	122·38 W
99	Petare (pĕ-tä′rĕ).......Ven. (In.)	10·28 N	66·48 W
90	Petatlán (pā-tä-tlän′).......Mex.	17·31 N	101·17 W
92	Petén, Laguna de (L.) (lä-gōō′nä-dĕ-pȧ-tān′) Guat. (Yucatan In.)	17·05 N	89·54 W
71	Petenwell Res..............Wis.	44·10 N	89·55 W
81	Peterborough (pē′tẽr-bŭr-ô)..Can.	44·20 N	78·20 W
160	Peterborough.............Austl.	32·53 S	138·58 E
110	Peterborough..............Eng.	52·35 N	0·14 W
116	Peterhead (pē-tẽr-hĕd′).....Scot.	57·36 N	3·47 W
81	Peter Pt...................Can.	43·50 N	77·00 W
86	Peter Pond L.(pŏnd).......Can.	56·03 N	109·23 W
64	Petersburg (pē′tẽrz-bûrg).Alaska	56·52 N	133·10 W
73	Petersburg..................Ill.	40·01 N	89·51 W
80	Petersburg.................Ind.	38·30 N	87·15 W
75	Petersburg...Ky. (Cincinnati In.)	39·04 N	84·52 W
79	Petersburg..................Va.	37·12 N	77·30 W
111	Petershagen (pĕ′tĕrs-hä-gĕn) Ger. (Berlin In.)	52·32 N	13·46 E
111	Petershausen (pĕ′tĕrs-hou-zĕn) Ger. (Munich In.)	48·25 N	11·29 E
95	Pétionville.................Hai.	18·30 N	72·20 W
82	Petitcodiac (pē-tē-kô-dyȧk′).Can.	45·55 N	65·11 W
93	Petite Terre I. (pē-tēt′târ′) N. A. (Le. & Wind. Is. In.)	16·12 N	61·00 W
95	Petit Goâve (pē-tē′ gô-ȧv′)...Hai.	18·25 N	72·50 W
73	Petit Jean Cr. (pē-tê′ zhäɴ′).Ark.	35·05 N	93·55 W
91	Petlalcingo (pĕ-tläl-sĕŋ′gô).Mex.	18·05 N	97·53 W
92	Peto (pĕ′tô)...Mex (Yucatan In.)	20·07 N	88·49 W
101	Petorca (pā-tōr′kȧ) Chile (Santiago In.)	32·14 S	70·55 W
80	Petoskey (pê-tŏs′kĭ)........Mich.	45·25 N	84·55 W
139	Petra......Jordan (Palestine In.)	30·21 N	35·25 E
152	Petra Velikogo, Zaliv (B.) (zä′lĭf pĕt-rä′ vĕ-lĭ′kô-vô) Sov. Un.	42·40 N	131·50 E
127	Petrich (pā′trĭch)...........Bul.	41·24 N	23·13 E
69	Petrified Forest Natl. Park (pĕt′rĭ-fīd fôr′ĕst).Ariz.	34·58 N	109·35 W
129	Petrikovka (pyĕ′trê-kôf-kä) Sov. Un.	48·43 N	34·29 E
129	Petrikov (pyĕ′trê-kô-v)..Sov. Un.	52·09 N	28·30 E
126	Petrinja (pā′trēn-yȧ).......Yugo.	45·25 N	16·17 E
136	Petrodvorets (pyĕ-trô-dvô-ryĕts′) Sov. Un. (Leningrad In.)	59·53 N	29·55 E
136	Petrokrepost′ (pyĕ′trô-krĕ-pôst) Sov. Un. (Leningrad In.)	59·56 N	31·03 E
80	Petrolia (pê-trō′lĭ-ȧ)........Can.	42·50 N	82·10 W
99	Petrolina (pĕ-trō-lē′nȧ).....Braz.	9·18 S	40·28 W
111	Petronell.......Aus. (Vienna In.)	48·07 N	16·52 E
129	Petropavlovka (pyĕ′trô-päv′lôf-κȧ) Sov. Un.	48·24 N	36·23 E
136	Petropavlovka.Sov. Un. (Urals In.)	54·10 N	59·50 E
134	Petropavlovsk (pyĕ-trô-päv′lôfsk) Sov. Un.	54·44 N	69·07 E
135	Petropavlovsk-Kamchatskiy (käm-chät′skĭ).Sov. Un.	53·13 N	158·56 E
100	Petrópolis (pȧ-trô-pô-lēzh′) Braz. (In.)	22·31 S	43·10 W
127	Petroseni.................Rom.	45 24 N	23·24 E
133	Petrovsk (pyĕ-trôfsk′)...Sov. Un.	52·20 N	45·15 E
129	Petrovskaya (pyĕ-trôf′skȧ-yȧ) Sov. Un.	45·25 N	37·50 E
133	Petrovskoye...........Sov. Un.	45·20 N	43·00 E
135	Petrovsk-Zabaykal′skiy (pyĕ-trôfskzä-bī-käl′skĭ) Sov. Un.	51·13 N	109·08 E
119	Petrozavodsk (pyä′trô-zȧ-vôtsk′) Sov. Un.	61·46 N	34·25 E
168	Petrus Steyn (pā′trōōs stān′) .S. Afr. (Johannesburg & Pretoria In.)	27·40 S	28·09 E

ăt; finăl; rāte; senâte; ärm; ȧsk; sofȧ; fâre; ch-choose; dh-as th in other; bē; êvent; bĕt; recĕnt; cratẽr; g-go; gh-guttural g; bĭt; ĭ-short neutral; rīde; κ-guttural k as ch in German ich;

PRONOUNCING INDEX Petseri–Plain City 251

Page	Name Pronunciation Region	Lat. °′	Long. °′
128	Petseri (pĕt'sĕ-rē) . . . . Sov. Un.	57·48 N	27·33 E
75	Pewaukee (pĭ-wô'kē) Wis. (Milwaukee In.)	43·05 N	88·15 W
75	Pewaukee L.. Wis. (Milwaukee In.)	43·03 N	88·18 W
75	Pewee Valley (pe wē) Ky. (Louisville In.)	38·19 N	85·29 W
132	Peza (R.) (pyâ'zȧ) . . . . . . Sov. Un.	65·35 N	46·50 E
122	Pézenas (pā-zē-nä') . . . . Fr.	43·26 N	3·24 E
120	Pforzheim (pfôrts'hīm) . . . . Ger.	48·52 N	8·43 E
142	Phalodi . . . . India	27·13 N	72·22 E
154	Phan Rang (p'hän'răng') . . . . Viet.	11·30 N	108·43 E
	Pharsalus, see Fársala		
78	Phenix City (fē'nĭks) . . . . Ala.	32·29 N	85·00 W
154	Phet Buri . . . . Thai.	13·07 N	99·53 E
78	Philadelphia (fĭl-ȧ-dĕl'phĭ-ȧ) . Miss.	32·45 N	89·07 W
84	Philadelphia Pa. (Philadelphia In.)	40·00 N	75·13 W
70	Philip (fĭl'ĭp) . . . . S. D.	44·03 N	101·35 W
	Philippeville, see Skikda		
155	Philippines (fĭl'ĭ-pēnz) . . . . Asia	14·25 N	125·00 E
156	Philippine Sea (fĭl'ĭ-pēn) . . . . . Asia	16·00 N	133·00 E
155	Philippine Trench . . . . Phil.	10·30 N	127·15 E
	Philippopolis, see Plovdiv		
81	Philipsburg (fĭl'ĭps-bērg) . . . . . Pa.	40·55 N	78·10 W
67	Philipsburg . . . . Wyo.	46·19 N	113·19 W
160	Phillip (I.) (fĭl'ĭp) . . . . Austl.	38·32 S	145·10 E
139	Phillip Chan. Indon. (Singapore In.)	1·04 N	103·40 E
81	Phillipi (fĭ-lĭp'ĭ) . . . . W. Va.	39·10 N	80·00 W
71	Phillips (fĭl'ĭps) . . . . Wis.	45·41 N	90·24 W
72	Phillipsburg (fĭl'lĭps-bērg) . . . Kans.	39·44 N	99·19 W
81	Phillipsburg . . . . Pa.	40·45 N	75·10 W
154	Phnom Penh (nŏm'pĕn') . . . Camb.	11·39 N	104·53 E
84	Phoebus (fē'bŭs) . Va. (Norfolk In.)	37·02 N	76·19 W
69	Phoenix (fē'nĭks) . . . . Ariz.	33·30 N	112·00 W
84	Phoenix . . . . Md. (Baltimore In.)	39·31 N	76·40 W
156	Phoenix Is. . . . . Oceania	4·00 S	174·00 W
84	Phoenixville (fē'nĭks-vĭl) Pa. (Philadelphia In.)	40·08 N	75·31 W
154	Phu Bia (Pk.) . . . . Laos	19·36 N	103·00 E
154	Phuket . . . . Thai.	7·57 N	98·19 E
148	P'i (R.) (pē') . . . . China	32·06 N	116·31 E
126	Piacenza (pyä-chĕnt'sä) . . . . It.	45·02 N	9·42 E
126	Pianosa (I.) (pyä-nō'sä) . . . . It.	42·13 N	15·45 E
121	Piatra-Neamt (pyä'trȧ-nä-ămts') Rom.	46·54 N	26·24 E
99	Piauí (State) (pyou'ē) . . . . . . Braz.	7·40 S	42·25 W
99	Piauí, Serra do (Mts.) (sĕr'rä dŏŏ pyou'ē) . Braz.	10·45 S	44·36 W
126	Piave (R.) (pyä'vā) . . . . It.	45·45 N	12·15 E
126	Piazza Armerina (pyät'sä är-mȧ-rē'nä) . It.	37·23 N	14·26 E
165	Pibor R. (pē'bôr) . . . . Sud.	7·21 N	32·54 E
71	Pic (R.) (pĕk) . . . . Can.	48·48 N	86·28 W
89	Picara Pt. (pē-kä'rä) . . . . . . Vir. Is. (U. S. A.) (St. Thomas In.)	18·23 N	64·57 W
78	Picayune (pĭk'ȧ yōōn) . . . . . . Miss.	30·32 N	89·41 W
126	Piccole Alpi Dolomitche (Mts.) (pē'k-kô-le-äl'pē-dô-lô'mē-tē'chĕ) It.	46·05 N	12·17 E
125	Pic du Midi d'Ossau (Mtn.) (pēk dü mē-dē' dôs-sō') . Fr.	42·51 N	0·25 W
73	Picher (pĭch'ẽr) . . . . Okla.	36·58 N	94·49 W
151	Pichieh . . . . China	27·20 N	105·18 E
101	Pichilemu (pē-chē-lĕ'mōō) Chile (Santiago In.)	34·22 S	72·01 W
91	Pichucalco (pē-chōō-käl'kô) . . Mex.	17·34 N	93.06 W
91	Pichucalco (R.) . . . . Mex.	17·40 N	93·02 W
71	Pickerel (L.) (pĭk'ẽr-ĕl) . . . . . . Can.	48·35 N	91·10 W
78	Pickwick (R.) (pĭk'wĭck) . . . Tenn.	35·04 N	88·05 W
74	Pico (pē'kō) Calif. (Los Angeles In.)	34·01 N	118·05 W
125	Pico de Aneto (Mtn.) (pē'kō-dĕ-ä-nĕ'tô) . Sp.	42·35 N	0·38 E
164	Pico I. (pē'kōō) . . . . . . Açores (In.)	38·16 N	28·49 W
99	Picos (pē'kōzh) . . . . Braz.	7·13 S	41·23 W
161	Picton (pĭk'tŭn) Austl. (Sydney In.)	34·11 S	150·37 E
83	Pictou (pĭk-tōō') . . . . Can.	45·43 N	62·44 W
143	Pidurutalagala Mt. (pē'dōō-rōō-tä'lȧ-gä'lȧ) . Ceylon	12·27 N	80·45 E
71	Pie (I.) (pī) . . . . Can.	48·10 N	89·07 W
101	Piedade (pyä-dä'dĕ) Braz. (Rio de Janeiro In.)	23·42 S	47·25 W
78	Piedmont (pēd'mŏnt) . . . . Ala.	33·54 N	85·36 W
65	Piedmont Calif.(San Francisco In.)	37·50 N	122·14 W
73	Piedmont . . . . Mo.	37·09 N	90·42 W
79	Piedmont . . . . S. C.	34·40 N	82·27 W
81	Piedmont . . . . W. Va.	39·30 N	79·05 W
124	Piedrabuena (pyä-drä-bwā'nä) . Sp.	39·01 N	4·10 W
101	Piedras, Punta (Pt.) (pōō'n-tä-pyĕ'dräs) Arg. (Buenos Aires In.)	35·25 S	57·10 W
76	Piedras Negras (pyä'dräs nā'gräs) Mex.	28·41 N	100·33 W
119	Pieksämäki (pyĕk'sĕ-mĕ-kē) . . Fin.	62·18 N	27·14 E
124	Piélagos (pyā'lä-gōs) . . . . Sp.	43·23 N	3·55 W
126	Piemonte (Reg.) (pyĕ-mô'n-tĕ) . It.	44·30 N	7·42 E
168	Pienaars R. . . . . S. Afr. (Johannesburg & Pretoria In.)	25·13 S	28·05 E
168	Pienaarsrivier . . . . S. Afr. (Johannesburg & Pretoria In.)	25·12 S	28·18 E
70	Pierce (pērs) . . . . Nebr.	42·11 N	97·33 W
81	Pierce . . . . W. Va.	39·15 N	79·30 W
84	Piermont (pēr'mŏnt) N. Y. (New York In.)	41·03 N	73·55 W
70	Pierre (pēr) . . . . S. D.	44·22 N	100·20 W
121	Piešťany (pyĕsh'tyä-nü') . . . Czech.	48·36 N	17·48 E
167	Pietermaritzburg (pē-tēr-mȧ-rĭts-bûrg) S. Afr. (Natal In.)	29·36 S	30·23 E
168	Pietersburg (pē'tẽrz-bûrg) S. Afr. (Johannesburg & Pretoria In.)	23·56 S	29·30 E
81	Pieton . . . . Can.	44·00 N	77·15 W
166	Piet Retief (pēt rĕ-tēf') . . . . S. Afr.	27·00 S	30·58 E
121	Pietrosul Pk. . . . . Rom.	47·35 N	24·49 E
126	Pieve di Cadore (pyā'vā dē kä-dō'rā) . It.	46·26 N	12·22 E
71	Pigeon (R.) (pĭj'ŭn) . . . Can.-Minn.	48·05 N	90·13 W
85	Pigeon Lake. Can. (Winnipeg In.)	49·57 N	97·36 W
73	Piggott (pĭg'ŭt) . . . . Ark.	36·22 N	90·10 W
91	Pijijiapan (pēkē-kē-ä'pän) . . . Mex.	15·40 N	93·12 W
111	Pijnacker. Neth. (Amsterdam In.)	52·01 N	4·25 E
72	Pikes Pk. (pīks) . . . . Colo.	38·49 N	105·03 W
79	Pikeville (pīk'vĭl) . . . . Ky.	37·28 N	82·31 W
120	Piła (pē'lȧ) . . . . Pol.	53·09 N	16·44 E
168	Pilansberg (pē'ȧns'bûrg) S. Afr. (Johannesburg & Pretoria In.)	25·08 S	26·55 E
101	Pilar (pē'lär) Arg. (Buenos Aires In.)	34·27 S	58·55 W
100	Pilar . . . . Par.	27·00 S	58·15 W
155	Pilar (pē'lär) . . . Phil. (Manila In.)	12·55 N	123·41 E
155	Pilar . . . . Phil. (Manila In.)	17·24 N	120·36 E
99	Pilar de Goiás (dĕ-gô'yȧ's) . . Braz.	14·47 S	49·33 W
65	Pilchuck (R.) . Wash. (Seattle In.)	48·03 N	121·58 W
65	Pilchuck Cr. (pĭl'chŭk) Wash. (Seattle In.)	48·19 N	122·11 W
65	Pilchuck Mtn.. Wash. (Seattle In.)	48·03 N	121·48 W
100	Pilcomayo (R.) (pēl-cō-mī'ō) . Par.	24·45 S	69·15 W
155	Pili (pē'lē) . . . . . Phil. (Manila In.)	13·34 N	123·17 E
121	Pilica R. (pē-lēt'sä) . . . . Pol.	51·00 N	19·48 E
65	Pillar Pt. (pĭl'ȧr) . Can. (Seattle In.)	48·14 N	124·06 W
65	Pillar Rock. . Wash. (Portland In.)	46·16 N	123·35 W
90	Pilón (R.) (pē-lōn') . . . . Mex.	24·13 N	99·03 W
73	Pilot Point (pī'lŭt) . . . . Tex.	33·24 N	97·00 W
	Pilsen, see Plzeň		
119	Piltene (pĭl'tĕ-nĕ) . . . . . . Sov. Un.	57·17 N	21·40 E
90	Pimal, Cerra (Mtn.) (sĕ'r-rä-pē-mäl') . Mex.	22·58 N	104·19 W
158	Pimba (pĭm'bȧ) . . . . Austl.	31·15 S	146·50 E
167	Pimville (pĭm'vĭl) . . . . S. Afr. (Johannesburg & Pretoria In.)	26·17 S	27·54 E
88	Pinacate, Cerro (Mtn.) (sĕ'r-rō-pē-nä-kä'tĕ) . Mex.	31·45 N	113·30 W
155	Pinamalayan (pē-nä-mä-lä'yän) Phil. (Manila In.)	13·04 N	121·31 E
133	Pınarbaşı (pē'när-bä'shĭ) . . . . . Tur.	38·50 N	36·10 E
94	Pinar del Río (pē-när' dĕl rē'ō) Cuba	22·25 N	83·35 W
94	Pinar del Río (State) . . . . Cuba	22·45 N	83·25 W
155	Pinatubo (Mtn.) (pē-nä-tōō'bō) Phil. (Manila In.)	15·09 N	120·19 E
73	Pinckneyville (pĭnk'nĭ-vĭl) . . . . . Ill.	38·06 N	89·22 W
121	Pińczów (pēn''chōōf) . . . . Pol.	50·32 N	20·33 E
101	Pindamonhangaba (pē'n-dä-mōnyä'n-gä-bä) Braz. (Rio de Janeiro In.)	22·56 S	45·26 W
127	Píndhos Oros (Mts.) . . . . Grc.	39·48 N	21·19 E
83	Pine, C (pīn) . . . . Can.	46·36 N	53·35 W
71	Pine (R.) . . . . Wis.	45·50 N	88·37 W
73	Pine Bluff (pīn blŭf) . . . . Ark.	34·13 N	92·01 W
71	Pine City (pīn) . . . . Minn.	45·50 N	93·01 W
158	Pine Creek . . . . Austl.	13·45 S	132·00 E
68	Pine Cr. . . . . Nev.	40·15 N	116·17 W
66	Pine Forest Ra. . . . . Nev.	41·35 N	118·45 W
132	Pinega (pē-nyĕ'gȧ) . . . . . . Sov. Un.	64·40 N	43·30 E
132	Pinega (R.) . . . . Sov. Un.	64·10 N	42·30 E
84	Pine Hill (pīn hĭl) N. J. (Philadelphia In.)	39·47 N	74·59 W
65	Pinehurst (pīn'hûrst) Wash. (Seattle In.)	47·56 N	122·13 W
79	Pine Is. . . . . Fla. (In.)	24·48 N	81·32 W
79	Pine Island Sd. . . . . Fla. (In.)	26·32 N	82·30 W
84	Pine Lake Estates (lăk ĕs-tāts') Ga. (Atlanta In.)	33·47 N	84·13 W
166	Pinelands (pīn'lănds) S. Afr. (Cape Town In.)	33·57 S	18·30 E
74	Pine Lawn (lôn) Mo. (St. Louis In.)	38·42 N	90·17 W
84	Pine Mountain (moun'tĭn) Ga. (Atlanta In.)	33·39 N	84·09 W
70	Pine Ridge Ind. Res. (rĭj) . . . S. D.	43·33 N	102·13 W
126	Pinerola (pē-nā-rô'lō) . . . . It.	44·47 N	7·18 E
77	Pines, Lake o' the . . . . Tex.	32·50 N	94·40 W
167	Pinetown (pīn'toun) S. Afr. (Natal In.)	29·47 S	30·52 E
74	Pine View Res. (vū) Utah (Salt Lake City In.)	41·17 N	111·54 W
78	Pineville (pīn'vĭl) . . . . Ky.	36·48 N	83·43 W
77	Pineville . . . . La.	31·20 N	92·25 W
154	Ping, Mae Nam (R.) . . . . Thai.	17·54 N	98·29 E
149	Pingchoupao. . China (Canton In.)	23·01 N	113·11 E
150	Pingchüan . . . . China	40·58 N	118·40 E
139	Pinggir . . . . Indon. (Singapore In.)	1·05 N	101·12 E
151	P'ingho (pĭng'hō') . . . . China	24·30 N	117·02 E
151	Pinghsiang . . . . China	27·40 N	113·50 E
150	Pingliang (pĭng'lyăng') . . . . . China	35·12 N	106·50 E
151	P'inglo (pĭng'lō') . . . . China	24·30 N	110·22 E
151	P'ingt'an . . . . China	25·30 N	119·45 E
150	Pingting (pĭng'tĭng') . . . . China	37·50 N	113·30 E
148	P'ingtu (pĭng'tōō') . . . . China	36·46 N	119·57 E
151	P'ingtung . . . . Taiwan	22·40 N	120·35 E
150	P'ingwu . . . . China	32·20 N	104·40 E
148	P'ingyuan (pĭng'yü-än') . . . . China	37·11 N	116·26 E
101	Pinhal (pē-nyà'l) Braz. (Rio de Janeiro In.)	22·11 S	46·43 W
125	Pinhal Novo (nô vōō) Port. (Lisbon In.)	38·38 N	8·54 W
124	Pinhel (pēn-yĕl') . . . . Port.	40·45 N	7·03 W
148	Pinhsien (pĭn'siän) . . . . China	38·29 N	117·58 E
150	Pinhsien . . . . China	45·40 N	127·20 E
154	Pini (I.) (pē'nē) . . . . Indon.	0·07 N	98·38 E
127	Piniós (R.) . . . . Grc.	40·33 N	21·40 E
68	Pinnacles Natl. Mon. (pĭn'ȧ-k'lz) Calif.	36·30 N	121·00 W
111	Pinneberg (pĭn'ĕ-bĕrg) Ger. (Hamburg In.)	53·40 N	9·48 E
65	Pinole (pĭ-nō'lē) Calif. (San Francisco In.)	38 01 N	122·17 W
94	Pinos, Isla de (I.) (ē's-lä-dĕ-pē'nôs) . Cuba	21·40 N	82·45 W
124	Pinos-Puente (pwān'tä) . . . . Sp.	37·15 N	3·43 W
90	Pinotepa Nacional (pē-nô-tā'pä nä-syô-näl') . Mex.	16·21 N	98·04 W
159	Pins, Ile des . . . . N. Cal.	22·44 S	167·44 E
121	Pinsk (pēn'sk) . . . . Sov. Un.	52·07 N	26·05 E
98	Pinta (I.) . . . . Ec.	0·41 N	90·47 W
85	Pintendre (pĕN-tăNdr') Can. (Quebec In.)	46·45 N	71·07 W
125	Pinto (pēn'tō) . . . Sp. (Madrid In.)	40·14 N	3·42 W
69	Pioche (pī-ō'chē) . . . . Nev.	37·56 N	114·28 W
126	Piombino (pyôm-bē'nō) . . . . It.	42·56 N	10·33 E
65	Pioneer (pī'ô-nēr') Wash. (Portland In.)	45·49 N	122·40 W
67	Pioneer Mts. . . . . Mont.	45·23 N	112·51 W
121	Piotrków Trybunalski (pyōtr'kōōv trĭ-bōō-nal'skē) . Pol.	51·23 N	19·44 E
78	Piper (pī'pẽr) . . . . Ala.	33·04 N	87·00 W
74	Piper . . . . Kans. (Kansas City In.)	39·09 N	94·51 W
127	Pipéri (I.) (pē'per-ē) . . . . Grc.	39·19 N	24·20 E
69	Pipe Spring Natl. Mon. (pīp sprĭng) . Ariz.	36·50 N	112·45 W
70	Pipestone (pīp'stōn) . . . . Minn.	44·00 N	96·19 W
71	Pipestone (R.) . . . . Can.	48·34 N	92·22 W
70	Pipestone Natl. Mon . . . . . . Minn.	44·03 N	96·24 W
82	Pipmaukin, L. (pĭp-mä-kän') Can.	49·36 N	69·55 W
80	Piqua (pĭk'wȧ) . . . . Ohio	40·10 N	84·15 W
101	Piracaia (pē-rä-kà'yä) Braz. (Rio de Janeiro In.)	23·04 S	46·20 W
101	Piracicaba (pē-rä-sē-kà'bä) Braz. (Rio de Janeiro In.)	22·43 S	47·39 W
101	Piraí (pē-rä-ē') Braz. (Rio de Janeiro In.)	22·38 S	43·54 W
101	Piraíba (R.) (pä-rä-ē'bä) Braz. (Rio de Janeiro In.)	21·38 S	41·29 W
134	Piramida, Gol'tsy (Mtn.) Sov. Un.	54·00 N	96·00 E
126	Piran (pē-rä'n) . . . . Yugo.	45·31 N	13·34 E
101	Piranga (pē-rä'n-gä) Braz. (Rio de Janeiro In.)	20·41 S	43·17 W
101	Pirapetinga (pē-rä-pĕ-tē'n-gä) Braz. (Rio de Janeiro In.)	21·40 S	42·20 W
99	Pirapora (pē-rä-pō'rȧ) . . . . . . Braz.	17·39 S	44·54 W
101	Pirassununga (pē-rä-sōō-nōō'n-gä) Braz. (Rio de Janeiro In.)	22·00 S	47·24 W
99	Pirenópolis (pē-rĕ-nô'pō-lēs) . Braz.	15·56 S	48·49 W
127	Pírgos . . . . Grc.	37·51 N	21·28 E
99	Piritu, Laguna de (L.) (lä-gōō'nä-dĕ-pē-rē'tōō) Ven. (In.)	10·00 N	64·57 W
120	Pirmasens (pĭr-mä-zĕns') . . . . . Ger.	49·12 N	7·34 E
120	Pirna (pĭr'nä) . . . . Ger.	50·57 N	13·56 E
127	Pirot (pē'rōt) . . . . Yugo.	43·09 N	22·35 E
69	Pirtleville (pûr't'l-vĭl) . . . . Ariz.	31·25 N	109·35 W
155	Piru (pē-rōō') . . . . Indon.	3·15 S	128·25 E
129	Piryatin (pēr-yä-tēn') . . . . Sov. Un.	50·13 N	32·31 E
126	Pisa (pē'sä) . . . . It.	43·52 N	10·24 E
98	Pisagua (pē-sä'gwä) . . . . Chile	18·43 S	70·12 W
84	Piscataway (pĭs-kȧ-tȧ-wā) Md. (Baltimore In.)	38·42 N	76·59 W
98	Pisco (pēs'kō) . . . . Peru	13·43 S	76·07 W
98	Pisco, Bahia de (B.) (bä-ē'ä-dĕ) Peru	13·43 S	77·48 W
81	Piseco (L.) (pĭ-sā'kō) . . . . N. Y.	43·25 N	74·35 W
120	Pisek (pē'sĕk) . . . . Czech.	49·18 N	14·08 E
139	Pissouri . . . . Cyprus (Palestine In.)	34·39 N	32·42 E
126	Pisticci (pēs-tē'chē) . . . . It.	40·24 N	16·34 E
126	Pistoia (pēs-tô'yä) . . . . It.	43·57 N	11·54 E
83	Pistolet B. (pĭs-tō-lā') . . . . Can.	51·40 N	55·43 W
124	Pisuerga (R.) (pē-swĕr'gä) . . . . Sp.	41·48 N	4·28 W
98	Pitalito (pē-tä-lē'tō) . . . . Col.	1·45 N	75·09 W
75	Pitcairn (pĭt'kârn) Pa. (Pittsburgh In.)	40·29 N	79·47 W
157	Pitcairn (I.) . . . . Oceania	24·30 S	133·00 W
112	Pite (R.) (pē'tĕ) . . . . Swe.	66·08 N	18·51 E
112	Piteå (pē'tĕ-ô') . . . . Swe.	65·21 N	21·10 E
127	Pitesti (pē-tĕsht'') . . . . Rom.	44·51 N	24·51 E
158	Pithara (pĭt'ărȧ) . . . . Austl.	30·27 S	116·45 E
122	Pithiviers (pē-tē-vyā') . . . . Fr.	48·12 N	2·14 E
84	Pitman (pĭt'mȧn) N. J. (Philadelphia In.)	39·44 N	75·08 W
93	Pitons du Carbet, Mt. Mart. (Le. & Wind. Is. In.)	14·40 N	61·05 W
66	Pit R. (pĭt) . . . . Calif.	40·58 N	121·42 W
167	Pitseng . . . . Leso. (Natal In.)	29·03 S	28·13 E
65	Pitt (R.) . . . Can. (Vancouver In.)	49·19 N	122·39 W
64	Pitt Pt. (pĭt) . . . . Alaska	70·48 N	152·00 W
65	Pittsburg (pĭts'bûrg) Calif. (San Francisco In.)	38·01 N	121·52 W
73	Pittsburg . . . . Kans.	37·25 N	94·43 W
65	Pittsburg . . . . . Ore. (Portland In.)	45·54 N	123·09 W
73	Pittsburg . . . . Tex.	32·00 N	94·57 W
75	Pittsburgh . . . Pa. (Pittsburgh In.)	40·26 N	80·01 W
73	Pittsfield (pĭts'fēld) . . . . Ill.	39·37 N	90·47 W
82	Pittsfield . . . . Maine	44·45 N	69·44 W
81	Pittsfield . . . . Mass.	42·25 N	73·15 W
81	Pittston (pĭts'tŭn) . . . . Pa.	41·20 N	75·50 W
148	P'itzuwo (Hsinchin) (pē'zhē'wŏ) (sĭn'jĭn) . China	39·25 N	122·19 E
101	Piũi (pē-ōō'ē) Braz. (Rio de Janeiro In.)	20·27 S	45·57 W
98	Piura (pē-ōō'rä) . . . . Peru	5·13 S	80·46 W
136	Piya (pē'yȧ) . . Sov. Un. (Urals In.)	58·34 N	61·12 E
74	Placentia (plă-sĕn'shĭ-ȧ) Calif. (Los Angeles In.)	33·52 N	117·50 W
83	Placentia . . . . Can.	47·16 N	53·59 W
83	Placentia B . . . . Can.	47·14 N	54·30 W
68	Placerville (plăs'ẽr-vĭl) . . . . . . Calif.	38·43 N	120·47 W
94	Placetas (plä-thä'täs) . . . . Cuba	22·10 N	79·40 W
81	Placid (L.) (plăs'ĭd) . . . . N. Y.	44·20 N	74·00 W
74	Plain City (plān) Utah (Salt Lake City In.)	41·18 N	112·06 W

ng-sing; ŋ-baŋk; N-nasalized n; nŏd; cŏmmit; ōld; ôbey; ôrder; fōōd; fŏŏt; ou-out; s-soft; sh-dish; th-thin; pūre; ûnite; ûrn; stŭd; circŭs; ü-as "y" in study; '-indeterminate vowel.

252 Plainfield–Port Bolivar PRONOUNCING INDEX

Page	Name Pronunciation Region	Lat. °′	Long. °′
75	Plainfield (plān'fēld) Ill. (Chicago In.)	41·37 N	88·12 W
75	Plainfield..Ind. (Indianapolis In.)	39·42 N	86·23 W
84	Plainfield...N. J. (New York In.)	40·38 N	74·25 W
73	Plainview (plān'vū).........Ark.	34·59 N	93·15 W
71	Plainview................Minn.	44·09 N	93·12 W
70	Plainview................Nebr.	42·20 N	97·47 W
72	Plainview..................Tex.	34·11 N	101·42 W
80	Plainwell (plān'wel)........Mich.	42·25 N	85·40 W
85	Plaisance (plě-zäNs') Can. (Ottawa In.)	45·37 N	75·07 W
95	Plana or Flat Cays (Is.) (plä'nä) Ba. Is.	22·35 N	73·35 W
122	Plan-de-Cuques (plä-dě-kük') Fr. (Marseille In.)	43·22 N	5·29 E
111	Planegg (plä'něg) Ger. (Munich In.)	48·06 N	11·27 E
73	Plano (plā'nō)..............Tex.	33·01 N	96·42 W
85	Plantagenet (pläN-täzh-ně') Can. (Ottawa In.)	45·33 N	75·00 W
79	Plant City (plånt sĭ'tĭ)..Fla. (In.)	28·00 N	82·07 W
77	Plaquemine (pläk'mēn')......La.	30·17 N	91·14 W
124	Plasencia (plä-sěn'thē-ä)......Sp.	40·02 N	6·07 W
136	Plast (plåst)..Sov. Un. (Urals In.)	54·22 N	60·48 E
82	Plaster Rock (plås'tēr rŏk)...Can.	46·54 N	67·22 W
152	Plastun (plås-to͞on').....Sov. Un.	44·41 N	136·08 E
100	Plata, R. de la (R.) (dālä plä'tä) Arg.-Ur.	34·35 S	58·15 W
126	Platani (R.) (plä-tä'nē)........It.	37·26 N	13·28 E
95	Plateforme, Pte.............Hai.	19·35 N	73·50 W
64	Platinum (plăt'ĭ-nŭm).....Alaska	59·00 N	161·27 W
98	Plato (plä'tō)...............Col.	9·49 N	74·48 W
90	Platón Sánchéz (plä-tōn' sän'chěz).Mex.	21·14 N	98·20 W
73	Platt Natl. Park (plăt)......Okla.	34·31 N	96·44 W
70	Platte (plăt)...............S. D.	43·22 N	98·51 W
73	Platte (R.).................Mo.	40·09 N	94·40 W
62	Platte (R.).................U. S.	40·50 N	100·40 W
71	Platteville (plăt'vĭl).........Wis.	42·44 N	90·31 W
73	Plattsburg (plăts'bûrg).......Mo.	39·33 N	94·26 W
81	Plattsburgh...............N. Y.	44·40 N	73·30 W
70	Plattsmouth (plăts'mŭth)...Nebr.	41·00 N	95·53 W
120	Plauen (plou'ěn)............Ger.	50·30 N	12·08 E
95	Playa de Guanabo (plä-yä-dě-gwä-nä'bô) Cuba (Havana In.)	23·10 N	82·07 W
95	Playa de Santa Fe (sä'n-tä-fě') Cuba (Havana In.)	23·05 N	82·31 W
69	Playas (L.) (plä'yås).....N. Mex.	31·50 N	108·30 W
91	Playa Vicente (vē-sěn'tå)....Mex.	17·49 N	95·49 W
91	Playa Vicente (R.).........Mex.	17·36 N	96·13 W
81	Pleasant (L.) (plěz'ănt).....N. Y.	43·25 N	74·25 W
65	Pleasant Hill Calif. (San Francisco In.)	37·57 N	122·04 W
73	Pleasant Hill..............Mo.	38·46 N	94·18 W
65	Pleasanton (plěz'ăn-tŭn) Calif. (San Francisco In.)	37·40 N	121·53 W
73	Pleasanton................Kans.	38·10 N	94·41 W
76	Pleasanton.................Tex.	28·58 N	98·30 W
75	Pleasant Plain (plěz'ănt) Ohio (Cincinnati In.)	39·17 N	84·06 W
75	Pleasant Ridge. Mich. (Detroit In.)	42·28 N	83·09 W
75	Pleasure Ridge Park (plězh'ēr rĭj) Ky. (Louisville In.)	38·09 N	85·49 W
74	Pleasant View (plěz'ănt vū) Utah (Salt Lake City In.)	41·20 N	112·02 W
84	Pleasantville (plěz'ănt-vĭl) N. Y. (New York In.)	41·08 N	73·47 W
159	Plenty, B. of (plěn'tê).N. Z. (In.)	37·23 S	177·10 E
67	Plentywood (plěn'tê-wo͝od).Mont.	48·47 N	104·38 W
128	Ples (plyěs).............Sov. Un.	57·26 N	41·29 E
128	Pleshcheyevo (L.) (plěsh-chă'yě-vô).Sov. Un.	56·50 N	38·22 E
82	Plessisville (plě-sē'vēl')......Can.	46·12 N	71·47 W
121	Pleszew (plě'zhěf)...........Pol.	51·54 N	17·48 E
123	Plettenberg (plě'těn-běrgh) Ger. (Ruhr In.)	51·13 N	7·53 E
127	Pleven (plě'věn)............Bul.	43·24 N	24·26 E
127	Pljevlja (plěv'lyä).........Yugo.	43·20 N	19·21 E
121	Płock (pwôtsk)..............Pol.	52·32 N	19·44 E
122	Ploërmel (plô-ěr-mêl')........Fr.	47·56 N	2·25 W
127	Ploești (plô-yěsht'')........Rom.	44·56 N	26·01 E
127	Plomárion (plô-mä'rĭ-ŏn).....Grc.	38·51 N	26·24 E
122	Plomb du Cantal (Mt.) (plôN'dükäN-täl'). Fr.	45·30 N	2·49 E
127	Plovdiv (Philippopolis) (plôv'dĭf) (fĭl-ĭp-ŏp'ô-lĭs).Bul.	42·09 N	24·43 E
91	Pluma Hidalgo (plo͞o'mä ē-däl'gō) Mex.	15·54 N	96·23 W
119	Plunge (plo͝on'gā).......Sov. Un.	55·56 N	21·45 E
116	Plymouth (plĭm'ŭth)........Eng.	50·25 N	4·14 W
80	Plymouth..................Ind.	41·20 N	86·20 W
81	Plymouth.................Mass.	42·00 N	70·45 W
75	Plymouth.....Mich. (Detroit In.)	42·23 N	83·27 W
81	Plymouth.................N. H.	43·50 N	71·40 W
79	Plymouth.................N. C.	35·50 N	76·44 W
81	Plymouth...................Pa.	41·15 N	75·55 W
93	Plymouth Montserrat (Le. & Wind. Is. In.)	16·43 N	62·12 W
71	Plymouth..................Wis.	43·45 N	87·59 W
128	Plyussa (R.) (plyo͞o'så)..Sov. Un.	58·33 N	28·30 E
120	Plzeň (Pilsen)............Czech.	49·46 N	13·25 E
126	Po, Bocche del (Mouth) (bô'chě-děl-pô').It.	44·57 N	12·38 E
126	Po, Fiume (R.) (fyo͞o'mě-pō)...It.	45·00 N	11·23 E
150	Poar.....................China	35·10 N	113·08 E
164	Pobé (pô-bā')..........Dahomey	6·56 N	2·32 E
73	Pocahontas (pō-kȧ-hŏn'tȧs)..Ark.	36·15 N	91·01 W
71	Pocahontas................Iowa	42·43 N	94·41 W
67	Pocatello (pō-kȧ-těl'ō)......Idaho	42·54 N	112·30 W
128	Pochěp (pô-chěp').......Sov. Un.	52·56 N	32·27 E
128	Pochinok (pô-chē'nôk)...Sov. Un.	54·14 N	32·27 E
132	Pochinski..............Sov. Un.	54·40 N	44·50 E
90	Pochotitán (pô-chô-tē-tä'n)..Mex.	21·37 N	104·33 W
91	Pochutla (San Pedro) (pō-cho͞o'tlä) (sän pā'drō).Mex.	15·46 N	96·28 W
81	Pocomoke City (pō-kō-mōk').Md.	38·05 N	75·35 W
81	Pocono Mts. (pō-cō'nō).......Pa.	41·10 N	75·05 W
101	Poços de Caldas (pō-sôs-dě-käl'dås) Braz. (Rio de Janeiro In.)	21·48 S	46·34 W
164	Poder (pô-dôr')..........Senegal	16·35 N	15·04 W
134	Podkamennaya (Stony) Tunguska (R.).Sov. Un.	61·43 N	93·45 E
136	Podol'sk (pô-dôl''sk) Sov. Un. (Moscow In.)	55·26 N	37·33 E
129	Podvolochisk...........Sov. Un.	49·32 N	26·16 E
126	Poggibonsi (pôd-jê-bôn'sê).....It.	43·27 N	11·12 E
128	Pogodino (pô-gô'dê-nô)..Sov. Un.	54·17 N	31·00 E
152	Pohai Str. (pō'hī').........China	38·05 N	121·40 E
152	P'ohangdong...............Kor.	35·57 N	129·23 E
148	Pohsien..................China	33·52 N	115·47 E
148	Pohsing (pō'hsĭng')........China	37·09 N	118·08 E
85	Pointe-a'-Gatineau (po͞o-ăNt'ă-gȧ-tē-nō') Can. (Ottawa In.)	45·28 N	75·42 W
93	Pointe-à-Pitre (pwăNt' à pē-tr') Guad. (Le. & Wind. Is. In.)	16·15 N	61·32 W
85	Pointe-aux-Pins (po͞o-ăNt' ō-pěN) Can. (Edmonton In.)	53·38 N	113·15 W
85	Pointe-aux-Trembles (po͞o-ăNt' ō-träNbl) Can. (Montreal In.)	45·39 N	73·30 W
85	Pointe Claire (po͞o-ăNt' klěr) Can. (Montreal In.)	45 26 N	73 50 W
85	Pointe Fortune (fôr'tûn) Can. (Montreal In.)	45·34 N	74·23 W
166	Pointe Noire............Con. B.	4·48 S	11·50 E
64	Point Hope (hōp).........Alaska	68·18 N	166·38 W
80	Point Pleasant (plěz'ănt)..W. Va.	38·50 N	82·10 W
65	Point Roberts (rŏb'ērts) Wash. (Vancouver In.)	48·59 N	123·04 W
123	Poissy (pwȧ-sē')....Fr. (Paris In.)	48·55 N	2·02 E
122	Poitiers (pwȧ-tyā')...........Fr.	46·35 N	0·18 E
142	Pokaran (pō'kŭr-ŭn).......India	27·00 N	72·05 E
150	Pok'ot'u (pō'kô-to͞o')......China	48·45 N	121·42 E
128	Pokrov (pô'krôf)........Sov. Un.	55·56 N	39·09 E
129	Pokrovskoye (pô-krôf'skô-yě) Sov. Un.	47·27 N	38·54 E
128	Pola (R.) (pō'lä)........Sov. Un.	54·44 N	31·53 E
124	Pola de Allade (dě-äl-yä'dě)...Sp.	43·18 N	6·35 W
124	Pola de Laviana (dě-lä-vyä'nä).Sp.	43·15 N	5·29 W
102	Poland (pō'lănd)............Eur.	52·37 N	17·01 E
155	Polangui (pô-läŋ'gē) Phil. (Manila In.)	13·18 N	123·29 E
136	Polazna (pô'làz-nȧ) Sov. Un. (Urals In.)	58·18 N	56·25 E
119	Polessk (pô'lěsk)........Sov. Un.	54·50 N	21·14 E
133	Poles'ye (Pripyat' Marshes) Sov. Un.	52·10 N	27·30 E
136	Polevskoy (pô-lě'vs-kô'ê) Sov. Un. (Urals In.)	56·28 N	60·14 E
121	Polgár (pôl'gär)...........Hung.	47·54 N	21·10 E
150	P'oli (pō'lĭ)...............China	45·40 N	130·38 E
126	Policastro, Golfo di (G.).......It.	41·00 N	13·23 E
123	Poligny (pō-lē-nyē')..........Fr.	46·48 N	5·42 E
127	Políkhnitos..................Grc.	39·05 N	26·11 E
155	Polillo (pô-lēl'yō).Phil. (Manila In.)	14·42 N	121·56 E
155	Polillo Is.......Phil. (Manila In.)	15·05 N	122·15 E
155	Polillo Str......Phil. (Manila In.)	15·02 N	121·40 E
128	Polist' (R.) (pô'lĭst).....Sov. Un.	57·42 N	31·02 E
126	Polistena (pō-lês-tä'nä)........It.	40·25 N	16·05 E
127	Poliyiros...................Grc.	40·23 N	23·27 E
134	Polkan, Gol'tsy (Mtn.)..Sov. Un.	60·18 N	92·08 E
125	Pollensa (pōl-yěn'sä).........Sp.	39·50 N	3·00 E
92	Polochic R. (pō-lô-chēk')...Guat.	15·19 N	89·45 W
129	Polonnoye (pô'lô-nô-yě)..Sov. Un.	50·07 N	27·31 E
128	Polotsk (pô'lôtsk).......Sov. Un.	55·30 N	28·48 E
101	Polpaico (pôl-på'y-kô) Chile (Santiago In.)	33·10 S	70·53 W
67	Polson (pōl'sŭn)...........Mont.	47·40 N	114·10 W
129	Poltava (pôl-tä'vä)......Sov. Un.	49·35 N	34·33 E
129	Poltava (Oblast)........Sov. Un.	49·53 N	32·58 E
128	Põltsamaa (pŏlt'så-mä)..Sov. Un.	58·39 N	26·00 E
128	Põltsamaa (R.).........Sov. Un.	58·35 N	25·55 E
136	Polunochnoye (pô-lo͞o-nô'ch-nô'yě) Sov. Un. (Urals In.)	60·52 N	60·27 E
134	Poluy (R.) (pôl'wê).....Sov. Un.	65·45 N	68·15 E
136	Polyakovka (pŭl-yä'kôv-kȧ) Sov. Un. (Urals In.)	54·38 N	59·42 E
132	Polyarnyy (pŭl-yär'nē)..Sov. Un.	69·10 N	33·30 E
101	Pomba (pô'm-bȧ) (R.) Braz. (Rio de Janeiro In.)	21·28 S	42·28 W
120	Pomerania (Reg.) (pŏm-ê-rā'nĭ-ȧ) Pol.	53·50 N	15·20 E
118	Pomeranian B. (pō'mě-rä-ny-än) Ger.	54·10 N	14·20 E
80	Pomeroy..................Ohio	39·00 N	82·00 W
167	Pomeroy (pŏm'ēr-roi) S. Afr. (Natal In.)	28·36 S	30·26 E
66	Pomeroy (pŏm'ēr-oi).......Wash.	46·28 N	117·35 W
125	Pomezia (pô-mě't-zyä) It. (Rome In.)	41·41 N	12·31 E
125	Pomigliano d'Arco (pô-mē-lyȧ'nô-d-ä'r-kô) It. (Naples In.)	40·39 N	14·23 E
70	Pomme de Terre (pôm dē těr') Minn.	45·22 N	95·52 W
74	Pomona (pô-mō'nȧ) Calif. (Los Angeles In.)	34·04 N	117·45 W
127	Pomorie...................Bul.	42·24 N	27·41 E
142	Pomo Tsho (L.)...........China	23·38 N	89·58 E
79	Pompano Beach (pŏm'pă-nô) Fla. (In.)	26·12 N	80·07 W
125	Pompeii Ruins....It. (Naples In.)	40·31 N	14·29 E
84	Pompton Lakes (pŏmp'tŏn) N. J. (New York In.)	41·01 N	74·16 W
92	Pomuch (pô-mo͞o'ch) Mex. (Yucatan In.)	20·12 N	90·10 W
70	Ponca (pŏn'kȧ).............Nebr.	42·34 N	96·43 W
73	Ponca City................Okla.	36·42 N	97·07 W
85	Ponce (pōn'sā) P. R. (Puerto Rico In.)	18·01 N	66·43 W
143	Pondicherry (pôn-dĭ-shěr'ē') (pŏn-dĭ-shěr'ê).India	11·58 N	79·48 E
124	Ponferrada (pôn-fěr-rä'dhä)...Sp.	42·33 N	6·38 W
86	Ponoca (pō-nō'cȧ)..........Can.	52·43 N	113·32 W
132	Ponoy..................Sov. Un.	66·58 N	41·00 E
132	Ponoy (R.).............Sov. Un.	65·50 N	38·40 E
164	Ponta Delgada (pôn'tȧ děl-gä'dȧ) Açores (In.)	37·40 N	25·45 W
100	Ponta Grossa (grō'sȧ).......Braz.	25·09 S	50·05 W
123	Pont-à-Mousson (pôN'tȧ-mo͞osôN') Fr.	48·55 N	6·02 E
99	Ponta Porã................Braz.	22·30 S	55·31 W
123	Pontarlier (pôN'tȧr-lyā')......Fr.	46·53 N	6·22 E
122	Pont-Audemer (pôN'tōd'mâr').Fr.	49·23 N	0·28 E
123	Pontcarré (pôN-kȧ-rā') Fr. (Paris In.)	48·48 N	2·42 E
77	Pontchartrain L. (pôN-shȧr-trăn') La.	30·10 N	90·10 W
126	Pontedera (pōn-tȧ-dā'rä)......It.	43·37 N	10·37 E
124	Ponte de Sor (pōŋ'tě dȧ sōr') Port.	39·14 N	8·03 W
110	Pontefract (pŏn'tê-frăkt)....Eng.	53·41 N	1·18 W
101	Ponte Nova (pô'n-tě-nô'vȧ) Braz. (Rio de Janeiro In.)	20·26 S	42·52 W
124	Pontevedra (pôn-tě-vě-drä)...Sp.	42·28 N	8·38 W
166	Ponthierville (pôN-tyā-vēl') Con. K.	0·28 S	25·19 E
80	Pontiac (pŏn'tĭ-ăk)...........Ill.	40·55 N	88·35 W
75	Pontiac.......Mich. (Detroit In.)	42·37 N	83·17 W
154	Pontianak (pôn-tê-ä'nȧk)..Indon.	0·04 S	109·20 E
139	Pontian Kechil Mala (Singapore In.)	1·29 N	103·24 E
122	Pontivy (pôN-tê-vē')..........Fr.	48·05 N	2·57 W
122	Pont-l'Abbe (pôN-lȧ-bā')......Fr.	47·53 N	4·12 W
123	Pontoise (pôN-twȧz') Fr. (Paris In.)	49·03 N	2·05 E
136	Pontonnyy (pôn'tôn-nyĭ) Sov. Un. (Leningrad In.)	59·47 N	30·39 E
78	Pontotoc (pŏn-tô-tŏk')......Miss.	34·11 N	88·59 W
126	Pontremoli (pôn-trēm'ô-lē).....It.	44·21 N	9·50 E
126	Ponza, Isole di (I.) (ê'sō-lě-dē-pōn'tsä)..........It.	40·55 N	12·58 E
116	Poole (po͞ol)................Eng.	50·43 N	2·00 W
84	Poolesville (poolěs-vĭl) Md. (Baltimore In.)	39·08 N	77·26 W
142	Poona (po͞o'nŭ)............India	18·38 N	73·53 E
98	Poopó, Lago de (L.) (lä'gô-dě-pō-ô-pô').Bol.	18·16 S	67·57 W
98	Popayán (pō-pä-yän')......Col.	2·21 N	76·43 W
67	Poplar (pŏp'lēr)...........Mont.	48·08 N	105·10 W
73	Poplar Bluff (blŭf)..........Mo.	36·43 N	90·22 W
80	Poplar Plains (plāns).........Ky.	38·20 N	83·40 W
85	Poplar Point.Can. (Winnipeg In.)	50·04 N	97·58 W
67	Poplar R..................Mont.	48·34 N	105·20 W
67	Poplar R., West Fork......Mont.	48·59 N	106·06 W
78	Poplarville (pŏp'lēr-vĭl).....Miss.	30·50 N	89·33 W
91	Popocatépetl (Mtn.) (pô-pô-kä-tā'pět'l) Mex. (Mexico City In.)	19·01 N	98·38 W
166	Popokabaca (pō'pô-kȧ-bä'kȧ) Con. K.	5·38 S	16·47 E
129	Popovka (pô'pôf-kȧ).....Sov. Un.	50·03 N	33·41 E
129	Popovka...............Sov. Un.	51·13 N	33·08 E
127	Popovo (pô'pô-vō)..........Bul.	43·23 N	26·17 E
142	Porbandar (pōr-bŭn'dŭr)....India	21·44 N	69·40 E
98	Porce (pôr-sě) (R.).....Col. (In.)	7·11 N	74·55 W
124	Porcuna (pôr-ko͞o'nä).........Sp.	37·54 N	4·10 W
64	Porcupine (R.)...........Alaska	67·00 N	143·25 W
86	Porcupine (R.)..............Can.	67·38 N	140·07 W
67	Porcupine Cr. (pôr'kû-pīn).Mont.	46·38 N	107·04 W
67	Porcupine Cr..............Mont.	48·27 N	106·24 W
126	Pordenone (pōr-dȧ-nō'nȧ)......It.	45·58 N	12·38 E
126	Poreč (pô'rěch)............Yugo.	45·13 N	13·37 E
119	Pori (Björneborg) (pô'rê) (byûr'nē-bôrgh)....Fin.	61·29 N	21·45 E
101	Poriúncula (po-rēo͞o'n-ko͞o-lä) Braz. (Rio de Janeiro In.)	20·58 S	42·02 W
112	Porjus (pôr'yo͞os)...........Swe.	66·54 N	19·40 E
128	Porkhov (pôr'Kôf).......Sov. Un.	57·46 N	29·33 E
98	Porlamar (pôr-lä-mär')......Ven.	11·00 N	63·55 W
122	Pornic (pôr-nēk')............Fr.	47·08 N	2·07 W
135	Poronaysk (pô'rô-nīsk)..Sov. Un.	49·21 N	143·23 E
120	Porrentruy (pô-räN-trüē')..Switz.	47·25 N	7·02 E
118	Porsgrunn (pôrs'gro͝on').....Nor.	59·09 N	9·36 E
98	Portachuelo (pôrt-ä-chwā'lô).Bol.	17·20 S	63·12 W
81	Portage (pôr'tåj)............Pa.	40·25 N	78·35 W
71	Portage...................Wis.	43·33 N	89·29 W
74	Portage Des Sioux (dē so͞o) Mo. (St. Louis In.)	38·56 N	90·21 W
85	Portage-la-Prairie (lä-prā'rĭ) Can. (Winnipeg In.)	49·58 N	98·18 W
86	Port Alberni (pōr äl-běr-nē').Can.	49·20 N	124·51 W
124	Portalegre (pôr-tä-lā'grě)....Port.	39·18 N	7·26 W
72	Portales (pôr-tä'lěs)......N. Mex.	34·10 N	103·11 W
82	Port-Alfred (ăl'frěd).........Can.	48·19 N	70·55 W
167	Port Alfred (Kowie) (kou'ĭ) S. Afr. (Natal In.)	33·36 S	26·55 E
86	Port Alice.................Can.	50·29 N	127·29 W
81	Port Allegany (ăl-ê-gā'nĭ).....Pa.	41·50 N	78·10 W
166	Port Ambim...............Ang.	11·01 S	13·45 E
66	Port Angeles (ăn'jē-lěs)....Wash.	48·07 N	123·26 W
95	Port Antonio...............Jam.	18·10 N	76·25 W
161	Portarlington Austl. (Melbourne In.)	38·07 S	144·39 E
87	Port Arthur (är'thŭr).......Can.	48·28 N	89·12 W
77	Port Arthur................Tex.	29·52 N	93·59 W
	Port Arthur, see Lüshun		
160	Port Augusta (ô-gŭs'tă)....Austl.	32·28 S	137·50 E
83	Port au Port B. (pôr'tō pōr').Can.	48·41 N	58·45 W
95	Port-au-Prince (prăNs')......Hai.	18·35 N	72·20 W
80	Port Austin (ôs'tĭn)........Mich.	44·00 N	83·00 W
83	Port-aux-Basques, Channel..Can.	47·36 N	59·09 W
166	Port Beaufort (bō'fērt).....S. Afr.	34·14 S	20·59 E
154	Port Blair (blâr)....Andaman Is.	12·07 N	92·45 E
77	Port Bolivar (bŏl'ĭ-vȧr).Tex. (In.)	29·22 N	94·46 W

ăt; finăl; rāte; senâte; ärm; åsk; sofȧ; fâre; ch-choose; dh-as th in other; bē; êvent; bět; recěnt; cratēr; g-go; gh-guttural g; bĭt; ĭ-short neutral; rīde; K-guttural k as ch in German ich;

ng-sing; ŋ-baŋk; N-nasalized n; nŏd; cŏmmit; ōld; ôbey; ôrder; fōōd; fŏŏt; ou-out; s-soft; sh-dish; th-thin; pūre; ûnite; ûrn; stŭd; circǔs; ū-as "y" in study; '-indeterminate vowel.

ăt; fĭnål; rāte; senåte; ärm; àsk; sofà; fåre; ch-choose; dh-as th in other; bē; ĕvent; bĕt; recĕnt; cratẽr; g-go; gh-guttural g; bĭt; ł-short neutral; rīde; κ-guttural k as ch in German ich;

PRONOUNCING INDEX Qezel Owzan–Raul Soares 255

Page	Name Pronunciation Region	Lat. °′	Long. °′
133	Qezel Owzan (R.)..........Iran	37·00 N	47·35 E
139	Qiblīya, el (cliff) U. A. R. (Palestine In.)	28·47 N	32·22 E
168	Qift (kêft).....U. A. R. (Nile In.)	25·58 N	32·52 E
168	Qinā (kä'nȧ)...U. A. R. (Nile In.)	26·10 N	32·48 E
139	Qiraiya (R.) U. A. R. (Palestine In.)	30·14 N	34·21 E
144	Qom.....................Iran	34·28 N	50·53 E
	Qomul see Hami		
81	Quabbin Res. (kwā'bĭn)....Mass.	42·20 N	72·10 W
73	Quachita, L. (kwä shĭ'tô)....Ark.	34·47 N	93·37 W
81	Quakertown (kwā'kẽr-toun)...Pa.	40·30 N	75·20 W
72	Quanah (kwä'nȧ)..........Tex.	34·19 N	99·43 W
151	Quang Ngai (kwăng n'gä'ê)..Viet.	15·05 N	108·58 E
151	Quang Ngai (Mtn.).........Viet.	15·10 N	108·20 E
154	Quang Tri (kwăng'trē')......Viet.	16·39 N	107·05 E
86	Qu'Appelle (R.) (kȧ-pĕl')....Can.	50·55 N	104·12 W
126	Quartu Sant' Elena (kwär-tōō' sänt a'lâ-nä) .It.	39·16 N	9·12 E
85	Quebec (kwê-bĕk') (kȧ-bĕk') Can. (Quebec In.)	46·49 N	71·14 W
87	Quebec (Prov.)............Can.	51·07 N	70·25 W
120	Quedlinburg (kvĕd'lēn-bōōrgh) Ger.	51·49 N	11·10 E
86	Queen Charlotte Is. (kwēn shär'lŏt) .Can.	53·40 N	132·50 W
86	Queen Charlotte Str. (strāt) .Can.	51·19 N	128·42 W
49	Queen Elizabeth Is. (ê-lĭz'ȧ-bĕth) Can.	78·20 N	110·00 W
86	Queen Maud G. (mâd)......Can.	68·27 N	102·55 W
47	Queen Maud Land.........Ant.	75·00 S	10·00 E
47	Queen Maud Mts..........Ant.	85·00 S	179·00 W
158	Queens Chan. (kwēnz)......Austl.	14·25 S	129·10 E
161	Queenscliff.Austl. (Melbourne In.)	38·16 S	144·39 E
159	Queensland (State) (kwēnz'lȧnd) Austl.	22·45 S	141·01 E
160	Queenstown (kwēnz'toun)..Austl.	42·00 S	145·40 E
167	Queenstown....S. Afr. (Natal In.)	31·54 S	26·53 E
124	Queija, Sierra de (Mts.) (sē-ĕ'r-rä-dĕ-kĕ'y-kä) .Sp.	42·08 N	7·23 W
100	Queimados (kā-mä'dôs).Braz. (In.)	22·42 S	43·34 W
166	Quelimane (kā lê-mä'nĕ)....Moz.	17·48 S	37·05 E
	Quelpart, see Cheju		
94	Quemado de Güines (kā-mä'dhä-dĕ-gwē'nĕs)...Cuba	22·45 N	80·20 W
151	Quemoy (Chinmen)......Taiwan	24·30 N	118·20 E
93	Quepos (kā'pôs)..........C. R.	9·26 N	84·10 W
93	Quepos, Punta (pt.) (pōō'n-tä).C. R.	9·23 N	84·20 W
166	Que Que (kwĕ'kwĕ)..........Rh.	18·49 S	29·45 E
90	Querétaro (kȧ-rā'tȧ-rō)......Mex.	20·37 N	100·25 W
124	Quesada (kȧ-sä'dhä).........Sp.	37·51 N	3·04 W
86	Quesnel (kā-nĕl')..........Can.	53·00 N	122·28 W
86	Quesnel (L.)..............Can.	52·28 N	121·40 W
98	Quetame (kĕ-tä'mĕ)....Col. (In.)	4·20 N	73·50 W
87	Quetico Provincial Park (kwĕ'tĭ-kô).Can.	48·29 N	91·50 W
142	Quetta (kwĕt'ȧ).........W. Pak.	30·19 N	67·01 E
92	Quezaltenango (kȧ-zäl'tȧ-näŋ'gō) Guat.	14·50 N	91·30 W
92	Quezaltepeque (kȧ-zäl'tȧ-pā'kȧ) Guat.	14·39 N	89·26 W
92	Quezaltepeque (kĕ-zäl'tĕ'pĕ-kĕ) Sal.	13·50 N	89·17 W
155	Quezon City (kā-zōn) Phil. (Manila In.)	14·40 N	121·02 E
98	Quibdo (kēb'dō)........Col. (In.)	5·42 N	76·41 W
122	Quiberon (kê-bē-rôN')........Fr.	47·29 N	3·08 W
92	Quiché (kē-shā')..........Guat.	15·05 N	91·08 W
111	Quicksborn (kvēks'bōrn) Ger. (Hamburg In.)	53·44 N	9·54 E
65	Quilcene (kwĭl-sēn') Wash. (Seattle In.)	47·50 N	122·53 W
101	Quilimari (kē-lē-mä'rē) Chile (Santiago In.)	32·06 S	71·28 W
86	Quill (L.) (kwĭl)..........Can.	52·10 N	103·34 W
122	Quillan (kê-yäN')............Fr.	43·53 N	2·13 E
101	Quillota (kêl-yō'tä) Chile (Santiago In.)	32·52 S	71·14 W
100	Quilmes (kēl'mās)......Arg. (In.)	34·28 S	58·16 W
143	Quilon (kwê-lōn')..........India	8·58 N	76·16 E
160	Quilpie (kwĭl'pê)..........Austl.	26·34 S	149·20 E
101	Quilpué (kēl-pōō ĕ') Chile (Santiago In.)	33·03 S	71·22 W
98	Quimbaya (kēm-bä'yä).Col. (In.)	4·38 N	75·46 W
122	Quimper (kăN-pĕr')..........Fr.	47·59 N	4·04 W
155	Quinabucasan Pt. (kē-nä-bōō-kä'sän) Phil. (Manila In.)	14·09 N	123·33 E
66	Quinalt R...............Wash.	47·23 N	124·10 W
66	Quinault Ind. Res.........Wash.	47·27 N	124·34 W
78	Quincy (kwĭn'sê)...........Fla.	30·35 N	84·35 W
73	Quincy....................Ill.	39·55 N	91·23 W
83	Quincy.......Mass. (Boston In.)	42·15 N	71·00 W
•80	Quincy...................Mich.	42·00 N	84·50 W
65	Quincy.......Ore. (Portland In.)	46·08 N	123·10 W
154	Qui Nhon (kwĭnyôn)........Viet.	13·51 N	109·03 E
66	Quinn R. (kwĭn)...........Nev.	41·42 N	117·45 W
124	Quintana de la Serena (kēn-tä'nä dā lä sȧ-rā'nä).Sp.	38·45 N	5·39 W
124	Quintanar (kēn-ta-nar').......Sp.	39·36 N	3·02 W
88	Quintana Roo (Ter.) (rô'ô)..Mex.	19·30 N	88·35 W
101	Quintero (kēn-tĕ'rô) Chile (Santiago In.)	32·48 S	71·30 W
90	Quiroga (kē-rô'gä)..........Mex.	19·39 N	101·30 W
124	Quiroga (kē-rô'gä)..........Sp.	42·28 N	7·18 W
78	Quitman (kwĭt'măn).........Ga.	30·46 N	83·35 W
78	Quitman...................Miss.	33·02 N	88·43 W
98	Quito (kē'tō)...............Ec.	0·17 S	78·32 W
99	Quixadá (kê-shä-dä').......Braz.	4·58 S	38·58 W
168	Qulūṣanā (kōō-lōōs'nä) U. A. R. (Nile In.)	28·22 N	30·44 E
167	Qumbu (kŏŏm'bōō) S. Afr. (Natal In.)	29·12 S	28·53 E
139	Qumran....Jordan (Palestine In.)	31·45 N	35·28 E
84	Quonset Point (kwŏn'sĕt) R. I. (Providence In.)	41·36 N	71·25 W
160	Quorn (kwôrn).............Austl.	32·20 S	138·00 E
168	Qūs (kōōs)....U. A. R. (Nile In.)	25·53 N	32·48 E
167	Quthing........Leso. (Natal In.)	30·35 S	27·42 E
159	Quvea (I.)..............N. Cal.	20·43 S	166·48 E
144	Quzvīn...................Iran	36·10 N	49·59 E
120	Raab R. (räp)............Aus.	46·55 N	15·55 E
112	Raahe (rä'ĕ)..............Fin.	64·39 N	24·22 E
126	Rab (I.) (räb)............Yugo.	44·45 N	14·40 E
154	Raba....................Indon.	8·32 S	118·49 E
121	Raba R.................Hung.	47·28 N	17·12 E
164	Rabat (rȧ-bät')...........Mor.	33·59 N	6·47 W
155	Rabaul (rä'boul).....N. Gui. Ter.	4·15 S	152·19 E
127	Rača (rä'chȧ)............Yugo.	44·13 N	21·01 E
71	Raccoon (R.) (ră-kōōn')......Iowa	42·07 N	94·45 W
95	Raccoon Cay (I.).........Ba. Is.	22·25 N	75·50 W
83	Race, C. (rās)............Can.	46·37 N	52·55 W
139	Rachado, C.Mala. (Singapore In.)	2·26 N	101·29 E
121	Racibórz (rä-chē'bōōzh)......Pol.	50·06 N	18·14 E
75	Racine (rȧ-sēn') Wis. (Milwaukee In.)	42·43 N	87·49 W
74	Raco (rȧ cō) Mich. (Sault Ste. Marie In.)	46·22 N	84·43 W
121	Rădăuti (rû-dû-ōōts'')......Rom.	47·53 N	25·55 E
110	Radcliffe (răd'klĭf).........Eng.	53·34 N	2·20 W
123	Radevormwald (rä'dĕ-fōrm-väld) Ger. (Ruhr In.)	51·12 N	7·22 E
79	Radford (răd'fẽrd)..........Va.	37·06 N	81·33 W
142	Rādhanpur...............India	23·57 N	71·38 E
74	Radio Center (ra'dĭ-ō cĕn'tẽr) Minn. (Minneapolis, St. Paul In.)	44·50 N	93·06 W
168	Radium (rā'dĭ-ŭm)........S. Afr. (Johannesburg & Pretoria In.)	25·06 S	28·18 E
116	Radnor Forest (răd'nôr)....Wales	52·11 N	3·25 W
121	Radom (rä'dôm)............Pol.	51·24 N	21·11 E
127	Radomir (rä'dô-mêr)........Bul.	42·33 N	22·58 E
121	Radomsko (rä-dôm'skô)......Pol.	51·04 N	19·27 E
129	Radomyshl (rä-dô-mēsh''l) Sov. Un.	50·30 N	29·13 E
127	Radoviš (rä'dô-vêsh).......Yugo.	41·39 N	22·28 E
118	Radöy (I.) (räd-ûê).........Nor.	60·43 N	4·40 E
129	Radul' (rä'dōōl).........Sov. Un.	51·52 N	30·46 E
119	Radviliškis (räd'vê-lēsh'kēs) Sov. Un.	55·49 N	23·31 E
144	Radwah, Jabal (Mtn.)...Sau. Ar.	24·44 N	38·14 E
121	Radzyń Podlaski (räd'zēn-y' pŭd-lä'skĭ).Pol.	51·49 N	22·40 E
79	Raeford (rā'fẽrd)..........N. C.	34·57 N	79·15 W
123	Raesfeld (răz'fĕld) Ger. (Ruhr In.)	51·46 N	6·50 E
158	Raeside (rā'sīd)...........Austl.	29·20 S	122·30 E
86	Rae Str. (rā)...............Can.	68·40 N	95·03 W
100	Rafaela (rä-fä-ĕ'lȧ).........Arg.	31·15 S	61·21 W
115	Rafah (rä'fä)...........U. A. R.	31·14 N	34·12 E
165	Rafai (rä-fī')......Cen. Afr. Rep.	4·59 N	23·58 E
144	Rafhā..................Sau. Ar.	29·43 N	43·13 E
67	Raft R. (răft).............Idaho	42·20 N	113·17 W
142	Raga....................China	29·31 N	85·52 E
155	Ragay (rä-gī').Phil. (Manila In.)	13·49 N	122·45 E
155	Ragay G.......Phil. (Manila In.)	13·44 N	122·38 E
133	Ragga.................U. A. R.	36·00 N	39·00 E
118	Ragunda (rä-gōōn'dä).......Swe.	63·07 N	16·24 E
113	Ragusa (rä-gōō'sä)............It.	36·58 N	14·41 E
	Ragusa, see Dubrovnik		
84	Rahway (rô'wā) N. J. (New York In.)	40·37 N	74·16 W
143	Raichur (rä'ê-chōōr')......India	16·23 N	77·18 E
142	Raigarh (rī'gŭr)...........India	21·57 N	83·32 E
69	Rainbow Bridge Natl. Mon. (rān'bō).Utah	37·05 N	111·00 W
88	Rainbow City............C. Z. (Panama Canal In.)	9.20·N	79·23 W
65	Rainier......Ore. (Portland In.)	46·05 N	122·56 W
66	Rainier, Mt. (rā-nēr')......Wash.	46·52 N	121·46 W
71	Rainy (L.) (rān'ê)....Can.-Minn.	48·50 N	93·06 W
71	Rainy (R.)..........Can.-Minn.	48·36 N	94·14 W
87	Rainy River.............Can.	48·42 N	94·29 W
142	Raipur (rä'jŭ-bōō-rê')......India	21·25 N	81·37 E
80	Raisin (R.) (rā'zĭn)........Mich.	42·00 N	83·35 W
84	Raitan (rā-tăn) N. J. (New York In.)	40·34 N	74·40 W
154	Raja, Bukit (Mtn.)........Indon.	0·45 S	112·11 E
143	Rajahmundry (räj-ŭ-mŭn'drê) India	17·03 N	81·51 E
154	Rajang, Balang (strm.).....Mala.	2·10 N	113·30 E
142	Rājasthān (State) (rä'jŭs-tän) India	31·20 N	72·00 E
142	Rājkot (räj'kôt)...........India	22·20 N	70·48 E
142	Rakers Tal (L.)...........China	30·42 N	80·40 E
121	Rakhov (rä'kôf)........Sov. Un.	48·02 N	24·13 E
136	Rakh'ya (räk'yȧ) Sov. Un. (Leningrad In.)	60·06 N	30·50 E
129	Rakitnoye (rä-kēt'nō-yĕ).Sov. Un.	50·51 N	35·53 E
120	Rakovník (rä'kôv-nyēk)...Czech.	50·07 N	13·45 E
128	Rakvere (räk'vĕ-rĕ).....Sov. Un.	59·22 N	26·14 E
79	Raleigh (rô'lȧ)............N. C.	35·45 N	78·39 W
79	Raleigh, B.................N. C.	34·50 N	76·15 W
93	Rama (rä'mä)...............Nic.	12·11 N	84·14 W
101	Ramallo (rä-mä'l-yô) Arg. (Buenos Aires In.)	33·28 S	60·02 W
123	Rambouillet (räN-bōō-yĕ') Fr. (Paris In.)	48·39 N	1·49 E
167	Rame Hd......S. Afr. (Natal In.)	31·48 S	29·22 E
136	Ramenskoye (rá'mĕn-skô-yĕ) Sov. Un. (Moscow In.)	55·34 N	38·15 E
144	Ramlat As Sab Atayn (Reg.) Sau. Ar.	16·02 N	45·30 E
139	Ramm, Jabal (Mts.) Jordan (Palestine In.)	29·37 N	35·32 E
143	Rāmnād.................India	9·13 N	78·52 E
90	Ramos (rä'mōs)............Mex.	22·46 N	101·52 W
76	Ramos Arizpe (ä-rēz'pȧ)....Mex.	25·33 N	100·57 W
64	Rampart (răm'pärt).......Alaska	65·28 N	150·18 W
84	Rampo Mts. (răm'pō) N. J.-N. Y. (New York In.)	41·06 N	72·12 W
142	Rāmpur (räm'pōōr)........India	28·53 N	79·03 E
142	Rāmpur-Boālia (bô-ä'lê-ä) E. Pak.	24·26 N	88·39 E
154	Ramree (I.) (räm'rē')........Bur.	19·01 N	93·23 E
85	Ramsayville (răm'zê vĭl) Can. (Ottawa In.)	45·23 N	75·34 W
110	Ramsbottom (rămz'bŏt-ŭm) Eng.	53·39 N	2·20 W
116	Ramsey (răm'zê).....Isle of Man	54·20 N	4·25 W
84	Ramsey....N. J. (New York In.)	41·03 N	74·09 W
117	Ramsgate (rămz''gāt).......Eng.	51·19 N	1·20 E
118	Ramsjö (räm'shû)..........Swe.	62·11 N	15·44 E
155	Ramu (R.) (rä'mōō)..N. Gui. Ter.	5·35 S	145·16 E
154	Ranau, L. (rä-nä'ōō)......Indon.	4·52 S	103·52 E
101	Rancagua (rän-kä'gwä) Chile (Santiago In.)	34·10 S	70·43 W
122	Rance (räNs)...............Fr.	48·17 N	2·30 W
142	Rānchi (rän'chē)..........India	23·24 N	85·18 E
95	Rancho Boyeros (rä'n-chô-bô-yĕ'rôs) Cuba (Havana In.)	23·00 N	82·23 W
84	Randallstown (răn'dȧlz-toun) Md. (Baltimore In.)	39·22 N	76·48 W
118	Randers (rän'ĕrs)..........Den.	56·28 N	10·03 E
167	Randfontein (rănt'fŏn-tān).S. Afr. (Johannesburg & Pretoria In.)	26·10 S	27·42 E
79	Randleman (răn'd'l-măn)...N. C.	35·49 N	79·50 W
83	Randolph (răn'dôlf) Mass. (Boston In.)	42 10 N	71·03 W
70	Randolph.................Nebr.	42·22 N	97·22 W
81	Randolph..................Vt.	43·55 N	72·40 W
83	Random I. (răn'dŭm).......Can.	48·12 N	53·25 W
118	Rands Fd. (räns' fyôr)......Nor.	60·35 N	10·10 E
82	Rangeley (rānj'lê).........Maine	44·56 N	70·38 W
81	Rangeley (L.)............Maine	44·55 N	70·40 W
76	Ranger (rān'jẽr)...........Tex.	32·26 N	98·41 W
142	Rangia...................India	26·32 N	91·39 E
154	Rangoon (răŋ-gōōn')........Bur.	16·46 N	96·09 E
142	Rangpur (rŭng'pōōr).....E. Pak.	25·48 N	89·19 E
139	Rangsang, Palau (I.) (räng'säng') Indon. (Singapore In.)	1·03 N	102·54 E
111	Rangsdorf (rängs'dōrf) Ger. (Berlin In.)	52·17 N	13·25 E
142	Raniganj (rä-nē-gŭnj')......India	23·40 N	87·08 E
86	Rankin Inlet (răŋ'kĕn)......Can.	62·45 N	94·27 W
128	Ranova (R.) (rä'nô-vȧ)..Sov. Un.	53·55 N	40·03 E
75	Ransomville (răn'sum-vĭl) N. Y. (Buffalo In.)	43·15 N	78·54 W
139	Rantau.....Mala. (Singapore In.)	2·35 N	101·58 E
154	Rantemario, Bulu (Mtn.)..Indon.	3·22 S	119·50 E
80	Rantoul (răn-tōōl').........Ill.	40·25 N	88·05 W
126	Rapallo (rä-päl'lô)..........It.	44·21 N	9·14 E
157	Rapa Nui (Easter) (I.) (rä'pä nōō'ê) (ēs'tẽr).Chile	26·50 S	109·00 W
101	Rapel (rä-päl') (R.) Chile (Santiago In.)	34·05 S	71·30 W
71	Rapid (R.) (răp'ĭd)........Minn.	48·21 N	94·50 W
70	Rapid City..................S. D.	44·06 N	103·14 W
119	Rapla (räp'lȧ)..........Sov. Un.	59·02 N	24·46 E
81	Rappahannock (R.) (răp'ȧ-hăn'ŭk).Va.	38·20 N	75·25 W
81	Raquette (L.) (răk'ĕt)......N. Y.	43·50 N	74·35 W
81	Raquette (R.)..............N. Y.	44·20 N	74·50 W
121	Rara Mazowiecka (rä'rä mä-zō-vyĕts'kä).Pol.	51·46 N	20·17 E
84	Raritan R. (răr'ĭ-tăn) N. J. (New York In.)	40·32 N	74·27 W
157	Rarotonga (rä'rō-tŏŋ'gȧ).Cook Is.	20·40 S	163·00 W
144	Ras Al Hadd (C.)....Mus. & Om.	22·29 N	59·46 E
139	Ra's an Naqb Jordan (Palestine In.)	30·00 N	35·29 E
163	Ras Dashan (Mtn.) (räs dä-shän') Eth.	12·49 N	38·14 E
119	Raseiniai (rä-syā'nyī)...Sov. Un.	55·23 N	23·04 E
144	Ra's Fartak (C.)..........S. Ar.	15·43 N	52·17 E
139	Rashayya....Leb. (Palestine In.)	33·30 N	35·50 E
168	Rashīd (Rosetta) (rȧ-shēd') (rô-zĕt'ȧ) U. A. R. (Nile In.)	31·22 N	30·25 E
168	Rashīd, Masabb (R. Mth.) U. A. R. (Nile In.)	31·30 N	29·58 E
136	Rashkina (rȧsh'kĭ-nȧ) Sov. Un. (Urals In.)	59·57 N	61·30 E
129	Rashkov (räsh'kôf)......Sov. Un.	47·55 N	28·51 E
144	Rasht....................Iran	37·13 N	49·45 E
127	Raška (räsh'kȧ)...........Yugo.	43·16 N	20·40 E
142	Ras Kuh Mt...........W. Pak.	34·03 N	65·10 E
144	Ras Madrakah (C.)..Mus. & Om.	18·53 N	57·48 E
133	Rasskazovo (räs-kä'sô-vô) Sov. Un.	52·40 N	41·40 E
144	Ra's Tannūrah..........Sau. Ar.	26·45 N	49·59 E
120	Rastatt (rä-shtät)..........Ger.	48·51 N	8·12 E
136	Rastes (rȧs'tĕs) Sov. Un. (Urals In.)	59·24 N	58·49 E
136	Rastunovo (rȧs-tōō'nô-vô) Sov. Un. (Moscow In.)	55·15 N	37·50 E
124	Ras Uarc (C.)............Mor.	35·28 N	2·58 W
142	Ratangarh (rŭ-tŭn'gŭr).....India	28·10 N	74·30 E
154	Rat Buri..................Thai.	13·30 N	99·46 E
77	Ratcliff (răt'klĭf)...........Tex.	31·22 N	95·09 W
120	Rathenow (rä'tĕ-nō).........Ger.	52·36 N	12·20 E
116	Rathlin (I.) (răth-lĭn).......Ire.	54·80 N	6·10 W
123	Ratingen (rä'tēn-gĕn) Ger. (Ruhr In.)	51·18 N	6·51 E
64	Rat Is. (răt)...............Alaska	51·35 N	176·48 E
142	Ratlam...................India	23·19 N	75·05 E
143	Ratnāgir.................India	17·04 N	73·24 E
72	Raton (rȧ-tōn')...........N. Mex.	36·52 N	104·26 W
66	Rattlesnake Cr. (răt''l snăk).Ore.	42·38 N	117·39 W
118	Rättvik (rĕt'vēk)...........Swe.	60·54 N	15·07 E
120	Ratzeburger See (L.) (rä'tzĕ-bōōr-gĕr-zā).Ger.	53·48 N	11·02 E
101	Rauch (rá'ōōch) Arg. (Buenos Aires In.)	36·47 S	59·05 W
118	Raufoss (rou'fôs)..........Nor.	60·44 N	10·30 E
101	Raúl Soares (rä-ōō'l-sōä'rĕs) Braz. (Rio de Janeiro In.)	20·05 S	42·28 W

ng-sing; ŋ-baŋk; N-nasalized n; nŏd; cŏmmit; ōld; ôbey; ôrder; fōōd; fŏŏt; ou-out; s-soft; sh-dish; th-thin; pūre; ūnite; ûrn; stŭd; circŭs; ü-as "y" in study; '-indeterminate vowel.

Page	Name Pronunciation	Region	Lat. °'	Long. °'
119	Rauma (rä´ōō-mä)	Fin.	61·07 N	21·31 E
119	Rauna (râŭ´-nä)	Sov. Un.	57·21 N	25·31 E
154	Raung, Gunung (Mtn.)	Indon.	8·15 s	113·56 E
119	Rautalampi (rä´ōō-tē-läm´pō)	Fin.	62·39 N	26·25 E
121	Rava-Russkaya (rä´vä rōōs´kä-yà)	Sov. Un.	50·14 N	23·40 E
126	Ravenna (rä-věn´nä)	It.	44·27 N	12·13 E
70	Ravenna (rà-věn´à)	Nebr.	41·20 N	98·50 w
80	Ravenna	Ohio	41·10 N	81·20 w
120	Ravensburg (rä´věns-bōōrgh)	Ger.	47·48 N	9·35 E
65	Ravensdale	Wash. (Seattle In.)	47·22 N	121·58 w
158	Ravensthorpe (rä´věns-thôrp)	Austl.	33·30 s	120·20 E
80	Ravenswood	W. Va.	38·55 N	81·50 w
142	Rawalpindi (rä-wŭl-pěn´dě)	W. Pak.	33·42 N	73·04 E
144	Rawāndūz	Iraq	36·37 N	44·30 E
120	Rawicz (rä´věch)	Pol.	51·36 N	16·51 E
158	Rawlinna (rôr-lēnä)	Austl.	31·13 s	125·45 E
67	Rawlins (rô´lĭnz)	Wyo.	41·46 N	107·15 w
100	Rawson (rô´sŭn)	Arg.	43·16 s	65·09 w
101	Rawson	Arg. (Buenos Aires In.)	34·36 s	60·03 w
110	Rawtenstall (rô´těn-stôl)	Eng.	53·42 N	2·17 w
83	Ray, C. (rā)	Can.	47·38 N	59·25 w
135	Raychikinsk (rī´chĭ-kēnsk)	Sov. Un.	49·52 N	129·17 E
110	Rayleigh (rā´lě)	Eng. (London In.)	51·35 N	0·36 E
86	Raymond (rā´mŭnd)	Can.	49·32 N	112·38 w
66	Raymond	Wash.	46·41 N	123·42 w
77	Raymondville (rā´mŭnd-vĭl)	Tex.	26·30 N	97·46 w
64	Ray Mts.	Alaska	65·40 N	151·45 w
77	Rayne (rān)	La.	30·12 N	92·15 w
90	Rayón (rä´yōn´)	Mex.	21·49 N	99·39 w
167	Rayton (rā´tŭn)	S. Afr. (Johannesburg & Pretoria In.)	25·45 s	28·33 E
74	Raytown (rā´toun)	Mo. (Kansas City In.)	39·01 N	94·48 w
77	Rayville (rā´vĭl)	La.	32·28 N	91·46 w
122	Raz, Pte. du (Pt.) (pwänt dü rä)	Fr.	48·02 N	4·43 w
129	Razdel'naya (räz-děl´na-yä)	Sov. Un.	46·47 N	30·08 E
152	Razdol'noye (räz-dôl´nô-yě)	Sov. Un.	43·38 N	131·58 E
127	Razgrad	Bulg.	43·32 N	26·32 E
127	Razlog (räz´lôk)	Bul.	41·54 N	23·32 E
122	Ré, Île de (I.) (ēl dē rā´)	Fr.	46·10 N	1·53 w
110	Rea (R.) (rē)	Eng.	52·25 N	2·31 w
85	Reaburn (rā´bŭrn)	Can. (Winnipeg In.)	50·06 N	97·53 w
110	Reading (rěd´ĭng)	Eng. (London In.)	51·25 N	0·58 w
83	Reading	Mass. (Boston In.)	42·32 N	71·07 w
80	Reading	Mich.	41·45 N	84·45 w
75	Reading	Ohio (Cincinnati In.)	39·14 N	84·26 w
81	Reading	Pa.	40·20 N	75·55 w
100	Realango (rě-ä-län-gō)	Braz. (In.)	22·25 s	43·25 w
165	Rebiana (Oasis)	Libya	24·10 N	22·03 E
152	Rebun (I.) (rě´bōōn)	Jap.	45·25 N	140·54 E
126	Recanati (rā-kä-nä´tě)	It.	43·25 N	13·35 E
158	Recherche, Arch. of the (rě-shärsh´)	Austl.	34·17 s	122·30 E
128	Rechitsa (ryě´chět-sà)	Sov. Un.	52·22 N	30·24 E
99	Recife (Pernambuco) (rā-sē´fě) (pěr-näm-bōō´kô)	Braz.	8·09 s	34·59 w
167	Recife, C. (rā-sē´fě)	S. Afr. (Natal In.)	34·03 s	25·43 E
100	Reconquista (rā-kŏn-kēs´tä)	Arg.	29·01 s	59·41 w
73	Rector (rěk´těr)	Ark.	36·16 N	90·21 w
78	Red (R.)	Tenn.	36·30 N	87·10 w
72	Red (R.), North Fk.	Tex.	35·20 N	100·08 w
63	Red. (R.)	U. S.	31·40 N	92·55 w
62	Red (R.)	U. S.-Can.	48·10 N	97·00 w
84	Redan (rě-dǎn´) (rěd´ăn)	Ga. (Atlanta In.)	33·44 N	84·09 w
84	Red Bank (băngk)	N. J. (New York In.)	40·21 N	74·06 w
68	Red Bluff (blŭf)	Calif.	40·10 N	122·14 w
76	Red Bluff Res.	Tex.	32·03 N	103·52 w
71	Redby (rěd´bě)	Minn.	47·52 N	94·55 w
71	Red Cedar (R.) (sē´děr)	Wis.	45·03 N	91·48 w
86	Redcliff (rěd´clĭf)	Can.	50·10 N	111·09 w
71	Red Cliff Ind. Res.	Wis.	46·48 N	91·22 w
160	Redcliffe (rěd´clĭf)	Austl.	27·20 s	153·12 E
72	Red Cloud (kloud)	Nebr.	40·06 N	98·32 w
86	Red Deer (dēr)	Can.	52·12 N	113·52 w
86	Red Deer (R.)	Can.	50·55 N	111·32 w
75	Reddick (rěd´dĭk)	Ill. (Chicago In.)	41·06 N	88·16 w
84	Redding (rěd´ĭng)	Ala. (Birmingham In.)	33·27 N	86·54 w
66	Redding	Calif.	40·36 N	122·25 w
101	Redenção da Serra (rě-děn-soun-dä-sě´r-rä)	Braz. (Rio de Janeiro In.)	23·17 s	45·31 w
70	Redfield (rěd´fēld)	S. D.	44·53 N	98·30 w
77	Red Fish Bar	Tex. (In.)	29·29 N	94·53 w
83	Red Indian L. (ĭn´dĭ-ǎn)	Can.	48·42 N	56·40 w
123	Redklinghausen (rěk´lĭng-hou-zěn)	Ger. (Ruhr In.)	51·36 N	7·13 E
87	Red Lake (lāk)	Can.	51·01 N	93·55 w
70	Red Lake (R.)	Minn.	48·02 N	96·04 w
70	Red Lake Falls (lāk fôls)	Minn.	47·52 N	96·17 w
70	Red Lake Ind. Res.	Minn.	48·09 N	95·55 w
74	Redlands (rěd´lǎndz)	Calif. (Los Angeles In.)	34·04 N	117·11 w
81	Red Lion (lī´ŭn)	Pa.	39·55 N	76·30 w
67	Red Lodge	Mont.	45·13 N	107·16 w
65	Redmond (rěd´mŭnd)	Wash. (Seattle In.)	47·40 N	122·07 w
120	Rednitz R. (rěd´nětz)	Ger.	49·10 N	11·00 E
70	Red Oak (ōk)	Iowa	41·00 N	95·12 w
122	Redon (rē-dôn´)	Fr.	47·42 N	2·03 w
100	Redonda, Isla (ē´s-lä-rě-dô´n-dä)	Braz. (In.)	23·05 s	43·11 w
93	Redonda I.	N. A. (Le. & Wind. Is. In.)	16·55 N	62·28 w
124	Redondela (rä-dhōn-dā´lä)	Sp.	42·16 N	8·34 w
124	Redondo (rä-dôn´dōŏ)	Port.	38·40 N	7·32 w
65	Redondo (rē-dôn´dō)	Wash. (Seattle In.)	47·21 N	122·19 w
74	Redondo Beach	Calif. (Los Angeles In.)	33·50 N	118·23 w
72	Red R., Prairie Dog Town Fk. (prā´rĭ)	Tex.	34·54 N	101·31 w
72	Red R., Salt Fk.	Tex.	35·04 N	100·31 w
146	Red R.	Viet.	22·25 N	103·50 E
67	Red Rock Cr.	Mont.	44·54 N	112·44 w
165	Red Sea	Afr.-Asia	23·15 N	37·00 E
67	Redwater Cr. (rěd-wô´těr)	Mont.	47·37 N	105·25 w
72	Red Willow Cr.	Nebr.	40·34 N	100·48 w
71	Red Wing	Minn.	44·34 N	92·35 w
65	Redwood City (rěd´ wōŏd)	Calif. (San Francisco In.)	37·29 N	122·13 w
71	Redwood Falls	Minn.	44·32 N	95·06 w
116	Ree, Lough (B.) (lŏk´rē´)	Ire.	53·30 N	7·45 w
80	Reed City (rēd)	Mich.	43·50 N	85·35 w
68	Reedley (rēd´lě)	Calif.	36·37 N	119·27 w
71	Reedsburg (rēdz´bûrg)	Wis.	43·32 N	90·01 w
66	Reedsport (rēdz´pôrt)	Ore.	43·42 N	124·08 w
78	Reelfoot (R.) (rēl´fŏŏt)	Tenn.	36·18 N	89·20 w
123	Rees (rēz)	Ger. (Ruhr In.)	51·46 N	6·25 E
74	Reese (rēs)	Utah (Salt Lake City In.)	41·15 N	112·09 w
160	Reeves, Mt. (rēv´s)	Austl.	33·50 s	149·56 E
78	Reform (rē-fôrm´)	Ala.	33·23 N	88·00 w
77	Refugio (rä-fōō´hyô) (rě-fü´jō)	Tex.	28·18 N	97·15 w
120	Rega (R.) (rě-gä)	Pol.	53·48 N	15·30 E
120	Regen R. (rä´ghěn)	Ger.	49·09 N	12·21 E
120	Regensburg(rä´ghěns-bōōrgh)	Ger.	49·02 N	12·06 E
126	Reggio (rě´jō)	It.	44·43 N	10·34 E
84	Reggio (rěg´jǐ-ō)	La. (New Orleans In.)	29·50 N	89·46 w
126	Reggio di Calabria (rě´jō dē kä-lä´brē-ä)	It.	38·07 N	15·42 E
121	Reghin (rå-gēn´)	Rom.	46·47 N	24·44 E
86	Regina (rē-jī´nä)	Can.	50·31 N	104·30 w
144	Registan (Reg.)	Afg.	30·53 N	64·42 E
95	Regla (rāg´lä)	Cuba (Havana In.)	23·08 N	82·20 w
120	Regnitz L. (rěg´nětz)	Ger.	49·50 N	10·55 E
124	Reguengos de Monsaraz (rå-gěn´gōzh dä mōn-sä-rázh´)	Port.	38·26 N	7·30 w
84	Rehoboth (rē-hō´bŏth)	Mass. (Providence In.)	41·50 N	71·13 w
166	Rehoboth	S. W. Afr.	23·10 s	17·15 E
139	Rehovoth	Isr. (Palestine In.)	31·53 N	34·49 E
120	Reichenbach (rī´kěn-bäк)	Ger.	50·36 N	12·18 E
79	Reidsville (rēdz´vǐl)	N. C.	36·20 N	79·37 w
110	Reigate (rī´gāt).Eng. (London In.)		51·12 N	0·12 w
122	Reims (răns)	Fr.	49·16 N	4·00 E
100	Reina Adelaida, Arch. (är-chě´-pyě´lä-gō-rä´nä-ä-dě-lī´dä)	Chile	52·00 s	74·15 w
71	Reinbeck (rīn´běk)	Iowa	42·22 N	92·34 w
86	Reindeer (L.) (rän´děr)	Can.	57·36 N	101·23 w
124	Reinosa (rä-ē-nō´sä)	Sp.	43·01 N	4·08 w
84	Reistertown (rēs´těr-toun)	Md. (Baltimore In.)	39·28 N	76·50 w
168	Reitz	S. Afr. (Johannesburg & Pretoria In.)	27·48 s	28·25 E
139	Rembau	Mala. (Singapore In.)	2·36 N	102·06 E
98	Remedios (rě-mě´dyōs)	Col. (In.)	7·03 N	74·42 w
94	Remedios (rě-mä´dhē-ōs)	Cuba	22·30 N	79·35 w
93	Remedios (rě-mě´dyōs)	Pan.	8·14 N	81·46 w
123	Remiremont (rē-mēr-môn´)	Fr.	48·01 N	6·35 E
139	Rempang I.	Indon. (Singapore In.)	0·51 N	104·04 E
123	Remscheid (rěm´shīt)	Ger. (Ruhr In.)	51·10 N	7·11 E
159	Rendova (I.) (rěn´dō-vä)	Sol. Is.	8·38 s	156·26 E
120	Rendsburg (rěnts´bōōrgh)	Ger.	54·19 N	9·39 E
81	Renfrew (rěn´frōō)	Can.	45·30 N	76·30 w
139	Rengam (rěn´găm´)	Mala. (Singapore In.)	1·53 N	103·24 E
101	Rengo (rěn´gō)	Chile (Santiago In.)	34·22 s	70·50 w
129	Reni (ran´)	Sov. Un.	45·26 N	28·18 E
160	Renmark (rěn´märk)	Austl.	34·10 s	140·50 E
159	Rennel (I.) (rěn-něl´)	Sol. Is.	11·50 s	160·38 E
122	Rennes (rěn)	Fr.	48·07 N	1·02 w
81	Rennselaer (rěn´sě-lâr)	N. Y.	42·40 N	73·45 w
68	Reno (rē´nō)	Nev.	39·32 N	119·49 w
126	Reno (R.) (rā´nō)	It.	44·10 N	10·55 E
81	Renovo (rě-nō´vō)	Pa.	41·20 N	77·50 w
80	Rensselaer (rěn´sě-lâr)	Ind.	41·00 N	87·10 w
74	Rentchler (rěnt´chlěr)	Ill. (St. Louis In.)	38·30 N	89·52 w
65	Renton (rěn´tŭn)	Wash. (Seattle In.)	47·29 N	122·13 w
71	Renville (rěn´vĭl)	Minn.	44·44 N	95·13 w
84	Republic (rē-pŭb´lĭk)	Ala. (Birmingham In.)	33·37 N	86·54 w
66	Republic	Wash.	48·38 N	118·44 w
72	Republican (R.), South Fk. (rē-pŭb´lĭ-kǎn)	Colo.	39·35 N	102·28 w
73	Republican (R.)	Kans.	39·22 N	97·14 w
159	Repulse B. (rē-pŭls´)	Austl.	20·55 s	149·22 E
124	Requena (rā-kā´nä)	Sp.	39·29 N	1·03 w
101	Resende (rě-sě´n-dě)	Braz. (Rio de Janeiro In.)	22·30 s	44·26 w
101	Resende Costa (kôs-tä)	Braz. (Rio de Janeiro In.)	20·55 s	44·12 w
129	Reshetilovka (ryě´ shě-tě-lôf-kà)	Sov. Un.	49·34 N	34·04 E
100	Resistencia (rā-sēs-těn´syä)	Arg.	27·24 s	58·54 w
127	Reşita (rå´shě-tä)	Rom.	45·18 N	21·56 E
87	Resolution (I.) (rěz-ō-lü´shŭn)	Can.	61·30 N	63·58 w
159	Resolution (I.) (rěz-ŏl-ûshŭn)	N. Z. (In.)	45·43 s	166·00 E
82	Restigouche (R.) (rěs-tē-gōōsh´)	Can.	47·35 N	67·35 w
98	Restrepo (rěs-trě´pô)	Col. (In.)	3·49 N	76·31 w
98	Restrepo	Col.	4·16 N	73·32 w
92	Retalhuleu (rä-täl-ōō-lān´)	Guat.	14·31 N	91·41 w
122	Rethel (r-tl´)	Fr.	49·34 N	4·20 E
126	Réthimnon	Grc. (In.)	35 21 N	24·30 E
111	Retie	Bel. (Brussels In.)	51·16 N	5·08 E
65	Retsil (rět´sǐl)	Wash. (Seattle In.)	47·33 N	122·37 w
47	Reunion I. (rā-ü-nyôn´)	Afr.	21·06 s	55·36 E
125	Reus (rā´ōōs)	Sp.	41·08 N	1·05 E
120	Reutlingen (roit´lĭng-ěn)	Ger.	48·29 N	9·14 E
136	Reutov (rě-ōōt´ôf)	Sov. Un. (Moscow In.)	55·45 N	37·52 E
	Reval, see Tallinn			
136	Revda (ryâv´dá)	Sov. Un. (Urals In.)	56·48 N	59·57 E
86	Revelstoke (rěv´ěl-stōk)	Can.	51·02 N	118·19 w
93	Reventazon, R. (rä-věn-tä-zōn´)	C. R.	10·10 N	83·30 w
83	Revere (rě-vēr´)	Mass. (Boston In.)	42·24 N	71·01 w
88	Revillagigedo, Islas De (I.) (ě´s-läs-dě-rě-věl-yä-hě´gě-dô)	Mex.	18·45 N	111·00 w
122	Revin (rě-văn´)	Fr.	49·56 N	4·34 E
142	Rewa (rä´wä)	India	24·41 N	81·11 E
142	Rewāri	India	28·19 N	76·39 E
67	Rexburg (rěks´bûrg)	Idaho	43·50 N	111·48 w
76	Rey, L. (rä)	Mex.	27·00 N	103·33 w
93	Rey, Isla del (I.) (ě´s-lä-děl-rā´ě)	Pan.	8·20 N	78·40 w
98	Reyes (rä´yěs)	Bol.	14·19 s	67·16 w
68	Reyes, Pt.	Calif.	38·00 N	123·00 w
102	Reykjanes (C.) (rā´kyä-něs)	Ice.	63·37 N	24·33 w
112	Reykjavik (rā´kyä-věk)	Ice.	64·09 N	21·39 w
76	Reynosa (rā-ē-nō´sä)	Mex.	26·05 N	98·21 w
144	Rezā´iyeh (Urmia) (rě-zī´) (ōōr´mě-à)	Iran	37·30 N	45·15 E
128	Rēzekne (rä´zěk-ně)	Sov. Un.	56·31 N	27·19 E
136	Rezh (rězh´)	Sov. Un. (Urals In.)	57·22 N	61·23 E
129	Rezina (ryězh´ě-ní)	Sov. Un.	47·44 N	28·56 E
126	Rhaetien Alps (Mts.)	It.	46·22 N	10·33 E
117	Rheden (rā´děn)	Neth.	52·02 N	6·02 E
123	Rheinberg (rīn´běrgh)	Ger. (Ruhr In.)	51·33 N	6·37 E
120	Rheine (rī´ně)	Ger.	52·16 N	7·26 E
120	Rheinland-Pfalz (Rhineland-Palatinate) (State)	Ger.	50·05 N	6·40 E
120	Rhein R. (rin)	Ger.	50·34 N	7·21 E
123	Rheydt (rě´yt)	Ger. (Ruhr In.)	51·10 N	6·28 E
71	Rhinelander (rīn´lǎn-děr)	Wis.	45·39 N	89·25 w
111	Rhin Kanal (Can.)	Ger. (Berlin In.)	52·47 N	12·40 E
111	Rhin R. (rēn)	Ger. (Berlin In.)	52·52 N	12·49 E
63	Rhode Island (State) (rōd ī´lǎnd)	U. S.	41·35 N	71·40 w
167	Rhodes (rōdz)	S. Afr. (Natal In.)	30·48 s	27·56 E
166	Rhodesia (rō-dē´zhǐ-à)	Afr.	17·50 s	29·30 E
127	Rhodope Mts. (rō´dô-pě)	Bul.	42·00 N	24·08 E
116	Rhondda (rŏn´dhä)	Wales	51·40 N	3·40 w
122	Rhône (R.) (rōn)	Fr.	45·14 N	4·53 E
111	Rhoon	Neth. (Amsterdam In.)	51·52 N	4·24 E
116	Rhum (I.) (rŭm)	Scot.	56·63 N	6·20 w
99	Riachão (rě-ä-choun´)	Braz.	7·15 s	46·30 w
74	Rialto (rē-äl´tō)	Calif. (Los Angeles In.)	34·06 N	117·23 w
124	Riaza (R.) (rě-ä´thä)	Sp.	41·25 N	3·25 w
124	Ribadavia (rē-bä-dhä´vě-ä)	Sp.	42·18 N	8·06 w
124	Ribadeo (rē-bä-dhä´ō)	Sp.	43·32 N	7·05 w
124	Ribadesella (rě´bä-dä-säl´yä)	Sp.	43·30 N	5·02 w
116	Ribble, R. (rǐb´ʼl)	Eng.	53·50 N	3·15 w
118	Ribe (rē´bě)	Den.	55·20 N	8·45 E
101	Ribeirão Prêto (rě-bä-roun-prě´tô)	Braz. (Rio de Janeiro In.)	21·11 s	47·47 w
72	Ribera (rē-bě´rä)	N. Mex.	35·23 N	105·27 w
98	Riberalta (rē-bä-räl´tä)	Bol.	11·06 s	66·02 w
71	Rib Lake (rǐb läk)	Wis.	45·20 N	90·11 w
68	Rice (rīs)	Calif.	34·05 N	114·50 w
81	Rice (L.)	Can.	44·05 N	78·10 w
74	Rice L.	Minn. (Minneapolis, St. Paul In.)	45·10 N	93·09 w
71	Rice Lake	Wis.	45·30 N	91·44 w
64	Richards I. (rǐch´ěrds)	Can.	69·45 N	135·30 w
74	Richards Landing (lǎnd´ǐng)	Can. (Sault Ste. Marie In.)	46·18 N	84·02 w
74	Richardson (rǐch´ěrd-sǔn)	Tex. (Dallas, Fort Worth In.)	32·56 N	96·44 w
65	Richardson	Wash. (Seattle In.)	48·27 N	122·54 w
86	Richardson Mts.	Can.	66·58 N	136·19 w
81	Richardson Park (pärk)	Del.	39·45 N	75·35 w
81	Richelieu (R.) (rěsh´lyü´)	Can.	45·05 N	73·25 w
74	Richfield (rǐch´fēld)	Minn. (Minneapolis, St. Paul In.)	44·53 N	93·17 w
75	Richfield	Ohio (Cleveland In.)	41·14 N	81·38 w
69	Richfield	Utah	38·45 N	112·05 w
81	Richford (rǐch´fěrd)	Vt.	45·00 N	72·35 w
73	Rich Hill (rǐch hǐl)	Mo.	38·05 N	94·21 w
82	Richibucto (rǐch-ǐ-bŭk´tō)	Can.	46·42 N	64·55 w
84	Richland (rǐch´lǎnd)	Ga.	32·05 N	84·40 w
66	Richland	Wash.	46·17 N	119·19 w
71	Richland Center (sěn´těr)	Wis.	43·20 N	90·25 w
159	Richmond (rǐch´mŭnd)	Austl.	20·47 s	143·14 E
161	Richmond	Austl. (Sydney In.)	33·36 s	150·45 E
65	Richmond	Calif. (San Francisco In.)	37·56 N	122·21 w
82	Richmond	Can.	45·40 N	72·07 w
85	Richmond	Can. (Ottawa In.)	45·12 N	75·49 w
75	Richmond	Ill. (Chicago In.)	42·29 N	88·18 w
80	Richmond	Ind.	39·50 N	85·00 w
80	Richmond	Ky.	37·45 N	84·20 w
73	Richmond	Mo.	39·16 N	93·58 w

PRONOUNCING INDEX Richmond–Rogoaguado 257

Page	Name Pronunciation Region	Lat. °′	Long. °′
77	Richmond . . . . . Tex.	29·35 N	95·45 W
167	Richmond . . . . . S. Afr. (Natal In.)	29·52 S	30·17 E
167	Richmond . . . . . S. Afr. (Natal In.)	33·44 S	26·36 E
67	Richmond . . . . . Utah	41·55 N	111·50 W
81	Richmond . . . . . Va.	37·35 N	77·30 W
65	Richmond Beach Wash. (Seattle In.)	47·47 N	122·23 W
74	Richmond Heights Mo. (St. Louis In.)	38·38 N	90·20 W
85	Richmond Hill (hĭl) Can. (Toronto In.)	43·53 N	79·26 W
78	Richton (rĭch'tŭn) . . . . . Miss.	31·20 N	89·54 W
80	Richwood (rĭch'wŏŏd) . . . . . W. Va.	38·10 N	80·30 W
111	Ridderkerk Neth. (Amsterdam In.)	51·52 N	4·35 E
81	Rideau L. (rē-dō') . . . . . Can.	44·40 N	76·20 W
85	Rideau R. . . . . . Can. (Ottawa In.)	45·17 N	75·41 W
84	Ridgefield (rĭj'fēld) Conn. (New York In.)	41·16 N	73·30 W
65	Ridgefield . . . Wash. (Portland In.)	45·49 N	122·40 W
81	Ridgeley (rĭj'lē) . . . . . W. Va.	39·40 N	78·45 W
75	Ridgeway (rĭj'wā) Can. (Buffalo In.)	42·53 N	79·02 W
81	Ridgeway . . . . . Pa.	41·25 N	78·40 W
84	Ridgewood (ridj'wŏŏd) N. J. (New York In.)	40·59 N	74·08 W
86	Riding Mountain Natl. Park (rīd'ĭng) . Can.	50·59 N	99·19 W
94	Riding Rocks (Is.) . . . . . Ba. Is.	25·20 N	79·10 W
167	Riebeek-Oos . . . S. Afr. (Natal In.)	33·14 S	26·09 E
120	Ried (rēd) . . . . . Aus.	48·13 N	13·30 E
120	Riesa (rē'zȧ) . . . . . Ger.	51·17 N	13·17 E
167	Riet (R.) (rēt) . . . . . S. Afr. (Johannesburg & Pretoria In.)	25·54 S	27·54 E
126	Rieti (rē-ā'tē) . . . . . It.	42·25 N	12·51 E
167	Rievleidam (L.) . . . . . S. Afr. (Johannesburg & Pretoria In.)	25·52 S	28·18 E
69	Rifle (rī'f'l) . . . . . Colo.	39·35 N	107·50 W
119	Riga (rē'gȧ) . . . . . Sov. Un.	56·55 N	24·05 E
119	Riga, G. of . . . . . Sov. Un.	57·56 N	23·05 E
144	Rīgān . . . . . Iran	28·45 N	58·55 E
85	Rigaud (rē-gō') Can. (Montreal In.)	45·29 N	74·18 W
67	Rigby (rĭg'bē) . . . . . Idaho	43·40 N	111·55 W
87	Rigolet (rĭg-ō-lā') . . . . . Can.	54·10 N	58·40 W
126	Rijeka (Fiume) (rĭ-yĕ'kȧ) . . . Yugo.	45·22 N	14·24 E
111	Rijkevorsel . . . . Bel. (Brussels In.)	51·21 N	4·46 E
111	Rijswijk . . Neth. (Amsterdam In.)	52·03 N	4·19 E
121	Rika R. (rē'kȧ) . . . . . Sov. Un.	48·21 N	23·37 E
122	Rille (R.) (rēl) . . . . . Fr.	49·12 N	0·43 E
144	Rimach, Wādī ar (R.) . . . . Sau. Ar.	26·17 N	41·13 E
121	Rimavska Sobota (rē'máf-skä sô'bô-tȧ) . Czech.	48·25 N	20·01 E
118	Rimbo (rēm'bŏŏ) . . . . . Swe.	59·45 N	18·22 E
126	Rimini (rē'mē-nē) . . . . . It.	44·03 N	12·33 E
127	Rîmnicu Sărat . . . . . Rom.	45·24 N	27·06 E
127	Rîmnicu Vâlcea . . . . . Rom.	45·07 N	24·22 E
82	Rimouski (rē-mōōs'kē) . . . . . Can.	48·27 N	68·32 W
90	Rincón de Romos (rēn-kōn dā rô-mōs') . Mex.	22·13 N	102·21 W
154	Rindjani, Gunung (Mtn.) . . Indon.	8·39 S	116·22 E
118	Ringkøbing (rĭng'kûb-ĭng) . . . Den.	56·06 N	8·14 E
118	Ringkøbing Fd . . . . . Den.	55·55 N	8·04 E
118	Ringsaker (rĭngs'äk-ĕr) . . . . . Nor.	60·55 N	10·40 E
118	Ringsted (rĭng'stĕdh) . . . . . Den.	55·27 N	11·49 E
112	Ringvassöy (I.) (rĭng'väs-ûê) . Nor.	69·58 N	16·43 E
161	Ringwood . Austl. (Melbourne In.)	37·49 S	145·14 E
88	Rio Abajo (rē'ō-ä-bä'kō) Pan. (Panama Canal In.)	9·01 N	78·30 W
90	Rio Balsas (rē'ō-bäl-säs) . . . . Mex.	17·59 N	99·45 W
98	Riobamba (rē'ō-bäm'bä) . . . . . Ec.	1·45 S	78·37 W
101	Rio Bonito (rē'ŏŏ bō-nē'tŏŏ) Braz. (Rio de Janeiro In.)	22·44 S	42·38 W
98	Rio Branco (rē'ŏŏ brăŋ'kŏŏ) . Braz.	9·57 S	67·50 W
100	Río Branco (riô blănĉô) . . . . . Ur.	32·33 S	53·29 W
99	Rio Branco (Ter.) . . . . . Braz.	2·35 N	61·25 W
101	Rio Casca (rē'ō-kȧ's-kä) Braz. (Rio de Janeiro In.)	20·15 S	42·39 W
99	Rio Chico (rē'ō chē'kŏ) . Ven. (In.)	10·20 N	65·58 W
101	Rio Claro (rē'ŏŏ klä'rŏŏ) Braz. (Rio de Janeiro In.)	21·25 S	47·33 W
100	Río Cuarto (rē'ō kwär'tō) . . . . Arg.	33·05 S	64·15 W
101	Rio das Flores (rē'ō-däs-flô-rĕs) Braz. (Rio de Janeiro In.)	22·10 S	43·35 W
100	Rio de Janeiro (rē'ŏŏ dā zhä-nâ'ê-rŏŏ) Braz. (In.)	22·50 S	43·20 W
99	Rio de Janeiro (State) . . . . . Braz.	22·27 S	42·43 W
93	Río de Jesús (rē'ō-dĕ-kĕ-sōō's) Pan.	7·54 N	80·59 W
164	Rio del Rey (rē'ō dĕl rā'ē) . . . Nig.	4·41 N	8·38 E
100	Río Dercero (rē'ō dĕr-sĕ'rô) . . Arg.	32·12 S	63·59 W
91	Rio Frío (rē'ō-frē'ō) Mex. (Mexico City In.)	19·21 N	98·40 W
100	Río Gallegos (rē'ō gä-lā'gōs) . . Arg.	51·43 S	69·15 W
100	Rio Grande (rē'ŏŏ grän'dĕ) . . Braz.	31·04 S	52·14 W
90	Rio Grande (rē'ō grän'dā) . . . Mex.	23·51 N	102·59 W
76	Riogrande (rē'ō grän'dā) . . . . . Tex.	26·23 N	98·48 W
69	Rio Grande (R.) (rē'ŏŏ grän'dĕ) Colo.	37·44 N	106·51 W
99	Rio Grande do Norte (State) (rē'ŏŏ grän'dĕ dŏŏ nôr'tĕ) . Braz.	5·26 S	37·20 W
100	Rio Grande do Sul (State) (rē'ŏŏ grän'dĕ-dô-sōō'l) . Braz.	29·00 S	54·00 W
98	Ríohacha (rē'ō-ä'chä) . . . . . Col.	11·30 N	72·54 W
93	Rio Hato (rē'ō-ä'tō) . . . . . Pan.	8·19 N	80·11 W
122	Riom (rē-ôɴ') . . . . . Fr.	45·54 N	3·08 E
163	Rio Muni (Reg.) (rē'ō mōō'nē) Equat. Gui.	1·47 N	8·33 E
98	Rionegro (rē'ō-nĕ'grō) . . . Col. (In.)	6·09 N	75·22 W
100	Río Negro (Prov.) (rē'ō nā'grō) Arg.	40·15 S	68·15 W
101	Río Negro (Dept.) (rē'ō-nĕ'grō) Ur. (Buenos Aires In.)	32·48 S	57·45 W
100	Rio Negro, Embalse del (Res.) (ĕm-bä'l-sĕ-dĕl-rē'ō-nĕ'grō) . Ur.	32·45 S	55·50 W
126	Rionero (rē-ō-nā'rô) . . . . . It.	40·55 N	15·42 E
101	Rio Novo (rē'ō-nô'vô) Braz. (Rio de Janeiro In.)	21·30 S	43·08 W
99	Rio Pardo de Minas (rē'ō pär'dō-dĕ-mē'näs) . Braz.	15·43 S	42·24 W
101	Rio Pombo (rē'ō pôm'bä) Braz. (Rio de Janeiro In.)	21·17 S	43·09 W
101	Rio Sorocaba, Represado (Res.) (rĕ-prĕ-sä-dô-rē'ō-sô-rō-kä'bä) Braz. (Rio de Janeiro In.)	23·37 S	47·19 W
98	Ríosucio (rē'ō-sōō'syō) . . Col. (In.)	5·25 N	75·41 W
125	Riou, Oued (R.) (ōō-ĕd rĭ-ōō) Alg.	35·45 N	1·18 E
139	Riouw Arch . Indon. (Singapore In.)	0·49 N	103·45 E
154	Riouw, Pulau-Pulau (Is.) . . Indon.	0·30 N	104·55 E
139	Riouw, Selat (Str.) Indon. (Singapore In.)	0·49 N	104·24 E
99	Rio Verde (vĕr'dĕ) . . . . . Braz.	17·47 S	50·49 W
90	Rioverde (rē'ō-vĕr'dā) . . . . . Mex.	21·54 N	99·59 W
110	Ripley (rĭp'lē) . . . . . Eng.	53·03 N	1·24 W
78	Ripley . . . . . Miss.	34·44 N	88·55 W
78	Ripley . . . . . Tenn.	35·44 N	89·34 W
125	Ripoll (rē-pōl'') . . . . . Sp.	42·10 N	2·10 E
71	Ripon (rĭp'ŏn) . . . . . Wis.	43·49 N	88·50 W
158	Ripon (I.) . . . . . Austl.	20·05 S	118·10 E
165	Ripon Falls . . . . . Ug.	0·38 N	33·02 E
159	Risdon (rĭz'dŭn) . . . . . Austl.	42·37 S	147·32 E
152	Rishiri (I.) (rē-shē'rē) . . . . . Jap.	45·10 N	141·08 E
139	Rishon-le-Zion . Isr. (Palestine In.)	31·57 N	34·48 E
80	Rising Sun (rīz'ĭng sŭn) . . . . . Ind.	38·55 N	84·55 W
118	Risor (rēs'ûr) . . . . . Nor.	58·44 N	9·10 E
98	Ritacuva, Alto (Mtn.) (ä'l-tô-rē-tä-kōō'vä) . Col.	6·22 N	72·13 W
75	Rittman (rĭt'măn) Ohio (Cleveland In.)	40·58 N	81·47 W
66	Ritzville (rĭts'vĭl) . . . . . Wash.	47·08 N	118·23 W
118	Riuvenfjell (Mts.) (rĭu-vĕn-fyĕl') Nor.	59·20 N	6·55 E
95	Riva (rē'vä) . . . . . Dom. Rep.	19·10 N	69·55 W
126	Riva (rē'vä) . . . . . It.	45·54 N	10·49 E
84	Riva (rĭ'vȧ) . . Md. (Baltimore In.)	38·57 N	76·36 W
92	Rivas (rē'väs) . . . . . Nic.	11·25 N	85·51 W
122	Rive-de-Gier (rēv-dē-zhē-ā') . . . Fr.	45·32 N	4·37 E
100	Rivera (rê-vā'rä) . . . . . Ur.	30·52 S	55·32 W
164	River Cess (rĭv'ĕr sĕs) . . . . . Lib.	5·46 N	9·52 W
75	Riverdale (rĭv'ĕr dāl) Ill. (Chicago In.)	41·38 N	87·36 W
74	Riverdale . Utah (Salt Lake City In.)	41·11 N	112·00 W
78	River Falls . . . . . Ala.	31·20 N	86·25 W
71	River Falls . . . . . Wis.	44·48 N	92·38 W
81	Riverhead (rĭv'ĕr hĕd) . . . . . N. Y.	40·55 N	72·40 W
160	Riverina (Reg.) (rĭv-ĕr-ē'nȧ) . Austl.	34·55 S	144·30 E
65	River Jordan (jôr'dăn) Can. (Seattle In.)	48·26 N	124·02 W
74	River Oaks (ōkz) Tex. (Dallas, Fort Worth In.)	32·47 N	97·24 W
75	River Rouge (rōōzh) Mich. (Detroit In.)	42·16 N	83·09 W
74	Riverside (rĭv'ĕr-sīd) Calif. (Los Angeles In.)	33·59 N	117·21 W
84	Riverside . N. J. (Philadelphia In.)	40·02 N	74·58 W
161	Riverstone . . . Austl. (Sydney In.)	33·41 S	150·52 E
86	Riverton (rĭv'ĕr-tŭn) . . . . . Can.	51·02 N	97·12 W
81	Riverton . . . . . Va.	39·00 N	78·15 W
67	Riverton . . . . . Wyo.	43·02 N	108·24 W
122	Rivesaltes (rēv'zält') . . . . . Fr.	42·48 N	2·48 E
79	Riviera Beach (rĭv-ĭ-ĕr'ȧ bēch) Fla. (In.)	26·46 N	80·04 W
84	Riviera Beach . Md. (Baltimore In.)	39·10 N	76·32 W
82	Riviere (rē-vyâr') . . . . . Can.	46·43 N	72·00 W
82	Riviere (R.) . . . . . Can.	49·05 N	72·04 W
85	Rivie're Beaudette (bō-dĕt') Can. (Montreal In.)	45·14 N	74·20 W
82	Rivière-du-Loup (rē-vyâr' dü lōō') Can.	47·50 N	69·34 W
85	Rivie're-Qui-Barre (rĕv-yĕr' kē-bär) Can. (Edmonton In.)	53·47 N	113·51 W
144	Riyadh . . . . . Sau. Ar.	24·31 N	46·47 E
133	Rize (rē'zĕ) . . . . . Tur.	41·00 N	40·30 E
127	Rizzuto, C. (rēt-sōō'tô) . . . . . It.	38·53 N	17·05 E
118	Rjukan (ryōō'kän) . . . . . Nor.	59·53 N	8·30 E
122	Roanne (rō-än') . . . . . Fr.	46·02 N	4·04 E
78	Roanoke (rō'ȧ-nōk) . . . . . Ala.	33·08 N	85·21 W
79	Roanoke . . . . . Va.	37·16 N	79·55 W
79	Roanoke (R.) . . . . . N. C.-Va.	36·17 N	77·22 W
79	Roanoke Rapids . . . . . N. C.	36·25 N	77·40 W
79	Roanoke Rapids, L. . . . . . N. C.	36·28 N	77·37 W
69	Roan Plat. (rōn) . . . . . Colo.	39·25 N	108·50 W
92	Roatan (rō-ä-tän') . . . . . Hond.	16·18 N	86·33 W
92	Roatan I . . . . . Hond.	16·19 N	86·46 W
166	Robben Island S. Afr. (Cape Town In.)	33·48 S	18·22 E
75	Robbins (rŏb'ĭnz) . Ill. (Chicago In.)	41·39 N	87·42 W
74	Robbinsdale (rŏb'ĭnz-dāl) Minn. (Minneapolis, St. Paul In.)	45·03 N	93·22 W
65	Robe (rōb) . . . . Wash. (Seattle In.)	48·06 N	121·50 W
159	Roberts, Mt. (rŏb'ĕrts) . . . . . Austl.	32·05 S	152·30 E
65	Roberts, Pt. (rŏb'ĕrts) Wash. (Vancouver In.)	48·58 N	123·05 W
83	Robertson (rŏb'ĕrt-sŭn) . . . . . Can.	51·05 N	59·07 W
164	Robertsport (rŏb'ĕrts-pōrt) . . . Lib.	6·45 N	11·31 W
82	Roberval (rŏb'ĕr-văl) (rô-bĕr-väl') Can.	48·32 N	72·15 W
80	Robinson (rŏb'ĭn-sŭn) . . . . . Ill.	39·00 N	87·45 W
83	Robinson's . . . . . Can.	48·16 N	58·50 W
160	Robinvale (rŏb-ĭn'văl) . . . . . Austl.	34·45 S	142·45 E
86	Robson, Mt. (rŏb'sŭn) . . . . . Can.	53·13 N	119·02 W
77	Robstown (rŏbz'toun) . . . . . Tex.	27·46 N	97·41 W
125	Roca, Cabo da (C.) (kȧ'bō-dä-rō'kä) Port. (Lisbon In.)	38·47 N	9·30 W
99	Rocas, Atol das (Atoll) (ȧ-tôl-dȧs-rō'kȧs) . Braz.	3·50 S	33·46 W
168	Rocca Littotorio Som. (Horn of Afr. In.)	7·00 N	47·30 E
96	Rocedos São Pedro E São Paulo (I.) (rô-zĕ'dôs-souɴ-pĕ'drô-ĕ-souɴ-päōō-lô) . Braz.	1·50 N	30·00 W
100	Rocha (rō'chȧs) . . . . . Ur.	34·26 S	54·14 W
110	Rochdale (rŏch'dāl) . . . . . Eng.	53·37 N	2·09 W
95	Roche à Bateau (rôsh ȧ bȧ-tō') Hai.	18·10 N	74·00 W
122	Rochefort (rôsh-fŏr') . . . . . Fr.	45·55 N	0·57 W
71	Rochelle (rô-shĕl') . . . . . Ill.	41·53 N	89·06 W
80	Rochester (rŏch'ĕs-tĕr) . . . . . Ind.	41·05 N	86·20 W
75	Rochester . . . . . Mich. (Detroit In.)	42·41 N	83·09 W
71	Rochester . . . . . Minn.	44·01 N	92·30 W
81	Rochester . . . . . N. H.	43·20 N	71·00 W
81	Rochester . . . . . N. Y.	43·15 N	77·35 W
75	Rochester . . . . Pa. (Pittsburgh In.)	40·42 N	80·16 W
71	Rock (R.) . . . . . Ill.	41·40 N	89·52 W
70	Rock (R.) . . . . . Iowa	43·17 N	96·13 W
65	Rock (R.) . . . . . Ore. (Portland In.)	45·34 N	122·52 W
65	Rock (R.) . . . . . Ore. (Portland In.)	45·52 N	123·14 W
84	Rockaway (rŏck'ȧ-wā) N. J. (New York In.)	40·54 N	74·30 W
161	Rockbank . Austl. (Melbourne In.)	37·44 S	144·40 E
85	Rockcliffe Park (rok'klĭf pärk) Can. (Ottawa In.)	45·27 N	75·40 W
75	Rock Cr. (rŏk) . . . Ill. (Chicago In.)	41·16 N	87·54 W
67	Rock Cr. . . . . . Mont.	46·25 N	113·40 W
66	Rock Cr. . . . . . Ore.	45·30 N	120·06 W
66	Rock Cr. . . . . . Wash.	47·09 N	117·50 W
84	Rockdale . . . . Md. (Baltimore In.)	39·22 N	76·49 W
77	Rockdale (rŏck'dāl) . . . . . Tex.	30·39 N	97·00 W
71	Rock Falls (rŏck fôlz) . . . . . Ill.	41·45 N	89·42 W
71	Rockford (rŏck'fĕrd) . . . . . Ill.	42·16 N	89·07 W
159	Rockhampton (rŏk-hămp'tŭn) Austl.	23·26 S	150·29 E
79	Rockhill (rŏk'hĭl) . . . . . S. C.	34·55 N	81·01 W
79	Rockingham (rŏk'ĭng-hăm) . . N. C.	34·54 N	79·45 W
110	Rockingham For. (rok'ĭng-hăm) Eng.	52·29 N	0·43 W
71	Rock Island . . . . . Ill.	41·31 N	90·37 W
66	Rock Island Dam (ī lănd) . . Wash.	47·17 N	120·33 W
85	Rockland (rŏk'lănd) Can. (Ottawa In.)	45·33 N	75·17 W
82	Rockland . . . . . Maine	44·06 N	69·09 W
83	Rockland . . . . . Mass. (Boston In.)	42·07 N	70·55 W
160	Rockland Res. . . . . . Austl.	36·55 S	142·20 E
78	Rockmart (rŏk'märt) . . . . . Ga.	33·58 N	85·00 W
74	Rockmont (rŏk'mŏnt) Wis. (Duluth In.)	46·34 N	91·54 W
80	Rockport (rŏk'pōrt) . . . . . Ind.	38·20 N	87·00 W
83	Rockport . . . . . Mass. (Boston In.)	42·39 N	70·37 W
73	Rockport . . . . . Mo.	40·25 N	95·30 W
77	Rockport . . . . . Tex.	28·03 N	97·03 W
70	Rock Rapids (răp'ĭdz) . . . . . Iowa	43·26 N	96·10 W
95	Rock Sd. . . . . . Ba. Is.	24·50 N	76·05 W
76	Rocksprings (rŏk sprĭngs) . . . . Tex.	30·02 N	100·12 W
67	Rock Springs . . . . . Wyo.	41·35 N	109·13 W
99	Rockstone (rŏk'stôn) . . . . . Guy.	5·55 N	57·27 W
85	Rockton (rŏk'tŭn) Can. (Toronto In.)	43·18 N	80·08 W
70	Rock Valley (văl'ĭ) . . . . . Iowa	43·13 N	96·17 W
80	Rockville (rŏk'vĭl) . . . . . Ind.	39·45 N	87·15 W
84	Rockville . . . . Md. (Baltimore In.)	39·05 N	77·11 W
84	Rockville Centre (sĕn'tĕr) N. Y. (New York In.)	40·39 N	73·39 W
73	Rockwall (rŏk'wôl) . . . . . Tex.	32·55 N	96·23 W
71	Rockwell City (rŏk'wĕl) . . . . . Iowa	42·22 N	94·37 W
85	Rockwood (rŏk-wŏŏd) Can. (Toronto In.)	43·37 N	80·08 W
82	Rockwood . . . . . Maine	45·39 N	69·45 W
78	Rockwood . . . . . Tenn.	35·51 N	84·41 W
67	Rocky Boys Ind. Res. . . . . . Mont.	48·08 N	109·34 W
72	Rocky Ford . . . . . Colo.	38·02 N	103·43 W
84	Rocky Hill (hĭl) N. J. (New York In.)	40·24 N	74·38 W
79	Rocky Mount . . . . . N. C.	35·55 N	77·47 W
72	Rocky Mountain Natl. Park . Colo.	40·29 N	106·06 W
49	Rocky Mts. (rŏk'ē) . . . . . N. A.	50·00 N	114·00 W
75	Rocky River . Ohio (Cleveland In.)	41·29 N	81·51 W
75	Rocky R., E. Br. Ohio (Cleveland In.)	41·13 N	81·43 W
75	Rocky R., W. Br. Ohio (Cleveland In.)	41·17 N	81·54 W
95	Rodas (rō'dhás) . . . . . Cuba	22·20 N	80·35 W
110	Roden (R.) (rō'dĕn) . . . . . Eng.	52·49 N	2·38 W
65	Rodeo (rō'dēō) Calif. (San Francisco In.)	38·02 N	122·16 W
76	Rodeo (rō-dā'ō) . . . . . Mex.	25·12 N	104·34 W
122	Rodez (rô-dĕz') . . . . . Fr.	44·22 N	2·34 E
115	Rōdhos . . . . . Grc.	36·24 N	28·15 E
115	Ródhos (I.) . . . . . Grc.	36·00 N	28·29 E
121	Rodnei, Muntii (Mts.) (rôd'nĕ-ê) Rom.	47·41 N	24·05 E
128	Rodniki (rôd'nê-kê) . . . . Sov. Un.	57·08 N	41·48 E
127	Rodonit, Kep I (C.) . . . . . Alb.	41·38 N	19·01 E
	Rodosto, see Tekirdağ		
84	Roebling (rōb'lĭng) N. J. (Philadelphia In.)	40·07 N	74·48 W
158	Roebourne (rō'bŭrn) . . . . . Austl.	20·50 S	117·15 E
158	Roebuck, B. (rō'bŭck) . . . . . Austl.	18·15 S	121·10 E
168	Roedtan . . . . . S. Afr. (Johannesburg & Pretoria In.)	24·37 S	29·08 E
117	Roermond (rōōr'mônt) . . . . . Neth.	41·11 N	5·59 E
117	Roeselare . . . . . Bel.	50·55 N	3·05 E
65	Roesiger (L.) (rōz'ĭ-gĕr) Wash. (Seattle In.)	47·59 N	121·56 W
87	Roes Welcome Sd. (rōz) . . . . . Can.	64·10 N	87·23 W
128	Rogachëv (rôg'ȧ-chyôf) . . Sov. Un.	53·07 N	30·04 E
127	Rogatica (rô-gä'tē-tsä) . . . . . Yugo.	43·46 N	19·00 E
121	Rogatin (rô-gä'tĭn) . . . . . Sov. Un.	49·22 N	24·37 E
73	Rogers (rŏj-ĕrz) . . . . . Ark.	36·19 N	94·07 W
80	Rogers City . . . . . Mich.	45·30 N	83·50 W
78	Rogersville (rŏj'ĕrz-vĭl) . . . . . Tenn.	36·21 N	83·00 W
122	Rognac (rŏn-yăk') Fr. (Marseille In.)	43·29 N	5·15 E
98	Rogoaguado (L.) (rō'gō-ȧ-gwȧ'dō) Bol.	12·42 S	66·46 W

ng-sing; ŋ-baŋk; ɴ-nasalized n; nŏd; cŏmmit; ōld; ôbey; ôrder; fōōd; fŏŏt; ou-out; s-soft; sh-dish; th-thin; pūre; ûnite; ûrn; stŭd; circŭs; ü-as "y" in study; '-indeterminate vowel.

258 Rogovskaya–Rybatskoye PRONOUNCING INDEX

Page	Name Pronunciation Region	Lat. °′	Long. °′
129	Rogovskaya (rô gôf′skȧ-yȧ) Sov. Un.	45·43 N	38·42 E
120	Rogózno (rô′gôzh-nô) Pol.	52·44 N	16·53 E
66	Rogue R. (rōg) Ore.	42·32 N	124·13 W
118	Röikenviken (rûē′kĕn-vêk-ĕn) Nor.	60·27 N	10·26 E
101	Rojas (rō′häs) Arg. (Buenos Aires In.)	34·11 S	60·42 W
91	Rojo, Cabo (C.) (rō′hō) Mex.	21·35 N	97·16 W
89	Rojo, Cabo (C.) (rō′hō) P. R. (Puerto Rico In.)	17·55 N	67·14 W
153	Rokkō-Zan (Mtn.) (rôk′kō zän) Jap. (Ōsaka In.)	34·46 N	135·16 E
120	Rokycany (rô′kĭ′tsȧ-nĭ) Czech.	49·44 N	13·37 E
98	Roldanillo (rôl-dä-nē′l-yō) Col. (In.)	4·24 N	76·09 W
73	Rolla (rŏl′ȧ) Mo.	37·56 N	91·45 W
70	Rolla N. D.	48·52 N	99·32 W
118	Rollag (rōō′lägh) Nor.	59·55 N	8·48 E
95	Rolleville Ba. Is.	23·40 N	76·00 W
160	Roma (rō′mȧ) Austl.	26·30 S	148·48 E
167	Roma Leso. (Natal In.)	29·28 S	27·43 E
125	Roma (Rome) (rō′mä) (rōm) It. (Rome In.)	41·52 N	12·37 E
126	Romagna (Reg.) (rô-mȧ′n-yä) It.	44·18 N	10·48 E
83	Romaine (rô-mĕn′) Can.	50·12 N	60·38 W
87	Romaine (R.) Can.	51·22 N	63·23 W
121	Roman (rō′män) Rom.	46·56 N	26·57 E
102	Romania (rō-mā′nê-ȧ) Eur.	46·18 N	22·53 E
79	Romano, C. (rō-mā′nō) Fla. (In.)	25·48 N	82·00 W
94	Romano, Cayo (I.) (kä′yō-rô-mȧ′nô) Cuba	22·15 N	78·00 W
136	Romanovo (rô-mä′nô-vô) Sov. Un. (Urals In.)	59·09 N	61·24 E
122	Romans-sur-Isère (rô-mäN′-sür-ē-sĕr′) Fr.	45·04 N	4·49 E
64	Romanzof, C. (rō′män zôf) Alaska	62·00 N	167·18 W
155	Romblon (rōm-blōn′) Phil. (Manila In.)	12·34 N	122·16 E
155	Romblon (I.) Phil. (Manila In.)	12·33 N	122·17 E
78	Rome (rōm) Ga.	34·14 N	85·10 W
81	Rome N. Y.	43·15 N	75·25 W
	Rome, see Roma		
80	Romeo (rō′mê-ō) Mich.	42·50 N	83·00 W
110	Romford (rŭm′fērd) Eng. (London In.)	51·35 N	0·11 E
122	Romilly-sur-Seine (rô-mê-yē′sür-sān′) Fr.	48·32 N	3·41 E
90	Romita (rō-mē′tä) Mex.	20·53 N	101·32 W
129	Romny (rôm′nĭ) Sov. Un.	50·46 N	33·31 E
118	Rømø (I.) (rûm′û) Den.	55·08 N	8·17 E
74	Romoland (rŏ′mō′lănd) Calif. (Los Angeles In.)	33·44 N	117·11 W
122	Romorantin (rô-mô-räN-täN′) Fr.	47·24 N	1·46 E
139	Rompin Mala. (Singapore In.)	2·42 N	102·30 E
139	Rompin (R.) Mala. (Singapore In.)	2·54 N	103·10 E
75	Romulus (rom′ū lŭs) Mich. (Detroit In.)	42·14 N	83·24 W
116	Ronaldsay, North (I.) Scot.	59·21 N	2·23 W
116	Ronaldsay, South (I.) (rŏn′ăld-s′ā) Scot.	59·48 N	2·55 W
67	Ronan (rō′nȧn) Mont.	47·28 N	114·03 W
99	Roncador, Serra do (Mts.) (sĕr′rȧ dōō rôn-kä-dôr′) Braz.	12·44 S	52·19 W
124	Roncesvalles (rôn-sĕs-vä′l-yĕs) Sp.	43·00 N	1·17 W
80	Ronceverte (rŏn′sê-vûrt) W. Va.	37·45 N	80·30 W
124	Ronda (rōn′dä) Sp.	37·45 N	5·10 W
98	Rondônia (Ter.) Braz.	10·15 S	63·07 W
86	Ronge, Lac la (L.) Can.	55·16 N	104·16 W
118	Rønne (rûn′ĕ) Den.	55·08 N	14·46 E
118	Ronneby (rōn′ĕ-bü) Swe.	56·13 N	15·17 E
42	Ronne Ice Shelf Ant.	77·30 S	38·00 W
72	Ront Ra. (Mts.) (rŏnt) Colo.	40·59 N	105·29 W
167	Roodepoort (rō′dĕ-pōrt) S. Afr. (Johannesburg & Pretoria In.)	26·10 S	27·52 E
73	Roodhouse (rōōd′hous) Ill.	39·29 N	90·21 W
168	Rooiberg S. Afr. (Johannesburg & Pretoria In.)	24·46 S	27·42 E
111	Roosendaal (rō′zĕn-däl) Neth. (Amsterdam In.)	51·32 N	4·27 E
69	Roosevelt (rōz″vĕlt) Utah	40·20 N	110·00 W
69	Roosevelt (R.) Ariz.	33·45 N	111·00 W
99	Roosevelt (R.) (rô′sĕ-vĕlt) Braz.	9·22 S	60·28 W
47	Roosevelt I. Ant.	79·30 S	168·00 W
75	Root R. (rōōt) Wis. (Milwaukee In.)	42·49 N	87·54 W
158	Roper (R.) (rōp′ēr) Austl.	14·50 S	134·00 E
136	Ropsha (rôp′shȧ) Sov. Un. (Leningrad In.)	59·44 N	29·53 E
122	Roquefort Fr.	43·59 N	3·00 E
98	Roques, Islas los (Is.) Ven.	21·25 N	67·40 W
101	Roque Pérez (rô′kĕ-pĕ′rĕz) Arg. (Buenos Aires In.)	35·23 S	59·22 W
125	Roquetas (rô-kā′täs) Sp.	40·50 N	0·32 E
98	Roraima (Ter.) (rô′rīy-mă) Braz.	2·00 N	62·15 W
99	Roraima, Mtn. (rô-rä-ē′mä) Ven.-Guy.	5·12 N	60·52 W
118	Röros (rûr′ôs) Nor.	62·36 N	11·25 E
120	Rorschach (rōr′shäk) Switz.	47·27 N	9·28 E
129	Ros′ (R.) (rôs) Sov. Un.	49·40 N	30·22 E
120	Rosa, Monte (Mt.) (mōn′tā rō′zä) It.	45·56 N	7·51 E
76	Rosales (rō-zä′lās) Mex.	28·15 N	100·43 W
155	Rosales (rô-sä′lĕs) Phil. (Manila In.)	15·54 N	120·38 E
90	Rosamorada (rō′zä-mō-rä′dhä) Mex.	22·06 N	105·16 W
91	Rosaria, Laguna (L.) (lä-gōō′nä-rô-sȧ′ryä) Mex.	17·50 N	93·51 W
101	Rosario (rô-zä′rê-ō) Arg. (Buenos Aires In.)	32·58 S	60·42 W
99	Rosario (rô-zä′rê-ōō) Braz.	2·49 S	44·15 W
90	Rosario Mex.	22·58 N	105·54 W
155	Rosario Phil. (Manila In.)	13·49 N	121·13 E
101	Rosario Ur. (Buenos Aires In.)	34·19 S	57·24 W
94	Rosario, Cayo (I.) (kä′yō-rô-sä′ryō) Cuba	21·40 N	81·55 W
100	Rosário do Sul (rô-zä′rê-ōō-dô-sōō′l) Braz.	30·17 S	54·52 W
99	Rosário Oeste (ō′ĕst′ĕ) Braz.	14·47 S	56·20 W
65	Rosario Str. Wash. (Seattle In.)	48·27 N	122·45 W
125	Rosas, Golfo de (G.) (gôl-fô-dĕ-rō′zäs) Sp.	42·10 N	3·20 E
123	Rosbach (rōz′bäĸ) Ger. (Ruhr In.)	50 47 N	7·38 E
76	Roscoe (rôs′kō) Tex.	32·26 N	100·38 W
70	Roseau (rô-zō′) Minn.	48·52 N	95·47 W
93	Roseau Dominica (Le. & Wind. Is. In.)	15·17 N	61·23 W
70	Roseau (R.) Minn.	48·52 N	96·11 W
66	Roseberg (rōz′bûrg) Ore.	43·13 N	123·20 W
67	Rosebud Cr. Mont.	45·48 N	106·34 W
70	Rosebud Ind. Res. (rōz′bud) S. D.	43·13 N	100·42 W
78	Rosedale (rōz′dāl) Miss.	33·49 N	90·56 W
65	Rosedale Wash. (Seattle In.)	47·20 N	122·39 W
75	Roselle (rō-zĕl′) Ill. (Chicago In.)	41·59 N	88·05 W
85	Rosemere (rōz′mēr) Can. (Montreal In.)	45·38 N	73·48 W
74	Rosemount (rōz′mount) Minn. (Minneapolis, St. Paul In.)	44·44 N	93·08 W
168	Rosendal (rô-sĕn′täl) S. Afr. (Johannesburg & Pretoria In.)	28·32 S	27·56 E
120	Rosenheim (rō′zĕn-hīm) Ger.	47·52 N	12·06 E
86	Rosetown (rōz′toun) Can.	51·37 N	108·10 W
	Rosetta, see Rashīd		
167	Rosettenville S. Afr. (Johannesburg & Pretoria In.)	26·15 S	28·04 E
68	Roseville (rōz′vĭl) Calif.	38·44 N	121·19 W
75	Roseville Mich. (Detroit In.)	42·30 N	82·55 W
74	Roseville Minn. (Minneapolis, St. Paul In.)	45·01 N	93·10 W
80	Rosiclare (rōz′ĭ-klâr) Ill.	37·30 N	88·15 W
99	Rosignol (rŏs-ĭg-nĕl) Guy.	6·16 N	57·37 W
127	Rosiorii de Vede (rô-shôr′ê dĕ vĕ-dĕ) Rom.	44·06 N	25·00 E
118	Roskilde (rôs′kêl-dĕ) Den.	55·39 N	12·04 E
128	Roslavl′ (rôs′läv′l) Sov. Un.	53·56 N	32·52 E
66	Roslyn (rŏz′lĭn) Wash.	47·14 N	121·00 W
129	Rosovka Sov. Un.	47·14 N	36·35 E
123	Rösrath (rûz′rät) Ger. (Ruhr In.)	50·53 N	7·11 E
75	Ross (rôs) Ohio (Cincinnati In.)	39·19 N	84·39 W
126	Rossano (rô-sä′nō) It.	39·34 N	16·38 E
85	Ross Cr. Can. (Edmonton In.)	53·50 N	113·08 W
66	Ross Dam Wash.	48·40 N	121·07 W
81	Rosseau (L.) (rôs-sō′) Can.	45·15 N	79·30 W
159	Rossel (I.) (rô-sĕl′) Austl.	11·31 S	154·00 E
85	Rosser (rôs′sēr) Can. (Winnipeg In.)	49·59 N	97·27 W
82	Rossignol (rô-sê-nyôl′) Can.	44·15 N	65·25 W
86	Rossland (rôs′lȧnd) Can.	49·00 N	118·08 W
129	Rossosh′ (rôs′sŭsh) Sov. Un.	50·12 N	39·32 E
167	Rossouw S. Afr. (Natal In.)	31·12 S	27·18 E
47	Ross Sea Ant.	76·00 S	178·00 W
47	Ross Shelf Ice Ant.	81·30 S	175·00 W
78	Rossville (rôs′vĭl) Ga.	34·57 N	85·22 W
120	Rostock (rôs′tŭk) Ger.	54·04 N	12·06 E
128	Rostov Sov. Un.	57·13 N	39·23 E
129	Rostov (Oblast) Sov. Un.	47·38 N	39·15 E
133	Rostov-na-Donu (rôstôv-nȧ-dô-nōō) Sov. Un.	47·16 N	39·47 E
112	Rösvatn (L.) (rûs-vät′n) Nor.	65·36 N	13·08 E
78	Roswell (rôz′wĕl) Ga.	34·02 N	84·21 W
72	Roswell N. Mex.	33·23 N	104·32 W
72	Rotan (rô-tăn′) Tex.	32·51 N	100·27 W
120	Rothenburg Ger.	49·20 N	10·10 E
110	Rotherham (rŏdh′ēr-ăm) Eng.	53·26 N	1·21 W
82	Rothesay Can.	45·25 N	65·59 W
116	Rothesay (rôth′sȧ) Scot.	55·50 N	3·14 W
110	Rothwell (rôth′wĕl) Eng.	53·44 N	1·30 W
154	Roti (I.) (rō′tê) Indon.	10·30 S	122·52 E
160	Roto (rō′tô) Austl.	33·07 S	145·30 E
111	Rotterdam (rôt′ĕr-däm′) Neth. (Amsterdam In.)	51·55 N	4·27 E
120	Rottweil (rōt′vīl) Ger.	48·10 N	8·36 E
122	Roubaix (rōō-bĕ′) Fr.	50·42 N	3·10 E
122	Rouen (rōō-äN′) Fr.	49·25 N	1·05 E
75	Rouge, R. Mich. (Detroit In.)	42·30 N	83·15 W
85	Rouge R. (rōōzh) Can. (Toronto In.)	43·53 N	79·21 W
75	Round Lake Ill. (Chicago In.)	42·21 N	88·05 W
83	Round Pd. (round) Can.	48·12 N	53·50 W
65	Round Top (Mtn.) (tŏp) Ore. (Portland In.)	45·41 N	123·22 W
67	Roundup (round′ŭp) Mont.	46·25 N	108·35 W
116	Rousay (I.) (rōō′zȧ) Scot.	59·10 N	3·04 W
87	Rouyn (rōōn) Can.	48·22 N	79·03 W
112	Rovaniemi (rô′vȧ-nyĕ′mĭ) Fin.	66·29 N	25·45 E
126	Rovato (rô-vä′tō) It.	45·33 N	10·00 E
129	Roven′ki (rô-vĕn′ki′) Sov. Un.	48·06 N	39·44 E
129	Roven′ki Sov. Un.	49·54 N	38·54 E
126	Rovereto (rō-vȧ-rā′tô) It.	45·53 N	11·05 E
126	Rovigo (rô-vē′gô) It.	45·05 N	11·48 E
126	Rovinj (rô′vên′) Yugo.	45·05 N	13·40 E
98	Rovira (rô-vē′rä) Col. (In.)	4·14 N	75·13 W
121	Rovno (rôv′nô) Sov. Un.	50·37 N	26·17 E
129	Rovno (Oblast) Sov. Un.	50·55 N	27·00 E
129	Rovnoye (rôv′nô-yĕ) Sov. Un.	48·11 N	31·46 E
83	Rowley (rou′lē) Mass. (Boston In.)	42·43 N	70·53 W
74	Roxana (rŏks′ăn-nȧ) Ill. (St. Louis In.)	38·51 N	90·05 W
154	Roxas (rô-xäs) Phil.	11·30 N	122·47 E
79	Roxboro (rŏks′ bŭr-ô) N. C.	36·22 N	78·58 W
72	Roy (roi) N. Mex.	35·54 N	104·09 W
74	Roy Utah (Salt Lake City In.)	41·10 N	112·02 W
94	Royal (I.) Ba. Is.	25·30 N	76·50 W
116	Royal Can. (roi-ȧl) Ire.	53·28 N	6·45 W
167	Royal Natal Natl. Pk. (roi′ăl) S. Afr. (Natal In.)	28·35 S	28·54 E
65	Royal Oak (roi′ăl ōk) Can. (Seattle In.)	48·30 N	123·24 W
75	Royal Oak Mich. (Detroit In.)	42·29 N	83·09 W
80	Royalton (roi′ăl-tŭn) Mich.	42·00 N	86·25 W
122	Royan (rwä-yäN′) Fr.	45·40 N	1·02 W
122	Roye (rwä) Fr.	49·43 N	2·40 E
84	Royersford (rô′ yērz-fērd) Pa. (Philadelphia In.)	40·11 N	75·32 W
78	Royston (roiz′tŭn) Ga.	34·15 N	83·06 W
110	Royton (roi′tŭn) Eng.	53·34 N	2·07 W
123	Rozay-en-Brie (rô-zā-ĕN-brē′) Fr. (Paris In.)	48·41 N	2·57 E
136	Rozhaya R. (rô′zhȧ-yȧ) Sov. Un. (Moscow In.)	55·20 N	37·37 E
121	Rožňava (rôzh′nyȧ-vȧ) Czech.	48·39 N	20·32 E
133	Rtishchevo (′r-tĭsh′chĕ-vô) Sov. Un.	52·15 N	43·40 E
167	Ruaha (R.) (rwä′hȧ) Tan.	7·51 S	37·00 E
159	Ruapehu (Mtn.) (rōō-ȧ-pā′hōō) N. Z. (In.)	39·15 S	175·37 E
139	Ruâq (R.) U. A. R. (Palestine In.)	29·48 N	33·59 E
134	Rubtsovsk Sov. Un.	51·31 N	81·17 E
64	Ruby (rōō′bê) Alaska	64·38 N	155·22 W
68	Ruby (L.) Nev.	40·11 N	115·20 W
68	Ruby Mts. Nev.	40·11 N	115·36 W
67	Ruby R. Mont.	45·06 N	112·10 W
144	Rūd-E-Kar (R.) Iran	33·15 N	47·31 E
118	Rudkøbing (rōōdh′kûb-ĭng) Den.	54·56 N	10·44 E
111	Rüdnitz (rüd′nētz) Ger. (Berlin In.)	52·44 N	13·38 E
142	Rudok (rōō′dôk) China	33·42 N	79·56 E
165	Rudolf, L. (rōō′dŏlf) Ken.-Eth.	3·43 N	35·49 E
117	Rudolstadt (rōō′dôl-shtät) Ger.	50·46 N	13·30 E
165	Rufa′a (rōō-fä′ä) Sud.	14·52 N	33·30 E
122	Ruffec (rü-fĕk′) Fr.	46·03 N	0·11 E
167	Rufiji (R.) (rōō-fē′jê) Tan.	8·29 S	37·39 E
164	Rufisque (rü-fēsk′) Senegal	14·41 N	17·13 W
66	Rufus Woods Wash.	48·02 N	119·33 W
110	Rugby (rŭg′bê) Eng.	52·22 N	1·15 W
70	Rugby N. D.	48·22 N	100·00 W
110	Rugeley (rōōj′lē) Eng.	52·46 N	1·56 W
120	Rügen (Pen.) (rü′ghĕn) Ger.	54·28 N	13·47 E
119	Ruhnu-Saar (I.) (rōōnōō-sȧ′år) Sov. Un.	57·46 N	23·15 E
120	Ruhr R. (rōōr) Ger.	51·18 N	8·17 E
90	Ruiz (rōōē′z) Mex.	21·55 N	105·09 W
98	Ruiz, Nevado del (Pk.) (nĕ-vȧ′dô-dĕl-rōōē′z) Col. (In.)	4·52 N	75·20 W
119	Rūjiena (rōō′yĭ-ă-nȧ) Sov. Un.	57·54 N	25·19 E
166	Rukwa (L.) (rōōk-wä′) Tan.	8·15 S	33·14 E
71	Rum (R.) (rŭm) Minn.	45·52 N	93·45 W
127	Ruma (rōō′mȧ) Yugo.	45·00 N	19·53 E
165	Rumbek (rŭm′bĕk) Sud.	6·52 N	29·43 E
95	Rum Cay (I.) Ba. Is.	23·40 N	74·50 W
82	Rumford (rŭm′fērd) Maine	44·32 N	70·35 W
139	Rummānah U. A. R. (Palestine In.)	31·01 N	32·39 E
110	Runcorn (rŭŋ′kôrn) Eng.	53·20 N	2·44 W
139	Rupat, Palau (I.) (rōō′pät) Indon. (Singapore In.)	1·55 N	101·35 E
139	Rupat, Selat (Str.) Indon. (Singapore In.)	1·55 N	101·17 E
67	Rupert (rōō′pērt) Idaho	42·36 N	113·41 W
87	Rupert (R.) Can.	76·27 N	77·47 W
127	Ruse (Russe) (rōō′sĕ) (rōō′sĕ) Bul.	43·50 N	25·59 E
71	Rush City Minn.	45·40 N	92·59 W
65	Rushton (rŭsh′tŭn) Wash. (Seattle In.)	47·18 N	122·30 W
73	Rushville (rŭsh′vĭl) Ill.	40·08 N	90·34 W
80	Rushville Ind.	39·35 N	85·30 W
70	Rushville Nebr.	42·43 N	102·27 W
77	Rusk (rŭsk) Tex.	31·49 N	95·09 W
65	Ruskin (rŭs′kĭn) Can. (Vancouver In.)	49·10 N	122·25 W
111	Russ (R.) Aus. (Vienna In.)	48·12 N	16·55 E
99	Russas (rōō′s-säs) Braz.	4·48 S	37·50 W
	Russe, see Ruse		
65	Russell Calif. (San Francisco In.)	37·39 N	122·08 W
86	Russell (rŭs′ĕl) Can.	50·47 N	101·20 W
85	Russell Can. (Ottawa In.)	45·15 N	75·22 W
72	Russell Kans.	38·51 N	98·51 W
80	Russell Ky.	38·30 N	82·45 W
159	Russell N. Z. (In.)	35·38 S	174·13 E
159	Russell Is Sol. Is.	9·16 S	158·30 E
78	Russellville (rŭs′ĕl-vĭl) Ala.	34·29 N	87·44 W
73	Russellville Ark.	35·16 N	93·08 W
78	Russelville Ky.	36·48 N	86·51 W
130	Russian S. F. S. R. Sov. Un.	61·00 N	60·00 E
68	Russian (R.) (rŭsh′ăn) Calif.	38·59 N	123·10 W
168	Rustenburg (rŭs′tĕn-bûrg) S. Afr. (Johannesburg & Pretoria In.)	25·40 S	26·15 E
77	Ruston (rŭs′tŭn) La.	32·32 N	92·39 W
129	Rutchenkovo (rōō-chĕn′kô-vô) Sov. Un.	47·54 N	37·36 E
124	Rute (rōō′tā) Sp.	37·20 N	4·34 W
68	Ruth (rōōth) Nev.	39·17 N	115·00 W
121	Ruthenia (Reg.) Sov. Un.	48·25 N	23·00 E
79	Rutherfordton (rŭdh′ēr-fērd-tŭn) N. C.	35·23 N	81·58 W
81	Rutland (rŭt′lănd) Vt.	43·35 N	72·55 W
110	Rutland (Co.) Eng.	52·40 N	0·37 W
84	Rutledge (rût′lĕdj) Md. (Baltimore In.)	39·34 N	76·33 W
166	Rutshuru (rōōt-shōō′rōō) Con. K.	1·13 S	29·15 E
126	Ruvo (rōō′vô) It.	41·07 N	16·32 E
163	Ruwenzori Ra. (rōō-wĕn-zō′rê) Afr.	0·53 N	30·00 E
128	Ruza (rōō′zȧ) Sov. Un.	55·42 N	36·12 E
121	Ruzhany (rōō-zhän′ĭ) Sov. Un.	52·49 N	24·54 E
166	Rwanda Afr.	2·10 S	29·37 E
136	Ryabovo (ryä′bô-vô) Sov. Un. (Leningrad In.)	59·24 N	31·08 E
128	Ryazan′ (ryä-zän″) Sov. Un.	54·37 N	39·43 E
128	Ryazan′ (Oblast) Sov. Un.	54·10 N	39·37 E
128	Ryazhsk (ryäzh′sk′) Sov. Un.	53·43 N	40·04 E
132	Rybachiy, P-Ov. (Pen.) Sov. Un.	69·50 N	33·20 E
136	Rybatskoye (rĭ-bät′skô-yĕ) Sov. Un. (Leningrad In.)	59·50 N	30·31 E

ăt; finăl; rāte; senåte; ärm; ȧsk; sofȧ; fâre; ch-choose; dh-as th in other; bē; êvent; bĕt; recĕnt; cratēr; g-go; gh-guttural g; bĭt; ĭ-short neutral; rīde; ĸ-guttural k as ch in German ich;

Page	Name	Pronunciation	Region	Lat. °'	Long. °'
128	Rybinsk	(ry-bǐ'nsk)	Sov. Un.	58·02 N	38·52 E
	Rybinsk, L., see Rybinskoye Vodokhranilishche				
128	Rybinskoye Vodokhranilishche (Rybinsk) (L.)		Sov. Un.	58·23 N	38·15 E
121	Rybnik	(rĭb'nĕk)	Pol.	50·06 N	18·37 E
129	Rybnitsa	(rĭb'nĕt-sà)	Sov. Un.	47·45 N	29·02 E
116	Ryde	(rid)	Eng.	50·43 N	1·16 W
84	Rye	(rī)	N. Y. (New York In.)	40·58 N	73·42 W
129	Ryl'sk	(rĕl'sk)	Sov. Un.	51·33 N	34·42 E
152	Ryōtsu	(ryōt'sōō)	Jap.	38·02 N	138·23 E
121	Rypin	(rĭ'pēn)	Pol.	53·04 N	19·25 E
156	Ryūkyū Rettō (Is.)	(ryōō'kyōō)	Asia	26·00 N	119·00 E
121	Rzeszów	(zhà'shōōf)	Pol.	50·02 N	22·00 E
128	Rzhev	('r-zhĕf)	Sov. Un.	56·16 N	34·17 E
129	Rzhishchëv	('r-zhǐsh'chĕf)	Sov. Un.	49·58 N	31·05 E
120	Saale R.	(sä'lĕ)	Ger.	51·14 N	11·52 E
120	Saalfeld	(säl'fĕlt)	Ger.	50·38 N	11·20 E
120	Saar (State)	(zär)	Ger.	49·25 N	6·50 E
120	Saarbrücken	(zähr'brü-kĕn)	Ger.	49·15 N	7·01 E
119	Saaremaa (Ezel) (I.)	(sä'rĕ-mä)	Sov. Un.	58·28 N	21·30 E
100	Saavedra	(sä-ä-vä'drä)	Arg.	37·45 S	62·23 W
127	Šabac	(shä'bàts)	Yugo.	44·45 N	19·49 E
125	Sabadell	(sä-bä-dhäl')	Sp.	41·32 N	2·07 E
154	Sabah (Reg.)		Mala.	5·10 N	116·25 E
93	Saba I.	(sä'bä)	N. A. (Le. & Wind. Is. In.)	17·39 N	63·20 W
154	Sabalana (I.)		Indon.	6·56 S	118·10 E
94	Sabana, Arch. de	(är-chē-pyē'lä-gô dĕ sä-bä'nä)	Cuba	23·05 N	80·00 W
93	Sabana, R.	(sä-bä'nä)	Pan.	8·40 N	78·02 W
95	Sabana de la Mar	(sä-bä'nä dä lä mär')	Dom. Rep.	19·05 N	69·30 W
99	Sabana de Uchire	(sä-bä'nä dĕ ōō-chē'rĕ)	Ven. (In.)	10·02 N	65·32 W
92	Sabanagrande	(sä-bä'nä-grä'n-dĕ)	Hond.	13·47 N	87·16 W
98	Sabanalarga	(sä-bä'nä-lär'gä)	Col.	10·38 N	75·02 W
98	Sabanas Páramo (Mtn.)	(sä-bä'näs pá'rä-mô)	Col. (In.)	6·28 N	76·08 W
91	Sabancuy	(sä-bän-kwē')	Mex.	18·58 N	91·09 W
154	Sabang	(sä'bäng)	Indon.	5·52 N	95·26 E
126	Sabaudia	(sä-bou'dĕ-ä)	It.	41·19 N	13·00 E
165	Sabderat	(säb-dà-rät')	Eth.	15·30 N	36·45 E
73	Sabetha	(sà-bĕth'à)	Kans.	39·54 N	95·49 W
166	Sabi (R.)	(sä'bē)	Rh.	20·18 S	32·07 E
119	Sabile	(sà-bē'lĕ)	Sov. Un.	57·03 N	22·34 E
76	Sabinal	(sà-bī'nál)	Tex.	29·19 N	99·27 W
94	Sabinal, Cayo (I.)	(kà'yō sä-bē-näl')	Cuba	21·40 N	77·20 W
88	Sabinas		Mex.	28·05 N	102·30 W
76	Sabinas, R.	(sä-bē'näs)	Mex.	26·37 N	99·52 W
76	Sabinas, Rio (R.)	(rē'ō sä-bē'näs)	Mex.	27·25 N	100·33 W
76	Sabinas Hidalgo	(ē-däl'gô)	Mex.	26·30 N	100·10 W
77	Sabine	(sà-bēn')	Tex.	29·44 N	93·54 W
47	Sabine, Mt.		Ant.	72·05 S	169·10 E
63	Sabine (R.)		U. S.	31·35 N	94·00 W
77	Sabine L.		La.-Tex.	29·53 N	93·41 W
155	Sablayan	(säb-lä-yän')	Phil. (Manila In.)	12·49 N	120·47 E
82	Sable, C.	(sä'b'l)	Can.	43·25 N	65·24 W
79	Sable, C.		Can.	25·12 N	81·10 W
122	Sablé-sur-Sarthe	(säb-lā-sür-särt')	Fr.	47·50 N	0·17 W
132	Sablya, Gora (Mtn.)		Sov. Un.	64·50 N	59·00 E
4	Sàbor (R.)	(sä-bōr')	Port.	41·18 N	6·54 W
73	Sac (R.)	(sôk)	Mo.	38·11 N	93·45 W
81	Sacandaga Res.	(sà-kän-dä'gà)	N. Y.	43·10 N	74·15 W
125	Sacavém	(sä-kä-vĕn')	Port. (Lisbon In.)	38·47 N	9·06 W
125	Sacavem (R.)		Port. (Lisbon In.)	38·52 N	9·06 W
71	Sac City		Iowa	42·25 N	95·00 W
120	Sachsen (Reg.)	(zäk'sĕn)	Ger.	50·45 N	12·17 E
81	Sacketts Harbor	(säk'ĕts)	N. Y.	43·55 N	76·05 W
82	Sackville	(säk'vǐl)	Can.	45·54 N	64·28 W
82	Saco	(sô'kō)	Maine	43·30 N	70·28 W
100	Saco (R.)	(sä'kō)	Braz.	22·20 S	43·26 W
82	Saco (R.)		Maine	43·53 N	70·46 W
100	Sacra Familia do Tinguá	(sä-krä fä-mä'lyä dô tēn-gwä')	Braz.	22·29 S	43·36 W
68	Sacramento	(säk-rà-mĕn'tō)	Calif.	38·35 N	121·30 W
76	Sacramento		Mex.	25·45 N	103·22 W
76	Sacramento		Mex.	27·05 N	101·45 W
68	Sacramento (R.)		Calif.	40·20 N	122·07 W
166	Sa'da Bandeira	(sä'dä bän-dā'rä)	Ang.	14·50 S	13·30 E
65	Saddle Mtn.	(săd''l)	Ore. (Portland In.)	45·58 N	123·40 W
145	Sadiya	(sŭ-dē'yä)	India	27·53 N	95·35 E
152	Sado (I.)	(sä'dō)	Jap.	38·05 N	138·26 E
124	Sado (R.)	(sä'dōō)	Port.	38·15 N	8·20 W
118	Saeby	(sĕ'bü)	Den.	57·21 N	10·29 E
153	Saeki	(sä'ä-kē)	Jap.	32·56 N	131·51 E
139	Safad	(sä'fäd)	Isr. (Palestine In.)	32·58 N	35·30 E
69	Safford	(săf'fĕrd)	Ariz.	32·50 N	109·45 W
164	Safi (Asfi)	(sä'fē) (äs'fē)	Mor.	32·24 N	9·09 W
133	Safid Rud (R.)		Iran	36·50 N	49·40 E
153	Saga	(sä'gä)	Jap.	33·15 N	130·18 E
153	Sagami-Nada (Sea)	(sä'gä'mē nä-dä)	Jap.	35·06 N	139·24 E
75	Sagamore Hills	(săg'à-môr hǐlz)	Ohio (Cleveland In.)	41·19 N	81·34 W
71	Saganaga (L.)	(sä-gà-nä'gà)	Can.-Minn.	48·13 N	91·17 W
142	Sagar		India	23·55 N	78·45 E
80	Saginaw	(săg'ǐ-nô)	Mich.	43·25 N	84·00 W
74	Saginaw		Minn. (Duluth In.)	46·51 N	92·26 W
74	Saginaw		Tex. (Dallas, Fort Worth In.)	32·52 N	97·22 W
80	Saginaw B.		Mich.	43·50 N	83·40 W
133	Sagiz (R.)	(sä'gēz)	Sov. Un.	48·30 N	56·10 E
69	Saguache	(sà-wäch') (sà-gwä'chĕ)	Colo.	38·05 N	106·10 W
69	Saguache Cr.		Colo.	38·05 N	106·40 W
95	Sagua de Tánamo	(sä-gwä dĕ tä'nä-mō)	Cuba	20·40 N	75·15 W
94	Sagua la Grande	(sä-gwä lä grä'n-dĕ)	Cuba	22·45 N	80·05 W
69	Saguaro Natl. Mon.	(säg-wä'rō)	Ariz.	32·12 N	110·40 W
87	Saguenay (R.)	(săg-ĕ-nā')	Can.	48·05 N	70·26 W
125	Sagunto	(sä-gōōn'tô)	Sp.	39·40 N	0·17 W
163	Sahara Des.	(sà-hä'rá)	Afr.	23·44 N	1·40 W
114	Saharan Atlas (Mts.)		Mor.-Alg.	32·51 N	1·02 W
142	Sahāranpur	(sü-hä'rŭn-pōōr')	India	29·58 N	77·41 E
74	Sahara Village	(sà-hä'rá)	Utah (Salt Lake City In.)	41·06 N	111·58 W
139	Saheira (R.)		U. A. R. (Palestine In.)	29·55 N	33·18 E
90	Sahuayo	(sä-wä'yō)	Mex.	20·03 N	102·43 W
164	Saïda	(sä'ê-dä)	Alg.	34·51 N	00·07 E
144	Sa'idābād	(sä'ê-dà-bät)	Iran	29·30 N	55·43 E
154	Saigon	(sä-ê-gôn') (sī-gôn')	Viet.	10·46 N	106·34 E
153	Saijō	(sä'ê-jô)	Jap.	33·55 N	133·13 E
119	Saimaa	(sä'ǐ-mä)	Fin.	61·24 N	28·45 E
90	Sain Alto	(sä-ēn' äl'tō)	Mex.	23·35 N	103·13 W
85	St. Adolphe	(sànt a'dôlf)	Can. (Winnipeg In.)	49·40 N	97·07 W
122	St. Affrique	(sän' tà-frēk')	Fr.	43·58 N	2·52 E
161	St. Albans	(sànt ôl'bànz)	Austl. (Melbourne In.)	37·44 S	144·47 E
110	St. Albans		Eng. (London In.)	51·44 N	0·20 W
81	St. Albans		Vt.	44·50 N	73·05 W
80	St. Albans		W. Va.	38·20 N	81·50 W
116	St. Albans Hd.		Eng.	50·34 N	2·00 W
85	St. Albert	(sànt ăl'bĕrt)	Can. (Edmonton In.)	53·38 N	113·38 W
122	St. Amand Montrond	(sän't à-män' môn-rôn')	Fr.	46·44 N	2·28 E
167	St. André, Cap (C.)		Malag. Rep.	16·15 S	44·31 E
78	St. Andrew, B.		Fla.	30·20 N	85·45 W
83	St. Andrew Chan.		Can.	46·06 N	60·28 W
82	St. Andrews	(ăn'drōoz)	Can.	45·05 N	67·03 W
116	St. Andrews		Scot.	56·20 N	2·40 W
85	St. Andrews East		Can. (Montreal In.)	45·33 N	74·19 W
85	Ste. Angele-de-Laval	(sànt' än-zhĕl'-dē-läväl')	Can. (Montreal In.)	45·33 N	73·42 W
85	St. Anicet	(sĕnt ä-nē-sĕ')	Can. (Montreal In.)	45·07 N	74·23 W
74	St. Ann	(sànt ăn)	Mo. (St. Louis In.)	38·44 N	90·23 W
82	Ste. Anne	(sănt' án') (sànt ăn')	Can.	46·55 N	71·46 W
85	Ste. Anne		Can. (Montreal In.)	45·24 N	73·57 W
75	Ste. Anne		Ill. (Chicago In.)	41·01 N	87·44 W
93	Ste. Anne		Grande Terre (Le. & Wind. Is. In.)	16·15 N	61·23 W
85	Ste. Anne, R.		Can. (Quebec In.)	47·07 N	70·50 W
85	Ste. Anne-de-Beaupré	(dĕ bō-prā')	Can. (Quebec In.)	47·01 N	70·56 W
82	St. Anne de la Pocatière	(dĕ là pô-kà-tyär')	Can.	47·24 N	70·01 W
85	Ste. Anne-des-Plaines		Can. (Montreal In.)	45·46 N	73·49 W
83	St. Anns B.	(ănz)	Can.	46·20 N	60·10 W
94	St. Ann's Bay		Jam.	18·25 N	77·15 W
85	St. Anselme	(săn' tăn-sĕlm')	Can. (Quebec In.)	46·37 N	70·58 W
83	St. Anthony	(săn ăn'thô-nĕ)	Can.	51·24 N	55·35 W
67	St. Anthony	(sànt ăn'thô-nĕ)	Idaho	43·59 N	111·42 W
155	St. Antonio, Mt.		Phil. (Manila In.)	13·23 N	122·00 E
85	St. Apollinaire	(săn' tà-pôl-ê-nâr')	Can. (Quebec In.)	46·36 N	71·30 W
123	St. Arnoult-en-Yvelines	(sän-tär-nōō'ĕn-nēv-lēn')	Fr. (Paris In.)	48·33 N	1·55 E
85	St. Augustin	(sànt ô'gŭs-tēn)	Can. (Montreal In.)	45·38 N	73·59 W
85	St. Augustin		Can. (Quebec In.)	46·45 N	71·27 W
79	St. Augustine	(sànt ô'gŭs-tēn)	Fla.	29·53 N	81·21 W
85	Ste. Barbe	(sànt bärb')	Can. (Montreal In.)	45·14 N	74·12 W
82	St. Barthélémy	(săn' bär-tā-lĕ-me)	Can.	46·09 N	73·10 W
93	St. Barthelemy I.		N. A. (Le. & Wind. Is. In.)	17·55 N	62·32 W
116	St. Bees Hd.	(sànt bēz' hĕd)	Eng.	54·30 N	3·40 W
85	St. Benoit	(sĕn bĕ-nōō-ä')	Can. (Montreal In.)	45·34 N	74·05 W
84	St. Bernard	(bĕr-närd')	La. (New Orleans In.)	29·52 N	89·52 W
75	St. Bernard		Ohio (Cincinnati In.)	39·10 N	84·30 W
85	St. Boniface	(bŏn'ĭ fàs)	Can. (Winnipeg In.)	49·53 N	97·06 W
116	St. Brides B.	(sànt brīdz')	Wales	51·17 N	4·45 W
122	St. Brieuc	(săn' brēs')	Fr.	48·32 N	2·47 E
85	St. Bruno	(brü'nō)	Can. (Montreal In.)	45·31 N	73·20 W
85	St. Canut	(săn' kà-nü')	Can. (Montreal In.)	45·43 N	74·04 W
82	St. Casimir	(kà-zē-mēr')	Can.	46·45 N	72·34 W
85	St. Catharines	(kăth'à-rǐnz)	Can. (Toronto In.)	43·10 N	79·14 W
93	St. Catherine, Mt.		Grenada (Le. & Wind. Is. In.)	12·10 N	62·42 W
122	St. Chamas	(săn-shä-mä')	Fr. (Marseille In.)	43·32 N	5·03 E
122	St. Chamond	(săn' shà-môn')	Fr.	45·30 N	4·17 E
85	St. Charles	(săn' shärlz')	Can. (Quebec In.)	46·47 N	70·57 W
75	St. Charles	(sànt chärlz')	Ill. (Chicago In.)	41·55 N	88·19 W
80	St. Charles		Mich.	43·20 N	84·10 W
71	St. Charles		Minn.	43·56 N	92·05 W
74	St. Charles		Mo. (St. Louis In.)	38·47 N	90·29 W
80	St. Clair	(sànt klâr)	Mich.	42·55 N	82·30 W
80	St. Clair (L.)		Mich.-Can.	42·25 N	82·30 W
80	St. Clair (R.)		Mich.-Can.	42·45 N	82·25 W
85	Ste. Claire		Can. (Quebec In.)	46·36 N	70·52 W
75	St. Clair Shores		Mich. (Detroit In.)	42·30 N	82·54 W
123	St. Claude	(săn' klôd')	Fr.	46·24 N	5·53 E
85	St. Clet	(sănt' klä')	Can. (Montreal In.)	45·22 N	74·21 W
79	St. Cloud	(sànt kloud')	Fla. (In.)	28·13 N	81·17 W
71	St. Cloud		Minn.	45·33 N	94·08 W
85	St. Constant	(kŏn'stănt)	Can. (Montreal In.)	45·22 N	73·35 W
167	St. Croix (I.)	(săn krwä)	S. Afr. (Natal In.)	33·48 S	25·45 E
89	Saint Croix (I.)	(săn kroi')	Vir. Is. (U. S. A.) (Puerto Rico In.)	17·40 N	64·43 W
82	St. Croix (R.)	(kroi')	Can.	45·17 N	67·32 W
71	St. Croix Ind. Res.		Wis.	45·40 N	92·21 W
71	St. Croix R.	(sànt kroi')	Minn.-Wis.	45·00 N	92·44 W
85	St. Damien	(sànt dā'mē-ĕn)	Can. (Quebec In.)	46·37 N	70·39 W
85	St. David	(dā'vǐd)	Can. (Quebec In.)	46·47 N	71·11 W
116	St. David's Hd.		Wales	51·54 N	5·25 W
123	St.-Denis	(săn'dē-nē')	Fr. (Paris In.)	48·26 N	2·22 E
123	St. Dié	(dê-ā')	Fr.	48·18 N	6·55 E
122	St. Dizier	(dê-zyä')	Fr.	48·49 N	4·55 E
85	St. Dominique		Can. (Montreal In.)	45·19 N	74·09 W
85	St. Edouard	(sĕn-tĕ-dōō-är')	Can. (Montreal In.)	45·14 N	73·31 W
64	St. Elias, Mt.	(sànt ê-lī'ăs)	Can.	60·25 N	141·00 W
85	St. Elzear	(sĕn-tĕl-zê-är')	Can. (Montreal In.)	45·36 N	73·44 W
85	St. Etienne	(săn' tā-tyĕn')	Can. (Montreal In.)	45·15 N	73·55 W
85	St. Etienne		Can. (Quebec In.)	46·39 N	71·19 W
122	St. Étienne		Fr.	45·26 N	4·22 E
85	Ste. Euphémie	(sĕnt û-fĕ-mē')	Can. (Quebec In.)	46·47 N	70·27 W
85	St. Eustache	(săn' tû-stäsh')	Can. (Montreal In.)	45·34 N	73·54 W
85	St. Eustache		Can. (Winnipeg In.)	49·58 N	97·47 W
85	St. Eustache sur le Lac	(sĕn tû-stäsh' sür lĕ läk)	Can. (Montreal In.)	45·33 N	73·54 W
93	St. Eustatius I.	(sànt u-stä'shŭs)	N. A. (Le. & Wind. Is. In.)	17·32 N	62·45 W
85	Ste. Famille	(sănt' fà-mē'y)	Can. (Quebec In.)	46·58 N	70·58 W
82	St. Félicien	(săn fä-lê-syăn')	Can.	48·39 N	72·30 W
82	Ste. Felicite		Can.	48·54 N	67·22 W
85	St. Féréol	(fa-rä-ôl')	Can. (Quebec In.)	47·07 N	70·52 W
126	St. Florent, Golfe de (G.)		Cor.	42·55 N	9·08 E
122	St. Florent-sur-Cher	(săn' flô-rän'sür-shär')	Fr.	45·02 N	2·15 E
122	St. Flour	(săn floor')	Fr.	45·02 N	3·09 E
85	Ste. Foy	(sànt fwä)	Can. (Quebec In.)	46·45 N	71·20 W
73	St. Francis (R.)	(sànt frän'sǐs)	Ark.	35·56 N	90·27 W
82	St. Francis (R.)	(frän'sǐs)	Can.	45·55 N	72·25 W
81	St. Francis L.	(săn frän'sǐs)	Can.	45·00 N	74·20 W
85	St. François	(săn'frän-swä')	Can. (Quebec In.)	47·01 N	70·49 W
122	St. Gaudens	(gō-däns')	Fr.	43·07 N	0·43 E
73	Ste. Genevieve	(sànt jĕn'ĕ-vēv)	Mo.	37·58 N	90·02 W
160	St. George	(sànt jôrj')	Austl.	28·02 S	148·40 E
82	St. George	(săn jôrj')	Can.	45·08 N	66·49 W
85	St. George	(zhôrzh')	Can. (Toronto In.)	43·14 N	80·15 W
79	St. George	(sànt jôrj')	S. C.	33·11 N	80·35 W
69	St. George		Utah	37·05 N	113·40 W
64	St. George (I.)		Alaska	56 30 N	169·40 W
83	St. George, C.		Can.	48·28 N	59·24 W
78	St. George, C.		Fla.	29·30 N	85·20 W
82	St. Georges	(jôrj'ĕs)	Can.	46·09 N	70·42 W
83	St. George's		Can.	48·29 N	58·26 W
99	St.-Georges		Fr. Gu.	3·48 N	51·47 W
93	St. Georges		Grenada (Le. & Wind. Is. In.)	12·02 N	61·57 W
83	St. George's B.		Can.	48·28 N	59·00 W
116	St. George's Chan.	(jôr-jĕz)	Eng.-Ire.	51·45 N	6·30 W
123	St. Germain-en-Laye	(săn' zhĕr-măn-än-lā')	Fr. (Paris In.)	48·53 N	2·05 E
85	St. Gervais	(zhĕr-vĕ')	Can. (Quebec In.)	46·43 N	70·53 W
122	St. Girons	(zhē-rôn')	Fr.	42·58 N	1·08 E
120	St. Gotthard Tun.	(sànt gôthärd') (săn gô-tär')	Switz.	46·38 N	8·55 E

ng-sing; ŋ-baŋk; N-nasalized n; nŏd; cŏmmit; ōld; ôbey; ôrder; fōōd; fŏŏt; ou-out; s-soft; sh-dish; th-thin; pūre; ûnite; ûrn; stŭd; circŭs; û-as "y" in study; '-indeterminate vowel.

ăt; finäl; rāte; senâte; ârm; àsk; sofá; fâre; ch-choose; dh-as in other; bē; ěvent; bět; recěnt; cratẽr; g-go; gh-guttural g; bĭt; ɨ-short neutral; rīde; ĸ-guttural k as ch in German ich;

PRONOUNCING INDEX

Salamat–Sand Springs 261

Page	Name Pronunciation Region	Lat. °′	Long. °′
165	Salamat, Bahr (R.) (bär sä-lä-mät') . Chad.	10·06 N	19·16 E
155	Salamaua (sä-lä-mä'wä) N. Gui. Ter.	6·50 S	146·55 E
98	Salamina (sä-lä-mē'-nä) . Col. (In.)	5·25 N	75·29 W
127	Salamis (săl'á-mĭs) Grc.	37·58 N	23·30 E
98	Salaverry (sä-lä-vä'rē) Peru	8·16 S	78·54 W
155	Salawati (I.) (sä-lä-wä'tē) W. Irian	1·22 S	130·15 E
157	Sala-y-Gómez (I.) Chile	26·50 S	105·50 W
95	Salcedo (säl-sā'dō) Dom. Rep.	19·25 N	70·30 W
98	Saldaña (R.) (säl-dá'n-yä) Col. (In.)	3·42 N	75·16 W
166	Saldanha S. Afr.	32·55 S	18·05 E
119	Saldus (sál'dŏŏs) Sov. Un.	56·39 N	22·30 E
160	Sale (sāl) Austl.	38·10 S	147·07 E
110	Sale Eng.	53·24 N	2·20 W
164	Salé (sá-lā') Mor.	34·09 N	6·42 W
85	Sale, Riviére (R.) (sál'rē-vyâr') Can. (Winnipeg In.)	49·44 N	97·11 W
132	Salekhard (sŭ-lyĭ-kärt) Sov. Un.	66·35 N	66·50 E
80	Salem (sā'lĕm) Ill.	38·40 N	89·00 W
143	Salem India	11·39 N	78·11 E
80	Salem Ind.	38·35 N	86·00 W
83	Salem Mass. (Boston In.)	42·31 N	70·54 W
73	Salem Mo.	37·36 N	91·33 W
83	Salem N. H. (Boston In.)	42·46 N	71·16 W
81	Salem N. J.	39·35 N	75·30 W
80	Salem Ohio	40·55 N	80·50 W
66	Salem Ore.	44·55 N	123·03 W
70	Salem S. D.	43·43 N	97·23 W
167	Salem S. Afr. (Natal In.)	33·29 S	26·30 E
79	Salem Va.	37·16 N	80·05 W
80	Salem W. Va.	39·15 N	80·35 W
126	Salemi (sä-lå'mē) It.	37·48 N	38·50 E
125	Salerno (sä-lĕr'nô) It. (Naples In.)	40·27 N	14·46 E
126	Salerno, Golfo di (G.) (gôl-fô-dē) It.	40·30 N	14·40 E
110	Salford (săl'fērd) Eng.	53·26 N	2·19 W
129	Salgir (R.) (sal'gēr) Sov. Un.	45·25 N	34·22 E
121	Salgótarján (shôl'gô-tôr-yän) Hung.	48·06 N	19·50 E
72	Salida (sá-lī'dá) Colo.	38·31 N	106·01 W
122	Salies (sá-lēs') Fr.	43·27 N	0·58 W
73	Salina (sá-lī'ná) Kans.	38·50 N	97·37 W
69	Salina Utah	39·00 N	111·55 W
126	Salina (I.) (sä-lē'nä) It.	38·35 N	14·48 E
95	Salina Pt. Ba. Is.	22·10 N	74·20 W
91	Salina Cruz (sä-lē'nä krōōz') Mex.	16·10 N	95·12 W
68	Salinas (sá-lē'nás) Calif.	36·41 N	121·40 W
90	Salinas Mex.	22·38 N	101·42 W
89	Salinas P. R. (Puerto Rico In.)	17·58 N	66·16 W
68	Salinas (R.) Calif.	36·33 N	121·29 W
91	Salinas (R.) (sä-lē'näs) Mex.	16·15 N	90·31 W
92	Salinas, Bahia de (B.) (bä-ē'ä-dĕ-sá-lē'nás) Nic.-C. R.	11·05 N	85·55 W
125	Salinas, Cape (sä-lĕnäs) Sp.	39·14 N	1·02 E
76	Salinas Victoria (sä-lē'näs vĕk-tō'rē-ä) Mex.	25·59 N	100·19 W
73	Saline (R.) (sá-lēn') Ark.	34·06 N	92·30 W
72	Saline (R.) Kans.	39·05 N	99·43 W
123	Salins-les-Bains (sä-lăN'-lā-băN') Fr.	46·55 N	5·54 E
166	Salisbury Rh.	17·49 S	30·52 E
116	Salisbury (sôlz'bē-rē) Eng.	50·35 N	1·51 W
82	Salisbury Can.	46·03 N	65·05 W
81	Salisbury Md.	38·20 N	75·40 W
73	Salisbury Mo.	39·24 N	92·47 W
79	Salisbury N. C.	35·40 N	80·29 W
87	Salisbury (I.) Can.	63·36 N	76·20 W
116	Salisbury Plain Eng.	51·15 N	1·52 W
164	Sal I. (säal) C. V. Is. (In.)	16·45 N	22·39 W
79	Salkehatchie (R.) (sô-kē-hăch'ē) S. C.	33·09 N	81·10 W
73	Sallisaw (săl'ĭ-sô) Okla.	35·27 N	94·48 W
67	Salmon (săm'ŭn) Idaho	45·11 N	113·54 W
66	Salmon Falls R. Idaho	42·22 N	114·53 W
158	Salmon Gums (gŭmz) Austl.	33·00 S	122·00 E
82	Salmon (R.) Can.	46·19 N	65·36 W
81	Salmon (R.) N. Y.	44·35 N	74·15 W
65	Salmon (R.) Wash. (Portland In.)	45·44 N	122·36 W
66	Salmon R. Idaho	45·30 N	115·45 W
66	Salmon R., Middle Fork Idaho	44·54 N	114·50 W
66	Salmon R., South Fork Idaho	44·51 N	115·47 W
66	Salmon River Mts. Idaho	44·15 N	115·44 W
123	Salon-de-Provence (sá-lôN-dē-prô-văNs') Fr.	43·48 N	5·09 E
121	Salonta (sä-lôn'tä) Rom.	46·46 N	21·38 E
133	Sal'sk (sälsk) Sov. Un.	46·30 N	41·20 E
69	Salt, (R.) (sôlt) Ariz.	33·28 N	111·35 W
73	Salt (R.) Mo.	39·54 N	92·11 W
100	Salta (säl'tä) Arg.	24·50 S	65·16 W
100	Salta (Prov.) Arg.	25·15 S	65·00 W
74	Saltair (sôlt'âr) Utah (Salt Lake City In.)	40·46 N	112·09 W
95	Salt Cay (I.) Turks & Caicos Is.	21·20 N	71·15 W
75	Salt Cr. (sôlt) Ill. (Chicago In.)	42·01 N	88·01 W
76	Saltillo (säl-tēl'yō) Mex.	25·24 N	100·59 W
74	Salt Lake City (sôlt lāk sĭ'tĭ) Utah (Salt Lake City In.)	40·45 N	111·52 W
101	Salto (säl'tō) Arg. (Buenos Aires In.)	34·17 S	60·15 W
100	Salto Ur.	31·18 S	57·45 W
101	Salto, Serra do (Mtn.) (sě'r-rä-dô) Braz. (Rio de Janeiro In.)	20·26 S	43·28 W
90	Salto (R.) Mex.	22·16 N	99·18 W
99	Salto Grande (grän'dä) Braz.	22·57 S	49·58 W
68	Salton Sea (sôlt'ŭn) Calif.	33·28 N	115·43 W
164	Saltpond Ghana	5·16 N	1·07 W
69	Salt River Ind. Res. (sôlt rĭv'ēr) Ariz.	33·40 N	112·01 W
95	Saltrou (sál-trōō') Hai.	18·15 N	72·00 W
118	Saltsjöbaden (sält'shû-bäd'ĕn) Swe.	59·15 N	18·20 E
79	Saltville (sôlt'vĭl) Va.	36·50 N	81·45 W

Page	Name Pronunciation Region	Lat. °′	Long. °′
136	Saltykovka (sál-tē'kôf-ká) Sov. Un. (Moscow In.)	55·45 N	37·56 E
88	Salud, Mt. (sä-lōō'th) Pan. (Panama Canal In.)	9·14 N	79·42 W
79	Saluda (sá-lōō'dá) S. C.	34·02 N	81·46 W
79	Saluda (R.) S. C.	34·07 N	81·48 W
126	Saluzzo (sä-lōōt'sō) It.	44·39 N	7·31 E
99	Salvador (Bahia) (säl-vä-dōr') (bä-ē'ä) Braz.	12·59 S	38·27 W
77	Salvador L. La.	29·45 N	90·20 W
94	Salvador Pt. Ba. Is.	24·30 N	77·45 W
90	Salvatierra (säl-vä-tyĕr'rä) Mex.	20·13 N	100·52 W
146	Salween R. (săl-wēn') Bur.	26·46 N	98·19 E
133	Sal'yany Sov. Un.	39·40 N	49·10 E
120	Salzburg (sälts'bŏŏrgh) Aus.	47·48 N	13·04 E
120	Salzburg (State) Aus.	47·30 N	13·18 E
120	Salzwedel (sälts-vā'dĕl) Ger.	52·51 N	11·10 E
168	Samālūt (sá-má-lōōt') U. A. R. (Nile In.)	28·17 N	30·43 E
95	Samaná (sä-mä-nä') Dom. Rep.	19·15 N	69·25 W
95	Samana, Cabo (C.) (ká'bô) Dom. Rep.	19·20 N	69·00 W
95	Samana or Atwood Cay (I.) Ba. Is.	23·05 N	73·45 W
155	Samar (I.) (sä'mär) Phil.	11·30 N	126·07 E
133	Samara (R.) Sov. Un.	52·50 N	50·35 E
129	Samara (R.) (sá-mä'rá) Sov. Un.	48·47 N	35·30 E
155	Samarai (sä-mä-rä'ē) Pap.	10·45 S	150·49 E
134	Samarkand (sá-már-känt') Sov. Un.	39·42 N	67·00 E
142	Sambalpur (sŭm'bŭl-pŏŏr) India	21·30 N	84·05 E
142	Sāmbhar (R.) India	27·00 N	74·58 E
121	Sambor (säm'bôr) Sov. Un.	49·31 N	23·12 E
101	Samborombón, Bahia (B.) (bä-ē'ä-säm-bô-rôm-bô'n) Arg. (Buenos Aires In.)	35·57 S	57·05 W
101	Samborombón (R.) Arg. (Buenos Aires In.)	35·20 S	57·52 W
117	Sambre (R.) (säNbr') Bel.	50·20 N	4·15 E
65	Sammamish, L. (sá-măm'ĭsh) Wash. (Seattle In.)	47·35 N	122·02 W
65	Sammamish (R.) Wash. (Seattle In.)	47·43 N	122·08 W
127	Samokov (sä'mô-kôf) Bul.	42·20 N	23·33 E
125	Samora Correia (sä-mô'rá-kôr-rě'yä) Port. (Lisbon In.)	38·55 N	8·52 W
134	Samorovo (sá-mä-rô'vô) Sov. Un.	60·47 N	69·13 E
127	Sámos (I.) (să'mŏs) Grc.	37·53 N	26·35 E
127	Samothráki (I.) Grc.	40·23 N	25·10 E
155	Sampaloc Pt. (säm-pä'lôk) Phil. (Manila In.)	14·43 N	119·56 E
118	Samsø (I.) (säm'sû) Den.	55·49 N	10·47 E
78	Samson (săm'sŭn) Ala.	31·06 N	86·02 W
152	Samsu (säm'sōō') Kor.	41·12 N	128·00 E
133	Samsun (sàm'sōōn') Tur.	41·20 N	36·05 E
133	Samtredia (sám'trě-dē-á) Sov. Un.	42·18 N	42·25 E
65	Samuel (I.) (sám'ū-ĕl) Can. (Vancouver In.)	48·50 N	123·10 W
133	Samur (R.) (sá-mōōr') Sov. Un.	41·40 N	47·20 E
164	San (sän) Mali	13·37 N	4·45 W
144	San'a (sän'ä) Yemen	15·45 N	44·00 E
164	Sanaga R. (sä-nä'gä) Cam.	4·33 N	11·50 E
96	San Ambrosio, Isla de (I.) (ē's-lä-dĕ-sän äm-brō'zē-ō) Chile	26·40 S	80·00 W
155	Sanana (I.) Indon.	2·15 S	126·38 E
144	Sanandaj Iran	36·44 N	46·43 E
68	San Andreas (săn ăn'drē-ăs) Calif.	38·10 N	120·42 W
65	San Andreas (L.) Calif. (San Francisco In.)	37·36 N	122·26 W
98	San Andrés (sän-än-drě's) Col. (In.)	6·57 N	75·41 W
91	San Andrés (sän än-dräs') Mex. (Mexico City In.)	19·15 N	99·10 W
91	San Andres, Laguna de (L.) Mex.	22·40 N	97·50 W
62	San Andres, Mts. (săn ăn'drē-ăs) U. S.	33·00 N	106·40 W
	San Andrés, see Petén, Laguna de		
101	San Andrés de Giles (sän-än-drě's-dě-gē'lěs) Arg. (Buenos Aires In.)	34·26 S	59·28 W
93	San Andres I. Col.	12·32 N	81·34 W
69	San Andres Mts. N. Mex.	23·45 N	106·40 W
91	San Andrés Tuxtla (sän-än-drā's-tōōs'tlä) Mex.	18·27 N	95·12 W
76	San Angelo (săn ăn'jĕ-lō) Tex.	31·28 N	100·22 W
126	San Antioco, I. di (ē'sō-lä-dē-sän-än-tyŏ'kō) It.	39·00 N	8·25 E
101	San Antonio (sän-än-tô'nyō) Chile (Santiago In.)	33·34 S	71·36 W
98	San Antonio Col. (In.)	2·57 N	75·06 W
98	San Antonio Col. (In.)	3·55 N	75·38 W
155	San Antonio Phil. (Manila In.)	14·57 N	120·05 E
74	San Antonio (săn ăn-tō'nē-ō) Tex. (San Antonio In.)	29·25 N	98·30 W
68	San Antonio (R.) Calif.	36·00 N	121·13 W
94	San Antonio, Cabo (C.) (kä'bô-sän-än-tô'nyō) Cuba	21·55 N	84·55 W
125	San Antonio Abad (sän än-tô'nyō ä-bädh') Sp.	38·59 N	1·17 E
77	San Antonio B. Tex.	28·20 N	97·08 W
101	San Antonio de Areco (dā ä-rā'kô) Arg. (Buenos Aires In.)	34·16 S	59·30 W
95	San Antonio de las Vegas (sän än-tô-nyō-dĕ-läs-vě'gäs) Cuba (Havana In.)	22·07 N	82·16 W
95	San Antonio de los Baños (dā lōs bän'yōs) Cuba (Havana In.)	22·08 N	82·30 W
100	San Antonio de los Cobres (dā lōs kō'bräs) Arg.	24·15 S	66·29 W
101	San Antônio de Pádua (dĕ-pá'dwä) Braz. (Rio de Janeiro In.)	21·32 S	42·09 W
99	San Antonio de Tamanaco (sän-än-tô-nyō-dĕ-tá-mä-nä'kō) Ven. (In.)	9·42 N	66·03 W

Page	Name Pronunciation Region	Lat. °′	Long. °′
100	San Antonio Oeste (sän-än-tō'nyō ô-ĕs'tä) Arg.	40·49 S	64·56 W
74	San Antonio Pk. (săn ăn-tō'nĭ-ô) Calif. (Los Angeles In.)	34·17 N	117·39 W
76	San Antonio R. Tex.	29·00 N	97·58 W
92	Sanarate (sä-nä-rä'tě) Guat.	14·47 N	90·12 W
77	San Augustine (săn ô'gŭs-tēn) Tex.	31·33 N	94·08 W
76	San Bartolo Mex.	24·43 N	103·12 W
91	San Bartolo (sän bär-tō'lô) Mex. (Mexico City In.)	19·36 N	99·43 W
126	San Bartolomeo (bär-tô-lô-mä'ô) It.	41·25 N	15·04 E
126	San Benedetto del Tronto (bā'nā-dět'tô děl trōn'tô) It.	42·58 N	13·54 E
77	San Benito (săn bě-nē'tô) Tex.	26·07 N	97·37 W
68	San Benito (R.) Calif.	36·40 N	121·20 W
74	San Bernardino (bûr-när-dē'nô) Calif. (Los Angeles In.)	34·07 N	117·19 W
68	San Bernardino Mts. Calif.	34·05 N	116·23 W
101	San Bernardo (sän běr-när'dô) Chile (Santiago In.)	33·35 S	70·42 W
90	San Blas (sän bläs') Mex.	21·33 N	105·19 W
78	San Blas, C. Fla.	29·38 N	85·38 W
93	San Blas, Cord. de (Mts.) (kôr-dĕl-yĕ'rä-dĕ) Pan.	9·17 N	78·20 W
93	San Blas, Golfo de (G.) Pan.	9·33 N	78·42 W
93	San Blas, Punta (Pt.) Pan.	9·35 N	78·55 W
65	San Bruno (sän brū-nô) Calif. (San Francisco In.)	37·38 N	122·25 W
76	San Buenaventura (bwā'nä-věn-tōō'rä) Mex.	27·07 N	101·30 W
65	San Carlos (săn kär'lŏs) Calif. (San Francisco In.)	37·30 N	122·15 W
100	San Carlos (sän-kä'r-lŏs) Chile	36·23 S	71·58 W
98	San Carlos Col. (In.)	6·11 N	74·58 W
91	San Carlos (sän kär'lōs) Mex.	17·49 N	92·33 W
76	San Carlos Mex.	24·36 N	98·52 W
93	San Carlos (sän-kä'r-lōs) Nic.	11·08 N	84·48 W
155	San Carlos Phil. (Manila In.)	15·56 N	120·20 E
98	San Carlos Ven.	9·36 N	68·35 W
100	San Carlos de Bariloche (sän-ká'r lŏs-dě-bä-rē-lô'chě) Arg.	41·15 S	71·26 W
69	San Carlos Ind. Res. (săn kär'lōs) Ariz.	33·27 N	110·15 W
69	San Carlos Res. Ariz.	33·05 N	110·29 W
93	San Carlos R. C. R.	10·36 N	84·18 W
99	San Casimiro (kä-sē-mē'rô) Ven. (In.)	10·01 N	67·02 W
126	San Cataldo (kä-täl'dō) It.	37·30 N	13·59 E
95	Sanchez (sän'chěz) Dom. Rep.	19·15 N	69·40 W
90	Sanchez, Río de los (R.) (rē'ō-dě-lôs) Mex.	20·31 N	102·29 W
90	Sánchez Román (Tlaltenango) (rô-mà'n) (tlä'l-tě-nän-gô) Mex.	21·48 N	103·20 W
124	San Clemente (sän klä-měn'tā) Sp.	39·25 N	2·24 W
68	San Clemente (I.) Calif.	33·02 N	118·36 W
95	San Cristobal (krēs-tô'bäl) Dom. Rep.	18·25 N	70·05 W
92	San Cristóbal Guat.	15·22 N	90·26 W
98	San Cristóbal Ven.	7·43 N	72·15 W
98	San Cristobal (I.) Ec.	1·05 S	89·15 W
159	San Cristobal (I.) Sol. Is.	10·47 S	162·17 E
126	San Croce, C. (krô'chā) It.	37·15 N	15·18 E
94	Sancti Spíritus (säŋk'tē spē'rē-tōōs) Cuba	21·55 N	79·25 W
122	Sancy, Puy de (Pk.) (pwē-dě-säN-sē') Fr.	45·30 N	2·53 E
65	Sand (I.) (sănd) Ore. (Portland In.)	46·16 N	124·01 W
71	Sand (I.) Wis.	46·03 N	91·09 W
168	Sand (R.) S. Afr. (Johannesburg & Pretoria In.)	28·09 S	26·46 E
153	Sanda (sän'dä) Jap. (Ōsaka In.)	34·53 N	135·14 E
154	Sandakan (sán-dä'kän) Mala.	5·51 N	118·03 E
116	Sanday (I.) (sănd'ā) Scot.	59·17 N	2·25 W
110	Sandbach (sănd'băch) Scot.	53·08 N	2·22 W
118	Sandefjord (sän'dě-fyôr') Nor.	59·09 N	10·14 E
65	San de Fuca (de-fōō-cä) Wash. (Seattle In.)	48·14 N	122·44 W
76	Sanderson (săn'dēr-sŭn) Tex.	30·09 N	102·24 W
78	Sandersville (săn'dērz-vĭl) Ga.	32·57 N	82·50 W
167	Sandflats (sănd-fläts) S. Afr. (Natal In.)	33·26 S	25·57 E
118	Sandhammar, C. (sänt'häm-mår) Swe.	55·24 N	14·37 E
70	Sand Hills (Reg.) (sănd) Nebr.	41·57 N	101·29 W
84	Sand Hook (sănd hŏŏk) N. J. (New York In.)	40·29 N	74·05 W
110	Sandhurst (sănd'hûrst) Eng. (London In.)	51·20 N	0·48 W
68	San Diego (săn dē-ā'gô) Calif. (San Diego In.)	32·43 N	117·10 W
76	San Diego Tex.	27·47 N	98·13 W
68	San Diego (R.) Calif.	32·53 N	116·57 W
90	San Diego de la Unión (sän dē-ā'gô dā lä ōō-nyōn') Mex.	21·27 N	100·52 W
77	Sandies Cr. (sănd'ēz) Tex.	29·13 N	97·34 W
74	San Dimas (săn dě'màs) Calif. (Los Angeles In.)	34·07 N	117·49 W
90	San Dimas (dē-mäs') Mex.	24·08 N	105·57 W
118	Sandnes (sänd'něs) Nor.	58·52 N	5·44 E
166	Sandoa (sän-dō'á) Con. K.	9·39 S	23·00 E
121	Sandomierz (sán-dô'myězh) Pol.	50·39 N	21·45 E
126	San Donà di Piave (sän dô-nä' dē pyä'vě) It.	45·38 N	12·34 E
146	Sandoway (sän-dô-wī') Bur.	18·24 N	94·28 E
66	Sandpoint (sănd point) Idaho	48·17 N	116·34 W
161	Sandringham (săn'drĭng-ăm) Austl. (Melbourne In.)	37·57 S	145·01 E
126	Sandrio (sä'n-dryô) It.	46·11 N	9·53 E
73	Sand Springs (sănd sprĭnz) Okla.	36·08 N	96·06 W

ng-sing; ŋ-baŋk; N-nasalized n; nŏd; cŏmmit; ōld; ôbey; ôrder; fōōd; fŏŏt; ou-out; s-soft; sh-dish; th-thin; pūre; ûnite; ûrn; stŭd; circŭs; ü-as "y" in study; '-indeterminate vowel.

ăt; fĭnăl; rāte; senăte; ârm; àsk; sofà; fâre; ch-choose; dh-as th in other; bē; êvent; bĕt; recĕnt; cratēr; g-go; gh-guttural g; bĭt; ɪ-short neutral; rīde; ᴋ-guttural k as ch in German ich;

PRONOUNCING INDEX San Miguel el Alto–Santiago del Estero 263

Page	Name Pronunciation Region	Lat. °′	Long. °′
90	San Miguel el Alto (ĕl äl′tô) . Mex.	21·03 N	102·26 W
168	Sanmur, Wadi (Val.) U. A. R. (Nile In.)	28·48 N	31·12 E
155	San Narcisco . . . Phil. (Manila In.)	15·01 N	120·05 E
155	San Narciso (sän när-sē′sô) Phil. (Manila In.)	13·34 N	123·33 E
101	San Nicolás (sän nē-kô-lá′s) Arg. (Buenos Aires In.)	33·20 S	60·14 W
155	San Nicolas (nê-kô-läs′) Phil. (Manila In.)	16·05 N	120·45 E
68	San Nicolas (I.) (săn nĭ′kô-lȧ) Calif.	33·14 N	119·10 W
90	San Nicolás (R.) . . . . Mex.	19·40 N	105·08 W
121	Sanok (sä′nôk) . . . . Pol.	49·31 N	22·13 E
65	San Pablo (săn păb′lô) Calif. (San Francisco In.)	37·58 N	122·21 W
155	San Pablo (sän-pä-blô) Phil. (Manila In.)	14·05 N	121·20 E
155	San Pablo . . . . . Phil. (Manila In.)	17·29 N	121·49 E
99	San Pablo (sän-pȧ′blô) . Ven. (In.)	9·46 N	65·04 W
65	San Pablo B. (săn păb′lô) Calif (San Francisco In .)	38·04 N	122·25 W
65	San Pablo Res. Calif. (San Francisco In.)	37·55 N	122·12 W
93	San Pablo R. (sän päb′lô) . . . . Pan.	8·12 N	81·12 W
155	San Pascual (päs-kwäl′) Phil. (Manila In.)	13·08 N	122·59 E
100	San Pedro (sän pā′drô) . . . . . . Arg.	24·15 S	64·51 W
101	San Pedro . Arg. (Buenos Aires In.)	33·41 S	59·42 W
74	San Pedro (săn pē′drô) Calif. (Los Angeles In.)	33·44 N	118·17 W
101	San Pedro (sän pĕ′drô) Chile (Santiago In.)	33·54 S	71·27 W
91	San Pedro (sän pā′drô) . . . . . . Mex.	18·38 N	92·25 W
100	San Pedro (sän-pĕ′drô) . . . . . . Par.	24·13 S	57·00 W
92	San Pedro (sän pā′drô) . . . . Sal.	13·49 N	88·58 W
	San Pedro, see Amusgos		
	San Pedro, see Pochutla		
69	San Pedro (R.) . . . . Ariz.	32·48 N	110·37 W
94	San Pedro (R.) (sän-pĕ′drô) . Cuba	21·05 N	78·15 W
91	San Pedro, Rio de (R.) (rê′ō-dĕ-sän-pĕ′drô) . Mex.	18·23 N	92·13 W
90	San Pedro, Río de (R.) . . . . . . Mex.	21·51 N	102·24 W
90	San Pedro (R.) (sän pā′drô) . Mex.	22·08 N	104·59 W
74	San Pedro B. (săn pē′drô) Calif. (Los Angeles In.)	33·42 N	118·12 W
76	San Pedro de las Colonias (dĕ-läs-kô-lô′nyäs) . Mex.	25·47 N	102·58 W
95	San Pedro de Macorís (sän-pĕ′drō-dȧ mä-kô-rēs′) Dom. Rep.	18·30 N	69·30 W
90	San Pedro Lagunillas (sän pā′drô lä-gōō-nēl′yäs) . Mex.	21·12 N	104·47 W
92	San Pedro R. (sän pā′drô) Guat. (Yucatan In.)	17·11 N	90·23 W
76	San Pedro R . . . . Mex.	27·56 N	105·50 W
92	San Pedro Sula (sän pā′drô sōō′lä) Hond.	15·29 N	88·01 W
	San Pedro y San Pablo, see Teposcolula		
126	San Pietro, I. di (ê′sō-lä-dē-sän pyā′trô) . It.	39·09 N	8·15 E
65	San Quentin (săn kwĕn-tēn′) Calif. (San Francisco In.)	37·57 N	122·29 W
155	San Quintin (sän kēn-tēn′) Phil. (Manila In.)	15·59 N	120·47 E
100	San Rafael (sän rä-fä-āl′) . . . . Arg.	34 30 S	68·13 W
65	San Rafael (săn rȧ-fĕl) Calif. (San Francisco In.)	37·58 N	122·31 W
98	San Rafael (sän-rä-fȧ-ĕ′l) Col. (In.)	6·18 N	75·02 W
69	San Rafael (R.) (săn rȧ-fĕl′) Utah	39·05 N	110·50 W
95	San Rafael, Cabo (C.) (kȧ′bô) Dom. Rep.	19·00 N	68·50 W
65	San Ramon (săn rä-mōn′) Calif. (San Francisco In.)	37·47 N	122·59 W
93	San Ramōn . . . . C. R.	10·07 N	84·30 W
126	San Remo (sän rā′mô) . . . . It.	43·48 N	7·46 E
121	San R . . . . Pol.	50·33 N	22·12 E
89	San Roman, C. (sän-rô-mă′n) Ven.	12·00 N	69·45 W
98	San Roque (sän-rô′kĕ) . . Col. (In.)	6·29 N	75·00 W
124	San Roque . . . . Sp.	36·13 N	5·23 W
76	San Saba (săn sä′bȧ) . . . . Tex.	31·12 N	98·43 W
76	San Saba R . . . . Tex.	30·58 N	99·12 W
92	San Salvador (sän säl-vä-dōr′) . Sal.	13·45 N	89·11 W
98	San Salvador (I.) . . . . Ec.	0·14 S	90·50 W
95	San Salvador (Watling) (I.) (săn săl′vȧ-dôr) . Ba. Is.	24·05 N	74·30 W
101	San Salvador (R.) (sän-säl-vä-dô′r) Ur. (Buenos Aires In.)	33·42 S	58·04 W
164	Sansanné-Mango (sän-sȧ-nā′ mäɴ′gô) . Togo	10·31 N	0·23 E
164	San Sebastian (sän sȧ-bäs-tyän′) Can. Is.	28·09 N	17·11 W
124	San Sebastian . . . . Sp.	43·19 N	1·59 W
99	San Sebastián (sän-sĕ-bäs-tyȧ′n) Ven. (In.)	9·58 N	67·11 W
125	San Sebastián de los Reyes (sän sā-bäs-tyän′dȧ lōs rā′yĕs) Sp. (Madrid In.)	40·33 N	3·38 W
126	San Severo (sän sĕ-vâ′rō) . . . . . . It.	41·43 N	15·24 E
150	San She (Mtn.) . . . . China	33·00 N	103·50 E
147	San Shui . . . . China	23·14 N	112·51 E
69	San Simon (R.) (săn sī-mōn′) Ariz.	32·45 N	109·30 W
74	Santa Ana (săn′tȧ ăn′ȧ) Calif. (Los Angeles In.)	33·45 N	117·52 W
90	Santa Ana (sän′tä ä′nä) . . . . . Mex.	19·18 N	98·10 W
92	Santa Ana . . . . Sal.	14·02 N	89·35 W
74	Santa Ana Mts. Calif. (Los Angeles In.)	33·44 N	117·36 W
74	Santa Ana R. Calif. (Los Angeles In.)	33·41 N	117·57 W
76	Santa Anna . . . . Tex.	31·44 N	99·18 W
100	Santa Anna, Cochilha de (Mts.) (kô-chê′lä dĕ sän-tä-nä) . Braz.	30·30 S	56·30 W
125	Sant' Antimo . . . . . It. (Naples In.)	40·40 N	14·11 E
101	Santa Bárbara (sän-tä-bȧ′r-bä-rä) Braz. (Rio de Janeiro In.)	19·57 S	43·25 W
68	Santa Barbara (săn′tȧ bär′bȧ-rȧ) Calif.	34·26 N	119·43 W
92	Santa Barbara (sän′tȧ bär′bä-rȧ) Hond.	14·52 N	88·20 W
76	Santa Barbara . . . . Mex.	26·48 N	105·50 W
68	Santa Barbara (I.) . . . . Calif.	33·30 N	113·01 W
68	Santa Barbara (Is.) . . . . Calif.	33·45 N	119·46 W
68	Santa Barbara Chan. . . . . Calif.	34·15 N	120·00 W
101	Santa Branca (sän-tä-brä′ɴ-kä) Braz. (Rio de Janeiro In.)	23·25 S	45·52 W
68	Santa Catalina (I.) . . . . Calif.	33·29 N	118·37 W
93	Santa Catalina, Cerro de (Mt.) (sĕ′r-rô-dĕ-sän-tä kä tä-lē′nä) Pan.	8·39 N	81·36 W
68	Santa Catalina, G. of (săn′tȧ kă-tȧ-lē′nȧ) . Calif.	33·00 N	117·58 W
76	Santa Catarina (sän′tȧ kä-tä-rē′nȧ) Mex.	25·41 N	100·27 W
	Sta. Catarina, see Loxicha		
	Sta. Catarina, see Yosonotú		
100	Santa Catarina (State) (sän-tä-kä-tä-rê′nȧ) . Braz.	27·15 S	50·30 W
90	Santa Catarina (R.) . . . . Mex.	16·31 N	98·39 W
65	Santa Clara (săn′tȧ klârȧ) Calif. (San Francisco In.)	37·21 N	121·56 W
94	Santa Clara (sän′tȧ klä′rȧ) . . Cuba	22·25 N	80·00 W
76	Santa Clara . . . . Mex.	24·29 N	103·22 W
100	Santa Clara . . . . Ur.	32·46 S	54·51 W
68	Santa Clara (R.) (săn′tȧ klă′rȧ) Calif.	34·22 N	118·53 W
92	Santa Clara, (Vol.) . . . . Nic.	12·44 N	87·00 W
94	Santa Clara, Bahía de (B.) (bä-ē′ä-dĕ-sän-tä-klä-rä) . . Cuba	23·05 N	80·50 W
88	Santa Clara, Sierra, (Mts.) (sē-ĕ′r-rä-sän′tȧ klä′rȧ) . Mex.	27·30 N	113·50 W
98	Santa Cruz (sän′tȧ krōōz′) . . . Bol.	17·45 S	63·03 W
100	Santa Cruz (sän-tä-krōō′s) . . Braz.	29·43 S	52·15 W
100	Santa Cruz . . . . Braz. (In.)	22·55 S	43·41 W
68	Santa Cruz (săn′tȧ krōōz′) . . Calif.	36·59 N	122·02 W
101	Santa Cruz . . . Chile (Santiago In.)	34·38 S	71·21 W
92	Santa Cruz . . . . C. R.	10·16 N	85·37 W
76	Santa Cruz . . . . Mex.	25·50 N	105·25 W
155	Santa Cruz . . . . . Phil. (Manila In.)	13·28 N	122·02 E
155	Santa Cruz . . . . . Phil. (Manila In.)	14·17 N	121·25 E
155	Santa Cruz . . . . . Phil. (Manila In.)	15·46 N	119·53 E
155	Santa Cruz . . . . . Phil. (Manila In.)	17·06 N	120·27 E
100	Santa Cruz (Prov.) . . . . Arg.	48·00 S	70·00 W
68	Santa Cruz (I.) (săn′tȧ krōōz′) Calif.	34·05 N	119·55 W
98	Santa Cruz (I.) (sän-tä-krōō′z) . Ec.	0·38 S	90·20 W
69	Santa Cruz (R.) (săn′tȧ krōōz′) Ariz.	32·50 N	111·30 W
100	Santa Cruz (R.) (sän′tȧ krōōz′) Arg.	50·05 S	66·30 W
92	Santa Cruz Barillas (sän-tä-krōō′z-bä-rê′l-yäs) Guat.	15·47 N	91·22 W
	Santa Cruz Chico, see Pedro Antonio Santos		
94	Santa Cruz del Sur (sän-tä-krōō′s-dĕl-sōō′r) . Cuba	20·45 N	78·00 W
164	Santa Cruz de Tenerife (sän′tä krōōz dȧ tā-nȧ-rē′fȧ) Can. Is.	28·07 N	15·27 W
159	Santa Cruz Is. . . . . Sol. Is.	10·58 S	166·47 E
65	Santa Cruz Mts. (săn′tȧ krōōz′) Calif. (San Francisco In.)	37·30 N	122·19 W
95	Santa Domingo, Cay (I.) . . Ba. Is.	21·50 N	75·45 W
126	Sant'Eufemia, Golfo di (G.) (gôl-fô-dē-sän-tĕ′ōō-fĕ′myä) . . It.	38·53 N	15·53 E
124	Santa Eugenia de Ribeira (sän-tä-ĕōō-hĕ′nyä-dĕ-rē-bĕ′y-rä) Sp.	42·34 N	8·55 W
125	Santa Eulalia del Rio (sän′ta ȧ-ōō-lä′lê-ä dĕl rē′ô) . Sp.	38·58 N	1·29 E
100	Santa Fe (sän′tä fā′) . . . . Arg.	31·33 S	60·45 W
94	Santa Fe (sän-tä-fĕ′) . . . . Cuba	21·45 N	82·40 W
69	Santa Fe (săn′tȧ fā′) . . . . . N. Mex.	35·10 N	106·00 W
124	Santafé (sän′tä-fā′) . . . . Sp.	37·12 N	3·43 W
100	Santa Fe (Prov.) (sän′tä fā′) . Arg.	32·00 S	61·15 W
99	Santa Filomena (sän-tä-fē-lô-mĕ′nä) . Braz.	9·09 S	44·45 W
88	Santa Genoveva, (Mtn.) (sän-tä-hĕ-nō-vĕ′vä) . Mex.	23·30 N	110·00 W
151	Sant'ai . . . . China	31·02 N	105·02 E
99	Santa Inés (sän′tä ē-nĕ′s) Ven. (In.)	9·54 N	64·21 W
100	Santa Inés (I.) (sän′tä ê-nās′) Chile	53·45 S	74·15 W
164	Santa Isabel (ê-sä-bĕl′) Equat. Gui.	3·43 N	8·42 E
159	Santa Isabel, (I.) . . . . Sol. Is.	7·57 S	159·28 E
94	Santa Lucia (sän′tȧ lōō-sē′ȧ) . Cuba	21·50 N	77·30 W
101	Santa Lucia (sän-tä-lōō-sê′ä) Ur. (Buenos Aires In.)	34·27 S	56·23 W
99	Santa Lucia . . . . Ven. (In.)	10·18 N	66·40 W
101	Santa Lucia (R.) (sän-tä-lōō-sê′ä) Ur. (Buenos Aires In.)	34·19 S	56·13 W
94	Santa Lucia B. (sän′tȧ lōō-sē′ȧ) Cuba	22·55 N	84·20 W
88	Santa Magarita (I.) (sän′tȧ mär-gȧ-rē′tȧ) . Mex.	24·15 N	112·00 W
100	Santa Maria (sän′tȧ mä-rē′ȧ) Braz.	29·40 S	28·45 W
68	Santa Maria (săn-tȧ mȧ-rē′ȧ) Calif.	34·57 N	120·28 W
126	Santa Maria (sän-tä mä-rē′ä) . . It.	41·05 N	14·15 E
155	Santa Maria (sän-tä-mä-rê′ä) Phil. (Manila In.)	14·48 N	120·57 E
	Santa Maria, see Huazolotitlán		
90	Santa Maria (R.) (sän′tȧ mä-rē′ȧ) . Mex.	21·33 N	100·17 W
95	Santa Maria, C . . . . Ba. Is.	23·45 N	75·30 W
124	Santa Maria, Cabo de (C.) (kȧ′bō-dĕ-sän-tä-mä-rê′ä) . Port.	36·58 N	7·54 W
94	Santa Maria, Cayo (I.) (kä′yō-săn′tȧ mȧ-rē′ȧ) . Cuba	22·40 N	79·00 W
90	Santa María del Oro (sän′tä-mä-rê′ä-dĕl-ô-rô) . Mex.	21·21 N	104·35 W
90	Santa Maria de los Angeles (dĕ-lôs-ȧ′n-hĕ-lĕs) . Mex.	22·10 N	103·34 W
90	Santa María del Rio (sän′tȧ mä-rē′ȧ dĕl rē′ō) . Mex.	21·46 N	100·43 W
90	Santa Maria de Ocotán (sän′tä-mä-rê′ä-dĕ-ô-kô-tȧ′n) Mex.	22·56 N	104·30 W
164	Santa Maria I. (sän-tä-mä-rê′ä) Açores (In.)	37·09 N	26·02 W
101	Santa Maria Madalena (sän-tä-mȧ-rê′ä-mȧ-dȧ-lĕ-nä) Braz. (Rio de Janeiro In.)	22·00 S	42·00 W
98	Santa Marta (sän′tȧ mär′tȧ) . Col.	11·15 N	74·13 W
74	Santa Monica (săn′tȧ mŏn′ĭ-kȧ) Calif. (Los Angeles In.)	34·01 N	118·29 W
74	Santa Monica Mts. Calif. (Los Angeles In.)	34·08 N	118·38 W
100	Santana (R.) (sän-tä′nä) Braz. (In.)	22·33 S	43·37 W
98	Santander (sän-tän-dĕr′) Col. (In.)	3·00 N	76·25 W
124	Santander (sän-tän-dâr′) . . . . . . Sp.	43·27 N	3·50 W
125	Sant'Angelo Romano (sän-tä′n-gzhĕ-lô-rô-mä′nô) It. (Rome In.)	42·02 N	12·45 E
125	Sant' Antimo . . . . . It. (Naples In.)	40·40 N	14·11 E
125	Santañy (sän-tän′yê) . . . . Sp.	39·21 N	3·08 E
68	Santa Paula (săn′tȧ pô′lȧ) . . Calif.	34·24 N	119·05 W
99	Santarém (sän-tä-rĕɴ′) . . . . . . Braz.	2·28 S	54·37 W
124	Santarém . . . . Port.	39·18 N	8·48 W
94	Santaren Chan. (săn-tȧ-rĕn′) Ba. Is.	24·15 N	79·30 W
69	Santa Rita (săn′tȧ rē′tȧ) . N. Mex.	32·45 N	108·05 W
101	Santa Rita do Passo Quatro (sän-tä-rê′tȧ-dô-pä′sô-kwȧ′trô) Braz. (Rio de Janeiro In.)	21·43 S	47·27 W
101	Santa Rita do Sapucai (sä-pōō-kȧ′ē) Braz. (Rio de Janeiro In.)	22·15 S	45·41 W
100	Santa Rosa (sän-tä-rô-sä) . . . . Arg.	36·45 S	64·10 W
68	Santa Rosa (săn′tȧ rō′zȧ) . . . Calif.	38·27 N	122·42 W
98	Santa Rosa (sän-tä-rô-sä) Col. (In.)	6·38 N	75·26 W
98	Santa Rosa . . . . Ec.	3·29 S	78·55 W
92	Santa Rosa (sän′tȧ rō′sȧ) . . . Guat.	14·21 N	90·16 W
92	Santa Rosa . . . . Hond.	14·45 N	88·51 W
72	Santa Rosa (săn′tȧ rō′sȧ) N. Mex.	34·55 N	104·41 W
155	Santa Rosa (sän′tȧ rō′sȧ) Phil. (Manila In.)	14·18 N	121·07 E
99	Santa Rosa (sän-tä-rô-sä) Ven. (In.)	9·37 N	64·10 W
98	Santa Rosa de Cabal (sän-tä-rô-sä-dĕ-kä-bä′l) Col. (In.)	4·53 N	75·38 W
101	Santa Rosa de Viterbo (sän-tä-rô-sȧ-dĕ-vē-tĕr′-bô) Braz. (Rio de Janeiro In.)	21·30 S	47·21 W
68	Santa Rosa Ind. Res. (săn′tȧ rō′zȧ′) . Calif.	33·28 N	116·50 W
88	Santa Rosalía (sän′tȧ rô-zä′lê-ȧ) Mex.	27·13 N	112·15 W
	Santa Rosalia, see Ciudad Camargo		
66	Santa Rosa Mts. (săn′tȧ rō′zȧ) Nev.	41·33 N	117·50 W
74	Santa Susana (săn′tȧ sōō-ză′nȧ) Calif. (Los Angeles In.)	34·16 N	118·42 W
	Santa Tecla, see Nueva San Salvador		
101	Santa Teresa (sän-tä-tĕ-rĕ′sä) Arg. (Buenos Aires In.)	33·27 S	60·47 W
99	Santa Teresa . . . . Ven. (In.)	10·14 N	66·40 W
100	Santa Vitória do Palmar (sän-tä-vē-tŏ′ryä-dô-päl-mȧr) Braz.	33·30 S	53·16 W
68	Santa Ynez (R.) (săn′tȧ ē-nĕz′) Calif.	34·40 N	120·20 W
68	Santa Ysabel Ind. Res. (săn-tȧ ĭ-zȧ-bĕl′) . Calif.	33·05 N	116·46 W
68	Santee (săn-tē′) Calif. (San Diego In.)	32·50 N	116·58 W
79	Santee (R.) . . . . S. C.	33·27 N	80·02 W
100	Santiago (sän-tyȧ′gô) . . . . Braz.	29·05 S	54·46 W
101	Santiago (sän-tê-ä′gô) Chile (Santiago In.)	33·26 S	70·40 W
93	Santiago . . . . Pan.	8·07 N	80·58 W
155	Santiago (sän-tyä′gô) Phil. (Manila In.)	16·42 N	121·33 E
124	Santiago . . . . Sp.	42·52 N	8·32 W
	Santiago, see Tejupan		
	Santiago, see Zacatepec		
101	Santiago (Prov.) (sän-tyȧ′gō) Chile (Santiago In.)	33·28 S	70·55 W
90	Santiago, Rio Grande de (R.) (rê′ō-grä′n-dĕ-dĕ-sän-tyȧ′gô) Mex.	21·15 N	104·05 W
155	Santiago (I.) . . . Phil. (Manila In.)	16·29 N	120·03 E
95	Santiago de los Cabelleros (sän-tyȧ′gô-dȧ lōs kȧ-bä-yā′rôs) Dom. Rep.	19·30 N	70·45 W
95	Santiago de Cuba (sän-tyȧ′gô-dā kōō′bȧ) . . . . Cuba	20·00 N	75·50 W
95	Santiago de las Vegas (sän-tyȧ′gô-dĕ-läs-vĕ′gäs) Cuba (Havana In.)	22·13 N	8 ·23 W
100	Santiago del Estero (sän-tē-ȧ′gō-dĕl ĕs-tā′rô) . Arg.	27·50 S	64·14 W

ng-sing; ŋ-baŋk; ɴ-nasalized n; nŏd: cŏmmit; ōld; ôbey; ôrder; fōōd; fŏŏt; ou-out; s-soft; sh-dish; th-thin; pūre; ûnite; ûrn; stŭd; circŭs; ü-as "y" in study; ′-indeterminate vowel.

Page	Name Pronunciation Region	Lat. °′	Long. °′
100	Santiago del Estero (Prov.) (sän-tē-ä'gō-dĕl ĕs-tā'rō) .Arg.	27·15 S	63·30 W
76	Santiago Mts. (sän-tē-ä'gō) .. Tex.	30·00 N	103·30 W
74	Santiago Res. Calif. (Los Angeles In.)	33·47 N	117·42 W
95	Santiago Rodriguez (sän-tyà'gô-rô-drē'gĕz) Dom. Rep.	19·30 N	71·25 W
91	Santiago Tuxtla (sän-tyà'gô-tōō'x-tlä) .Mex.	18·28 N	95·18 W
76	Santiaguillo, Laguna de (L.) (lä-ōō'nä-dĕ-sän-tē-ä-gēl'yō) Mex.	24·51 N	104·43 W
66	Santiam R. (săn'tyăm) ...... Ore.	44·42 N	122·26 W
124	Santisteban del Puerto (sän'tē stā-bän'dĕl pwĕr'tō) .Sp.	38·15 N	3·12 W
148	Santo (sän'tŏ) ...... China	32·49 N	119·39 E
99	Santo Amaro (sän'tōō ä-mä'rōō) Braz.	12·32 S	38·33 W
101	Santo Amaro de Campos (sän-tō-ä-mä'rô-dĕ-käm'pôs) Braz. (Rio de Janeiro In.)	22·01 S	41·05 W
101	Santo André (sän-tō-än-drā') Braz. (Rio de Janeiro In.)	23·40 S	46·31 W
100	Santo Angelo (sän-tō-ä'n-zhĕ-lō) Braz.	28·16 S	53·59 W
164	Santo Antão I. (sän-tō-än-tä-ō) C. V. Is. (In.)	17·20 N	26·05 W
166	Santo Antonio (sän'tōō än-tō'nē-ōō) .Ang.	6·10 S	12·25 E
101	Santo Antônio do Monte (sän-tō-än-tō'nyō-dō-môn'tĕ) Braz. (Rio de Janeiro In.)	20·06 S	45·18 W
94	Santo Domingo (sän'tō-dōmĭn'gō) Cuba	22·35 N	80·20 W
92	Santo Domingo (sän-tô-dô-mē'n-gō) .Nic.	12·15 N	84·56 W
155	Santo Domingo .Phil. (Manila In.)	17·39 N	120·24 E
95	Santo Domingo (sän'tô dô-mĭn'gô) Dom. Rep.	18·30 N	69·55 W
	Santo Domingo, see Zanatepec		
124	Santo Domingo de la Calzada (dä lä käl-thä'dä) .Sp.	42·27 N	2·55 W
124	Santoña (sän-tō'nyä) ...... Sp.	43·25 N	3·27 W
101	Santos (sän'tozh) Braz. (Rio de Janeiro In.)	23·58 S	46·20 W
101	Santos Dumont (sän'tôs-dōō-mô'nt) Braz. (Rio de Janeiro In.)	21·28 S	43·33 W
155	Santo Thomas (sän-tô-tō-mä's) Phil. (Manila In.)	14·07 N	121·09 E
155	Santo Tomas (Mtn.) Phil. (Manila In.)	16·23 N	120·32 E
100	Santo Tomé (sän-tô-tō-mĕ') .. Arg.	28·32 S	56·04 W
153	Sanuki (sä'nōō-kê). Jap. (Tōkyō In.)	35·16 N	139·53 E
101	San Urbano (sän-ōōr-bä'nô) Arg. (Buenos Aires In.)	33·39 S	61·28 W
100	San Valentin, M. (Mtn.) (sän-vä-lĕn-tē'n) .Chile	46·41 S	73·30 W
122	Sanvic (säN-vēK') ...... Fr.	49·34 N	0·08 E
101	San Vicente (sän-vē-sĕn'tĕ) Arg. (Buenos Aires In.)	35·00 S	58·26 W
101	San Vicente .. Chile (Santiago In.)	34·25 S	71·06 W
92	San Vicente (sän vē-sĕn'tä) ... Sal.	13·41 N	88·43 W
124	San Vincente de Alcántara (sän vē-thĕn'tā dā äl-kän'tä-rä) Sp.	39·24 N	7·08 W
126	San Vito (sän vē'tô) ...... It.	45·53 N	12·52 E
69	San Xavier Indian Res. (x-ä'vĭēr) Ariz.	32·07 N	111·12 W
151	Sanya ...... China	18·10 N	109·32 E
166	Sanyati (R.) (sän-yä'tē) ...... Rh.	17·08 S	29·11 E
149	Sanyüanli ..... China (Canton In.)	23·11 N	113·16 E
68	San Ysidro (sän ysĭ-drō') Calif. (San Diego In.)	32·33 N	117·02 W
101	São Bernardo do Campo (souN-bĕr-när'dô-dô-kä'm-pô) Braz. (Rio de Janeiro In.)	23·44 S	46·33 W
100	São Borja (souN-bôr-zhä) ... Braz.	28·44 S	55·59 W
101	São Carlos (souN kär'lōzh) Braz. (Rio de Janeiro In.)	22·02 S	47·54 W
99	São Cristovão (souN-krēs-tō-vouN) Braz.	11·04 S	37·11 W
101	São Fidélis (souN-fē-dĕ'lēs) Braz. (Rio de Janeiro In.)	21·41 S	41·45 W
99	São Francisco (souN frăN-sēsh'kōō) Braz.	15·59 S	44·42 W
99	São Francisco, Rio (R.) (rē'ō-sän-frän-sē's-kō) .Braz.	8·56 S	40·20 W
100	São Francisco do Sul (souN frăN-sēsh'kōō-dô-sōō'l) Braz.	26·15 S	48·42 W
100	São Gabriel (souN'gä-brē-ĕl') Braz.	30·28 S	54·11 W
101	São Geraldo (souN-zhĕ-rä'l-dô) Braz. (Rio de Janeiro In.)	21·01 S	42·49 W
100	São Gonçalo (souN'gōn-sä'lōō) Braz. (In.)	22·55 S	43·04 W
101	São Gonçalo do Sapucaí (souN-gôn-sä'lō-dô-sä-pōō-kī') Braz. (Rio de Janeiro In.)	21·55 S	45·34 W
101	São João da Barra (souN-zhôuN-dä-bà'rä) Braz. (Rio de Janeiro In.)	21·40 S	41·03 W
101	São João da Boa Vista (souN-zhôuN-dä-bôä-vē's-tä) Braz. (Rio de Janeiro In.)	21·58 S	46·45 W
125	São João das Lampas (soun zhô-oun' däzh län-päzh') Port. (Lisboa In.)	38·52 N	9·24 W
101	São João del Rei (souN zhô-ouN'dĕl-rä) Braz. (Rio de Janeiro In.)	21·08 S	44·14 W
100	São João de Meriti (souN-zhôuN-dĕ-mĕ-rē-tē) Braz. (In.)	22·47 S	43·22 W

Page	Name Pronunciation Region	Lat. °′	Long. °′
99	São João do Araguaia (souN zhô-ouN'dô-ä-rä-gwä'yä) Braz.	5·29 S	48·44 W
125	São João dos Lampas (souN' zhô-ouN' dōzh län-päzh') Port. (Lisboa In.)	38·52 N	9·24 W
101	São João Nepomuceno (souN-zhôuN-nĕ-pô-mōō-sĕ-nō) Braz. (Rio de Janeiro In.)	21·33 S	43·00 W
164	São Jorge I. (souN zhôr' zhĕ) Açores (In.)	38·28 N	27·34 W
101	São José do Rio Pardo (souN-zhô-sĕ'dô-rē'ō-pä'r-dō) Braz. (Rio de Janeiro In.)	21·36 S	46·50 W
99	São José do Rio Prêto (souN zhô-zĕ'dô-rē'ō-prĕ-tō) Braz.	20·57 S	49·12 W
101	São José dos Campos (souN zhô-zā'dōzh käN pōzh') Braz. (Rio de Janeiro In.)	23·12 S	45·53 W
100	São Leopoldo (souN-lĕ-ô-pôl'dô) Braz.	29·46 S	51·09 W
99	São Luis (Maranhão) (souN-lōōē's-mä-rän-youN'). Braz.	2·31 S	43·14 W
101	São Luis do Paraitinga (souN-lōōē's-dô-pä-rä-ē-tē'n-gä) Braz. (Rio de Janeiro In.)	23·15 S	44·18 W
99	São Mateus (souN mä-tā'ōōzh) Braz.	18·44 S	39·45 W
101	São Miguel Arcanjo (souN-mē-gĕ'l-är-kän-zhō) Braz. (Rio de Janeiro In.)	23·54 S	47·59 W
164	São Miguel I. ...... Açores (In.)	37·59 N	26·38 W
95	Saona (I.) (sä-ō'nä) ... Dom. Rep.	18·10 N	68·55 W
122	Saône (R.) (sōn) ...... Fr.	46·27 N	4·58 E
164	São Nicolau (souN' nê-kô-louN') C. V. Is. (In.)	16·19 N	25·19 W
101	São Paulo (souN' pou'lōō) Braz. (Rio de Janeiro In.)	23·34 S	46·38 W
99	São Paulo (State) (souN pou'lōō) Braz.	21·45 S	50·47 W
98	São Paulo de Olivença (souN'pou'lōōdâ ô-lê-vĕn'sä) Braz.	3·32 S	68·46 W
101	São Pedro (souN-pĕ'drô) Braz. (Rio de Janeiro In.)	22·34 S	47·54 W
101	São Pedro de Aldeia (souN-pĕ'drô-dĕ-äl-dĕ'yä) Braz. (Rio de Janeiro In.)	22·50 S	42·04 W
99	São Raimundo Nonato (souN' rī-mōō'n-do nô-nä'tōō) Braz.	9·09 S	42·32 W
101	São Roque (souN' rō'kĕ) Braz. (Rio de Janeiro In.)	23·32 S	47·08 W
99	São Roque, Cabo de (C) (kä'bo-dĕ-souN' rō'kĕ) . Braz.	5·06 S	35·11 W
166	São Salvador (souN säl-vä-dôr) Ang.	6·30 S	14·10 E
101	São Sebastião (souN sä-bäs-tē-ouN') Braz. (Rio de Janeiro In.)	23·48 S	45·25 W
101	São Sebastião, Ilha de (I.) (ēl'yä dâ souN' sä-bäs-tē-ouN') Braz. (Rio de Janeiro In.)	23·52 S	45·22 W
101	São Sebastião do Paraíso (souN-sĕ-bäs-tē-ouN-dô-pä-rä-ē'sō) . Braz. (Rio de Janeiro In.)	20·54 S	46·58 W
101	São Simão (souN-sē-mouN) Braz. (Rio de Janeiro In.)	21·30 S	47·33 W
164	São Tiago I. (souN tē-ä'gōō) C. V. Is. (In.)	15·09 N	24·45 W
164	São Tomé (souN tô-mä') ..... Afr.	0·16 N	6·44 E
101	São Tomé, Cabo de (C.) (kä'bō-dĕ-souN-tô-mĕ') Braz. (Rio de Janeiro In.)	22·00 S	40·00 W
164	São Tomé, Ilhade (I.) (ē'lä-dĕ) . Afr.	0·41 N	6·01 E
114	Saoura, Oued (R.) ...... Alg.	29·39 N	1·42 W
101	São Vicente (souN ve-se'n-tĕ) Braz. (Rio de Janeiro In.)	23·57 S	46·25 W
164	Sao Vincente I. (souN vē-sĕn'tā) C. V. Is. (In.)	16·51 N	24·35 W
124	São Vinente, Cabo de (C.) (kä'bō-dĕ-sän-vē-sĕ'n-tĕ) . Port.	37·03 N	9·31 W
164	Sapele (sä-pā'lā) ...... Nig.	5·57 N	5·22 E
128	Sapozhok (sä-pô-zhôk') .. Sov. Un.	53·58 N	40·44 E
152	Sapporo (säp-pô'rô) ...... Jap.	43·02 N	141·29 E
136	Sapronovo (säp-rô'nô-vô) Sov. Un. (Moscow In.)	55·13 N	38·25 E
101	Sapucaí (R.) (sä-pōō-kä-ē') Braz. (Rio de Janeiro In.)	21·07 S	45·53 W
101	Sapucaia (sä-pōō-kä'yä) Braz. (Rio de Janeiro In.)	22·01 S	42·54 W
101	Sapucaí Mirim (R.) (sä-pōō-kä-ē'mē-rēN) Braz. (Rio de Janeiro In.)	21·06 S	47·03 W
73	Sapulpa (sá-pŭl'pá) ...... Okla.	36·01 N	96·05 W
101	Saquarema (sä-kwä-rĕ-mä) Braz. (Rio de Janeiro In.)	22·56 S	42·32 W
65	Sara (sä'rä) .. Wash. (Portland In.)	45·45 N	122·42 W
127	Sara, Bahr (R.) (bär) Chad-Cen. Afr. Rep.	8·19 N	17·44 E
127	Sarajevo (sä-rä-yĕv'ô) (sà-rä'ya-vô). Yugo.	43·15 N	18·26 E
136	Sarana (sá-rä'nä) Sov. Un. (Urals In.)	56·31 N	57·44 E
81	Saranac Lake ...... N. Y.	44·20 N	74·05 W
81	Saranac L. (săr'á-năk) ...... N. Y.	44·15 N	74·20 W
100	Sarandi (sä-rän'dê) ..... Arg. (In.)	34·26 S	58·21 W
101	Sarandi Grande (sä-rän'dē-grän'dĕ) Ur. (Buenos Aires In.)	33·42 S	56·21 W
142	Sarangpur ...... India	23·39 N	76·32 E
132	Saransk (sá-ränsk') ...... Sov. Un.	54·10 N	45·10 E
136	Sarany (sá-rä'nĭ) Sov. Un. (Urals In.)	58·33 N	58·48 E
132	Sarapul (sá-rä'pōōl') ..... Sov. Un.	56·28 N	53·50 E

Page	Name Pronunciation Region	Lat. °′	Long. °′
79	Sarasota (săr-á-sōtá) .... Fla. (In.)	27·27 N	82·30 W
77	Saratoga (săr-á-tō'gá) ...... Tex.	30·17 N	94·31 W
65	Saratoga ...... Wash. (Seattle In.)	48·04 N	122·29 W
65	Saratoga Pass. Wash. (Seattle In.)	48·09 N	122·33 W
81	Saratoga Springs (springz) .. N. Y.	43·05 N	74·50 W
133	Saratov (sá rä'tôf) ...... Sov. Un.	51·50 N	45·00 E
151	Saravane ...... Laos	15·48 N	106·40 E
154	Sarawak (Reg.) (sá-rä'wäk) .. Mala.	2·30 N	112·45 E
121	Sárbogárd (shär'bô-gärd) ... Hung.	46·53 N	18·38 E
85	Sarcee Ind. Res. (sär'sē) Can. (Calgary In.)	50·58 N	114·23 W
164	Sardalas ...... Libya	25·59 N	10·33 E
126	Sardinia (I.) (sär-dĭn'ĭá) ...... It.	40·08 N	9·05 E
78	Sardis (sär'dĭs) ...... Miss.	34·26 N	89·55 W
70	Sargent (sär'jĕnt) ...... Nebr.	41·40 N	99·38 W
133	Sarikamis ...... Tur.	40·30 N	42·40 E
125	Sariñena (sä-rĕn-yĕ'nä) ...... Sp.	41·46 N	0·11 W
150	Sariwŏn (sä'rē-wŭn') ...... Korea	38·40 N	125·45 E
122	Sark (I.) (särk) ...... Guernsey	49·28 N	2·22 W
127	Şarkoy (shär'kû-ê) ...... Tur.	40·39 N	27·07 E
122	Sarlat (sär-lä') ...... Fr.	44·52 N	1·13 E
100	Sarmiento, Monte (Mt.) (mô'n-tĕ-sär-myĕn'tō) . Chile	54·28 S	70·40 W
80	Sarnia (sär'nē-á) ...... Can.	43·00 N	82·25 W
125	Sarno (sär'-nô) ... It. (Naples In.)	40·35 N	14·38 E
121	Sarny (sär'nê) ...... Sov. Un.	51·17 N	26·39 E
127	Saronikós Kólpos (G.) ...... Grc.	37·51 N	23·30 E
127	Saros Körfezi (G.) (sä'rôs) ... Tur.	40·30 N	26·20 E
121	Sárospatak (shä'rôsh-pô'tôk) Hung.	48·19 N	21·35 E
127	Šar Planina (Mts.) (shär plä'nê-na) . Yugo.	42·07 N	21·54 E
118	Sarpsborg (särps'bôrg) ...... Nor.	59·17 N	11·07 E
123	Sarrebourg (sär-bōōr') ...... Fr.	48·44 N	7·02 E
123	Sarreguemines (sär-gē-mēn') ... Fr.	49·06 N	7·05 E
124	Sarria (sär'ē-ä) ...... Sp.	42·14 N	7·17 W
92	Sarstun R. (särs-tōō'n) ...... Guat.	15·50 N	89·26 W
126	Sartène (sär-tĕn') ...... Fr.	41·36 N	8·59 E
122	Sarthe (R.) (särt) ...... Fr.	47·44 N	0·32 W
	Sartor, see Store Sotra		
120	Sárvár (shär'vär) ...... Hung.	47·14 N	16·55 E
133	Sarych, Mys (C.) (mĭs sä-rēch') Sov. Un.	44·25 N	33·00 E
134	Sary Ishikotrau, Peski (des.) (sä'rê ē' shĕk-ō'trou) . Sov. Un.	46·12 N	75·30 E
134	Sarysu (R.) (sä'rē-sōō) ... Sov. Un.	47·47 N	69·14 E
142	Sasaram (sŭs-ŭ-räm') ...... India	25·00 N	84·00 E
153	Sasayama (sä'sä-yä'mä) ...... Jap.	35·05 N	135·14 E
153	Sasebo (sä'sâ-bô) ...... Jap.	33·12 N	129·43 E
	Saseno, see Sazan		
120	Sašice ...... Czech.	49·14 N	13·31 E
86	Saskatchewan (Prov.) ...... Can.	54·46 N	107·40 W
86	Saskatchewan (R.) (săs-kăch'ĕ-wän) . Can.	53·30 N	103·41 W
86	Saskatoon (săs-ká-tōōn') ...... Can.	52·11 N	106·42 W
119	Saslauka (säs-lä'ŭ-kà) ... Sov. Un.	57·22 N	22·34 E
168	Sasolburg . S. Afr. (Johannesburg & Pretoria In.)	26·52 S	27·47 E
132	Sasovo (sás'ô-vô) ...... Sov. Un.	54·20 N	42·00 E
74	Saspamco (săs-păm'cō) Tex. (San Antonio In.)	29·13 N	98·18 W
164	Sassandra R. (sás-săn'drá) Ivory Coast	6·23 N	6·52 W
126	Sassari (säs'sä-rē) ...... It.	40·44 N	8·33 E
120	Sassnitz (säs'nēts) ...... Ger.	54·31 N	13·37 E
164	Satadougou (sä-tá-dōō-gōō') .. Mali	12·31 N	11·26 W
118	Säter (sĕ'tĕr) ...... Swe.	60·21 N	15·50 E
79	Satilla (R.) (sá-tĭl'á) ...... Ga.	31·15 N	82·13 W
136	Satka (sät'kà) . Sov. Un. (Urals In.)	55·03 N	59·02 E
121	Sátoraljaujhely (shä'tô-rô-lyô-ōō'yĕl') . Hung.	48·24 N	21·40 E
121	Satu-Mare (sà'tōō-mà'rĕ) ... Rom.	47·50 N	22·53 E
65	Saturna (să-tûr'ná) Can. (Vancouver In.)	48·48 N	123·12 W
65	Saturna (I.) . Can. (Vancouver In.)	48·47 N	123·03 W
118	Saude (sou'dĕ) ...... Nor.	59·40 N	6·21 E
112	Saudhárkrókur ...... Ice.	65·41 N	19·38 W
138	Saudi Arabia (sà-ōō'dĭ á-rä'bĭ-á) Asia	22·40 N	46·00 E
111	Sauerlach (zou'ĕr-läK) Ger. (Munich In.)	47·58 N	11·39 E
80	Saugatuck (sô'gá-tŭk) ...... Mich.	42·40 N	86·10 W
80	Saugeen Pen. (sô'gēn) ...... Can.	44·55 N	81·20 W
80	Saugeer (R.) (sô'gēr) ...... Can.	44·20 N	81·20 W
81	Saugerties (sô'gēr-tēz) ...... N. Y.	42·05 N	73·55 W
83	Saugus (sô'gŭs) . Mass. (Boston In.)	42·28 N	71·01 W
71	Sauk (R.) (sôk) ...... Minn.	45·30 N	94·45 W
71	Sauk Centre ...... Minn.	45·43 N	94·58 W
71	Sauk City ...... Wis.	43·16 N	89·45 W
71	Sauk Rapids (răp'ĭd) ...... Minn.	45·35 N	94·08 W
	Saulai, see Shyaulyay		
82	Sault-au-Mouton ...... Can.	48·34 N	69·20 W
74	Sault Ste. Marie (sōō sānt mà-rē') Mich. (Sault Ste. Marie In.)	46·29 N	84·21 W
95	Saumatre, Etang (L.) ...... Hai.	18·40 N	72·10 W
159	Saunders, C. (sôrn'dĕrs) . N. Z. (In.)	45·55 S	170·50 E
85	Saunders L. (sän'dērs) Can. (Edmonton In.)	53·18 N	113·25 W
65	Sausalito (sô-sá-lē'tô) Calif. (San Francisco In.)	37·51 N	122·29 W
122	Sausset-les-Pins (sō-sĕ'lā-păN') Fr. (Marseille In.)	43·20 N	5·08 E
65	Sauvie I. (sô'vē) Ore. (Portland In.)	45·43 N	123·49 W
127	Sava (R.) (sä'vä) ...... Yugo.	44·50 N	19·07 E
84	Savage (săv'ĕj) Md. (Baltimore In.)	39·07 N	76·49 W
74	Savage ...... Minn. (Minneapolis, St. Paul In.)	44·47 N	93·20 W
133	Savalan (Mtn.) ...... Iran	38·20 N	48·00 E
164	Savalou ...... Dahomey	7·58 N	2·00 E
71	Savanna (sá-văn'á) ...... Ill.	42·05 N	90·09 W
79	Savannah (sá-văn'á) ...... Ga.	32·04 N	81·07 W
73	Savannah ...... Mo.	39·58 N	94·49 W
78	Savannah ...... Tenn.	35·13 N	88·14 W
79	Savannah (R.) ...... Ga.-S. C.	33·11 N	81·51 W

ăt; finăl; rāte; senâte; ärm; àsk; sofá; fâre; ch-choose; dh-as th in other; bē; ēvent; bĕt; recĕnt; cratēr; g-go; gh-guttural g; bĭt; ĭ-short neutral; rīde; K-guttural k as ch in German ich;

PRONOUNCING INDEX Savanna la Mar–Sepik 265

Page	Name Pronunciation Region	Lat. °'	Long. °'
94	Savanna la Mar (så-văn'á lä mär') Jam.	18·10 N	78·10 W
120	Sávava R. Czech.	49·36 N	15·24 E
164	Savé (sä-vā') Dahomey	8·09 N	2·30 E
122	Save (R.) Fr.	43·32 N	0·50 E
166	Save, Rio (R.) (rē'ō-sä'vĕ) Moz.	21·28 S	34·14 E
123	Saverne (sá-vĕrn') Fr.	48·40 N	7·22 E
126	Savigliano (sä-vēl-yä'nô) It.	44·38 N	7·42 E
126	Savona (sä-vō'nä) It.	44·19 N	8·28 E
119	Savonlinna (sá'vôn-lēn'nà) Fin.	61·53 N	28·49 E
129	Savran' (säv-rän') Sov. Un.	48·07 N	30·09 E
154	Savu Sea (sä'vōō) Indon.	9·15 S	122·15 E
154	Sawahlunto Indon.	0·37 S	100·50 E
154	Sawankhalok Thai.	17·16 N	99·48 E
165	Sawda, Jabal as (Mts.) Libya	28·14 N	13·46 E
114	Sawfjjin, Wadi (R.) Libya	31·18 N	13·16 E
168	Sawhāj U. A. R. (Nile In.)	26·34 N	31·40 E
165	Sawknah Libya	29·04 N	15·53 E
154	Sawu (I.) Indon.	10·15 S	122·00 E
65	Sawyer (L.) (sô'yĕr) Wash. (Seattle In.)	47·20 N	122·02 W
164	Say (sä'ē) Niger	13·09 N	2·16 E
134	Sayan Khrebet (Mts.) (sŭ-yän') Sov. Un.	51·30 N	90·00 E
139	Sayda (Sidon) (sä'ē-dä) (sī'dŏn) Leb. (Palestine In.)	33·34 N	35·23 E
74	Sayers (sā'ĕrs) Tex. (San Antonio In.)	29·22 N	98·18 W
144	Sayhūt S. Ar.	15·23 N	51·28 E
72	Sayre (sā'ĕr) Okla.	35·19 N	99·40 W
81	Sayre Pa.	41·55 N	76·30 W
84	Sayreton (sā'ĕr-tŭn) Ala. (Birmingham In.)	33·34 N	86·51 W
84	Sayreville (sâr'vĭl) N. J. (New York In.)	40·28 N	74·21 W
146	Sayr Usa Mong.	44·51 N	107·00 E
91	Sayula (sä-yōō'lä) Mex.	17·51 N	94·56 W
90	Sayula Mex.	19·50 N	101·33 W
90	Sayula, Luguna de (L.) (lä-gōō'nä-dĕ) Mex.	20·00 N	103·33 W
144	Say'ūm S. Ar.	16·00 N	48·59 E
81	Sayville (sā'vĭl) N. Y.	40·45 N	73·10 W
127	Sazan (Saseno) (I.) Alb.	40·30 N	19·17 E
136	Sazhino (sáz-hē'nô) Sov. Un. (Urals In.)	56·20 N	58·15 E
118	Scäffle Swe.	59·10 N	12·55 E
138	Scandinavian Pen. Eur.	62·00 N	14·00 E
74	Scanlon (skăn'lŏn) Minn. (Duluth In.)	46·27 N	92·26 W
65	Scappoose (skă-pōōs') Ore. (Portland In.)	45·46 N	122·53 W
65	Scappoose (R.) Ore. (Portland In.)	45·47 N	122·57 W
85	Scarborough (skär'bĕr-ô) Can. (Toronto In.)	43·45 N	79·12 W
116	Scarborough (skär'bŭr-ô) Eng.	54·16 N	0·19 W
85	Scarborough Junction Can. (Toronto In.)	43·43 N	79·15 W
84	Scarsdale (skärz'dāl) N. Y. (New York In.)	41·01 N	73·47 W
165	Sceui Ghimira Eth.	7·13 N	35·49 E
111	Schaerbeek (skär'bāk) Bel. (Brussels In.)	50·53 N	4·23 E
120	Schaffhausen (shäf'hou-zĕn) Switz.	47·43 N	8·38 E
87	Schefferville Can.	54·52 N	67·01 W
117	Schelde, R. Bel.	51·04 N	3·55 E
81	Schenectady (skĕ-nĕk'tá-dē) N. Y.	42·50 N	73·55 W
111	Scheveningen Neth. (Amsterdam In.)	52·06 N	4·15 E
111	Schiedam Neth. (Amsterdam In.)	51·55 N	4·23 E
123	Schiltigheim (shēl'tegh-hīm) Fr.	48·48 N	7·47 E
126	Schio (skē'ô) It.	45·43 N	11·23 E
120	Schleswig (shlĕs'vēgh) Ger.	54·32 N	9·32 E
120	Schleswig-Holstein (State) (shlĕs'vēgh-hōl'shtīn) Ger.	54·40 N	9·10 E
120	Schmalkalden (shmäl'käl-dĕn) Ger.	50·41 N	10·25 E
75	Schneider (schnīd'ĕr) Ind. (Chicago In.)	41·12 N	87·26 W
71	Schofield (skō'fēld) Wis.	44·52 N	89·37 W
120	Schönebeck (shû'nĕ-bergh) Ger.	52·01 N	11·44 E
111	Schoonhoven Neth. (Amsterdam In.)	51·56 N	4·51 E
155	Schouten (I.) (skou'tĕn) W. Irian	0·45 S	136·40 E
120	Schramberg (shräm'bĕrgh) Ger.	48·14 N	8·24 E
81	Schroon (L.) (skrōōn) N. Y.	43·50 N	73·50 W
111	Schultzendorf (shōōl'tzĕn-dōrf) Ger. (Berlin In.)	52·21 N	13·35 E
70	Schuyler (skī'ler) Nebr.	41·28 N	97·05 W
81	Schuylkill (skōōl'kĭl) Pa.	40·35 N	76·10 W
120	Schwabach (shvä'bäk) Ger.	49·19 N	11·02 E
120	Schwäbische Alb (Mts.) (shvă'bē-shĕ älb) Ger.	48·11 N	9·09 E
120	Schwäbisch Gmünd (shvă'bēsh gmünd) Ger.	48·47 N	9·49 E
120	Schwäbisch Hall (häl) Ger.	49·08 N	9·44 E
120	Schwandorf (shvän'dôrf) Ger.	49·19 N	12·08 E
154	Schwaner Mts. (sKvän'ĕr) Indon.	1·38 S	111·08 E
120	Schwarzwald (For.) (shvärts' väld) Ger.	47·54 N	7·57 E
120	Schwaz Aus.	47·20 N	11·45 E
111	Schwechat (shvĕk'ät) Aus. (Vienna In.)	48·09 N	16·29 E
120	Schwedt (shvĕt) Ger.	53·04 N	14·17 E
120	Schweinfurt (shvīn'fōōrt) Ger.	50·03 N	10·14 E
123	Schwelm (shvĕlm) Ger. (Ruhr In.)	51·17 N	7·18 E
120	Schwenningen (shvĕn'ĭng-ĕn) Ger.	48·04 N	8 33 E
120	Schwerin (shvĕ-rēn') Ger.	53·36 N	11·25 E
120	Schweriner See (L.) (shvĕ'rē-nĕr zā) Ger.	53·40 N	11·06 E
123	Schwerte (shvĕr'tĕ) Ger. (Ruhr In.)	51·26 N	7·34 E
111	Schwielow L. (shvē'lōv) Ger. (Berlin In.)	52·20 N	12·52 E
120	Schwyz (shvēts) Switz.	47·01 N	8·38 E
126	Sciacca (shē-äk'kä) It.	37·30 N	13·09 E
116	Scilly (Is.) (sĭl'ē) Eng.	49·56 N	6·50 W
80	Scioto (R.) (sī-ō'tō) Ohio	39·10 N	82·55 W
83	Scituate (sĭt'ū-āt) Mass. (Boston In.)	42·12 N	70·45 W
67	Scobey (skō'bē) Mont.	48·48 N	105·29 W
65	Scoggin (skō'gĭn) Ore. (Portland In.)	45·28 N	123·14 W
85	Scotch R. (skŏch) Can. (Ottawa In.)	45·21 N	74·56 W
66	Scotia (skō'shá) Calif.	40·29 N	124·06 W
116	Scotland (skŏt'lănd) U. K.	57·05 N	5·10 W
70	Scotland S. D.	43·08 N	97·43 W
79	Scotland Neck (nĕk) N. C.	36·06 N	77·25 W
81	Scotstown (skŏts'toun) Can.	45·35 N	71·15 W
86	Scott, C. (skŏt) Can.	50·48 N	129·34 W
66	Scott, Mt. Ore.	42·55 N	122·00 W
65	Scott, Mt. Ore. (Portland In.)	45·27 N	122·33 W
74	Scott Air Force Base Ill. (St. Louis In.)	38·33 N	89·52 W
167	Scottburgh (skŏt'bŭr-ô) S. Afr. (Natal In.)	30·18 S	30·42 E
72	Scott City Kans.	38·28 N	100·54 W
84	Scottdale (skŏt' dāl) Ga. (Atlanta In.)	33·47 N	84·16 W
47	Scott Is. Ant.	67·00 S	178·00 E
47	Scott Ra. Ant.	68·00 S	55·00 E
70	Scottsbluff (skŏts'blŭf) Nebr.	41·52 N	103·40 W
70	Scotts Bluff Natl. Mon. Nebr.	41·45 N	103·47 W
78	Scottsboro (skŏts'bŭro) Ala.	34·40 N	86·03 W
80	Scottsburg (skŏts' bûrg) Ind.	38·40 N	85·50 W
160	Scottsdale (skŏts'dāl) Austl.	41·12 S	147·37 E
78	Scottsville (skŏts'vĭl) Ky.	36·45 N	86·10 W
80	Scottville Mich.	44·00 N	86·20 W
81	Scranton (skrăn'tŭn) Pa.	41·45 N	75·45 W
81	Scugog (L.) (skū'gôg) Can.	44·05 N	78·55 W
110	Scunthorpe (skŭn'thôrp) Eng.	53·36 N	0·38 W
	Scutari, see Shkodër		
127	Scutari (R.) (skōō'tä-rē) Alb.	42·14 N	19·33 E
79	Sea Is. (sē) Ga.-S. C.	31·21 N	81·05 W
65	Seabeck (sē'bĕck) Wash. (Seattle In.)	47·38 N	122·50 W
65	Seabold (sē'bōld) Wash. (Seattle In.)	47·42 N	122·33 W
84	Sea Bright (sē brīt) N. J. (New York In.)	40·22 N	73·58 W
77	Seabrook (sē'brŏŏk) Tex. (In.)	29·34 N	95·01 W
81	Seaford (sē'fērd) Del.	38·35 N	75·40 W
72	Seagraves (sē'grāvs) Tex.	32·51 N	102·38 W
86	Seal (R.) Can.	59·08 N	96·37 W
74	Seal Beach Calif. (Los Angeles In.)	33·44 N	118·06 W
95	Seal Cays (Is.) Turks & Caicos Is.	21·10 N	71·45 W
95	Seal Cays (Is.) Ba. Is.	22·40 N	75·55 W
166	Seal I. (sēl) S. Afr. (Cape Town In.)	34·07 S	18·36 E
77	Sealy (sē'lē) Tex.	29·46 N	96·10 W
166	Sea Point (sē point) S. Afr. (Cape Town In.)	33·55 S	18·23 E
73	Searcy (sûr'sē) Ark.	35·13 N	91·43 W
68	Searles (L.) (sûrl's) Calif.	35·44 N	117·22 W
82	Searsport (sērz'pōrt) Maine	44·28 N	68·55 W
66	Seaside (sē'sīd) Ore.	45·59 N	123·55 W
65	Seattle (sē-ăt''l) Wash. (Seattle In.)	47·36 N	122·20 W
92	Sebaco (sĕ-bä'kō) Nic.	12·50 N	86·03 W
82	Sebago (sĕ-bā'gō) Maine	43·52 N	70·20 W
88	Sebastion Vizcaino, Bahia (B.) (bä-ē'ä-sĕ-bäs-tyō'n-vēs-kä-ē'nô) Mex.	28·45 N	115·15 W
68	Sebastopol (sē-bås'tô-pôl) Calif.	38·27 N	122 50 W
154	Sebatik (I.) Indon.	3·52 N	118·14 E
127	Sebes Rom.	45·58 N	23·34 E
80	Sebewaing (se'bē-wăng) Mich.	43·45 N	83·25 W
128	Sebezh (syĕ'bĕzh) Sov. Un.	56·16 N	28·29 E
133	Sebinkarahisar Tur.	40·15 N	38·10 E
124	Sebkha bou Areg (Marsh) Mor.	35·09 N	3·02 W
125	Sebkhan d'Oran (L.) Alg.	35·28 N	0·28 W
120	Sebnitz (zĕb'nēts) Ger.	51·01 N	14·16 E
125	Seborbe (sĕ-bōr-dĕ) Sp.	39·50 N	0·30 W
114	Sebou, Oued R. Mor.	34·23 N	5·18 W
80	Sebree (sē-brē') Ky.	37·35 N	87·30 W
79	Sebring (sē'brĭng) Fla. (In.)	27·30 N	81·26 W
80	Sebring Ohio	40·55 N	81·05 W
126	Secchia (R.) (sĕ'kyä) It.	44·25 N	10·25 E
91	Seco (R.) (sĕ'kō) Mex.	18·11 N	93·18 W
73	Sedalia (sē-dā'lē-á) Mo.	38·42 N	93·12 W
122	Sedan (sē-däN') Fr.	49·49 N	4·55 E
73	Sedan (sē-dăn') Kans.	37·07 N	96·08 W
110	Sedgley (sĕdj'lĭ) Eng.	52·32 N	2·07 W
139	Sedom Isr. (Palestine In.)	31·04 N	35·24 E
65	Sedro Woolley (sē'drô-wŏŏl'ē) Wash. (Seattle In.)	48·30 N	122·14 W
119	Šeduva (shĕ'dŏŏ-vá) Sov. Un.	55·46 N	23·45 E
166	Seekoevlei (L.) (zā'kōōf-lī) S. Afr. (Cape Town In.)	34·04 S	18·33 E
111	Seestall (zā'shtäl) Ger. (Munich In.)	47·58 N	10·52 E
114	Sefrou (sē-frōō') Mor.	33·49 N	4·46 W
132	Seg (L.) (syĕgh) Sov. Un.	64·00 N	33·30 E
139	Segamat (sā'gá-mát) Mala. (Singapore In.)	2·30 N	102·49 E
164	Ségou (sā-gōō') Mali	13·24 N	6·20 W
98	Segovia (sĕ-gô'vēä) Col. (In.)	7·08 N	74·42 W
124	Segovia (sā-gō'vē-ä) Sp.	40·58 N	4·05 W
	Segovia, see Coco		
125	Segre (R.) (sā'grā) Sp.	41·54 N	1·10 E
64	Seguam (I.) (sē'gwâm) Alaska	52·16 N	172·10 W
64	Seguam P. Alaska	52·20 N	173·00 W
164	Séguela (sā-gā-lä') Ivory Coast	8·03 N	7·05 W
76	Seguin (sĕ-gēn') Tex.	29·35 N	97·58 W
64	Segula (I.) (sē-gū'lá) Alaska	52·08 N	178·35 E
125	Segura (R.) (sā-gōō'rä) Sp.	38·07 N	0·33 W
124	Segura, Sierra de (Mts.) (sē-ĕ'r-rä-dĕ) Sp.	38·05 N	2·45 W
124	Segura (R.) Sp.	38·24 N	2·12 W
142	Sehwān W. Pak.	26·33 N	67·51 E
95	Seibo (sĕ'y-bō) Dom. Rep.	18·45 N	69·05 W
119	Seinäjoki (sâ'ē-nĕ-yô'kē) Fin.	62·47 N	22·50 E
122	Seine, Baie de la (B.) (bī dĕ lä sân) Fr.	49·37 N	0·53 W
71	Seine (R.) (sân) Can.	49·04 N	91·00 W
122	Seine, Rivière (R.) (rēv-yâr') Fr.	49·21 N	1·17 E
85	Seine R. (sân) Can. (Winnipeg In.)	49·48 N	97·04 W
100	Seio do Venus (Mtn.) (sĕ-yô-dô-vĕ'nōōs) Braz. (In.)	22·28 S	43·12 W
125	Seixal (sâ-ê-shäl') Port. (Lisbon In.)	38·38 N	9·06 W
164	Sekondi-Takoradi (sĕ-kôn'dē tä-kô-rä'dē) Ghana	4·55 N	1·53 W
139	Selangor (State) (sâ-län'gōr) Mala. (Singapore In.)	2·53 N	101·29 E
127	Selanoutsi (sâl'ä-nôv-tsĭ) Bul.	43·42 N	24·05 E
155	Selaru (I.) Indon.	8·30 S	130·30 E
154	Selatan, Tandjung (C.) (så-lä'tän) Indon.	4·09 S	114·40 E
64	Selawik (sē-lå-wĭk) Alaska	66·30 N	160·09 W
118	Selbu (L.) (sĕl'bōō) Nor.	63·18 N	11·55 E
110	Selby (sĕl'bē) Eng.	53·47 N	1·03 W
64	Seldovia (sĕl-dō'vē-á) Alaska	59·26 N	151·42 W
135	Selemdzha (R.) (sâ-lĕmt-zhä') Sov. Un.	52·28 N	131·50 E
135	Selenga (R.) (sĕ lĕŋ gä') Sov. Un.	51·00 N	106·40 E
146	Selenge Gol (R.) Mong.	49·04 N	102·23 E
135	Selennyakh (R.) (sĕl-yĭn-yäk) Sov. Un.	67·42 N	141·45 E
123	Sélestat (sē-lē-stä') Fr.	48·16 N	7·27 E
164	Selibaby (sâ-lê-bà-bē') Mauritania	15·21 N	12·11 W
128	Seliger (L.) (sĕl'lē-gĕr) Sov. Un.	57·14 N	33·18 E
142	Seling Tsho (L.) China	31·55 N	89·00 E
142	Selipuk Gömpa China	31·37 N	82·42 E
128	Selizharovo (sâ'lē-zhä'rô-vô) Sov. Un.	56·51 N	33·28 E
86	Selkirk (sĕl'kûrk) Can.	50·13 N	97·07 W
86	Selkirk Mts. Can.	50·14 N	116·42 W
65	Selleck (sĕl'ĕck) Wash. (Seattle In.)	47·22 N	121·52 W
75	Sellersburg (sĕl'ĕrs-bûrg) Ind. (Louisville In.)	38·25 N	85·45 W
135	Sellya Khskaya, Guba (B.) (sĕl-yäk'sKá-yá) Sov. Un.	72·30 N	136·00 E
78	Selma (sĕl'má) Ala.	32·25 N	87·00 W
68	Selma Calif.	36·34 N	119·37 W
79	Selma N. C.	35·33 N	78·16 W
74	Selma Tex. (San Antonio In.)	29·33 N	98·19 W
111	Selsingen (zĕl'zĕn-gĕn) Ger. (Hamburg In.)	53·22 N	9·13 E
166	Selukwe (sē-lŭk'wē) Rh.	19·34 S	30·03 E
66	Selway R. (sĕl'wâ) Idaho	46·07 N	115·12 W
86	Selwyn (L.) (sĕl'wĭn) Can.	59·41 N	104·30 W
127	Seman (R.) Alb.	40·48 N	19·53 E
154	Semarang (sĕ-mä'räng) Indon.	7·03 S	110·27 E
154	Semarinda Indon.	0·30 S	117·10 E
	Semendria, see Smederevo		
129	Semënovka (sĕ-myôn'ôf-kà) Sov. Un.	52·10 N	32·34 E
65	Semiahmoo Ind. Res. Can. (Vancouver In.)	49·01 N	122·43 W
65	Semiahmoo Spit (sĕm'ĭ-å-mōō) Wash. (Vancouver In.)	48·59 N	122·52 W
64	Semichi Is. (sē mē'chī) Alaska	52·40 N	174·50 E
67	Seminoe Res. (sĕm'ĭ nō) Wyo.	42·08 N	107·10 W
73	Seminole (sĕm'ĭ-nōl) Okla.	35·13 N	96·41 W
79	Seminole Ind. Res. Fla. (In.)	26·19 N	81·11 W
79	Seminole Ind. Res. Fla. (In.)	27·05 N	81·25 W
78	Seminole, L. Fla.-Ga.	30·57 N	84·46 W
134	Semipalatinsk (sĕ'mē-pá-lá-tyĕnsk') Sov. Un.	50·28 N	80·29 E
64	Semisopochnoi (I.) (sĕ-mē-sá-pōsh' noi) Alaska	51·45 N	179·25 E
134	Semiyarskoye (sĕ'mē-yär'skô-yĕ) Sov. Un.	51·03 N	78·28 E
165	Semliki R. (sĕm'lē-kē) Con. K.-Ug.	0·45 N	29·36 E
	Semlin, see Zemun		
120	Semmering P. (sĕm'ĕr-ĭng) Aus.	47·39 N	15·50 E
133	Semnān Iran	35·30 N	53·30 E
99	Senador Pompeu (sĕ-nä-dōr-pôm-pĕ'ŏŏ) Braz.	5·34 S	39·18 W
78	Senatobia (sĕ-nȧ-tō'bē-á) Miss.	34·36 N	89·56 W
152	Sendai (sĕn-dī') Jap.	38·18 N	141·02 E
73	Seneca (sĕn'ĕ-ká) Kans.	39·49 N	96·03 W
78	Seneca S. C.	34·40 N	82·58 W
84	Seneca Md. (Baltimore In.)	39·04 N	77·20 W
81	Seneca (L.) N. Y.	42·30 N	76·55 W
81	Seneca Falls N. Y.	42·55 N	76·55 W
163	Senegal (sĕn-ĕ-gôl') Afr.	14·53 N	14·58 W
164	Senegal R. Senegal-Mauritania	16·45 N	14·37 W
168	Senekal (sĕn'ĕ-kál) S. Afr. (Johannesburg & Pretoria In.)	28·20 S	27·37 E
120	Senftenberg (zĕnf'tĕn-bĕrgh) Ger.	51·32 N	14·00 E
99	Senhor do Bonfim (sĕn-yôr dô bôN-fē'N) Braz.	5·21 S	40·09 W
126	Senigallia (sā-nē-gäl'lyä) It.	43·42 N	13·16 E
126	Senj (sĕn') Yugo.	44·58 N	14·55 E
112	Senja (I.) (sĕnyä) Nor.	69·28 N	16·10 E
123	Senlis (säN-lēs') Fr. (Paris In.)	49·13 N	2·35 E
165	Sennar (sĕn-när') Sud.	13·34 N	33·32 E
165	Sennar Dam Sud.	13·38 N	33·38 E
87	Senneterre Can.	48·20 N	77·22 W
128	Senno (syĕ'nō) Sov. Un.	54·48 N	29·43 E
122	Sens (säNs) Fr.	48·05 N	3·18 E
92	Sensuntepeque (sĕn-sōōn-tâ-pā'kå) Sal.	13·53 N	88·34 W
127	Senta (sĕn'tä) Yugo.	45·54 N	20·05 E
153	Senzaki (sĕn'zä-kē) Jap.	34·22 N	131·09 E
	Seoul, see Sŏul		
139	Sepang Mala. (Singapore In.)	2·43 N	101·45 E
100	Sepetiba, Baia de (B.) (bäē'ä dĕ sä-pā-tē'bá) Braz. (In.)	23·01 S	43·42 W
155	Sepik (R.) (sĕp-ēk') N. Gui. Ter.	4·07 S	142·40 E

ng-sing; ŋ-baŋk; N-nasalized n; nŏd; cŏmmit; ōld; ôbey; ôrder; fōōd; fŏŏt; ou-out; s-soft; sh-dish; th-thin; pūre; ûnite; ûrn; stŭd; circŭs; ü-as "y" in study; '-indeterminate vowel.

Page	Name Pronunciation	Region	Lat. ° ′	Long. ° ′
122	Septèmes-les-Vallons (sĕ-tăm′la-vä-ŏN′)			
		Fr. (Marseille In.)	43·25 N	5·23 E
95	Septentrional, Cordillera (Mts.) (kôr-dĕl-yĕ′rä sĕp-tĕn-tryŏ-nä′l)			
		Dom. Rep.	19·50 N	71·15 W
123	Septeuil (sĕ-tû′)	Fr. (Paris In.)	48·53 N	1·40 E
82	Sept-Iles	Can.	50·11 N	66·21 W
78	Sequatchie (R.) (sĕ-kwăch′ē)	Tenn.	35·33 N	85·14 W
65	Sequim (sē′kwĭm)			
		Wash. (Seattle In.)	48·05 N	123·07 W
65	Sequim B.	Wash. (Seattle In.)	48·04 N	122·58 W
68	Sequoia Natl. Park (sē-kwoi′à)			
		Calif.	36·34 N	118·37 W
117	Seraing (sē-răN′)	Bel.	50·38 N	5·28 E
155	Seram (I.)	Indon.	2·45 N	129 30 E
142	Sèrampore	India (Calcutta In.)	22·44 N	88·21 E
154	Serang (så-räng′)	Indon.	6·13 N	106·10 E
139	Seranggung. Indon. (Singapore In.)		0·49 N	104·11 E
	Serbia (Reg.), see Srbija			
133	Serdobsk (sĕr-dôpsk′)	Sov. Un.	52·30 N	44·20 E
121	Sered	Czech.	48·17 N	17·43 E
129	Seredina-Buda (sĕ-rå-dē′nå-bōō′då)	Sov. Un.	52·11 N	34·03 E
139	Seremban (sĕr-ĕm-bän′)			
		Mala. (Singapore In.)	2·44 N	101·57 E
166	Serenje (sē-rĕn′yĕ)	Zambia	13·12 S	30·49 E
168	Serenli (så-rĕn′lē)			
		Som. (Horn of Afr. In.)	2·28 N	42·15 E
	Seres, see Sérrai			
121	Seret	Czech.	48·17 N	17·43 E
121	Seret	Rom.	47·58 N	26·01 E
121	Seret R. (sĕr′ĕt)	Sov. Un.	49·45 N	25·30 E
134	Sergeya Kirova (I.) (sĕr-gyē′yå kē′rō-vå)	Sov. Un.	77·30 N	86·10 E
99	Sergipe (State) (sĕr-zhē′pĕ)	Braz.	10·27 S	37·04 W
132	Sergiyevsk (sĕr-gē′yĕfsk)	Sov. Un.	53·58 N	51·00 E
127	Sérifos	Grc.	37·10 N	24·32 E
127	Sérifos (I.)	Grc.	37·42 N	24·17 E
101	Serodino (sĕ-rô-dē′nō)			
		Arg. (Buenos Aires In.)	32·36 S	60·56 W
100	Seropédica (sĕ-rô-pĕ′dē-kà)			
		Braz. (In.)	22·44 S	43·43 W
136	Serov (syĕ-rôf′)			
		Sov. Un. (Urals In.)	59·36 N	60·30 E
166	Serowe (sĕ-rō′wĕ)	Bots.	22·18 S	26·39 E
124	Serpa (sĕr-pä)	Port.	37·56 N	7·38 W
128	Serpukhov (syĕr′pŏŏ-ĸôf) Sov. Un.		54·53 N	37·27 E
127	Sérrai (Seres) (sĕr′ĕs)	Grc.	41·06 N	23·36 E
76	Serranias Del Burro (sĕr-rä-nē′às dĕl bŏō′r-rō)	Mex.	29·39 N	102·07 W
99	Serrinha (sĕr-rēn′yä)	Braz.	11·43 S	38·49 W
124	Serta (sĕr′tà)	Port.	39·48 N	8·01 W
99	Sertânia (sĕr-tà′nyä)	Braz.	8·28 S	37·13 W
101	Sertãozinho (sĕr-toun-zē′n-yō)			
		Braz. (Rio de Janeiro In.)	21·10 S	47·58 W
139	Serting (R.) Mala. (Singapore In.)		3·01 N	102·32 E
100	Seruí (sĕ-rōō-ē′)	Braz. (In.)	22·40 S	43·08 W
126	Sesia (R.) (sâz′yä)	It.	45·33 N	8·25 E
125	Sesimbra (sĕ-sē′m-brä)			
		Port. (Lisbon In.)	38·27 N	9·06 W
167	Sesmyl (R.)	S. Afr.		
	(Johannesburg & Pretoria In.)		25·51 S	28·06 E
126	Sestri Levante (sĕs′trē lâ-vän′tà)			
		It.	44·15 N	9·24 E
136	Sestroretsk (sĕs-trô′rĕtsk)			
		Sov. Un. (Leningrad In.)	60·06 N	29·58 E
136	Sestroretskiy Razliv, Ozero (L.) (ô′zĕ-rô sĕs-trô′ rĕts-kĭ räz′lĭf)			
		Sov. Un. (Leningrad In.)	60·05 N	30·07 E
153	Seta (sĕ′tà)	Jap. (Ōsaka In.)	34·58 N	135·56 E
122	Sète (sĕt)	Fr.	43·24 N	3·42 E
99	Sete Lagoas (sĕ-tĕ lä-gô′ás)	Braz.	19·23 S	43·58 W
164	Setif (sā-tēf′)	Alg.	36·18 N	5·21 E
153	Seto (sĕ′tō)	Jap.	35·11 N	137·07 E
153	Seto-Naikai (Sea) (sĕ′tō nī′kī) Jap.		33·50 N	132·25 E
164	Settat (sĕt-ät′) (sĕ-tà′)	Mor.	33·02 N	7·30 W
166	Setté-Cama (sĕ-tĕ-kä-mä′)	Gabon	2·29 S	9·40 E
94	Settlement Pt. (sĕt′l-mĕnt)	Ba. Is.	26·40 N	79·00 W
168	Settlers (sĕt′lĕrs)	S. Afr.		
	(Johannesburg & Pretoria In.)		24·57 S	28·33 E
125	Setúbal (så-tōō′bäl)			
		Port. (Lisbon In.)	30·32 N	8·54 W
124	Setúbal, B. de (bä-ē′à)	Port.	38·27 N	9·08 W
87	Seul, Lac (L.) (lăk súl)	Can.	50·28 N	91·26 W
118	Sevalen (L.) (sĕ-vå-lĕn)	Nor.	62·19 N	10·15 E
133	Sevan (L.) (syĭ-vän′)	Sov. Un.	40·10 N	45·20 E
129	Sevastopol′ (Akhiar) (syĕ-vås-tô′pôl′) (ăĸ′yàr)			
		Sov. Un.	44·34 N	33·34 E
	Seven Is., see Shichitō			
110	Sevenoaks (sĕ-vĕn-ŏks′)			
		Eng. (London In.)	51·16 N	0·12 E
136	Severka R. (så′vĕr-kà)			
		Sov. Un. (Moscow In.)	55·11 N	38·41 E
87	Severn (R.) (sĕv′ĕrn)	Can.	55·21 N	88·42 W
116	Severn (R.)	Eng.	51·42 N	2·25 W
84	Severna Park (sĕv′ĕrn-à)			
		Md. (Baltimore In.)	39·04 N	76·33 W
132	Severnaya Dvina (Northern Dvina) (R.) Sov. Un.		63·00 N	42·40 E
130	Severnaya Zemlya (Northern Land) (Is.) (sĕ-vyĭr-nĭ′u zĭ-m′lyà′)		79·33 N	101·15 E
136	Severoural′sk (sĕ-vyĭ-rŭ-ōō-rälsk′)			
		Sov. Un. (Urals In.)	60·08 N	59·53 E
69	Sevier (L.) (sĕ-vēr′)	Utah	38·55 N	113·10 W
69	Sevier R.	Utah	39·25 N	112·20 W
69	Sevier R., East Fork	Utah	37·45 N	112·10 W
98	Sevilla (sĕ-vē′l-yä)	Col. (In.)	4·16 N	75·56 W
124	Sevilla (så-vēl′yä)	Sp.	37·23 N	5·59 W
75	Seville (sĕ′vĭl) Ohio (Cleveland In.)		41·01 N	81·54 W
127	Sevlievo (sĕv′lyĕ-vō)	Bul.	43·02 N	25·05 E
122	Sèvre Nantaise (R.)			
	(sà′vrĕ näN-tāz′)	Fr.	47·00 N	1·02 W

Page	Name Pronunciation	Region	Lat. ° ′	Long. ° ′
122	Sèvre Niortaise (R.) (sà′vr′ nyôr-tâz′)	Fr.	46·23 N	1·05 W
128	Sevsk (syĕfsk)	Sov. Un.	52·08 N	34·28 E
64	Seward (sū′ård)	Alaska	60·18 N	149·28 W
73	Seward	Nebr.	40·55 N	97·06 W
64	Seward Pen.	Alaska	65·40 N	164·00 W
100	Sewell (sē′ŏō-ĕl)	Chile	34·01 S	70·18 W
75	Sewickley (sē-wĭk′lē)			
		Pa. (Pittsburg In.)	40·33 N	80·11 W
91	Seybaplaya (sā-ē-bä-plä′yä)	Mex.	19·38 N	90·40 W
47	Seychelles (Is.) (sā-shĕl′)	Afr.	5·20 S	55·10 E
112	Seydhisfjördhur			
	(sā′dĕs-fyûr-dōōr′)	Ice.	65·21 N	14·08 W
92	Seyé (sĕ-yĕ′)	Mex. (Yucatan In.)	20·51 N	89·22 W
115	Seyhan (R.)	Tur.	37·28 N	35·40 E
129	Seym (R.) (sĕym)	Sov. Un.	51·23 N	33·22 E
80	Seymour (sē′mōr)	Ind.	38·55 N	85·55 W
71	Seymour	Iowa	40·41 N	93·03 W
72	Seymour	Tex.	33·35 N	99·16 W
167	Seymour (sē′môr)			
		S. Afr. (Natal In.)	32·33 S	26·48 E
167	Sezela	S. Afr. (Natal In.)	30·33 S	30·37 W
126	Sezze (sĕt′sā)	It.	41·32 N	13·03 E
127	Sfântul-Gheorghe	Rom.	45·53 N	25·49 E
164	Sfax (sfăks)	Tun.	34·51 N	10·45 E
111	's Gravenhage (The Hague) ('s krä′vĕn-hä′ĸĕ) (hāg)			
		Neth. (Amsterdam In.)	52·05 N	4·16 E
147	Sha (R.) (shä)	China	33·33 N	114·30 E
148	Sha (R.)	China	34·47 N	118·27 E
148	Sha (R.)	China	39·26 N	122·08 E
166	Shabani	Rh.	20·15 S	30·28 E
136	Shablykino (shäb-lē′kĭ-nō)			
		Sov. Un. (Moscow In.)	56·22 N	38·37 E
149	Shaching	China (Canton In.)	22·44 N	113·48 E
47	Shackleton Shelf Ice (shăk′′l-tŭn)	Ant.	65·00 S	100·00 E
84	Shades Cr. (shādz)			
		Ala. (Birmingham In.)	33·20 N	86·55 W
84	Shades Mtn.			
		Ala. (Birmingham In.)	33·22 N	86·51 W
144	Shagrā (shăg′rä)	Sau. Ar.	25·13 N	45·15 E
144	Shahdād	Iran	30·45 N	57·45 E
142	Shah Fuladi (Mt.)	Afg.	39·33 N	67·38 E
165	Shahhāt	Libya	32·49 N	21·46 E
142	Shāhjahānpur (shä-jŭ-hän′pōōr)			
		India	27·58 N	79·58 E
150	Shaho (shä-hō′)			
		China (Peking In.)	40·08 N	116·16 E
144	Shahrezā (shä-rä′zä)	Iran	31·47 N	51·47 E
133	Shahsavār (shä-sä′kĕr)	Iran	36·40 N	51·00 E
75	Shaker Hts. (shā′kĕr)			
		Ohio (Cleveland In.)	41·28 N	81·34 W
129	Shakhty (shäk′tē)	Sov. Un.	47·41 N	40·11 E
74	Shakopee (shăk′ō-pe)			
		Minn. (Minneapolis, St. Paul In.)	44·48 N	93·31 W
165	Shala L. (shä′lä)	Eth.	7·34 N	39·00 E
144	Sham, Jabal ash (Mtn.) Mus. & Om.		23·01 N	57·45 E
165	Shambe (shäm′bà)	Sud.	7·08 N	30·46 E
144	Shammar, Jabal (Mts.) (jĕb′ĕl shŭm′är) . Sau. Ar.		27·13 N	40·16 E
81	Shamokin (shá-mō′kĭn)	Pa.	40·45 N	76·30 W
72	Shamrock (shăm′rŏk)	Tex.	35·14 N	100·12 W
166	Shamva (shäm′vä)	Rh.	17·18 S	31·35 E
75	Shandon (shăn′dŭn)			
		Ohio (Cincinnati In.)	39·20 N	84·13 W
148	Shangch′eng (shäng′chĕng) . China		31·47 N	115·22 E
148	Shangchialin (shäng′jĭä′lin) . China		38·20 N	116·05 E
148	Shangch′iu (shäng′chĭō)	China	34·24 N	115·39 E
149	Shanghai (shäng′hī′)			
		China (Shanghai In.)	31·14 N	121·27 E
149	Shanghaihsien			
		China (Shanghai In.)	31·02 N	121·24 E
148	Shanghai Shih (City)	China	31·02 N	121·45 E
148	Shangho (shäng′hŏ)	China	37·18 N	117·10 E
151	Shangjao	China	28·25 N	117·58 E
148	Shangts′ai (shäng′zhī)	China	33·16 N	114·16 E
150	Shangtu	China	41·38 N	113·22 E
147	Shanhsi (Shansi) (Prov.)	China	37·31 N	111·30 E
148	Shanhsien (shän′hsyĕn′)	China	34·47 N	116·04 E
84	Shannon (shăn′ŭn)			
		Ala. (Birmingham In.)	33·23 N	86·52 W
116	Shannon R. (shăn′ŏn)	Ire.	52·30 N	9·48 W
146	Shanshan (shän′shän′)	China	42·51 N	89·53 E
	Shansi, see Shanhsi			
135	Shantar (I.) (shä.ı′tär) . Sov. Un.		55·13 N	138·42 E
151	Shant′ou (Swatow) (swä′tō′)			
		China	23·20 N	116·40 E
147	Shantung (Prov.)	China	36·08 N	117·09 E
151	Shantung Pantao (Pen.)	China	37·00 N	120·10 E
151	Shantung Pt. (shän′tōōng′)	China	37·28 N	122·40 E
151	Shaohsing	China	30·00 N	120·40 E
151	Shaokuan	China	24·58 N	113·42 E
148	Shaopo (shou′pō′)	China	32·33 N	119·30 E
148	Shaopo Hu (L.) (shou′pŏ′ hōō)			
		China	32·07 N	119·13 E
136	Shapki (shäp′kĭ)			
		Sov. Un. (Leningrad In.)	59·36 N	31·11 E
158	Shark B. (shärk)	Austl.	25·30 S	113·00 E
83	Sharon (shăr′ŏn)			
		Mass. (Boston In.)	42·07 N	71·11 W
80	Sharon	Pa.	41·15 N	80·30 W
72	Sharon Springs	Kan.	38·51 N	101·45 W
75	Sharonville (shăr′ŏn-vĭl)			
		Ohio (Cincinnati In.)	39·16 N	84·24 W
75	Sharpsburg (shärps′bûrg)			
		Pa. (Pittsburgh In.)	40·30 N	79·54 W
144	Sharr, Jabal (Mtn.)	Sau. Ar.	28·00 N	36·07 E
151	Shashih	China	30·20 N	112·18 E
66	Shasta, Mt.	Calif.	41·35 N	122·12 W
66	Shasta L. (shăs′tá)	Calif.	40·51 N	122·32 W
132	Shatsk (shätsk)	Sov. Un.	54·00 N	41·40 E
72	Shattuck (shăt′ŭk)	Okla.	36·16 N	99·53 W
86	Shaunavon	Can.	49·37 N	108·29 W

Page	Name Pronunciation	Region	Lat. ° ′	Long. ° ′
78	Shaw (shô)	Miss.	33·36 N	90·44 W
71	Shawano (shá-wô′nō)	Wis.	44·41 N	88·13 W
87	Shawinigan Falls	Can.	46·32 N	72·46 W
74	Shawnee (shô-nē′)			
		Kans. (Kansas City In.)	39·01 N	94·43 W
73	Shawnee	Okla.	35·20 N	96·54 W
80	Shawneetown (shô′nē-toun) . Ill.		37·40 N	88·05 W
151	Shayang	China	31·00 N	112·38 E
121	Shchara (R.) (sh-chä′rä) . Sov. Un.		53·17 N	25·12 E
136	Shchëlkovo (shchĕl′kŏ-vô)			
		Sov. Un. (Moscow In.)	55·55 N	38·00 E
129	Shchëtovo (shchĕ′tŏ-vô) . Sov. Un.		48·11 N	39·13 E
129	Shchigry (shchē′grĕ) . Sov. Un.		51·52 N	36·54 E
129	Shchors (shchôrs) . Sov. Un.		51·38 N	31·58 E
136	Shchuch′ye Ozero (shchōōch′yĕ ô′zĕ-rō)			
		Sov. Un. (Urals In.)	56·31 N	56·35 E
142	Sheakhala . India (Calcutta In.)		22·47 N	88·10 E
168	Shebeli R. (shä′bä-lē)			
		Eth. (Horn of Afr. In.)	6·07 N	43·10 E
71	Sheboygan (shē-boi′găn) . Wis.		43·45 N	87·44 W
71	Sheboygan Falls . Wis.		43·43 N	87·51 W
164	Shebshi Mts.	Nig.-Cam.	8·22 N	12·14 E
82	Shediac (shĕ′dē-ăk)	Can.	46·16 N	64·33 W
116	Sheelin (L.) (shēlĭn)	Ire.	53·46 N	7·34 W
110	Sheerness (shēr′nĕs)			
		Eng. (London In.)	51·26 N	0·46 E
78	Sheffield (shĕf′fĕld)	Ala.	35·42 N	87·42 W
85	Sheffield	Can. (Toronto In.)	43·20 N	80·13 W
110	Sheffield	Eng.	53·23 N	1·28 W
75	Sheffield	Ohio (Cleveland In.)	41·26 N	82·05 W
75	Sheffield Lake			
		Ohio (Cleveland In.)	41·30 N	82·03 W
148	Shehsien (shĕ′hsyĕn′)	China	36·34 N	113·42 E
116	Shehy, Mts.	Ire.	51·46 N	9·35 W
132	Sheksna (R.) (shĕks′nà) . Sov. Un.		59·50 N	38·40 E
135	Shelagskiy, Mys (C.) (shĭ-läg′skē)			
		Sov. Un.	70·08 N	170·52 E
73	Shelbina (shĕl-bī′nà)	Ark.	39·41 N	92·03 W
82	Shelbourne (shĕl′bûrn)	Can.	44·35 N	65·20 W
80	Shelburn (shĕl′bûrn)	Ind.	39·10 N	87·30 W
81	Shelburne	Can.	44·05 N	80·05 W
75	Shelby (shĕl′bē)			
		Ind. (Chicago In.)	41·12 N	87·21 W
80	Shelby	Mich.	43·35 N	86·20 W
78	Shelby	Miss.	33·56 N	90·44 W
67	Shelby	Mont.	48·26 N	111·50 W
79	Shelby	N. C.	35·16 N	81·35 W
80	Shelby	Ohio	40·50 N	82·40 W
80	Shelbyville (shĕl′bĕ-vĭl)	Ill.	39·20 N	88·45 W
80	Shelbyville	Ind.	39·30 N	85·45 W
80	Shelbyville	Ky.	38·10 N	85·15 W
78	Shelbyville	Tenn.	35·30 N	86·28 W
70	Sheldon (shĕl′dŭn)	Iowa	43·10 N	95·50 W
77	Sheldon	Tex. (In.)	29·52 N	95·07 W
135	Shelekhova, Zaliv (B.) . Sov. Un.		60·00 N	156·00 E
64	Shelikof Str. (shĕ′lē-kôf) . Alaska		57·56 N	154·20 W
67	Shelley (shĕl′lē)	Idaho	43·24 N	112·06 W
71	Shellrock (R.) (shĕl′rŏk)	Iowa	43·25 N	93·19 W
128	Shelon′ (R.) (shä′lŏn) . Sov. Un.		57·50 N	29·40 E
81	Shelton (shĕl′tŭn)	Conn.	41·15 N	73·05 W
72	Shelton	Nebr.	40·46 N	98·41 W
66	Shelton	Wash.	47·14 N	123·05 W
136	Shemakha (shĕ-må-kä′)			
		Sov. Un. (Urals In.)	56·16 N	59·19 E
133	Shemakha	Sov. Un.	40·35 N	48·40 E
73	Shenandoah (shĕn-ăn-dō′á) . Iowa		40·46 N	95·23 W
81	Shenandoah	Pa.	40·50 N	76·15 W
81	Shenandoah	Va.	38·30 N	78·30 W
81	Shenandoah Natl. Park	Va.	38·35 N	78·25 W
81	Shenandoah (R.)	Va.	38·55 N	78·05 W
148	Shenchiu (shenchĭō)	China	33·11 N	115·06 E
165	Shendi (shĕn′dē)	Sud.	16·44 N	33·29 E
148	Shengfang (shengfăng)	China	39·05 N	116·40 E
146	Shenhsi (Shensi) (Prov.) (shĕn′sē′) . China		35·04 N	108·45 E
148	Shenhsien (shen′sĭän′)	China	38·02 N	115·33 E
132	Shenkursk (shĕn-kōōrsk′) . Sov. Un.		62·10 N	43·08 E
150	Shenmu	China	38·55 N	110·35 E
	Shensi, see Shenhsi			
148	Shentse (shen′zhŏ)	China	38·12 N	115·12 E
150	Shenyang (Mukden) (shĕn′yäng′) (mōōk′dĕn) . China		41·45 N	123·22 E
142	Sheopur (shĕp′ŏŏr-tŭn)	India	25·37 N	78·10 E
85	Shepard (shĕ′pärd)			
		Can. (Calgary In.)	50·57 N	113·54 W
129	Shepetovka (shĕ-pĕ-tôf′kà)			
		Sov. Un.	50·10 N	27·01 E
160	Shepparton (shĕp′är-tŭn) . Austl.		36·15 N	145·25 E
83	Sherborn (shûr′bûrn)			
		Mass. (Boston In.)	42·15 N	71·22 W
81	Sherbrooke (shûr′brŏŏk)	Can.	45·25 N	72·00 W
110	Sherburn (shûr′bûrn)	Eng.	53·47 N	1·15 W
121	Shereshevo (shĕ-rĕ-shĕ-vô)			
		Sov. Un.	52·31 N	24·08 E
73	Sheridan (shĕr′ĭ-dăn)	Ark.	34·19 N	92·21 W
66	Sheridan	Ore.	45·06 N	123·22 W
67	Sheridan	Wyo.	44·48 N	106·56 W
73	Sherman (shĕr′măn)	Tex.	33·39 N	96·37 W
136	Sherna R. (shĕr′nä)			
		Sov. Un. (Moscow In.)	56·08 N	38·45 E
86	Sherridon	Can.	55·08 N	101·00 W
111	's Hertogenbosch (sĕr-tō′ghĕn-bôs)			
		Neth. (Amsterdam In.)	51·41 N	5·19 E
65	Sherwood (shûr′wŏŏd)			
		Ore. (Portland In.)	45·21 N	122·50 W
110	Sherwood For.	Eng.	53·11 N	1·07 W
116	Shetland (Is.) (shĕt′lănd)	Scot.	60·35 N	2·10 W
139	Sheva R.	Isr. (Palestine In.)	31·15 N	34·38 E
70	Sheyenne (R.) (shī-ĕn′)	N. D.	46·42 N	97·52 W
80	Shiawassee (R.) (shī-á-wôs′ē)			
		Mich.	43·15 N	84·05 W
144	Shibām (shĭ′bäm)	S. Ar.	16·02 N	48·40 E
168	Shibeli R . Som. (Horn of Afr. In.)		1·38 N	43·50 E

PRONOUNCING INDEX

Shibin al Kawn–Singapore Str. 267

Page	Name Pronunciation Region	Lat. °′	Long. °′
168	Shibīn al Kawn (shê-bēn'ĕl kōm') U. A. R. (Nile In.)	30·31 N	31·01 E
168	Shībin al Qanāṭir (kȧ-nä'têr) U. A. R. (Nile In.)	30·18 N	31·21 E
153	Shichitō (Seven Is.) (shê'chê-tō) Jap.	34·18 N	139·28 E
67	Shields R. (shēldz) .... Mont.	45·54 N	110·40 W
110	Shifnal (shĭf'năl) .... Eng.	52·40 N	2·22 W
148	Shih (R.) (shē hŏ) .... China	32·09 N	114·11 E
148	Shihchiangchen (shē'kĭăng'zhen) China	32·16 N	120·59 E
149	Shihch'iao.... China (Canton In.)	22·56 N	113·22 E
148	Shihchiu Hu (L.) (shē'jĭō'hōō) China	31·29 N	119·07 E
	Shihkiachwang, see Shihmen		
151	Shihlung .... China	23·05 N	113·58 E
148	Shihmen (Shihkiachwang) (shē mĕn) (shē'jĭä'zhŏŏäng) China	38·04 N	114·31 E
148	Shihohienfou .... China	31·27 N	117·51 E
144	Shihr .... S. Ar.	14·45 N	49·32 E
149	Shiht'ou...... China (Canton In.)	23·01 N	113·23 E
148	Shihts'un (shē'chōōen) ..... China	33·47 N	117·18 E
148	Shihtzu Shan (Mts.) (shē'jĕ shän) China	37·17 N	121·38 E
149	Shihwan...... China (Canton In.)	23·01 N	113·04 E
151	Shihwanta Shan (Mtns.) ... China	22·10 N	107·30 E
150	Shihwei Pk .... China	47·11 N	119·59 E
142	Shikarpur .... W. Pak.	27·51 N	68·52 E
153	Shiki (shê'kê) ... Jap. (Tōkyō In.)	35·50 N	139·35 E
153	Shikoku (I.) (shē'kō'kōō) ..... Jap.	33·43 N	133·33 E
135	Shilka (R.) (shĭl'kȧ) ..... Sov. Un.	53·00 N	118·45 E
142	Shilla (Mt.) .... India	37·18 N	78·17 E
142	Shillong (shêl-lông') .... India	25·39 N	91·58 E
74	Shiloh (shī'lō) .. Ill. (St. Louis In.)	38·34 N	89·54 W
153	Shimabara (shē'mä-bä'rä) .... Jap.	32·46 N	130·22 E
153	Shimada (shē'mä-dä) .... Jap.	34·49 N	138·13 E
153	Shimizu (shē'mê-zōō) .... Jap.	35·00 N	138·29 E
153	Shimminato (shêm'mê'nä-tô) . Jap.	36·47 N	137·05 E
153	Shimoda (shē'mô-dȧ) .... Jap.	34·41 N	138·58 E
143	Shimoga .... India	13·59 N	75·38 E
153	Shimonoseki (shē'mô-nō-sĕ'kê) (shê-mô-nô'sĕ-kĭ) . Jap.	33·58 N	130·55 E
153	Shimo-Saga (shê'mô sä'gä) Jap. (Ōsaka In.)	35·01 N	135·41 E
116	Shin, Loch (L.) (lŏk shĭn) ... Scot.	58·08 N	4·20 W
153	Shinagawa-Wan (B.) (shê'nä-gä'wä wän) Jap. (Tōkyō In.)	35·37 N	139·49 E
153	Shinano-Gawa (Strm.) (shê-nä'nô gä'wä) . Jap.	36·43 N	138·22 E
65	Shine (shīn) ... Wash. (Seattle In.)	47·52 N	122·40 W
153	Shingū (shĭn'gōō) .... Jap.	33·43 N	135·59 E
153	Shinji (L.) (shĭn'jê) .... Jap.	35·23 N	133·05 E
165	Shinko R. (shĭn'kô) . Cen. Afr. Rep.	6·37 N	24·31 E
166	Shinyanga (shĭn-yäŋ'gä) ..... Tan.	3·35 S	33·07 E
152	Shiono Misaki (C.) (shê-ô'nô mê'sä-kê) . Jap.	33·20 N	136·10 E
94	Ship Channel Cay (I.) (shĭp chă-nĕl kē) . Ba. Is.	24·50 N	76·50 W
110	Shipley (shĭp'lê) .... Eng.	53·50 N	1·47 W
82	Shippegan .... Can.	47·44 N	64·45 W
82	Shippegan (I.) .... Can.	47·50 N	64·38 W
81	Shippenburg (shĭp'ĕn bûrg) ... Pa.	40·00 N	77·30 W
82	Shipshaw (R.) (shĭp'shô) ..... Can.	48·50 N	71·03 W
139	Shiqma (R.) ... Isr. (Palestine In.)	31·31 N	34·40 E
153	Shirane-san (Mtn.) (shē'rä'nȧ-sän') . Jap.	35·44 N	138·14 E
152	Shira Saki (C.) (shê'rä sä'kê) . Jap.	41·25 N	142·10 E
166	Shirati (shê-rä'tē) .... Tan.	1·15 S	34·02 E
144	Shīrāz (shē-räz') .... Iran	29·32 N	52·27 E
166	Shire (R.) (shē'rȧ) .... Malawi	15·10 S	34·58 E
129	Shirokoye (shē'rô-kô-yĕ) . Sov. Un.	47·40 N	33·18 E
64	Shishaldin Vol. (shī-shăl'dĭn) Alaska	54·48 N	164·00 W
75	Shively (shīv'lê) Ky. (Louisville In.)	38·11 N	85·47 W
142	Shivpuri .... India	25·31 N	77·46 E
139	Shivta .... Isr. (Palestine In.)	30·53 N	34·38 E
69	Shivwits (Shebit) Ind. Res. (shĭv'wĭts) (shĕ'bĭt) . Utah	37·10 N	113·50 W
69	Shivwits Plat .... Ariz.	36·13 N	113·42 W
83	Shirley (shûr'lê) Mass. (Boston In.)	42·33 N	71·39 W
153	Shizuki (shĭ'zōō-kê) .... Jap.	34·29 N	134·51 E
153	Shizuoka (shē'zōō'ōkȧ) .... Jap.	34·58 N	138·24 E
128	Shklov (shklôf) .... Sov. Un.	54·11 N	30·23 E
127	Shkodër (Scutari) (shkô'dûr) (skōō'tȧrē) . Alb.	42·04 N	19·30 E
152	Shkotovo (shkô'tô-vô) ... Sov. Un.	43·15 N	132·21 E
73	Shoal Cr. (shōl) .... Ill.	38·37 N	89·25 W
80	Shoals (shōlz) .... Ind.	38·40 N	86·45 W
142	Shoapur .... India	25·53 N	76·45 E
153	Shodo (I.) (shō'dō) .... Jap.	34·27 N	134·27 E
143	Sholāpur (shō'lä-pōōr) ...... India	17·42 N	75·51 E
139	Shoniron ... Jordan (Palestine In.)	32·18 N	35·14 E
75	Shorewood (shōr'wŏŏd) Wis. (Milwaukee In.)	43·05 N	77·54 W
67	Shoshone (shô-shōn'ê) ...... Idaho	42·56 N	114·24 W
67	Shoshone L .... Wyo.	44·17 N	110·50 W
67	Shoshone R .... Wyo.	44·20 N	109·28 W
129	Shostka (shôst'kȧ) ...... Sov. Un.	51·51 N	33·31 E
148	Sh'ouchang (shō'zhäng) .... China	35·59 N	115·52 E
148	Shouhsien .... China	32·36 N	116·45 E
148	Shoukuang (shō'gōōäng) .... China	36·53 N	118·45 E
129	Shpola (shpô'lȧ) .... Sov. Un.	49·01 N	31·36 E
77	Shreveport (shrēv'pôrt) .... La.	32·30 N	93·46 W
110	Shrewsbury (shrōōz'bēr-ĭ) .... Eng.	52·43 N	2·44 W
83	Shrewsbury ... Mass. (Boston In.)	42·18 N	71·43 W
110	Shropshire (Co.) (shrŏp'shēr) . Eng.	52·36 N	2·45 W
94	Shroud Cay (I.) (shroud) .. Ba. Is.	24·20 N	76·40 W
150	Shuangch'eng .... China	45·18 N	126·18 E
148	Shuangho (shōōäng hŏ) ..... China	31·33 N	116·48 E
148	Shuanglunho (shōōäng'lōōĕn'hŏ) China	31·50 N	115·07 E
150	Shuangyang .... China	43·28 N	125·45 E
71	Shullsburg (shŭlz'bûrg) ...... Wis.	42·35 N	90·16 W
148	Shulyehehen (shōōlĭĕhŭhĕn) . China	36·08 N	114·07 E
64	Shumagin (Is.) (shōō'mȧ-gên) Alaska	55·22 N	159·20 W
151	Shunan (shōō'nän') .... China	29·38 N	119·00 E
64	Shungnak (shŭng'nȧk) ..... Alaska	66·55 N	157·20 W
150	Shuni (shōōn'yĭ') China (Peking In.)	40·09 N	116·38 E
146	Shunning (shŭ'nĭng') .... China	24·34 N	99·49 E
149	Shunte .... China (Canton In.)	22·50 N	113·15 E
136	Shunut, 'Gora (Mt.) (gȧ-rä shōō'nŏŏt) Sov. Un. (Urals In.)	56·33 N	59·45 E
144	Shuqrah .... S. Ar.	13·32 N	46·02 E
144	Shūrāb (R.) (shōō räb) ...... Iran	31·02 N	55·43 E
152	Shuri (shōō'rê) .... Ryūkyū Is.	26·10 N	127·48 E
133	Shur R. (shōōr) .... Iran	35·40 N	50·10 E
144	Shūshtar (shōōsh'tŭr) .... Iran	31·50 N	48·46 E
128	Shuya (shōō'yȧ) .... Sov. Un.	56·52 N	41·23 E
148	Shuyang (shōō yäng) .... China	34·09 N	118·47 E
145	Shweba .... Bur.	22·23 N	96·13 E
	Shyaulyay, see Šiauliai		
152	Siakin (L.) (sĭä'jĭn) .... China	42·25 N	132·45 E
139	Siak Ketjil (R.) Indon. (Singapore In.)	1·01 N	101·45 E
139	Siak Sri Indrapura (sê-äks'rĭ ēn'drȧ-pōō'rä) Indon. (Singapore In.)	0·48 N	102·05 E
142	Sialkot (sê-äl'kōt) .... W. Pak.	32·39 N	74·30 E
	Siam, see Thailand		
154	Siam, G. of (sī-ăm') .... Thai.	11·37 N	100·46 E
	Sian, see Hsian		
148	Siaowu Shan (Mts.) (sĭou'wōō shän) . China	39·48 N	114·52 E
127	Siátista (syä'tĭs-ta) .... Grc.	40·15 N	21·32 E
155	Siau (I.) .... Indon.	2·40 N	126·00 E
119	Šiauliai (Shyaulyay) (shê-ou'lê-ī) Sov. Un.	55·57 N	23·19 E
136	Sibay (sē'báy) . Sov. Un. (Urals In.)	52·41 N	58·40 E
126	Šibenik (shê-bā'nēk) .... Yugo.	43·44 N	15·55 E
138	Siberia (Reg.) .... Asia	57·00 N	97·00 E
154	Siberut (I.) (sē'bȧ-rōōt) .... Indon.	1·22 S	99·45 E
142	Sibī .... W. Pak.	29·41 N	67·52 E
166	Sibiti (sê-bê-tē') .... Con. B.	3·35 S	13·10 E
127	Sibiu (sê-bĭ-ōō') .... Rom.	45·47 N	24·09 E
70	Sibley (sĭb'lê) .... Iowa	43·24 N	95·33 W
154	Sibolga (sê-bō'gä) .... Indon.	1·45 N	98·45 E
145	Sibsagar (sêb-sŭ'gŭr) .... India	26·47 N	94·45 E
154	Sibuti .... Phil.	4·40 N	119·30 E
155	Sibuyan (I.) (sē-bōō-yän') Phil. (Manila In.)	12·19 N	122·25 E
154	Sibuyan Sea .... Phil.	12·43 N	122·38 E
154	Sicapoo (Mtn.) (sē-kä-pōō') .. Phil.	18·05 N	121·03 E
113	Sicily (I.) (sĭs'ĭ-lê) .... It.	37·38 N	13·30 E
92	Sico R. (sê'kô) .... Hond.	15·32 N	85·42 W
98	Sicuaní (sê-kwä'nē) .... Peru	14·12 S	71·12 W
165	Sidamo (Prov.) (sē-dä'mô) ... Eth.	5·08 N	37·45 E
126	Siderno Marina (sê-dĕr'nô mä-rē'nä) . It.	38·18 N	16·19 E
126	Sídheros, Akr. (C.) ... Grc. (Inset)	35·19 N	26·20 E
127	Sidhiró Kastron .... Grc.	41·13 N	23·27 E
125	Sidi-Aïsa .... Alg.	35·53 N	3·44 E
165	Sīdī Barrānī .... U. A. R.	31·41 N	26·09 E
164	Sidi-bel Abbès (sē'dē-bĕl ȧ-bĕs') Alg.	35·15 N	0·43 W
164	Sidi Ifni (ēf'nê) .... Ifni	29·22 N	10·15 W
47	Sidley, Mt. (sĭd'lê) .... Ant.	77·25 S	129·00 W
67	Sidney (sĭd'nê) .... Mont.	47·43 N	104·07 W
70	Sidney .... Nebr.	41·10 N	103·00 W
80	Sidney .... Ohio	40·20 N	84·10 W
78	Sidney Lanier, L. (lăn'yēr) .... Ga.	34·27 N	83·56 W
	Sidon, see Sayda		
121	Siedlce (syĕd''l-tsĕ) .... Pol.	52·09 N	22·20 E
123	Siegburg (zēg'bōōrgh) Ger. (Ruhr In.)	50·48 N	7·13 E
123	Siegen (zē'ghĕn) .. Ger. (Ruhr In.)	50·52 N	8·01 E
111	Sieghartskirchen . Aus. (Vienna In.)	48·16 N	16·00 E
120	Sieg R. (zēg) .... Ger.	50·51 N	7·53 E
121	Siemiatycze (syĕm'yä'tê-chĕ) . Pol.	52·26 N	22·52 E
121	Siemionówka (sêĕ-mēŏ'-nôf-kȧ) Pol.	52·53 N	43·50 E
154	Siem Reap (syĕm'rā'ȧp) ... Camb.	13·32 N	103·54 E
126	Siena (sê-ĕn'ä) .... It.	43·19 N	11·21 E
121	Sieradz (syĕ'rädz) .... Pol.	51·35 N	18·45 E
124	Siero (syā'rō) .... Sp.	43·24 N	5·39 W
121	Sierpc (syĕrpts) .... Pol.	52·51 N	19·42 E
76	Sierra Blanca (sē-ĕ'rȧ blaŋ-kȧ) Tex.	31·10 N	105·20 W
69	Sierra Blanca Pk. (blăn'kȧ) N. Mex.	33·25 N	105·50 W
163	Sierra Leone (sê-ĕr'rä lȧ-ō'nȧ). Afr.	8·48 N	12·30 E
74	Sierra Madre (mă'drē) Calif. (Los Angeles In.)	34·10 N	118·03 W
76	Sierra Mojada (sē-ĕ'r-rä-mô-kä'dä) . Mex.	27·22 N	103·42 W
127	Sífnos (I.) .... Grc.	36·58 N	24·30 E
118	Sigdal (sēgh'däl) .... Nor.	60·01 N	9·35 E
122	Sigean (sē-zhŏN') .... Fr.	43·02 N	2·56 E
71	Sigeurney (sē-gûr-nĭ) .... Iowa	41·16 N	92·10 W
121	Sighet (sê-gāt') .... Rom.	47·57 N	23·55 E
121	Sighisoara (sē-gê-shwä'rȧ) ... Rom.	46·11 N	24·48 E
112	Siglufjördhur .... Ice.	66·06 N	18·45 W
133	Signakhi .... Sov. Un.	41·45 N	45·50 E
74	Signal Hill (sĭg'năl hĭl) Calif. (Los Angeles In.)	33·48 N	118·11 W
98	Sigsig (sêg-sēg') .... Ec.	3·05 S	78·44 W
118	Sigtuna (sēgh-tōō'nȧ) .... Swe.	59·40 N	17·39 E
94	Siguanea, Ensenada de la (B.) (ĕn-sĕ-nä-dä-dĕ-lä-sê-gwä-nā'ä) Cuba	21·45 N	83·15 W
92	Siguatepeque (sē-gwȧ'tĕ-pĕ-kĕ) Hond.	14·33 N	87·51 W
124	Sigüenza (sē-gwĕ'n-zä) .... Sp.	41·03 N	2·38 W
164	Siguiri (sê-gê-rē') .... Gui.	11·30 N	9·04 W
154	Sihanoukville .... Camb.	10·40 N	103·50 E
133	Siirt (sĭ-ērt') .... Tur.	38·00 N	42·00 E
164	Sikasso (sê-käs'sō) .... Mali	11·15 N	5·43 W
73	Sikeston (sīks'tŭn) .... Mo.	36·50 N	89·35 W
135	Sikhote Alin', Khrebet (Mts.) (se-kô'ta a-lēn') . Sov. Un.	45·00 N	135·45 E
127	Sikinos (I.) (sĭ'kĭ-nōs) .... Grc.	36·45 N	24·55 E
142	Sikkim .... Asia	27·42 N	88·25 E
121	Siklós (sĭ'klōsh) .... Hung.	45·51 N	18·18 E
124	Sil (R.) (sê'l) .... Sp.	42·20 N	7·13 W
155	Silang (sê-läng'). Phil. (Manila In.)	14·14 N	120·58 E
90	Silao (sê-lä'ō) .... Mex.	20·56 N	101·25 W
142	Silchar (sĭl-chär') .... India	24·52 N	92·50 E
168	Silent Valley (sī'lĕnt vă'lē) . S. Afr. (Johannesburg & Pretoria In.)	24·32 S	26·40 E
79	Silcr City (sī'lĕr) .... N. C.	35·45 N	79·29 W
121	Silesia (Reg.) (sĭ-lē'shȧ) ...... Pol.	50·58 N	16·53 E
133	Silifke .... Tur.	36·20 N	34·00 E
115	Silistra (sê-lês'trȧ) .... Bul.	44·01 N	27·13 E
118	Siljan (R.) (sêl'yän) .... Swe.	60·48 N	14·28 E
118	Silkeborg (sĭl'kĕ-bôr') .... Den.	56·10 N	9·33 E
85	Sillery (sêl'-re') . Can. (Quebec In.)	46·46 N	71·15 W
73	Siloam Springs (sī-lōm) ...... Ark.	36·10 N	94·32 W
90	Silocayoápan (sē-lô-kä-yô-ȧ'pän) Mex.	17·29 N	98·09 W
77	Silsbee (sĭlz' bê) .... Tex.	30·19 N	94·09 W
119	Šilutė (shĭ-lōō'tȧ) .... Sov. Un.	55·23 N	21·26 E
101	Silva Jardim (sê'l-vä-zhär-dêN) Braz. (Rio de Janeiro In.)	22·40 S	42·24 W
65	Silvana (sĭl-vän'ȧ) Wash. (Seattle In.)	48·12 N	122·16 W
99	Silvânia (sēl-vȧ'nyä) .... Braz.	16·43 S	48·33 W
166	Silva Porto (sĭl'vȧ pôr'tŏŏ) ... Ang.	12·20 S	17·05 E
73	Silver (L.) .... Mo.	39·38 N	93·12 W
74	Silverado (sĭl-vēr-ä'dō) Calif. (Los Angeles In.)	33·45 N	117·40 W
95	Silver Bk .... Ba. Is.	20·40 N	69·40 W
95	Silver Bank Passage (Str.) . Ba. Is.	20·40 N	70·20 W
71	Silver Bay .... Minn.	47·24 N	91.07 W
69	Silver City (sĭl'vēr sĭ'tĭ) .. N. Mex.	32·45 N	108·20 W
93	Silver City .... Pan.	9·20 N	79·54 W
81	Silver Creek (crēk) .... N. Y.	42·35 N	79·10 W
69	Silver Cr .... Ariz.	34·30 N	110·05 W
75	Silver Cr..... Ind. (Louisville In.)	38·20 N	85·45 W
75	Silver Cr., Muddy Fk. Ind. (Louisville In.)	38·26 N	85·52 W
65	Silverdale (sĭl'vēr-dāl) Wash. (Seattle In.)	49·39 N	122·42 W
75	Silver Lake (lāk) Wis. (Milwaukee In.)	42·33 N	88·10 W
75	Silver L..... Wis. (Milwaukee In.)	42·35 N	88·08 W
84	Silver Spring (sprĭng) Md. (Baltimore In.)	39·00 N	77·00 W
65	Silver Star Mtn. Wash. (Portland In.)	45·45 N	122·15 W
69	Silverton (sĭl'vēr-tŭn) .... Colo.	37·50 N	107·40 W
75	Silverton.... Ohio (Cincinnati In.)	39·12 N	84·24 W
66	Silverton .... Ore.	45·02 N	122·46 W
167	Silverton .... S. Afr. (Johannesburg & Pretoria In.)	25·45 S	28·13 E
124	Silves (sēl'vĕzh) .... Port.	37·15 N	8·24 W
66	Silvies R. (sĭl'vēz) .... Ore.	43·44 N	119·15 W
168	Silwá (Baḥrī) .. U. A. R. (Nile In.)	24·43 N	32·58 E
136	Sim (sĭm) .... Sov. Un. (Urals In.)	55·00 N	57·42 E
80	Simcoe (sĭm'kō) .... Can.	42·50 N	80·20 W
81	Simcoe (L.) .... Can.	44·30 N	79·20 W
154	Simeuloee (I.) .... Indon.	2·27 N	95·30 E
129	Simferopol' (Akmechet) (sêm-fĕ-rô'pôl') (ȧk-mĕch'ĕt) Sov. Un.	44·58 N	34·04 E
115	Simi (I.) .... Grc.	36·27 N	27·41 E
65	Similk Beach (sē'mĭlk) Wash. (Seattle In.)	48·27 N	122·35 W
142	Simla (sĭm'lȧ) .... India	31·09 N	77·15 E
121	Simleul-Silvaniei (shêm-lā'ōōl-sêl-vä'nyĕ-ê) . Rom.	47·14 N	22·46 E
94	Simms Pt .... Ba. Is.	25·00 N	77·40 W
91	Simojovel (sê-mō-hô-vĕl') ... Mex.	17·12 N	92·43 W
119	Simola (sē'mô-lȧ) .... Fin.	60·55 N	28·06 E
101	Simonésia (sē-mô-nĕ'syā) Braz. (Rio de Janeiro In.)	20·04 S	41·53 W
166	Simonstown (sī'mŭnztoun) S. Afr. (Cape Town In.)	34·11 S	18·25 E
120	Simplon P. (sĭm'plŏn) (săN-plôN') Switz.	46·13 N	7·53 E
120	Simplon Tun .... It.-Switz.	46·16 N	8·20 E
71	Simpson (I.) .... Can.	48·43 N	87·44 W
158	Simpson Des. (sĭmp-sŭn) ... Austl.	24·40 S	136·40 E
86	Simpson Pen .... Can.	68·58 N	89·20 W
118	Simrishamn (sēm'rês-häm'n) . Swe.	55·35 N	14·19 E
136	Sim R........ Sov Un. (Urals In.)	55·00 N	57·42 E
77	Sims Bay, (sĭmz bī-yōō') . Tex. (In.)	29·37 N	95·23 W
135	Simushir (I.) (se-mōō'shēr) Sov. Un.	47·15 N	150·47 E
127	Sinaia (sĭ-nä'yȧ) .... Rom.	45·20 N	25·30 E
165	Sinai Pen. (sī'nī) .... U. A. R.	29·24 N	33·29 E
155	Sinait (sē-nä'ēt) . Phil. (Manila In.)	15·54 N	120·28 E
88	Sinaloa (State) (sē-nä-lô-ä) .. Mex.	25·15 N	107·45 W
152	Sinanju (sĭ'nän-jŏŏ') .... Kor.	39·39 N	125·41 E
133	Sinap .... Tur.	42·00 N	35·05 E
98	Sincé (sēn'sȧ) .... Col.	9·15 N	75·14 W
98	Sincelejo (sēn-sȧ-lā'hō) .... Col.	9·12 N	75·30 W
65	Sinclair Inlet (sĭn-klâr') Wash. (Seattle In.)	47·31 N	122·41 W
119	Sindi (sēn'dê) .... Sov. Un.	58·20 N	24·40 E
129	Sinel'nikovo (sē'nyĕl-nê'kô'vô) Sov. Un.	49·19 N	35·33 E
124	Sines (sē'nȧzh) .... Port.	37·57 N	8·50 W
165	Singa (sĭŋ'gȧ) .... Sud.	13·09 N	33·52 E
139	Singapore (sĭn'gȧ-pōr') Singapore (Singapore In.)	1·18 N	103·52 E
139	Singapore.... Asia (Singapore In.)	1·22 N	103·45 E
139	Singapore Str. Indon. (Singapore In.)	1·14 N	104·20 E

ng-sing; ŋ-baŋk; N-nasalized n; nŏd; cŏmmit; ōld; ôbey; ôrder; fōōd; fŏŏt; ou-out; s-soft; sh-dish; th-thin; pūre; ûnite; ûrn; stŭd; circŭs; ü-as "y" in study; '-indeterminate vowel.

268 Singaradjac–Solomon R. PRONOUNCING INDEX

Page Name Pronunciation Region Lat. °′ Long. °′

154 Singaradjac (sĭŋ'gȧ-rä'jä)..Indon. 8·15 S 115·03 E
127 Singitikós Kólpos (G.).......Grc. 40·15 N 24·00 E
146 Singu (sĭn'gŭ)..............Bur. 22·37 N 96·04 E
167 Singunyane (R.) Leso. (Natal In.) 29·35 S 28·08 E
129 Siniye Lipyagi (sēn'ê-ĕ lēp'yä-gê) Sov. Un. 51·24 N 38·29 E
126 Sinj (sēn')...............Yugo. 43·42 N 16·39 E
146 Sinkiang Uighur (Aut. Reg.) China 40·15 N 82·15 E
136 Sin'kovo (sĭn-kô'vô) Sov. Un. (Moscow In.) 56·23 N 37·19 E
99 Sinnamary.............Fr. Gu. 5·15 N 57·52 W
126 Sinni (R.) (sēn'nē)...........It. 40·05 N 16·15 E
168 Sinnūris.......U. A. R. (Nile In.) 29·25 N 30·52 E
100 Sino, Pedra do (Mtn.) (pĕ'drä-dô-sē'nô).Braz. (In.) 22·27 S 43·02 W
166 Sinoia (sĭ-noi'ȧ)............Rh. 17·17 S 30·09 E
111 Sint Niklaas...Bel. (Brussels In.) 51·10 N 4·07 E
77 Sinton (sĭn'tŭn)............Tex. 28·03 N 97·30 W
125 Sintra (sên'trȧ).Port. (Lisbon In.) 38·48 N 9·23 W
111 Sint Truiden...Bel. (Brussels In.) 50·49 N 5·14 E
152 Sinŭiju (sĭ'nŏŏĭ-jŏŏ).........Kor. 40·04 N 124·33 E
136 Sinyavino (sĭn-yä'vĭ-nô) Sov. Un. (Leningrad In.) 59·50 N 31·07 E
128 Sinyaya (R.) (sên'yȧ-yȧ).Sov. Un. 56·40 N 28·20 E
129 Sinyukha (R.) (sē'nyŏŏ-κȧ) Sov. Un. 48·34 N 30·49 E
120 Sion (sē'ôɴ')..............Switz. 46·15 N 7·17 E
70 Sioux City (sōō)...........Iowa 42·30 N 96·25 W
70 Sioux Falls (fôlz)..........S. D. 43·33 N 96·43 W
87 Sioux Lookout.............Can. 50·11 N 91·42 W
98 Sipí (sē-pē')..........Col. (In.) 4·39 N 76·38 W
86 Sipiwesk..................Can. 55·36 N 97·24 W
78 Sipsey (R.) (sĭp'sē).........Ala. 33·26 N 87·42 W
154 Sipura (I.)...............Indon. 2·15 S 99·33 E
90 Siqueros (sê-kā'rōs).........Mex. 23·19 N 106·14 W
93 Siquia, R. (sê-kē'ä)..........Nic. 12·23 N 84·36 W
113 Siracusa (sē-rä-koo'sä).........It. 37·02 N 15·19 E
142 Sirājganj (sĭ-räj'gŭnj).....E. Pak. 24·23 N 89·43 E
92 Sirama (sē-rä-mä)...........Sal. 13·23 N 87·55 W
158 Sir Edward Pellew Group (Is.) (pĕl'ū).Austl. 15·15 S 137·15 E
121 Siretul R.................Rom. 46·10 N 27·18 E
144 Sirhan, Wadi (R.).......Sau. Ar. 31·02 N 37·16 E
127 Síros (Ermoúpolis)..........Grc. 37·30 N 24·56 E
127 Síros (I.)..................Grc. 37·23 N 24·55 E
142 Sirsa......................India 29·39 N 75·02 E
119 Širvintos (shēr'vĭn-tôs)...Sov. Un. 55·02 N 24·59 E
91 Sisal (sê-säl')..............Mex. 21·09 N 90·03 W
126 Siska (sē'säk)...............Yugo. 45·29 N 16·20 E
68 Sisquoc (R.) (sĭs'kwŏk).......Calif. 34·47 N 120·13 W
70 Sisseton (sĭs'tŭn)............S. D. 45·39 N 97·04 W
144 Sistān, Daryacheh-ye (L.) Iran-Afg. 31·45 N 61·15 E
123 Sisteron (sēst'rôɴ')...........Fr. 44·10 N 5·55 E
80 Sisterville (sĭs'tēr-vĭl).....W. Va. 39·30 N 81·00 W
126 Sitía (sē'tĭ-ȧ)..........Grc. (In.) 26·10 N 35·09 E
64 Sitka (sĭt'kȧ).............Alaska 57·08 N 135·18 W
64 Sitka Natl. Mon...........Alaska 57·20 N 136·10 W
110 Sittingbourne (sĭt-ĭng-bôrn) Eng. (London In.) 51·20 N 0·44 E
133 Sivas (sē'väs)...............Tur. 39·50 N 36·50 E
129 Sivash (L.) (sē'väsh)....Sov. Un. 45·55 N 34·42 E
133 Siverek (sē'vĕ-rĕk)...........Tur. 37·50 N 39·20 E
119 Siverskaya (sē'vĕr-skȧ-yȧ) Sov. Un. 59·17 N 30·03 E
165 Sīwah (Oasis) (sē'wä)....U. A. R. 29·33 N 25·11 E
93 Sixaola R. (sē-κä-ō'lä) (sĕk-sȧ-ō'lä) C. R. 9·31 N 83·07 W
165 Sixth Cataract.............Sud. 16·26 N 32·44 E
118 Sjaelland (I.) (shĕl'lăn')......Den. 55·34 N 11·35 E
127 Sjenica (syĕ'nê-tsȧ).........Yugo. 43·15 N 20·02 E
129 Skadovsk (skä'dôfsk)....Sov. Un. 46·08 N 32·54 E
118 Skagen (skä'ghĕn)...........Den. 57·43 N 10·32 E
118 Skagen (Pt.)...............Den. 57·43 N 10·31 E
118 Skagerrak (Str.) (skä-ghĕ-räk') Eur. 57·43 N 8·28 E
65 Skagit B. (skăg'ĭt) Wash. (Seattle In.) 48·20 N 122·32 W
66 Skagit R..................Wash. 48·29 N 121·52 W
64 Skagway (skăg-wā)....... Alaska 59·30 N 135·28 W
118 Skälderviken (B.)..........Swe. 56·20 N 12·25 E
135 Skalistyy, Golets (Mtn.).Sov. Un. 57·28 N 119·48 E
65 Skamania (skȧ-mā'nĭ-ȧ) Wash. (Portland In.) 45·37 N 122·03 W
65 Skamokawa (skȧ-mȧ'nĭ-ȧ) Wash. (Portland In.) 46·16 N 123·27 W
118 Skanderborg (skän'ĕr-bôr')...Den. 56·04 N 9·55 E
81 Skaneateles (skăn-ĕ-ăt'lĕs)..N. Y. 42·55 N 76·25 W
81 Skaneateles (L.)...........N. Y. 42·50 N 76·20 W
118 Skänninge (shĕn'ĭng-ĕ)........Swe. 58·24 N 15·02 E
118 Skanör (skän'ûr)............Swe. 55·24 N 12·49 E
127 Skantzoúra (Is.) (skän'tsōō-rȧ) Grc. 39·03 N 24·05 E
118 Skara (skä'rȧ)..............Swe. 58·25 N 13·24 E
86 Skeena (R.)................Can. 54·31 N 129·21 W
167 Skeerpoort.............S. Afr. (Johannesburg & Pretoria In.) 25·49 S 27·45 E
167 Skeerpoort (R.)...........S. Afr. (Johannesburg & Pretoria In.) 25·58 N 27·41 E
99 Skeldon (skĕl'dŭn)..........Guy. 5·49 N 57·15 W
112 Skellefte (R.) (shĕl'ĕ-ftĕ).....Swe. 65·18 N 19·08 E
112 Skellefteå (shĕl'ĕf-tĕ-ȧ').......Swe. 64·47 N 20·48 E
118 Skern (R.) (skĕrn)...........Den. 55·56 N 8·52 E
116 Skerries (Is.) (skĕr'ēz)......Wales 53·30 N 4·59 W
136 Skhodnya R. (skôd'nyȧ) Sov. Un. (Moscow In.) 55·55 N 37·16 E
127 Skíathos (I.) (skē'ȧ-thôs)....Grc. 39·15 N 23·25 E
116 Skibbereen (skĭb'ĕr-ēn).......Ire. 51·32 N 9·25 W
77 Skidmore (skĭd'môr)........Tex. 28·16 N 97·40 W
118 Skien (skē'ĕn)..............Nor. 59·13 N 9·35 E
121 Skierniewice (skyĕr-nyĕ-vēt'sĕ) Pol. 51·58 N 20·13 E
114 Skikda (Philippeville)........Alg. 36·58 N 6·51 E
168 Skilpadfontein.............S. Afr. (Johannesburg & Pretoria In.) 25·02 S 28·50 E
127 Skíros......................Grc. 38·53 N 24·32 E
127 Skiros (I.).................Grc. 38·50 N 24·43 E
118 Skive (skē'vĕ)..............Den. 56·34 N 8 56 E
112 Skjalfandá (R.) (skyäl'fänd-ô) Ice. 65·24 N 16·40 W
112 Skjerstad (skyĕr-städ).......Nor. 67·12 N 15·37 E
126 Škofja Loka (shkôf'yȧ lō'kȧ) Yugo. 46·10 N 14·20 E
75 Skokie (skō'kê)..Ill. (Chicago In.) 42·02 N 87·45 W
65 Skokomish Ind. Res. (skŏ-kō'mĭsh) Wash. (Seattle In.) 47·22 N 123·07 W
121 Skole (skô'lĕ)...........Sov. Un. 49·03 N 23·32 E
127 Skópelos (I.) (skô'pȧ-lôs).....Grc. 39·04 N 23·31 E
128 Skopin (skô'pēn)........Sov. Un. 53·49 N 39·35 E
127 Skopje (skôp'yĕ)..........Yugo. 42·02 N 21·26 E
118 Skövde (shûv'dĕ)...........Swe. 58·25 N 13·48 E
135 Skovorodino (skô'vô-rô'dĭ-nô) Sov. Un. 53·53 N 123·56 E
82 Skowhegan (skou-hē'găn)..Maine 44·45 N 69·27 W
126 Skradin (skrä'dēn).........Yugo. 43·49 N 17·58 E
118 Skreia (skrā'ȧ)..............Nor. 60·40 N 10·55 E
118 Skudeneshavn (skōō'dĕ-nes-houn') Nor. 59·10 N 5·19 E
118 Skulerud (skōō'lĕ-rōōdh).....Nor. 59·40 N 11·30 E
69 Skull Valley Ind. Res. (skŭl).Utah 40·25 N 112·50 W
78 Skuna, (R.) (skû'nȧ).........Miss. 33·57 N 89·36 W
71 Skunk (R.) (skŭnk)........Iowa 41·12 N 92·14 W
119 Skuodas (skwô'dȧs).....Sov. Un. 56·16 N 21·32 E
118 Skurup (skû'rōōp).........Swe. 55·29 N 13·27 E
129 Skvira (skvē'rȧ)..........Sov. Un. 49·43 N 29·41 E
120 Skwierzyna (skvê-ĕr'zhĭ-nȧ)...Pol. 52·35 N 15·30 E
116 Skye (I.) (skī).............Scot. 57·25 N 6·17 W
65 Skykomish (R.) (skī'kō-mĭsh) Wash. (Seattle In.) 47·50 N 121·55 W
100 Skyring, Seno (B.) (sĕ'nô-s-krē'ng).Chile 52·35 S 72·30 W
118 Slagese....................Den. 55·25 N 11·19 E
154 Slamet, Gunung (Mtn.) (slä'mĕt) Indon. 7·15 S 109·15 E
127 Slanic (slŭ'nêk)............Rom. 45·13 N 25·56 E
71 Slate (I.) (slāt).............Can. 48·38 N 87·14 W
73 Slater (slāt'ĕr)..............Mo. 39·13 N 93·03 W
127 Slatina (slä'tē-nä)..........Rom. 44·26 N 24·21 E
72 Slaton (slā'tŭn).............Tex. 33·26 N 101·38 W
86 Slave (R.) (slāv)...........Can. 59·40 N 111·21 W
134 Slavgorod (sláf'gô-rôt)...Sov. Un. 52·58 N 78·43 E
127 Slavonija (Reg.) (slä-vô'nê-yä) Yugo. 45·29 N 17·31 E
126 Slavonska Požega (slä-vôn'skä pô'zhĕ-gä).Yugo. 45·18 N 17·42 E
127 Slavonski Brod (slä-vôn'skê brôd) Yugo. 45·10 N 18·01 E
129 Slavuta (slȧ-vōō'tȧ)....Sov. Un. 50·18 N 27·01 E
129 Slavyansk (slȧv'yänsk')..Sov. Un. 48·52 N 37·34 E
129 Slavyanskaya (slȧv-yȧn'skȧ-yȧ) Sov. Un. 45·14 N 38·09 E
70 Slayton (slā'tŭn)..........Minn. 44·00 N 95·44 W
110 Sleaford (slē'fērd)..........Eng. 53·00 N 0·25 W
71 Sleepy Eye (slēp'ĭ ī).......Minn. 44·17 N 94·44 W
77 Slidell (slī-dĕl')..............La. 30·17 N 89·47 W
111 Sliedrecht. Neth (Amsterdam In.) 51·49 N 4·46 E
116 Sligo (slī'gō)................Ire. 54·17 N 8·19 W
118 Slite (slē'tĕ)...............Swe. 57·41 N 18·47 E
127 Sliven (slē'vĕn)..............Bul. 42·41 N 26·20 E
84 Sloatsburg (slōts'bŭrg) N. Y. (New York In.) 41·09 N 74·11 W
119 Slobodka (slô'bôd-kȧ)....Sov. Un. 54·34 N 26·12 E
132 Slobodskoy (slô'bôt-skoi).Sov. Un. 58·48 N 50·02 E
119 Sloka (slô'kȧ)............Sov. Un. 56·57 N 23·37 E
121 Slonim (swō'nēm).........Sov. Un. 53·05 N 25·19 E
110 Slough (slou)..Eng. (London In.) 51·29 N 0·36 W
Slovakia, see Slovensko
126 Slovenija (Reg.) (slô-vĕ'nê-yȧ) Yugo. 45·58 N 14·43 E
121 Slovensko (Slovakia) (Prov.) (slô-vĕn'skô) (slô-vȧk'ĭ-ȧ).Czech. 48·40 N 19·00 E
121 Sluch' (R.)...............Sov. Un. 50·56 N 26·48 E
126 Sluderno (slōō-dĕr'nô).........It. 46·38 N 10·37 E
126 Slunj (slōōn')..............Yugo. 45·08 N 15·46 E
121 Slupsk (swōōpsk)............Pol. 54·28 N 17·02 E
128 Slutsk (slōōtsk)..........Sov. Un. 53·02 N 27·34 E
116 Slyne Head (slīn)...........Ire. 53·25 N 10·05 W
73 Smackover (smăk'ô-vēr)......Ark. 33·22 N 92·42 W
127 Smederevo (Semendria) (smĕ'dĕ-rĕ-vô) (sĕ-mĕn'drĭ-ȧ) Yugo. 44·39 N 20·54 E
127 Smederevska Palanka (smĕ-dĕ-rĕv'skä pä-län'kȧ).Yugo. 44·21 N 21·00 E
118 Smedjebacken (smĭ'tyĕ-bä-kĕn) Swe. 60·09 N 15·19 E
129 Smela (smyā'lȧ)..........Sov. Un. 49·14 N 31·52 E
129 Smeloye (smyā'lô-ĕ).......Sov. Un. 50·55 N 33·36 E
81 Smethport (smĕth'pōrt)........Pa. 41·50 N 78·25 W
128 Smiltene (smēl'tĕ-nĕ)....Sov. Un. 57·26 N 25·57 E
86 Smith (smĭth)................Can. 55·10 N 113·53 W
65 Smith (I.)....Wash. (Seattle In.) 48·20 N 122·53 W
72 Smith Center (sĕn'tēr).......Kans. 39·45 N 98·46 W
86 Smithers (smĭth'ērs)..........Can. 54·13 N 127·22 W
79 Smithfield (smĭth'fēld)........N. C. 35·30 N 78·21 W
74 Smithfield Tex. (Dallas, Fort Worth In.) 32·52 N 97·12 W
67 Smithfield...................Utah 41·50 N 111·49 W
80 Smithland (smĭth'lănd).........Ky. 37·10 N 88·25 W
77 Smith Point..........Tex. (In.) 29·32 N 94·45 W
67 Smith R....................Mont. 47·00 N 111·20 W
81 Smiths Falls (smĭths)..........Can. 44·55 N 76·05 W
83 Smith Sd.....................Can. 48·15 N 53·50 W
160 Smithton (smĭth'tŭn).........Austl. 40·55 S 145·12 E
74 Smithton......Ill. (St. Louis In.) 38 24 N 89·59 W
77 Smithville (smĭth'vĭl)........Tex. 30·00 N 97·08 W
167 Smits (R.).....S. Afr. (Natal In.) 31·45 S 26·33 E
166 Smitswinkel Flats S. Afr. (Cape Town In.) 34·16 S 18·25 E
68 Smoke Creek Des. (smōk crēk) Nev. 40·28 N 119·40 W
73 Smoky Hill (R.) (smōk'ĭ hĭl).Kans. 38·40 N 97·32 W
118 Smöla (I.) (smûlȧ)..........Nor. 63·16 N 7·40 E
128 Smolensk (smô-lyĕnsk')..Sov. Un. 54·46 N 32·03 E
128 Smolensk (Oblast).......Sov. Un. 55·00 N 32·18 E
127 Smyadovo....................Bul. 43·04 N 27·00 E
81 Smyrna (smûr'nȧ)...........Del. 39·20 N 75·35 W
84 Smyrna........Ga. (Atlanta In.) 33·53 N 84·31 W
64 Snag (snăg)................Can. 62·18 N 140·30 W
71 Snake (R.) (snāk).........Minn. 45·58 N 93·20 W
69 Snake Ra...................Nev. 39·20 N 114·15 W
67 Snake R., Henrys Fork.....Idaho 43·52 N 111·55 W
66 Snake R...................Wash. 46·33 N 118·18 W
66 Snake River Pln. (rĭv'ēr)...Idaho 43·08 N 114·46 W
94 Snap Pt....................Ba. Is. 23·45 N 77·30 W
69 Sneffels Pk. (snĕf'ĕlz).......Colo. 38·00 N 107·50 W
85 Snelgrove (snĕl'grōv) Can. (Toronto In.) 43·44 N 79·50 W
121 Sniardwy L. (snyärt'vĭ)......Pol. 53·46 N 21·59 E
118 Snöhetta (Mtn.) (snû-hĕttä).Nor. 62·18 N 9·12 E
65 Snohomish (snô-hō'mĭsh) Wash. (Seattle In.) 47·55 N 122·05 W
65 Snohomish (R.).Wash. (Seattle In.) 47·53 N 122·04 W
65 Snoqualmie (snō qwäl'mē) Wash. (Seattle In.) 47·32 N 121·50 W
66 Snoqualmie R...............Wash. 47·32 N 121·53 W
129 Snov (R.) (snôf).........Sov. Un. 51·38 N 31·38 E
116 Snowdon, Mt. (snō'dŭn)....Wales 53·05 N 4·04 W
81 Snow Hill (hĭl).............Md. 38·15 N 75·20 W
159 Snowy Mts. (snō'ê).........Austl. 36·17 S 148·30 E
72 Snyder (snī'dēr)............Okla. 34·40 N 98·57 W
76 Snyder.....................Tex. 32·48 N 100·53 W
110 Soar (R.) (sōr).............Eng. 52·44 N 1·09 W
165 Sobat R. (sô'bȧt)............Sud. 9·04 N 32·02 E
128 Sobinka (sô-bĭŋ'kȧ)......Sov. Un. 55·59 N 40·02 E
153 Sobo Zan (Mt.) (sô'bô zän)...Jap. 32·47 N 131·27 E
99 Sobral (sô-brä'l)............Braz. 3·39 S 40·16 W
121 Sochaczew (sô-κä'chĕf).......Pol. 52·14 N 20·18 E
146 Soch'e (Yarkand) (sō'chĕ) (yär-känt').China 38·15 N 77·15 E
133 Sochi (sôch'ĭ)............Sov. Un. 43·35 N 39·50 E
157 Society Is. (sô-sī'ĕ-tê) Fr. Polynesia 15·00 S 157·30 W
91 Socoltenango (sô-kôl-tē-näŋ'gō) Mex. 16·17 N 92·20 W
101 Socorro (sŏ-kô'r-rō) Braz. (Rio de Janeiro In.) 22·35 S 46·32 W
98 Socorro (sô-kôr'rō)..........Col. 6·23 N 73·19 W
69 Socorro...............N. Mex. 34·05 N 106·55 W
168 Socotra I. (sô-kō'trȧ) S. Ar. (Horn of Afr. In.) 13·00 N 52·30 E
124 Socuellamos (sô-kōō-āl'yȧ-môs).Sp. 39·18 N 2·48 W
68 Soda (L.) (sō'dȧ)...........Calif. 35·12 N 116·25 W
65 Soda Pk.....Wash. (Portland In.) 45·53 N 122·04 W
67 Soda Springs (sprĭngz)......Idaho 42·39 N 111·37 W
118 Söderhamn (sû-dĕr-häm''n)..Swe. 61·20 N 17·00 E
118 Söderköping................Swe. 58·30 N 16·14 E
118 Södertälje (sû-dĕr-tĕl'yĕ).....Swe. 59·12 N 17·35 E
150 Sodi Soruksum (Mtn.).....China 37·20 N 102·00 E
165 Sodo.......................Eth. 7·03 N 37·46 E
118 Södra Dellen (L.)...........Swe. 61·45 N 16·30 E
120 Soest (zōst)................Ger. 51·35 N 8·05 E
Sofia, see Sofiya
127 Sofiya (Sofia) (sô'fê-yȧ) (sô'fê-ȧ) Bul. 42·43 N 23·20 E
129 Sofiyevka (sô-fē'yĕf-kȧ)..Sov. Un. 48·03 N 33·53 E
153 Soga (sô'gä).....Jap. (Tōkyō In.) 35·35 N 140·08 E
98 Sogamoso (sô-gä-mô'sō)......Col. 5·42 N 72·51 W
118 Sogndal (sôghn'dȧl).........Nor. 58·20 N 6·17 E
118 Sogndal....................Nor. 61·14 N 7·04 E
118 Sogne Fd. (sôgn'ĕ fyôrd).....Nor. 61·09 N 5·30 E
128 Sogozha (R.) (sô'gô-zhȧ).Sov. Un. 58·35 N 39·08 E
122 Soissons (swä-sôɴ')...........Fr. 49·23 N 3·17 E
153 Sōka (sō'kä).....Jap. (Tōkyō In.) 35·50 N 139·49 E
121 Sokal (sô'käl')..........Sov. Un. 50·28 N 24·20 E
133 Soke (sû'kĕ).................Tur. 37·40 N 27·10 E
164 Sokodé (sô-kô-dā')..........Togo 8·56 N 1·08 E
121 Sokolka (sô-kōōl'kȧ).........Pol. 53·23 N 23·30 E
164 Sokolo (sô-kô-lō')...........Mali 14·51 N 6·09 W
164 Sokoto (sō'kô-tô)...........Nig. 13·03 N 5·14 E
164 Sokoto (Reg.)...............Nig. 12·29 N 6·34 E
121 Sokotów Podlaski (sô-kô-wōōf' pŭd-lä'skĭ).Pol. 52·24 N 22·15 E
91 Sola de Vega (San Miguel) (sō'lä dā vā'gä) (sän mê-gĕl') Mex. 16·31 N 96·58 W
155 Solana (sō-lä'nä) Phil. (Manila In.) 17·40 N 121·41 E
161 Solander, C....Austl. (Sydney In.) 34·03 S 151·16 E
155 Solano (sō-lä'nō) Phil. (Manila In.) 16·31 N 121·11 E
98 Soledad (sŏ-lĕ-dä'd)..........Col. 10·47 N 75·00 W
90 Soledad Díez Gutierrez (sô-lȧ-dhädh'dē'äz gōō-tyā'rĕz) Mex. 22·19 N 100·54 W
66 Soleduck R. (sōl'dŭk)......Wash. 47·59 N 124·28 W
92 Solentiname, Islas de (Is.) (ĕ's-läs-dĕ-sô-lĕn-tē-nä'mȧ).Nic. 11·15 N 85·16 W
110 Solihull (sō'lĭ-hŭl).........Eng. 52·25 N 1·46 W
136 Solikamsk (sô-lē-kȧmsk') Sov. Un. (Urals In.) 59·38 N 56·48 E
98 Solimões, Rio (R.) (rē'ō-sô-lē-mô'ĕs).Braz. 2·45 S 67·44 W
123 Solingen (zō'lĭng-ĕn) Ger. (Ruhr In.) 51·10 N 7·05 E
118 Sollefteå (sôl-lĕf'tĕ-ô)........Swe. 63·06 N 17·17 E
125 Sóller (sō'lyĕr).............Sp. 39·45 N 2·40 E
133 Sol'-Iletsk............Sov. Un. 51·10 N 55·05 E
122 Sologne (Reg.) (sō-lôn'yĕ).....Fr. 47·36 N 1·53 E
92 Solola (sô-lō'lä).............Guat. 14·45 N 91·12 W
159 Solomon Is. Prot. (sŏ'ô-mŭn) Oceania 8·50 S 157·52 E
156 Solomon Is.............Oceania 7·00 S 148·00 E
72 Solomon R..................Kans. 39·24 N 98·19 W
72 Solomon R., North Fk.......Kans. 39·34 N 99·52 W
72 Solomon R., South Fk.......Kans. 39·19 N 99·52 W

ăt; finăl; rāte; senâte; ärm; ȧsk; sofȧ; fâre; ch-choose; dh-as th in other; bē; ēvent; bĕt; recĕnt; cratēr; g-go; gh-guttural g; bĭt; ĭ-short neutral; rīde; κ-guttural k as ch in German ich;

Page	Name Pronunciation Region	Lat. °'	Long. °'
75	Solon (sō'lŭn) Ohio (Cleveland In.)	41·23 N	81·26 W
120	Solothurn (zô'lō-thōōrn) . . . . Switz.	47·13 N	7·30 E
132	Solov'etskiy (I.) . . . . Sov. Un.	65·10 N	35·40 E
126	Šolta (I.) (shôl'tä) . . . . Yugo.	43·20 N	16·15 E
144	Soltānābād . . . . Iran	28·06 N	55·24 E
120	Soltau (sôl'tou) . . . . Ger.	53·00 N	9·50 E
128	Sol'tsy (sôl'tsė) . . . . Sov. Un.	58·04 N	30·13 E
150	Solun (sô-lōōn') . . . . China	47·32 N	121·18 E
81	Solvay (sŏl'vā) . . . . N. Y.	43·05 N	76·10 W
118	Sölvesborg (sûl'vĕs-bôrg) . . . . . Swe.	56·04 N	14·35 E
132	Sol'vychegodsk (sôl'vê-chĕ-gôtsk') Sov. Un.	61·18 N	46·58 E
116	Solway Firth (sŏl'wāfûrth') Eng.-Scot.	54·42 N	3·55 W
163	Somali Republic (sō-mä'lē) . . . Afr.	3·28 N	44·47 E
127	Sombor (sôm'bôr) . . . . Yugo.	45·45 N	19·10 E
90	Sombrerete (sōm-brå-rā'tā) . . Mex.	23·38 N	103·37 W
99	Sombrero, Cayo (C.) (kä-yō-sôm-brĕ'rō) . Ven. (In.)	10·52 N	68·12 W
78	Somerset (sŭm'ēr-sĕt) . . . . Ky.	37·05 N	84·35 W
84	Somerset . . Mass. (Providence In.)	41·46 N	71·05 W
81	Somerset . . . . Pa.	40·00 N	79·05 W
74	Somerset . . Tex. (San Antonio In.)	29·13 N	98·39 W
167	Somerset East . S. Afr. (Natal In.)	32·44 S	25·36 E
82	Somersworth (sŭm'ērz-wûrth) N. H.	43·16 N	70·53 W
68	Somerton (sŭm'ēr-tŭn) . . . . . . Ariz.	32·36 N	114·43 W
83	Somerville (sŭm'ēr-vĭl) Mass. (Boston In.)	42·23 N	71·06 W
84	Somerville . . N.J. (New York In.)	40·34 N	74·37 W
78	Somerville . . . . Tenn.	35·14 N	89·21 W
77	Somerville . . . . Tex.	30·21 N	96·31 W
121	Somesul R. (sô-må'shōōl) . . . Rom.	47·43 N	23·09 E
125	Somma Vesuviana (sôm'mä vä-zōō-vê-ä'nä) It. (Naples In.)	40·38 N	14·27 E
122	Somme (R.) (sŏm) . . . . Fr.	50·02 N	2·04 E
111	Sommerfeld (zō'mĕr-fĕld) Ger. (Berlin In.)	52·48 N	13·02 E
161	Sommerville Austl. (Melbourne In.)	38·14 S	145·10 E
92	Somoto (sô-mō'tō) . . . . Nic.	13·28 N	86·37 W
100	Somuncurá, Meseta de (Plat.) (mĕ-sĕ'tä-dĕ-sô-mōō'n-kōō-rá') Arg.	41·15 S	68·00 W
142	Son (R.) (sōn) . . . . India	24·40 N	82·35 E
93	Soná (sō'nä) . . . . Pan.	8·00 N	81·19 W
152	Sŏnchŏn (sŭn'shŭn) . . . . Kor.	39·49 N	124·56 E
118	Sønderborg (sûn''er-bôrgh) . . Den.	54·55 N	9·47 E
120	Sondershausen (zôn'dērz-hou'zĕn) Ger.	51·17 N	10·45 E
151	Song Ca (R.) . . . . Viet.	19·15 N	105·00 E
166	Songea (sôn-gā'ä) . . . . Tan.	10·39 S	35·44 E
152	Sŏngjin (sŭng'jĭn') . . . . Kor.	40·38 N	129·10 E
154	Songkhla (sông'klä') . . . . Thai.	7·09 N	100·34 E
120	Sonneberg (sôn'ē-bĕrgh) . . . . . Ger.	50·20 N	11·14 E
68	Sonora (sō-nō'rȧ) . . . . Calif.	37·58 N	120·22 W
76	Sonora . . . . Tex.	30·33 N	100·38 W
88	Sonora (State) . . . . Mex.	29·45 N	111·15 W
88	Sonora (R.) . . . . Mex.	28·45 N	111·35 W
68	Sonora Pk. . . . . Calif.	38·22 N	119·39 W
124	Sonseca (sôn-sā'kȧ) . . . . Sp.	39·41 N	3·56 W
98	Sonsón (sôn-sōn') . . . . Col. (In.)	5·42 N	75·28 W
92	Sonsonate (sōn-sô-nä'tå) . . . . . . Sal.	13·46 N	89·43 W
155	Sonsorol Is. (sŏn-sô-rōl') Pac. Is. Trust Ter.	5·03 N	132·33 E
148	Soochow (Wuhsien) (sōō'jō) (wōō'sĭän) . China	31·19 N	120·37 E
65	Sooke Basin (sŏŏk) Can. (Seattle In.)	48·21 N	123·47 W
74	Soo Locks (sōō lŏks) . . . U. S.-Can.	46·30 N	84·30 W
98	Sopetrán (sô-pĕ-trä'n) . . . Col. (In.)	6·30 N	75·44 W
118	Sopot (sô'pôt) . . . . Pol.	54·26 N	18·25 E
120	Sopron (shŏp'rôn) . . . . Hung.	47·41 N	16·36 E
126	Sora (sô'rä) . . . . It.	41·43 N	13·37 E
118	Sör Aurdal (sûr äür-dål) . . . . . Nor.	60·54 N	9·24 E
124	Sorbas (sôr'bäs) . . . . Sp.	37·05 N	2·07 W
91	Sordo (R.) (sô'r-dō) . . . . Mex.	16·39 N	97·33 W
82	Sorel (sô-rĕl') . . . . Can.	46·01 N	73·07 W
160	Sorell, C. . . . . Austl.	42·10 S	144·50 E
126	Soresina (sō-rå-zē'nä) . . . . It.	45·17 N	9·51 E
124	Soria (sō'rê-ä) . . . . Sp.	41·46 N	2·28 W
101	Soriano (sŏ-rêä'nō) (Dept.) Ur. (Buenos Aires In.)	33·25 S	58·00 W
101	Sorocaba (sô-rô-kä'bȧ) Braz. (Rio de Janeiro In.)	23·29 S	47·27 W
129	Soroki (sô-rō'kē) . . . . Sov. Un.	48·09 N	28·17 E
155	Sorong (sō-rông') . . . . W. Irian	1·00 S	131·20 E
128	Sorot' (R.) (sō-rō'tzh) . . . Sov. Un.	57·08 N	29·23 E
165	Soroti (sō-rō'tē) . . . . Ug.	1·51 N	33·33 E
112	Söröy (I.) (sûr-ûê) . . . . Nor.	70·37 N	20·58 E
124	Sorraia (R.) (sôr-rī'ȧ) . . . . Port.	38·55 N	8·42 W
125	Sorrento (sôr-rĕn'tō) It. (Naples In.)	40·23 N	14·23 E
155	Sorsogon (sôr-sôgōn') . . . . Phil.	12·51 N	124·02 E
119	Sortavala (sôr'tä-vä-lä) . . Sov. Un.	61·43 N	30·40 E
150	Sŏsan (sŭ'sän) . . . . Korea	36·40 N	126·25 E
129	Sosna (R.) (sôs'nȧ) . . . . . . Sov. Un.	50·33 N	38·15 E
129	Sosnitsa (sôs-nê'tsȧ) . . . . . . Sov. Un.	51·30 N	32·29 E
134	Sosnogorsk . . . . Sov. Un.	63·13 N	54·09 E
121	Sosnowiec (sôs-nô'vyĕts) . . . . . Pol.	50·17 N	19·10 E
152	Sosunova, Mys (Pt.) (mĭs sŏ'sōō-nôf'ȧ) . Sov. Un.	46·28 N	138·06 E
136	Sos'va R. (sôs'vȧ) Sov. Un. (Urals In.)	59·55 N	60·40 E
132	Sos'va (R.) (sôs'vȧ) . . . . . Sov. Un.	63·10 N	63·30 E
90	Sota la Marina (sô-tä-lä-mä-rē'nä) Mex.	22·45 N	98·11 W
91	Soteapan (sō-tå-ä'pän) . . . . . . Mex.	18·14 N	94·51 W
90	Soto la Marina, Rio (R.) (rê'ō-sō'tō lä mä-rē'nä) . Mex.	23·55 N	98·30 W
92	Sotuta (sô-tōō'tä) Mex. (Yucatan In.)	20·35 N	89·00 W
99	Soublette (sŏ-ōō-blĕ'tĕ) . Ven. (In.)	9·55 N	66·06 W
126	Soúdhas, Kólpos (G.) . Grc. (Inset)	35·33 N	24·22 E
115	Soueïda . . . . Syr.	32·41 N	36·41 E
127	Souflion . . . . Grc.	41·12 N	26·17 E
93	Soufrière (sōō-frê-âr') St. Lucia (Le. & Wind. Is. In.)	13·50 N	61·03 W
93	Soufrière, Mt., St. Vincent (Le. & Wind. Is. In.)	13·19 N	61·12 W
93	Soufrière (Vol.) Basse Terre (Le. & Wind. Is. In.)	16·02 N	61·41 W
93	Soufrière Vol. Montserrat (Le. & Wind. Is. In.)	16·43 N	62·10 W
113	Souk-Ahras (sōōk-ȧ-räs') . . . . . Alg.	36·18 N	8·19 E
152	Sŏul (Seoul) . . . . Kor.	37·35 N	127·03 E
167	Sources, Mt. aux (mÔN'tō sōōrs') Leso.-S. Afr. (Natal In.)	28·47 S	29·04 E
124	Soure (sōr-ĕ) . . . . Port.	40·04 N	8·37 W
83	Souris (sōō-rē') . . . . Can.	46·20 N	62·17 W
86	Souris . . . . Can.	49·32 N	100·23 W
86	Souris (R.) . . . . Can.	48·46 N	101·32 W
77	Sourlake (sour'lāk) . . . . Tex.	30·09 N	94·24 W
164	Sousse (sōōs) . . . . Tun.	36·00 N	10·39 E
122	Soustons (sōōs-tôN') . . . . Fr.	43·46 N	1·22 W
79	South (R.) . . . . N. C.	34·49 N	78·33 W
167	South Africa . . . . . Afr. (Natal In.)	31·50 S	28·05 E
84	South Amboy (south'ăm'boi) N. J. (New York In.)	40·28 N	74·17 W
6	South America		
116	Southampton (south-ămp'tŭn) Eng.	50·54 N	1·30 W
87	Southampton I. . . . . Can.	64·38 N	84·00 W
154	South Andaman I. (ăn-dȧ-măn') India	11·57 N	93·24 E
138	South Arabia . . . . Asia	14·35 N	47·45 E
158	South Australia (State) (ôs-trā'lĭ-ȧ) . Austl.	29·45 S	132·00 E
95	South B. . . . . Ba. Is.	20·55 N	73·35 W
80	South Bend (bĕnd) . . . . Ind.	41·40 N	86·20 W
66	South Bend (bĕnd) . . . . Wash.	46·39 N	123·48 W
94	South Bight (B.) . . . . Ba. Is.	24·20 N	77·35 W
94	South Bimini (I.) (bē'mê-nê) Ba. Is.	25·40 N	79·20 W
83	Southboro (south'bŭr-ô) Mass. (Boston In.)	42·18 N	71·33 W
79	South Boston (bôs'tŭn) . . . . Va.	36·41 N	78·55 W
81	Southbridge (south'brĭj) . . . . Mass.	42·05 N	72·00 W
95	South Caicos (I.) (kī'kōs) Turks & Caicos	21·30 N	71·35 W
155	South C. . . . . Pap.	10·40 S	149·00 E
63	South Carolina (State) (kăr-ô-lī'nȧ) . U. S.	34·15 N	81·10 W
110	South Cave (cāv) . . . . Eng.	53·45 N	0·35 W
80	South Charleston (south chärlz'tŭn) . W. Va.	38·20 N	81·40 W
154	South China Sea (chī'nȧ) . . . . . Asia	15·23 N	114·12 E
161	South Cr. . . . . Austl. (Sydney In.)	33·43 S	167·00 E
62	South Dakota (State) (dȧ-kō'tȧ) U. S.	44·20 N	101·55 W
116	South Downs (dounz) . . . . Eng.	50·55 N	1·13 W
159	Southeast, C. . . . . Austl.	43·47 S	146·03 E
110	Southend-on-Sea (south-ĕnd') Eng. (London In.)	51·33 N	0·41 E
159	Southern Alps (Mts.) (sŭ-thûrn ălps) . N. Z. (In.)	44·08 S	169·18 E
158	Southern Cross . . . . Austl.	31·13 S	119·30 E
86	Southern Indian (L.) (sŭth'ērn ĭn'dĭ-ăn) . Can.	57·20 N	99·29 W
79	Southern Pines (sŭth'ērn pīnz) N. C.	35·10 N	79·23 W
116	Southern Uplands (ŭp'lȧndz) . Scot.	55·15 N	4·28 W
69	Southern Ute Ind. Res. (ūt) . Colo.	37·05 N	108·23 W
75	South Euclid (ū'klĭd) Ohio (Cleveland In.)	41·30 N	81·34 W
80	South Fox (I.) (fŏks) . . . . Mich.	45·25 N	85·55 W
74	South Gate (gāt) Calif. (Los Angeles In.)	33·57 N	118·13 W
96	South Georgia (I.) (jôr'jȧ) . Falk. Is.	54·00 S	37·00 W
80	South Haven (hāv''n) . . . . . . Mich.	42·25 N	86·15 W
81	Southington (sŭdh'ĭng-tŭn) . Conn.	41·35 N	72·55 W
159	South I. . . . . N. Z. (In.)	43·15 S	167·00 E
70	South Loup (R.) (lōōp) . . . . . Nebr.	41·21 N	100·08 W
83	South Merrimack (mĕr'ĭ-măk) N. H. (Boston In.)	42·47 N	71·36 W
75	South Milwaukee (mĭl-wô'kē) Wis. (Milwaukee In.)	42·55 N	87·52 W
94	South Negril Pt. (nā-grēl') . . . Jam.	18·15 N	78·25 W
84	South Norfolk (nôr'fŏk) Va. (Norfolk In.)	36·48 N	76·16 W
74	South Ogden (ŏg'dĕn) Utah (Salt Lake City In.)	41·12 N	111·58 W
82	South Paris (păr'ĭs) . . . . Maine	44·13 N	70·32 W
75	South Park (pärk) Ky. (Louisville In.)	38·06 N	85·43 W
74	South Pasadena (păs-ȧ-dē'nȧ) Calif. (Los Angeles In.)	34·06 N	118·08 W
72	South Pease (R.) (pēz) . . . . . . Tex.	33·54 N	100·45 W
65	South Pender (I.) (pĕn'dēr) Can. (Vancouver In.)	48·45 N	123·09 W
78	South Pittsburg (pĭts'bûrg) . Tenn.	35·00 N	85·42 W
62	South Platte (R.) (plăt) . . . . . U. S.	40·40 N	102·40 W
80	South Pt. . . . . Mich.	44·50 N	83·20 W
93	South Pt. Barb. (Le. & Wind. Is. In.)	13·00 N	59·43 W
160	Southport (south'pōrt) . . . . . Austl.	27·57 S	153·27 E
79	Southport . . . . N. C.	35·55 N	78·02 W
110	Southport (south'pôrt) . . . . . . Eng.	53·38 N	3·00 W
75	Southport . Ind. (Indianapolis In.)	39·40 N	86·07 W
82	South Portland (pōrt-lănd) . Maine	43·37 N	70·15 W
65	South Prairie (prā'rĭ) Wash. (Seattle In.)	47·08 N	122·06 W
74	South Range (rānj) Wis. (Duluth In.)	46·37 N	91·59 W
84	South River (rĭv'ēr) N. J. (New York In.)	40·27 N	74·23 W
84	South R. . . . . . . Ga. (Atlanta In.)	33·40 N	84·15 W
74	South St. Paul Minn. (Minneapolis, St. Paul In.)	44·54 N	93·02 W
74	South Salt Lake (sôlt lāk) Utah (Salt Lake City In.)	40·44 N	111·53 W
96	South Sandwich Is. (sănd'wĭch) Falk. Is.	58·00 S	27·00 W
96	South Sandwich Trench S. A.-Ant.	55·00 S	27·00 W
65	South San Francisco (săn frăn-sĭs'kô) Calif. (San Francisco In.)	37·39 N	122·24 W
86	South Saskatchewan (R.) (săs-kăch'ê-wăn) . Can.	50·29 N	110·25 W
116	South Shields (shēldz) . . . . Eng.	55·00 N	1·22 W
116	South Shropshire Hills (shrŏp'shīr) . Eng.	52·30 N	3·02 W
70	South Sioux City (sōō sĭt'ê) . Nebr.	42·28 N	96·26 W
159	South Taranaki Bght. (tä-rä-nä'kê) . N. Z. (In.)	39·27 S	171·44 E
74	Southton (south'tŭn) Tex. (San Antonio In.)	29·18 N	98·26 W
116	South Uist (I.) (ū'ĭst) . . . . Scot.	56·83 N	6·64 W
66	South Umpqua R. (ŭmp'kwȧ) . Ore.	43·00 N	122·54 W
110	Southwell (south'wĕl) . . . . Eng.	53·04 N	0·56 W
163	South West Africa (ăf'rĭ-kä) . . Afr.	19·30 S	16·13 E
159	Southwest C. . . . . N. Z. (In.)	47·17 S	167.12 E
65	South Westminster (wĕst'mĭn-stēr) Can. (Vancouver In.)	49·12 N	122·53 W
95	Southwest Pt. . . . . Ba. Is.	23·55 N	74·30 W
94	Southwest Pt. . . . . Ba. Is.	25·50 N	77·10 W
94	Southwest Pt. . . . . Ba. Is.	26·35 N	78·35 W
119	Sovetsk (Tilsit) (sô-vyĕtsk') Sov. Un.	55·04 N	21·54 E
135	Sovetskaya Gavan' (sŭ-vyĕt'skī-u gä'vŭn') . Sov. Un.	48·59 N	140·14 E
138	Soviet Union (sō-vĭ-ĕt') . . Eur.-Asia	60·30 N	64·00 E
110	Sow (R.) (sou) . . . . Eng.	52·45 N	2·12 W
152	Sōya Kaikyō (Str.) (sō'ya kī'kyō) Jap.-Sov. Un.	45·45 N	141·38 E
152	Sōya Misaki (C.) (sō'yȧ mē'sä-kē) Jap.	45·35 N	141·25 E
128	Sozh (R.) (sôzh) . . . . Sov. Un.	52·17 N	31·00 E
127	Sozopol (sôz'ô-pôl') . . . . Bul.	42·18 N	27·50 E
117	Spa (spä) . . . . Bel.	50·30 N	5·50 E
74	Spadra (spăd'rȧ) Calif. (Los Angeles In.)	34·03 N	117·48 W
102	Spain (spān) . . . . Eur.	40·15 N	4·30 W
70	Spalding (spôl'dĭng) . . . . Nebr.	41·43 N	98·23 W
65	Spanaway (spăn'ȧ-wā) Wash. (Seattle In.)	47·06 N	122·26 W
81	Spangler (spăng'lēr) . . . . Pa.	40·40 N	78·50 W
69	Spanish Fork (spăn'ĭsh fôrk) . Utah	40·10 N	111·40 W
163	Spanish Sahara (sȧ hä'rȧ) Afr.	23·05 N	15·33 W
94	Spanish Town . . . . Jam.	18·00 N	76·55 W
68	Sparks (spärks) . . . . Nev.	39·34 N	119·45 W
84	Sparrows Point (spăr'ōz) Md. (Baltimore In.)	39·13 N	76·29 W
78	Sparta (spär'tȧ) . . . . Ga.	33·16 N	82·59 W
73	Sparta . . . . Ill.	38·07 N	89·42 W
80	Sparta . . . . Mich.	43·10 N	85·45 W
78	Sparta . . . . Tenn.	35·54 N	85·26 W
71	Sparta . . . . Wis.	43·56 N	90·50 W
	Sparta, see Spárti		
84	Sparta Mts . N. J. (New York In.)	41·00 N	74·38 W
79	Spartanburg (spär'tăn-bûrg) . S. C.	34·57 N	82·13 W
124	Spartel (C.) (spär-tĕl') . . . . . . Mor.	35·48 N	5·50 W
127	Spárti (Sparta) . . . . Grc.	37·07 N	22·28 E
126	Spartivento, C. (spär-tê-vĕn'tō) . It.	37·55 N	16·09 E
126	Spartivento, C . . . . It.	38·54 N	8·52 E
128	Spas-Demensk (spȧs dyĕ-mĕnsk') Sov. Un.	54·24 N	34·02 E
128	Spas-Klepiki (spȧs klĕp'ê-kê) Sov. Un.	55·09 N	40·11 E
135	Spassk-Dal'niy (spŭsk'dâl'nyê) Sov. Un.	44·30 N	133·00 E
128	Spassk-Ryazanskiy (ryä-zän'skĭ) Sov. Un.	54·24 N	40·21 E
126	Spátha, Akr. (C.) . . . . Grc. (Inset)	35·42 N	23·45 E
84	Spaulding (spôl'dĭng) Ala. (Birmingham In.)	33·27 N	86·50 W
83	Spear, C. (spēr) . . . . Can.	47·28 N	52·30 W
70	Spearfish (spēr'fĭsh) . . . . S. D.	44·28 N	103·52 W
75	Speed (spēd) . Ind. (Louisville In.)	38·25 N	85·45 W
75	Speedway (spēd'wā) Ind. (Indianapolis In.)	39·47 N	86·14 W
111	Speicher L. (shpī'kĕr) Ger. (Munich In.)	48·12 N	11·47 E
80	Spencer (spĕn'sēr) . . . . Ind.	39·15 N	86·45 W
71	Spencer . . . . Iowa	43 09 N	95·08 W
79	Spencer . . . . N. C.	35·43 N	80·25 W
80	Spencer . . . . W. Va.	38·55 N	81·20 W
160	Spencer G. (spĕn'sēr) . . . . . . Austl.	34·20 S	136·55 E
111	Sperenberg (shpĕ'rĕn-bĕrgh) Ger. (Berlin In.)	52·09 N	13·22 E
127	Sperkhiós (R.) . . . . Grc.	38·54 N	22·02 E
116	Sperrin Mts. (spĕr'ĭn) . . . . . N. Ire.	54·55 N	6·45 E
120	Spessart (Mts.) (shpĕ'särt) . . . Ger.	50·07 N	9·32 E
116	Spey (L.) (spā) . . . . Scot.	57·25 N	3·29 W
120	Speyer (shpī'ēr) . . . . Ger.	49·18 N	8·26 E
168	Sphinx (Pyramid) (sfĭnks) U. A. R. (Nile In.)	29·57 N	31·08 E
111	Spijkenisse Neth. (Amsterdam In.)	51·51 N	4·18 E
126	Spinazzola (spê-nät'zô-lä) . . . . . . It.	40·58 N	16·05 E
66	Spirit Lake (spĭr'ĭt) . . . . Idaho	47·58 N	116·51 W
71	Spirit Lake (lāk) . . . . Iowa	43·25 N	95·08 W
86	Spirit River . . . . Can.	55·50 N	118·50 W
121	Spišská Nová Ves (spēsh'skä nō'vä vĕs) . Czech.	48·56 N	20·35 E
	Spitsbergen (Is.), see Svalbard		
120	Spittal (shpê-täl') . . . . Aus.	46·48 N	13·28 E
126	Split (splēt) . . . . Yugo.	43·30 N	16·28 E
66	Spokane (spōkăn') . . . . Wash.	47·39 N	117·25 W
66	Spokane R. . . . . Wash.	47·47 N	118·00 W
126	Spoleto (spô-lā'tō) . . . . It.	42·44 N	12·44 E
73	Spoon (R.) (spōōn) . . . . Ill.	40·36 N	90·22 W
71	Spooner (spōōn'ēr) . . . . Wis.	45·50 N	91·53 W

ng-sing; ŋ-baŋk; N-nasalized n; nŏd; cŏmmit; ōld; ôbey; ôrder; fōōd; fŏŏt; ou-out; s-soft; sh-dish; th-thin; pūre; ûnite; ûrn; stŭd; circŭs; ü-as "y" in study; '-indeterminate vowel.

Page	Name Pronunciation Region	Lat. °′	Long. °′
127	Sporádhes (Is.) Grc.	38·55 N	24·05 E
84	Spotswood (spŏtz′wŏŏd) N. J. (New York In.)	40·23 N	74·22 W
66	Sprague R. (sprāg) Ore.	42·30 N	121·42 W
154	Spratly (I.) (sprăt′lê) China	8·38 N	11·54 E
79	Spray (sprā) N. C.	36·30 N	79·44 W
120	Spree R. (shprā) Ger.	51·53 N	14·08 E
120	Spremberg (shprĕm′bĕrgh) Ger.	51·35 N	14·23 E
73	Spring (R.) Ark.	36·25 N	91·35 W
166	Springbok (spring′bŏk) S. Afr.	29·35 S	17·55 E
68	Spring, Cr. (spring) Nev.	40·18 N	117·45 W
77	Spring Cr. Tex.	30·03 N	95·43 W
76	Spring Cr. Tex.	31·08 N	100·50 W
73	Springdale (spring′dāl) Ark.	36·10 N	94·07 W
83	Springdale Can.	49·30 N	56·05 W
84	Springdale. Conn. (New York In.)	41·05 N	73·31 W
75	Springdale Pa. (Pittsburgh In.)	40·33 N	79·46 W
72	Springer (spring′ẽr) N. Mex.	36·21 N	104·37 W
72	Springfield (spring′fēld) Colo.	37·24 N	102·40 W
71	Springfield Minn.	44·14 N	94·59 W
66	Springfield Ore.	44·01 N	123·02 W
73	Springfield Ill.	39·46 N	89·37 W
80	Springfield Ky.	37·35 N	85·10 W
81	Springfield Mass.	42·05 N	72·35 W
73	Springfield Mo.	37·13 N	93·17 W
80	Springfield Ohio	39·55 N	83·50 W
78	Springfield Tenn.	36·30 N	86·53 W
81	Springfield Vt.	43·20 N	72·35 W
166	Springfontein (spring′fŏn-tīn) S. Afr.	30·16 S	25·45 E
82	Springhill (spring-hĭl′) Can.	45·39 N	64·04 W
68	Spring Mts. Nev.	36·18 N	115·49 W
167	Springs (springs) S. Afr. (Johannesburg & Pretoria In.)	26·16 S	28·27 E
85	Springstein (spring′stīn) Can. (Winnipeg In.)	49·49 N	97·29 W
84	Springton Res. (spring-tŭn) Pa. (Philadelphia In.)	39·57 N	75·26 W
161	Springvale Austl. (Melbourne In.)	37·57 S	145·09 E
68	Spring Valley Calif. (San Diego In.)	32·46 N	117·01 W
80	Springvalley (spring-văl′ĭ) Ill.	41·20 N	89·15 W
71	Spring Valley Minn.	43·41 N	92·26 W
84	Spring Valley N. Y. (New York In.)	41·07 N	74·03 W
69	Springville (spring-vĭl) Utah	40·10 N	111·40 W
161	Springwood Austl. (Sydney In.)	33·42 S	150·34 E
85	Spruce Grove (sprōōs grōv) Can. (Edmonton In.)	53·33 N	113·55 W
72	Spur (spûr) Tex.	33·29 N	100·51 W
81	Squam (L.) (skwôm) N. H.	43·45 N	71·30 W
126	Squillace, Gulfo di (G.) (gōō′l-fô-dē skwêl-lä′chā) It.	38·44 N	16·47 E
127	Srbija (Serbia) (Reg.) (sr bē-yä) (sẽr′bē-ä) Yugo.	44·05 N	20·35 E
127	Srbobran (s′r′bô-brän′) Yugo.	45·32 N	19·50 E
135	Sredne-Kolymsk (s′rĕd′nyĕ kô-lêmsk′) Sov. Un.	67·49 N	154·55 E
136	Sredne Rogartka (s′red′nä-ya) (rô gär′tkä) Sov. Un. (Leningrad In.)	59·49 N	30·20 E
136	Sredniy Ik (R.) (srĕd′nĭ ĭk) Sov. Un. (Urals In.)	55·46 N	58·50 E
136	Sredniy Ural (Mts.) (ŏŏ′rál) Sov. Un. (Urals In.)	57·47 N	59·00 E
121	Šrem (shrĕm) Pol.	52·06 N	17·01 E
127	Sremska Karlovci (srĕm′skê kär′lov-tsê) Yugo.	45·10 N	19·57 E
127	Sremska Mitrovica (srĕm′skä mē′trô-vê-tsä′) Yugo.	44·59 N	19·39 E
135	Sretensk (s′rĕ′tĕnsk) Sov. Un.	52·13 N	117·39 E
142	Srinagar (srē-nŭg′ŭr) India	34·11 N	74·49 E
121	Sroda (shrô′dà) Pol	52·14 N	17·17 E
146	Ssuch′uan (Szechwan) (Prov.) China	31·30 N	102·52 E
151	Ssuen China	24·50 N	108·18 E
148	Ssuhsien (sü′sĭän) China	33·29 N	116·57 E
146	Ssumao China	22·56 N	101·07 E
151	Ssunan China	27·50 N	108·30 E
150	Ssup′ing China	43·05 N	124·24 E
148	Ssushui (sĕ′sōōĭ) China	35·40 N	117·17 E
149	Ssut′uan China (Shanghai In.)	30·57 N	121·43 E
111	Stabroek Bel. (Brussels In.)	51·20 N	4·21 E
111	Stade (shtä′dĕ) Ger. (Hamburg In.)	53·36 N	9·28 E
112	Stadhur Ice.	65·08 N	20·56 W
118	Städjan (Mtn.) (stĕd′yän) Swe.	61·53 N	12·50 E
110	Stafford (stăf′fẽrd) Eng.	52·48 N	2·06 W
72	Stafford Kans.	37·58 N	78·37 W
110	Stafford (Co.) Eng.	52·45 N	2·00 W
111	Stahnsdorf (shtäns′dôrf) Ger. (Berlin In.)	52·22 N	13·10 E
	Stalin, see Varna		
	Stalinabad, see Dushanbe		
	Stalingrad, see Volgograd		
	Stalino, see Donetsk		
129	Stalino (Oblast) (stä′lĭ-nô) (ôb′lást) Sov. Un.	47·54 N	37·13 E
134	Stalino, Pik (Mtn.) Sov. Un.	39·00 N	72·15 E
	Stalinsk, see Novokuznetsk		
110	Stalybridge (stā′lē-brĭj) Eng.	53·29 N	2·03 W
71	Stambaugh (stăm′bô) Mich.	46·03 N	88·38 W
84	Stamford (stăm′fẽrd) Conn. (New York In.)	41·03 N	73·32 W
110	Stamford Eng.	52·39 N	0·28 W
72	Stamford Tex.	32·57 N	99·48 W
111	Stammersdorf (shtäm′ĕrs-dôrf) Aus. (Vienna In.)	48·19 N	16·25 E
73	Stamps (stămps) Ark.	33·22 N	93·31 W
73	Stanberry (stan′bĕr-ê) Mo.	40·12 N	94·34 W
168	Standerton (stăn′dẽr-tŭn) S. Afr. (Johannesburg & Pretoria In.)	26·57 S	29·17 E

Page	Name Pronunciation Region	Lat. °′	Long. °′
70	Standing Rock Ind. Res. (stănd′ing rŏk) N. D.	47·07 N	101·05 W
110	Standish (stăn′dĭsh) Eng.	53·36 N	2·39 W
78	Stanford (stăn′fẽrd) Ky.	37·29 N	84·40 W
167	Stanger (stăŋ-ger) S. Afr. (Natal In.)	29·22 S	31·18 E
118	Stangvik Fd. (stang′vêk fyôrd) Nor.	62·54 N	8·55 E
94	Staniard Creek Ba. Is.	24·50 N	77·55 W
68	Stanislaus (R.) (stăn′ĭs-lô) Calif.	38·10 N	120·16 W
82	Stanley (stăn′lê) Can.	46·19 N	66·45 W
100	Stanley Falk. Is.	51·46 S	57·59 W
70	Stanley N. D.	48·20 N	102·25 W
71	Stanley Wis.	44·56 N	90·56 W
165	Stanley Falls Con. K.	0·12 N	25·34 E
166	Stanley Pool (L.) Con. K.	4·15 S	16·00 E
142	Stanley Res. (stăn′lê) India	12·07 N	77·27 E
	Stanleyville, see Kisangani		
92	Stann Creek (stăn krēk) Br. Hond. (Yucatan In.)	17·01 N	88·14 W
135	Stanovoy Khrebet (Mts.) (stŭn-å-voi′) Sov. Un.	56·12 N	127·12 E
74	Stanton (stăn′tŭn) Calif. (Los Angeles In.)	33·48 N	118·00 W
70	Stanton Nebr.	41·57 N	97·15 W
76	Stanton Tex.	32·08 N	101·46 W
65	Stanwood (stăn′wŏŏd) Wash. (Seattle In.)	48·14 N	122·23 W
71	Staples (stā′p′lz) Minn.	46·21 N	94·48 W
127	Stara Planina (Balkan Mts.) Bul.	42·50 N	24·45 E
136	Staraya Kupavna (stä′rá-yá kû-päf′nà) Sov. Un. (Moscow In.)	55·48 N	38·10 E
128	Staraya Russa (stä′rá-yá rōōsà) Sov. Un.	57·58 N	31·21 E
127	Stara Zagora (zä′gô-rá) Bul.	42·26 N	25·37 E
85	Starbuck (stär′bŭk) Can. (Winnipeg In.)	49·46 N	97·38 W
120	Stargard Szczecinski (shtär′gärt shchĕ-chyn′skē) Pol.	53·19 N	15·03 E
128	Staritsa (stä′rê-tsà) Sov. Un.	56·29 N	34·58 E
79	Starke (stärk) Fla.	29·55 N	82·07 W
72	Starkville (stärk′vĭl) Colo.	37·06 N	104·34 W
78	Starkville Miss.	33·27 N	88·47 W
111	Starnberg (shtärn-bĕrgh) Ger. (Munich In.)	47·59 N	11·20 E
129	Starobel′sk (stä-rô-byĕlsk′) Sov. Un.	49·19 N	38·57 E
128	Starodub (stä-rô-drōōp′) Sov. Un.	52·25 N	32·49 E
121	Starograd Gdański (stä′rō-grad gdĕn′skē) Pol.	53·58 N	18·33 E
129	Staro-Konstantinov (stä′rô kôn-stán-tē′nôf) Sov. Un.	49·45 N	27·12 E
129	Staro-Minskaya (stä′rô mĭn′ská-yá) Sov. Un.	46·19 N	38·51 E
129	Staro-Shcherbinovskaya Sov. Un.	46·38 N	38·38 E
136	Staro-Subkhangulovo (stäro-sōōb-kan-gōō′lōvō) Sov. Un. (Urals In.)	53·08 N	57·24 E
136	Staroutkinsk (stá-rô-ōōt′kĭnsk) Sov. Un. (Urals In.)	57·14 N	59·21 E
129	Staroverovka Sov. Un.	49·31 N	35·48 E
116	Start Pt. (stärt) Eng.	50·14 N	3·34 W
121	Stary Sącz (stä-rê sôŋch′) Pol.	49·32 N	20·36 E
129	Staryy Oskol (stä′rê ôs-kôl′) Sov. Un.	51·18 N	37·51 E
120	Stassfurt (shtäs′fōōrt) Ger.	51·52 N	11·35 E
121	Staszów (stä′shōōf) Pol.	50·32 N	21·13 E
81	State College (stāt kŏl′ĕj) Pa.	40·50 N	77·55 W
74	State Line (līn) Minn. (Duluth In.)	46·36 N	92·18 W
84	Staten I. (stăt′ĕn) N. Y. (New York In.)	40·35 N	74·10 W
79	Statesboro (stāts′bŭr-ô) Ga.	32·26 N	81·47 W
79	Statesville (stāts′vĭl) N. C.	35·45 N	80·54 W
74	Staunton (stôn′tŭn) Ill. (St. Louis In.)	39·01 N	89·47 W
81	Staunton Va.	38·10 N	79·05 W
118	Stavanger (stä′väng′ẽr) Nor.	58·59 N	5·44 E
65	Stave (R.) (stāv) Can. (Vancouver In.)	49·12 N	122·24 W
110	Staveley (stāv′lē) Eng.	53·17 N	1·21 W
111	Stavenisse Neth.(Amsterdam In.)	51·35 N	3·59 E
133	Stavropol′ Sov. Un.	45·05 N	41·50 E
120	Stawno (swav′nō) Pol	54·21 N	16·38 E
72	Steamboat Springs (stēm′bōt′) Colo.	40·30 N	106·48 W
129	Steblëv (styĕp′lyôf) Sov. Un.	49·23 N	31·03 E
71	Steel (R.) (stēl) Can.	49·08 N	86·55 W
81	Steelton (stēl′tŭn) Pa.	40·15 N	76·45 W
111	Steenbergen Neth. (Amsterdam In.)	51·35 N	4·18 E
66	Steens Mts. (stēnz) Ore.	42·15 N	118·52 W
158	Steep Pt. (stēp) Austl.	26·15 S	112·05 E
165	Stefanie L. (stĕf-á-nē′) Eth.	4·46 N	37·31 E
75	Steger (stē′gẽr) Ill. (Chicago In.)	41·28 N	87·38 W
120	Steiermark (Styria) (state) (shtī′ẽr-märk) Aus.	47·22 N	14·40 E
86	Steinbach Can.	49·28 N	96·52 W
112	Steinkjer (stĕĭn-kyĕr) Nor.	64·00 N	11·19 E
65	Stella (stĕl′á) Wash. (Portland In.)	46·11 N	123·12 W
83	Stellarton (stĕl′ár-tŭn) Can.	45·34 N	62·41 W
120	Stendal (shtĕn′däl) Ger.	52·37 N	11·51 E
133	Stepanakert (styĕ′pän-á-kĕrt) Sov. Un.	39·50 N	46·40 E
160	Stephens, Port (stē′fĕns) Austl.	32·43 S	152·55 E
83	Stephenville (stē′vĕn-vĭl) Can.	48·31 N	58·38 W
84	Stepney Depot (stĕp-nê) Conn. (New York In.)	41·17 N	73·15 W
134	Stepnyak (styĭp-nyäk′) Sov. Un.	52·37 N	70·43 E
123	Sterkrade (shtĕr′krädĕ) Ger. (Ruhr In.)	51·31 N	6·51 E
167	Sterkstroom S. Afr. (Natal In.)	31·33 S	26·36 E

Page	Name Pronunciation Region	Lat. °′	Long. °′
72	Sterling (stûr′lĭng) Colo.	40·38 N	103·14 W
71	Sterling Ill.	41·48 N	89·42 W
72	Sterling Kans.	38·11 N	98·11 W
83	Sterling Mass. (Boston In.)	42·26 N	71·41 W
76	Sterling Tex.	31·53 N	100·58 W
136	Sterlitamak (styĕr′lĕ-ta-mák′) Sov. Un. (Urals In.)	53·38 N	55·56 E
121	Šternberk (shtĕrn′bĕrk) Czech.	49·44 N	17·18 E
	Stettin, see Szczecin		
120	Stettiner Haff (L.) (shtĕ′tē-nẽr häf) Ger.	53·47 N	14·02 E
86	Stettler Can.	52·19 N	112·50 W
80	Steubenville (stū′bĕn-vĭl) Ohio	40·20 N	80·40 W
65	Stevens (L.) (stē′vĕnz) Wash. (Seattle In.)	47·59 N	122·06 W
71	Stevens Point Wis.	44·30 N	89·35 W
67	Stevensville (stē′vĕnz-vĭl) Mont.	46·31 N	114·03 W
65	Steveston (stēvz′tŭn) Can. (Vancouver In.)	49·08 N	123·11 W
86	Stewart (R.) (stū′ẽrt) Can.	63·27 N	138·48 W
159	Stewart I. N. Z. (In.)	46·50 S	168·06 E
82	Stewiacke (stū′wē-ăk) Can.	45·08 N	63·22 W
168	Steynsrus (stīns′rōōs) S. Afr. (Johannesburg & Pretoria In.)	27·58 S	27·33 E
120	Steyr (shtīr) Aus.	48·03 N	14·24 E
86	Stikine (R.) (stĭ-kēn′) Can.	58·17 N	103·10 W
86	Stikine Mts. Can.	59·24 N	129·12 W
65	Stillaguamish (R.) Wash. (Seattle In.)	48·11 N	122·18 W
65	Stillaguamish (R.), South Fk. (stĭl-á-gwä′mĭsh) Wash. (Seattle In.)	48·05 N	121·59 W
74	Stillwater (stĭl′wô-tẽr) Minn. (Minneapolis, St. Paul In.)	45·04 N	92·48 W
67	Stillwater Mont.	45·23 N	109·45 W
73	Stillwater Okla.	36·06 N	97·03 W
68	Stillwater Ra. Nev.	39·43 N	118·11 W
66	Stillwater R. Mont.	48·47 N	114·40 W
127	Štip (shtĭp) Yugo.	41·43 N	22·07 E
116	Stirling (stûr′lĭng) Scot.	56·05 N	3·59 W
85	Stittsville (stĭts′vĭl) Can. (Ottawa In.)	45·15 N	75·54 W
118	Stjördalshalsen (styûr-däls-hälsĕn) Nor.	63·26 N	11·00 E
71	Stockbridge Munsee Ind. Res. (stŏk′brĭdj mŭn-sē) Wis.	44·49 N	89·00 W
111	Stockerau (shtô′kĕ-rou) Aus. (Vienna In.)	48·24 N	16·13 E
82	Stockholm (stŏk′hōlm) Maine	47·05 N	68·08 W
118	Stockholm (stôk′hôlm′) Swe.	59·23 N	18·00 E
110	Stockport (stŏk′pôrt) Eng.	53·24 N	2·09 W
68	Stockton (stŏk′tŭn) Calif.	37·56 N	121·16 W
116	Stockton Eng.	54·35 N	1·25 W
72	Stockton Kans.	39·26 N	99·16 W
71	Stockton (I.) Wis.	46·56 N	90·25 W
76	Stockton Plat Tex.	30·34 N	102·35 W
118	Stöde (stû′dĕ) Swe.	62·26 N	16·35 E
110	Stoke-on-Trent (stōk-ŏn-trĕnt) Eng.	53·01 N	2·12 W
121	Stokhod (R.) (stō-kōd) Sov. Un.	51·24 N	25·20 E
127	Stolac (stō′láts) Yugo.	43·03 N	17·59 E
135	Stolbovoy (Is.) (stôl-bô-voi′) Sov. Un.	73·43 N	133·05 E
121	Stolin (stô′lēn) Sov. Un.	51·54 N	26·52 E
123	Stommeln (shtō′mĕln) Ger. (Ruhr In.)	51·01 N	6·46 E
118	Stömstad Swe.	58·58 N	11·09 E
110	Stone Eng.	52·54 N	2·09 W
85	Stoneham (stōn′ăm) Can. (Quebec In.)	46·59 N	71·22 W
83	Stoneham Mass. (Boston In.)	42·30 N	71·05 W
116	Stonehaven (stōn′hā-v′n) Scot.	56·57 N	2·09 W
84	Stone Mountain (stōn) Ga. (Atlanta In.)	33·49 N	84·10 W
85	Stonewall (stōn′wôl) Can. (Winnipeg In.)	50·08 N	97·19 W
78	Stonewall Miss.	32·08 N	88·44 W
85	Stoney Creek (stō′nê) Can. (Toronto In.)	43·13 N	79·45 W
85	Stoney Ind. Res. Can (Calgary In.)	51·10 N	114·45 W
81	Stonington (stōn′ĭng-tŭn) Conn.	41·20 N	71·55 W
68	Stony Cr. (stō′nê) Calif.	39·28 N	122·35 W
85	Stony Mountain Can. (Winnipeg In.)	50·05 N	97·13 W
85	Stony Plain (stō′nê plān) Can. (Edmonton In.)	53·23 N	114·00 W
84	Stony Point. N. Y. (New York In.)	41·13 N	73·58 W
118	Storå (R.) Den.	56·22 N	8·35 E
132	Stora Lule (R.) (stōō′rá lōō′lĕ) Swe.	67·00 N	19·30 E
118	Stord (I.) (stōrd) Nor.	59·54 N	5·15 E
118	Store Baelt (Str.) Den.	55·25 N	10·50 E
112	Stören (stûrĕn) Nor.	62·58 N	10·21 E
118	Store Sotra (Sartor) (stô-rĕ-sō′-trá) (sär′tôr) Nor.	60·24 N	4·35 E
118	Stor Fd. (stôr fyôrd) Nor.	62·17 N	6·19 E
167	Stormberg (Mts.) (stôrm′bûrg) S. Afr. (Natal In.)	31·28 S	26·35 E
71	Storm Lake Iowa	42·39 N	95·12 W
89	Stormy Pt. (stôrm′ē) Vir. Is. (U. S. A.) (St. Thomas In.)	18·22 N	65·01 W
116	Stornoway (stôr′nô-wā) Scot.	58·13 N	6·21 W
121	Storozhinets (stô-rô′zhēn-yĕts) Sov. Un.	48·10 N	25·44 E
118	Storsjö (stôr′shû) Swe.	62·49 N	13·08 E
118	Storsjöen (L.) (stôr-syûĕn) Nor.	61·32 N	11·30 E
118	Storsjön (L.) Swe.	63·06 N	14·00 E
118	Storvik (stôr′vêk) Swe.	60·37 N	16·31 E
83	Stoughton (stō′tŭn) Mass. (Boston In.)	42·07 N	71·06 W
71	Stoughton Wis.	42·54 N	89·15 W
117	Stour (R.) (stour) Eng.	52·09 N	0·29 E
110	Stourbridge (stour′brĭj) Eng.	52·27 N	2·08 W
83	Stow (stō) Mass. (Boston In.)	42·56 N	71·31 W
75	Stow Ohio (Cleveland In.)	41·09 N	81·26 W

ăt; finăl; rāte; senâte; ärm; àsk; sofá; fâre; ch-choose; dh-as th in other; bē; ēvent; bĕt; recĕnt; cratẽr; g-go; gh-guttural g; bĭt; ĭ-short neutral· rīde; K-guttural k as ch in German ich;

Page	Name	Pronunciation	Region	Lat. °'	Long. °'
168	Straatsdrif (Johannesburg & Pretoria In.)		S. Afr.	25·19 s	26·22 E
116	Strabane (strá-băn')		N. Ire.	54·52 N	6·60 w
159	Stradbroke Is. (străd'brŏk)		Austl.	27·45 s	154·18 E
123	Straelen (shträ'lĕn)		Ger. (Ruhr In.)	51·26 N	6·16 E
159	Strahan (strä'ăn)		Austl.	42·08 s	145·28 E
120	Strakonice (strä'kŏ-nyĕ-tsĕ)		Czech.	49·18 N	13·52 E
127	Straldzha (sträl'dzhä)		Bul.	42·37 N	26·44 E
120	Stralsund (shräl'sŏŏnt)		Ger.	54·18 N	13·04 E
118	Strand (stränd)		Nor.	59·05 N	5·59 E
116	Strangford, Lough (B.) (lŏᴋ sträng'fĕrd)		Ire.·	54·30 N	5·34 w
118	Strängnas (strĕng'nĕs)		Swe.	59·23 N	16·59 E
116	Stranraer (străn-rär')		Scot.	54·55 s	5·05 w
123	Strasbourg (sträs-bōōr')		Fr.	48·36 N	7·49 E
80	Stratford (străt'fĕrd)		Can.	43·20 N	81·05 w
81	Stratford		Conn.	41·10 N	73·05 w
116	Stratford		Eng.	52·13 N	1·41 w
71	Stratford		Wis.	44·16 N	90·02 w
120	Straubing (strou'bĭng)		Ger.	48·52 N	12·36 E
120	Strausberg (strous'bĕrgh)		Ger.	52·35 s	13·50 E
69	Strawberry (R.)		Utah	40·05 N	110·55 w
66	Strawberry Mts. (strô'bĕr'ĭ)		Ore.	44·19 N	119·20 w
76	Strawn (strôn)		Tex.	32·38 N	98·28 w
80	Streator (strē'tĕr)		Ill.	41·05 N	88·50 w
70	Streeter		N. D.	46·40 N	99·22 w
85	Streetsville (strētz'vĭl)		Can. (Toronto In.)	43·34 N	79·43 w
127	Strehaia (strĕ-kä'yà)		Rom.	44·37 N	23·13 E
136	Strel'na (strĕl'nä)		Sov. Un. (Leningrad In.)	59·52 N	30·01 E
110	Stretford (strĕt'fĕrd)		Eng.	53·25 N	2·19 w
155	Strickland (R.) (strĭk'lănd)		Pap.	6·15 s	142·00 E
111	Strijen (strī'ĕn)		Neth. (Amsterdam In.)	51·44 N	4·32 E
127	Strimonikós Kólpos (G.)		Grc.	40·44 N	23·55 E
126	Strómboli (Vol.) (strŏm'bŏ-lē)		It.	38·46 N	15·16 E
136	Stromyn (strô'mĭn)		Sov. Un. (Moscow In.)	56·02 N	38·29 E
78	Strong (R.) (strông)		Miss.	32·03 N	89·42 w
75	Strongsville (strôngz'vĭl)		Ohio (Cleveland In.)	41·19 N	81·50 w
116	Stronsay (I.) (strŏn'sá)		Scot.	59·09 N	2·35 w
81	Stroudsburg (stroudz'bûrg)		Pa.	41·00 N	75·15 w
118	Struer (strŏŏ'ĕr)		Den.	56·29 N	8·34 E
128	Strugi Krasnyye (strŏŏ'gĭ krá's-ny'yĕ)		Sov. Un.	58·14 N	29·10 E
127	Struma (R.) (strŏŏ'mä)		Bul.	41·55 N	23·05 E
127	Strumica (strŏŏ'mĭ-tsä)		Yugo.	41·26 N	22·38 E
80	Struthers (strŭdh'ĕrz)		Ohio	41·00 N	80·35 w
111	Struvenhütten (shtrŏŏ'vĕn-hü-tĕn)		Ger. (Hamburg In.)	53·52 N	10·04 E
168	Strydpoortberg (Mts.) (Johannesburg & Pretoria In.)		S. Afr.	23·45 s	29·18 E
121	Stryy (strē')		Sov. Un.	49·16 N	23·51 E
121	Strzelce Opolskie (stzhĕl'tsĕ o-pŏl'skyĕ)		Pol.	50·31 N	18·20 E
121	Strzelin (stzhĕ'lĭn)		Pol.	50·48 N	17·06 E
121	Strzelno (stzhäl'nŏ)		Pol.	52·37 N	18·10 E
79	Stuart (stū'ĕrt)		Fla. (In.)	27·10 N	80·14 w
71	Stuart		Iowa	41·31 N	94·20 w
64	Stuart (I.)		Alaska	63·25 N	162·45 w
65	Stuart (I.)		Wash. (Vancouver In.)	48·42 N	123·10 w
158	Stuart Ra.		Austl.	29·00 s	134·30 E
154	Stung Treng (stŏŏng'trĕng')		Camb.	13·36 N	106·00 E
111	Stupava		Czech. (Vienna In.)	48·17 N	17·02 E
121	Stupsk (swŏŏpsk)		Pol.	54·28 N	17·02 E
71	Sturgeon (R.)		Mich.	46·43 N	88·43 w
71	Sturgeon Bay		Wis.	44·50 N	87·22 w
87	Sturgeon Falls		Can.	46·19 N	79·49 w
85	Sturgeon R. (stûr'jŭn)		Can. (Edmonton In.)	53·41 N	113·46 w
80	Sturgis		Ky.	37·35 N	88·00 w
80	Sturgis (stûr'jĭs)		Mich.	41·45 N	85·25 w
70	Sturgis		S. D.	44·25 N	103·31 w
158	Sturt Cr.		Austl.	19·40 s	127·40 E
75	Sturtevant (stûr'tĕ-vănt)		Wis. (Milwaukee In.)	42·42 N	87·54 w
167	Stutterheim (stŭrt'ĕr-hīm)		S. Afr. (Natal In.)	32·34 s	27·27 E
73	Stuttgart (stŭt'gärt)		Ark.	34·30 N	91·33 w
120	Stuttgart (shtŏŏt'gärt)		Ger.	48·48 N	9·15 E
112	Stykkisholmur		Ice.	65·00 N	21·48 w
121	Styr' R. (stĕr)		Sov. Un.	51·44 N	26·07 E
	Styria, see Steiermark				
165	Suakin (swä'kĕn)		Sud.	19·02 N	37·19 E
151	Suao (sŏŏ'ou)		Taiwan	24·35 N	121·45 E
142	Subarnarakha (R.)		India	22·38 N	86·26 E
119	Subata (sŏŏ'bà-tä)		Sov. Un.	56·02 N	25·54 E
155	Subic (sŏŏ'bĭk)		Phil. (Manila In.)	14·52 N	120·15 E
155	Subic B.		Phil. (Manila In.)	14·41 N	120·11 E
127	Subotica (sŏŏ'bŏ'tĕ-tsä)		Yugo.	46·06 N	19·41 E
84	Succasunna (sŭk'kà-sŭn'nà)		N. J. (New York In.)	40·52 N	74·37 w
121	Suceava (sŏŏ-chä-ä'và)		Rom.	47·39 N	26·17 E
121	Suceava R.		Rom.	47·45 N	26·10 E
121	Sucha (sŏŏ'kä)		Pol.	49·44 N	19·40 E
135	Suchan (sŏŏ-chän')		Sov. Un.	43·15 N	133·19 E
91	Suchiapa (soo-chĕ-a'pa)		Mex.	16·38 N	93·08 w
91	Suchiapa (R.)		Mex.	16·27 N	93·26 w
148	Such'ien (sŭ'chñän')		China	33·57 N	118·17 E
92	Suchitoto (sŏŏ-chē-tō'tō)		Sal.	13·58 N	89·03 w
	Süchow, see Hsüchou				
	Süchow, see Ipin				
65	Sucia Is. (sŏŏ'sĕ-á)		Wash. (Vancouver In.)	48·46 N	122·54 w
98	Sucio (R.) (sŏŏ'syŏ)		Col. (In.)	6·55 N	76·15 w
116	Suck (sŭk)		Ire.	53·34 N	8·16 w
98	Sucre (sŏŏ'krä)		Bol.	19·06 s	65·16 w
99	Sucre (State) (sŏŏ'krĕ)		Ven.	10·18 N	64·12 w
99	Suçuapara (sŏŏ-sŏŏä-pá'rä)		Braz.	16·57 s	48·47 w
95	Sud, Canal du (Chan.)		Hai.	18·40 N	73·15 w
85	Sud, Rivière du (rê-vyär'dü süd')		Can. (Quebec In.)	46·56 N	70·35 w
36	Suda (sŏŏ'dá)		Sov. Un. (Urals In.)	56·58 N	56·45 E
128	Suda (R.) (sŏŏ'dà)		Sov. Un.	59·24 N	36·40 E
144	Sudair (sŭ-dä'ĕr)		Sau. Ar.	25·48 N	46·28 E
163	Sudan		Afr.	14·00 N	28·00 E
163	Sudan (Reg.) (sŏŏ-dan')		Afr.	16·48 N	3·11 E
87	Sudbury (sŭd'bĕr-è)		Can.	46·28 N	81·00 w
83	Sudbury		Mass. (Boston In.)	42·23 N	71·25 w
120	Sudetes (Mts.)		Czech.	50·41 N	15·37 E
128	Sudogda (sŏŏ-dŏk-dà)		Sov. Un.	55·57 N	40·29 E
128	Sudost' (R.) (sŏŏ-dŏst')		Sov. Un.	52·43 N	33·13 E
139	Sudr (R.)		U. A. R. (Palestine In.)	29·46 N	32·57 E
129	Sudzha (sŏŏd'zhä)		Sov. Un.	51·14 N	35·11 E
125	Sueca (swä'kä)		Sp.	39·12 N	0·18 w
	Suez, see As Suways				
	Suez Canal, see Qana el Suweis				
168	Suez, G. of		U. A. R. (Suez In.)	29·53 N	32·33 E
84	Suffern (sŭf'fĕrn)		N. Y. (New York In.)	41·07 N	74·09 w
84	Suffolk (sŭf'ŭk)		Va. (Norfolk In.)	36·43 N	76·35 w
146	Sufu (Kashgar)		China	39·29 N	76·00 E
80	Sugar (Cr.)		Ind.	39·55 N	87·10 w
72	Sugar City		Colo.	38·12 N	103·42 w
74	Sugar Creek		Mo. (Kansas City In.)	39·07 N	94·27 w
73	Sugar Cr. (shŏŏg'ĕr)		Ill.	40·14 N	89·28 w
74	Sugar I.		Mich. (Sault Ste. Marie In.)	46·31 N	84·12 w
77	Sugarland Jct. (shŏŏg'ĕr-lănd)		Tex. (In.)	29·29 N	95·31 w
160	Sugarloaf Pt. (sŏŏgĕr'lŏf)		Austl.	32·19 s	153·04 E
142	Suget Pass (sŏŏ'gĕt)		China	36·35 N	77·40 E
120	Suhl (zŏŏl)		Ger.	50·37 N	10·41 E
148	Suhsien (sŏŏ'sĭän)		China	33·37 N	117·51 E
151	Suichuan (Mtn.)		China	26·25 N	114·10 E
148	Suichung (sŏŏī'jŏŏng)		China	40·22 N	120·20 E
135	Suifenho (swä'fŭn'hŭ')		China	44·47 N	131·13 E
150	Suihua (Peilintzu)		China	41·38 N	126·42 E
148	Suining (sŏŏ'ē-nĭng')		China	33·54 N	117·57 E
101	Suipacha (swē-pä'chä)		Arg. (Buenos Aires In.)	34·45 s	59·43 w
148	Suip'ing (sŏŏ'ē-pĭng)		China	33·09 N	113·58 E
116	Suir R. (sūr)		Ire.	52·20 N	7·32 w
65	Suisun B. (sŏŏ-ē-sŏŏn')		Calif. (San Francisco In.)	38·07 N	122·02 w
153	Suita (sŏŏ'ē-tä)		Jap. (Osaka In.)	34·45 s	135·32 E
150	Suite		China	37·32 N	110·12 E
84	Suitland (sŏŏt'lănd)		Md. (Baltimore In.)	38·51 N	76·57 w
146	Suiyuan (Prov.) (sŏŏ'ē-yän')		China	41·31 N	107·04 E
154	Sukabumi		Indon.	6·52 s	106·56 E
154	Sukadana		Indon.	1·15 s	110·30 E
153	Sukagawa (sŏŏ'kä-gä'wä)		Jap.	37·08 N	140·07 E
155	Sukarnapura (Hollandia)		W. Irian	2·30 s	140·45 E
128	Sukhinichi (sŏŏ'kē'nĕ-chĕ)		Sov. Un.	54·07 N	35·18 E
132	Sukhona (R.) (sŏŏ-kô'nä)		Sov. Un.	59·30 N	42·20 E
136	Sukhoy Log (sŏŏ'kôy lôg)		Sov. Un. (Urals In.)	56·55 N	62·03 E
133	Sukhumi (sŏŏ-kŏŏm')		Sov. Un.	43·00 N	41·00 E
142	Sukkur (sŭk'ŭr)		W. Pak.	27·49 N	68·50 E
136	Suksun (sŏŏk'sŏŏn)		Sov. Un. (Urals In.)	57·08 N	57·22 E
153	Sukumo (sŏŏ'kŏŏ-mô)		Jap.	32·58 N	132·45 E
153	Sukurai (sŏŏ'kŏŏ-rī)		Jap. (Osaka In.)	34·31 N	135·51 E
155	Sula (I.)		Indon.	2·20 s	125·20 E
129	Sula (R.) (sŏŏ-lä')		Sov. Un.	50·36 N	33·13 E
92	Sulaco R. (sŏŏ-lä'kŏ)		Hond.	14·55 N	87·31 w
142	Sulaiman Ra. (sŏŏ-lä-ē-män')		W. Pak.	34·22 N	69·10 E
133	Sulak (R.) (sŏŏ-läk')		Sov. Un.	43·30 N	47·00 E
154	Sulawesi (Prov.)		Indon.	1·30 s	120·22 E
118	Suldals Vand (L.) (sŭl-däls vän)		Nor.	59·35 N	6·59 E
136	Suleya (sŏŏ-lĕ'yá)		Sov. Un. (Urals In.)	55·12 N	58·52 E
111	Sulfeld (zŏŏl'fĕld)		Ger. (Hamburg In.)	53·48 N	10·13 E
129	Sulina (sŏŏ-lē'nä)		Rom.	45·08 N	29·38 E
112	Sulitjema (Mtn.) (sŏŏ-lē-t'yĕl'mä)		Nor.-Swe.	67·03 N	16·09 E
98	Sullana (sŏŏ-lyä'nä)		Peru	4·57 N	80·47 w
78	Sulligent (sŭl'ĭ-jĕnt)		Ala.	33·52 N	88·06 w
80	Sullivan (sŭl'ĭ-văn)		Ill.	41·35 N	88·35 w
80	Sullivan		Ind.	39·05 N	87·20 w
73	Sullivan		Mo.	38·13 N	91·09 w
126	Sulmona (sŏŏl-mō'nä)		It.	42·02 N	13·58 E
146	Sulo		China	41·29 N	80·15 E
146	Sulo Ho (R.)		China	40·53 N	94·55 E
73	Sulphur (sŭl'fŭr)		Okla.	34·31 N	96·58 w
73	Sulphur (R.)		Tex.	33·26 N	95·06 w
73	Sulphur Springs (sprĭngz)		Tex.	33·09 N	95·36 w
65	Sultan (sŭl'tăn)		Wash. (Seattle In.)	47·52 N	121·49 w
65	Sultan (R.)		Wash. (Seattle In.)	47·55 N	121·49 w
90	Sultepec (sŏŏl-tå-pĕk')		Mex.	18·50 N	99·51 w
154	Sulu Arch. (sŏŏ'lŏŏ)		Phil.	5·52 N	122·00 E
115	Suluntah		Libya	32·39 N	21·49 E
115	Suluq		Libya	31·41 N	20·23 E
154	Sulu Sea		Phil.	8·25 N	119·00 E
153	Suma (sŏŏ'mä)		Jap. (Osaka In.)	34·39 N	135·08 E
65	Sumas (sū'más)		Wash. (Vancouver In.)	49·00 N	122·16 w
139	Sumatera Tenga (Prov.)		Indon. (Singapore In.)	0·56 N	101·25 E
154	Sumatra (I.)		Indon.	2·06 N	99·40 E
154	Sumba (I.) (sŭm'bä)		Indon.	9·52 s	119·00 E
154	Sumbawa (I.) (sŏŏm-bä'wä)		Indon.	9·00 s	118·18 E
154	Sumbawa-Besar		Indon.	8·32 s	117·20 E
121	Sümeg (shü'mĕg)		Hung.	46·59 N	17·19 E
153	Sumida (R.) (sŏŏ'mĕ-dä)		Jap.	36·01 N	139·24 E
101	Sumidouro (sŏŏ-mê-dō'rŏŏ)		Braz. (Rio de Janeiro In.)	22·04 s	42·41 w
153	Sumiyoshi (sŏŏ'mê-yō'shè)		Jap. (Ōsaka In.)	34·43 N	135·16 E
66	Summer L. (sŭm'ĕr)		Ore.	42·50 N	120·35 w
82	Summerside (sŭm'ĕr-sīd)		Can.	46·25 N	63·47 w
79	Summerton (sŭm'ĕr-tŭn)		S. C.	33·37 N	80·22 w
79	Summerville (sŭm'ĕr-vĭl)		S. C.	33·00 N	80·10 w
75	Summit (sŭm'mĭt)		Ill. (Chicago In.)	41·47 N	87·48 w
84	Summit		N. J. (New York In.)	40·43 N	74·21 w
66	Summit Lake Ind. Res.		Nev.	41·35 N	119·30 w
69	Summit Pk.		Colo	37·20 N	106·40 w
65	Sumner (sŭm'nĕr)		Wash. (Seattle In.)	47·12 N	122·14 w
120	Šumperk (shŏŏm'pĕrk)		Czech.	49·57 N	17·02 E
78	Sumrall (sŭm'rôl)		Miss.	31·25 N	89·34 w
79	Sumter (sŭm'tĕr)		S. C.	33·55 N	80·21 w
129	Sumy (sŏŏ'mĭ)		Sov. Un.	50·54 N	34·47 E
129	Sumy (Oblast)		Sov. Un.	51·02 N	34·05 E
81	Sunbury (sŭn'bĕr-è)		Pa.	40·50 N	76·45 w
154	Sunda Is.		Indon.	9·00 s	108·40 E
118	Sundals Fd. (sŏŏn'däls)		Nor.	62·50 N	7·55 E
67	Sundance (sŭn'dăns)		Wyo.	44·24 N	104·27 w
142	Sundarbans (Swp.) (sŏŏn'dĕr-bŭns)		E. Pak.-India	21·50 N	89·00 E
154	Sunda Selat (Str.)		Indon.	5·45 s	106·15 E
154	Sunda Trench (sŏŏn'dä)		Indon.	9·45 s	107·30 E
167	Sundays (R.) (sŭn'dās)		S. Afr. (Natal In.)	33·17 s	25·14 E
158	Sunday Str. (sŭn'dā)		Austl.	15·50 s	122·45 E
118	Sundbyberg (sŏŏn'bü-bĕrgh)		Swe.	59·24 N	17·56 E
116	Sunderland (sŭn'dĕr-lănd)		Eng.	54·55 N	1·25 w
84	Sunderland		Md. (Baltimore In.)	38·41 N	76·36 w
118	Sundsvall (sŏŏnds'väl)		Swe.	62·24 N	19·19 E
78	Sunflower (R.) (sŭn-flou'ĕr)		Miss.	32·57 N	90·40 w
150	Sungari Res. (sŏŏng-gä-rē)		China	42·55 N	127·50 E
	Sungari, see Sung Hua (R.)				
149	Sungchiang		China (Shanghai In.)	31·01 N	121·14 E
147	Sung Hua (R.) (Sungari) (sŏŏn'gà-rē)		China	46·09 N	127·53 E
150	Sungtzu (Mtn.)		China	39·40 N	114·50 E
133	Sungurlu (sŏŏn'gŏŏr-lŏŏ')		Tur.	40·08 N	34·20 E
142	Sun Kosi (R.)		Nepal	27·13 N	85·52 E
74	Sunland (sŭn-lănd)		Calif. (Los Angeles In.)	34·16 N	118·18 w
118	Sunne (sŏŏn'ĕ)		Swe.	59·51 N	13·07 E
110	Sunninghill (sŭnĭng'hĭl)		Eng. (London In.)	51·23 N	0·40 w
74	Sunnymead (sŭn'ĭ-mēd)		Calif. (Los Angeles In.)	33·56 N	117·15 w
69	Sunnyside (sŭn'ĭ-sīd)		Utah	39·35 N	110·20 w
66	Sunnyside		Wash.	46·19 N	120·00 w
65	Sunnyvale (sŭn-nĕ-vāl)		Calif. (San Francisco In.)	37·23 s	122·02 w
65	Sunol (sŏŏ'nŭl)		Calif. (San Francisco In.)	37·36 s	122·53 w
67	Sun R. (sŭn)		Mont.	47·34 N	111·53 w
74	Sunset (sŭn-sĕt)		Utah (Salt Lake City In.)	41·08 N	112·02 w
69	Sunset Crater Natl. Mon. (krā'tĕr)		Ariz.	35·20 N	111·30 w
161	Sunshine		Austl. (Melbourne In.)	37·47 s	144·50 E
135	Suntar (sŏŏn-tär')		Sov. Un.	62·14 N	117·49 E
119	Suoyarvi (sŏŏ'ô-yär'vè)		Sov. Un.	62·12 N	32·29 E
69	Superior (su-pē'rĭ-ĕr)		Ariz.	33·15 N	111·10 w
72	Superior		Nebr.	40·04 N	98·05 w
74	Superior		Wis. (Duluth In.)	46·44 N	92·06 w
67	Superior		Wyo.	41·45 N	108·57 w
91	Superior, Laguna (L.) (lä-gōō'nä sŏŏ-pā-rê-ōr')		Mex.	16·20 N	94·55 w
63	Superior, L.		U. S.-Can.	47·38 N	89·20 w
74	Superior Village		Wis. (Duluth In.)	46·38 N	92·07 w
152	Sup'ung Res. (sŏŏ'pŏŏng)		Kor.-China	40·35 N	126·00 E
65	Suquamish (sŏŏ-gwä'mĭsh)		Wash. (Seattle In.)	47·44 N	122·34 w
139	Sür (Tyre) (sŏŏr) (tïr)		Leb. (Palestine In.)	33·16 N	35·13 E
144	Sür		Muscat and Oman	22·23 N	59·28 E
154	Surabaia		Indon.	7·23 s	112·45 E
168	Surad Ad (Mt.) (sŏŏ'răd-äd)		Som. (Horn of Afr. In.)	10·40 N	47·23 E
154	Surakarta		Indon.	7·35 s	110·45 E
121	Šurany (shŏŏ'rä-nŭ')		Czech.	48·05 N	18·11 E
160	Surat (sŏŏ-rät)		Austl.	27·18 s	149·00 E
142	Surat (sŏŏ'rŭt)		India	21·08 N	73·22 E
154	Surat Thani		Thai.	8·59 N	99·14 E
128	Surazh (sŏŏ-räzh')		Sov. Un.	53·02 N	32·27 E
128	Surazh		Sov. Un.	55·24 N	30·46 E
122	Surgères (sür-zhâr')		Fr.	46·06 N	0·51 w
134	Surgut (sür-gŏŏt')		Sov. Un.	61·18 N	73·38 E
154	Surin		Thai.	14·59 N	103·57 E
99	Surinam (Neth.) (sōō-rê-näm')		S. A.	3·45 N	56·30 w
99	Suriname (R.)		Sur.	4·15 N	55·38 w
119	Sur-Sari (I.) (sŏŏr-sä'rï)		Sov. Un.	60·04 N	26·55 E
153	Suruga-Wan (B.) (sŏŏ'rŏŏ-gä wän)		Jap.	34·52 N	138·36 E
165	Surt		Libya	31·14 N	16·37 E
115	Surt, Khalij (G.)		Afr.	31·30 N	18·28 E
126	Susa (sŏŏ'sä)		It.	45·01 N	7·09 E
153	Susa		Jap.	34·40 N	131·39 E
126	Susač (sŏŏ'shäts)		Yugo.	44·31 N	14·15 E
126	Sušak (sŏŏ'shäk)		Yugo.	45·20 N	14·24 E
126	Sušak (I.)		Yugo.	42·45 N	16·30 E
153	Susaki (sŏŏ'sä-kè)		Jap.	33·23 N	133·16 E
64	Susitna (sŏŏ-sīt'ná)		Alaska	61·28 N	150·28 w
64	Susitna (R.)		Alaska	62·00 N	150·28 w
81	Susquehanna (sŭs'kwĕ-hän'á)		Pa.	41·55 N	75·35 w
81	Susquehanna (R.)		Pa.	39·50 N	76·20 w
75	Sussex		Wis. (Milwaukee In.)	43·08 N	88·12 w
82	Sussex (sŭs'ĕks)		Can.	45·42 N	65·32 w
84	Sussex		N. J. (New York In.)	41·12 N	74·36 w
151	Susung (sŏŏ'sŏŏng)		China	30·18 N	116·08 E

ng-sing; ŋ-baŋk; ɴ-nasalized n; nŏd; cŏmmit; ōld; ŏbey; ôrder; fōōd; fŏŏt; ou-out; s-soft; sh-dish; th-thin; pūre; ûnite; ûrn; stŭd; circǔs; ū-as "y" in study; '-indeterminate vowel.

Page	Name Pronunciation Region	Lat. °′	Long. °′
154	Talakmau, Gunung (Mtn.) . Indon.	0·12 N	100·05 E
165	Tala Mt. . . . . Eth.	11·00 N	38·41 E
92	Talanga (tä-lä′n-gä) . . . . Hond.	14·21 N	87·09 W
98	Talara (tä-lä′rä) . . . . Peru	4·32 N	81·17 W
155	Talasea (tä-lä-sā′ä) . . N. Gui. Ter.	5·20 S	150·00 E
155	Talaud, Pulau-Pulau (Is.) (tä-lout′) . Indon.	4·17 N	127·30 E
124	Talavera de la Reina (tä-lä-vā′rä dā lä rå-ē′nä) . Sp.	39·58 N	4·51 W
74	Talbert (tôl′bûrt) Calif. (Los Angeles In.)	33·42 N	117·57 W
101	Talca (täl′kä) . Chile (Santiago In.)	35·25 S	71·39 W
101	Talca (Prov.) . Chile (Santiago In.)	35·23 S	71·15 W
101	Talca, Punta (Pt.) (pōō′n-tä-täl′kä) Chile (Santiago In.)	33·25 S	71·42 W
100	Talcahuano (täl-kä-wä′nō) . . Chile	36·41 S	73·05 W
128	Taldom (täl-dôm) . . . . Sov. Un.	56·44 N	37·33 E
134	Taldy-Kurgan (tal′dĭ-kŏŏr-gän′) Sov. Un.	45·03 N	77·18 E
91	Talea de Castro (San Miguel) (tä′lå-ä dā käs′trō) . Mex.	17·22 N	96·14 W
122	Talence (tå-lôɴs) . . . . Fr	44·48 N	0·38 W
146	Tali (tä′lē) . . . . China	26·00 N	100·08 E
155	Taliabu (tä-lê-ä′bōō) . . . . . . Indon.	1·30 S	125·00 E
148	Talichi (dä′lē′jē) . . . . China	33·47 N	117·47 E
148	Talien (Dairen) (dä′lĭän) . . . China	38·54 N	121·35 E
148	Talien Wan (B.) (wän) . . . . . China	38·55 N	121·50 E
155	Talim (I.) (tä-lēm′) Phil. (Manila In.)	14·21 N	121·14 E
155	Talisay (tä-lē′sī) . Phil. (Manila In.)	14·08 N	122·56 E
64	Talkeetna (tål-kēt′nå) . . . . . Alaska	62·18 N	150·02 W
133	Talkheh Rūd (R.) . . . . Iran	38·00 N	46·50 E
78	Talladega (tăl-å-dē′gȧ) . . . . Ala.	33·25 N	86·06 W
78	Tallahassee (tăl-ȧ-hăs′ê) . . . . . . Fla.	30·25 N	84·17 W
78	Tallahatchie (R.) (tal-ȧ hăch′ê) Miss.	34·21 N	90·03 W
78	Tallapoosa (tăl-ȧ-pōō′sȧ) . . . . . Ga.	33·44 N	85·15 W
78	Tallapoosa (R.) . . . . Ala.	32·22 N	86·08 W
78	Tallassee (tăl′ȧ-sê) . . . . Ala.	32·30 N	85·54 W
119	Tallinn (Reval) (tål′lên) (rā′väl) Sov. Un.	59·26 N	24·44 E
75	Tallmadge (tăl′mĭj) Ohio (Cleveland In.)	41·06 N	81·26 W
77	Tallulah (tă-lōō′lȧ) . . . . La.	32·25 N	91·13 W
93	Talmanca, Cord. de (Mts.) (kôr-dēl-yĕ′rä-dĕ-täl-mä′n-kä) C. R.	9·37 N	83·55 W
129	Tal′noye (tål′nô-yĕ) . . . . . Sov. Un.	48·52 N	30·43 E
165	Talōdi (tä-lō′dê) . . . . Sud.	10·41 N	30·21 E
143	Taloje Budrukh India (Bombay In.)	19·05 N	73·05 E
90	Talpa de Allende (täl′pä dā äl-yĕn′då) . Mex.	20·25 N	104·48 W
119	Talsi (tal′sĭ) . . . . Sov. Un.	57·16 N	22·35 E
100	Taltal (täl-täl′) . . . . Chile	25·26 S	70·32 W
129	Taly (täl′ĭ) . . . . Sov. Un.	49·51 N	40·07 E
71	Tama (tā′mä) . . . . Iowa	41·57 N	92·36 W
153	Tama (R.) . . . . . . Jap. (Tōkyō In.)	35·38 N	139·35 E
164	Tamale (tä-mä′lå) . . . . Ghana	9·16 N	00·53 W
129	Taman′ (tå-män′′) . . . . . . Sov. Un.	45·13 N	36·46 E
98	Tamaná, Cerro (Mtn.) (sĕ′r-rô-tä-mä-nå′) . Col. (In.)	5·06 N	76·10 W
99	Tamanaco (tä-mä-nä′kō) (R.) Ven. (In.)	9·32 N	66·00 W
164	Tamanr′aset R. (tä-män-räs′sĕt) Alg.	22·15 N	2·51 E
164	Tamanrasset . . . . Alg.	22·34 N	5·34 E
81	Tamaqua (tȧ-mô′kwă) . . . . Pa.	40·45 N	75·50 W
116	Tamar (R.) (tā′mär) . . . . Eng.	50·35 N	4·15 W
125	Tamarite (tä-mä-rē′tā) . . . . Sp.	41·52 N	0·24 E
167	Tamatave (tä-må-täv′) Malag. Rep.	18·14 S	49·25 E
90	Tamaulipas (State) (tä-mä-ōō-lē′päs′) . Mex.	23·45 N	98·30 W
90	Tamazula de Gordiano (tä-mä-zōō′lä dā gôr-dê-ä′nô) Mex.	19·44 N	103·09 W
91	Tamazulapan del Progreso (tä-mä-zōō-lä′päm-dĕl-prô-grĕ-sō) . Mex.	17·41 N	97·34 W
90	Tamazunchale (tä-mä-zŏŏn-chä′lå) Mex.	21·16 N	98·46 W
164	Tambacounda (täm-bä-kōōn′dä) Senegal	13·45 N	13·52 W
99	Tambador, Serra do (Mts.) (sĕ′r-rä-dô-täm′bä-dōr) . Braz.	10·33 S	41·16 W
153	Tambaichi (täm′bī′chê) Jap. (Ōsaka In.)	34·36 N	135·50 E
154	Tambelan, Pulau-Pulau (Is.) (täm-bå-län′) . Indon.	0·38 N	107·38 E
160	Tambo (tăm′bō) . . . . Austl.	24·50 S	146·15 E
133	Tambov (tåm-bôf′) . . . . . Sov. Un.	52·45 N	41·10 E
128	Tambov (Oblast) . . . . Sov. Un.	52·50 N	40·42 E
124	Tambre (R.) (täm′brā) . . . . Sp.	42·59 N	8·33 W
165	Tambura (täm-bōō′rä) . . . . Sud.	5·34 N	27·30 E
110	Tame (R.) (tām) . . . . Eng.	52·41 N	1·42 W
124	Tamega (R.) (tå-mā′gå) . . . . . Port.	41·30 N	7·45 W
90	Tamesí (R.) (tä-mĕ sē′) . . . . . Mex.	22·36 N	98·32 W
164	Tamgak, Monts (Mt.) (tam-gäk′) Niger	19·06 N	8·31 E
114	Tamgrout (täm-grōōt′) . . . . . . Mor.	30·12 N	5·46 W
164	Tamgue, M. du (Mt.) . . . . Gui.	12·13 N	12·28 W
91	Tamiahua (tä-myä-wä) . . . . . Mex.	21·17 N	97·26 W
91	Tamiahua, Laguna (L.) (lä-gŏŏ′nä-tä-myä-wä) . Mex.	21·38 N	97·33 W
79	Tamiami, can. (tă-mī-ăm′ĭ) Fla. (In.)	25·52 N	80·08 W
148	Taming (dä′mĭng) . . . . China	36·15 N	115·09 E
119	Tammela (tåm′ĕ-lå) . . . . Fin.	60·49 N	23·45 E
	Tammisaari, see Ekenäs		
79	Tampa (tăm′på) . . . . Fla. (In.)	27·57 N	82·25 W
79	Tampa B . . . . Fla. (In.)	27·35 N	82·38 W
112	Tampere (tåm′pĕ-rĕ) . . . . Fin.	61·21 N	23·39 E
91	Tampico (täm-pē′kō) . . . . Mex.	22·14 N	97·51 W
91	Tampico Alto (täm-pē′kō äl′tō) Mex.	22·07 N	97·48 W
139	Tampin . . . . Mala. (Singapore In.)	2·28 N	102·15 E
155	Tamrau (Mtn.) . . . . W. Irian	0·45 S	132·26 E
90	Tamuín (tä-mōō-ê′n) . . . . Mex.	22·04 N	98·47 W
160	Tamworth (tăm′wûrth) . . . . Austl.	31·01 S	151·00 E
110	Tamworth . . . . Eng.	52·58 N	1·41 W
167	Tana (R.) (tä′nä) . . . . Ken.	0·22 S	39·33 E
159	Tana (I.) . . . . New Hebr.	19·32 S	169·27 E
112	Tana (R.) . . . . Nor.-Fin.	69·20 N	24·54 E
153	Tanabe (tä-nä′bā) . . . . Jap.	33·45 N	135·21 E
153	Tanabe . . . . Jap. (Osaka In.)	34·49 N	135·46 E
64	Tanacross (tă′nå-crōs) . . . . . Alaska	63·20 N	143·30 W
64	Tanaga (I.) (tä-nä′gä) . . . . . Alaska	51·28 N	178·10 W
154	Tanahbala (I.) (tå-nä-bä′lä) Indon.	0·30 S	98·22 E
154	Tanahmasa (I.) (tå-nä-mä′sä) Indon.	0·03 S	97·30 E
142	Tanakpur (tǎn′ǎk-poor) . . . . . India	29·10 N	80·07 E
165	Tana L . . . . Eth.	12·09 N	36·41 E
158	Tanami (tå-nā′mê) . . . . Austl.	19·45 S	129·50 E
64	Tanana (tă′nå-nô) . . . . Alaska	65·18 N	152·20 W
64	Tanana (R.) . . . . Alaska	64·26 N	148·40 W
167	Tananarive (tå-nä-nä-rēv′) Malag. Rep.	18·51 S	47·40 E
126	Tanaro (R.) (tä-nä′rô) . . . . It.	44·45 N	8·02 E
155	Tanauan (tä-nä′wän) Phil. (Manila In.)	14·04 N	121·10 E
148	T′anch′eng (tän′chĕng) . . . . . China	34·37 N	118·22 E
152	Tanchŏn (tän′chŭn) . . . . Kor.	40·29 N	128·50 E
90	Tancítaro (tän-sē′tä-rō) . . . . . Mex.	19·16 N	102·24 W
90	Tancítaro, Cerro de (sĕ′r-rô-dĕ) Mex.	19·24 N	102·19 W
91	Tancoco (tän-kō′kō) . . . . Mex.	21·16 N	99·45 W
100	Tandil (tän-dēl′) . . . . Arg.	36·16 S	59·01 W
100	Tandil, Sierra del (Mts.) . . . . . Arg.	38·40 S	59·40 W
154	Tandjungbalai (tän′jông-bä′lå′) Indon.	2·52 N	99·43 E
139	Tandjungbalai Indon. (Singapore In.)	1·00 N	103·26 E
139	Tandjung Berakit (C.) Indon. (Singapore In.)	1·16 N	104·44 E
154	Tandjungpandan . . . . Indon.	2·47 S	107·51 E
139	Tandjungpinang (tän′jŏng-pē′näng) Indon. (Singapore In.)	0·55 N	104·29 E
153	Tanega (I.) (tä′nå-gä′) . . . . Jap.	30·36 N	131·11 E
164	Tanezrouft (Reg.) (tä′nĕz-rŏŏft) Alg.	24·17 N	0·30 W
148	T′ang (R.) (täng) . . . . China	33·38 N	117·29 E
167	Tanga (tăŋ′gå) . . . . Tan.	5·07 S	39·06 E
90	Tangancícuaro (täŋ-gän-sē′kwä rô) . Mex.	19·52 N	102·13 W
166	Tanganyika, L . . . . Tan.	6·00 S	30·15 E
148	T′angchiacha (tăng′jēä′jä) . . China	32·06 N	120·48 E
149	Tangchiaochen China (Shanghai In.)	31·13 N	121·30 E
164	Tanger (tăn-jēr′) . . . . Mor.	35·52 N	5·55 W
120	Tangermünde (täŋ′ĕr-mün′de) Ger.	52·33 N	11·58 E
150	Tangho . . . . China	32·40 N	112·50 E
148	T′anghsien (täng′sĭän) . . . . . China	38·09 N	115·00 E
77	Tangipahoa R. (tăn′jê-pȧ-hō′ȧ) La.	30·48 N	90·28 W
148	T′angku (täŋ′kōō′) . . . . China	39·04 N	117·41 E
142	Tangra Tsho (L.) . . . . China	30·38 N	85·40 E
148	Tangt′u (däng′tōō) . . . . China	31·35 N	118·28 E
148	Tangshan (täng′shän′) . . . . China	34·27 N	116·27 E
148	T′angshan . . . . China	39·38 N	118·11 E
155	Tanimbar, Pulau-Pulau (Is.) Indon.	8·00 S	132·00 E
139	Tanjong (C.) . Mala. (Singapore In.)	1·53 N	102·29 E
139	Tanjong Piai (I.) Mala. (Singapore In.)	1·16 N	103·11 E
139	Tanjong Ramunia (C.) Mala. (Singapore In.)	1·27 N	104·44 E
143	Tanjore (tăn-jôr′) . . . . India	10·51 N	79·11 E
131	Tannu-Ola (Mts.) . . . . Sov. Un.	51·00 N	94·00 E
155	Tañong (tän-yōn′) Phil. (Manila In.)	14·46 N	120·52 E
149	T′anpu . . . . China (Canton In.)	23·20 N	113·06 E
91	Tanquijo, Arrecife (Reef) (är-rĕ-sē′fĕ-tän-kê′kô) . Mex.	21·07 N	97·16 W
168	Ţanţā (tän′tä) . U. A. R. (Nile In.)	30·50 N	31·00 E
90	Tantoyuca (tän-tō-yōō′kä) . . Mex.	21·22 N	98·13 W
148	Tanyang (dän′yäng) . . . . China	32·01 N	119·32 E
152	Tanyang . . . . Kor.	36·53 N	128·20 E
163	Tanzania . . . . Afr.	6·48 S	33·58 E
152	Taoan (tä′ō-än′) . . . . China	45·41 N	123·00 E
148	T′aoch′ichen (tou′chē′jĕn) . . China	31·33 N	117·01 E
150	Taoerh (R.) . . . . China	45·40 N	122·00 E
150	Táo Ho′ (R.) (tä′ō hō′) . . . . China	35·30 N	103·40 E
148	Tao Hu (L.) (tou′hōō) . . . . . China	31·37 N	119·29 E
148	T′aok′ou (tou′kō) . . . . China	35·34 N	114·32 E
150	T′aonan (tä′ō-nän′) . . . . China	45·15 N	122·45 E
126	Taormina (tä-ôr-mē′nä) . . . . It.	37·53 N	15·18 E
69	Taos (tä′ôs) . . . . N. Mex.	36·25 N	105·35 W
164	Taoudenni (tä′ōō-dĕ-nê′) . . . . Mali	22·57 N	3·37 W
164	Taoudenni (Oasis) . . . . Mali	23·00 N	3·48 W
164	Taoulo (tä′ōō-lō) . . . . Lib.	6·30 N	8·49 W
164	Taourirt (tä-ōō-rērt′) . . . . Alg.	27·08 N	0·06 E
151	Taoyüan (tä′ō-yü-än′) . . . . . . China	29·00 N	111·15 E
119	Tapa (tå′på) . . . . Sov. Un.	59·16 N	25·56 E
92	Tapachula . . . . Mex.	14·55 N	92·20 W
150	Tapa Shan (Mts.) . . . . China	32·25 N	108·20 E
99	Tapajós (R.) (tä-pä-zhô′s) . . Braz.	3·27 S	55·33 W
101	Tapalqué (tä-päl-kĕ′) Arg. (Buenos Aires In.)	36·22 S	60·05 W
91	Tapanatepec (tä-pä-nä-tĕ-pĕk) Mex.	16·22 N	94·19 W
166	Tapepo (Mtn.) . . . . Tan.	7·57 S	31·28 E
151	Tapieh Shan (Mts.) . . . . China	31·40 N	114·50 E
148	Tapingi (dä′pĭng′yē) . . . . China	35·30 N	117·38 E
152	Tappi Saki (C.) (täp′pê sä′kê) Jap.	41·05 N	139·40 E
65	Tapps (L.) (tăpz) Wash. (Seattle In.)	47·20 N	122·12 W
142	Tāpti (R.) (täp′tê) . . . . India	21·38 N	74·10 E
149	Tapuhsü . . . . . . China (Canton In.)	23·17 N	113·34 E
99	Taquara, Serra de (Mts.) (sĕ′r-rä-dĕ-tä-kwä′rä) . Braz.	15·28 S	54·33 W
99	Taquari (R.) (tä-kwä′rĭ) . . . . Braz.	18·35 S	56·50 W
79	Tar (R.) (tär) . . . . N. C.	35·58 N	78·06 W
134	Tara (tä′rå) . . . . Sov. Un.	56·58 N	74·13 E
155	Tara (I.) (tä′rä) . Phil. (Manila In.)	12·18 N	120·28 E
134	Tara (R.) (tä′rå) . . . . Sov. Un.	56·32 N	76·13 E
139	T′arābulus (Tripoli) (tå-rä′bŏŏ-lōōs) Leb. (Palestine In.)	34·25 N	35·50 E
165	Tarābulus (Tripoli) . . . . Libya	32·50 N	13·13 E
165	Tarābulus (Tripolitania) (Prov.) Libya	31·00 N	12·26 E
154	Tarakan (Bunju) . . . . Indon.	3·17 N	118·04 E
124	Tarancón (tä-rän-kōn′) . . . . Sp.	40·01 N	3·00 W
126	Taranto (tä′rän-tô) . . . . It.	40·30 N	17·15 E
126	Taranto, Golfo di (G.) (gôl-fô-dē tä′rän-tô) . It.	40·03 N	17·10 E
98	Tarapoto (tä-rä-pô′tō) . . . . Peru	6·29 S	76·26 W
122	Tarare (tå-rär′) . . . . Fr.	45·55 N	4·23 E
122	Tarascon (tå-rås-kôɴ′) . . . . Fr.	42·53 N	1·35 E
122	Tarascon-sur-Rhône (tä-räs-kŏɴ-sür-rōn′) . Fr.	43·47 N	4·41 E
129	Tarashcha (tä′råsh-chå) . Sov. Un.	49·34 N	30·52 E
98	Tarata (tä-rä′tä) . . . . Bol.	17·43 S	66·00 W
126	Taravo (R.) . . . . Fr.	41·54 N	8·58 E
124	Tarazona (tä-rä-thō′nä) . . . . Sp.	41·54 N	1·45 W
124	Tarazona de la Mancha (tä-rä-zô′nä-dĕ-lä-mä′n-chă) . Sp.	39·13 N	1·50 W
116	Tarbat Ness (Hd.) (tår′båt) . Scot.	57·51 N	3·50 W
122	Tarbes (tårb) . . . . Fr.	43·04 N	0·05 E
79	Tarboro (tär′bŭr-ô) . . . . N. C.	35·53 N	77·34 W
165	Tarbū . . . . Libya	26·07 N	15·49 E
160	Taree (tă-rē′) . . . . Austl.	31·52 S	152·21 E
139	Tareifiya (R.) U. A. R. (Palestine In.)	29·34 N	33·41 E
75	Tarentum (tȧ-rĕn′tŭm) Pa. (Pittsburgh In.)	40·36 N	79·44 W
168	Tarfa, Wadi el (Val.) U. A. R. (Nile In.)	28·14 N	31·00 E
164	Tarhmanant (Well) (tăr-mä-nänt′) . Mali	24·32 N	4·58 W
124	Tarifa (tä-rē′fä) . . . . Sp.	36·02 N	5·35 W
98	Tarija (tär-rē′hä) . . . . Bol.	21·42 S	64·52 W
144	Tarīm (tå-rĭm′) . . . . S. Ar.	16·13 N	49·08 E
146	Tarim (R.) (tå-rĭm′) . . . . China	40·45 N	85·39 E
146	Tarim Basin (tå-rĭm′) . . . . . . China	39·52 N	82·34 E
167	Tarka (R.) (tä′kȧ) S. Afr. (Natal In.)	32·15 S	26·00 E
167	Tarkastad . . . . . S. Afr. (Natal In.)	32·01 S	26·18 E
129	Tarkhankut, Mys (C.) (mĭs tår-ĸän′kŏŏt) . Sov. Un.	45·18 N	32·08 E
73	Tarkio (tär′kĭ-ō) . . . . Mo.	40·27 N	95·22 W
164	Tarkwa (tärk′wä) . . . . Ghana	5·16 N	2·03 W
155	Tarlac (tär′läk) Phil. (Manila In.)	15·29 N	120·36 E
167	Tarlton (tärl′tŭn) . . . . S. Afr. (Johannesburg & Pretoria In.)	26·05 S	27·38 E
98	Tarma (tär′mä) . . . . Peru	11·26 S	75·40 W
122	Tarn (R.) (tärn) . . . . Fr.	44·03 N	2·41 E
121	Târnava Mica R. (tĕr-nä′vå mē′kŏ) . Rom.	46·17 N	24·20 E
121	Tarnów (tär′nŏŏf) . . . . Pol.	50·02 N	21·00 E
126	Taro (R.) (tä′rō) . . . . It.	44·41 N	10·03 E
164	Taroudant (tå-rōō-dänt′) . . . . Mor.	30·39 N	8·52 W
79	Tarpon Springs (tär′pŏn) Fla. (In.)	28·07 N	82·44 W
110	Tarporley (tär′pēr-lê) . . . . Eng.	53·09 N	2·40 W
95	Tarpum B. (tär′pŭm) . . . . Ba. Is.	25·05 N	76·20 W
126	Tarquinia (Corneto) (tär-kwē′nê-ä) (kôr-nā′tô) . It.	42·16 N	11·46 E
125	Tarragona (tär-rä-gō′nä) . . . . . . Sp.	41·05 N	1·15 E
84	Tarrant (tăr′ănt) Ala. (Birmingham In.)	33·35 N	86·46 W
125	Tarrasa (tär-rä′sä) . . . . Sp.	41·34 N	2·01 E
125	Tárrega (tä rå-gä) . . . . Sp.	41·40 N	1·09 E
125	Tarrejón de Ardoz (tär-rĕ-ĸô′n-dĕ-är-dôz) Sp. (Madrid In.)	40·28 N	3·29 W
84	Tarrytown (tăr′ĭ-toun) N. Y. (New York In.)	41·04 N	73·52 W
133	Tarsus (tår′sŏŏs) (tär′sŭs) . . . . Tur.	37·00 N	34·50 E
100	Tartagal (tär-tä-gå′l) . . . . Arg.	23·31 S	63·47 W
115	Tartous (tår-tōōs′) . . . . . . U. A. R.	34·54 N	35·59 E
128	Tartu (Dorpat) (tär′tōō) (dôr′pät) Sov. Un.	58·23 N	26·44 E
153	Tarumi (tä′rōō-mê) Jap. (Ōsaka In.)	34·38 N	135·04 E
128	Tarusa (tä-rōōs′å) . . . . Sov. Un.	54·43 N	37·11 E
74	Tarzana (tär-ză′ȧ) Calif. (Los Angeles In.)	34·10 N	118·32 W
148	Tashanchen (dä′shän′jĕn) . China	34·17 N	119·17 E
103	Tashauz (tŭ-shŭ-ōōs′) . . . Sov. Un.	41·50 N	59·45 E
142	Tashi-Chho Dzong (Thimbu) . Bhu.	27·33 N	89·42 E
134	Tashkent (tåsh′kĕnt) . . . . Sov. Un.	41·23 N	69·04 E
159	Tasman B. (tăz′măn) . N. Z. (In.)	39·11 S	173·22 E
159	Tasmania (I.) (tăz-mā′nĭ-ȧ) Austl.	41·28 S	142·30 E
160	Tasman Pen . . . . Austl.	43·00 S	148·30 E
156	Tasman Sea . . . . Oceania	29·30 S	155·00 E
90	Tasquillo (täs-kē′lyō) . . . . Mex.	20·34 N	99·21 W
164	Tassili-n-Ajjer (Plat.) (tås′ê-lê ä′jĕr) . Alg.	25·40 N	6·57 E
132	Tatar (A. S. S. R.) (tå-tär′) Sov. Un.	55·30 N	51·00 E
134	Tatarsk (tå-tärsk′) . . . . . . Sov. Un.	55·15 N	75·00 E
135	Tatar Str . . . . Sov. Un.	51·00 N	141·45 E
65	Tater Hill (Mtn.) (tāt′ĕr hĭl) Ore. (Portland In.)	45·47 N	123·02 W
153	Tateyama (tä′tê-yä′mä) . . . . . . Jap.	35·04 N	139·52 E
166	Tati (tä′tê) . . . . Bots.	21·18 S	27.43 E
121	Tatra Mts . . . . Czech.-Pol.	49·15 N	19·40 E

ng-sing; ŋ-banŋ; ɴ-nasalized n; nŏd; cŏmmit; ōld; ôbey; ôrder; fōōd; fŏŏt; ou-out; s-soft; sh-dish; th-thin; pūre; ûnite; ûrn; stŭd; circŭs; ü-as "y" in study; ′-indeterminate vowel.

Page	Name	Pronunciation	Region	Lat. °'	Long. °'
151	Tattien Ting (Mtn.)		China	22·25 N	111·20 E
151	Tatu Ho (R.)		China	29·20 N	103·30 E
101	Tatuí	(tä-tōō-ē′)	Braz. (Rio de Janeiro In.)	23·21 s	47·49 w
150	Tat'ung	(tä′ŏŏng)	China	40·00 N	113·30 E
101	Taubaté	(tou-bà-tā′)	Braz. (Rio de Janeiro In.)	23·03 s	45·32 w
120	Tauern Tun.		Aus.	47·13 N	13·17 E
165	Taufikia	(tou-fēk′yà)	Sud.	9·30 N	31·47 E
166	Taungs	(tä′ŏŏngs)	S. Afr.	27·25 s	29·45 E
84	Taunton	(tän′tŭn)	Mass. (Providence In.)	41·54 N	71·03 w
84	Taunton R.		R. I. (Providence In.)	41·50 N	71·02 w
117	Taunus (Mts.)	(tou′nōōz)	Ger.	50·15 N	8·33 E
159	Taupo, L.	(tä′ōō-pō)	N. Z.	38·38 s	175·27 E
119	Taurage	(tou′rà-gä)	Sov. Un.	55·15 N	22·18 E
	Taurus Mts., see Toros Dağlari				
124	Tauste	(tä-ōōs′tä)	Sp.	41·55 N	1·15 w
134	Tavda	(tàv-dä′)	Sov. Un.	58·00 N	64·44 E
132	Tavda (R.)		Sov. Un.	59·20 N	63·28 E
123	Taverny	(tà-věr-nē′)	Fr. (Paris In.)	49·02 N	2·13 E
91	Taviche	(tä-vē′chě)	Mex.	16·43 N	96·35 w
124	Tavira	(tä-vē′rá)	Port.	37·09 N	7·42 w
154	Tavoy	(tä-voi′)	Bur.	14·04 N	98·19 E
133	Tavşanli	(tàv′shän-lĭ′)	Tur.	39·30 N	29·30 E
77	Tawakoni (L.)		Tex.	32·51 N	95·59 w
153	Tawaramoto	(tä′wä-rä-mō-tō)	Jap. (Ōsaka In.)	34·33 N	135·48 E
80	Tawas City		Mich.	44·15 N	83·30 w
80	Tawas Pt.	(tô′wàs)	Mich.	44·15 N	83·25 w
148	Tawen (R.)	(dä′wěn)	China	35·58 N	116·53 E
154	Tawitawi Group (Is.)	(tä′wě-tä′wě)	Phil.	4·52 N	120·35 E
90	Taxco de Alarcón	(täs′kō dě à-lär-kō′n)	Mex.	18·34 N	99·37 w
116	Tay, Firth of	(fûrth ŏv tā)	Scot.	56·26 N	2·45 w
116	Tay (L.)		Scot.	56·25 N	5·07 w
116	Tay (R.)		Scot.	56·35 N	3·37 w
155	Tayabas B.	(tä-yä′bäs)	Phil. (Manila In.)	13·44 N	121·40 E
134	Tayga	(tī′gä)	Sov. Un.	56·12 N	85·47 E
135	Taygonos, Mys (Taigonos) (C.)		Sov. Un.	60·37 N	160·17 E
77	Taylor	(tā′lẽr)	Tex.	30·35 N	97·25 w
69	Taylor, Mt.		N. Mex.	35·20 N	107·40 w
80	Taylorville	(tā′lẽr-vĭl)	Ill.	39·30 N	89·20 w
144	Taymā		Sau. Ar.	27·45 N	38·55 E
135	Taymyr (Taimyr) (L.)	(tī-mír′)	Sov. Un.	74·13 N	100·45 E
134	Taymyr, P-Ov (Taimyr) (Pen.)		Sov. Un.	75·15 N	95·00 E
134	Tayshet (Taishet)	(tī-shět′)	Sov. Un.	56·09 N	97·49 E
154	Taytay	(tī-tī)	Phil.	10·37 N	119·10 E
151	Tayü		China	25·20 N	114·20 E
155	Tayung	(tä-yōōng′)	Phil. (Manila In.)	16·01 N	120·45 E
134	Taz (B.)	(tàz)	Sov. Un.	67·15 N	80·45 E
164	Taza	(tä′zä)	Mor.	34·08 N	4·00 w
134	Tazovskoye		Sov. Un.	66·58 N	78·28 E
133	Tbilisi	('tbĭl-yē′sē)	Sov. Un.	41·40 N	44·45 E
166	Tchibanga	(chē-bän′gä)	Gabon	2·48 s	10·50 E
121	Tczew	(t′chěf′)	Pol.	54·06 N	18·48 E
92	Teabo	(tě-ä′bō)	Mex. (Yucatan In.)	20·25 N	89·14 w
77	Teague	(tēg)	Tex.	31·39 N	96·16 w
91	Teapa	(tā-ä′pä)	Mex.	17·35 N	92·56 w
164	Tébessa	(tā′běs′à)	Alg.	35·27 N	8·13 E
139	Tebingtinggi, Palau (I.)	(teb′ĭng-tĭng′gä)	Indon. (Singapore In.	0·54 N	102·39 E
90	Tecalitlán	(tā-kä-lē̄′tlän′)	Mex.	19·28 N	103·17 w
90	Tecoanapa	(tāk-wä-nä-pä′)	Mex.	16·33 N	98·46 w
92	Tecoh	(tě-kō)	Mex. (Yucatan In.)	20·46 N	89·27 w
90	Tecolotlán	(tā-kō-lō-tlän′)	Mex.	20·13 N	103·57 w
91	Tecolutla	(tā-kō-lōō′tlä)	Mex.	20·33 N	97·00 w
91	Tecolutla (R.)		Mex.	20·16 N	97·14 w
90	Tecomán	(tā-kō-män′)	Mex.	18·53 N	103·53 w
91	Tecōmitl	(tě-kō′mětl)	Mex. (Mexico City In.)	19·13 N	98·59 w
90	Tecozautla	(tā′kō-zä-ōō′tlä)	Mex.	20·33 N	99·38 w
90	Tecpan de Galeana	(těk-pän′ dā gä-lā-ä′nä)	Mex.	17·13 N	100·41 w
91	Tecpatán	(těk-pä-tän′)	Mex.	17·08 N	93·18 w
90	Tecuala	(tě-kwä-lä)	Mex.	22·24 N	105·29 w
121	Tecuci	(ta-kōōch′)	Rom.	45·51 N	27·30 E
75	Tecumseh	(tě-kŭm′sě)	Can. (Detroit In.)	42·19 N	82·53 w
80	Tecumseh		Mich.	42·00 N	84·00 w
76	Tecumseh		Nebr.	40·21 N	96·09 w
73	Tecumseh		Okla.	35·18 N	96·55 w
116	Tees (R.)		Eng.	54·40 N	2·10 w
98	Tefé	(tě-fā′)	Braz.	3·27 s	64·43 w
153	Teganuna (L.)	(tā′gä-nōō′nä)	Jap. (Tōkyō In.)	35·50 N	140·02 E
92	Tegucigalpa	(tà-gōō-sē-gäl′pä)	Hond.	14·08 N	87·15 w
68	Tehachapi Mts.	(tě-hǎ-shä′pǐ)	Calif.	34·50 N	118·55 w
144	Tehrān	(tě-hrän′)	Iran	35·45 N	51·30 E
148	Tehsien	(dü′sǐän)	China	37·28 N	116·17 E
151	Tehua		China	25·30 N	118·15 E
91	Tehuacan	(tā-wä-kän′)	Mex.	18·27 N	97·23 w
91	Tehuantepec (Sto. Domingo)	(tà-wän-tà-pěk′) (sän-tō dô-mě′n-gō)	Mex.	16·20 N	95·14 w
88	Tehuantepec, Golfo de (G.)		Mex.	15·45 N	95·00 w
91	Tehuantepec, Istmo de (Isth.)	(ě′st-mô dě)	Mex.	17·55 N	94·35 w
91	Tehuantepec (R.)		Mex.	16·30 N	95·23 w
90	Tehuehuetla Arroyo (R.)		Mex.	17·54 N	100·26 w
90	Tehuitzingo	(tā-wě-tzǐŋ′gō)	Mex.	18·21 N	98·16 w
124	Tejeda, Sierra de. (Mts.)	(sē̄′r-rä dě tě-kě′dä)	Sp.	36·55 N	5·57 w
124	Tejo, Rio (R.)	(rê-ōtä′hōō)	Port.	39·23 N	8·01 w
91	Tejúpan (Santiago)	(tě-kōō-pä′n) (sän-tyä′gō)	Mex.	17·39 N	97·34 w
90	Tejúpan, Punta (Pt.)	(pōō′n-tä)	Mex.	18·19 N	103·30 w
90	Tejupilco de Hidalgo	(tä-hōō-pēl′kô dā ê-dhäl′gō)	Mex.	18·52 N	100·07 w
70	Tekamah	(tě-kä′má)	Nebr.	41·46 N	96·13 w
92	Tekax de Alvaro Obregon	(tě-kä′x dě à′l-vä-rô-brě′-gô′n)	Mex. (Yucatan In.)	20·12 N	89·11 w
127	Tekirdağ (Rodosto)	(tě-kěr′dägh′)	Tur.	41·00 N	27·28 E
92	Tekit	(tě-kě′t)	Mex. (Yucatan In.)	20·35 N	89·18 w
66	Tekoa	(tě-kō′à)	Wash.	47·15 N	117·03 w
92	Tela	(tā′lä)	Hond.	15·45 N	87·25 w
92	Tela, Bahia de (B.)	(bä-ē′ä dě)	Hond.	15·53 N	87·29 w
139	Telapa Burok, Gunong (Mt.)		Mala. (Singapore In.)	2·51 N	102·04 E
133	Telavi		Sov. Un.	42·00 N	45·20 E
139	Tel Aviv-Yafo	(těl-à-věv′jä′fà)	Isr. (Palestine In.)	32·03 N	34·46 E
86	Telegraph Creek	(těl′ê-gráf)	Can.	57·59 N	131·22 w
129	Teleneshty	(tyě-lê-něsht′i)	Sov.Un.	47·31 N	28·22 E
68	Telescope Pk.	(těl′ê skōp)	Calif.	36·12 N	117·05 w
99	Teles Pirez (R.)	(tě-lěs pē′rěz)	Braz.	8·28 s	57·07 w
139	Telesung		Indon. (Singapore In.)	1·07 N	102·53 E
92	Telica (Vol.)	(tä-lē′kä)	Nic.	12·38 N	86·52 w
146	Telii Nuur (L.)		China	45·49 N	86·08 E
80	Tell City	(těl)	Ind.	38·00 N	86·45 w
64	Teller	(těl′ěr)	Alaska	65·17 N	166·28 w
98	Tello	(tě′l-yô)	Col. (In.)	3·05 N	75·08 w
69	Telluride	(těl′ú-rīd)	Colo.	37·55 N	107·50 w
139	Telok Datok		Mala. (Singapore In.)	2·51 N	101·33 E
90	Teloloapan	(tā′lō-lô-ä′pän)	Mex.	18·19 N	99 54 w
132	Tel′pos-Iz, Gora (Mtn.)	(tyěl′pôs-ēz′)	Sov. Un.	63·50 N	59·20 E
139	Tel Sharuhea		Isr. (Palestine In.)	31·28 N	34·29 E
119	Telšiai	(těl′-shà′ê)	Sov. Un.	55·59 N	22·17 E
111	Teltow	(těl′tō)	Ger. (Berlin In.)	52·24 N	13·12 E
154	Telukbetung		Indon.	5·30 s	105·04 E
139	Telukletjak		Indon. (Singapore In.)	1·53 N	101·45 E
164	Tema	(tē′mà)	Ghana	5·45 N	0.00
90	Temascalcingo	(tā′mäs-käl-sǐŋ′gō)	Mex.	19·55 N	100·00 w
90	Temascaltepec	(tā′mäs-käl-tä pěk)	Mex.	19·00 N	100·03 w
92	Temax	(tě′mäx)	Mex. (Yucatan In.)	21·10 N	88·51 w
133	Temir	(tyě′měr)	Sov. Un.	49·10 N	57·15 E
134	Temir-Tau		Sov. Un.	50·08 N	73·13 E
82	Temiscouata (L.)	(tě′mĭs-kōō-ä′tä)	Can.	47·46 N	69·10 w
91	Temoaya	(tě-mô-ä-yä)	Mex. (Mexico City In.)	19·28 N	99·36 w
100	Temperley	(tě′m-pěr-lā)	Arg. (In.)	34·32 s	58·24 w
126	Tempio Pausania	(těm′pê-ō pou-sä′nê-ä)	Sard.	40·55 N	9·05 E
77	Temple	(těm′p′l)	Tex.	31·06 N	97·20 w
74	Temple City		Calif. (Los Angeles In.)	34·07 N	118·02 w
85	Templeton	(těm′p′l-tŭn)	Can. (Ottawa In.)	45·29 N	75·37 w
120	Templin	(těm-plēn′)	Ger.	53·08 N	13·30 E
90	Tempoal (R.)	(těm-pô-ä′l)	Mex.	21·38 N	98·23 w
129	Temryuk	(tyěm-ryōōk′)	Sov. Un.	45·17 N	37·21 E
100	Temuco	(tā-mōō′kō)	Chile	38·46 s	72·38 w
136	Temyasovo	(těm-yä′sô-vô)	Sov. Un. (Urals In.)	53·00 N	58·06 E
92	Tenabó	(tě-nä-bô′)	Mex. (Yucatan In.)	20·05 N	90·11 w
90	Tenamaxtlán	(tā′nä-mäs-tlän′)	Mex.	20·13 N	104·06 w
90	Tenancingo	(tà-nän-sēŋ′gō)	Mex.	18·54 N	99·36 w
91	Tenango	(tà-näŋ′gō)	Mex. (Mexico City In.)	19·09 N	98·51 w
154	Tenasserim	(těn-äs′ěr-ĭm)	Bur.	12·09 N	99·01 E
129	Tenderovskaya Kosa (C.)	(těn-dě-rôf′skà-yä kô-sä′)	Sov. Un.	46·12 N	31·17 E
	Tenedos, see Bozcaada				
164	Teneré. (Reg.)		Niger	18·45 N	11·16 E
164	Tenerife I.	(tä-nä-rē′fà) (těn-ěr-ĭf′)	Can. Is.	28·41 N	17·02 w
113	Ténés	(tā-něs′)	Alg.	36·28 N	1·22 E
148	T'enghsien	(těng′hsē-ěn′)	China	35·07 N	117·08 E
134	Tengiz (L.)	(tyĭn-gěs′)	Sov. Un.	50·45 N	68·39 E
153	Tenjin	(těn′jěn)	Jap. (Ōsaka In.)	34·54 N	135·04 E
166	Tenke	(těn′kà)	Con. K.	10·36 s	26·12 E
73	Tenkiller Ferry Res.	(těn-kĭl′ěr)	Okla.	35·42 N	94·47 w
164	Tenkodogo	(těŋ-kô-dō′gô)	Upper Volta	11·42 N	0·30 w
65	Tenmile (R.)	(těn mīl)	Wash. (Vancouver In.)	48·52 N	122·32 w
158	Tennant Creek	(těn′ănt)	Austl.	19·45 s	134·00 E
63	Tennessee (State)		U. S.	35·50 N	88·00 w
63	Tennessee (L.)		U. S.	35·35 N	88·20 w
78	Tennessee (R.)		U. S.	35·30 N	88·20 w
78	Tennille	(těn′ĭl)	Ga.	32·55 N	86·50 w
101	Teno	(tě′nô)	Chile (Santiago In.)	34·55 s	71·00 w
160	Tenora	(tě-nôrá)	Austl.	34·23 s	147·33 E
91	Tenosique	(tā-nô-sē′kà)	Mex.	17·27 N	91·25 w
153	Tenryū-Gawa (Strm.)	(těn′ryōō′gä′wä)	Jap.	35·16 N	137·54 E
77	Tensas R.	(těn′sô)	La.	31·54 N	91·30 w
78	Tensaw (R.)	(těn′sô)	Ala.	30·45 N	87·52 w
160	Tenterfield	(těn′těr-fēld)	Austl.	29·00 s	52·06 E
79	Ten Thousand, Is.	(těn thou′zănd)	Fla (In.)	25·45 N	81·35 w
90	Teocaltiche	(tā-ō-käl-tē′chä)	Mex.	21·27 N	102·38 w
91	Teocelo	(tā-ō-sä′lō)	Mex.	19·22 N	96·57 w
90	Teocuitatlán de Corona	(tā′ô-kwē′tä-tlän′ dā kô-rō′nä)	Mex.	20·06 N	103·22 w
99	Teófilo Otoni	(tě-ô′fē-lō′tō′nê)	Braz.	17·49 s	41·18 w
90	Teoloyucan	(tā′ô-lô-yōō′kän)	Mex.	19·43 N	99·12 w
91	Teopisca	(tā-ō-pēs′kä)	Mex.	16·30 N	92·33 w
91	Teotihuacán	(tě-ô-tē-wä-kä′n)	Mex. (Mexico City In.)	19·40 N	98·52 w
91	Teotitlán del Camino	(tā-ô-tē-tlän′ děl kä-mē′nô)	Mex.	18·07 N	97·04 w
90	Tepalcatepec	(tā′päl-kä-tä′pěk)	Mex.	19·11 N	102·51 w
90	Tepalcatepec (R.)		Mex.	18·54 N	102·25 w
90	Tepalcingo	(tā-päl-sēŋ′gō)	Mex.	18·34 N	98·49 w
90	Tepatitlan de Morelos	(tā-pä-tê-tlän′ dā mô-rā′los)	Mex.	20·15 N	102·47 w
91	Tepeaca	(tā-pā-ä′kä)	Mex.	18·57 N	97·54 w
90	Tepecoacuilco de Trujano	(tā′pä-kō′ä-kwēl′kō dā troō-hä′nô)	Mex.	19·15 N	99·29 w
90	Tepeji del Rio	(tā-pä-ʜe′ děl rē′ō)	Mex.	19·55 N	99·22 w
91	Tepelmeme	(tā′pěl-mā′mä)	Mex.	17·51 N	97·23 w
91	Tepetlaoxtoc	(tä′pä-tlä′ôs-tōk′)	Mex. (Mexico City In.)	19·34 N	98·49 w
90	Tepezala	(tā-pä-zä-lä′)	Mex.	22·12 N	102·12 w
90	Tepic	(tā-pēk′)	Mex.	21·32 N	104·53 w
148	Tep'ing	(dü′pǐng)	China	37·28 N	116·57 E
136	Teplaya Gora	(tyōp′lä-yä gô-rä)	Sov. Un. (Urals In.)	58·32 N	59·08 E
120	Teplice Sanov	(těp′li-tsě shä′nôf)	Czech.	50·39 N	13·50 E
91	Teposcolula (San Pedro y San Pablo)	(tā-pôs-kô-lōō′lä) (sän pā′drō ē sän pä′blō)	Mex.	17·33 N	97·29 w
98	Tequendama, Salto de (Falls)	(sä′l-tô dě tě-kěn-dä′mä)	Col. (In.)	4·34 N	74·18 w
90	Tequila	(tā-kē′lä)	Mex.	20·53 N	103·48 w
91	Tequisistlán (R.)	(tě-kē-sēs-tlä′n)	Mex.	16·20 N	95·40 w
90	Tequisquiapan	(tà-kēs-kē-ä′pän)	Mex.	20·33 N	99·57 w
125	Ter (R.)	(těr)	Sp.	42·04 N	2·52 E
124	Tera (R.)	(tā′rä)	Sp.	42·05 N	6·24 w
126	Teramo	(tā′rä-mô)	It.	42·40 N	13·41 E
123	Terborg	(těr′bôrg)	Neth. (Ruhr In.)	51·55 N	6·23 E
133	Tercan	(těr′jän)	Tur.	39·40 N	40·12 E
164	Terceira I.	(těr-sā′rä)	Açores (In.)	38·49 N	26·36 w
121	Terebovlya	(tě-rä′bôv-lyä)	Sov. Un.	49·18 N	25·43 E
133	Terek (R.)		Sov. Un.	43·30 N	45·10 E
136	Terenkul′	(tě-rěn′kōōl)	Sov. Un. (Urals In.)	55·38 N	62·18 E
99	Teresina	(těr-â-sē′ná)	Braz.	5·04 s	42·42 w
100	Teresópolis	(těr-ä-sô′pō-lězh)	Braz. (In.)	22·25 s	42·59 w
132	Teribërka	(tyěr-ê-byôr′kà)	Sov. Un.	69·00 N	35·15 E
133	Terme	(těr′mě)	Tur.	41·05 N	42·00 E
142	Termez	(tyěr′měz)	Sov. Un.	37·19 N	67·20 E
126	Termini	(těr′mê-nē)	It.	37·58 N	13·39 E
91	Términos, Laguna de (L.)	(lä-gōō′nä dě ě′r-mē-nôs)	Mex.	18·37 N	91·32 w
126	Termoli	(těr′mô-lê)	It.	42·00 N	15·01 E
110	Tern (R.)	(tûrn)	Eng.	52·49 N	2·31 w
155	Ternate	(těr-nä′tä)	Indon.	0·52 N	127·25 E
126	Terni	(těr′nê)	It.	42·38 N	12·41 E
121	Ternopol′	(těr-nō-pōl′)	Sov. Un.	49·32 N	25·36 E
152	Terpeniya, Zaliv (B.)	(zä′lĭf těr-pä′nǐ-yä)	Sov. Un.	49·10 N	143·05 E
135	Terpeniya, Mys (C.)		Sov. Un.	48·44 N	144·42 E
86	Terrace	(těr′ĭs)	Can.	54·36 N	128·38 w
126	Terracina	(těr-rä-chē′nä)	It.	41·18 N	13·14 E
83	Terra Nova Natl. Park		Can.	48·37 N	54·15 w
85	Terrebonne	(těr′bŏn′)	Can. (Montreal In.)	45·42 N	73·38 w
77	Terrebonne B.		La.	28·55 N	90·30 w
80	Terre Haute	(těr-ê hōt′)	Ind.	39·25 N	87·25 w
77	Terrell	(těr′ěl)	Tex.	32·44 N	96·15 w
65	Terrell		Wash. (Vancouver In.)	48·53 N	122·44 w
74	Terrell Hills	(těr′ěl hǐlz)	Tex. (San Antonio In.)	29·28 N	98·27 w
117	Terschelling (I.)	(těr-sкěl′ĭng)	Neth.	53·25 N	5·12 E
124	Teruel	(tā-rōō-ěl′)	Sp.	40·20 N	1·05 w
127	Tešanj	(tě′shän)	Yugo.	44·36 N	17·59 E
111	Teschendorf	(tě′shěn-dôrf)	Ger. (Berlin In.)	52·51 N	13·10 E
91	Tesecheacan	(tě-sě-chě-ä-kä′n)	Mex.	18·10 N	95·41 w
64	Teshekpuk (L.)	(tē-shěk′pŭk)	Alaska	70·18 N	152·36 w
152	Teshio Dake (Mt.)	(těsh′ê-ô-dä′kä)	Jap.	44·00 N	142·50 E
152	Teshio Gawa (R.)	(těsh′ê-ô gä′wä)	Jap.	44·35 N	114·55 E
86	Teslin (L.)		Can.	60·12 N	132·08 w
86	Teslin (R.)		Can.	61·18 N	134·14 w
146	Tesiin Gol (R.)		Mong.	50·14 N	94·30 E
164	Tessaoua	(těs-sä′ŏŏ-ä)	Niger	13·53 N	7·53 E
111	Tessenderlo		Bel. (Brussels In.)	51·04 N	5·08 E
116	Test (R.)	(těst)	Eng.	51·10 N	2·20 w
126	Testa del Gargano (Pt.)	(täs′tä děl gär-gä′nō)	It.	41·48 N	16·13 E

ăt; fĭnăl; rāte; senāte; ârm; àsk: sofá; fâre; ch-choose; dh-as th in other; bē; ēvent; bĕt; recĕnt; crātẽr; g-go; gh-guttural g; bĭt; ĭ-short neutral; rīde; к-guttural k as ch in German ich;

Page	Name Pronunciation Region	Lat. °′	Long. °′
166	Tete (tā'tĕ) Moz.	15·13 s	33·40 E
129	Teterev (R.) (tyĕ'tyĕ-rĕf) Sov. Un.	50·35 N	29·18 E
120	Teterow (tā'tĕ-rō) Ger.	53·46 N	12·33 E
127	Teteven (tĕt'ĕ-ven') Bul.	42·57 N	24·15 E
67	Teton R. (tē'tŏn) Mont.	47·54 N	111·37 W
164	Tétouan Mor.	35·42 N	5·34 W
127	Tetovo (tā'tô-vô) Yugo.	42·01 N	21·00 E
110	Tettenhall (tĕt'ĕn-hôl) Eng.	52·36 N	2·10 W
152	Tetyukhe-Pristan (tĕt-yōō'kĕ prĭ-stän') Sov. Un.	44·21 N	135·44 E
132	Tetyushi (tyĕt-yŏŏ'shĭ) Sov. Un.	54·58 N	48·40 E
111	Teupitz (toi'pētz) Ger. (Berlin In.)	52·08 N	13·37 E
126	Tevere (Tiber) (R.) (tā'vå-rā) (tī'bēr) It.	42·30 N	12·14 E
83	Tewksbury (tūks'bēr-ĭ) Mass. (Boston In.)	42·37 N	71·14 W
73	Texarkana (tĕk-sär-kăn'ȧ) Ark.	33·26 N	94·02 W
73	Texarkana Tex.	33·26 N	94·04 W
73	Texarkana Dam Tex.	33·18 N	94·09 W
62	Texas (State) U. S.	31·00 N	101·00 W
77	Texas City Tex. (In.)	29·23 N	94·54 W
90	Texcaltitlán (tās-käl'tê-tlän') Mex.	18·54 N	99·51 W
117	Texel (I.) (tĕk'sĕl) Neth.	53·10 N	4·45 E
91	Texcoco (tās-kō'kō) Mex. (Mexico City In.)	19·31 N	98·53 W
91	Texistepec (tĕk-sēs-tā-pĕk') Mex.	17·51 N	94·46 W
91	Texmelucan (tās-må-lōō'kän) Mex. (Mexico City In.)	19·17 N	98·26 W
73	Texoma, L. (tĕk'ō-mă) Okla.	34·03 N	96·28 W
167	Teyateyaneng Leso. (Natal In.)	29·11 s	27·43 E
128	Teykovo (tĕy-kô-vô) Sov. Un.	56·52 N	40·34 E
91	Teziutlán (tå-zê-ōō-tlän') Mex.	19·48 N	97·21 W
90	Tezontepec (tå-zōn-tå-pĕk') Mex.	19·52 N	98·48 W
90	Tezontepec de Aldama (dā äl-dä'mă) Mex.	20·19 N	99·19 W
142	Tezpur India	26·42 N	92·52 E
86	Tha-anne (R.) Can.	60·50 N	96·56 W
167	Thaba Putsua (Mtn.) Leso. (Natal In.)	29·44 s	27·58 E
168	Thabazimbi S. Afr. (Johannesburg & Pretoria In.)	24·36 s	27·22 E
138	Thailand (Siam) Asia	16·30 N	101·00 E
154	Thale Luang (L.) Thai.	7·51 N	99·39 E
110	Thame (tām) Eng. (London In.)	51·43 N	0·59 W
80	Thames (R.) (tĕmz) Can.	42·40 N	81·45 W
117	Thames, R Eng.	51·26 N	0·54 E
115	Thamit R Libya	30·39 N	16·23 E
143	Thāna (thä'nŭ) India (Bombay In.)	19·13 N	72·58 E
143	Thāna Cr India (Bombay In.)	19·03 N	72·58 E
146	Thang Ha Ri (Mts.) China	33·15 N	89·07 E
151	Thanh-Hoa (tän'hō'à) Viet.	19·46 N	105·42 E
123	Thann (tän) Fr.	47·49 N	7·05 E
123	Thaon-les-Vosges (tå-ŏN-lā-vōzh') Fr.	48·16 N	6·24 E
160	Thargomindah (thår'gō-mĭn'då) Austl.	27·58 s	143·57 E
127	Thásos (I.) (thă'sôs) Grc.	40·41 N	24·53 E
89	Thatch Cay (I.) (thăch) Vir. Is. (U. S. A.) (St. Thomas In.)	18·22 N	64·53 W
120	Thaya R. (tä'yà) Aus.-Czech.	48·48 N	15·40 E
73	Thayer (thâ'ēr) Mo.	36·30 N	91·34 W
	Thebes, see Thivai		
168	Thebes (Ruins) (thēbz) U. A. R. (Nile In.)	25·47 N	32·39 E
65	The Brothers (Mtn.) (brŭth'ērs) Wash. (Seattle In.)	47·39 N	123·08 W
66	The Dalles (dălz) Ore.	45·36 N	121·10 W
155	The Father, (Mtn.) N. Gui. Ter.	5·10 s	151·55 E
	The Hague, see 's Gravenhage		
142	Thelum W. Pak.	32·59 N	73·43 E
161	The Oaks Austl. (Sydney In.)	34·04 s	150·36 E
160	Theodore (thēō'dôr) Austl.	24·51 s	150·09 E
69	Theodore Roosevelt Dam (thê-ô-doř rōō-sȧ-vĕlt) Ariz.	33·46 N	111·25 W
70	Theodore Roosevelt Natl. Mem. Park N. D.	47·20 N	103·42 W
86	The Pas (pä) Can.	53·48 N	101·17 W
67	Thermopolis (thēr-mŏp'ô-lĭs) Wyo.	43·38 N	108·11 W
160	The Round Mtn Austl.	30·17 s	152·19 E
127	Thessalía (Reg.) Grc.	39·50 N	22·09 E
87	Thessalon Can.	46·11 N	83·37 W
127	Thessaloníki (thĕs-sà-lô-nē'kê) Grc.	40·38 N	22·59 E
82	Thetford Mines (thĕt'fērd mīns) Can.	46·05 N	71·20 W
167	The Twins (Mtn.) (twĭnz) Leso.-S. Afr. (Natal In.)	30·09 s	28·29 E
168	Theunissen S. Afr. (Johannesburg & Pretoria In.)	28·25 s	26·44 E
77	Thibodaux (tê-bô-dō') La.	29·48 N	90·48 W
86	Thickwood Hills (thĭk'wŏŏd) Can.	53·28 N	108·30 W
70	Thief (L.) (thēf) Minn.	48·32 N	95·46 W
70	Thief (R.) Minn.	48·18 N	96·07 W
70	Thief River Falls (thēf rĭv'ēr fôlz) Minn.	48·07 N	96·11 W
84	Thiells (thēlz) N. Y. (New York In.)	41·12 N	74·01 W
122	Thiers (tyâr) Fr.	45·51 N	3·32 E
164	Thiès (tê-ĕs') Senegal	14·43 N	16·56 W
146	Thimbu Bhu.	27·31 N	89·45 E
112	Thingvallavatn (L.) Ice.	64·12 N	20·22 W
123	Thionville (tyôN-vēl') Fr.	49·23 N	6·31 E
165	Third Cataract Sud.	19·53 N	30·11 E
118	Thisted (tēs'tĕdh) Den.	56·57 N	8·38 E
112	Thisti Fd. (tēs'têl) Ice.	66·29 N	14·59 W
160	Thistle (I.) (thĭs''l) Austl.	34·55 s	136·11 E
127	Thivai (Thebes) Grc.	38·20 N	23·18 E
112	Thjörsá (R.) (tyûr'sà) Ice.	64·23 N	19·18 W
111	Tholen Neth. (Amsterdam In.)	51·32 N	4·11 E
72	Thomas (tŏm'ăs) Okla.	35·44 N	98·43 W
81	Thomas W. Va.	39·15 N	79·30 W
78	Thomaston (tŏm'ăs-tŭn) Ga.	32·51 N	84·17 W
78	Thomasville (tŏm'ăs-vĭl) Ala.	31·55 N	87·43 W
79	Thomasville N. C.	35·52 N	80·05 W
86	Thompson (tŏmp'sŭn) Can.	55·48 N	97·59 W
73	Thompson (R.) Mo.	40·32 N	93·49 W
66	Thompson Falls Mont.	47·35 N	115·20 W
75	Thompsonville (tomp'sŭn-vĭl) Wis. (Milwaukee In.)	42·47 N	87·57 W
79	Thomson (tŏm'sŭn) Ga.	33·28 N	82·29 W
159	Thomson (R.) (tŏm-sŏn) Austl.	29·30 s	143·07 E
123	Thonon-les-Bains (tô-nôN'lå-băN') Fr.	46·22 N	6·27 E
112	Thórisvatn (L.) Ice.	64·02 N	119·09 W
110	Thorne (thôrn) Eng.	53·37 N	0·58 W
85	Thornhill (thôrn-hĭl) Can. (Toronto In.)	43·49 N	79·25 W
80	Thorntown (thôrn'tŭn) Ind.	40·05 N	86·35 W
85	Thorold (thō'rōld) Can. (Toronto In.)	43·13 N	79·12 W
122	Thouars (tōō-är') Fr.	47·00 N	0·17 W
81	Thousand Is. (thou'zănd) N. Y.-Can.	44·15 N	76·10 W
127	Thrace (Reg.) (thrās) Grc.-Tur.	41·20 N	26·07 E
110	Thrapston (thrăp'stŭn) Eng.	52·23 N	0·32 W
67	Three Forks (thrē fôrks) Mont.	45·56 N	111·35 W
80	Three Oaks (thrē ōks) Mich.	41·50 N	86·40 W
164	Three Points, C Ghana	4·27 N	2·29 W
80	Three Rivers Mich.	42·00 N	83·40 W
120	Thun (tōōn) Switz.	46·46 N	7·34 E
71	Thunder B. (thŭn'dēr) Can.	48·29 N	88·52 W
120	Thuner See (L.) Switz.	46·40 N	7·30 E
76	Thurber (thûr'bēr) Tex.	32·30 N	98·23 W
120	Thüringen (Thuringia) (former state or region) (tü'rĭng-ĕn) Ger.	51·07 N	10·45 E
116	Thurles (thûrlz) Ire.	52·44 N	7·45 W
110	Thurrock (thŭ'rŏk) Eng. (London In.)	51·28 N	0·19 E
159	Thursday (I.) (thûrz-dā) Austl.	10·17 s	142·23 E
85	Thurso (thŭr'sô) Can. (Ottawa In.)	45·36 N	75·15 W
116	Thurso Scot.	58·35 N	3·40 W
47	Thurston Pen. (thûrs'tŭn) Ant.	71·20 s	98·00 W
166	Thysville (tês-vēl') Con. K.	5·08 s	14·58 E
155	Tiaong (tê-ä-ông') Phil. (Manila In.)	13·56 N	121·20 E
100	Tibagi (tē-bà-zhē) Braz.	24·40 s	50·35 W
165	Tibasti, Sarir (Des.) Chad	24·00 N	16·30 E
	Tiber (R.), see Tévere		
139	Tiberias (tī-bē'rĭ-ăs) Isr. (Palestine In.)	32·48 N	35·32 E
139	Tiberias, L Isr. (Palestine In.)	32·53 N	35·45 E
165	Tibesti Massif (Mts.) Chad	20·43 N	17·16 E
146	Tibet, Plat. of (tĭ-bĕt') China	32·22 N	83·30 E
146	Tibeton Aut. Reg. (tĭ-bĕt'on) China	31·15 N	84·48 E
139	Tibnīn Leb. (Palestine In.)	33·12 N	35·23 E
65	Tiburon (tē-bōō-rōn') Calif. (San Francisco In.)	37·53 N	122·27 W
95	Tiburon Hai.	18·35 N	74·25 W
88	Tiburón (I.) Mex.	28·45 N	113·10 W
93	Tiburon, Cabo (C.) (kȧ'bô) Pan.	8·42 N	77·19 W
65	Tiburon I. Calif. (San Francisco In.)	37·52 N	122·26 W
155	Ticaco Pass (tê-kä-kô) Phil. (Manila In.)	12·38 N	123·50 E
155	Ticao (I.) (tê-kä'ō) Phil. (Manila In.)	12·40 N	123·30 E
110	Tickhill (tĭk'ĭl) Eng.	53·26 N	1·06 W
81	Ticonderaga (tī-kŏn-dēr-ō'gȧ) N. Y.	43·50 N	73·30 W
92	Ticul (tē-kōō'l) Mex. (Yucatan In.)	20·22 N	89·32 W
118	Tidaholm (tē'dà-hōlm) Swe.	58·11 N	13·53 E
110	Tideswell (tīdz'wĕl) Eng.	53·17 N	1·47 W
164	Tidikelt (Reg.) (tē-dê-kĕlt') Alg.	25·53 N	2·11 E
164	Tidjikdja (tê-jĭk'jä) Mauritania	18·37 N	11·30 W
150	T'iehling (tyå'lĭng) China	42·18 N	123·50 E
125	Tielmes (tyål-màs') Sp. (Madrid In.)	40·15 N	3·20 W
151	Tien Ch'ih (L.) (tyĕn) China	24·58 N	103·18 E
148	T'ienching (Tientsin) (tyĕn'tsĕn') China	39·08 N	117·14 E
111	Tienen Bel. (Brussels In.)	50·49 N	4·58 E
148	Tienerhwan (dĭăn'ĕ'hōōăn) China	31·39 N	114·08 E
148	Tienfou (dĭăn'fōō) China	31·53 N	117·28 E
148	T'ienma Shan (Mts.) (tĭăn'mă shăn) China	36·02 N	117·57 E
151	Tienmen (tyĕn'mĕn') China	30·40 N	113·10 E
151	Tienpai China	21·30 N	111·20 E
151	T'ienpao China	23·18 N	106·40 E
	Tien-Shan (Mts.), see Tyan' Shan'		
148	Tienshan Hu (L.) (dĭăn'shăn'hōō) China	31·08 N	120·30 E
150	T'ienshui China	34·25 N	105·40 E
150	T'ientsaokang China	45·58 N	126·00 E
	Tientsin, see T'ienching		
151	T'ientung China	23·32 N	107·10 E
118	Tierp (tyĕrp) Swe.	60·21 N	17·28 E
167	Tierpoort S. Afr. (Johannesburg & Pretoria In.)	25·53 s	28·26 E
91	Tierra Blanca (tyĕ'r-rä-blä'n-kă) Mex.	18·28 N	96·19 W
100	Tierra del Fuego (Reg.) (tyĕr'rä dĕl fwā'gô) Chile-Arg.	53·50 s	68·45 W
124	Tiétar (R.) (tê-ā'tär) Sp.	39·56 N	5·44 W
101	Tietê (tyā-tā') Braz. (Rio de Janeiro In.)	23·08 s	47·42 W
99	Tieté (R.) Braz.	20·46 s	50·46 W
80	Tiffin (tĭf'ĭn) Ohio	41·10 N	83·15 W
78	Tifton (tĭf'tŭn) Ga.	31·25 N	83·34 W
65	Tigard (tī'gärd) Ore. (Portland In.)	45·25 N	122·46 W
82	Tignish (tĭg'nĭsh) Can.	46·56 N	64·03 W
136	Tigoda R. (tē'gô-dà) Sov. Un. (Leningrad In.)	59·29 N	31·15 E
100	Tigre (tê'grĕ) Arg. (In.)	34·09 s	58·35 W
98	Tigre (R.) Peru	2·20 s	75·41 W
166	Tigres, Peninsula dos (Pen.) (pĕ-nê'ŋ-sōō-lä-dôs-tê'grĕs) Ang.	16·30 s	11·45 E
144	Tigris, R. Asia	34·30 N	44·00 E
139	Tîh, Gebel el (Mts.) U. A. R. (Palestine In.)	29·24 N	33·42 E
146	Tihua (Urumchi) (ōō-rōōm'chê) China	43·49 N	87·43 E
91	Tihuatlán (tê-wä-tlän') Mex.	20·43 N	97·34 W
68	Tijuana (tê-hwä'nä) Mex. (San Diego In.)	32·32 N	117·02 W
100	Tijuca, Pico da (Mtn.) (pē'kō-dä-tê-zhōō'kà) Braz. (In.)	22·56 s	43·17 W
92	Tikal (Ruins) (tê-käl') Guat. (Yucatan In.)	17·16 N	89·49 W
133	Tikhoretsk (tê kôr-yĕtsk') Sov. Un.	45·55 N	40·05 E
128	Tikhvin (têk-vēn') Sov. Un.	59·36 N	33·38 E
144	Tikrīt Iraq	34·36 N	43·31 E
135	Tiksi (têk-sē') Sov. Un.	71·42 N	128·32 E
111	Tilburg (tĭl'bûrg) Neth. (Amsterdam In.)	51·33 N	5·05 E
164	Tilemsi, Vallée du (Valley) Mali	18·09 N	0·02 W
135	Tilichiki (tyĭ-le-chĭ-kê) Sov. Un.	60·49 N	166·14 E
129	Tiligul (R.) (tē'lĭ-gûl) Sov. Un.	47·25 N	30·27 E
164	Tillabéri (tē-yà-bā-rē') Niger	14·14 N	1·30 E
66	Tillamook (tĭl'ȧ-mŏŏk) Ore.	45·27 N	123·50 W
66	Tillamook B. Ore.	45·32 N	124·26 W
118	Tillberga (tēl-bĕr'ghȧ) Swe.	59·40 N	16·34 E
80	Tillsonburg (tĭl'sŭn-bûrg) Can.	42·50 N	80·50 W
	Tilsit, see Sovetsk		
129	Tim (têm) Sov. Un.	51·39 N	37·07 E
159	Timaru (tĭm'à-rōō) N. Z. (In.)	44·26 s	171·17 E
129	Timashevskaya (tēmă-shĕfś-kă'yă) Sov. Un.	45·47 N	38·57 E
77	Timbalier B. (tĭm'bà-lēr) La.	28·55 N	90·14 W
65	Timber (tĭm'bēr) Ore. (Portland In.)	45·43 N	123·17 W
164	Timbo (tĭm'bō) Gui.	10·41 N	11·51 W
	Timbuktu, see Tombouctou		
118	Time (tē'mĕ) Nor.	58·45 N	5·39 E
164	Timimoun (tē-mê-mōōn') Alg.	29·14 N	0·22 E
164	Timiris, Cap (C.) Mauritania	19·37 N	17·38 W
127	Timiş (R.) Rom.	45·28 N	21·06 E
87	Timiskaming (L.) Can.	47·27 N	81·00 W
87	Timiskaming Station (tê-mĭs'kȧ-mĭng) Can.	46·41 N	79·01 W
87	Timmins (tĭm'ĭnz) Can.	48·25 N	81·22 W
164	Timmissao (tē-mê-sä'ō) Alg.	22·03 N	2·56 E
79	Timmonsville (tĭm'ŭnz-vĭl) S. C.	34·09 N	79·55 W
155	Timor (I.) (tê-mōr') Indon.	10·08 s	125·00 E
156	Timor Sea Asia	12·40 s	125·00 E
127	Timoşoara Rom.	45·44 N	21·21 E
69	Timpanogos Cave Natl. Mon. (tī-măn'ō-gŏz) Utah	40·25 N	111·45 W
77	Timpson (tĭmp'sŭn) Tex.	31·55 N	94·24 W
135	Timpton (R.) (têmp'tôn) Sov. Un.	57·15 N	126·35 E
168	Timsāh (L.) (tĭm'sä) U. A. R. (Suez In.)	30·34 N	32·22 E
95	Tina, Monte (Mtn.) (mô'n-tĕ-tē'nà) Dom. Rep.	18·50 N	70·40 W
167	Tina (R.) (tē'nă) S. Afr. (Natal In.)	30·50 s	28·44 E
99	Tinaguillo (tê-nä-gē'l-yô) Ven. (In.)	9·55 N	68·18 W
164	Tindouf (tên-dōōf') Alg.	27·43 N	7·44 W
139	Tinggi, Palau (I.) Mala. (Singapore In.)	2·16 N	104·16 E
148	T'ingho (dĭng'hŭ) China	37·45 N	118·29 E
148	Tinghsien (dĭng'sĭän) China	38·30 N	115·00 E
148	Tinghsing (dĭng'sĭng) China	39·18 N	115·50 E
149	Tinglin China (Shanghai In.)	30·53 N	121·18 E
98	Tingo María (tē'ngô-mä-rê'ä) Peru	9·15 s	76·04 W
118	Tingsryd (tĭngs'rüd) Swe.	56·32 N	14·58 E
148	Tingtzu Wan (B.) (ding'tze wän) China	36·33 N	121·06 E
90	Tinguindio Paracho (tēn-kê'n-dyō-pärä-chô) Mex.	19·38 N	102·02 W
101	Tinguiririca (R.) (tē'n-gē-rē-rê'kä) Chile (Santiago In.)	36·48 s	70·45 W
148	Tingyüan (tĭng'yü-än') China	32·32 N	117·40 E
75	Tinley Park (tĭn'lê) Ill. (Chicago In.)	41·34 N	87·47 W
118	Tinnosset (tên'nôs'sĕt) Nor.	49·44 N	9·00 E
118	Tinnsjö (tĭnnsyû) Nor.	59·55 N	8·49 E
100	Tinogasta (tē-nô-gäs'tä) Arg.	28·07 s	67·30 W
127	Tínos (I.) Grc.	37·45 N	25·12 E
145	Tinsukia (tin-sōō'kĭ-à) India	27·18 N	95·29 E
69	Tintic (tĭn'tĭk) Utah	39·55 N	112·15 W
165	Tin Toumma Steppe (Plat.) (tīn tōōm'à) Niger	16·16 N	13·06 E
139	Tioman (I.) Mala. (Singapore In.)	2·25 N	104·30 E
92	Tipitapa (tē-pê-tä'pä) Nic.	12·14 N	86·05 W
92	Tipitapa R. Nic.	12·13 N	85·57 W
78	Tippah Cr., (R.) (tĭp'pȧ) Miss.	34·43 N	88·15 W
80	Tippecanoe (R.) (tĭp-ê-kȧ-nōō') Ind.	40·55 N	86·45 W
166	Tipperary (tĭ-pē-râ'rê) Ire.	52·28 N	8·13 W
73	Tippo Bay. (tĭp'ō biōō') Miss.	33·35 N	90·06 W
110	Tipton (tĭp'tŭn) Eng.	52·32 N	2·04 W
80	Tipton Ind.	40·15 N	86·00 W
71	Tipton Iowa	41·46 N	91·10 W
127	Tiranë (tê-rä'nä) Alb.	41·18 N	19·50 E
126	Tirano (tê-rä'nō) It.	46·12 N	10·09 E
129	Tiraspol' (tê-räs'pôl') Sov. Un.	46·52 N	29·38 E
168	Tir'at el'Abbâsîya R. U. A. R. (Suez In.)	32·45 N	32·15 E
133	Tire (tē'rĕ) Tur.	38·05 N	27·48 E
116	Tiree (I.) (tī-rē') Scot.	56·34 N	6·30 W
127	Tîrgovişte Rom.	44·54 N	25·29 E
121	Tîrgu-Mureş Rom.	46·33 N	24·35 E
121	Tîrgu Neamt Rom.	47·14 N	26·23 E
121	Tîrgu-Ocna Rom.	46·18 N	26·38 E

ng-sing; ŋ-baŋk; N-nasalized n; nŏd; cŏmmit; ōld; ôbey; ôrder; fōōd; fŏŏt; ou-out; s-soft; sh-dish; th-thin; pūre; ûnite; ûrn; stŭd; circŭs; ü-a "y" in study; '-indeterminate vowel.

Page	Name Pronunciation Region	Lat. °′	Long. °′
121	Tîrgu Săcuesc..............Rom.	46·04 N	26·06 E
142	Tirich Mir (Mt.)............Afg.	41·06 N	71·48 E
136	Tirlyanskiy (tĭr-lyän′skĭ) Sov. Un. (Urals In.)	54·13 N	58·37 E
127	Tírnavos..................Grc.	39·50 N	22·14 E
121	Tîrnăveni.................Rom.	46·19 N	24·18 E
120	Tirol (State) (tê-rōl′)........Aus.	47·13 N	11·10 E
126	Tirso (R.) (tēr′sô)...........It.	40·15 N	9·03 E
143	Tiruchchirāppalli (tĭr′ŏŏ-chĭ-rä′pȧ-lĭ).India	10·49 N	78·48 E
143	Tirunelveli................India	8·48 N	77·49 E
143	Tiruppūr.. ....India	11·11 N	77·08 E
86	Tisdale (tĭz′dāl)............Can.	52·55 N	103·56 W
142	Tista (R.).................India	26·03 N	88·52 E
127	Tisza (R.) (tê′sä)...........Yugo.	45·50 N	20·13 E
121	Tisza R. (tē′sä)...........Hung.	46·30 N	20·08 E
142	Titagarh.....India (Calcutta In.)	22·44 N	88·23 E
98	Titicaca, Lago (L.) (lä′gô-tē-tê-kä′kä).Bol.-Peru	16·12 S	70·33 W
98	Titiribí (tē-tē-rē-bê′)....Col. (In.)	6·05 N	75·47 W
127	Titograd..................Yugo.	42·25 N	20·42 E
127	Titovo Užice (tê′tô-vô ōō′zhê-tsĕ) Yugo.	43·51 N	19·53 E
127	Titov Veles (tê′tôv vĕ′lĕs)..Yugo.	41·42 N	21·50 E
79	Titusville (tī′tŭs-vĭl)....Fla. (In.)	28·37 N	80·44 W
81	Titusville...................Pa.	40·40 N	79·40 W
123	Titz (tētz).......Ger. (Ruhr In.)	51·00 N	6·26 E
84	Tiverton (tĭv′ẽr-tŭn) R. I. (Providence In.)	41·38 N	71·11 W
125	Tívoli (tē′vô-lê)....It. (Rome In.)	41·58 N	12·48 E
92	Tixkokob (tēx-kō-kō′b) Mex. (Yucatan In.)	21·01 N	89·23 W
90	Tixtla de Guerrero (tē′x-tlä-dĕ-gĕr-rĕ′rô).Mex.	17·36 N	99·24 W
154	Tizard Bk. and Rf. (tĭz′ȧrd).China	10·51 N	113·20 E
92	Tizimín (tē-zē-mê′n) Mex. (Yucatan In.)	21·08 N	88·10 W
164	Tizi-Ouzou (tē′zê-ōō-zōō′)....Alg.	36·44 N	4·04 E
99	Tiznados (R.) (têz-nä′dôs) Ven. (In.)	9·53 N	67·49 W
164	Tiznit (têz-nēt)...........Mor.	29·52 N	9·39 W
154	Tjirebon..................Indon.	6·50 S	108·33 E
91	Tlacolula de Matamoros (tlä-kô-lōō′lä dā mätä-mō′rôs) Mex.	16·56 N	96·29 W
91	Tlacotálpan (tlä-kô-täl′pän).Mex.	18·39 N	95·40 W
90	Tlacotepec (tlä-kô-tȧ-pĕ′k)..Mex.	17·46 N	99·57 W
91	Tlacotepec...............Mex.	18·41 N	97·40 W
90	Tlacotepec...............Mex.	19·11 N	99·41 W
91	Tláhuac (tlä-wäk′) Mex. (Mexico City In.)	19·16 N	99·00 W
90	Tlajomulco de Zúñiga (tlä-hô-mōō′l-ko-dĕ-zōō′n-yē-gä) Mex.	20·30 N	103·27 W
90	Tlalchapa (tläl-chä′pä)......Mex.	18·26 N	100·29 W
91	Tlalixcoyan (tlä-lēs′kô-yän′).Mex.	18·53 N	96·04 W
91	Tlalmanalco (tläl-mä-nä′l-kô) Mex. (Mexico City In.)	19·12 N	98·48 W
91	Tlalnepantia (tläl-nĕ-pȧ′n-tyä) Mex. (Mexico City In.)	19·32 N	99·13 W
91	Tlalnepantla (tläl-nȧ-pȧn′tlä) Mex. (Mexico City In.)	18·59 N	99·01 W
91	Tlalpan (tläl-pä′n) Mex. (Mexico City In.)	19·17 N	99·10 W
90	Tlalpujahua (tläl-pōō-кä′wä).Mex.	19·50 N	100·10 W
	Tlaltenango, see Sanchez Román		
90	Tlapa (tlä′pä).............Mex.	17·30 N	98·09 W
90	Tlapa (tlä′pä).............Mex.	17·30 N	98·09 W
91	Tlapacoyan (tlä-pä-kô-yȧ′n).Mex.	19·57 N	97·11 W
90	Tlapaneco (R.) (tlä-pä-nĕ′kô) Mex.	17·59 N	98·44 W
90	Tlapehuala (tlä-pȧ-wä′lä)...Mex.	18·17 N	100·30 W
90	Tlaquepaque (tlä-kĕ-pä′kĕ)..Mex.	20·39 N	103·17 W
90	Tlatlaya (tlä-tlä′yä)........Mex.	18·36 N	100·14 W
90	Tlaxcala (tläs-kä′lä)........Mex.	19·16 N	98·14 W
90	Tlaxco (tläs′kō)............Mex.	19·37 N	98·06 W
91	Tlaxiaco Sta. Maria Asunción (tläk-sē-ä′kō sän′tä mä-rē′ä ä-sōōn-syōn′).Mex.	17·16 N	95·41 W
91	Tlayacapan (tlä-yä-kä-pȧ′n) Mex. (Mexico City In.)	18·57 N	99·00 W
164	Tlemcen (tlĕm-sĕn′).........Alg.	34·53 N	1·21 W
121	Tlumach (t′lû-mäch′)....Sov. Un.	48·47 N	25·00 E
95	Toa (R.) (tō′ä)............Cuba	20·25 N	74·35 W
67	Toano Ra. (Mts.) (tō-ȧ-nō′).Nev.	40·45 N	114·11 W
95	Toar, Cuchillas de (Mtn.) (kōō-chê′l-lyäs-dĕ-tô-ä′r).Cuba	18·20 N	74·50 W
89	Tobago (I.) (tô-bā′gō)......N. A.	11·15 N	60·30 W
124	Tobarra (tô-bär′rä)..........Sp.	38·37 N	1·42 W
134	Tobol (R.) (tô-bôl′).....Sov. Un.	56·02 N	65·30 E
134	Tobol′sk (tô-bôlsk′).....Sov. Un.	58·09 N	68·28 E
	Tobruk, see Tubruq		
98	Tocaima (tô-kä′y-mä)...Col. (In.)	4·28 N	74·38 W
99	Tocantinópolis (tō-kän-tē-nŏ′pō-lês) Braz.	6·27 S	47·18 W
99	Tocantins (R.)(tō-kän-tēɴs′).Braz.	3·28 S	49·22 W
78	Toccoa (tŏk′ô-ȧ).............Ga.	34·35 N	83·20 W
78	Toccoa (R.).................Ga.	34·53 N	84·24 W
153	Tochigi (tō′chē-gĭ)..........Jap.	36·25 N	139·45 E
148	T′ochi Tao (I.) (tōōŭ′jē dou) China	38·11 N	120·45 E
92	Tocoa (tō-kô′ä)...........Hond.	15·37 N	86·01 W
100	Tocopilla (tō-kô-pēl′yä).....Chile	22·03 S	70·08 W
99	Tocuyo de la Costa (tô-kōō′yō-dĕ-lä-kŏs′tä) Ven. (In.)	11·03 N	68·24 W
110	Todmorden (tŏd′môr-dĕn)...Eng.	53·43 N	2·05 W
118	Töfsingdalens (Natl. Park)...Swe.	62·09 N	13·05 E
153	Tōgane (tō′gä-nā)...........Jap.	35·29 N	140·16 E
163	Togo (tō′gō)................Afr.	8·00 N	0·52 E
136	Toguzak R. (tô′gōō-zák) Sov. Un. (Urals In.)	53·40 N	61·42 E
79	Tohopekaliga (L.) (tō′hô-pē′kȧ-lī′gȧ).Fla. (In.)	28·16 N	81·09 W
148	To′Hu (L.) (tōōŭ′hōō).....China	33·07 N	117·25 E
119	Toijala (toi′yȧ-lȧ)...........Fin.	61·11 N	21·46 E
153	Toi-Misaki (C.) (toi mê′sä-kê).Jap.	31·20 N	131·20 E
68	Toiyabe Ra. (toi′yă-bē).....Nev.	38·59 N	117·22 W
152	Tokachi Gawa (R.) (tō-kä′chê gä′wä).Jap.	43·10 N	142·30 E
121	Tokaj (tô′kô-ê)............Hung.	48·06 N	21·24 E
165	Tokar (tō′kär)..............Sud.	18·28 N	37·46 E
152	Tokara Guntō (Is.) (tō-kä′rä gōōn′tō′).Jap.	29·45 N	129·15 E
152	Tokara Kaikyo (Str.) (tô′kä-rä kī′kyô).Jap.	30·20 N	129·50 E
133	Tokat (tô-кät′).............Tur.	40·20 N	36·30 E
156	Tokelau Is. (tō-kê-lä′ōō)..Oceania	8·00 S	176·00 W
134	Tokmak (tôk′mȧk)......Sov. Un.	42·44 N	75·41 E
153	Tokorozawa (tô′kô-rô-zä′wä) Jap. (Tōkyō In.)	35·47 N	139·29 E
152	Tokuno (I.) (tô-kōō′nō)......Jap.	27·42 N	129·25 E
153	Tokushima (tō′kōō′shē-mä)...Jap.	34·06 N	134·31 E
153	Tokuyama (tō′kōō′yä-mä)....Jap.	34·04 N	131·49 E
153	Tōkyō (tō′kê-ō)..Jap. (Tōkyō In.)	35·41 N	139·44 E
153	Tōkyō (Pref.)....Jap. (Tōkyō In.)	35·42 N	139·40 E
153	Tōkyō-Wan (B.) (tō′kyō wän) Jap. (Tōkyō In.)	35·32 N	139·56 E
127	Tolbukhin..................Bul.	43·33 N	27·52 E
90	Tolcayuca (tôl-kä-yōō′kä)...Mex.	19·55 N	98·54 W
71	Toledo (tô-lē′dō)...........Iowa	41·59 N	92·35 W
80	Toledo....................Ohio	41·40 N	83·35 W
66	Toledo....................Ore.	44·37 N	123·58 W
124	Toledo (tô-lĕ′dô).............Sp.	39·53 N	4·02 W
124	Toledo, Montes de (Mts.) (mô′n-tĕs-dĕ-tô-lĕ′dô).Sp.	39·33 N	4·40 W
98	Tolima (Dept.) (tô-lē′mä) Col. (In.)	4·07 N	75·20 W
98	Tolima, Nevado del (Pk.) (nĕ-vä-dô-dĕl-tô-lē′mä).Col. (In.)	4·40 N	75·20 W
90	Tolimán (tô-lê-män′).......Mex.	20·54 N	99·54 W
110	Tollesbury (tōl′z-bĕrĭ) Eng. (London In.)	51·46 N	0·49 E
126	Tolmezzo (tôl-mĕt′sô).........It.	46·25 N	13·03 E
126	Tolmin (tôl′mên)..........Yugo.	46·12 N	13·45 E
121	Tolna (tôl′nô).............Hung.	46·25 N	18·47 E
154	Tolo, Teluk (B.) (tō′lō)....Indon.	2·00 S	122·06 E
124	Tolosa (tô-lō′sä).............Sp.	43·10 N	2·05 W
65	Tolt (R.) (tōlt).Wash. (Seattle In.)	47·13 N	121·49 W
80	Toluca (tô-lōō′kȧ)............Ill.	41·00 N	89·10 W
91	Toluca (tô-lōō′kȧ) Mex. (Mexico City In.)	19·17 N	99·40 W
91	Toluca, Nevado de (Zinántecatl) Mtn. (nĕ-vä-dô-dĕ-tô-lōō′kä) (zē-nä′n-tĕ-kä′tl) Mex. (Mexico City In.)	19·09 N	99·42 W
150	Tolun....................China	42·12 N	116·15 E
132	Tolyatti..............Sov. Un.	53·30 N	49·10 E
134	Tom′ (R.).............Sov. Un.	55·33 N	85·00 E
71	Tomah (tō′mȧ).............Wis.	43·58 N	90·31 W
71	Tomahawk (tŏm′ȧ-hôk)......Wis.	45·27 N	89·44 W
129	Tomakovka (tô-mä′kôf-kȧ) Sov. Un.	47·49 N	34·43 E
124	Tomar (tō-mär′)...........Port.	39·36 N	8·26 W
121	Tomashevka (tô-mȧ′shĕf-kȧ) Sov. Un.	51·34 N	23·37 E
121	Tomaszow Lubelski (tô-mä′shŏŏf lōō-bĕl′skĭ).Pol.	50·20 N	23·27 E
121	Tomaszów Mazowiecki (tô-mä′shŏŏf mä-zô′vyĕt-skĭ) Pol.	51·33 N	20·00 E
90	Tomatlán (tô-mä-tlȧ′n).....Mex.	19·54 N	105·14 W
90	Tomatlán (R.).............Mex.	19·56 N	105·14 W
99	Tombador, Serra do (Mts.) (sĕr′rȧ dōō tōm-bä-dôr′)..Braz.	11·31 S	57·33 W
78	Tombigbee (R.) (tŏm-bĭg′bê).Ala.	31·45 N	88·02 W
101	Tombos (tô′m-bōs) Braz. (Rio de Janeiro In.)	20·53 S	42·00 W
164	Tombouctou (Timbuktu) (tôm-bōōk-tōō′).Mali	16·52 N	2·53 W
69	Tombstone (tōōm′stōn).....Ariz.	31·40 N	110·00 W
118	Tomelilla (tô′mĕ-lēl-lä)......Swe.	55·34 N	13·55 E
124	Tomelloso (tō-mâl-lyō′sō).....Sp.	39·09 N	3·02 W
154	Tomini, Teluk (B.) (tô-mē′nê) Indon.	0·10 N	121·00 E
135	Tommot (tŏm-mŏt′).....Sov. Un.	59·13 N	126·22 E
134	Tomsk (tŏmsk).........Sov. Un.	56·29 N	84·57 E
91	Tonalá (tō-nä-lä′)..........Mex.	16·05 N	93·45 W
90	Tonala....................Mex.	20·38 N	103·14 W
91	Tonalá (R.)...............Mex.	18·05 N	94·08 W
75	Tonawanda (tôn-ȧ-wŏn′dȧ) N. Y. (Buffalo In.)	43·01 N	78·53 W
75	Tonawanda Cr. N. Y. (Buffalo In.)	43·05 N	78·43 W
110	Tonbridge (tŭn-brij) Eng. (London In.)	51·11 N	0·17 E
153	Tonda (tôn′dä)..Jap. (Ōsaka In.)	34·51 N	135·38 E
153	Tondabayashi (tôn′dä-bä′yä-shê) Jap. (Osaka In.)	34·29 N	135·36 E
155	Tondano (tôn-dä′nō)......Indon.	1·15 N	124·50 E
118	Tønder (tûn′nẽr)...........Den.	54·47 N	8·49 E
91	Tondlá....................Mex.	16·04 N	93·57 W
153	Tone (R.) (tō′nê) Jap. (Tōkyō In.)	35·55 N	139·57 E
153	Tone-Gawa (Strm.) (tô′nĕ gä′wa) Jap.	36·12 N	139·19 E
156	Tonga Is. (tŏŋ′gȧ).......Oceania	18·50 S	175·20 W
100	Tongoy (tōn-goi′)..........Chile	30·16 S	71·29 W
	Tongue of Arabat, see Arabatskaya Strelka (Spit)		
94	Tongue of the Ocean (Chan.) (tŭng ŏv thē ôshŭn).Ba. Is.	24·05 N	77·20 W
67	Tongue R. (tŭng).........Mont.	45·08 N	106·40 W
67	Tongue River Ind. Res.....Mont.	45·32 N	106·43 W
165	Tonj R. (tônj)..............Sud.	6·18 N	28·33 E
142	Tonk (Tŏŋk)..............India	26·13 N	75·45 E
73	Tonkawa (tŏŋ′kȧ-wô).......Okla.	36·42 N	97·19 W
151	Tonkin, Gulf of (tôn-kăn′)...Viet.	20·30 N	108·10 E
154	Tonle Sap (L.) (tôn′lā säp′).Camb.	13·03 N	102·49 E
122	Tonneins (tô-năɴ′)..........Fr.	44·24 N	0·18 E
120	Tönning (tû′nēng)..........Ger.	54·20 N	8·55 E
68	Tonopah (tō-nô-pä′)........Nev.	38·04 N	117·15 W
118	Tönsberg (tûns′bĕrgh).......Nor.	59·19 N	10·25 E
91	Tonto (R.) (tōn′tō).........Mex.	18·15 N	96·13 W
69	Tonto Cr..................Ariz.	34·05 N	111·15 W
69	Tonto Natl. Mon. (tôn′tô)...Ariz.	33·33 N	111·08 W
74	Tooele (tōō-ĕl′ê) Utah (Salt Lake City In.)	40·33 N	112·17 W
151	Toohsien.................China	25·30 N	111·32 E
160	Toowoomba (tōō wōōm′bȧ).Aust.	27·32 S	152·10 E
74	Topanga (tō′păn-gȧ) Calif. (Los Angeles In.)	34·05 N	118·36 W
73	Topeka (tô-pē′kȧ).........Kans.	39·02 N	95·41 W
91	Topilejo (tô-pē-lĕ′hô) Mex. (Mexico City In.)	19·12 N	99·09 W
121	Topol′čany (tô-pôl′chä-nü).Czech.	48·38 N	18·10 E
88	Topolobampo (tō-pō-lô-bä′m-pô) Mex.	25·45 N	109·00 W
127	Topolovgrad...............Bul.	42·05 N	26·19 E
66	Toppenish (tôp′ĕn-ĭsh).....Wash.	46·22 N	120·00 W
83	Torbay (tôr-bā′)............Can.	47·41 N	52·38 W
160	Torbreck, Mt. (tôr-brĕk)...Austl.	37·05 S	146·55 E
80	Torch (L.) (tôrch).........Mich.	45·00 N	85·30 W
118	Töreboda (tû′rĕ-bō′dä) .....Swe.	58·44 N	14·04 E
117	Torhout...................Bel.	51·01 N	3·04 E
98	Toribío (tô-rē-bê′ô).....Col. (In.)	2·58 N	76·14 W
153	Toride (tô′rê-dā).Jap. (Tōkyō In.)	35·54 N	140·04 E
126	Torino (Turin) (tô-rē′no) (tū′rĭn) It.	45·05 N	7·44 E
112	Torino (R.) (tôr′nĭ-ô)..Fin.-Swe..	67·00 N	23·50 E
124	Tormes (R.) (tōr′mās)........Sp.	41·12 N	6·15 W
112	Torne (R.) (tôr′nĕ).........Swe.	67·29 N	21·44 E
112	Torne Träsk (L.) (tôr′nĕ trĕsk) Swe.	68·10 N	20·36 E
87	Torngat Mts..............Can.	59·18 N	64·35 W
112	Tornio (tôr′nĭ-ô)............Fin.	65·55 N	24·09 E
82	Toro, Lac (L.).............Can.	46·53 N	73·46 W
127	Toronaíos Kólpos (G.).......Grc.	40·10 N	23·35 E
85	Toronto (tô-rŏn′tō) Can. (Toronto In.)	43·40 N	79·23 W
80	Toronto...................Ohio	40·30 N	80·35 W
76	Toronto, L. (lä′gô-tô-rô′n-tō) Mex.	27·35 N	105·37 W
128	Toropets (tô′rô-pyĕts)...Sov. Un.	56·31 N	31·37 E
133	Toros Dağlari (Taurus Mts.) (tô′rŭs).Tur.	37·00 N	32·40 E
125	Torote (R.) (tô-rō′tā) Sp. (Madrid In.)	40·36 N	3·24 W
118	Torp (tôrp)...............Swe.	62·30 N	16·04 E
	Torpen, see Åmot		
116	Torquay (tôr-kē′)...........Eng.	50·30 N	3·26 W
98	Torra, Cerro (Mtn.) (sĕ′r rô tŏ′r-rä).Col. (In.)	4·41 N	76·22 W
74	Torrance (tŏr′rănc) Calif. (Los Angeles In.)	33·50 N	118·20 W
125	Torre Annunziata (tôr′rā ä-nōōn-tsê-ä′tä) It. (Naples In.)	40·31 N	14·27 E
124	Torre de Cerredo (Mtn.) (tôr′rȧ dā thȧ-rā′dhō).Sp.	43·10 N	4·47 W
125	Torre del Greco (tôr′rȧ dĕl grā′kô) It. (Naples In.)	40·32 N	14·23 E
124	Torrejoncillo (tôr′rā-hōn-thē′lyō) Sp.	39·54 N	6·26 W
124	Torrelavega (tôr-rā′lä-vā′gä)..Sp.	43·22 N	4·02 W
126	Torre Maggiore (tôr′rā mäd-jō′rā) It.	40·41 N	15·18 E
160	Torrens, L. (tŏr-ĕns).......Austl.	30·07 S	137·40 E
125	Torrente (tôr-rĕn′tā).........Sp.	39·25 N	0·28 W
76	Torreon (tôr-rȧ-ōn′).........Mex.	25·32 N	103·26 W
125	Torre-Pacheco (tôr-rĕ-pä-chĕ′kô) Sp.	37·44 N	0·58 W
159	Torres Is. (tôr′rĕs) (tŏr′ĕz) New Hebr.	13·18 S	165·59 E
68	Torres Martinez Ind. Res. (tôr′ĕz mär-tē′nĕz).Calif.	33·33 N	116·21 W
124	Tôrres Novas (tôr′rĕzh nō′väzh) Port.	39·28 N	8·37 W
155	Torres Str. (tôr′rĕs)........Austl.	10·30 S	141·30 E
124	Tôrres Vedras (tôr′rĕzh vā′dräzh) Port.	39·08 N	9·18 W
125	Torrevieja (tôr-rā-vyā′hä).....Sp.	37·58 N	0·40 W
155	Torrijos (tôr-rē′hōs) Phil. (Manila In.)	13·19 N	122·06 E
81	Torrington (tŏr′ĭng-tŭn)....Conn.	41·50 N	73·10 W
70	Torrington...............Wyo.	42·04 N	104·11 W
124	Torro (tô′r-rō)..............Sp.	41·27 N	5·23 W
118	Torsby (tôrs′bü)............Swe.	60·07 N	12·56 E
118	Torshälla (tôrs′hĕl-ä)........Swe.	59·26 N	16·21 E
112	Tórshavn (tôrs-houn′)......Faer.	62·00 N	6·55 W
89	Tortola (I.) (tôr-tō′lä) Vir. Is. (Br.) (Puerto Rico In.)	18·34 N	64·40 W
126	Tortona (tôr-tō′nä)...........It.	44·52 N	8·52 W
125	Tortosa (tôr-tō′sä)...........Sp.	40·59 N	0·33 E
125	Tortosa, Cabo de (C.) (kȧ′bô-dĕ-tôr-tō-sä).Sp.	40·42 N	0·55 E
95	Tortue, Canal de la (Chan.) (tôr-tü′).Hai.	20·05 N	73·20 W
95	Tortue, Ile de la (I.)........Hai.	20·10 N	73·00 W
99	Tortuga, Isla la (I.) (ê′s-lä-lä-tôr-tōō′gä).Ven. (In.)	10·55 N	65·18 W
121	Toruń (tō′rōōn′)............Pol.	53·01 N	18·37 E
128	Tõrva (t′r′vȧ).........Sov. Un.	58·02 N	25·56 E
116	Tory (I.) (tō′rê).............Ire.	54·77 N	8·08 W
128	Torzhok (tôr′zhôk)......Sov. Un.	57·03 N	34·53 E
153	Tosa-Wan (B.) (tô′sä wän)...Jap.	33·14 N	133·39 E
126	Toscana (Reg.) (tôs-kä′nä)....It.	43·23 N	11·08 E
136	Tosna R.Sov. Un. (Leningrad In.)	59·38 N	30·52 E
136	Tosno (tôs′nô) Sov. Un. (Leningrad In.)	59·32 N	30·52 E
100	Tostado (tôs-tȧ′dô).........Arg.	29·10 S	61·43 W
133	Tosya (tôz′yȧ)..............Tur.	41·00 N	34·00 E
124	Totana (tô-tä-nä)............Sp.	37·45 N	1·28 W
132	Tot′ma (tôt′mȧ)........Sov. Un.	60·00 N	42·20 E
99	Totness....................Sur.	5·51 N	56·17 W

ăt; finăl; rāte; senâte; ärm; ȧsk; sofȧ; fâre; ch-choose; dh-as th in other; bē; êvent; bĕt; recĕnt; cratẽr; g-go; gh-guttural g; bĭt; ĭ-short neutral; rīde; ĸ-guttural k as ch in German ich;

PRONOUNCING INDEX Totonicapan–Tudela 277

Page	Name Pronunciation Region	Lat. °′	Long. °′
92	Totonicapán (tô-tō-nê-ᴋä′pän) Guat.	14·55 N	91·20 W
101	Totoras (tô-tô′räs) Arg. (Buenos Aires In.)	32·33 S	61·13 W
153	Totsuka (tōt′so͞o-kä)..........Jap.	35·24 N	139·32 E
110	Tottenham (tŏt′ĕn-ăm) Eng. (London In.)	51·35 N	0·06 W
153	Tottori (tô′tô-rê)..........Jap.	35·30 N	134·15 E
164	Touat (Oases) (to͞o′ät).......Alg.	27·22 N	00·38 W
164	Toubkal Pk..........Mor.	31·15 N	7·46 W
164	Touggourt (to͝o-go͞ort′) (to͞o-go͞or′) Alg.	33·09 N	6·07 E
114	Touil R. (to͞o-él′)..........Alg.	34·42 N	2·16 E
123	Toul (to͞ol)..........Fr.	48·39 N	5·51 E
82	Toulnustouc, Riviere (R.)...Can.	50·30 N	67·55 W
123	Toulon (to͞o-lôɴ′)..........Fr.	43·09 N	5·54 E
122	Toulouse (to͞o-lo͞oz′)..........Fr.	43·37 N	1·27 E
154	Toungoo (tŏ-o͝oŋ-go͞o′).......Bur.	19·00 N	96·29 E
	Tourane, see DaNang		
122	Tourcoing (to͞or-kwaɴ′).......Fr.	50·44 N	3·06 E
123	Tournan-en-Brie (to͞or-näɴ-ĕɴ-brē′) Fr. (Paris In.)	48·45 N	2·47 E
122	Tours (to͞or)..........Fr.	47·23 N	0·39 E
165	Toussidé, Pic (Pk.) (to͞o-sē-dā′) Chad	21·10 N	16·30 E
118	Tovdalselv (R.) (tôv-däls-ĕlv) Nor.	58·23 N	8·16 E
81	Towanda (tô-wän′dȧ)........Pa.	41·45 N	76·30 W
70	Towner (tou′nẽr)..........N. D.	48·21 N	100·24 W
83	Townsend (toun′zĕnd) Mass. (Boston In.)	42·41 N	71·42 W
67	Townsend..........Mont.	46·19 N	111·35 W
65	Townsend, Mt. Wash. (Seattle In.)	47·52 N	123·03 W
159	Townsville (tounz′vĭl)......Austl.	19·18 S	146·50 E
84	Towson (tou′sŭn) Md. (Baltimore In.)	39·24 N	76·36 W
154	Towuti, Danau (L.) (tô-wo͞o′tê) Indon.	3·00 S	121·45 E
76	Toyah (tô′yȧ)..........Tex.	31·19 N	103·46 W
153	Toyama (tō′yä-mä).........Jap.	36·42 N	137·14 E
153	Toyama-Wan (B.)..........Jap.	36·58 N	137·16 E
153	Toyohashi (tō′yô-hä′shê).....Jap.	34·44 N	137·21 E
153	Toyonaka (tō′yô-nä′kȧ) Jap. (Ōsaka In.)	34·47 N	135·28 E
114	Tozeur (tô-zûr′)..........Tun.	33·59 N	8·11 E
124	Trabancos (R.) (trä-bäŋ′kōs)..Sp.	41·15 N	5·13 W
133	Trabzon (trȧb′zôn)..........Tur.	41·00 N	39·45 E
68	Tracy (trā′sê)..........Calif.	37·45 N	121·27 W
70	Tracy..........Minn.	44·13 N	95·37 W
78	Tracy City..........Tenn.	35·15 N	85·44 W
124	Trafalgar, Cabo de (C.) (kȧ′bô-dĕ-trä-fäl-gä′r).Sp.	36·10 N	6·02 W
167	Trafonomby (Mtn.)..Malag. Rep.	24·32 S	46·35 E
86	Trail (trāl)..........Can.	49·04 N	117·56 W
111	Traisen (R.)....Aus. (Vienna In.)	48·15 N	15·55 E
111	Traiskirchen....Aus. (Vienna In.)	48·01 N	16·18 E
119	Trakai (trȧ-kȧy)........Sov. Un.	54·38 N	24·59 E
121	Trakiszki (trȧ-kē′-sh-kê).....Pol.	54·16 N	23·07 E
116	Tralee (trȧ-lē′)..........Ire.	52·16 N	9·20 W
118	Trälleborg (trĕl′ĕ-bôrg)......Swe.	55·24 N	13·07 E
118	Tranas (trän′ôs)..........Swe.	58·03 N	14·56 E
142	Tranbonsha (Mt.)..........China	35·27 N	86·25 E
124	Trancoso (träŋ-kō′so͝o)......Port.	40·46 N	7·23 W
155	Trangan (I.) (träŋ′gän)....Indon.	6·52 S	133·30 E
126	Trani (trä′nē)..........It.	41·15 N	16·25 E
103	Transcaucasia (Reg.)....Sov. Un.	41·17 N	44·30 E
85	Transcona (trăns-kō′nȧ) Can. (Winnipeg In.)	49·54 N	97·00 W
146	Trans-Himalays Mts. (trăns′hĭ-mä′lȧ-yȧ).China	31·15 N	81·56 E
166	Transvaal (Prov.) (trăns-väl′) S. Afr.	24·21 S	28·18 E
121	Transylvania (Reg.) (trăn-sĭl-vā′nĭ-ȧ).Rom.	46·30 N	22·35 E
	Transylvanian Alps (Mts.), see Carpatii Meridionali		
126	Trapani (trä′pä-nê)..........It.	38·02 N	12·34 E
123	Trappes (tràp).....Fr. (Paris In.)	48·47 N	2·01 E
160	Traralgon (tră′răl-gŏn).....Austl.	38·15 S	146·33 E
126	Trasimeno, Lago (L.) (lä′gō trä-sê-mā′nō).It.	43·00 N	12·12 E
124	Tras os Montes (Mts.) (träzh′ōzh môn′tāzh).Port.	41·33 N	7·13 W
124	Trasparga (träs-pär-gä).......Sp.	43·13 N	7·50 W
120	Traun R. (troun)..........Aus.	48·10 N	14·15 E
120	Traunstein (troun′stīn)......Ger.	47·52 N	12·38 E
70	Traverse, L. (trăv′ẽrs) Minn.-S. D.	45·46 N	96·53 W
80	Traverse City..........Mich.	44·45 N	85·40 W
126	Travnik (träv′nēk)........Yugo.	44·13 N	17·43 E
65	Treasure I. (trĕzh′ẽr) Calif. (San Francisco In.)	37·49 N	122·22 W
111	Trebbin (trĕ′bēn).Ger.(Berlin In.)	52·13 N	13·13 E
120	Třebič (t′rzhĕ′bēch).......Czech.	49·13 N	15·53 E
127	Trebinje (trȧ′bēn-yĕ).......Yugo.	42·43 N	18·21 E
121	Trebisov (trĕ′bê-shôf).....Czech.	48·36 N	21·32 E
120	Třeboň (t′rzhĕ′bôn′).......Czech.	49·00 N	14·48 E
159	Tregrosse Is. (trê-grōs′)....Austl.	18·08 S	150·53 E
100	Treinta y Tres (trȧ-ēn′tā ē trās′) Ur.	33·14 S	54·17 W
122	Trélazé (trā-lȧ-zā′)..........Fr.	47·27 N	0·32 W
100	Trelew (trē′lū)..........Arg.	43·15 S	65·25 W
116	Tremadoc B. (trĕ-mă′dŏk)..Wales	52·43 N	4·27 W
126	Tremiti, Isole di (Is.) (ê′sō-lĕ dē trā-mē′tē).It.	42·07 N	16·33 E
121	Trenčín (trĕn′chēn).......Czech.	48·52 N	18·02 E
154	Trengganu (State) (trĕng-gä′no͞o).Mala.	4·53 N	102·26 E
100	Trenque Lauquén (trĕn′kĕ-lȧ′o͝o-kĕ′n).Arg.	35·50 S	62·44 W
81	Trent (R.) (trĕnt)..........Can.	44·15 N	77·55 W
116	Trent (R.)..........Eng.	53·05 N	1·00 W
110	Trent and Mersey Can. (trĕnt) (mûr′zē).Eng.	53·11 N	2·24 W
126	Trento (trĕn′tô)..........It.	46·04 N	11·07 E
126	Trento (Reg.)..........It.	46·16 N	10·47 E
81	Trenton (trĕn′tŭn)..........Can.	44·05 N	77·35 W
83	Trenton..........Can.	45·39 N	62·40 W
75	Trenton......Mich. (Detroit In.)	42·08 N	83·12 W
73	Trenton..........Mo.	40·05 N	93·36 W
84	Trenton....N. J. (New York In.)	40·13 N	74·46 W
78	Trenton..........Tenn.	35·57 N	88·55 W
83	Trepassey (trê-păs′ê)........Can.	46·47 N	53·20 W
83	Trepassey B..........Can.	46·35 N	53·25 W
100	Tres Arroyos (trās′är-rō′yōs) .Arg.	38·18 S	60·16 W
101	Três Coraçoes (trĕ′s kō-rä-zô′ĕs) Braz. (Rio de Janeiro In.)	21·41 S	45·14 W
91	Tres Cumbres (trĕ′s ko͞o′m-brĕs) Mex. (Mexico City In.)	19·03 N	99·14 W
99	Três Lagoas (trĕ′s lä-gô′äs)..Braz.	20·48 S	51·42 W
99	Três Marias, Represa (Res.) (rĕ-prā′sä trĕs′ mä-rē′äs).Braz.	18·15 S	45·30 W
98	Tres Morros, Alto de (Mtn.) (ȧ′l-tō dĕ trĕ′s mô′r-rôs) Col. (In.)	7·08 N	76·10 W
101	Três Pontas (trĕ′s pô′n-täs) Braz. (Rio de Janeiro In.)	21·22 S	45·30 W
101	Três Rios (trĕ′s rê′ōs) Braz. (Rio de Janeiro In.)	22·07 S	43·13 W
111	Treuenbrietzen (troi′ĕn-brē-tzĕn) Ger. (Berlin In.)	52·06 N	12·52 E
126	Treviglio (trā-vē′lyô)..........It.	45·30 N	9·34 E
126	Treviso (trĕ-vê′sō)..........It.	45·39 N	12·15 E
146	Triangle, The (Reg.)........Asia	26·00 N	98·00 E
168	Trichardt (trĭ-ᴋärt′).......S. Afr. (Johannesburg & Pretoria In.)	26·32 S	29·16 E
126	Trieste (trê-ĕs′tā)..........It.	45·39 N	13·48 E
126	Trieste, G. of..........It.	45·38 N	13·40 E
124	Trigueros (trê-gā′rōs).........Sp.	37·23 N	6·50 W
142	Trigu Tsho (L.)..........China	28·47 N	91·37 E
127	Tríkkala..........Grc.	39·33 N	21·49 E
75	Trim Cr. (trĭm) . Ill. (Chicago In.)	41·19 N	87·39 W
143	Trincomalee (trĭŋ-kô-mȧ-lē′) Ceylon	8·39 N	81·12 E
110	Tring (trĭng)...Eng. (London In.)	51·46 N	0·40 W
98	Trinidad (trē-nê-dhädh′).....Bol.	14·48 S	64·43 W
72	Trinidad (trĭn′ĭ-dăd)........Colo.	37·11 N	104·31 W
94	Trinidad (trē-nê-dhädh′)....Cuba	21·50 N	80·00 W
101	Trinidad...Ur. (Buenos Aires In.)	33·29 S	56·55 W
94	Trinidad, Sierra de (Mts.) (sē-ĕ′r-rȧ dĕ trê-nê-dä′d).Cuba	21·50 N	79·55 W
99	Trinidad (I.) (trĭn′ĭ-dăd)....Trin.	10·00 N	61·00 W
89	Trinidad and Tobago (trĭn′ĭ-dăd) (tô-bā′gō).N. A.	11·00 N	61·00 W
96	Trinidade, Ilha da (I.) (ê′lä dă trê-nē-dä-dĕ).Braz.	21·00 S	32·00 W
88	Trinidad R. Pan. (Panama Canal In.)	8·55 N	80·01 W
91	Trinitaria (trē-nē-tä′ryä)....Mex.	16·09 N	92·04 W
93	Trinité Mart. (Le. & Wind. Is. In.)	14·47 N	61·00 W
83	Trinity (trĭn′ĭ-tê)..........Can.	48·22 N	53·24 W
77	Trinity..........Tex.	30·52 N	95·27 W
64	Trinity (Is.)..........Alaska	56·25 N	153·15 W
72	Trinity (R.), West Fk.......Tex.	33·22 N	98·26 W
73	Trinity (R.), East Fk.......Tex.	33·24 N	96·42 W
83	Trinity B..........Can.	47·55 N	53·30 W
66	Trinity Res..........Calif.	40·51 N	122·41 W
66	Trinity R..........Calif.	40·50 N	123·20 W
77	Trinity R..........Tex.	30·50 N	95·09 W
126	Trino (trē′nô)..........It.	45·11 N	8·16 E
78	Trion (trī′ŏn)..........Ga.	34·32 N	85·18 W
	Tripoli, see T′arābulus		
	Tripoli, see Tarābulus		
127	Tripolis (trĭ′pô-lĭs)..........Grc.	37·32 N	22·32 E
	Tripolitania, see Tarābulus		
70	Tripp (trĭp)..........S. D.	43·13 N	97·58 W
142	Tripura (Mts.)..........W. Pak.	28·38 N	91·37 E
47	Tristan da Cunha Is. (três-tän′dȧ ko͞on′yȧ).Atl. O.	35·30 S	12·15 W
99	Triste, Golfo (G.) (gôl-fô trē′s-tĕ) Ven. (In.)	10·40 N	68·05 W
84	Triticus Res. (trī tĭ-cŭs) N. Y. (New York In.)	41·20 N	73·36 W
143	Trivandrum (trê-vŭn′drŭm).India	8·34 N	76·58 E
121	Trnava (t′r′nȧ-vȧ)........Czech.	48·22 N	17·34 E
155	Trobriand Is. (trō-brê-ănd′)..Pap.	8·25 S	151·45 E
126	Trogir (trô′gēr)..........Yugo.	43·32 N	16·17 E
82	Trois Pistoles (trwä′ pês-tôl′).Can.	48.07 N	69·10 W
82	Trois-Rivières (rê-vyâr′)....Can.	46·21 N	72·35 W
136	Troitsk (trô′êtsk) Sov. Un. (Urals In.)	54·06 N	61·34 E
134	Troitsko-Pechorsk (trô′ĭtsk-ô-pyĕ-chôrsk′).Sov. Un.	62·18 N	56·07 E
129	Troitskoye..........Sov. Un.	47·39 N	30·16 E
118	Trollhättan (trôl′hĕt-ĕn).....Swe.	58·17 N	12·17 E
118	Trollheim (Mts.) (trôll-hĕĭm).Nor.	62·48 N	9·05 E
112	Tromsö (trôm′sû)..........Nor.	69·38 N	19·12 E
68	Trona (trō′nȧ)..........Calif.	35·49 N	117·20 W
100	Tronador, Cerro (Mtn.) (sĕ′r-rô trō-nä′dôr).Arg.	41·17 S	71·56 W
90	Troncoso (trôn-kô′sō).......Mex.	22·43 N	102·22 W
118	Trondheim (Nidaros) (trôn′hâm) (nē′dhä-rôs).Nor.	63·25 N	11·35 E
139	Troodos, Mt. Cyprus (Palestine In.)	34·56 N	32·52 E
118	Trosa (trô′sä)..........Swe.	58·54 N	17·25 E
87	Trout (L.)..........Can.	51·16 N	92·46 W
66	Trout Cr..........Ore.	42·18 N	118·31 W
65	Troutdale (trout′dāl) Ore. (Portland In.)	45·32 N	122·23 W
122	Trouville (tro͞o-vēl′)..........Fr.	49·23 N	0·05 E
78	Troy (troi)..........Ala.	31·47 N	85·46 W
74	Troy.........Ill. (St. Louis In.)	38·44 N	89·53 W
73	Troy..........Kans.	39·46 N	95·07 W
73	Troy..........Mo.	38·56 N	90·57 W
66	Troy..........Mont.	48·28 N	115·56 W
81	Troy..........N. Y.	42·45 N	73·45 W
79	Troy..........N. C.	35·21 N	79·58 W
80	Troy..........Ohio	40·00 N	84·10 W
127	Troy (Ruins)..........Tur.	39·59 N	26·14 E
122	Troyes (trwä)..........Fr.	48·18 N	4·03 E
	Trst, see Trieste		
127	Trstenik (t′r′stĕ-nêk).......Yugo.	43·36 N	20·00 E
128	Trubchëvsk (tro͝op′chĕfsk) Sov. Un.	52·36 N	32·46 E
138	Trucial States (tro͞o′shăl)....Asia	23·30 N	53·00 E
68	Truckee (trŭk′ê)..........Calif.	39·20 N	120·12 W
68	Truckee (R.).........Calif.-Nev.	39·25 N	120·07 W
161	Truganina.Austl. (Melbourne In.)	37·49 S	144·44 E
98	Trujillo (tro͞o-ᴋê′l-yō)...Col. (In.)	4·10 N	76·20 W
92	Trujillo (tro͞o-ᴋēl′yō)......Hond.	15·55 N	85·58 W
98	Trujillo..........Peru	8·08 S	79·00 W
124	Trujillo (tro͞o-ᴋê′l-yô)........Sp.	39·27 N	5·50 W
98	Trujillo..........Ven.	9·15 N	70·28 W
90	Trujillo (R.)..........Mex.	23·12 N	103·10 W
95	Trujin, L. (tro͞o-ᴋēn′)..Dom. Rep.	17·45 N	71·25 W
73	Trumann (tro͞o′măn)........Ark.	35·41 N	90·31 W
127	Trŭn (trŭn)..........Bul.	42·49 N	22·39 E
82	Truro (tro͞o′rō)..........Can.	45·22 N	63·20 W
116	Truro..........Eng.	50·17 N	5·05 W
84	Trussville (trŭs′vĭl) Ala. (Birmingham In.)	33·37 N	86·37 W
69	Truth or Consequences (tro͞oth ŏr kŏn′sê-kwĕn-sĭs) N. Mex.	33·10 N	107·20 W
120	Trutnov (tro͝ot′nôf).......Czech.	50·36 N	15·36 E
120	Trzcianka (tchyän′kȧ).......Pol.	53·02 N	16·27 E
120	Trzebiatow (tchĕ-byä′to͝o-v)..Pol.	54·03 N	15·16 E
146	Tsaidam Swp. (tsī′däm)....China	37·19 N	94·08 E
150	Ts′aiyü......China (Peking In.)	39·39 N	116·36 E
79	Tsala Apopka (R.) (tsä′lȧ ă-pŏp′kȧ).Fla.	28·57 N	82·11 W
148	Ts′anghsien (chäng′sĭän)...China	38·21 N	116·53 E
149	Ts′angmen....China (Canton In.)	22·42 N	113·09 E
	Tsangwu, see Wuchou		
148	Tsaochuang (jou′jo͝oäng)...China	34·51 N	117·34 E
148	Ts′aohsien (tsou′sĭän)......China	34·48 N	115·33 E
146	Tsast Bogda Ula (Mt.)....Mong.	46·44 N	92·34 E
65	Tsawwassen Ind. Res. Can. (Vancouver In.)	49·03 N	123·11 W
134	Tselinograd (tsĕ′lē-nô-gră′d) Sov. Un.	51·10 N	71·43 E
149	Tsengch′en...China (Canton In.)	23·18 N	113·49 E
136	Tsentral′nyy-Kospashskiy (tsĕn-träl′nyĭ-kôs-pȧsh′skĭ) Sov. Un. (Urals In.)	59·03 N	57·48 E
142	Tsethang..........China	29·20 N	91·49 E
166	Tshela (tshā′lȧ)..........Con. K.	4·50 S	13·05 E
166	Tshikapa (tshê-kä′pä)....Con. K.	6·29 S	20·53 E
166	Tshilongo (tshê-lôŋ′gō)...Con. K.	10·28 S	26·09 E
166	Tshuapa (R.)..........Con. K.	0·25 S	22·07 E
167	Tsiafajovona (Mtn.).Malag. Rep.	19·17 S	47·27 E
167	Tsiandra (tsē-än-drō′).Malag. Rep.	18·46 S	44·58 E
133	Tsimlyanskiy (Res.) (tsym-lyă′ns-kēê).Sov. Un.	47·50 N	43·40 E
139	Tsin (R.)......Isr. (Palestine In.)	30·52 N	35·05 E
148	Tsinan (Chinan) (je′nän)...China	36·40 N	117·01 E
146	Tsinghai (Prov.) (jĭng′hăĭ)..China	36·14 N	95·30 E
	Tsingtao, see Ch′ingtao		
167	Tsiribihina (R.) (tsē′rê-bē-hê-nä′) Malag. Rep.	19·45 S	43·30 E
167	Tsitsa (R.) (tsê′tsȧ) S. Afr. (Natal In.)	31·28 S	28·53 E
	Tsitsihar, see Ch′ich′ihaerh		
167	Tsolo (tsō′lō)..S. Afr. (Natal In.)	31·19 S	28·47 E
167	Tsomo........S. Afr. (Natal In.)	32·03 S	27·49 E
167	Tsomo (R.)....S. Afr. (Natal In.)	31·53 S	27·48 E
153	Tsu (tso͞o)..........Jap.	34·42 N	136·31 E
153	Tsuchiura (tso͞o′chê-o͞o-rä)....Jap.	36·04 N	140·09 E
153	Tsuda (tso͞o′dä)..Jap. (Ōsaka In.)	34·48 N	135·43 E
152	Tsugaru Kaikyō (str.) (tso͞o′gä-ro͞o kī′kyō).Jap.	41·25 N	140·20 E
166	Tsumeb (tso͞o′mĕb)....S. W. Afr.	19·10 S	17·45 E
153	Tsunashima (tso͞o′nä-shê′mä) Jap. (Tōkyō In.)	35·32 N	139·37 E
151	Ts′unghua..........China	23·30 N	113·40 E
148	Tsunhua (zho͞on′hooä).....China	40·12 N	117·55 E
153	Tsuruga (tso͞o′ro͝o-gä)........Jap.	35·39 N	136·04 E
153	Tsurugi San (Mtn.) (tso͞o′ro͝o-gê sän).Jap.	33·52 N	134·07 E
152	Tsuruoka (tso͞o′ro͝o-ō′kä).....Jap.	38·43 N	139·51 E
153	Tsurusaki (tso͞o′ro͝o-sä′kê)....Jap.	33·15 N	131·42 E
153	Tsu Shima (I.) (tso͞o shê′mä).Jap.	34·28 N	129·30 E
153	Tsushima Kaikyō (Str.) (tso͞o′shê-mä kī′kyō).Asia	33·52 N	129·30 E
153	Tsuwano (tso͞o′wȧ-nô′).......Jap.	34·28 N	131·47 E
153	Tsuyama (tso͞o′yä-mä′)......Jap.	35·05 N	134·00 E
124	Tua (R.) (to͞o′ä)..........Port.	41·23 N	7·18 W
65	Tualatin (R.) (to͞o′ȧ-lā-tĭn) Ore. (Portland In.)	45·25 N	122·54 W
157	Tuamotu (Low), Arch. (to͞o-ä-mō′to͞o).Fr. Polynesia	19·00 S	141·20 W
155	Tuao (to͞o-ä′ō) Phil. (Manila In.)	17·44 N	121·26 E
133	Tuapse (to͝o′ȧp-sĕ)......Sov. Un.	44·00 N	39·10 E
164	Tuareg (Reg.)..........Alg.	21·26 N	2·51 E
144	Tuayq, Jabal (Mts.).....Sau. Ar.	20·45 N	46·30 E
100	Tubarão (to͞o-bä-rouɴ′)....Braz.	28·23 S	48·56 W
120	Tübingen (tü′bĭng-ĕn).......Ger.	48·33 N	9·05 E
136	Tubinskiy (tû bĭn′skĭ) Sov. Un. (Urals In.)	52·53 N	58·15 E
165	Tubruq (Tobruk)..........Libya	32·03 N	24·04 E
99	Tucacas (to͞o-kä′käs)...Ven. (In.)	10·48 N	68·20 W
84	Tucker (tŭk′ẽr) Ga. (Atlanta In.)	33·51 N	84·13 W
69	Tucson (to͞o-sŏn′)..........Ariz.	32·15 N	111·00 W
100	Tucumán (to͞o-ko͞o-män′)....Arg.	26·52 S	65·08 W
100	Tucumán (Prov.)..........Arg.	26·30 S	65·30 W
72	Tucumcari (to͝o′kŭm-kâr-ê) N. Mex.	35·11 N	103·43 W
98	Tucupita (to͞o-ko͞o-pê′tä).....Ven.	9·00 N	62·09 W
99	Tucuruí (to͞o-ko͞o-to͝o-ē′)....Braz.	3·34 S	49·44 W
124	Tudela (to͞o-dhā′lä)..........Sp.	42·03 N	1·37 W

ng-sing; ŋ-baŋk; ɴ-nasalized n; nŏd; cŏmmit; ōld; ôbey; ôrder; fo͞od; fo͝ot; ou-out; s-soft; sh-dish; th-thin; pūre; ûnite; ûrn; stŭd; circŭs; ü-as "y" in study; ′-indeterminate vowel.

278 Tugaloo–Ueb Gestro R. PRONOUNCING INDEX

Page	Name Pronunciation Region	Lat. °′	Long. °′
78	Tugaloo (R.) (tŭg'ȧ-lōō) . Ga.-S. C.	34·35 N	83·05 W
167	Tugela (R.) (tōō-gel'ȧ) S. Afr. (Natal In.)	28·50 S	30·52 E
167	Tugela Ferry . . S. Afr. (Natal In.)	29·16 S	30·24 E
80	Tug Fork (R.) (tŭg) . . . . . . W. Va.	37·50 N	82·30 W
155	Tuguegarao (tōō-gā-gȧ-rä'ō) Phil. (Manila In.)	17·37 N	121·44 E
148	T'uhsich (R.) (tōō'hăĭ) . . . . . China	37·05 N	116·56 E
168	Tuinplaas . . . . S. Afr. (Johannesburg & Pretoria In.)	24·54 S	28·46 E
74	Tujunga (tōō-jŭŋ'gȧ) Calif. (Los Angeles In.)	34·15 N	118·16 W
136	Tukan (tōō'kȧn) Sov. Un. (Urals In.)	53·52 N	57·25 E
155	Tukengbesi, Palau-Palau (Is.) Indon.	6·00 S	124·15 E
165	Tukrah . . . . Libya	32·34 N	20·47 E
86	Tuktoyaktuk (tōōk-tō-yăk'tōōk) Can.	69·32 N	132·37 W
132	Tukum (tŏŏ'kŏŏm) . . . . . . Sov. Un.	57·00 N	22·50 E
119	Tukums (tŏŏ'kŏŏms) . . . . Sov. Un.	56·57 N	23·09 E
166	Tukuyu (tōō-kōō'yȧ) . . . . Tan.	9·13 S	33·43 E
65	Tukwila (tŭk'wĭ-lȧ) Wash. (Seattle In.)	47·28 N	122·16 W
90	Tula (tōō'lä) . . . . Mex.	20·04 N	99·22 W
128	Tula (tōō'lȧ) . . . . Sov. Un.	54·12 N	37·37 E
128	Tula (Oblast) . . . . Sov. Un.	53·45 N	37·19 E
90	Tula (R.) (tōō'lä) . . . . Mex.	20·40 N	99·27 W
159	Tulagi (I.) (tōō-lä'gē) . . . . . Sol. Is.	9·15 S	160·17 E
65	Tulalip (tū-lă'lĭp) Wash. (Seattle In.)	48·04 N	122·18 W
65	Tulalip Ind. Res. Wash. (Seattle In.)	48·06 N	122·16 W
90	Tulancingo (tōō-län-sĭŋ'gō) . . Mex.	20·04 N	98·24 W
68	Tulare (tōō-lä'rȧ) (tûl-âr') . . Calif.	36·12 N	119·22 W
68	Tulare Basin . . . . Calif.	35·57 N	120·18 W
69	Tularosa (tōō-lȧ-rō'zȧ) . . . N. Mex.	33·05 N	106·05 W
98	Tulcán (tōōl-kän') . . . . Ec.	0·44 N	77·52 W
129	Tulcea (tŏŏl'chȧ) . . . . Rom.	45·10 N	28·47 E
129	Tul'chin (tŏŏl'chĕn) . . . . . Sov. Un.	48·42 N	28·53 E
90	Tulcingo (tōōl-sĭŋ'gō) . . . . Mex.	18·03 N	98·27 W
68	Tule (R.) (tōō'lȧ) . . . . Calif.	36·08 N	118·50 W
167	Tuléar (tōō-lā-är') . . . Malag. Rep.	20·16 S	43·44 E
68	Tule River Ind. Res. (tōō'lȧ) Calif.	36·05 N	118·35 W
166	Tuli (tōō'lē) . . . . Rh.	20·58 S	29·12 E
72	Tulia (tōō'lĭ-ȧ) . . . . Tex.	34·32 N	101·46 W
91	Tulijá (R.) (tōō-lē-ĸȧ') . . . . . . Mex.	17·28 N	92·11 W
64	Tulik Vol. (tŏŏ'lĭk) . . . . Alaska	53·28 N	168·10 W
139	Tūl Karm (tōōl kärm) Jordan (Palestine In.)	32·19 N	35·02 E
78	Tullahoma (tŭl-ȧ-hō'mȧ) . . . Tenn.	35·21 N	86·12 W
116	Tullamore (tŭl-ȧ-mōr') . . . . Ire.	53·15 N	7·29 W
122	Tulle (tül) . . . . Fr.	45·15 N	1·45 E
111	Tulln (tŏŏln) . . . Aus. (Vienna In.)	48·21 N	16·04 E
111	Tullner Feld (Reg.) Aus. (Vienna In.)	48·20 N	15·59 E
165	Tulmaythah . . . . Libya	32·44 N	21·08 E
91	Tulpetlac (tōōl-pȧ-tlȧk') Mex. (Mexico City In.)	19·33 N	99·04 W
73	Tulsa (tŭl'sȧ) . . . . Okla.	36·08 N	95·58 W
98	Tuluá (tōō-lōō-ȧ') . . . . . . Col. (In.)	4·06 N	76·12 W
146	T'ulufan (Turfan) (tōō'lōō-fän') (tōōr-fän') . China	43·06 N	88·41 E
92	Tulum (tōō-lŏŏ'm) Mex. (Yucatan In.)	20·17 N	87·26 W
134	Tulun (tŏŏ-lōōn') . . . . Sov. Un.	54·29 N	100·43 E
69	Tumacacori Natl. Mon. (tōō-mä-kä'kō-rē) . Ariz.	31·36 N	110·20 W
98	Tumaco (tōō-mä'kō) . . . . Col.	1·41 N	78·44 W
92	Tuma R. (tōō'mä) . . . . Nic.	13·07 N	85·32 W
166	Tumba (L.) (tŏŏm'bä) . . . . Con. K.	1·03 S	18·28 E
98	Tumbes (tōō'm-bĕs) . . . . Peru	3·39 S	80·27 W
90	Tumbiscatío (tōōm-bē-skȧ-tē'ō) Mex.	18·32 N	102·23 W
65	Tumbo (I.) . . Can. (Vancouver In.)	48·49 N	123·04 W
150	T'umen (tōō'mĕn) . . . . China	43·00 N	129·50 E
152	Tumen (R.) . . . . China	42·08 N	128·40 E
99	Tumeremo (tōō-mȧ-rā'mō) . . . Ven.	7·15 N	61·28 W
99	Tumuc-Humac Mts. (tōō-mŏŏk'ōō-mäk') . S. A.	2·15 N	54·50 W
94	Tunas de Zaza (tōō'näs dā zä'zä) Cuba	21·40 N	79·35 W
116	Tunbridge Wells (tŭn'brĭj welz') Eng.	51·05 N	0·09 E
134	Tundra (Reg.) . . . . Sov. Un.	70·45 N	84·00 E
147	Tung (R.) . . . . China	24·13 N	115·08 E
148	Tunga (dōōng'ä) . . . . China	36·11 N	116·16 E
142	Tungabhadra Res . . . . India	15·26 N	75·57 E
151	T'ungan (tōōn'gän') . . . . China	24·48 N	118·02 E
148	T'ungch'engi (tōōng'chĕng'yē) China	36·21 N	116·14 E
147	T'ungchiang . . . . China	47·38 N	132·54 E
148	Tungeh'angshou (tōōng'chäng'shō) China	38·21 N	114·41 E
148	Tunghai (dōōng'hăĭ) . . . . China	34·35 N	119·05 E
150	T'ungho . . . . China	45·58 N	128·40 E
151	Tunghsiang . . . . China	28·18 N	116·38 E
150	Tunghsien . . . . . China (Peking In.)	39·55 N	116·40 E
148	Tung Hu (L.) (tōōng' hōō') . China	32·22 N	116·32 E
151	Tungjen (tŏŏng'jĕn') . . . . China	27·45 N	109·12 E
149	Tungkuan . . . . China (Canton In.)	23·03 N	113·14 E
150	T'ung-Kuan . . . . China	34·48 N	110·25 E
148	Tungkuang (dōōng'gōōäng) . China	37·54 N	116·33 E
151	T'ungku Chiao (Pt.) . . . . China	19·40 N	111·15 E
150	Tungliao (Payintala) . . . . China	43·30 N	122·15 E
148	Tungming (tŏŏng'mĭng') . . . . China	35·16 N	115·06 E
148	Tungpa (tōōng'bä) . . . . China	31·40 N	119·02 E
148	Tungpa . . . . China	35·56 N	116·19 E
150	T'ungpei (tōōng'pȧ) . . . . China	48·00 N	126·48 E
148	Tungping (tōōng'pĭng) . . . . . China	35·50 N	116·24 E
148	Tungp'ing Hu (L.) (hōō) . . . China	36·06 N	116·24 E
148	Tungt'antien (dōōng'tän'dĭän) China	35·26 N	116·54 E
151	Tungt'ing Hŭ (L.) (tōōng'tēng' hōō) . China	29·10 N	112·30 E
148	Tungwen (R.) (dōōng'wĕn) . China	36·24 N	119·00 E
150	Tunhua . . . . China	48·18 N	128·10 E
143	Tuni . . . . India	17·29 N	82·38 E
78	Tunica (tū'nĭ-kȧ) . . . . Miss.	34·41 N	90·23 W
164	Tunis (tū'nĭs) . . . . Tun.	36·59 N	10·06 E
113	Tunis, Golfe de (G.) . . . . Tun.	37·06 N	10·43 E
163	Tunisia (tû-nĭzh'ē-ȧ) . . . . Afr.	35·00 N	10·11 E
98	Tunja (tōō'n-hȧ) . . . . Col.	5·32 N	73·19 W
81	Tunkhannock (tŭnk-hăn'ŭk) . . Pa.	41·35 N	75·55 W
65	Tunnel (R.) (tŭn'ĕl) Wash. (Seattle In.)	47·48 N	123·04 W
68	Tuolumne (R.) (twô-lŭm'nē) . Calif.	37·35 N	120·37 W
135	Tuostakh (R.) . . . . Sov. Un.	67·09 N	137·30 E
99	Tupã (tōō-pȧ) . . . . Braz.	21·47 S	50·33 W
78	Tupelo (tū'pē-lō) . . . . Miss.	34·14 N	88·43 W
99	Tupinambaranas, Ilha (I.) (ē'lă-tōō-pē-năɴ-bă-ră'năs) . Braz.	3·04 S	58·09 W
98	Tupiza (tōō-pē'zä) . . . . Bol.	21·26 S	65·43 W
81	Tupper Lake (tŭp'ẽr) . . . . . . N. Y.	44·15 N	74·25 W
98	Tuquerres (tōō-kĕ'r-rĕs) . . . . . . Col.	1·12 N	77·44 W
134	Tura (tŏŏr'ȧ) . . . . Sov. Un.	64·08 N	99·58 E
103	Tura (R.) . . . . Sov. Un.	57·15 N	64·23 E
144	Turayf . . . . Sau. Ar.	31·32 N	38·30 E
90	Turbio (R.) (tōōr-byō) . . . . . . Mex.	20·28 N	101·40 W
98	Turbo (tōō'bō) . . . . Col.	8·02 N	76·43 W
121	Turciansky Svätý Martin (tōōr'chyȧn-skû'svă'tû' mär'tyĕn) . Czech.	49·02 N	18·48 E
121	Turda (tŏŏr'dȧ) . . . . Rom.	46·35 N	23·47 E
	Turfan, see T'ulufan		
146	Turfan Depression . . . . China	42·16 N	90·00 E
167	Turffontein . . . . S. Afr. (Johannesburg & Pretoria In.)	26·15 S	28·03 E
134	Turgay (tōōr'gī) . . . . Sov. Un.	49·42 N	63·39 E
103	Turgayka (R.) (tōōr-gī'kă) Sov. Un.	49·44 N	66·15 E
127	Tŭrgovishte . . . . Bul.	43·14 N	26·36 E
133	Turgutlu . . . . Tur.	38·30 N	27·20 E
119	Türi (tü'rĭ) . . . . Sov. Un.	58·49 N	25·29 E
124	Turia (R.) (tōō'ryä) . . . . Sp.	40·12 N	1·18 W
90	Turicato (tōō-rē-kä'tō) . . . . . . Mex.	19·03 N	101·24 W
94	Turiguano (I.) (tōō-rē-gwä'nō) Cuba	22·20 N	78·35 W
	Turin, see Torino		
121	Turka (tŏŏr'kȧ) . . . . Sov. Un.	49·10 N	23·02 E
134	Turkestan (tûr-kĕ-stăn') (tōōr-kĕ-stan') . Sov. Un.	42·40 N	65·00 E
130	Turkestan (Reg.) . . . . Sov. Un.	43·27 N	62·14 E
138	Turkey . . . . Eur.-Asia	38·45 N	32·00 E
71	Turkey (R.) (tûrk'ē) . . . . Iowa	43·20 N	92·16 W
130	Turkmen (S. S. R.) (tōōrk-mĕn') Sov. Un.	40·46 N	56·01 E
95	Turks I. Pass . . Turks & Caicos Is.	21·15 N	71·25 W
95	Turks Is. (tûrks) Turks & Caicos Is.	21·25 N	71·10 W
119	Turku (Åbo) (tŏŏr'kŏŏ) (ô'bô) . Fin.	60·28 N	22·12 E
68	Turlock (tûr'lŏk) . . . . Calif.	37·30 N	120·51 W
92	Turneffe I. (tûr-nĕf'fē) Br. Hond. (Yucatan In.)	17·25 N	87·43 W
74	Turner (tûr'nẽr) Kans. (Kansas City In.)	39·05 N	94·42 W
94	Turner Sd . . . . Ba. Is.	24·20 N	78·05 W
111	Turnhout (tŭrn-hout') Bel. (Brussels In.)	51·19 N	4·58 E
120	Turnov (tŏŏr'nôf) . . . . Czech.	50·36 N	15·12 E
127	Tŭrnovo . . . . Bul.	43·06 N	25·38 E
127	Turnu Măgurele (tŏŏr'nŏŏ mŭ-gōō-rĕ'ly') . Rom.	43·54 N	24·49 E
127	Turnu-Severin (sĕ-vĕ-rēn') . . Rom.	44·37 N	22·38 E
94	Turquino, Pico de (Pk.) (pē'kō dā tōōr-kē'nō) . Cuba	20·00 N	76·50 W
93	Turrialba (tōōr-ryä'l-bä) . . . . C. R.	9·54 N	83·41 W
127	Turski Trstenik . . . . Bul.	43·26 N	24·50 E
103	Turtkul' (tŏŏrt-kŏŏl') . . . . Sov. Un.	41·28 N	61·02 E
77	Turtle B. (tûr't'l) . . . . . . Tex. (In.)	29·48 N	94·38 W
70	Turtle Cr . . . . S. D.	44·40 N	98·53 W
70	Turtle Mountain Ind. Res . . N. D.	48·45 N	99·57 W
70	Turtle Mts . . . . N. D.	48·57 N	100·11 W
134	Turukhansk (tōō-rōō-ĸänsk') Sov. Un.	66·03 N	88·39 E
121	Turya R. (tŏŏr'yȧ) . . . . . . Sov. Un.	51·18 N	24·55 E
78	Tuscaloosa (tŭs-kȧ-lōō'sȧ) . . . . Ala.	33·10 N	87·35 W
66	Tuscarora (tŭs-kȧ-rō'rȧ) . . . . . Nev.	41·18 N	116·15 W
75	Tuscarora Ind. Res. N. Y. (Buffalo In.)	43·10 N	78·51 W
80	Tuscola (tŭs-kō'lȧ) . . . . Ill.	39·50 N	88·20 W
78	Tuscumbia (tŭs-kŭm'bĭ-ȧ) . . . . Ala.	35·41 N	87·42 W
151	Tushan (dōō'shän) . . . . China	25·50 N	107·42 E
148	Tushan . . . . China	31·38 N	116·16 E
136	Tushino (tōō'shĭ-nō) Sov. Un. (Moscow In.)	55·51 N	37·22 E
78	Tuskegee (tŭs-kē'gē) . . . . Ala.	32·25 N	85·40 W
148	T'ussuk'ou (tōō'sĕ'kō) . . . . . . China	36·19 N	117·37 E
74	Tustin (tŭs'tĭn) Calif. (Los Angeles In.)	33·44 N	117·49 W
128	Tutayev (tōō-tȧ-yĕf') . . . . Sov. Un.	57·53 N	39·34 E
110	Tutbury (tŭt'bẽr-ē) . . . . Eng.	52·52 N	1·51 W
143	Tuticorin (tōō-tē-kō-rĭn') . . . . India	8·51 N	78·09 E
91	Tutitlan (tōō-tē-tlä'n) Mex. (Mexico City In.)	19·38 N	99·10 W
99	Tutóia (tōō-tō'yȧ) . . . . Braz.	2·42 S	42·21 W
127	Tutrakan . . . . Bul.	44·02 N	26·36 E
73	Tuttle Creek Res . . . . Kans.	39·30 N	96·38 W
120	Tuttlingen (tŏŏt'lĭng-ĕn) . . . . . Ger.	47·58 N	8·50 E
78	Tutwiler (tŭt'wĭ-lẽr) . . . . Miss.	34·01 N	90·25 W
134	Tuva Aut. Oblast . . . . Sov. Un.	51·15 N	90·45 E
85	Tuxedo (tŭk-sē'dō) Can. (Winnipeg In.)	49·51 N	97·13 W
84	Tuxedo Park (tŭk-sē'dō pärk) N. Y. (New York In.)	41·11 N	74·11 W
110	Tuxford (tŭks'fẽrd) . . . . Eng.	53·14 N	0·54 W
90	Tuxpan (tōōs'pän) . . . . Mex.	19·34 N	103·22 W
91	Túxpan . . . . Mex.	20·57 N	97·26 W
91	Túxpan (R.) (tōōs'pän) . . . . . Mex.	20·55 N	97·52 W
91	Túxpan, Arrecife (Rf.) (är-rĕ-sē'fĕ-tōō'x-pä'n) . Mex.	21·01 N	97·12 W
91	Tuxtepec (tōōs-tȧ-pĕk') . . . . . Mex.	18·06 N	96·09 W
91	Tuxtla Gutiérrez (tōōs'tlä gōō-tyâr'rĕs) . Mex.	16·44 N	93·08 W
112	Tuy . . . . Sp.	42·07 N	8·49 W
99	Tuy (tōō'ē) (R.) . . . . Ven. (In.)	10·15 N	66·03 W
93	Tuyra R. (tōō-ē'rȧ) . . . . Pan.	7·55 N	77·37 W
151	Tuyün (tōō'yün') . . . . China	26·18 N	107·40 E
133	Tuz Gölü (L.) . . . . Tur.	39 00 N	33 30 E
127	Tuzla (tŏŏz'lȧ) . . . . Yugo.	44·33 N	18·46 E
118	Tvedestrand (tvĭ'dhĕ-stränd) . Nor.	58·39 N	8·54 E
118	Tveitsund (tvȧt'sŏŏnd) . . . . . . Nor.	59·03 N	8·29 E
	Tver, see Kalinin		
128	Tvertsa (L.) (tvĕr'tsȧ) . . . Sov. Un.	56·58 N	35·22 E
116	Tweed (R.) (twēd) . . . . Scot.	55·32 N	2·35 W
168	Tweeling (twē'lĭng) . . . . S. Afr. (Johannesburg & Pretoria In.)	27·34 S	28·31 E
75	Twelvemile Cr. (twĕlv'mīl) N. Y. (Buffalo In.)	43·13 N	78·58 W
85	Twenty Mile Cr. (twĕn'tĭ mīl) Can. (Toronto In.)	43·09 N	79·49 W
110	Twickenham (twĭk''n-ăm) Eng. (London In.)	51·26 N	0·20 W
83	Twillingate (twĭl'ĭn-gāt) . . . . . Can.	49·41 N	54·49 W
67	Twin Bridges (twĭn brĭ-jėz) . Mont.	45·34 N	112·17 W
67	Twin Falls (fôls) . . . . Idaho	42·33 N	114·29 W
75	Twinsburg (twĭnz'bŭrg) Ohio (Cleveland In.)	41·19 N	81·26 W
72	Two Butte Cr. (tōō būt) . . . . Colo.	37·39 N	102·45 W
71	Two Harbors . . . . Minn.	47·00 N	91·42 W
73	Two Prairie Bay. (prā'rĭ bī ōō') Ark.	34·48 N	92·07 W
71	Two Rivers (rĭv'ẽrz) . . . . Wis.	44·09 N	87·36 W
161	Tyabb . . . . Austl. (Melbourne In.)	38·16 S	145·11 E
121	Tyachev (tyä'chĕf) . . . . . . Sov. Un.	48·01 N	23·42 E
146	Tyan' Shan' (Tien-Shan) (Mts.) Sov. Un.-China	42·00 N	78·46 E
129	Tyasmin (R.) (tyȧs-mĭn') Sov. Un.	49·14 N	32·23 E
167	Tylden (tĭl-dĕn) . S. Afr. (Natal In.)	32·08 S	27·06 E
110	Tyldesley (tĭldz'lē) . . . . Eng.	53·32 N	2·28 W
70	Tyler (tī'lẽr) . . . . Minn.	44·18 N	96·08 W
77	Tyler . . . . Tex.	32·21 N	95·19 W
78	Tylertown (tī'lẽr-toun) . . . . . . Miss.	31·08 N	90·06 W
70	Tyndall (tĭn'dȧl) . . . . S. D.	42·58 N	97·52 W
135	Tyndinskiy . . . . Sov. Un.	55·22 N	124·45 E
116	Tyne (R.) (tīn) . . . . Eng.	54·59 N	1·56 W
116	Tynemouth (tīn'mŭth) . . . . . . Eng.	55·04 N	1·39 W
118	Tynest (tün'sĕt) . . . . Nor.	62·17 N	10·45 E
83	Tyngsboro (tĭnj-bûr'ō) Mass. (Boston In.)	42·40 N	71·27 W
	Tyre, see Sūr		
118	Tyri Fd. (tü'rē) . . . . Nor.	60·03 N	10·25 E
69	Tyrone (tī'rōn) . . . . N. Mex.	32·40 N	108·20 W
81	Tyrone . . . . Pa.	40·40 N	78·15 W
160	Tyrrell, L. (tir'ĕll) . . . . Austl.	35·12 S	143·00 E
113	Tyrrhenian Sea (tĭr-rē'nĭ-ȧn) . . . It.	40·10 N	12·15 E
119	Tyrvää (tür'vȧ) . . . . Fin.	61·19 N	22·51 E
133	Tyub-Karagan, Mys (C.) Sov. Un.	44·30 N	50·10 E
134	Tyukalinsk (tyŏŏ-kȧ-lĭnsk') Sov. Un.	56·03 N	71·43 E
135	Tyukyan (R.) (tyŏŏk'yȧn) Sov. Un.	65·42 N	116·09 E
133	Tyuleniy (I.) . . . . Sov. Un.	44·30 N	48·00 E
134	Tyumen' (tyōō-mĕn') . . . . Sov. Un.	57·02 N	65·28 E
134	Tyura-Tam . . . . Sov. Un.	46·00 N	63·15 E
92	Tzucacab (tzōō-kä-kä'b) Mex. (Yucatan In.)	20·06 N	89·03 W
148	Tz'uhsien (tsĕ'sĭän) . . . . China	36·22 N	114·23 E
151	Tzu Shui (R.) (tsōō) . . . . China	26·50 N	111·00 E
148	Tzuya (R.) (zhĕ'yä) . . . . China	38·38 N	116·31 E
148	Tzuyang (tsĕ'yäng) . . . . China	35·35 N	116·50 E
114	Uarc, Ras (C.) . . . . Mor.	35·31 N	2·45 W
98	Uaupés (wä-ōō'pās) . . . . Braz.	0·02 S	67·03 W
101	Ubá (ŏŏ-bȧ') Braz. (Rio de Janeiro In.)	21·08 S	42·55 W
163	Ubangi R. (ōō-băŋ'gē) . . . . Afr.	0·45 N	17·28 E
101	Ubatuba (ōō-bȧ-tōō'bȧ) Braz. (Rio de Janeiro In.)	23·25 S	45·06 W
124	Ubeda (ōō'bȧ-dä) . . . . Sp.	38·01 N	3·23 W
99	Uberaba (ōō-bȧ-rä'bȧ) . . . . . . Braz.	19·47 S	47·47 W
99	Uberlândia (ōō-bĕr-lȧ'n-dyä) . Braz.	18·54 S	48·11 W
166	Ubombo (ōō-bôm'bō) . . . . . . S. Afr.	27·33 S	32·13 E
154	Ubon Ratchathani (ōō'bŭn rä'chätá-nē) . Thai	15·15 N	104·52 E
129	Ubort' (R.) (ōō-bôrt') . . . . Sov. Un.	51·18 N	27·43 E
124	Ubrique (ōō-brē'kȧ) . . . . Sp.	36·43 N	5·36 W
146	Ubsa Nuur (L.) . . . . Mong.	50·29 N	93·32 E
98	Ucayali (R.) (ōō'kä-yä'lē) . . . . Peru	8·58 S	74·13 W
111	Uccle (ü'kl') . . . Bel. (Brussels In.)	50·48 N	4·17 E
136	Uchaly (û-chä'lĭ) Sov. Un. (Urals In.)	54·22 N	59·28 E
134	Uch-Aral (ŏŏch'ȧ-ral') . . . Sov. Un.	46·14 N	80·58 E
153	Uchiko (ōō'chē-kō) . . . . Jap.	33·30 N	132·39 E
153	Uchinoura (ōō'chē-nō-ōō'rȧ) . . Jap.	31·16 N	131·03 E
136	Uchinskoye Vodokhranilishche L. (ōōch-ēn'skô-yĕ vô-dô-ĸrȧ-nĭ'li-shchĕ) Sov. Un. (Moscow In.)	56·08 N	37·44 E
152	Uchiura-Wan (B.) (ōō'chē-ōō'rä wän) . Jap.	42·20 N	140·44 E
142	Uch-Korgon . . . . Sov. Un.	37·22 N	68·41 E
	Uch Turfan, see Wushih		
135	Uchur (R.) (ŏŏ-chŏŏr') . . . Sov. Un.	58·27 N	131·34 E
135	Uda (R.) (ŏŏ'dȧ) . . . . Sov. Un.	52·28 N	110·51 E
135	Uda (R.) . . . . Sov. Un.	53·54 N	131·29 E
142	Udaipur (ŏŏ-dŭ'ē-pōōr) . . . . . India	24·41 N	73·41 E
129	Uday (R.) (ŏŏ-dī') . . . . . . Sov. Un.	50·45 N	32·13 E
118	Uddevalla (ōōd'dĕ-väl-ȧ) . . . . Swe.	58·21 N	11·55 E
126	Udine (ōō'dē-nȧ) . . . . It.	46·05 N	13·14 E
134	Udmurt (A. S. S. R.) . . . . Sov. Un.	52·30 N	52·17 E
154	Udon Thani . . . . Thai.	17·31 N	102·51 E
135	Udskaya Guba (B.) . . . . . Sov. Un.	55·00 N	136·30 E
165	Ueb Gestro R. (wĕb gĕs'tro) . . Eth.	6·25 N	41·21 E

ăt; finăl; rāte; senâte; ärm; ȧsk; sofȧ; fâre; ch-choose; dh-as th in other; bē; ėvent; bĕt; recĕnt; cratẽr; g-go; gh-guttural g; bĭt; ǐ-short neutral; rīde: ĸ-guttural k as ch in German ich;

Page	Name Pronunciation Region	Lat. °′	Long. °′
75	Utica (ū'tĭ-kȧ) Ind. (Louisville In.)	38·20 N	85·39 W
81	Utica N. Y.	43·05 N	75·10 W
124	Utiel (ōō-tyâl') Sp.	39·34 N	1·13 W
75	Utika (ū'tĭ-kȧ) Mich. (Detroit In.)	42·37 N	83·02 W
92	Utila I. (ōō-tē'lä) Hond.	16·07 N	87·05 W
153	Uto (ōō'tō') Jap.	32·43 N	130·39 E
111	Utrecht (ū'trĕkt) (ü'trĕkt) Neth. (Amsterdam In.)	52·05 N	5·06 E
124	Utrera (ōō-trä'rä) Sp.	37·12 N	5·48 W
118	Utsira (I.) (ütsïrä) Nor.	59·21 N	4·50 E
153	Utsunomiya (ōōt'sōō-nō'mē-yȧ') Jap.	36·35 N	139·52 E
154	Uttaradit Thai.	17·47 N	100·10 E
142	Uttar Pradesh (State) (ōōt-tär-prä-dĕsh) India	34·19 N	78·40 E
110	Uttoxeter (ŭt-tôk'sē-tēr) Eng.	52·54 N	1·52 W
89	Utuado (ōō-tōō-ä'dhō) P. R. (Puerto Rico In.)	18·16 N	66·40 W
119	Uusikaupunki (Nystad) (ōō'sĭ-kou'pōōŋ-kĭ) (nü'stådh) Fin.	60·48 N	21·24 E
76	Uvalde (ū-văl'dē) Tex.	29·14 N	99·47 W
136	Uvel'skiy (ōō-vyĕl'skĭ) Sov. Un. (Urals In.)	54·27 N	60·22 E
166	Uvira (ōō-vē'rä) Con. K.	3·28 S	29·03 E
128	Uvod' (R.) (ōō-vôd') Sov. Un.	56·52 N	41·03 E
167	Uvongo S. Afr. (Natal In.)	30·49 S	30·23 E
153	Uwajima (ōō-wä'jē-mä) Jap.	33·12 N	132·35 E
83	Uxbridge (ŭks'brĭj) Mass. (Boston In.)	42·05 N	71·38 W
92	Uxmal (Ruins) (ōō'x-mä'l) Mex. (Yucatan In.)	20·22 N	89·44 W
136	Uy R. (ōōy) Sov. Un. (Urals In.)	54·05 N	62·11 E
136	Uyskoye (ûy'skô-yĕ) Sov. Un. (Urals In.)	54·22 N	60·01 E
98	Uyuni (ōō-yōō'nē) Bol.	20·28 S	66·45 W
98	Uyuni, Salar de (Salt Flat) (sä-lär-dĕ) Bol.	20·58 S	67·09 W
130	Uzbek S. S. R. (ōōz-bĕk') Sov. Un.	42·42 N	60·00 E
133	Uzen, Bol'shoy (R.) Sov. Un.	49·50 N	49·35 E
129	Uzh (R.) (ōōzh) Sov. Un.	51·07 N	29·05 E
121	Uzhgorod (ōōzh'gô-rôt) Sov. Un.	48·38 N	22·18 E
127	Uzunköpru (ōō'zōōn'kû-prū) Tur.	41·17 N	26·42 E
166	Vaal (R.) (väl) S. Afr.	28·15 S	24·30 E
168	Vaaldam (L.) S. Afr. (Johannesburg & Pretoria In.)	26·58 S	28·37 E
168	Vaalplaas S. Afr (Johannesburg & Pretoria In.)	25·39 S	28·56 E
168	Vaalwater S. Afr. (Johannesburg & Pretoria In.)	24·17 S	28·08 E
119	Vaasa (vä'sȧ) Fin.	63·06 N	21·39 E
121	Vác (väts) Hung.	47·46 N	19·10 E
95	Vache, Ile À (I.) (väsh) Hai.	18·05 N	73·40 W
112	Vadsö (vädh'sû) Nor.	70·08 N	29·52 E
118	Vadstena (våd'stĭ'nȧ) Swe.	58·27 N	14·53 E
120	Vaduz (vä'dōōts) Liech.	47·10 N	9·32 E
132	Vaga (R.) (va'gȧ) Sov. Un.	61·55 N	42·30 E
118	Vågsöy (I.) Nor.	61·58 N	4·44 E
121	Vah R. (väĸ) Czech.	48·07 N	17·52 E
142	Vaigai (R.) India	10·20 N	78·13 E
134	Vakh (R.) (våĸ) Sov. Un.	61·30 N	81·33 E
127	Valachia (Reg.) Rom.	44·45 N	24·17 E
85	Valcartier-Village (väl-kårt-yĕ' vē-läzh') Can. (Quebec In.)	46·56 N	71·28 W
128	Valdai Hills (vål-dī' gô'rĭ) Sov. Un.	57·50 N	32·35 E
128	Valday (Valdai) (vål-dī') Sov. Un.	57·58 N	33·13 E
125	Valdemorillo (väl-dȧ-mô-rēl'yō) Sp. (Madrid In.)	40·30 N	4·04 W
124	Valdepeñas (väl-dȧ-pān'yȧs) Sp.	38·46 N	3·22 W
124	Valderaduey (R.) (väl-dĕ-rä-dwĕ'y) Sp.	41·39 N	5·35 W
100	Valdés, Pen. (väl-dĕ's) Arg.	42·15 S	63·15 W
64	Valdez (văl'dĕz) Alaska	61·10 N	146·18 W
125	Valdilecha (väl-dē-lā'chȧ) Sp. (Madrid In.)	40·17 N	3·19 W
100	Valdivia (väl-dē'vä) Chile	39·47 S	73·13 W
98	Valdivia (väl-dē'vēä) Col. (In.)	7·10 N	75·26 W
87	Val-d' Or Can.	48·03 N	77·50 W
78	Valdosta (văl-dŏs'tȧ) Ga.	30·50 N	83·18 W
124	Valdovino (väl-dô-vē'nō) Sp.	43·36 N	8·05 W
66	Vale (vāl) Ore.	43·59 N	117·14 W
99	Valença (vä-lĕn'sȧ) Braz.	13·43 S	38·58 W
122	Valence-sur-Rhône (vä-lĕɴs-sür-rōn') Fr.	44·56 N	4·54 E
124	Valencia (vä-lĕ'n-syä) Port.	42·03 N	8·36 W
125	Valencia (vä-lĕn'thē-ä) Sp.	39·26 N	0·23 W
124	Valencia Sp.	39·34 N	7·13 W
99	Valencia (vä-lĕn'syä) Ven. (In.)	10·11 N	68·00 W
125	Valencia (Reg.) (vä-lĕn'thē-ä) Sp.	39·08 N	0·43 W
116	Valencia (I.) (vȧ-lĕn'shȧ) Ire.	51·55 N	10·26 W
99	Valencia, Lago de (L.) Ven. (In.)	10·11 N	67·45 W
122	Valenciennes (vȧ-läɴ-syĕn') Fr.	50·24 N	3·36 E
70	Valentine (vȧ lăɴ-tē-nyē') Nebr.	42·52 N	100·34 W
98	Valera (vä-lĕ'rä) Ven.	9·12 N	70·45 W
136	Valerianovsk (vȧ-lĕ-rĭ-ä'nôvsk) Sov. Un. (Urals In.)	58·47 N	59·34 E
128	Valga (väl'gȧ) Sov. Un.	57·47 N	26·03 E
167	Valhalla (väl-hăl-ȧ) S. Afr. (Johannesburg & Pretoria In.)	25·49 S	28·09 E
67	Valier (vă-lēr') Mont.	48·17 N	112·14 W
127	Valjevo (väl'yȧ-vô) Yugo.	44·17 N	19·57 E
129	Valki (väl'kē) Sov. Un.	49·49 N	35·40 E
92	Valladolid (väl-yä-dhô-lēdh') Mex. (Yucatan In.)	20·39 N	88·13 W
124	Valladolid (väl-yä-dhô-lēdh') Sp.	41·41 N	4·41 W
125	Vall de Uxo' (väl-dĕ-ōōx-ô') Sp.	39·50 N	0·15 W
98	Valle (Dept.) (vä'l-yĕ) Col. (In.)	4·03 N	76·13 W
68	Valle, Arroyo del (ä-rō'yō dĕl väl'yȧ) Calif.	37·36 N	121·43 W
125	Vallecas (väl-yä'käs) Sp. (Madrid In.)	40·23 N	3·37 W
76	Valle de Allende (väl'yä dä äl-yĕn'dȧ) Mex.	26·55 N	105·25 W
90	Valle de Bravo (brä'vô) Mex.	19·12 N	100·07 W
99	Valle de Guanape (vä'l-yĕ-dĕ-gwä-nä'pĕ) Ven. (In.)	9·54 N	65·41 W
98	Valle de la Pascua (lä-pä's-kōōä) Ven.	9·12 N	65·08 W
90	Valle de Santiago (sän-tē-ä'gô) Mex.	20·23 N	101·11 W
98	Valledupar (dōō-pär') Col.	10·13 N	73·39 W
98	Valle Grande (grän'dä) Bol.	18·27 S	64·03 W
65	Vallejo (vȧ-yä'hō) (vă-lā'hō) Calif. (San Francisco In.)	38·06 N	122·15 W
90	Vallejo, Sierra de (Mts.) (sē-ĕ'r-rä-dĕ-väl-yĕ'ĸô) Mex.	21·00 N	105·10 W
100	Vallenar (väl-yȧ-när') Chile	28·39 S	70·52 W
125	Vallerano (R.) (vä-lĕ-rä'nô) It. (Rome In.)	41·46 N	12·29 E
114	Valletta (väl-lĕt'ä) Malta	35·50 N	14·29 E
74	Valle Vista (văl'yȧ vĭs'tȧ) Calif. (Los Angeles In.)	33·45 N	116·53 W
70	Valley City N. D.	46·55 N	97·59 W
75	Valley City (văl'ĭ) Ohio (Cleveland In.)	41·14 N	81·56 W
73	Valley Falls Kans.	39·21 N	95·26 W
84	Valley Falls (fôls) R. I. (Providence In.)	41·55 N	71·23 W
85	Valleyfield (văl'ē-fēld) Can. (Montreal In.)	45·16 N	74·09 W
74	Valley Park (văl'ē pärk) Mo. (St. Louis In.)	38·33 N	90·30 W
84	Valley Stream (văl'ĭ strēm) N. Y. (New York In.)	40·39 N	73·42 W
126	Valli di Comácchio (L.) (vä'lē-dē-kô-mȧ'chyô) It.	44·38 S	12·15 E
95	Vallière (väl-yâr') Hai.	19·30 N	71·55 W
101	Vallimanca (R.) (väl-yē-mä'n-kä) Arg. (Buenos Aires In.)	36·21 S	60·55 W
125	Valls (väls) Sp.	41·15 N	1·15 E
86	Val Marie Can.	49·10 N	107·59 W
119	Valmiera (väl'myĕ-rȧ) Sov. Un.	57·34 N	25·54 E
122	Valognes (vå-lôn'y') Fr.	49·32 N	1·30 W
	Valona, see Vlorë		
101	Valparaíso (väl'pä-rä-ē'sô) Chile (Santiago In.)	33·02 S	71·32 W
80	Valparaiso (văl-pȧ-rā'zô) Ind.	41·25 N	87·05 W
90	Valparaiso Mex.	22·49 N	103·33 W
101	Valpariso (Prov.) Chile (Santiago In.)	32·58 S	71·23 W
122	Valréas (vȧl-rā-ä') Fr.	45·25 N	4·56 E
	Valsbaai, see False B.		
155	Valsch, Kap (C.) (välsh) W. Irian	8·30 S	137·15 E
168	Valsch R. S. Afr. (Johannesburg & Pretoria In.)	27·32 S	26·51 E
136	Valuyevo (vȧ-lōō'yĕ-vô) Sov. Un. (Moscow In.)	55·34 N	37·21 E
129	Valuyki (vȧ-lōō-ē'kē) Sov. Un.	50·14 N	38·04 E
74	Val Verde (văl vûr'dē) Calif. (Los Angeles In.)	33·51 N	117·15 W
95	Valverde (väl-vĕ'r-dĕ) Dom. Rep.	19·35 N	71·10 W
124	Valverde del Camino (väl-vĕr-dĕ-dĕl-kä-mē'nō) Sp.	37·34 N	6·44 W
142	Vambanād (R.) India	10·00 N	76·03 E
133	Van (vän) Tur.	38·04 N	43·10 E
73	Van Buren (văn bū'rĕn) Ark.	35·26 N	94·20 W
82	Van Buren Maine	47·09 N	67·58 W
80	Vanceburg (văns'bûrg) Ky.	38·35 N	83·20 W
65	Vancouver (văn-ĸōō'vēr) Can. (Vancouver In.)	49·16 N	123·06 W
65	Vancouver Wash. (Portland In.)	45·37 N	122·40 W
86	Vancouver I. Can.	49·47 N	128·23 W
80	Vandalia (văn-dā'lĭ-ȧ) Ill.	39·00 N	89·00 W
73	Vandalia Mo.	39·19 N	91·30 W
168	Vanderbijlpark S. Afr. (Johannesburg & Pretoria In.)	26·43 S	27·50 E
86	Vanderhoof Can.	53·59 N	124·10 W
	Van Diemen, see Ōsumi Kaikyō		
158	Van Diemen, C. (văndē'mĕn) Austl.	11·05 S	130·15 E
158	Van Diemen G. Austl.	11·50 S	131·30 E
75	Van Dyke (văn dīk) Mich. (Detroit In.)	42·27 N	83·01 W
90	Vanegas (vä-nĕ'gäs) Mex.	23·54 N	100·54 W
118	Vänern (L.) Swe.	58·52 N	13·17 E
118	Vänersborg (vĕ'nērs-bôr') Swe.	58·24 N	12·15 E
167	Vanga (väŋ'gȧ) Ken.	4·38 S	39·10 E
143	Vangani India (Bombay In.)	19·07 N	73·15 E
133	Van Gölü (L.) Tur.	38·45 N	43·00 E
80	Van Lear (văn lēr') Ky.	37·45 N	82·50 W
122	Vannes (vȧn) Fr.	47·42 N	2·46 W
74	Van Nuys (văn nīz') Calif. (Los Angeles In.)	34·11 N	118·27 W
119	Vantaan (R.) Fin.	60·25 N	24·43 E
80	Van Wert (văn wûrt') Ohio	40·50 N	84·35 W
118	Vara (vä'rȧ) Swe.	58·17 N	12·55 E
128	Varaklāni Sov. Un.	56·38 N	26·46 E
126	Varallo (vä-räl'lô) It.	45·44 N	8·14 E
142	Vārānasi (Banaras) India	25·25 N	83·00 E
112	Varanger Fd. (vä-räng'gĕr) Nor.	70·05 N	30·53 E
126	Varano, Lago di (L.) (lä'gō-dē-vä-rä'nô) It.	41·52 N	15·55 E
126	Varaždin (vä'räzh'dēn) Yugo.	46·17 N	16·20 E
126	Varazze (vä-rät'sä) It.	44·23 N	8·34 E
118	Varberg (vär'bĕrg) Swe.	57·06 N	12·16 E
127	Vardar (R.) (vär'där) Yugo.	41·40 N	21·50 E
118	Varde (vär'dĕ) Den.	55·39 N	8·28 E
112	Vardö (värd'û) Nor.	70·23 N	30·43 E
154	Varella, C. Viet.	12·58 N	109·50 E
119	Varėna (vä-rā'nȧ) Sov. Un.	54·16 N	24·35 E
85	Varennes (vȧ-rĕn') Can. (Montreal In.)	45·41 N	73·27 W
127	Vareš (vä'rĕsh) Yugo.	44·10 N	18·20 E
126	Varese (vä-rā'sȧ) It.	45·45 N	8·49 E
101	Varginha (vär-zhē'n-yȧ) Braz. (Rio de Janeiro In.)	21·33 S	45·25 W
119	Varkaus (vär'kous) Fin.	62·19 N	27·51 E
136	Varlamovo (vár-lȧ'mô-vô) Sov. Un. (Urals In.)	54·37 N	60·41 E
127	Varna (Stalin) (vär'nȧ) (stä'lĭn) Bul.	43·14 N	27·58 E
136	Varna Sov. Un. (Urals In.)	53·22 N	60·59 E
118	Värnamo (vĕr'nȧ mô) Swe.	57·11 N	13·45 E
120	Varnsdorf (värns'dôrf) Czech.	50·54 N	14·36 E
79	Varnville (värn'vĭl) S. C.	32·49 N	81·05 W
85	Vars (värz) Can. (Ottawa In.)	45·21 N	75·21 W
129	Varvaropolye (vår'vår'ô-pô-lyĕ) Sov. Un.	48·38 N	38·37 E
124	Vascongadas (Reg.) (väs-kôn-gä'däs) Sp.	42·35 N	2·46 W
132	Vashka (R.) Sov. Un.	63·20 N	47·50 E
65	Vashon (văsh'ŭn) Wash. (Seattle In.)	47·27 N	122·28 W
65	Vashon Heights (hītz) Wash. (Seattle In.)	47·30 N	122·28 W
65	Vashon I. Wash. (Seattle In.)	47·27 N	122·27 W
129	Vasil'kov (vȧ-sēl'-kôf') Sov. Un.	50·10 N	30·22 E
121	Vaslui (vȧs-lōō'ē) Rom.	46·39 N	27·49 E
80	Vassar (văs'ēr) Mich.	43·25 N	83·35 W
100	Vassouras (väs-sō'räzh) Braz. (In.)	22·25 S	43·40 W
118	Västanfors (vĕst'än-fôrs) Swe.	59·59 N	15·49 E
118	Västerås (vĕs'tĕr-ôs) Swe.	59·39 N	16·30 E
118	Väster-dalälven (R.) Swe.	61·06 N	13·10 E
118	Västervik (vĕs'tĕr-vēk) Swe.	57·45 N	16·35 E
126	Vasto (väs'tô) It.	42·06 N	12·42 E
134	Vasyugan (R.) (vȧs-yōō-gän') Sov. Un.	58·52 N	77·30 E
125	Vatican City (Cittádel Vaticano) (văt'ĭ-kăn sĭt'ē) (chē-tȧ'del vä-tē-kä'nô) Eur. (Rome In.)	41·54 N	12·22 E
126	Vaticano, C. (vä-tē-kä'nô) It.	38·38 N	15·52 E
112	Vatnajökull (Gl.) (vät'nȧ-yû-kōōl) Ice.	64·34 N	16·41 W
167	Vatomandry (vä-tōō-män'drē) Malag. Rep.	18·53 S	48·13 E
121	Vatra Dornei (vät'rȧ dôr'nâ') Rom.	47·22 N	25·20 E
118	Vättern (L.) Swe.	58·15 N	14·24 E
85	Vaudreuil (vô-drû'y') Can. (Montreal In.)	45·24 N	74·02 W
65	Vaugh (vôn) Wash. (Seattle In.)	47·21 N	122·47 W
72	Vaughn N. Mex.	34·37 N	105·13 W
98	Vaupés (R.) (vä'ōō-pĕ's) Col.	1·18 N	71·14 W
118	Vaxholm (väks'hôlm) Swe.	59·26 N	18·19 E
118	Växjo (vĕks'shû) Swe.	56·53 N	14·46 E
132	Vaygach (I.) (vī-gäch') Sov. Un.	70·00 N	59·00 E
99	Veadeiros, Chapadas dos (Mts.) (shä-pá'däs-dôs-vĕ-ä-dā'rōs) Braz.	15·20 S	48·43 W
118	Veblungsnares (vĭb'lōōngs-nĕs) Nor.	62·33 N	7·46 E
127	Vedea (R.) (vå'dyȧ) Rom.	44·25 N	24·45 E
101	Vedia (vĕ'dyä) Arg. (Buenos Aires In.)	34·29 S	61·30 W
80	Veedersburg (vē'dērz-bûrg) Ind.	40·05 N	87·15 W
91	Vega de Alatorre (vä'gä dā ä-lä-tōr'rå) Mex.	20·02 N	96·39 W
95	Vega Real (Mts.) (vĕ'gä-rĕ-ä'l) Dom. Rep.	19·30 N	71·05 W
112	Vegen (I.) (vĕ'ghĕn) Nor.	65·38 N	10·51 E
86	Vegreville Can.	53·26 N	112·27 W
143	Vehār L. India (Bombay In.)	19·11 N	72·50 E
101	Veinticinco de Mayo (vä-ēn'tē-sēn'kō dä mä'yō) Arg. (Buenos Aires In.)	35·26 S	60·09 W
124	Vejer (vā-kĕr') Sp.	36·15 N	5·58 W
118	Vejle (vī'lĕ) Den.	55·41 N	9·29 E
123	Velbert (fĕl'bĕrt) Ger. (Ruhr In.)	51·20 N	7·03 E
126	Velebit (Mts.) (vā'lĕ-bĕt) Yugo.	44·25 N	15·23 E
123	Velen (fĕ'lĕn) Ger. (Ruhr In.)	51·54 N	7.00 E
124	Vélez-Málaga (vā'lāth-mä'lä-gä) Sp.	36·48 N	4·05 W
124	Vélez Rubio (rōō'bē-ô) Sp.	37·38 N	2·05 W
126	Velika Kapela (Mts.) (vĕ'lē-kȧ kä-pĕ'lä) Yugo.	45·03 N	15·20 E
127	Velika Morava (R.) (mô'rȧ-vä) Yugo.	44·20 N	21·10 E
128	Velikaya (R.) (vå-lē'kȧ-yȧ) Sov. Un.	57·25 N	28·07 E
121	Velikiy Bychkov (vĕ-lē'kē bōōch-kôf') Sov. Un.	47·59 N	24·01 E
128	Velikiye Luki (vyē-lē'-kyē lōō'ke) Sov. Un.	56·19 N	30·32 E
132	Velikiy Ustyug (vå-lē'kĭ ōōs-tyōōg') Sov. Un.	60·45 N	46·38 E
128	Velikoye (vå-lē'kô-yĕ) Sov. Un.	57·21 N	39·45 E
128	Velikoye (L.) Sov. Un.	57·00 N	36·53 E
128	Velizh (vå'lĕzh) Sov. Un.	55·37 N	31·11 E
120	Velke Meziřičí (vĕl'kä mĕzh"r-zhyĭ-chĭ) Czech.	49·21 N	16·01 E
159	Vella (I.) (väl'yä) Sol. Is.	8·00 S	156·42 E
125	Velletri (vĕl-lā'trē) It. (Rome In.)	41·42 N	12·48 E
143	Vellore (vĕl-lōr') India	12·57 N	79·09 E
136	Vels (vĕls) Sov. Un. (Urals In.)	60·35 N	58·47 E
132	Vel'sk (vĕlsk) Sov. Un.	61·00 N	42·18 E
111	Velten (fel'tĕn) Ger. (Berlin In.)	52·41 N	13·11 E
136	Velya R. (vĕl'yȧ) Sov. Un. (Moscow In.)	56·23 N	37·54 E
98	Venadillo (vĕ-nä-dē'l-yō) Col. (In.)	4·43 N	74·55 W
90	Venado (vå-nä'dō) Mex.	22·54 N	101·07 W
100	Venado Tuerto (vĕ-nä'dô-tōōĕ'r-tô) Arg.	33·28 S	61·47 W
122	Vendée, Collines de (hills) (kō-lēn' dē väɴ-dā') Fr.	46·44 N	0·17 W
122	Vendôme (väɴ-dōm') Fr.	47·46 N	1·05 E
126	Veneto (Reg.) (vĕ-nĕ'tô) It.	45·58 N	11·24 E
128	Venëv (vĕn-ĕf') Sov. Un.	54·19 N	38·14 E
126	Venezia (Venice) (vå-nät'sē-ä) It.	45·25 N	12·18 E
126	Venezia, Golfo di (G.) (gôl-fô-dē-vå-nät'sē-ä) It.	45·23 N	13·00 E

ăr; finăl; rāte; senâte; ärm; åsk; sofȧ; fâre; ch-choose; dh-as th in other; bē; ēvent; bĕt; recĕnt; cratēr; g-go; gh-guttural g; bĭt; ĭ-short neutral; rīde; ĸ-guttural k as ch in German ich;

Page	Name	Pronunciation	Region	Lat. °′	Long. °′
96	Venezuela	(vĕn-ê-zwē′lá)	S. A.	8·00 N	65·00 W
98	Venezuela, Golfo de (G.)	(gól-fô-dĕ)	Ven.	11·34 N	71·02 W
64	Veniaminof, Mt.		Alaska	56·12 N	159·20 W
74	Venice	(vĕn′ĭs)			
			Calif. (Los Angeles In.)	33·59 N	118·28 W
74	Venice		Ill. (St. Louis In.)	38·40 N	90·10 W
	Venice, see Venezia				
123	Venlo		Neth. (Ruhr In.)	51·22 N	6·11 E
119	Venta (R.)	(vĕn′tá)	Sov. Un.	57·05 N	21·45 E
100	Ventana, Sierra de la (Mts.)				
		(sĕ-ĕ′r-rá-dĕ-lä-vĕn-tá′ná)	Arg.	38·00 S	63·00 W
168	Ventersburg	(vĕn-tĕrs′bùrg)			
			S. Afr. (Johannesburg & Pretoria In.)	28·06 S	27·10 E
168	Ventersdorp	(vĕn-tĕrs′dôrp)			
			S. Afr. (Johannesburg & Pretoria In.)	26·20 S	26·48 E
126	Ventimiglia	(vĕn-tê-mēl′yä)	It.	43·46 N	7·37 E
81	Ventnor	(vĕnt′nẽr)	N. J.	39·20 N	74·25 W
119	Ventspils	(vĕnt′spěls)	Sov. Un.	57·24 N	21·41 E
98	Ventuari (R.)	(vĕn-tōōä′rē)	Ven.	4·47 N	65·56 W
68	Ventura	(vĕn-tōō′rá)	Calif.	34·18 N	119·18 W
136	Venukovsky	(vĕ-nōō′kôv-skĭ)			
			Sov. Un. (Moscow In.)	55·10 N	37·26 E
90	Venustiano Carranza				
		(vĕ-nōōs-tyá′nô-kär-rä′n-zä)	Mex.	19·44 N	103·48 W
91	Venustiano Carranzo	(kär-rä′n-zô)	Mex.	16·21 N	92·36 W
100	Vera	(vĕ-rä)	Arg.	29·22 S	60·09 W
124	Vera	(vä′rä)	Sp.	37·18 N	1·53 W
88	Vera Cruz (State)	(vä-rä-krōō′z)	Mex.	20·30 N	97·15 W
91	Veracruz		Mex.	19·13 N	96·07 W
142	Verāval	(vẽr′ŭ-väl)	India	20·59 N	70·49 E
126	Vercelli	(vẽr-chĕl′lē)	It.	45·18 N	8·27 E
85	Verchères	(vẽr-shâr′)			
			Can. (Montreal In.)	45·46 N	73·21 W
69	Verde (R.)	(vûrd)	Ariz.	34·04 N	111·40 W
95	Verde, Cap (C.)		Ba. Is.	22·50 N	75·00 W
95	Verde, Cay (I.)		Ba. Is.	22·00 N	75·05 W
91	Verde (R.)		Mex.	16·05 N	97·44 W
90	Verde (R.)		Mex.	20·50 N	103·00 W
90	Verde (R.)		Mex.	21·48 N	99·50 W
155	Verde (I.)	(vĕr′dä)			
			Phil. (Manila In.)	13·34 N	121·11 E
155	Verde Island Pass.	(vĕr′dē)			
			Phil. (Manila In.)	13·36 N	120·39 E
74	Verdemont	(vûr′dĕ-mŏnt)			
			Calif. (Los Angeles In.)	34·12 N	117·22 W
120	Verden	(fĕr′dĕn)	Ger.	52·55 N	9·15 E
73	Verdigris (R.)	(vûr′dĕ-grēs)	Okla.	36·50 N	95·29 W
85	Verdun	(vĕr′dŭN′)			
			Can. (Montreal In.)	45·27 N	73·34 W
122	Verdun	(vâr-dûn′)	Fr.	49·09 N	5·21 E
168	Vereeniging	(vĕ-rä′nĭ-gĭng)	S. Afr.		
			(Johannesburg & Pretoria In.)	26·40 S	27·56 E
168	Verena	(vĕr-ēn a)	S. Afr.		
			(Johannesburg & Pretoria In.)	25·30 S	29·02 E
128	Vereya	(vĕ-rä′yá)	Sov. Un.	55·21 N	36·08 E
124	Vergara	(vẽr-gä′rä)	Sp.	43·08 N	2·23 W
124	Verin	(vä-rēn′)	Sp.	41·56 N	7·26 W
136	Verkhne Chusovskiye Gorodki				
		(vyẽrk′nyĕ chōō-sôv′skĭ-ye gä-rôd′ki)	Sov. Un. (Urals In.)	58·13 N	75·06 E
135	Verkhne-Kamchatsk				
		(vyẽrk′nyĕ kàm-chatsk′)	Sov. Un.	54·42 N	158·41 E
136	Verkhne Neyvinskiy	(nā-vǐn′skĭ)			
			Sov. Un. (Urals In.)	57·17 N	60·10 E
136	Verkhne Ural'sk	(ōō-ralsk′)			
			Sov. Un. (Urals In.)	53·53 N	59·15 E
129	Verkhneye	(vyẽrκ′nĕ-yĕ)			
			Sov. Un.	48·53 N	38·29 E
136	Verkhniy Avzyan				
		(vyẽrк′nyĕ àv-zyàn′)	Sov. Un. (Urals In.)	53·32 N	57·30 E
136	Verkhniye Kigi				
		(vyẽrк′nǐ-yĕ kǐ′gǐ)	Sov. Un. (Urals In.)	55·23 N	58·37 E
136	Verkhniy Ufaley	(ōō-fà′lä)			
			Sov. Un. (Urals In.)	56·04 N	60·15 E
136	Verkhnyaya Pyshma				
		(vyẽrк′nyä-yä pōōsh′mà)	Sov. Un. (Urals In.)	56·57 N	60·37 E
136	Verkhnyaya Salda	(säl′dà)			
			Sov. Un. (Urals In.)	58·03 N	60·33 E
134	Verkhnyaya Tunguska (Angara)				
		(R.)	(tōōn-gōōs′ká)	Sov. Un.	58·13 N	97·00 E
136	Verkhnyaya Tura	(tōō′rá)			
			Sov. Un. (Urals In.)	58·22 N	59·51 E
136	Verkhnyaya Yayva	(yäy′vá)			
			Sov. Un. (Urals In.)	59·28 N	59·38 E
136	Verkhotur'ye	(vyẽr-kô-tōōr′yĕ)			
			Sov. Un. (Urals In.)	58·52 N	60·47 E
135	Verkhoyansk	(vyẽr-ĸô-yänsk′)			
			Sov. Un.	67·43 N	133·33 E
135	Verkhoyanskiy Khrebet (Mts.)				
		(vyẽr-ĸô-yänsk′)	Sov. Un.	67·45 N	128·00 E
86	Vermilion	(vẽr-mĭl′yŭn)	Can.	53·19 N	110·53 W
82	Vermilion (R.)		Can.	47·30 N	73·15 W
80	Vermilion (R.)		Ill.	41·05 N	89·00 W
71	Vermilion (L.)		Minn.	47·49 N	92·35 W
71	Vermilion Ra.		Minn.	47·55 N	91·59 W
71	Vermilion (R.)		Minn.	48·09 N	92·31 W
70	Vermillion		S. D.	42·46 N	96·56 W
70	Vermillion (R.)		S. D.	43·54 N	97·14 W
77	Vermilion B.		La.	29·42 N	92·00 W
63	Vermont (State)	(vẽr-mŏnt′)			
			U. S.	43·50 N	72·50 W
67	Vernal	(vûr′nál)	Utah	40·29 N	109·40 W
166	Verneuk Pan (L.)	(vẽr-nŭk′)			
			S. Afr.	30·10 S	21·46 E

Page	Name	Pronunciation	Region	Lat. °′	Long. °′
74	Vernon	(vûr′nŭn)			
			Calif. (Los Angeles In.)	34·01 N	118·12 W
86	Vernon	(vẽr-nôɴ′)	Can.	50·18 N	119·15 W
85	Vernon		Can. (Ottawa In.)	45·10 N	75·27 W
80	Vernon	(vûr′nŭn)	Ind.	39·00 N	85·40 W
84	Vernon		N. J. (New York In.)	41·12 N	74·29 W
72	Vernon		Tex.	34·09 N	99·16 W
79	Vero Beach	(vē′rô)	Fla. (In.)	27·36 N	80·25 W
127	Véroia	(vä-rô′ná)	Grc.	40·30 N	22·13 E
126	Verona	(vä-rō′ná)	It.	45·28 N	11·02 E
65	Vernonia	(vûr-nō′nyá)			
			Ore. (Portland In.)	45·52 N	123·12 W
123	Versailles	(vẽr-sī′y′)			
			Fr. (Paris In.)	48·48 N	2·07 E
80	Versailles	(vẽr-sälz′)	Ky.	38·05 N	84·45 W
73	Versailles		Mo.	38·27 N	92·52 W
82	Verte, B.	(vûrt)	Can.	46·03 N	63·57 W
164	Vert, Cap (C.)		Senegal	14·52 N	17·49 W
167	Verulam	(vẽ-rōō-lăm)			
			S. Afr. (Natal In.)	29·39 S	31·08 E
117	Verviers	(vẽr-vyä′)	Bel.	50·35 N	5·57 E
129	Vesëloye	(vĕ-syô′lô-yĕ)	Sov. Un.	46·59 N	34·56 E
119	Vesijärvi (L.)		Fin.	61·09 N	25·10 E
123	Vesoul	(vĕ-sōōl′)	Fr.	47·38 N	6·11 E
112	Vester Aalen (Is.)	(vĕs′tẽr ô′lĕn)	Nor.	68·54 N	14·03 E
112	Vestfjord		Nor.	67·33 N	12·59 E
112	Vestmannaeyjar				
		(vĕst′män-à-ā′yär)	Ice.	63·12 N	20·17 W
125	Vesuvio (vesuvius) (Mtn.)				
		(vĕ-sōō′vyä)	It. (Naples In.)	40·35 N	14·26 E
128	Ves'yegonsk	(vĕ-syĕ-gônsk′)			
			Sov. Un.	58·42 N	37·09 E
121	Veszprem	(vĕs′präm)	Hung.	47·05 N	17·53 E
121	Vesztő	(vĕs′tû)	Hung.	46·55 N	21·18 E
128	Vetka	(vyĕt′ká)	Sov. Un.	52·36 N	31·05 E
118	Vetlanda	(vĕt-län′dä)	Swe.	57·26 N	15·05 E
132	Vetluga	(vyĕt-lōō′gä)	Sov. Un.	57·50 N	45·42 E
132	Vetluga (R.)		Sov. Un.	56·50 N	45·50 E
127	Vetovo	(vä′tô-vô)	Bul.	43·42 N	26·18 E
127	Vetren	(vĕt′rĕn′)	Bul.	42·16 N	24·04 E
168	Vet R.	(vĕt)	S. Afr.		
			(Johannesburg & Pretoria In.)	28·25 S	26·37 E
80	Vevay	(vē′vá)	Ind.	38·45 N	85·05 W
123	Veynes	(vän′′)	Fr.	44·31 N	5·47 E
122	Vézère (R.)	(vä-zer′)	Fr.	45·01 N	1·00 E
98	Viacha	(vēä′chä)	Bol.	16·43 S	68·16 W
126	Viadana	(vē-ä-dä′nä)	It.	44·55 N	10·30 E
73	Vian	(vī′ǎn)	Okla.	35·30 N	95·00 W
99	Viana	(vē-ä′ná)	Braz.	3·09 S	44·44 W
124	Viana del Bollo	(vē-ä′nä dĕl bôl′yô)	Sp.	42·10 N	7·07 W
124	Viana do Alentejo				
		(vē-ä′nd dōō ä-lĕN-tä′hōō)	Port.	38·20 N	8·02 W
124	Viana do Castélo	(dōō käs-tä′lōō)	Port.	41·41 N	8·45 W
124	Viar (R.)	(vē-ä′r)	Sp.	38·15 N	6·08 W
126	Viareggio	(vê-ä-rĕd′jô)	It.	43·52 N	10·14 E
118	Viborg	(vē′bôr)	Den.	56·27 N	9·22 E
126	Vibo Valentia	(vē-bô-vä-lĕ′n-tyä)	It.	38·47 N	16·06 E
125	Vicálvero	(vē-kà′l-vĕ-rô)			
			Sp. (Madrid In.)	40·25 N	3·37 W
100	Vicente López	(vē-sĕ′n-tĕ-lô′pĕz)			
			Arg. (In.)	34·15 S	58·29 W
126	Vicenza	(vē-chĕnt′sä)	It.	45·33 N	11·33 E
125	Vich	(vēch)	Sp.	41·55 N	2·14 E
128	Vichuga	(vē-chōō′gä)	Sov. Un.	57·13 N	41·58 E
122	Vichy	(vē-shē′)	Fr.	46·06 N	3·28 E
80	Vicksburg	(vĭks′bûrg)	Mich.	42·10 N	85·30 W
78	Vicksburg		Miss.	32·20 N	90·50 W
101	Viçosa	(vē-sô′sä)			
			Braz. (Rio de Janeiro In.)	23·46 S	42·51 W
101	Victoria	(vēk-tô′rĭ-á)			
			Arg. (Buenos Aires In.)	32·36 S	60·09 W
65	Victoria	(vĭk-tō′rĭ-á)			
			Can. (Seattle In.)	48·26 N	123·23 W
100	Victoria	(vēk-tô-rēä)	Chile	38·15 S	72·16 W
149	Victoria	(vĭk-tō′rĭ-á)	Hong Kong	22·10 N	114·18 E
98	Victoria	(vēk-tô′rēä)	Col. (In.)	5·19 N	74·54 W
164	Victoria	(vĭk-tō′rĭ-á)	Nig.	4·06 N	9·13 E
155	Victoria	(vēk-tô-ryä)			
			Phil. (Manila In.)	15·34 N	120·41 E
77	Victoria	(vĭk-tō′rĭ-á)	Tex.	28·48 N	97·00 W
79	Victoria		Va.	36·57 N	78·13 W
159	Victoria (State)		Austl.	36·46 S	143·15 E
158	Victoria (R.)		Austl.	17·25 S	130·50 E
146	Victoria, Mt.		Bur.	21·26 N	93·59 E
155	Victoria, Mt.		Pap.	9·35 S	147·45 E
166	Victoria (L.)		Tan.	2·00 S	32·16 E
94	Victoria de las Tunas				
		(vēk-tô′rĕ-á dä läs tōō′näs)	Cuba	20·55 N	77·05 W
166	Victoria Falls		Rh.	18·15 S	25·35 E
86	Victoria I.		Can.	70·13 N	107·45 W
47	Victoria Land		Ant.	75·00 S	160·00 E
92	Victoria Pk.	(vĭk-tō′rĭ′á)			
			Br. Hond. (Yucatan In.)	16·47 N	88·40 W
158	Victoria River Downs	(vĭc-tôr′ĭá)			
			Austl.	16·30 S	131·10 E
86	Victoria Str.	(vĭk-tō′rĭ-á)	Can.	69·10 N	100·58 E
82	Victoriaville	(vĭk-tō′rĭ-á-vĭl)	Can.	46·04 N	71·59 W
166	Victoria West	(wĕst)	S. Afr.	31·25 S	23·10 E
79	Vidalia	(vĭ-dä′lĭ-á)	Ga.	32·10 N	82·26 W
77	Vidalia		La.	31·33 N	91·28 W
127	Vidin	(vē′dēn)	Bul.	44·00 N	22·53 E
128	Vidzy	(vē′dzĭ)	Sov. Un.	55·23 N	26·46 E
100	Viedma	(vyäd′mä)	Arg.	40·55 S	63·03 W
100	Viedma (L.)		Arg.	49·40 S	72·35 W
92	Viejo R.	(vyä′hō)	Nic.	12·45 N	86·19 W
78	Vienna	(vē-ĕn′á)	Ga.	32·03 N	83·40 W
73	Vienna		Ill.	37·24 N	88·50 W
84	Vienna		Va. (Washington D.C. In.)	38·54 N	77·16 W

Page	Name	Pronunciation	Region	Lat. °′	Long. °′
	Vienna, see Wien				
122	Vienne	(vyĕn′)	Fr.	45·31 N	4·54 E
122	Vienne (R.)		Fr.	47·06 N	0·20 E
154	Vientiane	(vyän′tyän′)	Laos	18·07 N	102·33 E
89	Vieques	(vyä′kǎs)			
			P. R. (Puerto Rico In.)	18·09 N	65·27 W
89	Vieques (I.)	(vyä′kǎs)			
			P. R. (Puerto Rico In.)	18·05 N	65·28 W
168	Vierfontien	(vēr′fôn-tän)	S. Afr.		
			(Johannesburg & Pretoria In.)	27·06 S	26·45 E
123	Viersen	(fēr′zĕn)	Ger. (Ruhr In.)	51·15 N	6·24 E
120	Vierwaldstätter See (L.)		Switz.	46·54 N	8·36 E
122	Vierzon	(vyâr-zôɴ′)	Fr.	47·14 N	2·04 E
76	Viesca	(vē-ās′kä)	Mex.	25·21 N	102·47 W
76	Viesca, Laguna de (L.)				
		(lä-ōō′nä-dĕ)	Mex.	25·30 N	102·40 W
126	Vieste	(vyĕs′tä)	It.	41·52 N	16·10 E
139	Vietnam	(vyĕt′năm′)	Asia	18·00 N	106·20 E
155	Vigan	(vēgän)	Phil. (Manila In.)	17·36 N	120·22 E
126	Vigevano	(vē-jä-vä′nô)	It.	45·18 N	8·52 E
123	Vigny	(vēn-y′ē′)	Fr. (Paris In.)	49·05 N	1·54 E
124	Vigo	(vē′gô)	Sp.	42·18 N	8·42 W
119	Vihti	(vē′tĭ)	Fin.	60·27 N	24·18 E
	Viipuri, see Vyborg				
127	Vijosë (R.)		Alb.	40·15 N	20·30 E
112	Vik		Ice.	63·22 N	18·58 E
118	Vik	(vǐk)	Nor.	61·06 N	6·35 E
159	Vila		New Hebr.	18·00 S	168·30 E
166	Vila de João Belo				
		(vē′lä-dĕ-zho′uN-bĕ′lô)	Moz.	25·00 S	33·45 E
166	Vila de Manica	(vē′lä dä			
		mä-nē′ká)	Moz.	18·48 S	32·49 E
124	Vila de Rei	(vē′lä dä rā′ĭ)	Port.	39·42 N	8·03 W
124	Vila do Conde	(vē′lä dōō kôn′dĕ)			
			Port.	41·21 N	8·44 W
124	Vila Franca de Xira				
		(fräŋ′kä dä shē′rä)	Port.	38·58 N	8·59 W
166	Vila Henrique De Carvalho				
		(vē′lä-ĕn-rē′kĕ-dĕ-kär-vä′lô)	Ang.	9·25 S	20·30 E
122	Vilaine (R.)	(vē-làn′)	Fr.	47·34 N	0·20 W
166	Vila Luso	(vē′lä-lōō′sô)	Ang.	11·45 S	19·55 E
166	Vila Marechal Carmona				
		(mä-rĕ-zhäl-kär-mô′nä)	Ang.	7·30 S	15·05 E
166	Vilanculos	(vē-län-kōō′lôs)	Moz.	22·03 S	35·13 E
128	Vilāni	(vē′lä-nĭ)	Sov. Un.	56·31 N	27·00 E
124	Vila Nova de Fozcoa				
		(nô′vä dä fôz-kô′á)	Port.	41·08 N	7·11 W
124	Vila Nova de Gaia				
		(vē′lä nô′vä dä gä′yä)	Port.	41·08 N	8·40 W
124	Vila Nova de Milfontes				
		(nô′vä dä mēl-fôn′täzh)	Port.	37·44 S	8·48 W
124	Vila Real	(rä-äl′)	Port.	41·18 N	7·48 W
124	Vila Real de Santo Antonio				
		(vē′lä-rĕ-äl′-dĕ-sän-tô-än-tô′nyô)	Port.	37·14 N	7·25 W
166	Vila Rocadas	(rô-kä′däs)	Ang.	16·50 S	15·05 E
124	Vila Vicosa	(vē-sô′zá)	Port.	38·47 N	7·24 W
128	Vileyka	(vē-lā′ê-kä)	Sov. Un.	54·19 N	26·58 E
112	Vilhelmina		Swe.	64·37 N	16·30 E
119	Viljandi	(vēl′yän-dê)	Sov. Un.	58·24 N	25·34 E
168	Viljoenskroon		S. Afr.		
			(Johannesburg & Pretoria In.)	27·13 S	26·58 E
119	Vilkaviškis	(vēl-kä-vēsh′kés)			
			Sov. Un.	54·40 N	23·08 E
119	Vilkija	(vēl-kē′ēä)	Sov. Un.	55·04 N	23·30 E
134	Vil'kitskogo (I.)	(vyl-kēts-kōgô)			
			Sov. Un.	73·25 N	76·00 E
133	Vilkovo	(vĭl-kô-vô)	Sov. Un.	45·24 N	29·36 E
76	Villa Acuña	(vēl′yä-kōō′n-yä)			
			Mex.	29·20 N	100·56 W
76	Villa Ahumada	(ä-ōō-mä′dä)	Mex.	30·43 N	106·30 W
91	Villa Alta (San Ildefonso)				
		(äl′tä)	(sän ĕl-dä-fôn′sô)	Mex.	17·20 N	96·08 W
100	Villa Angela	(vēl′-yä ä′n-κĕ-lä)			
			Arg.	27·31 S	60·42 W
124	Villaba	(vēl-yä′bä)	Sp.	43·18 N	7·43 W
100	Villa Ballester	(vē′l-yä-bäl-yĕs-tĕr)			
			Arg. (In.)	34·18 S	58·33 W
98	Villa Bella	(bĕ′l-yä)	Bol.	10·25 S	65·22 W
164	Villa Bens	(bĕns)	Mor.	27·54 N	12·41 W
124	Villablino	(vēl-yä-blē′nô)	Sp.	42·58 N	6·18 W
124	Villacañas	(vēl-yä-kän′yäs)	Sp.	39·39 N	3·20 W
124	Villacarrillo	(vēl-yä-kä-rēl′yô)	Sp.	38·09 N	3·07 W
120	Villach	(fē′läκ)	Aus.	46·38 N	13·50 E
126	Villacidro	(vēl-lä-chē′drô)	It.	39·28 N	8·41 E
164	Villa Cisneros	(vēl′yä thēs-nä′rôs)			
			Sp. Sah.	23·45 N	16·04 W
101	Villa Constitución	(kôn-stē-tōō-syôn′)			
			Arg. (Buenos Aires In.)	33·15 S	60·19 W
76	Villa Coronado	(kô-rô-nä′dhô)			
			Mex.	26·45 N	105·10 W
91	Villa Cuauhtémoc				
		(vēl′yä-kōō-ǟōō-tĕ′môk)	Mex.	22·11 N	97·50 W
76	Villa de Allende				
		(vēl′yä dä äl-yĕn′dä)	Mex.	25·18 N	100·01 W
90	Villa de Alvarez				
		(vēl′yä-dĕ-ä′l-vä-rĕz)	Mex.	19·17 N	103·44 W
99	Villa de Cura	(dĕ-kōō′rä)			
			Ven. (In.)	10·03 N	67·29 W
90	Villa de Guadalupe				
		(dĕ-gwä-dhä-lōō′pä)	Mex.	23·22 N	100·44 W
90	Villa de Reyes	(dä rä′yĕs)	Mex.	21·45 N	100·55 W
100	Villa Dolores	(vēl′yä dô-lô′räs)			
			Arg.	31·50 S	65·05 W
90	Villa Escalante	(vēl′yä-ĕs-kä-lán′tĕ)			
			Mex.	19·24 N	101·36 W
125	Villafamés	(vēl′yä-fä-mäs′)	Sp.	40·07 N	0·05 E
91	Villa Flores	(vēl′yä-flô′räs)	Mex.	16·13 N	93·17 W
126	Villafranca	(vēl-lä-fräŋ′kä)	It.	45·22 N	10·53 E
124	Villafranca del Bierzo				
		(vēl′yä-fräŋ′kä dĕl byĕr′thō)	Sp.	42·37 N	6·49 W

Page	Name	Pronunciation	Region	Lat. ° '	Long. ° '
124	Villafranca de los Barros (vēl-yä-frän′kä dā lōs bär′rōs)		Sp.	38·34 N	6·22 W
125	Villafranca del Panadés (vēl-yä frän′kä děl pä-nä-dās′)		Sp.	41·20 N	1·40 E
90	Villa García (gär-sē′ä)		Mex.	22·07 N	101·55 W
124	Villagarcia (vēl′yä-gär-thē′ä)		Sp.	42·38 N	8·43 W
168	Villaggio Duca degli Abruzzi		Som. (Horn of Afr. In.)	2·40 N	45·20 E
76	Villagram (vēl-yä-gräm′)		Mex.	24·28 N	99·30 W
80	Villa Grove (vĭl′á grōv′)		Ill.	39·55 N	88·15 W
100	Villaguay (vē′l-yä-gwī)		Arg.	31·47 N	58·53 W
100	Villa Hayes (vēl′yä äyås)		Par. (häz)	25·07 S	57·31 W
91	Villahermosa (vēl′yä-ĕr-mō′sä)		Mex.	17·59 N	92·56 W
90	Villa Hidalgo (vēl′yä-ē-dàl′gō)		Mex.	21·39 N	102·41 W
125	Villajoyosa (vēl′yä-hō-yō′sä)		Sp.	38·30 N	0·14 E
76	Villaldama (vēl-yäl-dä′mä)		Mex.	26·30 N	100·26 W
76	Villa Lopez (vēl′yä lō′pěz)		Mex.	27·00 N	105·02 W
124	Villalpando (vēl-yäl-pän′dō)		Sp.	41·54 N	5·24 W
100	Villa María (vēl-yä-mä-rē′ä)		Arg.	32·17 S	63·08 W
124	Villamatín (vēl-yä-mä-tē′n)		Sp.	36·50 N	5·38 W
100	Villa Mercedes (měr-sä′dās)		Arg.	33·38 S	65·16 W
98	Villa Montes (vē′l-yä-mō′n-těs)		Bol.	21·13 S	63·26 W
90	Villa Morelos (mô-rě′lōs)		Mex.	20·01 N	101·24 W
98	Villanueva (vē′l-yä-nōō̆e′vä)		Col.	10·44 N	73·08 W
92	Villanueva (vēl′yä-nwä′vä)		Hond.	15·19 N	88·02 W
90	Villanueva (vēl′yä-nōō̆e′vä)		Mex.	22·25 N	102·53 W
124	Villanueva de Córdoba (vēl′-yä-nwē′vä-dä kôr′dô-bä)		Sp.	38·18 N	4·38 W
124	Villanueva de la Serena (lä sā-rā′nä)		Sp.	38·59 N	5·56 W
125	Villanueva y Geltrú (ēkēl-trōō′)		Sp.	41·13 N	1·44 E
91	Villa Obregón (vē′l-yä-ô-brě-gô′n)		Mex. (Mexico City In.)	19·21 N	99·11 W
76	Villa Ocampo (ô-käm′pō)		Mex.	26·26 N	105·30 W
90	Villa Pedro Montoya (vēl′yä-pě′drô-mǒn-tô′yä)		Mex.	21·38 N	99·51 W
123	Villard-Bonnot (vēl-yär′bôn-nô′)		Fr.	45·15 N	5·53 E
125	Villarreal (vēl-yär-rě-äl)		Sp.	39·55 N	0·07 W
100	Villarrica (vēl-yä-rē′kä)		Par.	25·55 S	56·23 W
124	Villarrobledo (vēl-yär-rô-blä′dhō)		Sp.	39·15 N	2·37 W
124	Villa Sanjurjo (vēl-yä-sän-kōō̆r′-kô)		Sp.	35·15 N	3·55 W
90	Villa Union (vēl′yä-ōō-nyōn′)		Mex.	23·10 N	106·14 W
98	Villavicencio (vē′l-yä-vē-sě′n-syō)		Col. (In.)	4·09 N	73·38 W
125	Villaviciosa de Odón (vēl′yä-vē-thē-ō′sä dä ō-dōn′)		Sp. (Madrid In.)	40·22 N	3·54 W
98	Villavieja (vē′l-yä-vē-ě′κä)		Col. (In.)	3·13 N	75·13 W
100	Villazón (vē′l-yä-zô′n)		Bol.	22·02 S	65·42 W
122	Villefranche-de-Lauragais (vēl-fränsh′dě-lô-rä-gä′)		Fr.	43·25 N	1·41 E
122	Villefranche-de-Rouergue (dě-rōō-ěrg′)		Fr.	44·21 N	2·02 E
122	Villefranche sur-Saône (sūr-sä-ōn′)		Fr.	45·59 N	4·43 E
123	Villejuif (vēl′zhüst′)		Fr. (Paris In.)	48·48 N	2·22 E
87	Ville-Marie		Can.	47·18 N	79·22 W
125	Villena (vē-lyā′nà)		Sp.	38·37 N	0·52 W
85	Villeneuve (vēl′nûv′)		Can. (Edmonton In.)	53·40 N	113·49 W
123	Villeneuve-St. Georges (sǎn-zhôrzh′)		Fr. (Paris In.)	48·43 N	2·27 E
122	Villeneuve-sur-Lot (sūr-lō′)		Fr.	44·25 N	0·41 E
77	Ville Platte (vēl plăt′)		La.	30·41 N	92·17 W
122	Villers Cotterêts (vē-ār′kô-trä′)		Fr. (Paris In.)	49·15 N	3·05 E
123	Villerupt (vēl′rüp′)		Fr.	49·28 N	6·16 E
98	Villeta (vē′l-yě′tä)		Col. (In.)	5·02 N	74·29 W
122	Villeurbanne (vēl-ûr-bän′)		Fr.	45·43 N	4·55 E
168	Villiers (vĭl′ĭ-ērs)		S. Afr. (Johannesburg & Pretoria In.)	27·03 S	28·38 E
120	Villingen (fĭl′ĭng-ěn)		Ger.	48·04 N	8·28 E
71	Villisca (vĭ-lĭs′ká)		Iowa	40·56 N	94·56 W
143	Villupuram		India	11·59 N	79·33 E
119	Vilnius (Wilno) (vĭl′pŭ-lä)		Sov. Un.	54·40 N	25·26 E
119	Vilppula (vĭl′pŭ-lä)		Fin.	62·01 N	24·24 E
111	Vilvoorde		Bel. (Brussels In.)	50·56 N	4·25 E
135	Vilyuy (R.) (vē-lyōō′ē)		Sov. Un.	65·22 N	108·45 E
135	Vilyuysk (vē-lyōō′ĭsk′)		Sov. Un.	63·41 N	121·47 E
118	Vimmerby (vĭm′ēr-bü)		Swe.	57·41 N	15·51 E
120	Vimperk (vĭm-pěrk′)		Czech.	49·04 N	13·41 E
101	Viña del Mar (vē′nyä děl mär′)		Chile (Santiago In.)	33·00 S	71·33 W
82	Vinalhaven (vī-nál-hā′věn)		Maine	44·03 N	68·49 W
125	Vinaroz (vē-nä′rōth)		Sp.	40·29 N	0·27 E
123	Vincennes (vǎn-sěn′)		Fr. (Paris In.)	48·51 N	2·27 E
80	Vincennes (vĭn-zěnz′)		Ind.	38·40 N	87·30 W
78	Vincent (vĭn′sěnt)		Ala.	33·21 N	86·25 W
112	Vindelälven (R.)		Swe.	65·02 N	18·30 E
112	Vindeln (vĭn′děln)		Swe.	64·10 N	19·52 E
142	Vindhya Ra. (vĭnd′yä)		India	22·30 N	73·50 E
81	Vineland (vīn′lǎnd)		N. J.	39·30 N	75·00 W
151	Vinh (vēn′y′)		Viet.	18·38 N	105·42 E
124	Vinhais (vēn′äs)		Port.	41·51 N	7·00 W
84	Vinings (vī′nĭngz)		Ga. (Atlanta In.)	33·52 N	84·28 W
73	Vinita (vĭ-nē′tá)		Okla.	36·38 N	95·09 W
127	Vinkovci (vēn′kŏv-tsě)		Yugo.	45·17 N	18·47 E
129	Vinnitsa (vē′nět-sä)		Sov. Un.	49·13 N	28·31 E

Page	Name	Pronunciation	Region	Lat. ° '	Long. ° '
129	Vinnitsa (Oblast)		Sov. Un.	48·45 N	28·01 E
136	Vinogradovo (vǐ-nô-grä′do-vô)		Sov. Un. (Moscow In.)	55·25 N	38·33 E
47	Vinson Massif (Mtn.)		Ant.	77·40 S	87·00 W
71	Vinton (vĭn′tŭn)		Iowa	42·08 N	92·01 W
77	Vinton		La.	30·12 N	93·35 W
143	Vinukonda		India	16·05 N	79·48 E
84	Violet (vī′ŏ-lět)		La. (New Orleans In.)	29·54 N	89·54 W
151	Virac (vē-räk′)		Phil.	13·38 N	124·20 E
119	Virbalis (vēr′bä-lěs)		Sov. Un.	54·38 N	22·55 E
86	Virden (vûr′děn)		Can.	49·48 N	101·00 W
73	Virden		Ill.	39·28 N	89·46 W
69	Virgin (R.)		Ariz.-Nev.-Utah	36·51 N	113·50 W
71	Virginia (vēr-jĭn′yá)		Minn.	47·32 N	92 36 W
168	Virginia		S. Afr. (Johannesburg & Pretoria In.)	28·07 S	26·54 E
63	Virginia (State)		U. S.	37·00 N	80·45 W
84	Virginia Beach..Va. (Norfolk In.)			36·50 N	75·58 W
68	Virginia City		Nev.	39·18 N	119·40 W
89	Virgin Is. (vûr′jĭn)		N. A.	18·15 N	64·00 W
119	Virmo (vĭr′mô)		Fin.	60·41 N	21·58 E
71	Viroqua (vĭ-rō′kwá)		Wis.	43·33 N	90·54 W
126	Virovitica (vē-rô-vē′tē-tsä)		Yugo.	45·50 N	17·24 E
127	Virpazar (vēr′pä-zär′)		Yugo.	42·16 N	19·06 E
119	Virrat (vĭr′ät)		Fin.	62·15 N	23·45 E
118	Virserum (vĭr′sě-rŏŏm)		Swe.	57·22 N	15·35 E
126	Vis (vēs)		Yugo.	43·03 N	16·11 E
126	Vis (I.)		Yugo.	43·00 N	16·10 E
126	Visa, Mt. (Mtn.) (vē′sä)		It.	45·42 N	7·08 E
143	Visākhapatnam (vē-zä′kä-pŭt′năm)		India	17·48 N	83·21 E
68	Visalia (vǐ-sā′lǐ-á)		Calif.	36·20 N	119·18 W
118	Visby (vĭs′bü)		Swe.	57·39 N	18·19 E
49	Viscount Mellville Sound (vī′kount′)		Can.	74·80 N	110·00 W
127	Višegrad (vē′shē-gräd)		Yugo.	43·45 N	19·19 E
136	Vishera R. (vǐ′shě-rä)		Sov. Un. (Urals In.)	60·40 N	58·46 E
136	Visim (vē′sĭm) .Sov. Un. (Urals In.)			57·38 N	59·32 E
118	Viskan (R.)		Swe.	57·20 N	12·25 E
128	Viški (vēs′kĭ)		Sov. Un.	56·02 N	26·47 E
127	Visoko (vē′sô-kô)		Yugo.	43·59 N	18·10 E
127	Vistonís (L.) (vēs′tô-nĭs)		Grc.	40·58 N	25·12 E
	Vistula, see Wisla				
127	Vitanovac (vē′tä′nô-väts)		Yugo.	43·44 N	20·50 E
128	Vitebsk (vē′tyepsk)		Sov. Un.	55·12 N	30·16 E
128	Vitebsk (Oblast)		Sov. Un.	55·05 N	29·18 E
126	Viterbo (vē-těr′bō)		It.	42·24 N	12·08 E
135	Vitim (vē′těm)		Sov. Un.	59·22 N	112·43 E
135	Vitim (R.) (vē′těm)		Sov. Un.	56·12 N	115·30 E
136	Vitino (vē′tĭ-nô)		Sov. Un. (Leningrad In.)	59·40 N	29·51 E
99	Vitória (vē-tô′rē-ä)		Braz.	20·09 S	40·17 W
124	Vitoria (vē-tô-ryä)		Sp.	42·43 N	2·43 W
99	Vitória da Conquista (-dä-kōn-kwē′s-tä)		Braz.	14·51 S	40·44 W
122	Vitré (vē-trā′)		Fr.	48·09 N	1·15 W
122	Vitrolles (vē-trôl′)		Fr. (Marseille In.)	43·27 N	5·15 E
122	Vitry-le-François (vē-trē′lě-frän-swä′)		Fr.	48·44 N	4·34 E
113	Vittoria (vē-tô′rē-ô)		It.	37·01 N	14·31 E
126	Vittorio (vē-tô′rē-ô)		It.	45·59 N	12·17 E
155	Vitu Is. (vē′tōō)		N. Gui. Ter.	4·45 S	149·50 E
124	Vivero (vē-vä′rō)		Sp.	43·39 N	7·37 W
77	Vivian (vĭv′ĭ-án)		La.	32·51 N	93·59 W
127	Vize (vē′zě)		Tur.	41·34 N	27·46 E
143	Vizianagram (vē-zē-ä-nŭ′grăm′)		India	18·10 N	83·29 E
111	Vlaardingen (vlär′dĭng-ěn)		Neth. (Amsterdam In.)	51·54 N	4·20 E
128	Vladimir (vlá-dyē′měr)		Sov. Un.	56·08 N	40·24 E
128	Vladimir (Oblast) (vlá-dyē′měr)		Sov. Un.	56·08 N	39·53 E
152	Vladimiro-Aleksandrovskoye (vlá-dyē′mē-rô â-lěk-sän′drôf-skô-yě)		Sov. Un.	42·50 N	133·00 E
121	Vladimir-Volynskiy (vlá-dyē′měr vô-lēn′skĭ)		Sov. Un.	50·50 N	24·20 E
135	Vladivostok (vlá-dē-vôs-tôk′)		Sov. Un.	43·06 N	131·47 E
127	Vlasenica (vlä′sě-nět′sä)		Yugo.	44·11 N	18·58 E
127	Vlasotinci (vlä′sô-tēn-tsě)		Yugo.	42·58 N	22·08 E
117	Vlieland (I.) (vlē′länt)		Neth.	53·19 N	4·55 E
117	Vlissingen (vlĭs′sĭng-ěn)		Neth.	51·30 N	3·34 E
127	Vlorë (Valona) (vlô′rŭ)		Alb.	40·28 N	19·31 E
120	Vltana R.		Czech.	49·24 N	14·18 E
132	Vodl (L.) (vôd′l)		Sov. Un.	62·20 N	37·20 E
167	Vogel (R.) (vô′gěl)		S. Afr. (Natal In.)	32·52 S	25·12 E
155	Vogelkop Pen. (fô′gěl-kôp)		W. Irian	1·25 S	133·15 E
126	Voghera (vô-gā′rä)		It.	44·58 N	9·02 E
167	Vohémar (vô-ā-mär′)		Malag. Rep.	13·35 S	50·05 E
65	Voight (R.)		Wash. (Seattle In.)	47·03 N	122·08 W
123	Voiron (vwä-rôn′)		Fr.	45·23 N	5·48 E
127	Voïviis (L.)		Grc.	39·34 N	22·50 E
129	Volchansk (vôl-chänsk′)		Sov. Un.	50·18 N	36·56 E
129	Volch′ya (R.) (vôl-chyä′)		Sov. Un.	49·42 N	34·39 E
133	Volga (R.) (vôl′gä)		Sov. Un.	47·30 N	46·20 E
133	Volga, Mouths of the		Sov. Un.	46·00 N	49·10 E
113	Volgograd (Stalingrad) (vôl′gō-grä′t)		(stá′lĭn-grat)	48·40 N	42·20 E
133	Volgogradskoye (Res.) (vôl-gō-grad′skô-yě)		Sov. Un.	51·10 N	45·10 E
128	Volkhov (vôl′kôf)		Sov. Un.	59·54 N	32·21 E
128	Volkhov (R.)		Sov. Un.	58·45 N	31·40 E
121	Volkovysk (vôl-kôvĭsk′)		Sov. Un.	53·11 N	24·29 E
85	Volmer (vôl′měr)		Can. (Edmonton In.)	53·43 N	113·40 W
136	Volodarskiy (vô-lô-där′skĭ)		Sov. Un. (Leningrad In.)	59·49 N	30·06 E
128	Vologda (vô′lôg-dä)		Sov. Un.	59·12 N	39·52 E

Page	Name	Pronunciation	Region	Lat. ° '	Long. ° '
128	Vologda (Oblast)		Sov. Un.	59·00 N	37·26 E
129	Volokonovka (vô-lô-kô′nôf-kä)		Sov. Un.	50·28 N	37·52 E
128	Volokolamsk (vô-lô-kôlámsk)		Sov. Un.	56·02 N	35·58 E
127	Vólos (vô′lôs)		Grc.	39·23 N	22·56 E
128	Volozhin (vô′lô ʒhĭn)		Sov. Un.	54 04 N	26 38 E
133	Vol′sk (vôl′sk)		Sov. Un.	52·10 N	47·00 E
164	Volta, L (vôl′tä)		Ghana	7·10 N	1·00 W
164	Volta R.		Ghana	8·15 N	0·57 W
101	Volta Redonda (vôl′tä-rä-dôn′dä)		Braz. (Rio de Janeiro In.)	22·32 S	44·05 W
126	Volterra (vôl-tě′rrä)		It.	43·22 N	10·51 E
126	Voltri (vōl′trē)		It.	44·25 N	8·45 E
126	Volturno (R.) (vôl-tōōr′nô)		It.	41·12 N	14·20 E
128	Volzhskoye (L.) (vôl′sh-skô-yě)		Sov. Un.	56·43 N	36·18 E
74	Von Ormy (vŏn ôr′mē)		Tex. (San Antonio In.)	29·18 N	98·36 W
128	Vôopsu (vōōp′-sôô)		Sov. Un.	58·06 N	27·30 E
111	Voorberg..Neth. (Amsterdam In.)			52·04 N	4·21 E
167	Voortrekkerhoogte (Johannesburg & Pretoria In.)		S. Afr.	25·48 S	28·10 E
168	Voortrekkerspos (vôr′trě-kěrs-pôs)		S. Afr. (Johannesburg & Pretoria In.)	24·12 S	27·00 E
128	Vop′ (R.) (vôp)		Sov. Un.	55·20 N	32·40 E
112	Vopnafjördhur (vôp′nä-fyûr′dhur)		Ice.	65·43 N	14·58 W
120	Vorarlberg (Prov.)		Aus.	47·20 N	9·55 E
118	Vordingborg (vôr′dĭng-bôr)		Den.	55·10 N	11·55 E
127	Voríai (Is.)		Grc.	39·12 N	24·03 E
127	Vorios Evvikós Kólpos (G.)		Grc.	38·48 N	23·02 E
132	Vorkuta (vôr-kōō′tä)		Sov. Un.	67·28 N	63·40 E
119	Vormsi (I.) (vôrm′sĭ)		Sov. Un.	59·06 N	23·05 E
133	Vorona (R.) (vô-rô′nä)		Sov. Un.	51·50 N	42·00 E
132	Voron′ya (R.) (vô-rô′nyä)		Sov. Un.	68·20 N	35·20 E
129	Voronezh (vô-rô′nyězh)		Sov. Un.	51·39 N	39·11 E
129	Voronezh (Oblast)		Sov. Un.	51·10 N	39·13 E
128	Voronezh (R.)		Sov. Un.	52·17 N	39·32 E
121	Voronovo (vô′rô-nô-vô)		Sov. Un.	54·07 N	25·16 E
136	Vorontsovka (vô-rônt′sôv-kä)		Sov. Un. (Urals In.)	59·40 N	60·14 E
128	Võrts-Järv (L.) (vôrts yärv)		Sov. Un.	58·15 N	26·12 E
128	Võru (vô′rû)		Sov. Un.	57·50 N	26·58 E
136	Vorya R. (vôr′yä)		Sov. Un. (Moscow In.)	55·55 N	38·15 E
123	Vosges (Mts.)		Fr.	48·09 N	6·57 E
136	Voskresensk (vôs-krě-sěnsk′)		Sov. Un. (Moscow In.)	55·20 N	38·42 E
118	Voss (vôs)		Nor.	60·40 N	6·24 E
132	Votkinsk (vôt-kěnsk′)		Sov. Un.	57·00 N	54·00 E
124	Vouga (R.) (vō′gä)		Port.	40·43 N	7·51 W
122	Vouziers (vōō-zyä′)		Fr.	49·25 N	4·40 E
118	Voxna älv (R.)		Swe.	61·30 N	15·24 E
132	Vozhe (L.) (vôzh′yě)		Sov. Un.	60·40 N	39·00 E
129	Voznesensk (vôz-nyě-sěnsk′)		Sov. Un.	47·34 N	31·22 E
130	Vrangelya (Wrangel) (I.).Sov. Un.			71·25 N	173·38 E
127	Vranje (vrän′yě)		Yugo.	42·33 N	21·55 E
127	Vratsa (vrät′tsä)		Bul.	43·12 N	23·31 E
126	Vrbas (v′r′bäs)		Yugo.	45·34 N	19·43 E
126	Vrbas (R.)		Yugo.	44·25 N	17·17 E
120	Vrchlabi (v′r′chlä-bě)		Czech.	50·32 N	15·51 E
168	Vrede (vrī′dě) (vrēd)		S. Afr. (Johannesburg & Pretoria In.)	27·25 S	29·11 E
168	Vredefort (vrī′dě-fôrt) (vrēd′fôrt)		S. Afr. (Johannesburg & Pretoria In.)	27·00 S	27·21 E
111	Vreeswijk..Neth. (Amsterdam In.)			52·00 N	5·06 E
127	Vršac (v′r′shäts)		Yugo.	45·08 N	21·18 E
121	Vrutky (vrōōt′ké)		Czech.	49·09 N	18·55 E
166	Vryburg (vrī′bûrg)		S. Afr.	26·55 S	29·45 E
166	Vryheid (vrī′hit)		S. Afr.	27·43 S	30·58 E
121	Vsetín (fsět′yēn)		Czech.	49·21 N	18·01 E
136	Vsevolozhskiy (vsě′vôlô′zh-skēē)		Sov. Un. (Leningrad In.)	60·01 N	30·41 E
94	Vuelta Abajo (Mts.) (vwěl′tä ä-bä′hō)		Cuba	22·20 N	83·45 W
111	Vught....Neth. (Amsterdam In.)			51·38 N	5·18 E
127	Vukovar (vōō′kô-vär)		Yugo.	45·20 N	19·00 E
80	Vulcan (vŭl′kăn)		Mich.	45·45 N	87·50 W
126	Vulcano (I.) (vōōl-kä′nô)		It.	38·23 N	15·00 E
127	Vŭlchedrŭm		Bul.	43·43 N	23·29 E
119	Vyartsilya (vyär-tsēl′yä)		Sov. Un.	62·10 N	30·40 E
132	Vyatka (R.) (vyät′ká)		Sov. Un.	58·25 N	51·25 E
152	Vyazemskiy (vyä-zěm′skĭ)		Sov. Un.	47·29 N	134·39 E
128	Vyaz′ma (vyäz′má)		Sov. Un.	55·12 N	34·17 E
132	Vyazniki (vyäz′ně-kě)		Sov. Un.	56·10 N	42·10 E
119	Vyborg (Viipuri) (vwē′bôrk)		Sov. Un.	60·43 N	28·46 E
132	Vychegda (R.) (vē′chěg-dá)		Sov. Un.	61·40 N	48·00 E
132	Vyg (L.)		Sov. Un.	63·40 N	35·00 E
132	Vym (R.) (vwēm)		Sov. Un.	63·15 N	51·20 E
136	Vyritsa (vē′rĭ-tsä)		Sov. Un. (Leningrad In.)	59·24 N	30·20 E
128	Vyshnevolotskoye (L.) (vŭy′sh-ně′vôlôt′s-kô′yě)		Sov. Un.	57·30 N	34·27 E
128	Vyshniy Volochëk (věsh′nyĭ vôl-ô-chěk′).Sov. Un.			57·34 N	34·35 E
120	Vyskov (věsh′kôf)		Czech.	49·17 N	16·58 E
120	Vysoké Mýto (vŭ′sô-kä mū′tô)		Czech.	49·58 N	16·07 E
128	Vysokovsk (vĭ-sô′kôfsk)		Sov. Un.	56·16 N	36·32 E
132	Vytegra (vŭ′těg-rä)		Sov. Un.	61·00 N	36·20 E
132	Vyur		Sov. Un.	57·55 N	27·00 E
117	Waal (R.) (väl)		Neth.	51·46 N	5·00 E
111	Waalwijk..Neth. (Amsterdam In.)			51·41 N	5·05 E
87	Wabana (wä bä-nä)		Can. (Newfoundland In.)	47·32 N	52·29 W
80	Wabash (wô′băsh)		Ind.	40·45 N	85·50 W
80	Wabash (R.)		Ill.-Ind.	38·00 N	88·00 W

PRONOUNCING INDEX Wabasha–Waukegan 283

Page	Name Pronunciation Region	Lat. °'	Long. °'
71	Wabasha (wä'bȧ-shô) Minn.	44·24 N	92·04 W
121	Wabrzeźno (vôṇ-bzĕzh'nô) Pol.	53·17 N	18·59 E
79	Waccamaw (R.) (wăk'ȧ-mô) S. C.	33·47 N	78·55 W
78	Waccasassa B. (wă-kȧ-să'sȧ) Fla.	29·02 N	83·10 W
111	Wachow (vä'kōv) Ger. (Berlin In.)	52·32 N	12·46 E
77	Waco (wā'kō) Tex.	31·35 N	97·06 W
153	Wadayama (wä'dä'yä-mä) Jap.	35·19 N	134·49 E
117	Waddenzee (Sea) Neth.	53·00 N	4·50 E
86	Waddington, Mt. (wŏd'dĭng-tŭn) Can.	51·30 N	125·23 W
165	Wadelai (wä-dĕ-lä'ē) Ug.	2·45 N	31·34 E
71	Wadena (wŏ-dē'nȧ) Minn.	46·26 N	95·09 W
79	Wadesboro (wādz'bŭr-ô) N. C.	34·57 N	80·05 W
139	Wadī Musa. Jordan (Palestine In.)	30·19 N	35·29 E
79	Wadley (wŏd'lē) Ga.	32·54 N	82·25 W
165	Wad Medani (wäd mĕ-dä'nē) Sud.	14·27 N	33·31 E
121	Wadowice (vȧ-dô'vēt-sĕ) Pol.	49·53 N	19·31 E
87	Wager B. (wā'jẽr) Can.	65·48 N	88·19 W
160	Wagga Wagga (wôg'ȧ wôg'ȧ) Austl.	35·10 S	147·30 E
73	Wagoner (wăg'ŭn-ẽr) Okla.	35·58 N	95·22 W
72	Wagon Mound (wăg'ŭn mound) N. Mex.	35·59 N	104·45 W
121	Wagrowiec (vôṇ-grô'vyĕts) Pol.	52·47 N	17·14 E
70	Wahoo (wä-hōō') Nebr.	41·14 N	96·39 W
70	Wahpeton (wô'pē-tŭn) N. D.	46·17 N	96·38 W
157	Waialua (wä'ē-ä-lōō'ä) Hawaii (In.)	21·33 N	158·08 W
157	Waianae (wä'ē-ȧ-nä'ä) Hawaii (In.)	21·25 N	158·11 W
120	Waidhofen (vīd'hôf-ĕn) Aus.	47·58 N	14·46 E
155	Waigeo (I.) (wä-ē-gā'ô) W. Irian	0·07 N	131·00 E
149	Waikang (wäī'käng) China (Shanghai In.)	31·23 N	121·11 E
159	Waikato (R.) (wä'ē-kä'to) N. Z. (In.)	38·00 S	175·47 E
160	Waikerie (wä'kẽr-ē) Austl.	34·15 S	140·00 E
157	Wailuku (wä'ē-lōō'kōō) Hawaii (In.)	20·55 N	156·30 W
157	Waimanalo (wä-ê-mä'nä-lô) Hawaii (In.)	21·19 N	157·53 W
157	Waimea (wä-ê-mā'ä) Hawaii (In.)	20·01 N	155·40 W
157	Waimea Hawaii (In.)	21·56 N	159·38 W
142	Wainganga (R.) (wä-ēn-gŭṇ'gä) India	20·24 N	79·41 E
154	Waingapu Indon.	9·32 S	120·00 E
64	Wainwright (wān-rīt) Alaska	74·40 N	159·00 W
86	Wainwright Can.	52·53 N	110·40 W
157	Waipahu (wä'ē-pä'hōō) Hawaii (In.)	21·20 N	158·02 W
74	Waiska R. (wȧ-ĭz-kȧ) Mich. (Sault Ste. Marie In.)	46·20 N	84·38 W
66	Waitsburg (wāts'bûrg) Wash.	46·17 N	118·08 W
153	Wajima (wä'jē-mȧ) Jap.	37·23 N	136·56 E
153	Wakamatsu (wä-kä'mät-sōō) Jap.	33·54 N	130·44 E
153	Wakasa-Wan (B.) (wä'kä-sä wän) Jap.	35·43 N	135·39 E
159	Wakatipu (R.) (wä-kä-tē'pōō) N. Z. (In.)	44·24 S	169·00 E
153	Wakayama (wä-kä'yä-mä) Jap.	34·14 N	135 11 E
156	Wake (I.) (wāk) Oceania	19·25 N	167·00 E
72	Wakeeney (wô-kē'nē) Kans.	39·01 N	99·53 W
85	Wakefield (wāk-fēld) Can. (Ottawa In.)	45·39 N	75·55 W
110	Wakefield Eng.	53·41 N	1·25 W
83	Wakefield Mass. (Boston In.)	42·31 N	71·05 W
71	Wakefield Mich.	46·28 N	89·55 W
70	Wakefield Nebr.	42·15 N	96·52 W
84	Wakefield R. I. (Providence In.)	41·26 N	71·30 W
79	Wake Forest (wāk fŏr'ĕst) N. C.	35·58 N	78·31 W
153	Waki (wä'kē) Jap.	34·05 N	134·10 E
152	Wakkanai (wä'kä-nä'ē) Jap.	45·19 N	141·43 E
166	Wakkerstroom (väk'ẽr-strōm) (wăk'ẽr-strōōm) S. Afr.	27·19 S	30·04 E
120	Wałbrzych (väl'bzhûk) Pol.	50·46 N	16·16 E
82	Waldoboro (wôl'dô-bŭr-ô) Maine	44·06 N	69·22 W
66	Waldo L. (wôl'dō) Ore.	43·46 N	122·10 W
84	Waldorf (wăl'dôrf) Md. (Baltimore In.)	38·37 N	76·57 W
74	Waldron (wôl'drŭn) Mo. (Kansas City In.)	39·14 N	94·47 W
65	Waldron (I.) Wash. (Vancouver In.)	48·42 N	123·02 W
64	Wales (wālz) Alaska	65·35 N	168·14 W
116	Wales U. K.	52·12 N	3·40 W
120	Wałez (välch) Pol.	53·16 N	16·30 E
160	Walgett (wôl'gĕt) Austl.	30·00 S	148·10 E
47	Walgreen Coast (wôl'grēn) Ant.	73·00 S	110·00 W
78	Walhalla (wŏl-hăl'ȧ) S. C.	34·45 N	83·04 W
71	Walker (wôk'ẽr) Minn.	47·06 N	94·37 W
68	Walker (R.) Nev.	39·07 N	119·10 W
65	Walker, Mt. Wash. (Seattle In.)	47·47 N	122·54 W
68	Walker L. Nev.	38·46 N	118·30 W
68	Walker River Ind. Res. Nev.	39·06 N	118·20 W
67	Walkerville (wôk'ẽr-vĭl) Mont.	46·20 N	112·32 W
66	Wallace (wŏl'ās) Idaho	47·27 N	115·55 W
161	Wallacia Austl. (Sydney In.)	33·52 S	150·40 E
66	Wallapa B. (wŏl ȧ pă) Wash.	46·39 N	124·30 W
160	Wallaroo (wŏl-ȧ-rōō) Austl.	33·52 S	137·45 E
110	Wallasey (wŏl'ȧ-sē) Eng.	53·25 N	3·03 W
66	Walla Walla (wŏl'ȧ wŏl'ȧ) Wash.	46·03 N	118·20 W
75	Walled Lake (wôl'd lăk) Mich. (Detroit In.)	42·32 N	83·29 W
165	Wallel, Tulu (Mt.) Eth.	9·00 N	34·52 E
110	Wallingford (wŏl'ĭng-fẽrd) Eng. (London In.)	51·34 N	1·08 W
81	Wallingford Vt.	43·30 N	72·55 W
156	Wallis Is. Oceania	13·00 S	183·50 E
77	Wallisville (wŏl'ĭs-vĭl) Tex. (In.)	29·50 N	94·44 W
66	Wallowa (wôl'ô-wȧ) Ore.	45·34 N	117·32 W
66	Wallowa Mts. Ore.	45·10 N	117·22 W
66	Wallowa R. Ore.	45·28 N	117·28 W
116	Walney (C.) (wôl'nē) Eng.	54·04 N	3·13 W
74	Walnut (wôl'nŭt) Calif. (Los Angeles In.)	34·00 N	117·51 W
73	Walnut (R.) Kans.	37·28 N	97·06 W
69	Walnut Canyon Natl. Mon. Ariz.	35·10 N	111·30 W
65	Walnut Creek Calif. (San Francisco In.)	37·54 N	122·04 W
74	Walnut Cr. Tex. (Dallas, Fort Worth In.)	32·37 N	97·03 W
73	Walnut Ridge (rĭj) Ark.	36·04 N	90·56 W
83	Walpole (wôl'pōl) Mass. (Boston In.)	42·09 N	71·15 W
81	Walpole N. H.	43·05 N	72·25 W
110	Walsall (wôl-sôl) Eng.	52·35 N	1·58 W
72	Walsenburg (wôl'sĕn-bûrg) Colo.	37·38 N	104·46 W
72	Walters (wôl'tẽrz) Okla.	34·21 N	98·19 W
83	Waltham (wôl'thǎm) Mass. (Boston In.)	42·22 N	71·14 W
110	Walthamstow (wôl'tǎm-stō) Eng. (London In.)	51·34 N	0·01 W
81	Walton (wôl'tŭn) N. Y.	42·10 N	75·05 W
110	Walton-le-Dale (lē-dāl') Eng.	53·44 N	2·40 W
166	Walvis Bay (wôl'vĭs) S. Afr.	22·50 S	14·30 E
71	Walworth (wôl'wŭrth) Wis.	42·33 N	88·39 W
165	Wamba (wăm'bȧ) Con. K.	2·15 N	28·05 E
166	Wamba (R.) Con. K.	6·45 S	17·51 E
73	Wamego (wŏ-mē'gō) Kans.	39·13 N	96·17 W
167	Wami (R.) (wä'mē) Tan.	6·31 S	37·17 E
84	Wanaque (wŏn'ȧ-kū) N. J. (New York In.)	41·03 N	74·16 W
84	Wanaque Res. N. J. (New York In.)	41·06 N	74·20 W
148	Wanchih (wän'chĭ') China	31·11 N	118·31 E
111	Wandsbek (vänds'bĕk) Ger. (Hamburg In.)	53·34 N	10·07 E
110	Wandsworth (wôndz'wûrth) Eng.	51·26 N	0·12 W
159	Wanganui (wôṇ'gȧ-nōō'ē) N. Z. (In.)	39·53 S	175·01 E
160	Wangaratta (wŏṇ'gȧ-răt'ȧ) Austl.	36·23 S	146·18 E
152	Wangching (wäng'chĕng) China	43·14 N	129·33 E
148	Wangch'ingt'o (wäng'chĭng'tōōŭ) China	39·14 N	116·56 E
120	Wangeroog I. (vän'gĕ-rōg) Ger.	53·49 N	7·57 E
151	Wanhsien (wän'hsyĕn') China	30·48 N	108·22 E
148	Wanhsien (wän'sĭän) China	38·51 N	115·10 E
166	Wankie (wăṇ 'kē) Rh.	18·27 S	26·30 E
110	Wantage (wŏn'tăj) Eng. (London In.)	51·33 N	1·26 W
151	Wantsai China	28·05 N	114·25 E
160	Waodoan (wŏd'ŏn) Austl.	26·12 S	149·52 E
80	Wapakoneta (wä'pȧ-kō-nĕt'ȧ) Ohio	40·35 N	84·10 W
71	Wapello (wŏ-pĕl'ō) Iowa	41·10 N	91·11 W
73	Wappapello Res. (wä'pȧ-pĕl-lō) Mo.	37·07 N	90·10 W
81	Wappingers Falls (wŏp'ĭn-jẽrz) N. Y.	41·35 N	73·55 W
71	Wapsipinicon (R.) (wŏp'sĭ-pĭn'ĭ-kŏn) Iowa	42·16 N	91·35 W
153	Warabi (wä'rä-bē) Jap. (Tōkyō In.)	35·50 N	139·41 E
143	Warangal (wŭ'räṇ-gȧl) India	18·03 N	79·45 E
158	Warburton, The (R.) (wŏr'bûr-tŭn) Austl.	27·30 S	138·45 E
139	Wardan (R.) U. A. R. (Egypt) (Palestine In.)	29·29 N	32·52 E
168	Warden (wôr'dĕn) S. Afr. (Johannesburg & Pretoria In.)	27·52 S	28·59 E
142	Wardha (wŭr'dä) India	20·46 N	78·42 E
75	Wardsworth (wôrdz'wûrth) Ohio (Cleveland In.)	41·01 N	81·44 W
80	War Eagle (wôr ē'g'l) W. Va.	37·30 N	81·50 W
120	Waren (vä'rĕn) Ger.	53·32 N	12·43 E
123	Warendorf (vä'rĕn-dōrf) Ger. (Ruhr In.)	51·57 N	7·59 E
166	Warmbad (värm'bäd) (wôrm'băd) S. W. Afr.	28·25 S	18·45 E
168	Warmbad S. Afr. (Johannesburg & Pretoria In.)	24·52 S	28·18 E
65	Warm Beach (wôrm) Wash. (Seattle In.)	48·10 N	122·22 W
66	Warm Springs Ind. Res. (wôrm sprĭngz) Ore.	44·55 N	121·30 W
66	Warm Springs Res. Ore.	43·42 N	118·40 W
118	Warnemünde (vär'nĕ-mün-dĕ) Ger.	54·11 N	12·04 E
66	Warner Ra. (Mts.) (wôrn'ẽr) Calif.-Ore.	41·30 N	120·17 W
120	Warnow R. (vär'nō) Ger.	53·51 N	11·55 E
160	Warracknabeal Austl.	36·20 S	142·28 E
161	Warragamba (R.) Austl. (Sydney In.)	33·55 S	150·32 E
159	Warrego (R.) (wôr'ē-gô) Austl.	27·13 S	145·58 E
73	Warren (wŏr'ĕn) Ark.	33·37 N	92·03 W
80	Warren Ind.	40·40 N	85·25 W
75	Warren Mich. (Detroit In.)	42·33 N	83·03 W
70	Warren Minn.	48·11 N	96·44 W
80	Warren Ohio	41·15 N	80·50 W
65	Warren Ore. (Portland In.)	45·49 N	122·51 W
81	Warren Pa.	41·50 N	79·10 W
84	Warren R. I. (Providence In.)	41·44 N	71·14 W
75	Warrendale (wŏr'ĕn-dāl) Pa. (Pittsburgh In.)	40·39 N	80·04 W
73	Warrensburg (wŏr'ĕnz-bûrg) Mo.	38·45 N	93·42 W
85	Warrenton (wŏr'ĕn-tŭn) Can. (Winnipeg In.)	50·08 N	97·32 W
79	Warrenton Ga.	33·26 N	82·37 W
65	Warrenton Ore. (Portland In.)	46·10 N	123·56 W
81	Warrenton Va.	38·45 N	77·50 W
164	Warri (wär'ē) Nig.	5·33 N	5·43 E
110	Warrington Eng.	53·22 N	2·30 W
78	Warrington (wŏr'ĭng-tŭn) Fla.	30·21 N	87·15 W
160	Warrnambool (wôr'nǎm-bōōl) Austl.	36·20 S	142·28 E
71	Warroad (wôr'rōd) Minn.	48·55 N	95·20 W
159	Warrumbungle Ra. (wôr'ŭm-bŭṇ-g'l) Austl.	31·18 S	150·00 E
73	Warsaw (wôr'sô) Ill.	40·21 N	91·26 W
80	Warsaw Ind.	41·15 N	85·50 W
81	Warsaw N. Y.	42·45 N	78·10 W
79	Warsaw N. C.	35·00 N	78·07 W
	Warsaw, see Warszawa		
110	Warsop (wôr'sŭp) Eng.	53·13 N	1·05 W
121	Warszawa (Warsaw) (vȧr-shä'vȧ) Pol.	52·15 N	21·05 E
120	Warta R. (vär'tȧ) Pol.	52·35 N	15·07 E
167	Wartburg S. Afr. (Natal In.)	29·26 S	30·39 E
160	Warwick (wŏr'ĭk) Austl.	28·05 S	152·10 E
82	Warwick Can.	45·58 N	71·57 W
116	Warwick Eng.	52·19 N	1·46 W
84	Warwick N. Y. (New York In.)	41·15 N	74·22 W
84	Warwick R. I. (Providence In.)	41·42 N	71·27 W
110	Warwick (Co.) Eng.	52·22 N	1·34 W
74	Wasatch Mts. (wô'săch) Utah (Salt Lake City In.)	40·45 N	111·46 W
69	Wasatch Plat. Utah	38·55 N	111·40 W
62	Wasatch Ra. U. S.	39·10 N	111·30 W
167	Wasbank S. Afr. (Natal In.)	28·27 S	30·09 E
167	Waschbank Pk. (Mtn.) (văsh'bȧnk) S. Afr. (Natal In.)	31·17 S	27·26 E
66	Wasco (wăs'kō) Ore.	45·36 N	120·42 W
71	Waseca (wô-sē'kȧ) Minn.	44·04 N	93·31 W
117	Wash, The (Est.) (wŏsh) Eng.	53·00 N	0·20 E
82	Washburn (wŏsh'bŭrn) Maine	46·46 N	68·10 W
71	Washburn Wis.	46·41 N	90·55 W
67	Washburn, Mt. Wyo.	44·55 N	110·10 W
84	Washington (wŏsh'ĭng-tŭn) D.C. (Washington D.C. In.)	38·50 N	77·00 W
78	Washington Ga.	33·43 N	82·46 W
80	Washington Ind.	38·40 N	87·10 W
71	Washington Iowa	41·17 N	91·42 W
73	Washington Kans.	39·48 N	97·04 W
73	Washington Mo.	38·33 N	91·00 W
79	Washington N. C.	35·32 N	77·01 W
75	Washington Pa. (Pittsburgh In.)	40·10 N	80·14 W
62	Washington (State) U. S.	47·30 N	121·10 W
81	Washington, Mt. N. H.	44·15 N	71·15 W
65	Washington, L. Wash. (Seattle In.)	47·34 N	122·12 W
71	Washington (I.) Wis.	45·18 N	86·42 W
80	Washington Court House Ohio	39·30 N	83·25 W
74	Washington Park Ill. (St. Louis In.)	38·38 N	90·06 W
72	Washita (R.) (wŏsh'ĭ-tô) Okla.	35·33 N	99·16 W
65	Washougal (wŏ-shōō'gȧl) Wash. (Portland In.)	45·35 N	122·21 W
65	Washougal (R.) Wash. (Portland In.)	45·38 N	122·17 W
121	Wasilkow (vȧ-sēl'kōōf) Pol.	53·12 N	23·13 E
123	Wassenberg (vä'sĕn-bĕrgh) Ger. (Ruhr In.)	51·06 N	6·07 E
68	Wassuk Ra. (wäs'sŭk) Nev.	38·58 N	119·00 W
74	Watauga (wȧ tō gā') Tex. (Dallas, Fort Worth In.)	32·51 N	97·16 W
89	Water (I.) (wô'tẽr) Vir. Is. (U. S. A.) (St. Thomas In.)	18·20 N	64·57 W
168	Waterberg (Mts.) (wôrtẽr'bûrg) S. Afr. (Johannesburg & Pretoria In.)	24·25 S	27·53 E
79	Waterboro (wô'tẽr-bûr-ō) S. C.	32·50 N	80·40 W
81	Waterbury (wô'tẽr-bĕr-ē) Conn.	41·30 N	73·00 W
82	Waterbury Vt.	44·20 N	72·44 W
95	Water Cay (I.) Ba. Is.	22·55 N	75·50 W
85	Waterdown (wô'tẽr-doun) Can. (Toronto In.)	43·20 N	79·54 W
79	Wateree (R.) (wô'tẽr-ē) S. C.	34·40 N	80·48 W
116	Waterford (wô'tẽr-fẽrd) Ire.	52·20 N	7·03 W
75	Waterford Wis. (Milwaukee In.)	42·46 N	88·13 W
167	Waterkloof S. Afr. (Johannesburg & Pretoria In.)	25·48 S	28·15 E
111	Waterloo Bel. (Brussels In.)	50·44 N	4·24 E
80	Waterloo (wô-tẽr-lōō') Can.	43·30 N	80·40 W
81	Waterloo Can.	45·25 N	72·30 W
73	Waterloo Ill.	38·19 N	90·08 W
71	Waterloo Iowa	42·30 N	92·22 W
84	Waterloo Md. (Baltimore In.)	39·11 N	76·50 W
81	Waterloo N. Y.	42·55 N	76·50 W
67	Waterton-Glacier Intl. Peace Park (wô'ter-tŭn-glā'shûr) Mont.-Can.	48·55 N	114·10 W
83	Watertown (wô'tẽr-toun) Mass. (Boston In.)	42·22 N	71·11 W
81	Watertown N. Y.	44·00 N	75·55 W
70	Watertown S. D.	44·53 N	97·07 W
71	Watertown Wis.	43·13 N	88·40 W
78	Water Valley (văl'ē) Miss.	34·08 N	89·38 W
82	Waterville (wô'tẽr-vĭl) Maine	44·34 N	69·37 W
71	Waterville Minn.	44·10 N	93·35 W
66	Waterville Wash.	47·38 N	120·04 W
81	Watervliet (wô'tẽr-vlēt') N. Y.	42·45 N	73·45 W
110	Watford (wŏt'fŏrd) Eng. (London In.)	51·38 N	0·24 W
	Watling I., see San Salvador I.		
110	Watlington (wŏt'lĭng-tŭn) Eng. (London In.)	51·37 N	1·01 W
72	Watonga (wŏ-tôṇ'gȧ) Okla.	35·50 N	98·26 W
86	Watrous Can.	51·40 N	105·32 W
165	Watsa (wät'sä) Con. K.	3·02 N	29·30 E
80	Watseka (wŏt-sē'kȧ) Ill.	40·45 N	87·45 W
75	Watson (wŏt'sŭn) Ind. (Louisville In.)	38·21 N	85·42 W
86	Watson Lake Can.	60·18 N	128·50 W
68	Watsonville (wŏt'sŭn-vĭl) Calif.	36·55 N	121·46 W
123	Wattenscheid (vä'tĕn-shīd) Ger. (Ruhr In.)	51·30 N	7·07 E
74	Watts (wŏts) Calif. (Los Angeles In.)	33·56 N	118·15 W
78	Watts Bar (R.) (bär) Tenn.	35·45 N	84·49 W
165	Wau (wä'ōō) Sud.	7·41 N	28·00 E
165	Wāu al Kebir Libya	25·23 N	16·52 E
70	Waubay (wô'bā) S. D.	45·19 N	97·18 W
79	Wauchula (wô-chōō'lȧ) Fla. (In.)	27·32 N	81·48 W
75	Wauconda (wô-kŏn'dȧ) Ill. (Chicago In.)	42·15 N	88·08 W
75	Waukegan (wŏ-kē'gǎn) Ill. (Chicago In.)	42·22 N	87·51 W

ng-sing; ŋ-baŋk; N-nasalized n; nŏd; cǒmmit; ōld; ôbey; ôrder; fōōd; fŏŏt; ou-out; s-soft; sh-dish; th-thin; pūre; ûnite; ûrn; stŭd; circŭs; ü-as "y" in study; '-indeterminate vowel.

284 Waukesha–Weymouth PRONOUNCING INDEX

Page	Name Pronunciation Region	Lat. °′	Long. °′
75	Waukesha (wô′kė-shô) Wis. (Milwaukee In.)	43·01 N	88·13 W
71	Waukon (wô kŏn)..........Iowa	43·15 N	91·30 W
65	Wauna (wȧ-nȧ) .Ore. (Portland In.)	46·09 N	123·25 W
71	Waupaca (wô-păk′ȧ)........Wis.	44·22 N	89·06 W
71	Waupun (wô-pŭn′)..........Wis.	43·37 N	88·45 W
72	Waurika (wô-rē′kȧ)........Okla.	34·09 N	97·59 W
71	Wausau (wô′sô).............Wis.	44·58 N	89·40 W
71	Wausaukee (wô-sô′kė).......Wis.	45·22 N	87·58 W
80	Wauseon (wô′sė-ŏn).........Ohio	41·30 N	84·10 W
71	Wautoma (wô-tō′mȧ)........Wis.	44·04 N	89·11 W
75	Wauwatosa (wô-wȧ-tō′sȧ) Wis. (Milwaukee In.)	43·03 N	88·00 W
117	Waveney (R.) (wāv′nė).....Eng.	52·27 N	1·17 E
167	Waverley......S. Afr. (Natal In.)	31·54 S	26·29 E
71	Waverly (wā′vēr-lė).........Iowa	42·43 N	92·29 W
78	Waverly...................Tenn.	36·04 N	87·46 W
80	Wawasee (L.) (wô-wô-sē′)....Ind.	41·25 N	85·45 W
77	Waxahachie (wăk-sȧ-hăch′ė)..Tex.	32·23 N	96·50 W
79	Waycross (wā′krôs)..........Ga.	31·11 N	82·24 W
78	Wayland (wā′lănd)..........Ky.	37·25 N	82·47 W
83	Wayland......Mass. (Boston In.)	42·23 N	71·22 W
75	Wayne.......Mich. (Detroit In.)	42·17 N	83·23 W
70	Wayne (wān)..............Nebr.	42·13 N	97·03 W
84	Wayne.....Pa. (Philadelphia In.)	40·03 N	75·22 W
79	Waynesboro (wānz′bŭr-ô).....Ga.	33·05 N	82·02 W
81	Waynesboro.................Pa.	39·45 N	77·35 W
81	Waynesboro.................Va.	38·05 N	78·50 W
81	Waynesburg (wānz′bûrg).....Pa.	39·55 N	80·10 W
78	Waynesville (wānz′vĭl).....N. C.	35·28 N	82·58 W
72	Waynoka (wā-nō′kȧ).......Okla.	36·34 N	98·52 W
74	Wayzata (wā-zä-tȧ)........Minn. (Minneapolis, St. Paul In.)	44·58 N	93·31 W
142	Wazīrbad..............W. Pak.	32·39 N	74·11 E
116	Weald, The (Reg.) (wēld)...Eng.	50·58 N	0·15 W
72	Weatherford (wĕ-dhēr-fērd) . Okla.	85·32 N	98·41 W
77	Weatherford...............Tex.	32·45 N	97·46 W
110	Weaver (R.) (wē′vēr).......Eng.	53·09 N	2·31 W
66	Weaverville (wē′vēr-vĭl)....Calif.	40·44 N	122·55 W
73	Webb City (wĕb)...........Mo.	37·10 N	94·26 W
74	Weber R. (wĕb′ēr) Utah (Salt Lake City In.)	41·13 N	112·07 W
83	Webster (wĕb′stēr) Mass. (Boston In.)	42·04 N	71·52 W
70	Webster..................S. D.	45·19 N	97·30 W
77	Webster..............Tex. (In.)	29·32 N	95·07 W
71	Webster City..............Iowa	42·28 N	93·49 W
74	Webster Groves (grōvz) Mo. (St. Louis In.)	38·36 N	90·22 W
81	Webster Springs (sprĭngz) . W. Va.	38·30 N	80·20 W
47	Weddell Sea (wĕd′ĕl)........Ant.	73·00 S	45·00 W
111	Wedel (vā′dĕl) Ger. (Hamburg In.)	53·35 N	9·42 E
82	Wedgeport (wĕj′pōrt).......Can.	43·46 N	65·58 W
110	Wednesbury (wĕd″nz-bŭr-ė) . Eng.	52·33 N	2·01 W
110	Wednesfield (wĕd″nz-fēld)...Eng.	52·36 N	2·04 W
66	Weed (wēd)...............Calif.	41·35 N	122·21 W
85	Weed Cr....Can. (Edmonton In.)	53·18 N	114·01 W
167	Weenen (vā′nĕn) S. Afr. (Natal In.)	28·52 S	30·05 E
117	Weert....................Neth.	51·16 N	5·39 E
111	Weesp....Neth. (Amsterdam In.)	52·18 N	5·01 E
87	Weggs, C..................Can.	62·14 N	73·43 W
121	Wegorzewo (vôŋ-gô′zhĕ-vô)...Pol.	54·14 N	21·46 E
121	Wegrow (vôŋ′grōōf)..........Pol.	52·23 N	22·02 E
148	Wei (R.) (wā).............China	35·47 N	114·27 E
150	Weich′ang (wā′chäng′).....China	41·50 N	118·00 E
148	Weifang..................China	36·43 N	119·08 E
148	Weihai (wa′hăī′)...........China	37·30 N	122·05 E
150	Wei Ho (R.)...............China	34·00 N	108·10 E
146	Weihsi (wā′hsē′)...........China	27·27 N	99·30 E
148	Weihsien (wā′hsyĕn′)......China	36·59 N	115·17 E
120	Weilheim (vīl′hīm′).........Ger.	47·50 N	11·06 E
120	Weimar (vī′mȧr)............Ger.	50·59 N	11·20 E
150	Weinan..................China	34·32 N	109·40 E
159	Weipa....................Austl.	12·25 S	141·54 E
80	Weirton (wēr′tŭn)........W. Va.	40·25 N	80·35 W
66	Weiser (wē′zēr)...........Idaho	44·15 N	116·58 W
66	Weiser R..................Idaho	44·26 N	116·40 W
148	Weishih (wā′shē)...........China	34·23 N	114·12 E
120	Weissenburg (vī′sĕn-bōōrgh) . Ger.	49·04 N	11·20 E
120	Weissenfels (vī′sĕn-fĕlz)......Ger.	51·13 N	11·58 E
121	Wejherowo (vā-hĕ-rô′vô).....Pol.	54·36 N	18·15 E
79	Welch (wĕlch)...........W. Va.	37·24 N	81·28 W
79	Weldon (wĕl′dŭn)..........N. C.	36·24 N	77·36 W
73	Weldon (R.)................Mo.	40·22 N	93·39 W
73	Weleetka (wė-lēt′kȧ).......Okla.	35·19 N	96·08 W
160	Welford (wĕl′fērd).........Austl.	25·08 S	144·43 E
168	Welkom (wĕl′kŏm).........S. Afr. (Johannesburg & Pretoria In.)	27·57 S	26·45 E
75	Welland (wĕl′ănd) Can. (Buffalo In.)	42·59 N	79·13 W
116	Welland (R.)...............Eng.	52·38 N	0·40 W
83	Wellesley (wĕlz′lė) Mass. (Boston In.)	42·18 N	71·17 W
158	Wellesley Is..............Austl.	16·15 S	139·25 E
160	Wellington (wĕl′lĭng-tŭn)...Austl.	32·40 S	148·50 E
110	Wellington................Eng.	52·42 N	2·30 W
73	Wellington...............Kans.	37·16 N	97·24 W
159	Wellington..........N. Z. (In.)	41·15 S	174·45 E
80	Wellington................Ohio	41·10 N	82·10 W
72	Wellington................Tex.	34·51 N	100·12 W
100	Wellington (I.) (ōōĕ′lēng-tŏn) . Chile	49·30 S	76·30 W
158	Wells (wĕlz)..............Austl.	26·35 S	123·40 E
86	Wells.....................Can.	54·11 N	121·40 W
80	Wells....................Mich.	45·50 N	87·00 W
71	Wells....................Minn.	43·44 N	93·43 W
66	Wells.....................Nev.	41·07 N	115·04 W
81	Wellsboro (wĕlz′bŭ-rô)........Pa.	41·45 N	77·15 W
80	Wellsburg (wĕlz′bûrg).....W. Va.	40·10 N	80·40 W
74	Wellston (wĕlz′tŭn) Mo. (St. Louis In.)	38·41 N	90·18 W
80	Wellston..................Ohio	39·05 N	82·30 W
73	Wellsville (wĕlz′vĭl)..........Mo.	39·04 N	91·33 W
81	Wellsville................N. Y.	42·10 N	78·00 W
80	Wellsville.................Ohio	40·35 N	80·40 W
67	Wellsville.................Utah	41·38 N	111·57 W
120	Wels (vĕls)................Aus.	48·10 N	14·01 E
116	Welshpool (wĕlsh′pōōl).....Wales	52·44 N	3·10 W
168	Welverdiend (vĕl-vēr-dēnd′) S. Afr. (Johannesburg & Pretoria In.)	26·23 S	27·16 E
110	Welwyn Garden City (wĕl′ĭn) Eng. (London In.)	51·46 N	0·17 W
110	Wem (wĕm)................Eng.	52 51 N	2·41 W
148	Wenan Wa (Swp.) (wĕn′än′ wä) China	38·56 N	116·29 E
66	Wenatchee (wė-năch′ė).....Wash.	47·24 N	120·18 W
66	Wenatchee Mts...........Wash.	47·28 N	121·10 W
151	Wench′ang..............China	19·32 N	110·42 E
151	Wenchou (wĕn′chō′).......China	28·00 N	120·40 E
150	Wenchüan (Halunrshan)...China	47·10 N	120·00 E
67	Wendorer.................Utah	40·47 N	114·01 W
85	Wendover (wĕn-dōv′ēr) Can. (Ottawa In.)	45·34 N	75·07 W
110	Wendover.....Eng. (London In.)	51·44 N	0·45 W
83	Wenham (wĕn′ăm) Mass. (Boston In.)	42·36 N	70·53 W
84	Wenonah (wĕn′ō-nā) N. J. (Philadelphia In.)	39·48 N	75·08 W
151	Wenshan.................China	23·20 N	104·15 E
148	Wenshang (wĕn′shäng).....China	35·43 N	116·31 E
148	Wenshussu (wĕn′shōō′sĕ)...China	31·55 N	114·47 E
146	Wensu (Aksu) (wĕn′sōō′) (äk′sōō′) China	41·45 N	79·54 E
117	Wensum (R.) (wĕn′sŭm)....Eng.	52·45 N	1·08 E
110	Went (R.) (wĕnt)...........Eng.	53·38 N	1·08 W
148	Wenteng (wĕn′tĕng′).......China	37·14 N	122·03 E
160	Wentworth (wĕnt′wûrth)...Austl.	34·03 S	141·53 E
166	Wepener (wē′pĕn-ēr) (vā′pĕn-ĕr) S. Afr.	29·43 S	27·04 E
111	Werder (vĕr′dĕr) . Ger. (Berlin In.)	52·23 N	12·56 E
123	Werl (vĕrl).......Ger. (Ruhr In.)	51·33 N	7·55 E
123	Werne (vĕr′nĕ)...Ger. (Ruhr In.)	51·39 N	7·38 E
111	Werneuchen (vĕr′hoi-ĸĕn) Ger. (Berlin In.)	52·38 N	13·44 E
120	Werra R. (vĕr′ä)............Ger.	51·16 N	9·54 E
161	Werribee..Austl. (Melbourne In.)	37·54 S	144·40 E
161	Werribee (R.) Austl. (Melbourne In.)	37·40 S	144·37 E
120	Wertach R. (vĕr′täk)........Ger.	48·12 N	10·40 E
123	Weseke (vĕ′zĕ-kĕ) . Ger. (Ruhr In.)	51·54 N	6·51 E
123	Wesel (vā′zĕl)....Ger. (Ruhr In.)	51·39 N	6·37 E
120	Weser R. (vā′zĕr)...........Ger.	53·08 N	8·35 E
76	Weslaco (wĕs-lā′kō).........Tex.	26·10 N	97·59 W
83	Wesleyville (wĕs′lē-vĭl)......Can.	49·09 N	53·33 W
158	Wessel (Is.) (wĕs′ĕl)........Austl.	11·45 S	36·25 E
168	Wesselsbron (wĕs′ĕl-brŏn) S. Afr. (Johannesburg & Pretoria In.)	27·51 S	26·22 E
70	Wessington Springs (wĕs′ĭng-tŭn) . S. D.	44·06 N	98·35 W
88	West, Mt C. Z. (Panama Canal In.)	9·10 N	79·52 W
75	West Allis (wĕst-ăl′ĭs) Wis. (Milwaukee In.)	43·01 N	88·01 W
74	West Alton (ôl′tŭn) Mo. (St. Louis In.)	38·52 N	90·13 W
77	West B..............Tex. (In.)	29·11 N	95·03 W
71	West Bend (wĕst bĕnd)......Wis.	43·25 N	88·13 W
142	West Bengal (State) (bĕn-gôl′) India	28·00 N	87·42 E
111	West Berlin (bĕr-lēn′) Ger. (Berlin In.)	52·31 N	13·20 E
78	West Blocton (blŏk′tŭn).....Ala.	33·05 N	87·05 W
83	Westboro (wĕst′bŭr-ô) Mass. (Boston In.)	42·17 N	71·37 W
83	West Boyleston (boil′stŭn) Mass. (Boston In.)	42·22 N	71·46 W
80	West Branch (wĕst brȧnch) . Mich.	44·15 N	84·10 W
110	West Bridgford (brĭj′fērd)...Eng.	52·55 N	1·08 W
110	West Bromwich (wĕst brŭm′ĭj) Eng.	52·32 N	1·59 W
82	Westbrook (wĕst′brōōk)....Maine	43·41 N	70·23 W
71	Westby (wĕst′bė)...........Wis.	43·40 N	90·52 W
95	West Caicos (I.) (käē′kō) (kī′kōs) Turks & Caicos	21·40 N	72·30 W
158	West Cape Howe (C.)......Austl.	35·15 S	117·30 E
75	West Chester (chĕs′tēr) Ohio (Cincinnati In.)	39·20 N	84·24 W
84	West Chester Pa. (Philadelphia In.)	39·57 N	75·36 W
75	West Chicago (chĭ-kȧ′gō) Ill. (Chicago In.)	41·53 N	88·12 W
79	West Columbia (cŏl′ŭm-bē-ȧ) . S. C.	33·58 N	81·05 W
77	West Columbia..............Tex.	29·08 N	95·39 W
77	West Cote Blanche B. (kōt blănch) La.	29·30 N	92·17 W
74	West Covina (wĕst kô-vē′nȧ) Calif. (Los Angeles In.)	34·04 N	117·55 W
71	West Des Moines (dē moin′) . Iowa	41·35 N	93·42 W
71	West Des Moines (R.)......Iowa	42·52 N	94·32 W
94	West End................Ba. Is.	26·40 N	78·55 W
110	Westerham (wĕ′stĕr′ŭm) Eng. (London In.)	51·15 N	0·05 E
111	Westerhorn (vĕs′tĕr-hōrn) Ger. (Hamburg In.)	53·52 N	9·41 E
111	Westerlo.......Bel. (Brussels In.)	51·05 N	4·57 E
81	Westerly (wĕs′tēr-lė).......Conn.	41·25 N	71·50 W
120	Western Alps (Mts.)....Switz.-Fr.	46·19 N	7·03 E
158	Western Australia (State) (ôs-trā′lĭ-ȧ) . Austl.	24·15 S	121·30 E
	Western Dvina, see Zapadnaya Dvina		
116	Western Downs.............Eng.	50·50 N	2·25 W
143	Western Ghats (Mts.).......India	22·09 N	74·15 E
81	Western Port (wĕs′tērn pōrt) . Md.	39·30 N	79·00 W
164	Western Region (Div.)......Nig.	8·54 N	3·30 E
156	Western Samoa..........Oceania	14·30 S	172·00 W
66	Western Shoshone Ind. Res. (wĕst′ērn shô-shōn′ė) . Idaho	42·02 N	115·49 W
130	Western Siberian Lowland Sov. Un.	63·37 N	72·45 E
80	Westerville (wĕs′tēr-vĭl).....Ohio	40·10 N	83·00 W
120	Westerwald (For.) (vĕs′tĕr-väld) . Ger.	50·35 N	7·45 E
84	Westfield (wĕst′fēld) Ala. (Birmingham In.)	33·29 N	86·57 W
81	Westfield...................Mass.	42·05 N	72·45 W
84	Westfield...N. J. (New York In.)	40·39 N	74·21 W
81	Westfield (wĕst′fēld)........N. Y.	42·20 N	79·40 W
83	Westford (wĕst′fērd) Mass. (Boston In.)	42·35 N	71·26 W
80	West Frankfort (frăŋk′fŭrt)...Ill.	37·55 N	88·55 W
110	West Ham.....Eng. (London In.)	51·30 N	0·00
81	West Hartford (härt′fērd)..Conn.	41·45 N	72·45 W
116	West Hartlepool (här′t′l-pōōl) Eng.	54·40 N	1·12 W
73	West Helena (hĕl′ĕn-ȧ)......Ark.	34·32 N	90·39 W
85	West Hill.....Can. (Toronto In.)	43·46 N	79·09 W
89	West Indies (Reg.) (ĭn′dēz) . N. A.	19·00 N	78·30 W
155	West Irian (ĭr′ē-ȧn).........Asia	3·05 S	135·00 E
74	West Jordan (jôr′dăn) Utah (Salt Lake City In.)	40·37 N	111·56 W
110	West Kirby (kûr′bė)........Eng.	53·22 N	3·11 W
80	West Lafayette (lä-fȧ-yĕt′)...Ind.	40·25 N	86·55 W
75	Westlake....Ohio (Cleveland In.)	41·27 N	81·55 W
168	Westleigh (wĕst-lē)........S. Afr. (Johannesburg & Pretoria In.)	27·39 S	27·18 E
71	West Liberty (wĕst lĭb′ēr-tĭ) . Iowa	41·34 N	91·15 W
65	West Linn (lĭn) . Ore. (Portland In.)	45·22 N	122·37 W
74	Westminster (wĕst′mĭn-stēr) Calif. (Los Angeles In.)	33·45 N	117·59 W
81	Westminster................Md.	39·40 N	76·55 W
78	Westminster...............S. C.	34·38 N	83·10 W
85	Westmount (wĕst′mount) Can. (Montreal In.)	45·29 N	73·36 W
83	West Newbury (nū′bēr-ė) Mass. (Boston In.)	42·47 N	70·57 W
75	West Newton (nū′tŭn) Pa. (Pittsburgh In.)	40·12 N	79·45 W
84	West New York (nû yŏrk) N. J. (New York In.)	40·47 N	74·01 W
73	West Nishnabotna (R.) (nĭsh-nȧ-bŏt′nȧ) . Iowa	40·56 N	95·37 W
84	West Norfolk (nôr′fŏk) Va. (Norfolk In.)	36·52 N	76·20 W
85	Weston (wĕs′tŭn) Can. (Toronto In.)	43·40 N	79·30 W
83	Weston.......Mass. (Boston In.)	42·22 N	71·18 W
80	Weston..................W. Va.	39·00 N	80·30 W
168	Westonaria...............S. Afr. (Johannesburg & Pretoria In.)	26·19 S	27·38 E
116	Weston-super-Mare (wĕs′tŭn sū′pēr-mā′rė) . Eng.	51·23 N	3·00 W
84	West Orange (wĕst ŏr′ĕnj) N. J. (New York In.)	40·46 N	74·14 W
79	West Palm Beach (päm bēch) Fla. (In.)	26·44 N	80·04 W
78	West Pensacola (pĕn-sȧ-kō′lȧ) . Fla.	30·24 N	87·18 W
65	West Pittsburg (pĭts′bûrg) Calif. (San Francisco In.)	38·02 N	121·56 W
73	Westplains (wĕst-plānz′).....Mo.	36·42 N	91·51 W
78	West Point.................Ga.	32·52 N	85·10 W
78	West Point................Miss.	33·36 N	88·39 W
70	Westpoint................Nebr.	41·50 N	96·00 W
84	West Point. N. Y. (New York In.)	41·23 N	73·58 W
74	West Point Utah (Salt Lake City In.)	41·07 N	112·05 W
81	West Point.................Va.	37·35 N	76·50 W
82	West Pt. (wĕst′ point).......Can.	49·53 N	64·35 W
84	Westport (wĕst′pōrt) Conn. (New York In.)	41·07 N	73·22 W
116	Westport..................Ire.	53·44 N	9·36 W
65	Westport (wĕst′pôrt) Ore. (Portland In.)	46·08 N	123·22 W
116	Westray (I.) (wĕs′trȧ)......Scot.	59·19 N	3·05 W
110	West Riding (Co.) (rīd′ĭng)..Eng.	53·37 N	1·30 W
74	West Riverside (wĕst rĭv′ēr-sīd) Calif. (Los Angeles In.)	33·59 N	117·24 W
74	West St. Paul (sȧnt pôl′)...Minn. (Minneapolis, St. Paul In.)	44·55 N	93·05 W
95	West Sand Spit (I.).......Ba. Is.	21·25 N	72·10 W
117	West Schelde (R.).........Neth.	51·25 N	3·30 E
69	West Tavaputs Plat. (wĕst tăv′ȧ-pōōts) . Utah	39·45 N	110·35 W
80	West Terre Haute (tĕr-ė hōt′) . Ind.	39·30 N	87·30 W
71	West Union (ūn′yŭn).......Iowa	42·58 N	91·48 W
75	Westview (wĕst′vû) Ohio (Cleveland In.)	41·21 N	81·54 W
75	West View...Pa. (Pittsburgh In.)	40·31 N	80·02 W
83	Westville (wĕst′vĭl).........Can.	45·35 N	62·45 W
80	Westville...................Ill.	40·00 N	87·40 W
63	West Virginia (State) (wĕst vēr-jĭn′ĭ-ȧ) . U. S.	39·00 N	80·50 W
68	West Walker (R.) (wôk′ēr)..Calif.	38·25 N	119·25 W
84	West Warwick (wŏr′ĭk) R. I. (Providence In.)	41·42 N	71·31 W
84	Westwego (wĕst-wē′gō) La. (New Orleans In.)	29·55 N	90·09 W
68	Westwood (wĕst′wōōd).....Calif.	40·18 N	121·00 W
83	Westwood.....Mass. (Boston In.)	42·13 N	71·14 W
74	Westwood. Kans. (Kansas City In)	39·03 N	94·37 W
84	Westwood..N. J. (New York In.)	40·59 N	74·02 W
160	West Wyalong (wī′alông)...Austl.	34·00 S	147·20 E
155	Wetar (I.) (wĕt′ȧr)........Indon.	7·34 S	126·00 E
86	Wetaskiwin (wĕ-tăs′kė-wŏn) . Can.	53·01 N	113·24 W
74	Wetmore (wĕt′mōr) Tex. (San Antonio In.)	29·34 N	98·25 W
123	Wettin (vĕ′tĕn)...Ger. (Ruhr In.)	51·23 N	7·23 E
78	Wetumpka (wė-tŭmp′kȧ).....Ala.	32·33 N	86·12 W
123	Wetzlar (vĕts′lär)...........Ger.	50·35 N	8·30 E
155	Wewak (wȧ-wäk′)...N. Gui. Ter.	3·19 S	143·30 E
73	Wewoka (wė-wō′kȧ).........Okla.	35·09 N	96·30 W
116	Wexford (wĕks′fērd).........Ire.	52·20 N	6·30 W
110	Weybridge (wā′brĭj) Eng. (London In.)	51·20 N	0·26 W
86	Weyburn...................Can.	49·31 N	103·50 W
116	Weymouth (wā′mŭth).......Eng.	50·37 N	2·34 W
83	Weymouth....Mass. (Boston In.)	42·44 N	70·57 W

ăt; finăl; rāte; senâte; ärm; ȧsk; sofȧ; fâre; ch-choose; dh-as th in other; bē; ėvent; bĕt; recĕnt; cratēr; g-go; gh-guttural g; bĭt; ĭ-short neutral; rīde; ĸ-guttural k as ch in German ich;

PRONOUNCING INDEX Weymouth–Winsford 285

Page	Name Pronunciation	Region	Lat. °′	Long. °′
75	Weymouth	Ohio (Cleveland In.)	41·11 N	81·48 W
94	Whale Cay (I.)	Ba. Is.	24·50 N	77·45 W
94	Whale Cay Chans	Ba. Is.	26·45 N	77·10 W
116	Wharfe (R.) (hwôr′fē)	Eng.	54·01 N	1·53 W
84	Wharton (hwôr′tŭn)	N. J. (New York In.)	40·54 N	74·35 W
77	Wharton	Tex.	29·19 N	96·06 W
71	What Cheer (hwŏt chēr)	Iowa	41·23 N	92·24 W
65	Whatcom, L. (hwät′kŭm)	Wash. (Portland In.)	48·44 N	123·34 W
75	Wheatland (hwēt′lănd)	Wis. (Milwaukee In.)	42·36 N	88·12 W
67	Wheatland	Wyo.	42·04 N	104·52 W
75	Wheaton (hwē′tŭn)	Ill. (Chicago In.)	41·52 N	88·06 W
84	Wheaton	Md. (Baltimore In.)	39·05 N	77·05 W
70	Wheaton	Minn.	45·48 N	96·29 W
69	Wheeler Pk. (hwē′lẽr)	Nev.	38·58 N	114·15 W
75	Wheeling (hwēl′ĭng)	Ill. (Chicago In.)	42·08 N	87·54 W
80	Wheeling	W. Va.	40·05 N	80·45 W
101	Wheelwright (ōōē′l-rē′gt)	Arg. (Buenos Aires In.)	33·46 S	61·14 W
65	Whidbey I. (hwĭd′bē)	Wash. (Seattle In.)	48·13 N	122·50 W
84	Whippany (hwĭp′á-nē)	N. J. (New York In.)	40·49 N	74·25 W
78	Whistler (hwĭs′lẽr)	Ala.	30·46 N	88·07 W
81	Whitby (hwĭt′bē)	Can.	43·50 N	79·00 W
110	Whitchurch (hwĭt′chûrch)	Eng.	52·58 N	79·00 W
81	White (L.)	Can.	45·15 N	76·35 W
71	White (L.)	Can.	48·47 N	85·50 W
73	White (R.)	Ark.	34·32 N	91·11 W
71	White (R.)	Can.	48·34 N	85·46 W
69	White (R.)	Colo.	40·10 N	108·55 W
80	White (R.)	Ind.	39·15 N	86·45 W
70	White (R.)	S. D.	43·41 N	99·48 W
70	White (R.), South Fork	S. D.	43·13 N	101·04 W
72	White (R.)	Tex.	36·25 N	102·20 W
81	White (R.)	Vt.	43·45 N	72·35 W
83	White B.	Can.	50·07 N	56·24 W
83	White Bear B.	Can.	47·28 N	57·55 W
74	White Bear Lake	Minn. (Minneapolis, St. Paul In.)	45·05 N	93·01 W
74	White Bear L.	Minn. (Minneapolis, St. Paul In.)	45·04 N	92·58 W
77	White Castle	La.	30·10 N	91·09 W
80	White Cloud	Mich.	43·35 N	85·45 W
86	Whitecourt	Can.	54·09 N	115·34 W
70	White Earth (R.)	N. D.	48·30 N	102·44 W
70	White Earth Ind. Res.	Minn.	47·18 N	95·42 W
71	Whiteface (R.) (whīt′fās)	Minn.	47·12 N	92·13 W
81	Whitefield (hwīt′fēld)	N. H.	44·20 N	71·35 W
67	Whitefish (hwīt′fĭsh)	Mont.	48·24 N	114·25 W
71	Whitefish (B.)	Mich.	46·36 N	84·50 W
71	Whitefish (R.)	Mich.	46·12 N	86·56 W
75	Whitefish Bay	Wis. (Milwaukee In.)	43·07 N	77·54 W
73	White Hall	Ill.	39·26 N	90·23 W
80	Whitehall (hwīt′hôl)	Mich.	43·20 N	86·20 W
81	Whitehall	N. Y.	43·30 N	73·25 W
116	Whitehaven (hwīt′hā-vĕn)	Eng.	54·35 N	3·30 W
65	Whitehorn, Pt. (hwīt′hôrn)	Wash. (Vancouver In.)	48·54 N	122·48 W
86	Whitehorse (whīt′hôrs)	Can.	60·39 N	135·01 W
84	White House	N. J. (New York In.)	40·37 N	74·46 W
77	White L	La.	29·40 N	92·35 W
68	White. Mt.	Calif.	37·38 N	118·13 W
82	White Mts	Maine	44·22 N	71·15 W
81	White Mts	N. H.	42·20 N	71·05 W
70	Whitemouth (L.) (hwīt′mŭth)	Can.	49·18 N	95·50 W
	White Nile, see El Abyad, Bahr			
71	White Otter (L.)	Can.	49·15 N	91·48 W
86	White P.	Alaska-Can.	59·35 N	135·03 W
84	White Plains	N. Y. (New York In.)	41·02 N	73·47 W
80	White R., East Fork	Ind.	38·45 N	86·20 W
66	White R.	Wash.	47·07 N	121·48 W
69	White River Plat.	Colo.	39·45 N	107·50 W
65	White Rock	Can. (Vancouver In.)	49·01 N	122·49 W
74	Whiterock Res. (hwīt′rŏk)	Tex. (Dallas, Fort Worth In.)	32·51 N	96·40 W
168	Whites (wīts)	S. Afr. (Johannesburg & Pretoria In.)	28·02 S	27·00 E
69	White Sands Natl. Mon.	N. Mex.	32·50 N	106·20 W
132	White Sea	Sov. Un.	66·00 N	40·00 E
74	White Settlement	Tex. (Dallas, Fort Worth In.)	32·45 N	97·28 W
67	White Sulphur Springs	Mont.	46·32 N	110·49 W
167	White Umfolosi (R.) (ŭm-fô-lō′zē)	S. Afr. (Natal In.)	28·12 S	30·55 E
79	Whiteville (hwīt′vĭl)	N. C.	34·18 N	78·45 W
71	Whitewater (whīt-wŏt′ẽr)	Wis.	42·49 N	88·40 W
70	Whitewater (L.)	Can.	49·14 N	100·39 W
79	Whitewater B.	Fla. (In.)	25·16 N	80·21 W
67	Whitewater Cr	Mont.	48·50 N	107·50 W
75	Whitewater R.	Ind. (Cincinnati In.)	39·19 N	84·55 W
78	Whitewell (hwīt′wĕl)	Tenn.	35·11 N	85·31 W
73	Whitewright (hwīt′rīt)	Tex.	33·33 N	96·25 W
116	Whitham (R.) (wĭth′ŭm)	Eng.	53·08 N	0·15 W
75	Whiting (hwīt′ĭng)	Ind. (Chicago In.)	41·41 N	87·30 W
83	Whitinsville (hwĭt′ĕns-vĭl)	Mass. (Boston In.)	42·06 N	71·40 W
83	Whitman (hwĭt′măn)	Mass. (Boston In.)	42·05 N	70·57 W
66	Whitman Natl. Mon	Ore.	45·58 N	118·10 W
79	Whitmire (hwĭt′mīr)	S. C.	34·30 N	81·40 W
68	Whitney, Mt.	Calif.	36·34 N	118·18 W
77	Whitney L. (hwĭt′nē)	Tex.	32·02 N	97·36 W
110	Whitstable (wĭt′stȧb′l)	Eng. (London In.)	51·22 N	1·03 E
159	Whitsunday (I.) (hwĭt′s′n-dā)	Austl.	20·16 S	149·00 E
74	Whittier (hwĭt′ĭ-ẽr)	Calif. (Los Angeles In.)	33·58 N	118·02 W
167	Whittlesea (wĭt′l′sē)	S. Afr. (Natal In.)	32·11 S	26·51 E
110	Whitworth (hwĭt′wŭrth)	Eng.	53·40 N	2·10 W
160	Whyalla (hwī-ăl′a)	Austl.	33·00 S	137·32 E
80	Wiarton (wī′ȧr-tŭn)	Can.	44·45 N	80·45 W
73	Wichita (wĭch′ĭ-tô)	Kans.	37·42 N	97·21 W
72	Wichita (R.)	Tex.	33·50 N	99·38 W
72	Wichita Falls (fôls)	Tex.	33·54 N	98·29 W
72	Wichita Mts.	Okla.	34·48 N	98·43 W
116	Wick (wĭk)	Scot.	58·25 N	3·05 W
84	Wickatunk (wĭk′á-tŭnk)	N. J. (New York In.)	40·21 N	74·15 W
84	Wickford (wĭk′fẽrd)	R. I. (Providence In.)	41·34 N	71·26 W
75	Wickliffe (wĭk′klĭf)	Ohio (Cleveland In.)	41·37 N	81·29 W
	Wicklow, see Cill Mantainn			
116	Wicklow Mts. (wĭk′lō)	Ire.	52·49 N	6·20 W
65	Wickup Mtn. (wĭk′ŭp)	Ore. (Portland In.)	46·06 N	123·35 W
81	Wiconisco (wĭ-kŏn′ĭs-kō)	Pa.	40·35 N	76·45 W
80	Widen (wī′dĕn)	W. Va.	38·25 N	80·55 W
110	Widnes (wĭd′nĕs)	Eng.	53·21 N	2·44 W
120	Wieden (vē′dĕn)	Ger.	49·41 N	12·09 E
121	Wieliczka (vyĕ-lēch′kȧ)	Pol.	49·58 N	20·06 E
121	Wieluń (vyĕ′lōōn′)	Pol.	51·13 N	18·33 E
111	Wien (Vienna) (vēn) (vē-ĕn′ä)	Aus. (Vienna In.)	48·13 N	16·22 E
111	Wien (State)	Aus. (Vienna In.)	48·11 N	16·23 E
120	Wiener Neustadt (vē′nĕr noi′shtät)	Aus.	47·48 N	16·15 E
111	Wiener Wald (For.)	Aus. (Vienna In.)	48·09 N	16·05 E
121	Wieprz, R. (vyĕpzh)	Pol.	51·25 N	22·45 E
77	Wiergate (wẽr′gāt)	Tex.	31·00 N	93·42 W
120	Wiesbaden (vēs′bä-dĕn)	Ger.	50·05 N	8·15 E
110	Wigan (wĭg′ăn)	Eng.	53·33 N	2·37 W
78	Wiggins (wĭg′ĭnz)	Miss.	30·51 N	89·05 W
116	Wight, Isle of (I.) (wīt)	Eng.	50·44 N	1·17 W
73	Wilber (wĭl′bẽr)	Nebr.	40·29 N	96·57 W
73	Wilburton (wĭl′bẽr-tŭn)	Okla.	34·54 N	95·18 W
160	Wilcannia (wĭl-cān-ĭȧ)	Austl.	31·30 S	143·30 E
111	Wildau (vēl′dou)	Ger. (Berlin In.)	52·20 N	13·39 E
111	Wildberg (vēl′bĕrgh)	Ger. (Berlin In.)	52·52 N	12·39 E
74	Wildomar (wĭl′dô-mär)	Calif. (Los Angeles In.)	33·35 N	117·17 W
70	Wild Rice (R.)	Minn.	47·10 N	96·40 W
70	Wild Rice (R.)	N. D.	46·10 N	97·12 W
74	Wild Rice L.	Minn. (Duluth In.)	46·54 N	92·10 W
120	Wild Spitze Pk.	Aus.	46·49 N	10·50 E
81	Wildwood (wīld′wŏŏd)	N. J.	39·00 N	74·50 W
72	Wiley (wī′lē)	Colo.	38·08 N	102·41 W
168	Wilge R. (wĭl′jē)	S. Afr. (Johannesburg & Pretoria In.)	25·38 S	29·09 E
168	Wilge R.	S. Afr. (Johannesburg & Pretoria In.)	27·27 S	28·46 E
155	Wilhelm, Mt.	N. Gui. Ter.	5·58 S	144·58 E
99	Wilhelmina Gebergte (Mts.)	Sur.	4·30 N	57·00 W
155	Wilhelmina-Top (Pk.) (vĕl-hĕl-mē′nȧ)	W. Irian	3·55 S	138·26 E
120	Wilhelmshaven (vĕl-hĕlms-hä′fĕn)	Ger.	53·30 N	8·10 E
111	Wilhemina, Kanal (can.)	Neth. (Amsterdam In.)	51·37 N	4·55 E
81	Wilkes-Barre (wĭlks′băr-ē)	Pa.	41·15 N	75·50 W
47	Wilkes Land	Ant.	71·00 S	126·00 E
65	Wilkeson (wĭl-kē′sŭn)	Wash. (Seattle In.)	47·06 N	122·03 W
86	Wilkie (wĭlk′ē)	Can.	52·29 N	108·50 W
75	Wilkinsburg (wĭl′kĭnz-bûrg)	Pa. (Pittsburgh In.)	40·26 N	79·53 W
66	Willamette R.	Ore.	44·15 N	123·13 W
80	Willard (wĭl′ȧrd)	Ohio	41·00 N	82·50 W
74	Willard	Utah (Salt Lake City In.)	41·24 N	112·02 W
69	Willcox (wĭl′kŏks)	Ariz.	32·15 N	109·50 W
98	Willemstad	Curaçao	12·12 N	68·58 W
110	Willenhall (wĭl′ĕn-hôl)	Eng.	52·35 N	2·03 W
110	Willesden (wĭlz′dĕn)	Eng. (London In.)	51·31 N	0·17 W
158	William Creek (wĭl′yăm)	Austl.	28·45 S	136·20 E
69	Williams (wĭl′yămz)	Ariz.	35·15 N	112·15 W
94	Williams (I.)	Ba. Is.	25·30 N	78·30 W
78	Williamsburg (wĭl′yămz-bûrg)	Ky.	36·42 N	84·09 W
75	Williamsburg	Ohio (Cincinnati In.)	39·04 N	84·02 W
79	Williamsburg	Va.	37·15 N	76·41 W
80	Williamson (wĭl′yăm-sŭn)	W. Va.	37·40 N	82·15 W
81	Williamsport (wĭl′yămz-pōrt)	Md.	39·35 N	77·45 W
81	Williamsport	Pa.	41·15 N	77·05 W
79	Williamston (wĭl′yămz-tŭn)	N. C.	35·50 N	77·04 W
79	Williamston	S. C.	34·36 N	82·30 W
80	Williamstown (wĭl′yămz-toun)	W. Va.	39·20 N	81·30 W
75	Williamsville (wĭl′yăm-vĭl)	N. Y. (Buffalo In.)	42·58 N	78·46 W
81	Willimantic (wĭl-ĭ-măn′tĭk)	Conn.	41·40 N	72·10 W
77	Willis (wĭl′ĭs)	Tex.	30·24 N	95·29 W
159	Willis Is.	Austl.	16·15 S	150·30 E
70	Williston (wĭl′ĭs-tŭn)	N. D.	48·08 N	103·38 W
75	Willoughby (wĭl′ô-bē)	Ohio (Cleveland In.)	41·39 N	81·25 W
67	Willow Cr. (wĭl′ô)	Mont.	48·45 N	111·34 W
66	Willow Cr.	Ore.	44·21 N	117·34 W
85	Willowdale (wĭl′ô-dāl)	Can. (Toronto In.)	43·47 N	79·25 W
84	Willow Grove	Pa. (Philadelphia In.)	40·07 N	75·07 W
74	Willowick (wĭl′ô-wĭk)	Calif. (Los Angeles In.)	33·45 N	117·55 W
75	Willowick	Ohio (Cleveland In.)	41·39 N	81·28 W
166	Willowmore (wĭl′ô-môr)	S. Afr.	33·15 S	23·37 E
75	Willow Run (wĭl′ô rŭn)	Mich. (Detroit In.)	42·16 N	83·34 W
68	Willows (wĭl′ōz)	Calif.	39·32 N	122·11 W
73	Willow Springs (sprĭngz)	Mo.	36·59 N	91·56 W
167	Willowvale (wĭ-lô′vāl)	S. Afr. (Natal In.)	32·17 S	28·32 E
77	Wills Point (wĭlz point)	Tex.	32·42 N	96·02 W
71	Wilmar (wĭl′mär)	Minn.	45·07 N	95·05 W
74	Wilmer (wĭl′mẽr)	Tex. (Dallas, Fort Worth In.)	32·35 N	96·40 W
75	Wilmette (wĭl-mĕt′)	Ill. (Chicago In.)	42·04 N	87·42 W
74	Wilmington (wĭl′mĭng-tŭn)	Calif. (Los Angeles In.)	33·46 N	118·16 W
84	Wilmington	Del. (Philadelphia In.)	39·45 N	75·33 W
75	Wilmington	Ill. (Chicago In.)	41·19 N	88·09 W
83	Wilmington	Mass. (Boston In.)	42·34 N	71·10 W
79	Wilmington	N. C.	34·12 N	77·56 W
80	Wilmington	Ohio	39·20 N	83·50 W
80	Wilmore (wĭl′mōr)	Ky.	37·50 N	84·35 W
110	Wilmslow (wĭlmz′ lō)	Eng.	53·19 N	2·14 W
	Wilno, see Vilnius			
73	Wilson (wĭl′sŭn)	Ark.	35·35 N	90·02 W
79	Wilson	N. C.	35·42 N	77·55 W
73	Wilson	Okla.	34·09 N	97·27 W
78	Wilson, L.	Ala.	34·45 N	86·58 W
78	Wilson (R.)	Ala.	34·53 N	87·28 W
161	Wilson, Pt.	Austl. (Melbourne In.)	38·05 S	144·31 E
74	Wilson, Mt.	Calif. (Los Angeles In.)	34·15 N	118·06 W
71	Wilson (I.)	Can.	48·48 N	87·23 W
67	Wilson Pk.	Utah	40·46 N	110·27 W
160	Wilson's Prom. (wĭl′sŭnz)	Austl.	39·05 S	146·50 E
74	Wilsonville (wĭl′sŭn-vĭl)	Ill. (St. Louis In.)	39·04 N	89·52 W
111	Wilstedt (vēl′shtĕt)	Ger. (Hamburg In.)	53·45 N	10·04 E
111	Wilster (vēl′stĕr)	Ger. (Hamburg In.)	53·55 N	9·23 E
84	Wilton (wĭl′tŭn)	Conn. (New York In.)	41·11 N	73·25 W
70	Wilton	N. D.	47·90 N	100·47 W
158	Wiluna (wĭ-lōō′nȧ)	Austl.	26·35 S	120·25 E
80	Winamac (wĭn′ȧ măk)	Ind.	41·05 N	86·40 W
169	Winburg (wĭm-bûrg)	S. Afr. (Johannesburg & Pretoria In.)	28·31 S	27·02 E
74	Winchester (wĭn′chĕs-tẽr)	Calif. (Los Angeles In.)	33·41 N	117·06 W
116	Winchester	Eng.	51·04 N	1·20 W
66	Winchester	Idaho	46·14 N	116·39 W
80	Winchester	Ind.	40·10 N	84·50 W
80	Winchester	Ky.	38·00 N	84·15 W
83	Winchester	Mass. (Boston In.)	42·28 N	71·09 W
81	Winchester	N. H.	42·45 N	72·25 W
78	Winchester	Tenn.	35·11 N	86·06 W
81	Winchester	Va.	39·40 N	78·10 W
81	Windber (wĭnd′bẽr)	Pa.	40·15 N	78·45 W
70	Wind Cave Natl. Park	S. D.	43·36 N	103·53 W
78	Winder (wīn′dẽr)	Ga.	33·58 N	83·43 W
116	Windermere (wĭn′dẽr-mēr)	Eng.	54·25 N	2·59 W
81	Windham (wĭnd′ăm)	Conn.	41·45 N	72·05 W
83	Windham	N. H. (Boston In.)	42·49 N	71·21 W
166	Windhoek (vĭnt′hŏŏk)	S. W. Afr.	22·05 S	17·10 E
75	Wind L.	Wis. (Milwaukee In.)	42·49 N	88·06 W
76	Wind Mtn.	N. Mex.	32·02 N	105·30 W
71	Windom (wĭn′dŭm)	Minn.	43·50 N	95·04 W
160	Windora (wĭn-dō′rȧ)	Austl.	25·15 S	142·50 E
67	Wind R.	Wyo.	43·17 N	109·02 W
67	Wind River Ind Res	Wyo.	43·07 N	109·08 W
67	Wind River Ra	Wyo.	43·19 N	109·47 W
161	Windsor (wĭn′zẽr)	Austl. (Sydney In.)	33·37 S	150·49 E
75	Windsor	Can. (Detroit In.)	42·19 N	83·00 W
82	Windsor	Can.	44·59 N	64·07 W
83	Windsor	Can.	49·00 N	55·39 W
72	Windsor	Colo.	40·27 N	104·51 W
110	Windsor	Eng. (London In.)	51·27 N	0·37 W
73	Windsor	Mo.	38·32 N	93·31 W
82	Windsor	Vt.	43·30 N	72·25 W
79	Windsor	N. C.	35·58 N	76·57 W
89	Windward Is. (wĭnd′wẽrd)	N. A.	12·45 N	61·40 W
95	Windward Pass	N. A.	19·30 N	74·20 W
73	Winfield (wĭn′fēld)	Kans.	37·14 N	97·00 W
87	Wingham (wĭn′gȧm)	Can.	43·48 N	81·23 W
67	Winifred (wĭn ĭ frĕd)	Mont.	47·35 N	109·20 W
76	Wink (wĭŋk)	Tex.	31·48 N	103·06 W
164	Winneba (wĭn′ē-bȧ)	Ghana	5·29 N	0·43 W
71	Winnebago (wĭn′ē-bā′gō)	Minn	43·45 N	94·08 W
71	Winnebago, L.	Wis.	44·09 N	88·10 W
70	Winnebago Ind. Res.	Nebr.	42·15 N	96·06 W
66	Winnemucca (wĭn-ē-mŭk′ȧ)	Nev.	40·59 N	117·43 W
68	Winnemucca (L.)	Nev.	40·06 N	119·07 W
70	Winner (wĭn′ẽr)	S. D.	43·22 N	99·50 W
75	Winnetka (wĭ-nĕt′kȧ)	Ill. (Chicago In.)	42·07 N	87·44 W
67	Winnett (wĭn′ĕt)	Mont.	47·01 N	108·20 W
77	Winnfield (wĭn′fēld)	La.	31·56 N	92·39 W
71	Winnibigoshish (L.) (wĭn′ĭ-bĭ-gō′shĭsh)	Minn.	47·30 N	93·45 W
85	Winnipeg (wĭn′ĭ-pĕg)	Can. (Winnipeg In.)	49·55 N	97·09 W
86	Winnipeg, L.	Can.	53·29 N	98·41 W
86	Winnipeg (R.)	Can.	50·30 N	95·34 W
86	Winnipegosis (wĭn′ĭ-pē-gō′sĭs)	Can.	51·40 N	100·01 W
86	Winnipegosis (L.)	Can.	52·19 N	101·40 W
81	Winnipesaukee (L.) (wĭn′ē-pē-sô′kē)	N. H.	43·40 N	71·20 W
77	Winnsboro (wĭnz′bŭr-ô)	La.	32·09 N	91·42 W
79	Winnsboro	S. C.	34·29 N	81·05 W
73	Winnsboro	Tex.	32·56 N	95·15 W
85	Winona (wĭ-nō′nȧ)	Can. (Toronto In.)	43·13 N	79·39 W
71	Winona	Minn.	44·03 N	91·40 W
78	Winona	Miss.	33·29 N	89·43 W
81	Winooski (wĭ-nōōs′kē)	Vt.	44·30 N	73·10 W
111	Winsen (Luhe) (vēn′zĕn)(lōō′hĕ)	Ger. (Hamburg In.)	53·22 N	10·13 E
110	Winsford (wĭnz′fẽrd)	Eng.	53·11 N	2·30 W

ng-sing; ŋ-baŋk; N-nasalized n; nŏd; cŏmmit; ōld; ôbey; ôrder; fōōd; fŏŏt; ou-out; s-soft; sh-dish; th-thin; pūre; ûnite; ûrn; stŭd: circŭs; ü-as "y" in study; '-indeterminate vowel.

286 Winslow–Yamasaki PRONOUNCING INDEX

Page	Name Pronunciation Region	Lat. °′	Long. °′
69	Winslow (wĭnz'lō) Ariz.	35·00 N	110·45 W
65	Winslow Wash. (Seattle In.)	47·38 N	122·31 W
81	Winsted (wĭn'stĕd) Conn.	41·55 N	73·05 W
110	Winster (wĭn'stẽr) Eng.	53·08 N	1·38 W
79	Winston-Salem (wĭn stŭn-sā'lĕm) N. C.	36·05 N	80·15 W
167	Winterberg (Mts.) S. Afr. (Natal In.)	32·18 S	26·25 E
79	Winter Garden (wĭn'tẽr gär'd'n) Fla. (In.)	28·32 N	81·35 W
79	Winter Haven (hā'vĕn) Fla. (In.)	28·01 N	81·38 W
79	Winter Park (pärk) Fla. (In.)	28·35 N	81·21 W
76	Winters (wĭn'tẽrz) Tex.	31·59 N	99·58 W
71	Winterset (wĭn'tẽr-sĕt) Iowa	41·19 N	94·03 W
123	Winterswijk Neth. (Ruhr In.)	51·58 N	6·44 E
120	Winterthur (vĭn'tẽr-tōōr) Switz.	47·30 N	8·32 E
167	Winterton (wĭn-tẽr-tŏn) S. Afr. (Natal In.)	28·51 S	29·33 E
82	Winthrop (wĭn'thrŭp) Maine	44·19 N	70·00 W
83	Winthrop Mass. (Boston In.)	42·23 N	70·59 W
71	Winthrop Minn.	44·31 N	94·20 W
159	Winton (wĭn-tŭn) Austl.	22·17 S	143·08 E
123	Wipperfürth (vē'pẽr-fürt) Ger. (Ruhr In.)	51·07 N	7·23 E
110	Wirksworth (wûrks'wûrth) Eng.	53·05 N	1·35 W
63	Wisconsin (State) (wĭs-kŏn'sĭn) U. S.	44·30 N	91·00 W
71	Wisconsin (R.) Wis.	43·14 N	90·34 W
71	Wisconsin Dells Wis.	43·38 N	89·46 W
71	Wisconsin Rapids Wis.	44·24 N	89·50 W
70	Wishek (wĭsh'ĕk) N. D.	46·15 N	99·34 W
121	Wisla (Vistula) R. (vês'wȧ) (vĭs'tū-lȧ). Pol.	52·48 N	19·02 E
121	Wisloka R. (vês-wô'kȧ) Pol.	49·55 N	21·26 E
99	Wismar (wĭs'mȧr) Guy.	5·58 N	58·15 W
120	Wismar (vĭs'mär) Ger.	53·53 N	11·28 E
70	Wisner (wĭz'nẽr) Nebr.	42·00 N	96·55 W
123	Wissembourg (vē-säN-bōōr') Fr.	49·03 N	7·58 E
166	Wissmann Pool (L.) Con. K.	3·18 S	17·28 E
73	Wister Res. (vĭs'tẽr) Okla.	35·02 N	94·52 W
168	Witbank (wĭt-băŋk) S. Afr. (Johannesburg & Pretoria In.)	25·53 S	29·14 E
110	Witham (wĭdh'ăm) Eng. (London In.)	51·48 N	0·37 E
110	Witham (R.) Eng.	53·11 N	0·20 W
75	Withamsville (wĭdh'ămz-vĭl) Ohio (Cincinnati In.)	39·04 N	84·16 W
79	Withlacoochee (R.) (wĭth-lȧ-kōō'chē). Fla. (In.)	28·58 N	82·30 W
78	Withlacoochee (R.) Ga.	31·15 N	83·30 W
74	Withrow (wĭdh'rō) Minn. (Minneapolis, St. Paul In.)	45·08 N	92·54 W
110	Witney (wĭt'nē) Eng. (London In.)	51·45 N	1·30 W
168	Witpoort S. Afr. (Johannesburg & Pretoria In.)	26·57 S	26·17 E
168	Witsieshoek (wĭt'sēz-hŏŏk) S. Afr. (Johannesburg & Pretoria In.)	28·33 S	28·48 E
80	Witt (vĭt) Ill.	39·10 N	89·15 W
123	Witten (vē'tĕn) Ger. (Ruhr In.)	51·26 N	7·19 E
120	Wittenberg (vē'tĕn-bĕrgh) Ger.	51·53 N	12·40 E
120	Wittenberge (vĭt-ĕn-bĕr'gē) Ger.	52·59 N	11·45 E
120	Wittlich (vĭt'lĭk) Ger.	49·58 N	6·54 E
167	Witu (wē'tōō) Ken.	2·18 S	40·28 E
167	Witwatersberg (Mts.) (wĭt-wôr-tẽrz-bûrg). S. Afr. (Johannesburg & Pretoria In.)	25·58 S	27·43 E
168	Witwatersrand (Ridge) (wĭt-wôr'tẽrs-rănd). S. Afr. (Johannesburg & Pretoria In.)	25·55 S	26·27 E
121	Wkra R. (f'krȧ) Pol.	52·40 N	20·35 E
121	Włocławek (vwô-tswä'vĕk) Pol.	52·38 N	19·08 E
121	Włodawa (vwô-dä'vä) Pol.	51·33 N	23·33 E
121	Włoszczowa (vwôsh-chô'vä) Pol.	50·51 N	19·58 E
83	Woburn (wōō'bŭrn) (wō'bŭrn) Mass. (Boston In.)	42·29 N	71·10 W
111	Woerden Neth. (Amsterdam In.)	52·05 N	4·52 E
110	Woking (wō'kĭng) Eng. (London In.)	51·18 N	0·33 W
110	Wokingham (wō'kĭng-hăm) Eng. (London In.)	51·23 N	0·50 W
74	Wolcott (wōl'kŏt) Kans. (Kansas City In.)	39·12 N	94·47 W
81	Wolf (I.) (wŏŏlf) Can.	44·10 N	76·25 W
78	Wolf (R.) Miss.	30·45 N	89·36 W
71	Wolf (R.) Wis.	45·14 N	88·45 W
120	Wolfenbüttel (vôl'fĕn-büt-ĕl) Ger.	52·10 N	10·32 E
75	Wolf L. Ill. (Chicago In.)	41·39 N	87·33 W
67	Wolf Point (wŏŏlf point) Mont.	48·07 N	105·40 W
111	Wolfratshausen (vōlf'räts-hou-zĕn) Ger. (Munich In.)	47·55 N	11·25 E
120	Wolfsburg (vôlfs'bŏŏrgh) Ger.	52·30 N	10·37 E
82	Wolfville (wŏŏlf'vĭl) Can.	45·06 N	64·02 W
120	Wolgast (vôl'gäst) Ger.	54·04 N	13·46 E
167	Wolhuterskop S. Afr. (Johannesburg & Pretoria In.)	25·41 S	27·40 E
111	Wolkersdorf Aus. (Vienna In.)	48·24 N	16·31 E
86	Wollaston (L.) (wŏŏl'ȧs-tŭn) Can.	58·03 N	105·00 W
86	Wollaston Pen. Can.	69·55 N	115·13 W
160	Wollongong (wŏŏl'ŭn-gŏng) Austl.	34·26 S	151·05 E
121	Wołomin (vô-wō'mēn) Pol.	52·19 N	21·17 E
110	Wolstanton (wŏŏl-stăn'tŭn) Eng.	53·02 N	2·13 W
111	Woltersdorf (vōl'tẽrs-dōrf) Ger. (Berlin In.)	52·07 N	13·13 E
110	Wolverhampton (wŏŏl'vẽr-hămp-tŭn). Eng.	52·35 N	2·07 W
168	Wolwehoek S. Afr. (Johannesburg & Pretoria In.)	26·55 S	27·50 E
152	Wŏnsan (wŭn'sän') Kor.	39·08 N	127·24 E
160	Wonthaggi (wŏnt-hăg'ē) Austl.	38·45 S	145·42 E
70	Wood (wŏŏd) S. D.	43·26 N	100·25 W
70	Woodbine (wŏŏd'bīn) Iowa	41·44 N	95·42 W
85	Woodbridge (wŏŏd'brĭj') Can. (Toronto In.)	43·47 N	79·36 W
84	Woodbridge. N. J. (New York In.)	40·33 N	74·18 W
86	Wood Buffalo Natl. Park Can.	59·50 N	118·53 W
74	Woodburn (wŏŏd'bûrn) Ill. (St. Louis In.)	39·03 N	90·01 W
66	Woodburn Ore.	45·10 N	122·51 W
84	Woodbury (wŏŏd'bĕr-ē) N. J. (Philadelphia In.)	39·50 N	75·14 W
74	Woodcrest (wŏŏd'krĕst) Calif. (Los Angeles In.)	33·53 N	117·18 W
65	Woodinville (wŏŏd'ĭn-vĭl) Wash. (Seattle In.)	47·46 N	122·09 W
68	Woodland (wŏŏd'lănd) Calif.	38·41 N	121·47 W
65	Woodland Wash. (Portland In.)	45·54 N	122·45 W
74	Woodland Hills Calif. (Los Angeles In.)	34·10 N	118·36 W
155	Woodlark (I.) (wŏŏd'lärk) Pap.	9·07 S	152·00 E
75	Woodlawn Beach (wŏŏd'lôn bēch) N. Y. (Buffalo In.)	42·48 N	78·51 W
74	Wood River Ill. (St. Louis In.)	38·52 N	90·06 W
158	Woodroffe, Mt. (wŏŏd'rŭf) Austl.	26·05 S	132·00 E
79	Woodruff (wŏŏd'rŭf) S. C.	34·43 N	82·03 W
75	Woodruff Place Ind. (Indianapolis In.)	39·47 N	86·07 W
158	Woods (L.) (wŏŏdz) Austl.	18·00 S	133·18 E
63	Woods, L. of the Can.-Minn.	49·25 N	93·25 W
74	Woods Cross (krŏs) Utah (Salt Lake City In.)	40·53 N	111·54 W
80	Woodsfield (wŏŏdz-fēld) Ohio	39·45 N	81·10 W
65	Woodson (wŏŏdsŭn) Ore. (Portland In.)	46·07 N	123·20 W
80	Woodstock (wŏŏd'stŏk) Can.	43·10 N	80·50 W
82	Woodstock Can.	46·09 N	67·36 W
110	Woodstock Eng. (London In.)	51·49 N	1·22 W
71	Woodstock Ill.	42·20 N	88·29 W
81	Woodstock Va.	38·55 N	78·25 W
81	Woodsville (wŏŏdz'vĭl) N. H.	44·10 N	72·00 W
78	Woodville (wŏŏd'vĭl) Miss.	31·06 N	91·11 W
77	Woodville Tex.	30·48 N	94·25 W
72	Woodward (wŏŏd'wôrd) Okla.	36·25 N	99·24 W
110	Woolwich (wŏŏl'ĭj) Eng. (London In.)	51·28 N	0·05 E
160	Woomera (wōōm'ẽrȧ) Austl.	31·15 S	136·43 E
84	Woonsocket (wōōn-sŏk'ĕt) R. I. (Providence In.)	42·00 N	71·30 W
70	Woonsocket S. D.	44·03 N	98·17 W
80	Wooster (wŏŏs'tẽr) Ohio	40·50 N	81·55 W
116	Worcester (wŏŏ-stẽr) Eng.	52·09 N	2·14 W
166	Worcester (wŏŏs'tẽr) S. Afr.	33·35 S	19·31 E
110	Worcester (Co.) (wŏŏ'stẽr) Eng.	52·24 N	2·15 W
83	Worcester (wôr'chĕs-tẽr) Mass. (Boston In.)	42·16 N	71·49 W
74	Worden (wôr'dĕn) Ill. (St. Louis In.)	38·56 N	89·50 W
116	Workington (wûr'kĭng-tŭn) Eng.	54·40 N	3·30 W
110	Worksop (wûrk'sŏp) (wûr'sŭp) Eng.	53·18 N	1·07 W
67	Worland (wûr'lănd) Wyo.	44·02 N	107·56 W
120	Worms (vōrms) Ger.	49·37 N	8·22 E
161	Worona Res. Austl. (Sydney In.)	34·12 S	150·55 E
75	Worth (wûrth) Ill. (Chicago In.)	41·42 N	87·47 W
74	Worth L. Tex. (Dallas, Fort Worth In.)	32·48 N	97·32 W
77	Wortham (wûr'dhăm) Tex.	31·46 N	96·22 W
116	Worthing (wûr'dhĭng) Eng.	50·48 N	0·29 W
80	Worthington (wûr'dhĭng-tŭn) Ind.	39·05 N	87·00 W
70	Worthington Minn.	43·38 N	95·36 W
155	Wowoni (I.) (wō-wō'nē) Indon.	4·05 S	123·45 E
110	Wragby (răg'bē) Eng.	53·17 N	0·19 W
64	Wrangell (răn'gĕl) Alaska	56·28 N	132·25 W
64	Wrangell, Mt. Alaska	61·58 N	143·50 W
64	Wrangell Mts. Alaska-Can.	62·28 N	142·40 W
116	Wrath, C. (răth) Scot.	58·34 N	5·01 W
72	Wray (rā) Colo.	40·06 N	102·14 W
101	Wreak (R.) (rēk) Eng.	52·45 N	0·59 W
159	Wreck Rfs. (rĕk) Austl.	22·00 S	155·52 E
110	Wrekin, The (Mt.) (rĕk'ĭn) Eng.	52·40 N	2·33 W
79	Wrens (rĕnz) Ga.	33·15 N	82·25 W
83	Wrentham (rĕn'thăm) Mass. (Boston In.)	42·04 N	71·20 W
110	Wrexham (rĕk'săm) Wales	53·03 N	3·00 W
75	Wrights Corners (rīts kôr'nẽrz) N. Y. (Buffalo In.)	43·14 N	78·42 W
79	Wrightsville (rīts'vĭl) Ga.	32·44 N	82·44 W
121	Wrocław (Breslau) (vrô'tsläv) (brĕs'lou). Pol.	51·07 N	17·10 E
110	Wrotham (rōōt'ăm) Eng. (London In.)	51·18 N	0·19 E
121	Września (vzhăsh'nyȧ) Pol.	52·19 N	17·33 E
151	Wuch'ang (wōō'chăng') China	30·32 N	114·25 E
150	Wuch'ang China	44·59 N	127·00 E
148	Wuchi (wōō'jē) China	38·12 N	114·57 E
148	Wuchiang (wōō'jĭăng) China	31·10 N	120·38 E
148	Wuch'iao (wōō'chĭou) China	37·37 N	116·29 E
150	Wuch'ing (wōō'chĭng') China (Peking In.)	39·32 N	116·51 E
151	Wu Chin Shan China	18·48 N	109·30 E
151	Wuchou (Tsangwu) (wōō'chō') China	23·32 N	111·25 E
151	Wuhan China	30·30 N	114·15 E
148	Wuhsi (wōō'sē) China	31·36 N	120·17 E
	Wuhsien, see Soochow		
151	Wuhsing China	30·38 N	120·10 E
148	Wuhu (wōō'hōō') China	31·22 N	118·22 E
151	Wui Shan (Mts.) China	26·38 N	116·35 E
152	Wulachieh (wōō'lä-kē'ā) China	44·08 N	126·25 E
	Wulanhata, see Ch'ihfeng		
154	Wu Liang Shan (Mts.) China	23·07 N	100·45 E
148	Wulitien (wōō'lē'dĭăn) China	32·09 N	114·17 E
111	Wünsdorf (vüns'dōrf) Ger. (Berlin In.)	52·10 N	13·29 E
69	Wupatki Natl. Mon. (wōō-păt'kē). Ariz.	35·36 N	111·45 W
151	Wup'ing (wōō'pĭng') China	25·05 N	116·01 E
123	Wuppertal (vŏŏp'ẽr-täl) Ger. (Ruhr In.)	51·16 N	7·14 E
151	Wu R. (wōō') China	27·30 N	108·00 E
111	Würm (R.) Ger.	48·50 N	11·17 E
120	Würm See (L.) (vürm zā) Ger.	47·58 N	11·30 E
123	Würselen (vür'zĕ-lĕn) Ger. (Ruhr In.)	50·49 N	6·09 E
120	Würzburg (vürts'bŏŏrgh) Ger.	49·48 N	9·57 E
120	Wurzen (vŏŏrt'sĕn) Ger.	51·22 N	12·45 E
146	Wushih (Uch Turfan) (wōō'shĭ) (ōōch' tōōr-făn'). China	41·13 N	79·08 E
111	Wustermark (vōōs'tĕr-märk) Ger. (Berlin In.)	52·33 N	12·57 E
111	Wustrau (vōōst'rou) Ger. (Berlin In.)	52·51 N	12·51 E
146	Wusu (Kweitun) (wōō'sōō') (kwā'tōōn'). China	44·28 N	84·07 E
149	Wusung (wōō'sōōng) China (Shanghai In.)	31·23 N	121 29 E
111	Wuustwezel Bel. (Brussels In.)	51·23 N	4·36 E
148	Wuwei (wōō'wā') China	31·19 N	117·53 E
148	Wuyang (wōō'yăng) China	33·16 N	113·37 E
148	Wuyuch'ang China	33·18 N	120·15 E
147	Wuyün (wōō-yün') China	48·51 N	130·06 E
75	Wyandotte (wī'ăn-dŏt) Mich. (Detroit In.)	42·12 N	83·10 W
110	Wye (wī) Eng. (London In.)	51·12 N	0·57 E
110	Wye (R.) Eng.	53·14 N	1·46 W
73	Wymore (wī'mōr) Nebr.	40·09 N	96·41 W
166	Wynberg (wĭn'bĕrg) S. Afr. (Cape Town In.)	34·00 S	18·28 E
158	Wyndham (wĭnd'ăm) Austl.	15·30 S	128·15 E
73	Wynne (wĭn) Ark.	35 12 N	90·46 W
73	Wynnewood (wĭn'wŏŏd) Okla.	34·39 N	97·10 W
73	Wynona (wī-nō'nȧ) Okla.	36·33 N	96·19 W
86	Wynyard (wĭn'yẽrd) Can.	51·48 N	104·13 W
75	Wyoming (wī-ō'mĭng) Ohio (Cincinnati In.)	39·14 N	84·28 W
62	Wyoming (State) U. S.	42·50 N	108·30 W
67	Wyoming Ra. Wyo.	42·43 N	110·35 W
110	Wyre Fon. (wīr) Eng.	52·24 N	2·24 W
121	Wysokie Mazowieckie (vê-sô'kyĕ mä-zô-vyĕts'kyĕ). Pol.	52·55 N	22·42 E
121	Wyszków (vêsh'kōōf) Pol.	52·35 N	21·29 E
79	Wytheville (wĭth'vĭl) Va.	36·55 N	81·06 W
94	Xagua, Banco (Bk.) (bä'n-kō-sä'gwä). Cuba	21·35 N	80·50 W
123	Xanten (ksän'tĕn). Ger. (Ruhr In.)	51·40 N	6·28 E
127	Xanthi Grc.	41·08 N	24·53 E
92	Xcalak (sä-lä'k) Mex. (Yucatan In.)	18·15 N	87·50 W
80	Xenia (zē'nĭ-ȧ) Ohio	39·40 N	83·55 W
90	Xicotencatl (sē-kô-tĕn-kät''l). Mex.	23·00 N	98·58 W
90	Xilitla (sē-lē'tlä) Mex.	21·24 N	98·59 W
99	Xingú (R.) (zhĕŋ-gōō') Braz.	6·20 S	52·34 W
90	Xochihuehuetlán (sô-chē-wĕ-wĕ-tlà'n). Mex.	17·53 N	98·29 W
91	Xochimilco (sō-chē-mēl'kô) Mex. (Mexico City In.)	19·15 N	99·06 W
151	Yaan China	30·00 N	103·20 E
121	Yablonitskiy Pereval (P.) (yáb-lô'nĭt-skĭ pĕ-rĕ-väl'). Sov. Un.	48·20 N	24·25 E
135	Yablonovyy Khrebet (Mts.) (yȧ-blô-nô-vê'). Sov. Un.	51·15 N	111·30 E
65	Yacolt (yă'kōlt) Wash. (Portland In.)	45·52 N	122·24 W
65	Yacolt (Mt.). Wash. (Portland In.)	45·52 N	122·27 W
78	Yacona (R.) (yă'cō nä) Miss.	34·13 N	89·30 W
100	Yacuiba (yä-kōō-ē'bä) Arg.	22·02 S	63·44 W
79	Yadkin (R.) (yăd'kĭn) N. C.	36·12 N	80·40 W
153	Yagi (yä'gē) Jap. (Ōsaka In.)	34·31 N	135·48 E
129	Yagotin (yä'gô-tēn) Sov. Un.	50·18 N	31·46 E
94	Yaguajay (yä-guä-hä'ē) Cuba	22·20 N	79·20 W
153	Yahagi-Gawa (Strm.) (yä'hä-gē gä'wä). Jap.	35·16 N	137·22 E
149	Yahu China (Canton In.)	23·19 N	113·17 E
90	Yahualica (yä-wä-lē'kä) Mex.	21·08 N	102·53 W
148	Yahungch'iao (yä'hōōng'chĭou) China	39·45 N	117·52 E
151	Yaihsien China	18·20 N	109·10 E
91	Yajalón (yä-hä-lōn') Mex.	17·16 N	92·20 W
136	Yakhroma (yäk'rô-mȧ) Sov. Un. (Moscow In.)	56·17 N	37·30 E
136	Yakhroma R. Sov. Un. (Moscow In.)	56·15 N	37·38 E
66	Yakima (yăk'ĭ-mȧ) Wash.	46·35 N	120·30 W
66	Yakima R. (yăk'ĭ-mȧ) Wash.	46·48 N	120·22 W
153	Yaku (I.) (yä'kōō) Jap.	30·15 N	130·41 E
135	Yakut A.S.S.R. Sov. Un.	65·21 N	117·13 E
64	Yakutat (yăk'ōō-tăt) Alaska	59·32 N	139·35 W
135	Yakutsk (yȧ-kŏŏtsk') Sov. Un.	62·13 N	129·49 E
152	Yal (R.) (yäl) China	48·20 N	122·35 E
80	Yale Mich.	43·05 N	82·45 W
73	Yale Okla.	36·07 N	96·42 W
66	Yale Res. Wash.	46·00 N	122·20 W
165	Yalinga (yȧ-lĭŋ'gȧ). Cen. Afr. Rep.	6·56 N	23·22 E
78	Yalobusha (R.) (yȧ-lô-bŏŏsh'ȧ) Miss.	33·48 N	90·02 W
129	Yalta (Krasnoarmeisk) (yäl'tȧ) (kräs-nô-är-măsk'). Sov. Un.	44·29 N	34·12 E
152	Yalu (Amnok) (R.) China-Kor.	41·20 N	126·35 E
146	Yalung Chiang (R.) (yä'lōōng') China	32·29 N	98·41 E
134	Yalutorovsk (yä-lōō-tô'rôfsk) Sov. Un.	56·42 N	66·32 E
153	Yamada (yä'mȧ-dȧ) Jap.	33·37 N	133·39 E
152	Yamagata (yä-mȧ'gȧ-tȧ) Jap.	38·12 N	140·24 E
153	Yamaguchi (yä-mȧ'gōō-chē) Jap.	34·10 N	131·30 E
134	Yamal, P-ov (Pen.) (yä-mäl') Sov. Un.	71·15 N	70·00 E
136	Yamantau, Gora (Mt.) (gȧ-rä' yä'măn-tȧw). Sov. Un. (Urals In.)	54·16 N	58·08 E
95	Yamasá (yä-mä'sä) Dom. Rep.	18·50 N	70·00 W
153	Yamasaki (yä'mȧ'sä-kē) Jap.	35·01 N	134·33 E
153	Yamasaki Jap. (Ōsaka In.)	34·53 N	135·41 E

ăt; finăl; rāte; senâte; ärm; àsk; sofȧ; fâre; ch-choose; dh-as th in other: bē: êvent; bĕt; recĕnt; cratẽr; g-go; gh-guttural g; bĭt; ĭ-short neutral; rīde; K-guttural k as ch in German ich;

Page	Name	Pronunciation	Region	Lat. °'	Long. °'
153	Yamashina	(yä'mä-shē'nä)	Jap. (Ōsaka In.)	34·59 N	135·50 E
153	Yamashita	(yä'mä-shē'tä)	Jap. (Ōsaka In.)	34·53 N	135·25 E
153	Yamato-takada	(yä'mä-tō tä'kä-dä)	Jap. (Ōsaka In.)	34·31 N	135·45 E
98	Yambi, Mesa de	(mĕ'sä-dĕ-yä'm-bē)	Col.	1·55 N	71·45 W
146	Yamdrog Tsho (L.)		China	29·11 N	91·26 E
146	Yamethin	(yŭ-mē'thĕn)	Bur.	20·14 N	96·27 E
65	Yamhill	(yăm'hĭl)	Ore. (Portland In.)	45·20 N	123·11 W
136	Yamkino	(yäm'kĭ-nô)	Sov. Un. (Moscow In.)	55·56 N	38·25 E
160	Yamma Yamma, L.	(yăm'ä yăm'ä)	Austl.	26·15 S	141·30 E
67	Yampa R.	(yăm'pá)	Colo.	40·29 N	108·12 W
135	Yamsk	(yämsk)	Sov. Un.	59·41 N	154·09 E
142	Yamuna (R.)		India	26·50 N	79·45 E
135	Yana (R.)	(yä'nä)	Sov. Un.	69·42 N	135·45 E
160	Yanac	(yän'äk)	Austl.	36·10 S	141·30 E
153	Yanagawa	(yä-nä'gä-wä)	Jap.	33·11 N	130·24 E
143	Yanam	(yŭnŭm')	India	16·48 N	82·15 E
144	Yanbu'al Bahr		Sau. Ar.	23·57 N	38·02 E
148	Yangch'eng Hu (L.)	(yäng'chĕng'hōō)	China	31·30 N	120·31 E
151	Yangchiang		China	21·52 N	111·58 E
148	Yangchiaokou	(yang'jēou'gō)	China	37·16 N	118·53 E
148	Yangchiat'an	(yäng'jēä'tän)	China	31·43 N	115·53 E
147	Yangchou		China	32·24 N	119·24 E
148	Yangch'uanchan		China	37·52 N	113·36 E
151	Yangch'un	(yäng'chōōn')	China	22·08 N	111·48 E
148	Yangerhchuang	(yäng'ē'jōōäng)	China	38·18 N	117·31 E
148	Yangho	(yäng'hŭ)	China	33·48 N	118·23 E
148	Yanghsin	(yäng'sín)	China	37·39 N	117·34 E
150	Yangkochuang		China (Peking In.)	40·10 N	116·48 E
148	Yangku	(yäng'kōō')	China	36·06 N	115·46 E
148	Yangsanmu	(yäng'sän'mōō)	China	38·28 N	117·18 E
147	Yangtze (R.)	(yäng'tsĕ')	China	30·30 N	117·25 E
152	Yangyang	(yäng'yäng')	Kor.	38·02 N	128·38 E
70	Yankton	(yănk'tŭn)	S. D.	42·51 N	97·24 W
	Yannina, see Ioánnina				
136	Yanychi	(yä'nĭ-chī')	Sov. Un. (Urals In.)	57·42 N	56·24 E
165	Yao	(yä'ō)	Chad	13·00 N	17·38 E
153	Yao		Jap. (Ōsaka In.)	34·37 N	135·36 E
164	Yaounde	(yä-ōōn-dā')	Cam.	3·58 N	11·45 E
156	Yap (yăp) (I.)		Pac. Is. Trust Ter.	11·00 N	138·00 E
95	Yaque del Norte (R.)	(yä'kä dĕl nôr'tä)	Dom. Rep.	19·40 N	71·25 W
95	Yaque del Sur (R.)	(yä-kĕ-dĕl-sōō'r)	Dom. Rep.	18·35 N	71·05 W
88	Yaqui (R.)	(yä'kē)	Mex.	28·15 N	109·40 W
99	Yaracuy (State)	(yä-rä-kōō'ē)	Ven. (In.)	10·10 N	68·31 W
160	Yaraka	(yä-räk'ä)	Austl.	24·50 S	144·08 E
132	Yaransk	(yä-ränsk')	Sov. Un.	57·18 N	48·05 E
165	Yarda (Well)	(yär'dä)	Chad	18·29 N	19·13 E
	Yarkand, see Soch'e				
142	Yarkand (R.)	(yär-känt')	India	36·11 N	76·10 E
82	Yarmouth	(yär'mŭth)	Can.	43·49 N	66·08 W
136	Yaroslavka	(yä-rô-släv'kä)	Sov. Un. (Urals In.)	55·52 N	57·59 E
128	Yaroslavl'	(yä-rô-släv''l)	Sov. Un.	57·57 N	39·54 E
128	Yaroslavl' (Oblast)		Sov. Un.	58·05 N	38·05 E
132	Yarra-to (L.)	(yä'rô-tō')	Sov. Un.	68·30 N	71·30 E
128	Yartsevo	(yär'tsyĕ-vô)	Sov. Un.	55·04 N	32·38 E
134	Yartsevo		Sov. Un.	60·13 N	89·52 E
98	Yarumal	(yä-rōō-mäl')	Col. (In.)	6·57 N	75·24 W
121	Yasel'da R.	(yä-syŭl'dä)	Sov. Un.	52·13 N	25·53 E
121	Yasinya		Sov. Un.	48·17 N	24·21 E
95	Yateras	(yä-tä'räs)	Cuba	20·00 N	75·00 W
73	Yates Center	(yäts)	Kans.	37·53 N	95·44 W
86	Yathkyed (L.)	(yăth-kī-ĕd')	Can.	62·38 N	97·12 W
153	Yatsuga-dake (Mtn.)	(yät'sōō-gä dä'kä)	Jap.	36·01 N	138·21 E
153	Yatsushiro	(yät'sōō-shē-rô)	Jap.	32·30 N	130·35 E
90	Yautepec	(yä-ōō-tä-pĕk')	Mex.	18·53 N	99·04 W
121	Yavorov	(yä'vô-rō'yĕ)	Sov. Un.	49·56 N	23·24 E
153	Yawata	(yä'wä-tä)	Jap. (Ōsaka In.)	34·52 N	135·43 E
153	Yawatahama	(yä'wä'tä'hä-mä)	Jap.	33·24 N	132·25 E
144	Yazd		Iran	31·59 N	54·03 E
78	Yazoo (R.)	(yă'zōō)	Miss.	32·32 N	90·40 W
78	Yazoo City		Miss.	32·50 N	90·18 W
154	Ye	(yā)	Bur.	15·13 N	97·52 E
84	Yeadon	(yē'dŭn)	Pa. (Philadelphia In.)	39·56 N	75·16 W
124	Yecla	(yā'klä)	Sp.	38·35 N	1·09 W
128	Yefremov	(yĕ-frä'môf)	Sov. Un.	53·08 N	38·04 E
128	Yegor'yevsk	(yĕ-gôr'yĕfsk)	Sov. Un.	55·23 N	38·59 E
148	Yehch'eng (Karghalik)	(yĕ'chĕng')	China	37·30 N	79·26 E
148	Yehhsien	(yĕ'sïän)	China	33·37 N	113·23 E
132	Yelabuga	(yĕ-lä'bōō-gä)	Sov. Un.	55·50 N	52·18 E
133	Yelan	(yĕ-län')	Sov. Un.	50·50 N	44·00 E
128	Yelcts	(yĕ-lyĕts)	Sov. Un.	52·35 N	38·28 E
136	Yelizavetpol'skiy	(yĕ'lĭ-za-vĕt-pôl-skĭ')	Sov. Un. (Urals In.)	52·51 N	60·38 E
135	Yelizavety, Mys (C.)	(yĕ-lyē-sä-vyē'tä)	Sov. Un.	54·28 N	142·59 E
116	Yell (I.)	(yĕl)	Scot.	60·35 N	1·27 W
78	Yellow (R.)	(yĕl'ō)	Fla.	30·33 N	86·53 W
86	Yellowknife	(yĕl'ō-nif)	Can.	62·29 N	114·38 W
	Yellow R., see Hwang Ho				
150	Yellow Sea		China	35·20 N	122·15 E
67	Yellowstone L.		Wyo.	44·27 N	110·03 W
67	Yellowstone Natl. Park	(yĕl'ō-stōn)	Wyo.	44·45 N	110·30 W
67	Yellowstone R.		Mont.	46·28 N	105·39 W
67	Yellowstone R., Clark Fk.		Wyo.	44·55 N	109·05 W
128	Yel'nya	(yĕl'nyä)	Sov. Un.	54·34 N	33·12 E
164	Yelwa	(yĕl'wä)	Nig.	8·57 N	9·44 E
136	Yemanzhelinsk	(yĕ-mán-zhä'lĭnsk)	Sov. Un. (Urals In.)	54·47 N	61·24 E
138	Yemen	(yĕm'ĕn)	Asia	15·45 N	44·30 E
132	Yemetsk		Sov. Un.	63·28 N	41·28 E
129	Yenakiyevo	(yĕ-nä'kĭ'yĕ-vô)	Sov. Un.	48·14 N	38·12 E
150	Yenan	(yĕ'nän')	China	36·35 N	109·32 E
146	Yenan (Fushih)		China	36·46 N	109·15 E
145	Yenangyaung	(yä'nän-d oung)	Bur.	20·27 N	94·59 E
148	Yench'eng	(yĕn'chĕng)	China	33·23 N	120·11 E
148	Yencheng	(yĕn'chĕng)	China	33·38 N	113·59 E
146	Yench'i	(yĕn'chī')	China	42·14 N	86·28 E
150	Yenchi		China	42·55 N	129·35 E
148	Yenchiaha	(yen'jēä'hŭ)	China	31·47 N	114·50 E
148	Yenchianchi	(yen'jēä'jē)	China	31·52 N	115·57 E
148	Yenching	(yĕn'jín)	China	33·09 N	114·13 E
148	Yenchuang	(yĕn'jōōäng)	China	36·08 N	117·47 E
164	Yendi	(yĕn'dē)	Ghana	9·21 N	0·02 E
133	Yenice (R.)		Tur.	41·10 N	33·00 E
134	Yenisei (R.)	(yĕ-nē-sē'ē)	Sov. Un.	67·48 N	87·15 E
134	Yeniseysk	(yĕ-nĭ-sā'ĭsk)	Sov. Un.	58·27 N	90·28 E
148	Yenling	(yĕn'líng')	China	34·07 N	114·12 E
148	Yenshan	(yĕn'shän')	China	38·05 N	117·15 E
150	Yenshou		China	45·25 N	128·43 E
148	Yent'ai (Chefoo)		China	37·32 N	121·22 E
158	Yeo (I.)	(yō)	Austl.	28·15 S	124·00 E
133	Yerevan	(yĕ-rĕ-vän')	Sov. Un.	40·10 N	44·30 E
116	Yerington	(yĕ'rĭng-tŭn)	Nev.	38·59 N	119·10 W
132	Yermak (I.)		Sov. Un.	66·30 N	71·30 E
124	Yeste	(yĕs'tä)	Sp.	38·23 N	2·19 W
122	Yeu, Île d' (I.)	(ēl dyü)	Fr.	46·43 N	2·45 W
129	Yevpatoriya	(yĕf-pä'tô-rĭ-yä)	Sov. Un.	45·13 N	33·22 E
129	Yeya (R.)	(yä'yä)	Sov. Un.	46·25 N	39·17 E
135	Yevrey Aut. Oblast		Sov. Un.	48·45 N	132·00 E
129	Yeysk	(yĕysk)	Sov. Un.	46·41 N	38·13 E
	Yg, see Yug				
127	Yiannitsá		Grc.	40·47 N	22·26 E
150	Yinch'uan (Ninghsia)		China	38·22 N	106·22 E
146	Yingchisha		China	39·01 N	75·29 E
150	Ying'ou	(yíng'kō')	China	40·35 N	122·10 E
149	Yinhang		China (Shanghai In.)	31·20 N	121·30 E
150	Yin Shan (Mtn.)	(yĭng'shän')	China	40·50 N	110·30 E
127	Yioúra (I.)		Grc.	37·52 N	24·42 E
127	Yíthion		Grc.	36·50 N	22·37 E
153	Ynasa	(yōō'ä-sä)	Jap.	34·02 N	135·10 E
77	Yoakum	(yō'kŭm)	Tex.	29·18 N	97·09 W
78	Yockanookany (R.)	(yŏk'á-nōō-kă-nī)	Miss.	32·47 N	89·38 W
153	Yodo-Gawa (Str.)	(yō'dō'gä-wä)	Jap. (Ōsaka In.)	34·46 N	135·35 E
151	Yog Pt.	(yŏg)	Phil.	14·00 N	124·30 E
86	Yoho Natl. Park	(yō'hō)	Can.	51·32 N	117·06 W
92	Yojoa, Lago de (L.)	(lä'gô dĕ yō-hō'ä)	Hond.	14·49 N	87·53 W
153	Yokkaichi	(yō'kä'ē-chē)	Jap.	34·58 N	136·35 E
153	Yokohama	(yō'kô-hä'mä)	Jap. (Tōkyō In.)	35·37 N	139·40 E
153	Yokosuka	(yô-ko'sōō-kä)	Jap. (Tōkyō In.)	35·17 N	139·40 E
153	Yokota	(yô-kō'tä)	Jap. (Tōkyō In.)	35·23 N	140·02 E
164	Yola	(yō'lä)	Nig.	9·13 N	12·27 E
93	Yolaina, Cord. de (Mts.)	(kôr-dĕl'yĕ'rä dĕ yō-lä-ē'nä)	Nic.	11·34 N	84·34 W
98	Yolombó	(yô-lôm-bō')	Col. (In.)	6·37 N	74·59 W
153	Yonago	(yō'nä-gô)	Jap.	35·27 N	133·19 E
152	Yonezawa	(yō'nĕ'zä-wä)	Jap.	37·50 N	140·07 E
152	Yŏngdŏk	(yŏng'dŭk')	Kor.	36·28 N	129·25 E
152	Yŏnghŭng	(yŭng'hŏong')	Kor.	39·31 N	127·11 E
152	Yonghŭng Man (B.)		Kor.	39·10 N	128·00 E
84	Yonkers	(yŏn'kĕrz)	N. Y. (New York In.)	40·57 N	73·54 W
122	Yonne (R.)	(yôn)	Fr.	48·18 N	3·15 E
153	Yono	(yō'nō)	Jap. (Tōkyō In.)	35·53 N	139·36 E
74	Yorba Linda		Calif. (Los Angeles In.)	33·55 N	117·51 W
78	York	(yôrk)	Ala.	32·33 N	88·16 W
158	York		Austl.	32·00 S	117·00 E
116	York		Eng.	53·58 N	1·10 W
73	York		Nebr.	40·52 N	97·36 W
81	York		Pa.	40·00 N	76·40 W
79	York		S. C.	34·59 N	81·14 W
159	York, C.		Austl.	10·45 S	142·35 E
49	York, Kap (C.)		Grnld.	75·30 N	73·00 W
160	Yorketown		Austl.	35·00 S	137·28 E
87	York Factory	(făk'tô-rĭ)	Can.	56·59 N	92·27 W
160	York Pen.		Austl.	34·24 S	137·20 E
116	Yorkshire Wolds (Hills)	(yôrk'shĭr)	Eng.	54·00 N	0·35 W
86	Yorkton	(yôrk'tŭn)	Can.	51·11 N	102·40 W
77	Yorktown	(yôrk'toun)	Tex.	28·57 N	97·30 W
79	Yorktown		Va.	37·12 N	76·31 W
156	Yoro	(yō'rô)	Hond.	15·09 N	87·05 W
156	Yoron (I.)		Jap.	26·48 N	128·40 E
68	Yosemite Natl. Park	(yō-sĕm'ĭ-tē)	Calif.	38·03 N	119·36 W
153	Yoshida	(yō'shē-dä)	Jap.	34·39 N	132·41 E
153	Yoshikawa	(yō-shē'kä'mä)	Jap. (Tōkyō In.)	35·53 N	139·51 E
153	Yoshino (R.)	(yō'shē-nō)	Jap.	34·04 N	133·57 E
153	Yoshiwara	(yō-shē'wä'rä')	Jap.	35·11 N	138·44 E
132	Yoshkar-Ola	(yôsh-kär'ô-lä')	Sov. Un.	56·35 N	48·05 E
91	Yosonotú (Santa Catarina)	(yō-sō-nô-tōō') (sän'tä kä-tä-rē'nä)	Mex.	16·51 N	97·37 W
152	Yŏsu	(yŭ'sōō')	Kor.	34·42 N	127·42 E
116	Youghal B.	(yōō'ôl) (yôl)	Ire.	51·52 N	7·46 W
116	Youhal		Ire.	51·58 N	7·57 W
165	Youkadouma	(yōō-kä-dōō'mä)	Cam.	3·29 N	15·04 E
160	Young	(yŭng)	Austl.	34·15 S	148·18 E
101	Young	(yô-ōō'ng)	Ur. (Buenos Aires In.)	32·42 S	57·38 W
65	Youngs (L.)	(yŭngz)	Wash. (Seattle In.)	47·25 N	122·08 W
75	Youngstown	(yŭngz'toun)	N. Y. (Buffalo In.)	43·15 N	79·02 W
80	Youngstown		Ohio	41·05 N	80·40 W
133	Yozgat	(yôz'gäd)	Tur.	39·50 N	34·50 E
75	Ypsilanti	(ĭp-sĭ-län'tĭ)	Mich. (Detroit In.)	42·15 N	83·37 W
66	Yreka	(wī-rē'kà)	Calif.	41·43 N	122·36 W
84	Yscloskey	(ĭs-klôs'kē)	La. (New Orleans In.)	29·51 N	89·42 W
76	Ysleta	(ēz-lĕ'tä)	Tex.	31·42 N	106·18 W
122	Yssingeaux	(ē-săn-zhō')	Fr.	45·09 N	4·08 E
118	Ystad	(ü'städ)	Swe.	55·29 N	13·28 E
118	Ytre Solund (I.)	(ü'trĕ sōō'lĕn)	Nor.	61·01 N	4·25 E
151	Yüan (R.)	(yōō'än)	China	28·50 N	110·50 E
151	Yüanan	(yōō'ä-nän')	China	31·08 N	111·28 E
151	Yüanling		China	28·30 N	110·18 E
148	Yüanshih		China	37·45 N	114·32 E
68	Yuba City	(yōō'bá)	Calif.	39·08 N	121·38 W
164	Yubi C.	(yōō'bē)	Mor.	28·01 N	13·21 E
74	Yucaipa	(yŭ-kà-ē'pá)	Calif. (Los Angeles In.)	34·02 N	117·02 W
88	Yucatan (State)	(yōō-kä-tän')	Mex.	20·45 N	89·00 W
88	Yucatán Chan.		Mex.	22·30 N	87·00 W
151	Yu Chiang (R.)	(yōō)	China	23·55 N	106·50 E
148	Yüch'eng	(yü'chĕng')	China	34·31 N	115·54 E
148	Yuch'eng		China	36·55 N	116·39 E
135	Yudoma (R.)	(yōō-dō'má)	Sov. Un.	59·13 N	137·00 E
148	Yüehchuang	(yüĕ'chĕng)	China	36·13 N	118·17 E
151	Yüehyang		China	29·25 N	113·05 E
132	Yug (R.)	(yōog)	Sov. Un.	59·50 N	45·55 E
102	Yugoslavia	(yōō-gô-slä-vǐ-à)	Eur.	44·48 N	17·29 E
148	Yühsien	(yü'sïän)	China	34·09 N	113·25 E
150	Yühsien	(yü'hsyĕn')	China	39·40 N	114·38 E
128	Yukhnov	(yōōk'-nof)	Sov. Un.	54·44 N	35·15 E
86	Yukon (Ter.)	(yōō'kŏn)	Can.	63·16 N	135·30 W
64	Yukon R.		Alaska	62·10 N	163·10 W
64	Yukutat B.	(yōō-kü tät')	Alaska	59·34 N	140·50 W
136	Yuldybayevo	(yōōld'-bä'yĕ-vô)	Sov. Un. (Urals In.)	52·20 N	57·52 E
151	Yulin		China	22·38 N	110·10 E
150	Yülin	(yōō'lĭn')	China	38·18 N	109·45 E
69	Yuma	(yōō'má)	Ariz.	32·43 N	114·40 W
72	Yuma		Colo.	40·08 N	102·50 W
95	Yuma, Bahia de (B.)	(bä-ē'ä-dĕ-yōō'má)	Dom. Rep.	18·20 N	68·05 W
95	Yuma (R.)		Dom. Rep.	19·05 N	70·05 W
146	Yümen	(yü'mĕn')	China	40·14 N	96·56 E
150	Yünch'eng	(yün'chĕng')	China	35·00 N	110·40 E
151	Yüngan	(yün'gän')	China	26·00 N	117·22 E
150	Yungch'ing	(yōōng'chíng')	China (Peking In.)	39·18 N	116·27 E
	Yungchow, see Lingling				
148	Yungnien	(yōōng'nían)	China	36·41 N	114·46 E
151	Yungshun	(yōōng'shōōn')	China	29·05 N	109·58 E
150	Yungting Ho (R.)	(yōōng'tíng'hŭ)	China	40·25 N	115·00 E
148	Yün Ho (R.) (Grand Canal)	(yün'hŭ)	China	34·23 N	117·57 E
151	Yünhsiao		China	24·00 N	117·20 E
150	Yünhsien		China	32·50 N	110·55 E
146	Yünnan (Prov.)	(yün'nän')	China	24·23 N	101·03 E
	Yünnanfu, see K'unming				
146	Yünnan Plat.		China	26·03 N	101·26 E
153	Yura	(yōō'rä)	Jap.	34·18 N	134·54 E
90	Yurécuaro	(yōō-rā'kwä-rô)	Mex.	20·21 N	102·16 W
98	Yurimaguas	(yōō-rē-mä'gwäs)	Peru	5·59 S	76·12 W
90	Yuriria	(yōō'rē-rē'ä)	Mex.	20·11 N	101·08 W
132	Yur'yevets		Sov. Un.	57·15 N	43·08 E
136	Yuryuzan'	(yōōr-yōō-zän')	Sov. Un. (Urals In.)	54·47 N	58·45 E
92	Yuscarán	(yōōs-kä-rän')	Hond.	13·57 N	86·48 W
151	Yüshan	(yōō'shän')	China	28·42 N	118·20 E
150	Yüshu		China	44·58 N	126·32 E
142	Yutien (Keriya)	(yōō'tĕn')	China	36·55 N	81·39 E
148	Yut'ien	(yü'tyĕn')	China	39·54 N	117·45 E
150	Yuty	(yōō-tē')	Par.	26·45 S	56·13 W
150	Yützu		China	37·32 N	112·40 E
148	Yuwangcheng	(yü'wäng'chĕng)	China	31·32 N	114·26 E
132	Yuzha	(yōō'zhä)	Sov. Un.	56·38 N	42·20 E
136	Yuzhnny Ural (Mts.)	(yōō'zhnĭ ōō-räl')	Sov. Un. (Urals In.)	52·51 N	57·48 E
135	Yuzhno-Sakhalinsk	(yōōozh'nô-sä-ĸä-lĭnsk')	Sov. Un.	47·11 N	143·04 E
136	Yuzhnoural'skiy	(yōōzh-nô-ōō-räl'skĭ')	Sov. Un. (Urals In.)	54·26 N	61·17 E
120	Yverdon	(ē-vĕr-dôn')	Switz.	46·46 N	6·35 E
122	Yvetot	(ēv-tō')	Fr.	49·39 N	0·45 E
114	Za R.		Mor.	34·19 N	2·23 W
91	Zaachila	(sä-ä-chē'lä)	Mex.	16·56 N	96·45 W
111	Zaandam	(zän'däm)	Neth. (Amsterdam In.)	52·25 N	4·49 E
139	Zabdani	(zäb-dä'nē)	Syr. (Palestine In.)	33·45 N	36·06 E
120	Zabkowice	(zaNb'kô-vē'tsĕ)	Pol.	50·35 N	16·48 E
121	Zabrze	(zäb'zhĕ)	Pol.	50·18 N	18·48 E
92	Zacapa	(sä-kä'pä)	Guat.	14·56 N	89·30 W
91	Zacapoaxtla	(sä-kä-pō-äs'tlä)	Mex.	19·51 N	97·34 W
90	Zacatecas	(sä-kä-tā'käs)	Mex.	22·44 N	102·32 W
88	Zacatecas (State)		Mex.	24·00 N	102·45 W
92	Zacatecoluca	(sä-kä-tä-kô-lōō'kä)	Sal.	13·31 N	88·50 W
90	Zacatepec	(sä-kä-tĕ'kō)	Mex.	19·12 N	98·12 W
91	Zacatepec (Santiago)	(sä-kä-tä-pĕk') (sän-tē-ä'gô)	Mex.	17·10 N	95·53 W
91	Zacatlán	(sä-kä-tlän')	Mex.	19·55 N	97·57 W
90	Zacoalco de Torres	(sä-kô-äl'kô dä tōr'rĕs)	Mex.	20·12 N	103·33 W
90	Zacualpan	(sä-kōō-äl-pän')	Mex.	18·43 N	99·46 W

288 Zacualtipan–Zywiec PRONOUNCING INDEX

Page	Name Pronunciation Region	Lat. °′	Long. °′
90	Zacualtipan (sȧ-kōō-äl-tē-pän′) Mex.	20·38 N	98·39 W
126	Zadar (zä′där) Yugo.	44·08 N	15·16 E
128	Zadonsk (zä-dônsk′) Sov. Un.	52·22 N	38·55 E
139	Za'farānah U. A. R. (Egypt) (Palestine In.)	29·07 N	32·38 E
120	Zagan (zhä′gan′) Pol.	51·34 N	15·32 E
125	Zagarolo (tzä-gä-rô′lô) It. (Rome In.)	41·51 N	12·53 E
119	Žagare (zhȧgȧrĕ) Sov. Un.	56·21 N	23·14 E
139	Zaghartā Leb. (Palestine In.)	34·24 N	35·53 E
164	Zaghouan (zȧ-gwäɴ′) Tun.	36·30 N	10·04 E
127	Zagorá (zä′gô-rȧ) Grc.	39·29 N	23·04 E
136	Zagorsk (zä-gôrsk′) Sov. Un. (Moscow In.)	56·18 N	38·08 E
126	Zagreb (zä′grĕb) Yugo.	45·50 N	15·58 E
144	Zagro Mts Iran	33·30 N	46·30 E
144	Zāhedān (zä′hȧ-dān) Iran	29·37 N	60·31 E
139	Zahlah (zä-lā′) Leb. (Palestine In.)	33·50 N	35·54 E
111	Zahorska-Ves Czech. (Vienna In.)	48·24 N	16·51 E
125	Zahrez Chergui (L.) Alg.	35·10 N	2·17 E
127	Zaječar (zä′yĕ-chär′) Yugo.	43·54 N	22·16 E
127	Zákinthos Grc.	37·48 N	20·55 E
127	Zákinthos (Zante) (I.) Grc.	37·45 N	20·32 E
121	Zakopane (zȧ-kô-pä′nĕ) Pol.	49·18 N	19·57 E
120	Zalaegerszeg (zŏ′lô-ĕ′gĕr-sĕg) Hung.	46·50 N	16·50 E
121	Zalău (zȧ-lŭ′ōō) Rom.	47·11 N	23·06 E
121	Zalew Wiślany (B.) (zälĕf vĭsh-lănĭ) Pol.	54·22 N	19·39 E
111	Zaltbommel Neth. (Amsterdam In.)	51·48 N	5·15 E
166	Zambezi (R.) (zȧm-bā′zē) Afr.	16·33 S	29·22 E
166	Zambia (zăm′bē-ȧ) Afr.	14·23 S	24.15 E
154	Zamboanga (säm-bô-aŋ′gä) Phil.	6·58 N	122·02 E
121	Zambrów (zäm′brōōf) Pol.	52·59 N	22·17 E
90	Zamora (sä-mō′rä) Mex.	19·59 N	102·16 W
124	Zamora (thä-mō′rä) Sp.	41·32 N	5·43 W
121	Zamość (zä′môshch) Pol.	50·42 N	23·17 E
91	Zanatepec (Sto. Domingo) (sä-nä-tȧ-pek′) (sän-tô dō-miŋ′gô) Mex.	16·30 N	94·22 W
111	Zandvoort Neth. (Amsterdam In.)	52·22 N	4·30 E
80	Zanesville (zānz′vĭl) Ohio	39·55 N	82·00 W
144	Zanjān Iran	36·26 N	48·24 E
167	Zanzibar (zăn′zĭ-bär) Tan.	6·13 S	39·12 E
167	Zanzibar (I.) Tan.	6·00 S	39·30 E
165	Zanzūr (zän-zōōr′) Libya	32·40 N	12·49 E
128	Zapadnaya Dvina (R.) (zä′pȧd-nȧ-yȧ dvē′nȧ) Sov. Un.	55·30 N	28·27 E
100	Zapala (zä-pä′lä) Arg.	38·53 S	70·02 W
119	Zapa-naya Dvina (R.) (zä′pȧd-nä-yȧ dvē nȧ) Sov. Un.	56·40 N	24·40 E
76	Zapata (sä-pä′tä) Tex.	26·52 N	99·18 W
94	Zapata, Ciénaga de (Swp.) (syĕ′nä-gä-dĕ-zä-pȧ′tä) Cuba	22·30 N	81·20 W
94	Zapata, Península de (pĕ-nē′n-sōō-lä-dĕ-zä-pȧ′tä) Cuba	22·20 N	81·30 W
92	Zapatera, Isla (I.) (ē′s-lä-sä-pä-tā′rō) Nic.	11·45 N	85·45 W
90	Zapopan (sä-pō′pän) Mex.	20·42 N	102·23 W
119	Zaporoshskoye (zȧ-pô-rôsh′skô-yĕ) Sov. Un.	60·36 N	30·31 E
129	Zaporozh'ye (zä-pô-rôzh′yĕ) Sov. Un.	47·53 N	35·25 E
129	Zaporozhye (Oblast) (zä-pô-rôzh′yĕ ôb′lȧst) Sov. Un.	47·20 N	35·05 E
90	Zapotiltic (sä-pô-tēl-tēk′) Mex.	19·37 N	103·25 W
90	Zapotitlán (sä-pô-tē-tlän′) Mex.	17·13 N	98·58 W
91	Zapotitlán, Punta (Pt.) Mex.	18·34 N	94·48 W
90	Zapotlanejo (sä-pô-tlä-nā′hô) Mex.	20·38 N	103·05 W
90	Zaragoza (sä-rä-gō′sä) Mex.	23·59 N	99·45 W
90	Zaragoza Mex.	22·02 N	100·45 W
125	Zaragoza (thä-rä-gō′thä) Sp.	41·39 N	0·53 W
121	Zărandului, Muntii (Mts.) Rom.	46·07 N	22·21 E
119	Zarasay (zä-rä-sī′) Sov. Un.	55·45 N	26·18 E
101	Zárate (zä-rä′tā) Arg. (Buenos Aires In.)	34·05 S	59·05 W
128	Zaraysk (zä-rä′ēsk) Sov. Un.	54·46 N	38·53 E
142	Zardālu W. Pak.	30·20 N	67·40 E
164	Zaria (zä′rē-ä) Nig.	11·08 N	7·45 E
133	Zarineh, Rūd-é (R.) Iran	36·40 N	46·35 E
139	Zarga (R.) Jordan (Palestine In.)	32·13 N	35·43 E
120	Zary (zhä′rē) Pol.	51·38 N	15·08 E
98	Zarzal (zär-zȧ′l) Col. (In.)	4·23 N	76·04 W
135	Zashiversk (zȧ′shĭ-vĕrsk′) Sov. Un.	67·08 N	144·02 E
121	Zastavna (zȧs-täf′nȧ) Sov. Un.	48·32 N	25·50 E
167	Zastron (zȧs′trŭn) S. Afr. (Natal In.)	30·19 S	27·07 E
120	Žatec (zhä′tĕts) Czech.	50·19 N	13·32 E
135	Zavitinsk Sov. Un.	50·12 N	129·44 E
121	Zawiercie (zȧ-vyĕr′tsyĕ) Pol.	50·28 N	19·25 E
144	Zāyantleh Rud (R.) Iran	32·16 N	50·48 E
134	Zaysan (zī′sȧn) Sov. Un.	47·43 N	84·44 E
134	Zaysan (L.) Sov. Un.	48·16 N	84·05 E
94	Zaza (R.) (zȧ′zȧ) Cuba	21·40 N	79·25 W
121	Zbarazh (zbä-räzh′) Sov. Un.	49·39 N	25·48 E
121	Zbruch R (zbrōōch) Sov. Un.	48·56 N	26·18 E
121	Zdolbunov (zdôl-bōō′nōōf) Sov. Un.	50·31 N	26·17 E
121	Zdunska Wola (zdōōn″skä vō′lä) Pol.	51·36 N	18·27 E
168	Zebediela S. Afr. (Johannesburg & Pretoria In.)	24·19 S	29·21 E
117	Zeebrugge (zā′brōōg′gĕ) Bel.	51·20 N	3·00 W
80	Zeeland (zē′lănd) Mich.	42·50 N	86·00 W
111	Zehdenick (tsā′dē-nēk) Ger. (Berlin In.)	52.59 N	13·20 E
111	Zehlendorf (tsā′lĕn-dôrf) Ger. (Berlin In.)	52·47 N	13·23 E
168	Zeila (zā′lä) Som. (Horn of Afr. In.)	11·19 N	43·20 E
111	Zeist Neth. (Amsterdam In.)	52·05 N	5·14 E
121	Zelechów (zhĕ-lĕ′ĸōōf) Pol.	51·48 N	21·55 E
119	Zelenogorsk (zĕ-lă′nô-gôrsk) Sov. Un.	60·13 N	29·39 E
120	Zella-Mehlis (tsȧl′ȧ-mā′lēs) Ger.	50·40 N	10·38 E
165	Zémio (za-myō′) Cen. Afr. Rep.	5·03 N	25·11 E
130	Zemlya Frantsa Iosifa (Franz Josef Land) (Is.) Sov. Un.	81·32 N	40·00 E
91	Zempoala, Punta (Pt.) (pōō′n-tä-sĕm-pô-ä′lä) Mex.	19·30 N	96·18 W
91	Zempoatlépetl (Mtn.) (sĕm-pô-ä-tlā′pĕt′l) Mex.	17·13 N	95·59 W
127	Zemun (Semlin) (zĕ′mōōn) (sĕm′lĭn) Yugo.	44·50 N	20·25 E
127	Zenica (zĕ′nēt-sä) Yugo.	44·10 N	17·54 E
153	Zeni-Su (Is.) (zĕ′nē sōō) Jap.	33·55 N	138·55 E
129	Zen'kov (zĕn-kof′) Sov. Un.	50·13 N	34·23 E
127	Žepče (zhĕp′chĕ) Yugo.	44·26 N	18·01 E
111	Zepernick (tsĕ′pĕr-nēk) Ger. (Berlin In.)	52·39 N	13·32 E
103	Zeravshan (R.) (zȧ-răf-shăn′) Sov. Un.	40·00 N	65·42 E
120	Zerbst (tsĕrbst) Ger.	51·58 N	12·03 E
111	Zerpenschleuse (tsĕr′pĕn-shloi-zĕ) Ger. (Berlin In.)	52·51 N	13·30 E
111	Zeuthen (tsoi′tĕn) Ger. (Berlin In.)	52·21 N	13·38 E
123	Zevenaar Neth. (Ruhr In.)	51·56 N	6·06 E
111	Zevenbergen Neth. (Amsterdam In.)	51·38 N	4·36 E
135	Zeya (zâ′yȧ) Sov. Un.	53·43 N	127·29 E
135	Zeya (R.) Sov. Un.	52·31 N	128·30 E
133	Zeytun (zā-tōōn′) Tur.	38·00 N	36·40 E
124	Zezere (R.) (zĕ′zȧ-rĕ) Port.	39·54 N	8·12 W
121	Zgierz (zgyĕzh) Pol.	51·51 N	19·26 E
129	Zgurovka (zgōō′rôf-kä) Sov. Un.	50·31 N	31·43 E
129	Zhdanov (zhdä′nôf) Sov. Un.	47·07 N	37·32 E
134	Zhelaniya, Mys (C.) (zhĕ′lä-nĭ-yȧ) Sov. Un.	75·43 N	69·10 E
135	Zhigalovo (zhē-gä′lô-vô) Sov. Un.	54·52 N	105·05 E
135	Zhigansk (zhē-gȧnsk′) Sov. Un.	66·45 N	123·20 E
142	Zhikatse China	29·22 N	88·57 E
129	Zhitomir (zhē′tô′mēr) Sov. Un.	50·15 N	28·40 E
129	Zhitomir (Oblast) Sov. Un.	50·40 N	28·07 E
128	Zhizdra (zhēz′drȧ) Sov. Un.	53·47 N	34·41 E
128	Zhizhitskoye (R.) (zhē-zhēt′skô-yĕ) Sov. Un.	56·08 N	31·34 E
129	Zhmerinka (zhmyĕ′rēŋ-kȧ) Sov. Un.	49·02 N	28·09 E
136	Zhukovskiy (zhōō-kôf′skĭ) Sov. Un. (Moscow In.)	55·33 N	38·09 E
158	Ziel, Mt. (zēl) Austl.	23·15 S	132·45 E
120	Zielona Góra (zhyĕ-lô′nä gōō′rä) Pol.	51·56 N	15·30 E
136	Zigazinskiy (zĭ-gazinskēē) Sov. Un. (Urals In.)	53·50 N	57·18 E
113	Zighouf Youcef Alg.	36·34 N	6·51 E
164	Ziguichor Senegal	12·28 N	16·27 W
136	Zilair (zē′lȧ-ĭr) Sov. Un. (Urals In.)	52·12 N	57·23 E
133	Zile (zē-lĕ′) Tur.	40·20 N	35·50 E
121	Žilina (zhē′lĭ-nä) Czech.	49·14 N	18·45 E
165	Zillah Libya	28·26 N	17·52 E
134	Zima (zē′mȧ) Sov. Un.	53·58 N	102·08 E
90	Zimapan (sē-mä′pän) Mex.	20·43 N	99·23 W
91	Zimatlán de Alvarez (sē-mä-tlän′ dā äl′vä-rāz) Mex.	16·52 N	96·47 W
127	Zimnicea (zêm-nē′chȧ) Rom.	43·39 N	25·22 E
91	Zinacatepec (zē-nä-kä-tĕ′pĕk) Mex.	18·19 N	97·15 W
	Zinántectl, see Toluca, Nevado de		
90	Zinapécuaro (sē-nä-pā′kwȧ-rô) Mex.	19·50 N	100·49 W
164	Zinder (zĭn′dēr) Niger	13·49 N	8·54 E
75	Zion (zī′ŭn) Ill. (Chicago In.)	42·27 N	87·50 W
69	Zion Natl. Park Utah	37·20 N	113·00 W
75	Zionsville (zīŭnz-vĭl) Ind. (Indianapolis In.)	39·57 N	86·15 W
98	Zipaquirá (sē-pä-kē-rä′) Col. (In.)	5·01 N	74·01 W
90	Zirandaro (sē-rän-dä′rō) Mex.	18·28 N	101·02 W
90	Zitacuaro (sē-tȧ-kwä′rō) Mex.	19·25 N	100·22 W
90	Zitlala (sē-tlä′lä) Mex.	17·38 N	99·09 W
120	Zittau (tsē′tou) Ger.	50·55 N	14·48 E
127	Zlatograd Bul.	41·24 N	25·05 E
136	Zlatoust (zlȧ-tô-ōōst′) Sov. Un. (Urals In.)	55·13 N	59·39 E
165	Zlitan Libya	32·27 N	14·33 E
121	Złoczew (zwô′chĕf) Pol.	51·23 N	18·34 E
128	Zlynka (zlēŋ′kȧ) Sov. Un.	52·28 N	31·39 E
129	Znamenka (znä′mĕn-kä) Sov. Un.	48·43 N	32·35 E
119	Znamensk (znä′mĕnsk) Sov. Un.	54·39 N	21·49 E
120	Znojomo (znoi′mô) Czech.	48·52 N	16·03 E
111	Zoetermeer Neth. (Amsterdam In.)	52·03 N	4·29 E
111	Zoeterwoude Neth. (Amsterdam In.)	52·03 N	4·29 E
111	Zohor Czech. (Vienna In.)	48·20 N	17·00 E
121	Zolochëv (zô′lô-chĕf) Sov. Un.	49·48 N	24·55 E
129	Zolotonosha (zô′lô-tô-nô′shȧ) Sov. Un.	49·41 N	32·03 E
152	Zolotoy, Mys (Pt.) (mĭs zô-lô-tôy′) Sov. Un.	47·24 N	139·10 E
166	Zomba (zôm′bȧ) Malawi	15·19 S	35·17 E
165	Zongo (zŏŋ′gô) Con. K.	4·19 N	18·36 E
133	Zonguldak (zôn′gōōl′dȧk) Tur.	41·25 N	31·50 E
111	Zonhoven Bel. (Brussels In.)	50·59 N	5·24 E
91	Zoquitlán (sô-kēt-län′) Mex.	18·09 N	97·02 W
124	Zorita (thō-rē′tä) Sp.	39·18 N	5·41 W
111	Zossen (tsō′sĕn) Ger. (Berlin In.)	52·13 N	13·27 E
128	Zubtsov (zōōp-tsôf′) Sov. Un.	56·13 N	34·34 E
125	Zuera (thwā′rä) Sp.	41·40 N	0·48 W
120	Zuger See (L.) (tsōōg) Switz.	47·10 N	8·40 E
120	Zugspitze Pk. Aus.-Ger.	47·25 N	11·00 E
124	Zújar (R.) (zōō′ĸär) Sp.	38·55 N	5·05 W
94	Zulueta (zōō-lōō-ĕ′tä) Cuba	22·20 N	79·35 W
166	Zululand (Reg.) (zōō′lōō-lănd) S. Afr.	27·45 S	31·29 E
166	Zumbo (zōōm′bōō) Moz.	15·32 S	30·30 E
71	Zumbro (R.) (zŭm′brō) Minn.	44·18 N	92·14 W
71	Zumbrota (zŭm-brō′tȧ) Minn.	44·16 N	92·39 W
90	Zumpango (sōōm-päŋ-gō) Mex.	19·48 N	99·06 W
111	Zundert Neth. (Amsterdam In.)	51·28 N	4·39 E
164	Zungeru (zōōŋ-gā′rōō) Nig.	9·45 N	6·13 E
69	Zuni (R.) Ariz.-N. Mex.	34·40 N	109·30 W
69	Zuni Ind. Res. (zōō′nē) N. Mex.	35·10 N	108·40 W
69	Zuni Mts N. Mex.	35·10 N	108·10 W
120	Zürich (tsü′rĭk) Switz.	47·22 N	8·32 E
120	Zürich See (L.) Switz.	47·18 N	8·47 E
153	Zushi (zōō′shē) Jap. (Tōkyō In.)	35·17 N	139·35 E
167	Zuurberg (Mts.) (zōō′bûrg) S. Afr. (Natal In.)	33·15 S	25·32 E
165	Zuwārah Libya	32·58 N	12·07 E
139	Zuwayzā Jordan (Palestine In.)	31·42 N	35·58 E
128	Zvenigorod (zvā-nē′gô-rôt) Sov. Un.	55·46 N	36·54 E
129	Zvenigorodka (zvā-nē′gô-rôt′kä) Sov. Un.	49·07 N	30·59 E
121	Zvolen (zvô′lĕn) Czech.	48·35 N	19·10 E
127	Zvornik (zvôr′nēk) Yugo.	44·24 N	19·08 E
165	Zwai L. (zwä′ē) Eth.	8·08 N	39·11 E
167	Zwartberg (Mtn.) (zvärt-bĕrk) S. Afr. (Natal In.)	30·08 S	29·34 E
120	Zwickau (tsvĭk′ou) Ger.	50·43 N	12·30 E
120	Zwiebrücken (tsvī-brük′ĕn) Ger.	49·16 N	7·20 E
117	Zwolle (zvôl′ĕ) Neth.	52·33 N	6·05 E
121	Zyrardow (zhē-rär′dōōf) Pol.	52·04 N	20·28 E
135	Zyryanka (zē-ryän′kȧ) Sov. Un.	65·45 N	151·15 E
134	Zyryanovsk (zē-ryä′nôfsk) Sov. Un.	49·43 N	83·52 E
121	Zywiec (zhĭ′vyĕts) Pol.	49·42 N	19·14 E

ăt; finăl; rāte; senâte; ärm; àsk; sofȧ; fâre; ch-choose; dh-as th in other; bē; ēvent; bĕt; recĕnt; cratẽr; g-go; gh-guttural g; bĭt; ĭ-short neutral; rīde; ĸ-guttural k as ch in German ich;

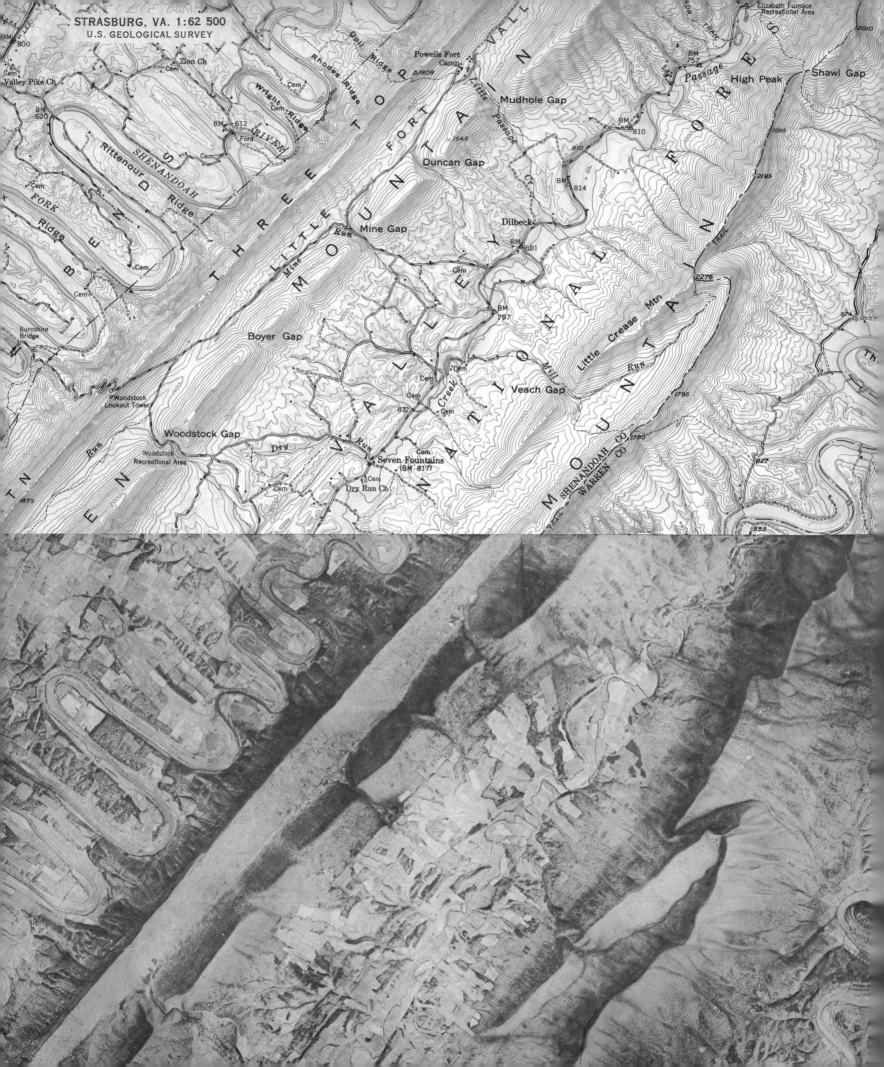